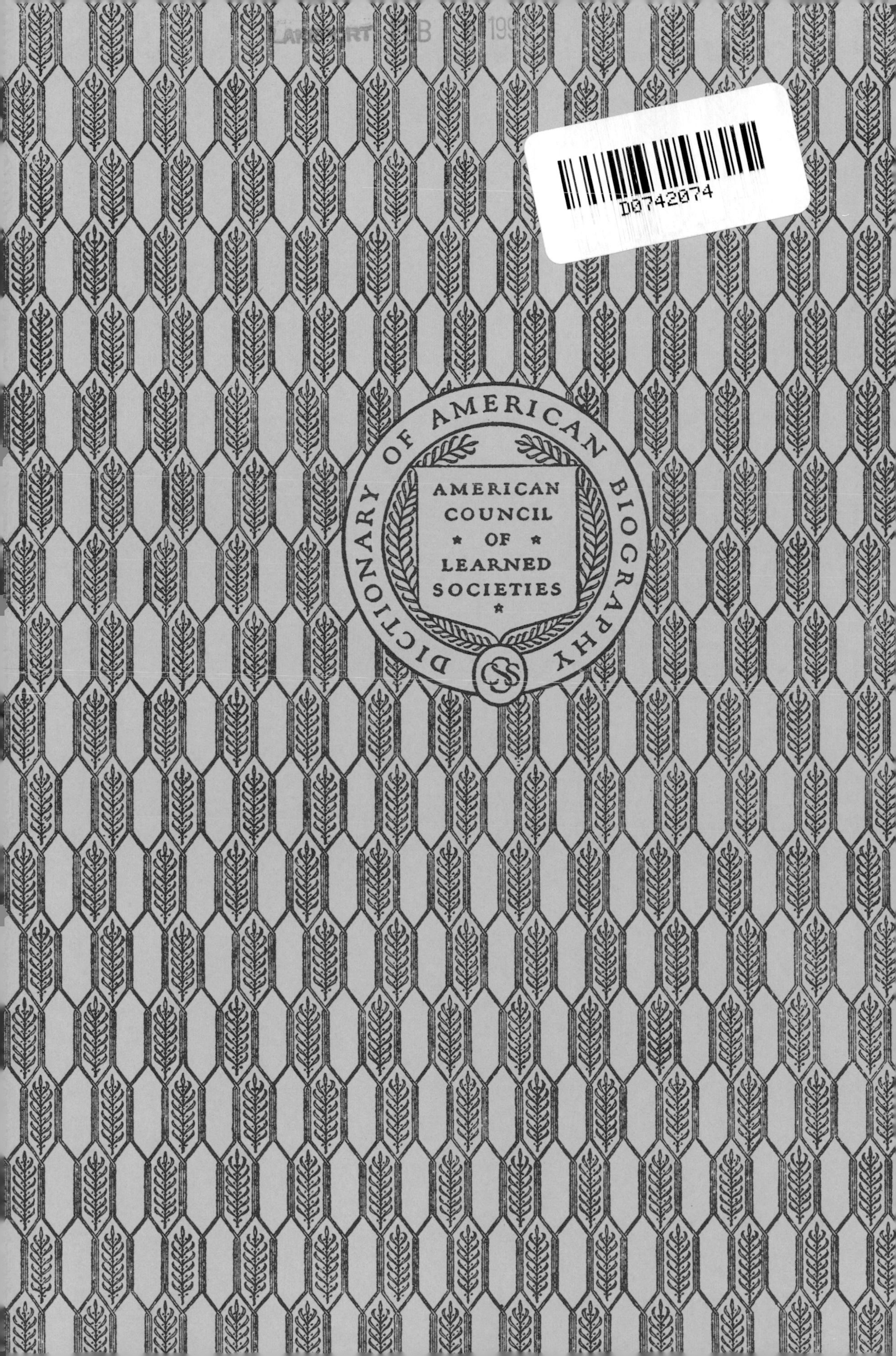

DICTIONARY OF AMERICAN BIOGRAPHY
AMERICAN
COUNCIL
OF
LEARNED
SOCIETIES
CSS
D0742074

DICTIONARY
OF AMERICAN BIOGRAPHY

The *Dictionary of American Biography* was published originally in twenty volumes. Supplementary volumes were added in 1944 and 1958. This edition of the work combines all twenty-two volumes.

The present Volume I (Abbe–Brazer) contains Volumes I and II of the original edition, but these are now denominated "Part 1" and "Part 2" of the Volume. Volumes II through XI are arranged similarly, the Second Part in each instance representing a volume of the original series. For ease in reference, although the articles follow one another in strict alphabetical order, each Second Part is preceded by a half-title page which relates that Part to its place in the original numbering of the volumes.

The Errata list at the head of Volume I contains corrections of fact and additional data which have come to the attention of the Editors from the first publication of the work up to the present. Minor typographical corrections have been made in many instances directly on the plates.

PUBLISHED UNDER THE AUSPICES OF THE AMERICAN COUNCIL OF LEARNED SOCIETIES

The American Council of Learned Societies, organized in 1919 for the purpose of advancing the study of the humanities and of the humanistic aspects of the social sciences, is a nonprofit federation comprising forty-five national scholarly groups. The Council represents the humanities in the United States in the International Union of Academies, provides fellowships and grants-in-aid, supports research-and-planning conferences and symposia, and sponsors special projects and scholarly publications.

MEMBER ORGANIZATIONS

AMERICAN PHILOSOPHICAL SOCIETY, 1743
AMERICAN ACADEMY OF ARTS AND SCIENCES, 1780
AMERICAN ANTIQUARIAN SOCIETY, 1812
AMERICAN ORIENTAL SOCIETY, 1842
AMERICAN NUMISMATIC SOCIETY, 1858
AMERICAN PHILOLOGICAL ASSOCIATION, 1869
ARCHAEOLOGICAL INSTITUTE OF AMERICA, 1879
SOCIETY OF BIBLICAL LITERATURE, 1880
MODERN LANGUAGE ASSOCIATION OF AMERICA, 1883
AMERICAN HISTORICAL ASSOCIATION, 1884
AMERICAN ECONOMIC ASSOCIATION, 1885
AMERICAN FOLKLORE SOCIETY, 1888
AMERICAN DIALECT SOCIETY, 1889
AMERICAN PSYCHOLOGICAL ASSOCIATION, 1892
ASSOCIATION OF AMERICAN LAW SCHOOLS, 1900
AMERICAN PHILOSOPHICAL ASSOCIATION, 1901
AMERICAN ANTHROPOLOGICAL ASSOCIATION, 1902
AMERICAN POLITICAL SCIENCE ASSOCIATION, 1903
BIBLIOGRAPHICAL SOCIETY OF AMERICA, 1904
ASSOCIATION OF AMERICAN GEOGRAPHERS, 1904
HISPANIC SOCIETY OF AMERICA, 1904
AMERICAN SOCIOLOGICAL ASSOCIATION, 1905
AMERICAN SOCIETY OF INTERNATIONAL LAW, 1906
ORGANIZATION OF AMERICAN HISTORIANS, 1907
AMERICAN ACADEMY OF RELIGION, 1909
COLLEGE ART ASSOCIATION OF AMERICA, 1912
HISTORY OF SCIENCE SOCIETY, 1924
LINGUISTIC SOCIETY OF AMERICA, 1924
MEDIAEVAL ACADEMY OF AMERICA, 1925
AMERICAN MUSICOLOGICAL SOCIETY, 1934
SOCIETY OF ARCHITECTURAL HISTORIANS, 1940
ECONOMIC HISTORY ASSOCIATION, 1940
ASSOCIATION FOR ASIAN STUDIES, 1941
AMERICAN SOCIETY FOR AESTHETICS, 1942
AMERICAN ASSOCIATION FOR THE ADVANCEMENT OF SLAVIC STUDIES, 1948
METAPHYSICAL SOCIETY OF AMERICA, 1950
AMERICAN STUDIES ASSOCIATION, 1950
RENAISSANCE SOCIETY OF AMERICA, 1954
SOCIETY FOR ETHNOMUSICOLOGY, 1955
AMERICAN SOCIETY FOR LEGAL HISTORY, 1956
AMERICAN SOCIETY FOR THEATRE RESEARCH, 1956
SOCIETY FOR THE HISTORY OF TECHNOLOGY, 1958
AMERICAN COMPARATIVE LITERATURE ASSOCIATION, 1960
AMERICAN SOCIETY FOR EIGHTEENTH-CENTURY STUDIES, 1969
ASSOCIATION FOR JEWISH STUDIES, 1969

DICTIONARY
OF
American Biography

VOLUME I
ABBE-BRAZER

Edited by

ALLEN JOHNSON

Charles Scribner's Sons *New York*

Prompted solely by a desire for public service the New York Times Company and its President, Mr. Adolph S. Ochs, have made possible the preparation of the manuscript of the Dictionary of American Biography through a subvention of more than $500,000 and with the understanding that the entire responsibility for the contents of the volumes rests with the American Council of Learned Societies.

ISBN 0-684-14138-8

Published simultaneously in Canada
by Collier Macmillan Canada, Inc.

17 19 B/C 20 18 16

Printed in the United States of America

The paper in this book meets the guidelines for
permanence and durability of the Committee on
Production Guidelines for Book Longevity of the
Council on Library Resources.

INTRODUCTION

TO THE FIRST VOLUME AS ORIGINALLY ISSUED

THE lack of an authoritative dictionary of national biography has been often deplored by American scholars. Encyclopedias and dictionaries of biography abound, but none are comparable in either scope or scholarship to the British *Dictionary of National Biography* edited by Sir Leslie Stephen and Sir Sidney Lee. It was this need that moved the newly organized American Council of Learned Societies to appoint a committee in 1922 to consider such a project. This committee, consisting of Dr. J. Franklin Jameson, chairman, Professor John Erskine, Professor Thomas W. Page, Professor Frederic L. Paxson, Professor Frederick J. Turner, and Dr. Robert S. Woodward, formulated plans for a comprehensive Dictionary of American Biography, contingent upon the raising of adequate funds. It was estimated that at least half a million dollars would be required to cover the cost of preparing the manuscript. Various plans to defray this initial cost were considered, but were found impracticable.

The committee then laid the whole project before Mr. Adolph S. Ochs, controlling owner and publisher of the New York Times. Mr. Ochs at once appreciated its significance and agreed on behalf of the New York Times Company to supply the required five hundred thousand dollars. This volume, therefore, and those that are to follow, owe their existence to his public spirit and generosity. Upon his initiative the New York Times Company entered into an agreement with the Council whereby ten yearly payments were to be made for the preparation of the manuscript of the Dictionary. The direction of the undertaking was vested in a Committee of Management of seven members, four of whom were to be appointed by the Council, two by the New York Times Company, and the seventh, to be editor-in-chief, by the other six. In February 1926 editorial offices were opened in Washington.

The selection of names for a dictionary of biography offers greater difficulties in the United States than in European countries. The very term American is not free from ambiguities. To restrict the term to persons resident in the original colonies and to citizens of the United States by birth or naturalization, would exclude many individuals of foreign birth who have identified themselves with the country and contributed notably to its history. The Committee of Management decided against any such limitation. Three other restrictions, however, were adopted: first, that no living persons should have biographies in the Dictionary; second, that no persons who had not lived in the territory now known as the United States should be eligible; and third, that no British officers serving in America after the colonies had declared their independence should appear in the Dictionary.

Positive qualifications were less easily defined. In general, only those are included in the following pages who have made some significant contribution to American life in its manifold aspects. The Dictionary cannot find space for average or merely typical figures, however estimable they may be. The observation of Sir Sidney Lee is quite to the point: "Actions, however beneficent or honourable, which are accomplished or are capable of accomplishment by many thousands of persons are actions of mediocrity, and lack the dimension which justifies the biographer's notice. The fact that a man is a devoted husband and father, an efficient school-master, an exemplary parish priest, gives him in itself no claim to biographic commemoration."

Earlier collections of biographies stressed, naturally enough, the lives of soldiers, statesmen, and clergymen whose conspicuousness, aside from their services, made them objects of interest. Physical science, however, has increased immeasurably the importance of the engineer, the technician, and the chemist in modern warfare; the new social sciences have bred ministering and administrative agents who now share the cure of souls; and even politicians now recognize the important rôle of the statistician and the economist in law-making. The modern age with its greater complexity and dependence upon new arts and sciences has brought into view less spectacular, and possibly less heroic, but certainly not less significant, figures. Within a half-century, industry, science, the fine arts, and literature have produced men and women whose special significance is not indicated by such traditional designations as merchant, naturalist, artist, and author. The currents of American life and expression have both widened and deepened.

A tentative list of names was first compiled from earlier works of reference, but it was deficient in the particulars just noted. A classification was then devised on the basis of occupations, trades, and professions, as likely under American conditions to bring to light significant figures in specialized fields of human endeavor. For each of these groups some authority was asked to supply a tentative list. Every such list was submitted to other specialists, or to groups of specialists, who dropped some names, added others, and attempted to make a rating of all. To avoid the possibility of names slipping through the meshes of this drag-net, necrologies of all sorts were carefully searched; and the proposed list of names in the first volume was printed and circulated three months before the volume was sent to the printers, in order to discover serious omissions.

Every effort has been made to secure fresh independent accounts of even well-known national figures and not mere compilations of preceding sketches. Contributors have been instructed to base their articles wherever possible upon original sources of information and to list their chief authorities in carefully considered bibliographies. They have been urged also not only to state but to appraise the circumstances and influences which shaped careers. So far as space and material permit, they have stressed such matters as ancestry, parentage, childhood experiences, educational advantages, physical and social environment. In the present chaotic condition of vital statistics in the United States, reliable information about the parentage and ancestry of lesser personages is often wanting; but wherever possible the names of parents and of husband, or wife, are given in each article. To insure accuracy in such details, a staff has been maintained at the Library of Congress to verify names, dates, and titles. To Dr. Herbert Putnam and his associates at the Library of Congress, contributors and editors alike have been under constant obligation for counsel and unremitting service. The American Antiquarian Society of Worcester, Massachusetts, through its Librarian, Mr. Clarence S. Brigham, has placed the resources of its library and its staff freely at the disposal of contributors to the Dictionary. Acknowledgment should be made, also, of the coöperation of many local historical societies and libraries, which have not only furnished detailed information at the cost of much time and effort, but have also directed contributors to unpublished manuscript sources. The Dictionary owes much to the generous interest of the publishers, who have desired to make it in form as well as substance a notable contribution to American scholarship and letters.

Finally, contributors have been urged not to rest content with a bare narrative of events, but so far as possible to leave the reader with a definite impression of the personality and achievements of the subject of each biographical sketch. At every point, however, limitations of space have necessitated terse, compact, direct statement, without rhetorical ornament. The length of an article has not been determined solely by the relative importance of the man, but also by the amount of available authentic material, by the nature of his career, and by the completeness of biographies already published. Quite apart from its usefulness as a general work of reference, the Dictionary should throw light upon the careers of men and women who, by the caprice of fortune, have been lost from view. A scarcely less important function is the re-interpretation of character and career made necessary by new sources of information and new points of view. So far as knowledge permits the Dictionary has endeavored to re-create and re-interpret the lives of the makers of American life and culture.

A BRIEF ACCOUNT OF THE ENTERPRISE

PREFIXED TO THE FINAL VOLUME IN THE ORIGINAL TWENTY-VOLUME ISSUE

I

The publication of the British *Dictionary of National Biography* (1885–1900) aroused in the minds of many Americans a desire that their own country should have a biographical dictionary of similar fullness and if possible of similar quality, prepared with an amount of scholarly labor not to be expected in the case of any book of reference whose total costs must not exceed the expected revenue from sales. No one of the existing scholarly organizations, however, felt that the task of compiling such a work was peculiarly incumbent upon it, and no one of them could command the necessary resources. In 1919, fortunately, plans were formed for a federation of such societies, and soon thereafter the American Council of Learned Societies Devoted to Humanistic Studies came into existence. At its first meeting, on Feb. 14, 1920, Professor Frederick J. Turner proposed that the Council should consider the possibility of undertaking the preparation of a cyclopedia of American biography. At the next annual meeting, in February 1921, he repeated the proposal, and it was resolved that a committee should be appointed to prepare a report on the subject. The Council had not then the means for rapid action, but in January 1922 the committee was appointed. Its members were Dr. J. Franklin Jameson, chairman, then connected with the Carnegie Institution of Washington, Professor Turner of Harvard University, Professors John Erskine of Columbia University, Thomas Walker Page of the University of Virginia, chairman of the United States Tariff Commission, Frederic L. Paxson of the University of Wisconsin, and Dr. Robert S. Woodward, who had lately retired from the presidency of the Carnegie Institution; before the committee was able to begin action, however, Dr. Woodward fell into an illness from which he never recovered, and the committee did not have the benefit of his wide knowledge of the history of American science and scientists.

It is now somewhat amusing to recall that the committee at first found a solid obstacle to its deliberations in the fact that the treasury of the Council did not contain the $500 necessary to defray the traveling expenses of the members of the committee in attending the meetings which were necessary before their report could be completed. It is proper to record here, with gratitude, the names of the ten gentlemen who, by equal contributions to a fund raised for the purpose, made possible the meetings of this planning committee: Messrs. Edward E. Ayer, Albert J. Beveridge, Hiram Bingham, Clarence M. Burton, Fairfax Harrison, William V. Kellen, Dwight W. Morrow, Conyers Read, John D. Rockefeller, Jr., and Henry D. Sharpe.

Brief Account of the Enterprise

After various deliberations, calculations, and studies, including studies of the great repertories of national biography published or in progress in other lands, the committee made its report to the Council at its annual meeting in January 1924. It is not inappropriate to quote from the report some passages that show upon what principles it was intended that the work should be conducted. The conclusions were:

"(1) That arrangements with any publishers should be deferred until money for the work of compilation was assured.

"(2) That the title should be *Dictionary of American Biography.*

"(3) That the character of the compilation should be kept up as nearly as possible to the level maintained in the *Dictionary of National Biography*; that the articles should be based as largely as possible on original sources; should be the product of fresh work; should eschew rhetoric, sentiment, and coloring matter generally, yet include careful characterization; should be free from the influence of partisan, local, or family prepossessions, striving to the utmost for impartial and objective treatment; should study compression and terseness; and should be written as largely as possible by the persons most specifically qualified, though the minor notices should be prepared 'in the office.' It was agreed that references to sources of information should be appended to the articles.

"(4) That living persons should be excluded; that in the main the compilation should be confined to American citizens, or, in the colonial period, to those having a corresponding position."

The plan as it finally emanated from the committee contemplated that about 15,000 persons should be treated, in twenty volumes of about 15,000 pages; that three volumes should be published each year, so that, allowing three years for preliminary preparations, the enterprise should be completed in ten years from the beginning of actual work; and that the editorial headquarters should be in Washington, where the work could draw upon the resources and liberality of the Library of Congress. It was calculated that the cost of preparing and editing the total manuscript, in the manner desired, would be $500,000. At the completion of the work in 1936, it may be noted that sketches of 13,633 persons have been published, in twenty volumes of more than 11,000,000 words, and that the last copy was in the hands of the printers ten years and seven months from the beginning of the enterprise, the last volume being published about two months later. The cost was a little more than $650,000.

The labors of the planning committee thus concluded in 1924, it fell to its chairman, who happened also to be a member of the Council's committee on ways and means, to find the half-million. The assignment seemed formidable, but, by one man's generosity and public spirit, was made unexpectedly easy. On the suggestion of Professor Turner, recourse was had to the publisher of *The New York Times*, Adolph S. Ochs, a man always ready to take a foremost part in all good works. The chairman invoked the good offices of his friend Dr. John H. Finley of *The Times*, who declared his belief that his chief's mind was ripe for the undertaking of another great public service, even one of the magnitude contemplated. One not very long letter and one brief interview sufficed. Mr. Ochs's rapid imagination saw at once the importance and public value of the service proposed, and his generosity rose at once to meet the opportunity. He immediately agreed that The New York Times Company should, in each year for ten years, advance fifty thousand dollars for the preparation and editing of the *Dictionary*, exclusive of any costs of printing and publication, which were to be arranged for by the Council with any publisher approved by *The Times*. Mr. Ochs, it would be needless to say to those who knew him, never sought any control, in the slightest particular, over anything that might appear in the *Dictionary*, and pointedly avoided responsibility for its contents. It is impossible not to lament that he should not have lived to see the completion of an enterprise so important, we hope, in the history of American letters, and so generously supported by his beneficence.

Brief Account of the Enterprise

On Dec. 6, 1924, at a special meeting of the American Council of Learned Societies held in the council room of *The New York Times*, an agreement under which the *Dictionary* has ever since been conducted was concluded between the Council and *The Times.* The agreement provided for a Committee of Management, consisting of seven persons, four of whom, including the chairman, should be appointed by the Council, and two, including the treasurer, by *The Times*, while the seventh should be the editor, to be chosen by the first six. It was provided also that the first volume should be published within three and a half years from the beginning of work, and that the royalties received by the Council from the publisher should be paid over to The Times Company till its advances had been repaid. The Council appointed to the Committee of Management Dr. J. Franklin Jameson, chairman, Professor Frederic L. Paxson, Carl Van Doren of the *Century Magazine*, and Charles Warren, formerly assistant attorney-general of the United States. *The Times* appointed Dr. John H. Finley and Mrs. Arthur H. Sulzberger (Iphigene Ochs Sulzberger). At a meeting held on Mar. 21, 1925, the Committee so constituted voted that the editorship of the *Dictionary* should be offered to Professor Allen Johnson of Yale University, commended to them and to all by his high reputation for scholarship in American history, his ability as a writer, and his distinguished success in the editing of the *Chronicles of America.* At the time of his election he was returning westward from the Orient, and the effort to correspond with him and, after his acceptance, to secure his release from Yale University, was attended with so much delay that it was not until Feb. 1, 1926, that his period of editorship formally began.

Meanwhile, Dr. Johnson had begun those fruitful and widespread consultations, as to subjects and as to writers, to which the *Dictionary* owes so much. Active interest in the new undertaking was manifested in many quarters, and much helpfulness encountered. Headquarters were established in the Hill Building in Washington, and Dr. Johnson began work, with the immediate editorial assistance of Dr. Harris E. Starr. In July 1927 a contract for printing and publishing was signed by the Committee of Management with the firm of Charles Scribner's Sons, whose helpfulness has run far beyond any contractual relations, and the first volume of the long-awaited *Dictionary* was published on Nov. 8, 1928. The occasion was celebrated by a dinner on Nov. 13 at the Hotel Roosevelt in New York, at which the generosity of Mr. Charles Scribner enabled the Council to act as host to nearly two hundred distinguished representatives of literature, learning, art, and science, and at which appropriate honor was paid to Mr. Ochs. Messages of congratulation were received from President Coolidge and other eminent Americans, and from the British Academy, the Institut de France, the six leading German and Austrian academies, and the Italian National Academic Union. It is believed that all who that evening heard Dr. Johnson's exposition of his ideals and policy in the conduct of the *Dictionary* were convinced that its direction had fallen into the right hands.

Another exposition of the principles on which Dr. Johnson conducted his work is to be found in his introduction to that first volume. It is not superfluous to quote here a paragraph from that introduction which sets forth a trait which any steady reader of the *Dictionary* will hardly have failed to observe, the catholicity with which its range has been extended, beyond the limits observable in most European repertories of the sort, to the inclusion of all the varied human elements that have made this composite America.

"Earlier collections of biographies stressed, naturally enough, the lives of soldiers, statesmen, and clergymen whose conspicuousness, aside from their services, made them objects of interest. Physical science, however, has increased immeasurably the importance of the engineer, the technician, and the chemist in modern warfare; the new social sciences have bred ministering and administrative agents who now share the cure of souls; and even politicians now recognize the important rôle of the statistician and the economist in law-making. The modern age with its greater complexity and dependence upon new arts and sciences has brought into view less spectacular, and possibly less heroic, but certainly not less significant, figures. Within a half-century, industry, science, the fine arts, and literature have produced men and women whose special significance is not indicated by such traditional designations as merchant, naturalist, artist, and author. The currents of American life and expression have both widened and deepened."

Dr. Johnson conducted the enterprise for almost exactly five years. The *Dictionary* is indebted in the highest degree to his devoted labors, his ripe judgment, his literary taste, and his fixed determination that the highest practicable standards of accuracy, truthfulness, and just portraiture should be maintained. His sense of the pressure of the work upon a constitution never robust had caused the Committee of Management to associate with him as editor on July 15, 1929, Professor Dumas Malone, then of the University of Virginia. Therefore when, on the evening of Jan. 18, 1931, an accident in the streets of Washington suddenly ended Dr. Johnson's life, it was possible for the work of the *Dictionary* to go on without interruption, under the direction of his junior colleague. On Feb. 2, 1931, Dr. Malone was formally elected sole editor, becoming a member of the Committee of Management, and the title of associate editor was conferred on Dr. Starr. Both have continued with the enterprise until its end. Volumes I–III were published under the editorship of Dr. Johnson, Volumes IV–VII under the editorship of Dr. Johnson and Dr. Malone, Volumes VIII–XX under that of Dr. Malone.

II

From the time that the plans of the *Dictionary* were first outlined, there has been continuity in its policy. The work of the editors has overlapped at so many points and in so many volumes that it is practically indistinguishable. However, as a rough approximation of the division of labors, it may be pointed out that up to July 15, 1929, when the present editor became connected with the enterprise, Dr. Johnson, besides creating a staff and directing the fundamentally important task of compiling the original list of names, had assigned almost half the articles, approximately the equivalent of nine volumes. During the next year and a half the work of making assignments to contributors proceeded with increased momentum, under two editors, provision being made for approximately six more volumes. Approximately five volumes were assigned after Dr. Johnson's death.

The securing of articles from contributors, which was properly regarded as the major editorial task during the first years of the enterprise, was accompanied with innumerable problems and complexities but proceeded rather more rapidly than had been anticipated. On the other hand, the preparation of these articles for press proved considerably more difficult than had been expected, partly because of their diversity and unevenness, and greatly delayed publication. The system of checking and literary editing that was instituted by Dr. Johnson was greatly extended by the present editor, who has borne the chief responsibility in the matter of publication.

The staff of the *Dictionary* from the beginning has been close-knit, with the greatest possible centralization of supervision and responsibility, and, in proportion to the size of the undertaking, has always been small. During ten and a half years approximately fifty persons have been members of the organization in one capacity or another, but the number at any given time has never exceeded fourteen or fifteen all told. Of the editorial group, Dr. Harris E. Starr, the present associate editor, has served longest. Joining the staff on Apr. 1, 1926, he shared with Dr. Johnson the task of compiling the original lists of subjects and contributors, and rendered invaluable aid in the work of assigning articles and, later, of preparing manuscripts for press. Furthermore, he has written more sketches (342), chiefly of educators and clergymen, than any other contributor. A generous share of credit for the establishment of the forms and usage of the work belongs to Dr. Ernest Sutherland Bates (Jan. 1, 1927–July 1, 1929), the first literary editor and also the author of 74 articles, chiefly on philosophic and literary figures. Second only to Dr. Starr in the number of sketches contributed is George H. Genzmer (335), more than seven years an assistant editor (Aug. 1, 1927–Sept. 1, 1934), whose articles on literary and miscellaneous figures have attracted the attention of many reviewers. Other assistant editors of fairly long service who were chiefly writers were Dr. John D. Wade (Oct. 1, 1927–July 31, 1928) and Frank Monaghan (Sept. 1, 1928–Sept. 30, 1929). Similar service was performed by W. J. Ghent (Feb. 1, 1927–Jan. 31, 1928) before the title of assistant editor was formally created.

It was originally estimated that approximately one-sixth of the articles in the *Dictionary* would be written by members of the staff, but the latter have actually contributed less than one-tenth. Within a few years it became apparent that greater reliance than had been expected would have to be placed on outside and often occasional contributors. The managerial tasks of the chief editors proved so exacting that, to their great disappointment, their personal contributions, while not unimportant, have been numerically slight. Also, it soon appeared that the funds available for staff purposes would have to be concentrated to a greater degree on the preparation of materials for press. Accordingly, the number of writing editors steadily declined and all later accessions to the staff consisted of library assistants and literary editors. During most of its life as an organization the *Dictionary* has trained its own workers.

Miss Eleanor R. Dobson (July 1, 1926 to the end) has had more to do with the preparation of materials for press than any other person. She was the first library assistant, and after the retirement of Dr. Bates was placed in charge of the literary editing, bearing the title of assistant editor from June 1929. Associated with her in this work were Miss Mildred B. Palmer (July 1, 1929–Nov. 30, 1934), who became an assistant editor on May 17, 1931, and Miss Dorothy Greenwald (June 18, 1934, to the end). Dr. Katharine E. Crane (Aug. 1, 1931, to the end), who has combined checking and editing and contributed a number of articles, became an assistant editor on Feb. 15, 1934. The proof for Volumes I, II, and part of III, IV, was read by H. W. Howard Knott (June 1, 1928–Apr. 30, 1930), who also contributed a large number of articles, chiefly on legal subjects. Mr. Knott, who was an assistant editor, died in September 1930 after a long illness. The rest of the proof for Volumes III, IV, was read by several persons, chiefly Mrs. Ethel B. Simonson (Jan. 1, 1929, to the end). The proof of the sixteen remaining volumes was read by Mrs. Simonson, with practically no assistance.

More than a score have served at one time or another as library assistants, working in the Library of Congress, the generosity and kindness of whose officials has been unbounded. Those of longest service were: Frank E. Ross (July 1, 1927–June 30, 1933), Miss Helen C. Boatfield (July 7, 1930, to end), Miss Katherine E. Greenwood (Feb. 1, 1931, to end), Miss Louise P. Blodget (Aug. 1, 1931–Feb. 29, 1936), Mrs. Margaret S. Ermarth (June 1, 1933, to end), who served during most of this period also as an editorial assistant, Miss Eleanor Poland (summer of 1932, and Mar. 1, 1934, to end), and Mrs. Catherine P. Mitchell (Mar. 1, 1930–July 15, 1932). Of the members of the clerical staff the services of Miss Ellen D. Fawcett (Feb. 8, 1926, to end), who from Sept. 1, 1927, was executive secretary, have been most memorable. Many of these persons have written articles, but their invaluable services have been chiefly anonymous and abundantly deserve mention here.

The cooperative nature of the *Dictionary* is nowhere more strikingly revealed than in the lists of contributors. To the original edition of the *Dictionary of National Biography*, which contains 29,120 notices and 27,195 substantive articles, 653 persons contributed. The *Dictionary of American Biography* contains 13,633 articles, less than half as many as its famous British predecessor, but its contributors number 2243, more than three times as many. So, in proportion to its size, the *Dictionary of American Biography* has six or seven times as many contributors. Coming from every one of the states of the Union and the District of Columbia, and from several foreign countries, these include, besides members of college and university faculties and other technical scholars, journalists, free-lance writers, antiquarians, lawyers, physicians, soldiers—representatives or students of all the diverse groups that are included in the *Dictionary* itself. Many of these contributors have died during the course of the work and themselves appear as the subjects of articles. Any distinction between them would appear invidious, but mention should be made of Dr. George P. Merrill, who aided in the preparation of the original list of geologists and before his death wrote more than 70 sketches.

Next to Dr. Starr and Mr. Genzmer, Carl W. Mitman of the Smithsonian Institution, United States National Museum, Washington, has written the largest number of articles (328), chiefly on inventors. Others who have contributed more than 100 articles, besides Mr. Knott, Mr. Ghent, and Dr. Wade, all members of the staff at one time or another, are: Professor Richard J. Purcell, of the Catholic University of America; Professor Allan Westcott, of the United States Naval Academy, Annapolis; William B. Shaw, formerly of the *Review of Reviews;* William H. Downes, formerly art critic of the *Boston Evening Transcript;* James Truslow Adams; Lieutenant-Colonel Thomas M. Spaulding and Colonel James M. Phalen of the United States Army. Approximately thirty other persons contributed upwards of fifty articles each. The number who have contributed twenty-five or more is naturally much greater, but a surprisingly large part of the work has been done by occasional contributors. Some of these are mentioned below, in the paragraphs that deal with the longer articles.

Early in the history of the enterprise the original plan was modified so that each volume of the *Dictionary* should consist of approximately 675 articles, ranging in length from 500 to 10,000 words, and totaling 500,000 words. The average of 675 articles has been maintained, but the average number of words in each volume has been more than 550,000, making a total of over 11,000,000 words. The work was planned as a collection of biographies, not as a register of names, and it was thought that persons about whom 500 words could not appropriately be written should be omitted altogether. While brief notices have been avoided, in practice some sketches, like many of those of Indians, have fallen below the minimum. In five cases, also, the maximum of 10,000 has been considerably exceeded. The names are given below in alphabetical order, though the longest of the articles is that on George Washington (16,500 words).

BENJAMIN FRANKLIN, by Prof. Carl L. Becker
THOMAS JEFFERSON, by Dr. Dumas Malone
ABRAHAM LINCOLN, by Prof. J. G. Randall
GEORGE WASHINGTON, by Dr. John C. Fitzpatrick
WOODROW WILSON, by Prof. Charles Seymour

These have seemed the Americans requiring most extensive treatment. The editors, however, have had no thought of estimating greatness on any strict arithmetical scale, or of attempting to establish any exact order of eminence. The space given to any particular person reflects in general the editorial judgment of his importance, but many other factors have had to be reckoned with. Among the more obvious of these are the length of any particular career, the controversies that have accompanied it, the amount of historical background that must be painted in, the new materials that have appeared, and the conciseness or prolixity of the author, the latter of which the editors have sometimes been unable to overcome. Obviously it is impossible to equate or compare in any arithmetical sense an artist and a statesman, a soldier and a philosopher. Even the sense of scale, which has come to be second nature with the editors, was itself the result of trial and error. It now appears that the earlier volumes, especially the first, are somewhat out of scale with the others, and many of the articles in them, if reconsidered, would be curtailed.

For these and other reasons a list of major articles in all the volumes in the exact order of length would have little value. Besides the five already mentioned, it seems sufficient to list below in alphabetical order the articles which run from approximately 5,000 to 10,000 words.

Charles Francis Adams (1807–1886), by Worthington C. Ford
Henry Brooks Adams, by Dr. Allen Johnson
John Adams, by Worthington C. Ford
John Quincy Adams, by Worthington C. Ford
Samuel Adams, by Prof. Carl L. Becker
Jean Louis Rodolphe Agassiz, by President David Starr Jordan and Jessie Knight Jordan
Nelson Wilmarth Aldrich, by Prof. Nathaniel W. Stephenson
Benedict Arnold, by Dr. Randolph G. Adams
George Bancroft, by M. A. DeWolfe Howe
Henry Ward Beecher, by Dr. Harris E. Starr
James Gillespie Blaine, by Prof. Carl Russell Fish
William Jennings Bryan, by Prof. John Spencer Bassett and Dr. Allen Johnson
William Cullen Bryant, by Prof. Allan Nevins
James Buchanan, by Prof. Carl Russell Fish
Aaron Burr, by Prof. Isaac J. Cox
John Caldwell Calhoun, by Prof. Ulrich B. Phillips
Andrew Carnegie, by Burton J. Hendrick
Salmon Portland Chase, by Prof. J. G. Randall
Henry Clay, by Prof. E. Merton Coulter
Samuel Langhorne Clemens, by Dr. Carl Van Doren
Stephen Grover Cleveland, by Prof. Frederic L. Paxson
James Fenimore Cooper, by Dr. Carl Van Doren
John Singleton Copley, by Frederick W. Coburn
Caleb Cushing, by Dr. Claude M. Fuess
Jefferson Davis, by Prof. Nathaniel W. Stephenson
Stephen Arnold Douglas, by Dr. Allen Johnson
Mary Morse Baker Eddy, by Dr. Allen Johnson
Jonathan Edwards, by Prof. Francis A. Christie
Charles William Eliot, by Prof. Ralph Barton Perry
Ralph Waldo Emerson, by Dr. Mark Van Doren
Abraham Alfonse Albert Gallatin, by Prof. David S. Muzzey
Elbridge Gerry, by Prof. Samuel Eliot Morison
Ulysses Simpson Grant, by Lieut.-Col. Christian A. Bach and Prof. Frederic L. Paxson
Horace Greeley, by Prof. Allan Nevins
Alexander Hamilton, by Prof. Allan Nevins
Warren Gamaliel Harding, by Prof. Allan Nevins
William Rainey Harper, by Prof. Paul Shorey
Nathaniel Hawthorne, by Dr. Carl Van Doren
John Milton Hay, by Prof. A. L. P. Dennis
Patrick Henry, by Prof. William E. Dodd
Oliver Wendell Holmes, by M. A. DeWolfe Howe

WASHINGTON IRVING, by Prof. Stanley T. Williams
ANDREW JACKSON, by Prof. Thomas P. Abernethy
HENRY JAMES (1843–1916), by Dr. Carl Van Doren
WILLIAM JAMES, by Prof. Ralph Barton Perry
ANDREW JOHNSON, by Prof. St. George L. Sioussat
JOHN LA FARGE, by Royal Cortissoz
ROBERT MARION LA FOLLETTE, by Prof. Frederic L. Paxson
BENJAMIN HENRY LATROBE, by Fiske Kimball
ROBERT EDWARD LEE, by Dr. Douglas S. Freeman
JAMES RUSSELL LOWELL, by M. A. DeWolfe Howe
JAMES MADISON (1750/51–1836), by Prof. Julius W. Pratt
JOHN MARSHALL, by Prof. Edward S. Corwin
JAMES MONROE, by Prof. Dexter Perkins
JOHN PIERPONT MORGAN, by Albert W. Atwood
THOMAS PAINE, by Prof. Crane Brinton
EDGAR ALLAN POE, by Hervey Allen
THEODORE ROOSEVELT, by Prof. Frederic L. Paxson
JOSIAH ROYCE, by Prof. Ralph Barton Perry
AUGUSTUS SAINT-GAUDENS, by Royal Cortissoz
WINFIELD SCOTT, by Lieut.-Col. William A. Ganoe
WILLIAM HENRY SEWARD, by Prof. Dexter Perkins
ALEXANDER HAMILTON STEPHENS, by Prof. Ulrich B. Phillips
JOSEPH STORY, by Prof. George E. Woodbine
CHARLES SUMNER, by Prof. George H. Haynes
WILLIAM HOWARD TAFT, by Henry F. Pringle
HENRY DAVID THOREAU, by Prof. Raymond William Adams and Dr. Henry Seidel Canby
DANIEL WEBSTER, by Prof. Arthur C. Cole
JAMES ABBOTT MCNEILL WHISTLER, by Royal Cortissoz
GEORGE WHITEFIELD, by Dr. Harris E. Starr
WALT WHITMAN, by Dr. Mark Van Doren

It may be argued that the greatest service of the *Dictionary* has been rendered in connection with shorter articles, which because of their number cannot be specifically mentioned here. Many of these add to the roster of memorable Americans names that have been overlooked hitherto, or little noted. A few minor but well-known names have been admitted because it was thought that a considerable number of persons would look for them, but in general there has been insistence on some significant contribution, achievement, or activity, whether or not this may have been long obscured. The discovery of these forgotten men and women, who upon inquiry have seemed significant, has been made possible only by a cooperation on the part of contributors and advisers that has surpassed even the most sanguine anticipation. It cannot be expected that the choice of names will meet with unanimous approval. No two men or groups of men would ever make exactly the same decisions. Furthermore, since the number of articles was determined almost in the beginning, the question of including certain names unavoidably involved that of omitting others. It is to be hoped that few really important persons have been left out and that the selection that was made is a truly representative one.

Until Jan. 1, 1935, when the lists for all the remaining volumes were closed, no definite deadline was ever established for admission to the *Dictionary*. The only requirement was that there must be time enough, after a person became eligible through death, for an article on him to be prepared and inserted in its proper place. Accordingly, until the last year and a half, part of the editor's task was the reading of current obituaries, from which hundreds of names were added. As a rule it may be assumed that, because of practical necessities, the list for any particular volume had to be closed approximately a year before the date of publication of that volume, though in the beginning, and in some cases later, the interval was shorter. The following table, showing among other things the dates of publication of all the volumes, will be useful in figuring the terminal date for admission to any one of them.

Vol.		*Contributors*	*Articles*	*Pages*	*Date of Publication*
I	Abbe—Barrymore	296	678	660	Nov. 8, 1928
II	Barsotti—Brazer	291	683	613	May 2, 1929
III	Brearly—Chandler	313	676	618	Nov. 15, 1929
IV	Chanfrau—Cushing	289	721	637	Feb. 26, 1930
V	Cushman—Eberle	261	691	616	June 20, 1930
VI	Echols—Fraser	262	660	604	Feb. 20, 1931
VII	Fraunces—Grimké	287	677	636	Sept. 21, 1931
VIII	Grinnell—Hibbard	324	663	612	Jan. 29, 1932
IX	Hibben—Jarvis	362	673	626	June 20, 1932
X	Jasper—Larkin	318	677	617	Jan. 20, 1933
XI	Larned—MacCracken	354	665	620	June 16, 1933
XII	McCrady—Millington	368	698	647	Nov. 24, 1933
XIII	Mills—Oglesby	415	706	649	Apr. 12, 1934
XIV	Oglethorpe—Platner	364	674	648	Sept. 14, 1934
XV	Platt—Roberdeau	363	687	647	Jan. 25, 1935
XVI	Robert—Seward	353	675	621	June 12, 1935
XVII	Sewell—Stevenson	363	682	636	Nov. 20, 1935
XVIII	Steward—Trowbridge	376	690	657	Jan. 31, 1936
XIX	Troye—Wentworth	363	680	659	Sept. 11, 1936
XX	Werden—Zunser	360	677	662	Dec. 10, 1936
		2243	13,633	12,685	

Unavoidably the policy of adding the names of persons recently deceased has worked to the disadvantage of those falling in the early part of the alphabet, and to the advantage of those in the latter. It has always been hoped that a supplementary volume, bringing the entire list to a definite terminal date, would redress the balance. For the sake of statistical completeness, figures from such a volume should be added to those given below, showing the distribution of the articles among the different letters of the alphabet. Interesting comparisons can be made between this table and the paragraph in "A Statistical Account," first published as a preface to the last volume of the original issue of the *Dictionary of National Biography,* showing the alphabetical distribution of notable names in Great Britain.

A	464	J	347	S	1432
B	1301	K	325	T	434
C	1014	L	662	U	34
D	632	M	1187	V	171
E	283	N	256	W	366
F	501	O	185	X	1
G	667	P	847	Y	55
H	1097	Q	25	Z	28
I	74	R	652		

Brief Account of the Enterprise

It has already been stated that the total expenses of the *Dictionary of American Biography* were a little more than $650,000, whereas the original estimate was $500,000. The additional cost has been chiefly due to the unexpected amount of time and money that it has been necessary to expend on the checking and editing of articles prior to publication. In so far as comparisons can be made with similar undertakings, the average cost of $32,500 per volume seems moderate, and an error of only a little more than five per cent in the calculation of the requisite time for the completion of the work seems slight. The additional financial needs were met by a further subvention of $32,500 from *The New York Times*, by a corresponding contribution from the publishers, and by appropriations made by the American Council of Learned Societies from its general funds and from special grants of the Rockefeller Foundation and the Carnegie Corporation.

From the beginning, those who have been charged with the management of the enterprise have tried to make the *Dictionary* in the broadest sense a national institution, identified with no one locality and no single group, except the associated scholars who have sponsored it, but comprehending all sects and sections, races, classes, and parties. It is hoped not only that this large collection of biographies will contribute to a better understanding of the chief actors on the stage of American history, but also that this vast common undertaking has furthered, and will continue to further, the spirit of scholarly cooperation throughout the land.

MEMOIR

OF

ADOLPH SIMON OCHS

March 12, 1858–April 8, 1935

PREFIXED TO THE FINAL VOLUME

IN THE ORIGINAL TWENTY-VOLUME ISSUE

Adolph Simon Ochs was born in Cincinnati, Ohio, the second and eldest surviving child of Julius [*q.v.*] and Bertha (Levy) Ochs. Both his parents were German, coming from well-connected Jewish families. The father, from Fürth near Nürnberg, had come to America in 1845; he engaged in teaching and business at various places, mostly in the South, and on Feb. 28, 1855, was married at Nashville, Tenn., to Miss Levy, who had been a refugee from Rhenish Bavaria after the revolution of 1848. This brilliant and forceful woman was to have a predominant influence in shaping the character of her son. Despite his long Southern residence and his wife's Southern sympathies, Julius Ochs served in the Civil War as a captain in the Union army; but after the war he removed his family to Knoxville, Tenn. The town, as he had foreseen, had a future, but Julius Ochs, cultured and impractical, failed to prosper with it, though he enjoyed the general esteem of his fellow citizens. His son Adolph had to go to work at the age of eleven as an office boy on the Knoxville *Chronicle*. Thereafter he worked pretty steadily; he got some local schooling, but as he afterward put it, "the printing office was my high school and university." It might be added that his parents were no bad substitutes for a more formal education.

In his teens Adolph Ochs tried various jobs in various places, but always came back to Knoxville and the newspaper business. Yet, he used to say in later years, he might never have made it his life work if, as printer's devil on the *Chronicle,* he had not had to work at night, and if his way home had not taken him past a graveyard. A young boy in a region not free from superstition, he preferred to stay in the office after his work was done till the foreman of the composing room could walk home with him; and, staying, he learned the newspaper business from the ground up. He had practised all its branches—news, business, and mechanical—when at the age of nineteen he moved to Chattanooga to take a job on a new paper there. This paper soon failed and its older rival, the *Chattanooga Times,* was on the verge of failure too. But Adolph Ochs foresaw the possibilities of Chattanooga, and of a paper which would print the news instead of catering to private interests. With $250 of borrowed money he bought the controlling interest in the *Times,* assuming its debts, and began his career as a newspaper publisher (1878) before he was old enough to vote.

The *Chattanooga Times* that he published from then until his death was the same kind of paper as *The New York Times* that he subsequently produced—"clean, dignified, and trustworthy," he described it in his New York salutatory in 1896; and to prove that such a paper could be made to earn its way, in the ragged-edge conditions of small-town journalism at the end of the seventies, was perhaps a greater feat than what he subsequently accomplished in New York. But it did earn its way; Chattanooga grew, and the publisher of the *Times* not only grew with it, but had more to do than anybody else with promoting its growth. Through nearly forty years of subsequent residence in New York, he remained a loyal Chattanoogan; and none of his public or academic honors pleased him so much as the title of Citizen Emeritus conferred on him in 1928 by the city where he had commenced his career half a century before.

He was married on Feb. 28, 1883, to Effie Miriam, daughter of Rabbi Isaac M. Wise [*q.v.*] of Cincinnati, the great leader of Reformed Judaism. To them some years later was born a daughter, Iphigene Bertha, who was married in 1917 to Arthur Hays Sulzberger. The Ochs household became increasingly a center of hospitality, for as Chattanooga grew the town attracted eminent visitors from all over the country, and by general consent the publisher of the *Times* was deputed to entertain them. He thus made friendships among men of national prominence which were to be valuable in his subsequent venture in New York; and further made himself known through his chairmanship (1891–94) of the Southern Associated Press, and later affiliation with the old (Western) Associated Press, from which developed the present nation-wide institution of that name.

Early in 1896, after an offer of the business managership of the New York *Mercury* had come to nothing, he was advised by a reporter on *The New York Times,* who had met him on a trip to Chattanooga some years before, of an opportunity to buy that paper. *The Times,* once prosperous and powerful, had been running down for years; by 1896 it had a circulation of only 9,000 and was losing $1,000 a day. A company organized by its editor, Charles R. Miller [*q.v.*], and some of his associates, which had bought it in 1893, was facing bankruptcy; and no New York newspaper executive believed that *The Times* could be salvaged. Ochs, upon investigation, thought otherwise; and after refusing an invitation to manage the paper for other men worked out a reorganization through which he became publisher, with full control, on Aug. 18, 1896 (*History, post,* pp. 178–86).

The plan was an ingenious harmonization of the interests of old and new investors, but for the new publisher it represented a tremendous gamble. If he succeeded in making the paper pay for three consecutive years he was to become its majority stockholder; but meanwhile he was sacrificing an assured position for a venture generally regarded as hopeless; he was leaving Chattanooga where he had been a great man to become a freshman in New York, and assume command over famous men who to the eyes of Chattanooga had seemed beings of a higher order (*Ibid.,* p. 206); and the $75,000 he had invested was mostly borrowed, for the bulk of his Chattanooga profits had been sunk in a premature real-estate boom. With a moribund property, a discouraged staff, and little working capital, he had to compete with papers either prosperous or backed by large fortunes; his prospects seemed so dark that it was widely believed that he was only a "front" for somebody else—perhaps friends of President Cleveland, with whose policies both he and the editors of *The Times* were in accord. Twenty years passed before he had completely dispelled the myth of outside influence on the paper which had been under his unrestricted control from the beginning.

To *The New York Times* he applied rigorously, in a situation which would have tempted a less scrupulous man to compromise, the principles he had practised in Chattanooga. He knew how to get out only one kind of paper, the reflection of his own personality; a strictly "news" paper, as he called it, in which editorial opinion was subordinate and the news was treated with a freedom from personal and partisan bias by no means general in those days. Nor was his exclusion of advertising which seemed to him fraudulent or improper, at a time when he needed all the advertising he could get, a common practice of the nineties. The eventual success of *The Times* invited imitation, and had a powerful influence in raising the standards both of news and of advertising; what he began to do in 1896, when it was unusual and hazardous, is what all respectable newspapers do today. But it was what he could not help doing, whether it succeeded or not; it seemed to him so obvious that he never fully appreciated the genius which enabled him to prove that decency and integrity could be profitable.

The profit was slow in coming, at first; *The Times* made headway, but was still "in the red"; there was a time when each week's payroll was a problem. Years later, when one of his executives left to become the proprietor of another paper, Ochs advised him against it—wisely, as the event proved. "You'll owe millions," he said, "and you're not used to it; you won't sleep of nights. I could never have got through my first years on *The Times* if I hadn't been used to being in debt, and to getting out of it." Equally serious problems, in the early years, were the belief of one or two advertisers that in a struggling paper they were buying more than advertising space; and one or two offers of large advertising or circulation revenue from political interests, which had to be refused for fear it might seem, to the offerers or to others, that they were getting a mortgage on *The Times*. Again and again he seemed to face a choice between compromise and disaster; but he never compromised.

New York morning journalism was then dominated by the fiercely competing "yellows," the *World* and the morning *Journal* (now the *New York American*), with enormous circulations built up at a sales price of one cent when the other papers sold for three. The much misinterpreted slogan, "All the News That's Fit to Print," which *The Times* has carried since Oct. 25, 1896, was really no more than a notice that *The Times* under its new management would continue to eschew the sensationalism of the "yellows." That meant no typographical pyrotechnics, no comic strips, no emphasis on crime and salacity. Ochs's definition of fitness was gradually somewhat modified as that old rivalry faded into history, but it remained a pervasive influence; twenty years later, the night city editor would tell a rewrite man, "Here's an incest story. Keep it clean."

Before *The Times,* slowly advancing, had found sufficient favor with readers whom the *World* and the *Journal* repelled, it was almost wrecked by the war with Spain. The tremendous expense of special correspondence entailed by a war conducted largely as a field for newspaper enterprise was beyond *The Times,* which was not yet breaking even; and the concomitant decline in advertising had brought the paper almost on the rocks by October 1898. Some of its executives, in the hope of emphasizing the appeal to a "quality public," proposed raising the price from three cents to five; whereupon Ochs had his most brilliant inspiration, and took his greatest gamble, by deciding instead to reduce it to one cent. At that time the price of a newspaper had a doctrinal implication; one cent was the badge of shame, the symbol of the "yellows," and he knew that if he went to that price people would be afraid that *The Times* was turning "yellow" too. But he was convinced, in the teeth of unanimous expert opinion, that many people bought the *World* and the *Journal* only because they were cheap, and would buy *The Times* instead if they could get it at the same price. He was right; within a year the circulation had trebled and the paper was making money; and the rest of his career is only a record of steadily increasing influence and prosperity.

The increase might not have been steady, however, if he had not treated *The Times* as a trust rather than a property, not only giving it his unremitting attention but putting most of his profits back into expansion. To the end of his life, unless out of town or ill, he was at the office every day, actively directing the paper. He retained ownership of the *Chattanooga Times,* directed by his brother Milton and his brother-in-law Harry C. Adler, and subsequently by his nephew Adolph Shelby Ochs; from 1902 to 1913 he owned the Philadelphia *Public Ledger,* edited by his brother George (see sketch of George W. Ochs Oakes); once or twice he contemplated buying other papers in New York, but eventually came to the conclusion that *The Times* was job enough for any man. His one serious outside professional interest was the Associated Press, which he served as director and member of the executive committee from its reorganization in 1900 till his death; in its councils no man had greater influence. He never held nor sought public office, except for a brief service on the Chattanooga school board in the eighties; and though, especially in his later years, he gave much time to various philanthropies and public causes, *The Times* remained his primary and predominant occupation.

The Ochs doctrine of news was implemented after 1904 by the genius of C. V. Van Anda, who as managing editor "seemed to get out *The Times* as if he were its only reader" (Alva Johnston, *The New Yorker,* Sept. 7, 1935, p. 28). Whatever interested Van Anda, which was everything from prize-fighting to Egyptology and the tensor calculus, became news as he played it up, and other papers had to keep pace with *The Times.* Yet for all Van Anda's immense contribution, and the contributions of other able men, *The Times* remained Ochs's personality reflected in print; and the men who had served it both before and after 1896 never doubted that he had been the single difference between failure and success. For years he was the least conspicuous, in the public eye, of New York newspaper owners; he sought no social or political career, and never used his paper for personal advancement. But that it was universally known to be his paper was proved by the fact that people who found fault with it always blamed him personally, and never anybody else.

A notable instance was an editorial (Sept. 16, 1918) favoring a cautious hospitality to the first

Austrian peace proposal. In retrospect it is unexceptionable, but in a hysterical time it provoked a hurricane of fury; thousands of people, by mail or telegraph, abused Ochs personally as a traitor. In fact he had been in the country, and because of a faulty telephone connection did not know the content of the editorial till he saw it in the paper. Asked later why he had not instantly disavowed it, he said that as he had got the credit for some of the achievements of his editors it was only fair to take the blame for their mistakes; adding that nobody would have accepted a second-day disavowal as genuine, after all that uproar. The blend of generosity and shrewd insight is characteristic, but most men who had to endure what he was enduring then would have tried to disavow it (Elmer Davis, *The New Yorker,* Nov. 21, 1925, p. 11).

As the excellence of *The Times's* war news raised the paper to preëminence, and post-war issues emphasized its conservatism, he became the target of further attacks from liberals and radicals. The good that he had done was by that time an old story, it had become the commonplace of newspaper practice; it was perhaps only natural that the *advocatus diaboli* should have his turn. But it was the primacy of *The Times* that made Ochs the target, rather than other newspaper owners who were more conservative but less successful; indeed at that time he was much less conservative than his principal editors (as some of his critics must have known), and had had the experience of being angrily denounced as a Socialist—on somewhat inadequate grounds, to be sure—at his own council table, by one of his employees working for a modest weekly wage.

All these criticisms, from the temperate and informed comments of Silas Bent (*Strange Bedfellows,* 1928, ch. xv) and Benjamin Stolberg (*Atlantic Monthly,* December 1926) to the grotesque embroiderings of Upton Sinclair (*The Brass Check,* 1919; *The Crimes of the Times,* 1921) are essentially complaints that he had not made *The Times* the sort of paper the complainants would have made it in his place. Whatever their merit as polemic against conservative doctrines or the principle of private newspaper ownership, as criticism of him and his paper they amount only to the contention that Adolph S. Ochs should not have been Adolph S. Ochs, but somebody else. His personality was reflected not only in the excellences of *The Times,* but in its respect for things as they are. Faith in the existing order was natural to a man whom that order had permitted to struggle up, by industry and ability unaided by any special luck, from impecunious obscurity to wealth and fame; and if he afterward emphasized the industry rather than the ability, ascribing his success to such virtues as any boy might learn at his mother's knee, that was the natural working of a mind which was intuitive rather than reflective, and of a genuine under-assessment of his own exceptional talent.

He was temperamentally convinced that there was much to be said on both sides of most questions, and that the taking of a firm editorial stand was often unwise. Perhaps, as Bent suggests (*Strange Bedfellows,* p. 233), early experience in a small town where his readers were also his friends had taught him to get out "a paper that hurt nobody's feelings"; but his peculiar political position was a factor too. He had been a Southern Democrat but he was also a Cleveland Democrat by conviction, as were his principal editorial writers. From 1896 on the disciples of Cleveland seldom dominated the party, so Ochs gradually came to feel that the Democrats were most useful in opposition, and that the support of a conservative paper (except when Bryan was their candidate) might tend to stabilize them. But he also believed in holding up the hands of the existing administration, whenever possible; so *The Times* usually found itself supporting in office Republicans whom it had opposed in the campaign. There was logic in that, once you could manage to follow it; those who knew him could not agree with the view that his Democracy was the mere rationalization of a Southern habit.

He never wrote editorials, in New York; though he presided over the daily editorial council and gave editorial policy its general direction he left his editorial writers about as much freedom as any newspaper owner ever could who concerned himself with editorial policy at all—this despite the fact that *The Times* was a platform for editorial opinion which he himself had built. His editorial writers often disagreed with him, and not infrequently were permitted to set forth their views in his paper, to the exclusion of his own. This to be sure did not occur on major issues, but there his successive editors-in-chief, Charles R. Miller [*q.v.*] and Rollo Ogden, were in harmony with him; and it is hard to see that a newspaper owner is under moral obligation to hire men who disagree with him, and to encourage them to use his paper for the dissemination of doctrines which he hates.

His mind worked by flashes of insight rather than slow reasoning; no doubt the inspirations that went right (as not all of them did) were usually based, subconsciously, on thorough knowledge; but his greatest inspiration, the discernment of a one-cent public for *The Times* of

1898, seems even yet to have been pure clairvoyance. Slower-witted men could not understand him any more than he understood himself, but affection did not have to wait for understanding; he was always most approachable on a personal basis, and the essence of his immense personal charm was a profound kindliness. That he pensioned superannuated employees, after he was able to afford it, may have been mere justice, but most newspapers turn them out into the street; and in a business whose attitude toward white-collar labor retains the Bohemian traditions of an art, *The Times* became exemplary in security of tenure and decent conditions of employment.

Some of his coreligionists never forgave him his opposition to Zionism; he believed in Judaism as a religion, not as a separatist racial culture. But it was no perfunctory faith expressed merely in benefactions; it colored his whole life. In later years he was happiest at his summer home on Lake George, surrounded by his family and a circle of old friends; but he died, as perhaps he would have wished, on a visit to Chattanooga.

[He left no writings except occasional speeches, reprinted from the newspapers in pamphlet form; and a voluminous correspondence, as yet unedited, which has not been used in this memoir. His own view of his achievement was published in *The New York Times* on his twenty-fifth anniversary as publisher, Aug. 18, 1921, and in Elmer Davis, *History of The New York Times* (1921), pp. viii–xxii. Part II of the *History,* where it treats of issues and policies of his critical years in New York, embodies his own recollection, often in his own words. The obituary in *The Times,* Apr. 9, 1935, incorporates the reminiscences of many associates of both his earlier and his later life. Virtually everything else so far published about him is commentary and appraisal, not source material.] ELMER DAVIS.

ERRATA

In making this reprinting of the Dictionary of American Biography, such corrections as have so far come to the attention of the editors will be found in the following list.

VOLUME I, PART 1

ABBE TO BARRYMORE

Page 13, column 2, line 13
ABBOT, HENRY LARCOM: *after* in command *insert* during the illness of Lieut. R. S. Williamson

Page 25, column 1, line 34
ABBOTT, LYMAN: *for* editors *read* editor *and omit* and Lawson Valentine

Page 140, column 2, line 21
ALCOTT, AMOS BRONSON: *for* south *read* northwest

Page 143, column 1, line 29ff.
ALCOTT, WILLIAM ANDRUS: *after* RAMBLER *omit comma and* probably the first . . . in this country

Page 178, column 2, line 17
ALGER, HORATIO: *for* Jan. 13, 1834 *read* Jan. 13, 1832

Page 227, column 1, line 12
ALPHONSA, MOTHER: *omit* and last surviving

Page 231, column 2, line 12
ALTGELD, JOHN PETER: *omit* [*q.v.*]

Page 284, column 2, line 55
ANDREWS, CHRISTOPHER COLUMBUS: *after* 1864 *insert* although news of his promotion, Jan. 4, had not yet reached him

Page 308, column 2, line 30
ANGELL, JAMES BURRILL: *insert* [*q.v.*] *after* John F. Swift

Page 311, column 1, line 8
ANSHUTZ, THOMAS POLLOCK: *for* W. Glacken *read* William Glackens

Page 332, column 1, line 11
APPLETON, NATHANIEL WALKER: *for* 1774, after which *read* 1776; in August 1774

Page 338, column 2, line 31
ARCHDALE, JOHN: *after* (1779). *insert* There are Archdale papers in the Library of Congress

Page 354, column 1, line 47f.
ARMSTRONG, JOHN: *omit* was again a delegate in 1787–88, and

Page 355, column 1, line 48
For (1720–95) *read* (1717–1795) [*q.v.*]

Page 359, column 2, line 47
ARMSTRONG, SAMUEL CHAPMAN: *omit* at Punahou

Page 359, column 2, line 49
After BECKWORTH *insert* Later, when Edward Beckworth became principal of the older school at Punahou, Armstrong transferred to that institution. *In the same line for* The school *read* The Royal School

Page 364, column 2, line 37
ARNOLD, BENEDICT: *for* Erie *read* Ontario

Page 378, column 1, line 13f.
ARTHUR, TIMOTHY SHAY: *for* It achieved . . . and *read* In 1853 it became a monthly, the HOME MAGAZINE, and as ARTHUR'S HOME MAGAZINE

Page 397, column 2, line 31–39
ASTOR, JOHN JACOB: *omit* About this time . . . netted Astor $50,000.

Page 399, column 2, line 7f.
Omit comma and from which he graduated in 1842

Page 400, column 1, line 56f.
For He graduated . . . foreign travel *read* He was enrolled as a special student in Harvard College from 1884 to 1887 and then spent some time in foreign travel

Page 401, column 1, line 10f.
ASTOR, WILLIAM BACKHOUSE: *omit* and the younger brother of John Jacob Astor the second

Page 407, column 1, line 49ff.
ATKINSON, EDWARD: *for* and he foresaw . . . manufacturing industry *read* but not the expansion of cotton manufacturing, which the Exposition none the less helped to promote

Page 414, column 2, line 15ff.
ATLEE, WASHINGTON LEMUEL: *omit* His love for surgery . . . Berlin.

Page 467, column 2, line 38
BACKUS, AZEL: *for* Dec. 9, 1817 *read* Dec. 28, 1816

Errata

Page 498, column 1, line 30
BAILEY, JACOB WHITMAN: *for* the son of Rev. Isaac *read* the son of Isaac

Page 523, column 2, line 26f
BAKER, LAURENCE SIMMONS: *for* Mary (Wynn) Baker *read* Mary Wynn (Gregory) Baker

Page 539, column 1, line 41
BALDWIN, JOSEPH GLOVER: *for* II *read* IX

Page 573, column 1, line 4
BANGS, FRANCIS NEHEMIAH: *for* LIFE *read* LIFETIME

Page 573, column 2, line 50
BANGS, JOHN KENDRICK: *after* periodicals. *insert* For the first half year of its existence, 1889, he edited MUNSEY'S WEEKLY.

Page 573, column 2, line 51ff.
Omit and the same year . . . before the year was up

Page 600, column 2, line 24f.
BARKER, ALBERT SMITH: *for* Graduating . . . duty *read* He graduated from the Naval Academy in the class of 1863 but was ordered to duty in 1861. He served

Page 617, column 1, line 21
BARNARD, DANIEL DEWEY: *for* East Hartford, Conn. *read* Sheffield, Mass.

Page 649, column 2, line 52
BARRON, JAMES: *for* 1769 *read* Sept. 15, 1768

VOLUME I, PART 2

BARSOTTI TO BRAZER

Page 29, column 2, line 20
BARUCH, SIMON: *for* as appendicitis *read* as a perforated appendix

Page 29, column 2, line 22
After America *insert* to be recorded

Page 52, column 2, line 40f.
BATES, JOSHUA: *for* with the exception . . . and Van Buren *read* except for a period beginning in the Jackson administration and ending in the summer of 1843

Page 76, column 2, line 33 f.
BAYLOR, GEORGE: *for* was born . . . of Virginia *read* was born at the country seat "Newmarket," in Caroline County, Virginia

Page 100, column 2, line 22f.
BEATTY, CHARLES CLINTON: *for* Three years later *read* In 1766

Page 109, column 1, line 20ff.
BEAUMONT, WILLIAM: *for* lived . . . eighty-three *read* died at St. Thomas de Jolliette in 1880

Page 119, column 2, line 47
BECKNELL, WILLIAM: *for* c. 1790–c. 1832 *read* c. 1796–Apr. 30, 1865

Page 119, column 2, line 48f.
For was possibly . . . in Missouri *read* was born in Amherst County, Va. In 1816–17 he was married and living in Howard County, Mo.

Page 120, column 1, line 38 f.
For His later life . . . in 1832 *read* About 1834 he went to Texas, where he acquired a plantation at Clarksville, Red River County. He recruited a company, known as the Red River Blues, which served in the Texas Revolution. In 1839 he acted as captain of Rangers against the Indians.

Page 120, column 1, line 51
After (1902). *Insert* See, also, copy of Mary Becknell's will in Records of Wills, Red River County, Tex., Book B, pp. 61–62; Muster Rolls, Tex. State Lib.; files of Clarksville NORTHERN STANDARD.

Page 122, column 2, line 34
BECKWOURTH, JAMES P.: *for* where he died about 1867 *read* dying about 1867 while on a visit to the Crow villages

Page 235, column 2, line 53ff.
BIBB, WILLIAM WYATT: *for* His mother . . . Sallie Wyatt *read* His mother, Sally Wyatt, was a descendant of the Rev. Hawte Wyatt, minister at Jamestown, and a daughter of Joseph and Sallie Wyatt

Page 282, column 1, line 26
BINNEY, HORACE: *for* son *read* grandson

Page 323, column 1, line 17
BLAINE, JAMES GILLESPIE: *after* been *insert* one of

Page 332, column 1, line 19f.
BLAIR, FRANCIS PRESTON: *for* Sir Christopher Gist *read* Christopher Gist

Page 365, column 1, line 3
BLEDSOE, ALBERT TAYLOR: *after* 1867 *insert comma and* having just completed THE PHILOSOPHY OF MATHEMATICS (1868), a work that attracted much attention and is still read,

Page 398, column 2, line 4ff.
BLUNT, GEORGE WILLIAM: *omit* In 1833 . . . the time of his death.

Page 400, column 1, line 8
BLY, NELLIE. [See SEAMAN, ELIZABETH COCHRANE, 1867–1922.] *Insert before* BLYTHE, HERBERT

Page 420, column 1, line 13
BOLLAN, WILLIAM: *for* c. 1776 *read* May 24, 1782

Errata

Page 420, column 2, line 36
Add for Bollan's date of death see a letter from his daughter, Mrs. Frances Shirley Western, to Francis Dana, Feb. 3, 1790, Dana Papers, Mass. Hist. Soc.

Page 444, column 2, line 29
BOOTH, AGNES: *for* of May Brooklyn *read* and it was given to Mary Brooklyn

Page 453, column 1, line 14
BOOTH, JUNIUS BRUTUS: *after* infancy. *insert* They were not divorced, however, until 1851.

Page 454, column 2, line 27
After particulars. *insert* Material on his first marriage and his divorce may be found in the Division of Manuscripts, Lib. of Cong.

Page 456, column 1, line 3
BOOTH, NEWTON: *after* Hittell. *insert* A most important source book is NEWTON BOOTH: HIS SPEECHES AND ADDRESSES (1894), by L. E. Crane.

Page 456, column 1, line 13f.
BOOTH-TUCKER, EMMA MOSS: *for* six children *read* eight children

Page 481, column 2, line 10
BOUQUET, HENRY: *after* Collection. *insert* There are Bouquet Papers in the Gage MSS., William L. Clements Lib., Univ. of Mich.

Page 509, column 2, line 4ff.
BOWIE, JAMES: *for* was born . . . in 1802 *read* was born in Logan County, Ky. His parents, Rezin and Elvira (Jones) Bowie, natives of Georgia, had moved to Tennessee about 1787, and thence, six or seven years later, to Kentucky. Four years after James's birth they removed to Missouri, but about 1802 went to Louisiana. James spent most of his childhood in Catahoula Parish (*De Bow's Review*, October 1853, p. 379).

Page 509, column 2, line 16
For Of his youth . . . is known *read* Of his earliest exploits little is known

Page 519, column 2, line 39f.
BOWLES, SAMUEL: *for* probably prepared by . . . E. P. Clark *read* written by O. G. Villard

Page 522, column 1, line 28
BOWNE, BORDEN PARKER: *after* was *insert* born in Leonardville, N. J.,

Page 607, column 1, line 45ff.
BRATTLE, THOMAS: *for* He is said to have been . . . MASSACHUSETTS, XIV]. *read* He was never elected a member of the Society, however, though that honor was conferred on his brother William [*q.v.*], largely that the Society might get possession of Thomas' scientific papers.

VOLUME II, PART 1

BREARLY TO CHANDLER

Page 53, column 2, line 19
BRISTED, CHARLES ASTOR: *for* John Jacob Astor II. *read* John Jacob Astor (1763–1848) [*q.v.*]

Page 128, column 2, line 33
BROWN, JOHN: *after* 1803), *insert* merchant,

Page 158, column 2, line 30ff.
BROWN, WILLIAM CARLOS: *for* Among them . . . city. *read* Among them were the rehabilitation and expansion of the system needed to meet modern conditions, the construction of the new Grand Central Terminal in New York City, and the electrification of the lines in and near that city. These, however, were initiated and carried through in large part by the chief engineer, later vice-president in charge of construction, during the regimes of the presidents Samuel R. Callaway [*q.v.*] and William H. Newman.

Page 187, column 2, line 45f.
BRUSH, GEORGE JARVIS: *for* On his return . . . in 1855, *read* In 1855, while he was still abroad, *omit* went once more abroad,

Page 212, column 1, line 5
BUCHANAN, JAMES: *for* embassies . . . Siam *read* an embassy from Japan

Page 212, column 1, line 39–50
For treasury, *read* treasury. *and omit* at whose suggestion . . . advantage.

Page 230, column 1, line 7ff.
BUCKLAND, RALPH POMEROY: *for* Ravenna . . . and *read* Leyden, Mass. His parents soon moved to Ravenna, Ohio,

Page 273, column 2, line 34
BURDICK, FRANCIS MARION: *omit* under Prof. Theodore Dwight

Page 424, column 1, line 15
CALLAWAY, SAMUEL RODGER: *after* Central, *insert* during which time bold measures were actively undertaken for the long-neglected rehabilitation, expansion, and modernizing of the system,

Page 433, column 2, line 42f.
CAMERON, ANDREW CARR: *for* Sept. 28, 1834–May 28, 1890 *read* Sept. 28, 1836–May 28, 1892

Page 434, column 2, line 27
Add and obituary in *Inland Printer*, June, 1892.

Page 482, column 1, line 13
CAPEN, NAHUM: *for* President James Buchanan *read* James Buchanan, then secretary of state

Errata

Page 506, column 1, line 30
CARNEGIE, ANDREW: *for* Thos. *read* Theodore

Page 563, column 1, line 38
CASS, LEWIS: *for* near the mouth of *read* on

Page 563, column 1, line 42
omit similarly located

Page 590, column 1, line 31
CHAFFEE, JEROME BONAPARTE: *for* JEROME BONAPARTE *read* JEROME B.

VOLUME II, PART 2

CHANFRAU TO CUSHING

Page 18, column 1, line 34
CHAPMAN, JOHN: *for* Nell Hillis's *read* Newell D. Hillis's

Page 66, column 2, line 9f.
CHILD, FRANCIS JAMES: *for* four daughters *read* three daughters and a son

Page 93, column 1, line 7ff.
CHOUTEAU, JEAN PIERRE: *for* the son . . . the given *read* the son of René Auguste Chouteau [*q.v.*] and Marie Thérèse (Bourgeois) Chouteau. The

Page 93, column 1, line 43
For half-brother *read* brother

Page 94, column 2, line 8ff.
CHOUTEAU, RENÉ AUGUSTE: *for* In 1757 . . . husband. *read* It is said that in 1757 she formed an unsanctioned union with Pierre Laclede [*q.v.*], by whom she had four children (Scharf, *post*, I, 179), but investigation of early records indicates that this tradition is false (ST. LOUIS GLOBE DEMOCRAT, Oct. 16, 1921; MISSOURI HISTORICAL REVIEW, July 1928), and that she later returned to her husband, since the four children bore Chouteau's name.

Page 94, column 2, line 13
After Laclede *insert comma and for* with his family *read* accompanied by Auguste,

Page 94, column 2, line 17
For his stepfather *read* Laclede

Page 94, column 2, line 33
For half-brother *read* brother

Page 105, column 1, line 55
CHURCHILL, THOMAS JAMES: *for* Mar. 10, 1905 *read* May 14, 1905

Page 105, column 2, line 1ff.
For Samuel Churchill . . . Albemarle County, Va. *read* Armistead Churchill, a native of Middlesex County, Va., who had moved to Kentucky about 1787.

Page 154, column 2, line 49ff.
CLARKE, JOHN: *for* of a Suffolk family . . . Bedfordshire *read* who like the Clarkes belonged to a Suffolk family

Page 156, column 1, line 19
After available. *insert* For geneal. data see NEW ENG. HIST. AND GENEAL. REG., Oct. 1921, pp. 273–301.

Page 170, column 2, line 23
CLAY, CLEMENT CLAIBORNE: *omit* under . . . John B. Minor

Page 185, column 1, line 53
CLAYTON, JOHN MIDDLETON: *for* His services . . . in 1828 *read* His loyalty to the Adams administration in 1828

Page 185, column 2, line 12f.
Omit comma and which left . . . to the former

Page 188, column 1, line 7ff.
CLAYTON, POWELL: *for* In 1897 . . . held *read* On Mar. 22, 1897, he was appointed minister to Mexico, and on Dec. 8, 1898, ambassador, holding

Page 207, column 2, line 16ff.
CLEVELAND, STEPHEN GROVER: *for sentence beginning* A rather short *substitute* He was a tall man—slightly over six feet—and when inaugurated weighed over 250 pounds.

Page 287, column 2, line 48
COLDEN, CADWALLADER: *for* South's *read* Smith's

Page 301, column 2, line 12
COLLES, CHRISTOPHER: *for* 1738 *read* May 8, 1739

Page 301, column 2, line 14f.
Omit probably in 1738. *Add* the son of Richard Colles of Dublin and his wife Henrietta Taylor. On Jan. 14, 1764, he married Anne Keogh (or Keough) of Kilkenny, by whom he had several children.

Page 302, column 2, line 10
Add at end of Bibliography See also the extensive article by John Austin Stevens in *Mag. Am. Hist.*, June, 1878, which includes a list of his writings. Family information supplied by Richard Colles Johnson.

Page 312, column 1, line 9
COLMAN, HENRY: *for* Congregational Church in Dedham, Mass. *read* Third Congregational Society (Unitarian), Hingham, Mass.

Page 361, column 2, line 15
CONWAY, ELIAS NELSON: *after* 1892) *insert comma and* governor of Arkansas,

Page 361, column 2, line 22
For He had only one son *read* His son *and omit* who

Page 361, column 2, line 28
For Here Thomas made his home *read* Here, later, he made his home

Page 361, column 2, line 30
After life. *insert* His daughters married sons of John Sevier [*q.v.*].

Errata

Page 361, column 2, line 30
For To him were born *read* Thomas had

Page 361, column 2, line 35f.
Omit The three daughters . . . Sevier family.

Page 410, column 1, line 40
COOPER, PETER: *for* Philipsburg, Pa., *read* Phillipsburg, N. J.

Page 414, column 1, line 27
COOPER, THEODORE: *after quotation insert* An unfortunate event of his later career was the collapse during construction of the Quebec bridge, for which he was consulting engineer, with a loss of seventy-four lives. A commission of inquiry held that he and the designing engineer had erred in judgment.

Page 414, column 1, line 30
After 1919 *insert semicolon and* ROYAL COMMISSION QUEBEC BRIDGE INQUIRY 1907 (2 vols., 1908)

Page 443, column 1, line 25
CORNELL, ALONZO B.: *after* Liberal *insert* Republican

Page 479, column 2, line 20f.
COX, LEMUEL: *for* between . . . the Charles River *read* the first bridge across the Charles River connecting Boston and Charlestown

Page 559, column 2, line 35ff.
CROKER, RICHARD: *for* He then married . . . Oklahoma. *read* He then married twenty-three-year-old Beulah Benton Edmondson, from Oklahoma, in whom there was a trace of Indian blood.

Page 560, column 2, line 18f.
CROLY, JANE CUNNINGHAM: *omit* probably the first American newspaper woman. She was

Page 589, column 1, line 48
CULLOM, SHELBY MOORE: *for* Santo Domingo *read* the Dominican Republic

Page 608, column 1, line 12
CURTIN, JEREMIAH: *for* 1840? *read* 1835

Page 608, column 1, line 14f.
For either . . . Wis. *read* at Detroit, Mich.

Page 608, column 2, line 43
After 1903–05. *insert* Birthplace and date of birth have been established by manuscripts in the lib. of the State Hist. Soc. of Wis.

VOLUME III, PART 1

CUSHMAN TO EBERLE

Page 19, column 2, line 26
DABLON, CLAUDE: *for* Onondaga . . . Liverpool, N. Y. *read* several Onondaga villages.

Page 76, column 2, line 44ff.
DARLING, FLORA ADAMS: *for* because she opposed . . . of the Board *read* because of her alleged refusal to recognize the authority of the Board

Page 142, column 1, line 50f.
DAVIS, PHINEAS: *after* CODORUS *insert comma and for* was launched . . . and *read* having been hauled to the river, was launched on the Susquehanna and subsequently

Page 167, column 2, line 50
DAYTON, WILLIAM LEWIS: *for* ser. 23 *read* ser. 2

Page 203, column 2, line 33f.
DE KAY, JAMES ELLSWORTH: *for* but the name and location . . . have not been preserved *read* where he prepared for college under the Rev. David Smith of Durham, and was a student at Yale from Apr. 26, 1810 until early in 1812, being dismissed, apparently, on a charge of disrespect to a tutor

Page 215, column 2, line 2f.
DE LANCEY, OLIVER: *for* cathedral church *read* minster

Page 267, column 1, line 15f.
DEWEES, WILLIAM POTTS: *for* founded by . . . Thomas Potts *read* founded by John Potts, half-brother of Thomas Potts, William's maternal grandfather

Page 281, column 2, line 59f.
DEXTER, TIMOTHY: *for* Continental currency *read* certificates of indebtedness

Page 281, column 2, line 61
For its *read* their

Page 282, column 1, line 36ff.
DEXTER, WIRT: *for* moved West, . . . at Dexter, Wis., *read* moved West and subsequently practised law at Dexter, Mich.,

Page 282, column 2, line 52
For practise *read* practice

Page 376, column 2, line 13
DOREMUS, ROBERT OGDEN: *for* Columbia College *read* the University of the City of New York

Page 376, column 2, line 14ff.
For at the University . . . in 1851 *read* from the medical department of which he received the degree of M.D. in 1851

Page 387, column 1, line 55
DORSEY, STEPHEN WALLACE: *omit* [*q.v.*]

Page 410, column 2, line 28ff.
DOW, LORENZO: *for* irregular preacher and inventor of camp-meetings *read* eccentric Methodist evangelist

Page 425, column 1, line 24ff.
DRAKE, CHARLES DANIEL: *for* he . . . resigning *read* he became a midshipman in the United States Navy, resigning in 1829

Errata

Page 549, column 1, line 20
DURHAM, CALEB WHEELER: *for* Presbyterian minister *read* merchant

Page 596, column 2, line 19f.
EARLE, RALPH: *omit* was made a member of the Royal Academy,

VOLUME III, PART 2

ECHOLS TO FRASER

Page 30, column 1, line 37
EDWARDS, JONATHAN (Oct. 5, 1703–Mar. 22, 1758): *insert* [*q.v.*] *after* Rev. Solomon Stoddard

Page 32, column 1, line 5f.
Insert [*q.v.*] *after* Israel Williams

Page 32, column 1, line 7
For 1729 *read* 1727

Page 79, column 1, line 16
ELIOT, JARED: *omit comma after* SAND *and insert* was

Page 79, column 1, 16
For comma after 1762 *insert period*

Page 79, column 1, line 16ff.
Omit was awarded . . . member of the society.

Page 81, column 2, line 18f.
ELIOT, SAMUEL ATKINS: *for* then . . . traveling *read* in 1823–24 traveled

Page 83, column 2, line 55
ELKINS, STEPHEN BENTON: *for* administration *read* admission

Page 94, column 2, line 22ff.
ELLIOTT, BENJAMIN: *for* In his pioneer pamphlet . . . peculiar institution *read* He collaborated in a small way with Edwin C. Holland [*q.v.*] in the preparation of A REFUTATION OF THE CALUMNIES CIRCULATED AGAINST THE SOUTHERN AND WESTERN STATES, RESPECTING THE INSTITUTION AND EXISTENCE OF SLAVERY AMONG THEM, published in 1822, which presents one of the earliest and ablest defenses of that institution.

Page 94, column 2, line 29ff.
Omit In the force of his logic . . . on the subject

Page 94, column 2, line 43ff.
Omit In addition . . . mentioned, *and for* he *read* He

Page 116, column 2, line 50f.
ELMER, JONATHAN: *for* on a printed thesis . . . Remediis," *read* on a thesis, DE SITIS IN FEBRIBUS CAUSIS ET REMEDIIS, published in 1771 and

Page 127, column 2, line 32
EMERSON, GEORGE BARRELL: *after* and *insert* the

Page 148, column 2, line 54
EMMETT, DANIEL DECATUR: *for* G. H. Odell *read* G. C. D. Odell

Page 194, column 1, line 21
EUSTIS, WILLIAM: *for* 1807 *read* 1809

Page 206, column 2, line 2
EVANS, LAWRENCE BOYD: *for* History *read* Historical

Page 206, column 2, line 25
EVANS, LEWIS: *for* in Pennsylvania and *read* in Llangwnadl Parish, Carnarvonshire, Wales. Emigrating to Pennsylvania, he

Page 207, column 1, line 49
After 1756. *Insert* Authority for place of birth is Evans' will, a copy of which is in the Hall of Records, New York City.

Page 266, column 2, line 50ff.
FANNING, EDMUND: *for* He was . . . but *read* He was agent for two expeditions under Pendleton and Palmer, that of 1820 during which Palmer Land (Palmer Archipelago) south of Cape Horn was discovered, and the ambitious expedition of 1829, in the course of which

Page 307, column 1, line 21
FAYSSOUX, PETER: *for* in the first British attack on America *read* during the British attack

Page 322, column 2, line 10
FENNER, ARTHUR: *omit* fourth

Page 384, column 1, line 21
FINCK, HENRY THEOPHILUS: *omit* the highest

Page 385, column 1, line 46
FINDLAY, JAMES: *for* on the . . . governor *read* for governor on a ticket supported by those opposed to President Jackson

Page 385, column 1, line 53
For As a *read* Until 1833 he was a

Page 385, column 1, line 54
Omit comma and he *and insert* and

Page 403, column 1, line 40
FISHBACK, WILLIAM MEADE: *omit* named for him *and commas preceding and following*

Page 474, column 1, line 45
FLINT, TIMOTHY: *omit* then a part of Fitchburg, Mass.,

Page 475, column 2, line 56
FLINT, WESTON: *for* Society *read* Association

Page 509, column 2, line 33ff.
FORBES, STEPHEN ALFRED: *for* origin, . . . MAYFLOWER *read* origin.

Page 514, column 2, line 57ff.
FORD, GORDON LESTER: *for* Ford's only literary production . . . (1882) *read* Ford is credited with no important literary production

Page 530, column 1, line 52ff.
FORREST, EDWIN: *omit*—except Boston, . . . Back Bay—

Errata

Page 531, column 1, line 34
For in New York . . . 1872 *read* in Boston in the latter part of 1872

Page 548, column 2, line 33f.
FOSTER, HANNAH WEBSTER: *for* is a prototype of *read* is, like

Page 551, column 1, line 11
FOSTER, JOHN WATSON: *for* University of Indiana *read* Indiana University

Page 551, column 2, line 56
For Santiago *read* Valparaiso

Page 559, column 1, line 39ff.
FOSTER, THEODORE: *omit* In 1785 . . . court of Admiralty.

Page 568, column 1, line 59ff.
FOX, GUSTAVUS VASA: *for* to the . . . midshipman *read* as midshipman in the United States Navy

Page 568, column 2, line 2
For For the next fifteen years *read* Subsequently,

VOLUME IV, PART 1

FRAUNCES TO GRIMKÉ

Page 21, column 2, line 48
FRÉMONT, JOHN CHARLES: *after* Couenga *insert* (Cahuenga)

Page 87, column 2, line 38
GAGE, THOMAS: *for* February *read* June

Page 88, column 2, line 24ff.
For comma after abilities *insert period and omit* but . . . was untenable.

Page 88, column 2, line 26
For He soon after resigned *read* He was soon after recalled

Page 88, column 2, line 52
For period after (1923) *insert semicolon and* Gage Papers in the William L. Clements Library, Ann Arbor, Mich.

Page 93, column 1, line 11f.
GAINES, EDMUND PENDLETON: *for* He was made adjutant-general and *read* He was made brigadier-general Mar. 9, 1814.

Page 93, column 1, line 12f.
For put . . . defended *read* Put in command of Fort Erie, he defended it

Page 93, column 1, line 14f.
For promoted . . . with *read* given

Page 100, column 1, line 20
GALES, JOSEPH: *for* and . . . year *read* in 1797 and two years later

Page 124, column 1, line 6ff.
GANNETT, HENRY: *for* His peculiar contribution . . . censuses *read* He was one of the editors of the statistical atlas published in 1883. He was statistical expert for the Cuban and Porto Rican censuses of 1899, assistant director for the Philippine census of 1903, and assistant director for the Cuban census of 1907

Page 124, column 1, line 40f.
For From 1903 to 1909 . . . editor *read* In 1908 and 1909 he was editor

Page 131, column 2, line 36
GARCELON, ALONZO: *for* the only . . . history *read* governor

Page 245, column 1, line 3
GIBBS, GEORGE: *for* from England . . . about 1670 *read* from England about 1670 and later went to Bristol, R. I.

Page 299, column 2, line 45f.
GILMAN, DANIEL COIT: *for* served as librarian . . . geography *read* served as professor of physical and political geography from 1863 to 1872; and he was assistant librarian of the University from 1856 to 1858, and librarian from 1858 to 1865

Page 335, column 2, line 1f.
GLYNN, MARTIN HENRY: *omit* From his keynote . . . war."

Page 335, column 2, line 5ff.
Omit and . . . (OUTLOOK, Nov. 15, 1916;

Page 335, column 2, line 7
Insert (*before* NEW YORK TIMES

Page 359, column 2, line 45
GOFF, JOHN WILLIAM: *for* One O'Reilly *read* John Boyle O'Reilly

Page 382, column 1, line 19
GOODE, GEORGE BROWN: *for* a founder *read* an early member

Page 476, column 1, line 3f.
GRAHAM, JAMES: *after* Windebank *insert comma and for* and had *read* his second wife, apparently, for in 1691 his daughter Isabella married Lewis Morris (1671–1746) [*q.v.*]. He had in all

Page 514, column 2, line 5f.
GRAY, ELISHA: *for* thus anticipating Gray *read* already in practical form

Page 545, column 1, line 41
GREEN, HENRIETTA HOWLAND ROBINSON: *for* HENRIETTA *read* HETTY

Page 619, column 1, line 9f.
GRIFFIN, CYRUS: *for* "Plan . . . Colonies" *read* plan of reconciliation

Page 619, column 1, line 47ff.
For presumably . . . patronage *read* partly because of Edmund Pendleton's refusal of the position and partly because of Washington's indebtedness to Griffin, who had lost his position in the Virginia privy council by serving on the Creek commission

Page 633, column 1, line 1ff.
GRIMKÉ, ARCHIBALD HENRY: *for comma after* affairs *insert period and omit* being made . . . entire organization

Errata

VOLUME IV, PART 2

GRINNELL TO HIBBARD

Page 108, column 1, line 4
HALE, NATHAN: *for* Cambridge *read* Charlestown

Page 119, column 2, line 9
HALL, CHARLES CUTHBERT: *after comma following parenthesis insert* Presbyterian minister,

Page 152, column 2, line 50f.
HALLET, ÉTIENNE SULPICE: *for* fl. 1789–1796 *read* Mar. 17, 1755–February 1825

Page 152, column 2, line 53
After building. *insert* He was born in Paris and died in New Rochelle, N. Y.

Page 154, column 1, line 21
After (1887). *insert* Information regarding places and dates of birth and death was supplied by Elima A. Foster, a great-granddaughter.

Page 154, column 1, line 23
HALLET, STEPHEN: *For* fl. 1789–1796 *read* Mar. 17, 1755–February 1825

Page 212, column 2, line 33f.
HAMPTON, WADE: *Insert period after parenthesis and omit* pursuing . . . "flax-breaker."

Page 212, column 2, line 36
For is not known *read* was Anne Preston

Page 274, column 1, line 34
HARLAND, HENRY: *for* New York City *read* St. Petersburg, Russia

Page 295, column 2, line 17ff.
HARRIGAN, EDWARD: *for* and in 1861 *read* about 1867. *Omit* was singing . . . and elsewhere

Page 315, column 2, line 11f.
HARRIS, JOSEPH: *for comma after* England *insert period and omit* near . . . Hastings.

Page 316, column 2, line 47
HARRIS, MERRIMAN COLBERT: *for* Wash., *read* Washington,

Page 316, column 2, line 48
Omit at

Page 317, column 2, line 4
After ADVOCATE *omit comma and insert* (New York),

Page 343, column 2, line 48
HARRISON, JAMES ALBERT: *for* Mary Thurston *read* Sidney Anne Norton

Page 360, column 2, line 25
HART, SAMUEL: *for* president *read* secretary

Page 360, column 2, line 27
Omit as secretary

Page 381, column 1, line 40
HASKELL, ERNEST: *for* Nov. 2 *read* Nov. 1; *for* July 30 *read* June 30

Page 413, column 2, line 51
HAWKINS, BENJAMIN: *for* 1818 *read* 1816

Page 481, column 2, line 24
HEAP, SAMUEL DAVIES: *omit* Graduating . . . in 1803,

Page 545, column 2, line 11
HENROTIN, CHARLES: *for* an active *read* a gold

VOLUME V, PART 1

HIBBEN TO JARVIS

Page 37, column 1, line 18
HILL, JAMES JEROME: *for* Mich. *read* in what is now the state of North Dakota.

Page 81, column 1, line 37
HITT, ROBERT ROBERTS: *after* Cleveland's *insert* proposed

Page 142, column 1, line 27f.
HOLLADAY, BEN: *for* on the Hudson . . . White Plains. *read* east of White Plains, N. Y.

Page 205, column 2, line 56f.
HOPE, JAMES BARRON: *for* That same year . . . Jamestown *read* At the celebration of the 250th anniversary of the settlement of Jamestown

Page 206, column 1, line 19
For he did newspaper work *read* he was connected editorially

Page 206, column 1, line 32ff.
For When death came . . . University. *read* He had been appointed by his state to act as poet at the laying of the cornerstone of the statue of General Lee in Richmond, October 1887, and had just completed his poem for that occasion, "Memoriae Sacrum," when death came to him.

Page 292, column 1, line 14
HOWE, JULIA WARD: *for* One night, while *read* After

Page 292, column 1, line 16f.
For too stirred . . . she *read* she awoke before dawn, and

Page 292, column 1, line 19
For dense *read* half

Page 292, column 1, line 20
Omit of her tent *and for* not *read* scarcely

Page 293, column 2, line 44
HOWE, MARK ANTHONY DEWOLFE: *omit* [*q.v.*]

Errata

Page 303, column 1, line 42f.
HOWELL, JOHN ADAMS: *For* at . . . class *read* second in his class

Page 504, column 2, line 31
IRVING, PETER: *after period following parenthesis insert* Birthdate is from family Bible.

VOLUME V, PART 2

JASPER TO LARKIN

Page 50, column 1, line 48
JENKINS, THORNTON ALEXANDER: *after* Va. *insert comma and* the son of William Jenkins.

Page 51, column 1, line 14f.
After first *insert comma and for* to a Miss Powers *read* about 1835, to Annie Power, daughter of John Power of Baltimore, Md.

Page 51, column 1, line 15
After second *insert comma and for* to a daughter . . . navy *read* in 1849, to Elizabeth A. Thornton, daughter of Francis A. Thornton, a paymaster in the United States navy

Page 51, column 1, line 23
After 1893. *insert* Information regarding name of father and marriages was supplied by Mrs. William G. Andrews, Washington, D. C.

Page 272, column 1, line 4
KEARNEY, PHILIP: *for* five *read* four *and after* children. *insert* He left her in 1855, however, and she divorced him in 1858, in which year he married Agnes Maxwell, by whom he had one son and two daughters.

Page 272, column 1, line 5ff.
For Kearny . . . later *read* Early in 1846 he resigned his commission. A month later

Page 272, column 1, line 28
After Kearny. *insert* From 1855 to 1857 he lived abroad.

Page 272, column 1, line 29
For however, he returned to *read* he was again in

Page 272, column 2, line 37
After (1913). *insert* Information regarding marriages was obtained from Thomas Kearny, *General Philip Kearny; Battle Soldier of Five Wars* (1937).

Page 274, column 2, line 1
KEARSLEY, JOHN: *for* In addition . . . designed *read* He also collaborated with Robert Smith [*q.v.*], the architect, in designing

Page 274, column 2, line 5
For designer's *read* designers'

Page 383, column 2, line 54f.
KING, CHARLES WILLIAM: *for* as an employee . . . Company *read* probably as an employee of his kinsman D. W. C. Olyphant [*q.v.*], who went out that year as agent for Thomas H. Smith.

Page 383, column 2, line 60
Omit (see sketch of D. W. C. Olyphant)

Page 398, column 1, line 47
KING, RUFUS: *for comma after* Congress *insert period and omit* then sitting at Trenton, N. J.

Page 398, column 1, line 48
After resolution *insert*—substantially the same as that proposed by Jefferson in the ordinance of 1784—

Page 417, column 1, line 25
KINNEY, ELIZABETH CLEMENTINE DODGE STEDMAN: *for* grandfather *read* great-grandfather

Page 417, column 1, line 25
For colonial poet *read* Rev.

Page 422, column 1, line 24f.
KINZIE, JOHN: *after* Detroit *omit* and there opened the first tavern

Page 520, column 2, line 22–31
LACLEDE, PIERRE: *for* In 1857 . . . husband. *read* The story that in 1757 he formed an unsanctioned union with Marie Thérèse Chouteau, mother of (René) Auguste Chouteau [*q.v.*] (Scharf, *post,* I, 179), by whom he had a son, (Jean) Pierre Chouteau [*q.v.*], and three daughters seems, in the light of early records, improbable (ST. LOUIS GLOBE DEMOCRAT, Oct. 16, 1921; MISSOURI HISTORICAL REVIEW, July 1928).

Page 520, column 2, line 34f.
For with his family read accompanied by young Auguste Chouteau

Page 520, column 2, line 41
For his young stepson *read* young Chouteau

Page 521, column 1, line 7f.
Omit of a great family . . . and

VOLUME VI, PART 1

LARNED TO MACCRACKEN

Page 21, column 1, line 28f.
LATROBE, BENJAMIN HENRY: *for* Nicholas James Roosevelt [*q.v.*] *read* Nicholas J. Roosevelt [*q.v.*]

Errata

Page 84, column 2, line 6f.
LEAVITT, HUMPHREY HOWE: *for* Anti-Slavery party *read* antislavery advocates

Page 108, column 2, line 41
LEE, HENRY: *omit period after* Calcutta *and insert* as agent for Patrick T. Jackson.

Page 118, column 2, line 12
LEE, RICHARD HENRY: *for* the first *read* one

Page 135, column 2, line 30
LEEDS, DANIEL: *for* Nottinghamshire *read* Leeds, Kent

Page 135, column 2, line 55
For second *read* first

Page 135, column 2, line 55f.
After almanac *omit comma and* that for the year 1688,

Page 136, column 1, line 41f.
For four *read* three *and omit* before he left England; second,

Page 136, column 1, line 43
For third *read* second

Page 136, column 1, line 45
For fourth *read* third

Page 136, column 2, line 8f.
For While . . . exist, *read* There is a complete file of Leeds's almanacs in the Pa. Hist. Soc., and

Page 136, column 2, line 25
After (1873). *insert* Information as to certain facts has been supplied by J. Henry Bartlett, Haverford, Pa., a descendant.

Page 194, column 2, line 40f.
LETTERMAN, JONATHAN: *for* Chancellorsville . . . Gettysburg *read* Antietam and Fredericksburg, and later at Chancellorsville and Gettysburg,

Page 232, column 1, line 22
L'HALLE, CONSTANTIN de: *omit* Several . . . name.

Page 232, column 1, line 24ff.
L'HALLE, NICOLAS BÉNOIT CONSTANTIN de: *omit* the whole cross reference

Page 281, column 1, line 26ff.
LINING, JOHN: *for* In 1739 . . . no children *read* On June 28, 1739 he had married Sarah Hill of "Hillsborough," a plantation lying across the Ashley River from Charleston; they left children whose descendants are numerous.

Page 310, column 2, line 28ff.
LIVINGSTON, EDWARD: *for comma after* 1806 *insert period and omit* who proved . . . maturity.

Page 312, column 2, line 6
For Academy of the Institute of France *read* Académie des Sciences Morales et Politiques

Page 332, column 2, line 20
LLOYD, HENRY DEMAREST: *Omit* until 1903. *For* party . . . supported *read* party, but for a number of years he supported

Page 347, column 1, line 45
LODGE, HENRY CABOT: *for period after* speeches *insert semicolon and* after his death there was issued SELECTIONS FROM THE CORRESPONDENCE OF THEODORE ROOSEVELT AND HENRY CABOT LODGE (2 vols., 1925).

Page 380, column 2, line 50
LONG. STEPHEN HARRIMAN: *after* Nov. 1923. *insert* The manuscript diary kept by Long on his journey into the Northwest in 1823 is in the Minn. Hist. Soc. library.

Page 447, column 2, line 48
LOW, JULIETTE GORDON: *for* was of Scotch descent *read* was born in Savannah, Ga., of Scotch descent

Page 450, column 2, line 43
LOWE, CHARLES: *for* as salutatorian of *read* in

Page 513, column 1, line 15–22
LYALL, JAMES: *for* While this invention . . . simultaneously *read* While it was believed at the time that this invention would revolutionize the manufacture of cotton goods throughout the world, that conviction was not justified.

Page 513, column 1, line 23
Omit enormous

Page 546, column 2, line 41
MCALLISTER, MATTHEW HALL: *after* identified *insert comma and* first,

Page 576, column 2, line 3
MCCAWLEY, CHARLES GRYMES: *omit* County

Page 589, column 2, line 38
M'CLINTOCK, JOHN: *for comma after* University *insert period*

Page 589, column 2, line 38f.
For both . . . he declined *read* The former election he declined, but he accepted the presidency of Troy conditionally and maintained a connection with it for several years, drawing up in the meantime a plan for the institution, which opened in 1858 and was compelled to close in 1862.

Page 618, column 2, line 5f.
MCCOY, ISAAC: *for* letters . . . Boston *read* letters in possession of Am. Baptist Foreign Missionary Soc., New York

VOLUME VI, PART 2

MCCRADY TO MILLINGTON

Page 10, column 1, line 31f.
MCCULLOUGH, JOHN: *for* McGuire's Theatre *read* Maguire's Opera House

Page 34, column 2, line 30
MCDUFFIE, GEORGE: *omit* near the Savannah River

Errata

Page 79, column 1, line 4
MCKEAN, SAMUEL: *for* Treasurer's *read* Secretary of the Treasury's

Page 144, column 2, line 19f.
MCMILLAN, JAMES: *for* Bland-Allison Act *read* Sherman silver-purchase law

Page 185, column 1, line 43ff.
MADISON, JAMES: *for* in order *read* although *and for* to have . . . slaves *read* he was "far from being determined ever to make a professional use of it"

Page 190, column 2, line 35
After Madison *insert comma and* elected over the Federalist candidate, Pinckney,

Page 287, column 1, line 13
MARKOE, ABRAHAM: *for* the first volunteer military association *read* one of the early volunteer military organizations

Page 337, column 1, line 31
MARTIN, HENRY AUSTIN: *for* Gen. *read* Lieut. Col.

Page 433, column 2, line 15
MAVERICK, SAMUEL: *for* (1876) *read* (1870)

Page 466, column 1, line 43
MAYO, WILLIAM WORRELL: *read* MAYO, WILLIAM WORRALL

Page 496, column 2, line 24ff.
MEEKER, MOSES: *for* was born . . . native state *read* was born in New Haven, N. J., the eleventh of the twelve children of Jonathan (*sic*) and Rachel (Denham) Meeker

Page 497, column 1, line 45
For period after (1881) *insert semicolon and* names of parents furnished by a granddaughter, Mrs. M. R. Wilkinson.

Page 613, column 1, line 50
MILES, JOHN. [See MYLES, JOHN, *c.* 1621–1683.] *insert before* MILES, MANLY

VOLUME VII, PART 1

MILLS TO OGLESBY

Page 13, Column 2, line 40f.
MILLS, ROBERT: *omit* in part

Page 13, column 2, line 42
Omit period after 1929 *and insert* and in ROBERT MILLS, ARCHITECT OF THE WASHINGTON MONUMENT (1935).

Page 32, column 1, line 6
MINTO, WALTER: *for* Cowdenham *read* Cowdenknowes

Page 32, column 1, line 7
For County Merse *read* district of the Merse

Page 32, column 1, line 7f.
Omit family . . . but his

Page 93, column 2, line 53
MONTEFIORE, JOSHUA: *omit* by Sir William Scott

Page 128, column 2, line 12
MOORE, JAMES: *after* vol. II. *insert* Authority for statement that Moore married Margaret Berringer may be found in S. C. HIST. AND GENEAL. MAG., July 1918, p. 156.

Page 170, column 2, line 21ff.
MORGAN, GEORGE: *for* esp. vol. I . . . (1921) *read* esp. vol. I (1903), ed. by H. W. Beckwith, vol. XI, "The New Régime" (1916), and vol. XVI, "Trade and Politics" (1921), both ed. by C. W. Alvord and C. E. Carter

Page 200, column 1, line 34f.
MORRILL, LOT MYRICK: *for* impeachment *read* conviction

Page 318, column 2, line 8ff.
MULFORD, PRENTICE: *omit* The quality . . . sage and seer."

Page 389, column 1, line 16
NASH, SIMEON: *omit* At the end of two years *and for* the *read* The

Page 389, column 1, line 18
After fraud *insert* (DOCUMENTS . . . FORTY-FOURTH GENERAL ASSEMBLY . . . OF OHIO, 1845–46, no. I)

Page 389, column 2, line 2
After period insert Date of death was furnished by Simeon Nash, a grandson, from tombstone at Gallipolis.

Page 422, column 1, line 43
NELSON, ROGER: *after period insert* She died about 1795 and on Feb. 2, 1797 he married Eliza Harrison, daughter of John and Catherine Contee Harrison of Prince Georges County, Md. There were four children by the first marriage and four by the second.

Page 422, column 1, line 59
After period insert Information regarding marriages was furnished by a great-granddaughter, Mrs. Byron E. Hamlin.

Page 459, column 1, line 43f.
NEWELL, ROBERT HENRY: *omit* (Artemus Ward, Mark Twain)

Page 486, column 1, line 45ff.
NICHOLAS, WILSON CARY: *omit* He became . . . in 1783.

Page 509, column 2, line 52
NICOLA, LEWIS: *after* France, *insert* or Ireland,

Page 510, column 2, line 61
For period after 1807 *insert semicolon and* W. H. Egle, "Names of Foreigners Who Took the Oath of Allegiance," PA. ARCHIVES, 2 ser., vol. XVII (1893); PA. ARCHIVES, see index vols.

Page 606, column 2, line 2
OBER, FREDERICK ALBION: *for comma after* Beverly *insert period*

Errata

Page 606, column 2, line 2f.
Omit on a grant . . . King.

Page 619, column 1, line 37f.
O'CONNOR, MICHAEL: *for* Rev. Joshua A. Young *read* Rev. Josue Maria Young [*q.v.*]

VOLUME VII, PART 2

OGLETHORPE TO PLATNER

Page 202, column 2, line 2f.
PARDOW, WILLIAM O'BRIEN: *omit* an heir of the Earl of Inchiquin,

Page 283, column 1, line 14
PARTRIDGE, JAMES RUDOLPH: *for comma after* Janeiro *insert period*

Page 283, column 1, line 14
Omit then known as Petropolis.

Page 302, column 2, line 7
PATTERSON, DANIEL TODD: *after semicolon insert* R. C. Archibald, CARLYLE'S FIRST LOVE: MARGARET GORDON LADY BANNERMAN (1910);

Page 309, column 2, line 10f.
PATTERSON, WILLIAM: *for* was born . . . Ireland *read* was born on Fanad, a peninsula in County Donegal, Ireland, at a townland known as Rosgarrow

Page 310, column 1, line 49
After semicolon insert R. C. Archibald, CARLYLE'S FIRST LOVE: MARGARET GORDON LADY BANNERMAN (1910);

Page 428, column 2, line 55
PENINGTON, EDWARD: *for* in the catalogue of Friends' books *read* in Joseph Smith's A DESCRIPTIVE CATALOGUE OF FRIENDS' BOOKS (1867)

Page 543, column 2, line 34
PHILLIPS, SAMUEL: *for* the earliest *read* one of the earliest

VOLUME VIII, PART 1

PLATT TO ROBERDEAU

Page 15, column 1, line 46ff.
PLUMLEY, FRANK: *for* He was lecturer . . . in 1888 *read* He was lecturer on constitutional law, commercial law, and social ethics from 1887 to 1893, and lecturer on international law from 1903 to 1911, at Norwich University. He was elected a trustee in 1888 and was later vice-president and acting president

Page 36, column 2, line 2
POLK, JAMES KNOX: *after* to *insert* immediate

Page 49, column 1, line 27
POLLARD, JOSEPH PERCIVAL: *for* dishonest *read* honest

Page 135, column 1, line 20f.
POTTER, WILLIAM JAMES: *omit* in the . . . a student *and insert* he entered Harvard College, from which he was graduated in 1854. He then enrolled

Page 211, column 2, line 56ff.
PRICE, ELI KIRK: *for* came . . . County *read* settled in Montgomery County in 1697

Page 254, column 1, line 31ff.
PRUYN, JOHN VAN SCHAICK LANSING: *for* It was . . . charities *read* It was at the suggestion of Pruyn that in 1867 Governor Fenton recommended the board of charities which the legislature established

Page 254, column 1, line 35
For commission *read* board

Page 295, column 1, line 15
QUANTRILL, WILLIAM CLARKE: *omit* comma *and for* women, and children were *read* were ruthlessly

Page 336, column 1, line 57f.
RAMÉE, JOSEPH JACQUES: *for* In 1811 . . . to New York; *read* in Hamburg, through the wealthy Breckwold family, Ramée made the acquaintance of the English merchant John Parish. The latter's son, David, invited Ramée to come to America in 1811 to design the layout of Parishville, a new settlement the Parishes were planning in part of their holdings in St. Lawrence County.

Page 336, column 2, line 6
For in *read* In

Page 337, column 1, line 33
For period after 1934 *insert*); *and* HAMBURGISCHES KUNSTLER LEXIKON (1854); Paul T. Hoffmann, NEUES ALTONA 1919-1929; ZEHN JAHRE AUFBAU EINER GROSSSTADT (1929).

Page 338, column 1, line 29ff.
RAMSAY, DAVID: *for* During . . . Continental Congress *read* From May 1782 to February 1783 and from May 1785 to May 1786 he was a delegate in the Continental Congress, and was for the last six months of his stay chairman of the Congress

Errata

Page 384, column 1, line 38
RAPP, WILHELM: *for* July 14, 1828 *read* July 14, 1827
Page 384, column 1, line 40
For Leonberg *read* Perouse
Page 384, column 1, line 55f.
For January, 1851 *read* June, 1850
Page 385, column 1, line 22
Add Birth certificate and other documents in Newberry Lib., Chicago.
Page 444, column 2, line 53f.
REDWOOD, ABRAHAM: *omit* Early in his eighteenth year, *and insert* On
Page 523, column 2, line 19
REZANOV, NIKOLAI PETROVICH: *omit* exclusive
Page 576, column 1, line 54
RICHARDSON, WILDS PRESTON: *omit* at Murmansk,
Page 576, column 1, line 56
For period after 1919 *insert comma, also* and effected the withdrawal of the American army from the Archangel fighting area.
Page 644, column 1, line 28
ROBB, JAMES: *for* a Meetkerk *read* Mary (Meetkerk) Robb
Page 644, column 2, line 22
For "His marriage . . . July 31, 1881) *read* His first wife, whom he married June 14, 1836, was Louisa Werninger, daughter of Augustus and Charlotte (Van Swearingen) Werninger of Morgantown, W. Va.; later, he married a Mrs. Craig, and still later, a Mrs. Stannard of Virginia.

VOLUME VIII, PART 2

ROBERT TO SEWARD

Page 48, column 1, line 47f.
ROBINSON, MONCURE: *after* Robinson *omit comma and* a merchant,
Page 85, column 1, line 49
ROE, FRANCIS ASBURY: *for* His mother, Hannah Drake, *read* His mother was Hannah Drake.
Page 85, column 1, line 49ff.
Omit was said . . . Sir Francis Drake.
Page 246, column 1, line 41ff.
RUSSELL, JOSEPH: *insert comma after* him *and omit* of the extraordinary . . . this vessel
Page 246, column 1, line 43
For that *read* which
Page 250, column 1, line 2
RUSSELL, WILLIAM: *for period insert comma and for* He *read* but
Page 250, column 1, line 3ff.
For comma insert period and omit because . . . at that time.
Page 372, column 1, line 37ff.
SARTAIN, JOHN: *omit* In 1885 . . . Armenia.
Page 372, column 2, line 5
For Schüssele *read* Schussele [*q.v.*]
Page 391, column 2, line 37f.
SAVAGE, THOMAS STAUGHTON: *for comma after* gorilla *insert period and omit* previously unknown.
Page 500, column 1, line 45
SCOTT, SAMUEL PARSONS: *for* Lobinger *read* Lobingier
Page 505, column 2, line 12f.
SCOTT, WINFIELD: *omit* of the clan Buccleuch

VOLUME IX, PART 1

SEWELL TO STEVENSON

Page 50, column 1, line 40f.
SHAYS, DANIEL: *for* then to Hadley, and Hatfield *read* then to Petersham
Page 62, column 2, line 46
SHELBY, JOSEPH ORVILLE: *for* Grantz *read* Gratz
Page 267, column 2, line 20
SMITH, FRANCIS MARION: *for* Two years later *read* A little more than a year later
Page 284, column 1, line 5f.
SMITH, JAMES: *for* Shortly after . . . he *read* Later he
Page 284, column 1, line 11
After life. *insert* He was admitted to the bar in 1752.
Page 284, column 1, line 56f.
For vigorously opposing *read* opposed to
Page 284, column 2, line 5ff.
For (1779) *read* (1780–81) *and for* as judge . . . controversy *read* and he was commissioned judge of the Pennsylvania high court of errors and appeals on Nov. 20, 1780, but resigned Mar. 20, 1781 and apparently never served

Errata

Page 361, column 1, line 27
SMITH, WILLIAM: *omit* Sir
Page 368, column 1, line 21
SMITH, WILLIAM SOOY: *for* Ohio *read* Ill.
Page 386, column 2, line 52f.
SNOW, LORENZO: *omit* although . . . forty years
Page 530, column 2, line 38
STARK, JOHN: *omit* County

VOLUME IX, PART 2

STEWARD TO TROWBRIDGE

Page 4, column 1, line 42f.
STEWART, ALEXANDER TURNEY: *for comma insert period and omit* and the current expenses . . . a year.
Page 113, column 1, line 23
STOUGHTON, EDWIN WALLACE: *for* Mary Fiske *read* Mary Fisk (Bound) Green
Page 176, column 1, line 12
STUART, ROBERT: *after* duties *omit* for *and insert* on imported furs and low duties on
Page 377, column 1, line 13
TERHUNE, MARY VIRGINIA HAWES: *omit comma and* the first
Page 377, column 1, line 14
For the first *read* an
Page 411, column 2, line 58ff.
THAYER, WHITNEY EUGENE: *for* Hollis . . . Churches *read* and Hollis Street churches, the First Church (Unitarian), Music Hall, where Theodore Parker's followers worshiped,
Page 463, column 1, line 29
THOMPSON, JOHN: *insert* [*qq.v.*] *after* Edwards Pierrepont
Page 505, column 2, line 50
THORNTON, WILLIAM: *for comma after* corner *insert period*
Page 505, column 2, line 51ff.
Omit in one . . . was signed.
Page 531, column 1, line 6ff.
TIEBOUT, CORNELIUS: *for* He is said . . . May 1830 *read* In 1826 he went to New Harmony, Ind., with William Maclure [*q.v.*], where he taught engraving in the community school. The engravings for the first parts of AMERICAN CONCHOLOGY by Thomas Say [*q.v.*] are by Tiebout. He died of tuberculosis at New Harmony and is buried in Wood's graveyard
Page 531, column 1, line 20
For period after (1910) *insert semicolon and* information from Workingmen's Institute, New Harmony, Ind.
Page 561, column 2, line 40f.
TINGLEY, KATHERINE AUGUSTA WESTCOTT: *for* Her father . . . in the Civil War, *read* Her father, an officer in the Civil War, was a large lumber merchant
Page 561, column 2, line 54
For stenographer *read* mechanical engineer
Page 561, column 2, line 57
For spiritualist medium *read* psychometric reader
Page 562, column 1, line 22f.
For "the Veiled Mahatma . . . Purple Mother," *read* "Purple," and "the Light of the Lodge,"
Page 562, column 1, line 38
For April *read* February
Page 562, column 1, line 39
For unseated *read* overthrew
Page 562, column 2, line 17
For comma after suits *insert period and omit* but
Page 562, column 2, line 18
For in *read* In
Page 562, column 2, line 23
For resided chiefly *read* spent an increasing amount of time
Page 574, column 2, line 25f.
TODD, SERENO EDWARDS: *for* the death of *read* a divorce from *and for* who left *read* by whom he had
Page 574, column 2, line 34
After Todd *omit period and insert* and information as to certain facts from a granddaughter, Mrs. W. V. D. Brigham.
Page 624, column 1, line 18
TRACY, NATHANIEL: *for* 120 sail of *read* many *and for* with 2225 *read* and
Page 624, column 1, line 20
For 110 *read* numerous
Page 624, column 1, line 24ff.
For semicolon after army *insert period and omit* his . . . worth $2,733,300
Page 624, column 1, line 26f.
Omit 120 *and for* $4,000,000 *read* a large sum
Page 629, column 2, line 25
TRAVIS, WALTER JOHN: *for* Lord Bishop *read* Archdeacon
Page 629, column 2, line 26
Omit Anglican

Errata

VOLUME X, PART 1

Troye to Wentworth

Page 300, column 1, line 28
WADDEL, MOSES: *for* Hampton-Sydney *read* Hampden-Sydney

Page 349, column 2, line 42
WALKER, JOHN GRIMES: *for* Henry G. Pickering *read* Henry W. Pickering

Page 349, column 2, line 43
For four *read* five

Page 395, column 2, line 44f.
WALTER, THOMAS: *omit* the A.M. degree and

Page 625, column 1, line 19
WELD, ARTHUR CYRIL GORDON: *after* descendant *insert* of Joseph Weld, a brother

Page 625, column 1, line 20f.
For After attending . . . in 1879 *read* In 1879 Arthur went abroad

VOLUME X, PART 2

Werden to Zunser

Page 284, column 2, line 40f.
WILLIAMS, OTHO HOLLAND: *for* battles *read* battle *and omit* and King's Mountain

Page 291, column 2, line 55
WILLIAMS, TALCOTT: *for* Congregational *read* Presbyterian

Page 291, column 2, line 56
After missionary *insert comma and for* and *read* was

Page 291, column 2, line 57ff.
For comma after [*q.v.*] *insert period and omit* was instrumental . . . Beirut.

Page 292, column 1, line 27
Omit as Philadelphia's leading critic

Page 414, column 1, line 16ff.
WINTHROP, JOHN: *omit* While . . . Royal Society.

Page 438, column 1, line 21f.
WITHERSPOON, JOHN: *omit* He was moderator . . . May 1789.

Page 555, column 2, line 60f.
WRIGHT, JAMES LENDREW: *Omit* In his late years . . . he had previously fought.

Page 583, column 2, line 40
WYMAN, JEFFRIES: *for* Capt. J. M. Forbes *read* Capt. R. B. Forbes

Page 589, column 1, line 49
XÁNTUS, JÁNOS: *for* Ignácznak *read* Ignácz

Page 589, column 2, line 9ff.
Omit At the conclusion . . . sand banks.

Page 589, column 2, line 31
For EJSZAKAMERIKÁBÓL *read* ÉJSZAKAMERIKÁBÓL

Page 589, column 2, line 44
For A *read* a

VOLUME XI, PART 1

First Supplement

Page 591, column 1, lines 55f.
OWEN, THOMAS MCADORY: *for* Susan Bankhead *read* Marie Susan Bankhead

Page 607, column 2, line 7
PRATT, ORSON: *for* September 1930 *read* September 1830

VOLUME I, PART 1

ABBE - BARRYMORE

(VOLUME I OF THE ORIGINAL EDITION)

CROSS REFERENCES WITHIN THIS AND THE SUCCEEDING VOLUMES ARE MADE TO THE VOLUME NUMBERS OF THE ORIGINAL EDITION.

CONTRIBUTORS
VOLUME I, PART 1

Contributor	Initials
Wilbur Cortez Abbott	W. C. A.
James Truslow Adams	J. T. A.
Randolph Greenfield Adams	R. G. A—s.
Robert G. Albion	R. G. A—n.
Carroll Storrs Alden	C. S. A.
Edmund Kimball Alden	E. K. A.
Edward Ellis Allen	E. E. A.
Horace Newton Allen	H. N. A.
William Henry Allison	W. H. A.
Dinsmore Alter	D. A.
Charles Henry Ambler	C. H. A.
Joseph Sweetman Ames	J. S. A.
John Clark Archer	J. C. A.
C. A. Bach	C. A. B.
Benjamin Wisner Bacon	B. W. B.
Theodore D. Bacon	T. D. B.
Ray Palmer Baker	R. P. Ba—r.
Hayes Baker-Crothers	H. B–C.
Charles Montague Bakewell	C. M. B.
Eugene Campbell Barker	E. C. B.
Viola Florence Barnes	V. F. B.
Claribel Ruth Barnett	C. R. B.
Harry McWhirter Barrett	H. M. B.
John Spencer Bassett	J. S. B.
Ernest Sutherland Bates	E. S. B.
Louis Agricola Bauer	L. A. B.
Arthur Grandville Beach	A. G. B.
Carl Lotus Becker	C. L. B.
Elbert Jay Benton	E. J. B.
Ralph Paul Bieber	R. P. Bi—r.
Frank Wilson Blackmar	F. W. B.
Edwin Howland Blashfield	E. H. B.
Theodore C. Blegen	T. C. B.
Roger S. Boardman	R. S. B.
Theodore Bolton	T. B.
Beverley W. Bond, Jr.	B. W. B—d.
Sarah G. Bowerman	S. G. B.
Charles N. Boyd	C. N. B.
William Kenneth Boyd	W. K. B.
Lilian Brandt	L. B.
Frederick Edward Brasch	F. E. B.
Edward Breck	E. B.
Howard Allen Bridgman	H. A. B.
Albert Perry Brigham	A. P. B.
Clarence Saunders Brigham	C. S. B.
Robert Preston Brooks	R. P. B—s.
Roscoe Conkling Ensign Brown	R. C. E. B.
Philip Alexander Bruce	P. A. B.
Solon Justus Buck	S. J. B.
James Aloysius Burns	J. A. B.
Walter Lincoln Burrage	W. L. B.
Charles Henry Butler	C. H. B.
Robert C. Canby	R. C. C.
Clarence Edwin Carter	C. E. C.
Hardee Chambliss	H. C.
Frank H. Chase	F. H. C.
Stanley P. Chase	S. P. C.
Francis Albert Christie	F. A. C.
Hubert Lyman Clark	H. L. C.
Robert Glass Cleland	R. G. C.
Frederick W. Coburn	F. W. C.
Charles F. Cochran	C. F. C.
James Fairbanks Colby	J. F. C.
Fannie L. Gwinner Cole	F. L. G. C.
Ellis Merton Coulter	E. M. C.
Stanley Coulter	S. C.
Avery O. Craven	A. O. C.
Nelson Antrim Crawford	N. A. C.
Laurence Murray Crosbie	L. M. C.
William James Cunningham	W. J. C.
Harrison Clifford Dale	H. C. D.
Arthur Burr Darling	A. B. D.
Herman J. Deutsch	H. J. D.
Fred H. Dewey	F. H. D.
Theodore Diller	T. D.
Charles Allen Dinsmore	C. A. D—e.
Gilbert H. Doane	G. H. D.
Eleanor Robinette Dobson	E. R. D.
Raymond Smith Dugan	R. S. D.
Clyde Augustus Duniway	C. A. D—y.
William Frederick Durand	W. F. D.
Harrison Griswold Dwight	H. G. D.
J. H. Easterby	J. H. E.
Edwin Francis Edgett	E. F. E.
Brother Edward	B. E.
Samuel Atkins Eliot	S. A. E.
Charles R. Erdman, Jr.	C. R. E., Jr.
Lawrence Boyd Evans	L. B. E.
Harold Underwood Faulkner	H. U. F.
John Alfred Faulkner	J. A. F.
Gustave Joseph Fiebeger	G. J. F.
Mantle Fielding	M. F.
G. Clyde Fisher	G. C. F.
Walter Lynwood Fleming	W. L. F—g.
Alexander Clarence Flick	A. C. F.
Worthington Chauncey Ford	W. C. F.
Harold North Fowler	H. N. F.
Douglas Southall Freeman	D. S. F.

Contributors

William Little Frierson . . . W. L. F—n.
Claude Moore Fuess . . . . C. M. F.
Raymond Garfield Fuller . R. G. F.
John F. Fulton . . . . J. F. F.
Francis Pendleton Gaines . F. P. G.
George H. Genzmer . . . . G. H. G.
W. J. Ghent . . . . W. J. G.
Frank A. Golder . . . . . . F. A. G.
Colin B. Goodykoontz . . . C. B. G.
Armistead Churchill Gordon, Jr. A. C. G., Jr.
Walter S. Grant . . . . . . W. S. G.
Charles Graves . . . . . . C. G.
Warren Grice. . . . . W. G.
George Gorham Groat. . . . G. G. G.
Byrne Hackett . . . . B. H—t.
LeRoy R. Hafen. . . . . . . L. R. H.
Robert Hale . . . . R. H.
Robert Edmond Ham. . . . . R. E. H.
J. G. de Roulhac Hamilton . J. G. de R. H.
Peter Joseph Hamilton . . . P. J. H.
Talbot F. Hamlin . . . . . T. F. H.
John Louis Haney . . . . . J. L. H.
Isaac S. Harrell . . . . . . I. S. H.
Benjamin Harrow . . . . . . B. H—w.
Louis C. Hatch . . . . L. C. H.
George Henry Haynes. . . . G. H. H.
Marshall DeLancey Haywood M. DeL. H.
John Donald Hicks . . . . . J. D. H.
Frank L. Hise . . . . F. L. H.
A. A. Hopkins . . . . A. A. H.
Arthur Hornblow . . . . . A. H.
Walter Hough . . . . W. H.
Leland Ossian Howard . . . L. O. H.
M. A. De Wolfe Howe . . . M. A. DeW. H.
William Jackson Humphreys . W. J. H.
Theodore Henley Jack . . . T. H. J.
Joseph Jackson . . . . J. J.
Edward Hopkins Jenkins . . E. H. J.
Allen Johnson . . . . A. J.
Edgar A. J. Johnson . . . . . E. A. J. J.
J. Wesley Johnston . . . . . J. W. J.
David Starr Jordan . . . . . D. S. J
Jessie Knight Jordan . . . . J. K. J.
Hope Frances Kane . . . . . H. F. K.
Marie A. Kasten . . . . . . M. A. K.
Herbert A. Kellar . . . . . H. A. K.
Louise Phelps Kellogg . . . L. P. K.
William Joseph Kerby . . . W. J. K.
Alfred Vincent Kidder . . . A. V. K.
Felix M. Kirsch. . . . . . . F. M. K.
Edgar Wallace Knight . . . E. W. K.
H. W. Howard Knott . . . . H. W. H. K.
Conrad H. Lanza . . . . . . C. H. L—a.
Charles Lee Lewis . . . . . C. L. L.
Charles H. Lincoln . . . . C. H. L—n.
Charles Ramsdell Lingley C. R. L.
L. Leland Locke . . . . . . L. L. L.
Frederick William Loetscher F. W. L.
Henry Miller Lydenberg . . H. M. L.
Lee Sullivan McCollester . L. S. M.
Thomas Denton McCormick . T. D. M.
Roswell Cheney McCrea . . R. C. M.
P. B. McDonald . . . . . . P. B. M.
Walter Martin McFarland . W. M. M.
John Hanson Thomas McPherson J. H. T. M.
William Harrison Mace . . . W. H. M.
Dumas Malone . . . . D. M.
Mary E. Manchester . . . . M. E. M.
Louis Leopold Mann . . . . L. L. M.
Frederick Herman Martens . F. H. M.
Thomas L. Masson . . . . . T. L. M.
Frank Jewett Mather, Jr. . F. J. M.
Shailer Mathews . . . . . . S. Ma—s.
David M. Matteson . . . . D. M. M.
Emil Mayer . . . . E. M—r.
Lawrence Shaw Mayo . . . . L. S. M.
Stewart Means . . . . . . S. Me—s.
George Perkins Merrill . . G. P. M.
Edwin Mims . . . . E. M—s.
Broadus Mitchell . . . . . B. M.
Carl W. Mitman . . . . . . C. W. M.
Robert E. Moody . . . . . . R. E. M.
Charles Moore . . . . . . C. M.
Samuel Eliot Morison . . . S. E. M.
William Alfred Morris . . . W. A. M.
Richard L. Morton . . . . . R. L. M.
Montrose J. Moses . . . . . M. J. M.
George Fulmer Mull . . . . G. F. M.
Paul H. Musser . . . . . . P. H. M.
H. R. Mussey . . . . H. R. M.
Edwin G. Nash . . . . E. G. N.
J. H. Nelson . . . . J. H. N.
Allan Nevins . . . . A. N.
Jeannette P. Nichols . . . . J. P. N.
Charles Noble . . . . C. N.
Henry Fairfield Osborn . . H. F. O.
James Harvey Osborne . . . J. H. O.
Frank L. Owsley . . . . . . F. L. O.
Francis Randolph Packard . F. R. P.
Victor Hugo Paltsits . . . . V. H. P.
Stanley M. Pargellis . . . . S. M. P.
William Belmont Parker . . W. B. P.
Fred Lewis Pattee . . . . . F. L. P—e.
Frederic Logan Paxson . . . F. L. P—n.
C. C. Pearson . . . . C. C. P.
Theodore Calvin Pease . . . T. C. P.
Donald C. Peattie . . . . . D. C. P.
Frederick Torrel Persons . F. T. P.
A. Everett Peterson . . . . A. E. P.
James M. Phalen . . . . . . J. M. P.
Henry Augustus Pilsbry . . H. A. P.
J. A. Pollard . . . . J. A. P.

Contributors

Julius W. Pratt . . . . . . J. W. P.
Waldo Selden Pratt . . . . W. S. P.
Edward Preble . . . . E. P.
Herbert Ingram Priestley . H. I. P.
Richard J. Purcell . . . . . R. J. P.
Milo Milton Quaife . . . . M. M. Q.
Arthur Hobson Quinn . . . A. H. Q.
Charles Henry Rammelkamp C. H. R.
Charles William Ramsdell . C. W. R.
P. Orman Ray . . . . P. O. R.
Jesse Siddall Reeves . . . . J. S. R.
Charles Dudley Rhodes . . C. D. R.
Irving Berdine Richman . . I. B. R.
Franklin Lafayette Riley . F. L. R.
William Alexander Robinson W. A. R.
Lindsay Rogers . . . . . . L. R.
George Rose, III . . . . . . G. R.
Frank Edward Ross . . . . . F. E. R.
Henry Kalloch Rowe . . . H. K. R.
Robert R. Rowe. . . . . . . R. R. R.
Dunbar Rowland . . . . . . D. R.
Dorothy Scarborough . . . D. S.
Joseph Schafer . . . . J. S.
Montgomery Schuyler. . . . M. S.
Jonathan French Scott . . . J. F. S.
Frank Hayward Severance . F. H. S.
George Dudley Seymour. . . G. D. S.
William Bristol Shaw . . . W. B. S.
Arthur MacC. Shepard . . . A. MacC. S.
Richard H. Shryock . . . . . R. H. S.
Kenneth C. M. Sills. . . . . K. C. M. S.
William Adams Slade . . . . W. A. S.
Charles Forster Smith . . . C. F. S.
David Eugene Smith . . . . D. E. S.
Edgar Fahs Smith . . . . . . E. F. S.
Gerald Birney Smith . . . . G. B. S.
Ralph C. Smith . . . . R. C. S.
George Franklin Smythe . . G. F. S.
John Kimball Snyder . . . . J. K. S.
Sherrod Soule . . . . S. S.
Charles L. Souvay . . . . . C. L. S.
James Alfred Spalding . . . J. A. S.
Thomas Marshall Spaulding T. M. S.
Mary Newton Stanard . . . M. N. S.
Harris Elwood Starr . . . . H. E. S.
Martha Tucker Stephenson M. T. S.
Nathaniel Wright Stephenson N. W. S.
William Oliver Stevens . . . W. O. S.
Witmer Stone . . . . W. S.
William Seneca Sutton . . . W. S. S.
Eben Swift . . . . E. S.
Edwin Platt Tanner . . . . E. P. T.
Frank A. Taylor . . . . . . F. A. T.
John R. M. Taylor . . . . . J. R. M. T.
Herbert Thoms . . . . H. T.
Charles Franklin Thwing . C. F. T.
Caroline Ticknor . . . . . . C. T.
Wilbur Fisk Tillett. . . . . W. F. T.
Alfred Charles True . . . . A. C. T.
Roland Greene Usher . . . R. G. U.
Paul van Dyke . . . . P. V-D.
Henry R. Viets . . . . H. R. V.
Jonas Viles . . . . J. V.
John Donald Wade . . . . . J. D. W.
Raymond Weaver . . . . . . R. W.
Frank Weitenkampf . . . . F. W.
Allan Westcott . . . . . . A. W.
George F. Whicher . . . . . G. F. W.
Charles Harris Whitaker . . C. H. W.
R. J. Wickenden . . . . . . R. J. W.
E. V. Wilcox . . . . E. V. W.
Harvey W. Wiley . . . . . H. W. W.
Stanley Thomas Williams . . S. T. W.
Samuel Williston . . . . . . S. W.
James Southall Wilson . . . J. S. W.
Otto Wilson . . . . O. W.
George Edward Woodbine . G. E. W.
Carter Godwin Woodson . . C. G. W.
Thomas Woody . . . . T. W.
William Loring Worcester . W. L. W.
Herbert F. Wright . . . . . H. F. W.
John J. Wynne . . . . J. J. W.
Edna Yost . . . . E. Y.
Clarence Clark Zantzinger C. C. Z.
Andrew C. Zenos . . . . . . A. C. Z.
Theodore A. Zunder . . . . T. A. Z.

DICTIONARY OF

AMERICAN BIOGRAPHY

Abbe — Barrymore

ABBE, CLEVELAND (Dec. 3, 1838–Oct. 28, 1916), astronomer, meteorologist, was descended from John Abbe, an Englishman born in 1613, who settled in Salem, Mass., in 1635. The latter's descendants were rather numerous, especially in New England. Joshua Abbe of the fourth generation was a leader of a Baptist sect that became known as Abbeites. One of the seventh generation, George Waldo Abbe, also a Baptist and a merchant in New York City, married Charlotte Colgate. Their eldest son, Cleveland, was born in New York City and received his education there in private schools, in the David B. Scott Grammar School, and in the New York Free Academy, now the College of the City of New York, where he was granted the degree of B.A. in 1857 and M.A. in 1860. During 1857–58 he was tutor of mathematics in Trinity Latin School, New York. In 1859 he was assistant professor of engineering in the Michigan Agricultural College, and in 1859–60 tutor in engineering at the University of Michigan, where, under the influence of Prof. Brünnow, he became an enthusiastic student of astronomy. In 1861 he tried to join the army in response to Lincoln's first call for volunteers, but after a few weeks' test at a training-camp was rejected because of excessive myopia. He then assisted Dr. B. A. Gould of Cambridge, Mass., in work, 1861–64, on longitude determinations for the United States Coast Survey. The next two years, during which he was a guest or supernumerary astronomer at the Observatory of Pulkowa in Russia, were, he said, among the happiest of his life. Here he felt the scientific urge of the famous Otto Struve, the charm of a hospitable home, and the courage of intellectual companionship. In 1867 he returned to the United States and accepted the position of aid in the United States Naval Observatory. On Feb. 1, 1868, he became director of the Cincinnati Observatory, Cincinnati, Ohio, and drew up for it the following plan of work: "If the director be sustained in the general endeavor to make the observatory useful, he would propose to extend the field of activity of the observatory so as to embrace, on the one hand, scientific astronomy, meteorology and magnetism, and, on the other, the application of these sciences to geography and geodesy, to storm prediction, and to the wants of the citizen and the land surveyor" (Humphreys, p. 473). All these things needed to be done, but the work outlined had no practical relation to the capacity of a one-man observatory that was used mainly to entertain the public. It was the plan of a dreamer who dreamed his life long, planning and often beginning things good within themselves but beyond the possibility of accomplishment with the means and time available. One of his friends says: "I remember, when living at his home, seeing him very early in the morning sitting in his library reading the *Encyclopædia Britannica.* He told me that he was reading it through consecutively" (*Ibid.*, p. 471). Such a remark gives a typical picture of Cleveland Abbe so universally interested as to be unmindful of time and obstacles.

Despite the comprehensiveness of his plans for the work of the Cincinnati Observatory, his interest turned more and more to meteorology, and especially to the issuing of warnings, based on telegraphic reports, of approaching storms. His weather reports or bulletins began to be issued on Sept. 1, 1869. Hence when the Weather Service of the United States was authorized on Feb. 9, 1870, and placed under the direction of the Signal Service, Abbe, and he alone in this country, was already experienced in drawing weather maps from telegraphic reports and in making forecasts therefrom. Naturally, he was offered an important position in this new service. This he accepted, beginning Jan. 3, 1871, and of course was often the official forecaster of the weather. His success in this rôle was indifferent. He was not one of the few that see a weather map in its entirety and quickly perceive its probable changes during the next twelve to thirty-six hours. He expected to resign at the end of three years, the term of appointment, but he had found his life's work and remained with it until forced to retire by protracted illness on Aug. 3, 1916. From August 1893, his chief duty was the congenial one of editing the meteorological journals of the United States Weather Bureau. This caused him to write to hundreds of scholars the world over—a pleasure to him, but a task to those who had to decipher his difficult chirography.

Abbe was not essentially a creative scholar. He made no important discovery, and published but little that contained anything new and original. He was primarily a teacher and a propagandist. He compiled in form convenient for use the best that was known about meteorological instruments, about climate and crops, and about the mechanics of the earth's atmosphere; published nearly 300 papers on meteorology and kindred subjects; and wrote many thousands of letters encouraging others to contribute something to our knowledge of the atmosphere and its phenomena. He was also one of the most active of those who worked for the adoption of standard time. He was a member of the National Academy of Sciences, and of many other organizations; and the recipient of the Symons Memorial Gold Medal bestowed by the Royal Meteorological Society of Great Britain in 1912 for eminence in meteorology, and the Marcellus Hartley Medal awarded by the National Academy of Sciences Apr. 18, 1916, for contributions to human welfare. His side interests were many: oriental archæology and ethnology, geology, botany, and music. His house in Washington entertained many guests. He was twice married: on May 10, 1870, to Frances Martha Neal of Cincinnati, Ohio, who died July 24, 1908, after their three sons had grown to manhood; and on Apr. 12, 1909, to Margaret Augusta Percival of Basseterre, St. Christopher, B. W. I.

[W. J. Humphreys, "Biog. Memoir of Cleveland Abbe," in *Nat. Acad. Sci. Biog. Memoirs,* VIII (1919); Cleveland Abbe and Josephine G. Nichols, *Abbe-Abbey Genealogy* (1916); *Lowell Courier-Citizen,* Mar. 1, 1928.]

W. J. H.

ABBETT, LEON (Oct. 8, 1836–Dec. 4, 1894), lawyer, governor of New Jersey, was born in Philadelphia, the son of Ezekiel and Sarah (Howell) Abbett. After graduating from the Central High School of Philadelphia in 1853, he entered a law office and was admitted to the bar in 1858. On Oct. 8, 1862, he married Mary Briggs of Philadelphia, moving immediately to Hoboken, N. J. In 1866 he moved to Jersey City, where he resided until his death. He began his political career in 1863, being appointed corporation attorney of Hoboken. The next year he was elected to the New Jersey Assembly, serving two terms, during both of which he was chairman of the Democratic caucus. In 1869 and again in 1870, he represented Jersey City in the Assembly. Elected Speaker both terms, he gave great satisfaction to the Democratic majority by his rulings. Senator from Hudson County 1875–77, and chosen as president of the Senate in 1877, he became a prominent candidate for the Democratic nomination for governor in 1877. He was defeated, however, by the tactics of his bitter political rival, Orestes Cleveland, who had the name of Gen. McClellan brought forward at the last minute, thereby stampeding the convention. Abbett retaliated three years later, preventing the nomination of Cleveland for governor by his audacious, if not unscrupulous, manipulation of the machinery of the convention from his vantage point of chairman.

Abbett's greatest public service was undoubtedly his successful fight to secure laws taxing railroad corporations. His fidelity to his party and the recognition of his services in the struggle to subject the railroad corporations to their share of the public tax burdens, led to his nomination for governor in 1883. His party platform contained among other things the proposal for equal taxation "on all properties within the state, whether that of individuals or corporations." Abbett was elected by a plurality of 6,800 and in his inaugural message struck out boldly at the railroads. "Our tax laws," he said, "demand immediate and radical reform. They impose unequal burdens. The only true rule in taxation is equality." Public opinion was aroused by the inaugural, and the legislature, in the face of bitter opposition, passed the famous tax laws (*New Jersey Public Laws,* 1884, pp. 142, 232), which imposed a state tax on railroad and other corporations, and to some extent equalized the burden of taxation.

On retiring from the governorship Abbett was nominated for the United States Senate by the Democratic caucus. The Democrats had a majority on joint ballot, so his election seemed certain. In one of the stormiest legislative sessions in the history of the state, however, the railroad lobby worked its revenge on Abbett. Four Democrats united with the Republicans to elect Rufus Blodgett, the superintendent of the Long Branch Railroad. Although defeated, Abbett came out of the contest stronger than ever, many Democrats feeling that he had been deprived of a reward justly due him. A mark of his popularity was shown in 1889 when he was again nominated for governor by acclamation, no other name being mentioned. He was elected by the unprecedented majority of 14,253. Abbett accepted a second term as governor with the view of winning the United States senatorship in 1893 and undoubtedly would have done so, had he not alienated the stanchest of his party supporters by his veto of a bill which would have legalized the combination of the Port Reading Company and the Jersey Central. Abbett's career was practically ended with this second defeat of his lifelong ambition. Appointed to the supreme court in 1893 by Gov. Werts, he served till his death a year later.

[*Docs. of the N.J. Leg.*, 1884–87, 1890–93, for Gov. Abbett's messages; W. E. Sackett, *Modern Battles of Trenton, 1868–94* (Trenton, 1895), for account of N.J. politics during this period; *N.J. Law Jour.*, XVII, 381, XVIII, 28; *The Record of Leon Abbett as Assemblyman, Senator and Governor* (Jersey City, 1889); F. B. Lee, *New Jersey as a Colony and as a State* (1902), IV.]

C. R. E., Jr.

ABBEY, EDWIN AUSTIN (Apr. 1, 1852–Aug. 1, 1911), historical and mural painter, was born at Philadelphia. To the father, William Maxwell Abbey, who passed unsuccessfully from business to business, little of the son's ability may be traced. The paternal grandfather, Roswell Abbey, was a pioneer in the application of electrotyping to printing and in the invention of the internal-explosion engine. Here we may suspect the origins of Edwin A. Abbey's executive and mechanical capacity. The paternal line is lost in the veteran of the Revolutionary War, Samuel. It was the family tradition that the stock was French. In the line of Abbey's mother, Margery Ann Kiple, English, Irish, and German blood mingled. She was a woman of fine taste in reading and of understanding disposition. The artist in Abbey apparently derives chiefly from her.

From mere infancy Edwin Abbey sketched what he saw. In the hope of making an Episcopal clergyman of him, the family put him in Henry D. Gregory's School, one of the best of its time in Philadelphia. In his fifteenth year they yielded to his evident vocation by giving him Saturday drawing lessons with Isaac L. Williams. At sixteen he was allowed to quit school and to study the art of drawing on box-wood for engraving, with Van Ingen and Snyder. At seventeen he was following the antique and life class of Christian Schussele at the Pennsylvania Academy. Sketches of this period reproduced in Lucas's biography show that Abbey's hand was already light and his sense of humorous characterization keen. As a correspondent to *Our Boys and Girls* he had shown signs of intellectual precocity. The episode brought him into relations with the future painters, Walter L. Palmer and Will H. Low. During this practice time Abbey fixed his taste permanently. It was paging over the English illustrated journals at Van Ingen's and Snyder's that brought before him as models, Millais, Rossetti, Pinwell, Arthur Boyd Houghton, and others. Abbey loved the precision of the work, as he did its frankly emotional content, and throughout his life, in a time when French and chiefly technical ideals were imposing themselves in America, Abbey remained unshaken in these early and fruitful admirations. He had also begun, under the influence of Eastlake's books, to frequent the old furniture shops.

Every ambitious young illustrator of the moment wished to get into *Harper's Weekly*. Abbey's début, preluded probably by many rejections, was the full-page picture "The Puritans' First Thanksgiving," published on Dec. 3, 1870. It was an appropriate beginning for an illustrator who was to make the British seventeenth and eighteenth centuries peculiarly his own field. The next year, being nearly nineteen, Abbey joined the illustrators' staff of Harper & Brothers, in Franklin Square, New York, with a salary of fifteen dollars a week. To the heavy duties of journalistic illustration young Abbey set himself resolutely under the kindly chieftainship of Charles Parsons and casual tutelage of the versatile C. S. Reinhart, an intelligent assimilator of the current English style. The work at Harper's was relentless. The big drawings, often worked up in the office by several draftsmen, had to be ready for the many woodcutters who collaborated on the big block regardless of the clock or the sun. It was a task to harden and coarsen the fibre of a young illustrator. In Abbey's case only the hardening resulted. For about five years with Harper's he made little impression. In these years he often did the hack work of redrawing other men's designs. The gusto and conscience he put into such work is well shown in the fantasy "Fire, Fire: A New Yorker's Nightmare" (from a sketch by Gray Parker), in the *Weekly* for Feb. 8, 1873.

His illustrations for several years still were uncharacteristic, mostly travel sketches from photographs, as in "Round by Propeller" (1872), where the sketches were his own. Indeed, we come upon the true Abbey rather suddenly in *Harper's Magazine* for May 1874, in the design for Herrick's poem "Corinna's Going A-Maying." It is charming, but Abbey, not finding it fit for the book, replaced it with another drawing. In 1874 he withdrew from Harper's, because they would not raise his salary from thirty-five to forty dollars a week, and set up as a free lance, sharing his studio with the most brilliant draftsman among the young illustrators, J. E. Kelly. The shift marks a considerable change in Abbey's manner of life. For four years he had been leading as much of a home life as a young artist could. His Brooklyn boarding-house was near his cousins, the Potters and Curtisses. There was good music and abundant merriment at their evening reunions, but Abbey's artist acquaintance was pretty well limited to Harper's staff. The move to his own studio, 35 Union Square, soon changed for the old University Building on Washington Square, brought Abbey into contact with many older artists and with the younger progressives who were one by one returning from Paris. His gift of friendship and charm soon won him that just affection and popularity among his peers which only increased to the end.

Abbey's year and a half of free-lancing were eventful. Working for *Scribner's,* he moved toward his true field, the seventeenth and eighteenth centuries. Such were his illustrations for Bryant and Gay's *Popular History of the United States* (1876–81). For its magazine appearance he did the drawing "John Nixon Reading the Declaration of Independence in the State House Yard, July 8th, 1776." It was not carried over into the book, but thirty-five years later Abbey repeated the theme in monumental form for the Pennsylvania State House. Again his illustrations for E. E. Hale's story "Philip Nolan's Friends," in *Scribner's,* marked a more accomplished antiquarianism. Already Abbey's lifelong habit of drawing true to his period was fixed. He bought, hired, or designed old costumes lavishly, at times spending on such archæological preparations as much as he got for the drawing. The Harpers continued to employ him and in the illustration of Dickens's *Christmas Stories,* a series used in part in the magazine, and in a volume of Harper's Household Edition of Dickens, they gave him the most congenial commission he had yet had. The *Christmas Stories,* Abbey's first illustrated book, was copyrighted in 1875. The English influence already pronounced was probably enhanced by a notable exhibition of British figure-painters in water-colors,—Fildes, Woods, Pinwell, and Du Maurier, in that year. The year before, Abbey exhibited at the American Water Color Society his painting, "Rustics Dancing in a Barn," and had the chagrin of being praised at the expense of his veteran colleague on *Harper's Weekly,* Winslow Homer. Characteristically, Abbey promptly paid him a visit of disavowal and homage.

Having tried his wings successfully, Abbey, in 1870, returned to the security of fifty dollars a week with Harper's. His position was still that of a valued general-utility man. For any kind of a short story he would make an acceptable illustration, while, when the popular C. S. Reinhart was not available, he did excellent decorations for poetry. He was pretty sure to appear in any article on American history. On the whole, Abbey's work from 1876 to 1878 is even and respectable, rather than brilliant, but now and then a fine cut heralds the coming master. He did much to improve the practice of Harper's art department, winning his associates to his own habit of working so far as possible from nature. In 1876 he did his first mural, a view of red roofs from a window, for a little panel in Harper's reception-room. He visited the Centennial Exhibition at Philadelphia, where he stood off from the general admiration for the French fine painters, preferring as ever the English. The next year he joined the Tile Club, that joyous band of young artists home from Europe—F. Hopkinson Smith, Augustus Saint Gaudens, J. Alden Weir, William M. Chase, Stanford White. Abbey's geniality made him a beloved member. Harper's now saw the expediency of giving Abbey the actual experience of that England which he had grasped only in imagination. The plan was for a simple visit, to sketch about Stratford-on-Avon and complete the Herrick drawings. Abbey hesitated to make the move. The financial arrangements were vague, and he now had his parents to support. With reassurances from Harper's he made what was probably his most momentous decision. In a commission for *Scribner's* just before he sailed, he first essayed what was to be a later specialty, the illustration of plays. He drew Charles Coghlan and others of Wallack's stock company in their costumes in the *School for Scandal.* In the same year he had done a fine illustration in *Harper's* for Thomas Bailey Aldrich's tragedy, *Mercedes.* On Dec. 7, 1878, the Harpers gave Abbey a breakfast at Delmonico's and delivered him alongside the *Germanic* in a four-in-hand.

To the English scene Abbey brought an extraordinary professional training, but in the new surroundings he found himself rather slowly. The sketches of Stratford-on-Avon for an article by William Winter, the ostensible reason for his trip, duly appeared in *Harper's Magazine* in April 1879. In New York they still regarded him as a general-utility man, proposing such tasks as the illustration of sketches by Mrs. Lillie; *The English Lakes,* by Moncure D. Conway; George H. Boughton's *An Artist's Rambles in Holland;* William Black's unsuccessful historical novel, *Judith Shakespeare;* James de Mille's trashy r

Abbey

mance, *A Castle in Spain.* At least this hack work kept Abbey on from month to month, and meanwhile he made good friends. Early in 1879 we find him in Bloomsbury, and, after several moves, joining forces with his friends, the Lillies, at South Kensington. He met Fred Barnard, George H. Boughton, and Alfred Parsons, whose decorative head and tail pieces were to grace many of his own books. He became a familiar of good drawing-rooms where he heard Brahms and George Henschel play. In June 1879, he saw the paintings at Paris, chiefly the old masters, opining of the most celebrated moderns that "Their subjects are not worth the immense amount of clever painting they put into them."

With the home office, relations were long unsatisfactory. It reproduced his delicate drawings badly, paid him by space,—extraordinary measure for a work of art,—and reduced his designs cruelly. Such issues were reasonably adjusted during a visit of some months to New York in 1881 and 1882. The year 1881 saw the appearance in *Harper's* of many of Abbey's best Herrick drawings, and the first mention of him in the table of contents. The next year he agreed to do twelve illustrations for Goldsmith's *She Stoops to Conquer.* Still the next year he made the first and perhaps the best designs—the drawings for "Sally in Our Alley"—for his loveliest book *Old Songs.* In 1882 had appeared the long-postponed *Selections from the Poetry of Robert Herrick,* surely the finest illustrated book that had appeared in America up to its time. Early in 1886 he undertook to illustrate the Comedies of Shakespeare. In 1889 the sixteen drawings for *Old Songs,* published that year as a book, won Abbey a first-class medal at the world's exhibition at Paris, and Joseph Pennell in a generous footnote to *Pen Drawing and Pen Draughtsmen* acclaimed him as "the greatest living illustrator."

Abbey's delicate and somewhat complicated lines usually suffered in the hands of the wood-engraver, and he frequently requested Harper's to be "processed." This was done in the case of *She Stoops to Conquer* (1886), and all his later books. The drawings for *She Stoops,* which had been in progress for four years, are larger in scale, less decorative, more fully pictorial than the Herrick illustrations. They reflect Abbey's growing interest in painting. The pen drawings are perhaps Abbey at his best, carefully studied without loss of grace and geniality. The evocation of the past is remarkable even for Abbey. Several large wash drawings were made for this book. They are highly competent, even brilliant, but they lack the compelling charm of the pen drawings. They suggest that Abbey's supremacy was with the pen, and that with any other instrument he was merely prominent among many able contemporaries. The Goldsmith drawings, published when he was thirty-four, made Abbey famous at home. They were really the occasion of his most lucrative commission, the Shakespeare illustrations, arranged with the Harpers during a brief visit to New York early in 1886. At the end of that year the Goldsmith sketches were successfully exhibited at the Grolier Club, New York, Abbey's first one-man exhibition.

Most collectors limited to a single book of Abbey would choose *Old Songs* (1889). Through six years of tranquil preparation he had culled these seventeenth and eighteenth century songs and thought over them. The illustrations represent many sure and happy moods. With one exception, the cuts are from pen drawings excellently processed. The variety of tone is amazing and always faultless. Lyrical rapture, mere waggishness; delicate sentiment, overt gallantry; dolor of lover offset by acid common sense or simple playfulness—such is the repertory. Abbey's pen moves with the exquisite assurance of a flutist's fingers, wreathing an appropriate visible music about these old words and melodies. No earlier book had been so fully his own.

Even more quintessential for Abbey is *The Quiet Life* (1890). To the handful of humorous or meditative poems from Marvell, Cowley, Pope, Praed, etc., Austin Dobson contributed a prologue and epilogue, while Abbey and Alfred Parsons fairly punctuated the stanzas and couplets with the most enticing drawings. The mood of a wise and genial serenity is perfectly maintained. The drawings are not only Abbey's sweetest but also his strongest. At times the line stands almost alone without shadow and again there is new and splendid massing of the lines in velvety structural blacks. The whole book well deserves Mr. Lucas's praise as "one of the most beautiful and satisfying works that the hand of man has devised."

From 1889 Abbey was fitfully engaged on the illustration of Goldsmith's *Deserted Village.* These plates were well printed in *Harper's* for 1902 and issued in an unsatisfactory book the same year. What should have been Abbey's maturest work was never adequately published. The beauty of the drawings may be appreciated from the selections in Mr. Lucas's biography.

Abbey's passage to the greater theme of Shakespeare's plays seems to mark a declension in his career as an illustrator. He began in 1886 with the Comedies. They were published ten years later in four handsome volumes. About Abbey of the *Old Songs* there can be only one critical opinion; about Abbey of the Shakespeare illustrations opinions will differ widely. While in the Comedies we have many of the old delightful pen drawings, we also have many paintings done in oils on a rather large scale. The work is highly skilful, the mood strenuous and self-conscious; one feels, what was absent from the previous work, a distinct sense of effort. Abbey continued with the Tragedies and Histories till his death, these illustrations, often in color reproduction, appearing in Harper's, but not in book form. As the task proceeded, it got farther and farther from book illustration. The pictures were conceived as units in many mediums and had no decorative relation to any conceivable book. We may evade the criticism of these very famous illustrations, made when Abbey's interest had passed from drawing to painting, because they are really only an aspect of his painting and subject to whatever appreciation it deserves.

Abbey was now thirty-seven years old. His ten English years had brought him wide fame and the beginning of fortune, and in these ten years virtually all of his best illustrations had been created. He had definitely chosen England as his home, and it had chosen him. In 1883 he was elected a member of the Royal Institute of Painters in Water-colours. In 1885 he moved to the charming Worcestershire village of Broadway, where he shared Russell House with Mr. and Mrs. Frank D. Millet, and had as close neighbors John S. Sargent and Henry James. There were occasional plunges into London gaiety from his own studio at 56 Bedford Gardens or from Sargent's at 33 Tite St., Chelsea, rarer European trips, short visits to New York in 1886 and 1889, and that longer and momentous visit to America, in 1890, whence he brought back Mary Gertrude Mead as his bride and the commission for the Grail series in the Boston Public Library. It was the beginning of a more spacious and ambitious life, if perhaps less complete from the point of view of art. The Abbeys set up their home in the delightful little country estate Morgan Hall, near Fairford, Gloucestershire. Abbey had his vast studio, which for a time he shared with his associate in the Boston work, John Sargent, his remarkable wardrobe of historic costumes, his chosen procession of guests, even his cricket team. His wife, a learned, cultured, and ambitious woman, aided in every way the new adventure in monumental painting.

In May 1890 Abbey signed the contract for a frieze 180 feet by 8 for the delivery-room of the Boston Public Library, the subjects to be of his own choice; the pay, a pittance, $15,000. An opportune chat between his fiancée and Saint Gaudens, the broad-minded response of Charles F. McKim to the sculptor's suggestion, and a noble confidence on the part of the trustees in an illustrator untried in monumental painting combined to give Abbey his great opportunity. He first considered an equal division of the four walls between panels celebrating the eight national poets. This was rejected in favor of that international legend of aspiration, the Quest of the Holy Grail. This he worked out in fifteen panels which were set up in 1902 after eleven years of unremitting labor. The setting, studied with archæological painstaking, was the twelfth century, and French. Early in the work Abbey described his intention with characteristic lucidity. "My idea is to treat the frieze not precisely in what is known as a decorative fashion, but to represent a series of paintings, in which the action takes place in a sort of procession (for lack of a better word) in the foreground. The background is there all the same but I try to keep it without incidental interest. Galahad's figure, in scarlet, is the brilliant recurring note, all the way around the room."

We may note the extraordinary care, not to say literalism, of procedure. Nothing was improvised. The many angels were a difficulty, humanity not supplying the type. Abbey writes: "I have a number of small lay figures—these are dressed in carefully cut dresses of thin white (old) cambric handkerchiefs, white pigeon wings, dried and stiffened in the right position and tacked to them; and drapery stiffened with stiff starch and arranged in folds." In all such matters Abbey developed an extraordinary efficiency. It is told that John Pettie advised the addition of the seated jester to the panel of the Round Table. Within a morning, Abbey tried out the new idea, designed a jester's costume, had it made in his wardrobe, and painted in the life-sized figure from the costumed model on the mural canvas.

It is doubtless the partial waiver of decorative quality, the retention of illustrative emphasis, and the plausibility of all the details that made the popular success of the Grail frieze. From the time that the first part of it was exhibited in Chicago in 1893 until the whole was in place in 1902 there had been no doubt of the popularity of these decorations. With the possible exception of Puvis's legend of St. Genevieve, no modern decorations are so much loved. All this makes criticism difficult. Abbey's own second thoughts are instructive. He came to regret the rigid twelfth-century setting, wishing he might have done it fifteenth-century, and more or less in Burne-Jones's manner. It never seems to have occurred to him that a remote legend need not have any period in an archæological sense. Later he wrote of the Grail frieze that he wished he might have it back in order that he might "make it simpler from beginning to end." One may share these critical reflections and yet be glad that the Grail frieze is what it is—an extension of Abbey's idealistic illustration to a mural scale and into a mystical field. A certain forcing of the idealism was almost inevitable. Abbey's twelfth century lacked the solid credibility of his seventeenth and eighteenth, and there had to be compensation in a general insistence on the emotional note. This has ever delighted the public, and the critics less so. In his later decorations Abbey set the scene either in nearer pasts or in no man's land, never desiring to repeat this greatest adventure in archæology.

In all this period honors were showered upon him. He was made an associate of the Royal Water Colour Society, an associate of the Société Nationale des Beaux Arts, a knight of the Legion of Honor, and a corresponding member of the Institute of France. Our National Academy, ever gingerly toward the expatriate artist, made him an associate in 1901, and an N.A. in 1902. Of all his honors Abbey especially valued his honorary membership in the Institute of American Architects, 1895, given in recognition of the Grail decorations.

While the Boston decorations were in progress Abbey steadily built up for himself a great reputation as a historical painter in oils. There was no abrupt break with the idyllic water-colors. His first oil painting at the Royal Academy, 1890, "Mayday Morning," was in the old vein. His decoration of the same year for the New Amsterdam Hotel, New York, merely renewed old studies of Knickerbocker Manhattan. Again the mural panel, "Fiammetta's Song," and its companion, "A Poet," with the similar canvas, "A Pavane," show Abbey merely extending the idealistic manner of the drawings for the Shakespeare Comedies to the decoration of New York houses. After the exhibition of the first half of the Grail series, in 1895–96, Abbey deals by preference with great and tragic themes. "Richard of Gloucester and the Lady Anne" was shown in the Royal Academy in 1896, the "Play Scene in Hamlet," which was to win Abbey gold medals at Paris, Vienna, and Berlin, in 1897, "King Lear's Daughters" in 1898, the "Trial of Queen Katharine" and the "Penance of Eleanor Duchess of Gloucester," in 1900. By his forty-eighth year, Abbey's claim to be regarded as the best historical painter of his day seemed incontestable. It was with entire logic that the Royal Exchange commissioned him in 1896 to do the mural panel, "The Reconciliation of the Skinners and Merchant Taylors before Richard III." And when in 1902 King Edward requested Abbey to do the Coronation picture, it was as much an act of artistic discretion as of international tact.

Abbey's capacity for work was extraordinary, and the vast studio at Morgan Hall saw an output comparable to that of a factory. "I have at least twenty paintings large and larger begun," he wrote in his fiftieth year. Among them must have been some of the preliminary studies for the decoration of the Pennsylvania State Capitol at Harrisburg. These were his last works. By 1907 the rotunda was complete. In the spandrels were four medallions, female figures on gold ground symbolizing Art, Law, Science, and Religion. The medallions are fourteen feet in diameter. In the collar of the dome are four lunettes 38 by 22 feet depicting the main industries of the state and her tradition of religious liberty:—"Science Revealing the Treasures of the Earth," "The Spirit of Vulcan," "Oil," "The Spirit of Religious Liberty Leading the Ships towards America." For these decorations Abbey adopted a blend of symbolism and actuality which has its precedent in Rubens and the Venetians. The light-bearing spirits rise in a flock across the tall scaffoldings of real oil wells. Vulcan presides over a modern steel works. Science with her attendants hovers over an actual mine opening. Behind Religious Liberty advancing in air, big square riggers swing easily over great favoring waves. In 1896 Abbey had offered this splendid design in competition for the Common Council Hall of Philadelphia and had lost to Joseph Decamp. In the four lunettes at Harrisburg he seems to have found the fit convention for his idealism, and they are certainly his finest achievement in mural painting. Oddly the historical subjects in the Hall of Representatives seem relatively a failure. The round ceiling, "The Hours," is decoratively perhaps his best piece, but the huge Apotheosis of Pennsylvania, the panels, "Penn's Treaty with the Indians" and "The Reading of the Declaration of Independence," exhibit a painful literalism. The "Washington at Valley Forge" is at best an oversized illustration. In short, the ambition to make decoration out of letter-perfect historical painting failed signally at the end as it had only partially succeeded all along. Which may suggest that the great illustrator in Abbey is what will longest be remembered.

Abbey did not live to finish the Harrisburg panels. After the rotunda was finished in 1906, he suffered a serious breakdown. He drew force from a trip to the Dolomites to keep going. He even continued his cricket week at Morgan Hall with elevens made up of artists. He developed characteristically clever ways of handling his great compositions, such as moving a figure about with the stereopticon and tracing the figure rapidly from the lantern image. He found energy to complete one of his most picturesque of historical paintings,

"Columbus in the New World," with its effective heraldic flight of flamingoes, and one of his most studied, "The Education of Isabella the Catholic."

Abbey had grown portly with the years, but carried his weight well and retained all of his old alertness and charm. One of his assistants, Mr. F. C. Cooper, writes: "Latterly I thought his expression became very noble looking, and he reminded me curiously of the portraits of Ingres at that age." His last illness came upon him in July 1911 in his Chelsea home, 42 Tite St. For ten days his bed was moved into the studio, where he directed his assistants. He died Aug. 1, 1911, aged fifty-nine years and four months. His body was cremated and the ashes buried in Old Kingsbury churchyard.

[The essential source is E. V. Lucas, *Edwin Austin Abbey, Royal Academician. The Record of His Life and Work* (1921), in two volumes, with 200 illustrations. Mr. Lucas fully exhausts all biographical matter, and his illustrations, being made from the original drawings by superior processes, are indispensable. Among critical estimates the most important are the following: Samuel Isham, *Hist. of Am. Painting* (1905), pp. 420–27, 550; Henry James, "Our Artists in Europe," *Harper's*, June 1889, pp. 54–57; N. N. (Mrs. Pennell), *Nation*, XCIV, 69, Jan. 18, 1912. On the Harrisburg murals: Royal Cortissoz, *Scribner's*, Dec. 1908, Jan. 1912. A few honors that have escaped Mr. Lucas are recorded in the *Am. Art Annual*, 1911, p. 307. The reader should be warned against the entirely apocryphal picture drawn by the late Elbert Hubbard in *Little Journeys to the Homes of Eminent Artists* (1902).]

F. J. M.

ABBEY, HENRY (July 11, 1842–June 7, 1911), poet, was born in Rondout, now a part of Kingston, N.Y., where doubtless he would have died, had not illness sent him in his last days to a sanitarium in Tenafly, N. J. All his life, except when a student, and the year 1862–63, when he was clerk in the office of the New York *Leader* and, later, editor of the Orange, N. J., *Spectator*, he made his native town his home, never journeying many miles beyond its borders. Kingston has beauty of situation and a lively trade in farm products, coal, cement, grain, and lumber. Abbey was destined to give the most of his time to its commerce, and what remained to enjoying its beauty, to study, and to writing poetry. He was the son of Stephen Abbey and Caroline Vail. Among his ancestors were the Scotch reformer, John Knox, and, according to tradition, the Indian chieftain, Massasoit. With the intention of entering college he attended Hedding Institute, and the Hudson River Institute. Financial reverses which came to his father about 1859 destroyed his hopes of a college education, but for a time he studied with the noted lawyer, John Norton Pomeroy, then practicing in Rochester, N.Y. After a period of editorial work on the Rondout *Courier* and the journalistic experiment in New York and Orange already mentioned, Abbey became teller in the Bank of Rondout, but soon left that institution to enter the feed, flour, and lime business conducted by his father and his brother. Thereafter, until his later years, he was closely identified with the commercial and banking activities of the town, making poetry his pastime and finding congenial companionship and literary inspiration in the New York Shakespeare Society and Authors Club. He is described as a quiet, square-headed, kindly-looking gentleman who talked nearly as well as he wrote, generously friendly at heart, but of a shy modesty and excessive fear of intrusion which often obscured his real sweetness and worth. He married in 1865 Mary Louise Dubois of Kingston. She died Nov. 3, 1889.

Abbey's first volume of poems *May Dreams* was published in 1862, when he was but twenty years old, and was dedicated by permission to William Cullen Bryant. This was followed by *Ralph and Other Poems* (1866); *Stories in Verse*, dedicated "to Richard Grant White with gratitude for his friendship, and with admiration for his elegant scholarship" (1869); *Ballads of Good Deeds*, dedicated to George William Curtis (1872); English edition of same with a few additions (1876); *Poems* (1879); *The City of Success and Other Poems* (1884); *Bright Things from Everywhere, Poems, Paragraphs, Wit and Wisdom selected by Henry Abbey* (1888); *Phaëthon* (1901); *The Poems of Henry Abbey* (1885), (1895), (1904); *Dream of Love* (1910).

Abbey's poetry was widely known in its day, being favorably received in England as well as in America. The simplicity, rhythm, and wholesomeness of his earlier poems won them a place in home papers and school readers, but the later and more elaborate did not achieve a like popularity. In form and sentiment both are typical of the last half of the nineteenth century. Often obtrusively didactic, they are permeated with the spirit of democracy, pride of country, and love of honor, justice, and kindness. They never rise to any great height of beauty, imagination, passion, or thought; neither do they sink very low. Some of them doubtless will live on in anthologies; the most of them will probably be forgotten.

[G. F. Bacon, *Kingston and Rondout, Their Representative Business Men and Points of Interest* (1892); *Biog. Dir. State of N.Y.* (1900); obituary notices of the Authors Club of N.Y. for 1911, *Bookman*, May 1912; *Who's Who in N.Y. City and State* (1904); *Who's Who in America*, 1910–11; *Manual of the Authors Club, N.Y.* (1912).]

H. E. S.

ABBEY, HENRY EUGENE (June 27, 1846–Oct. 17, 1896), theatrical and operatic manager, was the son of Elizabeth (Smith) Abbey and Henry Stephen Abbey, a Connecticut clockmaker, who migrated in 1835 to Akron, Ohio, then only a small village. After his son's graduation, with onors, from the Akron High School, the father ried to interest him in his jewelry business, but he younger Abbey's thoughts were turned toward he popular amusement field. Beginning as ticket-eller for the local opera house, of which, after wo years, he became lessee, in 1869 he brought, rom the Cleveland Academy of Music, John Ells-er's company, then playing *London Assurance* ith Clara Morris as ingenue. The next year he ook out his first "road company"—the Susan Gal-on Opera Troupe. In succeeding years Abbey rought to many of the smaller cities a better class f performances than they had customarily seen. Inder his management Lotta, Adams, and Ray-nond made extended tours. In 1876 he left Ak-on, formed a partnership with John B. Schoeffel, nd acquired the Academy of Music at Buffalo, .Y. After a year's trial the partners decided that ew York City was to be their field of operations nd undertook the management of the Park The-tre. That was the initial effort in a series of the-trical and operatic enterprises, some brilliantly uccessful and others disheartening failures, cov-ring a period of twenty years. It was Abbey who rought together the actors William H. Crane and Stuart Robson, who starred successfully for many easons. In New York the elder Sothern played long engagement in *The Crushed Tragedian* under Abbey's management. After managing sev-eral theatres in New York for three or four sea-sons, Abbey went to Europe in 1880 and made a contract with Sarah Bernhardt, then at the apex of her career, to give performances in the United States. It was a bold venture, but proved success-ful. Bernhardt played 164 times for $100,000 as her share of the proceeds, while Abbey, Schoeffel & Grau received an equivalent amount. This en-gagement gave Abbey his national reputation as a manager. Within three years he was in control of the Metropolitan Opera House, just opened in New York. The first two seasons of opera showed a loss of $250,000, which was quickly repaid to the creditors of the lessees; but Col. Mapleson's attempt to offer New York a rival program of grand opera made the success of either venture impossible. In 1889–90 Abbey managed the Amer-ican tours of Adelina Patti and the London Gaiety. Among the popular players who appeared under his management were Barrett, Sothern, Henry Irving, Coquelin, and Jane Hading. For one sea-son, in the earlier part of his career, he had Booth's Theatre and presented Edwin Booth himself in a Shakespearian repertoire. In 1891–92 he brought to the Metropolitan stage Jean and Edouard De Reszke and Emma Eames. The same year he se-cured Italian opera. The next year he introduced Calvé to America. He opened Abbey's Theatre in 1893, retaining the management of various other amusement places. In the season of 1895–96 he brought over a remarkable group of European opera singers, but financially the enterprise ended in failure. Before his death, however, a settlement had been obtained with the creditors of Abbey, Schoeffel & Grau. Abbey's distinction as an Amer-ican impresario was twofold: he was one of the first theatrical managers to present costly enter-tainments before audiences outside the largest cities and he was remarkably successful in cap-turing the best European talent, both histrionic and operatic, even when the financial investment seemed to make the undertaking hopeless. He was twice married, in 1876 to Kate Kingsley, who bore him two children and died in 1883, and in 1886 to Florence Gerard.

[S. A. Lane, *Fifty Years and Over of Akron and Sum-mit County* (1892); H. E. Krehbiel, *Chapters of Opera* (1908); *N. Y. Times, N. Y. Tribune,* Oct. 18, 1896.]

W. B. S.

ABBOT, BENJAMIN (Sept. 17, 1762–Oct. 25, 1849), educator, was descended from George Ab-bot, who left Yorkshire, England, in 1640, to set-tle in Andover, Mass., where for five generations the eldest son of the family was named John and farmed the original acres wrested from the wil-derness. Benjamin, son of the fourth John Ab-bot, entered Phillips Academy, Andover, in 1782. Here he was taught by Jeremiah Smith, later a prominent jurist of New Hampshire. From An-dover he went to Harvard, where he was gradu-ated with the degree of B.A. in 1788, delivering the salutatory oration. On Oct. 8, 1788, he was ap-pointed to the principalship of Phillips Exeter Academy, a position which he held for fifty years. Although assisted by young graduates from Har-vard, he carried the burden of the teaching in Latin, Greek, and mathematics. He was an enthu-siastic classical scholar and aroused the enthusi-asm of his students while at the same time he was very insistent on accuracy and thoroughness. As principal, he maintained a high standard of morals and manners in the school. Without resorting to corporal punishment,—the usual penalty for mis-demeanor being merely to carry wood or sweep the hall,—he nevertheless held his pupils under strict control. The father of Lewis Cass [*q.v.*], a rather unruly boy, said to Abbot, "If Lewis was half as afraid of the Almighty as he is of you, I should never have any more trouble with him." Other distinguished pupils were Daniel Webster, Edward Everett, Jared Sparks, and Francis Bow-en. On the occasion of Abbot's retirement, Aug. 23, 1838, hundreds of his old students were pres-ent, and Daniel Webster, in as brilliant a speech as he ever delivered, paid eloquent tribute to Abbot's training (Cunningham, pp. 29–30). Abbot was a man of medium height, dark complexion, and quiet manner. He was twice married: on Nov. 1, 1791, to Hannah Tracy Emery of Exeter, who died Dec. 7, 1793, at the age of twenty-two, leaving him with an infant son; and five years later to Mary Perkins of Boston, by whom he had two daughters and one son. His chief recreation was gardening. It is said that every year when the birds robbed his cherry trees, he would seize his gun and rush out, crying, "Those robins must be killed!" to return after a mild "Shoo! Shoo!" without having fired a shot. He lived on in the quiet of Exeter for eleven years after his retirement from teaching, and died there at the age of eighty-seven.

[J. G. Hoyt, "The Phillips Exeter Academy" in *North Am. Rev.*, July 1858; F. H. Cunningham, *Familiar Sketches of the Phillips Exeter Academy* (1883); C. H. Bell, *The Phillips Exeter Academy* (1883); *Exercises at the Centennial Celebration of Phillips Exeter Academy 1883* (1884); L. M. Crosbie, *The Phillips Exeter Academy: A History* (1923).] L. M. C.

ABBOT, EZRA (Apr. 28, 1819–Mar. 21, 1884), stands preëminent as a devoted, accurate scholar among those of American birth who have given themselves to the textual criticism of the New Testament. It was in a period marked by the famous discoveries of Tischendorf, no less than the patient industry of Tregelles, that Abbot made American scholarship for the first time deserving of recognition in this domain. Ultimately European scholars of the first rank recognized and gladly welcomed him as their peer. He was the eldest child and namesake of his father, a farmer of Jackson, Waldo County, Me. His mother, Phœbe Abbot, died when the child had reached the age of six. But to her influence may well be traced something of the character of the precocious lad, distinguished throughout life by Christian gentleness no less than scholarly attainment. During her married life of only seven years the young mother, besides forming her own little collection of theological works, acquired a knowledge of Greek sufficient for reading the New Testament.

Impressed, like the lad's teachers, with his "wonderful accuracy of knowledge," his mother's brother, Rev. Abiel Abbot of Peterboro, prevailed on his father to send the boy, at first destined to continue his father's calling, to Phillips Academy at Exeter, and subsequently to Bowdoin. At college his course was marked, as before, by a deeply religious spirit no less than by devotion to study, though throughout life he never lost his childhood's love of nature and out-door activity. After graduation in 1840 Abbot found a position as school-teacher in Maine, but continued his studies, receiving in 1843 the degree of M.A. from his alma mater. His first definite step toward an academic career was unconsciously taken at this time. Andrews Norton, professor of sacred literature at Harvard Divinity School, best known by his *Genuineness of the Gospels* (1837–44), was then reaching the summit of his fame as a fearless representative of the "liberal" school. His *Statement of Reasons for not believing the Doctrines of Trinitarianism concerning the Nature of God and the Person of Christ* (1833) reached the hands of the young school-teacher, who wrote to the author expressing delight in the work, stating that he had made an index of it, and adding some discriminating remarks. Pleased with the letter, Norton invited the writer to visit him. The result was that Abbot went to Cambridge, assuming in 1847 the position of teacher in the high school at Cambridgeport, and rendering years of editorial service to Norton.

The high-school task proved irksome. Abbot found relief from its monotony by preparing for the benefit of his pupils a work of some 250 printed pages entitled *A Classed Catalogue of the Library of the Cambridge High School,* published privately in 1853. This opened the doors to a new career. The *Catalogue* revealed surprising thoroughness and skill in dealing with the librarian's most difficult problem. It was a subject catalogue, dividing the 1,600 books of the high-school library according to their scientific or philosophical relations into thirty-one classes, with subdivisions, combining alphabetical arrangement with logical classification. It won for the author immediate recognition. He received a position on the library staff of the Boston Athenæum and of Harvard College, of which he became assistant librarian in 1856.

Long years of private study as teacher, editor, and librarian intervened before Abbot's services to New Testament research became fully known. In 1852 he became a member, in 1853 recording secretary, of the American Oriental Society, and in 1861 a member of the American Academy of Arts and Sciences. But it was not till 1871 that he at last obtained from Harvard an appointment as lecturer on the Textual Criticism of the New Testament, leading in 1872 to an election to the newly founded Bussey Professorship of similar title in the Divinity School. Meantime, in 1871, he had been chosen a member of the New Testament Committee for the Revision of the English Bible, where his services as a textual critic were invaluable; the papers which he prepared on disputed passages had great influence in determining the text finally adopted. His published work is largely hidden under others' names, as in the editing with copious notes and bibliography of several works for Prof. Norton, besides similar service for Alger's *Critical History of the Doctrine of a Future Life* (1864), and Lamson's *Church of the First Three Centuries* (1865). He also coöperated with his pupil, Prof. Caspar René Gregory, in bringing out the *Prolegomena* to Tischendorf's last critical edition of the Greek New Testament (1884), to which he contributed the chapter *De Versibus;* and with Prof. H. B. Hackett in the editing of the American edition of Smith's *Dictionary of the Bible* (1888), to which he contributed over 400 initialed additions. His signed work consists mainly of articles in various periodicals on subjects of biblical interest. Twenty of these were collected and published in 1888 by his successor, Prof. J. H. Thayer, under the title *Critical Essays selected from the Published Papers of Ezra Abbot.* They include his one venture into the field of the higher criticism, the well-known essay in defense of the traditional authorship of John entitled *The Authorship of the Fourth Gospel: External Evidences* (1880). This essay, however harmless against more recent critical views, had its effect against the overbold assertions of Tübingen critics. It still remains a model of scientific argument. But Abbot's best title to fame rests elsewhere. For a full generation he remained America's one great critic of the New Testament text. The *American Revised Version* is his chief monument.

[Obituaries in the leading religious periodicals at the time of Abbot's death, especially the *Unitarian Review* and the *Andover Review* for May 1884. *Ezra Abbot* (1884), containing memorial addresses by J. H. Thayer and others, gives biographical data and full bibliography.]

B.W.B.

ABBOT, FRANCIS ELLINGWOOD (Nov. 6, 1836–Oct. 23, 1903), Unitarian clergyman, philosopher, was the son of Joseph Hale Abbot, a teacher in Boston, and Fanny Ellingwood (Larcom) Abbot, descendant of Roger Conant of Salem. Bred in a family of intellectual energy and strenuous Puritanism, his youth was marked by brilliant scholarship and austerity of conscience. Prepared in the Boston Latin School and by private tuition, he graduated from Harvard College in 1859. He then married (Aug. 3) Katharine Fearing Loring, of Concord, Mass., and in November joined the Harvard Divinity School, but left it, in September 1860, to take charge of a girls' school in Meadville, Pa. At the same time he attended the Meadville Theological School, graduating from it in 1863. After a year in Beverly, Mass., he became pastor of the Unitarian church in Dover, N. H., June 1864. Basing faith on free present intuition, in the spirit of Emerson's Divinity School Address, he found a creedal limitation in the constitution of the National Unitarian Conference of 1865 which referred to its members as "disciples of the Lord Jesus Christ," and he strove in vain for the adoption of freer terminology. In 1867 he led in creating The Free Religious Association. Though an ardent theist sharing the main Christian ethical ideals, he held that historically "Christianity" meant subjection to the authority of Christ as Messiah and found definitive form in the authoritative system of Roman Catholicism. Free Religion must replace "God in Christ" by "God in Humanity" (*Freedom and Fellowship in Religion,* 1875, pp. 223–64). Doubting his ministerial prospects, he sought a chair of philosophy in the new Cornell University, failing despite strong recommendations. A similar appointment in Harvard, urged by Francis Bowen, 1866, had been barred by theological opposition. Constrained by logic and conscience, Abbot resigned his pastorate, Mar. 15, 1868, but a parish majority sought to retain him by changing their name from "The First Unitarian Society of Christians" to the "First Independent Religious Society." Legal action by the minority caused the majority, however, under legal advice, to claim the property under the former name, whereupon Abbot again resigned, Oct. 1. For a time he supported himself by tutoring, yet giving free public discourses in the City Hall. In September 1869 he accepted a call to the Independent Church in Toledo, Ohio, when to secure him it dropped the name Unitarian. There he edited the *Index,* a weekly journal championing Free Religion. This enterprise involving him in debt, he removed to Cambridge, Mass., 1873, editing the *Index* from Boston until 1880. After a teaching enterprise in New York, 1880, he established a classical school for boys in Cambridge, 1881, but relinquished it in 1892, when a legacy enabled him to devote his time to philosophical writing. From 1872 he had ardently fought a proposed amendment of the national constitution which would declare Christ the ruler and the Bible the control of the national life, organizing local resistant groups in 1876 into a National Liberal League. Of this he was president until 1878, resigning then because the League favored freedom of the mails for literature obnoxious to his ethical principles. In 1894 he became estranged also from The Free Religious Association on its refusal to avow independence of all historical religions (Abbot, *Free Church Tracts, No. 1,* Tacoma, Wash., 1895).

His philosophical power was early shown by widely admired articles in the *North American Review* (July, Oct. 1864, Oct. 1868), and by a thesis for a Harvard doctorate in 1881. His *Scientific Theism* (1885, 3rd ed. 1888) won European attention and appeared in a German translation (1893). This work sharply condemns the subjectivism of Idealism and on the basis of a realistic theory of knowledge argues that since science finds a self-existing, self-determining system of objectively real relations of objectively real things, and since only intelligence can create such relational systems, the universe must be itself intelligent, an infinite living self-consciousness. (For a valuable discussion of *Scientific Theism* see L. Carrau, *La Philosophie religieuse en Angleterre depuis Locke jusqu'à nos jours.*) Having served as substitute for Josiah Royce [*q.v.*] in Harvard in 1888, Abbot published a condensation of his lectures in *The Way Out of Agnosticism* (1890), an argument that philosophy compels faith in real personality, finite and relative in man, infinite and absolute in Nature. This was attacked by Royce in the *International Journal of Ethics* (Oct. 1890) with "a professional warning" against Abbot as an incompetent pretender in philosophy who, without logical ability or historical scholarship, based his thought on a crude misunderstanding of Hegel's theory of universals. This wound to a proudly conscientious man evoked from Abbot an indignant response which was denied publication. Without success he asked redress from the university authorities as being libeled by their appointee in his "professorial" capacity (*Prof. Royce's Libel, a Public Appeal to the Board of Overseers,* 1891, and *A Public Remonstrance to the Board of Overseers,* 1892). The episode was vigorously discussed by others in the *Nation* (Nov. 12, 19, 26, Dec. 3, 1891), and Royce's attitude evoked Mrs. Jack Gardner's celebrated remark that "One should be sure of his own manners before attacking another's morals." The next ten years Abbot devoted to the final elaboration of his thought in abstruse technical form in *The Syllogistic Philosophy.* Shortly after completing it, on the tenth anniversary of his wife's death, he was found dead upon her grave with signs of poison self-administered. *The Syllogistic Philosophy* was published in two volumes in 1906, was reviewed unfavorably in *Mind* (July 1907), the *Philosophical Review* (July 1907) and *Science* (May 31, 1907), and quickly dropped out of notice. Abbot's misfortune was to be twenty years ahead of his due time. His keen and subtle critique of idealism, so offensive to his American contemporaries, would later have proved most acceptable, while his insistence upon the unity of reason and experience, the inseparability of genus and specimen, and the objectivity of the syllogism would have received the attention they deserved. He undoubtedly owed more to Hegel than he himself supposed, and he was wont to underestimate the difficulties of his own view-point, but, for all that, he was a philosopher of parts.

[*Universal Religion,* vol. XI, no. 9 (Dec. 1903, memorial addresses); *Index,* June 24, 1880, Abbot's review of his career; *Ibid.,* June 10, 17, 1880; *Boston Transcript,* Oct. 24, 1903; *Christian Reg.,* Nov. 12, 1903.]

F. A. C.

ABBOT, GORHAM DUMMER (Sept. 3, 1807–Aug. 3, 1874), clergyman, educator, was the fourth in a family of seven children. Two brothers, Jacob Abbott [*q.v.*] and John Stevens Cabot Abbott [*q.v.*] preceded him, and two others, Charles Edward and Samuel Phillips, were born later. The last of these died at a comparatively early age, but the other four all achieved considerable eminence as teachers and writers. They were strikingly alike in gifts and tastes, but each had marked individuality of character, indicated in the case of the three oldest by the saying, "Jacob for advice; John for a speech; and Gorham for a prayer." When in college, for the sake of distinction, Jacob added a "t" to the family name, and the younger brothers adopted the same form, but Gorham soon returned to the original spelling. They were descended from a Yorkshire Puritan, George Abbot, who had emigrated to New England as early as 1640. Their father, Jacob Abbot 2nd, a pioneer in the development of southern Maine, moved from Concord, N. H., to that state in 1800, two years after his marriage to his second cousin, Betsey, daughter of Joshua and Elizabeth Chandler Abbot. Gorham was born in Brunswick, but spent his boyhood in the family home at Hallowell. He graduated from Bowdoin College in 1826, and studied at Andover Theological Seminary, but did not graduate. On Feb. 11, 1834, he married Rebecca S. Leach, daughter of Joseph Leach of South Natick, Mass. He was ordained in New York, Dec. 25, 1837, and from 1837 to 1841 was pastor of a Presbyterian church in New Rochelle, N. Y. The next two years he was connected with the literary department of the American Tract Society.

His chief interest, however, was in education, and especially in the higher education of women. After leaving the theological seminary, he had made a horseback journey for his health through the South, and had been impressed with the needs of public education. As a result, while pastor at New Rochelle, he was prominent in a movement to supply schools with libraries, suitable text-books, and educational journals. From 1831 to 1833 he had been associated with his brother Jacob in conducting the Mount Vernon School for girls in Boston, and in 1843 Gorham persuaded him to join with their other two brothers and himself in establishing a girls' school in New York. The enterprise "was a surprising success from the very beginning—one of the earlier movements for woman's better education which later led up to the woman's colleges, and woman's admission to the great universities" (Lyman Abbott, *Reminiscences,* 1923, p. 24). Charles withdrew in 1846 to open a boys' school in Norwich, Conn., and a little later Gorham took forty of the pupils and started what became known as Spingler Institute, which he conducted until 1870. It became widely known and drew students from all over the country and from Canada. The great aim of the institution, according to the catalogue of 1861, was "to provide for *daughters,* privileges of education equal to those of *sons* in our Universities, Colleges, and Halls. It had its origin in a careful examination of endowments, both in Europe and America. In many instances *hundreds of thousands of dollars,* and in some, MILLIONS, were invested in providing educational appliances, of every variety, and on the most ample scale, for *sons.* It did not appear that there was in the world a single institution for the education of *daughters,* with a well distributed endowment of *a hundred thousand dollars.*" Abbot's favorite text of Scripture, according to his students, was: "That our daughters may be as corner stones, polished after the similitude of a palace." He founded the school, he says, in the hope that such an institution in the metropolis would be imitated in every city of the Union. The soundness of his educational theories was widely recognized, and when Matthew Vassar was searching for some object to which he might devote his wealth, he met Abbot, who imbued him with his ideals of education for women (*New York Tribune,* May 19, 1899). His health failing he retired to South Natick, Mass., in 1870, where he died.

His publications include *Memoir of Nathan W. Dickerman,* American Tract Society (1830); an American edition, with improvements, of William Carpenter's *Scripture Natural History* (1833); *The Family at Home; or, Familiar Illustrations of the Various Domestic Duties* (1834); and *Mexico and the United States, Their Mutual Relations and Common Interests* (1869), a historical work of no great importance, strongly influenced by the author's political and religious views.

[Abiel Abbot and Ephraim Abbot, *Geneal. Reg. of the Descendants of George Abbot, etc.* (1847); Emma H. Nason, *Old Hallowell on the Kennebec* (1909); *Gen. Cat. Bowdoin Coll.* (1916); *Andover Theol. Sem. Cat. 1808–1908*; *N.Y. Evening Post,* Aug. 5, 1874.]

H. E. S.

ABBOT, HENRY LARCOM (Aug. 13, 1831–Oct. 1, 1927), army engineer, was a descendant of George Abbot, who emigrated from England in 1640 and of Mordecai Larcom, who came from France twelve years later. Two of his great-grandfathers served in the Revolutionary War: Maj. Abiel Abbot and Lieut. Joseph Hale. Henry L. Abbot was born at Beverly, Mass., the son of Joseph Hale and Fanny Ellingwood (Larcom) Abbot, and brother of Francis Ellingwood Abbot [*q.v.*]. He attended the Boston Latin School and then West Point Military Academy, where he was graduated in 1854. He was married in April 1858 to Mary Susan Everett of Cambridge, Mass. For two years after his graduation from West Point Abbot was assistant on the survey for a Pacific railroad, in command of the party which surveyed the route through California and Oregon which was later adopted. In 1857, then a lieutenant, he was appointed to the task of assisting Capt. A. A. Humphreys [*q.v.*] of the Corps of Engineers in an investigation of the questions of flood protection and channel improvements along the lower Mississippi. Their joint *Report upon the Physics and Hydraulics of the Mississippi River* (1861), which advocated the partial control of floods by means of levees, "was received by the engineers of the world as a most valuable contribution to the science of hydraulics, and remains a standard authority on the regimen of the Mississippi River" ("The Problem of the Mississippi," by Major-General W. M. Black, *North American Review,* December 1927). In 1869 further reports were submitted by Humphreys and Abbot on the same question.

During the Civil War Abbot served in the Eastern armies first as an engineer and later in command of the 1st Connecticut Heavy Artillery. He was wounded at the first battle of Bull Run, where he was serving on Gen. McDowell's staff. He acted as chief topographical engineer for Gen. Banks's New Orleans expedition. In the campaigns of 1864–65 he commanded the siege artillery brigade of both United States armies at Petersburg and Richmond. During the war he received seven brevets, the highest being that of major-general of Volunteers, "for gallant and meritorious conduct during the Rebellion." In September 1865 he was mustered out of the volunteer service and resumed his regular rank of major of the Corps of Engineers, U.S.A.

Following the war, Abbot was placed in command of the Engineer Battalion at Willett's Point, N.Y., where, with the encouragement of Gen. Humphreys, he developed the Engineer School of Application, making of it not only a post-graduate school, but a center of research in the problems of military engineering. At Willett's Point, during a period of some twelve years, he carried on the experiments in high explosives which resulted in the system of coast defense by submarine mines adopted for the United States. His voluminous *Report* was published in 1881 as No. 23 of the Professional Papers of the Corps of Engineers. He served on many engineering boards including the Board of Ordnance and Fortification. Three times he was sent to Europe as a member of special commissions: in 1870 to the Island of Sicily to observe the solar eclipse; in 1875 to make contracts for submarine mining cable and examine systems of torpedo defense adopted in Great Britain, Germany, Austria, and France; and again in 1883 as a member of a joint Army and Navy board to report on providing large steel cannon. His promotion as colonel in the Corps of Engineers came in 1886 and after his retirement in August 1895 he was promoted by Act of Congress to brigadier-general, U.S.A., retired.

After his retirement from active service he became consulting engineer (1895) to the company which built the harbor at Manitowoc, Wis., and established the much-used car ferry connecting that harbor with the Pere Marquette railroads in Michigan. He served as a member of the Comité Technique of the New French Panama Canal Company and later as its consulting engineer, residing in Paris and at the Isthmus part of the time. When in 1904 this property passed into the hands of the United States, he became a member of the American board of consulting engineers appointed by President Roosevelt to determine the plan of the Canal. The majority of the board recommended a sea-level canal, but the minority favored a lock-canal. Abbot's report was influential in the adoption by the Government of the minority's recommendation. He published in engineering journals numerous articles on the Canal question, and in 1905 *Problems of the Panama Canal* (2nd ed., London, 1907). He was also a member of the Panama Canal Slide Committee appointed by the National Academy of Sciences in 1915 at the request of the President. He was chairman of the Jury of Awards at the Atlanta Exposition in 1895. From May 1905 to July 1910 he was professor of hydraulic engineering on the faculty of graduate studies at George Washington University. Throughout his career he was a prolific writer; his articles and reports are scattered through the Professional Memoirs of the Corps of Engineers, the Printed Papers of the Essayons Club, the publications of the Engineer School, and periodicals.

[No adequate sketch of Abbot has yet been written. The record of his work is to be found in his publications and in the reports of the Chief of Engineers. His own account, *Early Days of the Engineer School of Application*, was published by the Engineer School in 1904 as No. 14 of its Occasional Papers. Biographical data are found in *Who's Who in America, Who's Who in Engineering*, and G. W. Cullum's *Biog. Reg.* (3rd ed. 1891).]

E. Y.

ABBOT, JOEL (Jan. 18, 1793–Dec. 14, 1855), naval officer, son of Joel and Lydia (Cummings) Abbot, of old Colonial stock, was born at Westford, Mass., and was bred to the sea. Volunteering for service at the outbreak of the second war with Great Britain, he was appointed a midshipman in the navy, June 18, 1812, and three days later, under Commodore John Rodgers in the frigate *President,* took part in the first action of the war, in which the British ship *Belvidera* escaped by superior speed after a sharp fight. In 1813, while acting as an officer in a prize ship, he was captured and taken to England, but was soon exchanged and attached to the squadron of Commodore Macdonough on Lake Champlain. His eagerness to serve is illustrated by a letter requesting that his exchange be quickly effected, to the end "that I may be enabled to return immediately to actual service, as I hope not always to remain a Midshipman." Ordered on a most hazardous and difficult duty, he entered the enemy's lines, disguised as a British officer, and succeeded in destroying a large number of spars and implements sorely needed by the British in the construction of vessels. He took part in the battle of Lake Champlain on Sept. 11, 1814, and was included in the thanks of Congress given to Macdonough and his officers, receiving at the same time one of the swords of honor conferred by Congress on the midshipmen of the victorious squadron. His promotion to lieutenant, Apr. 1, 1818, was no doubt partly in consequence of his conduct in this battle. In March 1822, while on duty at the Charlestown Navy Yard, he discovered a series of frauds upon the government, and, actuated in great measure by resentment at not having received leave of absence to visit his dying wife, he made very serious charges against the personal character of his commandant, Capt. Isaac Hull. Failing to prove these accusations when brought before a court-martial, Abbot was suspended from the naval service for the period of two years, after which he continued his otherwise distinguished career. He was commissioned captain, Oct. 3, 1850 (*United States Navy Register,* 1851), and in 1852 was chosen by Commodore M. C. Perry to command the frigate *Macedonian,* one of the vessels composing the fleet which carried out the famous expedition to Japan. During the fleet's sojourn in Pacific waters, Abbot was called upon by his chief to visit and report upon the Japanese, Bonin, and Philippine island groups, as well as Formosa. Upon Perry's return to the United States, Abbot became commanding officer of the fleet, in which position he gave proof of firmness and diplomatic qualities. He died at Hong Kong on Dec. 14, 1855, from the effects of the climate. He was twice married: in January 1820 to Mary

Wood of Newburyport, by whom he had one child, and who died Apr. 15, 1821; and on Nov. 29, 1825 to Laura Wheaton of Warren, R. I., by whom he had nine children.

[The chief sources of information concerning Joel Abbot are contained in the Office of Naval Records and Library, in the Navy Department at Washington, from which an account of his court-martial was published at Boston in 1822.]
E. B.

ABBOTT, AUSTIN (Dec. 18, 1831–Apr. 19, 1896), lawyer, author, was the second son of Jacob Abbott [*q.v.*] and brother of Benjamin Vaughan Abbott [*q.v.*], Edward Abbott [*q.v.*], and Lyman Abbott [*q.v.*]. He was born at Boston, his early education being obtained there and at Roxbury, Mass., and Farmington, Me. He became a student at New York University in 1847, where he graduated with high honors in 1851, delivering the English oration on that occasion. He then studied law, was admitted to the bar of New York City in 1852, and commenced practice there in partnership with Benjamin Vaughan Abbott under the firm name of "Abbott Brothers." Of his earliest literary efforts, two works of fiction, *Cone Cut Corners; the Experiences of a Conservative Family in Fanatical Times* (1855) and *Matthew Caraby* (1859), were written in collaboration with his brothers, Benjamin and Lyman, and published under the pseudonym "Benauly." In 1855 Austin and Benjamin jointly prepared the first volume of a series of *Reports of Practice Cases Determined in the Courts of the State of New York,* and thereafter for fifteen years, working in collaboration, produced legal text-books, reports, and digests, notable for variety, accuracy, scientific arrangement, and utility. During all this period Abbott continued in active practice and acquired a reputation for exceptional knowledge of legal principles combined with consistent untiring application. In 1865 he assisted the commissioners in preparing the codes of New York State. On the retirement of Benjamin Vaughan Abbott from the firm he practiced alone, and, after 1870, the brothers ceased to collaborate. Austin Abbott's first independent effort was *Reports of Decisions of the Court of Appeals of New York, 1850–69* in four volumes (1873–74), followed by the first volume of *New Cases, Courts of the State of New York* (1877), which ultimately extended to thirty-one volumes, covering the period 1876–94, the last volume appearing in 1894. He prepared a new edition of *Abbott's Digest of New York Statutes and Reports* in six volumes (1873), which he kept up to date by eight supplements, the last of which appeared in 1896. He published in 1880 *Trial Evidence, The Rules of Evidence Applicable on the Trials of Civil Actions*—"the most useful and widely circulated of his works"—according to W. I. Washburn. Then in succession he wrote a series of "Briefs," material for which he had been accumulating for years: *Brief for the Trial of Civil Issues before a Jury* (1885), *The Principles and Forms of Practice in Civil Actions* (2 vols., 1887–88), *Brief for the Trial of Criminal Cases* (1889), *Brief on the Mode of Proving the Facts most Frequently in Issue or Collaterally in Question on the Trial of Civil or Criminal Cases* (1891), and *Brief for the Argument of Questions Arising upon the Pleadings on the Trial of Issues of Law or Fact in Civil Actions* (1891), all of which obtained a wide circulation which was not confined to New York state. Supplementing these, he compiled *Select Cases on Code Pleading* (1893) and *Select Cases on the Law of Evidence as Applied During the Examination of Witnesses* (1895), thus completing his texts on the incidents of trials. He was retained in much heavy litigation, appearing in many notable cases. He was of government counsel in the prosecution of Guiteau for the assassination of President Garfield, and held a brief in the action brought by Madison Avenue Congregational Church, New York, which resulted in the ejection of Bishop Newman from its pastorate. He was of counsel for the defense in Tilton *vs.* Beecher, and his success in this celebrated case procured for him a national reputation. See his *Official Report of the Trial of Henry Ward Beecher* (2 vols., 1875). A lawyer's lawyer, as it was termed, his advice was frequently sought in conference by other members of the bar when they were faced with serious difficulties.

In 1891 he accepted the position of dean of the Law School of the University of New York with the professorship of Pleading, Equity, and Evidence. In this post he exercised a lasting influence. He altered the curriculum, making the courses less academic and more practical, instilled new vigor into the teaching, and materially raised the standard of the school. He died in New York City, Apr. 19, 1896. At the time of his death he had in preparation *Forms of Pleadings in Actions,* which was completed by C. C. Alden (1898–99).

Abbott was tall of stature, slender in physique, unobtrusive, and somewhat nervous in manner, a man of "undeviating integrity and lofty sense of duty" always interested in philanthropic movements. He was fond of music, played the organ, had a good t nor voice, and indulged at times in musical composition. As his life history shows he was a prodigy of systematic, indefatigable industry. He was married twice, in 1854 to Ella E. D. Gilman, and in 1879 to Mrs. Anna Rowe Worth.

[The "Memorial of Austin Abbott," prepared by W. I. Washburn in *Ass. of the Bar of N.Y.C., Report,* 1898,

p. 103, is authoritative, as is the obituary notice contained in *Am. Bar Ass., Report,* 1896, p. 668. Well-balanced appreciations will be found in *Case and Comment,* VII, 37, XIX, 70; *Am. Law Rev.,* XXX, 581, and *Hist. of the Bench and Bar of N.Y.,* ed. by D. McAdam *et al.* (1897), II, 8. See also Lib. Cat., Harvard Law School. For particulars of ancestry, see biography of Jacob Abbott.]
H. W. H. K.

ABBOTT, BENJAMIN (1732–Aug. 14, 1796), religious enthusiast, was an evangelist of unusual power, who "ploughed and seeded to Methodism much of southern New Jersey." His grandfather, James, had emigrated to Long Island from Somersetshire, England; his father, after whom he was named, upon becoming of age went to New Jersey and there married the daughter of John Burroughs, sheriff of Hunterdon County. Afterward, he returned to Long Island, but finally settled in Pennsylvania, where he bought a plantation of four hundred acres of good land, and lived with credit. Benjamin's birthplace is generally given as Long Island, but G. A. Raybold states that he was born in Pennsylvania (*Reminiscences of Methodism in West Jersey,* 1849, p. 15). His mother died of a nervous complaint when he was a lad, and six weeks later an attack of smallpox ended his father's career. In his will the latter stipulated that his sons should all be taught trades; accordingly, Benjamin was apprenticed to a hatter in Philadelphia. Breaking away from his master after a time, he went to work for his brother on a farm in New Jersey, and upon coming into possession of his share in his father's estate, he hired a farm and worked it. In Philadelphia he had fallen in with evil companions and had become addicted to card-playing, cock-fighting, and drinking. Being of powerful frame, and keenly relishing a fight, he went to fairs and other gatherings to display his prowess. When he had been drinking he was apt to be quarrelsome, and sometimes got into trouble with the authorities. There was nothing petty in his nature, however, and he was industrious and good to his family. He continued this manner of life until he was about forty, but professed himself a Presbyterian, attended meetings, and was often alarmed for his soul. From his mother, perhaps, who the night before she died startled the household by her hysterical cries for God's mercy upon it, he inherited a tendency to religious excitability. He was subject to fits of fear and remorse, and to vivid dreams in which he sometimes found himself in hell. Finally, after fearful mental struggles, influenced by the preaching of Abraham Whitworth, he was converted on Oct. 12, 1772, and became a Methodist.

Throughout the remaining years of his life he went about admonishing and exhorting with an effect seldom equaled; first, as a local preacher, speaking in homes chiefly, and later, having been made a deacon in 1790, and ordained elder in 1793, as a circuit preacher. With fanatical passion he attacked Calvinism and presented Methodism as teaching the only way of salvation. His appeal was to fear, and he so impressed his hearers that frequently they fell to the floor or shrieked in terror. Soldiers and others who came to molest him always changed their minds under his spell. He soon wore himself out and died in Salem, N.J., where he is buried. An ignorant zealot though he was, and possibly, as has been charged, on the verge of madness, he turned many from evil ways and contributed not a little to the spread of Methodism in this country.

[John Ffirth, *Experience and Gospel Labours of the Rev. Benjamin Abbott* (1820); W. B. Sprague, *Annals Am. Pulpit,* VII (1861); John Atkinson, *Hist. of the Origin of the Wesleyan Movement in America* (1896); J. M. Buckley, *Hist. of Methodists in the U.S.* (Am. Ch. Hist., vol. V, 1896); Robt. Southey, *Life of Wesley,* ed. by M. H. Fitzgerald (1925).]
H. E. S.

ABBOTT, BENJAMIN VAUGHAN (June 4, 1830–Feb. 17, 1890), lawyer, author, the eldest son of Jacob Abbott [*q.v.*], and brother of Austin Abbott [*q.v.*], Edward Abbott [*q.v.*], and Lyman Abbott [*q.v.*], was born at Boston. His early education was acquired under the supervision of his father, and in 1846 he entered New York University, graduating in 1850. He then spent a year at the Harvard Law School, completing his legal studies in New York City. On admission to the New York bar in 1852, he commenced practice in that city in partnership with his brother Austin. Of his earliest literary efforts, two works of fiction, *Cone Cut Corners; the Experiences of a Conservative Family in Fanatical Times* (1855) and *Matthew Caraby* (1859), were written in conjunction with his brothers, Austin and Lyman, and published under the pseudonym "Benauly." In 1855, at the instigation of John S. Voorhies, the law publisher, he and Austin Abbott prepared the first of a series of New York practice reports which developed into *Abbott's Reports of Practice Cases in the Courts of the State of New York,* in nineteen volumes covering the period 1854–65, and continued to 1876 in *Reports of Practice Cases, New Series,* in sixteen volumes, the last nine volumes being by Austin Abbott alone. For fifteen years the two brothers, in collaboration, assiduously wrote treatises, compiled digests, and prepared reports which placed them in the front rank of contemporary legal authors. In rapid succession they produced a volume of *Reports of Cases in Admiralty, United States District Court for Southern New York, 1847–50* (1857) and *A Collection of Forms of Pleadings in Actions* (1858). In 1860 appeared their *Digest of New York Statutes and Reports,* in five volumes, which in arrangement and method of treatment departed entirely from the form hitherto universally used. The cases were fitted into an analytical framework, showing the history of the law as developed by them; the addition of the state statutes was another novel feature. The work met with immediate success, and its plan has been followed in all subsequent legal digests. The first edition embraced cases and statutes to 1860, three supplements bringing it to November 1869, after which Austin Abbott continued it to January 1896. Their next joint production was *A Collection of Forms of Practice and Pleading in Actions* (1864), in two volumes, followed by a book of forms, *The Clerk's and Conveyancer's Assistant* (1866). In 1867 they issued the first volume of a work designed to do for the federal courts and laws what they had achieved for New York, *viz.*, a *Digest of the Reports of the United States Courts and Acts of Congress,* the first four volumes only of which were compiled by them jointly. Subsequently B. V. Abbott prepared four additional volumes bringing the work to 1880. Contemporaneously they prepared a volume of *Enactments Relative to the Federal Courts* (1869). The last works in which they collaborated were *General Digest of the Law of Corporations* (1869) and *A Treatise upon the United States Courts and their Practice* (1869), Volume II being by B. V. Abbott alone. In 1864, having withdrawn from active practice, he had been appointed secretary of the New York Code Commission and drafted a penal code which was placed before the legislature and became the basis of the existing law. In June 1870 he was appointed one of the commissioners to revise the Statutes of the United States, a work which occupied three years and resulted in the consolidation of sixteen volumes into one large octavo. The major part of this work was undertaken by him and he was recognized as the real author of the revision. He had the same year issued a *Digest of Reports of Indiana to the Year 1871,* followed by *Reports of Decisions Rendered in the Circuit and District Courts of the United States 1863–71* in two volumes (1870–71). He now devoted six years to a new *United States Digest,* which was issued in 1879 in fourteen volumes and subsequently kept up to date by nine annual supplements, the last being published in 1889. The year 1879 also saw the publication of his *Dictionary of Terms and Phrases used in American or English Jurisprudence* and *General Digest of English and American Cases on the Law of Corporations 1868–78.* His *Judge and Jury,* a popular exposition of leading legal topics, and *The Year Book of Jurisprudence,* a compend of general information, appeared in 1880, and a lighter work, *The Travelling Law School,* first lessons in government and law, four years later. In 1884 he also issued his *National Digest* of the decisions of United States courts up to that year in four volumes, subsequently continuing the digest to 1888 in a supplementary volume (1889). His last works were *The Patent Laws of all Nations* in two volumes (1886), *Decisions on the Law of Patents for Inventions, English Cases, 1662–1843* (1887) in three volumes, and *Addison on Contracts* with American notes (1888). For many years he contributed articles to the daily and weekly press and current periodicals, in addition to occasional editorial work for the Lawyers Co-operative Publishing Company of Rochester in connection with the *Central Reporter,* volumes I to III. The magnitude of his literary output necessarily engaged his undivided attention continuously, and he never actively interested himself in public life. Apart from his legal avocations his only interest was music, for which he had a discriminating taste, and which formed his only relaxation. He married in 1853 Elizabeth, daughter of John Titcomb of Farmington, Me., lived for the greater part of his life in Brooklyn, and died there Feb. 17, 1890.

[The fullest details of his life and work are contained in the *Green Bag,* II, 142, III, 1, where an excellent explanation of the novel features of his Digests is given. Notices will also be found in *Am. Law Rev.,* XXIV, 469 and *Hist. of the Bench and Bar of N.Y.,* ed. by D. McAdam *et al.* (1897), I, 245. Other information may be obtained from the various introductions to his works. The Lib. Cat. of the Harvard Law School contains a good and detailed (but not complete) list of his writings. For particulars of his ancestry see biography of Jacob Abbott.]

H. W. H. K.

ABBOTT, CHARLES CONRAD (June 4, 1843–July 27, 1919), naturalist, archæologist, and author, was the son of Timothy Abbott and Susan Conrad, both of Quaker stock, the ancestors of the former having come from England in 1680 and those of the latter from Germany, at about the same time. The family, however, in later years had left the Society of Friends. Charles Conrad, one of four children, was born at Trenton, N. J., and spent almost his entire life in that neighborhood, coming into possession in 1874 of the old Abbott homestead, "Three Beeches," a few miles south of the city on the banks of the Delaware. He was educated at the Trenton Academy (1852–58) and in 1860 began the study of medicine at the University of Pennsylvania, graduating in 1865, though he never practiced. He was married in 1867 to Julia Olden and was survived by a son and two daughters. From his earliest days Abbott was a devoted student of nature, inheriting this interest, perhaps, from his maternal grandfather, Solomon W. Conrad, a botanist of note. Much of his time in early life being spent at the Academy of Natural Sciences in Philadelphia, his contact with many scientists doubtless also had its influence upon his after life. He early became deeply interested in local archæology and Indian history of the Delaware Valley, and as early as 1875 was appointed field assistant to the Peabody Museum of Cambridge, Mass., to which institution he presented his extensive collection of early Indian material, numbering many thousand specimens. His volume on *Primitive Industry or Illustrations of Handiwork in Stone, Bone and Clay of the Native Races of the North Atlantic Seaboard* (1881) constitutes his most important contribution to science. Later he was connected for a time with the Museum of Science and Art of the University of Pennsylvania. The majority of his publications were short papers of a semi-popular character and more than one hundred of these appeared in the *American Naturalist, Popular Science Monthly, Science Gossip,* etc. In 1884 appeared *A Naturalist's Rambles about Home,* dealing with nature study in the vicinity of his delightful home on the Delaware, followed by *Days Out of Doors, Recent Rambles, Upland and Meadow, Travels in a Treetop,* etc. It is in connection with these works, which recall White's *Selborne,* that Abbott's name is most widely known. He also published, in later life, a number of sketches in *Lippincott's Magazine* and attempted some short stories and novels which were unsuccessful.

Abbott was short in stature with a square head, heavy drooping sandy mustache, deep-set eyes, and contracted brows. He was of rather combative disposition, expressing contempt for what he termed the "dry-as-dust-ical" closet naturalist. He stubbornly maintained his views in any argument even to insisting upon certain observations which subsequently were shown to be practically impossible. Perhaps this peculiarity of character came from his bluff Yorkshire antecedents or possibly from a certain embitterment due to the rejection of some of his earliest writings by scientific editors to whom they were submitted. To those who enjoyed the hospitality of the "Three Beeches" and who tramped with him over his home acres, where every spot was identified with some interesting meeting with beast, bird, or wild flower, he was an entirely different personality, and that is the Abbott whom one sees in his nature writings. His death occurred in Bristol, Pa., whither he had moved after the burning of his old home a few years before.

[*Who's Who in America,* 1920–21; biog. sketch, *Pop. Sci. Mo.,* Feb. 1887, p. 547; additional information from many years of personal acquaintance.] W. S.

ABBOTT, EDWARD (July 15, 1841–Apr. 5, 1908), Congregational and Episcopal clergyman, author, was the youngest son of Jacob Abbott [*q.v.*] and brother of Austin Abbott [*q.v.*], Benjamin Vaughan Abbott [*q.v.*], and Lyman Abbott [*q.v.*]. Born at Farmington, Me., he prepared for college there and in the city of New York, where he graduated with honors from New York University in 1860. He then took the three years' course in theology at Andover Seminary, spending some months during that period in the service of the United States Sanitary Commission with the Army of the Potomac. He entered the Congregational ministry in 1863. After acting as chaplain to various public institutions in Boston for two years, he organized and became pastor of the Pilgrim Congregational Church in Cambridgeport, Mass. Four years later he resigned and became assistant editor of the *Congregationalist* in Boston. While holding this position he published *The Baby's Things: a Story in Verse for Christmas Eve* (1871), *A Paragraph History of the United States* (1875), *A Paragraph History of the Revolution* (1876), and other writings of a popular character. He resigned in 1878 to become editor of the *Literary World,* a position which he held until 1888, and again from 1895 to 1903. He was disturbed by the current liberalism; and in Lent of the same year (1878) in which he left the *Congregationalist* he was confirmed in the Episcopal Church. "He believed in it, not as a merely human, but as a Divine Institution, with a divinely appointed threefold ministry, and divinely constituted Sacraments" (*St. James's Parish,* p. 118). The separation from his former fellowship was without bitterness on either side, and "he held always to many of the religious and doctrinal traditions of his Puritan ancestry" (*Ibid.,* p. 118). Almost immediately after his confirmation he was brought into service as a lay-reader in Episcopal churches. As such he was soon placed in charge of the parish of St. James in North Cambridge, then a home-missionary enterprise. As soon as the regulations of the Church permitted he was made rector, and here he remained, successful and beloved, for the rest of his life, becoming rector emeritus in 1908. In addition to the works already mentioned he published *Revolutionary Times; Sketches of Our Country, Its People and Their Ways One Hundred Years Ago* (1876); *Long Look Books* (3 vols., 1877–80); a memoir of his father, Jacob Abbott, included in the "Memorial Edition" of Jacob Abbott's *The Young Christian* (1882); and various other memoirs, sketches of places, and the like.

[*Who's Who in America,* 1906–07; *St. James's Parish, Cambridge,* by Edward Abbott, with Memorials on the Author (1909).] T. D. B.

ABBOTT, EMMA (Dec. 9, 1850–Jan. 5, 1891), dramatic soprano, was the daughter of Seth Abbott, son of Dyer Abbott, taverner of Concord,

N. H., and director of its Old South Choir. Seth married Almira Palmer of Woodstock, Vt., and eventually established himself as a vocal and instrumental teacher in Chicago, where his daughter Emma was born. In 1859 the child made her début in Peoria as a guitar-player and singer, before an audience of coal-miners, though she did not, as was later said, walk barefoot to the concert because of her family's extreme poverty. Giving lessons and singing in public, Emma in 1867 met Clara Louise Kellogg in Toledo, Ohio, and was by her encouraged to go to New York. There, about 1870, she studied with Errani, became the soprano of the Church of the Divine Paternity, and sang in concert with Ole Bull. In 1872, with the aid of the congregation and the blessing of Henry Ward Beecher (Martin, p. 28), she went to Europe to prepare herself for an operatic career, studying with Sangiovanni (Milan) and Delle Sedie (Paris), and appearing as Marie, in the *Daughter of the Regiment,* at Covent Garden, London, in 1876. After singing with Mapleson she returned to New York and formed her own company, managed by Eugene Wetherell of New York, whom she married in 1878. Thereafter, until her death in Salt Lake City, she toured the country, singing leading rôles in the Abbott English Opera Company. She began her operatic career with pietistic inhibitions which she was perforce obliged to drop by the way; tights in page rôles were justified by being "worn modestly"; her conscience finally allowed her to sing the "immoral" part of Traviata as "a woman who tried to be good"; proper motivation also sanctioned the fervor of the "Abbott kiss," renowned in its day though James Huneker (*Steeplejack,*1920, II, 155) said, "Emma Abbott and her famous 'kiss' do not impress me." Originally not very flexible, her voice, praised by Gounod, was pure and pleasant, but her singing was often mannered. George P. Upton's statement (*Musical Memories,* 1908, p. 117) that "she manufactured a very fluent technic out of this unbending voice by the hardest kind of work" may be accepted as valid. Among her famous leads were those in *Traviata, Romeo and Juliette, Paul and Virginia, Pinafore, Martha,* and *Sonnambula.* She was sincere, kind-hearted, impetuous, and though she committed artistic solecisms, did her share in popularizing opera in the United States. Clara Louise Kellogg (*Memoirs of an American Prima Donna,* 1913, p. 2) insists that Emma's "thirst for profits was the indirect means of her death," a cold caught in a primitive dressing-room in Ogden, Utah Territory, developing into pneumonia. But the initial friendship between the singers had cooled, and the opinions of one prima donna regarding another must always be taken with a grain of salt.

[Sadie E. Martin, *The Life and Professional Career of Emma Abbott* (1891), though sentimental and overlaudatory in describing the singer's achievement, may be accepted as generally reliable regarding the fact data. In addition to the works mentioned in the text, *Grove's Dict. of Music and Musicians, Am. Supp.* (1920), *Baker's Biog. Dict. of Musicians* (3rd ed., 1919), and *De Bekker's Music and Musicians* (rev. ed., 1925) contain brief notices.]

F. H. M.

ABBOTT, FRANK (Sept. 5, 1836–Apr. 20, 1897), dentist, was born in Shapleigh, York County, Me., of an English family which settled in Andover, Mass., in 1640. He was a farm boy, attending the schools of his native town until the age of sixteen, after which he "knocked about" the country for three years. At nineteen he began the study of dentistry with Dr. J. E. Ostrander, Oneida, N. Y., and three years later set up in practice in Johnstown, N. Y. In the Civil War, he served as first lieutenant in the 115th New York Volunteer Infantry, and was captured at Harper's Ferry in September 1862. On being exchanged, he returned to his practice in Johnstown. A year later he removed to New York City, where he matriculated as a medical student in New York University, receiving his M.D. degree in 1871. In 1866 he was appointed clinical lecturer in New York College of Dentistry; in 1868 professor of operative dentistry; in 1869 dean, serving until his death. At the close of the session of 1894–95 he demanded that the trustees establish a chair of pathology and bacteriology, with his son as incumbent. This was refused. He then sought to have the regents of the University of the State of New York withdraw the act of incorporation of the college and substitute a new charter from the regents. This also failed, as did other moves subsequently initiated.

Abbott will be remembered longest through the operative instruments he invented. These embraced forms for almost every phase of the dentist's work,—scalers, chisels, excavators, pluggers,—some of which still survive. His automatic mallet (patented Aug. 16, 1887) was the first with an effective back-action. He was the author of a text-book *Dental Pathology and Practice* (1896), was active in dental-society work, read many papers, and was president of the American Dental Association (1888) and of the National Association of Dental Faculties (1895). He was also a notable collector of rare prints, specializing in American history. Positive in his convictions, aggressive and imperious, he became a zealot in any cause he embraced. Something of a *poseur,* he liked applause. At a meeting of the New Jersey State Dental Society, at which the views he presented were rather badly manhandled, he seized his papers and, snapping out something about a "nest of hornets," left precipitately. (The members proudly adopted the epithet and for years termed themselves "hornets.")

Abbott was tall and was inclined to portliness; a decided blond, with regular features, luxuriant side-whiskers and mustache, a rather impressive figure. He was married in Johnstown to Catharine Ann Cuyler, who with three children survived him. A few of the more important papers he contributed were: "Light *vs.* Heavy Gold Foil and Crystal Gold," *Transactions of the American Dental Association,* 1870, pp. 130–33; "Indigestion, its Causes and Effects," *Transactions of the State Dental Society of New York,* 1875, pp. 39–48; "Caries of Human Teeth," *Dental Cosmos,* XXI, 1879, pp. 57–64, 113–25, 177–84; "Pericementitis (Periostitis), Its Causes and Treatment," *Dental Cosmos,* XXV, 1883, pp. 418–23; "Microscopical Studies upon the Absorption of the Roots of Temporary Teeth," *Transactions of the State Dental Society of New York,* 1884, pp. 45–53; "Hyperostosis of Roots of Teeth," *Transactions of the American Dental Association,* 1886, pp. 105–24; "Odontoblasts in Their Relation to Developing Dentine," *Ibid.,* 1888, pp. 112–22; "Growth of Enamel," *Ibid.,* 1889, pp. 39–53.

[*Trans. Am. Dental Ass.,* 1897, pp. 31–32; *Dental Cosmos,* 1897, pp. 514–15; *N.Y. Times,* Apr. 22, 1897; see also *Hist. of Dental Surgery* (1910), ed. by C.R.E. Koch.]

F.L.H.

ABBOTT, FRANK FROST (Mar. 27, 1860–July 23, 1924), classical scholar, was born at Redding, Conn., the son of Thaddeus Marvin and Mary Jane (Frost) Abbott. His father was a considerable landowner and a man of varied interests, who was actively concerned with religious and political questions, was probate judge at Redding, deacon in the Congregational church, and a representative in the state legislature. His mother was born and brought up in the city of New York and attended Miss Willard's School at Troy, N. Y. The son of these parents was brought up in an atmosphere of broad culture and in a region of much natural beauty. After obtaining the degree of A.B. at Yale University in 1882, he continued his studies and obtained the degree of Ph.D. at the same university in 1891. He was married, June 21, 1888, to Jane Harrison, of New Haven, a descendant of early settlers of Connecticut. Among her ancestors were soldiers of the Revolutionary War and several graduates of Yale College. In the year 1888–89 Abbott studied at the Universities of Berlin and Bonn and spent some time in Rome. He was tutor in Latin at Yale from 1884 to 1891, when he was chosen as the first member of the faculty of the newly founded University of Chicago. Here he drew up the first curriculum of the university, and his scholarship and constructive ability caused him to exert great influence upon the plans and policies of the young institution. He remained at Chicago as associate professor of Latin until 1894, then as professor of Latin until 1908, when he left Chicago to accept the Kennedy Professorship of Latin at Princeton University, a position which he retained until his death. He was professor of Latin in the American School of Classical Studies in Rome for the year 1901–02, and president of the American Philological Association in the year 1917–18. At the time of his death he was a trustee of the American Academy in Rome. He died at Montreux, Switzerland.

Professor Abbott was tall,—about six feet in height,—slender, and of delicate appearance, with dark hair and mustache. He was never robust, as he suffered from pulmonary trouble, and at one time, while he was in Chicago, he was obliged to give up teaching for a year; but he endured his long and discouraging illness cheerfully and without complaint, though it forced him to forego most of the social pleasures which he enjoyed. He was a delightful companion, a lover of literature and art with a keen appreciation and wide knowledge of both, full of delicate humor, and gifted with a keen but always kindly wit. One of his distinguishing characteristics was his invariable courtesy to every one with whom he came in contact.

As a scholar he was diligent, accurate, and conscientious. The trend of his mind was historical, and his chosen field was the life of the ancient Romans, its unbroken continuity through the centuries, and its connection with the life of the modern world. He devoted himself to the study of the political and social life of the Romans as expressed in their language, literature, political and social institutions. Though he was an original investigator he did not disdain to publish the results of his investigations, often combined with those of others, in such form as to appeal to those who are not professional scholars. He was an inspiring teacher, especially for the more mature students. His published works include, in addition to articles in American and foreign classical and philological periodicals, an edition of *Selected Letters of Cicero* (1897); *Repetition in Latin* (1900); *A History and Description of Roman Political Institutions* (1901); *The Toledo Manuscript of the Germania of Tacitus* (1903); *A Short History of Rome* (1906); *Society and Politics in Ancient Rome* (1909); *The Common People of Ancient Rome* (1911); *The Spanish Pleas of Alberico Gentili,* Volume I, Latin text with introduction; Volume II, Translation with introduction (1921); *Roman Politics* (1923); *Municipal*

Administration in the Roman Empire, published after his death with the aid of Allan Chester Johnson (1926).

[*Who's Who in America,* XII; *N.Y. Times,* July 28, 1924; private correspondence.] H. N. F.

ABBOTT, HORACE (July 29, 1806–Aug. 8, 1887), iron manufacturer, descended from George Abbott, who died in Rowley, Mass., 1647, was born in Sudbury, Mass., the fifth child of Alpheus and Lydia (Fay) Abbott. His opportunities for book education were of the slightest, and at the age of sixteen he was apprenticed to a blacksmith in Westboro, Mass. Here he served out his apprenticeship, after which he spent two years as a journeyman and then set up for himself as a country blacksmith at Westboro. In 1836, at the age of thirty, Horace and his equally capable brother, Edwin Augustus Abbott, moved to Baltimore. There he turned his attention to the manufacture of iron, secured the Canton Iron Works, then owned by Peter Cooper of New York, and for fourteen years specialized in the production of wrought-iron shafts, cranks, axles, and other necessities for steamboats and railroads. It was during this period that he forged the first large steamship shaft made in this country, a shaft designed for the Russian frigate *Kamtschatka,* built in New York for the Emperor Nicholas I. This and other manufacturing feats brought to his foundry well-deserved prestige. In 1850 Abbott constructed a rolling-mill which was believed to be capable of turning out the largest rolled plate in the United States. A second rolling-mill of the same size and capacity as the first was erected in 1857, a third large mill in 1859, and a fourth in 1861.

Abbott's rolling-mills proved of great value to the federal government during the Civil War. In them were made the armor plates for the *Monitor* and for nearly all of the vessels of the *Monitor* class built on the Atlantic coast. Ericsson when he designed the first monitor believed that it would be necessary to order the plates in Europe, and the ability of Abbott to produce them considerably speeded their completion. So essential was the service rendered by the Abbott mills that the employees were exempted from the draft, and Abbott himself was especially commended by Secretary of the Navy Welles for the rapidity of his execution of government orders. At the conclusion of the war in 1865 a group of capitalists purchased the Canton Iron Works, organized a stock company under the corporate name of the Abbott Iron Company of Baltimore, and elected Horace Abbott president. Abbott's interests, however, were not confined to iron manufacturing. He was a leader in the establishment of national banks in Baltimore, being one of the originators of the First National Bank, of which he was either a director or vice-president until his death, and a director of the Second National Bank. He was also a director of the Baltimore Copper Company and the Union Railroad of Baltimore.

Abbott was a man of distinguished presence and tireless industry. He lived to be eighty-one years of age, but partial paralysis had incapacitated him for eight years before his final collapse at "Abbottsford," his country seat on the outskirts of Baltimore. He had married in 1830 Charlotte Hapgood, by whom he had seven children, only one of whom survived him.

[Lemuel A. Abbott, *Descendants of George Abbott of Rowley, Mass.* (2 vols., 1906) II, 731–33, and the *Baltimore Sun,* Aug. 9, 1887.] H. U. F.

ABBOTT, JACOB (Nov. 14, 1803–Oct. 31, 1879), Congregational clergyman, educator, writer of children's books, son of Jacob Abbot 2nd and Betsey Abbot, and brother of Gorham Dummer Abbot [*q.v.*], and John S. C. Abbott [*q.v.*], was descended from George Abbot of Andover, who came to New England from Yorkshire as early as 1640. Jacob was born in Hallowell, Me., and after attending school in Brunswick, Me., and the Hallowell Academy, entered Bowdoin College, where he showed a leaning toward the physical sciences. While here he added an extra "t" to his name. He graduated in 1820, and in 1820–21 taught at Portland Academy, where Longfellow was one of his pupils, and in 1823 at Beverly, Mass. He studied theology at Andover Seminary in 1821–22 and 1824. In 1824–25 he was tutor, and in 1825 became professor of mathematics and natural philosophy at Amherst College. After being licensed to preach by the Hampshire Association, May 3, 1826, he occasionally supplied the pulpit in the college chapel and in the Congregational church of the neighboring town of Hatfield. He married Harriet Vaughan of Hallowell, Me., May 18, 1828, and removed soon afterwards to Boston, where he founded the Mount Vernon School, one of the pioneer institutions in America for the education of young women. Abbott here showed his unusual talent for the instruction and government of the young, and introduced many innovations which have now become part of our educational system. Throwing over traditional disciplinary methods, he appealed to the honor and conscience of his pupils by making the school largely self-governing. After several very successful years as principal of this school, Abbott found his interests turning more to preaching and authorship, and in 1833 he resigned and the following year became minister of the Eliot

Congregational Church in Roxbury, Mass. In 1835 he gave his pastoral charge to his brother, John S. C. Abbott, and, except for associating himself with his brothers in the founding and conducting of Abbott's Institution in New York City, from 1843 to 1851, and the short-lived Mount Vernon School for boys (1845–48), he devoted the remainder of his life to literary endeavor.

In 1832 Abbott published his first important work, *The Young Christian.* Its success was immediate, and it remained probably his most widely known book, went into many editions in America and the British Isles, and was translated into French and Dutch. The next volume in the same series, *The Corner Stone* (1834), raised considerable outcry in quarters hostile to Unitarianism, especially in England, where Abbott's emphasis upon practical Christianity was mistakenly thought to cover Arian leanings. The book even became the subject of one of the famous Oxford *Tracts for the Times* (No. 73) by J. H. Newman, although, after their meeting in the course of Abbott's first trip to Europe in 1843, the two men became cordial friends. In later editions of *The Corner Stone* Abbott changed certain equivocal passages to prevent further misapprehension of his views, which were substantially those of the more liberal Evangelicals of his period. He was a most prolific writer. A bibliography of his works lists 180 volumes of which he was sole author and thirty-one more of which he was joint author or editor, not to mention many articles in current periodicals. A number of these books were republished in England, Scotland, Ireland, Germany, Holland, France, and India, and secured for their author a wide contemporary reputation. They show a great diversity of subject-matter in religious, educational, literary, and historical fields. His famous *Rollo* series alone, begun in 1834, comprised twenty-eight volumes—*Rollo at Work, Rollo at Play, Rollo's Travels,* etc.—in which, in the form of simple stories, he attempted to provide rudimentary instruction for children in daily ethics, religion, natural science, travel, and similar subjects. Rollo and his companions belong to that inquisitive and edifying company in juvenile fiction which followed the Rousseauistic *Sandford and Merton* of Thomas Day and preceded the cheerful unregenerates of Thomas Bailey Aldrich and Mark Twain. Abbott thought of his books, not primarily as literary creations, but as instruments for the accomplishment of certain definite results in human life and character. With all their quaint formality and unconscious humor, these stories were read by an entire generation of American children, who were presumably benefited by the exemplary patterns of conduct, as they were certainly pleased by the author's gift for homely anecdote and illustration.

After his years of teaching and school management, Abbott continued to live in New York City until 1870, making several trips to Europe and writing many of the later *Rollo* books, the *Red Histories,* the *Science for the Young* series, etc. His wife had died in 1843, and in 1853 he married Mrs. Mary (Dana) Woodbury. The last years of his life were spent in quiet retirement at "Fewacres" in Farmington, Me., where he died.

[Short biog. by his son, Edward Abbott, prefixed to the Memorial Edition of *The Young Christian* (1882), bibliography appended; essay by Lyman Abbott, "Jacob Abbott, Friend of Children," in *Silhouettes of My Contemporaries* (1921); many manuscripts, journals, personal papers, etc., in the Abbott Room of the Bowdoin Coll. Lib.]

S. P. C.
J. K. S.

ABBOTT, JOHN STEVENS CABOT (Sept. 18, 1805–June 17, 1877), Congregational clergyman, historian, son of Jacob Abbot 2nd and Betsey Abbot, and brother of Gorham Dummer Abbot [*q.v.*] and Jacob Abbott [*q.v.*], was born in Brunswick, Me. Jacob and John added a "t" to the family name. The Abbot household represented the best and gentlest tradition of New England Puritanism. The boy received his schooling at Hallowell and Portland Academies, and entered Bowdoin College in the class of 1825, which included Nathaniel Hawthorne and Henry Wadsworth Longfellow. Upon graduation, he served for a year as principal of the academy in Amherst, Mass., and then for three years pursued a theological course at Andover Seminary, engaging also in the establishment of Sunday-schools along the southern shore of Cape Cod. Immediately following his graduation at Andover (1829), he entered upon his first pastorate, in Worcester, Mass., where he was ordained Jan. 28, 1830. On Aug. 17, 1830 he was married to Jane Williams Bourne of New Bedford, Mass. He held pastorates, successively, at the Central Calvinistic Church, Worcester (1829–34); the Eliot Congregational Church, Roxbury (1835–41); and the First Congregational Church, Nantucket (1841–43). A restless energy unfitted him for long-continued service in one place; it appeared also in his type of pulpit oratory—strongly evangelistic, little philosophical, but well supplied with historical illustrations and aiming chiefly at practical piety. His career as an author had begun, in 1833, with the publication of *The Mother at Home, or the Principles of Maternal Duty Familiarly Illustrated,* a compilation of a series of lectures before the mothers' association of his parish. In 1843 Gorham D. Abbot, with the coöperation of Jacob and Charles, founded a seminary for young ladies in New York

City. It was called by various titles—usually "Abbott's Institution" (*New York Tribune,* May 19, 1899). In December they were joined by John S. C. Abbott, who devoted himself chiefly to the affairs of this school for the next eight or ten years of his life. In 1853 he returned to Brunswick, to educate his son at Bowdoin, and to make use of the college library in completing his life of Napoleon, which was appearing in *Harper's Magazine* (1851–54) and was achieving for that periodical its initial success. The book, *The History of Napoleon Bonaparte,* was published in 1855 and enjoyed an enormous popularity, though it was also the most severely censured of his writings. It is marked by extravagant eulogy of Napoleon, whom Abbott portrays as "more than a hero, more than an Emperor," and again as "a man to whose name alone is attached inexhaustible admiration and imperishable remembrance." This strain of hero-worship, characteristic of Abbott's enthusiastic temperament, antagonized many American editors and critics,—among them, Horace Greeley and Charles A. Dana; it was even hinted that he had been bribed by French gold!

Returning to the active ministry in 1861, Abbott held for five years the pastorate of the Howe Street Church, New Haven, Conn. Meantime he continued with great energy his course of historical writing and publication. Of the numerous works which followed the life of Napoleon, the best-known were: *The Empire of Austria* (1859); *The Empire of Russia* (1860); *Italy* (1860); *Civil War in America* (2 vols., 1863, 1866); *History of Napoleon III* (1868); *Romance of Spanish History* (1869); and *History of Frederick the Great* (1871). In search of material, Abbott made two trips to France (the first before 1859, and the second in 1867), where he came into friendly relations with the Emperor Napoleon III. Although his principal effort was put into his European histories, he wrote copiously in other fields,—American history, biography, ethics, religion, popular science, and juvenile literature. Of his ethical works, *The Mother at Home* had a very considerable vogue both in the United States and in Europe, where it was translated into many languages; and *Practical Christianity* (1862) also was widely read. A didactic purpose is hardly less pervasive in the histories. In a late preface he says, "I have written fifty-four volumes. In every one it has been my endeavor to make the inhabitants of this sad world more brotherly,—better and wiser." His last literary work, a series called *Pioneers and Patriots of America,* was written at Fair Haven, Conn., where he was minister of the Second Church. In this his last pastorate (1870–74), his health began to fail, and after a prolonged illness he died, at Fair Haven, in his seventy-second year.

In Abbott's historical works quotations from such writers as Thiers, Alison, Napier, and Carlyle are numerous and extensive. His own writing abounds in exuberant rhetoric and melodramatic incident. To the discerning among his contemporaries it was plain that he was a florid writer, overfond of moralizing, and lacking independent authority; but to a large public who cared more for picturesque narrative than for sober interpretation the books were of absorbing interest, and undoubtedly they did much to popularize the reading of history.

[*Memorial of John S. C. Abbott,* by Rev. Horatio O. Ladd, his son-in-law (1878). The bibliography on pp. 24–25 is incomplete and inaccurate. Personal papers, etc., in the Abbott Room of the Bowdoin Coll. Lib.]

S. P. C.
R. E. H.

ABBOTT, JOSEPH CARTER (July 15, 1825–Oct. 8, 1881), journalist, politician, son of Aaron and Nancy (Badger) Abbott, was a descendant, in the seventh generation, of George Abbot of Andover, who came to New England from Yorkshire as early as 1640. He was born in Concord, N. H., graduated from Phillips Academy, Andover, and was admitted to the bar in Concord. He entered New Hampshire politics by the road of journalism. For five years he owned and edited the *Manchester Daily American.* His success in this venture brought him the editorship of the distinguished old "Whig organ of New England," the *Boston Atlas and Bee,* from 1859 to 1861. As adjutant-general of New Hampshire he was among the first to offer troops to President Lincoln in April 1861 (*Official Records,* ser. III, vol. I). By December he had become lieutenant-colonel of the 7th Regiment of New Hampshire Volunteers, and two years later he was made its colonel. In the operations around Petersburg he several times received favorable mention (*Ibid.,* ser. I, vol. XXXVI, pt. II). He commanded a brigade in the attack on Fort Fisher, and for his "gallant and meritorious service" there was brevetted brigadier-general, Jan. 15, 1865 (*Ibid.,* ser. I, vol. XLVI, pt. I). Thus far his public career had been marked by correct and well-balanced conduct and by remarkably good fortune.

Settling in North Carolina, at Wilmington, he reëntered journalism and politics and was soon recognized as a leader in the new Republican party of the state. His strength came primarily from the negroes, in whose capacity he apparently believed and whom he organized and counseled in ways that brought him blunt warnings from white Wilmingtonians. In the constitutional convention of 1868 he manifested neither chivalry nor idealism. His chief interests, aside from politics, were internal improvements and state finance. Next year, while in the legislature, he entered into the pay of a "ring" that had similar major interests (Wm. M. Shipp, *North Carolina Fraud Commission Report* (1872), p. 316). Elected to the federal Senate in 1868, he at once became, as was his custom, attentive and busy in that body. He spoke orthodoxly on suffrage matters (*Congressional Globe,* 40 Cong., 3 Sess., p. 980). He was helpful in handling the details of army administration. He strove earnestly for the improvement of the Wilmington harbor and hoped for a federal charter consolidating the railroads of the Carolinas and making them the eastern part of a southern transcontinental system. But his claim of altruistic service in the rebuilding of North Carolina obtained no favorable response. A duty on peanuts was his utmost achievement in the Senate (*Ibid.,*41 Cong., 2 Sess., pp. 2052, 3518, 3683, 4898). His party did not renominate him. For ten years more (1871–81) he lived on in Wilmington, a short, stout man of soldierly bearing and speech, thrice married but childless. Most of this time, as previously, he conducted a lumber manufacturing business and edited the *Wilmington Post.* The latter, a Republican weekly newspaper, compared favorably with its contemporaries. But, although during this period he was given campaign funds to disburse by political sympathizers outside the state and received federal office in Wilmington from Hayes as well as from Grant, he never recovered party leadership. The historians of the state even now mention him only to condemn him.

[J. G. de Roulhac Hamilton, *Reconstruction in N.C.* (1914) covers Abbott's Reconstruction activities thoroughly and mercilessly. An obituary was published in the *Wilmington Post,* Oct. 9, 1881, and reprinted in the *Raleigh Evening Visitor,* Oct. 10, 1881. There is a fairly accurate sketch in the *Cyc. Eminent and Representative Men of the Carolinas of the Nineteenth Century* (1892).]

C. C. P.

ABBOTT, LYMAN (Dec. 18, 1835–Oct. 22, 1922), Congregational clergyman, editor, author, was born in Roxbury, Mass., the son of Jacob Abbott [*q.v.*] and Harriet (Vaughan) Abbott. Before he was three years old, his parents transferred their residence to Farmington, Me. There, directly opposite the home of his paternal grandfather, on a pleasantly located ten-acre estate known as "Little Blue," Lyman Abbott, his two older brothers, and a younger brother, lived until the death of their mother in 1843, which led to the family's removal to New York City. Lyman prepared for college, first under his uncle Samuel, who, having acquired "Little Blue," had opened it as a school for boys; and then under his uncle Charles, in a similar school in Norwich, Conn. In 1849, at the age of fourteen, he entered New York University, where he was chiefly influenced by C. S. Henry, professor of philosophy, and Howard Crosby, professor of Greek. On graduation in 1853, he accepted the invitation of his brothers, Austin and Vaughan, to join their law firm already established in New York City. On Oct. 14, 1857 he married his second cousin, Abby Frances Hamlin. During the two following years, despite the fact that his reputation as a lawyer and the income from his practice were increasing, boyhood aspirations for the ministry revived. After much deliberation, he decided, July 13, 1859, to abandon the law. He prepared himself to preach, chiefly through his own reading and study, and through suggestions from his father and his uncle John S. C. Abbott [*q.v.*]. He was ordained at Farmington, Me., Mar. 12, 1860, and on Mar. 31 took charge of the Congregational church in Terre Haute, Ind. He remained there during the stirring years of the Civil War, adapting himself to the atmosphere of a mid-western city and ministering effectively to a church in which he was allowed a freedom of utterance somewhat unusual in those days, but essential to a man of his liberal spirit. He played an important part in clarifying the issues of the great contest and in comforting anxious and bereaved hearts. As the war drew to its end he, like Lincoln, sought to heal the wounds caused by internecine strife and to assist in the physical and moral reconstruction of the South, with whose peculiar problems Abbott sympathized keenly then and in all subsequent years. Despite the protests of devoted parishioners and other citizens of Terre Haute, he was led to resign his pastorate Feb. 27, 1865, and to become corresponding secretary of the American Union Commission, formed by a group of New York ministers and laymen to coöperate with the government in the work of reconstruction. He held this position four years. In connection with it he was pastor from 1866 to 1869 of the New England Congregational Church, just organized, on Forty-first St., New York City. Meanwhile, he had begun book reviewing for *Harper's Magazine,* and the connection thus made with the house of Harper & Brothers provided in considerable part, as it developed, the resources needed for the maintenance of his family during the early seventies. He also had charge of a church in Cornwall, where he built the home which was the center of the family's life during subsequent years.

His labors in the field of journalism and authorship grew more extensive and lucrative and led to his appointment in 1870, by the American Tract Society, as editor of its new periodical called

The Illustrated Christian Weekly. In this office he continued till 1876, when he became associated with Henry Ward Beecher in the editorship of the *Christian Union.* He had always been an admirer of Beecher, by whose vehement utterances in opposition to slavery he had been greatly influenced in pre-war days. With Beecher's withdrawal from the paper in 1881, Abbott became editor-in-chief and so continued after the name of the paper, in 1893, was changed to the *Outlook.* When Beecher died, Mar. 8, 1887, his great church, Plymouth Congregational in Brooklyn, turned to Abbott as his successor. Invited at first to act as temporary pastor, he was extended a call to the permanent pastorate on May 26, 1888 by a vote of 400 to 60 and was installed on Jan. 16, 1890 by a large council, unusual in that it included representatives of various denominations. He retired early in 1899, temporarily wearied with his double load as pastor and editor, but having maintained throughout the ten years the high pulpit standards of Plymouth Church and its prestige, membership, and influence. Henceforth he devoted himself chiefly to the development of the *Outlook* and to preaching and speaking in colleges and universities, on many platforms and on many different public occasions, where he advocated effectively important movements and reforms. The *Outlook* under his guiding hand became a powerful journal, the exponent of progressive and practical Christianity, distinguished for its enterprise, fairness, and literary qualities. Its success was furthered by Abbott's judicious selection, as associate editors, of Hamilton Mabie and Lawson Valentine. In 1912 it was one of the outstanding journals which supported, even at the cost of losing subscribers, the presidential candidacy of Theodore Roosevelt and the platform of the Progressive party. Later it advocated the early participation of the United States in the World War.

Slender, erect, energetic, of about the average height, Abbott impressed one as a man of force well under control and directed to definite ends. His long, flowing beard, whitening with the years, gave to his countenance a patriarchal appearance. His style was quiet and unadorned, though not lacking in fervor when emotions and convictions were deeply aroused. His strength was in his gift of analysis, comparison, and clear statement. Few equaled him in the ability to draw sharp and effective contrasts. He was a rapid and prolific writer, and his books were numerous. One of the most influential was *The Life and Literature of the Ancient Hebrews* (1901), in which while accepting the verdicts of modern Biblical scholarship he pointed out the abiding moral and spiritual values of the Old Testament. In his *Theology of an Evolutionist* (1897) he interpreted sympathetically the scientific conclusions of such men as Huxley, Tyndall, and Spencer and yet supported the essentials of the historic Christian faith. Two of his most widely circulated devotional books were *The Other Room* (1903) and *The Great Companion* (1904). His *Henry Ward Beecher* (1903) and *The Spirit of Democracy* (1910) represent other phases of his literary activity.

[Abbott's *Reminiscences* (1915), new ed. with an introduction by his son Ernest Hamlin Abbott covering his last years (1923), and *What Christianity Means to Me* (1921); the *Outlook,* Nov. 8, 1922, biographical number with character sketches by his associates and tributes from many distinguished Americans; the Abbott manuscript collection at Bowdoin Coll.]

H. A. B.

ABBOTT, SAMUEL WARREN (June 12, 1837–Oct. 22, 1904), physician, statistician, a pioneer leader of the American public health movement, was born in Woburn, Mass., the son of Ruth (Winn) and Capt. Samuel Abbott. He attended the Phillips Andover Academy and Brown University, taking his A.M. degree at the latter institution in 1858. He then began the study of medicine, first with Dr. Benjamin Cutter of Woburn, and later at the Harvard Medical School, where he received the M.D. degree in 1862. He was immediately appointed assistant surgeon in the federal navy, served in that capacity for two years, and was then transferred to the army. He saw much active service in Virginia as surgeon of the 1st Massachusetts Cavalry, 1864–65. In 1864 he returned temporarily from the front to marry Martha W. Sullivan of Woburn. At the conclusion of the Civil War he began the practice of medicine at Woburn and Wakefield. He established a moderate general practice but soon became especially interested in community health problems. He was probably the first physician in the state to establish standards for the production of a pure and reliable vaccine for use against smallpox; and in this connection he published a study of the "Uses and Abuses of Animal Vaccination" in the *Public Health Papers and Reports* (1882, vol. VIII). In 1886 he was appointed secretary of the Massachusetts Board of Health, the first real state board of health in the United States, and in this capacity he served until his death. Here his reputation as an outstanding leader of the public health movement was established. It was his good fortune to direct the board through the period when demography and bacteriology were first making a reality of preventive medicine. Abbott proved to possess, besides general medical ability, one notable characteristic of peculiar value to a man in his position; namely, a genius for the study of vital statistics. The science of demography was then making rapid progress in

Great Britain, and Abbott's potential ability in this field was doubtless stimulated by his contacts with the able British statistician, William Farr, whom he visited in England soon after his appointment to the Massachusetts State Board. Farr's standard work entitled *Vital Statistics* was published in London in 1885, and Abbott began in the following year to edit the annual *Report to the Legislature of Massachusetts Relating to the Registry and Return of Births, Marriages, and Deaths* (1887–91). He also edited *A Summary of the Vital Statistics of the New England States for the Year 1892* (1895). These two works became the model American statistical studies for the period. Some of the reports were of considerable value to the entire medical profession, notably the study of the "Influenza Epidemic of 1889–90," which appeared in the *Twenty-First Annual Report of the State Board of Health* (1890). Abbott's best-known work, however, was the fruit of his growing interest in the whole field of public health. This was his *Past and Present Condition of Public Hygiene and State Medicine in the United States* (1900). It was perhaps the first serious study of the development of the public health movement in this country.

[W. B. Atkinson, *Physicians and Surgeons of the U.S.* (1878); R. D. Leigh, *Federal Health Administration in the U.S.* (1927); R. F. Stone, *Biogs. of Eminent Am. Physicians and Surgeons* (1894); G. C. Whipple, *State Sanitation* (1917), containing photograph of Abbott, I, 207; personal recollections of Dr. Henry Walcott, of Cambridge, Mass., former president of the Mass. State Board of Health.]

R. H. S.

ABBOTT, WILLIAM HAWKINS (Oct. 27, 1819–Jan. 8, 1901), pioneer petroleum producer and refiner, the son of David and Hannah (Hawkins) Abbott, was born on his father's farm in Middlebury, New Haven County, Conn., the eldest of a family of twelve children. Until he was eighteen years of age Abbott helped with the farm work and completed the common-school curriculum, attending during the winter months. Then, with the approval of his father, he became a clerk in a general store at Watertown, Conn. He remained in this position until 1844, gaining a considerable amount of business experience and developing a character recognized for its industry and ambition. In September 1845 he was married to Jane Wheeler. When twenty-five years old, he removed to Newton Falls, Trumbull County, Ohio, where he entered the employ of a large general mercantile business. A year later, when the partners for whom he worked gave up this business relationship, Abbott joined with one of them and continued the store as Bronson & Abbott for another year. This partnership was dissolved a year later, both members continuing separate businesses. Another year passed and Abbott bought out his former partner as well as an established real estate business in Newton and continued the two on his own account with marked success until 1862. In 1859 Col. E. L. Drake had brought in the first oil well near Titusville, Pa., and partly from curiosity but mainly as a matter of business, Abbott visited there the following spring. What he saw prompted him to take a part interest in the lease of the near-by Parker farm, on which a well was being drilled. When this came into production some months later, Abbott, still a resident of Ohio, went to New York to establish a market for this oil and succeeded in selling 200 barrels at thirty-five cents a gallon to Schieffelin Brothers, an extensive drug and chemical house in New York. This deal may be said to mark the beginning of the oil trade. Abbott, too, was the moving spirit in the construction of the first refinery at Titusville, the plant beginning operations in January 1861. Throughout this year Abbott carried on his oil interests chiefly from his Ohio home, but in 1862 he moved with his family to Titusville, and during the same year brought the first coal for domestic use to Titusville and thus established the first retail coal business. Three years later he leased a large acreage of coal lands in Mercer County, Pa., and for years thereafter engaged successfully in coal mining. In 1865 he organized a company and built at a cost of $200,000 the Titusville and Pitt-Hole plank road. Meanwhile he was expanding his oil interests. In 1867 he formed with Henry Harley the Pennsylvania Transportation Company, the first of the great oil pipe-line consolidations, and finally in 1870 he was instrumental in reviving active interest in the earlier projected Union & Titusville Railroad Company, with the result that the road was opened in 1871. Thereafter until his death, Abbott divided his time generally amongst his various interests, including the presidency of the Citizens Bank of Titusville. From the time of his permanent residence in Titusville, because of his business ability, reliability, and far-sightedness, he was prominently identified with almost every civic development of the city.

[Lemuel A. Abbott, *Descendants of Geo. Abbott, of Rowley, Mass.* (1906); J. T. Henry, *The Early and Later Hist. of Petroleum* (1873); correspondence with Benson Memorial Lib., Titusville, Pa.]

C. W. M.

ABEEL, DAVID (June 12, 1804–Sept. 4, 1846), missionary of the Dutch Reformed Church, was born in New Brunswick, N.J., the son of Capt. David Abeel, U.S.N., "a man of strict morality and worth," and Jane Hassert, "a lady possessed of deep piety" and gentleness. At fifteen he applied for admission to West Point, but, owing to the number of prior applications, he shortly withdrew his own and turned toward medicine. Hardly had he entered upon his course of training for a medical career when religion thrust its claim upon him. He became overwhelmed by a sense of sin and the need of his complete surrender to the will of God. This conversion turned him toward the Christian ministry and he entered in 1823, without previous college training, the New Brunswick Seminary of his church. In 1826 he graduated, and in October of the same year was ordained at Athens, N. Y., where he entered upon a pastorate of two and one-half years. Ill health was destined to play a leading part in his ministry. It shortened his pastorate at Athens and went far toward determining the schedule and character of all his subsequent service. His affliction was early diagnosed as pulmonary tuberculosis. During the winter of 1828–29, which Abeel spent on the West Indian Island of St. John in quest of health, his mind turned definitely toward foreign missionary work, and he sought and received appointment as a chaplain of the Seamen's Friend Society, with an understanding also with the American Board. On Oct. 14, 1829, he sailed from New York on the ship *Roman,* arriving in Canton, Feb. 25, 1830. He took up the duties of his chaplaincy and set about the study of the Fukien colloquial. Having a good ear for tones he gradually acquired a fair control of the Chinese dialect. He later learned some Malay and Siamese in connection with his travels. After a year in the chaplaincy, he joined by previous agreement the service of the American Board and remained therein until his death in his forty-third year.

For various reasons, the times and his own health included, Abeel was not permitted to stay long at any one post. Leaving Canton at the end of December 1831, he visited Java, Malacca, Siam, and Singapore until finally ordered home to recuperate. Sailing from the East early in 1833 he found sufficient renewal of energy to allow him to tarry in England, Switzerland, France, Germany, and Holland, giving addresses and attending conferences in behalf of missions. While in England he helped to found the Society for Promoting Female Education in China and the East. He spent the years from 1835 to 1838 in America in efforts to renew his health and to enlist among the members of his own denomination enthusiasm and volunteers for missionary service. By the spring of 1839 he was again in the Far East. Finding the work in Canton hindered by the first Anglo-Chinese War, he journeyed again to the south visiting familiar fields and others in the Malay Archipelago. In October 1841 he returned northward along the China coast, establishing himself at Kolongsou, an island near Amoy. Upon the opening of Amoy as a treaty port he gave himself to the founding of the mission-station there. In January 1845 he was forced to leave Amoy on his last journey home. On arrival in America he lingered in rapidly failing health until his death in Albany, N.Y. Abeel's presence and his writings combined to make him an unusually influential figure in the early days of modern missions. Among his writings are: *To the Bachelors of India, by a Bachelor* (1833); *A Narrative of Residence in China* (1834); *The Claims of the World to the Gospel* (1838); various pamphlets and tracts, and many articles in the *Chinese Repository.*

[G. R. Williamson, *Memoir of the Rev. David Abeel* (1848); H.W.Pierson, *Am.Missionary Memorial*(1853); L. E. Smith, *Heroes and Martyrs of the Modern Missionary Enterprise* (1853); W. B. Sprague, *Annals of the Am. Reformed Dutch Pulpit* (1869); E. T. Corwin, *Manual of the Reformed Church in America* (1879); J. I. Good, *Famous Missionaries of the Reformed Church* (1903); Extracts from Abeel's Journal may be found in the *Missionary Herald,* vols. XXVII–XLII.]

J. C. A.

ABELL, ARUNAH SHEPHERDSON (Aug. 10, 1806–Apr. 19, 1888), journalist, was descended from Robert Abell, who came from England about 1630 to Rehoboth, now Seekonk, Mass. His father, Caleb, a quartermaster in the War of 1812, married Elona, daughter of Arunah Shepherdson; their son, named for his maternal grandfather, was born at East Providence, R. I. At fourteen the boy left school and worked for two years in the store of a dealer in West India goods. He wanted, however, to be a printer, and in October 1822 was apprenticed by his father to the *Providence Patriot.* After attaining his majority he worked as a journeyman and foreman in Boston. Later in New York he worked in the same office with William M. Swain and Azariah H. Simmons. The *New York Sun,* started as a one-cent paper in 1833, had set a new fashion in journalism. The three printers determined to found another "penny paper." Abell persuaded his associates that the New York field was occupied and that they should try Philadelphia, where all the newspapers sold for six cents. There they started the *Public Ledger,* which first appeared on Mar. 24, 1836. It consisted of four pages, fifteen-and-a-half by twenty-one-and-a-half inches, with meager general news and little local news, except police reports, but it furnished reading for artisans and in a year was paying dividends. Abell then proposed to start a similar paper in Baltimore, and his partners agreed on condition that he manage it. Accordingly on May 17, 1837, he issued the first number of the *Baltimore Sun,* of which he was to be the guiding spirit for the rest of his life, while the Philadelphia paper was chiefly managed by his partners, and after the death of Simmons, in 1855, by Swain alone.

With the *Sun* Abell made a departure. Avoiding the trivial and personal note of many of the early penny papers, he created a condensed but accurate and comprehensive journal, editorially independent without neutrality, free from religious or partisan political controversy, and never intemperate, vituperative, or wantonly disregardful of individual privacy. His paper always maintained sound business methods. When the managers of a fair for Southern relief after the Civil War objected to an advertising bill of $1,800, he insisted on payment, but then gave the money to the fund on condition of secrecy while he lived. He was a pioneer of modern impersonal journalism, and a pioneer in classification, in the systematic gathering of local news, and in the development of speedy general news service. In 1838 he brought the President's message by pony express from Washington a day in advance of his neighbors, who depended on copying it from the Washington papers. He repeated this exploit with President Harrison's inaugural address, issuing it the day of delivery. He established a pony express from Boston for foreign news; and when the Oregon question became acute, he organized with New York papers a special service from Halifax, covering the distance in less than sixty-three hours. His enterprise in the Mexican War increased the prestige of the *Sun*. He brought dispatches by a relay of riders from New Orleans in sixty hours, outstripping the mail by thirty hours, and frequently giving the government its first news of important movements, among them the fall of Vera Cruz. He scrupulously safeguarded his advance news from speculative use, instantly giving its substance to the government and the public. In 1847 he established a daily pony express from New Orleans, and he also used carrier pigeons for short distances, keeping between four and five hundred birds on Hampstead Hill. He assisted Samuel F. B. Morse in introducing the telegraph, and used it freely from the first. The President's message of May 11, 1846 on the Mexican War was telegraphed to the *Sun* and printed the next morning. His firm also invested in the enterprise of extending the subsidized Washington-Baltimore wire to Philadelphia. It was also eager for improvements in printing, and bought Hoe's first type-revolving cylinder press for the *Public Ledger* in 1846 (Robert Hoe, *Short History of the Printing Press,* 1902), and installed one in the *Sun* in 1853.

In the Civil War Abell had Southern sympathies. He printed the news and maintained editorial silence, but the *Sun* was watched by the authorities, and once an order to close it and arrest Abell was issued only to be withdrawn. He believed this attempt was incited by politicians, who presently offered to buy the paper on the plea of his precarious position. Increasing costs of publication caused disagreement in the firm. Since Swain was unwilling to increase the price of the *Public Ledger,* it was sold in 1864 to George W. Childs and Joseph W. and Anthony J. Drexel. The partners retained the *Sun,* with Abell in charge, and he raised the price to two cents. After the war he supported President Johnson's reconstruction policy and led in restoring the Democrats to power in Maryland, though he kept the *Sun* independent of the party organization. On the death of Swain, Feb. 16, 1868, Abell purchased his Baltimore interests and continued as sole proprietor of the *Sun* until its fiftieth anniversary, when he took into partnership his three sons, who inherited the paper by his will. He died in Baltimore on Apr. 19, 1888. In 1838 he married Mary, daughter of John Fox of Baltimore. She died in 1859, leaving three sons and five daughters. Abell was impressive in appearance, genial in disposition, and quietly masterful in execution.

[The Abell family records; H. E. West, *Hist. of the Sun,* published as a supplement to the *Sun,* May 14, 1922; J. T. Scharf, *Hist. of Baltimore City and County* (1881), pp. 617 ff.; Scharf and Westcott, *Hist. of Phila.* (1884), III, 2000; a sketch in the *Mag. of Western Hist.,* Jan. 1889; obituaries in *Baltimore Sun, Phila. Press,* and *N.Y. Tribune,* Apr. 20, 1888.]

R. C. E. B.

ABERCROMBY, JAMES (1706–Apr. 23, 1781), British general, belonged to a good Scottish family, the Abercrombys of Glassaugh, Banffshire, a cadet branch of the Abercrombys of Birkenbog. In his youth he followed the path blocked out for him by the career of his father, Alexander Abercromby, the previous laird of Glassaugh; he entered the army, was active in Banff affairs as commissioner of supply and justice of the peace, and was chosen member of parliament for Banff in 1734, a seat he held for twenty years. His mother was Helen, a daughter of George Meldrum of Crombie; he married his third cousin, Mary Duff of Dipple and Brace. Throughout his life he enjoyed two minor posts, as King's Painter in Scotland, and as deputy-governor of Stirling Castle. After passing through the lower ranks of the army, he became, in 1746, lieutenant-colonel of the first battalion of the Royal Scots, with the rank of colonel. He served in the same year as quartermaster-general in St. Clair's expedition, which was first designed for an attack upon Canada, but was diverted to a descent upon Port l'Orient. There he gained the intimate friendship of David Hume. The following year he was wounded in the fierce fighting at the relief of Hulst.

His military experience and his close friendship with Loudoun led to his selection in 1756 as second in command of the British forces in America. He was given the 44th Regiment, and promoted to the rank of major-general. Reaching Albany a month before his superior, Loudoun, he acted during that brief period as commander-in-chief, but took no decisive steps towards settling the various problems confronting him. As second in command, Abercromby proved himself an obedient and trustworthy officer. Loudoun put him in charge of the troops at Albany, where he performed his work adequately, since it involved no decisions of primary importance. He incurred no one's dislike; he won no one's admiration. He was a disciplinarian of the European school, and he gave his opinion upon colonial affairs, when asked, in favor of the most rigid interpretation of the royal prerogative.

Upon Loudoun's recall, Abercromby assumed, in March 1758, the supreme command of all British forces in America, and the colonelcy-in-chief of the Royal American Regiment. With Amherst's successful expedition against Louisburg, and Forbes's slow advance towards Fort Duquesne, he had nothing to do, for both offensives were planned by Pitt in England. To him was left the assault upon Ticonderoga, where his incapacity for chief command became apparent. His own second, Lord Howe, was unfortunately killed in a preliminary skirmish, and Abercromby, unable to make a decision by himself, trusted to the recommendations of his chief engineer, young Matthew Clarke, and attempted to carry by assault the almost impregnable French position. His forces were beaten back in one of the bloodiest battles in the history of British arms. So unnecessary a defeat turned both his own army and the provincials against him, and he was recalled in the fall of 1758. The provincials named him "General Nabbycromby." One of his medical officers wrote a succinct summary: "The General returns to Europe as little regretted as any man that ever left America. He had no resolution, no will of his own, was bullied into the favours he bestowed, made few friends thereby, created some enemies, and in short fell into universal contempt."

After his return to England, the usual rules of seniority brought him, in 1759, the rank of lieutenant-general, and in 1772, that of general. He spent a great portion of his last twenty-two years at Glassaugh. His daughter Jane succeeded to the property.

[For Abercromby's early career, some information may be found in A. and H. Tayler, *Book of the Duffs* (1914); *Records of the County of Banff* (1922), comp. by Jas. Grant; Jos. Foster, *Members of Parliament, Scotland* (2nd ed., 1882); and J. Hill Burton, *Life and Correspondence of David Hume* (1846). The chief sources for his commands in America are the Loudoun and Abercromby Papers in the possession of the Henry E. Huntington Lib. and Art Gallery, at San Marino, Cal. Some important letters are printed in the *Correspondence of Wm. Pitt* (1906), ed. by Gertrude Selwyn Kimball; while references are found in most of the chief collections of colonial source material.]

S. M. P.

ABERNETHY, GEORGE (Oct. 7, 1807–May 2, 1877), merchant, churchman, administrator, was born in New York City, not, as sometimes stated, in Aberdeen, Scotland. He was probably the son of William Abernethy, a shoemaker listed in the New York Directory of 1807. At any rate, he was trained for commercial pursuits, which he followed from an early age. On Jan. 21, 1830, he was married to Anne Cope (1811–84). In 1839, Rev. Jason Lee, superintendent of the Methodist mission of Oregon, while in the east to recruit the mission's funds and also its personnel, arranged with Abernethy to go to Oregon and assume the financial management of the mission's affairs. With his family, Abernethy sailed around the Horn on the *Lausanne,* which arrived in Oregon June 1, 1840, bringing also Mr. Lee and a strong reinforcement. This included farmers and craftsmen as well as mission workers. The *Lausanne* party may be said to have begun the American colonization of Oregon. They cultivated land to a considerable extent, opened an academy, built a mill, and started commercial activity in competition with the Hudson's Bay Company. In all of these enterprises Abernethy bore a leading part and remained for some years the outstanding American business man of the Pacific Northwest. His center of operations was Oregon City, where he is said to have erected, for warehouse purposes, the first brick structure built in the state. He also secured a printing-press and aided in establishing the first newspaper in Oregon. He encouraged lumbering and the fisheries, bought the settlers' wheat, and established commercial connections with Hawaii, California, and the Atlantic coast ports. Then came reverses. Some of his projects proved financially disastrous, and an unprecedented freshet in 1861 destroyed the bulk of his physical property, reducing him to very limited circumstances.

Until after the middle of the century, however, Abernethy, to most Oregonians, represented, on a smaller scale and under American auspices, what Dr. John McLoughlin and James Douglas represented, as agents of the British Fur Company, at Fort Vancouver. Yet, such was his address, courtesy, and business fairness that these magnates regarded him more in the light of a friend than a rival. Similarly, his conspicuous position with the mission failed to alienate from him the good will of those Americans, whose numbers rose with the successive annual overland immigrations, who were distrustful of the missionary influence in public affairs. His conciliatory disposition, his quiet dignity and ability to keep his own counsel, made him the natural compromise candidate for governor when, in 1845, the provisional government, begun in 1843, was reorganized with a single executive in place of the former executive committee. The election, though taking place during Abernethy's absence in Hawaii, resulted in giving him a majority of 98 out of a total of 504 votes cast. No adequate analysis of that vote is possible. At the election in 1847, however, when he was again a candidate, it was the votes from the district north of the Columbia, dominated by the Hudson's Bay influence, which secured him his small majority and enabled him to continue in the office until the provisional government was supplanted by the territorial government under Gen. Joseph Lane.

In November 1847 occurred the Whitman massacre, followed by the war against its perpetrators, the Cayuses, and the determined efforts to overcome the apathy of Congress in its attitude toward the Oregon region. The governor's responsibilities were thereby greatly increased, but he met them in a manner to win from his contemporaries, almost universally, the fame of being a just, wise, and capable public officer. Criticisms of Abernethy's character published in H. H. Bancroft's *History of Oregon* have been vigorously protested by pioneers who knew him intimately (especially Medorem Crawford, *Transactions of the Oregon Pioneer Society for 1886*), and these strictures fail of support in the public record of his words and acts. The criticisms implied, rather than stated, in Rev. George Gary's Diary (*Oregon Historical Quarterly,* XXIV, 270-71, 276) may be disregarded. When he died, Harvey W. Scott said of him (*Oregonian,* May 3, 1877): "Faithful, gentle, and obliging, devoted always to duty, and recognized as the impersonation of uprightness and honor, no man could be his enemy." Though written under circumstances which tempted to eulogy, these words are a truer index of his character than either the over-subtle inferences of the Bancroftian writer or the fault-finding of a harassed missionary.

Abernethy was a familiar figure in Portland, where he spent his declining years. In appearance he was at once unimpressive and decidedly pleasant. Short of stature, with kindly eyes, "soft brown hair," prominent sloping forehead, smooth upper lip and Quaker beard, he passed among western men for a Yankee and he had many of the traits which are common to Yankee and Scotchman alike. His letters and public papers disclose not only a good command of English but some skill in composition—as well as sound judgment in practical matters, and high motives.

[Dates of birth and marriage are given in a sketch of Wm. Abernethy, son of George, in Jos. Gaston, *Centennial Hist. of Ore.* (1912), IV, 72. La Fayette Grover, *Ore. Archives* (1853), and J. H. Brown, *Polit. Hist. of Ore.* (1892), contain Abernethy's public papers. One volume of his letter-press copy-book is in the Ore. State Hist. Soc. Lib. It deals with his business affairs in the years 1847 to 1850. For an account of the Ore. provisional government see Jos. Schafer, *A Hist. of the Pacific Northwest* (1918), pp. 156–97, and W. C. Woodward, *The Rise and Early Hist. of Polit. Parties in Ore. 1843–68* (1913).]

J. S.

ABRAMS, ALBERT (Dec. 8, 1863–Jan. 13, 1924), physician, was the founder of a system of universal diagnosis and treatment of disease, termed by him the Electronic Reactions of Abrams (E.R.A.), which was to prove "either a miracle or the greatest of fakes," and is at best regarded as an illusion well suited to commercial exploitation. Born in San Francisco, the son of Marcus and Rachel (Leavey) Abrams, he took his medical degree at Heidelberg (1882) and after extensive postgraduate studies in Europe settled in his home city, where he was sometime chief of the medical clinic at Cooper Medical School. His published works for this period comprise: *Manual of Clinical Diagnosis* (1891); *Diseases of the Heart* (1900); *The Blues (Splanchnic Neurasthenia)* five editions (1904–14); *Man and his Poisons* (1906), and *Diagnostic Therapeutics* (1910). Known for original research and prolific authorship he acquired an international reputation through his discovery of "Abrams's visceral reflexes." In 1910 his *Spondylotherapy; Spinal Concussion,* which went through five editions, sought to harmonize these discoveries with the claims and results in practice of the spinal-adjustments healing cults but departed more or less from the rigor of scientific medicine. In 1913 the assertion that disease causes changes in the electrical skin potential (see Arthur E. Baines and F. H. Bowman, *Electropathology and Therapeutics,* 1914) gave him the germ of the conception of electronic diagnosis and treatment, and his *New Concepts in Diagnosis and Treatment* (1916) maintained that the electron, the new unit of matter in general, was to supplant the cell as a biological unit; that disease is a disharmony of the electronic oscillations; that diagnosis must detect and measure the alteration—each disease has its own vibratory rate—and that treatment must restore equilibrium. Since all cures make use of this principle the new method must supplant all others. A drop of blood represents the entire individual and suffices for diagnosis, although it is necessary to place a healthy control subject in the electrical circuit and test his skin reactions, which conform to the vibratory rate of the disease. The apparatus comprised under fanciful names a condenser and a rheostat and ohmmeter for diagnosis, and for treatment a magnetic interrupter (oscilloclast). The book abounded in fantastic dogmatism to such an extent that the author's colleagues at first thought him unbalanced. But he was of established reputation, it was not easy to disprove his basic claims, and, as in all new systems of treatment, remarkable cures were not lacking. There was a possible crude foreshadowing of a revolutionary discovery.

After the interlude of the war Abrams seems to have abandoned professional for commercial methods, incidentally giving brief instruction courses and leasing apparatus, both at exorbitant prices, to physicians and laymen alike; so that by 1923 there were no less than 3,500 electronic practitioners in the world. He made increasingly extravagant claims in diagnosis, going far beyond the limits of disease, and his methods became more and more open to ridicule and exposure. The *Scientific American* began an investigation of E.R.A. in October 1923, not long before Abrams's death, which occurred with dramatic suddenness at the most critical period of his career. There has been considerable posthumous interest in Abrams in England, and the Royal Society of Medicine gave his doctrines an independent investigation; and despite his professional apostasy British medical men of the caliber of Sir James Barr insist that he was not only a genius but one of the outstanding medical figures of the last half-century.

[For the adverse report of the *Scientific American* committee, see the files of that journal from Oct. 1923 to Sept. 1924. Of recent British reports consult G. Laughton Scott, "*The Abrams Treatment" in Practice* (1924); *A Preliminary Communication Concerning the Electronic Reactions of Abrams* (the report of the Royal Society of Medicine Committee, Sir T. Horder, chairman, 1925) and *Abrams' Methods of Diagnosis and Treatment* (1925), ed. by Sir James Barr; biographical data from *Who's Who in America*, 1922–23.] E. P.

ACCAU (ACCAULT), MICHEL. [See Aco, MICHEL, fl. 1680–1702.]

ACKER, CHARLES ERNEST (Mar. 19, 1868–Oct. 18, 1920), inventor and manufacturer, was of Dutch descent. His parents were William James and Mercia (Grant) Acker, and his birthplace was Bourbon, Ind. He was educated at Wabash College and Cornell University, and, after his graduation (Ph.B., 1888), practiced as an electrical engineer in Chicago (1888–93). Here he began his career as an experimenter and inventor in electro-chemistry, perfecting in 1896 his process for producing caustic soda and chlorine from the electrolysis of molten salt, which won him the Elliott Cresson Gold Medal of the Franklin Institute in 1902. This invention was the basis of the Acker Process Company of Niagara Falls, of which Acker was vice-president and general manager for a number of years. His inventions, which were protected by over forty patents, American and foreign, covered a wide range in electro-chemistry and electro-metallurgy. They included processes for producing alkali metals, metallic alloys, and caustic alkalis, in 1899; three patents on caustic alkali and halogen gas processes, in 1900–01; patents on methods for producing stannic and stannous chlorids, other chlorine compounds of tin, with apparatus, in 1906; carbon-tetrachlorid process, in 1908; processes for nitrogen and other compounds, and for nitrides, in 1909; for producing oxygen, in 1911; for producing compounds of nitrogen and cyanogen, in 1912 and 1913; for obtaining various gases, in 1913; and for the electrolytic production of alkali and alkali-earth metals and nitrogen compounds, in 1915. He was the patentee, also, of improved electrodes and conductors for electric furnaces, in 1903, and of detinning processes and methods for treating detinned iron and residue, in 1907. He was the first in America to produce carbon and tin tetrachlorids on a commercial scale, as well as the actual founder of several special branches of electro-chemistry and electro-metallurgy. He was director of the American Electro-chemical Society (1905-10), a member of the American Institute of Electrical Engineers, the American Chemical Society, the Faraday Society, and the Society of Chemical Industry of London, and also a member of the New York State Historical Association. For a number of years he was a resident of Ossining, N. Y., where he was director of the Westchester County Bureau of Municipal Research, and where he died. His wife was Alice Reynolds Beal, whom he married in 1892.

[*Who's Who in America*, 1922–23; *N.Y. Times*, Oct. 19, 1920; records of the U.S. Patent Office.]

ACO, MICHEL (fl. 1680–1702), French explorer, was a native of Poitiers who in 1679–80 came into the Mississippi Valley in the train of La Salle. He is said by La Salle to have known the tongues of the Iroquois and of the Illinois tribes, and to have been able to communicate with the Iowa, the Oto, the Chippewa, and the Kickapoo. He, furthermore, says La Salle, was a man "prudent, courageous, and cool." In 1680 La Salle, who had determined to reconnoiter the upper Mississippi, sent on this errand three men, Aco, Antoine du Gay Auguel, called "the Picard" because of his home in Picardy, and Louis Hennepin, a Recollect friar, appointing Aco leader of the group. Near the Falls of St. Anthony the three men were seized by a large body of Sioux, who then left the river with their captives and struck out overland toward the Sioux villages about the Mille Lac. Hennepin was a man of large frame and it was hard for him to keep up with the rapidly moving Indians. To spur his steps, the friar relates that the "Indians set fire to the grass behind him and then taking him by the hands hurried him along in front of the flames." Aco and the Picard being smaller were able to proceed with less difficulty. While the Sioux were conducting their three captives to the Mille Lac neighborhood, they were encountered by the French *coureur de bois* and explorer, Du Lhut (Duluth). The latter, a man of power with the Sioux, rescued the three captives and escorted them down the Mississippi to the mouth of the Wisconsin River; thence they proceeded up the Wisconsin and down the Fox River to Green Bay and Mackinac. In the spring of 1681 the three men proceeded to Montreal. Here Aco and the Picard left Friar Hennepin (for whom Aco had little stomach) and busied themselves in disposing of a valuable store of furs which they had with them.

We now lose sight of Aco; but by the year 1693 he was again in the Mississippi Valley as a business partner of La Salle's associates, Tonty and La Forest. After the death of La Salle, Tonty built a fort in Illinois near the outlet of Lake Peoria. The fort became a center of trade and connected with this trade was Michel Aco. Near the fort lay a village of the Kaskaskia tribe under the chief Rouensa. Rouensa had a daughter seventeen years old, a devout convert to the Catholic faith. She took the name of Mary, and with her Aco fell desperately in love. At first Mary would not wed the white man, but in the end consented to do so in order to help forward conversions among her people to the Christian faith. In 1693 Aco and the Indian maiden were united by the local priest, Father Gravier. In 1695 there was born to Aco and Mary a son, named Pierre. In February 1702, another son was born, and named Michel after his father. Of the further life of Aco record is wanting.

[Margry, *Découvertes* (1877) II, 251 ff.; Louise P. Kellogg, *French Regime in Wis.* (1925); Tonty, "Memoir on La Salle's Discoveries" in Louise P. Kellogg's *Early Narratives of the Northwest, 1639–99* (1917); Francis Parkman, *La Salle and the Discovery of the Great West* (1869); J. C. Parish, "Michel Aco—Squaw Man" in the *Palimpsest,* June 1921; R. G. Thwaites, *The Jesuit Relations and Allied Documents,* LXIV, 280. Aco's name is spelled variously; the form given in this sketch is that which he himself used.]

I. B. R.

ACRELIUS, ISRAEL (Dec. 4, 1714–Apr. 25, 1800), Lutheran clergyman and author, was born in Öster-Åker, Sweden, the son of the local pastor Johan Acrelius and Sara Gahm. Before he was quite thirteen years old he began his studies at the University of Upsala, where he remained till his ordination in 1743. After serving for a while as a domestic chaplain he was appointed in 1745 to the pastorate of Riala, Kulla, and Norra Ljusterö.

Ever since 1696 the Swedish government had been sending missionaries to the expatriated Swedes who were settled in America along the Delaware River. These missionaries, their records show, were men of unusual character and ability. In the spring of 1749 Acrelius was appointed minister of the parish of Racoon and Pennsneck in the province of New Jersey. Before he was ready to leave for his post, news of the death of the Rev. Peter Tranberg, pastor at Christina (now Wilmington, Del.), reached the authorities, and at his own request Acrelius was named to the new vacancy. He sailed from Stockholm on July 20 and reached Christina early in November. He found that the Rev. Peter Tranberg had been revered as a saint—a fact that did not make the path easy for his successor. The congregation, too ignorant and illiterate to manage its own affairs, had entrusted its business to a Quaker, who possessed a decided talent for embezzling both money and real estate. Church discipline, during the absence of a regular pastor, had become indecently lax, and the "language difficulty," already a problem to the Lutheran Church in America, was acute. Acrelius set to work immediately. He put his own church in order. As provost of the Swedish clergymen he exercised a quickening influence over all the Swedish congregations. That he might minister to others besides his own countrymen he learned English, and one of his sermons, published by Benjamin Franklin in 1756, shows him the master of a chaste English style. He gave active help and sympathy to the German Lutherans of Pennsylvania and was on a friendly footing with their leader, the Rev. Henry Melchior Muhlenberg [*q. v.*]. His leisure he spent in making botanical, zoölogical, and geological collections for the Swedish chamberlain, Charles de Geer, and in gathering materials for his own excellent *History of New Sweden* (1759). Overwork, the miasmal climate, and perhaps the pioneer cuisine told severely on his health. After four years he requested to be relieved, but this action was delayed for several more years, and he did not leave until his successor was actually on the ground. His departure caused widespread sorrow. He preached farewell sermons in six different towns, and many followed him from one to another, "sorrowing most of all that they should nevermore behold his face."

He sailed for home Nov. 9, 1756, and after a sojourn of several months in England arrived in Stockholm in July 1757. Next year he was appointed pastor in Fellingsbro in the diocese of Westeras. His *annus mirabilis* was 1759: in that year he married Katarina Elisabet Strangh, the daughter of his predecessor at Fellingsbro, was made a rural dean, and published his history.

Scholarship, first-hand knowledge, and an admirably equitable temper made Acrelius a trustworthy historian of New Sweden. Three-fifths of his work treats of matters purely ecclesiastical, but the rest is a general history of the region under Swedish, Dutch, and English rule and a description of the land and people. His book is the chief literary monument of the Swedes on the Delaware.

[The best account of Acrelius is the article by the editor-in-chief in Bertil Böethius' *Svenskt Biografiskt Lexikon* (Stockholm, 1918). The *Hist. of New Sweden*, ably translated with valuable introduction and notes by W. M. Reynolds, forms vol. XI of the *Memoirs of the Hist. Soc. of Pa.* (Phila., 1874). *A Sermon Explaining the Duties of Christian Subjects to Their Sovereign* and another, *Der Todt als eine Seligkeit für diejenige, die in dem Herrn sterben* were published in Phila. by Benjamin Franklin in 1756. Cf. also A. L. Gräbner, *Geschichte der Lutherischen Kirche in America* (St. Louis, 1892).]

G. H. G.

ADAIR, JAMES (*c.* 1709–*c.* 1783), pioneer Indian trader, author, is said to have been born in County Antrim, Ireland. The dates given above are merely conjectural. The known facts of his life are few, gathered in the main from the personal incidents narrated in his book, *The History of the American Indians* (1775) and occasional references in South Carolina chronicles. A recent book, *Adair History and Genealogy* (1924), by J. B. Adair, gives many biographical details purporting to be based on family tradition, but few of them are verifiable by any available records. It is certain that Adair was highly educated. By 1735 he had come to America, probably entering at the port of Charleston, S. C. In that year he engaged in trade with the Catawbas and Cherokees, continuing with them until 1744. He then established himself among the Chickasaws, whose villages were on the headwaters of the Yazoo, in Mississippi, where he remained for about six years. During the latter part of this period he frequently visited the Choctaws, in an effort to counteract the influence of the French and to win them to an alliance with the English. The effort was successful, but it involved him in difficulties with other traders and with James Glen, royal governor of South Carolina from 1743 to 1756, which resulted, he asserts, in his financial ruin. In 1751 he moved to District Ninety-six (the present Laurens County), S. C., and resumed trade with the Cherokees, remaining there until about the end of 1759. His activities during these years covered a wide range. He was several times called in counsel by Gov. Glen, with whom he could never agree and whom he heartily detested. Among the Indians he was a diplomat and a peace-maker, but he was also a fighter—"a valiant warrior," says Logan; and when he could not compose their quarrels he not infrequently took sides in their wars. At various times he was engaged in conflicts with the French. In the Indian war of 1760–61 he commanded a band of Chickasaws under a commission as captain. From 1761 to 1768 he was again trading with the Chickasaws, receiving his supplies by way of Mobile. In 1769 he visited New York City. Either then or a few years later he probably voyaged to London. Of his later life nothing authentic is recorded. He was, as the conclusion of his book amply shows, a vigorous defender of the rights of the colonies, but there appears to be no mention of him in Revolutionary annals. He is said to have been married and to have had several children and also to have died in North Carolina shortly after the close of the Revolution.

Adair is chiefly known through his history of the Indians. Primarily it is an argument that the Indians are the descendants of the ancient Jews. The theory was accepted by Elias Boudinot, onetime president of the Continental Congress, who gave it hearty support in his book, *A Star in the West* (1816). Adair's work has outlived its thesis. Its account of the various tribes, their manners, customs, and vocabularies, its depiction of scenes and its narration of incidents in his own eventful career, give it a permanent value. It is a record of close and intelligent observation, and its fidelity to fact has been generally acknowledged. The book must have required many years of toil. In his preface he says that it was written "among our old friendly Chickasaws" (doubtless during his second period of residence with them) and that the labor was attended by the greatest difficulties. Though some passages may subsequently have been added, it was probably finished by the end of 1768. In the *Georgia Gazette*, of Savannah, Oct. 11, 1769, appeared an item dated Feb. 27 of that year, apparently copied from a New York newspaper, announcing the arrival of Adair in New York and saying that "he intends going to Europe in the ensuing summer where he proposes to print the Essays." The care with which the book is printed indicates that he gave it personal supervision through the press. From the dedication it is evident that he had the friendship of the noted Indian traders, Col. George Galphin and Col. George Croghan (with the former of whom he may for a time have been in partnership) and of Sir William Johnson; and from various references it is certain that he was highly respected by those who knew him. Logan credits him with the quick penetration of the Indian, audacity, cool self-possession, and great powers of endurance, and Volwiler says that he was one of the few men of ability who personally embarked in the Indian trade.

[J. H. Logan, *A Hist. of the Upper Country of S. C.* (1859); John Thos. Lee, letter in the *Nation*, Aug. 27, 1914; manuscript notes supplied by Robt. L. Meriwether; brief references in A. T. Volwiler, *Geo. Croghan and the Westward Movement, 1741–1782* (1926) and Edward McCrady, *Hist. of S. C. Under the Royal Government* (1899).]

W. J. G.

ADAIR, JOHN (Jan. 9, 1757–May 19, 1840), soldier, politician, was the son of a native-born Scotchman, Baron William Adair, who settled in the up-country of South Carolina. There, in Chester County, John was born in time to take part in the Revolutionary War, which devastated so thoroughly this part of the South. In the course of the struggle he was made prisoner and harshly treated. Following the inevitable course of the restless frontiersman, he migrated westward and settled in Mercer County, Ky., in 1786. In this restless and rapidly developing community he found a congenial atmosphere. In 1791 he enlisted in the enterprises against the Northwest Indians, conducted by Arthur St. Clair and James Wilkinson, and was made a major. From this time on until the Indians were definitely crushed by "Mad Anthony" Wayne he was much in evidence in fighting these scourges of Kentucky. In 1791, while in command of about a hundred men, he ran into a band of Indians near Fort St. Clair, led by the famous Miami chieftain Little Turtle, and was finally worsted in the engagement that took place. Despite this reverse he was recognized as a brave fighter and for his reward he was made a lieutenant-colonel the next year. Since a military record was the surest road to military preferment among vigorous frontiersmen, he was chosen as a representative from Mercer County in the legislature in 1793 and was frequently reëlected thereafter up to 1817, serving in all nine terms. He was the Speaker of the House from 1801 to 1803. His popularity at this time was attested by the fact that a county was laid off and named for him. In 1799 he served in the constitutional convention which made a second constitution for the state.

In 1805 Adair with other Kentuckians such as John Brown and Henry Clay became a willing listener to Aaron Burr on his trip through the state. To Adair, Burr was a patriotic advance-agent of the Federal Government on his way to arouse the West to take part in the contemplated war with Spain for the purpose of seizing the Southwest. Correspondence with James Wilkinson confirmed him in this view (Humphrey Marshall, *History of Kentucky*, II, 430). When therefore Burr was apprehended in Frankfort in 1806, a persistent but ineffectual effort was made to indict Adair also. In the hysteria that followed, Adair's reputation temporarily suffered. In 1805 he had been elected to fill out the unexpired time of John Breckinridge, but when in November of 1806, in the midst of the Burr trouble, he was defeated for the full term of six years, he immediately resigned.

The mellowing effect of a half-dozen years and the glamour of another war were necessary to restore Adair to the full affections of his fellow Kentuckians. On the outbreak of the War of 1812 he immediately volunteered and in the battle of the Thames the following year he served as an aide to Gov. Shelby. He received the praise of his superior officer and was rewarded with a brigadier-generalship in the state militia. But his particular glory came out of the battle of New Orleans, not so much because he led 1,100 Kentucky riflemen in the main conflict, as because when the struggle was over he defended another group of Kentuckians who were involved in the battle, against the charges of cowardice made by Gen. Jackson. For two years afterwards he fought Jackson in a heated correspondence and made himself an outstanding hero with Kentuckians (James Parton, *Life of Andrew Jackson*, II, 383–91). The people now proceeded to give him almost every important honor within their gift. In 1820 he was elected governor over three of the strongest men in the state, William Logan, Joseph Desha, and Anthony Butler. He was aided not only by his general popularity but by the position he took in the bitter struggle between the relief and anti-relief parties which had grown up during the past two years. He knew little about banks and money, but he was sure of his love for the common man. For the next four years, as the leader of the relief party, he helped to drag his state to the brink of destruction; but his broad sympathy for the people also led him into a strong advocacy of higher education, prison reform, and the abolition of imprisonment for debt. From 1831 to 1833 he was a member of the House of Representatives. He made only one speech during the two sessions and it was so inaudible that no one knew what he was advocating. The reporter guessed it was in favor of mounting some federal troops. Adair's career was not characterized by sound statesmanship but his genuine sympathy with the common people and his military exploits made him long a favorite. In 1872 the State brought his remains from Mercer County to the Frankfort Cemetery and there erected a marker to his memory.

[The facts concerning the life of Adair are scattering. In Lewis and Richard H. Collins, *Hist. of Ky.* (1882), there is a short sketch of his life. Humphrey Marshall, in his *Hist. of Ky.* (1824), a biased work in many respects, gives the best account of the Burr episode. Other works concerning his life are Jas. Parton, *Life of Andrew Jackson* (1860), vol II, and W. E. Connelley and E. M. Coulter, *Hist. of Ky.*, 2 vols. (1922).] E. M. C.

ADAMS, ABIGAIL (Nov. 11, 1744-Oct. 28, 1818), noted letter writer, wife of John Adams, second President of the United States, was born at Weymouth, Mass., where her father, the Rev. William Smith, was minister of the Congregational church. Her mother was Elizabeth Quincy, daughter of Col. John Quincy and grand-daughter of the Rev. John Norton. Of her childhood she writes: "I never was sent to any school. I was always sick" (*Familiar Letters*, preface, p. xi). Much of her time was spent in seclusion at the home of her grandparents at Mount Wollaston. Her grandmother, with a "happy method of mixing instruction and amusement together," took the place of school. The distance separating the homes of her relatives and friends was too great to permit of frequent social intercourse, so that letter writing became habitual among the young people. On Oct. 25, 1764 she was married to John Adams, and during the next ten years their four children were born—John Quincy, Thomas, Charles, and Abby. In the early part of the Revolution, when John Adams was much of the time in Philadelphia, Abigail was left with the entire care of the young family, exposed to many dangers. From the top of Penn's Hill, at the foot of which her house stood, she with her seven-year-old son watched the smoke of burning Charlestown. Later, she wrote, "The constant roar of the cannon is so distressing that we cannot eat, drink, or sleep" (*Letters*, pp. 31–32). She went through the trials of an epidemic and wrote her husband that there was sickness and death in nearly every household. During John Adams's absence in Europe she managed his affairs with great ability, at the same time attending to the farm, keeping up her keen interest in politics, and perpetuating in her letters a vivid picture of the times. After the signing of the treaty of peace, she joined her husband to spend the next eight months in Paris and then three years in London. Her letters during this period show her inimitable gift for brief and vivid description. Those from France are the more amiable; the English letters are thickly sprinkled with rather vindictive comments upon the people —although as she came to know the English better she liked them more, and long afterward could write to her son, "England, you know, is the country of my greatest partiality" (*Ibid.*, p. 368). With her return to America in 1787, and the election of Adams as vice-president, came what was perhaps the happiest period of her life. Her health, though delicate, had not yet given way, her husband was the second man in the nation, and about her was a remarkable society. But during the twelve years of public life in America her letters lose something of their sprightliness, due perhaps to increasing ill health. She was forced more and more to withdraw from the gayeties of the capital, and much of her time was spent at Quincy, as her home was now called. Nevertheless it was reported that she exercised great political influence over her husband. She fully shared the violent social and political feelings of the Federalist party. Gallatin, with a touch of malice, after Adams had become president, sneered at "Her Majesty," and interpreted her conversation as hostess to the effect that she was "Mrs. President not of the United States, but of a faction" (Henry Adams, *Life of Albert Gallatin*, 1879, p. 185). After 1801 practically all of her remaining life was spent in Quincy. There she and her family passed the years as tranquilly "as that bald old fellow, called Time" would permit. She wrote her son, "You will find your father in his fields, attending to his haymakers, and your mother busily occupied in the domestic concerns of her family." She resumed her "operations of dairy-woman" and she might be seen at five o'clock in the morning, skimming the milk, or going about the house with her pet dog Juno at her heels. The death of her daughter in 1813 cast a shadow over her last years, but as she said of herself, "My disposition and habits are not of the gloomy kind." Her grandson records that her cheerful nature "enlivened the small social circle around her." The key-note of this sunset of her life was her serene religious faith, joined with a never-failing disillusion about herself. "I bear no enmity to any human being; but, alas! as Mrs. Placid said to her friend, by which of thy good works wouldst thou be willing to be judged?" (*Ibid.*, p. 411). She died of typhoid fever in her seventy-fourth year.

[A proposal late in her life to publish her letters was laughed aside by Mrs. Adams. Her grandson, Charles Francis Adams, published two collections—*Letters of Mrs. Adams, the Wife of John Adams,* and *Familiar Letters of John Adams and his Wife During the Revolution*; each is prefaced by a memoir. A charming portrait of her as a young woman, by Blythe, is engraved in each collection. There is also a sketchy biography, *Abigail Adams and Her Times* (1917), by Laura Elizabeth Richards.] M. T. S.

ADAMS, ABIJAH (*c.* 1754–May 18, 1816), journalist, born in Boston, married Lucy Ballard, a widow, on July 11, 1790, and died in Boston, aged sixty-two years. His parents, and the exact date of his birth are not known; his relationship with the famous Braintree branch has not been traced. Trained as a tailor, he first came to public notice in 1799 when he was clerk and bookkeeper in the office of the *Independent Chronicle,* which since 1784 his younger brother, Capt. Thomas Adams, had controlled. The journal was the chief supporter in New England of Jeffersonian principles. When the General Court refused to support the Kentucky and Virginia Resolutions condemning the Alien and Sedition Acts because it had no right to decide upon the constitutionality of an act of Congress, the *Chronicle* declared (Feb. 18, 1799): "As it is difficult for common capacities to conceive of a sovereignty so situated that the sovereign shall have no right to decide on any invasion of his constitutional power, it is hoped for the convenience of those tender consciences who may hereafter be called upon to swear allegiance to the State, that some gentleman skilled in federal logic, will show how the oath of allegiance is to be understood, that every man may be so guarded and informed, as not to invite the Deity to witness a falsehood." Both brothers were arrested for libeling the General Court. Thomas was already under federal indictment for violating the Sedition Act. He was ill and was never tried on either charge. Abijah had merely sold the papers, but under the English common law was convicted of "publishing" the libel, and was sentenced to jail for thirty days. Thomas died shortly after and in 1800 the newspaper passed into the joint control of Abijah and Ebenezer Rhoades. Adams was called senior editor. Such a staunch supporter of the Virginia Dynasty and Mr. Madison's War was certain to continue in hot water in Boston. He was again convicted of libel in 1811, this time for comment upon the official conduct of Chief Justice Parsons. He was pardoned. His office was a gathering-place for federal office-holders and other prominent Republicans, men like Perez Morton and Benjamin Austin. The latter wrote often for the *Chronicle*. After Adams's death, his paper (May 23, 1816), after calling him an honest man, harked back to the libel suit as his chief reason for remembrance. "Mr. Adams displayed an heroism which nothing but his virtues could sustain.—One month he was imprisoned, . . . suffering under the utmost rigors of the Common Law, while others of the same profession were daily committing crimes of a more aggravated nature with impunity." In 1819 the paper was sold to Davis C. Ballard, his stepson.

[The few facts of Adams's private life are found in the local records only. The files of the *Independent Chronicle* are the main source on his position as a public man. Joseph T. Buckingham's *Specimens of Newspaper Literature with personal memoirs, anecdotes, and reminiscences* (1850), I, 248–87, deals with the paper and Adams's connection with it.]

D. M. M.

ADAMS, ALVA (May 14, 1850–Nov. 1, 1922), governor of Colorado, the son of John Adams of Kentucky and of Eliza (Blanchard) Adams of New York, was born in Iowa County, Wis., where he received the limited education of a common district school. On account of the ill health of a brother of Alva the family drove across the plains to Colorado in 1871, settling first near Colorado Springs. Alva Adams there obtained employment with a contractor engaged in hauling ties for the Denver & Rio Grande Railroad. Later he was employed as a clerk in a hardware store. He quickly showed his mettle by arranging to buy out the business with a partner. In 1872 he moved to Pueblo to open a branch of the business, separated from his partner, and continued by himself with success. He was married to Ella Nye in the same year. When the city government of South Pueblo was organized in 1873 he was elected a member of the first city council. He gave evidence of enterprise by establishing branch houses of his expanding business in Del Norte and Alamosa. The local prominence he had won brought about his election to the first legislature of the State in 1876. His qualities of leadership next made him the nominee of the Democratic party for governor in 1884. Defeated in that campaign, he was renominated and elected in 1886. His administration was signalized by constructive measures in the development of the young State's institutions of learning and correction. From 1889 to 1896 his attention was chiefly given to his business enterprises, during which time he became also a banker. In 1896 the Democrats of Colorado joined with the Silver-Republicans in nominating Adams for governor against a fusion of the local Populists and the National Silverites. Adams was elected by a large plurality. He was instrumental in bringing about the settlement of a long and disastrous strike of miners in Leadville. His last message before retirement in January 1899 made an earnest plea for radical reformation of the system of assessment and taxation under control of a state equalization board with adequate powers. He advocated an inheritance tax, an income tax, and royalties on corporate and municipal privileges. A third time, in 1904, he was a successful candidate for governor, taking office on Jan. 10, 1905. His rival, the retiring governor, Peabody, filed a contest, alleging gross frauds in city precincts. A partisan committee of the legislature, in a majority report, sustained Peabody. Enough Republicans dissented to block action until a "deal" was worked out to seat Peabody on his agreement to resign immediately and give place to the lieutenant-governor. Adams rejected the counsel of party friends who wished him forcibly to resist being supplanted. The remainder of his life was spent as a business man, but one interested in public matters. He was a member of the Democratic National Committee in 1908, and was a commissioner of the United States in 1915 to procure the participation of Australia, Java, Siam, Cochin China, New Zealand, and China in the Panama-Pacific exposition.

[*Who's Who in America,* 1920–21; Frank Hall, *Hist. of Colo.,* III (1891), pp. 52 ff.; *Rocky Mt. News,* Nov. 2, 3, 1922. For the election of 1904 see *Lit. Digest,* XXIX, 831, XXX, 85, 426; *World Today,* Mar. 1905; for that of 1896 see *Rocky Mt. News* and *Denver Republican,* Sept.–Nov. 1896.] C. A. D—y.

ADAMS, ALVIN (June 16, 1804–Sept. 1, 1877), pioneer in express business, was the ninth of eleven children born to Phebe (Hoar) Adams and Jonas Adams, descendant of Henry Adams of Braintree. Left an orphan at an early age, the boy was cared for by a guardian and older brothers who gave him a common schooling in his native town of Andover, Vt. At the age of sixteen, he set out to seek his fortune, working several years for a stage and hotel proprietor of Woodstock, Vt. Turning his hand to numerous employments, young Adams gained considerable experience, including marriage and bankruptcy, the former to Ann Rebecca Bridge of Boston, Nov. 10, 1831, the latter in the produce business during the bad year of 1837. Undaunted, he attempted the same business in New York City only to fail again. In 1840, associated with Ephraim Farnsworth, he established Adams & Company by purchasing two season railway tickets from New York to Boston and return. One day he would start from Boston to New York and his partner from New York to Boston, and vice versa on the following day. They contracted to carry valuables, securities, and bundles for delivery to either city and soon to intermediate points. Thus the express business began. As the ordinary delivery of valuables and parcels was tardy, unsafe, and unprotected, the convenience of Adams's service was appreciated by banks, merchants, and individuals making valuable shipments, and won general confidence which increased its clientage. The idea took hold, and Adams had the genius to develop it and the aggressive push to advance the business to large proportions. Farnsworth soon gave way to William B. Dinsmore, who struggled along with Adams in the creation of the huge express company. Their business union was cemented by the marriage of William B. Dinsmore, Jr., to Adams's daughter. In 1841 Adams & Company bought the Norwich route to Boston from William F. Harnden [*q.v.*] and four years later all his routes between Boston and New York. In 1842 Adams extended his agencies to Philadelphia, and later to Baltimore, Washington, Pittsburgh, Cincinnati, Louisville, and St. Louis, where he met the competition of Wells and Fargo. In 1849 he entered the California field, establishing within a year thirty-five offices in the towns and mining-camps and at least one station in Oregon. Three years later he started branch agencies and banking houses in Melbourne and Sydney, Australia. As this extension did not prove wise, the Australian houses were discontinued and the coast business was abandoned to such stout competitors as Wells and Fargo and the heavily capitalized Western freighters. Adams found competition in the East keen enough, but an amalgamation of express companies remedied the situation. The Adams Express Company was incorporated, 1854, with $10,000,000 capital and with Adams and Dinsmore in control as president and secretary-treasurer. The smaller concerns of Thomson & Company and Kingsley & Company were absorbed, as well as Harnden & Company, which through agencies in Liverpool, Paris, and Havre had developed a lucrative business with immigrants destined for America in the transfer of parcels and sale of money-orders and steamship and railway tickets. This combination was henceforth able to compete on equal terms with the American Express. During the Civil War the Adams Express Company reaped large profits in shipping arms, munitions, and supplies for the government, in delivering parcels from their homes to soldiers in camp or hospital, and in forwarding soldiers' pay and messages from the battle-field to the families at home probably in some out-of-the-way village or isolated Western farm. This was a service which won appreciation and merited reward. Aside from some interest in art during his late years and in his beautiful estate at Watertown, Mass., which he opened to the public one day a week, Adams apparently promoted no hobbies or charities. On his death he left few friends other than business associates, and no monument save the great express business which he founded and to which he gave his whole being.

[A. C. Hemenway, *Hist. of Andover, Vt.* (1886) containing an autobiographical account; Appleton's *Ann. Cyc.,* 1877; T. C. Quinn, *Mass. of To-day* (1892), p. 246; *Boston Transcript,* Sept. 3, 1877.] R. J. P.

ADAMS, ANDREW (Dec. 11, 1736–Nov. 27, 1797), jurist, the fourth son of Samuel and Mary (Fairchild) Adams, was born in Stratford, Conn. After attending Yale College, where he received his bachelor's degree in 1760, he studied law and began to practice in Stamford but in 1764 removed to Litchfield, which was his home for the rest of his life. He became a justice of the peace, judge of probate *pro tempore,* and king's attorney, for Litchfield County. In 1776 he was elected to the Connecticut General Assembly, of which he was Speaker during four sessions. The Colonial Records of the State indicate his prominence, as he was frequently placed on committees to investigate petitions to the Assembly. He was also a member of the Council of Safety; major, later colonel, in the militia; and, for a short time, served in the army under Gen. Wooster. In October 1777 he was appointed a delegate to the Continental Congress, and held this position for three years. He signed the Articles of Confederation and Perpetual Union. He was first nominated to the upper house of the Connecticut General Assembly in 1779, and three years later elected a member, holding this office until 1789, when he became an associate judge of the superior court, rising in 1793 to the position of chief justice which he held until his death. Learned in theology, as well as in law and in military affairs, he was a deacon of the church, and, in the absence of the minister, filled the pulpit on several occasions. He was married to Eunice, youngest daughter of Judge Samuel and Abigail (Peck) Canfield, of New Milford, Conn.

[F. B. Dexter, *Biog. Sketches of the Grads. of Yale Coll. 1745–63* (1896), p. 640; P. K. Kilbourne, *Biog. Hist. of the County of Litchfield, Conn.* (1851); Forrest Morgan, *Conn. as a Colony and as a State* (1904), II, 204; G. H. Hollister, *Hist. of Conn.* (1855), II, 624; Dwight Loomis and J. G. Calhoun, *Judicial and Civil Hist. of Conn.* (1895), p. 478; *Cat. of the Officers and Grads. of Yale Univ., 1701–1924* (1924).]

M. E. M.

ADAMS, BROOKS (June 24, 1848–Feb. 13, 1927), historian, youngest son of Charles Francis Adams and Abigail Brown (Brooks) Adams, was born at Quincy, Mass. After some years in English schools he entered Harvard College, graduated in 1870, and after a year in the Law School accompanied his father to Geneva, serving as his secretary during the Alabama Claims Arbitration. On his return he opened a law office in Boston, but like his brothers soon turned to historical investigation. His first work, *The Emancipation of Massachusetts* (1887), by its vigorous assault upon the accepted manner of dealing with early New England history, attracted attention, caused retort, and served as a wholesome protest against a somewhat blind acceptance of ancestor-worship. He then turned to a study of trade-routes and their influence upon the history of peoples and nations and published the *Law of Civilization and Decay* (1895), a work of a high order as history which laid down the principle that human societies differed among themselves in proportion as they were endowed by nature with energy, a principle later developed by Henry Adams. Since he supported the side of silver when the question of the free coinage of that metal was dividing the country, the merits of the book as an economic study were overshadowed by its political aspects. Having announced his principle that civilization follows exchanges, or commercial growth and decay, he sought to apply it to modern history and conditions. Could success have been attained, a means of forecasting the march of empire might have been given to the student of social movement; but his generalizations, brilliant and far-reaching as they were, did not lead to a universal law or even a suggestion of one, such as he desired. The domination of the bankers and the approaching collapse of social institutions were ever present to him and this neutralized in great part the usefulness of his work. In a series of volumes he stated and restated the problem and carried his "law" into a new field of experience. In *America's Economic Supremacy* (1900) he predicted the moving of the center of empire to America; in *The New Empire* (1902) he set forth the supremacy of America and in *Theory of Social Revolutions* (1913) he pointed out the ineffectiveness of the capitalist class in the United States in matters of government.

Becoming a lecturer in the Boston University School of Law in 1904, for seven years he illustrated the legal aspects of his economic studies and wrote with force on trusts and railroads as public agents. Elected a member of the Massachusetts constitutional convention in 1917, he favored the initiative and referendum. After the beginning of the World War, in which he saw a fulfilment of his predictions of the collapse of modern civilizations, he returned to social studies in his "Revolt of Modern Democracy against Standards of Duty" (*Proceedings of the American Academy of Arts and Letters,* vol. IX). He then wrote an elaborate preface to Henry Adams's "Letter to American Teachers of History," and published both, with additional material, under the title, *The Degradation of Democratic Dogma* (1920). He received recognition abroad, and *The Law of Civilization* was translated into French and German, the *Economic Supremacy* into German, and *The New Empire* into German and Russian. In whatever he wrote he showed a gift for generalization with a tendency to carry it beyond reasonable bounds. His chapters have substance and show sound and wide research, his explanations of social movement and disturbance are suggestive. He never held public office, nor did he ever seek it. He was the last to occupy the Adams house at Quincy, which on his death was devoted to public service as a memorial of the Adams family. He married, Sept. 7, 1889, Evelyn Davis, daughter of Admiral Charles Henry Davis and Harriette Blake Mills. She died Dec. 14, 1926. He himself died, at Boston, less than two months later.

[Memoir by W. C. Ford in *Harvard Grads. Mag.*, June 1927; also memoir in *Mass. Hist. Soc. Proc.*, LX, 345.]

W. C. F.

ADAMS, CHARLES (Dec. 19, 1845?–Aug. 19, 1895), soldier, diplomat, began life as Karl Adam Schwanbeck, son of Karl Heinrich and Maria J. (Markman) Schwanbeck of Pomerania, in Germany. Just prior to leaving the Old World he was graduated from the gymnasium with an enviable record. Soon after arrival in the United States he enlisted in a Massachusetts regiment and continued in service through the war, being twice wounded in battle. He then went west, joined the 3d United States Cavalry, and served two years against the Kiowa and Comanche Indians in New Mexico and Texas. In 1870 he was appointed brigadier-general of the Colorado militia by Gov. McCook and was subsequently appointed Ute Indian Agent upon recommendation of the same official. Before taking up his work at the Los Pinos Agency, Colorado, he was married to Mrs. Margaret Thompson Phelps, a sister of the wife of Gov. McCook. It was at her instance that his name was changed. Arriving at the Agency in June 1872, Adams and his wife found the Utes uneasy and fearful of attack, as reports were being circulated of Indian outrages. He succeeded in dispelling their suspicions and won their confidence. Soon he had a saw-mill running, hay being cured, their cattle cared for, and as winter approached he inaugurated a little school (*Report of Commissioner of Indian Affairs, 1872*, p. 289). During his two years at the Agency he became the warm personal friend of the great Ute chief, Ouray, and was respected by all the tribes,—factors of importance at a later date. In 1874 he resigned from the Indian service to become post-office inspector. When the Ute uprising of Sept. 29, 1879 resulted in the murder of Agent Meeker and his employees and the captivity of the white women, an emergency existed which called for a man of tact and of acknowledged influence among the Indians. Adams was called upon by the government. He proceeded immediately to the scene of hostilities and in coöperation with Chief Ouray secured the release of the white women. As one of a commission of three he investigated the tragedy and obtained the surrender of some of the leaders for trial. A delegation of Utes was then escorted to Washington, where they were induced to sign a treaty surrendering their land in Colorado and agreeing to remove to a reservation in Utah. President Hayes appointed Adams in 1880 minister to Bolivia. War then existed between Bolivia and Chile, and Adams acted as an arbitrator on the part of the United States in the conferences at Arica. In 1882 he left Bolivia and again became a post-office inspector. From this position President Cleveland removed him in 1885 for "offensive partisanship." Thereafter he engaged in business in Colorado, being interested in mining, glass manufacture, and mineral-water development. He met his death in an explosion at the Gumry Hotel, Denver.

[Sidney Jocknick, *Early Days on the Western Slope of Colo.* (1913) contains excellent material on Adams's dealings with the Utes, as does Frank Hall, *Hist. of Colo.* (4 vols., 1889–95). An excellent appraisal of his life-work appeared in the *Rocky Mt. News*, Aug. 20, 1895. Sidney Jocknick, Charles Tarbell, and Nathaniel Hunter have supplemented written data with their personal recollections of intimate associations with Adams.]

L. R. H.

ADAMS, CHARLES BAKER (Jan. 11, 1814–Jan. 18, 1853), naturalist, was born in Dorchester, Mass., the son of Charles J. Adams, and a descendant of Henry Adams of Braintree. As a boy he manifested a taste for scientific studies, and his parents, who had removed to Boston in 1818, gave up a room for his natural-history museum and chemical laboratory. Prepared for college at the Phillips Academy, Andover, he entered Yale in 1830, but transferred to Amherst the following year. He graduated at the head of the class of 1834. The average ability of that class should have been high, as Henry Ward Beecher stood at the foot! After spending some time at the Theological Seminary at Andover, Adams realized that science, not theology, was his vocation. He became assistant to Edward Hitchcock, then, in the summer of 1836, engaged in the geological survey of New York. Ill health caused Prof. Hitchcock to relinquish this work, and Adams became a tutor and lecturer on geology at Amherst. In 1837, recommended by Hitchcock to a new college that was being started at Marion, Mo., by Rev. Dr. Ely of Philadelphia, Adams went out there and taught for several months but received no salary and was obliged to send to his father for money on which to return home. In 1838 he was appointed professor of chemistry and natural history at Middlebury College, Vermont, and in 1845 he became state geologist. Four Annual Reports were published (1845–48) as well as an excellent chapter on invertebrate animals of the state in Zadock Thompson's *History of Vermont* (1842). In 1847 Adams was made professor of natural history and astronomy at Amherst, a position he held until his death.

He was popular and successful as a teacher, and is said to have been a terror to indolent students. He was married in February 1839 to Mary Holmes, daughter of Rev. Sylvester Holmes of New Bedford.

Adams's interest in tropical zoölogy began in the winter of 1843–44, which he spent in Jamaica. He had happened upon practically a virgin field, and was enchanted with the richness and diversity of the fauna, particularly the mollusks. Further visits were made in 1848–49, and in the following year Adams made a collecting trip by way of Jamaica to Panama. In December 1852 he sailed for St. Thomas, where he contracted yellow fever and died. His two chief works, *Contributions to Conchology* (1849–52) and *Catalogue of Shells collected at Panama* (1852) are counted among the classics of American conchology. They are still standard manuals, indispensable in the study of Antillean and Panamic mollusk faunas. While chiefly to be classed as descriptive zoölogy, the *Contributions* contain several essays dealing with major zoölogical problems. Adams was groping for the meaning of the varying degrees of relationship among species of animals, and for some rational explanation of their geographic distribution. He recognized the breakdown of the old concept of species—the immutable, specially created species of those pre-Darwinian days. He argued against the Lamarckian hypothesis of direct modification by environment, but he missed the explanation which Darwin was to give the world some years later.

[Thos. Bland, "Memoir of Chas. B. Adams," *Am. Jour. of Conchology*, July 1, 1865, with portrait; H.B. Adams, *Hist. of the Thos. Adams and T. Hastings Families of Amherst, Mass.* (1880), p. 18; Edward Hitchcock, *Reminiscences of Amherst Coll.* (1863), pp. 90–100; Wm. S. Tyler, *Hist. of Amherst Coll. during its first Half Century* (1873), pp. 366–68.]

H. A. P.

ADAMS, CHARLES FOLLEN (Apr. 21, 1842–Mar. 8, 1918), dialect poet, the ninth of ten children of Ira and Mary Elizabeth (Senter) Adams, was born in Dorchester, Mass. Though named after a German patriot and destined to become well known for his writings in German dialect, he was not of German descent. Both his parents were of pure New England stock, his father's and mother's families having been among the first to settle in the villages of Meredith and Center Harbor, N. H. Adams received a common-school education in Dorchester, and from his fifteenth to his twentieth year was employed by a firm of dry-goods merchants in Boston. In August 1862 he enlisted for a term of two years in the 13th Massachusetts infantry. He served with his regiment from the second battle of Bull Run until, on the first day of Gettysburg, he was wounded and taken prisoner. Three days later he was released by Union troops. After a period of convalescence, he was detailed for hospital duty in Washington for the remainder of his term of enlistment. He then returned to Boston and established himself for life as a dealer in dry and fancy goods. On Oct. 11, 1870 he married Harriet Louise Mills, daughter of James Mills of Boston. They had one son and one daughter. During the latter years of his life Adams made his home in Roxbury.

Authorship was never more than a diversion in Adams's busy life. About 1870 he commenced writing poems in German dialect, following the lead of Charles Godfrey Leland, whose "Hans Breitmann" ballads were then at the height of their vogue. He, however, should not be considered a mere imitator of Leland. He knew "scrapple English" from his own personal experience with Pennsylvania Dutch and German emigrant soldiers among the Union troops. Moreover, in place of the satire and extravaganza of the "Breitmann" ballads, he substituted the quieter humor and sentiment of familiar domestic happenings. If he followed Leland in the use of German dialect, he no less anticipated Field and Riley in his devotion to the nursery. His first poem in print, "The Puzzled Dutchman," was accepted by J. T. Trowbridge for *Our Young Folks* in 1872. Its favorable reception by the press paved the way for the appearance of other verses in the same vein contributed to various publications from Boston newspapers to *Scribner's Monthly*. In 1876 "Leedle Yawcob Strauss," first printed in the *Detroit Free Press* and copied over the length and breadth of the land, made Adams famous in his own right—he had often previously been confused with Charles Francis Adams—and created a steady demand for all the verse he cared to produce. A number of his later poems appeared in *Harper's Magazine;* others were sold to a newspaper syndicate and widely circulated. He was frequently called upon to give public readings in the vicinity of Boston, and the real sincerity and pathos of his recitation never failed to delight his hearers. Oliver Wendell Holmes wrote that "Leedle Yawcob Strauss" had "moistened thousands of eyes—these old ones of mine among the rest." Two collections of Adams's verses appeared in book form: *Leedle Yawcob Strauss, and Other Poems* (1877) and *Dialect Ballads* (1888). Both together were reprinted as *Yawcob Strauss and Other Poems* (1910).

[*Who's Who in America*, 1916–17; *One of a Thousand*, ed. by J. C. Rand (1890); *New Eng. Mag.*, n.s. XXXIII, 675–77, portr.; *N.Y. Times*, Mar. 9, 1918.]

G. F. W.

ADAMS, CHARLES FRANCIS (Aug. 18, 1807–Nov. 21, 1886), diplomat, was born at Boston, Mass., the son of John Quincy Adams [*q.v.*] and Louisa Catherine (Johnson) Adams. At the age of two years he was taken by his father to St. Petersburg and there he remained for six years, under no regular schooling but mastering French so thoroughly that he preferred to speak it rather than English. In the winter of 1815 his mother brought him by carriage from St. Petersburg to Paris, where they joined the father, recently appointed to the English mission. He was at Paris during the "Hundred Days" and remembered incidents of Napoleon's return. Two years followed at an English boarding-school, an experience of great value later, and, when the father returned to the United States to be secretary of state, the son passed through the Boston Latin School into Harvard College, where he graduated in 1825 at eighteen years of age. The following three years were spent in Washington without occupation. Determining to study law he returned to Boston and passed some weeks in the office of Daniel Webster, was admitted to practice in January 1829, and on Sept. 5, 1829, married Abigail Brown, daughter of Peter Chardon Brooks of Boston. He thus became closely connected with Rev. Nathaniel L. Frothingham and Edward Everett, who had also married daughters of Mr. Brooks. He early showed interest in the papers of John Adams and on John Quincy Adams's escape from the presidency urged him to undertake their arrangement and possible publication; but, not a little to his son's dislike, John Quincy determined to accept a nomination to Congress and for eighteen years continued to represent the Quincy district. Intensely engrossed in public affairs he could not turn to such a task, for which, indeed, he was not fitted, and the publication of John Adams's papers was postponed for a number of years. Charles Francis assumed the care of what little property his father possessed and by his deep devotion and unselfish service enabled the older man to accomplish what he did, freed from business anxieties. The younger Adams also turned to literature and wrote on American history for the *North American Review,* the leading literary quarterly in that day. At the suggestion and with the aid of the ex-President he wrote on presidential patronage, the question having arisen between Jackson and the encroaching Senate. Printed in two Boston journals, the essay was later issued as a pamphlet, *An Appeal from the New to the Old Whigs, by a Whig of the Old School* (Boston, 1835). The general political views of John Quincy Adams strongly influenced him, though he was not attracted by the example and methods of the older man.

On the supreme importance and general bearing of the slavery question he could not feel as did his father, nor could he accept the ideas of the abolitionists, then coming into sufficient prominence to alarm the South. Garrison and the *Liberator* in Boston provoked mob violence, but nothing of this drew the interest of Adams. He even disapproved of the course his father was pursuing in opening what was to be an intense struggle of thirteen years, though he noted "as he is in it, I must do my best to help him out" (Adams, *Charles Francis Adams,* p. 31). The victories gained by John Quincy Adams in the House came to have an attraction for the son and exerted an influence in gradually leading him to a better understanding of the issues at stake. He wrote upon slavery for the *Boston Advocate,* without taking a decided attitude, and as the contest at Washington over petitions became more severe his interest developed. Attending the meeting in Faneuil Hall in 1837 on the Lovejoy murder, the gross attack of Attorney General Austin on the abolitionists revolted him and "from that moment, I went with the meeting" (*Ibid.,* p. 36). On national questions connected with finance, the measures leading up to the crisis of 1837, he wrote much and independently without, as he felt, recognition or encouragement. Turning to the family papers in 1840, he published the letters of Abigail Adams with a brief biography which met with unlooked-for success.

Without strong party attachments, in 1840 he was elected to the Massachusetts legislature, receiving the highest vote on the Whig ticket, and served three years in the House and two years in the Senate. Not attracted by local questions, he devoted himself to the larger issues of policy such as the northeastern boundary, districting bill, the salary bill, the Latimer (slave) case, and the annexation of Texas, preparing elaborate statements showing the law and principles involved. A Democrat in 1836, he had become a Whig largely because of his views on slavery. Before he left the legislature he had placed the state in full opposition to slavery, a result which gave him much satisfaction.

Not pleased with the attitude of the Whig leaders, with Stephen Phillips, John G. Palfrey, Henry Wilson, and Charles Sumner, he established the *Boston Whig,* intended to express a form of opposition to slavery and Southern policy of which the recognized leaders of the Whig party in Massachusetts did not approve—leaders like Webster, Choate, and Winthrop; it pointed out that unless some great and unlikely change intervened the country must face the alternative of the total abolition of slavery or the dissolution of the Union. He was now one in sentiment with his father. Adams thus gave voice to the "conscience" against the "cotton" Whigs. Defeated in 1846, the "conscience" Whigs in 1848 could not support Taylor for president, a candidate without qualification for the office and selected merely for his military record. In Cass the Democrats had presented no better leader. An independent nomination seemed the only alternative. At Buffalo, in August, delegates from seventeen states met. With Adams as chairman they named Van Buren for president and Adams for vice-president, on a platform asserting a resolve to maintain the rights of free labor against the aggressions of the slave power, and to secure free soil for a free people. However high the character of the convention the candidates represented policies that could not be reconciled. The 291,263 votes they received, of which one-eighth came from Massachusetts, defeated Cass, which was all the Van Buren following desired.

Adams now took up seriously the publication of the *Works of John Adams* in ten volumes (1850–56), and prepared a biography which, quite apart from its merits, still holds a place for its wide reading and broad treatment. A wholly unbiased weighing of character could not be expected, but as written by a grandson the work has unusual qualities. Had more attention been given to the correspondence of John Adams and less space to his political writings, which had ceased to have interest, the contribution to history would have been greater. For eight years this work engrossed Adams and his participation in politics hardly went beyond the writing of a public letter (June 12, 1851) to the "Freedom Convention" at Ravenna, Ohio.

Meanwhile the changes in political parties gave him a new opportunity to enter public life. The compromise of 1850 had not settled the question of slavery and the breaking up of the Whig party gave rise to the Republican party. In 1858 Adams was nominated for Congress in his father's district and won the election by a handsome majority against two opposing candidates. As the presidential election of 1860 approached its importance increased, and the sectional contest between North and South became more bitter. Not burdened by engrossing committee appointments, Adams took measure of the House, in which the Republicans did not have a majority, observed his colleagues, on whom by his courtesy and moderation he made a marked impression, and studied the course of events. On May 31, 1860 he addressed the House, but the matter was intended for the campaign and was so circulated under the title "The Republican Party a Necessity." The immense property value of the slaves and the power of the owners to control all the political agencies of the government called, in Adams's judgment, for protective measures which only the Republican party as the party of reform could supply. The studied moderation of his speech in a time of violent passions was its strongest commendation. He favored the nomination of Seward for the presidency and, like so many leaders in the party, was not greatly pleased with Lincoln, though admitting his honesty and fair capability.

He campaigned in the Northwest with Seward, and, renominated in his own district without opposition, was elected to Congress by a majority more than twice as large as he had received two years before. In his second session he found himself admitted to the councils of the party and a recognized leader. The South had taken its stand, but the limit of its action could not be foreseen, and the border states hesitated. Without a definite policy the Republicans were divided and a part looked to Seward for leadership. Both houses appointed important committees on the state of the Union, and Adams took the lead in that of the House as Seward did in that of the Senate. The part assumed by Adams was to oblige the Southern members of the committee publicly to declare what they proposed to demand. So well did he accomplish this that the winter passed in proposals and discussion, with no more action than the secession of the Southern members from the committee. The Northern members were more united, the South had not gained advantage, and the new President was peaceably inaugurated. Misrepresented at the time as weak and yielding, Adams's management of the situation has come to be accepted as judicious and successful. His single speech, that of Jan. 31, 1861, received high praise for its statesmanship and its spirit of conciliation. One of its results was the termination of a long friendship with Sumner, who looked upon it as concession and therefore wholly wrong—unforgivable. Adams's friends pressed him upon Lincoln for a cabinet position—the Treasury being suggested—but at Seward's instance he was made minister to the Court of St. James's, at the time the diplomatic post of greatest importance. Visiting Washington to confer with Secretary Seward, Adams had his only meeting with the President and received an unfavorable impression that was lasting.

While he waited for his instructions the fall of Sumter brought on war. Leaving Boston, May 1, 1861, he arrived in London on the evening of the 13th, to learn from the newspapers of the following day that Great Britain had recognized the Confederacy as a belligerent, the very act which his predecessor, Dallas, and Adams himself were instructed to prevent by every means possible. Necessary from the British point of view for the safety of British commercial interests in the face of blockade and privateers, the step constituted for the United States a real grievance, which Seward pressed on every occasion. He regarded it as a measure hostile to the North and taken too hastily. The interval between the nomination and arrival of Adams at his post had allowed the British minister for foreign affairs to interview the Confederate commissioners, gain some knowledge of the Southern purpose, and in the face of events formulate a plan of action which would be neutral in theory and in fact, should no new circumstance —such as the dissolution of the Union—compel the adoption of a more active policy. Adams could not know that France and Great Britain had already agreed to act together, though he soon guessed the existence of such an agreement. Without means of judging how far it bound the two nations, he quickly recognized that the center of European relations with America would be in London.

His first meeting with Lord John Russell established personal relations which were permanent and on the whole favorable. Adams's English schooling came to his aid. He not only understood the English character, so much like his own, but his manner resembled their manner, reserved, logical, unimpassioned, and intelligent. In a frank interview between Russell and Adams each was gratified to see that he had a worthy opponent—for differences there were bound to be. Russell expressed later, what was for him a favorable judgment, that Adams was a "reasonable man." This reasonableness was a quality which events were to prove most essential in meeting the unexpected difficulties as they arose.

On his part Adams found a deep-rooted distrust of Seward in English official circles, due to a careless or jocose remark of his, interpreted as hostile to England. He also found English society quite pronounced in sympathy for the South, and, supported by material interests, ready to go to the full length of recognition. The Confederate agents, confident that time and the need of cotton would win the war, and for the moment content with the recognition given, worked against Adams by seeking influence which might embarrass his relations with the ministry. The general situation pointed to an almost assured eventual recognition of Southern independence. Adams shared in the opinion that the recognition of belligerency was ill-timed and ill-considered, but the very act gave him a certain advantage in his subsequent dealings, for under his protests the ministry was put on the defensive. At first the greater embarrassments came from America. Seward suggested a general war with Europe as a cure for the domestic civil strife, and but for the intervention of the President might have succeeded in producing serious international complications and possibly war. Even in its modified form the language of his dispatch to Adams of May 21 awakened in the latter the gravest apprehension in regard to the foreign policy of his government. It increased his sense of responsibility. He obeyed his instructions and read the dispatch to Earl Russell, softening as well as he could "its sharp edges." The leading point, that further intercourse with the Southern commissioners would be regarded as indication of a hostile spirit, was communicated and called out the statement from Russell that he did not expect to see them again. Seward's instructions had been fulfilled, and Adams had closed the door to any further intercourse between the British ministry and the Southern commissioners.

On another matter Adams was not so successful, more from a misunderstanding than from any neglect on his part. With other American ministers in Europe he was instructed to propose to the British government the accession of the United States to the Treaty of Paris of 1856, by which privateering would be abolished, neutral goods made exempt from capture, and blockades defined. The Buchanan administration had offered to accede to the treaty, if still further protection were given to private property on the seas in time of war; but the offer had not been accepted. As the United States was at war and the South threatened to send out privateers, the new offer made Europe suspect that another motive than the one apparent on the surface lay concealed in the offer. Adams made the proposal and understood that the question would be dealt with in Washington, as indeed it had been, for a chance capture of letters showed that the British government, through Lord Lyons in Washington, had approached the Confederacy on that very question and had secured its adhesion to the treaty. The British and French ministers at Washington then sought to interview Seward, but were rebuffed, and the question returned to Europe, accompanied by warnings from the French and British representatives. Adams, believing that negotiations were on foot in Washington, made no move until further instructions from Seward told him of the true situation. He then found Russell unwilling to enter into an agreement without an express exception applying to the Confederacy. The subject was allowed to drop and was not renewed during the war. It appeared later that Great Britain and France would have gladly accepted the adhesion of the United States, even with concessions on their own part. The delay and Seward's conduct produced a change of policy, but American interests did not suffer. The result made Adams more cautious in his dealings with Earl Russell, for he could not but interpret some of the steps taken as "miserable shufflings" showing strange "divergencies of recollection." Between the annoyance of this unsuccessful negotiation and the want of military success at home Adams did not find his position growing stronger.

In November the *Trent* affair aroused England almost to the point of war. The ministry, having in view the possibility of such an incident, had learned from its law advisers that the United States would be within its rights if it should stop and search the vessel on which the Southern emissaries to Europe were passengers, examine the mail, and even seize the vessel and take her into port for adjudication; but it could not take from her the emissaries and allow the ship to pursue her voyage. An American war-ship entered Southampton and the captain, Marchand, talked enough to lead the authorities to believe that he was there to intercept the *Nashville,* on which Mason and Slidell had intended to sail. The *Nashville* had taken and burned an American merchant ship in the British channel. Palmerston, in a friendly interview with Adams, asked about Marchand's purpose and strongly intimated the inexpediency of an attempt so offensive to the national flag. He could not see that any real advantage could be gained, for the Confederate ministers could not alter the policy already adopted by the British government. On the other hand, it could hardly fail to occasion much prejudice. Adams then told of Marchand's instructions, which were to look for the *Nashville,* and added that on his advice Marchand was watching a ship taking on arms and ammunitions for the South. Soon after, the news came of the seizure and the violation, through Capt. Wilkes's ill-judged act, of the protection offered by the British flag. The burst of jubilation that passed through the Northern States was met by the evidently serious protest of the British, accompanied by a demand for a suitable apology. When knowledge of the seizure reached London, Adams was passing a week-end with Richard Monckton Milnes at Fryston, in Nottinghamshire. On receiving a note from the legation announcing the fact, Adams realized the great danger of the crisis but made no move. He knew that Wilkes had placed the United States in opposition to its long-accepted policy of recognizing the rights of neutral nations in war-time; he was, indeed, one of the few Americans in public life who realized the extent of the crisis thus precipitated. On Dec. 14 the Prince Consort died, and on the 17th Adams received from Seward a statement that Wilkes had acted without instructions and the expression of a hope that the British government would consider the matter "in a friendly temper, and it may expect the best disposition" (*Ibid.,* p. 227) on the part of the American government. On the 19th Adams in a long interview with Russell learned that war might not follow, even if Lord Lyons should be recalled, and in a friendly spirit impressed himself on the British minister so far as to elicit the remark that if all matters were left to them Russell had little doubt they should soon agree. Adams added in his dispatch to Seward, "I expressed my assent" (*Ibid.,* p. 229). By no means relieved of his anxiety and fully aware of the excited condition of English opinion he could only await the issue, quite convinced that his stay in England would probably be short. Unaware of what was taking place in Washington, where almost to the last day concession was deprecated and a warlike outcome probable, he had done as much as could be done by writing confidentially to Seward that he hoped the United States would not invite the ill-will of Europe by not surrendering Mason and Slidell. On Jan. 8, 1862, he learned that the two emissaries had been surrendered. "The danger of war is at present removed," he noted in his diary, "and I am to remain in this purgatory a while longer" (*Ibid.,* p. 238).

The sentiment against the United States did not subside after the *Trent* affair but ebbed and flowed with the success or failure of the Federal military operations. Russell's colleague and chief, Palmerston, surprised the American minister by a personal note, characterizing in terms the opposite of diplomatic Butler's general order intended to put an end to the insults offered to the Federal troops by the women of New Orleans. Ignorant of the real situation and misinterpreting the scope of the order, Palmerston stated that "if the Federal government chooses to be served by men capable of such revolting outrages, they must submit to abide by the deserved opinion which mankind will form of their conduct" (*Ibid.,* p. 249). Adams's first thought was that Palmerston wished a quarrel; his second, that it might be connected with a desire for mediation, which had been rumored and which French activities seemed to confirm. Wishing not to give offense but to ascertain the real purpose of the criticism, Adams asked Palmerston whether it was "addressed to me in any way officially between us, or purely as a private expression of sentiment between gentlemen" (*Ibid.,* p. 251). He also took Palmerston's note to Russell, speaking of it as "entirely unprecedented"; but those words were not needed to impress Russell with its impropriety. What passed between him and Palmerston can only be conjec-

Adams

tured, but Palmerston's further communications with Adams placed him still more in the wrong. He had written as prime minister to the American minister and thus made it a public transaction; but he had by marking it "private and confidential" laid an injunction of secrecy on Adams, without his consent. A half-apology from Palmerston and the withdrawal of the implications contained in his note enabled Adams to close the incident in a manner greatly advantageous to himself, and to serve notice on the Premier that "I must hereafter, as long as I remain here in a public capacity, decline to entertain any similar correspondence" (*Ibid.*, p. 260). His position was distinctly stronger and once more he had shown his ability to handle a delicate situation to the credit of his government and himself. Russell throughout the incident had favored Adams and seemed more friendly. Speaking of an interview with Russell on June 19, 1862, Adams says: "I think it was the most kindly interview I have had" (*Ibid.*, p. 255).

Something more than kindness was needed. When Adams had arrived at his post in 1861, he had known no one in public life in England, and had met no one except Richard Cobden. While English feeling in general was against slavery and proved a strong obstacle to any connection with the South other than commercial, the cause of the North made no strong appeal to the ruling class in Great Britain or to the mercantile and industrial interests. A contest to preserve a union already in their opinion dissolved gave them no real issue. Neither trade nor industry had suffered to a marked degree as yet because of the war. The test of the feeling of the people was yet to come. London society reflected the official attitude and the American minister had little social recognition outside of a few who had volunteered acquaintance. Thurlow Weed and other well-intentioned Americans sought to aid him in fulfilling his duties, but they proved of little moment. The leading journals were hostile to the North and supercilious in their denial of any moral question in the contest. But W. E. Forster, a member of Parliament from Bradford, sought Adams, and throughout the contest was the firm defender of the United States and a warm friend of Adams. Cobden and Bright also came to his support, as did the Duke of Argyll, one of the few members of the government who were friendly to the North. Small as the number of such supporters might be, the weight in character influenced the result. The Southern commissioners, Mason and Slidell, and the Southern organ in London—the *Index*—attacked Adams by every means in their power, without gaining more than temporary success

The length and nature of the war in the South and the need of raw cotton in French and British manufactures brought about a crisis which Adams could feel without being able to measure its gravity. Mediation in any form had been excluded by Seward's firm policy, and interference with the blockade would bring a prompt declaration of war from the United States. The long lists of vessels that had run the blockade, prepared by Mason for use in Parliament, appeared formidable until the nature of the vessels was explained by the American minister. More difficult to combat was the growing conviction that the North could not win and that a further continuance of the war would be against humanity and the best interests of civilization. Still more potent arguments for ending the struggle were found in the suffering caused by the cotton famine. The large crop of 1860 and the large stocks of manufactured goods on hand in 1861 had given a certain appearance of prosperity to the industry, which speculative features tended to heighten as well as to discount. What could not be made good was the supply of raw cotton, for the South held almost a monopoly in that product and the growing need developed no other sources of supply. The great inducements the market offered (the price of raw cotton reaching sixty cents a pound) did not draw from all possible sources an appreciable fraction of the quantity hitherto supplied from the United States. A union of moral, political, and economic forces at this moment threatened to bring about the recognition of the Confederacy, the consequent raising of the blockade, and the undoing of all that had been so painfully secured in the foreign relations of the States.

Adams knew the influence which Mason had on certain members of Parliament, such as Roebuck and Lindsay, the one of whom had taken up the cause of the South for political and the other for commercial reasons. He had seen in the journals the speeches of members of Parliament to their constituents, utterances that became bolder in advocating interference in the American war and calling upon the government to act. He knew that the Emperor of the French was urging upon the British government positive measures of intervention or recognition which would quiet the real distress of the French cotton industry and pave the way for his own American projects in Mexico. Finally, Adams knew that the question had been formally raised in Parliament and a day appointed for taking a vote upon it. He could not know what had taken place between Slidell and Napoleon and the heavy inducements in cotton and alliance and Mexican policy offered by the South in return for Napoleon's aid. Nor could he know that Palmerston, Russell, and Gladstone, the three strong men in the cabinet, had resolved that the time had come to intervene, and, if the North rejected the offer, to recognize the Southern Confederacy. Adams had his instructions from Washington and used them indirectly so that their purport would be known to the ministry without the threat which a direct communication would carry. The cabinet took no action and the British and French policy remained as before. Yet in October and November 1862 the danger of intervention had been greater than ever before.

While Southern sympathizers had in that matter almost attained the end of their desire and had lost by so small a margin, the Emancipation Proclamation of President Lincoln reached England. The hatred of slavery, which the British so often, and even the French, had boasted was at the root of their own policy, should have led them to welcome the proclamation as a full indorsement of the long effort to suppress the slave trade and extend emancipation. But opinion in England had concluded that the North could not be successful and in that case the South certainly would pay no attention to so futile if not foolish an act. To Adams, who had led the anti-slavery policy in Massachusetts, the proclamation came as the consummation of his wishes. The war and its evils appeared to his mind "a just judgment upon the country for having paltered with the evil so long" (*Ibid.*, p. 295). He saw that in time emancipation would be accomplished and, as was his wont, he waited. After some weeks the force of abuse diminished and addresses to the President began to come to Adams, first from the workingmen, accompanied by deputations to give additional weight, then from societies and organizations, and early in February from the great meeting in Exeter Hall, London, proof to the minister that the sympathies of the middle classes had been aroused. He thought there could be little doubt that the popular current was in favor of the North, and noted the effect on newspapers and politicians. "It has closed the mouths of those who had been advocating the side of the South," wrote Cobden to Sumner, and he added assurance that no unfriendly act on the part of the government toward the cause of the North was to be apprehended (*Ibid.*, p. 301). The reception given to the proclamation in England proved to Adams the hollowness of the denunciations of America in the past for upholding slavery. "It is impossible for me to express the contempt I feel for a nation which exhibits itself to the world and posterity in this guise," he wrote in his diary. "It is a complete forfeiture of the old reputation for manliness and honesty" (*Ibid.*, p. 305).

While Adams was experiencing the sensation of victory, for such it was in reality, still another crisis was at hand, more serious than any he had yet met. That the government of Great Britain intended to remain neutral during the war until obliged or sufficiently interested to change its policy may be admitted as true. Yet from the beginning the South insisted that neutrality existed only in form; in effect the North had been greatly favored by Great Britain's accepting, however reluctantly, the fact of the blockade, and by the facilities which the North enjoyed in obtaining arms and munitions. The Confederates could buy, but they could not land arms in Southern ports. But in spite of the Foreign Enlistment Act, which prohibited the "fitting out, equipping, and arming of vessels for warlike operations" (*Ibid.*, p. 307), they could buy or build vessels in England, place guns and munitions upon them on the high sea or in a foreign port, and prey upon the commerce of the North. The *Nashville* had been such a cruiser and the *Florida* had been built for a Confederate agent. Their success led to another contract with the Lairds for a commerce-destroyer known officially as *290*, later as the *Alabama*. Launched in May 1862, time only was needed to man and equip her for service against Northern commerce. The purpose of the vessel was well known in Liverpool, and the United States consul at that place reported the progress made in the shipyard to Adams, who in turn laid the evidence before Russell. The depositions and other statements submitted by Adams to the Foreign Office were clear and conclusive and he had obtained opinion of leading counsel on the correctness of his position, that under the law the government could detain the vessel. The opinion of the law officers of the Crown rejected the evidence as insufficient to call for action, while the authorities at Liverpool were sympathetic with the Confederates and, when the ship was nearly completed, warned them of possible danger. Papers from the Foreign Office were sent to the Queen's Advocate, Sir John Harding, but he happened just then to have a nervous break-down ending in insanity, and they were overlooked. The ship under the name *Enrica* sailed from Liverpool on July 26 and five days later received her crew and guns and began her career as a privateer.

The Confederates in England had also contracted with the Lairds for two iron-clad vessels of the ram type, so greatly improved in destructiveness that no vessel in the Northern navy could meet them. Once released on the sea they could at their convenience raise the blockade and levy tribute upon Northern ports. The Confederacy saw in them a means of securing European recognition and of final success, and the authorities at Washington showed their sense of the situation by sending two representatives to England in an attempt to outbid the Confederates and purchase the rams for the United States. Of that intention Adams was not informed; a knowledge of it would have embarrassed him. He again bombarded the Foreign Office with detailed evidence of the serious nature of the violation of the intention of the Foreign Enlistment Act, and was again told by Russell that the government could not interfere. Not discouraged by his want of success in stopping the *Alabama,* Adams let no opportunity pass of calling attention to actual conditions, to the neglect in the past, and to the heavy responsibilities and damages likely to be incurred by a repetition of that neglect. In his long correspondence on the subject with Russell he proved his knowledge of essentials, his skill and force of statement, and his ability to construct a case against inaction. Seward had given him support by clearly outlining what might happen. If the British government, he wrote, could not enforce the plain intent of its law, the United States would protect its commerce at all hazard, and, should a "partial war" become a general one between the two nations, the responsibility would not fall upon the United States. The battle of Gettysburg and the opening of the Mississippi by the fall of Vicksburg greatly strengthened Adams's hand. At this juncture came the visit to Emperor Napoleon of the leading two parliamentary sympathizers with the South, Roebuck and Lindsay, their apparent success, and their misfortune when stating in Parliament that success. They awakened a temporary anxiety in Adams, who thought he could trace in that adventure the hand of Slidell, but by their own discomfiture they cleared the way for the outcome of Adams's duel with Russell. By September 1863 the rams were approaching completion and the operations of the *Alabama* were such as to leave little doubt as to what the rams could accomplish. To protect themselves from possible interference, the Confederates placed the ships in the name of a French firm ostensibly acting for the Egyptian government.

Steadily denying its power to act and leaving Adams in much the same position which he had occupied in the *Alabama* matter, the British government put him to the full test. He met it and knowing the responsibility of his act he wrote, Sept. 5, the dispatch containing the sentence "It would be superfluous in me to point out to your lordship that this is war" (*Ibid.,* p. 342). Three days later Russell notified him that orders had been given to prevent the departure of the rams. In the moment of this his greatest triumph Adams remained calm and merely noted: "I know not that even in the *Trent* case I felt a greater relief" (*Ibid.,* p. 344).

The narrative of these events does not measure the extent of the victory. With the stopping of the rams the efforts of the Confederacy in Great Britain ended and Mason withdrew to France. Peace with Europe ceased to be uncertain. The position of Adams was assured and the confidence of the American administration in his judgment and abilities was almost equaled by that of the British Foreign Office. In March 1868 when his name was mentioned in debate on the *Alabama* claims in the House of Commons, the House broke into cheers (*London Times,* Mar. 7, 1868). He had made the American representative more respected than he had been for many years and in so doing added reputation to the American name throughout Europe. The outcome of his mission has been compared to the military victories over the South and has not suffered by the comparison. He now conducted a long correspondence with the British government on its liability for losses to American commerce through rebel cruisers of British origin. He constructed the foundation of claims for which the British had made themselves liable morally and which stood the test of arbitration. With the end of war his anxieties were almost completely at rest. Diplomatic questions remained, but they had no such weight as those of the wartime. The activities of Fenians from America, claiming protection from the punishment of their crimes of violence on the ground of American citizenship, caused no little annoyance; and no little prejudice was aroused in political circles in the United States by the assumed neglect of Adams to do what the laws, treaties, or his position forbade.

Adams resigned and returned to the United States in June 1868. Parties and leaders had changed much, and no opening appeared for him in public life. Nor did he desire further service. He was offered the presidency of Harvard University, but declined it, and at Quincy resumed the life he had led before going on his mission. The unsettled disputes with England led to the negotiation of the Treaty of Washington and under it the reference of the *Alabama* claims to arbitration. Of five arbitrators two were to be chosen by the two nations concerned. The United States named Adams and Great Britain designated Sir Alexander Cockburn, chief justice of the Court of Queen's Bench. After a preliminary meeting at Geneva in December 1871, six months were given for study of the cases, and Adams traveled in Europe only to be recalled to Washington for consultation. Difficulties had arisen on the kind and limit of damages for which reparation was sought. In his correspondence with Russell, Adams had rested with direct damages. Sumner had developed claims for indirect damages of such an amount that they had ceased to be taken seriously, yet he had succeeded in having them inserted in the American case presented to the arbitration. The claims, impossible as they were, threatened to bring the arbitration to an end. Adams had knowledge of English feeling and its manifestation and had taken counsel at Washington. Cockburn, determined in his opposition to the indirect claims, could prevent arbitration. Adams took upon himself to have the indirect damages rejected as contrary to the principles of international law and thus prepared the way for a true arbitration on the direct damages. It was a personal as well as a national victory; for without such action arbitration would have failed.

While on the board of arbitration he was considered by the liberal Republicans—those who had been alienated from the party by the administration of Grant—as their candidate for the presidency. The final choice of Horace Greeley by the convention saved Adams, as his son expresses it, "from either a political defeat, or a presidency predestined from its commencement to failure." Adams turned to his family papers and published the full and untouched text of his father's diary, as *Memoirs of John Quincy Adams* (1874–77). This closed his active life. He died in Boston, Nov. 21, 1886.

With a mind less active and an experience less varied than his father's, Charles Francis Adams possessed a judgment better fitted to deal with the situations raised by the Civil War. Henry Adams speaks of his father as "singular for mental poise—absence of self-assertion or self-consciousness—the faculty of standing apart without seeming aware that he was alone—a balance of mind and temper that neither challenged nor avoided notice, nor admitted question of superiority or inferiority, of jealousy, of personal motives, from any source, even under great pressure" (*The Education of Henry Adams,* 1918, p. 37). In everything that Adams did this balance was shown and produced notable results. His directness and evident sincerity won the confidence even of his opponents. Greater than any office, elective or appointive, entrusted to him, he met the requirements of all in a manner to attract attention; but he had no capacity for political leadership and his following rested upon qualities above those required in party management. National in feeling, his highest accomplishments were on a national scale.

Apart from the volumes of family papers and diplomatic papers, Adams's published writings are as follows: *Appeal from the New to the Old Whigs* (1835); *Reflections upon the Present State of the Currency of the United States* (1837); *Further Reflections,* etc. (1837); "Report on North Eastern Boundary," *House Document, No. 44, Feb. 1841;* "Report on Petition of George Latimer," *House Document, No. 41, Feb. 1843; Report* of Massachusetts Committee on the Annexation of Texas, Massachusetts Senate, *No. 27* (1844); *Texas and the Massachusetts Resolutions* (1844); *How to Settle the Texas Question* (published anonymously, 1845); *What Makes Slavery a Question of National Concern* (1855); *Address on the Occasion of Opening the New Town Hall in Braintree, July 29, 1858;* "Republican Party a Necessity," speech in House of Representatives, May 31, 1860; *Conservatism and Reform* (1860); "On the Union," speech in House of Representatives, Jan. 31, 1861; *The Union and the Southern Rebellion, Farewell Address to His Constituents* (printed in London, 1861); *Struggle for Neutrality in America* (1871); *Address on Life, Character, and Services of William H. Seward* (1873); *Address before the Phi Beta Kappa* (1873); *Address at Amherst College before the Social Union* (1875); *Address before the Literary Societies of Colby University* (1875); and "Orations" on July 4, at Boston, 1843; Quincy, 1856; Fall River, 1860; and Taunton, 1876.

[*Charles Francis Adams,* by his son, Charles Francis Adams (1900); Frederic Bancroft, *Life of W. H. Seward* (1900); *Diplomatic Correspondence,* 1861–68; *Parliamentary Papers,* 1861–68; *Index,* London, 1862–64; E. D. Adams, *Great Britain and the American Civil War* (1925); Brooks Adams, "The Seizure of the Laird Rams," *Mass. Hist. Soc. Proc.,* vol. XLV, Dec. 1911.]

W. C. F.

ADAMS, CHARLES FRANCIS (May 27, 1835–Mar. 20, 1915), railroad expert, civic leader, historian, was born at Boston, Mass., the son of Charles Francis Adams [*q.v.*] and Abigail Brown (Brooks) Adams. His earlier years were passed between Boston and Quincy and by a preference for the latter he became identified with its history as a town. He remembered his grandfather, John Quincy Adams, as an old man, "always writing . . . with a perpetual inkstain on the forefinger and thumb of his right hand" (*Autobiography,* p. 9), and was impressed by his industrious and somewhat solitary life. From private schools the boy went through the Boston Latin School, entered Harvard University in the sophomore year, and graduated in 1856. Critical of his education and career, he looked back with pleasure on his Harvard days as a "period of rapid development and much enjoyment" (*Ibid.,* p. 31). After leaving college he studied law in the office of Richard

Henry Dana and Francis E. Parker, leading lawyers of their day; but though he was admitted to practice in 1858, he soon discovered that he had no great liking for the law. As what practice he had occupied but a small part of his time, he was in a position to form relations that developed his as yet unformed aptitudes. In 1848 he had accompanied his father to the Buffalo convention, and during the session of the convention Charles Sumner took him to Niagara Falls. He formed a close and admiring friendship for Sumner and later for Seward, with whom he and his father made a tour in the West in the campaign of 1860, where the young man made some speeches, which were well received. In Dana's office he met the best and took what was offered in the association. He grew up in an atmosphere of political discussion. His hours gave him time to write and he began, as had his father, with newspaper communications on public questions. Visiting his father in Washington in the winter of 1860, he eagerly made use of his opportunity to meet prominent men and gained in assurance as well as knowledge. Seeking a wider audience, he offered to James Russell Lowell, then editor of the *Atlantic Monthly,* an article on "The Reign of King Cotton," a subject of living interest. Its acceptance gave him encouragement. At this time he kept a diary, as his three forebears had done. Of this a few extracts only have been preserved, enough to cause regret that he destroyed the record in later years.

In February 1861 he again went to Washington, remained for nearly a month, and witnessed the inauguration of Lincoln, still widening his acquaintance with public men, observing, and studying the situation, only to admit in after years that, with almost every one concerned, he had failed to grasp the situation. His father and Seward seemed to him to have a policy "eminently sensible" (*Ibid.,* p. 73), that of holding the border states loyal until the secession movement should recede, the new administration be in power, and the Union reaction encouraged. Adams's vivid account of this interval, with its uncertainties, doubtings, and lack of coöperation, the coming of the President-elect and his loose utterances on the way, and the sentiments of Seward and Sumner, give proof of his gift of description.

Returning to Boston in March, the appointment of his father to the English mission laid upon him the care of the family property, and the outbreak of war made this a heavy responsibility. As all young men were in the militia, he was a member of the 4th Battalion of Massachusetts Volunteer Militia, learned the manual and how to march, and was in garrison in Fort Independence in Boston harbor. The training was elementary yet serviceable. He saw the first regiments leave for the South without a strong wish to follow them; he had five weeks of playing soldier at Fort Independence in April and May 1861; and in the following months he watched his friends take service. By the end of October his course of action was determined and he applied for a captaincy in the 1st Massachusetts Cavalry. He received a commission as first lieutenant in December and on the 28th of that month he started for South Carolina with his regiment. To Adams it proved a service of three and a half years, and five years passed before he was again a resident of Boston. Summing up his experience, he was inclined to regard his military life as educationally incomparably more valuable than his years in the university; it would have been even more valuable had he been a staff officer, as he more than once had the opportunity to become. A regimental officer, he records, "no matter how high his grade, sees nothing and knows nothing of what is going on—obedience, self-sacrifice, and patient endurance are the qualities most in demand for him; but as for any intelligent comprehension of the game in progress, that for the regimental officer is quite beyond his ken" (*Ibid.,* pp. 135–36). His family letters during his service have been printed in *A Cycle of Adams Letters, 1861–65* (1920) and have a quality of their own. Vivid in description, natural in expression, frank in opinion on men and events, they are shot through with the vein of introspection natural to an Adams. Sharing in two of the great battles, Antietam and Gettysburg, he gives a picture of camp and garrison service that is unmatched. Conscientious in the performance of duty and learning by experience the essentials of routine, he held an enviable reputation and Gen. Humphreys offered him the highest position on his staff. Adams, now a colonel, declined, feeling obliged to remain with his negro regiment—the 5th Massachusetts Cavalry. In August 1864 his health began to break down and in May 1865 he was a physical wreck. Mustered out in June of that year, he received the brevet of brigadier-general. He married at Newport, Nov. 8, 1865, Mary Hone Ogden, daughter of Edward and Caroline Callender Ogden of New York.

After eleven months in Europe in 1865–66 he returned, restored in health but without occupation. Realizing his unfitness for the law as a source of livelihood, he took to his pen and wrote on railroads, then the important feature in the economic growth of the country. The transcontinental lines were being built with government aid, and in Wall Street the greatest speculators were fighting for control of eastern roads. Adams, seeking for the broad principles that should apply to the development of railroad construction and management, had before him the best of examples. From 1866 to 1873 the building of roads had been overdone. They had been recklessly financed and made the object of stock gambling, involving good as well as doubtful undertakings. Adams analyzed the acts and intentions of the men seeking to gain possession of the Erie road, while wrecking it, and in a series of articles fearlessly attacked them and exposed the criminal acts to which they resorted. The papers attracted as great attention by their courage as by their grasp of some railroad problems of general application. Gathered into a volume—*Chapters of Erie and Other Essays* (1871)—they have kept a place in the literature of railroads and stock speculations. He also wrote a series of articles on the Tweed Ring, which were printed under the title, "An Episode in Municipal Government," in the *North American Review* (October 1874, January and July 1875, October 1875) over the name of C. F. Wingate, who had supplied some of the material and to whom Adams characteristically gave the full credit.

When Massachusetts took the lead in establishing a Board of Railroad Commissioners in 1869 Adams because of his evident fitness was appointed one of the three members. The youngest and most active, he performed the labor, controlled the proceedings, and in 1872 became the chairman. This position he held until 1879, producing a series of reports on railway accidents and policy that drew attention to the methods and utility of the board and led to the creation in other states of boards closely modeled after that of Massachusetts. The success of his administration rested upon a full and impartial public examination of facts and a frank presentation to the public of conditions and conclusions. He won the confidence of both operators and public; and the handling of the engineers' strike in 1877 proved the efficacy of his principles, for no other strike among railway operatives in Massachusetts occurred for twenty-five years. The subject was treated by him in 1902 in *Investigation and Publicity as opposed to Compulsory Arbitration* and his methods found favor but not acceptance. He left records of his railroad experience in *Railroads: Their Origin and Problems* (1878) and *Notes on Railroad Accidents* (1879). In 1878, through the influence of Carl Schurz, he became chairman of the government directors of the Union Pacific Railroad, visited the Pacific coast, and prepared the report. Later, in 1884, he became president of that road, a position forced upon him, only to be ousted from it after six years by Jay Gould and his following, who were none too friendly to Adams because of his exposure of the Erie. Adams foresaw the future importance of the road and from the verge of bankruptcy he raised it to a solvent and efficient system. The later financial situation and legislative measures hindered the completion of his administrative reforms. Through no fault of his own he was unable to meet the maneuvers of the speculative railroad wrecker. Still another recognition of his abilities in railroad affairs was his appointment to the Board of Arbitration of the Trunk Line Railroads, but he held the position for only three years, convinced that the time was not ready for such a board.

Living in Quincy, Mass., he and his brother John Quincy Adams served as moderators in town meetings for twenty years and directed the proceedings of the town government at a time when the place by its size was outgrowing that form of administration. Charles Adams had the more suggestive mind and the greater capacity for labor, but the two brothers left their impress in permanent form. Adams was a member of the school committee, a trustee of the public library, a park commissioner, and a commissioner of the sinking fund. In each of these positions he accomplished results that in retrospect pleased him. He found the school system antiquated and the methods of teaching so imperfect as to be of little value. The average graduate of the grammar school in 1870 could not read with ease, nor could he write an ordinary letter in good English in a legible hand. Uncertain what reforms were necessary, Adams proposed the employment of a trained superintendent and in 1875 gained his end. Out of this came the "Quincy System," which was widely studied and imitated throughout the land and for which Adams was almost wholly responsible. It substituted new methods for the old mechanical ones. In place of memorizing rules, children were to learn to read, write, and cipher as they learned to walk and talk, naturally and by practice. In reading and writing, a geography or history took the place of speller, grammar, and copybook. By 1880 the success of the system seemed assured and Adams's account of the reform—*The New Departure in the Common Schools of Quincy*—passed through six editions.

As the town possessed no public library, provision for one was made in 1871, the cost to be met by town and private subscription. Opened in that year, it proved a great success, and nine years later, through Adams's agency, the town gained the Thomas Crane library building, dedicated in 1882, Adams making the address. In 1874 the town had a debt of $112,000; after nine years of the Adams brothers' management this was reduced to $19,000 and disappeared shortly after. Owing to Adams's plans the town received Wollaston Park, historic as the site of Thomas Morton's Merry Mount. The union of the suggestive and the practical in Adams which had benefited the town by application trained him for wider fields, and in 1892 he was appointed to the state commission to devise a system of parks and public reservations in the vicinity of Boston. The work of this commission has surrounded the city with beautiful connecting roadways, saved Blue Hill from the quarrymen, and preserved the Middlesex Fells as public parks. He also served as chairman of a state commission to report upon the relations of street railways and municipalities, which caused him to study the subject in European cities and produced useful general legislation based upon his recommendations, which again was copied in other cities.

For twenty-four years from 1882 he was a member of the Board of Overseers of Harvard University and was prominent in many lines of its development. The nomination of visiting committees fell to him and he himself gave special attention to the English department. His elaborate reports on conditions produced some changes, but he was never satisfied that he had fully understood the situation and the remedy. To him the Harvard system was "radically wrong," and he expressed his views in two addresses which called out much controversy. His ideas on the education to be given by college and university were developed in *A College Fetich* (1883), a protest against the compulsory study of dead languages; and, in 1906, near the term of his long service as overseer, in *Some Modern College Tendencies,* in which he pointed out the complete separation of teacher and individual student and the absence of direction in studies and of the personal influence of instructors. A remedy he found in a group of colleges, each independent and each having its specialty, where the master should know every student. The university should supplement college training. Both papers were constructive in their suggestion and served their purpose of causing reëxamination of accepted methods.

Meanwhile another field had opened to him, by accident as he thought, when the citizens of Weymouth asked him to deliver an address on the 250th anniversary of its settlement. Without experience in historical investigation he accepted and in so doing entered upon forty years of historical writing, essentially his "aptitude," from which he derived his greatest pleasure and most lasting reputation. The address was given in 1874, and in the following year he was elected a member of the Massachusetts Historical Society, became a vice-president of it in 1890 and president in 1895, a position he held until his death. In that period he contributed many papers, broadened the scope of the society, and added greatly to its reputation. In 1883 he printed some six copies of *Episodes in New England History,* a study of the history of Quincy, which in 1892 appeared in an extended form in two volumes as *Three Episodes of Massachusetts History* and remains a model local history in its form and treatment. In the same year (1883) appeared his edition of Morton's *New English Canaan* and in 1894 his *Antinomianism in the Colony of Massachusetts-Bay, 1636–38,* elaborately annotated. He ventured into a somewhat new field in a biography of Richard Henry Dana (1890), and in a life of his father, Charles Francis Adams (1900), both of which have taken a high place in American biography.

Wishing to write a full biography of his father, Adams for a number of years gave close study to the political history of Massachusetts and the War of Secession and its results. Not a little of his material was used in occasional papers and addresses, the more important of which were side studies of his principal theme. In a group of papers he expressed his conception of secession and particularly the conduct of Gen. Lee: *"Shall Cromwell have a Statue?"* (1902), a plea for a statue to Lee in Washington; *Lee at Appomattox,* etc. (1902); *Constitutional Ethics of Secession* (1903); and *Lee's Centennial* (1907), a series that marked the waning of the animosities which had survived the war. Beginning with 1899 and for fifteen years thereafter he prepared a number of papers on the diplomatic history of the War of Secession, the larger part of which appeared in the *Proceedings of the Massachusetts Historical Society.* Drawing largely from the family papers, he was able to give valuable material hitherto unknown, and he enriched it by an interpretation which, always original and individual, often ran counter to accepted conclusions. In 1899 he printed "The Laird Rams," in the *Proceedings of the Massachusetts Historical Society,* vol. XXXIII; in 1901 he made an address in New York on *Before and after the Treaty of Washington* (published in 1902), and followed it by a number of essays on the British Declaration of Neutrality, the *Trent* Affair, the Rams, and British and French mediation. Becoming convinced that the story could not be fully told without having the contemporary English and French diplomatic papers, he went twice to England in 1913, the first visit being due to his appointment to deliver three lectures on American history at Oxford University. These lectures were printed in 1913 as *Trans-Atlantic Historical Solidarity.* He gained access to important collections in England, obtained much material, and returned to complete the life of his father. The new material led to a revision of his earlier studies in diplomatic history, but was never fully utilized.

All this does not measure the extent of his activities. He engaged in large business enterprises and with a measure of success. In the town of Lincoln, Mass., whither he removed from Quincy, he showed the same interest in town government as he had in Quincy. Throughout his whole career he was keenly alive to the course of political events, took an active share in reform and independent movements, and was an eager participant in the discussions of public policy, both state and national. He began as a Republican, but later became independent of party and remained so to the end. Except for the positions held in Quincy he never was a candidate for nor held an elective office. In 1883 he was offered a nomination for the governorship, but declined it on the ground that a third candidate would divide the party and make the defeat of Gen. Butler less certain. In dealing with public questions, he acted and wrote not as a partisan but in a large way—as had his ancestors before him. He spoke and published on ballot and electoral reform, proportional representation, free trade (he was in favor of a tariff for revenue), civil service reform, currency and finance, taxation, the abuses of the pension system, Panama tolls, the Philippines, and imperialism. To the end he remained active, individual, and suggestive. He died in Washington, Mar. 20, 1915.

"Always independent, sometimes recalcitrant . . . by nature inclined to believe that long-established practices of governments, institutions of education, and financial or industrial organizations were likely to be wrong, or at least capable of great improvement," was President Eliot's summary of his life-work (*Proceedings of the Massachusetts Historical Society,* XLVIII, 387). "Inheriting a great tradition of public service, he felt the obligations which it imposed, and to that patriotism which was born in the descendant of men who had done so much to found and preserve this nation was added the consciousness of what was due from the members of his family," added Moorfield Storey (*Ibid.,* XLVIII, 387). In his writing, so much of which was for special occasions, he has left a record of his own acts, opinions, and experience, expressed with detachment and independence. Possessing an inquiring and historical mind, with pronounced ability to investigate and present social and historical problems, progressive in matters of political or administrative improvement, yet conservative in action, he showed that he was near to John Quincy Adams in qualities of mind but wanting in the aggressiveness that distinguished the elder statesman. Passing a life largely in controversy, his absolute honesty of purpose and conviction was never questioned.

In addition to what has been mentioned Adams printed a number of historical addresses, of which the following are the more important: *Double Anniversary, '76 and '63* at Quincy (1869); *An Oration before the Authorities of Boston, July 4, 1872* (1872); *History of Braintree* (1891); *The Centennial Milestone, Quincy* (1892); *Massachusetts: its Historians and its History* (1893); *Sifted Grain and the Grain Sifters* (1900); and *"'Tis Sixty Years Since"* (1913). On politics he published *Individuality in Politics* (1880) and *Emancipation of the Voter* (1894). In 1911 he gathered into a volume a number of his papers—*Studies: Military and Diplomatic, 1775–1865*—and before 1912 he prepared an autobiography, published the year after his death.

[The chief sources are *Charles Francis Adams 1835–1915: an Autobiography,* with a "Memorial Address" by Henry Cabot Lodge (1916) and tributes in *Mass. Hist. Soc. Proc.,* XLVIII.]

W. C. F.

ADAMS, CHARLES KENDALL (Jan. 24, 1835–July 26, 1902), historian, college president, only son of Charles and Maria Shedd Adams, was born in the township of Derby, Vt. His grandfather was David E. Adams, and his earliest known ancestor William Adams, who emigrated from England in 1635. His father was a farmer and was assisted by his son. The latter attended the district school, and at the age of seventeen taught in a district school. In 1856 the family emigrated to Iowa, and there father and son worked together on a farm. His preparation for college, received at Denmark Academy, was so meager that when he applied for entrance at the University of Michigan he was admitted only, as he himself stated, through the leniency of his examiners. He was poor and had to work his way through college, but he was always diligent. In his freshman year he bought with his hard-earned savings a dozen good books in general literature. "By his maturity and weight of character, rather than by his scholarship, which was hampered by his slender preparation, he wielded a decided influence over his classmates," said President Angell. The chief influence of his college days was undoubtedly Andrew D. White [*q.v.*], professor of history, to whom, in the dedication of a book, he wrote: "To the inspiration of your lectures and your advice, more than to any other cause, I owe my fondness for historical study." It was due to the same influence that he was appointed to carry on the work in the chair of history when White resigned. After four years as assistant professor of history (1863–67), he was advanced to the full professorship, with leave of absence of a year and a half to study in German and French universities. He had been married Aug. 13, 1883, to a widow, Abigail Disbrow Mudge, and it was through her assistance chiefly, it was said, that he was enabled to study abroad.

His most important innovation at the University of Michigan was the introduction of the seminary method of instruction for advanced students. He was a stimulating and popular teacher, his lectures attracting citizens from the town until there was no longer space to receive them, and he was prominent on building committees and in other university activities. It was doubtless his success as a university lecturer and his general influence in the faculty that caused President White to invite him to give several successive courses of lectures at Cornell University (1881–85), and his success in these probably led to his nomination by White to succeed him in the presidency of Cornell (1885). Adams's first wife died at Cornell July 5, 1889, and July 9, 1890, he married Mary Mathews Barnes, the widow of Albert S. Barnes.

His seven years in the presidency of Cornell University were distinguished in several directions: the erection of the library and the chemical laboratory, the establishment of the law school, the President White School of History and Political Science, and the departments of architecture, civil engineering, and archæology. But the chief distinction of his administration was the appointment of eminent professors. Of sixty-three professors constituting the faculty when he left Cornell in 1892, thirty-two had been appointed during his administration. He was an extraordinary judge of character, and he never showed jealousy in having able scholars about him. He resigned from Cornell with the intention of devoting himself to literary work, but found the offer of the presidency of the University of Wisconsin too tempting to resist. This offer was doubtless due again to Andrew D. White, who, when his opinion was asked, is said to have replied: "My first choice would be Charles Kendall Adams, my second choice would be Charles Kendall Adams, my third choice would be Charles Kendall Adams."

His most successful work was done at Wisconsin. He was a building president, and had the gift of winning liberal appropriations from the legislature. Appropriations for three new buildings at Wisconsin had just been secured by his predecessor, but he set to work at once to secure a new library. This was completed at a cost of $750,000. It was the third university library he had helped to erect, and in many respects it may be considered the memorial of his administration. It is no wonder that at its dedication, as he walked along the white Ionic-columned front, he was heard to exclaim, "At last we have done something worthy of the state!" Altogether about a million and a half was expended in building during his ten years, and appropriations for other university needs were in proportion. He believed strongly in graduate work, and during his incumbency the Graduate School doubled its numbers.

After eight years of service his health broke down in January 1900, and after that he was never at the helm more than a day or two consecutively. His physicians sent him finally to Italy and Germany for recuperation. He returned from Europe in September 1901 seemingly much improved in health, but in the opening convocation address to the students the collapse came. His old trouble returned and serious illness followed. He realized that his health was broken, and as soon as the regents could be assembled he resigned (Oct. 11, 1901) and went to California. On the whole, his health seemed to improve there and he built a house at Redlands. "My wife looks forward with much pleasure to the new life," he wrote, "and I hope it will be in every way beneficial." They moved into their new residence on July 13, 1902, but on July 26 he died. His love of the University of Wisconsin was shown most significantly in the bequest of his whole property to it as a fellowship fund to promote graduate work in English, Greek, and history.

Adams was a man of distinguished presence; about six feet in height, one hundred and eighty pounds in weight, with steel-gray eyes and heavy eyebrows. His leonine head, that somewhat reminded one of Tennyson's, always attracted attention. Dean Birge described him as one of the first men of this country to catch the spirit and temper of true university work. Adams used to say, "The university is for the students," and "A university is chiefly an inspiration and an opportunity." These were key-notes of his policy, and he was always proud to feel that he "kept the team pulling together."

His first book was *Democracy and Monarchy in France* (1874). It was based on a university course of lectures, and attracted considerable attention, being translated into German. His *Manual of Historical Literature* (1882) passed through several editions. He edited also a collection of representative British orations, in three volumes, with biographical sketches and explanatory notes. After he assumed the presidency of Cornell University executive work left little time for writing except baccalaureate and other occasional addresses. To the Cornell period belongs his little volume, *Christopher Columbus* (1892). He was editor-in-chief of the revision of Johnson's *Cyclopædia*. *A History of the United States,* by Charles Kendall Adams and W. P. Trent, was published in 1903.

[Charles Forster Smith, *Charles Kendall Adams, a Life Sketch,* published by the Regents of the University of Wisconsin, 1924.]

C. F. S.

ADAMS, CHARLES R. (Feb. 9, 1834–July 4, 1900), opera singer, was born in Charlestown, Mass., the son of Charles and Eliza Ann (Runey) Adams—the father, who was a farmer, being a *Mayflower* descendant and the mother being descended from at least two previous generations of American-born. Both families had fought in the Revolution. Several of the eight children became choir singers and frequently sang together at home. Since Charles, the eldest, manifested unusual musical ability and possessed a voice of natural beauty, he began his musical studies at an early age, having as teachers, Edwin Bruce, Madame Arnault, and R. Mulder, all of Boston. His smooth, strong tenor voice made him a favorite concert singer and he decided to follow music as a profession. In 1856 he sang the tenor part in *The Creation* with the Handel and Haydn Society of Boston, and for the next five years he appeared in oratorio, as well as in concert, touring not only this country but the West Indies, where he sang also in opera. Mulder, recognizing the possibilities of his student, induced him to accompany him to Europe, where he studied with Barbière in Vienna and made such progress that he was called to the Vienna Opera to sing the tenor rôle in *La Sonnambula* with Mlle. Artot. He learned his rôle in three days and achieved a notable triumph. He toured Holland and Russia, after which he was given a three-year engagement at Budapest, though he did not complete the full period of his contract because of being called to a larger field—the Royal Opera in Berlin, where he remained three years. In 1867 he became the principal tenor at the Imperial Opera (Hofoper) in Vienna, where he remained until 1876—nine years. Besides this Vienna engagement he sang in opera for two seasons in Covent Garden, London, one season at the Royal Opera in Madrid, also one season at La Scala, Milan, and in the principal German opera houses. After gaining great success he came to America with the Strakosch Company for the season of 1877–78. He appeared in German opera with Madame Pappenheim and in Italian opera with Clara Louise Kellogg, Marie Litta, and Annie Louise Cary. He sang in the first American performance of *Rienzi.* His greatest rôles were Tannhäuser, Lohengrin, Rienzi, and Manrico. George Upton writes of him: "He was the most accomplished native tenor of his time and had not merely a very powerful voice, but a very sweet one and one of great range. He sang with dramatic expression and a peculiarly refined and artistic finish. His Tannhäuser and Lohengrin had made him a famous reputation both in this country and in Europe." He was without doubt the greatest American singer of his time. His naturally beautiful voice was excellently trained and under absolute control. Added to this, he had a splendid physique, regular, clear-cut features, and a commanding stage presence. He was as great an actor as he was a singer. From 1879 until his death he lived in Boston, devoting the last twenty years of his life to teaching, in which field he was also eminently successful. He taught many distinguished singers, among them Grace Hiltz, Nellie Melba, and Emma Eames. He died at his summer home at West Harwich, on Cape Cod, Mass.

[H. C. Lahee, *Famous Singers of Today and Yesterday* (1898); Geo. P. Upton, *Musical Memories* (1908); *Grove's Dict. of Music and Musicians, Am. Supp.* (1920); G. L. Howe and W. S. B. Mathews, *A Hundred Years of Music in America* (1889); additional information from Adams's intimate friend, Mr. Jacob Wachenheimer.]

F. L. G. C.

ADAMS, DANIEL (Sept. 29, 1773–June 8, 1864), physician, educator, was one of the many early New England doctors of broad interests, who were as active in serving the intellectual and moral needs of their communities as in ministering to the physical ailments of their patients. He was born in Townsend, Mass., the son of Daniel and Lydia Taylor Adams. His father was deacon in the church, a justice of the peace, and financially able to give his children ample educational advantages. Young Adams graduated from Dartmouth College in 1797, studied medicine under Dr. Nathan Smith of the Dartmouth Medical School, and is recorded as having received the degree of Bachelor of Medicine in 1799, and that of Doctor in 1822. Immediately upon receiving the first degree he began practicing in Leominster, Mass. Here at the memorial service for Washington, held Feb. 22, 1800, he delivered the eulogy, which the town ordered printed and "served to every legal voter." On August 17 of this year he married Nancy, the only daughter of Dr. Mulliken of Townsend. Together with Salmon Wilder he began publishing a weekly newspaper, called the *Telescope,* the first issue of which appeared Jan. 2, 1800. For want of sufficient encouragement it was discontinued, Oct. 14, 1802.

In the meantime he had become impressed by the lack of adequate text-books in the schools. The commonly used arithmetic, for example, was difficult and expensive. Accordingly, in 1801, Adams published *The Scholar's Arithmetic,* comparatively simple and reasonable in price. For many years it was used throughout New England. He also published not later than 1803, for a third edition with a preface of that date was issued in November 1805, *The Understanding Reader or Knowledge before Oratory.* In the preface he asks: "Do you who are parents wish for nothing more than that your children should acquire an easy volubility of tongues while their heads are left uncultivated as the bells in your churches?" His own reader was designed to arrest attention, excite curiosity, encourage reflection, and so cultivate understanding. This also had wide use. About 1805 he removed to Boston, where he taught a private school, and for a time edited the *Medical and Agricultural Register,* a monthly periodical designed to give "practical information in husbandry, cautions and directions for the preservation of health, management of the sick, etc."

His own health becoming somewhat impaired, Adams removed in 1813 to Mont Vernon, N. H., and resumed the practice of medicine. Soon he was one of the most prominent consulting physicians in that part of the state. His interest in schools and civic affairs continued, however, and it is said of him that he "wielded a controlling influence in behalf of temperance, education, and morality" (Chas. J. Smith, *History of the Town of Mont Vernon,* 1907). In 1838, 1839, and 1840, he was a member of the New Hampshire Senate. In 1846 he removed to Keene, N. H., where he died. Besides the text-books mentioned, he published: *Geography, or a Description of the World* (1814, 2nd ed., 1816); *The Thorough Scholar, or the Nature of Language* (1817, 4th ed.); *The Agricultural Reader* (1824); *Adams' New Arithmetic* (1827); *The Monitorial Reader* (1841); *Primary Arithmetic* (1848); *Bookkeeping* (1849). Biographical notices mention also a *Mensuration.*

[David Wilder, *Hist. of Leominster* (1853); Frank H. Whitcomb, *Vital Statistics of the Town of Keene, N. H.* (1905); Simon G. Griffin, *Hist. of the Town of Keene* (1904); *Dartmouth Coll. Gen. Cat.* (1900); G. T. Chapman, *Sketches of the Alumni of Dartmouth Coll. 1791–1854* (1867); *Records N. H. Med. Soc.* (1911).]

H. E. S.

ADAMS, DANIEL WEISSIGER (1820–June 13, 1872), lawyer, soldier, entered the Confederate Army from private life at the beginning of the Civil War, was a commanding officer in several of its severest battles, and at its close, having been three times wounded, returned to private life to survive but a few years. The son of George and Anna (Weissiger) Adams, he was born in Lynchburg, Va., but, while he was still a child, his father moved to Mississippi. Here the elder Adams was United States district attorney from 1830 to 1836, and United States district judge from 1836 to 1839. He is described by Reuben Davis, a member of the Mississippi bar (*Recollections of Mississippi and Mississippians,* 1890, p. 153), as "not great as to legal learning but was for justice and right, and his fine practical sense and good judgment enabled him to give general satisfaction." Young Adams was educated at the University of Virginia and became a lawyer, practicing in Louisiana, where he gained some reputation. In 1843 as a result of a quarrel over accusations of his father he killed editor James Hagan of Vicksburg under circumstances which suggested self-defense. He was tried for murder and acquitted.

In 1861 the governor of Louisiana appointed him one of three members of the military board to organize the state for war. Two regiments were formed, one of cavalry and one of infantry. Of the latter Adams was appointed lieutenant-colonel, and on Oct. 30, 1861 was commissioned colonel. The regiment was then at Pensacola, Fla., where preparations were being made to take Fort Pickens on Santa Rosa Island. The enterprise was abandoned, however, and in the spring of 1862 Adams and his men took part in the operations of the West. At Shiloh they were in Wither's division of the 2nd Corps under Gen. Bragg. Early in the first day's fighting, Apr. 6, the brigade commander was killed, and Adams succeeded him, leading his troops in the attack which, in spite of a heroic resistance, finally drove back and broke Prentiss's division on the Union left. In this engagement Adams lost an eye. On May 23 he was commissioned brigadier-general. Recovering from his wound sufficiently to take part in the Kentucky campaign, he commanded the Louisiana brigade of the Army of the Tennessee, in the wing under Gen. Hardee at Perryville, Oct. 8, 1862. Again, at Stone's River (Murfreesboro), Dec. 31 of the same year, Adams saw fierce fighting, his brigade being a part of the force sent to the support of Gen. Polk, and one of the two which attacked a Union force of fifteen guns supported by infantry. The Confederates were repulsed, having lost about a third of their men, and he was again wounded. He was able, however, to be at the battle of Chickamauga, Sept. 19, 1863, where his brigade was the first in contact with the Union army. On the second day, in the attack of Breckinridge's division, he fought his way to the rear of the Union intrenchments, but when reinforcements came up was driven back. Once more he was wounded. Gen. D. H. Hill, commenting on his gallantry, said, "It was difficult for me to decide which the most to admire, his courage in the field or his unparalleled cheerfulness under suffering" (quoted in biographical sketch of Adams in *Louisiana*, p. 23). Soon after recovering from his wounds, Adams was placed in command of a cavalry brigade operating in northern Alabama and Mississippi, and on Sept. 24, 1864, of the district of central Alabama. The conditions were those inevitable in the rear of any army when defeat is impending. Adams had to collect supplies, gather in deserters and malingerers, and suppress bushwhackers. On Mar. 11, 1865 he was given command of the entire state north of the Gulf department. He took part in the defense of Selma against Gen. Wilson, Apr. 2, 1865, and having evacuated Montgomery, fought a battle at Columbus, Ga., Apr. 16. He was paroled at Meridian, Miss., May 9, 1865, and resumed the practice of his profession at New Orleans, where he died. He left a widow, but no children. Brigadier-General Wirt Adams [*q.v.*] was his brother.

[*Official Records; Confed. Mil. Hist.* (1893–99); Alcée Fortier, *Louisiana,* sketches of parishes, towns, events, institutions and persons (1914); Dunbar Rowland, *Mississippi* (1907); *National Republican,* New Orleans, June 14, 1872.]

J. R. M. T.

ADAMS, DUDLEY W. (Nov. 30, 1831–Feb. 13, 1897), horticulturist, and leader in the "granger movement," was born in Winchendon, Mass., the son of Joseph Boynton and Hannah (Whitney) Adams, and a descendant in the eighth generation of Henry Adams of Braintree, Mass. When he was four years old his family moved to a small rocky farm, where he spent his boyhood and youth. He was bright and eager to learn, and after passing through the public schools became a teacher. When he was twenty-one years old he went west, and with his small savings took up a piece of government land, becoming one of the first settlers of Waukon, Ia. He learned surveying, and was for ten years the assessor of the county. In 1856 he established Iron Clad Nursery, and in a comparatively short time developed an orchard of 4,000 trees, which was one of the best in that section of the country. When the National Grange of the Patrons of Husbandry was organized he became one of its most active promoters, and in 1873 was elected its Master. He was the father of the first attempt at railroad-freight legislation, and had a hand in framing some of the proposals for fixing rates and forbidding discriminations, which were introduced into the Congress of 1873–74. No federal legislation was secured at that time, owing to opposition on the ground of unconstitutionality, but in Iowa a law embodying the ideas of the Grangers was passed, which was held constitutional. The result of the agitation which Adams helped to stimulate was the establishment of nation and state regulation of railroads. In 1875 he went to Florida, where he planted an extensive orchard of orange and other fruit trees, and did much to develop intelligent horticultural industry, as he had previously done in Iowa. He organized the State Horticultural Society and became its president, holding that office until his death. He was studiously inclined, of progressive tendencies, and a man of great energy. His service in organizing the farmers, awakening them to self-consciousness, and uniting them in efforts to promote their interests, especially with relation to railroad transportation, was of great importance.

[A. W. Adams, *Gen. Hist. of Henry Adams of Braintree, Mass., and his Descendants* (1898); L. H. Bailey, *Cyc. of Am. Ag.* (1904), IV, 548; O. H. Kelley, *Origin and Progress of the Order of Patrons of Husbandry in the U. S. 1866–73* (1875); E. W. Martin (James D. McCabe), *Hist. of the Grange Movement; or, the Farmers' War against Monopolies* (1874); T. C. Atkeson, *Semi-Centennial Hist. of the Patrons of Husbandry* (1916).]

E. H. J.

ADAMS, EBENEZER (Oct. 22, 1765–Aug. 15, 1841), educator, was reared on a farm in New Ipswich, N. H., the son of Ephraim and Rebecca Locke Adams. There were eighteen other children, and his father was a man of only moderate means. Opportunities for anything but work were therefore few, but he was an ambitious lad and not easily discouraged. A singing-school teacher once told him that his voice was so rasping that he "better save it to saw wood with"; nevertheless, he continued practicing and in time became a fairly good singer. He showed the same persistency in the matter of an education. Though he had to wait until he was twenty-one years old, he then began preparing for college at the local academy, the principal of which, John Hubbard, he was afterward to succeed as professor in Dartmouth College. Had he been born a hundred years later, his athletic prowess might have opened an academic career for him earlier, for at the age of nineteen he was chosen to defend the honors of New Hampshire in wrestling against three brothers who came over the line from Ashburnham, Mass. This he did conclusively. At the age of twenty-two he entered Dartmouth and graduated with honors in the class of 1791. The following year he became preceptor of the academy at Leicester, Mass., where he remained until 1806. He was no mere pedant, but a leading citizen of the town, serving as justice of the peace and as its first postmaster. On July 9, 1795, he married Alice, daughter of Dr. John Frink of Rutland, Mass., who died June 20, 1805, leaving five children. From Leicester he went to Portland, Me., where he taught in an academy. While here he married, May 17, 1807, Beulah, daughter of Timothy Minot of Concord, Mass., by whom he had two children. In 1808 he became the first professor of mathematics and natural philosophy at Phillips Academy, Exeter, N. H. Apparently the trustees of Dartmouth had had their eyes on him for some years, for in 1804 when they elected his former teacher, John Hubbard, professor of mathematics and philosophy, they stipulated that in case Hubbard declined, the chair was to be offered to Adams. In 1809 they elected the latter to the chair of languages, and at Hubbard's death, a year later, Adams became his successor. He remained at Dartmouth the rest of his life, relinquishing his chair to his son-in-law, Ira Young, in 1833, and becoming professor emeritus.

He is described by a pupil as "well-proportioned, broad-shouldered, with a commanding presence and amiable countenance. He was bold, earnest, energetic; persevering, artless, and honest as the day. He said exactly what he meant. His vision was clear, strong, and accurate. Imagination was never active; oratory was not his forte. Demonstrative evidence suited him best" (B. P. Smith, *History of Dartmouth College,* 1878, p. 244). During his term of service occurred the celebrated dispute between the State and the college. In 1816 the legislature passed an act amending the original charter, changing the name of the college to "Dartmouth University," increasing the number of trustees, and providing for state control through a board of overseers. Under the new arrangement certain of the old trustees were removed, President Francis Brown [*q.v.*] and Professors Adams and Shurtleff, the only two permanent professors, were deposed, and the "University" organized and opened. Although excluded from the college buildings, the old faculty held its ground and continued the college in a hired hall, contending that the action of the legislature was illegal. They were finally upheld by the United States Supreme Court in the famous "Dartmouth College Case." During this critical period Adams with his indomitable spirit and persistency was a tower of strength. Had he or his colleagues weakened, it is said, the original trustees would have surrendered. A hint at the extent of his activity may be derived from an entry in the diary of the Massachusetts printer, Isaiah Thomas (*Transactions and Collections of the American Antiquarian Society,* IX, 373–74), "Mr. Ebenr. Adams, one of the Professors of Dartmouth College, called on me. He is on a mission to collect a sum to enable the government of the College to defend their claims in the S. C. of the United States in Washington against the government of Dartmouth University." For more than two years during President Brown's sickness and after his death, he filled the office of president, although administrative work was not congenial to him. In addition to his varied services to the college, he found time for philanthropic and religious work, being president of the Bible Society in New Hampshire, interested in the Colonization Society, which he judged the only hope of removing the evil of slavery, and active in the cause of foreign missions and temperance.

[Geo. T. Chapman, *Sketches of the Alumni of Dartmouth Coll.*(1867); Emory Washburn, *Hist. Sketches of the Town of Leicester, Mass.*(1860); *New Eng. Hist. and Geneal. Reg.,* I; Chas. H. Chandler and Sarah F. Lee, *Hist. of New Ipswich, N.H.*(1914); Frederic Kidder and A. A. Gould, *Hist. of New Ipswich*(1852); John K. Lord, *Hist. of Dartmouth Coll.*(1913).]

H. E. S.

ADAMS, EDWIN (Feb. 3, 1834–Oct. 28, 1877), one of the most popular actors of his day and considered one of America's best light comedians, was born at Medford, Mass. He adopted the stage career in 1853, making his first appearance at the National Theatre, Boston, on Aug. 29 of that year, as Stephen in Sheridan Knowles's play *The Hunchback.* Two months later he appeared in the same city, at the Athenæum, as Bernardo in *Hamlet.* The following year, on Sept. 20, he acted the part of Charles Woodley in *The Soldier's Daughter* at the Chestnut Street Theatre, Philadelphia. But it was not until he was seen in Baltimore a few years later, when he scored a big hit, that he attracted any particular attention. His reputation now established, he became a star, making appearances in all the principal cities of the country. He was seen in *Hamlet* with Kate Bateman in 1860, and on Feb. 3, 1869 he played Mercutio to Edwin Booth's Romeo at the inauguration of the new Booth Theatre, New York City. During the engagement at Booth's Theatre, he was seen in *Narcisse,* as Raphael in *The Marble Heart,* and as Iago to Booth's Othello. The following week he played the Moor to Booth's Iago. Later, he was seen as Rover in *Wild Oats* and as Claude in *The Lady of Lyons,* and for some time continued as leading man at Booth's, his repertory including all the chief rôles in tragedy. On June 21 he was seen for the first time as Enoch Arden, in a dramatization of Tennyson's pathetic narrative poem. The play proved an enormous success and he appeared in it all over the United

States. Joseph Jefferson in his *Autobiography* writes concerning Adams's interpretation: "The animation of his face, the grace of his person, and, above all, the melody of his voice well fitted him for the stage. While he could not fairly be called a great artist, he was something more highly prized—a born actor, a child of nature if not of art, swayed by warm impulse rather than by premeditation. His Enoch Arden, so far as the character is related to the stage, was a creation entirely his own, and one, too, that touched the sympathies of his audience" (p. 323). Adams was the original in America of Ivan Khorvitch in Tom Taylor's drama *The Serf,* first performed at Philadelphia in September 1865, and he was also seen as Robert Landry in *The Dead Heart.* His last appearance as an actor was at the California Theatre, San Francisco, May 27, 1876, when he played Iago to the Othello of John E. McCullough. In 1877, when he was overtaken by ill health and misfortune, a series of benefit performances was given for him at the Academy of Music, New York City, in which McCullough participated, and netted $10,000. His last appearance in public was at the California Theatre, Feb. 12, 1877, when, at another benefit, he was unable to act himself but occupied a chair in the centre of the stage. William Winter writes of him: "Everybody loved Adams. Sothern (Edward A. Sothern) was devotedly attached to him. In his day he was one of the blithest spirits in all the bright world of the stage" (*Other Days,* pp. 192-93).

[William Winter, *Other Days* (1908); T. A. Brown, *Hist. of the Am. Stage* (1870); T. A. Brown, *Hist. of the N.Y. Stage* (1903).]

A.H.

ADAMS, ELIPHALET (Mar. 26, 1677–Oct. 4, 1753), clergyman, was an early New England divine of high standing and influence. He was born in Dedham, Mass., where his father, Rev. William Adams, was pastor. His mother was Mary, daughter of William Manning of Cambridge, Mass. A journal which Adams kept for a brief period opens with the following statements: "Anno 1677, March 26. I was born a sinner into an evil world. 1679, June 24. My mother died. 1685, August 17. My father left this evil world and left me an orphan to God's Providence and a wide world." Friends assisted him in getting an education and in 1694 he graduated from Harvard College. Where he received his theological training is not known, but under date of Nov. 20, 1696, his journal states: "I came first to Little Compton to preach among ym." The next two entries disclose the nature of the work in which he was next engaged: "1698, July 12. I was put in to be an Indian preacher by the Gentlemen who have the oversight of yt work. 1699, May. I preached my first sermon to the Indians in their own language with fears lest I should be a Barbarian to ym, but yy told me yy understood it well and accepted it thankfully." From 1701–3 he was assistant to Rev. Benjamin Colman at Brattle Street Church, Boston. His reputation became such that when Rev. Gurdon Saltonstall was elected governor of Connecticut, he was chosen to succeed him as pastor at New London, and was ordained to take charge of the church there on Feb. 9, 1708/9. In this capacity he continued for forty-three years. On Dec. 15, 1709, he married Lydia, daughter of Alexander and Lydia Pygan of New London, by whom he had six children. She died Sept. 6, 1749, and on Sept. 21, 1751 he was married by Mather Byles in Boston to Elizabeth Wass.

He was a man of discretion, well-balanced mind, and great stability of character, often resorted to for counsel by the churches of the colony when troubles arose. His own church he guided successfully through a stormy period. During it the Baptists founded their first society in New London; the Episcopalians formed a church out of his congregation; and the New Lights created much unrest; but with quietness, tact, and firmness he held to his course, stigmatized by the New Lights as "a dumb dog that would not bark." In addition to his pastoral duties, he took youths into his home and prepared them for the ministry. He also continued his activities among the Indians, acting as a missionary to the Pequots, Mohegans, and Niantics. From 1720 to 1738 he was a trustee of Yale College, and his influence upon the institution is said to have been great. In 1724 (F. B. Dexter, *Biographical Sketches of the Graduates of Yale College with Annals of the College History, 1701–1745,* 1885, pp. 289–90) the rectorship of Yale was offered him, and he was strongly urged to accept it. He laid the matter before a meeting of the town, Apr. 16, 1724, and declared his willingness to abide by its decision. The townspeople voted that they could not let him go, and he declined the appointment. He died in New London in his seventy-seventh year and was buried there.

[*Colls. Mass. Hist. Soc.* (1852), vol. I, 4th ser.; W. B. Sprague, *Annals Am. Pulpit* (1857), vol. I; Frances M. Caulkins, *Hist. of New London* (1852); W. H. Starr, *A Centennial Hist. Sketch of New London* (1876).]

H. E. S.

ADAMS, FREDERICK UPHAM (Dec. 10, 1859–Aug. 28, 1921), inventor, author, was born in Boston, Mass., and died at Larchmont, N. Y. His parents were John Spencer and Emeline

(Smith) Adams, the former a veteran of the Civil War and a mechanical engineer. To a general education in the public schools of Elgin, Ill., was added a thorough mechanical training under his father, which qualified him for several years' service (1880–83) as a machine designer in Chicago. In 1884, in collaboration with his father, he was granted letters patent on an electric-light tower—a lofty mast supporting a battery of arc-lamps—which for several years was widely used in the illumination of cities. His interest in street lighting led to his invention of an electric-lamp support in 1885, and of an electric-lamp post in 1889, the latter the standard structure since generally adopted. From electric lighting he turned to railroads, with special reference to designing rolling-stock for speed, and in January 1893 was granted seven letters patent on a railroad car and train, with suitable equipment and special housing for locomotive and tender. In 1900 an experimental train constructed from his designs for the Baltimore & Ohio Railroad proved capable of a sustained speed of over 100 miles per hour. A discussion of his theory and designs is found in his work, *Atmospheric Resistance and its Relation to the Speed of Railway Trains* (1892). In the meantime, Adams had established a reputation in journalism and authorship, but reappeared in the Patent Office, in 1914–15, with applications for an improved road-bed and leveler and a new type of vehicle tire.

Early in his journalistic experience, he developed marked interest in sociology and labor problems, which led to his service, during several years, as labor editor of the *Chicago Tribune*. He reported the anarchist uprising of 1886, and numerous labor strikes following it, and in 1893 founded a reform magazine, *The New Time*, which he conducted for several years. He was western press representative of the Democratic National Convention of 1892, and chief of the Democratic Library and Press Bureau in 1896. His only public service was in the office of chief of smoke inspection of Chicago, during 1894–97. As a writer on social and economic subjects, he early espoused the theory of direct legislation, which he advocated in his book, *The Majority Rule League of the United States* (1898). His other books, dealing principally with sociologic and political matters, are: *President John Smith* (1897), "the story of a peaceful revolution"; *The Kidnapped Millionaires* (1901), "a tale of Wall Street and the Tropics"; *John Burt* (1903), "a study of masterful character"; *Colonel Monroe's Doctrine* (1903); *How Cities are Governed in Great Britain* (1904); *John Henry Smith* (1905), a novel; *The Bottom of the Well* (1906), a tale of smugglers and anarchists; *The Revolt* (1907); *The Waters-Pierce Case in Texas* (1908); *The Oil War in Mexico* (1909); *The Plot that Failed* (1912), dealing with the alleged bribery activities of Edward Hines in securing the election of William Lorimer to the United States Senate; *The Conquest of the Tropics* (1914), the story of the United Fruit Company; *Woodrow Wilson vs. Woodrow Wilson* (1919); and *The Open Shop* (1919). In his later years, Adams gained recognition as an authority on aviation, a subject discussed by him in several series of newspaper articles. He was an expert, also, on bridge and other games of cards (see Stephen B. Ayres, *Bridge*, 1909). His wife was Alice Mary Whitaker, whom he married in 1884.

[*Who's Who in America* and general biog. colls.; *Bookm.*, July 1905, portr.; *N.Y. Times*, *N.Y. Tribune*, Aug. 30, 1921; records of the U. S. Patent Office.]

ADAMS, GEORGE BURTON (June 3, 1851–May 26, 1925), college professor, historian, was born at Fairfield, Vt. He was of old New England ancestry, a son of Emeline Nelson and Rev. Calvin Carlton Adams, a Congregational clergyman. He attended district schools but was prepared for college by his father, entering Beloit, where he took his A.B. in 1873, and his A.M. in 1876. Intending to enter the ministry, he took his B.D. at Yale in 1877; but went at once into teaching and was professor of history at Drury College from 1877 to 1888. With leave of absence from that post, he studied abroad, taking his Ph.D. in history at Leipzig in 1886. Two years afterward, in 1888, he was appointed professor of history in Yale College, where he spent the remainder of his life. He married Ida Mary Clarke of Beloit, July 1, 1878.

Adams's earliest publications did much to promote the study of medieval history in the United States. After editing Duruy's *History of the Middle Ages* (1891), he published in 1894 his own admirable survey of that period, *Civilization during the Middle Ages*, which went through many editions and greatly influenced the teaching and conception of the subject. He had earlier issued a preliminary study on *Mediæval Civilization* in 1883; and in 1899 he published a text-book of *European History*. Besides these he issued in 1896 a sketch of the *Growth of the French Nation*, which had wide circulation and influence. Interested at all times in the development of the imperial federation movement in the British Empire, he published *Rise of Imperial Federalism* (1896), *Origin and Results of Imperial Federation Movement in England* (1899), and *The British Empire and a League of Peace* (1917). But his main concern and contribution lay in the field of the English constitution. In 1905 he published his *History of England from the Norman Conquest to the death of John, 1066–1216,* as volume II of Hunt and Poole's *Political History of England*—the only American contribution to that series. After his retirement from the active work of instruction in 1917, he summed up the study of a lifetime in a series of volumes: a *Constitutional History of England* (1920); the *Origin of the English Constitution* (1920); an *Outline Sketch of English Constitutional History* (1918); and the summation of his studies in medieval English legal and constitutional history, *Council and Courts in Anglo-Norman England,* published posthumously in 1926. In this series of works lies his chief contribution to historical knowledge and his chief claim to the eminent position he achieved in scholarship in England and the United States.

His influence was not confined to his writings. He was an active and useful member of various learned bodies—corresponding member of the Royal Historical Society; Fellow of the American Academy of Arts and Sciences; member of the Colonial Society of Massachusetts and of the Massachusetts Historical Society; a leading member of the American Historical Association, a member of its executive council, an editor of the *American Historical Review* (1895–1913), and president of the Association (1907–8). Above all, perhaps, he was a great teacher. An admirable lecturer, clear, accurate, forcible; an exceptional and inspiring conductor of the work of more advanced students in his seminary, which was one of the chief centers of graduate instruction in his field in the United States; a most helpful and judicious adviser; had he written nothing his influence on his students would still have marked him as a leader of scholarship. Through many years he was a leading figure in Yale University, in whose affairs he took an absorbing interest, and in whose counsels he was one of the most weighty advisers. He was possessed of an unusually clear, logical, and analytical mind, extraordinary industry, wide and accurate knowledge. His scholarship within his chosen field was of the highest order; and, though no "literary historian," his writing partook of the quality of his mind in striking degree. His influence was great both upon scholarship and education in the field of history. Belonging as he did to the school of constitutional historians, he none the less, especially in his work on medieval civilization and that on imperial federation, entered the wider fields of cultural and political affairs, where he carried the same qualities which distinguished his special work, a peculiar sanity of judgment and clarity of exposition, which contributed to his eminent place in his profession.

[*Who's Who in America,* 1924–25; *Yale Alumni Weekly,* June 5, 1925; *New Haven Jour. Courier,* May 27, 1925; *N.Y. Times,* May 28, 1925.]

W.C.A.

ADAMS, HANNAH (Oct. 2, 1755–Dec. 15, 1831), compiler of historical information, was one of the Massachusetts Adamses, fifth in descent from Henry Adams of Braintree, and a distant cousin of President John Adams. She was born in Medfield, and from her father, Thomas, Jr., only son of a wealthy farmer, she seems to have derived many of her traits. He cared for nothing but books. Poor health deprived him of a college education, however, and he remained at home, marrying, in 1750, Elizabeth Clark. At his father's death he rented the farm to a man who sadly defrauded him, and opened a store for the sale of "English goods" and books. At storekeeping he was a failure, and he was soon reduced to poverty. A contemporary writes that he was a man of no thrift, but such a greedy devourer of books that he was commonly called "Book Adams." "He was altogether a curiosity, a locomotive library. He was much better than an index, for he could not only tell one where to find any fact in the multitude of voyages, travels, histories, and books of antiquities which he had read, but could recite for hours and days their various details. . . . His lean image on his lean walking or ambling pony, with a volume open before his eyes, and with his saddle-bags stuffed with his daughter's books to be distributed or vended, is still fresh in our recollections" (*American Monthly Review,* May 1832).

From childhood, Hannah had a frail constitution. She had also her father's avidity for knowledge, and his retentive mind. "I remember that my first idea of the happiness of Heaven," she writes, "was of a place where we should find our thirst for knowledge fully gratified." Though not quite so unpractical as her father, she was ridiculously absent-minded, and many stories circulated regarding her peculiarities. Her mother died when she was eleven and her father married again. She was too frail to go to school, but theological students whom her father boarded grounded her in Latin, Greek, geography, and logic. Thrown largely upon her own resources, she earned money during the Revolutionary War by making lace, and did some tutoring. A theological student introduced her to Broughton's *Dictionary of Religions,* which incited her to read widely on the subjects with which it deals. Disgusted with the lack of candor in the authors, she began to compile information about religion and sects and to attempt descriptions of them which would be accurate and unbiased. The result was her *Alphabetical Compendium of the Various Sects Which Have Appeared from the Beginning of the Christian Era to the Present Day* (1784). The book was a success, but the publisher got most of the proceeds. Encouraged, however, she determined to devote herself to similar work, and was probably the first woman in America to make writing a profession. "It was poverty," she says, "not ambition, or vanity, that first induced me to become an author, or rather compiler." A second edition, appearing in 1791, brought the author a considerable emolument. In 1799 she published *A Summary History of New England,* and in 1805 an abridgment of the same for school use. In the meantime her eyesight had failed, and she labored thereafter under this handicap. Her school history had been anticipated by one written by Rev. Jedidiah Morse, who, she claimed, had infringed upon her rights. A controversy ensued which enlisted many disputants and extended over a period of ten years (see *A Narrative of the Controversy Between the Rev. Jedidiah Morse, D.D. and the Author,* by Hannah Adams, 1814, and *An Appeal to the Public,* etc., by Jedidiah Morse, 1814). A number of prominent people, including Hon. Josiah Quincy, Stephen Higginson, and William S. Shaw, appreciating her literary services, settled a life-annuity upon her. In 1804 Miss Adams published *The Truth and Excellence of the Christian Religion.* This contains sketches of eminent laymen who have written in defense of Christianity and extracts from their writings. In 1812 appeared her *History of the Jews,* and in 1826, *Letters on the Gospels.* A portrait of her was painted by Chester Harding, and hung in the Boston Athenæum. She died in Boston and is buried in Mount Auburn Cemetery. While her works contain nothing original, they are compilations from many sources, carefully made, and woven together with skill, clear and readable. The usefulness of her *Dictionary of Religions* in its day is attested by the fact that it went through four editions in this country and was republished in England.

[The chief source of information is *A Memoir of Miss Hannah Adams,* written by herself and edited with additions by Mrs. Hannah F. Lee (1832). See also *A Geneal. Hist. of Henry Adams of Braintree, Mass., and his Descendants* (1898); Olive M. Tilden, "Hannah Adams," in the *Dedham Hist. Reg.,* July 1896; and Wm. S. Tilden, *Hist. of the Town of Medfield, Mass.* (1887). On the Adams-Morse controversy, in addition to references given, see Samuel T. Armstrong, *Remarks on the Controversy between Dr. Morse and Miss Adams* (1814).] H. E. S.

ADAMS, HENRY BROOKS (Feb. 16, 1838–Mar. 27, 1918), historian, was the great-grandson of John Adams, the grandson of John Quincy Adams, and the son of Charles Francis Adams who married Abigail Brown, third daughter of Peter Chardon Brooks. Though Henry Adams, for reasons best known to himself, dropped the Brooks from his name in the course of the seventies, that side of his ancestry was by no means negligible. At the time of his death Peter Chardon Brooks was reputed to be the wealthiest man in Boston and he left a goodly estate to be divided among his children. Henry Adams owed much to his maternal grandfather. Although he was born under the shadow of Boston State House on Beacon Hill, he always felt as a child that he belonged to Quincy, where his grandfather Adams lived and where the family spent their summers. He was less favored physically than his two elder brothers, falling behind them in stature "and proportionally in bone and weight"; and perhaps in consequence was less aggressive in temper. There may have been compensations, however, in greater emotional capacity and more delicate perceptions. He always believed his early education to have been singularly defective; but an education which permitted a boy of ten to hear the table-talk of men like John G. Palfrey, Richard Henry Dana, and Charles Sumner, frequent visitors at the house on Mt. Vernon St. when his own father was candidate for the vice-presidency on the Free-Soil ticket, was hardly defective, at least on its political side. In the intimate family circle there was much reading aloud—the emphasis falling rather heavily on political literature, though the children heard their father read also Longfellow and Tennyson. Dickens and Thackeray they read for themselves, and Henry found his father's library shelves full of the works of eighteenth-century poets and historians which he devoured. His happiest moments were those when he lay on a dusty heap of Congressional documents in the old homestead at Quincy, reading Walter Scott's romances. Of hours spent at Mr. Dixwell's School he had only bitter recollections. For Harvard College, where he matriculated as a matter of course—all young men of good families in Boston did—he had no particular aversion. It was a good school as schools went. he conceded, but it did not give him what he most needed. As for social contacts, Harvard contributed nothing which an Adams did not already possess.

Looking back through the haze of years, Henry Adams could recall only two potent influences at Harvard—Louis Agassiz, who lectured on glaciers and paleontology, and James Russell Lowell, who permitted him to read in his study. Lowell had brought back from the continent some perception of the educational value of friendly and intimate converse between instructor and student; and the alert mind of this Boston lad could hardly have failed to respond. The reading he did in Lowell's study counted for far less than this stimulating conversation on all manner of subjects. Small wonder that the routine of formal instruction in the class-room irked the boy. He made little effort to win scholastic honors; and, as he afterward learned, he was graded precisely in the middle of his class (*Education,* edition of 1918, pp. 59–60). He preferred to win distinction elsewhere and in a measure he succeeded. He wrote for college periodicals, made some addresses in literary societies, won a second prize for a dissertation in his senior year, and to his great surprise was chosen class orator.

It may have been one of those unscheduled conversations with Lowell that turned his thoughts to post-graduate study in Germany. He thought he would like to study the civil law in Berlin. Thither he went in November 1858 by way of London and Antwerp and matriculated at the university, only to find himself helpless for want of any mastery of the language. In the end German methods of instruction appealed to him as little as the ways of Harvard, and his enthusiasm for the civil law rapidly evaporated. He spent a second winter in Dresden and then, in the spring of 1860, frankly turned tourist and crossed the Alps to Florence and to Rome. At Naples the spirit of adventure took possession of him. Learning that Garibaldi and his thousand were threatening Palermo, he made up his mind to see these red-shirted revolutionists. He managed to secure permission from the American minister to serve as dispatch-bearer to the captain of an American war vessel in the harbor of Palermo, and so actually met Garibaldi face to face. In letters to the *Boston Courier* he has described this meeting and the *mise en scène* of this extraordinary revolution (two of these are reprinted in the *American Historical Review,* XXV, 241 ff.). A few more months spent in Paris with no very serious purpose completed this first European sojourn. In November he was back in Quincy again, not much wiser about the civil law, but richer by a good many emotional experiences.

Again putting the *Institutes* and *Pandects* aside, he went to Washington as his father's secretary during that memorable session of Congress in the winter of 1860–61. It was not his first visit to the Capital. As a boy of ten he had been taken to visit his grandmother Adams, and incidentally he had been taken to see President Taylor, feeling all the time, he said in after years, as though the White House belonged to the Adamses and never doubting that he himself would live there some day. He was less sure of his destiny in the Washington of 1861. Of the currents and counter-currents that swirled through the Capital in these winter months he wrote a vivid description, which, however, did not appear in print for fifty years (*Proceedings of the Massachusetts Historical Society,* XLIII, 656–87). Nevertheless life was not all politics and Adams had his part in the frivolities of the Capital. After the end of the session he returned to Boston and his lawbooks and might have found his vocation at the bar but for the firing on Fort Sumter.

While his brother Charles and many of his friends were enlisting in Massachusetts regiments, he yielded with no little reluctance to his father's wishes and set out for London as his secretary. He consoled himself with the thought that after all he was probably not cut out for a soldier, but the rout at Bull Run, which he took almost as a personal disgrace, made him think otherwise. He wrote passionately to Charles that he must have a commission—he could reach home in three weeks—he wishes it to be understood that he is in earnest—if Charles can't get a commission for him, he will try to get it by other means. To which the older brother replied coldly, "You are not particularly well-fitted for the army. Here is your field right before your nose . . . and you want to rush away to do what neither education nor nature fitted you for" (*Cycle of Adams Letters,* I, 30–31). This advice was so sound that Henry's bellicose mood vanished, leaving him dejected and despondent. His life seemed to him a failure. He had not found a career and he saw no prospect of finding one. He was tired of life. He had lost faith in himself (*Ibid.,* I, 112–13, 195–96). To which outpouring the elder brother replied, "I do wish you took a little more healthy view of life." By the time this letter reached its destination Henry was taking a more healthy view of life. Some months later, in almost a jubilant mood, he wrote to Charles that he had been in a party of eleven—Lytton, Browning, and others. "I had a royal evening; a feast of remarkable choiceness, for the meats were very excellent good, the wines were rare and plentiful, and the company was of earth's choicest" (*Ibid.,* II, p. 9). Doors opened to this young American on his own account and not merely because he was his father's son. He was a welcome guest in Devonshire House, at Sir Charles Trevelyan's where he met Sir Charles Lyell, and especially at Wenlock Abbey in Shropshire where the Gaskells dispensed a gracious hospitality.

As secretary his work was exacting and confining so long as the war continued. "My candles are seldom out before two o'clock in the morning," he wrote in July 1863, "and my table is piled with half-read books and unfinished writing" (*Ibid.*, II, 62). Yet he must have done a surprising amount of solid reading. John Stuart Mill and De Tocqueville he studied assiduously as "the two high priests of our faith," and he became an ardent follower, for a time, of Auguste Comte whose determinism fitted in well with his mood. The end of the Civil War and the prospect of an early return to the United States brought Adams face to face with the choice of a career. He was now twenty-seven and he had lost precious time if he were to continue the study of law. Occasionally he had written articles of timely interest for newspapers. He had a mind to try his hand at more serious writing. A chance meeting in London with John G. Palfrey, an old friend of his family, who had been editor of the *North American Review*, gave direction to his half-formed purpose. At Palfrey's suggestion he wrote the article on Captain John Smith which was published in the *North American Review*, January 1867. Encouraged by this success, he wrote two other articles, each costing several months of hard labor, which were accepted by the editor and published in successive numbers—"British Finance in 1816" (April 1867) and "The Bank of England Restriction of 1797–1821" (October 1867).

Meantime, Minister Adams was not recalled and his secretary stayed loyally by his side. An intimacy with the Lyells brought him inevitably into touch with the evolutionary views associated with Darwin and his *Origin of Species* and with the problems of geology. When Sir Charles Lyell brought out a new edition of his *Principles of Geology*, Adams undertook to review it for American readers. This article, too, was printed in the *North American Review* (October 1868). For the first time Adams caught the significance for human history of the evolutionary concept. As an old man he recalled how he had wrestled with these problems as he rambled over the hills of Shropshire, where Roman roads and ruins bore witness to the supersession of one civilization by another, and where fossils under foot told the tale of the evolution of vertebrates. Never again could Henry Adams return to absolute standards, as his Puritan forebears had held them. Seven years of English life had put him out of touch with American ways, as he found on his return in midsummer of 1868. After London, American society seemed to him "a long, straggling caravan, stretching loosely toward the prairies, its few score of leaders far in advance and its millions of immigrants, negroes, and Indians far in the rear" (*Education*, p. 237). Washington seemed on the whole the best substitute for London and a strategic point for a young journalist. Thither Adams went in the fall of 1868 to pick up what copy he could for an occasional letter to the *Nation* and for more substantial contributions to the reviews. He spent months preparing an article on finance which was finally published in the *Edinburgh Review* (April 1869) and then set himself to writing a review of the last Congress, borrowing his title from Lord Robert Cecil's annual review in the London *Quarterly*. "The Session" appeared in the *North American Review* of April 1869 and a second article in July 1870. Meantime, he had also written a trenchant article on Civil Service Reform (*North American Review*, October 1869), and an historical account of the Legal Tender Act (*Ibid.*, April 1870).

The attempt of Jay Gould to corner gold in 1869, and the political ramifications of the plot offered an intriguing subject which he wrote up in "The New York Gold Conspiracy" and sent to his friend Henry Reeve, never doubting that he would publish it in his *Edinburgh Review*. Shortly afterward he himself crossed the Atlantic again to enjoy the London season. Reeve declined to publish "The Gold Conspiracy"; so, too, did the editor of the *Quarterly*, but it was finally accepted by the editor of the *Westminster Review*. It was while he was in England that Adams received a letter from the new president of Harvard inviting him to become assistant professor of history. His first instinct was to decline the honor as wholly beyond the range of his interests and capacity. On reaching home, however, he found that he was to teach medieval history and at the same time to conduct the *North American Review*. An interview with President Eliot convinced him that he should try the new rôle. Either post alone would have conferred distinction; and, after all, what prospect was there for a young man of his training and intelligence in the stodgy world of Washington under the Grant régime? In *The Education of Henry Adams* (p. 332) he alludes to Senator Don Cameron as belonging to "the very class of American politician who had done most to block his intended path in life." It is the only intimation that as a young man he had looked forward to a political career. American politics in 1870 offered no career to talent; and Adams, partly from natural sensitiveness and shyness and partly from long residence in England, could not, or would not, make the necessary advances to those in party conclave who had offices and favors to confer. In July 1870 the *North American Review* printed his second article on

"The Session," essentially an indictment of the Grant administration. It was promptly reprinted by the Democratic National Committee and widely circulated as a campaign document.

In after years Adams had a poor opinion of his work as a college teacher. It was probably true, as he intimated, that nine out of ten students successfully withstood the impact of knowledge; but the tenth man responded, and Adams deliberately sought to cultivate this tenth mind. The little group that he interested in the origins of English constitutional law was the first historical seminar in the United States, though he would have repudiated the German appellation. One of this group recalls with satisfaction the meetings at the house which Adams subsequently occupied on Marlboro St. in Back Bay—"in the well-walled library with its open fire" (J. Laurence Laughlin in *Scribner's Magazine,* May 1921). These studies were printed in 1876 in *Essays in Anglo-Saxon Law.* The first of these, on "The Anglo-Saxon Courts of Law," was prepared by Adams. He looked back upon his life in Cambridge as "a social desert that would have starved a polar bear"; but he must have found compensations elsewhere, for, on June 27, 1872, he married Marian Hooper, a daughter of Robert William and Ellen Sturgis Hooper of Boston. Granted leave of absence for a year, he went abroad with his bride and on his return took up his residence in Boston.

After seven years of "laborious banishment" in Boston, Adams gave up his post at Harvard and once more turned to Washington, partly to write history, but chiefly to find companionship among his own kind. "So far as he had a function in life, it was as stable-companion to statesmen," he afterward said ironically. There he found his old friends William M. Evarts, now secretary of state, and John Hay, whom he had learned to know and love in the memorable winter of '61. Thither, too, for longer or shorter intervals, came Clarence King whom Adams had met in the Rockies in the summer of 1871. King, Hay, and Adams became inseparable. Some one named the little coterie of the Adamses, the Hays, and King "the Five of Hearts" (Thayer, *Life of John Hay,* II, 58). Never had there been a *salon* in the Capital, if Hay may be believed, like that over which Mrs. Adams presided with such rare charm (*Letters of Hay,* II, 98–99). Some one in this inner circle, so all Washington believed, must have written the novel *Democracy* which was published anonymously in 1880—some one who knew intimately the interlocking of politics and society at the National Capital. First King was suspected; then Hay; but the paternity belongs unquestionably to Adams (statement of the publisher, Henry Holt, in the *Unpartizan Review,* no. 29, p. 156; information from Mrs. Ward Thoron). From a literary point of view *Democracy* has no great merit, but it was a best-seller in its day, and is still read as a presentation of Washington life in the decade following the Civil War. Less known and seldom read is *Esther,* which Adams published in 1884, under the pseudonym Frances Snow Compton. Adams thought this the better of the two novels, but his opinion was not shared by the buying public. Meantime Adams was studying the beginnings of national government at Washington. The first fruits of this study were *The Life of Albert Gallatin* and *The Writings of Albert Gallatin* (3 vols.), published in 1879. A wealth of material had been put at his disposal by Gallatin's only surviving son and his greatest problem was one of selection. So far as possible Adams let Gallatin's own writings carry the narrative, reserving for himself only the task of clarifying the political background and of maintaining the sequence of events. The biography is marked by a fine restraint and an admirable sense of proportion. Restraint and proportion, however, are both wanting in *John Randolph,* which Adams wrote for the American Statesmen Series in 1882. Randolph was not a congenial subject and should never have been assigned to him. Having no liking for this wayward and eccentric Virginian, he took what material he could from Garland's biography and guessed at what information he did not find about Randolph's youth (see Wm. C. Bruce, *John Randolph of Roanoke,* 1922, preface and chapter III).

Freed from the tyranny of the class-room, possessed of an ample fortune, leisure, and social position, Adams could now follow his own bent and collect material for a thorough-going study of the Jeffersonian régime—that period in which his grandsire had played an unpopular but resolute rôle. Some of this material he edited and published in 1877—*Documents Relating to New England Federalism, 1800–1815.* It was a congenial task, and life was very agreeable, at Washington in winter and at Beverly Farms in summer. Both he and Mrs. Adams were fond of riding, and hours over books alternated with long rides in the country. The summer of 1885 bid fair to be one of more than ordinary interest, for H. H. Richardson was building adjoining houses for Adams and Hay on H St., which they would occupy in the course of the winter. Throughout the summer, however, Mrs. Adams suffered from ill health and on Dec. 6, 1885 she died suddenly under peculiarly tragic circumstances, leaving him to occupy the new house alone and to readjust his life as best he could. To escape from his grief and loneliness Adams went to Japan in the spring of 1886 with John La Farge as a companion. The Orient interested him mildly and diverted his mind after a fashion, but it only accentuated the mystery of life and death and hardly assuaged his grief. It gave him, however, the idea which he commissioned Saint-Gaudens to embody in bronze. The monument in Rock Creek Cemetery which Saint-Gaudens executed after five years is the most tangible result of Adams's contact with the East. "The whole meaning and feeling of the figure," he wrote in reply to a letter from R. W. Gilder (Oct. 14, 1896) "is in its universality and anonymity. My own name for it is 'The Peace of God.' La Farge would call it Kwannon."

Manfully he returned to Washington and began the task of completing his *History of the United States.* His friends rallied about him; his nieces ministered affectionately to him in their frequent visits; he was bound to admit, as time began its silent alchemy, that life was "not so disagreeable." Once again men of distinction and women of charm sought his house; and happy was he who was privileged to breakfast at 1603 H St. These breakfasts became almost an institution in Washington (Thayer, *Hay,* II, 61). Little by little the manuscript of the history grew under his hand, page after page written in a script that was as beautiful and perfect in its way as any that medieval chronicler ever penned. Following the custom he had begun with the first volumes, he had the manuscript privately printed as it was completed and sent these copies, interleaved and bound, to a few intimates in whose critical judgment he had confidence. (Two sets of these with marginal notes by George Bancroft and Charles Francis Adams are in the library of the Massachusetts Historical Society.) The first two volumes covering the first administration of Jefferson were published in 1889; the next four including the second administration of Jefferson and the first of Madison were published in 1890; and the last three on the second administration of Madison appeared in 1891. By general consent these volumes placed Adams in the first rank among American historians. What gave them an authoritative character was his mastery of the diplomatic background, based upon a first-hand acquaintance with the documentary material in foreign archives. Measured by latter-day standards, the history as a whole is deficient on the economic side. The emphasis is always on politics as they found expression in the conduct of the national government. Exception must be made, however, of the first six chapters of the first volume which described economic, social, and intellectual conditions in the United States at the turn of the century. Nothing better had been written and Adams himself never did any better historical writing.

The history finally off his hands, Adams sought rest and recreation in travel. With La Farge again as his companion he journeyed to Hawaii and thence from island to island in the South Sea, sketching a little under La Farge's tutelage and writing much to the friends and nieces at home. At Tahiti, he picked up many of the legendary tales of the island from the former Queen, which he printed privately in 1893 as the *Memoirs of Marau Taaroa, Last Queen of Tahiti.* This collection of tales he amplified and printed at Paris in 1901 (the binders' title is usually *Tahiti*). For many years he wandered whither the spirit listed, without any very clearly defined purpose. He spent a winter with Clarence King in Cuba, a summer with John Hay in the Yellowstone, several summers with the Camerons and with the Cabot Lodges in Europe. He traveled alone through Mexico and the islands of the Caribbean, and repeated the visit with the Camerons the following year. He went to Russia with the Lodges and then wandered off by himself through Sweden. He accompanied John Hay and his wife to Egypt and tried to enjoy Wagner at Baireuth with the Lodges. Always, however, he spent part of the year at his house in Washington, and more and more frequently he sought out Paris and France for seven or eight months of each year. Outwardly this was a singularly unproductive period in his life; spiritually it was the most significant and it bore fruit in the two works for which he will be longest remembered.

The current of Adams's life shifted, if we may trust his own account, after a summer (1895) with the Lodges in Normandy. Strangely enough, he seems never before to have visited Caen, Coutances, and Mont-Saint-Michel. "Through the medium of younger eyes and fresher minds," he now caught the atmosphere and spirit of the twelfth century, as his study of Anglo-Saxon law through German spectacles had never revealed it. He "drifted back to Washington with a new sense of history" (*Education,* p. 355). More and more dissatisfied with the sequences that are called history he sought some unit of measure for the movement of human society. The Paris Exposition of 1900 was a revelation to him. Facing the huge dynamo in the Gallery of Machines, "his historical neck," as he expressed it, "was broken by the irruption of forces totally new." As an expression of energy the dynamo was terrifying and mysterious, but not more mysterious than the

Virgin, he reflected, "the greatest force the western world ever felt." What if all life and thought could be measured in terms of Force? To measure man as a force, motion must be reckoned from a fixed point. Why not take that point of time "when man held the highest idea of himself as a unit in a unified universe"—the twelfth century? He then began what he called "a methodical survey of the century" (*Education,* p. 369), thinking later to make a study of twentieth-century multiplicity, so as to fix the acceleration of movement in human society between these points (*Education,* p. 423).

Such is Adams's own account of the origin of the folio which he printed privately in 1904 under the title *Mont-Saint-Michel and Chartres.* Few if any of his readers, however, suspected this underlying motive. The book was read, and is still read, by people of widely different interests, as a unique interpretative study of medieval life and philosophy, without a thought of its bearing on any dynamic theory of history. Only those who knew Adams intimately could understand the circircumstances that deflected his inner life and turned him from the age of Jefferson to that of Abelard and Saint Thomas Aquinas. He always gave La Farge credit for whatever emotional awakening he experienced in these latter years of his life. La Farge would often say, "Adams, you reason too much." "He should have blamed him," comments Adams, "for being born in Boston." La Farge had taught him much about color values, in the South Seas; and during a sojourn in France he had given Adams his first sense of values in medieval glass and a new interest in life (private letters). Summer after summer he had wandered among the cathedrals of Northern France, letting the Virgin reveal to him the creative spirit of the thirteenth century and then withdrawing "in ignorance and silence" to reflect upon "the eternal mystery of Force."

Adams never supposed that *Mont-Saint-Michel and Chartres* would have any wide appeal (*Letters to a Niece,* pp. 117-18). He printed only a limited number of copies which he presented to friends and to selected libraries (letter of July 19, 1910, in the *Yale Review,* October 1920). Request for copies became increasingly frequent, however, so that he was persuaded to reprint the book, which he did in 1912 after careful revision. By this time it had found so many readers among students of Gothic architecture that the American Institute of Architects through Mr. Ralph Adams Cram asked permission to publish an edition for general sale. Adams consented and the smaller quarto edition of 1913 was put within the reach of the general public. He did not take himself too seriously as a student of architecture or of medieval glass and literature. He acknowledged frankly his indebtedness to Viollet-le-Duc for what he knew about the structure of Gothic cathedrals; and he was equally ready to acknowledge the aid of scholars who knew far more than he did about the origin of the *Chanson de Roland,* the philosophy of Abelard, and the theological system of Saint Thomas Aquinas. To him *Chartres* was not a treatise on any of these subjects but a study of thirteenth-century unity—of the spirit that created Chartres, "the Court of the Queen of Heaven," Amiens, and the "Church Intellectual" of Saint Thomas Aquinas. There are informing chapters on towers and portals, roses and apses, twelfth-century glass and legendary windows, but also chapters of rare beauty and insight on "The Virgin of Chartres" and "The Miracles of Notre Dame." The unique value of the book does not consist in its scholarship, in the ordinary sense of that term, but rather in its interpretative quality, its suggestion of atmosphere, its intuitive glimpses into the medieval soul. "We are not studying grammar or archæology," Adams warns his readers, "and would rather be inaccurate in such matters, if, at that price, a finer feeling of the art could be caught."

Two years after the printing of *Chartres,* Adams presented his intimates with another privately printed folio bearing the title *The Education of Henry Adams.* When published by the Massachusetts Historical Society after his death, it carried the subtitle *An Autobiography.* Autobiography in the ordinary sense of the word it is not, however, and Adams would not have condoned the use of the word. To him it was "a study of twentieth-century multiplicity"—the correlative study to *Chartres* (Editor's Preface to the edition of 1918, which sounds indeed more like Adams than Henry Cabot Lodge). Henry Adams is to be regarded as no more than a manikin on which the toilet of education is draped, so that young men may see the faults of the patchwork fitted on their fathers (Preface). Nearly every one, nevertheless, persisted—and persists—in reading the intriguing volume as biography rather than as a contribution to the philosophy of history. Judgments of the book ran the whole gamut of emotions. There were those who took Adams at his word—adjudged him as indeed a failure, a disappointed Adams possessed of an inferiority complex and grown cynical of all the world; others were repelled by what they called his egotism, his dogmatism, his lack of faith in American democracy; still others were baffled by his reticences—his failure to record twenty years of his life, and mystified by his paradoxes. The younger generation sensed that he was one of them, a rebel against the conventions of education and an intrepid spirit daring to face this "sorry scheme of things entire." There was a degree of justification in all these points of view. Those who thought him self-contained and self-centered, however, found it hard to reconcile this characteristic with his fondness for children and with his capacity for enduring friendship. He was at his best at his own table. There, with those who knew him well, he could indulge his fondness for paradox, for exaggeration, for heresies of all sorts, with a twinkle in his eyes that encouraged retort and laughter. One who was frequently in this circle has said that Adams and his friends loved to play with ideas, to follow a lead regardless of consequences and often of logic—a game that had more of Gallic than American associations. All these characteristics appear in *The Education.* Any one who had seen Adams play with ideas knew that he was not always to be taken literally or even seriously. He exaggerated to provoke reaction. When he declared his education ended in 1871 and his life complete in 1890, he was obviously playing with ideas about life and education. Why fourteen more chapters, if futility is to be written across all the pages? Those who pronounce him a cynic and a misanthrope quite overlook his own statement that "he had enjoyed his life amazingly" (*Education,* p. 316). Yet there is an ironic quality in the book which is characteristic of the man. It is not the irony of an embittered soul, but the irony of one to whom "life was a cosmic exploration" (Thayer, *Life of Hay,* II, 54). He treated it as a great adventure, bore the buffetings of fate as best he could, laughed where he might, but never pretended to understand the meaning of it all.

The concluding chapters of *The Education* trace the steps by which he evolved his dynamic theory of history. The theory was more clearly formulated in the "Rule of Phase applied to History," an essay which he wrote in 1909 (printed by Brooks Adams in *The Degradation of the Democratic Dogma* in 1919). In 1910 Adams published and scattered widely a little volume which he called *A Letter to American Teachers of History.* Its style was designedly colloquial and its tone provocative. Assuming the validity of the second law of thermodynamics, that there is a universal tendency to the dissipation of mechanical energy, he pointed out the dilemma of teachers of history if they postulated a progressive evolution in human history toward some state of perfection, or tried to exempt mind from the operation of this law. What did they propose to do about it? Human thought should be considered as a substance passing from one phase to another, through a series of critical points which are determined by attraction, acceleration, and volume—the equivalents of pressure, temperature, and volume in mechanical physics. In short, the future historian who would interpret the movement called history would have to seek his education in the world of mathematical physics.

It was the fate of Adams to outlive both King and Hay. He closed the story of his education when Hay died in 1905. "It was time to go. The three friends had begun life together; and the last of the three had no motive—no attraction—to carry it on after the others had gone." Yet he lived on for fourteen years, not the least productive years of his life. In 1908 he helped Mrs. Hay make a selection of John Hay's letters which were privately printed; and in 1911 he published a little volume, *The Life of George Cabot Lodge,* an affectionate tribute to Bay Lodge, one of the group to whom he was always "Uncle Henry." In this same year, too, he made a careful revision of *Chartres.* In the following spring he suffered a shock which incapacitated him for some months and left him with impaired vision and strength. It was in these last years that he turned for diversion to the study of medieval songs, still intent upon wresting from life all that it had to offer. The end came while war clouds hung heavy in the spring of 1918. The newspapers of March 28, filled with reports of casualties, could find space only for the bare announcement that Henry Adams, a historian, had died.

[Whether or no *The Education of Henry Adams* (1907) was written as an autobiography, it remains the chief source of information about his intellectual life. It may be supplemented here and there by *A Cycle of Adams Letters* (2 vols., 1920), edited by W. C. Ford; by *Charles Francis Adams, 1835–1915; An Autobiography* (1916); by *The Degradation of the Democratic Dogma* (1919); by "A Niece's Memories" in *Letters to a Niece* (1920), by Mabel La Farge; by *The Life and Letters of John Hay* (2 vols., 1915), by W. R. Thayer. Letters of Henry Adams have been published by Mabel La Farge (*op. cit.*), by F. B. Luquiens and by A. S. Cook in the *Yale Review,* Oct. 1920. Access has been given to collections of letters owned by Joseph H. Schaffner and by Mr. and Mrs. Ward Thoron. To these sources of information should be added the personal recollections of Prof. J. Laurence Laughlin and of Mrs. Ward Thoron.] A. J.

ADAMS, HENRY CARTER (Dec. 31, 1851–Aug. 11, 1921), economist, statistician, was descended from William Adams, who came from Shropshire in 1628, and was the ancestor of a worthy succession, of which the fifth generation settled in New Ipswich, N. H., about the middle of the eighteenth century and developed a sturdy line of farmers, Congregational deacons, and selectmen. Of the eighth generation from the Shropshire yeoman, Ephraim Adams emerged in 1835 as a student at Phillips Academy, Andover, Mass., and was one of a group of fifty to leave the institution when the formation of an anti-slavery society in the Academy was forbidden. Graduated from Dartmouth in 1839, he studied for the ministry at Andover Theological Seminary and on completing his work there joined ten fellow students in 1843 in what became known as the Iowa Band—a group of leaders who devoted their lives to the erection of a Christian commonwealth west of the Mississippi. Marrying Elizabeth Douglass two years later, the young missionary preacher became identified with the building of Iowa (Grinnell) College. At Davenport, on Dec. 31, 1851, a son was born who was named Henry Carter Adams. The boy grew up in the new state without the kind of schooling that most of the youth of that day had, because delicate health made an outdoor life imperative. He did not know what the confinement of a schoolroom was until he was nineteen years of age. In due time, having been tutored by his father, he was ready to avail himself of such inspiration as the faculty of the struggling prairie college could impart, and in 1874 he received his A.B. degree. A year at Andover Seminary having sufficed to convince him that his father's profession was not for him, a mere chance turned his attention to the Johns Hopkins University, just opening at Baltimore, where he was awarded a fellowship. He devoted himself with enthusiasm to the studies in history and economics which he had begun in college. Within two years he received the degree of Ph.D., the first conferred by the young university, and one of the most significant, for it meant that American youths were beginning to think of careers in a field that had been neglected on this side of the Atlantic. He then spent two years in Europe, studying at Berlin and Heidelberg and also in France and England. Returning to America with an unusual equipment, for those days, he was appointed, in 1879, to a Cornell University lectureship in economics. Later he received a similar appointment at the University of Michigan and alternated courses of lectures between the two institutions.

During the strike on the Gould railroad system in 1886, Adams gave expression to views on the relations of capital and labor that displeased an influential member of the board of Cornell trustees and led to his separation from the university. His opinions, if voiced twenty years later, would have been accepted without serious question. They had chiefly to do with the principle of collective bargaining, in which he believed and which later was generally accepted as a basis of relations between corporations and their employees. Indeed within four years the Cornell trustees invited Adams to return, but by that time he had become unwilling to give up the professorship at the University of Michigan to which President Angell had called him immediately on the severance of his relations with Cornell. Meanwhile he had brought out a monograph on "The Relation of the State to Industrial Action" (*Publications of the American Economic Association,* vol. I, 1887), one of the early and effective protests from a growing group of American economists against the hitherto sacrosanct English dogma of laissez faire. In essential agreement with him were the younger men, headed by Prof. Richard T. Ely, of Johns Hopkins, who in the eighties were active in organizing the American Economic Association. Possibly realizing that his thinking in the field of social reform was in advance of his time, he devoted himself for several years to constructive work in public finance. His *Public Debts* appeared in 1887, *The Science of Finance* in 1898. Through Prof. Charles H. Cooley he was enabled to direct the statistical activities of the Interstate Commerce Commission almost from the beginning. He kept up his association with this work until 1911, a period of twenty-four years. He was in charge of the division of transportation of the Eleventh Census. For four years, beginning in 1913, he served as adviser to the Chinese Republic on the standardization of railway accounts. His book, *American Railway Accounting,* appeared in 1918.

In his development of economic theory Adams had ever in mind the progressive advancement of the race. He was far from being a pessimist. Yet his discussions of finance were free from any vague idealism. He was one of the first economists to write fully and authoritatively on the peculiar administrative conditions that exist in America. His influence, direct and indirect, on the students and teachers of economics did not seem to wane during the four decades of his active career. The small group of pioneers among whom he was a leader in 1881 had become by 1921 a great company, in which his primacy was still acknowledged. He was a man of fine presence and bearing, with a personal charm that won for him many warm friendships both within and without the circle of his colleagues and students. He was a lover of music and of good paintings. His artistic tastes, always ready to assert themselves but more or less repressed by the environment of his early years, found gratification in his mature life. He was married in 1890 to Bertha H. Wright of Port Huron, Mich.

[The Adams genealogy is given by Charles H. Chandler and Sarah F. Lee in *Hist. of New Ipswich, N. H., 1735–1914.* Within a few months after Adams's death, a tribute from his colleagues was published, *Jour. Pol.*

Econ., Apr. 1922. Addresses by members of the American Economic Association appeared in the *Am. Econ. Rev.*, Sept. 1922. In addition to the books noted in this article, Adams wrote many reviews and magazine articles. His official reports as statistician of the Interstate Commerce Commission were published continuously from 1887 to 1911. A bibliography of his publications (forty-one titles) compiled by Prof. I. L. Sharfman appeared in the *Jour. Pol. Econ.*, Apr. 1922.] W. B. S.

ADAMS, HENRY CULLEN (Nov. 28, 1850–July 9, 1906), congressman, was born in Oneida County, N. Y., the son of Caroline Shepard and Benjamin Franklin Adams, a professor of the classical languages in Hamilton College. During his early youth the family moved to southern Wisconsin. The boy, who was never vigorous, grew up in the midst of farm influences and thus acquired the devotion to the fields which was the *leit motif* of his whole life. Educated in country schools, he entered Albion College for one year and then spent three years in the University of Wisconsin. His fragile health gave way under the stress of study. On the advice of his physician he left and went to Colorado, where his health temporarily improved. On Oct. 15, 1878 he married Anne Burkley Norton, great-grand-daughter of Mary Smith, sister of Abigail Smith, the wife of President John Adams. Returning to his father's farm near Madison, Wis., he entered with enthusiasm into farm life. He was a leader in farmers' institutes under the auspices of the Wisconsin Agricultural College and became president of the State Horticultural Society and of the Dairymen's Association of Wisconsin. He was a member of the state legislature for two terms and was Dairy and Food Commissioner from 1895 to 1902. In the latter year he was elected to Congress by a plurality of 3,034 votes; in 1904 he was reëlected by a plurality of 7,508.

Adams's most important achievements occurred during his second term in Congress, when, with sadly weakened health and confined to his bed for days at a time, he nevertheless took a leading part in securing the passage of four great constructive measures. These were: the act admitting to statehood New Mexico and Arizona, the National Food and Drugs Act, the Meat Inspection Law, and the Adams Act, providing funds for agricultural researches. At that time the question of whether Arizona and New Mexico should be admitted into the Union as separate states or as one state was before Congress. In the vacation preceding the meeting of the Fifty-ninth Congress Adams made a journey to these two territories for the purpose of studying in person the problems of statehood. He became convinced that the two territories were so different in the character of their inhabitants and in the nature of their prospective duties as states that a combination of the two would be unwise. He therefore espoused dual statehood, and it was largely through his influence that the Fifty-ninth Congress admitted New Mexico and Arizona to the family of states as two distinct entities. The Meat Inspection bill was at first opposed by the packers, who hardly realized the benefit which would accrue to them as well as to the consumers through having at the time of slaughter a regular meat inspection which would insure the absence of trichina. Adams took an active part in bringing the packers and the proponents of the measure into harmony, and the prompt adoption of this measure was largely due to his good judgment in bringing the warring factions to one common purpose. There was no inherent opposition of any consequence to his pet measure, the Adams Act, but the United States had recently appropriated one hundred million dollars a year for the construction of new battleships, and the proposal to spend an additional million for the benefit of agriculture seemed to many a gross extravagance. But Adams succeeded so well in overcoming this opposition that, when the vote was taken, in both the House and the Senate practically unanimous approval was given to his plan. It is small wonder that all this extraordinary activity in legislation should have exhausted his vitality. In the full enjoyment of his victories he died on his way home at the end of the first session of the Fifty-ninth Congress.

[*Wis. Dairy and Food Commission Reports*, 1885 to 1902; *Jour. of Proc. of the Wis. Leg.* for 1883 and 1885; *Cong. Record*, 58 Cong. and 59 Cong., 1 Sess., debates on the Food and Drugs Act and the Adams Ag. Experiment Station Act; the *U.S. Office of Experiment Stations Bull. 184*, pp. 36 ff.; *U.S. Dept. of Ag. Year Bk.* (1906).] H. W. W.

ADAMS, HERBERT BAXTER (Apr. 16, 1850–July 30, 1901), college professor and promoter of historical studies, was born in Shutesbury, Mass., of farmer lineage. His father, Nathaniel Dickinson Adams, a descendant of Henry Adams of Braintree, moved to Amherst and died there in 1856, leaving a widow, Harriet (Hastings) Adams, and three sons with a small income for their support. Herbert Baxter, the youngest, graduated at the head of the class of 1872 at Amherst College, and took the degree of doctor of philosophy *summa cum laude* at Heidelberg in 1876. In that year Johns Hopkins opened its doors, a university founded on the Continental plan, led by a progressive president, and officered by European-trained instructors. It was Adams's good fortune to become one of these professors. He began his teaching by organizing a seminar on the German model. Soon afterwards he organized a "Johns Hopkins Historical and Political Science Association," and soon after that he began the publication of the *Johns Hopkins Studies in Historical and Political Science,* which Prof. Ely calls "the mother of similar series in every part of the United States"; and a few years later he planned and began to write a series of monographs on the history of education in the United States under the auspices of the federal Bureau of Education. He had a genius for organization and was happy when he could give it rein.

Many of his students became greater scholars than their master, and this despite his excellent record in college and university; but none of them had better than he the power to convert a new provincial into an aspiring and assured research student and writer of history. He never lost sight of his old students, writing many letters to them, always giving advice and making suggestions. None of them ever wrote book, pamphlet, or magazine article that he did not send a copy to the Master; nor was the copy received that was not duly presented to Adams's seminar with friendly comment.

Adams was more of a political scientist than historian. Although he took lectures at Heidelberg under Ihne on Roman institutions, Ihne did not attend his examination, which was conducted by Bluntschli and Knies, a political scientist and an economist. Adams's first writings in Baltimore show Bluntschli's influence. "The community," said Bluntschli, "is a preparatory school for the state. The structure of republics has its foundations in the independence of communities." This idea he instilled into Adams's mind, where it developed a new theory of New England social history. The Massachusetts town, Adams said, was but a development out of the English towns and parishes, which were in turn of Germanic origin. "These little communes," said Adams, following his teacher all too faithfully, "were the germs of our state and national life." He added that they were "the primordial cells of the body politic." These views he announced and expanded in three monographs, "The Germanic Origin of New England Towns," "Norman Constables in America," and "Saxon Tithingmen in America," all published in the first volume of the *Johns Hopkins Studies in Historical and Political Science* in 1882 and 1883. The treatment was quite objective and it shocked the old-school historians in New England, who were in the habit of regarding their history as an emanation of Puritan reverence. Others objected on the ground that what they called Adams's "germ theory of American history" did not sufficiently recognize the influence of "Americanism" in our history.

Adams was too much a man of action to devote himself to research, and he was too much interested in the life around him to find a chief interest in the past. The years 1883 and 1884 showed little literary activity, and after that he is seen turning to educational subjects, a phase of history that kept his interest as long as he lived. He wrote on the study of history, on university extension, on boys' schools, on civil service reform, and on the development of libraries,—sometimes in monographs, more often in shorter articles or reports. It was in this way that he wrote *The Study of History in American Colleges and Universities* (1887) with separate publications on history in Harvard, Yale, Columbia College, and William and Mary; also an interesting monograph on *Thomas Jefferson and the University of Virginia* (1888). In 1893 he published his *Life and Writings of Jared Sparks* in two volumes, the only long book that came from his pen. It was generally criticized for prolixity and lack of the critical spirit. Sparks was presented with a tender care of his frailties, of which he had many. Adams was not entirely able to defend his position; for as a leader of the new and more critical historians he could not be expected to apologize for Sparks's methods of softening or otherwise changing the text of letters Sparks edited. The diffuseness of Adams's style in this book, his glaring lack of perspective, aroused another group of critics. It was, they said, prepared by the "coal-shoveling method," notes and facts shoveled into the hopper without much idea of how they would sound or seem to the reader. The book, however, is replete with information about Sparks.

Next to his organization of the historical work at the Johns Hopkins University, and the training there of a corps of efficient students who soon distributed themselves among other institutions of learning, Adams's best work was the organization of the American Historical Association in 1884. It was he who suggested the idea, he who persuaded Moses Coit Tyler and Charles Kendall Adams to sign the call for the first meeting. He got it signed also by the president and secretary of the American Social Science Association, under whose "auspices" the proposed organization was to exist. But when the men came together their first act was to declare for an independent association. Adams became secretary of the association and held that position, so full of labor and opportunity, until declining health forced him to resign in 1900; and by his will he left it $5,000, its first considerable bequest.

[*Johns Hopkins Univ. Studies in Hist. and Pol. Sci.,* series 20, extra number, including, among other tributes, "The Life and Services of H. B. Adams," by R. T. Ely, and a biog. sketch by J. M. Vincent. The latter, revised and enlarged, is in H. W. Odum, *Am. Masters of Social Sci.* (1927). A bibliography of Adams's writings is in the Johns Hopkins volume cited above.] J. S. B.

ADAMS, ISAAC (Aug. 16, 1802–July 19, 1883), inventor of printing machinery, was born at Adams Corner, Rochester, N. H., the son of Benjamin and Elizabeth (Horne) Adams. His parents were poor and his chances of education were slight. His first work was in a cotton factory, and it is probable that the machinery in this mill gave him ideas which were later to prove of value in his inventions. At the age of eighteen he went to Sandwich, N. H., where he learned the trade of cabinet making. After a few years he went to Dover, where he remained until 1824, when he found work in a machine shop in Boston. Three years later he invented the famous printing-press which was to carry his name to every country where printing was carried on. With his brother, Seth Adams, he formed the firm of I. & S. Adams in 1836. Upon leaving Sandwich he had said that he would not return until he had money enough to buy the town, and he kept his word. When he ultimately retired from business he had a fortune variously estimated as from one to two millions. He bought up many farms and planted them with white pines.

The press of Isaac Adams went a long way toward developing the mechanical side of the art of printing. The machine was known as the "Adams Power Press." For more than fifty years it was the machine preferred for book printing, and as late as 1902, Theodore L. De Vinne stated that many Adams presses were still in use. The first ones had a wooden frame, but iron was later substituted. These presses would print sheets thirty by forty inches, printing this, then relatively large, surface beautifully at considerable speed. They sounded the death-knell of the hand press. When stereotyping began to be displaced by electrotyping, the cylinder press in time displaced the Adams press; for the speed was greater, the contact stronger, and an even larger sheet could be used.

[Robt. Hoe, *Short Hist. of the Printing Press and of the Improvements in Printing Machinery from the Time of Gutenberg to the Present Day* (1902); T. L. De Vinne, "Perfecting the Press," *Sci. Am. Supp.*, No. 1380, June 14, 1902, p. 22122; W. Kaempffert, *Pop. Hist. of Am. Invention* (1924), I, 247. For early accounts see Franklin McDuffee, *Hist. of Rochester* (1892); *Am. Encyc. of Printing*, ed. by J. L. Ringwalt (1891); *Am. Mech. Dict.*, ed. by E. H. Knight (1882).] A. A. H.

ADAMS, JAMES HOPKINS (Mar. 15, 1812–July 13, 1861), governor of South Carolina, was the grandson of one of the hardy Welsh pioneers who migrated from Virginia to the Carolinas during the latter half of the eighteenth century. He was the only child of Henry Walker Adams and Mary (Goodwyn) Adams. While he was still an infant both of his parents died, and he came under the care of his maternal grandparents, whose means were sufficiently ample to enable them to afford him unusual educational advantages. He first attended school at Minervaville Academy in Richland County near the place of his birth. At the age of fourteen he was sent to Capt. Partridge's Academy, Norwich, Conn., where he was prepared for Yale College, from which he graduated in 1831. Returning to South Carolina he engaged in cotton planting, by means of which he was able to augment considerably a substantial competence which had come to him through inheritance (E. D. English and B. M. Clark, "Richland County," *Bulletin of the University of South Carolina*, no. 136). In April 1832 he married Jane Margaret Scott.

Adams entered almost at once upon a long and somewhat turbulent career in politics. In 1832 he attached himself to the State-Rights party by warmly supporting the doctrine of nullification which was then under test. Thenceforth the chief tenet of his political creed was fixed; namely, a firm belief in the principles of state sovereignty. He came accordingly to act with that party in South Carolina which turned from nullification to secession, demanded disunion without success in 1851, and at length effected its purpose in 1860. He was a member of the local House of Representatives 1834–37, 1840–41, 1848–49, and of the Senate 1850–53. His affiliation with the Whig party after 1838 greatly increased the difficulty of securing election in his constituency, which was ordinarily Democratic, and competition between his own and the opposing faction became so keen that both were reduced to a frequent and open use of illegal methods. Adams himself confessed that he had spent $10,000 in the campaign of 1854 and had lost only because his opponent had spent $50,000.

Like the majority of those who followed a political career in *antebellum* South Carolina, he sought preferment in the state militia service, in which he rose to the rank of brigadier-general of cavalry when still in his twenties (*Charleston Mercury*, July 16, 1861). B. F. Perry, who personally admired Adams in spite of their political differences, describes him as "the finest-looking horseman in saddle, when in full uniform, that I ever saw, and the best rider."

In 1854 after his defeat for the state Senate, Adams was elected governor by a handsome majority (*Charleston Mercury*, Dec. 12, 1854). His administration, otherwise eminently conservative, was given a radical character at its very close by his proposal to reopen the African slave trade (T. D. Jervey, *The Slave Trade,* 1925, pp. 114–16). In spite of the presence in the South of a considerable sentiment in favor of the proposition, this official pronouncement shocked public sensibility, and the South Carolina legislature refused to indorse it (W. J. Carnathan, "The Proposal to Reopen the Slave Trade," in *South Atlantic Quarterly,* XXV, 410–30). In consequence of this and his advanced stand on the question of secession, Adams was defeated in his candidacy for the United States Senate in 1858 (E. Merritt, *James Henry Hammond,* 1923, p. 128). In the secession convention of 1860 he spoke eloquently in favor of immediate disunion. After the passage of the Ordinance of Secession he was elected one of three "Commissioners to the Federal Government at Washington" to negotiate for the transfer of United States property in South Carolina to the state government (*Journal of the Convention of the People of South Carolina, held in 1860–61,* pp. 59 ff.). His death occurred shortly after his return from this mission and while he was still a member of the convention.

[The nearest approach to an adequate account of the life of J. H. Adams is a brief but valuable sketch by B. F. Perry in his *Reminiscences of Public Men* (1883). A few of his private letters have been preserved in the Jas. H. Hammond MSS. in the Lib. of Cong., and two open letters on public questions were printed among papers by others in a pamphlet entitled, *An Appeal to the State Rights Party of S. C.* (1858). A eulogy by James D. Tradewell was published in the *Charleston Mercury,* July 22, 1861; obituaries in the *Columbia Guardian,* July 13, 1861, and *Charleston Courier,* July 15, 1861. A genealogy of the Adams family of South Carolina has been compiled by James Hopkins Adams, but has not been published.]

J. H. E.

ADAMS, JASPER (Aug. 27, 1793–Oct. 25, 1841), college president, was a good scholar, an unusually able administrator, and a man of great practical wisdom, energy, and determination, but a frail constitution necessitated his living in the South, where he worked under conditions which did not afford opportunity and recognition commensurate with his abilities. He was one of the numerous descendants of Henry Adams of Braintree, and was born in East Medway, Mass. His father was Major Jasper Adams, and his mother, whose first name is variously given as Ama, Anna, Amy, and Emma, was the daughter of Nathaniel and Elizabeth Rounds. He prepared for college under Rev. Luther Wright, graduated from Brown University in 1815, and then taught at Phillips Andover Academy for three years, during two of which he also studied at Andover Theological Seminary. After serving as tutor at Brown for a year, he was appointed, in 1819, professor of mathematics and natural philosophy. In 1820 he was ordained priest in the Episcopal Church. On May 16 of the same year he was married to Mercy D. Wheeler of Medway, who died Nov. 11, 1821. Some three years later he married a Miss Mayrant of Charleston, S. C. His principal educational work was done in connection with Charleston College, of which he was president from 1824 to 1836, except for an interim of about eighteen months. "From his accession the real greatness and true fame of the college seems to date" (*History of Charleston College,* 1896). It was then little more than a preparatory school, nearly bankrupt, without suitable buildings, and in ill repute. Almost single-handed, in the face of the pessimism and indifference of its trustees, he raised its standards, restored its reputation, and secured funds for an adequate building. Apparently discouraged by lack of support, in 1826 he accepted a call to become the first president of Geneva (Hobart) College, N.Y. The loss of his services awakened the trustees to an appreciation of his value, and in 1828 they summoned him back, offering him a practically free hand. Their assurances and the warmer climate led him to return, and he still further raised the standard of the institution, organized it into departments, put it on a business basis so that the tuition of students met all the expenses, and greatly increased its enrolment. After his resignation, in 1836, he engaged in literary work, and from 1838 to 1840 was chaplain and professor of geography, history, and ethics at the United States Military Academy, West Point. Returning to the South, he took charge of a seminary in Pendleton, S. C., in 1840, but died the following year. He published *Elements of Moral Philosophy* (1837), a practical rather than speculative work, based on the prevailing theology, and numerous sermons and addresses.

[Andrew N. Adams, *Geneal. Hist. of Henry Adams of Braintree, Mass., and His Descendants* (1898); E. O. Jameson, *Biog. Sketches of Prominent Persons in Medway, Mass.* (1886); *Hist. Cat. of Brown Univ.* (1905); *Hobart Coll. Gen. Cat.* (1897); *Am. Quart. Reg.,* XII, 164 (1829); Colyer Meriwether, "Hist. of Higher Educ. in S. C.," in *Contrib. to Am. Educ. Hist.,* vol. II (1889), U. S. Bureau of Educ.]

H. E. S.

ADAMS, JOHN (Oct. 19, 1735–July 4, 1826), second president of the United States, was of the fourth generation from Henry Adams, the first of the family to emigrate to America. This Henry was of yeoman stock, copyholder of the manor of Barton St. David, Somerset County, England. He married (*c.* 1609) Edith, daughter of Henry Squire of Charlton Mackrell, Somerset County, and for three generations after he came to Mount Wollaston (Braintree), Mass., about 1636, his descendants remained in that town, a line of "virtuous, independent New England farmers" (Morse, p. 4), undistinguished beyond the place where they lived. In the third generation John Adams (1691–1760) married Susanna Boylston, of a family prominent in the medical history of Massachusetts, and their eldest son was John, born at Braintree. On graduating from Harvard College in 1755 he taught school at Worcester with thoughts of becoming a minister; but "frigid John Calvin" was not to his liking and he had growing doubt on some "disputed points" of doctrine. So he took up the study of law under James Putnam, in the conviction that "the study and practice of law . . . does not dissolve the obligations of morality or of religion" (*Works,* I, 32). He was presented for admission to the Boston bar, Nov. 6, 1758, by Jeremiah Gridley, a leader in the profession, and attorney general of the province. His law practice grew slowly; he took an interest in town matters; and he wrote for the newspapers on public affairs. He married, Oct. 25, 1764, Abigail, daughter of Rev. William and Elizabeth (Quincy) Smith, of Weymouth, a marriage which greatly widened his connections with prominent families of Massachusetts. In mind and character Mrs. Adams was a worthy partner throughout his career. In 1765 he contributed to the *Boston Gazette* a number of essays, "written at random, weekly, without any preconceived plan," which were published as "A Dissertation on the Canon and Feudal Law" (*Ibid.,* IX, 332). The Stamp Act gave him his first real opportunity and the resolutions of protest he prepared for Braintree were followed throughout Massachusetts. This led to his association with Gridley and James Otis in presenting Boston's memorial against the closing of the courts and opened his long contest with the lieutenant-governor, Thomas Hutchinson. Adams disapproved of the Stamp Act riots, but opposed the act on legal grounds, arguing that it was invalid because the colonists had never consented to it. Early in 1768 he removed to Boston, occupying the "White House," Brattle Square, and was engaged to defend John Hancock, charged with smuggling; Corbet, on a question of impressment and manslaughter; and Capt. Preston, on a technical charge of murder. Such important cases connected him with the patriotic cause, and he declined an appointment as advocate general in the court of admiralty, rightly regarding it as a step to draw him from that association. His conduct was guided by law and he boasted that he had the only complete set of the British statutes-at-large in Boston, or even in the colonies.

Elected to the General Court as a representative of Boston he served a year and for reasons of health removed to Braintree in the spring of 1771, to pursue law and farming, but found it advisable again to take a house in Queen Street, Boston. Devoting himself to the law he soon occupied a leading place at the bar, but political events forced him into public life. The destruction of tea in Boston harbor he considered "the grandest event which has yet happened since the controversy with Britain opened" (*Ibid.,* IX, 333), yet he was again opposed to mob outbreaks. The Boston Port Act he condemned, and because of his general attitude on the controversy with Great Britain, he was chosen, June 17, 1774, one of the delegates from Massachusetts to the first Congress of the colonies, known later as the Continental Congress. His position on measures to be taken had not become fixed, though he saw independence as a possibility, and dreaded it. Before reaching Philadelphia he learned that Massachusetts was regarded as inclined to be dictatorial and infected with independence. Recognizing that the Congress would not take an extreme position and restraining publicly his impatience while recording it in his private letters, he served as a member of the committee to prepare a petition to the King; on a second to draft a declaration of rights, in which he urged unsuccessfully a recognition of "natural rights," and wrote the fourth section on taxation, representation, and consent to the regulation of external commerce; he favored non-importation. With not a little disappointment at the outcome of the Congress, Adams returned to Massachusetts, sat in the provincial congress, was chosen to the council, and for some months, indeed until the battle of Lexington, as "Novanglus" carried on a controversy in the press with Daniel Leonard ("Massachusettensis") on the origin of the dispute with Great Britain. "The language is rather energetic than elegant," wrote the grandson of Adams, "and the feeling is more cherished than the rhetoric" (*Ibid.,* I, 166).

In this interval he had opportunity to learn the disadvantages under which the province suffered from the want of an organized government, and in the second Congress, supported by instructions from the Massachusetts Assembly to concert measures for establishing American liberty on a permanent basis, secure from attack from Great Britain, he pointed out the probable necessity of forming a confederacy of separate states, each with its own government; but he found the Congress, while feeling the "spirit of war" more intimately than before, conservative and suspicious of New England, especially of Massachusetts. He opposed unsuccessfully another petition to the King, and served on committees to prepare an address to the people of Ireland, to draft instructions to Washington, for whose appointment to command he was largely responsible, to reply to Lord North's resolution of Feb. 20, 1775, and to consider equipping vessels to take enemy ships—the beginning of a navy. In July his policy had taken form: "We ought immediately to dissolve all Ministerial Tyrannies and Custom houses, set up Governments of our own like that of Connecticut in all the colonies, confederate together like an indissoluble Band for mutual defence, and open our Ports to all Nations immediately" (*Warren-Adams Letters,* I, 75). Encountering opposition, both in Congress and in his own delegation, he could not gain all he desired, and, accepted and feared by the conservatives as a leader for independence, he could only await the march of events which seemed to favor his propositions. His impatience became known through two intercepted letters, which proved for a time embarrassing without in the end reducing his influence. As colony after colony applied to Congress for advice on government Adams used the opening to advance his views, suggesting the adoption of a form as nearly resembling that which had existed as circumstances would permit, to be framed by colony conventions and submitted to the people if necessary. A governor, council, and representatives were familiar instruments and easily adaptable. In October he was appointed chief justice of the superior court of Massachusetts and accepted; but he never sat upon the bench and from pressure of occupation, Feb. 10, 1777, he resigned the office.

Early in December 1775 he obtained leave to return to Massachusetts, where he sat in the council and gained a knowledge of local opinion. He returned to Congress, Feb. 9, 1776. In that month appeared Paine's *Common Sense,* advocating a plan of government which Adams sought to counteract by his *Thoughts on Government,* originally prepared for the delegates of North Carolina, but published, at first anonymously, to meet a wider demand. In March he secured the adoption of recommendations to promote the production of flax, cotton, and wool, the establishing of societies for the improvement of agriculture, manufactures, and commerce, and for making steel and sail-cloth. By May Congress was persuaded to make a general recommendation, that where no adequate government had been established such a one should be adopted as in the opinion of the representatives of the people should "best conduce to the happiness and safety of their constituents in particular and America in general" (*Works,* I, 217). To this recommendation Adams prepared a preamble (*Journals of the Continental Congress,* IV, 357–58), which Duane called a "machine for the fabrication of independence," and which Adams thought was independence itself (*Works,* I, 18). The way was now open for the final act. Richard Henry Lee's motion for independence, foreign alliances, and a confederation was laid before Congress June 7 and seconded by Adams. Committees were provided for on June 11 to prepare a declaration of independence and a plan of treaties with foreign powers, and Adams was appointed on both. Of the plan of treaties, for trade and not alliance, he was the author, but not of the instructions to a negotiator under it. To the text of the declaration he contributed nothing of importance, but to him fell the severer task of defending it in its passage through Congress. "He was the pillar of its support on the floor of Congress," Jefferson wrote in 1813, "its ablest advocate and defender against the multifarious assaults it encountered" (*The Writings of Thomas Jefferson,* ed. by P. L. Ford, 1898, IX, 377–78). Stockton, of New Jersey, called him "the Atlas of American independence."

Meantime (June 13) he had been placed on the newly created Board of War, with engrossing duties; reported the (British) Articles of War, and rules for the navy; met Lord Howe at the Staten Island conference. He also drafted the credentials of the Commissioners to France and secured a committee to establish a military academy in the army. Worn down by continual application, anxious for the condition of his family, and wishing to confer with his constituents, he left Philadelphia Oct. 13, returning Feb. 1, 1777, when Congress was sitting in Baltimore. He served on a number of important committees—appeals, neutrality, Du Coudray, evacuation of Ticonderoga, Saratoga convention—and took part in the debates on currency, regulation of prices, French loan, foreign officers and confederation, trusted as a member free from the divisions which pervaded and hampered the Congress. Wearied by the disputes over promotions in the army, he expressed the hope to Greene that Congress would elect annually all the general officers, so that some great men should be obliged to serve their country in some other capacity, better adapted to their genius, a proposition cited against him many years after. The news of Burgoyne's surrender reached Congress Nov. 3, eight days after Adams had left that body never, as it proved, to return. He was not involved in the Conway cabal against Washington, but believed it wise to have a general ready, should any chance remove or incapacitate Washington.

On Nov. 21 Deane was recalled from France, and on the 28th Adams was elected commissioner to France. That did not prevent his reëlection on Dec. 4 to Congress. On Feb. 13, 1778, he embarked on the frigate *Boston* with his son, John Quincy Adams, then ten years old. After six weeks at sea they landed at Bordeaux, to learn that France had recognized the American States, entered into treaties of amity and commerce with them, and that war between France and Great Britain was regarded as inevitable. Adams reached Paris, Apr. 8, and took quarters in the same house with Franklin. He found the commissioners much divided by disputes which the recall of Deane had not ended, and sought to be neutral. "It is no part of my business to quarrel with anybody without cause; it is no part of my duty to differ with one party or another, let it give offence to whom it will" (*Works,* III, 139). He took upon himself to introduce orderly system in correspondence and accountability in money matters, lived simply, taking a somewhat exaggerated view of the expense of the other commissioners, and in May explained to Samuel Adams the need of an entirely new organization of the foreign mission of the States, framing a plan which would, if adopted, in all probability deprive him of office. Franklin agreed in his recommendations.

In the meantime a loan in France or Holland was considered necessary and Adams began the long series of letters on European affairs that form so large a part of his dispatches to Congress. In spite of the good resolutions he had brought with him to France, he conceived a jealousy—to ripen later—of French policy and its dangers to America, which colored his relations with that court, with his colleagues, and with their followers. Yet he confessed that the French ministry was reserved to all three of the commissioners and therefore could have no personal animus toward him. He became restive and distrustful of his associates. "There is no man here that I dare trust" (February 1779, *Works,* III, 188). Believing that common report belittled him, he belittled himself, and Deane's *Address to the People of America* (November 1778) roused him to fury; he wished to carry the matter to the French ministry, when he learned that Franklin had been appointed sole plenipotentiary, and that he himself had become a private citizen, his own suggestion having been adopted by Congress. Unwilling to remain in Europe without appointment, he embarked (Mar. 22, 1779), at Nantes on the *Alliance,* but was detained by the French government until the middle of June, that he might accompany the French minister to the United States in the *Sensible.* They arrived at Boston, Aug. 2, and seven days later he was chosen to represent Braintree in the convention called to frame a constitution for Massachusetts. The plan submitted to the convention was largely his, but he was called away before final action was taken. Congress, in response to an intimation from Gérard, the French minister, had spent much time on instructions for a minister to negotiate peace. On Sept. 25 both Adams and Jay were nominated, and on Sept. 26 both were also nominated to negotiate treaties with Spain; but on Sept. 27 Jay, believed to be not opposed to French plans, received the Spanish mission, and Adams, aided by a commendation of his conduct by Vergennes, the peace negotiation. Adams was also appointed to negotiate a commercial treaty with Great Britain and to represent the United States of America at the Court of St. James's.

Embarking on the *Sensible,* Nov. 13, with his two sons John and Charles, he landed at Ferrol Dec. 8, making the journey to Paris by land. He reached that city, Feb. 5, and the French ministry advised him, against his own judgment, to keep his mission secret for a time. Presented to the King, Mar. 7, Adams was again disappointed in not being publicly recognized. In his enforced inaction he wrote freely to Congress on European politics, contributed American news to the *Mercure de France,* and, at the instance of Vergennes, gave intelligence of American affairs direct to the minister. Neither Congress nor Adams had informed Franklin of the peace mission, and when Vergennes took exception to Adams's defense of a financial measure of Congress, deemed hostile to the interests of French holders of Continental paper, Adams found himself in a delicate situation, acting overzealously and independently of Franklin, and disavowed by Vergennes. He thought that Franklin had interfered with him instead of giving support, and his jealousy of French intentions increased. On his asking again that public announcement of his commission be made, Vergennes threatened to carry the question to Congress, thus strengthening Adams's suspicions of bad faith, since he knew that Vergennes could reach Congress through the French minister at Philadelphia and work against him. Adams gave to Vergennes his reasons for believing that Great Britain desired peace and added his conviction that greater naval and military exertions on the part of France would favor the Americans. So indiscreet a suggestion, made without instructions and on a matter clearly within Franklin's province, had the result that Vergennes ended all intercourse with Adams and sought to have his mission, at least in part, revoked. Without doubting his attachment to independence and the alliance, Vergennes thought a less unbending commissioner would be more promising in peace parleys.

Adams went to Holland (July 27) without the indorsement of the French court, to test the possibility of a loan for the States. A threat of war from Great Britain put an end to any hope of success; but he formed wide connections, wrote much on the situation of the Dutch, and gained useful knowledge of banking methods in that country. Congress had long been divided on foreign affairs and, while it indorsed the opinion of Vergennes on the inexpediency of communicating Adams's powers to Great Britain, refused to accede to the minister's wish that Adams be curbed and placed under the direction of France. On Dec. 29, 1780, it made Adams minister to the United Provinces in place of Laurens, and authorized him to join the newly formed league of armed neutrality. He could at that time hold out no hope of assistance in any shape from the Dutch republic, for he could not be recognized, French influence was against him, and his memorials were returned. Nor could the Americans expect any present advantage from the armed neutrality—a "sublime bubble" he termed it—however useful the principle of free ships making free goods might prove to a neutral America in the future.

Summoned to Paris by Vergennes in July 1781, he learned of a proposed peace or armistice with Great Britain through the mediation of Russia and Austria, and looked upon it as a clumsy trick. For Great Britain asked two preliminary and impossible conditions: that the United States should break with France, and that they should return to their obedience to their former ruler. Adams believed that the powers offering mediation should first acknowledge the independence of the States, or at least receive a minister plenipotentiary from them. Returning to Amsterdam in August, he received a new commission for peace (dated June 15, 1781), naming four associated commissioners; and later came a revocation (July 12) of his commission to treat with Great Britain on commerce. Welcoming the larger commission he regretted the revocation of his commercial powers as ill-judged, making it impossible in 1782 to take advantage of a liberal trade policy in the British ministry. The revocation had been moved in Congress by Madison and carried with only New England opposed. Adams was now laid low for weeks by a nervous fever and on recovery learned that Congress had, Aug. 16, commissioned him minister plenipotentiary to the United Provinces, with instructions to negotiate a treaty of alliance, but enjoining him on all occasions to confer in the most confidential manner with the French representative at The Hague. The peace commissioners were also directed ultimately to govern themselves by the advice and opinion of the French minister (Wharton, *Diplomatic Correspondence,* IV, 505). The measures in Congress and these instructions show how far Vergennes had succeeded in making the negotiations for peace subservient to French influence, and led Adams to consider resigning his mission. The surrender of Cornwallis and the arrogance of Great Britain turned the favor of the Dutch toward America, without, however, furthering a loan by the Dutch bankers. In October 1781, after months of effort, less than three hundred pounds had been subscribed and the bonds were held by not more than three persons. Encouraged by improved political conditions and with full sympathy of the French minister at The Hague, in January 1782 Adams demanded of the ministers of the republic and the deputies of the city a reply to his memorial of Apr. 19 asking for recognition. Three months later he was formally recognized, whereupon he submitted a plan of a treaty, which was signed in October, and made proposals for and secured the first loan.

While he was thus engaged, Great Britain had made at Paris advances toward peace, and, since June, Franklin and Jay had been in what they called the "skirmishing business" of their commission. Not until the end of September did the British representative, Oswald, show satisfactory powers to treat with the thirteen United States of America. Adams was then summoned to Paris. He arrived Oct. 26, and Jay, whose Spanish experience had made him suspicious of French designs, found him "a very agreeable coadjutor." Jay was willing and anxious to treat separately with Great Britain; Adams agreed with him; and Franklin, with some proper reluctance because of his closer ties with the French minister, accepted the decision. The articles of a treaty had been agreed upon before Adams's arrival, but his contributions to an agreement were essential. On the questions of boundaries, especially on the northeast, the claims of indemnity to the Loyalists and the fisheries, he prepared articles, and it was he who suggested that Congress recommend to the States to open their courts for the recovery of just debts, a suggestion welcomed by the British negotiators. Refusing to sign articles which did not meet his requirements as to the fisheries, he established, nevertheless, rights and liberties that were important for the new nation and essential to New England. On Nov. 30 the provisional articles were signed without the knowledge of the French court and in the event proved no hindrance to a general pacification or to the peace treaties of France or Spain. Not until August 1783 were the provisional articles ratified by Great Britain. Offered without change as a definite treaty, thus making any new concessions by the British ministry improbable, they were signed Sept. 3, 1783. Had a minister of the United States been then in London a fair agreement on a treaty of commerce might have been reached. Adams, with Jay and Franklin, had been appointed (May 1, 1783) to negotiate such a treaty, but a change of ministry prevented a favorable issue, and Adams, in England for his health, was obliged to return to Holland to negotiate a new loan, in which he was successful in spite of less favorable conditions. The return of Jay to America made a new commercial commission necessary and on May 7, 1784, Jefferson was added.

In the summer of 1784, Mrs. Adams and their daughter joining him, Adams took a house at Auteuil and on Feb. 24, 1785, he was appointed envoy to the Court of St. James's. He went to London in May, was received by the King, and had interviews with the Minister for Foreign Affairs on questions arising from the treaty—such as surrender of the Western posts, compensation for slaves and property, recovery of debts, and the treatment of refugees or Loyalists. The attitude of court and ministry discouraged advances, and the divided interests of the United States made it difficult for the British to have confidence in the execution of the treaty of 1783 or in the permanence of the confederation. The serious divisions in the States led Adams to study principles of government. Taking his text from a letter of Turgot to Dr. Price referring to the American States, he wrote in three volumes *Defence of the Constitutions of the United States of America against the Attack of Mr. Turgot* (1787). The first volume appeared in America while the convention for framing a constitution was assembling. Its timeliness gave it vogue; but it is chiefly remembered for the unjustifiable partisan interpretation given to it in later years as an attempt to favor a monarchy. Seeing no prospect of further success in England, Adams asked to resign and letters of recall were sent in February 1788. Congress thanked him for his "patriotism, perseverance, integrity, and diligence" (*Works,* I, 438).

Hardly had he landed in Massachusetts when he was elected to the Congress, but never took his seat in that dying body. In the new government under the Constitution Washington was unanimously chosen president, but the votes for vice-president were for political reasons scattered, and Adams, receiving 34 out of 69 votes, was chosen. Only after some years did Adams complain of the stratagem and of Hamilton's conduct of it. "My country has in its wisdom," he wrote to his wife, "contrived for me the most insignificant office that ever the invention of man contrived or his imagination conceived" (*Ibid.,* I, 460). An eager debater, he was reduced to silence, and he could exert influence only through the casting vote in a Senate equally divided, a vote he had occasion to exercise more frequently than any of his successors in office—no less than twenty times—and though not a party man, always on the Federalist side. Thus he decided the president's power of removal from office, commercial reprisal on Great Britain, and the policy of neutrality; supported Washington's administration; and aided Hamilton's financial measures, winning to that extent the favor of the Secretary of the Treasury, who had not concealed a certain want of confidence in the Vice-President. Watching the progress of the French Revolution Adams could see only failure in the want of proper government and in *Discourses on Davila,* published in the *United States Gazette* in 1791, he drew lessons from the past history of France. Not only did Hamilton disapprove of these essays, as tending to weaken the government, but Jefferson saw in them a leaning to hereditary monarchy and aristocracy, and to counteract the effect indorsed Paine's *Age of Reason.* Unknown to his father, John Quincy Adams answered Paine and widened the separation between Jefferson and John Adams, to whom the authorship of the reply was generally ascribed. In the second election (1792) Adams received the Federalist vote, becoming again vice-president; and in the election of 1796 Hamilton once more intervened, intending to make Thomas Pinckney president and to keep Adams in the vice-presidency. The plan failed of its purpose, but it drew sufficient votes to mortify Adams and to make Jefferson vice-president. Unnecessary as the act was, it exasperated Adams beyond possible reconciliation with Hamilton and was an unfortunate beginning for Adams's administration, which seemed to encounter Hamilton's hostility at every turn.

No change of cabinet officers followed Adams's accession to the presidency, nor was there made any sweeping change in the minor offices. The election brought Adams nearer to Jefferson than to Hamilton, for Adams had shown a sensibility to the candor of Jefferson's friends during the contest, and had learned of personal sentiments of Jefferson toward him of a conciliatory nature. Indeed Jefferson had written a friendly letter to Adams (Dec. 28, 1796. Jefferson, *Writings,* VII, 94) which Madison, to whose discretion it was entrusted, never delivered, though he allowed its general terms to become known. Hamilton compared this approach to the lying down together of the lion and the lamb, and was skeptical of the result; but added that he trusted Adams's real good sense and integrity would be a sufficient shield against his possible vanity (Hamilton, *Works,* 1851, VI, 206).

Adams's inaugural speech gave pledges to maintain the policy of his predecessor, but seemed "temporizing" to the Federalists. Relations with the French republic demanded immediate attention. Jay's treaty and the recall of Monroe had so worked upon the French Directory that it refused to receive or even to permit his successor, Charles C. Pinckney, to remain on French territory. Sincerely desirous of renewed relations between the two countries, Adams called upon Jefferson the day before inauguration to offer him the mission. Jefferson declined, nor did he warm to the suggestion of Madison in his place. The President immediately after inauguration consulted Wolcott and found that to pursue his plan would mean a break in his cabinet and its reorganization. Later Hamilton made the same suggestion, naming Jefferson or Madison, Pinckney, and Cabot, and favored an extraordinary mission as necessary to learn what redress the French expected. In spite of this apparent harmony in plan the Republicans felt that the administration of Adams might turn against them, surrounded as he was by ministers who had been made by Hamilton and who looked to him and not to the President as the leader of the party and of Federalist policy. Jefferson thought the followers of Hamilton to be only a "little less hostile" to Adams than to himself; but it cannot be shown that the Jeffersonians excited Adams's suspicions against Hamilton, nor that they were to be held responsible for Pickering's dismissal, as the latter claimed. At the same time the Jefferson party became more and more antagonistic to Adams's administration and almost from its beginning opposed its measures and the man held responsible for them.

A special session of Congress was called for May 15, but before it assembled news came that the French Directory had declared pirates all Americans serving on British vessels. On Apr. 14 Adams framed questions for his cabinet on the situation with France, and on the 15th other questions on his message to be submitted to Congress (Gibbs, I, 501, 502). McHenry sent both lists to Hamilton who prepared replies (Steiner, *Life and Correspondence of James McHenry,* 1907, pp. 216, 213), which McHenry practically made his own (*Ibid.,* p. 222). The cabinet was against war, and united in support of a new mission and measures of defense in case negotiation should fail. The message to Congress was firm and dignified, favoring peace and means of defense in militia and navy, and received general approbation. Adams wished one member of the mission to be taken from the opposition and suggested Gerry, but met with no support from his cabinet. The names first sent to Congress were Pinckney, Marshall, and Dana; when Dana declined to serve, Gerry was added. William Vans Murray was appointed minister to The Hague in place of John Quincy Adams, a measure later to prove important. The commission sailed for France, there not to be admitted to an audience with the Directory, and to be met by a demand of a bribe and loan, impossible conditions which led to the return of Marshall and Pinckney; Gerry remained. Wishing to be prepared for a failure of negotiation, the President, Jan. 24, 1798, asked his cabinet to advise on war, an embargo, or changed relations with European powers. McHenry, as before, sent the questions to Hamilton and his reply seems to have formed the opinion of Wolcott, Pickering, and McHenry (*McHenry,* p. 291), recommending a vigorous policy and also closer connections with Great Britain. The latter Adams could not accept. The first intimation of the situation in France reached the United States in March 1798; the failure of the mission was announced to Congress Mar. 19, and Gerry was directed to return but delayed. On June 21, after Marshall's arrival, Adams sent a message to Congress saying: "I will never send another minister to France, without assurances that he will be received, respected and honored, as the representative of a great, free, powerful and independent nation" (Adams, *Works,* IX, 159). The country was aroused.

Without declaring war, Congress declared the treaties with France null and void, increased the army, ordered the construction or purchase of new ships, and created a navy department. The President, having in mind a defensive system, favored a navy, but Congress, under the influence of Hamilton, planned a large provisional army in case of actual invasion (May 28), and, in imitation of British acts, passed the Alien (July 6) and Sedition (July 14) laws, of doubtful expedience or necessity. For the command of the provisional army only one person was considered. On July 2 the President nominated Washington, and the Senate confirmed the nomination on the following day. The Secretary of War went to Mount Vernon with the commission and arranged that the general officers should be such as were acceptable to Washington. Pickering urged Hamilton for the second place and, after some hesitation between Pinckney and Knox, Washington named the three in the following order, Hamilton, Pinckney, Knox, and the Senate so confirmed them. The President believed that by right Knox should come first and Pinckney second, and sought to rank them thus. On Washington's threat to resign, Adams yielded, but from that time he distrusted the two members of the cabinet—Pickering and McHenry—who were closest to Hamilton. By defeating the appointment of Adams's son-in-law, William S. Smith, to the army, Pickering did not fail to invite the displeasure of the President. While this difference continued—it was not settled till the end of September—addresses from all parts of the country poured in upon the President, and his replies, all of his own composition, kept the public feeling awakened to the dangers of the situation.

Gerry landed at Boston, Oct. 1, and made report of his mission to Adams, then at Quincy. Not only did he convince the President that he was without blame in remaining, but he brought intimation of a wish on Talleyrand's part to renew diplomatic intercourse. From Murray, at The Hague, was received about the same time a message to the same effect, which had been sent by Talleyrand to Pichon, the French representative in the Netherlands, and was intended for Murray's notice. Not yet willing to meet these indirect advances, the President asked Pickering to consult the cabinet on two points: whether it would be expedient for the President to recommend to the consideration of Congress a declaration of war against France; and whether any further proposals of negotiation could be made with safety, or with any advantage, in Europe or America. Might not the President say, in order to keep the channels of negotiation open, that he would nominate a minister to the French republic, ready to embark on proper assurances from that country? The President wished in his message to say that he was ready at all times to appoint or receive a minister to treat of the differences between France and the United States. The cabinet note, prepared in consultation with Hamilton, sought to shut off all possibility of a new mission. Adams modified his wish so as to read: "But to send another minister without more determinate assurances that he would be received, would be an act of humiliation to which the United States ought not to submit" (*Ibid.*, IX, 130), and outlined in general terms the steps necessary to restore intercourse. The door was left open for a peaceful solution, but vigorous preparations for war were essential. Not satisfied with this outcome, Hamilton exerted his influence on Congress. By this time Adams was quite conscious of Hamilton's dominance in the party, cabinet, and Congress, and of his effort to bring about war with France, a large standing army, and an attack upon Spanish America. Without consulting any one, but acting wholly within his right, on Feb. 18, Adams sent to the Senate the nomination of W. Vans Murray, then minister to the Netherlands, to be minister to the French republic. The cabinet felt outraged. The Senate intended to reject the nomination and Sedgwick, of the committee reporting on it, took the unusual step of personally remonstrating with the President, a step he was unable to defend on correct principles. To meet some of the objections raised and before action was had on Murray, Adams proposed a peace commission of three members, not to depart on their mission without further instructions. This bold and unexpected act brought to his support the press of the country and neither Hamilton nor Congress could oppose it, however ardently the Federalists resented it. Adams realized that he could place little confidence in two of his cabinet—Pickering and McHenry—now completely under the influence of Hamilton, and for his own good he should have replaced them. Instead of this he said he counted upon their coöperation and to his cost permitted them to remain in office. By his long absence at Quincy he gave them full opportunity to work against his policy. Fries's rebellion in March was a local incident which in the event produced feeling against Adams; and the Alien and Sedition laws, for which he had no direct responsibility and which he refused to enforce as the Federalists wished, added to his unpopularity. To be prepared for probable concessions by France, in August he agreed with his cabinet on instructions to the commissioners, but in his absence the cabinet determined to suspend the mission until he could be personally consulted. They believed the restoration of the Bourbons at hand; Adams had no faith in such a prediction. Arriving, Oct. 10, at Trenton, to which place the government had retired because of the infection at Philadelphia, the President found there his cabinet, Ellsworth of the French mission, and Hamilton, and felt that a struggle for control was at hand. Knowing that France would receive the mission, he went over the instructions with his cabinet on the evening of the 15th, and the next day gave orders for the completion of the papers and for the departure of the mission by Nov. 1. Again he had surprised his advisers through an independent act by which they believed themselves to have been deceived and outraged. By so doing he antagonized Hamilton's influence, prevented a war with France, preserved the neutrality of the United States, and lost a renomination, which he did not then desire and for which he had laid no plans. Regarding him as a traitor to the party, the leaders sought means to win the election without him. At last convinced that he could no longer retain certain members of his cabinet bent upon thwarting his policy and plotting his exclusion, Adams had a stormy interview with McHenry, the least efficient member, who promptly resigned. A few days later, Pickering, the chief sinner in disloyalty to his chief, was given an opportunity to resign, but refused it and on May 12 was discharged from office. Wolcott, as much involved as his colleagues, was not suspected and remained, serving as an informer. In the appointment of John Marshall and Samuel Dexter the cabinet gained, but nothing could prevent the bitter war made upon Adams by the Federalist leaders, now implacably bent not only upon defeating but upon discrediting him to the limit of their power. The pardon of three men condemned to death for participation in the Pennsylvania "insurrection" increased the Federalist animus. Hamilton's illogical and ill-judged *Letter concerning the Public Conduct and Character of John Adams* displayed at large his own animosity and the division in the party. It was based upon information derived from Wolcott, had been first submitted for his revision, and appeared in the last week of October, too late to permit of reply before election. Adams, with no party behind him, received 65 to Jefferson's 73 votes, and Hamilton was obliged to admit that the body of the people of New England favored him. Hamilton's tactics had merely resulted in the election of Jefferson whom he disliked far more than Adams. Immediately after the election Wolcott sent in his resignation, to take effect at the close of the year; but he in no wise abated his intrigues against the President, to serve under whom, he said, would be "incompatible with honor and a suitable respect" to his own character (Wolcott to Pickering, Dec. 28, 1800, Gibbs, II, 461). He even obtained from the State Department material to enable Pickering to attack his chief. Adams never knew or suspected Wolcott's hostility, or treachery, and appointed him to a judgeship in the circuit court of the United States. Peace with France was concluded at Morfontaine, Sept. 30, 1800, and was, with the exception of one article, accepted by the Senate. One of the last acts of Congress reorganized the national judiciary system and created a large number of life appointments. The President made the appointments on grounds of public policy and by so doing incurred the increased enmity of Jefferson.

On the expiration of his term of office and after twenty-six years passed in public employment, in a great variety of important services, Adams retired to Quincy under a weight of odium which he could not accept as merited. The legislature of Massachusetts welcomed him, however, as did the town of Quincy. Never a strong partisan, he saw the Federalists lose their influence as a party and their opponents attain almost unquestioned power, and he was held to be the cause of the defeat of the one and the success of the other. After a quarter of a century of great and varied activity he was doomed to as long a period of almost complete isolation from public affairs. His active mind refused to rest, retaining an interest in public questions, which grew in strength as he sympathetically watched the career of his son, John Quincy Adams. At times he was aroused to take part in political discussions and corresponded freely with a few of his friends. The affair of the *Chesapeake* in June 1807 brought both the Adamses to the support of the administration in maintaining the rights of America, and from the elder a vigorous examination of *The Inadmissible Principles of the King of England's Proclamation of Oct. 16, 1807,* on the impressment of seamen from neutral vessels. The younger Adams's vote for the embargo proved that the son was no more of a partisan than the father, and led to a series of letters from the latter to the *Boston Patriot,* a newspaper recently established, in explanation and defense of his own past acts, diplomatic and executive. A part of this correspondence, which extended over a period of three years, was gathered into a volume, *Correspondence of the late President Adams* (1809). Loosely constructed and carelessly printed in the columns of a newspaper at a time when party feeling ran high, and without arrangement or fit explanation, the series did preserve, nevertheless, important documents; but it is marked by intemperate denunciation of Hamilton and others as unjust to them as to the writer. The appointment by Madison of John Quincy Adams, regarded by the Federalists as a Republican, to be minister of the United States at St. Petersburg seemed to John Adams almost a recognition of himself, who had been so harshly dealt with by the party in power. Through the agency of Benjamin Rush he renewed relations with Jefferson, and the letters which passed between these men whom political circumstances had so often placed in opposition have an extraordinary interest. Adams turned to the history of the past and wrote on the men and events of his day, with uncertain memory, but with much that is valuable for personal characters and historical fact. Though the death of Mrs. Adams, Oct. 28, 1818, deprived him of a loved companion and saddened his later years, he was made happier by the changing public attitude. In 1820 he attended the state constitutional convention and was received with honors. As the years passed he gained in general estimation; Quincy became a place of visit, with him as its leading character. He died, July 4, 1826, a few hours after Jefferson.

His grandson, Charles Francis Adams, has described John Adams as "not tall, scarcely exceeding middle height, but of a stout, well-knit frame, denoting vigor and long life, yet as he grew old, inclining more and more to corpulence. His head was large and round, with a wide forehead and expanded brows. His eye was mild and benignant, perhaps even humorous, when he was free from emotion, but when excited, it fully expressed the vehemence of the spirit that stirred within. His presence was grave and imposing, on serious occasions, but not unbending. He delighted in social conversation, in which he was sometimes tempted to what he called rhodomontade. . . . His anger, when thoroughly roused, was, for a time, extremely violent, but when it subsided, it left no trace of malevolence behind." In 1783, on learning of Adams's appointment on the peace commission, Jefferson wrote: "He has a sound head on substantial points and I think he has integrity. . . . His dislike of all parties and all men, by balancing his prejudices, may give the same fair play to his reason as would a general benevolence of temper" (Jefferson, *Writings,* ed. by Ford, III, 309–10). Four years later and after more than seven months of intimacy, he added: "He is vain, irritable, and a bad calculator of the force and probable effect of the motives which govern men. This is all the ill which can possibly be said of him. He is as disinterested as the being who made him; he is profound in his views and accurate in his judgment, except where knowledge of the world is necessary to form a judgment. He is so amiable, that I pronounce you will love him if ever you become acquainted with him. He would be, as he was, a great man in Congress" (*The Writings of Thomas Jefferson,* ed. by H. A. Washington, 1871, II, 107). Men most hostile to Adams have united in praise of his abilities, integrity, high intentions, and unquestioned patriotism. His diplomacy showed initiative clogged by influences he had himself aroused; his administration showed statesmanship and independence. His mind was stored with much learning, usable at will; though often intemperate and extravagant in language, he was cool in action. Of undoubted courage and ambition, careful of his independence and jealous of others, he stood much alone, and so largely lost the benefit of acting with others.

Of his published writings the following are the more important: 1. *Essay on Canon and Feudal Law* (London, 1768) appended to *The True Sentiments of America;* also to *Collection of State Papers* (The Hague, also London, 1782; reprinted at Philadelphia, 1783). 2. *Thoughts on Government* (Philadelphia, 1776; Boston, 1776 and 1788). 3. *Mémoire à leurs Hautes-Puissances les Seigneurs États-Généraux des Provinces-Unies des Pays-Bas* (1781; also in English, Leyden, 1781). 4. *A Collection of State Papers* (The Hague, 1782; reprinted at London, 1782). 5. *History of the Dispute with America,* an abridgment of his replies to Leonard (written in 1774, published at London, 1784. Both series were not printed in full until 1819, as *Novanglus and Massachusettensis.* A Dutch edition of the *History* appeared at Amsterdam, 1782). 6. *Letters* (to Dr. Calkoen, privately printed, 1786; reprinted as *Twenty-Six Letters, upon Interesting Subjects,* in two editions, New York, 1789). 7. *A Defence of the Constitutions of Government of the United States of America* (the first volume, London, 1787, reprinted, Boston, New York and Phila., 1787; with Volumes II and III, London, 1787–88; again in two editions, London, 1794, one with title *History of the Principal Republics of the World;* Paris, 1792; Phila., 1797). 8. *A Selection of the Patriotic Addresses to the President of the United States, together with the President's Answers, presented in the year 1798* (Boston, 1798). 9. *Four Letters* (John and Samuel Adams, Boston, 1802). 10. *Discourses on Davila* (Boston, 1805). 11. *The Inadmissible Principles of the King of England's Proclamation* (Boston, 1809). 12. *Correspondence . . . concerning the British Doctrine of Impressment* (Baltimore, 1809). 13. *Correspondence of the late President Adams* (originally published in the *Boston Patriot,* Boston, 1809). 14. *Correspondence between the Hon. J. Adams and the late William Cunningham* (Boston, 1823. This publication was a gross violation of decency, by the son of Cunningham, who sought favors of Adams and, when denied, printed in 1811 *A Letter to a Great Character* abusive of the former President and based upon the letters to the father). 15. *Letters of John Adams, addressed to his Wife* (1841, being Volumes III and

IV, supplementing *Letters of Abigail Adams,* 1841; the two series republished as *Familiar Letters of John Adams and his wife Abigail Adams,* Boston, 1876). 16. *Works,* 10 vols. (1850–56). 17. "Letters to Mercy Warren," *5 Massachusetts Historical Society Collections,* IV, 1878. 18. "Letters" in *Bulletin of the New York Public Library,* April 1906. 19. "Warren-Adams Letters," 2 vols., *Massachusetts Historical Society Collections,* LXXII, LXXIII (1917, 1925). 20. *Correspondence of John Adams and Thomas Jefferson,* 1812–26, selected by Paul Wilstach (1925). 21. *Statesman and Friend,* letters to Dr. B. Waterhouse (1927).

[Charles Francis Adams, *Life,* being vol. I of the *Works;* John T. Morse, Jr., *John Adams* (1885); John Wood, *Hist. of the Administration of John Adams* (1802, repub. 1846), and *A Correct Statement of the various Sources from which the Hist. was compiled* (1802), being a reply to James Cheetham's *A Narrative of the Suppression by Col. Burr of the Hist. of the Administration of John Adams* (1802); Geo. Gibbs, *Memoirs of the Administration of Washington and Adams,* 6 vols.; J. H. A. Doniol, *Histoire de la Participation de la France à l'Établissement des États Unis d'Amérique* (1886–99); Correa M. Walsh, *Political Science of John Adams* (1915); C. Warren, *John Adams and Am. Constitutions* (1927). A catalogue of his library was printed by the Boston Public Library in 1917.]

W. C. F.

ADAMS, JOHN (Sept. 18, 1772–Apr. 24, 1863), fourth principal of Phillips Academy, Andover, was born in Canterbury, Conn., the eldest of ten children of Capt. John Adams, a Revolutionary soldier, and Mary (Parker) Adams. His forebears were simple farming folk, but he traced his ancestry back to Henry Adams, from whom the two Presidents of the United States were also descended. As a boy, he worked hard in the fields, but he was enabled, through the painful economy of his parents, to enter Yale College, where he graduated in 1795. After some experience in teaching at Canterbury, at Plainfield Academy, and at Bacon Academy, Colchester, Conn., he was offered in 1810 the principalship of Phillips Academy, then at the lowest point in its history. There he found only twenty-three pupils and a complete lack of discipline. Under his firm rule, however, conditions quickly improved, and the academy was soon in good standing. The number of students gradually increased until in ten years it was over a hundred, the faculty having meanwhile been enlarged to four. Although he was naturally conservative and did not disturb the predominance of Latin and Greek, he somewhat modified the curriculum; of the twenty subjects required for a diploma in 1820, however, thirteen were classical and two mathematical. He set a high standard of scholarship, and his boys did well in college. Among his pupils were Nathaniel P. Willis, Josiah Quincy, and Oliver Wendell Holmes. Adams's influence was exerted most vigorously in the field of morals and religion. He was "by all his views, habits, and impulses a *revival* man," and he aimed "to lay as securely as possible in the character of every pupil the foundation of Christian manhood." He held frequent prayer-meetings and accomplished many conversions; indeed he boasted that one out of every five of his pupils later entered the ministry. He was a handsome and imposing figure, with the bearing of an autocrat. As he walked down the aisle in church, his ivory-headed cane ringing against the floor, he seemed to dominate the assemblage. Holmes, in his poem *The School Boy,* gave his impression of Adams in the lines:

"Supreme he sits. Before the awful frown
That bends his brows the boldest eye goes down."

After 1825 Adams seems to have loosened his grip on school affairs, with the result that the attendance gradually fell off and he lost the confidence of the trustees; in 1832, when he was sixty, he resigned at their request. During the remaining thirty-one years of his life, he struggled bravely against poverty, first as principal of an academy in Elbridge, N. Y., then as president of a female seminary in Jacksonville, Ill., and finally as agent of the American Sunday-school Union in the Middle West; for twelve years he drove from village to village in an open carriage, organizing Sunday-schools and winning the title of "Father Adams." In 1854 Yale made him a Doctor of Laws.

Adams was twice married, first to Elizabeth Ripley, in 1798, by whom he had ten children. After her death, in 1829, he married Mrs. Mabel Burritt, of Troy, N. Y. One of his sons, William Adams, became president of Union Theological Seminary. Principal Adams is commemorated at Andover by a tablet in the Chapel, the gift of his grand-daughter, Mrs. John Crosby Brown, and also by a dormitory, erected in 1912 and known as Adams Hall. He was buried in Jacksonville, Ill., under a granite monument with the epitaph, "A Lover of Children, A Teacher of Youth, A Sinner Saved by Grace."

[*The Story of John Adams* (1890), by M. E. B. (Mrs. J. C. Brown) and H. G. B. (Helen Gilman Brown); *An Old New Eng. School,* by Claude M. Fuess (1917); articles in the *Phillips Bull.,* the quarterly publication of Phillips Acad., Andover.]

C. M. F.

ADAMS, JOHN (July 1, 1825–Nov. 30, 1864), Confederate soldier, was the son of parents who came to the United States in 1814 from Ulster, Ireland, following the example of a relative, John Adams, who had prospered as a banker in New York City. In 1817 they moved to Nashville, Tenn., and there John Adams was born. Shortly afterwards his father moved to Pulaski, where he died before his son entered the U. S. Military Academy at West Point in 1841. Adams graduated in the class of 1846 and was appointed second lieutenant in the 1st Dragoons, United States Army. He served in that regiment during the Mexican War and was brevetted for gallantry in the assault of Santa Cruz de Rosales, Chihuahua, Mar. 16, 1848. Duty on the frontier followed. In 1848–49 he served at Santa Fé and Taos, N. Mex. Then came expeditions against the Utah and Apache Indians with the consequent skirmishes and hard marching. In 1850–51 he served at Rayado and Las Vegas, N. Mex., and reached his first lieutenancy. The following year he was stationed at Fort Snelling, Minn., where he married Georgia McDougal, the daughter of a distinguished army surgeon. In 1853 he acted as aide-de-camp for the governor of Minnesota with the rank of lieutenant-colonel. During 1854–56 he served at Fort Leavenworth, Kan.; Fort Craig, Fort Union, and Santa Fé in New Mexico; Fort Massachusetts in Colorado. In 1856 he received his captaincy in the Dragoons, and this was followed by two years of recruiting duty. The outbreak of the Civil War found him serving at Fort Crook, Cal. This life in command of small units, of operations against Indians, and of incessant movement, all under the most general instructions, had given him, like so many of his contemporaries, a military training whose results were to be made manifest in the coming conflict.

Capt. Adams resigned from the army May 31, 1861 and proceeded to New York by sea, arriving there in August. Gen. Scott, in command of the army, ordered his arrest as a political prisoner but he avoided this and made his way back to Tennessee, where he was appointed a captain of cavalry in the Confederate Army and placed in command of Memphis. By May 1862 he had reached the grade of colonel and was assigned to duty as acting brigadier-general, commanding a force operating about Huntsville. On Dec. 29, 1862 he was appointed brigadier-general. On May 16, 1863, on the death of Gen. Lloyd Tilghman, Gen. Johnson placed him in command of Tilghman's brigade of six regiments of Mississippi infantry. In command of this force, which served at least in part as mounted infantry, he took part in the operations for the relief of Vicksburg and in those about Jackson, Miss. Then he marched under Gen. Polk to Resaca, Ga., where his brigade joined the Army of the Tennessee and participated in the battles of the campaign from Dalton to Atlanta, where it especially distinguished itself. After the fall of Atlanta, he led the advance of Gen. Hood's army much of the time, and grew to be marked as one of those men who, like Gen. Forrest of the same army, compelled devotion. At the battle of Franklin, Nov. 30, 1864, he was wounded early in the day but refused to give up his command. In the great assault which, like a wave, swept upon the Union works, Adams, still mounted, led his brigade, cheering on his men charging behind him. When the wave broke and drew back, he was found mortally wounded, beneath his dead horse on the crest of the Union parapet.

[*Confed. Mil. Hist.*(1899), VIII; *Official Records;* W. W. Clayton, *Hist. of Davidson County, Tenn.* (1880); G. W. Cullum, *Biog. Reg.* (1891), II.]

J. R. M. T.

ADAMS, JOHN COLEMAN (Oct. 25, 1849–June 22, 1922), Universalist clergyman, author, was a descendant of Henry Adams of Braintree, Mass., and numbered among his ancestors John Alden and Col. James Barrett, who commanded the militia at Concord Bridge. His father was John Greenleaf Adams, also a Universalist clergyman and author; and his mother, Mary Hall (Barrett) Adams. He was born in Malden, Mass., prepared for college in the public schools, graduated from Tufts, in 1870, and from the theological school connected with that college in 1872. He then became pastor of the Universalist church in Newton, Mass., where he remained until 1880, leaving there to take charge of the First Universalist Church in Lynn. On July 18, 1883 he married Miriam P. Hovey of Newton, Mass. In 1884 he was called to St. Paul's Church, Chicago. In 1890 he began an eleven years' pastorate in Brooklyn, N. Y., at the close of which he went to All Souls' Church, Hartford, Conn., and remained there until his death.

He was a man of cultivation, fine taste, and transparent sincerity. During his long pastorate in Hartford his intellectual strength and personal charm caused his professional associates to give him the title "Dean of the Hartford Ministry." A progressive liberal, firm in his convictions, he had great charity, nevertheless, for all who differed with him. Young men were especially attracted to him, and in his later years he became the beloved champion of those whose interpretations of theology and life were at variance with those of their fathers. He had an irenic spirit and a quiet humor which always quieted a conference excited over questions of theology, ecclesiastical policies, or the attitude of the church toward matters of state. He was fond of out-of-door life and found much time for recreation. His nature studies show keen appreciation of beauty, an eye for delicate details, and originality of description. The following is a list of his publications: *The Fatherhood of God* (1888); *Christian Types of Hero-*

ism (1889); *The Leisure of God* (1895); *Nature Studies in Berkshire* (1899); *William Hamilton Gibson* (1901); *Hosea Ballou and the Gospel Renaissance of the Nineteenth Century* (1902); *An Honorable Youth* (1906); *Short Studies in the Larger Faith* (1907); *Santa Claus's Baby and other Christmas Stories* (1911); *Universalism and the Universalist Church* (1915); "The Universalists," in *The Religious History of New England* (1917).

[*Who's Who in America*, 1922–23; O. F. Adams, *Dict. of Am. Authors* (4th ed., 1901); *Men of Mark in Conn.*, II (1906), ed. by N. G. Osborn; *Hartford Daily Courant*, June 23, 1922; personal information.] L. S. M.

ADAMS, JOHN QUINCY (July 11, 1767–Feb. 23, 1848), eldest son of John and Abigail (Smith) Adams, was born at Braintree (now Quincy), Mass. With little early schooling he accompanied his father to France in 1778, already keeping a journal which developed into one of the most famous of diaries. He had a short training in French and Latin in an academy at Passy. Returning to America he went to France again in 1779 and attended the Latin School at Amsterdam. He matriculated into Leyden University in January 1781, but soon went to St. Petersburg as secretary to Francis Dana, United States minister to Russia. In 1783 he returned to The Hague and resumed his classics under Dumas, the editor of Vattel, again to be called away to serve as secretary to his father during the peace negotiations. On the father's appointment to the London mission the son determined to return to America, entered Harvard College a junior sophister, graduated in 1787, studied law at Newburyport under Theophilus Parsons, afterwards chief justice of Massachusetts, and was admitted to practice July 15, 1790. Law as a profession did not attract him and he readily turned to political discussion. In 1791 he wrote, under the name of "Publicola," a reply to Paine's *Rights of Man*, and the authorship was ascribed to his father in London and Edinburgh reissues. He contributed to and translated for a French newspaper in Boston and in a series of essays signed "Marcellus," "Columbus," and "Barneveld," he so dealt with Genet and neutrality as to attract the notice of Washington, who commissioned him (May 30, 1794) minister to the Netherlands. He arrived at his post as the French occupied the country, but remained to study, observe, and report upon European conditions. On July 26, 1797, while in England on diplomatic business he married Louisa Catherine, daughter of Joshua Johnson, of a Maryland family. He was named for the mission in Portugal, but his destination was changed to Berlin, where he negotiated a treaty and found abundant leisure for reading. He made a visit to Silesia and printed a volume of letters describing it. His foreign mission ended in September 1801, he resumed his law practice in Boston. He was nominated for Congress, but was defeated on Nov. 3, 1802, by W. Eustis, who received a majority of 59 votes in a total of 3,699. Though without party affiliations, Adams had been previously elected to the state Senate in April 1802. On the first opportunity he showed his want of respect for party lines by proposing in caucus that two or three of the governor's council be "of opposite politics to our own, by way of conciliatory procedure," but his suggestion was rejected. In February 1803 he was elected to the United States Senate, with Timothy Pickering as a colleague, and took his seat in October while the bill for taking possession of Louisiana was under consideration. On Oct. 26 he asked its supporters where in the Constitution they found authority for vesting in persons appointed by the President the military, civil, and judicial powers exercised "by the existing government of Louisiana." He proposed to amend the bill "consistently with the Constitution," but his motion, not being in order, could not be considered. On Nov. 3 he voted in favor of an appropriation for carrying into effect the purchase treaty, which other Federalist senators opposed, and on Jan. 10, 1804 he introduced two resolutions against taxing the inhabitants of Louisiana without their consent, neither of which was accepted by the Senate. He also opposed a bill for the temporary government of the territory. He was never reconciled to the course of legislation taken at that time, but believed the acquisition of Louisiana to have been "accomplished by a flagrant violation of the Constitution."

His report on Senator John Smith, who was implicated in the Burr plot, his attitude on the impeachment of Judge Pickering, his apparent support of the administration in regard to British aggressions against neutrals and the affair of the *Chesapeake*, and finally his votes on the Embargo of 1807, where he chose to favor embargo as an alternative to war, proved his want of party allegiance and aroused the full hostility of Pickering. The latter denounced him at home, secured a premature election of a new senator from Massachusetts, and thus forced Adams to resign, on June 8, 1808. He was now regarded by the Federalists as an apostate, was shunned by his old associates, and shared in the odium heaped upon his father. He had in 1806 been appointed to the chair of rhetoric and oratory in Harvard College and even in that position was made to feel the dislike of his social equals. During his term as senator the tendency of the Federalists to condone the insults and injuries inflicted upon American commerce, that peace might be kept with Great Britain, had led Adams to draw away from that party; and its secret maneuvers, with Pickering as a leader, to form closer relations, if not more, with England shocked his devotion to the Union. Unable to induce the Federalists of Boston to pledge full support to the government after the affair of the *Chesapeake,* he accomplished his end in a meeting of Republicans. Yet he was not a Republican nor a full supporter of the administration, and refused an offer from Republicans of a nomination to Congress. An independent, he was regarded with suspicion by both parties.

When Madison became president he nominated Adams to be minister at St. Petersburg, and in October 1809 the new minister was at his post. His experience at other capitals proved of service in Russia, the only country of Europe which refused to comply with the commercial decrees of Napoleon and thus the only outlet for the trade of the United States. On friendly terms with the Tsar, respected by his diplomatic colleagues, participating in the social life of the capital though without being able properly to reciprocate favors, he widened his knowledge and, even against the English representative, furthered the interests of his country with results that were to be gratefully remembered fifty years later. During his absence (February 1811) he was nominated and confirmed to the Supreme Court of the United States, an appointment which he immediately declined. He saw Russia invaded by Napoleon because of her refusal to close her ports and he saw the United States declare war against Great Britain at the very time when Russia was combining with that nation against France. An offer from Russia to mediate the differences between England and the United States led to the appointment of peace commissioners by the latter, and Adams, James A. Bayard, and Albert Gallatin were named (Apr. 17, 1813) and dispatched, too hastily, it proved, as Great Britain had not agreed to the mediation, and the Senate rejected Gallatin (July 19, 1813). Growing weary of the war, Great Britain expressed a willingness to negotiate, but not under Russian mediation, and the United States again named the same agents and added to the mission Jonathan Russell and Henry Clay (Jan. 18, 1814). In a commission composed of such incongruous personalities differences in opinion were certain to arise. Adams was the first in authority by his appointment, but he required Gallatin's tact and criticism to temper his too ardent sensibility and in the end the credit for success may be divided between those two members. The British commissioners were by no means the equal in ability of the Americans, and by their demands and arrogant manner of making them created a situation unfavorable to agreement. Adams drafted the papers of the American commissioners and complained somewhat overmuch that his colleagues revised them in a hostile spirit. Clay specially irritated him, for they differed in temperament as well as in interests. To Adams the fisheries were immeasurably important; to Clay the navigation of the Mississippi. Clay favored a continuance of war, Adams looked for peace. The course of the negotiation and the part played by each commissioner are related in Adams's diary. While failing to obtain all their instructions called for, they succeeded in making peace (Dec. 24, 1814) and either postponed undetermined questions or provided for their settlement in future instruments.

Adams was in Paris on the return of Napoleon and during the greater part of the "Hundred Days." He was made minister to the Court of St. James's, thus repeating the father's experience in being the first minister to that court after a war, and, still in succession, took part in discussing a commercial treaty. For two years Adams had abundant opportunity to complete his diplomatic education. Never quite congenial with the English, he carried on negotiations with the cabinet of the King on questions still at issue between the two countries, without reaching agreement. He lived at Ealing, in the neighborhood of London, and took but little part in the social life around him, though he formed many agreeable connections, and educated his sons in English schools. Official functions he endured, rather than enjoyed, and he indulged his tastes as a reader and student.

He was invited by Monroe, in March 1817, to be secretary of state in his cabinet and took up his duties Sept. 22. No more congenial office could have fallen to him, and his previous training and experience eminently fitted him to fill it. Politically, it was a period of calm. The war for independence and the organization of a federal government had been accomplished; a new generation, with new problems, had come forward and Adams, though inheriting and easily imbibing prejudices, brought to the conduct of his office wide experience and knowledge, great industry, and political independence. At times, it is true, his direct method seemed aggressive and unnecessarily forceful in cabinet discussion. He soon learned, too, that the apparent "era of good feeling" was largely neutralized by a contest among many for the presidency, in succession to Monroe. Clay had opposed Adams's appointment to the State Department, deeming that he had himself better claims and he opposed the administration because of his disappointment. Crawford and Calhoun, in the cabinet, laid their plans for succession and the last four years of Monroe's term were passed in maneuvering for political position.

The questions before the Department of State were many and of grave moment. The revolting Spanish colonies in America fitted out many privateers in the United States, a practice defended by Clay, who severely criticized both Monroe and Adams for their more cautious and correct policy. The Floridas, still Spanish territory, afforded a refuge for Indians and malefactors, and Spain could not protect the United States from raids and retreats, accompanied by murder and rapine. Jackson, placed in command, went against the Seminole Indians, pursued them into Spanish territory, hanged some of them, executed two British subjects, deposed one governor and named another, and left a garrison in occupation. Thus to invade the territory of a nation in time of peace created serious liabilities. Monroe and all his cabinet, except Adams, believed the general had exceeded his instructions and had done what could not in law be defended. Calhoun would have punished him. Adams took the ground that, as Spain had proved incapable of policing her territories, the United States was obliged to act in self-defense, and so far and so ably justified Jackson's conduct as to silence protests either from Spain or Great Britain. Congress debated the question, with Clay as the leading opponent of Jackson, but would not disapprove of what Jackson had done. It was strange that Jackson's later hatred of Adams, his ablest defender, should have been greater than his hatred of Clay and Calhoun, his critics.

The most delicate and important negotiation conducted by Adams was the treaty for the cession of the Floridas by Spain. Not only were the western bounds of the territory in doubt, but the delays and trickiness of Spanish diplomacy complicated the agreement. Huge grants of land to court favorites, not mentioned, or concealed by false dates, nearly trapped Adams in serious errors. He had secured (1818) a postponement of the Oregon question by an agreement with Great Britain for a joint occupation for ten years, and to obtain Florida and quiet Spanish claims he gained an acknowledgment from Spain of a line of boundary to the South Sea, a proposal wholly his, in which he took natural pride. Giving up Texas with the consent, if not at the instance of Monroe, he obtained a treaty of cession (1819) which later was declared by his opponents a deliberate sacrifice of territory. Jackson approved of the treaty, and Clay again opposed what had been done, but without success.

While the Spanish treaty was in the making Missouri applied for statehood and a struggle arose on the exclusion of slavery. Adams approved of the Missouri Compromise and believed the measure excluded slavery in territories and in states formed from territory north of the dividing line. He saw clearly that the principle involved momentous possibilities, and might even lead to the dissolution of the Union. To him the controversy over Missouri was the "title-page to a great tragic volume." His opposition to slavery was pronounced and in his diary he pictured a life devoted to the problem of emancipation as "nobly spent or sacrificed."

The Spanish colonies in America obtained recognition of their independence from Monroe in March 1822. Already Adams had questioned the claims of Great Britain on the Pacific Ocean, and soon after, in contesting a Russian ukase regarding the same ocean, he laid down the principle that "the American continents are no longer subjects for any new European colonial establishments." Russia acquiesced. Great Britain feared that the United States would take Cuba and that France, if allowed to interpose in Spain, might control the Spanish empire in America. Acting on a suggestion of Adams that the interests of the United States and Great Britain were the same, Canning proposed a joint declaration against a forcible subjection of the colonies to Spain and against acquisition by cession or conquest of American territory by any European power. Both Jefferson and Madison favored this proposal, though it recognized the leadership of England and opposition to the Holy Alliance; but Adams wished to remonstrate against interference of European powers by force with South America, to disclaim all interference with Europe, and to make an American policy. The President's message of Dec. 2, 1823, embodied those principles. Striking out his own references to European questions, such as the invasion of Spain by France and the Greek revolt, Monroe asserted that the American continents "are henceforth not to be considered as subjects for future colonization by any European power"; that "any attempt on their part to extend their system to any portion of this hemisphere" would be regarded as "dangerous to our peace and safety," and "we could not view any interposition for the purpose of oppressing them [the late Spanish possessions], or controlling in any other manner their destiny, by any European power in any other light than as the manifestation of an unfriendly disposition toward the United States."

Known as the Monroe Doctrine, and with credit equally divided between the President and the Secretary, it has proved of great importance in the history of American diplomacy.

As the time of the presidential election approached Adams was one of four candidates. His office had by custom come to be regarded as the stepping-stone to the presidency, but in his term of service he had done little directly to advance his prospects by conciliating his rivals or the politicians. He stood upon his public services, and was the only Northern candidate. When the returns were known Jackson had received 99 votes; Adams, 84; Crawford, 41; and Clay, 37. Adams's support had come from New York and New England. With Crawford broken in health the decision in the House rested with Clay and his pronounced dislike of Jackson made a support of Adams natural. Adams, receiving the votes of thirteen states to Jackson's seven, was declared elected. The contest left a long train of consequences materially affecting the later careers of the two candidates, and Adams himself wished that a nearer approach to unanimity could have been reached, even had it been necessary for him to refuse the office in order to permit a new choice. Before the House had acted it was charged that Clay had entered into a corrupt bargain with Adams by which Adams would be president and Clay secretary of state. Though without any basis of truth the charge gained plausibility when Clay was appointed secretary. In the hands of Jackson and his followers it became a weapon which served to check Clay's success during his life and to defeat Adams in 1828. Three years before that election Jackson was again nominated for the presidency by the legislature of his State; he accepted and announced his platform, the essence of which was the denunciation of the alleged bargain between Clay and Adams.

President Adams in his inaugural stated his broad plan of internal improvements, and, in his annual message, his ideas of directing government powers to promote the arts and sciences, a national university, astronomical observatories, and scientific enterprises, in short, to whatever would improve the people. Not only were Northern strict constructionists astonished at the proposal that the federal government should exercise such extensive powers but Southerners were alarmed, fearing slavery might be abolished under them. Opposition in Congress took shape and was first directed against the proposed Panama mission—the sending of commissioners to attend a congress of the republics, lately Spanish colonies. In the course of the debate John Randolph uttered his famous characterization of the "coalition of Blifil and Black George—the combination, unheard of till then, of the Puritan with the blackleg." Adams's own faith in any success from the Congress was not strong and he gauged the weakness of the republics better than did Clay. In the end circumstances prevented the United States from being represented.

The mid-term elections of 1827 to Congress gave, for the first time in the history of the government, a large majority against the administration. By the union of the Crawford and Jackson forces the South was consolidating its influence against Adams. With no great difference in policy to justify contests of parties the agitation for political vantage turned upon personalities. Adams removed no man for political opinion or even for political activity against himself, and so little of the politician did he have in his make-up that he wished to retain Crawford in the cabinet and to appoint Jackson to the War Department. He refused to break with McLean, the postmaster general, though cognizant of his activities in behalf of Jackson. Such restraint in the exercise of a power to secure followers by the use of patronage alienated friends and encouraged enemies. During his administration only twelve removals from office were made, yet in 1826 he was arraigned for abuse of patronage and an effort was made to transfer a good share of the appointments from the President to congressmen. Few campaigns have equalled that of 1828 for its license and bitter personalities. For want of a party of his own to check the attacks of the well-organized opposition, Adams and his policy of centralized government were defeated. In the electoral college he received only 83 votes while to Jackson were given 178.

He returned to Massachusetts, where the old-time Federalists showed much the same opposition to him that they had shown to his father. By the publication of a Jefferson letter in the last days of the campaign Giles of Virginia fixed upon Adams the charge of giving Jefferson knowledge of the disunion proposals by the leaders of the party in 1804. To a demand for names and particulars by thirteen leading Federalists of Massachusetts Adams made a reply which did not satisfy, and the questioners published a letter (expressive of their deep resentment against him) which they believed to be conclusive (see *Correspondence between John Quincy Adams and Several Citizens of Massachusetts*, 1829). Keenly feeling the attitude and language of his opponents, among whom were some of the most influential men in the state, he prepared a reply, which was first published in 1877 (*Documents*

Relating to New England Federalism, ed. by Henry Adams). As a controversial document it stands high and as an explanation of the somewhat obscure movements of Pickering and others, it must be accepted as final.

Retiring to Quincy, ostracized by the Federalists and deeming his defeat an unjust return for his long public service, Adams expected to repeat the years of practical banishment endured by his father. Books, of which he had collected many in Europe, offered some refuge from memories of the past, his farm required attention, and he planned writing history or biography. Before he could fall upon any settled and engrossing task, however, he was asked to be the representative in Congress from the Plymouth district. Without definite party support he was elected to the Twenty-second Congress (Mar. 4, 1831) by a large majority and was returned for eight successive Congresses—a period of seventeen years lacking ten days. At the time of his election no member had sat in the House who possessed such varied experience and appropriate qualities. He was familiar with the inside political history of forty years abroad and at home. His remarkable memory of events was supplemented by a remarkable diary, the general accuracy of which could hardly be questioned, however colored it might be by temperament and prejudice. Industrious and conscientious in the discharge of his public duties in Congress, he served on many important committees and prepared reports which covered many questions of public policy. As a debater he was listened to with respect and, when aroused, with nearly as great fear; for his integrity was unquestioned, his information vast and ready, and his utterances direct, forceful, and at times tipped with gall. Altogether he entered upon years of influence and combat which made his congressional service unique and quite the most important part of his career.

His first appointment, chairman of the committee on manufactures, which he held for ten years, brought him into indirect connection with South Carolina nullification. For Calhoun he had no warm feeling, having received no support from him in Monroe's cabinet and only opposition in the presidency; but he thought that some concessions in the protective tariff might be made to placate South Carolina. Though it was not his committee that devised tariffs, he presented from it a minority report censuring the course of the administration. Jackson's proclamation he commended, but he believed in the event too much had been yielded to the nullifiers by a compromise which postponed instead of deciding the issue. To him any compromise on that particular question would lead to "final and irretrievable dissolution of the Union," an ever present thought in his view of public affairs.

In the discussion of the question of slavery Adams did not take a prominent part before 1835 and even then leadership was thrust upon him by force of circumstances. In 1805 he had proposed to lay a duty upon imported slaves, but only four senators had voted with him. As secretary of state he had dealt with the suppression of the slave-trade and not with the question of slavery. Atrocious as he considered that traffic, he considered the right of search by foreign officers of American vessels upon the seas in time of peace a still greater evil (*Memoirs,* VI, 37). When Haiti had become free and could be recognized in 1826, as president he had acted with caution and had found reasons for withholding an acknowledgment of independence. Clay's influence had led him to evade the question in the proposed Panama Congress, as both Haiti and Cuba furnished "near and dangerous examples," against the contagion of which "all means necessary to the security" of the United States should be employed. Now in Congress the question assumed a new form. In the first weeks of his first session he had presented petitions on slavery. In 1834 the attempts of the upholders of slavery to suppress the right of petition had been successful. For Congress to refuse to receive appeals from individuals and associations was bad enough from any point of view; to treat with contempt resolutions from the legislature of a State, no matter what the subject, involved an extraordinary exercise of power, even more indefensible. Adams, whether armed with resolutions of the legislature of Massachusetts, or with his "bundles" of petitions, kept the question before the House, greatly exasperating the majority, who were always ready to enforce the gag principle.

When president he had made a fruitless attempt to obtain Texas from Mexico by cession; but now when the annexation of Texas was first brought forward he opposed it and in a speech delivered May 25, 1836—"by far the most noted speech that I ever made," he wrote in the following year—he "opened the whole subject of the Mexican, Indian, negro, and English war." A Spanish translation was printed in Mexico and Miss Martineau used it in her volume upon America. On the general reception given to it, assailed in the South and West and applauded in the North and East, he felt that his opportunity had come. "This [the extension of slavery] is a cause upon which I am entering at the last stage of life, and with the certainty that I cannot advance in it far; my career must close, leaving the cause at the threshold. To open the way for others is all that I can do. The cause is good and great" (*Memoirs,* IX, 298). His position, the same as that he had taken on the admission of Louisiana, was on the broadest lines. In June 1838, it was expressed in the following language: "That the power of annexing the people of a foreign government to this Union has not been delegated to the Congress nor to any Department of the Government of the United States, but has been reserved to the people. That any attempt by Act of Congress or by treaty to annex the republic of Texas to this Union would be an usurpation of power, which it would be the right and the duty of the free people of the Union to resist and annul" (*Memoirs,* V, 20). On that proposition he occupied the "morning hour" from June 16 to July 7, 1838, preventing a vote on annexation; and in 1843 he united with twelve other members of Congress in a protest declaring that annexation would mean the dissolution of the Union (*Niles' Register,* LXIV, 173–75). Territory, they held, could be acquired by treaty, but there was no power to transfer a man from one country to another without his consent. Adams embodied the conviction that the Texas question involved the sacrifice of Northern freedom to slavery and the South, and the purchase of Western support by the plunder of the public lands. His opposition to annexation and to the war with Mexico brought to him petitions against annexation as well as on slavery in the District of Columbia and on slavery in general and they came to him in increasing numbers. His management of these "incendiary papers" was at first guided by the unanimous support of the Massachusetts members of the House of Representatives (*Memoirs,* IX, 443), but he acted more and more independently.

Wearied if not frightened by the number of petitions relating to slavery, some of which had been presented through Adams, the House entertained a proposition (December 1836) that no such petitions should be read, printed, committed, or in any way acted upon by the House. This took final shape in the rule that all such petitions should, without reading or printing, or any other action of the House upon them, be laid upon the table. As a motion to lay on the table admitted no debate, all discussion was precluded. Each year, from 1836 to 1844, Adams opposed without success the adoption of this rule. Such a "gag" on free discussion, he charged, was a direct violation of the Constitution, of the rules of the House, of the rights of his constituents, and, as he said in after years, of his right to freedom of speech as a member of the House. On Dec. 3, 1844, the "gag" resolution was at last defeated. While the right of petition was to Adams the real issue, he became the channel through which petitions on slavery streamed in large numbers. He was not an abolitionist, and suffered from the attacks of the abolitionists as well as from their opponents; but he recognized, as few of his day did, that a denial of the right to discuss a public question of such character threatened the continuance of the Union. Further, he early expressed (1836) the conviction that should the South become the seat of a war, "civil, servile, or foreign, from that instant the war powers of the Congress [would] extend to interference with the institution of slavery in every way by which it can be interfered with" (*Register of Debates in Congress,* vol. XII, pt. IV, p. 4047), a sweeping proposition which implied an assertion of an even stronger power; *viz.,* that slavery could be abolished by the exercise of the treaty-making power (1841) and still later, that in a state of war the military authority—president or commander of the army—might order the universal emancipation of slaves (Apr. 14, 1842. See C. F. Adams, "John Quincy Adams and Emancipation through Martial Law" in *Proceedings of the Massachusetts Historical Society,* 2nd ser., vol. XV). To check Adams's continued presentation of petitions, Southern members proposed to discipline and even to expel him, but he proved capable of holding his positions and of putting his critics in the wrong. Thus in February 1837 he asked if the gag resolution would cover a petition he had received from twenty-two persons who declared themselves to be slaves, and in the confusion that followed various motions from censure to expulsion were offered. When permitted to speak, Adams, by stating that the petition favored slavery, turned the tables on his opposers, who rounded out a somewhat ridiculous policy of suppression by gravely proposing to censure Adams for "creating an impression and leaving the House under that impression" that the petition in question was for the abolition of slavery (*Letters from John Quincy Adams to his Constituents,* 1837, p. 16); also for "giving color to the idea that slaves have the right of petition" and for being ready to serve as their organ (*Ibid.,* p. 19). The petition was probably a hoax, intended to embarrass Adams. His final speech silenced his critics and proved his ability to meet, almost single-handed, the forces of the South.

His course in the House showed what was regarded at the time as strange inconsistency. He debated and voted with complete independence, to the great confusion of those who counted upon his support. When assurance was made by those in charge of the bill for the admission of Arkansas as a State that no proposition concerning slavery would be made in the debate, Adams remarked that if no other member would offer such a proposal he would, and kept his promise. The fact that he had not been on speaking terms with President Jackson and had received insult at his hands did not prevent his supporting him—"at the hazard of my own political destruction"—in Jackson's quarrel with France, in his controversy with South Carolina, and in other critical periods of his administration. Yet he opposed Jackson's bank policy, submitting a minority report in protest against the proceedings of the committee of inquiry of which he was a member. A speech upon Jackson's removal of the public moneys from the Bank of the United States was not delivered but was published and served its purpose. From the committee on manufactures he also submitted (February 1833) a report which reviewed the claims of the South for the protection of slavery, the proposed disposal of the public lands, and the doctrine of nullification. To none of these would he yield a particle. Only one other member of the committee signed this report.

His personal influence and ability to deal with a crisis were shown in December 1839, when the House assembled to find itself unable to organize because of the arbitrary action of its clerk. So equally were parties divided in it that the members from New Jersey, whose election was contested, would decide the political complexion of the House, the Speaker, and the committees. The clerk, himself the clerk of the last House, without authority to do anything but list the members offering proper credentials, and depending for his own reëlection on the issue of the contest, refused to name the contested seats, producing a state of complete inaction difficult to meet. After three days of futile effort, Adams appealed to the members to organize and stated his determination himself to put to the meeting the question of ordering the clerk to read the names of the New Jersey members holding the governor's credentials. He was elected chairman, and for eleven days presided over a body not yet formally organized and torn by a partisan difference, on which depended the large rewards of committee appointments and their influence on legislation. Belonging to no party and entirely familiar with parliamentary practice, he controlled the stormy sessions and brought the extraordinary situation to a successful issue.

When the Whigs controlled the House in the Twenty-seventh Congress Adams was made chairman of the Committee on Foreign Affairs, for which he was eminently fitted. He could not escape attack, however, and his position in the matter of the *Creole,* a vessel captured by its cargo of slaves and taken to Nassau, where the slaves were set free by the authorities, invited it. A petition from Georgia for his removal engaged the House for some days; the Southern members of the Committee on Foreign Affairs resigned from it, unwilling, as they said, to serve with a chairman in whom they had no confidence, and others appointed asked to be excused. If the objectors planned to replace Caleb Cushing in the chairmanship, they failed; but Adams was not reappointed to that committee in the next Congress.

In January and March 1841, for the first time since 1809, Adams appeared before the Supreme Court of the United States. On the earlier occasion he had argued in defense of certain rights in which many of his fellow citizens had much property at stake; on the later he presented an elaborate argument vindicating the right to freedom of the *Amistad* captives, fifty-three negroes who had been taken at sea by a vessel of the United States, after they had revolted, killed the captain, and obtained possession of the vessel in which they and their masters were sailing for their destination. They were charged with murder and piracy. The Spanish owners claimed the negroes, the Spanish minister claimed both ship and negroes under the treaty of 1795, and the United States officer called for salvage. The United States circuit court held that it had no jurisdiction of a crime committed on the high seas in a Spanish vessel, but would not release the negroes claimed as property by the Spaniards. Adams was asked to defend the slaves and made an argument which Justice Story described as "extraordinary, for its power, for its bitter sarcasm, and its dealing with topics far beyond the record and points of discussion" (W. W. Story, *Life and Letters of Joseph Story,* 1851, II, 348). The decision of the Court declared the negroes to be free. Adams's published argument was a plea for justice, but it also served once more to express his views upon slavery.

In 1842 another occasion arose in the House of Representatives for action against Adams. He had presented (Jan. 24) a petition from citizens of Haverhill, Mass., praying that for sectional reasons the Union of the States be peaceably dissolved, and moved its reference to a select committee with instructions to report against it. The document may be regarded as a satire on the proposed dissolution of the Union. Days were spent in discussing resolutions prepared in a caucus of Southern members and presented by Marshall of Kentucky, stating that Adams had disgraced his country, might well be expelled from the national councils, and should receive their "severest censure." After eleven days of excitement, with Adams as the center of the storm, he offered to drop the subject if the resolution of censure were tabled, ending a scene that was dramatic and sensational and ending also all attempts to suppress the offender by threats of censure.

Science had interested him, though he was too absorbed in public duties to be able to pursue the study. When in Russia he had given some attention to Russian weights and measures and, shortly after becoming secretary of state, the Senate (March 1817) called upon him for a full report. The House did not act until December 1819, when it made the same requisition. On receiving the Senate's call Adams began a report, but had made little progress before that of the House was received. Devoting six months to the subject he completed the document—"a fearful and oppressive task"—and in February 1821 it was printed by Congress. Elaborate and thorough for the time and containing definite recommendations for permanent and universal uniformity of standards, it remained without influence in legislation or in advancing an agreement among nations on the subject. It was reprinted in 1871 and is still of value for reference. In another direction he left a permanent record. He was chairman of the committee to report upon the power of Congress to accept the fund left by the Englishman, James Smithson, to the United States, to establish at Washington an institution for the "increase and diffusion of knowledge." Adams not only reported that Congress was competent to accept the bequest, but he made recommendations for employing it and was instrumental in preventing its diversion to local and temporary objects. He wished to establish in the United States "the most complete astronomical observatory in the world," but Congress was unwilling to act. From the receipt of the fund in 1838 until 1846 Adams jealously watched the proposed uses, made four elaborate reports upon its disposition, provided for restoring the fund when wasted by bad investment in state bonds, and saw success in the end—a permanent fund and a national observatory. In the Smithsonian Institution his foresight and labor have been justified. It was in recognition of his efforts to encourage the study of astronomy that he was invited in 1843 to lay the corner-stone of the Cincinnati Observatory.

On Sept. 17, 1842, Adams gave to his constituents a full statement of his conduct during his service in Congress in the form of an examination of the administration under the successive presidents in that time (*Address of John Quincy Adams to his Constituents of the Twelfth Congressional District*). It embodied his conception of what the South and the slave power had done or wished to do, and how far their policy had been aided by a sacrifice of principle by the North. Entirely characteristic in form and expression it contains an excellent picture of the great political acts of twelve years by a leading actor in them. It was the last political paper prepared by Adams and may serve as his political testament. A minority report supporting resolves of the legislature of Massachusetts which proposed to amend the Constitution of the United States so as to abolish the representation of slaves was made by him in April 1844, signed also by Giddings. Occasional addresses, of more or less political cast, and debates in Congress on the annexation of Texas and the Oregon question, occupied his attention and called out his accustomed vigor and acumen. On Nov. 19, 1846, he was stricken with paralysis while walking in the streets of Boston, but recovered sufficiently to take his seat in the House on Feb. 16, 1847. A year later, Feb. 21, 1848, shortly after responding to the call of his name he fell in a second stroke and, carried to the Speaker's room in the Capitol, he died there on the evening of Feb. 23 without having recovered consciousness. Mrs. Adams died on May 15, 1852.

Of unquestioned patriotism, Adams believed that the nation should contribute to the happiness of all, and that no nation should "regulate its conduct by the exclusive or even the paramount consideration of its own interest." He saw and criticized the faults of policy or administration even more readily than he praised conduct that was based on the performance of duty. From his early years he studied political institutions, especially those of his own country, applying his knowledge to national and international questions as they came before him. Too much engrossed by immediate problems, he did not formulate a policy and thus appears inconsistent in his conduct, as if swerved by temporary considerations. Yet it was recognized in his day that one sentiment ran through all his life, an intense love of freedom for all men, and an invincible belief in the inalienable rights of man. The American Constitution was to him but a stage in the political development of those rights, not creating but accepting them, and must itself, therefore, be interpreted as a means rather than an end. As his father had done before him, he went back to natural law for the origin of rights, and, because the Constitution embodied "compromises," he accepted and defended it only so far as its principles rested upon natural right. In his long and bitter controversy over slavery this conception of the Constitution and its failure to embody the higher forms of freedom and rights of man gave him a weapon of great power. "Slavery and democracy," he wrote, "especially a democracy founded, as ours is, on the rights of man—would seem to be incompatible with each other; and yet, at this time, the democracy of the country is supported chiefly, if not entirely, by slavery."

In the contest with the slave power he acted almost alone. Independence of party was a "duty" imposed upon him, for his service belonged to the nation. Even as a representative in Congress from Massachusetts he was not influenced by the peculiar interests of that State, unless support of a protective tariff can be instanced to the contrary, a tariff that in form was framed for the whole country. To him a majority meant nothing, unless it acted oppressively—and he worked for the individual or a number, for the slave or the free man, for women or men, with the same zeal and detachment, intent only on defending the cause he had at heart. No other man of his day came to represent as he did the essence of the right of petition, and his persistence and courage won admiration even from those who thought him a madman or incendiary, and condemned his methods and the principle for which he was contending.

His many writings and speeches contain much that is autobiographical and much that is historical, for he dwelt on past and present history, and both utilized his own experience to the full and rested upon documents. His state papers and controversies suffered from the wealth of reference which his early studies, wide reading, extraordinary memory and application supplied. His readiness in debate and his bitterness of speech, which seemed at times almost too strongly colored by vindictiveness, made his attack something to be feared. Fond of combat and of controversy, his career was marked by an assertiveness amounting to pugnacity. Conscientious to a fault, he left no argument without exhausting its possibility. From his early days surrounded by enemies, as he believed, his gift of contention was developed and leaned toward offense. Yet he kept himself under restraint in the face of great provocation. He avoided the mean and tricky: he was always an honorable foe. No man judged his own acts more severely than he, and his diary, described as a "treasury of damnations," dealt with his own thoughts and acts more contritely than the occasion demanded. Harsh as his judgments on men and deeds appear, they show an ability to touch upon character and motives that makes them in part true. He had a deeply religious feeling and became a Unitarian, but never worked out a system of theology, any more than he did a system of politics. Only in his great fight on freedom did he approach a philosophy of the latter subject.

To him his generation gave the title of "the old man eloquent." Yet Theodore Parker thought him "seldom eloquent" and what oratorical ability he had to be of late development. In his manner of speaking there was little dignity and no grace, though sometimes there was a terrible energy and fire and "invective was his masterpiece of oratoric skill." Emerson, who heard him in his later years, spoke of his reputation as a fine reader: "No man could read the Bible with such powerful effect" (*Works,* 1904, VIII, 122). Of the fine voice broken by age he declared that the "wonders he could achieve with that cracked and disobedient organ showed what power might have belonged to it in early manhood" (*Ibid.*).

Simple in his tastes, and disliking the exposure to flattery that high position in the state brings, Adams was known as a man of social talent, a good talker, admired for his richness of recollection and apt illustration. Even his enemies, of whom he had an abundance, recognized that side of him and wondered. His family letters are of a quality different from his public papers, and his admiration for his father and his ambitions for his son, Charles Francis Adams, led to free confidences which reveal a softer and more lovable nature and a conscience that smote him when he thought himself most obliged to oppose or punish. Theodore Parker, not sparing in his opinion of others, wrote on the death of Adams, "The one great man since Washington, whom America had no cause to fear" (*Works,* 1908, vol. VII).

The more important writings of John Quincy Adams are: *Memoirs,* 12 vols., edited by Charles Francis Adams (1874–77); *Life in a New England Town,* diary as a law student, 1787–88, edited by Charles Francis Adams, Jr. (1903); *Documents Relating to New England Federalism,* edited by Henry Adams (1877); *Writings,* edited by W. C. Ford, 7 vols. (1913); *Oration at Plymouth, Mass.,* Dec. 22, 1802 (repr., 1820); *Letters on Silesia* (London, 1804; Paris, trans. by J. Dupuy, 1807); *Inaugural Oration* (1806); *Letter to H. G. Otis* (1808); *American Principles, a Review of the Works of Fisher Ames* (1809); *Lectures on Rhetoric and Oratory,* 2 vols. (1810); *Correspondence, 1811–14* (1913); *Report on Weights and Measures* (1821); *Duplicate Letters, the Fisheries and the Mississippi* (1822; 2nd ed., Louisville, 1823); *Correspondence between John Quincy Adams and Several Citizens of Massachusetts, concerning the Charge of a Design to Dissolve the Union* (1829); *Eulogy on James Monroe* (1831); *Dermot MacMorrogh, or the Conquest of Ireland* (1832); *Letters to Wm. L. Stone . . . upon the Subject of Masonry and Antimasonry* (1833); *Letters to Edward Livingston* [on Freemasonry] (1833); *Oration on Lafayette*, Dec. 31, 1834 (1835); *Eulogy on James Madison* (1836); *Letters to his Constituents* (1837); *Character of Hamlet: a letter to J. H. Hackett* (1839); *Speech upon Right of Petition*, June–July, 1838; *Jubilee of the Constitution* (1839); *China Question* (1841); *New England Confederacy of MDCXLIII* (1843); *Oration, Cincinnati Astronomical Society* (1843); *Letters on the Masonic Institution* (1847); *Poems of Religion and Society* (1848); and *Orations*, 4th of July, at Boston, 1793; Quincy, 1831; and Newburyport, 1837.

[W. H. Seward, *Life and Public Services of John Quincy Adams* (1849); Josiah Quincy, *Memoir of the Life of John Quincy Adams* (1858); John T. Morse, *John Quincy Adams* (1882).]

W. C. F.

ADAMS, JOSEPH ALEXANDER (1803–Sept. 11, 1880), wood engraver, inventor, was born in New Germantown, Hunterdon County, N. J. He was largely self-taught, under the encouragement of Dr. Alexander Anderson, America's first wood engraver. His apprenticeship to the printing business, which took place at an early age, was directed by three successive masters. When he became twenty-one, he went to New York, where he worked for three weeks as a journeyman printer. While still an apprentice, he had made his first attempt at engraving, a cut of a boot which could be used for a newspaper advertisement. In his own words he worked as follows: "I intensely blackened the block with India ink, then marked the outlines of the subject with a point and cut away at it. I had not then even heard of finished drawings being made on the wood. In this manner I worked for about six months" (Linton, p. 12). One day Samuel Wood, a publisher of juvenile works, advised him to go to see Dr. Alexander Anderson. "After walking several times to and fro in front of his house," Adams wrote, "I ventured to knock at the door. I found him very pleasant and communicative. He showed me a block he was then working upon and to my astonishment I found the whole design was neatly washed on the block complete with India ink alone. This was entirely a new idea to me. The Doctor gave me many hints, such as lowering parts of the block after the manner of Bewick, so as to print faintly. He also sent me customers occasionally. He laid before me several of Bewick's works which I had never heard of before and also showed me many other specimens of cuts done by English and old German artists" (*Ibid.*, p. 12). Books were not profusely illustrated in Adams's time, and what illustration was used was generally copperplate: nevertheless, in 1831, he was financially able to make a voyage to England, probably incited to do so by the coming to this country in 1829 of Abraham J. Mason, an English engraver on wood, from whom he may have had introductions to Thompson, Bonner, and others.

In 1833 some of his work appeared in the *Treasury of Knowledge* and in the *Cottage Bible*. His "Last Arrow" was engraved in 1837 for the *New York Mirror*. But it was his sixteen hundred illustrations for Harper's *Illuminated Bible*, published in 1843, which constituted his greatest achievement. He is said to have been the first electrotyper in America and to have invented several improvements in the process. Linton commends his work for its firm, honest exactness and clearness, and for his graver drawing, mechanism of the art, disposition and perfection of lines. He died in New Jersey at the age of seventy-seven.

[William James Linton, *Hist. of Wood Engraving in America* (1882); J. Henry Harper, *The House of Harper* (1912), pp. 79–81; *Am. Art Rev.*, Oct. 1880.]

R. C. S.

ADAMS, NEHEMIAH (Feb. 19, 1806–Oct. 6, 1878), Congregational clergyman, was born in Salem, Mass., the son of Nehemiah Adams, deacon of the Tabernacle Congregational Church, and Mehitable Torrey Adams. He was educated at Salem Latin School, Harvard College, and Andover Theological Seminary; was ordained and installed as co-pastor with Dr. Abiel Holmes at the Shepard Church (First Congregational) in Cambridge, Mass., in 1829, and on the retirement of Dr. Holmes in September 1831 was made sole pastor. He served in this position until Mar. 14, 1834, and was installed pastor of the Essex Street or Union Congregational Church of Boston, Mar. 26, 1834. He remained pastor of the Boston church until his death. He was given the degree of D.D. by Amherst in 1847. In 1869 he suffered a paralytic shock from which he never fully recovered. Accompanied by his two daughters, he made a trip around the world, 1869–70, in the ship *Golden Fleece*, commanded by his son. The experiences of this trip are recorded in his book, *A Voyage Around the World* (1871), republished in enlarged form as *Under the Mizzen Mast* (1873). During the Unitarian controversy Adams figured prominently as an upholder of Evangelical orthodoxy. His works in this connection are *Remarks on the Unitarian Belief* (1832), *A Letter to Rev. Ezra S. Gannett, occasioned by his tract on atonement* (1840), *Injuries done to Christ* (1841), a pamphlet in reply to Prof. Henry Ware for strictures on the same (1841), "Why am I a Trinitarian Congregationalist?" in *Pitts Street Chapel Lectures* (1858). He produced, in all, sixteen volumes and more than fifty other publications. Among his books are *The Life of John Eliot* (1847); *The Friends of Christ in the New Testament* (1853); *The Communion Sabbath* (1856); *Agnes and the Key of her Little Coffin* (1857); *Bertha and her Baptism* (1857). He edited the *Autobiography of Rev. Thomas Shepard* (1832), and compiled a hymnal, *Church Pastorals* (1864). In the winter of 1854 he visited the South and his hospitable treatment led him to write his best-known book, *A South-side View of Slavery* (1854). This was not a defense of slavery, but it recognized the better side of the institution and deplored the excesses of the Northern abolitionists. Its author believed that if unmolested the South would peacefully abolish slavery. The book subjected Adams to bitter criticism. A resolution of disapproval was offered at a meeting of his church, but it was laid on the table. In 1861 he replied to his critics in another book on slavery, *The Sable Cloud,* which was largely suppressed by his friends. His last work on this subject was a volume of sermons, *At Eventide* (1877), whose publication was requested by ten clergymen of Charleston, S. C., for the promotion of better feeling between North and South.

Hon. Rufus Choate, a parishioner and strong admirer of Adams, praised him for "the daily beauty of his life, his consistency, steadiness, affection, sincerity, taste and courage." Dr. James Hamilton of London called him "the Washington Irving of sermon writers." Dr. Austin Phelps commended "his broad reach in adaptation to different classes of mind." Addison and Jeremy Taylor are said to have been his models in literary style.

Adams married Martha Hooper of Marblehead, Mass., Jan. 11, 1832. She died Dec. 23, 1848. On May 15, 1850 he married Sarah Williston Brackett of Easthampton, Mass. He was the father of seven children by his first marriage and of two by his second. Two sons and three daughters survived him. He was a member of the American Tract Society, a corporate member of the American Board of Foreign Missions for forty-one years, and of its Prudential Committee for thirty-two years. Portraits of him are found in the *Memorial Volume,* issued by the Essex Street Church in 1860, and in *At Eventide;* there is also an oil portrait in Union Congregational Church, Boston.

[*Congregational Yr. Bk.* (1879); *Congregationalist,* Oct. 16, 1878; *N.Y. Observer,* Oct. 17, 1878; *Ministries that Never End,* by his successor, Rev. F. A. Warfield (1878); *Boston Advertiser, Statesman, Zion's Herald,* Oct. 9, 11, and 17, 1878; Anniversary publications of Union Church, 1860, 1897, and 1922.]

F. T. P.

ADAMS, ROBERT (Feb. 26, 1846–June 1, 1906), lawyer, legislator, son of Robert and Matilda Hart Adams, was a native of Philadelphia. The family was important in Pennsylvania history as appears from the State's muster-rolls and Robert's membership in various colonial and Revolutionary societies. He began his education at Claymont, Del., prepared for college at the Philadelphia Classical Institute, and graduated from the University of Pennsylvania, with the degrees A.B. 1869, A.M. 1872. He studied law with George W. Biddle of Philadelphia and was admitted to the bar in 1872. While at college he had taken courses in geology under Prof. Ferdinand V. Hayden, who in 1867 began his explorations in the government's western territories, and in 1871 he joined Hayden in his Yellowstone researches leading to the withdrawal of 3,575 square miles for a national park. During these four years of investigation, Adams was special correspondent for two New York and two Philadelphia newspapers, and developed the ability to interest the average reader in subjects demanding intimate knowledge and accurate description. Upon the completion of this scientific work he resumed the study of law and politics, although retaining his membership in the United States Geological Survey. He graduated from the Wharton School of the University of Pennsylvania in 1884 with the degree B.F., and represented a Philadelphia district in the state Senate 1882–86. On Apr. 1, 1889 President Harrison appointed him minister to Brazil, where he remained until July 1, 1890, devoting much money and time to a thorough examination of consular work in Spanish America. Upon election to Congress in 1893 he framed a measure for consular reform, which after twelve years of vigorous support he was to see become law.

In Congress Adams represented an important business district of Philadelphia which returned him in 1904 by 41,724 votes to 7,393 for all other candidates. His particular fields of activity during his thirteen years of service were foreign relations, internal improvements, and Pennsylvania interests. He was familiar with the resources of Spanish America and saw clearly the effects of Spanish misgovernment in Cuba, from which he reasoned that Spain would not long hold her colonial empire together and that the United States could not guarantee her against loss. When therefore President McKinley on Apr. 11, 1898 asked Congress for authority to end hostilities in Cuba,

Adams, as acting chairman of the House Committee on Foreign Affairs, conducted through the House, and had charge in conference with the Senate, of the resolution by which at 3 a. m. Apr. 19 Congress declared Cuba independent. With like energy he drafted, introduced, and forced through the House in one hour the congressional resolution of Apr. 25 declaring war against Spain. After the power of Spain had collapsed, Adams, as a representative of America's commercial interests, favored the retention of the Philippines by the United States. At about this time he began to meet with increasing financial difficulties. Weakened by failing health, he was subjected to extra work as acting chairman of the House Committee on Foreign Affairs in the absence of his chief. Not until May 31, 1906 did his diplomatic and consular measure pass the House. Then, as he wrote Speaker Cannon, he felt warranted in abandoning his official position, and the next morning died by his own hand. Congress dispensed with the usual memorial addresses, as he had written: "I have never been in sympathy with the latter custom." Adams was never married but had been a bachelor leader in Philadelphia and Washington society.

[*Cong. Record,* 1893–1906; H. E. Flack, "Spanish-American Diplomatic Relations Preceding the War of 1898," in *Johns Hopkins Univ. Studies in Hist. and Pol. Sci.,* ser. XXIV, nos. 1–2; Woodrow Wilson, *Hist. of the Am. People* (1918), esp. vols. IX and X; obituaries in *N.Y. Evening Post,* June 1, 1906, and *N.Y. Herald, Phila. Public Ledger, Phila. Inquirer,* June 2, 1906.]

C. H. L—n.

ADAMS, SAMUEL (Sept. 27, 1722–Oct. 2, 1803), Revolutionary statesman, was descended from Henry Adams, who came from England, and settled in Mt. Wollaston (Braintree), Mass. Of two grandsons of Henry Adams, one, Joseph Adams, was the grandfather of John Adams, second president of the United States. The other was John Adams, a sea captain, whose second son was Samuel Adams, born May 6, 1689, in Boston. Samuel Adams married Mary Fifield, and to them were born twelve children. One of these was Samuel Adams, who was born in Purchase St., Boston. Little is known of his mother, except that she was a woman "of severe religious principles" (Wells, I, 3). His father was of sufficient prominence so that in Harvard College his son ranked socially, fifth in a class of twenty-two. His Purchase St. residence was accounted a fine one, and besides other real estate he owned a thriving brewery. He was a deacon in Old South Church, and instrumental in establishing (1715–17) New South Church, one of the ministers of which, Samuel Checkley, was a relative and the father-in-law of his famous son. At different times Adams was justice of the peace, selectman, and member from Boston in the House of Representatives. William Gordon says, on what authority is not known, that as early as 1724 the elder Adams and others "used to meet, make a caucus, and lay their plans for introducing certain persons into places of trust and power" (*History of the Rise, Progress, and Establishment of the Independence of the United States,* 1788, I, 365).

Of the youth of Samuel Adams little is known. According to Wells (*Life of Samuel Adams,* I, 5), who probably relies on family tradition, he studied under Mr. Lovell, principal of the Boston Grammar School. In 1736 he entered Harvard College, where he acquired a knowledge of Greek and Latin, and learned to admire the classical heroes as seen through the eyes of Plutarch. It is said that the college authorities admonished him once—for over-sleeping. He graduated in 1740, and three years later came back to receive the degree of Master of Arts, arguing affirmatively the thesis: "Whether it be lawful to resist the Supreme Magistrate, if the Commonwealth cannot be otherwise preserved" (*Ibid.,* p. 10). Upon leaving college in 1740 he studied law to please his father, but gave it up to please his mother (*Ibid.,* pp. 11–12). He then entered the counting-house of Thomas Cushing, only to leave it after a few months in order to establish himself in a business of his own, for which purpose his father advanced him £1,000. Half of this sum Adams loaned to an impecunious friend who could not repay it; the other half he soon lost on his own account. He then joined his father in the brewery, where it may be supposed he did little good for lack of capacity, and little harm from lack of responsibility. His father died in 1748, and shortly after, upon the death of his mother, he inherited one-third of the property, including the Purchase St. house and the brewery. This fair estate was gradually dissipated, and Adams found himself embarrassed by obligations which he could not meet. In 1758 an attempt was made to serve a sheriff's attachment on the Purchase St. house for the benefit of the creditors of the Land Bank, dissolved by Act of Parliament in 1741 (*14 George II, ch. 37*), of which the elder Adams had been one of the principal stockholders. The action was successfully resisted (Wells, I, 26–27); but meantime, as tax collector from 1756 to 1764, Adams fell into arrears in his collections until he was obligated to the Town of Boston to the extent of about £8,000 for back taxes. During these years he was twice married: in 1749 to Elizabeth Checkley, who died in 1757, leaving two children, and in 1764 to Elizabeth Wells. In the latter year, the year of the Sugar Act and the beginning of the quarrel with Great Britain, Adams was forty-two years old, in debt, living in the run-down Purchase St. house, his family often dependent for food and clothes upon the strict economies of his wife, or the casual gifts of neighbors.

Unable to manage his own affairs, Adams had already shown some talent for managing local politics. According to Wells (I, 15–16), he helped in 1747 to found a political club, dubbed by its opponents the "Whipping Post Club"; and he was probably one of the contributors to the *Independent Advertiser* which the club established in 1748 (Isaiah Thomas, *History of Printing in America,* 1810, II, 235). At least as early as 1763 he was a member of the influential "Caucus Club," which, according to John Adams, "meets . . . in the garret of Tom Dawes. . . . There they smoke tobacco . . . drink flip, I suppose, . . . choose a moderator, who puts questions to the vote regularly; and selectmen, assessors, . . . and representatives, are regularly chosen before they are chosen in the town" (*Works of John Adams,* II, 144). By 1764 Adams's influence in local politics must have been considerable, and his ability as a writer well known, since in that year he was given the task of drafting the instructions from the Town of Boston to its representatives (Cushing, *Writings of Samuel Adams,* I, 1). His effective career really began, however, with the year 1764; for it was the quarrel with Great Britain that first offered him both an adequate opportunity for the exercise of his political talents and an adequate excuse for neglecting the private business for which he had neither inclination nor capacity.

After 1764 Adams devoted even less time than formerly to making a living. He is a "universal good character," said his cousin, John Adams, "unless it should be admitted that he is too attentive to the public, and not enough to himself and his family" (*Works of John Adams,* II, 164). He told John Adams that "he never looked forward in his life; never planned, laid a scheme, or formed a design for laying up anything for himself or others after him" (*Ibid.,* p. 238). About the time of the first Continental Congress (1774) one unknown friend built him a new barn, another repaired his house; others fitted him out for his journey to Philadelphia with a new suit, new wig, new shoes, new silk hose; and one man "modestly enquir'd of him whether his finances want rather low than otherways. He reply'd it was true that was the case, but he was very indifferent about these matters, so that his *poor* abilities was of any service to the publick; upon which the Gentleman oblig'd him to accept of a purse containing about 15 or 20 Johannes" (*Proceedings of the Massachusetts Historical Society,* VIII, 340). To a man who could receive so much for his services to the public and retain his self-respect, it was essential that the public business should be always pressing and of vital importance. Temperament and circumstances combined to give Samuel Adams but one occupation—the public business; temperament and circumstances combined to furnish him with a passionate and unquestioned faith in the virtue of the cause he served. This is perhaps the principal key to the quality and the success of all his labors.

Adams was associated with the popular party which for some years before 1764 had been opposed to that small group of wealthy, interrelated, and socially exclusive families that virtually governed the province. Of this group the outstanding figure was Thomas Hutchinson [*q.v.*], lieutenant-governor, member of the Council, and chief justice. Adams had personal reasons for disliking Hutchinson, because of the latter's part in getting the Land Bank dissolved, and because he regarded Adams as having "made defalcation" in failing to collect the taxes (so Hutchinson refers to Adams in his *History of Massachusetts Bay,* III, 294–95). Until 1764 the popular party had made but little headway against the "aristocracy"; but Adams and his friends seized upon the issue raised by the Sugar Act and the Stamp Act as admirably calculated to discredit them. Hutchinson was opposed to both the Sugar Act and the Stamp Act, it is true; but he regarded them as unwise merely, never as unconstitutional, and he was especially opposed to the radical scheme of resisting the application of the Stamp Act by "doing business as usual without stamps." The radicals therefore denounced the Hutchinsonian conservatives as "enemies of liberty" who secretly sympathized with British measures of oppression. Special odium fell upon Hutchinson, not only because of his resistance to the radical program, but also because his brother-in-law, Andrew Oliver, had accepted the office of stamp distributor. During the riots of 1765 Oliver was burned in effigy, and Hutchinson's town house was gutted by the mob.

Adams never openly countenanced violence, but he was a leading influence in turning popular hatred against the conservatives. In 1765 he again wrote the instructions for the "Boston Seat" (*Writings,* I, 7). On Sept. 27 he was elected to fill the vacancy in the House occasioned by the death of Oxenbridge Thatcher; and as a member of the House he prepared the "Answer...to the Governor's Speech" and the "Resolutions of the House" setting forth its theory of American rights (*Ibid.,* pp. 13, 23). Entrenched in the Caucus Club and the "Sons of Liberty," Adams and his colleagues made political capital out of the popular hatred of the conservatives, with the result that in 1766 the radicals elected a majority of the House of Representatives and excluded from the Council five prominent conservatives, including Hutchinson and his relatives, Andrew and Peter Oliver. Adams himself was reëlected in 1766, and continuously thereafter until 1774, serving also during those years as clerk of the House. Thus from 1766 the General Court was largely controlled by the radical party, and of this party Samuel Adams rapidly rose to be the outstanding leader. Under cover of "restricting the executive power," he used his influence in the House and out of it to make the position of Gov. Bernard untenable, and when Bernard was recalled in 1769 he directed his hostility to Lieutenant-Governor Hutchinson (*Ibid.*, pp. 114 ff.). He directed the opposition to the Townshend Acts (*Ibid.*, pp. 134 ff.), helped to organize the Non-Importation Association of 1768, drafted the famous "Circular Letter" to the assemblies of the other provinces (*Ibid.*, p. 184) and that for the "Convention" of the patriot party held in Boston in 1768. Above all he kept up a running fire of opposition to the Commissioners of the Customs sent to Boston to collect the Townshend duties, and was probably more influential than any other person in stirring up the popular hatred of the British troops which ended in the Boston Massacre of 1770 (*Writings*, I, 248, ff.; Hosmer, *Adams*, pp. 109, 160 ff.)

Adams's influence was due, not only to his unrivalled skill as a local politician, but also to his skill as a polemical writer. As clerk of the House, he drafted most of the official papers of that body. He also wrote many letters on his own account to prominent persons in England and America, and contributed to the *Boston Gazette* and other journals numerous articles signed, according to the custom of the time, "Candidus," "Vindex," "Poplicola," etc. (*Writings*, I, *passim*). While it has been asserted that Adams aimed at separation from Great Britain as early as 1768 (Wells, I, 207; Hosmer, *Adams*, p. 119), there is no clear evidence in his contemporary writings that such was the case. But as early as 1765 he formulated the basic premises from which could easily be deduced the conclusions which Jefferson reached in the Declaration of Independence. "The leading principles of the British Constitution have their foundation in the Laws of Nature and universal Reason. Hence . . . British Rights are in great measure, unalienably, the Rights of the colonists, and of all Men else" (*Writings*, I, 64). Since the British Constitution accorded Englishmen the right of being taxed only by representatives of their own choosing, the Stamp Act was unconstitutional, inasmuch as the colonists were not, and in the nature of the case could not well be, represented in the British Parliament. In 1768 Adams went a step farther by maintaining that the colonial legislatures were "subordinate" but not "subject" to Parliament. (1) The British Constitution, like the constitution of all free peoples, is "fixed in the law of Nature and of God"; (2) The British Constitution provides for a "supreme," in the sense of a supervising, legislature (Parliament), and many "subordinate," in the sense of local, legislatures (colonial assemblies); (3) None of these legislatures, since they all derive their authority from the Constitution, can change the Constitution without "destroying their own foundations"; (4) Among the powers conferred by the Constitution upon the subordinate legislatures is that of guaranteeing the natural and constitutional rights of Americans (*Ibid.*, pp. 134, 150, 156, 161, 175, 185, 190). The theory is important, not only because its argumentative ingenuity (much needed at the time) gave Adams an intercolonial reputation, but because the underlying conception of many legislatures limited by a "fixed" constitution was later applied to the federal system of the United States.

For two years following the repeal of the major part of the Townshend duties (Apr. 7, 1770, *10 George III, ch. 17*), the controversy with Great Britain died down, and Adams's popularity and influence declined. The "Merchants" (conservative wing of the Patriot party) gladly abandoned the Non-Importation Association in its extreme form. Hancock, irritated by the rumor that he had been "led by the nose," quarrelled with Adams and devoted himself to commercial ventures. John Adams, incurring some unpopularity for having defended the soldiers implicated in the Massacre, retired in disgust from politics. When Hutchinson succeeded Bernard as governor in March 1771 the trend of opinion was distinctively conservative, and in November 1772 Adams himself was elected to the House by a much smaller vote than usual. Yet it was during these years of declining interest that Adams made what was perhaps his chief contribution to the Revolution by keeping the dying controversy alive. Finding the House less amenable than formerly, he turned to the press, contributing some forty articles to the Boston newspapers, in which he made a grievance of the facts that the General Court had been removed from Boston to Cambridge, that the judges held office by independent tenure, that Hutchinson received his salary from the crown instead of the General Court. But the chief significance of Adams's writings in these years is not the matter but the manner. He wrote with concentrated bitterness, in the manner of a Jeremiah denouncing the sinister aims and wicked conduct of those in high places, warning the people of the concealed conspiracy intended to deprive them of their liberty, and repeatedly pointing out that the chief danger was in thinking that there was no danger. In the years when most people were disposed to think their liberties secure, it was the supreme rôle of Samuel Adams to proclaim that they were by insidious arts being made slaves unaware (*Writings,* II, *passim.* See especially pp. 172, 198, 245, 249, 250, 266, 270, 273, 287, 308).

Not content with warning the people against the approach of tyranny, Adams set about constructing an organization for resisting it. In November 1770 the House had appointed a committee, of which Adams was a member, to correspond with the similar committees in other colonies (Wells, I, 373). Although this committee was once renewed, in June 1771 (*Ibid.,* p. 406), nothing effective came of the project until it was revived by the Virginia House of Burgesses in 1773. But in 1772 Adams initiated what may be regarded as the origin of the revolutionary government in Massachusetts. On Nov. 2, 1772, the Boston Town Meeting, on Adams's motion, appointed "a committee of correspondence . . . to state the rights of the Colonists and of this Province in particular, as men, as Christians, and as Subjects; and to communicate the same to the several towns and to the world" (*Ibid.,* p. 496). On Nov. 20 the committee reported to the Town a declaration of rights, a list of grievances, and a letter of correspondence addressed to the several towns. As a member of the committee, Adams drafted the declaration of rights (*Writings,* II, 350). Meantime, by private correspondence, he had prepared the towns for the coming project, and now urged them to follow the lead of Boston in appointing committees (*Ibid.,* pp. 340, 346, 348).

Upon the publication of the Boston declaration of rights, in which Adams laid greater stress than formerly on natural rights and affirmed with less qualification America's legislative independence of Parliament, Gov. Hutchinson felt it necessary to take part in the controversy. He was alarmed at the apparently reviving influence of Adams, whom he regarded as the chief source of trouble. In 1771 he said of Adams: "I doubt whether there is a greater incendiary in the King's dominion or a man of greater malignity of heart" (Hosmer, *Hutchinson,* p. 215). He had already procured writers to answer Adams's articles in the newspapers (*Ibid.,* p. 224). The "correspondence Committees" he regarded as "glaringly unconstitutional," and the Boston declaration of rights as too mistaken in point of law to be allowed to pass without correction. Accordingly, on Jan. 6, 1773, the Governor presented to the General Court a carefully articulated argument on the thesis that no line could be drawn "between the supreme authority of Parliament and the total independence of the colonies" (*Ibid.,* pp. 363, 367). To this address the House made an elaborate reply which was probably in large part the work of Samuel and John Adams in collaboration (for the authorship of this paper, see Wells, II, 31 ff.; *Works of John Adams,* II, 310; Frothingham, *Joseph Warren,* p. 223; Hutchinson, *History,* III, 374). Hutchinson's address may have had some effect in temporarily checking the formation of the correspondence committees, as he himself thought (*Massachusetts Archives,* XXVII, 451); but whatever influence the Governor may have had was shortly lost by the publication of the "Hutchinson Letters."

Of all the "enemies of liberty" Adams had long regarded Hutchinson as the chief; had long believed that his private letters to friends in England would if known prove his hostility to the American cause. Fortunately for Adams, six letters, written by Hutchinson in 1768–69 to some one in England, came "by a singular accident" (R. H. Lee, *Life of Arthur Lee,* 1829, I, 233; P. O. Hutchinson, *Diary and Letters of Thomas Hutchinson,* I, 81 ff.; Hosmer, *Hutchinson,* p. 273) into the possession of Benjamin Franklin, and were by him transmitted to Cushing, Speaker of the Massachusetts House, with the statement that they might be shown to proper persons, but were to be neither copied nor printed. They were shown to Samuel Adams, John Adams, Hawley, and Hancock. On June 2, 1773, Samuel Adams read the letters to the House in secret session, first pledging the members to observe the conditions imposed by Franklin. Hutchinson, learning that letters of his, alleged to have been written with a design to "subvert the constitution," were in possession of the House, demanded to see them. The House gave the governor the dates of the letters, asking him to furnish copies of letters written by him on those dates (Hutchinson, *History,* III, 401–2). Hutchinson refused to furnish the copies, whereupon the House appointed a committee to consider means by which it could become honorably possessed of the letters; and on June 10 Hawley for the committee reported "that Mr. Adams had acquainted them that, having conversed with the gentleman from whom he received the letters, he is authorized to inform the House that the said gentleman consents (as he finds that copies of said letters are already abroad, and have been publicly read) that the House should be fully possessed of them to print, copy, or make whatever use of them they please" (Wells, II, 76). The letters were then printed and circulated to the committees of correspondence (for the letters, see Hosmer, *Hutchinson,* p. 429). The letters were conservative in tone, and hostile to the radical fashion, but they revealed nothing of Hutchinson's views not already well known. Nevertheless, Hutchinson said, "had they been Chevy Chase, the leaders would have made them (the people) *believe* it full of evil and treason" (*Ibid.,* p. 278).

Meantime, on May 10, Parliament passed Lord North's Tea Act (*13 George III, ch. 44*). The traditional account is that Adams, perceiving the importance of the Tea Act, began at once to work for a continental congress (Wells, II, 81; Hosmer, *Adams,* p. 237). The Virginia House of Burgesses had already (Mar. 12) revived Adams's own former scheme for intercolonial committees. Adams welcomed the proposal (*Writings,* III, 25), and on May 28, on Adams's motion, the Massachusetts House responded by appointing a committee of fifteen of which Adams was a member (Wells, II, 71). An article in the *Boston Gazette* of Sept. 27, signed "Observation" and attributed by Wells to Adams, proposed that "a congress of American States be assembled as soon as possible; draw up a Bill of Rights; ... choose an ambassador to reside at the British court to act for the united colonies; appoint where the congress shall annually meet," etc. (*Ibid.,* p. 90). Cushing did not include this article in Adams's collected works; and aside from this article there is little evidence that Adams was seriously interested in a continental congress at this time. Writing to Arthur Lee Apr. 9, 1773, he said: "Should the Correspondence proposed by Virginia produce a Congress; and that an *Assembly of States,* it would require the Head of a very able Minister to treat with so respectable a Body. This is perhaps a mere fiction in the mind of a Political Enthusiast" (*Writings,* III, 21). An ironical aside, rather than a serious proposal? If Adams did indeed appreciate the importance of the Tea Act and seriously desire a continental congress before October 1773, it is difficult to explain his inactivity as a member of the Massachusetts Committee of Correspondence appointed May 28. That committee did nothing until June 28, when it appointed a sub-committee of five, with Adams as chairman, to draft a circular letter to the various provinces. The letter was not reported until Oct. 20, and, as finally adopted the day following, it was a brief communication, mentioning the Tea Act only casually, making no suggestion for a congress (*Writings,* III, 62, 63, note).

By November, at all events, Adams was aware that the arrival of the tea ships might be used to precipitate a crisis. On Nov. 2, the North End Caucus, with the Boston Committee of Correspondence present by request, voted "that the tea shipped by the East India Company shall not be landed" (Frothingham, *Life of Warren,* p. 240). On Nov. 3, a committee of the Sons of Liberty, Adams being one, requested the consignees of the tea to resign (*Diary of John Rowe,* pp. 252–53). Failing to obtain their resignation, a Boston town meeting, Nov. 5, adopted resolutions, drafted by Adams, declaring all who aided in landing or selling the tea to be "enemies of America" (*Writings,* III, 69). On Nov. 29, the day following the arrival of the first of the tea ships (the *Dartmouth*), a mass meeting (not a legal Town Meeting, but a so-called "Body Meeting") assembled in Faneuil Hall and, on Adams's motion, resolved that the tea "shall be returned to the place from which it came at all events" (Wells, II, 111, quoting *Boston Gazette,* Dec. 6, 1773). Adams gives the number assembled at 5,000 (*Writings,* III, 74). John Rowe says 1,000 (*Diary,* p. 256). On Nov. 30 the body met again and appointed a directing committee, of which Adams was one (*Diary of John Rowe,* p. 256), and undoubtedly the leading influence. During the next two weeks there were frequent Body Meetings, excitement ran high, and there was some rioting. Adams and his associates endeavored to force the ships to return with the tea; and arrangements had been made, just how is not known (see Wells, II, 124–25; Hosmer, *Adams,* p. 245), to destroy the tea in case an attempt should be made to land it. On Dec. 16, the day on which the customs laws require the cargo of the *Dartmouth* to be either entered or confiscated, Adams presided at a mass meeting which assembled at ten o'clock and remained in session until about six in the evening, when Rotch arrived saying that Gov. Hutchinson still refused the clearance which would permit the ships to return to England. Adams then arose and said: "This meeting can do nothing more to save the country." It was doubtless a signal agreed upon, since the "Mohawks" present immediately repaired to the wharf and threw the tea into the harbor (Wells, II, 122, quoting *Boston Gazette,* Dec. 20, 1773; for Adams's account, see *Writings,* III, 75).

The tea episode brought on that crisis which Adams had helped to make inevitable by thinking it so. "If the British administration and government," he wrote, "do not return to the principles of moderation and equity, the evil which they profess to aim at preventing . . . will the sooner be brought to pass, viz.:—*the entire separation and independence of the colonies*" (*Writings,* III, 100). When the news of the Coercive Acts arrived, Adams took the lead in organizing resistance. On May 13 a Boston town meeting, with Adams as moderator, approved of the adoption of strict non-intercourse measures, and instructed Adams to transmit the vote to the "sister colonies," which he did with a request that they adopt similar measures (Wells, II, 162; *Writings,* III, 109). Personally, he thought an intercolonial congress could "not be had speedily enough to answer for the present emergency" (*Ibid.,* p. 115). On June 5 the Boston Committee adopted a "Solemn League and Covenant," effective Oct. 1, for the suspension of commercial intercourse with Great Britain, which was circulated by the correspondence committees and, in spite of opposition from the "Merchants," was generally subscribed to (Wells, II, 172, 183; Peter Force, *American Archives,* 4th series, I, 397). Meantime, learning that other colonies were unwilling to adopt non-intercourse measures except in concert (see letter from New York, May 23, *Ibid.,* p. 297), Adams concluded that a congress was an "absolute necessity" (*Writings,* III, 126). On June 17, in the House of Representatives, with the door locked to prevent Gage from dissolving the General Court, Adams moved to appoint delegates to the congress "to deliberate and determine upon all measures." With only twelve dissenting voices, five delegates, Adams being one, were chosen, whereupon the door was unlocked and the last General Court of Massachusetts Bay was dissolved (Wells, II, 176).

Before leaving for Philadelphia, Adams was active in organizing the convention which, by adopting the famous "Suffolk Resolves" on Sept. 9, virtually placed Massachusetts in a state of rebellion (*Ibid.,* pp. 206, 226–28). At Philadelphia the Massachusetts delegates, suspected of too great rashness, shrewdly kept in the background (*Works of John Adams,* II, 382, note) and Adams moved that Duché, an Episcopal clergyman of Philadelphia, be asked to offer the opening prayers (*Ibid.,* p. 369). He must certainly have used his influence to commit the Congress to the three crucial measures—approval of the Suffolk Resolves, repudiating of Galloway's Plan, and adoption of the Association. Galloway, at least, thought Adams played a decisive part (*Historical and Political Reflections on the Rise and Progress of the American Rebellion,* 1780, pp. 66–67). Elected to the second Congress, and avoiding arrest by the British troops sent to Lexington, Adams returned to Philadelphia in May 1775. He favored immediate independence, proposed (January 1776) a confederation of such colonies as were ready for independence, supported the resolution for the formation of independent state governments, and voted for and signed the Declaration of Independence (Wells, II, 296, 358, 432).

As Adams's effective career began only with the opening of the quarrel with Great Britain, so it may be said to have ended with the final breach. Essentially a revolutionary agitator, he possessed little talent as a constructive statesman. Nevertheless, for twenty-five years of declining popularity and influence he played his minor rôle without blemish if without distinction. He served in Congress until 1781, a member of many committees, notably the committee to draft the Articles of Confederation (*Journals of the Continental Congress,* ed. by W. C. Ford, 1906, V, 433). He seconded John Adams's speech in behalf of Washington as commander-in-chief (*Works of John Adams,* II, 417); favored giving him dictatorial powers (Wells, II, 458); and while often impatient with the General's Fabian tactics, he was not, as charged by Hancock, implicated in the Conway Cabal (*Ibid.,* pp. 505 ff.). Always suspicious of the concentration of power, he opposed the creation of the (undoubtedly needed) executive departments of Finance, War, and Foreign Affairs (*Ibid.,* III, 127 ff.).

In April 1781 Adams returned to Boston, where he lived in "honorable poverty" until his death. In his own state he never recovered his former influence. He was a delegate to the convention which drafted the Massachusetts Constitution (1779–80). He drafted the "Address of the Convention . . . to their Constituents"—a document which best expresses his mature reflections on government (*Ibid.,* pp. 80–97). Under the new government, Adams served as senator and member of the Council. In 1788 he was defeated for Congress by Fisher Ames; and the unrivalled popularity of Hancock, which astonished as much as it irritated him, precluded his being elected governor during Hancock's lifetime. Elected lieutenant-governor (1789–93), he became governor upon Hancock's death, and was subsequently elected to the office (1794–97). In spite of his popular sympathies, Adams was unable to appreciate the economic grievances which led to Shays's rebellion, and vigorously aided the suppression of that movement. His ingrained suspicion of Great Britain led him to sympathize with the "Jacobin" movement, and to oppose Jay's Treaty. As a member of the Convention called in 1788 to ratify the Federal Constitution, he was at first opposed to that instrument. "As I enter the building I stumble on the threshold. I meet with a National Government, instead of a Federal Union of Sovereign States" (*Writings,* IV, 324). But in the end he gave his support, or was by an ingenious maneuver (Wells, III, 260), induced to give his support to the Constitution, with proposed amendments (*Ibid.,* pp. 248 ff.)

Adams died Oct. 2, 1803. On the following day William Bentley wrote in his diary: "Samuel Adams persevered through life in his Republican principles without any conformity to parties, influence or times. He was feared by his enemies, but too secret to be loved by his friends. He did not put confidence in them, while he was of importance to them. . . . He preserved the severity of Cato in his manners, and the dogmatism of a priest in his religious observances" (*Diary of William Bentley,* III, 49).

[The chief sources of information about Samuel Adams are the following: *The Writings of Samuel Adams,* ed. by H. A. Cushing, 4 vols. (1904–8); *The Life and Public Services of Samuel Adams . . .,* by Wm. V. Wells, 3 vols. (1865); *Samuel Adams* (American Statesmen Series), by James K. Hosmer (1885). Wells was a grandson of Adams. His work is highly laudatory, but based on careful and full research. He attributed to Adams many unsigned articles in newspapers which Cushing rejected. Hosmer follows Wells in the main, but he is more discriminating, and would have been still more so if he had written this work after his life of Hutchinson. *Samuel Adams, Promoter of the American Revolution,* by Ralph Volney Harlow (1923) is a "Freudian" interpretation which aims to be realistic, but ends by being as biased against Adams as Wells is in favor of him; it is not always accurate in detail. Aside from the above, the most useful works are: vol. II of *The Works of John Adams,* ed. by C. F. Adams (1850–56); Hosmer's *Life of Thomas Hutchinson* (1896); vol. III of Hutchinson's *Hist. of the Province of Mass. Bay* (1828); Richard Frothingham, *Life and Times of Joseph Warren* (1865); Wm. Tudor, *Life of James Otis* (1823); M. C. Tyler, *Lit. Hist. of the Am. Rev.* (1897).] C. L. B.

ADAMS, WILLIAM (Jan. 25, 1807–Aug. 31, 1880), Presbyterian clergyman, was the son of John Adams and Elizabeth Ripley. On his father's side he was descended from Henry Adams of Braintree, and on his mother's from William Bradford of Plymouth. He was born in Colchester, Conn., where his father was preceptor of Bacon Academy, but in 1810, on the appointment of the latter to the principalship of Phillips Academy, he was taken to Andover, Mass. He was a precocious child, beginning the study of Latin at six. To earn money for his college expenses he taught in a private school in Norwich, Conn., where he succeeded admirably in spite of his extreme youth. Entering the sophomore class of Yale College in December 1824, he graduated in 1827, first in classical scholarship. Returning to Andover, while a student in the Theological Seminary where he graduated in 1830, he assisted his father in teaching. He was ordained and installed pastor of the Congregational church in Brighton (now a part of Boston) on Feb. 2, 1831. In July 1831 he married Susan P. Magoun of Medford, Mass. In 1834 he resigned his pastorate owing to the illness of his wife, who died on May 22. He was installed pastor of the Central Presbyterian Church, Broome St., New York, on Nov. 13. In August 1835 he married Martha B. Magoun, a sister of his first wife. In 1836 he was one of the group who founded Union Theological Seminary. In 1853 the major portion of his congregation established the Madison Square Presbyterian Church, taking their pastor with them. Having declined in 1840 and 1871 offers of the presidency of Union Theological Seminary, carrying with it the chair of sacred rhetoric, he accepted the position in 1874. Adams's last six years, spent at Union, constituted the most useful period of his life. He was influential in securing large endowments for the seminary, and the strength and independence of this institution were largely the result of his work (A. P. Stokes, *Memorials of Eminent Yale Men,* 1914, I, 105). In the interest of Presbyterian unity he favored the granting to the General Assembly a veto power in the appointment of professors, but was opposed to any greater measure of ecclesiastical control.

Adams is often rated as the leading Presbyterian clergyman of his time. At the division of that church in 1837, he became a leader of the New School party, being moderator of its General Assembly which met in Washington in 1852. He was also a foremost advocate of reunion, being chairman of the New School Committee of Conference from 1866 till the union was consummated in 1870. He was an eminent leader in the Evangelical Alliance, and his welcome to the representatives of foreign Protestantism at the Alliance meeting of 1873 is counted one of the ablest addresses of his life. He was a corporate member of the American Board of Foreign Missions with which the New School Presbyterians were largely affiliated, was president of the Presbyterian Foreign Board after the reunion, and was active in many other religious and philanthropic organizations. In 1871 he visited Russia at his own expense to plead the cause of the Protestant dissenters in the Baltic provinces. An orthodox Evangelical according to the theological standards of his day, he was nevertheless broad-minded and truly liberal.

Although an accurate scholar, he had little taste

for authorship. His most characteristic book is *Thanksgiving. Memories of the Day: Helps to the Habit* (1867). Others are *The Three Gardens, Eden, Gethsemane, and Paradise* (1856) and *Conversations of Jesus Christ with Representative Men* (1868). In addition he published many single addresses and sermons.

[*Obit. Record of the Grads. of Yale Coll., Deceased from June, 1880 to June 1881*; *New Eng. Hist. and Geneal. Reg.*, Apr. 1894; A. N. Adams, *A Geneal. Hist. of Henry Adams of Braintree, Mass., and His Descendants* (1898). Adams's connection with Union Seminary is set forth in *The Union Theol. Sem. in the City of N.Y.: Hist. and Biog. Sketches of the First Fifty Years* (1889), by G. L. Prentiss. A sketch of his life appeared in the *N.Y. Observer* Sept. 2, 1880, and a funeral address by Dr. Roswell D. Hitchcock was published in the *Evangelist*, Sept. 9, 1880. There is an oil portrait of him in the possession of Union Theol. Sem.]

F. T. P.

ADAMS, WILLIAM LYSANDER (Feb. 5, 1821–Apr. 26, 1906), Campbellite preacher, editor, physician, connected on the paternal side with the Adams family of Massachusetts, on the maternal with the Allens of Vermont, was born of Vermont parents, at Painesville, Ohio. His frontier-loving parents kept on moving, and the boy received his early education at Galesburg, Ill. His college training was secured at Bethany, W. Va. Under Alexander Campbell's instruction he became a Campbellite and planned to preach. Tradition says he excelled in the classics and in Hebrew. In 1848 he married Frances O. Goodell at Galesburg, Ill., went to Oregon, bought a farm, and for about seven years divided his time between farming and teaching school, doing much preaching on the side and also writing for the newspapers. One of Adams's contributions, "A Melodrame entitled 'Treason, Stratagems, and Spoils,' in five acts, by 'Breakspear,'" which was published in the Portland *Oregonian* in February and March 1852, and also in a thirty-two page pamphlet, constitutes his best title to distinction as literary artist and political satirist. In 1855 he bought the defunct *Spectator* at Oregon City and began the publication of the *Oregon City Argus*, of which he continued as editor till his appointment by Lincoln to be collector of customs at the port of Astoria (date of confirmation July 27, 1861). In 1873 he studied medicine at Philadelphia, afterwards practicing first in Portland and then for many years in connection with a sanitarium established by him at Hood River, Ore., where he died in 1906. To the last generation he was known as "Doctor Adams," to an earlier one as either "Parson Adams" or "Editor Adams." His intellectual brilliancy was manifested in all of these departments but his most permanent results were obtained as political editor and stump speaker. In these capacities he ranked among the leading public men of Oregon, and he is generally placed first among the founders of the Republican party in that state.

Adams's bitterest fight was against the so-called "Salem Clique" of which for some years Federal Judge O. C. Pratt was local boss and Asahel Bush, editor of the *Salem Statesman*, the foremost political writer and policy molder. The "Melodrame" mentioned above was a merciless caricature of the acts, plans, and supposed plots of that clique. The author imputes to them the treasonable design of detaching Oregon territory from the United States, and charges a secret purpose to adopt Mormonism, to conquer California, and to make Brigham Young king over a Pacific empire. Some of his avowed suspicions have hardly the usual partisan basis of fact or assumed fact; yet, by shrewd inference and innuendo he imparts to them a certain plausibility. As Republican editor he was more feared and more hated than any man in his day in Oregon,—"dreaded by his foes and not greatly beloved by his friends" (H. W. Scott, *History of the Oregon Country*, 1924, V, 292).

[The chief source of Adams's editorial career is the file of the *Argus* in possession of the Ore. Hist. Soc. The Society also has the only known original copy of the pamphlet edition of "Treason, Stratagems, and Spoils." A biographical sketch, approved by Adams, was published by Geo. H. Hines in the *Ore. Hist. Soc. Quart.*, III, 356–58. There is also some biographical information in *An Illustrated Hist. of the State of Ore.* (1893).]

J. S.

ADAMS, WILLIAM TAYLOR (July 30, 1822–Mar. 27, 1897), writer of juvenile stories under the name "Oliver Optic," the son of Capt. Laban Adams and Catherine (Johnson) Adams, and a descendant of Henry Adams of Braintree, was born in Bellingham, Mass. His father was proprietor of the Lamb Tavern, Boston. In 1838 the family moved to a farm in West Roxbury. Here the boy found it difficult to take time from farm work to keep up his schooling. Winter nights he studied late in a room so cold that he could hardly keep his blood in circulation and turned the pages with a mittened hand. But he succeeded in leading his classes in almost every subject, especially composition. His parents were so proud of his ability that they managed to have him continue his studies under a private tutor, for two years after leaving school. Then followed a period of travel through the Northern and Southern states during which he took voluminous notes, which later stood him in good stead. After a brief experience in helping his father manage the first Adams House, on the site of the Lamb Tavern, he turned to teaching. In 1846 he married Sarah Jenkins of Dorchester, by whom he had two daughters. He continued to teach in the public schools of Boston for twenty years, resigning in 1865 to devote himself to writing. For fourteen years he served as a member of the school committee of Dorchester; and one year, 1869, he was a member of the state legislature, but declined a renomination.

He had already written for periodicals, chiefly without pay; but his first book (1853) was a story, *Hatchie, the Guardian Slave; or the Heir of Bellevue.* This brought him $37.50. His next venture, however, *Indoors and Out* (1855), a collection of stories, was more sucessful; and he then attempted a book for boys, *The Boat Club* (1855), which proved so popular that he followed it with five more in the *Boat Club* series. The initial volume, *The Boat Club,* ran through sixty editions. Other series followed fast: *Great Western, Lake Shore, Onward and Upward, Yacht Club, Riverdale Story Books, Woodville Stories,* etc. He made about twenty visits not only to all parts of Europe but to Asia and Africa as well. These furnished material for the *Young America Abroad* and *All Over the World* series, the latter comprising twelve volumes. The Civil War bore fruit in many stories grouped under *Army and Navy* and *Blue and Gray* series, besides a biography of Grant. Nothing, short of death, could stop his writing. The sum of all his output totaled 126 books, of which far over a million copies have been sold. As if these were not enough, he wrote about a thousand short tales for periodicals, edited at various times *The Student and Schoolmate, Oliver Optic's Magazine,* and *Our Little Ones.* He was most successful with the magazine that bore his pen name.

Although he is known as "Oliver Optic," it was not his only pseudonym. He took the name from a character in a play that appeared in Boston, "Doctor Optic," adding "Oliver." But he wrote love stories as "Irving Brown," travel sketches as "Clingham Hunter, M.D.," and he sometimes signed himself "Old Stager." He never wrote over his own name. He was most methodical, keeping "plot" books and other note-books crammed with incidents, anecdotes, and observations. He wrote regularly five hours a day. He had a real gift for story telling and his familiarity with boats, farming, and practical mechanics, to which must be added a genial personality that won friends among boys in every walk of life, gave him a wide range of knowledge. At first the public libraries refused his books because his heroes accomplished too many improbable feats. That, however, was no defect to his boy readers, whom he counted by the million. His motto in writing was, "First God, then Country, then Friends." He died at his home in Dorchester (Boston).

[Obituaries in *N.Y. Evening Post, N.Y. Herald,* and *N.Y. Press,* Mar. 27 and 28, 1897; F. A. Munsey, *Munsey's Mag.,* Oct. 1892; Allan Eric, *Midland Mo.,* Dec. 1897.]

W. O. S.

ADAMS, WILLIAM WIRT (Mar. 22, 1819–May 1, 1888), Confederate soldier, a son of Judge George Adams and Anna (Weissiger) Adams, was born at Frankfort, Ky. Judge Adams was an intimate friend and correspondent of Henry Clay. In 1825 he moved from Kentucky and located at Natchez, Miss.; from 1836 to 1839 he was judge of the United States court for Mississippi. William Wirt Adams was educated at Bardstown, Ky. On his return from college in 1839, he enlisted as a private in Col. Burleson's command for service to the Republic of Texas and soon afterwards was made adjutant of the regiment and was in the campaign against the Indians in northeast Texas. In the autumn of 1839 he returned to Mississippi. In 1850 he was married to Sallie Huger Mayrant at Jackson, Miss., and engaged in planting and banking at Jackson and Vicksburg. From 1850 to 1861 he was occupied in a successful business career and served two sessions in 1858 and 1860 as a member of the Mississippi legislature. When Mississippi withdrew from the Union in 1861, he was appointed commissioner from Mississippi to Louisiana and assisted in securing the withdrawal of that state from the Union. In February 1861, upon the formation of the Confederate States of America at Montgomery, Ala., he was called to Montgomery by President Jefferson Davis and offered the cabinet position of postmaster general, which he felt compelled to decline. As soon as he had settled his banking interests, he raised a cavalry regiment and enlisted it in the Confederate Army as the 1st Mississippi Cavalry. It was also officially known as Wirt Adams's Regiment of Cavalry. The regiment was organized at Memphis, in August 1861. The command was ordered to Columbus, Ky., in September, and in October to the headquarters of Gen. Albert Sidney Johnston at Bowling Green. The regiment was the rear-guard in the retreat from Kentucky to Nashville and Corinth. At the battle of Shiloh Adams's regiment was stationed upon the extreme right, near Greer's Ford of the Tennessee River, and accompanied the infantry line into battle. During the Corinth campaign the regiment was on outpost duty. After the retreat to Tupelo four companies of the regiment had a spirited engagement with the enemy near Booneville, "charging, routing, and pursuing two miles a Federal regiment" under command of Maj. Phil Sheridan (*Mississippi,*

I, 32). Col. Adams with his own and Slemons's Arkansas regiment was at Iuka with Gen. Price, and near Burnsville captured a train-load of Federal troops sent out from Corinth. He was then ordered to Washington County, Miss., guarding the plantations and observing the movements against Vicksburg. When Sherman advanced against Jackson after the fall of Vicksburg, Adams, with his regiment and the 28th Mississippi Cavalry, harassed his advance, skirmishing all the way. He was commissioned brigadier-general in September 1863, and in November was assigned to the command of a brigade composed of his own regiment and Col. Logan's command. In February 1864, he was ordered to meet Sherman's advance on Meridian. When the end came he was operating with Gen. Forrest in north Alabama. Adams's brigade was surrendered near Ramsey Station, Sumpter County, Ala., May 4, 1865. His farewell address was delivered to his command May 6, 1865. His parole is dated Gainesville, Ala., May 12, 1865. After the war Gen. Adams resided at Vicksburg and later in Jackson. He was appointed state revenue agent in 1880, and resigned in 1885 to become postmaster at Jackson by appointment of President Cleveland. On May 1, 1888, in a street encounter with John Martin, a Jackson editor who had bitterly criticized Adams in his paper, both Adams and Martin were killed.

[The best sources of information concerning William Wirt Adams are: his papers in the possession of Mrs. Norvelle Adams Beard of Jackson, Miss.; a sketch in *Mississippi* (1907) ed. by Dunbar Rowland, I, 31–35: "Mil. Hist. of Miss." in the *Miss. Official and Statistical Reg. of 1908*, pp. 770–82. A good oil portrait of Adams hangs in the Miss. Hall of Fame in Jackson.]

D. R.

ADDICKS, JOHN EDWARD O'SULLIVAN (Nov. 21, 1841–Aug. 7, 1919), promoter, political adventurer, was born in Philadelphia, the son of John Edward and Margaretta (McLeod) Addicks. The father was a local politician of some prominence and for a time held the place of health officer of the port of Philadelphia. The son attended the public schools until he was fifteen and then went to work in a wholesale dry-goods house. At nineteen he entered the flour business of Levi Knowles, and two years later, on attaining his majority, was made a partner in the firm. His next venture was in real estate. The panic of 1873 left him bankrupt, but he soon regained a commercial footing. He married Laura Butcher of Philadelphia, and in 1877 moved to Claymont, Del. He first came to the general notice of the business world when he introduced Minnesota spring wheat to the farmers of the east. He soon turned to the then infant industry of producing water gas for illuminating purposes, and though occasionally speculating in railroad stocks, devoted most of his time to the promotion of gas companies. He built gas works in Jersey City, Brooklyn, and Chicago, making large profits through the manipulation of contracts. In 1882 he was the prime mover in organizing what was known as the Chicago Gas Trust. Two years later he organized and became president of the Bay State Gas Company, and by his subsequent legerdemain with its securities, according to Thomas W. Lawson, he "made Boston look like the proverbial country gawk at circus time" (*Frenzied Finance,* 1905, p. 65). His activities in this field caused him to be known as "Gas Addicks" and the "Napoleon of Gas." He was also associated with Lawson in the promotion of the Amalgamated Copper Company. In 1892 he bought a majority interest and became president of the Brooklyn Gas Company. Six years earlier he had moved to Boston, deeding his Claymont house to his wife, who in turn deeded it, at his suggestion, to a Mrs. Ida Carr Wilson, later to figure prominently in the Addicks romance.

In Philadelphia Addicks had dabbled lightly in local politics. He was now to enter the national field, in a long and fiercely contested effort to be elected senator from Delaware. It is said that the first prompting in this direction came to him in New York City on a day in December 1888, just after his return from Europe, where he had made a million dollars by a coup in Siberian railroads. Reading in a morning newspaper that the Delaware legislature was deadlocked in a contest over a senatorship, he immediately summoned his Boston political agent, and on the latter's arrival they started together for Dover. On Jan. 1, 1889, conspicuously overdressed, he appeared with this agent and two or three other followers at the Hotel Richardson, Dover, and announced to the newspaper correspondents that he was a candidate for senator. Then began a campaign unique in American history. He established a residence at the house of Mrs. Wilson, and for seventeen years thereafter, at a cost believed to have reached $3,000,000, he strove by every means that he could employ to obtain a majority of the Delaware legislature. His first move was to win supporters for himself by paying the tax bills of citizens, and as no delinquent taxpayer in the state could then vote he soon had a following. In time he built up a formidable faction, known as the Union Republicans, in the Republican party, and several times he came near to success. In 1895 the joint ballot resulted in a tie; in 1899 he obtained a plurality, and at other times, unable to win for himself, he prevented an election In the Fifty-fourth and

Fifty-sixth Congresses Delaware was represented by but one senator, and in the Fifty-seventh, was unrepresented. This spectacular campaign aroused deep interest throughout the country, and denunciation of Addicks became a hackneyed theme in the press. The end came in 1906. The Republicans, reunited and led by the du Ponts, had obtained a large majority in the legislature. The vote for senator in the two houses on June 12 was 36 for Col. Henry A. du Pont and 2 for Addicks, the 18 Democrats expressing no choice.

Financial disasters to Addicks followed almost immediately. The decline in the price of copper had wrecked his fortune, and his operations in gas were now to entangle him in costly litigation. In 1907, on the plea of stockholders who alleged fraud, George Wharton Pepper, later a senator from Pennsylvania, was appointed receiver for the Bay State Gas Company. About the same time a federal court awarded a judgment against Addicks for $4,000,000. He was soon hiding from subpœna and attachment servers. At one time he was found in a cheap tenement in Hoboken without light or heat. He escaped and was not again apprehended until 1913. Taken into custody, he was released on $2,000 bail, which he forfeited. Two years later he was again arrested. The last four years of his life are believed to have been spent in extreme poverty. He died in an apartment-house in New York City.

Addicks was married three times. His second wife was Rosalie Butcher, a sister of his first wife. In 1894 she sued him for divorce, naming Mrs. Wilson as co-respondent. Addicks contested this divorce, but, on a change in the character of the complaint, made no further opposition. The divorce was granted in 1896 and Addicks thereupon married Mrs. Wilson.

There is no evidence that Addicks had any of the qualities fitting one for the office of United States senator. "Coarse" and "common" were the terms usually applied to him, and no responsible witness has recorded anything greatly to his credit. His idea of a senatorship was evidently that of a commodity that could be bought in the open market and is well illustrated by the declaration he is credibly reported to have made at a dinner in Georgetown, Sussex County, after the sweeping Republican victory of 1894: "Well, boys, we've won! . . . I've bought it; I've paid for it, and I'm going to have it. It has cost me $140,000" (*Outlook*, Feb. 14, 1903).

[Information regarding Addicks is scattered through the newspapers and periodicals over a period of many years. The three articles by George Kennan, "Holding Up a State: The True Story of Addicks and Delaware," in the *Outlook* of Feb. 7, 14, and 21, 1903, are especially valuable. Obituaries in N. Y. *Sun, N.Y. Herald*, and *N.Y. Times* of Aug. 8, 1919, of which the first-named is the most copious in details, give much additional information.]

W. J. G.

ADEE, ALVEY AUGUSTUS (Nov. 27, 1842–July 5, 1924), diplomat, a New Yorker accidentally born in Astoria, as he put it, was the fifth and youngest child of Fleet Surgeon Augustus Adee, U.S.N., and Amelia Kinnaird Graham. His father belonged to a solid Westchester family with a Huguenot strain. His mother's father was David Graham, Irish patriot of Scotch affiliations, Pittsburgh preacher, and New York lawyer, whose interest in Robert Emmet occasioned his removal to this country. Among other accidents of Adee's life, two of the earliest had a profound influence upon his career. An attack of scarlet fever permanently impaired his hearing; and the death of his father in 1844, followed in 1864 by that of his mother, left him a competency. Thus he who received an honorary A.M. from Yale in 1888 never went to school or college, and at an age when most young men seek a livelihood he was able to continue his studies. He happened to be of those uncommon mortals who combine a talent for letters and languages with a taste for mathematics. He traveled abroad, became an accomplished linguist and a distinguished Shakespearean, contributed prose and verse to the press (*e.g.* "The Life-Magnet," in vol. VIII of Scribner's *Stories by American Authors,* 1885), and set out to be a civil engineer—under the tutelage of his uncle Charles Kinnaird Graham, surveyor of the port of New York. It was through another uncle, however, that he stumbled upon his true profession. A firm friend and conspicuous client of the criminal lawyer John Graham was Major-General D. E. Sickles, whom President Grant in 1869 made minister to Spain. And the not too happy warrior invited Adee to go with him as his private secretary.

The eight years he spent in Madrid, where the congenial secretary of legation he succeeded in 1870 chanced to be a young man named John Hay, laid the foundation of Adee's vast diplomatic experience. At five different times during this stormy period he acted as chargé d'affaires *ad interim.* He was not in charge when the *Virginius* affair threatened war in 1873 (*Foreign Relations of the United States,* 1874–76). He was, however, when Boss Tweed of New York, having escaped from the guard in whose company he was enjoying an airing out of Ludlow Street Jail, set sail from Cuba in 1876, under an assumed name, for Vigo. We then had no extradition treaty with Spain. But the chargé who spoke Spanish so well and steered so tactfully between revolutions had established a position for himself; and at his request the Spanish authorities made him a present of the mysterious passenger on the *Carmen*—who was promptly returned to Ludlow Street on board an American frigate. The tactful chargé was the first to suggest the Extradition Convention and Protocol of 1877 (Malloy's *Treaties, Conventions . . . and Agreements between the United States and Other Powers,* II, 1665).

In August 1877 Adee handed over his legation to James Russell Lowell and returned to America. He had intended to retire to private life, for his strenuous years in Spain had told upon his health and he now contemplated the care-free life of a banker. Among the dispatches on every conceivable subject which he signed at the rate of one a day for every day he was in charge, those on currency and exchange prove that a Shakespearean may not be incapable of fathoming the mysteries of high finance. But Madrid was not the only place where he had established a reputation. His tact, his diligence, his dignified style, not to speak of his skill in apprehending fugitives from justice, had been noted by Secretary Hamilton Fish, who doubtless mentioned them to his successor W. M. Evarts. At any rate, Secretary Evarts offered Adee a "temporary" position in the Department of State, where he would be relieved of responsibility and free to exercise his special talent for drafting state papers—or to resign. Thus began, accidentally once more, the second stage of a career which was to become legendary in the annals of Washington. In 1878 Evarts made him chief of the Diplomatic Bureau, in charge of correspondence with legations. In 1882 President Arthur appointed him third assistant secretary of state. In 1886 he was promoted to be second assistant secretary, which he was for thirty-six years. He might have gone higher yet. He preferred a post less conspicuous but less subject to political and social pressure. As it was he frequently assumed the duties of acting secretary, and in September 1898 spanned as secretary of state *ad interim* the interval between the departure of Justice Day and Hay's arrival. The only time he ever consented to appear at an international conference was in 1914. Happening to be in France, on his vacation, he accepted an emergency assignment to the conference on Spitzbergen, then sitting at Oslo. His credentials were dated the day before the assassination of the Archduke Ferdinand, and the conference rose on July 30 (*Foreign Relations,* 1914, p. 974). Unable to cross the German frontier, Adee spent a fortnight in helping disentangle the legation at Copenhagen from the confusion which beset every diplomatic establishment in those troubled days, and finally succeeded in making his way to the north of Scotland. He was then in his seventy-second year. He continued to serve the department for ten years longer, remaining at his desk until a week before his death.

During this unprecedented period of nearly fifty-five consecutive years of service, forty-seven of them in Washington, he set upon the department a stamp no other one man has left. Time worked in his favor, of course, as did his private circumstances. He never married; and his deafness, which gradually cut him off from general conversation, made official society irksome to him. He preferred that of his lawyer brother, with whom he lived, of his nephews and nieces, and of his books. It was, therefore, the easier for him, at seasons of special stress, to install a cot in his office and to remain at his post day and night. He was no mere official bookworm, however. To keep himself fit he long rode a bicycle, taking it nearly every spring to Europe for an unconventional tour, and in his later years he kept a canoe on the Potomac. He also took a scientific interest in lenses, acquiring the proficiency of a professional with the camera and the microscope. With their aid he became an expert in the study of diatoms, of which he discovered several new species. It was perhaps this interest in scientific and mechanical things which caused him who had spent so many painful hours with a pen, to introduce typewriters into the department in the eighties, and in the nineties to permit the innovation of typing a diplomatic note. But his conscientiousness and his versatility would have availed little without his wide reading, his immense experience, his prodigious memory, his intimacy with the records, workings, and personalities of the department, his quick wit, his gift for the turn and tone of a phrase. He was human enough to have a temper, as rash or stupid subordinates knew to their cost, and journalists found him a far from loquacious informant; yet no one could be more appreciative of good work, more urbane, or readier to turn off an importunate question with a laugh. At the time of the Boxer uprising he was asked what had passed at a momentous interview between the secretary and Wu Ting Fang. "Well," he replied, "Mr. Hay was rather hazy and Mr. Wu was rather woozy." Hay's nickname for him was "Semper Paratus"! Students often complained of the rigor with which he edited the annual volumes of *Foreign Relations* and controlled access to the archives of the department. It was not that he believed in secret diplomacy. It was rather that they had to pay for the indiscretions of yellow journalists, of petty politicians, of publicity-seekers, of sensation-mongers, for whom he had a profound distaste. He disliked the tendency of amateur diplomats to burst into print. He himself kept a diary for years, but never entered in it a syllable that had to do with his official life. The only book he ever published was an edition of *King Lear* (1890), being Volume X of The Bankside Shakespeare (1888–1906), published by the Shakespeare Society of New York, of which he was long a member. On the other hand, in a government tender to the spoils system and to the theory of rotation in office, he gave consistency to the policies and methods of the State Department. And at a time when the tradition of English as written and spoken in America was undergoing radical changes, not always for the best, he set a standard of style and held the department to it. For thirty years scarcely a written communication went out until he had passed upon it. Of those communications a fabulous number were written by himself, although many of them were signed by other men. He drafted treaties, wrote notes and instructions, reprimanded the erring and commended the praiseworthy, composed proclamations, invented formulas, solved intricate problems of procedure or precedence. He had to a remarkable degree the ability to summarize a lengthy document in a paragraph, and to indicate in a word the manner of reply to be drafted. The department's files are full of the slips of green paper on which he wrote his comments or directions in red ink—sometimes tart, often witty, always informed and to the point. Of his facility in drafting, a classic example is President McKinley's reply to the ambassadors of the five Great Powers, who on the eve of the Spanish War counselled moderation and delay (*Foreign Relations,* 1898, p. 741). Having got wind of what was to come, Adee wrote it in ten minutes, while the ambassadors were all but at the door of the White House. And before the hastily penciled original could be put on record, it had to be retrieved from a presidential waste-basket. He also had a hand in the important correspondence relating to the Open Door in China and the situation resulting from the Boxer Rebellion (*Foreign Relations,* 1899–1902).

[No biography of Adee as yet exists. The records of his life, like his works, are scattered in the archives of the department, to which the writer has generously been allowed access. He has also drawn upon the recollections of relatives and associates. Outlines of Adee's career may be found in *Who's Who in America,* XIII, and in the *Reg. of the Dept. of State* (1924). *Foreign Relations,* from 1871 onward, contains much printed material by or relating to him, while Moore's *Digest of Internatl. Law* (1906) indexes five pages of state papers from his pen (VIII, 221; see also vol. II, p. 668). Among many press notices may be cited "Adee the Remarkable" by E. G. Lowry, *Harper's Weekly,* Nov. 18, 1911; "The Anchor of the State Department" by "Vieillard," the *Nation,* Aug. 5, 1915; and obituaries in the *N.Y. World* and *Tribune* and the *Phila. Public Ledger* for July 6, the *Outlook* for July 16, and the *World's Work* for September 1924. W. R. Thayer, *Life and Letters of John Hay* (1915) contains brief but interesting references, notably in vol. II, p. 186.]

H. G. D.

ADGATE, ANDREW (d. 1793), musician, for about ten years prior to his death was an active and useful promoter of rudimentary musical education in Philadelphia. Nothing positive is known of his origin or training. But if he is to be identified (as by the bibliographer Charles Evans) with the "Absalom Aimwell" who purports to be the author of *The Mechanics Lecture* (1789) and also of *The Philadelphia Songster* in the same year, with an appended *Mechanic's Song* (words and music), he was "a native of the United States" and "the son of a mechanic." His importance lies in his having opened in 1784 an Institution for the Encouragement of Church Music, which in 1785 took the name of the Free School for Spreading the Knowledge of Vocal Music, and in 1787, under a more elaborate plan of organization, that of The Uranian Academy. Among the names on the board of directors of this last we find the lawyer-composer Francis Hopkinson and the physician Benjamin Rush. The Academy seems to have continued until after 1800. As early as 1785, if not before, Adgate set about giving occasional choral concerts, at which various tunes and anthems by Lyons, Billings, Tuckey, and others already active in America were given, besides even the Hallelujah Chorus from Handel's *Messiah.* His most ambitious undertaking in this line was on May 4, 1786, when for a concert at the German Church he gathered a chorus of 230 voices and a band of fifty players. A résumé of his extant programs, as well as of his plans for systematic instruction, is given in O. G. Sonneck's *Early Concert-Life in America, 1731–1800* (1907), pp. 103–120. Though the scope of his pedagogical work was naturally limited by the circumstances of the time, what he says of his projects implies enterprise and thoughtful purpose. For the Academy he published about a half-dozen books in 1785–88, of which the *Rudiments of Music* and the *Philadelphia Harmony* ran through eight editions from 1788 to 1803, and a *Selection of Sacred Harmony* through five before 1797, besides the *Lecture* and the *Songster* above named as possibly his. His death occurred in the yellow fever epidemic of 1793.

[The account in Sonneck is by far the fullest. It also gives many references to contemporary newspapers Other references are: Charles Evans, *Am. Bibliog.* (1903–25), vols. VII and VIII; Gould, *Hist. of Ch. Music in America* (1853); Holyoke, *Harmonia Americana* (1791).]

W. S. P.

ADLER, GEORGE J. (1821–Aug. 24, 1868), philologist, the son of John J. Adler, was born in Leipzig. He was brought to the United States in 1833, was valedictorian of the class of 1844 at New York University, and was appointed professor of modern languages in that institution in

1846. He had begun teaching in the college while still an undergraduate. During the next few years he published several excellent German text-books, but most of his time and energy was devoted to the *Dictionary of the German and English Languages* (1849) for which his name is remembered. The significance of this work as a scholarly achievement can be appreciated only when one recalls that it was written in the New York of Poe's *Literati,* by a scholar who was still in his twenties and before Sanders and the Grimms had laid the foundation of modern German lexicography. As his basis Adler used Flügel's dictionary, but he subjected the whole book to a thorough revision, adding almost 30,000 new terms (chiefly loan words) and several hundred brief articles on synonyms. He had nothing to do with the smaller English-German volume, which was a mere reprint "under the auspices of the publisher" of Flügel. Adler's dictionary, which has been a boon to several generations of American students of German, was for its author a calamity, for the unaided, unremitting drudgery of its compilation shattered his health, and he was thenceforward intermittently insane.

In October 1849, his health temporarily restored, he sailed for Europe for a year of study and travel. On the wharf George Duyckinck introduced him to a fellow-traveler, Herman Melville [*q.v.*]. The two instantly became friends, spending the long days of the voyage in discussing philosophy, and meeting again in London and Paris. In his diary Melville affords us a pleasant glimpse of his companion and characterizes him as "an exceedingly amiable man and a fine scholar, whose society is improving in a high degree."

On his return to New York, Adler resumed his duties at the university, meanwhile studying assiduously. In the summer of 1853 hallucinations and delusions of persecution began again to assail him; on Oct. 5 he had a violent outbreak and two days later was taken to the Bloomingdale Asylum. In the shelter of the asylum, he completed, among other text-books, an interesting Latin grammar on Ollendorfian principles (1858). Later he lectured on Roman literature, Arabian poetry, and Goethe's *Faust,* and supported himself by giving private lessons in Latin and German. Other able works from his pen were a translation of Fauriel's *History of Provençal Poetry* (1860), *Notes on Certain Passages of the Agamemnon of Æschylus* (1861), *Wilhelm von Humboldt's Linguistic Studies* (1866), and *The Poetry of the Arabs of Spain* (1867). He died at the Bloomingdale Asylum, and was buried from St. Michael's Episcopal Church in Bloomingdale Road.

[The few facts known about Adler must be pieced together from a brief account in Duyckinck's *Cyc. of Am. Lit.* (rev. ed. 1875), a sketch in *Universities and Their Sons: N. Y. Univ.* (1901), ed. by J. L. Chamberlain, the *N.Y. Univ. Gen. Alumni Cat.* (1906), the prefaces to Adler's books and his pamphlet *Letters of a Lunatic* (privately printed, N. Y., 1854), Raymond Weaver's *Herman Melville* (1921), the death notice and editorial comment in the *N.Y. Times,* Aug. 25, 1868.]

G. H. G.

ADLER, SAMUEL (Dec. 3, 1809–June 9, 1891), rabbi, was born at Worms, Germany. He received his first instruction in Hebrew and Biblical literature from his father, Isaac Adler, rabbi at Worms, but when he was thirteen years of age, his father died, leaving his widow and five children destitute. Although very poor, Samuel carried on his studies assiduously at the Worms Yeshibot, or Talmudical Academy, and later at Frankfort-on-the-Main. Having completed his preliminary studies, he entered the University of Bonn in 1831, and from there went to Giessen, where the Ph.D. degree was awarded him in 1836. He was elected rabbi at Worms and remained there until 1842, when he became chief rabbi at Alzey. In 1843 he was married to Henrietta Frankfurter. During these years he toiled to lift the civil disabilities of the Jews and to introduce in the lower and higher schools the teaching of Jewish religion on a par with Protestant and Catholic teachings. In 1857 he was offered and accepted the position of rabbi of Emanu-El Congregation at New York. Entering upon his new duties in March 1857, he now had greater opportunity of giving full practical scope to his genius. He sought, above all, to lift the deadening weight of tradition from his people and to stimulate in them a higher Jewish consciousness. With this in mind, he devoted himself strenuously and ardently to the religious training of the young, to extending the fullest equality in all religious matters to women as well as men, to reconciling Jewish doctrines with the needs of modern life, particularly with reference to the Sabbath Day, and to reforming the ritual and making the liturgy more acceptable to the modern mind. He undertook the revision of the prayer-book, which his predecessor, Dr. L. Merzbacher, the first rabbi of Emanu-El Temple, had arranged, and so well was his work done that this book later became the pattern for most of the other reform prayer-books in American Judaism. He helped in the founding of the Hebrew Orphan Asylum of New York City and several other charitable institutions.

Adler was a man of vast learning concerning the life and literature of his people. He combined within himself the old Jewish training and viewpoint with the modern critical analysis and method, which he had learned at the German universities. He attended the three Rabbinical Reform Conferences, held in Brunswick in 1844, in Frankfort-on-the-Main in 1845, and in Breslau in 1846. These three conferences laid the foundation of Reform Judaism, and made it possible to build the Jewish faith for the future. In all of his work for reform, he sought to buttress his labors on the principles of Judaism as an everlasting revelation of God's purposes. His was a flaming passion for religion as an instrument in man's struggle for emancipation from ignorance and the forces which hinder progress. He left numerous monographs on subjects pertaining to Jewish learning, such as *The Day of Atonement According to the Bible—Its Origin and Meaning, A Biblio-Critical Study of the Passover, The Levitical Tithe, Karaitic Questions, Phariseeism and Sadduceeism.*

["Samuel Adler," by Rabbi Joseph Silverman, in the *Yr. Bk. of the Central Conference of Am. Rabbis,* XIX; *Sontagsblatt der New Yorker Staatszeitung,* June 21, 1891; *N.Y.Times, N.Y.Herald, N.Y.Tribune,* June 11, 1891.]

L.L.M.

ADLUM, JOHN (Apr. 29, 1759–Mar. 1, 1836), pioneer in viticulture, the son of Joseph and Catherine Adlum, was born in York, Pa. He served as a soldier in the Revolution and as a major in the Provisional Army. Later he was appointed brigadier-general in the state militia. Experience as a surveyor led to his employment in various surveys undertaken by the state and to his appointment by state authority to study the navigation of the Susquehanna and Schuylkill rivers. In 1795 he became associate judge of Lycoming County, Pa., and served in this capacity for three years. But these various engagements were of only passing importance to him. His life-long interest and his greatest service were in the cultivation, study, and improvement of American grapes. He established a farm and nursery at Georgetown, D. C., which ultimately contained over 200 acres. A portion of it was on the present site of the Bureau of Standards. If not the first, he was among the first to urge the federal government to give support to research institutions for the special benefit of agriculture; a movement which, after repeated efforts, was successful some ninety years later. His effort to have the federal government establish an experimental farm being unsuccessful, he made his own farm experimental, as far as his limited means permitted. His correspondence with Thomas Jefferson and his earlier acquaintance and friendship with Dr. Joseph Priestley, the celebrated English natural philosopher, living at Northumberland, Pa., were of great value to him in applying their knowledge to his farming operations. His special interest lay in the study of the grape and of wine making, and in this work he became an American pioneer. At first he grew a considerable number of European and American varieties, but, sharing Jefferson's opinion that it was wiser to attempt the improvement of native sorts than to introduce those of foreign origin, he ultimately rejected the latter, confining his study to between twenty and thirty native varieties. From cuttings obtained from one of these he propagated what he first named the Tokay but later the Catawba grape. This variety he propagated extensively and secured its distribution and cultivation. It has maintained its wide use and popularity to this day. His work he summarized in two books. One of them, *A Memoir on the Cultivation of the Vine in America and the Best Mode of Making Wine,* was published in 1823. An enlarged edition was issued in 1828. The other publication, *Adlum on Making Wine,* was issued in 1826. In 1813 he married Margaret Adlum, a cousin, by whom he had two daughters. He died at "The Vineyard" near Georgetown, D. C.

Adlum devoted his energy and means to a worthy and useful public service more than to advancing his personal interests. The Catawba grape—and its products—is a fitting memorial to him. A more humble memorial is a plant, the climbing fumitory, *Adlumia,* which was named in his honor. Personally he was tall, a man of muscular frame and great energy, lovable himself and loving to help the needy and unfortunate.

[*Records of the Columbia* [*D.C.*] *Hist. Soc.,* X, 38; Bailey's *Cyc. of Am. Ag.,* IV, 549.]

E.H.J.

ADRAIN, ROBERT (Sept. 30, 1775–Aug. 10, 1843), mathematician, was of Huguenot stock,—at any rate such is the tradition in the family. Born in Carrickfergus, Ireland, he received as good an education as his father could afford, but was thrown upon his own resources at the age of fifteen. He then began teaching, seemingly with success, but his Irish career was terminated when, having joined the Irish revolutionists, he was left for dead on the battle-field. He recovered, however, and with his wife (Ann Pollock) and child he escaped to America and here resumed his work as a teacher. He was successively a master in the academy at Princeton, N. J.; and principal in similar schools in York, Pa., and in Reading, Pa. In 1809 he became professor of mathematics at Queen's College (afterward Rutgers College) in New Brunswick, N. J. Four years later he became a professor in Columbia College (afterward Columbia University, New York City), his work there apparently including at different times mathematics, natural history, natural philosophy, and astronomy. After thirteen years at Columbia he resumed his former professorship in New Brunswick, but a year later he was called to the University of Pennsylvania. In 1828 he became vice-provost, but apparently owing to his failure in matters of discipline he found it advisable to sever his connection with the university in 1834. Of the next nine years, four were spent in New York as teacher in the Columbia College grammar school, and the rest apparently on his farm in New Brunswick, N. J. Of his teaching, Dr. Benjamin Haight of the University of Pennsylvania, class of 1828, gave the following account: "If one was thoroughly prepared in his recitation, all was well, but if a student was in doubt or needed a word of explanation in a difficult problem, he not only did not get assistance, but was sent down with some remark of the sort, 'If you cannot understand Euclid, dearie (a term he frequently used when out of temper) I cannot explain it to you.' The consequence was that only a small portion of his class could keep up with his course . . . in my class not more than one-fifth of the number" (Coolidge, *post*).

Adrain was the most outstanding mathematician in America in his time. His contributions began in a humble way in 1804 by problems sent to the *Mathematical Correspondent.* He soon, however, suggested a curve which he called the *catenaria volvens* and which, upwards of a half-century later, was rediscovered and attracted much attention in mathematical circles. He also wrote upon Diophantine algebra; founded a short-lived journal, the *Analyst, or Mathematical Companion* (1808); prepared an American edition of Hutton's *Course of Mathematics* (1812); attempted to revive the *Analyst* (1814); established *The Mathematical Diary,* which ran irregularly from 1825 to 1833, and edited a revised edition (1832) of Keith's *A New Treatise on the Use of Globes,* which had first appeared in England in 1805. His greatest mathematical achievement, however, was his consideration of the exponential law of error which Gauss demonstrated a year later and which generally bears the latter's name. Adrain gave two proofs, each of which has often been surpassed in elegance and clearness, a fact which does not, however, lessen the honor of priority which is due to him. If, instead of being a self-made mathematician, he had come under the influence of men like Laplace, Legendre, and Gauss, he might have been a great leader. As chance had it, he was lost in a mathematical desert.

[The leading source of information is an address "Robt. Adrain, and the Beginning of Am. Math.," by Prof. Julian L. Coolidge of Harvard Univ., pub. in the *Am. Mathematical Mo.,* XXXIII, 61, where the earlier biographical articles are listed.] D. E. S.

AFFLECK, THOMAS (July 13, 1812–Dec. 30, 1868), agricultural writer, was born in Dumfries, Scotland, the son of Thomas Affleck, a merchant, and Mary (Hannay) Affleck. After finishing school he was employed in the National Bank of Scotland, in Dumfries, of which bank his uncle, Alexander Hannay, was the managing agent. In 1832 he gave up his position with this bank for the purpose of moving to the United States, where he felt there would be better opportunities for success in the agricultural vocation which he desired to follow and for which he had prepared himself by attending agricultural lectures under Prof. Low of Edinburgh. He set sail from Liverpool and arrived in New York on May 4, 1832, and a few months later declared his intention of becoming a citizen of the United States. After some months in New York and Pennsylvania, he went to Indiana, engaging in business there for a few years. In 1840 he became junior editor of the *Western Farmer and Gardener,* in Cincinnati, Ohio. The next year he made an extensive tour through Mississippi and Louisiana, an account of which was given in his paper. On Apr. 19, 1842, he married Mrs. Anna (Dunbar) Smith of Washington, Miss., daughter of Isaac Dunbar and Elizabeth (Wilkinson) Dunbar, and widow of Calvin Steven Smith. After his marriage he took up his residence at Ingleside, near Washington, Miss. Here he established a commercial nursery (one of the earliest in the South) called the "Southern Nurseries" and also entered business life as a planter on an extensive scale. He imported many plants from Europe and carried on an extensive series of experiments. At this time he gave up the editorship of the *Western Farmer and Gardener.*

Realizing the political unrest in the country and that the lower Mississippi River, in case war should come, would be the hotbed of contention, he disposed of his interests in Mississippi and in 1857 moved to Texas, where he bought land in the county of Washington. He lost no time in improving the holding which he acquired. In addition to constructing a commodious dwelling and large plantation quarters, he erected a saw-mill, grist-mill (the only one in Texas for a number of years), cotton-gin, corn-mill, and a large sorghum-mill. His energies were also devoted to the cultivation of the usual field crops grown in that section. He established a nursery under the name of the "Central Nurseries," most of the trees and plants for which were supplied from his former nurseries in Mississippi. He did much, too, for the development of the better grades of livestock. During the Civil War his saw-mill manufactured wheel-barrows and other implements from lumber for the Confederate army. He was among the first in Texas to take the "amnesty oath" after peace was declared and he at once set to work in helping to rebuild the state. He made several trips to Europe for the purpose of encouraging English and Scotch emigrants to settle in Texas. One of his great undertakings, which failed, however, of materialization because of his death in 1868, was the establishment of a large beef-packing plant in Texas to be financed with European capital. European capitalists became interested in the project and it was planned that the proposed company should operate its own line of steamers between Texas and Europe. Affleck established an office in Galveston to look after this business in addition to his other interests. His death occurred just when these plans seemed on the eve of maturity.

Through his writings and his business undertakings Affleck did much for the agricultural advancement of the South. He was one of the early advocates of diversified farming in the Southern states. He edited *Norman's Southern Agricultural Almanac for 1848* (New Orleans, B. N. Norman) and later published for several years (beginning with 1851) an almanac entitled *Affleck's Southern Rural Almanac and Plantation and Garden Calendar.* He was the author of *Bee Breeding in the West* (1841) and *Hedging and Hedging Plants in the Southern States* (1869), as well as author of two useful and popular account-books, *The Cotton Plantation Record and Account Book,* and *The Sugar Plantation Record and Account Book.*

[The chief sources of information about Thomas Affleck are (1) his letters, diaries, books, etc., in the possession of his grandson, Mr. T. D. Affleck, of Galveston, Tex., and (2) his articles in various agricultural publications. A brief reference to him appears in an article by R. L. Allen in the *Cultivator,* vol. VIII, no. 7, July 1841, p. 114. An account of a visit to his plantation in Washington, Miss., is given by Solon Robinson in the *Ohio Cultivator,* vol. V, no. 7, Apr. 1, 1849, pp. 101–2. Obituaries in the *Am. Farmer,* Feb. 1869, *Cultivator and Country Gentleman,* Jan. 21, 1869, *Southern Planter,* Mar. 1869, and *Houston Telegraph,* Jan. 3, 1869.]

C. R. B.

AGASSIZ, ALEXANDER (Dec. 17, 1835–Mar. 27, 1910), zoologist, oceanographer, and mine operator, was the son of Jean Louis Agassiz [*q.v.*], the geologist and zoologist, and of Cécile Braun of Baden, Germany, sister of the eminent botanist Alexander Braun, for whom the younger Agassiz was named. She possessed marked skill as an artist, many of the finest plates in her husband's *Poissons Fossiles* being by her hand. Maximilian Braun, another brother, was an eminent mining engineer. Agassiz's paternal grandfather was a gifted pastor, of French Swiss Protestant stock, whose wife possessed a very strong, practical turn of mind, coupled with much Swiss astuteness.

Alexander Agassiz was born at Neuchâtel, Switzerland, a district which within a short span of time produced the elder Agassiz, the younger Agassiz, Pasteur, and Cuvier. The intellectual level of the times and the community was high, and was an excellent culture in which to produce a young man with a taste for natural history. From boyhood the younger Agassiz was trained to the study of animals, particularly aquatic animals, and was accustomed to observe and to draw practically anything he saw. His boyhood education was largely in his father's hands. Shortly after his mother's death and his father's departure for America, Agassiz left, in June 1849, for the New World. He was educated in the public high school at Cambridge, Mass., and graduated with the degree of A.B. from Harvard in 1855. Two years later he received the degree of B.S. in Engineering from the Lawrence Scientific School, where he had studied engineering and mining, neither of which led directly to a career as a naturalist, but ultimately proved of great worth to him in the practical side of marine exploration and in amassing a fortune. He returned immediately to Harvard to study chemistry, intermittently working there till he received the degree of B.S. in Natural History from Harvard in 1862.

In the meantime he had employed himself in teaching in the Agassiz school for girls, conducted by his stepmother, Elizabeth Cabot (Cary) Agassiz [*q.v.*], whom his father had married in 1850, and in 1859 he had attached himself to the United States Survey of the Washington Territory boundaries, and utilized the opportunity to collect marine animals from Panama to San Francisco, and north in the Columbia River and Puget Sound. In this year appeared his first scientific paper, on the mechanism of flight in the Lepidoptera (butterflies). In 1860, though having neither money nor very good health, he married one of the pupils from his mother's school for girls, Anna Russell of a well-known Boston family. Now began active publication in systematic zoology upon the marine invertebrates. His *North American Acalephae* (1865) was illustrated with 360 drawings by his own pen, and his *Embryology of the Starfish* (1865), not less completely illustrated, was the first of his embryological researches which shed so much light upon the phylogeny of the marine fauna.

In 1865 he was temporarily engaged in coal-mining in Pennsylvania, was in charge of the Harvard Museum during Louis Agassiz's absence in Brazil, and published with his stepmother a popular work, *Seaside Studies in Natural History*. In the following year he paid two visits to Calumet, on the Michigan shore of Lake Superior, through his interest in a copper mine, the existence of which was largely due to his father's geological reconnaissances in the Lake Superior districts. In March 1867, he became superintendent of the mine and took up his residence in Calumet. The mine was unprofitable when he came to it; at the time of his death, when he was its president, it was not only the greatest copper mine in the world in output, but declared the largest dividends for its investors which any metal mine in the world has ever divided. Agassiz in those early days of his mining career worked fourteen hours a day, was tireless in his energy and inventiveness, and made himself beloved by all the workers. He instituted pension and accident funds, safety devices, sanitary measures for the communities, modern and large mining machinery. On the occasion of a great fire breaking out in the mine he hastily produced from such chemicals as he had at hand enough carbonic acid gas to smother the flames immediately. Throughout his life he never lost touch with the industry under his ownership, making himself so highly regarded that the workmen raised over a thousand dollars as a gift to his museum. The years of mining experience were probably, however, permanently damaging to his health.

In search of rest and refreshment, and with the purpose of seeing all the specimens of Echini of value, Agassiz and his wife went to Europe in 1869, there forming social and scientific contacts of ultimate value. By 1872 he was able to begin issuing the great work of his life, from the point of view of systematic zoology, a *Revision of the Echini,* in which his father took great pride, and of which Jeffries Wyman said that it would live as long as anything the author's father ever did. The elder Agassiz was not to see the completion of this scientific monument, as he died in 1873, and the younger Agassiz's wife caught pneumonia while attending her father-in-law, and died eight days later. The double tragedy overwhelmed Agassiz, whose devotion to his father was almost religious, and to his wife was such that he was never able to speak of her death to his friends. His buoyant and genial nature was crushed by these losses. For a little while he carried on very unwillingly his father's summer school on the island of Penikese which the elder Agassiz had begun with such high hopes but about which his son had always had misgivings. The owner of the island lost interest in the school, an effort to subscribe public funds for its maintenance failed, and Agassiz paid out of his pocket its indebtedness and closed this first American experiment in a field laboratory. He immediately opened a private laboratory at Newport, R. I., however, and there, with everything in the way of the most modern and flawless equipment, he entertained ten biologists at a time, among whom were such famous men as Fewkes, Whitman, Brooks, and his warm friend Count Pourtalès whose marine faunal dredgings on the *Corwin* had already drawn Agassiz's attention to the delights and rewards of marine exploration. In 1874 he was made curator of the unfinished University Museum which his father had so optimistically begun to build, and he immediately set about its completion, giving $25,000, and raising $310,000 by popular subscription. Ultimately he devoted about $1,000,000 of his own to its construction and maintenance, dedicating the work to his father's memory.

Seeking distraction from his cares and sorrow he traveled along the west coast of South America in 1875. His letters at this time bear witness to terrible depression of spirit, but he found comfort in his studies. He discovered a recent coral reef at 3,000 feet above sea-level, which confirmed his suspicion that Darwin's theory of coral reefs and atolls as fringes around sinking volcanoes was untenable. His father had been a strong anti-Darwinian, and though the younger Agassiz was presumed to accept evolution as a fact, he carried on some of the hereditary opposition to Darwin's ideas, averring that Darwin had explained the survival of species, but not their origin. Against Darwin's theory of atoll formation Agassiz at this time began a vigorous attack, continuing his studies for twenty-five years. Before leaving South America, he chartered the only steamer on Lake Titicaca and collected all the animals and plants in that mysterious lake, making besides a complete chart of its deep bed.

In 1877, the year in which he issued his *North American Starfishes,* he embarked on the *Blake,* a government vessel under Lieutenant Commander S. D. Sigsbee, and began the first of his marine explorations. The government with great foresight authorized Sigsbee and subsequent commanders of the federal vessels on which Agassiz sailed to give the scientist free rein in directing the movements of the boats. The voluminous and costly reports of these expeditions, however, were published at Agassiz's expense, chiefly in the bulletins and memoirs of the Harvard Museum of Comparative Zoology. The *Blake* on its first voyage explored the course of the Gulf Stream in American waters. In 1878 Agassiz was again aboard her in a West Indian cruise, and in 1880 on a further exploration of the Gulf Stream's course. The coral reefs of the Hawaiian Islands were privately visited by Agassiz in 1885, and in 1891 he was aboard the *Albatross* when it explored the waters of the Pacific from Panama to the Galapagos and north to the Gulf of California. A friend loaned the *Wild Duck,* a small but excellent craft, for exploration of the waters and corals of the Bahamas in 1892, and as a result of this voyage Agassiz concluded that the Bahamas are formed of æolian rock, thinly overlaid with recent coral formation, a view then revolutionary. His private explorations of the Bermudas and the Florida barrier reefs in 1894 led him to the same conclusions, though probably he was in error as regards the mainland rocks about Miami, Fla.

The trip to the Great Barrier Reef of Australia in 1896 was largely a failure, owing to the fact that Agassiz had not counted on the trade winds which made navigation so difficult that science did not prosper, but in the years following he profited by this lesson and visited thousands of Pacific atolls in the hot still season. In 1899–1900 he was aboard the *Albatross,* Jefferson Moser commander, in its explorations of the region between San Francisco and the Marquesas. Over this vast basin, as large as the United States, which he named the Moser Deep, he made thousands of soundings and dredgings, bringing up siliceous sponges from 4,173 fathoms, the deepest haul that had ever been made. His survey of this marine desert, over which the British biologists in the *Challenger* had passed without solving the riddle of the countless sharks' teeth imbedded in concreted oozes, led him to the conclusion that not later than Tertiary times the floor had been raised nearly to the surface, providing the warm shallow sea in which sharks abound. Again with the *Albatross,* in 1904, he explored the sea from Peru to Easter Island and its mysterious monoliths, making a special study of the Humboldt current, showing that life abounded in its cold waters, but fell off rapidly on its western edges, though the waters of the bordering deep were warmer. While these marine explorations were not the first, they were the most extensive that had ever been made. The late Prince of Monaco attributed to Agassiz the larger part of the present knowledge of the configurations of the ocean beds and continental shelves, and Sir John Murray accredited him with making the marine fauna of the West Indies and the Gulf Stream better known than that of any similar area in the world. All of his findings were tirelessly reported and magnificently illustrated.

As he had an aversion to theories as such, and to speculation and metaphysics, he did not state his conclusions on the subject of his life work in the study of coral reefs, in any definitive, descriptive law. Indeed, a certain diffusion of purpose and even obscurity of meaning sometimes mark his work. He probably proved his negative conclusion—that Darwin was unsupported by the evidence in his theory of the formation of coral atolls. His own study of thousands of reefs and atolls prevented him from uttering any generalities on the subject; each case presented special problems to him, and it was his belief that the ordinary agencies of wind, wave, rain-water, and the normal habits of corals were sufficient to account for the varied structure of coral formations, without reference to elevation or subsidence of land or ocean level. A popular work on coral formations was three times written, and on the eve of his death was about to be scrapped in favor of a fourth beginning; as a consequence his final views will never be known. The close of his life was marked by his presiding over the International Congress of Zoologists at Boston in 1907, by his pleasure trip to the Great Lakes of Africa in 1908, and by his recreational visit to Europe in 1910. A few days from the coast of England, aboard the *Adriatic,* he died in his sleep. His honors were many, but Harvard University was the only American institution which signalized its recognition, by awarding him the degree of LL.D. in 1885. In 1898 he was made an Officer of the Legion of Honor. In 1902 he became a Knight of the Order of Merit of Prussia, though in his youth, with characteristic democracy, he had deliberately insulted a Prussian officer by refusal to salute him. The Victoria Research Medal was awarded him in 1909. He had previously (1878) been given the Prix Serres by the Paris Academy. At various times he was an Overseer of Harvard, at other times a Fellow. The only popularly elected office which he held was on the committee of the Cambridge public schools, a small duty into which he put much conscientious labor.

He ever remained something of a foreigner, thinking in French, though undoubtedly his simple and democratic temperament was well adapted to American life. In his relations to his employees in the mines he was a model of kindness and forethoughtfulness. His position in the Harvard Museum, and aboard the vessels in which his marine exploration was conducted, was that of a benevolent despot. His private wealth, his great generosity, his obvious superiority to his associates as a scientist and organizer quite naturally made him an autocrat in the museum as at sea. He did very little classroom teaching in his life, but his generosity toward young scientists and his interest in them gave him an influence which extended far beyond the classroom. From his mother perhaps he inherited a swift anger, but he had no animosities or sullenness. He has been compared in features to Bismarck, and like that organizer he planned his trips with such precision that he knew exactly where he would be on almost every day in the following year. All mishaps were allowed for, the time of his return was known to the day and very hour, and punctually at that hour he was in his museum office, writing the first words of the report of his expedition. His previous reading and his collections were so highly organized that his writing could proceed with perfect sequence as soon as he returned.

[*Letters and Recollections of Alexander Agassiz* (1913) by his son George Agassiz. For more impersonal accounts, with extended notices of his works, see A. G. Mayer in *Ann. Rep. Smithsonian Inst.* for 1910, pp. 447–72 (reprinted from *Pop. Sci. Mo.*, vol. LXXVI, no. 5); H. P. Walcott in *Proc. Am. Acad. Arts & Sci.*, XLVIII, 31–44; and Sir John Murray in *Bull. Mus. Comp. Zool. Harvard*, XLIV, 139–58.]

D. C. P.

AGASSIZ, ELIZABETH CABOT CARY (Dec. 5, 1822–June 27, 1907), educator, born in Boston, the daughter of Thomas Graves Cary and Mary (Perkins) Cary, grew up, one of a large family, in the intellectual group of the Boston of that day. In the letters of her girlhood there was revealed already a nature sprightly, humorous, and warm-hearted. The event of the year 1846 in Boston was the arrival of the naturalist, Louis Agassiz. Shortly after he came, his wife died in Europe, and in Boston, on Apr. 25, 1850, he married Elizabeth Cary. A year later the young wife accompanied him to Charleston, S. C., where she enjoyed the life of the seaside laboratory on Sullivan's Island. By 1856 she was back in Cambridge, Mass., with her husband, conducting a girls' school in order to increase the family income. As a pioneer in the higher education of women, she proved herself a tactful supporter of a cause highly unpopular in that conservative society. She taught little, but was rather the directress and the embodiment of the school's enthusiastic spirit. In 1863 the institution, for her, had fulfilled its mission and was abandoned, but in it there was the promise of later and greater achievement. A member of Agassiz's expedition to Brazil in 1865, Mrs. Agassiz kept a record of the trip and his daily lectures. *A Journey in Brazil* was published in 1868 as a collaboration, the final literary mold being Mrs. Agassiz's part in the book. In 1871 the two sailed around Cape Horn; the record she kept of this expedition has never been completely published. The blow of her husband's death fell on Dec. 14, 1873; courageously rallying, Mrs. Agassiz set about collecting all papers in regard to his life and work. In 1885 she published *Louis Agassiz: His Life and Correspondence,* admirably edited, pardonably eulogistic, but by its impersonal tone leaving the reader's interest rather unsatisfied concerning his private life. Nevertheless, her service to science as Agassiz's amanuensis and biographer cannot be exaggerated.

Her diary for Feb. 11, 1879 records a "meeting about Harvard education for women." With Mr. and Mrs. Arthur Gilman, William James, President Eliot, and others, she was a founder of the institution that ultimately became Radcliffe College in Cambridge. Her influence was thrown upon the side of granting to the students the same courses as were offered at Harvard and by the same instructors. At a time when the close proximity of a girls' college to an institution for men was viewed with doubt, her faith in the self-reliance of the women students was firm. From the outset she threw her heart into the enterprise and at the age of seventy-two accepted the presidency of the college, remaining until 1902 when she resigned. Her relation as stepmother to Agassiz's gifted children was one of great tenderness. To Alexander Agassiz she was especially close, and with him in 1865 published *Seaside Studies in Natural History,* in which her literary gift is evident. She died in 1907 at Arlington Heights, Mass., as a result of a paralytic stroke.

[*The Life of Elizabeth Cary Agassiz* was written by Lucy Allen Paton in 1919; it is highly satisfactory as a personal picture and as a record of Mrs. Agassiz's work and influence. For the founding of Radcliffe College see Arthur Gilman's account in the *Harvard Grads. Mag.*, Sept. 1907.]

D. C. P.

AGASSIZ, JEAN LOUIS RODOLPHE (May 28, 1807–Dec. 14, 1873) was born at Motier-en-Vuly, Canton Fribourg, near the edge of the Vaud, in French Switzerland. The house of his birth, then a pretty parsonage set amid orchard and vines, is still standing and bears a commemorative tablet. The family background must have been one of simple comfort and culture. From his father, the last of a line of Protestant clergymen, the boy seemingly inherited some of those traits which were to make him in after years the incomparable teacher. The life-long sympathy and understanding of his wise mother, Rose Mayor, many of whose charming qualities he also repeated, evoked in him a corresponding devotion. At Cudrefin, under the ample rooftree of kind grandpapa Mayor, a country physician generally respected and beloved, Louis, his younger brother, Auguste, and two sisters passed many delightful holidays. His uncles, Dr. Mathias Mayor and Mr. François Mayor, were, respectively, a leading physician of Lausanne and a successful business man at Neuchâtel. The apparent destiny of the lad, who must necessarily prepare to earn a livelihood, but who yearned for a scholar's career, thus hung for some time between business and medicine, with medicine temporarily winning. Nevertheless, Louis showed himself from the beginning an inveterate lover of nature, with wonderful gifts of observation,—an endowment not to be permanently denied.

At the age of ten he was sent to school at Bienne, and at fifteen to the College of Lausanne, where to his delight he had access to the natural history museum directed by Professor Chavannes, an entomologist. Wandering around Bienne and Lausanne, he especially studied the local fresh-water fishes and memorized their Latin names, even while still floundering (he said) "in the rudiments of many desperate studies at Bienne." In 1824 he entered upon his medical training at the University of Zurich, where he made warm friends among the professors carrying on original research. It was during this period also that a wealthy gentleman, attracted by his uncommonly engaging personality, proposed to adopt and educate him for life. Neither father nor son, however, felt it wise to accept the offer, though a friendly correspondence between Louis and his new acquaintance was kept up for years.

In the spring of 1826 he matriculated at Heidelberg; while there, his interest in natural history increased under the influence of Professors Leuckart, Tiedemann, Bronn, and Bischoff. In 1827, however, he turned to the University of Munich with its larger scope for his genius and sat at the feet of Ignaz von Döllinger, a pioneer embryologist. He once said, "I lived three years under Döllinger's roof and my scientific training goes back to him and to him alone." To be another like Döllinger was his great ambition, and he kept steadily at work. Frequently when a group of students were starting on a pleasure jaunt he would refuse to join them, saying, "Sie gehen alle mit den Anderen." ("They all go with the other fellows.") Agassiz never went with "the other fellows" when matters of his own occupied his attention.

At the same time, he had already made a few intimate friendships, notably with Alexander Braun and Karl Schimper, young botanists of brilliant promise, his inseparable comrades at Heidelberg. The early affection between him and Braun was further cemented in October 1833 by Louis's marriage to Alexander's sister, Cécile, a natural-history artist whose rare ability appears in some of the best drawings in her husband's two monumental series, the one on fossil fishes, the other on fresh-water fish forms. Early in 1828, also, he formed a close relationship with the gifted Joseph Dinkel, who for many years was constantly occupied in making most of the fine illustrations in the two great works just mentioned, as well as the pictures in lesser monographs and small papers by Agassiz. In Munich Dinkel passed many hours a day in the room shared also by Weber (another animal artist in Agassiz's employ) as well as by Schimper and Braun. This amazingly cluttered studio, Agassiz sometimes explained, "was bedroom, library, drawing-room, fencing-room, all together. Students and professors used to call it 'the little academy.'" In that "little academy" some of the most important discoveries of the time were made. There first were discussed the distribution of Baltic fishes, the anatomy of the lamprey and, most important (by Schimper and Braun), the law of phyllotaxy, "the marvelous rhythmical arrangement of the leaves of plants," as their host described it.

Agassiz's crowning effort at Munich was his work on Brazilian fishes dedicated to Cuvier. Two eminent naturalists, J. B. von Spix and K. F. Ph. von Martius, had returned from Brazil in 1821 loaded with rich booty. After the death of Spix in 1826, von Martius turned the fish collection over to Agassiz, then only twenty-one years of age. *The Fishes of Brazil* with many excellent colored plates appeared in 1829. It was an admirable piece of work and the most important account of a local fish-fauna which had been published to that time. In the spring of 1829 Agassiz took his Ph.D. degree at Erlangen—for reasons of convenience—partly because von Martius felt that it would lend dignity to the title-page of *The Fishes of Brazil.* During the following winter Agassiz planned and inaugurated his superb *Recherches sur les Poissons fossiles* (1833–44). Yet at the end of 1830, when he left Munich with his degree of Doctor of Medicine, he felt no confidence that a life of scholarly investigation rather than the practice of medicine could be realized. Nevertheless, at quiet Concise, where his parents were then living, he continued to carry on ichthyological pursuits, meanwhile looking after such few neighborhood patients as sought his help.

Happily, by the autumn of 1831, means had been found to take him to Paris, a center of zoological and medical research, where he arrived in December, accompanied as usual by Dinkel. Still pursuing medical studies, he also gave a portion of his long day to the fossil fish collection in the Museum of Natural History of the Jardin des Plantes, and won almost at once the affectionate interest of Cuvier, the master of comparative anatomy. Cuvier's mission was to make the classification of animals not an arbitrary scheme of convenience but a reflex of their structure. Before him, each different kind, very uncritically described, had been called a species and flung into its particular genus as into a pigeonhole. In large degree Agassiz's attitude was a continuation of that of Cuvier, whose mantle was said to have fallen on him.

Up to that time only eight fossil-fish generic types had been even named in formal publications. Agassiz, however, had studied the problems involved since 1829, while Cuvier had been gathering notes and materials for a future work on the subject. Now, Cuvier graciously turned over to Agassiz the whole matter, including his own data and collections. Thus, though harassed by financial anxieties,—living on 200 francs a month, 125 of which went to Dinkel,—and without a presentable coat in which to make calls, Agassiz labored incessantly to reconstruct fossil forms from the rocks in which their skeletons were imbedded. Collateral investigations took him finally to all the other museums and important collections of Europe. His colossal monograph, when completed, contained descriptions of about 340 new genera, illustrated by 1,290 splendid plates. Begun in 1830, it appeared successively in five quarto volumes, with folio "atlas," and laid the foundation of our knowledge of the fish-fauna of primitive seas, even though the higher groupings were necessarily rather crude. Indeed, until after this work was finished, the fossil fishes of the rest of the world remained unrecorded.

Agassiz's workshop in the Jardin des Plantes was thus described by Theodore Lyman, one of his old students: "Those little low rooms, in the old building propped up at one end with timbers, they should be the Mecca of scientific devotees! Perhaps every great zoologist of the past hundred years has sat in them and discussed the problems which are always awaiting solution and are never solved. Cuvier, Humboldt, Johannes Müller, Von Baer—they have all gone. . . . Everywhere in these galleries and laboratories it is the same. You are surrounded by the traditions of science. The spirits of great naturalists still haunt these corridors and speak through the specimens their hands have set in order."

It was in Paris that Agassiz first met Humboldt, who had grown interested in the youth. On coming to Paris, the distinguished explorer sought him out in the Latin Quarter and took him to lunch at a celebrated café. The acquaintance afterward became one of sympathetic intimacy, and of enduring gratitude on the part of Agassiz. Indeed, Humboldt's spontaneous "advance" of a thousand francs in the spring of 1832 made it possible for Agassiz to continue his researches in Paris. Humboldt's interest was again shown by his help in securing for his young protégé, at Neuchâtel in 1832, a specially established professorship in natural history.

The inauguration of Agassiz's labors at Neuchâtel marks his definite entrance on the most compelling phase of his life. Up to that time he had been primarily student and investigator. Now, on a salary of only eighty louis (about $400) a year, he showed the same ardor for teaching and tireless energy which later characterized his career in America. With boundless enthusiasm he gathered about him a group of coöperating colleagues, students, and fellow-citizens, so that "the little town suddenly became a center of scientific activity." A Natural History Society was organized with Agassiz as secretary. For friends and neighbors he instituted a series of informal lectures on topics which interested him. He enticed to his side groups of children whom he led in fair weather about the country, instructing them in geology, physical geography, and botany. For indoor lessons every child had before him a specimen of the thing under discussion; and occasionally the meeting ended with a feast, even if meager, of bananas, dates, etc. More enduring material went home to build up each one's private collection. Mature students enjoyed the same methods of field instruction on frequent gay out-of-door excursions.

But for six years, unfortunately, the professorship remained on an insecure basis of three years' tenure only, once renewed with salary increase of $200. In 1838, however, the King of Prussia (under whose sovereignty the canton remained until 1846) guaranteed 10,000 louis yearly for a period of ten years for public instruction in Neuchâtel, at which time Agassiz's position was confirmed as professor of "the Academy."

Meanwhile the youthful professor's extraordinary achievements in zoological research brought him general fame in Europe, with offers of material and coöperation from workers and museum men in many quarters, including America. The great treatise on *The Fishes of Brazil* had been immediately followed by a study of those of the Lake of Neuchâtel, ultimately extended into a *History of the Fresh Water Fishes of Central Europe*. This publication, illustrated by many beautiful colored lithographic plates, was put out between 1839 and 1842 by Agassiz's own printing-press established at Neuchâtel in 1838. Between 1837 and 1845 Agassiz printed the results of his investigations on living and fossil mollusks, culminating (1840–45) in his *Études critiques sur les Mollusques fossiles,* with nearly 100 plates. His large quarto, *Nomenclator Zoologi-*

cus, appeared in successive instalments between 1842 and 1846. This tremendously laborious, invaluable work comprised years of patient research. In 1844–45 he published an important *Monograph on the Fossil Fishes of the Old Red or Devonian of the British Isles and Russia,* based mainly on the famous Hugh Miller's collection from Cromarty, Scotland. Other museum and private collections had also been generously placed at his disposal by friends in Britain, where he had visited in 1834 and again the following year. His life-long attachments for Buckland, Lyell, Sir Philip Egerton, Lord Cole, and others, began at this time. To them he was deeply indebted for financial aid as well as for scientific assistance.

With the close of 1835, Agassiz's modest home was gladdened by the birth of his son Alexander, named for his best friend and brother-in-law, Braun. Later came two daughters, Ida (1837) and Pauline (1841). To these children Madame Cécile gave the best of care. Manifestly it was impossible that she should at the same time, and hampered by desperately insufficient means, continue to assist her husband with drawings and work on manuscript.

The summer of 1836 was one of deep significance to Agassiz. Passing it with his wife and child at Bex, near the home of his friend Jean de Charpentier, "a rare and perfect type of savant," he now became a convinced adherent of the glacial theory previously expounded in several papers by the civil engineer Venetz and by de Charpentier. Not only so. With amazing perspicacity, his mind soon leaped to the conclusion that probably a portion of Europe far greater than the Rhône Valley had been subjected to a period of extreme cold. To designate this "glacial epoch," he afterward employed the brief term, "Ice Age," coined by Schimper,—with whom he had long discussions on the new problem. On returning to Neuchâtel he found plain evidences of glacial action in that region and about Bienne. During the winter he gave a public lecture on the subject and the following summer delivered his famous "Discourse" at Neuchâtel, at the opening of the conference of the Helvetic Society of Natural Science, of which he was president. The address contained some erroneous hypotheses, finally abandoned by their author; but it was of great value in that it extended and illuminated de Charpentier's observations, at the same time presenting a tremendous new idea, that of glacial action from the North Pole to the Mediterranean and the Caspian Seas.

Undismayed by the storm of criticism which ensued, Agassiz now inaugurated a notable series of investigations of glacial phenomena in Europe. These continued throughout the succeeding decade, according to an elaborate plan in which his intimate friend, the noted geologist, Arnold Guyot, his secretary-collaborator, Édouard Desor, and several other associates were engaged. The combined results now confirmed in detail the debated general hypothesis of glacial action and distribution. To supplement these conclusions with more specialized data, Agassiz in 1840 established headquarters in the so-called Hôtel des Neuchâtelois on the great median moraine of the lower Aar glacier. This shelter had for roof the projecting surface of a large boulder, with a stone wall on one side and a blanket door. From that picturesque base and its more roomy successors were computed year after year the rate of motion of the glacier as a whole, the difference in rate of upper, middle, lower, and side portions, the amount of annual melting, and numerous allied phenomena. The changing relative positions of eighteen prominent rocks on the glacier and of a crosswise series of stakes set upright in the ice entered into many of the calculations. The huge mass, it was found, behaved somewhat like a viscid fluid, for the stakes in the middle of the glacier moved the most rapidly (even though very slowly) and as they moved they slanted forward. It was thus apparent that gravity controlled the glacier,—also that it traveled fastest in the middle and at the surface, and was not shoved on, as had been asserted, by the freezing of water underneath.

In the summer of 1841 Agassiz caused himself to be lowered into one of the glacier "wells," a perilous undertaking in which he was able to observe clearly the interesting blue-banded (laminated) structure of the ice to a depth of over eighty feet. Other observations of extreme interest were launched and completed. Agassiz's first comprehensive discussion of the subject as a whole, *Études sur les Glaciers,* in two volumes, appeared toward the end of 1840. This was followed in 1846 by the *Système Glaciare,* and in 1847 by *Nouvelles études et expériences sur les Glaciers actuels.* In 1844, also, Agassiz allowed Desor to publish a popular account of the work in the High Alps, with an excellent paper by the leader himself.

In the autumn of 1840, in company with his good friend, Dr. Buckland, Dean of Westminster, Agassiz started out on a "glacier hunt" in Great Britain. The resulting discoveries sufficiently vindicated his expanding theory of general glacial action wherever the earth's surface bears drift material and polished or striated erratic boulders. Buckland, hitherto in only partial agreement, now publicly adhered to this doctrine, having also previously brought Lyell over to Agassiz's side. Humboldt, strangely, never became convinced; and he tried to induce Agassiz to abandon the "icy" researches, which nevertheless continued for many more years, proving the glaciation of a large part of both hemispheres, and leading finally to the tracing by others of several distinct glacial periods. The substance of Agassiz's permanent conclusions has now been universally accepted, although much additional information has since been gathered by others from mountain chains and plateaux the world over.

Certain matters, meanwhile, had been going badly at Neuchâtel. Affairs at the great lithographic establishment, too pretentious by far, had become increasingly involved, and in 1845 it was closed of necessity. In Agassiz's other multiform undertakings, also, his impetuosity, which for a time seemingly overcame all obstacles, much more than exhausted his slender resources, while frequent gifts from outside failed to ward off impending disaster. Dinkel and Vogt (the latter had acted as his assistant for five years) both left Neuchâtel in 1844. In 1845 the situation made it imperative for Agassiz's relatives to extricate him from serious financial embarrassment. In the meantime his wife, a frail, sensitive woman, overburdened by cares and sorely tried by the presence of Desor and Vogt in the household, longed to go back to her old home. The public announcement of a gift from the King of Prussia to defray Agassiz's expenses in a previously projected trip to America allowed this move to be made in May 1845. Except for a brief visit to Carlsruhe before his departure for the United States, Agassiz never saw his first wife again, for later when conditions might otherwise have permitted their reunion, she had already (1848) passed away, a victim of tuberculosis. In due time, however, the three children joined him in Cambridge, where, as will be seen, they grew up in fortunate surroundings.

During Agassiz's fourteen brilliant years at Neuchâtel he had refused several complimentary offers elsewhere, namely, to Heidelberg, Lausanne, and Geneva. Now, however, his departure in March 1846 was clouded in the minds of all by the well-founded conviction that, though ostensibly only temporary, his absence would be permanent, and it must have been with deep emotion on both sides that he took leave of the manifold associations into which he had prodigally poured himself. In Paris, at a meeting of the Geological Society of France, he so carefully and eloquently expounded the glacial theory as to leave no ground for the former French opposition. At the Jardin des Plantes, at work as of old, this time on echinoderms, he conquered everything and every one by his enthusiasm, "sometimes raised to perfect rapture." In England he met again with pleasure the scientific leaders, among them especially Lyell, who had been the means of arranging for the Lowell Institute lectures he was to give soon after his arrival in Boston. At the end of September 1846, embarking from Liverpool, he left the Old World for the New with its untried fields—"a land," as he afterward said, "where Nature was rich, but tools and workmen few and traditions none." A great adventure it turned out to be, lasting until his death, and one that put America permanently in his debt. In the words of Jules Marcou, "American natural history had found its leader."

Though mentally despondent and burdened by financial obligations it took many years to fulfil, Agassiz threw himself with customary avidity into the new environment. The interval between landing and the beginning of his lecture engagement he employed in making the acquaintance of a number of scientific workers in Boston and along the Atlantic seaboard, his journeys taking him as far south as Washington. Institutions, collections, people, manners, and customs compelled his interest, frequently his admiration. On the other hand he was disappointed to find so little official scientific activity at Washington, where the Smithsonian Institution had not yet begun to function. His first lecture at once revealed to a large, enthusiastic audience those charms of intellect and personality which soon endeared him not only to Boston but to all New England. Again it was the same story. Absolute absorption in his calling, coupled with an engaging spirit of democracy, brought rich and poor alike to his side wherever he went. A contagious enthusiasm and warmth surrounded him like an atmosphere. The remark, "One has less need of an overcoat in passing Agassiz's house than by any other in Cambridge," expressed afterward a common feeling. His early establishment, however, shared by several old associates who now had joined him, assumed more the character of a laboratory than a home. It was again "a hive of industry," but to support it financially required too many lectures on the part of the host. As a result Agassiz soon suffered his first serious illness, an attack of nervous prostration.

The summer of 1847, with his first trip on a Coast Survey steamer as guest of the government, opened up a fascinating new world to the mountain-bred naturalist. It was followed by many other similar excursions, including one from Boston around the Horn to San Francisco in 1872. The generous coöperation and friendship of Dr. Alexander Dallas Bache, then head of the Coast Survey and a founder of the National Museum, played a part in inducing Agassiz to remain in the United States. Disturbed political conditions abroad, with the ending of his service to the King of Prussia, were also important factors in the decision. In the spring of 1848 Agassiz accepted the chair of natural history in the recently organized Lawrence Scientific School at Harvard. From that time on, despite highly tempting though belated offers from Europe, this land increasingly claimed him for her own. The new position brought him into intimate relations with the distinguished circle of scholars, both literary and scientific, then grouped around the college. The *Evening Traveller* of Boston printed his local lectures of 1848–49, in full, the day following their delivery, reprinted each such issue, and finally published them in pamphlet form. A fortunate fact, for the expenses of his growing household made heavy demands upon his purse, always emptied in advance. His roof as usual sheltered a long succession of workers, twenty-three in all, twenty-two of whom came from Neuchâtel. Meanwhile he had taken his customary place in the scientific activities of the country at large. Almost immediately, moreover, he began to gather, in an old shanty set on piles by the Charles River, the collections which formed the basis of the great Harvard Museum of Comparative Zoology, his enduring monument.

In the summer of 1848 he led a party of seventeen to the northern and eastern shores of Lake Superior. At night Agassiz habitually talked upon some outstanding feature of the day; with a piece of black canvas, chalk, and a specimen he was always sufficiently provided for a lecture. The results of this important expedition were embodied in a fine volume, beautifully illustrated, which appeared in March 1850 and served in some sense as model for succeeding publications of the kind in America. Early in 1850, he married Elizabeth Cabot Cary of Boston, sister-in-law of his dear friend Prof. C. C. Felton, a woman of superior parts who proved a tower of strength and devotion to him and his. Young Alexander had already arrived in Cambridge; the two daughters were soon brought over by Agassiz's kindly cousin, Auguste Mayor, for many years a resident of Brooklyn. In 1856, feeling the pressing need of additional means for the household, Mrs. Agassiz, with her husband's enthusiastic coöperation, opened a select school for girls. In this highly successful venture of eight years' duration, she had the help of his two older children. Not only did the enlarged income relieve Agassiz from the strain of public lectures but it also enabled him to pay off his European debts.

At the beginning of 1851, Agassiz headed a ten weeks' exploration of the Florida Reefs, inaugurated by Prof. Bache in the interests of the Coast Survey. The complete report of this investigation was published in 1882 by Alexander Agassiz. It was accompanied by very fine plates made under the author's supervision. In December 1851 Agassiz began his winter lectures as professor of comparative anatomy at the Medical College of Charleston, S. C. The climate, unfortunately, proved unsuited to him, and he therefore reluctantly resigned at the end of two years. On the way north in 1852 he gave a course of lectures at the Smithsonian Institution, with whose distinguished secretary, Prof. Joseph Henry, he was already on intimate terms. Later, as one of the board of regents of the institution, Agassiz interested himself deeply in its welfare.

Toward the close of his first decade in the United States, another work of colossal proportions began to shape itself in Agassiz's brain. This was to consist of *Contributions to the Natural History of the United States,* in ten volumes, each complete in itself. The response to an appeal for public subscription was astounding, 2,500 people promising to buy the set at a rate of twelve dollars a volume. Four only were finally completed, and of these only Part I, the *Essay on Classification,* had popular interest, the rest being of a highly specialized character. The *Essay* Marcou regards as "by far the most important contribution of Agassiz to natural history during his life in America," more exactly, to the philosophical aspects of the subject. But its most valuable point is the recognition that "the changes which animals undergo during their embryonic growth coincide with the order of succession of the fossils of the same type in past geological ages." Already Karl Ernst von Baer had shown that, as a rule, the life history of the individual repeats the history of the type. Agassiz now threw back this generalization into geologic time. The *Essay* may be regarded as the culmination of the thought of those who, with Cuvier, noted the succession of types in geological history but saw no genetic connection, one with another, between any of the four great classes then recognized—Vertebrates, Articulates, Mollusks, and Radiates. Later studies have broken down the supposed barriers between these types and between geological ages as well. The four classes, we now know, are tied together in the simple basal forms from which they diverge; and one geologic era was not marked by the sweeping away of all living forms before the onset of the next.

Agassiz's championship of Cuvier's views, now wholly belated, led him to oppose persistently the Darwinian conception of evolution with natural selection as the moving force. Furthermore, always essentially an idealist, he regarded his own investigations not as studies of animals and plants as such, but as glimpses into the divine plans of which their structures are the expression. To his mind, divine ideas were especially embodied in animal life, the species being the "thought unit." The marvel of structural affinity—unity of plan—in creatures of widely diverse habits and outward appearance, he took to be a result of the association of ideas in the divine mind, not proofs of common descent. "Life seemed to him controlled by something more than the mechanism of self-adjusting forces." That "material form is the cover of the spirit" was to him "fundamental and self-evident."

Referring to his early work on fossil fishes, Agassiz once said to David Starr Jordan: "At that time I was on the verge of anticipating Darwinism, but I found that the highest fishes were those that came first." That is, the sharks, the most primitive in some respects, had the largest brains, the most specialized teeth and muscular system. Judging from the nervous system alone, therefore, they should be regarded as the highest of fishes. But he had fallen into the error of supposing that evolutionary divergence could be measured in terms of "progress." Sharks in most regards are primitive as compared with the welter of bony fishes which followed them. Natural selection while bringing about progress in certain lines—or increased specialization through more varied relation to environment—by no means involves universal or even general progress.

The four large quarto issues of *Contributions to the Natural History of the United States* included (besides the *Essay on Classification*) an exhaustive study of the embryology of American turtles, dedicated to Döllinger, as well as two volumes on "radiate" animals, all four illustrated by many extremely fine plates. These monographs constitute Agassiz's last elaborate additions to biological knowledge. The ravages of ill health, added to increasing absorption in other interests, put a stop to further undertakings in the great series projected. Agassiz's fiftieth birthday, May 28, 1857, saw the completion of the first volume—a consummation to which he had passionately devoted himself. The event was furthermore marked by a charming tribute on the part of his students. This consisted of a midnight program of delightful music, supplemented by flowers and affectionate congratulations. The following evening, at a special dinner given Agassiz by the famous "Saturday Club," to which he and many other distinguished men belonged, Longfellow contributed the well-known poem, "The Fiftieth Birthday of Agassiz," full of tender feeling. The summer of 1859 Agassiz passed in Europe with his wife and younger daughter, renewing family ties and professional associations. In London, Paris, and Geneva he was received with acclaim by the scientific groups; he refused a brilliant offer in connection with the Museum of Natural History in the Jardin des Plantes, and other glowing possibilities. In September he returned to America, having meanwhile secured important additions for the institution at Cambridge which had already begun to engross his attention. His plan was to establish a splendid zoological museum, where enormous working collections for the specialist, as well as scientifically arranged displays for general instruction, could be safely housed, with the specimens so placed as to reveal their comparative relations in structure, together with their distribution in time and space. During the prosecution of this scheme, Agassiz, by his iron determination in the face of difficulties, achieved the apparently impossible. The official attitude was strikingly emphasized in a remark by one of the members of the Massachusetts legislature: "I don't know much about museums but I, for one, will not stand by and see so brave a man struggle without aid." Harvard College gave the necessary site; the corner-stone was laid in June 1859; state appropriations and private gifts, a large part of the latter from members of Agassiz's own family, provided for the continuance and development of the museum until it was turned over to Harvard University. Its profound influence during all these years, as a center of scientific research and study, can hardly be estimated.

Agassiz's entrance into the faculty of Harvard College, moreover, marked the beginning of a new era in American education as a whole. He has been called our first university builder, because of his unprecedented emphasis on advanced and original work as factors in mental training. To know something well is "the backbone of education." He laid great stress on the direct study of nature; and the classes in biology became crowded with eager disciples. Some of

Agassiz

his associates took alarm at this. It was "making the college lop-sided," they complained. Even broad-minded Emerson suggested that "something should be done to check the rush towards natural history." Agassiz replied that "the remedy is not to cut off the vigorous growth, but to stimulate the rest. I, for one, would be willing to run a race with any of my colleagues." Each of his students spread his educational idea far and wide. Indeed, during the latter part of the last century there was hardly an active naturalist in America or Japan who had not either studied under Agassiz or been a pupil of one of his students. He also took a vigorous interest in the work of the lower schools. The science they taught was mostly of the routine order, "fourteen weeks" of memorizing in one subject after another. Whenever opportunity arose he strenuously urged a better method. In speaking before teachers he always displayed the actual material with which he had to deal. "There will never be good teaching in natural science," he said, "nor in anything else until similar methods are brought into use." He also insisted that a year or two of natural history would give the best kind of training for any sort of mental work. Referring to the prescribed "classical course," he used to say that "Harvard is a respectable high school where they teach the dregs of education."

The spring of 1865 brought to fulfilment the long-cherished dream of exploration in Brazil. The expedition of nineteen months, shared by Mrs. Agassiz, six assistants, and as many more volunteers, was primarily financed by Nathaniel Thayer of Boston, a close friend of the leader. Additional aid extended by government and steamship officials led Agassiz to say that he felt "like a spoiled child of the country" and that he hoped God would give him "strength to repay in devotion to her institutions, and to her scientific and intellectual development, all that her citizens had done for him." (As evidence of this desire, he had already, at the beginning of the Civil War, become a naturalized citizen of the United States.) In Brazil, distinguished courtesies from the enlightened Emperor, Dom Pedro, as well as other marked favors, lent an air of almost triumphal progress to the trip. Enormous collections were made and brought back to the Museum; certain observations, also, strengthened Agassiz's conception of the universality of the Ice Age, though his conclusions as to the Amazon Valley have not been accepted. A detailed account of daily doings is to be found in *A Journey in Brazil* (1868) written mainly by his wife, with certain additions by Agassiz.

The next few years were devoted to routine occupations broken, as always, by outside efforts. These included an opportunity (1868) to study glacial phenomena in the Rocky Mountain and contiguous regions; a course of lectures as non-resident professor at the infant Cornell University (1868), accompanied by observations on the interesting local ice-action; an important Coast Survey dredging-expedition (1869) in Cuban and adjacent waters under the leadership of the competent Count de Pourtalès, Agassiz's one-time pupil at Neuchâtel, now colleague and co-worker; and an admirably exhaustive memoir on Humboldt's life and influence, delivered at the Humboldt Centennial Celebration (1869) fathered by the Boston Society of Natural History. By the fall of 1869 the strain had been too heavy, and Agassiz suffered a serious attack of apoplexy which prevented his return to the Museum until November 1870. There, however, under the able administration (since 1865) of his son, assisted by a distinguished corps of adult workers, both American and foreign, and a group of ardent students, affairs had gone well. In December 1871 apparently quite restored, Agassiz, accompanied again by his wife, embarked on the Coast Survey vessel *Hassler* for the long trip to California. De Pourtalès and Dr. Franz Steindachner, the latter an authority on ichthyology from Vienna and a member of the Museum staff, served as scientific assistants on the voyage. Results from the deep-sea dredging, on which Agassiz had distinctly counted, were disappointing, because of defective apparatus. On the other hand, he was rewarded by acquaintance with the impressive glaciers and clear evidences of past glaciation around Magellan Strait and among the Chiloë Islands, remarking later that those observations alone amply repaid him for all his trouble and fatigue. This was far greater than had been expected. In San Francisco, for example, he felt too weary to undertake a trip to Yosemite Valley or to the Giant Sequoias of Calaveras County. What a pity that Nature's flaming apostle should have missed, by so narrow a margin, two of her finest manifestations!

It was to bring sound methods into general nature study in America that Agassiz, only a few months before his death, took up with old-time ardor the then novel idea of a summer school of science where teachers should be trained to see nature and to teach others how to see it. Through the generosity of John Anderson of New York, who deeded his island of Penikese in Buzzard's Bay and added an endowment of $50,000, the Anderson School of Natural History was opened in July 1873. From the hundreds who applied for admission Agassiz selected about thirty men and twenty women—teachers, students, and naturalists of various grades. These fifty, he thought, would carry back to their schools and laboratories right views of scientific teaching. Each center would then radiate influence until proper methods in science should gradually spread throughout the educational system. The one new building on the island served a double purpose of laboratory and dormitory, while an old barn had been made into dining and lecture room. At the head of one of the tables Agassiz sat, a blackboard by his side, so that he would often lecture during the meal about a fish the remains of which lay upon the plates.

Agassiz's daily talks at Penikese covered a wide range of subjects: the personalities of European naturalists, the history of geology, the glacial system, methods of teaching. Eloquent in the best sense, though occasionally quaint in diction and aberrant in accent, they embodied to some extent his general confession of faith. He cared little for dogma and ceremonial, but found in Nature a constant revelation of his God. "I feel more vexed at impropriety in a scientific laboratory than in a church," said he. "The study of Nature is intercourse with the Highest Mind. You should never trifle with Nature. At her lowest her works are the works of the highest powers, the highest something in the universe, in whatever way we look at it. . . . This is the charm of study from Nature herself; she brings us back to absolute truth whenever we wander." Subtle distinctions of theology did not concern him in the least. "In Europe," he once remarked, "I have been accused of deriving my scientific ideas from the church. In America I have been called an infidel because I will not let my church-going friends pat me on the head."

His inherent friendliness captured every one. His robust, well-proportioned figure, somewhat above medium height though then slightly bent with years, was surmounted by a superb head. Beautiful, keen, brown eyes lighted up a large, round face, olive in color, while his rather sparse hair retained to considerable extent its original chestnut tone. One could still easily see that in youth he must have been extremely strong and handsome.

In October 1873 Agassiz commenced his final course of lectures at the Museum. His last article, one of several projected under the title, "Evolution and Permanence of Type," a justification of his attitude toward the current trend in biology, appeared shortly after his death, in the *Atlantic Monthly*. He died in Cambridge on Dec. 14, 1873. The funeral was attended by a large concourse of distinguished people and devoted friends, in addition to all of the great scholastic body he had honored by his presence. His grave at Mount Auburn is marked by a huge boulder taken from the Aar Glacier, not far from the site of the "Hôtel des Neuchâtelois," and is shaded by pines brought from the heights above Neuchâtel.

[Elizabeth Cary Agassiz, *Louis Agassiz, His Life and Correspondence*, 2 vols. (1885), especially important for the inclusion of many letters to and from eminent men of science; Jules Marcou, *Life, Letters, and Works of Louis Agassiz*, 2 vols. (1896), a comprehensive work, valuable for the range and accuracy of details, including an annotated list of American and European publications concerning Agassiz, also a complete catalogue of his scientific papers, 425 in number; Arnold Guyot, *Memoir of Louis Agassiz* (1879); Lane Cooper, *Louis Agassiz as a Teacher* (1917), a very useful little book especially for its inclusion of the testimony of early students as to Agassiz's methods; C. F. Holder, *Agassiz* (1910); B. G. Wilder, "Louis Agassiz, Teacher," *Harvard Grads. Mag.* (1907); Theodore Lyman, "Recollections of Louis Agassiz," *Atlantic Mo.*, XXXIII, 1874; David Starr Jordan, "Agassiz at Penikese," *Pop. Sci. Mo.*, XL, 1892, reprinted, with additions, in *Sci. Sketches* (1895); David Starr Jordan, "Anderson School at Penikese," in *Days of a Man*, I (1923); David Starr Jordan, "Louis Agassiz, Teacher," *Sci. Mo.*, Nov. 1923.]

D. S. J.
J. K. J.

AGATE, ALFRED T. (Feb. 14, 1812–Jan. 5, 1846), miniature painter, illustrator, was born at Sparta, N. Y., a son of Thomas and Hannah Agate, natives of England; he was a brother of the artist Frederick Styles Agate [*q.v.*]. Trained as a miniaturist at New York, he became in 1832 an associate of the National Academy of Design. He joined the scientific corps of the Wilkes Exploring Expedition, his name appearing on the roster of the *Relief* as "portrait and botanical artist." Capt. Charles Wilkes, writing of the personnel of the expedition, said: "To Messrs. Drayton and Agate, the Artists of the Expedition, I feel it due to make known how constantly and faithfully they have performed their duties. The illustrations of these volumes will bear ample testimony to the amount of their labors, and the accuracy with which they have been executed." Examination of the publications that followed the expedition, in which many of Agate's drawings of flora and fauna are included, show that Capt. Wilkes's appreciation of them was not fulsome; they are beautifully and delicately made. Agate's membership in the National Academy was changed from "associate" to "honorary" in 1840, probably on account of his change of residence. He died at Washington, D. C., according to the *Academy Register*, which, mistakenly, gave his age as twenty-eight. The Academy's permanent collection contains one of Agate's little pictures, "Cocoanut Grove," dated 1840 and given in 1902 by James D. Smillie. Agate was married to Elizabeth Hill Kennedy, but left no children.

[The chief sources of information regarding Alfred T. Agate are the *Reg. of the Natl. Acad. of Design* (N.Y.); the collections of the Naval Records and Library, Navy Dept., Washington, D. C.; J. T. Scharf, *Hist. of Westchester County, N.Y.* (1886). A sketch in the *Allgemeines Lexicon der Bildenden Künstler, von der Antike bis zur Gegenwart* (1907) by Edmund von Mach, is inadequate and inaccurate.]

F. W. C.

AGATE, FREDERICK STYLES (Jan. 29, 1803–May 1, 1844), painter, brother of Alfred T. Agate [*q.v.*], was the son of Thomas and Hannah Agate, who were born at Shipley, England (manuscript letter of E. Agate Foster, M.D.) and settled at Sparta, Westchester County, N.Y. As a boy he made notable drawings of animals and at the age of fifteen he was sent to New York to study with John Rubens Smith, an English mezzotinter, who, settling in America, had become a popular teacher of drawing and painting. Agate at once showed himself a careful and correct draughtsman. In 1825 he and his fellow student Thomas S. Cummings [*q.v.*], afterwards treasurer of the National Academy and its historian, left Smith to paint in oil and copy from the antique under S. F. B. Morse at the Academy of Fine Arts. Finding at this academy "no liberal and accommodating spirit," they organized a coöperative class to meet at the members' rooms. The New York Historical Society soon extended to them the use of a room, and thus was the National Academy of Design "initiated and managed exclusively by the artists." In 1827 Agate set up at 152 Broadway as historical and portrait painter. He had already shown two pictures at the National Academy's first exhibition, May 1826. Thereafter, down to his death, he was a regular exhibitor, in 1829 contributing fifteen paintings, and in several other years ten or more. His "Ugolino" and the "Old Oaken Bucket" of 1834 were especially popular. His success with them encouraged Agate to go abroad. In 1834 he went to Paris and thence to Florence, where he made copies for his friend and patron James Boorman. He started a large canvas "Jesuit Missionaries among the Indians" on which he was working at Rome when seized with a severe and nearly mortal illness. His health continuing poor, he sailed from Leghorn to New York in 1835. Despite advancing tuberculosis, Agate continued to paint and send pictures to the National Academy exhibitions. In the winter of 1843–44 several New York artists met frequently to criticize each other's compositions. While attending one of these meetings on a stormy evening, Agate was fatally stricken, and was sent to his parents' home at Sparta, where "he lingered until about the beginning of May." On his death, the National Academy passed a resolution of regret in which it was stated: "We do not believe he ever had an enemy or was ever jealous of another's successes."

Agate's works belonged to a period in which the mission of art was generally held to be moralistic as well as esthetic, and he himself, a profoundly religious man, was "of opinion that mind should have precedence of mere skill and manner; that simple imitations of what is called nature, without aiming at that which awakens a responsive feeling in the heart, ought to be viewed in no other light than as a curious display of human dexterity." But his own compositions, earnestly fashioned in the light of this conception, have not stood the test of time. They are now regarded as of antiquarian rather than artistic interest.

[A comprehensive account by F. W. Edmonds, *Knickerbocker Mag.*, XXIV, 157 ff.; brief biog. by H. T. Tuckerman, *The Book of the Artists* (1867); references to Agate's professional activities and exhibition pictures in T. S. Cummings, *Hist. Annals of the Natl. Acad. of Design* (1865). The correct date of the artist's birth, sometimes given as 1807, is established by a headstone in the Sparta cemetery.]

F. W. C.

AGNEW, CORNELIUS REA (Aug. 8, 1830–Apr. 18, 1888), New York ophthalmologist and medical organizer, was of Huguenot, Scotch, and North of Ireland ancestry. His grandfather came to America in 1786, settling first in Philadelphia but moving soon to New York City, where he was engaged in the tobacco and shipping business, a member of a firm which was continued by his son William, who married Elizabeth Thomson, daughter of a Pennsylvania surveyor. Their son Cornelius was educated in private schools and entered Columbia College at the age of fifteen. Upon graduating in 1849 he studied medicine with J. Kearny Rodgers, surgeon to the New York Eye and Ear Infirmary and professor of anatomy in the College of Physicians and Surgeons, the medical department of Columbia. Young Agnew went through this school, took his M.D. in 1852, served as "walker" or interne in the New York Hospital, and in 1854 began practice in a small mining settlement on Lake Superior. A year there and he returned to New York to accept the position of surgeon to the Eye and Ear Infirmary with the proviso that he first go abroad to make a special study of the diseases of the eye and ear. In Dublin he was under William Wilde; in London, William Bowman; in Paris, Sichel and Desmarres. When he returned to his native city he began general practice, married (1856) Mary Nash, daughter of Lora Nash, a merchant, and served as surgeon to the Eye and

Ear Infirmary until April 1864. Previous to the opening of the Civil War (1858) Gov. Morgan appointed Agnew surgeon-general of the militia of the state and when the war began, medical director of the New York State Hospital for Volunteers. It was in this position that he gave evidence of the unusual executive ability which characterized him through life. He was one of the organizers of the famous United States Sanitary Commission, which did so much for the soldiers during the war. In conjunction with Dr. Wolcott Gibbs and Dr. William H. Van Buren, Agnew prepared the plans for the Judiciary Square Hospital at Washington, the model for the pavilion system of hospitals. Other evidences of his gift for organization were the Union League Club in New York, which he and three others started; the School of Mines at Columbia (1864); an ophthalmic clinic at the College of Physicians and Surgeons; the Brooklyn Eye and Ear Hospital, and the Manhattan Eye and Ear Hospital. From 1869 until his death Agnew was clinical professor of the diseases of the eye and ear at the College of Physicians and Surgeons. As a lecturer he was fluent and practical. He wrote a moderate amount for the medical press; he devised an operation for divergent strabismus (squint) that was described in the *Transactions of the American Ophthalmological Society* for 1886, and his "operation for thickened capsule" was used widely by operators in this field of medicine. He was a man of medium height, of slender build, dark complexion, and black hair. He had a dignified bearing and an engaging smile.

[Sketches by R. French Stone in *Biogs. of Eminent Am. Surgeons* (2nd ed., 1898) and by Thos. Hall Shastid in *Am. Medic. Biogs.* (1920), ed. by Kelly and Burrage; W. B. Atkinson, *Physicians and Surgeons of the U.S.* (1878); *Universities and Their Sons* (1898–1900), ed. by J. L. Chamberlain, II (1899).]

W. L. B.

AGNEW, DAVID HAYES (Nov. 24, 1818–Mar. 22, 1892), surgeon, teacher of anatomy and surgery, was born in Lancaster County, Pa., of a family which, it was said, could be traced through many generations of North of Ireland and Scotch ancestry to Norman progenitors. In America the Agnews had been prominent in the history of Pennsylvania for nearly two centuries. Agnew's father, Robert, was a physician, his mother had married as first husband the Rev. Ebenezer Henderson. The son was educated at Moscow College in Chester County, at Jefferson College at Canonsburg, and for a year at Delaware College, Newark, Del. He studied medicine with his father and was graduated from the medical department of the University of Pennsylvania in 1838, before he had attained his majority. He then went into general practice near Nobleville, in Chester County. In 1841 he was married to Margaret, daughter of Samuel Irwin, an iron-founder in the same county. When he had been five years in a country practice, and had found his ambition to study anatomy and surgery ungratified, he joined with his brothers-in-law to establish the iron-founding firm of Irwin & Agnew; but it failed in 1846, through lack of proper transit facilities and a general business depression. He then returned to the practice of medicine in Chester and Lancaster Counties and after two years moved to Philadelphia, where in 1852 he bought and resuscitated the decadent Philadelphia School of Anatomy. There he worked early and late, sometimes being in the school from twelve to eighteen hours a day, lecturing and demonstrating to ever-growing classes who held him in affectionate regard. At one time when the quarters in Chant St. had been enlarged, the class numbered 267, the students coming from the University of Pennsylvania and from the Jefferson Medical College, near at hand, and from the South. Agnew had the capacity of the Scot for hard labor, and the pertinacity,—and he acquired the reputation of being the clearest and most practical lecturer and demonstrator of the time. For ten years he maintained this school—often personally securing much of the material for dissection—and eventually he organized a school of operative surgery. In 1854 he was made a surgeon to the Philadelphia Hospital where he could teach clinical surgery, and be assistant to Henry H. Smith, professor of surgery at the University. At the opening of the Civil War, Agnew, then at the age of forty-two, was known as an able operator and a sound consultant. During the war he served chiefly as surgeon in charge of the Hestonville Hospital and as consulting surgeon at the Mower General Hospital, though he was employed also by the government elsewhere. He became an expert in gun-shot wounds. In 1863 he was elected surgeon to the Wills Eye Hospital; in 1865, surgeon to the Pennsylvania Hospital; in 1867, surgeon to the Orthopædic Hospital; in 1870, professor of clinical surgery, and in the following year professor of surgery in the University of Pennsylvania, retaining the last position until 1889, when he retired as professor emeritus.

Agnew grew constantly in skill and reputation. His clinics were crowded, as was his waiting-room; he was the chief consultant in the case of President James A. Garfield when he was shot by Guiteau, in 1881; in 1888 he was given a complimentary banquet, attended by over 200 physicians, in the foyer of the Academy of

Music, at which J. M. Da Costa and Lewis A. Sayre spoke and Weir Mitchell read a poem; and next year he was elected president of the Philadelphia College of Physicians, a crowning honor. His writings comprise some sixty-six titles, including, besides addresses on sundry occasions, *Practical Anatomy; A New Arrangement of the London Dissector* (1856); *Anatomy in its Relations to Medicine and Surgery* (1859–64); *Clinical Reports* (1859–71); and his *magnum opus, Treatise on the Principles and Practice of Surgery,* the three successive volumes of which bear the dates 1878, 1881, and 1883. This book set forth his enormous experience, embraced every department of surgery, and was written in a clear, judicial manner so that his well-balanced consideration of points in diagnosis, his lucid explanations of the surgical anatomy of diseases and injuries were of the highest value to the student.

Agnew was six feet tall and possessed a splendid physique. As an operator he was calm, never flurried in the face of emergencies; he could handle the knife with either hand, ambidextrousness having been acquired early in life when a finger on his right hand had a runround; so that spectators marveled at the exactness of his operating and at his judgment. As a consultant he was most courteous to his brother practitioners, quickly ferreting out the important facts in the case, and advising appropriate treatment. His calm, well-balanced disposition endeared him to all, for he was never irritable, even in the operating-room. When he himself suffered acutely with angina pectoris in late life, he bore the pain with equanimity. Active to the last he died of arteriosclerosis of the heart complicated by kidney disease and diabetes, in his seventy-fourth year.

[J. Howe Adams, *Hist. of the Life of D. Hayes Agnew* (1892); J. Wm. White, "Memoir of D. Hayes Agnew," *Trans. Coll. of Physicians, Phila.* (1893), XV, 29–65; De Forest Willard, "Biog. Sketch of D. Hayes Agnew," *Internatl. Medic. Mag.* (1893), I, 1–8.]

W. L. B.

AGNEW, ELIZA (Feb. 2, 1807–June 14, 1883), missionary, daughter of James and Jane Agnew, was born in New York City, which was the place of her education and her residence for nearly thirty-two years. On Dec. 28, 1823, she was converted during a revival meeting and joined the Orange Street Presbyterian Church. From her school days she cherished the resolve to enter mission work, but until her thirty-third year she devoted herself to service in her home, in the "Sabbath-school," and in the distribution of Scripture and tracts. By 1839 her only close home ties had been severed by the death of her parents, and she turned to the American Board of Boston and secured appointment to their Ceylon Mission. She sailed from Boston on July 30, 1839, on the *Black Warrior,* and arrived at Jaffna, Ceylon, Jan. 17, 1840. In 1842 she was stationed at Oodooville (Uduvil), just north of Jaffna, as "teacher" in the Female Boarding School. Here she spent forty-three years without furlough, save for one brief vacation in South India. She was a pioneer in Ceylon in work for girls and women. *The Missionary Herald* (September 1883, p. 330) said of her, "It is largely owing to the work she was permitted to do that female education is more advanced here (Ceylon) than in almost any other heathen land." Owing to her presence the religious history of the school was truly remarkable. She was a woman of prayer and was much concerned for the spiritual welfare of her charges. They in turn trusted her and accepted her example and guidance. Out of 1,000 individuals of three generations who passed under her influence, more than 600 adopted the Christian faith. She visited the graduates and ex-pupils in their homes, counseling them in matters of housekeeping and in affairs of the spirit. In 1879 she resigned as principal of the school and removed to Manepay, a town to the west, to pass her remaining years with the Christians there. The last two years of her life were spent in the home of the Misses M. and M. W. Leitch, missionaries in Manepay of the American Board. In June 1883 she had a paralytic stroke and died. She was buried in Oodooville near the school over which she had presided.

[Annie Ryder Gracey, *Eminent Missionary Women* (1898); M. and M. W. Leitch, *Seven Years in Ceylon* (1890); *Missionary Review of the World* (1890–97).]

J. C. A.

AGNUS, FELIX (May 5, 1839–Oct. 31, 1925), Union soldier, newspaperman, was born in Lyons, France, the son of Étienne and Anne (Bernerra) Agnus. After attending for a while the College of Jolie Clair near Montrouge, he went to sea and in the course of four years sailed around the globe, visiting St. Helena, the west coast of Africa and the Cape of Good Hope, Madagascar, Chile, and Peru, and returning to France by way of Cape Horn. For three years he studied sculpture. During the war with the Austrians he served in the 3rd Regiment of Zouaves, took part, May 20, 1859, in the battle of Montebello, and later was detailed to Garibaldi's corps in the Italian lakes region. Then he came to America, settling first in Newport, R. I., and later finding a place with Tiffany & Co. in New York as a sculptor and chaser. On May 9, 1861, less than a month after the bombardment of Fort Sumter, the young Frenchman donned the bright-hued uniform he had worn under Garibaldi and enlisted in the 5th New York Infantry. A month later, on June 10, he was in the battle of Big Bethel and distinguished himself by saving the life of Capt. Judson Kilpatrick. For this piece of gallantry he was shortly after made a second-lieutenant. At Gaines's Mill, June 27, 1862, he was shot through the right shoulder. The injury caused the loss of the joint. In Baltimore, where he was sent to recuperate, he was the guest of Charles C. Fulton, proprietor of the *Baltimore American*, whose daughter Annie he married Dec. 13, 1864. She died in March 1922. With other convalescent officers he raised the 165th New York Zouaves, in which he was captain of the color company. This regiment garrisoned New Orleans and Baton Rouge in the winter of 1862–63. On May 27, 1863, he was wounded during an assault on Port Hudson, and for his bravery during the action was later promoted to major. He was one of those who volunteered for the proposed final effort to take Port Hudson by storm. Still later, as lieutenant-colonel, he commanded the 165th New York in the Shenandoah Valley under Sheridan, was brevetted colonel and brigadier-general on Mar. 13, 1865, and was sent with his regiment to occupy Savannah and to dismantle various Confederate forts in South Carolina, Georgia, and Florida. He was then twenty-six years old. On July 26, 1865, he resigned his commission. Soon afterward he went to work for his father-in-law and on July 4, 1869, was made business manager of the *American*. He managed the property successfully and on Fulton's death in 1883 became, under a deed of trust, publisher and sole manager. Under his direction the paper was long a power in Baltimore and throughout Maryland. On Aug. 17, 1908, Agnus launched an evening paper, the *Star*. In November 1920 he sold both papers to Frank A. Munsey [*q.v.*] and retired from active business. In the controversy over the relative deserts of Admirals Sampson and Schley he attracted national attention by his ardent championship of his friend Schley, whom he had met in front of Port Hudson forty years before. He was active in Republican politics, though never a candidate for office, served twice as a member of the Board of Visitors to West Point, was chairman of the Chesapeake and Delaware Canal Commission, and was a member of the commission that made itself famous by building and furnishing the Baltimore Court-house with the money appropriated for the building alone. He wrote short stories and was fond of dispensing the hospitality of his country estate in Green Spring Valley.

[*A Hist. of the City of Baltimore* (1902); *Baltimore Sun*, Oct. 31, 1925; *Who's Who in America*, 1924–25; *Official Records*, ser. I, vols. II, XI, XXVI, XXXVII, LIII.]

G. H. G.

AIKEN, CHARLES AUGUSTUS (Oct. 30, 1827–Jan. 14, 1892), educator, was all his life prominent in academic circles, and as teacher, administrator, writer, and translator contributed both to the intellectual life of his day and to the development of its educational institutions. He was a precocious lad and early gave proof of unusual mental ability. No obstacles made difficult the preparation for his career. The surroundings of his boyhood were favorable, and the best which this country and Europe offered was within his reach. His father, John, of old New Hampshire Scotch-Irish stock, was a successful lawyer and man of means, a promoter of the textile industries of Lowell, Mass., and was associated with the management of several educational and religious organizations; his mother, Harriet, was the daughter of Prof. Ebenezer Adams [*q.v.*] of Dartmouth College. Although born in Manchester, Vt., his early years were spent in Lowell, Mass., where he attended the public schools. At the age of twelve he was ready for college, but his father put him into one of his mills, where he got a training in business which was of service to him later. In spite of this interruption he graduated from Dartmouth at nineteen. After three years' teaching in Lawrence Academy, Groton, Mass., and in Phillips Andover Academy, he entered Andover Theological Seminary in 1849. His course here was broken by two years' study at Berlin, Halle, and Leipzig, where his linguistic ability attracted notice. Returning to this country, he graduated from Andover in 1853. On Oct. 17, 1854, he married Sarah Elizabeth, daughter of Daniel and Eleanor Noyes of Andover, and two days afterward was ordained pastor of the Congregational Church, Yarmouth, Me., resigning five years later to become professor of Latin language and literature at Dartmouth. In 1866 he accepted a similar chair at the College of New Jersey, Princeton. From 1869 to 1871 he was president of Union College, Schenectady, N.Y. Relinquishing that office on account of his wife's health, he returned to Princeton to become the first Archibald Alexander Professor of Christian Ethics and Apologetics in the Seminary, where he remained until his death.

As a teacher he was uncommonly successful, having had the reputation at Dartmouth of being able to do twice as much with students in an hour as any one else could accomplish. His business ability was such that he was given a large share in the administrative work of the institutions with which he was connected. The range of his scholarship may be inferred from the different names given to the chair he occupied at Princeton,—Christian Ethics, and Relations of Philosophy and Science to the Christian Religion. He was most distinguished in philology, and was a prominent member of the American Committee on the revision of the Bible, and the translator and editor of Zockler's "The Book of Proverbs" (1870), in Volume X of the Schaff-Lange series of commentaries. While he was not a maker of many books, his literary activity was unceasing. The first year the *Presbyterian Review* was founded, he acted with Dr. Charles A. Briggs [*q.v.*] as managing editor, and during the nine years of its existence, with the exception of the 1884 issues, there was no number to which he did not make a contribution. His association with the *Presbyterian and Reformed Review* was also practically that of editor. To the *Princeton Review* and *Bibliotheca Sacra* he was a frequent contributor. A portrait of him may be found in the first volume of Andrew V. Raymond's *Union University* (1907).

[*Princeton Theol. Sem. Necr. Reports,* 1892; *Andover Theol. Sem. Necrology,* 1890–91; *Presbyt. and Reformed Rev.,* Apr. 1892; *Cat. of the Class of 1846 in Dartmouth Coll.; N.Y. Tribune,* Jan. 15, 1892; *N.Y. Times,* Jan. 15, 1892.] H. E. S.

AIKEN, DAVID WYATT (Mar. 17, 1828–Apr. 6, 1887), Confederate soldier, agricultural editor, congressman, was born in Winnsboro, S. C. After establishing himself in South Carolina during the eighteenth century, William Aiken of Ireland persuaded his mother and his seven brothers and sisters to try their fortunes in America likewise. David, the youngest of these, ultimately settled in Winnsboro, where he became a prosperous merchant and farmer. He married Nancy Kerr, like himself a native of County Antrim, Ireland; and David Wyatt was the seventh of his nine children. David Wyatt Aiken was educated at Mount Zion Institute and at the South Carolina College, graduating from the latter in 1849. For the next two years he taught at Mount Zion Institute, but in 1852 turned to agriculture. He was married during the same year to Mattie Gaillard. Following her death, which occurred shortly after marriage, he married Virginia Smith of Abbeville. In 1858 he removed from Winnsboro to Cokesbury in Abbeville District, where he became the proprietor of Stony Point Farm. At the beginning of the Civil War he enlisted as a private, but was soon appointed adjutant of the 7th South Carolina Regiment of Volunteers, which subsequently became a part of the 4th (Kershaw's) Brigade, 2nd Division, Army of Northern Virginia. Upon the reorganization of the regiment in the spring of 1862, he was elected colonel. Being severely wounded in the battle of Antietam, Sept. 17, 1862 (for an account of his gallant conduct in this action see *Official Records,* ser. I, vol. XIX, pt. II, p. 866), he was unable to rejoin his command until June 1863. After participating in the Gettysburg campaign, he was declared unfit for further active service, and was assigned to duty as commandant of the troops and defenses at Macon, Ga. He held this post for one year and was then discharged on account of ill health (*Official Records,* see Index).

From 1864 to 1866 Aiken represented Abbeville District in the state House of Representatives (*Journals of the South Carolina Legislature,* 1864, 1865, 1866). After the establishment of the rule of the Republican party in South Carolina he zealously promoted the rehabilitation of Southern economy. Through the *Rural Carolinian* he defined the economic problems of reconstruction and discussed their solution. This agricultural journal was founded in Charleston, S. C., in October 1869. From January 1870 to December 1875 Aiken was part owner and correspondent, and during the last year of its publication (1876) he was sole owner and editor. The work of the *Rural Carolinian* was carried on for several years after its discontinuance, through an agricultural department in the *News and Courier* (Charleston, S. C.) of which Aiken was editor. In 1872 he was appointed deputy-at-large of the National Grange, Patrons of Husbandry, for the Southern States, and in the next year was made a member of its executive committee. By October 1872 he had succeeded in organizing a state grange in South Carolina, of which he was first made secretary and then master (1875–77). In the campaign which accomplished the overthrow of the carpet-bagger régime in South Carolina (1876), Aiken was elected to Congress from the third congressional district (J. S. Reynolds, *Reconstruction in South Carolina,* 1905, pp. 347, 361, 394). He continued during the last decade of his life to occupy a seat in the House of Representatives where he was a leading spokesman of the militant agrarian interests. His death occurred a few weeks after his retirement from public life.

[Yates Snowden, *Hist. of S. C.* (1920) and D. A. Dickert, *Hist. of Kershaw's Brigade* (1899) contain brief but fairly reliable sketches of Aiken's life. The most considerable body of printed material dealing with his career is contained in the *Rural Carolinian.* An obituary was published in the *News and Courier,* Apr. 7, 1887.] J. H. E.

AIKEN, GEORGE L. (Dec 19, 1830–Apr. 27, 1876), actor and playwright, was born in Boston, and made his début on the stage as Ferdinand in

The Six Degrees of Crime in Providence, R. I., in June 1848. His *Orion, the Gold Beater,* a dramatization of the novel, was produced at the National Theatre, New York, Jan. 15, 1851. A manuscript exists in the Players Club, New York. His chief claim to remembrance, however, is his dramatization of Mrs. Stowe's *Uncle Tom's Cabin.* After more than one unsuccessful attempt had been made by other hands, Aiken wrote his play at the suggestion of George C. Howard, manager of the Museum, Troy, N. Y., who believed that the characters of Eva and Topsy were suited to the talents of his daughter, Cordelia, and his wife, who was Aiken's cousin. Aiken acted the dual parts of George Shelby and of George Harris, the mulatto, in his own version, which opened at the Troy Museum, Sept. 27, 1852, ran 100 nights, and was taken to Purdy's National Theatre, New York, July 18, 1853, where it was performed 325 consecutive times. This version was played in Philadelphia in 1853–54, in Detroit in 1854, and in Chicago in 1858. When the play was revived on Nov. 24, 1924, at the Triangle Theatre, New York, the production was based on Aiken's version. Aiken followed the novel closely in his plot, beginning in Kentucky, then taking Uncle Tom to New Orleans and finally to his death at Legree's plantation. All the sentimental features of the novel are emphasized, and little Eva is taken almost bodily to a better world. Yet poor as the play is from a dramatic standpoint, it was one of the most potent forces in the abolition movement. According to H. P. Phelps (*Players of a Century,* 1880), Aiken dramatized a number of stories from the *Ledger,* including "The Gun Maker of Moscow" and "The Mystic Bride," during the season of 1856–57. He also continued to write for the National or Chatham Theatre in New York. On Nov. 3, 1856, his play of *The Old Homestead,* a dramatization of Ann S. Stephens's novel, was performed, and on May 18, 1858, *The Emerald Ring. The Doom of Deville; or The Maiden's Vow* had its production at Barnum's Museum, New York, Nov. 28, 1859. These seem to have perished. *Uncle Tom's Cabin; or, Life Among the Lowly. A Domestic Drama in Six Acts* was published by Samuel French, New York. The records of that house fail to reveal any date. A play, *Josie; or, Was He a Woman?* was copyrighted in 1870, by title. To Aiken have also been attributed stories, *The Household Skeleton* (1865) and *Cynthia, The Pearl of the Points,* a tale of New York (1867), *Chevalier, the French Jack Sheppard* (1868), and *A New York Boy among the Indians* (1872). He was acting in Philadelphia in 1860 at the Arch Street Theatre, and in 1859 and again in 1861 was house dramatist at Barnum's Museum in New York. In 1862 he was associate manager of the Troy Theatre. Aiken retired from the stage in 1867 but continued writing fiction and making dramatizations, living in Brooklyn, N. Y., until 1875. He died in Jersey City, N. J.

[A brief notice of Aiken appears in T. Allston Brown's *Hist. of the Am. Stage* (1870), and another in F. C. Wemyss's *Chronology of the Am. Stage* (1852). A detailed account of *Uncle Tom's Cabin* appears in T. A. Brown's *Hist. of the N.Y. Stage* (1903), I, 312–19. The date of his death, given incorrectly by Brown, has been established by the Registrar of the Board of Health and Vital Statistics of Hudson County, N.J. Information has also been furnished by letters from Mrs. Cordelia Howard Macdonald, who created the part of Eva in 1852, and by Mrs. Viola Aiken Baker. Scattered references are also found in *Records of the N.Y. Stage,* by J. N. Ireland (1866). See also A. H. Quinn's *Hist. of the Am. Drama from the Beginning to the Civil War* (1923).]

A. H. Q.

AIKEN, WILLIAM (Jan. 28, 1806–Sept. 6, 1887), planter, statesman, philanthropist, was born in Charleston, S. C. At about the time that the Articles of Confederation were being replaced by the "more perfect" plan of union embodied in the Federal Constitution, William Aiken, Sr., a native of County Antrim, Ireland, settled in Charleston. He became a merchant, sat for several years in the state legislature, and at the time of his death (1831) was serving as the first president of the South Carolina Canal and Railroad Company and was said to be one of the wealthiest men in Charleston (*Charleston Mercury,* Mar. 7, 1831). He married Henrietta Wyatt, and William Aiken was his only son. The latter received his early education in the schools of Charleston (*In Memoriam William Aiken,* 1887). He then entered the South Carolina College from which he graduated in 1825. After a period of extensive travel he returned to Charleston, and on Feb. 3, 1831, married Harriett Lowndes (G. B. Chase, *Lowndes of South Carolina,* 1876, p. 23). The untimely death of his father as the result of an accident the next month brought him at once into the possession of a large fortune and considerable business responsibilities. Agriculture, however, held more attractions for him than commerce, and he was soon developing a great rice plantation on Jehossee Island, near Charleston, which through his careful and skilful management came to be a model of its kind. (For a description of this plantation as it appeared in 1850 see *DeBow's Review,* IX, 201 ff.)

Aiken's political career began in 1838, when he was sent to the lower house of the legislature by the parishes of St. Philip's and St. Michael's (city of Charleston). He was reëlected in 1840, and two years later was elevated to the state Senate by the same constituency. In 1842, before the expiration of his term in the Senate, he was chosen governor by the legislature after three ineffectual ballots (*Charleston Courier,* Dec. 9, 1844). His administration (1844–46) was marked by no unusual incident, and his efforts were mainly directed toward the development of the economic interests of the state, particularly the railroads (see his annual messages in the *Journals of the Legislature*). After a short period of retirement from public life, he was induced in 1850 to offer for Congress (*Charleston Mercury,*Oct. 12, 1850). He was elected by a handsome majority, and took his seat in the House of Representatives on Dec. 1, 1851. He was returned without opposition to the Thirty-third and Thirty-fourth Congresses. He seldom took part in debate, but through his position on leading committees he exerted an important influence on legislation. His freedom from violent party and sectional bias and his reputation as a man of sterling character admitted him to the councils of all factions (see Howell Cobb's estimate of him in "The Correspondence of Toombs, Stephens, and Cobb," *American Historical Association Reports,* 1911, vol. II, pp. 358–59). Accordingly, after the House of the Thirty-fourth Congress had spent two months in futile efforts to elect a Speaker, Aiken was brought forward as a compromise candidate. The resolution by which his name was proposed met with so favorable a response that it appeared that he might be elected. On the following day, Feb. 2, 1856, it was agreed that, if after three further ballots no candidate had secured a majority, then on the fourth the member receiving the largest number of votes should be declared Speaker. No decision was reached on the first three ballots in spite of the fact that Aiken gained the solid support of the Democrats and the votes of most of the Southern Know-Nothings. The final ballot, the 133rd since the beginning of the contest, was then taken. The count stood: 103 for Nathaniel P. Banks, the Republican candidate; 100 for Aiken; and 11 for all others. An effort to have this decision thrown out on technical grounds was defeated by Aiken and others, and Banks was escorted to the chair by his defeated rival and two other members (*Congressional Globe,*34 Cong., 1 Sess., pp. 334 ff.).

Aiken declined a fourth term in Congress and retired again to private life. He had steadfastly opposed disunion, and it was with regret and no little misgiving as to the consequences that he saw the Southern States secede from the Union in 1861. During the war which ensued, however, he contributed materially to the Southern cause by the donation of supplies and by making large subscriptions to Confederate loans. In June 1865 he was arrested by the federal authorities and taken to Washington, but was released on parole immediately upon his arrival. He was soon after elected to Congress by his old constituency, but was denied his seat by the action of the Northern members (J. S. Reynolds, *Reconstruction in South Carolina,* 1905, p. 20). He did not participate further in public life other than to perform the duties of a trustee of the Peabody Educational Fund. His death occurred at Flat Rock, N. C., ten years after his state had resumed its normal position in the Union.

[The private papers of William Aiken were lost in a fire which destroyed his plantation home at Jehossee Island, and no biographical sketch has ever been written. An excellent obituary, however, was published in *The News and Courier* (Charleston, S. C.), Sept. 8, 1887. A portrait of him in later life, painted by John Stolle after a photograph, is in the possession of the Rhett family of Charleston. Yates Snowden's *Hist. of S. C.* (1920) contains a brief account of the genealogy of the Aiken family.]

J. H. E.

AIKENS, ANDREW JACKSON (Oct. 31. 1830–Jan. 22, 1909), editor, publisher, was born among the Vermont hills, in the town of Barnard, to parents of rugged ancestry. His father, Warren Aikens, was of Scotch descent, while his mother, Lydia, was directly descended from John Howland of the *Mayflower.* At the age of fifteen, he started his life career by becoming a printer's apprentice. After some experience as editor of country newspapers in Woodstock and Bennington, Vt., and North Adams, Mass., he was employed in Boston in the state printing office. In 1853, he became the special western correspondent of the *New York Evening Post.* During his travels in connection with this position, he made the acquaintance, in Milwaukee, of Editor Cramer of the *Wisconsin* (still issued as the *Evening Wisconsin*) and was persuaded to assist in editing that paper, an evening sheet which was, according to a contemporary, "noted for its enterprise and generally popular for its miscellaneous intelligence and family reading" (A. C. Wheeler, *The Chronicles of Milwaukee,* 1861, p. 287). It gave its influential support to the Union during the Civil War. Aikens became its business manager in 1857 and one of its proprietors in 1868, continuing his connection with it until his death.

His chief claim to remembrance, however, is due to the fact that the Western Newspaper Union of to-day, with a central office in Omaha and branch offices in thirty-seven cities throughout the United States, is the outgrowth of his genius. In 1864, the proprietors of the *Wisconsin,* under Aikens's leadership, devised a plan of coöperative advertising, an adaptation of the "patent insides" idea. They furnished a ready-print page, the new and financially successful feature of which was the columns of advertising matter. This made an immediate appeal to country weekly newspapers and, in 1870, Cramer, Aikens, and Cramer established the Chicago Newspaper Union. With his characteristic enterprise, Aikens, in the same year, carried his idea to New York and with George P. Rowell and Samuel French launched the New York Newspaper Union. The next step (*c.* 1874) was the formation of the American Newspaper Union, which included the Unions above mentioned, and branch offices in Fort Wayne, Ind., Sioux City, Ia., Nashville, and Cincinnati. Of the 1,700 country weeklies using ready-print pages in 1875, this Union claimed to be supplying 1,100. Aikens did not live to see the greater merger, in 1912, which brought into existence the present Western Newspaper Union.

[G. P. Rowell, *Forty Years an Advertising Agent* (1906); J. W. Watrous, *Memoirs of Milwaukee County* (1909); D. B. E. Kent, "One Thousand Men of Vermont," *Proc. Vermont Hist. Soc.*, 1913–14. A paragraph is given to the *Evening Wis.* (Aikens's paper) in *Cat. of Newspaper Files in the Lib. of the State Hist. Soc. of Wis.* (1911). Obituaries appear in the *Evening Wis.*, Jan. 22, 1909, *Fourth Estate*, Jan. 30, 1909, *Editor and Publisher*, Jan. 30, 1909, *Printers' Ink*, Feb. 3, 1909; in the first three portraits accompany the notices.]

A. E. P.

AIME, VALCOUR (1798–Dec. 31, 1867), pioneer sugar planter, was born in the parish of St. Charles in Louisiana. In spite of his boast that, like Napoleon, his "nobility" began with himself, the family was an old one in Louisiana, of sturdy French beginnings. His father, François Aime, came from a family long resident in Dauphiné and his mother was the daughter of one Col. Fortier, whose ancestors dwelt in St. Malo. Young Aime early acquired a plantation in the parish of St. James above New Orleans, married Josephine Roman, sister of André Roman, twice governor of the state of Louisiana, and by careful and skilful effort built for himself one of the great "refineries" of the state. On this plantation, under his supervision, sugar, for the first time, was refined in the United States. To-day in the old Cabildo in New Orleans Valcour Aime's portrait hangs beside that of Étienne de Boré, who established the sugar industry in Louisiana.

But Aime's contribution to the agriculture of his section was wider than this single accomplishment. His plantation diary, kept from the late 1820's, shows that he was continually experimenting with new things in the effort to improve both the growing and manufacturing ends of his business. And each improvement was passed on to his neighbors through the agricultural papers of the day. As early as 1829 he had applied steam power to his machinery; in 1831 he proved the superiority of the new Archibald's process to the old one; he quickly adopted new kinds of boiling-kettles as they appeared and was the leading advocate of the Rillieux apparatus from its first introduction. In 1845 he made a trip to Cuba to observe sugar methods there, and two years later sent one of his men to France and England "to take farther lessons" from their refiners. In the growing of sugar-cane he was equally progressive. He experimented with cane planted at varying distances; he used peas and clover on his lands; he early adopted fertilizers, especially guano, and ever urged the Southern planter to diversify his crops to the point of complete self-sufficiency.

Aime's own success justified his teachings. In 1852 his St. James plantation contained 9,500 acres, worked by 215 slaves and valued at over $700,000. The annual income ran well over $100,000 and his great house, surrounded by a garden filled with tropical plants, was instinctively called by a people familiar with seventeenth-century France, "The Little Versailles." A generous social life was matched by an equally generous charity, which became the dominating interest in the years following the death of the only son and heir. He gave freely to the churches of his own parish and New Orleans; to Jefferson College, also, he gave liberally; and common men, both black and white, constantly benefited by his generosity. But the keen business ability never slackened, and neither the losses suffered from the Civil War nor those from the freeing of his slaves threw him into debt or forced the division of the estate. Returning from Christmas mass in 1867 he contracted a sickness that brought him to his death on the last day of that year. He was buried in the little grave-yard of the St. James church near the great "refinery," which soon crumbled away in the hands of others less intelligent and less enterprising.

[*Plantation Diary of the Late Mr. Valcour Aime* (1878), and scattered writings in *DeBow's Rev.*, vols. IV and V.]

A. O. C.

AINSLIE, HEW (Apr. 5, 1792–Mar. 11, 1878), poet, was born at Bargeny Mains, Ayrshire, Scotland, a dozen miles from the birthplace of Burns. He was the only son of George Ainslie, a farmer employed on a large but somewhat barren estate. The boy grew up on the wild banks of the river Girvan and along the rocky southwestern coast of Scotland. This had been a famous smuggling shore, and in Ainslie's boyhood many of the old mariners were still living, though retired from their adventurous profession (notes to *Scottish Songs, Ballads, and Poems*, 1855, pp. 201–6). Young Ainslie had the poetic temperament, and reveled in the beauty of the region and in the romantic tales of the surroundings. His mother sang many ballads to the boy. In his father's library he found the works of Ramsay, Fergusson, and Burns. He was first given private instruction at home, then attended the Ballantrae parish school and later the Ayr Academy, but he was taken from school because of fears as to his health. He participated in amateur plays, among other rôles taking the part of Jenny in Ramsay's dramatic pastoral, *The Gentle Shepherd.* This part, containing numerous lyrics, stimulated Ainslie's poetic faculties, and shortly thereafter he first began to write verse (notes to *Scottish Songs, Ballads, and Poems,* p. 210).

In 1809 the Ainslie family moved to Roslin. The eighteen-year-old youth was sent to Glasgow to study law, but, disliking it, returned home. A year later he was given a position as copyist in the Register House, Edinburgh, where he met Jamieson the translator, Pringle the poet, and other literary figures. He held this position for twelve years, except for a brief period when he acted as amanuensis to Prof. Dugald Stewart. In 1812 he was married to his cousin, Janet Ainslie. A trip through Ayrshire in 1820 with two friends resulted in his first book, *A Pilgrimage to the Land of Burns,* published anonymously in 1822. The work is an informal, somewhat exuberant travel diary, containing a number of original lyrics in Scottish dialect. "The Land of Burns," as a popular name for Ayrshire, is attributed to Ainslie's title (*Memoir of Hew Ainslie,* p. xiv).

In 1822, Ainslie sailed for America, leaving his family behind until he should make a new home for them. After three unsuccessful years of farming near Hoosick, N.Y., he went to New Harmony, Ind., and spent a year as a member of Robert Owen's colony. His family rejoining him, he entered the brewing business, but flood and fire successively destroyed his establishments. Thereafter he followed the business of erecting breweries and distilleries for others. His real interest, however, was in poetry, and he wrote numerous verses, principally in dialect. In 1855 a collection of some eighty of his poems was published in New York under the title, *Scottish Songs, Ballads, and Poems.* His work met with favor in his native country, and when he returned for a visit in 1862 he received a hearty welcome from literary people. After a trip through Europe, he returned to the United States and spent the rest of his life with his children, at Louisville, Ky. Here he devoted himself to gardening, writing little if any poetry. His tallness and his tousled hair and beard made him a conspicuous figure in the city, while his sociability endeared him to a wide circle of acquaintances. Ainslie's poetry is for the most part light verse. It possesses sentiment, humor, and often rollicking rhythm. Certain of his poems are invested with a vague humanitarianism. His work shows a joyous, honest spirit rather than emotional intensity.

[The only detailed biography of Hew Ainslie is the "Memoir," by Thomas C. Latto, prefixed to *A Pilgrimage to the Land of Burns,* published by Alexander Gardner, London, in 1892. There are certain autobiographical data in the notes written by Ainslie for *Scottish Songs, Ballads, and Poems* (1855). An obituary appeared in the *Louisville Courier-Journal,* Mar. 13, 1878.] N. A. C.

AITKEN, ROBERT (1734–July 15, 1802), printer, publisher, engraver, was born in Dalkeith, Scotland, and appeared in Philadelphia as a bookseller in 1769. He returned to Scotland the same year, but in 1771 he again opened a bookstore in Philadelphia, adding bookbinding, a craft he had learned in Edinburgh, to his business. Two years later he made his first venture as a publisher, issuing *Aitken's General American Register, and the Gentleman's and Tradesman's Complete Annual Account Book, and Calendar, for the Pocket or Desk, for the Year of Our Lord, 1773.* Sabin says this was "the first attempt of its kind in the American Colonies" (Joseph Sabin, *A Dictionary of Books Relating to America,* vol. I, p. 68); it must have proved successful, for it was issued again in 1774. From January 1775 to June 1776, Aitken published the *Pennsylvania Magazine, or American Monthly Museum,* having Hopkinson, Witherspoon, and Thomas Paine as contributors. Isaiah Thomas says that on at least one occasion Aitken found it necessary to seat Paine at a table, supply him with paper and brandy, and insist that he stay there until the contribution was forthcoming. Thomas adds that "what he penned from the inspiration of the brandy was perfectly fit for the press without any alteration or correction," and comments that "Aitken was a man of truth, and of an irreproachable character. This anecdote came from him some years before his death." (*History of Printing in America,* 2nd ed., 1874, II, 152.) For the *Pennsylvania Magazine* Aitken engraved the title-page vignette, after a design by Pierre E. du Simitière, and a number of maps, plans, and other illustrations, among them some of the first views ever engraved of military operations of the Revolution. The check-lists given by Fielding and Stauffer include: "A New and Correct Plan of the Town of Boston and Provincial Camp," "Exact Plan of General Gage's Lines on Boston Neck in America," "A Map of the Present Seat of War on the Borders of Canada," "Machine for Saving Life at Fires," "A Perspective View of the Salt Works in Salisbury, New England." While done on copper, the work is crude, plainly showing an unpracticed hand, though in the *Pennsylvania Eve-*

ning Post, May 22, 1777, he advertises "All Kinds of Engraving done in the Neatest Manner at R. Aitken's Book Store."

Aitken's single enterprise of greatest interest was "the Aitken Bible, the first complete English Bible printed in America and bearing an American imprint, and the only one authorized and approved by Congress to this day (June 1902)" (note in Library of Congress Catalogue). Numerous attempts to publish the Bible in America had been made previously, but none were successful. When the outbreak of war stopped the importation from England of the usual supply of Bibles the problem seemed grave enough to be brought before the Government. A memorial was presented to Congress by its chaplain and some others, asking that Congress import suitable types and paper for the production of an American edition of the Bible, or "import 20,000 Bibles from Holland, Scotland, or elsewhere, into the different parts of the States of the Union" (quoted by John Wright, *Early Bibles of America,* 1894, p. 55), and Congress resolved to direct its committee to make such an importation. The agitation of the subject encouraged Robert Aitken to issue an edition of the New Testament in 1777, followed by others in 1778, 1779, and 1781. The reception accorded them was such that in 1781 Aitken ventured to undertake the printing of an edition of the entire Bible, and presented a petition to Congress seeking support and sanction. A favorable report by the committee (Messrs. Duane, McKean, and Witherspoon) to whom the petition had been referred, and by the chaplains of Congress, whose advice had been sought, resulted in the passage on Sept. 21, 1782, of the desired authorization. The resolutions appear following the title-page of the Bible, which was issued in 1782, as a small duodecimo, usually bound in two volumes. The venture was not a success financially. In spite of organized encouragement—the Synod of Philadelphia in 1783 voted to buy none but Aitken Bibles for distribution among the poor—Aitken lost more than 3,000 pounds (Wright, p. 64).

By this time, however, he was a printer of repute. Jeremy Belknap, seeking a publisher for his *History of New Hampshire,* was advised by Ebenezer Hazard that "Robert Aitken has the most taste of a printer of any man in this city; and were I to have a book printed here it should be done by him" (letter of Apr. 10, 1782, "Belknap Papers," in *Collections of the Massachusetts Historical Society,* ser. V, vol. II). As a result of this and subsequent recommendations Aitken received Belknap's fourteen-year-old son as an apprentice in the autumn of 1783, and in 1784 published the first volume of Belknap's *History.* In 1783 he contemplated publishing a literary weekly which never materialized. Isaiah Thomas says of Aitken: "He was industrious and frugal. His printing was neat and correct. In his dealings he was punctual, and he acquired the respect of those who became acquainted with him." After his death "Jane Aitken, his daughter, continued his business. . . . She obtained much reputation by the productions which issued from her press." (Thomas, I, 267.)

[Additional references: D. M. Stauffer, *Am. Engravers upon Copper and Steel* (1907); *A Descriptive Cat. of an Exhibition of Early Engraving in America* (Museum of Fine Arts, Boston, 1904); Mantle Fielding, *Am. Engravers upon Copper and Steel* (1917).] R. C. S.

AKELEY, CARL ETHAN (May 19, 1864–Nov. 17, 1926), taxidermist, inventor, naturalist, explorer, was born on a farm in Clarendon, Orleans County, N. Y., the son of Daniel Webster and Julia (Glidden) Akeley. "By all the rules of the game," he wrote, "I should have been a farmer, but for some reason or other, I was always more interested in birds and chipmunks than in crops and cattle." At about the age of thirteen he saw in the *Youth's Companion* an advertisement of a book on taxidermy and later he was able to borrow a copy from one of the older boys of the neighborhood. The book was probably a determining factor in his life. At the age of nineteen, he entered Ward's Natural Science Establishment at Rochester, N. Y., where he began work at three dollars and a half a week. At that time Ward's was a famous institution for the collection and distribution of specimens for museums and for the training of museum curators. It was the headquarters of taxidermy in America. In 1887 he obtained a position in the Milwaukee Museum and established a shop of his own in the town. In the Museum he made a group of a reindeer being driven by a Lapp in his sledge over the snow, the first habitat group he ever built. Later he mounted a group of orang-utans, and then a habitat group of muskrats, the latter of which still stands, after more than thirty-five years, as good as new. After eight years in Milwaukee, Akeley went to the Field Museum of Natural History in Chicago. While here he made his first expedition to Africa, starting in 1896. After his return he spent a great deal of time for four years mounting the four seasonal groups of the Virginia deer, now in the Field Museum. These four years mark the period of greatest development in the Akeley method, which is now in use in all of the great museums of the world. Taxidermy had been hitherto merely a trade; Akeley raised it to the dignity of an art.

In 1905, he made his second expedition to Africa, when he collected the elephants for "The Fighting Bulls," now the dominant group in the Stanley Field Hall of the Field Museum of Natural History. In 1909 he started on his third expedition to Africa, this time for the American Museum of Natural History. Among other things he collected the elephants for the great group called "The Alarm." On this trip he formulated his dream of African Hall for the American Museum, which is now in the process of preparation. In 1921–22 he made his fourth expedition to Africa and collected the animals for the "Gorilla Group." At this time he made the first motion-pictures ever taken of wild gorillas in their natural surroundings. On his fifth and last expedition to Africa, he died and was buried on the slopes of Mount Mikeno.

As a sculptor Akeley produced among other pieces, "The Wounded Comrade," "Stung," "The Charging Herd," and "The Nandi Spearmen." While at the Field Museum he invented the Akeley Cement Gun, which is now widely used over the world. In recognition he received the Scott Gold Medal of the Franklin Institute. After his third expedition to Africa he invented the Akeley Camera, which is considered to be the best naturalists' motion-picture camera ever made. The first model was patented in 1916. In recognition of this invention he was voted the John Price Wetherell Medal by the Franklin Institute. When the World War came on, he was past the age to enlist, but he gave his entire time to the government in mechanical research and investigation, especially in his contribution to concrete construction and in his improvement of large search-lights. He was instrumental in securing the establishment by King Albert of Belgium of the Parc National Albert in the Belgian Congo, the first wild life sanctuary established in Central Africa. He was twice married: on Dec. 23, 1902, to Delia J. Denning of Beaver Dam, Wis., from whom he was divorced in March 1923; and on Oct. 18, 1924 to Mary L. Jobe of New York City.

[Carl E. Akeley, *In Brightest Africa* (1923); "Carl Akeley and His Work," by Clyde Fisher, *Sci. Mo.*, Feb. 1927; the entire number of the *Mentor* for Jan. 1926 is devoted to C. Akeley and includes autobiographical notes; the Akeley Memorial Number of *Natural History* (Mar.–Apr. 1927) contains articles by Baron de Cartier de Marchienne, Kermit Roosevelt, James Earl Fraser, F. Trubee Davison, George H. Sherwood, William M. Wheeler, Frederic A. Lucas, Mary Hastings Bradley, and Henry Fairfield Osborn.] G. C. F.

AKERMAN, AMOS TAPPAN (Feb. 23, 1821–Dec. 21, 1880), lawyer, public official, was one of a number of New England youths who, prior to 1860, settled in Georgia, became a part of the warp and woof of their adopted state, and gained honors in their new home. The son of Benjamin Akerman, a land surveyor, and Olive (Meloon) Akerman, he was born at Portsmouth, N.H. He attended Phillips Exeter Academy, and graduated from Dartmouth in 1842. Shortly thereafter he went to Georgia, at first teaching school near Augusta. In 1846 he was engaged by Hon. John McPherson Berrien of Savannah as tutor of the latter's children. While thus employed, he studied law under Berrien, and was licensed to practice at Clarksville, the summer home of his legal preceptor. Soon thereafter he located at Elberton, practicing in partnership with Robert Hester. He married Martha Rebecca, the daughter of Rev. Samuel Galloway, a native of Bethlehem, Pa., but then residing in Georgia. Though opposed to the wisdom of secession as a remedy for what the South considered her wrongs, he followed his state into the Confederacy, serving first in the brigade under Gen. Robert Toombs, and later in the quartermaster's department. In thus aligning himself with the new government, he did that which almost every son of the North did who at the time was a resident of the South. In early life an old-line Whig and a Union man, his political convictions made him a Republican during the political readjustments following the struggle, and he remained a firm adherent of that party.

Akerman's most valuable service to his adopted state was as a member of the state constitutional convention of 1868. It was held at a time when the greater part of the intelligence and character of the state was disfranchised by the federal authorities; fully a third of its membership was composed of ignorant negro ex-slaves, and nearly all of the others were mere adventurers—"carpet-baggers"—from the North who had drifted into the state following the close of hostilities. Fortunately there was a small minority of men of high character who acted as a check upon this irresponsible majority, and to Akerman and a few others like him was due the fact that the constitution was not more radical than it was. In 1869, he was appointed United States district attorney, and the Senate confirmed the appointment, but as he refused to take the test oath, his disabilities had to be removed by Congress before he would assume the office.

In July 1870 President Grant appointed him attorney general of the United States. Under certain bounties granted by Congress in 1862 and 1864 to certain trans-continental railways, one or more of these roads attempted to obtain large amounts of additional lands. The Secretary of the Interior, Columbus Delano, referred the matter to the Attorney General. He denied the right, and advised the Secretary to reject the claim. He was asked by the Secretary to reconsider the question, and did so, with the result that he became more convinced than ever that the claim of the railroads was illegal. The railroad magnates, Gould and Huntington, began a campaign against the Attorney General, and put heavy pressure on the President to remove him. Delano owned the *Baltimore American,* and that organ "opened fire" on Akerman. Finally, the President was persuaded to ask for his resignation, doing so in a letter dated Dec. 13, 1871, marking it "Confidential." The letter read: "Circumstances convince me that a change in the office you now hold is desirable, considering the best interests of the government, and I therefore ask your resignation. In doing so, however, I wish to express my appreciation of the zeal, integrity, and industry you have shown in the performance of all of your duties, and the confidence I feel personally by tendering to you the Florida Judgeship, now vacant, or that of Texas. Should any foreign mission at my disposal without a removal for the purpose of making a vacancy, better suit your tastes, I would gladly testify my appreciation in that way. My personal regard for you is such that I could not bring myself to saying what I say here any other way than through the medium of a letter. Nothing but a consideration for public sentiment could induce me to indite this. With great respect, Your obedient servant, U. S. Grant." Akerman resigned, and George H. Williams of Oregon, friendly to the Pacific railroad companies, was appointed to succeed him. Declining the sops offered by the President, Akerman retired to private life. He moved to Cartersville, Ga., about 1870, and continued actively in the practice of the law until his death ten years later.

[I. W. Avery, *Hist. of Ga.* (1881); *Memoirs of Ga.* (1895); L. L. Knight's *Ga. and Georgians* (1917); extended biographical sketch by (Mrs.) Ex-Senator Felton in the *Cartersville* [Ga.] *Courant;* unpublished diary of Akerman; additional information furnished by members of his family.]

W. G.

AKERS, BENJAMIN PAUL (July 10, 1825–May 21, 1861), sculptor, was the eldest of the eleven children of William Akers of Saccarappa, Me. When he was still a boy his family moved to Salmon Falls, where his father kept a wood-turning shop or, according to some accounts, a sawmill. Sent to school in Norwich, Conn., Benjamin was intensely homesick and only too glad when he could return to work with his father, showing considerable ability in ornamental woodwork. His youth was characterized by a tendency to reverie and by a love of nature, particularly of the scenery of his native district. In search of broader intellectual fields, he went to Portland to work as a printer and even considered taking up writing, an occupation he occasionally indulged in later, as essays in the *Atlantic Monthly* and the *Crayon* testify. His final choice of sculpture as a profession, whether inspired by a cast seen in Norwich, by a marble bust by Brackett in a Portland shop, or by Chantrey's "Washington," seems to date from this period. In 1849, at any rate, he went to Boston and learned plaster-casting from Joseph Carew, after which he returned home and tried his hand at a medallion, a bust, and a head of Christ. Some months later he and Tilton, a landscape painter, opened a studio in Portland. Among his commissions were busts of Longfellow, Samuel Appleton, and John Neal. After two years of this work he spent a year of study in Florence, there producing two bas-reliefs, "Night" and "Morning." On his return to Portland he made his first statue, "Benjamin in Egypt," which was later destroyed by fire. The winter he spent in Washington doing several busts—President Pierce, Judge McLean, Linn Boyd, Gerrit Smith, Edward Everett—and a medallion head of Sam Houston. He then went to Rome, where he produced his best-known works—"Una and the Lion," "St. Elizabeth of Hungary," the "Dead Pearl Diver" (now in Portland), and a head of Milton. His works exemplify the taste of the period—a cold neo-classicism with its accompanying meticulous finish. His Roman stay was broken by a trip through Switzerland, Germany, France, and England. Owing to failing health he returned home for a year. On his way back to Rome he was taken seriously ill at Lyons, but managed to continue his journey. He was again forced to return to America in 1860 and in August of that year married a minor poet, Mrs. Elizabeth (Chase) Taylor of Portland, Me. (See Elizabeth Chase Akers.) He was too ill to do much work, and his bust of John Frothingham was completed with the help of his brother Charles. Advised to go to Philadelphia for the winter, he died there of tuberculosis in the following spring.

[The most important notices of Akers, which are not always in agreement, are those of H. T. Tuckerman in his *Book of the Artists* (1867), and Leila Usher in the *New Eng. Mag.* for Dec. 1894.]

E. G. N.

AKERS, ELIZABETH CHASE (Oct. 9, 1832–Aug. 7, 1911), author, was born in Strong, Franklin County, Me., the daughter of Thomas Chase, a lawyer, whose grandfather, Thomas Chase, sea fighter under Paul Jones, came to Livermore, Me., from Tisbury, Martha's Vineyard, in 1790. One of her books, *Sunset Songs,* is dedicated "to the dear memory of my mother, who in her girlhood was Mercy Fenno Barton, who died in her youth." After her mother's death she lived in Farmington, Me., and in June 1851 she married Marshall S. M. Taylor, son of a Presbyterian minister of Sheldon, Vt. Their life together was not a happy one and they were divorced. In 1855 she became assistant editor of the Portland *Transcript.* Her first volume of poems, *Forest Buds from the Woods of Maine,* was published in 1856, under the pseudonym, Florence Percy. It proved a financial success, and enabled her to travel on the Continent, where, apparently, she met the sculptor, Benjamin Paul Akers [*q.v.*], also a native of Maine, whom she married in Portland in 1860. He was then in failing health, however, and died the following year. She resumed her former editorial position and in 1865 married E. M. Allen, a New York merchant. From 1866 to 1873 their home was in Richmond, Va. Returning to Maine, she became, in 1874, literary editor of the *Portland Daily Advertiser,* and served that paper in various capacities for about seven years. During the latter part of her life her home was near Tuckahoe, N. Y., where she died. Her body was cremated, and a funeral address was given by Mary Riley Smith, poet, and president of Sorosis.

Besides *Forest Buds,* her published works include *Poems* (1866–68); *Queen Catherine's Rose* (1885); *The Silver Bridge* (1886); *The Triangular Society, Leaves from the Life of a Portland Family,* prose (1886); *Two Saints, a Tribute to the Memory of Henry Bergh* (1888); *"Gold Nails" to Hang Memories on, a Rhyming Review Under Their Christian Names of Old Acquaintances in History, Literature, and Friendship* (1890); *The High-Top Sweeting* (1891); *The Proud Lady of Stavoren* (1897); *The Ballad of the Bronx* (1901); *The Sunset Song and Other Verses* (1902); *Sheaf of Acrostics,* privately printed (1914). Her poetry has fertility of fancy, but little originality of thought or form. The fact that it expresses the emotions which ordinary people experience, together with its melodiousness and sentimentality, made her one of the favorite household poets of her day. The only one of her poems now generally remembered is "Rock Me to Sleep," first printed anonymously in the Philadelphia *Saturday Evening Post* in 1860, and included later in *Poems,* but it should not be taken as a fair example of her best work.

[Only fragmentary accounts of her career are available. See Grael Washburn, Jr., *Notes, Hist., Descriptive and Personal of Livermore, Me.* (1874), pp. 25–28; *Lit. World,* XVI, 137; *N. Y. Tribune,* Aug. 12, 1911; *Who's Who in America,* 1910–11; *Portraits and Biogs. of Prominent Am. Women,* ed. by Frances E. Willard and Mary A. Livermore (rev. ed. 1901). Reviews of her work may be found in the *Nation,* Oct. 18, 1866, and Dec. 16, 1886. The authorship of "Rock Me to Sleep" was disputed. Mrs. Akers's claim is vindicated in the *N. Y. Times,* May 27, 1867. See also *Atlantic Mo.,* Aug. 1867. Information regarding her first marriage was furnished by the Me. Hist. Soc.]

H. E. S.

AKO, MICHEL. [See Aco, Michel, *fl.* 1680–1702.]

ALARCÓN, HERNANDO DE (*fl.* 1540), Spanish explorer, was perhaps born at Trujillo in 1500. He is first definitely heard of in 1540 in connection with the celebrated expedition of Coronado sent out by Antonio de Mendoza, Viceroy of New Spain, in search of the Seven Cities of Cíbola. By order of the Viceroy, Coronado pursued an overland course northward along the west border of Mexico. To support him two vessels under Alarcón were sent up the Mexican coast from San Blas (Santiago). At a port called Aguaiavale (Altata west of Culiacán), Alarcón was joined by a third ship with provisions. Entering the Gulf of California, he made his way, at times laboriously amid flats and shoals, until the gulf narrowed to a breadth of five or six miles. Ahead, the Colorado (Río del Tizón or Fire Brand River) entered the gulf through broad, low, mud bottoms. On Aug. 26, the expedition, coming to "the very bottome of the Bay," encountered the tidal wave or "bore" which rushes up and down the Colorado River with a thunderous noise. In order to make better progress, Alarcón now left his ships and proceeded up the river with twenty men in two boats. On the banks of the river he met some Cocopa Indians. From the Indians he heard reports of Cíbola, which, he was told, lay at a distance of thirty days' journey. A little later he heard that there had arrived at Cíbola men like himself, armed with "things which did shoote fire" and with swords, who called themselves Christians. These were the advance forces of Coronado. Alarcón sought to persuade his soldiers to carry to Coronado the news of his own proximity, but none of them would consent to go except a negro slave, who, however, was not sent. Later still Alarcón heard from the Indians further accounts of Coronado. Fearing now for his own safety, Alarcón set forth down the Colorado (which he names the Buena Guia or Good Guide) to his ships. The ascent of the river had taken over two weeks, but the journey back was accomplished in two days and a half. Determined, if possible, to join Coronado, he started up the river again on Sept. 14. He advanced farther than before, reaching about 34° (F. S. Dellenbaugh, *The Romance of the Colorado River,* 1902, pp. 27, 164), a point not far below the beginning of the Grand Canyon (Edward Channing, *History of the United States,* 1905, I, 83). Here he erected a cross, and at its foot secreted letters which were subsequently found by Coronado's lieutenant, Melchior Diaz. Having rejoined his ships, Alarcón made frequent landings in a vain attempt to find Coronado. On reaching Colima, he delivered a report of his expedition and sailed away that night. The following year the Viceroy directed him to renew the attempt to communicate with Coronado, but the expedition never sailed. A substantial achievement of the expedition of Alarcón was a map of the Gulf of California by the pilot Don Domingo del Castillo (Winsor, *Narrative and Critical History of America,* II, 444). By this map (1541) the gulf was fully demonstrated to be a gulf and not a passage. So California was not an island as it was suspected of being. "But because your Lordship commanded mee," writes Alarcón, "that I should bring you the secret of that gulfe, I resolved that although I had knowen I should have lost the shippes, I would not have ceased for anything to have seene the head thereof" (Hakluyt, p. 279).

[Herrera, *Historia General,* and other sources not in English, as cited by F. W. Hodge, Introduction to "Narrative of the Expedition of Coronado," *Spanish Explorers in the Southern U. S., 1528–43* (1907); "Relation of Captaine Fernando Alarcon," Hakluyt, *Voyages* (MacLehose, 1904), IX; W. Lowery, *The Spanish Settlements in the U. S.* (1901), I; Justin Winsor, *Narr. and Crit. Hist. of America,* II (1886), 443, 481, 486.]
I. B. R.

ALBEE, ERNEST (Aug. 8, 1865–May 25, 1927), philosopher, was born at Langdon, N. H., the son of Solon and Ellen Lucillia (Eames) Albee. He graduated from the University of Vermont in 1887. Specializing in psychology, he naturally went for his post-graduate work first to Clark University, where he held a fellowship in 1891. The ensuing year, as his major interest shifted to philosophy, he went to Cornell, where he also held a fellowship and where he obtained the degree of Ph.D. Already, in 1892, he had become a member of the faculty of the Sage School of Philosophy in which he continued to teach (instructor 1892–1902, assistant professor 1902–07, professor after 1907) until his death thirty-five years later. He was married in 1911 to Emily Humphreys Manly. From January 1903 to January 1909 he was associated with J. E. Creighton and James Seth as one of the editors of the *Philosophical Review,* and was again a co-editor of this magazine from 1924 to May 1927. Albee's most important work, however, was in the history of English Utilitarianism. Attracted early in his career to this relatively neglected field, he clung to it with singular tenacity. His doctoral thesis, *The Beginnings of English Utilitarianism,* which dealt with the movement in the eighteenth century, ran through the *Philosophical Review* between May 1895 and July 1897 and was later greatly expanded by the additional treatment of nineteenth-century writers until it became *The History of English Utilitarianism* (1902). Besides being far more comprehensive than Leslie Stephen's *The English Utilitarians* (1900), its only rival, it differed from the latter also in emphasizing the strictly philosophical rather than the social significance of the Utilitarian movement. Albee was the first duly to bring out the importance of Richard Cumberland as the founder of the movement and the first to establish the significance of Paley and the theological Utilitarians in the movement as a whole. Accurate, temperate, appreciative and yet keenly critical, his work was definitive for the period and school which it covered. It constitutes one of the few American contributions to the history of philosophy.

[*Who's Who in America,* vol. XIV; *Phil. Rev.,* July 1927; *N.Y. Times,* May 27, 1927.]
E. S. B.

ALBRIGHT, JACOB (May 1, 1759–May 18, 1808), religious leader, was the son of Johann Albrecht and his wife, German immigrants who had settled near Pottstown, Montgomery County, Pa., where Jacob was born. They were Lutherans, and he was baptized, and later confirmed, in the Lutheran Church. He had but little education, and for a number of years followed his father's calling of brick-and-tile maker. When he was twenty he married one Catharine Cope and moved to Lancaster County, where he earned for himself the nickname of the Honest Tiler. His religious nature was not fully awakened until, in 1790, he was afflicted by the loss of several of his children. The sermon at their funeral awoke in him a sense of sinfulness, and, after a severe inward struggle, he was converted to the Methodist faith. In 1796 he began to preach as an "exhorter." He was particularly concerned about his fellow Germans, who were largely without pastoral care, and went about among them preaching with flaming enthusiasm, calling men to immediate repentance and conversion, and insisting on the duty of entire sanctification (sinlessness) for all believers. He traveled about through Eastern Pennsylvania, Maryland, and Virginia, preaching in barns, log-cabins, schoolhouses, and the like. He met with opposition but made converts here and there. As most of them spoke nothing but German, there were no churches in which they could find a congenial home; so, after nearly four years, he ventured to form three classes, Methodist fashion, each with its class-leader, for such of his converts as were near enough together for this purpose. There were but twenty all told. Two years later there were forty members and more classes, and in 1803 a council from these classes ordained him a minister. That he had but little education and no theological training was a recommendation rather than a drawback in their eyes, as they regarded all education with suspicion and spoke of theological seminaries as "preacher factories." This was due, in large part, to what they felt to be the lethargy and lax moral standards of the Lutheran Church, which they ascribed to the rationalism with which their pastors had become imbued in German universities. Two young enthusiasts came to Albright's assistance, and in 1807 the number of converts was sufficient to admit of holding an Annual Conference, which adopted temporarily the name of "The Newly Formed Methodist Conference," and elected Albright as its bishop. It was Methodist in doctrine and polity, but it was an entirely independent movement, which the Methodists refused to recognize on the ground that the German language would not long continue in this country. The movement, however, continued, the name being changed, first to "The so-called Albrights," and later to "The Evangelical Association." But this, Albright himself did not live to see, for six months after his election as bishop he died, worn out with his exertions.

[R. Yeakel, *Albright and His Co-laborers* (1883) ; *Hist. of the Evangelical Ass.* (1892) ; S. P. Spreng, "The Evangelical Ass.," in the Am. Ch. Hist. Series (1894), vol. XII, pp. 385–439.] T. D. B.

ALBRO, LEWIS COLT (Feb. 6, 1876–Mar. 1, 1924), architect, son of Lewis Kinley Albro and Mary Lewis (Colt) Albro, was born in Pittsfield, Mass. While still a boy he became deeply interested in architecture and at the age of eighteen was sent by his parents to New York, where he studied for a year in the Metropolitan Art School. He then entered the office of McKim, Mead & White, first as student draftsman, and later as full draftsman and designer, remaining with the firm for nine years. He was closely associated with the design for the Columbia Library, and other Columbia work, and toward the end was in charge of such important commissions as the New York house of Charles Dana Gibson. It was through this connection that he decided to enter independent practise, his first commission being the Gibson house at Newport. In 1906 Albro and another graduate from the McKim, Mead & White office, Harrie T. Lindeberg, formed a partnership that lasted until 1914. They rapidly gained reputation as designers of the highest type of residential work, their houses being generally of English or Colonial inspiration, but never strictly archeological, and always characterized by freshness of conception, picturesqueness of outline, and a sensitive feeling for materials. In 1914 the partnership of Albro and Lindeberg was dissolved by mutual consent, and from then until his death Albro practised independently, producing a series of houses of marked distinction, in which his restraint, his delicacy of invention, and his inherent classicism received a continually growing expression. The most characteristic were those for George Arents, Jr., Rye, N. Y.; Jerome Mendleson, Albany, N. Y.; Dr. M. E. Johnston, Lexington, Ky.; John L. Bushnell, Springfield, Ohio; and that which was his favorite work, the group of Farm Buildings for Ernest Fahnestock, Putnam County, N. Y. In this group of houses Albro's genius attained a synthesis of originality, sensitiveness to tradition, simplicity and directness of plan, restraint sometimes almost austere, grace, and honesty of expression that rank him among the very best of modern American domestic architects. He knew styles, but was never a slave to stylism; without being fantastic or self-conscious, he infused freshness and personality into all of his designs. He was married in 1914 to Mrs. Groner of Richmond, Va. For the greater portion of his life he lived in New York City, but in his later years owned a small estate in Wingdale, N. Y., on which he lavished much affection.

[These facts of Albro's life are given on the authority of Mrs. Lewis Colt Albro, who based them upon manuscript notes prepared by herself and her husband shortly before his death. A short biography appeared in the *Architectural Rec.*, May 1924, which gives the date and place of birth as Feb. 4, 1876, Paris, France. Albro's work is illustrated in *Architectural Rev.*, Oct. 1911, Oct. 1912, and in *Lewis Colt Albro*, a monograph published by the Architectural Cat. Co., N. Y.] T. F. H.

ALCORN, JAMES LUSK (Nov. 4, 1816–Dec. 20, 1894), governor of Mississippi, senator, was descended from a poor immigrant from the North of Ireland, a lastmaker by trade, who settled in Philadelphia, Pa., in 1721. His grandson, William Alcorn, a native of Georgia, was a millwright. He and his wife (Sarah McLean Alcorn) with their son James and his wife (Louisa Lusk Alcorn) removed from South Carolina to Kentucky in 1810. The younger Alcorn became a boatman on the Mississippi River and was captain, first of a barge and then of a steamboat. He enlisted in the War of 1812 as lieutenant in a boatman's company and took part in the battle of New Orleans. Later, he was sheriff of Pope County, Ill., and of Livingston County, Ky. James L. Alcorn, eldest of eight children of James Alcorn, was born near Golconda, Ill., reared in Kentucky, and educated in Cumberland College. After teaching a short time in Jackson, Ark., he became deputy sheriff of Livingston County, Ky. Four years later (1843) he resigned this office and served one term in the Kentucky legislature. Meantime he was admitted to the bar, and in 1844 he began the practise of law and the operation of a small plantation in Coahoma County, Miss. In his impressionable college days in Kentucky he became a convert to the political doctrines of Henry Clay, and was an ardent Whig as long as that party existed.

He was a member of the Mississippi Senate, 1848–56; representative, 1846, 1856, 1865; and author and foremost champion of the legislation establishing the levee system along the Mississippi River. He was for many years president of the Mississippi Levee Board. As a delegate to the Mississippi convention of 1851, called by Gov. Quitman to crystallize sentiment in favor of secession, Alcorn was among the majority who defeated the movement. In the presidential campaign of 1852 he was an elector at large on the Scott ticket. Five years later he declined a nomination for governor from the Whig and Know-Nothing parties, but accepted their nomination for representative in the lower house of Congress. He was defeated by his brilliant Democratic opponent, L. Q. C. Lamar, after a joint canvass of the district which was largely Democratic. Alcorn then returned to his law practise and planting interests, and soon accumulated great wealth. In the Mississippi secession convention (1861) he and Lamar again engaged in a spirited conflict, this time over the Ordinance of Secession, which was drafted and reported to the convention by Lamar as chairman of a special committee of fifteen. The result of this contest is given in Alcorn's own words on the floor of the convention: "I have thought that a different course . . . should have been adopted, and to that end I have labored and spoken. But the die is cast—the Rubicon is crossed—and I enlist in the army that marches to Rome." The convention elected him one of the brigadier-generals of the army of Mississippi, all of whom, except Alcorn, had been officers in the Mexican War and had gained military reputations. He raised a brigade and served under Generals Polk and Clark until he was taken prisoner at Helena, Ark. At the expiration of his parole he volunteered as a private, but was appointed colonel of a detached force for special service on the Mississippi River. His military career covered a period of about eighteen months, and was not at all conspicuous. After the fall of the Confederacy he was elected to the legislature that undertook to reorganize the state government. That body elected him and Judge William L. Sharkey to the United States Senate (1865), but they were not allowed to take their seats. He counseled his people to take no part in the Johnson convention that met in Philadelphia in 1866, and urged them to "make no alliances," and to "stand aloof from all entanglements of party." Again in 1867 he admonished them not to resist congressional reconstruction. He entered the Republican party with the hope that he might utilize the negro vote for the best interests of his state, little realizing that carpet-bag leaders would bid for the same support. Most of the former leaders of the state not only opposed congressional reconstruction, but denounced Alcorn and his policies. On the other hand, Alcorn's contest for the colored vote and his defense of Republican rule led him far afield, and somewhat obscured his purpose to shield his people against the harsh policies of the radical leaders in Congress.

In 1869 he was elected governor of Mississippi by the radical party aided by many former Democrats. This office he resigned (Nov. 30, 1871) to enter the United States Senate, as the successor of Hiram R. Revels, the first colored man to occupy a seat in that august body. Senator Alcorn urged the removal of the political disabilities of his people and resisted all efforts to enforce social equality by federal legislation (*Congressional Globe,* 42 Cong., 2 Sess., pp. 246–47); he denounced the federal cotton tax as robbery (*Ibid.,* pp. 2730–33) and defended separate schools for both races in Mississippi. Although a former slaveholder, he characterized slavery as "a cancer upon the body of the Nation" and expressed the gratification which he and many other Southerners felt over its destruction (*Ibid.,* p. 3424). His most bitter controversy in the Senate was with Gen. Adelbert Ames, his colleague, May 20–21, 1872 (*Ibid.,* pp. 3701–04, & app., pp. 393–96, 402–11). In 1873 they both sought vindication by entering the race for governor of Mississippi. Ames was supported by the extreme radicals, who controlled the colored vote, and was elected by a vote of 69,870 to 50,490. Although he had met the bitterest disappointment of his life, Alcorn remained in the Senate until Mar. 3, 1877. He then retired to his palatial plantation home, "Eagle's Nest," in Coahoma County. His last public service was rendered as a delegate to the Mississippi constitutional convention of 1890, in which he supported the disfranchising clause of the new constitution which broke the political power of the colored race in the state. He was twice married: in 1839 to Mary C. Stewart of Lexington County, Ky., who died in 1849; and in 1850 to Amelia Walton Glover of Alabama.

[The principal sources of information on the life of James L. Alcorn are the newspapers of Mississippi from 1846–94 and the *Cong. Globe* for 42nd to 44th Congresses, inclusive. Most of his public and private papers were lost in the burning of the home of Col. J. F. H. Claiborne, who at the time was putting the finishing touches on the second volume of his *Miss. as a Province, Territory, and State,* which was also lost. A manuscript copy of Claiborne's preface, in which he passes judgment on Alcorn's reconstruction policies escaped destruction, and will be found, with a sketch of Alcorn's life in *Biog. and Hist. Memoirs of Miss.* (1891), I, 291–95. Many important facts will be found in J. W. Garner, *Reconstruction in Miss.* (1901); Franklin L. Riley, *Pubs. of the Miss. Hist. Soc.*, vols. I–XIV (1898–1914); Edward Mayes, *Lucius Q. C. Lamar, His Life, Times, and Speeches* (1896); Dunbar Rowland, *Mississippi* (1907), I, 62–71.]

F. L. R.

ALCOTT, AMOS BRONSON (Nov. 29, 1799–Mar. 4, 1888), educator, author, mystic, was the most transcendental of the Transcendentalists. His father was Joseph Chatfield Alcox, a corruption of Alcocke, the name borne by the earliest definitely known ancestor, who came to Massachusetts in 1630 with the elder Winthrop. His mother was Anna Bronson, a daughter of Amos Bronson, a Connecticut sea-captain. Alcott, who owed the spelling of his surname to his own choice, was born on a large farm at Spindle Hill near Wolcott, Conn., in the same log-house in which his father was born before him. His formal education was of the meagerest, derived mainly from the district school and a few months of private instruction under two clergymen of the neighborhood. He desired to go to Yale, but being the eldest of eight children felt that he must help support the family,—although throughout life he always turned out to be a financial liability rather than asset to those whom he would benefit. At nineteen he went to Virginia, hoping to teach school, but failing to secure a position he took up peddling. For four and a half years he offered his wares to Virginia and the Carolinas with as scant success as he was later to meet in offering ideas to the North. But his time was not wasted. To the example of the Virginia planters he owed something of the courtliness of manner for which he was later noted, and to the North Carolina Quakers he owed that faith in individual inspiration which became the corner-stone of his life and work. In March and April 1823 he read Penn, Barclay, Fox, Clarkson, and Law, and soon returned to New England with his mind bent on higher things than peddling.

The next ten years established Alcott's lifelong habit of spiritual success and temporal failure, the one largely the cause of the other. They were years of teaching—in the small Connecticut towns of Bristol, Wolcott, and Cheshire (1823–27), in Boston (1828–30), and in Germantown, Pa. (1831–33). Although recognized as personally an able teacher, he worked out an educational program too far in advance of anything then known in America for it to be permissible. It was directed toward the harmonious development of the physical esthetic, intellectual, and moral natures, with especial emphasis on the imagination. To this end Alcott introduced in his schools organized play, gymnastics, the honor system, and juvenile libraries; minimized corporal punishment; beautified the school-rooms; and presented instruction and study as activities pleasant in themselves rather than as the means to discipline or acquisition of learning. These extraordinary changes everywhere aroused doubts of the schoolmaster's fitness, which were increased by only too well-founded suspicions of religious heresy. In fact, during this period, Alcott was writing in his diary: "I hold that the Christian religion is the best yet promulgated, but do not thence infer that it is not susceptible of improvement; nor do I wish to confound its doctrines with its founder, and to worship one of my fellow-beings." Such sentiments, however guardedly expressed, were highly offensive to the majority of Alcott's countrymen and together with his radical educational views were sufficient to defeat his work.

The situation was made no easier by the development of Alcott's general philosophy. His stay in Germantown was marked by the reading of Plato and Coleridge, under whose influence, later intensified by that of the Neo-Platonists, Alcott reached an extreme transcendental idealism which viewed the world as the visionary creation of the fallen soul of man, itself a distant emanation of the deity. The notion of preëxistence, which most of the transcendentalists merely played with, became to Alcott a fundamental tenet. Spirit, temporarily imprisoned in the illusions of matter, could be freed, he thought, through its intuitive self-knowledge and utter devotion to its own inspirations. This philosophy Alcott integrated thoroughly with his personality, and without being given to trance or vision he lived in a state of quiet ecstasy which illuminated his whole being. Lacking all sense of humor, he was never willing, like Emerson, to compromise in the slightest degree with facts.

Thus when he opened a new school in the Masonic Temple in Boston on Sept. 22, 1834, it was of even more radical character than his previous ones. To his earlier reforms he now added great emphasis upon moral education cultivated by a conversational method of question and answer through which he endeavored to elicit from the children those rational ethical ideas which he believed innate in every one. The method was open to criticism as tending to develop habits of introspection far too early, but it was not this point which eventually aroused the wrath of Boston. *The Record of a School, Exemplifying the General Principles of Spiritual Culture* (1835), judiciously edited by Alcott's assistant, Elizabeth Peabody, was followed by *Conversations with Children on the Gospels,* Volume I (1836), Volume II (1837), less judiciously edited by Alcott himself. These works made it all too plain that Alcott was stimulating his pupils to independent thinking in religious matters. A single passage, however, constituted the cardinal offense: "A mother suffers when she has a child. When she is going to have a child, she gives up her body to God, and he works upon it, in a mysterious way, and with her aid, brings forth the Child's Spirit in a little Body of its own" (*Conversations,* I, 229). This modest attempt to supplant the legend of the stork was promptly stigmatized as blasphemous and obscene by two prominent Boston newspapers, the *Daily Advertiser* and the *Courier.* Replies in Alcott's support by Emerson and James Freeman Clarke proved of no avail, and the attendance at the school dropped to one-third of its former numbers. Alcott fell deeply in debt, to cover which the furniture and school library were sold at auction in April 1837. The school itself lingered on, moving about from place to place until 1839 when it finally gave up the ghost owing to the refusal of various parents to permit their children to associate with a young colored girl who had been admitted.

He had married on May 23, 1830, Abigail May, sister of a distinguished Unitarian clergyman, and he was now the impoverished father of a growing family. Early in March 1840 the Alcotts moved their few belongings to Concord, where they took a small cottage at an annual rental of $50; with it went an acre of ground which Alcott proposed to till. The spectacle of a philosopher at the plough was very inspiring to Channing and others of Alcott's friends but less so to Alcott himself. Constant attendance at innumerable reform meetings—anti-slavery, vegetarian, temperance—interfered with his success as a farmer. For several years he had been in correspondence with a group of Englishmen, James Pierrepont Greaves, John Heraud, Charles Lane, and Henry Wright, who had founded near London a school which they called "Alcott House," and on May 8, 1842, with money supplied by Emerson, Alcott set sail to visit his spiritual offspring. He remained in England until October, during which time he had two interviews with Carlyle, who was plainly bored but sent to Emerson this immortal description: "The good Alcott; with his long, lean face and figure, with his gray worn temples and mild, radiant eyes; all bent on saving the world by a return to acorns and the golden age; he comes before one like a venerable Don Quixote, whom nobody can laugh at without loving." Alcott returned to America with a large collection of books on mysticism and with three living mystics, Henry Wright, Charles Lane, and his son William, who were to form the nucleus of a Utopian community.

The numerous coöperative communities which sprang up in America during the decade 1830–40 were largely inspired by a hatred of industrialism with its accompanying over-specialization and by a determination to return to larger and simpler modes of living. Their ultimate intent was sane, but they were ruined by the eccentricities so likely to develop in small minority movements. Of them all, however, none failed so swiftly and ignominiously as Bronson Alcott's Fruitlands. During the winter of 1843–44 he kept Wright and the Lanes at his house in Concord, where they worked out the plans for the new enterprise. In the spring Lane invested all his savings (about $2,000) in a hundred-acre tract near the village of Harvard, thirty miles south of Boston. Thither the party moved in June 1844. Others joined the community from time to time during the summer; at its largest it embraced eleven persons, for all of whom Mrs. Alcott acted as an unbelieving but faithful slave. The organization was based on strictly vegetarian principles; the eating of flesh, fish, or fowl, eggs, milk, cheese, or butter was forbidden; the labor of horses was dispensed with; the use of manure was disdained. In his zeal for spirituality, Alcott is said to have drawn a distinction between the "aspiring vegetables" which grow upward and those degraded forms which burrow in the earth; the former alone received the doubtful compliment of being eaten. The crops were planted late and carelessly; at harvest time the men left to attend a reform meeting, and Mrs. Alcott and her daughters rescued what they could from an impending storm. By winter the Lanes and Alcotts, sole remaining members of the community, were on the brink of starvation. In January 1845 the undertaking was finally abandoned.

The Alcotts returned to Concord to continue their long war with poverty, not to be ended until 1868, when the success of *Little Women* by Louisa M. Alcott [*q.v.*] placed her parents in comfortable circumstances. During the intervening years, in Concord 1845–47, in Boston 1848–54, in Walpole, N. H., 1855–57, and again in Concord after 1857, the family was supported mainly by the efforts of Mrs. Alcott and Louisa in sewing, teaching, or domestic service, supplemented by the assistance of various friends. Meanwhile Alcott gradually developed a system of attractive but not particularly remunerative "conversations"—informal lectures and discussions—with which after 1853 he repeatedly toured the old Northwest. He was a brilliant, though rambling, talker, somewhat after the manner of Coleridge. On one occasion when Theodore Parker was present, he asked Alcott to define his terms. "Only God defines," replied the seer, "man can but confine." "Well, then, will you please confine," said Parker. But Alcott refused to confine or be confined; he soared above rational distinctions in the true mystic manner. Only in the field of education was he ever able to harness his inspiration to a definite program. Appointed superintendent of the dozen schools of Concord in 1859, he introduced into the curriculum singing, calisthenics, and the study of physiology, and advocated the introduction of dancing, hours of directed conversation, and a course of readings aloud. He organized an informal parent-teachers club. His three school reports were models of sane educational thinking. In 1879 the Concord Summer School of Philosophy and Literature was modestly started in Alcott's library. Later it was more adequately housed and continued to flourish as a center of belated transcendentalism until his death in 1888. Alcott's direct service in connection with it terminated in 1882, as on Oct. 24, while writing two sonnets on Immortality, he was stricken with paralysis from which he never fully recovered.

Alcott's publications included *Observations on the Principles and Methods of Infant Instruction* (1830); *The Doctrine and Discipline of Human Culture* (1836); the mystical "Orphic Sayings" contributed to the *Dial* (1840); *Tablets* (1868); *Concord Days* (1872); *Table Talk* (1877); *New Connecticut,* a poetical autobiography covering his boyhood and youth (privately printed in 1881, published 1887); *Sonnets and Canzonets,* in memory of his wife, who died in 1877 (1882); *Ralph Waldo Emerson* (privately printed in 1865, revised and published in 1882, together with Alcott's finest poem, "Ion"). Alcott's verse has ease and melody, while his prose, at its best, possesses an oracular quality almost equal to that of Emerson. But he was never able for long to communicate the glow of his personality to the printed page, and his writings as a whole are undoubtedly tedious. Hence a later generation has been at a loss to account for his influence over such men as Emerson, Thoreau, Hawthorne, Channing, and W. T. Harris. The loftiness which they found in his serene unworldly spirit can now only be glimpsed, as it were, between the lines; while it is also between, not in, his deeds, that one senses a nature much too sweet and simple for this complex world.

[F. B. Sanborn and W. T. Harris, *A. Bronson Alcott, His Life and Philosophy* (1893), containing copious excerpts from Alcott's letters and diary; R. W. Emerson, sketch in the *New Am. Cyc.* (1858); Clara Endicott Sears, *Bronson Alcott's Fruitlands* (1915), containing also a reprint of *Transcendental Wild Oats* by Louisa M. Alcott, whose personal animus against Lane is to be discounted; a brief but exceptionally discriminating estimate of Alcott by H. C. Goddard in *Cambridge Hist. of Am. Lit.* (1917), I, 336–39; a more diffuse but still valuable discussion by O. B. Frothingham, *Transcendentalism in New England* (1876), ch. X; a sympathetic account of Alcott's educational career by Honoré Willsie Morrow, *The Father of Little Women* (1927).]

E. S. B.

ALCOTT, LOUISA MAY (Nov. 29, 1832–Mar. 6, 1888), author, was the second daughter of Amos Bronson Alcott [*q.v.*] and Abigail (May) Alcott. She was born in Germantown, Pa., but her childhood and youth were passed mainly in Boston and Concord, Mass. She obtained her education almost entirely from her father, although Thoreau was an early instructor, and she received friendly guidance and inspiration from Emerson and Theodore Parker. At the age of sixteen she began to write for publication, and produced her first book, *Flower Fables,* which was not published for six years. In her efforts to assist her family she tried teaching, sewing, and even domestic service. At the age of seventeen, having shown some talent in amateur theatricals, she contemplated a stage career. "I like tragic plays, and shall be a Siddons if I can," she confided to her diary (Cheney, p. 63). She wrote a number of melodramatic plays, such as *The Bandit's Bride* and *The Captive of Castile; or, The Moorish Maiden's Vow,* one of which, *The Rival Prima Donnas* was accepted by Barry of the Boston Theatre, but never produced. She had more success, however, with poems and short stories and by 1860 her work began to be published in the *Atlantic Monthly.* During the Civil War she became a nurse in the Union Hospital at Georgetown where she rendered efficient service until her health broke down. Her letters to her family, in a revised form and under the title "Hospital Sketches," were published by Frank B. Sanborn in the *Commonwealth* in 1863 and later in the same year brought out in book form. They excited widespread interest, and were followed, in 1864, by her first novel *Moods.* In 1865 she visited Europe, and on this trip made the acquaintance of a Polish youth, who was the original of Laurie in *Little Women.* In 1867 she became editor of *Merry's Museum,* a magazine for children.

The first volume of *Little Women,* founded on her own family life, was written in 1868; its success was immediate and its popularity so great that she promptly produced a second volume (1869); both were translated into several languages and had a phenomenal sale. From this time she was able to make her family financially independent. In 1870 *An Old Fashioned Girl* was published and she again visited Europe. It was during this sojourn that *Little Men* (1871) was written. *Work* (1873), which recounts her own early experience, was followed by *Eight Cousins* (1875); *Rose in Bloom* (1876); *Silver Pitchers* (1876); *A Modern Mephistopheles* (1877); *Under the Lilacs* (1878), written during her mother's last illness; *Jack and Jill* (1880); *Aunt Jo's Scrap-Bag* (6 vols., 1872–82); *Proverb Stories* (1882); *Spinning-Wheel Stories* (1884); *Lulu's Library* (3 vols., 1886–89); *Jo's Boys* (1886); and *A Garland for Girls* (1888). Much of her work was done in Boston where the climate suited her better than in Concord; there she spent her last years, and wrote her final books. She died on Mar. 6, 1888, two days after the death of her father.

In appearance she was striking, her well-proportioned figure indicating strength and activity. She possessed ardent sympathies. A born champion of persons and causes dear to her heart, she espoused both woman's suffrage and the temperance movement. Literature was to her always a means to moral edification rather than an esthetic end in itself. Nevertheless, her books, after half-a-century, still retain their appeal to youthful readers. Their charm lies in their freshness, humor, and true understanding of the feelings and pursuits of boys and girls. Her characters are full of the buoyant, free, and hopeful spirit characteristic of their creator.

[Ednah D. Cheney, *Louisa May Alcott, Her Life, Letters, and Journals* (1889); Maria S. Porter, *Recollections of Louisa M. Alcott, etc.* (1893); F. B. Sanborn, *Recollections of Seventy Years* (1909); Clara Endicott Sears, *Fruitlands* (1915); Gamaliel Bradford, *Portraits of Am. Women* (1919).]

C. T.

ALCOTT, WILLIAM ANDRUS (Aug. 6, 1798–Mar. 29, 1859), educator and pioneer in physical education, was born in Wolcott, Conn. His grandfather, John Alcox, was the original settler here in the year 1731, and his mother, Anna (Andrus) Alcox, was a descendant of William Andrus, a first settler in the adjoining town of Waterbury, Conn. He was educated at the district school with his cousin, Bronson Alcott (with whom he decided to change the spelling of his family name), and for a short time with the parish minister, who kept a sort of high school during the winter months. The interest of William Alcott in popular education manifested itself at an early age. When he was fourteen years old, he formed a juvenile library with several of the boys of his town. At the age of eighteen he was appointed to teach school in his district, and for four successive winters he was employed as a teacher in parts of Litchfield and Hartford counties. When he was twenty-two, he made a journey to the South with Bronson Alcott. Their plan was to teach school in the Carolinas, but this was unsuccessful, and after journeying on foot from Charleston to Norfolk, Va., they reached home the next year. At the age of twenty-four William Alcott was again teaching—boarding around, as was the prevalent custom. From this time on the serious purpose of his life continuously manifested itself. He became a true missionary of education. When not actually engaged at his school-house, he spent his time instructing the children—and incidentally the parents—in their own homes. One of his first school reforms was the bettering of the condition of the school-room. The crude benches for the smaller children were supplanted by seats with backs, and he inaugurated a system of ventilation,—a subject which, until that time, had been almost entirely neglected. His devotion and enthusiasm for his calling were such that every waking hour was spent in labor. He was literally on his feet from morning until night—arising at dawn, hastening away to school to sweep his own floor and light his own fire. His experiences at this time are portrayed in detail in his book *Confessions of a Schoolmaster,* written twenty years later. The effects of his strenuous life, however, brought on a serious decline in health, from which he never fully recovered. This illness, which was accompanied with emaciation, sweats, and fever, speaks only too clearly of tubercular infection. It was at this time that he determined to study medicine. His idea was not to relinquish teaching for medicine but to gain a knowledge of physiology and the laws of health that would aid his usefulness in his own profession.

During four months of the winter of 1824–25 he had charge of the Central School in Bristol, Conn., and in his spare hours studied medicine. During the next winter he attended a regular course of lectures at the Yale Medical School in New Haven, and in the following March he received a diploma to practise medicine and surgery. After leaving college, more determined than ever to devote his life to education, he made application for the Central School in his home, at Wolcott, Conn. It had long been his ambition to establish a model school and he now set out to do this. To the usual curriculum he added grammar and geography, and in his school-room were to be seen flowers, plants, maps, and other appurtenances designed to inculcate cultural habits in his pupils. Not long after the inception of this unique school, another setback to his health occurred. His pulmonary disturbance, which had no doubt been aggravated by his close attention to study at the medical college, became so threatening that he was obliged to abandon his educational project. He became a sort of itinerant physician, practising medicine in his native district, making calls on horseback—a complete change to outdoor life, from which he was so benefited that he attempted once more to teach—this time in Southington, Conn. The attempt was followed by another serious decline in health. His discouragement at this time was so great that he made up his mind to give up all idea of teaching or practising medicine, and to devote his life to farming. While preparing to do this, he met Rev. William C. Woodbridge of Hartford. Woodbridge, who formerly had been associated with Pestalozzi, invited Alcott to assist him in establishing in the vicinity of Hartford a sort of "miniature Fellenberg school." The offer was accepted. It was during this engagement that Alcott began to write voluminously. His essay on the construction of school-houses was awarded a premium by the American Institute of Education. He began to publish small volumes on educational subjects, and by means of his pen and lectures his name gradually became known throughout this country. In 1831 he accompanied Woodbridge to Boston, where he assisted him in the work of the *Annals of Education,* and for the next two years he was also engaged as editor of the *Juvenile Rambler,* probably the first magazine for children published in this country. At the end of this time, S. G. Goodrich (Peter Parley) invited him to become editor of *Parley's Magazine.* This connection lasted four years, during which time he contributed to other publications. The *Annals of Education,* the *Watchman and Traveller* of Boston, and the *Boston Medical and Surgical Journal* all shared in his contributions. Unquestionably, there was no individual of his time better informed on educational subjects. Essay after essay, volume after volume issued from his pen, all preaching the betterment of education and the importance of healthful living. A classification of his works is as follows: educational—nineteen volumes; medical, physical education, and health—thirty-one volumes; books for the family and school library—fourteen volumes; books for the Sabbath-school library—forty-four volumes. Among these may particularly be mentioned: *Confessions of a Schoolmaster* (1839); *Lectures for the Fireside* (1852); *The Home Book of Life and Health* (1856); *Forty Years in the Wilderness of Pills and Powders* (1859). To one interested in the influence of Alcott's medical training upon his career, the medical writings are the most interesting. While written almost exclusively for the lay reader, with a view to popularizing the laws of health, they nevertheless give an excellent insight into the keen medical mind of the writer.

In 1836 Alcott married Phebe Bronson of Bristol, Conn., by whom he had two children. His last years were spent in the town of Newton, Mass. Here he died of pleurisy, and was buried in the Newton cemetery. His dying message to his son—then a college student—was characteristic of the man, "Tell William to live for others, not for himself."

[Amos Bronson Alcott, *New Conn.* (1887); T. Dwight, *Travels in New Eng. and N.Y.* (1821); S. Orcutt, *Hist. of Wolcott, Conn.* (1847); *Am. Jour. Ed.*, 1857, IV, 629–56.]

H. T.

ALDEN, EBENEZER (Mar. 17, 1788–Jan. 26, 1881), medical historian, bibliophile, and genealogist, born in Randolph, Mass., was an only son of Dr. Ebenezer Alden, Sr. (1755–1806), by his wife, Sarah Bass. Dr. Alden, Sr., was born in Stafford, Conn., and moved to Randolph in 1781. As a physician he is said to have been "remarkably prudent, attentive, and successful." Through both his father and his mother, Ebenezer Alden was descended from John Alden of the *Mayflower.* He was graduated from Harvard College with the class of 1808 and received the degree of M.B. from Dartmouth Medical School in 1811, and M.D. from the University of Pennsylvania (1812). At the latter institution he came under the stimulating influence of Benjamin Rush, Caspar Wistar, and Benjamin S. Barton. While at Dartmouth he had been a pupil of Nathan Smith. After completing his medical education he returned to his native town (Randolph) and there passed, almost without interruption, the remaining seventy years of his life. Little information is obtainable concerning his professional career other than that it was successful and that it brought him and his family a comfortable livelihood. He is chiefly noted for his interest in the history of American medicine. An active member of the Massachusetts Medical Society, he early attracted attention by writing an interesting and scholarly history of that venerable medical institution (*Historical Sketch of the Origin and Progress of the Massachusetts Medical Society,* 1838), which was read as the "Annual Discourse" for 1838. In 1847 he was offered the presidency of the society, but he declined to serve, though he was for many years a regular attendant at its meetings. Alden's second important historical contribution, *The Early History of the Medical Profession in the County of Norfolk, Mass.,* was published in Boston in 1853. It is a well-written account of early practitioners in the various towns of Norfolk County (including part of Boston).

Alden's professional contributions were not numerous. The most notable, the *Medical Uses of Alcohol,* was read to the executive board of the Massachusetts Temperance Association in 1868. His conclusions may be set forth in his own words: "In view of the preceding facts and arguments, permit me to renew my adhesion to the principles of Temperance Reform; and, as a physician, to express my deliberate conviction, that in the treatment of disease in coming years, new and more successful methods will be discovered than we now possess, in which alcoholic narcotics will rarely find a place" (p. 16).

Alden was a great collector of books and pamphlets, and his library may be ranked among the important collections made in this country in the nineteenth century. It was especially rich in items relating to the Civil War and to the ecclesiastical history of New England. Alden had also strong antiquarian and genealogical interests, being an active member of the New England Historical and Genealogical Society. His memoir of his own ancestors (*Memorial of the Descendants of the Hon. John Alden,* 1867) is exemplary of careful genealogical research. In 1818 he married Anne, daughter of Capt. Edmund Kimball of Newburyport, and by her had six children, three of whom survived him. During the last six years of his life, he was totally blind owing to cataract.

[Obituary in the *Boston Medic. and Surgic. Jour.*, CIV, 116–17; W. L. Burrage, sketch in *Am. Medic. Biogs.* (1920); W. L. Burrage, *Hist. of the Mass. Medic. Soc., 1781–1922* (1923); *New Eng. Hist. and Geneal. Reg.* for 1881, p. 213, portr.] J.F.F.

ALDEN, HENRY MILLS (Nov. 11, 1836–Oct. 7, 1919), editor and author, was one of the last representatives in American letters of the old New England type. He was born in the small village of Mt. Tabor, Rutland County, Vt., the son of Ira Alden, eighth in descent from John Alden the Pilgrim, and Elizabeth Packard Moore, niece of Zephaniah Moore, second president of Williams and first president of Amherst. His father's small farm was located amidst the Green Mountains in a wild region where children went to school through woods still frequented by bears. In Alden's seventh year, however, the family moved to the manufacturing town of Hoosick Falls, N. Y. This was in the heyday of American democracy, when factory-labor and child-labor were alike respectable; Alden had two uncles employed in the cotton-mills, and he at once became a "bobbin-boy," working from dawn till eight at night. There were occasional bright vacations from work when he went to school, but most of his time up to the age of fourteen was spent as a factory hand. He then decided to prepare for college and entered Ball Seminary, where he earned his tuition by sweeping out the rooms and building fires. The principal, Rev. Charles J. Hill, encouraged his ambition and, in 1853, the lad left the Seminary in a blaze of valedictorian glory and entered Williams. It was at a time when Williams was particularly flourishing, under the presidency of Mark Hopkins; among Alden's fellow-students were James Garfield, Horace Scudder, and Washington Gladden; he found there abundant intellectual stimulus and sympathy. His trend of mind may be inferred from his nickname of "Metaphysics," although most of his actual study was in the classics, to which he sacrificed his chance of college honors rather than divert his attention to the necessary courses in mathematics. During this period he taught every year for a few months in various district schools of Vermont and New York.

Upon graduation from Williams in 1857, he went to Andover Theological Seminary in pursuance of his mother's desire that he enter the ministry and attracted by its large library of Greek literature. He was graduated in 1860, and occasionally supplied vacant pulpits for a time, but his voice was weak, the work was none too congenial, and he decided not to be ordained. At Andover he had made the acquaintance of Mrs. Harriet Beecher Stowe, who had become interested in a manuscript poem, "The Ancient Lady of Sorrows," and through her kind offices two articles on the Eleusinian Mysteries were accepted by Lowell for the *Atlantic.* The next winter Alden spent at home caring for an invalid father, but April 1861 saw him arriving in New York to seek his fortune with two dollars in his pocket. When the Civil War broke out, he endeavored to enlist but could not pass the physical examination. He then found teaching positions, first in a girls', then in a boys' school, rooming meanwhile with his friend, Horace Scudder. By July he was making seven dollars a week and on the basis of this substantial income was married to Susan Frye Foster, whom he had met in Andover and by whom he later had four children. Further contributions to the *Atlantic* gained the attention of James T. Fields, Emerson, and Wendell Phillips, through whom Alden received an invitation to deliver twelve lectures on "The Structure of Paganism" before the Lowell Institute, Boston, in the winter of 1863–64. In August 1863 he accepted a position to collaborate with Dr. Alfred H. Guernsey in writing *Harper's Pictorial History of the Great Rebellion* and to assist him in editorial work. Thus began a connection with the Harpers which was to last for over fifty years.

Alden was managing editor of *Harper's Week-*

ly 1863–69 and editor of *Harper's Magazine* from 1869 until his death. His conscientiousness in reading manuscripts, his recognition of talent, his unfailing courtesy became a legend. Under his editorship *Harper's Magazine* was the most widely circulated periodical in the country. His colleague, W. D. Howells, said of him that he was "an editor perfect in his time and place." His function was not so much to initiate new policies as to maintain and improve the old. *Harper's Magazine* was committed to its rôle as a family magazine, refusing to publish anything which "could not be read aloud in the home." This limitation brought Alden into some embarrassing situations during the serial publication of Hardy's *Jude the Obscure* and Henry James's translation of Daudet's *Port Tarascon,* when he was forced to insist upon the omission of certain chapters that were quite justified from his own literary standpoint, but his tact and personal liberalism enabled him to accomplish the task without offending either authors or readers. Meanwhile, year after year, he had a medium for personal expression in the department of the Editor's Study. He also found time to publish three volumes: *God in His World* (1890); *A Study of Death* (1895); *Magazine Writing and the New Literature* (1908). There was a strong religious quality in all his literary work, expressing itself in devotion to the personality of Christ and in a mystical nature worship, two themes which he strove to blend poetically rather than rationally. He believed in the innate goodness of human nature and in the innate depravity of dogmas. Although vaguely perturbed by the growth of mediocrity in America, he remained loyal to his early faith in democracy and progress, and could write in 1908, "It is a fortunate era we have reached." Despite their dates, his writings express the spirit of New England of 1840, its vague but deep religiosity, its moral idealism, its innocence of evil.

In person, also, Alden was the late New Englander, rugged, angular, bearded, low of voice, deliberate of speech, animated always by an impressive kindliness. He was no ascetic; an inveterate smoker, fond of cards, and fond of people. He was twice married; his first wife died in 1895, and he was married again in 1900 to Ada Foster Murray, a Virginia poet. He died in New York City when almost eighty-three years old.

[A short biographical account in *The House of Harper* by J. Henry Harper (1912); obituaries by W. D. Howells, *Harper's Mag.,* CXL, 133, and by James Lane Allen, *Bookman,* L, 330;; *Reader Mag.,* IV, 96; *Rev. of Revs.,* LX, 542; *Lit. Dig.,* Oct. 25, 1919; *Nation,* CIX, 516; *Commemoration Tribute* by Robt. Underwood Johnson (Am. Acad. of Arts and Letters, 1922); private information from Mrs. Ada Murray Alden.]

E. S. B.

ALDEN, ICHABOD (Aug. 11, 1739–Nov. 11, 1778), Revolutionary soldier, was born in Duxbury, Mass., a descendant of John Alden of Plymouth and the son of Samuel and Sarah (Sprague) Alden. Appointed lieutenant-colonel in 1775, he was assigned to the 25th Continental Infantry Jan. 1, 1776, and promoted to be colonel of the 7th Massachusetts on Nov. 1 of that year. A brave and honorable man but inexperienced in warfare and especially in Indian methods, he was appointed to command in Cherry Valley, N. Y. This was a prosperous frontier community south of the Mohawk. On this valley fell one of the most fearful blows of the war, due, it is said, to a desire for retaliation on the part of Butler and the Indians. Alden received on Nov. 8, 1778 a letter from Fort Schuyler giving warning of an attack, through information obtained from an Oneida Indian. He was unconcerned, discouraged those of the inhabitants who wished to take refuge in the fort, and promised assurance of safety. He commanded about 200 or 300 soldiers, and dispatched scouts in the direction of possible danger. The attacking party was led by Walter Butler and Brant, and consisted of about 600 Indians, and about 200 Tories and British. It proceeded from Tioga Point, and surprised Alden's scouts, who had imprudently built a fire and fallen asleep. Good information was obtained regarding the position of the officers and the general condition of affairs, and the attack on the valley—Nov. 11, 1778—had the usual features of an Indian surprise, and was marked by appalling acts of atrocity. A considerable number of the garrison and of the dwellers in the valley perished in the massacre or were made prisoners. Alden in attempting to escape from the house to the fort was killed by an Indian. The blame for his share in the disaster was only partially offset by the excuse of his unfamiliarity with frontier warfare. His body was buried within the fort.

[F. W. Halsey, *Old N.Y. Frontier* (1901); W. W. Campbell, *Annals of Tryon County* (1831, 4th ed. 1924); W. L. Stone, *Life of Joseph Brant* (1838).]

E. K. A.

ALDEN, JAMES (Mar. 31, 1810–Feb. 6, 1877), naval officer, was born in Portland, Me., the son of James and Elizabeth (Tate) Alden. His father being a ship-owner and fifth in direct line from the *Mayflower* Pilgrim, John Alden, whose descendants numbered many merchant seamen in colonial and revolutionary times, young James quite naturally sought a career in the rising American Navy. Appointed midshipman in 1828, he made his first cruise on the *Concord* in the Mediterranean; and in 1838–42 served as a lieutenant in the Wilkes, or South Sea Exploring Expedition, which cruised along the Antarctic continent and later among the Samoan, Hawaiian, and Fiji islands. In the latter group, a landing party was attacked by natives, and Alden led a boat expedition to the rescue; though arriving too late to save two brother officers, he averted the massacre of the rest. In 1844–46 he made a second voyage around the world, in the famous *Constitution,* and met another exciting adventure commanding a boat expedition which cut out several war junks under the guns of the fort in Zuron Bay, Cochin China. The Mexican War found him attached to the Home Squadron, with which he served at the captures of Vera Cruz, Tuspan, and Tobasco. Commissioned commander in 1855, at the outbreak of the Civil War he was put in command of the *South Carolina,* with which he reënforced Fort Pickens. He commanded the *Richmond* in the passage of Forts Jackson and St. Philip below New Orleans, as well as in the running of the Vicksburg batteries and the action at Port Hudson. He was promoted to the rank of captain in 1863, and commanded the *Brooklyn* at the van of the column of wooden ships in the battle of Mobile Bay. Appalled by the sudden sinking of the monitor *Tecumseh* and the report of torpedoes ahead, he stopped his ship and began backing. His action threw the fleet into disorder but evoked Farragut's decisive dash in the *Hartford* to the head of the column, and his historic profanity, "Damn the torpedoes! Go ahead!" Alden's conduct was the object of some courteous animadversion in Farragut's official report and aroused considerable controversy. There is little doubt that he was guilty of indecision and perhaps overcautiousness. Yet his fault has been kindly treated, and the matter is well summed up by a brother officer and naval historian: "A good seaman, a skilful officer, whose battle-record attests his bravery, his hesitation . . . must needs be ascribed to an error in judgment . . ." (F. A. Parker, *Battle of Mobile Bay,* 1878, p. 29). He rounded his war service by participating in the attacks on Fort Fisher, and was commissioned commodore in 1866. He rose to the rank of rear admiral, and after a brief command of the European Squadron retired in 1872. He was a man of fine appearance, and is described as courtly and accomplished. He died in San Francisco. The destroyer *Alden* was named after him.

[Official reports and correspondence by and relating to Alden may be found carefully indexed in the multi-volumed *Official Records.* See also Alden's official service record, Navy Dept., and a sketch in the *Army and Navy Jour.,* Feb. 10, 1877. For family history, see *New Eng. Hist. and Gen. Reg.,* July 1877, p. 363.] A. MacC. S.

ALDEN, JOHN (*c.* 1599–Sept. 12, 1687), one of the *Mayflower* Pilgrims, was born in or about 1599. There are no absolute proofs regarding his ancestry. A similar name occurs in Domesday Book, and Aldens have been found from early times in the eastern counties of England. The first definite statement concerning John Alden is the familiar one by Bradford, that he was hired at Southampton as a cooper; this was possibly due to the requirement of an Act of Parliament (1543), which provided that a vessel carrying beer beyond sea should have the services of a cooper, to make good the loss of "barrel-stock." He was one of the signers of the *Mayflower* Compact, and evidently gained an honorable standing in the community; for in 1627 he was one of the eight bondsmen or "undertakers," responsible for assuming the colonial debt. In this same year, or possibly a few years later, he removed from Plymouth to Duxbury, acquiring a farm of about 169 acres; and to this grant there was later added one in Bridgewater. Standish, his neighbor in Duxbury, was his friend and associate; the two were joint arbitrators in disputed claims between the Indians and settlers of Sandwich, and Alden was frequently engaged in determining bounds.

Alden was employed as an agent for the colony, for example at the trading-post on the Kennebec in 1634. He held various public offices; surveyor of highways; on the local committee for raising a force against the Indians; deputy from Duxbury —nearly continuously—from about 1641 to 1649; on the local council of war in 1675; and a member of the colony's council of war in 1646, 1653, 1658, and 1667; treasurer (elected for 1656–58). To the important position of governor's assistant he was first chosen on Jan. 1, 1632/33, and thereafter through 1640–41, and again continuously from 1650 to 1686. Twice he was "deputy-governor," in 1664–65, and in 1677 (following the critical King Philip's War).

Alden married Priscilla Mullens (or Molines), a daughter of one of the Pilgrims, about 1623, or possibly in 1621. Near the site of his Duxbury home a house has been occupied by his descendants from early colonial days, and is now owned by the Alden kindred. According to tradition he was tall, blond with blue eyes, of the Saxon type. Tradition also emphasizes his reputation as a speaker, and his interest in military matters. The famous story used by Longfellow in the *Courtship of Miles Standish* is unfounded, except as it rests on Timothy Alden's *Epitaphs and Inscriptions* (1812–14). Equally without foundation is the claim that Alden was the first of the Pilgrims to land on Plymouth Rock.

Alden died in Duxbury, the last surviving signer of the *Mayflower* Compact, and was buried in the little graveyard in South Duxbury, near his friend Standish, but the exact spot has not been identified. There were—according to Bradford—eleven children, from whom are descended the greater number of those who bear the name Alden.

[Wm. Bradford, *Hist. of Plymouth Plantation* (edition of 1912); *Records of the Colony of New Plymouth* (1855–61); Augustus E. Alden, *Pilgrim Alden* (1902); Chas. H. Alden, *Eliab Alden, Ancestors and Descendants* (1905); Ebenezer Alden, *Memorial of the Descendants of the Hon. John Alden* (1867); Justin Winsor, *Duxbury* (1849); Azel Ames, *The Mayflower and Its Log* (1901.) For the date of his birth, see *Records of the Colony of New Plymouth*, VII, 256.]

E. K. A.

ALDEN, JOHN FERRIS (Mar. 19, 1852–Feb. 27, 1917), civil engineer, a direct descendant of John Alden and son of Sidney and Harriet Webster Alden, was born in Cohoes, N. Y. His early education was received at private schools in Albany and at the age of twenty he was graduated with honors from the Rensselaer Polytechnic Institute with a degree in civil engineering. In 1885 he married Mary E. Bogue of Brooklyn. His life was devoted to bridge-building and iron and steel construction of other kinds. After serving as assistant engineer, under Charles Hilton, on the construction of a railroad bridge for the tracks of the New York Central over the Hudson River at Albany, he accepted a position with the Leighton Bridge & Iron Works at Rochester, N. Y. He became a member of the firm in 1878, but in 1881, with Moritz Lassig as partner, he leased the Leighton Bridge & Iron Works in both Rochester and Chicago, and they went into business for themselves. After four years the partnership was dissolved, and Alden purchased the interests of the firm in Rochester, reorganizing it under the name of the Rochester Bridge & Iron Works. In 1901 he sold his business to the American Bridge Company but retained an interest in this company until his death.

Many of the steel and iron bridges in use to-day in both the United States and Canada were built by Alden during his active connection with the Rochester Bridge & Iron Works. Among them are bridges for the Delaware & Hudson, the Chicago, Milwaukee & St. Paul, and the Buffalo, Rochester & Pittsburgh Railroads; also the bridge over the Columbia River at Pasco, Wash., the viaducts at Los Angeles, the Upper Suspension Bridge at Niagara Falls, the Driving Park Avenue Bridge at Rochester, and part of the elevated railroads in New York City. He constructed many large buildings in New York, Chicago, and other cities, including the tower and elevator in the Parliament Buildings at Ottawa, Ont., Canada; and he furnished most of the iron and steel work for the buildings at the Columbian Exposition in Chicago.

[Material for this biographical sketch has been obtained from the files of the Am. Soc. of Civil Engineers, especially from vol. LXXXI of their *Transactions*.]

E. Y.

ALDEN, JOSEPH (Jan. 4, 1807–Aug. 30, 1885), educator, author, began his career as a teacher at the age of fourteen in a district school and finished it with a fifteen-year term as principal of a normal school, having been in the meantime a professor and college president. He was a descendant in the sixth generation of John Alden of Plymouth, and was born in Cairo, N.Y., the son of Eliab and Mary (Hathaway) Alden. He entered Brown University but transferred to Union College, where he graduated in 1829 (*Union University Centennial Catalogue, 1795–1895,* elsewhere given as 1828). For two years he studied at Princeton Theological Seminary and was subsequently a tutor at Princeton. In 1834 he was ordained pastor of the Congregational Church, Williamstown, Mass., but resigned after a few months to accept a professorship at Williams College. Thereafter, although acting as a supply and as college pastor, he gave his entire time to educational work and writing. At Williams, where he served from 1835 to 1852, he was first professor of Latin, and then of English language and literature, political economy, and history. In the latter year he accepted the chair of mental and moral philosophy at Lafayette College, leaving there in 1857 to take the presidency of Jefferson College, which office he held for five years. From 1867 to 1882 he was principal of the State Normal School at Albany, N. Y. He was twice married: first, in 1834, to Isabella, daughter of Rev. Gilbert R. Livingston; and second, June 30, 1882, to Amelia, daughter of George W. Daly, of Tompkinsville, Staten Island. He left a son, William Livingston Alden [*q.v.*].

He was more highly regarded as a teacher than as an administrator and was best-known perhaps as an author. His success in the class-room was largely due to his ability to clarify a subject quickly and reveal the essential facts. A clear thinker himself, he trained his students to think logically. For generalities or splurge he had no tolerance, and was likely to make one who indulged in them feel ridiculous. His lesser success as an official was due to the impression of impatience and condescension he gave to those who had dealings with him, his habit of pointing out errors for the pleasure of correcting them, and a tendency to lose his balance and make ill-advised remarks. "He was a man of fine presence, about five feet ten inches tall, and well-proportioned, with massive head well-rounded, hair a little thinned on top and turned to iron grey, and whiskers of the Burnside order" (J. W. Wight-man, *History of the Jefferson College Class of 1860,* 1911).

His published writings, which number more than seventy, disclose tireless industry and a wide range of interests. They are chiefly of a didactic nature, many of them books for Sunday-school libraries, others intended to be used in the classroom. His was the practical type of mind and he wrote with a view to getting results in every-day life, whether his subject was philosophy, government, or religion. Among these writings are: *The Aged Pilgrim* (1846); *Alice Gordon, or the Uses of Orphanage* (1847); *The Lawyer's Daughter* (1847); *Anecdotes of the Puritans* (1849); *Christian Ethics* (1866); *Elements of Intellectual Philosophy* (1866); *Elizabeth Benton, or Religion in Connection with Fashionable Life* (1846); *The Example of Washington Commended to the Young* (1846); *The Jewish Washington, or Lessons in Patriotism and Piety Suggested by the History of Nehemiah* (1846); *Studies in Bryant,* with introduction by W. C. Bryant (1876); *A Textbook of Ethics* (1867); *Thoughts on the Religious Life,* with introduction by W. C. Bryant (1879); *Self-Education: What to Do and How to Do It* (1880); *First Principles of Political Economy* (1879); *Introduction to the Use of the English Language* (1875); *Science of Government* (1866); *Normal Class Outlines* (1900).

[Calvin Durfee, *Williams Biog. Annals* (1871); *Gen. Cat. Wms. Coll.* (1910); *Princeton Theol. Sem. Necr. Report,* 1886; *An Hist. Sketch of the State Normal Coll. at Albany, N.Y., 1844–1894*; *N.Y. Herald, N.Y. Tribune* Aug. 31, 1885; *N.Y. Observer,* Sept. 3, 1885.]

H. E. S.

ALDEN, RAYMOND MACDONALD (Mar. 30, 1873–Sept. 27, 1924), philologist, was born at New Hartford, N. Y., the son of Gustavus R. and Isabella (Macdonald) Alden. His father was a Presbyterian minister; his mother was known to an army of Sunday-school scholars, with outposts in Armenia and Japan, as "Pansy," the author, ultimately, of about seventy-five volumes of juvenile fiction persuasively written to make "observance of the Golden Rule a pleasure." Over her son's education and literary taste she exercised a guiding influence, to which other influences were added later. Alden studied for a time at Rollins College at Winter Park, Fla., attended Columbian (now George Washington) University 1892–93, and for his last year went to the University of Pennsylvania. Apparently unhampered by these changes, he took active part in student affairs, made the winning speech in a Cornell-Pennsylvania debate, and graduated as valedictorian of the class of 1894. He then taught for a year at Columbian University, took his A. M. at Harvard in 1896 and was assistant in English there 1896–97, took his Ph.D. at Pennsylvania in 1898 with a dissertation on *The Rise of Formal Satire in England under Classical Influence* (1899), and stayed on as fellow in English 1898–99 and as instructor 1899–1901. He then went to Leland Stanford Jr. University as assistant professor. He married Barbara G. Hitt of Alhambra, Cal., May 24, 1904, by whom he had five children. He was made associate professor in 1909, went to the University of Illinois as full professor in 1911, but returned to Stanford with full rank in 1914. He taught in summer sessions at Chicago in 1910, at Harvard in 1912, and at Columbia in 1916 and 1919. A man of unusual urbanity and charm, he was liked by most, and by those who could appreciate the range and accuracy of his knowledge, the lucidity and balance of his thinking, he was admired. As a prosodist and as a Shakespearean he had, at least in America, no indisputable superiors. The peculiar quality of his scholarship was its entire freedom from crotchets, from strained hypotheses, and from glimmering intuitions doing duty as ascertained facts. He was therefore eminently successful as the author of handbooks such as *English Verse* (1903), *An Introduction to Poetry* (1909), *Alfred Tennyson—How to Know Him* (1917), and *Shakespeare* (1922), and as the editor of *Beaumont's Knight of the Burning Pestle* and *A King and No King* (both in one volume, 1910), and of the *Sonnets* in the Tudor Shakespeare (1913). His full powers show best perhaps in his variorum edition of *The Sonnets of Shakespeare* (1916), a masterly performance, and in various shorter articles and reviews (*e.g.,* "The Punctuation of Shakespeare's Printers," *Publications of the Modern Language Association,* XXXIX, 557–80) in which whole batteries of fact and argument are deployed in order to demolish the structures of less cautious scholars. His diligence as a scholar and editor of text-books did not lead him to slight his work in classroom and seminar; he was an energetic and stimulating teacher. He also wrote verse, won a $1,000 prize in a short-story contest in 1905, and was the author of several children's books. In 1924, while absent on sabbatical leave from Stanford, he was visiting professor at Swarthmore College and at Columbia University. A disease of the nerves, long held in abeyance, at this time took an acute turn, but he persisted with his work until April, and in September after months of suffering bravely endured he died in Philadelphia.

[*Who's Who in America,* 1924–25; *Cat. of Columbian Univ. 1892–93* (1893); *Gen. Alumni Cat. of the Univ. of Pa.* (1917); *Stanford Univ. Bull., 34th Ann. Reg. 1924*–

25; F. E. Schelling, "Introductory Note" in R. M. Alden, *A Shakespeare Handbook* (1925); *Phila. Public Ledger*, Sept. 29, 1924; personal information.] G. H. G.

ALDEN, TIMOTHY (Aug. 28, 1771–July 5, 1839), Congregational clergyman, college president, antiquarian, was a descendant in the sixth generation of John Alden of Duxbury, who came to this country in the *Mayflower* in 1620. He was the son of Sarah (Weld) Alden and of Timothy Alden, who graduated from Harvard in 1762 and was for fifty-nine years pastor of the Congregational church at Yarmouth. At the age of eight, he went to live with his uncle, Joshua Alden, a well-to-do farmer of Bridgewater. Here he remained seven years. He was, however, bent upon receiving a liberal education and was much more interested in his Latin grammar than in the tasks of the farm, and, on his uncle's advice, was allowed to give up farming and prepare for college. He began his preparatory studies with his father, continued them with the Rev. John Mellen, of Barnstable, and completed them at Phillips Academy, Andover. He then entered Harvard College, graduating with high rank in 1794, having distinguished himself especially by his proficiency in the classical and the oriental languages. After graduation, he began to study for the ministry under David Tappan, professor of theology, at Harvard. He then taught in an academy at Marblehead, at the same time completing his theological studies. It was here that he met and married Elizabeth Shepard Wormsted, daughter of Capt. Robert Wormsted. (She died in 1820 and in 1822 he married Sophia L. L. Mulcock.) In the fall of 1799 he accepted a call to the South Congregational Church of Portsmouth, N. H., as colleague pastor with the Rev. Samuel Haven. But his heart was always more in teaching than in preaching, and, even while serving as assistant pastor at Portsmouth, his time was largely given to teaching and historical research. His sermons were rather dull; he approached eloquence only when his subject gave him the opportunity to dwell on the history and heroes of his country; but he was an exceptionally gifted teacher. In 1805 he resigned his pastorate, and then for a number of years was engaged in teaching in various girls' schools.

On a trip to Cincinnati he had been much impressed by the opportunities of the West and the need of a higher institution of learning. He was caught by the vision of a college rising on the western frontier, a vision aptly portrayed in the original seal of the college he later founded, where (the description is Alden's) "the sun is represented as just rising and darting its beams across the distant Alleghany and other mountainous ridges by which it is flanked upon the wilderness of the west." He determined to bring about the realization of this vision and planned a settlement to be named Aldenburg in the Alleghany Valley about ninety miles from Pittsburgh with the college in its midst, but having a cousin, Maj. Roger Alden, living in Meadville, Pa., he selected that town, instead, as the site. The citizens of Meadville entered into the scheme with enthusiasm, subscribed $6,000 and then sent Alden to tour the East in search of further endowments, one of the many trips undertaken for that purpose. He came back with $461, some land of uncertain value, and a goodly collection of books, a collection soon to be augmented by further benefactions until it comprised 7,000 volumes, making it one of the most valuable college libraries of the time. Thus Allegheny College was launched. Alden was made president and professor of oriental language and of ecclesiastical history, and was inaugurated July 28, 1817. As there were for some years no college buildings, the president received the students in his own home. The years that followed were years of hardship and repeated disappointments. Often for lack of funds the entire burden of instruction rested on the shoulders of the president, who served without salary. In face of all obstacles, however, Alden held steadfastly to his high ideals of scholarship, and when in 1831, for lack of funds, he was forced to turn the key of the one building that had been erected, and close the college (which was to be opened two years later under the auspices of the Methodists), he had established high traditions which lived on in the reëstablished college.

His life on leaving Meadville was uneventful. For a time he kept a boarding-school at Cincinnati. Then he moved to Pittsburgh to take charge of an academy in the suburb known as East Liberty. In the last year of his life, he officiated as stated supply at Pine Creek Congregational Church in Sharpsburg.

While living at Meadville Timothy Alden devoted what time he could spare from college duties in the summer months to missionary work with the Seneca and Munsee tribes of Indians, being led to undertake this work as much from an admiration of their character as from a sense of their spiritual needs; and he left interesting and historically valuable records of his experiences. He had at first volunteered in this service, but later received an appointment from the Society for Propagating the Gospel among the Indians and Others in North America. He assisted in the organization of the American Antiquarian Society. It had been his habit from early youth, whenever he visited any town, to spend much time in its old burial ground, transcribing the epitaphs of the worthies of former days and using these as texts for brief articles, giving such information as he could gather about their lives and characters, which he later published in five volumes as *A Collection of American Epitaphs and Inscriptions* (1814). During his sojourn in Boston, he was appointed librarian of the Massachusetts Historical Society and prepared for publication a catalogue of its books and pamphlets, and later performed the same service for the New York Historical Society.

[The chief sources of information are: *The Diary of William Bentley* (1905–14); Elisha Thayer, *Family Memorial* (1835); *Alleghany Mag.* (1816–17); E. A. Smith, *Allegheny—A Century of Education* (1916); Ebenezer Alden, *Memorial of Descendants of John Alden* (1867); and two unpublished MSS. accounts in the possession of his descendants. A sketch of his life was published in W. B. Sprague's *Annals of the Am. Pulpit*, vol. II (1857).]

C. M. B.

ALDEN, WILLIAM LIVINGSTON (Oct. 9, 1837–Jan. 14, 1908), journalist, was the son of Rev. Joseph Alden [*q.v.*], by his first wife, Isabella Graham, daughter of Rev. Gilbert R. Livingston of Philadelphia. He was born at Williamstown, Mass., where his father was pastor of the Congregational church and held the combined chairs of rhetoric, political economy, and history in Williams College. Alden's choice of an institution of higher learning was determined by his father's advancement in 1853 to the professorship of mental and moral philosophy in Lafayette College, Easton, Pa., and five years later to the presidency of Jefferson College (now Washington and Jefferson College) at Canonsburg, Pa. After three years at the former college, Alden completed his course at Jefferson with the class of 1858. He then went to New York City to study law in the office of William M. Evarts, was admitted to the New York bar on May 2, 1860, and practised until 1865. In that year he married Agnes M. McClure and gave up the law for journalism.

In a magazine article written late in life (*Putnam's Monthly*, III, 554–58), Alden sketched the state of literary society as he first knew it. Like Stedman and the Stoddards, whom he met at Anne Swift's boarding-house on Tenth St., he kept somewhat aloof from the Bohemian circle of Pfaff's and equally aloof from the well-established coterie of the Century Club, composed of writers of an older generation. Eventually he joined with others of the middle group in founding the Lotos Club. He was employed for a short time as editorial assistant on the *Citizen* under Charles G. Halpine, and then settled into harness as leader writer for the *Times, World, Graphic,* and other papers. His humorous skits in the "sixth column" of the *Times* won him reputation as a clever writer. The nature of these productions is indicated by one of his formulas for manufacturing them, which ran: "First invent a German and then let him invent something." Two collections appeared in book form. Alden also wrote, during the eighties, a popular life of Columbus and contributed half a dozen volumes to Harper's Young People's Series. After 1885 he lived much abroad. During Cleveland's first administration he held the post of United States consul-general at Rome, and upon his retirement, in 1890, he received the decoration of Knight of the Crown of Italy from King Humbert. Until 1893 he remained in Paris as leader writer for the Paris edition of the *Herald*. He then moved to London and for the last fifteen years of his life wrote humorous stories for a variety of magazines besides acting as literary correspondent for the *New York Times*. He died at the home of his daughter in Buffalo, N. Y.

Alden's favorite recreation was canoeing. Shortly after McGregor and Baden-Powell had popularized the sport in England, he introduced it into the United States. His articles on canoeing in the *Times* (1871) and in *Scribner's Monthly* (Aug. 1872) attracted wide attention. He designed a successful cruising canoe, the "Shadow," founded the New York Canoe Club in 1870, and was the first commodore of the American Canoe Association. One of the cruises in which he participated with three companions is described in *Canoeing in Kanuckia* (1878), by Charles Ledyard Norton and John Habberton. The list of his works includes such varied titles as *Domestic Explosives* (1877), *Shooting Stars* (1878), *The Cruise of the Canoe Club* (1883), *Trying to Find Europe* (1889), *Among the Freaks* (1896), *Cat Tales* (1905).

[*Who's Who in America*, 1908; *N.Y. Times*, Jan. 16, 1908; private information.]

G. F. W.

ALDRICH, EDGAR (Feb. 5, 1848–Sept. 15, 1921), jurist, was born at Pittsburg, N. H., the son of Ephraim and Adaline (Haynes) Aldrich, and a descendant of George Aldrich, who came from Derbyshire, England, in 1631. Having obtained his early education in the common schools, Edgar Aldrich went in 1862 to Colebrook Academy. In 1865 he commenced the study of law at Colebrook, subsequently proceeding to the University of Michigan, where he obtained his law degree in 1868. He was called to the New Hampshire bar in August 1868 and started practise at Colebrook. He was appointed solicitor for Coos County in 1872 and again in 1876. In January 1881 he removed to Littleton, which he made his permanent home. In 1884 he was elected to the legislature as representative for Littleton. Though without legislative experience he was elected Speaker and displayed conspicuous ability in that position. This was his only term in the legislature. His law practise was extensive, but, having a distaste for office routine, he confined himself almost exclusively to court work, holding briefs in most of the important local litigation of his time. On Feb. 20, 1891, he was commissioned United States district judge of the district of New Hampshire, a position which he held for over thirty years. The judicial qualities he developed, combined with a natural dignity and courtesy, procured for him universal confidence and respect, and he was frequently called upon to sit in the circuit court of appeals for the first judicial district. In 1907, during the famous Eddy litigation, he was appointed Master to inquire whether Mrs. Eddy was capable of intelligently managing her financial interests (see Michael Meehan's *Mrs. Eddy and the Late Suit in Equity,* Concord, 1908). As a delegate from Littleton he attended the constitutional convention at Concord in December 1902. "His commanding presence, intimate knowledge of every subject which came before the assembled delegates, together with the great esteem and confidence in which he was held, made him a powerful factor" (*Granite Monthly,* XXXIV, 17). His impressive speech upon trusts and combinations and against "the slavery of criminal monopoly," had great influence in inducing the convention to propose an amendment empowering the legislature to regulate trusts, which was subsequently approved by the electorate and incorporated in the constitution. In his leisure moments Aldrich devoted much time to historical research, contributing papers to the New Hampshire Historical Society (see *Proceedings of the New Hampshire Historical Society,* vols. II, III).

[Sketches of his life are contained in Conrad Reno, *Memoirs of the Judiciary and the Bar of New Eng.,* pt. III (1901), and *Geneal. and Family Hist. of N.H.* (1908), ed. by E. S. Stearns, pp. 1157–58. A short notice of his career prior to his appointment to the bench appears in *N.H. Men,* by G. H. Moses (1893). The official *Report of the N.H. Constitutional Convention of 1902* contains full details of his participation and a valuable verbatim report of the discussions.]

H. W. H. K.

ALDRICH, LOUIS (Oct. 1, 1843–June 17, 1901), actor, was born in Ohio. His real name was Lyon. His youth, spent in Cleveland, was beset with hardship, but having some talent for recitation, he early took to the stage as a boy actor, appearing as Richard III with such success that he afterward toured the country as the "Ohio Roscius." Later, under the various names of Master Moses, Master McCarthy, Master Kean, he appeared as a boy star in such rôles as Richard III, Macbeth, Shylock, Claude Melnotte, Young Norval, and Jack Sheppard. In 1857 he left the stage and entered White Water College, Wayne County, Ind. The following year he returned to the boards as a star, using for the first time the name Aldrich. Becoming a member of the juvenile Marsh players in St. Louis, he remained with that organization five years and married Clara Shropshire, one of the members of the troupe. In 1863, the Marsh players having disbanded, he proceeded to San Francisco and joined the company at Maguire's Opera House, where he remained until 1866. The following year he was in Boston playing in *Leah the Forsaken,* in support of Kate Bateman. Later, he was seen in New York acting with Charles Kean during that player's farewell to America. Returning to Boston, he resumed his position at the Museum, where he remained seven seasons. While there, he gained a reputation as an actor of rare versatility, acting leading rôles in support of Forrest, Booth, Cushman, and other noted stars. During the season 1873–74 he was leading man in Mrs. John Drew's company at the Arch Street Theatre, Philadelphia. In 1877 he played the Parson in McKee Rankin's production of Joaquin Miller's play *The Danites,* and two years later, Sept. 16, 1879, he was first seen as Joe Saunders in Bartley Campbell's *My Partner,* one of the most popular American plays ever written. Aldrich continued to play this piece for six years and it brought him an independent fortune. His later ventures, *In His Power* (1877), *The Kaffir Diamond,* and *The Editor* (1890), were less successful. In June 1897 he was elected president of the Actors' Fund of America, a position he held for four years. Noted for his charities to his fellow actors, he was the first to suggest the building and endowment of a home for destitute aged players, a suggestion realized later in the present Actors' Home on Staten Island, N.Y. He died at Kennebunkport, Me.

[*Dramatic Mirror,* June 29, 1901; T. A. Brown, *Hist. of the N.Y. Stage* (1903).]

A. H.

ALDRICH, NELSON WILMARTH (Nov. 6, 1841–Apr. 16, 1915), statesman, financier, man of business, was the son of Anan E. Aldrich and Abby (Burgess) Aldrich. He was born in the town of Foster, R. I., on a farm that belonged to his mother's people, who were descended from Roger Williams. His temperament included a luxurious and art-loving bent that may well have come to him from his father, while from his mother he inherited an iron will, practical resourcefulness, and indomitable energy. As his character matured, he developed great personal charm, which enabled him in later life to be on terms of close intimacy with confirmed political enemies. During his youth New England passed through the severe final stage of the industrial revolution when its fine old farming and seafaring communities were transformed into manufacturing communities. His parents were involved in the general hardship that overtook so many of the native stocks. Despite straitened circumstances, however, they gave him a common-school education in the town of East Killingly, and later a year at East Greenwich Academy. At seventeen he was at work in Providence. Soon afterward he entered the employ of the leading wholesale grocers of the state. His promotion was so rapid that at twenty-four he was a junior partner.

Meanwhile he had seen service in the 10th Rhode Island Volunteers, which was called to Washington when the capital was threatened in 1862. An attack of typhoid fever was followed by his discharge and return to Providence the same year. He was married in 1866 to a lovely and accomplished girl, Abby Chapman, who inherited what in that day was considered wealth. Aldrich showed his rooted independence of character by refusing to accept any of his wife's money as part of their family income. Mrs. Aldrich met his views in this respect and their scale of living was adjusted rigorously to what he could himself make. So successful was he that his business interests rapidly expanded; before many years had passed he was a millionaire. A fine natural taste was well served by his wealth, with the result that he became a discriminating if not an extensive collector of works of art. During his later years one of his chief interests was the beautiful estate which he developed near Warwick, R. I. In the full maturity of his fortunes he had extensive investments in banking, sugar, rubber, traction, gas, and electricity. His acumen as a man of business, had he not given most of his time to politics, would doubtless have placed him in the front rank of the millionaires of his day. His marked success led to bitter misrepresentation when subsequently his political power made him an object of attack.

Aldrich entered politics in 1869, standing for the common council of Providence as an independent Republican in a Democratic ward. He continued in the council until 1875. There followed two terms in the state legislature. At this time the Republican party in the state was divided into two factions, each bidding against the other for promising recruits. In 1877 the more powerful faction, headed by Senator Henry B. Anthony, offered Aldrich the nomination for governor. He declined it, fearing that it would merely put him on the shelf. The next year the Anthony faction offered him a nomination to Congress which he accepted. He sat in the Forty-sixth Congress, an attentive, thoughtful legislative apprentice. In 1880 he was reëlected. Before the next Congress met, Gen. Burnside, who had been Anthony's associate in the Senate, died. Aldrich made an independent campaign for the vacant seat and despite the rather cool attitude of the regular machine captured the prize. In October 1881 Anthony formally introduced him to the Senate. From that day until he retired thirty years later he was the master in Rhode Island politics. His local position was strengthened by the death of Anthony three years later. The Anthony following became the Aldrich following. In the Senate he was promptly recognized as a coming man. In 1886, at forty-five, he had overridden all local competition and won a second election to the Senate.

During the next few years he was drawn into a group of senatorial leaders who eventually formed a singular inner coterie, acting almost like a privy council, hardly paralleled in our history. They were men who like himself were sure of their constituencies, who therefore could act without trimming in a way that the senators of more variable states could not. The older senators, around whom this coterie gathered, were attracted by Aldrich's personality—serene, unresentful, humorous, ironic, stedfast, masterful. His first term had established his reputation for having a mind of extraordinary range and grasp. A thoroughgoing protectionist, he took position among the ablest defenders of the doctrine in the discussions of 1883. Though an effective party man in all the controversies of the Cleveland administration, it was not until 1888 that he definitely stepped up out of the rank of the competent senators and into the rank of the distinguished senators. When the Mills Bill focused in Congress the tariff issue, Aldrich was one of those Republicans who rose immediately to the challenge. The counter bill brought forward in the Senate as a party program was largely his work. It was in this connection that he made the first complete exhibition of his genius as a parliamentarian—a rôle in which it is doubtful whether he has ever been excelled. He possessed a lucidity of mind, a sense of humor, and a perfect freedom from vindictiveness that rendered him a most unusual judge of human nature. He also had the gift of absorbing himself in parliamentary strategy as if it were a game pure and simple. Like the true whist-player, he judged his result not by the tricks taken but by the possibilities discovered in his hand. No one ever surpassed him in subtle use of the strategic retreat. As a consequence, in after days he would issue frequently from what had seemed to be predestined ruin, with some measure of triumph.

Scope for these talents was found in the complicated bargaining and diplomacy of the famous measures of 1890—the Silver Purchase Act, the Anti-Trust Act, the Force Act, and the McKinley Tariff. In all his politics he had dealt directly with individuals—the senators, the party managers, the spokesmen of business interests. He had not dealt with crowds behind the men. His strength was not as a public speaker. The institutional influences that had contributed to form him had all worked in the same direction. He was the product of a stable state, of constant tendencies. His temperament had fitted him to respond to such influences. At fifty he stood revealed—the embodiment in politics of the creative business forces of his time. Furthermore, his temper was fixed in a smiling indifference both to the applause and the condemnation of the multitude. A splendid directness, joined with a contempt for changeable emotions which led him at times to miss the significance of mob psychology, was to be his characteristic to the end.

In the legislation of 1890 the Republicans were skating over thin ice. It broke under them in the elections at the close of the year. The Democrats swept the variable states and the Republican senators from those states began to disappear. In 1892, not content with their capture of the variable states, his opponents paid Aldrich the compliment of sending their strongest speakers into Rhode Island. This was the year of his third senatorial election. He was the conspicuous symbol of the stable states of the North, where the Republicans had a hold analogous to that of the Democrats in the South. But Aldrich was too well entrenched in his own field to be shaken by the storm. He was one of the few Republican senators who survived. It was inevitable that his group—the heart of the coterie of the elder statesmen—should become the sure foundation of Republican power in the upper house. All that had been needed to make them the inevitable masters of their party was the political execution by popular fickleness of their weaker brethren in the Democratic victories of 1892. From that time until the end of the chapter, eighteen years later, they were the irreducible minimum of Republican power. Among them, all that while, Aldrich was a major figure, and during most of the time the central figure.

Aldrich's strong position was due to personal and business connections as well as to political power in the narrow sense. He was now rich. This was made a charge against him in 1892. In framing the tariff of 1890 he had supported a rise in the duty on refined sugar. He had investments in sugar. In the desperate efforts to unseat him, his opponents began that campaign of innuendo, which was to become still more reckless in after days, to develop from innuendo to vituperation. His scornful silence in 1892 on the subject of his investments was characteristic. It was at this period also that the Republican senatorial coterie drew together socially in an unusually close way. Aldrich was a leading member in a little card club that is certain to become historic. It was called playfully "The School of Philosophy." Composed at first entirely of senators, it included later a few important cabinet members. Senator McMillan is credited with being the incomparable host who held together this unique male salon. He and Aldrich became close friends and their friendship seems to have included business as well as political interests. In no other period of his senatorial career had Aldrich as much time for business as during the enforced inactivity of the party eclipse and he appears to have made good use of it.

A second event of marked significance in this period of Republican eclipse was the panic of 1893. Rhode Island weathered the panic comparatively well. Aldrich appears to have attributed this to its compact social-economic system which exemplified fairly completely the Hamiltonian conception of an industrial hierarchy with prosperity percolating automatically from the governing group at the top downward through all the layers. Such was his social conception ever after. The third significant event of the period of the eclipse was the breaking of party lines in the Senate over the repeal of the Silver Purchase Act, and still more surprisingly over the Wilson-Gorman Tariff, in 1894. It had long been evident that the parties were inconsistently based, partly upon actual economic interests, partly upon sentimental traditions of doubtful vitality. The fact of this double affiliation in both the parties was glaringly demonstrated when the protection Democrats under Gorman and the protection Republicans led by Aldrich coöperated to enact a tariff that was nominally a Democratic measure but essentially Republican.

The accident of the next two years enabled Aldrich and other Republican leaders of similar views to accomplish the great feat of bringing this double affiliation to an end. The silver movement gave them their opportunity. Aldrich did his full part in that relentless attack upon the silver Republicans which split his party, but served also indirectly to split the Democratic party, and divided the nation for the first time since the Civil War on a clear-cut issue based on true affiliations unclouded by sentimentality. With the election of 1896, the Republican party issued from its eclipse and entered upon that period of unshakeable predominance which lasted until the disastrous schism of 1910. Its *pronunciamento* for the new day was the Dingley Tariff, in the adoption of which Aldrich became in the popular mind the protectionist senator *par excellence.*

There was an element of irony in the popular delusion. In his three great tariff battles, Aldrich stood twice, in 1897 and again in 1909, not so much for protection in and of itself as for the *status quo.* In both these instances he believed that a new chapter was beginning, that more important legislation lay immediately ahead, and that any radical interference with the existing conditions was dangerous. In 1897 the further legislation which he had in mind concerned those monetary issues which were not by any means settled with the election of McKinley. It seems clear that in 1897 he was on the whole in favor of slight reductions below the rates of 1890, rather than material increases. Here, however, as again in 1909, his chief purpose was the unification of the party. He was the target of such a bombardment by special interests that it filled him with contempt for "the trooping of the beggars" through his committee room. Having worked out a compromise tariff and thus solidified the party, he turned to the less distasteful but equally difficult task of final adjustment of monetary problems, which was at last accomplished in the Gold Standard Act of 1900. The delay in bringing this about was due to the fact that not until then could the Senate Finance committee be delivered from the domination of its silver majority.

In 1897 the Senate crossed a dividing line in its history. Of the Republican members who had disappeared in the dark days of the eclipse, few ever returned. Their places were taken by men who were new to the intricacies of senatorial procedure and who, with the exception of Hanna, were not sure of their position in national politics. Inevitably the small group of senators who had weathered the storm became the central figures in the transformed party, the authoritative link between its present and its past. Within this group there was still an inner group which might, with some justice, be called the heart of hearts in Republican policy from 1897 to 1905. It was composed of four senators—Allison of Iowa, Platt of Connecticut, Spooner of Wisconsin, and Aldrich. It is frequently asserted that Hale of Maine formed a fifth, but there is little evidence in support of the contention and much against it. The "Big Four," as they have been labeled (the "Big Five" by those who include Hale), formed a unique political coterie which acted with almost complete unanimity and may be said to have dominated the Senate until their fraternity was broken up by the death of Platt in 1905. Spooner withdrew from the Senate in 1907. The death of Allison in 1908 left Aldrich at the height of his power, master of the Senate, but without that sympathetic inner group to sustain him.

No statesman ever did less in the way of explaining his purposes than Aldrich. It seems to be safe, however, to attribute to him about 1897 a definite conception of American society. He appears to have perceived in it three large elements, to have concluded that two, capital and labor, had similar interests, while both were being threatened by the rise of a meddling and hysterical bourgeoisie. There was much to justify him in his estimate of that wave of hysteria which swept the country in 1898 and was the first popular manifestation with which the Four had to deal in the period of their eminence. They struggled hard to prevent the war with Spain. It seemed, almost to the last moment, that they were going to succeed, that they would bring about an amicable solution of the Cuban difficulties. And then President McKinley, hitherto their ally, suddenly changed front and threw them for a moment into the minority. War came. They gave to its conduct the support they considered obligatory, while deliberating what to do next. At this juncture the temper of Aldrich was a decisive factor. Nothing was more deeply rooted in him than a humorous acceptance of the accomplished fact; no attribute of his mind was more conspicuous than the power to discern just when the inevitable had arrived. His conclusion, ten months later, that the Spanish War had made imperialism unavoidable—specifically, that the President's peace treaty must be accepted, with its acquisition of the Philippines—became the conclusion of the Four. In the words of Spooner, they saw that they had to make the best of "the bitter fruits of victory." Following the peace, Aldrich became a member of Platt's committee on Cuban affairs. He visited Cuba in company with Platt and took a main part in enacting "the Platt Amendment" (to the Army Appropriation Bill of 1901) which established permanent relations between Cuba and the United States.

The peak of the influence of the Four was about the time of the reëlection of McKinley, with whom they were now entirely in accord. The accession of Roosevelt produced no apparent change in their position. They welcomed him cordially. He consulted them all in drawing up his first message, in which at places the hand of Aldrich seems to be apparent. The Four gave him steady support during his difficult first Congress. Roosevelt had inherited from McKinley a number of reciprocity treaties which had been negotiated under a clause of the Dingley Act. Whether it was ever intended to take them seriously is a question. On the advice of Aldrich, Roosevelt let the treaties drop out of view. The Hay-Pauncefote treaty, which had come before the Senate the previous year, had been opposed by Aldrich in its original form. Since then, Hay had negotiated a new treaty. This was promptly sent to the Senate by Roosevelt and was ratified with Aldrich's support. The preëminent problem of the first half of 1902 was reciprocity with Cuba. The lobbies of conflicting sugar interests wrangled furiously at Washington. The matter was complicated by insidious charges against Gen. Wood, the temporary governor of the island. The Four stood firmly by the President in support of the policy which resulted eventually in the Cuban reciprocity convention.

By the summer of 1902, the Four appear to have concluded that it was desirable to reach a clear understanding with the President as to what should be the official position of the party in the approaching elections. In August the President visited New England and spent a day with Aldrich at his country place near Warwick. Almost immediately after returning to Washington, Roosevelt invited the Four, together with Lodge and Hanna, to an informal conference at Oyster Bay which took place Sept. 16 (Roosevelt Engagement Book, Library of Congress). The upshot of their deliberations was expressed in the speeches of the President on his western tour which immediately followed, especially in his speech at Logansport (Roosevelt to Allison, Sept. 27, 1902, Roosevelt Papers). During the remainder of Roosevelt's first administration, the Four may be ranked as, in the main, administration senators. They steadily supported the President with regard to Panama.

Aldrich's relations with Roosevelt fall into three distinct stages, and an aftermath. A second stage began with the election of 1904 and extended until the summer of 1906. Meanwhile, Roosevelt made his bold attempt at personal government—or something equivalent to that—and instantaneously converted Aldrich from the administration leader to the leader of opposition. In these eighteen months, he was the Senate's general in its battle royal with the President for the dominant place in the governmental system. The President boldly brought the matter to a head by his foreign policy of early 1905. His proposed arbitration treaties vesting in the Executive large powers of international negotiation, and his proposed receivership for San Domingo were promptly rejected by the Senate. Thereupon Roosevelt touched his peak in audacious defiance of the Senate, accomplishing his purpose without the formality of a treaty. It was this notice to the Senate that its wishes in foreign policy were to count for nothing, that formed the background of the great duel between Aldrich and Roosevelt in 1906.

The Hepburn Rate Bill had been designed with a view to giving the Interstate Commerce Commission the power to initiate railway rates and to make them binding until, if ever, the roads might bring about a reversal through the slow process of legal proceedings. To repair losses incurred by a road in the case of a rate finally abrogated by the Supreme Court, no provision was made. In fact the wording of the bill laid it open to the charge that it was designed to make appeal to the courts impossible. This famous measure, like so many of the measures of that day, has been all overclouded in popular apprehension by the significance imputed to it by its enemies. It was not—at least as it came before the Senate—an attempt at government management of railways; it was something which in the eyes of Aldrich was much more objectionable. It was an attempt to compel the railways to obey a dictation which did not accept any responsibility for the results it might produce, and which was vested in a commission not answerable to Congress. The bill contained other radical features, but the crux of it all was this creation of a dictatorship over business, with the hardship of its practices thrown altogether upon the corporations involved. It had the approval of the President and was hailed by a whole army of the literary propagandists as a revolutionary measure of first importance. Aldrich concentrated opposition upon this one phase of the bill. He drew in powerful Democratic support, and contrived to have Tillman report the bill from the Interstate Commerce Committee to the Senate. After a long and furious parliamentary battle, in which La Follette began his persistent denunciation of Aldrich, the administration forces were beaten and the dictatorship provision was eliminated by conferring "express jurisdiction upon the Circuit Courts in suits to enjoin, set aside, or suspend orders of the Commission" (Ripley, *Railway Problems,* p. 545). Aldrich then permitted the amended bill to pass.

Even in the height of their political duel, Aldrich and Roosevelt did not come to an open break. Concerning the tariff, at least, Roosevelt continued to take advice from "the Aldrich Group." In one respect, he and Aldrich were alike—in their genius for recognizing the inevitable. Their relations took on a new aspect with the Senate's victory over the Rate Bill. Thereafter, Roosevelt, the radical, pursued his ends, broadly speaking, outside of Congress, while in his relations with Congress he blended radical temper with conservative purpose. Here we have the third stage of Aldrich-Roosevelt relations, when again Aldrich was virtually the administration leader in the Senate. At the close of the administration, these two strong men parted company with profound respect. "He is the greatest politician we have had," Aldrich said of Roosevelt, who wrote to Lodge, "My intercourse with Aldrich gave me a steadily higher opinion of him" (*Correspondence of Roosevelt and Lodge,* II, 337, 346).

In 1908, after contributing to the nomination of Taft, Aldrich went abroad in order to make a thorough study of modern banking. He was chairman of the National Monetary Commission. It had been created under an act he had sponsored,—the Aldrich-Vreeland Act, an emergency measure caused by the panic of 1907. Hitherto, he had accepted as a fixed American tradition the old system of the National Bank Act of 1862. Even the Aldrich-Vreeland Act did not show evidence of a change of front. Such a change took place with sweeping completeness in the course of the investigations which, in company with the Monetary Commission, he made this year. A leading New York banker, who had hitherto thought of Aldrich as wedded to the American tradition, was amazed shortly after the return of the Commission, when Aldrich said to him, "I am going to have a central bank in this country" (memorandum of Paul M. Warburg, *Warburg Papers*). He had discovered his final purpose which remained his inspiration until the day of his death. An omnivorous reader in economics and finance, he had gradually taken the career of Sir Robert Peel as the model that stirred him most. His aim henceforth was to close his own career by making a permanent contribution to the economic system of his country. He had ceased to think in terms of mere measures and had begun to think in terms of institutions.

The campaign promises of 1908 had committed the Republicans to a downward revision of the tariff. Bills to that end were in preparation when Taft called Congress in extra session in 1909. The ensuing controversy was an intricate tangle of party strategy, private ambition, and sectional and class fury. Confronting it, Aldrich, whose inner thought was on other things, made the crucial mistake of his career. He gave too much weight to the intrigues for place of a group of Republican senators from the West, and failed to realize that behind them were new popular forces he did not understand. These dissatisfied Western senators were all young men, from the senatorial point of view, who had grown restless under Aldrich's domination. Some of them were genuine radicals, like La Follette, while others, like Dolliver of Iowa, were wavering between the main chance in obedience to Aldrich and the popular demands of their constituencies calling them to martyrdom, or at least to revolt. La Follette was the leader without, as yet, a following, who was trying to bring this group together to create an insurgent *bloc.* Hitherto his efforts had been futile. Whether he could have succeeded in 1909 if Aldrich had made no mistake in generalship is not certain. But Aldrich made his mistake and La Follette was quick to take advantage of it.

Aldrich considered the Western outcry over the tariff as of no importance, and looked upon the whole matter as merely a problem in party unity; he had no deeper purpose than to get the subject out of the way on any terms that would unite the party and would enable him to throw its massed strength behind the financial legislation upon which his real interest now centered. Believing Dolliver to be of little actual consequence, he contrived his exclusion from the Finance committee. Dolliver sought La Follette, and, after dwelling for three hours upon his wrongs, pulled himself together and vowed war to the knife upon Aldrich and all his works (La Follette, *Autobiography,* p. 433). An "Insurgent" *bloc* was quickly formed around these two. It was frankly sectional, as was the Eastern *bloc* with which it was soon at sword's points. Its aim was not a genuine reduction of the tariff but a rearrangement of rates in the interests of the West, the highest sort of protection for commodities which the West produced, with ruthless reduction of duties upon commodities which the East produced and the West had to buy.

The Insurgents allied themselves with the Democrats by proposing to splice upon the tariff bill an income tax. As Aldrich was known to be opposed to such a tax, this seemed to them a way of tying him up to an impossible program. They had reckoned without their host. Just when the opposition had become formidable, he took the wind out of its sails by bringing forward, with the support of the President, a proposed amendment to the Constitution, empowering Congress to lay income taxes. The Democrats deserted the Insurgents and the opposition began to melt away. By similar tactics he forced the voting upon various isolated provisions. The President coöperated with him and at last, as the conclusion of one of the most tortuous and apparently contradictory battles of Congressional history, the Payne-Aldrich Tariff was enacted. All the high rates demanded by the Westerners had been cut down, a few Eastern demands had been reduced; but in the main, duties had not been materially lowered.

Aldrich turned to the problem of a new system of banking and currency without apparently any suspicion how serious was the rift in the party which had been opened by his defeat of the Insurgents. They now started a campaign to drive the old leaders from power. It was a campaign of vilification. The authors of what has been called the literature of protest and certain powerful newspapers, eager to sow dissension among the Republicans, made common cause with La Follette and Dolliver, whose vindictiveness knew no bounds. As a consequence, the Democrats carried the elections of 1910. The senatorial prestige established in 1897 had crumbled to the dust. As early as 1906, Aldrich had made up his mind not to stand again for reëlection, and the next spring, after thirty years of continuous service, he left the Senate. He was now absorbed in his new line of institutional thinking. While the ground was being cut from under him by the schism in the party, he was holding private conferences with leading bankers and working gradually toward the formation of what was known later as "the Aldrich Plan." This was a scheme of banking reform that was published early in 1911, received a wide variety of criticism, and was republished in amended form late that same year. It provided for a system of emergency currency based on the rediscounting of commercial paper; it contemplated the creation of a national reserve association that was to have functions suggested at least by those of the great central banks of Europe, but which was to operate through fifteen regional branches. He became the central figure in a nation-wide campaign to convert the country to the general idea of sweeping reform in banking, with a view to creating a flexible currency that would expand and contract in volume as the necessities of business might dictate. In this he had the hearty coöperation of the American Bankers Association, of many of the ablest individual bankers of the country, as well as of the leading economists and of a specially formed organization, the National Citizens League. The campaign was brilliantly successful. In November 1911, the Convention of American Bankers, in session at New Orleans, indorsed the Aldrich Plan. A bill based upon it was drawn up by the Monetary Commission and submitted to Congress.

The Democrats had now taken possession of the House. Aldrich thus found himself in a position he had not foreseen when he left the Senate. The bill of the Monetary Commission was quietly set aside. Aldrich's last hope that he might participate in putting the new banking system into practise vanished with the election of 1912. Thereafter, he could do nothing but stand aside while the victorious party, laboring hard to make the country believe they were not continuing his work, brought the reform movement to a conclusion by establishing the system of the Federal Reserve. It was not altogether a conclusion he could approve. Woodrow Wilson, before election, had said that the Aldrich Plan was "sixty or seventy per cent correct" (Willis, *The Federal Reserve System,* p. 140). Apparently, almost every plan suggested by any one had just about that margin of the dubious in every mind except the author's. While the Federal Reserve Act was under discussion, both in Congress and in the press, Aldrich joined its critics. In an address before the Academy of Political Science, in October 1913, he praised the bill as being based, in the majority of its provisions, on sound economic principles. Such disapproval as he expressed was concentrated on two points: its provisions for the issue of government notes and the subjection of the entire system to the control of a political board to be appointed by the president. In publishing the address the next year, after the bill had assumed its final form as the Federal Reserve Act, he expressed still greater satisfaction, adding the comment, very significant of the man, "Whether the measure will meet the expectation of its friends will depend largely upon the manner in which it is administered."

His brief remaining time was spent in political retirement. Almost the last event of his life was a reconciliation with Roosevelt, whose course in 1912 had inevitably reproduced the relations of 1905 and 1906. In the bitter days of the first stage of the World War, Roosevelt and Aldrich met by prearrangement at the house of Mr. Cornelius Vanderbilt. They had a long conversation by themselves, and parted with great cordiality. Two days later occurred Aldrich's sudden death at the age of seventy-four.

[The reliable published materials, except for the episode of the Federal Reserve, which is comprehensively reviewed in H. P. Willis's *The Federal Reserve System* (1923), and in a sharply partisan way by Carter Glass, *An Adventure in Constructive Finance* (1927), are obvious and scant; they are scattered through the *Congressional Record,* hearings before committees of the Senate, memoirs and lives of contemporaries such as *La Follette's Autobiography* (1913), the *Correspondence of Theodore Roosevelt and Henry Cabot Lodge* (1925). H. Croly, *Marcus Alonzo Hanna* (1912), L. A. Coolidge. *An Old Fashioned Senator—Orville H. Platt of Conn.* (1910), etc. Newspapers and periodicals contain a great deal of Aldrich matter, but as a rule it is too partisan to be accepted at face value. His bitterest newspaper opponent was the *N. Y. World,* while the N. Y. *Sun* might be almost regarded, at least for the Roosevelt and Taft administrations, as the Aldrich organ. The Aldrich Papers include a valuable collection of interviews with participants in the events of his career by J. P. Nicholls, who has also made an exhaustive exploration of numerous small bodies of private papers as well as the great manuscript collections that contain Aldrich matter. Chief among the latter are his own papers at Warwick, R. I.; the Allison Papers at Des Moines; the Andrew Papers at Gloucester; the Holls Papers at Columbia University; the Chandler Papers at Concord; the Foraker Papers at Cincinnati; the Platt Papers at Hartford; the Roosevelt Papers in the Library of Congress; the Taft Papers in the Library of Congress; the Warburg Papers in New York City. A biography by N. W. Stephenson is in progress.]

N. W. S.

ALDRICH, THOMAS BAILEY (Nov. 11, 1836–Mar. 19, 1907), poet, story-writer, editor, the son of Elias Taft Aldrich and Sarah Abba (Bailey) Aldrich, was born at Portsmouth, N. H. His ancestry on both sides was of New England colonial stock: on the father's side he was descended from George Aldrich who came to Massachusetts Bay in 1631; on the mother's side he traced his ancestry to a John Bailey who, about 1620, was living at Grantham, England. "I could boast," wrote Aldrich in 1854, "of a long line of ancestors, but won't. They are of no possible benefit to me, save it is pleasant to think that none of them were hanged for criminals or shot for traitors" (Greenslet, p. 6). His father's family were men with something of the wanderer in their blood; his mother came of a gentler and less adventurous stock. Elias Aldrich had all the restlessness of his race and, though he died when his son was only thirteen, he had wandered so actively that Aldrich used to say that as a child he had visited every state in the Union. During the earlier years of this period the family home was in New York and during the later years in New Orleans, where Mrs. Aldrich was living when the news came of her husband's death, Oct. 6, 1849. The boy had already returned to the maternal home in Portsmouth, known to all readers of *The Story of a Bad Boy* as the Nutter House, where he slipped with inherited ease into the ways of the New England household and there continued for three happy years. It seemed then and sometimes later as if the sojourn in the South had made no mark, but in the course of the years the effect showed deeply in his work and in his ways—in a fondness for subjects touched with a southern sun and in a blithe assurance of manner that never grew in a New England air.

When he was sixteen his uncle, Charles Frost, found him a clerkship in his office in New York, and there Aldrich and his mother went to live. It was the New York of N. P. Willis, Halleck, Bryant, and George P. Morris, and a group of literary bohemians—a New York where poetic standards were far less severe than in the Boston of Longfellow, Lowell, Holmes, Emerson, and Whittier. Aldrich was probably fortunate in trying his poetic wings upon the lesser heights. Before he was fifteen, verses from his pen had appeared in the poet's corner of the *Portsmouth Journal,* and now, under the stimulus of the metropolis, he entered on a period of rapid and facile production which the duties assigned him in his uncle's office were not arduous enough to check. He declared afterward that he "wrote a lyric or two every day before going down town" (*Ibid.,* p. 21). By 1855, when he had been three years in New York, he had become known as a writer of graceful, sentimental, and ironical verse and had gathered enough work to make a volume which appeared under the title of *The Bells.* It is interesting to note that not a single title from this volume survived in his collected works. But in the same year he wrote *The Ballad of Babie Bell,* the first of his more lasting achievements.

He resigned his clerkship to give himself definitely to a literary career and was offered the modest post of junior literary critic of the *Evening Mirror,* thus beginning that career of editorship which was to last, with interruptions, for thirty-five years. The year had not closed before he moved on to be sub-editor of the *Home Journal,* then the popular literary journal of New York with N. P. Willis at its head. He had meantime been forming friendships with men of letters—Bayard Taylor, Stedman, William Winter, R. H. Stoddard, and a group of lesser figures who constituted the literary Bohemia of the time. When some of this group joined in 1858 to establish the *Saturday Press* he became associate editor. During its brief span of life it was a vivacious journal which enjoyed the admiration and support of the young literary men of the country. It expired in 1860, and with its death Aldrich returned for a period to the precarious but exhilarating life of authorship. The outbreak of the Civil War in the following year took the poet's mind for a time far from rhymes. He had ground for expecting an appointment, first in the army and then in the navy, but, his hopes in both services proving vain, in the fall he applied for work as a war correspondent. Thus, though he fired no shot, he saw some of the realities of war that gave convincing quality to the poems and stories which it inspired him to write. When he returned to New York in 1862 he resumed his editorial work first as literary adviser to a publishing firm and later as managing editor of the *Illustrated News.* This proved to have but a short span of life remaining to it, but its demise daunted Aldrich not a whit, though he had lately become engaged, to Lilian Woodman of New York. Rather he set himself more energetically to his poetry and produced within a year two of his longest poems, *Judith and Holofernes* and *Friar Jerome's Beautiful Book.*

The year 1865 marked not merely a turning point, but a complete dividing line in Aldrich's life, separating the earlier from the later period. In this year he changed his residence from New York to Boston, took a new post as editor of *Every Saturday,* and was married to Lilian Woodman. All the changes were validated by experience. He continued to edit *Every Saturday* for the seven years of its existence; he made Boston his home as long as he lived, and in 1905 he was writing, "Tomorrow Lilian and I shall have been married forty years! Forty happy years" (*Ibid.,* p. 77). He took quick root in Boston, as was proper to one of his birth and lineage. He was soon as much at home in its spiritual as in its physical atmosphere. His first poetic inspiration had been drawn from Longfellow; now he came under the immediate influence of the master and found him friendly. The genial Autocrat had already welcomed him to the company of poets; Lowell had not forgotten the author of that "fine poem" *Pythagoras,* which he had accepted in a generous note five years earlier. "I don't think," Aldrich wrote to Hamilton Mabie on Dec. 4, 1897, "that any four famous authors were ever so kind to an obscure young man as Hawthorne, Whittier, Lowell, and Holmes were to me" (*Ibid.,* p. 200). Aldrich was not merely a poet, he was young, handsome, graceful, witty, and the husband of a wife as young and charming as himself. It was as near Paradise as a mortal may expect to attain and in these idyllic conditions his powers expanded and matured. In 1868 he finished what is on the whole his best piece of prose work, *The Story of a Bad Boy* (1870), and in the same year were born his twin boys about whom the family life largely revolved for the next twenty years.

With the success of *The Story of a Bad Boy,* Aldrich was launched upon a course of prose in which he won a success hardly less than he had won in poetry. For some years to come his larger work was in prose and when in 1874 *Every Saturday* ceased and he was able to devote himself wholly to writing, it was chiefly in prose that he worked. His novels *Prudence Palfrey* (1874), *The Queen of Sheba* (1877), and *The Stillwater Tragedy* (1880) give the full measure of his achievement as a writer of fiction. But when the record is complete, the verdict must be that not the novel, but the short story was his proper medium. Nothing that he wrote in this form exceeded in charm the exquisite story, *Marjorie Daw,* finished in 1873. For five years, from 1875 to 1880, Aldrich had freedom from editorial duties. The time came opportunely. He was now at the height of his powers. He had written much, and had enjoyed the inestimable advantages of a position at the editor's desk. He was equipped with the results of a long practise of criticism, was familiar with the requirements of editors, and had a sure knowledge of the literary market. Making the best of his advantages, he was able to turn all his efforts to good effect and to make this half-decade the most productive in his career. He found leisure for travel, too, and in 1875 he and Mrs. Aldrich made a journey to Europe, the first of many, visiting England, France, and Italy, whence he returned, as he wrote Fields, "chock-full of mental intaglios and Venetian glass and literary bric-a-brac generally" (*Ibid.,* p. 119). In 1878 the death of Bayard Taylor, a friend of a quarter-century, brought him one of the great sorrows of his life and drew from him the elegy which, like those on Holmes, Lowell, Wendell Phillips, and Booth, disclosed his capacity to express the deeper as well as the lighter emotions.

With 1881 began another period of Aldrich's life to which all that had gone before was a preparation. Howells retired from the editorship of the *Atlantic Monthly,* and Aldrich was chosen to succeed him. Then followed nine years, from 1881 to 1890, during which Aldrich exerted his greatest influence on American letters. The delicacy, charm, and precision of workmanship which were associated with his name gave him authority in the matter of literary taste which few Americans had possessed before him. It followed then that under his editorship, taste, distinction of form, excellence of craftsmanship became characteristic of the *Atlantic,* so that it was described by one of the London journals as "the best edited magazine in the English language" (*Ibid.,* p. 147). Though Aldrich, no more than his fellows, could bear comparison with the first editor of the *Atlantic,* lacking Lowell's scholarship and range of power, and though he lacked also Lowell's wide interest in affairs, it is probable that during his control of the magazine there was no truer touchstone of taste to be found on this continent. One has only to glance at the list of contributors to see how naturally he drew around him the best exemplars of literary taste and literary workmanship then living. In the field of poetry Longfellow and Lowell, Holmes and Whittier could still be called upon. There were Parkman, Fiske, Marion Crawford, Henry James, Thomas Hardy, George E. Woodberry, Edward Rowland Sill, and a score of others. In the long run, to be sure, Aldrich's somewhat restricted field of interest, his lack of concern in great political, economic, and social movements resulted in a contraction of the circle of readers so that the Aldrich régime was not the most successful in the *Atlantic* history. It contributed greatly to fixing standards of taste, but it tended to make the famous monthly a miscellany rather than a magazine, and was for the cultivated rather than the general reader.

In 1890 Aldrich relinquished his editorial authority and for the rest of his life was a man of letters and leisure. There remained to him seventeen years of such lettered ease as is often dreamed of and seldom realized. He traveled, made several journeys to Europe and two voyages around the world, and, as the muse commanded, wrote. In fact the body of work produced in these years of professed idleness is substantial. It includes stories and essays which formed four volumes, *An Old Town by the Sea* (1893), *Two Bites at a Cherry* (1894), *A Sea Turn and Other Matters* (1902), and *Ponkapog Papers* (1903); it includes the preparation for the stage and the successful production of his dramatic poem, *Mercedes* (1894), as well as the more arduous task of dramatizing *Judith and Holofernes* for Nance O'Neill, who first appeared in it under its revised title, *Judith of Bethulia,* on Oct. 13, 1904. Finally it includes, in addition to the editing of his collected works, a group of new poems which enhanced his reputation—*Elmwood, Unguarded Gates, Santo Domingo,* the *Shaw Memorial Ode,* and *Longfellow,* the poem written for the Longfellow centenary. This was his last work; it was finished only a short time before his death, and, with touching appropriateness, was read at his funeral. It was singularly fitting that Aldrich's tribute to the master from whom he had drawn his earliest inspiration should have afforded his own requiem.

Aldrich died on Mar. 19, 1907, after a brief illness following upon an operation. The last few years of his life had been clouded with sorrow. On the 6th of March, 1904, his son Charles had died of tuberculosis after three years of the hopes and fears that characterize the course of the disease, and Aldrich never fully rallied from the blow. In 1905 he and Mrs. Aldrich went to Egypt and he returned in good health, but the zest was gone from life. Yet to one who knew him in his later years, Aldrich still seemed a peculiarly vital creature. His erect, alert figure, his jaunty step with a hint of a swagger rather of the sea than of the army, his eye, glinting with mischief, his manner of confident assurance, just short of arrogance, were signs of a magnetic personality that seemed possessed of inexhaustible youth. As a poet Aldrich was more craftsman than creator. He will not challenge the masters for a place on the heights. His level is rather with the Lovelaces, Sucklings, and Dobsons. But as a craftsman he deserves high rank. His ear for the felicitous word, the inevitable phrase, was true, and he was not sparing of toil to fit and finish his work. We may be sure that so long as there is a love of American verse of delicacy and charm there will be lovers of such poems as *Fredericksburg, Nocturne,* and *Elmwood.*

[Ferris Greenslet, *Life of Thomas Bailey Aldrich* (1908), containing bibliography; Lilian W. Aldrich, *Crowding Memories* (1920); personal recollections.]

W. B. P.

ALDRIDGE, IRA FREDERICK (*c.* 1805–Aug. 10, 1867), negro tragedian, was probably born in New York City, although his birthplace is also given as Belair, near Baltimore, Md. The accounts of his early life are conflicting. His father, Joshua Aldridge, is variously described as a negro ship-carpenter and as a full-blooded African chieftain who had been brought to the United States, educated, and settled as a pastor over a colored church. It is stated that young Aldridge was educated at Schenectady, N. Y., and Glasgow, Scotland (Fountain Peyton, *post*). According to the usual account, when Edmund Kean made his first visit to America, Ira Aldridge became his personal attendant and later accompanied him back to England, where, encouraged by Kean, he studied for the stage. He made his début in 1826 as Othello at the Royalty Theatre, London, with considerable success. Highly praised by Kean, and nicknamed the "African Roscius," he was next seen at the Coburg and other metropolitan theatres, afterward touring the English and Irish provinces. At Belfast, Charles Kean played Iago to his Othello. At some time subsequent to 1830 Aldridge appeared unsuccessfully at the "Mud Theatre" in Baltimore. Returning to London, he played at Covent Garden (1833), the Lyceum, and the Surrey. His last London engagements were in 1858 and 1865. Among his rôles were Othello, Lear, Macbeth, Aaron (*Titus Andronicus*), Zanga (*The Revenge*), Gambia (*The Slave*), Rolla (*Pizarro*), and Mungo (*The Padlock*). The critic of the London *Athenæum* in 1858 particularly drew attention to one novel feature of his performance of Othello: "He dispenses," says the writer, "with the black gloves usually worn by the Othello of the theatre and displays his own black hands with his finger-nails expressly apparent." He was generally regarded as one of the ablest and most faithful interpreters of Shakespeare of his day. In 1853 he went to the Continent, visiting Switzerland and Germany, in which latter country he stayed three years. In Germany he acted in English, while his supporting players spoke their lines in German. Crowded houses greeted him everywhere, princes and people eager to see the colored tragedian. Honors, orders, and medals were showered upon him. The King of Prussia wrote him an autograph letter accompanying the first-class medal for art and science. The Emperor of Austria conferred on him the Grand Cross of Leopold. At Berne he received the Medal of Merit. He was a member of the Imperial and Archducal Order of Our Lady of the Manger in Austria, and an honorary member of the Imperial Academy of Beaux Arts in St. Petersburg. For the last ten years of his life he played mainly on the Continent, where he accumulated a considerable fortune. His wife was a white woman. He died in Lodz, Poland, while on his way to fill an engagement in St. Petersburg.

[Fountain Peyton, *A Glance at the Life of Ira Frederick Aldridge* (1917); memoir in *Theatrical News* (Lond.), Apr. 15, 1848; accounts of Covent Garden appearance in *London Times, Globe, Standard, Morning Post,* Apr. 11, 1833; mention in Tallis's *Drawing Room Table Book of Theatrical Memoirs and Anecdotes* (*c.* 1851), p. 14; T. A. Brown, *Hist. of the Am. Stage* (1870); Dutton Cook, *On the Stage* (1883).] A. H.

ALEMANY, JOSÉ SADOC (July 13, 1814–Apr. 14, 1888), Dominican missionary, archbishop, was originally a Catalonian from Vich, in Spain, was educated partly in his native country, and, after taking the habit of the order of St. Dominic, studied in Italy. There at Viterbo he was ordained priest, Mar. 27, 1837. Four years later he became a missionary to the western states of America, where the Dominicans were established in Kentucky and Ohio. The extension of the West, at the close of the Mexican War, brought the former Mexican province of Upper California into the jurisdiction of the United States, while the secularization of the Franciscan missions in that region created a serious problem for the Catholic Church. While Alemany was at Rome on a pilgrimage he was consecrated bishop of Monterey, June 30, 1850. He immediately left for his diocese, taking with him a priest and nun of his order to begin educational institutions. Since he went by way of the Isthmus of Panama, then crowded with gold seekers, it was December before he reached San Francisco, where the Irish pioneers gave him a hearty welcome. At Monterey he found that his diocese contained about twenty-one adobe churches; some of them in the ruined mission premises, served by twelve secular and fourteen regular clergy. His knowledge of Spanish assisted him with the older population; while the white cassock of his order, which he always wore, was a harbinger of peace wherever he went. After two and a half years at Monterey, Alemany was called to the more exacting duties of the newly erected see of San Francisco, of which he was the first archbishop. The problem of support for the many churches needed to serve the rapidly growing population was a pressing one. While still bishop, Alemany had appeared before the United States commission for settling private land claims, and had successfully supported the cause of the missions, obtaining their land in fee simple. This emboldened him to a further effort to obtain church property. At the Monterey bishopric he had found a bundle of papers and documents relative to the "Pious Fund of the Californias," which had been begun in the seventeenth century for the benefit of the missions of lower and upper California. Upon the suppression of the Jesuits, the fund passed into the hands of the State, which held it in trust, and as such upon the independence of Mexico, it continued. In 1842 President Santa Anna sequestered the fund, promising to pay the interest thereafter to the missions. This had been paid rather irregularly until the cession of California to the United States in 1848. Alemany submitted the documents to a San Francisco lawyer, who aided him in an appeal to the Mexican government, which was denied. The case was then presented to the State Department at Washington, which after several years submitted the matter to the arbitration of the Mixed Commission. Sir William Thornton, the third arbitrator, then made a large award to the California church, consisting of one-half of the amounts of interest from 1848 to the date of the award. The successful issue of this case enabled Alemany to promote the cause of Catholicism on the Pacific coast, and to develop educational and charitable institutions. When Mexico refused to continue annual payments the final settlement of the case by the Hague Tribunal in 1902 did not come within the administration of Alemany; nevertheless it was due to his insistence that the case was presented and finally brought to a successful issue. In 1883 he received Father Patrick Riordan of Chicago as his coadjutor, and the next year, at his own earnest solicitations, he was permitted to retire and spend his last days in his native land. Singularly gentle and reposeful in manner, Alemany had the reverence of his subordinates, the affection of his people, and the respect of the entire community.

[Z. Engelhardt, *Missions and Missionaries of Cal.* (1915), IV, 666 ff.; J. P. Young, *Hist. of San Francisco* (*c.* 1912), vol. I, *passim.* On the Pious Fund see 57 Cong., 2 Sess., *House Doc.* I, app., Serial 4442 (1903). General conditions of the see are discussed in J. G. Shea, *Hist. of the Cath. Ch. in the U. S.* (1892), IV, 356.] L. P. K.

ALEXANDER, ABRAHAM (1717–Apr. 23, 1786), Revolutionary patriot, was a member of one of the seven Scotch-Irish families, bearing the surname Alexander, who landed at New York during the eighteenth century. One family remained there, the others moving on to New Jersey and then to Maryland. About 1745 these six families left Maryland for North Carolina, settling on the Catawba River not far from the South Carolina boundary. Of one of these the head was Abraham Alexander, the others being his brothers, Adam, Charles, and Ezra, and two cousins, Hezekiah and John McKnitt, who were also brothers. In course of time Abraham Alexander, whose residence was three miles northwest of Charlotte, became one of the influential and prominent leaders in the affairs of his community. He was for years an elder in the Presbyterian Church at Sugar Creek. In 1762 he was appointed by Gov. Dobbs a justice of the peace for the county of Mecklenburg, established that year, and one of the commissioners for erecting a court-house and other public buildings; and in 1766 he was one of the commissioners for establishing the town of Charlotte. In 1769 and 1770 he represented Mecklenburg in the North Carolina Assembly, and in the latter year he was one of the trustees of Queen's Museum, an educational institution at Charlotte, the charter of which was disallowed by the Crown because the trustees were Dissenters; but the institution functioned without a charter until 1777, when it was incorporated as Liberty Hall, Abraham Alexander again appearing as a trustee. In the agitation resulting in the Revolution he was active, being a member of the Committee of Safety of Mecklenburg County. On May 31, 1775, he was chairman of a public meeting at Charlotte which adopted resolutions declaring that as King George III by his address to Parliament in the preceding February had suspended the constitution of the colonies, the people of Mecklenburg should adopt certain regulations for the government of the county. This was a declaration that independence was the result of British not American policy, and it was the first step in all the colonies toward establishing a government independent of England. The records of the meeting passed into the possession of John McKnitt Alexander (1738–1817), and when they were destroyed by fire in 1800 he attempted to recast them from memory; in that effort he wrote into the resolutions the spirit and some of the language of the Declaration of Independence adopted by the Continental Congress in 1776, and also made the date of the meeting May 20. Thus arose the controversy as to the historicity of the resolves of May 20.

[There is a brief and inaccurate sketch of Abraham Alexander in George W. Graham's *Mecklenburg Declaration of Independence* (1905). This must be supplemented by the *Lineage and Tradition of the Family of John Springs* (Atlanta, 1921) and references in the *Colonial Recs. of N.C.*, VI–IX, XXIII, XXIV. W. H. Foote's *Sketches of N.C.* (1846) contains the best account of the Scotch-Irish settlements and W.H. Hoyt's *Mecklenburg Declaration of Independence* (1907) gives the best presentation of the controversy over the documents bearing that name.]

W. K. B.

ALEXANDER, ARCHIBALD (Apr. 17, 1772–Oct. 22, 1851), Presbyterian clergyman, educator, author, was named for his grandfather, Archibald Alexander, a well-educated Ulster Scot, who about 1736 migrated from County Derry in Ireland to Pennsylvania, and after some years moved south and organized a settlement of his fellow countrymen near Lexington, in the present county of Rockbridge, Va. There his son William, a merchant and farmer, and an influential elder of the Presbyterian Church, married Ann Reid, the daughter of a prosperous landholder of the same community. Of the nine children of this union, the subject of this sketch was the third. The Alexanders were noted for their love of liberty, their intellectual vigor and ambition, and their devotion to evangelical religion. Archibald knew his Shorter Catechism at seven; began his Latin even earlier; used his own rifle at eleven; and in his early teens became an expert swimmer and horseman. At Liberty Hall (later Washington College) he studied the classics under the Rev. William Graham, a graduate of the College of New Jersey. At seventeen, when about to take his bachelor's degree, he interrupted his studies to accept a tutorship in the family of Gen. Posey, near Fredericksburg. There was a season of religious awakening in the community, and in the fall of 1789 Alexander made a public profession of his faith. On his return to Lexington he began theological studies under Graham, who encouraged him to "exercise his gifts" in preaching. His maiden effort was prophetic of his later reputation as an extemporaneous preacher. "Although," he himself testifies in 1843, "I did not know a single word which I was to utter"—he had been called on unawares—"I began with a rapidity and fluency equal to any I have enjoyed to this day" (*Life*, p. 86). Licensed by the Lexington Presbytery at the early age of nineteen, he spent some months in a missionary tour in Virginia and North Carolina with extraordinary success. On Nov. 7, 1794, he was ordained as pastor of the churches of Briery and Cub Creek, in Charlotte County. His preaching was both awakening and edifying and resulted in many conversions. As president of Hampden-Sidney College, a position which he accepted in 1796 and resigned in 1801 in order to be free to make an extended trip to New England, and which he held a second time from 1802 to 1807, he exerted great influence not only by his teaching but also by his preaching in the many churches that sought him as a supply. On Apr. 5, 1802, he married Janetta Waddel, daughter of the celebrated "Blind Preacher," Dr. James Waddel of Louisa County. Of the seven children of this marriage—six sons and one daughter—two sons became noted lawyers and three became eminent ministers—James W., Joseph A., and Samuel D. [*q.v.*].

In the spring of 1807 Alexander was installed over the Pine Street Church of Philadelphia, one of the largest congregations in the metropolis of the nation. The same year he was chosen moderator of the General Assembly, being one of the youngest ministers ever elected to this office. The next year he preached the opening sermon on the text, "Seek that ye may excel to the edifying of the church" (1 Cor. XIV, 12), in which he crystallized the growing sentiment in the denomination in favor of establishing a theological seminary. In 1812 the Assembly resolved to locate the institution in Princeton, and by an almost unanimous vote elected Alexander as the first professor (June 2, 1812). Inaugurated the following August, he not only organized all the courses, but himself conducted the whole work of instruction. With the coming of Dr. Miller in 1813 as the second professor, he devoted himself to the teaching of didactic and polemic theology. In 1840 his chair was changed to that of pastoral and polemic theology and in 1851, the year of his death, the subject of church government was also entrusted to him. In this period of thirty-nine years he put the stamp of his scholarly attainments and his fervent piety upon the whole life of the seminary. This was also the period of his literary productivity. His most important works, besides numerous theological essays, reviews, tracts, and sermons, were *A Brief Outline of the Evidences of the Christian Religion* (1825); *The Canon of the Old and New Testaments* (1826); *Suggestions in Vindication of Sunday Schools* (1829); *The Lives of the Patriarchs* (1835); *Thoughts on Religious Experience* (1841); *Biographical Sketches of the Founder and Principal Alumni of the Log College* (1845); *History of Colonization on the Western Coast of Africa* (1846); *Outlines of Moral Science* (1852). Small and rather slight in build, he had in his prime a clear complexion, dark piercing eyes, abundant hair, a flute-like voice, and an extraordinary vivacity in speech and gesture. Simple in his tastes, affable and hospitable, he was venerated and beloved for his "singular attainments in holiness."

[The admirable *Life* by his son, James W. Alexander (1854), is based on original sources. *Cf.* W. B. Sprague, *Annals of the Am. Pulpit*, III, 612–26, and John DeWitt, "Archibald Alexander's Preparation for His Professorship," in *Princeton Theo. Rev.*, Oct. 1905.] F. W. L.

ALEXANDER, BARTON STONE (Sept. 4, 1819–Dec. 15, 1878), Union soldier, was born in Nicholas County, Ky., the eldest of the ten children of John and Margaret (Davidson) Alexander. His father was a farmer of small means, but "made considerable exertions to give to his promising son an education rather above his condition" (unpublished letter of Garrett Davis, then a young lawyer practising near by). Alexander entered West Point in 1838, and on his graduation in 1842 was commissioned in the Corps of Engineers. From then until the Civil War he was engaged almost constantly in the construction of coast fortifications, of certain buildings at West Point, and of the Soldiers' Home at Washington, then just established; in alterations of the Smithsonian Institution; and, most notable of all from an engineering standpoint, in the erection of a stone lighthouse on Minot's Ledge to replace the iron one destroyed in the great storm of 1851. "The first difficulty encountered was to cut the rock for the foundation stone, which could be done only in a perfectly smooth sea, and at the lowest spring tides. Though the work was prosecuted with all possible diligence, it was more than three years before the ledge could be cut to receive the first stone. This accomplished, the building went on more rapidly, but it required six years before it was completed" (Cullum, II, 119). At the outbreak of the Civil War, Alexander was sent to Washington to assist in the planning and execution of the defenses of the city. He accompanied the advance of the federal troops across the Potomac in May 1861, and supervised the construction of some of the hasty intrenchments which were the beginning of the great chain of forts that eventually surrounded the city. Three times he left Washington for service in the field, taking part in the first battle of Bull Run, the Peninsular Campaign, and a part of Sheridan's campaign in the Shenandoah Valley, always, after brief absences, resuming his work on the fortifications. At first as assistant, and later as chief engineer, he had a greater part in the construction of this defensive system than any other man except Gen. Barnard. Of the works which he personally designed the best known at present is Fort McPherson, which, on account of its location in Arlington National Cemetery, remains in perfect preservation. During the war he was promoted to be major of engineers, and held the temporary rank of lieutenant-colonel. He was brevetted brigadier-general in 1865. In 1867 he was promoted to lieutenant-colonel in the regular service, and with that rank continued on engineering duties until his death. Alexander was a man of great height and bulk, somewhat rough and uncouth in manner; but possessing excellent judgment and high professional qualifications. He was notable for his fondness for children and theirs for him.

[G. W. Cullum, *Biog. Reg.* (3rd ed. 1891), II, 117–21; J. G. Barnard, in *Report on the Defenses of Washington* (1871), describes the fortifications with some incidental mention of Alexander's share in their execution; Alexander's own account of the construction of the Minot's Ledge Lighthouse is in *Trans. Am. Soc. Civil Engineers,* VIII, 83–94; good obituary by Gen. Barnard in *Bull. Ass. Grads. U.S. Mil. Acad., 1879,* pp. 55–68.] T. M. S.

ALEXANDER, DE ALVA STANWOOD (July 17, 1845–Jan. 30, 1925), congressman, historian, belonged to a distinguished line which traced its ancestry back through William Alexander, the pioneer of 1719, to Somerled, Lord of the Isles in Scotland in 1135 (D. A. S. Alexander, *The Alexanders of Maine,* 1897). He was born at Richmond, Me., the son of Stanwood and Priscilla (Brown) Alexander. When he was seven years old, his father died and his mother moved to Ohio where the boy grew up. In 1862 he enlisted—at sixteen—in the 128th Regiment, Ohio Volunteer Infantry. He served as a private until the close of the war, then returned to his native state and entered the Edward Little Institute at Auburn to prepare for college. From here he passed to Bowdoin College, graduating in 1870 with the degree of A.B. It is recorded that he had an excellent record, particularly in English. Soon after leaving college, he for a time taught in the public schools of Fort Wayne, Ind.; a little later he acquired an interest in the *Daily Gazette,* and was its editor at a period when it was a leading organ of the Republican party in that state. In 1874 he sold out his interest and went to Indianapolis, where he acted as staff correspondent of the *Cincinnati Gazette.* About this time he served also as secretary of the Republican state committee. He studied law under Senator McDonald, was admitted to the bar in 1877, and formed a law partnership with Stanton J. Peelle of Indianapolis, in after years chief justice of the court of claims in Washington. After four years of legal practise, on the recommendation of his friend Senator Benjamin Harrison, he was appointed auditor in the United States Treasury Department. In 1885 he removed to Buffalo, N. Y., and formed a partnership with a former college friend, James A. Roberts, who subsequently was comptroller of the State of New York. In June 1889 President Harrison appointed him United States district attorney for the northern district of New York. He discharged the duties of this office with fidelity and distinction until December 1893, when he resigned.

In 1896 he was elected on the Republican ticket to represent his district in Congress. It is a striking tribute to his efficiency that he was nominated eight times in succession without opposition. For fourteen years he faithfully served his constituents, winning his way to a commanding place in the House. His service was conspicuously valuable as chairman of the Rivers and Harbors Committee. During his chairmanship the port of Buffalo was granted $8,500,000 in appropriations. In 1910 the Republican party was disrupted by a revolt against the so-called "old guard." One result of the split-up was Alexander's defeat by his Democratic opponent by one vote. This led to his retirement from public life.

While still in Congress he had begun his *Political History of the State of New York.* The first two volumes were published in 1906, a third in 1909, and a supplementary volume, entitled *Four Famous New Yorkers,* in 1923. Believing that the history of a state or nation is largely the history of a few leading men (Preface, Vol. I), he made his narrative center around those picturesque figures from Clinton to Platt, who successively occupied the stage of New York politics. If there is little suggestion of underlying forces which may have shaped policy and conduct, the story is always told interestingly, often dramatically, and with a desire to do even-handed justice to politicians of all parties. *The History and Procedure of the House of Representatives* (1916) is an informing account of parliamentary procedure, interspersed with many brief character sketches. It was a congenial task for which his fourteen years of service in the House fitted him admirably.

Alexander was twice married, first, in September 1871, to Alice Colby of Defiance, Ohio; second, in December 1893, to Anne Bliss of Buffalo, who survived him. In the ordinary relations of social life he was distinguished by a cordial urbanity of manner which made him a welcome member of a great variety of groups. He was to an unusual degree an example to the younger generation of that fine combination of dignity and courtesy with which it is customary to designate "a gentleman of the old school."

[This sketch is based on an obituary written for the *Quart. Jour. of the N. Y. State Hist. Ass.,* Apr. 1925; also on an intimate acquaintance of many years.] F. H. S.

ALEXANDER, EDWARD PORTER (May 26, 1835–Apr. 28, 1910), Confederate artillerist, author, was born at Washington, Ga., the son of

Leopold and Sarah (Gilbert) Alexander. He was appointed to West Point from his native state in 1853. Graduating in 1857, he became brevet lieutenant of engineers and was assigned to duty as an instructor in the Military Academy. From October 1857 to March 1858 he served in this capacity, obtaining leave of absence to accompany the expedition sent to Utah in 1858 to compel the Mormons to recognize the authority of the United States. He crossed the plains as far as Fort Bridger, where news was received of Brigham Young's submission. From the autumn of 1858 to 1860, Alexander taught in the Military Academy, becoming head of the department of fencing and target practice in 1859. His first important assignment came in the latter year, when he was detailed to study the Myer army signals offered to the United States government. Alexander tested the proposals and the result of his experiments was the evolution of the "wig-wag" system, which marked a great advance in the art of military signaling and which was used by both sides in the Civil War. He also sat on a board of officers engaged in experimenting with breech-loading rifles, then being developed. In 1860 he was ordered to Washington Territory, which was then usually reached by crossing the Isthmus of Panama and ascending the Pacific shore in a coasting vessel. He paused long enough to marry Bettie Mason, of King George County, Va., and then set out with his wife for his new post, following the usual route. He reached Washington in September 1860 and spent the winter there. He was then ordered to Alcatraz Island, San Francisco, on engineer duty. The Civil War, however, was now rapidly approaching. McPherson, in command at Alcatraz Island, besought Alexander to remain on the Pacific coast; but the latter decided that he must go with his state and, when Georgia seceded, he resigned from the United States Army. Returning east, he was commissioned captain of engineers in the Confederate army on June 3, 1861.

Alexander was, however, destined to see other service than engineering. President Davis knew of him as the developer of the army signal service and assigned him to duty on Beauregard's staff as engineer and chief of the signal service. In this capacity he was present at the first battle of Manassas. On July 22, 1861, he was appointed chief of ordnance to Beauregard's command and shortly after became chief of ordnance to the Army of Northern Virginia with the rank of major. His duties embraced the supplying of arms and ammunition to the troops in the field. In this capacity he served in the Peninsular Campaign and at Seven Pines. During the Seven Days he was engaged in supervising the distribution of ammunition to the various commands and was also in charge of a signal balloon which was captured by the Unionists. He continued to serve as chief of ordnance in the second Manassas and in Lee's Maryland campaign. When the Army of Northern Virginia was reorganized in November 1862, Alexander was appointed to the command of a battalion of artillery in Longstreet's corps. In December 1862 he became colonel of artillery. At the battle of Fredericksburg he commanded the batteries on Marye's Heights and so swept the plain below with his guns that every charge of the Unionists at that point broke down with heavy loss. At Chancellorsville he accompanied Jackson's famous flanking march around Hooker and in the night of May 2 posted the batteries that opened Stuart's attack on the following morning. Alexander accompanied the army to Gettysburg as commander of the reserve artillery of Longstreet's corps. On July 2 his batteries followed Longstreet's movement against the Union right and were engaged in the Peach Orchard. On July 3 the duty fell to him of suppressing the opposing Union batteries in order to prepare the way for Pickett's charge. Noting the slackening of the Union fire, he sent Pickett word at 1:40 p. m., "For God's sake come quick. The 18 guns have gone. Come quick or my ammunition will not let me support you properly." Shortly after the dispatch of this message, Longstreet joined Alexander and sought to draw from him an opinion that he could not defeat the Union artillery, in order to secure an excuse to hold Pickett back, but Alexander did not commit himself. Pickett then charged, but his effort was not efficiently aided and failed.

In September 1863 Alexander accompanied Longstreet to Georgia, but arrived just too late to take part in the battle of Chickamauga. He went with Longstreet to Knoxville and thence into the Tennessee mountains, returning with his commander to Lee's army early in 1864. On Feb. 26, 1864, he was made brigadier-general, and became chief of artillery of Longstreet's corps. He was in the thick of the fighting at Spottsylvania in May 1864 and at Cold Harbor. His was the first artillery to arrive from Lee's army at Petersburg when Beauregard was holding the town against the assaults of Grant's overwhelming forces. On June 30, 1864, he surmised that the Unionists were mining under the Confederate works and informed Lee of the matter, with the result that the Confederates countermined but failed to tap the Union tunnels. Being wounded, he was absent from the front for some time. In the last part of the war his duties included the command of Drewry's and Chaffin's Bluffs and the defense of the James River. He accompanied the army on the retreat from Petersburg, acting chiefly as an engineer. Thrown much with Lee in these final days, he counseled his chief on Apr. 8 to disperse the army instead of surrendering, but Lee declined to follow his recommendation. He was included among those surrendered on Apr. 9, 1865.

Alexander's career after the Civil War was busy and distinguished. From 1866 to 1869 he was professor of engineering in the University of South Carolina. Going into business, he was president of the Columbia Oil Company from 1869 to 1871 and then took up railroading. He held several important positions, and from 1887 to 1893 was president of the Georgia Railroad & Banking Co. During the early nineties, he purchased North and South Islands, off the coast of South Carolina, and engaged in rice-planting. He entertained many friends there, with long-remembered hospitality, one of his frequent visitors being Grover Cleveland, with whom he often went duck hunting.

Ardent and energetic, a man of imposing military bearing, he found time for other things besides business. He served as an arbitrator of a boundary dispute between Costa Rica and Nicaragua, was a member of the Capitol commission of Georgia (1883–88) and of the boards of navigation for the Columbia River and the Chesapeake-Delaware ship-canal (1892–94). From 1885 to 1887 he was a government director of the Union Pacific Railroad. He also did much writing. His works on transportation include *Railway Practice* (1887) and many shorter publications. In 1888 appeared his intimate *Catterel Ratterel (Doggerel)*. After a number of preliminary articles on the Civil War, published chiefly in the *Southern Historical Society Papers,* he brought out in 1907 his *Military Memoirs of a Confederate,* a work much more comprehensive than its title indicates. It is, in fact, a critical study of the operations of the Army of Northern Virginia for the whole period of the war and of the Army of Tennessee in its final stages. Based on a careful study of the records as well as on personal observation, his conclusions are recognized by all authorities on the Civil War as carrying great weight.

Alexander's first wife preceded him to the grave by many years. In 1901 he married Mary L. Mason. During his presidency of the Georgia Railroad & Banking Co. he resided in Augusta, Ga., but his home in later years was Savannah.

[*Confed. Mil. Hist.*, VI, 389–91; obituaries in the *Savannah Morning News* and the *Augusta Chronicle,* Apr. 29, 1910.] D. S. F.

ALEXANDER, FRANCIS (Feb. 3, 1800–*c.* 1881), portrait painter and lithographer, was born at Killingly, Conn. In an autobiographical letter to William Dunlap, he thus sketched his early life: "From the age of eight up to twenty I laboured almost incessantly, the eight warm months of the year, upon my father's farm. The other four months in the year I went to a country district school till I was seventeen" (Dunlap, II, 427). He then records the fact that, during an illness, he occupied himself with making water-color pictures, the first of these being of a string of fish he had caught. "I had been to Providence," he continues, "had seen signs there, and those were the only marvels in painting that I saw till I was twenty except two very ordinary portraits that I had seen at some country inn" (*Ibid.*, II, 482). He managed to get to New York about the year 1820 and studied under Alexander Robertson at the Academy of Fine Arts, also copying portraits by Trumbull and Samuel Waldo. He then set up as a portrait painter in Providence, removing after two years to Boston, where he remained until October 1831. Then, having married Lucia Gray Swett, daughter of Col. Samuel Swett of Boston, a "lady of exceptional beauty and wealth," he immediately started upon a trip to Italy. He returned to the United States in 1832. In 1835 he painted a portrait of Daniel Webster now at Dartmouth College. Other portraits he painted were of Benjamin R. Curtis and Mrs. Daniel Webster. He also drew on stone what were probably the first attempts at portrait lithography in America.

His early work was rather good in color and careful in drawing, but during his trip to Italy he changed his manner. Although his later work became less colorful and was executed with a rapidity that was almost careless, it was so much what his sitters in Boston wanted that he became popular. He was a shrewd, business-like man and carried his faculty for driving a bargain to such an extent that his associates called him the "Art Jockey." French tells the story of his going out in a boat in Boston harbor, in 1845, to meet the steamer upon which Charles Dickens arrived from England, and asking for a sitting as soon as he met the novelist. Dickens granted the request and later remarked: "The impertinence of the thing was without limit; but the enterprise was most astonishing, and deserved any kind of reward demanded" (French, p. 63). He finally took up his residence in Florence. During the last years of his life he was not active in his profession. He contemplated returning to the United States in 1878. It is not certain that he ever returned, and he is supposed to have died in Florence.

[W. J. Dunlap, *Hist. of the Rise and Progress of the Arts of Design in the U. S.*(1834) ; *McClure's Mag.*, May 1897, p. 622 (illus.) ; H. W. French, *Art and Artists in Conn.* (1879) ; H. T. Tuckerman, *Book of the Artists* (1867) ; Mantle Fielding, *Dict. of Am. Painters, Sculptors and Engravers ; Boston Mo. Mag.*, Dec. 1825.]

T. B.

ALEXANDER, GROSS (June 1, 1852–Sept. 6, 1915), Methodist clergyman, born in Scottsville, Ky., was the son of Dr. Charles Holliday Alexander, a practising physician, and of Eliza (Drane) Alexander. He was named after the eminent surgeon, Dr. Samuel Gross. When he was fifteen, the family moved to Louisville, where he entered the city high school, from which he graduated in 1871 with the A.B. degree. So satisfactory was his work as a student in this school that immediately following his graduation he was offered a place in the faculty which he accepted and held for two years. He next filled for two years (1873–75) the professorship of Latin and Greek in Warren College, a newly established institution located at Bowling Green, Ky. At the end of his second year in this college, having received what he interpreted as a divine call to the Christian ministry, he resigned his professorship for the purpose of pursuing at Drew Theological Seminary a course of study preparatory to entrance into the ministry of the Methodist Episcopal Church, South. Just before going to Drew Seminary, he was married to Helen M. Watts of Louisville. In connection with his studies at Drew (1875–77), he served as pastor of the Methodist Church at Mohonk Lake, N. Y. Having graduated with the B.D. degree, he entered in the autumn of 1877 upon the active work of the ministry in the Louisville Annual Conference. His first appointment was to Portland, a suburb of Louisville, where he remained for two years. His very successful pastorate in this place was memorable for the conversion, through his public ministry and personal influence, of a noted gambler named Steve P. Holcombe, whose later career as a social worker and evangelist was in turn so successful and remarkable that it called forth from his spiritual father a volume entitled *Steve P. Holcomb, the Converted Gambler: His Life and Work* (1888). Following his ministry at Portland, Alexander spent a year of travel in Europe, after which he was pastor, first at Anchorage, and then at Russellville, Ky., from which place he was transferred in the fall of 1884 to the Tennessee Conference and appointed to the pastorate of West End Methodist Church in Nashville, serving at the same time as chaplain of Vanderbilt University. At the end of this year he became professor of New Testament Greek in the university, which chair he filled successfully until 1902, when he resigned, and returned to ministerial work in the Louisville Conference, serving as presiding elder of the Louisville district for four years. In the meantime his wife had died in the fall of 1885, leaving two children, a son and a daughter. He was again married in 1887, to Arabel Wilbur of Chicago, by whom he also had a daughter and a son. At the General Conference of 1906, which met in Birmingham, Ala., Alexander was elected official book editor of the publications of the Methodist Episcopal Church, South, and also editor of the *Methodist Quarterly Review,* published at Nashville, which office he filled with marked ability until his death. He died suddenly in 1915 during a visit to Long Beach, Cal. His published works include a translation and annotation of *Chrysostom's Homilies on Galatians and Ephesians* (1889); *The Son of Man* (1889), a devout and scholarly interpretation of the person and work of Christ; *History of the Methodist Episcopal Church, South* (1894); *The Epistles to the Colossians and to the Ephesians* (1910), one of the Bible for Home and School series of brief New Testament commentaries. He wrote various articles for *Hastings' Bible Dictionary,* and was a member of the Commission that prepared the commemorative tercentenary edition of the Authorized Version of the English Bible, known as "The 1911 Bible."

[Obituary by Rev. Robert W. Browder in *Minutes Ann. Conf. M. E. Ch., South, for 1915*, pp. 66–69 ; an extended and sympathetic appreciation by Dr. Frank M. Thomas in the *Meth. Quart. Rev.*, Jan. 1916 ; "Memoir," by Bishop H. M. DuBose in the *Jour. Eighteenth Gen. Conf. M. E. Ch., South*, pp. 497–501.]

W. F. T.

ALEXANDER, JAMES (1691–Apr. 2, 1756), lawyer, politician, statesman, and patriot, was born in Scotland, a descendant of the Earls of Stirling, and heir to the title. He was trained as an engineer officer, receiving a good education in mathematics and kindred sciences, in which he early showed a proficiency. Although a Whig in politics, as a good Scotsman he formed Jacobite connections and served with some distinction in the forces of the Old Pretender during the Rebellion of 1715. Upon the defeat of this cause, with the consequent peril to its supporters, he fled to America. Just as he had not hesitated to support the exiled Stuarts against one regarded as an usurper, so in this country he did not fail to attack autocratic power. It is thought that he received the patronage of some influential figure, possibly John, Duke of Argyle, the hereditary friend of his family. This is borne out by the fact that he continually received the favors of the colonial representatives of the House of Brunswick, although he frequently was numbered among its opponents. Owing to his mathematical ability and experience he was appointed, Nov. 7, 1715, surveyor-general of the Province of New Jersey, and later of New York. In 1718 he became recorder of Perth Amboy, N. J., where he had taken up his residence. He engaged at this time in the study of law and was admitted to the provincial bar of New Jersey in 1723. In 1718 he was also appointed deputy-secretary of New York. In March of the following year he was made a commissioner to run the boundary between New York and New Jersey. In 1721 he became a member of the Council of New York, and a member of the Council of New Jersey in 1723. In the latter year he also became attorney-general of New Jersey.

In 1725 he made a motion in the Council of New Jersey for legal reform which shows him to have been clear-sighted as to incumbrances which impeded and thwarted justice and as to the necessity for a change. In this motion he set forth the great delays to practitioners of law in demurrers, special pleadings, and special verdicts. Due to them the practise was then managed in such a way that it was commonly two years before any judgment could be had. He was ordered to prepare a bill remedying such delay, but nothing seems to have come of it. In 1727 he resigned as attorney-general of New Jersey. He declared that he remembered only once having taken fees from the acquitted, as was the practise of his predecessors, and offered to return any money thus received. In this he showed a higher conception of his duty and the requirements of his office than that which was held by most of his contemporaries. In 1732 Gov. Cosby asked for his removal from the Council of New York and after much correspondence succeeded in securing it. In his letters to the Lords of Trade and to the Duke of Newcastle he spoke of Alexander as the only one who had caused him any uneasiness, and stated that he thought he was unworthy to serve His Majesty. Lady Cosby is said to have expressed the wish that Alexander might be done away with, he had opposed the Governor so constantly. Mr. Clarke, President of the Council, accused him of being near treason in working the people up to the pitch of rebellion. In 1735 he was removed from the Council of New Jersey.

Alexander obtained his greatest prominence in the case of Peter Zenger. This man, printer and publisher, "whose paper was the vehicle of invective and satire against the governor and his adherents," was charged with libel and with inviting sedition. Copies of his paper were ordered to be burned by the common hangman, but the magistrates of the quarter would not suffer the order to be entered. Nevertheless, Zenger was thrown into jail. William Smith and Alexander volunteered to serve as his counsel. They secured a writ of habeas corpus, and argued against his reincarceration. Zenger swore that he was not worth more than forty pounds above his exemptions for raiment and tools, yet bail was exacted in penalty of 800 pounds. The grand jury refused to indict; the attorney-general, however, proceeded by information against him. Zenger's counsel took exception to the judges' commissions, wherefore the latter declared Smith and Alexander to be in contempt, and struck their names from the roll of attorneys. Mr. Hamilton of Philadelphia was secured to represent their client, and obtained a verdict for Zenger. Later Smith and Alexander were permitted to present their brief and argue the matter of their exceptions before a committee on grievances. They were given no relief, and it was not until two years later that they were reinstated as members of the bar. With the change of administration on the death of Cosby, Alexander was recalled to the Council of New York, and was considered as still a member of the Council of New Jersey. About this time he removed to New York. In the succeeding years he continued to be active in the councils but his practise absorbed most of his energy. In 1756 there was proposed a ministerial scheme oppressive to the colonists. Although he was suffering from gout at the time, Alexander hurried to Albany to oppose it. There he experienced a paroxysm of his disease, contracted a cold, and died Apr. 2, 1756.

He was regarded as the foremost lawyer in New Jersey, although he was not admitted to the bar until the same day that he was made attorney-general. He was one of the founders of the American Philosophical Society, and had frequent correspondence with prominent scientists of his day. Soon after his arrival in America he married a widow of a prosperous merchant named Provoost, and had by her five children. His wife had continued her first husband's business after his death with much success, and her second marriage did nothing to interfere with it. Their only son, William Alexander [*q.v.*], later known as Lord Stirling, became a prominent general in the American Revolutionary War.

[*Docs. Rel. to the Colonial Hist. of N.J.*, series I, vols. XI, XIV, XV, XVI; *Docs. Rel. to Colonial Hist. of N.Y.*, vols. V, VI; F. B. Lee, *N. J. as a Colony and as a State* (4 vols., 1902); C. A. Ditmas, *Life and Service of Maj.-Gen. Wm. Alexander* (1920); Wm. Smith, *Hist. of the Late Province of N. Y.* (1829); *N. Y. Gazette or Weekly Post Boy*, Apr. 5, 1756.]

G. R.

ALEXANDER, JOHN HENRY (June 26, 1812–Mar. 2, 1867), scientist, was born in Annapolis, Md., the youngest child of William Alexander and his wife Mary Stockett. His father was a merchant of Scotch-Irish descent, and his mother came from an old Maryland family which settled near Annapolis in 1642. Alexander received his education, a typical classical one, at St. John's College, Annapolis, taking his degree at the age of fourteen. He began the study of law shortly after, but soon turned aside from this, being attracted into the new field of applied science. It was the day of the beginning of railroad development and of the organization of coal-mining operations. His first work was in connection with a survey for a railway, but he saw a larger problem, the need of a complete topographical survey of Maryland in connection with a geological survey; and, having urged its importance upon the legislature and convinced its members of the great value of the project, he was appointed, while not yet twenty-one, to make a preliminary study of the question. In 1834 the office of state topographical engineer was created, to which he was appointed. This position he held until 1841. His work in this time was largely preparatory; in the first four years he had constructed a map sufficiently good for the representation of the geology of the state; but he determined not to proceed upon accurate surveys till the time should come when he could work in conjunction with the United States Coast Survey. In the meanwhile he became interested in the coal deposits of Maryland and was one of the first to draw attention to the vast coal fields in Allegany County. He was one of the founders of the George's Creek Coal & Iron Company, and its president from 1836 to 1845.

His primary interest was, however, in scientific work, and the subject of the standardization of weights and measures attracted his attention very early. He urged upon the state legislature the desirability of supplying each county with copies of the standards supplied the state by the federal government; and in 1842 he was given charge of this undertaking. His *Report on Standards of Weight and Measure for the State of Maryland* (1845) was notable for the account given of his researches and for the accuracy of the results obtained. From this time till his death he was a valued coadjutor of the Coast Survey. In 1850 he published *A Universal Dictionary of Weights and Measures, Ancient and Modern,* characterized as "one of the most complete and exact works of the kind ever published" (Hilgard, p. 221). In 1857 he was sent to Europe by the national government on a mission dealing with the unification of coinage, and he was about to be appointed director of the mint in 1867, when he died.

Alexander held many academic positions, being at various times professor of mining and civil engineering at the University of Pennsylvania, professor of natural history in St. James's College, and at the time of his death professor of natural philosophy in the University of Maryland. He was a notable linguist, a student of philosophy, and a writer of pure English prose. A sincere churchman, he was a vestryman of his church for many years and at different times treasurer and secretary of the diocese. His diverse interests are suggested in the bibliography appended to Hilgard's memoir, which includes, among published works, two volumes of religious poetry, *Introïts* (1844) and *Catena Dominica* (1855), and in manuscript, a "Dictionary of the Language of the Lenni-Lenape," a "Handy Book of Parliamentary Practice," and a monumental "Dictionary of English Surnames." He was married in 1836 to Margaret Hammer, the daughter of a Baltimore merchant. She survived him with five sons and one daughter.

[J. E. Hilgard, "Memoir of John H. Alexander," *Nat. Biog. Memoirs,* I (1877), 213–26; Wm. Pinkney, *Memoir of John H. Alexander* (Md. Hist. Soc., 1867); *Biographic Memoir of John Henry Alexander* (1868).]

J. S. A.

ALEXANDER, JOHN WHITE (Oct. 7, 1856–May 31, 1915), painter, was born in Allegheny, Pa., the son of John and Fanny (Smith) Alexander. Left an orphan at the age of five, he lived with his maternal grandparents until twelve years old, when he left school and became a messenger boy in the office of the Atlantic and Pacific Telegraph Company. The president of the company, Col. Edward Jay Allen, became so interested in him that he took the boy to his own home. While still a lad, Alexander "did some remarkably good work in wash drawings for the periodicals" (J. H. Harper, *The House of Harper*), and when about eighteen, he obtained regular employment with Harper & Brothers under Charles Parsons, manager of their art department. In 1877 the "Great Strike" in Pittsburgh offered in its drama and tragedy an opportunity which the young illustrator seized with avidity and used with graphic appreciation. In three years Alexander saved at the Harpers $300, a fortune which floated him to Europe, and became the basis of a career of singularly consecutive successes. Paris disappointed the student by reason of a temporary closing of the École des Beaux Arts; Munich dissatisfied him by the rigidity of its academic routine. The little art colony at Pölling suited his temperament better, and his memories of Edwin A. Abbey, Stanley Reinhart, and Arthur B. Frost as illustrators upon the staff of *Harper's* were further supplemented by his new comradeship with painters, Currier, DeCamp, Shirlaw, and Ross Turner, in the little Bavarian village. In the course of the years spent in Munich and Pölling, there was awarded to him a bronze medal, the first of a whole downpour which later years were to bring. After Pölling, came Frank Duveneck and Florence, Whistler and Venice, great artists as influences, great backgrounds as stimuli. Meantime America paid the bills, through the Harpers, black and white work being sent them, since the $300 had presumably been spent. From the Lagunes Alexander went to the Ohio River, still in magazine service, for the two houses of Harpers and the Century played a large rôle in his early life; and after a term of New York studio work, he went again abroad, once to Spain, once to draw a series of heads of famous Europeans. In 1887 he married Elizabeth Alexander, a lady not related to him by family though of the same name, but related indeed to him in interests of every kind, stimulating through her mentality, and helpful through her social graces to such an extent that his marriage must have been one of his greatest titles to success. And success was his in a fulness diminished only by the tenuous character of his physical strength.

Three years after his marriage he went to Paris with Mrs. Alexander to recuperate from a seriously weakening case of grippe, and he remained there eleven years, reaping honors, cultivating his genius for making friends, and becoming a full member of the Société Nationale des Beaux Arts on the strength of his ability in portraiture, which by this time had shown itself to be his solid and admirable asset. In 1901 he came to New York and here his natural capacity for constructive social work was at once almost as much to the fore as his capacity for painting. Rarely has there been a more many-sided official. He was not only president consecutively of several societies, but could at need, as it were, conduct a whole quadriga of art institutions at once. The arduousness of these public and semi-public duties, and the strenuous physical labor involved in the painting of his larger canvases were not backed by physical robustness; nose and throat trouble called for several painful and not too successful operations which he bore gallantly. Already in 1891 his health had been seriously impaired by grippe poison and after that he was, though intensely active, not really strong. In the winter of 1914–15 his physical vicissitudes grew more and more frequent and on the 31st of May, 1915, the end came.

As is the case with any first-rate artist, both the spirit of his art and its technique were interesting. If we take the spirit and technique in combination perhaps our first impression of the man as artist is that he was by nature, almost by instinct, essentially decorative in everything that he touched. He was an able realist with each portrait as long as the importance of getting a likeness was concerned, but once that was achieved—and it was easily achieved in his case—he let himself loose in the direction of decorativeness, basing it upon his facile and delightful use of great curves in long sweeping lines. Some of his pictures, as for instance "A Butterfly," are in composition almost like calligraphic flourishes but the result is lovely. He was keenly perceptive of the value of simplicity and the fact that much can be done with little, and that economy of effort may even be an enhancement. These *multum in parvo* pictures of his have at once great inter-resemblance and excellent variety—they are homogeneous and vivid manifestations of his personality and in summing up their effect both individually and in the mass, the word that covers them best is charm. In such delightful canvases—usually containing one or two figures at most—as those named "Peonies," "Sunlight," "A Quiet Hour," "The Blue Robe," "The Ring," "Autumn," "Memories," one finds Alexander at nearly his highest point doing exactly the things he loved best to do, untrammeled by any conditions save those proper to all art. He needed only to have a pretty woman clad in sympathetic material, and he would make the latter billow all over the canvas, sweeping it into curving folds and leaving wide spaces of focal light with an almost complete eschewal of complicated modeling. With the long skirt he obtained beautiful results, sometimes treating it balloonwise as in "The Divan" or again like the tail of a comet. Considering all these elements of a single figure picture, and adding the fact that in the faces of his sitters he always fixed charm and dignity if he found it, and that in his finding he preferred to give the benefit of a doubt rather than wreak himself upon a peculiarity, it is not at all difficult to discover good reason for his immense vogue and solid success as portrait painter.

As in Sargent's instance some of his works appeared to be impressions from first to last; in reality with both artists they were much more than that, but Sargent's swiftness, at any rate in his more elaborate compositions, was a result, after many experiments, while Alexander's seemed more like improvisation. When he was painting the main panel of his extensive series for the Carnegie Institute in Pittsburgh, he was asked by one of his comrades "Where are your sketches and studies for the panel?" and he replied, "I didn't make any, I just went ahead." Such a method seems ideal to that part of the public which likes to think of an artist as throwing a work upon a canvas beginning at one side and painting right onward to the other. But it has not been a usual method of mural painters from Botticelli to Michelangelo and onward to Puvis de Chavannes. Although Alexander's disclaimer was a modest and smiling one probably not to be taken *au pied de la lettre,* his remark did reflect his tendency toward improvisation, and it would perhaps seem that he had hardly done enough mural painting to adopt a settled preliminary procedure.

In his art taken as a whole, refinement rising to distinction was one of its most obvious qualities. Pattern and lighting seemed to interest him particularly, and by good pattern is here meant such a treatment of the lines and masses as would insure the picture's being handsome in effect even if it were seen upside down. This carrying power of harmonious pattern is especially desirable in large mural panels which so often have to be seen at great distances, where had they not at once grace and force of line they would appear confused, even blurred. Alexander had good knowledge of all this and used it skilfully. He loved simplicity and thought simply in his painting and was happiest in his treatment of single figures. It was peculiarly in these that his sense of pattern never failed him. He was very personal in his lighting, which was simple and large, yet often exceedingly picturesque as well, in its arrangement. Its effect was not a little enhanced by his predisposition toward masses of reflected light which he used with great skill. Restraint, which was in many cases pronounced sobriety, marked most of his color. He liked to use a warm gray in wide planes and then to strike into it one or two rich or brilliant passages. This predilection reminded one not a little of Giovanni Battista Tiepolo. Probably his striking use of chiaroscuro in large masses would count in his artistic baggage immediately after his grace of line.

In one picture—"The Ring"—now in the Metropolitan Museum, he attains an almost Jack-o'-lantern effect of spots of sunlight which one feels as though they were in actual motion playing about his model. Thus he used the light to enliven the sober key of color which he preferred, and he did not seek for transparent depths, nor for the sustained subtility of a Chardin as shown in the latter's still life pictures. Instead he preferred to strike reflected color back into semi-opaque shadows, and his surfaces, when not the result of direct painting laid on and then let alone, had the effect rather of scumbled than of glazed passages.

Portrait painting on the whole remains the backbone of his achievement and to it he brought excellent characterization, expressed by a skilful, swift, correct yet graceful drawing, and he gave it rounded existence and background by the ingenious and charming use of chiaroscuro cited above. Perhaps the "Portrait Gris" and the "Portrait Noir"—as well indeed as the "Portrait Jaune"—all of them shown in Paris in 1892, and their following of two portraits at the Grafton Gallery in London with five at the exhibition of the Société Nationale des Beaux Arts of Paris in June 1894, were the productions of his psychological moment in portraiture. But both before and after this he showed himself a born portraitist in his capacity for quick seizing of character and a swiftness of execution which saved his sitter from the fatigue which is so apt to induce a fidgety unrest, or worse, a hardening into expressionlessness. In sum, although he was a great deal besides, he was probably first and last a portrait painter—and his output in that direction was prodigious. The Century Company noting his quality sent him abroad to draw, for full-page publication, portraits of men who at that time were of special interest to Americans. These, together with many others drawn a little before or after on this side of the Atlantic, were the vanguard of the army of portraits which marched into our magazines and on to our walls. To name only a portion of Alexander's models calls up memories of the stage, the pulpit, the rostrum, and the salons of the eighties, the nineties, and the first fifteen years of the twentieth century. From the stage we have Joe Jefferson as Bob Acres, Gilbert as Sir Peter Teazle, Miss Maude Adams as L'Aiglon, Miss Annie Russell as Elaine, and Salvini as Lear (a sketch). Among the artists are Rodin, Whittredge, Frost, Thaulow, and many others; and be it noted that while in these Alexander loses the aid of trailing garments and of the "special sense of feminine grace" which Arthur Hoeber so happily attributes to him, he nevertheless stands up sturdily both as appreciator and executant. The universities appear in his male portraits, Princeton being to the fore with McCosh, Patton, and Henry van Dyke, while we have also Van Amringe of Columbia, John F. Weir of Yale, Alexander C. Humphreys, and others. John Hay and Grover Cleveland may stand for the rostrum, Andrew Carnegie for the market; while there is a whole constellation of the literary folk: Howells, Mark Twain, Gilder, Stockton, Booth Tarkington, George Bancroft, Alphonse Daudet from over the seas, with Robert Louis Stevenson, Thomas Hardy, and Austin Dobson as a British contingent; and perhaps best known of them to New Yorkers the Walt Whitman of the Metropolitan Museum.

Alexander contributed to the Library of Congress in Washington six lunettes entitled the "Evolution of the Book." They were rather slight in character, background being almost eliminated and the color remaining somewhat neutral. Later, Pittsburgh honored him with one of the largest commissions both as to extent and remuneration that have ever gone to a mural painter. He was chosen to decorate the entire grand staircase of the Carnegie Institute Building, and he selected for his subject "The Crowning of Labor" as an apotheosis of Pittsburgh. The principal group is at the second floor of what the French aptly call the *cage d'escalier*. A man in steel armor, typical enough of the city of foundries, stands poised against clouds with his drawn sword in his hand and is apparently the focal hero of the apotheosis. In a sort of semicircle before him but always swaying among clouds are young women symbolizing Peace, Prosperity, Luxuries, and Education, making graceful obeisance to him. Again a line of women blow long slender trumpets in his honor. Below, around, and above these figures, smoke and steam curl and mount with the stories of the staircase, not only offering a presence appropriate to Pittsburgh but also affording a medium of the utmost value to the creator of the decoration since it enables him to dissemble the figures wherever he pleases and concentrate them in groups at the points of real vantage. In type these women are always pretty, sometimes handsome, but hardly noble; they do not in that respect equal the types as studied and developed in his portraits where he never let any beauty or dignity that existed in the sitter pass him by. His young men, stripped to the waist, handling chains and cranes and buckets or bending over their levers, are the finest part of the decoration, and the artist used with admirable arrangement and effect the naked human back in muscular action. In the twelve panels of one of the walls to the staircases there are said to be 400 figures of men, women, and children, the people from the streets of Pittsburgh. The mere volume is extraordinary and, if Mrs. Alexander is quoted correctly as saying that everything even to the painting of the vast planes of steam and smoke is by the hand of Alexander himself, one feels rather appalled at the strain put upon such a fragile physique as his and feels that the result was quite as much the crowning of the painter's devotion as it was "The Crowning of Labor" in any other sense.

During Alexander's last years, a great deal of his time—too much in the life of a man valuable in such special directions—was taken away from his painting and given to public service. Toward leadership he gravitated inevitably, and in it he established himself solidly, using the experience of one official position to affirm that of another, touching the circle of the Arts at many points of its circumference. In this synthetizing he worked first, say, as a member of the Board of the Metropolitan Museum of Art at increasing and caring for the Museum's treasures; next as an officer of the School Art League he worked to provide intelligent appreciation of those treasures, appreciation planted in the minds of the children of the city to grow till it should reward the Museum's effort with understanding adult and trained. And he did not leave it there, but after showing art objects of many kinds to these young seekers, he followed them to their East Side clubs and schools and catechized them, and when he noted what they had best remembered, he encouraged them to try experiments of their own in painting and modeling and stimulated them by prizes which he adjudged. To such an instinctive maker of pictures as he, the plastic presentation of the drama naturally called loudly; to its costuming, lighting, and color he gave enthusiastic attention, aided almost always by Mrs. Alexander. It was an easy progression for him from his canvases to the moving pictures of a pageant or a play. Miss Maude Adams and he reacted upon each other most sympathetically in such directions. They both had summer places in Onteora and at the time when Miss Adams was planning her Harvard pageant of Jeanne d'Arc one met them not unoften, all three pondering their problems and climbing the hills as they talked. Of course the organizers of charity bazaars sought Alexander as arranger of tableaux. "If you have a frame and some gauze," he said, "you have no idea how much you can do in a moment with a few colored rags." He was so smiling and kindly that one sometimes did not realize how much his ready service must often have tired him.

In "A Few Words of Appreciation" prefixed to the *Catalogue of Paintings of the John White Alexander Memorial Exhibition* (1916) we are told that at the time of his death he was either officer or member of twenty different art societies. Of many of these he was president: of the National Academy of Design, the National Institute of Arts and Letters, the School Art League of New York, the National Academy Association and the MacDowell Club. He was a director of the American Federation of Arts in Washington; vice-president of the Mural Painters; a member of the American Academy of Arts and Letters, the American Fine Arts Society, the Architectural League of New York, the Fine Arts Federation of New York, the National Association of Portrait Painters, the American Academy in Rome, the Royal Society of Fine Arts of Brussels, the International Society of Painters and Gravers, London; an honorary member of the American Institute of Architects, the Society of Illustrators, the Royal Society of British Artists, the Secession of Munich and Secession of Vienna. In 1901 he was made a Knight of the Legion of Honor by the French government. He received from the Pennsylvania Academy of Fine Arts the Temple Gold Medal and Gold Medal of Honor in 1897 and 1904; a first-class medal at the International Exhibition at the Carnegie Institute, Pittsburgh; gold medals of honor at the Exposition Universelle of Paris, 1900, Pan-American Exposition of Buffalo, 1901, St. Louis Universal Exposition in 1904, San Francisco Panama-Pacific International Exposition in 1915; the Carnegie Prize by the Society of American Artists in 1901; in 1903 the Corcoran Prize by the Society of Washington Artists. Among all his honors there was not one which he took more to heart than the presidency of the National Academy of Design which he held for many years during a season of especial storm and stress, since the Academy at that time was trying persistently, though unavailingly, to obtain larger quarters which should be accessible and well-lighted. It was his dream to succeed in this quest and the effort contributed not a little to the wearing out of his physical endurance.

[J. W. McSpadden, *Famous Painters of America* (1916); *Address of John G. Agar . . . and Resolutions Adopted at the Testimonial of John W. Alexander under the Auspices of the Fine Arts Federation of New York, May 28, 1916; Commemorative Tributes to John White Alexander*, by E. H. Blashfield, G. B. Post, Thomas Hastings, Bronson Howard, and Augustus Thomas (1922); articles by Armand Dayot, *Harper's*, Oct. 1899, Gabriel Mourey, *Int. Stud.*, Aug. 1900, C. H. Caffin, *World's Work*, Jan. 1905, P. T. Farnsworth, *Craftsman*, Apr. 1906, Arthur Hoeber, *Int. Stud.*, May 1908, E. F. Baldwin, *Outlook*, May 28, 1910, E. H. Blashfield, *Art World*, Sept. 1917; other articles in *Appleton's Booklover's Mag.*, Apr. 1904, *World's Work*, Mar. 1905, *Outlook*, Mar. 6, 1909, *Outlook*, June 9, 1915, *Scribner's*, Sept. 1915.]

E. H. B.

ALEXANDER, JOSEPH ADDISON (Apr. 24, 1809–Jan. 28, 1860), educator and author, the third son of Archibald [*q.v.*] and Janetta (Waddel) Alexander, was born in Philadelphia, his father being at the time pastor of the Pine Street Church. When he was four years old, the family moved to Princeton, N. J. Addison received most of his early education from his father. He was a precocious boy, astonishing all who knew him by his extraordinary versatility and his amazing powers of concentration, memory, and understanding. He early revealed remarkable linguistic gifts. As soon as he could read English fluently, he took up the study of Latin. At six he knew the Hebrew alphabet, and at ten he read the Old Testament in the original. At fifteen he entered the junior class of Princeton College, graduating with the highest honors in 1826. After spending two years in private study, mainly of oriental tongues, he became adjunct professor of ancient languages and literature in Princeton College (1830–33), and, after a year of study and travel in Europe, successively instructor (1834), associate professor (1838), and professor of oriental and Biblical literature (1840–51) in Princeton Seminary. In 1851 he was transferred to the chair of Biblical and ecclesiastical history, and from 1859 to his death he was professor of Hellenistic and New Testament literature. He contributed numerous articles—linguistic, textual, exegetical, historical, and theological—to the *Biblical Repertory*, of which he was for some years an editor; was a singularly original and impressive preacher, being much in demand in metropolitan pulpits (*Sermons*, 2 vols., 1860); and was the author of several Biblical commentaries, which established his reputation in Europe as well as America (*The Psalms*, 1850, 3 vols.; *Isaiah*, 1846–47, 2 vols.; *Acts*, 1857, 2 vols., 3d ed. 1860, with later reprints; *Mark*, 1858; and *Matthew*, posthumous, 1861). His scholarly attainments were almost incredible. His biographer (*Life*, pp. 862 ff.) credits him with a thorough mastery of seven tongues, with ability to read and write fourteen more, and with a reading knowledge of five others—a total of twenty-six. He had no special fondness or aptitude for metaphysical discussions, but otherwise the versatility and vigor of his mental faculties were the more astonishing because of their symmetrical and harmonious development. His sermons, his elaborate articles on oriental poetry, and even his letters, especially those in which he narrates his travels, reveal imagination and keen powers of observation, while his critical reviews show sobriety and candor of judgment. As a teacher, he was inclined, in his early years, to underestimate the difficulties of average students, many of whom dreaded his severity and his occasional sarcasm, though all admired the range and thoroughness of his scholarship. He was specially successful in stimulating students in scholarly research. He never married. He was diffident in large social gatherings but brilliant in conversation with congenial acquaintances; and was very fond of children, whom he delighted to entertain with oral and written tales of adventure. Until he was stricken with diabetes, he was of stout figure and florid complexion. His head impressed many with its likeness to that of Napoleon.

[*Life* by Henry C. Alexander, New York, 1870, 2 vols.]

F. W. L.

ALEXANDER, SAMUEL DAVIES (May 3, 1819–Oct. 26, 1894), Presbyterian clergyman and author, the fifth son of Archibald [*q.v.*] and Janetta

(Waddel) Alexander, was born in Princeton, N. J. He was prepared for college chiefly by his two older brothers, James and Joseph Addison Alexander [*q.v.*]. He graduated from the College of New Jersey in 1838. He then spent two years as a resident graduate in Princeton, assisting Prof. Henry; three years as a civil engineer; and one year in studying law. Having determined to devote his life to the ministry, he now took the regular course in Princeton Seminary (1844–47). Ordained by the Second Presbytery of Philadelphia on Nov. 16, 1847, he served the Richmond Church of Philadelphia till 1849, when he accepted the position of assistant secretary of the Board of Education of the Presbyterian Church. In the year 1851 he began a five years' pastorate of the church at Freehold, N. J. In 1856 he accepted a call to the Fifteenth Street Church of New York City, later known as the Phillips Church. His service here, the main work of his life, continued to 1889, when he became pastor emeritus. He continued to reside in New York until, in the seventy-sixth year of his age, he succumbed to an attack of pneumonia. He was unmarried.

Faithful and beloved as a pastor, he had unusual resources of scholarship with which to sustain his ministry in a metropolitan pulpit. As stated clerk of the Presbytery of New York he commanded the respect and admiration of his fellow presbyters by reason of his knowledge of Presbyterian law, his accuracy and thoroughness in keeping the records, and his self-sacrificing spirit. Besides contributing the last four chapters to his father's work on the *History of Colonization on the Western Coast of Africa* (1846), and numerous articles in the *Princeton Review* (see especially his "Editions of Pilgrim's Progress" in the volume of 1859, pp. 232–257), he was the author of the following works: *Life Sketches from Scottish History* (1855); *History of the Presbyterian Church in Ireland, Condensed from the Standard Work of Reid and Killen* (1860); *Princeton College during the Eighteenth Century* (1872) —mainly a biographical dictionary of alumni; and *The Presbytery of New York 1738 to 1888*, even yet a valuable work of reference. Alexander possessed capacity for painstaking, scholarly research but lacked originality and had an imperfect grasp of the principles underlying historical facts. His writings were devoid of literary charm.

[*Princeton Theo. Sem. Biog. Cat.*, ed. by Joseph H. Dulles (1909), gives the main facts of Alexander's life; see also *Princeton Theo. Sem. Necrological Rep.*, 1895, p. 314.]

F. W. L.

ALEXANDER, STEPHEN (Sept. 1, 1806–June 25, 1883), astronomer, was the son of Alexander Alexander, a descendant of Scotch Presbyterians, who had settled in Schenectady, N. Y., in a mercantile career in which he proved successful. He died at the age of forty-four years, leaving a widow, Maria, and two small children. Little is known of Stephen's mother except that she had the qualities necessary to dominate the circumstances now facing the future of the young boy and girl. She gave special attention to the education of her son, who was delicate in physique, quiet and sensitive in disposition, and very studious and observant. His early education was thorough, and with the natural habit of study he completed the academic course at Union College with honors at the age of eighteen. Subsequently he taught in the academy at Chittenango, N. Y. In 1830, his sister, Harriet, married her cousin, Joseph Henry [*q.v.*], who was then entering upon a distinguished career at the Albany Academy as an investigator in magneto-electricity and related problems. Alexander gave up his teaching and became associated with his cousin-brother-in-law. Just what position he held is not known, but he was soon at work upon astronomical problems. His observations upon star occultations and solar eclipses in 1830 and 1831 were communicated to the Albany Academy. In the latter year he made an expedition to Maryland to observe an annular eclipse of the sun, which was in those days a scientific event of note. The next year, 1832, was the turning-point of his life, for the trustees of the New Jersey College at Princeton extended an invitation to Henry to become the professor of natural philosophy, and Alexander accompanied him. He entered the Theological Seminary, but in 1833 accepted an appointment as tutor in mathematics, thereby beginning a long and distinguished service to the college. In 1834 he was advanced to adjunct professor in the same department, in 1840 he became professor of astronomy and, with several later changes of title, he remained on the faculty until his retirement in 1877. He was twice married: on Oct. 3, 1826 to Louisa Meads of Albany, who died in 1847, leaving three daughters; and on Jan. 2, 1850 to Caroline Forman of Princeton, by whom he had two daughters.

In conjunction with Henry, he published his observations of terrestrial magnetism in the *American Journal of Science*, April 1832, and his determination of the difference of longitude by the fall of meteors in the *Proceedings of the American Philosophical Society*, December 1839. We find him directing a large party to Labrador to observe the solar eclipse of 1860, the scientific results being published in the *United States Coast and Geodetic Survey Report* of that year. In 1869 he was chairman of the committee appointed by the National Academy of Sciences to organize the observation of the solar eclipse at Ottumwa, Ia. In 1838, 1854, 1865, and 1875 he observed the annular eclipses of the sun of those years, as well as a partial eclipse and a transit of Mercury. He terminated his astronomical observations of more than fifty years in December 1882 by observing with great interest and care the transit of Venus. Aside from his strictly scientific work Alexander carried on his duties as college professor with exactitude, and found time to publish many scholarly papers upon subjects bordering on the philosophy of the sciences. The most important of these were as follows: "On the Origin of the Forms and the Present Condition of Some of the Clusters of Stars and Several of the Nebulæ," *Astronomical Journal,* Mar. 13–July 10, 1852, II, Nos. 12–20; "Lecture on the Vastness of the Visible Creation," *Smithsonian Institution Annual Report,* 1857; "Lecture on the Relation of Time and Space," *Smithsonian Institution Annual Report,* 1861; *Address by Prof. Stephen Alexander, LL.D. with an Account of the Subsequent Proceedings at the Laying of the Corner Stone of the Astronomical Observatory of the College of New Jersey,* June 27, 1866; "Statement and Exposition of Certain Harmonies of the Solar System," *Smithsonian Contributions to Knowledge,* 1875, XXI, art. 2. Alexander was elected a member of the American Philosophical Society in 1839, and a Fellow of the American Academy of Arts and Sciences in 1850. He received the degree of LL.D. from Columbia University in 1852; in 1859 he became president of the American Association for the Advancement of Science, and in 1862 he was selected as one of the original fifty members of the National Academy of Sciences.

[C. A. Young, "Memoir of Stephen Alexander," *Natl. Acad. Sci. Biog. Memoirs,* 1886, II, 249–59; *Am. Acad. Arts & Sci. Proc.,* 1884, XIX, 504–11; *A Memorial of Joseph Henry* (Smithsonian Institution, 1880); *Princeton. Theol. Sem. Necr. Report,* 1884.]

F. E. B.

ALEXANDER, WILLIAM (1726–Jan. 15, 1783), Revolutionary soldier, was better known as Lord Stirling. Sir William Alexander, from whose family he claimed descent, was a court poet and favorite of James I, from whom he received an immense grant of land in North America. The grant, afterward enlarged, included Nova Scotia, Long Island, and a large part of Canada, but was never carried into effect. The favorite was created Earl of Stirling, and the peerage became extinct with the death of the fifth Earl in 1739. William Alexander's father, James Alexander [*q.v.*], was a Jacobite who emigrated to America after the unsuccessful rising of 1715. He became a lawyer, and held various public offices. The son was born in New York City, was well educated, and, like his father, an excellent mathematician and astronomer. He was associated with his mother as a merchant in New York, and in the early stages of the French and Indian War he was a commissary, and aide and secretary to Gov. Shirley. He accompanied that unfortunate commander to England in 1756, and defended him, the next year, as a witness before the House of Commons. During this visit Alexander expended considerable money and time in the attempt to assert his claim to be the sixth Earl of Stirling. "Chiefly on the deposition of two old men, who affirmed, his descent from John Alexander 'uncle of the first earl,' a jury at Edinburgh, on the 24th March 1759, served him heir-male of Henry, fifth Earl of Stirling" (Charles Rogers, *Memorials of the Earl of Stirling,* 1877, I, 282). "The memorial was . . . remitted to the House of Lords. On the 10th March 1762, the Lords' Committee of Privileges resolved that he had not established his claim" (*Ibid.,* I, 283). Alexander had returned to America the previous year, assuming the title Lord Stirling.

A man of wealth, and social prominence, having married the sister of Gov. Livingston, he held various offices prior to the Revolution, surveyor-general of New Jersey, member of the Council, and assistant to the governor. He promoted farming, manufacture, and mining. His New York house was sold before the war, but he owned a fine mansion at Basking Ridge, N. J. (burned in 1920). His interests in other lines are shown by his report on the transit of Venus in 1769 (in the New York Historical Society Library), and by the fact that he was one of the early governors of Kings (Columbia) College.

As the Revolution came on, Stirling opposed the Stamp Act, and organized a company of grenadiers. He conducted a stormy correspondence with the Loyalist Gov. Franklin, who suspended him from the Council. On Nov. 7, 1775, he was made colonel of the 1st New Jersey Regiment, and he raised and equipped two regiments in the state. His first opportunity for distinction came in January 1776. With forty volunteers in a pilot boat he captured at Sandy Hook the British transport *Blue Mountain Valley.* For this exploit he received the thanks of Congress, and on Mar. 1, 1776, the commission of brigadier-general in the Continental army. Appointed to the chief command in New York City, he prepared for the imminent British invasion. Under his direction Forts Lee and Washington were built, and other fortifications were constructed in Harlem and on Long Island. Fort Stirling on Brooklyn Heights bears his name. The strategic importance of the

Hudson Highlands was becoming recognized, and Stirling reported to Washington on their defenses.

It is with the battle of Long Island, Aug. 27, 1776, that his name is chiefly associated. Under the direction of Putnam, his immediate superior, he was put at the head of the American right wing, charged with the defense of the coast road. His brigade consisted of Delaware, Maryland, and Pennsylvania troops, about 1,500 to 2,000 in number. There were no fortifications; it was the earliest meeting of an American army with its opponent in open field. The line was near the junction of the present Twentieth St. and Third Ave. in Brooklyn, extending thence to Battle Hill in Greenwood Cemetery. His opponent was Gen. Grant, with far superior forces. After a conflict of several hours with Grant, he was exposed to attack in the rear by a detachment under Lord Cornwallis. Stirling's main body escaped by fording Gowanus Creek and passing over a causeway, while Stirling himself with a part of the Maryland regiment held Cornwallis in check for a short time. Then superior numbers told, the mass of Stirling's small force was cut down, and he surrendered to the German De Heister. It was this part of the battle which Washington witnessed from the neighboring heights, and which drew from him his lament at the sacrifice of his soldiers.

Stirling was commended for his bravery by the British as well as by Washington, to whom he had written an account of the battle. He was exchanged in time to take part in the campaign for Westchester County, and in the retreat through the Jerseys. He guarded various points in New Jersey and along the Delaware River, and fought with distinction at the battle of Trenton, which he described in a letter two days later to Gov. Livingston. His services led to his promotion to major-general Feb. 19, 1777. When Howe renewed his invasion of New Jersey from Amboy in the summer, Stirling was opposed to Cornwallis June 26; there was fighting near the present Metuchen, Westfield, and Plainfield, in which Stirling lost three field-guns. Cornwallis's advance was halted at Westfield, and the expedition was recalled.

Gen. Stirling served for a short time in the Highlands during the summer of 1777, led a division under Sullivan at the battle of Brandywine, and commanded the reserves at Germantown. He was one of the minority of officers who favored an attack on Philadelphia. In the succeeding melancholy winter at Valley Forge there occurred the Conway Cabal, in the exposure of which Stirling had a share. While at Reading he heard some remarks by the notorious Wilkinson, who quoted Conway's letter to Gen. Gates, and these remarks Stirling reported to Washington. His last important battle was Monmouth, where he commanded the left wing, and was distinguished by his handling of artillery and in repelling a flank attack. Lee's conduct in that battle led to a court-martial, over which Lord Stirling presided.

In the following year "Light Horse Harry" Lee made his attack on Paulus Hook, and Stirling received the thanks of Congress for the manner in which he had supported Lee's advance and covered the retreat. In the record-breaking winter of January 1780, when the bays and sounds near New York were frozen over, Stirling led an expedition across the ice from Elizabeth to Staten Island; but the British had received warning, and the enterprise was a failure. In the following autumn Arnold's treason took place, and Stirling served on the court of inquiry to determine André's fate. Later he was stationed in New Jersey and Pennsylvania, but chiefly at Albany. While there he prepared a plan of resistance at Saratoga to St. Leger's expected invasion by way of Ticonderoga, but the end of active warfare was at hand. Among his last military reports was a letter to Gov. Clinton (Sept. 10, 1781) giving news about the fleet of De Grasse, and one to the Commander-in-Chief, with details of recent events in the northern department.

Stirling was soldierly in bearing; according to one writer, "of the most martial appearance of any general in the army save Washington himself." He was brave, intelligent, energetic and yet cautious; a good organizer and military engineer; "a great acquisition to the army," in the words of a contemporary. He was highly esteemed by Washington, and after his death Lady Stirling received a letter of tribute from the General.

[Charles Rogers, *Memorials of the Earl of Stirling and of the House of Alexander* (1877); C. A. Ditmas, *Life and Services of Major-General Wm. Alexander* (Kings County, N. Y., Hist. Soc., 1920); W. A. Duer, *Life of William Alexander* (1847); Ludwig Schumacher, *Earl of Stirling* (1897); C. F. Adams in *Am. Hist. Rev.* (1896); T. W. Field in *Memoirs of the Long Island Hist. Soc.*, vol. II.]

E. K. A.

ALEXANDER, WILLIAM DEWITT (Apr. 2, 1833–Feb. 22, 1913), historian and scientist, was born at Honolulu, the son of William Patterson and Mary Ann (McKinley) Alexander. His father, who was a Kentuckian by birth, had come to Hawaii as a missionary in 1832. Alexander had his early education at the Punahou School, Honolulu, and, after the long voyage around the Horn which was necessary in those days, completed his preparation for college in Harrisburg, which had been his mother's home. He graduated at Yale in 1855, taught for a time at Beloit College and at an academy near Vincennes, Ind., and returned to Hawaii in 1858. Soon after he married Abigail, daughter of Dwight Baldwin of Lahaina. He was professor of Greek at the Punahou School for six years, and president of the institution from 1864 to 1870. (The corporate name of the group of schools at Punahou is Oahu College; it is now rarely used, except in legal documents, and does not indicate a "college" in the usual American sense.) In 1872 he became surveyor-general of the kingdom, and continued in that position for the rest of his active life. His interests were scholarly and varied. He was a founder of the Hawaiian Historical Society, one of the original members of the Polynesian Society of New Zealand, a fellow of the Royal Geographical Society, and a member of the Astronomical Society of the Pacific. He wrote a grammar of the Hawaiian language and numerous scientific papers and reports. But it is as a historian that he is chiefly remembered. His *Brief History of the Hawaiian People,* first published in 1891, though intended as a school text-book, still serves as a useful introduction to the subject for mature students. An account of recent political events prepared in 1893 for presentation to the American commissioner (Blount) was expanded into his *History of Later Years of the Hawaiian Monarchy and the Revolution of 1893,* and published in 1896. Though the work of one who frankly avows that he does not write as a neutral (he was a supporter of the revolution, and was sent to Washington to represent the interests of the provisional government), it is judicious in reasoning and temperate in tone. It must always remain of prime importance in the study of this period. In 1884 he was appointed to the privy council, once an important element in the government, but now performing little more than nominal functions. Membership, therefore, was merely honorary, but his long service on the board of education involved more exacting duties. He was active in religious work, too, throughout his life. Probably the ablest scholar that Hawaii has yet produced, and of attainments that won him recognition far beyond the limits of his native country, he was a quiet, unassuming man, with the faculty of winning both the respect and the love of all his associates. He died in Honolulu, and was buried in the yard of Kawaiahao church,—the old building of coral rock which king and people labored together to erect in the early days of island Christianity.

[There is an extended obituary in the *Honolulu Advertiser,* Feb. 24, 1913, and a short one in the *Ann. Report, Hawaiian Hist. Soc.* for 1912, published in 1913. See also *Who's Who in America,* 1912–13.]

T. M. S.

ALFONCE (ALFONSE), JEAN. [See ALLEFONSCE, JEAN, *c.* 1482–1557.]

ALGER, CYRUS (Nov. 11, 1781–Feb. 4, 1856), iron-master, inventor, was born at Bridgewater, Mass., the son of Abiezer Alger and Hepsibah (Keith) Alger. His father, a man of sagacity and energy, was prominent in local affairs and successful in business, owning iron foundries in West Bridgewater, Easton, and Titicut. Cyrus, after a partial preparation for college at the nearby town of Taunton, entered the iron-foundry business with his father at Easton, where he thoroughly mastered the existing knowledge of that industry. At the solicitation of Gen. Winslow, with whom he formed a partnership, Cyrus Alger moved to South Boston in 1809 and there established an iron-foundry. The partnership was dissolved five years later, but Alger continued in the same business on a new site. The receipt from the government of large orders for cannon-balls during the War of 1812 and the profits derived therefrom insured the success of the new venture and definitely launched Alger upon a notable career. At the conclusion of the war his fortunes were further improved by a bold real estate speculation. The South Boston Association (an organization which had taken over the town lands after the annexation of that town to Boston) by building a sea-wall had partly reclaimed the flats lying west of Dorchester Ave. Alger now purchased these lands lying between the North Free Bridge and Fifth St., being careful that the deed should include all the flats in front of the sea-wall to the channel or low-water mark. Being paid liberally for the rest, the association without hesitation threw in this parcel. Alger now improved the sea-wall, filled in the flats within the wall, laid out roads, built his own factory and house in this section and induced others to do the same. Eventually the flats outside the wall were raised, wharves built, and the section became an important manufacturing and mercantile section. No individual contributed more to the rapid development of South Boston. Associating himself in 1827 with George C. Thacher, William H. Howard, and Caleb Reed, Alger formed the South Boston Iron Company, built a new plant on Foundry St., and rapidly extended his works until they became the largest and best-equipped in the United States. He also in 1829, in connection with several capitalists of Halifax, built, near Annapolis, the first smelting furnace in the British provinces, manufacturing the machinery in his South Boston plant and installing it with his own mechanics.

Although Alger thus showed throughout his life unusual executive capacity, he was known quite as widely as an inventor and metallurgist. The patent records up to 1839 record at least five inventions to his credit, including a malleable cast-iron plow, a cast-iron cannon, and casting rollers for casting iron. He designed the first cylinder stoves in 1822, and the first gun ever rifled was turned out of his shop in 1834. As a metallurgist he developed a process by which he could purify cast iron so as to give it more than triple the strength of ordinary cast iron, "the process consisting in removing impurities from the metal while in a fluid state and causing it to be much more dense" (Simonds, p. 255). He improved the reverberatory furnaces for melting iron and "first introduced and patented the method of making cast iron chilled rolls, by which the part subject to wear should be hard, while the necks remain unchanged as to hardness and strength—these being cast in sand, while the body is cast in a chill, or iron cylinder" (*Ibid.*, p. 256). Nor was Alger's interest confined to iron. His plant turned out the first perfect bronze cannon ever made for the United States Government and for the State of Massachusetts. Ordnance, in fact, after the War of 1812, was with him a primary interest, and his superior methods of casting iron brought to his foundry so many government contracts that for many years he was chiefly employed in making guns. He made improvements in the composition of fuses for bombshells and cast the mortar gun, "Columbiad," the largest gun cast in America up to 1850.

As the chief land owner in South Boston and the proprietor of the largest factory in the community, Alger, following the older New England tradition, took an active part in local politics. He was a member of the common council the first year of the city government of Boston (1822) and represented South Boston as alderman during a portion of 1824 and in 1827. His interest in the development of South Boston was unflagging, and the great respect in which he was held by his fellow townsmen made his influence potent. For his time Alger was an enlightened employer; he was the first man in South Boston to introduce the ten-hour system, his wages were always paid in cash, and he did not hesitate to put men on half time at some sacrifice to himself in order to insure continuous employment. His benefactions were many and his private life unblemished. He was twice married: in 1804 to Lucy Willis (1782–1830), by whom he had seven children; and in 1833 to Mary Pillsbury. The Cyrus Alger Primary school erected in 1881 on West Seventh St. was named after him.

[The fullest account is in T. C. Simonds, *Hist. of South Boston* (1857), pp. 251–60. A condensation of this, with frontispiece of Cyrus Alger, is in Arthur M. Alger's *Geneal. Hist. of That Branch of the Alger Family which Springs from Thomas Alger of Taunton and Bridgewater in Mass, 1665–1875* (1876). See also Toomey and Rankin, *Hist. of South Boston* (1901), which contains a picture of Alger (p. 226) and of his foundry (pp. 232–33). See also Francis Alger, *Claim of the Late Cyrus Alger for Remuneration for the Use by the U. S. of Certain Inventions Relating to Fuses and Shells* (1862), and J. L. Bishop, *Hist. of Am. Manufactures* (1861–64), II, 660–63 and index.]

H. U. F.

ALGER, HORATIO (Jan. 13, 1834–July 18, 1899) was the most successful writer of boys' stories in the whole of American literature. An entire generation was indoctrinated by him in the comforting assurance that virtue is always rewarded by wealth and honor. His voluminous epics on the moral conquest of poverty exercised an influence on the formation of American youth comparable to that exercised on our British cousins by Henty's demonstrations of Anglo-Saxon superiority. He was born in Revere, Mass., the son of Olive (Fenno) Alger and the Rev. Horatio Alger, a rather sanctimonious Unitarian clergyman, who was determined that his son should follow in his footsteps. As a boy the future author was known as "Holy Horatio." He was educated at Gates Academy and at Harvard, where he distinguished himself in the classics and in French. At this time an early marriage was prevented by the interference of his father. After three years in teaching and journalism, Alger became a student at the Harvard Divinity School, supporting himself the while by tutoring and writing for the press. Having graduated in 1860, he showed no immediate inclination for the ministry but instead spent in Paris a year marked by futile indiscretions and equally futile remorse. He then returned to Cambridge as a private tutor. On Dec. 8, 1864, he was, however, at last ordained minister of a Unitarian church, in Brewster, Mass., but he resigned two years later and moved to New York to devote himself to literature. There he continued to live until 1896, with the exception of two visits to the Pacific coast in search of copy and another trip to Paris in the course of a frenetic amour which left him temporarily insane. He never married. After 1896 he made his home with his sister in Natick, Mass., until his death in 1899.

Although he had written several earlier works, *Bertha's Christmas Vision* (1856), *Nothing to Do, a Tilt at Our Best Society* (1857), *Frank's Campaign, or What a Boy Can Do* (1864), and *Helen Ford, a Novel* (1866), it was not until

Alger's residence in New York that he found his real vocation. Through his charitable interest in the work of the Newsboys' Lodging House, founded by Charles Loring Brace [*q.v.*], he formed an enduring friendship with its superintendent, Charles O'Connor, and became informally identified with the management of the institution. Most of his time he spent in the Lodging House, to which he brought a rescued Chinese foundling, Wing, whom he practically adopted until the boy's death beneath the feet of a runaway horse. By his warm-heartedness and sympathy Alger won the confidence of the street gamins, made innumerable friends among them, and came to know their life in all its details. This life, highly idealized and sentimentalized, henceforth formed the subject of a steady stream of works from his pen. The first of these, *Ragged Dick,* a serial story that appeared in Oliver Optic's magazine, *Student and Schoolmate,* in 1867, became at once enormously popular. A. K. Loring, a Boston publisher, immediately contracted on liberal terms for six other stories of the same kind. Thus came into existence a whole series of *Ragged Dick,* to be followed by further series, *Luck and Pluck* (1869) and *Tattered Tom* (1871), no less than eight volumes being required to remove all of Tom's tatters and establish him in perfectly safe respectability. Still other works followed, and although none of the later Alger heroes quite equaled the prototypal Dick in popularity, all of these volumes sold widely. Alger also wrote biographies of self-made American statesmen, such as *From Canal Boy to President* (1881), *From Farm Boy to Senator* (1882), *Abraham Lincoln, the Backwoods Boy* (1883), and he brought out a volume of poems, *Grand-'ther Baldwin's Thanksgiving* (1875), some of which did not fail to acquire popularity as a medium for public recitations. Writing with extraordinary rapidity, having on one occasion completed an entire book within two weeks, Alger produced all in all 119 works. The enormous income from his writings was, however, owing to his spendthrift habits, insufficient to prevent his dying poor. He was generous to the point of prodigality and was often imposed upon by his ragged protégés. The bold and frank heroes of his fancy seem to have been created as a compensatory substitute for a personality naturally weak and timorous. He suffered from a sickly conscience, and, yearning hopelessly to write a really serious novel, was tortured by a sense of frustration. With a new generation of sophisticated boys such as he never knew, his popularity is dwindling. His works may be counted upon to disappear, but none the less they will have left a stronger mark upon the American character than the works of many a greater writer.

[Herbert R. Mayes, *Alger* (1928), containing bibliography; obituaries in *N. Y. Herald, N. Y. Post, N. Y. Tribune,* July 19, 1899; *Munsey's Mag.,* Oct. 1892; Grace W. Edes, *Annals of the Harvard Class of 1852* (1922); *Who's Who in America,* 1899–1900.]

E. S. B.

ALGER, RUSSELL ALEXANDER (Feb. 27, 1836–Jan. 24, 1907), governor of Michigan, commander-in-chief of the Grand Army of the Republic, and secretary of war during the blundering campaign of 1898 against Spain, was born in the log cabin of his parents, Russell and Caroline (Moulton) Alger, in the Western Reserve of Ohio, and was obliged to make his own way from an early age. In 1859 he became a lawyer in Ohio, but he removed in that year to Grand Rapids, Mich., in search of an outdoor life. Here he laid the foundation of his large fortune in lumber, and married, in 1861, Annette Henry, who bore him nine children. With five of them, she survived him.

He entered the Civil War as a private soldier, was wounded several times, and was in the autumn of 1864 commanding his regiment with rank of colonel in the Virginia Valley campaign under Sheridan. He was later able out of ample means and a generous heart to assist Sheridan with a gift of $10,000. Apparently inconsistent with this friendship was a discovery which Charles A. Dana of the *Sun* flaunted against Alger to block the latter's aspirations for the presidency in 1892 (N. Y. *Sun,* Feb. 11, 1892). Dana alleged that, with the approval of Sheridan, Alger had been recommended for dismissal from the army. Alger had indeed been discharged, upon resignation, Sept. 20, 1864; and he had subsequently been given brevet rank, for gallantry, as brigadier-general and then as major-general of volunteers. The dismissal papers, however, included the original charge of absence without leave made by Gen. Custer, indorsed in succession by Merritt, Torbert, Sheridan, and the adjutant-general of the army. Alger's story was one of sickness in August 1864, hospitalization at Annapolis, assignment to court-martial duty in Washington, and honorable discharge upon his own request. The two stories were never adequately reconciled; but upon the eve of Alger's selection for a place in McKinley's cabinet they were studied by Senator J. C. Burrows of Michigan, who guaranteed that Alger's military record would pass muster (W. D. Orcutt, *Burrows of Michigan and the Republican Party,* 1917, II, 102). Dana himself seems to have become satisfied that his exposé was without validity. After the Civil War, Alger settled in Detroit, where his fortune and his personal popularity grew to large dimensions. He defeated "Uncle Josiah" W. Begole, when the latter with fusion indorsement ran for reëlection as governor of Michigan in 1884. As Republican governor, Alger gained some eminence among the statesmen of the Middle West. He returned to business after a single term, was a "favorite son" in the Republican nominating convention of 1888, and received from his comrades of the war their highest honor in the command of the Grand Army of the Republic, in 1889.

Alger was secretary of war from March 1897 until July 1899 when he resigned at the request of President McKinley. The responsibility for the army and for the War Department as he found them rests squarely upon the people of the United States, indifferent in this period to both military preparation and efficiency of administration. The posts of command in the regular army were filled with elderly officers, generally near their age for retirement. The bureaus of the War Department were encrusted with the routine of an army of 25,000, and there were deep jealousies between the officers of the line and the bureaus that governed them. There was nothing resembling a general staff, and no systematic study had been given to any of the problems that must certainly arise in the event of war. Alger administered the War Department in a kindly, routine way, inheriting the antagonism that usually existed between the department and the commanding general. When Congress, on Mar. 9, 1898, appropriated the President's fund of fifty millions "for the national defense, and for each and every purpose connected therewith," Alger neither secured an allotment for such last-hour preparations as might have been practicable, nor resigned his post. "No part of this sum was available for offensive purposes —even for offensive preparation," he subsequently declared, without apparently realizing that such an interpretation of the law by the President ought to have led to his own immediate withdrawal from the cabinet. Not until after the actual declaration of war were there funds available for the preparation of an expeditionary force; and then events moved so rapidly that, with the inadequate and red-tape-bound departmental organization, all preparation was hit-or-miss. The degree to which the President interfered with the fighting of the war lessened the personal liabilities of his subordinates. Alger, however, was the one who prevented Gen. Miles, the commander-in-chief, from going to Cuba, and who secured the command of the expedition for a Michigan officer, W. R. Shafter, who was obese to start with and physically incapacitated during much of the Santiago campaign. As the short war progressed a wave of criticism was directed against Secretary Alger. In the commissary and hospital services the inadequacies were flagrant. As soon as the fighting was over, President McKinley created a voluntary commission, with Gen. Grenville M. Dodge as president, to survey the conduct of the war. Its report, supplemented by that of the "embalmed beef" commission, and by the court-martial proceedings in the case of Commissary-General Charles P. Eagan, presents a bitter picture of war administration.

Through the winter of 1898–99 McKinley retained Alger in the cabinet, feeling the increasing political burden of his presence. The President appears to have refused to let Alger retire under fire; but he called for his resignation a few weeks after it was suggested that his Secretary would become a candidate for the United States Senate, with the support of Gov. Pingree, upon an anti-trust platform. Alger became senator from Michigan in 1902, and died before the expiration of his term.

[Alger left a long trail through the newspapers and the critical literature relating to the war with Spain. In 1900 he gave to Henry C. Campbell of the *Milwaukee Jour.* a confidential interview which that paper printed on the evening of his death, Jan. 24, 1907. There are the usual obituaries, but there is no good biography. Much can be read between the lines of his apologia, *The Spanish-American War* (1901).]

F. L. P—n.

ALGER, WILLIAM ROUNSEVILLE (Dec. 28, 1822–Feb. 7, 1905), Unitarian clergyman, author, was born in Freetown, Mass., the son of Nahum and Catherine Sampson (Rounseville) Alger. His father was a man of ability, but "unfortunate in his affairs." When ten years of age young Alger went to Boston and worked first in a grocery store and later in a broker's office. Subsequently he secured employment in a cotton-mill at Hooksett, N. H. His Huguenot ancestry conferred on him intellectual ambitions and aptitude, however, and he gave his early morning hours and evenings to study, and even while at his work, it is said, memorized pages of history and grammar and worked out problems in arithmetic. Such preparation finally enabled him to enter an academy at Pembroke, N. H., and at twenty-two he enrolled in the Harvard Divinity School, graduating in 1847. He was immediately ordained and became pastor of All Souls' Unitarian Church, Roxbury, Mass. This same year, 1847, he married Anne Langdon Lodge. On Jan. 7, 1855, he was installed as pastor of Bulfinch Street Church, Boston. Later he made a name for himself by an extended period of theatre preaching. In 1868 he was appointed chaplain of the Massachusetts House of Representatives. It was then the custom, it is said, for most of the members to remain outside the chamber till the prayer was over. Alger made short prayers and had a full attendance. From 1874 to 1878 he was pastor of the Church of the Messiah, New York, and later held brief pastorates in Denver, Colo., and Portland, Me. He was a favorite on the lyceum platform, and much in demand as a speaker for special occasions. At these times he did not hesitate to say what he thought ought to be said even though it brought him into temporary disfavor. Thus in 1857, chosen to deliver the Fourth of July oration in Boston, he criticized the pro-slavery attitude of the people so strongly that the city refused to publish the oration or give the customary vote of thanks. Seven years later, however, it made amends.

He lived more in the world of literature than of action. His memory was unusually retentive and he became familiar with a wide range of literature. *The Poetry of the East* (1856), consisting of translations of Persian, Sanskrit, and Arabic poems, went through several editions, although his acquaintance with these literatures was only through French and German translations. His *Life of Edwin Forrest, the American Tragedian* (1877), is a notable work, elaborate, painstaking, and exact, but diffuse and full of digressions; his *Critical History of the Doctrine of a Future Life* (1864), written after twelve years of patient labor, is a scholarly work of much value. Besides the books mentioned he published: *History of the Cross of Christ* (1851); *The Nature, Grounds, and Uses of Faith* (1853); *The Christian Theory of Life* (1855); *An American Voice on the Late War in the East* (1856); *The Charities of Boston* (1856); *The Genius and Future of America* (1857); *The Historic Purchase of Freedom* (1859); *Public Morals* (1862); *The Solitudes of Nature and of Man* (1867); *The Friendships of Women* (1868); *Prayers in the Massachusetts House of Representatives* (1868); *The School of Life* (1881).

[Biographical material is sparse. Arthur M. Alger's *Geneal. Hist. of That Branch of the Alger Family which Springs from Thomas Alger of Taunton and Bridgewater in Mass.* (1876) contains an informative sketch. See also obituary notices in the *Boston Transcript,* Feb. 8, 1905, and *Boston Globe* of same date. A good idea of the value and style of some of his writings may be had from reviews in the *Nation,* Nov. 29, 1866, Mar. 14, 1867, Aug. 23, 1877, and in the *Atlantic Mo.,* Feb. 1864.]

C. G.

ALISON, FRANCIS (1705–Nov. 28, 1779), Presbyterian clergyman, educator, was born in the parish of Leck, county of Donegal, Ireland. After preparation under the Bishop of Raphoe he entered the University of Glasgow. He came to America in 1735, settling first in Talbot County, Md., then at New London, Chester County, Pa. He married Hannah Armitage of New Castle, Del.; of their children the most prominent was the physician, Dr. Francis Alison, Jr. In 1752 he removed to Philadelphia, where he lived and labored till his death.

In Maryland, Alison was tutor in the home of Samuel Dickinson. At New London, having been licensed to preach, he was inducted into the local church May 25, 1737, and continued there till called to Philadelphia. Educational facilities were meager; "there was not a College, nor even a good Grammar School in four provinces, Maryland, Pennsylvania, Jersey, and New York" (Ezra Stiles, p. 431). To remedy the lack, he opened a school (1743), which was officially recognized and subsidized by the Synod of Philadelphia (1744). Such noted men as Charles Thomson, Thomas McKean, and George Read were educated at Alison's school, and, when removed to Newark, Del., it became the foundation of Delaware College. The fame of the master spread abroad and, at the sudden death of the rector of the new academy in Philadelphia, he was referred to as "a gentleman of good learning" who might be secured for the place. Though, at first, "diffident" about undertaking the Latin School, he finally accepted the post at £200 per annum. In 1754 he and Dr. Smith proposed the "advantage" of being allowed to confer degrees on properly qualified students. A clause granting this privilege was drawn up at the trustees' suggestion and subsequently approved. On Mar. 7, 1755, Alison was chosen vice-provost of the "new institution"—the college—and his name, with that of Dr. Smith, inserted in the draft of the new charter.

Of this long service (1752–79) most favorable judgments were passed by students and trustees. Provost Ewing said "he had an unusual fund of learning and knowledge" which fitted him for "the painful instruction of youth in the College" (Wm. B. Sprague, *Annals of the American Pulpit,* III, 76). His only weakness as a teacher was "proneness to anger." Of his scholarship there was great praise. Ezra Stiles avowed he was "the greatest classical scholar in America, especially in Greek." Franklin thought him "a Person of great Ingenuity and Learning" (Ezra Stiles, p. 4). That he knew several fields, is suggested by the fact that (1756) it was agreed that he should teach, besides classics, "Logic, Metaphysicks and Geography" and "other arts and sciences. . . ." While vice-provost of the College he continued to serve as assistant pastor of the First Presbyterian Church of Philadelphia. In the religious turmoil of the day he championed the "Old Side." In 1758, May 24 and 25, he preached two remarkable sermons on *Peace and Union Recommended* before the Synods of New York and Philadelphia; no other published work is extant. These sermons, *An Address to the Rev. Dr. Alison* (1765), *An Address of Thanks to the Wardens of Christ Church and St. Peters* (1764), and several letters give fleeting glimpses of a mind well informed and keenly active in the religious, educational and political affairs of the day. His philanthropic bent led him to found the Presbyterian Society for the Relief of Ministers and their Widows.

In his later years, in spite of vexatious events and illness, he did not cease to labor in public and private. On July 20, 1775, he "entertained the Congress at church and meeting. Such a Fast was never before observed in this city; Sunday was never so strictly kept" (*Connecticut Historical Society Collections,* II, 292). In 1777 he signed, with others, a protest to the Council of Safety against the "interruptions [quartering of soldiers] which we have met with in the important Business of Education." While ill, he continued teaching at his house, asking that wood be sent there till he was "sufficiently recovered to attend his duty in College. . . ." Later (Mar. 16, 1779) he prayed the trustees to consider that "double the nominal sum" of his former salary was not adequate. His death occurred shortly after the hostile legislature had set aside the charter of the institution to which he had given the best of his life.

[The most reliable, though fragmentary, sources of information about Francis Alison are: the unpublished Minutes of Trustees of the College, Academy, and Charitable Schools and the unpublished Archives of the Univ. of Pa. (1740–90); *Extracts from the Itineraries and other Miscellanies of Ezra Stiles, 1755–1794, with . . . Correspondence,* ed. by Franklin B. Dexter (1916); Leonard Allison Morrison, *Hist. of the Alison or Allison Family in Europe and Am. 1135–1893* (1893); J. S. Futhey and Gilbert Cope, *Hist. of Chester Co.* (1881); Thos. H. Montgomery, *Hist. of the Univ. of Pa.* (1900).]

T. W.

ALLAIRE, JAMES PETER (1785–May 20, 1858), master mechanic, engine builder, was of French Huguenot descent. Emigrating from La Rochelle, France, in the seventeenth century, Alexander Allaire settled in 1680 at what is now New Rochelle, N. Y. "Among the inhabitants of this town [New Rochelle] in 1710 were Alexander Allaire and Jane, his wife, with their children, Peter, Philip, Jean, and Isaac" (Bolton, I, 678). James P. Allaire was a great-grandson of Alexander and Jane Allaire through their son, Peter. As a young man he was one of the few skilled workmen in America capable of assembling the engines, marine and others, that were being shipped from England. In 1813 he began business as a brass founder in New York City. At the time, Robert Fulton had his engine shop in Jersey City, and in 1815 Allaire leased the Fulton shop, transferring its business the following year to his brass foundry on Cherry St., New York City, thus founding the oldest steam-engine works in New York. Under the patronage of Fulton and others he became the leading manufacturer of steam-engines, boilers, etc., of his day. The name of the Allaire Works became famous and was to be seen on a vast number of engines, particularly steam-boat engines, still in use in this country toward the latter half of the nineteenth century. When the Works were in their prime Allaire heard of the presence of iron ore in the bogs of Monmouth County, N. J. He went prospecting and found not only iron ore but a forest nearby suited for charcoal, then essential in smelting. He purchased, in all, about 8,000 acres of woodland and set about erecting furnace, smelter, and finishing mill, and then an ideal town (later called Allaire) to take care of his workmen. The erection of these works, called the Howell Works, began in 1831. The Squan River furnished water power. Allaire had a canal dug to enable flatboats and barges to float up to the Works. He constructed a tiny railroad to shunt the ore to the smelter. There was every evidence of permanent prosperity. His works were said to be worth $250,000. Then iron ore with soft coal beds in close proximity was discovered in Pennsylvania. Charcoal became valueless. The new ore-beds were near railroads. Allaire could be but a feeble competitor when the competition came. His business dwindled and when he died he was "land poor." But "the excellent steam machinery turned out at his extensive foundry carried his name to every part of the world" (Bolton, I, 678). Some of the boats for which the Allaire Works built engines were the *Henry Eckford, Sun, Post Boy, Commerce, Pilot Boy, Swiftsure, Chancellor Livingston, Savannah, North River, Panama, Bay State,* and *Monita Puritan.* Allaire built the first compound-type engine ever applied to marine purposes in any country. He also had constructed in New York City in 1833 the first house designed exclusively for many tenants, a four-story building with each floor designed for but one family. He was twice married: first to Frances Roe, and later to Calicia Tompkins.

[Robert Bolton, *Hist. of the Several Towns, Manors, and Patents of the County of Westchester* (2 vols., 1881); C. H. Haswell, *Reminiscences of an Octogenarian* (1896); W. T. Bowman, *New York—The World Metropolis* (n. d.); and the *N. Y. Herald,* Nov. 3, 1901, all contain material on the Allaire Works and James P. Allaire; additional information from Miss Louise Allaire of Brooklyn, a distant cousin of James P. Allaire.]

E. Y.

ALLAN, JOHN (Jan. 3/14, 1746/7–Feb. 7, 1805), Revolutionary soldier, the eldest of the eight children of William and Isabella (Maxwell)

Allan, was born in Edinburgh Castle, Scotland. His father, a British soldier, took his family in 1749 to the newly founded town of Halifax, Nova Scotia, later settling on a tract of land, vacated by the Acadians in 1756, near Fort Cumberland. In early manhood, young Allan occupied such public positions as justice of the peace, clerk of the sessions, and clerk of the supreme court, meanwhile carrying on an agricultural and mercantile business. From 1770 to June 28, 1776 he was a member of the provincial Assembly. His sojourn in Massachusetts, where he had been sent sometime during his youth to complete his education, apparently led him to sympathize with the colonial cause. He became so active in organizing sentiment, particularly among the Indians, against the British government, that steps were taken to apprehend him on the charge of treason. Forced thus to flee the country, he arrived in Machias, Me., Aug. 13, 1776, leaving his wife, Mary Patton, whom he had married Oct. 10, 1767, and five children to suffer many hardships before they were allowed to join him. Later a reward of £100 was offered for his capture.

The Council of Massachusetts had already recognized the possibility that Nova Scotia might be induced to join its cause (Massachusetts Archives, CCXI, 435; CXLIV, 365). The Council in November 1776 and the Continental Congress in January 1777 received Allan sympathetically, the latter body appointing him its agent to the Eastern Indians. Under the general direction of the Massachusetts Council a plan was formulated (1) to protect the settlements in eastern Maine, (2) to prevent the British in Nova Scotia from communicating with those in Canada through the St. John River, (3) to free Nova Scotia from British control (*Documentary History of Maine*, XIV, 419; see also "Proposals for an attack on Nova Scotia" in *Nova Scotia Historical Society Collections*, II, 11–16). The St. John Expedition of June–August 1777 under Allan's leadership was a failure as a military movement because of lack of support. As an attempt to secure the friendship of the Indians, however, it was of value. Allan's knowledge of Indian character and dialects, and of French, gained in the course of trade, added to his resourcefulness, courage, and faith in the cause he represented, made him an ideal agent to the Indians. For the remainder of the war, Allan made his headquarters at Machias, of the garrison of which Massachusetts in September 1777 appointed him colonel. Though faced with extreme difficulties—lack of men, ammunition, and supplies for the Indian trade which would alone prevent the Indians from deserting to the British with disastrous effect to the Americans—he managed affairs with such skill that Machias remained the eastern outpost of the United States until the close of the war. To Allan's success must be attributed, in part at least, the fact that our northeast boundary is now the St. Croix and not the Kennebec.

Resigning his commission Apr. 15, 1783, Allan engaged in mercantile business on Allan's Island in Passamaquoddy Bay from 1784 to 1786, when he retired to Lubec Mills, where he lived until his death. He is buried on Allan's Island.

[Documents from the Mass. Archives are printed in the *Colls. Me. Hist. Soc., Second Ser., Documentary Hist.*, XIV–XX (1910–14). Frederic Kidder, *Military Operations in Eastern Me. and Nova Scotia during the Revolution* (1867), is a mine of source material. See also Papers of the Continental Cong. (Lib. of Cong.), *Jours. of the Continental Cong., Acts and Resolves of the Province of Mass. Bay, 1776–80; Sprague's Jour. of Me. Hist.*, II; *New Eng. Hist. and Geneal. Reg.*, XXX (1876), pp. 353–59.] R. E. M.

ALLEFONSCE, JEAN (*c.* 1482–*c.* 1557), French navigator, was born at Saintonge near Cognac. In 1534 Jacques Cartier, under orders from Francis I to discover a passage to Cathay, had visited the North American coasts of Newfoundland and Labrador. On a further voyage (1535) he had followed the St. Lawrence River as far as Hochelaga (Montreal). Determining to erect the newly discovered region into a viceroyalty, the King in 1540 selected Jean François de la Roque of Picardy, known as Roberval, to be virtual viceroy. Roberval set forth for America perhaps in April 1542, taking Jean Allefonsce with him as chief pilot, and reached Newfoundland June 8.

To Allefonsce fell the duty of exploration incident to finding, if possible, the much sought Western Passage. He entered the Gulf of St. Lawrence and may have ascended the St. Lawrence River to the Saguenay. Of the coasts visited, and of other coasts, he made sketch maps which have come down to us. These appeared in 1545 in a little manuscript treatise (*Cosmographie*) prepared for the King. The sketches include the Gulf of St. Lawrence and the region northward to Iceland, a portion of the St. Lawrence River, and the Saguenay as a strait leading into a great sea. "I think," says Allefonsce, "the same runs into the Sea of Cathay." Some of the sketches relate to the southern part of Newfoundland and the New England coast with the river Norumbega. A sketch shows the coast of Florida with the West Indies and part of South America. Allefonsce, it is interesting to note, makes mention of "the Isle St. Brandon and a large island called the Seven Cities, forming one large island; and there were many persons who have seen it, as well as myself, and can testify, but I do not know how things look in the interior for I did not land upon it. It is in 28° 30′ north latitude."

As a navigator Allefonsce was thought to possess unusual skill. But he was something of a corsair, adventurous, haughty, and apt to incur trouble. In 1559 there was published posthumously his *Voyages Avantureux,* and from this volume we learn that he met his death in a naval engagement "with Menendez, the Spaniard, near the reef of Rochelle."

[Voyages of Cartier 1534–40, Hakluyt, *Voyages* (MacLehose 1904), VIII, 183–274; same with "Voyage by John Alphonce chiefe Pilote to M. Roberval, 1542," VIII, 275–82, and "Voyage of John Francis de la Roche to . . . Camden, 1542," VIII, 283–89; Voyages of Cartier from Hakluyt, *Early English and French Voyages* (1906), ed. by H. S. Burrage; Justin Winsor, *Cartier to Frontenac* (1900), index under "Allefonsce," "Roberval" and "Cartier"; Benjamin F. De Costa, "Jacques Cartier and His Successors" (citing Henry Harrisse and others), in Winsor's *Narr. and Crit. Hist.,* IV, with Critical Essay by Justin Winsor, chap. II; consult index under "Allefonsce." For the sketch maps by Allefonsce, see Winsor, *Narr. and Crit. Hist.,* IV, 74–78; Francis Parkman, *Pioneers of France* (ed. 1901), index under "Roberval" and "Alphonsce"; E. G. Bourne, *Spain in America* (1904), chap. X, with bibliog. p. 333; J. P. Baxter, *Memoir of Jacques Cartier* (1906).]

I. B. R.

ALLEN, ALEXANDER VIETS GRISWOLD (May 4, 1841–July 1, 1908), Episcopal clergyman, educator, author, was born at Otis, Mass., the son of Ethan and Lydia Child (Burr) Allen. His father, who had been a teacher and had not been ordained until he was forty years old, was rector of a little Episcopal church there on a salary of $200 a year and free firewood. From here, when Alexander was about four years of age, he went to St. Paul's parish, Nantucket. There as elsewhere in this country at that time the Oxford movement was making trouble, and after ten rather unhappy years he took charge of a small church at Guilford, Vt. Under these straitened and, from most points of view, unpromising conditions, young Alexander grew up. Both father and mother were strongly evangelical, and in the mother there was a deep vein of mystical piety, which perhaps left traces in her son, though he was of a more intellectual type. How, when, and where he got his early education, except perhaps from his father, it is hard to imagine; but at the age of eighteen he entered the sophomore class of Kenyon College, Gambier, Ohio. This was then a strongly evangelical or Low Church institution, with the consequent limitations and disadvantages which belonged to the later period of the evangelical movement. Here may be said to have been the real beginning of Allen's intellectual life. He graduated at the head of his class in 1862 and the same year entered Bexley Hall, the theological seminary at Gambier, where he spent two years. During this period of his life his reaction from the evangelical party, as it was then represented, began. So strong was it that in 1863 he seems to have been almost on the point of rejecting historical Christianity. But he found help and relief in the study of S. T. Coleridge, the guide of so many ardent spirits tormented by the hardness and unreality of popular theology. Partly to escape from the conditions at Gambier, and partly for other reasons, he went to the Andover Theological Seminary. Here he found a different and more stimulating atmosphere, in which his intellectual horizon broadened. While a student at Andover he was made deacon by Bishop Eastburn of Massachusetts, in Emmanuel Church, Boston, July 5, 1865. On June 24, 1866, in St. John's Church, Framingham, he was ordained priest, and became rector of St. John's, Lawrence. In 1867 he was called to be instructor in church history in the new theological school at Cambridge, Mass., and became full professor in 1869. Here he remained until his death.

In 1872 he married Elizabeth Kent Stone, who died in 1892, and in 1907 he married Paulina Cony Smith. He was of medium size, rather inclined to stoutness, with soft light hair turning to gray in his later years, a sandy mustache, side whiskers, and a broad forehead over a pair of eyes almost hidden by glasses. His voice was peculiar in its softness, low and almost muffled, but flexible, expressive, and well adapted to the classroom. He was not a great scholar in the European sense of the word, but, judging by the almost unanimous testimony of his pupils, he was a great teacher. His first real appeal to the thinking world was his *Continuity of Christian Thought* (1884). It is his most original and distinctive work. He approached the subject from a standpoint new to most modern writers, beginning with Clement of Alexandria, rejecting the entire Latin tradition, and following the Greek entirely. As a consequence, his treatment of the great Latin theologians was not only sometimes wanting in justice, but even in understanding. He is also widely known for his *Life and Letters of Phillips Brooks* (2 vols., 1900). In addition to many contributions to magazines, he also published *Jonathan Edwards* (1889); *Religious Progress* (1894); *Christian Institutions* (1897); *Freedom in the Church* (1907).

[Charles Lewis Slattery, *Alexander Viets Griswold Allen, 1841–1908* (1911); C. J. Palmer, *The Life Work of Prof. A. V. G. Allen as Influenced by His Early Environment* (in MS.).]

S. Me—s.

ALLEN, ANDREW (June 1740–Mar. 7, 1825), Loyalist, second son of William Allen [*q.v.*], chief justice of Pennsylvania, and Margaret Hamilton Allen, was born at Philadelphia. He graduated from the University of Pennsylvania in 1759, studied law under Benjamin Chew and later in England (1761), and was admitted to practise before the Pennsylvania Supreme Court Apr. 20, 1765. He married Sally, eldest daughter of William Coxe of New Jersey, Apr. 21, 1768. On Nov. 4, 1769 he became attorney-general of the province, thus confirming his political and social position in Philadelphia. Before 1776 public opinion in Pennsylvania advanced slowly toward American independence. The Allens were influential advocates of a just administration with local self-government under the Crown. Recorder of Philadelphia in 1774 and elected to the Committee of Safety June 30, 1775, Allen was well fitted to serve his province. In the elections to the Assembly of May 1776, he tied for second place among the four members chosen by the city; but when in the Continental Congress he faced the question of American independence under a national government he hesitated, and later opposed the Declaration of 1776. This attitude curtailed his influence. Elected to Congress on Nov. 3, he resigned in December and sought Lord Howe's protection at Trenton. It has been assumed that this act was due to Washington's defeat at New York, and fear that the American cause was lost. In "A Letter from Philadelphia" Allen had already (1775), however, been termed "A Sworn Advocate for George III," and it is probable that his loyalty was due to conscientious scruples and family traditions. His preference for the British, his reported selection by Howe as lieutenant-governor of Pennsylvania, and his return to Philadelphia with that general on Dec. 26, 1777 destroyed Allen's standing among the Whigs; and when the tide favored the Americans he was attainted (March 1778), and his property confiscated by the state. With the close of the Revolution Loyalists were more kindly regarded, and in 1792 Allen was pardoned and revisited Philadelphia. Under the Jay Treaty of 1794 he attempted to recover money paid the state by his early debtors. Failing in this, Allen returned to England to live the remainder of his life with one of his seven children. He received a yearly pension of £400 from the Crown, dying in London Mar. 7, 1825, an English gentleman faithful to the tenets and teachings of his fathers.

[Allen Manuscripts in the Hist. Soc. of Pa.; *Pa. Arch.*, especially the first two series; Thompson Westcott, "Hist. of Phila." (section published in the *Sunday Dispatch*, May 2, 1875); C. P. Keith, *The Provincial Councillors of Pa.* (1883); J. H. Martin, *The Bench and Bar of Phila.* (1883); C. P. Keith, "Andrew Allen," in *Pa. Mag. of Hist. and Biog.*, vol. X; E. F. De Lancey, "Chief Justice Wm. Allen" in *Pa. Mag. of Hist. and Biog.*, vol. I.]

C. H. L—n.

ALLEN, ANTHONY BENEZET (June 24, 1802–Jan. 12, 1892), farmer, writer, manufacturer and dealer in farm machinery, the son of Ruth (Falley) Allen and Samuel Allen, was born in Hampshire County, Mass. The family later moving to New York, he received his education in the schools of that city. In 1833 he took up his residence in Buffalo, where he devoted himself to farming and the breeding of livestock. Of large stature, hazel eyes, fair, slightly florid complexion and expansive forehead, he was a striking figure. On a visit to England in 1841 he was impressed with the superiority of English livestock and at once resolved to import some of the best blood to start herds of pure blood stock in the United States and to begin a campaign of education in better breeding methods. To carry on such a campaign it was necessary to have a more effective means of reaching the public eye and ear. He therefore founded the *American Agriculturist* in 1842 in connection with his brother, Richard L. Allen [*q.v.*], and with contributions from his other brother, Lewis F. Allen [*q.v.*]. For fourteen years he was editor and owner of this paper, moving to New York City at the close of the first year. In 1852 he was married to Mary E. Butterworth. In 1856 he sold his paper to Orange Judd and devoted himself to the business of manufacturing and selling farm machinery. A warehouse for this purpose had been opened at 189 Water St., New York, in 1847. His trade rapidly extended all over the United States and even to the West Indies and South America. During his career as a manufacturer he took out many patents, chiefly for improvements in mowers, reapers, and plows. Farm machinery when he began business had been largely limited to crude cast-iron plows, a rough sort of harrow, hoes, and shovels. In 1867 he made another trip to England and also toured the continent of Europe studying farm methods to be used in improving American agriculture. All this time he supplied a constant stream of articles on a great variety of agricultural topics from plows to pigeons and from county fairs to rural schools. In 1870 he bought a farm on Toms River in Ocean County, N. J., where he passed his summers for the rest of his life, spending the winters at Flushing, L. I. But this Toms River adventure was by no means a retirement. A friend who visited him in his eighty-second year speaks of his tall, erect, elastic figure and of the numerous experiments he had in progress on his farm. He knew the history of every tree on his place and kept on planting more as if he should live forever to enjoy them. Perhaps the first impetus to the use of polled cattle in this country was given by Allen and he was also instrumental in introducing the improved Berkshire swine and pointing out their value and importance. Indeed between 1840 and 1892 his pen was seldom at rest, warning others of his mistakes, telling them about his successes, and always suggesting the possibility of still better crops, better livestock, better farm homes and more rural happiness. In fact, he never laid down his hoe or his pen till pneumonia, the arch enemy of old age, seized upon him in his ninetieth year.

[Obituary in the *Cultivator and Country Gentleman*, Jan. 21, 1892, p. 50; article by Geo. Thurber in *Am. Agriculturist*, Nov. 1884, p. 509; brief note in *N. Y. Tribune*, Jan. 13, 1892, p. 7.]

E. V. W.

ALLEN, CHARLES (Apr. 17, 1827–Jan. 13, 1913), jurist, was the son of Sylvester Allen who in 1812 established himself in business at Greenfield, Franklin County, Mass., where he became one of the leading merchants, and married Harriet, sister of George Ripley [*q.v.*], a woman of unusual refinement and intellectual keenness. Charles Allen was born at Greenfield, attended school there and at Deerfield Academy, and proceeded thence to Harvard (A.B., 1847). He entered the Harvard Law School, Sept. 9, 1848, but did not graduate, leaving in 1849 to study law with George T. Davis at Greenfield, by whom on his admission to the Northampton bar in 1850 he was taken into partnership. He remained at Greenfield for eleven years, engaging in general practise and actively interesting himself in local and municipal matters. In January 1861 he was appointed reporter to the supreme judicial court of Massachusetts and accordingly removed to Boston. His reports, covering the cases from January Term, 1861, to January Term, 1867, are of a high order, being distinguished for accuracy, clearness of diction, and simplicity of statement, and are always cited by his name (*Allen's Massachusetts Reports*, vols. I–XIV). In April 1867 he was elected attorney-general of Massachusetts and retained the position till 1872. In the latter year he resumed private practise in Boston. Despite the fact that he was retained in much important litigation, he edited a selection of *Telegraph Cases Decided in the Courts of America, Great Britain and Ireland* (1873). He was appointed chairman of the commission to revise the general statutes of Massachusetts, Apr. 13, 1880.

In 1881 he declined a position on the federal bench, but in response to the public sentiment of the bar, accepted an appointment as associate justice of the supreme judicial court of Massachusetts, Jan. 23, 1882. "Sitting at *nisi prius* his rulings were characterized by that accuracy and promptness which result from years of service as an advocate. Without being a martinet . . . the conduct of counsel and parties before him was held in firm restraint. He brooked no altercation and permitted no brow-beating. . . . When necessary his reprimand was swift and its effect final. . . . His words from the bench were few but they went to the bottom of the thing in hand" ("Memorial of Boston Bar Association," *214 Mass. R.*, 613). Though eligible for retirement in 1897 on attaining his seventieth birthday, he remained on the bench till Sept. 1, 1898, when he resigned. In 1900 he published *Notes on the Bacon-Shakespeare Question*, a volume of 284 pages, in which from the lawyer's standpoint he analyzed the evidence and maintained with great force that Bacon could not have written the plays. He experienced a paralytic stroke in June 1907, from which he never recovered, remaining a confirmed invalid till his death at Boston, Jan. 13, 1913. He was unmarried.

[Particulars of his ancestry and details of his life at Greenfield are contained in F. M. Thompson's *Hist. of Greenfield* (1904). A résumé of his career and an appreciation of his judicial work are embodied in the "Memorial" cited above. See also article in the *Green Bag*, XXV, Feb. 1913. Details of his work as attorney-general of Mass. are contained in the *Reports of the Attorney General* for the years 1867–71. His opinions while on the bench—some 700 in number—are contained in *CXXXII–CLXXI, Mass. Reports.*]

H. W. H. K.

ALLEN, DAVID OLIVER (Sept. 14, 1799–July 19, 1863), Congregational missionary, the son of Moses and Mehitable (Oliver) Allen and brother of Nathan Allen [*q.v.*], was born in Barre, Mass. He was educated in the academies of New Ipswich, N. H., and New Salem, Mass., in Williams, Union, and Amherst Colleges, and in Andover Theological Seminary. He graduated from Amherst in 1823 and from Andover in 1827. Toward the end of his senior year at Andover he was ordained at Westminster, Mass., to the Congregational ministry and foreign missionary service; at about the same time he was married to Myra Wood of Westminster. They sailed from Boston on June 5, 1827, and on Nov. 27 arrived at Bombay, where Allen was destined to serve conspicuously for a quarter-century. His first years in India were devoted of necessity to a study of language. In the use of Marathi he acquired considerable skill. He took upon himself at once such mission duties as he could perform and early showed marked capacity for leadership. After the death of his first wife on Feb. 5, 1831, he went frequently "on tour," leaving their small son Myron in the care of friends. His most significant work, however, was done in the city of Bombay. From 1827 to 1832 he was secretary of the Bombay Tract and Book Society. The following twenty years he was identified with the work of the British and Foreign Bible Society, serving for twelve years as secretary of its Bombay branch. He took an interest in the work of the Seaman's Friend Society, the Bombay Education Society, the Bombay District Benevolent Society, and for a brief period edited the *Temperance Advocate*. He was a member of the Royal Society and of the American Oriental Society. For the Mission itself he served for ten years as superintendent of its press and gave much time to the translation, revision, and publication of Scripture. He himself translated the books of Samuel and aided in the revision of previous versions of the New Testament. By Mar. 1, 1847, all of the books of the Bible had been rendered into Marathi. Thereafter, as "principal editor" on behalf of the Bible Society, Allen was chiefly engaged in the bringing out of the Marathi Bible in one volume in uniform type and improved version. After the actual printing of this edition (finished in 1855) had proceeded through II Samuel, he was forced to retire from active service because of broken health. On Feb. 12, 1853 he took final leave of India. His last three years were spent in Lowell, Mass., where his death occurred in his sixty-fourth year. He was married four times. Seven years after the death of his first wife, he married, Feb. 22, 1838, Orpah Graves who died June 5, 1842; on Dec. 12, 1843, he married Azuba Condit who died June 11, 1844; and on May 3, 1858 he married Mrs. Mary S. Barnes who survived him. In addition to his work as translator and editor, Allen was the author of several Marathi tracts, including a revision (1832) of Gordon Hall's *On the Worship of God;* a *Summary of the Holy Scriptures* (1833) after an original by Samuel Newell; an abridgment of the *Summary on Prayer* (1834), intended for children; and *A History of Our Saviour* (1834). He kept a voluminous journal, and wrote a worthy and comprehensive volume on *India, Ancient and Modern* (1856).

[Information may be found in Allen's Journal (see the *Missionary Herald*, 1832–42); *Am. Board Reports*, 1828–54; R. Anderson, *India Mission of the Am. Board* (1874); *Memorial Papers Am. Marathi Mission* (1882); *Centennial Volume Am. Marathi Mission* (1913); *Biog. Rec. Alumni Amherst Coll.* (1883).]

J. C. A.

ALLEN, ELISHA HUNT (Jan. 28, 1804–Jan. 1, 1883), congressman, diplomat, was the son of Samuel Clessen Allen, congressman, and Mary (Hunt) Allen, member of an influential family of the Connecticut Valley. He entered Williams College at fifteen, graduated second in his class, studied law with his father, and practised for a short time in Brattleboro, Vt. Late in 1828 he moved to Bangor and in a few years formed a partnership with John Appleton, subsequently chief justice of Maine. In 1835 he was elected to the Maine House of Representatives and served for five years, one as speaker. It was the time of the Northeastern Boundary controversy and Allen took a prominent part in urging a vigorous support of the rights of Maine. In 1840 he was elected a representative in Congress on the Whig ticket, defeating his personal friend, Hannibal Hamlin. In Congress he joined frequently in the debates, defending the Whig principles in regard to banking and protection. In 1846 he moved to Boston and in 1849 represented the city in the legislature. He then accepted a nomination as consul at Honolulu thinking that a few years in the tropics might benefit his health. The position of consul was one requiring much tact as the whale ships made Honolulu a rendezvous and there was often friction between the sailors and the natives, but Allen managed affairs with excellent judgment and his activity and eloquence were of great assistance in restoring order after Honolulu had for two days been in possession of a furious mob of between two and three thousand sailors. On the expiration of his consulship the King of Hawaii offered him the post of minister of finance, which he accepted and held until 1857, when he became chancellor and chief justice with a seat in the cabinet. He retained these positions for twenty years. A well-read lawyer and naturally of a judicial temperament, he discharged his judicial duties well, but the great object of his career was to secure the closest relations between Hawaii and the United States. While consul he carried a treaty of annexation with certain limitations to Washington but it was not accepted. As a Hawaiian official he made various similar attempts sometimes in person and sometimes by deputy and in 1876 had the pleasure of seeing the final conclusion of a treaty of reciprocity which also prevented Hawaii from granting similar privileges to any other nation or in any manner alienating any of its territory. In 1876 he was obliged to return to the United States because of the health of his wife. He was appointed Hawaiian minister and served for the remainder of his life, becoming by virtue of seniority dean of the diplomatic corps. He died suddenly at the President's New Year's reception on Jan. 1, 1883. He was twice married: his first wife was Sarah E. Fessenden of Brattleboro, Vt.; his second, Mary Harrod Hobbs of Bangor.

[The principal authority for Allen's life is a long sketch written by his son Frederick and a friend in Hawaii, Samuel E. Damon, and published in the *Biog. Encyc. of Me. of the Nineteenth Cent.* (1885), ed. by Henry Clay Williams; there is also a long obituary in the *Washington Post*, Jan. 2, 1883.]

L. C. H.

ALLEN, ELIZABETH CHASE AKERS. [See AKERS, ELIZABETH CHASE, 1832–1911.]

ALLEN, ETHAN (Jan. 10, 1737/8–Feb. 12, 1789), Revolutionary soldier, author, though identified with the history of Vermont, was born in Litchfield, Conn. His father, Joseph, great-grandson of Samuel Allen, who died in Windsor, Conn., in 1648, married Mary Baker, aunt of Remember Baker of Vermont fame. Ethan was their oldest son. Of his youth very little is known. He is said to have been preparing for college when his father died in 1755 (E. C. Starr, *History of Cornwall, Conn.*, 1926, p. 254). He served in the French and Indian War at Fort William Henry in 1757 (*Connecticut Historical Society Collections*, IX, 247). By 1769 he was probably resident in the New Hampshire Grants, as Vermont was then called, over the control of which New York and New Hampshire were having a lively controversy. As a result of this dispute the Green Mountain Boys were organized in 1770, with Allen as "colonel commandant" (Ira Allen, *Natural and Political History of the State of Vermont*, 1798, pp. 26–27). By December 1771 Allen had made his leadership so felt that Gov. Tryon of New York offered a reward of twenty pounds for his capture (E. B. O'Callaghan, *Documentary History of the State of New York*, 1851, IV, 749–50). In March 1774 this reward was increased to one hundred pounds (*Ibid.*, pp. 871–73). At the Westminster (Vt.) meeting in April 1775 he was appointed, with others, to draw up a remonstrance to the King, but the news of the battle of Lexington momentarily quieted affairs in Vermont, and Allen received instructions from Connecticut to capture Fort Ticonderoga. Consequently at dawn on May 10, 1775, he entered the fort, with Col. Arnold by his side, and demanded its immediate surrender (*Connecticut Historical Society Collections*, vol. I). In September he went on the expedition against Canada, where he was captured by the British in a foolhardy attempt to surprise Montreal. For over two years he was held prisoner, being finally exchanged at New York, May 6, 1778, for Col. Archibald Campbell. Immediately afterward he received from Gen. Washington the brevet rank of colonel (F. B. Heitman, *Historical Register*, p. 67). He returned at once to Vermont and was soon actively engaged in local affairs. In September 1778 he presented the Vermont claims to the Continental Congress without success. Soon afterwards he was given command of the Vermont militia with rank of major-general, and commenced a petty warfare against the New York settlers.

In July 1780 Allen received a letter from Col. Beverly Robinson which opened a correspondence with Gen. Haldimand, commander of the British forces in Canada. Together with his brothers Ira [*q.v.*] and Levi Allen he was deeply implicated in an attempt to negotiate a treaty with Great Britain, which would have made Vermont a province of that country. Whether the Allens actually wanted this, or were merely trying to force Congress to recognize Vermont as a separate state, has never been determined. Ethan, however, took no further part in the Revolution, but gave his attention to Vermont affairs and the management of his farms. In 1787 he settled in Burlington, where, two years later, he died of apoplexy. A granite shaft, erected in 1855, stands near his grave. Allen was a man of strong physique, courageous, impulsive in all his actions, prone to daring exploits, and inclined to appeal to force rather than reason. No portrait is known to exist, but there are idealistic statues by Mead in Montpelier and Washington. He was twice married: first, in 1762, to Mary, daughter of Cornelius and Abigail (Jackson) Bronson, who died at Sunderland, Vt., in 1783, having borne him five children; second, in 1784, to Mrs. Frances (Montresor) Buchanan, by whom he had three more children.

Allen was the author of several books and pamphlets, as well as many controversial contributions to various New England newspapers: 1. *A Brief Narrative of the Proceedings of the Government of New York Relative to Their Obtaining the Jurisdiction of that Large District of Land to the Westward from Connecticut River* (Hartford, 1774). 2. *An Animadversory Address to the Inhabitants of the State of Vermont* (1778). 3. *A Vindication of the Opposition of the Inhabitants of Vermont to the Government of New York* (1779). 4. *A Narrative of Col. Ethan Allen's Captivity* (1779), of which many editions were printed. In it Allen fails to mention Arnold's share in the capture of Ticonderoga, and is vituperative about the British. 5. *A Concise Refutation of the Claims of New Hampshire and Massachusetts Bay to the Territory of Vermont* (1780). 6. *The Present State of the Controversy Between the States of New York and New Hampshire on the One Part and the State of Vermont on the Other* (1782). 7. *Reason the Only Oracle of Man; Or, A Compenduous System of Natural Religion* (Bennington, 1784), a curious book, of which this first edition is excessively rare, most of it having been destroyed by fire at the printer's, and practically all of the remainder having been burned by the printer because of its "atheistic" content.

[Authorities in addition to those cited: Wm. Slade, *State Papers* (1823); *Recs. of the Council of Safety and Gov. and Council of the State of Vt.*, vols. I–III (1873–

75); *Vt. Hist. Soc. Coll.* (1870–71); Ethan Allen Papers (MSS.), and Stevens Papers (MSS.), in Montpelier; B. H. Hall, *Hist. of Eastern Vt.* (1858); Hiland Hall, *Hist. of Vt.* (1868); Samuel Williams, *Natural and Civil Hist. of Vt.* (1794). There is no satisfactory biography, but Hugh Moore's *Memoir of Col. Ethan Allen* (1834), Jared Sparks's *Life of Col. Ethan Allen* (1858), Henry W. DePuy's *Ethan Allen and the Green Mountain Heroes of '76* (1853), and Henry Hall's *Ethan Allen, the Robin Hood of Vt.* (1892) should be mentioned. There is a bibliography in M. D. Gilman's *Bibliog. of Vt.* (1897), pp. 5–7.] G. H. D.

ALLEN, FREDERIC DE FOREST (May 25, 1844–Aug. 4, 1897), classical scholar, was born at Oberlin, Ohio, of old New England stock. The family can be traced from Samuel Allen, who settled in Braintree, Mass., about 1629, and whose daughter Sarah married Josiah, the son of Miles Standish. Frederic's father, George Nelson Allen, set out for Ohio in 1832 under the influence of his pastor, Lyman Beecher. He was taken ill and kindly cared for at Hudson, Ohio, where the Western Reserve College had been recently established, and there he studied at the preparatory school and the college for five years, at the end of which he went to Oberlin, where he was graduated in 1838. Three years later he married Mary Rudd, who had just received the degree of bachelor of arts. She and two classmates were the first women to receive that degree at Oberlin and were probably the first women in the world to receive the degree in course. Her father, Hezekiah Rudd, is said to have conducted a school for boys at Stratford, Conn. Her mother, Maria De Forest Rudd, was descended from a French family which had been among the first settlers of Harlem, N.Y. She was a woman of marked scholarly tastes and great strength of mind and character. In the year of his marriage, George N. Allen was appointed instructor in Oberlin College, where he taught music and natural science until 1871. Frederic Allen was, therefore, bred in an atmosphere of intellectual culture amid the rural and intensely religious surroundings of the small college and village of the Oberlin of that time. He was graduated from the College in 1863, at nineteen years of age. In his undergraduate days he showed no strong inclination for classical studies, but read widely in the best French literature. He taught school in one or more of the long winter vacations, on one occasion in the small village of Brecksville, near Cleveland. After his graduation he taught for about two years in a school at Sewickley, Pa., and for a few months at the Blind Asylum in St. Louis. During this time he turned eagerly to the study of the classics, and in 1866 was appointed professor of Greek and Latin at the University of East Tennessee, at Knoxville. In 1868 he obtained leave of absence and went to Leipsig to study under Georg Curtius. Here he remained two years, taking active part in the work of Prof. Curtius's Grammatische Gesellschaft and winning the respect of the scholars of the University. He obtained the degree of doctor of philosophy in 1870, with a dissertation *De Dialecto Locrensium,* which gives clear signs of his ability as a philological investigator.

Returning to Knoxville, Allen resumed his former position, but in 1873 he was called to Harvard University as tutor in Greek. The next year he was called to the newly founded University of Cincinnati. Here, although chiefly occupied with the work of his department, he found time to prepare his excellent edition of the *Medea* of Euripides, a treatise on the meter of Homer, and his *Remnants of Early Latin,* a small but important book. In 1879 he accepted a call to the chair of Greek in Yale University; but he remained there only one year, for in 1880 he was called to be professor of classical philology at Harvard, a position which gave him relatively few hours of classroom teaching, and most of those with graduate students. Here he was in his element and could bring to bear upon his daily work his wide and profound knowledge of the ancient languages, and of the literature, life, and thought of the Greeks and Romans. The academic year 1885–86 he spent in Greece as director of the American School of Classical Studies at Athens; but his health was so poor that he had to relinquish his plans for excursions in the country. His eldest daughter, then his only child, died at Athens. He had been married on Dec. 26, 1878, to Emmeline Laighton of Portsmouth, N. H., of a well-known family of that state. She was a charming woman, with great love of music, which was also Allen's chief recreation. He composed the music for the *Phormio* of Terence and for a pantomime and an operetta of his friend Prof. James B. Greenough. After his death the manuscript of an operetta, with words and music complete, was found in his desk. Few scholars have understood Greek music as well as he.

Allen was never robust, for he suffered severely at various times from sciatica and asthma, and during the latter part of his life from hay-fever, and, worst of all, from violent sick-headaches. To escape from hay-fever he used to go to the White Mountains, where he tramped and climbed among the heights for several weeks of each summer. While riding a bicycle from Cambridge toward Portsmouth, Aug. 4, 1897, he was stricken with apoplexy and died without recovering consciousness.

Allen's published work is for the most part in the form of articles in periodicals and encyclopedias. His only books are *Remnants of Early*

Latin (1880); a revision, with many changes and additions, of Hadley's *Greek Grammar* (1884); and editions of the *Medea* of Euripides (1876) and the *Prometheus Bound* of Æschylus (1891). In the last the notes and introduction are translated from the German of N. Wecklein. Of his numerous articles perhaps the most important is "On Greek Versification in Inscriptions," in the *Papers of the American School of Classical Studies at Athens,* Volume IV, 1888, pp. 37–204. At the time of his death he had been working for some years on an edition of the scholia of Plato.

[Thos. D. Seymour, "Frederic De Forest Allen," in *Am. Jour. of Philology,* XVIII, 373–75; Jas. B. Greenough, "Memoir of Frederic De Forest Allen," in *Harvard Studies in Classical Philology,* IX, 27–36, with portrait and bibliography.]

H. N. F.

ALLEN, GEORGE (Dec. 17, 1808–May 28, 1876), educator, Episcopal clergyman, author, was the son of Sarah (Prentiss) Allen and Heman Allen, a successful lawyer, distinguished judge, and member of Congress. Though born at Milton, Vt., George Allen considered himself "a native of Burlington." His first steps toward scholarship followed a well-marked path. "My earliest instruction in Greek and Latin," he wrote, "was given partly by students in my father's office, by students of the University of Vermont, such as may have happened to keep our district school of winters, and partly by the principal of an academy at Burlington . . ." (*Penn Monthly,* Aug. 1876, p. 648). At sixteen he was sent to Canada, where he studied French in the household of Father Consigny and acquired a sympathetic understanding of Roman Catholicism. In 1823 he entered the University of Vermont, where, he wrote, "the classical instruction was at first miserable, contemptible. . . . My best studies I made by myself . . ." (*Ibid.,* p. 649). Nevertheless he was influenced by Robertson, Porter, and Marsh, the latter, particularly, awakening his interest in Coleridge, Wordsworth, and the German Romanticists. He graduated in 1827.

He began his teaching in an academy at Georgia, Vt. Of this experience he later wrote, "You will laugh to hear me say that I even taught Mathematics and Natural Philosophy, quite furiously." From 1828 to 1830 he filled a vacancy in Languages, which was the occasion for beginning serious classical study. He said, "I did five years' reading during those eighteen months." During 1830 he studied law and was admitted to the bar in 1831. On July 7 of the same year he married Mary Hancock Withington. After his father was elected to Congress, he gave some attention to the law office, but soon slighted it for a newly awakened interest in religion and the church. In 1832 he was confirmed and began to study Hebrew and theology, while he taught classics at the Vermont Episcopal Institute. In May 1834 he was ordained and began to preach. Because of ill health, the strenuous combination of two professions was relinquished, and he accepted the rectorship of a church in St. Albans, where he spent three happy and significant years. With the practise in sermon writing, he experienced a "reawakening of a literary spirit, more intense and enthusiastic . . . than I had ever known before. . . ." The reawakening bore fruit in an article, "The Study of Works of Genius," published in the *New York Review,* and in his justly celebrated "Critical Review" of McVickar's edition of Coleridge's *Aids to Reflection* (*Churchman,* Mar. 7 to May 9, 1840).

In 1837 he returned to teaching, and continued in that profession till his death. For eight years he was professor of Languages in Delaware College, whence he was called in 1845 to the chair of Latin and Greek at the University of Pennsylvania. In 1864 he was made professor of Greek. About the middle of the century a movement began having as its objective a greater university with curtailment of the college. This found expression in a much-discussed "Letter and By-Laws," reported by the trustees Nov. 3, 1852. To the views of the letter and its proposals Allen raised vigorous objections in a closely reasoned statement covering twenty-one pages. In 1847 he startled, and even alienated, some of his friends by becoming a Catholic. This sudden and superficially inexplicable change was due to several factors,—notably, his life and study in the household of Father Consigny, the secession of a number of the Oxford group to join the Roman church, and the fact that he had defended Mr. Hoyt, former associate and close friend, who had taken a similar action a year earlier. Allen served, for a time, as counsel in Philadelphia for Pope Pius IX.

Besides classical literature, Allen cultivated an interest in music, chess, and military science. His published works include *The Remains of W. S. Graham* (1849); *The Life of Philidor* (1863); *The History of the Automaton Chess Player in America* (1859), and many articles for the *United States Service Magazine,* edited by Coppée. His chess collection, about 1,000 volumes, was the best in the United States when, at his death, it was purchased by the Library Company of Philadelphia. Though his scholarly attainments were well known and recognized by such men as Hadley, Felton, and Woolsey, he published no contribution to classical scholarship. As a teacher, however, he had few rivals. His colleagues united in saying of him: "He wanted no one of the qualities of the finished gentleman, the polished scholar, the efficient instructor . . . he taught with brilliant success . . . [and] as a scholar, especially in Greek literature, he combined the nicest accuracy with a broad range of attainment . . ." (*Penn Monthly,* July 1876, p. 574).

[The best accounts of George Allen are: *An Autobiographical Fragment,* in the *Penn Mo.,* Aug. 1876; a sketch by R. E. Thompson, *Penn Mo.,* July 1876; and W. G. Smith's *George Allen: An Address to the Soc. of Alumni of the Univ. of Pa.,* June 13, 1900. The Archives of the Univ. of Pa., especially 1849–64, contain significant letters, which, with unpublished essays and lectures, help to form an accurate estimate of his work. For family hist. see C. J. F. Binney, *Hist. and Geneal. of the Prentice, or Prentiss, Family in New Eng.* (1883), p. 306.]

T. W.

ALLEN, HARRISON (Apr. 17, 1841–Nov. 14, 1897), anatomist and physician, was born at Philadelphia, the son of Samuel Allen and his wife, Elizabeth Thomas. After graduating from the Philadelphia Central High School he began the study of dentistry under Dr. Josiah Foster Flagg [*q.v.*], a cultivated man of great artistic ability, who had graduated in medicine at Harvard but had subsequently devoted himself to dentistry. Flagg had done considerable work in anatomical illustration, and although Allen only remained in his office for one year he was undoubtedly greatly influenced by Flagg throughout his subsequent career. Allen studied medicine at the University of Pennsylvania and at the end of the necessary two years' course received his degree of M.D. in 1861. He then served for one year as a resident physician in the Philadelphia Hospital. In 1862 he was appointed an acting assistant surgeon in the United States Army and a few months later was commissioned assistant surgeon. His duties during the Civil War were chiefly in hospitals in Washington or its vicinity. Dr. Horatio C. Wood [*q.v.*], who served under Allen when the latter was in command at a military hospital in Alexandria, Va., pays a high tribute to the executive ability he manifested in this capacity. Allen resigned from the Army in 1865 with the brevet rank of major and began practising medicine in Philadelphia, devoting himself to diseases of the nose and throat.

As one of the pioneer American laryngologists he acquired great eminence in his special field, particularly for his dexterity as an operator, but his real calling was comparative anatomy and his most important contributions dealt with it. Every minute that he could spare from his practise was spent at the Academy of Natural Sciences or in the Philadelphia School of Anatomy. In 1864 the Smithsonian Institution published his very important *Monograph of the Bats of North America,* which was republished in 1893, and is still regarded as authoritative on that subject. From 1865 until the last year of his life the *Proceedings* of the Academy of Natural Sciences of Philadelphia contained numerous communications from his pen. In 1869 he published his *Outlines of Comparative Anatomy and Medical Zoology,* of which a second edition appeared in 1877. In 1875 he published *Analysis of the Life Form in Art,* a work which possessed great value for artists and was duly appreciated by them. His *System of Human Anatomy, Including Its Medical and Surgical Relations* (1884) was greatly esteemed by other anatomists, but was too erudite and elaborate to achieve general success. He did an immense amount of work on craniology, making comparative studies of skulls from the Florida mounds, the Hawaiian Islands, and elsewhere, and deducing many valuable conclusions from his investigations. These studies were published in the transactions of various societies and have never been collected in book form. H. C. Wood in the bibliography appended to his *Memoir of Allen* lists ninety-seven (non-medical) scientific articles from his pen. In 1865 Allen was appointed professor of zoology and comparative anatomy in the Auxiliary Faculty of Medicine at the University of Pennsylvania, and in 1879 professor of the institutes of medicine in the same institution. This chair he resigned in 1885 to resume his previous position as professor of zoology and comparative anatomy. Allen was also professor of anatomy and surgery in the Pennsylvania Dental College from 1866 to 1878, and was at one time or another on the staff of the Philadelphia Hospital, the Wills Eye Hospital, and St. Joseph's Hospital. He was one of the founders of the American Laryngological Association and a member and at one time president of the Association of American Anatomists and the Anthropomorphic Society. He was a Fellow of the College of Physicians of Philadelphia and a member of the Pathological Society and a constant attendant at their meetings. Of a modest, retiring disposition, he inspired affection and respect in his colleagues, patients, and friends. He was married in December 1869 to Julia A. Colton, daughter of S. W. Colton of Massachusetts.

[Horatio C. Wood, memoir in *Trans. Coll. Physicians of Phila., 1898,* vol. XX, 3rd series; B. G. Wilder, memoir in the *Proc. Ass. of Am. Anatomists,* Dec. 1897; C. R. Bardeen, biog. sketch in Kelly and Burrage, *Am. Medic. Biogs.* (1920); personal recollections. There is an excellent oil painting of Allen in the Hall of the College of Physicians in Philadelphia.]

F. R. P.

ALLEN, HENRY WATKINS (Apr. 29, 1820–Apr. 22, 1866), Confederate soldier, governor of Louisiana, the son of Dr. Thomas and Ann (Watkins) Allen, was born in Prince Edward County, Va. In 1833, Dr. Allen removed to Kay County, Mo., with his then motherless children. He placed Henry in a store in Lexington, Mo., with the intention of making him a merchant. The boy, however, finding business distasteful, entered Marion College, Mo., where he remained for two years. Running away from college at the age of seventeen, he established himself as a teacher in Grand Gulf, Miss. His nights were given to the study of law, and he soon entered that profession. He was gaining a practise when his legal career was interrupted by a call for volunteers for the Texas army issued by President Houston in 1842. Romantically inclined, Allen joined the rush of Southern boys for Texas and remained there for six months, showing a marked aptitude for military affairs. Returning to Grand Gulf and the law, he fell in love with Salome Crane, the young daughter of a Mississippi planter. Parental opposition led to an elopement and a duel in which Allen was seriously wounded. Crane eventually forgave his daughter and established the young couple on a plantation in Claiborne County, Miss. Here Allen lived happily for several years until the death of his wife. He then removed to Tensas Parish, La., and in 1852 to West Baton Rouge, La. He was in ill health for some time but eventually recovered. In 1853 he was elected to the Louisiana legislature. In the following year he went to Harvard to study law. Still romantic, his sympathies were so engaged in the Italian struggle for freedom that he sailed with the intention of enlisting under Garibaldi. On reaching Europe he found that the war was over and he then made an extensive tour of the continent. The result of his experiences was a book, *The Travels of a Sugar Planter* (1861).

While away from home he was reëlected to the legislature. On his return to Louisiana he engaged in various public matters and gained a wide popularity. He seemed destined for a successful career in politics when the opening of the Civil War changed his life. He enlisted at the very beginning as a private but was quickly elected lieutenant-colonel of the 4th Louisiana Regiment. His first service was as commander of a part of the regiment at Ship Island off the Mississippi coast. Here he suppressed an incipient mutiny and drilled his troops into efficiency. In March 1862 he became colonel of the 4th Louisiana, which was ordered to join Beauregard in Tennessee. He led his regiment at Shiloh, on Apr. 6, 1862, and was wounded in the face but refused to leave the field. In the defense of Vicksburg in 1862 he played a conspicuous part. He accompanied Breckinridge in the expedition against Baton Rouge, then held by the Unionists, as the commander of a Louisiana brigade. In the attack on Baton Rouge, on Aug. 5, 1862, Allen distinguished himself by his gallantry but was badly wounded by a shell fragment which shattered his right leg. He refused to have the limb amputated and succeeded in saving it, but at the cost of terrible suffering and eventually of his health. Although virtually incapacitated for field duty he was appointed a brigadier-general in September 1863 and ordered to the Trans-Mississippi Department. Soon after his arrival at Shreveport he was elected governor of Louisiana, almost by acclamation.

Allen's opportunity had arrived. When he was inaugurated on Jan. 25, 1864, he found the state in a desperate condition. East of the Mississippi it was overrun by the Unionists and lost; west of the river the people were starving. Everything was in chaos. Allen immediately went to work to save the almost hopeless situation. Gathering sugar and cotton, he exported them to Mexico and exchanged them for the commodities of which the state stood in dire need: dry-goods, cotton and woolen cards, machinery, and many other things. Luxuries were rigidly excluded. He established a system of state stores, factories and foundries, and a dispensary where medicines were sold at a low price. Some of them were manufactured by Allen himself: he had a turpentine distillery, a castor-oil works, and a place for making carbonate of soda. Importing iron ore from Texas, he made various articles of iron. By accepting Louisiana money at the state stores, he largely restored its value; and Confederate currency, almost worthless elsewhere, had purchasing power west of the Mississippi. Quantities of ordnance stores and army supplies were brought from Mexico in mule wagons driven by Mexicans and negroes. Food and clothing were distributed to the suffering. The state actually advertised for the names of disabled Louisiana soldiers who needed support. The sale of alcoholic beverages was stopped in Allen's realm. The distillation of grain was permittted only in the state distillery, and the alcohol was used only for medicinal purposes. Such of the state charitable institutions as continued to exist were supported by cotton sales. In brief, Allen rescued the population of west Louisiana from the direst straits and in some degree restored industry.

One of his greatest services came after Lee's surrender. The Trans-Mississippi Department was actually stronger in 1865 than it had been before. The Confederates had defeated every effort of the Unionists to penetrate into west Louisiana and Texas, and were obtaining supplies of all kinds from Mexico. Kirby Smith, the military commander, contemplated continuing the war. His army was still intact and, materially, was in good condition. When first summoned by the Unionists to surrender, he prepared a message of defiance. Allen persuaded Smith not to send this message but to wait. His judgment was justified by circumstances. So great was the confidence felt in him that he was empowered by Texas, Arkansas, and the Confederate governor of Missouri to conduct negotiations for surrender. Soon the army began to break up and then the military authorities gave up the contest. It is probable that but for Allen's stand for peace, Louisiana would have suffered invasion and devastation.

With the struggle over, Allen felt that he could no longer remain in Louisiana; his prominence both as a military commander and a war governor marked him out for punishment. Accordingly, like many other Confederates, he decided to try his fortunes in a foreign land. The decision was stern, for he was almost penniless and in bad health, as he had never recovered from his wounds. Borrowing a few hundred dollars from a friend, he made his way to Mexico, where he was well received by Maximilian. His popularity in Louisiana remained so great that he was proposed for governor in October 1865, although ineligible and an exile. In Mexico City Allen established an English newspaper that gave every promise of permanency. But his health soon gave way completely and most of his career in Mexico was a battle with death. He thought of going to Europe for medical aid but died in Mexico City on Apr. 22, 1866. Allen was the single great administrator produced by the Confederacy. His success in Louisiana indicates that he might have changed history to some extent if his talents could have been utilized by the Confederate government on a large scale.

[*Confed. Mil. Hist.*, vol. X (1899); S. E. Dorsey, *Recollections of Henry W. Allen* (1866); H. E. Chambers, *Hist. of La.* (1925).] D. S. F.

ALLEN, HORATIO (May 10, 1802–Dec. 31, 1899), civil engineer, inventor, was born in Schenectady, N. Y. His father, Dr. Benjamin Allen, was professor of mathematics and natural philosophy at Union College from 1800 to 1809; his mother was Mary Benedict Allen, a woman of superior culture and high social standing. When he was eight years old his father became principal of a large preparatory school at Hyde Park, N. Y.; and it was from there that young Allen entered Columbia College. He received his A.B. degree with the class of 1823, attaining high honors in mathematics. Immediately thereafter he began the study of law, but within a year decided that an engineering profession was more to his liking, and, after a year spent with the Chesapeake & Delaware Canal Company at St. George's, Del., he joined the engineering staff of the Delaware & Hudson Company as a resident engineer. In this capacity he assisted in the construction of a portion of the company's canal, and apparently showed marked ability as an engineer and unusual resourcefulness, for in 1828, when the company decided to use locomotives at the western terminus of the canal, Allen, although not yet twenty-six years of age, was delegated to go to England as the company's representative to purchase them. He was given certain specifications for the locomotives, but many points of considerable importance were left to his discretion. When it is recalled that there was no steam locomotive in service in the United States at that time and that Allen did not have the ready means of communicating with his superiors that exist to-day, the importance of the commission entrusted to him may be realized. Four locomotives were contracted for and when the first was tried out at Honesdale, Pa., Aug. 9, 1829, Allen operated it. "Thus," he wrote, "on this first movement by steam on railroad on this continent, I was engineer, fireman, brakeman, conductor, and passenger." In September of that year Allen accepted the position of chief engineer of the South Carolina Railroad Company to construct its railroad from Charleston to Augusta, Ga. He was influential in introducing locomotives as the motive power on this railroad, making the following quaint contention, "There is no reason to expect any material improvement in the breed of horses in the future while, in my judgment, the man is not living who knows what the breed of locomotives is to place at command." Under Allen's direction, the West Point Foundry in New York City built a locomotive (the first ever constructed for sale in the United States) for the railroad company and, after its christening as the "Best Friend of Charleston," it was put in service in December 1830.

Allen remained in Charleston until 1835 when he and his wife, Mary Moncrief Simons, daughter of Rev. James Dewar Simons, of Charleston, whom he had married in 1834, went abroad and spent three years in foreign travel. On their return they settled in New York City. Allen almost immediately was appointed assistant principal engineer of the Croton Aqueduct. He was also at the same time a consulting engineer for the New York & Erie Railroad Co. In 1842 he became one of the proprietors of the Novelty Iron Works in New York City, the firm being known as Stillman, Allen & Co. This company specialized in the building of marine engines and during the Civil War employed about 1,500 men; it constructed many of the engines of American-built steamships of that time and later. Allen continued as consultant for the Erie Railroad for many years and was its president in 1843. He retired from active business in 1870 but continued as a consulting engineer for a number of years thereafter. His most important services in this connection were in the construction of the famous Brooklyn Bridge and the Panama Railroad.

Allen's interests covered a wide range of subjects. He devoted much time in his later years to the subject of education, particularly to the teaching of astronomy. He published *Astronomy in its General Facts and Relations, Taught by Aid of Mechanical Presentation and Illustration* (1877) and constructed many instruments to facilitate the teaching of it in the schools. While connected with the Novelty Iron Works he devoted considerable time to the improvement of the cut-off valve mechanism of steam-engines and received three United States patents, nos. 2,227, 2,597, and 18,837 between the years 1841 and 1857. He also patented a rotary steam-valve. He was one of the founders of the Union League Club of New York City, and took an active interest in philanthropic and charitable matters. He was honored with the presidency of the American Society of Civil Engineers in 1872, and was one of the organizers of the New York Gallery of Art. He died at his residence "Homewood," near South Orange, N. J., leaving a widow, three daughters, and a son.

[*A Century of Progress: Hist. of the Del. & Hudson Co.* (1925); *Railroad & Engineering Jour.*, vol. LXIV, nos. 2, 3, and 4; *Cassier's Mag.*, Oct. 1896; Recs. of the U. S. Museum; Recs. of the U. S. Pat. Office.]

C. W. M.

ALLEN, IRA (May 1, 1751–Jan. 15, 1814), Vermont political leader, the youngest son of Joseph and Mary (Baker) Allen, was born at Cornwall, Conn. Of his youth and education practically nothing is known. By 1772 he, together with his brothers Ethan [*q.v.*], Heman, Heber, and Levi, was actively interested in the affairs of the New Hampshire Grants (*i. e.* Vermont), where he had received grants of land, and was a member of the regiment of Green Mountain Boys. He was not by nature a soldier; consequently after his first participation in the Dorset Convention of July 1776 as the representative of the town of Colchester, he devoted by far the greater part of his time to the political affairs of the embryo state. His rise to political power was rapid, due to his keen mind and love of statecraft. He took a prominent part in the Windsor Convention, where he, with Thomas Chittenden and others, was selected to draw up the constitution of the state, which had declared its independence on Jan. 17, 1777. He wrote the preamble of that document, the remainder of which was copied from the Pennsylvania constitution with a few additions. At the same time he was made secretary of the Council of Safety, virtually sharing the powers of the president of that body. Under the constitution, which was adopted in December 1777, he was elected a member of the Governor's Council and first treasurer of the state in March 1778. He was, after that, many times the official representative of the state in its negotiations with New Hampshire and other states for the recognition of Vermont's independence. As recognition was not forthcoming from the Continental Congress, Allen, with his brother Ethan, who had been approached in 1780 in the matter by Col. Beverly Robinson, a Loyalist, became interested in the possibility of a separate peace and alliance with Great Britain. Ostensibly to negotiate for the exchange of prisoners, Allen went to Isle aux Noix early in May 1781 to meet Gen. Haldimand's representative, Maj. Dundas. While there he had a secret conference with Capt. Justus Sherwood, a Loyalist in the service of Haldimand, regarding a treaty, under the terms of which Vermont was to become a British province, with her borders guarded by British troops.

Conclusive evidence as to Allen's motive in this affair has never been forthcoming. On the face of it the Allens seem to have entered the negotiations in the hope of forcing the Continental Congress to recognize the independence of Vermont (*Vermont Historical Society Collections,* II, 104–5); ultimately they appear to have become convinced that a British alliance was necessary to insure the autonomy of the territory, since the New York representatives were still powerful enough to prevent Congress from coming to terms (*Records of the Governor and Council of the State of Vermont,* I, 472–74). The proclamation of the cessation of hostilities in April 1783 put a stop to active negotiation on the part of the British, whose interest in Vermont had been for the most part a strategic one, but the Allens, particularly Levi, who had in 1779 been publicly condemned by Ethan as a Loyalist (William Slade, *Vermont State Papers,* p. 563), continued to foster the idea of making Vermont a British province, mainly for commercial reasons, as Vermont was then virtually an independent republic and remained so until she was admitted to the Union as a state in 1791. Levi Allen was in London in 1789–91, not, however, as the accredited representative of the state, attempting to bring about the alliance. He returned to Vermont in 1791, and died in jail ten years later, having been imprisoned for debt (*American Historical Review,* XXI, 547–60; *Records of the Governor and Council,* III, 399–410).

Meanwhile, Ira was negotiating for commercial treaties with Quebec, and furthering other interests of the same kind. In 1789 he gave land valued at £4,000 to assist the founding of the University of Vermont. In 1795 he went to England to buy arms for the Vermont militia, of which he was then major-general. He bought his munitions in France, however, and sailed for home with them in the *Olive Branch,* which was captured by the British in November 1796. A long litigation ensued and Allen spent large sums in carrying the fight through the British courts, which finally decided in his favor. A question was raised regarding the purpose for which the arms were purchased, but Allen's explanation was accepted. He published, in London, in 1798, his *Natural and Political History of the State of Vermont,* which, although not strictly accurate, is valuable in that it was written by one of the principal pioneers of the state. In the same year he issued the *Particulars of the Capture of the Ship Olive Branch.* In 1801 he returned to America to find that his party had lost power, and that much of his property had been seized. He was immediately arrested and thrown into prison in Burlington, but was released by order of the legislature and granted immunity from arrest for one year. He fled to Philadelphia, where he spent the remainder of his life, attempting to recuperate his fortune, revising and reissuing his account of the *Olive Branch* affair, and revising his *History* (which was never reissued). He died there of "retrocedent gout" on Jan. 15, 1814 (*Vermont Historical Society Proceedings,* 1917–18, pp. 180–81). He had married, about 1789, Jerusha, daughter of Gen. Roger and Jerusha (Hayden) Enos, who bore him three children, of whom only Ira H. survived to maturity (*Ibid.,* p. 144, note regarding supposed early marriage to Lucinda Miner, and issue by her). Allen was a man of medium stature, polished in his appearance, and inclined to the niceties of good living, although he could and did endure the hardships of pioneer life. He published in addition to the books mentioned several controversial pamphlets, which are listed in M. D. Gilman's *Bibliography of Vermont* (1897), pp. 8–9.

[In addition to the references given above, see the various histories of Vermont cited under Ethan Allen, Ethan Allen MSS., and Stevens MSS., in Montpelier; Canadian Archives, series Q, in Ottawa; Clinton Papers, in Ann Arbor; Colonial Papers in Pub. Rec. Office, London; Allen letters published in *Vt. Hist. Soc. Proc.,* 1917–18, pp. 144–89; geneal. details in O. P. Allen, *The Allen Memorial,* 2nd ser. (1907), pp. 54–56.]

G. H. D.

ALLEN, JAMES LANE (Dec. 21, 1849–Feb. 18, 1925), novelist, short-story writer, the seventh and youngest child of Richard and Helen (Foster) Allen, was born on a farm near Lexington, Ky. On his father's side he was descended from Virginia pioneers of English blood, on his mother's from Scotch and Irish ancestors. His early days were passed happily on the farm, but after 1860, with the coming of hostilities between North and South, the Allens suffered heavy misfortunes, encountering the hardships of both Civil War days and Reconstruction. For years Allen knew poverty, hard work, a struggle to get an education. As a student in Transylvania College he wore, instead of an overcoat, an old shawl, and during one winter, at least, he had no hat save a dilapidated one made of straw (manuscript article by M. A. Cassidy). Throughout these years of distress older people around him continually reminded the youth of happier conditions prevailing in the South before the war. Like Thomas Nelson Page and others, he fell heir to a belief in the chivalrous ideals of plantation society—an inheritance which in part explains his predilection, later, for aristocratic heroines and gallant lovers, and his high evaluation of good breeding. His mind played fondly over the idealized past of the South. His first instruction was from his mother, who directed his reading as well as stimulated his interest in Kentucky birds, flowers, and woodland scenery. At about the age of ten he began attending a neighboring school, then at seventeen the Academy of Transylvania College, and in 1868 Transylvania College itself (known at the time as Kentucky University). Graduating with honors in 1872, he forthwith entered upon a varied career as schoolmaster and college professor. For a year he taught in the district school at Fort Springs, Ky., for another in the high school at Richmond, Mo.; next, in 1875, he established a private school at Lexington, Mo., but, abandoning this enterprise, he returned to his native state, and reëntered his Alma Mater to work for the M.A. degree, at the same time acting as tutor to the Whitney family near Lexington. In 1878 he accepted the principalship of Transylvania Academy, a position he held until offered the chair of Latin at Bethany College, West Virginia, in 1880. Here he was professor during the academic year 1881–82 and during most of 1882–83; then he resigned the post and returned to Lexington, once more to open a private school. This school was his last;

closing its doors two years later, he gave up teaching altogether. During these years in the schoolroom, however, he had been serving his true apprenticeship. Continuing at his studies, receiving the M.A. from Transylvania in 1877 and an honorary M.A. from Bethany in 1880, he had extended the scope of his reading, especially among French and British novelists. He had also become engrossed in scientific study, and was particularly interested in the theories of Darwin and Huxley. Most important of all, he had been practising the art of writing, so that when presently he ventured to address the editors, he was master of a deft and euphonious style.

His first significant contributions were to the *Continent, Harper's, Atlantic Monthly, Independent, Critic*—articles on Keats, Heine, Pepys, Hawthorne. *Harper's* for March 1884 contained his poem "Midwinter." "Too Much Momentum," his first story, appeared in *Harper's* for April 1885, and "Beneath the Veil," another poem, in the *Atlantic Monthly* for September 1885. By 1886 he was well on the way to establishing himself. Real success came in 1891, with the publication of his first book, *Flute and Violin, and Other Kentucky Tales and Romances*, distinctive short stories reprinted from the magazines. This was followed by *The Blue Grass Region of Kentucky, and Other Kentucky Articles* (1892), essays also reprinted from the magazines. Allen's reputation was now made. He left Kentucky, where except for occasional sojourns elsewhere he had lived since his birth, and in 1893 settled permanently in New York City. After this removal, his work became more pretentious, for like so many other successful American story writers, he turned novelist. In 1893 appeared *John Gray,* a slight novel subsequently expanded; in 1894 and 1895 respectively, *A Kentucky Cardinal* and *Aftermath,* idyllic accounts of two lovers in a Kentucky garden, and Allen's masterpieces; in 1896, *Summer in Arcady,* a handling of the sex problem, severely criticized in its day; in 1897, *The Choir Invisible,* an expansion of *John Gray,* and withal a strong piece of fiction, with historical facts as a basis; in 1900, *The Reign of Law,* reflecting the author's interest in science and theology; and in 1903, *The Mettle of the Pasture,* dealing with the question of the "double standard." From this point on, Allen's popularity declined somewhat, although he continued to be highly esteemed both at home and abroad. Critics were less consistently favorable, some of them seeing only confusion in *The Bride of the Mistletoe* (1909) and *The Doctor's Christmas Eve* (1910), parts of an ambitious trilogy never completed. His later volumes are small and comparatively unimportant: *The Heroine in Bronze* (1912), *The Last Christmas Tree* (1914), *The Sword of Youth* (1915), *A Cathedral Singer* (1916), *The Kentucky Warbler* (1918), *The Emblems of Fidelity* (1919), *The Alabaster Box* (1923). At the time of his death he was collecting his last magazine stories, published posthumously as *The Landmark* (1925); for this work he had intended an autobiographical preface and an introduction, dealing with the short story, but unfortunately these were left as brief fragments.

Allen's closing years were apparently uneventful. They were years of retirement, hard work, study, and devotion to an invalid sister. He was never married. In 1894, 1900, 1909, and perhaps other years, he was in Europe; but after settling in New York he returned but once to Kentucky—because, as he said, of the painfulness of noting the inevitable changes in city and district (unpublished letter to M. A. Cassidy). He was frequently asked to lecture upon his works, but whereas in earlier years he had sometimes done so, later he consistently refused. He appears to have been very sensitive, avoiding publicity and furnishing the outside world few facts about himself. Those who knew him personally, however, agree that as a man he was most engaging. His friend, George Folsom Granberry, writes that he was "most dignified, formal, adhering strictly to the highest ideals of personal conduct, extremely kind-hearted; to his intimate friends, all that was genial and considerate; inaccessible to 'lion-hunters,' and entirely devoid of any feeling for personal display" (manuscript note from G. F. Granberry). He is buried in Lexington.

Among American writers, Allen holds a secure place. The best stories in *Flute and Violin,* and *A Kentucky Cardinal, Aftermath,* and *The Choir Invisible,* written in pure, sonorous English, have permanent worth as expressions of the quieter, more spiritual experiences of the race. Without being narrow or provincial in outlook, Allen was at his best when utilizing the life and scenery of his native state; and more than any other author he made the Blue Grass Region of Kentucky known to both his countrymen and Europeans.

[No adequate biog. of Allen exists, although much valuable information is to be found in John Wilson Townsend's little volume, *James Lane Allen* (Louisville, 1927). Among numerous criticisms and sketches the best are those in the *Lib. of Southern Lit.*, I, 41–46 (by I. F. Marcosson); J. W. Townsend's *Kentucky in Am. Letters,* II, 4–10; J. B. Henneman's *Shakespearean and Other Papers,* pp. 115–67; *Book News,* XXIV, 753 (by E. C. Litsey); *Bookman,* I, 303 (by Nancy H. Banks). Passages in *The Blue Grass Region* are autobiographical, as are also the opening paragraphs of Allen's essay on H. M. Alden (*Bookman,* L, 330–36), remarks in several of his prefaces, and the introduction to the Hugh Thomson ed. of *A Kentucky Cardinal* and *Aftermath.* The facts here recorded have been verified, whenever possible, by reference to newspaper files, coll. records, material in the *Critic,* several unpublished letters of Allen, and information furnished by J. T. C. Noe, M. A. Cassidy, G. C. Knight, all of Lexington, and G. F. Granberry of New York, Allen's literary executor.] J.H.N.

ALLEN, JEREMIAH MERVIN (May 18, 1833–Dec. 29, 1903), engineer and pioneer in steam-boiler insurance, was seventh in descent from Samuel Allen, an early colonist who settled in Cambridge, Mass., in 1632. Among the descendants of Samuel was Gen. Ethan Allen, and the Allen family intermarried with that branch of the Adams family which gave Samuel and John Adams to the Revolution. A taste for science and mechanics seems to have been common in the family. One of the Allens was an astronomer and issued *Allen's New England Almanac.* Another was perhaps the earliest in this country to engage in the manufacture of telescopes and microscopes; others were contractors and builders. Jeremiah M. Allen was born in Enfield, Conn., the son of Jeremiah V. Allen and Emily Pease. He remained at Enfield until twelve years of age, attending the primary schools of that place, and then studied for two years at Rev. Dr. Lawton's school at Longmeadow, Mass., after which he spent four years at Westfield Academy, in studies directed toward his becoming a civil engineer. Subsequently he taught school for four years, improving himself in the meantime with reading and study. In 1865 he became connected in Hartford, Conn., with the insurance business, thus making his first contact with the field of activity which was later to become his life-work. In the year 1857 there had been formed by a few young men in Hartford an association known as the "Polytechnic Club," with the purpose of discussing matters of science in relation to every-day life. Among other subjects discussed at meetings of this Club was that of steam-boiler explosions and their causes. As these discussions developed, the subject became one of special interest, and in the environment of Hartford, with its large insurance activities, these early beginnings led, in 1866, to the organization of a company "to inspect steam-boilers and to insure their owners against loss or damage arising from boiler explosion." With his deep interest in the subject itself, his taste for mechanical and engineering matters, and his previous experience in the insurance business, Allen was chosen to lead in this new enterprise, and from 1867 to his death was president and general manager of the company.

Allen's interests were wide, and in one way or another he was connected with most of the leading movements in his community. Among many other duties and activities he served as president of the Hartford board of trade, member and president of the board of trustees of the Hartford Theological Seminary and non-resident lecturer in the Sibley College of Mechanical Engineering, Cornell University. He was active in the work of the Y. M. C. A. and served a term as president. He was likewise a member of many societies and organizations, scientific, technical, and historical. His lasting contribution to industrial and social progress, however, is to be found in his work in the field of steam-boiler inspection and insurance. This was distinctly a pioneer movement in its recognition of both the social and economic value of human life and in the taking of measures calculated to reduce the hazards and minimize the loss both of life and property due to steam-boiler explosions. Through the system of boiler inspection which was inaugurated under Allen's direction, as well as through the promulgation of carefully framed rules and regulations for design and operation, the hazards of steam-boiler operation were enormously reduced. In 1856 Allen married Harriet S. Griswold of Ellington, Conn., by whom he had two children. He died at the age of seventy, active in his many interests to the last, loved and honored by associates and friends.

[Biog. sketches in *Trans. Am. Soc. Mech. Engineers,* XXV, 1121, and in the *Locomotive* (a technical periodical founded by Allen) for Jan. 1904; see also O. P. Allen, *The Allen Memorial,* 2nd ser. (1907); obituaries and editorials in *Hartford Courant,* Dec. 30, 1903, *Hartford Times,* Dec. 29, 1903.] W.F.D.

ALLEN, JOEL ASAPH (July 19, 1838–Aug. 29, 1921), zoologist, author, came of early New England stock; on the side of his father, Joel Allen, he was a descendant in the seventh generation of Samuel Allen, who settled in Windsor Conn., in 1640. His mother, Harriet (Trumbull) Allen, was descended from John Trumbull, great-grandfather of Gov. Jonathan Trumbull, who migrated from Newcastle-on-Tyne to Roxbury, Mass., in 1639. The father of Joel Asaph Allen was a farmer, carpenter, and house-builder in his early days, and young Allen was the only member of his family to show the traits of the born naturalist, which were favored by the early surroundings of his birthplace on the old farm not far from Springfield. Only during the winter session could he be spared from farm work to attend the nearest school, a mile distant. At the age of fourteen he made his first collection of birds, which he described, attempted to draw and color, and even named, totally in ignorance of written works which could have enlightened him. Soon afterward a new world opened to him in the discovery of the volumes of Wilson, Nuttall, and Audubon, which led to his ambition, at the age of twenty, to write a history of the "Birds of New England." During three years' attendance at

Wilbraham Academy, Springfield, he made natural-history collections of all kinds which he later (1861) reluctantly sold to the Academy in order to go to Harvard University to study under Louis Agassiz. In 1865 he accompanied his great teacher to Brazil. Growing talent led to his selection as Curator of Birds in the Harvard Museum of Comparative Zoology (1867–85). Actively exploring in Illinois, Indiana, Michigan, Florida, on the Great Plains, in the Rocky Mountain region, Wyoming, Colorado, Dakota, Missouri, he showed unprecedented ability as a collector. The great West was then in primitive condition, wild life of all kinds still abounding, and he observed the American bison in its prime. A distant journey to the Yellowstone River beyond Bismarck took him into a region infested with hostile Indians. With health impaired by long exposure, from 1876 to 1882 he devoted his time wholly to writing, producing his two monographs, *The American Bisons, Living and Extinct* (1876) and *History of North American Pinnipeds* (1880), the latter a volume of 800 pages.

The second stage of his life was the call to the American Museum of Natural History, New York, 1885, as head of the department of birds and mammals, which he administered with great distinction and success; during this time the collections grew apace and several of the most talented young naturalists of America came to work under him. From the year 1889 he was editor-in-chief of all the zoological publications of the Museum, and thirty-seven volumes of the *Bulletin* and twenty-two *Memoirs* passed through his hands. Honors from American and foreign scientific societies came thick and fast; he received the Humboldt scholarship from Harvard, the degree of Ph.D. from the University of Indiana, the Walker Grand Prize from the Boston Society of Natural History, the Linnæan Society (London) medal, and, above all, the veneration and love of his colleagues and associates. As a man his distinguishing characteristics were sincerity and consideration for others, but he was impatient of careless work and of generalizations based on insufficient data. His enthusiasm for research led him constantly to overtax his physical resources, yet in spite of a frail physique he was actively engaged in writing and research till within a few weeks of his death. He was twice married: in 1874 to Mary Manning Cleveland, who died in 1879; and in 1886 to Susan Augusta Taft.

[The chief sources of information are *Autobiog. Notes and a Bibliog. of the Scientific Pubs. of Joel Asaph Allen* (1916), written at the instance of the president of the Am. Museum of Natural Hist.; the tribute of his colleague and successor, Curator Frank M. Chapman, in the *Auk*, Jan. 1922, vol. XXXIX, no. 1, and the sketch in *Nat. Acad. of Sci. Memoirs*, vol. XXI, 1st memoir.]

H.F.O.

ALLEN, JOHN (Nov. 4, 1810–Mar. 8, 1892), dentist, the son of Nirum Allen, physician and farmer, of the family that had produced Gen. Ethan Allen in the preceding century, was born on his father's farm in Broome County, N.Y. While he was still a small boy, his family removed to Ohio. At nineteen he began the study of dentistry with Dr. James Harris of Chillicothe, Ohio. A year later he removed to Cincinnati and began to practise. He also studied medicine at the medical college of that city, receiving the degree of M.D. In 1853 or 1854 he removed to New York City, where he continued to practise dentistry until his death from general debility in 1892, at his home in Plainfield, N.J. He was twice married: in 1835 to Charlotte Dana, by whom he had one son, Charles D. Allen, who became his father's partner and successor in practise; in 1846, to Mrs. Cornelia Reeder, by whom he had one daughter.

Allen's chief service was in the invention of new denture. The highest type of artificial denture then known was formed of porcelain teeth, singly or in blocks, ground and fitted together and riveted or soldered to gold plates swaged to fit the mouth. There was no way to prevent the seeping of the oral secretions into the interstices between the teeth, and there was no adequate means of restoring the contour of the face where it had shrunken or fallen in because of absorption of the tissues. Allen first devised what he called "plumpers," forms adapted to fill out shrunken parts, to be attached to the denture. For this device he was awarded by the American Society of Dental Surgeons in 1845 a suitably engraved gold medal. Later he took out a patent (Dec. 16, 1845). Then began the major task, the devising of the denture itself. First he acquired a thorough knowledge of the making of porcelain teeth. He soon found that gold, the commonly accepted base for artificial dentures, melted at a temperature so low that no porcelain that would resist the oral fluids could be fused upon it. Platinum, only, afforded the necessary characteristics. Several years devoted to the working out of formulas for porcelain bodies and methods of procedure developed "continuous gum," then and still the highest type of artificial denture. The "gum" is represented by porcelain suitably colored, embracing the porcelain teeth, attaching them to the platinum plate, and continued to cover its lingual surface without seam or crevice. It allows any desired arrangement of the teeth, and is immune to the action of the oral fluids. A patent was granted Dec. 23, 1851, and almost immediately there began the first patent litigation in which dentists were interested. Allen sued Dr. William M. Hunter, who had been working along the same lines, for infringement. After several years of acrimonious controversy, legal and literary, the case was decided in favor of Hunter. During his professional career of more than sixty years, Allen wrote many papers, covering almost the entire range of dental literature. He became a member of the first dental society in the world (American Society of Dental Surgeons) at its second annual session (1841); was active in the founding of the second dental college (Ohio College of Dental Surgery, 1845), in which he filled a professorship for several years; and helped to establish the New York College of Dentistry (1865).

[*Hist. of Dental Surgery* (1909), ed. by Chas. R. E. Koch; J. E. Dexter, *Hist. of Dental and Oral Science in America* (1876); *Dental Reg.*, Apr. 1874; *Internat. Dental Jour.*, Apr. 1892; *Dental Cosmos*, May 1892.]

F. L. H.

ALLEN, JOHN F. (1829–Oct. 4, 1900), engineer, inventor, was born in England. When twelve years old he was brought to this country, where he early interested himself in mechanical affairs. As a young man he was an engineer on the propeller *Curlew*, a freight boat running on Long Island Sound between New York and Providence, using a Corliss engine. There was a defect in this engine which caused it to race furiously when the Sound was rough; Allen invented a new valve motion which he hoped would remedy the defect, but found that he was unable to use it successfully on the Corliss engine. In 1860 he was recommended as an expert engineer by Thurston and Gardiner, engine builders of Providence, R. I., to Henry A. Burr, manufacturer of felt-hat bodies in New York City, who was having trouble with a pair of engines built by the Providence firm. Allen soon had the engines running satisfactorily. One day he accidentally met Charles T. Porter, who was the inventor of a form of engine governor, and Allen told him the details of the valve motion he had invented. Porter immediately saw its application to a high-speed engine and asked to be allowed to attempt its introduction. The result was the Allen engine, later improved and known as the Porter-Allen engine, a pioneer in steam-engines of the so-called high-speed type. It made possible high rotative speeds and good economy, and reduced the weight and size of the engine. In order to help finance the Porter-Allen engine-building shops Allen mortgaged his home in Tremont, N. Y. Within a few years he had invented an inclined tube vertical water-tube boiler which was also being successfully introduced. But he seemed incapable of retaining much interest in his inventions after they were successfully placed on the market, so he sold out his stock in the Porter-Allen Company in the early seventies and built a shop of his own at Mott Haven. Here he originated an important system of pneumatic riveting in its two methods, by percussion and by pressure, and began the manufacture of air compressors and pneumatic riveters. At the time of his death he was doing a small business in this kind of manufacturing in New York City.

[*Trans. Am. Soc. Mechanical Engineers*, 1901, XXII, 1149; *Engineering News*, 1900, XLIV, 396; *Am. Machinist*, 1900, XXIII, 46; C. T. Porter, *Engineering Reminiscences* (1908).]

E. Y.

ALLEN, JOHN JAMES (Sept. 25, 1797–Sept. 18, 1871), jurist, was the grandson of Robert Allan, who settled at Carlisle, Pa., in 1757, and the son of James and Jean (Steele) Allen. His father, who adopted the name "Allen," practised law in the Shenandoah Valley and became judge of the 17th Virginia judicial district. John James Allen was born in Woodstock, Shenandoah County, Va., and received his education at Washington College, Va., and Dickinson College, Pa. He then read law with his father, and was admitted as an attorney in 1818. He at first opened an office at Campbell Court House, Va., but in 1819 removed to Clarksburg, where he practised for seventeen years. He early evinced an active interest in politics and in 1827 was elected to the state Senate, serving for three years. In his law business he had had experience of the insecurity of the title to land in Trans-Alleghany Virginia, arising from the looseness with which the regulations governing settlers had been drafted and administered since 1777, and he prepared and procured the passage through the legislature of a bill for the purpose of quieting titles in that district which was of inestimable benefit to the frontier settlers. In 1833 he was elected a representative in the Twenty-third Congress, and served for two years, but failed of reëlection. In 1834 he had been appointed state attorney for the counties of Harrison, Lewis, and Preston, and in 1836 the acting governor of Virginia, Wyndham Robertson, appointed him judge of the 17th judicial district, the position which his father had previously held. He was comparatively unknown to the people of the district, and some discontent was voiced at the appointment, but his dignity and courtesy on the bench and the facility with which he conducted the proceedings of the court soon attracted the confidence of the public and the profession. Removing to Botetourt, the court seat, he resided there during the remainder of his life. In 1840 he was nominated for the United States Senate but no election took place, no candidate having the necessary votes. Immediately afterward, a vacancy occurred on the court of appeals and he was elected thereto without opposition, Dec. 12, 1840. When the court was reorganized in compliance with the reformed constitution of 1851, he became its president, a rank equivalent to that of chief justice. Though not of any pronounced learning and inclined to be reserved in manner, he possessed great intellectual force and on the bench was always competent, eminently painstaking, and firmly maintained the best traditions of the judiciary. He resigned in April 1865, being then in his sixty-eighth year, having nearly completed thirty years' judicial service of which twenty-five had been spent on the appellate court bench. He was a strong supporter of the Southern cause, and prepared a brilliant and trenchant defense of the attitude of Virginia, which was adopted as a preamble to a resolution, advocating secession, passed at a Botetourt meeting, Dec. 10, 1860. The preamble and resolution were published in *Southern Historical Society Papers,* I, 13, January 1876. He died at Botetourt. In 1824 he had married a near relative of "Stonewall" Jackson. His judicial decisions are found in *11, 12 Leigh, 1, 2 Robinson,* and *1–16 Grattan.*

[An adequate sketch of his career appeared in an article by S. S. P. Patterson, "The Supreme Court of Appeals of Va.," in the *Green Bag,* V, 310, 362; see also Henry Hammond, *Hist. of Harrison County, West Va.* (1909); J. W. Wayland, *A Hist. of Shenandoah County, Va.* (1927).] H. W. H. K.

ALLEN, JOSEPH HENRY (Aug. 21, 1820–Mar. 20, 1898), Unitarian clergyman, author, editor, was born in Northboro, Mass. His father, Joseph Allen, was minister of the First Church in Northboro for fifty-six years; his mother was a daughter of that Rev. Henry Ware whose appointment as Hollis Professor of Divinity in Harvard created consternation among the stricter orthodox brethren of the day. Joseph Henry was prepared for college in the noted school which his father established and for many years maintained in the Northboro parsonage. He graduated from Harvard at the age of twenty, ranking third in his class, and without delay entered upon the course in divinity, graduating in 1843. In October of that year he was ordained minister of the First Congregational Society of Jamaica Plain. On May 22, 1845, he married Anna Minot Weld, who bore him three sons and three daughters. In 1847 he took charge of the Unitarian church in Washington, D. C., and in 1850 became minister of the church in Bangor, Me. He seems not to have possessed those features of temperament which make the so-called successful preacher. Meditatively rather than socially inclined, he found it difficult to adjust himself to the peculiar social demands of a parish. He was of too judicial and discerning a temperament to become an aggressive advocate of partisan measures, and he lacked the positive manner of address expected from the pulpit. But at no time did he ever leave his hearers in doubt as to where he stood on questions of importance. While it was contrary to his nature to become a member of anti-slavery organizations, he spoke unreservedly and plainly for abolition at a time when it would have been profitable to have been, at least, non-committal. His scholarly and critical temper and his preference for the study rather than the parlor probably made it inevitable that he should drift out of the active ministry.

In 1857 he took up the calling of teacher in Jamaica Plain, Northboro, and West Newton. During this period (1857–66) he became active in the field of Unitarian periodical literature in various editorial capacities. He was associate editor of the *Christian Examiner,* 1863–65, to which he had begun to contribute as early as 1844. In 1878 he was appointed, on recommendation of Rev. F. H. Hedge, lecturer on ecclesiastical history in Harvard, a position he held for four years. From 1887 to 1891 he was editor of the *Unitarian Review.* During these years he did not entirely sever his connection with the ministry, and was ready to respond to frequent calls to supply pastorless pulpits. Though refusing to accept any permanent settlement, he ministered to churches in Ann Arbor, Mich., 1877–78, Ithaca, N.Y., 1882–83, and San Diego, Cal., 1884. He died in Cambridge, Mass., on Mar. 20, 1898, survived by his wife and five of his six children.

Allen is most widely known for his Latin manuals. He prepared a *Latin Primer* (1870) and, in association with his brother W. F. Allen[*q.v.*], *A Latin Reader* (1869); a *Manual Latin Grammar* (1868), and others. In collaboration with Prof. J. B. Greenough he prepared that series of Latin manuals which made his name familiar to every high school scholar of the generations just past. His contributions to distinctively Unitarian literature, apart from his writings in Unitarian periodicals, include: *Our Liberal Movement in Theology* (1882); *Christian History in Its Three Great Periods* (1883); *Historical Sketch of the Unitarian Movement* (1894).

[The chief printed sources for the life of Joseph Henry Allen are an article by Rev. John W. Chadwick, *N. Y. Evening Post,* Mar. 21, 1898; an article by Rev. Francis Tiffany, *Christian Register; Pub. Colonial Soc. Mass.* (1902), V, 310–14.] C. G.

ALLEN, LEWIS FALLEY (Jan. 1, 1800–May 2, 1890), stock breeder, farm writer, was born in Westfield, Mass., the son of Samuel and Ruth (Falley) Allen and brother of Anthony Benezet Allen [*q.v.*] and Richard L. Allen [*q.v.*]. In 1825 he married his first cousin, Margaret Cleveland, daughter of William and Margaret (Falley) Cleveland and aunt of President Grover Cleveland. After trying his fortune in New York City, Norwich, Conn., and Sandusky, Ohio, he moved to Buffalo, N. Y., in 1830, becoming a permanent resident of that city from 1836 to his death. His acquaintances describe him as a strong, frank, and positive character, of keen wit and generous sentiment. Among his intimate friends he counted Daniel Webster, Gen. Winfield Scott, and Henry Clay, all of whom were frequent guests at his home. His chief life-work was as a breeder and improver of cattle. He founded and for forty years was the editor of the *American Shorthorn Herdbook.* With his brother, A. B. Allen, he was connected with the *American Agriculturist* from its origin. A voluminous writer, contributing frequently to the *Genesee Farmer, Country Gentleman, American Farmer,* and other journals, he still found time to write *Rural Architecture* (1852), *American Cattle* (1868), and *History of the Shorthorn Cattle* (1872), besides serving in the New York legislature and as president of the New York State Agricultural Society. His 600-acre farm and the neighboring settlements on Grand Island in the Niagara River became the center not only of breeding operations with Shorthorn and Devon cattle and Southdown sheep, but also of experiments in coöperative human societies, some of the results of these studies being recorded in his paper on the "Founding of the City of Ararat" (*Buffalo Historical Society Publications,* I, 305–28). While in the legislature of his state, he was active in furthering the interests of agriculture and particularly in the construction and maintenance of canals as a means of transporting farm products to market. Even these many-sided activities failed to absorb all of his time and strength, for he was constantly busy with the civic affairs of Buffalo, with which his interests became more and more closely identified during his long participation in its history. At the time of his death he was engaged in a controversy with an Ohio admirer of Shorthorns who had taken Allen to task for proving false to his first love for Shorthorns and bestowing too much praise on Guernseys. But he stoutly maintained that, though fourscore and nine years were creeping upon him, he was still able to judge of merit in cattle and that the Guernseys were a coming milk breed. And he was still working on agricultural architecture, plans for farm buildings and for landscaping the grounds about farm homesteads, the treatment of clay land meadows, the place of dogs and bees on farms, and the construction of farm fences.

[Long and very full obituary in *Buffalo Express,* May 3, 1890; editorial comment and portrait in same journal, May 4, 1890; references in J. N. Larned, *Hist. of Buffalo* (1911).]

E. V. W.

ALLEN, NATHAN (Apr. 25, 1813–Jan. 1, 1889), physician, was born in Princeton, Mass., the son of Moses Allen by his wife, Mehitable Oliver, of Barre, Mass., and brother of David Oliver Allen [*q.v.*]. A graduate of Amherst College in 1836, Allen later (1841) received the degree of M.D. from the University of Pennsylvania Medical College, after which he returned to Lowell, Mass., where he practised medicine until his death. He was for many years an active member of the staff of St. John's Hospital in that city. After he had come into prominence through his writings, he was made a member of the state board of charities, and in 1872 attended as an American delegate the International Congress on Prison Reform. He was twice married: on Sept. 24, 1841, to Sarah H. Spaulding of Wakefield, Mass., who died in April 1856; and on May 20, 1857, to Annie A. Waters of Salem, Mass.

While a medical student in Philadelphia, Allen improved his financial circumstances by association with the well-known press of Adam Waldie as proof-reader, correspondent, and "hack" writer. This post brought him into contact with important men of his time—Horace Mann, Charles Caldwell, George Combe—and it led to his being appointed editor of the newly established *American Phrenological Journal and Miscellany* at the early age of twenty-six (1839). Phrenology—being then still a sister study to "mental philosophy"—had attracted to its pursuit certain of the best intellects of that period. For three years Allen (still a medical undergraduate) contributed extensively to this journal in letters, editorial comments, and numerous book reviews. His contributions, which reveal familiarity with general literature, ancient and modern, were always well written, but one observes a marked improvement in his literary style during the three years of his editorship. Apart from training his pen, which in later life was ever scholarly and prolific, this experience as an editor marked the beginning of Allen's active interest in problems of human behavior and of insanity. His graduation thesis, *An Essay on the Connection of Mental Philosophy with Medicine,* which was published by Waldie in 1841 (32 pp.), was a well-argued plea for the consideration of the influence of mental states upon bodily ailments, and was apparently well received. Following the publication of this thesis, Allen severed his connection with the *Phrenological Journal.* He will be remembered chiefly for two important contributions: *The Physiological Laws of Human Increase* (Philadelphia, 1868 and 1870; also *Quarterly Journal of Psychology and Medicine,* N.Y., 1868); *Changes in the New England Population* (Lowell, 1877; also *Popular Science Monthly,* vol. XXIII, 1883). In the former he sought to establish a "great general law of propagation applicable to all organic life" by demonstrating that the over-activity of any organ tends to the impairment of other organs and to the diminishment of fertility. In the latter, which aroused wider public interest, he endeavored to prove that the lowering birth-rate of native New England stock (as contrasted with immigrants) was due to impaired physical condition. Other important works were: *The Intermarriage of Relations* (1869), *Physical Degeneracy* (1870), and *The Treatment of the Insane* (1876).

[*New Eng. Medic. Mo.,* III, 215–19 (portr.); W. L. Burrage in *Am. Medic. Biogs.* (1920); *Boston Medic. and Surgic. Jour.,* 1889, vol. CXX; W. B. Atkinson, *Physicians and Surgeons of the U.S.* (1878); R. F. Stone, *Eminent Am. Physicians and Surgeons* (1894); W. L. Montague, *Biogs. of Recent Alumni of Amherst 1821–1871* (1883). An extensive though not wholly complete list of Allen's works is to be found in the Index Cat. Lib. Surgeon General's Office, vols. I of series 1 and 2.]

J. F. F.

ALLEN, NATHAN H. (Apr. 14, 1848–May 9, 1925), musician and composer, was born at Marion, Mass., the son of Henry M. Allen, a captain of packet-ships between New York and Liverpool, and Matilda E. Clark, whose ancestry ran back to Thomas Clark of Plymouth and Henry Butler Bridgman of the vicinity of Limerick, Ireland. His middle name was either 'Hale' or 'Henry,' as it was written in both ways without protest on his part. His regular signature was 'N. H. Allen' simply. He attended public schools in Providence and for a time studied at Phillips Andover Academy. His musical aptitude was early displayed and he aspired to become a singer. An illness affected his voice, however, and he then turned to the organ, taking lessons for two years in Providence. In 1867 he went abroad and had three years at Berlin under the famous organist Haupt, and the equally famous Grell, the conductor of the Singakademie. Returning in 1870, he became organist at the First Unitarian Church in New Bedford, Mass. In 1877 he married Elizabeth Macy, a descendant of an early settler in Nantucket. In 1878 he removed to Hartford, Conn., as organist at the Park Congregational Church and from 1880 at community services at South Manchester, Conn. From 1883 till 1906 he held his most distinguished post as organist of the First or Center Church in Hartford. For some years thereafter he was at Piedmont Church in Worcester, Mass., about 1915 returning to live at Hartford. For at least fifty years he was steadily occupied in teaching piano, organ, singing and theory, besides other activities noted below.

He was an expert and effective player, and was invited to serve as recitalist at the Buffalo, St. Louis, and San Francisco Expositions. Among his many able organ pupils were R. P. Paine of Norfolk, Conn., and W. C. Hammond of Holyoke, Mass. For a time he conducted the Musurgia Club of Hartford, a select chorus of trained voices which he organized. He was greatly interested in the choral projects of Carl Stoeckel at Norfolk, acting often as conductor for the Litchfield County Festival Chorus. He was an original member of the New York Manuscript Society, a founder of the American Guild of Organists, and for years taught theory at Mount Holyoke College, as well as later at the Hartt School in Hartford. He was a facile and even brilliant writer, contributing valuable critical and historical articles to papers and magazines, and in 1888 (with Leonard Woolsey Bacon) he published *The Hymns of Martin Luther,* in which he dealt with the musical side of the subject. His interest in colonial history led him for years to elaborate a *History of Music in a New England State, 1630–1900,* pertaining chiefly to Connecticut, the manuscript being left at his death to the Watkinson Library in Hartford. Of his compositions, vocal and instrumental, numbering perhaps 150, may be mentioned the cantatas *The Apotheosis of St. Dorothy* (1891) and *The New-Born King* (1904), a *Fantasie-Impromptu* and *Winter Sketches* for piano, a *Pièce Symphonique,* a *Symphonic Fantasia* and many shorter works for organ, *In Memoriam* for organ, piano, and strings, etc., some fifty published anthems, a set of *Forty Liturgical Responses* (1915), and many songs. His breadth and delicacy of conception were everywhere combined with notable technical skill.

[*Internatl. Who's Who in Music* (1918); *Musical Courier,* Dec. 7, 1898; *Commemorative Biog. Rec. of Hartford Co., Conn.* (1901); *Hartford Daily Times,* May 11, 1925; *Hartford Courant,* May 10, 11, 1925; *N. Y. Times,* May 11, 1925; additional information from Mr. Frank B. Gay.]

W. S. P.

ALLEN, PAUL (Feb. 15, 1775–Aug. 18, 1826), editor, poet, was born in Providence, R. I., the son of Paul and Polly (Cooke) Allen. His mother was a daughter of Nicholas Cooke, governor of the state from 1775 to 1778. He graduated from Rhode Island College (Brown University) in the class of 1793. The subsequent course of his career cannot be traced in detail. At college he had gained some reputation as an orator, and on Nov. 22, 1792, had delivered an oration in the chapel on the death of a classmate, Roger Williams Howell, which at the request of the students was published. At least six other published orations delivered in Providence or vicinity between 1796 and 1806 are in existence. He studied for the bar, but no one probably was ever more unfitted to practise law than was he, for he was full of simplicity, credulous as a child, and irresolute in the extreme. Nothing was so easy for him as writing; accordingly that became his only occupation. In 1801 he published *Original Poems, Serious and Entertaining,* a collection of rather graceful verse, obviously patterned after English models. He removed to Philadelphia and was a contributor to the *United States Gazette,* and to the *Port Folio,* conducted by Joseph Dennie and Nicholas Biddle. In behalf of the latter he supervised the printing of the *History of the Expedition, under the Command of Captains Lewis and Clark,* which appeared in 1814. The last twelve years of his life were spent in Baltimore. Here he was a contributor to the *Portico.* John Neal [*q.v.*] wrote of him: "He is rather below the middle size—say about five feet six—dark eyes, dark hair—face deeply marked, a plain looking, nay, an ordinary looking man . . . with a character of sluggishness, slovenly inaptitude, and moroseness, all about him. Yet there is not a better natured fellow on the earth—bating a momentary petulance here and there with a far off politician in the way of trade, or a little fermentation at home, when he has been pestered by popinjays a little too long; nor a man that will write more, with less substantial information, on any subject, in the same time. He is near sighted; reads with his nose on the paper—and such reading! Lord—I can imagine nothing more dismal than the reading of his own poetry by Paul Allen. It is a continual whine—nasal and barbarous, beyond all conception." For a time he edited the *Federal Republican and Baltimore Telegraph,* but disagreed with his associates and left. There followed, according to Duyckinck (*Cyclopedia of American Literature,* 1855, I, 643), a period of poverty when he was imprisoned for a debt of thirty dollars. His friends started the *Journal of the Times* to give him an editorial position. This was succeeded in 1818 by the *Morning Chronicle,* which he edited till 1824, when he assumed management of the *Saturday Evening Herald.* He also published the *Morning Post.* He projected a *History of the American Revolution,* the most of which, owing to his irresponsibleness, was written by his friends Neal and Watkins. This appeared in 1819. In 1821, he published *Noah,* in five cantos. "John Neal," says Duyckinck, "did his friend another equally good service by reducing his poem of *Noah,* it having been submitted to his revision, to one-fifth its original dimensions."

[*Biog. and Hist. Dict.* (2nd ed. 1832); John Neal, *Randolph* (1823), I, 135–37; II, 181, 227; J. T. Scharf, *Hist. of Baltimore City and County* (1881); *Vital Record of R. I.,* ed. by Jas. N. Arnold, ser. 1, vol. II (1892); *Baltimore Am. and Commercial Daily Advertiser,* Aug. 21, 1826.]

H. E. S.

ALLEN, PHILIP (Sept. 1, 1785–Dec. 16, 1865), manufacturer, governor of Rhode Island, senator, was born in Providence, R. I., the son of Capt. Zachariah Allen, a West India trader and dealer, and Nancy (Crawford) Allen. He was educated at Taunton Academy, at the celebrated school of Robert Rogers in Newport, and at the Latin School under Jeremiah Chaplin, afterward president of Waterville College. In 1799 he entered Rhode Island College (later Brown University), from which he was graduated in 1803, at the age of eighteen. His father having died in 1801, he took over the business. His ability was soon recognized by his fellows and within three years of his graduation from college he was elected to the directorate of the Providence Insurance Company. He had a decided bent for things mechanical. The first steam-engine ever built in Providence was constructed by him, on the improved Watt and Boulton plan, featuring detachable puppet-valves. Having in 1812 begun to engage in the manufacture of cotton cloth, he obtained the best machinery available and was the first manufacturer to import the improved bobbin and fly frames that later came into general use, as well as the lapping machine for cotton cards. In 1831 he began printing calicoes, and the Allen calicoes soon became widely known. He was married, in January 1814, to Phœbe Aborn, by whom he had eleven children.

His career in public life began in 1819 when he was elected to the General Assembly from Providence, which he continued to represent until 1821. In 1827, Seth Wheaton, president of the Rhode Island branch of the United States Bank and disbursing agent of Revolutionary pensions, asked that Allen be appointed as his successor. This position Allen held until the second United States Bank wound up its affairs in 1836. He did not again hold public office until 1851. On Feb. 20 of that year he was nominated for governor by the Democratic State Convention and in the election of Apr. 2 he defeated Josiah Chapin, the Whig candidate, by a majority of 887. He was twice renominated by the Democrats and won the elections of Apr. 7, 1852, and Apr. 6, 1853, by substantial majorities. The most important feature of his administration was his fight with Thomas W. Dorr for the control of the Democratic party in Rhode Island. At the time of the Dorr Rebellion (1842), Allen had been an "Algerine," or Law and Order man, and far from sympathizing with Dorr he had purchased arms and raised a company known as the Rhode Island Carbineers for the defense of the state. Now the Democrats had returned to power and Dorr sought to have the legislature pass an act restoring him to civil and political privileges. Dorr himself prepared a bill for this purpose that reversed and annulled the decision of the supreme court of Rhode Island of June 25, 1844, which had sentenced Dorr to imprisonment. Allen refused what Dorr asked as a matter of right and the bill as finally passed placed the restoration on the ground of clemency (*Providence Daily Journal,* May 10, 1851). Thus Allen obtained complete control of his party in Rhode Island. As the *Providence Daily Journal* (Jan. 13, 1853), leading organ of the Whig party in Rhode Island, remarked: "... he [Allen] holds the Democratic party in his pocket: he *owns* it.... When, on the first of January, he makes up the inventory of his large estate, he puts down in the list: 'Item: one Democratic party'..."

On May 4, 1853, the two houses of the General Assembly met in Grand Committee and elected Allen to the seat in the Senate that had been vacant for some months, during which the Democratic state Senate had refused to meet the Whig House in Grand Committee. During his first four years in the Senate Allen's activities were confined to local matters. He was chairman of the Committee on Agriculture and served on the committees on Commerce and Naval Affairs. On Mar. 3, 1854, when the Senate voted on the Kansas-Nebraska Bill, he was absent, having been called home by the illness of his son, but his colleague, Senator James, announced that, if present, Senator Allen would vote against the bill (*Congressional Globe,* 33 Cong., 1 Sess., p. 532). In 1857, however, Allen became one of the leaders of his party in the Senate, and, although he was unusually free from party dictation, this perhaps influenced his attitude, so that on May 3, 1858, he voted to admit Kansas into the Union under the Lecompton (slave) Constitution (*Congressional Globe,* 35 Cong., 1 Sess., p. 1899). In 1859 he retired to private life. His independence is shown by his numerous clashes with his party. In 1836 he was vigorously opposed to Jackson on the removal of the deposits from the United States Bank. In 1848 he supported Martin Van Buren for the presidency and gave his money and influence in aid of the Free-Soilers. Finally, Allen was always a Tariff Democrat.

[James N. Arnold, *Vital Records of Rhode Island, 1636–1850,* vols. XIII (1903), p. 112, XIV (1905), p. 465, XV (1906), p. 469, XVII (1908), p. 33; *Providence Daily Jour.,* Dec. 18, 1865; *Biog. Cong. Dir. 1774–1911* (1913), p. 436; Thomas W. Bicknell, *History of the State of Rhode Island and Providence Plantations,* vol. III (1920), p. 1146; Arthur M. Mowry, *The Dorr War* (1901), pp. 257–58.]

F. E. R.

ALLEN, RICHARD (Feb. 14, 1760–Mar. 26, 1831), founder and first bishop of the African Methodist Episcopal Church, was born a slave in Philadelphia, and at an early age was sold to a farmer near Dover, Del. Reaching manhood at the time of the increasing toleration and religious liberty granted such sects as the Quakers, Presbyterians, Methodists, and Baptists, he early manifested interest in religion. He was converted under the influence of the Methodists and immediately became a religious worker. Impressed with his deep piety, his master permitted Allen to conduct religious services in his home, was himself converted at one of the meetings, and made it possible for Allen and his family to obtain their freedom. Allen educated himself by private study. While working at such occupations as wood-cutting and hauling he embraced every opportunity for preaching to both whites and blacks. He traveled through various parts of Delaware, New Jersey, Pennsylvania, and Maryland; and at the meeting of the first general conference of the Methodist Church in Baltimore, in 1784, was accepted by that hierarchy as a minister of promise. He then traveled with Richard Watcoat and Bishop Asbury, who gave him appointments to preach. Coming to Philadelphia in 1786, he was asked to preach occasionally at the St. George Methodist Church. He began also to conduct prayer-meetings among his own people. He immediately thought of making a special appeal to the negroes by establishing for them a separate place of worship, but both the whites and the blacks objected. When, however, the forceful preaching of Allen attracted to the church a large number of negroes, the white members objected to their presence, pulled them from their knees one Sunday when in an attitude of prayer, and ordered them to the gallery. Rather than submit to the insult, the negroes withdrew and established in 1787 an independent organization known as the "Free African Society." Out of this body some few went with Absalom Jones to establish the African Protestant Episcopal

Church, but Richard Allen influenced the majority to organize an independent Methodist church. The church thus founded was dedicated by Bishop Asbury in 1794. Allen was ordained deacon in 1799, and elder in 1816. In the meantime, other negro churches, separated from the whites in the same way in New York, New Jersey, Delaware, and Maryland, offered the opportunity for national organization. This was effected by sixteen congregations in 1816, and Allen was chosen bishop. Thus began the African Methodist Episcopal Church, which is one of the strongest organizations ever effected by negroes. Allen labored incessantly for the promotion of this cause until he died in 1831. By that time he had finally succeeded in impressing the public and had won national standing for his denomination. It was not allowed to expand in the South after the supposed connection of certain of its members with the Denmark Vesey plot in Charleston, S. C., in 1822; but the work had found its way into the Northern states east of the Mississippi River. In 1836, five years after Allen's death, the churches numbered eighty-six. There were four conferences, two bishops, and twenty-seven ministers. These served 7,594 members, and controlled $125,000 worth of property. Allen had made the Church not only an agency for religious uplift; but, forced into the anti-slavery movement and the Underground Railroad effort, the institution had become a factor in the battle for freedom.

[*The Life, Experience, and Gospel Labors of the Rt. Rev. Richard Allen, Written by Himself* (1793, repub. 1888); Absalom Jones and Rich. Allen, *Narr. of the Proceedings of the Black People, during the Late Awful Calamity in Phila. in the year 1793* (1794); sketch in R. R. Wright's *Centennial Encyc. of the African M. E. Ch.* (1916), pp. 5–6; a treatment of Allen's contribution to the development of the Church in C. G. Woodson, *Hist. of the Negro Ch.* (1921) in the chapter entitled "The Independent Ch. Movement," pp. 71–99.]

C. G. W.

ALLEN, RICHARD LAMB (Oct. 20, 1803–Sept. 22, 1869), agriculturist, editor, and manufacturer, was born in Westfield, Mass., being a son of Samuel Allen and Ruth (Falley) Allen and a grandson of Capt. Richard Falley, a soldier in the colonial war against Canada and in the American Revolution. He was educated at the Academy at Westfield, Mass. He first engaged in mercantile business in New York City and then in literary pursuits and the study of law at Baltimore, Md. Ill health compelled him to take up a more active life in 1832. He acquired possession of a large tract of woodland on the Niagara River, near Buffalo, N.Y., where he cleared land, cultivated crops, and bred various kinds of improved livestock. In later years he was a larger owner of real estate at Manitowoc, Wis. He was married on Dec. 30, 1834 to Sally O. Lyman of Northampton, Mass. In April 1842 with his older brother, Anthony B. Allen [*q.v.*], he founded the *American Agriculturist* in New York City. At the end of that year he retired from the editorship but was a frequent contributor and in 1849 again became a co-editor, in which capacity he continued until this journal was sold to Orange Judd in 1856. The great demand for improved agricultural implements, which was created in part by the wide circulation of this paper, led the two brothers to create the firm of A. B. Allen & Co. and open on Jan. 1, 1847, an agricultural-implement warehouse in Water St., New York. Soon afterward extensive agricultural-implement works were added in Brooklyn. Success attended these ventures and the business was afterward carried on by R. H. Allen, a son of R. L. Allen.

In 1846 Richard Allen published *A Brief Compend of American Agriculture.* This book of 436 pages dealt broadly with plant and animal production, farm equipment, and animal diseases. It was dedicated "to the young farmers of the United States." The author thought of it as having a definite educational mission. In the introduction he showed his great interest in agricultural education by declaring that it was "the duty of each of the largest States of the Union, liberally to endow and organize an Agricultural College," connected with which should be laboratories and farms for experimental investigations. The following year that portion of the *Compend* which dealt with animals was revised and made into a separate book, entitled *Domestic Animals.* This contained a "History and description of the horse, mule, cattle, sheep, swine, poultry and farm dogs, with directions for their management, breeding, crossing, rearing, feeding and preparation for a profitable market, also their diseases and remedies, together with full directions for the management of the dairy." In 1849 a revised and illustrated edition of that part of the *Compend* relating to plant production and farm equipment was issued as *The American Farm Book.* The entire *Compend* was reissued in 1869 as the *New American Farm Book* and, revised by the author's brother Lewis F. Allen [*q.v.*], was again republished in 1883.

Richard L. Allen had a love of history, belles-lettres, science, and art. He traveled extensively in the United States and in Europe for the year and a half before his death, which occurred at Stockholm, Sweden. The obituary notice in the *American Agriculturist* of January 1870 states that he was "of an uncommonly amiable disposition, with pleasing, winning manners—erect and noble in person, active and youthful for his years." He was an elder in the Presbyterian Church and was liberal in his support of religion and education.

[*Last Letters of Rich. L. Allen* (1871); S. H. Perry, *Hist. of the City of Buffalo and Erie County* (1884), I, 701.] A. C. T.

ALLEN, ROBERT (July 1812–Aug. 5, 1886), Union soldier, was born in Ohio. He graduated from West Point in 1836, was commissioned in the 2nd Artillery, and served with it in the Florida War and elsewhere for some years. In 1846, he accepted appointment as captain and assistant quartermaster. In the Mexican War he was at first on duty as a quartermaster with Gen. Taylor's army. He was transferred to Gen. Scott's in time to be present at the siege of Vera Cruz, and served with it until after the capture of the City of Mexico. From then until the Civil War his service was chiefly on the Pacific coast, as treasurer of the military government of California and as chief quartermaster of the military command. In 1861 he was promoted major and sent to St. Louis as chief quartermaster of the department. In the early days of any war of the United States, habitually unprepared as it is, the task of the quartermaster's department is a herculean one. Allen's situation would have been difficult at best, but it was rendered doubly so by the aberrations of Gen. Frémont, the department commander, whose administration took no account of law, regulations, or the state of the treasury. Allen had no choice but to carry out the orders of his chief, but wrote in October, "If the reckless expenditures in this department are not checked by a stronger arm than mine, the Quartermaster's Department will be wrecked in Missouri alone" (*Official Records,* ser. I, vol. III, p. 549). Nevertheless, he survived the ordeal, brought order out of chaos, and continued throughout the war to act as the chief quartermaster for the armies in the west. He was given temporary rank as colonel in 1862, and appointed brigadier-general of volunteers, May 23, 1863. With headquarters first at St. Louis and later at Louisville, he provided stores and transportation for the operations against Donelson and Corinth, for the Vicksburg and Atlanta campaigns, and for many other expeditions from eastern Tennessee westward to New Mexico. His task was an immense one, efficiently performed. Gen. Meigs said of him that "no more faithful or more able officer is in the service of the Government" (*Ibid.,* ser. III, vol. IV, p. 897). He became colonel in the regular army in 1866, and until his retirement from active service in 1878 was stationed in Washington and San Francisco. He then traveled extensively in Asia and Europe. He died in Geneva.

[G. W. Cullum, *Biog. Reg.* (3rd ed., 1891), I, 651–53; *Bull. Ass. Grads. Mil. Acad.,* 1887, pp. 16–21.] T. M. S.

ALLEN, THOMAS (Aug. 29, 1813–Apr. 8, 1882), railroad builder, congressman, the son of Jonathan and Eunice (Larned) Allen, was born at Pittsfield, Mass. His father was a member of both houses of the Massachusetts legislature; through his grandmother he was a descendant of William Bradford. Graduating from Union College in 1832, he studied law in an office in New York City, supporting himself by writing for the *Family Magazine,* and was admitted to the bar in 1835. But he never practised law actively. In 1837 he started at Washington the *Madisonian,* an anti-Van Buren Democratic paper, which supported Harrison in 1840. The *Madisonian* was to be the organ of the new administration, but on Harrison's death Allen sold the paper and in 1842 removed to St. Louis. His real career began in 1848–49, when he was a prime mover in the National Railroad Convention at St. Louis, writing the preliminary publicity, the memorial to Congress, and the address to the public. He took a leading part in securing the charter of the Pacific Railroad and in 1850 was elected to the state Senate. Here he was largely responsible for the initiation of the policy of state loans to the railroads, securing a loan of two million dollars for the Pacific road; his elaborate report of 1852 was later very closely followed and was the basis of the earlier railroad system of the state. In 1854 he resigned the presidency of the Pacific Railroad, which he had held since 1851, and withdrew from politics. In 1858 he organized the banking-house of Allen, Copp & Nisbet, prominent in the early railroad financing in Missouri and Illinois. When at the close of the war the bankrupt, state-aided railroads were reorganized, Allen purchased the Iron Mountain, then eighty-six miles in length, and by further purchases and the construction of a hundred miles a year built up by 1874 the St. Louis, Iron Mountain & Southern system of 686 miles. He retained control of it until he sold out to Jay Gould in 1881. He was also interested in the St. Louis street-railway developments. Save for an unsuccessful campaign for Congress in 1862 on the Union ticket, he had taken no active part in politics for many years, but in 1880 he was elected to Congress on the Democratic ticket. He died in Washington on Apr. 8, 1882.

Allen was a man of definite objectives, strict standards of personal conduct, great force and determination. His strong sense of community interests and obligations was evidenced by his organization of the Missouri Horticultural Society, the endowment of the Allen Professorship of Mining and Metallurgy at Washington University, and the gift of a free library and building to his native town. He built the Missouri Building at the Centennial Exposition at his own expense when state funds were not available. He was married in 1842 to Ann Russell, daughter of William Russell of St. Louis.

[L. U. Reavis, *St. Louis, the Future Great City of the World* (1875), pp. 261–69, portr.; Richard Edwards and M. Hopewell, *Edwards's Great West* (1860), pp. 437–39; J. T. Scharf, *Hist. of St. Louis City and County* (1883), pp. 638–41, portr.; J. L. Jenkins, *Sermon Preached at the Funeral of Hon. Thomas Allen in the First Church, Pittsfield, Mass., Apr. 11, 1882*; "Memorial Address on the Life and Character of Thomas Allen," *48 Cong., 1 Sess., H. R. Misc. Doc. No. 47.*]

J.V.

ALLEN, THOMAS M. (Oct. 21, 1797–Oct. 10, 1871), pioneer minister of the Disciples in Kentucky and Missouri, and promoter of educational institutions, was born in Shenandoah, now Warren County, Va. He was of Presbyterian ancestry and received his early education from Presbyterian ministers and from John S. McNamara, considered in his day an exceptional mathematician. He entered the army before he was seventeen years old and served six months in a Virginia regiment. In 1816, while he was riding through a forest, lightning struck a tree, which fell, killing a young woman riding with him, crushing his own horse, and so injuring him that thereafter his left arm was practically useless. Removing to Kentucky in 1819, he married Rebecca Russell of Fayette County, studied law at Transylvania University, and later practised for a short time in Bloomington, Ind.

Coming under the influence of Barton W. Stone [*q.v.*], however, he was converted to the religious views of that leader, was baptized by him in 1823, and returned to Kentucky, where in 1825 he was ordained by Stone at "Old Union" Church, Fayette County, which Allen and five others had established two years before. Soon he was prominent in the councils and activities of the Christians, and planted churches of that order in Paris, Antioch, Clintonville, and Cynthiana. He was one of those instrumental in bringing about the union between the followers of Stone and those of Alexander Campbell [*q.v.*] which was effected in 1832. In 1836 he removed to Boone County, Mo.

Here he became a person of extensive influence. He was six feet tall, of commanding person, always dressed in faultless taste, an easy speaker, and an accomplished gentleman. He possessed ample means and the farm which he purchased, worked by slaves so well cared for that the most of them remained with him after the emancipation, became one of the best estates in the county. His home was noted for its hospitality, and he was intimate with the leading men of the state. He was frequently urged to become the Whig candidate for governor, and declined an appointment to Congress to fill an unexpired term. Although a slave-holder, he was opposed to secession, and at a meeting of citizens of Boone County, held May 6, 1861, he urged them to maintain an armed neutrality within the Union, and not be driven away by passion and prejudice into the dangerous experiment of revolution and anarchy. His chief interest always was the extension of religion and education, and to this he gave himself untiringly almost to the day of his death. He went where there were no churches, preaching in court-houses, schoolhouses, barns, and groves, and he is credited with having done more than any other one man to establish the Disciples of Christ in Missouri. It was largely through his efforts that Boone County subscribed more than any other county toward the founding of the University of Missouri in 1839, in consideration of which generosity the institution was located at Columbia. He was a member of its first board of curators, and president of the board in 1839, 1841, and again in 1864. He was among the first advocates in the state of equal educational advantages for women, and one of the founders of Christian Female College, of the governing board of which he was many years a member.

[Robt. Richardson, *Memoirs of Alex. Campbell* (1870), II; *Hist. of Boone County, Mo.* (1882); Thos. P. Haley, *Hist. and Biog. Sketches of the Early Churches and Pioneer Preachers of the Christian Ch. in Mo.* (1888); Errett Gates, *The Disciples of Christ* (1905); W. T. Moore, *A Comprehensive Hist. of the Disciples of Christ* (1909).]

H. E. S.

ALLEN, TIMOTHY FIELD (Apr. 24, 1837–Dec. 5, 1902), homeopathic physician, botanist, son of Dr. David and Eliza (Graves) Allen, was born in the village of Westminster, Vt. Reared amidst the beauties of the Connecticut Valley, the boy absorbed a love of nature which proved a vital factor in his later life. In those days the only profession that offered any opportunity for a born naturalist was that of medicine, hence Timothy Allen, like Asa Gray, turned to it for a livelihood. He prepared for college at East Windsor Hill, Conn., and went from there to Amherst. Here he came under the stimulating influence of Edward Hitchcock, Charles U. Shepard, and W. S. Clark. He was graduated in 1858 with the degree of A.B. and went at once to New York, where he became a student in the Medical Department of the University of the City of New York (now New York

University), receiving the degree of M.D. in 1861. He was married on June 3, 1861, to Julia Bissell of Litchfield, Conn. Soon after he had begun the practise of medicine in Brooklyn, his career was interrupted by the Civil War, and he became acting assistant-surgeon in the United States Army at Point Lookout, Md. On being released from his duties there, he resumed his practise in Brooklyn, but in 1863 he removed to New York City, where he remained for the rest of his life.

After his establishment as a successful practitioner in New York, his activities extended into three different fields and his achievements in each proved him a man of unusual ability. His most notable accomplishments were in connection with the development of homeopathy, and his practise and writings contributed largely to the establishment of that school of medicine. From 1867 on, he was professor of materia medica and therapeutics in the New York Homeopathic Medical College and from 1882 to 1893, he was dean of that institution. In 1874, he began the publication of his most important work, an *Encyclopedia of Materia Medica* which extended to ten volumes. In the field of ophthalmic surgery his achievements were little less notable and in 1884 he became surgeon to the New York Ophthalmic Hospital. Later, his interest in that institution led to his being for some years president of its board of trustees. His volume on *Ophthalmic Therapeutics*(1876) is his chief publication in this field. Soon after his establishment in New York, he became associated with the famous botanist, Dr. John Torrey, and for the remainder of his life botany was a major interest. He was one of the founders of the Torrey Botanical Club in 1871 and for many years was one of its vice-presidents. The club published in 1870–76 a *Flora of New York City* to which he was one of the chief contributors. Soon after this he began to devote himself to the stoneworts (*Characeæ*), a group of curious fresh-water plants to which little attention had been paid in America. He quickly made himself master of this field, published a number of important papers, and accumulated an extraordinary collection of stoneworts from all over the world, which in 1891 he gave to the New York Botanical Garden.

[Memoirs by N. L. Britton, *Bull. Torrey Bot. Club*, XXX, 173–77, containing bibliography of Allen's botanical writings; *Jour. N. Y. Bot. Garden*, III, 232; *Amherst Coll. Biog. Recs. Grads. & Non-Grads.*, 1927, p. 199; *N. Y. Tribune*, Dec. 7, 1902.]

H. L. C.

ALLEN, WILLIAM (Aug. 5, 1704–Sept. 6, 1780), merchant, jurist, was a member of the Allen family of Philadelphia, Presbyterians from Dungannon, Ireland, who were prominent in that Scotch-Irish group which brought Pennsylvania into the national manner of thinking in time for the American Revolution. William Allen, Sr., died in 1725, but not until his son had secured at London a legal training valuable throughout his future life. Upon his father's death William returned to America, where family loyalty impelled him to neglect his chosen profession and maintain the important and remunerative mercantile business created by his father. In 1727 he entered the Philadelphia Council and for nearly fifty years his influence in political affairs is easily followed. His prestige was enhanced by his marriage, Feb. 16, 1733/4, to Margaret, daughter of Speaker Andrew Hamilton, and by the family alliances of their six children. First came his leadership of Philadelphia when it petitioned the Assembly in 1729 to be allowed to erect a "State House." The legislature, guided by Allen and Hamilton as trustees of the purchasing and building funds, established its first permanent home at Philadelphia, in October 1735, instead of at Chester, as the Quaker Party, to be distinguished from the religious Society of Friends, had desired. For the rapid completion of this future "Independence Hall" despite labor troubles, Allen advanced considerable money from his private purse, some of which was not repaid until 1761.

Meanwhile Allen's influence extended. He was member of the Assembly 1731–39, was elected Grand Master of Freemasons in 1732, and became mayor of Philadelphia in 1735. Chosen recorder of the city in 1741, he joined Franklin in defending the western frontier and in advancing provincial self-government, especially during the terms of his brother-in-law Governor James Hamilton 1748–54 and 1759–63. These activities, his initial aid to the College of Philadelphia, and his furtherance of many charities mark Allen's breadth of character. His reputation when justice of various lower courts 1737–50 and as chief justice of the province 1750–74 proves his legal ability, although the texts of few decisions have been preserved. His position in the American Philosophical Society and upon the board of trustees of the University of Pennsylvania shows his literary interests. Allen's value to province and to country was demonstrated when he recommended Franklin for deputy postmaster-general of America(1751), and served on the Maryland-Pennsylvania boundary commission (1750–51) to adjust the dispute between so-called "Penn pertinacity and Baltimore pugnacity." In 1765, being owner of a large estate in Northampton County, Pa., he laid out the town of Northampton, afterward named Allentown.

Allen felt keenly the grievances of America against Great Britain. When in England in 1763, he obtained a postponement of the sugar duties, and later, in 1766, joined Franklin in securing a repeal of the Stamp Act. But for the next decade "the great giant," as he was described, remained an advocate of compromise when wiser statesmen were realizing the necessity of effective colonial union. A member of the Proprietary party in 1774, he could not follow Franklin into American nationalism; thus, when his plan for reconciliation outlined in *The American Crisis* (1774) failed, his active service for Pennsylvania ended and he resigned his judicial position. When the Constitution of 1776 was adopted and his son James wrote, "Peace is scarcely thought of," Allen retired to England to await a reconsideration. He died on Sept. 6, 1780, after revisiting Philadelphia in 1779 and freeing his slaves by a codicil to his will dated Dec. 1 of that year. Later opinion has recognized the difficulties of Allen's position and judged more kindly than did his contemporaries in 1776 this promoter of Pennsylvania's welfare during sixty years of loyal service.

[Allen MSS. in the Hist. Soc. of Pa.; the *Pa. Mag. of Hist. and Biog.*, I, 202–10, XXXVIII, 385–406; *The Writings of Benj. Franklin*, Smyth ed., 10 vols. (1922); C. H. Lincoln, *The Revolutionary Movement in Pa.* (1901); J. H. Martin, *The Bench and Bar of Phila.* (1883); Scharf and Westcott, *Hist. of Phila.* (1884); Isaac Sharpless, *Hist. of Proprietary Government in Pa.* (1896).]

C. H. L—n.

ALLEN, WILLIAM (Jan. 2, 1784–July 16, 1868), clergyman, educator, author, was well known in New England during the first half of the nineteenth century as one of the most learned scholars of the time, an effective preacher, an able college president, and a writer of poetry. He is now remembered chiefly as the compiler of the *American Biographical and Historical Dictionary* (1809), one of the earliest undertakings of its kind, though the same year John Eliot published his *Dictionary of Eminent Characters in New England*, a less comprehensive work. The first edition of Allen's dictionary contained approximately 700 names; the 1832 edition, 1,800; and the 1857 edition, 7,000.

He was born in Pittsfield, Mass., the son of Rev. Thomas Allen and Elizabeth Lee, daughter of Rev. Jonathan Lee of Salisbury, Conn. On his father's side he was a descendant of Samuel Allen, a native of England, who died in Windsor, Conn., in 1648; and on his mother's, of Gov. Bradford of Plymouth. His father was for forty-six years pastor of the First Congregational Church, Pittsfield. An ardent Jeffersonian, vigorously partisan in the pulpit and out, with no gift or taste for conciliation, he aroused much violent antagonism. His son grew up to hold the same political views and to display a like tendency to provoke opposition, though not with respect to matters political. He graduated from Harvard College at the age of eighteen, studied theology under Rev. John Pierce of Brookline, Mass., and was licensed to preach by the Berkshire Association in 1804. From 1805 to 1810 he was assistant librarian and regent at Harvard. It was while here that he prepared the first edition of his dictionary. In 1810 his father died, and on Oct. 10 of that year he was ordained to succeed him as pastor at Pittsfield. Here he remained until 1817. On Jan. 28, 1813 he married Maria Malleville Wheelock, only daughter of President Wheelock of Dartmouth College, by whom he had eight children. His pastorate, though less stormy than his father's, was not untroubled. He is described as impassive, inflexible, stately, and stiff, but just, kind, and faithful; "more learned than apt to teach; a good ruler for all but the unruly" (*General Catalogue of Bowdoin College*, 1894). He insisted upon strict compliance with the letter of the law and his unyielding disposition and rigorous enforcement of church discipline made him many enemies.

A son-in-law of President Wheelock, a pronounced Democrat, and a firm believer in the desirableness of a close union between college and state, he was a natural choice for a place on the Dartmouth University faculty when the New Hampshire legislature altered the charter of Dartmouth College, and attempted to reorganize that institution. Upon the death of President Wheelock in 1817 he was made his successor. During two years of litigation, with the college and university existing side by side, he administered the affairs of the latter as best he could, until it went out of existence as a result of the decision of the United States Supreme Court. In December 1819 he was chosen president of Bowdoin College. Here he gathered about him a strong faculty, established the Medical School of Maine, and broadened the curriculum, especially with respect to modern languages, of which Henry W. Longfellow was made professor. The personal characteristics previously mentioned finally brought him into serious conflict with his trustees, however, and, in 1831, with a view to getting him out of office a piece of special legislation was enacted by the state (*Public Acts of the State of Maine*, 1831, chapter DXVII), which provided that no person holding the office of president of any college in the state should hold that office beyond the day of the next commencement unless reëlected by the trustees, and that he must receive two-thirds of all the votes given on the question of his election. Allen failed of reelection but took the legality of the act of the legislature before the federal circuit court, which declared it unconstitutional (decision of Justice Story, Allen *vs.* McKean, *1 Sumner's Reports*, 276). The litigation extended over two years during which time he did not perform the duties of president. He resumed them in 1833, but increasing unpopularity with the students, together with the prejudice against him among the trustees, caused him to tender his resignation in 1838, to take effect the following year. The rest of his life was spent in literary activity at Northampton, Mass. His wife had died in 1828, and on Dec. 2, 1831, he married Sarah Johnson Breed, daughter of John McLaren and Rebecca Walker Breed of Norwich, Conn.

In addition to the *Biographical Dictionary* and numerous sermons and addresses, he published *Accounts of Shipwreck and of Other Disasters at Sea, Designed to be Interesting and Useful to Mariners* (1823); *Junius Unmasked, or Lord George Sackville Proved to be Junius* (1828); *Lectures to Young Men* (1830); "An Account of Arnold's Expedition Against Quebec in 1775" (in *Collections of the Maine Historical Society*, I, 1831); *Psalms and Hymns for Public Worship* (1835); *Memoir of John Codman, D.D.* (1853); *Wunnissoo, or the Vale of Hoosatunnuk, a Poem* (1856); *A Book of Christian Sonnets* (1860); *Poems of Nazareth and the Cross* (1866).

[Wm. B. Sprague, *A Discourse Delivered in the First Cong. Ch. in Northampton, Mass., on the 26th of July, 1868*, etc. (1868); *N.E. Hist. and Genealogical Reg.*, vol. XXIII (1869); J. E. A. Smith, *Hist. of Pittsfield* (1876); John K. Lord, *Hist. of Dartmouth Coll.* (1913); Hist. sketch in *Gen. Catalogue of Bowdoin Coll.* (1894).]

H. E. S.

ALLEN, WILLIAM (Dec. 18, 1803–July 11, 1879), congressman, governor of Ohio, was descended from Quaker forebears who were among the earliest settlers of Pennsylvania. In the eighteenth century a branch of the family removed to North Carolina, where it separated itself from the Society of Friends and engaged actively in the American Revolution. Nathaniel Allen, the father of William, was an officer in the Revolutionary army and later a member of the North Carolina convention which ratified the Federal Constitution. William, the issue of Nathaniel's third marriage, to one Sarah Colburn, was born in Edenton, N.C. Deprived of both his parents at an early age, and, through a technicality of the law, of his share in the large estate of his father, he was reared under the tutelage of his half-sister, a woman of great force and of some education, who had become the wife of the Rev. Pleasant Thurman. After a short residence in Lynchburg, Va., as an apprentice to a saddler, Allen determined to hazard his fortunes in the West, whither his sister and her family had already gone. In 1819 the sixteen-year-old boy arrived at the home of his sister in Chillicothe, Ohio, after a perilous journey on foot, in midwinter, across the ice-clad Alleghanies. After two years of preparation in Chillicothe Academy, supplemented by a course of general reading under the direction of his sister, he began the study of law in the office of Col. Edward King, the son of Rufus King. Three years later, at the age of twenty-one, he was admitted to the practise of law and became at once a partner of Col. King. Riding the circuit, in accordance with frontier custom, Allen soon became a noted local figure; his large stature and commanding presence, his fluency of speech and skill in debate won for him a reputation throughout the section of the state in which he traveled,—a reputation which induced the Jackson Democrats of his district to nominate him as their candidate for Congress. The district was normally Republican by a majority of 1,500 to 2,000, but after an exciting contest the youthful Allen carried it by a majority of 1 against Gen. Duncan McArthur, whose only daughter, Mrs. Effie (McArthur) Coons, he subsequently married (1842). He served one term in the House, from 1833 to 1835, without particular distinction, and was defeated for reëlection. But the Democratic party sent him to the Senate in 1837 to succeed Thomas Ewing, and again for a second term in 1843. He was an ardent expansionist and a frequent declaimer on the Senate floor for the rights of the United States in Oregon and for the annexation of Texas. In his second term he was chairman of the important Committee on Foreign Relations and became the spokesman of President Polk during the war with Mexico. In the confusion of public opinion in the late forties and fifties Allen was unable to perceive the significance and weight of the Free-Soil element in the Democratic party. After his defeat by Salmon P. Chase (1849) he went into retirement on his large 1,400 acre farm, "Fruit Hill," near Chillicothe, where he remained for the next twenty-five years. During the Civil War he was an anti-war Democrat and an outspoken critic of the Lincoln administration. For his stand on the war he was severely criticized. Toward the end of his life he made a spectacular reappearance in state politics in his election to the governorship of Ohio in 1873. Although he served acceptably in this office, he failed to be reëlected, his espousal of the Greenback panacea contributing largely to his defeat. In 1876 his name was presented to the Democratic National Convention for the presidency. He died at "Fruit Hill" three years later. Allen did not reach the higher levels of statesmanship. A partial explanation of his failure is found in his provincial and partisan outlook, his attachment to lost causes, and his inability to weigh accurately new and unexpected issues. But he voiced at all times what he believed to be aspirations and ideals of the West. His essential honesty was never questioned.

[Reginald C. McGrane's *William Allen, A Study in Western Democracy* (1925) is an authoritative biography. This study is thoroughly documented and the accompanying bibliography contains a classified list of sources. The most important of these are twenty-one volumes of the MSS. of William Allen in the Lib. of Cong.]

C. E. C.

ALLEN, WILLIAM FRANCIS (Sept. 5, 1830–Dec. 9, 1889), classical scholar, was born at Northboro, Mass., the son of Joseph Allen, Unitarian clergyman, and Lucy Clarke Ware of Cambridge, Mass. He was prepared for college in a school kept by his parents in the Northboro parsonage, with one year at the Roxbury Latin School, and was graduated from Harvard College in 1851. For three years he was tutor in a private family in New York; then, in 1854, he went to Europe, where he studied one semester at Göttingen and one in Berlin, after which he went to Italy, arriving in Rome in November 1855. Here he spent three months mainly in studying the topography of the ancient city, then went to Naples and to Greece. He returned to Boston in June 1856. From 1856 to 1863 he was associate principal of the English and Classical School at West Newton, Mass., and here, July 2, 1862, he married Mary Tileston Lambert. In November 1863, accompanied by his wife, he went, in the employ of the Freedmen's Aid Commission, to begin the education of the freedmen at St. Helena Island, S. C. He came north in July 1864, and in September went as agent of the Sanitary Commission to Helena, Ark., where he remained until February 1865. His wife died on Mar. 23 of that year, leaving an infant daughter, Katherine. After a service of some months as assistant superintendent of the schools of Charleston, S. C., Allen went as professor of ancient languages to Antioch College, Yellow Springs, Ohio, but remained there only one year, after which he taught for a year in a military academy at Perth Amboy, N. J. In 1867 he was called to the chair of ancient languages and history in the University of Wisconsin, and here he remained until his death. On June 30, 1868, he married Margaret Loring Andrews, of Newburyport, Mass.. who bore him three sons.

Allen was a pioneer in the teaching of history by the topical system of study and the examination of original sources. His published writings show great versatility and prodigious industry. Those which appeared as books are the following: *Slave Songs of the United States,* compiled in conjunction with Charles P. Ware and Lucy M. Garrison (1867); *A Latin Reader,* with his brother J. H. Allen [*q.v.*] (1869); *Latin Lessons,* with J. H. Allen (1869); *Manual Latin Grammar,* with J. H. Allen (1868); six volumes of Latin texts and selections, with J. B. Greenough and J. H. Allen, known as the "Allen and Greenough" series, to which he furnished the historical and mythological notes and introductions (1873, 1874, and 1875); *An Introduction to Latin Composition* (1870); the *Germania and Agricola of Tacitus* (1880); the *Annals of Tacitus,* Books 1–4 (1890); and a *Short History of the Roman People* (1890), the manuscript of which was finished the evening before his death. The last is his most important single work and his only book dealing entirely with his special subject. His further writings comprise more than 900 articles and reviews on classical, historical, political, and various other subjects.

[C. L. Smith, *Classical Rev.,* IV, 426–28; J. D. Butler, *Trans. Wis. Acad. Sciences, Arts and Letters,* VIII, 439–41; D. B. Frankenburger, *Essays and Monographs, Memorial Volume,* with memoir, pp. 1–21, and bibliography, pp. 351–82 (1890).]

H. N. F.

ALLEN, WILLIAM FREDERICK (Oct. 9, 1846–Nov. 9, 1915), railroad expert, was born in Bordentown, N. J., the son of Joseph Warner and Sarah (Norcross) Allen. His father, a civil engineer, was drowned off Hatteras Inlet, Jan. 15, 1862, on the Burnside expedition, in command of his regiment, the 9th New Jersey Volunteers. The son was educated at the Bordentown Model School and at the Protestant Episcopal Academy at Philadelphia. In 1862 he became a rodman on the civil-engineering force of the Camden & Amboy Railroad, was made assistant engineer in 1863, and served as resident engineer from 1868 to 1872. On Apr. 20, 1871, he was married to Caroline Yorke of Salem, N. J., by whom he had four sons. In October 1872 he became a member of the staff of the *Official Guide of the Railways and Steam Navigation Lines,* and remained until his death with the company that published it, acting as president after 1914. This connection brought him in contact with many railroad men and with many forms of railroad activity, and thus led to his most important contribution,—his work in connection with the adoption of standard time for the railways. In those days every railroad fixed the time of its train schedules as it chose, usually taking it from that of its home city or the most important town on its line. Over fifty different standards were in use, with much resulting confusion. Beginning in 1872, various efforts had been made to arrange time schedules for through trains from one system to another. In that year, a General Time Convention had been organized, and in 1877 a Southern Railway Time Convention began to serve the southern roads. From 1875 until his death Allen acted as secretary and treasurer of the General Time Convention and of the American Railway Association, formed later by the consolidation of the two Conventions. In 1881 the organization referred to him the problem of standardization of time, and as a result of his report submitted on Apr. 11, 1883, the fifty differing systems melted into four at high noon on Nov. 18, 1883. Various schemes of standardization had been suggested by others before this, and these earlier efforts undoubtedly influenced the final plan. The difference between them and Allen's suggestion lay in the fact that they usually assumed adoption of meridians an even hour apart, while Allen adapted and adjusted his points of change to the territory in question. His scheme was practical, rather than theoretical, with the advantage of suggestion by a man perfectly acquainted with the difficulties to be overcome, the means to be used, conditions to be met, and the point of view of the railroad operating man. In 1904 he edited a *Short History of Standard Time and Its Adoption in North America in 1883.*

[A collection of manuscript and printed material connected with the movement for standard time, gathered by Allen as work progressed, is in the Manuscript Division of the New York Public Library. The *American Railway Association Proceedings,* vol. I and an *Historical Statement* issued by the Association in 1921 serve as official records of his connection with the Association; see also R. E. Riegel, "Standard Time in the United States," *Am. Hist. Rev.,* XXXIII, 84–89. There is a memoir by C. A. Hammond in *Trans. Am. Soc. Civil Engineers,* LXXX, 2244–48; other biographical references are *Who's Who in America, 1914–15; Biog. Dir. Railway Officials of America,* ed. by H. G. Lane (1913); *N. Y. Times,* Nov. 10, 1915; *Railway Age Gazette,* Nov. 12, 1915, p. 919.]

H. M. L.

ALLEN, WILLIAM HENRY (Oct. 21, 1784–Aug. 18, 1813), naval officer, born in Providence, R. I., was the son of Gen. William Allen of Revolutionary distinction, his mother being Sarah, a sister of William Jones, at one time governor of Rhode Island. Appointed a midshipman in the United States Navy Apr. 28, 1800, his first service was in the frigate *George Washington,* under Capt. William Bainbridge, who, like his later commanders, Barron and Rodgers, gave him proofs of their trust in his enterprise and seamanship. After several years of service in the Mediterranean, he was ordered as third lieutenant to the frigate *Chesapeake,* and commanded a gun division on board that ill-fated vessel when she was attacked and severely damaged by the British ship *Leopard* on June 22, 1807, after a refusal by Commodore James Barron [*q.v.*] to give up certain alleged deserters from the British navy. The surrender of the *Chesapeake* by Barron without striking a blow, although ample time was given the American commander to clear his ship for action, aroused the indignation of his officers, and especially of Lieut. Allen, who, the day following the action, drew up a petition to the Secretary of the Navy for the arrest and punishment of Commodore Barron, which was signed by six officers of the *Chesapeake.* Only a single shot was fired by the *Chesapeake,* according to Allen, who wrote in a letter, "I was at the galley (the camboose) and, snatching up a coal from the flames, fired the only gun, which went through the wardroom of the English ship." Three of the *Chesapeake's* crew were killed and eighteen wounded. Barron, though acquitted of cowardice, was suspended from the service for five years without pay, on the charge of not clearing his ship for action.

Allen's sense of duty and justice was repeatedly brought out during his short life by his refusal to ask special favor either for himself or his friends. When requested by his own father to protect certain persons from the consequences of flouting the Embargo Act, he replied, "Nothing, my dear Sir, could give me more pleasure, . . . but, Sir, had this been *your* vessel, her situation would have been precisely the same. It is impossible that I can be of the least service." Promoted to be first lieutenant, he joined the frigate *United States* under Commodore Decatur in 1809, and on Oct. 25, 1812, took a prominent part in the fierce action between his ship and the powerful British frigate *Macedonian,* 49 guns, which lasted for nearly two hours and resulted in the surrender of the *Macedonian,* so crippled by the accuracy of the American fire that it was doubtful if she would continue to float. "Her two principal masts were secured and a jurymast rigged by Mr. Allen . . . who was put in charge of her, with great ingenuity. . . . Mr. Allen was promoted to the rank of master-commandant, and he received due credit for the steady discipline that the ship's company had displayed" (J. F. Cooper, *History of the Navy,* 1839, II, 180).

Receiving the command of the *Argus,* sloop-of-war of 20 guns, Allen sailed for France on June 18, 1813, with Mr. Crawford, the newly appointed American minister to France, on board, and, having landed his passenger safely at l'Orient, proceeded on a cruise, the object of which was the difficult one of harrying British commerce in the Irish Channel. After various successes the *Argus* fell in with the British brig *Pelican,* 21 guns, a short and sharp fight resulting, during the first few minutes of which Capt. Allen's leg was carried off by a round shot. Refusing to go below, he soon fainted from loss of blood and was carried down, together with one of his lieutenants, Watson, who was struck in the head. The *Argus* continued to be gallantly fought by the other lieutenant, William Howard Allen, but so devastating was the fire of the *Pelican* that the American brig hauled down her colors. Allen died of his wound in the hospital of Mill Prison, and was buried by the enemy with the honors of war. "Capt. Allen," says Cooper (*Ibid.*, p. 267), "was esteemed one of the best officers of his class in the navy. A thorough man-of-war's man, he was of mild and gentlemanlike deportment, a fine, martial personal appearance, and of respectable mental attainments. His influence over the crews with which he sailed was very great, and it is not possible to say now what might have been the result of the combat in which he fell, had he not been so early killed. He was unmarried."

[Records of the Office of Naval Records and Lib., Navy Dept., Washington, D.C.; J. H. Brown, *Am. Naval Heroes* (1899).] E.B.

ALLEN, WILLIAM HENRY (Mar. 27, 1808–Aug. 29, 1882), college president, son of Jonathan and Thankful (Longley) Allen, was born at Readfield, now Manchester, Me. To parentage and rigorous early training in the harsh environment of the Maine country he owed the sturdy nature that served him well throughout an active life. He attended district school, Kent Hill Seminary, and Bowdoin College. After graduating from the latter in 1833, he taught Latin and Greek in the Oneida Methodist Conference Seminary, Cazenovia, N. Y. (1833–36), and was principal of the high school in Augusta, Me., for six months. From Augusta he was called in 1836 to the chair of chemistry and natural history at Dickinson College, which he occupied with distinction for ten years, being then transferred to philosophy and English literature. For nearly a year he was acting president of the institution. He was elected to the presidency of Girard College in 1849, took office the following year, and gave twelve years of whole-hearted, effective service. In 1862, chiefly because of a policy of retrenchment adopted by the directors, he resigned the presidency but continued lecturing and writing. From these pursuits he was called in 1865 to the presidency of the Pennsylvania Agricultural College. After two years of valuable service, he left this post, being urged to resume the headship of Girard College. The next fifteen years there were most gratifying to him and most valuable to those for whom he labored. Recognition of his services is found in the declaration of the directors that he had "performed the duties of his position with a decidedness that won our regard and endeared him not only to pupils but the officials of the institution and to all connected with the college" (resolution of the directors, Aug. 29, 1882, *In Memoriam,* p. 5). Throughout life, Allen identified himself closely with religious work. While at Bowdoin, he professed Christianity, and it was his recognized religious leadership and high personal character that secured his election to the presidency of Girard College. At Dickinson College, he contributed numerous articles to the *Methodist Quarterly Review;* at Girard, his religious contribution lay in his upright example, preparation of a manual of devotional services, and carefully studied lectures to the boys. In 1872, he became president of the American Bible Society. He was married four times: to Martha Ann Richardson, who died in 1839; to Ellen Honora, sister of Andrew G. Curtin, governor of Pennsylvania; after her early death, to Mary Frances Quincy, daughter of Samuel Quincy of Boston, and finally, in 1858, to Mrs. Anna (Dunton) Gamwill, who survived him. Besides successful work as teacher and administrator, Allen acquired a considerable reputation as lecturer and orator. His addresses covered many fields, such as "Peace," "The Bible," "Public Welfare," "Labor," "Temperance," "Farm Life," "Economic Conditions," "Popular Education," and the "Waste of Intellect"; but his most polished and complete efforts were "Our Country's Mission in History" and his *Eulogy on Daniel Webster,* published in Philadelphia, 1853.

[C. A. Herrick, *Hist. of Girard Coll.* (MS.); *In Memoriam: In Commemoration of the Death of William H. Allen* (1883); *Girard Coll. Rec.*, vol. I, no. 6, pp. 1–2; *Alumni Rec. Dickinson Coll.* (1905); *Autobiography, Memories and Experiences of Moncure Daniel Conway* (1905), I, 43–45; *First Fifty Years of Cazenovia Seminary* (1877); C. F. Himes, *Dickinson Coll.* (1879), p. 106; *Phila. Public Ledger*, Aug. 30, Sept. 2, 1882; *N. E. Hist. and Geneal. Reg.*, Jan. 1883, p. 98.] T.W.

ALLEN, WILLIAM JOSHUA (June 9, 1829–Jan. 26, 1901), jurist, congressman, was born in Wilson County, Tenn. His father was Willis Allen, of Scotch-Irish descent, son of John Allen, who fell at New Orleans; his mother was Elizabeth Joiner, a North Carolina girl of Welsh descent. In 1830 Willis Allen migrated to the part of Illinois which later became Williamson County; he sat in the Illinois General Assemblies of 1838, 1844, and 1846 and served in Congress, 1851–55, as a Democrat. William Joshua Allen studied law in his father's office and at Louisville, Ky., and began the practise of law in 1849 at Metropolis, Ill. In 1853 he removed to Marion, where he formed a partnership with John A. Logan, was elected to the General Assembly in 1854, and was appointed United States district attorney in 1855. His support of Stephen A. Douglas after the latter's break with the administration led the Attorney-General to seek excuse to remove him. Allen soon after resigned. In 1859 he was elected judge of the circuit court succeeding his father in that office.

Allen's course at the outbreak of the Civil War was equivocal. He endeavored to counteract the effect of a disunionist meeting held Apr. 15, 1861, at Marion (Erwin, p. 260). By 1862 Allen was concerned in a movement to separate southern Illinois from the state and the Union and was an active Knight of the Golden Circle. He was arrested in August 1862, held prisoner for some months at Cairo and in the "Old Capitol Prison" at Washington and then released. In the summer of 1863 a local federal officer posted a guard on his residence (Cole, pp. 302, 309). Allen was, however elected to the constitutional convention of 1862, to fill Logan's unexpired term in the Thirty-seventh Congress, and to succeed himself in the Thirty-eighth Congress (1863–65). In 1864 he was beaten for reëlection largely by the influence of his old associate, Logan, who returned from the army to denounce him for treasonable conduct (*Ibid.*, pp. 327, 328).

After the war, Allen practised first at Cairo, then at Carbondale, Ill. He served in the constitutional convention of 1870, serving on the committee on the judiciary and as chairman of the committee on the bill of rights. In 1876 as special state's attorney he prosecuted those concerned in the Williamson Vendetta, which first gave the county the nickname of "Bloody Williamson." In 1886 he moved to Springfield and formed a partnership with C. C. and Stuart Brown. In April 1887 he was appointed United States district judge for southern Illinois. He died at Hot Springs, Ark., Jan. 26, 1901. In 1858 he had married Anna McKeen of Maryland, who died Aug. 17, 1892; three sons and two daughters survived them.

[J. M. Palmer, *Bench and Bar of Ill.* (1899), I, 211–14; obituaries in the *Ill. State Reg.*, *Ill. State Jour.*, and *Chicago Tribune*, Jan. 27, 1901; an unidentified clipping dated Apr. 18, 1887, in A. W. Snyder's coll. in the Ill. State Hist. Lib., Springfield. The account in the *Cong. Directory* is short and quite inaccurate; Milo Erwin, *Hist. of Williamson County, Ill.* (1876), is also untrustworthy. Allen's Civil War record is adequately treated in A. C. Cole, *The Era of the Civil War* (1919).]

T. C. P.

ALLEN, WILLIAM VINCENT (Jan. 28, 1847–Jan. 12, 1924), Populist senator, was born in Midway, Madison County, Ohio, the son of Rev. Samuel and Phœbe (Pugh) Allen. When he was but ten years old his family removed to Iowa, where they lived the normal life of pioneers. They were abolitionists and participated in the activities of the "Underground Railroad," and from them doubtless young Allen imbibed the views which led him to enlist at fifteen in the Union army. He served to the end of the war—certainly one of the youngest soldiers on the Northern side. This army experience he regarded as "the better part of his education," but at the close of the war he attended Upper Iowa University, and later he read law. He was married, in 1870, to Blanche Mott of Fayette, Ia., was admitted to the bar in Iowa, and practised there until 1884, when he removed to Madison, Nebr. There he soon took rank as a leading attorney, fell in with the Farmers' Alliance, turned Populist in 1890, and next year was elected district judge. When, in 1893, the Populists in the Nebraska legislature found it possible for them to dictate the choice of a United States senator, they turned to Allen, and with the help of Democratic votes elected him. A powerful man physically, and well endowed mentally, Allen distinguished himself early in his senatorial career by speaking continuously for fifteen hours during a filibuster against the repeal of the Sherman Silver Purchase Act. His speech did not prevent the repeal, but it marshaled the arguments for free coinage in a forceful way, and it marked Allen as a man of unusual resourcefulness. He made a strong argument, also, to prove unconstitutional the action of Secretary Carlisle in issuing bonds for gold under authority of the Resumption Act. On many other matters his voice was raised, and his opinions were received with respect. Allen's ability to hold his own in the Senate against great odds gave boundless joy to the Populists, and won much admiration from men outside third-party circles. He was acclaimed as "the intellectual giant of Populism." Although not reëlected in 1899, he returned to the Senate by appointment of the Governor to serve in the place of his successor-elect, who died without taking office. He remained in the Senate until 1901. Allen was one of those who favored fusion with the Democrats in 1896, and as chairman of the Populist nominating convention of that year he did much to further this end. When Populism waned he became a Democrat, and after his retirement from the Senate he again served as district judge; but in his later years he was not a strict partisan. He continued to live at Madison until the time of his death in January 1924.

[A short biography of Allen, self-inspired, appears in Albert Watkins and J. S. Morton, *Hist. of Nebr.* (1913), III, 493–94. There is an enthusiastic sketch by Albert Shaw in *Rev. of Revs.*, X, 32–42. Allen's senatorial career is reviewed by T. W. Tipton, "Forty Years of Nebr., in *Nebr. State Hist. Soc. Coll.*, ser. 2, vol. IV, 362–85. His speech on free silver is in the *Cong. Rec.*, 53 Cong., 1 Sess., app., pp. 289–340.]

J. D. H.

ALLEN, YOUNG JOHN (Jan. 3, 1836–May 30, 1907), Methodist missionary, educator, was born in Burke County, Ga., and died in Shanghai, China, with a record of nearly half a century of service in that eastern city. He was early left an orphan—his father, Young John, died shortly before the son's birth, and his mother, Mary Wooten, soon thereafter—but being endowed with vigor of body and mind, he developed an unusual store of self-reliance. His boyhood was spent in Meriwether County in the home of his aunt, Mrs. Wiley Hutcheson. From the Starrsville (Ga.) High School he went to Emory and Henry College (Va.) and then to Emory College (Ga.), securing his B.A. from the latter in 1858. He came early under the influence of the fervent Methodism of his surroundings, and was converted during his high-school days. At college he decided upon the ministry and received a license to preach. Upon graduation from Emory he was ordained and admitted to the Georgia Conference of his church, the Southern Methodist. In the same year he was married to Mary Houston, who had finished in July her course at Georgia Wesleyan. They both responded eagerly to an opportunity which came the following year to enter upon foreign service. In December 1859, with his wife and their five-months-old daughter—there were ultimately ten children in all—he sailed from New York for Shanghai to be Georgia's first missionary ambassador to China. He had himself raised the funds for passage.

Allen's resourcefulness and capacity came into full play soon after arrival in China in July 1860. The interruption of the American Civil War threw him upon his own support. For fifteen years, in fact, he provided not only for himself but for the Mission. While never abandoning missionary work he served as teacher and translator under the Chinese government. As translator of some ninety volumes he did much to satisfy the Chinese desire, newly awakened by the treaty of 1858 with England, for knowledge of world history, politics, and literature. He also edited for the government an *Official News Gazette*. In 1867 he founded his *Review of the Times*, a weekly magazine in Chinese devoted to the interpretation of the West, a periodical which became later the organ under his editorship of the China Christian Literature Society. He made himself the standard-bearer for forty years of the modern newspaper in Chinese and won distinction as a pioneer of Christian journalism in the East. Although he spent eighteen years in the employ of the Chinese government, toward the end of that period we find him giving more and more attention to specifically mission work. In 1881 he severed all official connection with the government and became superintendent of the China Mission of his church. Prior to assuming this new office he had built up a church congregation of over fifty in Shanghai and had opened several schools for boys. His chief educational monument was the Anglo-Chinese College in Shanghai—later incorporated into Soochow University (see article on D. L. Anderson)—which he founded in 1882 to train English-speaking Chinese for government and commercial posts. He was also directly concerned in the founding of the McTyeire School for girls. Among his original writings in English may be cited *The War Between China and Japan,* in connection with the writing of which Li Hung Chang gave him access to government papers, and his magnum opus, *Women in All Lands; or, China's Place Among the Nations.* He was twice sent to the General Conference of his church in America as delegate from the China Mission, and once represented his communion in an ecumenical conference in London.

Of flashing eye, giant frame, and great mustache and beard, Allen was a striking figure. With booming voice, keen mind, and facile pen, he was forceful upon platform, in council hall, or in the study. He attacked foot-binding vigorously, and championed the cause of China's womanhood. In his efforts to nationalize Christianity in China he addressed himself to the men of greatest influence, the scholars and rulers. He did all his work with care and punctuality, leaving at his death no writing unfinished, no letter unanswered, and no bill unpaid.

[*Chinese Recorder*, July 1907; *Work and Progress of the M. E. Ch., South, in China*(1907); *Ann. Rept. Board of Missions M. E. Ch., South* (1908); E. F. Cook, *Young J. Allen* (1910); L. H. Hammond, *Missionary Heroes* (1925); and James Cannon, *Hist. of Southern Meth. Missions* (1926).] J. C. A.

ALLEN, ZACHARIAH (Sept. 15, 1795–Mar. 17, 1882), scientist, inventor, author, reformer, was born, resided, and died in Providence, R. I. His parents were Zachariah and Anne (Crawford) Allen, the former an importer of cotton goods and a pioneer in calico printing in America; both were representatives of colonial families. In his youth, Allen was devoted to experiments in chemistry and physics, subjects which claimed his attention throughout life. After graduation from Brown University, in 1813, he read law in the office of James Burrill of Providence, and was admitted to the bar in 1815; he also pursued a course in the Brown Medical School which brought him a certificate of proficiency. He married Eliza Harriet Arnold in 1817. In 1822 he was a member of the town council of Providence, where his influence was effective in introducing the first fire-engine and hose equipment, in place of the hand-buckets previously used. Later, in spite of popular indifference, he projected and accomplished the construction of the city waterworks. He founded the village of Allendale, where he built a mill and storage reservoirs, said to be the first in the United States chartered for hydraulic purposes. As an inventor his work was various and notable. In 1821 he constructed the first central furnace system for heating houses by hot air, and later devised the method of transmitting power by leather belting, in place of the gear, or "cog wheel," connections previously employed. His contributions to textile manufacture included: cloth-napping machines (patented 1829, 1830), a dressing and finishing machine (1830), and a machine for spooling wool (1839). Preëminent, however, was his invention of the automatic steam-engine cut-off, controlled by the centrifugal ball-governor, or regulator (patented 1834), which is still used in substantially the original form (Stephen Roper, *Engineer's Handy Book,* 1881). He was the originator, also, of the methods for testing explosive oils, since widely adopted by legislation, and he devised the system of mutual fire insurance for manufacturing property, which requires underwriters to study methods for preventing fires and estimate premiums on the adequacy of the safety equipment installed. Beginning with the Manufacturers' Mutual Fire Insurance Company, which he founded in 1835, his scheme has been followed by numerous companies to the present time. Allen's sympathies were pronounced, particularly in behalf of the working classes. He promoted the first free evening school in New England, in 1840; led the movement to establish the Providence Association of Manufacturers and Mechanics; and endowed the city's public library. His various writings on the wrongs done the American Indians brought him official letters of acknowledgment from the Ojibway and Potawatomi of Canada, in 1877. He aided, also, the erection of monuments to King Philip and Massasoit.

Allen was a constant writer of newspaper and magazine articles, the most notable perhaps being "On the Volume of the Niagara River" (*American Journal of Science,* April 1844), in which he calculated, it is said for the first time, the volume of Niagara Falls. He was also the author of numerous books, addresses, and monographs including *The Science of Mechanics, as Applied to the Present Improvements in the Useful Arts* (1829); *Philosophy of the Mechanics of Nature and the Source and Modes of Action of Natural Motive-Power* (1852); *Memorial of Roger Williams* (1860); *Improvements in Transmission of Power from Motors to Machines* (1871); *Bi-Centenary of the Burning of Providence in 1676. Defense of the Rhode Island System of Treatment of the Indians, and of Civil and Religious Liberty* (1876); *The Conditions of Life, Habits and Customs, of the Native Indians of America and Their Treatment by the First Settlers* (1879); *Solar Light and Heat: the Source and the Supply* (1881).

[Amos Perry, *Memorial of Zachariah Allen* (1883); *Providence Jour.* and *Boston Advertiser,* Mar. 20, 1882; records of the U. S. Patent Office.]

ALLERTON, ISAAC (c. 1586–February 1658/9), Pilgrim father, trader, was one of the six most important Pilgrims during the Leyden period and third in importance during the first ten years at Plymouth. The rejection of his later policies and his withdrawal from Plymouth in disgrace cost him his place in history. A deposition of his established the date of his birth as "about" 1586 (*Mayflower Descendant,* IV, 109). He was a tailor in London, but moved to Leyden in 1608 before the Scrooby contingent arrived. He joined their congregation at once and in 1611 married Mary Norris, another member of it. In 1614 he became a citizen of Leyden. When the emigration to America was decided upon, he was one of four to complete the arrangements at Leyden and was one of those who bought and equipped the *Speedwell.* In it, he, his wife, and three children sailed in 1620, transferring later to the *Mayflower.* When Bradford was elected governor on the death of Carver in 1621, Allerton was elected assistant and was for three years the only other officer. The crisis in the colony's life came in 1625. They learned that the merchants who had originally financed the venture had decided to do no more. It was to Allerton that the Pilgrims turned to effect a settlement of their problems. In successive trips to England, he reached a settlement with the first merchants for the repayment of the original expense of equipping the colony (1626); borrowed money to purchase much-needed supplies of goods and cattle which ended the extreme poverty at Plymouth; arranged for the emigration of the remainder of the Leyden congregation (1629); induced many able people to emigrate who later became prominent at Plymouth and much strengthened the colony; interested a new group of English merchants; and secured the Patent of 1630 which at last gave the Pilgrims a title to their lands and property. These are among the most important achievements in the history of the colony. Thereafter its future was no longer in doubt.

In 1630 Allerton became convinced that trading ventures could be pursued with such profit and certainty that the colony might soon become rich. He borrowed further sums of money; the new English associates loaned more; he equipped a ship to trade and sailed back in another with a large consignment of goods which they had not ordered him to buy. He had wittingly exceeded his authority and had more than doubled their indebtedness; they therefore declined to accept his acts on their behalf and renounced him altogether as their agent (1631). Allerton's first wife had died in 1621 and he had married, at some time between 1623 and 1627, Fear, the daughter of Elder Brewster. He seems to have left Plymouth at once in 1631, though he was taxed there until 1634 and his name was carried on the list of Freemen until 1637 (Goodwin, *Pilgrim Republic*, p. 341). His second wife remained behind and died at Plymouth, in 1634. All his children by both marriages also remained behind. His daughter Mary, who died at Plymouth in 1699, was the last survivor of the *Mayflower* passengers.

Allerton's faith in trading was unquenchable and he now himself embarked in the elaborate series of ventures proposed. Many disasters overtook him, but on the whole he made money and became, as he had predicted, a rich man for those days. Some time before 1644 he married again and settled at New Haven. His will (*Mayflower Descendant*, II, 155–57) proves that he was trading with the Dutch at Manhattan on a large scale, with Delaware Bay, with Virginia, and with the West Indies. He died at New Haven.

[The chief authority is Bradford's *Hist.* Most documents to 1623 are printed in E. Arber's *Story of the Pilgrim Fathers* (1897). See also Dexter's *England and Holland of the Pilgrims* (1905) and R. G. Usher, *The Pilgrims and Their Hist.* (1918). Allerton's autograph is given in facsimile in the *Mayflower Descendant*, XXV, 97. We have no idea of his personal appearance.]

R. G. U.

ALLERTON, SAMUEL WATERS (May 26, 1828–Feb. 22, 1914), capitalist, was born at Amenia Union, Dutchess County, N. Y., the son of Samuel Waters Allerton (who traced his descent from Isaac Allerton, one of the *Mayflower's* passengers) and Hannah (Hurd) Allerton. His father had operated a woolen-mill, but failing in business moved west with his family, settling in Dubuque, Ia., in 1837. Ill health and further reverses caused a return to the East. In 1842 he rented a farm in Yates County, N. Y., and six years later moved to a farm in Wayne County, which he bought.

The son had begun to shift for himself at the age of twelve. Two years later, with his brother Henry, he rented a farm in Yates County, on which they cleared $1,500. This sum they gave in partial payment for a farm in Wayne County, assuming an indebtedness of $3,000. Here also they prospered, and at about the age of twenty-four Samuel, with $3,200 of savings, moved to Newark, where he engaged in the purchase and sale of livestock. About 1856 he moved to Illinois, starting a stock farm in Fulton County and selling his cattle in Chicago. Ill health and disasters due to the panic of 1857 prompted him to return to Newark, where for a time he kept a store. Two years later he was back in Illinois, and in March 1860 made Chicago his home. On July 1, 1860, he was married to Pamilla W. Thompson of Peoria. A few months later he made his formal entrance into the business world of Chicago by the unprecedented act of cornering the pork market, a transaction that brought him a large profit. He was the chief factor in organizing (May 1863) the First National Bank of Chicago, of which for many years he was a director. In 1865, by means of a series of articles in the *Tribune*, he began the movement for the establishment of a union stockyard, which in the following year was brought to success. He founded the Allerton Packing Company and was for many years its president. In 1880–82 he brought about the adoption in Chicago of the street-railway cable car, which he had seen in operation while on a visit to San Francisco.

His fortune grew rapidly. He invested largely in the stockyards of Pittsburgh, Baltimore, and Jersey City and later in the yards at St. Joseph and Omaha; and he bought large tracts of farming lands in Illinois, Ohio, Iowa, Nebraska, and Wyoming. Near Monticello, Ill., he acquired a tract of 19,000 acres, which he converted, under the management of his son Robert, into a model stock and crop farm. He also acquired extensive land and elevator interests at Allerton, Ill., and was a large stockholder in the Allerton State Bank. He was deeply concerned in all affairs relating to the city and for a time was active in politics. He was a Republican, and in 1893 was the party's candidate for mayor against Carter Harrison (the elder), who defeated him. With the coming of old age he gradually withdrew from participation in business and spent much of his time at the winter home which he established in South Pasadena, Cal. After the death of his first wife he was married (Mar. 15, 1882) to her sister, Agnes C. Thompson. He died at his California home, of diabetes.

Allerton was one of the builders of the modern Chicago. "He could rightfully lay claim," said the *Tribune*, at the time of his death, "to more work for making the greater Chicago than almost any other citizen." He was a man of large and powerful physique. His manner derived from the rough school in which he graduated, was somewhat brusque and assertive. He was an operator of great initiative and energy and an administrator of exceptional executive ability. Business success, however, he believed to be predominantly a matter of character; and his advice to the young, for which he seems to have been frequently asked, always stressed this quality. With an established character in business, he maintained, one could always obtain credit, and with credit one could hardly fail of success. A number of benevolences are recorded of him, one of them, in coöperation with Henry E. Weaver, having been the establishment of the St. Charles Home for Boys.

[Obituaries in the *Tribune* and the *Record-Herald* of Chicago, Feb. 23, 1914; biog. sketch in J. S. Currey, *Chicago: Its Hist. and Its Builders,* vol. V (1912).]

W.J.G.

ALLIBONE, SAMUEL AUSTIN (Apr. 17, 1816–Sept. 2, 1889), literary lexicographer and librarian, born in Philadelphia, was descended from French Huguenots and English Quakers. His paternal ancestor, Benjamin Allibone of Pennsylvania, was said to have been a descendant of Sir Richard Allibone who sat on the trial of the Seven Bishops. His maternal forebears were Thomas and Agnes Croasdale, who accompanied William Penn to Pennsylvania in 1682. At the age of twenty, Samuel Austin Allibone was baptized and confirmed in St. Andrew's Protestant Episcopal Church of Philadelphia. He married Mary Henry, the daughter and youngest child of Alexander Henry, a noted merchant and philanthropist of Philadelphia. His active life began in mercantile pursuits and for ten years he helped to shape the policy of the Insurance Company of North America, in Philadelphia. But from boyhood he had been a book-lover; his temperament destined him to the life of letters. In 1852 appeared his first printed publication, *A Review by a Layman of a Work Entitled "New Themes for the Protestant Clergy."* He then devoted himself to *A Critical Dictionary of English Literature and British and American Authors.* George W. Childs, book-publisher of Philadelphia, encouraged this project and became the original publisher of the *Dictionary,* bringing out through the firm of Childs & Peterson the first volume in 1858. Two more volumes were published by J. B. Lippincott & Company in 1871. The three volumes have often been reissued. They contain accounts and critical judgments of the productions of 46,499 authors, with forty classified indexes of subjects, filling 3,140 printed royal octavo pages. From 1867 to 1873, and from 1877 to 1879 he was editor of publications and corresponding secretary of the American Sunday School Union. His publications in this connection include: *An Alphabetical Index to the New Testament* (1868); *Explanatory Questions on the Gospels and the Acts* (1869); *The Divine Origin of the Holy Scriptures* (1869), which was the first part, published separately, of *The Union Bible Companion* (1871). He also prepared for publication by Lippincott three works: *Poetical Quotations from Chaucer to Tennyson* (1873); *Prose Quotations from Socrates to Macaulay* (1876); *Great Authors of all Ages,* selections (1880).

In May 1879 at the request of James Lenox, founder of the Lenox Library, he removed to New York City, where for nine years he was librarian, working on a descriptive catalogue and entertaining visitors by talks on book treasures. He prepared a card catalogue written in his own hand, and furnished copy for *The Contributions to a Catalogue of the Lenox Library* (monographs on Bunyan, Shakespeare, Milton, and Walton). In 1886 he was invited to join James Grant Wilson and George William Curtis in the editorship of the projected *Appletons' Cyclopædia of American Biography.* He declined the offer, but contributed biographical articles on George Bancroft, Alexander H. Everett, Edward Everett, William Hickling Prescott, George Ticknor, and perhaps others. On retiring from the Lenox Library, in May 1888, he went to Europe to travel and rest; but soon died, at Lucerne, Switzerland, where he was buried. "His beautiful face, his gracious manner, the invincible sweetness of his temper, his charm as a companion, his skill as a *raconteur,* his quips and jests and dainty whimsies—these were parts of the furnishing of the man" (S. D. McConnell, pp. 21–22).

[S. D. McConnell, *In Memory of S. Austin Allibone,* a paper read before the Hist. Soc. of Pa., Dec. 8, 1890; O. B. Stebbins, sketch in *New Eng. Hist. and Geneal. Reg.* (1892), XLVI, 283; Wm. Henry Eldridge, *Henry Genealogy* (1915), p. 174; MS. of the *Dictionary,* given by Allibone to Anthony J. Drexel and by him to the Lib. Co. of Phila.; Allibone correspondence in the Henry E. Huntington Lib.; personal recollections of the writer.]

V.H.P.

ALLINE, HENRY (June 14, 1748–Feb. 2, 1784), revivalist, was born in Newport, R. I., to which place his parents William and Rebecca (Clark) Alline, had moved from Boston, their native town. There seems to be no authority for spelling his name "Allen," as has been the custom in works of reference from the time of Hannah Adams's *Dictionary of Religions* (1814) down to the present. In his *Journal* he himself writes it "Alline," and in the marriage records of Boston his father's name is so written. When Henry was twelve years old his parents joined in the migration from New England to Nova Scotia then going on, and settled in Falmouth. From boyhood the subject of religion had been uppermost in his mind, but it was not until his twenty-seventh year, after fierce inner conflicts lasting over a long period, that he became assured of his conversion. With this assurance came the conviction that he was called to be a preacher. For some time he hesitated to obey the summons, because of his scanty education, for though he had thought and read much he had had little schooling. Finally, however, he began to preach in Falmouth, and there followed an itinerant ministry that had a profound effect on the people. His view and methods were in the main those of the New Light movement, and he has been called "the Whitefield of Nova Scotia." Old churches, "churches of antichrist," their ministers "unconverted," he styled them, were divided; and new ones formed. On Apr. 6, 1779, he was ordained by lay representatives of churches he had helped to found. After some eight years of exhausting evangelistic labors, while on a visit to New England, he died in North Hampton, N. H., at the home of Rev. David McClure.

Although Alline had not the learning or saintliness of David Brainerd [*q.v.*], the lives of the two present striking similarities. Both were of the neurotic type, subject to periods of elevation and of miserable depression, both had in them the seeds of tuberculosis from which they died at an early age, both wore themselves out by their self-ignoring devotion, and both left journals of their travels and inner experience. It is commonly said that Alline founded a short-lived sect known as the Allenites. It is true that he promulgated more or less fantastic views regarding the genesis of souls and the relation of the spiritual and physical worlds, which were set forth in *Two Mites Cast into the Offering of God for the Benefit of Mankind,* an edition of which was published in Boston in 1804; but his real significance lies in the fact that he produced a New Light awakening in Nova Scotia, the effects of which are still to be discerned. His *Life and Journal* was published in Boston in 1806, and his *Hymns and Spiritual Songs* in 1802.

[Arthur W. H. Eaton, *Hist. of Kings County, Nova Scotia* (1910); David Benedict, *Gen. Hist. of the Baptist Denomination in Amer.* (1813, 1848); Duncan Campbell, *Nova Scotia* (1873); Geo. Punchard, *Hist. of Congregationalism,* IV (1880). A refutation of Alline's views was published in Halifax in 1784 by Rev. Jonathan Scott under the title, *A Brief View of the Religious Tenets and Sentiments Lately Published and Spread in the Province of Nova Scotia, etc.*]

H. E. S.

ALLIS, EDWARD PHELPS (May 12, 1824–Apr. 1, 1889), manufacturer, was born at Cazenovia, N. Y., the son of Jere Allis and Mary White. His ancestors on both sides had been among the settlers of Hatfield, Mass., in the Connecticut Valley. Young Allis was reared in conditions of comfort and moderate prosperity, as the terms were understood in those times in rural New York. He attended Union College at Schenectady, from which he was graduated in 1845, during the presidency of Dr. Eliphalet Nott. At first intending to prepare himself for the law, he changed his plans soon after graduation from college, went to Milwaukee two years before Wisconsin's admission as a state, and engaged in the leather business. In 1848 he was married to Margaret Watson of Geneva, N. Y., by whom he had twelve children. He built extensive tanneries at Two Rivers, Wis., but in 1854 disposed of his holdings and for seven years confined his operations to banking and real estate. In the first year of the Civil War, having an opportunity to buy a small iron-foundry in Milwaukee, he established the Reliance Iron Works, which he built up in his lifetime into one of the largest industrial plants in the Middle West. In 1869, when the city of Milwaukee was installing a water-system, the Allis Company by underbidding competitors obtained the contract for piping, which it filled, although when the contract was awarded the company had no machinery for making pipe. It then installed the necessary pumps and engines for the Milwaukee service and within a few years became known as one of the largest machine-shops in the country. Its products were shipped in later years to Europe, Japan, South America, and Australia. When the roller process was adopted by American flour-millers the Allis works made the new machinery that was required in hundreds of mills throughout the country. Saw-mill and mining machinery and heavy pumps were also made at the Milwaukee plant. The famous Corliss engines were built there, under the direction of a graduate of the works at Providence, R. I. Before the owner's death, in 1889, the business amounted to $3,000,000 a year, with 1,200 employees. All this had been developed within a period of twenty-eight years, which included the serious business depression of 1873. In those years Allis became a convert to the Greenback faith and was that party's candidate for governor of Wisconsin in 1877. He cultivated good relations with his employees and was prompt to reward diligence and efficiency. He became a patron of art and was known as a man of genuine culture. In Milwaukee he was remembered as a pioneer who had contributed to the city's fame as an industrial center. In his own lifetime the spindles of cotton-mills in New England, the home of his ancestors for seven generations, were driven by engines that were fabricated in his works on the western shore of Lake Michigan—a region that was only one remove from a wilderness when he migrated to it in his youth.

[The ancestry of Edward Phelps Allis is given in *Genealogy of William Allis of Hatfield, Mass., and Descendants, 1630–1919*, by Horatio D. Allis (n.d.) ; and in *Memorials of Elder John White, One of the First Settlers of Hartford, Conn., and of His Descendants*, by Allyn Stanley Kellogg (1860). An obituary appeared in the *Milwaukee Sentinel*, Apr. 2, 1889.] W. B. S.

ALLISON, WILLIAM BOYD (Mar. 2, 1829–Aug. 4, 1908), congressman, was born in Perry township, Ashland County, Ohio, the son of John and Margaret (Williams) Allison. His parents gave him a strong constitution; and life about the log cabin and on the farm developed him into a sturdy, dignified youth of some five feet, eight inches, with a broad frame and a bushy shock of hair. Some of that restless ambition which brought his Scotch-Irish forebears from Ireland to Pennsylvania sent their descendant searching from one early institution to another for his educational equipment. "Professor Parrot's School," two years of Wooster Academy, one of Allegheny College, an interlude of school-teaching, and a final year of life at Western Reserve constituted his academic experience. Back in Ashland County again, he gained admission to the bar at twenty and launched himself upon his legal and political career forthwith. He was twice married: in 1854, to Anna Carter who died in 1860, and in 1873 to Mary Nealley.

Like many another Ohioan of those days, Allison abandoned the Whigism of his father to unite with Democrats in the new Republican venture. They made Chase governor (1855); but Allison felt a degree of disappointment because he himself failed of election as district attorney. In this mood he set his face westward, first toward Chicago and thence by chance to Galena and across the Mississippi to Dubuque, Ia. The Dubuque of those days was a place to stir the imagination—the chief city between St. Louis and St. Paul, thriving on river commerce, and optimistic about becoming a railroad center to tap the rich hinterland westward. Here Allison stopped and remained. He entered the law firm of Samuels & Allison, but politics proved a more engaging profession. The aggressiveness of the Middle West found expression in the Allison of the next ten years. From that stronghold of the Democrats, Dubuque, he set forth to help unite the Republican organization of the state sufficiently to elect Kirkwood governor in 1859. At Chicago in 1860 he switched from futile support of his friend Chase to Lincoln as the candidate, giving the party more assurance. As a special aid on Kirkwood's staff in 1861, he raised and equipped four regiments in northeastern Iowa, securing important coöperation from Major-General Baker. Finally the congressional Republican organization recognized him in 1862 with a nomination to Congress from the newly created third district, and a combination of absentee soldier votes and local personal effectiveness made Allison a member of the Iowa delegation in the Thirty-eighth Congress, a place he retained four terms. Thus, he passed under the tutelage of Thaddeus Stevens at the same time as did Blaine and Garfield.

As a representative, Allison labored for harmony between loyalty to his party and loyalty to his section, a balancing feat incumbent upon all successful congressmen. He usually avoided a vindictive attitude toward his associates, cultivating a normal friendliness instead. As a Republican from the inception of the party, he gave his vote to the Lincoln administration for new loans, continuance of the bounty system, amendment of the National Bank Act, and the Thirteenth Amendment, and acted with the majority in the House on the impeachment of Johnson and the Wade-Davis reconstruction program. As a midwestern representative he at all times advocated Mississippi improvements and increased transportation largess; and he sometimes voted with the inflationists on the currency issue. His current tariff pronouncements urged the lowering of wool and iron schedules to give the Middle Border less costly clothing and cheaper iron rails. It was his uneven record on the currency (*Palimpsest,* VI, 274) and his urgency for lowered schedules throughout his congressional period that made Allison's reputation as a moderationist—a reputation which was to cling to him through his thirty-five years in the Senate and to determine his peculiar function and unique importance in that body. By 1869 Allison felt that his constituents, for whom he had fought many a battle in the Ways and Means Committee, should place him in the Senate. Disappointment came then, and again in 1870. Eastern tariff interests propagandized the state against him; his chief competitor for the nomination, James Harlan, was more widely known at home than he; and Allison's entanglement with Blaine and others in railroad-construction projects lessened his availability (*Atlantic,* LXX, 549; Oberholtzer, *History of the United States* (1922), II, 545, 602 ff.; T. C. Smith, *Life and Letters of James Abram Garfield* (1925), pp. 528 ff.). It is significant of this period in American development that Allison's career, like that of two of his coadjutors, Garfield and Henry Wilson, suffered no permanent ill effects from the disclosures. He simply put the matter behind. him, enjoyed a European trip (1871) which gave him contacts with foreign students of finance, and returned to ride into the Senate on a wave of anti-Harlanism (1872).

Allison ran as a Grant supporter and yet enjoyed the favor of the liberals. A curious ability to unite opposing groups had become his forte; and he employed it so effectively throughout the next three decades that the erratic state of Weaver, of Larrabee, and of Cummins returned him to the Senate five times successively. He employed as senator a personal technique of rare effectiveness: an invariable friendliness in manner of approach which brought liking without dangerous intimacy; an unobtrusiveness and a lack of great wealth which allayed jealousy; a ready expression of sympathy for younger politicians and an avoidance of controversy which maintained his leadership of the delegation at Washington; a moderation of speech and of outward attitude which gave conservative constituents a sense of security and radical constituents a gleam of hope. And one thing more—the capstone to the whole edifice of his local and national success—Allison had become identified with the nation-wide, expansive business urge of the time, especially in the fields of manufacturing and transportation. He chose the two highest official committees with the result that he was chairman of Appropriations for twenty-seven years (1881–1908), and had a place on Finance during thirty years. Also as senior senator he inherited from Sherman in 1897 the highest unofficial place in the Senate, chairmanship of the caucus. These powerful committeeships of course ramified influentially into the committee on committees and the steering committee, and brought Allison into close harmony with the other dominant beneficiaries by seniority, Aldrich, O. H. Platt, Spooner, and Hale. Allison's special function in the joint leadership was best described by its dominant personality, Senator Aldrich, as that of "a master of the arts of conciliation and construction." Such he was in currency legislation, when his amendment emasculated Bland's bill (1878) but stayed the appetite of Silverites by substituting, for remonetization, limited silver purchase and a bimetallic conference (*Congressional Record,* 45 Cong., 2 Sess., H. R. No. 1093). Again (1892), to gain time for the passing of the silver craze he acted as chairman of the Brussels Monetary Conference. In Cleveland's second term he actively offset the silver majority of the Finance Committee and Senate. The Gold Standard Act (1900) followed upon careful preliminary coöperation between Allison, Platt, and Aldrich. Rooseveltian tendencies toward currency expansion were forestalled by united action between Allison, Aldrich, O. H. Platt, and Cannon. Thus Allison became one of the few western men popular with eastern financiers, who felt that his conservatism bore evidence of genius.

The tariff gave Allison the special school and theatre of his powers. As party harmonizers, he and Morrill and Aldrich united the Republican caucus behind that substitute for the Mills bill which brought Republican victory in 1888 and acknowledged its commitments in 1890 in the form of the McKinley tariff. In his rôle of moderate protectionist he often won encomiums from local constituents, while national protective organizations were lauding his work with Aldrich for drastic enforcement of customs regulations (1888–90). Democrats demonstrated a like confidence in him, particularly as regards the sugar schedule of 1894. The burden of reconciling conflicting importunities, especially on lumber, coal, and silver, for the so-called Dingley bill (1897) was shouldered by Allison. In the days of Roosevelt the result of the united efforts of Allison, Platt, and Aldrich is summed up in the fact that the Roosevelt administration postponed settlement of the tariff until the days of its successor.

Transportation legislation was Allison's greatest problem. He sympathized fully with railroad needs as voiced by Perkins, Hughitt, Fish, and Dodge and always worked hard to justify their faith in him. Yet he realized the closeness of the subject to everyday life, to legislative usage, to campaign exigencies; seeing intervention inevitable he sought to guide it into safe channels. From 1885, when Cullom as chairman of the Interstate Commerce Committee found Allison the safe man to follow, until the era of Hepburn's bill (1906), when Roosevelt utilized an amendment bearing Allison's name for reaching an agreement with conservative opponents, Iowa's senior senator was balancing the railroad problem for many Republicans. In the words of Depew, "He could grant to an adversary an amendment with such grace and deference to superior judgment that the flattered enemy accepted a few suggestions from the master as a tribute to his talents. The post-mortem revealed his mistake" (*Congressional Record,* 60 Cong., 2 Sess., p. 1988).

When death took Allison he was the senior, by eight years, of any colleague left in the Senate; he was a national institution; and by reason of that fact the Republican party stood in immense debt to this moderationist. Not a campaign from 1880 on but he had helped to correlate the concrete necessities of the national committee with congressional performance. Not a party split from the days of Conkling and Garfield to those of Aldrich and Roosevelt but he served as a go-between. Scarcely a legislative tangle but what this most modest and benignant of drill-sergeants, almost first on the roll-call, beckoned pleasantly for the faithful to follow. His political value was further enhanced by his disinclination to demand that his party pay him in kind. Cabinet honors he declined from Garfield, Harrison, and McKinley. He continued the even tenor of his way, enjoying with three or four others control through the Senate of the political affairs of the expanding republic.

[The chief available source in general is the *Cong. Rec.* with accompanying docs. Iowan background is furnished by the *Annals of Ia.*, ser. 3; *Ia. Hist. Rec.; Ia. Jour. of Hist. and Politics;* the *Palimpsest;* D. E. Clark, *Kirkwood* (1917); J. E. Briggs, *Hepburn* (1913); J. Brigham, *Harlan* (1913); F. E. Haynes, *Third Party Movements* (1916); O. B. Clark, *Politics of Ia.* (1911); and S. J. Buck, *Granger Movement* (1913). Allison's personal and private papers are available only under restrictions in the Hist., Memorial, and Art Dept. of Ia.]

J. P. N.

ALLOEZ (ALLOUES), CLAUDE JEAN. [See ALLOUEZ, CLAUDE JEAN, 1622–1689.]

ALLOUEZ, CLAUDE JEAN (June 6, 1622–Aug. 27, 1689), Jesuit missionary, was born at Saint-Didier, Haute Loire, France. He graduated in his seventeenth year from the college at Le Puy, where one of his masters was the famous missionary François Regis, from whom he acquired his own missionary zeal. In 1639 he entered the Jesuit novitiate at Toulouse, pursuing his clerical studies in the same city and later at Billom and Rodez. He was ordained priest in 1655, and in 1658 went to Canada with the newly appointed governor of New France, Pierre d'Argenson. After three years of labor among Indian tribes along the St. Lawrence, he became superior at Three Rivers. Whilst there July 21, 1663, he was appointed vicar general for all the natives and traders of the northwest. This office required him to visit the tribes in that territory, to obtain missionaries, to regulate the relations of the traders with the natives, and to open new missions.

He set out for Lake Superior in 1664, but missing the canoe flotilla for that year, he was obliged to wait until Aug. 8, 1665. The Indians, who did not want his company, thrice abandoned him, and finally only consented to his presence on his doing his share of the paddling and portages. He arrived on Sept 2 at Lake Superior, or, as he named it, Lac de Tracy, and on Oct. 1 at Chequamegon (Ashland) Bay, where, at La Pointe on Madeline Island, he found a large village with a force of 800 warriors, the aggregation of seven different tribes. On May 6, 1667, he left for Lake Nipigon, a distance, allowing for detours, of about 1,500 miles. At that place he found many Christian Indians, particularly the Nipissiriniens, who had taken refuge there after the slaughter by the Iroquois of the various tribes in the Ontario country. After two weeks, Allouez returned to his people at La Pointe. There he persuaded the "Queues Coupées" (the Kiskakon clan of Ottawas) to renounce their superstitions and polygamy. To satisfy the need thus created for new missionaries, he carried the news to Quebec, where the superiors, not having heard from him for over two years, had given him up for dead. After remaining for only two days, he returned to his western missions.

In 1669 he was back in Quebec with a number of Iroquois captives whom he had ransomed. After a brief stay he again returned to the west, this time to the Potawatomi, near Green Bay, then the Baie des Puants, with whom he spent the winter. On Apr. 16, 1670, he left them in order to go to the Outagamies. His diary of this journey contains observations on natural history, and an account of the eclipse of the sun which occurred on Apr. 19. On that day he reached Lake Winnebago, which he called St. Francis Xavier. The next day, Sunday, he celebrated mass on the site of the present city of Oshkosh. On Apr. 25 he established St. Mark's Mission (location uncertain). He left St. Mark's on Apr. 27 and two days later came among the Miamis and the Mascoutens, and founded the mission of St. James. He next spent some months at Sault Ste. Marie, leaving there with Father Dablon in September, for the Green Bay missions. On June 4, 1671, he was the orator of the day at the Sault when the northwest territory was solemnly declared to be subject to the King of France by M. de Saint Lusson, delegated for that purpose by the Governor at Quebec. The same year, when Marquette and Joliet started on the search for the Mississippi, Allouez returned to Green Bay to establish the Mission of Rapides des Pères, now De Pere (Wisconsin), on Fox River, where the State Historical Society of Wisconsin has built a monument to him near the site of the house and chapel which he occupied. In 1674 there were over 2,000 Christian Indians at this mission. A fine monstrance presented to the mission by Nicholas Perrot in 1686 was plowed up at the site in 1802.

When news came of Marquette's death, May 18, 1675, Allouez was ordered to continue Marquette's work among the Illinois. He started in October 1676, but owing to the severity of the winter could not reach his mission until the following March. On the way, on the eve of St. Joseph's Day, Mar. 18, he reached Lake Michigan, which he called St. Joseph. He canoed over seventy-six leagues to the Illinois country, where he was well received and conducted to the wigwam at Kaskaskia. After prospecting for a central mission station, he came back to Green Bay, but returned in 1678 to the Illinois, where he passed the rest of his life, eleven years, until his death among the Miamis, near the site of Niles, Mich. Father Dablon styled him a second Francis Xavier. He is said to have baptized fully 10,000 Indians and to have preached to about 100,000. The citizens of Niles erected a huge granite cross on the supposed site of his grave.

[R. G. Thwaites, *Jesuit Relations and Allied Docs.* (1896–1901), Allouez's contributions being found in the *Relations* of 1666–67, 1669–70, 1672–73, 1673–74, 1679; T. J. Campbell, *Pioneer Priests of North America* (1911), vol. III; J. S. La Boule, *Claude Jean Allouez, the Apostle of the Ottawas* (Parkman Club Pubs., no. 17, Milwaukee, 1897); Chrysostom Verwyst, *Missionary Labors of Fathers Marquette, Menard and Allouez* (1886).]

J. J. W.

ALLSTON, ROBERT FRANCIS WITHERS (Apr. 21, 1801–Apr. 7, 1864), planter, governor of South Carolina, was descended from John Alston, son of William Alston, Gentleman, of Hammersmith, Middlesex, England, who began in 1682 a seven-year apprenticeship to a certain James Jones, merchant of Charles Town (A. S. Salley, Jr., "John Alston," *South Carolina Historical and Genealogical Magazine,* VI, 114–16). This first Alston in South Carolina seems to have preferred the spelling "Alston," but during the first three generations that form was replaced by "Allston." Late in the eighteenth century, however, one branch of the family, by reverting to the earlier spelling, introduced a now recognized division into double and single "l" Alstons (Lionel Creswell, *Stemmata Alstoniana,* 1905, and J. A. Groves, *Alstons and Allstons,* 1901). John Alston, the immigrant, prospered, acquired wide lands, and became the founder of a family whose members were, for the most part, planters of the "low country." In the course of time Waccamaw Neck, All Saints' Parish, became the chief seat of the Allstons (H. A. M. Smith, "Hobcaw Barony," *South Carolina Historical and Genealogical Magazine,* XIV, 61–80).

Robert F. W. Allston, of the fifth generation, was of the Alston blood both by his father, Benjamin Allston, and his mother, Charlotte Anne Allston, who were second cousins. The fifth of six children, he was born at Brookgreen Plantation in All Saints' Parish, S. C. His early education was received at Waldo's School in Georgetown. At the age of sixteen he entered West Point Military Academy and graduated in June 1821. He was appointed lieutenant in the 3rd Artillery and assigned to duty with the Coast Survey. After taking part in the survey of the harbors of Plymouth and Provincetown, Mass., and the entrance of Mobile Bay, he resigned his commission (February 1822) in order to assume the management of the plantation of his now widowed mother. In this occupation he did not abandon, however, the profession of civil engineer and was elected in 1823 to the office of surveyor general of South Carolina. In 1828, after two terms as surveyor general, he was elected from the parish of Prince George, Winyah, to the lower house of the General Assembly. In the legislature he acted with the State-Rights party which was then evolving the doctrine of nullification. In 1830 he was reëlected as a candidate of that party, but was defeated in 1832 by a Unionist. In the next month, however, he ran successfully for the state Senate (see files of *Charleston Courier* and *Charleston Mercury,* 1828, 1830, 1832). He was regularly returned to this body until his election as governor in 1856, and from 1847 to 1856 he was its presiding officer. He continued in his support of state-rights principles, but was inclined to favor coöperation on the part of the slaveholding states in preference to separate state action (MS. notes on the Nashville Convention). During the nullification episode he was made colonel of the militia and subsequently deputy adjutant-general. In 1832 he married Adele Petigru, sister of James Louis Petigru [*q.v.*]. With the latter his relations were in every way cordial, but such was the independence of his mind that he seems not to have been deflected from his political views by Petigru's ardent championship of the Union. In fact, the Petigrus regarded this tall, "good-looking" Allston as a trifle "obstinate." In 1842 he was nominated, against his wishes, to oppose J. H. Hammond in the election for governor. In 1850 he was a delegate to the Nashville Convention. His term as governor, 1856–58, occurred in one of the rare intervals of comparative quietude in the political history of ante-bellum South Carolina, a fact which enabled him to employ talents for organization and administration which he possessed in an eminent degree. His energies were expended upon the development of railroads, improvement of agricultural methods, and correction of the inefficient public-school system. A report on the last prepared by Allston in 1846 was made the basis of reform (*Reports and Resolutions of General Assembly,* 1847, pp. 210–43).

This long and active public career was made possible by the harmony existing between the social and political life in ante-bellum South Carolina. Allston had come to be, chiefly through his own efforts, one of the foremost planters and slave-owners in the state. He was one of the last of the rice barons of the "low country." In the reclaiming of swamp land, in the ditching and diking of rice-fields, his knowledge of engineering served him well. The results of some of his experiments were set forth in two elaborate treatises: *A Memoir of the Introduction and Planting of Rice in South Carolina* (1843) and *An Essay on Sea Coast Crops* (1854). The fact that the former is still regarded as the most authoritative treatment of the subject would seem to justify the praise of a contemporary reviewer: "Such essays do more for the advancement of agricultural science than can well be conceived" (*DeBow's Review*, I, 356). Indeed, it is upon his success as a planter and scientific agriculturist that Allston's claim upon the memory of posterity, in the main, must rest. He died in the midst of the Civil War. He was engaged at the time in cultivating his lands in order to contribute foodstuffs to his Confederate countrymen.

[The chief source of information about Allston is a great mass of undigested manuscript material in the possession of his daughter, Mrs. C. A. Hill. Another daughter, Mrs. Elizabeth W. A. Pringle, has given an intimate account of her father in her *Chronicles of Chicora Wood* (1922). A sketch of Allston's life appeared in *DeBow's Rev.*, XII, 574–75. Obituaries were published in the *Charleston Mercury*, Apr. 23, 1864, and in the *Charleston Courier*, Apr. 12, 1864.]

J. H. E.

ALLSTON, WASHINGTON (Nov. 5, 1779–July 9, 1843), artist and author, was a member of a prominent South Carolina family. On Jan. 19, 1775, Capt. William Allston, Gentleman, was married to Rachel Moore, a colonial beauty of three-quarter French Huguenot extraction. The family trees of both Rachel and her widower husband bristled with governors and doughty warriors against the Indians. In 1781, upon his return from the battle of Cowpens, Capt. Allston was seized with a mysterious illness: poisoned, according to a persistent rumor, by a trusted servant. His wife, left with three infants, of whom Washington was the second, later married Henry C. Flagg, chief of the medical staff of Greene's army. Though Dr. Flagg was viewed by Widow Allston's people as a mere Yankee adventurer, Rachel declared that she had "married once to please her family"; she was "now determined to please herself."

Washington Allston early betrayed what was deemed a deplorable knack for drawing. Before the age of six, according to his own account, he locked himself in his room and commenced a picture in oils of the eruption of Vesuvius; and his family was so distressed by its excellence that they feared he might disgrace them all by becoming an artist. He was shipped by his stepfather to Newport, "in order that his nervous and high-strung organization might be recruited by a more bracing air." With a fatal instinct, he here sought out as one of his earliest associates a certain Mr. King who made quadrants and compasses and occasionally painted portraits. The youngster haunted the quadrant shop—but not to look at compasses. He remained in Newport until 1796, when, at the age of seventeen, he entered Harvard. Although undistinguished in scholarship, he was inordinate in his interests and curiosities. He admired Southey's poetry, and the Della Cruscans, whom he soon abandoned, however, "for the manliness of Churchill" (Flagg, p. 27). On his own part he took to writing verse, and was chosen to declaim on occasions both public and private. Of the theatre, dancing, and wine, he was exceedingly fond; and when old Major Brattle, prince of epicures, invited him to dinner, he celebrated the prospect by a day of preliminary fasting. By his classmates he was nicknamed "Count." Not only did he exhibit a flair for caricature, but his landlord, Don Clark, bore witness to other of his peculiarities: "He has painted a woman, stark naked, going into the water to wash herself. It is as natural as life. Mr. Allston, sir, is quite a genius" (*Ibid.*, pp. 23–24). Though morbidly shy with women, by his junior year he had become engaged to be married to the sister of his fellow student, William Ellery Channing. It was, however, to be a protracted engagement.

In August 1800, after his graduation, Allston came to terms with his stepfather, who wanted to make a physician of him, and wrote to his mother that he was resolved to stake his career upon painting. This step taken, he returned to Carolina; sold hastily and at a sacrifice, so it is said, "a considerable patrimonial estate"; and sailed for London in May 1801. For three years he was a student at the Royal Academy, under Benjamin West. In November 1803 he migrated to Paris, where he painted in the Louvre for several months, and thence, by way of Switzerland, into Italy, where he spent what were, perhaps, the four richest years of his life. He stopped first in Siena to learn Italian, then visited Venice, and spent a year studying and painting in the galleries of Florence. In March 1805 he entered the Eternal City. Raphael, Michelangelo (then fallen into disrepute), and the Venetians, so Allston recognized in Italy, were his authentic masters. In Rome began his long and close friendship with Coleridge and with Washington Irving. Years later, Allston said: "To no other man do I owe so much intellectually as to Mr. Coleridge who has honored me with his friendship for more than five and twenty years"; and Coleridge to Allston:

"Had I not known the Wordsworths [I] should have esteemed and loved you first and most; and, as it is, next to them I love and honor you." Between Irving and Allston a young man's intimacy immediately took place. Together they rambled about the city, and before each new recurrent wonder, according to Irving, Allston's "eyes would dilate; his pale countenance would flush; he would breathe quick, and almost gasp in expressing his feelings." But all the while, Ann Channing awaited Allston's return to Newport. In 1808 he left Rome for Boston and marriage. It was Benjamin West's conviction that this was a fatal step. There survives no evidence that Allston felt for his bride any of the vivid enthusiasm so variously expressed for his friends and for his art. His old classmate, Jarvis, reports: "I found him, on the morning after his nuptials, at his usual hour, engaged in his customary occupations."

After two years in Boston, Allston, his wife, and his young friend and pupil, S. F. B. Morse [*q.v.*], sailed for Liverpool, to be joined six months later by Charles R. Leslie [*q.v.*]. Throughout the War of 1812, this group, though enemy aliens, resided peaceably and unmolested in England. Allston painted with feverish absorption, producing at this time what is perhaps the greatest of his paintings, *Dead Man Revived by Touching the Bones of the Prophet Elisha,* a prize picture, bought for $3,500 by the Pennsylvania Academy of Art. His career was now interrupted, however, by an illness from which he never completely recovered. During his convalescence he painted the famous portrait of Coleridge, and saw through the press a volume of verse, *The Sylphs of the Seasons with other Poems* (1813)—verse sentimental and satirical, praised by Wordsworth and Southey. Rapidly upon his own illness followed the death of his wife, and a period of morbid depression, insomnia, and horrid thought. He completed *The Agony of Judas,* in his own judgment "the finest head I ever painted." But he destroyed it "lest it might some time have an immoral effect upon some perverted imagination." He was confirmed an Episcopalian, and from thence on devoted himself to an intensive cultivation of the Christian virtues. But despite illness, bereavement, insomnia, and a hypersensitive regard for purity and piety, his artistic productivity was at its apex. *Uriel in the Sun* and *Jacob's Ladder* had increased his reputation, and no other man in England was so competent and eligible to succeed Benjamin West, then aged and infirm, as president of the Royal Academy. At this juncture, he learned that "through the mismanagement and dishonesty of his agent in South Carolina his patrimony was exhausted." Faced with this misfortune, he made what was the most momentous decision of his life. He decided to return to America. And with this resolve, his career as an artist terminated.

He returned to America in 1818, and again made Boston his home. In ill health, worried by debts, without stimulus but what he found in himself, with prosaic surroundings, his studio a badly lighted barn, without models or means for his art, he started to work revising the huge canvas of *Belshazzar's Feast* which, in England, he had all but finished. Ten friends contributed $1,000 each to be paid for this picture upon its completion. But year after year dragged itself out, and the painting, endlessly refusing to realize itself to his satisfaction, grew to be both an obsession and an incubus. At his death twenty-five years later it was still unfinished. Allston remarried, and moved to Cambridgeport. His wife, Martha R. Dana, was the cousin, on the maternal side, of his first wife, and sister of his college friend Richard Henry Dana [*q.v.*]. The circles in which he moved were content to admire him as a Christian without making any critical demands upon him as an artist. In August 1841 he published *Monaldi*—"not with the pretensions of a Novel," as he says in the Introductory Note, "but simply as a Tale." It had been written in 1822, for the short-lived serial of Dana, *The Idle Man.* The scene is Italy; the hero is an artist; the villain, a defeated man of letters. It is a story of jealousy, envy, and revenge, after the manner of Mrs. Radcliffe, whom Allston especially admired. At Cambridgeport he also began the preparation of a course of lectures on art, only four of which he completed, and none of which he ever delivered. They were published posthumously by R. H. Dana, Jr. Allston died in Cambridge, July 9, 1843. Whether due to his illness, to the unstimulating environment of America, to the incompatibility between his art and his pietistic religion, or to some deeper defect of personality, certain it is that the productions of his later years had failed to bear out his earlier promise.

[The official life of Washington Allston was to have been written by Richard Henry Dana. The latter's notes and unfinished manuscripts passed into the hands of Jared B. Flagg, whose *Life and Letters of Washington Allston* (1892) is the fullest account in existence. Flagg's biography, if supplemented by M. F. Sweetser's *Allston* (1879), is invaluable. Typical of the contemporary moral adulation of Allston are Charles Sumner's Phi Beta Kappa address, *The Scholar, the Jurist, the Artist, and the Philanthropist* (1846), and the sermon by J. A. Albro, *The Blessedness of Those Who Die in the Lord* (1843).]

R. W.

ALLYN, ROBERT (Jan. 25, 1817–Jan. 7, 1894), educator, was a direct descendant in the eighth generation of Capt. Robert Allyn, one of the early settlers of New London, Conn. He was born on a farm at Ledyard, Conn., received the customary district-school training, and in 1837 entered Wesleyan University. Here he distinguished himself in both mathematics and the languages, and was voted the best student in his class. Graduating in 1841, he was married on Nov. 18 of the same year to Emeline Denison. For two years he taught mathematics in Wesleyan Academy at Wilbraham, Mass. He had entered the New England Conference of the Methodist Church in 1842, and from 1843 to 1845 he was stationed at Colchester, Conn. His first wife died in 1844, leaving him with two children, and on June 22, 1845, he married Mary Budington, by whom he later had three children. He became principal of Wesleyan Academy in 1846 and principal of the Providence Conference Seminary at East Greenwich, R. I. in 1848. Through his interest in abolition and prohibition he was drawn into politics and was twice elected to the legislature. His chief service to the state, however, was as commissioner of public schools, 1854–57, when he founded and edited the *Rhode Island Schoolmaster,* an excellent educational magazine which continued until 1875, when it was merged in the *New England Journal of Education.* His contributions to this magazine, as well as to others, such as the *Methodist Quarterly Review,* and his educational reports as commissioner, particularly his *Special Report on Truancy and Absenteeism in Rhode Island* (1856), were notable for their lucidity, thoroughness, and practicality. In September 1857 he resigned the commissionership to become professor of ancient languages in Ohio University at Athens, Ohio. Two years later he was elected president of Wesleyan Female Academy at Cincinnati. In 1863 he became president of McKendree College in Illinois. He was active in the establishment of the Southern Illinois State Normal University and was its first president (1874–92).

Allyn united dignity and ease in his personal bearing and in his educational work. Much influenced by Pestalozzi, he emphasized the importance of interest, without, however, sacrificing discipline. A distinct liberal, he strove to infuse the experimental spirit into education. He labored through writings, addresses, and meetings to educate parents at the same time as their children. His whole life was devoted to the school and the church.

[Biog. sketch in John Williston Cook's *Educational Hist. of Ill.* (1912), pp. 235–37; *Alumni Record of Wesleyan Univ.*(1911); Chas. Carroll, *Public Ed. in R. I.* (1918).]
E. S. B.

ALMY, JOHN JAY (Apr. 24, 1815–May 16, 1895), naval officer, the son of Samuel Almy, was born in Newport, R. I. Losing his parents at an early age, he was allowed by his guardian, an elder brother, to follow his boyish bent, which led him while still a child into the navy. Warranted midshipman at fourteen, he served his apprenticeship in the *Concord* on the Mediterranean Station (1830–32), and in the next twenty years cruised over half the globe in ships of the old sailing navy. He served as lieutenant on the *Ohio* during the Mexican War, and commanded the *Fulton* off Nicaragua in 1857, when the filibuster, Gen. Walker, surrendered to Admiral Paulding. That officer in his report said: "Lieutenant Commander Almy performed his part of the work exceedingly well, and is an officer who can be relied upon at all times" (L. R. Hamersly, *Records of the Living Officers of the U. S. Navy and Marine Corps,* 1894, p. 16). Though denied the honor of participating in notable engagements during the Civil War, he was assigned the equally important, arduous, and exacting service of maintaining the blockade of Confederate ports. He not only performed this service with high efficiency but wrote of it in fresh, incisive language. In his official reports and in a narrative of later years, the sea-worn life of the blockading cruisers is vividly described. That the months of hardship off the gale-swept coasts were lightened by hours of thrilling triumph is also shown by Almy's record. While commanding the *Connecticut* in 1864, he captured four noted blockade-runners and destroyed four others. The captured vessels were adjudged worth $1,063,352.49, or more than four per cent of the adjudicated value of the prizes taken during the war. In his career following the conflict, Almy personally substantiated the claim that naval officers are the real diplomats of the State Department. Serving on distant stations, in the successive grades of captain, commodore, and rear admiral, he cultivated and won by tactful services and courtesies the friendship of the rulers and peoples of Brazil and Hawaii. While commanding the Pacific Squadron in 1873, he landed a body of seamen in Panama during a violent revolution, maintained order, and kept the railroad across the Isthmus running until the end of hostilities. For these services he was thanked by the business men and the corps of foreign consuls of Panama. Retiring in 1877, he set the record of the longest sea service, twenty-seven years and ten months, of any officer since the founding of the navy. He passed the years of his retirement and died in Washington, D. C. A typical seaman in appearance, he was a gentleman of the finest tact and courtesy.

[Almy's official reports during the Civil War are found in the *Official Records.* See also his "Incidents of the Blockade" in *War Papers of the Mil. Order of the Loyal*

Legion of the U.S., D.C. Commandery. For further material his official service record, Navy Dept., and sketches in the *Army and Navy Jour.* and *Army and Navy Reg.*, both of May 18, 1895, should be consulted.]

A. MacC. S.

ALOES (ALOUES) CLAUDE JEAN. [See ALLOUEZ, CLAUDE JEAN, 1622–1689.]

ALPHONCE (ALPHONSE), JEAN. [See ALLEFONSCE, JEAN, *c.* 1482–*c.* 1557.]

ALPHONSA, MOTHER (May 20, 1851–July 9, 1926), philanthropist, religious superior, was Rose, youngest and last surviving child of Nathaniel and Sophia (Peabody) Hawthorne. She was born at Lenox, Mass., but in her third year the family moved to Liverpool where Hawthorne served as consul. Subsequently they traveled extensively in Europe, returning to the United States in 1861. Hawthorne died at Plymouth, N. H., May 18, 1864, when Rose was thirteen years of age. In 1868 Mrs. Hawthorne returned to Europe with her three children Julian, Una, and Rose. She died in England in 1871 when Rose was twenty years of age. Shortly thereafter the latter was married to George Parsons Lathrop [*q.v.*] in London. Both were converted to the Roman Catholic faith in 1891. Lathrop died in 1898.

Rose Hawthorne inherited rich literary and cultural traditions from her parents. Her education had been carefully supervised by them and she shared the enriching experience of travel and the distinguished friendships which played so large a rôle in the lives of her parents. She was alert, widely informed, thoroughly cultured, forceful, and kindly. She published a little volume of verse *Along the Shore* in 1888. The files of *St. Nicholas* contain a number of short sketches from her pen. Her *Memories of Hawthorne* appeared first serially in the *Atlantic Monthly*, being published as a volume in 1897. A second edition appeared in 1923 with a Prelude by Maurice Francis Egan. Mr. and Mrs. Lathrop published as joint authors in 1894 *A Story of Courage*, a history of the Georgetown Visitation Convent, based on a study of its archives.

In 1896 Mrs. Lathrop became interested in the victims of incurable cancer and opened a small home for the care of them. As the work grew she determined to consecrate her life to it, founding a religious Sisterhood known as Servants of Relief for Incurable Cancer and taking the name of Sister Alphonsa, as a member of the Community. The work was permanently established at Rosary Hill Home, Hawthorne, N. Y., in 1901. A second Home known as St. Rose's was opened in New York City in 1912. Only victims of incurable cancer, without friends and utterly without resources, were received, no distinction as to race or creed being known among the patients cared for. Such sympathy with suffering was traditional in the Hawthorne family. Mother Alphonsa's sister, Una, spent her last years in caring for destitute children in London, where she died in 1877. Mother Alphonsa's own vision, which brought the victims of cancer within the embrace of her sympathy, rested on a profound spiritual insight and corresponding impulse toward self-effacing service. It is said that she succeeded in maintaining a spirit of wholesome joy among those whom she served, in spite of the dreadful realities of suffering with which she dealt. Her death on July 9, 1926, brought forth unusual tributes from the American press.

Mother Alphonsa's literary activity practically ceased when she gave herself up to the care of her cancer patients. She wrote, however, a general introduction to a limited edition of Hawthorne's works in 1900 and an admirable preface for the new edition of *Memories of Hawthorne* in 1923. While this volume consists in large measure of the letters of her gifted mother, the author's text reveals extraordinary powers of insight and description, and the style takes on at times a quality of haunting beauty.

[Some details of the childhood of Rose Hawthorne are found in *Hawthorne and His Wife* (1885) by Julian Hawthorne, her brother; this work, however, contains practically no information about Mother Alphonsa after her childhood. Her *Memories of Hawthorne* furnishes good insight into the temperament, associations, and culture of the author. See also obituaries and appreciations in *Catholic World*, Aug. 1926; *Outlook*, July 21, 1926; *Lit. Digest*, May 15, 1926 and July 31, 1926. The archives of the Rosary Hill Home contain little personal information.]

W. J. K.

ALSOP, GEORGE (b. 1638), author, owes his narrow escape from total oblivion to a single book, boasting one of the longest titles on record: *A Character of the Province of Mary-Land, wherein is Described in four distinct Parts, (Viz.) I The Scituation, and plenty of the Province. II The Laws, Customs, and natural Demeanor of the Inhabitant. III The worst and best Usage of a Mary-Land Servant, opened in view. IV The Traffique and vendable Commodities of the Countrey. Also a small Treatise on the wilde and naked Indians (or Susquehanokes) of Mary-Land, their Customs, Manners, Absurdities, & Religion. Together with a Collection of Historical Letters* (Lond., 1666). The little that is known of Alsop's life is derived almost entirely from this book. After an apprenticeship of two years to some unknown trade in London, he left England in 1658, owing, according to his own account, to his hatred for the Puritans, and became an indented servant for four years to Thomas Stockett, one of four brothers who came out in this same year to Baltimore County, Md. Alsop was kindly treated by his master, and being of an enthusiastic temperament, conceived an unbounded admiration for the new colony. At the close of his period of servitude he was seriously ill, and soon after returned to England, published his book, and disappeared from history, unless he was the author of a volume of *Sermons* brought out later by some one of the same name.

Alsop's book bears internal evidence of being written for the purpose of stimulating emigration to America. He had the modern salesman's ability to see only the virtues of the thing he advertises and to go into a fine moral indignation against any who belittle it. As a result his work is more trustworthy as a record of the permanent psychology of publicity than as a strict historical account. Written in a high-flown and exaggerated style it eulogizes indiscriminately every phase of the Maryland colony. "Neither do I think there is any place under the Heavenly altitude, or that has footing or room upon the circular Globe of this world, that can parallel this fertile and pleasant piece of ground" (1902 ed., p. 32). Nevertheless as one of the earliest and fullest descriptions of Maryland it retains considerable value as a historical source, particularly with regard to the Susquehanna Indians, although even here some of its statements such as that "Their skins are naturally white, but altered from their originals by the several dyings of Roots and Barks" (*Ibid.*, p. 77) will hardly bear too close a scrutiny.

[The original edition of Alsop's *Maryland* was "Printed by T. J. for Peter Dring at the sign of the Sun in the Poultrey," Lond. 1666. A reprint edited by J. G. Shea was published in 1869 (reissued 1880). Another reprint, with introduction and notes by N. D. Mereness, was published in 1902. All contain Alsop's portrait, in which Shea fancied he perceived the character of a "rollicking roysterer."]

E. S. B.

ALSOP, RICHARD (Jan. 23, 1761–Aug. 20, 1815), satirist, poet, was one of the few millionaires of his generation, and was also, in many ways, the most gifted of the "Hartford Wits," among whom, says his friend, Elihu Hubbard Smith, he was the moon shining among lesser lights. He was the oldest son of Richard and Mary (Wright) Alsop. From his father, a prominent merchant of Middletown, Conn., he inherited a taste for business, an affectionate disposition, and a shaping force in his life—a passionate love of books. Against the tumultuous days of the new republic, Alsop, though no recluse, appears as a gentleman-financier of conservative Connecticut, possessing beneath a playfully humorous manner a rare aptitude for writing. His verse had a tincture of learning. One of his four sisters testifies to his early erudition acquired both at home and from tutors (*The Charms of Fancy,* 1856, pp. viii–ix), and it is probable that he entered Yale College in the class of 1778, a class distinguished by Noah Webster and Joel Barlow (*Catalogus Recentium in Collegio Yalensi,* 1774). Of his connection with Yale little is known save that he received in 1798 the degree of M.A. Whatever the sources, his acquaintance with classical literature was apparent even in boyhood; stories survive of his dramatic impersonations of the *Iliad.* His absorption in books, however, begot in him less learning than a rich culture which found expression in skill with modern languages and in poetry based on old legends. His leisure, his cultivation, and his talent for fluent poetry make him seem a precursor of Longfellow, the poet of a more tranquil age. Alsop translated from French, Spanish, and from the Scandinavian, the last-named study influencing his epic, "The Conquest of Scandinavia" (published in part in Elihu Hubbard Smith's *American Poems,* Litchfield, 1793). All his writings attributed to this early period and unpublished (a Greek poem on the Trojan War; translations from Silius Italicus and from the French of Florian and the Italian of Monti) proclaim him a poet deeply in debt to European culture. This remains true, despite his interest in field sports, natural history, taxidermy, and shrewd trading on the Connecticut River.

As part of his talent for literature Alsop adapted himself readily to the prevalent mode in writing satire. Like Freneau and Odell, he won fame by jests at the foibles of his time, but, unlike these, his pen was more playful than caustic. He had no part in the Revolution, but his letters are full of his concern with contemporary events; full also of good-humored derision at fools and Jacobins,—he thought them identical. Alsop wrote frequently in collaboration with David Humphreys, Joel Barlow, and Dr. Lemuel Hopkins, but he probably had no part in composing the mock-heroic poem "The Anarchiad." Wittier and more distinctive was "The Echo," which appeared in twenty numbers of the *American Mercury,* between 1791 and 1805. The origins of "The Echo," and thus indirectly of a later burlesque, "The Political Greenhouse," recreate perfectly the temper of Alsop in this mild flagellation of John Hancock, Samuel Adams, and Judge Hugh Brackenridge. In an office at Hartford he read, with Theodore Dwight and Mason Cogswell, a flamboyant newspaper account of a thunderstorm in Boston, and, amid laughter, volunteered a satire. His gibes struck home; there were fresh couplets; and the group, with others, was soon known as "The Hartford Wits."

This edge in Alsop sharpens a literary output which sometimes appears hopelessly bookish. The *American Poems* published at Litchfield in 1793 seem mere relicts of scholarship. Not less conventional is *A Poem: Sacred to the Memory of George Washington* (1800), in which Alsop, though stirred by the President's death, is an extremely orthodox mourner. Such writing (including inoffensive works like *The Enchanted Lake of the Fairy Morgana,* from the Italian of Boiardo, *The Geographical, Natural, and Civil History of Chili,* from the Italian of Molina, and even *The Charms of Fancy,* so reminiscent of Akenside's *Pleasures of the Imagination*), simply reiterates Alsop's ideal of following intently the acknowledged masters. Fortunately he occasionally strays off the beaten path. Though formal, the "Hymn to Peace" and the "Inscription for a Family Tomb" betray real emotion. The true Alsop, kindly, social, brilliant, comes out also in the remaining years of his life. These (1800–15) he spent in Middletown; in Hartford, where he is said to have conducted a bookstore; and in New York, where he frequently visited Isaac Riley, the bookseller, his brother-in-law. He wrote for Charles Brockden Brown's periodical, the *Monthly Magazine and American Review,* and the tale persists that Alsop, the "Hartford Wit," mingled with the New York coterie, Brown, William Dunlap, S. L. Mitchill, and Philip Freneau. He was now famous; he admitted modestly that "The Political Greenhouse" had awakened "considerable curiosity in this country." It had indeed; it was quoted in Congress to demonstrate that Connecticut was entangling the United States in a war with France! Alsop died suddenly at Flatbush, Long Island (where his ancestors had first settled). In the very year of his death he edited a curious volume, the *Narrative of the Adventures and Sufferings of John R. Jewitt, Only Survivor of the Ship Boston, During a Captivity of Nearly Three Years Among the Savages of Nootka Sound.* Though unlike his standard writings, this book, an imitation of Defoe, reminds us again of Alsop's love of remote lore, his respect for proven literary models, and what his contemporaries called his "ingenious fancy."

[The most reliable source of information concerning Alsop is the biog. sketch by Theodore Dwight, prefixed to *The Charms of Fancy* (1856). Important manuscript material consists of letters in the N. Y. Hist. Soc., the Yale Univ. Lib., and the N. Y. Pub. Lib.; other references to Alsop, more or less significant, may be found in *The Conn. Wits* (1926), ed. by V. L. Parrington; *Cyc. of Am. Lit.* (1856), ed, by E. A. and G. L. Duyckinck; *Specimens of Am. Poetry* (1829), by S. Kettell, II, 54–57; *The Conn. Wits* (1920), by H. A. Beers; "The Lit. of Conn.," by S. T. Williams, in *A Hist. of Conn.* (1925), ed. by N. G. Osborn, II, 509–10.]

S. T. W.
J. A. P.

ALSTON, JOSEPH (*c.* 1779–Sept. 10, 1816), lawyer, planter, statesman, was the eldest child of Mary (Ashe) Alston, daughter of Gen. John Ashe of North Carolina, and of Col. William Alston (1756–1839), rice-planter of All Saints' Waccamaw, "sometime captain" in the command of Gen. Francis Marion, and founder of the single "l" branch of the Alston family of South Carolina (J. A. Groves, *Alstons and Allstons,* 1901, pp. 75–79). He was probably born in All Saints' Parish, South Carolina. Prepared for college, it appears, by private tutors, he entered the junior class of Princeton in 1795, but left the next year without graduating (Princeton College Faculty Minutes, 1795, 1796). He then studied law in the office of Edward Rutledge, but soon after being admitted to the bar abandoned the profession for planting and an active career in politics.

He entered the lower house of the South Carolina legislature in 1802, and continued, with the exception of the session of 1804, to occupy a seat in that body until 1812. For the greater part of the period from 1805 to 1809 he served as speaker. In 1812, after a bitterly contested campaign, he was elected governor and entered at once upon an administration, 1812–14, which was distinguished by its vigorous measures in support of the War of 1812. On Feb. 2, 1801, he had married Theodosia Burr [*q.v.*], the talented daughter of Aaron Burr. The influence of father upon son-in-law has been greatly overemphasized in what has been written about the former (*e.g.,* J. Parton, *Life and Times of Aaron Burr,* 1864, I, 298), but it is not to be denied that the connection with the Burrs was in the end the determining factor in Alston's life. In 1806 he was drawn into "Burr's Conspiracy," a fact which his enemies never forgot (E. S. Thomas, *Reminiscences of the Last Sixty-five Years,* 1840, II, 69–82). If, however, Burr actually entertained thoughts of dismembering the Union, it is improbable that Alston was cognizant of them. It is true that in his haste to deny that he had been party to treasonable designs, he was led into a somewhat unbecoming repudiation of Burr (W. H. Safford, *Blennerhassett Papers,* 1864, pp. 227–30); but at the moment he had good grounds to suspect the latter of double-dealing, and he later made amends by zealously aiding the Colonel to establish his innocence. According to Harman Blennerhassett, whose fortune was swept away by the failure of Burr's schemes, Alston had guaranteed him against losses to the extent of $50,000 but later refused to reimburse him beyond the amount of $12,-

500 (*Ibid.*, pp. 533–38). Blennerhassett, however, never produced convincing proof of his claim, though he several times threatened a public exposure. In June 1812 Alston's only child, Aaron Burr Alston, died; early the next year Theodosia perished at sea; and less than three years later Alston himself was dead.

[Sources of information concerning Joseph Alston are surprisingly few. There is slight possibility that any of his private papers are extant, and no adequate sketch of his life has ever been written. Nor is any portr. or other likeness of him known to exist. In the "Diary of Edward Hooker, 1805–08," *Am. Hist. Ass. Reports,* 1896, I, 842–929, is given a description of his personal appearance and an account of some of his activities in the S. C. Leg., by a contemporary observer. A few of his letters are to be found in such places as M. L. Davis, *Memoirs of Aaron Burr,* 2 vols. (1836–37), and W. H. Safford, *Blennerhassett Papers* (1864), and at least three of his printed speeches are preserved. It is no longer to be doubted that Alston wrote the "Agrestis Pamphlet," which appeared during Burr's trial; his authorship is established by the *Blennerhassett Papers* (see pp. 337–41). The references to Alston in the general histories and in works dealing with Aaron and Theodosia Burr are for the most part inaccurate and prejudiced. An obituary was published in *The Times* (Charleston, S. C.), Sept. 16, 1816.]

J. H. E.

ALSTON, THEODOSIA (BURR). [See BURR, THEODOSIA, 1783–1813.]

ALTER, DAVID (Dec. 3, 1807–Sept. 18, 1881), physician, physicist, was a grandson of Johan Jacob Alter, who came to America on the *Beulah,* from Amsterdam, in 1753, immediately took the oath of allegiance to Pennsylvania, and during the Revolutionary War served with a Pennsylvania regiment. John Alter, the father of David, was born in 1771 and in 1800 moved to Westmoreland County in western Pennsylvania. David's mother was Eleanor Sheetz, of Swiss descent, whose grandfather had come to America in 1740. The boy's early formal schooling was poor, but a life of Benjamin Franklin, given him when nine, and a little later a book on electricity, supplemented by a few simple electrical devices, seem to have shown him very early where his chief interest was to lie. When twenty-one, he entered the Reformed Medical College in New York City, graduating three years later. He was twice married, first in 1832 to Laura Rowley, and in 1844 to Elizabeth A. Rowley. There were eleven children by these two marriages.

Throughout his life Alter devoted himself to physical experiments, showing remarkable ability despite the handicaps of his position, his apparatus even to prisms and lenses being almost entirely home-made. Among many minor inventions and discoveries were a successful electric clock, a method of purifying bromine, and the model of an electric locomotive. More important, however, were an electrical telegraph, early discoveries in spectrum analysis, and a method of obtaining coal-oil from coal; the last was apparently the only project which he considered commercially, and its chances of enriching him were destroyed by the drilling of the first Pennsylvania oil-well. His telegraph, invented in 1836, which seems to have been among the first successfully used, consisted of seven wires, each deflecting a needle. Combinations of deflections spelled the messages. Although it was in actual use between his house and barn, a patent was apparently refused on the ground that such an invention was absurd. Claims have been made that this was the first telegraph, but another, likewise not used commercially, seems to have been invented in Alabama in 1828.

A controversy has raged over Alter's discoveries in spectrum analysis. It is certain that far more credit is due him than was at first generally recognized, but, on the other hand, the assertion that he anticipated Kirchhoff's greatest discovery is without foundation. The fundamental principles of spectrum analysis are grouped in three laws commonly called Kirchhoff's Laws. The first of these had been common property for years. Alter and the great European physicist Angstrom independently and almost simultaneously discovered and published the second, *i. e.*, that the various elemental gases have spectra peculiar to themselves. This law made possible the determination of the chemical nature of gases by means of the spectroscope and was an extremely important advance. The publication of Alter's results in an American journal did not call to them the full recognition that they deserved, but Kayser in his great handbook has reviewed them thoroughly, reproducing Alter's maps of twelve metal spectra and concluding with the statement: "Man sieht dass Alter ein recht guter Beobachter war, der etwas denselben Standpunkt auf dem Gebiete der Emission erreicht hat, wie Angstrom. Interessant ist bei ihm der Hinweis auf die astronomischen Anwendungen." The third of Kirchhoff's laws, that of absorption spectra, while it is the most important of the three, was not known either to Angstrom or to Alter. It is unfortunate that at least two biographers have made charges of theft against Kirchhoff. Certainly Alter made no such charges.

[Sketches by Frank Cowan in G. D. Albert's *Hist. of the County of Westmoreland, Pa.* (1882), and by James B. Laux in the *Pa. German,* Mar. 1910; E. Stieren, "Auf Alter als einer der Entdecker der Spectral-Analyze," Poggendorf *Annalen* (1867), CXXXII; early abstracts of Alter's spectral analysis in *Chemico-Jahresberichte, 1854, L'Institute, 1856, Archives des sciences physiques et naturelles,* Geneva, 1855, XXIX; Kopp and Will's *Ann. Rep. of Chem. for 1859,* p. 107; H. G. Kayser, Jr., *Handbuch der Spectroscopie,* I, pp. 67–68. Angstrom's work is given on pp. 62–67 of the same volume.]

D. A.

ALTGELD, JOHN PETER (Dec. 30, 1847–Mar. 12, 1902), the first Democratic governor of Illinois after the Civil War, was the son of an illiterate and unsuccessful German immigrant, John Peter Altgeld, and Mary his wife. He was born at Nieder Selters in Nassau, and while an infant was brought by his parents to Richland County, Ohio, where he grew to maturity with little formal education and much grinding labor. Until he was twenty-one he worked for his father, with only the short intermission of temporary service in an Ohio volunteer regiment in 1864. In 1869 he left home, drifted west, and worked as common laborer, school-teacher, and student of law. He was elected state's attorney for Andrew County, Mo., in 1874. Even so late as his removal to Chicago in 1875, he was still obliged, as he confessed, to look at the dictionary for one word in five to know that he had spelled it correctly. Yet he ultimately mastered the English language and the law, wrote a treatise on oratory and practised it with effect, and in 1886 was elected to the superior court of Cook County (Chicago), Ill. When he resigned from the bench in 1891 he was chief justice of this court.

His little treatise on crime, *Our Penal Machinery and Its Victims* (1884), was early evidence of a belief that the poor and unfortunate had less than a fair chance in American life. In 1892 his influence among Illinois Democrats was such that he was nominated for governor on the first ballot in their convention; his ensuing election to a four-year term in that office came as a part of the wave of Democratic success that, having arisen in 1890, now swept Grover Cleveland into the presidency for his second term.

The public reputation of Altgeld as governor was established in 1893, a few weeks after his inauguration, by his action upon an appeal for clemency on behalf of certain anarchistic agitators who were in jail, under conviction of complicity with the murders in the Chicago Haymarket riot of May 4, 1886. Four of their associates had been hanged in November 1887. In studying the case, Altgeld came to the belief that the trial jury had been packed, that the judge had been prejudiced, and that the conviction of any one for "constructive" conspiracy to incite to murder was a miscarriage of justice. His brief of reasons, accompanying the pardons on June 26, 1893, has gained in weight with years; but at the time it outraged public opinion, and led to a wide, panicky, and scurrilous disposition to brand Altgeld as an anarchist and defender of crime. His Republican opponents made much of this alleged alliance of Democracy and revolution. When in July 1894 Altgeld protested the action of President Cleveland in sending the regular army to maintain order in Chicago during the Pullman strike, the critics ignored the constitutional basis of the protest, misrepresented the degree of disorder, and redoubled their attacks upon him. When he accepted the doctrine of free silver, and helped to steer the Democratic party toward a 16:1 plank in 1896, he gave the cue for an attack upon Bryan as the nominee of repudiation and anarchy. Broken in health, Altgeld was renominated for the office of governor in 1896 and although defeated by John R. Tanner [*q.v.*], the Republican candidate, he nevertheless ran ahead of the Democratic presidential ticket. It was generally believed that, save for the constitutional inhibition of his alien birth, he would have been the Democratic candidate for the presidency instead of William Jennings Bryan.

Altgeld died suddenly in 1902, after a speech in advocacy of Boer independence. Before this time, he had lost the large fortune which he had accumulated chiefly through speculation in Chicago real estate. He was survived by his wife, Emma Ford, a friend of his childhood and a graduate of Oberlin College. His unattractive appearance, and his attacks upon complacent position and wealth limited the number of friends, but his intimates developed a permanent devotion to him.

[Altgeld deliberately destroyed his biog. papers. Most of his writings were official or argumentative. *Live Questions, Including Our Penal Machinery and Its Victims* (1890) was republished in 1899 with a collection of his speeches, messages, and interviews as governor, "and a statement of the facts which influenced his course on several famous occasions." *The Cost of Something for Nothing* (1904) was printed after his death. The only important biog. is that of Waldo R. Browne, *Altgeld of Illinois: A Record of His Life and Work* (1924), but there are passages that throw light upon his character in Brand Whitlock, *Forty Years of It* (1914); Henry James, *Richard Olney and His Public Service* (1923); Caro Lloyd, *Henry Demarest Lloyd* (1912). There is also a good obituary in the *Outlook*, LXX, 696–97. Vachel Lindsay's widely quoted poem, "The Eagle That Is Forgotten," may most easily be found in his *Collected Poems* (1923). In the daily press, during Altgeld's term as governor, he was discussed and condemned with wholehearted bitterness. The *Chicago Tribune* was chief among his journalistic critics.]

F. L. P—n.

ALTHAM, JOHN (1589–Nov. 5, 1640), Jesuit missionary, connected with the founding of Maryland, is believed to have been a native of Warwickshire. His early life is obscure, and it is not certain whether his real name was Altham or Gravenor (possibly Grosvenor). His colleague, Father Andrew White, speaks of him as Altham (*Maryland Historical Society, Fund Publication No. 7*, p. 33), while in his latter years he was always mentioned as Father Gravenor. He is believed to have entered the Jesuit order in 1623; whether he was of Roman Catholic parentage or not, his career in England must necessarily have been difficult, since in 1585 all Jesuits and Seminary priests were by Parliamentary decree expelled from the kingdom. If educated at one of the Jesuit seminaries for the English on the continent at Douay, or elsewhere, he had been sent to his native land, and had been in ministry in Devonshire and London before joining the Maryland colonists.

Altham and White boarded at the Isle of Wight the *Dove* and the *Ark,* carrying the twenty gentlemen and 200 servants whom Leonard Calvert was taking to colonize the proprietorship of his brother, Lord Baltimore, in the New World. They set sail in the late autumn of 1633, and went by way of the West Indies. Upon arrival at Chesapeake Bay in March of 1634, where they held the first mass on Lady's Day, Calvert took Father Altham as his comrade on an initial exploration of the Potomac River. After the settlement of St. Mary's, Altham served in the fort; but soon asked permission to visit and preach to the Indians. For, although weak in health, he had "a bent for the hard missionary life." He thereupon was sent to Kent Island, where by 1640 he had made so deep an impression on the local chief that the latter and his wife were baptized as "Charles" and "Mary" in honor of the English sovereigns, and were married by clerical rites. Kent Island, where it was hoped trade might be drawn from the "Grand Lake of Canada," was the seat of a Virginia settlement, and the rivalry between the two groups of colonists lasted during the remainder of Father Altham's life. Through illness, he lost the use of his feet, but recovered sufficiently to accompany some of his Indian converts to St. Mary's, where he finally died, not, however, before Maryland had been reenforced by other Jesuit missionaries to continue his work.

[T. A. Hughes, *Hist. of the Soc. of Jesus in North America* (1907), I, 269; Cardinal Gibbons, "Sketch of the Cath. Ch. in Md.," in *Cath. Red Bk. of Western Md.* (1909), pp. 25–26; W. P. Treacy, *Old Cath. Md. and Its Early Jesuit Missionaries* (Swedesboro, N. J.), pp. 13–22; B. U. Campbell, "Early Christian Missions among the Natives of Md.," in *Md. Hist. Mag.*, I, 293–316; J. G. Shea, *Hist. of the Cath. Ch. within the Limits of the U. S.* (1886), I, 42; Clayton Hall, "Narr. of Early Md.," in Original Narr. of Early Am. Hist. Series (1910), pp. 44, 116, 124, 131–32.]

L. P. K.

ALTMAN, BENJAMIN (July 12, 1840–Oct. 7, 1913), merchant, philanthropist, art patron, was the son of Phillip and Cecilia Altman, Bavarian Jews from near Nuremberg, who came to New York about 1835, settling in the lower East Side. There, on Attorney St., Benjamin was born, the second of three children. The boy attended a public school near his home, and may have completed the grammar-school course, but this was the extent of his schooling. Phillip Altman conducted a small store near his home, and here, we may assume, Benjamin received his first training as a salesman. In these humble surroundings he learned honesty, thrift, and perseverance. His father died when Benjamin was still young, and from this time the boy's history is obscure. One report states that he strayed down to Clarksville, Va., and worked for a time in a general store. Most of his experience was gained in small Newark and New York dry-goods shops. In these he gathered also the capital to open, in 1865, at the age of twenty-five, a similar store of his own on Third Ave., near Tenth St. His success and ambition are attested by his removal in 1870 to Sixth Ave., where his brother Morris was for a time his partner. Morris later withdrew to engage in an independent enterprise, but on his death, in 1876, Benjamin Altman took over his brother's business and established himself at Sixth Ave. and Nineteenth St. David Frankenberg became his partner temporarily, but soon Benjamin Altman as sole owner of the business could give full play to his dreams and his determination to develop a large and distinctive department-store enterprise. After thirty years of progress at the Sixth Ave. location, in 1906 Altman moved his store to the northeast corner of Fifth Ave. and Thirty-fourth St., being a pioneer in the trend of big business to up-town Fifth Ave. By this time Michael Friedsam had become his partner and the firm was known as B. Altman & Co., the name it still retains. Successive additions after 1906 enabled the firm finally to occupy the entire block bounded by Fifth and Madison Aves., Thirty-fourth and Thirty-fifth Sts. The business was incorporated in 1913.

John Wanamaker, himself a leader among merchants, placed Altman first among the retail merchants of New York, and called him an excellent organizer. Another fellow merchant attributed his success to "ability and hard work—a lot of ability and a lot of hard work." Altman also possessed health, keen discernment, and balanced judgment. He took a constant interest in the welfare of his employees and was among the first to establish for his workers luncheon, rest, and medical service. Shortly before his death, he established the Altman Foundation to promote their welfare and to aid other New York philanthropical enterprises.

Another side of Altman's life is revealed by his esthetic tastes. At an early age a love for the beautiful began to assert itself and in 1882 he began a collection of Chinese enamels and porcelains. This led to interest in other fields of art, until the treasures housed in his Fifth Ave. residence consisted of some thousand articles of remarkable rarity and beauty, including porcelains, enamels, tapestries, rugs, furniture, sculpture, and paintings. William Bode, the German art critic, wrote that he had never seen a finer private collection of paintings. Altman made an extended tour of the Old World in 1888–89, using a keen eye and excellent judgment for rare and worthy art objects. Shorter trips to Europe were made in 1890 and 1909. He also acquired a valuable art library, familiarizing himself with the history of his acquisitions. During his later years he devoted himself more and more to these various collections, leaving business affairs largely in the hands of his partner. He never married and cared little for social life. "I doubt if 100 persons in New York City knew him by sight," commented a friend after his death.

He died, after a brief illness, on Oct. 7, 1913, at his residence, 626 Fifth Ave., New York. His will disbursed property to the value of approximately $35,000,000. There was a substantial legacy to the National Academy of Design, to foster American painting, which he had always encouraged. His entire art collections, appraised at $20,-000,000, were given to the Metropolitan Museum, New York, where they constitute the largest individual gift, "notable alike for their wide range of interest and the uniformly high quality of their contents."

[No biog. of Benjamin Altman has been published, and material for this sketch has been secured largely from representatives of the Altman Foundation of New York. Obituaries appeared in all leading New York dailies of Oct. 8, 1913, and immediately succeeding days. Later issues contain notices of Altman and his bequests. The full text of his will appeared in the *N. Y. Times* of Oct. 15, 1913. A *Handbook of the Benjamin Altman Coll.* was issued by the Metropolitan Museum of Art in 1914 (revised ed. 1915). It gives a brief record of Altman's career as collector and a full description of his donations.]

R. S. B.

ALTSHELER, JOSEPH ALEXANDER (Apr. 29, 1862–June 5, 1919), editor, author, was a prolific writer of novels, whose stories of adventure, with their background of American history, gave wholesome enjoyment and knowledge of their country to numberless youths. A Kentuckian, descended on his mother's side from Virginia and Kentucky borderers, he was born in Three Springs, Hart County, the son of Joseph and Lucy Snoddy Altsheler. Books were not plentiful in that part of the state, he says, and such as found their way there were passed from family to family, but he read Scott, Dickens, and Thackeray, and heard at first hand the legends of the Kentucky pioneers, and tales of the Civil War from both Union and Confederate veterans. The former had a great fascination for him and he would lie on his back in the woods for hours recalling them (Annie Carroll Moore, *Joseph A. Altsheler and American History,* 1919). After studying at Liberty College, Glasgow, Ky., and at Vanderbilt University, in 1885 he joined the staff of the Louisville *Courier-Journal,* serving as dramatic critic, assistant city editor, commercial editor, and editorial writer. In 1892 he became associated with the New York *World,* and finally took charge of the tri-weekly edition of that paper. During the annexation period in 1898 he was the correspondent for the *World* in Honolulu. He married Sarah Boles of Glasgow, Ky., on May 30, 1888. At the outbreak of the World War he and Mrs. Altsheler were in Germany and the difficulties they encountered getting home so weakened him that he never recovered his strength.

He became a story-writer almost by chance. Desiring a serial for his paper and being unable to secure one, he himself wrote a story of adventure for boys which was well received. His interest in history led him to turn to that field for material, and in 1897 he published *The Sun of Saratoga, a Romance of Burgoyne's Surrender.* Between then and 1919 he wrote more than forty other novels. The majority of these belong to some one of six series: the French and Indian War Series; the Great West Series; the Young Trailers Series; the Texas Series; the Civil War Series; and the World War Series. They are the work of one who had a natural gift for story telling, good descriptive ability, love for nature, a sense of humor, and skill in character portrayal. He tried to make the historical background of his tales truthful by study of the best authorities and found inspiration in the writings of Francis Parkman. The exploits of his characters are such as to captivate the heart of any robust lad. In 1918 he was the most popular of the authors of books for boys in the public libraries (*Bookman,* November 1918).

[In addition to the sources mentioned above, some biog. material may be found in the *Book Buyer,* Sept. 1900; *N. Y. Times,* June 7, 1919; *Louisville Courier-Jour.,* June 7, 1919; and *Who's Who in America,* 1918–19.]

H. E. S.

ALVARADO, JUAN BAUTISTA (Feb. 14, 1809–July 13, 1882), governor of Mexican California, was born in Monterey, Cal., the son of a Spanish sergeant, José Francisco Alvarado, and his wife Maria Josefa Vallejo, sister of Mariano Guadalupe. His father died when Bautista was three months old, and his mother later married Ramón Estrada. Early schooling from invalided sergeants and his mother was supplemented by Gov. Sola, who assisted the boy with reading; Alvarado had a *flair* for contraband literature, being excommunicated for indulging in Fénelon's *Télémaque*. Clerical positions with foreign traders and in the custom-house led to public life in 1827, when the boy became secretary of the territorial *diputación;* he held this post till 1834, meantime adding that of territorial treasurer. Active as a *diputado,* he was president in 1836, and with José Castro unseated Gov. Gutierrez, the centralist. Alvarado assumed the governorship in December as a result of this move for local control under the federalism of 1824. Perhaps actuated by fear of foreigners, chiefly Americans, he adhered to the Mexican departmental system after gaining the power, the "sovereign state" of California being overlooked. He organized the Department, which included Lower California, into districts and subdistricts under prefects and subprefects, with town councils in the larger towns. The Los Angeles region had to be subjected by arms and arguments, but submitted before February 1837. The jealousies of the Carrillo family, Carlos Carrillo having obtained an appointment to the governorship, had also to be eliminated. This was done by sending Andrés Castillero to Mexico, and Alvarado was made proprietary governor in November 1838. The personal jealousies of Mariano Vallejo in Sonoma, of Pio Pico in the South, and of Castillero occupied much of the executive's attention. The expulsion of Isaac Graham, who had a brandy distillery at Branciforte, and a crew of followers who were thought to be plotting revolt, caused a flurry of interest almost international; the Graham party was sent to Mexico, but in 1842 was released and returned.

Under Alvarado came John A. Sutter, to establish himself at the present Sacramento as a citizen defender of the frontier against Americans and Indians. Sutter bought the establishment of the retiring Russians from Gov. Kostromitinoff, the Department accepting the obligation, as Sutter had no funds. During Alvarado's term the ex-missions were inspected by William P. Hartnell, in a vain effort to stop the decay into which they had been falling since secularization in 1834. Alvarado's measures have been called destructive, but the resuscitation had become impossible. There was an attempt to establish a superior court, but the civil arm had no material with which to do this; better was the ecclesiastical court begun by the bishop, Father Francisco Garcia Diego y Moreno, after the Department became a bishopric in 1840. In September 1841 the governor became ill, and surrendered his office to the president of the departmental junta until Jan. 1, 1842. In October came Commodore T. A. C. Jones, palpitating lest Great Britain anticipate him in seizing California, and overzealously raising the American flag at Monterey, only to haul it down with apologies. In December at his own request Alvarado handed the government over to Gen. Manuel Micheltorena, sent by Santa Anna to govern; his office was established at Los Angeles because of the Jones incident. After retiring, Alvarado received a commission as colonel; in 1844–45 he and Castro led a short revolt which unseated Micheltorena, Alvarado serving under Gov. Pio Pico as administrator of customs in Monterey. In 1845 he was elected to Congress, but neither he nor the treasury had money enough to send him to Mexico. Alvarado was married to Martina Castro in 1839 by proxy in Santa Clara; they resided at Monterey until 1848, and afterward at San Pablo. There were several children of this marriage, and natural daughters born before it.

[Mexican California is best presented in R. H. Dana, *Two Years Before the Mast* (1840); Alfred Robinson, *Life in Cal.* (1846; repr. ed. by Thos. C. Russell, 1925); and E. Duflot de Mofras, *Exploration du Territoire de l'Orégon, des Californies, et de la Mer Vermeille* (1844); Alexander Forbes, *California* (1839), the first English book on the area. See also H. H. Bancroft, *Hist. of Cal.* (1884–90), especially his "Pioneer Register," and T. H. Hittell, *Hist. of Cal.* (4 vols., 1885–97), and Fr. Zephyrin Engelhardt, *The Missions and Missionaries of Cal.* (4 vols., 1908–15); for added bibliography, R. E. Cowan, *A Bibliography of the Hist. of Cal.* (1914); and C. E. Chapman, *A Hist. of Cal.: The Spanish Period* (1921).]

H. I. P.

ALVEY, RICHARD HENRY (Mar. 6, 1826–Sept. 14, 1906), jurist, was born in St. Mary's County, Md., the eldest son of George and Harriet (Wicklin) Alvey, the family having lived in the county from the time of Lord Baltimore's colonization. He went to the little school taught by his father. At the age of eighteen he entered the clerk's office of Charles County, where he was a deputy until 1850. He had been reading law, and was admitted to the bar in 1849. On quitting the clerk's office, he moved to Hagerstown to practise. In briefless years he was profoundly affected by study of Tucker's addenda to Blackstone, dealing with American law, in which Jeffersonian principles were espoused. He had been in Hagerstown only a year when he ran for the state Senate as a Democrat. Though Washington County was strongly Whig, the vote was a tie, and a second election went in favor of his opponent, Judge French, by only forty votes. Alvey first came to wide notice when as a Pierce elector in 1852 he spoke throughout the state, the ticket receiving Maryland's vote. He was married in 1856 to Mary Wharton, who died four years later. In 1862 he married Julia I. Hays, of Washington County, by whom he had nine children. In January 1861, just after Lincoln's election, a meeting was held in Hagerstown to express the opinion of the county on the secession issue. Alvey, then thirty-five years old, was named chairman of the committee on resolutions. He headed a minority report which leaned to the state-rights view. This "Alvey Resolution" attracted much attention, and spoke for the sympathies of certainly half the people of Maryland. It is believed that this incident was responsible for his arrest as soon as Federal troops entered Hagerstown, the charge that he was holding communication with the enemy lacking proof. For a year, until February 1862, he was held prisoner, first at Fort McHenry, Baltimore, next at Fort Lafayette, New York, and last at Fort Warren in Boston Harbor, where were also Severn Teackle Wallis and other Marylanders. Returning home on parole, he resumed his practise, for a time being associated with Judge J. T. Mason, and later being the partner of Hon. William T. Hamilton.

After the war, Alvey labored for the restoration of normal conditions. He particularly forwarded the return of the franchise to those deprived of it through factional differences, and being elected to the legislature in 1867 fathered the law putting the selection of juries immediately under the eye of the court instead of leaving the choice to partisan sheriffs. At first made local to Washington, Carroll, and Frederick Counties, this jury law was soon extended throughout the state. Alvey was a delegate to the constitutional convention held the same year, being active as chairman of the committee on representation. In 1867 under the new constitution he was elected chief judge of the fourth judicial circuit for the counties of Washington, Allegany, and Garrett, thus becoming a member of the Maryland court of appeals. He was reëlected in 1882. The following year, on the retirement of Judge James L. Bartol, he was commissioned by Gov. Hamilton chief judge of the highest Maryland court, in response to a public demand which the reluctant executive could not dismiss. Alvey's opinions as associate judge appear in volumes XXVIII–LX of the *Maryland Reports,* and those as chief judge in volumes LX-LXXVII.

Alvey was a large, stout man, clean-shaven, and with a shining bald head, reminding one of a priest. When he came to the bench he was known for his irascible temper, the story being told that once in Hagerstown, while arguing a case, he threw a law book at the head of opposing counsel. But in his judicial office he developed repose, having learned, say those who knew him, from his association with Judge Bartol, who was eminently suave. He was of the old school, a thorough student of the English Common Law, and one who would have lamented the sympathetic bending of legal theory to meet social exigency. In his thirty-eight years on the bench he wrote some 3,000 opinions, which show his mastery and veneration of the law as a science. He never employed a stenographer or permitted himself the informality of even a lead pencil; ". . . all of his opinions as filed are autographic, and written in the neatest chirography, and with the slightest bearing on the pen, as though he wanted to be gentle, and level and calm even with the instrumentalities he involved in the transfer of his thoughts to paper." In a period in which echoes of the Civil War were vibrant and distrust of government was common, Judge Alvey, in spite of his supposed partisanship, was even-handed and a lesson in reflection. When the District of Columbia court of appeals was organized in 1893, President Cleveland appointed him chief justice. Here, until his retirement from failing health in 1904, he was responsible for laying down the rules of practise of the new tribunal, and he made it answer to expectations. In 1896 he was appointed by Cleveland to serve on the commission which determined the boundary line between Venezuela and British Guiana, discharging his judicial duties at the same time. He lectured at the National University in Washington on branches of the law, serving also as chancellor of the institution. Never wishing public notice, and rarely accepting social invitations, he spent his last years in the quiet of his family circle. He died at Hagerstown, and was buried in sight of the mountains which always gave him pleasure.

[For biographical sketches see the *Baltimore Sun* and the *Baltimore American,* Sept. 15, 1906; *Men of Mark in Md.* (1907), pp. 34–37; *Bench and Bar of Md.* (n.d.), pp. 474, ff. Three meetings of bench and bar were held in honor of Judge Alvey, the first when he resigned from the Maryland Court of Appeals (reported in *76 Md.,* xxviii–xxxix), the second when he sat for the last time in the District Court of Appeals (reported in *24 App. Cas.* (D.C.), xvii–xxi), and the third at his death (reported in *28 App. Cas.* (D.C.), xxiii). Though mainly eulogistic, all throw light upon his character and attainments; the second includes biographical material.]

B.M.

ALVORD, BENJAMIN (Aug. 18, 1813–Oct. 16, 1884), Union soldier, was born at Rutland, Vt., son of William and Lucy (Claghorn) Alvord, and sixth in descent from Alexander Alvord, who came from the southwest of England to Windsor, Conn., about 1645 (S. M. Alvord, pp. 123, 225). Upon his graduation from West Point in 1833 he was commissioned in the 4th Infantry, and, except for brief periods of detached service and a two years' tour of duty as instructor at the Military Academy, served with it for twenty-one years. He took part in the Florida War, in the battles of Palo Alto and Resaca de la Palma, and in the guerrilla fighting of Lally's command which convoyed supplies from Vera Cruz to the city of Mexico in the summer and fall of 1847. In 1854 he accepted an appointment as paymaster with the rank of major. At the outbreak of the Civil War he was chief paymaster in Oregon. Some experienced officer was needed for the command of that remote district, and to this duty Alvord was assigned, being made a brigadier-general of volunteers in 1862, and continuing in Oregon until 1865. Thus no opportunity for distinction in the field came to him, but his services, though unspectacular, were not unimportant. In the early days of the war his influence was effectively exerted to keep the people of the territory loyal to the Union and to overcome the secessionist sympathies which were active in some places. Throughout the whole period he had the difficult task of protecting settlers from the attacks of hostile Indians, and peaceable Indians from the aggression of rascally white men. He seems to have performed it with impartial justice. The government showed its approval of his conduct of affairs by conferring three brevets. From 1872 until his retirement in 1880, he was paymaster-general of the army, at first with the rank of colonel, and after 1876 with that of brigadier-general.

Although the greater part of Alvord's life was spent in places remote from facilities for study, his attainments in several branches of science were considerable, and he wrote extensively for learned publications. His monograph on "The Tangencies of Circles and of Spheres" (*Smithsonian Contributions to Knowledge,* vol. VIII, 1856) and its sequel, "The Intersection of Circles and the Intersection of Spheres" (*American Journal of Mathematics,* March 1882) formed original contributions to mathematical knowledge. He was the first to classify the compass plant botanically. Among other published papers are "Winter Grazing in the Rocky Mountains" (*Bulletin of the American Geographical Society,* 1883), and several on mathematical subjects and on the American Indians. A kindly, unassuming, studious man, his interests were scholarly, and his abilities of a sort little appreciated in an army whose duties lay chiefly on the frontier. He was married in 1846 to Emily Louise Mussey of Rutland, Vt., by whom he had six children.

[G. W. Cullum, *Biog. Reg.* (3rd ed., 1891), I, 553–58; *Official Records,* vol. L, pts. 1, 2; *Genealogy of the Descendants of Alexander Alvord,* comp. by S. M. Alvord (1908); additional information from Alvord's son, Brig.-Gen. Benjamin Alvord, Jr.] T. M. S.

ALVORD, CLARENCE WALWORTH (May 21, 1868–Jan. 24, 1928), historian, was born in Greenfield, Mass., the son of Daniel Wells and Caroline Betts (Dewey) Alvord, and a descendant of a long line of New England ancestry. He attended the schools of Northampton, Mass., and Phillips Academy, Andover, and was graduated from Williams College in 1891. After teaching in Milton Academy (Mass.) for two years, he began his graduate work in history, spending the years 1893–95 at Friedrich Wilhelm University in Berlin and part of the following year at the University of Chicago. In 1897 he became an instructor in the preparatory school of the University of Illinois and, four years later, instructor in history in the university proper. For nineteen years he remained at Illinois, receiving a Ph.D. degree there in 1908 and becoming a full professor in 1913.

Alvord's discovery in 1905 of the records of the old French settlements of Cahokia and Kaskaskia in Illinois, long believed lost, resulted in his appointment by the State Historical Library as general editor of the *Illinois Historical Collections.* Under his editorship fourteen volumes of the *Collections* were published, making accessible a wealth of original documents relating to western history and setting a high standard for the editing of historical materials. Of five of these volumes he was also special editor. His introduction to the *Cahokia Records* (1907) is a brilliant study (143 pages) of "The County of Illinois" created by Virginia in 1778. In 1909 Alvord was appointed director of the Illinois Historical Survey, created in the university as a research bureau; and in 1913 he was selected by the Illinois Centennial Commission as editor of the *Centennial History of Illinois.* Of this five-volume work, he wrote the first (1920), a notable contribution to the history of the Middle West. That his historical interests were far from being confined to a narrow field was demonstrated by a work published in 1912 in collaboration with Lee Bidgood on *The First Exploration of the Trans-Allegheny Regions by Virginians, 1650–1674,* and by his *Mississippi Valley in British Politics* (2 vols., 1917). The latter work, which treated the period from 1763 to 1774, was recognized by scholars at home and abroad as an outstanding contribution to the history of England and of the causes of the American Revolution as well as to that of the Mississippi Valley. It was awarded the Loubat prize for the best work on American history published in five years.

Alvord's influence and counsel were important factors in shaping the policies of the Mississippi Valley Historical Association, organized in 1907. It was due largely to his efforts that the association became not merely a confederation of historical societies, but an association of scholars bent upon promoting scientific study and research. In 1914 he brought about the establishment by the association of a quarterly magazine, *The Mississippi Valley Historical Review,* of which he was managing editor, 1914–23. In 1920 he resigned his positions in Illinois to become professor of history in the University of Minnesota. Three years later he determined to devote his time to research and writing, and his remaining years were spent abroad. In 1925 he delivered the annual Raleigh lecture before the British Academy, and in 1926 he was chosen as the first American to deliver the Creighton lecture at the University of London. He was married in 1893 to Jennie Kettell Blanchard (*née* Parrott), who died in 1911. In 1913 he was married to Idress Head. He was of slender build and dark complexion and wore a Van Dyke beard. His incisive intellect, genial personality, and wide range of interests contributed to his strong influence upon mature students.

[An outline of Alvord's career may be found in *Who's Who in America,* 1926–27. The present writer was in close touch with him from 1910 to 1923 and has drawn largely upon personal recollections and correspondence files. He is preparing a longer sketch, with a bibliography of Alvord's works, for publication in the *Mississippi Valley Hist. Rev.* for Dec. 1928. For an account and evaluation of Alvord's work at Illinois, see D. R. Fox, "State Hist. II," in *Polit. Sci. Quart.,* XXXVII, 99–118, and Allan Nevins, *Illinois* (1917), p. 341.]

S. J. B.

ALVORD, CORYDON ALEXIS (May 12, 1813–Nov. 28, 1874), printer, was born in Winchester, Conn., the son of John and Experience (Webb) Alvord. He went to Hartford at the age of fifteen and served an apprenticeship at the printer's trade, subsequently becoming foreman in the house of Case & Tiffany. On Sept. 6, 1836, he married Mary Ann Buckland of New Hartford, by whom he had ten children. In 1845 the opportunities of a large city lured him to New York, where he commenced business for himself, first at 51 John St. (*N.Y.Dir.,* 1845–46), then 29 Gold St., and finally at 15 Vandewater St. (*N.Y.Dir.,* 1857). Those familiar with his Vandewater Street establishment tell of a very unusual equipment, fonts of old-style type, and of ancient and oriental letters, old engravings, stereotype plates, with immense underground storage rooms separated by thick walls and connected by iron doors. If any one had an unusual piece of printing to be done, Alvord was equipped to do it. Many books of the period which carry "Privately Printed" on the title-page show "C. A. Alvord, Printer" modestly tucked away somewhere. "Limited Editions," too, came from his shop; *e.g.,* Thomas Dring, *Recollections of the Jersey Prison-Ship* (1865), James Parton, *Life and Times of Benjamin Franklin* (1865), Fitz-Greene Halleck, *Fanny: A Poem* (1866).

Alvord was one of the first presidents of the Typothetæ (organized, 1862), and when that organization of employers assembled at the Astor House, Jan. 29, 1869, on the occasion of the first great printers' strike, he spoke in opposition to the high wage demand of Typographical Union No. 6 and presented resolutions which were unanimously adopted (*N. Y. Times,* Jan. 30, 1869). In 1867, he bought a residence in Hartford and moved his family thither; he continued, however, to carry on his business in New York. In the spring of 1871, there came a merger of several printing firms, including Alvord's, into the New York Printing Company, Alvord accepting a position as superintendent. This printing company, the most extensive of its kind in the city, with over 2,000 employees, was controlled by the "Tweed Ring," and the "fancy prices" charged for the "Corporation printing" were already under suspicion (*N.Y.Times,* Dec. 28, 1871). In 1870, the Common Council had voted "to prepare for the press the ancient records of the City of New Amsterdam and those of the City of New York, prior to 1850" (*Ordinances Approved by the Mayor,* xxxviii, 197). Presswork on this job (in which old-style type was used and copy strictly followed) had been started under Alvord's supervision when the "Committee of Seventy" appointed to investigate Tweed's activities (*N. Y. Times,* Sept. 5, 1871) found reason to take possession of the company's properties. Comptroller Andrew H. Green reported that the work on the records as projected would have involved an outlay of more than half a million dollars, and produced 240,000 volumes, enough to fill a room 24x24 feet, and 13 feet high, from floor to ceiling (*Proceedings of the Board of Aldermen* (1873), cxxix, 129). No discredit attaches to Alvord in this matter; he appears simply to have been carrying on the printing business for extravagant and unscrupulous employers. He retired to Hartford and indulged his taste for historical and genealogical research. A manuscript which he "incurred much expense to prepare" is the basis of the *Genealogy of the Descendants of Alexander Alvord,* finally published in 1908. Articles of his appeared in the *Winsted Herald* and *Hartford Courant* during the last two years of his life.

[Alvord's life work is portrayed by the books he printed; the card catalogue in the "Reserve" room of the N. Y. Pub. Lib. enables one to find examples of his best workmanship. The obituary in the *Hartford Daily Courant,* Nov. 30, 1874, contains the best account of his career.]

A. E. P.

ALVORD, HENRY ELIJAH (Mar. 11, 1844–Oct. 1, 1904), educator, specialist in dairy husbandry, was born at Greenfield, Mass., the eldest son of Daniel Wells Alvord, a prominent lawyer, and Caroline (Clapp) Alvord. He was prepared for college in the public schools of Greenfield and entered Norwich University in Vermont in 1860, but joined the Union Army in his junior year. He served in Rhode Island and Massachusetts volunteer cavalry regiments, becoming a major in 1865. For a brief period he was with the Freedman's Bureau and then served five years in the 10th Cavalry Regiment of the regular army, attaining the rank of captain. During this period he studied and wrote on the cattle industry of the Southwest. For his article on "American Beef for the British Markets" he was awarded the grand medal of the Royal Agricultural Society of England. He was the first army officer detailed as military instructor at a land-grant college, performing this service at the Massachusetts Agricultural College from 1869 to 1871. There he also studied agriculture under Stockbridge and Goessmann. During the next eight years his time was divided between teaching in the scientific department at Williston Seminary, Easthampton, Mass., and other educational and agricultural enterprises. He had married, on Sept. 6, 1866, Martha Scott Swink, daughter of William Swink of Virginia, and from about 1871 their home was on her family estate, known as "Spring Hill Farm," near the Great Falls of the Potomac, in Fairfax County, Va., although residence there was often interrupted by Alvord's public duties. At this Virginia home he conducted a dairy farm and established a herd of registered Jersey dairy cattle, one of the first in the state. He wrote much for the agricultural press and delivered public addresses on agricultural subjects. He was the author of the American chapters published in *Sheldon's Dairy Farming*. He managed the Chautauqua "School of Farming" and prepared "what was probably the first correspondence course in agriculture." He helped to organize the Carlisle training school for Indians and served at times as special Indian commissioner in the Southwest. From about 1876 he was a pioneer and leader in the establishment of the coöperative creamery system, particularly in New England, and himself established the first creamery east of the Hudson River. When in 1880 Lawson Valentine started the Houghton Farm near Mountainville, Orange County, N.Y., with an experiment department, he made Alvord general manager of the enterprise. Interesting practical and scientific experimental work was carried on there for five years.

In 1886 and 1887 Alvord was professor of agriculture at the Massachusetts Agricultural College. After this until 1893 he was president of the Maryland Agricultural College where he organized the Maryland Agricultural Experiment Station, and then for brief periods he was president of the Oklahoma Agricultural and Mechanical College and professor of agriculture at the New Hampshire College of Agriculture and Mechanic Arts. His connection with these land-grant colleges gave him the opportunity of broad leadership in the nation-wide promotion of the interests of such institutions through his activities connected with the Association of American Agricultural Colleges and Experiment Stations (now the Association of Land-Grant Colleges and Universities). At the convention of representatives of these institutions at Washington in 1885 Alvord was chairman of the committee which supervised its proceedings and helped materially to pave the way for the permanent organization of the Association effected in 1887. He was then made chairman of its executive committee, which dealt with the relations of the Association with the federal government and otherwise promoted its interests at and between its conventions. In this capacity he served seven years and among other things was active in helping to put into effect the Hatch Agricultural Experiment Station Act of 1887 and to secure the passage of the Morrill Land-Grant College Endowment Act of 1890. In recognition of his important services he was elected president of the Association in 1894. When a Dairy Division was created in the Bureau of Animal Industry of the United States Department of Agriculture in 1895 Alvord was appointed its chief and held that position until his death. The division was at first organized to collect and disseminate information regarding the condition of the dairy industry, but in 1902 it established research laboratories.

Alvord was a fellow of the American Association for the Advancement of Science, twice president of the Society for the Promotion of Agricultural Science, honorary member of the Royal Agricultural Society of England, and "Officer" of the National Order of Merite Agricole of France. He had a strong and attractive personality, was exact and systematic in business and authoritative in manner and procedure. Among his friends he was cordial, generous, and unselfish. Through his writings and public addresses he achieved a high reputation as an authority on animal husbandry and dairying. Among these may be mentioned "The Dairy Herd: Its Formation and Management" (*United States Department of Agriculture Year Book*, 1894); "Dairy Development in the United States" (*Ibid.*, 1899); Dairying at Home and Abroad" (*Ibid.*, 1902); and (with R. A. Pearson) "The Milk Supply of Two Hundred Cities and Towns" (*Bureau of Animal Industry Bulletin 46,* 1903).

[The chief sources of information are: S. M. Alvord, *A Genealogy of the Descendants of Alexander Alvord* (1908); G. M. Dodge and W. A. Ellis, *Norwich Univ., 1819–1911* (3 vols., 1911); *Proc. Ass. Am. Ag. Colls. and Experiment Stations,* 1887–95, and the reports and bulletins of the Bureau of Animal Industry, 1895–1904. Brief biogs. are contained in *Proc. Soc. for the Promotion of Ag. Sci.,* 1905, and L. H. Bailey's *Cyc. Am. Ag.* (1909), vol. IV.]

A. C. T.

AMADAS, PHILIP (fl. 1584–85), English navigator, was one of Raleigh's commanders. On Mar. 25, 1584, there was granted to Sir Walter Raleigh by Queen Elizabeth a patent empowering him to "discover, search, find out and view . . . heathen and barbarous lands . . . the colonists to have all the priviledge of Denizens and persons native of England." By April Raleigh had fitted out two vessels, one under the command of Philip Amadas of Hull, and the other under that of Arthur Barlowe. On Apr. 27, 1584, the ships "departed the West of England." Their course led them first to the Canary Islands and thence to the West Indies. Turning northward, on July 2, they entered shoal water, "wher we smelt so sweet and so strong a smel as if we had bene in the midst of some delicate garden abounding with all kinde of odoriferous flowers by which we were assured that the land could not be farre distant." On July 4 the ships reached the coast of what is now North Carolina. Sailing along the coast 120 English miles they entered an inlet. They then "manned their boats and went to view the land next adjoyning." Of this land they took possession in the name of the Queen. It proved to be an island twenty miles long and about six miles broad—"the isle of Wokokon" over against Pamlico Sound (chart by John White, 1585 or 1586, in *Early English and French Voyages,* p. 248). The island was found to be "full of grapes" and to contain "goodly cedar trees," deer, hares, and wild fowl. In a few days the explorers were visited by forty or fifty Indians "as mannerly and civill as any of Europe." Among the visiting Indians were "some women of colour yellowish and their haire black for the most part, and yet," says the account, "we saw children that had very fine aburne and chestnut coloured haire," descendants, it has been conjectured, of white men wrecked on the coast some twenty-six years before. In return for these visits the English made a journey to Ohanoak (Roanoke) Island, distant from the harbor by which they entered, "seven leagues." Here was found a village of nine houses surrounded by a stockade, some of the houses containing five rooms. The visitors were treated to a foot-bath and given a feast of venison, melons, etc. They heard of places such as "Pomeyooc" (west of the present site of Engelhard, N. C.), "Nomopana" (the Chowan River), and "Sequotan"—a position apparently near Blount Bay (*Ibid.*, pp. 227 ff. and notes). "When," says the account, "we first had sight of this countrey, some thought the first land we saw to bee the continent; but after we entred into the Haven, we saw before us another mighty long Sea: for there lyeth along the coast a tracte of Islands, two hundreth miles in length, adjoyning to the Ocean sea, and betweene the Islands, two or three entrances . . . We brought home also two of the Savages being lustie men whose names were Wanchese and Manteo." By September the ships were back in England, and their report, written by Barlowe, so pleased Elizabeth that she stood god-mother to the new colony, naming it Virginia. In 1585 Raleigh furnished seven ships to take permanent possession of the country discovered by Amadas and Barlowe, and Sir Richard Grenville was sent out as admiral with Ralph Lane as governor of the colony. With Grenville went Capt. Amadas, whom Hakluyt sets down as "Admirall" of Virginia. Amadas, with others, now passed over to the mainland, "victualled for eight dayes," on a tour of discovery during which the party actually set eyes upon "Pomeyooc" and "Sequotan." Under the government of Ralph Lane, Amadas, says Hakluyt, remained in Virginia "one whole yeere."

["Captain Arthur Barlowe's Narrative" in *Hakluyt's Voyages* (MacLehose, 1904), VIII; H. S. Burrage, *Early English and French Voyages, 1534–1608* (1906).]

I. B. R.

AMATEIS, LOUIS (Dec. 13, 1855–Mar. 16, 1913), sculptor, a son of Gen. Paolo and Carolina Amateis, came to America when twenty-eight years old. His training in sculpture had been received in various places. He had studied in Paris in 1878. In his native Turin he had been Gold Medalist at the Royal Academy of Fine Arts and in 1880 was graduated from the Institute of Technology there. In the same year he had received honorable mention at the National Exhibition. The following year found him at Milan and two years later he set sail for New York, where he continued his profession. Much of his work here was in the nature of architectural sculpture, largely done for the firm of McKim, Mead & White. In New York also he was married on Feb. 24, 1889, to Dora Ballin. In 1893 he was made professor of fine arts in the department of architecture at George Washington University, then known as Columbian University. He remained there for ten years and even after his retirement continued to reside in Washington. His best-known work is the pair of bronze doors, together with the transom above them, for the west entrance of the Capitol; these have never been hung, because their installation would require some minor structural changes, but they are on exhibition at the north entrance of the New National Museum Building in Washington. Most of Amateis's monumental works were made, however, for the state of Texas. In Galveston are the Henry Rosenberg monument to the Texas heroes of the War of 1836 and a statue of Rosenberg in front of the Rosenberg Library. In Houston is an "Angel of Peace," and in Corsicana "The Call to Arms." Among his other works are "Father Rhine" in Mobile, the Heirrich mausoleum in Washington, and the memorial monument of Nathan A. Baldwin in the cemetery at Milford, Conn. This last, made in 1899, recalls distinctly Amateis's Italian birth and training, for it would be quite appropriate in such a place as the Campo Santo at Genoa. Besides these monumental works he did numerous portrait busts, among them those of President Arthur, James G. Blaine, Gen. Hancock, Gen. Logan, Secretary Bayard, and Andrew Carnegie. He was a member of the National Art Society and an exhibitor at the National Academy of Design in New York and at the Art Society in Philadelphia. For the Pan-American Exposition at Buffalo in 1901 he made a group called "El Caney." He was likewise represented at the Louisiana Purchase Exposition at St. Louis in 1904. The example of his life and work was not lost on his own children, for of his four sons two became architects and one a sculptor.

[Written sources of information about Louis Amateis are entirely lacking aside from a brief and incomplete notice in *Who's Who in America,* 1910–11, and an obituary in the *Washington Evening Star,* Mar. 17, 1913.]

E. G. N.

AMBLER, JAMES MARKHAM MARSHALL (Dec. 30, 1848–Oct. 30, 1881), military surgeon, explorer, was born at "The Dell," Markham, Fauquier County, Va., the son of Dr. Richard Cary and Susan (Marshall) Ambler. He was a descendant of Richard Ambler of Yorkshire, who settled in Virginia early in the eighteenth century. His mother, characterized by one of his biographers as "a wise and great-hearted woman," was a niece of Chief Justice Marshall and a grand-daughter of Robert Morris. He attended the neighborhood schools until his sixteenth birthday. Then he enlisted in the 12th Virginia Cavalry of the Confederate Army, where he served during the last months of the war. He entered Washington College (now Washington and Lee University) for the school year 1865–66 and remained there until 1867, when he went to the University of Maryland to study medicine. After graduating he took the government examinations and in April 1874 was commissioned an assistant surgeon in the United States Navy. During the remainder of the year and a part of the year following he served on the *Mayflower* and the *Kansas,* of the North Atlantic fleet, and was then transferred to the training ship *Minnesota.* In 1877 he was made a passed assistant surgeon and transferred to the Naval Hospital at Norfolk. It was while there that a telegram came to him from Lieut. George W. De Long [*q.v.*] asking him to accept the post of surgeon on the *Jeannette,* then being fitted out for its historic voyage in the Arctic regions. He immediately left for his old home to consult with his mother. They both agreed that it was his duty to go, and he accepted.

From the time the *Jeannette* sailed (July 8, 1879), until Sept. 6, when the ship was solidly frozen in, his duties were those of ordinary routine. From then until the released ship sank (June 1881) and on until the final tragedy he bore an increasingly arduous part in the attempt to ward off disaster. Though he could not foresee the cases of lead poisoning that were to come from the soldering of the food cans, it was due to his vigilance that no case of scurvy appeared. In the effort to reach land after the retreat from the ship he acted as roadmaster, having charge of the bridging and rafting, and also had the duty of husbanding and apportioning the meager food stores of the party. After the separation of the three boats off the shores of the Lena delta in the storm of Sept. 16, the party of De Long, Ambler, and eleven others landed and struggled on buffeted by storms and worn down by hunger and cold. On Oct. 9, when the store of food was almost exhausted, two men, subsequently rescued by a native, were sent ahead for succor. Ambler declined the offer to go. In his journal he relates the incident and says: "I thought my duty required me with him (De Long) and the main body for the present." His last entry, dated Oct. 20, addressed to his brother and containing a tender message to his mother, tells of the suffering endured by the party. The end came ten days later. De Long, Ambler, and Ah Sam, the Chinese cook, forged somewhat ahead of the remainder of the party and then, exhausted, lay down and expired. To Chief Engineer Melville, who discovered the bodies Mar. 23, 1882, it was evident that Ambler had been the last to die. The remains were brought to New York Feb. 20, 1884, and Ambler's body was buried at Markham, his birthplace.

[John Cropper Wise, "James Markham Marshall Ambler," *Jour. Ass. Mil. Surgeons of the U. S.,* May 1906; Wm. Taylor Thom, *A Notable Beta of Yesterday* (pamphlet, 1921); Wm. Williams Keen, "Story of the Three Tablets," *Mil. Surgeon,* Jan. 1918; Geo. W. Melville, *In The Lena Delta* (1885); Emma De Long, *Voyage of the Jeannette* (1883).]

W. J. G.

AMENT, WILLIAM SCOTT (Sept. 14, 1851–Jan. 6, 1909), Congregational clergyman and missionary, was born at Owosso, Mich., the son of Winfield Scott and Emily (Hammond) Ament, of Dutch, French Huguenot, and English ancestry. He was educated in the Owosso public schools where he excelled in baseball, being known as "Home-run Ament." In 1867 he entered Oberlin Academy and two years later Oberlin College, graduating in 1873. In college he preferred sports and athletics to study, but was active in debating and in conducting religious services in the villages of the neighborhood. After a year of teaching school at Richfield, Ohio, he entered Union Theological Seminary in 1874, changed to Andover Seminary in 1876, and graduated there the following year. He was married on Aug. 23, 1877, to Mary Penfield, daughter of an Oberlin professor, was ordained on Sept. 5, and in October he sailed as a missionary to China. He was first stationed at Pao Ting Fu but in May 1880 was transferred to Peking. In March 1885 he returned to America and for two years was pastor of a church in Medina, Ohio, where he was active in the work of the Gospel Temperance Union. In August 1888 he went back to China, and the rest of his life, with the exception of brief trips to America in 1897 and 1901, was passed as a missionary in Peking.

The nature of Ament's achievement as a missionary was determined partly by his preparation and partly by his own temperament. He had made no particular study of Chinese culture before he entered upon his work, and he never seems to have made much effort to understand the native religions. He was four years in China before he learned that Taoism possessed any temples; the ritual of Buddhism was to him mere "rigmarole" (Porter, *post,* p. 61); he regarded the non-Christian Chinese very simply as "heathen" to be saved. To this task of salvation he brought unusual ardor, energy, and devotion. During the first year he learned the Chinese language sufficiently well to preach effectively, and later edited a monthly paper, *The North China News,* written in Mandarin. He traveled thousands of miles on foot and mule-back, strewing the country with small missions. At the outbreak of the Boxer War, he proved his dauntless courage, when the American Minister could not spare marines for the service, by going alone as an escort with twenty carts which brought in the refugees from Tung-Chow. During the siege of Peking he was active in providing for the helpless converts who had fled into the city. After the siege was lifted he went about among the native villages, without military attendance, and succeeded in raising indemnities to rebuild burned chapels, and to take care of the widows and orphans of slaughtered converts. He found many occasions to protect the villagers from marauding expeditions of the foreign soldiery. Meanwhile an inaccurate account of an interview with him, published in the New York *Sun* on Dec. 24, 1900, led to strictures on his conduct by several eastern newspapers and to a hasty indictment by Mark Twain in the *North American Review* for February and April 1901, in which he openly accused Ament of looting and extortion. Upon more careful investigation the charges fell to the ground, and Mark Twain rather than Ament was left in need of exoneration. The latter's indefatigable labors in the missionary cause ended in 1909, when after five months' illness he succumbed to an abscess of the brain.

[H. D. Porter, *Wm. Scott Ament* (1911), containing copious extracts from Ament's correspondence and a full account of the Boxer episode; Ament's own discussion of the latter, *Independent,* May 9, Sept. 12, Sept. 19, 1901; "In Memoriam, Rev. Wm. Scott Ament," by G. D. Wilder, in the *Chinese Recorder,* May 1909, pp. 276–81.]

E. S. B.

AMES, CHARLES GORDON (Oct. 3, 1828–Apr. 15, 1912), Baptist and Unitarian clergyman, editor, was born in Dorchester, Mass. A foundling, he was adopted when about three years old by Thomas and Lucy (Foster) Ames, and was brought up on a farm near Canterbury, N. H., with few educational advantages. Emotionally religious by nature, he was less affected by "the long sermons and long prayers, uttered from a high pulpit by a venerable pastor" in the Congregational meeting house, than by the preaching of a Freewill Baptist revivalist, "a man of prayer and tears, of dark and solemn aspect, and a son of thunder" (*Charles Gordon Ames: A Spiritual Autobiography,* p. 13). In October 1842 he was baptized into the Freewill Baptist Church, and the April following he left the farm to work in a printing establishment operated by his denomination at Dover, N. H. This served him as "a sort of religious school" (*Ibid.,* p. 21). He early decided to be a preacher, and was still under eighteen when licensed to preach. From 1847 to 1849 he studied at Geauga Seminary near Cleveland, and in November of the latter year, when barely twenty-one, he was ordained. He was twice married, first to Sarah Jane Daniels of Dover, N. H., Mar. 28, 1850, and second, in 1863, to Julia

Frances Baker of Cincinnati. In the summer of 1851 the Home Missionary Society of his church sent him to St. Anthony, Minn. (Minneapolis), where he founded the first Freewill Baptist church in that place. His services to this growing community were numerous and varied, for he was a man of practical common sense, and took an active interest in all civic affairs. On July 4, 1854, he was secretary of the meeting that marked the birth of the Republican party in Minnesota, and became the first editor of the *Minnesota Republican,* ancestor of the *Minneapolis Tribune,* serving in that capacity from 1855 to 1857. In 1856 he was elected first recorder of deeds for Hennepin County.

During his five years' pastorate in Minneapolis he found so much in the faith and attitude of his people which ran counter to his understanding and love of human life, that he withdrew from it, and for a time from the ministry. In 1859, however, he returned to New England and became a member of the Unitarian Church of the Disciples in Boston. Declining an invitation to the Unitarian pulpit in Quincy, Mass., he accepted a call from Bloomington, Ill., to spend a month organizing a Unitarian Society there. Instead of a month, he gave three years to this work. Brief ministries in Cincinnati, Ohio, and Albany, N. Y., followed. During the Civil War he was an ardent supporter of the North. When rejected for military service because of physical disabilities, he insisted upon paying for a substitute out of his slender resources. He went about preaching the righteousness of the Northern cause, and the superior wisdom and uprightness of Abraham Lincoln, with whom he had become acquainted in Bloomington. He was also tireless in relief work, and by speeches in the camps did what he could to keep up the morale of the soldiers. In 1865 the American Unitarian Association sent him to make a survey of religious conditions on the Pacific coast, and he was engaged in missionary work there until 1872, when he became pastor of a church in Germantown, Pa. A plan presented by him at a meeting in Philadelphia dealing with the poverty and distress of the winter of 1873, resulted in one of the first organized societies of charity in the United States. After five years' service in Germantown he resigned to become editor of the *Christian Register,* but in 1880 returned to the active ministry and spent eight years in organizing and developing the Spring Garden Church, Philadelphia. At the age of sixty he was called to succeed James Freeman Clarke at the Church of the Disciples, Boston, remaining there as pastor and pastor-emeritus until his death. In his active and varied life he found time to write, *George Eliot's Two Marriages* (1885); *As Natural as Life* (1894); *Sermons of Sunrise* (1901); *Poems* (1898); *Five Points of Faith* (1903); *Living Largely* (1904).

[Sources are meager. *Charles Gordon Ames: A Spiritual Autobiography with an Epilogue by Alice Ames Winter* (1913); *Who's Who in America,* and obituary in *Boston Transcript,* Apr. 16, 1912.]

C. G.

AMES, EDWARD RAYMOND (May 20, 1806–Apr. 25, 1879), Methodist bishop, was a descendant of William Ames, who came to Braintree, Mass., from England in 1643. His grandfather, Sylvanus, was a graduate of Harvard in the class of 1767, and died at Valley Forge while serving as chaplain in Washington's army. Edward's father, also Sylvanus, was born in Bridgewater, Mass., in 1771, and in 1795 married Nabby Lee Johnson. Two years later they migrated westward and finally settled in what is now Adams County, Ohio, at a place later called Amesville. Here Edward was born and amid rough frontier conditions was reared. His father soon became a leader in the county, serving as sheriff, colonel of the militia, trustee of Ohio University, representative in the legislature, and, from 1813 to 1823, associate judge. In his home, which was the resort of the politicians of southern Ohio and a favorite stopping place for public men on their long trips from East to West, young Ames had opportunity to see many prominent people and hear much about the political movements of the day. His formal education was meager, but he made good use of the local Western Library Association, later the Coonskin Library, said to have been the first public library founded in the Northwest Territory, though not the first incorporated, in which his father was one of the original stockholders. For two or three years he attended Ohio University, supporting himself by teaching and other work. While there, Bishop Robert R. Roberts induced him to attend a session of the Illinois Methodist Conference, and here he met two men who persuaded him to open a seminary at Lebanon. The school was a success, and was the beginning of McKendree College. In 1830 he joined the Illinois Conference, and became an itinerant minister. Ten years later the General Conference elected him corresponding secretary of the Missionary Society for the South and West. During the four years that he filled this office he traveled some 25,000 miles. On one trip he passed over the entire frontier from Lake Superior to Texas, camping out during almost the entire trip, at one period, it is said, so destitute of provisions that for two days the only nourishment he and his companions had was a little moistened maple sugar (Walker, pp. 422–23). His task was to systematize the missionary work, take an inventory of the property, and obtain land grants from the government for educational work among the Indians. In 1844 he returned to the itinerancy and in 1848 was elected to succeed Matthew Simpson as president of Indiana Asbury University, but declined. In 1852 he was made bishop. His episcopal residence was Indianapolis, and during the Civil War he was energetic in behalf of the Union. He was the only Methodist bishop appointed chaplain in the army, and during the winter of 1861 preached to the soldiers in the various camps. In January 1862, with the Hon. Hamilton Fish, he was appointed by the War Department as commissioner to visit Union prisoners at Richmond and provide for their comfort at the expense of the United States. The appointment of the commission aroused indignation in the South, and Bishop Ames's presence upon it seems to have given special offense. Prof. William W. Sweet quotes from a letter from a Confederate officer, an ex-Methodist minister, to Jefferson Davis, warning him not to allow Ames to enter the lines, characterizing him as an "astute politician, who in the garb of a Christian minister and with the specious plea of 'Humanity' upon his lips, would insinuate himself into the very heart of that Government whose very foundation he would most gladly sap and destroy" (Sweet, p. 154). The commission was not permitted to enter Richmond. Ames had a clear, practical mind and business ability of a high order. He was strong in his convictions, imperious in manner, and sometimes dealt with a heavy hand. His sermons were usually conversational in style, but he was capable of impassioned oratory, and was at his best when addressing the thousands who gathered at Western camp meetings. His talent as an organizer and administrator was of great value to the church. The last years of his life were spent in Baltimore, where he died at the age of seventy-three.

[Chas. M. Walker, *Hist. of Athens County, Ohio* (1869); H. N. Herrick and W. W. Sweet, *Hist. of the North Indiana Conference* (1917); Wm. W. Sweet, *The M. E. Church and Civil War* (1912); J. M. Reid, *Missions and Missionary Societies of the M. E. Church* (1879); *Gen. Conf. Jour.* (1880); Matthew Simpson, *Cyc. of Methodism* (1878); *Methodist* (N. Y.) May 3, 1879.]

J. W. J.

AMES, EZRA (May 5, 1768–Feb. 23, 1836), portrait painter in oils and miniature, was an artist of slender education but remarkable talent. He ministered to the esthetic needs of his generation in nearly every field from the painting of carriages to the portraiture of statesmen. His father, Jesse Emes or Ames, a farmer, was the fifth son and tenth child of Henry Emes and Ruth (Newton) Emes of Framingham, Mass.; his mother, who died on Feb. 14, 1776, had been Bette Bent also of Framingham, where Ezra Ames was born, the youngest of six children. Some time during his childhood the family moved to a farm at Staatsburg, N. Y. Ezra apparently left home at an early age and returned to Massachusetts, where in 1790 we find him established as a furniture and carriage painter in Worcester. From a memorandum book now in the possession of the New York Historical Society we learn that he was by this time already painting miniatures. Between the years 1790 and 1798 he records the sale of twenty-five miniatures, none of which has been located, although one was of so important a person as Gov. Clinton of New York. On Oct. 6, 1794, Ames was married to Zipporah Wood, daughter of Joseph Wood of Upton, Mass., and in the ensuing year they settled permanently in Albany, N. Y. Besides his work as a carriage painter and miniaturist during these years, Ezra Ames gilded frames, painted furniture, lettered clock faces, decorated flags; and, during 1797–98 engraved spoons, rings, and Masonic emblems. He first emerges as a painter in oils with the portrait of a Mr. Glen for which he received four pounds sterling on Feb. 22, 1794. The portrait by which he gained the widest reputation was not done until 1812: a full length painting of Gov. Clinton, which was exhibited at the Pennsylvania Academy of Fine Arts in that year and a replica of which was ordered by the State of New York the following year. Ames also painted a bust portrait of Clinton, which was engraved by Maverick. A bust portrait of Alexander Hamilton, engraved by Leney and by Hoogland, is now lost. Besides these, Ames painted portraits of Solomon Allen, engraved by Tanner and by Jones; Clarkson Crolius (1773–1843), Charles Genet and Leonard Gansevoort, the last three owned by the Albany Institute; Gen. William Irvine (1741–1804), which is now lost but can be identified by the copy at the New York Historical Society; Mrs. James King; Allan Melville (1782–1832) and Mrs. Allan Melville, *née* Gansevoort (1791–1872), the parents of Herman Melville, both reproduced in the catalogue of the Thomas B. Clarke sale, New York 1919; Catherine Van Schaick, later Mrs. Peter Gansevoort (1751–1831), loaned to the Metropolitan Museum in 1919; and a self portrait which was engraved by H. B. Hall. Six miniatures by Ames are owned by the Albany Institute.

[Dorothy C. Barck, "Ezra Ames," in *N. Y. Hist. Soc. Quart. Bull.*, Jan. 1927; W. Dunlap, *Hist. of the Rise and Progress of the Arts of Design in the U. S.* (1834); D. M. Stauffer, *Am. Engravers upon Copper and Steel* (1907); T. Bolton, *Early Am. Portr. Painters in Minia-*

ture (1921); *N. Y. Times Mag.*, Sept. 5, 1926. For information as to the Clinton portrs. see C. W. Bowen, *Centennial of the Inauguration of George Washington* (1892). Six portrs. by Ames are reproduced in M. L. Sutliff, *Record of the Ancestors and Descendants of Betsy M. Sutliff* (1897).]

T. B.

AMES, FISHER (Apr. 9, 1758–July 4, 1808), statesman and publicist, was descended from William Ames (not the author of *Medulla Theologiæ*, but a Somersetshire yeoman who emigrated to Plymouth in 1626), and from Capt. Daniel Fisher, who arrested Gov. Andros in the revolution of 1689. He was born in Dedham, Mass., third in a family of five, to Deborah (Fisher) and Nathaniel Ames [*q.v.*], 1708–64, innkeeper, astronomer, physician. After the death of Nathaniel in 1764 his medical practise and almanac business were taken over by his eldest son, Nathaniel Ames, whose diary records political opinions diametrically opposed to those of his more gifted brother. Fisher Ames showed such early promise of scholarship that his mother, who carried on the family tavern, had him "fitted" by the age of twelve for the class of 1774, Harvard College, where he was an active member of a new debating club (the Institute of 1770), a leading scholar, and (what his early biographers considered more remarkable) a spotless youth. From 1774 to 1779 he lived at home, occasionally teaching in the district schools, once turning out with the militia for a short tour of duty, but for the most part reading deeply in ancient history, Latin, and English classics, and Greek classics in translations. In 1779 he was received as a law pupil in a Boston office, and in 1781 was admitted to the Suffolk bar. He never liked the law, but practised it successfully.

Elected as delegate to the Concord convention for regulating prices (1781), he argued against the wisdom of price-fixing. As "Lucius Junius Brutus," in the *Boston Independent Chronicle* on Oct. 12, 1786, when Shays's Rebellion was at its height, he struck a note of stern repression; his "Camillus" essays of March 1787 furthered the movement for a federal convention, and fixed his reputation as a publicist. "Anarchy and government are both before us, and in our choice. If we fall, we fall by our folly, not our fate." In the autumn he was elected a delegate from Dedham to the Massachusetts ratifying convention, where he delivered a powerful speech in favor of biennial elections "as a security that the sober, second thought of the people shall be law." The trend of his political thought was revealed by the declaration, "We cannot live without society. . . . The liberty of one depends not so much on the removal of all restraint from him, as on the due restraint upon the liberty of others. Without such restraint, there can be no liberty."

Fisher Ames was now a local celebrity, and a young man whom the Federalists trusted. In April 1788 he was chosen a representative of Dedham in the General Court of Massachusetts, and in the following winter was elected to Congress, obtaining 818 votes against 521 for Samuel Adams. He was reëlected to the Second, Third, and Fourth Congresses (1791–97) with a larger majority and a heavier total vote. He was not a monarchist, even in the sense that John Adams was. His model was that ideal Roman republic which never existed in fact. Like Hamilton, he believed that the Federal Government was inherently weak. It must lean on an aristocracy of talent and virtue, reach out for power, and acquire popular prestige by a vigorous, energetic policy. He expected to find Congress a group of like-minded gentlemen and was dismayed at the "yawning listlessness" of many, and the adherence of some to what he considered the mischievous nonsense that the best government is that which governs least. During the first session he labored, and not in vain, to adjust the tariff bill to New England interests, to uphold the President's power of removal, and to strike out discrimination in the first tonnage act between British and French vessels. Ames shared the opinion of leading Boston merchants that their profitable commerce with England must not be placed in jeopardy by retaliation. Hamilton's appointment to the Treasury Department provided both the leader and the vigorous impulse that Ames wanted, and he became one of the Secretary's consistent supporters in the House, though never his intimate friend. Ames had a large share in shaping important legislation. He endeavored to fix an organic connection between Congress and the executive, considering the heads of departments as a recognized ministry, "imparting a kind of momentum to the operations of the laws." The creation of a ways and means committee in 1795 broke the connection, and led Ames to predict that in consequence "our government will be, in fact, a mere democracy, which has never been tolerable, nor long tolerated" (R. V. Harlow, *History of Legislative Methods,* 1917, p. 146).

As brilliant intellectually as Hamilton, Ames was wholly devoid of vanity, a most fortunate circumstance for his effectiveness in debate. Erect in stature, pleasing in voice and appearance, conciliatory in manner, he impressed the House as much by candor as by ardor, and with wealth of knowledge no less than oratorical grace. His lively imagination drew forth striking metaphors, which his good taste kept within bounds. The intellectual contempt that he felt for many of his fellow members was reserved for confidential letters, and Attic salt was sprinkled through his speeches in such a way as to arouse the admiration rather than the resentment of Bœotian colleagues. His formal speeches were concise and pointed, well supplied though never overloaded with facts, and often reserved for the close of a debate when they could clear a confused issue.

In a letter of remarkable penetration (Nov. 30, 1791, *Works,* I, 103) Ames analyzed the "equally unpleasant and lasting" causes of party difference; but he never questioned that what Hamilton and New England wanted was good for the whole country. Peace and prosperity, he hoped, would reconcile the South to the Federalist system. Jefferson considered Ames one of the "paper men" in Congress, and the Republican press denounced him as a speculator, financially interested in the funding system. Ames retorted that the interest on the Massachusetts members' funds would not pay for the oats of the Southern members' coach horses. The *Boston Columbian Centinel,* Oct. 22, 1794, stated that Ames had invested his savings in twelve shares of the Bank (of which he was a director for a short time) and in $600 worth of public funds, and had neither bought nor sold other securities. In 1796, he sold eight of the Bank shares for $4,149.60, and used the money for East India ventures (*Proceedings American Antiquarian Society,* 1927). His income was derived largely from these ventures, his law practise, and the property of his wife (Frances, daughter of Col. John Worthington of Springfield, Mass., whom he married on July 15, 1792).

The British spoliations, and other Anglo-American incidents of 1793–94 aroused a resentment against Great Britain which culminated in Madison's resolutions proposing to inaugurate a commercial war. In his speech of Jan. 27, 1794, Ames exposed the spurious economics of this policy and the doubtful diplomacy of endeavoring to "quarrel ourselves into their good will," ending with the words, "I hope we shall show, by our vote, that we deem it better policy to feed nations than to starve them, and that we shall never be so unwise as to put our good customers into a situation to be forced to make every exertion to do without us." In consequence of this speech, Fisher Ames was burned in effigy in Charleston, S. C., together with Benedict Arnold, and the Devil (Madison, *Writings,* 1865, II, 9). But a more important result was that the speech made possible Jay's mission and treaty.

Ames's speech on Jay's treaty (Apr. 28, 1796) was "one of the greatest speeches ever made in Congress" (Channing, *History of the United States,* 1917, IV, 145). The previous summer, he had been prostrated by a malady (diagnosed by contemporary physicians as marasmus, or atrophy), from which he never entirely recovered. Coming to Philadelphia in February 1796 at great hazard, he sat silent during the debate as to whether Jay's treaty, duly ratified, should be executed or nullified by the House. Near the conclusion, summoning all his strength, he arose to speak, tottering, faint in voice, and cold in diction. As he warmed to the subject, it seemed to call forth latent energies, until his physical equaled his mental powers. Dr. Priestley, who was present, and who had heard the great English and Irish orators, called it "the most bewitching piece of parliamentary oratory he had ever listened to" (Charles Caldwell, *Autobiography,* 1855, p. 114). "He addressed himself to every faculty of the mind, and awakened every feeling and emotion of the heart. . . . The effect produced was absolute enchantment" (*Port Folio,* 3rd ser., vol. I, p. 12). It was necessary for the treaty opponents to carry an adjournment in order to break the spell, but the next day the House by a majority of three voted to execute the treaty.

Declining reëlection in 1796, Ames retired to Dedham at the end of Washington's administration. The only office he held subsequently was a seat on the governor's council in 1799–1801. In 1805 the Harvard Corporation broke the clerical tradition of the Harvard presidency by electing him to that office, which he declined on the ground of his feeble health and "advancing age" of forty-seven. "Squire" Ames was a cheerful neighbor, easy of access, interested in town affairs. A liberal in religion, he joined the local Episcopal church, partly to escape the theological contentions in the Congregational parish, partly because ritual meant good order. His estate, with a model piggery, dairy, and orchard, was constantly improved; his house a center of hospitality and good conversation. Popular rumor made Fisher Ames a member of the Essex Junto; George Cabot and Christopher Gore were his closest friends; but henceforth his political rôle was largely that of a sage.

Ames shared John Adams's view of the French Revolution, and the poisonous effect of Gallomania on American politics. Hence he hailed the dispute of 1797–98 with France as an occasion to purify the country of "Jacobinism," and strengthen the Federal Government by a bold and spirited policy. Although in 1794 he would have dealt with "self-created societies" by "the gentle power of opinion," in 1798 he highly approved the Sedition Act, and was instrumental in the prosecution of David Brown for erecting a liberty pole at Dedham with a "seditious" inscription (*Report of the American Historical Association,* 1912, pp. 122–25). The President's peace mission of 1799 disappointed him, but he refused to be drawn into the intrigue against the reëlection of Adams.

After Jefferson's election Fisher Ames became the slave of a fixed idea, that catastrophic theory of democracy which was common to other New England leaders, and to Federalists elsewhere such as Carroll, Hamilton, Morris, and Rutledge. Since the "wise and good and opulent" had lost power to jealous, ignorant, and enthusiastic democracy, the Republic must sink into anarchy, from which military despotism would emerge. Jefferson's early moderation was vain or delusive; "Brissot will fall by the hand of Danton, and he will be supplanted by Robespierre." "It is the almost universal mistake of our countrymen, that democracy would be mild and safe in America." "The most ferocious of animals when his passions are roused to fury and uncontrolled, is man; and of all governments, the worst is that which never fails to excite, but was never found to restrain those passions, that is, democracy. It is an illuminated hell. . . ." These quotations are from Ames's essay on "The Dangers of American Liberty," written in 1805, and published posthumously by his friends as the best expression of their faith and fear. His other published essays struck the same note. Their style is clear and precise, nervous and vigorous, illuminated by vivacity and imagination.

On the side of practical policy, Fisher Ames declared in a letter of 1802: "The Federalists must entrench themselves in the State governments, and endeavor to make State justice and State power a shelter of the wise, and good, and rich, from the wild destroying rage of the Southern Jacobins"—in other words, they must endeavor to maintain a solid block of Federalist states, and prevent the Jeffersonian infection from debauching New England. Ames devised no constitutional doctrine of state rights, and rejected Pickering's secession proposals of 1804: but his writings did much to build up a sectional consciousness which almost became New England nationalism. That the British navy was the only remaining barrier against French conscription of American boys for Santo Domingo was roundly asserted in Ames's last essay, "The Dangerous Power of France." He died at Dedham on July 4, 1808, too soon to witness the revival of Federalism after Jefferson's embargo acts. His imposing funeral at Boston was a political demonstration and his works were promptly published as a political testament.

Fisher Ames stands out from other New England Federalists as a man of singularly pure and unselfish character, humble in spite of his great talents, zealous and active through chronic illness. As an orator he had no equal in the generation between Patrick Henry and Henry Clay. On the formative period of the Federal Government he had a strong and wholesome influence; but his very virtues were a bane to New England. An intellect enriched but not disciplined by scholarship, accepted from the legacy of Rome and Greece only a political formula, invalid for American society.

[*Works of Fisher Ames,* 2 vols. (1854), ed. by Seth Ames, supersedes the edition of 1809; *Speeches of Fisher Ames in Cong.* (1871), ed. by P. W. Ames, includes additional matter, but not everything found in the *Annals of Cong.* Henry Ewbank, *The Influences of Democracy on Liberty, Property, and the Happiness of Society* (London, 1835), a selection of Ames's works, with a hortatory preface, was pointedly reviewed in the *Quart. Rev.,* vol. LIII, pp. 548–73 (1835). Additional letters are found in most of the lives of contemporary Federalists, especially in G. Gibbs, *Memoirs of the Administrations of Washington and Adams* (1846). The Dedham Hist. Soc. possesses many MS. letters and business documents, and the diary of Nathaniel Ames (1741–1822), extracts from which are printed in the *Dedham Hist. Reg.,* vols. I–XIV (1890–1903). Samuel Dexter's funeral oration (*Boston Gazette,* July 11, and *Repertory,* July 8, 1808) is the foundation of most subsequent biog. articles, of which the best is in the *Analectic Mag.,* III, 309–33 (Phila., 1814). J. Q. Adams, *Review of Works of Fisher Ames* (1809), presents the opposition view. A memoir by Ames's pastor, Rev. Wm. Montague, in the *Diocesan Reg. and New Eng. Calendar for 1812* (Dedham, 1811), pp. 238–48, is the best account of his character and private life; further details have been collected by J. B. Thayer in *Homes of Am. Statesmen* (Hartford, 1855), pp. 275–97.]

S.E.M.

AMES, FREDERICK LOTHROP (June 8, 1835–Sept. 13, 1893), capitalist, born at North Easton, Mass., was the son of Oliver Ames, Jr. [*q.v.*], and Sarah (Lothrop) Ames. He was educated at Phillips Exeter and Harvard (1854), and on June 7, 1863, was married to Rebecca, daughter of James Blair of St. Louis, by whom he had six children. He entered Oliver Ames & Sons in 1863, becoming treasurer in 1876. A cold, forceful, unostentatious man, he carried almost as many business burdens as his sire. A director or official in threescore of railroads, an officer of banks and trusts, an authority on railroads, a fellow of Harvard College, one of the heaviest owners of Boston realty including the Ames Building, Frederick Ames was a power in industrial circles. Yet he gave the same care to the Home for Incurables of which he was president, to the Unitarian Society, to the Massachusetts School for the Blind, the Perkins Institute, the McLean Insane Asylum, and the Children's Hospital as to his lucrative business connections. His diversion was horticulture, and for thirty years he was a leader in the Massachusetts Horticultural Society and a willing contributor to the Arnold Arboretum of Harvard University. This austere capitalist and executive had an enlightened interest in all things human save political preferment, but even there his neighbors in his absence nominated and elected him to a term in the state Senate (1872).

[*Report, Class of 1854, Harv. Univ.* (1894); *Representative Men of Mass.*, ed. by W. F. Moore (1898); *Boston Transcript*, Sept. 13, 14, 1893.] R. J. P.

AMES, JAMES BARR (June 22, 1846–Jan. 8, 1910), educator and legal writer, the only son of Samuel T. Ames, a Boston merchant, and Mary H. (Barr) Ames, was born in Boston, but soon after his birth his parents moved to the neighboring town of Medford. There young Ames received his earliest education. His parents returning to Boston in 1856, he attended successively the Brimmer School and the Boston Latin School until he entered Harvard College in 1863. After his first term as a sophomore he was compelled by ill health to leave college and spent most of the time until March 1866 on a farm in New Ipswich, N. H., thereby gaining a love of farming which he retained for the rest of his life. He then joined as a sophomore the class of 1868 at Harvard, and was graduated with that class. He was distinguished in college as captain of the university baseball nine, for social popularity, and for high scholarship. After graduation he taught in Boston for a year in the private school of E. S. Dixwell. Then, after a year in Europe, he became tutor, 1871–72, in French and German in Harvard College, and, 1872–73, supplied the place of Henry Adams in teaching medieval history. Meanwhile he had entered the Harvard Law School in 1870, and was studying law while serving as college instructor. As a law student he made such an impression upon his teachers that, after graduation and a year of post-graduate study, he was appointed in 1873 assistant professor of law. The experiment of appointing as a teacher of law one who had never practised the profession was novel, but proved so successful that when, in 1877, on some intimation that his lack of practise might preclude a permanent appointment, he resigned and was about to go into practise, the Corporation of the University appointed him professor without limit of tenure. His life-work thereafter was bound up with the Harvard Law School.

It is to Ames's success in adapting the idea of his teacher, C. C. Langdell [*q.v.*], that the triumph of the system of teaching law by the study of reported cases is largely due. Though Langdell's name will rightly always be connected with a system of study and teaching which has revolutionized methods in the principal law schools of the United States, and has had wide influence in other departments of study, Ames's collections of cases and his skill in using them, were important factors in bringing about this result. He prepared successively case books on torts, pleading, bills and notes, trusts, partnership, admiralty, suretyship, and equity jurisdiction. The annotations in these books, as well as Ames's essays and lectures, have had formative influence in more than one department of the law. A love for history acquired in college study led Ames almost from the beginning of his work as teacher to read the earlier sources of English law. In the course of some years during summer vacations on his farm at Castine, Me., he read through the *Year-Books* which contain a great mass of early judicial decisions reported in abbreviated Norman-French. He noted the salient points discovered in this reading, and he was thus enabled in two essays on "The History of Assumpsit" (*Harvard Law Review,* II, 1, 53) to give the answer to a problem that had heretofore puzzled lawyers and legal historians—what were the sources from which was developed the law of simple contracts, and the action of assumpsit by which such contracts were enforced. These essays at once gave Ames a high reputation as a legal scholar and historian not only throughout the United States, but in Europe.

Ames's encouragement and support were instrumental in the founding and early development of the *Harvard Law Review*. This periodical, founded by students in 1887 and since then edited entirely by students, soon became recognized as one of the leading legal periodicals in the English-speaking world, and served as a model for a number of similar periodicals subsequently started in other law schools. Most of Ames's legal writing appeared in the pages of this journal, and as the articles were on crucial questions, they have had an influence out of proportion to their number. Since Ames's death they have been collected and republished, together with the substance of a course of lectures on legal history which he delivered shortly after the publication of his essays on the history of assumpsit (*Lectures on Legal History and Miscellaneous Legal Essays,* by James Barr Ames, with a Memoir, 1913).

As a teacher, Ames was markedly successful. His method was an adaptation of that of Socrates, and though his reading had made him profoundly learned in the law, he never presented his learning to students as something to be memorized. His knowledge of legal principles was freely drawn upon, as was his intimate acquaintance with the historical development of any doctrine under consideration, but in the class-room he rarely entered into detailed discussion of authorities. He was an idealist in law, and his supreme gift as a scholar and a teacher was his constructive legal imagination. He believed it to be the function of the lawyer, and especially of the teacher of law, to weld from the decisions a body of principles not only just but mutually consistent and coherent. It was his constant effort to lead his students to exercise their reasoning powers to this end. In 1895 Ames followed Langdell as dean of the Harvard Law School as a natural successor, since for many years previously he had been Langdell's chief lieutenant. During the years of Ames's leadership the standards of scholarship required for admission to the school and for securing its degree were continuously made more severe. His faith that excellence would always win recognition was unquestioning and inspiring. He had no hesitation in requiring a college degree as a requisite for admission to the school, and was not surprised when this requirement was soon followed by a large growth in numbers. His personal contact with students was always intimate, and though his sympathy was controlled by a keen sense of justice, and he never hesitated to tell the truth merely because it was disagreeable, his influence over them was very great. Though not of striking appearance, he had not only character but the gift of manners, and no one was long associated with him without being impressed with his quality. Many universities recognized his distinction with honorary degrees. On June 29, 1880, he married Sarah Russell, daughter of George Russell and Sarah (Shaw) Russell of Boston, who with two sons survived him.

[*Centennial Hist. Harv. Law School* (1918); *Harv. Law Rev.*, XXIII, 321–38; *Reports Sec. Harv. Class of 1868*; *Harv. Grads. Mag.*, XVIII, 401, 518.] S. W.

AMES, JAMES TYLER (May 13, 1810–Feb. 16, 1883), mechanic, manufacturer, was born at Lowell, Mass., the son of Nathan Peabody Ames and Phœbe (Tyler) Ames. He was endowed to a high degree with the mechanical skill possessed both by his father and his more famous brother, Nathan Peabody Ames, Jr. [*q.v.*]. In his father's shop at Lowell and later in his brother's factory at Cabotville (now Chicopee) he received a thorough and practical training as a mechanic. Although in later years he devoted his chief attention to the business aspect of his great factory, there were few men in his employ superior to him as a practical craftsman.

The Ames family, at the urgent behest of Edmund Dwight, had removed in 1829 to Chicopee Falls, where success had come quickly. Under the leadership of Nathan P. Ames, Jr., the Ames Manufacturing Company was organized in 1834 and new factories built down the river upon the site of the present Chicopee. Specializing in cutlery and tools, the Ames Company speedily branched into the manufacture of brass cannon, military accoutrements, and many other products, and gained reputation in operating the first sword factory in this country. James Tyler Ames so thoroughly demonstrated his ability and integrity that upon the untimely death of his brother in 1847 he became head of the Ames Company, the direction of which he maintained until 1874. Under his control the Ames Company greatly extended its interests. It began in 1849 the manufacture of cotton-machinery, of lathes, planes, and turbine water-wheels. It not only participated in the growth of the great textile development of New England but took contracts for manufacturing the Eldredge Sewing Machine and the first Victor and Eagle bicycles. Just before the Civil War the concern became interested in bronze castings, and from its forges were turned out the "Crawford Doors" on the East Wing of the Capitol and many statues, including the equestrian statue of Washington in the Boston Public Gardens, the Minute Man at Concord, and the Lincoln Monument at Springfield, Ill. During the Civil War the Ames plant was one of the largest munition factories in the North, manufacturing sabers, Springfield rifles, and a thousand cannon for the Federal Government. The factory also executed large saber contracts for Turkey during the Russo-Turkish War and for France during the Franco-Prussian War. Among Ames's own inventions was a cannon-ball perfected with the aid of Gen. James of Providence, from which grew the necessity of rifled cannon. Ames also invented the special machinery for the manufacture of these cannon.

He was an enlightened employer, popular with his men. Throughout his life he was an active and liberal supporter of the Third Congregational Church of Chicopee. He was particularly interested in mineralogy and his private collection was a notable one. This interest in natural science led Amherst College to grant him in 1863 the honorary degree of M.A. He was married in 1838 to Ellen Huse of Newburyport (1809–1902), by whom he had three children.

[A sketch of the life and work of the Ames brothers, with pictures of both, can be found in Louise Johnson, *Chicopee Illustrated* (1896). See also A. M. Copeland, *Hist. of Hampden County* (1902), III, 503, and J. L. Bishop, *Hist. of Am. Manufacturers* (1861–64), II, 686–87. A collection of products manufactured by the Ames Company and many mementoes of the Ames brothers are in the museum connected with the Ames Family School at Chicopee. For an excellent account of the Ames Manufacturing Company, see *Springfield Republican*, Jan. 15, 1899.] H. U. F.

AMES, JOSEPH ALEXANDER (1816–Oct. 30, 1872), portrait painter, was born at Roxbury, Mass., and died in New York City. The names of his parents are not recorded. He early set his mind upon becoming an artist and copied a portrait while he was still a boy. The copy was good enough for him to receive professional orders that kept him occupied in his native town until he was disposed to try his fortune in Boston. He soon established himself and although self-taught did his best work as a young man. Accumulating enough money to further his studies, he sailed for Italy in 1848 and settled in Rome. His portrait of Pope Pius IX was painted at this time. When his period of study ended, he returned to Boston. His well-known full-length portrait of Daniel Webster, representing Webster standing with a long walking-stick and wearing a felt hat, was painted in 1852. This was the last portrait painted from life of Webster, who was at that time seventy years old. Ames also painted nine or more bust portraits of Webster, but not all of these are from life. Ames lived in Baltimore during 1870 on account of his health, but the change proving without benefit he moved the same year to New York and was almost immediately elected a member of the National Academy of Design. He gained a reputation both as a genre and as a portrait painter and was constantly employed. Tuckerman noted: "Ames paints on an average seventy-five portraits in a year; of course they often lack high finish; but his fresh and bright tints and frequent success in likeness—even the rapidity of his execution—contribute to his prosperous activity." He died of brain fever after a short illness, leaving upon his easel a portrait of Adeline Ristori, the actress, in the character of "Medea." The National Academy exhibition for that year contained two portraits of his, one of them of Ross Winans of Baltimore. Besides the portraits mentioned above, Ames painted President William Conway Felton of Harvard, Rufus Choate, William H. Seward, Ralph Waldo Emerson, and Marietta Gazzaniga, the singer. Some of his other works are "Maud Muller," "The Old Stone Pitcher," "The Last Days of Daniel Webster at Marshfield." A steel engraving of the latter was popular in its day. His wife and daughter were both artists.

[H. T. Tuckerman, *Book of the Artists* (1867); *McClure's Mag.*, May 1897, illus.; Thieme-Becker, *Allgemeines Lexikon der Bildenden Künstler;* obituaries in *Boston Transcript*, Nov. 1, and *N.Y. Times*, Nov. 2, 1872.]

T. B.

AMES, MARY CLEMMER. [See CLEMMER, MARY, 1831–1884.]

AMES, NATHAN PEABODY (Sept. 1, 1803–Apr. 3, 1847), metal-worker, manufacturer, was born at Chelmsford, Mass., the eldest son of Nathan Peabody Ames and Phœbe (Tyler) Ames. He early displayed the mechanical skill which was to make him famous in later years, and which was probably inherited from his father, who manufactured edged tools and cutlery at Chelmsford and was reported to have been the first to use water-power at that place. The elder craftsman gave his sons a thorough mechanical grounding in his shop, and in 1829, when his health was failing, he turned over the cutlery business in Chelmsford to the management of Nathan, Jr., whose brother James Tyler Ames [*q.v.*] was associated with him. A curious chance occasioned their removal in the same year to Chicopee Falls, near Springfield, Mass. The elder brother on a stage-coach journey formed a chance but lifelong friendship with Edmund Dwight, who owned a mill at Chicopee Falls and who offered the Ames brothers space in his mill if they would transfer their business thither. They accepted this generous offer, and occupied a portion of the Dwight mill, for which the owner would take no rent, for about four years; success came immediately, and in 1834 the Ames Manufacturing Company was organized, with a capital of $30,000. A factory was constructed a mile farther down the Chicopee River, at "the Lower Privilege," where Dwight also built extensive mills, around which grew up a new community called Cabotville (now Chicopee). For a half-century after its organization the Ames Company was a leader in the manufacturing development of western Massachusetts. Although many kinds of metal goods were produced, the concern in its early days specialized in cutlery and tools. The Ames Company operated the first sword factory in the United States; it received contracts for sabers from the government as early as 1830. Both of the brothers were themselves skilled mechanics, representing the highest type of Yankee ingenuity and integrity, and the products of the Ames factory were widely known for their quality and beauty. So famous were they that one English concern was known to have copied their models and stolen their trademark with the hope of obtaining some of their American business. Not content with cutlery and tools, the Ames Company in 1836 began the founding of brass cannon and later the manufacture of leather belting, military accoutrements, bells, and turbine water-wheels. With the development of textile manufacturing in New England the concern devoted much attention to the production of every type of cotton-machinery. Nathan Ames invented numerous mechanical improvements, such as the rotary bell-clapper, but did not patent them. In 1840 he went to Europe with a commission for the United States Ordnance Department to inspect and study arsenals and gun factories. While there he contracted a cold, which, aggravated by poisoning from an amalgam paste, inserted in his teeth by a London dentist, brought on serious illness, several years of intense suffering, and an early death at the age of forty-three. Ames was slightly above the average in height, slim in stature, with dark hair and deep-set brown eyes. His expression of openness and honesty won him immediate respect and confidence which his life did not belie. Always greatly interested in the church, he had given in 1834 half his fortune to aid in building the Third Congregational Church of Chicopee and was an active worker in that congregation until his death. Believing at one time during his illness that he was on the road to recovery, he had married Mary Bailey of Newburyport, but left no offspring.

[For sources of information see Ames, James Tyler.]

H. U. F.

AMES, NATHANIEL (July 22, 1708–July 11, 1764), almanac-maker and physician, was the son of Nathaniel Ames first and the father of Nathaniel third. The family was descended from Richard Ames of Bruton, Somersetshire, England, whose son William emigrated to Massachusetts and settled at Braintree as early as 1640. Capt. Nathaniel Ames, father of our subject, lived at Bridgewater and there married Susannah Howard, Dec. 2, 1702 (*New England Historical and Genealogical Register,* XXI, 226). Six children were born to them, of whom Nathaniel second was the eldest son (Fisher Ames, p. 3). The father is said to have been learned in astronomy and mathematics. Nothing is known of his son's education, but he became a physician, probably without other medical training than apprenticeship to some country doctor. In 1725 he published the first annual number of his almanac, which was to become famous and remain the standard New England almanac for a half-century. At this time, he was still living at home in Bridgewater, and although the almanac bears on the title-page "by Nathaniel Ames, Jr.," it may well be that the boy, then only seventeen years old, received some help from his mathematical parent. He is said to have moved to Dedham in 1732 (Briggs, p. 23) and his name is entered from that place on the list of subscribers to Prince's *Chronology,* to which most of the subscriptions were made in 1728 (*New England Historical and Genealogical Register,* VI, 189). On Sept. 14, 1735, he married Mary, daughter of Capt. Joshua Fisher of Dedham, by whom, Oct. 24, 1737, he had a son, Fisher Ames, who died less than a year later, Sept. 17, 1738, surviving his mother, however, who had died Nov. 11, 1737. She had had a residuary interest in certain property and the situation gave rise to one of the famous lawsuits of New England, Ames claiming inheritance according to the Province Law against others who claimed it under the Common Law. Ames won, and thus established an exception to the rule of inheritance in Massachusetts. In 1740 (Oct. 30), he married for second wife Deborah, daughter of Jeremiah Fisher, by whom he had five children, the eldest being Nathaniel third, and the third son being Fisher Ames [*q.v.*]. In this year, 1740, he was also one of the subscribers to the celebrated Land Bank (*Ibid.,* L, 191). In addition to his duties as local doctor and as publisher of the almanacs, Ames for many years ran the well-known "Sun" tavern. The contemporary entry in Whiting's Diary: "Jan. 25, 1750, Dr. Ames began to keep tavern," seems to settle the date of this venture as against those given by Briggs (p. 23) and Kittredge (p. 264). He continued to live at Dedham until his death in 1764.

His chief importance is as founder and editor of his almanacs, the publishing of which his son, Nathaniel third, continued for ten years after his father's death. The father issued the first number, 1725, three years before James Franklin started his in Rhode Island and eight years before Benjamin Franklin inaugurated *Poor Richard.* Ames must have been a household word throughout New England, for it is said that the circulation of his almanac ran to 60,000 copies (Briggs, p. 20). Moses Coit Tyler considered it as superior to Franklin's, which it resembled in many ways. Besides the astronomical observations, Ames published short articles, extracts from the English poets, such as Milton and Pope, and used the same pithy and witty maxims as made the reputation of Franklin, such as:

"All Men are by Nature equal,
But differ greatly in the sequel."

He had taste for good literature and considerable wit, though some of it seems a trifle forced to-day, and the quality rather improved than otherwise when the almanac was continued by his somewhat abler son. Ames, however, undoubtedly did much to bring, if only in brief allusions and extracts, some knowledge of the better English authors to innumerable New England farmhouses.

[There are brief allusions to Ames in *The Old Farmer and His Almanac,* by G. L. Kittredge (1904). "The Diary of John Whiting," *New Eng. Hist. and Gen. Reg.,* LXIII, contains references to both the second and third Nathaniels. A number of letters between father and son appear in "The Two Nathaniel Ames," by J. H. Tuttle, *Pubs. Coll. Soc. Mass.,* XIX. A few facts may be picked up in *A Bit of Ames Genealogy,* by Fisher Ames (1898). The *Almanacs* have been reprinted, with a brief biog. introduction, by S. Briggs, *The Essays, Humor, and Poems of Nathaniel Ames* (1891). They are discussed in the standard histories of American literature of the colonial period.]

J. T. A.

AMES, OAKES (Jan. 10, 1804–May 8, 1873), manufacturer, capitalist, and politician, the son of Oliver Ames [*q.v.*] and Susannah Angier, was born in Easton, Mass. He received a district-school education, supplemented at sixteen by a few months in Dighton Academy. Entering his father's shovel factory as a laborer, he became familiar with every process, was made a superintendent, and soon became his father's main reliance. He showed zeal, business acumen, and marked inventiveness. In 1844 his father retired, turning the business over to Oakes and his brother Oliver Ames, Jr. [*q.v.*], who carried it on under the name Oliver Ames & Sons. The two brothers rapidly expanded the business. The discovery of gold in California in 1848 lent it marked impetus, and Oakes Ames was responsible for the sale of large consignments to California merchants and adventurers upon credit. Heavy losses were ultimately sustained upon these ventures, but were more than recouped through the gold rush to Australia and the agricultural development of the Northwest. The Ames shovel was declared to be "legal tender in every part of the Mississippi Valley," and was known even in South Africa (*Appleton's Annual Cyclopædia,* 1873, article "Oakes Ames"; E. L. Sabin, *Building the Pacific Railway,* 1919, p. 71). At the beginning of the Civil War the business was valued at $4,000,000, and the war enormously increased its prosperity.

Ames became known in the late fifties as an ardent Free-Soiler, a director of the Emigrant Aid Company during the Kansas conflict, and an adherent of the Republican party. In 1860 he was made a member of the executive council of Massachusetts, and Gov. Andrew relied heavily upon his business experience. In 1862 Ames was urged by influential men to run for the national House, was elected for the second Massachusetts district, and took his seat in the Thirty-eighth Congress. He was reëlected four times, serving till his death. His position in Congress was not conspicuous. He rarely made a speech; his most important committees were those on manufactures and the Pacific Railroad. His knowledge of business, however, and his shrewd judgment made him a valued working member and gave him the confidence of President Lincoln.

In 1865 Ames was drawn with his brother Oliver into connection with the Crédit Mobilier, a company formed to carry on the construction of the Union Pacific Railroad. The Crédit Mobilier was promoted by T. C. Durant, vice-president of the Union Pacific, to keep in the hands of a small group all the profits derivable from building the road. Durant became president, the two Ames brothers were prominent among the subscribers, and largely through Oakes Ames's efforts the capital by Sept. 21, 1865, was brought up to $2,500,000. After the line had been completed to the 100th meridian, the managers of the Crédit Mobilier split into two hostile factions, one led by Durant and the other by Ames. The upshot was an arrangement by which Oliver Ames became president of the Union Pacific, and Oakes Ames took virtual control of the Crédit Mobilier's work. On Aug. 16, 1867, when only 247 miles had been built, he contracted in his own name to build 667 miles more, at prices varying from $42,000 to $96,000 a mile, according to the terrain. He then (Oct. 15, 1867) executed legal papers assigning these contracts, which aggregated some $47,000,000, to seven trustees (*Congressional Globe,* 42 Cong., 3 Sess., p. 1724). These trustees acted for the stockholders of the Crédit Mobilier, and the profits were to be paid to holders of the Crédit Mobilier stock. Upon this basis the remainder of the Union Pacific line was built and turned over to the Union Pacific company. Though this method of building the transcontinental railway was vicious, exhausting the company's endowment of government grants, and by excessive costs and profits loading it with debt, it was the accepted method of building railways in 1860–80. Ames merely used the tools at hand. His purpose, he later said, was "to connect my name conspicuously with the greatest public work of the present century" (*Ibid.,* p. 1724).

Unfortunately, at a critical moment, Ames resorted to improper acts. When Congress opened on Nov. 21, 1867, it was evident that the Union Pacific-Crédit Mobilier arrangement might come under fire. The statutes required that the Union Pacific stock be paid for in actual cash; but as a matter of fact, it was issued to Ames and other Crédit Mobilier men "who paid for it at not more than thirty cents on the dollar in roadmaking" (Wilson Investigative Report, p. iii). An inquiry would be embarrassing. Moreover, on Dec. 9, C. C. Washburn of Wisconsin introduced in the House a bill to regulate by law the rates on the Union Pacific. Ames took what he deemed a fair precautionary step by selling shares of the Crédit Mobilier to other members of Congress. He had 343 shares issued him for the purpose. "I shall put [these]," he wrote from Washington on Jan. 25, 1868, "where they will do the most good to us. I am here on the spot and can better judge where they should go" (Poland Investigative Report, p. 4). By Jan. 30 he was able to write: "I don't fear any investigation here. I have used this [the Crédit Mobilier shares] where it will produce most good to us, I think. In view of . . . Washburn's move here, I go in for making our bond dividend in full" (*Ibid.*, p. 5). The stock was sold at par value, with interest from the previous July. Later evidence indicated that at this time Ames himself considered the stock worth at least double the par value. In fact, he wrote on Feb. 22, 1868, that some holders considered it worth \$300–\$350 a share (*Congressional Globe*, 42 Cong., 3 Sess., p. 1718). In all, later investigators traced contracts for the delivery of 160 shares to members of Congress. When some men hesitated, Ames assured them that "we are not coming to Congress to ask any favors" (*Ibid.*, p. 1718). He later admitted, however, that he did wish the negative favor of non-interference. "I have found," he said, "there is no difficulty in inducing men to look after their own property" (*Ibid.*, p. 1719).

The revelation of the stock sales came about through a quarrel between Ames and Col. H. S. McComb of Delaware, an associate who alleged that an unfilled subscription entitled him to \$25,000 worth of stock which he had not received. Ames resisted the claim. Col. McComb finally threatened to use, in a way to create a scandal, certain letters which Ames had writtten during the distribution of the stock. To this blackmailing gesture Ames refused to yield. McComb then filed affidavits in a Pennsylvania court in the summer of 1872 alleging Ames's misuse of stock. The result of the affidavits was that the letters of Ames which McComb held were published in full in the New York *Sun* of Sept. 4, 1872, under the caption "The King of Frauds: How the Crédit Mobilier Bought Its Way into Congress." The presidential campaign was at its height and the effect was stupendous. Congressmen who had accepted the stock and were standing for reëlection seemed panic-stricken. Many who had called themselves friends of Ames and begged for favors now denied any connection with him or the company and left him to face the storm alone.

At the opening of Congress in December 1872 two committees of inquiry were appointed by the House, one under Luke P. Poland of Vermont to ascertain if any member had given or received bribes, and another under Jeremiah M. Wilson of Indiana to discover if the government had been defrauded (Rhodes, vol. VII, ch. 1). Public pressure forced the removal of the rule of secrecy from the hearings, and the disclosures day by day riveted national attention. Several congressmen—Senator Henry L. Wilson of Massachusetts and Representatives H. L. Dawes and G. W. Scofield—had first accepted shares and then feeling the impropriety had returned them. Other members received shares to be paid for from dividends. Representative B. M. Boyer of Pennsylvania, who had bought seventy-five shares for his wife, stood almost alone in maintaining that his purchase was "both honest and honorable, and consistent with my position as a member of Congress" (Poland Investigative Report, p. 208). Those most discreditably involved were Senator Patterson of New Hampshire and Representatives James Brooks of New York and Schuyler Colfax of Indiana. Between Ames and Representative James A. Garfield of Ohio arose a sharp issue of veracity (J. A. Garfield, *Review of the Transactions of the Crédit Mobilier Company*, 1873). The Poland Committee formally reported Ames "guilty of selling to members of Congress shares of stock in the Crédit Mobilier of America for prices much below the true value of such stock, with intent thereby to influence the votes and decisions of such members in matters to be brought before Congress for action" (*House Reports*, 42 Cong., 3 Sess., No. 77, p. 19). It recommended that he and James Brooks be expelled. In debate Representative Poland led the attack upon Ames with much effectiveness. Ames replied in a long speech, read by the clerk, attempting a justification of his actions. He declared that his motive had been purely patriotic, that he had taken staggering financial risks, and that the stock had not been worth more than par when he sold it. Financially, he asserted, he would have been better off if he had never heard of the Union Pacific, for at its completion the railroad was in debt about \$6,000,000, the burden of which fell upon himself and others. The Wilson Committee had reported that the Crédit Mobilier had defrauded the government. Ames denied this, saying that the Crédit Mobilier profits were less than \$10,000,000 upon \$70,000,000 of expenditures. Partly because the Judiciary Committee threw grave doubt upon the right of the House to expel a member for offenses committed so long previously, partly because expulsion was felt to be too harsh a punishment, the House dropped that penalty. It instead took up a resolution declaring that it "absolutely condemns the conduct of Oakes Ames" (*Congressional Globe*, 42 Cong., 3 Sess., p. 1832). This was passed by a vote of 182 to 36. At once Ames's seat was surrounded by members who assured him that they had acted with reluctance and that they felt the warmest confidence in the rectitude of his intentions (Oberholtzer, II, 607). The consensus of historical opinion has been that Ames's action was highly improper, but that he had not contemplated bribery. He was a product of his time, and his ethical perceptions, like those of other business men of the day, were blunt. He declared that he believed his sales of stock to Congressmen were the "same thing as going into a business community and interesting the leading business men by giving them shares." His steps had been selfish and unethical, but not consciously corrupt.

Returning broken and dispirited to his North Easton home, Ames was given a hearty reception by his constituents, while plans were made by Boston business men for a complimentary dinner. But business worries (including grave financial difficulties through which the Easton manufactory had passed in 1870) and political disgrace had undermined his health. He was stricken by paralysis and lived but four days. His death was followed by a revulsion of feeling in his favor. The dedication of a memorial hall in his honor in North Easton, Nov. 17, 1881, evoked tributes from Gov. John D. Long, George S. Boutwell, E. E. Hale, Blaine, Evarts, Tilden, and others, and the Massachusetts legislature in 1883 passed a resolution of vindication. A monument had meanwhile been erected to him by the Union Pacific at Sherman Summit, Wyo.

In personality Oakes Ames was rugged, laborious, taciturn, and kindly. He was of simple and abstemious habits, with many homely traits which dated back to his early days as a workman. In his time he was known as a temperance advocate, and had other Puritanical qualities. But business shrewdness and keenness, allied with a speculative bent, were his salient characteristics.

[A brief anonymous sketch was published in 1883, *Oakes Ames, A Memoir*. The two volumes on *The Crédit Mobilier of America* by J. B. Crawford (1880) and R. Hazard (1881) both defend Ames. For the Poland and Wilson Reports see *House Reports,* 42 Cong., 3 Sess., Nos. 77, 78, and *Senate Reports,* 42 Cong., 3 Sess., No. 519. A few items of information may be found in J. P. Davis, *The Union Pacific Railway* (1894), and E. L. Sabin, *Building the Pacific Railway* (1919). The relations of Ames and Garfield are treated in T. C. Smith, *Life and Letters of James A. Garfield* (1925), vol. I, ch. 15. Good general accounts of the Crédit Mobilier scandal are offered by J. F. Rhodes, *Hist. of the U.S.,* vol. VII (1906), ch. I, and E. P. Oberholtzer, *Hist. of the U.S.,* vol. II, (1922), pp. 600 ff. Some interesting pages, not altogether accurate, occur in George F. Hoar, *Autobiography of Seventy Years* (1903), vol. I, ch. 22.] A. N.

AMES, OLIVER (Apr. 11, 1779–Sept. 11, 1863), pioneer manufacturer, was descended from William Ames, an English colonist of Braintree, Mass. (1638). John Ames (1738–1803), blacksmith, Revolutionary captain and major, and manufacturer of rude guns and shovels for the patriot forces, was the first outstanding member of the family. Oliver Ames, son of Capt. John and Susanna (Howard) Ames, was born at West Bridgewater, Mass., learned the primitive trade of shovel-maker, and later served an apprenticeship as a gunmaker under his older brother David, a foundryman commissioned by Washington as first superintendent of the Springfield armory. Leaving the armory, Oliver took up his father's business on the latter's death, and moved the shop from Bridgewater, Mass. to North Easton, Mass. (1803). The embargo and War of 1812, removing foreign competition, gave the shovel factory an impetus. In 1814 Oliver established a plant to manufacture cotton goods and machinery, but it was soon destroyed by fire. Thereafter he gave his whole attention and inventive genius to the manufacture of shovels, which he made lighter and less durable than the heavy implement of the time, in the belief that iron and shovels were cheaper than muscle and more easily replaced. In 1823 he built branch shops at Braintree and in 1844 at Canton, Mass. About this time he turned over his business, worth about $200,000, reorganized as Oliver Ames & Sons, to his boys, Oakes and Oliver. The senior Oliver was a man of standing, fair to labor, which in turn served him loyally, the founder of the local Unitarian Society, for four years a representative of his town in the legislature, and the builder of the thriving factory town of North Easton. Married early in life to Susannah Angier, daughter of Oakes Angier, a prominent attorney of Bridgewater, he was the father of two daughters and six sons, of whom Oakes Ames [*q.v.*] and Oliver Ames [*q.v.*] gained distinction as industrial leaders and railroad builders.

[W. L. Chaffin, *Hist. of the Town of Easton, Mass.* (1886); *Representative Men and Old Families of Southeastern Mass.* (1912).] R. J. P.

AMES, OLIVER (Nov. 5, 1807–Mar. 9, 1877), manufacturer, railroad promoter and official, was born at Plymouth, Mass., the son of Oliver Ames [*q.v.*] and Susannah (Angier) Ames, and was educated in the local school of North Easton, whither the family removed during his childhood, and in the Franklin Academy of North Andover. His first intention was to enter the law, but illness forced him to abandon legal study. He then went into his father's shovel factory as an apprentice, learning the business from the ground up before the management of the company, about 1844, was assigned to him and his brother Oakes Ames [*q.v.*]. In the meantime he married Sarah, a daughter of the Hon. Howard Lothrop of Easton, by whom he had two children, Helen Angier and Frederick Lothrop Ames [*q.v.*]. Business was booming. Irish immigrants afforded cheap labor and an enlarged production, though in turn this was not great enough to meet the increased demand for shovels on the construction work widely undertaken throughout the country. The opening of the California gold diggings brought heavier orders and profits so huge that the shovel manufacturers easily pocketed a loss of a million dollars through the failure of coast merchants. For a short time (1854–71), Oliver Ames & Sons manufactured hinges, nails, and even shoes in a string of separate plants, but meanwhile they never slackened in manufacturing and improving shovels. Luck, cheap but well-treated labor, and managerial genius enabled the concern to increase its business to a virtual monopoly.

In 1852 and 1857 Oliver Ames was elected to the state Senate as a Whig and Republican, but sought no further political career, preferring to give undivided attention to business and money-making. In 1855 he joined Oakes in building the Easton Branch Railroad, which turned the brothers toward railroad development. The Civil War brought heavy government contracts for swords and shovels, possibly greater because Oakes served in Gov. Andrew's executive council and later in Congress. The wealth of the concern jumped from four to eight million dollars during this period when shrewd business men easily accumulated fortunes. Their auspicious prosperity turned Oakes and Oliver toward bigger things, for under the capable management of their sons its own momentum enabled their business to expand. They were caught by the vision of a Union Pacific road connecting the East with the coast and enmeshed in the Crédit Mobilier company which, along with others, they incorporated to build and finance the transcontinental railway. Oliver was not involved in the subsequent congressional investigation, as he was not personally concerned with the alleged corruption of congressmen or the unlawful means of obtaining legislative favors and aid.

He was acting president of the Union Pacific 1866–68, president, succeeding Gen. John A. Dix, 1868–71 during the period of construction and trials, and a director until his death. In 1870 he saw Oliver Ames & Sons facing bankruptcy, though the shovel works had assets of fully fifteen million dollars and liabilities of only eight million. Building the Union Pacific had been a desperate business. Oliver obtained an extension of time from his creditors and as head of the concern on the death of Oakes (1873) brought about order with the aid of his nephew, also an Oliver Ames [*q.v.*]. Few men were better known in the industrial world: his business acumen was at the service of the Atlantic and Pacific, Kansas Pacific, Denver Pacific, Colorado Central, Old Colony, and other railroads in which he was a director. Finance he knew quite as well as railroading, through his promotion schemes and close supervision, if not ownership, of the Easton and Bristol National Banks. He also had other interests. Together with Oakes, he donated the site of the first Catholic church in North Easton (1850) and gave small amounts to a number of small colleges and schools in Massachusetts or in the new West. He left a fund for a town library, for the schools of North Easton, and for the improvement of local roads. He was long vice-president of the Massachusetts Total Abstinence Society and for twenty years a trustee of the Taunton Insane Asylum. A Unitarian in belief, he erected a church and parsonage for the society of which his father was a charter member, but this did not prevent him from donating a meeting house to the Methodists of his neighborhood. He was beloved by his townsmen whose prosperity was so largely dependent upon his factories and the employment which they afforded. The town was silent when he died, Mar. 9, 1877. The shops and schools were closed. A special train from Boston brought about forty business and railroad men of national importance, but it was to the employees of twenty-five to fifty years' standing that his remains were confided to be carried to the grave. The man and his labors are commemorated by a huge truncated pyramid at Sherman, Wyo., the highest point on the Union Pacific, dedicated to Oakes and Oliver Ames, railroad builders.

[Boston Jour.'s *Commonwealth of Mass.* (1883); *Representative Men and Old Families of Southeastern Mass.* (1912); *Memorial of Oliver Ames* (n.d.); Appleton's *Annual Cyc.*, 1877; *Easton Jour.*, Mar. 17, 1877; *Brockton Gazette*, Mar. 15, 1877; *Boston Transcript*, Mar. 13, 1877; *Oakes Ames, a Memoir* (1883).] R. J. P.

AMES, OLIVER (Feb. 4, 1831–Oct. 22, 1895), capitalist, governor of Massachusetts, was born at North Easton, Mass., the second son of Oakes Ames [*q.v.*] and Evelyn (Gilmore) Ames. Educated in the local public schools and the academies of North Attleboro and Leicester, he commenced his apprenticeship in the Oliver Ames & Sons shovel works. Injured at work, he was sent to Brown University where he came under the instruction of the learned President Wayland. After a year he reëntered the shovel works. As a young man he was active in the state militia advancing from second-lieutenant to lieutenant-colonel, although resigning before the Civil War commenced. For his "pusillanimous war record," he was severely criticized during his canvass for the governorship. Ames explained that he had hired a substitute and had given thousands of dollars in support of the Union cause. The actual explanation may have been his marriage, in 1860, to Anna

Ray, adopted daughter of William Hadwen of Nantucket, a lady of old English lineage, by whom he had six children.

In 1863, on the death of his grandfather, Oliver Ames[*q.v.*], the young Oliver received a ninth interest in the huge shovel works and became an active partner at a time when the war contracts and profits were tremendous. For several years he was personally in charge of the mechanical department, where he displayed an inventive skill in perfecting tools and processes which improved the product and increased the output. Under his skilled direction, sales were greatly enlarged. Ten years later, he was given the additional burden of straightening out his deceased father's entangled estate and taking over his numerous directorates and varied business responsibilities. The Crédit Mobilier investigation and the panic of 1873 had left Oakes Ames's estate of about $6,000,000 so involved that Oliver was compelled to pledge his private fortune to satisfy the creditors. His capable management and a rehabilitation of railroads, as times grew better, bridged the crisis. Soon he was able to settle all debts and pay a legacy of $1,000,000 bequeathed by his father to various philanthropies. Ere long, on the death of his uncle, Oliver Ames, Jr.[*q.v.*], he became the dominant figure in the business of Oliver Ames & Sons. In addition he was for a time president of the Union Pacific Railroad and a director of a long list of railroads, banks, savings companies, and land companies. Indeed, the numerous activities of Oliver Ames quite rivaled those of his plunging father. His most spectacular speculation was the purchase at auction of stock in the Central Kansas branch of the Union Pacific at twenty-five cents a share and its later sale at $250 to Jay Gould when the latter was consolidating the Union Pacific and Kansas Pacific roads. This deal netted about a million dollars, bringing his estate well over eight million by 1892. And he weathered the panic of 1893 with little loss as he retrenched and clung tenaciously to his bonds and stocks.

Always a staunch Republican and protectionist and chairman of the local Republican organization, he did not enter politics actively until 1880 when he was elected to the state Senate, where he served two years. In 1882, he was elected lieutenant-governor under the Democratic governor, Benjamin Butler, with whom he got along successfully despite political differences and his efforts to check some of the governor's erratic political impulses. He was reëlected to second, third, and fourth terms under the Republican governor, George D. Robinson. He served the state, though not without subjecting himself to violent criticism, by arranging the sale of its interests in the New York and New England Railroad at some loss and its heavy holding of stock in the Troy and Greenfield road and Hoosac Tunnel at less than a third of the par value of the stock. Time demonstrated the wisdom of this action and brought commendation, but for the moment the opposition made much capital out of the apparent loss of several million dollars. Robinson declining another nomination, Ames was nominated by the Republican convention and elected with a plurality of 8,000 over John F. Andrew, son of the noted war governor. In 1887, he was reëlected by a majority of 17,000 over H. B. Lovering in spite of a vicious campaign in which his war record was violently attacked. The "Maintes," too, were in the opposition; for while Gov. Ames had been actively interested in the Massachusetts Temperance Society, he was opposed to legislative restriction. His donation of $1,000 to Holy Cross College (Roman Catholic) was said to have injured him in Worcester County, a result which he regarded, perhaps rightly, as showing contemptible narrowness on the part of voters who cut his ticket. Yet in 1888, he was again reelected, defeating William E. Russell by 28,000.

Ames made a good governor. He brought business methods into the state administration and made judicious appointments on the basis of merit as far as political considerations would permit. He sought to improve the public schools so that private schools could not compete, rather than curb private schools by hostile legislation as many of his supporters favored. He urged that savings banks be separated from national banks to prevent the transfer of assets to meet the audit of public examiners and he proposed that claims against the state be handled by the superior court, not by the legislature. In both reform policies, the legislature agreed by translating his recommendations into law. During his administration, the legislature voted to enlarge the state house, and before retiring he had the satisfaction of laying the corner-stone. And in an expenditure of $3,000,000 there was no breath of the scandal so usual in such building projects.

In January 1890, Gov. Ames retired in the belief that the customary limit of three terms in the governorship should be maintained. Thereafter he gave his time to business affairs, to European travel, cultural interests, charities, and family. His retirement was splendid—a winter home in Boston, a grand summer residence at Martha's Vineyard, and the palatial show house and grounds at North Easton. He spent much time in reading, and in collecting books for his library and the works of old masters for his gallery. As an owner of Booth's Theatre in New York, he had a considerable interest in the drama, and his love of art merited the presidency of the Boston Art Club which he cherished more than a similar leadership in the Boston Merchants' Club. A custodian of great wealth, Ames was no niggard in his private charities or in his treatment of the employees of the family industry. At North Easton, on whose school committee he served a score of years, he joined with his brothers in building the Oakes Ames Memorial Hall and donated to the town a high school which was dedicated shortly after his death.

[W. R. Cutter, *Encyc. of Mass.*(1916) ; *Boston of Today*, ed. by R. Herndon(1892), pp. 125–26 ; D. P. Toomey, *Mass. of Today*, ed. by T. C. Quinn(1892), p. 42 ; *Representative Men of Mass.*, ed. by W. F. Moore(1898), pp. 379–81 ; G. A. Marden, *Government of the Commonwealth of Mass.*(1880), pp. 239–42 ; Appleton's *Annual Cyc.*, 1895, pp. 941–43 ; Alanson Borden, *Our County and its People, a Descriptive and Biog. Rec. of Bristol County, Mass.*(1899) ; *Springfield Republican*, Oct. 23, 1895 ; *Boston Transcript*, Nov. 5, 7, 9, 1887, Oct. 22, 1895.]

R. J. P.

AMES, SAMUEL (Sept. 6, 1806–Dec. 20, 1865), jurist, was descended from one Robert Ames (or Eames) who settled at Boxford, Mass., about 1650. Fourth in descent from this Robert Ames was a Samuel Ames, storekeeper in Providence, married to Anne Checkley (Chichele). Samuel, their eldest son, was born at Providence, and received his early education there and at Phillips Academy, Andover. Proceeding thence to Brown University, he graduated in 1823 at the early age of seventeen. He then attended the law school at Litchfield, Conn., and, on being admitted to the Rhode Island bar in 1826, opened an office in Providence. As a young man, it is said, his distinguishing characteristics were a positive manner, athletic figure, and careful dress. Despite a keen enjoyment of social amenities he was an insatiable student and rapidly forged to the front. In 1832 he assisted Joseph K. Angell [*q.v.*] in the preparation of the latter's authoritative treatise on corporation law. Although not greatly interested in politics, he was an extremely effective speaker, took an active part in public affairs, and several times served in the city council. In 1841 he was elected representative for Providence in the General Assembly, and, with brief intermissions, continued a member of the legislature till February 1851. During the so-called "Dorr Rebellion" in 1842 he adhered to the *status quo*, serving as quartermaster-general of the state troops, despite the fact that he had married, June 27, 1839, Mary Throop Dorr, sister of Thomas Wilson Dorr [*q.v.*]. His law practise had been steadily growing, and he became the recognized leader of the Rhode Island bar, on several occasions being retained before the United States Supreme Court. In 1853 the legislature appointed him state representative to adjust the boundary between Rhode Island and Massachusetts. In October 1854 he became chairman of the commission to revise the state laws—which resulted in the first complete restatement of the statutory law of Rhode Island. In May 1856 he was elected chief justice of the supreme court of Rhode Island and reporter. Unsettled constitutional questions of vital importance came up for solution shortly after his appointment, and his judgment in Taylor *vs.* Place (*4 R. I. Reports*, 324), declaring that the exercise by the General Assembly of judicial power as a court of appeal from the supreme court of Rhode Island was unconstitutional, is a masterpiece of constitutional law and reasoning. In 1861 he attended as a representative of Rhode Island the futile Peace Conference at Washington. He died at Providence, Dec. 20, 1865. On the bench he enjoyed the confidence of the bar and of the public to a remarkable extent, and his judgments were accorded a respect which was not confined to the state itself. His strong alert mind and quick logical perception made him at times somewhat impatient in dealing with men of less capacity. He seldom reserved a decision, and his reasons for judgment were usually brief. The extent of contemporaneous admiration is indicated by the name applied to him of "The Great Chief Justice."

[An account of Ames's life and genealogy is given in *New Eng. Families*(R. I. ed. p. 13). The best biography is that by Chief Justice Stiness in *Great Am. Lawyers*, V, 293. A more intimate sketch by his former law partner, Abraham Payne, appears in the latter's *Reminiscences of the R. I. Bar*(1885). A full report of the Proceedings in the Supreme Court on the announcement of his death will be found in *8 R. I. Reports*, 581.]

H. W. H. K.

AMHERST, JEFFERY (Jan. 29, 1717–Aug. 3, 1797), British soldier, was born at Riverhead in the parish of Sevenoaks, Kent County, England. He was the second son of Jeffery and Elizabeth (Kerril) Amherst, both of whom were of Kentish antecedents. His father and grandfather were barristers ; his great-great-grandfather was an Anglican clergyman (A. T. Ritchie and R. Evans, *Lord Amherst and the British Advance Eastwards to Burma*, 1894, pp. 9–10). Not far from Riverhead, at "Knole," resided Lionel Cranfield Sackville, the first Duke of Dorset. This propinquity, coupled with more or less association between the two families, led to Jeffery Amherst's early employment as a page in the Sackville household, and thence to his entering the army in 1731. In the War of the Austrian Succession he served as aide-de-camp to Gen. John Ligonier and took part in the battles of Dettingen and Fontenoy (F. H. Skrine, *Fontenoy and Great Britain's Share in the War of the Austrian Succession,* 1906, pp. 164–65). On Dec. 25, 1745 he was made lieutenant-colonel (*Army List for 1754,* p. 8) and placed in command of a company in the 1st Battalion of the 1st Regiment of Foot Guards. In 1747 he was aide-de-camp to the Duke of Cumberland and was present at the battle of Laffeldt. After the Peace of Aix-la-Chapelle he continued his association with the Duke of Cumberland, being appointed Groom of the Bedchamber.

When the outbreak of the Seven Years' War was impending, the British government employed 8,000 Hessians to protect the Electorate of Hanover, and in February 1756 Amherst was sent to Germany to take charge of their commissariat. After a few weeks on the Continent he was ordered to return to England, bringing with him a portion of the Hessian subsidiaries. Soon after his arrival he was promoted to the colonelcy of the 15th Regiment of Foot (*Army List for 1757,* p. 6), but this was virtually a sinecure and Amherst continued in charge of the Hessians. In the spring of 1757 Cumberland was dispatched to the Continent to defend Hanover, and Amherst accompanied him as commissary. He was present at the battle of Hastenbeck, July 26, in which Cumberland's army was defeated by the French.

In January 1758, while still in Germany, Amherst received orders to return to England, whence, with the rank of major-general, he was to proceed to America in command of an army of over 14,000 men to capture the French stronghold of Louisburg on Cape Breton Island. This promotion is attributable to Sir John Ligonier (*Additional MS.* No. 32876, in the British Museum), who had been appointed commander-in-chief of all the forces in Great Britain. Amherst sailed for Halifax in March, but did not reach the coast of Nova Scotia until May 28. The army sent to capture Louisburg was supplemented by a fleet under Boscawen. The combined forces began their siege of the town about June 1 and the French surrendered it on July 27 (Francis Parkman, *Montcalm and Wolfe,* 1884, vol. II, ch. XIX). This was the first British victory in the Seven Years' War, and great rejoicing spread throughout the empire. Towns in Massachusetts and New Hampshire were named in honor of Amherst, and likewise a county in Virginia (Lawrence Shaw Mayo, *Jeffery Amherst,* 1916, pp. 117–18). Pitt, who had taken charge of the war in June 1757, had hoped that Amherst might capture both Louisburg and Quebec in the campaigns of 1758, but this prospect was frustrated by Abercromby's failure to take Ticonderoga. In consequence of Abercromby's disastrous defeat, Amherst deferred the attack on Quebec until another season and devoted the remainder of the summer to securing his hold upon the Gulf of St. Lawrence, including Prince Edward Island. Toward the end of August he and five regiments sailed for Boston, and thence made their way overland to Albany. He agreed with Abercromby that another movement against Ticonderoga in that year would be unwise, and retired to New York for the winter.

The British success at Louisburg was due in part to the brilliant work of Brigadier-General Wolfe; consequently Pitt gave him a semi-independent command for the campaign of 1759 and ordered him to take Quebec. Amherst, now commander-in-chief in North America, was to push northward from Albany, drive the French from their posts on Lakes George and Champlain, and, if possible, join forces with Wolfe before Quebec. Owing to unfavorable weather and the late arrival of the provincial troops, Amherst's progress was slow, but he captured Ticonderoga on July 27 and Crown Point on Aug. 4 (Parkman, *op. cit.,* II, ch. XXVI). Instead of advancing at once toward Quebec he spent much time in constructing a strong fort at Crown Point, and the burden and glory of taking Quebec settled upon Wolfe alone. Amherst reached the northern end of Lake Champlain about the middle of October, and, learning that Quebec had fallen, closed his campaign. In recognition of his services at Louisburg, Ticonderoga, and Crown Point, George II appointed him to the sinecure governorship of Virginia (W. M. Torrens, *History of Cabinets from the Union with Scotland to the Acquisition of Canada and Bengal,* 1894, II, 515–16).

Montreal remained to be captured, and upon it Amherst converged a triple campaign in 1760. Murray ascended the St. Lawrence from Quebec, Haviland pushed northward from Lake Champlain, and Amherst came down the river from Oswego. The combination was well-timed and entirely successful. On Sept. 8, 1760, Montreal surrendered, and Canada was added to the British Empire (Parkman, *op. cit.,* II, ch. XXX). In May 1761 Amherst was appointed a Knight of the Bath. In the following year an expedition commanded by his younger brother, William Amherst, captured Newfoundland.

Amherst returned to England in the winter of 1763–64. In 1768 George III decided to have the governor of Virginia reside in that colony, and gave Amherst his choice of going to America or resigning the office. The general resigned, but took offense and threw up his military appointments as well. After three or four months he was placated by an additional military commission and a grant of 20,000 acres in the province of New York. In 1770 he was appointed to the sinecure governorship of Guernsey. When the American situation became acute in the winter of 1774–75, George III urged Amherst to take command of the British forces in New England, but the general declined (Mayo, *op. cit.*, pp. 278–80). As a military adviser to the cabinet, however, he served his country during the war, and in 1776 was raised to the peerage with the title of Baron Amherst. When France entered the war in 1778, he was made commander-in-chief of all British forces in England (*Gentleman's Magazine,* March 1778, p. 140). In this capacity he showed efficiency in his suppression of the Gordon Riots in 1780 (J. Paul de Castro, *The Gordon Riots,* 1926, pp. 69–85, 112–14, *et passim*). After the American war he retired to his seat, "Montreal," at Sevenoaks, Kent; but when war with France was approaching in 1793 he once more took command of the army in Great Britain and held it until relieved in February 1795. In the following year he was given the rank of field-marshal, the highest military office in the British army. He died on Aug. 3, 1797.

In appearance, Amherst was tall and spare; his complexion was florid, and his nose large and aquiline. There is a portrait of him by Reynolds; also a sketch by the same artist. Other likenesses include a Blackburn (1758) in the possession of Herbert L. Pratt, Esq., of Glen Cove, Long Island; a Gainsborough in the National Portrait Gallery, London; a detail in Copley's "Death of Chatham"; and a crude engraving in the *London Magazine,* February 1782. Although in Blackburn's portrait Amherst has a genial expression, at least one contemporary found him "grave, formal, and cold" (N. W. Wraxall, *Historical and Posthumous Memoirs,* ed. by H. B. Wheatley, 1884, I, 406–7).

[The works cited in the text above will be found especially useful; also Gertrude Selwyn Kimball, *Correspondence of Wm. Pitt with Colonial Governors* (1906); J. W. Fortescue, *Hist. of the Brit. Army,* vol. II (1899), vol. III (1902); *Hist. MSS. Commission's Rept. on the MSS. of Mrs. Stopford-Sackville,* vol. I; Beckles Willson, *Life and Letters of James Wolfe* (1909); Horace Walpole, *Letters; Grenville Papers,* ed. by W. J. Smith (1852–53), vols. III and IV; *Pol. Reg.,* Sept. 1768; and W. B. Donne, *Correspondence of King George the Third with Lord North* (1867), vol. I. Amherst's letters to Gen. Robert Monckton, Nov. 1758 to Sept. 1763, are preserved in the "Northcliffe Coll." in the archives at Ottawa.]

L. S. M.

AMMEN, DANIEL (May 16, 1819–July 11, 1898), naval officer and writer, was the son of David and Sally (Houtz) Ammen, both of Swiss-German ancestry, and the brother of Jacob Ammen [*q.v.*]. Daniel Ammen was a boyhood playmate of U. S. Grant, their early intimacy developing into a close friendship in Washington after the Civil War. Following his appointment as midshipman, July 7, 1836, he spent three months in special study at West Point, where his brother was a graduate instructor. From then until the Civil War his life was passed chiefly in long cruises, including a voyage in Commodore Biddle's squadron to China and Japan, 1845–47, a surveying expedition up the Paraguay River, 1853–54, and a cruise in the Pacific, 1857–60. In 1849–50 he enjoyed a tour in Germany and Italy. His reputation as a resolute and dependable ship commander in the Civil War is suggested in the phrase of a brother officer, "that grim, true-hearted fighting man, Daniel Ammen." His special experience was in monitors and new types of ordnance. In the gunboat *Seneca* he took part in the attack on Port Royal, Nov. 7, 1861, hoisted the flag next day on Fort Beauregard, and won Admiral Du Pont's commendation for "intelligent and energetic conduct" of subsequent operations on the St. John's River, Fla. In the monitor *Patapsco* he participated in the bombardment of Fort McAllister, Mar. 3, 1863, and in the unsuccessful attack on Charleston in the next month. During the summer he was on sick-leave, but in the autumn he was again off Charleston in Admiral Dahlgren's flagship. On May 15, 1864, in charge of 220 naval recruits from New York to Panama on the merchant vessel *Ocean Queen,* he suppressed a mutinous outbreak by shooting down two of the leaders. In command of the steam sloop *Mohican* he took part in the two attacks on Fort Fisher in the winter of 1864–65.

After the war Ammen was called from sea duty to Washington through President Grant's influence, and from 1868 until his retirement as rear admiral, June 4, 1878, he was in charge, first of the Bureau of Yards and Docks for three years, and then of the Bureau of Navigation. As secretary of the Isthmian Canal Commission, 1872–76, he became an earnest and leading advocate of the Nicaragua canal route. He represented the United States at the Interoceanic Canal Congress in Paris, 1879, helped to organize a company which secured temporary concessions from Nicaragua, and in the period 1880–92 published seven pamphlets in its advocacy. His range of interest appears also in his books: *The Atlantic Coast* (1883), in the Navy in the Civil War series; *Country Homes and Their Improvement* (1885); and an entertaining volume of reminiscences, *The Old Navy and the New* (1891). His mechanical bent is seen in the invention of a cask life-raft used in the navy, and the design of the "Ammen ram," a small coast-defense type, of which only one was completed, the *Katahdin* (accepted for service Jan. 4, 1896). Of medium height, thin and active, fond of horseback-riding and country life, Rear Admiral Ammen lived after about 1870 on his estate "Ammendale," in the suburb still so named thirteen miles north of Washington. His first wife was Mary Jackson, daughter of an English army officer. He was survived by his second wife, Zöe Atocha, a Louisianian of distinguished French-Spanish descent whom he married Apr. 11, 1866, and by whom he had five children.

[In addition to his autobiography, *The Old Navy and the New* (1891), see *Official Records*, especially vols. VI–XVI on the Atlantic Blockade (fully indexed); "Daniel Ammen," by G. E. Belknap, *Cassier's Mag.*, XIV, 267; and articles by Ammen on "The Nicaragua Canal Route" and "Recollections and Letters of Grant" in *N. Am. Rev.*, Oct. and Nov. 1885. Obituaries in the July 16, 1898, issues of the *Army and Navy Jour.* and the *Army and Navy Reg.*]

A. W.

AMMEN, JACOB (Jan. 7, 1807–Feb. 6, 1894), Union soldier, was born at Fincastle, Va., the son of David and Sally (Houtz) Ammen, and the brother of Daniel Ammen [*q.v.*]. When he was ten years old his parents removed to Ohio, and he was appointed from that state to the Military Academy. He graduated in 1831, was commissioned in the 1st Artillery, and served six years in the army. During most of his time he was an instructor at West Point, but a short tour of duty in Charleston harbor made him a witness of the nullification proceedings in South Carolina. Resigning from the army in 1837, he became professor of mathematics at Bacon (now Transylvania) College, in Kentucky. He taught there and elsewhere—three years at Indiana University—until 1855, when he took up the practise of civil engineering. When Fort Sumter was bombarded, he immediately volunteered for service, was appointed captain in the 12th Ohio, and raised a company. He was quickly promoted to be lieutenant-colonel of the regiment, and was appointed colonel of the 24th Ohio in June 1861. After participating in the West Virginia campaign in the fall of that year, his regiment joined the Army of the Ohio. He was in command of a brigade at Shiloh when that army came up in time to avert the threatened disaster to Grant; the division commander (Nelson) wrote: "The cool, wary and vigorous method in which he fought his brigade gave me a profitable lesson in the science of battle" (*Official Records*, ser. I, vol. X, pt. I, p. 325). Ammen's gallantry and good conduct were noted by Gen. Buell in his report. He continued with the army through the siege of Corinth and for some months after, but illness took him away in September 1862. He had meanwhile (July 16) been appointed brigadier-general of volunteers. The state of his health prevented service in the field, and, though he was not long absent from duty, he was assigned to commands in the North. In April 1864 he took charge of the district of East Tennessee. This was a debatable land, with a population containing both unionist and secessionist sympathizers, harried by guerrillas, and occasionally invaded by organized forces of one party or the other. Ammen's task was largely an administrative one, varied by a little active campaigning. It involved much disagreeable work and no glory. He performed it to the satisfaction of his superiors for several months, and then, in October, offered his resignation, on account of "my pecuniary interests at home, which if not attended soon may subject me to very considerable loss." Some time elapsed before it was found possible to dispense with his services, and it was not till Jan. 14, 1865, that he relinquished his command and returned to civil life. He resumed civil engineering in Ohio, but abandoned it in 1872 and became a farmer near Beltsville, Md., a few miles outside of Washington. He was a member of a commission sent to Central America in 1874 to investigate proposed isthmian canal routes. He removed in 1891 to Lockland, Ohio, where he died, after two years of blindness. He was twice married, first to Caroline L. Pierce, and then to Martha Beasley (*Cincinnati Times-Star*, Feb. 7, 1894, p. 5).

[G. W. Cullum, *Biog. Reg.* (3rd ed., 1891), I, 475–76; *Bull. Ass. Grads. Mil. Acad.*, 1894, pp. 57–61; *Official Records*, see Index; unpublished War Dept. Records.]

T. M. S.

AMMONS, ELIAS MILTON (July 28, 1860–May 20, 1925), ranchman, governor of Colorado, son of Jehu and Margaret (Brendle) Ammons, both of whom traced their ancestry back to colonial forebears, was born in Macon County, N. C. For four years following the removal of the family to Colorado in 1871, the boy worked as ranch-hand and teamster; but, thanks to training received at home from a cultured mother and a father who had been educated for the Baptist ministry, he was able quickly to make up the time lost when he returned to school in 1875. His formal education closed in 1880, when he was graduated from the East Denver High School. Already he had entered on a journalistic career, having become a reporter on the *Denver Times* in 1879; by 1885, when failing eyesight forced him to abandon newspaper work, he had risen to the post of associate editor. Since outdoor life seemed advisable, he went into the cattle business in 1886 in partnership with Thomas F. Dawson. Until his death he retained his interest in this industry and in all forms of agriculture, as is shown by his long membership in the Grange and on the State Board of Agriculture, and by his activity in the establishment of the Colorado Cattle and Horse Growers' Association and the National Western Stock Show at Denver.

Although not strong physically, and nearly blind, Ammons was a man of great vitality and energy. His political career began in 1890 with his appointment as clerk of a district court. Within a few months he resigned to take a seat in the lower house of the Colorado legislature, of which body he was made speaker two years later. When the Republican party committed itself to the gold standard in 1896, he withdrew from its ranks and helped organize the Silver Republican party in Colorado. It was as a "Teller Silver Republican" that he was elected to the state Senate in 1898. The transition to the Democratic party was easily made; in 1904 and 1906 he was its unsuccessful candidate for lieutenant-governor, but in 1912 he carried the gubernatorial election by a plurality of nearly 48,000 votes (*World Almanac,* 1914). As governor he sponsored non-partizan legislation such as improvements in the public utilities, insurance, and banking laws, a revision of the tax system, provision for coal-mine inspection, and a more comprehensive plan for state highways. Both preceding and during his term as governor he opposed vigorously the Reservation policy then followed by the Federal Government, on the ground that it would deprive the people of the West of their right to develop the natural resources of their states (*Senate Document 650,* 61 Cong., 2 Sess.) The most perplexing problem during his administration was the great strike in the Colorado coal fields (1913–14), which became so serious after the "Ludlow battle" between the strikers and the state militia on Apr. 20, 1914, that federal troops were called in to restore order. Ammons was accused of grossly favoring the mine owners throughout the struggle, and a motion calling for his resignation was introduced in the legislature but defeated by a vote of 26 to 4. After his term of office expired (1915), he continued to give freely of his time to business and civic enterprises. He was president of the Farmers' Life Insurance Company (1911–25), of the Denver Chamber of Commerce (1923–24), and of the State Historical and Natural History Society (1922–25). He was survived by his wife, Elizabeth (Fleming) Ammons, to whom he was married on Jan. 29, 1889.

[The best sketch of his life is in W. F. Stone, *Hist. of Colo.* (1918), II, 32–38; his inaugural and farewell addresses as governor may be found in the *Rocky Mountain News* (Denver), Jan. 15, 1913, and Jan. 9, 1915; obituary in the *Rocky Mountain News,* May 21, 1925; facts about his personal life furnished by his sister, Mrs. James E. McLaughlin of Boulder, Colo.] C. B. G.

AMORY, THOMAS (May 1682–June 20, 1728), merchant, was born in Limerick, Ireland. His grandfather was a member of the "Merchant Venturers" of Bristol; his father Jonathan Amory, married to Rebecca Houston, was a merchant of Dublin. Thomas was taken as an infant to the West Indies and in 1786 to Charleston, S. C., where his father became a landowner, speaker of the colonial assembly, advocate general and "Receiver for the Public Treasury." In 1694 the boy was sent to relatives in London to be educated; but the statement that he attended Westminster School cannot be substantiated. Five years later he was bound out as an apprentice to a French merchant of London, Nicolas Oursel, who sent him, at the expiration of the indenture in 1706, as his factor to Terceira in the Azores. There he established himself as a merchant trading with Portugal, England, Holland, and America. His precise letter books, written in French, English, and Portuguese, contain the records of his transactions. In 1712, in company with Andrew White and with William Fisher, the richest merchant of the island, he purchased a French prize ship and went to Europe to dispose of her. He had intended to wind up his affairs in the Azores and remove to Charleston, S. C., but the loss of part of the cargo, poor markets, and the cost of repairing the vessel at Amsterdam, forced him to return to the islands to make up his losses. The confidence that he inspired, notwithstanding the failure of this venture, is shown by the willingness of his partner to join in fresh ventures, and by his appointment as consul by the Dutch, French, and English governments. In 1719 he resigned these offices, sailed for Boston and thence to Charleston, where he intended to settle and to marry Sarah, the daughter of Mrs. William Rhett, administratrix of his property since the death of his father in 1699. But he found that the daughter was promised to another, and that Mrs. Rhett was unwilling to relinquish the property except as the result of prolonged but finally successful litigation. In the spring of 1720 he visited Rhode Island, Pennsylvania, and New York in search of an opening for trade, but decided to settle in Boston, where he purchased land and built a wharf and still-house. A bold and able merchant, Amory rapidly extended his business to the other English colonies, the West Indies, the Azores, England, Ireland, and Europe; developed inland trade; invested in ship-building; and distilled rum and turpentine in Boston. He was a man of prodigious activity, scrupulous in the protection of his business reputation, yet not above evading the Acts of Trade. On May 9, 1721, he married Rebecca Holmes, daughter of Francis Holmes, who owned the "Bunch of Grapes" tavern in Boston, although, as he writes, "Her fortune in it is but £500." After his death, caused by falling into the cistern of his still-house, Mrs. Amory carried on the importing business and supervised the management of the distillery for nearly fifteen years.

[The principal records of Thomas Amory's life are contained in his pocket book (1699) and his five-volume letter books (1711–14 and 1717–28), extracts from which are reproduced in Gertrude E. Meredith's *The Descendants of Hugh Amory* (1901). His Boston property is shown in the Boston property records and on Bonner's 1722 map of Boston. The account of Thomas Amory in *Amor y amistad* (1856), a pamphlet by T. C. Amory, is correct in outline but unreliable in detail, and Joseph Johnson's Amory tradition in his *Traditions and Reminiscences Chiefly of the Am. Rev.* (1851) is entirely untrustworthy. W. B. Weeden used the Amory letter books in preparing his *Econ. and Social Hist. of New Eng.* (1891), which presents a full and critical account of Amory's career.]

E. A. J. J.

ANAGNOS, MICHAEL (Nov. 7, 1837–June 29, 1906), Greek patriot, American educator of the blind, was born at Papingo, a mountain village of Epirus. He was of peasant origin, though his surname, Anagnostópoulos, shows that either his father, Demetrios, or his grandfather was Reader in the community at a time when the ability to read was a distinction. The lad himself had such a thirst for knowledge that he once trudged sixteen hours to Janina where he won an academic scholarship. Then he spent four years at the University of Athens, his major studies being the classics and philosophy. From the Greek poets and orators he imbibed the love of liberty and the vehement patriotism and poetic style which afterward characterized his speeches and writings. He read law but later chose journalism and became editor of a daily paper. Certain bitter polemics of his having brought him imprisonment, and his zeal for annexing Crete being disapproved of by his staff, he resigned his position. He was thirty years old when, on Dr. Samuel G. Howe's going to Greece with relief for the Cretan refugees, Anagnos (as he thereafter called himself) gave his services as secretary and interpreter and later obtained this Philhellene's consent to accompany him to Boston and to Perkins Institution of which he was director and executive head. When Anagnos had learned English he became Dr. Howe's assistant and loyal understudy, married his daughter Julia, whose mother was Julia Ward Howe, and upon Dr. Howe's death in 1876 succeeded him. The election of one whose abundant curly black beard and broken English marked him as a foreigner was not without misgivings. His prompt raising of a printing fund in memory of his predecessor, however, both put misgivings aside and showed Anagnos his own forte, the raising of money in behalf of blind children. Indeed, in this he far excelled Dr. Howe. Having rapidly increased the school's stock of embossed books and appliances, he gathered a museum of stuffed objects and specimens for object teaching, as well as a special reference library on blindness and the blind, both hitherto found in European institutions only. Perhaps his greatest contribution to the cause of the blind was a kindergarten for little blind children, the first, largest, and best appointed in this country if not in the world. Within twenty years he had raised $1,000,000 for it. Alike in that and in introducing Swedish gymnastics and sloyd he showed his progressiveness. Nevertheless he was always set against any new proposal irreconcilable with the Perkins tradition. He chose assistants discriminatingly and, holding them responsible for results, was freed to read and study and to write voluminous though cogent annual reports. It was said of him that his devotion to Greece constituted a real religion. The Greeks of this country chose him president of their union, formed through his eloquence to promote Pan-Hellenism and national liberty. But he had another means of helping Greece. His investments and his thrift had made him a comparatively rich man. He deposited in a bank at Athens $25,000 to found in Papingo the Kallinean Free Schools, named for Kallina, his mother, and by his will left them one-sixth of the residue of his estate, and five-sixths to establish in Epirus a classical high school. It was while leisurely traveling in the Near East in the interests of his health and of these schools that he died. Civic exercises in his memory were held in Boston at which the governor of Massachusetts, the mayor of the city, and other prominent men spoke. A card announcing his death bore the inscription: "A deep thinker, a wise counsellor, a prophet of good, a great-hearted lover of mankind, a true and far-seeing leader of the blind along the higher paths." The former pupils of the kindergarten affectionately erected in its court a bronze bust of Anagnos. Every year, on Founder's Day (his birthday), his memory is revived by exercises at which his personality is described and his deeds rehearsed.

[*Michael Anagnos, 1837–1906,* issued by Perkins Inst (1907), containing portrs., a memoir, tributes, resolutions, press notices (those from Greek papers translated), and memorial exercises in full—all reprinted from the *75th Ann. Report* of Perkins Inst.; the *Ann. Reports,* 1876–1905, written by Anagnos (that for 1913 telling in twenty-seven pages the story of the kindergarten); *Μιχαηλ 'Αναγνωστόπουλος*, by D. and G. Anagnostópoulos, Athens, 1923; Anagnos's will. All of these may be consulted at Perkins Inst., Watertown, Mass.]

E. E. A.

ANDERSON, ALEXANDER (Apr. 21, 1775–Jan. 17, 1870), engraver, was the son of John Anderson, a Scotch printer, and of Mary, his wife, living near Beekman's Slip, New York City. While still a boy he came in contact with some Hogarth engravings "which," he says in his diary, "determined my destiny." He was sent to a classical school where he learned to read Latin fluently, but he spent almost as much time in copying engravings with India ink. Having discovered indirectly through a cyclopedia how they were produced, he made his first prints etched on copper plates manufactured from pennies rolled out for him by a friend, his first graver being the sharpened backspring of a pocket-knife. Thus at the age of twelve he began the practice of the engraver's art. It may be said that he was self-taught, his knowledge coming from close observation of the work of others. His first engraving was the head of Paul Jones printed with red oil-paint, but soon acquiring better tools he began cutting small plates which he sold to the newspapers. Anderson's father, not having faith in the profession of engraving as a means of livelihood, determined that his son should study medicine, a thing which the boy reluctantly consented to do. At fourteen he entered the office of Dr. Joseph Young and studied hard for the next four or five years. But he never entirely gave up his favorite pursuit, soon became proficient in cutting initial letters, and before he was eighteen years old was frequently employed by printers and publishers. At nineteen he engraved a commencement ticket for Columbia College and later made the illustrations for more than a hundred volumes of English classics. On type-metal he engraved illustrations for *The Pilgrim's Progress,* for *Tom Thumb's Folio,* for different editions of *Dilworth's Spelling Book* and later on for *Webster's Spelling Book.* Early in 1794 he had the chance to peruse a sketch of Bewick's life and works and to see some of his illustrations of birds and quadrupeds. From this eminent English wood-engraver Anderson received a new revelation which he at once put to use. His first attempt on wood was a tobacco-stamp (1793), but a year later he tried more elaborate work. He had already engraved on type-metal the illustrations for *The Looking Glass of the Mind* (1794); he now set about reproducing them on wood. Thus in 1794, while still under twenty, Anderson became the first engraver on wood in America.

He received a license to practise medicine in 1795 and was offered a position in Dr. Young's office, which he declined in favor of a small private practise. During this year the yellow fever broke out and the young doctor abandoned everything in order to work in Bellevue Hospital. He took his medical degree in 1796, but he eventually gave up medicine, which had become increasingly repugnant to him. In April 1797 he married Ann Van Vleck, a young Moravian. In the same year he became an independent publisher, a step which was a failure. In 1798 he drew and engraved on wood a full-length human skeleton from *Albinus' Anatomy.* During this year the fever broke out again and he lost almost every member of his family, including his wife and infant son. He took a trip to the West Indies, and on returning devoted himself entirely to the practise of his art. Some time after this he married again, a sister of his first wife. In 1800 he made fifty-two cuts for *Emblems of Mortality.* He was called in the draft of the War of 1812 but soon found a substitute and on his return to New York was employed to engrave plates for the small paper money issued in 1814 and 1815. He continued to be a faithful student of Bewick and re-drew and engraved 300 of the latter's illustrations for the first American edition of Bewick's *General History of Quadrupeds* (1804). He also made cuts for Irving and Paulding's *Salmagundi* (1814). Among other of his engravings are those for the American Tract Society. In the London *Art Journal* for September 1858, when he was eighty-four, his own picture appeared engraved by himself in his "best style." For ten years more he was constantly at work, and at ninety-three he cut a picture of the "Hudson County Court House and Jail" for Barber's *Historical Collections of New Jersey* (1868), this being the last work he did for a publisher. In 1868 he moved to Jersey City, where he died. Anderson's engravings all exhibit a most careful execution and attention to detail. He was modest and conscientious and would never consent to receive more than he thought his work was worth. He was also a good miniaturist and in early life was often employed in that capacity. He shrank from publicity but numbered among his friends many prominent men. He belonged to the Academy of Fine Arts, and when the Academy of Design was founded he was immediately made a member.

[Frederic M. Burr, *Life and Works of Alexander Anderson* (1893); Benson J. Lossing, *Memorial of Alexander Anderson* (1872); "Diary of Alexander Anderson" in lib. of Columbia Coll., N.Y.; W. J. Linton, *Hist. of Wood Engraving in America* (1882).] M.F.

ANDERSON, DAVID LAWRENCE (Feb. 4, 1850–Feb. 16, 1911), Methodist missionary, educator, the son of J. H. and Mary Margaret Adams Anderson, was born in Summerhill, S. C., of a family of some local prominence. When ready for higher education he entered in September 1866 Washington College (now Washington and Lee), Va., in the days of the presidency of Gen. Lee. After two years he withdrew and served for a time as a bookkeeper in the office of the *Atlanta Constitution,* of which his father was a founder. This post, however, he soon relinquished in order to devote himself to the ministry. He rose in a few years to a presiding eldership in the North Georgia Conference of Southern Methodism. On Dec. 31, 1879, he married Mary Garland Thomson, of Huntsville, Ala. While in charge of the work in his mountain area he heard the call to foreign service, applied to his Board of Missions, and was appointed to China. His first year there was spent in the Shanghai neighborhood. The next year (1884) he was appointed to Soochow, where he made his home, reared his family, and did his work as a missionary and educator. His application, regard for details, and orderliness indicated at once his administrative capacity. When in 1886 the China Mission Conference of his church was organized he was put in charge of the Soochow district. He succeeded well in this office and bore his full share of the burdens of the Conference. When thoughtful Chinese realized through the disastrous war with Japan their need of new learning, Anderson responded to the unique opportunity by opening an Anglo-Chinese school in 1894. Although the Boxer uprising five years later interrupted the progress of the new venture, the ultimate result was the death of the old educational régime. In the very midst of the uprising, Anderson was planning for the new order. When in 1899 the Mission committed itself to a reorganization of its educational work, it fell to Anderson's lot to found the university of which he and others had dreamed.

Soochow University was formally opened in March 1901 under the presidency of Anderson and with the generous support of the Soochow gentry and the home church. Beginning in the old buildings of the Mission's Buffington Institute, the new establishment acquired new buildings almost immediately and projected literary, theological, and medical departments. For ten years Anderson gave himself heartily to his new work. In February 1908 the school granted its first B.A. degree. The following year there were three graduates in Arts and three in Medicine. By that time some 350 students were enrolled. The University continued to grow, and upon Anderson's death Dr. Allen's Shanghai Anglo-Chinese College was merged with it. Owing to his late coming to China, Anderson never mastered spoken Chinese. He had marked success, however, in understanding the educational problems of the East and in dealing with his students and the Chinese community. Several times he represented the China Mission at General Conferences in America. His last visit to America was in 1910. Upon his return to China in the fall he assumed unusually heavy burdens under which his health broke, and when pneumonia came upon him it took his life.

[*Ann. Reports Board of Missions M. E. Ch., South,* especially for the year 1912; A. P. Parker, "In Memoriam. Dr. D. L. Anderson," in the *Chinese Recorder,* May 1911.]

J. C. A.

ANDERSON, ELIZABETH MILBANK (Dec. 20, 1850–Feb. 22, 1921), philanthropist, was born in New York City, the daughter of Jeremiah and Elizabeth (Lake) Milbank. She grew up under the best cultural and social advantages available to her generation, and in a home atmosphere of benevolence and public spirit. In 1887 she married Abram A. Anderson, the portrait painter. She traveled extensively, crossing the Atlantic some sixty times and visiting Japan in 1918. She owned notable paintings and a fine collection of Chinese porcelains. From her father she inherited (1884) a considerable fortune, and it was greatly increased in her hands by wise management. She had an alert mind, sound business judgment, buoyant spirits, a keen sense of humor, strong likes and dislikes, decided and independent opinions. Loyalty and fearlessness she placed high in the list of virtues. Insincerity roused her scorn. A portrait near the close of her life shows a head daintily and reliantly poised; delicate features under a high crown of soft white hair; eyes that seem to look through surfaces and pretensions with kindly penetration and interest; a mouth half smiling in tolerant sympathy, with perhaps a touch of amusement.

Barnard College owes a great deal to her interest in its critical early period. She became a trustee in 1894, and was vice-chairman of the Board from 1899 until her death. In 1896 she gave the administration building (Milbank Hall); and in 1903, at the cost of $1,000,000, the tract of three blocks which was developed as the Milbank Quadrangle. She provided funds for a dormitory on this site (Brooks Hall); contributed liberally to the general and special funds of the College; and helped many of its students with financial aid and personal friendship. Medical missions in China, negro schools in the South, the tuberculosis research laboratory at Saranac Lake, were other educational projects which received her help. In the field of social work her interest was primarily in applying the results of research to the prevention of poverty and suffering, especially that due to ill health. In 1904 she gave to the New York Association for Improving the

Condition of the Poor a building on East Thirty-eighth Street to be used for public baths, and for many years it served as a model and stimulated the provision of bath houses by the city. Through the same Association she provided hot lunches in over thirty public schools, until the city assumed responsibility for the work. In 1909 she gave land, buildings, and endowment to the value of $1,000,000 to the Children's Aid Society of New York City, for a convalescent home for children at Chappaqua, N. Y. By a promise of $50,000 a year for ten years she made possible the establishment, in 1913, of the Department of Social Welfare of the New York Association for Improving the Condition of the Poor. She indulged freely in what she called "unconventional giving," of which no record remains except in the memories of its beneficiaries. During and after the World War she made generous gifts to France and Belgium, and to the children of Serbia and Central Europe. For her services to France she was decorated with the ribbon of the *Légion d'honneur* in 1918.

As a tribute to her father and mother, Mrs. Anderson founded in 1905 the Memorial Fund Association, to which she transferred securities from time to time, and which she used increasingly as a medium for her benefactions. At her death in 1921 the endowment had reached nearly $8,000,000. By the terms of her will it was increased to about $10,000,000, and the name was changed to the Milbank Memorial Fund. With characteristic far-sightedness she left the directors unhampered by limitations or detailed instructions, specifying only that the income be used to "improve the physical, mental, and moral condition of humanity, and generally to advance charitable and benevolent objects."

[The principal sources of information in print are: *Annual Reports of the Milbank Memorial Fund*, 1922–25, especially the sketch on pages 65–69 in the *Report* for 1922; and an article by John A. Kingsbury in the *Survey* for Mar. 26, 1921, entitled "A New Foundation and its Donor."]

L. B.

ANDERSON, GALUSHA (Mar. 7, 1832–July 20, 1918), Baptist clergyman, college president, was descended from a Scotch family which came to Hingham, Mass., in 1701. Born at Clarendon, N. Y., the seventh child of Seneca and Lucy (Webb) Anderson, he spent his early years on his father's farm at Bergen, Genesee County, N. Y. His mother was a woman of unusual energy and ability, and he inherited many of her characteristics. His father was a deacon in the Baptist church, and was an ardent believer in the abolition of slavery and in total abstinence which were then unpopular and even dangerous causes. Like him, the son was noted throughout his life for his unflinching courage and uncompromising determination. Deciding to enter the Christian ministry, he studied at Alfred Academy, going from there to the University of Rochester, where he received the bachelor's degree in 1854. From 1854 to 1856 he was a student in Rochester Theological Seminary. His first pastorate (1856–58) was in the First Baptist Church of Janesville, Wis., where his ability was immediately evident. In 1858 he was called to the pastorate of the Second Baptist Church of St. Louis. This was at the time the largest church in the denomination, west of the Mississippi. His pastorate continued until after the close of the Civil War. He was outspoken in his convictions on the slavery question, and when the war broke out devoted himself with unsparing vigor to the task of helping to keep Missouri in the Union. Inevitably he encountered strong opposition. Many influential members of his church repudiated him. For a time his life was in danger. In 1863 his health broke under the strain; but after a vacation spent in Europe, he returned to his post. His influence in Missouri at this critical period was very great. The story is told vividly in his *A Border City during the Civil War*.

In 1866 he was called to Newton Theological Institution as professor of sacred rhetoric, church polity, and pastoral duties. After seven years of teaching, he returned to the pastorate, serving the Strong Place Baptist Church, Brooklyn, N. Y., 1873–76, and the influential Second Baptist Church of Chicago, 1876–78. In 1878 he was elected president of the old University of Chicago. The institution was hopelessly in debt, and he heroically undertook the task of placing it on its feet. He succeeded in paying off the floating indebtedness, but was unable to meet the mortgage obligations and was compelled to see the University close its doors in 1885 in spite of his devoted efforts. He took the pastorate of the First Baptist Church of Salem, Mass., in 1885. In 1887 he was elected president of Denison University, Granville, Ohio, where he remained for three years. He was called to the chair of homiletics, church polity, and pastoral duties, in the Baptist Union Theological Seminary at Morgan Park, Ill., in 1890. When this school was taken over as the Divinity School of the new University in 1892, Anderson came with the rest of the faculty and continued his teaching. But he was a convinced conservative in theology and did not sympathize with the prevailing liberal tendencies of the Divinity School. This attitude somewhat restricted his influence. After his retirement in 1904, he lived in Massachusetts, engaged in writing. Anderson was married to Savina Dorr in 1856. In 1860 she and their three sons died within a period of six months. In April 1861, he married Mary Eleanor Roberts, by whom he had five children. His publications include *Notes on Homiletics* (1891); *Ancient Sermons for Modern Times* (1904); *The Story of a Border City during the Civil War* (1908); *Hitherto Untold* (1910); *When Neighbors Were Neighbors* (1911); *Science and Prayer* (1915); *Poems and Biography of Mary Eleanor Anderson* (1917).

[*Who's Who in America,* 1918-19; H. S. Louthan, *Am. Bapt. Pulpit* (1903), p. 710; *The Standard,* Aug. 3, 1918; *Univ. of Chicago Rec.,* N. S., IV, 188; Minutes of the Board of Trustees of the Univ. of Chicago, Sept. 10, 1918; letters from Anderson's son, Frederick L. Anderson of Newton Center, Mass.; conversations with Dr. T. W. Goodspeed, intimately acquainted with Anderson during his work in Chicago; personal recollections of the writer.]

G. B. S.

ANDERSON, GEORGE THOMAS (Mar. 3, 1824–Apr. 4, 1901), Confederate soldier, was a native of Georgia. His parents were Joseph Stewart and Lucy (Cunningham) Anderson. Beyond his service as second-lieutenant Georgia Mounted Volunteers, 1847–48, and captain 1st Cavalry, 1855–58, no events of his life before the Civil War are recorded. At its beginning he was made colonel of the 11th Georgia Regiment, and served throughout the war. He commanded with distinction a brigade in the Seven Days' conflicts in the Peninsula. He continued to see service in the remaining great battles of 1862, Second Manassas, in which he was wounded, Antietam, where he was conspicuous for bravery, and Fredericksburg. He was commissioned brigadier-general on Nov. 1, 1862. In the organization of the Army of Northern Virginia, as of June 1, 1863, he commanded a brigade in Hood's division of Longstreet's corps. He may easily be confused with the more noted Gen. R. H. Anderson of the same army, who commanded a division in the corps of Gen. A. P. Hill (Doubleday, *Chancellorsville and Gettysburg* (1885), Appendix B). Still more easily is he confounded with the Confederate Gen. George B. Anderson (1831–62), also serving in the Peninsula, and also commanding a brigade at Turner's Gap. In the ensuing battle of Gettysburg George T. Anderson was prominent in the struggle for Round Top, and was severely wounded in the attack at Devil's Den. After Gettysburg he went with Gen. Longstreet to join the army near Chattanooga, and participated in the siege of Knoxville. The following year (1864) he was again in Lee's army, and was present in all the great struggles, Wilderness, Spottsylvania, Cold Harbor, down to the surrender at Appomattox. In later years he held a number of offices in the South, among others that of chief of police of Atlanta, and died in Anniston, Ala.

[*Confed. Veteran* (1901), p. 418; *Confed. Mil. Hist.* (1899), VI, 391–93; M. J. Wright, *Gen. Officers of the Confed. Army* (1911); J. B. Young, *Battle of Gettysburg* (1913).]

E. K. A.

ANDERSON, HENRY TOMPKINS (Jan. 27, 1812–Sept. 19, 1872), clergyman, scholar, translator of the New Testament, from his earliest years had little interest in anything but the study of the Bible. A minister of the Disciples of Christ, he was for comparatively short periods pastor of churches in Hopkinsville, Ky., Louisville, and Washington, D. C., but it was for his exposition of the Scriptures that he was commended as a preacher, while for parish details he had no great relish. He taught in several schools in Kentucky, because his extensive knowledge of the classics created a demand for his services, and more particularly because he needed money to support a rather large family, but he found teaching irksome. "The Lord made man upright," he wrote a friend, "but he hath 'sought out many inventions,' boarding schools being one of them." Even more important offices did not appeal to him. "The presidency of a college in Iowa has been offered me," he states, "and my wife is inclined to that region. The presidency of a college presents no pleasing anticipation to me. I have no desire to accept." The state in which he felt he could be content he thus describes: "Give me a few acres with good garden, a small forest and lasting spring. I would go to my little place in the country, read Hebrew and Greek, translate, write notes and essays, and beautify the little thirty-acre plot with trees, flowers, and shrubbery, and whatsoever is pleasant to the eyes and good for food." (Marshall Wingfield, *A History of Caroline County, Va.,* 1924). The visible fruits of thirty years of Bible study, carried on, not under these ideal conditions, but in spite of many distractions, was his *New Testament, translated from the original Greek,* and published in 1864.

He was born in Caroline County, Va., where his ancestors had been extensive land owners since the days of Richard Anderson, who came there from England in 1635. His father was John Burbage Anderson. His mother, Martha Tompkins, a woman of unusual attainments, gave him his education in Latin and Greek. At the age of twenty-one he was ordained by his brother, Dr. Benjamin Anderson, a physician, and elder in the Church of the Disciples. While pastor at Hopkinsville, he met and married Henriette Ducker. It was not until 1861, when the war had closed the schools, that he had opportunity to begin his long-anticipated translation. The war also swept away what little property he had, but he was a man of childlike simplicity and implicit faith in the providence of God. Believing that his wants would be supplied, he went on with the work, and he was not disappointed. "The Lord raised me up friends," he said in 1863. "Some from a distance sent me a few dollars. Two worthy sisters paid one hundred and twenty dollars each last year. Those near me have, some of them, remembered my wants, and generously supplied me with food and clothing" (W. T. Moore, *Living Pulpit of the Christian Church,* p. 70.) His translation was completed about the time of Tischendorf's discovery of the *Codex Sinaiticus,* and he at once began a translation of the Sinaitic manuscript, which he barely finished before his death. It was published in 1918. He died in comparative poverty in Washington, where he had secured a position in the Land Office. The *Christian Standard,* Sept. 28, 1872, contains an appeal for contributions to save his family from want.

His translation of the New Testament is dedicated "to all lovers of the truth," and was intended to open and illuminate the Scriptures for the masses. To this end the translator endeavored to express the thought of the original in "the English language as now spoken." Some of the stateliness and beauty of the common version is sacrificed, but the work is done with restraint and good taste, and has dignity as well as clarity.

[Practically the only available sources of information are those mentioned above. Both the *Hist. of Caroline County* and the *Living Pulpit* contain portrs.]

H. E. S.

ANDERSON, JAMES PATTON (Feb. 12, 1822–Sept. 1, 1872), Confederate soldier, was born in Franklin County, Tenn. He studied and practised medicine in Hernando County, Miss. There during the Mexican War he raised the first battalion of Mississippi Rifles, which he commanded as lieutenant-colonel. As it was raised after the capture of the City of Mexico it was employed only in garrison duty, probably at Tampico. After the war Anderson seems to have taken up the profession of politics. In 1850 he was elected a member of the Mississippi legislature; in 1853 President Pierce appointed him United States marshal for the territory of Washington; in 1855 he was elected its first territorial delegate to Congress. Apparently he was not much interested, however, in the development of the new territory, for the outbreak of the Civil War found him in Florida, where he was a member of the state convention and where he promptly raised a company of volunteers which was later absorbed by the 1st Florida Regiment, of which he became colonel. His regiment served at Pensacola under Bragg and there in the autumn of 1861 it took part in the night attack on the encampment of the Wilson Zouaves of New York. On Feb. 10, 1862, he was commissioned brigadier-general and soon after he accompanied Bragg to Corinth, Miss., where he was assigned a brigade in Bragg's division. After the battle of Shiloh, Bragg said of him: "Brigadier General Patton Anderson was among the foremost where the fighting was hardest, and never failed to overcome whatever resistance was opposed to him. With a brigade composed almost entirely of raw troops his personal gallantry and soldierly bearing supplied the place of instruction and discipline" (*Confederate Military History,* XI, 196). Although but a brigade commander, Anderson was assigned to the command of a division in Bragg's invasion of Kentucky and as division commander took part in the battle of Perryville. In the battle of Murfreesboro or Stone River he commanded Walthall's brigade of Wither's division which distinguished itself by a desperate charge and the capture of Union artillery on the first day and by covering the retreat of Breckinridge's corps on the last day. Of the latter event Bragg says in his report: "Brig. Gen. J. Patton Anderson for the coolness, judgment, and courage with which he interposed his brigade between our retreating forces and the enemy, largely superior to him, . . . and saved our artillery, is justly entitled to special mention" (*Official Records,* ser. I, vol. XXIX, p. 670). During the battle of Chickamauga, Anderson was for some time in command of Hindman's division, and after the battle, in which Hindman was wounded, he commanded it in the battle of Chattanooga, where it was engaged in the defense of Missionary Ridge. On Feb. 17, 1864, he received the commission of major-general, which he had well earned. About this time a Union column landed at Jacksonville, Fla., in order to recapture that state, and Anderson was directed to assume command of the district of Florida and direct its defense. After Hood's unsuccessful attacks on Sherman in front of Atlanta, July 21 and 22, 1864, Bragg, then chief of staff of the Confederate armies, sent the following telegram from Columbus, Ga., to the Confederate adjutant-general: "After learning the result of yesterday's operations at Atlanta, I have ordered Maj. Gen. Patton Anderson to report to Gen. Hood. It is important he should go immediately." On rejoining the army Anderson was assigned to the command of Hindman's division in Gen. Stephen D. Lee's corps and was in the engagements of Ezra Church and Utoy Creek. In the battle of Jonesboro he was badly wounded and forced to give up active service. Against the advice of his surgeon, when Johnston's army was in North Carolina he rejoined it and was assigned to the command of Taliaferro's division. He was with the army when it surrendered at Greensboro, N. C.

Anderson's career indicates a versatile and adventurous character. In battle he exposed himself recklessly and was in the thick of the fight; for this reason men followed him willingly, even when he was only in temporary command, as was frequently the case. That he was at times a strict disciplinarian is indicated by his prompt execution of a deserter. Gen. Bragg, who was noted for making enemies rather than friends, manifested his esteem for him in many ways. After the war Anderson settled in Memphis, where he conducted a paper devoted to agriculture and was collector of state taxes for Shelby County.

(*Official Records,* see Index; *Confed. Mil. Hist.*(1899), XI, 15, 32, 82, 195–97; *Biog. Cong. Dir.*, 1913; *Mexican War Veterans* (1887), compiled by W. H. Robarts.]

G. J. F.

ANDERSON, JOHN ALEXANDER (June 26, 1834–May 18, 1892), Presbyterian clergyman, college president, congressman, was descended from two generations of clergymen. His father, the Rev. William C. Anderson, son of the Rev. John Anderson, married the daughter of Col. John Alexander, a soldier of the Revolutionary War. John Alexander Anderson, born in Washington County, Pa., was educated at Miami University, Oxford, Ohio, where he graduated in 1853. While in college, Benjamin Harrison, afterward President of the United States, was his room-mate Anderson studied theology, and began his pastoral work in Stockton, Cal., in 1857, where he had opportunity for experimental work in a frontier community. He was associated with the Rev. Thomas Starr King [*q.v.*] in the reform of the charitable institutions of the state, and in 1860 was appointed a trustee of the Insane Asylum. At the call of President Lincoln for volunteers, in 1862, he entered military service as chaplain of the 3rd California Infantry and accompanied Gen. Connor on his expedition to Salt Lake City. Through the influence of King, he was made California representative on the United States Sanitary Commission. Subsequently he was transferred to the central office of the Commission at New York, where he was assigned to the duty of relief agent in the 12th army corps. In 1864, when Grant entered upon his Wilderness campaign as an approach to Richmond, Anderson was given the important position of superintendent of transportation. At the close of the campaign, he served for a time as assistant superintendent of the Canvas and Supply Department at Philadelphia. Here he edited a paper called the *Sanitary Bulletin.* Subsequently he was transferred to the History Bureau at Washington, where he remained one year gathering statistics and writing the history of the sanitary work. For the next two years he was statistician for a Citizens' Reform Association movement in Pennsylvania. In 1868, deciding to return to the ministry, Anderson accepted a call to the First Presbyterian Church at Junction City, Kan. While his ministerial work was a success, his inquisitive, alert mind sought a wider range of usefulness. Apparently he could not keep out of public affairs. In 1873 he was appointed president of the Kansas State Agricultural College, a position which he held for five years. In this position he made his greatest contribution as a citizen of Kansas. The school had as a foundation the Blue Mound College, which after the manner of the small college of the day was a weak attempt at a school of liberal arts. Anderson worked a complete reform, laying a foundation for the industrial and mechanical arts, including agriculture, thus fulfilling the purpose of the federal land grant of 1862. In 1878 he was elected to Congress, a position which he filled for six successive terms, retiring Mar. 4, 1891. In Congress, Anderson served his state and nation with conscientious vigor. He was interested in the railroad land grants, and succeeded in getting measures for their regulation including the taxation of a large amount of land that had hitherto escaped. He favored two-cent letter postage, and is credited with being the author of the bill providing it. But his chief endeavor was to make the Agricultural Department a full federal department with a secretary in the cabinet. In 1891 he was appointed consul-general at Cairo, Egypt. The next year, on the return voyage, he died at Liverpool, England. His wife, Nannie (Foote) Anderson, whom he had married in 1864, had died in 1885.

[Records in the Kan. State Hist. Soc. at Topeka; Geo. W. Martin, "John A. Anderson," in the *Push,* Nov. 1902, repr. in *Trans. Kan. State Hist. Soc.*, VIII; Wm. E. Connelly, *Standard Hist. of Kan.* (1918), III; *Hist. of Kan. State Ag. Coll.* (1909); Hill P. Wilson, *Eminent Men of Kan.* (1901); Frank W. Blackmar, *Kansas* (1912), I.]

F. W. B.

ANDERSON, JOSEPH (Nov. 5, 1757–Apr. 17, 1837), jurist, senator, was born at White Marsh, Philadelphia County, Pa., the second son of William and Elizabeth (Inslee) Anderson. At the age of nineteen, in May 1776, he entered the 3rd New Jersey Regiment, Continental establishment, as ensign. He was commissioned second-lieutenant in July 1776, first-lieutenant in the following November, and captain in October 1777.

At the time of his promotion to captain, he was made regimental paymaster, and remained such until the end of the war, revealing a financial capacity to be later disclosed more fully. He was with Sullivan in his expedition against the Iroquois, was made brevet major, Sept. 30, 1783, and a month later took part in the siege of Yorktown. After the war, he practised law in Delaware until he was appointed by President Washington on Feb. 25, 1791, one of the judges in the territory of the United States south of the Ohio River, which was to become the State of Tennessee. In 1796, while still judge of the territory, he was elected a delegate from Jefferson County to the first constitutional convention of Tennessee. The convention assembled on Jan. 11, 1796, and Anderson played a very important part (*Journal of the Constitutional Convention, passim*). In 1797 he was appointed United States senator from Tennessee, to fill the unexpired term of William Blount, who had been expelled (*Annals of Congress,* 5 Cong., I, 470). This was the beginning of a long period of service in this office ending in the year 1815. During this time he made a reputation as a man of good judgment and fair dealing and was appointed on most of the finance committees and many other important committees. He was made president *pro tempore* of the Senate when Aaron Burr resigned and also on one or two other occasions when the president was absent (T. H. Benton, *Abridgment of the Debates of Congress,* III, 165, 169, 170). He very ably championed the demand of the West in regard to the right of deposit at the mouth of the Mississippi (*Annals of Congress,* 7 Cong., 2 Sess., pp. 208–15). In 1809 he demonstrated his popularity by being reëlected to the Senate over John Sevier, who had been one of Tennessee's most beloved leaders, having held the office of governor for six terms. In 1815 President Madison, in recognition of Anderson's experience and great ability in public finance, appointed him comptroller of the United States Treasury, which office he held until July 1, 1836. As comptroller, his knowledge of law, court procedure, and legal decisions was very valuable. He held this position over two of the stormiest periods of American finance, during the panic of 1819 and the beginning of the panic of 1837 (accounts of his official duties are found in his reports in the *American State Papers,* Class III, Finance, vols. II, V, *passim*). Anderson was married in 1797 at the age of forty to Only Patience Outlaw, aged fifteen, a daughter of Col. Outlaw of Revolutionary fame, and became the father of seven sons. Anderson County, named for him, was created by the General Assembly on Sept. 21, 1801. He was a trustee of Blount College and of Washington College (Tenn.) and was one of the charter members of the Delaware State Society of the Cincinnati.

["Personal Recollections of Captain Enoch Anderson," by H. H. Ballas, *Del. Hist. Soc. Papers,* 1896, vol. XVI; "A History of the Delaware State Society of the Cincinnati," by H. H. Ballas, *Del. Hist. Soc. Papers,* 1895, vol. XV; "The Honorable Joseph Anderson and Some of His Distinguished Relatives and Descendants," by Mrs. Henley in *Am. Hist. Mag.,* July 1898, III, 240–59.]

F. L. O.

ANDERSON, JOSEPH REID (Feb. 6, 1813–Sept. 7, 1892), Confederate soldier, and manufacturer, was the son of William Anderson, son of Robert Anderson, a Scotch-Irishman who landed in Philadelphia in 1756. His mother was Anna (Thomas) Anderson, daughter of a planter of Frederick County, Md. Joseph Reid Anderson was born at his father's home, Walnut Hill, near Fincastle, Botetourt County, Va. On July 1, 1832, he entered West Point, graduated fourth in his class, and on July 1, 1836, was commissioned a second-lieutenant of the 3rd Artillery. The next year he was transferred to the Corps of Engineers, in which he acted as assistant engineer in building Fort Pulaski, Ga. He resigned from the army in September 1837. Upon entering civil life he was for a short time assistant engineer of the State of Virginia. From 1838 to 1841 he was chief engineer of the Valley Turnpike Company, and built the great highway between Staunton and Winchester. He was a member of the Virginia House of Delegates from 1852 to 1855. Meanwhile he was becoming more and more engaged in what was to prove the main activity of his life. As early as March 1841 he was agent of the Tredegar Iron Company at Richmond. In November 1843 he leased the works, and in January 1848 became their owner. Under his management the Tredegar Works developed into one of the leading iron manufactories of the country, building over forty locomotives for various Southern railroads and supplying the United States Government with 1,200 cannon as well as chain cable, shot, shell, boilers, and naval machinery. Upon the outbreak of the Civil War the removal of the Confederate capital to Richmond was largely dictated by the necessity of holding the Tredegar Works, and the same necessity largely governed Confederate military strategy throughout the war.

Upon the election of Lincoln in November 1860, Anderson, who was a Secessionist, initiated agreements with several of the Southern states to supply them with cannon and ammunition. Anxious, however, for field service, he arranged also to enter the Confederate Army, with the understanding that if his personal supervision were needed, he would return to the Tredegar plant. Commissioned brigadier-general on Sept. 3, 1861, he reported to Brigadier-General Gatlin, commanding the Department of North Carolina, for duty in connection with coast-defense, and was assigned to command the district of Cape Fear, with headquarters at Wilmington. On Mar. 15, 1862, he relieved Gatlin in the command of the Department, and nine days later was himself succeeded by Major-General Holmes, who assigned him to command the 3rd brigade. On Apr. 22–23, 1862, as McClellan's Peninsular campaign developed, Anderson's brigade was transferred from North Carolina to Fredericksburg, to oppose McDowell. His line of communications threatened by the arrival on May 24, 1862, of McClellan's right at Mechanicsville, at the end of May he fell back to the Chickahominy under orders from Gen. J. E. Johnston (*Battles and Leaders of the Civil War,* vol. II, pt. I, "The Peninsular Campaign," McClellan, p. 174; "Manassas to Seven Pines," Johnston, p. 211). As a part of Hill's division, Anderson's brigade crossed the Chickahominy, and participated in the battle of Mechanicsville on June 26, and the battle of Gaines's Mill on June 27. The brigade recrossed the Chickahominy on June 29, and on June 30 participated in the battle of Frazier's Farm, being thrown into the action as a last reserve, about dark, and winning the approbation of Gen. Hill. In this engagement Anderson was wounded, and was obliged to relinquish command of the brigade. On July 15, 1862, in accordance with previous agreement, he resigned his commission as brigadier-general, and returned to the Tredegar Works, where he was more needed than in the field.

It is here, rather than in his comparatively limited experience of military activity, that Anderson claims attention, because of the masterly way in which as a business man and manufacturer he grappled with, and solved, the larger and more complicated problems connected with war industry. The Tredegar Works became nothing less than the mainstay of the Confederacy in the matter of munitions. From 1861 to 1863 they constituted practically the sole source of heavy guns; they were the laboratory for Confederate experiment; they formed the nucleus from which sprang the government shops at Richmond and down the coast to Selma, Ala. The activity in production of guns was equaled by the activity in the production of projectiles, gun-carriages, plates for iron-clads, wheels and axles for railroad rolling-stock, furnace machinery for iron-furnaces destroyed by Federal troops, and other products of the foundry and rolling-mill for Confederate munitions factories and navy-yards. The government repeatedly refused Anderson's request that it take over the Works, because it saw that they were being run at the top of their efficiency. In solving the grave problems connected with labor, raw material, food, clothing, transportation, and finance, that had to be met in sustaining this activity, Anderson displayed imperturbable resourcefulness and in the face of all discouragements never suspended operations until April 1865.

Confiscated by the Federal Government at the close of the war, the plant was soon released, and in 1867 the Tredegar company was reorganized with Anderson as president. From 1876 to 1878 the company was in the hands of a receiver, Anderson holding that office, after which he resumed his place at its head, retaining this position until his death. He was successful and enterprising; his advice in state and municipal matters was sought and esteemed. In 1874 he was elected president of the Chamber of Commerce of the city of Richmond, and was reëlected in 1875. He was a member of the Common Council of Richmond. He died on the Isles of Shoals, N. H. In 1837 he had married Sally Archer, daughter of a United States army surgeon; and on her death, Mary Pegram, who, together with five children by his first wife, survived him.

[The historical record of the Tredegar Iron Works and their importance to the Confederacy were definitely established by Dr. Kathleen Bruce in her monograph "Economic Factors in the Manufacture of Confederate Ordnance," *Army Ordnance,* VI, nos. 33, 34. *The Annual Cyc.,* New Series, XVII, 532, contains a brief sketch of Anderson's life. His Civil War service can best be discerned in the *Official Records.* A brief account of the Tredegar Works may be found in J. C. Wise, *The Long Arm of Lee* (1915), I, 50–51.] W. S. G.

ANDERSON, MARTIN BREWER (Feb. 12, 1815–Feb. 22, 1890), college president, was born in Brunswick, Me., where his grandfather, Jacob Anderson, a Revolutionary soldier of Scotch-Irish descent, had cleared a farm. Martin, son of Jacob, fought in the War of 1812. It was a sturdy ancestry of farmers and mechanics that gave its heritage to Martin Brewer Anderson, son of Martin. His mother was Jane Brewer, of the neighboring town of Freeport. She was of English descent, a woman of force and character, deeply religious, and a zealous promoter of temperance. When the boy was three years old, his parents removed to Freeport, and thirteen years later to Bath, where the father was a school-teacher. The son matured rapidly and determined to acquire a good education, although through his father's ill health he was compelled to aid in the support of the family. While employed in a shipyard, he prepared himself for college and saved what he could toward his future expenses. He entered

Waterville (now Colby) College, Me., in 1836, where his natural gifts soon made him a leader. To eke out his living he served as commissary in college commons. At the age of eighteen he had become interested in personal religion, and had joined the Baptist church in Bath. At the end of his college course he went to the Newton Theological Institution in Massachusetts to prepare for the ministry, but after a year returned to Waterville as instructor in Greek, Latin, and mathematics. A winter vacation spent in Washington for his health gave him opportunity to supply the pulpit of a church so satisfactorily that he was invited to remain as pastor; he declined, however, and returned to his college, where he served as professor of rhetoric from 1843 to 1850. On a visit to New York he made the acquaintance of Elizabeth Gilbert, member of a family of social prominence, and in 1848 they were married. Two years later he became editor and proprietor of the *New York Recorder,* a denominational weekly. Through the columns of this paper he discussed with a fearless and trenchant pen the religious issues of the day: foreign missions, Bible translation, educational matters in the State of New York—all to such good purpose that he gained a steadily increasing influence over Baptist thought.

When the University of Rochester was founded in 1853 to supplant Madison University located inconveniently at Hamilton off the main routes of travel, Anderson was called to be its first president. Within ten years under his leadership the growth of the college required a new building, and the president undertook the task of raising funds, including an attempt to secure a state appropriation. The task was uncongenial to one sensitive to rebuffs, but he succeeded in raising the outside amount necessary to obtain a state allowance of $25,000, enabling the theological department of the institution to be separated from the college. After the custom of those days President Anderson taught psychology, metaphysics, and ethics. He was in sympathy with the scientific method, and believed in the historical method of research and criticism, which became a hobby with him. He required in each department of the college the historical development of every subject. Versatile in his learning, acquainted with literature, art, politics, and law, he also lectured on economics in his own institution, and on various subjects to a wider public. He was one of the editors of *Johnson's Cyclopædia,* working faithfully at the tiresome details of the undertaking. During the years of his college activities he still took part in the activities of his religious denomination. For three years he was president of the American Baptist Missionary Union, and for a shorter time of the American Baptist Home Mission Society. His health broke down in 1877, although, by limiting his engagements and taking time to recuperate in Florida, he was able to retain the presidency of the college until 1888. In 1889 he took up his permanent residence at Lake Helen, Florida, where he died in the following year.

[A. C. Kendrick, *Martin B. Anderson*(1895); H. C. Vedder, "Martin B. Anderson: an Appreciation," in the *Baptist Quart. Rev.*, XII, 206–227; James Ricker, *Personal Recollections* (1894), pp. 296–313.]

H. K. R.

ANDERSON, RICHARD CLOUGH (Jan. 12, 1750–Oct. 16, 1826), Revolutionary soldier, the son of Robert and Elizabeth (Clough) Anderson, was of Scottish and Welsh ancestry. He was born in Hanover County, Va., where he received little schooling other than that of the great outdoors. When he was sixteen, much against his father's will, he accepted the patronage of a rich merchant, Patrick Coots, and tried his fortune in the lines of trade. At various times he shipped as supercargo on merchant vessels and was in Boston when the tea was thrown overboard into the harbor. Soon after the outbreak of the Revolution he entered the service as captain of a Hanover County company and three months later was transferred to the same rank in the 5th Virginia Continentals. On the night before the battle of Trenton he crossed the river and alarmed the Hessians, killing a sentry, and has sometimes been held as having come near causing Washington's plans to miscarry. But his reconnaissance was made under orders of a superior and seems in reality to have deceived the British into thinking that the Americans consisted of only a few scouts. Anderson took part also in the battles of Germantown, Brandywine, and Monmouth. In 1778 he was made a major, and the next year he aided in the misdirected attempt to capture Savannah. In an assault, he received a sword-wound through the shoulder, but was not so badly injured as to prevent him from administering to the last wants of Pulaski, who was mortally wounded there. For this kindness the grateful Pole presented him with his sword. After the withdrawal from Savannah, Anderson was stationed at Charleston and was captured when that city fell into the hands of the British. He remained a prisoner for nine months. Upon his release he joined Gen. Morgan and remained with him until Washington ordered him to report to Lafayette in Virginia. Anderson acted as a messenger to bring "Mad Anthony" Wayne to the rescue of Lafayette, who was now being hard-pressed by Cornwallis. When the latter retreated into the Yorktown peninsula and the trap was set for him, Anderson was detailed to the Governor to organize the Virginia militia, and so was not present at the battle of Yorktown. Before the end of the war he was made a lieutenant-colonel.

With the war over, in 1783 Anderson was selected to act as surveyor-general to divide the lands reserved by Virginia in the West for her Continental troops. He now crossed the mountains to Kentucky and settled near Louisville, married Elizabeth Clark, a sister of George Rogers Clark, and built a home which he called "Soldier's Retreat." His first wife having died in 1795, two years later he married Sarah Marshall, a daughter of William Marshall. He was the head of a remarkable family consisting of Richard Clough, Jr. [*q.v.*], Larz, Robert [*q.v.*], William Marshall, John, and Charles. Although without political ambitions, he served in the Kentucky constitutional convention of 1788, was an elector for state officials in 1792, and was a presidential elector the next year. His home became famous for its hospitality; President Monroe, Andrew Jackson, and Simon Kenton were visitors there in 1817.

[E. L. Anderson, *Soldier and Pioneer; A Biog. Sketch of Lt. Col. Richard C. Anderson of the Continental Army* (1879); *Niles' Reg.*, vol. XXXI; *Richmond Enquirer*, Nov. 7, 1826; *National Intelligencer* (Washington, D. C.), Nov. 2, 1826.]

E. M. C.

ANDERSON, RICHARD CLOUGH (Aug. 4, 1788–July 24, 1826), statesman, diplomat, born at Louisville, was the son of Richard Clough Anderson [*q.v.*], a Virginia Revolutionary officer who removed to Jefferson County, Ky., and of Elizabeth (Clark) Anderson, a sister of the renowned frontier fighter, George Rogers Clark. Fortunate in his connections on both sides of his family, Richard was given the best education the frontier afforded and was then sent to William and Mary College in Virginia. Here he was graduated in 1804, and immediately thereafter was prepared for the law by Judge St. George Tucker, Sr. He returned to Louisville and began a private practise, but opportunities in politics for one so well prepared were compelling. He was a member of the state House of Representatives in 1812, 1814, and 1815. Two years later he climbed a rung higher and entered the House of Representatives at Washington where he served two consecutive terms. Here he showed an uncommon ability and polish in debate and in general contact with his colleagues. During his second term he was chairman of the Committee on Public Lands. Throughout his congressional career he took a prominent part in the proceedings of the House. He was in sympathy with the Spanish colonies fighting for their independence and recognition, and he spoke at length in the Missouri Compromise debate, favoring the admission of the state with slavery. On the expiration of his second term, he chose Kentucky politics in preference to national affairs, and, returning to Louisville, was elected to the state House of Representatives in 1821 and 1822, becoming speaker at the latter time and using throughout both terms his influence against the radicalism of the rising New Court heresies. The United States having recognized the independence of the South American republics about this time, President Monroe appointed him minister plenipotentiary to Colombia in 1823. Now for a second time he left Kentucky, and taking with him his wife and children, he sailed for South America. He was received at Bogotá with such enthusiasm and esteem as almost to overwhelm him. Toasts were drunk to him, to Kentucky, and to Henry Clay. In October 1824 he negotiated the first treaty the United States ever made with a South American republic, and in May 1825 this was ratified by the Senate and proclaimed by President Adams. In this year, his wife dying, he returned to Kentucky to place his children in school. In October he again sailed for Colombia, taking with him his brother Robert Anderson [*q.v.*], later to become famous as the defender of Fort Sumter. In the following July he was appointed one of the American delegates to the Panama Congress. On his way to Cartagena, the point of embarkation, he fell ill and died at the small town of Turbaco on July 24, 1826. Anderson was a brilliant and courtly man whose promise of greater things thus cut short was likened to that of William Lowndes. He had literary tastes, and had begun a history of Colombia which he did not live to finish. The year after his death Kentucky named a new county in his honor.

[*Niles' Reg.*, Aug. 30, 1823, Mar. 13, 1824; L. and R. H. Collins, *Hist. of Ky.* (1874); *Treaties and Conventions Concluded between the United States of America and other Powers since July 4, 1776* (1871). For Anderson's work in Congress, see *Annals of Congress*, 15th and 16th Congresses.]

E. M. C.

ANDERSON, RICHARD HERON (Oct. 7, 1821–June 26, 1879), Confederate soldier, the son of Dr. William Wallace Anderson and Mary (Mackenzie) Anderson, was born at Statesburg in Sumter County, S. C. His grandfather was Richard Anderson who fought through the Revolutionary War as an officer of the Maryland Line. It was perhaps from this ancestor that he inherited his taste for the military profession. He entered the Military Academy at West Point, July 1, 1838 and graduated four years later. Among his classmates were James Longstreet, Lafayette McLaws, and D. H. Hill, with all of whom he was later closely associated in the Army of Northern Virginia. Upon graduating from the Academy he was assigned to the Dragoons, in which he served until his resignation in March 1861. With the exception of the Mexican War practically his entire service was on the western frontier. As a second-lieutenant of the 2nd Dragoons he took part in Gen. Scott's operations from Vera Cruz to the City of Mexico and received the brevet of first-lieutenant for gallant and meritorious conduct in an engagement with the enemy at San Augustin. In accordance with a resolution of the legislature of the State of South Carolina ten years later he was presented by the Governor with a sword inscribed "South Carolina to Capt. Richard Heron Anderson, a memorial of gallant conduct in service at Vera Cruz, Cherubusco, Molino del Rey, Mexico."

When South Carolina seceded he resigned his commission and became colonel of the 1st South Carolina Regiment of infantry. During the siege of Fort Sumter his regiment supported the artillery, and, when Beauregard went north to command the Army of Virginia, Anderson succeeded to the command of Charleston. On July 19, 1861, he was commissioned brigadier-general in the Confederate army, and in August he was sent to Pensacola as principal assistant to Gen. Bragg. In October he directed the only engagement in that territory—the night attack on the encampment of the Wilson Zouaves of New York near Fort Pickens. The more important operations in Virginia and Tennessee caused the withdrawal of the Confederate forces from Pensacola early in 1862, and Anderson was sent to Virginia to command a brigade in the division of his classmate Longstreet. In the Confederate retreat from Yorktown he was assigned four brigades and directed to halt the advance of the Union troops at Williamsburg to allow the withdrawal of the army; this he did so successfully as to receive commendation from Longstreet. Of the battle of Seven Pines in front of Richmond in which Longstreet commanded his own division and that of D. H. Hill, the former says: "The attack of the two brigades under Gen. R. H. Anderson . . . was made with such spirit and regularity as to have driven back the most determined foe. This decided the day in our favor" (*Official Records,* ser. I, vol. XI, pt. I, p. 940). In his report of the Seven Days' fighting in front of Richmond Longstreet says: "There was more individual gallantry displayed upon this field than any I have ever seen. Conspicuous among those gallant officers... Brig. Gen. R. H. Anderson" (*Ibid.,* pt. II, p. 758). On July 14, 1862 Anderson was commissioned major-general and placed in command of the division formerly commanded by Huger.

When McClellan's army withdrew from the Peninsula and Longstreet followed Jackson northward to operate against Pope, Anderson's division was left to cover Richmond until Lee was assured that McClellan would not return. Anderson was then directed to join the army and reached it just in time to take part under Longstreet in the last day's operations of the second battle of Bull Run or Manassas in which the Union army was driven from the field. When the Confederate army crossed the Potomac and reached Frederick, the divisions of McLaws and Anderson were detached by Longstreet to invest Harper's Ferry on the north and assist Jackson in capturing its garrison. In these operations it became necessary for Anderson's division to check the advance of the Union columns through Crampton's Gap until the surrender of Harper's Ferry. This it did successfully with the aid of some of McLaws's brigades. After the fall of Harper's Ferry, McLaws and Anderson crossed the river at that point and moved up the south bank of the Potomac, reaching Sharpsburg, after a long march, on the morning of the battle of Antietam. Here Anderson's division reinforced the division of D. H. Hill at the "Bloody Lane," but Anderson himself took little part in the battle, as he was wounded immediately after his arrival. Before the battle of Fredericksburg he had resumed command, but as he occupied the extreme left of the Confederate line his division was not attacked. During the battle of Chancellorsville in the spring of 1863, Longstreet being in southern Virginia with two of his four divisions, those of McLaws and Anderson remained under the direct command of Lee. With these two divisions Lee held the left of the Union army in check while Jackson made his famous march to attack its extreme right. Anderson and McLaws took part in the final operations of the day and assisted in winning the battle. While the Union army was intrenching its position on the south bank of the Rappahannock, Anderson and McLaws went to the assistance of Early who was being attacked by the 6th corps which crossed the river below Fredericksburg. The combined counter-attack forced this corps to recross the river. Of his conduct in this battle Lee says: "Maj. Gen. R. H. Anderson was also distinguished for the promptness, courage, and skill with which he and his division executed every order" (*Ibid.,* vol. XXV, pt. I, p. 803).

After the battle of Chancellorsville, in which Jackson was mortally wounded, Lee decided to reorganize his army into three corps, and in his letter to President Davis recommended Ewell and A. P. Hill to be the new corps commanders. In this same letter he said: "R. H. Anderson and J. G. Hood are also capital officers. They are improving too and will make good corps commanders if necessary" (*Ibid.,* p. 811). In the reorganization of the army Anderson's division was detached from Longstreet's corps and assigned to that of A. P. Hill. This was probably because Lee considered Hood, Anderson, and Early his best division commanders and desired one in each corps. In the battle of Gettysburg, Hill's corps was the first to reach the field, but as Anderson's division formed the rear of his column it was employed only as a reserve in the first day's fighting. On the second, however, it was to engage with Longstreet's two divisions in the great advance of the Confederate right wing. For this purpose it was moved forward in the morning to Seminary Ridge and drove back the regiments of the 3rd Union corps which had been sent forward to the ridge later occupied by Longstreet. This enabled Longstreet to bring up and deploy his troops before his presence was discovered by any of the Union commanders. About noon Anderson was in position ready to attack, but was obliged to wait several hours for Longstreet to get into position. When Longstreet made his attack four brigades of Anderson's division formed his left. Anderson's attack was made over practically the same ground covered by Pickett's on the following day, but in front of him were two Union lines—Humphreys's division of the 3rd corps reinforced by two regiments of the 2nd corps along the Emmitsburg Road, and in their rear on Cemetery Ridge two divisions of the 2nd corps. Notwithstanding the obstinate defense of Humphreys's division, one of Anderson's brigades actually reached the batteries on Cemetery Ridge, but being nearly surrounded was soon compelled to retreat. On the third day Anderson's brigades supported the attack of the divisions of Pickett and Pettigrew.

In the battle of the Wilderness which opened the campaign of 1864 Longstreet was badly wounded on May 6, and as Hood had been transferred from his corps, Lee selected Anderson to command it until Longstreet was able to return to duty. On the afternoon of May 7 Lee learned that Grant was sending his trains southward and was probably preparing to move his army in that direction. He therefore directed Anderson, whose corps was on the right, to move to Spottsylvania. Gen. Pendleton, who was Lee's chief of artillery, volunteered to go to Anderson and show him the road he was to follow. Pendleton says he learned from Anderson that the movement was ordered to begin at 3 a. m., May 8, but he was ready to move at 11 p. m., May 7. Probably assured that Lee would approve, he started the movement at once and thus secured for Lee the important position of Spottsylvania. In his memoirs Grant says: "It is impossible to say now what would have been the result if Lee's orders had been obeyed as given; but it is certain that we would have been in Spottsylvania and between him and his capital. My belief is that there would have been a race between the armies to see which could reach Richmond first, and the Army of the Potomac would have had the shorter line" (*Memoirs,* II, 212). Under Anderson, Longstreet's corps sustained its high reputation at Spottsylvania, Cold Harbor, and in the various battles around Petersburg and Richmond until Longstreet returned to duty in October. In accordance with his duties Anderson was commissioned with the temporary rank of lieutenant-general, May 31, 1864.

After Longstreet's return, Anderson took over the command of the divisions of Hoke and Bushrod Johnson which had been under Beauregard, but as Hoke's division was soon sent to North Carolina his command was reduced to a single division occasionally reinforced by a division from one of the other corps. When the final retreat began on the night of Apr. 2, 1865, Anderson was on the extreme right of the Confederate army in command of the divisions of Pickett and Johnson and Fitz Lee's cavalry. On Apr. 5 the Confederate army was concentrated at Amelia Court House and on the afternoon of that day began its further retreat; the corps of Longstreet and Hill, under Longstreet, with the cavalry, formed the van, followed by Anderson, Ewell, and Gordon. The trains were to follow a road to the north. That same night the 2nd, 5th, and 6th corps of the Army of the Potomac with Sheridan's cavalry were at Jetersville, seven miles west of Amelia Court House and only half that distance from the Confederate line of retreat, with orders to move on Amelia Court House in the morning. By a night march Longstreet's command reached Rice Station, twelve miles west of Jetersville, without meeting any opposition. Anderson, who was following, was not so fortunate. Being discovered on the morning of Apr. 6, and attacked by Sheridan's cavalry, he halted his command to beat off the attack and protect the trains passing in his rear. Since no such delay had been contemplated by Lee, a gap was opened between the corps of Longstreet and Anderson which enabled Sheridan with the greater part of his corps to cut across the line of retreat. When the trains had passed and Gordon's corps had come up and followed the trains, Anderson, followed by Ewell, proceeded on his way and crossed Sailors' Creek. Here in the afternoon Anderson and Ewell were attacked in front and flank by Sheridan and in rear by the 6th corps. As the Confederates were greatly outnumbered and had no artillery the issue was not long in doubt. Ewell was obliged to surrender with his entire command; Anderson's two divisions were badly shattered, but about two-thirds of his men managed to reach Longstreet. At Farmville the Confederate army was reorganized and Anderson's troops were assigned to Longstreet and Gordon; therefore his name does not appear on the rolls of the Army of Virginia, which surrendered two days later.

As a brigade and division commander Anderson showed marked ability, as Generals Lee and Longstreet both testified in their reports. As a corps commander Lee apparently ranked him below his other corps commanders, since he entrusted the defense of Petersburg mainly to A. P. Hill and sent Early to exercise independent command in the Shenandoah Valley. As a military leader Anderson lacked both the magnetism and the striking personality which win the loyalty of officers and men, and he failed to cultivate this loyalty, as did Longstreet, by reports of engagements and battles in which attention was called to the gallantry and achievements of organizations and individuals entitled to special mention. The only report of Longstreet's corps while under his orders is a colorless diary of its operations, but possibly he was too modest to claim credit for the deeds of a corps whose division and brigade commanders had been trained by Longstreet and whose high esprit de corps was due to him.

After the war Anderson was employed by the South Carolina Railroad until appointed state inspector of phosphates, which position he retained until his death, June 26, 1879. In 1850 he married Sarah Gibson, daughter of John B. Gibson, chief justice of Pennsylvania, and by her he had two children; she died in 1872 and in 1874 he married Martha Mellette, who survived him.

[Cornelius I. Walker, *Life of R. H. Anderson* (1917); *Battles and Leaders of the Civil War;* G. W. Cullum, *Biog. Reg.*]

G. J. F.

ANDERSON, ROBERT (June 14, 1805–Oct. 26, 1871), Union soldier, was the son of Richard Clough Anderson, Sr. [*q.v.*] and Sarah (Marshall) Anderson, and half-brother of Richard Clough Anderson, Jr. [*q.v.*]. His father, a lieutenant-colonel in the Continental Army, removed from Virginia to Kentucky after the Revolution and Robert Anderson was born near Louisville. He graduated at West Point in 1825 and was commissioned in the 3rd Artillery. After a few months as private secretary to his brother, who was minister to Colombia, he served at various stations on artillery or ordnance duty; took part in the Black Hawk and Florida wars, receiving a brevet for gallantry in action; and was for three years assistant adjutant-general of the Eastern Department. He served as a captain under Gen. Scott in the campaign of 1847 against the City of Mexico, until wounded at the battle of Molino del Rey. For his conduct here he received another brevet. From then until 1860 he was engaged in routine duties and also served on important boards relating to artillery matters. He translated certain French texts on artillery, which were used in instruction in the army. It was partly through his efforts that the Soldiers' Home was established. He was promoted major in 1857.

When secession became imminent Anderson was sent to take command of the forts in Charleston Harbor, S. C. His selection for the post was due to both military and political considerations. He was an able officer of unquestioned loyalty. He was also a Virginian by ancestry, a Kentuckian by birth, pro-slavery in principles, and was married to a Georgian (Elizabeth, daughter of Gen. D. L. Clinch). It was to be expected, then, that while faithful and efficient in his command, he would likewise be tactful and considerate in his dealing with the local authorities. Of the three forts designed to protect the harbor, but one (Fort Moultrie) was garrisoned. Here Anderson remained for some five weeks, meanwhile urgently calling upon the War Department to reinforce him, and representing that Fort Moultrie by itself could not be held against attack. From his government he received only vague and conflicting instructions, but no assistance in men or munitions. On Dec. 20, South Carolina passed the ordinance of secession. Satisfied that hostile acts were imminent, he proceeded on Dec. 26 to a "dramatic, bold and self-reliant act, one for which the country owes a debt to this upright and excellent commander" (F. E. Chadwick, *Causes of the Civil War,* 1906, p. 211). Making his preparations with such secrecy that his own officers did not suspect his design until its execution was ordered, he spiked the guns at Fort Moultrie and shifted its garrison to Fort Sumter, which, rising from a shoal in the harbor, could not be approached by land.

Personally loyal though he was, Anderson, like many other Union men in those days, believed that separation was inevitable; the most he hoped for was that the seceding states might "at some future time be won back by conciliation and justice" (Crawford, *post,* p. 291). His earnest desire was to keep the peace until his government should be ready to evacuate the posts and turn them over to the seceding states. This is the key both to his boldness in occupying Sumter and to his inaction when the *Star of the West* entered the harbor on Jan. 9, 1861, bearing the reinforcements for which he had pleaded. Sumter was occupied, not as an aggressive movement, but to prevent the outbreak of civil war. "Nothing will be better calculated to prevent bloodshed," wrote Anderson, "than our being found in such an attitude that it would be madness and folly to attack us" (*Official Records,* ser. I, vol. I, p. 75). When the *Star of the West* was fired upon by the South Carolina batteries, she was not supported by fire from Fort Sumter, and turned back. Anderson was not wholly to blame. As he told the governor of South Carolina some days before, he "could get no information or positive orders from Washington," and was left to act upon his "own responsibility alone" (Crawford, p. 111). When confronted on Apr. 11 with a formal demand for the surrender of his post, he showed no hesitation or weakness, but "defended Fort Sumter for thirty-four hours, until the quarters were entirely burned, the main gates destroyed by fire, the gorge walls seriously injured, the magazine surrounded by flames"; and then, accepting the terms offered, marched out "with colors flying and drums beating . . . saluting my flag with fifty guns" (*Official Records,* ser. I, vol. I, p. 12).

He was appointed brigadier-general in the regular army, May 15, 1861, and for a short time commanded in Kentucky, where he helped to save the state for the Union. His health giving way, he was relieved in October 1861. He never completely recovered, and performed little duty between that time and the date of his retirement from active service on Oct. 27, 1863. He was brevetted major-general of volunteers in 1865, and was sent to raise the flag over Fort Sumter on Apr. 14, four years from the date he lowered it. He died at Nice, Oct. 26, 1871. He was an excellent officer, through industry and a high sense of duty, rather than brilliancy; deeply religious; considerate and kindly in his relations with all; a just and popular commander.

[*An Artillery Officer in the Mexican War 1846–47; Letters of Robert Anderson,* with preface by his daughter Eba Anderson Lawton (1911); S. W. Crawford, *Genesis of the Civil War* (1887); *Official Records,* ser. I, vol. I; G. W. Cullum, *Biog. Reg.* (3rd ed., 1891), I, 347–52.]

T.M.S.

ANDERSON, WILLIAM (December 1762–December 1829), soldier, legislator, though distinguished as a citizen of Pennsylvania, was a Virginian by birth. One of his ancestors, William Anderson of Accomac County, was a member of the Virginia House of Burgesses, 1685–88. During the French War, 1756–63, a later William Anderson was fighting for America in the field and appears also as a taxable in Londongrove, Pa., in 1753, a member of the Masonic Lodge at Philadelphia in 1759, and a resident of Londongrove following the war. The available records, including the somewhat uncertain statements of the first United States census, support the contention that our William Anderson, son of this later William, was born in Accomac County, Va., in December 1762, and that a few years afterward the family had settled upon lands which it owned about 200 miles farther north in Chester County, Pa. In Londongrove William passed his youth, but had little time for books. In his fifteenth year he joined the Continental Army, becoming a member of Major-General Lafayette's staff at Brandywine, Sept. 11, 1777, and serving at Germantown, at Valley Forge, and until after the surrender of Cornwallis, Oct. 19, 1781, at Yorktown. Following a short period as colonel in the Pennsylvania militia, Anderson returned to Chester County, where he maintained a residence until his death. In 1785 he was admitted to the Philadelphia bar. In September 1796 he purchased the Columbia House at Chester in which Lafayette's wounds had been dressed when Anderson was on his staff and which the latter had occupied for several years. A short time later he built the Anderson mansion at Fifth and Welsh Sts., which soon became a social center for Chester and Delaware Counties.

His political importance increased when on Aug. 29, 1807, he headed the movement from Delaware County throughout the state to allow districts unrepresented in the legislative caucus to elect delegates having a right to vote therein. Following this political activity he was elected to various local positions and in 1808 to the national House of Representatives, serving in the Eleventh, Twelfth, Thirteenth, and Fifteenth Congresses. His name is associated with no prominent legislation at this time, although the marriage of his daughter Evelina to Commodore David Porter may have aroused the interest in naval affairs shown by his speech of Jan. 25, 1810, upon the Navigation Act. Throughout the War of 1812 he was a Jeffersonian, but his advocacy of Pennsylvania's interests and his friendship for the navy injured his popularity with the Southern wing of his party. His disregard for petty enmities caused disfavor at home but increased his capacity for service at Washington, where strict party lines were being replaced by sectional groupings. He failed of reëlection in 1818, and his later political positions came by appointment. During the Marquis de Lafayette's visit to America in 1824, Anderson, on behalf of various local committees, welcomed him to Pennsylvania, and to Delaware County. He was selected as judge of the Delaware County court in Pennsylvania, Jan. 5, 1826. Upon his resignation of this position in 1829, he was appointed United States Collector of Customs at Chester, where he died a few months later at the age of sixty-seven. The exact date of his death was probably Dec. 15, 1829, although it is also given as Dec. 13, 14, and 16. He was married to Elizabeth Dixon of Virginia, by whom he had two daughters and one son.

[*Annals of Cong.*, vols. XI, XII, XIII, and XV, esp. XI and XIII (1853–55); H. G. Ashmead, *Hist. of Delaware County, Pa.* (1884); J. S. Futhey and Gilbert Cope, *Hist. of Chester County, Pa.* (1881); *Pa. Archives*, ser. V, vols. V and VII; *Pa. Mag. of Hist. and Biog.*, vols. XIII, XXXI, XXXII, and XXXVIII; Pa. contemporary press, esp. the *Aurora*, Sept. 4, 23, 1807, and the *Norristown Herald and Free Press*, Jan. 5, 1830; W. G. Stanard, *Colonial Va. Reg.* (1902); *Heads of Families in Va. 1782, according to Census of 1790* (1908).]

C. H. L—n.

ANDRÉ, LOUIS (May 28, 1631 or 1623–Sept. 19, 1715), Jesuit missionary, Indian linguist, arrived in Canada on June 7, 1669, after having served for nineteen years as a teacher in southern France, where he was born at St. Remy, on the Rhone. His appointment to New France gratified his desire to carry the gospel message to the Indians. Almost at once he was sent to the Northwest, where, on June 14, 1671, he assisted at the ceremony of taking possession of the western country for Louis XIV (*Wisconsin Historical Collections*, 1888, XI, 26–29). André's first mission was to the wandering tribes of Lake Huron; the following year he came to Wisconsin and with Allouez built at the modern De Pere the mission of St. François Xavier. He was assigned to duty among the tribes about Green Bay, and for several years spent all his time preaching and singing in the villages of the Menominee, Potawatomi, Winnebago, and other tribesmen. He carried with him a flute, and taught the Indian children to sing Christian songs to its accompaniment. More than once his cabin was burned in severe winter weather by hostile Indians; he suffered also greatly from gout and was obliged to secure a dog team to draw him over the icy swamps. "Such crosses," he wrote, "are the delight of missionaries." He made use of religious pictures to impress his neophytes, and was more successful with women and children than with chiefs and warriors. With the latter he had many disputes concerning the nature of the devil, and endeavored to substitute the crucifix for their idolatrous emblems. In all he baptized about 500, mostly children, during his ten years of ministration around Green Bay. His letters are those of a garrulous, cheerful, intrepid, and tireless enthusiast, willing to dare and suffer for his beliefs (Thwaites, *Jesuit Relations*, LVI, 129–39; LVII, 265–301; LVIII, 273–89; LX, 201–5).

After one year (1682–83) at Mackinac, André was recalled to Quebec, where he taught in the Jesuit College for several years. He was later (1691–92) a missionary on the lower St. Lawrence above Tadousac, and in 1695 at Seven Islands in the lower river. During all the period after his return from the West he was occupied with linguistic labors and left three manuscripts: "Preceptes, Phrases et Mots de la Langue Algonquine Outaouise pour un Missionaire Nouveau"; "Dictionaire Algonquin"; "Homilies in the Montagnais Language." A small catechism in the native tongue was printed in 1693. He never returned to France, but died at Quebec.

[The best biog. is by Father Arthur Jones in *U. S. Cath. Hist. Mag.* (1890), pp. 26–40. This is abbreviated in James C. Pilling, *Bibliography of Algonquian Languages* (1891), pp. 12–16, with an account of André's linguistic MSS. A brief sketch is in R. G. Thwaites, *Jesuit Relations and Allied Docs.* (1895–1901), LVII, 318; in the same volume is a facsimile of André's Ottawa writings. Brief mention of his work appears in L. P. Kellogg, *French Régime in Wis. and the Northwest* (1925), pp. 162–65, 169–70.]

L. P. K.

ANDREIS, ANDREW JAMES FELIX BARTHOLOMEW DE (Dec. 12, 1778–Oct. 15, 1820), pioneer priest, was the oldest son of Maurice De Andreis, a registrar of deeds in the town of Demonte, near Cuneo in Piedmont. That at the end of his college course, taken partly at home and partly at Cuneo, he, who was endowed intellectually far above the average, sought admittance into a religious congregation devoted to the work of country missions and the training of the clergy, is an early evidence of the desire for obscurity which was one of the outstanding traits of his character. He began his term of novitiate at Mondovi on Nov. 1, 1797, was ordained priest in December 1801, and, after brilliantly completing his theological studies in Alberoni College in the summer of 1802, was appointed professor in that institution. But his state of health necessitating a change to a milder climate, he was, in February 1806, transferred to Monte Citorio, the central house of the congregation in Rome. Here, in addition to his duties as professor of dogmatic theology to his young confrères and to the students of the College of the Propaganda, he conducted missions in the little towns of the neighboring dioceses and to the herdsmen of the Roman Campagna. His reputation as a scholar and a preacher soon reached higher authorities. Pope

Pius VII was quoted as saying, "Keep an eye on this young man: for the likes of him are those who ought to be promoted to bishoprics." This remark alarmed De Andreis and no doubt fanned to new flame the embers never grown cold of former yearnings for the foreign missions. Only in 1815 were his hopes to be fulfilled. In the first days of September the administrator-apostolic of the diocese of Louisiana, the Very Rev. Louis William Valentin Du Bourg arrived in Rome. Happening to hear Father De Andreis address a gathering of men, he sought an interview which ended to the satisfaction of both; De Andreis agreed to follow the American prelate, if his superiors consented. The latter, however, tenaciously resisted Du Bourg's entreaties, until the Pope, to whom the prelate appealed, positively declared it his will that the missionary should go to Louisiana.

On Dec. 15, with three companions, he started by stage for Bordeaux, which he reached, after a fatiguing journey over the Alps, on Jan. 30, 1816. After a long delay, on June 12 the whole company, composed of thirteen persons, boarded the *Ranger,* bound for Baltimore, where she arrived on July 26. Seven weeks the missionaries waited at St. Mary's Seminary; finally, on Sept. 10, they set out by stage on the trying journey to Pittsburgh, whence a flatboat took them to Louisville. At Bishop Flaget's suggestion, they determined to wait at St. Thomas's Seminary, Bardstown, Ky., until Du Bourg's arrival. There for nearly a year De Andreis found congenial employment in teaching theology, meantime pursuing the study of English and doing mission work among the neighboring Catholic congregations. On receiving intelligence of Du Bourg's landing at Annapolis with a numerous company, Flaget and De Andreis set out for Upper Louisiana. De Andreis was left in charge of the parish of St. Genevieve, Mo. Du Bourg arrived at St. Genevieve on Dec. 30, 1817, and, accompanied by De Andreis, whom he had appointed his vicar-general before sailing for France, made, on Jan. 5, 1818, his entry into St. Louis.

De Andreis became the rector of the cathedral, at the same time taking care of the theological training of the clerics who taught in the college established by Bishop Du Bourg, and for a while directing the novitiate of the Congregation inaugurated at the episcopal residence. For nearly three years, despite his very precarious health, he labored untiringly, ever hoping for the day when he could bring the gospel to the Indians of Missouri, whose language meanwhile he learned; until, on Oct. 15, 1820, he died of "putrid bilious" (probably typhoid) fever. Short as had been his sojourn in Missouri, his virtues left there an impression which, as it seemed confirmed by remarkable signs, led the ecclesiastical authorities to take steps toward the public recognition of his holiness which have been sanctioned by Rome, Pope Benedict XV issuing (June 25, 1918) a decree formally introducing his Cause of Beatification.

[The many MSS. left by De Andreis are the main source of information for his life. They consist of letters to his family, his superiors, or members of his Congregation; private notes chiefly of a spiritual nature; a collection of intimate reflections written in America under the title: "Ad quid venisti et cur Europam reliquisti?" and a large MS. of Sermons. These must be supplemented by the letters (for the most part unpublished) of Bishops Du Bourg and Rosati. His biog., written in French mainly from personal recollections by Bishop Rosati, his pupil, friend, and companion to America, was completed and rendered into Italian by G. B. Semeria, but never published until Rev. Francis Burlando, C.M., translated it into Eng. under the title, *Life of the Very Rev. Felix De Andreis, C.M.* (1861). By far the best and most complete work is that compiled by Very Rev. Raffaele Ricciardelli, C.M., *Vita del Servo di Dio Felice De Andreis* (Rome, 1923).]

C. L. S.

ANDREW, JAMES OSGOOD (May 3, 1794–Mar. 2, 1871), bishop of the Methodist Episcopal Church, South, was born in Wilkes County, Ga. His father, the Rev. John Andrew, was the first native Georgian that ever entered the itinerant ministry of the Methodist Church (1789); but after only three years in the traveling connection he located and became a country school-teacher. His wife, whose maiden name was Mary Cosby, is described as a woman of many domestic virtues, of more than ordinarily strong intellect, fine taste, and deep piety. Their son's educational opportunities were limited to what he could get in country schools and from reading such books as a home of severe poverty made possible. He was converted and joined the church when he was fifteen years of age. Taking up the duties of an assistant "class-leader" soon after, he exhibited, in spite of his youth, such gifts of religious leadership as indicated his fitness for the ministry. With considerable hesitation he took out a license to preach when he was eighteen; during the ensuing months he preached often to negroes, and in the latter part of the same year applied for and obtained admission on trial to the South Carolina Annual Conference of the Methodist Episcopal Church. During his first twenty years in the ministry he served various charges in Georgia and the Carolinas, from the humblest country circuit to the largest city stations. He proved himself efficient both in pulpit and pastoral work and in leadership, so that when the General Conference met in Philadelphia in 1832 and decided to elect two bishops, he was speedily chosen as the first of the two.

It is not often that marriage so seriously affects a man's public career as it did Bishop Andrew's. He was married three times: first, in 1816, to Ann Amelia McFarlane, who was the mother of three daughters and one son, and died in 1842; second, in 1844, to Mrs. Leonora Greenwood, who died in 1854; third, to Mrs. Emily Sims Childers. Through marriage he became a slaveholder. His first wife inherited from her mother a negro boy, who on the death of this wife became the property of the bishop. He at once declared that although the laws of Georgia did not permit owners to free their slaves if they remained in the state, the boy was at liberty to leave the state and locate elsewhere as soon as he chose to do so under conditions which would guarantee that he would be well taken care of. But the bishop became further, and more seriously, involved when he married his second wife, a cultured and estimable woman, who was the owner of slaves inherited from her former husband. Immediately following this marriage he executed legal papers renouncing for himself all personal property rights in the ownership and control of these slaves. But when the General Conference met in New York, in May 1844, so intense was the feeling of the Northern delegates against a bishop's owning slaves, or being the husband of a wife who owned them, that after several days of strenuous debate in the Conference, a resolution was passed by a vote of 110 to 68 to the effect that Andrew should desist from the exercise of his episcopal office until his connection with the ownership of slaves should cease.

From the beginning of the controversy he had expressed a perfect willingness to resign his episcopal office, but the entire body of Southern delegates were a unit in their insistence that he should not do so, declaring in justification of their position that such a surrender to Northern anti-slavery opinion would be disastrous to the church in the South, where a large proportion of the influential ministers and members of all religious denominations were themselves slaveholders. It was in every way desirable, they contended, that the church through its ministry should have free access both to slave-owners and their slaves; this access, it was declared, would be denied to them, or greatly limited, by the owners of the slaves throughout the South if Bishop Andrew should be forced to resign his office under the pressure of Northern abolition and anti-slavery sentiment. The Southern delegates in the main, as their speeches indicated, agreed fully with the delegates from the North in regarding slavery as a social and moral evil that should be abolished, but they took the position that slavery in the Southern section of the Union was not only a moral and religious, but also a political, social, and economic question. An evil of this nature, they held, could be best dealt with by helping to create and develop public sentiment until the growing opposition to slavery would find expression in a nation-wide demand for emancipation. But until that time should come, the Southern leaders contended, the church should adapt itself in the South to existing conditions, and go on with its work in the slaveholding states, preaching alike to slave-owners and their slaves after the manner suggested by Saint Paul in his Epistle to Philemon. In holding these views Bishop Andrew and other Southern leaders in the General Conference were true representatives and exponents of the attitude and sentiment that prevailed among religious people generally in the Southern states.

The result was that a "Plan of Separation" and division of the Church was drawn up and passed by the General Conference, looking to the organization of all the Annual Conferences in the slaveholding states into an independent and self-governing Southern church as soon as it should be determined that this was the desire of the ministers and members of the Methodist Episcopal Church residing in these states. In keeping with this "Plan" representatives from all the Southern Annual Conferences met in a convention in Louisville, Ky., in May 1845, and formed an organization under the name of the Methodist Episcopal Church, South. This convention was presided over in turn by Bishop Joshua Soule and by Bishop Andrew. The first session of the General Conference of the newly organized Methodist Episcopal Church, South, was held (obedient to the action of the Louisville Convention) at Petersburg, Va., in May 1846; when the episcopal credentials of Joshua Soule and James Andrew were duly recognized, and they thus became the first bishops of the Southern Church. Bishop Andrew continued in the active exercise of his office until the meeting of the first General Conference held after the close of the Civil War, in New Orleans in May 1866, when he requested and was granted a superannuated relation, and retired from active work. On a visit to New Orleans in the early spring of 1871 he was prostrated by a sudden attack and died after being removed to the home of his daughter, the wife of the Rev. J. W. Rush, in Mobile, Ala. Bishop Andrew was a frequent contributor to the religious weekly papers of the Church. He published an excellent treatise on *Family Government* (1847). His volume of *Miscellanies* (1855) contains his "Letters of Travel," extending over many years, several addresses on missions, and various other papers, including an extended biographical sketch of his first wife.

[In addition to the condensed but informing sketches found in Matthew Simpson, *Cyc. of Methodism* (1878) and in McClintock and Strong, *Biblical, Theological and Ecclesiastical Cyc.* (1885–87), particular mention should be made of the "Memoir," found in *Gen. Minutes Ann. Conferences M. E. Ch. South,* 1874, pp. 643–44; *Jour. Seventh Gen. Conference M. E. Ch. South,* 1874, p. 576; G. G. Smith, *Life and Letters of Bishop Jas. Osgood Andrew* (1883); Gross Alexander, *Hist. of the M. E. Ch. South* (1894); J. N. Norwood, "The Schism in the M. E. Church, 1844: A Study of Slavery and Ecclesiastical Politics," *Alfred Univ. Studies,* vol. I, 1923.]

W. F. T.

ANDREW, JOHN ALBION (May 31, 1818–Oct. 30, 1867), governor of Massachusetts, was born at Windham, Me., of Massachusetts stock, his earliest ancestor of whom we have record, Robert Andrew, having come as it appears from England, settled in what is now Boxford, and died there a prosperous landowner in 1668. Robert's son, Joseph, moved to Salem, where the main stem of the Andrews continued to live. Jonathan Andrew, the father of the future governor, moved to Windham, Me., in 1807, established a general store, married Nancy Green Pierce, prospered, and became the leading man of the village. On John Andrew's education unusual pains were lavished. His mother, a woman of attainments and force of character, had been a school-teacher and for a time taught the boy herself. Later, when the family was larger, finding the district school inadequate, the parents built a tiny school-house near their own door and here John, his brother, and two sisters were carefully grounded in the rudiments. The next stage, following the custom of the time, was the local academy and in due course the boy attended for a brief time the academies at Portland, North Yarmouth, and Bridgton. Late in 1831, when he was in his fourteenth year, the serious illness of his mother, to whom he was much attached, called him home and he remained there until her death in the early spring of 1832. Soon afterward he returned to his studies, this time at Gorham Academy, where he prepared for college, entering Bowdoin in 1833. As a student he ranked among the lowest in his class. He spent more time in social fellowship than in study and graduated with more competency in argument and public speaking than in any other field. As a boy he had been stirred by the Anti-Slavery movement; he had now become a determined foe of slavery and his conviction on this issue was to shape his political course.

He was not yet twenty when he arrived in Boston in 1837, and entered the law office of Fuller & Washburn as a student, and he was still very youthful in appearance in 1840 when he was admitted to the bar. His progress in the profession was gradual, partly because he was of a slow-maturing type, partly because of his incurably sociable temperament which was always leading him away from the paths of legal preferment. He was active in the Unitarian Church and assistant editor of the church paper, secretary for many years of the Boston Port Society, and one of the most devoted visitors to the prisons, where he was to be found every Sunday afternoon and whence he derived more law cases than fees. It was said of him at this period, "No one who had a 'hard case,' with no money to pay for legal assistance, was ever turned away from his office for that reason; and no one however guilty was denied whatever assistance his case was fairly entitled to receive" (Chandler, p. 79). His father, with his younger son and two daughters, had removed from Maine to Massachusetts and settled at Boxford not far from Boston so as to be near the elder son. There the family hearth continued and the family life was maintained, Andrew returning constantly to recount his experiences in the city and to renew his strength in the atmosphere of love and admiration. So a decade passed while he established relations, made friends, set the foundations for the career which lay hidden before him. In 1847 he became engaged to Eliza Jones Hersey and in 1848 was married.

During all this time, Andrew's interest in the Anti-Slavery movement never wavered. His association with the members of James Freeman Clarke's church and other reforming and aspiring groups had deepened the religious and humanitarian side of his nature. When the slavery question again became a burning issue he took a leading part in its discussion. Though he rejected the extreme positions of Garrison and Wendell Phillips, he maintained the firm and uncompromising opposition to slavery which represented the best spirit of Massachusetts. He took part with Bowditch, Howe, Sumner, Theodore Parker, Charles Francis Adams, and others in the fugitive slave case of the brig *Ottoman* in the summer of 1846 and read the resolutions at the Faneuil Hall meeting where John Quincy Adams, then in his eightieth year, presided. From this time on he was drawn into closer relations with Sumner and Howe and the Young Whigs. Politics, which had always fascinated him, now took a larger part of his thought. The campaign of 1848 stirred him deeply. He was one of the organizers of the Free-Soil party with its platform "Free Soil, Free Speech, Free Labor, and Free Men," and he gave himself whole-heartedly to the campaign. With the Know-Nothing movement which swept over Massachusetts four years later he had little in common, and it was not until the Republican party appeared that he was again able to engage with full conviction. In 1857 he was nominated and elected on the Banks or Republican ticket to the legislature. There in the session of 1858 he won distinction by a speech so brilliant and effective that it made him at once one of the leaders of the party. Though he declined reëlection his place was established and his popularity grew.

John Brown's raid, his capture, trial, and death had an effect that could not have been predicted upon Andrew's career. When the raid failed and Brown was made prisoner, Andrew took a leading part in raising funds for his defense. When sentence had been pronounced, he took part in a public meeting to raise funds for Brown's family and on that occasion used the words, "John Brown himself is right," which aroused a storm of enthusiasm among anti-slavery men everywhere. When at the instance of the Southern senators a committee was set up to investigate the raid, Andrew was cited to appear and testify. His bearing and testimony before the committee, which had the widest publicity, gave lively satisfaction to anti-slavery men, especially to Massachusetts anti-slavery men. The episode made him more popular than before and in consequence he was almost unanimously chosen delegate to the Republican National Convention at Chicago and made chairman of the delegation. He shared in the nomination of Lincoln, went to Springfield to see him, and brought back a lofty but just opinion of the great leader. One honor led to another. It had long been growing evident that Andrew was one to whom his fellow citizens were well disposed. In the month of July, 1860, a well-informed observer described him as "the most popular man in Massachusetts." In the following month occasion offered a proof. Gov. Banks, whose renomination was taken for granted, suddenly declined, five days before the nominating convention. The "machine" had settled upon Henry L. Dawes, a Conservative. But no sooner was it known that Andrew's nomination was a possibility than a legion of friends hastened to his support and he was nominated on the first ballot by a great majority. By an even greater majority—in fact the greatest popular majority in the history of the state up to that time—he was elected governor on the same ticket on which Lincoln became President.

Andrew was now at his utmost vigor of mind and body. Forty-two years of age, strong and sturdy of build, full of energy, capable of great effort and equal to unusual strains of endurance, he was ready for the great labors before him. The crisis was swift in appearance. He had not written his inaugural address before warnings reached him from Adams and Sumner that the government at Washington was in danger. He at once took steps to put the state militia in a position of readiness. Other warnings followed and within a month he had obtained from the legislature an emergency fund of $100,000, with which to arm, equip, and transport the militia if needed for the defense of Washington. Then came the firing on Fort Sumter and Lincoln's call for troops. Andrew so labored that the Massachusetts regiments were ready and went forward before those of any other state. The 6th Massachusetts was the only armed regiment to reach Washington on that critical 19th of April before the city was cut off from the North—as it remained for nearly a week. As the war went on, the Governor came to be more and more the embodiment of the patriotic spirit of the State. His short, rotund, figure, once ridiculed, became beloved. The upper circles of society found him an agreeable guest. The chorus, still remembered in Massachusetts, made to rally the pro-slavery mobs

"Tell John Andrew
Tell John Andrew
Tell John Andrew
John Brown's dead"

would now have brought him votes in any town in the state. There was no longer any question about his reëlection. The state felt that he was enlisted for the war.

In 1862, when the first fine enthusiasm was over, when the tale of deaths and wounds, losses and defeats chilled the spirits and the delay of emancipation discouraged the most ardent, the governors of several northern states united in what has been called the Altoona Conference to urge upon the President the emancipation of the negroes and a more vigorous prosecution of the war. Andrew was a member of the Conference. By a singular coincidence President Lincoln issued his Emancipation Proclamation the day before the Conference met, but the governors went on to Washington, conferred with the President, and doubtless contributed something to that increased vigor which became apparent from then on. With emancipation secured there was one other thing that Andrew had at heart. This was to give the negro the full standing of a man by making him a soldier and admitting him to the army. He urged that the negroes be organized into separate corps and regiments. Nothing that he ever undertook appealed to him more powerfully and when he finally had the consent of the War Department and got his first negro regiment, the 54th, organized he felt it a great achievement. "I stand or fall," he declared, "as a man and a magistrate, with the rise and fall in history of the 54th Massachusetts Regiment." It was a great venture for, without some such test, one may doubt whether the negro would have achieved his citizenship in the United States.

At the election of 1864 Andrew was reëlected governor. The end of the war was now in sight. Andrew, absorbed with the problems which would come with peace, labored to establish the negro in his rights and to provide for coöperation between the North and the South. In his farewell message delivered in January 1866, he advocated a lenient and friendly policy toward the Southern states and reconstruction without retribution. When he retired from office, at the close of 1866, it became apparent that the war had worn him out. His friends had already noted that he had overdrawn his physical resources, and he had been warned to husband his strength. Through the greater part of 1867 he continued, however, to take an active interest in public affairs; he worked for reform in the usury laws and in the divorce law, and took a prominent position in opposing the principle of total prohibition. He resisted several minor attacks of ill health and worked on at his legal business, but finally, on October 29, he was stricken with apoplexy and died on the following day amid the general grief of the city.

[Henry Greenleaf Pearson, *The Life of John A. Andrew* (1904); Peleg W. Chandler, *Memoir of Gov. Andrew* (1880); Albert Gallatin Browne, *Sketch of the Official Life of John A. Andrew* (1868); *A Memorial Volume Containing the Exercises of the Dedication of the Statue of John A. Andrew* (1878); Elias Nason, *Discourse on the Life and Character of the Hon. John Albion Andrew* (1868); Samuel Burnham, "Hon. John Albion Andrew" in *New Eng. Hist. and Geneal. Reg.*, Jan. 1869; Moorfield Storey, *Life of Charles Sumner* (1900), pp. 52, 192, 209, 271, 295.]

W. B. P.

ANDREW, SAMUEL (Jan. 29, 1656–Jan. 24, 1738), Congregational clergyman, one of the founders of Yale College, and from 1707 to 1719 its acting rector, was born in Cambridge, Mass., the son of Samuel and Elizabeth (White) Andrew. He graduated from Harvard in 1675, and later was for some years connected with that college as tutor or fellow. The General Court of Massachusetts, May 24, 1682, ordered that fifty pounds be paid to him and John Cotton for their pains and diligence in carrying on the president's work after the death of Mr. Oakes. On Nov. 18, 1685, he was ordained pastor of the Congregational Church in Milford, Conn. The town made him a grant of land, and his salary was £100 a year, paid in provisions, with twelve pounds for firewood. In 1710 it was raised to £150. In Milford, he married Abigail, daughter of Robert Treat [*q.v.*], from 1689 to 1698 governor of Connecticut. She died Dec. 25, 1727, and a tombstone in the Milford cemetery shows that he married a second Abigail, whose last name is not given.

During his fifty-three years' pastorate at Milford he became one of the most prominent and influential ministers in the Connecticut colony. Preëminently a scholar, he seldom went out of his study, leaving all pastoral work to his deacons. He was noted for singular acuteness of mind, and his counsel was highly valued. He was one of the twelve ministers who, with four laymen, constituted the Saybrook Synod, which met Sept. 9, 1708, and formulated the famous Saybrook Platform. According to President Thomas Clap, "The Design of founding a College in the Colony of Connecticut was first concerted by the Ministers; among which the Rev. Mr. Pierpont of New Haven, Mr. Andrew of Milford, and Mr. Russel of Branford were the most forward and active" (*The Annals or History of Yale College*, 1766, p. 2). He was one of the ministers who met in Russel's parsonage at Branford about the 1st of October, 1701, and founded the college by promising, according to tradition, to give to it a number of books; and was one of its charter trustees. Upon the death of its first rector, Abraham Pierson, in 1707, he was made rector *pro tempore* and continued to act in that capacity until his son-in-law, Timothy Cutler, was elected rector twelve years later. The site of the college had not been finally determined, and Andrew taught the senior class in the parsonage at Milford and supervised the instruction of the other classes, which was carried on by tutors at Saybrook. He was a good teacher, but was somewhat lacking in energy and administrative ability, and displayed little leadership. He served as rector, against his inclination, in order to save the college from being abandoned as a result of controversy among the trustees. The Yale University library contains two manuscripts by him: one a letter to Tutor Samuel Johnson, dated July 23, 1717, printed in F. B. Dexter's *Documentary History of Yale University* (1916), and the other a small volume of his sermons preached in Milford, 1691–92, written in shorthand which has not been deciphered.

[The *Vital Records of Cambridge, Mass. to 1850* (1914), give the date of Andrew's birth as Jan. 29, 1655, in accordance, no doubt, with the old legal and ecclesiastical calendar. In addition to references above, see Ebenezer Baldwin, *Annals of Yale Coll. . . . from its Foundation to the Year 1831* (1831); J. L. Kingsley, "A Sketch of the Hist. of Yale Coll.," *Am. Quart. Reg.*, VIII, 1835–36; E. R. Lambert, *Hist. of the Colony of New Haven* (1838); T. D. Woolsey, *An Hist. Discourse* (1850); John L. Sibley, *Biog. Sketches of Grads. of Harvard Univ.*, II (1881); *Proc. at the Celebration of the 250th Anniv. of the First Ch. of Christ in Milford* (1890); John H. Treat, *The Treat Family* (1893); Edwin Oviatt, *The Beginnings of Yale* (1916).]

H. E. S.

ANDREWS, ALEXANDER BOYD (July 23, 1841–Apr. 17, 1915), railroad promoter, was conspicuous among the men who built up the South in the half-century following the Civil War. For more than a generation he was one of its leading figures in railroad development. Born near Franklinton, N. C., he was the son of William J. Andrews, fourth in line from William Andrews who came to North Carolina from Virginia in 1749, and Virginia (Hawkins) Andrews, a descendant of the Hawkins family famous in Elizabethan England. At seventeen he finished his education at the Henderson Male Academy and immediately took up work in transportation, an uncle giving him a responsible position in the building of a South Carolina railroad. Then came the war, and young Andrews enlisted in the 1st North Carolina Cavalry. He served under the dashing commands of J. E. B. Stuart and Wade Hampton. In 1862 he was made captain. But active service ended in September 1863, when he was almost mortally wounded in an action at Jack's Shop, Va. At the close of the war, penniless and with shattered health, he took up courageously the task of earning a livelihood. Observing that the railroad bridge across the Roanoke River had been destroyed, he entered into a contract to ferry over passengers and freight. His long career as an operator and builder of railroads began two years later. In 1867 he accepted an offer of the position of superintendent of the Raleigh & Gaston Railroad, and a year later he also became superintendent of the Chatham Railroad. His capacity in directing these roads and building extensions was recognized by the Richmond & Danville Railroad Company, and when that expanding system leased the North Carolina Railroad, running between Charlotte and Goldsboro, he was made superintendent of that line. Under the Richmond & Danville his responsibilities steadily increased. While still holding his original position he became successively assistant to the president of the system, third vice-president, and second vice-president. During these years he was also busy with the building of many short lines, controlled by the Richmond & Danville, and was president of many of them. His most noted single achievement was probably the building of an extension of the Western North Carolina Railroad almost to the western state line, opening up the mountainous western section. Against immense physical, financial, and political handicaps he fulfilled a pledge he had made to complete the line if the state should furnish certain convict labor and carry out other promises. When the Richmond & Danville was merged in the Southern Railway in 1894 Andrews became first vice-president of the latter company and held that position until his death. Multifarious as they were, his railroad duties did not engross all his attention. He was interested in other business enterprises and held several official positions, among them that of state commissioner to the Chicago World's Fair. He married, in 1869, Julia Johnston, daughter of Col. William Johnston of Charlotte. His portrait shows him to have been a man of large build, with full face and heavy mustache.

[S. A. Ashe, Sketch in *Biog. Hist. of N. C.* (1905), I, portr.; *Hist. of N. C.* (1919), V; *Confed. Mil. Hist.* (1899), IV, 359; *Cyc. Eminent Men of the Carolinas* (1892), II; *News and Observer* (Raleigh), Apr. 18, 1915.]

O. W.

ANDREWS, CHARLES (May 27, 1827–Oct. 22, 1918), jurist, was born at New York Mills, Whitestown, Oneida County, N. Y., the sixth child of John and Polly (Walker) Andrews. After attending public school and Cazenovia Seminary he studied law at Syracuse, where, on being admitted to the bar in January 1849, he commenced practise. His ability was early recognized and in 1853 he was elected district attorney of Onondaga County, holding the position for three years. He was mayor of Syracuse in 1861, 1862, and 1868. As delegate-at-large to the constitutional convention at Albany, June 4, 1867, he assisted in framing the "judicial article" which reconstituted the court of appeals and was subsequently adopted. He was elected associate judge of the New York court of appeals, May 17, 1870, being appointed chief justice, Nov. 19, 1881. In 1882, as Republican nominee for this position, he suffered defeat in the wave which swept Grover Cleveland and the whole Democratic ticket into office; but on the expiration of his term as associate justice in 1884 he was reëlected on the nomination of both parties. In November 1892, again on a joint nomination, he was elected chief justice. He retired, Dec. 31, 1897, having reached the age limit of seventy years. Admirably equipped for the appellate court, he had become an outstanding figure in the judicial life of the state. To an independent yet tolerant mind was added a thorough knowledge of the principles of equity. Having maintained a close connection with Syracuse throughout his career, he spent his long years of retirement there, dying Oct. 22, 1918, in his ninety-second year. "Judge Andrews was a great judge and a great citizen. . . . He was loved and honored not only by his associates on the bench but by all the people whom he had served so well and he was hailed by them as the First Citizen of Syracuse." (Franklin W. Chase, *Syracuse and its Environs,* II, 52). Travel, fishing, and riding had been his main forms of relaxation, and advancing age did not altogether debar him from the open-air life. Indeed, it is said that when he was ninety years old Mrs. Andrews made him a present of a horse! He had married, May 17, 1855, Marcia, daughter of Judge Shankland, and one of his sons, William Shankland Andrews, became judge of the New York supreme court.

[Alfred Andrews, *Geneal. Hist. of John and Mary Andrews* (1872); Franklin W. Chase, *Syracuse and Its Environs* (1924); D. H. Bruce, *Memorial Hist. of Syracuse* (1891); Charles Z. Lincoln, *Constitutional Hist. of N.Y.* (1906), vol II.] H. W. H. K.

ANDREWS, CHARLES BARTLETT (Nov. 4, 1836–Sept. 12, 1902), jurist, was the son of Almira (Bartlett) Andrews and Rev. Erastus Andrews, pastor of a church in North Sunderland, Mass., and a descendant of William Andrews, one of the earliest settlers of Hartford, Conn. He prepared for college at Franklin Academy, Shelburne Falls, Mass., and taught while studying. He was graduated from Amherst College in 1858, studied law while teaching school in Sherman, Conn., and was admitted to the bar in Fairfield County. He began practise in Kent, Conn. John H. Hubbard, a leader of the bar in Litchfield, was elected to Congress in 1863 and invited the young attorney in Kent to be associated with him in Litchfield and to take charge of his large practise while he was in Washington. Andrews proved deserving of the faith placed in him, advanced rapidly, and himself became a leader of the bar of the county. The April following his removal to Litchfield he argued six cases before the state supreme court. One of these was the famous case of Webster *vs.* Harwinton (32 *Conn.* 131). During the Civil War the town of Harwinton had voted to pay a certain sum to each man drafted from the town. A taxpayer petitioned for an injunction, claiming that the town did not have the power to make such an appropriation. Andrews, arguing for the defendant, claimed that under our government ultimate sovereignty is in the people and that the towns as the simplest organizations had all powers except those which had been expressly granted away. He was defeated but gained a wide reputation because of his remarkably learned and powerful argument. When he had been in Litchfield about five years he was elected to the state Senate and later to the state House of Representatives; in each body he served on its judiciary committee. He was governor of Connecticut from 1879 to 1881. In the latter year he was appointed a judge of the superior court by Gov. Bigelow. Some of the most important cases in the history of the state came before the court while he was a judge. His opinion in the case of State *ex rel.* Morris *vs.* Bulkley (61 *Conn.* 287) is well known. Luzon B. Morris [*q.v.*] had received a majority of twenty-six votes over all other candidates in the election for governor in 1890. On several past occasions a Democratic candidate had received more votes than any other candidate but not a majority over all, and the Republicans in the General Assembly had exercised the constitutional privilege of electing a governor. In 1891 the Senate was controlled by the Democrats and the House by the Republicans, and questions arose over certain votes which had been rejected. A deadlock ensued. Finally, the state's attorney brought an action of *quo warranto* on behalf of Morris against Morgan G. Bulkley [*q.v.*], the Republican governor, who was holding over. Andrews in his opinion stated that a declaration by the General Assembly is the only authentic evidence of the result of the election, and as there was no such declaration in this case, Morris was not governor. He also indicated that the General Assembly had power to go back of the returns and pass upon the validity of the ballots cast. Andrews's last public service was as chairman of the constitutional convention of 1902, to which he was unanimously elected by the people of Litchfield. He was a man of tireless industry, remarkable energy, and extensive knowledge of men as well as books; personally he was genial, a good conversationalist and story-teller. He was twice married: in 1866 to Mary J. Carter of Kent, Conn., who died the following year; and in 1870 to Mrs. Sarah (Wilson) Osborn of Bethlehem, Conn.

[Geo. M. Woodruff, obituary in 75 *Conn.* 729; F. C. Norton, *Governors of Conn.* (1905), p. 301; *Biog. Rec. Alumni of Amherst Coll., 1821–71* (1883), p. 322; N. G. Osborn, *Hist. of Conn. in Monographic Form* (1925), III, 239; D. C. Kilbourn, *Bench and Bar of Litchfield County, Conn.* (1909); *Cat. of the Officers and Grads. of Yale, 1701–1924*, ser. 21, no. 5 (1924).] M. E. M.

ANDREWS, CHAUNCEY HUMMASON (Dec. 2, 1823–Dec. 25, 1893), mine operator, railroad builder, manufacturer, was born in Vienna, Trumbull County, Ohio, the son of Norman Andrews, a native of Connecticut, and of Julia (Hummason) Andrews. Since the schooling provided at that time for the children of New England families settling in Ohio attempted little beyond "the three R's," young Andrews had to content himself with a rudimentary education. In his twenties he explored the coal deposits of the Mahoning Valley, finding much bituminous coal of comparatively low grade. These deposits had not been worked, and needed only improved railroad connection to become profitable. In 1857 Andrews opened a mine which in nine years produced 500,000 tons of coal. He formed a partnership with William J. Hitchcock and opened other mines in the '60's, which were worked at a profit for some years but finally were exhausted. Because of his mining operations Andrews became a railroad builder and did much to develop the transportation facilities of the Mahoning Valley. In 1871 he helped to project and build the Mahoning Coal Railroad, which gave an outlet to Lake Erie, and in 1876 he was one of the promoters and organizers of the Pittsburgh & Lake Erie. Other lines that he helped to develop were the Pittsburgh, Youngstown & Chicago, and the Pittsburgh, Chicago & Toledo, which were later absorbed into trunk systems. He was also president of the Wood Mower & Reaper Manufacturing Company at Youngstown. Foreseeing the decline of the coal industry in that part of eastern Ohio, Andrews and his partner extended their operations to Pennsylvania, opening mines in Mercer County and establishing furnaces and rolling-mills. In 1879 they organized the Imperial Coal Company, which soon attained importance in western Pennsylvania, owning 3,000 acres of coal-bearing land and mining 1,000 tons a day. Andrews was an alert, aggressive pioneer industrialist. Having adopted a plan of campaign, he would leave no stone unturned to secure its success. Those who thought to contest with him a right-of-way for one of his railroad lines were always caught napping. The rails were laid as he wished them to be and they were not removed. Firm decisions, with abounding energy to enforce them, marked his career as an executive. He must also be credited with keen foresight. The city of Youngstown, which was a place of minor importance in 1842, when Andrews and his father became residents of it, grew within his lifetime into a railroad and industrial center for northeastern Ohio, largely because of enterprises that he had initiated or brought to fruition. Within thirty years after his death Youngstown had become a city of 150,000 inhabitants, with huge investments in the steel industry and other manufactures. He interested himself in Republican politics, national and local, and held for a time a controlling interest in one of the Youngstown newspapers. He was a delegate to the National Republican Convention of 1884. On July 1, 1857, he married Louisa Baldwin.

[*Youngstown Telegram*, Dec. 26, 1893; Jos. G. Butler, Jr., *Hist. of Youngstown and the Mahoning Valley, Ohio* (1921), III, 529; *Cleveland Plain Dealer*, Dec. 26, 1893; Alfred Andrews, *Geneal. Hist. of John and Mary Andrews Who Settled in Farmington, Conn., 1640* (1872).]

W. B. S.

ANDREWS, CHRISTOPHER COLUMBUS (Oct. 27, 1829–Sept. 21, 1922), lawyer, author, was descended through Ammi Andrews, one of Arnold's lieutenants in the Quebec campaign of 1775, from Robert Andrews, a Norwich Englishman who settled in Ipswich, Mass., in 1635. Ammi's grandson Luther, a farmer of Hillsboro, N. H., married Nabby Beard, and Christopher was the youngest of their four children (H. F. Andrews, *History of the Andrews Family*, 1890, p. 103). Three terms at Francestown Academy prepared this son for studies in law offices and at Harvard Law School preliminary to his admission to the bar in 1850. Of a restless disposition, he began to practise in Newton, Mass., then moved to Boston, and in 1854 joined the rush of settlers to Kansas. From Fort Leavenworth he wrote letters to Northern newspapers encouraging free-state immigration; and after six months he went to Washington, D. C. His fellow-townsman, President Pierce, appointed him to a clerkship in the Treasury Department in 1855, but the next year Andrews again went West, this time to Minnesota. His letters to the *Boston Post*, vividly describing his journey up the Mississippi in the *Lady Franklin* to St. Paul and by stage-coach to the frontier town of Crow Wing, later appeared in book form (*Minnesota and Dacotah*, 1857). This excursion led to the resignation of his clerkship, and in 1857 he went to Minnesota to practise law in St. Cloud. In the same year he brought out his *Digest of the Opinions of the Attorney Generals of the United States* and in 1858 *A Practical Treatise on the Revenue Laws of the United States*. Law led to politics, and in 1859 he was elected to the state Senate; and the next year, as a Douglas Democrat, he held more than thirty joint political debates with Stephen Miller, later governor. In 1861 he helped to found and for a short time was joint editor of the *St. Cloud Union*, but resigned because of the pro-slavery views of his associate, S. B. Lowry. Upon the outbreak of the Civil War he enlisted as a private, but his energy and ability soon won his promotion. At Murfreesboro in 1862 the colonel of his regiment, the 3rd Minnesota Volunteer Infantry, surrendered to Gen. Forrest over Andrews's vigorous protest. Three months in Southern prisons gave Andrews, now a captain, leisure to read Plutarch and Shakespeare and to write a book of *Hints to Company Officers on Their Military Duties* (1863). His exchange gave him an opportunity to apply his theories in action (*My Experiences in Rebel Prisons*, 1893). He was with the reorganized 3rd Minnesota at Vicksburg; he commanded the regiment in the Arkansas campaign of 1863; as brigadier-general he led a decisive charge at Fitzhugh Woods in 1864; and in the Mobile campaign, now brevetted major-general, he participated in the storming of Fort Blakely.

After the collapse of the Confederacy he was in command of several southern districts, the last of which was that of Houston. He returned to Minnesota in August 1865 and was mustered out on Jan. 15, 1866. A year later he published a comprehensive *History of the Campaign of Mobile;* and he contributed a full account of his own regiment to the two-volume history, *Minnesota in the Civil and Indian Wars,* brought out by the state under his editorship (1890–92).

After his return to St. Cloud, he soon became prominent in state politics. He was a delegate to the Republican convention that nominated Grant in 1868, and in that year was the regular Republican candidate for Congress in the second Minnesota district, but because of a party split lost the election. In 1869 President Grant appointed him minister to Sweden and Norway. He took up his duties at Stockholm in July 1869 and served eight and one-half years. A noteworthy feature of this service was the preparation of a series of more than thirty remarkable reports on conditions in Norway and Sweden that were published in government documents and in many cases reprinted. Among the more important were those on industrial classes, pauperism and poor laws, emigration, public instruction, agriculture, Swedish forest culture, commerce, iron production, and manufactures. A discriminating study of *Life and Manners in Sweden and Norway* (n.d.) was privately published. After his retirement in 1877 he returned to Minnesota; in 1880 he supervised the census in the third Minnesota district; and in the same year he served as editor of the *St. Paul Dispatch.* He was appointed consul-general to Brazil by President Arthur and held this office at Rio de Janeiro from 1882 to 1885, when he was recalled by Cleveland. His book *Brazil, Its Condition and Prospects* (1887) includes a charming narrative of his own experiences. Two other publications of the eighties were a study of *Spring Wheat Culture in the Northwest* (1882), and a political brochure on *Administrative Reform* (1888) in which he advocated the extension of the civil service. In 1890 he edited a coöperative *History of St. Paul, Minn.,* of the commercial type. Andrews was a pioneer in advocating the application of European forestry principles to American conditions, and the latter part of his career was devoted to this field of interest. He was chief warden and forest commissioner of Minnesota from 1895 to 1911 and secretary of the state forestry board from 1911 until his death in 1922. He was influential in the movement for establishing forest reserves in the state; and his sixteen annual reports as warden and commissioner are valuable compendiums of forestry data. Andrews married Mary Frances Baxter of Central City, Colo., in December 1868. He died at his home in St. Paul, after an illness of a few months.

[The Minn. Hist. Soc. possesses a large collection of Andrews Papers, including correspondence and miscellaneous MSS.; it also has a mass of archives from the office of the chief fire warden during Andrews's incumbency. Andrews's autobiography, written in his later years, has recently been published as *Recollections: 1820–1922* (1928). Biog. information in many of the works cited in the foregoing sketch may be supplemented by a *Report of the Mil. Services of C. C. Andrews* (1872); an autobiog. fragment, "In the Early Days," in W. B. Mitchell, *Hist. of Stearns County, Minn.* (1915), ch. 14; "Sketch and Public Record of Christopher C. Andrews" in *Our Representatives Abroad* (1874); an undated leaflet (issued after 1911) under the title *Short Sketch of Gen. C. C. Andrews;* long obituary in *St. Paul Pioneer Press,* Sept. 22, 1922.]

T. C. B.

ANDREWS, EDWARD GAYER (Aug. 7, 1825–Dec. 31, 1907), Methodist bishop, was born in New Hartford, Oneida County, N. Y., the son of George and Polly Andrews, and the fifth in a family of eleven children. His father was a mill superintendent until 1839, when he went to live on a farm he had purchased in Onondaga County. Edward was brought up in a Methodist home, under rigorous discipline. From early childhood he showed more than usual susceptibility to religious influences and joined the church when but ten years old. Encouraged by his parents to get what education he could, he prepared for college at Cazenovia Seminary, and graduated from Wesleyan University, Middletown, Conn., in the class of 1847. Almost immediately he was appointed to supply the Morrisville Circuit in the Oneida Methodist Conference, and in July 1848 was admitted to the Conference, ordained by Bishop Janes, and appointed to Hamilton and Leesville. In 1851 he married Susan Matthews Hotchkiss, daughter of Sherlock Hotchkiss of Cheshire, Conn. After several pastorates his voice failed, and in 1854 he took a position as teacher in Cazenovia Seminary. A few months later he became president of Mansfield Female College, Ohio, but in a year's time returned to Cazenovia to succeed Dr. Henry Bannister as principal. For nine years he managed the institution with great success, and became prominent among the educators of central New York. In 1864 his voice having recovered sufficiently to warrant his return to the pulpit, he became pastor of the Methodist church in Stamford, Conn. From Stamford he went to Brooklyn, N. Y., where he first served at Sands Street Church, then at St. John's, finally at Grace Church, of which he was pastor when, May 24, 1872, he was elected bishop. His first episcopal residence was in Des Moines, Ia. Early in 1876 the Board of Bishops and the Board of Foreign Missions realized that a more perfect form of organization was necessary in the Methodist churches in Europe and India. They also appreciated that to gather into annual conferences independent, scattered congregations and churches, to place over them responsible ministers, and to bring about a recognition of episcopal control without disturbance or friction, was a task requiring the utmost tact and delicacy. They therefore chose Bishop Andrews for this mission and in the performance of it he visited Sweden, Norway, and India. In 1880 he was transferred from Des Moines to Washington, where his advice on public questions was sought by many of the national leaders. From 1888 to 1904, the time of his retirement, his residence was in New York. In 1907, although eighty-two years old, he crossed the continent to attend a meeting of the bishops at Spokane, Wash., but overtaxed his strength and died, in Brooklyn, shortly after his return.

Bishop Andrews was of substantial frame, with a well-chiseled face, high forehead, genial, intelligent eyes, and benign countenance. As a preacher he had a high reputation. Though cautious and conservative, he was open-minded, more tolerant toward modern theological tendencies than many in his church, and liberal in his attitude toward the troublesome question of amusements. During a long and important period in the history of the denomination, he was one of its wisest and most influential leaders.

[Francis J. McConnell, *Edward Gayer Andrews* (1909); *Who's Who in America,* 1906–7, Matthew Simpson, *Cyc. of Methodism* (1878); *Jour. of Gen. Conference,* 1908.]

J. W. J.

ANDREWS, ELISHA BENJAMIN (Jan. 10, 1844–Oct. 30, 1917), college president, was of a New England stock which from the beginning was concerned with education. The first of whom there is record, William Andrews of Hartford, Conn., was engaged at a town-meeting in April 1643, to "teach the children in the Scoole one yere next ensewing from the 25 of March," and was subsequently reëngaged for the same purpose in succeeding years. Later, for a period of eight years, he served as town clerk. The descendants of William Andrews were frequently teachers; sometimes they were ministers; occasionally they held public office. One of them, Israel Andrews, who lived a century later than William, was for a time a seafaring man, and afterward a teacher and a surveyor. Israel had a son Elisha, who before reaching eighteen was a teacher and a surveyor, and at twenty-five a Baptist minister. The Rev. Elisha Andrews gained a considerable reputation for his theological writings and for his acuteness in controversy; he was also known for his love of books, and for his accomplishments, though self-instructed in Greek, Latin, Hebrew, and German. His son Erastus Andrews was also self-instructed, and also became a Baptist minister. He served two terms in the Massachusetts House of Representatives, and one in the Massachusetts Senate. On May 10, 1829, he married Almira Bartlett, a country school-teacher, a daughter of John and Martha Bartlett of West Boylston, Mass., and the youngest of eleven children. The children born to Erastus and Almira Bartlett Andrews also numbered eleven. The second child, Charles Bartlett Andrews [*q.v.*], was successively governor of Connecticut, judge of the superior court, and chief justice of that state. The eighth child was Elisha Benjamin Andrews.

He was born in Hinsdale, N. H., where his father was supplying the pulpit of the Baptist church. In the summer of 1844, when Elisha Benjamin was barely six months old, the Rev. Erastus Andrews returned to his former pulpit in Sunderland, Mass., and took up his residence in Montague, near the Sunderland line. Here Elisha Benjamin spent his early boyhood, and here he received his earliest education in the small schoolhouse, a mile or more away. Often, in winter, when the roads were blocked with snow and ice, Almira Andrews taught the children at home. Ten of them had survived infancy; the record is preserved of the mother's force of mind and character, and of her wisdom and energy in bringing up her large family on the small salary of a country minister. Vigor and independence of thinking are also among the qualities attributed to her. In 1858, the Rev. Erastus Andrews accepted the pastorate of the First Baptist Church on Zion's Hill, in Suffield, Conn., attracted by the educational opportunities for his younger children that Suffield afforded. Shortly after the removal to Zion's Hill, Elisha Benjamin injured his left foot so severely that for a time he was in danger of losing his leg, and over two years passed, marked by much suffering, before he was able to take up his studies in regular course. He was still crippled and still using crutches when, in September 1860, he entered the Connecticut Literary Institute, in Suffield, to prepare for college. His preparatory studies were, however, to suffer a long interruption. In April 1861 the Civil War began. On May 23, Elisha Benjamin, then a boy of seventeen, enlisted as a private in the 4th Connecticut Infantry, shortly afterward reorganized as the 1st Connecticut Heavy Artillery. On the muster rolls his name is given as Benjamin Andrews, the name by which his intimates in later years always knew him.

His regiment is said to have been the earliest

volunteer regiment mustered in for a three years' service. It took part in engagements at Yorktown, Hanover Court House, Gaines's Mill, Chickahominy, Golden Hill, Malvern Hill, and elsewhere. The early months of the war were, for Andrews, the harder because of the condition of his leg, despite which he had been accepted for service. His comrades, witnessing his discomfort and frequent pain, paid warm tribute to his pluck. Nor did they themselves complain when, as the head of a squad, he worked the men hard, for he worked as hard as they, with equal energy, and with equal exposure to the enemy's fire. On Apr. 18, 1862, he was promoted to be a corporal; on Jan. 21, 1863, to be a sergeant; on Sept. 7, 1863, to be a second-lieutenant. In the summer of 1864 he was in the siege of Petersburg, and on the fateful June 30, when the mine laid by the Union forces was exploded, went through the Crater. On Aug. 24, he was seriously wounded. A fellow member of his regiment, Bennett Rowe, came to his assistance and perhaps saved his life. The wound resulted in the loss of his left eye; on Oct. 29, he was discharged from military service, incapacitated.

He immediately enrolled in the Powers Institute in Bernardston, Mass., and studied there a year. The next year was spent at the Wesleyan Academy, in Wilbraham, Mass., from which he was graduated in 1866, the class valedictorian. He had now decided to study theology and to enter the ministry. In September 1866, he registered in Brown University. From the beginning, he was prominent in his class. In his freshman year, he was the class president; in his senior year, he gave the Address to the Undergraduates—a student honor highly prized. Always a ready and witty speaker, he is recalled by one of his hearers as seemingly giving it *extempore*. He was seasoned by war, maturer than many of his mates, and devoted to his studies. He was graduated in 1870, the fourth in his class. On Nov. 25, he married in Newton, Mass., Ella Allen, the daughter of the Rev. Ralph Willard Allen and Mary (Tower) Allen. Before taking up his theological course, he served for two years (1870–72) as principal of the Connecticut Literary Institute, now called the Suffield School. From 1872 to 1874 he studied at the Newton Theological Institution; in the latter years he was ordained, and in the same year became minister of the First Baptist Church, in Beverly, Mass. One of his congregation was the Bennett Rowe who had come to his aid on the battlefield in 1864. After a successful pastorate of one year, Andrews received an unexpected call to the presidency of Denison University, and, on the advice of some of his closest friends, coupled with his own growing conviction that his place was in the field of education, decided to accept the call. Hereafter, he continued in that field. His vocation had found him.

The *Memorial Volume of Denison University* tells that the four years of his administration were "virile and inspiring." In connection with the presidency he held the chair of moral and intellectual philosophy. The innumerable stories of his influence as a teacher and his extraordinary power over men begin with his days at Denison, if not with those earlier at Suffield. Among the teachers at Denison was an instructor in Greek and Latin, William R. Harper [*q.v.*], who had come there with disconcerting youthfulness, for he was only twenty, to be a tutor in the preparatory school, and who shortly afterward became its principal. Ernest De Witt Burton [*q.v.*] was a member—the youngest member—of the class of 1876. John D. Rockefeller was a member of the Board of Trustees. All three were to be closely identified with the University of Chicago; Andrews's friendship with all three was life-long. President Harper, looking back upon his Denison period, recalled Andrews as "his inspired friend," "his exemplar," "his intellectual father." President Burton called Andrews the greatest teacher in his experience.

From 1879 to 1882 Andrews was professor of homiletics and pastoral theology in Newton Theological Institution. In the latter year, during the illness of President Robins of Colby College, he arranged also to conduct the latter's classes in philosophy. In 1881, the death occurred of J. Lewis Diman, professor of history and political economy in Brown University, widely known as a brilliant teacher, and for seventeen years one of the lights of Brown. Andrews, on being invited to succeed him, spent a year of study in Berlin and Munich, and in 1883 entered upon his new work at Brown, retaining his professorship there until 1888. The opportunity was one that gave ample play to his teaching powers, and the man himself was magnetic, brimming with life, and immensely popular. The enthusiastic response to him on the part of the undergraduates doubtless had much to do with his later election to the headship of Brown. Outside of the University there was some opposition, when it was learned that he was a free-trader, and the opposition to some extent became vocal, but the particular economic views that Andrews held proved no very serious obstacle when, after a year as professor of political economy and finance at Cornell (1888–89), he was recalled to Brown to succeed Ezekiel Gilman Robinson as president.

The modern period in the history of Brown

begins with the accession of Andrews. A statistical summary of the achievements of his administration (1889–98) tells of the results, not of the quality, of his leadership, though suggesting something of the exceptional and strong personality in command. An expansion took place with a rapidity that was remarkable. The number of undergraduate men increased from 276 to 641; the number of graduate students, which at the opening of this era was only three, to 117; and the total registration, including the undergraduate students in the Women's College, from 549 to 908. The officers of instruction increased from twenty-two to seventy-three; all the old departments were enlarged, and new departments were created. The Women's College, founded in October 1891, was largely Andrews's creation, and, since, at the beginning, none of the funds of the university were applicable to its purpose, he personally bore the financial responsibility for the undertaking until 1895, when relieved of it by a committee of women. In November 1897 the women's department was accepted by the Corporation and officially designated the Women's College in Brown University.

The change that had come over Brown was, however, not merely quantitative. At bottom it was qualitative, "a spirit and a life, of which the growth in size was only a result. The primary source of this new life was the President" (Walter C. Bronson, *History of Brown University*, 1914). The President kept regular office hours, and was accessible to all members of the college community; he customarily led the daily chapel service; he conducted courses, at first in philosophy, later in "practical ethics." "Bennie," the students called him—the diminutive was the expression of their complete affection. He seemed to know all of them and to be able to call each one by name. None was without a contribution to the rich fund of anecdote that grew up about him, of counsel or admonition imparted, sometimes with racy humor, sometimes with blunt sarcasm, sometimes with a small personal loan. He was in the line of Arnold and Jowett, of Wayland and Nott and Hopkins. For him, the work at Brown accorded with his desires. While in the service of his *alma mater* an offer came to share the presidency of the University of Chicago with Dr. Harper, but the claims of Brown predominated and the offer was declined.

One essential for the work at Brown was, however, lacking. The rapid expansion had continued without the accompanying increase in invested funds that the new situation demanded. In his report for 1891–92, President Andrews called for "a million dollars within a year, and two million more in ten years." But in the years that followed not even the first million was forthcoming. In 1896, Andrews, overworked, and worn with the weight he was carrying, was allowed a year's leave of absence, which he spent abroad. In June 1897, shortly before his return to Providence, the Corporation, at its regular meeting entered into a discussion of the financial affairs of the University, and, in the same connection, into a discussion of the economic views of Dr. Andrews, the opinion being advanced that his stand on the silver question had stood in the way of additions to the endowment fund. The discussion was concluded with the adoption of a resolution appointing a committee "to confer with the President in regard to the interests of the University." President Andrews reached Providence at the end of June. The committee of the Corporation transmitting their statement to Dr. Andrews, in writing at the latter's request, informed him that it "signified a wish for change in only one particular, having reference to his views upon . . . the free coinage of silver. . . . The change hoped for by them is not a renunciation of these views . . . but a forbearance . . . to promulgate them." The statement of the committee is dated July 16. On July 17 Andrews tendered his resignation, believing himself unable to meet the wishes of the Corporation as explained by the committee "without surrendering that reasonable liberty of utterance which my predecessors, my faculty colleagues and myself have hitherto enjoyed, and in the absence of which the most ample endowment for an educational institution would have but little worth."

The resignation of President Andrews precipitated a heated controversy. During it, although much was said about his views on silver, the actual issue, namely, the President's "reasonable liberty of utterance," was forced to its rightful priority. That Andrews had long believed in international bimetallism, there was no question. He had written and made speeches favoring a freer use of silver under international agreement, and he had served as one of the commissioners from the United States to the International Monetary Conference at Brussels in 1892. Prior to 1896, he had argued that any attempt to resume the free coinage of silver by the United States alone would be harmful both for this country and for the cause of bimetallism, but by that year a new element had entered into his thinking, and he had come to believe, largely because of the increased production of gold, that the United States should freely coin silver at a ratio of sixteen to one, and that if the United States were to do this, other nations would follow the example and international bimetallism be thereby secured. But, despite the impression to the contrary then existing, President Andrews had published nothing and made no speech advocating the free coinage of silver by the United States alone. He had done no more than to state his views in a few personal letters, which were printed in the newspapers without his consent, and in one instance without his knowledge.

The actual issue involved in the resignation of Andrews was defined in "An open letter addressed to the Corporation of Brown University by members of the faculty of that institution," dated July 31. This letter, now known to have been from the hand of Prof. J. F. Jameson, was signed by twenty-five members of the faculty, and combated the proposition that official action tending to restrain Dr. Andrews's expressions on public affairs was to be justified, either on the lower ground of pecuniary necessity, since Brown University had only been sharing in the adverse circumstances that had beset the other colleges of New England, or otherwise "when considered from that higher point of view from which the educational institutions of a great country ought always to be regarded," for, as the letter concluded, "we are convinced that the life-blood of a university is not money, but freedom." The Corporation was also petitioned by over 600 alumni, representing classes from 1838 to 1897, asking it to "take that action upon the resignation of President Andrews which will effectually refute the charge that reasonable liberty of utterance was or even is to be, denied to any teacher of Brown University." Another petition, of similar tenor, was presented by forty-four out of the forty-nine women graduates. A general memorial was made to the Corporation, signed by college presidents,—among them President Gilman of Johns Hopkins and President Eliot of Harvard,—college professors, business men, and others, urging "such action on the part of the Corporation as might naturally lead to the withdrawal of the resignation of President Andrews." With these documents, a special memorial of economics was presented, headed with the signature of Prof. Taussig of Harvard and Prof. Seligman of Columbia, setting forth to the Corporation a "brief statement of opinion," as follows: "We hope that no action will be taken by you that could be construed as limiting the freedom of speech in the teaching body of our universities. We believe that no questions should enter except as to capacity, faithfulness, and general efficiency in the performance of appointed duty. To undertake inquiry as to the soundness of opinions expressed on any question, or set of questions, must inevitably limit freedom of expression, tend to destroy intellectual independence and to diminish public respect for the conclusions of all investigators."

At its meeting Sept. 1, the Corporation unanimously adopted an address, five members not voting, affirming that its action in June was occasioned by the fear that the views of the President on the silver question might perhaps in some degree be assumed to be representative and not merely individual, disclaiming any intention to administer any official rebuke, or to restrain the President's freedom of opinion, or "reasonable liberty of utterance," and asking the President to withdraw his resignation. Andrews, by this date, had accepted an offer from the proprietor of the *Cosmopolitan Magazine,* John Brisben Walker, to direct a scheme of educational advancement through directed reading. A release being obtained from Mr. Walker, Andrews withdrew his resignation, writing to the committee of conference that the action of the Corporation "entirely does away with the scruple which led to my resignation."

Andrews remained at Brown one more academic year. On July 15, 1898, he resigned the presidency to accept the position of superintendent of schools in Chicago, soon to become engaged in a fight, from which he emerged the winner, whereby he won from the board of education a decision to vest the superintendent with the power to nominate and promote teachers in the public schools. This decision, said the *Chicago Times-Herald* (Dec. 16, 1898), "is something more than a personal victory for Dr. Andrews. It is a victory for the public schools of Chicago." In 1899 he declined the presidency of the State Agricultural School of Colorado; in 1900 he accepted the chancellorship of the University of Nebraska. Here, during the eight years of his administration, he repeated on a larger scale his successes at Brown. The faculty was doubled in size, and the appropriations nearly trebled; new buildings were added; a school of medicine, a teachers' college, and a law department were established; the agricultural department was notably expanded, and the state farm re-created. Behind all these was the chancellor's vigorous personality. For several years he gave a course in practical ethics, to which the students thronged. Sometimes he addressed the students in a body. He could rejoice with them over an athletic victory, or he could, if need be, give them forthright counsel. "You should go home," he told them on one occasion, "and enter your closets, and shut the door; and kneeling down you should ask God in his great mercy to vouchsafe to you one original idea." For Andrews, "intellectual vigor and moral integrity were the indispensable beginnings of all worthy education" (William F. Dann of the University of Nebraska in *Denison Alumni Bulletin,* 1917–18). His services as a public speaker were frequently sought, and he lectured widely. He wrote much, and he engaged in much public activity. He kept politics out of the university when politics threatened, and made no truce with the policies of favoritism. Approaches were made to see whether he would consider a transfer of his services to the University of Wisconsin, but he was adverse to the change. The Regents of the University of Nebraska at this time added $1,000 to his annual salary. Andrews's reply to the Regents was explicit. "So long as the University is compelled to the rigid economy it now exercises," he begged permission to continue "to be paid at the old rate."

In 1903, Andrews confounded the friends of silver by his blunt acknowledgment that he had been in error for a number of years in his conclusions regarding the production of gold. His statement had all of the frankness of his earlier utterances in the same connection. Basing his reports on the conclusions of geologists, he said, "I believed that the greatest output of gold was passed. I have to admit that it was an astounding mistake, and that I was in great and inexcusable error. I now believe that the heavy output of gold will continue" (*New York Evening Post,* May 25, 1903; *Springfield Republican,* May 26, 1903). In 1907 he was granted a retiring allowance by the Carnegie Foundation for the Advancement of Teaching, but, despite failing health, he managed to continue in his position until Dec. 31, 1908, when his physical condition at last compelled him to resign. Subsequently the Regents created for him the title of chancellor emeritus. A two years' trip around the world, which included several months in South Africa, failed to restore Dr. Andrews's health, nor was it restored after the return to Lincoln. In 1912 he was so ill that he had to be removed to West Palm Beach, in Florida, and the next year to Interlachen, in that state. His naturally robust frame was now all but worn out, but still he studied, and thought, and wrote. He died at Interlachen, Oct. 30, 1917, and was buried in Granville, Ohio, on the campus of Denison University.

Andrews was six feet in height and weighed in his prime nearly 180 pounds. His well-shaped head, his smooth-shaven face, his clear-cut features could have served in making a die for a coin. Tempted by his native strength and exceptional constitution, through all his active years he drew heavily on his physical store, with long hours of sustained labor, which at the end had exhausted it when it should have had years to serve. His personality was not a complex one; on the contrary, it was unusually simple and straightforward. In matters of consistency and convention he was apt to be a non-conformist, though in reality holding to the higher consistency that convention tends to conceal. His many writings, produced in the midst of constant time-consuming activities, show a diversity of absorbing interests, an eager and searching intellectual curiosity, a keen analytical power, and the vigor that was preëminently his in all things. His interest in ethics readily passed over to an interest in human relations as the subject-matter of economics and history. A certain choice of titles, as *An Honest Dollar* (1889) and *Wealth and Moral Law* (1894) obviously suggests this preoccupation with the ethical, but that factor is not allowed to overbalance the economic, and both books are written with penetration and power. *The History of the United States,* in six volumes (1913), bears the marks of writing done under pressure. *The History of the Last Quarter-Century in the United States* (1896), enlarged under the title *The United States in Our Own Time* (1903), is, however, a vivid, picturesque narrative full of the stir of the national life of the period. An earlier work, used as a text-book, but of too important content to escape notice, the *Brief Institutes of General History* (1887), is a presentation, really a precipitation, of essential facts, and an achievement of condensation that either saddened the indolent of successive student generations, or else inspired the industrious to unroll its tight involutions and gain a genuine notion of the groundwork of history. *The Call of the Land* (1913) deals partly with agricultural subjects, and represents Andrews's self-devotion to the interests stimulated by his residence and official position in a great agricultural state. His other works include *A Private's Reminiscences of the First Year of the War* (1886); *Brief Institutes of Our Constitutional History, English and American* (1886); *Institutes of Economics* (1889); *The Economic Law of Monopoly* (1890); *Syllabus of Lectures . . . upon the Rise and Growth of the Government of the United States* (1891); *The Duty of a Public Spirit* (1892); *Eternal Words and Other Sermons* (1894); *The Sin of Schism* (1896).

[W. C. Bronson, *Hist. of Brown Univ. 1764–1914* (1914); W. McDonald, "President Andrews: as Seen by the Brown Men of His Time," and other articles in *Memories of Brown,* ed. by R. P. Brown and others (1909); *Providence Journal,* June–Sept. 1897, June 22, 28, 1898, July 14, 18, 1898, Sept. 7, 8, 1898, Oct. 31,

1917; *An Open Letter Addressed to the Corporation of Brown University by Members of the Faculty of that Institution*(1897); Letter from Prof. Henry B. Gardner in *N.Y.Tribune*, Aug. 3, 1897; also Index Volumes to *N.Y.Tribune, Springfield Republican*, and *Brooklyn Eagle; New Eng.Mag.*, Sept. 1897; *Chicago Times-Herald, Tribune*, and other Chicago newspapers, July 14, 1898, Nov.–Dec. 1898; *Brooklyn Citizen*, Dec. 6, 1898; *Semi-Centenn.Anniv.Bk., the Univ. of Nebr. 1869–1919*(1919); *Nebr. State Jour.*, Sept. 23, 1900, Oct. 2, 1902, May 13, 1911, Oct. 31 and Nov. 1, 1917; Alexander Meiklejohn, "A Leader in Freedom," in *Freedom and the Coll.* (1923); *Memorial Vol. Denison Univ. 1831–1906*(1907); *Denison Alumni Bull.*, 1917–18; *Alumni Records of Brown Univ.*; Letters from Mrs. E. Benjamin Andrews, Interlachen, Fla., Profs. Walter C. Bronson and Wilfred H. Munro of Brown Univ., Rev. Jesse F. Smith of the Suffield School, and Bennett Rowe of Beverly, Mass.; personal knowledge.] W. A. S.

ANDREWS, GARNETT (May 15, 1837–May 6, 1903), lawyer, soldier, was a descendant of the family which settled in Virginia in 1635, when James Andrews received an extensive grant of lands in that colony. John Andrews was a Revolutionary soldier who, soon afterward, removed to Georgia. His wife was Ann Goode of Virginia, and their son, Garnett Andrews, was a judge of one of the superior courts of Georgia for twenty-seven years and married Annulet Ball. Judge Andrews's son, Garnett, was educated in the Male Academy at Washington, Ga., and had just graduated from the law school at the University of Georgia when the state seceded in 1861. He was the first man in his county to enter the Confederate service, was made a lieutenant in the 1st Georgia Regulars, served actively in Virginia and North Carolina, both as a staff officer and in command of a regiment, and was twice severely wounded. In 1864, detailed to organize a regiment by means of the voluntary enlistment of foreigners among the Federal prisoners, he raised such a regiment, officially known first as the "Second Foreign Legion" and later as the "8th Confederate Battalion of Infantry," but soon popularly known as the "Galvanized Yankees." On Apr. 11, 1865, Andrews, with his "Galvanized Yankees," was ordered to hold Salisbury, N. C., against the advance of Gen. Stoneman. Seizing a railroad train and manning it with men from his troops, he entered the town on one side as Stoneman was entering it on the other. A bloody battle, fought in ignorance of Lee's surrender on Apr. 9, ensued, in which Andrews was again severely wounded.

At the close of the war, after recovering from his wounds, he went to Yazoo City, Miss. Deciding to locate there, he began the practise of law, which he continued with marked success until his removal from the state in 1882. At that time his law partner was John Sharp Williams, then a young man, but afterward a distinguished senator. While living in Mississippi, Andrews commanded a militia company known as the Yazoo Rifles, edited the *Yazoo Herald* and served in the legislature in 1879 and 1880. In 1884, he published *Andrews' Digest of the Decisions of the Supreme Court of Mississippi.* On Aug. 23, 1867, he married Rosalie Champe Beirne of Monroe County, W. Va., a grand-daughter of Col. Andrew Beirne, a native of Ireland, who came to this country in 1793, was afterward a member of Congress, and commanded a regiment, equipped at his own expense, in the War of 1812. In 1882, Andrews removed to Chattanooga, Tenn., where he soon enjoyed a lucrative practise and a high place at the bar. He was elected mayor of Chattanooga in 1891, and served one term of two years, declining to be a candidate for reëlection. Tall, handsome, and always faultlessly dressed, with something of the soldier in his bearing, he was a striking figure in any company. Courtly in demeanor, impatient with anything like dishonesty, and with an abundance of physical and moral courage, he was a gentleman of the old school.

[Family records in the possession of Andrews's son, Mr. Garnett Andrews of Chattanooga; George Brown Goode, *Va. Cousins: a Study of the Ancestry and Posterity of John Goode of Whitby, a Va. Colonist of the Seventeenth Cent.* (1887), pp. 175, 307–9; *Chattanooga Daily Times*, May 7, 1903.] W. L. F—n.

ANDREWS, GEORGE LEONARD (Aug. 31, 1828–Apr. 4, 1899), Union soldier, was born at Bridgewater, Mass., the son of Manasseh and Harriet (Leonard) Andrews. After graduating from the State Normal School at Bridgewater, he entered West Point, and graduated there in 1851, at the head of his class. For four years he served as a lieutenant of engineers, and then resigned from the army to take up private practice as a civil engineer. At the outbreak of the Civil War he was appointed lieutenant-colonel of the 2nd Massachusetts Infantry, the colonel of which was also a former officer of the regular army, and under their training the regiment quickly acquired a reputation for steadiness and discipline which it maintained to the end. The colonel being absent commanding the brigade, the charge of the regiment devolved upon Andrews from the beginning of its service in field operations against the enemy. He led it during Gen. Banks's campaign in the Shenandoah Valley, and afterward as colonel (having been promoted, June 13, 1862) at the battles of Cedar Mountain and Antietam. He was then designated for service with Gen. Banks's expedition to Louisiana, and after some weeks at the port of embarkation, supervising shipments, he joined the command and was appointed its chief of staff. As such he took part in the campaign which culminated in the siege and capture of Port Hudson. He was then placed in command of the territorial district about Baton Rouge, and was also charged with the organization and training of a large force of colored troops. There had been a few regiments of negroes received into the service before this time, but with the secure occupation of a large area in the extreme South, their enlistment on a considerable scale was begun. Under their original fanciful designation of Corps d'Afrique, and afterward as plain regiments of United States colored troops, Andrews continued in command of these organizations, and also of his district, until early in 1865. He took part in the attack on Mobile, and after some further staff service was mustered out of the army in August. He tried life as a planter in Mississippi until 1867, and then returned to Massachusetts, where he served as United States marshal for four years, and is said to have incurred the pronounced enmity of Benjamin F. Butler. In 1871 he was appointed professor of French at West Point, and when the departments of French and Spanish were merged in 1882, he became head of the new department as professor of modern languages, which place he held until his retirement in 1892. From then until his death he resided in Brookline, Mass., writing occasional papers on military historical topics. He was imposing in appearance, dignified and formal in manner, studious, and well-read. He made few intimate friends, and as a commander was one to inspire confidence rather than devotion.

[G. W. Cullum, *Biog. Reg.* (3rd ed., 1891), II, 436–37; *Official Records,* see Index; *Bull. Ass. Grads. Mil. Acad.*, 1900, pp. 21–28; private information.] T. M. S.

ANDREWS, GEORGE PIERCE (Sept. 29, 1835–May 24, 1902), jurist, traced his descent in a direct line from Robert Andrews of Norwich, England, who emigrated in May 1635, settling at Ipswich, Mass. A descendant, Capt. Abraham Andrews—a minute-man at Lexington and participant in Arnold's Quebec expedition—moved to Maine, and his grandson, Solomon Andrews, entered the lumber business at North Bridgton, Me. There he married Sibyl Ann Farnsworth. Their son, George Pierce, was born at Bridgton. The future judge received his early education at Bridgton and at St. Johnsbury, Vt., subsequently attending Williston Seminary, Easthampton, and Dudley's Institute, Northampton, Mass. He entered Yale in 1854, graduating in 1858 with the honor of "class orator." He then studied law with Senator Fessenden at Portland, Me., but in 1859 went to Louisiana as a private tutor, continuing, however, his law reading. In 1860 he entered the office of the United States district attorney for the southern district of New York and was admitted to the New York bar in May of that year. He became well known through his connection with the famous Gordon case. A federal statute of 1820 had made slave-trading an act of piracy punishable by death, but no person had hitherto been condemned for an infraction of this law. Gordon was master of the ship *Erie* in August 1860, when she was captured off the west coast of Africa with 890 slaves on board. Gordon was indicted for piracy and the trial attracted great public attention. Andrews took charge of the prosecution, pressed it with much ability, and obtained a conviction; Gordon was hanged Feb. 21, 1862 (United States *vs.* Gordon 25 *Fed. Cas.* 15, 231; 5 *Blatchford* 18). In 1863 Andrews was appointed first assistant district attorney. In this capacity it fell to him to conduct for the national government a large number of difficult prize cases. In 1869 he resigned and commenced private practise. Fortunate in the confidence of Cornelius K. Garrison, who was a power in marine and financial circles in New York, he was retained in much heavy corporation litigation. He was appointed first assistant corporation counsel to the City of New York in December 1872, becoming corporation counsel in 1882. In 1883 he was elected associate justice of the supreme court for the first judicial district of New York, serving the full term of fourteen years. He failed of reëlection, but the following year was elected for a second term, continuing to hold office till his death. Bringing to the bench a rich and varied experience in every phase of municipal and corporation business, he was recognized as a high authority on the law appertaining to these subjects. His opinions on complicated questions arising under the tax laws were of exceptional value. "Judge Andrews . . . was thoughtful and reserved, but very genial in a quiet way and full of devotion to those he loved. He was a great reader of literature, especially French. . . . He had a strong temper, but even under most trying circumstances rarely showed it. . . . No Judge on our Bench was more courteous and kind to the bar, especially to its younger members. He was the most humane of Judges and the most judicial of men" (John H. Judge, "Memorial"). In 1889 he married Mrs. Catherine M. Van Anken, daughter of his old client, Cornelius K. Garrison. The mural portrait bust in bronze, life-size, which stands in the county court-house, New York City, was presented by his widow.

[Full particulars of the ancestry of Judge Andrews are contained in *Hist. of the Andrews Family—a Genealogy of Robert Andrews and His Descendants, 1635–1890,* by H. Franklin Andrews (1890). The "Memorial of George P. Andrews," by John H. Judge, in *Ann. Rept. of the Bar of the City of N. Y.*, 1904, p. 18, and the brochure, *George Pierce Andrews* (n.d.), prepared by his widow, are authoritative though brief and not altogether satisfying. Details of his work at the bar and on the bench must be sought for in the various N.Y. State Law Repts., covering the period 1860–1902.] H.W.H.K.

ANDREWS, ISRAEL WARD (Jan. 3, 1815–Apr. 18, 1888), college president, was born at Danbury, Conn., the son of Sarah (Parkhill) Andrews and Rev. William Andrews, a descendant of one of the first settlers of New Haven. In 1833 he entered Amherst College, where he spent one year; later he became a student at Williams College, of which Mark Hopkins had recently become president, and he was graduated there in 1837. After a year spent as principal of an academy at Lee, Mass., he was called to Marietta College, Ohio, on the recommendation of President Hopkins. Here he spent the rest of his life as instructor in mathematics, 1838, professor of mathematics and natural philosophy, 1839–55, president 1855–85, and professor of political science, 1855–88. As a teacher he was remarkable for thoroughness and clearness. As an executive he guided the young college successfully through the years when it had practically no endowment and was a pioneer enterprise in a new country. It was said that he knew personally every graduate of the college during its first fifty years. He was also active in the general educational work of Ohio, serving as president of the Ohio Educational Association and as a member of its executive committee and being for many years an associate editor of the Ohio *Journal of Education.* He was one of the original members of the National Teachers' Association and a member of the National Council of Education. His work as a scholar and author was largely in the fields of education and political science. One especially notable paper was read before the National Union Association of Cincinnati, June 2, 1863, on "Why Is Allegiance Due and Where Is It Due?" which was widely copied by newspapers and became an important factor in forming public opinion on the relation of the states to the Union. His most valuable contribution in the field of political science was his *Manual of the Constitution* (1874), which was used for many years as a textbook in colleges and universities. His death occurred at Hartford, where he was visiting, after delivering an address in Boston before the New England Historical and Genealogical Society on "The Marietta Colony of 1788" (published in the *New England Historical and Genealogical Register*, Oct. 1888). He was twice married: on Aug. 8, 1839, to Sarah Clarke of Danbury, Conn., who died in 1840; and on Aug. 24, 1842, to her sister, Marianne Clarke.

[Memoir by John Eaton, *New Eng. Hist. and Geneal. Reg.*, Oct. 1888; *Cincinnati Times-Star,* May 7, 1888; *Marietta Reg.*, Apr. 19, 1888; *Mag. of Western Hist.*, June, 1888.] A.G.B.

ANDREWS, JOHN (Apr. 4, 1746–Mar. 29, 1813), Episcopal clergyman, educator, was born in Cecil County, Md., of Scotch ancestry. His parents, Moses and Letitia Andrews, were sufficiently well-to-do to give him a satisfactory education at the Elk School, which was a near-by Presbyterian institution, and at the College of Philadelphia, where he graduated with high honors in 1764, although, owing to the absence of the Provost, he did not receive his degree until the following year. He spent the interim in teaching in the Grammar School connected with the college. He then took charge of a classical school at Lancaster, Pa., where he also studied theology under the Rev. Thomas Barton, an Anglican clergyman. In 1767 he went to London for his ordination, after which he was appointed by the Society for Propagating the Gospel in Foreign Parts, a "missionary" to Lewes, Del. Here he remained for three years and then, his health suffering from the climate, he removed to York, Pa. In 1772 he married Elizabeth Callender, " a lady of fine domestic qualities and great general excellence of character" (Sprague, V, 247), by whom he had ten children. His salary proving insufficient for the support of his increasing family, he accepted a position as rector of St. John's in Queen Anne's County, Md., where he remained until after the Declaration of Independence. Doubting the expediency of separation from the mother country and deploring patriot outrages against Loyalists, he now returned to the quieter atmosphere of York and started a classical school there. At this time he made the acquaintance of the unfortunate Major André, who was in York on his parole, and the British officer and the most pronounced friends of the American cause often met amicably in the house of this scholar, whose spirit was above the battle. But in 1782 Andrews returned to Maryland as rector of St. Thomas's in Baltimore County and two years later was a prominent member of the convention which organized the Protestant Episcopal Church of Maryland as independent of British jurisdiction. Shortly afterward, as member of a conference of important Episcopalians and Methodists, he vainly urged the union of these two religious bodies, on the ground that there was not sufficient difference between them to justify their separation. In 1785 he became head of the Protestant Episcopal Academy in Philadelphia, and in 1791, when this institution was absorbed in the University of Pennsylvania he was elected to the office of vice-provost (provost 1810–12), which included the chairs of moral philosophy and the classics. In 1798 one of Andrews's children was burned to death and his wife died from the shock of the news—a double loss which, it is said, he never mentioned without tears. Henceforth he devoted himself almost entirely to his two major interests—religion and the classics. His attitude toward religion was one of classical moderation and his attitude toward the classics was one of religious fervor. He saw much of Joseph Priestley, the famous Unitarian, during the latter's visits to Philadelphia, when Andrews would patiently listen to his arguments and then after his departure reëxamine the doctrine of Christ's divinity and become more convinced of it than ever. Unquestionably one of the best classical scholars in the country, he was reasonably proud of his learning. Classical scholarship in America, however, had not yet reached the productive stage and Andrews's only published works, aside from a few sermons, were two textbooks, *A Compend of Logick* (1801) and *Elements of Rhetorick and Belles Lettres* (1813). In person, he was tall and portly with a square face and ruddy complexion. "His manners were those which became a clergyman, and the Provost of a University" (*Ibid.*, p. 249).

[W. B. Sprague, *Annals of the Am. Pulpit* (1859), V, 246–51; the *Port Folio*, ser. 3, I, 425–41; H. M. Lippincott, *The Univ. of Pa.* (1919), pp. 97–98; H. W. Smith, *Life and Corresp. of the Rev. Wm. Smith* (1880), I, 365.]

E. S. B.

ANDREWS, JOSEPH (*c.* 1805–May 7, 1873), engraver, was the son of Ephraim and Lucy (Lane) Andrews, and a descendant in the eighth generation of Thomas Andrews who settled in Hingham prior to 1635. He was apprenticed at an early age (1821) to Abel Bowen, a Boston engraver, from whom he learned to engrave upon wood. His instructions in intaglio or copperplate engraving were received from William Hoogland, one of the early American bank-note engravers, who, at that time, was working with Abel Bowen. In 1827 (or 1829) he became a member of the firm of Carter, Andrews & Company of Lancaster, Mass. This firm did a very prosperous engraving, printing, and publishing business, as many as fourteen engravers being employed at one time, most of whom were engravers on wood. The firm failed as a result of the panic of 1833.

"The Wicked Flee Where No Man Pursueth" is the title of what is said to have been Andrews's first steel plate. This he engraved in 1829, after the painting by Alvan Fisher. Six years later, in 1835, he went to London, where he received instructions from the engraver, Joseph Goodyear. During the nine months he was thus engaged, he engraved, among other works, "Annette de l'Arbre," after W. E. West. He went to Paris with his instructor and while there engraved a head of Benjamin Franklin from the Duplessis portrait now in the Boston Public Library, for the *Works of Franklin*, edited by Jared Sparks. He returned to the United States, but again visited Europe in 1840. During this absence, which lasted two years, he engraved six portrait plates, for the *Galerie Historique de Versailles*, published in Paris under the auspices of Louis Philippe. One of these portraits was that of Cardinal Tencin. At Florence he began the "Duke of Urbino," after Titian, which he finished in the United States. In 1853 he went to Paris for the third time. In 1855 he commenced his chief plate, "Plymouth Rock, 1620," engraved after the painting by Peter Frederick Rothermel. This plate occupied nearly half of his time for fourteen years. His other works include portraits of George Washington, after Gilbert Stuart; Oliver Wolcott, after Trumbull; John Quincy Adams; Zachary Taylor; Jared Sparks, after Stuart; Amos Lawrence, after Harding; Abbot Lawrence, engraved in conjunction with Thomas Kelly for the *Whig Review*, and James Graham, both after G. P. A. Healy; Charles Sprague; Thomas Dowse, after M. Wright; "Crossing the Ford," after Alvan Fisher; "The Panther Scene," after George Loring Brown; "Bargaining for a Horse," after William S. Mount; "Parson Wells and His Wife"; "Christiana and Her Children in the Valley of Death," after Daniel Huntington; "Saul and the Witch of Endor," after Washington Allston; and "Pilgrim's Progress," after Billings.

Andrews is classed among the best American line-engravers and excelled especially in portrait work. From his signed plates it is apparent that he had various business associates during his career in the United States, such as Thomas Kelly, Stephen A. Schoff, H. Wright Smith, W. H. Tappan, and C. E. Wagstaff. He was twice married. The place of his death is given as Boston, Mass., by one authority, and as Hingham, Mass., by another.

["Memoir of Joseph Andrews," by his friend, Sylvester R. Koehler of the Museum of Fine Arts, Boston, in the *Rept. of Proc. at the Memorial Meeting in Honor of the Late Mr. Joseph Andrews*, May 17, 1873; sketch by Mantle Fielding, *Pa. Mag. of Hist. and Biog.*, Jan. 1907; check-list of engravings by Mantle Fielding, *Mag. of Hist. and Biog.*, Apr. 1907. See also C. E. Clement and Laurence Hutton, *Artists of the Nineteenth Century and Their Works* (1879); W. S. Baker, *Engravers and Their Works* (1875); D. M. Stauffer, *Am. Engravers upon Copper and Steel* (1907); Mantle Fielding, *Am. Engravers on Copper and Steel* (1917).]

R. C. S.

ANDREWS, LORIN (Apr. 1, 1819–Sept. 18, 1861), college president, was the son of Alanson and Sally (Needham) Andrews, both originally of Massachusetts but, at the time of his birth, among the earliest settlers of Ashland, Ohio. Born in a log cabin, he acquired such education as the local schools could furnish, taught a country school, and in 1837 entered the preparatory department of Kenyon College, at Gambier, Ohio. In 1838 he entered the college in the same class with Rutherford B. Hayes, but withdrew in 1840, owing to lack of money. On Oct. 30, 1843, he married Sarah Gates of Worcester, Mass., by whom he had three children. He taught at Ashland Academy, and at Mansfield, Ohio; then was called back to Ashland as principal of the Academy; then became superintendent of the newly organized "union school" of Massillon, Ohio. He was one of the founders of the Ohio State Teachers' Association, in 1847, and became chairman of its executive committee. In order to devote himself wholly to this work he resigned his teaching position in 1851 (*Ohio Educational Monthly*, Nov. 1861, new series, II, 356 ff.). It was his influence, more than that of any other one man, that secured the adoption of the excellent "School Law of 1853," and through his incessant lecturing before teachers' institutes he showed the teachers how their work should be done, and filled many of them with enthusiasm for their profession. Under the new school law a state school commissioner was to be elected; Andrews was the unanimous choice of the teachers, but failed to obtain the nomination. Thereupon, in 1853, the trustees of Kenyon College elected him president of that institution. Here his success was remarkable; he brought up the college, both in number of students and in financial strength, to the most prosperous condition it had ever known. In 1861, immediately upon President Lincoln's call for volunteers, he enlisted, and is believed to have been the first volunteer in Ohio. His example was followed by hundreds of teachers and other men, who had become accustomed to look to him for leadership. He raised, in Knox County, Ohio, a company of soldiers that was soon incorporated into the 4th Ohio Volunteer Infantry, of which he was made colonel. In the summer of 1861, before the regiment had seen much service, he was taken with "camp fever" in West Virginia, and was carried home to Gambier, Ohio, where he died. Great numbers of people from all parts of the state attended his funeral and saw his body laid to rest in the college cemetery, where a marble obelisk now marks his grave.

[Alfred Andrews, *Geneal. Hist. of John and Mary Andrews* (1872); G. W. Hill, *Hist. of Ashland County* (1880), pp. 208–10; an article by O. T. Corson in C. B. Galbreath's *Hist. of Ohio* (1825), I, 462; Geo. F. Smythe, *Kenyon Coll., Its First Century* (1924), p. 154; memorial sermon by Rev. Samuel Clements in the *Western Episcopalian*, Oct. 3, 1861; and Bishop C. P. McIlvaine's remarks to the convention of the Diocese of Ohio, printed in the jour. of the convention of 1862, p. 29.]

G. F. S.

ANDREWS, LORRIN (Apr. 29, 1795–Sept. 29, 1868), missionary, educator, was born in a Congregational home in East Windsor (now Vernon), Conn. After finishing the work of local schools, he studied in Jefferson College (now Washington and Jefferson), Pa., and received his B.A. Having decided meanwhile upon the ministry as a career, he entered Princeton Theological Seminary and finished his course there in 1825. He was ordained on Sept. 21, 1827, at Washington, Ky. In the autumn of 1827 the American Board, of Boston, commissioned a reinforcement of sixteen persons for the Hawaiian Islands Mission. The company sailed from Boston on Nov. 3, aboard the *Parthian*, Capt. Blinn, and passing around Cape Horn reached Honolulu, Mar. 30, 1828. Among the number were Andrews and Mary Wilson, his new bride. Within a month of his arrival he was assigned to the station at Lahaina, on the western shore of the island of Maui. He undertook his work in the spirit of a previous meeting of the Hawaiian missionaries which had decided that their service was "for life." For a while, language study took much of his time. In 1829 the first stone church on the islands was completed at Lahaina, 104 by 50 feet in size, and dedicated at the request of Hoapili, the governor, with the name "Ebenezer."

In 1831 the Mission decided to put into operation a high school for the training of teachers, the Hawaiian government coöperating in the enterprise. This school, accordingly, was opened in September of the same year at Lahainaluna, or "Upper Lahaina," two miles inland and 700 feet above the port. Andrews was assigned to the principalship of the school, an office which he held for ten years. The first year of the new "missionary seminary" began with twenty-five young men enrolled and closed with sixty-seven. A course of four years was projected. It was the school's design not only to prepare native school-teachers, but also promising natives to become assistant teachers and ministers of religion, "to disseminate sound knowledge through the islands," and to render the population "a thinking, enlightened and virtuous people," in the words of the Board's official report. Within a few years industrial training became a feature of the school. Printing was undertaken. On Feb. 14, 1834 Andrews published the first Hawaiian newspaper. He taught himself from books the process of copperplate engraving and established, at his own cost, a considerable engraving enterprise, begging copper at first from passing ships.

For a time the new station of Lahainaluna was part of the old Lahaina, but in 1835 it had grown to independence, and Andrews was the senior missionary. Along with his work as teacher and industrialist, he gave attention to translation of the entire Bible into the Hawaiian tongue. He also acted for a time (1837) as teacher and interpreter for certain Hawaiian chiefs, having obtained from the Mission "conditional dismission" therefor. He had already considered the matter of teaching both the king and the chiefs politics, law, and political economy. In 1841 he offered the Board his unconditional resignation, and turned eventually to government service in which he saw a wider and more congenial field of labor. The immediate occasion for the resignation was his objection to the receipt by the Mission Board of contributions from slaveholders. For a time he filled the post of seaman's chaplain at Lahaina. In 1845 he removed to Honolulu and accepted appointment as judge in the government court in cases involving foreigners. Constitutional government had previously been established and the independence of the islands recognized by the powers. In 1846 he was made a member of the privy council, serving for several years as secretary and keeping the records both in English and Hawaiian. In 1848 he was appointed a member of the superior court of law and equity, and in 1852 became first associate justice of the supreme court. He resigned in 1855 from the supreme court and was made judge of the court of probate and divorce with jurisdiction throughout the islands. In 1859 he retired on a government pension of $1,000 yearly. The last years of his life were devoted to research and authorship. His research into ancient meles, or songs, and the traditions of the Hawaiian people is said to have been probably more extensive than that of any other missionary. In 1865 he published a Hawaiian dictionary of some 17,000 words, the collection of which he had begun as early as 1835. He was the author also of a Hawaiian grammar. He was, according to island testimony, "a thorough and profound scholar." He had wide interests, was well read, extremely conscientious, and though diffident was highly respected by all. Shortly before his death he became nearly blind, but continued his work through an amanuensis. He died in Honolulu, leaving, in the words of the American Board report for 1869, "a noble record."

[Hiram Bingham, *A Residence of Twenty-One Years in the Sandwich Islands* (1847), pp. 325 ff.; Rev. and Mrs. O. H. Gulick, *The Pilgrims of Hawaii* (1918); Rufus Anderson, *Hist. of the Sandwich Islands Mission* (1870), pp. 362–63; Rufus Anderson, *The Hawaiian Islands* (1864), pp. 70, 181, 187, 261–68; *The Centennial Bk. One Hundred Years of Christian Civilization in Hawaii* (1920), pp. 40–41.]

J. C. A.

ANDREWS, SAMUEL JAMES (July 31, 1817–Oct. 11, 1906), clergyman in the Catholic Apostolic Church, was born and brought up in an atmosphere of piety. His father, William, was one of the earliest graduates of Middlebury College, Vt., and an influential Congregational minister in various churches in that state. By his wife, Sarah Parkhill, of Massachusetts, he had six sons, of whom five became distinguished clergymen. Samuel, born in Danbury, brought up in Cornwall, graduated from Williams College in 1839, studied law, and was admitted to the bar in Connecticut, Ohio, and New York, and opened an office in New York City. After a year of practise he turned to the ministry, taking a year or more of study in Lane Theological Seminary, Cincinnati, and was licensed to preach in 1846. He supplied the Congregational Church in Terryville, Conn., for a year and in 1848 was ordained pastor of the Congregational Church in East Windsor, Conn., where he served seven years without special incident. His resignation was the result of his accepting the doctrine and beliefs of the Catholic Apostolic Church, an organization which had grown out of the "speaking with tongues" and other spiritual manifestations in Edward Irving's church in London 1830–32, and which looked forward to the second coming of Christ in the immediate future. Andrews was probably influenced by the similar step taken by his eldest brother, William Watson Andrews [*q.v.*], in the previous year. He continued to support this religious body with tongue and pen until the end of his life. For more than thirty years he was an angel (*i. e.* pastor) of a parish in Hartford, Conn. He was also at various times an instructor in philosophy in Trinity College, Hartford. His published works include *The Life of Our Lord Upon the Earth* (1862); *William Watson Andrews: A Religious Biography* (1900); *Christianity and Anti-Christianity in Their Final Conflict* (1898); *God's Revelation of Himself* (2nd ed., 1901); *Man and the Incarnation* (1905); *The Church and its Organic Ministries*, an open letter to the Right Rev. John Williams, P. E. Bishop of Conn. He was an able and active member of the Society of Biblical Exegesis and Literature. His appearance and air were those of the scholar. He was married to Catherine Augusta Day of Hartford, Apr. 15, 1850.

[*Hartford Courant*, *Hartford Times*, Oct. 12, 1906; *Williams Record* (Williams Coll.), Oct. 18, 1906.]

S. S.

ANDREWS, SHERLOCK JAMES (Nov. 17, 1801–Feb. 11, 1880), lawyer, congressman, was born at Wallingford, Conn., the son of a distinguished physician, Dr. John Andrews. He was educated at Cheshire Academy and at Union College, graduating at the latter in 1821. After studying law he settled in Cleveland, Ohio, in 1825, and was married in 1828 to Ursula McCurdy Allen, who also came of a well-known Connecticut family. His marked ability speedily won him a distinguished position at the bar. Of a distinguished presence, witty and learned, with a remarkable vocabulary, he achieved an enviable reputation as an orator. He took a prominent part in the early development of Cleveland, serving as the first president of the city council and of the public-library board, as one of the original promoters of the Cleveland & Pittsburgh Railway, and as a leader in many other undertakings. His public career began in 1840 when he was elected to Congress on the Whig platform. Ill health compelled him to resign his seat in May 1842, but not until he had definitely taken his stand beside John Quincy Adams in the fight against the suppression of anti-slavery petitions. In 1848 he was appointed judge of the superior court of Cleveland, an office he filled with distinction until it was abolished. In the Ohio constitutional convention of 1850–51 he was an influential member, and fought especially for the rights of the colored race. The situation was a critical one, for, with the Democrats in control of the convention, there was real danger that the "Black Code" of Ohio might be restored. Leading the fight against a proposal to prohibit the immigration of free negroes into Ohio, Andrews made a speech that was a model of its kind, voicing the determined opposition of the Western Reserve to the proposed measure, yet recognizing the view-point of southern Ohio. Such moderate and tactful leadership won the day, and the measure was voted down (*Official Reports, Ohio Constitutional Convention,* 1851, p. 1227). In the next struggle, in favor of granting the negro the suffrage, Andrews found the opposition too powerful (*Ibid.*, pp. 1256–58). He was chosen as one of the attorneys to defend the men who rescued a negro, John Price, from the slave catchers, at Wellington, Ohio, in 1859 (*Publications of the Western Reserve Historical Society,* No. 101, p. 156). His last public office was that of delegate to the constitutional convention of 1873. Here his long experience and his high standing throughout Ohio made him easily a leader, and he became chairman of the important committee on the judicial department. Under his leadership important and extensive judicial reforms were drawn up and incorporated in the proposed constitution. The electorate did not see fit to ratify the new frame of government, but Andrews's committee had led the way for future legislation upon the judiciary.

[*In Memoriam, Sherlock James Andrews* (1880); *Bench and Bar of Ohio,* ed. by George Irving Reed (1897), II, 100–3; James H. Kennedy, *Hist. of the City of Cleveland, 1796–1896* (1896); Samuel P. Orth, *Hist. of Cleveland* (1910), vol. I, *passim;* Harvey Rice, "Western Reserve Jurists," *Mag. of Western Hist.*, June 1885.]

B. W. B—d.

ANDREWS, SIDNEY (Oct. 7, 1835–Apr. 10, 1880), journalist, was the oldest of four children born to Charles Henry Andrews and Nancy (Noble) Andrews. His early years were spent in Sheffield, Mass., where his father followed the trade of carpenter and joiner until his death in 1846. After the father's death young Andrews left Massachusetts to join a relative in Dixon, Ill. He attended the University of Michigan 1856–59 but was forced to withdraw before he received his degree, owing to the failure of the bank in which he had placed his earnings. From the age of thirteen he had written for the press, and upon leaving college he served as assistant editor and later as editor of the *Daily Courier,* Alton, Ill. In the early mining days he followed the gold rush to Colorado, but during the Civil War drifted to Washington where he became an attendant in the Senate. In Washington he made valuable friends and had a successful career as a journalist. From 1864 to 1869 he was special correspondent for the *Chicago Tribune* and the *Boston Advertiser,* writing under the name "Dixon." September–November 1865 he visited the Carolinas and Georgia as special correspondent, and his letters to the Boston and Chicago papers were brought together in 1866 in a 400-page volume—*The South Since the War,* his most notable achievement. Andrews's observations in the South were intelligent and orderly and the book furnished valuable information on the social and political conditions in the states he visited. His conclusions were, however, flavored with anti-Southern sentiment. (For review see the *Nation,* Apr. 26, 1866, II, 532–33.) In January and February 1869 he wrote a series of five letters to the *Boston Advertiser* on the treaty with Denmark, then before the Senate, for the purchase of St. Thomas and St. John Islands, contending that in view of the initiative taken in the negotiations by the State Department the Senate should ratify the treaty. These letters were so pleasing to the Danes, who were urging ratification, that they were published in pamphlet form by Gen. C. T. Christensen, Danish consul at New York (*The St. Thomas Treaty —A Series of Letters to the Boston Advertiser,*

1869). A severe illness in 1869 compelled Andrews to give up his newspaper work in Washington. During his convalescence he removed to Boston. In 1870 he contributed two articles on the Chinese as immigrants—"Wo Lee and His Kinsfolk" and "The Gods of Wo Lee"—to the *Atlantic Monthly* (XXV, 223, 469). For six months (1871) he was on the staff of *Every Saturday.* In 1872 he was appointed private secretary to Gov. William Washburn with whom he had formed a friendship in Washington. In 1874 he was made secretary to the Massachusetts Board of State Charities and held that position until the office was abolished in 1879. His death occurred the next year. Andrews was of medium height, had dark-brown hair, brown eyes, and wore a beard. He was twice married: to Hila Maria Breeze, November 1866; to Sarah Lucretia Washburn, a distant connection of Gov. Washburn, November 1873.

[Biography above based on information from Mrs. Andrews; obituaries in *Boston Transcript* and *Boston Daily Advertiser,* Apr. 12, 1880. L. M. Boltwood, *Hist. and Geneal. of the Family of Thomas Noble*(1878), p. 479, and Allibone's *Dict. of Authors*(1899), vol. I, supp., p. 41, give brief, inaccurate sketches.] I. S. H.

ANDREWS, STEPHEN PEARL (Mar. 22, 1812–May 21, 1886), reformer and eccentric philosopher, was born in Templeton, Mass., the youngest of the nine children of the Rev. Elisha Andrews and Wealthy Ann (Lathrop) Andrews. The strong moral energy characteristic of the family, shown by his father and brothers (see W. B. Sprague, *Annals of the American Baptist Pulpit,* 1860, pp. 268–76) and above all by his nephew, Elisha Benjamin Andrews [*q.v.*], appeared in Stephen Pearl Andrews as a more radical reforming spirit. At the age of nineteen he joined his elder brother, Thomas, in New Orleans, studied law, and was admitted to the bar. Both of the brothers were ardent abolitionists; Thomas aided the cause by marrying a Southern lady of wealth and carrying her and her slaves to the free soil of Illinois, while Stephen Pearl worked out a plan of manumission by purchase from a fund to be controlled by the government. He was married in New Orleans in 1835. Removing to Houston, Tex., in 1839, within three years he rose to an outstanding position at the bar but became very unpopular because of his fearless opposition to slavery. In 1843 his house was mobbed, and he, with his wife and infant son, managed to escape only by a dangerous twenty-mile night drive across flooded prairies. He immediately went to England in the endeavor to raise there the money necessary for the purchase of the slaves in the form of a loan from Great Britain to Texas. Lord Aberdeen, Lord Palmerston, and other influential men were at first favorably inclined toward his project but dropped it when Andrews was repudiated by Ashbel Smith, Texan Chargé d'Affaires.

If Andrews's efforts on behalf of anti-slavery had thus failed, there were at least other philanthropic enterprises to be undertaken. During his stay in England, he became enthusiastically interested in the short-hand system of Isaac Pitman and determined to introduce it in America. He returned to Boston and at once opened a school of phonography. In 1847 he moved to New York, added spelling reform to the list of his interests, edited two magazines printed in phonetic type, the *Anglo-Saxon* and the *Propagandist,* and, in collaboration with Augustus F. Boyle, compiled and published *The Comprehensive Phonographic Class-Book* (1845) and *The Phonographic Reader* (1845) each of which ran to sixteen editions within ten years. A linguist of amazing ability, reputed to be master of thirty-two languages, including Hebrew, Sanskrit, and Chinese, he was active in stimulating interest in foreign languages at a time when little progress had been made by American schools in that direction. In 1854 he brought out his *Discoveries in Chinese; or, the Symbolism of the Primitive Characters of the Chinese System of Writing as a Contribution to Philology and Ethnology and a Practical Aid in the Acquisition of the Chinese Language;* later he devised an international language that he called Alwato—a forerunner of Volapük and Esperanto (*Primary Grammar of Alwato,* 1877).

So far were these various undertakings from exhausting Andrews's energies, however, that in his own view they were all entirely subsidiary to his great achievement, the establishment of nothing less than "Universology," a deductive science of the universe. He had worked at this intermittently ever since his Louisiana days, and it was at last formulated in *The Basic Outline of Universology* (1877), a vast chaotic volume which remains one of the curiosities of philosophical literature. Because of the semi-anarchistic character of the ideal society of which he dreamed—which he called the "Pantarchy"—Andrews, in his later years, became a leader among the radical groups in New York City. The Colloquium, a society for free discussion, was started by him in 1882 and he was a prominent figure in the Manhattan Liberal Club. He died still deeming himself the founder of the most important of all the sciences, still supposing that the social millennium, for which he had striven in such various ways, was close at hand.

[*Appleton's Annual Cyc. for 1886*(1887); *N.Y. Tribune, N.Y. Herald,* May 23, 1886; Jesse S. Reeves, *Am.*

Diplomacy under Tyler and Polk (1907), p. 126; Ephraim D. Adams, *Brit. Interests and Activities in Texas* (1910), p. 137; *Brit. Diplomatic Correspondence Concerning the Republic of Tex.*, ed. by Ephraim D. Adams, pp. 261–62; [575] Cor. on Slave Trade, 1843, enc. in No. 454, *Parl. Papers* (1844), vol. XLIX; Julius E. Rockwell, *The Teaching Practice and Literature of Shorthand* (1884); John T. Trowbridge, "A Reminiscence of the Pantarch," in the *Independent*, Feb. 26, 1903; Laura Stedman and Geo. M. Gould, *Life and Letters of Edmund Clarence Stedman* (1910), vol. I, ch. 7.]

W. B. S.
E. S. B.

ANDREWS, WILLIAM LORING (Sept. 9, 1837–Mar. 19, 1920), bibliophile, was born in New York City, where he lived for above eighty years. He was the son of Loring and Caroline (Delamater) Andrews, a grandson of Constant A. Andrews, and a direct descendant of William Andrews, one of the Davenport Company which sailed from Boston in 1638 and settled the Town of Quinnipiac which they afterward called New Haven. Educated at private schools because of delicate health, Andrews engaged in his father's long-established leather business which prospered under his active management. He became in time a director of the Continental Fire Insurance Company, a trustee of the Bank for Savings, and a trustee of New York University. He acquired an enviable position in the business world, where his ability, character, and trustworthiness secured for him success and general confidence. On Oct. 17, 1860 he was married to Jane E. Crane, daughter of Theodore Crane of New York City. He retired from active business in 1877. The next year he became a trustee of the Metropolitan Museum and helped to found its library. For eleven years he was one of the managers of the House of Refuge on Randall's Island. At his residence on Feb. 5, 1884, the name Grolier was adopted for the famous Book Club of which he was one of the moving spirits. In 1895 he founded the Society of Iconophiles of New York. Long a lover of books, throughout his life he busied himself in collecting rarities in English and American literature, and in 1865 began the publication of his deservedly famous printed editions of the books from his own pen, published in his own taste, through his own direction, and marked by exquisite taste in type, paper, illustration, and binding. He engaged in their production the services of E. D. French and S. L. Smith as engravers and the active interest of Walter Gilliss and Theodore De Vinne in their printing. From 1865 up to 1908 he had issued thirty-six volumes of which all but ten were from his own pen. Many of them were important and all of them distinguished by the beauty and appropriateness of their format. Among the more important titles were *Roger Payne and His Art* (1892); *Jean Grolier* (1892); *Among My Books* (1894); *An Essay on the Portraiture of the American Revolutionary War* (1896); *A Journey of the Iconophiles Around New York* (1897); *New Amsterdam, New Orange, New York* (1897); *Gossip About Book-Collecting* (1900); *Paul Revere and His Engravings* (1901); *New York as Washington Knew It After the Revolution* (1905); *An English XIXth Century Sportsman* (1906).

["In Memoriam William Loring Andrews," *Year Bk. of the Grolier Club, 1921*, with appendix containing bibliography of Andrews's books; *Cat. William Loring Andrews Coll. Early Books in Yale Univ.* (1913); A. Growall, *Am. Bk. Clubs* (1897); William T. Bonner, *N. Y. the World's Metropolis* (1924), pp. 474, 724; James Grant Wilson, *Memorial Hist. of the City of N. Y.* (1893), IV, 126; *N. Y. Times, N. Y. Tribune*, Mar. 21, 1920.]

B. H—t.

ANDREWS, WILLIAM WATSON (Feb. 26, 1810–Oct. 17, 1897), clergyman in the Catholic Apostolic Church, descended from William Andrews, one of the first settlers of New Haven, Conn., was the son of William Andrews, a Congregational minister of Connecticut, and Sarah (Parkhill) Andrews, of Massachusetts. He was the eldest of six sons and was born in Windham, Conn. At the age of fourteen he was ready to enter Yale, but his youth and family financial limitations turned him for a time toward teaching. In 1828 he entered Yale as a sophomore, a classmate of Noah Porter, with whom a close and lifelong friendship was formed. He graduated in 1831 with high standing in scholarship, especially in English and debate. During his last year he came under special religious influence which turned him from the law to the ministry. After three years of teaching, and of studying divinity under his father, he was ordained on May 21, 1834 as pastor of the Congregational Church in Kent, Conn., where he remained for fifteen years. His resignation was due to his departure from the religious denomination of his father and brothers. For a number of years he had been interested in and attracted to a religious movement in Great Britain, whose adherents were commonly called "Irvingites," from the name of its foremost advocate, but later and better known as the Catholic Apostolic Church. The founders believed its form of organization would conduce to the union of Christendom and that their body was a special receptacle and instrument of the presence and power of the Holy Spirit. The imminent and visible coming of Christ was the chief tenet. Into this movement Andrews cast his lot sincerely and unreservedly. A pastorate of eight years in Potsdam, N. Y., was followed by thirty or more years of labor as an evangelist, requiring extensive traveling in the United States and Canada. Even with his eloquence and earnestness the results were negligible, but he never lost faith in his beliefs or despaired of their ultimate triumph, although disappointed at its delay. The latter part of his life he resided in Wethersfield, Conn. His published works comprise more than thirty sermons, addresses, books and magazine contributions, mainly pertaining to the Catholic Apostolic Church. He was twice married: on July 24, 1833, to Mary A. Given; and in July 1858, to Elizabeth Byrne Williams.

[*Yale Obit. Record* (1898); S. J. Andrews, *William Watson Andrews: A Religious Biog.* (1900); *Hartford Times,* Oct. 18, 1897.] S. S.

ANDROS, SIR EDMUND (Dec. 6, 1637–February 1714), is best known to American history as a colonial governor, having served first as the Duke's appointee in New York, then as royal governor of the consolidated northern colonies, and finally as governor of Virginia. His military training and experience made him a very valuable official at a time when defense of the colonies was one of England's chief concerns, but the background of his life somewhat unfitted him for understanding certain colonial conditions. The son of Amice Andros and Elizabeth (Stone) Andros, he belonged to the feudal aristocracy of Guernsey, where his family held many positions of authority. Upon the death of his father in 1674 he became bailiff of the island and lord of the seigneurie of Sausmarez. A few years later he added to his estates the island of Alderney. He began his colonial career by serving as major in Sir Tobias Bridge's regiment of foot sent in 1666 to the West Indies to protect the islands against the Dutch. Through the influence of the Earl of Craven, a relative of his wife, he was made landgrave in Carolina in 1672 under that most aristocratic of colonial governmental schemes, the Fundamental Constitutions. He received four baronies, an estate of about 48,000 acres of land, but he appears to have shown no further interest in this enterprise. He is next heard of as a friend of the Duke of York. After the restoration of the Duke's New York propriety by the Dutch in 1674, Andros was appointed governor of the province and captain of a company of 100 foot soldiers. He handled very skilfully the chief problems of government—defense, boundary disputes with Connecticut, and post-war political and racial readjustments—but certain discrepancies in his financial reports caused the Duke to send over a special commission to investigate his administration. Andros was exonerated and a decidedly favorable report made to the Duke. Although he was not sent back to New York as governor he received many marks of favor at court. He was knighted about 1681, made Gentleman of the Privy Chamber to the king in 1683, and in 1685 was appointed lieutenant-colonel of the Princess of Denmark's regiment of horse under the command of the Earl of Scarsdale.

Meanwhile, James II was completing the plan begun under Charles II for consolidating the New England colonies into one royal province. The king's long struggle to curb the growing independence of Massachusetts had ended in 1684 in the annulling of that colony's charter, leaving the path open for a more comprehensive colonial policy than was possible with so many small separate colonies. Such a policy was badly needed, particularly for defense. Commercial expansion had made France and England each jealous of the other's American colonial possessions and eager for control of the fur trade of North America, which centered in the Five Nations strategically situated on the New York frontier. Each was alert to snatch any advantage which might be offered, yet at the same time reluctant to take the offensive. In such a critical situation, defense of the New York and New England frontiers was of paramount importance, a fact which the little individualistic New England colonies could not see. It therefore behooved England to take such action as would bring the military forces of those colonies under a single command and make available their combined resources for concentration on the weakest spots. Massachusetts; Maine, once the property of the Massachusetts Bay Company; New Hampshire, a royal province; Plymouth, an independent but charterless colony; and King's Province (the old Narragansett Country), were all now in the king's hands. Rhode Island and Connecticut were needed to make the plan complete, but they were legally protected by their charters against such action. Flaws in their fulfilment of charter obligations were sought and found, and they submitted to regulation without defending their charter at law. These seven provinces comprised the Dominion of New England. The king now sought a man for royal governor whose military experience would enable him to build up a strong defense against the French. Sir Edmund Andros, whose latest service had been to lead a troop of horse against the rebels in Monmouth's rebellion, was chosen. Upon his arrival at Boston in December 1686 he took over the reigns of government from Joseph Dudley, who had been put temporarily in charge of the Dominion.

The most conspicuous feature of this new province was the absence of a representative assembly, the administration of government being entrusted to the governor and a council consisting of royal appointees from every colony included in the Dominion. That this body should tax the community seemed, to the supporters of charter rule, contrary to Magna Charta. The first levy met with resistance in Essex County, Mass., Ipswich being the chief transgressor. This mutiny in the new ship of state Andros put down with firmness and severity. The New England frontier was for the most part quiet after he assumed control, but New York was still harassed by the French and their Indian allies. The governor's urgent appeals for help brought the Lords of Trade to sudden decision in 1688 to abandon the idea of forming a second group of colonies consisting of New York, the Jerseys, Pennsylvania, and Maryland, and instead, to add the two former to the Dominion of New England. Danger to the security of the Dominion, however, lay less in the menace of the French than in the discontent of the theocrats of the Puritan colonies, who fanatically expected the Lord to restore their "judges." Sir Edmund had at the outset the support of the merchants and large landowners throughout the Dominion because they wished to inaugurate a régime of commerce and business. Unfortunately, he alienated the merchants by his too vigorous enforcement of the navigation acts and conservative financial policy, at the same time stirring the landowners against him by his introduction of the English system of landholding and by his lack of sympathy with their schemes for land speculation. Loss of their support made possible the success of a movement against the Dominion. Under the leadership of Cotton Mather and other Puritan divines, a plot was hatched at Boston, probably instigated by Increase Mather, then in England seeking reforms of government. Upon hearing of the landing of William of Orange, the people of Boston rose and seized all of the Dominion officers who could be found, including Andros himself. Plymouth, Connecticut, and Rhode Island followed Massachusetts in resuming charter government, while New Hampshire and Maine were again brought under the rule of Massachusetts. The revolt spread to New York by way of Long Island and soon the Dominion was completely at an end. The prisoners after a long delay were sent to England for a hearing, but were acquitted, the agents of Massachusetts having refused to sign the charges.

That Sir Edmund's reputation with the Crown did not suffer from his New England experience is shown by his appointment as governor of Virginia in 1692, a post which he filled with success. Randolph reported in 1693 that Virginia "of all the Gomts I have passed thro' has the onely face of peace & Good Gomts" (Goodrick, *Edward Randolph,* VII, 433). To be sure, Commissary Blair complained that Andros was indifferent to the needs of the Anglican Church and the new college of William and Mary, but no charge of mismanagement of government was brought against him. In 1697 Sir Edmund resigned his post and returned to England. In 1704 he was made lieutenant-governor of Guernsey, an appointment against which the jurats of the court of the island protested because he already held the office of bailiff. They declared that to have "the whole power as well civil as Military" lodged in the same person was "an infringement of their Rights." In 1706 Sir Edmund retired from office and spent the rest of his days in London, where he died in February 1714.

His personality has been little understood because attention has always been focused on the policies of his administration which were distasteful to the theocrats, policies which, for the most part, were not of his own choosing but dictated by the Lords of Trade. He was essentially a soldier, and where soldierly qualities were needed his rule was excellent; but he lacked understanding of business affairs and of Puritan psychology. His aristocratic background allowed him little faith in democratic institutions, and his experience with the contentious Dominion council led him often abruptly to silence lengthy and unprofitable debates. He was impatient and at times brusque, but one does not hear of him such tales of violence as are associated with many other colonial governors of his day. There is no evidence of his ever having turned his position of authority to personal profit. To his friends he was a person of great charm, but he never understood or enjoyed the humbly born. That England valued his services is shown by his long years in office and his appointment to difficult posts. Though not popular with advocates of democratic government, nevertheless he was one of the ablest English colonial governors of the seventeenth century.

[The best short life of Sir Edmund Andros is that by W. H. Whitmore in vol. I of the *Andros Tracts.* A detailed account of his administration of government in New England may be found in Viola F. Barnes, *Dominion of New England* (1923). For a thorough knowledge of his whole career it will be well to consult the following source material: *Docs. Rel. to the Col. Hist. of N.Y.* vol. III (1853), ed. by E. B. O'Callaghan; "Andros Records," ed. by Robert Toppan in *Proc. Am. Antiquarian Soc.,* n. s., XIII, 237–68, 463–99; *Laws of New Hampshire,* I (1904), ed. by A. S. Batchellor (containing Andros's commission and instructions as governor of New England, and the laws passed by the Dominion Council); *Andros Tracts* (Prince Soc., 1868), three vols.; *Calendar of State Papers, Colonial Series; Edward Randolph,* ed. by Robert Toppan (Prince Soc., 1898–99).]

V.F.B.

ANGEL, BENJAMIN FRANKLIN (Nov. 28, 1815–Sept. 11, 1894), lawyer, diplomat, the son of Benjamin and Abigail (Stickney) Angel, was a descendant of Thomas Angell, who came to Boston with Roger Williams in 1631. He was born at Burlington, Otsego County, N. Y., and received his early education there and at Exeter. In 1830 he entered the Livingston County High School at Geneseo, N. Y., but weak eyesight compelled him to abandon the hope of a university course. He taught school for a short time and in 1834 commenced the study of law at Hudson, N. Y. At a comparatively early age he had taken an active interest in politics on the Democratic side and was appointed surrogate of Livingston County, Mar. 23, 1836, serving four years in that position and being admitted to the bar in 1837. Though young, he proved an extremely efficient official and after the presidential election of 1844, when the Democratic party regained power in the state, he was reappointed surrogate, continuing to hold office until, under the constitution of 1846, his duties were merged in those of the county judge. In 1848 he was appointed master in chancery and supreme court commissioner. He was a delegate to the National Democratic Convention at Baltimore in 1852. At about this period his health gave way and in 1853, in the hope of benefiting by a change of climate, he accepted an appointment by President Pierce as United States consul at Honolulu. He went to his post in June 1853 and remained there eighteen months, but the United States Senate failed to ratify the appointment. In 1855, accordingly, the President sent him to China as special envoy and commissioner to settle if possible a controversy between the Chinese customs officials and some American merchants who had refused to pay customs export duties. After executing this mission satisfactorily, he returned to the United States by way of the East Indies, making an extended tour in Egypt and Europe. He described his experiences in letters to the press which aroused great interest. In 1856 he was the Democratic nominee from Livingston County for Congress. Though defeated, his party was successful nationally, and one of the first acts of President Buchanan was to appoint him minister resident to Norway and Sweden. He remained in this post till the change of administration in 1861, returning home in 1862. He did not resume practise but took up farming on a large scale at Geneseo. His last appearance in the political arena was as a delegate to the National Democratic Convention at Chicago in 1864. He was president of the New York State Agricultural Society in 1873. His latter years were spent in retirement on his Geneseo estate, where he died. He was married twice and was survived by three children.

[James Hadden Smith, *Hist. of Livingston County, N.Y.* (1881), p. 392; L. L. Doty, *Hist. of Livingston County, N. Y.* (1876); obituaries in the N. Y. press of Sept. 13, 1894, most of them containing inaccuracies.]

H. W. H. K.

ANGELA, MOTHER (Feb. 21, 1824–Mar. 4, 1887), educator and religious superior, christened Eliza Maria Gillespie, was descended from Neal Gillespie, who was probably born in Argyleshire, Scotland, and Eleanor Dougherty of County Donegal, Ireland, both Catholics, who came to America, and settled in Pennsylvania about 1777. Eliza was born near Brownsville, Pa. From her parents, John Purcell Gillespie and Mary Madeleine Miers, she drew much of her deep devotion to religion and charity. A frail and delicate child, she displayed unusual talents from her earliest years. She attended a select school at home, and then was sent to the school of the Dominican Sisters at Somerset, Ohio. After her father's death, her mother, having removed to Lancaster, Ohio, where she had relatives, married William Phelan, a wealthy landowner. In 1841, at the age of seventeen, Eliza, with her cousin Ellen Ewing, the future Mrs. W. T. Sherman, was sent to the Visitation Convent school at Georgetown, D. C. Here the young girl formed friendships with many who later became distinguished women at home or abroad. Graduating in 1842, she taught for a while at an Episcopalian seminary in St. Mary's County, Md., and then organized a Catholic school at her home town of Lancaster.

Intellectual culture, charity, and religious devotion were the dominating ideals of her life. In 1853 she set out for Chicago, determined to devote herself unreservedly to the pursuit of these ideals by becoming a Sister of Mercy. On the way she stopped to see her brother Neal, a seminarian at Notre Dame, Ind., where Father Edward Sorin [*q.v.*], recognizing at a glance her superior qualities, persuaded her to remain and join the Sisters of the Holy Cross, who had established a convent and academy a few miles away at Bertrand, Mich. After a novitiate in France, she returned within a year and became the head of the academy. For almost thirty years, as Mother Mary of St. Angela, she remained the superior of the Sisters of the Holy Cross in the United States. With the cooperation of Father Sorin, the ecclesiastical superior, she raised the Community from its humble beginnings to the position of one of the strongest religious organizations of Catholic women in the country. She knew how to attract and train religious-minded young women, and she gradually widened the opportunities for educational, charitable, and religious work. Removing the academy and mother-house from Bertrand to a beautiful property near the historic La Salle Portage, a mile west of Notre Dame University, she set to work to develop there, in St. Mary's Academy, a school that should be second to none in the higher education of girls. Contrary to the prevailing view and practise, she believed that this education ought to be fully equal to that of boys, and therefore not only encouraged painting and other fine arts, but also strongly emphasized the development of intelligence and reason. While thus engaged, she found time and means to establish numerous other academies modeled upon St. Mary's; she supplied teachers to parish schools, edited a series of Catholic school books, and cooperated with Father Sorin in the founding of the *Ave Maria,* for which she wrote and translated.

In pursuance of her ideals of charity, Mother Angela founded several important hospitals. Her greatest opportunity in this direction came with the outbreak of the Civil War, during which, while continuing to direct the educational and religious activities of the Community, she was busily engaged in supervising the work of her Sisters in military hospitals at Paducah, Louisville, Memphis, Cairo, Mound City, Washington, and other places, as well as their employment on river transports and hospital boats. The services of Mother Angela and her Sisters in the hospitals and on the battle-fields of the Civil War formed one of the brightest chapters in the record of the ministrations of mercy and charity during the great struggle.

[In the archives of the mother-house, St. Mary's, Notre Dame, Ind., there are a number of important MSS. relating to Mother Angela which have been consulted in preparing the above sketch, chief among them being "A Geneal. Sketch of the Gillespies," by John G. Ewing (twelve pages); "Items relating to the Life of Mother Mary Angela" (eighty pages); "Memoir of Mother Angela," by Eleanor Ewing Brown (eight folio typewritten pages), containing biog. material derived from Mother Angela and persons close to her; "Mother Angela" (two pages), chiefly chronological data. The booklet, *In Memoriam—Mother Mary of St. Angela,* is important for her views and work as an educator and her Civil War services. An excellent sketch of her as a religious superior is to be found in *A Story of Fifty Years,* an hist. account of the Sisters of the Holy Cross. An account of the growth and work of the Community is also to be found in *The Cath. Ch. in the U. S. of Am.* (1914), II, 249–60; also in the *Cath. Encyc.* (1913), VII, 405.]

J. A. B.

ANGELL, GEORGE THORNDIKE (June 5, 1823–Mar. 16, 1909), reformer, was born in Southbridge, Mass., the son of Rev. George Angell and Rebekah (Thorndike) Angell. His mother was left a widow when their only child was four years old. As her financial resources were small, she became a teacher in private schools, the boy being kept during the next ten years in the homes of relatives and friends in various parts of New England. His employment at fourteen in a dry-goods house in Boston was followed by attendance at a boarding-school in Meriden, N. H. In 1842 he entered Brown University, but changed a year later to Dartmouth College. On graduation in 1846 he went to Boston, where he taught school and studied law until 1851, when he was admitted to the bar and began to practise. For a short time he was in partnership with Benjamin F. Brooks and for a longer time with Samuel E. Sewall. In 1868 he retired with sufficient capital for his ordinary needs and enough to spare to enable him to contribute largely to the philanthropic enterprises which from now on engaged most of his attention.

Stirred by accounts of a race in which two horses had been driven to death over rough roads from Brighton to Worcester, he appealed in the newspapers for help in taking hold of "this business," as he called it, and putting an end to it. He was joined by Mr. and Mrs. William Appleton and other prominent citizens, and at a meeting in his office the Massachusetts Society for the Prevention of Cruelty to Animals came into existence. Though Angell regarded Mrs. Appleton as co-founder, her name was not used in the articles of incorporation, for "public opinion had not then reached the point when it was deemed judicious to make this use of a lady's name." The Society was successful in securing legislation and actively assisted in law enforcement. Its educational functions were later taken over by the American Humane Educational Society, through which Angell conducted a varied and incessant campaign to further the ideas expressed on its shield: "Glory to God, Peace on Earth, Kindness, Justice and Mercy to Every Living Creature." He established a periodical, *Our Dumb Animals* (vol. I, no. 1, June, 2, 1868). The Society published the first American edition of *Black Beauty* and in all distributed more than a million copies. It also published *Beautiful Joe,* winner of a prize-story contest conducted by the Society. Angell was especially concerned to bring his gospel to children in the public and Sunday schools and to this end encouraged and aided the organization of local Bands of Mercy. He believed that humane education in childhood would prove the solution of many social ills, not only procuring better treatment of dumb animals but preventing crimes and wars. Through legislation and otherwise he helped to effect reforms in connection with the transportation of cattle, their care in the markets, and the methods employed in slaughter-houses. He denounced Theodore Roosevelt both as a hunter and as a militarist. Though opposed to vivisection, he did not entirely satisfy some of the more extreme foes of the practise; he wished "to confine it within the narrowest and most merciful limits." Angell waged war on the adulteration of foods and on the use of poisonous materials in the manufacture of cooking utensils and wall-papers; he wrote and lectured on peace, and declared that "if Christian churches would do their duty there would never be another war between Christian nations." He traveled extensively in this country, addressing meetings, organizing societies. In 1869 he went to Europe, assisted the British Royal Society for the Prevention of Cruelty to Animals in establishing a journal called *The Animal World,* aided the Baroness Burdett-Coutts in forming the Ladies' Humane Educational Committee of England, and took an active part in the world congress of animal-protection societies at Zurich. In 1872, at the age of forty-nine, he married a widow, Mrs. Eliza (Mattoon) Martin. In 1882 he formed the American Band of Mercy and in 1889 the American Humane Education Society. When he died the funeral procession in which his body was borne from Boston to Mount Auburn Cemetery, Cambridge, was rendered unique by the presence of thirty-eight splendid horses following the hearse in double line.

[Angell's *Autobiog. Sketches and Personal Recollections,* pub. in several editions without date by the Am. Humane Education Soc., is the chief source, but the material in it on the last two decades of his life is meager and unsystematic. An excellent and reliable sketch by Guy Richardson appeared in *Zion's Herald,* June 1923. Other sources are Sydney H. Coleman, *Humane Soc. Leaders in America* (1924), and obituary in *Boston Transcript,* Mar. 16, 1909.]

R. G. F.

ANGELL, ISRAEL (Aug. 24, 1740–May 4, 1832), Revolutionary soldier, a descendant of one of the original settlers who came to Rhode Island with Roger Williams, was born in Providence, the son of Oliver and Naomi (Smith) Angell. He had a good education, and was particularly interested in scientific subjects. At the beginning of the war he was a major of Rhode Island troops and served nearly to the end. He was successively promoted: major of the 11th Continental Infantry 1776, lieutenant-colonel of the 2nd Rhode Island, Jan. 1, 1777, and shortly afterward colonel. Angell's services were at the siege of Boston, at the battles of Brandywine, Red Bank, Monmouth, and Springfield; in Valley Forge, and at various points in Rhode Island, New Jersey, and the Hudson Highlands, particularly at Peekskill and West Point. He gained distinction especially in the almost forgotten battle at Springfield, N. J., June 23, 1780, where he held an important command, by withstanding the British advance at the bridge. His value in this engagement was recognized in the correspondence between Washington and Greene. Retiring from the army, Jan. 1, 1781, Angell settled in Johnston, R. I., as farmer and cooper. He was a man of medium height, fair complexion, and military bearing. He was married three times: to (1) Martha Angell, his second cousin; (2) Susanne Wright, or Wight; (3) Sarah Wood. He had seventeen children and was courting a fourth lady when he died at Smithfield, R. I., in his ninety-second year.

[*Diary of Col. Israel Angell* (1899), ed. by Edward Field, covers, in part, the years 1778–81; L. L. Lovell's *Israel Angell, Colonel of the 2nd R. I. Regiment* (1921), seems to be based on family papers; see also A. F. Angell's *Geneal. of the Descendants of Thos. Angell* (1872) and F. B. Heitman's *Hist. Reg.* (1893).]

E. K. A.

ANGELL, JAMES BURRILL (Jan. 7, 1829–Apr. 1, 1916), journalist, college president, diplomat, was a member of an old Rhode Island family. His ancestor, Thomas Angell, one of the founders of Providence, R. I., came from England in the *Lion* with Roger Williams in 1631. He was a signer of the Compact in 1636 and a deputy to the General Court in 1652. A son, John Angell (1646–1720), was a soldier in King Philip's War. Eighth in descent from the settler Thomas, and seventh from John, was James Burrill Angell (named for James Burrill, senator from Rhode Island, 1817–20), the eldest of eight children, his father being Andrew Aldrich Angell (1802–65), his mother, Amy, daughter of Richard Aldrich. So far as is known none of Angell's forebears came from other than colonial stock, originally English: "They have been found chiefly in the ranks of plain farmers, mechanics and tradesmen, gaining by industry and integrity an honest living, but winning no particular distinction" (*Reminiscences,* p. 3). His birthplace, near Scituate, was the farm upon which Thomas Angell, grandson of the first Thomas, had settled in 1710. The highway between Providence and Norwich ran through it, and in 1810 Angell's grandfather, Charles Angell, justice of the peace and local man of affairs, built near the road a large house which was conducted as a tavern by him and his son down through Angell's boyhood. In this combined farmhouse and tavern the town meetings and justice's court were held.

The farm lad grew up in an atmosphere of public affairs, and learned his letters from the old lawbooks of his grandfather. His first instruction was at the primitive district school, but a Quaker, Isaac Fiske, established in the neighborhood a private school which the boy attended from the age of eight to twelve. He then went for one term to Seekonk Academy, near Providence, and from there, for two years, to Smithville Academy in the town of Scituate, five miles from his home. There followed another year spent upon the farm, after which it was decided by his father that the boy should have a college education. For better preparation in the classics Angell spent the academic year 1844–45 at the then recently established Brown University Grammar School in Providence. There he came under the influence of Henry S. Frieze [*q.v.*], a classical scholar whom he was later to find on his faculty when he became president of the University of Michigan. "Contact with this inspiring teacher," Angell asserted, "formed an epoch in my intellectual life. He represented the best type of the modern teacher at once critical as a grammarian, and stimulating with the finest appreciation of whatever was choicest in the classic masterpieces" (*Ibid.*, p. 17).

In 1845 Angell entered Brown University, from 1827 to 1855 under the presidency of Francis Wayland [*q.v.*], who introduced a new educational program of the first importance, which embraced a broadening of the curriculum and an abandonment of the prevailing idea that a college education was for the few preparing for the ministry or the law. He was thus the prophet of higher education for the many, in the realization of which Angell was later to become an effective instrument. Throughout his four years at Brown, Angell maintained an excellent record in scholarship, graduating as valedictorian. Yet he was no recluse. In his freshman year he organized a debating society which survived for several years. He was a member of the Psi Upsilon fraternity and Phi Beta Kappa. Even more than the instruction he received, which was well above the average of that of the colleges of the time, Angell prized the opportunities offered by the college library. His chief interests lay in mathematics, English literature, and modern languages. After graduation he spent part of the year 1849–50 as an assistant in the college library, during which time he was able to gratify his taste for wide reading.

A serious affection of the throat, from which he never entirely recovered (explaining the fact that in his public utterances his voice was soft and conversational, making its impression by clearness and distinctness of enunciation rather than by force and volume), induced him in the late autumn of 1850 to join his friend and classmate, Rowland Hazard, in a horseback trip through the Southern states. For nearly eight months the two young men had unusual opportunities to witness the operation of the slave system. These impressions, as well as those of the South generally, were later of direct value to Angell in his journalistic work. He had planned to enter Andover Theological Seminary in the autumn of 1851, but his throat continuing weak, he was advised against any occupation which involved public speaking. Aiming to secure work that would keep him out of doors, he entered the employment of a civil engineer in Boston, with whom he remained for about five months, when, again upon the solicitation of Hazard, he sailed for Europe, where he remained for nearly two years, spending most of the time in the study of modern languages and literature, principally at Paris and Munich. His scheme of studies looked toward the acquisition of a speaking knowledge of French and German and a general insight not only into literature but into history and science, a training cultural rather than professional.

In the spring of 1852 Wayland offered Angell his choice of two chairs at Brown, the one of Civil Engineering, the other of Modern Languages. Angell chose the latter, spent the next year in further preparation, and returned to Providence in the autumn of 1853, to enter upon his professorship as the youngest member of the faculty. Fresh with the inspiration from foreign study, he took up his work with enthusiasm. He developed his advanced courses, planned to return to Europe for further study, and sought an outlet for the beginnings of productive scholarship in a number of contributions upon literary subjects to the *North American Review*. But in 1855 Wayland resigned, and his successor, Sears, sought to return to the traditional college course. Angell soon found himself limited to elementary instruction. Fortunately the classroom did not absorb all of his time or energy. In 1857 he revised and edited Chambers's well-known *Handbook of French Literature*. In 1858 an acquaintance, Henry B. Anthony, editor and principal owner of the *Providence Journal*, was elected to the United States Senate and asked Angell to contribute leading articles to the *Journal* during his own absence in Washington. During 1859 Angell wrote the more important editorials, giving particular attention to European and international politics. In the summer of 1860 he resigned his chair at Brown in order to assume the editorship of the paper, a position which he held until the summer of 1866.

The *Providence Journal*, established before 1800, had long been a daily paper, and under Anthony's direction it had exerted an important influence. Its policy had been strongly Republican and such it continued to be after Angell became editor. Although the *Journal* at first accepted the nomination of Lincoln with only mild approval, it soon undertook to arouse popular enthusiasm for the Republican candidate. Threats by southern states to secede were dismissed lightly, with consequent surprise at the secession ordinances which followed Lincoln's election. During the Civil War the *Journal* consistently supported the Administration, and there seems to have been no disagreement as to policy between Anthony, the owner, at Washington and Angell, the editor, at Providence. Angell's editorials were easy, clear, and restrained in style, temperate in judgment, and accurate in their statement of facts. Written in haste, they gave the impression of deliberate preparation. Upon international politics and questions involving international law Angell was at his best. These were the subjects in which he had come to have the greatest interest. In this editorial experience he acquired readiness and accuracy in writing and learned to avoid diffuseness. Even more important for his later work, he came to know men and to mingle with them without aloofness or intellectual pride. The six years thus spent without respite during a period of great stress told seriously upon his health. Having attempted unsuccessfully to purchase the *Journal* from Anthony, he came to the conclusion that further drafts upon him as an employee would be deadening to his ambitions. Hence he accepted the offer of the presidency of the University of Vermont in August 1866.

The University of Vermont had been chartered by the state legislature in 1791, but the state gave it no financial support. The Civil War had seriously affected the attendance in all departments. In the Literary College, when Angell became president, there were but thirty students. To undertake the administration of such an institution and to make something out of it required a man of abundant faith and courage. Such Angell soon proved himself to be. His first task was that of raising necessary funds. He visited all parts of Vermont as well as Boston, New York, and Washington, speaking before public meetings and soliciting contributions from groups and individuals. As a result of his canvass nearly $100,000 was raised, by which a laboratory was equipped, a professorship endowed, the old college building remodeled, and a house built for the president. Angell's policy, afterward successfully developed at Michigan, was to arouse an interest in the institution among the people of the state, so that they would come to regard the state university as an integral and necessary part of the public educational system. But at the outset he met with exceptionally adverse conditions. Vermont was relatively poor as a state, and privately endowed New England institutions competed with the University for students, prestige, and financial support. Angell had an uphill task. He was forced to supply deficiencies of equipment by his own personal exertions. "As we had not funds enough to complete our faculty, I set myself to teach the branches not provided for, namely, Rhetoric, History, German, and International Law" (*Ibid.*, p. 123), a statement which sufficiently emphasizes both the poverty of the institution and the intellectual resourcefulness of its president.

Angell was offered the presidency of the University of Michigan in the autumn of 1869. He went to Ann Arbor and was inclined to accept the offer. Upon returning to Burlington, however, he found so much insistence upon his remaining that he felt a moral obligation to stay at Vermont some time longer. His declination was not regarded at Ann Arbor as final. The regents apparently did not attempt to find another man, but continued negotiations with Angell for more than a year, until on Feb. 7, 1871, he was formally elected president. The university to which he came was at this time one of the largest of American educational institutions, having a college, law, and medical departments, and offering instruction in engineering and pharmacy. Its curriculum was liberal, its faculty relatively large and well selected. Coeducation had recently been introduced and a system of accredited high schools established. The state was committed to a policy of financial support, although the equipment of the university was inadequate and its salary scale greatly below that obtaining in the older institutions of the East.

Angell's inaugural address, delivered in June 1871 (*Selected Addresses*, pp. 3–33), was an able, brilliant, and, for the time, novel appeal to his audience and to the people of Michigan by which he sought to create an ideal for the state by setting forth an ideal for the University. In an era of *laissez-faire,* when the Spencerian conception of state functions was fashionable, he proposed for the state "the higher positive office of promoting by all proper means the intellectual and moral growth of the citizens." By establishing a university the assumption had been made that it was "just and wise for the State to place the means of obtaining generous culture within the reach of the humblest and poorest child upon its soil." This meant that "the University must interpret its vital connection with the State as a call to the largest and best work obtainable with its means. In that call it must find the stimulus to all strenuous endeavor. It may determine the culture, the civilization, nay, it may save the very life of the State and is justly held responsible for the faithful discharge of its sacred duty." The horizon of the University must not be limited to the boundaries of the state. To perform its work it "must be a part of the great world of scholars. It hospitably flings its gates wide open to all seekers after knowledge, wherever their home." Otherwise the University could not render its highest service to the state which had created it. Such was the ideal set forth by Angell, one, it is believed, never before expressed as the aim of a working system of public instruction. He had in mind a university in its widest sense—a college and professional schools, and, in addition, the providing of facilities for advanced study. "Either the State or the University will be unworthy the vantage ground which has been gained here with so much money and toil, if this is not the first of the Western schools to satisfy the demands for the highest order of university work. . . . Till that end is reached, our opportunities are not seized. Nothing less than that must content us." And then a note of most relevant warning: "It needs still however to be remembered in this country that calling an institution a university does not make it so. Neither do buildings, however imposing, nor endowments, however splendid, constitute a university. Nor does it convert a college into a university to abolish recitations and give all the instruction by lectures. I fear that the public do not sufficiently understand that the essential thing in a university is *men;* both in the students' seats and in the professors' chairs."

With such an ideal before him, Angell entered upon the duties of the presidency, and, thanks to his natural tact, soon entered into friendly relations with the members of his faculty, with many of whom he came to be on terms of intimate friendship. An Eastern man with Eastern training, he was without prepossessions in favor of those institutions with which he had been in contact. He did not handicap himself by making comparisons of the new with the old. He had intellectual curiosity and sympathy. Coeducation was alien to his experience, yet he viewed the experiment with an open mind, justified its logical position in the public school system of the state, and soon became its enthusiastic advocate. He came with no startling program of reformation or of remodeling. He set out to understand every phase of the university's activities; he visited the laboratories and talked with the men about the work in hand, he attended the classrooms to observe methods of instruction. He never lost sight of the fact that he was himself a teacher. As he said in his inaugural, "when a man stops acquiring knowledge, it is time for him to stop teaching." Notwithstanding the great increase in his executive duties due to the growth of the institution, he continued to conduct courses in international law and in the history of treaties. He made it a point to establish personal contacts with the students, acting for many years as the dean of the College of Literature, Science, and the Arts. As long as practicable he even performed the duties of a registrar, personally attending to the formalities of the registration of freshmen and conducting the university correspondence by letters written by himself. For nearly a decade he knew every student and called him by name. He was genial and sociable, approachable at all times and fond of social intercourse. The President's house became the center of a social life important to members of the faculty. In this he was greatly assisted by his wife (Sarah Swope, daughter of Alexis Caswell, professor at Brown and its sixth president, 1868–77), whom he had married at Providence in 1855.

Angell had no false pride as to the office of university president. He was not a dictator, because he was not an egotist. He never sought to impose a policy upon his faculty, or to make some new departure upon a mere majority vote. In one of his earliest annual reports he stated that radical changes should not be undertaken except with the substantial unanimity of the faculty. Even with the students he had no desire to be a driver—"A collegiate course cannot be wisely shaped with primary reference to driving drones to work. It should provide every manly and noble incentive to worthy achievement" (*President's Report,* 1873, p. 10). He was willing to experiment, but he was far from having the illusion that with the keys of the University had been acquired educational omniscience. It was by a quiet examination of the existing, by the tentative suggestion of the possible, by step-by-step improvement that Angell proceeded, bringing his constituency along with him, bridging the gaps between the university and the high schools yet raising the standards of admission, creating a larger clientele among the people of the state, arousing their interest, urging their support, and relying upon their approval of his policies as set forth in dignified and well-considered utterances. Thus he came to be regarded as an essential part of the institution of which he was the head, and as the leader of the new work of higher popular education.

With the adoption in 1873 of a millage tax for the University, specific appropriations in large amounts for buildings were not usually asked for. As a result, Angell's presidency left no great edifices at Ann Arbor as monuments of his administration. In current matters the administration was frugal, the salary scale remained rather low, and the teaching load large. The net result of his policy during nearly forty years was thus not a striking liberality on the part of the state but a regular support coming to be acquiesced in as a matter of course. When he retired the millage tax had been increased from one-twentieth to three-eighths of a mill. The returns therefrom increased from $15,000 to $650,000. Materially the improvement of the University had fallen relatively behind that of several rival state universities, so that by 1910 its equipment was inadequate and its buildings unprepossessing if not dingy. Angell's achievements were along other lines. He sought to broaden the college curriculum, to make possible a college education for those who had not had classical preparation, to enlarge the range of elective studies, and to extend the certificating privileges under university inspection to secondary schools in other states (1884). He established the first permanent system of admission requirements for medical schools (1874), the first professorship in the science and art of teaching (1879), the first instruction in the science of forestry (1882). He recommended (1877) comprehensive examinations at the end of the senior year as a part of the requirements for the bachelor's degree. He advocated (1882) a separation in methods of instruction between the sophomore and junior years, giving to the first two years the character of what has come to be known as the junior college and to the last two that of advanced university work. This was in part adopted, but Angell was too far in advance of his time and after about ten years the plan was abandoned.

So also he was hopelessly in advance of the state on the matter of the importance of graduate study and research. He saw that unless adequate aid were provided for graduate work the state universities would fall seriously behind the endowed universities. In October 1896 he said: "The question therefore with which this University and the other large State Universities is confronted is this,—are the states willing to furnish the means for providing this kind of instruction? . . . Upon the answer to be given to this question, it depends whether the state universities are to have their development arrested at their present stage, and so are to fall behind the universities which depend for their support upon private endowments" (*Proceedings of the Board of Regents, 1891–96*, pp. 660–61). But the people of Michigan remained unconvinced. The organization of graduate studies into a separate school was delayed until 1910. By that time other state universities had begun to devote considerable sums for fellowships and for publications. Michigan reluctantly followed rather than joyously led in this important development.

The administration of the University during the years 1871–1909 was not all plain sailing. When Angell came, the legislature had been insisting upon the establishment of a school of homeopathic medicine. Angell did not welcome but neither did he oppose an additional and rival medical faculty. A man of a different type, questioning the possibility of two rival routes for the acquisition of truth, might have resisted this increment of university responsibility. But modern scientific medicine had not yet received a recognized position. If there were two ways of training for a profession, why should not the state provide both ways? Public opinion seemed to demand it, the legislature was insistent, and the school was established, with irritating conflicts between the two faculties and with results not infrequently embarrassing to the University as a whole.

Meanwhile came occasional but important national diplomatic service. Angell's first diplomatic mission was to China in 1880. The liberal Burlingame Treaty in 1868 had allowed free entry of Chinese nationals into and residence within the United States. Subsequent congressional legislation excluding the Chinese, had been vetoed by President Hayes, who felt, however, that some modification of the treaty was necessary to forestall further congressional action which might amount to a breach of treaty obligations. Angell had been recommended to the President by Senator Edmunds of Vermont, and was appointed in the spring of 1880 as minister to China and also as one of the commission of three (the other members being John F. Swift of California, and W. H. Trescot of South Carolina) to negotiate a new immigration treaty. He was opposed to complete prohibition of Chinese immigration, but felt that existing abuses might be corrected by wise regulation and restraint. Swift favored total exclusion, while Trescot agreed with Angell. Their instructions allowed for some discretion. The negotiations were largely guided by Angell, whose benign dignity and bland manner made a favorable impression upon the Chinese plenipotentiaries. A treaty was signed, Nov. 17, 1880 (ratification advised by the Senate, May 5, 1881, and effective until 1894), by which China agreed that the United States might "regulate, limit or suspend," but not "absolutely prohibit" the entry and residence of Chinese laborers. On the same day a commercial treaty was signed, after a period of negotiation unprecedented for brevity, the most important article of which prohibited the importation, transportation, purchase, or sale of opium in China by American nationals or American ships, thus reverting to the position taken in the Cushing Treaty of 1844. The negotiations thus concluded, Angell remained in Peking as minister until October 1881, resuming his academic duties in February 1882.

Although a Republican, Angell was asked by

President Cleveland in October 1887 to serve upon the Anglo-American Northeastern Fisheries Commission, the other American members of which were Secretary of State Bayard and William L. Putnam. The negotiations, held in Washington, resulted in the treaty of Feb. 15, 1888, rejected by the Senate on party lines on Aug. 21, 1888. Of even date with the treaty was the protocol embracing a *modus vivendi* for two years, proposed by the British commissioners and agreed to by the United States. This, although never submitted to the Senate, continued, with recurrent renewals, to regulate the activities of the two countries in the fisheries.

In his second administration, Cleveland reiterated his confidence in Angell by appointing him to the Canadian-American Deep Waterways Commission with John E. Russell of Massachusetts and Lyman E. Cooley of Illinois. This Commission presented a report in 1897, but no congressional action followed its recommendations.

Angell's last diplomatic experience was as minister to Turkey. He was appointed by McKinley in 1897 and served until August 1898, thus representing the United States during the Spanish-American War. During his eleven months at Constantinople the matters claiming attention, in addition to those constantly under discussion with the Porte, were connected with the relations of belligerent and neutral. As to the success of his mission opinions differ. Oscar S. Straus, who succeeded Angell, gave a decidedly unfavorable judgment of it (*Under Four Administrations,* 1922, *passim*), while Bryce (*International Relations,* 1922, p. 150), characterized Angell as, with one possible exception, "the best ambassador any Power had during many years sent to the exceptionally difficult post at Constantinople."

Angell was a regent of the Smithsonian Institution, one of the founders of the American Historical Association, 1884, and its president, 1893–94. He contributed an essay upon the diplomatic history of the United States to Winsor's *Narrative and Critical History of America,* vol. VII (1888). He retired from the presidency of the University of Michigan in 1909 but continued to occupy the president's house upon the campus until his death in 1916.

Angell was about five feet eight in height, slender in early life, increasing in weight in later years. His hair was brown, his eyes strikingly blue and apt to twinkle with merriment. From at least the period of the Civil War he carried a beard with upper lip and chin shaven in the style adopted by Horace Greeley. His cheeks were unlined, his speech was soft, his manners gentle. Yet his whole figure radiated vitality. Even as an old man, he bore himself erect, walking with an easy stride good to look upon. The personal devotion which he inspired was due to an active eager spirit intent upon accomplishment through ways of kindliness and moderation. Of all the great American college presidents, he was probably the most modest. In one of his last speeches at the University of Michigan he took to himself the dying words of Cecil Rhodes—"so little done, so much remains to do." His accomplishment was what it was largely because it was so little in his own eyes.

[The chief source of information about Angell (and the best for his early life) is his *Reminiscences* (1911), but his administration at Michigan is inadequately treated in one chapter. For his connection with Brown University, see W. C. Bronson, *Hist. of Brown Univ.* (1914). For the period of his presidency at Vermont, see *U. S. Bureau of Education, Circulars of Information,* 1900, pp. 138–69. For the period of his presidency at the University of Michigan the best sources are his annual reports printed in the *Proc. of the Board of Regents of the Univ. of Mich.,* 1871–1909. See also Wilfred Shaw, *Univ. of Mich.* (1920). For the China Mission, see *Foreign Relations of the U. S.,* 1881, pp. 168–318; upon the Fisheries Treaty Commission, *Sen. Ex. Doc., 127,* and *House Ex. Doc. 434,* 50 Cong., 1 Sess.; upon the Waterways Commission, "Report of U. S. Deep Waterways Commission," *House Doc. 192,* 54 Cong., 2 Sess.; upon the Turkish Mission, *Foreign Relations of the U. S.,* 1898, pp. 1086–1120. Angell's *Selected Addresses* (1912) contain his principal public utterances. Genealogical information may be found in Avery F. Angell, *Geneal. of the Descendants of Thos. Angell* (1872).]

J. S. R.

ANGELL, JOSEPH KINNICUTT (Apr. 30, 1794–May 1, 1857), legal writer, was the only son of Amey (Kinnicutt) and of Nathan Angell, a storekeeper of Providence, R. I. He was descended from Thomas Angell, one of "the thirteen original proprietors," who came from England with Roger Williams in 1631. He was born at Providence, entered Brown University in 1809, graduated in 1813, and then attended the Law School, Litchfield, Conn., being admitted to the Rhode Island bar in March Term, 1816. Three years later he went to England to claim an estate under the will of William Angell, brother of his paternal ancestor Thomas Angell, but his suit terminated adversely on a technicality (Angell *vs.* Angell, 1 *Simons & Stuart,* 83). He returned home in 1822 and devoted himself to writing on legal subjects. His first book was *The Common Law in Relation to Watercourses* (1824), followed by *The Right of Property in Tide Waters* (1826), both being well received. Chancellor Kent said that no intelligent lawyer could well practise without them. In rapid succession Angell wrote treatises on *Adverse Possession* (1827) and *The Limitation of Actions* (1829). In 1829 he also edited the first volume of *The United States Law Intelligencer and Review.* He was assisted by Samuel Ames [*q.v.*] in the preparation of his next book, *The Law of Private Corporations Aggregate* (1832), which became a standard authority. The appearance of his *Law of Assignment* (1835) was followed by a period mainly occupied in revision necessitated by the demand for new editions of his previous works. In 1847 he was appointed reporter in the supreme court of Rhode Island—the first to hold that office. He issued one number of the *Reports* in July of that year, and prepared a second, but resigned in September Term, 1849. In the same year he wrote *The Law of Carriers.* His last work to appear during his lifetime was *The Law of Insurance* (1854). He died in Boston "as he had lived, without an enemy; distinguished through life by the simplicity of his character, by his kindly feelings toward all around him, by his attachment to his friends, by his freedom from prejudice, and by the total absence of all malevolence of spirit." He had at the time partially prepared *The Law of Highways,* which was subsequently completed by Thomas Durfee [*q.v.*]. He was unmarried. His portrait hangs in Rhode Island Hall, Brown University.

[Sources of information about J. K. Angell are few. Important material is contained in a "Memoir," prepared by Sidney S. Rider for insertion in a reprint of the *R. I. Reports,* vol. I, which latter contains memoranda relative to Angell's official connection with the court. This memoir is reproduced in *R. I. Hist. Tracts,* No. 11 (1880). Incidental references occur in Abraham Payne, *Reminiscences of the R. I. Bar* (1885). A brief sketch and details respecting his claim to the Angell fortune in England are in Avery F. Angell, *Geneal. of the Descendants of Thomas Angell* (1872).]

H. W. H. K.

ANGELL, WILLIAM GORHAM (Nov. 21, 1811–May 13, 1870), inventor, manufacturer of screws, was born in Providence, R. I., the son of Enos Angell, a carpenter, and Catherine (Gorham) Angell. Several years of his youth were devoted to learning his father's trade, but an intense interest in machinery drew him to its field instead. His educational advantages were few; he acquired the mere rudiments of a common-school education. He was married to Ann R. Stewart, and one of their two children, Edwin Gorham, succeeded him as president of the American Screw Company. Angell had what his associates described as an intuitive perception of the capabilities of a machine; and he used it to good advantage. In his early twenties he became a partner in a reed-making business. Meanwhile he engaged in experiments on the construction of machinery for making iron screws to be used in woodwork. The American market at the time was supplied with English screws, rough and clumsy, and no one seemed to be dreaming of an American screw to compete with the English one. Angell's inventive mind found ways for the improvement of screw-making machinery and when, in 1838, the Eagle Screw Company was formed, he became its agent and manager. They made a gimlet-pointed screw which, by a careful analysis of facts, he was able to persuade American merchants to buy. No artifice was needed as his product was superior to the English product. The Eagle Screw Company, after twenty successful years in business, united with the New England Company to form the American Screw Company. Angell became its president and manager.

Along with his inventive ability and sound business sagacity, Angell was an excellent draftsman and an architect and builder of no mean capacity. This trait helped invaluably in the construction of buildings which would stand the strain of heavy machinery necessary in his business. He had a keen interest in patents and patent laws, particularly as they applied to screw machinery, and he was frequently called upon to act as a referee in settling conflicting claims on different patents. Believing that a man could do but one thing well, he concentrated on his business to the exclusion of everything else. He joined no church, had no interest in politics, and gave little or no time to amusement. He was, however, a man of warm personal sympathies, and contributed liberally though inconspicuously to the relief of suffering among the poor and unfortunate.

[Avery F. Angell, *Geneal. of the Descendants of Thomas Angell* (1872); *Providence Morning Jour.,* May 17, 1870.]

E. Y.

ANSHUTZ, THOMAS POLLOCK (Oct. 5, 1851–June 16, 1912), painter, was the son of Jacob Anshutz, born in Strasbourg, Alsace, and of Jane Abigail Pollock, born at Wheeling, (then) Va., of New England and Scotch-Irish stock. He was born at Newport, Ky., where he spent his early childhood, going thence to Wheeling and afterward to New York, in 1873, to study at the National Academy of Design under L. E. Wilmarth. Among his fellow students were Joseph Boston, Charles Vanderhoof, Kelly the sculptor, C. Y. Turner, and Carl Hirshberg. In 1875 he went to Philadelphia and entered the classes of the Pennsylvania Academy of Fine Arts under Thomas Eakins and Christian Schussele, and six years later became a member of its faculty. In September 1892 he married Effie Schriver Russell, of Wheeling, W. V ., and sailed for Paris, where he remained a year under the instruction of Doucet and Bouguereau at the Julian Academy. He then returned to Philadelphia to resume his professorship in the Academy schools, which he held for the remainder of his life. He had a house and studio at Fort Washington, Pa. A basic knowledge of anatomy and other sciences increased his remarkable efficiency as a teacher.

His method was to consider carefully the native tendencies in each pupil, and to develop these upon a foundation of the essential elements in art training. His success as "a maker of painters" is evident in the number of eminent American artists who benefited by his instruction—Robert Henri, George Luks, Edward W. Redfield, Hugh H. Breckenridge, John Sloan, W. Glacken, W. E. Schofield, Daniel Garber, and others.

While devoting his attention to this task, he still found time to produce many pictures. One of his first exhibits was a "View of the Ohio River" with the old Mississippi steamboats, based on early impressions. He painted landscape with much feeling, but it was in figures and portraits, for which his studies thoroughly prepared him, that he achieved his greater successes. His painting exemplified in its technical soundness the principles he taught. Appreciation of his ability as a painter existed for some years before he received more concrete recognition. Honorable mention was awarded him in 1901 at the Philadelphia Art Club's exhibition; in 1904, a silver medal at the St. Louis Exposition; and in 1909 the Gold Medal of Honor at the Pennsylvania Academy's exhibition—a distinction shared with Whistler and Sargent. The Walter Lippincott Prize for meritorious painting followed for "The Tanagra," now in the Pennsylvania Academy's permanent collection, a gift from his pupils and admirers. At the Buenos Aires International Exposition in 1911, his painting "Shadows" received a gold medal. Two other paintings—beside "The Tanagra"—"Becky Sharp" and "In a Garret," are in the Pennsylvania Academy collection. At the Corcoran Gallery at Washington is "The Dutchman"; at the National Academy of Design, New York, "The Breaker," and his own portrait presented on his election as an associate member. In the Thomas B. Clarke Collection is "Noontime at the Mill," besides many pictures and portraits i private collections.

He was president of the Philadelphia Sketch Club, a member of the Philadelphia Art and Water Color Clubs, of the New York Water Color Club, and also of the Union Internationale des Beaux-Arts et Belles-Lettres. In 1909 he succeeded William M. Chase as head of the faculty of the Pennsylvania Academy of Fine Arts. He died at Fort Washington, Pa. Writing in the *Philadelphia Record* (May 29, 1910) John Cournos thus describes his appearance: "His body, tall and slightly stooped, suggests strongly both in repose and in motion the man of thought; while the blue eyes that gaze abstractly from the depths of a virile and truly noble head reveal the dreamer."

[John Cournos, "A Great Art Instructor: His Methods and Ideas," *Phila. Record,* May 29, 1910; "A Maker of Painters," *Boston Evening Transcript,* Feb. 10, 1912; obituaries in the *Public Ledger, North American, Evening Telegraph,* all of Phila., June 17, 1912; *Who's Who in America,* 1912–13; information supplied by Mrs. Effie Schriver Anshutz.]

R. J. W.

ANSON, ADRIAN CONSTANTINE (Apr. 17, 1852–Apr. 14, 1922), baseball player, son of Henry and Jeannette (Rice) Anson, was born at Marshalltown, Ia. Attracting attention in 1871 as a member of the Forest City team of Rockford, Ill., Anson filled his first important professional engagement in the next year with the Philadelphia Athletics. He was married in 1876 to Virginia Fiegel of Philadelphia. In the same year he was induced by his friend, A. G. Spalding, to sign a contract with the Chicago Club of the newly formed National League, with which he remained until 1897, when he retired from league baseball. As first-baseman, captain, and manager he guided the Chicago team to league championships in 1880, 1881, 1882, 1885, and 1886. During this period the blue uniforms and white hose of Anson's men became established as symbols of victory. Anson was one of the greatest batsmen of his day. Always standing high in the batting averages, he four times led his league. For his twenty-two seasons with Chicago he had the remarkable grand average of .331. A blond giant standing well over six feet and weighing 195 pounds, he was a terror to pitchers. Smiting every kind of ball with equal success, he was never more dangerous than at critical stages of the game. Though apparently rather awkward in the field, he was also a remarkably steady and successful first-baseman. His greatest strength, however, lay in his burly power of leadership. Never puffed up over his own importance, he strove constantly for his team. Aggressive in disposition, "he had a voice in his impassioned moments like a hundred Bulls of Bashan" (*New York Times,* Apr. 17, 1922, p. 16). It was this fighting spirit which attracted and amused lovers of baseball, friends and foes alike. He took part in two trips abroad as an American baseball player, one of these being the famous tour of the world in 1888 by a National League party. After retiring from baseball, he interested himself in other sports, especially billiards and golf. He served in public office as city clerk of Chicago 1905–07, but he was not fitted for political life. Because of his genial character, his unexpected humor, and his remarkable generosity, Anson was greatly loved. Always called "Captain" or "Cap" and later "Pop," he was the hero of numerous anecdotes. His rather sudden death brought deep grief to all sportsmen. It is said that he wished as his epitaph, "Here lies a man that batted .300."

[Obituaries in leading American newspapers following Anson's death; excerpts in the *Lit. Dig.*, May 6, 1922, pp. 62 ff. Anson's character and work are referred to in A. G. Spalding, *America's National Game* (1911); J. J. McGraw, *My Thirty Years in Baseball* (1923), and F. C. Richter, *Hist. and Records of Baseball* (1914).]

E. P. T.

ANTES, HENRY (1701–July 20, 1755), religious leader among the German-Americans of Pennsylvania, was born in Freinsheim in the Rhenish Palatinate and was the son of Philip Frederick and Anna Catherine Antes; his ancestor, Baron von Blume, from Mainz, had hellenized his German name to the Greek equivalent Antes in order to escape persecution during the Thirty Years' War. The elder Antes emigrated to Pennsylvania about 1720; and in 1726 his son married Christina Elizabeth, daughter of William De Wees, by whom he had eleven children. He settled in Frederick, in the present Montgomery County, became a partner with his father-in-law in a paper and flour mill, and acquired property. He is described as a man of powerful frame, strong, with the versatility of a pioneer: mechanic, farmer, hunter, guide, a trusted counsellor skilled in the drawing of legal documents. His place in history depends upon his religious leadership, and especially on his association with the United Brethren, and his strivings for union. At first he was a member of the Reformed Church at Falkner Swamp, and a friend of its minister Boehm. He was soon a leader and a lay preacher, unusually broad-minded, being "singularly free from prejudice and bigotry." In Philadelphia and the back country there were Germans of various denominations, Mennonites, Dunkers, Lutherans —with whom he wished to fraternize—and members of his own Reformed Church, and to these were added new arrivals, Moravians or United Brethren. Antes and several others formed a group called the "Associated Brethren of Skippack," which met in conferences until 1740. His house was a rendezvous for German immigrants, and with the new-comer Spangenberg (later Moravian bishop) he discussed religious unity. His projected union was wider than the "Brethren of Skippack." He welcomed as an ally the great Moravian leader Zinzendorf, who had recently landed, and on Dec. 15, 1741, he issued a call for a meeting of Christians to be held at Germantown, Jan. 1, 1742. At this meeting Antes presided, and in the subsequent conferences he took an active part. The union, a sort of federation, "Congregation of God in the Spirit" "so grand in its conception, so exalted in its purposes," nevertheless failed of fulfilment (J. H. Dubbs, *History of the Reformed Church, German,* in vol. VIII, 1895, of the American Church History Series).

Antes had left the Reformed Church in 1740, and not long afterward he joined the Moravians. In 1741 acting as their agent he bought for £400 a tract of 500 acres along the Lehigh River, which became the nucleus of the town of Bethlehem. He removed thither in 1745, and his house and farm in Frederick were used as a school for boys. He served as business manager for the Moravians—to which office he was regularly appointed in 1748—built a noted mill and other works, was appointed justice of the peace by the governor, and investigated the grievances of the Indians. When the Moravians were attacked he defended them, and acted as the trustee of their property in Philadelphia. Two further instances may be given: he received a license to run a ferry on the Lehigh River, and when the Moravians launched a vessel of their own, it was registered in Antes's name. His services were of "immense value," and his position was shown by his friendship with such religious leaders as Zinzendorf, Spangenberg, Muhlenberg, and Whitefield.

In 1750 Antes left Bethlehem and the Moravians, and returned to Frederick. He objected to certain innovations, especially to the rule that the minister should wear a white surplice at the Eucharist. It has been stated that he withdrew from membership in the Moravian Church (questioned by Levering, pp. 251–52). However this may be, he continued his activity in Moravian affairs at Bethlehem and elsewhere. In 1752–53, with others, he made a trying journey to North Carolina, exploring in the interests of the church; 100,000 acres were purchased near the Yadkin River, which became the Moravian colony of Wachovia. Antes was made justice of the peace in Philadelphia County in 1752. He defended the loyalty of the Pennsylvania Germans in a letter written to the provincial secretary, and died soon after at Frederick, leaving a legacy to the Moravians. His daughter, Ann Margaret, married the Moravian Bishop, Benjamin Latrobe, and became the mother of the architect Latrobe who designed the central part of the Capitol.

[Henry S. Dotterer, "Family Record of Henry Antes," *Perkiomen Region,* Dec. 1894, and "Henry Antes," *Ibid.,* Oct., Nov., Dec., 1899; Edwin McMinn, *A German Hero* (1886) and *On the Frontier with Col. Antes* (1900); Jos. M. Levering, *Hist. of Bethlehem, Pa.* (1903); L. T. Reichel, "Early Hist. of the Ch. of the United Brethren," in *Moravian Hist. Soc. Trans.,* III (1888); J. Taylor Hamilton, *Hist. of the Unitas Fratrum, or Moravian Ch. in the U. S.,* in vol. VIII (1895) of the Am. Ch. Hist. Ser.; John Henry Clewell, *Hist. of Wachovia in N. C.* (1902).]

E. K. A.

ANTHON, CHARLES (Nov. 19, 1797–July 29, 1867), classical scholar, was born in New York, the son of Dr. George Christian Anthon and Genevieve Jadot (for parents see Anthon, John). He grew up in a large family of intelligent young people, with five brothers and two sisters, and inherited the persistent industry of the German and the quick perception of the French. He attended the best schools of the city and in 1811 entered Columbia College, where he was awarded so many distinctions that his name was withdrawn from competition and therefore is not found among those of the recipients of honors at graduation. He studied law for four years in the office of his brother John, and in 1819 was admitted to the bar of the supreme court of the state. During these years he spent his spare time in reading Greek and Latin and in studying French and German.

In 1820 he was chosen adjunct professor of Greek and Latin in Columbia College, and thus entered upon his life-work. While preparing for the bar he had adopted the habit, which he retained for many years, of rising at 4 a. m. and devoting the early hours of the morning to his literary labors. His college duties occupied a large part of the day, and the rest was carefully divided, with a liberal allowance for modern languages. His Saturdays were spent in careful and exhaustive preparation for the next week's classes. According to the system then in vogue, the memorizing of inflections and rules of syntax formed a great part of the work which he demanded of his students, and he was an exacting teacher, even in his later years, when he had adopted a different system of instruction. In 1830 Anthon was put in charge of the Grammar School of Columbia College, and about the same time, when the professorship of Greek and Latin in the College was divided, he was made Jay Professor of the Greek Language and Literature. As Professor in the College Anthon was greatly liked, chiefly because of his faculty of uniting with the text under discussion a series of facts artfully grouped so that they remained fixed in the memory of his pupils. In the grammar school he was too much feared to be generally liked. He often raised a laugh at the expense of his pupils, and employed Greek, Latin, and English nicknames in ridicule of delinquents. His own nickname among the boys was "Bull."

Anthon was a large, strongly built man, of imposing presence. His head was large, his forehead high and massive, his eyes black and deeply set. The lower part of his face was square, massive, and firm. His voice was clear and sonorous. He was always carefully dressed, and his manuscripts were models of neatness. Though brilliant in conversation and of a cheerful disposition, he had few familiar friends and almost never appeared in general society or in places of public amusement. His walks for exercise were usually taken after dark or within the college grounds. He never married, but was devotedly attached to his sisters, who lived with him. He had no religious or political associations, though during the Civil War he exhibited warm patriotism. He visited libraries and bookstores rarely, but knew and bought books from catalogues. His library was large and well chosen. For years he never left New York City. Once only, in 1831, he visited his mother's birthplace, Detroit, returning by way of Montreal, Quebec, and the White Mountains. Even after the first attack of the illness which finally caused his death, he would not give up his work, but returned to his classes and continued to conduct them until prevented by a second attack. He rallied slightly after this, but grew more and more feeble, and died July 29, 1867.

One of Anthon's earliest works was the first American edition of *Lemprière's Classical Dictionary.* In this he did not change the text, but made many additions. In a subsequent edition, finished in 1833, which still bore the name of Lemprière, almost every article was rewritten or enlarged, and many additions were made, especially in the field of geography. The third edition, published in 1842, was again greatly changed, and was called *Anthon's Classical Dictionary.* He also edited and revised *Smith's Dictionary of Greek and Roman Antiquities,* and *Smith's Dictionary of Greek and Roman Biography, Mythology, and Geography, Zumpt's Latin Grammar,* and the *English-Latin Lexicon* of Riddle and Arnold. He was the author of *A System of Latin Prosody and Metre* (1838) and *A System of Ancient and Mediæval Geography for the Use of Schools and Colleges* (1850). Anthon was one of those who introduced into the United States the results of foreign, chiefly German, scholarship. He was the first American to prepare a critical and exegetical edition of a classical author with learned prolegomena, critical notes, and ample commentary. This was his *Horatii Poemata,* or "larger Horace," published in 1830, a large octavo volume of more than 1,000 pages. Almost immediately after his appointment to his professorship he began to prepare text-books which should aid the student to understand the ancient authors. By these he was chiefly known, judged, and misjudged. Anthon edited the texts on the basis of foreign, chiefly German, editions, and added copious explanatory notes, often translating entire sentences or even longer passages. For this reason his editions, in spite of the scholarship which they exhibit, were more popular with pupils than with teachers. He continued for thirty years to prepare at least a volume annually, editing for school and college use the works, in whole or in part, of Homer, Xenophon, Cæsar, Cicero, Horace, Juvenal, Sallust, Tacitus, and Virgil. Each of his text-books passed through several editions, and for some thirty years, about the middle of the nineteenth century, his influence upon the study of the classics in the United States was probably greater than that of any other one man.

[*Charles Anthon, A Commemorative Discourse,* prepared and delivered at the request of the Trustees and Alumni of the College by Dr. Henry Drisler (1868); "Reminiscences of Dr. Anthon," by Robert D. Nesmith, in the *Galaxy,* vol. IV, Sept. 1867; obituary in *N.Y. Times,* July 30, 1867.]

H. N. F.

ANTHON, CHARLES EDWARD (1823–June 7, 1883), educator, numismatist, was born in New York, the son of a prominent lawyer, John Anthon [*q.v.*], and nephew of Charles Anthon [*q.v.*], eminent classical scholar. He graduated from Columbia in 1839, spent some years in study and travel in Europe, and upon his return was elected to the chair of history in St. John's College, Annapolis, Md. In 1852 he was appointed professor of history and belles-lettres in the New York Free Academy, which later became the College of the City of New York. Here he remained until ill health forced him to resign in March 1883. He went abroad in May, but died in Bremen the following June.

He became interested in numismatics sometime about 1865, in which year he made his first purchase of coins at the Chilton sale. To these he added until he had acquired an extensive collection containing many rare pieces. For a series of sales from his cabinet he made catalogues, so carefully and thoroughly prepared, "that they will long serve as books of reference for students and collectors" (*American Journal of Numismatics,* July 1883). From 1869 until his death he was president of the American Numismatic and Archæological Society of New York, and from May 1867 until April 1870 he was an editor of the *American Journal of Numismatics.* He published *A Pilgrimage to Treves, through the Valley of the Meuse and the Forest of Ardennes in the Year 1844* (1845), a brief but excellently written descriptive and historical sketch; *The Son of the Wilderness* (1848), a translation of a dramatic poem by Friedrich Halm; *Narrative of the Settlement of George Christian Anthon in America* (1872); *The Gloriam Regni* [Gloriam Regni Tui Dicent 1670] *or Silver Louis of 15 Sous, and of 5 Sous, Struck for Circulation in French America* (1877); and in the *Proceedings of the New York Law Institute in Accepting the Donation of the Bust o' the Late John Anthon* (1876), there is printed a letter of presentation signed by him.

[For ancestry see Anthon's own *Narrative,* mentioned above, and Marie M. G. Anthon, *The Ancestry of Genevieve Jadot Anthon* (1901); obituary notices appeared in *N.Y. Times,* June 9, 1883, *N.Y. Tribune,* June 9, 1883, and the *Am. Jour. of Numismatics,* July 1883. The contents of his collection at his death are listed in *Cat. of the Late Prof. Anthon's Numismatic Cabinet* (1884).]

H. E. S.

ANTHON, JOHN (May 14, 1784–Mar. 5, 1863), lawyer, was born at Detroit. His father, George Christian Anthon, a native of Salzungen in the Duchy of Saxe-Meiningen and a surgeon in the Dutch West Indian trade, having been captured by a British privateer was landed in New York in 1753. He became an assistant surgeon with the British army, and served in the West, being stationed permanently at Detroit after 1767. There he married as his second wife Genevieve Jadot. John was their second surviving son. In 1786 the family moved to New York, where Dr. Anthon acquired a prominent position professionally and socially. John received a good classical education. He graduated from Columbia in 1801 at the head of his class, studied law, was admitted to the New York bar in 1805, and commenced practise in New York City about 1807. He practised at first principally in the mayor's court, and he drafted the act by which this court —which had been the municipal court of New York City for 156 years—was merged in the court of common pleas (*Ch. 62, Sess. 44,* 1821). His untiring industry, and the high quality of his work are indicated by the fact that in 1829 he argued no less than forty-two reported causes on appeal (Hall's *New York Superior Court Reports*). "He was the horse in the legal mill. If he had been absent a week, the Courts would have stopped trying causes" (J. W. Gerard, *Address before the New York Law Institute,* Apr. 4, 1863). He assisted in founding the New York Law Institute, and after its incorporation in 1830 continued actively interested in its affairs. Elected second vice-president Apr. 8, 1839, he became president in 1852—an office which he held till his death.

Anthon had the reputation of being the best practitioner at the New York bar. Although somewhat brusque in manner and possessed of a displeasing voice, he showed great skill in marshalling facts and in legal exposition and analysis. His leisure hours were devoted to horticulture, the reading of Greek and Latin classics, and the study of Italian. He was the author of *American*

Precedents and Declarations (1810), *Digested Index to the Reported Decisions of the United States Court* (1813), and *The Law of Nisi Prius* (1820). He also left in manuscript three volumes of literary criticisms to which he had given the name "Neo-Photius," and a volume on "Characteristics of Books and Men." He was married in 1810 to Judith Hone. Two of his sons attained some degree of eminence, William Henry as a lawyer and Charles Edward as a professor in the College of the City of New York.

[Charles Edward Anthon's *Narrative of the Settlement of George Christian Anthon in America* (1872) contains particulars of the family history. No adequate material, however, exists for a detailed memoir of John Anthon. The only printed matter available consists of a biog. notice by E. Patterson in his sketch prefixed to *The Cat. of the Lib. of the Law Institute* (1874), an address by J. W. Gerard, reported in *Proc. on the Occasion of the Death of John Anthon* (N. Y. Law Institute, 1863), and a letter written by Prof. C. E. Anthon, Jan. 3, 1876, printed in *Proc. of N. Y. Law Institute in Accepting a Bust of John Anthon* (1876). The N. Y. Pub. Lib. possesses in the Stuart Coll. a copy of a *Cat. of the Private Lib. of the Late John Anthon,* prepared for the sale which took place after his death. It contains no less than 1,423 items, embracing the whole field of classical and modern literature. A plaster bust of Anthon, made about 1826 by John Browere, stands in the vestible of the Law Institute Lib. in N. Y. City.] H. W. H. K.

ANTHONY, ANDREW VARICK STOUT (Dec. 4, 1835–July 2, 1906), wood engraver, was born in New York City, the son of John and Eliza (Stout) Anthony. He was named after his maternal uncle Andrew Varick Stout, and was of English stock on his father's side, and of Dutch on his mother's. The latter was the daughter of Elsie Van Varick, of the family of Richard Varick, mayor of New York. Andrew's desire to be an artist not being approved by his father, the boy ran away from home at the age of eleven. He had "a sketchy schooling," but later became "singularly well informed on a vast variety of subjects." He studied art with T. S. Cummings and wood engraving under T. W. Strong. Before he was twenty, "with some wild scheme," wrote S. G. W. Benjamin, "of coining mahogany into dollars by exporting it from Mexico," he sailed to Honduras and was shipwrecked. Then he succumbed for a time to the lure of California, but eventually returned to New York. An early engraving on a small broadside—*Hutchings' California Scenes: The Mammoth Tree* (1854)—is signed "Anthony & Baker Sc." In 1857 appeared *The Indian Fairy Book* of Cornelius Mathews, with designs by John McLenan, engraved by Anthony. He also engraved drawings by D. C. Hitchcock of scenes and incidents in Central America, and wrote articles on Honduras, "Scraps from an Artist's Note Book," published in *Harper's Magazine,* 1856–57. On Dec. 24, 1858, he married, in New York, Mrs. James M. Warner, *née* Mary Aurelia Walker. In 1860, in charge of the engraving department of the *New York Illustrated News,* he went to England for that paper to "scoop" the Heenan-Sayers prize-fight. His large and hurried engraving of the event, after a drawing by Thomas Nast, was done in part on the *Vanderbilt* during his passage home, and appeared in the "Championship Number" (May), with a note on the engraver and his portrait. The first important work in which he had a hand was *Folk Songs* (1860), edited by John W. Palmer. Then began the activity by which he became best known. From 1866 to 1889 he superintended, with delicate taste, the production of fine editions for Ticknor & Fields; Fields, Osgood & Co.; and James R. Osgood & Co., in Boston. Both Linton and Koehler state that this work had much influence on the art of wood engraving. Among the editions he superintended were those of Whittier's *Snow Bound* (1866), in which most of the engravings, after Harry Fenn, were his own—"of his best," writes Linton, "subjects and drawings well suited to his graver,—honest while refined"; and Longfellow's *Building of the Ship* (1870), engravings by Anthony and Linton; Longfellow's *Skeleton in Armor* (1877), illustrations by Mary A. Hallock, later Mrs. Foote. He wrote the text for W. T. Smedley's drawings of *Life and Character* (1899), and his unfinished paper on "An Art That Is Passing Away" forms part of the volume *Wood Engraving: Three Essays by A. V. S. Anthony, Timothy Cole and Elbridge Kingsley,* published by the Grolier Club in 1916. From 1894 until his death he was connected with the literary department of Harper & Brothers. He died at West Newton, Mass., leaving a widow and one daughter; his son Ripley Osgood, who showed talent as an artist and painted a portrait of his father, had died some years before.

[Anthony's daughter, Mrs. Henry P. Perkins, furnished notes accompanying the gift of her father's engravings and engraving tools to the N. Y. Pub. Lib. His friend S. G. W. Benjamin devoted a chapter to him in *Our Am. Artists, for Young People,* 2nd ser. (1881), with a portr. of Anthony and a picture of him at work, engraving. Clement and Hutton's *Artists of the Nineteenth Cent.* (1884) quotes newspaper criticisms. Critical estimates of his engraving appear in W. J. Linton's *Hist. of Wood Engraving in Am.* (1882) and in S. R. Koehler's chapter on the United States, in *Holzschnitt der Gegenwart* (Vienna, 1887).] F. W.

ANTHONY, GEORGE TOBEY (June 9, 1824–Aug. 5, 1896), governor of Kansas, was the youngest of five children. His parents, Benjamin and Anna (Odell) Anthony, ardent members of the Society of Friends, lived on a farm near Mayfield, Fulton County, N. Y., where George was born. Benjamin Anthony died when this son was five years of age. Four years later the family moved to Greenfield, N. Y., where the boy attended school in the winter months and "worked out" on the farms in the neighborhood during the remainder of the year. At the age of sixteen he was apprenticed to a tinner at Union Springs, N. Y. At the conclusion of his apprenticeship he opened a small tinshop and hardware store at Medina, N. Y. He was proprietor, merchant, and tinner, doing all of the work in the establishment. In 1852 he was married to Rosa A. Lyon at Syracuse. Subsequently, at an uncertain date, he moved to New York City and entered the commission business, which he followed until President Lincoln's call for volunteers, on July 2, 1862. Gov. Morgan, in response to the call, organized the state of New York, for the purpose of recruiting, into territorial divisions, over each of which was a committee in charge. The committee supervising the sub-division which included Genesee, Orleans, and Niagara counties was composed of Ex-Gov. Church, Noah Davis, Jr., and George Tobey Anthony. Anthony recruited and organized the New York independent battery and entered the service as its captain. The battery served with credit throughout the war, Anthony remaining with it until mustered out, June 12, 1865. He was brevetted major of volunteers for distinguished service.

Anthony and his wife arrived in Leavenworth, Kan., in November 1865, when he began the second and more important period of his life. He became editor of the *Daily Bulletin* and the *Daily Conservative,* positions which he held for two and one-half years. He was editor and proprietor of the *Kansas Farmer* for six years. It was in this capacity that he made his influence especially felt in Kansas. He had a practical knowledge of thorough farming in New York, a foremost state in sound agricultural theory and practice. This was in contrast with the slipshod methods prevailing in Kansas at that time. He admonished the farmers to diversify crops, to rotate them in order to preserve the soil, to care for farm machinery, to care for livestock and to improve the breed, to economize farm management, and to improve home conditions on the farm. In December 1867 he was appointed assistant assessor of Internal Revenue and in the following year collector of Internal Revenue for the United States. He was president of the state Board of Agriculture for the three years 1874–76 and a member of the Board of Managers of the Centennial Exposition. In 1876 he was elected governor of Kansas on the Republican ticket. He failed to be reëlected for a second term. During his administration he recommended that the legislature provide for a reformatory for young criminals separate from the penitentiary, was instrumental in subduing refractory Indians, put down a riot caused by striking railway employees, and recommended that the legislature take action to compel railroads to fulfil their obligations to the public in cases where citizens had voted bonds to build the roads. Anthony met all the duties of the executive office with good judgment and firmness. Indeed, he was aggressively honest and rather militant in his attitude toward those whom he deemed in the wrong; hence he made political enemies. In 1881 he was appointed general superintendent of the Mexican Railway; in 1885 he represented Leavenworth County in the legislature; in 1889 he was appointed a member of the state Board of Railroad Commissioners; in 1892 he was nominated for Congress by the Republican party, but failed of election.

[Collected material in the lib. of the Kan. State Hist. Soc.; *Trans. Kan. State Hist. Soc.,* VI, 202, VII, 253; *Portr. and Biog. Album of Leavenworth, Douglas and Franklin Counties* (1899); Wm. E. Connelly, *Standard Hist. of Kan.* (1918); Frank W. Blackmar, *Kansas* (1912), I; Chas. L. Anthony, *Geneal. of the Anthony Family* (1904); obituary in the *Leavenworth Standard,* Aug. 6, 1896.]

F. W. B.

ANTHONY, HENRY BOWEN (Apr. 1, 1815–Sept. 2, 1884), journalist, politician, a descendant of John Anthony of Hampstead, England, who came to Boston in 1634 and removed to Rhode Island about 1640, was born at Coventry, R. I. His father was William Anthony and his mother was Eliza Kinnicutt Greene. Both his father and his maternal grandfather, James Greene of Warwick, were Quakers. His father was a cotton manufacturer and the part of the town in which they lived was called Anthony. There the boy attended village school and the Friends' meeting-house. Most of his life was spent, however, in Providence, where he fitted for college at a private school and entered Brown University in 1829. He made a good, though not brilliant, record in college and graduated with his class in 1833, carrying with him a very definite leaning toward letters. Although he went into business, to which he gave five years, partly in Providence and partly in Savannah, Ga., literature remained his major interest. In 1837 he married Sarah Aborn, daughter of Christopher Rhodes. A year later, when he was twenty-three years old, he was invited by a kinsman who owned the *Providence Journal* to take the editorship during an interim of a few weeks. He exhibited such a surprising gift and aptitude for the editorial duty that what began as a mere stop-gap became permanent. So skilfully did he guide the fortunes of the paper and so general was the respect and influence it attained under his direction that he was soon seen to be indispensable. Thus it came about that he was in charge of the paper—the most influential journal in the state—in 1842 during the Dorr Rebellion, one of the crises in the modern history of the old commonwealth. During that time of turbulence and disorder, the newspaper office became the center and rallying-point of the conservative interests of the state and its editor rose to a position of exceptional authority. To Anthony the paper owed not only its political power but very largely also its excellent literary style. Examples of his skill in verse are the mock heroic poems, "The Dorriad" and "The Chepachet Campaign," satirizing Dorr and his partizans, which appeared in the *Journal* in 1843 (republished in *The Dorr War,* by Arthur M. Mowry, 1901). Throughout his life and even up to within a week or two of his death he continued to exercise a guiding influence over the *Journal,* writing paragraphs and articles which were marked by urbanity, charm, and a shrewd knowledge of men and affairs.

Naturally enough then, when in 1849 a conservative candidate was sought for the governorship, Anthony was named and elected governor of the state, was reëlected in 1850 and was urged to run again in 1851, but declined. His administration as governor fulfilled the expectations of his friends and gave him a reputation both for talent and sagacity in the conduct of public affairs. It was, therefore, a matter of course that when he was nominated in 1858 for the Senate he was elected with little opposition. The atmosphere of the Senate was particularly congenial to Anthony's tastes and abilities. His personal charm and dignity, his knowledge of affairs, his acquaintance with public men, his natural ease and kindliness of manner, all fitted him to fill his part in the upper chamber with distinction and success. There he was chosen president *pro tempore* on many occasions, in 1869, 1870, 1871, and for the last time in 1884, when he declined to serve on the score of ill health. It was no wonder that he was returned by his loyal state time after time until he had become the "Father of the Senate"; he was still a member when he died, full of honors and greatly admired both by his associates and his constituents.

Anthony was one of the type of senators whose services lie rather in the exercise of judgment and practical wisdom than in any definite contribution either to law or practise. He was a member, however, of important committees: Claims, Naval Affairs, Mines and Mining, Post Office and Post Roads, and finally that of Public Printing, on which he served for more than twenty-two years and there labored to reduce the extravagance and waste, to restrict public printing to the legitimate demands of the various government departments, and to make the *Congressional Record* a faithful transcript of congressional proceedings. In these endeavors he was only partly successful; they were such desirable ends, however, that they have been pursued, and some of them attained, by others. Similarly as a member of the Committee on Naval Affairs, a post which he filled from 1863 to 1884, he exerted always a sound and moderating influence. He was conservative by constitution: he voted for the impeachment of Johnson, was a steadfast supporter of a protective tariff, and was no less firm in support of a sound currency. He brought to the Senate the character and attainments of a gentleman, a profound and sympathetic knowledge of the state he represented, and an urbanity and courtesy which made him a valued associate in the upper chamber.

[*Henry Bowen Anthony, A Memorial* (1885); George Frisbie Hoar, *Autobiography of Seventy Years* (1903), vol. II; letters and papers of Justin S. Morrill.]

W. B. P.

ANTHONY, JOHN GOULD (May 17, 1804–Oct. 16, 1877), zoologist, was born in Providence, R. I. His parents, Joseph and Mary (Gould) Anthony, were of old New England stock, the Anthonys going back to John Anthony (or Anthonie) of London, who settled in Rhode Island in 1634. Several members of this American branch of the family became widely known for public services, military, politico-social, or scientific. When John was twelve years of age, his parents moved to Cincinnati. The boy's schooling seems to have been of the briefest and he went into business. On Oct. 16, 1832, he was married to Anna W. Rhodes. In those days a group of enthusiastic naturalists had arisen in Ohio. Anthony made the acquaintance of Jared Kirtland and others of this circle, and became deeply interested in natural history. He was apparently able to devote considerable time to the collection and study of fresh-water mollusks, for which the Ohio River is famous. From 1835 on, he corresponded extensively with mollusk students in the East and in Europe. In his delightfully frank letters to Louis Agassiz, S. S. Haldeman, and others, we have glimpses of the human and personal side of the scientific workers of the time. Serious eye trouble in 1849 interrupted Anthony's activities for a year, and in 1851 he retired from business.

In 1853 he made a pedestrian tour of Kentucky, Tennessee, and Georgia. His aims, the restoration of health and the collecting of mollusks, were successfully achieved. The materials gathered were worked up and published in his papers from 1854 to 1860, and in L. Reeve's great British work *Conchologia Iconica* (1843–68). In 1863 Agassiz placed Anthony in charge of the mollusk collections of the Museum of Comparative Zoology at Cambridge, and in 1865 he was included in the scientific staff of the expedition to Brazil. His later years were devoted to the classification and arrangement of the great collections at Cambridge, and, as a side issue, gathering data for a history of the Anthony family. Personally he was a rather short and slender man, with well-shaped head, full beard, and brilliant, dark eyes. His letters were written in a small, regular, copperplate hand, beautiful if somewhat ornate. His labels, to be found in all the older museums, are unmistakable. As an author he was not prolific. His papers were mainly descriptive and had no great scientific influence; but in his letters a wider horizon is often seen, and he supplied material for important monographs by others.

[Chas. L. Anthony, *Geneal. of the Anthony Family* (1904); unpublished letters in Academy of Natural Sciences, Phila.]
H. A. P.

ANTHONY, SISTER (1814–Dec. 8, 1897), nurse in the Civil War, known as "the angel of the battlefield" and "the Florence Nightingale of America," originally Mary O'Connell, daughter of William and Catherine (Murphy) O'Connell, was born in Limerick, Ireland, but came to the United States in early childhood and was educated at the Ursuline Academy in Charlestown, Mass. In 1835 she entered the novitiate of the American Sisters of Charity at St. Joseph's Valley. In 1837 she was transferred to Cincinnati, where her work as a Sister of Charity was carried on for forty-five years. In 1852 the Sisters organized the first modern hospital established in the city. It was called St. John's Hotel for Invalids, and Sister Anthony was placed in charge. The hospital was begun in a building previously used by Harriet Beecher Stowe for a private school. The hospital staff was formed from the faculty of the Ohio Medical College. Sister Anthony was brought into relation with Dr. George C. Blackman, president of the Ohio Medical College, and Dr. John Shaw Billings, then an interne in the hospital. Both Dr. Blackman and Dr. Billings achieved unusual distinction as surgeons during and following the Civil War. Their friendship for Sister Anthony and appreciation of her character and services are significant features of the recognition which she earned in the medical history of the state. She and other members of her community served as nurses in Civil War camps and battlefields at Camp Dennison, Winchester, Cumberland, Nashville, Richmond, New Creek, Gallipolis, Culpeper Court House, Murfreesboro, Pittsburg Landing, Lynchburg, and Stone River. They brought boat-loads of wounded soldiers up the Ohio River, and St. John's Hospital was given over entirely to the care of them. The Sisters also accompanied wounded soldiers on flat cars from Cumberland to Washington. In their field nursing they faced every difficulty with the greatest courage and performed services reserved to the supreme reaches of sympathy and spiritual consecration. The *Medical and Surgical History of the War of the Rebellion* (pt. III, vol. I, p. 910) refers to their services "in terms of highest praise." In recognition of the work of Sister Anthony, two citizens of Cincinnati, neither a member of the Catholic Church, purchased the United States Marine Hospital and presented it to her to be used as a hospital under the direction of the Community. In 1873 one of the donors presented to Sister Anthony property to be used as a maternity hospital. The records of the Hebrew Southern Relief Board contain a tribute to her for her work during the outbreak of the yellow fever in 1877. In 1880 she retired from active service. She celebrated her golden jubilee in 1885 and died in 1897. Her death brought forth extraordinary tributes of appreciation and affection from the press and public. The fundamental qualities in her character were self-effacement, profound human sympathy, quick understanding, resourcefulness, and fearless devotion. She had a remarkable gift for inspiring general confidence. The records show that even Jefferson Davis trusted her implicitly when her duties brought her into contact with him. On one occasion a Union general, in compliance with an appeal from Sister Anthony, spared the life of a Confederate soldier who had crossed the lines and incurred the penalty of death. Her personal influence was recognized as of the greatest help by army surgeons in their work with wounded soldiers who were under their charge.

[Much information concerning Sister Anthony is found in Sister Mary Agnes McCann, *The Hist. of Mother Seton's Daughters* (1917–23); in Lieut.-Col. Fielding H. Garrison, *Dr. John Shaw Billings* (1915); in Otto Juettner, *Daniel Drake and His Followers* (1909); and in J. F. Maguire, *The Irish in Am.* (1868), pp. 480 ff.]
W. J. K.

ANTHONY, SUSAN BROWNELL (Feb. 15, 1820–Mar. 13, 1906), reformer, was a descendant of John Anthony, Jr., who came to America from Hampstead, England, in 1634. She was born in Adams, Mass., where her well-to-do Quaker father was a pioneer cotton manufacturer. The Anthony family had produced strong-minded women, not afraid to face the public, before Susan's day. Her father's mother had been given an exalted place on the high seat in the meeting, and his sister, Hannah, had been a Quaker preacher. Susan grew up in an atmosphere of independence and moral zeal. Daniel Anthony had married Lucy Read, passionately fond of music and dancing, in defiance of the meeting. Much to the annoyance of his patrons, he discontinued the sale of liquor at the store he conducted in conjunction with his mill. He permitted none but Quaker preachers to smoke or drink in his home; was so opposed to slavery that he tried to get cotton for his mills which had not been produced by slave labor; encouraged his daughters to be self-supporting, ignoring the criticism of his neighbors; and finally was "read out of meeting" for permitting the young people of the town to dance on the top floor of his house, instead of over the tavern, though his own children were allowed the rôle of spectators only. His remark when told that the men would not come to the "raising" of tenement houses he had decided to build, unless he furnished them with gin, had in it the same grim determination which his iron-willed daughter later displayed: "Then the houses will not be raised."

Susan was a precocious child, learning to read and write at the age of three, endowed with an unusual memory, and eager for knowledge. When she was six years old, the family moved to Battensville, N. Y. Here she attended the district school and later a school which her father established in his home for his own children and those of his neighbors. This training, supplemented by a year at Deborah Moulson's boarding-school at Hamilton, near Philadelphia, qualified her for good positions in the teaching profession, the best and last of which, head of the Female Department of Canajoharie Academy, she held from 1846 to 1849.

Her early letters reveal a straight-laced, prudish young woman, serious-minded, with very rigid moral standards, and prone to criticize her elders with more than the ordinary assurance of conceited youth. She writes to her uncle, rebuking him for drinking ale and wine at yearly meeting; and after commenting sharply upon President Van Buren's patronage of the theatre, and revelings in the tents of luxury and "all-debasing wine," asks if there can be hope of less dissipation among the people, when one who practises such abominable vices "(in what is called a gentlemanly manner) is suffered to sit at the head of our Government." She was not without admirers of the other sex in those days, but there is no evidence that her passions were ever stirred. She never felt it her mission to be a home-maker. When nearing thirty she was in the family of a cousin when the latter gave birth to a child, and wrote home rather disgustedly that in her opinion there were some drawbacks to marriage which made a woman quite content to remain single. Later her views of amusements and life in general broadened, and she lost much of her priggishness. It was to reform, however, that she gave her heart, and in its service that she found an outlet for her emotions, pouring into it the devotion, loyalty, and self-sacrifice which most women give to their families.

Interest in the great issues of the day and a growing passion to join in the fight against injustice and vice had made her restless in the narrow confines of the school-room, and by 1850 she was back in the family home, now near Rochester, N. Y. It had become a rallying-place for reformers and about its table gathered such men as Garrison, Phillips, Pillsbury, Channing, and Frederick Douglass. Soon she became acquainted with Amelia Bloomer, Lucretia Mott, Lucy Stone, and Elizabeth Cady Stanton with whom she formed a life-long alliance, which in the face of seemingly insurmountable difficulties did much to force the woman suffrage movement on to ultimate success.

Her first public work was in behalf of temperance. In 1852 she was a delegate to a meeting held by the Sons of Temperance in Albany. Upon arising to speak on a motion, she was informed that "the sisters were not invited there to speak but to listen and learn." As a result of this treatment she and others organized the Woman's State Temperance Society of New York, the first of its kind ever formed. She continued her efforts for temperance in conventions and elsewhere, but all the time meeting violent prejudice against women's participation in public affairs, she became increasingly convinced that only through equal rights could women become effective workers for social betterment. She also attended teachers' conventions, where she demanded for women all the privileges enjoyed by men. She took a radical abolitionist stand, and in 1857–58 campaigned under the banner "No Union with Slaveholders." After the war she was one of the first to advocate negro suffrage. When the Fourteenth Amendment was under discussion, she attempted to have included a provision insuring the franchise to women as well as to male blacks but was unsuccessful. In 1852 with some reluctance she joined her friend Amelia Bloomer and others in wearing the short skirt and Turkish trousers, known as the Bloomer costume. In about a year she abandoned it. "I found it a physical comfort," she said, "but a mental crucifixion. The attention of my audience was fixed upon my clothes instead of my words. I learned the lesson then that to be successful a person must attempt but one reform."

Any chronological record of Miss Anthony's life would be one of unending lecture tours and the direction of campaigns in one state after another. In 1868 in association with Mrs. Stanton and Parker Pillsbury she published a periodical known as *The Revolution,* radical and defiant in tone. "We said at all times," Mrs. Stanton declares, "just what we thought, and advertized nothing we did not believe in" (Theodore Stanton and Harriot Stanton Blatch, *Elizabeth Cady Stanton,* 1922, I, 215). In 1869 the National Woman Suffrage Association was organized to secure a sixteenth amendment to the Federal Constitution, enfranchising women. Mrs. Stanton was made president and Miss Anthony chairman of the executive committee. Owing to some division in sentiment, the American Woman Suffrage Association was formed the same year, with Henry Ward Beecher as president and Lucy Stone chairman of the executive committee. It worked chiefly to secure suffrage through amendments to state constitutions. In 1890 the two societies were merged under the name National American Woman Suffrage Association and Mrs. Stanton was elected president and Miss Anthony vice-president at large. In 1892 Miss Anthony was elected president and served until 1900, when she retired at the age of eighty.

In 1872, in a plan to test the legality of woman suffrage under the Fourteenth Amendment, she registered with fifteen other women and voted at the November elections in the city of Rochester. Two weeks later she was arrested for having violated the law. Her trial was postponed and she voted again in the city elections the following March. Since the trial of the United States *vs.* Susan B. Anthony was to be a jury trial, she and her associates spent the weeks and months preceding it in an intensive lecture campaign aimed to educate the voters from among whom the jury would have to be selected. She was most ably defended at the trial by Henry R. Selden and John Van Voorhis. At its conclusion Judge Ward Hunt delivered a written opinion, written before the trial had taken place, which directed the jury to bring in a verdict of guilty. In the face of Miss Anthony's counsels' objections to this questionable procedure, Judge Hunt refused to allow the jury to be polled and discharged them without permitting them to consult together. He then imposed a fine of $100 on Miss Anthony. She told him she would never pay a dollar of the penalty and she never did. Courts and laws meant nothing to her, if they conflicted with what she thought was right. She "would ignore all law to help the slave," she once declared, and "ignore it all to protect an enslaved woman."

Throughout the many years of Miss Anthony's strenuous career she encountered opposition of almost every kind. She met hisses and clamor, rotten eggs and vegetables, press comments that were vile and all but obscene, but sustained by an unshakable confidence in the justice of her cause, she never wavered, and before her death she was rewarded with respect and honor rarely bestowed upon woman, and had the satisfaction of seeing equal suffrage granted in four states, and a measure of suffrage granted in others. At international congresses of women in London and Berlin (1899 and 1904), her appearance called forth demonstrations of exceptional regard.

When she was about thirty-five she was described by a newspaper reporter as having "pleasing rather than pretty features, decidedly expressive countenance, rich brown hair very effectively and not at all elaborately arranged, neither too tall nor too short, too plump nor too thin—in brief one of those *juste milieu* persons, the perfection of common sense physically exhibited." In her later years her face was lined, angular, and somewhat austere, but lighted with the spiritual beauty which life-long devotion to high purposes often imparts. She was of the militant type, and being engaged in a desperate fight, she not infrequently displayed some of the less pleasant characteristics which such warfare is likely to produce in a soldier. She had amazing physical vigor, was aggressive and bold. She spoke her mind with great frankness, and occasionally used strong epithets, but no stronger than those hurled at her. There was little of the conciliatory or diplomatic in her disposition. As is often the case with those who are obsessed with one idea, she showed little appreciation for the complexity of social and personal problems, and had difficulty in being altogether fair to points of view different from her own. These, however, were the faults of the qualities which gave her power, and she ranks high among the notable array of reformers, male and female, of her day. She died in Rochester, N. Y., one month after reaching her eighty-sixth year, leaving her small fortune of $10,000 for the cause to which she had given her life.

[Material for this sketch has been found in Ida H. Harper's three-vol. work, *The Life and Work of Susan B. Anthony* (vols. I, II, 1899; vol. III, 1908). These vols. contain much newspaper and mag. comment, giving a wide range of editorial opinion on her work and personality. See also M. A. De Wolfe Howe, *Causes and Their Champions* (1926); Don C. Seitz, *Uncommon Am.* (1925); Sherwood Eddy and Kirby Page, *Makers of Freedom* (1926); United States *vs.* Susan B. Anthony, in Blatchford, *Reports of Cases in the Circuit Court,* XI, 200–12. Elizabeth Cady Stanton, *Eighty Years and More* (1898), contains two chapters on Miss Anthony.

With Mrs. Stanton and Mrs. Matilda Gage, Miss Anthony prepared a *Hist. of Woman Suffrage,* 3 vols. (1881–87), and in 1900, in conjunction with Mrs. Ida Husted Harper, she prepared a fourth vol., which closed the century.]
H. E. S.

ANTOINE, PÈRE (Nov. 18, 1748–Jan. 19, 1829), Capuchin friar and parish priest of New Orleans, was a storm center of controversy during his life and has remained so ever since. Opinion in regard to his character has varied all the way from John G. Shea's view that he was "the scourge of religion in Louisiana" (*Catholic Church in the United States,* 1888, II, 548) to C. W. Bispham's judgment that he "did more for New Orleans, morally and spiritually, than any other known person" (*Louisiana Historical Quarterly,* 1919, II, 37). What is certain, however, is that he eventually became the most popular figure of his day in Louisiana.

He was born at Sedella in Granada (Spain), the son of Pedro Mareno and Ana of Arze, and was baptized by the name of Francisco Ildefonse Mareno. "He was made Priest by the Bishop of Guadix in the convent of the Capuchins of Granada, Dec. 21, 1771 . . . came to the Mission of Louisiana in the year 1780 . . . was Auxiliary Vicar 1787 . . . was also instituted Curé of the Parish of St. Louis of New Orleans Nov. 25, 1785" (*Vie abregée du Père Antoine,* 1829, quoted by Bispham, p. 25). As early as 1787 Gov. Miro suspected Père Antoine of a design to establish the Inquisition in Louisiana (Correspondence quoted by Bispham, p. 26), a measure likely to arouse the hostility of the French inhabitants of the province and to interfere with further immigration. Friction had also developed between Père Antoine and Bishop Cyril and by 1790 had reached such a point that the latter requested him to return to his monastery in Spain (F. L. Gassler, *Catholic Historical Review,* 1922, II, 60). Gov. Miro gladly agreed to supply the necessary sailing facilities and on Apr. 28, 1790 notified the friar that the arrangements for his departure were completed. Antoine now refused to leave and not only produced a royal order of the previous December appointing him Supreme Officer of the Holy Inquisition of Cartagena in Louisiana, but demanded that the Governor should make ready immediately to furnish him with troops "at any hour of the night" to carry this order into effect. He repeated this demand in even more peremptory terms the following day (*Ibid.,* p. 61). With matters thus brought to a crisis, it was decided that the friar be returned at once to Spain for "canonical reasons" (*Ibid.,* p. 62). "On a stormy night [he] was bound in irons and sent back" (*Louisiana Historical Quarterly,* II, 384).

After his return to Spain, Père Antoine disappears from view for five years, but in August 1795 he reappears, bearing the new title of Honorary Preacher to His Majesty and reinstated in his parish in New Orleans by order of the King (*Ibid.,* pp. 27, 374). During the confusion attendant upon the rapid transfer of Louisiana first to France and then to the United States, Antoine was frequently accused of political and ecclesiastical intrigues. The accusations were believed by Archbishop Carroll of Maryland, who was in ultimate charge of the area of New Orleans, by Secretary of State Madison, and, apparently by Gov. Claiborne. At this distance it is impossible fully to determine the actual facts. Carroll's jurisdiction over New Orleans, although later confirmed, was at this time still doubtful, and the legality of his appointments may have been sincerely questioned by Antoine. The friar was evidently a high-spirited man, indisposed to avoid enmity. He seems to have regarded the welfare of his own parish as more important than harmony with his fellow ecclesiastics. In 1805 a dispute arose between him and the Rev. Patrick Walsh, Vicar-General of Louisiana, who suspended the friar from his offices and appointed the Convent of the Ursuline Nuns as the only place in the parish where the sacraments could be administered. Antoine defied Walsh's authority, and claimed that the church was the property of the citizens of New Orleans; and the Catholics of the city held a meeting which elected a body of wardens who in turn chose Père Antoine as their parish priest (*Ibid.,* p. 29). Antoine further appealed to the Spanish King, who once more supported his claim (*Propaganda Arch. Congreg. particolari,* CXIV, 71 ff., a document which proves that the Spanish King even after the cession of the territory to the United States, made use of the prerogatives granted by the Popes in matters of ecclesiastical territory). After Walsh's death his successors continued the assault on the friar, but Antoine maintained his position successfully. From 1813 to 1816 he acted as a secret political agent for the Spanish government, communicating to its war department news of various filibustering conspiracies against Mexico (correspondence quoted, *Louisiana Historical Quarterly,* II, 385–92).

If in his political and ecclesiastical activities Antoine was unnecessarily assertive, the record of his relations with his parishioners shows entire devotion and unselfishness. When in 1819, with his position definitely established, he was offered the bishopric of New Orleans by Du Bourg, he modestly declined on the score of age and incapacity (letter, Antoine to Du Bourg,

Louisiana Historical Quarterly, II, 33). He continued to live a life of poverty in a little wooden hut in the rear of the church. During the frequent epidemics of yellow fever, he always remained in the city and ministered to the sick (A. Lavasseur, *Lafayette in America,* II, 231). He devoted to the care of the poor all the gifts which he received from the 3,500 marriages which he performed. In 1816 he established a confraternity for instructing negroes in the Catholic faith. His funeral in 1829 was more of a triumph than a funeral. Both houses of the legislature, in accordance with the public sentiment, adjourned for the day and assisted at the interment. The courts likewise suspended their sessions, and the judges joined in the procession. The members of the City Council did likewise and wore crape for thirty days (*Louisiana Advertiser,* New Orleans, Jan. 24, 1829). The Masons of all lodges were asked to walk in the procession, and a special notice was given to the members of the Lodge L'Étoile Polaire to take part (*Louisiana Gazette, The Bee,* both of New Orleans, Jan. 22, 1829). The date-palm tree that overshadowed the hut in which Antoine lived and died, became, in memory of the friar, a famous landmark in New Orleans. The centenary of the appointment of Antoine as Pastor of New Orleans, Nov. 29, 1885, was solemnly celebrated at the Cathedral, and a book, *Centenaire du P. Antoine,* was published to commemorate the event.

[In addition to the sources cited above, see Fredegand Callaey in *Analecta O. M. Cap.,* XLI (Rome, 1925); Otto Jeron, "The Capuchins in the U. S.," in *Hist. Recs. and Studies of the U. S. Cath. Hist. Soc.;* Marie Louise Points in *Cath. Encyc.* (1911), XI, 8–11. The statement of Shea (*Cath. Ch. in the U. S.,* II, 548–49) that it was charged that Antoine "was sent to Spain for having killed a man in a quarrel concerning a woman" rests upon a doc. that has never been found.]

F. M. K.

ANZA, JUAN BAUTISTA DE (b. 1735), Spanish explorer and founder of San Francisco, was born at the Spanish port of Fronteras in Sonora, Mexico. At an early age he became a lieutenant and in 1760 was made captain of the Presidio of Tubac, though not confirmed in the position. An official said of him that by reason of his "activity, valor, zeal, intelligence, and notable unselfishness he was an all-round good officer" (C. E. Chapman, *Founding of Spanish California,* 1916, pp. 150–52).

Spain at this period (1769–76) was more or less constantly planning to occupy the Pacific coast of North America as far as the Bay of Monterey and beyond, in order to anticipate possible occupation by the Russians or the English (*Ibid.,* ch. VIII). In 1770 a mission had been planted at Monterey itself by members of the Franciscan Order under Fr. Junipero Serra, and in 1771 there had been planted San Gabriel Mission near the present Los Angeles. As for Monterey, it was thought by Anza that supplies could more successfully be transported thither overland from Sonora than up the coast by ship. In pursuance of this idea, and of permission granted by the Viceroy of New Spain, Antonio Maria Bucarely, Anza on Jan. 8, 1774, set forth from his Presidio of Tubac with twenty-one soldiers, thirty-five loads of provisions, munitions, etc., pack animals and cattle. His course was by way of the Presidio of Altar and of Caborca Mission northwest to the junction of the Gila and Colorado Rivers. From this junction he proceeded to the foot of the San Jacinto mountains, and from the San Jacinto mountains by San Carlos pass to the Mission of San Gabriel. Much of the journey lay across the Colorado Desert and was accomplished only with great suffering. Quitting San Gabriel on Apr. 10, Anza took the road for Monterey. There he made a short stop and then started back to the Presidio of Tubac whence he had set out, arriving May 26, 1774. In recognition of his expedition to Monterey, which had proved the practicability of the route, Anza on Oct. 4, 1774, was made a lieutenant-colonel.

Straightway a second California expedition was decided upon by Viceroy Bucarely, and Anza was instructed to explore the land about San Francisco Bay and to place at some suitable point a presidio, for the site "ought to be occupied in order to advance the Spanish conquests." The expedition set forth from Tubac on Oct. 23, 1775. It consisted not only of a body of troops but of the wives, children, and servants of the soldiers—some 240 persons. California was not merely to be occupied in a military sense but was to be colonized. The route was north to the Gila, then down that stream to the Colorado. Anza reached San Gabriel, Jan. 4, 1776. From San Gabriel he set forth for Monterey on Feb. 21, where he arrived Mar. 10. Attended by his chaplain and cartographer, Pedro Font, he explored the site of San Francisco, marched around the lower end of the bay, and ascended for a short distance the San Joaquin River. In April he departed for Sonora and the City of Mexico, leaving the final dispositions to be made by Lieut. José Joaquin Moraga. On Sept. 17, 1776, there was celebrated the founding (on the site chosen by Anza) of the San Francisco presidio, and on Oct. 9, the founding of the Mission of San Francisco. In June 1777 Anza was made governor of New Mexico, so that he might bring about communication between California and Santa Fé. In

1780 colonies were established on the Colorado River, but in 1781 they were overwhelmed by an attack of the Yuma Indians. For this disaster Anza was criticized, as in the reports of his California expeditions he had spoken highly of the pacific disposition of the Yumas. In 1787 he was put forward for governor of Texas but failed of the office, and in 1788 was relieved of his governorship of New Mexico. Thenceforth he disappears from view.

[H. H. Bancroft, *Hist. of Cal.*, I (1884), chs. IX, X, XII, XIII; I. B. Richman, *Cal. under Spain and Mexico* (1911), ch. VI; C. E. Chapman, *Hist. of Cal.—The Spanish Period* (1921), chs. XXIII, XXIV—ch. XXIII containing an interesting portr. of Anza; Z. S. Eldredge, *The Beginnings of San Francisco from the Expedition of Anza*, 2 vols. (1912). A reproduction of a chart by Pedro Font, showing the route of Anza on his second expedition (1775–76), may be found in Bancroft, I, 263. Exact reproductions of various charts by Font, as contained in his manuscript diary, are to be found in *San Francisco Bay and Cal. in 1776*, John Carter Brown Lib. (1911).]
I. B. R.

APES, WILLIAM (b. Jan. 31, 1798), Pequot Indian, missionary and author, was born in the woods near Colrain, Mass. His father was a half-breed who joined the natives and married a descendant of King Philip. During his childhood the boy's parents led a roving life as basketmakers, and his early years were passed with his grandparents, who treated him with great brutality. At some time during his fifth year, after his arm had been broken by his grandmother, he was rescued by an uncle who called in a neighboring white man to his assistance. Brought up and Christianized by the whites, he ran away at the age of fifteen and enlisted in the army. He took part in Gen. Hampton's abortive campaign against Canada, in Gen. Wilkinson's attack on Montreal, and in the battle of Lake Champlain. Soon after his discharge he married a white woman. He now became a Methodist preacher, but being refused a license by the Methodist Episcopal Conference, he joined the Methodist Society, instead, by which he was regularly ordained in 1829.

Four years later when visiting the Marshpee Indians on Cape Cod he found them very discontented with their lot. Unjustly taxed, receiving neither police protection, education, nor religious instruction—the white missionary appointed by Harvard College received 400 acres of Indian land but devoted all his attention to his own countrymen—the Indians endured in silence for lack of a leader to voice their complaints. This leader they now found in Apes, who became a member of the tribe, and boldly encouraged them to adopt rather high-handed resolutions, dismissing their white overseers and *fainéant* missionary, and forbidding the whites to cut wood on their plantation. Presently Apes was arrested for forcibly unloading a wagonload of wood collected by one Sampson in defiance of the Indian notification; he was tried on the charge of inciting to riot and sentenced to thirty days in jail. The case attracted attention throughout the state and was widely commented upon in the newspapers. Apes was at liberty in time to make one of the Indian deputation which petitioned the next legislature. Largely influenced by his sincerity and eloquence, the legislature adopted measures removing most of the Indian grievances. Apes brought libel suits against three of his detractors and compelled apologies. After these victories, his career is unrecorded.

He was the author of four works: *A Son of the Forest* (1829), a delightfully naive autobiography, containing a long appendix on the Indian character; *The Experiences of Five Christian Indians: or the Indian's Looking-Glass for the White Man* (1833); *Indian Nullification of the Unconstitutional Laws of Massachusetts Relative to the Marshpee Tribe: or, the Pretended Riot Explained* (1835), a full, well-documented account of the whole Marshpee affair, put into its final shape by William J. Snelling; *Eulogy on King Philip* (1836), a convincing evidence of Apes's oratorical power.

[In addition to the above see *Hist. of Barnstable County, Mass.*, ed. by Simeon L. Deyo (1890) and *Laws of the Commonwealth of Mass., Passed by the Gen. Court*, 1834, ch. CLXVI, 1836, Ch. CLXXIX.]
E. S. B.

APPENZELLER, HENRY GERHARD (Feb. 6, 1858–June 11, 1902), Methodist missionary to Korea, was descended from Jacob Appenzeller, who came to Philadelphia in 1735 from Appenzell, Switzerland, and was secured as a tenant farmer by a Mr. Thomas, of Suderton, Pa. Jacob was thrifty and eventually acquired the farm. Gideon, of the fourth generation, married Maria Gerhard, of Mennonite stock. Henry, the second of their three sons, was born on the Suderton farm. His mother never mastered English, and she and her son always conversed in "Pennsylvania Dutch." After a public school education, he attended the West Chester Normal School, graduated from Franklin and Marshall College at Lancaster, Pa., in 1882, and then attended Drew Theological Seminary at Madison, N. J. He had been "converted" in 1876, while attending Presbyterian revival services at West Chester, but in 1879 had joined the Methodist Church at Lancaster, and, being licensed to preach, had filled sundry small pulpits during his college and seminary days. At Drew he "excelled in Greek" (Griffis, p. 76), and became private secretary to one of the professors. On Dec. 17, 1884, he married Ella Dodge, who had removed to Lancaster from Berlin, N. Y., in 1879. She had been reared a Baptist, but, like her future husband, had joined the Methodist Church at Lancaster. While on their honeymoon at the home of his parents the Christmas holidays brought them their appointment as missionaries to Korea. The faculty and students of Drew accompanied them to their train, singing hymns. Appenzeller was ordained at San Francisco, Feb. 1 or 2, 1885, and sailed on the latter date, accompanied by Dr. Scranton and family, Methodist missionaries, and the Rev. Horace Underwood, Presbyterian; all bound for Korea. The Appenzellers and Mr. Underwood arrived at Chemulpo on Apr. 5, 1885. The century-old opposition to Christianity still made missionaries unwelcome in Korea, and, because of the disturbed conditions following the bloody *émeute* of Dec. 4, 1884, official advice was against taking ladies to Seoul. The Appenzellers therefore returned temporarily to Japan but were back in Chemulpo in June 1885, and settled at Seoul in July. Their daughter, Alice R., was born that year—the first white child born in Korea. Two other daughters were also born there.

Appenzeller soon acquired a knowledge of the language and assisted in the translation of the Scriptures; Matthew and Mark, First and Second Corinthians being assigned to him. He aided in the establishment of the Methodist printing house by the Rev. Mr. Ohlinger, whom he assisted in editing the *Korean Repository*. He later became the editor of this valuable magazine under its new title *Korean Review*. In 1886 he established the Pai Chai School for boys, the brick building for which was completed in 1887. In 1895 he realized the fulfilment of a fond dream in the laying of the corner-stone of a brick church building on the Methodist premises at Seoul. In a regrettable encounter, in May 1902, with some Japanese workmen engaged in the construction of the Seoul-Fusan Railway, he and Bishop Moore and the Rev. Mr. Swearer, were injured. This delayed his intended departure for the South on mission work, so that he was obliged to take a following steamer, the *Kumagawa,* sailing from Chemulpo June 11, 1902. That evening his ship was wrecked in collision with the *Kisawaga* near Kunsan. His body was not recovered. Being dressed, he might have saved himself, as did others, had he not gone forward to rescue a native mission girl entrusted to his care.

[Wm. E. Griffis, *A Modern Pioneer in Korea* (1912); Jas. S. Gale, *The Vanguard* (1904), *Korean Sketches* (1898); Daniel L. Gifford, *Every-Day Life in Korea* (1898); L. H. Underwood, *Underwood of Korea* (1918); Horace Grant Underwood, *Modern Education in Korea* (1926); Isabella B. Bishop, *Korea and Her Neighbors* (1898); Horace N. Allen, *Chronological Index of Korea* (1891), *Things Korean* (1908), *Korean Fact and Fancy* (1904). The above sketch has been checked and elaborated by the personal recollections of the biographer, and by correspondence with the M. E. Board of Foreign Missions.]

H. N. A.

APPLE, THOMAS GILMORE (Nov. 14, 1829–Sept. 17, 1898), theologian, educator, born at Easton, Pa., the seventh son of Andrew and Elizabeth (Gilmore) Apple (or Appel), came of German, English, and Irish ancestry. He graduated at Marshall College, Mercersburg, Pa., in 1850, under the presidency of the celebrated theologian, Dr. John W. Nevin. During his college course and for several years thereafter he studied theology and in 1852 was ordained as a minister of the (German) Reformed Church in the United States. On Aug. 27, 1851, he married Emma Matilda Miller, of Easton, Pa., by whom he had eleven children. In 1865 he became president of Mercersburg College, a new institution, established upon the physical foundations of old Marshall College, which in 1853 had been merged in Franklin and Marshall College at Lancaster, Pa. On June 27, 1871 he was elected professor of church history and New Testament exegesis in the Theological Seminary, which in this year was also moved from Mercersburg to Lancaster. In 1877 he was elected president of Franklin and Marshall College and assigned to the chair of philosophy, which he occupied for twelve years in conjunction with his professorship in the Theological Seminary. From 1868 to the end of his life he was editor of the *Mercersburg Review,* later changed in title to the *Reformed Church Quarterly Review* as the organ of the denomination for Christological, historical, and positive theology. In its pages will be found his most important writings, particularly his contributions to the system of thinking which in this country came to be identified with the institutions at Mercersburg and hence was called "Mercersburg Theology." He also took an active part in the legislative and executive affairs of the church, and was instrumental in the organization of some and the reorganization of other enterprises which profited by his administrative abilities. He was a member of the committee which framed the *Order of Worship* (1866). He was a leading member of the so-called "Peace Commission" which finally settled the liturgical question upon a satisfactory basis in the form of a *Directory of Worship,* authorized for use in 1887. In the matter of doctrine, he drew a sharp line between religion as a challenge to faith and theology as a science. "He held firmly to the historic faith of the church, and yet he never refused to accept any new light that was shed upon the old faith by modern critical research" (*Reformed Church Messenger,* vol. LVI, no. 39). His writings are marked by clear thinking, intellectual honesty, and lucid expression. He had a constructive mind and contributed much of permanent value to the religious and educational history of his time.

[Joseph Henry Dubbs, *Hist. of Franklin and Marshall Coll.* (1903); *Franklin and Marshall Coll. Obit. Rec.,* vol. I, no. 3; *Reformed Ch. Messenger,* Sept. 22, 29, 1898; Theodore Appel, *Life and Work of John Williamson Nevin* (1889), see Index; *Proc. Gen. Council Presbyt. Alliance,* 1880; "Mercersburg Theology" in the *New Schaff-Herzog Encyc. of Religious Knowledge;* files of the *Reformed Church Quart. Rev.; Lancaster Daily New Era,* Sept. 17, 1898.]

G. F. M.

APPLEBY, JOHN FRANCIS (May 23, 1840–Nov. 8, 1917), inventor, was born at Westmoreland, Oneida County, N. Y., the son of James and Jane Appleby who had but recently come to New York from England. In 1845 the parents continued their migration to try a fresh start in the newer country of Wisconsin, where they established their farm home in Walworth County. Here Appleby grew up, obtaining a district school education in the infrequent intervals when he was not needed for work at home or on some neighbor's farm. It was when only eighteen, in the employ of a farmer in Iowa County, that he first conceived the idea of a binder. He was assisting in the trial of a new reaping machine, binding the sheaves as the grain was cut, when it occurred to him that a machine could be made to do this work. His suggestion was received with jeers from his employer. Nevertheless, during the ensuing year he constructed a model of a twine binder which contained the essential elements of the Appleby Knotter which binds nine-tenths of the grain grown in the world to-day. Lack of funds prevented Appleby from further developing his knotter and when the Civil War started he volunteered and served in the 23rd Wisconsin Infantry. While in the trenches before Vicksburg, he had time to whittle out a new device for rifles. This mechanism provided a magazine for cartridges and an automatic feed device. He received a patent for this the next year (1864) which he sold for $500, only to see it resold for $7,000. This incident, besides supplying funds necessary to continue experimentation, impressed Appleby with the value of invention and made him an inventor for life. In 1867 he was able to demonstrate his first complete machine at Mazomanie, Wis. The demonstration was unsuccessful and earned him the reputation of being a crank. He was encouraged, however, by one spectator, Dr. E. D. Bishop, who invested $1,500 in the binder. In 1872 Appleby connected himself with Parker & Stone of Beloit, Wis., and built in their factory a wire binding machine which was successful as a binder, but failed because of the farmers' prejudice against wire as a binding material. In 1874 he organized the Appleby Reaper Works to build self-rake reapers at Mazomanie. The following winter he renewed his experiments with the twine binder at the factory of Parker & Stone, and the next year rebuilt the machine which was then entirely satisfactory. On July 8, 1878, and Feb. 18, 1879, patents were issued covering the perfected machine and binder. In the winter of 1878, William Deering, of the firm of Gammon & Deering, recognized the possibilities of the binder and purchased the rights to substitute it for a wire binder which the company had been using on the Marsh Harvester. This was the first manufacture of the Appleby Knotter on a large scale, and marked the beginning of its general adoption on harvesters. The McCormick, Champion, and Osborn companies procured rights and began the manufacture of this type of binder and all others were soon outdistanced by its superiority. It remains to-day the most popular binding machine. Appleby was married at Mazomanie, Wis., in 1867, and was the father of three children.

[R. L. Ardrey, *Am. Agricultural Implements* (1894); Merritt Finley Miller, *The Evolution of Reaping Machines* (1902); Herbert N. Casson, *The Romance of the Reaper* (1908); V. D. Stockbridge, *Digest of Patents Relating to Breech-Loading and Magazine Small Arms* (1874); F. B. Swingle, "Unbending Backs at Harvest Time" in *Wis. Agriculturist,* July 14, 1923, repub. as "The Invention of the Twine Binder" in *Wis. Mag. of Hist.,* X, 35; U. S. Patent Office Records; obituaries in *Chicago Herald, Chicago Tribune,* Nov. 9, 1917, *Implement Age,* Nov. 17, 1917, *Implement and Tractor Trade Jour.,* Nov. 24, 1917. Appleby's first knotter is in the Wis. State Hist. Museum at Madison.]

F. A. T.

APPLEGATE, JESSE (July 5, 1811–Apr. 22, 1888), surveyor, legislator, publicist, was the youngest son of Daniel, a New Jersey Revolutionary soldier, and Rachel (Lindsey) Applegate. He was born in Kentucky but the family moved to Missouri when he was ten years old. In 1827–28 he attended Rock Spring Seminary (afterward Shurtleff College), in Shiloh, Ill., where he made noteworthy progress in mathematics and surveying under the tuition of John Messenger. Later, while teaching school, he continued these studies privately under the direction of Justus Post. He then secured a clerkship in the surveyor general's office at St. Louis under Col. McRee and soon became deputy surveyor-general, doing field work for a number of years in western Missouri. He settled in the Osage Valley on a farm. In 1832 he was married to Cynthia Parker. In 1843, owing to hard times and the menace of slavery in his region, he joined the "great emigration" to Oregon and, having one of the largest herds, was elected captain of the "cow-column." He brought his company safely to the Columbia with their wagons, opened a farm in the Willamette Valley not far from the Columbia, built a mill, and also performed much public work as surveyor. He was leader of the party which in 1845 opened the southern road into Oregon by way of Rogue River, Goose Lake, and the Humboldt River to Fort Hall.

In 1845 he was a member of the legislative committee of the Provisional Government and succeeded in effecting a complete revision of that government, also in securing the adherence to it of the managers of the British Hudson's Bay Company, thus for the first time unifying the Oregon settlement politically. The government thus established endured till Oregon became a Territory of the United States in 1849. Applegate was a member of the state constitutional convention in 1857 but refused to remain till its work was completed. He was deficient in the spirit of coöperation, had a somewhat dictatorial temper, and succeeded best when his leadership was unchallenged. He was a Whig and then a Republican in politics, while Oregon, to 1860, was controlled by the Democrats His influence was powerful in securing Lincoln's election and in maintaining the national cause during the Civil War. In 1849 he had removed to southern Oregon, settling on a large ranch near the California trail in the Umpqua Valley, at a place he named Yoncalla. His chief business was raising beef cattle which he drove to the mines. Here he built his "great house," dispensed a generous hospitality to all comers, and entertained men of national distinction. Schuyler Colfax and Samuel Bowles visited him in 1865. He assembled a good private library and remained through life a student, and a writer on public questions for the newspapers. His literary style was distinguished, as witness the appeal of the Provisional Government to Congress in 1847, the report of the American commission to settle the claims of the Hudson's Bay Company under the treaty of 1846, and especially *A Day with the Cow-Column in 1843,* which ranks as a western classic. He also wrote for Schuyler Colfax, and published locally, a treatise on the subject of reconstruction. This reveals his grasp of constitutional problems, also his extreme reliance on logic and corresponding disregard of human prejudices. Applegate was a large factor in promoting the construction of the Oregon and California railroad, yet it is said he refused to accept a United States senatorship on terms which would have made him subservient to the railroad interest. He was aggressively independent, looked like an old Roman, and had many of the Roman virtues. A frontiersman in the simplicity of his life, he was physically of the mountaineer type—above medium height, thin, wiry, resilient, capable of walking sixty miles a day. He was gifted intellectually and was a good conversationalist but shrank from public speaking. He molded opinion through the press, through resolutions drafted for general organizations, through a wide correspondence with prominent men, and through direct personal appeal.

[Letters to M. P. Deady, MS. in the Deady Collection, Ore. Hist. Soc.; Views of Ore. Hist., MS. comments on Mrs. Victor's *River of the West,* Bancroft Lib., Univ. of Cal.; Jos. Schafer, "Jesse Applegate, Pioneer and State Builder," *Univ. of Ore. Bull.,* n. s., vol. IX, no. 6, Feb. 1912, containing a unique portrait which is reproduced also in Jos. Schafer's *Hist. of the Pacific Northwest* (1918); J. M. Peck to Gen. Jos. Lane, giving an account of Applegate's success as a student at Rock Spring Seminary, *Quart. Ore. Hist. Soc.,* XV, 208–9; obituary, *Morning Oregonian,* Oct. 24, 1888.]

J. S.

APPLETON, DANIEL (Dec. 10, 1785–Mar. 27, 1849), publisher, son of Daniel and Lydia (Ela) Appleton, was born at Haverhill, Mass. After a limited schooling he started in business in his native town, keeping a general store. He married Hannah Adams of Andover, Mass., May 4, 1813: there were in all six sons and two daughters. Some years later he sought Boston as a larger field of endeavor and sold "English goods" at 21 Broad St. (*Boston Directory,* 1826). New York, however, in 1826, with a population of about 165,000, was four times as large as Boston and just the place for this man of ambition and energy. The *New York Directory* of 1827 reads: "Daniel Appleton, merchant, 15 Water St." During these years the "English goods" which Appleton imported began to include books, and there are many allusions to the ruddy-faced proprietor picturesquely dressed "in blue coat with bright buttons, a light buff vest and blue pants, and looking not unlike Daniel Webster" (Overton, p. 28), giving careful heed to the requests of his book-loving patrons. His young son, William H. Appleton [*q.v.*], was encouraged to build up a "book department," and soon both father and son were ready to risk their futures on the book business alone. Book publishing was first undertaken in 1831, and W. Mason's *Crumbs from the Master's Table,* a microscopic volume (see photographs, actual size, in Overton, *op. cit.,* pp. 28, 29) appeared with the imprint, "D. Appleton." Another tiny affair with the title *Gospel Seeds* was published in the same year, and a third, in

1832, bore the title *The Refuge Containing the Righteous Man's Habitation in the Time of Plague and Pestilence.* The firm name "D. Appleton & Co." dates from Jan. 27, 1838, when Daniel took William H. into partnership. The desire which the father expressed at that time that the firm name should continue forever unchanged has been respected. An entirely new line of books that Appleton was one of the first to put out was for children's use. Books in Spanish, particularly for South American countries, began to be published by him in the forties and found a ready sale. In the choice of his publications Appleton had, as his contemporaries testify, "a scrupulous regard for the interests of Religion and Morality" (Resolutions in *N. Y. Tribune,* Mar. 31, 1849). He retired from business in 1848 and died one year later.

[*The House of Appleton* (1916), and G. M. Overton, *Portrait of a Publisher*(1925)are informing, although dates and locations for the beginning of Appleton's business in N. Y. are in conflict with the Boston and N. Y. *Directories* from 1825 to 1830. There is an historical collection in the library of the firm, containing first editions of many publications.] A. E. P.

APPLETON, JAMES (Feb. 14, 1785–Aug. 25, 1862), reformer, was one of the first to propose state prohibition as a remedy for intemperance. He was born in Ipswich, Mass., a descendant of Samuel Appleton, who came there from England in 1635. His father also bore the name Samuel. His mother, Mary, was the daughter of Rev. Timothy White of Haverhill, Mass. He had only ordinary educational advantages, but possessed business ability and a gift for public speaking. Removing to Gloucester, Mass., he engaged in the jewelry business and also kept a public house. Here, Nov. 19, 1807 (*Vital Records of Gloucester, Mass.;* Nov. 15, according to Waters's "Genealogy of the Ipswich Descendants of Samuel Appleton," in *Publications of the Ipswich Historical Society,* XV), he married Sarah, daughter of Rev. Daniel and Hannah Bowers Fuller, by whom he had ten children. Though a Federalist in politics, as soon as the government had committed itself to war with England in 1812 he volunteered for service in the field. As lieutenant-colonel of the Gloucester regiment, "he twice, at the engagements of Sandy Bay and of Gallup's Folly, in 1814, repelled attacks of the British fleet under Sir George Colier upon the city and forts of Gloucester, for which service he was borne as of the same rank upon the rolls of the Regular Army of the United States. He subsequently was promoted Colonel and Brigadier-General of the First Brigade, Second Division, of the Massachusetts Line" (*The Diary of the Revd. Daniel Fuller,* ed. by D. F. Appleton, 1894, pp. 5, 6). He represented Gloucester in the General Court in 1813 and 1814. In 1832 he prepared and presented to that body a petition asking for a law prohibiting sales of liquor in less quantities than thirty gallons. In reply to opposition, he wrote three letters, which were published in the *Salem Gazette* during February 1832. This pioneer attempt to secure state prohibition failed, and the following year he left Massachusetts for Portland, Me. In 1836 he was elected a member of the legislature of that state and the following year he was chairman of a special committee appointed to consider the license system. Its report, which was written by him, was, according to Neal Dow [*q.v.*], "the first official document in the history of Maine in which prohibition is suggested as the true method of dealing with the liquor traffic" (*Reminiscences,* 1898, p. 243). In 1838 he was chairman of a similar committee which presented a bill in favor of prohibition and provided for the submission of the matter to popular vote. In the legislature of 1839 he was again chairman of the committee on license laws and sought, without success, to secure the passage of a prohibitory law.

His interest was not confined to temperance reform, however; he was also an ardent antislavery advocate. Among the tracts published by the New England Anti-Slavery Tract Association is one (No. 3) written by him on the Missouri Compromise. In 1842, 1843, and 1844 he was the candidate of the Liberty party for governor of Maine. In his later years he returned to Ipswich and lived on the ancestral farm, but continued his interest in public affairs. He was active in his support of war measures during 1861, but died without seeing the cause for which he had labored victorious. His portrait shows clear-cut features, a high forehead, thick, waving hair, keen but kindly eyes with the suggestion of the dreamer in them, and a mouth and jaw indicative of grim determination. He is described as belonging "to the class of men known as fanatics. From business he turned to politics that he might encourage legislation to remedy a number of social ills. . . . He indorsed Birney's views on slavery, advocated generous and systematic relief of the pauper and championed the cause of popular education. But his real hobby was temperance" (J. A. Krout, *The Origins of Prohibition,* 1925).

[*Origin of the Maine Law and of Prohibitory Legislation,* with a brief memoir of James Appleton, pub. by the National Temp. Soc., New York, 1886—this contains the letters pub. in the *Salem Gazette;* John J. Babson, *Hist. of the Town of Gloucester* (1860); Austin Willey, *Hist. of the Anti-Slavery Cause in State and Nation* (1886); John G. Woolley and Wm. E. Johnson, *Temperance Progress of the Century* (1903); D. L. Colvin, *Prohibition in the U. S.*(1926).] H. E. S.

APPLETON, JESSE (Nov. 17, 1772–Nov. 12, 1819), theologian, educator, born at New Ipswich, N. H., was the fourth son of Francis and Elizabeth (Hubbard) Appleton, and a descendant of Samuel Appleton, who came to this country from Suffolk, England, in 1635. His father was a farmer, so limited in means that he felt unable to give Jesse an education and planned to make a mechanic of him. His interest in books was such, however, that a brother promised to aid him, and he prepared for college at a local academy. Entering Dartmouth at the age of sixteen, he graduated in the class of 1792, and spent the next two years teaching at Dover, N. H., Aurean Academy, Amherst, N. H., and Leominster, Mass. He studied theology under Dr. Joseph Lathrop of West Springfield, Mass., supplied different churches for some time, was called to the church at Leicester, Mass., but finally accepted the pastorate of the Congregational Church at Hampton, N. H., where he was ordained Feb. 22, 1797. His salary was ninety pounds a year and the keep of his horse, twenty pounds to be paid in provisions with corn reckoned at three shillings a bushel, and pork and beef at three pence and two pence per pound respectively. Later it was increased to ninety-five pounds with house and firewood, and provision for a horse, two cows, and six sheep. In 1800 he married Elizabeth Means, daughter of Col. Robert Means of Amherst, N. H., by whom he had six children. The third of these, Jane, became the wife of Franklin Pierce, president of the United States.

Appleton was pastor at Hampton ten years. Extremely thorough and methodical in everything, he carefully planned out each day's work, allowing ample time for study. In his agreement with the church he had stipulated that he be permitted to exchange frequently that he might not have to write but one sermon a week. Soon he had acquired a reputation for sincere devotion, kindly spirit, sound judgment, and extensive learning. Although not a controversialist, he came to be regarded as a leader of the conservative element in the church. He was one of the group, which included David Sewall, Joseph Buckminster, and Benjamin Abbot, who initiated *The Piscataqua Evangelical Magazine,* and was put forward as a candidate by the conservatives of the Harvard Corporation when Dr. Henry Ware was elected to the Hollis Professorship of Divinity. He was also a frequent contributor to the *Panoplist,* founded by those who were broadly Calvinistic rather than Hopkinsian.

In 1807 Appleton was elected president of Bowdoin College. At this time he was thirty-five years old, and is described as a little under six feet in height, of commanding figure, his head very bald and of brilliant whiteness, his complexion remarkably fair. To the difficult work of his office he gave himself unsparingly. Besides struggling successfully with the financial problems of the day, he had a large share in the work of instruction, and prepared himself in minute detail for every recitation. Tutors contemplating the ministry were instructed by him. For long periods he allowed himself but four hours a day for sleep and ate a scant diet that the need of physical exercise might be lessened. He had an almost morbid sense of responsibility for the religious and intellectual welfare of the students, which increased his labors and anxiety. Under the strain he broke down physically, and died of a pulmonary affection at the age of forty-seven.

Appleton's publications were chiefly sermons and addresses. Many of these and a bibliography of all may be found in *The Works of Rev. Jesse Appleton, D.D., with a Memoir of His Life and Character,* by Alpheus S. Packard, 2 volumes (1837).

[Benj. Tappan, *A Sermon Delivered at the Interment of the Rev. Jesse Appleton* (1819); Wm. B. Sprague, *Annals Am. Pulpit,* II (1857); I. A. Jewett, *Memorial of Sam. Appleton of Ipswich, Mass., with Geneal. Notices of Some of His Descendants* (1850); G. T. Chapman, *Sketches of the Alumni of Dartmouth Coll.* (1867); *Gen. Cat. of Bowdoin Coll.,* with hist. sketch by Geo. T. Little (1894); Jos. Dow, *Hist. of the Town of Hampton, N. H.* (1893).]

H. E. S.

APPLETON, JOHN (July 12, 1804–Feb. 7, 1891), lawyer, the son of John and Elizabeth (Peabody) Appleton, was born in the village of New Ipswich, N. H. His forebears had come from a position of prominence in Suffolk, England; the first American ancestor, Samuel Appleton, took the freeman's oath in Massachusetts in 1636; his descendants were prominent throughout the seventeenth and eighteenth centuries. The boy's mother died when he was four years of age, and he was brought up in his native village by an aunt. His early education was in the schools and academy of New Ipswich. At fourteen he entered Bowdoin College, where he graduated in 1822. After a short period of school-teaching, he studied law in the offices of George Farley of Groton, Mass., and of his relative, Nathan Dan Appleton, of Alfred, Me. Admitted to the bar in 1826, he practised in the small towns of Dixmont, Penobscot County, and Sebec, Piscataquis County, until 1832, when he moved to Bangor and entered into partnership with Elisha H. Allen, who was elected to Congress in 1840. His subsequent partners were John B. Hill and his cousin, Moses Appleton.

Appleton's work was as a trial lawyer and from the outset he was a success. He had the physical and intellectual vigor and toughness which the trial lawyer needs. He was a hard worker, a zealous student of law, and an able advocate. These qualities placed him in a few years at the top of his profession in the state. His practise was large and, as times went, lucrative. In 1852 Gov. Hubbard recognized his capacities by nominating him associate justice of the supreme judicial court. Appleton served in this capacity from May 11, 1852, till Oct. 24, 1862, when he was elevated to the office of chief justice. He was reappointed at the expiration of each seven-year term until his retirement on Sept. 20, 1883, at the age of seventy-nine. Thereafter he lived in Bangor. Personally Appleton was a man of wide friendships and warm affections. He enjoyed recreation as well as work, liked a hand at whist, and was a great reader. He was married in 1834 to Sarah N. Allen, who died Aug. 12, 1874. On Mar. 30, 1876, he married Annie Greely.

The monuments of Appleton's judicial labors are to be found in the *Maine Law Reports*. His opinions begin with the case of Larrabee *vs.* Lumbert (34 *Maine* 79), and end with his opinion in State *vs.* Garing (75 *Maine* 591). They are characterized by a ready and lucid legal style, and though his language is sometimes rather more florid than is approved by modern taste, his is perhaps the most valuable single contribution to the legal literature of his state. Important and lengthy as were Judge Appleton's services on the bench, his most distinctive contribution to his times was probably as a legal reformer. He was chairman of a legislative commission which reported on a reconstruction of Maine's judicial system, and it was through his efforts that the legislature in 1852 abolished the district court and gave its jurisdiction to the supreme judicial court. But his best efforts as a student of legal theory were bent upon the abolition of the principle of common law that a party might not be a witness in his own behalf in either civil or criminal cases. In his effort in this direction, Appleton was a confessed disciple of Bentham. His articles on the Law of Evidence first published in *The Jurist,* beginning in 1833, were collected and published in Philadelphia in 1860 under the title, *The Rules of Evidence*. In 1856 he had the satisfaction of seeing the Maine legislature enact a law that no person should "be excused or excluded as a witness in any civil suit or proceeding at law or in equity, by reason of his interest in the event of the same as party or otherwise." Eight years later this principle was extended to criminal cases.

[Chas. Hamlin, article in *Great Am. Lawyers,* ed. by W. D. Lewis, IV (1908); L. C. Hatch, *Maine* (1919); *Green Bag,* VII, 510–16; H. C. Williams, *Biog. Encyc. Maine* (1885); and, most important of all, the *Maine Law Reports* mentioned in the text.]

R. H.

APPLETON, JOHN (Feb. 11, 1815–Aug. 22, 1864), congressman, diplomat, was born at Beverly, Mass., a son of John W. and Sophia (Williams) Appleton, and a descendant in the direct line from Samuel Appleton of Ipswich, Mass. During most of his boyhood the Appletons lived in Portland, Me., and John gravitated in the natural course of events to Bowdoin College whence he graduated in 1834. He then returned to Portland and took up the study of law in the office of George W. Pierce. In the summers of 1835 and 1836 he attended the Harvard Law School and later worked in the law office of Willis & Fessenden in Portland. Admitted to the Cumberland County bar on June 20, 1837, he started to practise with Edward Fox who had been his fellow student and who was later United States district judge. Appleton had not been long in practise, however, before he was seized with political ambitions. On July 4, 1838, the young man delivered the oration of the day at the largest Democratic gathering that Portland had ever seen, while John Neal harangued the Whigs near by on Munjoy's Hill. The *Daily Eastern Argus* of the following day records that there were 130 Democratic speeches, 116 of which were by volunteers! Appleton's oration was described as "all that could have been wished." The same journal observed nothing in the speech which "could offend the most refined and delicate taste . . . while the principles of democracy were enforced and defended with an energy which evinced how deeply they were felt and sacredly believed by the orator." In view of this effusion it is not surprising to learn that the orator of the day became shortly after attached to the editorial staff of the *Daily Eastern Argus*. He was later appointed by Gov. Fairfield to be register of probate for Cumberland County, but this service apparently did not prevent his going on with his editorial work. On Nov. 27, 1840, he was married to Susan L. Dodge of Salem. In 1845, at the invitation of George Bancroft, then secretary of the navy, Appleton became chief clerk in the Navy Department, and there he remained until 1848 when he was transferred to the State Department then headed by James Buchanan. He was there for a few weeks only when President Polk appointed him to the inconspicuous and uncoveted post of chargé d'affaires in Bolivia. On his way to fulfil his new mission, Appleton was shipwrecked and narrowly escaped death. The journey inland was on horseback over mountains, and the post proved on arrival scarcely more agreeable than the journey thither. Living conditions were unattractive, diplomatic amenities were few, and there was little work to attend to. Appleton projected a book on the young republic, then closing the first generation of its independence. But his ambition flagged, and on the accession of Zachary Taylor to the presidency, he resigned (May 4, 1849) and returned to Portland to take up the practise of law with Nathan Clifford. In 1851 Appleton successfully opposed William Pitt Fessenden for the Thirty-second Congress. His majority was 40 votes in 12,000 cast. He was not highly conspicuous in Congress, and congressional life seems not to have been wholly to his liking. He retired at the end of his first term on Mar. 3, 1853. In 1855 he accepted an appointment as secretary of the legation at London under his old chief, James Buchanan, now minister to the court of St. James's. Buchanan retired a few months after Appleton's arrival and procured Appleton's appointment as chargé d'affaires ad interim. Appleton did not elect to remain longer, however, and returned to take an active part in Buchanan's successful campaign for the presidency. The election over, Appleton took charge for a few months in 1857 of an administration paper known as the *Washington Union,* but this he was obliged to relinquish for reasons of health. On Apr. 4, 1857, he accepted the assistant secretaryship in the State Department, where he remained for the three succeeding years until June 8, 1860. Here he seems to have worked hard and effectively. There is considerable evidence that the most important dispatches of the day came from his pen. In 1860 he accepted the post of minister to Russia and took up his residence at St. Petersburg. Upon Lincoln's election the following November, he resigned and returned to Portland. The severity of the Baltic winter had aggravated an old tendency to tuberculosis. He lived on in Portland for nearly four years of lingering illness. Appleton was a staunch friend of the Union and of the federal constitution. His last years were oppressed by the thought that by remaining in Washington in the closing days of Buchanan's administration he might have exercised some influence toward averting the war.

[*Colls. Me. Hist. Soc.,* ser. 2, II, 337; *Cong. Globe,* 32 Cong., 1851–52; *U. S. State Dept. Reg.,* 1874.]

R. H.

APPLETON, NATHAN (Oct. 6, 1779–July 14, 1861), manufacturer, banker, politician, was the seventh son of Isaac Appleton of New Ipswich, N. H., and Mary (Adams) Appleton. He was prepared for Dartmouth College, but preferred to go into trade in Boston with his brother Samuel [*q.v.*]. Their partnership, established in 1794, prospered, and continued until 1809; then Nathan organized another company with his brother Eben. This firm was dissolved on account of the war with Great Britain, but Nathan Appleton was frank to say: "The war, however, added considerably to our profits." In 1813 he invested $5,000 in Francis C. Lowell's power-mill for making cotton cloth at Waltham; two years later his firm became the sales agent on commission for the factory. Appleton and his associates had established the principles of the American textile industry—power machinery with cheap female labor and a separate selling organization. So successful were the pioneers at Waltham that they bought water-rights on the Merrimac River, founded the industrial city of Lowell, and by 1840 had mills in operation with a capital of $12,000,000. In like manner, they built up the manufacturing centers of Manchester, N. H., and Lawrence, Mass. Appleton attributed much of their success to the fact that they invested only two-thirds of their capital in mills and machinery and kept one-third free to carry on the business (*Introduction of the Power Loom, and Origin of Lowell,* 1858, p. 30). But to him success meant not only handsome profits from large-scale production but also attractive working conditions for the employees and decreasing cost of the goods to the consumers.

The same conception of responsibility to the public guided Nathan Appleton in his banking enterprises. He championed the Suffolk system, by means of which a group of Boston banks checked rural issues of paper money, because, as he said: "The only proper basis of bank circulation is a large monied capital, exclusively appropriated to the business of banking.... Public security requires, that the issue of a bank should bear a small proportion to its capital" (*An Examination of the Banking System in Massachusetts,* 1831, p. 46).

He was elected to Congress in 1830 for the Boston district, as a representative of the manufacturing interest, in preference to Henry Lee, candidate for the merchants. John Quincy Adams accordingly called upon him to assist in framing the protective tariff of 1832; and Appleton defended it in May 1832 against the attacks of McDuffie of South Carolina, who argued that a duty on imports was a tax on exports and especially discriminatory against the Southern industry of cotton planting (*Congressional Register,* 22 Cong., 1 Sess., pp. 3119 ff.). But Appleton did not argue for his own mills; they were already producing on a large scale and able to compete in foreign markets (see his articles, as "Statist," in the *Philadelphia Banner of the Constitution,* 1831). He asserted that protective tariffs were for the interest of the whole nation; they would increase the consumption of Southern cotton by Northern mills, replacing the foreign with a domestic market; they would encourage competition among American mills, and thus reduce the cost of cotton goods to domestic consumers. He opposed Clay's compromise tariff of 1833 as "abandonment" of protection; he warmly commended President Jackson's proclamation against the "semi-rebellion" of South Carolina.

Seeing that the controversy over the Bank of the United States was a question of "the bank or no bank," Appleton supported Biddle and Clay against Jackson, for he believed that a national bank was essential. But acting with a group of New York bankers, he resisted Biddle's policy of contracting and expanding the bank's loans after the denial of a new charter and the "removal of the deposits" by Jackson's administration; and, following the panic of 1837, Appleton and his allies in New York opposed Biddle's wishes, secured gold from the Bank of England, and resumed the payments of specie in the spring of 1838. When Clay proposed another central bank with a national charter, Appleton wrote his masterly pamphlet, *Currency and Banking* (1841), to discuss the principles of sound finance and to show "the danger from an institution of so great power." He recommended a national bank with a capital of only ten millions. Experience with Biddle's bank had obliged him to modify his principle that a large capital was essential to success, at least when applied to the interests of the whole nation: "It was a power too great to be intrusted to any one man."

Slavery, to Nathan Appleton, was a local problem, with which fortunately New England was no longer cursed. Moreover, the greater part of the United States was developing without it; the interests of the nation should not be hampered because slavery was present in the South. Placing the Constitution and the Union above all else, Appleton would have nothing to do with that "fanatical monomaniac," William Lloyd Garrison (*Letter to the Hon. W. C. Rives of Virginia,* 1860; *Correspondence between Nathan Appleton and John G. Palfrey,* 1846), and he firmly asserted his right to vote for Zachary Taylor in 1848, in defiance of Charles Sumner's charge that there was an "unhallowed union" between "the lords of the lash and the lords of the loom" (see transcripts of letters between Charles Sumner and Nathan Appleton, in the Boston Pub. Lib.). But in 1860, when the South came to the verge of secession, Appleton plead with his Southern friend, W. C. Rives, that the Southern states should abandon political competition with the free states and be content to stay within the Union, even if in a minor position. Why could they not see that a "peaceable separation" was impossible?

In 1806 Appleton married Maria Theresa Gold of Pittsfield. Six years after her death in 1833 he married Harriet Coffin Sumner of Boston. His family of seven children was reared in an aristocratic mansion on Beacon St., with the advantages of fine schooling, travel abroad, and contact with the cultured manners and the intellectual interests of their father. Although engrossed in business, finance, and politics, Appleton still had time for an interest in science; he was one of the organizers of the Boston Athenæum and its treasurer from 1816 to 1827; he was active in the Massachusetts Historical Society and was associated with many similar organizations. He cherished, almost as a fetich, his reputation as a man of scrupulous honesty; and he especially charged his friend, Robert C. Winthrop, to make clear in the memorial of his life that money-making had not been his aim; he would have been content, he declared, with the $200,000 which he had made in trade; he had gone into the cotton industry by chance: "Accident and not effort," he said, "has made me a rich man." His quality was manifest in his religious views. He was not satisfied with attendance in the congregation of William Ellery Channing or, occasionally, in King's Chapel; Christian theology, he said, was a favorite study with him. He could not hold, however, to any theological system, for all doctrines were "mere human opinions" and knowledge went no further than understanding; for himself, he must subordinate moral sense and affection, however strong, to reason (see his correspondence with Rev. W. E. Heygate, printed as *The Doctrines of Original Sin and the Trinity* . . ., 1859). Reason did not dictate to him a belief in the immaculate conception, the Athanasian Trinity, or Calvinistic dogmas, the utter iniquity of slavery, or the wickedness of possessing riches; but the spirit within him commanded Nathan Appleton to live in frankness and candor and to face the unknown with quiet courage. When word came that his daughter, Mrs. Henry Wadsworth Longfellow, had met a horrible death, he remarked with no outward display of emotion: "She has gone but a little while before me." A few days later he was buried beside her in Mount Auburn.

[The chief sources of information are Appleton's "Sketches of Autobiography," written about 1855, which

R. C. Winthrop quoted at length in his "Memoir," *Mass. Hist. Soc. Proc.* (1861), V, 249–306, portr., p. 249. There is a collection of Appleton papers, 29 vols., in the Mass. Hist. Soc. For geneal., see I. A. Jewett, *Memorial of Samuel Appleton of Ipswich, Mass.*, 1850.]

A. B. D.

APPLETON, NATHANIEL WALKER (June 14, 1755–Apr. 15, 1795), physician, was the son of Nathaniel Appleton, a Boston merchant, and Mary (Walker) Appleton. He received his A.B. from Harvard in 1773 and his A.M. in 1774, after which he moved to Salem, Mass., to become a student of medicine. He chose as his preceptor—for these were the days before the beginnings of medical schools in New England—his father's cousin, the celebrated centenarian, Edward Augustus Holyoke. After his novitiate, Appleton returned to Boston, and on May 24, 1780, married Sarah Greenleaf, by whom he had seven children. Though a diffident man of an impersonal frame of mind, Appleton appears to have acquired a large practise, but his reputation has come down to us chiefly through his activities in the early Massachusetts Medical Society (founded in 1781). James Thacher, as quoted by Burrage, said of him: "When we consider that he was an incorporator of the Massachusetts Medical Society and its recording secretary for the first ten years of its existence; that he attended every meeting of the society and council during that time, writing and signing a record for every one, through all those years fostering the infant organization, Appleton deserves to have the meager facts of his life transmitted to future generations." He did for this early medical society much what Henry Oldenburg had done for the Royal Society of London in its early days. He aroused interest in the meetings, kept copious notes of the proceedings, and often recorded the outside activities of the members of its council. In many instances our only information concerning the early members of the Society is derived from Appleton's carefully penned minutes and records. He was also chairman of the committee which in 1790 brought out the first volume of *Medical Communications,* the official channel of publication for the members of the Massachusetts Medical Society—a journal which continued to be issued regularly for 124 years. As far as is known, Appleton's professional contributions were only two in number, published in the *Medical Communications.* The first was entitled, "An Account of the Successful Treatment of Paralysis of the Lower Limbs, Occasioned by a Curvature of the Spine" (1790, vol. I, ser. 1, p. 56); the second, "History of Hæmorrhage from a Rupture of the Inside of the Left Labium Pudendi" (vol. I, ser. 3, p. 24).

[For our knowledge of Appleton we are indebted largely to recent investigations of Dr. W. L. Burrage recorded in his work, *Hist. of the Mass. Medic. Soc., with Brief Biogs. of the Founders and Chief Officers, 1781–1922* (1923). See also: Burrage's "Life" of Appleton in Kelly and Burrage's *Am. Medic. Biogs.* (1920); Letters of Nathaniel Walker Appleton to his classmate, Eliphalet Pearson, 1773–84, ed. by Wm. Coolidge Lane, *Pubs. Colonial Soc. of Mass.*, VIII (1906); Rev. John Clarke's *Discourse Delivered at the First Ch., in Boston, 19th April, A.D. 1795, the Lord's-day after the Interment of Nathaniel W. Appleton, M.D.*, Boston, 1796.]

J. F. F.

APPLETON, SAMUEL (June 22, 1766–July 12, 1853), merchant, philanthropist, was descended from Samuel Appleton of Suffolk County, England, who settled at Ipswich, Mass., in 1636. His son, Samuel, became a commander in King Philip's War and an opponent of Sir Edmund Andros. The grandson of this militant colonial went inland to New Ipswich, N. H.; there, his son, Isaac Appleton, grew to manhood and married Mary Adams of Concord; there, Samuel Appleton was born, the third of their twelve children. The hardships so common in the American frontier town were Appleton's early education, giving him perhaps an appreciation of values from the meagerness of his own opportunities; except for a few intervals during the Revolution, between his tenth and sixteenth years, he received no schooling; then, he himself became the district teacher. At twenty-two he helped to establish a new township in Maine, and labored for two summers to clear his farm. But the propensity for trading, so typical of New Englanders, was uppermost in him, and after storekeeping ventures in Ashburnham and New Ipswich, he went in 1794 with his brother, Nathan Appleton [*q.v.*], to open a shop in Boston. By 1799 their business had so developed that a trip to England for merchandise seemed worth while; and until 1819 Samuel Appleton was often abroad on such business. In spite of the Jeffersonian Embargo and the War of 1812, he prospered; he accumulated enough capital to invest with Nathan Appleton in the new cotton industry; he acquired valuable real estate in Boston; he soon had funds to subscribe to the railroad projects of the thirties.

Samuel Appleton never led in politics, although he sat in the state legislature from 1828 to 1831, and served as a presidential elector for Daniel Webster in 1836. He was numbered among the merchants who controlled the currency and finance of New England from State St. As these conservatives turned their capital from shipping and importing to the manufacture of cotton and woolen goods, they deserted the free-trade doctrines of the mercantile aristocracy for protective principles. They dropped their objections to the Second Bank of the United States and, following

Daniel Webster, became its defenders. With them, in opposition to Jacksonian Democracy, Samuel Appleton moved from the Federalist to the National Republican and later to the Whig party.

At the age of fifty-three he married Mrs. Mary Gore. They had no children; but their mansion on Beacon St. was a joyous open house to their nieces and nephews. When he reached the age of sixty, Appleton retired from business with the avowed purpose of spending his income upon philanthropies. He became a benefactor and trustee of the Massachusetts General Hospital; he gave to the Boston Female Asylum, New Ipswich Academy, and Dartmouth College; he was a patron of the Boston Athenæum and the Massachusetts Historical Society. Besides providing for his widow, her nieces, and her sister, for the descendants of his four brothers and two sisters, for his servants, and for his friend, Rev. Ephraim Peabody, his will allotted industrial stocks worth about $200,000—nearly a fifth of his fortune—to scientific, literary, religious, and philanthropic endeavors. Knowing his wishes, his executors distributed most of these stocks among the American Academy of Arts and Sciences, Massachusetts Historical Society, Boston Athenæum, Sailors' Snug Harbor, Massachusetts General Hospital, New Ipswich Academy, and Amherst, Dartmouth, and Harvard Colleges. With its share, Harvard built Appleton Chapel in honor of the benefactor. The portrait by Healey, now in the Boston Athenæum, of this man who began life with no wealth and few advantages, depicts him as a ponderous gentleman of culture and ease, prosperous and benign.

[The principal source of information is a memorial by his friend, Ephraim Peabody, in the *New Eng. Hist. and Geneal. Reg.*, Jan. 1854, VIII, No. 1. Additional material may be found in a memoir by W. C. Bates in the *Memorial Biogs.* (1881), II, 62, of the same soc., and another by S. K. Lathrop in the *Mass. Hist. Soc. Proc.* (1855), III. Appleton's will was published in 1853 with remarks by N. I. Bowditch, one of his executors. Broadsides, issued in 1853 and 1854, listed the industrial and railroad stocks and the real estate of Samuel Appleton which were sold at pub. auction in the old State House at Boston. His portr. by Healey is reproduced in the *Athenæum Centenary* (1907), p. 136. For geneal., see I. A. Jewett, *Memorial of Samuel Appleton of Ipswich, Mass.* (1850).]

A. B. D.

APPLETON, THOMAS GOLD (Mar. 31, 1812–Apr. 17, 1884), essayist, poet, and artist, was a prominent member of the literary coterie which made Boston famous in the middle of the nineteenth century. His presence there was due not so much to his achievements in literature or art, as to his social graces and the brilliance of his talk. Holmes said of him that he "has spilled more good things on the wasteful air in conversation than would carry a 'diner-out' through half a dozen London seasons," and he so impressed Emerson that when the formation of the famous Saturday Club was under way, and possible members were being discussed, that sage declared him to be "desirable in a superlative degree."

His father was Nathan Appleton, a wealthy merchant of Boston, one of the founders of the textile industry of Lowell, and for two sessions a member of Congress; his mother, Maria Theresa Gold of Pittsfield, Mass. They had four other children, one of whom, Frances Elizabeth, married Henry W. Longfellow. Thomas was born in Boston, had Wendell Phillips and John Motley for playmates, spent a year at the Boston Latin School, but prepared for college at the Round Hill School, Northampton, Mass., then conducted by Joseph Cogswell and George Bancroft. He entered the sophomore class at Harvard in 1828 and graduated in 1831. In compliance with his father's wish, he continued at Cambridge a year studying law, though he had no taste for the work.

Appleton never had any fixed occupation. He felt himself lacking in the qualities that had given his father business success, and unfitted for the monotonous life of a profession. He loved to roam and was passionately fond of beauty both in nature and in art. Much of his time was spent in traveling about Europe and in its galleries and theatres. He collected books and works of art. At the same time he keenly enjoyed being with people. Nothing that was lovely or amusing escaped him. He was an habitual diner-out, and his original mind, lively fancy, and quick wit were such as to give his sayings the reputation of being the best Boston had heard since Mather Byles. His ambition was to excel in literature and art but it was not realized. He could not write as he talked, and his essays are but pleasant reading for an idle hour; his poems, formal and uninspired. His sympathies were keen and he was generous with his wealth. During the Civil War both by word and money he was a staunch supporter of his friend, Gov. Andrew. He was actively interested in the growth and improvement of Boston, and was a trustee of the Athenæum, Public Library, and Museum of Fine Arts. To the fund that insured a suitable building for the latter institution he was one of the three largest subscribers, and to both the museum and the library he donated valuable art collections.

His published works are as follows: *Faded Leaves,* poems (1872); *Fresh Leaves,* poems (privately printed, 1874); *A Sheaf of Papers,* essays (1875); *A Nile Journal,* travel (1876); *Syrian Sunshine,* a journal of travel (1877);

Windfalls, essays (1878); *Chequer Work,* essays (1879).

[Susan Hale, *Life and Letters of Thos. Gold Appleton* (1885); E. W. Emerson, *The Early Years of the Saturday Club* (1918); *Memories of a Hostess,* ed. by M. A. DeWolfe Howe (1922); O. W. Holmes, "Thomas Gold Appleton," *Atlantic Mo.,* LIII, 848–50.]

H. E. S.

APPLETON, WILLIAM HENRY (Jan. 27, 1814–Oct. 19, 1899), publisher, was born at Haverhill, Mass., the son of Daniel Appleton [*q.v.*] and Hannah Adams. His schooling ceased at sixteen, when he entered his father's business and was given an opportunity to build up a book department. The first of many business trips to Europe was taken at the age of twenty-one. Thus early, he made acquaintance with the publishers, Longmans, Murray, and Tauchnitz, also with Thomas Moore and the youthful Thackeray. A very formal and businesslike contract is still preserved (in the possession of Mary Appleton, his grand-daughter), which marks the formation of a partnership with his father, in 1838, under the firm name "D. Appleton & Co." Caution that ever characterized the father was thrown to the winds, or at any rate to one side, by the dash and enterprise of the son, and the firm of brothers, organized under William's leadership on their father's retirement in 1848, expanded the publishing business with amazing rapidity. It is said that the revival of the *Webster Spelling Book* kept one press busy all the time for several years, the sales in a single year (1866) totalling 1,596,000 (Overton, p. 44). There were hundreds of other books of an educational character, such as the *Perkins Arithmetics,* the *Cornell Geographies,* the *Quackenbos Histories.* Appleton's was the medium through which the scientific ideas of Darwin, Huxley, and Spencer came to the American public. The *Popular Science Monthly* of to-day is traceable to this enthusiasm for things scientific, the first issue coming from the Appleton press in 1872. The first *Appleton's Cyclopedia of Biography* appeared in 1856. Travelers' guides began also in this decade, one of the earliest being *Navigation Guide for United States and Canada* (1852). In the period following the Civil War the firm was keen to realize the popular veneration of the war hero, and books about Farragut, Porter, Grant, Sheridan, Sherman, and many other commanders, bore the Appleton imprint. Later, Confederate leaders became accepted authors, *e.g.,* Jefferson Davis, *The Rise and Fall of the Confederate Government.* Printing that was formerly done on the outside had now become an integral part of the firm's business. An early printing plant in Franklin St., New York City, was outgrown and a factory covering the larger part of a city block was erected (1868) in Williamsburg; over 600 workmen were employed there. Enlarged sales quarters had also become necessary and the Society Library Building at 346 Broadway was purchased and remodeled. *Gleason's Pictorial Drawing-Room Companion* (Boston), June 24, 1854, pictures and describes the retail salesroom on the ground floor with its "fourteen Corinthian columns in imitation of Sienna marble" and its "book-cases and shelving of plain oak, in length 270 feet."

Appleton was an earnest and active advocate of international copyright and was president of the American Publishers Copyright League in 1887. The Appleton Church Home at Macon, Ga., erected and endowed by him, is evidence of his interest in the church and in humanity. He married Mary Worthen of Lowell, Mass., Apr. 16, 1844, and had two sons and two daughters. The Appleton Mansion, which he occupied in the latter part of his life in the Riverdale section of Bronx Borough, is still standing (A. E. Peterson, *Landmarks of New York,* 1923, pp. 118, 122–23).

[G. M. Overton, *Portr. of a Publisher* (1925) gives much information, with reproductions of title-pages, photographs and letters of authors, newspaper advertisements, etc. A hist. coll. in the company's lib. contains letters from Darwin, Wm. H. Lecky, Huxley, James Buchanan, and other authors, also first editions of many titles including *Webster's Spelling Book,* first Appleton edition of 1855. Obituaries in the *Herald* and other N. Y. papers of Oct. 20, 1899.]

A. E. P.

APPLETON, WILLIAM WORTHEN (Nov. 29, 1845–Jan. 27, 1924), publisher, was born in Brooklyn, N. Y., a son of William H. Appleton [*q.v.*] and Mary Worthen. With no education beyond private elementary and secondary schools in New York, he entered the "House of Appleton" and became a partner at the age of twenty-three. Literary and editorial interests were his from the first. He showed an uncanny ability to gauge the public's taste. Thus he was responsible for the inclusion in the company's list of English translations of Louisa Mühlbach's historical novels which sold by hundreds of thousands; for the American editions of Carroll's *Alice's Adventures in Wonderland,* and Disraeli's *Lothair,* the latter selling up to 80,000; for the addition to the list of Appleton authors of Joel Chandler Harris in fiction and William T. Osler in medicine. "Mr. Willie," a name which suggests the fondness felt toward him by every one in the organization, gave a great deal of attention to the "International Scientific Series," inaugurated in 1873 under the editorship of E. L. Youmans, in which Draper's *History of the Conflict between Religion and Science* appeared in

1875. In later years Appleton spent much time in acquainting himself with the leaders of thought in the universities of the country. This he did by extensive travel, "stopping here and there in college centers, always developing new lines of contact and bringing back suggestions for publishing enterprises" (*Publishers Weekly,* Feb. 2, 1924). An evidence of this activity is the "International Education Series" under the editorship of Dr. W. T. Harris; nearly every great educational leader of Europe and America in the late nineteenth century contributed a volume to this series. Other evidence is the long line of Appleton texts for colleges.

William W. continued his father's advocacy of the rights of literary property and gave important aid in securing the Copyright Act of 1891; later, as president of the Publishers' Copyright League, he worked hard but unsuccessfully to have the United States join the International Copyright Union. He took an active interest in the circulating library idea. When the "Sewing Circle" of Grace Church started in 1870 a little circulating library of 500 books, Appleton was invited to be one of "an advisory committee of gentlemen" (*History of the New York Public Library,* 1923, p. 201). In the following year the New York Free Circulating Library came into existence with Appleton chairman of the Committee on Library and Reading Rooms. Subsequently this library was consolidated with the New York Public Library and he was appointed a trustee of that institution and made chairman of the Committee on Circulation. His great interest made him a frequent visitor to all the branches and many librarians testify to his sympathy and generous support. For many years he was senior warden of St. Bartholomew's Church and a trustee of the Institute for the Blind, and at the time of his death was one of the trustees of the endowment fund of the American Library Association. He resided in his later years at 571 Park Ave. In 1881 he married Anna Sargent, by whom he had two sons and two daughters.

[G. M. Overton, *Portrait of a Publisher* (1925), the first twenty-five pages with portrait; collection of letters in the firm's library; obituary, also portrait, in *Publishers Weekly,* Feb. 2, 1924; other notices in the *Times, Tribune, Sun,* and other N.Y. papers of Jan. 28, 1924. Additional information from *Hist. of the N.Y. Pub. Lib.*(1923)and from Pub. Lib. officials and friends of the family.]

A. E. P.

APTHORP, WILLIAM FOSTER (Oct. 24, 1848–Feb. 19, 1913), music critic, was born in Boston, the son of Robert and Eliza (Hunt) Apthorp. He was the product of intellect and culture that dated back to pre-Revolutionary days, when several of the family, officers of the crown and of the British army and navy, were stationed in Boston. One of his ancestors, a crown official, Charles Apthorp, a merchant and an Eton scholar, was paymaster of the navy, the most distinguished of whose eighteen children was the Rev. East Apthorp, the founder of Christ Church, Cambridge. William Foster Apthorp was born into a home of culture and refinement. In the autumn of 1856, when he was but eight years of age, his parents took him to Europe for the purpose of giving him the best opportunity for studying languages and art, feeling that his latent talents lay in the latter field. In France he attended a day school; in Dresden the Marquardt'sche Schule, at the same time studying drawing with Frenzel and beginning the study of music; in Berlin he was a student in the Friedrich Wilhelm'sches Progymnasium; in Rome, in the École des Frères Chrétiens. Since he had manifested some ability for drawing, his study in Rome included drawing and painting under Guglielmi and Garelli, in order to ascertain whether he had enough talent to choose painting as a life work. He studied art also in Florence and was a fellow student with John Singer Sargent. Returning to Boston in 1860, he fitted for college at the school of E. S. Dixwell and was graduated from Harvard in 1869. In his senior year he was conductor of the Pierian Sodality. Soon after his return from Europe, he became increasingly interested in music and in 1863 he gave up painting and studied piano, harmony, and counterpoint with J. K. Paine until 1867, when Paine went to Europe. He then studied piano with B. J. Lang for several years, but his theoretical work was self-directed. He was fully aware that the dream of his devoted parents—that he would become a great painter or a great pianist—would never be realized and he was quite content to take up teaching as a profession. In 1872 and 1873 he taught piano and theory at the National College of Music in Boston. When that institution closed, he joined the New England Conservatory, where for the next thirteen years he taught piano, harmony, counterpoint, fugue, and general theory, besides having classes in esthetics and musical history in the College of Music of Boston University. In 1886 he severed his connection with both institutions.

Not until 1872 did he begin his work as music critic, in which capacity he was destined to achieve his greatest success. William Dean Howells, then editor of the *Atlantic Monthly,* founded a music department in the magazine and engaged him as musical editor, which position he held until the department was discontinued. From this beginning, he occupied successively the following positions: in 1876 music critic of the *Sunday Courier;* in 1878 both music and dramatic critic of the *Traveller;* and finally, in 1881, music and dramatic critic of the *Transcript,* collaborating with F. H. Jenks, holding both positions until 1903, when he gave up all active work. Besides his regular work as critic, he contributed articles to the *Atlantic Monthly, Dwight's Journal of Music, Scribner's Magazine,* and occasional correspondence to the *New York Tribune.* In 1880 he delivered a course of lectures at the Lowell Institute in Boston, repeating the same in New York, Brooklyn, and the Peabody Institute in Baltimore. From 1888 to 1890 he was critical editor of Scribner's *Cyclopedia of Music and Musicians,* 3 volumes, collaborating with John Denson Champlin, Jr. From 1892 to 1901 he edited the program books of The Boston Symphony Orchestra. He was undoubtedly one of the greatest critics America has produced. His work was strikingly individual and independent, and always constructive. His intimate acquaintance with the languages and his deep knowledge of literature and philosophy contributed largely to his success as a writer. He was an incessant worker and ceased his labors only because of failing eyesight. He bore this affliction, however, with the greatest fortitude and never lost his contagious humor. Notwithstanding a certain educated pride of family and position, he was very democratic, though his exceeding diffidence was often misunderstood by those who did not know his natural shyness. He was married in 1876 to Octavie Loir Iasigi. He died in Vevey, Switzerland, whither he had gone in 1903 after giving up active work. His most important published works are *Musicians and Music Lovers* (1894); *By the Way* (1898); *The Opera, Past and Present* (1901); *Some of the Wagner Heroes and Heroines* (1889); also several translations, *Hector Berlioz—Selections from His Letters, and Æsthetic, Humorous and Satirical Writings* (1879); *Jacques Damour* and other smaller works from Zola (1895). He also edited three volumes of the songs of Robert Franz.

[*Grove's Dict. of Music and Musicians, Am. Supp.; One Hundred Years of Music in America,* ed. by G. L. Howe and W. S. B. Mathews (1889); obituaries in the *Boston Herald,* Feb. 22, 1913, *Boston Transcript,* Feb. 20, 1913.]

F. L. G. C.

ARBUCKLE, JOHN (1839–Mar. 27, 1912), merchant, was the son of Scotch parents, Thomas and Margaret (MacDonald) Arbuckle, who had settled in western Pennsylvania. He was born at Pittsburgh and obtained in the public schools of Allegheny City all the formal education that he was to have. In company with his brother, Charles, he built up at Pittsburgh a business of roasting and grinding coffee and selling it in packages. In 1871 the brothers went to New York, where they greatly expanded their enterprise, soon gaining for it a national scope and reputation. This was made possible by Arbuckle's invention (in which he was aided by associates) of machinery for weighing, packing, and sealing the ground coffee. After some years (Charles Arbuckle having died in 1890) an arrangement was made with the Havemeyers, then the leading sugar refiners, to sell a part of their product in packages. Sales by the Arbuckle method were pushed rapidly, and the profits became so large as to attract the attention of the Havemeyer interests, which canceled the selling arrangements with Arbuckle and proceeded to take to themselves the profits from package sales. Then began (in 1896) a dramatic episode in the sugar industry; for Arbuckle, in open defiance of the Sugar Trust (American Sugar Refining Company), himself built a large refinery in Brooklyn and entered the sugar market as a formidable competitor, cutting sugar prices almost to cost. In retaliation the Havemeyers went into the coffee trade. The fight lasted five years and at the end of that period, after millions had been lost by both sides, it was not Arbuckle who capitulated—his refinery was still operating and the sugar magnates had withdrawn from the coffee business; but an armistice was declared. Arbuckle became one of the leading importers of the country and his ships were known in many ports. At the time of his death, in 1912, he was believed to be the largest individual owner of shipping under American registry. His extensive interests on the sea led him to give attention to the raising and salvaging of ships. He invented important machinery for that purpose, which was employed in raising several vessels of the United States Navy. In order to make a fuller use of the harbor tugs that he owned and employed about New York he went into the business of towing canal boats between New York and Albany, cutting the rates for that service.

He was a rugged, farmer-like man in personal appearance, six feet tall, with a slight stoop. He remained all his life extremely simple and unpretentious in his habits. In 1868 he was married to Mary Kerr of Pittsburgh. He resided in Brooklyn, where as a young man he had come under the influence of Henry Ward Beecher, and in the latter years of his life he gave much thought to plans for a Beecher memorial to be associated with Plymouth Church and to be a sort of clubhouse for young men and women, where evening classes could be maintained for vocational instruction. His will made provision for such a memorial and a few years after his death the Arbuckle Institute was opened in Brooklyn, adjacent to Plymouth Church.

[Obituary and editorial in *Brooklyn Daily Eagle,* Mar. 27, 1912; obituary in *N. Y. Evening Post,* Mar. 27, 1912; character sketch by Samuel E. Moffett in *Cosmopolitan Mag.,* Sept. 1902.] W. B. S.

ARCHBOLD, JOHN DUSTIN (July 26, 1848–Dec. 5, 1916), capitalist, was born at Leesburg, Ohio. His father, the Rev. Israel Archbold, was a Methodist preacher of Irish descent; his mother, Frances (Dana) Archbold, was a daughter of the Massachusetts Dana family who migrated to Marietta, Ohio, in the early days of that settlement. After a few years of schooling Archbold began work in a country store at Salem, a few miles from the Pennsylvania oil region. As an eleven-year-old boy he had known something of the excitement that followed the discovery of petroleum near Titusville in 1859. By the time he had reached his eighteenth year he was ready to cast in his lot with the nondescript horde of fortune-hunters in the oil fields, where a new frenzy of speculation followed the close of the Civil War. Young Archbold quickly proved himself able to hold his own with experienced men in the rough give-and-take of trade under conditions not unlike those of the California gold rush in 1849. He was soon to come off winner in a hotly contested race with a group of master minds in the new industry. The South Improvement Company, in which John D. Rockefeller and other Standard Oil men were members, blocked the advance of the Pennsylvania producers and refiners, including Archbold, by obtaining from the railroads freight rebates which put the Pennsylvanians out of the running as competitors. Even in those cut-throat days, Archbold was able to unite the leading oil men of the Titusville region against an outside foe that threatened the business life of the community. He was successful; the Cleveland combination was thwarted in its plans; it acknowledged defeat—for the moment—and took the victorious young leader into its own camp, where his brains and talents were needed in working out a national organization to control the oil industry. The launching of Archbold's Acme Oil Company was followed by the expansion of the Standard Oil Company, with Archbold on its directorate.

From 1882 to the day of his death there was no question of the dominance of Archbold in Standard Oil policy and counsels. In the various investigations made from time to time by Congress and the state governments, when facts were disclosed, Archbold usually acted as spokesman for the company. He often disarmed criticism by his frankness. Asked before the Industrial Commission of 1900 whether Standard Oil was enabled by its great power to secure prices somewhat above those that were competitive, he replied, "Well, I hope so" (United States Industrial Commission, *Preliminary Report on Trusts and Industrial Combinations,* 1900, I, 569). In the period of the Standard Oil Company's rapid growth and absorption of independent companies, Archbold as vice-president was one of its most aggressive officers. After 1896, when John D. Rockefeller, although still president, had comparatively little to do with the corporation's affairs, Archbold was the real genius of the organization. Stabilization, combined with steady improvement of product, was his goal. He bent his energies to the creation of an efficient system of distribution, including the control of pipe-lines and the location of refineries at points convenient to markets; to the perfection of plants, and to the economical utilization of by-products. Thus an organization was developed that was soon beyond the reach of effective competition. In 1908 copies of letters addressed by Archbold to men in public life, notably Senators Quay and Penrose of Pennsylvania and Foraker of Ohio, were stolen from his office files and published. Although these letters did not point to actual corruption, they seemed to mark their writer as a corporation officer who had no hesitancy in calling upon men in the government service to do his bidding (*Independent,* New York, Oct. 8, 29, Nov. 5, 1908). As a result of the United States Supreme Court decision of 1911, dissolving the Standard Oil Company, Archbold became president of the Standard Oil Company of New Jersey and held that office at the time of his death. He was married in 1870 to Annie Mills of Titusville, Pa.

[*House Report No. 3112,* 50 Cong., 1 Sess. (1888); *Proc. of the Special Committee on Railroads* (Hepburn Committee, N. Y. Assembly, 1879); Ida M. Tarbell, *Hist. of the Standard Oil Company* (1904); G. H. Montague, *Rise and Progress of the Standard Oil Company* (1905); J. D. Archbold, "Effect of Trusts on Labor," *Independent,* Mar. 15, 1900, and "Petroleum: A Great Am. Industry," *Ibid.,* Mar. 5, 1908; *N. Y. Times,* Dec. 6, 8, 19, 30, 1916.] W. B. S.

ARCHDALE, JOHN (*c.* May 5, 1642–*c.* July 4, 1717), colonial governor, was born in England, the son of Thomas and Mary (Nevill) Archdale and grandson of Richard Archdale, who in 1604 and 1628 acquired the manors of Loakes and Temple Wycombe in Buckinghamshire. Sons of the Archdale family were regularly educated at Wadham College, Oxford, but John was an exception and received no college training. His first connection with America came through the marriage of his eldest sister to Ferdinando Gorges, who disputed with Massachusetts Bay Colony the ownership of Maine. In the autumn of 1664 Archdale was sent to New England to make good the Gorges claim. He landed at Piscataqua and carried a letter from Charles II, requiring the Bay Colony to cede the Maine government or to show reason to the contrary. Massachusetts answered that Maine was a part of its grant and that its claims would not be given up except by consent of the General Court (*Massachusetts Bay Colony Records,* vol. IV, pt. 2, p. 247). This unfavorable reply did not deter Archdale, who, assiduous in the proprietor's interest and zealous in the pursuance of his duties, visited every town in Maine and granted commissions to individuals who ruled independently of Massachusetts. The contest continued until the arrival of the King's agents in 1665 and the suspension of the authority of Massachusetts. But this defeat was not a triumph for Archdale, for he was ignored, and his authority set aside, so that shortly afterward he left the province (W. D. Williamson, *History of the State of Maine,* 1832, I, 414). With the withdrawal of the King's commissioners Massachusetts quietly resumed its authority in 1668, and the Gorges claim was settled by purchase in 1678.

After the return of Archdale to England, he married Ann (Dobson) Cary, a widow, in December 1673, by whom he had four children. He became identified with the Society of Friends, and it was perhaps influenced by his beliefs that he accepted a commission in 1682 from the Carolina proprietors to collect their rents in North Carolina where numbers of Quakers had settled. In this occupation he continued through 1683 (*Collections of the Historical Society of South Carolina,* I, 105–6, 110). His next connection with the American colonies occurred in 1694. Due to trouble in Carolina the resident governor had appealed to the proprietors to send out one of their number as governor. Archdale was appointed to this office, as he had supposedly bought the Carolina claim of the widow of Sir William Berkeley, but the title was clouded, hence his status was defined as "being in the nature of a proprietor." He went to Carolina by way of Virginia and was nearly a year in reaching his destination. He reported that on his arrival all was in confusion, with every faction appealing to him for relief and that "I appeased them with kind and gentle Words and so soon as possible call'd an Assembly" (Carroll, II, 101–3). His first assembly was soon dissolved because of a dispute over land questions. During the next assembly a temporary solution was secured by passing an act regulating prices, rents, and the conveyance of land. His administration was notable for the passage of the colony's first recorded liquor law, which forbade the sale of liquors under the quantity of one gallon except by license of the governor and put into effect the English law governing abuses and disorders of taverns (*Statutes at Large of South Carolina,* 1837, II, 113). His Quaker principles were revealed in the law which he secured from his assembly exempting Quakers from serving in the militia and in his policy of friendship toward the Indians (*Ibid.,* p. 108).

In 1698 he was elected member of Parliament for Chipping Wycombe, Buckinghamshire. Again he showed himself a man of strong religious principles in declining as a Quaker to take the oath, and the House refused to seat him. After this he retired from public life. In 1707 he published *A New Description of the Fertile and Pleasant Province of Carolina with a Brief Account of Its Discovery and Settling and the Government thereof to the Time, with Several Remarkable Passages of Divine Providence during my Time.*

[The chief sources for Archdale's career in America are his own account, "Archdale's Description," etc., in B. R. Carroll, *Hist. Colls. of S. C.* (1836); and Josselyn's "Chronological Observations of America" in *Mass. Hist. Soc. Coll.,* 3rd series, vol. III. A short sketch of his life is in the *Dict. of Nat. Biog.* and an account of his public career in Carolina in E. McCrady, *S. C. under Proprietary Govt.* (1897). See also W. J. Rivers, *Sketch of the Hist. of S. C.* (1856); A. Hewatt, *Hist. of S. C.* (1779).]

H. B–C.

ARCHER, BRANCH TANNER (1790–Sept. 22, 1856), political leader in the Republic of Texas, was a native of Virginia. His father was a Revolutionary soldier, Maj. Peter Field Archer, of Henrico and Powhatan Counties; his mother was Frances, daughter of Branch Tanner. According to one biographer, Archer "studied medicine in Philadelphia, and for some years was a physician and politician in his native state, where he served one or two terms as a member of the legislature" (Fulmore, p. 103). It is said that his departure from Virginia followed a duel in which he shot and killed his cousin, Dr. Crump. He arrived in Texas in 1831, and immediately identified himself with a small group of malcontents who were impatient with Mexico's bungling political experiments. Brazoria was the headquarters of this group, and Archer's first public service in Texas was to represent a mass meeting of Brazoria in demanding modification of objectionable port regulations. He represented the district of Brazoria in the convention of April 1833, which adopted a provisional constitution and petitioned the Mexican Congress for the admission of Texas to the Mexican Confederation as a co-state. In November 1835 he again represented Brazoria in the consultation which was called originally for settling on a policy to be followed with regard to the changes which Santa Anna was making in the federal constitution of 1824. Before the consultation met, war had already been precipitated by the demand of the military commandant for a cannon which the colonists had at Gonzales. Archer was elected chairman of the consultation, and made a speech at the beginning of the session, urging the members to disregard factional irritation and to devote themselves solely to the best interests of Texas (*Journal of Consultation,* pp. 6–9). The fundamental question to be settled by the consultation was, "What are we fighting for?" The answer tentatively adopted on Nov. 7 was, "For the republican principles of the constitution of 1824." On this question Archer voted aye, though he favored independence. But whether the Texans were fighting to uphold the federal constitution of Mexico or for independence, it was apparent that they would need assistance. Therefore Archer, with Stephen F. Austin [*q.v.*] and William H. Wharton, was appointed a commissioner to the United States to solicit men, money, and supplies. The three commissioners arrived at New Orleans in January 1836, and negotiated loans there for $250,000. They aroused much sympathy for the Texan cause in their progress up the Mississippi River, and were indirectly responsible for the movement of a considerable number of "emigrants" to Texas to assist in the war for independence which was declared on Mar. 2, 1836. At Washington, though Archer was related to William S. Archer [*q.v.*] who long represented Virginia in Congress, and though both Austin and Wharton had influential friends, the commissioners were unable to commit the government of the United States in any way to the policy of recognizing or aiding the new Republic of Texas. It was probably due to Archer that the personal relations of the commissioners were harmonious and cordial, for Austin and Wharton had not previously been friends. Archer and Wharton took the lead in nominating Austin for the presidency of Texas, and supported him against Henry Smith and Sam Houston. A member of the first Congress of Texas, Archer was at the second session elected speaker of the lower house. His last public service was in the cabinet of President Lamar, where he served as secretary of war. A newspaper at the time of his death speaks of his "stalwart form and Cato-like look." His portrait shows a handsome, striking face—long, lean, broad of forehead, with piercing eyes, and clearly chiseled nose, lips, and chin.

[Eugene C. Barker, *Life of Stephen F. Austin* (1925); Texas State Lib., *Calendar of the Papers of Mirabeau Buonaparte Lamar* (1914); H. S. Foote, *Texas and the Texans,* 2 vols. (1841); Z. T. Fulmore, *Hist. and Geography of Texas as Told in County Names* (1915); H. P. N. Gammel, *Laws of Texas,* I (1898); files of *Texas State Hist. Ass. Quart.*; A. M. Williams, *Sam Houston* (1893); *New Orleans Daily Picayune,* Sept. 30, 1856; Geneal. of the Archer family prepared by Wm. G. Stanard, in the *Richmond Critic,* May 8, 1889; information from Mrs. Mary Newton Stanard.]

E. C. B.

ARCHER, FREDERIC (June 16, 1838–Oct. 22, 1901), organist, was the only child of Martha (Costa) and James Archer, clergyman and professor of Latin at Magdalen College, Oxford. He was born at Oxford, and became a chorister at All Saints' Church, London, at the age of nine. Five years later he returned to Oxford as organist of St. Clement's Church and Merton College. His musical education was continued in Oxford, London, and Leipzig. His career as an organ recitalist began with engagements at the Panopticon and the Alexandra Palace, London; at the latter he gave over 2,000 recitals. Meanwhile he became active as church organist, choral conductor, and lecturer. In 1878–80 he conducted the Glasgow Select Choir, for which he composed and edited a series of part-songs. He was also conductor of the Blanche Cole Opera Company. His first trip to America was in 1881, and one of the results was his engagement as organist at Plymouth Church, Brooklyn, where Henry Ward Beecher was pastor. Later he removed to the Church of the Incarnation, New York, thence to Boston, where he conducted the Boston Oratorio Society (1887–88). In 1885 he founded, and for a time edited a musical paper, *The Keynote.* From Boston he went to Chicago, where he became organist at St. James Roman Catholic Church, and was active in musical projects connected with the World's Fair. He left Chicago to become organist and director of music at Carnegie Institute, Pittsburgh, where he was engaged from 1895 to his death, giving two organ recitals weekly in the Music Hall, and officiating (1896–98) as conductor of the Pittsburgh Orchestra.

Archer was one of the first players to popularize the organ recital in America. His wide experience in England with giving recitals before large audiences and with ordinary concert surroundings was in strong contrast to the severe and churchly associations of the average American organ recital fifty years ago. His first program at Carnegie Institute, Pittsburgh, was typical of the player. It contained Merkel's second Sonata, a Bach Toccata and Fugue, Lemmen's *Storm Fantasy,* the Air and variations from Moszkowski's first orchestral suite, Gounod's *Funeral March of a Marionette* (written for one of Archer's London orchestral concerts), and Meyerbeer's overture *Star of the North,* with smaller pieces. Such programs he played throughout this country and Canada on his many and extended tours. This type of program, as well as its performance, helped greatly in awakening popular appreciation of organ recitals.

Of more than ordinary stature, and of commanding appearance, Archer was favored by nature for organ playing. He had fingers of unusual length, and in consequence could achieve organ effects impossible for normal hands. A real virtuoso, his manipulation of the instrument was masterly, and his registration notable for its variety and brilliance. He was a remarkable sight reader, sometimes playing in recital from orchestral scores; it is possible that he occasionally depended too much upon this facility in reading music. He was a man of great energy and constant activity. Among his published works are *The Organ, The Collegiate Organ Tutor,* and a number of organ compositions, piano pieces, songs, and choruses. His writings on musical subjects were published in English and American magazines. He was married in 1859 to Harriet Rothschild, a niece of Baron Alfred de Rothschild of England.

[Much of the above information is from a sketch written by Archer, in the possession of his family. A rather extended obituary note is in the *Musical Times* (London), Dec. 1901. See also *The Organ and its Masters* (1902) by Henry C. Lahee.]

C. N. B.

ARCHER, JAMES J. (Dec. 19, 1817–Oct. 24, 1864), Confederate soldier, was a native of Stafford in Harford County, Md. In the earlier part of his career he has been confused (*Confederate Military History,* II, 171) with John Archer also from Maryland and a graduate of West Point (class of 1826). Gen. Archer, who was not a West Point graduate, was educated at Princeton and at Bacon College in Georgetown, Ky., and became a lawyer. He served in the Mexican War, and was brevetted major for gallantry in the battle of Chapultepec, and received from the legislature of his state a vote of thanks. Returning to civil life in 1848, he reëntered the army as captain in 1855. He entered the Confederate army in 1861, and was commissioned brigadier-general June 3, 1862. The phrase "Archer's brigade" occurs frequently in the annals of the Army of Northern Virginia, for instance in the narrative of Longstreet (*From Manassas to Appomattox,* 1896). He was present in all the noteworthy engagements of 1862 and 1863, the Seven Days, Cedar Mountain, Second Manassas, Antietam, Fredericksburg, Chancellorsville—where he was with Jackson in the flanking march—and Gettysburg. He has been credited with a prominent part in the counter-attack at Antietam. In the campaign of Gettysburg he was in the division of Gen. Heth, and on July 1, he was attached to that portion of the army which began the three days' battle. This was in the part of the field where Reynolds and Doubleday were in command. Archer was "captured by a flank movement" (*Battles and Leaders of the Civil War,* III, 1888, p. 352), and with him were taken many in the brigade. He was a prisoner for over a year, was sent southward and exchanged, but died soon after his release.

[*Biog. Cyc. of Md., and the D. C.* (1879); M. J. Wright, *Gen. Officers* (1911); F. B. Heitman, *Hist. Reg.* (1890); C. A. Evans, ed., *Confed. Mil. Hist.* (1899), II, 171–72; *Tercentenary Hist. of Md.* (1925), I, 757.]

E. K. A.

ARCHER, JOHN (May 5, 1741–Sept. 28, 1810), medical teacher, founder of the Medical and Chirurgical Faculty of Maryland, was born near the present village of Churchville, Harford County, Md. His father, originally a farmer from Rathmelton, County Donegal, Ireland, was then an agent for the local iron works. John was educated at the West Nottingham Academy and at Princeton College, where he received his A.B. in 1760 and his A.M. three years later. Meanwhile he had begun the study of theology under Presbyterian auspices and had preached a trial sermon; then he turned his attention to medicine, becoming a pupil of John Morgan and beginning attendance at the courses of lectures at the Philadelphia College of Medicine, which later became the University of Pennsylvania Medical Department. The degree of Bachelor of Medicine was conferred on him June 21, 1768, the first medical degree, involving attendance at lectures, to be bestowed in this country. Even before Archer obtained his degree he had begun to practise in Newcastle County, Del.; it is said he declined an offer from Dr. Morgan to go into partnership; at all events he returned to his native county in July 1769 and began a practise which lasted nearly forty years. During the Revolution he was a member of the local committees from November 1774, and in December of the same year was captain of a militia company, becoming major in January 1776. That August he was a member of the convention which framed the Maryland constitution and bill of rights.

During his many years of practise Archer gave instruction to some fifty medical students, following the custom of the time that a student should remain as assistant to a well-known practitioner for a period of three years, this novitiate serving in lieu of a degree in medicine. His assistants formed a sort of medical society, the minutes of which are preserved in the library of the Medical and Chirurgical Faculty of Maryland at Baltimore, the state medical society which Archer helped to found in 1799. He was on its examining board and a member of the executive committee. In 1801 he was a presidential elector and served as a representative in Congress from that date until 1807. He contributed a few papers to the *Medical Repository* of New York and introduced senega as a remedy in the treatment of croup. His health began to fail at the time of the completion of his service in Congress; he had a partial paralysis and gave up active pursuits. He died suddenly, probably from another cerebral hemorrhage, while sitting in his chair at his home in Harford County.

Archer was married in 1766 to a daughter of Thomas Harris, of the family that founded Harrisburg, Pa., by whom he had ten children, of whom five studied medicine. Several portraits of him are extant; one in the court-house at Belair, Harford County, Md., a second in the hall of the Medical and Chirurgical Faculty at Baltimore, and a third in the State House at Annapolis, Md.

[The chief sources of information are the *Medic. Annals of Md.* (1903); articles by Eugene F. Cordell in the *Johns Hopkins Hospital Bull.* (1899 and 1902); J. Carson, *Hist. of the Medic. Dept. of the Univ. of Pa.* (1869); *Biog. Cong. Dir. 1744–1911* (1913); *Am. Archives,* ser. 4, vol. I, p. 403; vol. IV, p. 737; ser. 5, vol. II, p. 637.]

W. L. B.

ARCHER, SAMUEL (1771–Apr. 14, 1839), merchant, philanthropist, was born near the village of Columbus, Burlington County, N. J., and went to Philadelphia about 1794. In 1797 he married Elizabeth West, who was a member of the Society of Friends, and nine years his senior. The same year he began business in Philadelphia under the firm name of Archer & Newbold, described in the Philadelphia Directory as merchants. The following year he was engaged in the retail dry-goods trade, but in another twelvemonth was in the importing business. In 1804 he took in Robert L. Pittfield, an accountant, as partner, and the firm name was changed to Samuel Archer & Company, which, a few years later, became Archer & Bispham, Stacy B. Bispham entering the firm as the successor of Pittfield, who retired. Between the years 1800 and 1812, the greater part of the business in importations from India and China was transacted through Philadelphia and Archer's firm was among the largest importers of muslins from the East Indies. These goods were not then manufactured in this country. The house was also noted as an extensive importer of Chinese manufactures, but a great deal of Archer's business was in textiles of British make. So large a buyer was he and so scrupulous in all his business dealings, that it was currently said his credit in Europe was unlimited. "The business for the house in that day was immense, having reached in a single year over two million of dollars in amount" (Simpson, p. 20). In 1810–11 Archer made a visit to Europe to purchase goods. The War of 1812, which began soon after his return home, cut off the bulk of the foreign trade of the house, but after hostilities had ceased, with rare courage and business sagacity, he began to export to China American-made fabrics, the manufacture of which was just beginning here. He is credited with having been the first American merchant to export extensively American-made cotton goods to Asia. While fortune smiled upon many of his daring enterprises, it also, occasionally, frowned upon him, and he suffered several serious reverses, owing, it is said, to his generous disposition to place too much confidence in some concerns and men with whom he engaged in business. He took an active interest in the financial institutions of his adopted city, and was one of the original managers of the Philadelphia Saving Fund Society (1816), the first of its kind in the United States; and the same year he was elected a director of the Insurance Company of North America, the first marine insurance company organized in this country. In 1817 he was one of four wealthy men who presented a lot on which was erected the Philadelphia Orphan Asylum; his partner at that time, Robert Ralston, was another of the quartet. William D. Lewis, who furnished the sketch of his life which appeared in Simpson's book, wrote of him (p. 21) that he "held a prominent place among the enterprising merchants of our city for near half a century. When basking in the sunshine of great riches and prosperity, he possessed much simplicity of manners and an utter absence of all display. . . . Charity, benevolence, and uprightness seemed to be the natural qualities of his character exhibited through life." His portrait, painted by Anna C. Peale, and engraved by Samuel Sartain, pictures him in the quiet simplicity of the Quakers, whose ideals he made his own, although he was not a member of that religious society at the time of his marriage. He was buried, however, in a Friends' burial-ground in Philadelphia.

[Henry Simpson, *Lives of Eminent Philadelphians Now Deceased* (1859), portr.; Abraham Ritter, *Phila. and Her Merchants* (1860), p. 145; Jas. M. Willcox, *A Hist. of the Phila. Saving Fund Soc.* (1916); T. H. Montgomery, *A Hist. of the Insurance Company of North America* (1885). Manuscript records of the Society of Friends in Philadelphia are authority for some of the statements made.]

J. J.

ARCHER, STEVENSON (Oct. 11, 1786–June 26, 1848), jurist, the son of John Archer [*q.v.*], was born at "Medical Hall," Harford County, Md., within a few hundred yards of the birthplace of Edwin Booth. He attended school in Baltimore, entered the sophomore class of Princeton College, graduated in 1805, and studied law first in the office of John Montgomery at Belair and later with Chancellor Johnson at Annapolis. Soon after coming to the bar he was elected to the legislature as an Independent, 1809, and the next year was reëlected as a Democrat. He married in 1811 Pamelia Barney Hays, whose father owned the adjoining farm. She was a capable woman, who in her husband's absence on court business took active control over hundreds of acres. Archer was elected to Congress the year of his marriage, and was twice reëlected to succeed himself. In these war years he was a reliance of the administration, and in 1817, declining a fourth term, was appointed, by President Madison, judge of Mississippi Territory. He held court at St. Stephens on the Alabama River, and also exercised gubernatorial powers of a broad character. Though he had ordered a flatboat built at Wheeling to bring his family and effects down, he concluded in less than a year to return to Harford, whence in 1819 he was again sent to Congress. His law practise had widened to embrace Harford, Cecil, and Kent Counties when, in 1824, he was appointed chief judge of the 6th judicial district, embracing Baltimore and Harford Counties. This appointment made him associate justice of the Maryland court of appeals, of which, on the death of Judge Buchanan in 1844, Gov. Pratt appointed him chief judge.

He was a tall man, of strong frame, and his portraits show a kindly, thoughtful countenance. During his twenty-five years on the bench he was deliberate and painstaking in judgment and considerate in manner. His opinions display industry and patience in details. It is said of him that "his amenity won the universal respect of the bar, while his sound judgment and . . . legal attainments commanded for his decisions entire confidence." He presided in courts on both the western and eastern shores, and during a summer session at Easton, in the flat country, contracted a fever of which, after a few days' illness, he died at his home in Harford.

[*Biog. Cyc. Rep. Men of Md. and D. C.* (1879); James McSherry, "Former Chief Judges of the Court of Appeals of Md.," in *Rept. Ninth Meeting Md. Bar Ass.*, 1904, pp. 120–21; *Bench and Bar of Md.* (n. d.), pp. 291–92; *Baltimore Sun* and *Baltimore American*, June 27, 1848; *Green Bag*, VI, 232; *Biog. Cong. Directory, 1774–1903* (1903).]

B. M.

ARCHER, WILLIAM SEGAR (Mar. 5, 1789–Mar. 28, 1855), congressman, came of a family whose emigrant ancestor, George Archer, was living in Henrico County, Va., in 1665. During the Revolution all of the Archers were warm supporters of the American cause. An uncle and several first cousins of William S. Archer were officers in the army and this uncle, Col. William Archer, was captured and died in a British prison ship. Col. Archer's son, Lieut. Joseph Archer, was killed in the battle of Brandywine and two other sons, John and Peter Field, were majors. Dr. Branch T. Archer [*q.v.*], a son of Peter Field, played a distinguished part in the early history of Texas. William Segar Archer, the son of Maj. John Archer (brother of Col. William Archer just referred to) and Elizabeth (Eggleston) Archer, was born in Amelia County, Va. He was graduated from William and Mary College in 1806, studied law, was admitted to the bar, and practised his profession during the rest of his life. He was elected to the Virginia house of delegates in 1812 and was reëlected every year till 1819 (E. G. Severn and John W. Williams, *Register of the General Assembly of Virginia*, 1918). He was a Whig and was a member of the United States House of Representatives from January 1820 to March 1835, and of the United States Senate from Mar. 4, 1841 to Mar. 3, 1847 (*Biographical Congressional Directory 1774–1911*, p. 444). Archer was nominated for the Senate on anti-Bank grounds and the success of the Whigs carried him into office. In debate in reference to the Bank, Senators Archer and Rives opposed Henry Clay, whom they charged with attacking President Tyler. Finally, however, Archer voted in support of the bank. In a letter dated June 18, 1841, Henry A. Wise wrote to Beverley Tucker: "Archer is *obliged* to be with us, or perhaps he would not be. He is weak, but not wicked. For instance, I am told that he is sophomore enough to say if Clay's plan is presented to Tyler, he must veto, but then *resign!*" (Lyon G. Tyler, *The Letters and Times of the Tylers*, 1885, II, 47). Archer was an ardent advocate of the annexation of Texas, as his printed speeches show. At the time of the annexation he was chairman of the Committee on Foreign Relations. A tall, dark man of refined appearance and gentle manner, he never married, but built for himself in Amelia County a charming home which he named "The Lodge" and which is now a picturesque ruin. There he lived with two devoted maiden sisters till death overtook him at the age of sixty-six. His epitaph in Amelia declares that: "This monument is erected to the memory of William S. Archer by his affectionate sisters to whom he stood almost throughout their lives in the double relation of father and brother."

[*Richmond Whig,* Mar. 10, 1840; *Richmond Enquirer,* Mar. 4, 1841; for Archer's speeches in Cong. see *Annals of Cong.,* XXXVI–XLII (1820–24), *Reg. of Debates,* I–XI (1825–35), *Cong. Globe,* IX–XVIII (1841–47). Dates of birth and death from his tomb.] M. N. S.

ARDEN, EDWIN HUNTER PENDLETON (Feb. 4, 1864–Oct. 2, 1918), actor, manager, playwright, was born in St. Louis, Mo., the son of Arden Richard and Mary Berkeley (Hunter) Smith. After a common-school education he went West and became successively mine-helper, cowboy, railroad brakeman, clerk, reporter, and theatre manager. He made his début as an actor in Chicago in 1882 as a member of Thomas W. Keene's Shakespearian company. During the three years following, he played in stock as member of the Boston Museum and Madison Square Theatre (New York) companies. On Feb. 21, 1883, he was married to Agnes Ann Eagleson Keene. At about this time he wrote several plays, some in collaboration, among the most successful of which were *The Eagle's Nest, Raglan's Way,* and *Barred Out.* He starred in these plays for nine seasons and then, in 1895, joined the company of William H. Crane, taking among other leading rôles that of Mason Hix in *The Governor of Kentucky.* Then came a season with the Julia Arthur company, when he played Sir John Oxen in *A Lady of Quality* in support of the star. In 1898, he played Oliver West, the young husband in *Because She Loved Him So,* and the following year returned to starring in a play from his own pen called *Zorah.* On Oct. 22, 1900, he appeared with Maude Adams at the Knickerbocker Theatre, New York City, playing Prince Metternich in that actress's production of Rostand's *L'Aiglon,* his acting as the famous Austrian diplomat attracting much attention. The following year he acted with Sadie Martinot in *The Marriage Game* and was also seen in the Bellew-Mannering revival of *The Lady of Lyons.* During the season of 1902 he appeared in *The Ninety and Nine,* and also in the all-star cast of *Romeo and Juliet* at the Knickerbocker Theatre, New York. In 1904, he was with Bertha Kalich, playing the rôle of Louis in *Fedora,* and the year following he was with James K. Hackett in *The House of Silence.* After a short time spent in vaudeville, he again appeared as a star at the Powers Theatre, Chicago, in the drama *Told in the Hills.* Later, he had his own stock company in Washington, D. C.

[Walter Browne, *Who's Who on the Stage* (1908); T. A. Brown, *Hist. of the N. Y. Stage* (1908); *Who's Who in America* (1918–19); *Who's Who in N. Y.* (1918); *N. Y. Times,* Oct. 3, 1918.] A. H.

ARENTS, ALBERT (Mar. 14, 1840–May 15, 1914), metallurgist, was born at Clausthal, Germany, becoming one of that group of German mining school graduates who, in the seventies and early eighties, took so active a part in the metallurgical development of the Rocky Mountain region, particularly in lead-silver smelting. His education was typical of this school of young German engineers. He had two years at the University of Berlin and his technical training at the Royal Mining Academy, Clausthal. He came to America in 1865 under engagement to a small lead mine in Massachusetts and later found employment with the Eureka Consolidated Company, Eureka, Nev. The most primitive character of smelting operations greeted Arents and his associates at Eureka, the first furnace used there having been an adobe affair with only natural draft, not actually a blast-furnace. Nevertheless, Eureka may well be considered as the birthplace of American lead smelting, for Arents was responsible for many of the most important features and his "siphon lead-well" was, in fact, revolutionary in its effect upon lead blast-furnace practise. Prior to the use of his device it had been necessary to periodically "tap" the lead from the furnace, but with his improvement the lead continually overflowed from the furnace crucible, gradually as it was reduced from the ore, thus avoiding the noxious operation of "tapping" large volumes of such highly heated lead, besides materially improving all of the blast-furnace conditions. The metallurgical progress was so great that when, in the next few years, smelting spread into Utah and Colorado, the practise, except for automatic feeding and the much smaller furnaces, was practically the same as present-day operations. Arents's siphon lead-well was not a manufactured device upon which his name could be distinctly displayed, but was merely the manner of placing the brick-work in the furnace crucible, and yet universally, from general manager down to most menial workman, it was spoken of as "Arents's lead-well." Prior to 1885 Arents removed to Alameda, Cal., which remained his home until his death. That he did not altogether relinquish pyrometallurgy is shown by an indefinitely worded patent (No. 321,780, July 7, 1885) of a revolving roaster, some of its features remaining in its prototype, the widely used cement kiln of the present day. Arents devoted himself to prospecting and study of geology and mineralogy of the adjacent counties, having added "partzite" to the mineralogical list. It seems unfortunate that one, having, in so brief a time, made such an impress upon American lead-silver smelting practise, should so soon have abandoned this particular field, but his contemporaries, and those who have followed him, have left no uncertain testimony in the technical literature as to the benefits which he conferred upon the art.

[*Trans. Am. Inst. Mining Engineers*, I, II, IV, XXII; *Engineering and Mining Jour.*, XCVII, 1216; Carl Schnable, *Handbook of Metallurgy* (1898); H. F. Collins, *Metallurgy of Lead and Silver* (1899–1900); personal recollections and letter from Arents's daughter.]

R. C. C.

ARGALL, PHILIP (Aug. 27, 1854–Mar. 19, 1922), engineer, metallurgist, son of Philip and Sarah Argall, was born in Newtownards, near Belfast, Ireland. His ancestry was predominantly Celtic and endowed him with an enthusiastic and adaptable nature. Growing up among mines and metallurgical works, he finished grammar school and obtained a grounding in Latin, but at sixteen was laboring ten hours a day for a penny an hour in a mill of the Wicklow copper-mining district, south of Dublin. At seventeen he worked eight hours a day in a mine and had two hours of daily instruction in mathematics and surveying from an ex-officer of ordnance. He profited by association with the professors of a small technical college in Dublin, forty miles away. Using second-hand chemical apparatus found at an abandoned mine, he made analyses for copper and sulphur in ores. At the age of nineteen he was promoted to shift-boss in the Cronebane mine. Two years later he was assistant manager, with the Cornish title of captain. At this early age, with little formal education, he wrote two papers on ore deposits and copper precipitation that were published by the Royal Dublin Society. In 1876 he married Frances Ellen Oates of Ovoca, Ireland, daughter of Capt. George Oates, a Cornish mining man. At twenty-five he took charge of a small metallurgical plant in Swansea, South Wales, at that time the leading metallurgical center of the world, and during a year and a half there he took a course in metallurgy. In quick succession, he was manager for an iron-ore company in Ireland, manager of a mine near Newquay in Cornwall, manager of an antimony smelter in London, and finally in 1884, at the age of thirty, went to New Zealand as manager of gold mines at Coromandel for the Kapanga Gold Mining Company. After a year in New Zealand and Australia, he returned to England and then went to Mexico as superintendent of mines in Sonora, but a year later was back in Ireland building a successful concentrating mill for an iron-ore company and acting as consulting engineer for a silver-lead company in France. All these engagements contributed to the development of his versatility and taught him not to become discouraged even though his employers went bankrupt.

In 1887, at the age of thirty-three, he came to the United States as manager of the La Plata smelter at Leadville, Colo. The smelter soon had to close because of intense competition by a number of others that were bidding for the available ore. In 1889 Argall became a naturalized American citizen. Reports began to reach America of the new cyanide process being developed in South Africa for extracting gold from ore. Many American mining men were incredulous of the new process, but a few small plants were built and experiments begun in adapting the little-understood technique to the difficult ores of Colorado. In 1894 Argall went to Cripple Creek to investigate the failure of a small cyanide plant. The Moffat railroad interests encouraged the building of the first large custom-plant to treat Cripple Creek gold ores by cyanidation. This was done by the Metallic Extraction Company whose mill Argall designed, erected, and managed. By 1895 this mill was treating 3,000 tons of ore a month, and two years later 10,000 tons a month. These telluride ores presented many problems. The clay or talc in dry-crushed ore could not be wetted; the fine ore would not leach. Argall briquetted 15 to 20 per cent of the ore and roasted it prior to cyanidation. Later he patented apparatus for separating the dust from the sand, and a method of crushing in alkaline solution. The cost of treating Cripple Creek gold ores by wet methods was reduced from $15 a ton to $3.50 in 1898 and to $1.38 in 1913. Argall advocated cyanidation, rather than chlorination, of Cripple Creek ores as simpler and cheaper. He engaged in several such metallurgical controversies, including those on dry and wet crushing, roasting and non-roasting, sliming and non-sliming. In 1906 he became consulting engineer for the British owners of the famous Stratton's Independence mine at Cripple Creek. This mine had a large amount of dump ore containing about $3 per ton, but custom mills were charging $5.50 for treating low-grade ore. Argall estimated that he could treat this ore for $1.52 per ton for an extraction of 74.22 per cent. Results for six years on 671,665 tons showed a cost of $1.5138 and an extraction of 74.57 per cent, a remarkable record. In 1905 and 1906 he had charge of the field work of the Zinc Commission appointed by the government of Canada to investigate the zinc resources of British Columbia and test the ores for metallurgical processes. He introduced the eight-hour day in Colorado mills in 1899. In 1903 he received a gold medal from the Institution of Mining and Metallurgy (London) for a paper on "Sampling and Dry

Crushing in Colorado." With two sons, he maintained an office in Denver; for a time he was consulting metallurgist for the American branch of the MacArthur-Forest Company, well-known British engineers who invented the cyanide process in Glasgow in 1887. At his death, ten children survived him; his wife died in 1903. In appearance Argall was stocky and wore a mustache; he showed Cornish and Irish characteristics with western-American adaptations.

[The best source is an interview entitled "Philip Argall and Metallurgical Progress" by T. A. Rickard, in the *Mining and Scientific Press,* Jan. 22, 1916; see also long obituary in the *Rocky Mt. News,* Mar. 20, 1922.]

P. B. M.

ARGALL, SIR SAMUEL (fl. 1609–1624), adventurer, deputy governor of Virginia, first appears in history in 1609 when he was selected to discover a short route to Virginia. The usual course led by way of the Canaries to the Island of Porto Rico in the West Indies, a long, circuitous pathway peculiarly exposed to the attacks of pirates and the interference of Spain. Argall was instructed to steer, after leaving the Canaries, straight across the Atlantic Ocean, in the hope that the reports of dangerous seas in that quarter could be proven false, and thus a far shorter pathway westward be opened up. It required only nine weeks to finish this memorable voyage; and of these, two were spent in a dead calm. Following the same route on his return, Argall reached England in October of the same year, after an absence of only five months. By this conspicuous achievement he gained lasting fame as one of England's maritime pioneers.

When, in the spring of 1610, Lord Delaware arrived in Virginia to take possession of his post of governor general, he was accompanied by Argall, probably to point out the northerly route, which he had the year before shown to be practicable. Delaware had been in the colony only a few days when he sent Sir George Somers and Argall to Bermuda to get a supply of hogs to take the place of those which had been devoured by the starving colonists at Jamestown, during Percy's rule. Somers died during the voyage, and Argall, having either accidentally or purposely missed the Bermudas, went on to Cape Cod, where he secured a cargo of fish for the immediate relief of the Virginia colony. He then aided Lord Delaware by expeditions to the Rappahannock and Potomac in search of grain, which the Indians were ready to sell for English merchandise that appealed to their fancy. On the occasion of one of these voyages, he was able to bring back to Jamestown a cargo of 1,000 bushels of corn. It was said at this time that it was chiefly through him that the disease-wracked and disheartened community there was preserved. He endeavored to advance the culture of wheat in Virginia by securing a supply of seed during a voyage to Canada; and from that remote country he also brought back to Jamestown a considerable number of horses, mares, and colts. But not all his voyages to the far North were actuated solely by a desire to replenish the live stock of Virginia, or to furnish its inhabitants with seed for new crops, or to fill their spindling larders with large quantities of dried fish from the Banks. From some points of view, the most memorable event in his career was his part in breaking up the French settlements on the coast of Maine. In 1611, although the English had by this time founded Jamestown and taken permanent possession of Virginia, Louis XIII granted all the territory lying on the Atlantic Ocean between the mouth of the St. Lawrence and Florida to a French Jesuit mission, which soon undertook to convert the Indian inhabitants to their faith. Argall was in London when news arrived of these letters-patent by an alien power. From his reputation for boldness and skill, he was selected to expel the intruders from the soil claimed by England. He promptly set out in 1613 for Mt. Desert; captured the missionaries who had established themselves there and at St. Croix and Port Royal; burned down their houses; and carried off the priests to Virginia. This was not his sole achievement in an expedition which preserved New England for English occupation, a few years later. He stopped, in the course of his voyage, at the Dutch settlement on the Hudson, and forced the Dutch governor to declare his allegiance to England.

Hardly less important was Argall's capture of Pocahontas in the previous year in one of the villages on the Potomac, where she had been living since Capt. John Smith's departure from Virginia. Argall, on hearing of her presence, while he was foraging for grain in the neighborhood, perceived at once that through her a lasting peace might be established by a formal agreement between her father, Powhatan, and the English. By connivance with the chief of the tribe with whom she was staying, he cunningly induced her to come on board of his vessel; and after a few hours of entertainment, the unsuspecting princess was carried off to Jamestown. Here she was detained; but in a spirit of so much kindness, that she became reconciled to her situation, was converted to Christianity, married John Rolfe, and accompanied Gov. Dale, Argall, and her husband, to England in the spring of 1616.

In 1617, Argall was appointed to the office of deputy governor of Virginia. His conduct, during his administration, has been a subject of controversy. At his arrival, the colony was in a state of prosperity. The cattle were numerous; the tenants were profitably at work in the public garden; and the granaries were full of corn. His first measures were further promotive of this happy condition. He required that each householder should cultivate two acres in grain to provide bread; he reserved all the hay for the cattle; he experimented in the production of wheat; he conserved the supply of powder and shot; he enforced the law relating to church attendance; and he rebuilt the governor's residence. But before the close of his administration, a different spirit was exhibited by him. The Divine and Military Laws of Dale and Gates were still in force, and Argall seems to have taken advantage of this fact. He refused to grant freedom to the tenants whose terms were up; he converted to his own use the grain from the public garden; he killed the public cattle for their hides for his private sale; he sold the tobacco belonging to the magazine to shipmasters and sailors, leaving none to pay for the adventurers' merchandise; he neglected to compel the Indians to pay their usual tributes of maize; and he permitted the rule requiring the cultivation of two acres in grain to fall into abeyance. Apparently, at the end of his government, all the public property had been dispersed or devoured, and the colony, as a whole, had fallen into a state of great poverty.

To crown the delinquencies with which he was charged, he, at the instance of the Earl of Warwick, sent the ship *Treasurer* to the West Indies, ostensibly for goats and salt, but in reality to ravish the commerce of Spain in those waters. The vessel later sailed to the Bermudas with a cargo of slaves snatched in a piratical manner. This incident led to Argall's departure from Virginia in order to justify his conduct, which, through Warwick's powerful influence at Court, he was able to do. In 1620, he was in command of the *Golden Phœnix,* which was attached to the English fleet in the Mediterranean; and, in 1625, he was an admiral in a great naval force which sailed from Plymouth and succeeded in capturing £100,000 worth of prizes. He became a member of the New England Royal Council, and was knighted for his services. But, in 1624, he was defeated in his candidacy for the governorship of Virginia. His death occurred at some time previous to 1641.

[Capt. John Smith, *Hist of Va.* (1627); Wm. Stith, *Hist. of Va.* (1747); Alexander Brown, *Genesis of U.S.* (1891); Purchas, *Pilgrimes* (1625), pt. 4; Neill, *Eng. Colonization of America* (1871), p. 187; Ralph Hamor, *True Discourse* (1615); J. A. Doyle, *Eng. Colonies* (1882); Peter Force, *Coll. of Hist. Docs. 1836–46;* P. A. Bruce, *Econ. Hist. of Va. in the Seventeenth Century* (1896).]

P. A. B.

ARMISTEAD, GEORGE (Apr. 10, 1780–Apr. 25, 1818), soldier, was born in New Market, Caroline County, Va. He was the son of John and Lucy (Baylor) Armistead. The family was known in England from the days of Queen Elizabeth, and according to one tradition it originated in Hesse, Germany. Armistead entered the United States Army as second-lieutenant, and was commissioned major of the 3rd Artillery Mar. 3, 1813. In October 1810 he was married to Louisa Hughes, sister of Christopher Hughes of Baltimore, chargé d'affaires in Denmark, Norway, and Sweden. Armistead was distinguished at the capture of Fort George in Upper Canada on May 18, 1813, but his reputation is chiefly based on his successful defense of Fort McHenry. After the burning of Washington, Aug. 24, 1814, the British fleet under Admiral Cochrane and the army under Gen. Ross sailed up Chesapeake Bay with the purpose of capturing Baltimore. While the fleet entered the Patapsco River, Ross with about 3,000 men landed at Northern Point, Sept. 12, 1814, and advanced toward the city. The mayor and citizens had made rapid preparations. Militia guarded the hastily built intrenchments, and sailors manned the batteries. The troops, inclusive of officers, present for duty numbered about 13,900, under command of Major-General Samuel Smith. Armistead was appointed to command Fort McHenry, a small fortification, but the chief defense of the harbor. He had under him about 1,000 men, regulars, volunteers, and sailors. He was the only man, so it is stated, aware of the alarming fact that the powder magazine was not bombproof. The advance by land under Ross was opposed by about 3,000 militia under Gen. Stricker. They were placed unskilfully and were routed, but the British suffered the great loss of their general. Proceeding the next day, Sept. 13, to a point within sight of Baltimore, the enemy planned a night attack, but in the meantime the bombardment of Fort McHenry and other defenses had failed. The larger vessels of Cochrane's fleet were unable to make a near approach on account of shallow water and sunken ships. Fort McHenry was but little injured, and the loss was small. The British army retreated, and the fleet returned down the bay. Maj. Armistead was brevetted lieutenant-colonel, to date from Sept. 12, and the citizens of Baltimore presented to him a salver, goblets, and a silver bowl shaped like a bombshell. The "Hero of Fort McHenry" survived the event a few years only, dying in Baltimore in 1818. The most celebrated incident associated with the defense is, of course, the writing of the *Star Spangled Banner* by Francis Scott Key.

[Mrs. Virginia Garber, *Armistead Family* (1910). The Confederate Gen. Lewis Armistead [*q.v.*] was a member of the same family. Armistead's Report is given in *Niles' Register,* VII, 40. For the defense of Baltimore see Henry Adams, *Hist. of the U.S.* (1889–1891), VIII, 166–73.]

E. K. A.

ARMISTEAD, LEWIS ADDISON (Feb. 18, 1817–July 3, 1863), Confederate soldier, came of a prominent Virginia family. The first of the Armisteads to arrive in America was settled in Virginia about 1635. Although he came from England, tradition ascribes a German origin to the family, and the Virginia estate was accordingly named "Hesse" (G. N. Mackenzie, *Colonial Families of the United States,* 1907, I, 12). One branch of the family developed a strong taste for the military career. Five sons of John Armistead were officers of the army. One of these was killed in action at Fort Erie in 1814; one was that George Armistead who defended Fort McHenry against the attack of the British fleet; the youngest, Walker Keith Armistead, was a member of the second class to be graduated from West Point, was colonel of the 3rd Artillery and was brevet brigadier-general at the time of his death. The subject of this sketch, son of the last named and Elizabeth (Stanley) Armistead, was born at Newbern, N. C. He was admitted to West Point as a cadet in 1834, but failed in his studies on account of insufficient preparation, and returned to school to lay a more solid foundation of education. On July 10, 1839, he was appointed, from Virginia, a second-lieutenant in the 6th Infantry. He remained a member of that regiment throughout his service, and in due course was promoted first-lieutenant in 1844 and captain in 1855. He was married to Cecelia Lee Love, daughter of Richard H. Love of Fairfax County, Va. During the Mexican War he distinguished himself at Contreras, Churubusco, and Molino del Rey, and received two brevets. The rest of his service was chiefly on the frontier. He "went with his state" in 1861, resigning his commission on May 26, and making his way overland from the Pacific coast, along with several other ex-officers, the most notable of whom was Albert Sidney Johnston. Armistead was appointed to the colonelcy of the 57th Virginia Regiment, in the Confederate army, and commanded it for a few months in West Virginia and North Carolina. Upon his appointment as brigadier-general, on Apr. 1, 1862, he was assigned to the command of a brigade in what later became Pickett's division of the Army of Northern Virginia. He joined it in time to take part in the Peninsula Campaign, and with it he remained until his death, winning a reputation for distinguished courage. On the third day of the battle of Gettysburg he led his brigade in the final assault on the Union center—a conspicuous figure, noted by many witnesses. With his cap raised on the point of his sword, cheering on the handful of men who had survived the long advance across the open fields, he entered the Union position and fell mortally wounded within the lines. The monument on this spot marks the "high tide" of the Confederacy.

[F. B. Heitman, *Hist. Reg.* (1903), I, 169; *Confed. Mil. Hist.* (1899), III, 576–77; *Battles and Leaders of the Civil War* (1887–88), III, 354; *Official Records,* ser. I, vols. XI (pts. 1, 2, 3), XIX (pts. 1, 2), XXVII (pts. 1, 2), L (pt. 1); unpublished War Dept. records.]

T. M. S.

ARMOUR, PHILIP DANFORTH (May 16, 1832–Jan. 6, 1901), meat packer and grain dealer, was born at Stockbridge, Madison County, N.Y., the son of Danforth and Julia Ann (Brooks) Armour. His father was of Scotch-Irish and his mother of Puritan stock. Soon after their marriage, at Union, Conn., in 1825, they moved to a farm near Stockbridge. Of their eight children six were boys, five of whom were afterward to be associated in the packing and grain industry. Philip attended the district school and the Cazenovia Seminary, afterward working on the farm. In the spring of 1852, with a company of thirty men from Oneida, he started overland for California. On his arrival he found work as a miner and later was engaged in constructing sluices. With earnings of several thousand dollars he returned home in 1856. Farm life no longer interested him, and he again started west, going first to Cincinnati and then to Milwaukee, where he formed a partnership with a friend, Frederick B. Miles, in the wholesale grocery and commission business. In 1862 he married Malvina Belle Ogden, of Cincinnati. The partnership with Miles was successfully carried on until 1863, when it was dissolved. In the same year he joined with John Plankinton under the firm name of Plankinton, Armour & Co., in the business of grain dealing and meat packing. His first notable stroke in the business world was his operation in pork in the closing days of the Civil War. The price was then about $40 a barrel, with for a time an upward tendency. Confident that the Confederacy was toppling and that prices would fall heavily, he went to New York, then the chief trading market, offering to sell pork for future delivery in any quantity. He found plenty of buyers. The series of Union victories caused prices to sag, and so far had they fallen during the ninety days of his stay that he was able to buy for $18 what he had agreed to deliver for from $30 to $40. The transaction, which ruined many traders, is said to have netted him at least two millions.

About the time of his return to Milwaukee he became financially interested in the grain commission house of H. O. Armour & Co., established in Chicago three years earlier by his brother, Herman Ossian (1837–1901). The business was enlarged by the addition of a pork-packing plant in 1868, and in 1870 it took the name of Armour & Co. The Armour interests had been gradually concentrated in Chicago, and in 1875 Philip moved there and assumed the headship of the firm.

Before any of the packers (except Nelson Morris) later to gain a world-wide celebrity reached Chicago, that city had superseded Cincinnati (1861–62) as the pork-packing center of the nation. Slaughtering and dressing were then done mainly on nearby farms, and as refrigeration was hardly known, the bulk of the shipments was made in cold weather. Armour is said to have been one of the first packers to bring live hogs to the city and to supervise his own slaughtering. Also he is said to have been one of the first to note the enormous waste in slaughtering and to plan the utilization of waste products. He was a systematizer and an innovator of methods resulting in great economies, and others were not slow in following his example. The great expansion of the industry, however, waited the discovery of a sure method of refrigeration. There is dispute as to who first made refrigeration practicable, Armour having given the credit to his brother Joseph and others having apportioned it variously. Not until 1880 was it in general use. With its adoption the industry took on a new life. Armour now bought his own cars and even established distributing plants in the eastern cities. About this time he also began on a large scale the preparation of canned meats. He next turned his attention to the export trade (though in this venture he seems to have been preceded by Gustavus Swift) and began to send refrigerated beef and pork to England and later to France and Germany. With sleepless energy he continued to extend the range of his operations. In 1879 the Armour Brothers' bank was established in Kansas City, and the fifth brother, Andrew Watson (1829–92), was brought from the New York farm to be its president. Philip Armour figured in many spectacular contests on the exchange, particularly the bear raid on pork in 1879 and the wheat deal of 1882, in each case supporting the market and making large winnings. In the panic of 1893, when runs were made on the Chicago banks and the credit of both the city and the Exposition was threatened, he bought $500,000 in gold in Europe and offered help to the big houses of the city. His last notable operation was that of breaking the "corner" in wheat attempted by Joseph Leiter in 1897. The growth of his enterprises, which in 1892 had been consolidated, was constant, and his wealth reached a total of perhaps $50,000,000. During his last five years he employed an average of 15,000 workers, and his pay-roll ran from six to ten millions a year.

The prestige of his house, as well as that of the other packing-houses, was considerably dimmed by the "embalmed beef" scandals of 1898–99. Complaints regarding the condition of the meat bought from the packing-houses and served to the troops had been made at various times during the summer of 1898. They were supported by the report (Oct. 1) of an inspector in the Chickamauga training camp and further supported by the testimony (Dec. 21) of Gen. Miles before the War Investigation Commission. President McKinley thereupon appointed a court of inquiry to examine the charges. Its report, made public on May 7, 1899, asserted that the charge made against the packers of having treated the meat with chemicals was "not established," that such instances of tainted meat as had been disclosed were due to tropical weather conditions and the injury of the containers by transportation, and that the quality of the meats served to the troops was the same as that sold to the trade. It was a report that satisfied no one and was generally regarded as a political document. Public excitement was for a time intense, and the press teemed with charges against the packers, including the allegation of bribery of government officials. It is the testimony of the friends of Armour that the scandal affected him deeply, one of them asserting that he never rallied from the shock. He steadfastly upheld the quality of his products and denied that he had ever countenanced the expenditure of a single dollar for bribery or corruption.

In the spring of 1899 his health began to fail. He sailed for Germany, took the baths at Nauheim and traveled for a time in Switzerland. On his return he spent the winter in Pasadena. Here his son, Philip D., Jr., visited him, but succumbed to a sudden attack of pneumonia, dying on Jan. 29, 1900. Armour later returned to Chicago, but was not again active in business. He died at his home of myocarditis following an attack of pneumonia.

Armour was broad-shouldered, of medium

height and heavy build, though not fleshy. The familiar portrait of his later years represents him with a bald crown, side whiskers, and no mustache. His hair was red or "sandy," and he used sometimes, says Gunsaulus, to stress the importance of "sandy-haired" men and women in history. There was no man in Chicago whose face and figure were better known. He walked "like a man intent on getting somewhere." His dress was plain, his home simple, and his art treasures were few. He spent little on himself, but much on others. He founded the Armour Mission on a bequest of $100,000 left by his brother Joseph, adding to the fund large sums of his own. He built the Armour flats for workingmen's families, and he founded the Armour Institute of Technology, opened in 1893, to which he gave between three and four millions. His bounty knew no limits, and his closest associates believed that he gave away a fortune at least the equal of that which he left. He had faith in the improvability of humankind, and his field of experimentation was the young. "I like to turn bristles, blood, bones, and the insides and outsides of pigs and bullocks into revenue now," he is reported to have said, "for I can turn the revenue into these boys and girls, and they will go on forever." He is credited with being a liberal, too—an upholder of freedom of opinion, undisturbed by the newer theories regarding the social control of property. "If the next twenty-five years make Armours impossible," he once said to Gunsaulus, president of the Armour Institute, ". . . I want these young people to be prepared for it. Don't ever let me or my business get in the way of your work." His attitude toward his employees was, however, the patriarchal one. His eulogists praise him as a kindly employer, who paid more than a living wage. It is certain, however, that he opposed collective bargaining and the organization of labor, and he seems to have believed that the "good employer" was the solution of the labor problem.

[*Who's Who in America,* 1899–1900; Howard Copeland Hill, "The Development of Chicago as a Center of the Meat Packing Industry," *Mississippi Valley Hist. Rev.,* Dec. 1923; Philip D. Armour, "The Packing Industry," in *One Hundred Years of Am. Commerce* (1895), ed. by Chauncey M. Depew; Charles Edward Russell, *The Greatest Trust in the World* (1905); Rept. of Military Court of Inquiry, *N. Y. Times,* May 8, 1899; Frank W. Gunsaulus, "Philip D. Armour: A Character Sketch," *Rev. of Rev.,* Feb. 1901; H. I. Cleveland, "Philip Armour, Merchant," *World's Work,* Mar. 1901; obituaries in the *N. Y. Times, N. Y. Tribune,* and *Chicago Tribune* of Jan. 7, 1901.]

W. J. G.

ARMSBY, HENRY PRENTISS (Sept. 21, 1853–Oct. 19, 1921), agricultural chemist, the son of Lewis and Mary (Prentiss) Armsby, was born at Northbridge, Mass. After primary education in the schools of that town he graduated from the Worcester Polytechnic Institute with the degree of B.S. in 1871. He continued his studies at the Sheffield Scientific School of Yale University, graduating in 1874 with the degree of Ph.B. In the following year he studied in Germany at the University of Leipzig, devoting special attention to the subject of animal nutrition. Returning in 1877 he served for two years as chemist in the recently established Connecticut Agricultural Experiment Station. On Oct. 15, 1878, he married Lucy A. Harding. After two years' service as vice principal and professor of agricultural chemistry in the Storrs (Conn.) Agricultural School, he became professor of agricultural chemistry in the University of Wisconsin, doing work in the Agricultural Station, of which, in 1886, he was made associate director. In 1887 he was called to organize the Pennsylvania station, and served as its director for twenty years; from 1890 to 1902 he was also dean of the school of agriculture. In 1907 an Institute of Animal Nutrition was established at the Pennsylvania station to carry on and extend the investigations which he had planned and begun. He was then relieved of his other duties and left free to devote himself to research work as director of the Institute. In this he continued active until near the time of his death.

Armsby's study and thought bore its first fruit during his service at the Connecticut station. He began a translation of Wolff's *Feeding of Farm Animals* to supply the lack of any adequate work on the subject in English; but he soon realized that many changes and additions would be necessary to adapt it to American conditions and to include the most recent work. He therefore wrote, instead, *A Manual of Cattle Feeding, a Treatise on the Laws of Animal Nutrition* (1880), making free use of Wolff's book and all other sources of information. This work, long used as a text-book, was the first presentation in English of the results of the studies of animal nutrition which had been made abroad and of the methods by which they had been obtained. The work had great influence in awakening attention and starting a study of the subject in this country.

When he became professor of agricultural chemistry in Wisconsin, Armsby began his life work of research on animal nutrition in connection with agricultural stations, which continued without interruption till his death forty years later. For fourteen years, in Wisconsin and Pennsylvania, he carried out a variety of feeding experiments. Of these he wrote, "Fourteen years' experiments in animal feeding and study of experimental results elsewhere confirm the belief of the writer in the urgent need of further investigation into fundamental physiological laws governing animal nutrition. Only by such investigations can we obtain the solid and indispensable basis of rational practise." As early as 1890 he suggested his view that the study of the fuel and energy value of foods would furnish a simpler method of comparing food values than the one then in use. In 1907, with the establishment of the Institute referred to above, came his opportunity to develop this thought and to begin the classic research which made him preëminent as a leader in nutrition studies.

He and his fellow workers, with the financial help of the United States Bureau of Animal Industry, developed a respiration calorimeter of sufficient size for observation on farm animals. It was an instrument of great precision with the help of which could be determined the energy value of any kind of food consumed, its loss in all the various excreta of the body, and the amount which was utilized for maintenance and production; the "net energy" of the ration. With it Armsby made the first demonstration of the validity of the principle of the conservation of energy in cattle, as it had been previously made by Rübner on the dog and by Atwater and Benedict on man. Quantitatively the principal function of food is to supply energy, hence knowledge of the relative amounts of energy which can be recovered in various methods of utilization is of prime importance in food conservation. Armsby fixed the net energy of the chief American feeding stuffs and methods of using them in compounding rations. He studied the efficiency of different types and ages of animals as converters of "waste" into animal foods. He disclosed the great waste that may be involved in the conversion of vegetable into animal foods through the agency of live stock, proving that to feed to farm animals agricultural products which can be used directly for human sustenance involves a great economic loss.

The results of Armsby's work are set forth in the following of his writings: *The Principles of Animal Nutrition with Special Reference to the Nutrition of Farm Animals* (1903); *The Nutrition of Farm Animals* (1917); *The Conservation of Food Energy* (1918); *The Animal as a Converter of Matter and Energy* (prepared after his death by his collaborator, C. R. Moulton, 1925, in the monograph series of the American Chemical Society). In recognition of his services honorary degrees came to him from the University of Wisconsin, Yale, and the Worcester Polytechnic Institute. He was elected a member of the Royal Society of Arts of Great Britain in 1911, foreign member of the Royal Academy of Sweden in 1912 and member of the National Academy of Science in 1920.

Armsby was a man of slight physique, rather retiring in nature, but with broad interests, generous in his helpfulness to others, tolerant, patient, and persistent in pursuit of his ideals. Valuable in counsel, he held office in the prominent agricultural organizations of this country. In the fall of 1918 he was sent to Europe by the United States as a member of the Inter-allied Scientific Food Commission, which rendered valuable service during the World War.

[*U. S. Dept. of Ag. Experiment Station Rec.*, vol. XLV, Nov. 1921.]

E. H. J.

ARMSTRONG, DAVID MAITLAND (Apr. 15, 1836–May 26, 1918), painter, worker in stained glass, was born at "Danskammer," near Newburgh, N. Y. He was the son of Edward Armstrong and the grandson of Col. William Armstrong, a Scotchman in the British army during the Revolutionary War. His mother was Sarah Hartley Ward, daughter of Col. John Ward of South Carolina. He entered Trinity College, Hartford, in 1854, graduating with the degree of A.B. in 1858. He then read law in New York City with the view of becoming a lawyer, was admitted to the bar in 1862, and practised law for several years, but turned finally to painting as a career. He had already studied painting both in Rome and Paris, where he had Luc Olivier Merson as his instructor. Friendships formed in Europe led him to become interested in diplomatic affairs, and friends obtained for him the position as consul in the Papal States. He received this appointment in March 1869 and held the position three years. Upon the formation of the Paris Exposition in 1878, he was appointed director of the American department, a position he filled with such success that he was made a chevalier of the Legion of Honor for his services. For the World's Fair in Chicago, in 1893, he frescoed the exterior of the Machinery Hall in a renaissance manner and was also associated in a general way with the exposition. Working in stained glass occupied much of his time during his later years. Examples of his work in glass are to be found in All Souls' Chapel, Biltmore, N. C.; in the home of Mrs. O. H. P. Belmont, New York City; and in the Columbia University Chapel. In the spring of 1877 Armstrong returned to "Danskammer," remodeled an old house near his paternal acres, and lived there for about twenty years. He settled finally in New York City. In 1866 he had married Helen Neilson, a niece of Hamilton Fish. His reminiscences, entitled *Day before Yester-*

day, reflect a society-loving artist and a tireless worker. He was a great clubman and at the Century Club he frequently met Augustus Saint Gaudens, Stanford White, Charles Follen McKim, and F. Hopkinson Smith. He was a member of the American Artists Society and the Architectural League. He was elected an Associate National Academician in 1906.

[David Maitland Armstrong, *Day before Yesterday*, N. Y. (1920); *N. Y. Times*, May 27, 1918; *Who's Who in America*, 1918–19.] T. B.

ARMSTRONG, FRANK C. (Nov. 22, 1835–Sept. 8, 1909), Confederate soldier, was born at the Choctaw Agency, Indian Territory, the son of Frank W. and Anne (Millard) Armstrong. His mother later married Gen. Persifor F. Smith. Armstrong was educated at Holy Cross Academy and College. Because of distinguished conduct in an Indian fight, while accompanying his stepfather on an expedition to New Mexico, he was commissioned second-lieutenant in the 2nd Dragoons, June 7, 1855. He accompanied Gen. Albert Sidney Johnston's expedition to Utah; was promoted captain June 6, 1861, and resigned Aug. 13, 1861. As a volunteer aide he was with McCulloch at Wilson's Creek, Aug. 12, 1861; and with Col. James McIntosh at the fight at Chustenahlah, Cherokee Nation, on Dec. 26, 1861. As a lieutenant he was an assistant adjutant-general at Pea Ridge, Mar. 6–8, 1862; and then inspector-general of Steen's Brigade in Arkansas. He was elected colonel of the 3rd Louisiana Infantry and accompanied the Army of the West, under Price, to Tupelo, Miss., in the spring of 1862. Detailed acting brigadier-general on July 7, 1862, in command of Price's cavalry, he won renown by raids on Courtland, Ala., on July 25, 1862, and in West Tennessee, about one month later. He was in command of the cavalry in the operations of Price and Van Dorn against Grant and Rosecrans in the Iuka operations, Sept. 13–20, and in the battle of Corinth, Oct. 3–4, 1862. He subsequently operated under cavalry division or corps commanders, such as Forrest, Wheeler, W. H Jackson, W. T. Martin, S. D. Lee, and Chalmers. These operations were those conducted while Bragg and Rosecrans were confronting each other at Tullahoma and Murfreesboro during the spring of 1863; those involved in the retreat of Bragg from Tullahoma, and in the ensuing battle of Chickamauga, on Sept. 19–20, 1863; the operations of Longstreet against Burnside at Knoxville, Nov. 17–Dec. 4, 1863; those of Johnston and Hood against Sherman, from Dalton to Atlanta, during the summer of 1864; Hood's campaign against Schofield and Thomas, resulting in the battle of Franklin on Nov. 30, and the Confederate defeat at Nashville on Dec. 15–16, 1864; the retreat from Nashville; and the operations against Gen. J. H. Wilson, previous to the capture of Selma by the latter on Apr. 2, 1865. Repeated recommendations gained for Armstrong, on Apr. 23, 1863, a commission as brigadier-general, to date from Jan. 20, 1863. His military character was marked by the exercise of prudence, discretion, and good sense; by stubbornness and gallantry in action; by a disposition to "march to the sound of the guns." After the close of the war he was in the Overland Mail Service; then a United States Indian inspector; and later assistant commissioner of Indian Affairs. He died at Bar Harbor, Me. He had married, first, Maria Polk Walker, daughter of Knox Walker of Tennessee; and second, Charlotte McSherry (born Combs) of St. Mary's County, Md.

[Succinct accounts of Armstrong's career may be found in the *Confed. Mil. Hist.*, VIII, 288; *Who's Who in America*, 1908–9, p. 48. A brief biog. is contained in the *New International Yr. Bk.*, 1909, p. 52. For record of his Regular Army service, see T. H. S. Hamersly, *Complete Regular Army Reg. of the U. S., 1779–1879*, p. 265. Detailed accounts of his participation in Forrest's operations are contained in John A. Wyeth, *Life of Gen. Nathan Bedford Forrest* (1889). The most complete account of his Civil War service is contained in the *Official Records*. For contemporary recognition of his ability as an organizer, and cavalry leader, see *Battles and Leaders of the Civil War*, II, pt. II. Obituaries in *N. Y. Times*, Sept. 9, 1909, and *Washington Evening Star*, Sept. 9, 13, 1909.] W. S. G.

ARMSTRONG, GEORGE BUCHANAN (Oct. 27, 1822–May 5, 1871), reconstructor of the railway mail service in the United States, was born in County Armagh, Ireland. Of his parents little is recorded except that his mother was a Buchanan, distantly related to President Buchanan, and that they emigrated to the United States in 1830, living for three years in Newark, N. J., then moving to Virginia and later to Maryland. The youth is first heard of in Baltimore as a clerk in a commission house. About 1846 he married Julia H. W. McKee. An attraction to the postal service prompted him to apply for a clerkship, and through the influence of his noted kinsman he was appointed to a place in the Post Office Department in Washington, about 1852. Two years later, on the recommendation of his superior, he was transferred to Chicago. He resigned in 1856, to engage in business, but after two years his firm failed. In 1858 he was appointed assistant postmaster. During the Civil War Gov. Oglesby appointed him a colonel of the Illinois volunteers, but the title was probably honorary, as he seems to have continued with the Post Office.

He early became interested in the matter of a

more systematic handling of the mails. In February 1864, he personally laid before the Post Office Department proposals for a thorough-going reform of the service, his main suggestion being the abandonment of the distributing offices then in use and the sorting of the mails on trains. On July 1, after repeating his proposals by letter, he was authorized by Postmaster General Blair to make an experiment on any railroad that would grant him the privilege. The first trial was made on Aug. 28, on the Chicago & Northwestern, between Chicago and Clinton, Ia., and was soon followed by trials on other lines. By the end of the year the "traveling post office," or "post office on wheels," was regarded as a success, and in December Armstrong was appointed a special agent of the department to organize the system. By the act of Mar. 3, 1865, Congress formally recognized the innovation and authorized its further development by the Postmaster General, who thereupon divided the service, appointing Armstrong as special agent of the western section and Harrison Park of the east. At the beginning of Grant's administration a Bureau of Railway Mail Service was established, and on Apr. 4, 1869, Armstrong was appointed general superintendent, with headquarters in Washington. His remaining two years were spent in developing the service. In the spring of 1871 he returned to Chicago. On May 3 he resigned his office, and two days later he died.

Through contributions from the railway mail clerks of the country a statue to his memory, naming him as the "founder of the railway mail service in the United States," was erected on the grounds of the Federal Building in Chicago, and on May 19, 1881, was dedicated with a eulogy by Schuyler Colfax. The event brought on a spirited controversy as to Armstrong's right to the distinction given him. It was shown that the idea of the "traveling post office" had been suggested by H. A. Burr, topographer of the Post Office Department, as early as 1853, and that in the fall of 1862 William A. Davis, superintendent of mails on the Hannibal & St. Joseph railway, had tried the experiment of sorting westbound overland mail on the cars. The controversy served to confirm the theory that most inventions and innovations are the joint contribution of many minds, but also confirmed the claim made for Armstrong that it was he who elaborated the project of the railway post office, brought it to the attention of the department, obtained its adoption in spite of many formidable obstacles, and spent his last years in making it a practical success. He is eulogized by Colfax as a man of indomitable will, with a mind of great originality and force, remarkable executive ability, and a nobility of character that impressed all who came in contact with him.

[*Hist. of the Railway Mail Service* (1903); W. J. Dennis, *The Travelling Postoffice* (1916); *The Beginnings of the True Railway Mail Service* (1906), ed. by Geo. B. Armstrong, Jr.; Jas. E. White, *A Life Span and Reminiscences of Railway Mail Service* (1910); A. T. Andreas, *Hist. of Chicago* (1885), II, 391; *Chicago Tribune*, May 20, 1881.]

W. J. G.

ARMSTRONG, GEORGE DOD (Sept. 15, 1813–May 11, 1899), Presbyterian clergyman and controversial writer, was born in Mendham, Morris County, N. J., where his father, Rev. Amzi Armstrong, was pastor of the Presbyterian church. He was one of ten children, and the youngest of three sons, the other two being Amzi, who attained some prominence in New Jersey as a lawyer and politician, and William, clergyman and promoter of missionary activity in the Presbyterian denomination. On his father's side he was of Irish descent, his ancestors having emigrated to this country about 1730; through his mother, Polly, daughter of Aaron and Sarah Dod, he was of Puritan extraction. After graduating from Princeton in 1832, he taught school for a time, and in 1836 entered Union Theological Seminary, Prince Edward County, Va. In 1838 he became professor of chemistry and mechanics in Washington College, Lexington, which position he held for thirteen years, resigning to become pastor of the First Presbyterian Church, Norfolk, Va., where he remained until his death. During the yellow-fever epidemic there in 1855, he ministered to the afflicted tirelessly and without regard for his own welfare. Four of his household died, including his wife and oldest child, and he himself was taken sick and reported dead, but recovered. In 1856 he published a vivid account of the epidemic under the title, *The Summer of the Pestilence*.

Puritan in rigidness of convictions and performance of duty, he was Irish in his love of combat. Sympathizing with the views on slaveholding held in the South, and aroused by the attempt of Dr. Albert Barnes [*q.v.*] to "wrest the Scriptures respecting slavery," he published in 1857 *The Christian Doctrine of Slavery*, a detailed exposition of the teachings of Christ and the Apostles regarding that institution. This book aroused a controversy, and it was followed in 1858 by *A Discussion on Slaveholding; Three Letters to a Conservative by George D. Armstrong, D.D., of Virginia, and Three Conservative Replies by C. Van Renselaer, D.D., of New Jersey*. In 1857 he published *The Doctrine of Baptism*, an examination of the Scriptures with a view to controverting the teachings of the Baptists. The most of this is included in a more ambitious work, *The Sacraments of the New Testament as Instituted by Christ,* issued in 1880, which combats Roman Catholic as well as Baptist doctrines. *The Two Books of Nature and Revelation Collated* (1886) is essentially a defense of the Biblical view of the world as against that of modern science. These writings, though narrow in outlook, show painstaking study and a keen mind. In addition he published: *Politics and the Pulpit* (1856); *The Theology of Christian Experience* (1858); *"The Good Hand of Our God Upon Us," a Thanksgiving Sermon Preached on the Occasion of the Victory of Manassas* (1861).

[Alfred Nevin, *Encyc. of the Presbyt. Ch. in the U.S.A.* (1884); *Gen. Cat. of Princeton Univ.* (1908); *Centennial Gen. Cat. . . . of Union Theol. Sem. in Va. 1807–1907.* For ancestry, see W. B. Sprague, *Annals Am. Pulpit* IV (1859), "Amzi Armstrong."] H. E. S.

ARMSTRONG, GEORGE WASHINGTON (Aug. 11, 1836–June 30, 1901), pioneer in the express business, was a descendant of a family of emigrants from the North of Ireland, who settled about 1722 in the Scotch-Irish stronghold of Londonderry, N. H., but later moved to Windham, N. H. George Armstrong, son of David and Mahalia (Lovering) Armstrong, was born in Boston, where his father labored as an artisan in the shipyards. The boy's schooling in the noted Old Hawes Grammar School was cut short on the death of his father in 1851. With a legacy of eighty-three dollars, a strong constitution, pluck, and the racial characteristic of aggressive tenacity, he struck out for himself. Penny postman in South Boston, office boy for the *South Boston Gazette,* newsboy on State St., and news agent for nine years on the Boston & Worcester Railroad with occasional relief as a brakeman, baggage handler, and conductor, mark the rungs of his rising ladder. In 1863, he purchased a half-interest in the restaurant at the Boston terminal of the Boston & Albany Railroad. Eight years later, he was able to buy out his partner. In 1865, he purchased King's Express, which operated over the Boston & Worcester Railroad, changing the name to Armstrong's Transfer. With a couple of coaches and a Berlin carriage, Armstrong's men transferred baggage and passengers from the Boston & Worcester station to the North End terminals. In 1869, the restaurant and news concession on the Fitchburg division were taken over. Soon the Armstrong Company controlled the transfer, news, and lunchroom service on the Boston & Albany, the Old Colony, the eastern section of the Boston & Maine, and the Boston, Revere & Lynn Railroads. The employees numbered several hundred. Armstrong did a prosperous business. Travelers appreciated his reliable service and reasonable rates, and rewarded him with an ever increasing patronage. In 1882, the concern, with a virtual monopoly of business on the New England railways, was reorganized as the Armstrong Transfer Company with George W. Armstrong as president. With Yankee intuition, he had found a new line of endeavor and developed a tremendous business.

Armstrong was twice married: in 1868 to Louise Marston of Bridgewater, N. H., who died in 1880; and in 1882 to Flora E. Greene, daughter of a distinguished Boston physician, Dr. Reuben G. Greene; he had two children by each wife. His later years were spent in his Brookline residence, where he had gathered a good library and a rich collection of antiques and bric-a-brac, and in a quiet summer cottage at Centre Harbor, N. H. Yet his business cares were heavy, for in addition to the Armstrong Transfer, he was a director of the Worcester, Nashua & Rochester Railway, the Manchester & Lawrence Railroad, and the United States Trust Company. His gift of the Armstrong Memorial Building commemorates the family name in Windham, with which town he retained a close association.

[*Representative Men of Mass.* (1898), ed. by W. F. Moore; *Men of Progress in Mass.* (1896), ed. by E. M. Bacon; *Boston of Today* (1892), ed. by R. Hernden; D. P. Toomey, *Mass. of Today* (1892); *Granite Mo.,* VIII, 191–200, XXIII, 157–63, XXVII, 22; *Boston Transcript,* July 1, 1901.] R. J. P.

ARMSTRONG, JOHN (Oct. 13, 1717–Mar. 9, 1795), Pennsylvania soldier and politician, son of James Armstrong, was born in Brookborough Parish, County Fermanagh, Ireland, and was married to Rebecca Lyon of Enniskillen in the same county. They settled in the Cumberland district of Pennsylvania, a hilly region on the border. In his capacity as surveyor Armstrong laid out the town of Carlisle. The entire frontier of the middle colonies was in constant peril from Indian attacks, after Braddock's disastrous defeat in 1755; and Armstrong, who seems to have acquired early the confidence of the authorities, was commissioned captain in January 1756 and lieutenant-colonel in May, and was sent by the governor in the following year with 300 men against Kittanning. This was a town of the Delawares on the upper course of the Allegheny River, a headquarters for scalping parties. The enterprise was completely successful; the town was taken by surprise in a night attack on Sept. 8, 1756; and Armstrong, who had been wounded in the battle, received from Philadelphia "thanks, medal, and plate." It was, in fact, one of the few outstanding British successes in the early part of the French and Indian War. Henceforth Armstrong was often styled the "Hero of Kittanning." Two years later he was the senior officer of Pennsylvania troops in the expedition under Forbes and Washington, and had the honor of raising the flag over Fort Duquesne. He served in Pontiac's War, and for many years was judge of the court of common pleas.

When the Revolution began, experienced officers were in demand. On Mar. 1, 1776, Armstrong was commissioned brigadier-general, and was sent to take command at Charleston, S. C., receiving his instructions from Gen. Lee. He arrived in April, and commanded the South Carolina troops at Haddrell's Point. The actual defense, however, was conducted by others. He returned to the northern army, and in the dark days which preceded the battle of Trenton he was sent on a mission to his own part of the state "to stir up the people."

In the critical year of 1777 Armstrong, now a major-general, was influential in state affairs prior to and after the British invasion, as is evidenced from Joseph Reed's letter to Washington (Jared Sparks, *Correspondence of the American Revolution,* 1853, I, 389–90). He commanded the left wing below the ford of the Brandywine, but was not actively engaged in that battle. Subsequently he held the line of the Schuylkill, in the effort to delay the advance on Philadelphia. Three weeks later, at Germantown, he led a division, about 1,000 of Pennsylvania militia, and in the plan of the attack it was intended that he should support Generals Wayne and Sullivan, and fall upon the British left and rear; but this scheme failed of accomplishment, one of the various factors in that day's fiasco. Armstrong resigned that same year, but was present at a council in Valley Forge in 1778, and was sent to Wyoming Valley after the massacre. On the whole, though Armstrong's name appears frequently in the military annals of the Revolution, it does not appear that his actual achievements measured up to his reputation gained in the Seven Years' War. He was elected to the Continental Congress in 1778, and served in 1779–80, obtaining leave of absence in the latter year. He was again a delegate in 1787–88, and died at Carlisle, Pa. His occasional letters to Washington show his views on political and other subjects.

[*Jour. of the Continental Cong.* (1904–22); Wm. S. Stryker, *Battles of Trenton and Princeton* (1898); Charlemagne Tower, *Lafayette* (1895); Henry B. Carrington, *Battles of the Am. Rev.* (1876); *Chronicles of the Armstrongs* (1902), ed. by James L. Armstrong; *Papers Read before the Lancaster County Hist. Soc., Dec. 3, 1897,* containing a notice of Armstrong and a letter from him to Washington, as well as a sketch of Armstrong by F. R. Diffenderffer; narrative of the battle of Germantown in a letter from Armstrong to Thomas Wharton, Jr. (President of Pa.), Oct. 5, 1777, *Pa. Archives,* 1853, V, 645–46. The date of birth is on the authority of J. W. King, in *Western Pa. Hist. Mag.,* July 1927. 1725 is commonly given by other authorities.]

E. K. A.

ARMSTRONG, JOHN (Apr. 20, 1755–Feb. 4, 1816), soldier, explorer, son of Thomas Armstrong of Donagheady, County Tyrone, Ireland, by Jane, his wife, daughter of Michael Hamilton of Tully, County Londonderry, was born in New Jersey. As an officer of the 12th and 3rd Pennsylvania regiments in the Revolution he won distinction by his abilities and bravery, and immediately afterward (1783–84) was an officer under the state in its conflict with the Connecticut claimants at Wyoming. The active part he took there is by most writers confused with that taken by Maj. John Armstrong, author of the Newburgh Addresses. On the organization of a standing army, in August 1784, he received a commission, and thereafter was constantly engaged in arduous duties on the Ohio frontier, becoming one of the best-known woodsmen, explorers, and military characters of the early West. He was commandant at Fort Pitt, 1785–86, and in the latter year was transferred to the remote frontier. The hero of several thrilling episodes in border history, incident to his duties in the army, he at the same time, with uncommon faith in the early and rapid settlement of the regions north of the Ohio, voluntarily assumed duties looking to the future welfare of the pioneers. Col. Francis Johnston, receiver general of the land office at Philadelphia, wrote him (1790): "Your passion for improving the Ground by planting fruit Trees of various kinds & making Gardens where ever you go will redound much to your credit, & I will add to the real emolument of mankind."

In 1790, when the government had determined to attempt a secret exploration into the Spanish territory, and up the Missouri River, Armstrong was entrusted with the hazardous enterprise. Such profound secrecy veiled this undertaking, the forerunner of the Lewis and Clark expedition, that little is known of it beyond the guarded letters that passed between Gen. Harmar, Gov. St. Clair, and Knox, the Secretary of War, and a few memoranda made by Armstrong himself. A biographical sketch (1844) by his son, William Goforth Armstrong, who was intimately familiar with his father's career, states that "he proceeded up the Missouri some distance above St. Louis, not with . . . an escort, but entirely alone! It was his intention to examine the country of the upper Missouri and cross the Rocky Mountains," but owing to intertribal Indian wars he was obliged to abandon the undertaking. He was then detailed to explore the Wabash River and its communications with Lake Erie, and, although it was the very eve of a war with the savages, he made this exploration through the heart of the Indian country with only two friendly Indians as companions. In Harmar's expedition, in October 1790, the first organized effort of the Federal Government to drive the Indians back from the frontier, Armstrong commanded the only regulars engaged in the initial encounter of that campaign, and with them, when deserted by the militia, stood his ground until all but seven of his men were slain. His escape from the field forms a remarkable chapter in the history of western adventure and woodsmanship. He served also in St. Clair's campaign (1791), and as commandant of Fort Hamilton, which was built chiefly under his direction. Resigning from the army in 1793, soon after his marriage to a daughter of Judge William Goforth, one of the most influential men in the formation of the Ohio commonwealth and champion of popular education, Armstrong settled at Columbia, near Cincinnati. From 1796 to the close of the territorial period he servd as treasurer of the Northwest Territory, besides holding local offices. He removed, in 1814, to Armstrong's Station, on the Ohio, which he had founded in 1796, one of the first American settlements on Indiana soil. There he died on Feb. 4, 1816.

[*Original Jours. of the Lewis and Clark Expedition,* ed. by R. G. Thwaites, VII (1905); Chas. Cist, *Cincinnati Miscellany,* I (1845); *Pa. Archives,* ser. I, 1852–56; *Am. State Papers, Mil. Affairs,* I; Jas. McBride, *Pioneer Biog.,* I (1869).]

C.F.C.

ARMSTRONG, JOHN (Nov. 25, 1758–Apr. 1, 1843), soldier, diplomat, was descended from Johnnie Armstrang or Armstrong of Gilnockie, a hero of the Scottish border in the early sixteenth century, and through him from Thomas Armstrong, Lord of Morgarten, Roxburghshire, Scotland, in the fifteenth century (*Journal of American Genealogy,* I, 149–53). A grandson of Johnnie Armstrong, a partisan of Charles I in the Civil Wars, settled in northern Ireland, near Enniskillen, County Fermanagh, where his son Edward married into the Irish house of the Maguires. A grandson of Edward, John Armstrong (1720–95), emigrated from Ireland to Pennsylvania between 1745 and 1748, and settled at Carlisle. He participated as a soldier in the French and Indian War and the war against Pontiac, and during the Revolution became a major-general in the Pennsylvania service. His wife, Rebecca Lyon, was also, it would appear, a native of northern Ireland. Their son, John Armstrong, was born at Carlisle, Pa.

When the Revolutionary War began, John Armstrong was a student at Princeton. Leaving college in 1775, he entered the colonial army and served successively on the staffs of Generals Mercer and Gates. He participated in the Saratoga campaign and was present at the surrender of Burgoyne. When hostilities ended he was serving as aide-de-camp to Gates, with the rank of major. In March 1783, while the army was camped at Newburgh on the Hudson, and while discontent was rife at the failure of Congress to meet arrears of pay, Armstrong, at the instigation of Gates, composed the notorious "Newburgh Letters," calling a meeting of the field officers and representatives of the officers of each company to consider measures of relief, and suggesting that, as its petitions to Congress had gone unheeded, the army threaten to take matters into its own hands if Congress failed to meet its just demands. The authorship of these letters, though not generally known at the time, was later expressly avowed by Armstrong. They exhibited a facility in caustic and rather sophistical reasoning, mixed with skilful emotional appeal, for which their author enjoyed a lifelong reputation. The harsh opinion which Washington at this time expressed of the letters and their anonymous author he withdrew in a letter to Armstrong fourteen years later, declaring that he had "since had sufficient reason for believing, that the object of the author was just, honorable, and friendly to the country, though the means suggested by him was certainly liable to much misunderstanding and abuse" (Jared Sparks, *Writings of George Washington,* VIII, 551–66).

When the army was disbanded with the coming of peace, Armstrong returned to Pennsylvania and promptly found political employment as secretary of the Supreme Executive Council of the State. In the summer of 1784 the Council placed him in command of 400 militia and sent him to restore order in the Wyoming Valley on the Susquehanna, where hostilities had broken out between settlers from Connecticut and the agents of a group of Pennsylvania land speculators. Instead of taking a neutral position, as he should have done, Armstrong played directly into the hands of the Pennsylvania party, treating the Yankees with bad faith and with characteristic ruthlessness. The state made amends to the Connecticut settlers, but Armstrong kept his position as secretary and was also made adjutant-general of Pennsylvania (Charles Miner, *History of Wyoming,* 1845, chaps. 21–23). He continued to act as secretary of the Council even after his election in 1787 as a delegate to Congress (*Minutes of the Supreme Executive Council of Pennsylvania,* XV, 194–95).

In 1789 Armstrong married Alida Livingston, a sister of Chancellor Robert R. Livingston of New York, and moving to Red Hook, Dutchess County, N. Y., devoted himself for eleven years to agriculture. When he again entered public life it was as a member of the Livingston clan, which in 1800 by an alliance with the Clintons carried New York for the Republican party. Armstrong, like the Livingstons, had been a Federalist, but with them, when their merits were not sufficiently recognized by Washington, Hamilton, and Adams, he had gone over to the party of Jefferson. It was characteristic of the man that his first political service to the Republicans was the composition of an anonymous petition for the repeal of the Alien and Sedition Laws, "written with his usual ability and in his usual unequalled style of bitterness and severity." This proved a useful campaign document, particularly through the publicity arising from the arrest of at least one prominent person who helped to circulate it (Jabez D. Hammond, *History of Political Parties in the State of New York,* 1842, I, 131).

The Republican victory of 1800 made George Clinton governor of New York, but the Livingston family was generously rewarded with offices. "Happy was the man who had married a Livingston," remarks a recent writer. John Armstrong's portion of the spoils was a seat in the United States Senate, to which he was chosen in November 1800 by an almost unanimous vote of the legislature (*Ibid.,* pp. 153–54). In February 1802 he resigned his seat, thus making way for De Witt Clinton. When Clinton in turn resigned from the Senate in November 1803 to become mayor of New York, Gov. George Clinton appointed Armstrong to fill his place, and he served until June 30, 1804, when he again resigned to become minister to France in place of his brother-in-law, Robert R. Livingston. Presumably this diplomatic appointment was due to the influence of the Livingstons, though it might be argued that it was Jefferson's way of disposing of a too independent senator (Henry Adams, II, 157).

There was little glory to be won by an American minister at Napoleon's court between 1804 and 1810, the years in which Armstrong resided there. It was a period of futile hopes and futile protests—hopes of securing Florida from Spain through the good offices of Napoleon, and protests against French confiscation of American shipping under the Decrees of Berlin, Milan, and Rambouillet. It is to Armstrong's credit that he objected to the subservient attitude of the American administration. He had no faith in expressions of good will by Napoleon or his ministers, and he advised his government, if it wanted Florida, to take it by force and expect no aid from Napoleon. He evidently considered discussions with the French ministers a waste of breath, and his lack of communicativeness led Napoleon to complain that Armstrong was "a morose man with whom one cannot treat," and to request his recall (*Ibid.,* 228–29, 251–52). The closing event of his ministry at Paris was a famous note handed him by Cadore, the French foreign minister, on Aug. 5, 1810. The object of this note was, without really committing France to any change of policy, to convince the United States that Napoleon had revoked the Berlin and Milan decrees, and thereby to induce the United States to take hostile steps against England if the latter refused to make similar concessions. This note, with its apparent yielding to the United States, gave Armstrong an opportunity to retire from his mission in triumph, and he did so, without making any effort to probe into the true nature of the new French policy. By this bit of negligence he contributed materially to the success of Napoleon's scheme, and must thus bear part of the responsibility for the ensuing quarrel with England and the War of 1812 (*Ibid.,* V, 259–61). He left Paris for America Sept. 12, 1810.

Armstrong returned from France in a mood none too friendly to President Madison. When the War of 1812 opened, De Witt Clinton of New York, though a Republican, resolved to run for the presidency against Madison on an anti-war platform appealing to Federalists and dissatisfied Republicans. He expected Armstrong's support in his campaign, but Armstrong disappointed him by coming out in favor of Madison and accepting (July 6, 1812), a commission of brigadier-general with the command of New York City and its defenses (Alva De S. Alexander, *A Political History of the State of New York,* 1906, I, 216). In this position he used such generous means for encouraging enlistments for local service as to call forth criticism from Albert Gallatin, secretary of the treasury, who feared that his measures would interfere with the recruiting of the regular army (Albert Gallatin, *Writings,* 1879, I, 530).

In January 1813 President Madison nominated him for the post of secretary of war. Eustis had demonstrated his own incompetency for that position and had resigned in December 1812. Madison had asked James Monroe, secretary of state, to fill the office temporarily, and had wished to have him keep it, as Monroe would probably have liked to do, but northern jealousy of Virginia forbade this course. Virtually compelled to select a northern man, Madison was urged by Judge Ambrose Spencer and Gov. Tompkins of New York to name Armstrong, and made the nomination accordingly, though without liking for or great confidence in the nominee, who had made no secret of his dislike for the Virginia school of statesmanship. The Senate confirmed the nomination by a small majority, the Virginia senators absenting themselves, and Armstrong took charge of the War Department on Feb. 5, 1813.

About Armstrong's merits as secretary of war there has been much controversy. The verdict of history has been for the most part adverse, and there seems no reason to alter that verdict. Allowances must be made for the serious if not insuperable difficulties that confronted him —the deficiency in troops and war material resulting from the niggardly measures of Congress, the untrained and generally incompetent men who held generals' commissions, and the bitter fight, amounting almost if not quite to disloyalty, waged against him from the beginning by Monroe, who rightly regarded him as a rival candidate for the presidency. In the face of these difficulties Armstrong accomplished one notable achievement: he vastly strengthened the army by the promotion of Generals Andrew Jackson, Jacob Brown, Winfield Scott, and other officers. In making a major-general of the Quaker farmer, Jacob Brown, Armstrong displayed discernment and courage. But over against this service must be set an array of mistakes and failures. With Gen. Harrison in the West he interfered too much; with Gen. Dearborn on Lake Ontario he interfered too little. Armstrong's plan for a spring campaign on Lake Ontario in 1813 was promising; in place of it he allowed Gen. Dearborn and Commodore Chauncey to substitute one of their own which had nothing to commend it and which ended in disaster. Even more discreditable to Armstrong was the autumn campaign of the same year against Montreal. Armstrong went himself to Sackett's Harbor on Lake Ontario, in order to mediate between the two generals, Wilkinson and Hampton, who were personal enemies. He started the two (Wilkinson from Sackett's Harbor and Hampton from Lake Champlain) on a campaign for Montreal which he plainly knew must fail, and then returned to Washington, leaving Wilkinson and Hampton to bear the responsibility for failure (Adams, vol. VII, ch. 8). In the following summer, when 11,000 British veterans were threatening an invasion of New York via Lake Champlain, he ordered Gen. Izard, with 4,000 men from Plattsburg on Lake Champlain to Lake Ontario, leaving only 2,000 troops to man the defenses at Plattsburg. Many attempts have been made to fix the blame for the capture of Washington by the British, Aug. 24, 1814. Responsibility has been variously placed upon Gen. Winder, who commanded the district, Secretary Armstrong, and President Madison. The fairest conclusion seems to be that there is discredit enough for all three, and that all must share in the responsibility. Winder unquestionably was ill provided with troops and equipment, but he failed completely in using what he had. Armstrong was culpable in his failure to heed Winder's complaints, and must bear much of the blame for failure to erect even the simplest fortifications despite ample warning that the British were coming. Armstrong's criticism of Jackson's defense of New Orleans may well be turned against himself in relation to the defense of Washington. "Had the General been better acquainted with military history," wrote Armstrong in his *Notices of the War of 1812,* II, 177, "he would not have suffered a single day, of the twenty he had for preparation, to have passed, without forming one or more entrenched camps for the protection of the city." Finally, Madison was responsible for the appointment of Winder, an incompetent, over Armstrong's protest, and in a more general way, as commander-in-chief of the army, was responsible for all that was done or left undone. Armstrong stated truly that he had carried out all Madison's orders, but Madison replied as truly that in other matters Armstrong had shown enough, and sometimes too much, initiative. Each of the three exhibited, in this affair, an almost incredible degree of incompetence.

Armstrong had never been popular in Washington, and he now received the chief blame for the disaster. "Universal execration follows Armstrong," wrote a Washington lady, Aug. 30, 1814 (Mrs. S. H. Smith, *The First Forty Years of Washington Society,* 1906, p. 115). Monroe and his friends insisted that Armstrong must leave the cabinet. In an interview of Aug. 29, Madison told him that, although his resignation was not desired, he could no longer direct military affairs within the District of Columbia. Armstrong agreed to leave the city, ostensibly to pay a visit to his family in New York, and to remain until the excitement in Washington should blow over (James Madison, *Writings,* Hunt edition, VIII, 300–4), but from Baltimore he mailed his resignation to the President (Sept. 3, 1814), at the same time giving to the press a letter defending his conduct (*Niles' Weekly Register,* VII, 6-7).

The Washington disaster, coupled perhaps with Armstrong's flirtations with the Federalists while in office (*Life and Correspondence of Rufus King,* V, 370–71), put an end to his political career. His friend, Judge Spencer of the New York supreme court, tried in 1815 to secure his election to the United States Senate but was unable to secure the requisite support. Armstrong retired to Red Hook, N. Y., and there devoted the remainder of his life to agriculture with occasional ventures in authorship. The most important of his publications, *Notices of the War of 1812* (1836), is chiefly an attempted vindication of his record in the War Department. In this and other published works, as well as in some of his MS. letters still extant, he showed the same command of a caustic pen which had distinguished the author of the "Newburgh Letters." He contributed a "Life of Richard Montgomery" and a "Life of Anthony Wayne" to the *Library of American Biography* (1st series, 10 vols., 1834–38) edited by Jared Sparks, and in 1839 published in book form as *A Treatise on Agriculture* a series of articles which he had written for the Albany *Argus.*

"His disposition was eminently pugnacious," says Martin Van Buren (*Autobiography,* in *American Historical Association Report,* 1918, p. 42). This quality, together with the leaning to indolence and intrigue with which he was justly charged, did much to vitiate the fruits of his unquestioned ability, and, together with the opposition of powerful rivals, rendered his public life of slight value to his country.

[There is no biog. of John Armstrong. A great deal of information about his career in France and in the War Dept. is contained in Henry Adams, *Hist. of the U. S. during the Administrations of Jefferson and Madison,* 9 vols. (1889–91). Much of his official correspondence during the same periods is printed in *Am. State Papers: Foreign Relations,* vols. II and III, and *Mil. Affairs,* vol. I. An important critical account of his failure to take adequate measures for the defense of Washington in 1814 is E. D. Ingraham, *A Sketch of Events which Preceded the Capture of Washington, by the British on the 24th of August, 1814* (1849), while Armstrong's own view is presented in his *Notice of Mr. Adams' Eulogium on the Life and Character of James Monroe* (1832).]

J. W. P.

ARMSTRONG, PAUL (Apr. 25, 1869–Aug. 30, 1915), playwright, was born in Kidder, Mo., the son of Richard and Harriet (Scott) Armstrong. His parents removing to Bay City, Mich., where his father engaged in the steamship business, he began and ended his education by attendance at public schools in that city. At twenty-one, he secured a license to be master of steam-vessels and for a short time was purser on a steamer plying between Chicago and St. Joseph, Mich. Numerous short stories which he wrote were uniformly rejected by the publishers, but, undiscouraged, he decided to enter literature by the back-door of journalism. He went to Buffalo and wrote for the *Express,* the *Courier,* and the *News* until 1896, one of his first assignments on the *Express* being a murder mystery which he unexpectedly helped to solve. He next worked for two years on the *Chicago Times-Herald* and the *Inter-Ocean,* after which he moved to New York and under the pen-name of "Right Cross" wrote on sports and pugilism for several New York newspapers. Meanwhile he had become interested in writing for the theatre. His first play, *Just a Day Dream,* was favorably read in manuscript by Joseph Jefferson and was produced by a Boston stock company, but Armstrong tried in vain to interest any New York manager in it. Three later plays, *The Superstition of Sue, St. Ann,* and the first version of *Society and the Bull Dog* were staged about 1904 without success. The reward of perseverance came, however, in 1905, with the triumphant production of *The Heir to the Hoorah.* For the next eight years Armstrong was one of the most popular of American playwrights, and his fecundity under the stimulus of success was remarkable. There appeared from his pen: *Ann Lamont* (1905), a revision of *St. Ann; In a Blaze of Glory* (1906), one act; *Salomy Jane* (1907), adapted from Bret Harte's story, "Salomy Jane's Kiss"; *Society and the Bull Dog* (1908), revised version; *Going Some* (1908), farce written in collaboration with Rex Beach; *Via Wireless* (1908), melodrama in collaboration with Winchell Smith; *Blue Grass* (1908), revision of an early curtain-raiser; *The Renegade* (1909); *For a Woman* (1909); *Alias Jimmy Valentine* (1909), written in a single week, and his most successful work, prompting a long series of imitative "crook plays" by others; *The Deep Purple* (1910), pseudo-scientific mystery play, in collaboration with Wilson Mizner; *A Romance of the Underworld* (1911), revision of *For a Woman; The Greyhound* (1912), in collaboration with Wilson Mizner; *The Escape* (1912); *A Love Story* (1913); *Woman Proposes* (1913), vaudeville sketch; *To Save One Girl* (1913), vaudeville sketch. About 1913 Armstrong's health began to fail and his work to lose its grip. *The Bludgeon* (1914) and *The Heart of a Thief* (1914) were less successful than their predecessors. *Mr. Lorelei,* a folk-comedy, was merely published posthumously in *Smart Set,* January 1916.

Armstrong was twice married. His first wife was Rella Abell, of Kansas City, whom he married in London, July 24, 1899. On Dec. 10, 1913 Mrs. Armstrong secured a divorce with alimony for herself and her three daughters, and on Dec. 12 Armstrong married Kittie Cassidy, of Baltimore, who had starred in several of his plays and who later, as Catharine Calvert, became a prominent moving-picture actress. They had one son. Armstrong died from heart-failure at his home in New York City on Aug. 30, 1915. His plays were ephemeral, written solely for the stage with slight regard for literary merit. Nevertheless he was an effective story-teller, adept in producing crisp, pungent dialogue, with grim humor and strong climaxes. At a time when the American stage gave promise of better things he devoted his talent mainly to melodrama and was one of the last writers to compete successfully in this field with the moving-picture theatre.

[Obituaries in N.Y. newspapers of Aug. 31, 1915, also in *N. Y. Dramatic Mirror,* Sept. 8, 1915; article on Armstrong's personality by Chas. W. Collins, *Green Book* (XI, 651–66); portrait, *Green Book* (XI, 651). *Who's Who in America,* 1916–1917, gives date of Armstrong's death incorrectly as Aug. 29.]

J. L. H.

ARMSTRONG, ROBERT (Sept. 28, 1792–Feb. 23, 1854), soldier, belonged to a military family, his father, Trooper Armstrong, being a Revolutionary soldier of fine physique and great strength, and two brothers, Frank and William, each attaining the rank of major. He was born in Abingdon, Va., but early in life removed with his family to east Tennessee. Later he returned to Abingdon for his education, which ended when the country went to war in 1812. At Nashville he enlisted, becoming a sergeant, and later, when Andrew Jackson led an army against the Creek Indians, he served with it as a lieutenant of artillery. In a campaign marked by several battles, shortage of provisions, and mutiny, he cemented a close friendship with the indomitable leader of the little army. At the battle of Enotochapko, on Jan. 24, 1814, he was shot through the left hip while courageously standing by his guns. This wound, however, was not so severe as to keep him from serving gallantly on Jackson's staff at the battle of New Orleans. The life that followed these stirring times was for the most part comparatively quiet. In June 1814 he married Margaret Nichol, daughter of a Nashville merchant, and settled in that city. President Jackson appointed him postmaster there in 1829, a place which he held for sixteen years, and in 1836, when the second Seminole War broke out, appointed him brigadier-general in command of two regiments of volunteers. The short Florida campaign, ending in the battle of Wahoo Swamp, was effective though not brilliant, and the prestige of Armstrong's command made him the candidate of the Jackson-Van Buren party for governor in 1837. But the tide was running heavily against Jackson and Van Buren in Tennessee at that time, and Armstrong was decisively defeated. Appointed consul at Liverpool by Polk in 1845, he served there for four years. After his return to this country he became proprietor of the *Washington Union,* and in its columns gave steady support to Democratic policies during the three years of life that remained to him. His political papers were marked by the stately dignity that characterized the writings of the time, and betray no particular originality of thought.

[John H. Calender, "A Leaf from History. A Portrait of Gen. Robert Armstrong," *Tenn. Hist. Mag.,* July 1919; speech of Robert Ewing before Tenn. Hist. Soc., *Nashville Tennessean,* Nov. 18, 1918; John T. Moore and Austin P. Foster, *Tennessee, the Volunteer State, 1769–1923* (1923), I, 408, 415–16; Will T. Hale and Merritt Dixon, *Hist. of Tennessee and Tennesseans* (1913), II, 432, 489, III, 839; Zella Armstrong, *Notable Southern Families* (1926), III, 1-15; editorials in *N.Y. Times,* Feb. 24, 1854, and *Washington Union,* Feb. 24, 26, 28, 1854.]

O. W.

ARMSTRONG, SAMUEL CHAPMAN (Jan. 30, 1839–May 11, 1893), educator, was born on the Island of Maui in the Hawaiian Islands. His parents, Richard and Clarissa Armstrong, were missionaries of the American Board, people of the pioneer type, of keen intelligence, sincere piety, and great bodily endurance. Richard Armstrong was of Scotch-Irish descent and of vivacious and demonstrative temperament. Clarissa Armstrong was of New England Puritan stock, practical, reserved, and devout. In 1840 the Armstrongs moved to Honolulu where Richard Armstrong became the pastor of the First Church. He soon added to his missionary work many other public responsibilities. He was made a member of the King's privy council and then minister of public instruction, and later president of the board of education.

Samuel Armstrong grew up in a large family of brothers and sisters. He was a high-spirited boy, full of fun, and a proficient horseman, swimmer, and sailor. He was expert in all forms of bodily exercise, took great delight in out-of-door life and mingled in friendly fashion with the natives and in the social, political, and religious activities that centered at his father's house. He attended the Royal School at Punahou, which was under the charge of the brothers Edward and George Beckwith. The school in 1855 became Oahu College, and Armstrong finished the first two years of the college course which prepared him to enter the junior class at Williams College. His father died suddenly in 1860, and it was to carry out the father's hope for the education of his son that Samuel Armstrong sailed in the autumn of that year for the United States. Williams College was then under the charge of Dr. Mark Hopkins, and during his first winter Armstrong formed an intimate friendship with the son of the president and was invited to share his room at Dr. Hopkins's house, thus beginning a life-long and inspiring connection. The excitements of the opening days of the Civil War changed everything for the young student. Armstrong had no particular interest in the issues of the war for he had lived quite remote from the discussions and was not an American citizen. Nevertheless, he could not but share the convictions and ardors of his associates. His classmates were enlisting almost in a body and he finally accepted a captain's commission in the 125th New York Regiment. He recruited his own company at and about Troy, N. Y., and on Aug. 30, 1862, started with his regiment for the front. The regiment had a somewhat unexciting part in the campaigns of the succeeding year, and Gettysburg was its first real battle. Armstrong distinguished himself for skill and valor. He was promoted to the rank of major and soon after, though not yet twenty-five years old, he was commissioned colonel of the 9th Regiment, United States colored troops. He took over this charge without enthusiasm but soon became keenly interested in the men of his command and in proving the capacity of the colored troops. The regiment took part in the operations before Petersburg, but at the time of the assault Armstrong was in the hospital at Fortress Monroe, very near to the scenes of his later life-work. At the end of the war he received the brevet rank of brigadier-general and commanded brigades for some months in Virginia and Texas.

The Freedmen's Bureau had come into existence in response to the crying needs of the emancipated negroes, and Armstrong, who had been conspicuously successful as a commander of colored troops, was appointed an agent of this Bureau. In March 1866 he took charge of a great camp of negroes in and about the village of Hampton, Va., and made his headquarters in an old mansion on the shore of Hampton Creek. His thoughts were more and more directed toward the need of industrial education for the freedmen. "The north," he wrote, "generally thinks that the great thing is to free the negro from his former owners; the real thing is to save him from himself."

Armstrong's early experience in Hawaii came right to hand. In his youth he had seen the development of the plan of the Hilo Manual Labor School for native Hawaiians. This was a boarding school for Hawaiian boys where they paid the expenses of their tuition by working at carpentry, housework, gardening, etc. Armstrong set himself to discover the way in which selected negro young men and women could be trained to be teachers and leaders of their own people. The plan of combining mental and manual training exactly fitted the needs of the situation. In 1867 Armstrong wrote to the American Missionary Association, which was interested in negro education, recommending that the estate upon which he was then living, covering 159 acres, be purchased as the foundation of an industrial school for negro teachers. Through the Association and by the gift of one benefactor, the estate was secured and the Hampton Normal and Industrial Institute was opened in 1868. By personal solicitation among friends in the Northern states Armstrong raised the money for the first school buildings. A great institution was gradually upbuilt, and its successful administration has had a profound effect on the educational life of America. It sprang from a creative, though not a wholly original, conception, and it has been the source and inspiration of many schools which represent the same idea.

Armstrong was twice married: in 1869 to Emma Dean Walker of Stockbridge, Mass.; and in 1890 to Mary Alice Ford of Lisbon, N. H. He was a man of fascinating personality and exceptional gifts of leadership. He possessed a large measure of the warmth and vehemence of his father, and at the same time the Puritan traits of practical sagacity and indomitable persistence derived from his New England mother. The two elements in his nature made a strong and significant combination, the union of the moralist and the seer, the alliance of imagination and tenacity. He described and advocated the fundamental essential of education—education of head, heart, and hand alike—education for life; and then he made the special application and illustration of that principle at Hampton Institute.

[Edith Armstrong Talbot, *Samuel Chapman Armstrong* (1904); F. G. Peabody, *Education for Life* (1918), a history of Hampton Institute; the series of Founder's Day Addresses delivered in successive years at Hampton on Armstrong's birthday.]

S. A. E.

ARMSTRONG, SAMUEL TURELL (Apr. 29, 1784–Mar. 26, 1850), publisher, banker, statesman, was born in Dorchester (now a part of Boston), Mass. His parents, John and Elizabeth, both died before he was thirteen. The new century found the youth a printer's apprentice with Manning & Loring in Boston. His appenticeship completed, he formed a partnership with Joshua Belcher and conducted a printing business at 70 State St. After a few years the partnership was dissolved and he moved to Charlestown, where from his printery appeared monthly the *Panoplist and Missionary Magazine United* (still current as the *Missionary Herald*) beginning with June 1808. Returning to Boston (1811), he located his business at 50 Cornhill. His publications were generally of a religious character, such as Thomas Scott's *The Holy Bible Containing the Old and New Testaments, with Explanatory Notes* (1824), Worcester's edition of Watts's *Psalms and Hymns*, and Claudius Buchanan's *Christian Researches in Asia* (1811). Of a religious nature, too, was the publisher himself, a deacon in the Old South Church (H. A. Hill, *History of the Old South Church*, 1890, II, 489), and member of the American Board of Commissioners for Foreign Missions (*Boston Recorder*, Sept. 18, 1835). His connection with the Old South Church accounts for his discovery, in 1816, in the tower of the church, of "the third volume of the History of New England in the original MS. of the author, John Winthrop, the first governor of the Massachusetts Bay" (*New England Historical and Genealogical Register*, VII, 364; *Winthrop's Journal*, 1908, I, 16). A man of civic spirit as well, Armstrong headed the subscription list "for the preservation of the Plymouth Rock," June 1835 (*Chronicles of the Armstrongs*, p. 391). This same spirit led him to accept public office; he was representative to the General Court from the City of Boston (May 1822 to May 1823; May 1828 to May 1829), lieutenant-governor (1833–35) and governor succeeding Gov. Davis after Mar. 4, 1835, when the latter went to the United States Senate. A Whig in politics, he had Anti-Masonic support, but he was not in the favor of Daniel Webster, Massachusetts Whig leader, who scorned this self-made man "of the common people" (*Boston Morning Post*, Jan. 15, 1836). Hence in the gubernatorial election of November 1835 Armstrong ran unsuccessfully as an Independent in the same field with Edward Everett, Webster's nominee. In the municipal election of the following month, however, his fellow citizens of Boston elected him mayor for the ensuing year. His administration was marked by the erection of an iron fence for the enclosure of three sides of the Common, and the extension of the mall through the burial grounds of Boylston St. His last public office was that of state senator in 1839. He continued his connection with his publishing business in the latter years of his life, but the moderate fortune he had amassed (Abigail, *née* Walker, his widow, is mentioned by Forbes and Green, *Rich Men of Massachusetts*, 1852, as being worth $150,000) enabled him to give considerable time to European travel.

[A short sketch of Armstrong, written by his contemporary and partner, Uriel Crocker, appears in *Memorial Biogs. of the New Eng. Hist. and Geneal. Soc.* (1880), I, 232–36. A similar sketch accompanied by a portr. is in vol. XLIV of the Society's *Register*, pp. 137–39. A. B. Darling, *Pol. Changes in Mass., 1822–48* (1925), refers to his pol. career, as do also John Koven, *Boston 1822 to 1922* (1923); the *Boston Recorder*, Feb. 27, Mar. 6, Dec. 13, and Dec. 18, 1835; P. R. Frothingham, *Edward Everett, Orator and Statesman* (1925), pp. 128–29; and *Memoirs of J. Q. Adams*, IX, 242–43. Obituaries in *Boston Transcript*, Mar. 27, 1850, and the *Liberator*, Apr. 5, 1850.]

A. E. P.

ARNOLD, AZA (Oct. 4, 1788–1865), inventor, was born in Smithfield, near Pawtucket, R. I., the son of Benjamin and Isabel (Greene) Arnold and a descendant of Thomas Arnold, who with his family joined the English colonists in 1635 and settled in Providence, R. I., in 1661. Arnold's mother died when he was two years old and after his father's second marriage young Arnold was left to shift more or less for himself. He attended the village school, but began working as soon as he was able, first learning the carpenter's trade and then the machinist's. At the age of twenty he entered the employ of Samuel Slater in his wool and cotton machinery manufacturing plant in Pawtucket, but left after a few years to engage in the manufacture of woolen blankets. This venture proving unsuccessful, he next became associated with Larned Pitcher and P. Hovey in the operation of a machine shop in Pawtucket. Here he remained until 1819. In this year he moved with his family to Great Falls, N. H., where he built and operated a cotton-mill. Within a few years he was again back in Rhode Island, this time in North Providence, where he established a machine of his own for the manufacture of textile machinery. While with Pitcher and Hovey in Pawtucket he devised a machine for separating wool, in carding, into slivers so that it could be spun from the cards. It was a form of "endless" roving, roving previously having been in short rolls which had to be pieced together. Whether the device was patented is not known, but on Jan. 21, 1823, Arnold obtained a patent for a roving machine for spinning cotton in which he introduced a differential motion applied to the speeder. The result was a valuable improvement in cotton-roving machines, increasing both quantity and quality of product. It was introduced into England in 1825 and was characterized as being one of the most important machines for spinning cotton. While some American manufacturers acknowledged this invention and paid Arnold royalties, others, especially those outside of Rhode Island, refused to do so, and, in the course of the infringement suits which Arnold brought, the whole code of patent laws was repealed and the new code of 1836 was passed, but Arnold received no redress for the infringements. In 1838 he gave up his machine shop and moved with his family to Philadelphia, where he operated the Mulhausen Print Works. Here he remained for about twelve years, when he went to Washington, D. C., established himself as a patent attorney, and continued in this capacity until his death. Arnold's last known invention was a "self-setting and self-raking saw for sawing machines," for which patent No. 15,163 was granted him on June 24, 1856. While it is said that he invented a machine for cutting files about 1812, no record of this invention is to be found in the Patent Office. Arnold married Abigail Dennis of Newport, R. I., on July 28, 1815.

[*Vital Record of R. I.*, VII (1895), ed. by Jas. N. Arnold; *Representative Men and Old Families of R. I.* (1908); *Hist. of Providence County* (1891), ed. by Rich. M. Bayles; *Hist. Sketch of the Town of Pawtucket* (1876), by Massena Goodrich; Patent Office Records.]

C. W. M.

ARNOLD, BENEDICT (Jan. 14, 1741–June 14, 1801), Revolutionary patriot and traitor, was born at Norwich, Conn., the son of Benedict and Hannah King (*née* Waterman) Arnold. The Arnolds had for several generations been a family of education and position in New England, an ancestor of the same name having been several times governor of Rhode Island in the seventeenth century (*American Historical Association Report*, 1906, vol. II, pp. 331–32). Arnold's training was under the influence of the strictest kind of New England religious thought, against which he displayed a distinct spirit of revolt. Biographers have extolled the fine qualities of his mother, but in the light of modern psychology it seems likely that her unwise efforts at restraint may have been responsible for much in his later character. At the age of fourteen he ran away from home to join the colonial troops then starting out for the French and Indian War. At the instance of his mother he was brought back, but he ran away a second time for the same purpose, joined the provincial troops, and saw service on Lakes George and Champlain. When the charm of the soldier's life had vanished, Arnold deserted and returned home, alone, through the wilderness. Only his youth saved him from the serious consequences of his act. At the age of twenty-one he moved to New Haven and became a druggist and bookseller. As he grew more prosperous, he invested money in the West India trade, and traveled himself between Quebec and the West Indies, selling horses and mules to the plantations in the sugar islands. On Feb. 22, 1767, he married Margaret Mansfield of New Haven, by whom he had three sons, Benedict (1768), Richard (1769), and Henry (1772). He was soon a person of some consequence in New Haven and became a captain in the Connecticut militia. His personality made a lasting impression upon observers. His black hair and dark complexion were remarked by all who tried to describe him, although his eyes were light. Thick set and well proportioned, he possessed unusual physical strength and agility, and was capable of great endurance.

When the news of the fight at Lexington reached New Haven, Arnold called his company together and asked for volunteers to aid the patriot cause. With the approval of Gov. Trumbull the company started out and reached Cambridge on Apr. 29, 1775. Since the great problem was how to fight a war without either gunpowder or artillery, Arnold told the Committee of Safety of Massachusetts that Fort Ticonderoga, on Lake Champlain, held eighty cannon left over from the French and Indian War, and he volunteered to go and get them (Force, *American Archives*, 4th ser., vol. II, p. 450). The committee promptly gave him a colonel's commission, power to enlist troops, and an order to go and take Fort Ticonderoga (*Ibid.*, p. 485). At the same time this idea occurred to some other Connecticut people, and Arnold found himself en route to Ticonderoga in company with another expedition led by Ethan Allen of Vermont. Neither was the type of man to yield precedence to the other, but the importance of their joint expedition seems to have impressed them with the necessity for some compromise. It was agreed that Allen should issue commands jointly with Arnold (J. H. Smith, *Our Struggle for the Fourteenth Colony*, I, 132). Together they assaulted and captured the fort on May 10, 1775, Allen reporting to the Albany Committee, "Col. Arnold entered the fortress side by side with me." The controversy over who was really in command continued after the victory, which tradition has usually assigned to Allen. Shortly Arnold's own troops, whom his subordinates had enlisted, joined him. He promptly left Allen at Fort Ticonderoga and sailed to the extreme northern end of the Lake and captured the fort at St. Johns. Having destroyed that post and the boats with which British reinforcements might pursue him, he returned to the south, where he was reinforced with more troops under Col. Hinman. There were now quarrels among Hinman, Allen, and Arnold as to the chief command, complicated by the conflicting jurisdictions and authority of four governments, Massachusetts, Connecticut, New York, and the Continental Congress. Arnold had the mortification of seeing his signal services rewarded only by his being "investigated" and superseded, whereupon in July 1775 he returned to Connecticut, decidedly disgruntled.

In spite of the fact that he had drawn upon his personal savings and his credit for the public service, he was so badly treated by the Massachusetts authorities, in their failure to reimburse him, that even the Continental Congress, with all its poverty, voted him $800. To add to his distress, his wife died on June 19, 1775, while he was absent at the Lakes. His misfortunes, however, did not prevent him from laying before Congress an even more ambitious scheme for securing supplies for the Continental Armies. He proposed an attack on Canada. In furtherance of this he went to Cambridge, where Washington had now taken command of the armies. In the new commander-in-chief he found a sympathetic listener, and one who was already thinking of a new route for an attack on Quebec. The usual course of warlike expeditions in past campaigns had been by way of Lake George and Lake Champlain. Washington had news of a newer route by way of the Kennebec River (Maine) and the Chaudière River, leading straight to Quebec itself (*Maine Historical Society Collections,* ser. I, vol. I, p. 447). With the coöperation of Schuyler, who was now in command at Ticonderoga, two expeditions to Canada were planned. One under Schuyler was to follow the old route of the Lakes, and capture Montreal, while the other under Arnold was to take the new route through the lakes, forests, and rivers of Maine, and secure Quebec. On Sept. 19 Arnold's command left Newburyport, Mass., for Maine. Going up the Kennebec they found waiting the 200 bateaux which had been ordered ahead of time. The journey through the Maine woods is a classic in American military history; for perseverance under the utmost hardships, it is almost unparalleled. About a fourth of the army turned back, for which their leader, Enos, was promptly court-martialed on his return to Cambridge. Arnold struggled on through snow-storms and icy water, and the vanguard of his party reached the St. Lawrence opposite Quebec on Nov. 8. He found the garrison weak, but he was even weaker. It would have been madness to attempt an assault with his force decimated by disease and starvation. He therefore withdrew his troops twenty miles up the river and waited. Meantime Montgomery, who on Schuyler's illness had taken the command, had followed the Lake route and captured Montreal. He joined Arnold on Dec. 2. Quebec had a garrison of about 1,200 men by this time, while the combined forces of Arnold and Montgomery were less than a thousand. In a blinding snow-storm, they made the assault on the night of Dec. 31, 1775. Despite the most heroic conduct the attack failed utterly, Montgomery being killed and Arnold wounded. While still badly injured, Arnold took command of the shattered remnants of the army and placed them so as to blockade Quebec on the west side, while the ice blockaded it on the east until spring came. On Jan. 10, 1776, Congress made him a brigadier-general (*Journals of the Continental Congress,* L. C. ed., IV, 47). As spring came the British obtained reinforcements by sea, and it was apparent that Gen. Carleton, the British commander, would soon be in a position to drive the Americans from Canada. In June Arnold sent his army back to Crown Point from Montreal, and followed in the last boat, just as the advance guard of the British army came in sight.

At Crown Point he immediately set to work to prepare for the contest for the control of the Lakes which was bound to come. Carleton left Quebec in pursuit of Arnold and mobilized his forces at St. Johns. Schuyler was now in command of the northern department, but Arnold was entrusted with building a fleet to resist Carleton's armament. The British plan of campaign for 1776 was that Howe should capture New York, while the army under Carleton or Burgoyne was to move south from Canada and join Howe, thus cutting the New England states from the middle colonies. This plan might well have been fatal to the American cause, and had far better chances of success in 1776 than in the following summer. Only one thing prevented its execution, and that was the work of Benedict Arnold. His extraordinary foresight and industry in building a fleet made it necessary for Carleton to delay and prepare a more ambitious expedition than he had originally planned, including the knocking down of war vessels in the St. Lawrence and transporting them in parts overland to be reërected on Lake Champlain. At St. Johns Carleton gathered a force of 12,000. Arnold met him with a fleet which was a curious assortment of schooners, galleys, and gondolas, which were open boats mounting but a single gun each. The two fleets met on Oct. 11, 1776, on Lake Champlain. Arnold had drawn his force up behind Valcour Island in such fashion that the British got between him and Fort Ticonderoga. The first day's contest was exceedingly hard fought and was a drawn battle when evening fell. Arnold realized he must get away, for another such fight would probably ruin him. With remarkable daring and skill he sailed the remains of his fleet straight through the British lines at night and was out of sight when Carleton realized what had happened. The British pursued and on Oct. 13 another desperate battle occurred just below Crown Point. Arnold's fleet was worsted, but he managed to run his own schooner and five gondolas ashore and burn them to prevent their falling into the hands of the British. He then withdrew his force overland to Crown Point and thence to Ticonderoga. The effect of Arnold's fierce resistance completely upset Carleton's calculations, so that the British commander realized it was impossible to go on and attack, not to say, capture, Fort Ticonderoga that summer. His force retreated to Canada. The principal naval authority has said, "The little American navy on Champlain was wiped out; but never had any force, big or small, lived to better purpose or died more gloriously, for it had saved the Lake for that year" (A. T. Mahan, p. 25).

By November of 1776, his private affairs having become involved in his absence, Arnold received permission from Gen. Gates (now in command of the northern army) and also the consent of Washington to go home. He passed the winter in New England. On Feb. 19, 1777, occurred one of the first events which embittered him against the American cause. Congress promoted five brigadier-generals to be major-generals, all of whom were junior in rank to Arnold (*Journals of the Continental Congress,* VIII, 133). He was beside himself with indignation—but he was not less angry than the commander-in-chief, who immediately demanded an explanation from Congress and emphasized the extraordinary character of Arnold as a leader of men (Sparks's *Washington,* IV, 351). Congress gave the lame excuse that Connecticut already had two major-generals, upon which Washington commented "this is a strange mode of reasoning." Arnold was dissuaded from resigning by a personal plea from the commander-in-chief. It is not too much to say that for the sake of the common cause, Arnold swallowed an injustice which others would not have tolerated (Ford, *Writings of Washington,* V, 270–71 n., 403–6).

In the spring of 1777 he was about to start for Philadelphia to defend himself before Congress, when he heard of the invasion of Connecticut by Gen. Tryon. The object of the expedition was the destruction of the military stores at Danbury. The militia were rallied but did not arrive in time to save the arsenals. Arnold rode to the scene of action, gathered what troops he could, met the enemy at Ridgefield, and opposed his 500 militia against 2,000 British. As usual he was in the thick of the action, and his horse fell dead, hit by nine bullets. Arnold drew off his troops with great skill and followed Tryon on to Norwalk, where, having been reinforced by artillery, he again attacked. The British got back to their ships just in time to avoid capture. This action drew from the Continental Congress warm praise and secured for Arnold the delayed promotion to a major-generalship, without, however, restoring his rightful rank above that of the five previously appointed. Arnold went to Philadelphia, where the Continental Congress was considering some charges which had been made against him. They were proved groundless, the result of personal spite on the part of a fellow officer who had had a grievance against Arnold since the days of Fort Ticonderoga. Congress exonerated Arnold, but still failed to restore his rank above the five. Washington wrote the President of Congress expressing his pleasure at the promotion but again bringing up the question of rank. The delay was probably due to another investigation under way as to Arnold's accounts and his actions as to private property at Montreal. An officer in command of starving troops in an enemy's country might, one would have supposed, be permitted some latitude, but Arnold's enemies in Congress declined to consider the circumstances. Not receiving the satisfaction which was certainly due him, Arnold finally sent in his resignation. Congress received it in July on the same day that it received a letter from Washington telling them that Burgoyne had started south on his momentous expedition from Canada and that Arnold must be sent at once to help block him. Arnold, again upon the personal request of Washington, withdrew his resignation and left for the northern headquarters, where his services were so sorely needed.

The British campaign of 1777 involved three elements. Burgoyne was to march south from Canada. Howe was to march north from New York and join him at Albany. St. Leger was to go up Lake Erie to Oswego and come down the Mohawk Valley, meeting the other two at Albany. The American hopes for defending the Mohawk Valley depended on holding Fort Stanwix. By Aug. 3 St. Leger had surrounded that fort. On Aug. 12 Arnold reached Schuyler's headquarters and was immediately sent off with 800 men to relieve Fort Stanwix. With fewer men than St. Leger, he rushed forward with the utmost audacity, and sent on ahead a half-crazy man and a friendly Indian to tell St. Leger he was coming with an immense army. The speed of his approach and the wild story of his messenger had the effect of driving St. Leger's Indians and Tories away in confusion. When Arnold arrived the siege was raised and St. Leger was in full flight back to Oswego. This almost bloodless victory demonstrated the terror which Arnold's name held for the British.

Without waiting a moment he turned his army about and hurried back to Schuyler, now superseded by Gates. In September Burgoyne was face to face with the American army. Arnold's command participated in the battles of Sept. 19 and Oct. 7, at Freeman's Farm and Bemis Heights, which sealed the fate of Burgoyne's expedition. A distinct impression has been left with posterity that the fire and dash of Arnold in those battles had as much to do with the American victory as had the careful disposition of troops by Gates. Arnold's biographer, Isaac N. Arnold, has put the extreme case for his subject, giving him the principal credit for the triumph of the American arms (*Arnold,* pp. 163–212). This has been questioned by F. D. Stone (*Pennsylvania Magazine,* IV, 389) and by J. A. Stevens (*Magazine of American History,* IV, 181–91). Possibly Arnold was not present at the battle of Sept. 19, but there can be no doubt that he led the troops in person and was wounded on Oct. 7, although probably acting as a volunteer. There can also be no doubt that Burgoyne thought in terms of Arnold as much as he did in terms of Gates. After Burgoyne's surrender, Arnold was carried home to Connecticut where his own people were warm in their recognition of a "fighting general," and Congress belatedly restored to him his proper rank in the army.

In May of 1778 he was sufficiently recovered to rejoin the army under Washington at Valley Forge. In June the British evacuated Philadelphia, and at Washington's order Arnold became the commander at that city. Here he met and fell in love with Margaret Shippen, at that time the darling of Philadelphia society. He married her in April 1779, and took her to "Mt. Pleasant," a magnificent country seat which he purchased upon the banks of the Schuylkill. Philadelphia society was accustomed to the gaiety and extravagance of the British army, and Arnold seems to have felt obliged to keep up an appearance of social activity which was impossible on the small pay of a Continental officer. He was soon seriously in debt. During the period of his command at the headquarters in Philadelphia, he got into trouble with the civil authorities in Pennsylvania on several minor points. In addition it was now charged against him that he utilized his military office for private gain, and that he had made use of soldiers of the Pennsylvania militia for menial services and for his own personal work. These charges, which seem to have resulted from a combination of Arnold's hasty temper and the oversensitiveness of the Pennsylvania authorities, were brought to the attention of Congress, who referred certain of them to the commander-in-chief. Arnold demanded a court martial to clear him of the allegations. The court martial was ordered in May of 1779, but to his irritation was delayed until December. The court, while finding him not guilty of most of the charges, decided that he had violated the articles of war in permitting a vessel to leave a port in the possession of the enemy and enter a port in the United States, and further that he had been imprudent in the use of the military forces for his private purposes. For this they recommended a reprimand by the commander-in-chief. Washington's execution of the recommendation of the court martial was a model of combined firmness and regard for Arnold's better nature and his feelings.

At the time of his trouble with the Pennsylvania authorities, Arnold began actively to enter into that betrayal of the American cause indelibly associated with his name. There seems no reason to doubt that his treasonable correspondence with Sir Henry Clinton began in May or June of 1779. His motives seem to have been fourfold: (1) anger at the repeated slights of Congress, (2) resentment at the actions of the Pennsylvania authorities which culminated in his court martial, (3) the need for ready money to maintain his position and repay himself for the sacrifices and expenses to which the war had put him and for which he had received no adequate recompense from Congress, and (4) a real and sincere indignation at the French alliance, which, as a New England Protestant, and as an inheritor of the traditions of the colonial wars, he could not abide. Historians have in the past attempted to add the motive of his actually being won over to the British cause by the Tories with whom he associated in Philadelphia after becoming commander there. It has, however, been pretty well established that the Shippens of Philadelphia were not all Loyalists in the Revolution, that Edward Shippen, his father-in-law, was more favorable to the American than to the British cause, and that the stories of Margaret Shippen's flirtation with the British officers during the occupation of Philadelphia had no very serious political aspect at that time. Whether, as Arnold subsequently alleged, he was sincerely converted to the British cause, it is difficult to say (*Pennsylvania Magazine,* XXIV, 424).

There can be no doubt that he gave military information of the highest importance to the British throughout the summer of 1779 and the following year. He opened with the British headquarters an avenue of communication, the ramifications and extent of which were not dreamed of until the coming of the British Headquarters Papers to America in the winter of 1926. Information as to troop movements, numbers of forces, dispositions of supplies, the coming and the strength of the French fleet and army was all sent regularly to Sir Henry Clinton's headquarters. Elaborate ciphers were employed and a perfect net-work of spies. It is difficult now to avoid the conclusion (which up to this time few historians have been willing to accept) that Mrs. Arnold certainly handled some of the secret dispatches, and that the same spies who carried the dispatches were also used to carry personal messages to André and the other British officers whom she had known in the winter of 1778 in Philadelphia. A document in Clinton's own handwriting, dated Nov. 14, 1792, says "his wife obtained for her services, which was very meritorious, 350 pounds."

By the early summer of 1780, Arnold had obtained from Washington the command of the American post at West Point—the key to the American positions above New York. According to his own words, "I have accepted the command at West Point as a post in which I can render the most essential services"(Arnold to André, July 12, 1780). The price offered by Clinton for Arnold's treason and the surrender of West Point and its garrison was considerable, but not definite. Arnold demanded £20,000 if he succeeded in his treachery, and £10,000 if he came over without being able to betray the fort. A meeting was arranged between Arnold and Maj. John André, the British adjutant-general, who assumed the guise of "Mr. John Anderson." They finally met at a point between the British and American lines on Sept. 21, 1780, and arranged the details of the surrender of West Point. Meantime the British war vessel, *Vulture,* which had brought André up the river was compelled to fall several miles further down because it was fired upon by the American artillery. The result was that André had to ride many miles overland to rejoin his ship while Arnold returned to West Point. In direct violation of Sir Henry Clinton's positive orders, André had changed his uniform for a disguise and carried compromising papers in his stocking. The trip back was long and circuitous and Sept. 23 found André still in the saddle trying to reach the British lines. He was furnished with a pass from Arnold, with which he got by successive American pickets, but on the morning of the 23rd, while still some distance above Dobbs Ferry, on the eastern bank of the Hudson, he was stopped by a party of irregulars. They searched him, found the papers, and suspected his errand. He was taken to the nearest American outpost, where the commander sent a note to Arnold, notifying him of the capture of "Mr. John Anderson," but sent the papers to Gen. Washington, who was at the time approaching West Point for an inspection. Arnold realized he had lost, and fled, leaving his wife in hysterics. He galloped to the river, secured a boat and rowed to the *Vulture,* leaving André to his fate. The unfortunate British adjutant-general was court-martialed, found guilty of being a spy, and executed on Oct. 2, 1780.

Upon arriving at New York, Arnold reported to Clinton, and was received into the British army with the rank of brigadier-general of provincial troops. One of his first acts was to write a vindication of his conduct and an appeal to the American army to follow his example. This was published as a broadside. The British commander sent Arnold off on a marauding expedition into Virginia in December of 1780, which he conducted with skill and ruthlessness. Gov. Jefferson of Virginia offered a reward of 5,000 guineas to any one who would capture Arnold, and several private efforts were made by American officers to kidnap him during the remainder of his stay in America. He returned to New York in June of 1781. In September Clinton tried desperately to create a diversion which would keep the French and Americans away from their projected attack on Cornwallis. He sent Arnold on another marauding expedition to New London in Connecticut. Here Arnold blackened his name still further by attacking his old neighbors, and although he is probably not to blame for the massacre of the American defenders at Fort Griswold, he may fairly be charged with responsibility for the burning of New London, which was an unforeseen result of his intentional setting fire to the public buildings there. In the next month, Cornwallis surrendered at Yorktown, and Great Britain's chances of subduing her former colonies were over.

Mrs. Arnold had gone from West Point to her father in Philadelphia, but she was ordered out by the authorities and joined her husband in New York. In December of 1781 Arnold sailed with his family for England. Upon his arrival there he was consulted upon the conduct of the war and drew up a very able memorandum for the continuance of the conflict. But it was too late. The party of North and Germain, under which he had been induced to desert, went out of power, and Arnold found himself exceedingly unpopular in England. The scorn in which he was held led to some slurring remarks about him by Lord Lauderdale in the House of Lords, and Arnold challenged the offender to a duel. They met in July of 1792, but neither was injured. Lauderdale said something which Arnold took as an apology, and the affair was closed (*Pennsylvania Magazine,* XXV, 169). Of the rest of his life we are well informed by the pathetic letters of his wife. Failing to procure active military service under the new régime, he attempted a number of commercial speculations, which proved in the main unfortunate. He was often absent from England, coming to Canada and to the West Indies as his business dictated. On one occasion he may have visited Detroit (*Diaries of Washington,* IV, 136). He made desperate efforts to secure further rewards from the British for his past services, in which Sir Henry Clinton seconded his demands. Pitt certainly took the matter under consideration, but little was done. The total sum Arnold received from Clinton for the actual treason was £6,315. This he felt was not adequate. There exist letters from Mrs. Arnold to Clinton in which she explains their desperate straits and begs his intercession. She was loyal to her husband, if not to her country, and endured his disgrace with all the troubles which it brought. She and Arnold had four sons and one daughter. All of Arnold's sons served with distinction in the British military and civil services. In 1797 he was granted 13,400 acres of land in Canada, but these appear to have profited him very little. As the Napoleonic Wars grew more serious, he tried again in 1798 to get active service in the British army—but without success. The remainder of his life was unhappy and tragic. He died in London of "dropsy and a disease of the lungs."

[The principal biog. study remains I. N. Arnold's *Life of Benedict Arnold* (1880). Jared Sparks's *Life and Treason of Benedict Arnold* (vol. III of his Lib. of Am. Biog., 1848) was written while personal feeling against Arnold still ran high. Shorter biogs. are G. C. Hill's *Life of Benedict Arnold* (1858) and C. B. Todd's *The Real Benedict Arnold* (1903). J. H. Smith's *Arnold's March from Cambridge to Quebec* (1903) contains Arnold's "Jour. of the Expedition to Canada." Arnold's letters on this expedition are in vol. I of the *Me. Hist. Soc. Colls.* (1865). J. H. Smith's *Our Struggle for the Fourteenth Colony* (1907) is the final word on the Ticonderoga and Quebec campaigns. J. J. Henry, one of the survivors, wrote an *Account of Arnold's Campaign against Quebec* (Albany, 1877). The campaign on the Lakes is best studied in A. T. Mahan's *The Major Operations of the Navies in the War of Am. Independence* (1913). The *Proc. of a Gen. Court Martial for the Trial of Major General Benedict Arnold* was printed in only fifty copies (Philadelphia, 1780), but was later reprinted (N.Y., 1865). Pennsylvania's case against Arnold will be found in *Proc. of the Supreme Executive Council of the State of Pennsylvania, in the Case of Major General Arnold* (Philadelphia, 1779). The *Jours. of the Continental Cong.* (L. C. ed.), vols. I–XVIII, enable us to follow his conflicts with that body. Both the Sparks and Ford editions of Washington's works should be consulted. The most detailed study of the treason is Wm. Abbatt's *The Crisis of the Revolution* (1899). One of the accomplices told his own story in Joshua Hett Smith's *Authentic Narrative of the Causes which led to the Death of Major André* (London, 1808; N.Y., 1809). H. B. Dawson's *Rec. of the Trial of Joshua Hett Smith* (Morrisania, N.Y., 1866) goes into further detail on the same points. *The Proc. of André's Court-Martial* were printed, Philadelphia, 1780; N. Y., 1780; Providence, n.d.; Albany, 1865. Winthrop Sargent's *Life and Career of Major John André* (1861) is still standard. Surprisingly little attention has been paid to L. B. Walker's "Life of Margaret Shippen, the Wife of Benedict Arnold," which is a mine of source material and includes both the Margaret Shippen and the Edward Shippen Correspondence. This large work ran through the *Pa. Mag. of Hist. and Biog.* (1900, 1901, 1902). The same magazine contains much other material about Arnold. Barbé-Marbois studied the treason in his *Complot d'Arnold et de Sir Henry Clinton* (Paris, 1816, reprinted, 1831), which was translated by Robert Walsh in the *Am. Reg.* for 1817, vol. II. James Wilkinson's *Memoirs of My Own Times* (1816) and M. L. Davis's *Memoirs of Aaron Burr* (1855) must be used with caution. Arnold's proclamation *To the Inhabitants of America* (N.Y., 1780) was also printed in the *Royal Gazette* (N. Y., Oct. 11, 1780). Of manuscript material there are the papers found at West Point after Arnold's flight, now in transcript at the Lib. of Cong., the Schuyler and Morgan Papers at the N. Y. Pub. Lib., the Gates Papers at the N.Y. Hist. Soc., and the Papers of the British Headquarters under Sir Henry Clinton, now at the W. L. Clements Lib., University of Michigan.]

R. G. A—s.

ARNOLD, GEORGE (June 24, 1834–Nov. 9, 1865), poet, was born in Bedford St., New York City. Presumably the Rev. George B. Arnold, listed in the city directory of that year as living at No. 119 was his father, but nothing definite is known of his family. From Arnold's third to his fifteenth year his parents lived in Alton, Ill. They then settled at Strawberry Farms, Monmouth County, N. J., near a Fourierite phalanstery, which at the time was in process of dissolution. Arnold was educated at home. His country boyhood made him familiar with aspects of nature which he later turned to account in his serious poetry. Contact with the Fourierites seems to have given him a bent for independent speculation, though he was never in active sympathy with any sect of reformers. In the autumn of 1852 he entered the studio of a portrait painter in New York City, but within two years found his true vocation in literature. His training in painting was not wasted, however, since it enabled him to write art criticism for the press and to illustrate his lighter verse with comic drawings. His caricature of himself in the character of "McArone" is reproduced in the preface to his *Poems* (1886), and another of the sculptor Launt Thompson is included in Ferris Greenslet's *Thomas Bailey Aldrich* (1908). According to William Winter, Arnold was for a short time employed as the sub-editor of a story paper. He soon, however, became a free lance, contributing a large quantity of fluent writing to various newspapers and magazines. He turned out stories, sketches, essays, poems, comic and satirical verse, criticisms of books and paintings, editorial articles, jokes and pointed paragraphs with equal facility. Most of them were published anonymously or under such pseudonyms as "Graham Allen," "George Garrulous," "Pierrot," and "The Undersigned."

His greatest success was attained with a series of papers signed "McArone," begun in *Vanity Fair,* Nov. 24, 1860, continued in the *Leader,* and concluded in the *Weekly Review,* Oct. 14, 1865. The sunny and preposterous absurdity of these burlesques, dealing first with the Italian campaign of 1860, then with the Civil War and miscellaneous topics, delighted the reading public at a time when spontaneous gaiety was at a premium. Arnold's lighter verse, particularly "The Jolly Old Pedagogue," also enjoyed a wide circulation. During the Civil War he served for some time with troops stationed at one of the forts on Governor's Island, N.Y. Early in 1865 his health gave way, and he died at Strawberry Farms on Nov. 9, 1865. A poem by E. C. Stedman commemorates the poet's burial in Greenwood Cemetery.

Arnold was closely associated with the "Bohemians" of Pfaff's beer-cellar, marshaled by Henry Clapp of the *Saturday Press,* and including FitzHugh Ludlow, William Winter, Fitz James O'Brien, and other young writers and artists. Stedman, Aldrich, Whitman, and "Artemus Ward" were occasional visitors at Pfaff's. "Those who met George Arnold," writes Winter, "saw a handsome, merry creature, whose blue eyes sparkled with mirth, whose voice was cheerful, whose manners were buoyant and winning, whose courtesy was free and gay." Among the not always harmonious "Bohemians" he was universally beloved. The Bohemian pose, however, was fatal to one of his easy temper. It encouraged him to take the attitude of a *farceur* and to make no effort to improve his position as an author. He never collected any of his work for book publication and his career from first to last was marked by ineffectiveness.

He contributed a few acting proverbs to Frank Cahill's *Parlor Theatricals* (1859). A comic *Life and Adventures of Jeff. Davis,* by "McArone" appeared in 1865 (chap-book). Two volumes of Arnold's poetry were edited by William Winter: *Drift: a Sea-Shore Idyl and Other Poems* (1866) and *Poems Grave and Gay* (1867). Both together were reissued as *The Poems of George Arnold, Complete Edition* (1886).

[The Memoir and Preface by William Winter in the *Complete Edition* are the chief sources of information. An obituary was published in the *N.Y. Tribune,* Nov. 10, 1865. Other references are W. Winter, *Old Friends* (1909), pp. 52–106, 350; Ferris Greenslet, *Thomas Bailey Aldrich* (1908), p. 38; L. Stedman and G. M. Gould, *Life and Letters of Edmund Clarence Stedman* (1910), I, 365; E. Halloway, *Whitman* (1926), pp. 157, 193.]

G. F. W.

ARNOLD, ISAAC NEWTON (Nov. 30, 1815–Apr. 24, 1884), lawyer, congressman, historian, was born at Hartwick, Otsego County, N.Y. He was the son of Dr. George Washington Arnold and his wife, Sophia M. Arnold, both born in Rhode Island. His grandfather was Thomas Arnold, a soldier of the Revolution. Isaac was educated at local schools. Thrown on his own resources at fifteen he taught school and studied law in the offices of Richard Cooper and Judge E. B. Morehouse at Cooperstown. In 1835 he was admitted to the bar; after a year's practise he came to Chicago in 1836, the year before its incorporation as a city (*Chicago Tribune,* Apr. 24, 1884). Here he formed a law partnership with Mahlon D. Ogden, also a New Yorker, which lasted till 1847 (A. T. Andreas, *History of Chicago,* I, 435–36). His legal practice, both criminal and civil, was large and important. In 1841 he was concerned in the case of Bronson *vs.* Kinzie decided by the United States Supreme Court (1 *Howard,* 311) in accord with his contention that the state stay law (allowing relief from foreclosure if land did not bring two-thirds its appraised value at auction) was unconstitutional (*Illinois State Historical Society Journal,* vol. VII, no. 2, p. 25). As a Democratic politician he opposed repudiation of the state's indebtedness in 1842; he was one of the persons among whom is to be shared the credit for the plan that finally extricated the state from debt. He served in the General Assembly, 1842–45, where he was chairman of the house committee on finance. He was presidential elector for Polk in 1844.

Arnold took an active part in the Free-Soil movement of 1848, going as a delegate to the national and state conventions. He was one of the Chicago committee appointed to draw resolutions of protest against the Fugitive Slave Law in October, 1850 (J. Seymour Currey, *Chicago: Its History and Its Builders,* 1912, I, 415). He was elected to the General Assembly in 1856 as a Republican. In 1860 he was elected to Congress and at once assumed a position of prominence. In December 1861, as chairman of the committee on defense of lakes and rivers, he pressed a measure for enlarging the Illinois and Michigan Canal to permit the passage of warships from the Mississippi to the Lakes. In this connection he was active in securing a National Canal Convention at Chicago in 1863. In January 1865 his measure finally passed the House but failed in the Senate (Arthur C. Cole, *Era of the Civil War,* 1919, pp. 354–56). In his second term he was chairman of the roads and canals committee (*Congressional Globe,* 38 Cong., 1 Sess., p. 18). His record continued to be one of out-spoken hostility to slavery. On Mar. 24, 1862, he introduced a bill to prohibit slavery in every place subject to national authority, which became a law June 19, 1862 (*Ibid.,* 37 Cong., 2 Sess., p. 1340; App., p. 364). He made an able speech in support of the second confiscation act, May 23, 1862 (*Ibid.,* 37 Cong., 2 Sess., App., p. 182). On Feb. 15, 1864, he moved the amendment abolishing slavery in the United States (*Ibid.,* 38 Cong., 1 Sess., p. 659). He served as auditor of the treasury for the Post Office Department, 1865–66.

As his political career ended, his literary career began. In 1866 he published *The History of Abraham Lincoln and the Overthrow of Slavery.* In 1880 he published a *Life of Benedict Arnold.* At his death in 1884 he was on the point of finishing his *Life of Abraham Lincoln.* This is the best known of his historical works. Although frankly eulogistic, it was for some time the best biography available, and has of course to-day the value of a source. Arnold's literary style was clear, simple, and enjoyable. Compared with the standards of his time, his historical workmanship is generally competent. Arnold was one of the founders of the Chicago Historical Society and had procured its charter when a member of the General Assembly in 1857 (Currey, III, 218). He delivered the address dedicating its building, Nov. 19, 1868, and on Dec. 19, 1876, he was elected its president. A series of papers given by him before the Society has been published by it. He was twice married: first, to Catherine E. Dorrance of Pittsfield, Mass., who died Oct. 30, 1839, leaving one child; and second, to her sister, Harriet Augusta Dorrance, by whom he had nine children.

[In addition to the references given above, something is to be gleaned from Arnold's reminiscent addresses: *Abraham Lincoln,* paper read before the Royal Hist. Soc., London, June 16, 1881 (Chicago, 1881); Addresses before Chi. Hist. Soc., Nov. 19, 1868 (1877); *W. B. Ogden; and Early Days in Chicago,* paper read before Chi. Hist. Soc., Dec. 20, 1881 (1882); *Recollections of the Early Chi. and Ill. Bar,* lecture before Chi. Bar Ass., June 10, 1880; *Reminiscences of Lincoln and of Congress during the Rebellion,* lecture before N.Y. Geneal. and Biog. Soc., Apr. 15, 1882; *The Layman's Faith,* paper read before the Chi. Philosophical Soc., Dec. 10, 1883. The *Memorial Address* by E. B. Washburne for the Chi. Hist. Soc., 1889, has to be used with caution due to Washburne's consistent inaccuracy. There is a good but brief sketch by John M. Palmer, in *The Bench and Bar of Illinois,* 1889, vol. I.] T. C. P.

ARNOLD, JONATHAN (Dec. 3, 1741–Feb. 1, 1793), Revolutionary patriot, was born at Providence, R. I. He was descended from a family of early colonists believed to be of Welsh origin. In the Revolutionary assembly of the colony Arnold became a leading member; the decisive event in the birth of the new state was the statute, May 4, 1776, which repealed the oath of allegiance to England, and the original draft of this law is said to be in Arnold's handwriting. This vital statute has been described as a "solemn, deliberate, desperate act of popular sovereignty," and was followed by Rhode Island's coöperation with the other states.

Arnold's services were not confined to legislation. He had studied medicine, and in 1776 he organized the Revolutionary Hospital of Rhode Island, and was its surgeon 1776–81. During the years 1782–84 he was a delegate from Rhode Island to the Continental Congress. This was the period of the unsuccessful effort to strengthen the Articles of Confederation by laying an impost. Rhode Island was a persistent objector, and Arnold's name occurs frequently in the record of the controversy. More significant was his defense in Congress of the new State of Vermont against the claims of New York and New Hampshire, which led to his future career in the Green Mountain State. It must have been in recognition of Arnold's action, that Gov. Chittenden of Vermont in 1776 granted to him and his associates a large tract of land in Orange County (now included in Caledonia County). Thither he removed in 1787, and became the leading founder of St. Johnsbury. His own portion of the grant was 3,900 acres, and he began the settlement, working personally in the cutting of timber, surveying, and building of roads and bridges. Among his other activities, he was a judge in the court of Orange County, one of the early trustees of the University of Vermont, and one of twelve councilors who in 1791 attended the session of the Vermont General Assembly which voted to accept the Federal Constitution of the United States.

Arnold was distinguished in appearance; "of sanguine temperament, independent mind, and positive opinions"; highly respected, and obviously a natural leader. He died at St. Johnsbury, leaving a record of considerable versatility and of unquestionable value in the development of two states. By a singular coincidence he played a prominent part in the history of the last of the original thirteen to ratify the Constitution, and in that of the first of the new states to enter the Federal Union.

[Samuel G. Arnold, *Hist. of R. I.* (1859–60); Edward T. Fairbanks, *Town of St. Johnsbury, Vt.* (1914).]

E. K. A.

ARNOLD, LAUREN BRIGGS (Aug. 14, 1814–Mar. 7, 1888), dairy husbandman, was the eighth child of George and Elizabeth (Grimes) Arnold. He was born in Fairfield, N.Y., where his father came from Rhode Island in 1798 and took a fifty-acre farm. After ending his study in the public school in 1833, Lauren Arnold taught in the winter and did mechanical work in the summer. With limited opportunities he was bent on getting a college education and continued his study at Fairfield Academy. At the age of twenty-seven he entered Union College in the junior class, graduating in 1843. He planned to be a teacher, but his father persuaded him to take over the farm which he operated for a term of years. Here he became specially interested in dairying and spent the rest of his life in the discovery and teaching of better methods of dairy practise. He studied not only the handling of milk and its products but all that related to its production in the care of dairy stock. To facilitate this study he built a model cheese factory on his farm in 1867 and an excellent dairy laboratory. He published his conclusions in *American Dairying* (1876) which was for some time the leading authority on this subject. Some of his opinions met with strong opposition at the time and further studies have shown errors in them, but in the main his work stands justified by experience and is a contribution of great permanent value to the industry. Specially useful were his improvements in the manufacture of cheese, which were extensively adopted in this country and Canada and also in Scotland. He was active in forming the Little Falls Farmers' Club, one of the first in western New York, which acquired a wide reputation. In the meetings of this club he trained himself to become a ready and fluent speaker. In 1874 his health failed and he moved to a farm of five acres near Rochester, N.Y. He wrote extensively for agricultural papers and his services as a teacher and lecturer were often called for in this country and in Canada. In 1885, by invitation of the British Dairymen's Association, he was a delegate from the United States to a conference in London of delegates from nearly all the countries of Europe. In 1876 he was an expert judge in the dairy section at the Centennial Exposition at Philadelphia. He was one of the founders of the Society for the Promotion of Agricultural Science. In 1852 he married Melissa Bishop, who died in 1866. He afterward married Mrs. Elizabeth Woodward, who died about 1881. Two sons survived him.

[*Cultivator and Country Gentleman*, Mar. 15, 1888, p. 214; *Farm Jour.*, May 1888; L. H. Bailey, *Cyc. of Am. Ag.* (1904), IV, 551; *Proc.*, Ninth Ann. Meeting Soc. for the Promotion of Ag. Sci., 1888, p. 11.]

E.H.J.

ARNOLD, LEWIS GOLDING (Jan. 15, 1817–Sept. 22, 1871), Union general, was born in New Jersey and appointed to the Military Academy from that state. Upon his graduation in 1837 he was commissioned in the 2nd Artillery and served with it in the Florida War, in the removal of the Cherokee Nation to the West, and at various northern stations. Accompanying Gen. Scott's army in its campaign against the City of Mexico, he was wounded slightly at the siege of Vera Cruz and severely in storming the bridge-head at Churubusco, and was twice brevetted for gallantry in action. He had further field service against the Seminoles during the hostilities of 1853–56. The beginning of 1861 found him stationed at Fort Independence, in Boston harbor. Just at this time the Washington government showed a flash of spirit, and took measures to hold the southern forts which had not already fallen into secessionist hands. Arnold was sent to Florida to occupy Fort Jefferson, in the Dry Tortugas, which, though commonly referred to in swelling phrases as the Gibraltar of America and the key of the Gulf, was still an unfinished work, ungarrisoned, and with no guns mounted. By tremendous exertions Arnold put it into a state of defense, bringing guns over from Key West, where there was a considerable surplus. As Fort Jefferson was never attacked, its very existence is now generally forgotten; but if the Confederacy had developed a strong navy, or had concluded an alliance with a naval power, the possession of this fortress would have been of high importance to the United States. This should be remembered in estimating the merit of Arnold's achievement. He was promoted to major in May, and in August was transferred to Fort Pickens, which had remained in Unionist hands from the beginning, although the city of Pensacola was held by the enemy. Though a regiment of undisciplined volunteers, largely officered by incompetents, made up the greater part of the garrison, a Confederate raid on Santa Rosa Island, where the fort is situated, was beaten off in October. Arnold was appointed brigadier-general of volunteers, Jan. 24, 1862, and was soon after assigned to the command of the department of Florida. Transferred to New Orleans in October, he drew near to service in the field, but was stricken with apoplexy while reviewing his troops, and on Nov. 10, 1862, was granted sick leave from which he never returned to duty. He was promoted to lieutenant-colonel in the regular army in August 1863, but as it became evident that he was permanently paralyzed he was placed on the retired list, Feb. 8, 1864. Arnold was a cheerful, companionable man, with a strong sense of humor and (as a friend wrote) "a laugh peculiar to himself." He was a strict disciplinarian, but careful and considerate of his men. The high estimate held of him by his superiors suggests that he would have attained distinction in the war if the opportunity had come to him.

[Josiah H. Shinn, "Fort Jefferson and Its Commander," in *Jour. of the Mil. Service Institution,* XLV, 487–97, XLVI, 121–33; G. W. Cullum: *Biog. Reg.* (3rd ed., 1891), I, 669–70; *Official Records,* ser. I, vols. I, VI, XV.]

T. M. S.

ARNOLD, RICHARD (Apr. 12, 1828–Nov. 8, 1882), soldier, born at Providence, R. I., was the son of Sally (Lyman) Arnold and Lemuel Hastings Arnold, governor of Rhode Island, and a descendant of Thomas Arnold who was established in New England by 1635. He entered West Point in 1846, was graduated in 1850, and was commissioned in the artillery. He served with his battery in Florida and California, and was engaged for two years in exploration and road-building in the Northwest. In 1854 he was promoted to first-lieutenant, and the next year was assigned to duty as aide-de-camp to Gen. Wool, with whom he served until his promotion to a captaincy at the beginning of the Civil War. He joined his battery at Washington, and a few days later took it into action at Bull Run, his first battle. Though heavily engaged through the day, the battery was not infected with the general panic. With other troops which preserved their cohesion and discipline, it covered the retreat of the demoralized army, and in doing so was compelled to sacrifice all its guns. "The loss of well-served guns in the defense of a position, or in close support of the other arms, is honorable" (*Drill Regulations for Field Artillery,* 1911, p. 300). Arnold began the Peninsular Campaign, next spring, as chief of artillery in Gen. Franklin's division, and at the very outset was noted for his energy and ability in getting his guns ashore. Through the greater part of the campaign, however, he was not with the artillery, but serving on the staff of the 6th corps, with which he was present at the battles of Savage Station, Glendale, and Malvern Hill. After the withdrawal of the army from the peninsula, illness kept him from the field for some months. He was then selected as chief of artillery of the Department of the Gulf, was appointed brigadier-general of volunteers (Nov. 29, 1862), and departed for New Orleans. His duties in his new position, for a great part of the time, were administrative, but he was in the field during the campaign which ended with the siege and capture of Port Hudson in 1863, and again during the disastrous Red River Expedition in the spring of 1864. In this expedition he was temporarily assigned to duty with the cavalry, and commanded the cavalry division for two months. Immediately afterward he was sent to assist in the siege of Fort Morgan, in Mobile Bay, and with its surrender in August 1864 his field service ended. He was mustered out of the volunteers a year later, and returned to battery duty. Promoted to major in 1875, he served with his regiment for a time, and then on staff duty at Governor's Island, where he died. His promotion to a lieutenant-colonelcy had fallen due only a few days before.

[G. W. Cullum: *Biog. Reg.* (3rd ed., 1891), II, 416–17; *Bull. Ass. Grads. Mil. Acad.* (1883), pp. 52–55; *Official Records,* ser. I, vols. II, XI (pt. 1), XV, XXVI (pt. 1), XXXIV (pts. 1, 2, 3, 4), XLI (pt. 2).]

T. M. S.

ARNOLD, RICHARD DENNIS (Aug. 19, 1808–July 10, 1876), physician, politician, was born in Savannah, Ga., the son of Capt. Joseph Arnold of Rhode Island and Eliza (Dennis) Arnold of New Jersey. After private training in Savannah, he was sent North to complete his education, first at a boarding-school near his mother's home in New Jersey, and later at Princeton College, from which he graduated in 1826. He then went to Philadelphia to take up the study of medicine and graduated with distinction in 1830 from the Medical School of the University of Pennsylvania. From 1830 to 1832 he was resident physician in Blockly Hospital, Philadelphia. In 1832 he returned to Savannah to begin the practise of his profession, and in the same year he was married to Margaret Baugh Stirk.

During the early thirties, while his practise was still relatively small, he became the owner and editor of the Savannah *Georgian,* a Democratic journal, and this position involved him in local and state politics. He soon became a leader of the "Union Democrats" of lower Georgia, taking a strong stand in his paper against the nullification movement of 1833. In 1839 he represented Chatham County in the House of Representatives at Milledgeville, and in 1842 was elected to the state Senate. He held many municipal offices, being four times elected mayor and serving at various times as city health officer, chairman of the board of aldermen, and chairman of the board of education. Because of his professional duties he consistently refused to enter the broader field of national politics. He did serve, however, as a delegate to several national Democratic conventions and maintained personal contacts with many national party leaders. He supported the secession movement in 1860, as a last resort against northern aggression. As mayor of Savannah he surrendered that city to Gen. Sherman in December 1864, and immediately took an open stand for peace, in order to prevent further unnecessary bloodshed. He became one of the "peace party" leaders of the state, and in the spring of 1865 led a delegation to Washington to request of President Johnson the establishment of a provisional government for Georgia.

Meanwhile, however, Arnold's professional interests always received his first consideration—he himself regarding his political activities as "mere episodes, not to be followed out." He carried on a large personal practise, was a contributor to medical journals, and an active worker in all fields of interest to his profession. His chief scientific studies related to the yellow and "bilious" fevers, and he rendered especially heroic service to Savannah in the terrible yellow-fever epidemic of 1854. He was one of the directors of the municipal hospital and served for fifteen years as president of the local medical society. With several other physicians he established in the forties the Savannah Medical College, in which he was professor of theory and practise for some twenty years, during which time he strove earnestly against a tendency to lower the standards of medical education. In 1846 he helped to found the American Medical Association, of which he became the first secretary, and in which he was also a member of the first committee on professional ethics. In 1851 he was elected vice-president of the Association. In the same year he helped to organize and himself wrote the constitution of the Medical Association of Georgia. In his personal life he displayed great devotion to his immediate family and never entirely recovered from the loss of his beloved wife in 1850. He died in Savannah, in the same room in which he was born.

Arnold was tall but far from handsome, popular in society, something of a *bon vivant,* and a connoisseur of old wines. He was widely read, rationalistic in his religious thinking, and a member of a small Unitarian group in Savannah,—an unusual type of person in the South of his day. Personally unselfish, he suffered several severe financial losses as a result of a too generous confidence in his associates,—as he himself put it, he "was always a fool in money matters."

[Sketch in *Trans. Am. Medic. Ass.,* XXIX, 615–18; Charles C. Jones, O. F. Vedder, and Frank Weldon, *Hist. of Savannah* (1890), pp. 439–41; Adelaide Wilson, *Historic and Picturesque Savannah* (1889), pp. 128, 153, 158; *Savannah Morning News,* July 11, 12, 1876.]

R. H. S.

ARNOLD, SAMUEL (*c.* 1838–1906). [See Booth, John Wilkes.]

ARNOLD, SAMUEL GREENE (Apr. 12, 1821–Feb. 13, 1880), historian, was born in Providence, R. I., at the corner of South Main and Planet Sts., in the house said to have been the rendezvous of the patriots who burned the *Gaspée*. He was the son of Samuel Greene Arnold and Frances (Rogers) Arnold, and was descended from Thomas Arnold, one of the earliest settlers of Providence. The family's wealth, his father and grandfather both being prominent Rhode Island merchants, permitted him to enjoy the advantages offered by private tutors, private schools in Providence, and Dr. Muhlenberg's school at Flushing, N. Y. Although ill health prevented his remaining at Brown University, which he entered in 1836, a trip to Europe, in company with the Rev. Dr. Hague, contributed to his education until he was able to return to the completion of his college course, which he finished in 1841. Following a short period spent in the counting-house of James T. Rhodes, he visited St. Petersburg, Russia. Thence he returned to Harvard Law School, secured the degree of LL.B. in 1845, and was admitted to the Rhode Island bar. A gentleman of wealth and leisure, he spent a great deal of his time in travel, including Europe, the North Cape, Egypt, Syria, and South America. In England and France he examined and copied records and state papers relative to Colonial history, having already planned, while in law school, to write the history of Rhode Island. This work, entitled *History of Rhode Island and Providence Plantation* (1859), while written in a heavy style, was scholarly and thorough.

Arnold's services to his state included three terms as lieutenant-governor, the last interrupted, however, by his selection as senator to complete an unexpired term. Although an ardent champion of freedom and union, he went as a delegate to the Peace Conference of 1861. The attempt at compromise having failed, he served throughout the war as aide-de-camp to Gov. Sprague with the rank of colonel, commanding a battery of light artillery. Always interested in public charities, he acted as trustee for the state reform school and for Butler Hospital, and contributed largely to the Charitable Baptist Society, of which he was president. His later years, mainly devoted to historical research and writing, were spent in his home, "Lazy Lawn," at Middletown, R. I. His historical addresses, read upon various commemorative occasions and before the Rhode Island Historical Society, which he served also as president, were of conspicuous merit, especially his *Memorial Papers on A. C. Greene, William Staples, and Usher Parsons.* Other works worthy of note were his *Historical Sketch of Middletown* (1880), and the centennial addresses on Providence and on the First Baptist Meeting House.

[Sketch by Edwin M. Stone in *R. I. Hist. Soc. Proc.,* 1879–80, pp. 93–96; see also *Biog. Cyc. of R. I.,* and *Providence Daily Jour.,* Feb. 16, 17, 1880. Arnold's photograph, many of his literary contributions, his autograph, and the many memorials published at his death, are in the Rider and Church Colls. of the John Hay Lib. in Brown Univ.]

H. F. K.

ARRINGTON, ALFRED W. (Sept. 17, 1810–Dec. 31, 1867), lawyer, poet, was third in the line of descent from Maj. Arrington, an ex-British army officer, who had purchased a large estate in North Carolina and whose descendants continued to be associated with that state for many years. His father, H. Archibald Arrington, a Methodist minister, married Miss Moore, a lady of Highland Scotch origin. Alfred Arrington was born in Iredell Co., N. C. He received a good education, and absorbed while still young an extraordinary amount of miscellaneous knowledge. In 1819 he accompanied his father to Arkansas, then almost a wilderness, and in 1828 became an itinerant Methodist preacher. Possessing a natural gift of eloquence, he met with great success. For five years he traveled, preaching through Arkansas, Indiana, and Missouri, but being assailed with doubts as to the truths of religion, he abandoned the ministry in 1834 and commenced to study law. He was admitted to the Missouri bar in 1835, but moved to Arkansas, where he acquired a flourishing practise, and was elected a member of the state legislature. He had no interest in politics, however, and on completion of his term went to Texas. In 1847 he visited the East, and, using the pseudonym "Charles Summerfield," published *The Desperadoes of the South West,* an eloquently written but lurid picture of lynch law drawn from personal experience. He remained in Boston and New York for two years, contributing *Sketches of the South and South West* to the newspapers and writing *The Mathematical Harmonies of the Universe,* a somewhat abstruse essay which was translated into French and German. Returning to Texas in 1849, he was elected judge of the 12th (Rio Grande) judicial district of that state in 1850. This position he retained for five years, but the climate commenced to affect his health and he was compelled to resign in 1856. He moved to New York, engaged in literary work, and published *The Rangers and Regulators of the Tanaha* (1856), again using the pseudonym "Charles Summerfield." This novel, in which he essayed to give a picture of the transition stage of Southwestern life, was somewhat heavy in style and sentiment, occasionally relieved by brilliance of language. In 1857 he went to the Northwest, settled in Chicago, and there resumed the practise of law. His ornate oratory appealed to Western audiences and juries, whilst his thorough knowledge of law and innate dialectical skill enabled him to achieve outstanding success before the appellate tribunals, particularly in constitutional cases. "Although sometimes eccentric, his briefs were models and his arguments cogent" (John M. Parker, *The Bench and Bar of Illinois,* 1899, II, 162). He died in Chicago, having shortly before abandoned his skepticism and been received into the Catholic faith. During his later years, as a relaxation from professional work and with no idea of publication, he had composed a number of poems, and these were collected and published after his death under the title, *Poems by Alfred W. Arrington* (1869). Of brilliant ability and altogether exceptional powers of oratory, he was a disappointment as far as actual attainment was concerned. The greater part of his life was passed upon the frontier. He disliked the restraints of society and lived, as far as an active professional career would permit, a solitary life, and the instability of purpose which distinguished him up to middle age was an effective obstacle to his attainment of definite eminence in either literature or law.

[The chief authority for the incidents of his career is the memoir written by his wife and prefixed to the posthumous edition of his *Poems.* This work also contains a somewhat labored estimate of his character as a lawyer and poet by C. C. Bonney; see also Usher F. Linden, *Reminiscences of the Early Bench and Bar of Ill.* (1879), p. 234, and J. M. Wilson, *Memorial to Alfred W. Arrington* (1869).]

H. W. H. K.

ARTHUR, CHESTER ALAN (Oct. 5, 1830–Nov. 18, 1886), President of the United States, was born at Fairfield, Franklin County, Vt., the oldest son among the seven children of Rev. William Arthur [*q.v.*] of Ballymena, County Antrim, Ireland, a Scotch-Irish Baptist clergyman. After his succession to the presidency, an unfriendly writer, A. P. Hinman, went to much pains in compiling a little book, *How a British Subject Became President of the United States* (1884). The argument of Hinman was that the clerical father, who practised variously as parson and teacher and who had married a Vermont girl, Malvina Stone, was in the habit of taking positions indifferently on either side of the Vermont-Canadian boundary. Hinman alleged that the oldest son of William and Malvina Arthur was born in Canada in 1828; and that a second son, who died in infancy, was born in Fairfield, Vt., in 1830. He further alleged that Chester A. Arthur, who was the elder son, and hence a Canadian by birth, had appropriated the birthday of his younger brother; and that the appropriation took place definitely after the nomination of Arthur for the office of Vice-President in 1880, when he made a secret trip to Canada to make sure that no conflicting public records were there to disprove his story. No opinion appears to have been affected by this attack; and Chauncey M. Depew, who ought to have known of it, declared in 1927 that he had never even heard of it.

Young Arthur attended Union College at Schenectady, N. Y., where he was graduated in 1848. He taught school and studied law, and was a successful practitioner in New York City before the opening of the Civil War. He had meanwhile married in 1859 Ellen Lewis Herndon (1837–80), daughter of an officer of the U. S. Navy. Arthur had no record of service with troops during the Civil War, but he performed administrative duties that were rated highly. An active Republican from the organization of the party, he was closely associated with the war governor of New York, Edwin D. Morgan, and held by appointment of the latter the posts of engineer-in-chief, inspector-general, and quartermaster-general of the State of New York. In the last capacity he had to carry heavy burdens that called for administrative skill and honesty. The volunteers for the army of the United States enlisted locally, and the states were called upon to receive and equip them in the first instance. Later they were turned over to the United States, and eventually the states were reimbursed for their outlay for clothing and maintenance. The largest single group of volunteers came from New York, and Arthur as quartermaster-general was called upon to organize and administer an extensive service. With this done, he turned over to his Democratic successor in 1863 a running department; and retired to private life with a detailed knowledge of personal and political matters affecting his whole state. He did not share in the attack upon and exposure of the Tweed ring, but held for a time an office created by it. In November 1871 President Grant recognized his importance as a working part of the Republican organization by making him collector of the Port of New York, where for seven years he was responsible for the honest handling of most of the customs revenue of the United States, and for the political utilization of above 1,000 employees who by long precedent had been the effective units of the Republican organization of the city and state.

It was Arthur's misfortune to have been trained in a school of practical politics that came under fire as American standards changed between 1869 and 1883. No trace of scandal attached itself to his private life or his capacity as a public servant. But he believed and practised, with his contemporaries, the theory that underlay the spoils system. The New York Custom House was honestly run, but it was over-staffed with clerks and laborers who recognized the obligation upon them to attend party caucuses and conventions, and to get out the vote upon election days; and who thought it no sin to slack on the government job from which they derived their pay. Arthur was incapable of poor administration; during his incumbency the turnover of employees for political reasons was lessened far below its average of the preceding decade; and yet he, like his predecessors, viewed the Custom House as a branch of the New York political machine whose leader was Senator Roscoe Conkling. Its virtues as a political establishment, however, suddenly became a liability when in 1876 the Republican party nominated and seated in the presidency Gov. Rutherford B. Hayes of Ohio, who knew neither Conkling nor the professional Republican politicians, and whose mind and heart were filled with desires for a merit system in the conduct of the Government of the United States. John Sherman, who became secretary of the treasury, and thereby Arthur's chief, was under no impulse to uphold the power of the Conkling crowd, and was genuinely interested in removing some of the worst results of politics from the Federal civil service. An investigation of the New York Custom House was undertaken early in the new administration; and in June the tenor of the régime was indicated by Hayes's executive order directing civil servants to refrain from participation in the management of parties and campaigns. Alonzo B. Cornell, Naval Officer of the Port of New York, and Arthur's associate there, was also state chairman of the Republican organization. He resigned neither post. Senator Conkling, who was abroad on vacation, hurried home to help Cornell and Arthur fight the President and defend their party machine. And in the Republican state convention, held in September 1877, open defiance to the program of Hayes was declared.

Hayes met the opposition firmly. The commission investigating the Custom House reported its over-supply of help, and its political activity. The President accordingly nominated to the Senate in November a set of new officers for the Custom House. He was restrained from removing Arthur and Cornell out of hand by the Tenure of Office Act (1867) that Congress had enacted to hobble Andrew Johnson. Conkling succeeded in defeating the confirmation of the new appointees on Dec. 12, 1877. Hayes was forced to accept the fact of defeat, but he did not yield to it. Immediately upon the adjournment of Congress in the following July he exercised his legal right to suspend Arthur and Cornell, and to appoint substitutes to act until the Senate should have had a chance to reject or confirm them. The next session of the Senate overrode Conkling's pleas for senatorial courtesy, and permitted Hayes to fill the Custom House places with men of his own choice. Arthur and Cornell became martyrs to their political devotion. New York as a state supported

Conkling's contention that the New York jobs were perquisites of the New York senators; it elected Cornell to the governorship and reëlected Conkling to the Senate in 1879; and two years later elected as Conkling's junior associate in the Senate his political lieutenant, Thomas Collier Platt.

At the Republican National Convention in 1880 the New York group of "stalwarts" labored long and firmly for the renomination of Gen. U. S. Grant. Defeated in this, they at least made impossible the nomination of any of Grant's avowed rivals; although Garfield, the winner, came from the "half-breed" faction which had originally been divided in the convention between Blaine and Sherman. To sweeten the dose of defeat for the followers of Gen. Grant, Arthur was nominated as vice-president. So far from being placated by the recognition accorded him in the person of the martyr of the Custom House, Conkling remained lukewarm through the canvass of 1880, and gave only a grudging support to the ticket of Garfield and Arthur, which was none the less installed at Washington, Mar. 4, 1881. In three weeks the battle of the patronage was on again, as Garfield tried to make nominations to the same Custom House posts to please himself, while Conkling used every effort to maintain his privilege to dictate appointments within his state. He now had Platt in the Senate to help him; and Arthur in the chair of the vice-president. The latter was much in the chair,—so much that he did not vacate it during the short Senate session in March 1881, nor give an opportunity for the Republican majority of one to elect a president *pro tempore*. On May 14, 1881, Conkling resigned his seat in the Senate, and appealed to the legislature of his state against the claim of the President to the right to appoint. Platt, hardly settled in his seat, resigned as well, gaining thereby the nickname "me too" as he followed his chief to the test of strength. He followed him as well to private life, for in spite of the fact that Vice-President Arthur accompanied Conkling and Platt to Albany and worked for their vindication and reelection, the legislature filled their places with other men. While the contest was on, Garfield was murdered by a crazy office-seeker, who further muddied the political situation by declaring noisily that he was a "stalwart" and had committed the murder in order to make Arthur President. Garfield lingered between life and death from July 2 until Sept. 19, when Arthur took over the powers and duties of the presidency, burdened by the scandal of Garfield's assassination, and by the wide belief that he was only a spoilsman and machine politician.

The presidential administration of Arthur was dignified, honorable, and as intelligently constructive as the even division of politics would permit. He looked the part of President, as few have done. Six feet two in height, well-proportioned and heavily built, with the shaven chin and side whiskers that his generation affected, he carried himself with constant dignity. He dressed with scrupulous care, and at times had the newly imported epithet of "dude" hurled against him. He was also, said the *World* (June 9, 1880), "one of the best salmon fishers in the country." His wife having died during the preceding year, the White House was directed for him by a sister, Mrs. John E. McElroy. For the first time since the Civil War it became the center of generous and stately hospitality. Those who had expected that the Custom House crowd would make the White House a loafing-place were happily deceived; while, as the months wore on, the members of the old organization came to feel themselves betrayed. They could not understand why Arthur did not bring into the national government the spoils system of his earlier political experience. When, instead of this, he gave immediate support to a proposed reform of the civil service, and consistent backing to the bill that was passed in 1883, they were at first bewildered and then indignant.

It was not an easy administration to direct. Arthur reconstructed the cabinet during the winter of 1881–82, but his personal appointees did not act as partisans in office. In neither house of Congress was there a good working Republican majority, and, in fact, after the election of 1882 the Democrats controlled the House of Representatives, electing John G. Carlisle, a Kentucky tariff reformer, as speaker. The most pressing questions had to do with the large and embarrassing surplus revenue in the national treasury, the rising interest in tariff reform, the movement for civil service reform which was much accentuated by the death of Garfield, and the pending prosecutions of the Star Route thieves, the willingness of Congress to spend lavishly upon local improvements, the control of immigration, and the rebuilding of the American navy. The surplus in the treasury was the product of the high tariff that had hung over from the Civil War, and the swollen importations that had come when financial stability and resumption of specie payments arrived in 1877. This surplus, for the four fiscal years 1879–82, averaged over eighty millions a year. Even before the resumption of specie payments a movement for tariff reform, based upon the idea of free trade, had made its appearance. The Democratic party, generally disposed to attack the protective tariff, made the existence of a large surplus a ground of special grievance. A tariff commission was created early in 1882, to report in December upon a reduction of revenue without changing the fundamental theory of the tariff. By the date of its report the elections of 1882 had shown a popular swing toward the Democratic party, and the need for a genuine revision became great, if only for party reasons. But the lobbies of the protected interests were so effective that the tariff act of 1883 accomplished little in the way of drawing off Democratic fire; and the issue ripened for the campaign of 1884.

The Star Route frauds, hinted at while Hayes was president, were uncovered before the death of Garfield; and the latter had dismissed from the service of the United States the post office official within whose jurisdiction they had been committed. They involved a complicated plot to juggle the mail contracts upon the horse-drawn mail routes (known in post-office language as the "Star Routes") and to readjust the tables of compensation so that the corrupt contractors might receive unwarranted profits. A ring of contractors was uncovered; showing that great numbers of the contracts were let to political bidders who subsequently sublet the actual carriage of the mails while dividing among themselves the illicit profits. The secretary of the Republican national committee, an ex-senator named Dorsey, was implicated in the prosecutions, and since he had in 1880 hurried to Indiana in the closing days of the campaign to carry that state for Garfield and Arthur it was easy to make it appear that the Republican victory of that year had been aided by successful corruption. A banquet had been given Dorsey (*New York Herald,* Feb. 12, 1881), with Gen. Grant in the chair, and with Vice-President-elect Arthur there to raise a smile about the secret means by which Dorsey carried Indiana. The men under suspicion defended themselves not only in their trials but before public opinion. They threatened, if prosecuted, to carry down with them the reputation of Garfield and to show who were the beneficiaries of their work. The trials were continued under Arthur, with vigor but without effective convictions. The criminals escaped, but attention was drawn to the scandalous condition of the civil service and of the national government in which frauds could occur. Arthur's earnestness in the prosecutions and in reform was enough to lose him his former followers, but failed to secure for him the support of the leaders of the reform movement. By 1882, in New York, he was offering for governor his secretary of the treasury, Charles J. Folger, and fighting his old associate, Alonzo B. Cornell, who still had the backing of the Conkling machine. Folger gained the Republican nomination, but was defeated for election by the Democratic candidate, Grover Cleveland of Buffalo.

In other matters of administration, Arthur showed independence and conscience. He vetoed a Chinese exclusion bill that ran counter to an existing treaty agreement with China. He vetoed also a river and harbor appropriation bill in 1882 because of its wasteful allotment of public funds for improper local purposes. This was passed over his veto by a Congress impatient with reform, and lessened Arthur's hold upon the professional political group. In non-contentious matters, he gave his approval to the early laws by which the first steps were taken for the building of a modern American navy to supersede the obsolete navy of Civil War construction.

The natural desire to succeed himself and to receive from his party and the people a vote of approval for his course led Arthur to hope that he might gain the Republican nomination for president in 1884. Lacking the enthusiastic support of the reform element, which turned finally to Senator Edmunds of Vermont, or any support from the Blaine element, which was able to dominate the convention, his candidacy never progressed beyond its early and hopeful stages. He was later accused, unjustly it seems, of working against the party ticket in the canvass. He left office with the respect if not the affection of the people, and died early in the administration of his successor.

[There are no good materials for a biog. of Arthur. A few unimportant papers are in the Lib. of Cong., but most of his correspondence is supposed to have been destroyed. Autograph collectors have found it hard to discover his holograph letters. The tendency of the historians, in gen. works, has been to treat him better than his contemporaries did. A friendly eulogy is William E. Chandler's *Address on the Occasion of the Completion . . . of a Monument and Tablet to Mark the Birthplace of President Chester A. Arthur* (Concord, N. H., 1903). The reports of the Custom House investigation are in *House Ex. Doc. 8,* 45 Cong., 1 Sess., and *House Ex. Doc. 25,* 45 Cong., 2 Sess.] F. L. P—n.

ARTHUR, PETER M. (1831–July 17, 1903), labor leader, arrived in America from Paisley, Scotland, in 1842 at the age of eleven years. His boyhood was passed on an uncle's farm in New York, where he received only a meager common school education. He began independent work on a farm at six dollars a month. Later he bought a horse and went into the carting business in Schenectady, but this proved hardly more lucrative. At eighteen he secured work as an engine wiper with the New York Central Railroad and was soon promoted to locomotive engineer. His family name was Peter McArthur, but through an error it was entered on the pay-roll as Peter

M. Arthur and so it remained. As an engineer he became active in his union, held local offices, and was delegate to several national conventions. He was associated with the Brotherhood of Locomotive Engineers from its inception in 1863. In 1874 he was elected Grand Chief of the order, an office he held continuously until his death. He built up the Brotherhood into one of the strongest and most conservative of labor unions. It always maintained independence of other unions and selected its own policies, at the same time establishing cordial relations with others. Consequently, among Arthur's critics were the more radical leaders who accused him of playing into the hands of his employers and "capitalists" generally; and the officials of the American Federation of Labor, who said that his "chief mistake consisted in his policy of isolation from the general labor movement" (*American Federationist,* Sept. 1903, p. 840). At the time of his taking office the Brotherhood had been little more than a benevolent and insurance society. Arthur made it an aggressive agent for collective bargaining. In general he declared against strikes; but there were strikes and successful ones. In every case he had to be convinced that a strike was necessary. Consequently he went into a strike with the full support of his followers. No unsuccessful strikes are attributed to him. He was known, therefore, as "an able organizer and a formidable fighter." An associate editor of *The Labor Movement: The Problem of Today* (1887), prepared under the editorship of George E. McNeill, he contributed to the volume an article entitled "The Rise of Railroad Organization." Through real-estate speculations in the city of Cleveland he acquired a comfortable fortune in his later years. His death came suddenly. At a district convention in Winnipeg he was responding to the presentation of a floral tribute when he was stricken with heart failure and died in the middle of a sentence.

[*Lit. Digest,* Aug. 1, 1903, p. 127; *Outlook,* July 25, 1903, p. 725; *Independent,* July 23, 1903, p. 1710; *Locomotive Engineers Mo. Jour.,* Aug. 1903, pp. 568–72, Sept. 1903, p. 630.]

G. G. G.

ARTHUR, TIMOTHY SHAY (June 6, 1809–Mar. 6, 1885), editor and author, the grandson of Timothy Shay, a Revolutionary officer, was born on a farm near Newburgh, Orange County, N. Y. The family was large and his parents' means limited. While he was an infant they removed to the vicinity of West Point, and his first recollections were of Fort Montgomery on the Hudson. In 1817 occurred another removal, this time to Baltimore. The boy was placed in the public schools, but proved exceedingly dull and slow, requiring several months to master the principle of simple addition. Upon his teacher's advice, he was taken from school and apprenticed to a watchmaker. Except for a brief attendance at night school his formal tuition now ceased, but he became an omnivorous reader. Before completing his apprenticeship, the combination of bench work and night reading so injured his sight that he never entered his trade. A friend obtained him light employment as a clerk in a Baltimore counting-room, and his ample leisure he employed in scribbling verse and sketches. Meanwhile, he had joined the first temperance society in Maryland, and, though not himself a teetotaler, had become a convinced enemy of saloons. In 1833 seeking to improve his income, he went west as agent for a Baltimore bank, but was recalled by its failure. By now he had begun to find that writing was a vocation rather than an avocation. Baltimore was the seat at that time of two distinct literary groups. One, the older, was led by John P. Kennedy, William Gwynn, and Lambert A. Wilmer. The younger group included Arthur, Dr. Nathan C. Brooks, Rufus Dawes, and W. H. Carpenter. Both groups had contacts with Edgar Allan Poe, who was in Baltimore 1831–35. Arthur therefore did not lack encouragement and advice in his early literary efforts (Hervey Allen, *Israfel: The Life and Times of Edgar Allan Poe,* 1926, I, 353). After his return from the West he became editor of the short-lived *Baltimore Athenæum.* We then hear of him as having editorial charge of a succession of ephemeral literary enterprises. He followed Poe's friend John H. Hewitt as editor of the *Baltimore Saturday Visitor;* later (1838–39) he was associated with Carpenter and J. N. McJilton in editing the *Baltimore Book* and the *Baltimore Literary Magazine;* in 1840 Duff Green placed him in charge of the *Baltimore Merchant,* a Harrison campaign daily.

Arthur's contributions to *Godey's Lady's Book* had begun in the late thirties, and he had found a ready market in it and other magazines for domestic tales of a moralizing tendency. Leaving Baltimore in 1841, he went to Philadelphia and began pouring tales, essays, and verse into *Godey's, Graham's Magazine,* the *Saturday Courier,* and the newspapers. He was now fully enlisted in the rising temperance movement, and his first book of importance (1842) was *Six Nights with the Washingtonians: A Series of Original Temperance Tales.* In 1845 he ventured to establish a monthly literary magazine called *Arthur's Ladies' Magazine,* which by the standards of the time had some genuine merit, but failed to attain a large circulation, and was soon abandoned. His pen had meanwhile never stopped. In 1845 he brought out *Married and Single: or Marriage and Celibacy Contrasted,* a story to prove that celibacy is "opposed to every law of God and Man," and results in misery. In 1847 appeared *The Lady at Home,* and in 1848 *The Maiden,* the latter a novelette demonstrating that girls may pay a fearful price if they do not investigate carefully the moral antecedents of the men they marry. His ambitions in the magazine world remained strong, and in 1850 he began the publication of a weekly, devoted half to fashion and half to letters, called *Arthur's Home Gazette.* It achieved a warm public favor; in 1853 it became a monthly, *Arthur's Home Magazine,* and Arthur was still editing it at his death. Just after the Civil War (1867) he began the publication of the *Children's Hour,* an illustrated juvenile periodical which also attained a high circulation. Arthur was considered to have a marked talent for juvenile tales. From time to time he embarked upon other magazine enterprises. Thus he attempted in 1869 an eclectic review, *Once A Month,* modeled after *Littell's Living Age,* which lasted only a year. He at once followed it by *The Workingman,* a monthly journal for farmers and mechanics, which was intended to give these readers moral tales and instructive articles as a substitute for such "sensation" magazines as *Bonner's New York Ledger.* It gained a following, but Arthur shortly sold it. Such business ventures did not check the steady flow of didactic books, some of them astonishingly popular, from his pen. By 1875 there was a list of some seventy titles. *Pride and Prudence, or The Married Sisters,* in 1850, employed his favorite device of contrast. So did *Sparing to Spend; or, The Loftons and Pinkertons* (1853). These were tracts against extravagance, vanity, worldliness, and disregard of the precepts of religion. In *The Wedding Guest: A Friend of the Bride and Bridegroom,* he presented another anticipation of the Laura Jean Libbey school of sugared advice upon matters of domestic felicity. The flow of temperance stories was constant, and he edited such collections as *The Crystal Fount, For All Seasons* (1850), two volumes of tales and verse. But his greatest success was achieved in 1854 with *Ten Nights in a Barroom and What I Saw There.*

This volume at once leaped to an enormous circulation. Its sale in the fifties was second only to that of *Uncle Tom's Cabin.* Like Mrs. Stowe's book it was dramatized and played throughout much of the country with great success; indeed, it is still sold and played. It satisfied the appetite for the sensational and lurid, and yet was endorsed by all the clergy. Dealing with a once-happy village, it narrated the sad ruin wrought by the "Sickle and Sheaf," Simon Slade's tavern. Its characters included the drunkard, Joe Morgan; his noble wife, Fanny, and angelic little daughter Mary; Gambler Green, who met a dark and terrible death; Judge Hammond, wrecked by drink; and Frank Slade, who in a drunken passion killed his father. Few Sunday-school libraries were considered complete without a copy. It was supplemented in 1872 with *Three Years in a Mantrap,* which describes the evils of drink in a great city. The beginnings of the Woman's Christian Temperance Union crusade brought forth *Woman to the Rescue* (1874), a characteristic story of saloons closed by praying church-workers. Among Arthur's later publications in this field were *Strong Drink: The Cause and the Cure,* the first part of which was fiction and the second part a sketchy history of the temperance movement; and *The Strike at Tivoli Mills* (1879), a product of the industrial upheaval of 1877, which traced the workingman's chief miseries to drink. Arthur's other books covered a wide range, from such didactic works as *The Old Man's Bride; or, The Lesson of the Day,* to the "cabinet histories" of various states which he and W. H. Carpenter hastily compiled from obvious sources and published between 1850 and 1856. In *Cast Adrift* (1873) he included an attack upon the continuance of the lottery evil in American cities. From first to last he was an advocate of temperance by education rather than temperance by prohibitory legislation, and he did not support coercive enactments upon the subject. But for thirty years following 1840 his influence in the movement against liquor was powerful, and he accomplished quite as much with his pen as men like John B. Gough did from the platform.

At Arthur's death in Philadelphia he was still actively engaged in writing and editing. He had married, in 1836, Ellen Alden, a daughter of Capt. James Alden of Portland, Me., and a sister of Rear Admiral James Alden of the United States Navy. To them were born five sons and two daughters, of whom four sons and one daughter survived their father. The death in 1862 of the older daughter had been a sorely felt affliction. Arthur was a leading member of the Swedenborgian Church of Philadelphia. At times he occupied minor civic positions, being a member of the executive committee of the Centennial Exhibition in 1876. But his title to remembrance rests upon his temperance fiction, and above all upon his *Ten Nights in a Barroom.*

[The above is based largely on family information. Arthur prefaced a "brief autobiography" to his *Lights and Shadows of Real Life* (1867). A pamphlet sketch, *T. S. Arthur, His Life and Work, by One Who Knows Him,* was published in 1873. There are short sketches in

Scharf and Westcott, *Hist. of Phila.* (1888), II, 1157–58, and in E. P. Oberholtzer, *Lit. Hist. of Phila.* (1906), p. 233. The best obituary appeared in the *Phila. Public Ledger,* Mar. 7, 1885. An etched portr. of Arthur is published in Hervey Allen's *Israfel* (1926), I, 353.]

A. N.

ARTHUR, WILLIAM (Dec. 5, 1797–Oct. 27, 1875), Baptist clergyman, antiquarian, was born at "The Draen" near Ballymena, County Antrim, Ireland, the only son of Alan and Eliza McHarg Arthur. After a thorough preliminary training, he entered Queen's College, Belfast, and was graduated from that institution at the early age of eighteen. Deciding to seek a career in the United States, he sailed from Liverpool to New York, and from there went to Vermont, where he attempted to earn a living by teaching school, at the same time studying law in the office of Cornelius P. Van Ness at Burlington. He soon resolved, however, to prepare himself for the ministry and began preaching in various Baptist churches. On Apr. 12, 1821, he married Malvina Stone, by whom he had seven children, of whom the second, Chester Alan Arthur [*q.v.*], future President of the United States, was born at Fairfield, Vt. Family tradition interestingly pictures William Arthur's early efforts as a Baptist preacher in this town. He at first preached in the district school-house, but his ability and eloquence soon led to a change because the building was too small to hold the crowds that gathered to hear him. A spacious barn in the neighborhood was secured, and here the young Irishman preached to a congregation seated on slabs placed on the barn floor, while the deacons and older men sat in the stalls for the horses and cattle, and the young people were grouped on the edges of the haymows above. Arthur continued to preach in various Vermont churches—Burlington, Jericho, Williston, Richford, Pownal, Waterville, and Hinesburgh—until 1835, when he removed to New York. Here he labored in the ministry successively at York, Perry, Greenwich, Schenectady, Lansingburgh, Hoosic, West Troy, and Albany. In the last city, he was pastor of the State Street Baptist Church from 1857 to 1864, when he retired, to reside at Newtonville, N. Y., and to devote the remainder of his life chiefly to literary pursuits. Here he died on Oct. 27, 1875.

Arthur was a student of the classics, especially of antiquities. When living in Schenectady he began the publication of a magazine with the lengthy title of *The Antiquarian, and General Review: comprising Whatever is Useful and Instructive in Ecclesiastical or Historical Antiquities; Serving as a Book of Useful Reference, on Subjects of Research and Curiosity.* This work he edited through four volumes, the last two being published at Lansingburgh. It contained articles quoted from historical and antiquarian reviews, accounts of recent discoveries, and some original contributions of merit, especially those written by himself on Irish antiquities and on the derivation of proper names. In 1857 he published *An Etymological Dictionary of Family and Christian Names, with an Essay on their Derivation and Import,* a scholarly work much in advance of anything written on the subject up to that time.

[The main source for his biog. is the excellent obituary in the *Albany Evening Jour.,* Oct. 29, 1875. The various Vermont and New York county histories have brief references to his pastorates, and the biogs. of his noted son, President Arthur, contain material regarding the father.]

C. S. B.

ASBOTH, ALEXANDER SANDOR (Dec. 18, 1811–Jan. 21, 1868), Union soldier, was born in Keszthely in the county of Zala, Hungary. He served in the Austrian army, and was engaged later in engineering and in the law. In the great Hungarian insurrection of 1848–49 he fought under Kossuth, shared with him his exile and internment, and accompanied him to the United States. Like many other central European revolutionary exiles, he became an American citizen, and at the beginning of the Civil War he was appointed an officer by reason of his military experience. In the autumn of 1861 he was on the staff of Gen. Frémont, and in the following winter he commanded a division under Gen. Curtis in the campaign along the borders of Missouri and Arkansas. He was wounded at the battle of Pea Ridge, March 1862, and despite his wound was in action the next day at the head of his division (*Battles and Leaders,* II, 328). The same month he was commissioned brigadier-general of volunteers. After this he was in command at Columbus, Ky., and at Fort Pickens, Fla. At Marianna in Florida in 1864 he was severely wounded in the arm and in the cheek-bone, and from the effects of these wounds he never recovered. He left the army, with the brevet of major-general, in 1865, and was appointed United States minister to Uruguay and Argentina, dying at Buenos Ayres not long after his arrival.

[M. Force, *From Fort Henry to Corinth* (1861); *Appleton's Annual Cyc.* (1868); F. B. Heitman, *Hist. Reg.* (1903).]

E. K. A.

ASBURY, FRANCIS (Aug. 20/21, 1745–Mar. 31, 1816), pioneer Methodist preacher and bishop, was born on the edge of the colliery district, near the foot of Hamstead Bridge four miles from Birmingham, England. His parents, Joseph Asbury and Elizabeth Rogers, were in humble circumstances. The father was a tenant-farmer, or gardener for two well-to-do families in the parish—a hard-working yeoman; the mother was of Welsh stock with much of the traditional emotional susceptibility of the race. It was the mother who left the greater impress upon the son. The death of an infant daughter had plunged her into the deepest melancholy for several years, until "God was pleased to open the eyes of her mind." Hitherto a worldly woman, she now turned for consolation to religion, seeking the company of religious people, attending services, and poring for hours over devotional books. Her house became a rendezvous for "people of God." Before the birth of her son, according to a family tradition (Asbury, *A Methodist Saint,* p. 1), she had a vision in which God appeared to her, announcing that her child would be a boy and would become a great religious leader. Cherishing this vision, she lavished upon the boy all the affection which the infant daughter had inspired. Francis grew up under the sheltering care of this emotional woman and developed a mother-love which seems to have inhibited, with one possible exception, every normal inclination toward the other sex. If his own account may be trusted (Tipple, *The Heart of Asbury's Journal,* p. 70), he was always a serious lad with "a particular sense of the being of God," greatly fearing both an oath and a lie, abhorring fighting and quarreling, and never imbibing the vices of his wicked companions. He had a very limited schooling and at the age of thirteen and a half was apprenticed to learn "a branch of business," which may have been that of blacksmith (Tipple, *Francis Asbury,* p. 47). He remained an apprentice for some six years, meantime at the age of fourteen experiencing a religious awakening. An interest in Methodism seems to have been kindled by his mother, who sent him to the neighboring village of Wednesbury to hear itinerant preachers. It was indeed a new experience for a lad brought up in the established church to hear a preacher preach without a sermon book and pray without a prayer-book. For the first time he saw men and women on their knees, shouting their Amens in an ecstacy of religious devotion. "This was not the Church, but it was better," he concluded.

From this time on he consorted more and more with Methodists, meeting with them for reading and prayer and even holding devotional exercises in his father's house. He also accompanied his mother to fortnightly meetings of women, where he read the Scriptures at first and then ventured "to expound and paraphrase a little on the portion read." Before long he was a full-fledged local preacher, visiting the surrounding shires and at the same time pursuing his calling. So he labored until he was twenty-one, when he went to London and was admitted to the Wesleyan Conference. Four years of itinerant preaching followed on different circuits; and then in 1771, at the Conference at Bristol, he and Richard Wright volunteered to go as missionaries to America. The reasons for this eventful decision have seemed to Methodist biographers too obvious to need elaboration. Are they not contained in the entry which he made in his Journal, after he had been eight days at sea? "Whither am I going? To the New World. What to do? To gain honor? No, if I know my own heart. To get money? No; I am going to live to God, and to bring others so to do" (Tipple, *Asbury's Journal,* p. 2). There is some evidence, however, that he had formed an attachment to a young woman which was not favored by his mother (Tipple, *Francis Asbury,* p. 316), and this disappointment may have made it easier to plunge into the wilderness. This seems to be the only suggestion of romance in his life. He never married. There may have been, too, just a little alloy mixed with the pure gold of his resolve to live to God and to bring others so to do. The assistant of the Staffordshire circuit once taxed Asbury with not obeying instructions and playing the "dictator" (Asbury, *A Methodist Saint,* p. 17). It is a note sounded more than once by those who worked with the future bishop. "Passion for superiority and thirst for domination" were always characteristic of him, according to one who knew him well (*Ibid.,* p. 16). Was it possible that America appealed to him because there, unhampered by conventions, he could make others live unto God, in *his* own way—carve out a unique career in this New World? When he embarked for America, he resolved to keep a journal, for his own satisfaction (Tipple, *Asbury's Journal,* p. 71). Ten years later, he gave another motive: the Journal when published would let his friends and the world see "how I employed my time." "People unacquainted with the causes and motives of my conduct," he wrote still later, "will always more or less judge of me improperly" (*Ibid.,* p. 547). His Journal was to be the attestation of his missionary career—if need be, his vindication (Tipple, *Francis Asbury,* p. 86).

Methodism in America did not begin with the arrival of Asbury in Philadelphia. Other missionaries had preceded him, but an overwhelming sense of responsibility for this vast country oppressed him. On the day of his arrival, he fortified his soul by praying five times, reading three chapters from Revelation, a hundred pages of Wesley's *Sermons,* and a hundred pages of Edwards's account of New England revivals. The following week he started out on the first of his itineraries to join Richard Boardman. There is much that is significant for his whole career in his first experiences. Though he was only a helper under Boardman, who was his senior in years and service, he took himself and his work very seriously. He found much to criticize in New York: he thought the discipline lax; he did not approve of preachers staying in town; he believed frequent changes of circuit desirable "to avoid partiality and popularity." He determined to set an example. On Nov. 24, 1771, without asking leave of Boardman, he started off on a borrowed horse through the villages of Westchester County, preaching wherever chance offered—in taverns, in jails, by the wayside. He spared neither himself nor his mount; and as winter approached he defied rain and snow. As yet unacclimated, he took a severe cold but continued to preach even when suffering from chills and fever. He finally collapsed and had to take to his bed for three weeks. He was still weak when he resumed his preaching and from this time on he seems never to have had good health.

In October 1772, Asbury received a letter from Wesley, appointing him general assistant or superintendent in America, and with this authority he carried out his own ideas of discipline. He did not hesitate to shut offending brothers and sisters out of meeting, in spite of protests. "While I stay," he wrote in his Journal, "the rules must be attended to and I cannot suffer myself to be guided by half-hearted Methodists" (Tipple, *Asbury's Journal,* p. 19). But in June 1773 he had to surrender his authority to Thomas Rankin, newly arrived from England. He was never a good subordinate, however, and he was soon out of sympathy with his superior, who, it is true, never fully understood the colonial attitude toward the mother country and continually gave offense. In the end Rankin complained to Wesley, who summoned Asbury to return home (Mar. 1, 1775).

It was a critical moment in Asbury's career. With a prescience of coming events, he determined to stay on, believing that it would be "an eternal dishonor" to leave 3,000 souls in this time of danger (*Ibid.,* p. 87). There may also have been in his mind the unuttered thought that if Rankin and others departed eventually, as seemed likely, he would have a unique place in the upbuilding of a Methodist organization. There was rebellion in the air. Keener observers than Asbury scented independence as the goal of the colonies. As yet, in the words of Jesse Lee, the Methodists "were only a religious society, not a church" (Jesse Lee, *A Short History of the Methodists,* p. 47); but Strawbridge and Southern preachers were already administering the sacraments as though they were a separate organization. Two revolutions thus seemed imminent (Tipple, *Francis Asbury,* ch. VI). With the political revolution Asbury had no concern, except as it interfered with his supreme object. He attended the third Conference in Philadelphia while the Second Continental Congress hard by was wrestling with temporal problems, and he noted with apprehension that the minds of men were "full of sin and politics."

For various reasons, for which Wesley, Rankin, and his associates were chiefly responsible, the Methodists fell quite generally under suspicion as Loyalists during the Revolution and suffered some persecution. Asbury himself refused to take the oath of allegiance required by the State of Maryland and was forced to take refuge in Delaware. There he remained for the space of twenty months (1777-78) while Rankin and his colleagues fled the country. He had tried to remain neutral in the struggle between his native land and her colonies, but the logic of events drove him on. He was convinced that England could never subdue the rebellious colonists and that independence was inevitable. With no little misgiving he made his choice and became a citizen of Delaware (Strickland, *The Pioneer Bishop,* pp. 115–16).

Though Asbury made this enforced sojourn in Delaware a means of bringing some 1,800 souls into the Methodist fold, he was temporarily in eclipse. The sacramental controversy brought him again to the fore and gave him the opportunity of winning personal control of the Methodist societies at the most critical point in their history. The Southern preachers being now pretty thoroughly committed to the administration of the sacraments, as the Church of England lost its cohesion in the rebellious colonies, Asbury built up a following among the Northern preachers and got them thoroughly committed to the Wesleyan view. A split in the Methodist organization seemed inevitable after the Southern Conference took its stand in the Conference at Fluvanna in 1779. In the negotiations that followed, Asbury proved himself an adept at conciliation, procrastination, and compromise. The wisdom of the serpent was oddly mingled with the harmlessness of the dove in his composition. Prayer and practical politics went hand in hand (Asbury, *A Methodist Saint,* pp. 129–30). The outcome was a complete victory for the Northern party and a personal triumph for Asbury, who now in all but title became the head of the Methodist organization. The Baltimore Conference of 1782 confirmed his position and put an end once for all to the sacramental controversy. A month later, down in Virginia, Asbury heard "the good news" that Britain had acknowledged the independence of America (Tipple, *Asbury's Journal,* p. 209).

To deal with this new situation, Wesley resolved in 1784 upon a course which he had long had under consideration. He sent to the United States the Rev. Thomas Coke, a presbyter of the Church of England who had espoused Methodism, with instructions to act with Asbury in joint superintendence of the Methodist societies. Coke met Asbury for the first time in Barratt's Chapel in Kent County, Del. Extended conferences followed. Again Asbury evinced his practical shrewdness. Sensing correctly the temper of his associates, he insisted that he should receive his appointment not from Wesley, but from a regular conference, and he had his way. At a memorable Conference in December 1784, at Baltimore, Coke and Asbury were chosen joint superintendents; and the abridged prayer-book, liturgy, and discipline sent over by Wesley were adopted as the foundation of the Methodist Episcopal Church in the United States. On successive days, Asbury was ordained deacon and elder, and consecrated as superintendent—not bishop. Almost at once, however, he began to refer to himself as bishop (Asbury, *A Methodist Saint,* p. 163), a course which Wesley deprecated strongly, but the title stuck and appeared in the Conference minutes of 1787. Theoretically, he shared his episcopal functions with Coke, but the frequent absences of the latter left practical control and direction of the organization to his American colleague. Theoretically, too, he was the servant of the Methodist Conference, but between sessions he ruled as autocratically as any Pope of Rome. With an eye single to the glory of God he appointed preachers without the slightest regard to their wishes or to the preference of parishioners. There were often loud complaints and more than once his autocratic power was challenged. It was not until his strength failed and he was obviously unable to carry his burden that he accepted Richard Whatcoat as an associate bishop (1800), who became, however, little more than his understudy. It was Asbury who planned those great campaigns which sent preachers to fight the great Adversary not only in the remote parts of the old states but over the Alleghanies on the hazardous frontiers of Kentucky and Ohio. He was a master of religious strategy. It was not an idle gesture when he and Coke presented a congratulatory address, drafted by Asbury, to the newly inaugurated President, Gen. Washington, and thus secured recognition for the Methodists as the first religious body to profess allegiance to the new government (*Ibid.,* p. 201).

A master of strategy usually stays behind the lines. Not so Bishop Asbury. He asked no more of his skirmishers and shock-troops than he was himself prepared to undergo. He sought out the Adversary for personal combat in every field from New Hampshire to Georgia, not once but many times. It has been said that he traveled all told nearly 300,000 miles. "My horse trots stiff," he wrote in his Journal, "and no wonder when I have ridden him upon an average of 5,000 miles a year for five years successively." Much of this incessant traveling was over roads that beggared description and under physical tension that would have speedily worn down a man of less resolute will. And Asbury was at no time a well man. He suffered from all sorts of maladies which he undoubtedly aggravated by injudicious treatment. Blood-letting and blistering were his favorite remedies for nearly every complaint from boils and worse skin-diseases to intestinal disorders. His condition was made worse by bad food, exposure, and lack of ordinary sanitation in the frontier cabins where he took refuge. In all these long years, he had no fixed abiding place that could be called home; and, except when sheer exhaustion forced him to a sick-bed, no rest from his labors. Yet he gloried in his sufferings and desired posterity should know what he had undergone for the salvation of souls. He was a familiar figure as he journeyed through Methodist America—a tall spare man with fine forehead and keen eyes, dressed in a plain frock-coat and small clothes, and wearing a low-crowned broad-brimmed hat. He always had a serious, almost austere, aspect to which in later life his flowing white locks added a patriarchal dignity. With the election of William McKendree as bishop to succeed Whatcoat, who died in 1806, the reins of government began to slip from Asbury's hands. More and more he left details to his "assistant bishop" as he persisted in calling his associate. Yet to the very end, when his frame was racked by a consumptive cough and he had to be lifted in and out of his sulky, he kept to the road and he died in Virginia as he was making all possible haste to reach Baltimore for the Conference of 1816.

Asbury was not a learned man. He read much by the way, to be sure, but his intellectual curiosity was easily satisfied. Life was to him only a temporary abode for a soul in transit. He was essentially an ascetic, devoid of interest in temporal affairs. He flagellated his mind as he did his body, taking a grim satisfaction in doing the hard thing. Nor was he a great preacher, from all accounts. There is no evidence that he threw his hearers into those religious frenzies in which his itinerant preachers saw the working of Providence. Yet he preached on the same themes with profound conviction—sin and redemption with hope of Heaven and fear of Hell. It is as an organizer rather than as a preacher that Asbury has a primacy in the annals of American Methodism.

[The earliest biog. of Asbury is W. P. Strickland's *The Pioneer Bishop: or the Life and Times of Francis Asbury* (1858), and the latest is Herbert Asbury's *A Methodist Saint* (1927), a critical study of the first importance. Between these extremes are numerous lives written with varying degrees of denominational fervor. The best of these is *Francis Asbury, the Prophet of the Long Road* (1916), by E. S. Tipple, who has drawn upon manuscripts in the Emory Coll. in the Drew Theological Seminary. The same author has edited selections from Asbury's *Journal* under the title *The Heart of Asbury's Journal* (1904). *An Extract from the Journal of Francis Asbury* (Aug. 7, 1771 to Dec. 29, 1778) was published in 1792; and a continuation (to Sept. 3, 1780) in 1802. The entire *Journal* was published in three volumes in 1821. Jesse Lee, *A Short History of the Methodists, in the United States of America* (1810) is valuable as an account by a contemporary who was often in sharp opposition to Asbury. Valuable too are Henry Boehm's *Reminiscences* (1865), and *The Substance of a Funeral Discourse . . . on the Death of the Rev. Francis Asbury* (1819) by Ezekiel Cooper.]

A. J.

ASCH, MORRIS JOSEPH (July 4, 1833–Oct. 5, 1902), laryngologist, soldier, was born in Philadelphia, the second son of Joseph M. and Clara (Ulman) Asch. His early education was mainly under private tutors. He entered the University of Pennsylvania in 1848, graduated in 1852, and the same year entered the Jefferson Medical College, from which he graduated as M.D. in 1855. Soon thereafter he was appointed clinical assistant to Dr. Samuel Gross. On the outbreak of the Civil War he was appointed assistant surgeon in the United States Army. He was on duty at the surgeon-general's office from August 1861 to August 1862; subsequently became surgeon-in-chief to the artillery reserve of the Army of the Potomac, medical inspector of the Army of the Potomac, medical director of the 24th army corps, medical inspector Army of the James and staff surgeon of Gen. Philip H. Sheridan from 1865 to 1873. He participated in battles at Chancellorsville, Mine Run, Gettysburg, and Appomattox Court House. On Mar. 13, 1865, he was brevetted major for faithful and meritorious services during the war. While on the staff of Gen. Sheridan, he was assistant to the medical director, Department of the Gulf, and medical director at department headquarters and was most prominent and active in two great epidemics in New Orleans, cholera in 1866, and yellow fever in 1867. The latter epidemic under control, Sheridan was relieved and ordered to Fort Leavenworth, Asch accompanying him, but at St. Louis Asch fell ill with yellow fever. On his recoverey he joined Sheridan at the new station. His success in caring for the wounded and sick during the unprecedented cold of the winter campaign of 1868–69 against the plains Indians was often remarked by the officers in command. When Sheridan was promoted to the grade of lieutenant-general, he took Asch with him to his new headquarters in Chicago, where the latter continued rendering invaluable services, until he resigned in 1873.

On his retirement, he practised medicine in New York City, devoting himself, though not exclusively, to laryngology. He was one of the founders of the American Laryngological Association, and was appointed surgeon to the throat department of the New York Eye and Ear Infirmary and the Manhattan Eye and Ear Hospital. He soon had a large and lucrative practise and took an active part in the scientific advances in his chosen specialty, contributing largely to medical journals and often presenting special articles in text-books. Among these contributions was "A New Operation for Deviation of the Nasal Septum" (*New York Medical Journal,* LII, 1890). This came to be known as the "Asch operation" and it was, up to that time, the most successful method employed, and was performed both in this country and abroad.

Asch was tall, handsome, of commanding presence, genial and conscientious. Always young in heart, he loved to have his juniors with him, feeling that he could correct his perspective through their fresher vision. He was unmarried, and when attacked with cerebral embolism, he made his home with his sister, where he was surrounded with every comfort, until he died.

[*Trans. Am. Laryngol. Ass.,* 1902, pp. 246–51; *Medic. News* (N.Y.), LXXXI, 715, 944; *Medic. Record,* LXII, 585; *N.Y. Medic. Jour.,* LXXVI, 642; the *Laryngoscope* (St. Louis), XIII, 17–22, Jan. 1903, containing partial list of Asch's scientific publications.]

E. M—r.

ASHBURNER, CHARLES ALBERT (Feb. 9, 1854–Dec. 24, 1889), geologist, one of nine children of Algernon Eyre Ashburner, of English descent, and Sarah (Blakiston) Ashburner, was born in Philadelphia. He was educated first at the Friends' Central School in that city, then at the High School, and at the Towne Scientific School of the University of Pennsylvania, entering the university at the early age of sixteen and graduating as civil engineer, first in his class, in 1874. As a student he showed great ability in appreciation of form and structure; he was accurate, and a born artist, "seeing what he drew and drawing what he saw" (Lesley, *post*). He showed also unusual mathematical ability. As an undergraduate he took part in a survey of the raft channel of Delaware River between Easton and Trenton and was one of the organizers of the Engineers' Club of Philadelphia in 1873. While in the university he attracted the attention of J. P. Lesley [*q.v.*], then professor of geology, through whose perhaps unconscious influence he was induced to give up the engineering profession and enter upon his life work as a geologist. On the organization of the Second Geological Survey of Pennsylvania, Lesley was appointed director and selected Ashburner as an assistant, commissioning him and his classmate C. E. Billin, to assist in the survey of the fossil iron-ore belt of the Juniata Valley. Ashburner soon acquired sufficient skill to work independently and wrote the report on the Aughwick Valley and East Broad Top coal-basin published in *Report F* in 1878. He was commissioned in 1876 to survey the counties of McKean, Elk, Cameron, and Forest, one of the most difficult as well as the most important oil districts of the state. This survey occupied two years. Realizing the importance of topography, as a first step he made a good topographic map, "contouring it with the eye of an artist who knew the geological significance of every feature and every curve" (*Ibid.*). The generalization which he was able to deduce from this work was of great economic value, enabling him to fix the limit of the oil-bearing strata and to place the calculation of the depth of well boring upon a scientific basis. In 1880, with the organization of the survey of the anthracite field, Ashburner was placed in control and produced what his chief described as a "*chef d'œuvre* of geology as an applied science." He knew and did exactly what was to be done. "He selected his assistants, taught them and worked with them, inspired them with his own zeal and lifted their work to the standard of his own" (*Ibid.*). He conducted the survey of 1880–86, resigning in the fall of the latter year to accept an engagement as scientific expert with the Westinghouse firm at Pittsburgh. To this work he devoted the rest of his life, traveling extensively and enduring hardship and exposure that brought about severe illnesses and finally an untimely death in 1889. He was a member of the American Philosophical Society, American Institute of Mining Engineers, Philadelphia Academy of Natural Sciences, Franklin Institute and several other organizations of similar character. In 1881 he married Roberta M. John of Pottsville, by whom he had two children.

[Sketch by J. P. Lesley in *Trans. of the Am. Institute of Mining Engineers,* XVIII, 1889–90; another by Arthur Winslow, containing full bibliography, in *Am. Geologist*, VI, 69–78.]

G. P. M.

ASHBY, TURNER (Oct. 23, 1828–June 6, 1862), Confederate soldier, was born at his father's home, "Rose Bank," near what is now Markham, Fauquier County, Va. His father, Col. Turner Ashby, who married Dorothy Green of Rappahannock County, was an officer in the War of 1812; his grandfather, Capt. Jack Ashby, an officer in the Revolution. He himself never married. His education was obtained from his mother, tutors, and in Maj. Ambler's private school. He entered commercial pursuits, then bought a place near "Rose Bank," and engaged in farming. Stirred by John Brown's raid on Oct. 16, 1859, Ashby, who was enterprising, fearless, a splendid horseman, and a natural leader, gathered some mounted men and rode north. They arrived late on Oct. 19 at Charlestown, where Brown had been jailed. In January 1860, they returned home after several months spent in picketing the Potomac. Ashby believed in slavery but not in secession. But when Virginia seceded, Apr. 17, 1861, he again rode with his company of horsemen to Harper's Ferry. With his command augmented by infantry, and Imboden's artillery, he took post opposite Point of Rocks, performing bridge-guard and scouting duty (*Rebellion Records,* ser. I, vol. II, pp. 861, 868, 881, 894). In June 1861, he marched with his company to Winchester, where it was incorporated in the 7th Virginia Cavalry which Col. McDonald was officially organizing for the defense of the upper Potomac border (*Ibid.,* p. 952). From June 18, 1861, to early March 1862, he was engaged in picket and scouting duty, and in minor operations, in the Romney-Bath-Martinsburg-Harper's Ferry region, except for a short time in July, when with part of the 7th, he coöperated with Stuart's cavalry in masking Johnston's withdrawal from Winchester to Manassas (*Battles and Leaders of the Civil War,* I, 230). He was commissioned lieutenant-colonel about July 23, 1861. Under official authority he organized Chew's Horse Battery on Nov. 13, 1861, which formed a part of his command. In November or December he succeeded McDonald in command of the regiment. From Mar. 4, 1862, when Banks entered Charlestown, to the latter part of April, Ashby, promoted colonel about Mar. 14, covered Jackson's retreat to Swift Run Gap, participating with great credit in the battle of Kernstown. During Jackson's movement against Milroy in early May, Ashby, with part of his command, watched Banks at Harrisonburg and followed him during his retreat to Strasburg. Leaving a few companies opposite Banks, Ashby, with the remainder, joined Jackson in his march toward Front Royal; moved off and attacked the Federal detachment at Buckton Station; joined Jackson again at Front Royal; and moving on his left toward Middletown, struck Banks's column on the flank in retreat. He took part in the engagement at Winchester, on May 25, and in the subsequent pursuit of Banks toward Harper's Ferry. On May 27, he received his commission as brigadier-general. During Jackson's subsequent retreat up the Valley, on June 6, Ashby, while commanding the cavalry brigade, and fighting a rear-guard action, a few miles south of Harrisonburg, was shot by the enemy.

[The statement by R. L. Dabney in his *Life and Campaigns of Jackson* (1866) that, at Winchester, Ashby had undertaken an "independent enterprise," is well refuted in Avirett's *Memoirs of Gen. Turner Ashby and His Compeers* (1867), which gives a detailed account of Ashby's life. Clarence Thomas in *Gen. Turner Ashby* (1907) proves that Ashby was more than a partisan leader. G. F. R. Henderson, in *Stonewall Jackson* (1898), while not failing to comment on Ashby's early ignorance of military drill and discipline, shows how his coolness under fire, his daring horsemanship, his skill in handling his command, and his power of gaining devoted followers, won for him the affection and admiration of his own troops and of the Southern people.]

W. S. G.

ASHE, JOHN (*c.* 1720–October 1781), soldier and politician of North Carolina, was the son of Elizabeth (Swann) and John Baptista Ashe, an Englishman of good family who settled in the eastern part of the colony and became a member of His Majesty's Council of North Carolina in 1733. The son was probably born at Grovely, Brunswick County, N. C., in 1720 (A. M. Hooper and S. J. Mcree, *North Carolina University Magazine,* October 1854), although John H. Wheeler claims that he was born in England in 1721 (*Historical Sketches,* II, 279). He was well educated, perhaps in England, and had a good library. Early in life he married his cousin, Rebecca Moore, sister of Judge Maurice Moore and Gen. James Moore. He was an officer of militia in the French War, and became a popular leader against the Crown. He was speaker of the Colonial Assembly 1762–65, and a leader in the Stamp Act agitation. Either he or his nephew, John Baptista Ashe [*q.v.*], siding against the anti-government Regulators in 1771, was taken prisoner by them, tied to a tree, and whipped (Hooper and Mcree, *supra*). John Ashe was, however, a strong Whig, was a member of the Committee of Correspondence, and of the Provincial Congress, and of the Committee of Safety, and led the successful attack on Fort Johnston near Wilmington in the opening year of the Revolution. He was made a colonel in 1775, and brigadier-general of North Carolina troops in 1776. He was a good public speaker, graceful in appearance, with "popular manners."

Highly regarded for character and patriotism, Ashe was nevertheless an unskilled and inexperienced commander, as was shown too clearly in the unfortunate affair with which his name is chiefly connected. He had been sent by Gov. Caswell of North Carolina in 1778 to reinforce Gen. Lincoln who commanded in Charleston, and he led a regiment recruited from the eastern counties of his state. Detached by Lincoln to pursue the English leader, Col. Campbell, he crossed the Savannah River with about 1,200 militia and some Georgia Continentals, inadequately armed. Lincoln's plan involved an attack by his whole army, and Ashe's coöperation was essential. Descending the river, Ashe occupied a strong position at Briar Creek, but neglected to defend an exposed flank, and was lacking in vigilance. Col. Prevost, brother of the English general, by a circuitous march gained the rear of the American army and took it by surprise; Elbert, a subordinate officer, and some of the troops fought well, but the bulk of the army gave way, and Prevost won a complete victory. Ashe was unable to rally the fugitives, many of whom perished in their flight to the swamps and the Savannah River. The loss was estimated at about 150 or 200, that of the enemy being trifling; many officers were among the prisoners, and a large part of the arms, ammunition, colors, and baggage fell to the English. The defeat was decisive, securing Georgia to the enemy, opening communications between that state, the Carolinas, and the Indians, and protracting the war.

Ashe was apparently inactive during the battle. It has been asserted that he neglected to supply the troops with cartridges, and he was even charged with cowardice. He was brought before a court of inquiry over which Gen. Moultrie presided. Acquitted of cowardice, he was censured "for want of sufficient vigilance"; "having," in the words of one historian, "neither judgment, skill, foresight, nor self-reliance" (William B. Stevens, *History of Georgia,* 1859, p. 197). The language of the court of inquiry was that he "did not take all the necessary precautions which he ought to have done" (William Moultrie, *Memoirs of the American Revolution,* 1802, I, 337, ff.). He was greatly depressed by these events, and was soon after in hiding during the occupation of the eastern part of the state by the English. Betrayed to the enemy in 1781, he was freed on parole, but died of smallpox in Sampson County, N. C.

[Samuel Ashe, in *Biog. Hist. of N. C. from Colonial Times to the Present,* IV (1905), 36–52; Hugh McCall, *Hist. of Ga.,* II (1816), 220–24; David Schenck, *N. C. 1780–81* (1889), p. 34; Frank Moore, *Diary of the Am. Rev. from Newspapers and Original Docs.,* II (1859), 138–41; John H. Wheeler, *Hist. Sketches of N. C. from 1584 to 1851* (1851), I, 50–51, 58, 65, 74, 79, 85, 88, II, 279–80.]

E. K. A.

ASHE, JOHN BAPTISTA (1748–Nov. 27, 1802), soldier and politician of North Carolina, was born at Rocky Point in that state, the eldest son of Samuel and Mary (Porter) Ashe, and grandson of John Baptista Ashe. He belonged to a family prominent in the commonwealth. His grandfather was a member of His Majesty's Council of North Carolina, his father was governor, and his uncle—with whom he is sometimes confused—was Gen. John Ashe [*q.v.*]. John Baptista Ashe married early in life Eliza Montfort, daughter of Col. Joseph Montfort of Halifax, N. C. She was the lady who later made the famous if doubtfully courteous retort to Col. Tarleton when he was an unwelcome guest in the home of her sister, Mrs. Willie Jones. Tarleton had been wounded at the battle of Cowpens by Col. William Washington. He commented upon the illiteracy of Col. Washington. Mrs. Ashe replied, glancing at Tarleton's scarred hand, "But you will at least agree that Col. Washington can at any rate make his mark." Serving throughout the Revolutionary War, in 1776 Ashe became a captain, and later rose to the rank of lieutenant-colonel. At the battle of Eutaw Springs, Sept. 8, 1781, the last important conflict of the far South, he was lieutenant-colonel of a battalion of regulars, in the brigade of Gen. Sumner who was stationed on the right. In this capacity he aided in covering the retreat of the North Carolina militia. The brigade "bore itself nobly, fighting with the coolness and resolution of veterans" (see letter of Gen. Greene, published in the *New Jersey Gazette,* Oct. 24, 1781).

After the war Ashe held nearly every political office in his state. He was a member of the House of Commons, of the state Senate and of the Continental Congress 1787–88. When the belated convention of North Carolina met in 1789 to ratify the Federal Constitution, he was one of the leading delegates. He represented his state in the House of Representatives in the First and Second Congresses 1789–93. His final political honor was election to the governorship in 1802, but before he could take office he died at Halifax, N. C.

[David Schenck, *N. C. 1780–81* (1889), pp. 25, 437, 451; Stephen B. Weeks, in *Biog. Hist. of N. C. from Colonial Times to the Present* (1917), VIII, 26–29; John H. Wheeler, *Hist. Sketches of N. C. from 1584 to 1851,* I, 80, II, 199, 281; R. D. W. Connor, *Hist. of N. C.* (1919), I, 316, II, 47.]

E. K. A.

ASHE, SAMUEL (1725–Feb. 3, 1813), jurist, governor, was born near Beaufort and died in Rocky Point, N. C. His father, John Baptista Ashe, speaker of the colonial Assembly at the time of Samuel's birth, removed soon after that event to the environs of the Cape Fear River. The boy's mother having already died, the death of his father in 1734 gave his rearing into the hands of his uncle, Sam Swan. This uncle, a vigorous advocate of popular sovereignty, was speaker of the colonial Assembly for twenty-five years. Hostility to British rule was insistent in the North Carolina of Samuel's youth, but he found himself not unwilling upon completing his education in the North and returning home to the Wilmington district, to become assistant attorney for the Crown. He was esteemed by the royal governor, who, as a fugitive some years later, singled him out with one Samuel Johnson as the only two men of integrity in the entire North Carolina Council of Safety. For all his imperial attachments, he was among the earliest Republicans, and beginning in 1774 he furthered his theories by his activities as a propagandist, and as a member of many Revolutionary organizations. In 1776 he became president of the state Council of Safety, and in 1779 he was captain of a troop of light horse. He was perhaps the most substantial lawyer in the state who unreservedly identified himself with the more aggressive implications of the Revolution. He was one of a committee of twenty-four appointed in 1776 to prepare a state constitution, and he held the first court ever conducted under that instrument. Speaker of the Senate in the first state legislature, he was elected presiding judge of the first state supreme court, an office which he retained till 1795. As judge, he championed the legislature against a group of lawyers who were defending the property claims of persons who had sympathized with England in the late war, and he also, in the case of Bayard *vs.* Singleton, took part in the decision, which asserted the right of judicial review of legislative enactments on the ground of alleged conflict with the constitution. He was "independent," he wrote to some lawyers, "in principle, in person, and in purse, and should neither court their love, nor fear their enmity" (Ashe, *Samuel Ashe,* p. 22). Made governor in 1795, he served in that office for three one-year terms. He was Jeffersonian in policies, an extremist for state rights, but in times of what he considered national crisis he would subordinate his own views to the views of his opponents in control at Washington. He was president of the board of trustees of the University of North Carolina. He was married twice, first to his cousin,

Mary Porter, and next, to another cousin, a widow, Elizabeth Merrick. His two sons who had reached maturity at the time of the Revolution were both soldiers, and later took part in local public affairs. The younger of these sons, Samuel, an ardent Federalist, is notable for having actively arrayed himself in the first decade of the nineteenth century as the leader of Federalist forces pitted against the contrary forces led by his father.

[*Cyc. of Eminent and Successful Men of the Carolinas in the 19th Cent.* (1892); S. A. Ashe, "Samuel Ashe," *Biog. Hist. of N. C.*, VIII (1917); S. B. Weeks, *Colonial and State Records of N. C.*; J. Sprunt, *Chronicles of the Cape Fear River* (1914); J. H. Wheeler, *Hist. Sketches of N. C.* (1851); G. J. McRee, *Life and Correspondence of Jas. Iredell* (1858); *South in the Building of the Nation*, XI (1909); R. D. W. Connor, *Hist. of N. C.*, I (1919); F. X. Martin and J. Haywood, *N. C. Reports*, pp. 42–48 (2nd ed. 1843); J. B. Thayer, *Cases on Constitutional Law*, I, pp. 78 ff. (1895).]

J. D. W.

ASHE, THOMAS SAMUEL (July 19, 1812–Feb. 4, 1887), legislator, was a member of the Ashe family which, long of consequence in Wiltshire, England, became prominent in North Carolina very early in the eighteenth century, and contributed numerous men of note to the history of the state. Thomas, the son of Pasquale Paoli Ashe and Elizabeth Strudwick, was born at his maternal grandfather's home, "The Hawfields," in Orange County. He lived as a boy at "The Neck," the Ashe home on the Cape Fear River, in New Hanover (now Pender) County. While he was still a youth the family removed to Alabama, but he returned later to North Carolina to attend the Bingham School in Orange County and the University of North Carolina, where he graduated in 1832, and of which he was, later, an active trustee for more than thirty years. After graduation he studied law in Hillsboro, N. C., under Chief Justice Thomas Ruffin and in 1836 began practise at Wadesboro, N C. In 1842 he was elected as a Whig to the House of Commons. In 1848 the legislature elected him solicitor and he served for four years. In 1854 he was again elected to the legislature, this time as a member of the Senate. In 1859 he declined to accept a nomination to Congress. In February 1861 the legislature submitted to the people of the state the question of a convention, providing for the election of delegates at the same time. Ashe was chosen as a Union candidate, but the people refused to ratify the call and the delegates never assembled. Although originally a Union man, Ashe held that North Carolina should tolerate no attempt on the part of the United States to coerce the seceded states, and when the call for troops came he advocated secession. In November 1861 he was elected to the Confederate Congress and served one term as a consistent supporter of the administration. On Dec. 9, 1864, he was elected to the Confederate Senate, defeating Edwin G. Reade, who was supported by the peace party in the state, but before his term began the Confederate Congress had ceased to exist.

In 1868 at the first election under the Reconstruction constitution, he was nominated by the conservative party for governor. Although he was prevented by Gen. Canby's orders from voting in the election, he accepted the nomination and made an active campaign against the ratification of the new constitution. He was defeated by William Woods Holden. In 1872 he was elected a member of the Forty-third Congress, and served two terms. In his second term as a member of the judiciary committee he aided in drawing up the articles of impeachment against William Worth Belknap, secretary of war, and in the deliberations concerning the electoral commission bill. He also took some part in the investigation of James G. Blaine at the time of the Mulligan Letters exposé. The principle of rotation in office being then widely accepted in his state, he was not a candidate for renomination, but returned to the practise of law. In his profession, indeed, was to be found his major interest, and his nomination by the Democratic party, in 1878, for associate justice of the supreme court of the state opened to him the career for which by training, temperament, and taste he was best fitted. He served with credit in a court which had high standards, and his opinions rank well. Elected the first time to fill a vacancy, he was reëlected in 1880 and again in 1886.

Ashe was possessed of rather striking beauty. He was tall and imposing, with a fine head of abundant dark, later gray, hair, smiling gray eyes, firm mouth, and clear, ruddy skin. Quietly and simply religious, he was for many years a vestryman in the Episcopal Church. He married in 1837 Caroline, daughter of George W. B. Burgwin of "The Hermitage," New Hanover County.

[The chief sources of information are the N. C. newspapers; *Jour. First Confed. Cong., 1862–64*; and *Cong. Rec. 1873–77*. Ashe's judicial opinions in *N. C. Reports*, 80–95. Sketch by P. M. Wilson in the *Biog. Hist. of N. C.* (1917), vol. VIII.]

J. G. de R. H.

ASHE, WILLIAM SHEPPERD (Sept. 14, 1814–September 1862), congressman, railway president, was the son of Samuel and Elizabeth (Shepperd) Ashe, both representatives of families long prominent in North Carolina. His grandfather was Samuel Ashe, governor of that state and judge of its first supreme court. He was born in Rocky Point and died there, or near there. He attended college at Washington (later Trinity) College, Hartford, Conn., and studied law in North Carolina under the supervision of Judge John De Rossett Toomer. He was married to Sarah Anne Green of Brunswick County, N. C., in January 1836, a few days before he was admitted to practise as an attorney. In the same year he was elected county solicitor for four counties on the Cape Fear River, but his planting interests, and his social disposition which, according to his son, "was at variance with the exactions of a professional life" (S. A. Ashe, p. 30) led him to abandon his activities as a lawyer. He found time, however, to read widely, especially in the field of politics. In 1846 and 1858 he was in the state Senate, and in 1848 he was elected both to that body and to the national Congress. As a state legislator he is memorable for his opposition to schemes for making alien Charleston the normal railway outlet for the products of all western North Carolina. For it was largely through his influence that certain new traffic lines of his state were built in general eastward to Wilmington rather than southward to Charleston. During his two terms in Congress at Washington (December 1849–August 1852) he maintained the extreme Democratic view-point except when it conflicted with interests which were more immediately local. He had little hope of efforts to compromise sectional difficulties, and felt that only secession could better the condition of the South. He knew, nevertheless, when he was seeking Federal appropriations for North Carolina river improvements, how to cajole away from the House enough of his Democratic colleagues to let his bill be voted through by his friends among the Whigs, who, fortunately, had declared no policy against bills of that kind (*Ibid.*, p. 33). Becoming in 1854 president of the Wilmington & Weldon Railroad, he filled his office with aggressive energy, and to the profit of the organization. He was a member of the state convention of 1861, but resigned at the request of his friend Jefferson Davis to assume charge, first as major and then colonel, of Confederate government transportation between New Orleans and Richmond. After a year's service in this capacity, he turned his attention in the summer of 1862 to raising a legion of soldiers of which he was to be commander. These plans were cut short. One evening, in great distress over a report that one of his two sons—both of whom were soldiers—had been wounded, he set out immediately for his home some fifteen miles distant in the hope of gaining further information. He had not gone far when the hand-car which he had commandeered was run down by an unlighted train. He survived his injuries for three days.

[*Cyc. of Eminent and Representative Men of the Carolinas in the 19th Century,* II (1892); S. A. Ashe, "William Shepperd Ashe," *Biog. Hist. of N. C.*, VIII (1917); U. B. Phillips, *Hist. of Transportation in the Eastern Cotton Belt to 1860* (1908); R. D. W. Connor, *Hist. of N. C.* (1919); *Biog. Cong. Dir.* (1903).]

J. D. W.

ASHER, JOSEPH MAYOR (Sept. 23, 1872–Nov. 9, 1909), rabbi, was born in Manchester, England, the son of Rabbi Aaron Asher and Betsey (Jacobs) Asher. He was descended from Russian rabbis, among whom were to be found some of the greatest masters of the Torah or Jewish Law, and his heritage strongly influenced him in the selection of his profession. He was sent for his training to the Jews School, Grammar School, Technical School, and Owens College, then one of the constituent colleges of Victoria University, where he took his B.A. and M.A. degrees and where he received a scholarship and fellowship, the latter for excellence in philosophy. While at Trinity College, Cambridge, he came under the spell of that great scholar Dr. Solomon Schechter, who kindled in him a burning ardor for rabbinical study and research. Resolved to embark upon the career of a rabbi, and seeking to acquaint himself with German methods of scholarship, he matriculated at Bonn University in Germany. Having learned what he wanted at Bonn, he left for Russia and there entered the Yeshibot at Kovno. He remained in Russia long enough to complete his rabbinic studies and to secure his diploma as rabbi from Rabbi Katzenellenbogen of Suwalko. Returning to his native city, Manchester, he devoted himself whole-heartedly to the cause of Jewish education and all interests pertaining to orthodox Judaism. He organized the Talmud Torah schools, where studies in the lore and religion of the Jew might be ardently pursued.

Upon the reorganization of the Jewish Theological Seminary of America, in 1902, Asher was asked to serve as professor of homiletics and to take charge of the department of philosophy and ethics. Soon after his arrival in this country, he was appointed rabbi of Congregation B'nai Jehurum of New York City. He served with distinction in this position for a number of years and then went to Congregation Orach Chaim, also of New York City. He remained as rabbi of this congregation until his death. By his eloquence in the pulpit Asher made a name for himself, not only in New York but in other communities. His popular expositions on Jewish thinkers were marked contributions to the Jewish cultural life of the time. He was equally learned in the subtleties of Talmudic disquisitions, the Maimonidean philosophy, or the reasoning of Immanuel Kant. Little opportunity was given him for writing, because of the exacting nature of his professorial and ministerial duties, but he contributed an article on Jewish food and health laws to the *Encyclopedia Americana* (1907 edition, vol. IX; 1925 edition, vol. XVI) as well as reviews in the *International Journal of Ethics* and the *Critical Review.* His unceasing labors exhausted him, and he died at the age of thirty-seven.

[*Am. Jewish Year Bk.,* 1903–04, p. 42; *Am. Hebrew* (N.Y.), Nov. 12, Dec. 24, 1909; *Jewish Exponent* (Phila.), Nov. 12, Nov. 19, 1909; *Jewish Comment* (Baltimore), Nov. 12, 1909; *Jewish Tribune* (Portland, Ore.), Nov. 19, 1909; *Jewish Chronicle* (London), Nov. 26, 1909; *N.Y. Herald,* Nov. 10, 1909.] L. L. M.

ASHHURST, JOHN (Aug. 23, 1839–July 7, 1900), surgeon and author, was born in Philadelphia. He was the son of John Ashhurst and his wife, the daughter of Manuel Eyre, an East India merchant. As a boy his health was poor, and perhaps largely on account of his inability to partake in outdoor sports he early developed studious habits. Taught to read before he was four years old, by the age of sixteen he had accumulated a library of 3,000 volumes. He became proficient in Greek, Latin, and mathematics, and was also a skilful pianist. Throughout his life these tastes remained with him. He received his B.A. degree from the University of Pennsylvania in 1857, having made the highest average ever attained there, and in 1860 graduated from the Medical Department and received also the degree of M.A. He served first as resident physician in the Pennsylvania Hospital and later, during the Civil War, as an acting assistant-surgeon in the Chester (Pa.) United States General Hospital and as executive officer in the Cuyler United States Hospital at Germantown, Pa. In 1877 he was elected professor of clinical surgery in the University of Pennsylvania and in 1888 succeeded Dr. Agnew as professor of surgery in that institution. He was surgeon to the Pennsylvania, Episcopal, and Children's Hospitals of Philadelphia and to the Hospital of the University of Pennsylvania, and president of the Pathological Society of Philadelphia (1870–71) and of the College of Physicians of Philadelphia (1890–1900).

Ashhurst's contributions to medical literature were many and valuable. He wrote nearly all the surgical reviews in the *American Journal of the Medical Sciences* from 1867 to 1877. His monograph *Injuries of the Spine* (1867) was one of the first applications of the statistical method in medical investigation. In 1871 he published *Principles and Practise of Surgery,* which went through many editions, a justly popular textbook. As editor of the *International Encyclopædia of Surgery* (1881–86) he gained a solid reputation in Europe. He was one of the greatest authorities on the history of his profession. As a surgeon he was bold but conservative, and above all possessed sound judgment. He was wont to follow up his cases with the most scrupulous care, regarding the after-care as of equal importance with the performance of an operation. He was a deeply religious man. Of somewhat austere aspect he rather overawed younger men when they first came in contact with him, but this first impression soon melted away before his genuine kindheartedness.

Dr. Ashhurst suffered from a cerebral hemorrhage in August 1898, which paralyzed his left side. Though bedridden, his mind remained clear until his death, July 7, 1900. He had married in 1864 Sarah Stokes Wayne. They had seven children, of whom two, William and Astley Paston Cooper, became physicians.

[R. H. Harte, "John Ashhurst, Jr.: A Memoir," in *Trans. Coll. of Phys. of Phila.,* XXIV, 1902; biog. by his son A. P. C. Ashhurst, in *Am. Medic. Biogs.,* ed. by H. A. Kelly and Walter L. Burrage (1920); personal recollections. Portraits in Coll. of Phys. of Phila. and Medic. Laboratories of the Univ. of Pa.] F. R. P.

ASHLEY, JAMES MITCHELL (Nov. 14, 1824–Sept. 16, 1896), congressman, counted ancestors among the early English settlers of Virginia—the name of Capt. John Ashley appearing in the Virginia Charter of 1609. For nearly two centuries the descendants of Capt. Ashley resided in and near Norfolk. One branch of the family drifted to the frontier of Pennsylvania, settling near Pittsburgh in the early years of the nineteenth century. James Mitchell, the oldest of several children of John C. and Mary Kilpatrick Ashley, was born in Allegheny County, Pa.; shortly thereafter the family removed to Portsmouth, Ohio. Both his father and grandfather were itinerant ministers of the church founded by Alexander Campbell. He had no schooling, his early education being acquired at home, chiefly under the guidance of his mother. From his ninth to his fourteenth year he frequently accompanied his father, who preached in a circuit extending through the border counties of Kentucky and western Virginia. Here the boy glimpsed something of the system of slavery, and early came to detest it. At the age of sixteen, rebelling against the austere regulations established by his father for the government of his household, he ran away from home and secured employment as a cabin-boy and later as a clerk upon an Ohio river steamboat. A still more deep-seated abhorrence of slavery was acquired through his experiences on the southern rivers. Time and again he saw negroes, with safe-conducts of passage, sold back into slavery; the cruel treatment of slaves on board; and the utter disregard of their persons all through the country. Abandoning his work on the river, Ashley wandered through a number of southern states, visiting, among other places, the Hermitage, an event which he subsequently asserted made a profound impression upon him. While in Virginia, his expressions in opposition to slavery were so violent that he was told to leave the state.

Shortly after his return to Ohio, Ashley entered the printing office of the *Scioto Valley Republican* (1841), and subsequently was employed in various printing offices until he became editor of the *Democrat* in Portsmouth, Ohio (1848). During his experience as an editor he studied law with Charles O. Tracy, under whom he prosecuted his studies until he was admitted to the bar (1849), shortly after which he relinquished his connection with the *Democrat*. The ensuing two years were passed in Portsmouth in the work of boat construction. In 1851 he was married to Emma J. Smith of Kentucky, and in the same year removed to Toledo, where he engaged for a few years in the wholesale drug business.

He was by this time keenly interested in the political issues of the day. Hitherto a Democrat, his intense antagonism to slavery swept him into the Free-Soil party (1848) and shortly thereafter into the Republican party (1854). He assisted in the formation of the latter in the Toledo district, and was a delegate to the Republican National Convention at which John C. Frémont was nominated for the presidency (1856). Two years later he was himself nominated as the Republican candidate for Congress from his district and was elected. To this position he was consecutively reëlected in 1860, 1862, 1864, and 1866. Among the more important measures introduced or advocated in the House by Ashley was that of minority representation, a bill being reported by him looking to the introduction of that principle in the territorial governments—his speech in support of his bill being the first on that subject made in Congress. During the extra session of July 1861 he prepared the first measure for the reconstruction of the southern states presented to Congress, and as chairman of the Committee on Territories, reported it to the House (Mar. 12, 1862). The bill was tabled by a vote of 65 to 56, and the subject was not again revived at that session, but the ideas contained in the bill and the line of policy it outlined were embodied in the reconstruction measures finally adopted and carried into effect. In connection with Lot M. Morrill of Maine, Ashley drew up and had charge of the bill to abolish slavery in the District of Columbia (Apr. 11, 1862). He introduced the first proposition to amend the Constitution of the United States, so as to abolish slavery (Dec. 14, 1863), but the measure was at first defeated in the House. On a reconsideration Ashley succeeded in converting twenty-four border and northern Democrats and secured the passage of the measure (Jan. 31, 1865). He considered this the greatest achievement of his life.

It was on the initiative of Ashley that the move for the impeachment of President Johnson was begun (Jan. 7, 1867). Like many others of the extreme radicals, he dropped from political life after the trial and acquittal of the President. He was defeated in the ensuing fall election and left Congress Mar. 3, 1869. He was appointed by President Grant territorial governor of Montana, but was removed within a year on account of his sharp criticisms of the President's policies. The final act of his political career was his active participation in the Liberal Republican convention of 1872 and his support of Greeley for the presidency in the ensuing campaign. Ashley's political principles were not formed by logical mental processes, but by sentiment aroused by personal experiences. Puritan in habit, suspicious, uncharitable of opposition and somewhat vain, he was a born radical. His personal courage, his hatred of oppression, and his love of liberty drew him into the emancipation cause—first for the negro and then, as he believed, by his warfare on Johnson, for the whole American people.

After his political career was over, he became interested in the possibility of a railroad extending from Toledo across to the Michigan Peninsula which would furnish an outlet for about 300 miles of country. He purchased valuable terminals at Toledo entirely on credit and proceeded to build the road north to Lake Michigan, which became the Toledo, Ann Arbor & Northern Michigan Railroad. He was its president from 1877 to 1893. This work illustrates perhaps better than any other the characteristic feature of his life—his pertinacity.

[*Orations and Speeches by J. M. Ashley of Ohio* (1894), ed. by Benjamin W. Arnett and published by the Afro-Am. League of Tenn., is the chief source of information. The *Cong. Globe* and the files of the *Toledo Blade* are indispensable sources for the period of Ashley's pol. career. His connection with reconstruction is detailed in "An Ohio Congressman in Reconstruction," a manuscript thesis prepared by his grand-daughter, Margaret Ashley Paddock, at Columbia Univ. James G. Blaine's *Twenty Years of Cong.* (1884) contains numerous estimates of Ashley's services from the viewpoint of a partisan Republican. Ashley's lib., containing his collection of private papers, was destroyed by fire during his lifetime.]

C. E. C.

ASHLEY, WILLIAM HENRY (*c.* 1778–Mar. 26, 1838), fur trader, explorer, congressman, was born in Powhatan County, Va. He received a fair schooling, and acquired business interests in his native state that demanded his personal attention for years. Settling in Missouri at some time between 1803 and 1805, he engaged in the extraction of saltpeter at Ashley's Cave, Texas County, and in the manufacture of gunpowder at Potosi, where, in partnership with Andrew Henry, he also undertook lead-mining ventures, which, like the manufacture of gunpowder, had received a considerable impetus from the War of 1812. He served on the board of trustees of Potosi Academy and advanced in the territorial militia from the rank of captain in 1813, through that of colonel in 1819, to a generalship in 1822. In 1820 he was elected lieutenant-governor of the newly formed state of Missouri. Abandoning lead mining for the more promising venture of fur trading, in which Henry had had considerable experience, Ashley and Henry in 1822 and 1823, in the face of active hostility from the Arikara Indians in the latter year, dispatched successive expeditions up the Missouri River to the Yellowstone, where they established a post. Accompanying them was Hugh Glass, whose remarkable adventures have been justly celebrated (Neihardt, *Song of Hugh Glass,* 1915). Another Ashley party, which actually broke new ground, was that of Smith and Fitzpatrick, which set out from a trading post named Fort Kiowa in southern South Dakota in September 1823 and pushed west—in the following February or March crossing South Paso and entering Green River Valley. From 1824 Ashley continued the business on his own account under a new plan of operations, substituting for the fixed trading post or fort the annual rendezvous, which could be conducted at any accessible point and which enormously extended the range of operations of the men in the field. By using horses on the more direct westward route by land, he also avoided the dangerous and decidedly circuitous water route up the Missouri. To transport supplies to the men who had been left in the mountains, 1823–24, and to bring out their furs, Ashley set out, Nov. 3, 1824, from Fort Atkinson (the site of the present Calhoun, Nebr., some seventeen miles north of Omaha), following the valleys of the Platte, the South Platte, and the Cache la Poudre to the vicinity of Long's Peak, Colo. Traveling in the dead of winter and with insufficient feed for his horses, he accomplished the difficult feat of crossing the eastern Rockies and the lofty and barren plateau of southern Wyoming, reaching Green River near the mouth of the Sandy early in April 1825. The first to embark on the Green, which has been navigated less than half a dozen times and usually with specially constructed craft, he descended its turbulent waters in buffalo-skin boats. "As we passed along between these massy walls, which in a great degree excluded from us the rays of heaven and presented a surface as impassable as their body was impregnable, I was forcibly struck with the gloom which spread over the countenances of my men. They seemed to anticipate (and not far distant, too) a dreadful termination of our voyage, and I must confess that I partook in some degree of what I supposed to be their feelings, for things around us had truly an awful appearance" (Ashley narrative, *Ashley-Smith Explorations,* p. 145). Continuing to a point fifty miles below the Uintah River he retraced his course to the mouth of that stream, where, procuring horses from the Ute Indians, he proceeded by land to the confluence of Henry's Fork with the Green, where he conducted the first rendezvous. Leaving immediately with the accumulated furs, Ashley returned to St. Louis by way of South Pass, the Big Horn, and the Missouri. Again going west in the spring of 1826, he reached the vicinity of Great Salt Lake, where he conducted the annual rendezvous, returning this year by land, covering the distance from Salt Lake to St. Louis in the brief space of seventy days. Retiring from active participation in the fur trade he continued to supply goods to his successors in the business.

After suffering defeat for governor in 1824, Ashley ran for the United States Senate in 1829, but was again defeated. In 1831, however, he was elected to Congress on an anti-Jackson ticket to fill a vacancy caused by the death of a congressman in a duel. Reëlected twice, he retired from national politics in March 1837. Throughout his career in Congress he proved himself an active champion of western measures. On the House Committee on Indian Affairs, he consistently opposed the policy of temporizing with the Indians, "buying peace," as he called it. In 1836 he was again defeated for the governorship of Missouri. Failing health induced him to leave his magnificent residence in north St. Louis to seek change of climate at the home of his father-in-law, Dr. J. W. Moss, in Cooper County, where he died of pneumonia. He was married three times. His first wife, Mary Able, died Nov. 7, 1821. His second wife, Eliza Christy, whom he married Oct. 26, 1825, died June 12, 1830. In October 1832 he married Mrs. Elizabeth (Moss) Wilcox, who survived him.

[The most extensive account of Ashley's career is in Harrison Clifford Dale, *Ashley-Smith Explorations and the Discovery of a Central Route to the Pacific* (1918).

Short biog. sketches are available in Wm. F. Switzler, "Gen. Wm. Henry Ashley," *Am. Mo. Mag.*, 1908, XXXII, 318–30; J. T. Scharf, *Hist. of St. Louis City and County* (1883), pp. 196–97; *Encyc. of Va. Biog.* (1915), II, 264; D. M. Grissom in *Encyc. of the Hist. of St. Louis* (1899), I, 53–55. The narrative of his significant expedition of 1824–25 is printed in full in Dale.]

H. C. D.

ASHMEAD, ISAAC (Dec. 22, 1790–Mar. 1, 1870), printer, son of Jacob and Mary (Naglee) Ashmead, was born at Germantown, Pa. He was well connected, and belonged to a family which had come to Philadelphia in the opening year of the colony. Ashmead's father served in the Revolution and he himself in the War of 1812. He was apprenticed to a Philadelphia printer, William Bradford, and about 1821 he established a business of his own which he conducted until his death. In 1828 he married Belina Farren, daughter of Jacob Farren of East Haven, Conn. He was prosperous in business, and a pioneer in various technical matters relating to his trade. He was the first to introduce the composition roller, and the hydraulic press for smooth-pressing wet sheets; the first also—in Philadelphia—to use the power printing press. He was active in church affairs and in establishing evening schools, and was manager of the Philadelphia Institute for apprentices. Probably his most important accomplishment was in connection with Sunday-schools. In 1819 he founded the Sunday and Adult School Union, a body which developed into the widely known American Sunday School Union. This organization, with nationwide activities, distributed a variety of publications, and Ashmead was its printer. He was a man of wide reading, of scrupulous integrity, and was held in general esteem.

[Geo. F. Wiswell, *Sermon: Legacy of a Good Man* (Mar. 13, 1870); *Phila. Pub. Ledger*, Mar. 3, 1870.]

E. K. A.

ASHMEAD, WILLIAM HARRIS (Sept. 19, 1855–Oct. 17, 1908), entomologist, was the son of Capt. Albert and Elizabeth (Graham) Ashmead and came of excellent colonial ancestry on both sides. Born in Philadelphia, he early in life entered the publishing house of J. B. Lippincott Company, of that city, and as soon as he felt that he had had sufficient experience went to Jacksonville, Fla., and, with a brother, founded a printing house for the publication of agricultural and other books. He established an agricultural daily and weekly newspaper, the *Florida Dispatch,* in which he soon started a scientific department and was drawn to the study of injurious insects. His earlier articles in the *Dispatch* were rather crude, but he was a far-sighted young man and a great worker. He began to contribute to the scientific journals in 1879, and these contributions increased rapidly in number and importance so that at the time of his death his bibliography comprised more than 250 titles. In 1887 he was appointed special field agent of the United States Department of Agriculture, and the following year was made entomologist to the State Agricultural Experiment Station at Lake City, Fla., publishing in this capacity one of the first entomological bulletins issued by any of the state agricultural experiment stations under the so-called Hatch Act. In 1889 he was made an assistant in the Division of Entomology of the Department of Agriculture at Washington. The winter of 1890–91 he spent as a student in Berlin. In 1895 he was made assistant curator of the Division of Insects in the United States National Museum, and held this position until shortly before his death. His large private collection was donated to the Museum in 1898. When he came to Washington in 1889 he was a wealthy man, but a disastrous fire in Jacksonville destroyed the bulk of his property. The great majority of his published papers were of taxonomic character. His two great works were his *Monograph of the North American Proctotrypidæ,* published as Bulletin 45 of the United States National Museum (1893), and his *Classification of the Chalcid Flies or the Superfamily Chalcidoidea,* published by the Carnegie Museum of Pittsburgh in 1904. The preparation of these two volumes would have been enough to have monopolized the working lifetime of any ordinary man, but in addition to these he described many hundreds of new genera and species (607 genera and 3,100 species) and published a number of papers of a broad classificatory nature, several of which revolutionized the views then accepted. The greater part of his work dealt with North American insects, but he studied and described many forms from South America and Japan and, after the Spanish War, very many from the Philippines. He held many offices in scientific societies. There was much in his work of lasting value. He had a keen eye and remarkable judgment in estimating the relative value of structural characters. It was fortunate that his principal interest lay in the parasitic Hymenoptera, since the value of that group in the practical control of insect pests has become more and more evident. It is probable that his admirers did not overestimate the value of his work when they called him "a genius in taxonomy." Personally he was of genial temperament, fond of whist and billiards. In 1878 he married Harriet Holmes.

[*Proc. Entomological Soc. Washington,* X, 126–56, including lists of Ashmead's writings and of his new genera and species, and accompanied by portrait. Shorter sketches in the *Canadian Entomologist,* XL, 437–38, *Entomological News,* XIX, 397–98, portr.]

L. O. H.

ASHMORE, WILLIAM (Dec. 25, 1824–Apr. 21, 1909), Baptist missionary, was born in Putnam, Ohio, of Scotch-Irish parentage. He was educated in the local schools, in Granville College (now Denison University), from which he received the B.A. degree in 1845, and in the Western Baptist Theological Institute in Covington, Ky. Upon graduation from the seminary in 1848 he entered upon a pastorate in Hamilton, Ohio. In 1849 he received appointment to the China Mission, toward which he set out the following year with his wife, Martha Ann Sanderson. At that time the Mission's chief work for the Chinese was conducted at Bangkok, Siam. Ashmore assumed charge of the Chinese department of the Siam Mission, giving his chief attention to learning Chinese and to personal evangelism. At the end of 1858 in Hongkong he planned the opening of a station in Swatow. Another, however, actually began the work, as Ashmore was forced to return to America by illness. At home he recovered his health and in 1861 married a second wife, Eliza Dunlevy, his first wife having died in 1858. Upon his return to China, the China war was over and Swatow open. He took up his work at the new station which in time became the center of the South China Mission. In 1872 upon the death of Mr. Johnson, who had established the station, Swatow passed into the care of Ashmore. Having at first preferred evangelism as "the more scriptural kind of labor," he became increasingly aware of the need of schools to train a Chinese ministry. To this end he conducted a "theological class," which led to the establishment in 1892 of the Biblical Training School for Men, which ultimately became the Ashmore Seminary in 1905.

Ashmore was often interrupted in his direct missionary work. At home in 1875–76 for his wife's sake, he rendered effective service through articles in the *Journal and Messenger* and addresses before the churches. For three years from 1881 he suffered from partial blindness. At home again in 1885 for the health of his wife, who died despite the furlough, he was elected home secretary of the American Baptist Missionary Union. He actually served in this capacity only during the year 1889, after a further stay in Swatow. From 1890 he not only exercised general oversight of Swatow but was charged by the executive committee at home with inspection of other fields as well. During a visit to Japan he married Mrs. Charlotte A. Brown of that Mission. With one year in America delivering masterly addresses at church gatherings, the next in China at the Swatow Bible Training School, again at home in 1899, he made his last trip to the East with the understanding that he would shortly withdraw from the foreign field and "devote the remainder of his days to service among the home churches." Coming home in 1903 he located in Wollaston, Mass., and for a time wrote constantly for the *Journal and Messenger.* His eightieth birthday was celebrated by his Board with a service in Tremont Temple and by himself with a gift, $10,000 in value, to the Swatow mission. By this gift the seminary which bears his name became possible. He continued its official head until his death.

[*Ann. Reports of the Am. Bapt. Missionary Union,* 1852–1909; "In Memoriam: Wm. Ashmore" in *Bapt. Missionary Mag.,* June 1909; "In Memoriam: Wm. Ashmore" in the *Chinese Recorder and Missionary Jour.,* Aug. 1909; G. W. Hervey, *The Story of Bapt. Missions in Foreign Lands* (1892), pp. 539, 868, 940–41; W. S. Stewart, *Early Bapt. Missionaries and Pioneers* (1926), II, 105–26.]

J. C. A.

ASHMUN, GEORGE (Dec. 25, 1804–July 17, 1870), congressman, was born at Blandford, Mass., the son of Eli Porter Ashmun. His mother was a daughter of the Rev. John Hooker, of Northampton, Mass. To a surprising extent his career duplicated that of his father, who was also born in Blandford, became a lawyer, served several terms in each branch of the Massachusetts legislature, and became a member of the United States Senate, 1816–18. George Ashmun was graduated from Yale College in 1823, studied law, and in 1828 began practise in Springfield, where he continued to make his home until his death. From 1834 to 1851 he was associated in practise with Reuben A. Chapman, later chief justice of the supreme court of Massachusetts. He served five terms in the Massachusetts House of Representatives, in the last (1841) being elected speaker. In 1838 and 1839 he was a member of the Massachusetts Senate. Elected to Congress as a Whig, he represented his district in three successive terms, 1845–51. He early took a strong stand against the extension of slave territory. On Feb. 3, 1846, he offered a resolution (upon which action was prevented) calling upon the President for information "whether the army or navy or any part of either, had been ordered to move toward that Republic [Mexico], and what occurrences had come to the knowledge of the President to require such a movement" (*Congressional Globe,* 29 Cong., 1 Sess., p. 299). When Polk's message (May 11, 1846) announced to Congress, "War exists, and notwithstanding all our efforts to avoid it, exists by the act of Mexico," Ashmun made a bold speech, citing official documents to prove that the war with Mexico "has been brought upon us by the men who are administering the offices of Government, in disregard of the principles of the Constitution and of their duties to the people of the country" (*Ibid.,* 29 Cong., App., 1 Sess., July 27, 1846, pp. 809–12). He was one of the fourteen who voted against the army supply bill of May 13, 1846. During his years in Congress he served on committees on the Judiciary, on Indian Affairs, and on Rules. He interested himself in efforts to curb the President's power of patronage, and to restrict the immigration of persons liable to become a public charge. He was a great admirer of Daniel Webster, although he did not follow him in abandoning the Wilmot Proviso. Aside from his protests against the Mexican War, he made his strongest impress upon the country by his passionate defense of Webster in two speeches, the first in reply to C. J. Ingersoll (*Ibid.,* 29 Cong., 1 Sess., App., pp. 729–33), and the second in response to a storm of abuse from Charles Allen, following the "7th-of-March Speech" (*Ibid.,* 31 Cong., 2 Sess., p. 687). Through these speeches he won a national reputation, but they caused him to share in Webster's unpopularity, and this led to his retirement from Congress. In 1852 he was chairman of the committee on resolutions in the Whig Convention. In 1860 he was made permanent chairman of the Republican National Convention at Chicago, and "presided over the excited and enthusiastic assemblage with dignity, tact, and ability" (Henry Wilson, *History of the Rise and Fall of the Slave Power in America,* 1874, II, 691). President Lincoln often sought his advice. Within a few hours after the fall of Sumter, Ashmun persuaded Stephen Douglas to go with him to the White House (Apr. 14) where in a long conference Douglas pledged to the President hearty support in efforts to preserve the Union, maintain the government, and defend the capital. In 1866 Ashmun was chosen a delegate to the National Union Convention in Philadelphia, but took no part in its proceedings. For some time he was a director of the Union Pacific Railroad. He was a man of commanding presence and great personal magnetism, eloquent in speech, of fine literary taste and unusual social charm. In western Massachusetts he was unmatched in his profession, and was held in high regard as a clear-headed statesman of conscience and courage. He married Martha E. Hall of Springfield, in 1828.

[The most authoritative data are to be found in *Obit. Rec. Grads. Yale Univ.,* 1870–80, p. 17, and in an extended article in the *Springfield Republican,* July 18, 1870, attributed to his life-long friend, Samuel Bowles.]

G. H. H.

ASHMUN, JEHUDI (Apr. 21, 1794–Aug. 25, 1828), colonial agent, remembered chiefly for his heroic and vital connection with the colonizing of Liberia, was the second son of Samuel Ashmun, and one of a numerous family of scanty means in the backwoods settlement of Champlain, N.Y. He nevertheless succeeded in gaining a classical education; after three years at Middlebury College and one at the University of Vermont, he was graduated at the latter institution in 1816. He entered the Congregational ministry and became principal and organizer of the Maine Charity School at Hampden, the germ of the Bangor Theological Seminary. Success was crowning two years' hard work when misunderstandings arising from a hasty marriage on Oct. 7, 1818 to Miss C. L. Gray, led to his resignation. Almost penniless and without prospects, he went by sea to Baltimore and engaged in several unsuccessful journalistic ventures. These, however, led to employment in Washington as editor of the *Theological Repertory,* a monthly periodical of the Episcopal Church, which he later joined. He kept the *Repertory* on its feet for several years, contributing himself a number of able articles. Among these were several in support of the work of the American Colonization Society, whose Liberian enterprise had captured his imagination. He also wrote a sympathetic biography of the Rev. Samuel Bacon, one of the agents of the society who had gone over with the first colonists.

This interest led to his appointment as a representative of the United States Government on a mission to the colony, and so determined his destiny. In 1819 an appropriation had been made by Congress to provide a station in Africa for the return of smuggled slaves rescued by revenue officers. The fund had already been drawn upon to establish a colony in Liberia. Now a few "recaptured Africans" were to be sent back from Baltimore on the brig *Strong.* Thirty-seven new colonists of the Society were given passage. Ashmun was put in charge. He expected to return on the *Strong,* and his wife accompanied him. They landed Aug. 9, 1822. He found the colony in a desperate situation. Of the 114 settlers sent over in 1820 and 1821 many had succumbed to fever; nearly all the survivors were on the sick-list; their supplies were exhausted; the rainy season had set in; the white agents appointed to protect them had deserted; and, worst of all, the native chiefs were threatening an attack. Heroically determining to remain, Ashmun assumed leadership in caring for the sick and preparing for the attack. Only twenty-seven men were capable of bearing arms. A few small field-pieces formed his main reliance. The expected assault was delayed, permitting earthworks to be thrown up, trees and brush cleared away, and the little force drilled. But the fatiguing labor brought on fever. Ashmun was prostrated; his wife sickened and died before his eyes; at one time scarcely a man in the colony was well. At length on Nov. 11 just before daybreak 800 savages attacked. In a desperate contest the colonists finally succeeded in bringing a brass field-piece to bear upon the dense ranks. The effect at such short range was decisive. "Every shot literally spent its force in a solid mass of human flesh. Their fire suddenly terminated. A savage yell was raised . . . and the whole host disappeared" (Ashmun, *post,* p. 29). A second attack on Dec. 2 was decisively repulsed, supplies and ammunition having been replenished by a chance English vessel on the very day before. The unusual sound of a midnight cannonade attracted another vessel, of the English navy, having on board the experienced African explorer, Capt. Laing. Through Laing's tactful mediation a peace with the native chiefs was arranged and the crisis passed. In May 1823 a new agent Dr. Ayres, arrived. In the emergency Ashmun had without authority assumed the position of agent. He now found himself superseded, his arrangements upset, his sacrifices unappreciated, his drafts dishonored, and his motives questioned. After stirring up the colony to the point of insurrection, Ayres at a touch of fever betook himself to America. The colonists, again deserted by their official protectors, turned to Ashmun who forgot his wrongs in redoubled efforts. In 1824 the Rev. R. R. Gurley, secretary of the Society, was sent over to investigate the charges against Ashmun. He not only exonerated him, but became his warmest admirer and ultimately his biographer. Ashmun, now fully authorized agent, remained the vigorous and successful head of the enterprise until 1828. In 1826 was published his *History of the American Colony in Liberia from December, 1821 to 1823.* His health failing in 1828, he sought, in vain, relief in the West Indies, whence he sailed for New Haven, which he reached on Aug. 10. On Aug. 25 he died.

[R. R. Gurley, *Life of Jehudi Ashmun, Late Colonial Agent in Liberia* (1835); Ashmun's articles, letters, and reports in the *Am. Colonization Soc. Reports,* the *African Repository,* and the *Theological Repertory;* J. H. T. McPherson, "Hist. of Liberia," *Johns Hopkins Studies* (1891); Sir Harry Johnston, *Liberia* (1906), I, 129–51, II, 813; Leonard Bacon, *A Discourse Preached in the Center Church, in New Haven, Aug. 27, 1828, at the Funeral of Jehudi Ashmun, Esq.* (New Haven, 1828).]

J. H. T. M.

ASPINWALL, WILLIAM (May 23, 1743–Apr. 16, 1823), physician, son of Thomas and Joanna (Gardner) Aspinwall, was descended from Peter Aspinwall, one of the 4,000 Puritans of 1630 who followed the *Mayflower.* He was born on the ancestral farm in Brookline, Mass., in the house which had been built by Peter in 1660. He was educated by a clergyman, the Rev. Amos Adams, obtained his degree at Harvard in 1764, and then studied medicine, first with Dr. Benjamin Gale of Killingworth, Conn., author of *A Treatise on Small Pox Inoculation,* and later with Dr. William Shippen of Philadelphia, who gave him a certificate for skill in 1769. He was in the ranks at the battle of Lexington and carried from the field the body of Isaac Gardner, whose daughter, Susanna, he later married. Immediately after Lexington he applied for a commission in the Continental army but was persuaded by Dr. Joseph Warren to enter the military medical department, in which he was appointed brigade surgeon and deputy director to an army hospital at Jamaica Plain, Mass. After peace was declared, Dr. Aspinwall opened at Brookline, Mass., an inoculation hospital for small-pox, the second of its kind in America. The "business," as it was called, prospered until the coming of vaccination in which Aspinwall recognized a method superior to that which he had been using: he thereupon closed the doors of his hospital. "This new inoculation . . . is no sham," he wrote. "As a man of humanity, I rejoice in it, although it will take from me a handsome annual income." His private practise, however, remained large, and in going his rounds on horseback he often covered as much as forty miles in one day. Although slated for appointment in a new "Massachusetts College of Physicians," he withdrew his name from the petition for a charter on becoming convinced that the proposed institution would injure the already well-established medical department at Harvard. He was a leader in the town affairs of Brookline as treasurer, warden, representative to the General Court, state senator, and member of the governor's council. An accident in youth lost him the use of one eye, and late in life he was afflicted with a cataract in the other, so that, despite an operation, total blindness resulted. He was married in 1776 to Susanna Gardner, by whom he had seven children. A portrait by Gilbert Stuart, hanging in the house of his abolitionist son-in-law, Lewis Tappan of New York, is said to have been spared by anti-slavery rioters because they mistook it for a picture of George Washington.

[A. A. Aspinwall, *Aspinwall Geneal.* (1901); James Thacher, *Am. Medic. Biog.* (1828), I, 91–95; W. L.

Burrage in *Am. Medic. Biogs.* (1920), pp. 44–45; J. M. Toner, *Medic. Men of the Revolution* (1876), pp. 11, 96; Ebenezer Alden, *Boston Medic. and Surgic. Jour.*, Oct. 19, 1853.]

J. A. S.

ASPINWALL, WILLIAM HENRY (Dec. 16, 1807–Jan. 18, 1875), merchant, was born in New York City, a posthumous son of John Aspinwall, merchant and son of a sea-captain. His mother was Susan Howland. On receiving a common school training he was apprenticed to his uncles, G. G. and S. Howland, sons of a New London whaler, who had built up a leading business house in New York, which carried on a heavy trade with Mexico, England, and the Mediterranean countries. In 1832, Aspinwall was admitted as a partner with a fourth interest which meant an annual profit of about $15,000. In 1837 the older men turned the business over to William Edgar Howland and Aspinwall with a capital of $200,000. Howland and Aspinwall withstood the panic of that year, continuing to handle the largest general trading, exporting, and importing business of any house in New York. The years following 1837 were treacherous ones for a newly established mercantile house. The credit for successful carrying on was probably due to the well-established reputation of the Howlands as much as to the executive ability and far-sightedness of their young successors. At any rate, the firm retained its heavy trade with England and the Mediterranean lands and remained without a rival in the Pacific trade and scarcely an equal in the West and East Indies shipping. Favored by the president of Venezuela, Howland and Aspinwall had almost a monopoly of the American trade with that republic. With this and the Mexican business as an entering wedge, the concern made great strides in the Latin-American countries. Its fleet of clipper ships was well known in the chief ports; and its profits were rapidly making Aspinwall a leading merchant and capitalist of New York.

Affected by the gold fever of 1849–51, he resigned active leadership in the firm to enter the Pacific Railroad & Panama Steamship Company. In 1850, largely through his efforts, the New York legislature granted a charter for the Panama Railroad incorporated at $1,000,000. He and his associates, Lloyd Aspinwall, a brother, Samuel W. Comstock, Henry Chauncey, and John L. Stevens, obtained from New Granada the privilege of building a railway across the isthmus, and within five years the forty-nine miles of road were completed under the engineers George M. Totten and John C. Trautwine. The town at the eastern terminal was named Aspinwall in honor of the man who more than any one else was responsible for the success of the hazardous undertaking. In 1848, Aspinwall, Chauncey, Richard Alsop, the Howlands, and Edwin Bartlett founded the Pacific Mail Steamship Company, incorporated under a New York statute for twenty years. This was considered highly speculative for such a conservative investor as Aspinwall, and its failure was generally predicted. California gold soon decided otherwise. Two years later, its capital was increased from $400,000 to $2,000,000, so large were the returns from carrying by way of Panama men and supplies to California and gold back to the East. With the completion of the railroad, the Aspinwall interests had control of a through water-rail route from New York to San Francisco and a monopoly of the carrying trade until the completion of the Union Pacific Railroad (1869). By 1859, the railroad alone had netted about $6,000,000. When Aspinwall resigned the presidency of this corporation (1856), he was one of the richest men of New York.

During the Civil War, he was an active supporter of the Lincoln policies, a founder and vice-president of the Union League Club, and, along with John M. Forbes a secret emissary of the President to urge the British Government to stop the building and outfitting of iron-clad rams under construction at the Laird shipyards for the Confederacy. After this time, Aspinwall was not actively engaged in business, though he or a representative of his house held a place on innumerable boards of directors of railroads, shipping concerns, banks, and insurance companies. Indeed, Howland & Aspinwall had become more of a banking and brokerage than trading firm. Aspinwall never sought or held political office, though his interest in politics was keen. He was long a leader in the Chamber of Commerce, active in social life, a trustee of the Lenox Library, a charter member of the Society for the Prevention of Cruelty to Animals (1866), a patron of the drama and of fine arts, and owner of one of New York's finest art galleries, which he opened to the public. He was married to Anna L. Breck of Bristol, Pa. His later years were spent in his town house, which his hospitality made a social center, in his show place near Tarrytown on the Hudson, and in extended travel. On his death, the wealthy old merchant could be described as a good man, generous if not open-handed, lenient to debtors, and willing to meet bankrupt merchants more than halfway.

[*Diary of Philip Hone* (1889), ed. by Bayard Tuckerman, I, 101, 283, 360, II, 82, 243, 245, 270; J. A. Scoville, *Old Merchants of N.Y.C.* (1862), pp. 306–14; J. G. Wilson, *Memorial Hist. of the City of N.Y.* (1893), III, 422, 490, IV, 88, 369, 451; *N.Y. the World's Me-*

tropolis (1924), ed. by W. T. Bonner, p. 723; Moses Yale Beach, *Wealth and Pedigree of the Wealthy Citizens of N.Y.C.* (4th ed., 1842), p. 4; *N.Y. Times, N.Y. Tribune,* Jan. 19, 1875.] R. J. P.

ASTOR, JOHN JACOB (July 17, 1763–Mar. 29, 1848), fur trader, capitalist, was born in the village of Waldorf, Duchy of Baden, Germany. His father, Jacob, according to Parton, was "a jovial, good-for-nothing butcher, . . . much more at home in the beer-house than at his own fireside," and though his mother was industrious, saving, and capable, the family was often in want. Of the three older sons, George and Henry left home at an early age, the former establishing himself in a musical-instrument house in London and the latter in a butcher's shop in New York City. After the death of the mother and the advent of a stepmother, the third son, John Jacob, decided to shift for himself. A strong, healthy lad of about seventeen, with enough schooling to enable him to read, write, and cipher, and with a crown or two in his pocket, he started afoot for the Rhine. On his way he is said to have sat down under a tree and made three resolutions—to be honest, to be industrious, and not to gamble. He got work on a timber raft, and by the time it reached the mouth of the river he had earned enough to pay his passage to England. On his arrival in London he found employment with his brother. He remained there about three years, saving money, studying the language, and learning everything he could about the land of his dreams, the United States. On the news of the signing of the Treaty of Paris in the fall of 1783 he decided to cross the Atlantic. He embarked in November, with about twenty-five dollars in money, a merchandise stock of seven flutes, and a passage paper entitling him to a berth in the steerage with sailor's fare of salt beef and biscuit. The vessel entered Chesapeake Bay early in January, but before a landing could be made was frozen in, to remain ice-bound for more than two months. Among the passengers whose acquaintance he made was a German immigrant who had been in America before and had successfully traded for furs with the Indians. Astor questioned this man persistently regarding everything connected with the fur trade, and by the time the vessel was freed he had chosen his future occupation.

He arrived in New York City in March 1784, and was welcomed by his brother Henry. Of his first years in the city the accounts are conflicting. There is a story that he served for some time as an apprentice to a baker, George Dieterich, for whom he peddled cakes, and another that his brother Henry got him a place as a helper, at two dollars a week and board, in the fur store of Robert Bowne, an aged and benevolent Quaker. Both Irving and Chittenden, on the other hand, imply that he became at once a factor in the trade and assert that in the same year (Chittenden says in the early summer) he returned with a cargo of furs to England. In 1786 he had his own place of business, a small shop in Water Street, where for a time he also sold musical instruments. In the same year (or possibly in 1785) he married Sarah Todd, a connection of the Brevoorts, who brought him $300 in cash, a clear head for business, and an especially keen sense in the valuation of furs. He worked hard, constantly planned new ventures, and bought and sold with a talent for bargaining which always kept in view, says Parton, "the simple object of giving the least and getting the most." Often he made trips to the nearby frontiers, once at least going as far as Mackinaw. The Jay treaty, with the sequent evacuation of the frontier forts by the British in the summer of 1796 and the modifying of trade restrictions between the United States and Canada, greatly increased his opportunities. By an arrangement with the Northwest Company he was now able to add to his stock by direct importations from Montreal. His energy was tireless, and his business continued to expand. By 1800, when he had amassed a quarter of a million dollars, he was acknowledged to be the leading factor in the trade.

About this time he began to ship to the Orient. On one of his visits to London an official in the East India House, whom he had known as a boy, had given him a ship license to trade freely in any port monopolized by the East India Company. A merchant friend in New York was induced to fit out a vessel which, carrying this license, voyaged to Canton and back, making profits that netted Astor $50,000. About this time, also, he began to make large purchases of city real estate, which later was to form the bulk of the Astor fortune. He now emerged from the somewhat squalid quarters in which he had dwelt, and the year 1801 saw the family handsomely housed near the corner of Broadway and Vesey St., later to become famous as the location of the Astor House.

The Louisiana Purchase opened to him illimitable vistas of the extension of the fur trade; and the reports that followed the return of Lewis and Clark in the fall of 1806 set in motion his energies toward the penetration of the West. In the following year he began to contest the hold of the Mackinaw Company, a Canadian organization, in the Upper Mississippi Valley. On Apr. 6, 1808, he incorporated, through a charter granted by the New York legislature, all his widespread interests in the American Fur Company, of which he was the sole owner. He would doubtless at this time have entered the Far West through St. Louis, but the hostility of the traders of the frontier capital made the project hazardous. His plans were slowly forming, and by another year they had crystallized into a colossal project—a scheme, says Chittenden, "as feasible as it was magnificent." He would plant a central establishment at the mouth of the Columbia, with subordinate posts at various points in the interior. Furs would thus be gathered where they were most abundant and collected at the point at once nearest to the sources and to the richest market, China. A fleet of ships would carry them to Canton, there sell and reload, again sell and reload in Europe, and finally return to New York, while an annual ship from New York would supply the establishment with trading goods for the Indians and white trappers. Another year was spent in preliminaries, and on June 23, 1810, articles of agreement forming the Pacific Fur Company were signed by Astor and four others, three of whom were British subjects formerly with the Northwest Company. To forestall competition this company had been offered by Astor a one-third interest in the new organization. It had declined the offer, however, in the belief that it could itself control the territory, and it immediately planned a descent upon the Oregon country. Astoria was founded in the spring of 1811. But though the enterprise was begun with high hopes and prosecuted with great energy, it was destined to a brief life. The vessel that had carried the pioneers was lost, with all its crew, in June through an Indian massacre and an explosion; a party from the Northwest Company arrived shortly afterward to contest the territory, and in January 1813 came news that war had broken out between England and America and that the post was in imminent danger of capture. On Oct. 23 the post and property were sold by Duncan McDougall, temporarily in charge, to representatives of the Northwest Company for $58,000, a mere fraction of their value. On Nov. 30 a British naval vessel arrived, and on Dec. 12 its captain took possession of all the territory and rechristened the post Fort George.

But though Astor suffered reverses during the war he enjoyed more than compensating gains. His Manhattan real estate continued to increase in value. From the Government also he added enormously to his wealth. During the first two years of the war, said Greeley's *Tribune,* he loaned the Government only small sums; but in 1814, when its desperate need compelled it to pay ruinous toll for whatever money it could raise, he combined with Girard and Parish of Philadelphia to buy a large block of loan bonds at from eighty to eighty-two cents on the dollar, paying for them in bank notes worth approximately only half their face value. With the signing of peace, Astor turned again to the plan of reaching the trans-Mississippi region from the East. Through his efforts Congress was persuaded to pass the act of Apr. 29, 1816, which excluded, except by executive permit, aliens from engaging in the fur trade other than as employees. By 1817 Astor was in possession of all the Mississippi Valley posts of the Northwest Company as well as of the Southwest Company (the latter a reorganization of the old Mackinaw Company, in which he had bought a controlling interest before the war). Against the bitter opposition of the St. Louis traders he now pushed his operations toward the Missouri. In the winter of 1821–22 he succeeded in getting Congress to abolish the government trading posts which had been begun in 1796, and in the spring of 1822 he established in St. Louis the western department of the American Fur Company. Its chief competitor, the Columbia Fur Company, was absorbed in 1827, and through its field organization, the Upper Missouri Outfit, it soon monopolized the territory, afterward pushing to the west and south and putting itself in direct competition with the Rocky Mountain Fur Company of Fitzpatrick, Sublette, and Bridger. It was a bold and vigorously maintained campaign, but the returns were disappointing. The company's losses from Indians were heavy, the Rocky Mountain men were the superiors of its own men both as trappers and traders, and, moreover, the fur trade, due to changes in fashion, had begun to decline. Astor grew tired of the business, and on June 1, 1834, he sold all his fur interests. He did not again engage in commerce, but spent the remainder of his days, assisted by his son, William Backhouse Astor [*q.v.*] in administering his estate. He died in his New York home, by far the richest man in America. He had piled up a fortune conservatively estimated at $20,000,000, and all of it, except some two millions distributed in bequests, went to his son. Most of the bequests were to members of the family. He left $400,000 for the founding of a library, and to his faithful employee of many years, Fitz-Greene Halleck, the poet, he left a meager annuity of $200.

Astor is described by the *Tribune* as stout and square built, about five feet nine inches in height, with a high, square forehead and somewhat heavy features. Either he was good-natured or he held command of his passions, for his manner was urbane. He "wrote a wretched scrawl, setting spelling and grammar equally at defiance," and yet everything he wrote revealed the virile force of the man. He never overcame his marked German accent. Regarding his character there is disagreement. Irving was his eulogist and ascribes to him both benevolence and public spirit; in fact, his frequent laudation of the man prompted the charge that he was a paid retainer, but it seems to have been baseless, Irving himself declaring that he had never accepted the slightest pecuniary aid from the magnate. Other contemporaries saw Astor in a different light. "He has exhibited at best but the ingenious powers of a self-invented money-making machine," said Bennett's *Herald* on his decease, while Greeley's *Tribune* was equally uncomplimentary. Parton, though viewing him as "one of the ablest, boldest, and most successful operators that ever lived," found him selfish, grasping, and ruthless. The stories of his extreme parsimony as well as of his exacting acquisitiveness as creditor and landlord are many, and his merciless aggression in prosecuting the fur trade is attested by official documents that cannot be questioned. His influence at Washington, combined with his great wealth and his extensive organization, enabled him to carry on his operations with a high hand. His employees on the frontier (it was reported from Green Bay about 1818), if interfered with by government agents, threatened them with dismissal; and with his increasing monopolization of the field they grew more arrogant and lawless. "They entertain, as I know to be a fact," wrote an agent in a letter to Secretary of War Cass, dated St. Louis, Oct. 31, 1831 (quoted by Myers), "no sort of respect for our citizens, agents, officers or the Government or its laws or general policy." His men shared with other traders, and of course with his approval, in the work of debauching the Indians with liquor in order to get their furs more cheaply. The amassing of wealth was his ruling passion, and few devices that could contribute to that end were neglected by him. Though in his later days he wished to be portrayed as a broad-minded patriot and even a humanitarian, there is evidence that this ruling passion still possessed him at the close.

[James Parton, *Life of John Jacob Astor* (1865); Pierre M. Irving, *The Life and Letters of Washington Irving* (1857); H. M. Chittenden, *The Am. Fur Trade of the Far West* (1902); Gustavus Myers, *Hist. of the Great Am. Fortunes* (1910); Elizabeth L. Gebhard, *The Life and Ventures of the Original John Jacob Astor* (1915); Grace Flandrau, *Astor and the Ore. Country* (pamphlet, n.d.); Stella M. Drumm, "More About Astorians," *Ore. Hist. Soc. Quart.*, XXIV, 4 (1923); Sydney and Marjorie Greenbie, *Gold of Ophir* (1925); Walter Barrett (J. A. Scoville), *The Old Merchants of N. Y.C.* (1863); *Sen. Doc. 60*, 17 Cong., 1 Sess. (1821–22); *Sen. Doc. 90*, 22 Cong., 1 Sess. (1831–32); the *N. Y. True Sun*, Mar. 30, 1848; the *N. Y. Weekly Tribune*, Apr. 8, 1848; the *N. Y. Herald*, Apr. 5, 1848.]

W. J. G.

ASTOR, JOHN JACOB (June 10, 1822–Feb. 22, 1890), capitalist, the third of the name in America, was born in New York City, the son of William Backhouse and Margaret (Armstrong) Astor. After graduating from Columbia College in 1839 he studied at the University of Göttingen. Later he entered the Harvard Law School, from which he graduated in 1842. Shortly afterward he married Charlotte Gibbes, of a prominent but somewhat impoverished South Carolina family. At the end of a year spent in the practise of law he entered upon what was to be his lifework in the office of the family estate. At the beginning of the Civil War he enlisted and was made a colonel. His main service was on the staff of Gen. McClellan. He is said to have been a devoted student of military affairs. In later life, when he made a practise of regularly attending the meetings of the Loyal Legion, he often spoke of his army days as the best period of his life.

On leaving the army he resumed his employment in the office of the estate. Of his career thereafter few outstanding events are recorded. Like his father and grandfather, he abstained as a rule from political activities, and his one deviation from the rule is not to his credit. In 1871, when the Tweed ring was at the height of its power, Astor and five other prominent business men—Moses Taylor, Marshall O. Roberts, E. D. Brown, George K. Sistare, and Edward Schell—were induced to make a perfunctory examination of Controller Connolly's books and to hand in a report highly commending Connolly for his honesty and faithfulness to duty. It is hardly credible that either Astor or any other of these men could have been unaware of the gigantic frauds then being committed; and the collapse of the Tweed ring three years later placed all of them in a somewhat sorry light. The death of his father in 1875 brought Astor to the headship of the more important part of the estate, which required the greater administrative care. He continued the policy of buying urban real estate and always kept on deposit a large sum of money, so as to be able to take instant advantage of bargains offered. He never insured his houses, believing that he could better afford the occasional loss by fire of a whole block of buildings than the payment of the large sums required for insurance policies. He had a few business interests outside of his real estate; he became a director in the Western Union and in several banks, but it is unlikely that these affiliations engaged much of his time. He had few ambitions apart from business. It is said that President Hayes offered him the post of minister to Great Britain and that the offer did not interest him. The fostering of the Astor Library was his chief public concern. For some years he served as its treasurer. In 1879 he deeded the institution three lots on Lafayette Place, on which he subsequently erected the extension known as the North Library Building at a cost of $250,000. The last ten years of his life were uneventful. He died at his home in New York City, of angina pectoris.

Astor was about six feet tall. His eyes were gray, and the complexion of his full and somewhat rounded face was ruddy. His later portraits show a mustache and flowing side whiskers, worn in English style. His manner, though reserved, was courteous. Like his father he was extremely methodical. Though generous in large matters, in small ones he was calculating and even parsimonious; he would take time to rewrite a telegram in order to save a word. For many years he practised, with his wife, an extreme simplicity of household management. About the time of the death of his father, it is said, his wife persuaded him that the matter of simplicity had been somewhat overdone. After that, though display of all kinds was carefully avoided, there came lavish expenditures for entertainments, paintings, furniture, and books. A first-class chef was employed, and Astor became known as a connoisseur of wines and cigars. Mrs. Astor's collection of old laces, presented to the Metropolitan Museum in 1887, after her decease, must have cost what most persons would regard as a fortune. Both Astor and his wife expended large amounts in charities and public benefactions. The sum contributed to the Astor Library probably totaled $450,000. Large sums were given to the New York Cancer Hospital, St. Luke's Hospital, and the Metropolitan Museum, while the Children's Aid Society was sufficiently financed to make it one of the foremost institutions of practical benevolence in the country. Trinity Church, of which for many years Astor was a vestryman, was a special object of his favor. There were also private benevolences of many kinds, which are believed to have amounted to several hundred thousand dollars. The fortune left by Astor is estimated at from $75,000,000 to $100,000,000.

[*Ann. Cyc.*, 1890; Morgan Dix, "Mr. J. J. Astor and His American Ancestry," *N. Y. Geneal. and Biog. Record*, July 1891; Gustavus Myers, *Hist. of the Great Am. Fortunes*, I (1910); obituaries in the metropolitan press, Feb. 23, 1890, of which those in the *Tribune, Sun*, and *Times* are the best.]

W. J. G.

ASTOR, JOHN JACOB (July 13, 1864–Apr. 15, 1912), capitalist, inventor, and the fourth of the name in America, was born at Rhinebeck, N. Y., the son of William and Caroline Webster (Schermerhorn) Astor. He graduated at Harvard, with the degree of B.S., in 1888. The next two years he spent in foreign travel. In 1891 he returned to the United States to assume the management of the family estate and shortly afterward was married to Ava Lowle Willing of Philadelphia, by whom he had one son and one daughter. For two years (1895–96) he served on the staff of Gov. Levi P. Morton, with the rank of colonel. In 1897 he built the Astoria section of the palatial Waldorf-Astoria Hotel. At the beginning of the Spanish War in 1898 he was one of the first to offer his services to the government. He placed his palatial yacht, the *Nourmahal,* at the disposal of the Navy Department and equipped at his own expense a battery of artillery for service in the Philippines. Commissioned a lieutenant-colonel of volunteers, he assisted Major-General Breckinridge, inspector-general of the army, in the inspection of camps and troops at Chickamauga. He was later assigned to the staff of Major-General Shafter and served in the operations ending in the surrender of Santiago. At the close of the war he was recommended by Shafter for promotion to the brevet rank of colonel on account of "faithful and meritorious services," and this rank was later conferred.

Astor nourished for a time a literary ambition, and in 1894 published a semi-scientific novel, *A Journey in Other Worlds.* But his major interest apart from his business lay in the field of mechanics. He spent much time in experimenting with new devices, and invented, among other things, a bicycle brake, a pneumatic road improver (which seems to have been too fancifully conceived to be of practical use), and an improved turbine engine. In a letter published in the *Scientific American,* Nov. 8, 1902, he reported that all his applications for patents on marine turbines had been granted and that he dedicated them to the public. While his work as manager of the family estate was intermittent, during 1902 and 1903 he devoted himself to it assiduously and proved himself an able administrator. He had other business interests as well, being a director in the Western Union, the Equitable Life, the Illinois Central, and the Mercantile Trust Company. Astor and his first wife were divorced on Nov. 8, 1909. On Sept. 9, 1911, he married Madeline Talmage Force of New York City. Later, with his wife, he traveled in Europe. Beginning their return, they took passage on the ill-fated *Titanic,* which in mid-seas struck an iceberg and went down. Mrs. Astor was rescued, but Astor was drowned. The testimony of many survivors bears witness that in the catastrophe he showed a disregard of self and displayed great coolness and courage.

[*Who's Who in America,* 1912–13; H. H. Lewis, "The Quiet Control of a Vast Estate," *World's Work,* Nov. 1902; R. H. Greene, "Col. John Jacob Astor," *N.Y. Geneal. and Biog. Record,* Jan. 1913; *N.Y. Times,* Apr. 16, 1912, and N. Y. *Sun,* Apr. 17, 1912.]

W.J.G.

ASTOR, WILLIAM BACKHOUSE (Sept. 19, 1792–Nov. 24, 1875), capitalist, was born in New York City, the son of John Jacob Astor [*q.v.*] and Sarah (Todd) Astor and the younger brother of John Jacob Astor the second. Until the age of sixteen he attended the public schools, helping his father at the store after school hours and in vacation times. He was then sent to Heidelberg, and after two years to Göttingen, where he chose as his tutor a fellow-student, von Bunsen, later known as "the Chevalier," with whom for a time he traveled. In 1815 he returned to America and was taken into partnership by his father under the firm name of John Jacob Astor & Son. In 1818 he married Margaret, daughter of Gen. John Armstrong of Rhinebeck, N. Y., secretary of war under Madison, and thus became allied with one of the first families of the state. His part in the operations of the firm and of its chief subsidiary, the American Fur Company, though important, was always subordinate. Though he seems to have been nominally the head of the fur company during the last four or five years of the Astor ownership, the father, aided by Ramsay Crooks [*q.v.*], continued to dictate policies and methods, and it was the father who decided upon the sale of the company and the terms of purchase. The son's share in laying the foundations of the estate was thus hardly more than that of an industrious and faithful head clerk. All the bold plans by which it was built up were originated by the father. It is as his father's efficient coadjutor that the son is best known and after the father's death as the administrator and augmentor of the Astor millions.

Through a legacy of $500,000 left him by his uncle, Henry Astor, and his own share of the income of the Astor business, he became a man of great wealth. On the death of his father in 1848 he succeeded to the rank of the richest man in the United States. The elder son, John Jacob, was feeble-minded, and the bulk of the fortune—some $18,000,000 out of $20,000,000—was left to William, the remainder having been distributed in various bequests. The father's policy of buying real estate in the section of New York City south of Fifty-ninth St. between Fourth and Seventh Aves. was continued by the son until the greater part of the fortune was invested in land and buildings. He thus became commonly known as the "landlord of New York." The rapid growth of population in the metropolis greatly increased land values and brought to him a constantly augmenting rent-roll. The pressure for living quarters soon converted many of the Astor buildings into crowded tenements, for which they were wholly unfitted. Complaints of the foul and reeking condition of these habitations became general. For many years Astor was unmoved and steadfastly opposed every proposal for building and street improvements, but by 1861 he had come to adopt a wiser policy. During the next twelve years he demolished many of the old rookeries and erected in their place simple and substantial buildings appropriate to the various localities. The improvements made, however, could have constituted little more than a patch on a great social sore. Most of Astor's time was spent in close application to his business. He was extremely methodical, and for many years made a practise of leaving his home exactly at nine and walking to his place of business. Up to four days before his death he was at his desk daily, hard at work. He died at his home in New York City, of pneumonia.

Astor in his seventy-sixth year was described by a contemporary, Matthew Hale Smith, as "a tall, heavy built man, with a decided German look, a countenance blank, eyes small and contracted, a look sluggish and unimpassioned, unimpressible in his feelings, taciturn and unsocial" (*Sunshine and Shadow in New York,* 1868, p. 186). Others have portrayed him as a man of dignified culture, a student of books and affairs, and one who, though he made no new literary friends, retained as associates the scholars and penmen who had been the friends of his father. There is word also of his many and generous benefactions, of his liberality to his tenants, and of his high sense of honor. Certain it is that he corrected at once some of the niggardly bequests of his father. He raised, for instance, the annuity of Fitz-Greene Halleck from $200 to $1,500. Also, he gave $50,000 to St. Luke's Hospital. He made the Astor Library his particular care. Under his direction the edifice was completed in May 1853. Two years later he presented to the trustees an adjoining lot, and he erected thereon a similar structure, completed in 1859. His various gifts to the library totalled about $550,000. His fortune, estimated to have been from $45,000,000 to $50,000,000, he divided equally between his sons, John Jacob and William.

[The long obituaries in the New York newspapers, the *World, Tribune, Times,* and *Sun,* give a great deal of what purports to be information, but much of it is conflicting. The accumulation of the Astor fortunes and their later management is treated at length by Gustavus Myers, *Hist. of the Great Am. Fortunes,* I (1910). See also *Ann. Cyc.,* 1875.]

W.J.G.

ASTOR, WILLIAM WALDORF (Mar. 31, 1848–Oct. 18, 1919), capitalist, journalist, was born in New York City, the son of John Jacob Astor, 1822–90 [*q.v.*], and Charlotte (Gibbes) Astor. From his mother he derived a taste for intellectual pursuits. He was trained by private tutors and later was graduated from Columbia Law School. For a time he was associated with a law firm. Later he was employed under his father in the management of the family estate, but he soon tired of the work and withdrew. Persuaded, against the family tradition, to enter politics, he was elected (1877) to the Assembly as a Republican. Two years later he was elected to the Senate. He was twice a candidate for Congress, but each time was defeated. He was married on June 6, 1878, to Mary Dahlgren Paul of Philadelphia. In August 1882 he was appointed by President Arthur minister to Italy, a post which he retained for three years. A period of literary activity followed. In 1885 he published *Valentino: An Historical Romance of the Sixteenth Century in Italy;* in 1889 *Sforza, a Story of Milan;* in 1900 *Pharaoh's Daughter and Other Stories.*

On the death of his father in February 1890 he succeeded to the management of the family estate, with a personal fortune estimated at $100,000,000. He erected the Waldorf section of what ultimately became the Waldorf-Astoria Hotel. By now he had come to feel a strong dislike for his native land. It was induced, according to report, partly by his political experiences and partly by the contest waged between his wife and his aunt for the leadership of what was then known as the "four hundred" of metropolitan society. It was said further that his wife, excited over newspaper accounts of kidnappers, had come to be alarmed for the safety of her children. In September 1890 he removed with his family to England and took up his residence in an imposing mansion in London. In 1893 he bought the liberal daily newspaper, the *Pall Mall Gazette,* with its weekly edition, *The Budget,* and changed the two journals into conservative organs. The same year he established a monthly periodical, the *Pall Mall Magazine.* He then grew tired of journalism, and though from time to time contributing an article or an editorial, he rarely visited his office. Years later (1911) he bought, for some unknown reason, a Sunday newspaper, *The Observer.* Three years later he disposed of all his publications, the daily and the Sunday journals going to his son, Maj. Waldorf Astor, who shortly afterward sold them.

In 1899 he became a British subject. His dislike of his former compatriots appears in much that he wrote and said. An article on his famous grandfather, published in the *Pall Mall Magazine* for June 1899, served as a vehicle for a particularly vigorous criticism of American character and customs. Despite this antipathy he was keenly sensitive to American opinion. In July 1892, in an effort to learn what Americans thought of him, he caused a false report of his death to be published here. He was not to be enlightened, for the hoax was discovered before any obituary had appeared. His life in England was characterized by vast expenditures, a somewhat obtrusive effort to win social recognition, and a series of quarrels and squabbles over insignificant matters. He bought several estates, one of them embracing the Ann Boleyn castle at Hever, Kent, and he entertained lavishly. The Hever castle he restored at a cost said to be more than $10,000,000. On Jan. 1, 1916, he was made a peer, with the title Baron Astor of Hever Castle, and on June 3 of the following year was made a viscount. He had achieved a desired social distinction, but not without strong opposition. A considerable part of the English press denounced his elevation to the peerage as an act of recompense for financial support to the party then in power.

His estimated wealth shortly before his death was $80,000,000. On his removal to England he had reinvested a large part of his funds in London real estate. In August 1919, presumably to avoid the inheritance tax, he conveyed all his property in America to a trust in favor of his sons, Maj. Waldorf and Capt. J. J. Astor. His temperament was eccentric and his disposition irascible. He was both vain and contentious. "A strange, crotchety man," he was dubbed. His numerous quarrels culminated in the episode in which an affront was offered to Admiral Sir Berkeley Milne, which brought about a strong reaction against him in English social circles. After that he gradually retired from society. He died at Western House, Brighton.

[The basic data appear in the Am. and the British *Who's Who;* articles in many journals and periodicals over the whole period from 1890 to 1919 inclusive; obituaries in the *London Times, N. Y. Times,* N. Y. *Sun,* and *N.Y. World* of Oct. 20, 1919. A genealogical table published by Astor in the *Pall Mall Mag.* for June 1899, traced the family to Jacques d'Astorga, a Spanish cavalier who came to France in 1085. This genealogy was investigated by Lothrop Withington, a competent genealogist, and his report, declaring the table a fabrication, was published in the N. Y. *Sun* (under the erroneous signature of "Lathrop Wittington"), July 30, 1899.]

W. J. G.

ATCHISON, DAVID RICE (Aug. 11, 1807–Jan. 26, 1886), lawyer, senator, was born at Frogtown, Ky. His parents, William and Catherine (Allen) Atchison, intending their son for the ministry, named him after a pioneer Presbyterian minister. But upon his graduation from Transylvania University, young Atchison entered, instead, upon the study of law in the office of Charles Humphreys, at the same time attending the law school in Lexington. Shortly after his admission to the Kentucky bar, in 1830, he moved to Missouri and began the practise of law in Liberty County. In 1833, along with three other Missouri lawyers, he was retained by the Mormons of Jackson County to defend them in their troubles with Gentile neighbors. Moving to Clay County, he was elected to the lower branch of the Missouri legislature in 1834 and again in 1838, but failed of reëlection in 1840. During the legislative session of 1839, he was made chairman of a special committee to investigate and report upon certain statements in the report of Gen. Zachary Taylor that reflected unfavorably upon the conduct of Missouri troops serving in the Seminole War. During these and the following years, Atchison was closely identified with the military service of the state, rising from the rank of captain to that of major-general. After removal to Platte County on Missouri's western border, he was appointed judge of the newly created circuit court for that county, in February 1841. Two years later (October 1843), upon the death of Senator L. F. Linn, Atchison, already a man of influence and distinction, was appointed to the United States Senate (W. B. Stevens, *Centennial History of Missouri*, II, 185; *Missouri Historical Review*, Apr. 1916, X, 177–79) and in January 1849 was reëlected for a full term which expired in March 1855. As senator, Atchison held the chairmanship of the important Committee on Indian Affairs, and actively promoted land-grant legislation in aid of Missouri railroads, believing that later they would form important links in a transcontinental system. He was elected president *pro tempore* of the Senate sixteen times between August 1846 and November 1854, when he resigned the office. By virtue of this position, it has been asserted that Atchison became President for one day, when the 4th of March, 1849, fell on Sunday and Zachary Taylor did not take the oath of office until the day following. But this has been shown to be without substantial foundation (G. H. Haynes, *American Historical Review*, XXX, 308–10).

While a member of the Senate, Atchison was the most powerful man in the Democratic party in Missouri, next to Thomas H. Benton. The latter's defeat for reëlection to the Senate in 1850 was due mainly to the efforts of Atchison and other leaders of the pro-slavery faction. Later, in 1852–53, Benton declared himself a candidate to succeed Atchison in 1855, and there ensued a senatorial campaign of intense factional and personal bitterness. In order to strengthen his hold upon the slave-owners of western Missouri in 1853, Atchison repeatedly pledged himself in speeches to work for and support a bill establishing territorial governments in the region immediately west of Missouri, and, in connection therewith, to bring about, if possible, the repeal of the Missouri Compromise. At the following session of Congress (1853–54), he was an important, though inconspicuous, influence in the passing of the Kansas-Nebraska bill; and afterward claimed credit for the provisions of that act repealing the Missouri Compromise. Both Atchison and Benton, however, failed of reëlection in 1855, and this defeat appears to have closed Atchison's political career.

At all events, little is known of his subsequent activities further than that he was a prominent leader of the Missouri "border ruffians" in their raids into Kansas Territory in 1855–56; that he supported the Confederate cause and was in Texas during the Civil War; and that, after the war, he returned to Missouri and resided at Gower, in Clinton County, where he was engaged in farming until his death. In February 1870 his residence was destroyed by a fire which also consumed his valuable library and collection of manuscripts (*History of Clinton County, Mo.*, 1881, pt. II, 182). The latter is said to have included a history of the Missouri Compromise repeal and of the troubles in Kansas.

A contemporary describes Atchison as "a man of imposing presence, six feet two inches high and straight as an arrow, florid complexion, and weighing about 200 pounds" (W. F. Switzler, quoted in W. B. Stevens, *op. cit.*, II, 832). His speeches were characterized by a simplicity and directness in striking contrast to the ornateness and pomposity of those of his rival, Benton. Although a Presbyterian, he indulged in intoxicants, in profanity, and in incitements to violence against the free-state settlers in Kansas. The county of Atchison, Mo., and the city of Atchison, Kan., were both named after him.

[No biog. of Atchison has been published. A very brief sketch, published during his lifetime, appears in W. B. Davis and D. S. Durrie's *Illustrated Hist. of Mo.* (1876), p. 466. Fragmentary material may be gleaned from various state and local histories, especially W. F. Switzler's *Illustrated Hist of Mo.* (1879); *The Provinces and States*, ed. by W. A. Goodspeed (1904), IV; and W. M. Paxton's *Annals of Platte County, Mo.* (1897). The Atchison-Benton senatorial contest and Atchison's connection with the Kansas-Nebraska Act are traced in detail in P. O. Ray's *Repeal of the Mo. Compromise: Its Origin and Authorship* (1909), which quotes extensively from Atchison's speeches as reported in Mo. newspapers and the *Cong. Globe*. L. W. Spring's *Kansas* (rev. ed., Boston, 1907) brings out briefly Atchison's connection with the Kansas border troubles, 1854–56.]

P.O.R.

ATHERTON, CHARLES GORDON (July 4, 1804–Nov. 15, 1853), lawyer, politician, was born in Amherst, N. H., the son of Charles Humphrey and Mary Ann (Toppan) Atherton. Both his father and grandfather were prominent and successful New Hampshire lawyers. He graduated from Harvard in 1822, was admitted to the bar in 1825, and began practise at Dunstable (later Nashua), N. H. In 1828 he was married to Ann Barnard Clark. He represented Dunstable in the legislature in 1830, was clerk of the Senate 1831–32, and again served in the lower house 1833–36, being speaker during the last three terms. He was elected to Congress in 1836, serving three terms as representative, afterward entering the Senate in 1843 for the full term. His political career began contemporaneously with a new alignment in New Hampshire parties, and he became a Jacksonian Democrat of the straitest sect. He opposed internal improvements, denounced the tariff as a method of "taxing the many for the benefit of the few," and was an ardent supporter of the independent treasury scheme as against a national bank. His strict constructionist view of the Constitution was well expressed in the famous "gag resolutions" which he introduced in the House on Dec. 11, 1838 (*Congressional Globe,* 25 Cong., 3 Sess., pp. 23 ff.). These resolutions, which made his name anathema to the abolitionists, provided for laying on the table without consideration all memorials relating to slavery, declaring that on the constitutional basis of state equality the national government even in territory subject to its jurisdiction could take no action against slavery which might tend toward the destruction of that institution in the states. Atherton spoke frequently in Congress and among his notable addresses were those on the civil and diplomatic appropriation bill of 1840—a savage arraignment of Whig policies (*Ibid.,* 26 Cong., 1 Sess., pp. 405–12); against the apportionment bill of 1842 (*Ibid.,* 27 Cong., 2 Sess., App., pp. 350–51); on the tariff (*Ibid.,* 28 Cong., 1 Sess., pp. 544–48); and on the financial policy of the government during the Mexican War (*Ibid.,* 30 Cong., 1 Sess., pp. 410–15). Throughout his service in the House he was a member of the Ways and Means Committee, and during his last two years in the Senate, chairman of the Finance Committee, when the vigor with which he resisted riders to appropriation bills excited the approval of Senator Benton. On his retirement in 1849 he resumed professional work in Nashua and built up what was reputed to be the most extensive and lucrative practise in the state. He was a member of the constitutional convention of 1850, serving as chairman of the committee on the legislature and exercising great influence throughout the proceedings. The many democratic innovations submitted by this convention were, however, rejected at the polls. In November 1852 he was again elected to the Senate for the six-year term beginning Mar. 4, 1853. Because of his close personal and political association with President Pierce he was expected to be an influential figure in the Thirty-third Congress, an expectation disappointed by his sudden death three weeks before the session began.

[Charles H. Bell, *Bench and Bar of N. H.* (1894); Daniel F. Secomb, *Hist. of the Town of Amherst*(1883); *N. H. Patriot,* Nov. 23, 1855; *Biog. Cong. Dir.* (1913).]

W. A. R.

ATHERTON, GEORGE WASHINGTON (June 20, 1837–July 24, 1906), college president, son of Hiram and Almira (Gardner) Atherton, was born at Boxford, Mass., a descendant of the well-known Atherton family which settled in Massachusetts before 1630. Left by the death of his father totally dependent upon his own resources at the age of twelve, he worked his way through Phillips Exeter Academy and later through Yale College, receiving his degree at the latter in 1863. Enlisting as first-lieutenant in the 10th Connecticut Volunteers, he served with that regiment in its campaign in North Carolina and was promoted to captain after the battle of Newbern, but was forced to resign from the service because incapacitated by sickness. Four years of teaching followed in the Albany Boy's Academy, New York, and in St. John's College, Annapolis, and then in 1868 Atherton was elected a member of the first faculty of what is now the University of Illinois. Here he obtained a vision of the possibilities of the land-grant college, a vision which in a way ruled the rest of his life. A year later he was called to the new chair of political economy and constitutional law at Rutgers College, New Jersey, where he remained for nearly fourteen years. With no neglect of his college duties, he threw himself with characteristic energy into many activities both state and national. He became a member of the board of visitors to the United States Naval Academy; he was one of the commission appointed by President Grant to investigate the Red Cloud Indian Agency; he served the state on its board of tax revision, and once he ran unsuccessfully for Congress. His continued championship of the new land-grant college idea, his paper on the subject of federal aid for colleges before the National Educational Association, his numerous articles and addresses, brought him in 1882 the presidency of the Pennsylvania State College, to which he gave with untiring activity and enthusiasm the remainder of his life. In many ways he may be counted as the real founder of the college. When he took the presidency the school was regarded by the people of the state as an experiment that had failed. There were but two buildings, one of them a mere shed, and there were but thirty-three students in the college classes. The state, having accepted the land grant, had abandoned the college seemingly for good. When Atherton died after an administration of twenty-two years there were more than thirty buildings and 1,200 students, in five thoroughly organized schools. He was married on Dec. 25, 1863, to Fannie W. L. Washburn of Plymouth, Mass.

[*Obit. Rec. Grads. Yale Univ.* (1907); *Triennial Meeting and Biog. Rec. Class of Sixty Three Yale Coll.* (1869); *Who's Who in America,* 1901–02; *Phila. Press, Phila. Public Ledger,* July 25, 1906.]

F. L. P—e.

ATHERTON, JOSHUA (June 20, 1737–Apr. 3, 1809), lawyer, Loyalist during the Revolution, early anti-slavery leader, was born in the town of Harvard, Worcester County, Mass., the second son of Peter and Experience (Wright) Atherton. Educated in the common schools and under the tuition of a clergyman, at the age of twenty-one he entered Harvard College, from which he was graduated in 1762. He studied law under James Putnam of Worcester, the King's attorney-general for the province. In 1765 he was married to Abigail Goss, of Bolton, Mass. Locating in southern New Hampshire, he practised his profession in the towns of Litchfield and Merriman from 1765 until 1773, when having been appointed register of probate for the County of Hillsborough, he removed to its shire town, Amherst, which was his home during the rest of his life. His rise at the bar of the province, which now seemed assured, was soon halted by the outbreak of the American Revolution. Hillsborough County early became a stronghold of the Sons of Liberty, but, apparently because of his natural conservatism and strong belief that the liberties of the colonies would be best insured by their remaining subject to Great Britain, Atherton firmly refused to join them. Becoming at length a "suspect," he was arrested on Aug. 21, 1777, as a "disaffected person" whose presence at large would be dangerous to the liberties of the country, and he was confined in jail until June 5, 1778. In January 1779, probably convinced by the surrender of Burgoyne and the American alliance with France that it was useless longer to oppose the independence of the United States, he took the oath of allegiance to the State of New Hampshire and was admitted to practise in its courts.

After the establishment of peace, the marked personality, legal ability, and strong character of Atherton soon sufficed to dispel the prejudice created by his record as a Tory. His law practise rapidly grew, and he was repeatedly elected to important public positions. He was a member of the convention which drafted the first permanent constitution of New Hampshire, that of 1784, and also of the convention of 1792, the first summoned to revise that organic law. In each of these bodies he took a leading part and had large influence in shaping both the substance and form of the present constitution of the state. In 1788 he was the leader of the opposition in the state convention called to act upon the adoption of the proposed Federal Constitution. The most memorable event in its debates was his strong and impassioned argument against ratification of the proposed constitution without its prior amendment prohibiting the slave trade, allowed by Article 1, section 9, till 1808. His opposition contributed to delay the final action of the convention for three months, until on June 21, 1788, ratification was carried by a narrow margin. In 1792 and again in 1793 Atherton was a member of the state Senate, then a body of only twelve, in which he sought, though unsuccessfully, to remedy existing defects in the state law by investing the superior court of judicature with the powers and jurisdiction of a court of equity. The high position which Atherton now had won at the bar led to his appointment by Gov. Josiah Bartlett on June 11, 1793 to the office of attorney-general of the state. Four years later, when only sixty years of age, he began to suffer from an organic affection of the heart which gradually so impaired his powers that he was forced to resign this office in 1801 and also to withdraw from the private practise of his profession. He passed the remainder of his life with his family and books, gracefully dispensing, after the manner of an aristocratic country gentleman, his habitual hospitality to members of the bench and clergy and to distinguished visitors.

[C. H. Atherton, *Memoir of the Hon. Joshua Atherton* (1852); D. F. Secomb, *Hist. of Amherst, 1728–1882* (1883); C. H. Bell, *Bench and Bar of N.H.* (1894); J. B. Walker, *Hist. of N. H. Convention for Ratification of Federal Constitution* (1888).]

J.F.C.

ATKINS, JEARUM (fl. 1840–1880), inventor, was born in Vermont and like many another son of that region went west as a young man to seek his fortune. As early as 1840 he was plying his trade as a millwright in northern Illinois near Chicago. Two years later a fall from a wagon inflicted serious spinal injuries and he did not walk again for twenty-four years. Confined to bed he turned his attention to mechanical invention but for a considerable period met with only moderate success. The first decade of Atkins's illness coincided with the introduction and development of reaping machinery in the west. On numerous occasions he had heard farmers complain because of the hard manual labor involved in raking the severed grain from the platforms of reapers, and it occurred to him that if he could eliminate the man used for the purpose and substitute a mechanical device, he would not only increase the efficiency of such machines but perhaps make his fortune as well. Day after day, lying upon his back with a drawing-board suspended above his head, Atkins gave thought to this problem, and finally in the spring of 1852 achieved sufficient progress to justify the construction of an experimental appliance. This was attached to a reaper and tried in the harvest. The apparatus worked surprisingly well and Atkins at once applied for a patent which was granted on Dec. 21, 1852. This ingenious and complicated apparatus, known as Atkins's automaton or self-rake, was designed to imitate the motion of human arms. The favorable result of the first trial attracted the attention of John S. Wright, editor of the *Prairie Farmer* of Chicago, and after investigation he applied for and obtained the right to build and attach them to a reaper for which he had secured a construction license. Forty machines were manufactured and sold in 1853, and 300 the next year, distributed among twenty states. The automaton by now had proved a sensation. Its ingenious mechanism wherever it was exhibited drew curious and wondering crowds. Despite bitter attacks from competing manufacturers, most of whom still made the old hand-raking reapers, the craze, as they termed it, for Atkins's automaton persisted. Orders poured in so fast that although construction was quadrupled for 1855, and rose to nearly 5,000 in 1856, it fell short of the demand. Newspapers and the agricultural press both here and abroad widely discussed its merits and faults. Scientific and agricultural societies vied with each other in awarding premiums to Atkins, the machine, and the manufacturer. It is said that over three hundred medals, cups, and diplomas were won by them between 1853 and 1856. At the height of its fame Atkins's automaton disappeared from the market almost overnight. In the attempt to expand manufacture too rapidly the machines of 1856 were made of green wood and poor materials. As a consequence they broke down everywhere and were returned to Wright in such numbers that he went into bankruptcy, and dragged Atkins down with him, the latter receiving only $7,000 for an invention reputed to have had a commercial value during the life of the patent of over $2,000,000. Walter Wright of Chicago, who succeeded to the control of the patent, set too high a price for licenses to build, with the result that manufacture was never again resumed. Atkins might have retrieved his misfortunes in part by selling or licensing the rights to the extension of his original patent after 1866, but through a misunderstanding the Commissioner refused to renew it. Congress corrected the error by special legislation in 1871 but the renewal only had two years to run and the gesture was too late to be of value to Atkins. Manufacturers by that time had taken up other types of self-rakes and were no longer interested in his device. As a last resort Atkins appealed to Congress for $100,000 as a partial return for his contribution to agricultural advancement. Congress refused to listen, and thenceforth Atkins dropped from sight.

[Items relating to Atkins and his invention are scattered through the *Prairie Farmer,* 1852–57; *Northwestern Farmer and Cultivator,* 1852–57; *Mich. Farmer,* 1852–57; *Ohio Cultivator,* 1852–57; *Country Gentleman,* 1852–57; *Am. Agriculturist,* 1853–57; *Genesee Farmer,* 1852–57; *Am. Farmer,* 1852–57; *Southern Planter,* 1852–57. See also the Catalogues of John S. Wright, 1853–56; and the *Memorial for the Relief of Jearum Atkins* (1880).]

H. A. K.

ATKINSON, EDWARD (Feb. 10, 1827–Dec. 11, 1905), industrialist, economist, was a descendant of John Atkinson who was born about 1640, whether in England or America is not known, but who, according to tradition, was a son of Henry Atkinson, barrister, who came with his brother Theodore to America and settled in Newbury, Mass. A great-grandson of John, Lieut. Amos Atkinson, was one of the minutemen at Lexington and Concord. His son, Amos Atkinson, married Anna G. Sawyer, and was the father of Edward Atkinson, who was born in Brookline, Mass. After attending private schools in Brookline and Boston, Edward went to work as a boy of fifteen, for a Boston textile commission house, doing chores which ranged from the building of fires, sweeping of floors, and packing of goods, to the more responsible work of confidential clerk. He gave five years to general apprenticeship of this type, advancing in 1848 to more important clerical and financial responsibilities, until he assumed the treasurership of several textile-manufacturing companies. In 1855 he was married to Mary Caroline Heath.

In the eighties Atkinson turned his attention as a business man to factory mutual insurance. He helped to establish the Boston Manufacturers Mutual Insurance Company, of which he later became chief executive. Its central feature was the now well recognized one of mutual insurance in a restricted field, in which the factor of "exposure" was greatly reduced. Both hazard and loss were diminished by insisting on safeguards governing construction and use, and making precaution the corner-stone of the plan. Textile factories, cordage plants, paper-mills, machine-shops, and wood-working establishments were made better risks from the standpoint of the underwriter than the average public building. The industrial architecture of the country improved appreciably as a result. In a number of articles and pamphlets, Atkinson developed the ideas underlying these innovations. In his own judgment, his greatest single contribution to future well-being was the invention of the Aladdin oven, the outgrowth of an interest revealed and expanded in *The Science of Nutrition* (1896), which went through ten editions. The oven was a fully insulated piece of apparatus with heat applied from a common lamp in which a little over two pints of kerosene oil would do the work of 120 pounds of coal burned in an ordinary cooking stove. In the middle nineties it was a hobby with Atkinson to entertain in his house guests who dined on sumptuous viands prepared in their presence through the use of his invention. It was characteristic of him that he did not patent it.

A diligent statistician, gifted public speaker, economist, financier, and industrious and prolific writer, Atkinson left a long list of published works, among which the following are the more important: *Cheap Cotton by Free Labor* (1861); *Our National Domain* (1879); *Labor and Capital Allies not Enemies* (1880); *Railroads of the United States* (1880); *Cotton Manufacturers of the United States* (1880); *What is a Bank?* (1881); *The Railway and the Farmer* (1881); *Distribution of Products* (1885); *Facts and Figures, the Basis of Economic Science* (1904). He wrote many pamphlets and delivered numerous addresses on wages, fire loss, nutrition, banking, economic legislation, peace and war, and many other questions of social concern. The Cotton Exposition at Atlanta in 1881 had its inception in an address by him in that city a few years earlier. He advised more widely diversified agriculture for the South, and he foresaw and encouraged the development of the Southern cotton-manufacturing industry. In 1887 he served, by special appointment of President Cleveland, as special commissioner to report upon the status and prospects of bi-metalism in Europe. This appointment was due to Atkinson's consistent advocacy of sound money as a basis of honest commercial practise.

Physically, Atkinson was of massive build, in appearance impressive, dignified yet benign, in manner genial yet urbane, in expression positive often to the point of obstinacy. But he was always fortified with facts which under the spur of a vigorous sense of justice in human relations, gave his opinions unusual force. He was a consistent free trader, sound-money advocate, pacifist and anti-imperialist.

[The materials for this sketch were obtained mainly from a scrutiny of Edward Atkinson's published writings, from a statement made by Henry Mandell Atkinson, of Atlanta, Ga., and from geneal. data furnished by the N.Y. Geneal. and Biog. Soc. A striking obituary editorial will be found in the *Commercial and Financial Chronicle,* Dec. 16, 1905; other obituaries in *N.Y. Times, N.Y. Herald, Brooklyn Eagle, Boston Journal, Boston Daily Globe, Boston Post,* and *Boston Daily Advertiser,* all of Dec. 12, 1905.]

R. C. M.

ATKINSON, GEORGE FRANCIS (Jan. 26, 1854–Nov. 15, 1918), botanist, son of Joseph and Josephine (Fish) Atkinson, was born in Raisinville, Monroe County, Mich. He attended both Olivet College and Cornell, and graduated at the latter in 1885. In 1885–86 he was assistant professor of entomology and zoology in the University of North Carolina, and in the latter year was promoted associate professor; in 1888 professor of botany and zoology in the University of South Carolina; in 1889 professor of biology and botany at the Alabama Polytechnical Institute; in 1892 assistant professor of botany at Cornell, where in four years he rose to be head of the department, remaining such until his death. He was the first president of the American Botanical Society, and in 1905 was sent as a delegate to the International Botanical Congress at Vienna, and again represented his country before the Brussels meeting of 1910. He was the author in all of 150 scientific papers. An examination of their titles, chronologically arranged, reveals not only a great variety of biological interests, but a transition in his field of work. Beginning as a zoologist, he early turned his attention to parasitic animals, winning his scientific spurs with a study of the nematode so injurious to field crops, *Heterodera radicicola.* The animal parasites drew his interest to the parasitic plants, and he became a mycologist of the first rank. His early mycological work was a survey of the fungi of the high mountains of North Carolina; rapidly this broadened into an interest in the entire field of mycology, covering the physiology, economic importance, systematic classification, and theoretical relationships of the fungi. He was especially interested in the evolution of the various families of fungi and the outline of their family trees, and, mindful of the law that embryology mirrors life stages of evolution, he gave more attention to the early life stages of the higher fungi than had any other American botanist. In his *Studies of American Fungi* (1900), Atkinson accomplished the first successful attempt to write a book on the higher fungi which would be at once thoroughly popular and irreproachably scientific. His *Biology of Ferns* (1893), a gem of natural-history study, has also delighted more readers than the purely scientific. For the most part his work did not take book form, however, but appeared in multitudinous short papers in strictly botanical publications. As an inspirer of students and a tireless contributor to the record of scientific detail, Atkinson takes rank among the first two or three mycologists of this country. The passing of a delightful figure evoked more than perfunctory expressions of grief, and though really in the sixties, he was thought of as one who died young; such was the vigor of his personality and the momentum of his work. His death occurred under peculiarly tragic circumstances. In the summer of 1918, lured by the rich fungus flora of the rainy Northwest coast, he explored the slopes of Mount Rainier. As autumn drew on, his students and assistants returned to other duties, and alone, late in the season, Atkinson returned from a storm in the alpine regions in a condition of exhaustion, and was removed to a hospital at Tacoma, Wash., where influenza was followed by pneumonia. In his delirium he attempted to dictate his mycological observations to his nurse; he died quite alone, his friends unknowing that he was even ill. Students hastened to Tacoma when word of his death was received, and cared for his collections and valuable notes.

[No life of Atkinson has yet been written; at the time of his death friends and students wrote brief articles in technical journals, but these are appreciations rather than biogs. or critical estimates of his work; *vide* W. A. Murrill in *Jour. N.Y. Bot. Gard.*, XIX, 314–15; H. H. Whetzel, in *Bot. Gazette*, LXVII, 366–68; H. M. Fitzpatrick in *Science*, XLIX, 371–72.]

D. C. P.

ATKINSON, GEORGE HENRY (May 10, 1819–Feb. 25, 1889), Congregational clergyman, educator, community builder, the son of William and Anna (Little) Atkinson, was born at Newbury, now Newburyport, Mass. He attended Bradford Academy; Dartmouth College, graduating in 1843; and Andover Theological Seminary, graduating in 1846. In the latter year he married Nancy Bates of Springfield, Vt. In the winter of 1847–48 he sailed from Boston "around the Horn" as a representative to the Pacific Northwest of the American Home Missionary Society, an organ of the Congregational churches. Settling in Oregon City, he organized one of the first Congregational churches in Oregon and continued as its pastor for fifteen years. He then became pastor of the First Congregational Church of Portland, remaining till 1872. Thereafter, until the date of his death, he was engaged in missionary activities in both Oregon and Washington.

He was a natural enthusiast—this trait emerging with special clearness in his attitude toward the subject of education. The Home Missionary Society, concerned about the development of academies and colleges, gave him encouragement toward their establishment. The Society also provided him with an equipment of school books valued at $2,000, which he brought with him to Oregon. He promptly started a school for girls at Oregon City and, learning about the beginnings of academic instruction already made at Forest Grove, he at once joined in organizing Tualatin Academy which grew into Pacific University, of which Atkinson was a life-long trustee and a powerful supporter. When Gov. Joseph Lane arrived at Oregon City to set up the territorial government in March 1849, Atkinson impressed upon him the need of a general system of public schools. He drafted the section of the governor's first message on that subject, advocating the Massachusetts system, with some modifications. The framework of that system was ultimately provided for Oregon. Development was retarded by circumstances, but the state was permanently benefited by the educational ideas which Atkinson injected during the formative period.

In his missionary service he traveled widely through the interior and took the opportunity to gather specimens of soils which later were subjected to chemical analysis. He became convinced that millions of acres of hill land in Oregon and Washington would grow wheat in place of bunch grass. Fortified with comparative analyses of the soils of wheat areas in this and other countries, he spread his propaganda far and wide by means of conversations, lectures, newspaper articles, and pamphlets. He called the process he advocated "reclaiming this interior basin from mere pastures to farm lands" (*The Northwest Coast*, p. 45). He worked out and presented the principles of "dry farming" applicable to the inland empire wheat lands. He prevailed on individual settlers to experiment with wheat planting. In a word, he was the prophet and the pioneer scientist of a movement which rescued that region from an almost exclusively pastoral economy and transformed it into one of the world's great wheat areas. His detailed knowledge respecting the Northwest as the potential home of a vast population caused him to be much sought by railway engineers and promoters. He published a pamphlet on the Northwest Coast consisting of "a series of articles upon the Northern Pacific Railroad in its relations to the Basins of the Columbia and of Puget's Sound." Legislation by Congress favorable to the railroad was one object of the publication.

Atkinson has been described as the ideal "booster," because he was wholly unselfish, his opinions were based on careful research, and he favored no particular localities as against others. He had the reputation, for many years, of knowing more about the Pacific Northwest than any other man and by his standing in eastern communities, where he delivered lectures, he was able to advance the interest of the Northwest in that quarter. In theology he was strictly orthodox, but his nature was so generous that he was able to live on terms of close friendship with men of all shades of belief. This was one secret of his success in promoting favorite causes. Eager interest, a fine presence, and splendid voice coupled with knowledge of the subjects he discussed, coöperated to render his advocacy successful. He was a community builder after the grand manner. His sermons were usually carefully prepared written discourses, delivered in conversational tone. His lectures were apt to be more charged with imagination and more rhetorical. But whether in the pulpit, on the rostrum, in convention hall or parlor, he was always impressive, persuasive, and usually convincing.

[The *Biog. of Rev. G. H. Atkinson* (1893), compiled by Nancy Bates Atkinson and prepared for the press by Rev. Myron Eells, contains his jour. of the voyage to Oregon in 1848, selected addresses, printed articles, and a particular account of his church work in the Pacific Northwest. His quasi-scientific writing is illustrated by *The Northwest Coast* (Portland, 1878). His "Occasional Address" on the subject of Oregon Pioneers of 1848, *Oregon Pioneer Ass.*, 1880, affords a sample of his oratory. The best account of his educ. work is in J. R. Robertson, "A Hist. of Pacific Univ.," *Oregon Hist. Soc. Quart.*, VI, 114–23. There is an account of his personality, his preaching, his coöperative spirit, his gospel of wheat growing, his appearance, by George H. Himes, in a letter of Feb. 28, 1927, addressed to Joseph Schafer, and filed in the State Hist. Lib. of Wisconsin.]

J. S.

ATKINSON, GEORGE WESLEY (June 29, 1845–Apr. 14, 1925), author, lecturer, jurist, was born on a farm in Kanawha County, Va., now West Virginia, son of James and Miriam (Rader) Atkinson. A product of the "old field" schools of his state, he received his higher education in Ohio Wesleyan University, from which he was graduated, A.B., 1870, M.A., 1873. The following year he graduated in law from Howard University, Washington, D. C., and was admitted to the bar of his native state in 1875. Subsequently he took a graduate course in literature in Mount Union College, Alliance, Ohio, from which he received the doctorate, *pro merito,* in 1885. Literary interests occupied an important place in his life, as is attested by an impressive list of works from his pen, including: *History of Kanawha County* (1876); *West Virginia Pulpit* (1878); *After the Moonshiners* (1881); *Hand Book for Revenue Officers* (1881); *A. B. C. of the Tariff* (1884); *Dont's or Negative Chips from Blocks of Living Truths* (1887); *Prominent Men of West Virginia,* jointly with A. F. Gibbens (1895); *Psychology Simplified* (1897); *Public Addresses* (1901); and *Bench and Bar of West Virginia* (1919). Atkinson also contributed to the press, being editor of the *Evening Standard* (Wheeling) 1877–78, and subsequently for a period of nine years, joint editor of the *West Virginia Journal.* Throughout West Virginia he was in demand as a public lecturer on the Sunday-school, prohibition, and literary themes. He was, however, best known politically. Before he graduated from college he was a member of the board of education of Charleston, W. Va., which city he served as postmaster from 1876 to 1881. As United States marshal for the District of West Virginia, 1881–85, he won temporary publicity because of his war on moonshiners. He was Federal collector of internal revenue, 1878–81. Meanwhile, he moved to Wheeling, and in 1888 was elected to Congress as a Republican. He declined renomination and practised law until 1896, when he was elected the first Republican governor of West Virginia in a quarter century. As governor he was vigorous and constructive, standing, among other things, for better public schools, permanent roads, reforms in state election laws, the right of labor to organize, and encouragement of immigration (*Public Addresses,* pp. 74, 211, 523). Almost immediately after the expiration of his term as governor, he became United States district attorney for southern West Virginia, which office he filled until Apr. 15, 1905, when President Roosevelt appointed him judge of the United States Court of Claims. On Apr. 17, 1916, he retired to private life. He was twice married: first, on Dec. 2, 1868, to Ellen Eagan of his native county, by whom he had five children, and who died in 1893; and second, on June 24, 1897, to Mrs. Myra (Hornor) Camden, widow of Judge G. D. Camden of Clarksburg, W. Va.

[*Charleston* (W. Va.) *Daily Mail,* Apr. 4, 15, 1925; Jas. Morton Callahan, *Hist. of W. Va., Old and New* (1923); Atkinson's *Public Addresses* (1901).]

C. H. A.

ATKINSON, HENRY (1782–June 14, 1842), soldier, was born in North Carolina. Concerning his parentage and youth no records are available. He entered the army, July 1, 1808, as a captain in the 3rd Infantry. He was made colonel of the 45th Infantry, Apr. 15, 1814, and a week later transferred to the 37th Infantry. On the reorganization of the army after the War of 1812 he was appointed (May 17, 1815) colonel of the 6th Infantry. In 1819 he was assigned to the command of the "Yellowstone expedition," a grandiose project, fathered by the secretary of war, John C. Calhoun, for taking an army of 1,100 men to the mouth of the Yellowstone, as a warning to the Indians and the British fur traders. In September, Atkinson and a part of his force reached Old Council Bluffs, in the present Nebraska, where a post was established, named Camp Missouri, later renamed Fort Atkinson and still later Fort Calhoun. Nothing further came of the project except the exploratory journeys, in the summer of 1820, of Maj. Stephen H. Long to Pike's Peak and of Capt. Matthew J. Magee to the mouth of the Minnesota. Returning to St. Louis, Atkinson was put in command of the right wing of the Western Department, with the rank of brigadier-general (appointed May 13, 1820), but on the revision of army ratings in 1821 he was reappointed colonel of the 6th Infantry, with his brigadier-generalship reduced to a brevet.

On the authorization by Congress in 1824 of another expedition to the upper Missouri he was assigned to the command and was also appointed one of two commissioners (his colleague being Benjamin O'Fallon, the Indian agent) to make treaties with the Indians. With a force of 476 men he left St. Louis on Mar. 20, 1825, held councils with a number of tribes, and arrived at the mouth of the Yellowstone on Aug. 17, where he met Gen. Ashley, returning from the Rockies with his first cargo of furs. A few days later, giving safe escort to Ashley, he started for home, and after halting at several points to make treaties, arrived in St. Louis on Oct. 20, without the loss of a boat or a man. He selected the site for the historic post of Jefferson Barracks, ten miles south of St. Louis, which was occupied July 10, 1826, and which subsequently became his home. Early in 1827 he dispatched Col. Henry Leavenworth to choose a site for a new post on the Kansas frontier—a mission that resulted in the establishment of Fort Leavenworth (May 8) and the abandonment of Fort Calhoun. In July, on the news of a serious outbreak among the Winnebagos, he hurried to Prairie du Chien, and by a swift concentration of troops, restored peace. He was in general command of the troops in the Black Hawk war of 1832 and in immediate command on the second day's fight at Bad Axe, Aug. 2, when the Sauk chief's forces were almost annihilated. In 1840 he supervised the earlier stages of the removal of the Winnebagos from Wisconsin to the Neutral Ground in Iowa, where a post was established May 31, in the following spring, named Fort Atkinson. His remaining days were spent at Jefferson Barracks, where he died.

Atkinson was married in Louisville, Ky., Jan. 16, 1826, to Mary Ann Bullitt, who with a son, Edward Graham Atkinson, survived him. He was highly regarded by those who knew him, and his funeral was largely attended by volunteer companies and private friends from St. Louis. He is praised by Chittenden for his uniform exhibition of practical good sense. Though the first Yellowstone expedition was a fiasco, the fault is charged to the officials of the War Department, by whom it was "smothered in an elaboration of method." His second expedition, planned by himself, was in every way a conspicuous success. His name is inseparably connected with the earlier period of the conquest of the frontier, and the part he bore is equaled in importance by that of no contemporary with the possible exception of William Clark.

[F. B. Heitman, *Hist. Reg.* (1903); H. M. Chittenden, *The Am. Fur Trade of the Far West* (1902); Bruce E. Mahan, *Old Fort Crawford and the Frontier* (1926); "Jour. of S. W. Kearny, 1820," in Mo. Hist. Soc. *Colls.*, III, 1 and 2 (1908); manuscript notes supplied by Miss Stella M. Drumm.]

W. J. G.

ATKINSON, JOHN (Dec. 6, 1835–Dec. 8, 1897), Methodist clergyman and historian, was born at Deerfield, N. Y. His educational advantages were restricted to the country school. He early developed an oratorical gift, and at the age of eighteen became a preacher. He joined the New Jersey Conference of the Methodist Episcopal Church in 1853. In 1856 he married Catharine O'Hanlon. He held pastorates in numerous small towns in New Jersey, in Newark, in Jersey City, in Chicago, in Bay City, Mich., and again in Newark, and in Jersey City. At the time of his death he was pastor in Haverstraw, N. Y. Beecher-like in appearance, tall, with large smooth face, long hair, and splendid voice, he was a strong and popular preacher, fervent, sometimes fiery, inclined to speak everywhere as though addressing a congregation. His first books were the outcome of his work as pastor: *The Living Way* (1856), *The Garden of Sorrows* (1868), and *The Class Leader* (1875). Permanently important were his histories. *Memorials of Methodism in New Jersey* (1860) unearthed interesting facts and incidents. *The Cen-*

tennial History of American Methodism, 1784–1816 (1884) was unfortunate only in its title, suggested by the celebration of the centennial organization of the church. For the first time from a Methodist Episcopal hand the facts and their true interpretation were recorded. This notable book has not received the attention it deserves. More elaborate is *The Beginnings of the Wesleyan Movement in America 1766–73* (1896), where the story is told with a devotion, particularity, historical sense, and investigation worthy of all praise. In literary skill Atkinson is behind Stevens but he has searched the facts more critically. He was also something of a poet, and his hymn "Shall We Meet Beyond the River?" is known in all English-speaking countries.

[H. A. Buttz in *Minutes of the Newark Conference, 1898*, pp. 80–82; J. M. Buckley in *Christian Advocate*, Dec. 16, 1897, p. 2; private letters.] J. A. F.

ATKINSON, THOMAS (Aug. 6, 1807–Jan. 4, 1881), Episcopal bishop, the son of Robert and Mary Tabb (Mayo) Atkinson, was born on his father's plantation, Mansfield, in Dinwiddie County, Va. After due preparation in the schools of Petersburg (near his home) he entered Yale College, but in his junior year transferred to Hampden-Sidney College in Virginia. From the latter institution he graduated with the honors of his class at the age of eighteen. He first entered the legal profession, after pursuing his studies under Judge Henry St. George Tucker of Winchester, Va. In 1828 he was licensed to practise law and successfully followed that profession for eight years. He then abandoned the law to enter the ministry. At Christ Church, Norfolk, Va., Nov. 18, 1836, he was ordained deacon by the Right Rev. William Meade, then assistant bishop (later diocesan bishop) of Virginia. He was advanced to the priesthood in St. Paul's Church, Norfolk, May 7, 1837, by the Right Rev. Richard Channing Moore, bishop of Virginia. During his diaconate he was assistant rector of Christ Church, Norfolk; and, after his elevation to the priesthood, became rector of St. Paul's Church, in the same city, where he remained until 1843. In the year last named, he was elected rector of St. Peter's Church, Baltimore. He and some of the parishioners of St. Peter's withdrew and built Grace Church, Baltimore, soon after 1850, and he remained there until 1853, when he was elected bishop of North Carolina. While rector of Grace Church he was twice elected bishop of Indiana, and twice declined. He was consecrated bishop of North Carolina on Oct. 17, 1853. On his removal to North Carolina he at first lived in Raleigh, but two years later removed to Wilmington. He aided in efforts to establish the University of the South at Sewanee, Tenn., before the Civil War, but that institution could not be built until after the war. The religious enlightenment of the negroes had a strong advocate in Bishop Atkinson. After the outbreak of the war, the diocese of North Carolina withdrew from its former union with the Northern dioceses and allied itself with the "Protestant Episcopal Church in the Confederate States of America." Bishop Atkinson, a devoted Southerner, loyally upheld the government of the Southern Confederacy. After the surrender of Gen. Lee, and the consequent end of the war, he was instrumental in effecting a union between the Northern and Southern branches of the Church. In 1866 Bishop Atkinson made a six months' tour of Europe (June–December) for the benefit of his health. Almost immediately upon his arrival he was invited by the Archbishop of Canterbury to take part in the consecration of some English colonial bishops, but circumstances forced him to decline. He was also present by invitation at an Anglican Conference in York. In 1867 he attended and participated in the First Lambeth Conference at Lambeth Palace. In 1873 Bishop Atkinson was given an assistant bishop in the person of the Rev. Dr. Theodore B. Lyman, who became diocesan bishop upon Atkinson's death, which occurred in Wilmington, N. C., Jan. 4, 1881.

[M. De Lancey Haywood, *Lives of the Bishops of N.C.* (1910), pp. 143–204; Bishop J. B. Cheshire, *The Ch. in the Confed. States* (1912); obituaries in the *Sun* (Baltimore), Jan. 5, 1881, *News and Observer* (Raleigh), Jan. 6, 1881.] M. DeL. H.

ATKINSON, WILLIAM BIDDLE (June 21, 1832–Nov. 23, 1909), obstetrician and medical biographer, was the son of Isaac S. and Mary (Biddle) Atkinson. His ancestors were among the earliest settlers of Burlington, N. J., but he was born at Haverford, Pa. After graduating from the Philadelphia Central High School, he received his M.D. from Jefferson Medical College in 1853. During the Civil War he was an acting assistant-surgeon. He was a very successful obstetrician, serving in that capacity on the staff of the Howard Hospital, but his chief claim to distinction is as the author of a large work on American medical biography entitled *The Physicians and Surgeons of the United States,* the first edition of which appeared in 1878, and the second two years later. This book is of great value as a work of reference. Atkinson edited or assisted in editing various medical journals. He was a frequent contributor to medical periodicals and wrote two other books, *Hints in the Obstetric Proceeding* (1875) and *Therapeutics of Gynecology and Obstetrics* (1880). He also edited the

Medical Registry and Directory of Philadelphia. For many years he was secretary of the Medical Society of the State of Pennsylvania and of the American Medical Association. In 1877 he was elected professor of sanitary science and pediatrics in the Medico-Chirurgical College of Philadelphia. He was for some years a medical inspector for the State Board of Health of Pennsylvania. Owing to his connection with the state and national medical societies he had a very large acquaintance with the members of his profession, which with his literary experience peculiarly qualified him as the biographer of American physicians. He was twice married, first to Jennie R. Patterson, and after her death to Miss S. J. Hutchinson, both of Philadelphia.

[Sketches in *Biog. of Eminent Am. Physicians and Surgeons* (1894), ed. by R. French Stone; *Physicians and Surgeons of Am.* (1896), ed. by Irving A. Watson; Kelly and Burrage, *Am. Medic. Biogs.* (1920); *Phila. Pub. Ledger,* Nov. 24, 1909; personal recollections.]

F. R. P.

ATKINSON, WILLIAM YATES (Nov. 11, 1854–Aug. 8, 1899), governor of Georgia, was the son of John Pepper Atkinson, 1804–73, born in Brunswick County, Va., educated at Oxford, N. C., who moved in 1853 to Georgia and established himself as a well-to-do farmer at Oakland. His mother was Theodora Phelps Ellis, of Putnam County. He was the sixth of eight children. Born on the farm, up to his seventeenth year he shared in all phases of farm work, attending irregularly the county schools and taught at home by his parents. Thrown upon his own resources by his father's death, he earned money to complete his education and, prepared in part at a local private school of some reputation kept by Wm. T. Revill, and in part by his elder brother, a teacher, and by his brother-in-law, he entered the University of Georgia, where, after a brief elective course in the academic department, he transferred to the law school and was graduated in 1877. The following year he began the practise of law at Newnan, Ga. Gov. Colquitt appointed him solicitor of the county court, and a successful career began. He married on Feb. 23, 1880, Susie Cobb Milton, a direct descendant of Christopher, brother of John Milton the poet, and member of a family which had included John Milton (1740–1804) the first secretary of state of Georgia, John Milton [*q.v.*], governor of Florida, and Senator W. H. Milton.

The young county solicitor took naturally to politics and in 1888 was elected to the state House of Representatives. He developed skill in political leadership and was twice reëlected, in his third term becoming speaker. In 1890 he served as president of the state Democratic convention and as chairman of the state executive committee. Among the measures which he championed in the General Assembly were bills making the office of commissioner of agriculture elective, placing telegraph and express companies under the regulative control of the railroad commission, limiting the pay of oil inspectors to $1,500 a year, and creating the State College for Women at Milledgeville. In 1894 he became a candidate for governor against Gen. Clement A. Evans, a popular and eloquent Confederate veteran and Methodist preacher. It was deemed a triumph of Atkinson's popularity and political ability when Evans foresaw defeat and withdrew before the election. It is said to have been the first time an ex-Confederate was ever defeated by a civilian in Georgia. Gov. Atkinson later appointed Evans to a post on the prison commission. He was reelected in 1896 without opposition. His administration was without salient features, but his popularity steadily increased and he exercised a dominant influence on the policies of his party. On the expiration of his second term in 1898 he resumed law practise at Newnan, where he died the following year. He was a man of considerable ability, a good speaker, and an astute political leader. He was not robust physically, but possessed powers of endurance and courage. In appearance he was tall and spare, with regular features, high brow, and crisply curling dark hair.

[*Men of Mark in Ga.*, ed. by W. J. Northen (1910), IV, 377; Lucian Lamar Knight, *Ga.'s Landmarks, Memorials, and Legends* (1914); *Hist. of Ga.* (1926), ed. by Howell Clarke; Lucian Lamar Knight, *Standard Hist. of Ga. and Georgians* (1917); *Atlanta Jour.*, Aug. 8, 1899.]

J. H. T. M.

ATKINSON, WILMER (June 13, 1840–May 10, 1920), journalist, was born on a farm in Warwick township, Bucks County, Pa., the third child of Thomas and Hannah (Quinby) Atkinson. His parents were Quakers, opposed to slavery and to drinking, and sympathetic with the woman's rights movement, then just starting. He attended a rural school and Foulke's Quaker Boarding School, Gwynedd, Pa., and then spent a year in Freeland Seminary, Collegeville, Pa. He took much interest in writing and speaking. After leaving Freeland, he taught a country school near his home and also helped his father on the farm. In 1862 he and Howard M. Jenkins, who later married Atkinson's sister, purchased the *Norristown Republican,* a weekly newspaper. They were barely started in the publishing business when Pennsylvania was threatened with invasion by Lee's Confederate army. The two youths enlisted to resist the expected attack. When the danger was past, they were discharged and returned to their paper. Atkinson's work was interrupted twice more by army service, and before his final discharge he became a second-lieutenant. In 1864 he sold his interest in the *Republican.* Two years later he and Jenkins went to Wilmington, Del., and founded the *Wilmington Daily Commercial,* the first daily newspaper in the state. The same year Atkinson was married to Anna, daughter of Samuel Allen of Philadelphia. While living in Wilmington, he served on the Board of Education. In 1876 he sold his interests and moved to Philadelphia.

Here he began the enterprise that was to absorb the rest of his life—the publication of a monthly agricultural paper, the *Farm Journal.* The first number appeared in March 1877. Atkinson dedicated his journal to "practical, not fancy farming." He filled the publication with crisp, compact articles, and concise, often epigrammatic paragraphs. "Ginger" and "gumption" were favorite words of his, and he put into his work the qualities for which they stand. His writing also had much of the shrewdness and humor traditionally characteristic of the farmer. Atkinson followed Orange Judd, publisher of the *American Agriculturist,* in excluding doubtful advertising, and the *Farm Journal* was the first periodical in America specifically to bar advertisements of patent medicines. The paper announced in its first number that it would "refuse quack medical advertisements at any price." In 1880 it inaugurated the first guaranty ever instituted by any publication against fraudulent practises by its advertisers. The *Farm Journal* grew rapidly, attaining eventually a circulation of more than a million. In 1910 Atkinson started a farm almanac under the title of *Poor Richard's Almanac Revived.* He edited it personally for five years, then turned over the direction of it to a member of his staff. In 1915 he was elected president of the Pennsylvania Men's League for Woman Suffrage and directed a vigorous but unsuccessful campaign for a suffrage amendment to the state constitution. In 1917 he retired from the editorship of the *Farm Journal* after forty years' service. He devoted the last part of his life to writing his autobiography, which was almost completed when he died. He was a force not only for better agriculture, but for a more satisfying rural life. His advocacy of rural free delivery of mail, postal savings banks, protection of birds, and modernization of farm homes was especially effective.

[*Wilmer Atkinson, An Autobiography* (1920); *Who's Who in America,* 1903–21; *Farm Journal,* June 1920; *How It Works* (n. d.), a pamphlet issued by the *Farm Journal,* discusses the guaranty of advertising inaugurated by Atkinson, and its results. Atkinson seldom signed anything in his paper, but a large proportion of its contents, especially in the early days, was written by him, and his personality appears clearly throughout the files of the publication during his editorship.]

N. A. C.

ATLEE, JOHN LIGHT (Nov. 2, 1799–Oct. 1, 1885), surgeon, the son of Col. William Pitt Atlee and Sarah Light, was born in Lancaster, Pa., where he passed almost his entire life. He received his early education in Lancaster except that in the winter of 1813–14 he attended the Gray and Wylie Academy of Philadelphia, a noted school of its day. He intended to enter college; but his plans were upset by the death of his father, who left his widowed mother with six children, of whom John was the eldest. At an early age he began the study of medicine in Lancaster under Dr. Samuel Humes, who later became the first president of the State Medical Society. At the age of eighteen, Atlee entered the medical department of the University of Pennsylvania, but, being too young for graduation the following year, he continued his studies with Dr. Humes, under whose direction in the winter of 1818–19 he attended many cases of variola, this being the first time the disease had made its appearance in America after the discovery of vaccination. He attended another course of lectures at the University of Pennsylvania in the winter of 1819–20 and in the spring of 1820 received the degree of Doctor of Medicine. He immediately began his medical career in his native town, and practised there without interruption until the day of his death sixty-five years later. Although a general practitioner of medicine, Atlee's reputation was gained chiefly in surgery and obstetrics. He performed no less than 2,125 important operations, mainly on the eye, ear, and nose, and attended 3,264 parturitions. Operations of ovariotomy had been successfully performed 1809–13 by Dr. Ephraim McDowell, but the method had been looked upon with general disfavor. Impressed by an account of McDowell's procedure, Atlee revived the operation in 1843. Altogether he performed it seventy-eight times, with a mortality rate of eighteen per cent, a very creditable showing when it is considered that Sir Spencer Wells's estimated mortality of these cases before 1860 was fifty per cent. Cholera made its appearance in Lancaster in 1855. Atlee was an active member of the Sanitary Commission of Lancaster County which was formed to combat it. The deaths were but twenty-six (considered a small number at the time), due largely to the precautions taken by the Commission. Medical organizations greatly interested Atlee from the beginning of his career. He was one of the founders of the Lancaster County Medical Society in 1844, was present at the birth of the State Medical Society in 1848, and in 1882 was made president of the American Medical Association. He was a man of singular probity of character, with dignified bearing, which at once commanded attention and respect. He was for forty years a member of the public school board, a promoter of Franklin and Marshall College, a trustee of the State Lunatic Asylum at Harrisburg and a vestryman of St. James's Church of which he was a regular attendant. On Mar. 12, 1822, he married Sarah Howell Franklin, daughter of Judge Walter Franklin of Lancaster County.

[John L. Atlee, *Address Delivered before the Medic. Soc. of the State of Pa.* (1858); Washington Atlee, "A Table of all the Known Operations of Ovariotomy," in *Trans. Am. Medic. Ass.* (1851); J. L. Ziegler, *Report to the Sanitary Committee of Lancaster, May 26, 1855;* "John Light Atlee," in the *Practitioner,* Jan. 1883; B. H. Detwiler, "Personal Recollections of Doctors John L. and Washington L. Atlee" in *Penn. Medic. Jour.,* Oct. 1904; E. A. Barber, *Geneal. Recs. Atlee Family* (1884).]

T. D.

ATLEE, WASHINGTON LEMUEL (Feb. 22, 1808–Sept. 6, 1878), surgeon, brother of John L. Atlee [*q.v.*], was born in Lancaster, Pa., the youngest of six children of William Pitt Atlee and Sarah Light. His father was a son of the Hon. W. A. Atlee, an active Whig in the Revolutionary War and a judge of the supreme court of Pennsylvania from 1777 until his death in 1793; his maternal grandfather, Maj. John Light, was also an officer in the Revolutionary War. When he was seven years of age, his father died and he went to live with his grandparents. At fourteen he was clerk in a dry-goods and grocery store. At sixteen he entered the office of his brother John and began the study of medicine. It was apparent at an early age that he was an earnest student; for with meager opportunities he acquired several languages and developed a fondness for chemistry and botany and later for practical anatomy. During his apprenticeship he worked in the Lancaster County Hospital. After the customary two full years at Jefferson Medical College, he graduated in the spring of 1829. While a student at Jefferson he became a private pupil of the distinguished surgeon, George McClelland. He was now twenty-one; and armed with his medical diploma, he settled in Mt. Joy, a substantial village about twelve miles from Lancaster. We have no record of his early practise, but it may be surmised that he was not wholly occupied by it when we learn that he collected 400 botanical specimens, to which he attached written descriptions, and that he delivered a temperance lecture and one on "Falling Stars." The next year he married Ann Eliza Hoff, by whom he had ten children. In 1834 he moved to Lancaster, his native town, and soon thereafter was elected to the staff of the hospital. In 1837 he was made treasurer of the Commissioners of Lancaster County. For several years he instructed private classes in chemistry. He was active in the organization of the Lancaster Conservatory of Arts and Sciences and gave lecture courses in hygiene. He was one of the founders of the Lancaster County Medical Society in 1844; and the same year accepted an invitation to fill the chair of medical chemistry in the Medical College of Philadelphia. He continued in this position until 1852 when he resigned to devote his entire time to a growing surgical practise. His love for surgery had probably been fired by his brother John, who the year before had returned from two years' study in Paris and Berlin.

No date can be set for the beginning of his surgical career, but soon after he settled in Lancaster in 1834 he performed an operation for vesical calculus. In 1843 he assisted his brother John in the latter's first ovariotomy operation. He performed his own first operation for ovariotomy the next year on a patient in Lancaster, with fatal result. His second operation was performed later in the same year, and a third was done in 1849. Shortly after the first operation, he encountered the disapproval of his colleagues, some going so far as to say that he committed murder and others, less violent, saying the operation was untried and did not have the approval of the medical profession. Possessing argumentative ability and gifted with ready speech, Atlee ably defended himself. After a time, Gross, Chapman, McClelland, and other leading surgeons of Philadelphia indorsed him, and the opposition faded away. In 1851 Atlee prepared a notable paper in which he exhibited in tabulated form all the operations of ovariotomy from 1701 to 1851, comprising in all 222 cases. Dr. J. M. Toner wrote in 1878 that Washington Atlee himself had at that time performed 378 ovariotomies which he believed, with the exception of one other surgeon, was the largest number done by any living operator. In 1861, while he was performing an operation in Williamsport, on the second floor of a frame building, surrounded by an eager group of colleagues, the floor gave way and the patient, operator, and onlookers, were precipitated to the floor below. In the midst of the confusion, unmindful of the discomfort of his audience, Atlee calmly completed the operation. Like his brother John, he was a medical organization man, and president of the Pennsylvania State Medical Society in 1874, and vice-president of the National Society in 1875.

[*Lecture Introductory to the Course of Medic. Chemistry in the Medic. Dept. of Pa. College by W. L. Atlee* (1844); W. L. Atlee, "A Table of all the Known Operations of Ovariotomy," *Trans. Am. Medic. Ass.* (1851); J. M. Toner, *Biog. Sketch of Washington L. Atlee* (Lancaster, 1878); E. A. Barber, *Geneal. Rec. Atlee Family* (1884); *Phila. Inquirer,* Sept. 10, 1878.] T. D.

ATTUCKS, CRISPUS (*c.* 1723–Mar. 5, 1770) was the leader of the mob which precipitated the so-called "Boston Massacre." Almost nothing is known definitely of his life previous to the event which brought him prominence and death. It is possible that he was a sailor on a whaling-ship. There had been a period of "unrest" in Boston, due to the presence of British troops, and relations were visibly strained. On the evening of Mar. 5, 1770, Attucks at the head of a crowd of fifty or sixty men, mostly sailors, marched from Dock Square to the present State Street, a figure, according to John Adams, "almost a giant in stature" (J. B. Fisher, "Who was Crispus Attucks?" in the *American Historical Record,* I, 1872). A collision ensued with a small group of British troops under Capt. Preston. Shots were fired, and three citizens—including Attucks—were killed, and two others mortally wounded. In the trial which followed, Attucks's name was necessarily often mentioned, and he is the one most prominently associated with the "Massacre."

In the common accounts Attucks is described as a mulatto, supposed to have been owned by Deacon William Browne of Framingham, Mass., who advertised for the recovery of a runaway slave named Crispus in the *Boston Gazette,* Oct. 2, Nov. 13, Nov. 20, 1750 (the advertisement is reprinted in the *New England Historical and Genealogical Register,* XIII, 300). The belief that Attucks was a mulatto or negro underlay the proceedings at the unveiling of the monument on Boston Common in 1888, where the chief speaker was John Fiske and the poet was John Boyle O'Reilly. On the other hand J. B. Fisher argues strongly that Attucks was an Indian, probably of the Natick tribe from the neighborhood of Framingham. Frederick Kidder, in his *History of the Boston Massacre* (1870) suggests that he was of mixed Indian and negro blood. In the *Works of John Adams* (II, 322), under date of July 19, there is cited a denunciatory address in the name of Attucks, to the royal governor, Hutchinson, which, according to a footnote by C. F. Adams, "seems to have been intended for publication in a newspaper."

[In addition to the references above, see *Attucks Memorial* (1889); J. H. Semple, *Hist. of Framingham, Mass.* (1887); Geo. Livermore, "An Historical Research Respecting the Opinions of the Founders of the Republic on Negroes as Slaves, as Citizens, and as Soldiers," in *Mass. Hist. Soc. Proc.,* ser. I, vol. I.] E. K. A.

ATWATER, CALEB (Dec. 25, 1778–Mar. 13, 1867), pioneer, author, was born at North Adams, Mass., the son of Ebenezer and Rachel (Parker) Atwater and a descendant of David Atwater, one of the first settlers of New Haven. His father was a carpenter. His mother died when he was about five years old, and he was then placed in the home of a Mr. Jones, a neighbor, who reared him. He entered Williams College, from which he graduated in 1804 with the degree of B.A. Removing to New York City, he kept a school for young women, at the same time studying theology, and later becoming a Presbyterian minister. He married Diana Lawrence, who lived only about a year after the wedding. His health failing, he gave up the ministry. He then studied law and after a few months was admitted to the bar. On Apr. 3, 1811, he married Belinda Butler, of Pompey, N.Y. A business venture proving disastrous, he resolved to go west, and in 1815 settled in Circleville, Ohio. For the next six years he practised law, giving his spare time to the study of the earthworks and other antiquities of the state. In 1820 he contributed to the American Antiquarian Society a paper on the subject, published in *Archæologia Americana,* vol. I, the Transactions for that year.

In 1821 he was elected to the lower house of the legislature, where he at once became prominent through his advocacy of digging canals, improving highways, and providing for popular education. As chairman of the committee on school lands and later of a state board to formulate a system of education he carried on a vigorous campaign for public schools. He was an unsuccessful candidate for Congress in 1822, and the following year he served on the Circleville school board. The election of 1824 registered a notable victory for his public policies and marked the beginning of Ohio's school system and fostering of internal improvements. In May 1829, he was appointed by President Jackson one of three commissioners to treat with the Winnebago and other Indians in the vicinity of Prairie du Chien, Wis. The treaties were promptly concluded and were carried by him to Washington, where in December they were ratified by the Senate. An account of the episode, with descriptions of the regions traversed and a discussion of the relations of the government to the Indians was published by him two years later. In 1833 the paper on antiquities and the account of the trip to Prairie du Chien and thence to Washington, with some additional matter, were published in a volume entitled *The Writings of Caleb Atwater.* In

1838 he published *A History of the State of Ohio, Natural and Civil,* which except for the brief historical sketch introducing Salmon P. Chase's compilation of Ohio laws, was the first published history of the state. In 1841 appeared *An Essay on Education,* characterized by C. L. Martzolff as "the best thing he ever wrote" and a treatise which "makes good pedagogical reading even at this time." His later years were spent quietly at his home among his books. He died at Circleville, where he had lived for fifty-two years.

Atwater was one of the intellectual and social pioneers of the Middle West. He lived and died poor, too deeply concerned in questions of science and of human welfare to bother about making money. He was perhaps the first advocate of forest conservation; he was one of the first to predict the success of the railway; he was the first historian of his state and the founder of her school system. It was his fate to have outlived his time and to have been forgotten by his contemporaries a full decade before his death.

[L. Martzolff, "Caleb Atwater," *Ohio Archeol. and Hist. Quart.,* July 1905; Francis Atwater, *Atwater Hist. and Genealogy,* II (1907); R. L. Rusk, *The Lit. of the Middle Western Frontier* (1925).]

W. J. G.

ATWATER, LYMAN HOTCHKISS (Feb. 3, 1813–Feb. 17, 1883), clergyman, educator, was widely known in his day as a versatile scholar and able controversialist. A descendant of David Atwater, one of the original planters of New Haven, Conn., he was born in Cedar Hill, then a suburb of that city, the son of Lyman and Clarissa (Hotchkiss) Atwater. He prepared for college under Dr. H. P. Arms, a Congregational minister, entered Yale at the age of fourteen, where he formed a life-long intimacy with his classmate, Noah Porter, graduated with honors in 1831, taught the classics for a year at Mount Hope Seminary, Baltimore, and then pursued the prescribed course in the Yale Divinity School, during the last two years of which he also served as tutor in Yale College. On July 29, 1835, he was ordained pastor of the First Congregational Church, Fairfield, Conn., where he remained for nineteen years. For the rest of his life he was a professor in the College of New Jersey, Princeton. His original appointment was to the chair of mental and moral philosophy, but when Dr. James McCosh became president, Atwater consented to the transfer of those subjects to him, while he himself took the chair of logic and moral and political science. He married, Oct. 7, 1835, Susan, the daughter of Elihu and Susan Howell Sanford, of New Haven, by whom he had four sons and a daughter.

He was a prolific writer of articles of a polemic nature. The most of these, more than a hundred, appeared in the *Princeton Review,* with the editorship of which he was long connected. They cover a wide range of subjects, including doctrine and apologetics, biography, history, education, metaphysics, ethics, political economy, and finance. His chief interest, however, was in philosophy and theology. This had been greatly stimulated in his youth by his reading of Coleridge, to whom he confessed great indebtedness (see article on Coleridge, *Princeton Review,* April 1848). Coleridge's effect upon him in the end, however, was to stiffen his orthodoxy, and he became one of the ablest champions of the old order as against the theological and social changes which characterized the middle of the nineteenth century. His first contribution to the *Princeton Review,* "The Power of Contrary Choice," October 1840, was a defense of the old-school Calvinism, and an arraignment of the theory of personal responsibility advanced by Dr. Nathaniel W. Taylor [*q.v.*], his old pastor and professor. For Horace Bushnell [*q.v.*] as a man and preacher he professed great admiration, but deemed him poorly fitted to try to reconstruct theology, and lamented that he did much "to undermine and confuse the true conception of the Trinity, Incarnation, Atonement, of language, logic, and creeds" (*Presbyterian Review,* January 1881). The tendency of the new theology to create the form of preaching advocated by Dr. Charles G. Finney [*q.v.*], which would "multiply converts with unexampled rapidity," was abhorrent to him ("Revivals," *Princeton Review,* January 1842). Naturally he combated the philosophy of Herbert Spencer, and repudiated the evolutionary hypothesis, exulting that in so doing he had Agassiz on his side ("Herbert Spencer's Philosophy," *Ibid.,* April 1865). In his political and social views he was equally orthodox. True progress he said must be based, not on skepticism, but on "stability," *i. e.* adherence to the fundamental truths revealed in the Bible ("The True Progress of Society," *Ibid.,* January 1852). Civil government, the family, and tenure of property, he termed "great ordinances of God for the social regulation of man." The woman's-rights movement he characterized as a "mad enterprise." No less conservative was he in his views on education, criticizing adversely the freedom given to students at Harvard under President Eliot, and supporting the policies favored by his friend President Porter ("Proposed Reforms in Collegiate Education," *Ibid.,* July 1882). Although sharp in his criticisms and sometimes given to strong invectives, he was extremely fair in stating the arguments of his opponents, appreciative of their excellences, and uniformly kind in spirit. His writings are still of value, both because of the information and wisdom which, in spite of their conservatism, they contain, and also because of the light which they shed upon the intellectual and religious movements going on during the period in which they were written. He published also several addresses and one book, *Manual of Elementary Logic* (1867).

[The best sources of information are a series of addresses delivered by Noah Porter, James McCosh, Archibald A. Hodge, and Wm. M. Taylor, published under the title, *Addresses Delivered at the Funeral of Lyman Hotchkiss Atwater* (1883). See also *Princeton Theol. Sem. Necrological Report*(1883); *Princeton Univ. Gen. Cat.* (1906); Francis Atwater, *Atwater Hist.* (1901).]

H. E. S.

ATWATER, WILBUR OLIN (May 3, 1844–Sept. 22, 1907), pioneer in agricultural chemistry, the son of William Warren and Eliza (Barnes) Atwater, was born at Johnsburg, N.Y. He was educated at the public schools, studied at the University of Vermont for two years (his father was a minister in Burlington), and obtained his bachelor's degree at Wesleyan University, Middletown, Conn., in 1865. The chance acquaintance of several unusually intelligent farmers who had thought much about scientific agriculture, turned his attention from engineering to agricultural chemistry; and upon their advice he went to Yale to study under Dr. Samuel W. Johnson. He remained there until 1869, when he received his Ph.D. degree on a thesis dealing with the chemical composition of maize, a paper which for the first time showed the possibilities of the application of modern chemical methods to American food materials. For the next two years he studied at Leipzig and at Berlin, obtaining the most advanced chemical information that could then be given, and becoming acquainted with agricultural experiment stations in Europe. On his return to America he taught first at the University of Tennessee and then at the Maine State College (now the University of Maine). He was married in 1873 to Marcia Woodard of Bangor, Me. In the same year he was appointed professor of chemistry at Wesleyan University, and here he remained until his death, developing agricultural chemistry in this country as it had never been developed before. In 1875, largely through the pleadings of Atwater and his former teacher Johnson, the Connecticut legislature established at Middletown the first state agricultural station in the United States. For the next two years the agricultural station had its quarters in Middletown, and Atwater was the director; then in 1877 it was moved to New Haven, its present quarters, and Atwater gave place to Johnson. But the removal of the experiment station did not lessen Atwater's desire to carry on agricultural investigations. He inaugurated an ambitious program to study fertilizers, and by 1881 was in a position to draw one very important conclusion from these investigations: that free atmospheric nitrogen is assimilated by leguminous plants. Largely through Atwater's efforts, Congress passed the Hatch Act of 1887, which provided that every state should be allowed $15,000 a year for the maintenance of at least one experiment station. He impressed upon people the importance of regarding such stations not merely as testing laboratories for fertilizers but as places in which fundamental work in agriculture could be carried out. "The future usefulness of the stations," he wrote, "will depend upon what they discover of permanent value, and this must come largely from the most abstract and profound research; to forget this will be fatal."

In a sense, the turning point in Atwater's career came from a visit to Voit's laboratory in Munich in 1887, where he came in contact not only with Voit himself, but with Voit's chief assistant, Max Rubner. It was through these men that he became interested in calorimetry; and it was this interest which led him, in conjunction with E. B. Rosa, then professor of physics at Wesleyan University, to build what has since become the famous Atwater-Rosa calorimeter. This was begun in 1892 and not completed until five years later. With the help of his calorimeter, Atwater demonstrated that the law of the conservation of energy is valid for human beings as it is for everything else: the quantity of heat produced by an individual is no more and no less than the amount of heat produced when the foods he consumes are oxidized. Another important result of his interest in calorimetry was the preparation of elaborate tables giving the calorific value of various foodstuffs—tables first published in 1896 and still used everywhere. In 1888 Atwater became founder and chief of the Office of Experiment Stations, United States Department of Agriculture. This position was merely an addition to his professorial duties, and was undertaken primarily to foster research. Not long before Atwater's death, the Carnegie Institution of Washington decided to endow the work in calorimetry and to build a special laboratory for him. It was also during these days, when the laboratory sponsored by the Carnegie Institution was taking shape, that he conceived the notion of experiments on an international scale, involving relations between the diet, labor power, and the success and health of nations; and in this scheme he was more encouraged by his European than by his American colleagues. He was in the very midst of these activities when he died.

Atwater's work was recognized in Europe to an extent which was unusual for that period. Many of his articles were translated into French by Armand Gautier and Paul Heger, into Russian by Likhacher and Smolenski, and into Swedish by Tigerstedt. "In Berlin, the center of German thought in the field of metabolism and problems of nutrition," writes F. G. Benedict, "Atwater's work is most fully appreciated. Magnus-Levy in his book on the physiology of metabolism suggests certain fundamental problems in nutrition that can be solved only with the aid of the apparatus possessed by America" (meaning the apparatus devised by Atwater and still further refined by Benedict).

References to some important individual papers by Atwater (the total number runs into several hundred) are: "On the Acquisition of Atmospheric Nitrogen by Plants" (*American Chemical Journal,* 1885, VI, 365–88); "Investigations on Metabolism in the Human Organism: Experiments on the Income and Outgo of the Body with Different Food Materials" (with C. D. Woods and F. G. Benedict, *Annual Report, Storrs Agricultural Station,* 1896, p. 163); "A Respiration Calorimeter and Experiments on the Conservation of Energy in the Human Body" (with E. B. Rosa, *Ibid.,* 1897, p. 212); the following, published by the United States Department of Agriculture, Office of Experiment Stations: "The Chemical Composition of American Food Materials" (*Bulletin XXVIII,* 1896 and 1899), "Report of Preliminary Investigations on the Metabolism of Nitrogen and Carbon in the Human Organism, with a Respiration Calorimeter of Special Construction" (with C. D. Woods and F. G. Benedict, *Bulletin XLIV,* 1897), "Description of a New Respiration Calorimeter and Experiments on the Conservation of Energy in the Human Body" (with E. B. Rosa, *Bulletin LXIII,* 1899), "Experiments on the Metabolism of Matter and Energy in the Human Body" (with F. G. Benedict and others, *Bulletin LXIX,* 1899); "A Respiration Calorimeter with Appliances for the Direct Determination of Oxygen" (with F. G. Benedict, *Carnegie Institution of Washington, Publication No. 42,* 1905); "Dietetics" (*Encyclopædia Britannica,* 1902).

[Much of the material in the above account was derived from Miss Helen W. Atwater, editor of the *Jour. of Home Economics,* and from Dr. F. G. Benedict, of the Carnegie Institution of Washington. There are good sketches of Atwater in *Science,* Oct. 18, 1907, and in *Obit. Rec. Grads. Yale Univ.* (1908); portrait in *Pop. Sci. Mo.,* Dec. 1907; articles by Prof. Graham Lusk and Dr. Charles A. Browne in the *Jour. Am. Chemic. Soc.* (1926), vol. XLVIII; good descriptions of the Atwater-Rosa calorimeter in Graham Lusk, *The Elements of the Science of Nutrition* (1906) and in T. B. Robertson, *Principles of Biochemistry* (1920); a very complete discussion of energy metabolism in *Practical Physiological Chemistry* (1926) by P. B. Hawk and Olaf Bergeim.]

B. H—w.

ATWOOD, CHARLES B. (May 18, 1849–Dec. 19, 1895), architect, son of David and Lucy (Bowles) Atwood, was born in Charlestown, Mass. His architectural interest began early; already at seventeen he was studying architecture, and in 1868 he entered the course in architecture at the Lawrence Scientific School of Harvard University, remaining there two years. From Harvard he entered the office of Ware & Van Brunt, then one of the few firms of architects of high professional standing in the country, where he remained until 1872, when he opened his own offices in Boston. During a three-year period of independent practise, Atwood's work was largely in the neighborhood of Worcester, near which, at Millbury, his family then resided. His most important works of this time were the Merchants Fire Insurance Building at Worcester, and the Five Cent Savings Bank at Lowell. He was also the successful prize winner in various minor competitions. In 1875 he was called to New York to take charge of the architectural work of Herter Brothers, the well-known fashionable decorators. While with them he designed the twin Vanderbilt houses on Fifth Avenue between Fifty-first and Fifty-second Streets. Later, he left the employ of Herter Brothers, and again entered independent practise, designing, among others, the Twombly and Webb houses, and a great deal of work on the estate of Mrs. Mark Hopkins at Great Barrington.

In 1890, D. H. Burnham's partner, John W. Root, had died, and Burnham was in a quandary as to his successor, for it would have been impossible for Burnham to do by himself the immense amount of work thrust on him by his position as chief of construction and consulting architect for the contemplated Chicago World's Fair. William R. Ware (of Ware & Van Brunt), then professor of architecture in Columbia College, at once suggested Atwood, and, despite the doubts expressed by C. F. McKim, Burnham selected him. By the spring of 1891 the reorganization was completed, and Atwood thus became "Designer-in-Chief" of the Chicago World's Fair. Moore states that he designed "more than sixty of the Fair buildings besides various ornamental features." The most important were the combination of Music Hall, Peristyle, and Casino, in one composition, and the Art Building, the artistic crown of the Exposition and Atwood's undoubted *chef-d'œuvre.* Augustus Saint-Gaudens said that the Art Building had been "unequaled since the Parthenon" and Burnham that "his Art Building in design was the most beautiful building I have ever seen."

In 1893 Burnham originated a new firm, D. H. Burnham & Co., with Atwood in control of "all artistic matters . . . including making designs." Among the buildings which Atwood designed under this arrangement was the Ellicut Building in Buffalo. After the completion of the World's Fair work, however, he seems never to have been completely happy in the Burnham firm. At first a genial, companionable person, he grew more and more peculiar as the years drew on, more and more a recluse. Moore notes that Atwood lacked certain qualities needed for success in commercial undertakings; moreover, the state of his health prevented steady work. His artistic skill was the product of an intense artistic temperament, which had many of the peculiarities and deficiencies that occasionally accompany it. He resigned on Dec. 10, 1895, and died, somewhat under a cloud, on Dec. 19.

[Charles H. Moore's *Daniel H. Burnham* (1921) contains many references to Atwood and his work, as well as a portrait, and a charming description of his appearance and personality. An extended notice of his death appeared in the *Am. Architect and Building News,* Dec. 28, 1895, and shorter notices in *N.Y. Herald,* Dec. 20, 1895, and *Chicago Tribune,* Dec. 21, 1895.]

T. F. H.

ATWOOD, DAVID (Dec. 15, 1815–Dec. 11, 1889), editor, politician, was born in Bedford, N. H. David Atwood, his father, was a Presbyterian and of English stock; his mother, Mary (Bell) Atwood, was Scotch-Irish. His early training was that of the average boy on a New England farm. At seventeen he apprenticed himself to a printing house at Hamilton, N.Y., in which his brother had an interest. The death of the other partner left the firm in financial straits, and to meet the difficulty David undertook to market an eight-volume digest of Federal and state court decisions, *The American Common Law.* The work entailed traveling by horse and democrat through the Middle Atlantic states and the Old Northwest. The next five years David spent in Hamilton in journalistic work with his brother. In 1840 and 1844 he supported the Whigs, and his labors in the second contest so injured his health that in 1845 he migrated to the West where two years of farming in Stephenson County, Ill., ruined him financially but restored him physically. He decided to establish himself in Wisconsin Territory, which had been authorized to form a state constitution. Coming to Madison in 1847, he immediately secured a position on the *Madison Express,* the only Whig paper at the capital. His most important duty was reporting the proceedings of the constitutional convention. In October 1848, he became a partner in a firm that bought the *Express* and changed the title to the *Wisconsin Express.* This journal supported the Free-Soil wing of the Whig party, while a rival Whig paper, the *Statesman,* founded in the spring of 1850, favored the Fillmore administration and the Compromise of 1850. A consolidation of these papers into the *Palladium* was effected in 1851, but it soon collapsed and Atwood alone in September 1852 established the *Wisconsin State Journal,* which for a quarter century played an important part in Wisconsin political life. First Whig and then Republican, it remained strictly regular both in state and national politics. Though partisan, its news was accurate; a correspondent of a Chicago paper says that its record was considered by out-of-town reporters as reliable as the legislative journals. Atwood was an active supporter of Coles Bashford in the latter's contest for the governorship in 1855–56. In 1861 he represented Madison district in the lower house of the state legislature, and in 1862 was appointed United States internal revenue assessor for the second congressional district. In 1866 he was removed from office after his paper had strongly opposed President Johnson. Mayor of Madison, 1868–69, he was elected to Congress in 1870 to fill the unexpired term of Benjamin F. Hopkins, deceased. He was for many years president of the Madison Mutual Insurance Company, also president of the Madison Gas Light & Coke Company, and director in several railroad enterprises. Well-proportioned medium stature, good features, and, in later years, a full flowing white beard gave him an impressive appearance. Conscious of this and of his prominence, Atwood was vain, always formal and immaculate in dress, and extremely distant in public. In more intimate relations, however, he was kind and courteous. He was married on Aug. 23, 1849, to Mary Sweeney.

[Horace Rublee, "Gen. Atwood" in *Proc. Wis. Press Ass.* (1890), pp. 63–71; R. G. Thwaites, "Gen. David Atwood" in the *Mag. of Western Hist.* (Feb. 1887). A sketch that Atwood himself published is in H. A. Tenney and D. Atwood, *Memorial Rec. of the Fathers of Wis. containing Sketches of the Lives and Careers of the Members of the Constit. Conventions of 1846 and 1847–48, with a Hist. of Early Settlement in Wis.* (1880), pp. 294–95.]

H. J. D.

ATWOOD, LEWIS JOHN (Apr. 8, 1827–Feb. 23, 1909), inventor, manufacturer, was born in Goshen, Conn., the son of Norman and Abigail (Woodward) Atwood. One of nine children, he was compelled to assume his share of the family support at an early age. When but fifteen he entered the employ of Amos Gridley, a merchant of Watertown, Conn., from which position he went to Waterbury, Conn., in 1845 to continue in mercantile activities for a short time before starting the manufacture of brass buckles and buttons with Samuel Maltby in that city. When this enterprise failed from lack of capital, Atwood entered the employment of Holmes, Booth & Haydens, brass-manufacturers. It was at this time (1855) that petroleum came on the market and increased the demand for lamps. To meet this demand there was a movement by brass-manufacturers to adapt sheet brass to the making of lamps and their fittings. Atwood and Hiram W. Hayden [*q.v.*] were the two men who led in the successful invention and use of sheet-brass lamp burners, Atwood himself obtaining some fifty patents in this field. Because of this activity he is credited by some as having done "more to develop the science of domestic lighting" than any other mechanic. It is certain that his inventions enabled his company to take a leading place in brass-manufacturing and did as much for the American industry, in general, as did the tariff. Atwood also devised a scrap-metal press which has been used in the trade to the present day. This press accomplished the work known as "cabbaging," or the compacting of scrap metal preparatory to remelting. This work formerly was accomplished by hand, the metal being pounded with sledges into a cast-iron mortar. In 1869 Holmes left Holmes, Booth & Haydens and organized the Holmes, Booth & Atwood Manufacturing Company (afterward changed to Plume & Atwood), in which Atwood became a stockholder and officer and later (1890) its president. This new firm bought a brass-mill in Thomaston, Conn., which had been organized to roll metal for clocks, and also a small concern in Waterbury, and became one of the important factors in the trade. The company was essentially a remanufacturing concern, and by means of control of patents and the trade that it had in certain specialties it enjoyed a large, non-competitive business. When the American Brass Company was formed in 1899 as a merger of brass-sheet, rod, and wire mills, Plume & Atwood remained outside the amalgamation as one of the larger independent concerns. Atwood remained in Waterbury as president of the company until the time of his death. He was active in many public-welfare enterprises, being especially interested in the Y.M.C.A.; he was chairman of the committee having in charge the construction of the Waterbury branch of which he was president for five years. He was married on Jan. 12, 1852 to Sarah Platt, by whom he had three children.

[Joseph Anderson, *The Town and City of Waterbury, from the Aboriginal Period to the Year 1895* (1896); Joseph W. Roe, *Eng. and Am. Tool Builders* (1916); *Metal Industry,* Mar. 1909; *U. S. Pat. Office Recs.*]

F. A. T.

ATZERODT, GEORGE A. (*c.* 1832–1865). [See BOOTH, JOHN WILKES.]

AUCHMUTY, RICHARD TYLDEN (July 15, 1831–July 18, 1893), philanthropist, was born in New York City and received the first and middle names of his father, an officer in the United States Marine Corps, through whom he inherited the Scotch blood and family name of the Auchmutys of Fifeshire. The first Auchmuty of the line to settle in America was Robert [*q.v.*]. Samuel [*q.v.*], the second son of Robert, was rector of Trinity Church, New York City, before and during the early part of the Revolutionary War, in which three of Samuel's sons served with the British army. One of them, Robert Nicholas Auchmuty, returned to New York City at the close of the war; he was the father of Richard Tylden Auchmuty, Sr., who married Mary Allen, great-grand-daughter on the paternal side of Chief Justice Allen of Pennsylvania and, on the maternal side, of Philip Livingston, one of the signers of the Declaration of Independence. Richard Tylden Auchmuty, Jr., entered Columbia College at the age of sixteen, withdrawing in his junior year on account of ill health and spending some months in European travel. On coming home he studied architecture in the office of James Renwick and in a few years was admitted to partnership. At the outbreak of the Civil War he was commissioned a captain in the Federal army, and as an officer of the 5th army corps took part in a number of important battles. Colonel by brevet for gallantry at Gettysburg, he was transferred, because of impaired health, from field service to duty in the War Department at Washington, assisting the next year (1864) in the defense of the city against Early's attack. The war over, he resumed residence in New York City, but established a summer home in Lenox, Mass., where he interested himself in local affairs and held various public offices. He was one of the pioneer members of the summer colony there, and his influence contributed much to its growth.

Retiring from the architectural profession, Auchmuty gave more and more of his time to his interests in Lenox and to the trade school which in 1881 he opened in New York City. In establishing this school the founder sought to provide an opportunity for mechanically inclined young men in poor circumstances to learn a trade without having to submit to the conditions imposed by the labor unions in the matter of apprenticeship. He felt that the length of the apprenticeship period and the limited number of apprentices allowed by the unions were keeping many young men out of fields, particularly in the building trades, of which immigrants trained in Europe were taking possession. The curriculum of the New York Trade School combined theoretical instruction and shop practise in a manner which was then new to American education. Until 1892 the institution was maintained solely through the liberality of Auchmuty and his wife (formerly Ellen Schermerhorn). In this year it was incorporated under the state laws and a board of trustees appointed. J. Pierpont Morgan donated a large sum to the endowment, and the school is still operating under its original charter, with nominal tuition fees, "neither in the interest of, nor in opposition to, any trade organization, whether it be employers or journeymen" (*Forty-sixth Annual Catalogue,* 1926–27).

From available accounts Auchmuty seems to have been a man of strong opinions and vigorous personality, conservative in belief and conscientious in speech and action. In addition to these qualities his friends found in him a strain of gentleness. He was a vestryman of Trinity Church, New York City, and likewise held lay offices in Trinity Church, Lenox. He died at Lenox, at the age of sixty-two.

[The latest annual catalogue of the New York Trade School contains a few historical paragraphs regarding the school, of which an account may also be found in Frederick William Roman, *The Industrial and Commercial Schools of the United States and Germany* (1915). An appreciation of Auchmuty is found in *A Sermon Preached in Trinity Church, Lenox, on Sunday, July 23, 1893, Being the Sunday Following the Funeral Services of Richard Tylden Auchmuty,* by William M. Grosvenor. Obituaries in the *N.Y. Times, N.Y. Tribune,* July 19, 1893.]

R. G. F.

AUCHMUTY, ROBERT (d. 1750), colonial jurist, was born in Scotland. He studied law in London, being admitted to the Middle Temple, Apr. 5, 1705, and was called to the English bar Nov. 23, 1711. Some time later he came to America, won prominence as a lawyer in Boston, and was judge of admiralty in Massachusetts 1733–41. He was sent to England in 1741 as the agent for his colony in a boundary dispute with Rhode Island, and he acted in the settlement of various boundary controversies. In 1744, or possibly earlier, he wrote a pamphlet advocating an expedition to Louisburg (the one which was carried out in 1745), and thereby the historian Smollett gained the wrong impression that Auchmuty originated the project. He left a reputation for wit and shrewdness. In the words of his younger contemporary, John Adams, he "sits up all night at his bottle—Argues to admiration the next day" (Adams, *Works,* II, 357). In 1733 he bought an estate in Roxbury (now included in Boston), a part of which descended to his son and had notable associations.

[E. A. Jones, *Am. Members of the Inns of Court* (1924), p. 10; Francis S. Drake, *The Town of Roxbury* (1878); Emory Washburn, *Sketches of the Judicial Hist. of Mass.* (1840); "Diary of Samuel Sewall" in *Mass. Hist. Soc. Colls.,* ser. 5, vols. V, VI, VII.]

E. K. A.

AUCHMUTY, ROBERT (d. November 1788), colonial jurist and Loyalist, was born in Boston, the son of Judge Robert and the brother of Samuel Auchmuty [*q.v.*], rector of Trinity Church. He was privately educated. Like his father he became a prominent lawyer in Boston, learned and successful, and was associated with the group of which Otis, Quincy, and John Adams were members. In 1767 he was appointed judge of vice-admiralty for Massachusetts and New Hampshire. With Adams he was counsel for Capt. Preston in the case of the so-called "Boston Massacre" in 1770. Adams, an unfriendly critic, describes him as heavy and dull, voluble and addicted to repetitions, but flat in wit, and he wonders why such a speaker should be considered a leader of the bar (Adams, *Works,* II, 198). Returning to the subject he writes that Auchmuty "maintains the air of reserve, design, and cunning" (*Ibid.,* II, 364).

Auchmuty received from his father a part of his estate in Roxbury (Boston), and on it he built a house about 1761. This mansion had a noteworthy history. It was a rendezvous for officers of the Crown, Hutchinson, Bernard, and others. Thither Gov. Bernard summoned a council, and in it were quartered British officers during the siege of Boston. It was confiscated in 1779, and after the war it was occupied for a time by Gov. Increase Sumner. Auchmuty, like his brother, was an ardent Loyalist, and his letters written to correspondents in England were sent to America by Franklin in 1773, being considered in the same category with Hutchinson's letters. (One of them was published with the Hutchinson letters in the *Copy of Letters sent to Great Britain,* Boston, 1773.) He removed to England in 1776, and belonged to the New England Club of Loyalists, formed that year in London. Since his property was confiscated, he was greatly reduced in means during his later years. His library in 1784 was sold at Boston by order of the authorities. From the British government he received a pension of £100 (A. C. Flick, *Loyalism in New York,* 1902, p. 202).

[F. S. Drake, *Town of Roxbury* (1878); Justin Winsor, *Memorial Hist. of Boston* (1881), II, 343; Lorenzo Sabine, *Biog. Sketches of Loyalists of the Am. Rev.* (1864); John Adams, *Works* (1850–56); Emory Washburn, *Sketches of the Judicial Hist. of Mass.* (1840).]

E. K. A.

AUCHMUTY, SAMUEL (Jan. 26, 1722–Mar. 4, 1777), Anglican clergyman, Loyalist, the son of Judge Robert Auchmuty [*q.v.*], was graduated at Harvard in 1742, was admitted to holy orders by the Bishop of London in 1747, and in the following year became assistant minister of Trinity Church, New York. Here his duties embraced the reading of prayers, the assisting of the rector in his parochial work, and the serving as catechist to the colored population. By reason of faithful service he became rector in 1764. He won the respect of his community, and received the degree of S.T.D. from Oxford in 1766, and from Kings (Columbia) in 1767. The parish in his time had two assistants, and under his auspices St. Paul's Chapel was completed and opened for service in 1766. In 1771 he wrote an address to the Virginia Episcopalians, favoring an American Episcopate. He was a High Churchman, and in the Revolution a strong Loyalist, like most of the Anglican clergy in America. His attitude at the outbreak of the war is indicated by these extracts from a letter addressed to him: "They[parishioners]recollect a Sermon, in which you strongly inculcated the Doctrine of Non-Resistance and Passive Obedience . . . I am very sorry to find you such an enemy to Congresses, 'to Hancock, Adams, and their followers.' Whatever you may think of them, Sir, the Wise and Virtuous now applaud their Conduct . . . 'We have lately been plagued with a rascally Whig mob' is hardly a decent Expression for a Clergyman to use, and your Reflection on our worthy Magistrates is exceedingly illiberal . . . I would recommend to you . . . to avoid Party Spirit and Party Prejudice" (*Letter to the Rev. Dr. Auchmuty,* signed C. J., and incorrectly dated Mar. 12, 1775, bound with the *Hazard Pamphlets,* XXX, in the Library of Congress; it is evidently a reply to *Dr. Auchmuty's Letter to Capt. Montresor, Chief Engineer, at Boston,* dated Apr. 15, 1775, to be found in the Massachusetts Broadsides, Manuscripts Division, Library of Congress). Trumbull in his satirical poem *McFingal* refers to Auchmuty in these lines:

> "What warnings had ye of your duty
> From our old rev'rend Sam. Auchmuty."
>
> "While mitres fall, as 'tis their duty,
> On heads of Chandler and Auchmuty."

He was ill and absent in New Brunswick, N. J., at the time of Washington's occupation. Soon after occurred the great fire of September 1776, which destroyed Trinity Church, the charity school, and the parish tenements, and Auchmuty's house and library. His personal loss was heavy, and destruction of church property was estimated at about £22,200. Services were carried on in the chapels, but Auchmuty did not long survive the disaster, his death being hastened perhaps by the fire and the circumstances of the war. He was married in December 1749 to "Mrs. Tucker, widow of the late Capt. Tucker" (Dix, I, 250), and was the father of Sir Samuel Auchmuty, who fought on the royal side during the Revolution, and later was a distinguished English general.

[*Hist. of the Parish of Trinity Ch.,* ed. by Morgan Dix (4 vols., 1898–1906), I; Wilkins Updike, *Hist. of the Episc. Ch. in Narragansett, R. I.* (1907); Lorenzo Sabine, *Biog. Sketches of Loyalists of Am. Rev.* (1864); Chas. C. Tiffany, *Hist. of the P. E. Ch. in the U. S.* (1895); *Memorial Hist. of the City of N.Y.,* ed. by Jas. Grant Wilson (1892–93).]

E. K. A.

AUDSLEY, GEORGE ASHDOWN (Sept. 6, 1838–June 21, 1925), architect, organ designer, author, son of John James Audsley, was born in Elgin, Scotland. He received his architectural education in his birthplace, being apprenticed at an early age to A. & W. Reid, who at that time had a considerable reputation in Scotland. At the age of eighteen he went to Liverpool, where he worked under John Weightman, the borough surveyor; a little later he went into partnership with one John Cunningham, and later still with his talented younger brother, W. J. Audsley—a partnership which continued until the latter's death. Entering the practise of architecture in the heyday of the Gothic Revival, and at a time of much building throughout Great Britain, he established an early reputation that brought him and his brother many important commissions, among which may be mentioned the Welsh Church, St. Margaret's Church, Christ Church, and the Racquet Club in Liverpool, and, in association with N. S. Joseph, the West End Synagogue in London (biographical notice by Hall Caine, *Biograph,* vol. V. no. 26, pp. 198–206). Later, Audsley moved to London, and lived there, confining himself to writing, until 1892, when he and his family (he was married to Mary Maclellan) came to New York, in the neighborhood of which he passed the rest of his life, especially in Yonkers, Plainfield, and Bloomfield. In New York he and his brother opened offices for the active practise of architecture. Especially notable among their works in America were the old Bowling Green Building (now destroyed), the Milwaukee Art Gallery (Audsley's favorite work), and the Catholic Church of St. Edward the Confessor in Philadelphia. During his latter years Audsley became enthralled by an interest in organ building, which had begun in his apprentice days, and which had grown rapidly through constant attendance at W. T. Best's recitals on the great organ of St. George's Hall in Liverpool. This interest culminated in the construction of an organ for his own home, built with his own hands over a period of seven years, which included many innovations in the usual practise of the time. This organ, though of only nineteen registers, sold at auction, when their English home was broken up, for 5,000 guineas; it is now, slightly altered, the property of Lord Dysart, at Ham House, Petersham. Audsley's reputation as an expert in organ construction led to his selection as designer of the great organ in the Festival Hall of the St. Louis Exposition, an organ now in the John Wanamaker Store in Philadelphia.

As with so many artists and architects, particularly in England, the enthusiasm of the Gothic Revival led Audsley to a careful study of ornament, and especially of polychrome ornament. This study found expression in a long list of scholarly and lavishly produced books on ornament and illumination which form, even more than his work as practising architect, the foundation of his wide reputation. A list of his books is given below; in addition he was a frequent contributor to art and musical periodicals and especially to the *American Organist,* to whose editor, T. Scott Buhrman, he left his valuable library of organ literature—some ten thousand volumes, now constituting the Audsley Memorial Library. As an architect, he was one of the sanest of the Gothic Revivalists, willing to depart from Gothic where necessary (as in the Bowling Green Building). His design is careful and scholarly. Color interested him particularly, as is evident in the polychrome marble treatment of the chancel of his Philadelphia church, or the organ case designed by himself for the Church of Our Lady of Grace, in Hoboken. Strongly under the influence of Ruskin, his fullest interest lay in ornament, in craftsmanship, in a loving care of detail, that made him, at enormous expense of time and money, supervise every process in the making of the color plates for his books, and made even his manuscripts, handwritten in pencil, works of art. At the time of his death he had not yet completed a valuable work on the *Pointed Architecture of England,* to be illustrated with many photographs taken by himself. His published works, several of them in collaboration with his brother, include: *Guide to the Art of Illuminating and Missal Painting* (1861); *Taste Versus Fashionable Colours, a Manual on Colour in Dress* (1863); *Handbook on Christian Symbolism* (1865); *Notes on Japanese Art* (1872); *Keramic Art of Japan* (1875); *Influence of Decorative Art and Art Workmanship in Household Details* (1876); *Outlines of Ornament in All Styles* (1881); *The Art of Chromolithography* (1883); *The Ornamental Arts of Japan* (perhaps his *magnum opus,* 1884); *The Practical Decorator* (1887); *The Art of Organ Building* (1905); *Guide to the Art of Illuminating on Vellum or Paper* (1911); *Artistic and Decorative Stencilling* (1911); *Amateur Joinery in the Home* (1912); *The Organ of the Twentieth Century* (1919); *Organ Stops and their Artistic Registration* (1921); *The Temple of Tone* (published posthumously, 1925).

[A sketch by T. Scott Buhrman as an appendix to *The Temple of Tone* (1925); *Am. Organist,* July 1925; *Diapason,* July 1, 1925.]
T. F. H.

AUDUBON, JOHN JAMES (Apr. 26, 1785–Jan. 27, 1851), artist and ornithologist, perhaps the most popular naturalist of America, has so long been a figure of sentiment and idealism, and as a man and a scientist has suffered so from the touching up of enthusiastic biographers, that it has been difficult to divorce the romance of fiction from that of truth in what was in any case a most colorful and adventurous life. The facts of Audubon's birth and parentage, long obscured by the haze of legend, have been established through the researches of Prof. Herrick. Audubon's father, Jean Audubon, a native of Les Sables d'Olonne on the Bay of Biscay, from boyhood had followed the sea. In 1770 he entered the Santo Domingo trade, and from 1774 captained his own ship. Captured by the British in 1779, he was held a prisoner in New York for several months. A short time after his release he was placed in command of the *Queen Charlotte,* with which in October 1781 he joined the fleet of De Grasse before Yorktown. After commanding successively several armed and trading vessels, in 1783 he was engaged by a firm of colonial merchants at Nantes to take charge of their West Indian trade, which centered at Les Cayes, Santo Domingo. He resided almost continuously at Les Cayes for a period of six years, and as merchant, planter, and dealer in slaves amassed a considerable fortune. During these years his wife, Anne Moynet Audubon, whom he had married in 1772, remained in France.

On his father's plantation at Les Cayes the future naturalist was born. Little is known of his mother except that she was called "Mlle. Rabin" and was "a Creole of Santo Domingo" (Herrick, I, 52); it is probable that she died within a year after her son's birth. In 1789 Jean Audubon with the boy, who was called Fougère, or sometimes Jean Rabin, and his younger half-sister called Muguet, the daughter of another Creole, returned to France, where he settled in Nantes and became a prominent local figure in the Revolution. His wife received the children tenderly, and in 1794 they were legalized by a regular act of adoption in the presence of witnesses as the children of Jean and Anne Moynet Audubon. On Oct. 23, 1800, at Nantes, Fougère, "adoptive son of Jean Audubon . . . and of Anne Moynet his wife" was baptized Jean Jacques Fougère Audubon. Confusion has been caused to biographers by the fact that young Audubon adopted for a time the fanciful name La Forest; some of his bird drawings of 1805–07 and possibly others of later date, are signed "J. L. F. A." or "J. J. L. Audubon," but he used the La Forest only sporadically, and later dropped it (*Ibid.*, p. 61).

Audubon's education was that of a well-to-do young bourgeois; he was instructed in mathematics, geography, music, and fencing, but his father, occupied with the affairs of the Republic, left the supervision of the boy's studies to the indulgent stepmother, with the result that the formal schooling was sometimes neglected. Audubon, years afterward, regretted that as a boy he had had no drill in writing his native tongue. He did, however, absorb the atmosphere of the revival of interest in nature which Rousseau, Buffon, and Lamarck had made popular, and by the time he was fifteen had begun a collection of his original drawings of French birds. Recognizing the boy's lack of discipline, his father put him into a military school for a year, but the experience did not have much permanent effect, and, having always encouraged the lad's taste for natural history and drawing, in 1802–03 Jean Audubon enabled him to study drawing for a few months under David at Paris.

In the autumn of 1803 young Audubon left France for America. Early in 1804 he reached the estate which his father had bought in 1789, "Mill Grove," near Philadelphia, where for a time he lived the life of a country gentleman, essentially free from money cares, hunting with dog and gun, a sentimental and enthusiastic observer of nature. The Audubon Societies that now form a league of bird protection over the country have created a picture of Audubon as a passionate protector of wild life. In his early years, at least, he was, by his own admission, a great sportsman, killing for amusement as well as food, and he remained a hunter even after he had achieved a reputation as an ornithologist. Only to the middle period of his life, too, belongs the familiar picture of Audubon as a pioneer; in his early years he roamed the placid Pennsylvania countryside in satin pumps and silk breeches. Nevertheless, it was during this period that he began his studies of American bird life. Peewees nesting in a cave attracted his attention; he took the cave for a study, and "it must be set down to Audubon's credit that in the little cave on the banks of the Perkioming, in April 1804, he made the first 'banding' experiment on the young of an American wild bird." He fastened a light silver thread to the legs of some of the baby peewees, and the next spring found that two of them had returned to the region and were nesting a little way up the creek from their place of birth. "Little could he or anyone else then have thought that 100 years later a Bird Banding Society would be formed in America to repeat his test on a much wider scale, in order to gather exact data upon the movements of individuals of all migratory species in every part of the continent" (*Ibid.*, pp. 107–8).

In 1804, also, he met and became engaged to Lucy, daughter of William Bakewell, an Englishman settled on a neighboring estate. Early in 1805, having quarrelled with his father's agent, who owned an interest in a lead mine at Mill Grove, and was acting as Audubon's guardian, he walked to New York, obtained money to pay his passage from Benjamin Bakewell, the uncle of his fiancée, and went back to France. After a year, during which he may have served for a time in the French navy, in 1806 he formed a partnership with Ferdinand Rozier, the son of one of his father's business associates, and returned to America. For a time they tried without success to operate the lead mine, then sold the Audubon interest in Mill Grove; Rozier found a position in Philadelphia, and Audubon entered Benjamin Bakewell's counting-house in New York. In August 1807 the partners decided to seek their fortunes in the West, bought a stock of goods in New York, and went to Louisville, where they opened a general store. Although the business suffered somewhat as a result of the Embargo Act, Audubon went to Philadelphia in June 1808, married Lucy Bakewell, and took her back to Louisville.

In Kentucky, then almost a wilderness, Audubon's penchant for natural history had fresh scope and encouragement, and, entirely out of touch with other ornithologists, working as an artist and a lover of nature more than as a scientist, he went on with his bird paintings. But his interest in mercantile affairs was not sufficient to win success against competition in the growing town of Louisville, so in the spring of 1810 he and Rozier loaded their goods on a flatboat and floated 125 miles down the Ohio to Henderson, Ky. Here history was repeated; "during their stay in Henderson Rozier was in his habitual place behind the counter and attended to what little business was done, while Audubon with a Kentucky lad named John Pope, was was nominally a clerk, roamed the country in eager pursuit of rare birds, and with rod and gun bountifully supplied the table" (*Ibid.*, p. 237).

At Henderson and in other parts of Kentucky to which business vicissitudes or whimsy removed him, Audubon gathered a rich store of the flavor and the personalities of pioneer life on the Ohio, which formed the basis of the sketches of western life scattered throughout the *Ornithological Biography*. His acquaintance with Daniel Boone has perhaps been overstressed by some biographers, and has gone far to tinge with the color of the great huntsman and explorer the really very different personality of Audubon. During these Kentucky years he was visited by some famous personages, and each visit has built up the curious picture of Audubon which tradition has left. Possibly the most famous of these episodes is the chance meeting, in 1810, with Alexander Wilson, the foremost ornithologist of America at that time, over the counter of Audubon's store. The two had never met nor heard of one another before, and the interview was not cordial. Audubon, out of jealousy, as he admits (*Audubon and His Journals*, vol. II, p. 200), did not subscribe for a set of Wilson's ornithological works, and found the little Scotch stranger dour and secretive, while Wilson records of his visit that "science or literature has not one friend in this place" (*American Ornithology*, IX, 39). This meeting and the charges of plagiarism growing out of it formed the basis for a feud, revived and nurtured in later years by George Ord, the friend and biographer of Wilson. Another episode, the visit of Constantine Samuel Rafinesque in 1818, is an exhibition of the prankish and unpredictable character of our artist-naturalist, but unfortunately had consequences not foreseen at the time. Rafinesque was gullible in the extreme, and Audubon could not resist the temptation to sketch for him, in all solemnity, fishes and birds most marvelous and mythical, which Rafinesque proceeded to publish as new species, much to the bewilderment of later zoologists. Here and in some of his own bird drawings, Audubon showed a carelessness of the veracity that science demands which has done irreparable hurt to his reputation as a naturalist.

The business partnership with Rozier was not a success, so after another fruitless venture it was dissolved, though the friendship continued. Audubon then, in association with his brother-in-law, Thomas Bakewell, and others, attempted successively several different enterprises, the last being a steam grist and lumber mill, at Henderson, which was too elaborate for the needs of the new country and failed in 1819. Audubon, the heaviest loser, was jailed for debt, but was released on the plea of bankruptcy with only the clothes he wore, his gun, and his original drawings. This disaster ended his business career. Turning to account his artistic skill, for a time he did crayon portraits at five dollars a head, then, in the winter of 1819–20, he took his family to Cincinnati, where he became a taxidermist in the new Western Museum, just founded by Dr. Daniel Drake. Some time in 1820 the possibility of publishing his bird drawings occurred to him, and thereafter his life had a definite aim. In October of that year he started down the Ohio and Mississippi rivers, exploring the country for birds, and paying his expenses by portraits. After a period in New Orleans, where Audubon worked as tutor and drawing teacher, and even painted street signs, Mrs. Audubon obtained a position as governess and took upon her shoulders the burden of the needy family—a burden she sustained for some twelve years.

In 1824 Audubon made a journey to Philadelphia, in search of a publisher. He was encouraged by C. L. Bonaparte, and by Thomas Sully, who gave him lessons in the use of oils, but encountered the opposition of the friends of Alexander Wilson, under the leadership of George Ord. Bonaparte and the engraver Fairman advised him to seek a publisher in Europe, where he would find a greater interest in his subject, and the requisite skill to reproduce his drawings. He returned to the West by way of Niagara Falls and the Great Lakes, and spent the next year with his wife at St. Francisville, La., teaching music and drawing to her pupils. In the summer of 1826, with the funds raised in this way added to Mrs. Audubon's savings, he took his drawings to Europe. He was favorably received at Liverpool, where he obtained his first subscribers, and he was lionized in Edinburgh. He formed a pleasant acquaintanceship with Sir Walter Scott, and in March 1827 was elected to the Royal Society of Edinburgh. The man of the hour in Scotland, he continued, as during the lean years in America, to pay his expenses by painting, though copies in oils of his birds had superseded portraits. In 1827 he went to London, with many letters of introduction but was not so enthusiastically received as he had been at Edinburgh, though at last the king subscribed for his books and set the fashion in his favor.

Wm. Lizars, the Edinburgh engraver who had undertaken the work of publishing the birds, gave it up after producing ten plates, and Audubon was forced to find another engraver. He finally reached an agreement with Robert Havell, Jr., of London, "who, through eleven years of the closest association with his new patron became one of the greatest engravers in aquatint the world has ever seen" (Herrick, I, 362).

The *Birds of America,* in elephant folio size, began to appear in 1827, in parts: it occupied in its serial publication and subsequent reprintings eleven years, and necessitated frequent trips to and from America. During all this time Audubon was engaged in obtaining subscribers, a task more favorable in Europe with a ready scientific audience, than in America. Among the people whom he approached was the famous Baron Rothschild, with whom Audubon had, as he relates it, an unpleasant dealing, discreditable to the Baron's honesty. Whatever the rights of the case may be, it is evident that as success crowned his work, Audubon became by turns increasingly vain, touchy, and buoyantly good-natured. He has been called egotistic, but there was nothing so ponderous in his character; he had, rather, an almost womanish vanity, that extended to his handsome face, his clothes, at first elegant, then consciously rustic, and to the long backwoodsman ringlets which he would wear, no matter where he went.

In October 1830 he and Mrs. Audubon settled temporarily in Edinburgh, where he began the work on the text of his *Birds of America,* to be called *Ornithological Biography.* He had considered asking William Swainson, with whom he had become intimate, to collaborate on the text, but finally made connection with Wm. MacGillivray, than whom "a better trained or more competent helper . . . could hardly have been found in Great Britain or elsewhere" (*Ibid.,* I, 438). Edinburgh publishers would offer nothing for the first volume, so it was published in 1831 at Audubon's expense, and although several competing works appeared at about the same time, "was well received and drew forth immediate and unstinted praise from many sources" (*Ibid.,* I, 445).

Having achieved a European reputation, Audubon returned to America in 1831 acclaimed the foremost naturalist of his country. His first American notice had appeared in the *American Journal of Science* in 1829; in November 1830, upon nomination of Edward Everett, he was elected a Fellow of the American Academy, and in 1832 was the subject of the first of a series of able articles by W. B. O. Peabody in the *North American Review.* There were controversies and criticisms, of course—Charles Waterton was the most persistent heckler—but on the whole the stay in America between 1831 and 1834 was a pleasant and fruitful one. The year of his return Audubon met John Bachman [*q.v.*] in Charleston, and began what was to be a life-long friendship, cemented in 1837 and 1839 by the marriage of Audubon's sons to Bachman's daughters. He went on several expeditions, in the company of his younger son, his friend and patron Edward Harris, and others, exploring the dunes and lagoons of the Texas coast, the palmetto groves of Florida, and the wild coast of Labrador, where the destruction of the gannets in their rare breeding-grounds awoke from him a passionate cry of protest that still rings with the appeal and authority of great poetry. His Labrador Journals are stirring reading, and distinctly the best contributions to natural history among his diaries.

In 1834 he went back to Edinburgh to continue his work on the *Ornithological Biography.* Havell issued the last part of the *Birds of America* in June 1838, completing the work begun in Edinburgh in 1826; the concluding volume (vol. V) of the *Ornithological Biography* appeared in May of the next year, followed, in the summer, by the *Synopsis of the Birds of North America,* a methodical catalogue of the birds then known, prepared with the efficient help of MacGillivray.

The great work finished, Audubon returned to America, began work on a "miniature edition" of the *Birds,* and almost immediately undertook the preparation, in collaboration with John Bachman, of the *Viviparous Quadrupeds of North America.* In 1841 he bought land on the Hudson, and the next year settled finally on his estate, "Minnies's Land," which is now Audubon Park, New York City. With old age came a kindly attitude toward his former rivals; he was the adviser and encourager of young scientists (notably Spencer F. Baird [*q.v.*], who had begun a correspondence with Audubon at the age of seventeen), the revered and adored sage, and patron saint of the birds. His latter years, indeed, accorded closely with the popular legend that has grown up about him, so that at the time of his death in January 1851 the real man was already merged in the traditional Audubon of romance. His powers had failed in the last few years, and the completion of the *Quadrupeds* for which he had finished about half of the large drawings was left to his sons. The colored plates (originals by J. J. and J. W. Audubon) were published in two volumes (1842–45), and the text in three volumes (1846–54).

The legacy of Audubon's work must be judged by a dual standard—as art and as science. Artists have thought him too photographic, scientists find his work too emotional and impressionistic. Though Cuvier said of the drawings that they were "la plus magnifique monument que l'art ait encore élevé à la science," others have thought his work greatly overpraised, and even an admirer like Coues admits that many of his birds are posed in attitudes anatomically impossible. Where Audubon was interested in a bird he would lavish on its representation a microscopic detail satisfying to the most critical scientist. In other cases he washed in his colors with an eye only to the impressionistic effect produced by the bird in some strained pose caught in a split second of time. His passion for representing birds in violent action had obvious advantages and defects, but it bears witness to the fact that he studied and painted birds in life, not stuffed in museum cases. Audubon was above all an out-of-doors naturalist; he possessed no formal scientific training and no aptitude for books or taxonomy, nor did he care particularly about describing new species of birds, though he certainly observed numerous such. The Latin nomenclature and the scientific identification of most of the species in the *Birds of America,* is largely the work of MacGillivray, whilst most of what may be called systematic science in the *Quadrupeds of America* is probably due to Bachman, Audubon supplying the brilliant drawings, the fund of incident and personal observation, and the peculiar literary flavor of the biographical part, which is sometimes sentimental but always vivid. Weighed with all detractions in the balance, however, Audubon remains, with Alexander Wilson, at the head of early American ornithology. Contrasted with the work of Wilson, Audubon's ornithology had a greater general usefulness in that it included many birds that Audubon had never seen but merely knew by report, while Wilson confined himself to his own observations, which had been more limited than Audubon's in any case. As a pioneer manual of American ornithology, Audubon's work stands out preëminently, whilst the earlier work of his great rival Wilson was more original, more steadily scientific, and more circumscribed. As to the literary style and the magnificence of the illustrations, there can be no choice between the work of the two men; the honors go to Audubon even when all his inaccuracies and mannerisms have been acknowledged.

[F. H. Herrick, *Audubon the Naturalist,* two vols. (1917), is the product of much careful research, and contains an extensive bibliography. Another valuable work is M. R. Audubon, *Audubon and His Journals, with . . . Notes by Elliott Coues,* two vols. (1897). For source material, see bibliography in Herrick. Lucy Audubon, *The Life of John James Audubon, the Naturalist*(1869), is a reproduction of an earlier work by Robert Buchanan, which, though based on materials supplied by Mrs. Audubon, is not very reliable.]

D. C. P.
E. R. D.

AUGUR, CHRISTOPHER COLUMBUS (July 10, 1821–Jan. 16, 1898), Union soldier, son of Ammon and Annis (Wellman) Augur, was sixth in descent from Robert Augur who came from England and was living at New Haven, Conn., in 1673. He was born at Kendall, N. Y., moved in 1821 with his widowed mother to Michigan, and was appointed as a cadet to the United States Military Academy in 1839. He graduated in 1843, standing sixteenth in a class of thirty-nine members, which included U. S. Grant and a dozen others who distinguished themselves on one side or the other during the Civil War. In 1844 he was married to Jane E. Arnold of Ogdensburg, N. Y. Assigned to the 4th Infantry, he served with credit in the Mexican War at the battles of Palo Alto and Resaca de la Palma under Gen. Zachary Taylor, and as aide-de-camp for several brigade commanders. He had active service on the frontier in the new territories of Washington and Oregon, during the years 1852–56, in campaigns against the Yakima and Rogue River Indians, with engagements at Two Buttes, Big Bend of Rogue River, and Sohomy Creek. At the beginning of the Civil War, he had reached the grade of major and was serving as commandant of cadets at the West Point Military Academy, with the *ex-officio* rank of lieutenant-colonel. He was promoted to brigadier-general of volunteers in November 1861, and placed in command of the advance defenses of Washington until March 1862. This was followed by active service on the Rappahannock and the first capture of Fredericksburg by his command March–July 1862.

When Gen. Pope took command of the Army of Virginia, Augur was given Sigel's division of Banks's 5th corps on Aug. 9, which was ordered in a few days to threaten Gordonsville on the Virginia Central Railroad. Pope brought up the remaining corps, but did not place them at supporting distance. Banks thought that he was ordered to advance and attack the enemy, and in doing so found himself in the presence of Jackson's entire force, about four times as great as his own, at Cedar Mountain. He was driven back with great loss. Augur was severely wounded late in the day and the other division commanders were wounded or captured. The rank of major-general of volunteers and of brevet-colonel in the regular army was conferred upon him for "gallant and meritorious services" on this occasion, one of the few commissions given for specific acts during the war. In the fall of 1862, when Banks organized his expedition to New Orleans, at his request Augur was assigned as second in command. He commanded the district of Baton Rouge for some months; commanded in the action at Port Hudson Plains, May 21, 1863; commanded the left wing of the army in the siege of Port Hudson until the surrender of the Confederate force under his classmate, Frank Gardner, in July. It was a long and tedious siege with much fighting. He opposed in council the disastrous assault of May 27 as premature and without proper study of the ground. He was ill and on leave of absence and president of the Warren court of inquiry and other military commissions until Oct. 13, 1863, when he was assigned to the command of the Department of Washington and the 22nd army corps, which he maintained until the end of the war. He was brevetted brigadier-general in 1865 for gallant and meritorious service at Port Hudson and major-general for services in the field during the war. He was mustered out of volunteer service in 1866, reverted to his position as colonel of the 12th Infantry in the regular army, and was promoted to brigadier-general by Gen. Grant to fill one of the vacancies created by his own election to the presidency in 1869.

In the years following the Civil War there were many new problems requiring solution by military commanders. The building of the Union Pacific Railroad and the migration of thousands of home seekers to the West aroused the Indian tribes to the defense of their hunting-grounds. Augur commanded various military departments during that period and directed operations against nearly every one of the hostile tribes in the years from 1867 to 1885. While in command of the Department of the Gulf during the reconstruction days of 1876, when opposing factions were on the verge of open war because of the disputed election of that year, he settled the affair without bloodshed. He retired from active service July 10, 1885, and died Jan. 16, 1898, at Georgetown, D. C.

[Edwin P. Augur, *Family Hist. and Geneal. of the Descendants of Robert Augur* (1904), pp. 83, 138–46; *Ass. Grads. U. S. Mil. Acad., Ann. Reunion* (1898); *Official Records,* vols. LXXXIV, CII, CIV; G. W. Cullum, *Biog. Reg.; Papers of the Mil. Hist. Soc. of Mass.,* II (1895); *Campaigns of the Civil War,* vol. IV (1881), vol. VIII (1882); John Codman Ropes, *Story of the Civil War,* II (1898).]

E. S.

AUGUR, HEZEKIAH (Feb. 21, 1791–Jan. 10, 1858), sculptor, was one of eight children born to Hezekiah Augur and his second wife, Lydia Atwater. The father was a house carpenter and joiner in New Haven, where the young Hezekiah was born. The boy learned to use his father's tools and early devised various machines, but his father was unwilling to have him continue his own trade and apprenticed him, at nine years old, to a grocer. After four or five years of this work, he was set to learn the apothecary's trade. To qualify he had to study anatomy and this, though he continued it only one year, was of use to him later on. At sixteen he was placed, as clerk, in a mercantile house and at nineteen he became acting partner in a business concern. A few years later he became a partner in a dry-goods business of which he acted as sole manager. He came successfully through the difficult business years of 1815 and 1816, but in December of the latter year, as the result of a misunderstanding, the partnership was dissolved and Augur found himself a bankrupt. Not only did he find that his original capital had disappeared but also that, for some inexplicable reason, he was in debt as well. His father and some of his relatives became indebted for him. This financial catastrophe preyed upon him and he became somewhat of a recluse; for many years his one desire was to free himself from a situation for which he was not to blame. At first he assisted his father, but after four or five months borrowed $200 and set up a small fruit and cigar stand which he kept for about two years. Previously he had carved the frame of a harp and when he had taken it to be varnished it had attracted sufficient attention to encourage him to continue, so after he had sold his fruit stand he opened a carving establishment. His business grew and he soon added mirrors to his output. From this period came one of his numerous inventions—an improvement on the artificial leg. After having relieved his relatives by annual payments from their indebtedness for him, he was at last able, in 1823, to make a final settlement with his former partner. It required, however, the selling of his mirror establishment and left him in somewhat straitened circumstances. In this same year he began, at the suggestion of S. F. B. Morse, to carve in marble the head of the Apollo Belvedere. It was finished the following year and was much praised at the time. Since his father had died in 1818 he now felt free to follow his own bent and continued to interest himself in sculpture. He did a head of George Washington and a Sappho. One of the few public commissions he received was for the bust of Oliver Ellsworth in the Supreme Court room in the Capitol at Washington. Another of his early works is the bust of Prof. Alexander M. Fisher, made in 1827 and presented to Yale College by members of the professor's class. Though carved in marble it shows the technique of wood-carving. Another bust—an idealized subject, called "Resignation," —is now in the possession of a member of his family in Portland, Ore. His principal work, "Jephthah and His Daughter," consists of two separate small statues. Though executed sometime in the thirties, they still recall the technique of the wood-carver, particularly in the folds of the drapery. They show, however, artistic imagination and a degree of characterization and emotional expression rare in works of that period. After its completion, sometime before the end of 1837, the group was acquired by the Trumbull Gallery at Yale. Previously the college had, in 1833, bestowed upon the sculptor the honorary degree of Master of Arts. Up to the year 1837 Augur had been living with his mother and sister, but after the death of the former in that year he moved into bachelor quarters. The following year he was commissioned to design the bronze medals for the two hundredth anniversary of the settlement of New Haven. According to his diary, he made, in 1840, a monument for Miss Ogden, but all trace of it has apparently disappeared. His sculpture, however, seems not to have been very remunerative, for in 1845 he was forced to sell his effects at auction. Among the items sold of which all trace has been lost were an Apollo and a Washington in marble, probably the ones previously mentioned, a Franklin and a "Sleeping Cupid." It was a disheartening period for Augur. In his diary he speaks of a single ray of light, which refers possibly to a carving machine which he perfected at about this time. He patented it and became a member of a company for exploiting it in New England. It was perhaps the most important of his various inventions, among which were a machine for making worsted lace, and the bracket-saw. His financial difficulties seem to have emphasized his somewhat reserved and unassuming manners. They likewise prevented him, except at rare intervals, from indulging his fastidious taste in dress. He was a small man and in stature resembled his mother's family. In features he is said to have resembled portraits of Jefferson. Considering all the obstacles he had to face in his career as sculptor—paternal objection, financial difficulty, entire lack of training—his accomplishment is praiseworthy and, though exercising no influence, he remains an interesting figure in early American sculpture.

[Edwin P. Augur, *Family Hist. and Geneal. of the Descendants of Robert Augur* (1904); *Am. Hist. Mag.* (New Haven), I, no. 2; H. W. French, *Art and Artists in Conn.* (1879); Lorado Taft, *Hist. of Am. Sculpture* (1903), pp. 24–28.]

E. G. N.

AUGUSTUS, JOHN (1785–June 21, 1859), philanthropist, was a self-appointed pioneer probation officer and friend of the unfortunate, in Boston, Mass., for more than twenty years. In 1841 he was a humble shoemaker in Boston, employing several assistants. Present in the police court one day that year, he became interested in a man charged with being a common drunkard. At Augustus's request and offer of bail, sentence was deferred for three weeks and the man released. At the end of that short probation the man was able to convince the judge of his reformation, and received a nominal fine. Thereafter, Augustus was present daily, at first in the police, and later in the municipal court, acting as counsel for prisoners, and furnishing bail. He also found homes for juvenile offenders, and made possible a fresh start in life for men and women who through intemperance or vice had gone wrong. He is described as a thin man, of medium height, his face somewhat wrinkled, and his features of a benevolent expression. Hurrying about on his errands in a chaise, he became one of the familiar sights of the city. He was warm-hearted, impulsive, and direct of speech, often in trouble with court officials, sometimes because they thought him presumptuous and a hindrance to the transaction of business, and often because his activities lessened their fees. Between 1842 and 1858, according to the court records, he bailed 1,946 persons, making himself liable during that period to the extent of $243,235.

For five years after taking up this work, Augustus conducted his shoe shop, often working all night, he says, to make up the time spent in court. All he earned he devoted to his philanthropies. Others voluntarily contributed, though never large amounts, his receipts for five years averaging $1,776. In 1846 he gave up his business, having acquired, apparently, a meager income upon which to support himself. He was never the agent of any sect or society and never received salary or remuneration. When seventy-four years of age he died from a general prostration due to overtaxing his powers. The sentiments and convictions which underlay his activities have won general approval, and work similar to his is now carried on widely by institutions private and public.

[Information regarding Augustus's antecedents and early life is lacking. A good idea of the man and his work may be derived from *A Report of the Labors of John Augustus* (1852) and *Letter Concerning the Labors of Mr. John Augustus, from One Who Knows Him* (1858). See also obituary notice in *Boston Herald*, June 22, 1859.]

H. E. S.

AUSTELL, ALFRED (Jan. 14, 1814–Dec. 7, 1881), financier, was born near Dandridge in East Tennessee. His father, William Austell, a farmer of that region, and his mother, Jane Wilkins) Austell, were of English descent. Growing up without educational advantages except of the most limited sort, Austell found himself, at twenty-two, engaged in merchandising and farming with his brother at Campbellton, a village near Atlanta, Ga. The two brothers located there in 1836. The elder brother died early, but Alfred, whose business acumen was of a high order, prospered and became the leading merchant and farmer in his section. In 1853 he was married to Franchina Cameron of La Grange. In 1858 he closed out his business at Campbellton and moved to Atlanta. Though the future capital of Georgia had at the time less than 10,000 inhabitants, its location at the junction point of three important railroads convinced Austell that it was destined to be an important city. In the stirring political controversies of the period he took no active part. He was, however, an ardent Unionist and anti-secessionist and used his influence on the side of conservative action. With secession an accomplished fact, he supported the Confederacy and was an important factor in the industrial and financial aspects of the war. The title "General," by which he was universally known, dated back to Campbellton days when he was a brigadier in the state militia. On the collapse of the Confederacy Andrew Johnson, a personal friend, urged on him the appointment as provisional governor of Georgia, but Austell declined. Again in 1868 tradition has it that Austell could have received the Democratic nomination for governor. He preferred, however, to continue his quiet efforts toward material rehabilitation and declined to be drawn into the political maelstrom.

His name is associated in the history of Georgia and the South with the great task of laying the foundations of a stable economic structure to take the place of the old regime. He realized that the primary needs were strong financial institutions and more extensive railroad development. In September 1865 he organized the Atlanta National Bank, the first Southern institution chartered under the National Banking Act of 1863. As its first president (he held the position until his death) Austell created one of the strongest of the Southern commercial banks, one that has played a large part in the development of Atlanta. At a time when the extension of credit was on a less impersonal basis than at present, Austell established a reputation as a remarkably keen judge of character and business ability. As a railroad builder he also achieved much. He was associated with a number of railroad enterprises, the most important of which was the Atlanta & Charlotte Air Line (now part of the Southern system). This road, 265 miles long, provided a direct connection with Washington. Austell was the first chairman of its board, acted as its financial agent, and was its vice-president for ten years. In addition to these activities in the banking and railroad worlds, Austell organized the cotton firm of Austell & Inman, later Inman, Swann & Company, one of the greatest cotton commission houses in the country. These ventures, invariably managed with conspicuous ability and success, brought to Austell a commanding position in the world of Southern business. He was a leader in that army of enterprisers who rebuilt the South after the ruin of the Civil War. His wealth, large for the period, he freely gave to all deserving causes.

[Lucian Lamar Knight, *Standard Hist. of Georgia and Georgians* (1917), VI, 3040–43; Bernard Suttler, "Alfred Austell," in *Men of Mark in Ga.*, ed. by Wm. J. Northen (1911), III, 357–65.]

R. P. B—s.

AUSTEN, PETER TOWNSEND (Sept. 10, 1852–Dec. 30, 1907), chemist, was born at Clifton, Staten Island, the son of John H. and Elizabeth (Townsend) Austen, and a descendant of Peter Townsend of Sterling Iron Works who in 1776 had introduced into America from Germany a new process for the manufacture of steel (Benjamin F. Thompson, *History of Long Island,* 3rd ed., II, 351). Peter Townsend Austen, after attending a local private school and the Columbia School of Mines, went abroad for three years' further study. In 1876 he received the degree of Ph.D. from the University of Zurich and returned to America to become instructor in chemistry at Dartmouth. Two years later he went to Rutgers as full professor of general and applied chemistry. This connection continued for thirteen years, during which he served also on the faculty of the New Jersey Science School, as state chemist, and as adviser to various state and municipal boards. As a pioneer in university extension work he was a pleasing and popular lecturer who obtained much satisfaction from public speaking, a taste possibly derived from his father, a well-known auctioneer. Austen left Rutgers expecting to devote himself thenceforth to private practise, but he soon resumed college work at the Brooklyn Polytechnic Institute. A few years later (1896) he gave up educational work altogether and established a consulting office and laboratory in New York City. He belonged to a number of chemical societies at home and abroad and was at one time chairman of the New York section of the American Chemical Society. His pleasing personality, his keen insight into technical problems, and his facility as a speaker won for him recognition among his fellow chemists. During a comparatively short scientific career he published a number of text-books, one of the best-known of which was his translation and revision of Adolph Pinner's *Introduction to the Study of Organic*

Chemistry (1883). He was the author of about fifty scientific papers which appeared in the *American Chemical Journal* and in the *Proceedings of the Chemical Society of Berlin.* But his interests were not confined to pure science. They included the popular presentation of the subject and the practical applications of chemistry to the arts and industries. His lectures on "Science Teaching in the Schools," "Scientific Speculations," and "The Chemical Factor in History" aroused much interest as did also his article entitled "Harnessing the Sun," which appeared in the *North American Review,* June 1895. He invented several manufacturing processes used in dyeing and bleaching (see Patent Indexes, 1880–1900), and was a frequent contributor to chemical trade journals. He was married in 1878 to Ellen M. Monroe.

[*Am. Men of Science* (1906), ed. by J. M. Cattell and *Who's Who in America* for the same year contain the most reliable information, since the data were probably supplied by Austen himself. Obituary in *N.Y. Tribune,* Jan. 1, 1908.]

H. C.

AUSTIN, BENJAMIN (Nov. 18, 1752–May 4, 1820), political leader, was born in Boston, the son of Elizabeth (Waldo) Austin and Benjamin Austin, merchant and member of the Council of Massachusetts. The Waldos were mostly Tories; the Austins belonged to a small group of mercantile families in eastern Massachusetts who became ardent disciples of Samuel Adams, and were unable to understand that the formulas of 1775 were inadequate if not mischievous in 1785 and 1795. Benjamin Austin, Jr., made a tour of Europe in 1783, and was married to Jane Ivers in 1785. During the war he had written patriotic orations in the Boston press, but he gained his reputation in 1786 by a series of *Observations on the Pernicious Practice of the Law* signed "Honestus," exposing the evil conditions of legal procedure in the Commonwealth, and demanding the abolition of lawyers and the exclusion of English common law. In their stead he proposed (1) that petty cases be decided by referees, (2) the adoption of a plain and simple law code that any educated citizen could understand, (3) that parties be required to do their own pleading in civil cases, or be represented by a friend who must declare on oath that he is receiving no fee, (4) that the Commonwealth appoint an advocate general to appear on behalf of all persons indicted by the attorney-general (*Independent Chronicle,* Apr. 20, 1786). The last proposal foreshadows the public defender of modern law reformers; and Austin's suggestions were not unfitted for the needs of the times, but the lawyers of course assailed him, and accused him of fomenting Shays's Rebellion, which broke out shortly after. The injustice of this charge turned Austin's zeal to bitterness, and his courage to contentiousness. He succeeded Sam Adams as favorite of the Boston mob, and was elected to the state Senate in 1787, and from 1789 to 1794. J. Q. Adams describes his flooding the town meeting with 700 men "who looked as if they had been collected from all the Jails on the continent, with Ben. Austin like another Jack Cade at their head" (*Proceedings of the Massachusetts Historical Society,* 2nd ser., IV, 63). By 1790 he was opposing Washington's administration, and his local faction for which he accepted the name Democratic (*Independent Chronicle,* May 14, 1795) was one of the urban groups whose adherence Jefferson accepted with some misgivings. "Aristocracy," "monarchical influence," "the Essex Junto," "the British Treaty," were phrases that Austin used like bludgeons. "Lank Honestus with his lanthorn jaws," was a terror to the Federalists and the target of their satire, for which his violent, demagogic manner of speaking, and his business of rope-making rendered him singularly vulnerable. His probity, however, was unquestioned, and throughout the period of Federalist ascendancy he occupied positions of trust such as Overseer of the Poor, and manager of the Harvard College lotteries. He was a leader in the Boston Constitutional Club, one of the "self-created societies" of 1794 that interfered with the authorities, promoted riots, frightened property-holders, and quickly brought conservative reaction. He was defeated for the state Senate in 1795, and although returned on Apr. 4, 1796, he definitely lost political control of Boston three weeks later at a town meeting on Jay's treaty, and was not again reëlected.

"Every attempt to restore the liberties of mankind, or to check the progress of arbitrary power, is now styled Jacobinism," wrote Austin in 1797 (*Constitutional Republicanism,* p. 52). He kept Republican principles before the people in frequent newspaper articles, the republication of which in 1803 was followed shortly by a presidential appointment as commissioner of loans. His caustic tongue on one occasion got him a beating by a Federalist editor, and on another had tragic consequences. Having accused T. O. Selfridge, a Federalist lawyer, of barratry, Austin failed to give satisfaction when the charge was proved false. Selfridge posted him in the Boston *Gazette* as a coward, liar, and scoundrel. That afternoon, Aug. 4, 1806, Austin's son Charles, a Harvard student, assaulted Selfridge with a hickory stick and was shot dead. The trial of Selfridge for manslaughter developed into a contest of strength between Federalists and Republicans; his acquittal by a Federalist jury, following a charge by Justice Parker, added bitterness to the party conflict. Although regarded as a dangerous radical, Austin was essentially a conservative always opposing local improvements and changes. He liked the political vintage of 1775 too well to accept the new wine of Federalism.

[Benjamin Austin, Jr., *Constitutional Republicanism, in Opposition to Fallacious Federalism; as Published Occasionally in the Independent Chronicle*, Boston, 1803. The "Honestus" articles of 1786 ran in the Boston *Independent Chronicle* from Mar. 9 to June 15; a digest of them was published in a pamphlet, *Observations on Pernicious Practice of Law* (Boston 1786, 2nd ed. 1819). Austin's other newspaper pseudonyms were "Brutus" (during the Revolution), "Old South" (after 1795), and "Examiner" (after 1812). For political satire, see *The Democratiad* (Phila., 1795); J. S. J. Gardiner, *Remarks on the Jacobiniad* (Boston, 1795, 1798); and files of the *Chronicle* and *Federal Orrery*. For the Selfridge case, see *Trial of Thomas O. Selfridge . . . for Killing Charles Austin* (Boston, 1807); T. O. Selfridge, *Correct Statement of the Whole Preliminary Controversy between Tho. O. Selfridge and Benjamin Austin* (Charlestown, 1807); B. Austin, *Memorial on the Grounds of Excusable Homicide to the Leg. of Mass.* (1806); A. E. Morse, *Federalist Party in Mass.* (1909).]

S. E. M.

AUSTIN, DAVID (Mar. 19, 1759–Feb. 5, 1831), Congregational clergyman, widely known in his day because of his predictions and writings regarding the millennium, was born in New Haven, Conn., a descendant of John Austin, and the son of David, a prosperous merchant, and Mary (Mix) Austin. He graduated from Yale in 1779, studied theology under Dr. Joseph Bellamy [*q.v.*] of Bethlehem, Conn., and was licensed to preach by the New Haven Association of Congregational Ministers, May 30, 1780. In 1781 he went to Europe and spent nearly a year in travel. Upon his return he supplied several churches, and while at Norwich, Conn., became engaged to Lydia, daughter of Dr. Joshua Lathrop, whom he married June 5, 1783. On Sept. 9, 1788, he was ordained and installed pastor of the Presbyterian church in Elizabeth, N. J.

While here he undertook several literary enterprises, editing *The Christian's, Scholar's and Farmer's Magazine*, a bi-monthly, the first number of which was for April and May 1789. He also published by subscription *The American Preacher*, containing sermons by living divines without respect to denomination. The first three volumes of this appeared in 1791 and the fourth in 1793. He was a man of great energy, lively imagination, and excitable temperament, regarded from boyhood as brilliant but erratic. As early as 1791 he had become interested in the study of prophecy and was soon convinced that the millennium was at hand. This belief became an obsession. A severe attack of scarlet fever in 1795 aggravated his eccentricities. Thereafter, he thought of little but the second advent, and finally predicted that May 15, 1796, would be the date of its occurrence. With a crowd of excited people he awaited the event in church, but as the day wore on and nothing unusual happened, he finally arose and preached from the text, "My Lord delayeth his coming." His ingenuity found excuses for his mistake, and his faith in the imminence of the advent was more ardent than ever. At length his church felt obliged to ask the presbytery to dissolve the pastoral relation, at which request he withdrew from the Presbyterian denomination. His subsequent career was a checkered one. Returning to New Haven he expended his fortune in building houses, stores, and wharfs for the Jews who he believed would assemble there on their way to the Holy Land to await the Messiah. He affiliated himself with the Baptists for a while, spent considerable time in New York, Washington, and New Jersey where he sought unsuccessfully to get reinstated in the Presbyterian Church. Finally, in 1815, he became pastor of the Congregational church in Bozrah, Conn., and remained there until his death.

His publications include: *The Millennium; or, The Thousand Years of Prosperity, Promised to the Church of God, in the Old Testament and the New, Shortly to Commence, and to be Carried on to Perfection* (1794); *The Voice of God to the People of These United States* (1796); *A Prophetic Leaf* (1798); *Masonry in Its Glory; or Solomon's Temple Illuminated* (1799); *The Millennial Door Thrown Open* (1799); *The Dance of Herodias, through the Streets of Hartford, on Election Day, to the Tune of the Stars of Heaven, in the Dragon's Tail; or A Gentle Trip at the Heels of the Strumpet of Babylon* (1799); *A Discourse on the Occasion of the Death of George Washington* (1800); *The Dawn of Day* (1800); *The National "Barley Cake"* (1802); *Republican Festival* (1803); *Proclamation for the Millennial Empire* (1805); *The Rod of Moses Upon the Rock of Calvary* (1816). He also edited Jonathan Dickinson's *The True Scripture Doctrine* (1793) and Jonathan Edwards's *History of Redemption* (1793).

[E. F. Hatfield, *Hist. of Elizabeth, N. J.* (1868); Wm. B. Sprague, *Annals of the Am. Pulpit*, II (1857); F. B. Dexter, *Biog. Sketches of the Grads. of Yale Coll.*, IV (1907).]

H. E. S.

AUSTIN, HENRY (Dec. 4, 1804–Dec. 17, 1891), architect, son of Daniel and Adah (Dorman) Austin, was born at Mt. Carmel, Conn. A carpenter at fifteen, he was then for some years in the office of Ithiel Town, who about 1810 opened an office for the practise of architecture in New Haven. Town had what was undoubtedly the finest collection of books on architecture at that time in this country. Austin made the most of his opportunities, opened an office of his own in 1836, and, on account of the number of men trained in his office in the fifty-five years of his professional life, became locally known as the "Father of Architects." In 1842 he was commissioned to design a library for Yale College, a design, everything considered, never surpassed by any building erected by Yale. Modeled, it is said, after King's College Chapel at Cambridge, England, it had the charm of relative smallness of scale. In designing this building, Austin was assisted by Henry Flockton, an Englishman then employed in his office. Another notable design of Austin's, happily unaltered, is the massive brown-stone gateway (1845–48), in the Egyptian style, of the historic Grove Street Cemetery, New Haven. Of excellent proportions and large enough to be imposing, this is an impressive design, with its bold inscription, "The Dead Shall be Raised." In 1861 Austin was commissioned to design a City Hall for New Haven, in which he was assisted by David Russell Brown of his office. This building, in the Italian Gothic style, with its bold tower, was greatly admired, and gains much from its location but is inferior, as a design, to the other designs mentioned.

Among Austin's other buildings were the old Railway Station at the intersection of Union and Chapel Sts. with a clock-tower rising 140 feet above the pavement; the old New Haven House (now replaced by the Hotel Taft), of which it was said, "Even the garret chambers were good enough for a Prince"; the Cutler and Hoadley Buildings (the latter now demolished); the Yale, Tradesmen's, Mechanics, and New Haven Savings Banks; Eaton School; a bank in Springfield; Trinity Church Home. He built so many private residences that it was said that almost every street in New Haven bore marks of his taste. Most of these were in the then fashionable so-called Tuscan or Italian style, with flat roofs; they had dignity and solidity, were extremely well-planned, and were eminently gentlemanly. Austin also built many churches throughout the state and elsewhere, tidy, well proportioned, spired, of which the most notable was the "Pride of Danbury," in 1857, burned down in 1907. In constructing the spire, rising to a height of 210 feet, he attempted to emulate Town, who constructed the spire of Center Church on the level in one piece within the tower and raised it by an ingenious system of windlasses to its final position; but after Austin's spire had been raised to within some few inches of its final position, one of the guy ropes gave way and the spire turned up-side-down and crashed through the roof of the building. The spire was rebuilt *in situ.* Austin also designed the monument erected in 1846 in Coventry, Conn., to the memory of Nathan Hale, the youthful hero of the Revolutionary War.

Austin's work was done in what may be viewed as the worst period of American architecture; he had neither the genius nor the opportunities of training of Town, his master: but his designs were for the most part restrained, sound, and had the exceptional merit of attachment to their sites. It would be difficult to class him as a stylist, so eclectic was he in his taste. In personal appearance, he was below middle height, stocky. In his later years, he wore a brown wig, contrasting oddly with a very wrinkled face. Customarily, he wore a black broadcloth frock-coat. A man of fine personal qualities, he was genial, generous, large-minded, helpful. He was twice married.

[On his death, in 1891, Austin left a large library containing many books from the library of Town, but his books and drawings were, unfortunately, dispersed. The Yale University Library contains two volumes of his designs, and the full plans and specifications of one of his houses. Representations of the College Library and of the Grove Street Cemetery Gateway will be found in Mrs. L. C. H. Tuthill's *Hist. of Architecture* (1848).]

G. D. S.

AUSTIN, JAMES TRECOTHICK (Jan. 10, 1784–May 8, 1870), lawyer, Massachusetts politician, was born in Boston, the son of Jonathan Loring and Hannah (Ivers) Austin. He prepared for college first under Caleb Bingham, next at Andover, and finally at the Boston Latin School. He entered Harvard College in April 1799, at the third quarter of the freshman year, and graduated third in his class in 1802. Studying law with the Hon. William Sullivan, he was admitted to the bar in 1805, and on Oct. 3, 1806, he married Catherine, daughter of Elbridge Gerry. In 1807 Gov. Sullivan appointed him county attorney for Suffolk County, which office he held until 1832. Two years later he became town advocate and in 1811 was appointed a director of the state prison, serving in the latter capacity for a number of years. In 1816 President Madison appointed him as public agent under the terms of the Treaty of Ghent. Four years later Austin was a delegate to the convention that met to revise the state constitution and in 1826 he became a member of the Harvard Board of Overseers. He represented Boston in the state Senate for several terms. In 1828 he was appointed by Gov. Levi Lincoln as commissioner to settle the boundary line between Massachusetts and Connecticut east of the Connecticut River, and in

1832 Gov. Lincoln appointed him attorney-general of Massachusetts, which office he held by successive appointments until 1843, when the office was abolished. The most striking incident of his career as attorney-general was the case of the Commonwealth *vs.* Abner Kneeland (20 *Pickering,* 206). Later Austin returned to private practise, in which he was recognized as being one of the leading lawyers of the day in Massachusetts. He was president of the Suffolk County Bar Association in 1835. In politics he was a stanch Republican, a decided opponent of the Federalists, and later a Whig. He was very much opposed to the anti-slavery agitation, as he considered slavery to be permanently established. In this connection his greatest effort was his speech at the memorial meeting for the Rev. Elijah Lovejoy, Dec. 8, 1837, in which he compared the Alton mob with the patriots of the Boston Tea Party and demanded to know what Lovejoy had done to merit the distinction of being commemorated by a meeting in historic Faneuil Hall (*Boston Daily Advocate,* Dec. 9, 1837). A rather fertile writer, he was editor of the Boston *Emerald,* an ephemeral magazine of light literature (1806–8); published, in 1811, a series of articles over the name "Leolin" in the *Boston Patriot* on the subject of resistance to the laws of the United States; wrote *The Life of Elbridge Gerry* (1828–29); furnished a life of his father to *The Hundred Boston Orators . . . 1770 to 1852* (1852); and in 1853 published his *Remarks on Dr. Channing's Slavery.* He also contributed numerous articles to the *Christian Examiner* and the *Law Reporter.* He is described as having a face well-molded, long, exceedingly expressive, with piercing eyes, and something of a sandy complexion. In his later years his mind was impaired. He died at his home in Tremont St. at the age of eighty-six.

[Jas. S. Loring, *The Hundred Boston Orators . . . 1770 to 1852* (1852), pp. 470–76; *Necrology of Harvard Coll., 1869–72* (1872), pp. 5–7; scattering references in the *Memoirs of John Quincy Adams . . . 1795 to 1848,* 12 vols. (1874–77); Wm. H. Channing, *The Life of Wm. Ellery Channing* (1880), pp. 503–7, 557–63; *Boston Daily Jour.* and *Boston Daily Evening Transcript,* May 9, 1870.]

F. E. R.

AUSTIN, JANE GOODWIN (Feb. 25, 1831–Mar. 30, 1894), author, was a writer of stories and novels, the best known of which are descriptive of early New England life. Her interest in this field sprang from the fact that she herself was a *Mayflower* descendant, and that all her immediate ancestors had been born and reared in Plymouth. Her father, Isaac Goodwin, was a lawyer, antiquarian, and authority on Pilgrim history; her mother, Elizabeth Hammatt, a writer of poems. At the birth of Jane (named by her parents Mary Jane), they were living in Worcester, Mass., to which place they had gone from Plymouth, carrying with them many old traditions and records. When Jane was very young her father died, and her mother went to live in Boston. Browsing about in the family records as she grew up she was inspired to write stories, at first for her own amusement, and later for publication. At the age of nineteen, however, she married Loring Henry Austin of Boston by whom she had three children, and there followed a period of some thirteen years when she did no writing. She then began to contribute stories to the *Atlantic Monthly, Harper's Magazine, Putnam's Magazine, Emerson's Magazine,* and the *Galaxy,* a collection from which is to be found in *David Alden's Daughter and Other Stories* (1892). Thereafter, she was constantly engaged in literary work.

The most of Mrs. Austin's life was spent in the vicinity of Boston. For a time she lived in Concord and was on friendly terms with Emerson, Louisa Alcott, and the Hawthornes. She was a woman of instinctive graciousness, and in her later years her rooms were the weekly resort of admirers, and especially of those who were of direct Pilgrim descent. Her summers were spent in Plymouth gathering material for her stories. The "Pilgrim Books" constitute a series, the proper sequence of which is *Standish of Standish* (1889), *Betty Alden* (1891), *A Nameless Nobleman* (1881), *Dr. Le Baron and His Daughters* (1890). They cover a period from the landing of the Pilgrims to 1775. She had planned a fifth and completing volume which she did not live to write. They afford an excellent idea of the atmosphere, customs, and characters of early New England days. It was her practise, Mrs. Austin states in her preface to *David Alden's Daughter,* to put nothing down as a fact which she had not carefully determined to be such.

Besides the books already mentioned, Mrs. Austin published: *Fairy Dreams* (1859); *Dora Darling, the Daughter of the Regiment* (1865); *The Novice* (1865); *The Tailor Boy* (1865); *Outpost* (1867); *Cipher, A Romance* (1869); *The Shadow of Moloch Mountain* (1870); *Moonfolk* (1874); *Mrs. Beauchamp Brown* (1880); *The Desmond Hundred* (1882); *Nantucket Scraps* (1883); "Safe in Purgatory" (in *Vignettes: Real and Ideal,* ed. by Frederic Edward McKay, 1890); *It Never Did Run Smooth* (1892); *Queen Tempest* (1892); *The Twelve Great Diamonds* (1892).

[*Boston Transcript,* Mar. 30, 1894; *Boston Herald, Boston Journal,* Mar. 31, 1894; *Lit. World,* XXV, 111;

Book Buyer, n. s. XI, 194. See also Mary LeBaron Stockwell, *Descendants of Francis LeBaron of Plymouth, Mass.* (1904).]

H. E. S.

AUSTIN, JONATHAN LORING (Jan. 2, 1748–May 10, 1826), was a younger brother of Benjamin Austin [*q.v.*]. Born in Boston, he graduated from the Latin School and Harvard College (1766) and became successively a merchant at Kittery, Me., major in a volunteer New Hampshire regiment (1775), secretary to the Massachusetts Board of War (Nov. 21, 1776) and official messenger to convey the news of Burgoyne's surrender to the American commissioners at Paris. He sailed on the snow *Penet* from Boston on Oct. 31, 1777, arrived at Nantes on Nov. 30, and delivered the dispatches to Franklin at Passy on Dec. 4. On Jan. 31, 1778, Franklin sent Austin on a secret mission to London, in order to supply the opposition leaders with information that would enable them to demonstrate the uselessness of continuing the war. Austin moved about London freely, dined with Lord Shelburne and Dr. Price, visited his Loyalist cousins near Bristol, and left for France on Mar. 23, 1778, when warned by the French ambassador that communications would soon be closed. The American commissioners to France employed him in secretarial work until September, when he left for home via Holland, where he engaged in some sort of speculation (Franklin MSS., XI, 152), sailing about Nov. 15, and finally arriving at Virginia, via St. Eustatius, in April. He was recommended by the commissioners to the generosity of Congress, which rewarded him by assuming a debt for 130 louis d'or that he had borrowed from Franklin (*Jours. of Congress,* June 26, 1779). The State of Massachusetts-Bay sent him abroad in January 1780 to raise a loan of £150,000. He was captured by a Jersey privateer, was released through the exertion of his English friends, and pursued his mission with no other success than the purchase on credit of £3,000 worth of military clothing in Holland (Massachusetts Archives, CCLXXXVIII, 126–55; CLXXXVII, 305–17). Returning to Boston in the summer of 1781, he married Hannah Ivers, a sister of his brother Benjamin's wife, became his brother's partner, and a merchant. Until the party division of 1793, when the "Honesti" were ostracized by Federalists and confined to the society of the few gentlefolk who became Republicans, Austin was a man of fashion. He was elected to the state Senate from Boston in 1801, to the House from Cambridge in 1803 and 1806; served as secretary of the commonwealth under Gov. Sullivan (1806–8) and as treasurer under Gov. Gerry (1811–12), whose daughter married his son, James T. Austin [*q.v.*]. He died in Boston, on May 10, 1826.

[Austin's MS. journal of his journey to Paris and London—extracts printed in E. E. Hale, *Franklin in France* (1887) and in Francis Wharton, *Revolutionary Diplomatic Correspondence of the United States* (1889); Benjamin Franklin Stevens, *Facsimiles of Manuscripts in European Archives Relating to America,* III (1890), XXI (1894), XXII (1894); *Acts & Resolves of Province of Mass. Bay,* XXI (1922). A highly imaginative memoir of J. L. Austin in the *Boston Mo. Mag.,* II, 57–66, probably by J. T. Austin, is the basis of several biog. notices.]

S. E. M.

AUSTIN, MOSES (Oct. 4, 1761–June 10, 1821), merchant and mine owner, son of Elias and Eunice Austin, was descended from Richard Austin, who landed at Boston from the south of England in 1638. In 1674 Anthony, a son of Richard, became the first town clerk of Suffield, Conn. About the middle of the eighteenth century, Elias, a grandson of this Anthony, crossed the state to Durham and became there the father of Moses. Part of Moses Austin's boyhood was passed at Middletown, Conn., where, during the American Revolution, important lead-mining and smelting operations were carried on. It is probable that his attention was attracted there to the industry that occupied much of his mature life. In 1783, with the return of peace, Austin became connected in some way with the firm of Manning, Merrill & Co. at Philadelphia, and, in his own words, "commenced the importation of dry goods from England." His older brother, Stephen, was also a member of the Philadelphia firm, and in 1784 the two brothers seem to have reorganized and expanded the business, the older brother remaining at Philadelphia, while the younger established a branch under the name of Moses Austin & Company at Richmond, Va. By 1789 the Richmond firm had acquired the Chiswell lead mines in southwestern Virginia, and shortly thereafter Moses Austin moved to the mines, though the business at Richmond was continued. There is no authentic history of these mines. They were an important asset to the patriot government during the Revolution, but there are no figures on their output either before or after the Austins got possession. That the output was large is indicated by a reference to the accumulation of slag, which they were resmelting in 1801. Stephen Austin wrote then, "there still remains sufficient for your children and grandchildren." The Austins worked the mines with slave labor and cultivated adjacent farms to provide food for the slaves and the animals. When not absorbed by his other enterprises Moses Austin turned an odd penny by acting as a land scout for dealers in Virginia bounty warrants.

During the winter of 1796–97 Austin made a

reconnaissance of the great lead fields in southeastern Missouri. He recorded in his diary that the mineral was encountered within three feet of the surface, "in great Plenty and better quality than I have ever seen either from the Mines of England or America." Forming a strategic partnership with two local officials, he applied for and received a grant to a league of land, including the old workings known as Mine à Burton. On or near this grant he established the town of Potosi, to which his own contribution was an improved furnace, a shot-tower and a plant for making sheet lead, a saw-mill and flour-mill, a store, and a house for his family. For the next twenty years he carried on the variegated, miscellaneous business that characterized the frontier, most of it conducted by barter and credit. In 1812 he estimated that his property was worth $160,000, the mines being valued at $150,000; but the turnover in his various ventures was very slow, collections were uncertain, and his debts were chronically pressing. In 1816 he joined with others in organizing the Bank of St. Louis, and its subsequent failure wiped out his whole estate. The depression in the West which preceded and followed the panic of 1819 left him no heart to struggle against adverse fortune in Missouri. He turned his eyes again toward the frontier.

In December 1820 he appeared at San Antonio, Tex., and applied to the Spanish governor for a permit to establish 300 familes in Texas. Though details of his plan are lacking, it was evidently his intention to charge colonists a small fee for the privilege of settling in his grant. The permit was given by the commandant-general of the Eastern Interior Provinces on Jan. 17, 1821; but Austin died before concluding his arrangements for moving to Texas.

Moses Austin embodied the characteristic qualities of the westward movement. He was intelligent, enterprising, energetic, sanguine, and persevering. He enjoyed the confidence and esteem of the government and of the citizens wherever he lived. He was captain of his militia district in Virginia, and was presiding judge of the first court organized in the St. Genevieve district after the purchase of Louisiana by the United States. In 1784 he married Maria Brown in Philadelphia—descended on the mother's side from two of the Quaker proprietors of New Jersey—and left at his death a daughter and two sons, one of whom, Stephen F. Austin [*q.v.*] was to carry out successfully the colonization of Texas.

[The chief sources of information about Moses Austin are *The Life of Stephen F. Austin* (1925) by Eugene C. Barker, and "The Austin Papers," in *Am. Hist. Ass. Report*, vol. I (1919), vol. II (1924). *The Bates Papers* (2 vols., 1926), ed. by Thomas Maitland Marshall, are a valuable source for frontier conditions in Missouri.]

E. C. B.

AUSTIN, SAMUEL (Oct. 7, 1760–Dec. 4, 1830), Congregational clergyman, prominent in the theological and political controversies of his day, was born in New Haven, Conn., the son of Samuel and Lydia (Wolcott) Austin. After the Revolutionary War, in which, although but sixteen years old, he served as a substitute for his father, he taught school and later studied law with Judge Charles Chauncey of New Haven. When twenty-one years old he entered the sophomore class at Yale, graduating in 1783. His interest having turned from law to religion, he studied theology under Jonathan Edwards, the younger, then a pastor in New Haven. For a time he was principal of a newly formed academy in Norwich, Conn. Called to the Fair Haven Church, New Haven, in 1786, he was ordained its pastor Nov. 9. On Sept. 14, 1788, he married Jerusha, daughter of Rev. Samuel Hopkins of Hadley, Mass. His stay in New Haven was short. Dissatisfied with conditions in his church and especially with its adherence to the half-way covenant to which he was vigorously opposed, he asked for dismissal, which was granted by ecclesiastical council, Jan. 19, 1790. Immediately he was called to Worcester, Mass., where he was pastor of the First Congregational Church for twenty-five years. In 1815 he was persuaded to accept the presidency of the University of Vermont, which had been closed during the war with Great Britain. His church first granted him leave of absence, but on Dec. 23, 1818, the pastoral relation was dissolved. For six years he worked with reasonable success to rehabilitate the University, but he was not happy out of the ministry, and, resigning in March 1821, he took charge of the Congregational church in Newport, R. I. In 1825, his health failing, he resigned, and later sank into a condition of religious melancholy which resulted in his death.

His most important work was done in Worcester, but his influence extended beyond the city. He was instrumental in organizing the General Association of Massachusetts Ministers and the Massachusetts Missionary Society. Tall, erect, well-proportioned and courtly in appearance, with a face quickly expressive of his emotions, widely informed and with unusual command of language, animated and often vehement in delivery, he became known as one of the ablest preachers of his day. Theologically he was of the school of Jonathan Edwards [*q.v.*] and Samuel Hopkins [*q.v.*], and none was a more effective champion of orthodoxy against the Unitarian heresy which threatened to spread over the commonwealth (Samuel W. S. Dutton, *History of the North Church in New Haven,* 1842, pp. 77–83). The views of the Baptists he combated in *An Examination of the Representations and Reasonings Contained in Seven Sermons Lately Published by the Rev. Daniel Merrill, on the Mode and Subjects of Baptism* (1805); in *Mr. Merrill's Defensive Armor Taken from Him* (1806); and in *A View of the Economy of the Church of God . . . Particularly in Regard to the Covenants* (1807). In sermons delivered on special occasions, he took a decided political stand. *A Sermon Preached at Worcester on the Annual Fast, April 11, 1811* (1811), severely arraigns Thomas Jefferson, and *The Apology of Patriots, or the Heresy of the Friends of the Washington and Peace Policy Defended* (1812), is a defense of those who disagreed with the policies of the party then in power, especially respecting war with Great Britain. Numerous other sermons and addresses of his were published. (For a full list see F. B. Dexter, *Biographical Sketches of the Graduates of Yale College,* 1907, vol. IV, pp. 248–57.) He was the author of *Dissertations upon Several Fundamental Articles of Christian Theology* (1826), and editor of *The Works of President Edwards,* eight volumes (1808–9), to which is prefixed a memoir of Edwards's life, and annotations. He also published an American edition of Rev. Thomas Haweis's *Impartial and Succinct History of the Revival and Progress of the Church of Christ.*

[Besides references above, see Sam. S. Riddel, "Memoir of Rev. Samuel Austin, D.D.," *Amer. Quart. Reg.,* Feb. 1837; Wm. B. Sprague, *Annals of the Am. Pulpit,* II (1857); Wm. Lincoln, *Hist. of Worcester, Mass.* (1837), 174–374, *passim.*] H. E. S.

AUSTIN, STEPHEN FULLER (Nov. 3, 1793–Dec. 27, 1836), founder of Texas, was born at the lead mines (now in Wythe County) on the southwestern frontier of Virginia. His father was Moses Austin [*q.v.*], and his mother was Maria (Brown) Austin, descended on the maternal side from two of the Quaker proprietors of New Jersey. When the Austins moved to Missouri in 1798 the total population of that territory did not exceed 4,000—mostly French and Spanish, but with a sprinkling of adventurous Anglo-Americans who had responded during the past four years to Carondelet's liberal bid for immigrants. Austin was familiar from childhood, therefore, with the mingled social types that must be harmoniously combined later in the successful colonization of Texas. His incidental training for his life-work was nearly perfect. During the impressionable years from eleven to fourteen he was a student at Colchester, Conn., in the severe atmosphere of Yale College. The next two years until April 1810, he was at Transylvania University, Lexington, Ky., in the genial atmosphere of Henry Clay at his prime. Then back to a varied experience in Missouri—storekeeper, manager of the lead mines, director of the ill-fated Bank of St. Louis, adjutant of militia, member of the territorial legislature (1814–20). When the family fortunes collapsed in Missouri, Austin followed the frontier into Arkansas, where, in June 1820, the governor appointed him judge of the first judicial circuit. He qualified, but probably never held court, for he proceeded immediately to New Orleans and began the study of law, while assisting in the editorial department of the *Louisiana Advertiser.* With training and experience of such breadth and versatility, and with intimate knowledge of frontier life, Austin at twenty-seven was well prepared to be the founder and patriarchal ruler of a wilderness commonwealth.

Austin yielded with some reluctance to his father's sanguine enthusiasm for the Texas venture, but, having yielded, he spent himself in singular devotion to the task. He visited Texas in 1821; obtained the governor's consent to settle the 300 families stipulated in the grant to Moses Austin; selected for the colony a fertile and well-watered site, bordering on the Gulf; and in January 1822 planted the first legal settlement of Anglo-Americans in Texas. In the meantime, Mexico had established its independence, and belated doubts occurred to the governor concerning his authority to sanction Austin's enterprise, which had been authorized by the Spanish régime. The governor's doubts sent Austin to Mexico City, and the turbulent confusion which accompanied the birth-pangs of the new republic kept him there a year, but he returned to Texas with his grant fully confirmed. His sojourn in the capital had been trying but valuable, having given him a practical knowledge of the language, a profound insight into the national psychology, and powerful friends.

Austin returned to Texas with extraordinary powers. Until 1828, speaking broadly, he was executive, law-maker, supreme judge and military commandant. He had, in addition, absolute authority to admit immigrants to his grant or to exclude them from it; and, acting with a representative of the government, he could invest settlers with land titles. His political functions passed after the organization of constitutional government in Texas, but his influence remained great both with the settlers and with the superior authorities, and in effect he continued to direct the local government until 1832.

By 1825 Austin had settled the 300 families permitted by his original grant, when the legislature of Coahuila and Texas, acting under a federal statute, opportunely passed a general colonization law. The system established by this law was the same as that under which Austin had settled his first colony, and was substantially that which Spain had employed in Louisiana. It permitted immigration agents, known as *empresarios,* to contract for the introduction of multiples of a hundred families, and provided that for this service they should receive generous land bounties from the government and fees from the immigrants. Each married settler was entitled to a league of land (4,428 acres) at a total cost of less than $200 on easy terms. Under the state law Austin made contracts in 1825, 1827, and 1828 for 900 families, and settled some 750 of these before the last contract expired in 1834. Other *empresarios* obtained contracts aggregating many thousands of families, and several of them partially fulfilled their contracts. Austin alone, however, was conspicuously successful; and it seems obvious that, without his wise management and the results of his success to lean upon, the others would have accomplished little or nothing.

Austin's conception of his task was expressed in a striking comparison which he made in 1832: "Such an enterprise as the one I undertook in settling an uninhabited country must necessarily pass through three regular gradations. The first step was to overcome the roughness of the wilderness, and may be compared to the labor of the farmer on a piece of ground covered with woods, bushes, and brambles, which must be cut down and cleared away, and the roots grubbed out, before it can be cultivated. The second step was to pave the way for civilization and lay the foundation for lasting productive advancement in wealth, morality, and happiness. This step might be compared to the ploughing, harrowing, and sowing the ground after it is cleared. The third and last and most important step is to give proper and healthy direction to public opinion, morality, and education . . . to give tone, character, and consistency to society, which, to continue the simile, is gathering in the harvest and applying it to the promotion of human happiness." To another correspondent he wrote: "My ambition has been to succeed in redeeming Texas from its wilderness state by means of the plough alone, in spreading over it North American population, enterprise, and intelligence; in doing this I hoped to make the fortunes of thousands and my own amongst the rest. . . . My object is to build up, for the present as well as for future generations."

It would be impossible to exaggerate the importance of Austin's labors during the early years of the colonization of Texas. He once complained that too much of his time was consumed in settling "neighborhood disputes about cows and calves," but it was the patience with which he devoted himself to minutiæ as well as his intelligence and ability in larger things that accounts for his success. He fixed the land system; pushed back the Indians; mapped the province and charted its bays and rivers; promoted commerce with the United States, and kept a steady stream of immigrants flowing in; encouraged the erection of gins and sawmills and the establishment of schools; and exercised a most remarkable influence at the state and federal capitals in matters affecting Texas. To mention only the more important instances of his influence with the government: he was responsible in large measure for the liberal terms of the colonization law; his arguments prevented the constitutional abolition of slavery in 1827 and obtained the contract labor law of the next year permitting the continued introduction of slaves in the form of indented servants; in 1829 he induced the legislature to pass a sweeping homestead law to protect colonists from suits to collect debts contracted before immigration; and in 1830 he induced the federal authorities to sanction the continued settlement of colonists from the United States in his own and DeWitt's grants, though an act passed by Congress on April 6 of that year plainly meant to stop such settlement. A judiciary law which he outlined in 1824, providing appellate courts and trial by jury in Texas, was passed by the legislature in 1834. He was a member of the legislature of Coahuila and Texas, 1831–32, and was elected for the term beginning in 1835, but as appears below, was unavoidably prevented from serving.

The attraction of immigrants to Texas was a matter that caused Austin little concern. The restless surge of the Westward Movement had carried the American frontier to the borders of Texas before his first colony was established. Economic conditions in the Mississippi Valley, produced by the establishment of the Second United States Bank, the panic of 1819, and the abolition of credit in the public land system, were sufficient to push an increasing stream of settlers into Texas as the news spread that Austin could give them valid land titles at relatively low cost. The problem, rather, that taxed all Austin's skill was that of maintaining, on the one hand, among the swelling tide of settlers, an attitude of tolerant patience toward the habitual political bungling of the Mexicans, and that, on the other hand, of holding the confidence of Mexican statesmen and soothing their growing fear of the ultimate absorption of Texas by the United States. His success with both colonists and Mexicans proves him a great leader and a great diplomat. Much of his influence with Mexican officials is attributable to his loyalty. When he moved to Texas he transferred his whole-hearted allegiance to Mexico. Writing to his confidential friend and secretary in 1831, Austin said: "You are well aware that in my intercourse with this govt. I have followed a few fixed rules.... In the first place, I came with pure intentions. I bid an everlasting farewell to my native country, and adopted this, and in so doing I determined to fulfill rigidly all the duties and obligations of a Mexican citizen." This declaration is abundantly supported by facts. Until 1830, at least, Austin believed without reservation that the surest road to happiness and prosperity for Texas lay through its development as a Mexican state. The liberal land system and the hope of free trade with England, in contrast with the land policy and protective tariff of the United States, were the chief reasons for this belief. During the next few years his faith in the ultimate stability of Mexico wavered; but when he thought—as he sometimes did—of the possible necessity of secession, he favored independence rather than annexation to the United States.

Aloofness from party contests was the very keystone of Austin's political policy. In discussing the reason for this in 1831, when Guerrero and Pedraza were fighting for the presidency, he explained that Mexican parties were not clearly defined, had no fixed character, nor permanency of purpose; if the colonists took part in the scramble, they would be "like children in a mob, and as likely to be trodden upon by friends as by foes." "Play the turtle," he more than once enjoined, "head and feet within your own shell." If they were ever compelled to make a declaration, they must say, "that they will do their duty strictly as Mexican citizens—that they will adhere to Mexico and to the federal and state constitution, and resist any unjust attacks upon either, by any or by all parties."

Despite the well-tried wisdom of this policy, attested by its happy results, grinding, inescapable necessity compelled a declaration for Santa Anna in July 1832. Thereafter catastrophe was not to be long held back. In April 1833 a convention, assembled against Austin's better judgment, petitioned for separation of Texas from Coahuila and the erection of state government in Texas. Austin was in full accord with the object but doubted the expediency of the method. Despite his hesitation, he was sent to Mexico as the man best qualified to obtain the government's approval of the petition. He took the position with Congress and the vice-president, Gomez Farias, that elevation of Texas to statehood was the only way to save it to Mexico; that the people did not want to secede, but that they were determined to separate from Coahuila and assume control of their own local government. By pressing his arguments too impetuously he offended Gomez Farias, and was imprisoned on the vague and wholly baseless charge of attempting to revolutionize Texas and annex it to the United States. After a year in prison, followed by six months' detention under bond, he was released by a general amnesty law in July 1835, without having been brought to trial. On his arrival in Texas Austin found the people at the verge of revolt; a convention had been called to adopt a policy toward Santa Anna's evident design to centralize the republic. Austin was still opposed to a declaration of independence, because he did not believe that Texas yet had the resources either to win or maintain independence. Expediency, he thought, pointed rather to alliance with the Liberal party which was opposing Santa Anna in Mexico. To effect this end he exerted himself, as chairman of a central committee of safety and correspondence, to make the coming convention a truly representative body, able to speak for all the people. Before the date set for the meeting, however, the war of the Texas revolution was precipitated. Austin was first called to the command of the volunteer army; then, in December 1835, was sent by the provisional government—with William H. Wharton and Branch T. Archer—to the United States to negotiate loans and credit, enlist sympathy, and test the sentiment of the Jackson Government toward recognition and eventual annexation. This mission—through no fault of Austin and his colleagues—was only partially successful. Austin returned from the United States in June 1836; was defeated for the presidency of the Republic of Texas by Sam Houston in September; accepted office with Houston as secretary of state in October; and died in December at the age of forty-three.

But for the extraordinarily tactful work done by Austin prior to 1825 the settlement of Texas from the United States would have been impossible, or at the least greatly delayed. It was he, and no other, who opened the door and by leadership of high order held it open. The colonists were sometimes impatient at his cautious, temporizing policy with Mexican officials; but to himself, at least, the answer was sufficient: "It was my duty to steer my precious bark [the colony] through all the shoals and quicksands regardless of the curses and ridicule of the passengers. I knew what I was about—they did not." For seven years the government of the American settlements was absolutely in his hands; for the remaining eight years of his life no important step was ever taken by the colonists without his counsel and concurrence.

There is no definite contemporary description of Austin. He was evidently a small, slight man. One gathers the impression that he was about five feet five or six and weighed around 135 pounds. His portraits, of which there are several, show a fine, strong face, with firm chin, thin lips, prominent nose, good eyes, and a high, intellectual forehead. His hair, of which a lock exists, was dark brown, with a tinge of bronze, worn long, and inclined to wave. In spite of slight stature and severe illnesses, his constitution was naturally wiry and resilient. He was a grave, gentle, kindly man, charitable, tolerant, affectionate and loyal, naturally impetuous but restrained by habit, sensitive, and lonely. Though he enjoyed social companionship, his position set him apart from the colonists and made close friendships with them difficult and rare. He smoked, danced, loved music, and drank moderately. He was well educated, widely read for his opportunities, and a clear thinker and writer. His letters in their straightforward precision and naturalness remind one of Franklin. He worked incessantly, unselfishly, and generally most patiently. He never married, and the only representatives of his branch of the family now living are the descendants of his sister.

[Besides numerous editorials and articles contributed to the *Texas Gazette,* Austin published in 1829, *Translation of the Laws, Orders and Contracts on Colonization . . . with an Explanatory Introduction to the Settlers of What Is Called Austin's Colony in Texas*—seventy pages. This was the first bk. published in Texas. In January 1835 he published in Mexico City, *Esposición al Público sobre los Asuntos de Tejas,* a pamphlet of thirty-two pages—translated by Ethel Zively Rather in *Texas State Hist. Ass. Quart.,* VIII, 232 ff. "The Austin Papers," comprising Austin's collected writings as well as correspondence and documents received by him, edited by Eugene C. Barker, is published in the *Am. Hist. Ass. Reports* for 1919, 1922 (issued 1924, 1928), with a concluding volume by the Univ. of Texas Press (1927). The only biog. of Austin is that by Eugene C. Barker (1925).] E. C. B.

AUSTIN, WILLIAM (Mar. 2, 1778–June 27, 1841), author, came of ancestors who had been prominent in the affairs of Charlestown, Mass., since 1651. The burning of the town during the battle of Bunker Hill drove his father, Nathaniel, to Lunenburg, Worcester County, Mass., where William was born. Soon after his birth the family returned to Charlestown, and there he spent the most of his life. Nathaniel was a pewterer by trade, but through speculation in real estate acquired some wealth. On Nov. 19, 1766, he had married Margaret Rand, daughter of Deacon Isaac Rand of Charlestown. They had six children of whom William was the third. Though her husband was a staunch patriot, Margaret was a spirited Tory, and never failed to characterize each observance of Bunker Hill Day as "the celebration of a defeat." Political differences, however, seem never seriously to have disturbed the peace of the Austin family, for in later years William, an ardent Jeffersonian Republican, and his brother, Nathaniel, a strong Federalist, ran against each other for a seat in the General Court of Massachusetts with no lessening of their regard for each other.

William prepared for college at Rev. John Shaw's school, Haverhill, and graduated from Harvard in the class of 1798. He early became imbued with the philosophy of Rousseau, and in his senior year wrote *Strictures on Harvard University,* criticizing the official restraints on college life. When older, however, he acknowledged that his prejudices had been unfounded. He declined an election to Phi Beta Kappa, because he was opposed to secret societies, and also because he thought an injustice had been done one of his classmates. In 1802–03 he studied law at Lincoln's Inn, London, having secured the necessary means by serving as schoolmaster and chaplain on the United States frigate *Constitution.* Austin is said to have been the first chaplain appointed in the navy by government commission. While in England he wrote *Letters from London,* which were published by William Pelham, a Boston bookseller. They attracted a good deal of notice in their day and are still of interest as illustrating the attitude of a New England Republican toward English institutions and manners.

Returning to Charlestown in 1803, Austin soon built up a large law practise, took an active part in civic and political affairs, and represented the town in the General Court in 1811, 1812, 1816, 1827, and 1834, and the County of Middlesex in the Senate in 1821, 1822, and 1823. He was also a delegate in the convention of 1820 for revising the constitution of Massachusetts. He was twice married and had fourteen children. His first wife was Charlotte Williams, daughter of Deacon Isaac Williams, whom he married June 17, 1806. Charlotte died, Dec. 10, 1820, and on Oct. 3, 1822, he married Lucy Jones, daughter of Peter Jones of Charlestown.

Austin was fervent in his convictions, independent, impulsive, quickly stirred to indignation by any apparent injustice, and blunt and forceful in the expression of his feelings. These characteristics, involved him in a duel, March 31, 1806, with James Henderson Elliot. Capt. Joseph Loring, Jr., an officer in the militia, and a Democrat, was tried for alleged disobedience of orders. He was acquitted, but the court was sworn not to divulge its findings until they were approved or disapproved by Gen. Simon Elliot. The latter did nothing for several months. Political feeling was running high at the time, and all appeals to Gen. Elliot and the Governor, who were Federalists, failed to get Loring out of prison. Austin wrote a letter, signed "Decius," which was published in the *Independent Chronicle* of March 17, 1806, violently attacking the general for his part in the affair, and the latter's son, James, sent a challenge to the writer. Since duelling was forbidden in Massachusetts, the event took place near Providence, R. I. So bitter was the feeling that the parties fired three shots although the articles of agreement called for but two. Austin was wounded in the neck and thigh, but Elliot was uninjured.

Austin's varied activities left him little freedom for literature, and writing was more or less a pastime with him. Of the five stories which he wrote, one, however, not only had great popularity in its day, but has lived, and is of significance in the history of American fiction, "Peter Rugg, the Missing Man," published in the *New England Galaxy* for Sept. 10, 1824. The scene is laid in 1820, and the story is that of a man who, driving toward Boston with his little daughter, fifty years before, with a storm threatening, had sworn he would reach home that night or never see home again. All the intervening years he had been seeking it in vain, and his old-fashioned chaise drawn by a galloping white-footed black horse, always heralding a storm, had become a frequent sight on the roads. With the exception of "Rip Van Winkle," it is perhaps the most original and imaginative American tale before the days of Poe and Hawthorne. The latter confessed that it made a deep impression upon him, and to the method of its art some critics have thought him indebted (see Thomas W. Higginson in the *Independent,* Mar. 29, 1888). The other stories are of less interest, but show imaginative ability, sense of humor, and the morality and mysticism of New England Puritanism.

The following is a list of Austin's publications: *Strictures on Harvard University* (1798); *Oration before the Artillery Company, Charlestown, June 17, 1801* (1801); *Letters from London* (1804); *Essay on the Human Character of Jesus Christ* (1807); "Peter Rugg, the Missing Man," *New England Galaxy,* Sept. 10, 1824; continuation, *Ibid.,* Sept. 1, 1826; Jan. 19, 1827; "The Sufferings of a Country Schoolmaster," *Ibid.,* July 8, 1825; "The Late Joseph Natterstrom," *New England Magazine,* July 1831; "The Origin of Chemistry, a Manuscript Recently Found in an Old Trunk," *Ibid.,* Jan. 1834; "The Man with the Cloaks: a Vermont Legend," place and date of publication uncertain; "Martha Gardner; or Moral Reaction," *American Monthly Magazine,* Dec. 1837.

[The principal sources of information are *Literary Papers of William Austin, with a Biog. Sketch,* by his son, James Walker Austin (1890); and *William Austin,* by Walter Austin (1925). The latter contains a copious bibliography of references to Austin and his writings, and all the stories except "The Sufferings of a Country Schoolmaster."]

H. E. S.

AVERELL, WILLIAM WOODS (Nov. 5, 1832–Feb. 3, 1900), Union soldier, was born in Cameron, Steuben County, N. Y. The family's first American ancestor appears to have been William Avery or Averell, who, marrying Abigail Hinton of Oxford, England, emigrated to Ipswich, Mass., about the year 1637. William Woods Averell's great-grandfather, Solomon Averell, was born in Preston, Conn., in 1719, and had four sons who took part in the American Revolution (*Landmarks of Steuben County, N. Y.,* ed. by Harlo Hakes, 1896, II, 331); his grandfather was Ebenezer Averell, born in Preston, Conn., in 1762, who moved to New York in 1791; while his father was Hiram Averell (born in Harpersfield, N. Y., in 1795) and his mother, Huldah Hemenway of Greenwood, N. Y. Hiram Averell was for some time constable and collector of the town of Addison, N. Y., and in his later years was postmaster and justice of the peace in Cameron (Clara A. Avery, *The Averell-Averill-Avery Family,* 1914, p. 347). After a common school education, young Averell became a drugclerk in the village of Bath, N. Y., until opportunity came to receive an appointment to the United States Military Academy at West Point, July 1, 1851. After four years of thorough training as a soldier, he was graduated number twenty-six in a class of thirty-four. He was immediately commissioned brevet second-lieutenant of mounted rifles, and during the next few years underwent experiences in the West which were to prepare him in many ways for the nation's great struggle which followed. His first army station was at Jefferson Barracks, Mo.—then regarded as the frontier, and there he remained with his regiment during the years 1855 and 1856, when he received his full commission as second-lieutenant of mounted rifles. The young officer, energetic and ambitious, felt the need of advanced instruction in duties not covered by the curriculum at the Military Academy, for we find him next as a student-officer at the Cavalry School for Practice, Carlisle, Pa. This training completed in the year 1857, he was ordered to

New Mexico, where he received full measure of arduous field service; escort duty for the commanding general, Department of New Mexico; participant in the Navajo Expedition of 1858; in a skirmish with Kiowa Indians; and in additional skirmishes during 1858 with hostile Kyatanos and at the so-called "Puerco of the West," where he was severely wounded in an Indian night attack. Reluctant to give up his field duties, it was only after an additional Indian engagement in the year 1859 that he was persuaded to take an extended leave of absence on account of wounds, —an absence which was prolonged until the beginning of the Civil War. During this formative period in Averell's military career, he gained a deserved reputation for bravery, energy, and good judgment as an Indian fighter. Then came the great war between the states, with all its sudden opportunities and responsibilities.

With the initial organization of what later became the Army of the Potomac, there was a crying need for experienced officers. Early in the summer of 1861, Averell became an assistant adjutant-general on the staff of Gen. Andrew Porter, and as such the young officer participated in the hastily planned first battle of Bull Run. After that discreditable experience for the poorly trained Union army, Averell was placed on provost duty in the city of Washington. On Aug. 23, 1861, his abilities were recognized by his appointment as colonel of the 3rd Pennsylvania Cavalry, United States Volunteers, and he was placed in command of a cavalry brigade in front of the defenses of Washington. Here he remained until the following spring, when, on Mar. 9–10, he and his cavalry were honored with leading the advance on Manassas of Gen. McClellan's newly organized army. Thereafter, he followed the army's fortunes in the severe Peninsular Campaign, and participated actively in the siege of Yorktown (Apr. 5–May 4); the battles of Williamsburg (May 4–5), Fair Oaks (June 1), and Malvern Hill (July 1); and in skirmishes at Sycamore Church (Aug. 2) and at White Oak Swamp (Aug. 5, 1862). These arduous battle experiences were followed by a short illness (Sept. 5–24), but Averell's ability as a cavalry commander was rewarded, Sept. 26, 1862, by his appointment as brigadier-general, United States Volunteers, at less than thirty years of age. Meanwhile (July 17, 1862), he was commissioned to a captaincy in the regular army. Events moved rapidly, and in the month of November, we find Averell and his cavalry scouting and skirmishing along the upper Potomac, and in small engagements with the Confederate forces at Upperville, Markham, Corbin's and Gaines's Cross Roads, and at Amissville (Nov. 2–10, 1862). The Army of the Potomac then embarked on the sanguinary Rappahannock campaign, and Averell's command took part in the battle of Fredericksburg (Dec. 13, 1862). Following this disaster for the Union army, Averell and his cavalry initiated a series of small raids into Virginia, the nature of which is shown in part by a short extract from one of the cavalry commander's despatches: "Dec. 21, 1862.—My column has marched, climbed, slid, and swum, 340 miles since Dec. 8!"

From Feb. 22 to May 4, 1863, Averell took over command of the important 2nd cavalry division. Beginning with a small skirmish at Hartwood, Feb. 25, the division's operations reached a climax in the great cavalry combat at Kelly's Ford, Mar. 17, 1863—an engagement which military experts agree to have been brilliant in conception and in execution. The battle really *made* the Union cavalry, and changed the hitherto contemptuous assertion of "Who ever saw a dead cavalryman!" into a spirit of confidence and faith in the mounted arm, which formed the basis, later, of Gen. Sheridan's great cavalry achievements. At the time, Gen. Butterfield characterized the battle at Kelly's Ford as "the best cavalry fight of the war." And although Gen. Hooker thought Averell overcautious in alleged inaction after the engagement, Secretary of War Stanton sent Hooker the following characteristic dispatch: "I congratulate you upon the success of Averell's expedition. It is good for the first lick. You have drawn first blood. . . . Give my compliments and thanks to Averell and his command." For "gallant and meritorious services" in the battle of Kelly's Ford, Averell was awarded the brevet of major in the regular army. The cavalry division was not long idle, and soon after Kelly's Ford, Averell and his command took part in the famous "Stoneman's Raid" toward Richmond (Apr. 29–May 8, 1863). On the latter date, however, Averell was transferred to West Virginia for operations of the 4th separate brigade, and with characteristic energy, engaged hostile forces at Beverly (July 1), Hedgeville (July 19), Moorfield (Aug. 7), Rocky Gap (Aug. 26), and at Droop Mountain (Nov. 6, 1863). For the last named action, he received the brevet of lieutenant-colonel. After a short rest, his cavalry took part in the important "Salem Raid," which cut the Tennessee railroad, and destroyed large quantities of Longstreet's clothing, rations, and equipment. Every effort was made by the enemy to capture or destroy this bold raiding party, but, eluding every Confederate column, Averell rejoined the Union lines with 200 prisoners and 150 horses. For this brilliant achievement, he was brevetted a colonel in the regular army. After a short sick-leave in the early part of the important year 1864, he assumed command of the 2nd cavalry division, and engaged in a series of cavalry actions under Sheridan, which materially affected the collapse of the Confederacy. The most important of these were Winchester (July 24), Opequan (Sept. 19), Fisher's Hill (Sept. 22), and Mount Jackson (Sept. 23). These engagements rounded out, in large part, Averell's fine military career. On Mar. 13, 1865, he was made brevet brigadier-general, United States Army, for his services during the entire war; and on the same date, was honored with brevet major-general, United States Army, for gallant services at the battle of Moorfield, Va.

He resigned on May 18, 1865, and was appointed by the President consul-general for British North America at Montreal, which office he held for three years. He then returned to private life. On Sept. 24, 1885, he was married to Kezia Hayward. Until 1888, he was interested in engineering and in manufacturing. Among other things, he invented a system of conduits for electric wiring, and also secured valuable patents for asphalt paving. In the year 1898, after twenty years of litigation, the Supreme Court awarded him infringement damages of $700,000 in his suit against the Barbour Asphalt Paving Company. Meanwhile, after having been reappointed by Congress a captain on the army retired list, Averell had been made assistant inspector-general of the Soldiers' Home at Bath, N. Y., holding this office for ten years. In 1898, his patents having made him financially independent, he resigned his inspectorship and prepared to enjoy a well-earned rest. But after a lingering illness, he died at Bath, Feb. 3, 1900, leaving uncompleted the manuscript of reminiscences of an eventful life.

[*Rep. Ass. Grads. U. S. Mil. Acad.*, 1900; Cullum's *Biog. Reg.* (3rd ed. 1891), II; *Battles and Leaders of the Civil War* (1887–88); C. D. Rhodes, *Hist. of the Cavalry of the Army of the Potomac* (1900); Jacob B. Cooke, *Battle of Kelly's Ford* (1887); John Bigelow, *Campaign of Chancellorsville* (1910); *Officers of the Army and Navy in the Civil War* (1894).]

C. D. R.

AVERY, BENJAMIN PARKE (Nov. 11, 1828–Nov. 8, 1875), journalist, diplomat, was born in New York City, the son of Samuel Putnam and Hannah (Parke) Avery, and brother of Samuel Putnam Avery [*q.v.*]. His father, a hotel keeper, died during the cholera epidemic of 1832, leaving a widow and six children in poverty. Mrs. Avery is credited with unusual capabilities of mind and character. Benjamin often spoke of her in after years as his "polar star" and as a mother who taught her family the highest principles of honor. Though the boy early developed a taste for literature and the plastic arts, he had no opportunities for formal education. He learned the trade of bank-note engraving, and was so employed when news of the gold discovery at Sutter's Mill fired him with a determination to go to California. On the sailing ship *Orpheus,* which rounded the Horn, he arrived at San Francisco July 8, 1849. For several years he vainly followed prospecting, and was often destitute and ill. In 1856, with savings earned as a druggist and general storekeeper, he started a weekly newspaper, the *Hydraulic Press,* at North San Juan, Nevada County. It was a Republican and anti-slavery organ, and the community was hostile. In 1860 he moved to Marysville and with Noah Brooks established the *Appeal,* the first daily newspaper in the state outside of San Francisco. In 1861 he married Mary A. Fuller, of Michigan. In September of the same year he was elected state printer, and at the end of his two-years term moved to San Francisco. He now became editor of the *Bulletin,* a post which he retained for ten years. During this period he organized the San Francisco Art Association and spent much time in writing and speaking in its behalf. Failing health caused him to retire from daily journalism, and in January 1874 he accepted the editorship of the *Overland Monthly.* A few months later he was appointed by President Grant minister to China, and in August sailed for Peking. Among several diplomatic achievements he is credited with an important share in composing the differences between China and Japan, then at the verge of war. He died at Peking. The body was embalmed by the surgeon of the Russian embassy and after impressive ceremonies was carried by the U.S.S. *Monocacy* from Tientsin to Yokohama. It was there transferred to the *City of Tokio* and was then brought to San Francisco, where on Jan. 26, 1876, after a largely attended memorial meeting, it was interred.

The portrait of Avery shows a refined and sensitive face. He had the quality of inspiring the warm regard and admiration of those with whom he was most closely associated. "He appears to me," said the historian John S. Hittell, at his funeral, "the best man I ever knew, without exception." Of his influence in his own community the tribute of Samuel Williams, who succeeded him as editor of the *Overland Monthly,* bears striking witness: "Perhaps no one person did so much to educate the people of the state in the right direction—to lift the thoughts of men above the sordid interests of the hour and the mean ambition of personal gain." His one separately published work, *Californian Pictures in Prose and Verse,* which appeared posthumously in 1878, hardly justifies the praise that has been given to him as a writer. The verse is mediocre, and the prose, though indicative of a feeling for the beauty and grandeur of the physical world, has few qualities of distinction. Among his literary remains was an unfinished work on "Art and Its Uses."

[The chief sources of information are the *Geneal. Rec. of the Dedham Branch of the Avery Family in America* (1893) and the pamphlet, *In Memoriam, Benjamin Parke Avery, 1875.* The latter, which carries no publication place or date but was evidently printed in San Francisco in 1876, is a collection of tributes from intimate friends. The biog. matter included reveals many discrepancies as to dates and events. A brief biog. sketch, with a woodcut portrait, appeared in *Harper's Weekly,* May 2, 1874, and other sketches are given in various reference books.]

W. J. G.

AVERY, ISAAC WHEELER (May 2, 1837–Sept. 8, 1897), Confederate soldier, journalist, politician, was born in St. Augustine, Fla., the son of Isaac Wheeler and Mary Moore (King) Avery. On his father's side he was descended from Gov. Winthrop of Massachusetts. He was educated at Oglethorpe University, and studied for the bar. Enlisting in the 8th Georgia, he fought from the first battle of Bull Run nearly to the close of the war, and reached the rank of colonel and the command of a brigade. For a short time he was a prisoner, having been captured by Gen. Sheridan, and in 1864 while serving under Gen. Johnston he was severely wounded at the battle of New Hope Church. Of his conduct in this engagement the commander-in-chief wrote: "Although desperately wounded in the onset Col. Avery, supported in his saddle by a soldier, continued to command, and maintained the contest until the arrival of forces capable of holding the ground" (J. E. Johnston, *Narrative of Military Operations,* 1874, p. 328). The wound injured his spine so that for years afterward he used crutches. After the war he practised law, and was active in the politics and journalism of the Reconstruction era in Georgia. He married Emma Bivings, Jan. 1, 1868. For a number of years he was editor-in-chief of the *Atlanta Constitution* and for a short time owned the *Atlanta Herald.* He was a delegate to the National Democratic Convention of 1872 and held at one time a position in the United States Treasury Department. He was one of the leaders in the South in promoting direct trade between the United States and other countries, particularly with the lands to the south. His *History of the State of Georgia from 1850 to 1881* (1881) is mainly political. As a writer he was associated with the *National Cyclopædia of American Biography.* His death removed "one of the old cavaliers of the old south. He was a type that is now growing so rare" (*Atlanta Constitution,* Sept. 10, 1897). His resemblance to this "type" is emphasized in his own dictated statement, that he had taken part in four "affairs of honor."

[Maj. Chas. Hubner, in *Nat. Cyc. of Am. Biog.* (1891), III, 238, from data furnished by Avery; E. M. and C. H. T. Avery, *The Groton Avery Clan* (1912).]

E. K. A.

AVERY, JOHN (Sept. 18, 1837–Sept. 1, 1887), linguist, was born at Conway, Mass., the son of Joseph and Sylvia (Clary) Avery, but was left at an early age dependent on his own resources. He was fitted for college at Williston Seminary and graduated from Amherst in the class of 1861. He then taught at Leicester Academy for a year and in 1862 was a tutor at Amherst. In 1863 he entered upon a four years' course of study in philology at Yale College under Prof. Whitney and for the last two years of that time was also tutor in physics in the Sheffield Scientific School, teaching what was to him a distasteful subject in order to be able to pursue the study of his favorite languages. On Aug. 21, 1866 he was married to Cornelia M. Curtiss of New Haven, Conn., by whom he had one child. From 1867 to 1868 he studied Sanskrit and Zend at Berlin and Tübingen, in Germany. For the remainder of his life his scholarly interests were chiefly concerned with the languages and literature of India. He was elected a member of the American Oriental Society in 1870, and furnished papers at each of its meetings. From the year 1875 until his death he was assistant editor of the *American Antiquarian and Oriental Journal.* He was the first American to be admitted to the Royal Asiatic Society of London. It is said that he was master of fifteen languages. For over twenty years he devoted himself to the antiquities, ethnology, and philology of the ancient tribes of northern India and at the time of his death he was engaged upon a book on the aboriginal tribes of India (never published). From 1870 to 1871 he was professor of Latin and from 1871 to 1877 professor of Greek at Iowa College, Grinnell; and from 1877 to 1887 professor of Greek at Bowdoin. As a teacher he was industrious and conscientious rather than inspiring, while his erudition was sometimes over the heads of college boys. In June 1887 he retired from his professorship in order to devote himself to his favorite study of Sanskrit, but died in the ensuing September, at North

Bridgeton, Me., from a disease contracted in nursing his only son.

[*Obit. Rec. Grads. Amherst Coll.*, 1888; *Lewiston* (Me.) *Evening Jour.*, Sept. 5, 1887; address of President William DeWitt Hyde, Bowdoin College Chapel, Sept. 18, 1887, in *Bowdoin Orient*, Sept. 28, 1887.]

K. C. M. S.

AVERY, SAMUEL PUTNAM (Mar. 17, 1822–Aug. 11, 1904), art connoisseur, philanthropist, was born in New York City, the son of a leather merchant, Samuel Putnam Avery and of Hannah (Parke) Avery. His parents were both of good Massachusetts stock. In 1832 the father died of the cholera, and his son, ten years of age, with a younger brother and three sisters, inherited the father's name—and little else. School days were cut short; but so far as Samuel was concerned self-training and culture continued for seventy years. A passion for the beautiful turned the lad's thought and effort to the art of engraving on wood and copper. There were years of apprenticeship to a calling that brought slight material rewards, but laid the foundation of a long career that in the passing of time led step by step to an appreciation of much in the world of art which America before his day had overlooked or neglected. At first he learned to engrave on copper and was employed by the American Bank Note Company; but he turned from that to wood engraving for publishers and printers. An edition of *Chevalier Bayard*, by W. G. Simms, was illustrated by Avery for Harper & Brothers in 1847. It was not long before this self-taught descendant of English Puritans was a collector of rare paintings and etchings, advising Americans who had money to spend in the importation of such works from the galleries of Europe. These well-to-do Americans with artistic interests gave Avery the opportunity to accumulate a fortune. They encouraged him in starting an art business in New York, in which he prospered because of his skill in appraisal and the confidence that buyers reposed in his discrimination. When the International Exposition at Paris was opened in 1867, Avery already had a recognized standing among the few Americans whose judgment in matters of art was generally respected. It was natural that he should be appointed United States Commissioner at that exposition and that his attendance there should notably widen his acquaintance among European art-lovers, and open to him doors that otherwise might have remained closed. Relationships thus formed continued unbroken to the end of his life. He was interested especially in old Dutch paintings and in romantic French landscapists. Two American buyers who were influenced profoundly by him were William T. Walters of Baltimore, and William H. Vanderbilt of New York. As one of the founders of the Metropolitan Museum in New York City, he induced Vanderbilt to place his valuable collection of paintings in that institution. As a memorial to his son, Henry O. Avery, he gave to the Columbia University Library a collection of 15,000 volumes on art and architecture, long regarded as the best architectural library in the United States. To the New York Public Library he gave his priceless collection of engravings and etchings—17,000 in number—containing many Whistlers and artists' proofs of other great etchers (the series of Flameng, for example, is more complete than that in Paris). Avery's public spirit is indicated by the munificence of his gifts. He was married in 1844 to Mary Ann Ogden, who survived him. His eldest son, Samuel Putnam Avery, followed the calling of art collector and died in 1920.

[T. L. De Vinne, in *N.Y. Geneal. and Biog. Rec.*, XXXVI, 1–4; *Who's Who in America* 1903–05; S. P. Avery, *The Avery, Fairchild, and Park Families* (1919); *Editorials and Resolutions in Memory of Samuel Putnam Avery* (privately printed, 1905); *N.Y. Times*, Aug. 13, 14, 1904; *N.Y. Tribune*, Aug. 14, 1904; *35th Ann. Rept. of Metropolitan Museum of Art, N.Y.* (1905); R. Sturgis, "Samuel Putnam Avery," in *Columbia Univ. Quart.*, VII, 14–23.]

W. B. S.

AVERY, WILLIAM WAIGSTILL (May 25, 1816–July 3, 1864), lawyer, was born in Burke County, and died in Morganton, N. C. He was descended from Christopher Avery, who came to Massachusetts from England in 1631, and from Waigstill Avery, who, going south in 1769, soon after his graduation from Princeton, became one of the prominent Revolutionary patriots of North Carolina. His father was Isaac Thomas Avery, a rich planter of literary tastes, and his mother Harriet Eloise Erwin, a representative of a family long distinguished in local public affairs. Entering the University of North Carolina in 1833, he found his preparation so inadequate that it was necessary for him to remain there in study for two years without any vacation. He was graduated at the head of his class in 1837, and in 1839 he was admitted to the bar. A year later he was an unsuccessful candidate for the state legislature, but he was elected to that body in 1842, and served for one term before retiring to his already important law practise. His political convictions were largely those of John C. Calhoun. In 1846 he was married to Corinna Mary Morehead, daughter of Gov. John Motley and Ann Elizabeth (Lindsay) Morehead. He was a state legislator in 1850 and 1852. In 1856 and in 1860 he was a state senator, and head of the North Carolina delegation to the National Democratic Convention. On the election of Lincoln as president, he advocated that North Carolina secede immediately. He was a member of the Confederate Provisional Congress throughout its existence. Having procured authority from Jefferson Davis, he planned in 1862 to recruit a regiment for the Confederate army, but gave over this project out of regard for his domestic status—he was married and had five children—and out of regard also for his aged father, three of whose sons were already in military service. In the summer of 1864 he went with a hastily organized body of citizens in pursuit of an irregular organization of hostile troops which had advanced into North Carolina from Tennessee. A skirmish ensued and he was shot. Brought home, he died of his wounds three days later. He was the third of his father's sons to be killed in battle within one year.

[E. M. and C. H. T. Avery, *Groton Avery Clan* (1912); K. P. Battle, *Hist. Univ. N. C.* (1907); S. A. Ashe, *Biog. Hist. N. C.*, VII (1908); J. P. Arthur, *Western N. C., a Hist.* (1914).]

J. D. W.

AWL, WILLIAM MACLAY (May 24, 1799–Nov. 19, 1876), alienist, was born in Harrisburg, Pa., the son of Samuel Awl, lawyer and senator, and Mary (Maclay) Awl. He began the study of medicine at the age of eighteen under a physician of his home town. Two years later he entered the medical department of the University of Pennsylvania, but did not graduate. He began to practise in Harrisburg, Pa.; tramped with a knapsack to Lancaster, Ohio, in 1826; practised his profession successively in several towns in that state; and finally took root in Columbus in 1833, to remain there for the rest of his life. In his early career he devoted himself to anatomy and surgery, gaining the reputation of being the first surgeon west of the Alleghanies to tie the left common carotid artery (*Lancaster Gazette,* Mar. 20, 1827; *Western Medical and Physical Journal,* October 1827). After reaching Columbus he gravitated toward the treatment of mental diseases. He had a knack in the management of the insane that was quite unusual. He was a tall, slender individual of fair complexion and blue eyes but afflicted with a spasmodic wry neck. Every few moments his head gave a sudden twist to one side. He boasted that if he could once fix his eyes on those of even the most violent lunatic he could control him without difficulty. Some of the scoffing onlookers believed that as he was unable to fix his own eyes he could not rivet the attention of the mentally unbalanced. But as a matter of fact he did; and he often appeared in court as an expert in cases of doubtful sanity. He was a member of the legislature with Marmaduke B. Wright, another prominent medical man of the time. They promoted a bill to place the insane of Ohio in the care of the state. The bill became law in 1835 and the "State Hospital" was opened in 1838 with Awl as superintendent. In the same year he became president of the Association of Superintendents of Asylums for the Insane of the United States and Canada, retaining the position until 1851. He drew the bill for the founding of the schools for the education of the blind and the feeble-minded in Ohio. In 1846 he joined with Daniel Drake and other leading members of the profession in establishing the Ohio State Medical Society. He was married on Jan. 28, 1830, to Rebecca Loughey.

[*Trans. Ohio State Medic. Soc.*, 1877, pp. 67–80; *Trans. Am. Medic. Ass.*, 1880, pp. 1009–11; Otto Juettner, *Daniel Drake and His Followers* (1909), pp. 176, 207, 434.]

W. L. B.

AXTELL, SAMUEL BEACH (Oct. 14, 1819–Aug. 6 or 7, 1891) lawyer, politician, jurist, was born on a farm in Franklin County, Ohio, the fourth child of Samuel Loree and Nancy (Sanders) Axtell. He graduated in 1844 from Western Reserve College (now Adelbert College of Western Reserve University), studied law, and was admitted to the Ohio bar. He married Adaline S. Williams of Summit County, Ohio, Sept. 20, 1840, and in 1843 moved to Mt. Clemens, Mich. In 1851, two years after the discovery of gold in California, he joined the great migration to the Pacific Coast. Not long after his arrival in California, he began a political career of some distinction. Upon the formation of Amador County in 1854 he became its first district attorney and held office for three successive terms. In 1860 he removed to San Francisco and six years later was elected to Congress on the Democratic ticket and served two terms (Fortieth and Forty-first Congresses). Axtell gave up his Democratic affiliation while in Congress and definitely aligned himself with the Republican party. For several years after his return from Washington, he was more or less active in California politics; and in 1874 President Grant appointed him governor of Utah. Because of the bitter controversy between Mormon and anti-Mormon factions in the territory, Axtell's tenure of office was brief and somewhat stormy. His failure to identify himself vigorously with the anti-Mormon party led to much criticism and is sometimes given as the reason for his failure to retain the governorship. He left this office in June 1875, but was appointed governor of New

Mexico almost immediately thereafter. In this new office Axtell again found numerous disturbances. A violent feud among the cattlemen was intensified by the presence in the territory of many desperate characters who had fled from near-by states, and had found a safe refuge in the thinly populated territory of New Mexico. It was these conditions that later gave rise to the "Lincoln County War." Axtell remained governor of New Mexico until 1878, when he was succeeded by Gen. Lew Wallace. Four years later he was made chief justice of the supreme court of New Mexico and served from 1882 till 1885. He exercised considerable influence upon the legal development of the Territory and sometimes in the discharge of his duty was called upon to face personal danger. During a criminal trial at Las Vegas a search of attendants and spectators revealed no less than forty-two revolvers which had been brought into the court-room (R. E. Twitchell, *Leading Facts of New Mexican History,* 1912, II, 419). In 1890 Axtell became chairman of the territorial Republican committee of New Mexico. He died at Morristown, N. J., the former home of his family.

[H. H. Bancroft, *Hist. of Utah* (1889); O. F. Whitney, *Hist. of Utah* (1892–1904); *Biog. Cong. Dir., 1774–1911* (1913); *Gen. Cat. of . . . Adelbert Coll. 1826–95; Appleton's Ann. Cyc. 1891; The Axtell Record,* ed. by E. S. Axtell (1886).] R. G. C.

AYALA, JUAN MANUEL DE (fl. 1775), Spanish navigator, appears just once in American history. In connection with the occupation by the Spanish of the Bay of Monterey (1770) as an outpost against the Russians, the Viceroy of New Spain, Antonio Maria Bucarely, by way of preparation for a land expedition under Juan Bautista de Anza [*q.v.*] gave orders (1774–75) for a naval exploration of the Bay of San Francisco. To this end he sent northward a ship, the *San Carlos,* charged with the duty of exploring the bay, but also carrying provisions for Monterey. Of this ship Juan Manuel de Ayala, replacing an officer who had just "gone mad," was made commander. The *San Carlos* set sail from the port of San Blas in March 1775. The ship reached Monterey June 27 and about July 24 left for the Bay of San Francisco. Ayala spent August and much of September in exploring the bay, and on Nov. 9 reported to the Viceroy that it was the best port he had seen northward from Cape Horn. He had found that the bay had a practicable entrance and not merely one port but many. He returned to Monterey, arriving Sept. 22, and reached San Blas on Nov. 6, having accomplished his task of exploration. Of the results the viceroy wrote that the place was well adapted to settlement. There was plenty of fresh water, fire-wood, and stone. The climate was cold but healthful, and free from the fogs which beset Monterey! In his survey of the bay through his two pilots, José Canizares and Juan Bautista Aguirre, Ayala makes mention of points familiar to us such as Angel Island, Round Bay (San Pablo), and Mission Bay.

[H. H. Bancroft, *Hist. of Cal.,* I (1884), ch. XI; I. B. Richman, *Cal. under Spain and Mexico* (1911), p. 109, with chart of the bay of San Francisco, by Ayala, pp. 110–11, and with a subsequent map of the bay pp. 112–13; and see p. 421 n. 66; C. E. Chapman, *Founding of Spanish Cal.* (1916), pp. 238–39, 243, 314, 326–27.] I. B. R.

AYCOCK, CHARLES BRANTLEY (Nov. 1, 1859–Apr. 4, 1912), governor of North Carolina, was born in Wayne County, N. C., the youngest of ten children of Benjamin Aycock and Serena (Hooks) Aycock. His early years were passed when opportunities for public education were meager almost everywhere in the South. In such private schools as were accessible he received preparation sufficient for admission to the state university, where he promptly attained a position of leadership. He was graduated in the class of 1880. A year later he married Varina (Davis) Woodard who died in 1890, and in 1891 he married Cora Woodard, a younger sister of his first wife. Immediately after graduation he began the practise of law in Goldsboro. In 1888 he canvassed his congressional district as presidential elector for Grover Cleveland and gained distinction as an orator and political debater. He was elector-at-large on the Cleveland ticket four years later and in 1893 received appointment as United States attorney for the eastern district of North Carolina, a post which he held until 1897. In the spring of 1900 he was unanimously nominated for governor by the Democratic state convention, and became the leader in a notable campaign to secure an amendment to the state constitution requiring literacy as one of the qualifications for suffrage. In August of that year he was elected by the largest majority that had ever been received by any candidate in the state. He served from 1901 to 1905, when he returned to Goldsboro to resume the practise of his profession, moving to Raleigh in 1909. In 1911 he yielded to a widespread demand and became a candidate for the Democratic nomination to the United States Senate, but he died before the campaign opened.

Aycock's greatest achievement was in the cause of popular education. In this he early became interested. As a boy he had seen his mother make her mark to a deed and the incident greatly impressed him with the failure of his state to provide schools. Educational conditions were inadequate when he reached manhood. Throughout the South the principle of public education had not yet been practically accepted. Economic desolation, racial conflicts, defective school arrangements, and the blight of partisan politics were among the obstacles which stood in the way of substantial social progress. Conflicts over the elimination of the negro vote were fierce and demoralizing. As candidate for governor on a platform of white supremacy and education, Aycock led the movement which took the ballot from the illiterate negro until he could be prepared by education and training for its proper use, thus committing the state to a program of universal education. When he was inaugurated governor in 1901 the annual school term of the state was less than four months, the monthly salary of teachers was only $25, the schoolhouses were inferior, and nearly a thousand districts had no schoolhouses. Most of the teachers were poorly trained. There was almost no professional supervision. One-fifth of the white population above ten years of age was illiterate. Aycock gave the prestige of his office to a movement to improve these conditions. He organized and led campaigns to arouse the people to the need for increased school funds for longer terms, increased salaries for teachers, better schoolhouses, improved school teaching and management, and other features of improved public educational work. Wide publicity was given to the state's educational needs, through the press, by meetings in court-houses, schoolhouses, churches, and wherever the people could be assembled. Educational rallies were held in each county. Public men of almost every calling followed Aycock's leadership and liberally gave their services as speakers and workers in behalf of better schools. Improvements appeared almost immediately. Larger legislative appropriations were made, increased local taxes were voted, the school term was lengthened, facilities for the training of teachers were provided, the salaries of teachers were established, illiteracy was gradually reduced, provision was made for the establishment of rural high schools (1907), all as a result of the movement inspired and led by Aycock.

[The chief source of information is Connor and Poe, *The Life and Speeches of Charles B. Aycock* (1912); a sketch of his life and an account of his educational influence in Connor, *The Program of Exercises for North Carolina Day* (State Dept. of Pub. Instruction, Raleigh, 1912); a sketch of his life to 1905 in *Biog. Hist. of N. C.*, ed. by Samuel A. Ashe (Greensboro, 1905), I, 76–82. His educational influence has been appraised by Edgar W. Knight, in *Pub. School Educ. in N. C.* (1916); by E. A. Alderman in a chapter in *Southern Pioneers*, ed. by H. W. Odum (1925); and by French Strother, in "N. C.'s Dreams Come True," *World's Work*, Nov. 1924. In the *Rept. of the N. C. Bar Ass.*, 1912, is an account of his legal career. His state papers are in the *Pub. Docs. of N. C.* (1901-5).]

E. W. K.

AYER, EDWARD EVERETT (Nov. 16, 1841–May 3, 1927), railway lumberman, bibliophile, collector, was born at Kenosha, Wis., the son of Elbridge Gerry and Mary (Titcomb) Ayer. The son of a pioneer of Wisconsin, as a boy he had but little schooling. At the age of eighteen he joined an overland expedition to California. He stopped in Nevada, where he found a job in a quartz mill, working twelve hours a day, but as soon as possible he went on to San Francisco, where he arrived with twenty-five cents in his pocket. Here he found work in a planing-mill, where he remained until the outbreak of the Civil War. He enlisted in the First California Cavalry, company E, and during the following three years served in Arizona and New Mexico, winning the rank of lieutenant. Mustered out in the summer of 1864, he returned to his home in Harvard, Ill., and with the gift from his father of a third interest in a general store he settled down and began his business career. On Sept. 7, 1865, he was married to Emma Augusta Burbank. Within a brief period he began buying timber, first for the use of the Chicago & Northwestern Railway, and later furnishing ties and telegraph poles for most of the western roads, including the Union Pacific, the Santa Fé, and the Mexican Central. About the year 1880 he came to Chicago, and in 1893, together with John B. Lord, formed the Ayer & Lord Tie Company.

While a soldier in Arizona he had chanced upon a copy of Prescott's *Conquest of Mexico.* The book fascinated him and opened to him a new world. He became a student of history; later, as wealth came to him, a collector of historical books and manuscripts, and still later a collector of antiquities of many kinds. He gradually built up one of the finest private libraries in the United States, particularly noteworthy for its source material on the native races of North America, the Hawaiian and the Philippine Islands. This library, containing more than 17,000 printed books, 4,000 manuscripts, and thousands of maps, prints, drawings, and photographs, he gave, in 1911, to the Newberry Library of Chicago, where it is separately housed and administered as the Edward E. Ayer Collection on the North American Indian.

Ayer was one of the founders of the Field Museum of Natural History of Chicago. He, probably more than any other person, aroused the enthusiasm of Marshall Field in the proposal to utilize the remarkable and choice collections left from the World's Fair in Chicago as the nucleus of a great museum, and it was he who, more than any one else, persuaded the merchant prince to give his millions for endowment and thus made the dream of a great natural-history museum in Chicago an actuality. Ayer was its first president, serving from 1893 to 1898, when he resigned, but remained a trustee to the end of his life. When the old Fine Arts Building of the World's Fair became the Field Museum he presented to it his large collection of Indian paraphernalia and his fine library of illustrated books on ornithology, besides many antiquities from Italy, Egypt, and other lands.

Ayer was a trustee of the Newberry Library from 1892 to 1911, a trustee of the Art Institute, president of the Archæological Society, a member of the State Historical Society of Wisconsin, the American Historical Association, the American Anthropological Association, the Chicago Historical Society, and numerous others. During many years, with his wife, he made extensive tours abroad, one of which—a journey in Northern Africa—was narrated by Mrs. Ayer in *A Motor Flight Through Algeria and Tunisia* (1911). In the midst of his other activities he found time to serve (1912–18) on the Board of Indian Commissioners, and in 1913 made a personal investigation of the Menominee Reservation in Wisconsin. Besides his home in Chicago, he maintained a summer home on Lake Geneva, Wis., and during the last fifteen years spent much time in California, where he was particularly identified with the effort to save the redwood forests. He died in Pasadena, Cal., and was buried in Harvard, Ill.

[*Who's Who in America,* 1916–17; Charles Moore, *Daniel H. Burnham, Architect, Planner of Cities* (1921), I, 123–24, 232, 236–39, II, 148; Donald Wilhelm, "A Lumberman Bibliophile," *Outlook,* Aug. 25, 1915; J. C. Bay, "Edward Everett Ayer," *Am. Collector,* July 1927; *Chicago Tribune, Chicago Evening Post,* May 4, 1927; additional information from Mrs. Ayer and from George B. Utley, Librarian of the Newberry Lib., Chicago.]

W. J. G.

AYER, FRANCIS WAYLAND (Feb. 4, 1848–Mar. 5, 1923), advertising agent, was the ninth in descent from John Ayer, who emigrated from England to Massachusetts in 1636 and became one of the founders of Haverhill. He was born in Lee, Mass., the son of Nathan Wheeler and Joanna B. (Wheeler) Ayer. His father, a graduate of Brown University, was admitted in 1852 to the Massachusetts bar, but preferred to make his living by school-teaching. Ayer passed his boyhood and youth in western New York, where he taught district schools for five years and attended the University of Rochester for another year. Early in 1869 he came to Philadelphia, where his father had opened a girls' school. He found employment as advertising solicitor for a religious paper, liked the work, and on Apr. 1, 1869, started business for himself under the firm name of N. W. Ayer & Son, the firm consisting of himself and his father, a book-keeper, and $250 in cash. The remaining fifty-four years of Ayer's life saw American advertising grow from a small, unintelligent, less than reputable craft into a well organized business that exerted a powerful influence on the national life. To that growth Ayer probably contributed as much as any one man. When he first took up the work, the advertising agent played a catch-as-catch-can game for his profits, making as much as he could out of both the advertiser and the publisher whose space he sold, and feeling little regard for the welfare of either. By his "open-contract" plan of operation Ayer made himself the responsible agent of the advertiser. Not only did he account to his clients for how their money was spent, but he spent their money so as to bring them the greatest possible returns. He developed trade-marks, slogans, pictorial displays, and all the other paraphernalia of the business as it is now conducted—a business that incidentally made possible the modern newspaper and popular magazine. A by-product of the firm's activities was the well-known *American Newspaper Annual and Directory*. Himself of irreproachable honor, he did much for the ethical standards of advertising men. As his business expanded, he showed excellent judgment in selecting employees who ultimately became his partners. Ayer's interests, however, extended into other fields. He was president of the Merchants' National Bank of Philadelphia from 1895 till 1910, when it was merged with the First National. Ordered by his doctor to spend as much time as possible in the open air, he developed a farm of 2,000 acres at Meredith, N. Y., imported pure bred Jersey cattle, and went into the butter, milk powder, and stock-raising business on a large scale. Fine dairy cattle from his farm were shipped to all parts of the United States, and even to South America, China, Japan, and India. His thirty-five years as a dairy farmer and stock breeder was in itself a distinguished career. A devout Baptist, he gave freely of his time, money, and judgment to the Baptist Church. For a half century he was superintendent of the Sunday-school of the North Baptist Church of Camden, N. J., where he made his home, was president of the New Jersey State Convention of Baptists for more than twenty-five years, was president of the Northern Baptist Convention, and held other important positions in the work of the church. He likewise gave generous support to the Y. M. C. A. He was married twice: on May 5, 1875, to Rhandena Gilman, who died Oct. 3, 1914, and on Apr. 21, 1919, to Martha K. Lawson.

[*Who's Who in America*, 1922–23; B. C. Forbes, "The Man Who Led Advertising Out of the Darkness," in *Forbes*, July 21, 1923; C. A. Barbour, "F. W. Ayer: An Appreciation," in the *Watchman Examiner*, Mar. 22, 1923; *F. Wayland Ayer 1848–1923* (privately printed, n. d.); *F. Wayland Ayer, Founder* (privately printed, 1923); J. W. Jordan, ed., *Encyc. of Pa. Biog.*, XIII (1921); statement by W. W. Fry, senior partner of N. W. Ayer & Son; G. P. Rowell, *Forty Years an Advertising Agent* (1906); *N. Y. Times*, Mar. 6, 17, 1923; *Vital Records of Lee, Mass., to the Year 1850* (1903).]

G. H. G.

AYER, JAMES COOK (May 5, 1818–July 3, 1878), physician, patent-medicine manufacturer, capitalist, was born at Ledyard, Conn., where his father, Frederick Ayer, owner of a saw and grist mill, died when the child was seven years old. The widow, born Persis Cook, moved to the adjacent town of Preston at which her father operated a small flannel-mill. In this factory James Cook Ayer had his first mechanical training. He also attended school at Preston and Norwich. Then he was sent to his uncle, James Cook, a manufacturer and one of the early mayors of the newly established city of Lowell, Mass. Under Cook's supervision the boy's studies were continued at the Lowell High School, whence he desired to enter college but met with opposition from his relatives. He accordingly entered the apothecary shop of Jacob Robbins and simultaneously began to study medicine with Dr. Samuel L. Dana, a local practitioner. This preparation enabled young Ayer to gain his M.D. degree from the University of Pennsylvania.

In 1841 Ayer bought the Robbins drugstore for $2,486.61 with money borrowed from his uncle which he repaid in three years. He devised a remedy, reputed to be beneficial for pulmonary troubles, which he placed on the market as "Ayer's Cherry Pectoral," a pioneer among the now multifarious American patent medicines. Discovering that advertising pays, the young physician-manufacturer pushed the sales of this first preparation, added sugar-coated pills (1854), extract of sarsaparilla (1855), an ague cure (1857), and "Ayer's Hair Vigor" (1869). A brother, Frederick Ayer, was admitted to partnership in 1855. The company at first occupied various rented quarters, but in 1857 it bought the property between Middle and Market Sts., Lowell, at which location the manufacture is still, in 1928, conducted. In his shop Ayer was master of every process. His versatility and mechanical ingenuity were remarkable; there was scarcely a machine in the entire establishment outside of the printing department which was not wholly invented by Dr. Ayer or improved by his changes and additions.

Ayer married, Nov. 14, 1850, Josephine Mellen Southwick. He bought an old stone tavern on Pawtucket St., a historic structure and landmark, which became the family residence, and which is now the Ayer Home for Young Women and Children, endowed by Mrs. Ayer and Frederick Fanning Ayer. A fast-growing bank account enabled Ayer to invest in textile enterprises, in several of which he became the largest shareholder. In their management he took little interest until 1857, when the collapse of companies at Lowell and Lawrence led to his investigating the conduct of their officers. An exposure was written by "Historicus" (Charles Cowley) from material furnished by Ayer. Feeling ran high, and a personal encounter ensued between Ayer and Richard S. Fay, treasurer of the Middlesex Company. In 1863 Ayer published *Some of the Usages and Abuses in the Management of Our Manufacturing Corporations*. He personally combined the Tremont and Suffolk Mills at Lowell, which, under a treasurer of his choice, entered on a period of prosperity. A feud concerning freight rates subsisting between Ayer and the Boston & Lowell Railroad led to his building the Lowell & Andover Railroad, connecting with the Boston & Maine and providing a parallel and competing service between Lowell and Boston. This was opened Dec. 1, 1874.

Ayer had meantime become interested in mining. In 1865 he was awarded patents for ore-reducing processes. He bought into the Lake Superior Ship Canal & Railroad & Iron Company, which he successfully financed. He acquired timber lands in Florida and erected on them saw-mills which he operated from Lowell. He made two European journeys, after the first of which he presented to his city, in 1866, the Victory monument now standing before the Lowell city hall. In his honor the town of Groton Junction, Mass., was renamed on Mar. 6, 1871. The Ayer town hall, dedicated in 1876, was a gift of the Ayer family to this town. A project to build an interoceanic canal over one of eight proposed routes located between Panama and Tehuantepec was cut short by Ayer's death, which occurred at Winchendon, Mass., July 3, 1878, as the result of many years of continuous overwork. After an elaborate funeral service at Huntington Hall, he was buried in the Lowell Cemetery, where a massive lion marks his grave. Mrs. Ayer, who outlived her husband many years, became a prominent figure in New York and Paris society.

[Charles Cowley, *Reminiscences of James C. Ayer and the Town of Ayer* (1879) is an authentic memorial biog.; F. W. Coburn, *Hist. of Lowell and Its People* (1920), has a sketch of Ayer with portr. and, in the narrative part of the hist., accounts of the controversy with the manufacturing corporations and of the dedication of the Victory monument. Ayer's home life is eulogistically described in *Josephine Mellen Ayer, a Memoir* (1900); his benefactions to the town of Ayer are set forth by G. J. Burns in vol. II of D. H. Hurd's *Hist. of Middlesex Co.* (1890).]

F. W. C.

AYLLON, LUCAS VASQUEZ DE (*c.* 1475–Oct. 18, 1526), Spanish explorer, a native of Toledo, was one of the group who came to Hispaniola (Santo Domingo) in 1502 with Gov. Nicolas de Ovando. In no sense a warrior, "never having donned a corselet or borne a sword to earn his wages therewith" (Oviedo, quoted in Lowery, p. 154), he is said to have had a talent for "conversation." He was of good character, intelligent, and well educated, and received from Ovando various offices. Made a judge of the supreme court of Hispaniola, he was granted 400 Indians in *repartimientos,* or fiefs, and was therefore considered rich. He was, however, not so rich as not to care to become richer. Countries of fabulous wealth, islands or a mainland, were said to lie to the west and north. So Ayllon formed a partnership with the clerk of the Audiencia of Hispaniola, and in 1520 sent a ship under Francisco Gordillo as captain and Alonzo Fernandez Sotil as pilot with orders to sail northward until they should reach land.

Near the island of Lucayoneque, Gordillo fell in with Pedro de Quexos, who had been sent out from Hispaniola by another judge, Juan Ortiz de Matienzo, in quest of Caribs to sell as slaves. The commanders decided to go north together on a search for land, and incidentally for slaves as well. In June 1521, according to Quexos, the two ships came upon land in latitude 33° 30′ at the mouth of a considerable river to which was given the name of San Juan Bautista (the Peedee? J. G. Johnson, *Georgia Historical Quarterly,* 1923, p. 340, n. 5). The Indians are thought to have called the country Chicora. On June 30, 1521, Gordillo and Quexos took possession of the newly discovered country and by help of a native guide made exploration into the interior. Gordillo, contrary to instructions from Ayllon, lured to his ship 150 Indians and with them sailed for Hispaniola. On his return he was brought before a commission under Diego Columbus which freed the captives and ordered their return to their people.

Ayllon, soon after this, proceeded to Spain to secure his discovery by royal grant. With him he took a native of the new country who had been baptized as "Francisco Chicora" and who had learned to speak Spanish. In his own country, said Chicora, there dwelt a race of men with long flexible tails which obliged them to pierce holes in the seats where they wished to sit down. He said, too, that the region was one of great treasures, with numerous islands of which the royal grant mentions the names of nineteen. On June 12, 1523, Emperor Charles V issued a decree conferring upon Ayllon and his descendants the titles of *adelantado* and governor. By this decree Ayllon was empowered to navigate the coast for 800 leagues in vessels furnished at his own cost. In particular he was to search for an interoceanic strait leading to the Spice Islands. He was required to start on his expedition the following year, 1524, and was allowed three years from the day his fleet left Hispaniola in which to complete it.

His grant secured, Ayllon returned to the West Indies with the intention of following up his undertaking. He was, however, embarrassed by a *residencia* (a public and official investigation of his conduct) and by the non-appearance of vessels from Spain bringing the armament for his ships. While thus delayed, he, in 1525, sent to the new land two ships under Pedro de Quexos, probably Matienzo's former pilot. Quexos explored the coast for 250 leagues, taking possession in the King's name and returning the same year to Hispaniola. He brought back with him some gold and silver and a few pearls. In June or July 1526, Ayllon was himself able to go to the new land and begin the planting of his colony. He sailed from La Plata in Hispaniola with a fleet of "three large vessels" and some lesser ones. He took with him from the West Indies five or six hundred men and women and eighty or ninety horses in addition to the necessary outfit for the colony. The pilot Quexos again accompanied him. Among the colonists were three Dominican friars, one of whom, Fr. Antonio Montesino, became world famous as first to preach against the enslavement of the natives. Ayllon landed at the mouth of a river (33° 40′) which one of his pilots named the Jordan (the Cape Fear? J. G. Johnson, p. 344; Lowery, p. 165). On entering the river Ayllon lost a ship but saved the crew. Meanwhile some of his captains explored the interior, while others followed up the coast searching for a strait. Francisco Chicora, who was with the expedition, deserted and returned to his people.

Thereupon Ayllon turned southwestward for about 115 miles until he came to a great river (Gualdape) which Lowery (p. 166) thinks may have been the Peedee, but which Johnson is confident was the Santee. John Gilmary Shea (Winsor, p. 241), thinking Ayllon's course to have been northward, believed the Gualdape to be the James (Virginia), as does Edward Channing (p. 61); while Henry Harrisse (*The Discovery of North America*, 1892, p. 213) identifies it with the Cape Fear River between Wilmington and Smithville. On the Gualdape, in any event (above 33°), was begun the settlement of San Miguel de Gualdape. The region was flat and marshy and the settlement did not prosper. Many of the colonists sickened and died. Ayllon himself died on St. Luke's Day, 1526. His survivors, 150 in number, placed his body on a tender and set sail for Hispaniola; but the boat foundered and the ocean became his sepulchre, "where," observes Oviedo, "have been and shall be put other captains and governors" (Lowery, p. 168).

[Oviedo, Herrera, Navarrete, and in gen. the sources in Spanish cited by W. Lowery, *Spanish Settlements in the U. S.*, 1513–61 (1901), esp. Appendix H; J. G. Shea, "Ancient Florida," in Justin Winsor, *Narr. and Crit. Hist. of America* (1886), II, ch. IV; E. G. Bourne, *Spain in America* (1904), ch. X; Edward Channing, *Hist. of the U. S.* (1905), I, ch. III; sketch map of the Tierra of Ayllon, Lowery, *supra*, ch. II.]
I. B. R.

AYLWIN, JOHN CUSHING (*c.* 1780–Jan. 28, 1813), naval officer, the son of Thomas Aylwin, a merchant of Boston, and Lucy (Cushing) Aylwin, a sister of William Cushing, justice of the Supreme Court of the United States, was born in Quebec, whither his parents had removed at the time of the siege of Boston. Receiving an excellent education, the lad, who manifested a love for the sea, was rated on board a frigate in the British navy; but the odious system of impressment pursued by England at that time producing in him a strong aversion, he took service aboard a vessel engaged in the London trade, with the stipulation that he should enjoy six months' tuition at a naval academy. This promise, however, was not kept, and young Aylwin was forced to continue in the West Indian trade. His progress in seamanship was so rapid that he was promoted to be mate of his ship at the age of fifteen. Some dispute having arisen between him and the captain, the latter connived at the kidnapping of the youth by a press-gang. Aylwin was forced to serve aboard a gun-brig, where every artifice was employed to cause him to enter the British navy voluntarily. The lad, however, steadfastly refused, with the result that he continued his enforced service in the navy for six years. It was only when his health temporarily declined and his usefulness consequently diminished that he was allowed his freedom, when he immediately rejoined his parents in Boston, to which they had meanwhile returned from Canada. Recovering his health, he served as captain of several merchant ships out of Boston, and, at the outbreak of war in 1812, he was appointed sailing-master with the rank of lieutenant of the frigate *Constitution*, under Capt. Hull, in which capacity he earned a large share of the credit for this famous vessel's escape from the powerful British fleet, after a chase of sixty hours. Continuing his service as sailing-master in the *Constitution* under Capt. Bainbridge, he took a prominent part in the battle which resulted in the capture of the British frigate *Guerrière*, and heroically ended his career and his life during the fight of the *Constitution* with the *Java*, living long enough to witness the latter's capture. Bainbridge gave the following account of Aylwin's share in these events: "In the action with the *Guerrière* he stood on an elevated situation, by the side of his brave comrades, Morris and Bush, at the time the two vessels came in contact, and was wounded in the left shoulder with a musket ball. . . . In the late action [with the *Java*] he commanded the forecastle division, and his bravery and marked coolness throughout the contest gained him the admiration of his commander, and all who had an opportunity of witnessing him. When boarders were called to repel boarders, he mounted the quarter-deck hammock cloths, and, in the act of firing his pistols at the enemy, received a ball through the same shoulder. Notwithstanding the serious nature of his wound, he continued at his post until the enemy had struck; and even then did not make known his situation until all the wounded had been dressed. His zeal and courage did not forsake him in his last moments, for, a few days after the action, although laboring under considerable debility and the most excruciating pain, he repaired to quarters, when an engagement was expected with a ship. . . . He bore his pain with great and unusual fortitude, and expired without a groan."

[The best account of Aylwin's short but eventful life is his biog. in Isaac Bailey's *Am. Naval Biog.* (1815), pp. 242–47.]
E. B.

AYRES, ANNE (Jan. 3, 1816–Feb. 9, 1896), original member of the Sisterhood of the Holy Communion, was the first woman in this country to become a Protestant Sister. For many years she was prominently associated with the philanthropic work of Dr. William Augustus Muhlenberg [*q.v.*], rector of the Church of the Holy Communion, New York. At her death she left the request that all her journals and writings which would tend to perpetuate her memory be destroyed, in order that her work might be known only as a part of Dr. Muhlenberg's.

Born and educated in London, England, she came to New York with her father, Robert

Ayres, when she was twenty years old. There she secured pupils from families of social prominence, among whom was a niece of Dr. Muhlenberg. Upon hearing him preach a sermon on "Jephtha's Vow," in the chapel of St. Paul's College, College Point, N. Y., she was moved to devote her life to religious service, and was by him consecrated a Sister of the Holy Communion on All Saints' Day, 1845. At this time no Protestant orders of the kind existed, either in this country or in England. Other women joined her later, and the sisterhood was formally organized in 1852. Sister Anne conducted a parish school and worked among the poor. During the epidemic of 1849, she rendered valuable aid in the cholera hospitals. She conducted an infirmary in the rear-tenement of an alley near the church, which was the real beginning of St. Luke's Hospital, also one of Dr. Muhlenberg's projects. The patients were moved from the tenement to the memorial home of the Sisterhood, given by Mr. and Mrs. John H. Swift in 1853, and in 1858, from there to St. Luke's, where Sister Anne and her associates were put in charge of the nursing. Here she died thirty-eight years later. During her life of modest and unselfish ministry, she found time to write *Evangelical Sisterhoods, In Two Letters to a Friend* (1867), edited by W. A. Muhlenberg, and *The Life and Work of William Augustus Muhlenberg,* a carefully prepared and interesting biography, which first appeared in 1880 and has passed through several editions.

[Considerable information about Sister Anne and her work may be gleaned from her life of Dr. Muhlenberg. See also Henry C. Potter, *Sisterhoods and Deaconesses* (1873); *The Living Church,* Feb. 22, 1896; and obit. notice in the *N. Y. Herald,* Feb. 12, 1896.]
H. E. S.

AYRES, BROWN (May 25, 1856–Jan. 28, 1919), college president, was born in Memphis, Tenn., the son of Samuel W. and Elizabeth (Cook) Ayres. After attending private schools in Memphis and New Orleans, he studied engineering at Washington and Lee University in Virginia, and graduated (1878) at Stevens Institute of Technology. He was one of the remarkable group of Fellows who went to Johns Hopkins in the later 'seventies, the attraction for him being the well-known physicist, Prof. Rowland. In 1880 he was elected professor of physics and electrical engineering at Tulane University, and twenty years later professor of physics and astronomy. As dean of the College of Technology from its organization in 1894 till 1900 he displayed such administrative ability that he was elected dean of the academic department and vice-chairman of the faculty, and in 1904 acting president of the university.

He served as president of the Southern Association of Schools and Colleges (1904–05) and as a member of the faculty of the first large summer school in the South, at the University of Tennessee. He was recognized as the logical successor of Charles W. Dabney when the latter resigned the presidency of the University of Tennessee in 1904. Ayres held this position until his death, Jan. 28, 1919. Like most state universities in the South, the university had been only nominally a state institution; it had only a small faculty and student body and almost no income from appropriations for maintenance or buildings. Ayres began at once to arouse the people of the state to their duty and obligations. In 1917 a conference was called of leading citizens to put before the legislature a program of expansion. The result was that in that year a half-mill tax was levied for the maintenance of the university and a million-dollar bond issue was made for buildings. Tennessee was thus the first state in the South to put its university upon a financial basis that made unnecessary many special appropriations. With the agricultural, engineering, law, and academic departments at Knoxville, the medical and dental departments at Memphis, and demonstration and extension departments at other points in the state, plans were made by Ayres that resulted in a progressive institution, the head of the educational system in reality as well as in name. While many had a part in the work of reorganization, to Ayres must be given the credit for outlining the plans and seeing the vision. He was far removed from the emotional agitator or crusader, but he appealed to reasonable men by his scientific method, practical sense, and zeal for higher education. His influence was not confined to Tennessee. He was president of the national Association of State Universities (1909–10) and vice-president of the Association of Land Grant Colleges the year of his death.

[*Who's Who in America,* 1918–19; *Knoxville Jour. & Tribune,* Jan. 29, 30, 31, 1919; additional information in an unpublished paper prepared by the Trustees of the Univ. of Tenn.]
E. M—s.

AYRES, ROMEYN BECK (Dec. 20, 1825–Dec. 4, 1888), Union soldier, was born in Montgomery County, N. Y., the son of a country physician, who took a strong interest in the education of his sons. That young Ayres was regarded as an authority on Latin by his classmates at the Military Academy, does not, of course, indicate any great attainments, but does show that at least some part of what he had learned clung to him in the unclassical atmosphere of West Point. Graduating in 1847, about the middle of his class, he was commissioned in the artillery and sent to Mexico, but was too late to take part in any of the active operations of the war. He served at many posts, from Maine to California, on routine duties, and was promoted to captain just at the outbreak of the Civil War. He commanded a battery at the first battle of Bull Run, and was with the Army of the Potomac from its organization until the end of the war. As chief of artillery of a division and later of a corps, he served in the Peninsular campaign, at Antietam and at Fredericksburg. Then and for many years after, the artillery was regarded as a kind of necessary appendage to the real army, and it was the usual thing for the chief of artillery of a large command to be, like Ayres, only a captain. Even the chief of artillery of the Army of the Potomac never ranked higher than brigadier-general. So when Ayres was appointed brigadier-general of volunteers (Nov. 29, 1862), he was soon removed from artillery duties and assigned to the command of a brigade, as being an employment suitable to his rank. As a brigade and division commander in the 5th corps, he fought at Chancellorsville, Gettysburg, the Wilderness, Spottsylvania, Petersburg, and Five Forks. He was repeatedly brevetted for gallantry in action and for meritorious services, and his appontment as major-general of volunteers was under consideration when the war ended. His muster out of the volunteer service left him once more a captain of artillery, but on the reorganization of the army in 1866 he was appointed lieutenant-colonel. He was promoted to the colonelcy of the 2nd Artillery in 1879, and died at Fort Hamilton, N. Y., while still in active service. Ayres was a tall man, of distinguished presence, erect and soldierly. Like a good many military men of his type, he was somewhat vain of his appearance and meticulous as to dress. He was by no means a mere show soldier, however, but an energetic, determined, hard-fighting commander. The rank he attained and the responsibilities he carried all came to him as the result of faithful and efficient service.

[G. W. Cullum, *Biog. Reg.* (3rd ed. 1891), II, 325–29; *Battles and Leaders of the Civil War* (1887–88), II, 259; *Official Records*, ser. I, vols. I, XI (pts. 1, 2), XIX (pt. 1), XXI, XXV (pts. 1, 2), XXVII (pts. 1, 3), XXIX (pts. 1, 2), XXXIII, XXXVI (pts. 1, 2, 3), XL (pts. 1, 2, 3), XLII (pts. 1, 2, 3), XLVI (pts. 1, 2, 3), LI (pt. 1).]

T. M. S.

AZARIAS, BROTHER (June 29, 1847–Aug. 20, 1893), educator, author, was born near Killenaule, County Tipperary, Ireland, the eldest son of Thomas and Margaret (Ryan) Mullany. His baptismal name was Patrick Francis. The family emigrated to Deerfield, N. Y., in 1851, leaving Patrick behind for a few years, owing to his delicate health. After his arrival in the United States he attended the Union School of Deerfield, and later, the Christian Brothers' Academy of Utica. There he fell under the magnetic influence of the late Brother Justin, and at the age of fifteen, desiring to become a religious and a teacher, he successfully applied for admission to the Brothers of the Christian Schools, a society of lay religious educators, founded in France in 1861 by Saint John Baptist De La Salle, and conducting schools in most parts of the world. Brother Azarias was further educated in the training schools and academies of the society. Subsequently he taught in Albany, New York, and Philadelphia. His natural abilities and devotion to study are evidenced by his call at the age of nineteen to the professorship of mathematics and literature at Rock Hill College, Ellicott City, Md. Here he laid under contribution the ready and convenient library resources of Washington and Baltimore, pursued literary and philosophical studies, cultivated the acquaintance of neighboring scholars, taught his classes, lectured occasionally before learned societies, and began his career of independent authorship. In 1877, somewhat broken in health, he went to Europe for rest and recuperation, but the occasion gave him his first opportunity to visit the great libraries of the Old World and so to lay the foundation for extensive reading and research which he was to use to full advantage some ten years later. In 1879, he was named to the presidency of Rock Hill College, a position that he held with marked success till 1886, when, his constitution shattered by sickness and intense literary work, he again sought health in Europe. On his return to the United States, somewhat restored, he went to De La Salle Institute, New York City, and continued to occupy himself partly in teaching, but mainly in collating and extending the materials gathered abroad. An attack of pneumonia, following a series of lectures on education at the Catholic Summer School, Plattsburg, N. Y., of which he was one of the founders, caused his death.

Singularly modest and almost shy, Brother Azarias was, however, an inspiring teacher and a fascinating lecturer. A peculiar merit of his work may be found in his presentation of the literary, educational, and philosophical claims of the Roman Catholic Church in a style free from the bitterness of controversy, and appealing to non-Catholics and Catholics alike. His chief works are: *An Essay Contributing to a Philosophy of Literature* (1874); *The Development of Old English Thought* (1879); *Aristotle and the Christian Church* (1888); *Books and*

Reading (1890); *Phases of Thought and Criticism* (1892); *Essays Educational, Essays Philosophical, Essays Miscellaneous* (1896), gathered and published after his death.

[J. T. Smith, *Brother Azarias* (1897); *Addresses and Letters Read at the Memorial Meeting in Honor of Brother Azarias* (1894); J. A. Mooney, *Memoir of Brother Azarias* (1901).] B. E.

BABBITT, BENJAMIN TALBOT (1809–Oct. 20, 1889), inventor, manufacturer, was born at Westmoreland, Oneida County, N. Y. His father, Nathaniel Babbitt, a farmer and blacksmith, had migrated as a young man from Connecticut and had married Betsey Holman, the daughter of another Connecticut immigrant. Oneida County in the first decade of the past century represented the newest frontier, and Benjamin's boyhood was characterized by a minimum of educational advantages and a maximum of labor. Arduous work on the farm and in the blacksmith shop, relieved by hunting and trapping expeditions, laid the foundations of a strong physique and at the same time whetted the appetite of the boy for larger opportunities. At the age of eighteen he left the farm, but so valuable had he become to his father that the parental objections were overcome only by an agreement whereby the boy consented to pay his father $500 annually for five years. This money he obtained by hiring out in the winter as a lumberman, and in the summer as a mechanic.

Babbitt was a mechanical genius and intensely eager to learn. His application made him, within three years, an expert wheelwright, steam-pipe fitter, file maker, blacksmith, and general mechanic. He persuaded some of his fellow workmen to rise an hour earlier so that they might quit work an hour sooner two days a week, and induced a professor from Hamilton College at Clinton, N. Y., to come to Utica on those days and conduct a class in chemistry and physics. This was Babbitt's introduction to chemistry. By the time he was twenty-two he had acquired not only a foundation knowledge of mechanics, but enough money to establish a machine-shop at Little Falls. Here he labored for twelve years manufacturing pumps, engines, and various kinds of farm machinery. Among his products at this time was one of the first workable mowing machines in this country. After his mill had been twice destroyed by floods, Babbitt left for New York, leaving accounts amounting to $5,000, which owing to the dishonesty of his agent he never received.

Arriving in New York in 1843, he turned his restless brain for a moment from mechanics to chemistry, developed an original and cheaper process of making salaratus, put it on the market in convenient packages, and eventually became the dominant figure in the manufacture of salaratus. He soon added a yeast baking-powder, one of the earliest baking-powders made, a soap powder, and various brands of soap. He also manufactured soda and potash. "Babbitt's Best Soap" became a household word, and his soap business brought him an immense fortune. His interest in soap manufacture never flagged; he was taking out patents in this field as late as 1886, and practically all of the apparatus in his factories was of his own invention. Improved methods of putting up caustic alkali, extracting glycerine, bleaching palm-oil, and boiling soap are among the inventions to his credit. His early factory was in New York, but the plant was later moved to New Jersey.

Babbitt's interests were as diverse as his brain was ingenious. Between 1842 and 1889, 108 patents were issued to him for his own inventions, and these covered almost every conceivable field. His first patent (Oct. 7, 1842) was for a pump and fire engine, his second (1846) for a brush-trimming machine, his third for a car ventilator. Like other inventors and manufacturers, he turned his attention during the Civil War to ordnance and armor-plates, and this interest remained with him all his life, one of his latest patents being an improvement in ordnance. He patented an ordnance projector and a mould for casting gun-barrels, and spent much time in designing an "armoured fighting craft with steam controlled steering gear and the vitals protected by coal bunkers" with a "screw at the bow and stern so that the vessel might be propelled in either direction or turned almost in the center" (Leonard, p. 872). After the war Babbitt became absorbed in the steam-engine. He was granted six patents for the use of steam, and eight for new types of steam-boilers. In the same field he patented an automatic boiler feeder, an apparatus for cleaning a steam-generator, a rotary engine, and a balance-valve. He also experimented on gas-engines. In his later life he became interested in the use and control of air, inventing an air-pump, an air compressor, wind motors, pneumatic propulsion of various types, and air-blasts for forges. He likewise turned his attention to new methods for steering and propelling vessels, for which he obtained several patents. In 1882 he patented a plan for an elevated railroad structure over the Erie Canal, upon which engines could draw the canal boats.

Unlike many inventive geniuses, Babbitt possessed an interesting personality. With curly hair, broad face, large features, and ready smile, he left an impression of high intelligence and a capacity for human enjoyment and friendship. A close friend of P. T. Barnum, he has often been compared with him as an advertising genius. He was one of the first to advertise by giving his products away, and to adopt the custom of advertising on stage curtains. He also knew how to obtain much free advertising; his six immense kettles for boiling soap, with an aggregate capacity of 3,500,000 pounds and requiring $216,000 worth of materials to fill them, were long one of the sights of New York. Babbitt was the typical ingenious Yankee carried to the *n*th degree—a jack of all trades and a master of most. He was married to Rebecca McDuffie, by whom he had two daughters.

[W. B. Browne, *The Babbitt Family Hist., 1643–1900* (1912); J. W. Leonard, *Hist. of the City of New York 1609–1909* (1910), pp. 869–72; *N.Y. Tribune* and *N.Y. Times,* Oct. 21, 1889.]

H. U. F.

BABBITT, ISAAC (July 26, 1799–May 26, 1862), inventor, son of Zeba and Bathsheba (Luscombe) Babbitt, was descended from Edward Bobet, who was the founder of the Babbitt family in America and who joined the Plymouth colony in 1643. Babbitt's branch of the family settled in Taunton, Mass., where he was born. He had very little schooling but by the time he was twenty-four years old he was a full-fledged goldsmith. About this time britannia ware was being imported into the United States from England, so Babbitt with his knowledge of alloys began experimenting with the idea of manufacturing britannia ware to compete with the imported metal. His first products were marketed in 1824 and were the first of the kind produced in the United States. After satisfying himself that he could make an alloy and cast it, he entered into partnership with a friend, William Crossman. They made and sold on a small scale such articles as inkstands, cups, and shaving-boxes, and received awards from numerous exhibitions for their products. In 1827 they had a brick factory built in Taunton, and two apprentices, Henry G. Reed and Charles Barton, were employed. Successful competition with imported britannia ware was apparently short-lived, for in a few years Babbitt and Crossman sold their holdings to their apprentices. The latter continued the manufacture of britannia ware, later substituting silverware, and Reed & Barton silver plate has been made and sold continuously since that time.

Following this venture, Babbitt went to Boston in 1834 and obtained employment as superintendent of the South Boston Iron Works, sometimes known as Alger's Foundry and Ordnance Works. Here he succeeded in making the first brass cannon ever cast in the United States. It was also while with this company that Babbitt invented a journal-box and received United States patent No. 1,252 for it on July 17, 1839. The specifications for this patent contained an incidental suggestion that a good lining for the box to serve as the bearing surface for a journal or an axle could be had by melting up fifty parts of tin, five of antimony, and one of copper. This alloy was found subsequently to be so satisfactory and was used so extensively that Babbitt's name became and has continued to be associated with it. The popularity and great utility of this alloy so overshadowed the journal-box invention that the latter was all but forgotten and there developed the general popular belief that Babbitt had invented a bearing-metal, something that was never in his mind. On May 15, 1840, he received British patent No. 9,724 for his journal-box, and in 1847 the idea was patented in Russia. Probably his largest award for the invention was that of $20,000, granted by Congress in 1842. The Secretary of the Navy in that year made a tentative agreement with Babbitt to purchase for $20,000 the rights to use his patented journal-box and "anti-attrition" metal in the United States navy. The agreement, together with letters of recommendation as to the value of the idea, including one from the prominent engineer, John Ericsson, was presented to Congress by Secretary Upshur during the third session of the Twenty-seventh Congress, and appears in *House Executive Document No. 163.* Just how long Babbitt continued with the Alger Foundry in the manufacture of journal-boxes is not known. Toward the close of his career he became associated with a relative, B. T. Babbitt [*q.v.*] in the manufacture of soap. He was twice married: first to Sally Leonard, who gave birth to five children who all died in infancy and who herself died nine years after marriage; and second, to Eliza Barney, who bore him three daughters and a son. Overwork and the overstraining of an unusual brain eventually necessitated his commitment to the McLean Asylum, at Somerville, Mass., where he died in his sixty-third year.

[Wm. Bradford Browne, *The Babbitt Family Hist., 1643–1900* (1912); Edward W. Byrn, *Progress of Invention in the Nineteenth Cent.* (1900); *U. S. Pat. Office Recs.*]

C. W. M.

BABCOCK, GEORGE HERMAN (June 17, 1832–Dec. 16, 1893), engineer, inventor, was the son of Asher M. and Mary E. (Stillman) Babcock. He came by his mechanical aptitude naturally from both sides of the family, his father being a well-known mechanic and inventor, and his mother coming from a family of mechanics. He was born at Unadilla Forks near Otsego, N. Y., but moved to Westerly, R. I., when he was twelve. He there became the friend of his future partner, Stephen Wilcox. He did not at once take up engineering but devoted himself to daguerreotypy and newspaper work, which last in connection with job printing was his vocation until 1854. Then followed the invention, with his father, of the first polychromatic printing-press, which was ahead of its time, and of a job printing-press which was commercially successful and is still manufactured. In 1860, Babcock moved to Brooklyn, N. Y., where he was engaged for several years in the office of T. D. Stetson, patent solicitor. In the evenings he gave instruction in drawing at Cooper Institute, N. Y. He was employed for a time at the Mystic Iron Works and then became chief draftsman of the Hope Iron Works at Providence, R. I. Here he fell in again with Wilcox, and they invented and brought out the Babcock and Wilcox steam-engine, one of the early automatic cut-off engines of excellent design and much utility. It was manufactured in Providence and Baltimore until the expiration of the early Corliss patents flooded the market with cheap engines with which the Babcock and Wilcox engine could not compete in price. During this association at Providence, the two inventors formed a partnership and secured a patent for a boiler. Wilcox had patented a safety water-tube boiler in 1856, and the joint patent of 1867 is based, in principle, on the earlier one. The primary idea of the boiler was the ability to withstand high pressures and safety against disastrous explosion, which made possible a far more powerful machine than had previously been used. In 1868 the partners moved to New York to carry on the manufacture of the boiler. They had other manufacturing interests also, but by 1878 the boiler business took all their time, and in 1881 the firm was incorporated, with Babcock as president. He appears to have devoted himself mainly to the exploitation of the merits of the boiler by lectures at technical institutes and colleges, attendance at technical societies, and the business end of affairs, Wilcox giving his special attention to design, invention, manufacture, and experiment. The boilers were built, at first, at Elizabethport, N. J., and later at the specially designed plant at Bayonne, N. J.

Babcock was a devoutly religious man, a member of the Seventh-Day Baptists, to whose interests he devoted much of his time and means. He was president of the board of trustees of Alfred University, to which he contributed liberally during his lifetime and by bequest. He was a resident for many years of Plainfield, N. J., and was active in civic affairs, being president of the Board of Education and of the Public Library. He was president of the American Society of Mechanical Engineers for 1887, and was a constant contributor to its proceedings. His versatility is shown by his acquiring a working acquaintance with French when he was nearly sixty. He was a man of commanding presence and attractive personality, a good friend and a considerate employer. He was married four times.

[*Trans. Am. Soc. Mech. Engineers,* vol. XV (1894); obituaries in *N.Y. Tribune, N.Y. Herald,* Dec. 18, 1893; additional information from relatives.] W. M. M.

BABCOCK, JAMES FRANCIS (Feb. 23, 1844–July 19, 1897), chemist, born in Boston, was the son of Archibald D. and Fannie (Richards) Babcock, and a direct descendant of early Puritan settlers (Stephen Babcock, *Babcock Genealogy,* 1903, p. 512). He attended the English High School and was a student in the Lawrence Scientific School at Harvard in 1860–61. He then established a private office and laboratory in his native city. He became so well known as a chemical analyst and investigator that he was frequently called upon for expert testimony in criminal cases, and was often consulted in food investigations and patent suits. Later (1869–74) he served as professor of medical chemistry in the Massachusetts College of Pharmacy; then for six years in a similar position at Boston University. During this latter period his work on alcoholic beverages was begun and it was this work as state assayer of liquors (1875–85), together with his later attention to the milk problem of Boston, which made him celebrated as a chemist. Babcock is credited with having brought about the introduction into the Massachusetts Statutes of the "three per cent limit" as defining an intoxicating liquor. As city inspector of milk he established rigid enforcement of the laws against the adulteration of milk and other dairy products; his methods finding favor in other cities. That he possessed some versatility is shown by the fact that he was a skilful analyst, a recognized investigator, a public lecturer, and the inventor of the Babcock fire-extinguisher. With the exception of official reports concerning pure foods and sanitation he wrote only an article, "Blood Stains," which appeared in Hamilton's *Legal Medicine,* and a brochure entitled *Laboratory Talks on Infant Foods* (1896). His interest in medicines and drugs appears to have been continuous, for in later life (1894) we find him president of the

Druggists' Association of Boston. He was twice married: on Mar. 28, 1869, to Mary P. Crosby of Boston, who died in 1890; and on Aug 24, 1892, to Marion B. Alden, also of Boston.

[*Hist. Reg. Boston Univ.* (1891), p. 25; *Am. Druggist and Pharmaceut. Rec.*, Aug. 10, 1897, p. 86; *Boston Morning Jour.*, July 21, 1897.] H. C.

BABCOCK, JAMES WOODS (Aug. 11, 1856–Mar. 3, 1922), psychiatrist, was born in Chester, S. C., the son of Dr. Sidney E. Babcock and Margaret (Woods) Babcock. His father was a surgeon in the Confederate army and a practitioner of medicine in Chester before and after the Civil War. Babcock was educated at Phillips Academy, Exeter, N. H., and Harvard College, where he was graduated in 1882. Four years later he received his M.D. degree from the Harvard Medical School. After his graduation he was appointed assistant physician to the McLean Hospital, then located in Somerville, Mass., where he remained from 1887 to 1891. In the latter year he accepted the superintendency of the State Lunatic Asylum, Columbia, S. C., a position which he held until 1914. He was professor of mental diseases at the South Carolina Medical College from 1915 until his death. During his residence in the South Carolina State Hospital for the Insane, as it was later called, Babcock did most of his important work. He not only made his institution one of the best in the country, but also investigated or stimulated investigation in many important problems of psychiatry and of the care of the insane. In 1894, in a timely paper, he called attention to the prevalence of tuberculosis in hospitals for the insane and outlined a sound scheme for prevention of this disease (*American Journal of Insanity*, 1894–95, LI, 182). The next year he made a plea, which had far-reaching effects, for the better care of the colored insane (*Alienist and Neurologist*, 1895, XVI, 423). His most important work, however, was with pellagra. Patients with pellagra were observed at his hospital in 1907, and the next year Babcock and others presented to the South Carolina State Board of Health a report on nine cases and a careful review of the literature of the subject, the first comprehensive account of the disease to be published in this country (*Journal of the South Carolina Medical Association*, 1908, IV, 64). In 1910, he collaborated with Dr. C. H. Lavinder in a translation into English of Dr. A. Marie's *La Pellagre*, a book which was used extensively in this country and, combined with Lavinder's later reports for the Public Health and Marine Hospital Service, served to establish the disease here as a clinical entity. Babcock founded the National Association for the Study of Pellagra and through this organization vigorously conducted a fight against this malady, especially in the southern states.

In 1892 he married Katharine Guion of Lincolnton, N. C., a graduate of the Massachusetts General Hospital Training School for Nurses, by whom he had three daughters. He was a great lover of literature and old books. In addition, he made a remarkable collection of antique furniture, which was much admired by his numerous friends from both the North and the South, who often enjoyed the hospitality of his home. He died Mar. 3, 1922, of heart disease.

[The principal sources of information about Babcock's life are to be found in the obit. notices in the *Jour. S. C. Medic. Ass.* (1922), XVIII, 338 (by J. H. Taylor), and the *Am. Jour. of Psychiat.*, 1921–22, I, 709 (by Herbert B. Howard). An important estimation of the value of his work on pellagra appeared in the *Rivista Pellagrologica Italiana*, Apr. 1922; see also the *Trans. Nat. Ass. for the Study of Pellagra*, 1909 and 1912.] H. R. V.

BABCOCK, JOSEPH WEEKS (Mar. 6, 1850–Apr. 27, 1909), congressman, was the grandson of Joseph Weeks of Massachusetts, who migrated to Vermont, sat for that state in the Twenty-fourth and Twenty-fifth Congresses, and became the father of Mahala Weeks, who married Ebenezer Wright Babcock. Joseph was born in Swanton, Vt., but at the age of five he was taken to Iowa, where his education was irregular. He was successful in business. After 1872 he was continuously interested in lumber, as employee, partner, and owner; first, at Dubuque, Ia., and later at Necedah, Wis., where the rich forests of the upper valley of the Wisconsin River were yielding great rewards to the pioneer lumbermen. In 1896 his firm is said to have cut 25,000,000 feet of lumber. He served for two terms in the Wisconsin Assembly, during the political upset of 1890, which broke the old Republican control of the state. In the new alignment for the election of 1892 (for the Republicans had carried only one of the nine congressional districts of the state in 1890), Babcock secured nomination and election to Congress from the third Wisconsin district; and in Congress, among the thin ranks of the Republican minority, he took a prominent position from the day of his entrance. He was assigned to the Committee on the District of Columbia, becoming its chairman after the Republican victory of 1894, and remaining throughout his service a leader in matters affecting the government of the National Capital. He was named as the Wisconsin member of the Republican Congressional Campaign Committee when it organized in the autumn of 1893. The resignation of its chairman in the following spring brought him into unexpected prominence as acting chairman, and then as chairman of the committee. He had full charge of the campaign of the Republican party in 1894, showing himself to be adroit and patient, with a head for detail. He gained the confidence of his associates and retained the chairmanship through five ensuing campaigns. Under his direction the control of Congress was taken from the Democratic party, and thereafter it was a question only of the size of the Republican majority. In his state relationships he was contestant for the United States Senate, to succeed John L. Mitchell, but was defeated by a Republican rival, Joseph V. Quarles. He was induced by this defeat to give his support to Robert M. La Follette, who was then fighting the regular organization of the Republican party, and who was elected governor in 1900. But he broke with La Follette before the next election in 1902, and with the latter ascendant had difficulty in securing renomination in 1902 and 1904. In 1906, at the first test of the new primary election law, he won his eighth consecutive nomination; but he was defeated in the election by a Democrat to whom the La Follette progressives gave many votes. In 1900 and 1901 Babcock was greatly alarmed by the big business mergers, and he advocated a repeal of the protective duties upon steel products a year before the so-called Iowa Idea was launched. After his defeat in 1906 he removed his residence further north in Wisconsin, into Vilas County; and thereafter he divided his time between his new home and Washington, where he died in 1909.

[The best sketches of his life are his obituary in the *Milwaukee Sentinel,* Apr. 28, 1909, and an article by Bessie A. Safford in *The Vermonter,* Mar. 1902.]

F. L. P—n.

BABCOCK, MALTBIE DAVENPORT (Aug. 3, 1858–May 18, 1901), Presbyterian clergyman, author, was born in Syracuse, N. Y. He was of good stock, had remarkably varied gifts, and was afforded ample opportunity to develop them. His father, Henry Babcock, traced his descent from James Babcock, an Englishman who settled in Portsmouth, R. I., in 1642, and his mother, Emily Maria Maltbie, was the daughter of Rev. Ebenezer Davenport Maltbie, and the grand-daughter of Henry Davis, second president of Hamilton College. He prepared for college in the public schools, his character, varied talents, and athletic prowess early winning him popularity and leadership. Graduating from Syracuse University in 1879, he at once entered Auburn Theological Seminary, where he finished his course in 1882. At college he took high rank as a student, was leader of the glee club, director of the orchestra, and president of the baseball team. His interest in sports lasted throughout his life; he loved the out-door world, and was an enthusiastic fisherman. Had he chosen, he could have had a successful career as a musician, for he was a singer of more than ordinary ability, and a proficient player of several instruments, among them the organ, for which he composed a number of works of merit. He wrote some excellent poetry, mostly of a religious nature, could impersonate with marked success, was clever at drawing, and had a knack with tools. Yet despite his versatility and the ease with which he seemed to do whatever he attempted, he was industrious and methodical in the extreme.

As soon as he had completed his theological training, he was called to the First Presbyterian Church of Lockport, one of the most important churches in western New York. Here he was ordained by the Presbytery of Niagara, July 13, 1882. On Oct. 4, following, he was married to Katherine Eliot Tallman, daughter of Judge John P. H. Tallman of Poughkeepsie. After five years' ministry in Lockport he became pastor of the Brown Memorial Church, Baltimore, where he soon became greatly beloved for his unselfish service to all classes, and achieved a reputation as a preacher which travelled far. When in 1899 he resigned his charge to become the successor of Dr. Henry van Dyke at the Brick Presbyterian Church of New York, it was in the face of a vigorous protest from the whole city of Baltimore. His success in New York was immediate, the church was filled to the doors and even the steps of the pulpit covered with hearers. Unfortunately his ministry here was brief. On a trip to the Holy Land in 1901 he was stricken with Mediterranean fever at Naples and taken to the International Hospital there. Some fifteen years before, in Lockport, he had suffered for six months from acute melancholia. A second attack now visited him, during which, while his nurse was out of the room, he cut the arteries of his wrists and drank corrosive sublimate.

Maltbie Babcock was not a theologian, or even a deep thinker. His reasoning frequently will not stand the test of rigid logic. Toward the Bible and doctrine his attitude was not critical, but he presented spiritual and ethical truths with freshness and effect. He had an agile mind, a wide range of information, dramatic ability, fluency of speech, and a magnetic personality. His physical characteristics contributed to his power. He was tall, broad-shouldered, sinewy, and graceful in form and gesture, with a face remarkably expressive of the emotions, and a voice vibrant and sympathetic. His sermons were full of original illustrations, touches of humor, which were never in bad taste, and pungent epigrams. His main interest was in life and the needs and possibilities of men and women and in an extraordinary degree he was able to inspire his hearers with hope, courage, and the will to overcome. In this power, and as much, perhaps, in his own personal goodness, lay the secret of his success.

Babcock himself published nothing, but after his death there appeared, *Thoughts for Everyday Living from the Spoken and Written Words of Maltbie Davenport Babcock* (containing collection of poems), edited by Katherine Tallman Babcock and Mary R. Sanford (1901); *Three Whys and Their Answer* (1901); *Letters from Egypt and Palestine* (1902); *The Success of Defeat* (1905); *Fragments that Remain,* selections from sermons, reported and arranged by Jessie B. Goetschius (1907); *The Joy of Work,* reprinted chapters from *Fragments that Remain* (1910).

[Charles E. Robinson, *Maltbie Davenport Babcock* (1904); John T. Stone, *Footsteps in a Parish* (1908); *N. Y. Times,* May 19, 20, 1901; *Baltimore Sun,* May 20, 21, 1901.]

H. E. S.

BABCOCK, ORVILLE E. (Dec. 25, 1835–June 2, 1884), engineer, soldier, the son of Elias Babcock, Jr., and Clara Olmstead, was born at Franklin, Vt., a small town on the Canadian border close to Lake Champlain. His military career began in 1861 with his graduation from West Point and his assignment to the engineer corps as a second-lieutenant. At the opening of the Civil War he assisted in organizing and instructing a battalion of engineers, in which he commanded a company. On June 13, 1861, he was ordered to the headquarters of the Department of Pennsylvania, in July to the Department of the Shenandoah, and in November to the Army of the Potomac. In 1862 Gen. W. B. Franklin, then in charge of the left grand division of the Army of the Potomac, placed Babcock on his staff. In January 1864, Babcock was made acting chief engineer of the Department of the Ohio, with headquarters at Knoxville, Tenn., to have entire charge of positions, defenses, bridges, and so forth. Shortly afterward he was attached to Grant's staff as an aide-de-camp. During his advance in rank from the position of a second-lieutenant in 1861 to that of a brigadier-general by brevet in 1865, Babcock apparently enjoyed the enthusiastic approval of his superiors. In 1861, Gen. J. G. Barnard mentioned his "great gallantry"; Gen. Patterson referred to his "efficient" work; and Gen. McClellan in 1862 noted that his work was "splendidly" done and urged his promotion. Grant used Babcock in a wide variety of circumstances to carry orders and counsel, to gather information, and to survey positions. Thus in 1864 he sent Babcock to observe Sherman's army and then to Secretary Stanton to convey news and information that might be useful. The tenacity with which Grant later shielded his staff officer against attacks becomes understandable in the light of these experiences in the field, as when Grant sent Babcock—"in whom I have great confidence"—to Burnside during the operations about Spottsylvania Court House, with instructions to give every assistance in his power. On June 6, 1865, Grant recommended promotion "for meritorious services in the defense of Knoxville, Tenn., and especially for gallant conduct in the defense of Fort Sanders, ... gallant conduct in the battle of the Wilderness, ... gallant conduct in the battles in front of Petersburg, and in the pursuit and capture of the Army of Northern Virginia."

Just after the close of the war, on Nov. 8, 1866, Babcock was married in Galena, Ill., to Annie Eliza Campbell. For several years he was private secretary to President Grant, and superintendent of buildings and grounds in the city of Washington. While holding the former office he visited Santo Domingo (1869) in the interest of Grant's attempt to annex the island. At this time Babcock became associated with a group of men in the Internal Revenue Service who were defrauding the government of great sums of money. In particular, he was friendly with John McDonald, supervisor of Internal Revenue at St. Louis, known to be one of the leaders of the "Whisky Ring," and had received costly presents from McDonald. On Dec. 9, 1875, the grand jury at St. Louis returned a true bill against Babcock "for conspiracy to defraud the revenue." Grant found it impossible to believe that his old army friend and aide had been guilty of such practises. He accordingly volunteered a deposition to the effect that he knew of nothing suggesting guilt on Babcock's part, and that he believed his secretary innocent. Subsequently, in February 1876, the court returned a verdict of not guilty, and Babcock returned to his duties at the White House for a short time, but soon left permanently. He retired to private life and was drowned at Mosquito Inlet, Fla., on June 2, 1884.

[A sketch appears in the *Babcock Genealogy* (1903), pt. 2. His mil. career may be followed in the *Official Records* (1880–1901). On the Whisky Ring, see *House Misc. Docs.,* 44 Cong., 1 Sess., no. 186 (1876). See also works on the period of Civil War and Reconstruction, by James F. Rhodes, W. A. Dunning, and E. P. Oberholtzer; G. W. Cullum, *Biog. Reg.* (3rd ed. 1891), II, 771; *Times-Union* (Jacksonville, Fla.), June 4, 1884; and the several biographies of Grant, esp. that by L. A. Coolidge (1917).]

C. R. L.

BABCOCK, WASHINGTON IRVING (Sept. 26, 1858–Aug. 7, 1917), naval architect, was born at Stonington, Conn., the son of Capt. David S. and Charlotte (Noyes) Babcock. When he was seven, his parents moved to Brooklyn, where in 1876 he graduated from the Polytechnic Institute. He studied for two years in Rensselaer Polytechnic Institute, and on graduation, in 1878, secured a position with the Morgan Iron Works, New York. A year later he joined the staff of the Tehuantepec Interocean Railroad Company. More valuable than this experience was the training which he received at the Delaware Iron Shipbuilding and Engine Works, Chester, Pa., during 1880–85. In the latter year he became assistant superintendent of the Providence and Stonington Steamship Company and, in 1887, superintendent of the Union Drydock Company, Buffalo. He then turned promoter. The result was the organization, in 1889, of the Chicago Shipbuilding Company, of which he became manager and later president. When it was absorbed by the American Shipbuilding Company in 1900, he began practise as a naval architect in New York, forming a partnership with Henry Penton in 1907.

Fair-haired and well-proportioned, with an easy manner and a pleasant disposition, he differed little in appearance or address from any prosperous manufacturer. Nevertheless, he made notable advances in naval design and construction. Incited by recurrent difficulties with the riveters in the yards at Chicago, he invented a mechanism which made it possible to employ pneumatic tools. He also introduced the mould system of construction, which has since become universal. His most important innovations, however, were connected with lake carriers. Since the eight steel vessels on the St. Lawrence route in 1886 were Clyde-built and unsuited for inland traffic, he constructed the *Owego,* a typical freighter, in 1887, and in 1895 designed and launched the first lake vessel 400 feet over all. Intended for the bulk trade, his *Victory,* which was one of the earliest ships laid down on the channel system, was arranged so that the entire space between the living quarters and the engine rooms, fore and aft, was reserved for cargo. Babcock was also a pioneer in the development of the passenger type represented by the *Manitou.* He was the author of various technical papers on naval architecture. He died at his home in New York, Aug. 7, 1917.

[The only sketch of Babcock is that in Henry B. Nason, *Biog. Rec. Officers and Grads. Rensselaer Polytechnic Inst.* (1887). His most notable achievements, however, are treated in his papers in the *Trans. Soc. Naval Architects and Marine Engineers,* vols. VI, pp. 29–35, VII, pp. 173–82, XIII, pp. 187–94. An obituary appeared in vol. XXV, pp. 341–43.] R. P. Ba—r.

BACHE, ALEXANDER DALLAS (July 19, 1806–Feb. 17, 1867), physicist, was the great-grandson of Benjamin Franklin, and the grandson of Richard Bache, Franklin's successor as postmaster general from 1776 to 1782; on his mother's side he was the grandson of Alexander James Dallas, secretary of the treasury in President Madison's cabinet. His grandmother, Sarah (Franklin) Bache, was the "Sally" Bache, so well known for her ministrations to the soldiers during the Revolution. He was born in Philadelphia, the oldest child of Richard and Sophia (Dallas) Bache. Having completed his studies in a classical school, he was permitted, because of unusual mental ability, to enter the United States Military Academy at the early age of fifteen years. He graduated at the age of nineteen with highest honors and with the rare record of not having received a single mark of demerit during his entire course. Following his graduation he served three years, first as assistant professor in the Academy and then as lieutenant of engineers in the construction of Fort Adams, Newport, R. I. On Sept. 16, 1828, he was appointed professor of natural philosophy and chemistry at the University of Pennsylvania, and resigned from the army. About this time he married Nancy Clarke Fowler of Newport, who proved a helpful companion throughout their married life. In Philadelphia he quickly made his influence felt in the newly-established Franklin Institute, the chief research work of which was placed in his charge, and in the American Philosophical Society, founded in 1727 by his great-grandfather. On his thirtieth birthday he became the first president of Girard College and was sent abroad for two years to study educational institutions. On his return he prepared a voluminous report on *Education in Europe,* published in 1839, which did much to improve educational methods in this country. Owing to delay in opening the college, he spent three years in reorganizing the public schools of Philadelphia so successfully that his system became a model for other cities. The opening of Girard College being still further delayed, Bache resumed in 1842 his former professorship in the University of Pennsylvania, but the following year, on Dec. 12, 1843, as the result of recommendations of leading learned societies and other influence, he became superintendent of the United States Coast Survey, which position he held until his death. He was eminently well-fitted to build on the foundation laid by Hassler, the first superintendent, and to impress Congress with the needs of the Survey; with added funds he expanded its operations, and by his own enthusiasm and achievements in devising instruments and methods, he stimulated the efforts of his staff. He was also a member of the Lighthouse Board and superintendent of weights and measures, a subject in which he had long been interested.

Throughout his career, in spite of interruptions and the cares of administrative office, Bache kept up his interest in scientific research and a long list of papers and reports attests his many-sided activities. Stimulated by the work of the two famous German magneticians, Gauss and Weber, he became interested in terrestrial magnetism and in 1830 began making observations in a small building attached to his house. From time to time during the rest of his life he continued to make magnetic observations, both at home and abroad; his published results contributed effectively to the elucidation of fundamental facts. Chiefly through his instrumentality the first magnetic observatory in this country was established at Girard College; it was in operation from 1840 to 1845, following a program of work conforming to that of about thirty similar institutions in different parts of the globe. In the summers of 1840–43, he made a detailed magnetic survey of Pennsylvania and adjacent parts. Later he saw to it that magnetic work was made an important part of the regular operations of the Coast Survey. In 1846 he was made regent of the Smithsonian Institution. In the founding of the National Academy of Sciences, of which he was the first president, he took a leading part, and he bequeathed to it $42,000 for research. From learned institutions at home and abroad he received many honors and marks of distinction. During the Civil War he served his country as adviser to the President and his war secretaries and was vice-president of the Sanitary Commission. He also planned the defenses of Philadelphia. In appearance we are told that he was of medium height and had a particularly pleasing expression; his portrait shows a kind, intellectual face, that of a man not lacking in a sense of humor. He wore his waving hair rather long and had a full, somewhat pointed beard.

["Address in Commemoration of Alexander Dallas Bache," by B. A. Gould, *Proc. Am. Ass. for Advancement of Sci.* (1869), pp. 1–47, to which a bibliography is appended, pp. 48–56; "Eulogy on Prof. Alexander Dallas Bache," by Prof. Joseph Henry, *Smithsonian Institution Report* for 1870, pp. 91–116, and in *Nat. Acad. Sci., Biog. Memoirs,* vol. I (1877), pp. 181–212, also containing bibliography; *Coast Survey Reports,* 1844–66; *Centennial Celebration U. S. Coast and Geodetic Survey,* Washington, D. C., 1916.] L. A. B.

BACHE, BENJAMIN FRANKLIN (Aug. 12, 1769–Sept. 10, 1798), one of the most prominent journalists in the early history of the Democratic-Republican party, was born at Philadelphia. His mother, Sarah Bache, was the only daughter of Benjamin Franklin; his father, Richard Bache, was a Whig merchant. As a boy he accompanied Franklin to Europe, studied in France and Geneva, and, after his return, in the college at Philadelphia. In Paris he learned the rudiments of his trade in the printing-house of Didot.

Bache's career began in 1790 with the founding of the Philadelphia *General Advertiser,* better known later under the name the *Aurora.* He announced the plan of the journal on Oct. 4 of that year, and put as a heading his motto, "Truth, Decency, Utility." Political parties were taking shape during Washington's first term, and each side felt the need of an organ. The Federalists had Fenno's *United States Gazette,* and the mouthpiece of the Republicans was the *National Gazette,* edited by Philip Freneau. When the latter periodical suspended, because of the epidemic of yellow fever, the *Aurora* succeeded to its influence. Among the subscribers at one time were Jefferson and the President himself. It was a newspaper quite catholic in its scope in some respects; it contained, for those days, extended accounts of European affairs, and published quite fully the proceedings of Congress and papers by the Executive. But its notorious feature was the virulent personal abuse for which that decade of journalism was famous. Washington wrote, "The publications in Freneau's and Bache's papers are outrages on common decency" (*Writings,* edited by Jared Sparks, X, 359). Bache, nicknamed "Lightning-Rod Junior," usually maintained the anonymous editorial attitude. Often the columns were open to contributors, as when a "Calm Observer" charged that the President had overdrawn his salary and was a common defaulter. Other examples of the paper's treatment of Washington are found in the issues of 1796, when the accusation was made that he had violated the Constitution, when a burlesque poem was printed for his birthday, and when the *Aurora* reprinted forged letters of Washington, originally issued by the British in 1776.

In the summer of 1795 there was knowledge in the United States that Jay had signed a treaty with England, but the details were unknown beyond the circle of the President and Senate. Before Washington made public the text of the treaty, Senator Mason of Virginia sent an advance copy to Bache. The latter printed the substance in the *Aurora* of June 29, and published the full treaty in pamphlet form on July 1. The excitement was intense; as the *Aurora* said on July 4, "The fountains of the great deep are broken up." Another instance of Bache's actions was at the time of the election, near the close of 1796, when he opened his columns to the French minister Adet. This diplomatist sent four notes to Pickering, secretary of state, and copies of them simultaneously to the *Aurora;* they contained a decree of the Directory, an address to the French in America, and sentimental appeals. Bache's final utterance concerning the administration was his abusive "valedictory," when Washington retired from office in March 1797: "If ever there was a period for rejoicing, this is the moment—every heart in unison with the freedom and happiness of the people, ought to beat high with exultation that the name of *Washington* from this day ceases to give a currency to political iniquity, and to legalize corruption."

The *Aurora's* early commendation of President Adams soon changed to severe attacks. The bitterness at that time was intense, as is shown by the fact that Bache on a visit to the shipyard in Philadelphia was beaten by Humphreys, the son of the builder of the frigate *United States;* this act, it was alleged, was in return for newspaper abuse. The Federalists, in turn, charged that the editor was in the pay of the Directory, a charge which Bache denied. The same year 1798 was that of the XYZ sensation, and of the Sedition Act. Jefferson had noted in a letter to Madison dated Apr. 26 that the "*Aurora* was particularly named" in preparing the Sedition bill. On June 26 Bache was arrested on the charge of libeling the President and Executive, but was released on parole. He had just printed, June 16, Talleyrand's note to the United States Commissioners, and, June 20–23, their reply. The circulation of his journal fell off during the XYZ excitement, and his own activities were nearly over. He fell a victim to yellow fever in Philadelphia, Sept. 10, 1798. On Nov. 17, 1791, he had married Margaret Hartman Markoe, of a Danish family. She carried on the paper after his death and married Duane, who had been associate editor.

[See the files of the *Aurora* 1794–98; *Remarks Occasioned by the Late Conduct of Mr. Washington* (1797); *Truth Will Out* (1798), a pamphlet giving Bache's version of the circumstances in the issuing of the Talleyrand letter; J. T. Scharf and T. Westcott, *Hist. of Phila.* (1884); *The Franklin Ancestry and Descendants in the Col. Louis Bache Line to 1889* (1889); *New Eng. Hist. and Geneal. Reg.*, VIII, 374; *Writings of George Washington* (ed. by Jared Sparks, 1836), X, 359, XI, 183.] E.K.A.

BACHE, FRANKLIN (Oct. 25, 1792–Mar. 19, 1864), teacher, chemist, physician, was the great-grandson of Benjamin Franklin. His parents were Benjamin Franklin Bache and Margaret (Markoe) Bache. He was born in Philadelphia. In 1810 he received the degree of A.B. from the University of Pennsylvania, in 1814 the degree of M.D. In 1811 he published in the Philadelphia *Aurora* (established by his father) a contribution on the composition of hydrochloric acid in which he contended that chlorine is simple and by its union with hydrogen gives hydrochloric acid. He contributed three excellent papers to the *Memoirs of the Columbian Chemical Society* (1813), bearing the titles, "An Inquiry into what circumstance will warrant us justly to reckon a substance a principle of a common property of any set of bodies"; "An Inquiry whether M. Berthollet was warranted, from certain experiments, in framing the Law of Chemical Affinity, 'that it is directly proportional to the quantity of Matter'"; "Thoughts on the Expediency of changing parts of the chemical nomenclature." These papers were valuable contributions to the development of chemical theory in America.

The War of 1812 temporarily interrupted his scientific activities. He enlisted as an assistant-surgeon in the army in 1813, was promoted to surgeon in 1814, and resigned in 1816. In 1819 there appeared Bache's *System of Chemistry for the Use of Students in Medicine.* In 1821, with Robert Hare [*q.v.*], he edited an edition of Andrew Ure's *Dictionary of Chemistry,* in 1823 he prepared a supplementary volume to William Henry's *Elements of Experimental Chemistry,* and in 1825 he published an anonymous edition of James Cutbush's *System of Pyrotechny,* while during 1826–31 he conducted the *North American Medical and Surgical Journal.* He was professor of chemistry in the Franklin Institute from 1826 to 1832, and in 1830 revised the *Pharmacopœia of the United States;* he also at this time began his excellent *Dispensatory of the United States of America,* which passed through eleven editions during his life. He was made Fellow of the College of Physicians, Philadelphia, 1829, and acted as its vice-president, 1855–64. From 1831 to 1841 he was professor of chemistry in the Philadelphia College of Pharmacy and Science. In 1836 he edited the third edition of Robert Hare's *Compendium of the Course of Chemical Instruction in the Medical Department of the University of Pennsylvania,* and between 1819 and 1841 brought out four American editions of Edward Turner's *Elements of Chemistry.*

In 1841 he assumed the professorship of chemistry in Jefferson Medical College, delivering a notable introductory lecture whose tenor is indicated by the lines: "But here, gentlemen, let me stop to inquire is chemistry in its applications to medicine and pharmacy worthy of your regard? This is an important preliminary question; for if you follow the ensuing course under the erroneous impression that you can be reputable physicians without being chemists your attention will flag." Similar introductory addresses were delivered by him in 1843, in 1844, in 1848, in 1849, and in 1852. For eighteen years he was secretary of the American Philosophical Society, vice-president for ten years, and finally president (1853–55). In 1818 he had married Aglae Dabadie, who entered heartily into her husband's literary and scientific pursuits, but died in 1835, leaving him "as her best legacy, a young family of sons and daughters to give exercise to his affections and comfort to his declining years." He was regarded by his colleagues as a man of excellent reason and judgment, clear in thought and correct in conclusion; in mental action, as in bodily movements, slow and deliberate; a delightful companion because of his faculty of humor. His writings and teachings were marked by simplicity, clearness, and accuracy.

[J. T. Scharf and T. Westcott, *Hist. of Phila.*(1884); G. B. Wood, *Biog. Memoir of Franklin Bache* (1865); Edgar F. Smith, *Franklin Bache, Chemist* (1922).]

E. F. S.

BACHE, RICHARD (1737–July 29, 1811), a merchant of New York City, was born in Settle in the West Riding of Yorkshire, England. According to William B. Bache, *The Franklin Ancestry and Descendants in the Col. Louis Bache Line* (1889), the date of birth was Feb. 23; according to Oscar E. Schmidt, *Smaller New York and Family Reminiscences* (1899), and Thomas E Satterthwaite, *Biographical and Historical Sketches* (1923), it was Sept. 12. The family traced its origin to the Middle Ages, one tradition carrying it back to the Norman Conquest. The name was originally Bêche, or de la Bêche (beech), and—according to one statement—the anglicized pronunciation was *Beech*. Richard was a younger brother of Theophylact Bache [*q.v.*]. Their parents were William and Mary (Blyckenden) Bache. In 1765 Richard followed his brother to New York, becoming his business partner. He removed to Philadelphia, made the acquaintance of Benjamin Franklin, and in 1767 married Franklin's daughter Sarah. His firm had an extensive business with foreign lands, including the West Indies and Newfoundland; in addition, Bache issued private insurance policies, as these were the years prior to the formation of regular companies of life insurance. The opening of the war, leading to a divergence of political sentiment between the brothers, caused the dissolution of their partnership, though not the severance of their personal relations. Richard Bache adhered to the Whigs; he was a member of the Committee on Non-Importation Agreements, of the Committee of Correspondence, and was on the Board of War. He succeeded his father-in-law, Franklin, as postmaster general, and remained in that office until 1782. Sarah Bache, as was natural for a daughter of Franklin, played a patriotic part during the contest; in the gloomy days of 1780 she was active in collecting money and clothing for the destitute soldiers. In later years, the family retired to their farm on the banks of the Delaware River.

[In addition to the works mentioned above, see obituary in *N. Y. Columbian*, Aug. 2, 1811, and numerous references in J. T. Scharf and T. Westcott, *Hist. of Phila.* (1884). A number of Bache's letters are listed in the *Calendar of tha Papers of Benj. Franklin in the Lib. of the Am. Phil. Soc.* (1908).]

E. K. A.

BACHE, THEOPHYLACT (Jan. 17, 1734/35–Oct. 30, 1807), a merchant of New York City, son of William and Mary (Blyckenden) Bache, was a native of Settle in Yorkshire, England. He came to New York City in 1751, and was soon associated in business with his uncle by marriage, Paul Richard, mayor of New York from 1735 to 1739. A few years later the uncle died, and Bache inherited the business, goodwill, and £300. When his brother Richard [*q.v.*] arrived, he was taken into partnership. The business of the firm was chiefly with the West Indies and Newfoundland, and Bache was also agent for transatlantic packets. His standing in the mercantile community is shown by the fact that he was a Royal Incorporator of the Marine Society of New York in 1770, as well as by his election to the presidency of the New York Chamber of Commerce; he was chosen to that office in 1773, and later served as vice-president, 1788–92. When the Revolution began he was at first inclined toward the Whigs, but by 1776 was classed as a Loyalist, though he wrote to Philip Livingston denying that he was hostile to American rights. A. C. Flick (*Loyalism in New York,* 1901, p. 34 note) states that he belonged to the following class, "With nothing to lose and everything to gain, policy made them Loyalists." The brothers dissolved partnership, but they continued to be friendly. Theophylact Bache was cited to appear before the provincial congress, but wrote a letter declining to do so. He soon passed within the British lines, and had a narrow escape from capture. During the occupation of New York and western Long Island by the enemy, Bache resided either in the city or in Flatbush. While living in his country house, he was captured one night in 1778, members of his family were severely treated, and the house was plundered; Bache was hurriedly taken to Morristown, N. J., but was soon exchanged. The incident does not appear to have affected his conduct, for he had a reputation for unusual humanity during the war. After its termination, he resumed business; but the times were unsettled, especially as the contests of the French Revolution and Napoleonic period disturbed American trade, and Bache, like other merchants, suffered severe losses in his last years.

Socially he was well connected, and was highly esteemed as a courteous gentleman. He was married on Oct. 16, 1760, to Ann Dorothy Barclay, daughter of Andrew Barclay and Helena Roosevelt, by whom he had fifteen children. For many years he was vestryman of Trinity Church, and his tomb is in the churchyard, next to that of Hamilton. He was governor of New York Hospital, and president of its board, and from 1788 to 1799 he was president of the St. George's Society. He died in New York City.

[See works mentioned under Richard Bache; also Lorenzo Sabine, *Biog. Sketches of Loyalists of the Am. Rev.* (1864); *Mem. Hist. of the City of N.Y.* (1893), ed. by Jas. Grant Wilson; Jos. Bucklin Bishop, *Chamber of Commerce of the State of N.Y.* (1890), comp. by Geo. Wilson.]

E. K. A.

BACHELDER, JOHN (Mar. 7, 1817–July 1, 1906), inventor, manufacturer, was born at Weare, N. H., the son of William and Mary (Bailey) Bachelder, and directly descended from the Rev. Stephen Bachiler, the non-conformist who founded the town of New Hampton, N. H. His father was variously a lumberman and a blacksmith, successful enough to afford John a common school and academic education. Bachelder taught school for three years, went to Boston, worked as an accountant for a transportation company operating on the Middlesex Canal, and shortly after formed a partnership and engaged in the same business until the completion of the railroad to Manchester caused him to suspend. In 1843 he was married to Adaline Wason. He engaged in the dry-goods business at Boston and in 1846 visited England to establish connections for the successful importing business that he organized as Bachelder, Burr & Company. In the winter of 1847 Bachelder became interested in the sewing-machine as it had been developed by Elias Howe, believing that it could be materially improved. Becoming more and more interested, he bought a small machine-shop, retired from business, and devoted his time to mastering the machinist's trade. He spent five years' time and $16,000 before achieving success, but at the end of that time (1849) had developed the continuous feed, the vertical needle, and the horizontal table, all features of the modern sewing-machine. The importance of these inventions is indicated by the statement that "the patents of Howe, Bachelder, and Wilson cover all the fundamental principles of the sewing-maine," a statement indorsed by all well-informed men within the industry. The importance of these devices is further reflected in the marked reduction in the price of sewing-machines that was made when the patents expired. From this reduction their actual value has been estimated at $100,000,000. Unfortunately he was forced to sell his patents immediately, realizing but little more than enough to pay his debts. With this experience as an inventor Bachelder turned to manufacturing and with help from friends was able to buy (1852) a cotton-factory at Lisbon, Conn., but a disastrous fire so reduced his resources that he was unable to weather the depression following the war and was forced to sell his interest in this and other mills. He served as postmaster and town treasurer at Lisbon, and was a director of the First National Bank of Norwich and a trustee of the Chelsea Savings Bank. In 1875 he went to Napa, Cal., and established a manufacturing plant only to be caught in the panic of 1877–78 and forced to retire from active business. While in Napa he became interested in library work and was trustee and president of the board of the Public Library. He wrote one book, *A. D. 2050* (1890), suggested by Bellamy's *Looking Backward.* Returning to the east, he spent his later years in Milwaukee, Wis. He died at Houghton, Mich.

[Sketch in *Boston Globe,* June 24, 1916; E. W. Byrn, *Progress of Invention in the Nineteenth Cent.* (1900); F. C. Pierce, *Batchelder, Batcheller Geneal.* (1898); F. M. Caulkins, *Hist. of Norwich, Conn.* (1866); records of Singer Manufacturing Co.; information from Bachelder's son, Mr. Chas. S. Bachelder of Napa, Cal.]

F. A. T.

BACHER, OTTO HENRY (Mar. 31, 1856–Aug. 16, 1909), etcher and illustrator, was born in Cleveland, Ohio, the son of Henry and Charlotte Bacher. He began his art studies under De Scott Evans, but in 1878, in company with Willis S. Adams and Sion L. Wenban, he went to Munich. Later he studied under Carolus Duran, Boulanger, and Lefebvre. By 1880 he was one of the group of young Americans working with Duveneck in Venice. He came also under the influence of Whistler, to whom he pays warm tribute in his *With Whistler in Venice* (1908), drawing a sympathetic picture of the famous artist making etchings and pastels from the windows of Bacher's quarters and using the younger man's press. In Venice, Duveneck and others of the group took up monotype, painting upon a plate with burnt sienna or ivory black, and printing on Bacher's press; the product they called "Bachertype." At the first exhibition of the Royal Society of Painter Etchers, London, 1881, Bacher was represented by seventeen etchings. Late in 1883 he left Venice for America, via London and Paris; in 1885–86 he revisited London. His life thenceforth was passed in New York City and in Bronxville, where he settled in October 1896. At the Pan-American Exposition (Buffalo, 1901) he was awarded honorable mention, and at the Louisiana Purchase Exposition (St. Louis, 1904) a silver medal. He drew many illustrations, especially of still life for *Harper's* and the *Century.* He was a member of the Royal Society of Painter Etchers (London), the New York Etching Club, the Society of Illustrators, and the Society of American Artists where he occasionally exhibited a painting; in 1906 he became an associate of the National Academy of Design. He was married to Mary Holland in Cleveland, 1888, and died in Bronxville, 1909, leaving a widow and four sons. A memorial exhibition of his etchings was held at the Cleveland Museum of Art in 1921.

Bacher's etchings date from his early sojourn in Bavaria, when the *Danube* series was produced. Such plates as *Auf Stauffa-Bruck* and *Schwabelweiss* show a style already free, though more restrained than that of his later Venetian work. In the latter, says Koehler, "his manner o'erleaped itself and degenerated into wildness. And yet it is impossible to close oneself against the telling effect of these plates. A stormy life surges in them." Of this Venetian set Sir Seymour Haden writes, "The whole of it, accessories and all, evinces a strong artistic feeling. Bold and painter-like treatment characterizes it throughout." Bacher gave the effect of tone with comparatively few lines, placed with almost impetuous irregularity. He later took up illustrating in pen-and-ink "with more pleasure," he said (*New York Times,* Feb. 16, 1907), "than any other form of black-and-white work." He became one of the leading American pen-and-ink artists of the eighteen-nineties. "W. H. Drake and O. H. Bacher rendered arms and armor . . . in an excellent manner," writes Pennell; "no American artists have done as good work in rendering the play of light on old silver, or jeweled caskets, or bronze, or ivories."

[Facts verified by Mrs. Bacher, widow of Otto Bacher; obituaries *N.Y. Evening Post* and *N.Y. Times,* Aug. 18, 1909, *Am. Art News,* Sept. 20, 1909, and *Am. Art Ann.,* VII, 1909–10; criticisms by S. R. Koehler, *Am. Art Rev.* (1881), II, 51, 231, and *Die Radirung der Gegenwart* (Vienna 1892); J. R. W. Hitchcock, *Etching in America* (1886); Mrs. M. G. Van Rensselaer, in *Century Mag.,* Feb. 1883, and Joseph Pennell, *Pen Drawing* (1920).]

F. W.

BACHMAN, JOHN (Feb. 4, 1790–Feb. 24, 1874), naturalist, Lutheran clergyman, was born in the village of Rhinebeck, Dutchess County, N. Y., the youngest son of Jacob Bachman, a farmer. The Bachman family is traditionally supposed to have come to Pennsylvania with William Penn seven generations earlier, though this is not a matter of precise record. The family took its origin in the canton of Berne, Switzerland, and one of its members, Lieut. Bachman, was killed with the Swiss guards who died in the defense of the Tuileries in 1789. John Bachman's father fought in the American Revolution; his mother's family came from Würtemberg. "From my earliest childhood I had an irrepressible desire for the study of Natural History," Bachman testified, but it was not encouraged and he pursued his studies surreptitiously. By catching beavers and skinning them he earned enough money to buy some coveted natural-history books. While yet a boy he was made secretary to Knickerbocker in an exploring expedition and embassy to the Oneida Indians. It is said that he entered Williams College at an early age (Haskell-Bachman; name not in college catalogues) and that his close application to study resulted in a menacing collapse of health which forced him to leave his college work uncompleted. For some time he lived out-of-doors, studying the Bible and Luther.

His first contact with men of science was his meeting in Philadelphia with the ornithologist, Alexander Wilson, who gave him an introduction to the great explorer and naturalist, Baron von Humboldt, then visiting this country. Bachman taught school at Ellwood, Pa., and later in Philadelphia, and in 1813 he was licensed to preach in the Lutheran Church. His first charge was "Gilead Pastorate," composed of three churches near Rhinebeck. He was ordained in December 1814. His call to the Lutheran pulpit of St. John's in Charleston, S. C., brought him in 1815 into what was, for his time and denomination, a religious frontier, and at the same time it threw him in with the group of naturalists gathered about the old medical school of Charleston in the first half of the nineteenth century. In 1816 he married Harriet Martin, daughter of a German Lutheran minister of Charleston. For many years he was tireless in building up his congregation, giving especial attention and benevolence to the negroes. He initiated the Lutheran Synod of South Carolina, was its first president, and founded South Carolina's Lutheran theological seminary. As a religious leader he was undoubtedly a persuasive figure, swaying an adoring congregation and known to every one of all creeds throughout his state. His chief religious tract was *A Defense of Luther and the Reformation* (1853), brought forward in answer to alleged attacks by local Catholics. His sermons when re-read even to-day, appear liberal, as well as gracefully eloquent and forthright.

As a naturalist, Bachman was very modest about his attainments. His celebrated association with Audubon, the great ornithologist and painter, began in October 1831, when Audubon spent a month under his roof. His letters to Audubon often reveal rather more scientific caution and acumen than Audubon himself sometimes showed, and his judgment of the two great rivals, Audubon and Wilson, was kind yet discerning and candid. At first too busy with religious duties to give much attention to natural history, by 1835 he had begun to show himself of indispensable service to Audubon by his collections of southern animals and his trustworthy studies of their habits and habitats. He wrote monographs on squirrels and hares, and took, besides, a warm interest in botany and agriculture. He practically founded the State Horticultural Society in 1833, contributing studies on useful animals and plants, and in 1834 he prepared *A Catalogue of the Phænogamous Plants and Ferns Native and Naturalized, Found Growing in the Vicinity of Charleston, S. C.*

Bachman is best known for his collaboration with Audubon upon *The Viviparous Quadrupeds of North America,* three volumes (1845–49), with its sequels and re-editions. According to Witmer Stone ("Audubon," in Jordan's *Leading American Men of Science,* p. 83), Bachman "wrote a large portion and edited all of the work"—a monumental task. The two friends were further united by the marriage of two of Audubon's sons to Bachman's daughters. In 1838 Bachman took a vacation in Europe, traveling about the British Isles with Audubon, and visiting Humboldt at Berlin, where the university gave him the degree of Ph.D.

The Civil War and the approach of the evolutionary controversy gave great disturbance to Bachman, personally, intellectually, morally. His book *The Unity of the Human Race* (1850) was a criticism of and exegetical retort to Nott and Gliddon's *Types of Mankind.* As against his opponents, he maintained that humankind is all of one species, a point of view now upheld by the best anthropologists. In dignified terms, by no means devoid of good scientific thinking, he tried, unsuccessfully, to reconcile Scripture and Science. In the hostility between the states of the North and South he was equally unsuccessful in his efforts at a middle course. During the Nullification agitation he was noted for his Unionist views, yet when at last South Carolina met to enact an ordinance of secession it was he who opened the meeting with prayer. Throughout the war he was a soldier of mercy, giving his entire time to the sick and dying. Much against his will he was persuaded to escape from Charleston by the last train before the evacuation of the town, as his part in the Secession meetings marked him for Northern hatred. He did not escape indignities and loss of property. His death by paralysis occurred in Columbia, S. C. Thousands came to view his body, especially negroes who had known his kindness, and hundreds of children were lifted to kiss the face of a leader especially beloved. In person he was at once simple and urbane. Thoroughly American, there was something about him so *hertzlich* as to recall his foreign origin. His letters and sketches deserve to be better known, for they have, if not real literary pretensions, a powerful sense of the picture and the moment, an easy flow of the best words, and a bubbling humor and heartiness.

[At Bachman's death a scant and perhaps not wholly accurate unsigned article was published about him in *Am. Acad. Arts and Sci.,* IX (o. s.), 330–31 (1874). The only other source is a detailed compilation and sketch of 463 pages, *John Bachman, the Pastor of St. John's Church, Charleston, S. C.: Letters and Memories of His Life* (1888). It was begun by J. B. Haskell, a kinsman, and completed by Miss C. Bachman. Cf. also H. E. Jacobs, *Hist. of the Evangelical Lutheran Church in the U.S.* (1893).]

D. C. P.

BACKUS, AZEL (Oct. 13, 1765–Dec. 9, 1817), Congregational clergyman and first president of Hamilton College, son of Jabez and Deborah (Fanning) Backus, was born in a section of Norwich, Conn., which later became the town of Franklin. He was brought up by a pious mother and a step-father "distinguished neither by industry, prudence, nor probity." Asked in after years what education his step-father gave him, Backus replied, "He took me with him to steal hoop-poles." The piety of the mother could not prevail against other influences, and the boy early declared himself an infidel. At the age of seventeen, however, he went to live with his uncle, the Rev. Charles Backus, pastor of the Congregational Church at Somers, Conn., whose wise treatment of the lad resulted in his conversion. In 1787 he graduated from Yale, where he ranked high as a scholar and was popular with his fellows. Inclined to enter the ministry, he hesitated, fearing that his buoyancy of spirit and love of fun unfitted him for sacred duties. Finally he decided to go into the army, but once more his uncle dissolved his doubts, and he prepared for the ministry under the former's tuition. On Feb. 7, 1791, he married Melicent Deming, and on Apr. 6 of the same year he was installed as pastor of the Congregational Church at Bethlehem, Conn., succeeding the noted Dr. Joseph Bellamy. That his misgivings about his fitness for the ministry had some foundation is shown by the fact that the only serious criticism of his preaching was that he could not keep his drolleries out of the pulpit, and that his witticisms were not always in good taste. He combined humor and pathos in his preaching and was frank and emphatic in his utterances. After supplying a neighboring pulpit he was asked if he dared preach that way at home, and replied, "The sermon you have heard is a hazel switch; when I am at home I use a sled-stake." His qualities made him much sought after as a preacher for special occasions. He took interest in civil affairs and was passionately opposed to what he deemed the atheism and license of Jefferson and his following. Invited to preach the election sermon in 1798, with Absalom as an example he portrayed the character of the demagogue in such a way as to leave no doubt as to what living politician he had in mind. The sermon was published (1798), and is said to have been twice republished in England. Some years later, for alleged libelous statements made about President Jefferson, he was arraigned in the United States district court (*Connecticut Courant,* Oct. 1, 1806; Sept. 30, 1807). The case aroused much excitement; lawyers volunteered their services in his behalf, and friends offered financial aid. The case never was tried.

He was almost as well known as a teacher. At Bethlehem he carried on a preparatory school and enjoyed a high reputation as a wise and kindly disciplinarian. Boys hard to manage were frequently put under his care, and he had great success with them. In September 1812, he was elected president of Hamilton College. He supervised the young institution in a paternalistic way and with reasonable success, but his career was cut short by a fever contracted while watching over a sick tutor. His publications include *A Sermon Delivered at the Funeral of His Excellency Oliver Wolcott, Governor of the State of Connecticut, Dec. 1, 1797; Absalom's Conspiracy* (1798); *An Inaugural Discourse Delivered in the Village of Clinton, Dec. 3, 1812, by Rev. Azel Backus, D.D., on the Day of His Induction into the Office of President of Hamilton College* (1812); *The Importance of Ministerial Fidelity* (1813), a sermon at the ordination of John Frost; *A Sermon at the Ordination of John B. Whittlesey* (1814).

[F. B. Dexter, *Biog. Sketches Grads. of Yale Coll.* (1907); F. W. Bailey, *Early Conn. Marriages* (1898); *Hist. of the Town of Kirkland, N. Y.* (1824); Pomroy Jones, *Annals and Recollections of Oneida County, N.Y.* (1851); W. B. Sprague, *Annals Am. Pulpit,* vol. II (1857); Wm. Cothren, *Hist. of Ancient Woodbury, Conn.* (1854).]

H. E. S.

BACKUS, ISAAC (Jan. 9, 1724–Nov. 20, 1806), Separatist and Baptist minister, historian, champion of religious liberty, was born in the village of Yantic in the town of Norwich, Conn. The first paternal ancestor of whom we have information was Stephen Backus, one of the original settlers of Norwich (1660). His grandson Joseph represented Norwich in the colonial legislature for several years. A consistent opponent of the Saybrook Platform of 1708, when the Norwich church accepted the Platform, he and others withdrew and set up their own public service, a foretoken of the important Separatist movement of a generation later. The church censured the group, reporting the matter to the legislature, which expelled Joseph Backus and Richard Bushnel, another representative who had acted with him in this controversy. Later Joseph Backus made a visit to the Mathers in Boston and to John Wise in Ipswich in the interest of the conservation of a pure Congregationalism. Joseph's son, Samuel, was a farmer who owned the only industry in Yantic, the Iron Works, which were greatly developed by his son, Capt. Elijah Backus. The Backus Iron Works, making all kinds of iron products for domestic purposes, became especially important and prosperous during the Revolution. Here and in important land holdings in the Delaware and Susquehanna Purchases is found the economic basis for the extensive travels of Isaac Backus, who evidently was never dependent upon his pastoral field for his financial support. Samuel Backus married Elizabeth Tracy, a descendant of Edward Winslow of the *Mayflower,* a woman of genuine piety and moral courage. Of this marriage Isaac Backus was the fourth child. The extant correspondence between mother and son shows mutual esteem and affection, and on the part of the son an appreciation of his mother's influence in shaping his own religious feelings and convictions.

Writing in 1768 (*A Fish Caught in His Own Net,* pref., p. ix), Backus says he "is a person of very little note in the learned world and never was a member of their schools," referring to colleges and theological seminaries. He may have studied under Dr. Lord, the minister at Norwich; as a ministerial tutor might not have had so much interest in the minutiæ of learning as in its broader scope, this conjecture is in harmony with the striking paradox of Isaac's intellectual equipment. When only in his eighteenth year he considered himself well grounded in doctrine, yet his journals and letters abound in misspelling and in awkward and incorrect grammar. He was not, however, unaware of qualities of literary style; in his MS. account of his debate with Mr. Scales (1769) he discusses the use of a neuter noun and quotes from the "British Grammer" (*sic*). He was included in a committee of the Warren Association (1782) to bring out a new spelling book; he served for thirty-four years on the Board of Rhode Island College, and in 1797 was honored with its degree of Master of Arts. The lapses and crudities in his style are transcended by a native strength of intellect and precision of aim.

In June 1741, the Great Awakening reached Norwich with the preaching of Dr. Eleazar Wheelock. But it was not till the arrival of James Davenport in early August that Isaac entered into the experience typical of the Awakening—heart-searchings, obsession by the sense of original sin, and consciousness of overt transgression. "As I was mowing alone in the field, Aug. 24, 1741, all my past life was opened plainly before me, and I saw clearly that it had been filled up with sin" (MS. Autobiography, 1724–56, p. 16; Hovey, *Memoir*, p. 39). It was two days before he recognized this experience as conversion. Already he was dissatisfied with conditions in the Norwich church and it was not until the following year (1742) that he joined it, "concluding to bear those things as a burden and to hope for a reformation" (MS. Autobiography, p. 22). For several years he remained in a quiescent attitude, content to stay in the background. In 1745 he heard Whitefield preach in five different towns. When the church voted to admit to membership some who made no claim of any change of heart and when the minister gave his support to the Saybrook Platform, which the church had repudiated at the time of his settlement, a large minority withdrew—forming, with some additions, a New Light Church, July 16, 1746. It is not surprising to find the Backus family in this group. The trials and tribulations of the Norwich Separatists have been frequently described. Some years after Isaac had left home his pious mother and brother were cast into prison. In a letter dated Nov. 4, 1752, she wrote: "Your brother Samuel lay in prison twenty days. October 15, the collectors came to our house, and took me away to prison, about nine o'clock, in a dark, rainy night. . . . We lay in prison thirteen days, and were then set at liberty, by what means I know not" (*Memoir*, p. 28).

For a decade Isaac Backus is numbered among the Separatists of New England Congregationalism. In September 1746, he had an experience which he interpreted as a call to preach, and almost immediately he started out upon the first of a long series of preaching tours. At least eight of these can be distinguished in the next twelve months, including one to Rehoboth, Mass., where he first met Susanna Mason, who was to become his wife. Late in 1747 he visited Rev. Joseph Snow, a Separatist pastor in Providence, who told him of a needy field in Massachusetts. This was the precinct of Titicut, lying partly in Bridgewater and partly in Middleborough. Here Snow and Backus preached alternately twenty-four times in ten days, and the precinct committee invited Backus to remain as minister, after examination and approval by the neighboring ministers. He expressed his willingness to be thus examined, but refused to submit to the ministers or to the committee his own right to preach. Although not yet twenty-four years of age, he had come to a definite position in regard to the call to preach and the civil control of the church. In February, a group of people asked Backus to draw up articles of faith and a covenant, which he did. In March, they invited him to become their minister and on Apr. 13, 1748, he was ordained. A visit of a few days was to be prolonged to a residence of almost sixty years.

A little later we find him refusing to pay a tax of five pounds for support of the standing order; he was arrested but the statement that he was imprisoned does not seem well founded; in the crisis, Capt. Eleazar Edson paid the tax. In season and out, Backus was insistent in carrying on the recognized duties of a New Light minister. This involved constant preaching and pastoral calling in the home field with evangelistic tours and visitations to other Separatist flocks where counsel might be needed or opportunity for preaching afforded. His sermons contained much doctrinal discussion and exhortation; he relied largely upon the inspiration of the hour. His diaries frequently admit that he was "straitened in spirit" or acknowledge that he had "delightful liberty." Although he made eight journeys beyond his parish during the first year of his pastorate, totaling almost 800 miles, the membership of his own church about doubled. The next year he entered in all conscientiousness into marriage. "We solemnly covenanted together in July, were published in September, and were married on Nov. 29, 1749. Thus Susanna Mason of Rehoboth became the companion of my life, and the greatest temporal blessing which God ever gave me, for nearly fifty-one years, for which I trust I shall praise him to eternity" (MS.

Autobiography, p. 69. Cf. also *Memoir,* p. 81, for his own account of the simple marriage ceremony). At about this time he purchased a small farm in Middleborough which was his home for the rest of his life.

The most striking aspect of Backus's pastorate was its controversies, the details of which are readily accessible (*Memoir,* chaps. VII and VIII). The most disturbing of them was over the question of baptism. The Half-Way Covenant had been repudiated by the New Lights as inconsistent with the principles of a regenerate church membership. Was not infant baptism likewise inconsistent with this principle? While Backus was on a visit to his old home, two leading members of his church declared that they had adopted Baptist principles (Aug. 7, 1749). Upon his return, Backus was perplexed, but was suddenly carried over and preached a sermon holding the immersion of believers as the only true baptism. Within a few days he abandoned this view, but the question continued to agitate his mind. In July 1751 he again announced his conviction that infant baptism lacked scriptural warrant, and on Aug. 22, he and his wife and five others of his church were immersed by the Baptist elder, Benjamin Pierce of Warwick, R. I. Then began the great period of controversy, involving discipline and fellowship, the holding of ecclesiastical councils, the exclusion of Backus by a majority of the church, and the final consideration of the questions by a general council of New Lights at Exeter, R. I., in May 1753. This council favored mixed communion, and the church and Backus were virtually committed to what to-day would be considered "open membership." When he baptized three members "whom others thought had been baptized before," it was construed as his official repudiation of infant baptism, and further sharp contention arose. For a year and a half, the factions could not meet for communion. This led Backus directly to the logical principle of close communion, and with a few of the New Lights, on Jan. 16, 1756, he organized a Baptist church in Middleborough, and was ordained its pastor on June 23. This office he held for the rest of his life.

Again Backus must build an ecclesiastical organization. It was over a year before they could erect a church building, upon which Backus worked with his own hands as well as upon clearing a road to it. There is no indication of any change in his conception of his duties as a minister, but he was now in a position where he could apply more consistently the conclusions he had reached regarding the Christian life, the church, and its place in human society. Except during the last few years of his long pastorate, he attended to the routine duties of his work, his diaries and some of his published writings giving occasional glimpses of his experiences. He continued his itinerant missions, finding in the rapidly growing Baptist denomination opportunity for his constructive ability. His tours may be viewed as somewhat apart from his pastorate, for he kept a separate record of them, but they were a vital part of his ministry. He compiled a summary of his journeys from his arrival in Titicut, beginning with January 1748 and extending through December 1802, showing 918 trips exceeding ten miles in length, aggregating over 68,600 miles. This was for the most part on horseback. He combined various objectives in these tours. Numerous trips to Connecticut usually permitted visits to his old home and transaction of personal and family business there; in passing through Providence he had frequent consultation with President James Manning [*q.v.*]; he visited Harwich and other places where there were difficulties with the standing order; he was called from home by councils of ordination and associations; on a journey to New Hampshire (1769), he engaged in an interesting debate on Baptism with Mr. Scales, the minister of the church at Hopkinton. From the time he began to work upon his *History,* he was indefatigable in seeking information, locating and copying records, letters, and other documents. He was ever alert to advance the cause of the freedom of the Church from civil control; but the primary object of most of his journeys was to preach the gospel and to promulgate Christian doctrine as he understood it. He did not tarry so much as did his friend Hezekiah Smith [*q.v.*] of Haverhill for the distinct purpose of organizing Baptist churches, though many of these were in part the product of his preaching tours. These activities disclose a broad interest which lifts Backus out of his rôle as pastor, although his leadership there made Middleborough the strongest Baptist community in Massachusetts during his lifetime, and the fifty years' pastorate should not be underestimated. But it was in three fields not circumscribed by parish boundaries that the place of Backus in history is found.

In the realm of ecclesiastical polity in the second half of the eighteenth century, his was perhaps the keenest mind in America. Amid complicated situations, he safeguarded the independence of the local church and its democratic control. Although he served as clerk at the first meeting of the Warren Association, his church waited three years before joining and then came in "upon the express condition that no complaint should ever be received by the Association against any particular church that was not of the Association, nor from any censured member of any of our churches." Here is evidence of his alertness in the field of polity. He was from this time a recognized leader, in influence the peer of Hezekiah Smith and James Manning. In 1771 he was made agent to represent Baptist interests in relation to the civil government, involving duties yet to be considered. In 1773, at the request of Manning, he journeyed to Connecticut, where he was instrumental in attaching some Separatist churches to the Baptist cause (Backus MS.). As late as 1788, when the Baptists of Virginia sent to the Warren Association for assistance and advice, that body turned to Backus for this important mission, necessitating the longest journey in his career. Sailing from Newport on Jan. 2, 1789, he landed in North Carolina. Although he gave a report of this tour to the Warren Association on his return, we have very few details of his activities; but he attended a number of Associations and in about five months "travelled on horseback 1,251 miles . . . and preached 117 sermons" (*Memoir*, p. 272).

It was as a protagonist of religious liberty, however, that Isaac Backus has his chief claim to a fame which will probably increase as the strategic position of his contribution to what is now recognized as a triumphant cause becomes more fully known. Though many others joined in the protest against civil control of religion and there were other leaders in the effort to secure separation of Church and State, no individual in America since Roger Williams stands out so preëminently as the champion of religious liberty as does Isaac Backus. Long before he became a Baptist he had grasped the distinction between toleration and religious freedom. Through his first-hand acquaintance with affairs at Norwich, he knew the disadvantages from establishment in Connecticut, while his experience and observation in Massachusetts showed him a cause worthy of the best endeavors of the strongest years of his ministry. At a meeting of the Warren Association before the Middleborough church joined, Backus was named on a committee to collect information concerning the difficulties under which the Baptists were laboring, and for years he served on this Committee on Grievances. In 1772, he became Agent for the Association and from that time was considered the chief spokesman of the Massachusetts Baptists in all relations with the state. Through visitation and correspondence, he amassed a wide and accurate knowledge of affairs, and drafted reports and other documents through which the Baptists expressed their protests against the existing system of control. He was a conscientious objector against the system of certification by which Baptists might obtain remission of ministerial rates, and denied the legal right of the tax as well. He was largely instrumental in winning the Warren Association to this view in 1773 and himself drafted the *Appeal to the Public,* which in over sixty pages indicts the blend of civil and ecclesiastical authority in Massachusetts and justifies the Baptist insistence upon separation of Church and State.

The public career of Backus is nowhere more on the defensive than in connection with his mission to the First Continental Congress in the fall of 1774, for this was represented as an intention to embarrass the Massachusetts delegation and even to sow discord in the Congress itself. Backus went only at the earnest solicitation of several leaders of the denomination, including President Manning, who himself went to Philadelphia and presented the Baptist memorial at a conference with some of the delegates. The attitude of Backus was decidedly moderate. The whole broad field of liberty was being tilled at Philadelphia and the Baptists feared lest one important part should be neglected. In letters in the press later, Backus vindicated his own attitude and action. On the Sunday following the conflict at Lexington, Backus took a definite stand, justifying the Americans (MS. Diary), and from that time on through the Revolution his patriotism was beyond reproach.

While Backus was frequently occupied in efforts to improve the status of the Baptists, special opportunity came in connection with the adoption of the Massachusetts constitution in 1780 and with the ratification of the Federal Constitution in 1788. The Congregational standing order was virtually continued through Article III of the Declaration of Rights in the Massachusetts constitution. Backus had a considerable part in the discussion of this Article and became involved in controversy in the newspapers. His signing a certificate at this time was assailed as inconsistent, but he pointed out that his act was not in conformity to any law, for the certificate law was not then in force; while Article III, which forbade "subordination of any one sect to another," precluded the reënactment of such a law. He gives the essential facts in the *History* (edited by Weston, II, 225–31).

Backus was himself a member of the Massachusetts convention called to consider the ratification of the Federal Constitution. When the town of Middleborough selected its four delegates, he was the first named. "When I was first informed of it on Dec. 20," he wrote in his diary (*Ibid.*, II, 335), "I thought I should not go, but as religious liberty is concerned in the affair, and many were earnest for my going, I consented." He testifies to the liberty of discussion in the convention and to his own reception of light upon public affairs; although two-thirds of upward of twenty Baptist members present voted against ratification, he himself voted for it. "The exclusion of any hereditary, lordly power, and of any religious test, I view as our greatest securities in this constitution" (*Ibid.*). His criticism of the Massachusetts legislature for indifference toward the first amendment implies interest in the latter, but he himself took no active part in securing its adoption.

The third field in which Backus appears with a wider horizon than his parish is that of his literary activities. Here he does not rise to high level except in his historical work. The few sermons in print do not disclose any remarkable homiletic power. His earliest published discourse, *Nature and Necessity of an Internal Call to Preach* (1754), and one of his latest, *The Liberal Support of Gospel Ministers* (1790), set forth two important aspects of his views on the ministry. His controversial temper may be studied in his famous reply to Rev. Joseph Fish, in *A Fish Caught in His own Net* (1768), and in his *Reply to a Piece . . . by Mr. Israel Holly* (1772). His most important printed contributions to the cause of religious liberty were *A Seasonable Plea for Liberty of Conscience* (1770); *A Letter to a Gentleman in the Massachusetts General Assembly Concerning Taxes to Support Religious Worship* (1771); *Appeal to the Public* (1773); and, above all, the work popularly known as his "History of the Baptists."

Reference has already been made to the thoroughness of Backus in his search for documents and every other source of information for his *magnum opus*. More than the dominant majority realized, there was significance in the title which he framed. It was indeed *A History of New England, with Particular Reference to the Denomination of Christians Called Baptists* (vol. I, 1777; vol. II, 1784; vol. III, 1796. Revised, edited by David Weston, 2 vols., 1871). His style is often turgid and diffuse; he indulges in preachments and presents much from a partisan point of view; yet he never intentionally misrepresents, and much that his partisanship pointed out was being completely ignored by his opponents. Every interpreter of New England history of the colonial period and through the eighteenth century in all matters pertaining to the Church and religion and their relation to civil government must use the documentary evidence which Backus brought forth and pay some heed to his strictures upon the prevailing system of control.

In physique Isaac Backus was a man of large proportions in features and in body. While occasionally his diaries refer to rheumatism and other ailments, only a robust constitution could have borne the fatigue of his long journeys and an indomitable spirit have endured the trials of his long life.

[There is only one biog. of Isaac Backus, *A Memoir of the Life and Times of the Rev. Isaac Backus, A.M.*, by Alvah Hovey, D.D. (Boston, 1859). This is based primarily upon the manuscript diaries, accounts of journeys, letters, and other papers, to be be found in the New Eng. Bapt. Lib., Ford Building, Boston. These MSS. and a few others at Brown Univ. Lib. are listed somewhat in detail in W. H. Allison, *Inventory of Unpublished Material for Am. Religious Hist. in Protestant Ch. Archives and Other Repositories* (Carnegie Institution of Washington, 1910). A few MSS. will be found in the Samuel Colgate Bapt. Hist. Coll., Hamilton, N. Y., and in private possession at Norwich, Conn. The *Minutes* of the Warren Bapt. Ass. to 1806 are important. David Weston, *The Bapt. Movement of a Hundred Years Ago* (1868) and D. B. Ford, *Hist. Discourse on the Dedication of the Backus Monument* (1893) give information not otherwise easily accessible.]

W. H. A.

BACKUS, TRUMAN JAY (Feb. 11, 1842–Mar. 25, 1908), educator, the son of Mercy (Williams) Backus and the Rev. Jay Spicer Backus, a Baptist clergyman, was born at Milan, N. Y. As his father later moved to New York City with his family, Truman Backus received his early education there. He then attended the University of Rochester, from which he graduated with honors in 1864. At the close of the Civil War he organized a school for colored people in Richmond, Va., while that city was still under martial law. He later returned to Rochester and completed work for the degree of Master of Arts. On Jan. 9, 1866, he married Sarah Glass of Syracuse, N. Y. In 1867 he accepted a call to Vassar College to teach rhetoric and English. Vassar, the earliest American college for women, was then in its infancy; and Backus rendered effective pioneer service to the cause of the education of women in coöperating with Dr. John Howard Raymond, its first president, and Miss Maria Mitchel, professor of astronomy, in planning the work of the institution. He was offered a professorship of English at Harvard University, as well as the presidency of Vanderbilt University, both of which he declined. While he was teaching at Vassar his first wife died; and in 1883 he married Helen Hiscock of Syracuse, a graduate of Vassar in the class of 1873 and until her marriage a member of the English department of that institution. In 1883 he accepted the presidency of the Packer Collegiate Institute of Brooklyn, a well-known educational institution for girls and young women, partly preparatory, partly collegiate in character. He continued in the presidency until his death. As an administrator he combined a grasp of detail with an ability to eliminate unessentials and to solve the larger problems. Above all, his joyous spirit infected the whole institution. "Lugubriousness was a quality he could not bear. There was so little for it to feed upon under his directorship that it soon disappeared." Despite the pressure of teaching and administrative work, Backus found time for literary, civic, and other activities. He revised Thomas B. Shaw's *New History of English Literature* (1884) and was himself the author of *The Great English Writers from Chaucer to George Eliot* (1889) and the *Outlines of Literature, English and American* (1897). He served as civil service commissioner in Brooklyn under two mayors. He held office, also, as president of the board of managers of the Long Island State Hospital, president of the Head Masters Association of New York City, and president of the Association of Colleges and Preparatory Schools of the Middle States and Maryland.

[Obituaries in the *Brooklyn Daily Eagle* and the *N.Y. Tribune*, Mar. 25, 1908; *Who's Who in America*, 1908; *Minutes of the Trustees of the Packer Collegiate Institute* (transcribed on their permanent records); letter from Miss Cornelia Raymond of Vassar Coll. to the writer.]

J.F.S.

BACON, ALICE MABEL (Feb. 6, 1858–May 1, 1918), writer, teacher, lecturer, was born in New Haven, Conn., the youngest daughter of Catherine (Terry) Bacon and of Leonard Bacon [*q.v.*], and educated at private schools in that city. She passed the Harvard examinations for women in 1881. Her interest in other races took her to Hampton Institute, where she taught from 1883 to 1888. Japanese friends then made possible the extraordinary experience of teaching in the conservative and anti-foreign Peeress's School under the management of the Imperial Household. For a year she lived an almost completely Japanese life, sharing a house with three Japanese teachers and several Japanese girls. Her observations and experiences in this environment, and later in another school, were the subject of books and lectures in which she attempted to interpret Japanese civilization to Americans. In letters to her brothers and sisters, collected in *Japanese Girls and Women* (1891) and in *A Japanese Interior* (1893), she describes the domestic life and the customs, the popular beliefs and superstitions, of all classes, whom she was particularly well able to observe. She was a familiar guest in many Japanese households, and her contact with ladies almost untouched by foreign influence was very close. Returning to America in 1889, she taught again at Hampton until 1899, and founded the Dixie Hospital for the training of colored nurses in 1890. In 1896, in connection with the Atlanta Exposition, she published a survey and evaluation of the development of the colored race. But Japan called her once more in 1899 and she crossed the Pacific to teach for two years at the Higher Normal School in Tokyo. Again in America, she was a teacher for one year in Miss Capen's school in Northampton, Mass. Until shortly before her death she spent her summers in managing Deep Haven camp in Holderness, N. H., where for successive years large numbers of her friends gathered.

Her published works are *Japanese Girls and Women* (1891, republished in 1902, in a revised and enlarged edition, with illustrations by Keishu Takanouchi); *A Japanese Interior* (1893); *The Negro and the Atlanta Exposition* (*Occasional Papers*, No. 7, published by Trustees of the John F. Slater Fund, Baltimore, 1896); *In the Land of the Gods* (1905). She edited *Human Bullets, A Soldier's Story of Port Arthur,* by Tadayoski Sakurai (1907).

[The sources of information are Miss Bacon's own published writings; *Who's Who in America*, 1912–13; *Woman's Who's Who in America*, 1914–15; *New Haven Jour.-Courier*, May 3, 1918; Thomas W. Baldwin, *Michael Bacon of Dedham, 1640, and His Descendants* (1915).]

M.A.K.

BACON, AUGUSTUS OCTAVIUS (Oct. 20, 1839–Feb. 14, 1914), lawyer, senator, was born in Bryan County, Ga., though his parents were residents of Liberty County. On one side his progenitors were among the earliest settlers of Virginia, on the other they were of the colony of Puritans who settled in Dorchester, Mass., in 1630, whose descendants later in a body emigrated to South Carolina, and in 1753 moved to Georgia and founded what was known as the Midway Colony. He was named for his father who died four months before the son was born; his mother, Mary Louisa (Jones) Bacon, died before he was a year old. He was reared by his grandmother, a daughter of Dr. Henry Holcombe, an eminent Baptist minister. At the age of sixteen he entered the University of Georgia, receiving the A.B. degree in 1859 and the following year his law degree. He selected Atlanta as the place to practise his profession, but soon after joined the Confederate army and was made adjutant of the 9th Georgia Regiment. Afterward, with the rank of captain, he was assigned to general staff duty. He was married Apr. 19, 1864, to Virginia Lamar, in Macon, Ga., which city after the war became his permanent residence. He at once took high standing as a lawyer and commanded a large clientele. Notwithstanding the demands of his law practise, and the exactions of a long and brilliant service in the state legislature, he published in 1872 a digest of the decisions of the supreme court of Georgia. His advent in politics came in 1868, when he was nominated by the state Democratic convention for presidential elector. Two years afterward he was elected a member of the Georgia House of Representatives. He was reëlected to that body continuously for a period of twelve years, and was subsequently again elected for a term of two years. He was speaker *pro tempore* for two years, and speaker for eight years. In 1883, he was a candidate for the governorship of his state, and in the Democratic convention he lacked but one vote of receiving the nomination which would have been equivalent to an election.

In 1894 he was chosen United States senator by the General Assembly of Georgia. In 1900 he was nominated at a Democratic state primary for the Senate, and was afterward unanimously elected by the legislature. In 1906 he was again indorsed in the state Democratic primary, having no opposition, and was again unanimously elected to the Senate. He was the first Georgian to be elected to a third consecutive full term in the Senate. In 1912 he was again renominated in the state Democratic primary. Before the legislature convened, the change in the method of selecting senators had become effective. When the legislature met, it promptly provided machinery for the election of a senator by the people, and Senator Bacon had the distinction of being the first member of the United States Senate elected under the operation of the Seventeenth Amendment to the Constitution. He was elected president *pro tempore* in the Sixty-second Congress. In 1913 he became Chairman of the Committee on Foreign Relations. At the time of his death he had served but one year of his fourth term as United States senator.

In the Senate he was a frequent debater, discussing practically every important subject that came before Congress during his service of about nineteen years. He was especially strong in debate on constitutional questions and matters of foreign relations. One of his most notable efforts was in opposition to the acquisition of the Philippines. He introduced a resolution "declaring the purpose of the United States not permanently to retain the islands, but to give the people thereof their liberty." The vote was a tie, the resolution being defeated by the vote of the vice-president. The debate on this resolution between Senator Bacon and Senator Spooner of Wisconsin has justly been characterized as one of the great debates in the history of the Senate. No senator took a more active part in the debates when the Dingley tariff bill was before the Senate, and later, in 1909, when the Payne-Aldrich bill was under discussion. He had a deep concern for the proprieties of the Senate and was sensitive as to its rights and jealous of its constitutional prerogatives.

The time when Congress was not in session he usually spent in foreign travel. He was interested in public education and was for many years a trustee of the University of Georgia and a regent of the Smithsonian Institution. He was of medium size, physically strong and vigorous, dignified in carriage and deportment. He died in Washington after a brief illness, on Feb. 14, 1914. In his will, after making bequests to his kindred, he donated to the city of Macon, Ga., as a public park and recreation ground, his home "Baconsfield" and a valuable tract of land surrounding it on the Ocmulgee River.

[L. L. Knight, *Landmarks, Memorials, and Legends* (1914); I. W. Avery, *Hist. of the State of Georgia from 1850 to 1881* (1881); James Stacy, *Hist. of the Midway Congreg. Ch., Liberty County, Ga.* (1903); *Cong. Rec.* 1895–1914; *Recs. in Court of Ordinary, Bibb County, Ga.;* Hull, *Hist. of the Univ. of Ga.* (1894); memorial addresses in the Sen., Dec. 17, 1914, and in the House, Feb. 21, 1915, in *Cong. Rec.*, 63 Cong., 3rd Sess., pp. 296–303 and 4244–55.]

W. G.

BACON, DAVID (Sept. 4, 1771–Aug. 27, 1817), Congregational clergyman and missionary, was born at Woodstock, Conn. His father, Joseph Bacon, was a direct descendant of Michael Bacon, who came to Massachusetts from England in 1640; his mother was Abigail Holmes. His son, Rev. Leonard Bacon [*q.v.*], tells us that in David's early life, a "deep and thorough religious experience" brought him into special sympathy with David Brainerd, the famous missionary to the Indians whose life was written by Jonathan Edwards. He had slight educational opportunities; learned and practised the trade of a wheelwright; but must have been something of a student, for he was also a teacher. He married Alice Parks, at a date not recorded, and was led, perhaps by his interest in David Brainerd, to give himself to the ministry, studying theology, according to the custom of the time, with a clergyman. His teacher, Rev. Levi Hart, seems to have been a classical scholar, as his translations of Virgil are named in the catalog of the Library of Congress.

In August 1800, Bacon was commissioned by the Connecticut Missionary Society to "explore and experiment" among the Indian tribes beyond Lake Erie; and made the journey "alone, on foot, luggage strapped upon his back." The next year, accompanied by his young wife, and her fourteen-year-old brother (Beaumont Parks), he entered on his missionary work on Mackinac Island. Alarmed by the expense, the trustees directed him to return to Hudson in the Western Reserve, then sometimes called New Connecticut; and here he learned that his drafts had been protested, and it was necessary for him to return to Connecticut. Again, on foot, alone, he made the journey, met the trustees, triumphantly vindicated himself, and received full payment for his protested drafts and reappointment to remain in Hudson and give half time to the church there. Here he conceived the idea of a community built from the beginning upon the foundation of New England Puritanism. Returning to Connecticut, he contracted with Benjamin Tallmadge of Litchfield for his interest in a township in the Western Reserve: about 12,000 acres at $1.50 each. In 1807 Bacon came, the pioneer, built his log cabin and surveyed and plotted the town of Tallmadge. By 1809, twelve families had arrived, and in his cabin a Congregational church was organized; but Bacon was not to share in the further growth of church and town. Hard times, Jefferson's embargo and bank failures, checked emigration. He returned to Connecticut, tried unsuccessfully to meet his obligations, and died at Hartford, in August 1817.

[T. W. Baldwin, *Michael Bacon of Dedham and His Descendants* (1915); biog. sketch by E. N. Sill, and address by his son, Rev. Leonard Bacon, both in *Proc. in Commemoration of the Fiftieth Anniversary of the Settlement of Tallmadge* (1857); Charles Whittlesey, *Sketch of the Settlement and Progress of Tallmadge* (1842); E. O. Randall, "Hist. Sketch of the Settlement of Tallmadge," in *Ohio State Archæol. and Hist. Soc. Quart.*, vol. XVII, 1908, no. 3.] C. N.

BACON, DELIA SALTER (Feb. 2, 1811–Sept. 2, 1859), author, daughter of Rev. David Bacon [*q.v.*] and Alice (Parks) Bacon, was born in the log cabin which constituted the first house in Tallmadge, Ohio. A year later her heroic father's pioneering enterprise had failed, and he returned with his family, broken-hearted, to Connecticut. His death in 1817 left his wife and six children in utter poverty. Delia was charitably brought up by Mrs. Delia Williams of Hartford, where she attended the excellent school of Catharine Beecher [*q.v.*] until she was fifteen. Obliged at this early age to become self-supporting, and embarrassed by constant ill health, she endeavored unsuccessfully for four years, in conjunction with an elder sister, to establish a school of her own, at Southington, Conn., at Perth Amboy, N. J., at Jamaica, N. Y. She also published a collection of short stories, called *Tales of the Puritans* (1831), and later a closet drama, *The Bride of Fort Edward* (1839). Meanwhile she had found a source of income in lecture courses upon literature and history which she delivered with remarkable success in the larger eastern cities. Fair, slight, and graceful, she made upon her audiences an impression of radiant enthusiasm.

It was this fatal gift of enthusiasm, an inherited trait, which determined her later life. Having become convinced by 1852 that the Shakespearian plays were the work of a literary coterie, headed by Bacon, Raleigh, and Spenser, who produced the plays in order to set forth a liberal political philosophy which they could not present openly, she henceforth devoted all her energy and talent to the establishment of this strange thesis. Emerson, who seems to have been temporarily converted, encouraged her, and in May 1853 she sailed for England to prosecute her studies there. Carlyle, to whom she carried a letter of introduction from Emerson, at first warmly befriended her, but she turned a deaf ear to his suggestions of original sources, preferring to follow her inner illumination stimulated by the historical scenes about her. She lived in and near London for three years in shabby, unheated quarters with barely enough food to sustain life, quite alone and voluntarily friendless. *Putnam's Magazine,* after virtually contracting for a series of articles, published one and refused to accept the rest. Emerson, after being indirectly responsible for the loss of a bundle of her manuscripts, visibly cooled toward the whole enterprise. Her brother, Rev. Leonard Bacon [*q.v.*], pastor of the First Church, New Haven, who had had from the first no sympathy with her undertaking, offered to pay her way home if she would abandon it, but otherwise practically washed his hands of her. In these circumstances she found a needed friend in Nathaniel Hawthorne, then consul at Liverpool. With little faith in her thesis, he thought that it at least deserved a hearing, secured an English publisher for her book, loaned her money, and bore with her subsequent ingratitude when her mind began to fail. In the spring of 1856 she became obsessed with the idea that certain documents which would finally prove her theory were buried in the tomb of "Lord Leicester's stable-boy," as she habitually called Shakespeare. Going to Stratford, she had actually succeeded in making arrangements to have the tomb opened, when she seems to have been overcome with doubts. Her indications were not sufficiently clear; perhaps the documents were buried in Bacon's tomb or Raleigh's rather than Shakespeare's. Her *Philosophy of the Plays of Shakspere Unfolded* appeared in April 1857. It was greeted by the critics with ridicule and contempt, but of this Delia Bacon was happily unaware. Her mind, long unhinged, definitely gave way shortly after the publication of her book and she became violently insane. Through the ministrations of Hawthorne she was cared for in England until April 1858, when her nephew, George Bacon, returning from China, took her home with him. She died a few months later. Her book, containing a few pages of valuable criticism amid a mass of prolixity, remains one of the curiosities of literature. Hawthorne in later years averred that he had met one man who had read it through; there is no record of another. But to its author remains the credit, or discredit, of having first inaugurated the most absurd, and, in other hands, the most popular, of literary heresies.

[Theodore Bacon's *Delia Bacon* (1888) is a thorough and entirely satisfactory biog. See also Hawthorne's "Recollections of a Gifted Woman" in *Our Old Home* (1863), and Mrs. John Farrar's *Recollections of Seventy Years* (1866), ch. XL.]

E. S. B.

BACON, EDWARD PAYSON (May 16, 1834–Feb. 16, 1916), grain trader, was born in the town of Reading, Steuben (now Schuyler) County, N. Y., the eldest son of Matilda (Cowles) Bacon and Joseph F. Bacon, a tailor, both of early New England families. In 1838 the father, because of ill health, gave up his business and took the family to a farm near Geneva, N. Y. When Bacon was fifteen he was spared from the farm and entered the Collegiate Institute, Brockport, N.Y., to prepare for the ministry. Unfortunately, his father's health failed completely, and Bacon, to aid in supporting the family, obtained a position as freight and ticket clerk with the New York & Erie Railroad, at Hornellsville, N. Y. After four years (1851–55) with this company, he became chief clerk of its freight department in New York City. In 1855 he accepted a similar position in the new Chicago office of the Michigan Southern & Northern Indiana Railroad. The next year he began a nine-year connection with the Milwaukee & Mississippi Railroad. The systems of accounts and the method of conducting the freight and passenger departments as originated here by Bacon were adopted generally by the western roads, and the equipment which he devised for handling coupon tickets in the passenger department is in general use to-day. In 1865 he left the railroad in order to organize at Milwaukee the firm of Bacon & Everingham, grain traders. Successful from the start, he organized, in turn, the firm of E. P. Bacon & Company, and the E. P. Bacon Company, extended his operations to Chicago and Milwaukee, and became known as the leading grain trader of the Middle West. In this connection, and as a member and official of the Milwaukee Chamber of Commerce, he was able to institute many important changes in grain trading methods. The most important public work in which he engaged was a successful campaign for the enlargement of the powers of the Interstate Commerce Commission. He personally convinced President Roosevelt of the need for legislation, appeared before Congressional committees, was a delegate to the Conference of Commercial Organizations at Chicago, November 1899, and was chairman of the executive committees of the Interstate Commerce Law Conventions of 1900, 1904, and 1905. The result of these activities was the enactment of the law of 1906 empowering the Interstate Commerce Commission to determine reasonable rates and, after full hearing, to substitute the reasonable for the existing rates, the new rates to continue in effect until reversed by the courts. This is considered one of the most far-reaching acts of legislation intended to promote trade, and more credit for its realization is due Bacon than any other man. He had a large part in the founding of the Milwaukee Y.M.C.A., of which he was president from 1889 to 1891, and he was vice-president of the board of trustees of Beloit College, where he founded the Bacon Fellowships. He was married in 1858 to Emma Hobbs of Paterson, N. J., who died in 1892, and to Mrs. Ella C. Baird of Pelham Manor, N. Y., in 1895. He died at the age of eighty-two in his winter home at Daytona, Fla.

[*Grain Dealer's Jour.*, Mar. 10, 1916; Beloit Coll. Recs.; *Beloit Daily News*, Feb. 26, 1916; *Who's Who in America*, 1909.]

F. A. T.

BACON, EDWIN MUNROE (Oct. 20, 1844–Feb. 24, 1916), journalist, author, was born in Providence, R. I., of good Scotch and English ancestry on both sides, being the son of Henry Bacon, a Universalist clergyman, and of Eliza Ann (Munroe) Bacon. After an education at private schools in Providence, Philadelphia, and Boston, rounded off with a few months at an academy in Foxboro, Mass., he started, at nineteen, his career as a journalist, beginning as a reporter on the *Boston Daily Advertiser*. He rapidly advanced through various subordinate positions, securing additional experience by working for a year with the *Illustrated Chicago News* and (1868–72) with the *New York Times* as assistant night editor and news editor. In 1873 he was appointed editor of the *Boston Globe*, resigning, however, in 1878 over a matter of policy. He then returned to the *Daily Advertiser,* of which he became chief editor in 1883. In May 1886 he took over the editorial control of the *Boston Post,* holding the position until 1891, when he withdrew because of impaired health. He was married, Oct. 24, 1867, to Gusta E. Hill, daughter of Ira Hill of Boston, by whom he had one daughter.

After abandoning active newspaper work, Bacon devoted himself chiefly to the preparation of books descriptive of Boston and of New England. In succession he published *A Dictionary of Boston* (1886), *Boston Illustrated* (1893), *Historic Pilgrimages in New England* (1898), *Literary Pilgrimages in New England* (1902), *Boston: A Guide Book* (1903), *The Connecticut River and the Valley of the Connecticut* (1906), and *Rambles Around Old Boston* (1914), the last being a very pleasant volume, attractively illustrated with drawings by Lester G. Hornby. Bacon knew Boston as few of its residents have known it, and no one has written better than he about interesting spots in that city. He died, Feb. 24, 1916, in Cambridge, being survived by both his wife and his daughter.

Bacon was described by a fellow newspaper man as "a journalist of the old conscientious school," a man who "wrought his personality into every line of the newspaper at whose head he stood." Many younger men were trained under him to be thorough and accurate. Although he was not in any marked degree either original or brilliant, he insisted on high standards in his profession and he set a fine example for others to follow. By realizing the responsibility of his editorships and making the most of the opportunities which they offered, he performed an important service in his community.

[Obituaries in *Boston Transcript, Boston Globe,* and *Boston Herald,* Feb. 25, 1916; *Who's Who in America,* 1916–17; private information.]

C. M. F.

BACON, FRANK (Jan. 16, 1864–Nov. 19, 1922), actor and playwright, was born in Marysville, Cal., the son of Lyddell and Jane (McGren) Bacon. Leaving school in San José at the age of fourteen, he became successively a sheep-herder, an advertising solicitor, a photographer, a newspaper writer, and a candidate for the California legislature. He began his stage career after he had reached maturity; joining a stock company at the Garden Theatre in San José in 1890 he made his first appearance there as Sample Switchell in *Ten Nights in a Barroom* and acted over six hundred rôles during his ensuing seasons in that city. For a time he managed a company of his own in Portland, Ore., and then he began a long season at the Alcazar Theatre in San Francisco, where he further enlarged his repertory by acting a different character each week. After the San Francisco earthquake he came east with his wife, Jennie Weidman, whom he had married June 27, 1885, and they with their son and daughter played vaudeville engagements on the way. Arriving in New York, he was successful in securing first-class engagements, among them being the parts of William Carr in *Stop Thief,* Sam Graham in *The Fortune Hunter* (his tours in that play later taking him back to San Francisco), Hiram Higgins in *The Miracle Man,* and Jerry Primrose in *The Cinderella Man.* In collaboration with Winchell Smith he wrote *Lightnin',* which was based on a vaudeville sketch of his own entitled *Truthful James,* its principal character being especially constructed to fit his own manner and temperamental qualities. It opened in Washington, Jan. 28, 1918, and on Aug. 26, 1918, began its long run at the Gaiety Theatre in New York, where it continued uninterruptedly, with the exception of a few days when the theatre was closed on account of the actors' strike, through to Aug. 27, 1921, a total of 153 weeks and 1,291 performances. Bacon died suddenly in Chicago, where he was playing at the Blackstone Theatre. After his death, the play was performed with success in many American cities and also in London. The character of Lightnin' Bill Jones, so called ironically because he was leisurely in speech and action, gained the affection of an audience through its homely simplicity and humor, and through Bacon's quaint personality and natural style of acting. Among his other works for the stage was his collaboration with James Montgomery in the writing of *Me and Grant,* in which Bacon acted another Bill Jones, and with Freeman Tilden in the authorship of *Five O'Clock.* A play entitled *Everybody's Friend* was all his own.

[References are scattered through many periodical sources, and include notices of the plays in which he acted and interviews with him. A brief biog. sketch appears in *Who's Who in the Theatre,* ed. by John Parker, 4th ed., 1922. Long obituaries in *N. Y. Times, Tribune, Herald,* Nov. 20, 1922.]

E. F. E.

BACON, HENRY (Nov. 28, 1866–Feb. 16, 1924), architect, the son of Henry and Elizabeth (Kelton) Bacon, both of Massachusetts, was a direct descendant of Michael Bacon who settled in Dedham, Mass., in 1640. His father, a civil engineer, was employed in the early development of the Illinois Central Railroad, and it was while he was living in Watseka, Ill., that his son Henry was born. In the later practise of his profession the father moved from place to place, finally settling in Wilmington, N. C. as government engineer in charge of the Cape Fear River improvements. Henry Bacon went to school in Wilmington and at the age of fifteen was sent north to enter the Chauncy Hall School in Boston. He also attended the University of Illinois for one year. His architectural studies began in the office of Chamberlain & Whidden, in Boston, but he soon left to enter the office of McKim, Mead & White, in New York City. In 1889 he won the Rotch Traveling Scholarship for architectural students and this gave him two years of study and travel in Europe. On his return he went back to the office of McKim, Mead & White which was then at work on designs for certain of the buildings for the World's Fair in Chicago. Bacon soon found himself actively at work on these plans and he was later sent to Chicago in connection with their execution. There he met Daniel H. Burnham [*q.v.*], with whom a lifelong friendship ensued. On Apr. 27, 1893, he married Laura Calvert, daughter of the British consul at the Dardanelles.

In 1897 Bacon left the office of McKim, Mead & White to found, with James Brite, also of New York, a new partnership. The firm won the competition for the Jersey City Public Library and thereafter built a number of public buildings and private houses. The partnership was dissolved in 1902 and Bacon practised under his own name until his death. His connection with McKim, the winning of the Rotch Scholarship, and other circumstances which brought him intimately into the sphere of Greek culture, contributed toward the formation of his architectural predilections. He was a devoted adherent of the theory of Greek architecture and his work is profoundly marked by that influence. If his technique was somewhat austere, it sufficed to win him such laurels as few architects have enjoyed during their life. The history of American architecture records no more impressive occasion than that in May 1923, when Bacon stood, under the evening sky, on the steps of the Lincoln Memorial, his crowning work, at Washington, and received from President Harding the Gold Medal of the American Institute of Architects, the highest distinction it was in the power of his fellow craftsmen to confer. Very early in his career Bacon had become interested in monumental work, the designing of pedestals, and the accompanying architectural settings for statues. He collaborated with various sculptors and executed a great deal of work jointly with Augustus Saint-Gaudens and Daniel Chester French, all of which seemed to lead logically to his final achievement at Washington.

He designed, among others, the following buildings: Public Library, Paterson, N. J.; Memorial Day Nursery, Paterson, N. J.; Halle Brothers Department Store, Cleveland, Ohio; Railroad Station, Naugatuck, Conn.; Waterbury General Hospital, Waterbury, Conn.; Memorial Bridge, Naugatuck, Conn.; Union Square Savings Bank, New York City; Chelsea Savings Bank, Chelsea, Mass.; National City Bank, New Rochelle, N. Y.; Citizens & Manufacturers National Bank, Waterbury, Conn.; Court of the Four Seasons, Panama-Pacific Exposition, San Francisco; Electrical Society Building, Middletown, Conn.; Astronomical Observatory, a dormitory, and the general plan of the University in connection with its future extension, Middletown, Conn.; gates for the University of Virginia, Charlottesville, Va.; First Congregational Church (alterations), Providence, R. I.; Woodmere High School, Woodmere, N. Y.; Public Bath, Brooklyn, N. Y. In collaboration with Daniel Chester French there were designed some fifty memorials and monuments, of which the principal ones are: Parkman Monument, Jamaica Plain, Mass.; Melvin Monument, Concord, Mass.; Oglethorpe Monument, Savannah, Ga.; Marshall Field Monument, Chicago, Ill.; Spencer Monument, Atlanta, Ga.; Lincoln Monument, Lincoln, Nebr.; Draper Monument, Milford, Mass.; Longfellow Monument, Cambridge, Mass.; Spencer Trask Memorial, Saratoga Springs, N. Y.; Lafayette Monument, Brooklyn, N. Y.; Republic Monument, Chicago, Ill.; Du Pont Fountain, Washington, D. C.; War Memorial for the State of Massachusetts, St. Mihiel, France. With Saint-Gaudens there were designed the Parnell Monument, Dublin, Ireland; Hanna Monument, Cleveland, Ohio; Whistler Monument, West Point, N. Y.; Magee Memorial, Pittsburgh, Pa.; Gov. Flower Memorial, Watertown, N. Y.

[See C. H. Whitaker, "Five Architects and One Truth," *Jour. of the Am. Inst. of Architects,* Sept. 1924; *N. Y. Times* and *N. Y. Tribune,* Feb. 17, 1924. At Wesleyan University there is to be a Memorial Room, a duplicate of Bacon's private office, in which will be placed his library, together with the furnishings of his office and all his original drawings and architectural sketches.]

C. H. W.

BACON, JOHN (Apr. 9, 1738–Oct. 25, 1820), Congregational clergyman, legislator, the son of John and Ruth (Spaulding) Bacon, and a descendant of Michael Bacon who emigrated to America in 1640, was born at Canterbury, Conn. He was graduated from the College of New Jersey (Princeton) in 1765, was licensed to preach by the presbytery at Lewes, Del., and preached for some time in Somerset County in that state. On Sept. 25, 1771, he was installed as pastor of the Old South Church, Boston. Two months later he married Elizabeth Goldthwaite, the widow of his predecessor, Rev. Alexander Cumming. Trouble soon arose in his parish. His training as a Presbyterian may have made it difficult to enter into the traditions of the Congregationalists of Massachusetts, while his severe manner, tenacious opinions, and fondness for argument created opposition. Furthermore, he offended patriot sentiment by publicly reading Gov. Hutchinson's proclamation calling upon the people to observe a day of thanksgiving particularly for the preservation of their civil and religious liberty. Hence his parishioners were all the more ready to criticize his theological views, and on Feb. 8, 1775, he was dismissed from the pastorate. In 1781, at Bacon's request, the parish gave him a testimonial of its confidence and respect and stated that its only differences with him related to the doctrine of the Atonement and the practise of the Half-way Covenant. Upon leaving the Old South he removed to Stockbridge, where he became a farmer and resided until his death. The constitution submitted to the voters of Massachusetts in 1778 excluded "negroes, Indians, and Molattoes" from the suffrage. Bacon opposed this on the ground that such persons would then be taxed without representation and "would be justified in making the same opposition against us which we are making against Great Britain." The provision was retained but the constitution was rejected by the people and that adopted in 1780 contained no race discrimination. Although not a lawyer, Bacon served as associate judge of the court of common pleas of Berkshire County from 1779 to 1807 and as presiding judge from 1807 to 1811. He was twice a member of the General Court and served twelve terms in the Massachusetts House of Representatives and ten in the Massachusetts Senate. In national politics he was a Jeffersonian Democrat and as such served in the national House of Representatives from 1801 to 1803 and was a presidential elector in 1804.

[Accounts of Bacon appear in Electa F. Jones, *Stockbridge, Past and Present, Records of an Old Mission Station* (1854), p. 257, and in the *New Eng. Hist. and Geneal. Reg.*, Jan. 1890, pp. 122–23. The controversy at Old South Church which led to his dismissal is described in Hamilton Andrews Hill, *Hist. of the Old South Church (Third Church) Boston, 1669–1884* (1890), II; Benjamin Blydenburgh Wisner, *Hist. of the Old South Church in Boston* (1830), p. 53; and Leverett W. Spring, "A Case of Church Discipline in the Berkshires," *Proc. Mass. Hist. Soc.*, XLIX, 96.] L. B. E.

BACON, LEONARD (Feb. 19, 1802–Dec. 24, 1881), Congregational clergyman, was born at Detroit, Mich., the son of Rev. David Bacon [*q.v.*] and Alice (Parks) Bacon. In his sixth year the family removed to Tallmadge, Ohio, and one of the boy's first memories was of a school exhibition in the neighboring town of Hudson in which he and John Brown, later of Harper's Ferry fame, conducted a dialogue. At the age of ten, after his missionary father's defeat and poverty-stricken return to Connecticut, the boy was put under the care of an uncle, whose name he bore, in Hartford. So well was he trained at the Hartford Grammar School that at fifteen he entered the sophomore class of Yale College. Although maintaining a good rank, he fell below the expectations of his classmates, and, at the end of the course (1820), one of them, Theodore D. Woolsey, reproved him because "he had not studied enough and was in danger of hurting himself by superficial reading." This warning and a maturing sense of responsibility so influenced his habits in Andover Theological Seminary, which he entered in the autumn of 1820, that upon graduation he was assigned the principal address. On Sept. 28, 1824, he was ordained as an evangelist by the Hartford North Consociation; it being his intention to go as a missionary to the Western frontier. The next day brought a letter from the ecclesiastical society of the First Church of New Haven, asking him to supply their vacant pulpit. After preaching fourteen sermons he was called by the society with a vote of 68 to 20 to become its minister at a salary of $1,000. He was installed over this noted church on Mar. 9, 1825, when he was twenty-three years of age. The young man was rather appalled by the weight of his responsibilities. In the pews before him sat Noah Webster, the lexicographer, James Hillhouse, senator, Eli Whitney, inventor of the cotton-gin, and many of the faculty of the college. The congregation was accustomed to a high order of ministerial ability. His immediate predecessor was Nathaniel W. Taylor, whose sermons were an intellectual event; before him, Moses Stuart, distinguished for scholarship and effective speech, had been the pastor. Evidently Leonard Bacon did not at first fulfil the hopes of his parish, for after some months a committee waited upon him, intimating that his sermons were not worthy of the high place he held. His answer was, "Gentlemen, they shall be made worthy." With the years he grew in power and gained hold upon the affections of his people. They were proud of his unusual influence in the city, of the commanding position he occupied in Congregational councils, and of the reputation which extended beyond the boundaries of the denomination. He was the sole and active pastor of the First Church for forty-one years, and pastor emeritus until his death. When it became known that he was leaving the active ministry the corporation of Yale offered him a chair in the Divinity School, and he was acting professor of revealed theology from 1866 to 1871, when he became lecturer on church polity and American church history, holding this position until his death in his eightieth year. He was twice married: in July 1825, to Lucy Johnson of Johnstown, N. Y., and in June 1847, to Catherine E. Terry of Hartford, Conn. Fourteen children were born to him.

Bacon was not primarily a great preacher. Although his sermons were always solid and dignified, they could be on ordinary Sabbaths very dull. But no occasion of unusual significance found him unequal to his task. As a theologian he was in sympathy with the system of thought known as the "New Haven School," yet he held his convictions in a spirit of abundant charity. His style in writing was the clear expression of a practical understanding, glowing with moral earnestness. At times it was made graceful by phrases of rare felicity. A gift of genuine poetic sentiment found expression in several hymns used in the churches of his order. The one beginning

"O God, beneath Thy guiding hand,"

written in 1838 for the second centennial of New Haven and of his church, sprang into immediate popularity and has secured a permanent place in American hymnology.

A natural controversialist, he was never so completely awake and self-possessed as in public debate with no moment available for preparation. Yet he fought as a champion, not as a gladiator. He engaged in no warfare which did not engage his conscience. "He inherited in large measure," wrote a friend, "the old Puritan zeal for making things straight in this crooked world, for compelling magistrates to rule justly, and for beating down the upholders of demoralizing institutions and customs." Yet he was a controversialist who sought to quell controversy. Two theological battles convulsed the Congregational churches of Connecticut during the early years of his ministry. The first was the famous Taylor-Tyler dispute on certain doctrines concerning man's freedom of choice. After the conflict had become so bitter that the followers of Dr. Tyler founded a new theological seminary at East Windsor, since removed to Hartford, Bacon wrote an *Appeal to the Congregational Ministers of Connecticut against a Division* (1840), in which he showed that the two warring factions agreed on twenty-six points; as these more than covered the essential tenets of the Christian religion, he urged that, although the differences might be of importance to the science of theology, they afforded no occasion for brethren to renounce each other. The next pronounced disquiet grew out of the revolutionary teachings of Horace Bushnell [*q.v.*]. In 1847 Bushnell published his *Christian Nurture* in which he rejected the prevalent view of the necessity of conscious conversion and advanced the opinion that a child in a Christian household should "grow up a Christian," be trained in the Christian faith, and at the proper time be received into the church without experiencing a dramatic conversion. This was followed in 1849 by a still more unsettling book entitled *God in Christ,* in which was advanced what has since become known as the "moral influence" theory of the Atonement, in opposition to the prevailing substitutionary or governmental explanation. Bushnell, fiercely attacked, was defended by the Hartford Central Association. So intense was the feeling that fifty-one ministers petitioned the General Association of the state to exclude the Hartford Association from fellowship. Bacon, though not holding Bushnell's views, was influential in passing an ambiguous or mollifying resolution which prevented a division. If he was regarded as the most formidable polemical writer and speaker in the American Congregationalism of his day, he was equally distinguished for the soundness of his judgment. During the Beecher-Tilton controversy, a council of churches called by Beecher's opponents in 1874 chose Bacon as moderator, while a later council held in Plymouth Church in 1876, the largest advisory council of its kind ever convened, also elected him moderator.

Perhaps Bacon's chief service to his denomination was his work in arousing Congregationalism to self-consciousness and confidence in its polity. In his early ministry the churches of this order were in a slough of self-distrust. A form of semi-presbyterianism was common among them, and a "Plan of Union," entered into with Presbyterianism, hindered Congregational polity from entering into the developing West. Bacon, as one of the editors of the *Christian Spectator* from 1826 to 1838, as one of the founders and editor for a score of years of the *New Englander,* by his speeches at conventions and his influence in national missionary societies, and by his historical studies, did more than any other to awaken the churches of this faith to the value of their heritage. In 1839 he published *Thirteen Historical*

Discourses, but his most elaborate and permanent work, *The Genesis of the New England Churches* (1874), was the fruit of his old age. In this he told the story of the beginnings of Congregationalism in England, its establishment at Plymouth, Mass., and its struggle until success was assured. It is worthy of note that this successor of John Davenport was much more in sympathy with the principles and polity of the Pilgrims than with those of the Puritans.

Bacon's most conspicuous claim for remembrance rests on his leadership in the anti-slavery cause. In his student days at Andover he wrote a report *On the Black Population of the United States* (1823) which was extensively circulated in New England, and its severest passages quoted even in Richmond. On going to New Haven he organized a society for the improvement of the colored people of that city. With Garrison and the extreme abolitionists he had no sympathy, and he received from them malignant attacks. In 1846 he published a volume entitled *Slavery Discussed in Occasional Essays.* This fell into the hands of a comparatively unknown lawyer in Illinois, Abraham Lincoln. A statement in the preface made a profound impression on the future emancipator: "If that form of government, that system of social order is not wrong,—if those laws of the southern states, by virtue of which slavery exists there and is what it is, are not wrong, nothing is wrong." The sentiment reappeared in Lincoln's famous declaration, "If slavery is not wrong, nothing is wrong." In 1848 the name of Leonard Bacon appears as one of the founders and the senior editor of the *Independent,* which asserted as a motto, "We stand for free soil." Bitter opposition resulted from his anti-slavery work, even in his own church, but looking back on that epoch, he said: "I make no complaint—all reproaches, all insults endured in a conflict with so gigantic a wickedness against God and man, are to be received and remembered, not as injuries but as honors." During the Civil War he was a steadfast supporter of the administration.

In appearance Bacon was of slight and sinewy frame, with a massive head, bushy hair and beard, a face suggestive of thought and intense energy, blue-gray eyes, lips mobile for wit, yet set in firmness, the whole figure denoting a man of vital force expressing itself in intellectual strength.

[Williston Walker, *Ten New England Leaders* (1901); *Leonard Bacon, Pastor of the First Church in New Haven* (1882); S. A. W. Duffield, *English Hymns* (1866); *Congreg. Yr. Bk.* 1882, pp. 18–21; *New Haven Evening Register,* Dec. 24, 25, 1881.]

C. A. D—e.

BACON, LEONARD WOOLSEY (Jan. 1, 1830–May 12, 1907), Congregational clergyman, known chiefly for his historical and controversial writings, was born in New Haven, Conn., the son of Rev. Leonard Bacon [*q.v.*] and Lucy (Johnson) Bacon. After graduating from Yale in 1850 he went abroad with his father and traveled in Europe and the East. Upon his return he studied theology for two years at Andover Seminary and for another at the Yale Divinity School, graduating from the latter in 1854. He then studied medicine, and in 1856 received the degree of M.D. from the Yale Medical School, but on Oct. 16 of the same year was ordained to the Congregational ministry at Litchfield, Conn. On Oct. 7, 1857, he married Susan, daughter of Nathaniel and Almira (Selden) Bacon. He served the church in Litchfield until 1860, and for the next eleven years was successively state missionary of the general association of Connecticut, and pastor in Stamford, Brooklyn, and Baltimore. The next five years he spent abroad, during a part of which time he was pastor of the American Church in Geneva. From 1878 to 1892, his pastorates took him from the Park Church, Norwich, Conn., to Philadelphia, where he had charge of the Woodland Presbyterian Church, then to Savannah, where he served the Ancient Independent Presbyterian Church, and finally back to Norwich, where from 1887 to 1892 he was at the Second Congregational Church. The next ten years he devoted to study and writing, but from 1902 to 1906 he again engaged in pastoral work, this time at Assonet, Mass. His first wife died in 1887, and on June 26, 1890, he married Letitia Wilson Jordan.

He was a restless, intense man, brilliant but erratic, widely informed and versatile, with a taste for historical investigation, a forceful speaker, and a vigorous, slashing writer. His lack of tact, frankness in speaking his mind, and polemic spirit were not conducive to long pastorates. A born controversialist, he scented opportunity for combat from afar, and his essays on "Two Sides of a Saint" (St. Francis de Sales) and "William Lloyd Garrison" in *Irenics and Polemics* (1895) reveal with what relish he corrected perversions of history and discredited popular idols. His own bias is always apparent in his writings, but he sought diligently for facts and endeavored to be fair. Interest in the Old Catholic movement led him to publish several volumes of translations from Père Hyacinthe in 1869, 1870, and 1871, and in the following year, *An Inside View of the Vatican Council.* He also published another translation, *The Abbé Tigrane* (1875).

Bacon

His *History of American Christianity* (1897) is the final volume in the American Church History series, and sums up what is described in the preceding volumes without adding much that is new. *The Congregationalists* (1904) is a brief popular work. Other writings of his include *Fair Answers to Fair Questions* (1868); *Church Papers* (1876); *A Life Worth Living, Memorial to Emily Bliss Gould* (1879); *The Sabbath Question* (1882), with G. B. Bacon; *The Simplicity that is in Christ* (1886); *Norwich, The Rose of New England* (1896); *Young People's Societies* (1900), with C. A. Northrop; *Anti-Slavery before Garrison* (1903). He also edited several hymnbooks and wrote much for periodicals.

[*Obit. Record Grads. of Yale 1900–1910* (1910); *Who's Who in America*, 1906–7; *Cong. Yr. Bk.* 1908; T. W. Baldwin, *Bacon Geneal.* (1915).]

C. N.

BACON, NATHANIEL (Jan. 2, 1647–October 1676), colonial leader, celebrated in history as the Rebel, was the son of Thomas Bacon of Friston Hall, Suffolk, and a cousin of Lord Chancellor Francis Bacon. Educated at Cambridge University and at Gray's Inn, he afterward traveled widely on the Continent; married Elizabeth, daughter of Sir Edward Duke; emigrated to Virginia; and settled at Curl's Neck on James River. His talents and kinship to the astute senior Nathaniel Bacon of the Council led to his appointment to a seat in that body soon after his arrival in Virginia. From the beginning, his sympathies were with the people at large; and he chafed under the wrongs which they were made to suffer. In 1676, when Gov. Berkeley's failure to check the Indian invasion brought the popular discontent to a head, Bacon was chosen by the people to lead them in an excursion against the common foe. Having lost an overseer by the tomahawk and resenting the Governor's delays, he entered the campaign with fierce ardor. But the conquest of the savages was not the limit of his plans. He aimed at a reform of the whole system of colonial laws in order to remove the grinding inequalities that existed. At the head of a small army, he penetrated the forest domain of the Pamunkey Indians without waiting for Berkeley to give him a commission; and he next forced the Governor to summon a new assembly to exact the reform measures so generally desired. Before this assembly convened, Bacon, with a strong following, assaulted the forts of the Susquehannocks and Occaneechees in the Fork of Roanoke River, and having dispersed these tribes, returned to the settlements. He was soon elected a member of the projected reform assembly and, with an escort, sailed down the river to Jamestown. On arriving there, his sloop was seized, and he and his companions were brought before Berkeley, who, after violent reproaches, pardoned him, and readmitted him to the Council.

Fearing secret plots against his life, Bacon deserted Jamestown at night; then returning with a large body of incensed supporters, he held a stormy interview with the infuriated Governor, and extorted from him a commission to march against the Indians. The Falls in the James was named as the rendezvous; but hardly had his soldiers assembled there, when news arrived that Berkeley was riding up and down the country trying to raise a force to put down "the rebels." The cry arose: "To Jamestown"; but before Bacon could get there, the Governor had fled to the Eastern Shore. Bacon now, by proclamation, called upon the principal planters of the colony to coöperate with him in restoring peace and reforming the laws. He next seized the colony's guard-ship in order to transport commissioners across the bay and to demand the Governor's surrender. But Berkeley, instead of being captured by these commissioners, was successful in capturing them. In the meanwhile, Bacon had invaded the villages of the Pamunkey Indians. While this expedition was in progress, Berkeley returned in triumph to Jamestown. Informed of this fact, Bacon made a rush for that place with a large force, and after a sharp battle on its outskirts, captured it, and burnt it to the ground. Berkeley again fled to the Eastern Shore.

Withdrawing to Green Spring near the town, Bacon drafted an oath of fidelity to himself which he compelled every citizen in his power to sign. All opposition to his supremacy having ceased, he became conciliatory in spirit, so as to consolidate his support; but before he could fully develop this statesmanlike policy, he was taken ill in Gloucester County, died, and was buried in the waters of one of its rivers. The spot of his interment has never been known down to the present day. With the withdrawal of his guiding hand, the rebellion gradually collapsed.

[The only formal biog. of Nathaniel Bacon in existence was written by Mrs. Mary Newton Stanard, *The Story of Bacon's Rebellion* (1907). There is, however, an extraordinary wealth of original material relating to the events of his life. The following are among the most authoritative: "The Beginning, Progress, and Conclusion of Bacon's Rebellion in Va.," by Thos. Mathew in Force's *Tracts*, vol. I (1835); *Strange News from Va.* (1677); "True Narrative of the Rise, Progress, and Cessation of the Late Rebellion in Va.," *British Colonial Papers*, XLI, 79; "Grievances of the Several Counties," *British Colonial Papers*, republished in the *Va. Mag. of Hist. and Biog.*, vols. I, II, III, and the

William and Mary College Quart. Mag., vols. II, III, IV, VIII, IX, XI. Proc. of Courts Martial, W. W. Hening, *Statutes at Large*, vols. II, III. There are valuable reprints in the *Mass. Hist. Coll.*, 4th ser., IX, 177–84; also numerous reprints in John Burk, *Hist. of Va.*, vol. II (1805).] P. A. B.

BACON, ROBERT (July 5, 1860–May 29, 1919), banker, diplomat, soldier, came of a line of sturdy Puritans. The emigrant ancestor, Nathaniel Bacon of Stratton in Cornwall, arrived at Barnstable, Mass., in 1639. Admitted a freeman in 1646, he subsequently held several town offices of trust, was one of the seven assistants to the governor, and a member of the Council of War. His wife was Hannah, daughter of the Rev. John Mayo. Nathaniel Jr. married Sarah, daughter of Thomas Hinckley, governor of Plymouth Colony. The grandfather of Robert, Daniel Carpenter Bacon, shipped before the mast in 1809 and was in command of a ship when just over twenty. Later he was a shipowner and merchant. William Benjamin, his second son, was the father of Robert. After graduation from Harvard, he went to China as supercargo and later with his elder brother became a member of the firm of Daniel G. Bacon & Company. His second wife was Emily Crosby Low, a noted beauty. Robert Bacon, the second son of that marriage, was born at Jamaica Plain, Mass. He went to Hopkinson's School and Harvard, graduating in June 1880, the youngest man of a class which included Theodore Roosevelt, of whom he was always a devoted friend and follower. His closest friend at college was Dr. Henry Jackson, who writes of him: "He was singularly blessed by nature with a superb physique to which was added a manly beauty; he may well be chosen as a type of the perfection of manhood at its best." His superb physique placed him in a position to excel in any sport. He was a member of the freshman football team; first base and captain of the freshman baseball team; member of the University football team, and one year its captain; winner in heavy-weight sparring, 100-yard dash, and quarter-mile run; and number seven in the university crew.

After a trip around the world, he settled down to a business career with the firm of Lee, Higginson & Company, whom he left in 1883 to become a partner in the firm of E. Rollins Morse & Brother. On Oct. 10 of this same year he married Martha Waldron Cowdin of New England ancestry, but then living in New York. He remained with the Morse firm until 1894, when he accepted a partnership in J. P. Morgan & Company. Three of the most important enterprises in which Bacon took part in the latter firm are given by Dr. James Brown Scott, his biographer, as: the relief of the Government in the panic of 1895; the formation of the United States Steel Corporation in 1901, and the negotiations resulting in the Northern Securities Company. He resigned from the firm in 1903.

In July 1905, Elihu Root was offered the secretaryship of state by President Roosevelt to succeed John Hay. In carrying out his own and Hay's policies, Root needed an assistant secretary who could understand and help to execute them and he offered the position to Robert Bacon. During Root's absence at the Pan-American Conference at Rio de Janeiro in the summer of 1906 and his subsequent trip through South America, Bacon was acting secretary. Early in 1909, Root resigned and was succeeded on Jan. 27 by Bacon for the few remaining weeks of Roosevelt's administration. President Taft appointed him ambassador to France in December 1909, but he resigned in January 1912, to become Fellow of Harvard, of which he had been an Overseer. At the request of the Carnegie Endowment he made a trip to South America in 1913. His addresses on this trip were published in a volume entitled, *For Better Relations with Our Latin American Neighbors: A Journey to South America* (1915).

From the outbreak of the World War Bacon realized its seriousness and that ultimately the United States would be forced to take part. As early as August 1914, he sailed for France, and while Mrs. Bacon was raising funds for the "American Ambulance," he was personally helping the work and even driving an ambulance at the front. Toward the end of 1915 he made a hasty trip to the United States, where he threw himself into the campaign for preparedness and attended the military training camp at Plattsburg, N. Y., which he entered as a private. In the summer of 1916, he announced his candidacy for the United States Senate on a platform of support for the Allies and preparedness. Although not running as a candidate of the regular organization, he polled an enormous vote in the primaries (144,366 of a total of 297,739), even with the handicap of being a last-minute candidate.

In May 1917, he was commissioned a major in the quartermaster corps of the Army and sailed for France with Gen. Pershing. His military service was distinguished and as Chief of the American Military Mission at British General Headquarters his work was most valuable. Shortly before the Armistice he was promoted to be a lieutenant-colonel of infantry and left Paris for home in March 1919, a physical wreck from over-exertion and strain. On May 29 of the same year he died. Never a great man, he was of the highest type of sportsman, business man, and public servant. His entire devotion to his country, his integrity, his patriotism and sacrifices for the Allied cause were notable.

[The chief source of information is *Robert Bacon. Life and Letters* (1923), by James Brown Scott, an admirable and sympathetic biog. by a competent scholar and warm friend. Bacon's important papers while secretary of state and his dispatches to the department while ambassador to France may be found in *Foreign Relations of the U. S.*, 1906–12, and in the MS. archives of the State Dept.]

M.S.

BACON, THOMAS (*c.* 1700–May 24, 1768), clergyman of the Church of England in Maryland, leader in educational and philanthropic activity there, was born on the Isle of Man. He was a brother of Sir Anthony Bacon, who was a graduate of the University of Dublin, a London shipping merchant with Maryland connections, and later a resident of Glamorganshire. Mention is made of another brother who kept a coffee-house in Dublin ("Callister Papers," quoted in *Maryland Historical Magazine,* VI, 219). Thomas acquired a good education, and if the British Museum catalogue is correct in this instance, he was "of the Custom House, Dublin" in 1736–37, when he published *A Compleat System of the Revenue of Ireland, in Its Branches of Import, Export, and Inland Duties.* On Sept. 23, 1744, having previously studied under Thomas Wilson, Bishop of Sodor and Man, he was by him ordained deacon at Kirk Michael; and on Mar. 10, 1744/5 he was made priest "in order to go into the Plantations" (John Keble, *The Life of the Right Reverend Father in God, Thomas Wilson,* 1863, II, 920). He arrived at Oxford, Talbot County, Md., in October of the same year, having been appointed domestic chaplain to the Proprietary, an honorary office apparently, though it seems to have ensured his support of the Proprietary, a support which later made him many enemies who did not hesitate to attack his character, and interfere with his projects (see *Archives of Maryland,* IX, "Correspondence of Gov. Horatio Sharpe," ed. by Wm. H. Browne, 1890, p. 417; also Ethan Allen, "Rev. Thomas Bacon," *Quarterly Church Review,* XVII, 448). He was appointed curate of St. Peter's parish, and at the death of the incumbent, a few months later, he became rector. In 1747 he made Dover his residence.

A man of varied ability, social proclivities, and musical talent, he soon became popular and influential. Although himself a slaveholder, he was a pioneer in the education of the negro. He preached two sermons to slaves addressing them as "my dear black brothers and sisters," and assuring them as large a share in the kingdom of heaven as the greatest man alive, if they behaved themselves aright (*Two Sermons Preached to a Congregation of Black Slaves at the Parish Church of S. P. In the Province of Maryland, By an American Pastor,* London, 1749). The motive of their publication, he says, was to "raise a spirit of emulation among his brethren to attempt something in their several parishes toward bringing home so great a number of wandering souls to Christ." They were followed by *Four Sermons upon the Great and Indispensable Duty of All Christian Masters and Mistresses to Bring up Their Negro Slaves in the Knowledge and Fear of God,* London (1750), which was placed in the list of books for distribution by the Society for Promoting Christian Knowledge in England. In 1750 he inaugurated a movement which resulted in the establishment of a Charity Working School, a free manual-training school, in which there was no distinction of sex, race, or condition of servitude. Troubles came to him in his later years. His wife died in 1755, and his only son was drowned at sea. The same year a mulatto, Rachel Beck, charged him with an offense against law and morals. He seems to have been acquitted, or the case dropped, for later he sued her successfully for slander. In 1757 he married Elizabeth, daughter of Col. Thomas Bozman of Oxford Neck, whom in 1755 he had united to Rev. John Belchier. The latter proved to be an adventurer with a wife living in England. For not publishing the banns or securing licenses in either case, Bacon was heavily fined. Nevertheless, in 1759, he was appointed reader at All Saints, Frederick, the most valuable living in the Province, and in 1762 was inducted as rector. Here also he exerted himself in behalf of popular education. After years of painstaking labor, and in the face of political opposition, he finally published in 1765, a work of much importance, *Laws of Maryland at Large,* etc., a compilation of all the laws of the Province, beginning with the first legislation in 1638. It was printed in Annapolis, and "in many particulars it formed the most elaborate and laborious piece of editorial work until that time undertaken in America," and "it happens also to have been a specimen of typography which was not exceeded in dignity and beauty by any production of a colonial press" (L. C. Wroth, "The Reverend Thomas Bacon, and His Edition of the Laws of Maryland at Large," *A History of Printing in Colonial Maryland,* 1922). Bacon died in Frederick but his burial place is now unknown.

[In addition to references above, see S. A. Harrison and O. Tilghman, *Hist. of Talbot County, Md.,* I (1915); B. C. Steiner, *Hist. of Education in Md.* (1894); *Md. Hist. Mag.* (1911); W. B. Sprague, *Annals of the Am. Pulpit,* V (1859).]

H.E.S.

BADEAU, ADAM (Dec. 29, 1831–Mar. 19, 1895), author, soldier, diplomat, the son of Nicholas Badeau, a descendant of a French Huguenot family, was born in New York City, received a secondary-school education at Tarrytown, N. Y., and wrote articles for newspapers. He then procured an appointment as clerk in the State Department. At the outbreak of the Civil War, Badeau became an aide on the staff of Gen. T. W. Sherman, and in 1862 on that of Gen. Q. A. Gillmore. On Apr. 8, 1864, Gen. Grant announced the appointment of "Lt. Col. Adam Badeau" as a military secretary on his staff. Grant seems to have relied heavily on Badeau's abilities, and on Feb. 20, 1865, recommended that he be made colonel by brevet. During these two years began the friendship that so completely made the remainder of Badeau's life—he became attached to the person and fortunes of Grant. He continued on Grant's staff until March 1869, retiring in May with the rank of brigadier-general by brevet. After Grant's inauguration as president, Badeau became secretary of the legation at London, and in May 1870 was appointed consul-general at that port. He remained in London almost all the time until 1881 except as he accompanied Grant for a time on his travels. In 1881 he was nominated by Garfield to be chargé d'affaires at Copenhagen, but the nomination met opposition in the Senate. In 1882 he accepted the position of consul-general at Havana, where he busied himself, in addition to his ordinary duties, in making a report on the defenses of Havana, and in writing an article for the *Century* (February 1884) on "Lieut.-Gen. Sheridan." In 1884 Badeau disagreed with the administration policy in regard to Cuba, on the ground that the interests of Americans there were being "grossly neglected"; and he declared also that "culpable frauds" had been committed at the Havana consulate. When the state department failed to investigate the accusation, Badeau resigned (Badeau, *Grant in Peace,* 1887, pp. 535, 542, 549, 552, 556–57, 559, 560). On his return to America, he collaborated with Grant on an article about the battle of Shiloh, and at the latter's suggestion went to live at Grant's house to aid in the preparation of the General's *Memoirs.* His connection with this task ended in May 1885. After Grant's death in the same year Badeau wrote many articles on military and other subjects. He died at Ridgewood, N. J., Mar. 19, 1895. The career of Badeau was to an unusual degree concerned with the activities of a single associate—Gen. Grant. His *Military History of Ulysses S. Grant* (in 3 vols., 1868, 1881) is a technical work of high order (J. K. Hosmer, *Outcome of the Civil War,* 1907, p. 308; Henry Adams, *The Education of Henry Adams,* 1907, p. 263). Badeau's *Grant in Peace* (1887) is a detailed study of Grant's activities and characteristics, and not least informing are Badeau's admissions concerning the weaknesses of President Grant. Cabinet appointments were determined upon, he asserts, partly because Grant liked the appointees as companions or as personal friends, and in part because Grant was unwilling to have any "rivals near the throne." As a whole, the volume deserves a high place in the literature of the period of political reconstruction.

[The best source of information about Badeau is his volume *Grant in Peace* (1887), esp. the coll. of letters in ch. 50. See also *Mil. Hist. of Ulysses S. Grant* (1868, 1881), II, 19–20. Other writings of Badeau are *The Vagabond* (1859), *Conspiracy: A Cuban Romance* (1885), *Aristocracy in England* (1886). See J. D. Cox in J. N. Larned, *Lit. of Am. Hist.* for estimates of the *Mil. Hist.;* W. H. Powell, *List of Officers of the Army of the U. S. 1779–1900;* obituary in *N. Y. Evening Post,* Mar. 20, 1895; *Ann. Cyc.* 1895 (1896).]

C. R. L.

BADGER, GEORGE EDMUND (Apr. 17, 1795–May 11, 1866), jurist, secretary of the navy, senator, was born in New Bern, N. C. His father, Thomas Badger, a native of Windham, Conn., after attending Yale, went to New Bern, where he studied law and, in 1793, married Lydia, a daughter of Richard Cogdell, a Revolutionary leader. He died early, after attaining some distinction at the bar, leaving a widow and several children. George, the first child and only son, attended a local academy and was for two years a student at Yale, but was forced, on account of poverty, to leave without graduating. Returning to New Bern he studied law and was admitted to the bar at the age of nineteen, and soon thereafter, by appointment, became solicitor for his district. In 1814 he served for a short time as aide with the rank of major in the militia which was called out to repel a threatened British invasion. Two years later he was elected to the House of Commons by the borough town of New Bern, and at the conclusion of the session he moved to Hillsboro to take the practise of Thomas Ruffin, who had been elevated to the superior bench. There he remained several years, moving finally to Warrenton, the home of his wife, Rebecca, daughter of Gov. James Turner. In 1820 he was elected a judge of the superior court and served five years, resigning to begin the practise of law in Raleigh. His first wife having died, he married Mary, daughter of Col. William Polk, and sister of Leonidas Polk, later bishop and Confederate general. Upon her death he married a widow, Delia Williams, daughter of Sherwood Haywood of Raleigh, who survived him.

Born and educated a Federalist, Badger separated from the party during the War of 1812, and was in 1828 an ardent supporter of Jackson, who was confidently expected to appoint him attorney-general. He broke with Jackson in 1832, by 1836 had become a Whig, and in 1841 was appointed secretary of the navy by President Harrison. As he resigned when the cabinet broke up under President Tyler, he had, as secretary, little opportunity to make any lasting contribution to the navy. He recommended, however, a home squadron to patrol the Caribbean and the Gulf, and he secured authority for the construction of two steam vessels. In 1846 he was elected to the United States Senate and served until 1855. Entering in the midst of the Mexican War, he strongly opposed the policies of the administration. He combated the Wilmot Proviso but believed it constitutional. He was in favor of all the compromise measures of 1850 except the abolition of the slave trade in the District of Columbia. His influence, with that of his colleague, Willie P. Mangum, secured the success of the compromise advocated by Daniel Webster in the Seventh-of-March speech. Badger refused to accept the doctrine of "squatter sovereignty," but he voted for the Kansas-Nebraska Act, later regarding this as the greatest mistake of his political life. A nationalist in theory, he was nevertheless in practise in full accord with his section in questions having a bearing upon slavery. Shortly before he left the presidency, Fillmore, after the Senate had been polled as to confirmation, nominated Badger for associate justice of the Supreme Court. But the Senate failed to act; Badger's residence outside the circuit where the vacancy was, and the control of the Senate by the Democrats, combined to defeat him. When he retired, two years later, the Senate paid him the tribute of a unanimous resolution of regret.

Upon his retirement, Badger continued the practise of law. He served for a number of years as regent of the Smithsonian Institution and he was chairman of the county court of Wake. His only other public service was in the crisis of 1860–61, when he took an active and leading part in the organization of the Constitutional Union party and was a candidate for elector on the Bell and Everett ticket. In February 1861 the legislature submitted to the people the question of a convention and provided for the election of delegates at the same time. Badger was elected as a Union candidate, but the people refused the call and the delegates, in consequence, never met. In May he was also elected to the convention called for the purpose of seceding. A nationalist as ever, he could not accept secession as a constitutional doctrine, and he offered in the convention a declaration of independence. After its rejection, however, he finally voted for the ordinance of secession and later signed it. During the duration of the convention (1861–62) he supported the war with vigor, if not enthusiasm. His health failed in 1863, but he lingered for three years afterwards.

A wide reader, Badger had unusual capacity to assimilate and use what he learned. He was a combination of scholar, orator, lawyer, and humorist, with more than a touch of statesmanship added. In appearance he was impressive with a fine figure and striking head and face. In spite of his brilliance in law and politics, he lacked something of power, the humorous flippancy which characterized him being, perhaps, a good index to the reasons for the deficiency. His chief success was at the bar. His presentation was at once brilliant and persuasive. He won distinction and success in the trial courts by his power with a jury, and in the courts of appeal by his powerful exposition of the law. The peer of any in North Carolina in a day of great lawyers, he ranked before the Supreme Court of the United States with Webster, Crittenden, Berrien, and Cushing.

[The *Cong. Globe*, 1849–55, and the various newspapers of the time, are the most important sources. Wm. A. Graham's *Discourse in Memory of the Life and Character of the Hon. Geo. E. Badger* (1866) is the most extended study and is valuable as the view of a close pol. and personal friend. A sketch by S. A. Ashe appears in the *Biog. Hist. of N. C.* VII, 35–44, and a somewhat exaggerated estimate of Badger's work as secretary of the navy, by P. M. Wilson, is in the *N. C. Booklet*, vol. XV, no. 3.]

J. G. de R. H.

BADGER, JOSEPH (Mar. 14, 1708–1765), colonial portrait painter, was unknown to Dunlap, Tuckerman, and other early historians of American art. He first received his rightful recognition through the researches of Frank W. Bayley (*Proceedings of the Massachusetts Historical Society*, XLIX, 259–61) and Lawrence Park (*Ibid.*, LI, 158–201). Only a few references to him had previously been made, as in *The Diary of William Bentley* (vol. III, 1911, p. 368), in which portraits of Rev. Otis Gray of the Brick Church, Boston, are said to be "both by Badger." Beginning with little definite information, the investigators recovered a fairly complete story of a painter many of whose portraits are of historic importance. Park prepared a list of about eighty canvases attributed by him to Badger, this including several works formerly attributed to Copley, Blackburn, and Smibert. Badger was born at Charlestown, Mass., a son of Stephen Badger, tailor, and Mary (Kettell) Badger. He was baptized and called into full communion of the First Church of Charlestown, Jan. 21, 1728. He married, June 2, 1731, Katharine, daughter of Samuel and Katharine (Smith) Felch of Reading. About 1733 Mr. and Mrs. Badger seem to have moved into Boston, for Brattle Square Church records show baptisms of four of their children, the first on Jan. 20, 1734. Badger is recorded variously as painter and glazier, his portraiture presumably occupying only a portion of his time. Dedham town records show that he painted a house there in 1739. It is reasonably conjectured that he was poor and of slight social consequence. He died intestate in the summer of 1765, and his widow was appointed administratrix of his insolvent estate, on Aug. 23, 1765. She later was given by the court permission to sell his small house of three rooms on the west side of Temple St. to pay his debts. An inventory set the value of his estate at £140 10s., including "a Coat-of-Arms," "a chaise Body and Carriage" and "pots, brushes, stones, etc."

From whom Badger learned to paint is unknown. His works were not signed. He apparently had low prices, even as estimated by eighteenth-century standards. In 1758 he received £5 each for the large portraits of Timothy Orne and wife. In 1764 he was paid by George Bray £12 for making five pictures. His talent was not that of a sensitive and highly competent painter. He had well-defined mannerisms. The heads were placed high on the canvas; in color they were often livid and unlovely. The hands were badly drawn. The best Badger portraits nevertheless have the charm of sincere, stiff, archaic work. His children are peculiarly naive. From about 1748, when Smibert's health was failing, until about 1760, when the vogue of John Singleton Copley was beginning, Badger was the principal portrait painter in Boston. That he taught Copley to paint has been conjectured by Park, though without evidence other than that of a general resemblance between the Badger portraits and the earliest of Copley's works. The Pelhams and Badgers were near neighbors in Boston, but Peter Pelham, painter and engraver, was himself capable of instructing the boys of his household, Copley and Henry Pelham, both of whom became artists. Among notable portraits by Badger are those of James Bowdoin (Bowdoin College), Rev. William Cooper (Massachusetts Historical Society), Rev. Ellis Gray and Rev. Thomas Prince (American Antiquarian Society, Worcester), Mrs. Norton Quincy (Worcester Art Museum), Miss Mary McIntosh Royall (New England Historical and Genealogical Society, Boston).

[In addition to the references above, a brief account of Badger is given in the supplementary list of artists in William Dunlap's *Hist. of the Rise and Progress of the Arts of Design in the United States* (Bayley and Goodspeed ed., 1918), III, 282.] F. W. C.

BADGER, JOSEPH (Feb. 28, 1757–Apr. 5, 1846), pioneer missionary, was a descendant, in the fourth generation, of Giles Badger, who came from England about the year 1635 and settled in Newbury, Mass. He was the son of Henry and Mary (Langdon) Badger. Born in Wilbraham, Mass., he was brought up in rural remote Peru, Mass., without educational advantages. Three weeks after the battle of Lexington, when eighteen years old, he enlisted. He engaged in the battle of Bunker Hill and later was with the expedition to Canada. His versatility is evidenced by his being called to act as nurse, physician, and cook, in addition to making mechanical comforts for the sick and wounded. Honorable discharge was granted after two years' service and he came to Connecticut just at the time the British burned Danbury, only to reënlist and serve a year as orderly sergeant. Hiring out as a weaver in New Preston, Conn., he proved himself rapid and expert. To improve his limited education he became a boarder in the family of Rev. Jeremiah Day, the Congregational pastor, father of President Day of Yale College, then a six-year-old boy and as advanced as Badger was in his twenty-second year. He prepared for Yale, supporting himself during his course by manual labor, teaching day and singing schools and doing college chores. In his senior year he constructed a planetarium for which the Corporation awarded him $100. He graduated creditably in 1785. Two years later he was ordained pastor of the Congregational Church in Blandford, Mass., and served with success for thirteen years. In 1800 he was appointed by the Missionary Society of Connecticut as one of the earliest missionaries to Ohio. For a year he labored as itinerant preacher to the sparse wilderness settlements and even to the Indians through an interpreter. He founded the first church on the Western Reserve at Austinburg. Convinced of the future development and importance of this territory he returned to Massachusetts and placing wife, six children, and a few necessary articles of household furniture in a covered wagon he started westward. The trip took over two months, as they encountered snow, mud, streams, and forests. The next twenty-five years were spent in arduous, often perilous, missionary pilgrimages, and the peace and prosperity of the churches in those new settlements during that period were largely due to his indefatigable toil, wise counsel, and earnest preaching. During the War of 1812 he was invited to visit the forces sent to guard the frontier and without consent or consultation was appointed by Gen. Harrison as brigade chaplain. In his seventieth year, when the task of travel and toil became too great, he received a pension of ninety-six dollars as a Revolutionary soldier and planned retirement. The ruling spirit, still strong, however, could not refuse an invitation from a small group of immigrants in Gustavus, Ohio. He organized a church, became the settled pastor, and served eight years. His long and constantly used voice grew feeble and he was dismissed at his own request on June 26, 1835. His declining days he spent with his only surviving daughter at Perrysburg, Ohio, where he died in his ninetieth year. He was twice married: in October 1784 to Lois Noble, who died Aug. 4, 1818; and in April 1819 to Abigail Ely of North Wilbraham, Mass.

[Badger's autobiography in *Am. Quart. Reg.,* XIII, 317–28 (also in H. N. Day, *Memoir of Joseph Badger,* 1851), gives in fulness and detail four-score years of his life. In Wm. B. Sprague, *Annals of the Am. Pulpit,* III (1858), the editor completes the life, followed by two appreciations, one written by President Pierce of Western Reserve Coll. See also F. B. Dexter, *Biog. Sketches Grads. Yale Coll.,* IV (1907), and *Conn. Courant,* Apr. 21, 1846. Letters of Badger were published in the *Am. Pioneer,* June, Aug. 1843, and in the *Conn. Evangelical Mag.,* Dec. 1800, Mar., Sept. 1801, Feb., Sept. 1803, Mar. 1804, Feb. 1806.]

S. S.

BADGER, OSCAR CHARLES (Aug. 12, 1823–June 20, 1899), naval officer, was the son of Albert Allen and Asenath (Crosby) Badger, and eighth in descent from Giles Badger, one of the original settlers of the town of Newbury, Mass., in 1635. He was born at Mansfield, Conn., and was appointed to the Naval Academy in 1841 by his cousin, George E. Badger of North Carolina, at that time secretary of the navy. In 1843, as a midshipman on board the *Saratoga,* he took part in the destruction of the Berribee villages on the west coast of Africa, and in 1855 he commanded a landing party from the *John Adams,* which attacked and destroyed the town of Vutia, Fiji Islands, both of these expeditions being punitive in character. During the Mexican War he served on board the frigate *Mississippi.* During the winter and spring of 1862, while in command of the gunboat *Anacostia,* he was engaged in a number of attacks on the Confederate batteries in the Potomac River and Aequia Creek, as well as in the shelling of Yorktown, Va., and the defenses at Gloucester Point. In different attacks on Forts Wagner, Gregg, and Sumter he commanded with distinction the ironclads *Patapsco* and *Montauk* in the summer of 1863. On Sept. 1 of that year, while he was acting as fleet captain on board the *Weehawken* during a night bombardment of Forts Moultrie and Sumter, his right leg was shattered by an iron splinter driven by a round shot which struck the *Weehawken's* turret. The commander-in-chief, Admiral John A. Dahlgren [*q.v.*], in his report to the secretary of the navy dated Sept. 2, said, "I shall feel greatly the loss of Capt. Badger's services at this time; he has been with me for more than eight years, and his sterling qualities have rendered him one of the very best ordnance officers in the Navy" (*Official Records,* ser. I, vol. XIV, pp. 532–33). From this wound Badger never fully recovered. He was promoted to be commander July 25, 1866, captain Nov. 25, 1872, and commodore Nov. 15, 1881. His last duty was from 1882 to 1885 as commandant of the navy yard at Boston, and he retired on Aug. 12, 1885. He was considered one of the most brilliant officers in the navy, and an authority on ordnance. He was married on Oct. 27, 1852, to Margaret, daughter of Capt. Z. M. Johnston, and had two children, Annie Mansfield, who became the wife of Major-General G. F. Elliott, and Rear Admiral Charles J. Badger. The destroyer *Badger* was launched and named in his honor in 1918.

[See publications of the Office of Naval Records and Library, Navy Dept., Washington, as well as manuscripts preserved there; Daniel Ammen, *The Atlantic Coast,* being the second volume of the series, "The Navy in the Civil War" (1883), pp. 128, 134.]

E. B.

BADIN, STEPHEN THEODORE (July 17, 1768–Apr. 19, 1853), missionary, had the distinction of being the first Roman Catholic priest to be ordained within the United States, whither he had come in 1792, fleeing from the dangers of the revolutionary party in France. A native of Orleans, and the eldest son of the family, he had been destined for the church and educated at Collège Montaigu, Paris, and at the Sulpician Seminary in Orleans. After arrival in America, he continued his studies at Baltimore, where, on May 25, 1793, he received from Bishop Carroll the order of priesthood. Soon thereafter he was appointed to the new state of Kentucky where he estimated there were about three hundred Catholics, widely scattered. En route to his missionary parish he visited the French settlement at Gallipolis, where he baptized several children. His first mass in Kentucky was celebrated in a private house; and for several years Badin's home was the saddle, as he traveled from one isolated community to another, cheering, comforting, exhorting, advising the members of his scattered flock. He was imperfectly acquainted with the language of his parishioners, knew nothing of backwoods life, and suffered many hardships, often being hungry, cold, and weary.

He built for himself a small log shelter in the present Marion County, fifty-seven miles south of Louisville, which he called St. Stephen's; and by the end of the century had founded six or seven small log chapels, and was vicar-general for Kentucky. The first Catholic chapel in Lexington was built in 1800, and a brick Gothic church dedicated there by Father Badin May 19, 1812 (George W. Ranck, *History of Lexington, Ky.*, 1872, pp. 190–92). At Louisville he built the first chapel, named for St. Louis, in 1811. His people were poor, and so was the priest; yet his wit, learning, and good temper made him popular, and he made friends among the Protestants of his region, notably with Col. Joseph Daviess, after whose death at the battle of Tippecanoe, Father Badin composed a Latin elegy in his honor ("Epicedium," translated in Martin J. Spalding, *Sketches of the Catholic Missions of Kentucky,* 1844, Appendix). Another poem, "Carmen Sacrum," was written on the appointment of his early friend, Benedict J. Flaget, as bishop of Bardstown. Not long afterward, however, Father Badin had a disagreement with the Bishop on land titles, and in 1819 retired to his native land. There he remained for nine years, employed in collecting funds for his American missions, in a visit to Rome, and in serving parishes in France and Belgium.

In 1828 the call of America grew so loud that Badin determined to return, all the more that his younger brother, François Vincent Badin, was a priest on the northern frontier, and his Sulpician colleague, Gabriel Richard, was preaching in Detroit. Arrived at this place Father Stephen Badin accepted a parish of French Canadians at Monroe, on River Raisin, where he officiated about eighteen months. Then came a call to an Indian mission in western Michigan, where the Potawatomi lived and retained memories of Father Claude Allouez [*q.v.*], who a century and a half earlier had lived and died in this locality. The Chief Pokagon received Badin into his own cabin, and the priest labored zealously to reclaim those of the redmen that had listened to Baptist teachings. He was present at the treaty of 1832 and wrote from the treaty grounds letters asking a land grant for his services (*American Catholic Historical Researches,* 1911, XXVIII, new series, VII, 197–202). He obtained at about this time, either by purchase or grant, the land upon which the University of Notre Dame is built at South Bend, Ind.; thither his remains were removed in 1904, and a replica of his first log church on this site now stands on the University grounds, containing a memorial tablet to his memory.

While among the Potawatomi Badin visited the village of Chicago, where he performed several baptisms and said mass in private houses. After leaving the Indian mission he became a peripatetic priest, visiting many of his old parishes, serving for a few months here and there throughout the West. He grew somewhat eccentric with age, but for the sake of his services in the past he was everywhere received with loving devotion. He died at the house of Bishop Purcell in Cincinnati. Tall, slender, wiry, and indefatigable in efforts for his people, Badin was a well-known figure in the West for over half a century. A colleague said on seeing his portrait, "I never saw him quiet before."

[The best life is that of W. J. Howlett in *U.S. Cath. Hist. Soc., Hist. Records and Studies,* IX, 101–146. Badin's own book, *Origin et Progrès de la Mission du Kentucky, Etats Unis d' Amérique par un Témoin Oculaire,* was published in Paris, 1821, and gives a vivid account of his early Kentucky mission; several of Badin's letters from the Potawatomi mission are in *Annales de la Propagation de la Foi,* XXIII, 154–77. See also Ben J. Webb, *Centenary of Catholicity in Kentucky* (1884); and Martin J. Spalding, *Sketches of Cath. Missions of Kentucky* (1844), written with the assistance of Badin; there is a brief sketch in *Ill. Cath. Hist. Mag.,* IV, 155; and an account of his tomb at South Bend, *Ibid.,* V, 223.]

L. P. K.

BAER, GEORGE FREDERICK (Sept. 26, 1842–Apr. 26, 1914), lawyer, railroad president, the son of Maj. Solomon Baer and Anna (Baker) Baer, was descended from a German immigrant who arrived prior to 1740 and settled in Northampton County, Pa., in 1743. Born near Lavansville, Somerset County, Pa., Baer received some schooling at the Somerset Institute and the Somerset Academy and at thirteen became a "printer's devil" in the office of the *Somerset Democrat.* After working there for two years he entered Franklin and Marshall College at Lancaster. In 1861 he and his brother Henry became owners of the *Democrat.* Its political policy aroused resentment, and at one time a mob attempted to wreck the plant, but was beaten off. About this time Henry enlisted as a soldier, and George was left to manage the paper alone. He set type, wrote articles, and looked after the business generally, and at odd hours studied law. In the summer of 1862 he organized a company, of which he was elected captain, for the 133rd Pennsylvania Volunteers. The regiment was assigned to Humphreys's division of the Army of the Potomac and joined the army at the time of the second battle of Bull Run. Capt. (afterward Maj.) Baer served through the Antietam, Fredericksburg and Chancellorsville campaigns and was then detailed as adjutant-general of the 2nd brigade. At the end of a year's service he returned to Somerset and resumed the study of law. He was admitted to the bar in April 1864. On June 14, 1866, he was married to Emily Kimmel.

Two years later he removed to Reading, where he soon built up a lucrative practise. He successfully conducted several damage suits against the Philadelphia & Reading Railway Company, and the energy and ability which he displayed in this work brought about, in 1870, his employment by the company as counsel. He invested his earnings in various manufacturing enterprises, in many of which he became a director, and he was also chosen a director of the Reading company. Early in his business career he formed an association with John Pierpont Morgan as the magnate's local representative and coöperated with him in his plan of uniting all the coal-carrying roads with terminals in New York City. The plans of the Reading company, under the presidency of Angus McLeod, for the invasion of the territory of the New Haven railroad, then dominated by Morgan, were opposed by Baer, who withdrew from the company. Morgan later gained control of the Reading properties, and in the reorganization that followed (1901) Baer was made president of each of the three Reading companies and was later placed at the head of the Central company.

Under his administration the Reading properties are said to have prospered. But early in May 1902, came the great strike declared by the United Mine Workers of America throughout the anthracite region—a strike in which 147,000 wage-earners were thrown out of employment and an invested capital of $500,000,000 went idle. From the beginning the owners maintained a stubborn refusal to deal with the strikers. Morgan declined to be drawn into the controversy, and Baer at once became the leader of the interests resisting the strike. "We will give no consideration," he declared, in June, in a statement to the press, "to any plan of arbitration or mediation or to any interference on the part of any outside party." He was brought into instant and nation-wide fame by the publication of a letter dated July 17, and signed "Geo. F. Baer," addressed to W. F. Clark, of Wilkes-Barre, who had appealed to him to end the strike. "The rights and interests of the laboring man," read one of the sentences, "will be protected and cared for—not by the labor agitators, but by the Christian men to whom God in his infinite wisdom has given the control of the property interests of the country, and upon the successful management of which so much depends." A storm of jeering and denunciatory comments followed the appearance of the letter. The time was one of great popular dissatisfaction with the policies of the monied interests, and this inept expression of an obstinate and anti-social attitude served only to array public sentiment more solidly against the owners. For a time, however, they ignored the warning. As late as Sept. 16 Baer gave out a statement that the operators would not yield. President Roosevelt, however, now intervened, and on Oct. 3 brought together representatives of both sides in a conference. Eleven days later the President announced that the operators were willing to arbitrate. Under a provisional agreement the miners resumed work Oct. 23, and a commission, during the following winter, settled, for the time being, the outstanding issues of the conflict.

Baer's later life was uneventful. He was a student and spent much time with his books. Occasionally he spoke at public dinners. In mental characteristics it was said of him that he was more like Morgan than any other man with whom the great magnate was ever associated, both having to a superlative degree the qualities of determination, confidence, and self-control. His manner was quiet, and though he was sometimes brusque in business contracts he is said to have been always genial to friends. He is reported to have had a keen sense of humor, but the evidence is not conclusive. He was about five feet six inches in height, of wiry build, slight and erect, and with a well-poised head. "He had," writes one observer, "almond eyes, like those of an Oriental." All his portraits show a mustache and short beard. He left a fortune estimated at $15,000,000.

[Comment upon Baer's character and policies will be found in many of the newspapers and periodicals of the summer and fall of 1902. A number of biog. sketches have appeared. A "character sketch" by W. C. Hollister in the *Cosmopolitan* for Dec. 1902, except for certain errors in details, will be found helpful. The long obituaries in the *Sun* (N. Y.) and the *N. Y. World* for Apr. 27, 1914, give much information, though not all of it is dependable. The brief sketch that appeared in *Who's Who in America* during the last twelve years of his life corrects some of the blunders as to events and dates appearing elsewhere. An interesting light on the fiscal manipulations of the Reading companies is given by Charles Edward Russell, in *Railroad Melons, Rates and Wages*(1922). The biog., *Henry Demarest Lloyd*(1912), by Caro Lloyd (later Mrs. George H. Strobell), gives a vivid account of some phases of the coal strike and of the work of the commission. It contains also (vol. II, opp. p. 190) a facsimile of the letter which made Baer for a time famous. On his seventieth birthday, nearly ten years after the letter was published, Baer denied its authenticity. He did not allege that a forgery had been committed, but only that words had been ascribed to him which he had not used. In just what sense his disavowal of the letter is to be accepted cannot be determined. The document bears every sign of genuineness.]

W. J. G.

BAERMANN, CARL (July 9, 1839–Jan. 17, 1913), teacher of music, pianist, was the fourth of his family to attain distinction as a musician. His grandfather, Heinrich Joseph, born at Potsdam Feb. 14, 1784, was one of the greatest clarinet players of all time, an intimate friend of Mendelssohn and von Weber, both of whom, inspired by his masterly playing, wrote compositions for him. Having attracted the interest of Prince Louis Ferdinand of Prussia, he was placed in the regiment of guards at Berlin, and later went to the court band at Munich. He toured Germany, England, France, Italy, and Russia, and was everywhere acclaimed a great artist. He died in Munich, July 11, 1847, leaving not only a fame (to quote von Weber) as "a truly great artist and a glorious man," but many compositions for clarinet which are still in the repertoire of every great clarinettist. An elder brother of Heinrich was a celebrated bassoonist. Karl, son of Heinrich, who was born at Munich in 1820 and died there in 1885, like his father was a clarinettist, and became equally great. With the added prestige of his father's reputation, he toured Europe with the greatest success, though he later took a regular place in the court band at Munich, in which he had played frequently since early boyhood. Carl Jr., son of the preceding, was born in Munich and at a very early age began the study of the piano under the best teachers of his native city, among whom was Franz Lachner. Later he studied with Liszt and became one of his really favorite students. His friendship with Liszt remained unbroken and he corresponded with the master, as his father and grandfather did with von Weber, Mendelssohn, and Moscheles. He became well known through his concert performances and was appointed teacher at the Royal Music School at Munich, King Ludwig of Bavaria a little later conferring on him the title of professor. Here he taught many American students and in 1881 he obtained leave of absence to visit America, where he expected to remain two years. He decided, however, to settle in Boston and for the next twenty-four years became a large factor in the musical development of the country. He appeared as recitalist and as soloist with various symphony orchestras, but his chief influence was as a teacher. His students were numerous, the most distinguished being Mrs. H. H. A. Beach, Frederick L. Converse, and, in later years, Lee Pattison. His compositions are not numerous (only a few, including a set of twelve piano studies, having been published), but all are of high order. He married in Munich, in 1865, Beatrice von Dessauer, member of a fine Bavarian family. He returned to Europe at various times for concertizing and also to attend the performance of an orchestral work, a Festival March, in Munich. He adhered to the classical ideal both in teaching and in writing and did much to guide the musical taste of the land of his adoption. He died in Newton, Mass.

[Louis C. Elson, *Hist. of Am. Music* (1925); *Boston Transcript*, Jan. 18, 1913; *Boston Sunday Post*, Jan. 19, 1913; *Grove's Dict. of Music and Musicians*, vol. I, also *Am. Supp.*] F. L. G. C.

BAGBY, ARTHUR PENDLETON (1794–Sept. 21, 1858), governor of Alabama, senator, diplomat, fourth in descent from James Bagby, a Scotchman who settled in Jamestown about 1628, was born in Louisa County, Va., in 1794, the son of Capt. James Bagby and Mary Jones of Gloucester County. Well educated for the times and enjoying the prestige of a fine Virginia name, he was induced by the unfavorable economic conditions in his home state to migrate westward as a young man. Traveling on foot, with all of his worldly goods in a pack on his back, he reached Alabama in 1818 and settled at Claiborne, in Monroe County, a distributing point for immigrants and at that time one of the most important towns in Alabama, where he found a number of fellow Virginians, read law, and was admitted to the bar in 1819. He was twice married, first to Emily Steele, of Georgia, second (1828) to Anne Elizabeth Connell, of South Carolina. His majestic personality and striking physical appearance, the fluency and grace of his speech, his growing reputation as a criminal lawyer attracted the attention of his fellow citizens, and he was soon a notable figure in that vigorous frontier community. With a penchant for politics he entered the lower house of the state legislature in 1821 and made so favorable an impression on his colleagues that, on reëlection in 1822, he was chosen speaker, the youngest man ever to hold that office in Alabama. While continuing his legal career, Bagby was again in the House in 1824, in the state Senate in 1825, and in the House again in 1834, 1835, and 1836, serving once more as speaker in the latter year.

Although he was originally a National Republican and a supporter of John Quincy Adams, a change in his political faith appeared in 1831 when he opposed the proposal to commit Alabama to the support of a national bank. When Jackson issued his proclamation against nullification in 1832 Bagby came to his support and henceforth was a Jackson Democrat. As a result of his adherence to the Jackson cause he was nominated by the Democrats in 1837 for the governorship and elected over S. W. Oliver, Whig, of Conecuh County, by 21,800 to 17,663. Two years later he was reëlected practically without opposition. In a series of able state papers, he urged readjustment and reform in the financial system of Alabama which was suffering from the panic of 1837 and from an inefficient and corrupt banking system. His personal influence and political prestige, however, could not avail against corrupt politics and his actual accomplishments in remedying financial conditions were small. Bagby secured the establishment of chancery courts, forced the creation of a penitentiary system, and brought about a satisfactory settlement of the irritating boundary dispute with Georgia. He advocated the improvement of river navigation, lent his support to the Bestor movement for a good system of public schools, and consistently urged support for higher education. He secured the passage of a law providing for the general ticket system of electing representatives in Congress, which scheme he advocated later in the federal Senate.

On the expiration of his term as governor (1841), Bagby was elected to the United States Senate to fill an unexpired term and in 1842 was reëlected for a full term. Here his support of the movement for the annexation of Texas created some dissatisfaction among the Democrats of Alabama, but he successfully met the opposition to his course. He opposed Tyler's aspirations for a Democratic nomination for the presidency, and, on Polk's election, became a strong administration man. Polk rewarded him in the summer of 1848 with an appointment as minister to Russia, where he served acceptably but without particular distinction from June 16, 1848, to May 14, 1849, resigning when party control changed in national politics. On his return to Alabama, he served on the committee to codify the laws of the state, his last public duty. In 1856 he removed to Mobile, where he died in 1858 during an epidemic of yellow fever. His public career was seriously marred by his utter carelessness and inefficiency in his personal financial affairs and he was constantly in great financial difficulties.

[Wm. Garrett, *Reminiscences of Public Men in Ala.* (1872), and Willis Brewer, *Ala.: Her Hist., Resources, War Record, and Public Men* (1872), are the most valuable sources of information. Accounts of Bagby's public career are in Thos. M. Owen, *Hist. of Ala. and Dict. of Ala. Biog.* (1921), and Wm. Garrott Brown, *Hist. of Ala.* (1900). Bagby's defense of his course on the Texan question may be found in his *Letter to the People of Ala.* (1845). Benj. Perley Poore, *Perley's Reminiscences of Sixty Years in The National Metropolis* (1886), gives a description of his personality and appearance and contains extracts from his speech against the nomination of Tyler.]

T. H. J.

BAGBY, GEORGE WILLIAM (Aug. 13, 1828–Nov. 29, 1883), author, editor, the eldest son of George and Virginia (Evans) Bagby, was born in Buckingham County, Va., but spent his early years in Lynchburg, where his father was a merchant. His mother died when he was a lad of six and he was sent to a boarding-school at Prince Edward Court House and to the Edgehill School at Princeton, N. J. He attended Delaware College for two years and then the University of Pennsylvania as a medical student, where he graduated in 1849. For a short time he had an office in Lynchburg, but after the success of a series of articles in the Lynchburg *Virginian* he was drawn more and more into literary work, assisting James McDonald, editor of the *Virginian,* and soon abandoning entirely the idea of practising medicine. With George Woodville Latham he purchased the Lynchburg *Express* and for two or three years during the fifties kept it going in spite of poor business management. He was later a newspaper correspondent in Washington, D. C., until 1859. In 1860 he succeeded John R. Thompson as editor of the *Southern Literary Messenger* in Richmond. At the outbreak of the Civil War, Bagby promptly joined the Confederate army, but his health, which was never robust, suffered from camp life and he was fortunately detailed for clerical work at headquarters, until he was discharged on account of ill-health. He returned to the editorship of the *Messenger,* which he retained until January 1864, but he was busy chiefly as a correspondent for papers throughout the South. His vivid pen gave a truthful picture of the Southern capital. He married in 1863 Lucy Parke Chamberlayne of Richmond by whom he had ten children. After the close of the war, he went to New York as a journalist, but the weakness of his eyes forced him to return to Virginia and undertake a career as a popular lecturer. He had tried himself out some years before with his lecture, "An Apology for Fools." His success in Virginia in 1865–66 with a new humorous lecture, "Bacon and Greens," was immediate; and later "Women Folks" and "The Disease Called Love" were equally popular. When in 1867 he became part owner of the *Native Virginian,* which he edited at Orange, Va., he continued his lectures. Three years later his friend James McDonald secured his appointment as custodian of the State Library and he held the position for three administrations. Meantime, besides contributing articles to magazines and newspapers, he traveled through Virginia giving his most famous lectures, "The Old Virginia Gentleman" and "The Virginia Negro." His *John M. Daniels'*

Latch Key (1868), published in Lynchburg, and *Canal Reminiscences* (1879), a pamphlet published in Richmond, were characteristic sketches of Virginia just after the Civil War. So popular that every educated Virginian of Bagby's generation was familiar with them were *What I Did with My Fifty Millions: by Moses Adams* (1874) and *Meekins's Twinses* (1877). Bagby's reputation during his latter days rested largely upon these slight publications, his newspaper writings, and his lectures; but it is no exaggeration to say that if he was little known outside of his native state, within it his fame was universal. He had never published a collection of his writings, but in a rural state, although lectures were usually free and money painfully lacking, he could always be sure of an audience. He died in Richmond, Va., Nov. 29, 1883. Soon after his death, his widow prepared one volume of *Selections from the Miscellaneous Writings of Dr. George W. Bagby* (1884), with a sketch of Bagby by Edward S. Gregory; a second volume followed the next year; both were privately printed in limited edition.

Bagby was the portrayer of old Virginia. The intensity of his localism is both his strength and his weakness. His pictures and his humor are so intimately a part of one place and one time that they have little universality of appeal. To Virginians who know the spirit or the memory of the life he portrayed, he is the truest as he is the most representative interpreter of the old order in their state. He was in the details of his writing a realist, but the intensity of his devotion to a passing civilization touched much that he wrote, even of humor or satire, with a feeling so intense that the spirit of his writing and its effect are idealistic. His most widely known piece is *Jud Browning's Account of Rubenstein's Playing.* His humor was homely and fresh but never subtle. His serious writing was often sentimental but always vivacious and nervously alive, and sometimes full of tender power and beauty. *The Old Virginia Gentleman, The Virginia Editor, Bacon and Greens, Flize,* and *Meekins's Twinses* are among his most characteristic writings.

[Edward S. Gregory's biog. sketch in the 1884–85 edition of the *Selections from the Miscellaneous Writings* is the usual source of the biog. accounts that have been printed. Gregory's sketch was reprinted, somewhat altered, in the edition of *The Old Virginia Gentleman and Other Sketches* (1910), ed. with an introduction by Thos. Nelson Page. The best short account, however, is by Churchill Gibson Chamberlayne in the *Lib. of Southern Lit.*, I (1909). The only full biog. is that by Jos. Leonard King, *Dr. Wm. Bagby, a Study of Virginian Lit., 1850–80* (1927).]

J. S. W.

BAILEY, ANN (1742–Nov. 22, 1825), a scout and messenger on the Virginian border, was a native of Liverpool. Her maiden name was Ann Hennis. Her father had been a soldier in the campaigns of the Duke of Marlborough. She came to America in 1761, and her life henceforth was identified with the frontier. Her first husband was Richard Trotter, a pioneer in the Shenandoah Valley. He was one of the survivors of Braddock's expedition of 1755, and, serving in Lord Dunmore's war against the Indians, was killed at the battle of Point Pleasant, Oct. 10, 1774. After his death his widow assumed male costume, and became noted as a scout and messenger along the frontier, and especially in the valley of the Kanawha. Her second husband, John Bailey, was also a border leader. She was an excellent shot, horsewoman, and an adept in woodcraft. Many stories were told of the marvellous adventures and narrow escapes from the Indians of the "White Squaw of the Kanawha." Her most famous exploit was in 1791. Fort Lee, on the site of Charleston, West Va., was besieged by Indians, and the supply of ammunition ran low. Ann Bailey made a solitary ride of about a hundred miles through a forest wilderness to the fort on the site of Lewisburg, and returned to Fort Lee with a supply of powder. The siege was raised, and the achievement has been retold in prose and in indifferent verse. To her other occupations she added those of letter carrier and express messenger. After her husband's death she lived with her son, removed with him to Ohio, and died in Gallia County in that state.

There is a dubious version of her earlier life, according to which she was born in 1700, and was kidnapped (Mrs. James R. Hopley, in *Ohio Archæological and Historical Quarterly,* 1907, pp. 340–47). If this version be credited, she performed her noted exploits in extreme old age, and lived to be 125 years old.

[Virgil A. Lewis, *Life and Times of Anne Bailey* (1891); *Ann Bailey: Thrilling Adventures of the Heroine of the Kanawha Valley* (1907), ed. by Mrs. Livia Simpson-Poffenbarger, containing accounts by Virgil A. Lewis, and by Mrs. Lillian R. Messenger.]

E. K. A.

BAILEY, ANNA WARNER (October 1758–Jan. 10, 1851), heroine of two incidents in American wars, was a native of Groton, Conn. She was an orphan, and was brought up in the family of her uncle Edward Mills. On the day of the battle of Groton Heights, Sept. 6, 1781, she missed her relative, and walked from the farm to the scene of fighting. How she found her uncle who was desperately wounded, how she returned to the farm and conducted the wife and children to the bedside of the dying man, became one of the cherished stories of the period. Soon afterward she married Capt. Elijah Bailey, the postmaster; and in the War of 1812 "Mother Bailey" again appeared on the scene. In the summer of 1813 the British fleet was off the coast of Connecticut, blockading Commodore Decatur's vessels, and raiding or threatening attacks upon the towns. Among the soldiers at Groton who had assembled for the defense of the coast, there was a shortage of flannel, which was needed in those days as wadding for cartridges. In partial remedy for this need, Mrs. Bailey contributed her flannel petticoat, and the "martial petticoat" has become celebrated in song and story. A local chapter of the Daughters of the American Revolution bears her name.

[N. H. Burnham, *Battle of Groton Heights* (1907), pp. 277–78, contains a portr. and a sketch; Frances M. Caulkins, *Hist. of New London, Conn. . . . 1612 to 1852* (1895), pp. 631–32, also gives the "flannel" story.]

E.K.A.

BAILEY, EBENEZER (June 25, 1795–Aug. 5, 1839), educator, was the son of Paul Bailey, a thrifty farmer, and Emma (Carr) Bailey. Though the youngest of four children, he was the only one sent to college. He entered Yale in 1813 and graduated four years later with honor. He then purchased, one knows not how, the goodwill and fixtures of a private school in New Haven. At the same time he started to study law. But the double work proving too much, he went to Richmond, Va., to become private tutor in the family of Col. Carter. In his journal he recorded appreciation of Southern hospitality but disapproved of Southern "frivolity." After a year in Virginia he returned to Massachusetts and established a private school for young ladies in Newburyport. In 1823, however, he left to become headmaster of the Franklin Grammar School for boys in Boston. In 1825 he married Adeline Dodge, daughter of a merchant of Newburyport. Early in the year 1826 the Girls' High School of Boston was opened and Bailey was made principal. The first high school for girls in Massachusetts and one of the first in the United States, it was looked upon as a doubtful experiment, and in 1827 the mayor, Josiah Quincy, pronounced it an "entire failure." In a *Review of the Mayor's Report* Bailey indignantly denied the mayor's assertion; and many citizens shared his indignation. The truth seems to be that the school's "failure" was that it had succeeded too well. Far more girls applied for admission the second year than limited accommodations could permit to enter. The question therefore arose whether the accommodations of the High School should be extended or the curriculum of the lower schools be advanced to meet the girls' demands. The latter alternative was chosen and the Girls' High School died. In December 1827 Bailey opened the Young Ladies' High School, a private institution which he conducted with extraordinary vigor, enthusiasm, and success. The crisis of 1837, however, brought its collapse. Pupils were withdrawn, bills remained unpaid; and Bailey, who had been generous and hospitable rather than thrifty, had to sell the school and its appurtenances. Unfortunately the man to whom he sold died insolvent after the papers had been signed but before a single payment had been made. There was nothing left for Bailey but to start life over again. This he did, opening a school for boys in Roxbury in 1838. The following year he transferred this school to Lynn. Prospects for happiness and success seemed bright once more. But toward the end of July he met with an accident and contracted lockjaw. During his brief but terrible illness his chief anxiety seems to have been, not for himself, but for his family. He was undoubtedly one of the most brilliant teachers of his day, but his abundant energies found outlet also in other channels than teaching. He was one of the founders of the American Institute of Instruction, a member of the Common Council of Boston, and a director of the House of Reformation. A writer of repute, he contributed frequently to the *Courier* and was the author of a number of poems better known in his own day than in ours. His text-books included: *The Young Ladies' Class Book*, *Bakewell's Philosophical Conversations* (1833) and the very popular *First Lessons in Algebra* (1833).

[Barnard's *Am. Jour. of Ed.*, XII, 215, 429–52, XIII, 243–58; E. E. Brown, "The Girls' High School of Boston," *School Review*, VII, 286–94; A. J. Inglis, *The Rise of the High School in Mass.* (1911).]

J.F.S.

BAILEY, FRANCIS (*c.* 1735–1815), printer, journalist, was the son of Robert Bailey (1708–98) and his wife Margaret McDill, early settlers in Lancaster County, Pa. On Dec. 4, 1766, Robert obtained from Thomas and Richard Penn a patent for over 230 acres of land in Sadsbury township. Meanwhile Francis, one of six children, had been bred a carpenter but had acquired from Peter Miller, the Dunkard printer at Ephrata since 1745, familiarity with making and setting type. He came forward in this occupation in 1771 when he began to publish his quarter-century series of the *Lancaster Almanac*, at first with Stewart Herbert, but after 1772 from his own shop, with the assistance of his brother Jacob and sister Abigail. In 1773 Bailey bought out

William Goddard and by Sept. 18, 1777, had completed the purchase from Christian Ilgnes of the land upon which his shop stood. Among his Lancaster issues were the almanacs mentioned, *A Sermon on Tea* (1774), a fourth edition of Paine's *Common Sense* (1776), *The Articles of Confederation and Perpetual Union* (1777), *Das Pennsylvanische Zeitungs-Blat* (Feb. 4–June 24, 1778), and reprints of various foreign and domestic publications. In 1777 Bailey was also coroner of Lancaster County, and when his father joined the Whig Associators Francis served as brigade-major of state troops at Valley Forge 1777–78. In April 1778 Bailey was one of the officers charged with conducting prisoners from Winchester, Va., to Lancaster. Later in 1778 Hugh Henry Brackenridge persuaded him to join in the publication at Philadelphia of the *United States Magazine*. The first number appeared in January and the last in December 1779, but the move was important. On Jan. 13, 1780, Bailey sought patronage from the Continental Congress for an edition of its *Resolves*. This was not granted, but later in the year, following the death of his brother Jacob, the Congress authorized Bailey to publish *The Constitutions of the Several Independent States of America, The Declaration of Independence, and The Treaties between His Most Christian Majesty and the United States of America*. These made a 226-page volume of which 200 copies were printed in 1781, and other editions in 1783. Bailey became official printer for Congress and the State of Pennsylvania, with his main office at Market above Third St., Philadelphia.

On Apr. 25, 1781, Bailey began to edit *The Freeman's Journal or the North American Intelligencer*, a weekly "open to all parties but influenced by none." This journal justified its motto and became a successful paper to which all parties resorted. It supported George Bryan [*q.v.*] and the Pennsylvania constitution and helped toward a stronger national government. Prominent contributors were Bryan himself, Philip Freneau, George Osbourne, Jonathan Sergeant, and James Wilson. During this decade Bailey was also active with special imprints, including an edition of Freneau's poems, and with the invention and presentation to Washington of a style "of marginal figures for notes, certificates, etc., which could not by the ingenuity of man be counterfeited" (Washington's Diary in *Pennsylvania Magazine of History and Biography*, XX, 44). He served also in the state militia during the critical period 1783–87 before the adoption of the national Constitution. Busy in Philadelphia, he retained his Lancaster property until 1805, and when the state legislature held its sessions there, Bailey continued his state printing at his old shop.

On Oct. 19, 1797, Robert Bailey and wife conveyed the Sadsbury estate to Francis, who erected there a large stone printing office and thenceforth divided his work between Sadsbury, Philadelphia, and his small country residence at Octoraro, fourteen miles east of Philadelphia, where the Acts of Assembly 1804–05 were printed. Gradually he withdrew from the printing business in favor of his son Robert, whose widow, Lydia Bailey [*q.v.*], carried it on after Francis's death in 1815.

[J. T. Scharf and T. Westcott, *Hist. of Phila.* (1884); *Pa. Mag. of Hist. and Biog.*, XXI, 363; Alexander Harris, *Biog. Hist. of Lancaster County* (1872); Isaiah Thomas, *Hist. of the Art of Printing* (1810), with William McCulloch's additions in *Am. Antiq. Soc. Proc.*, Apr., 1921; E. P. Oberholtzer, *Lit. Hist. of Phila.* (1906); *Jour. of the Continental Cong.*, Lib. of Cong. ed. (1904–22); *Annals of Cong.*, 1789–1815; Phila. Directories to 1816; Phila. contemporary press, esp. the *General Advertiser*, the *Aurora*, the *Freeman's Journal*, Oswald's *Independent Gazetteer*, *Pa. Archives and Colonial Records*; additional help from the Librarian of the Hist. Soc. of Pa.]

C. H. L—n.

BAILEY, FRANK HARVEY (June 29, 1851–Apr. 9, 1921), engineer, naval officer, son of James and Sarah (Hurd) Bailey, was born at Cranesville, Pa. He was educated in the public schools of Gowanda, N. Y., at Scio College, Scio, Ohio, and at the United States Naval Academy, where he was in the third class of two-year cadet engineers, graduating in 1875 at the head of his class. Then followed the alternation of duty at sea and on shore usual in the navy, with promotion through the various grades. Bailey was professor of marine engineering at Cornell University 1885–88, where he gained the respect of all for his ability in his own specialty as well as his broad knowledge of engineering. In 1896 he was promoted to the position of chief engineer. Having come into the navy at a time of profound peace, most of his sea service was uneventful, but he took part under Admiral Dewey in the Battle of Manila Bay, May 1, 1898, where he was chief engineer of the *Raleigh*. Probably his most important achievement was as chief designer of the Bureau of Steam Engineering for eight years under Melville, where his ability took shape in the machinery of the famous flyers *Columbia* and *Minneapolis*, which were the fastest large vessels of their day (1890–1900). On the amalgamation of the engineer corps with the line of the navy, he became a lieutenant commander and passed through the various grades, to rear admiral. He was inspector of engineering and ordnance material for the New York district for two years and completed his active duty by two years of service as inspector general of engineering under the Bureau of Engineering. He retired for age in 1913, but during the World War was recalled to active duty, and assigned to the design division of the Bureau of Engineering, where his ripe experience and sound judgment enabled him to render valuable service. After the war he returned to the retired list. He died suddenly of heart failure while on a visit in Arizona.

Although an engineer by genius as well as occupation, Bailey was devoted to the Service as a whole and was one of the earliest to recognize the progress of the evolution which made inevitable the amalgamation of the line and the engineer corps, with the future naval officer what Roosevelt called a "fighting engineer." This was the greatest change in naval personnel since the latter part of the seventeenth century, and the favorable attitude of Bailey and other progressive officers was an important factor in overcoming the inertia and prejudice of such a conservative organization as the navy.

Bailey was married on Dec. 28, 1881, to Anna J. Markham by whom he had three sons and one daughter. He was a handsome man, tall and portly, of amiable and engaging personality. With an unusual fund of information, he was modest to a fault, tolerant of opinions that differed from his, and always ready to listen to suggestions.

[Walter M. McFarland, "Rear Admiral Frank Harvey Bailey, U. S. N.," in *Jour. Am. Soc. Naval Engineers,* May 1921, pp. 373–76.]

W. M. M.

BAILEY, GAMALIEL (Dec. 3, 1807–June 5, 1859), journalist, anti-slavery agitator, was born at Mount Holly, N. J., the son of Rev. Gamaliel Bailey, a Methodist clergyman. Soon after his son's birth, his father removed to Philadelphia, where the boy, after attending private schools, entered the Jefferson Medical College, graduating in 1827. For a few months he taught in a New Jersey country school. Then, suffering in health, he shipped before the mast on a trading vessel bound for China. At Canton so much sickness developed among the sailors that he became temporarily ship's surgeon. On returning to America he opened a physician's office, but was soon installed as editor, in Baltimore, of the *Methodist Protestant,* the short-lived organ of the sect so styled—an unusual appointment considering that Bailey had then no experience in writing and was not a church-member. This position soon failing him, he departed to St. Louis to join an expedition to Oregon, only to find the venture a fraud. Practically penniless, he walked back to Cincinnati. Here a severe epidemic of cholera broke out soon after his arrival (1831), and through friendly influence he became physician in charge of the "Hospital for Strangers," where by his heroic work he gained favorable introduction to the city. In 1833 he married Margaret Lucy Shands of Virginia. In 1834 occurred the Lane Seminary debates on slavery, which immediately enlisted the interest of Bailey, who was lecturing there on physiology. After due reflection he became an ardent abolitionist and associated himself (1836) with J. G. Birney in editing the *Cincinnati Philanthropist,* the first anti-slavery organ in the West. A year later Bailey became sole editor and proprietor. The influence of his pen in the ensuing years is evidenced by the fact that his office was thrice mobbed; on one occasion printing outfit and building were entirely destroyed but three weeks later new presses were turning out the *Cincinnati Philanthropist* as usual—a remarkable accomplishment for that time. The third assault (1843) was suppressed by the police and a reaction in Bailey's favor followed; on the strength of this he launched a daily, the *Herald.* When the American and Foreign Anti-Slavery Society decided to publish a national periodical in Washington he was the logical choice for editor-in-chief. Disposing of his Cincinnati journals, he assumed his new duties at the nation's capital in January 1847, and for twelve years efficiently served the Anti-Slavery cause through the *National Era,* a weekly journal, of which during the Frémont campaign of 1856 Bailey issued a daily edition at considerable personal sacrifice. In 1848 he again faced a mob, which for three days threatened his printing-plant and even his house, the rioters erroneously assuming his connection with the escape of certain slaves. His conduct at this time was thoroughly characteristic. Unarmed he appeared at the door of his house, and calmly entered on a frank statement of his innocence of the charge preferred and his right as an American citizen to complete freedom of utterance. His angry auditors yielded to his persuasive logic and, as he finished his appeal, dispersed. He was not molested again.

The career of the *Era* was remarkably successful. Whittier, Theodore Parker, Mrs. Southworth, Grace Greenwood, and particularly Mrs. Stowe, with *Uncle Tom's Cabin,* were contributors, but the directing mind and will were Bailey's. He exerted a wide moral and political influence for the Anti-Slavery movement, the more so because, besides integrity, good business judgment, and determination, he possessed literary ability and a fair-minded tolerance that compelled the respect even of opponents. He condemned the Know-Nothing movement, though it cost him money and friends.

Physically he was delicate-looking, but possessed a good physique, with well-shaped head, intellectual face, and magnetic manner. Political and social Washington flocked to the gatherings at the Bailey home, where the charm and wit of host, hostess, and guests added friends to their cause. In 1853 his health necessitated a trip to Europe, and in 1859, again ill, he embarked on a second voyage thither. He died at sea but his body was brought back to Washington for burial.

[*The Atlantic Monthly,* June 1866, XVII, pp. 743–51, contains an anonymous article "A Pioneer Editor," dealing with Bailey's career. A more intimate sketch is "An American Salon," by Grace Greenwood, in the *Cosmopolitan,* Feb. 1890, VIII, 437–47. The files of the *National Era* (1847–59) reflect the mind and heart of the man. His obituary appeared in the issue of June 30, 1859, and an account of his funeral in that of July 7, 1859, with a tribute by Whittier entitled "Gamaliel Bailey."]

R. S. B.

BAILEY, JACOB (1731–Mar. 22, 1818), pioneer missionary of the Church of England in Maine, Loyalist, was born in Rowley, Mass., a descendant of James Bailey, one of the first settlers of that town. His parents, David and Mary (Hodgkins) Bailey, were poor, and as a boy he had to work long days on the farm, but he shortened his sleeping hours in order to read and write. An early distaste for democratic conditions seems to have been created in him by the disfavor with which such efforts to elevate oneself were viewed by his fellows; for in after years he referred with feeling to the "ignorance, narrowness of mind, and bigotry" which prevailed in his native town, where a boy was "whipped for saying Sir to his father," and "nothing could be more criminal than for one person to be more learned, religious, or polite, than another" (William S. Bartlet, *The Frontier Missionary: A Memoir of the Life of the Rev. Jacob Bailey,* 1853, p. 3). A composition of his fell into the hands of the village parson, Rev. Jedediah Jewett, who, impressed by its excellence, prepared the author for college. At Harvard, where he was a member of the class of 1755, he was supported largely by the gifts of the charitably inclined, and on the class list, arranged according to the social standing of its members, his name was at the bottom. For several years after graduating he taught school, first, in Kingston and Hampton, N. H., and later in Gloucester, Mass.

Although he had been licensed to preach, June 4, 1758, by the Association of Congregational Ministers in Exeter, N. H., his temperament inclined him toward the established church, and in 1759 he wrote to Dr. Caner of King's Chapel, Boston, acknowledging the loan of *Potter on Church Government,* and saying: "I have carefully perused it, with Bennet's Abridgment, and find all the objections against Episcopal Ordination, and Conformity to the Church of England, answered entirely to my satisfaction" (W. B. Sprague, *Annals of the American Pulpit,* V, 202). To secure ordination, he set sail for England on the British gunship *Hind,* and after a trying trip of twenty-eight days, reached his destination, and on Mar. 16, 1760, was ordained priest by Dr. Terrick, Bishop of Peterborough. The Society for Promoting the Gospel in Foreign Parts, appointed him Itinerant Missionary on the Eastern Frontier of Massachusetts.

This frontier extended up the Kennebec River to Canada on the north and indefinitely to the east. Arriving on the field, July 1, 1760, he fulfilled his mission faithfully for nineteen years. He brought there as his wife Sally, daughter of Dr. John Weeks of Hampton, N. H., whom he married in August 1761. He lived first in the barracks of Fort Shirley, afterward in Fort Richmond, and later in Pownalborough, the county seat of Lincoln County, where St. John's Church and parsonage were built for him in 1770. He traveled among the widely scattered people on foot, horseback, by canoe, and when the river was frozen, by sleigh, frequently suffering from hunger and exposure, and in the summer "afflicted with extreme heat, and assaulted with armies of flies and musketoes" (Bartlet, p. 91). When the Revolution came he remained loyal, refusing to read the Declaration of Independence in church, to take the oath of allegiance to Congress, or to refrain from praying for the King. He was subjected to all manner of persecution, and frequently had to go into hiding to save his life. Writing in 1776, he says: "My Presbyterian neighbors were so zealous for the good of their country that they killed seven of my sheep,—and shot a fine heifer as she was feeding in my pasture" (Bartlet, p. 111). His name was placed on the list for transportation, but in town meeting the people voted to strike it off. He was summoned before the Committee of Safety and tried on several counts, but defended himself well, and was not convicted. Finally, on the plea of poverty, since, as he said, the magistrates would not consider the plea of conscience, he procured permission of the Council at Boston to remove to Nova Scotia. After much difficulty he succeeded in chartering a schooner, and with his family and some of his effects escaped to Halifax, thankful when he reached that place that he was in a land of freedom. He settled at Annapolis, Nova Scotia, where he served as rector until his death.

Considering the strenuous life which Bailey led, he was a prolific writer, publishing little, if anything, but leaving behind sermons, extensive journals, a "History of New England," a "Description of the Present Province of New Brunswick," an "Account of the Suffering of the American Loyalists," dramatic sketches of a political nature, poems, and text-books. "Observations and Conjectures on the Antiquities of America by Rev. Jacob Bailey of Annapolis-Royal in Nova Scotia" is printed in *Collections of the Massachusetts Historical Society for the Year 1795,* and his description of the burning of Falmouth, Me., is in the *Collections of the Maine Historical Society,* V (1857).

[In addition to the authorities mentioned above, see Chas. E. Allen, *Rev. Jacob Bailey; His Character and Works* (1895); Marguerite Ogden, *One Hundredth Anniv. of the Diocese of Me.* (1920); Arthur H. W. Eaton, *Hist. of Kings County, Nova Scotia* (1910); Wm. A. Calnek, *Hist. of the County of Annapolis,* ed. by A. W. Savary (1897).]

H. E. S.

BAILEY, JACOB WHITMAN (Apr. 29, 1811–Feb. 27, 1857), botanist, chemist, geologist, was the son of Rev. Isaac and Jane (Whitman) Bailey of Ward (now Auburn), Mass. He early gave evidence of a taste for scientific studies, a taste which seems to have come by direct inheritance from both branches of his ancestral lines, his great-grandmother Whitman having been especially distinguished for her work in botany and astronomy, and his great-grandfather, Rev. Ralph Emerson, also having been a lover of science. Owing to the limited resources of the family he was, at the age of twelve, placed in a circulating library and bookstore in Providence, R. I. In this position he was so earnestly studious as to attract the attention of John Kingsbury, secretary of Brown University, who invited him to spend certain evenings of the week in his house for the purpose of studying Latin. The remaining evenings of the week were spent in the study of French. During these years he also found time to make a large collection of shells and insects. In July 1828 he received an appointment as cadet at West Point, graduating, fifth in his class, in 1832. After serving at various posts as second-lieutenant of artillery, he was, in 1834, appointed assistant professor of chemistry at West Point, serving in that capacity until 1838, at which time he was made incumbent of the newly created chair of chemistry, mineralogy, and geology, a position held until the time of his death in 1857. Among his earlier scientific passions was that for botany, and throughout his life, even though his chair was in a different field, he continued its study. While he did noteworthy work in chemistry and geology, his distinction as a scientist rests mainly upon his botanical research. He was the pioneer worker with the microscope in this country and it was through his knowledge and mastery of it that he won a distinctive place in the botanical world.

Bailey was especially distinguished for his researches among the minor algæ and especially the diatomaseas (which he was the first to detect in a fossil state in this country); for his microscopical investigations concerning the crystals contained in the tissues of plants, and for the detection of vegetable structures in the ashes of anthracite. His numerous scientific papers are all clear, explicit, and as unpretending as they are thorough, and every one of them embodies some direct and positive contribution to science.

He was married on Jan. 23, 1835, to Maria Slaughter of West View, Va. Her tragic death, along with that of his only daughter, in the burning of the steamer *Henry Clay* near Yonkers in July 1852, shadowed his later years. He was modest and reserved in manner, except to those to whom he had given his friendship; bright and sparkling in his intercourse with the chosen few; of a rich poetic taste, strong in his hate of wrong; faithful and painstaking in duty. To fully appreciate his work, it must be remembered that his was the task of breaking paths in hitherto untrodden fields; that he worked without assistance, without literature, without appliances save those devised by his own ingenuity; that while thus working, he was filling with distinction his chair in the Military Academy at West Point. Yet, this pioneer in American science, in the midst of his duties, with all the new world he had discovered to explore, found leisure to draw hundreds of carefully finished sketches of knights and ladies, castles and palaces for the amusement of an invalid son.

[Stanley Coulter, "Jacob Whitman Bailey," *Bot. Gazette,* XIII, 118–24; see also address of A. A. Gould, Aug. 19, 1857, *Proc. Am. Ass. for the Advancement of Science,* 1857–58, pp. 1–8; and G. W. Cullum, *Biog. Reg.*]

S. C.

BAILEY, JAMES ANTHONY (1847–Apr. 11, 1906), showman, was a native of Detroit. His parentage and early childhood are obscure, and his boyhood seems to have been passed in poverty, with little education. He worked his way upward and while still a very young man became connected with a circus. At one time during the Civil War he was a sutler's clerk at the front. He reëntered the circus field, and developed an extraordinary advertising talent and business capacity. In 1872 the firm of Cooper & Bailey was founded, and Bailey was soon in the front rank of his "profession." An achievement unusual at that time was his conducting, with his show, a tour around the world, in the course of which he visited South America, India, Australia, and islands of the Pacific. He had become a serious competitor of P. T. Barnum [*q.v.*], but in 1881 the two showmen wisely abandoned the contest, united forces, and exhibited the combined shows in New York. He was already proprietor of the Great London Show, and in 1890 he bought the Forepaugh circus. In the united Barnum & Bailey shows he had a large part in the management. Many of the special features of note were his projects, for instance the "Ethnological Congress," the spectacle "Nero," and—particularly—Jumbo. This renowned and gigantic elephant was purchased by Bailey in England from the Royal Zoological Society. His transfer to the United States excited some resentment, and the matter became for a time an "international incident."

Bailey exhibited his show in England, France, Germany, and various European countries. In Germany many thrifty citizens, having seen the parade in the mornings, declined to attend the regular performances of the circus as paying patrons; whereupon Bailey discontinued the parades for that country. In the course of his journeys he had made a considerable collection of works of art, which were placed in his house in Mount Vernon, N. Y. He died suddenly at Mount Vernon, shortly after building his house. He left the reputation of a man kind to his many employees, and decidedly more retiring than his famous partner. "Mr. Bailey never subscribed to this sentiment ['the public likes to be humbugged']. His motto was: 'Give the people the best—spare no expense in doing it—and they'll reward you'" (*New York Times*, Apr. 12, 1906). He was married to Ruth Louisa McCaddon of Zanesville, Ohio, who survived him; there were no children.

[N. Y. *Sun, Times, Tribune*, Apr. 12, 1906. According to the *Tribune*, Bailey's name was McGinness.]

E. K. A.

BAILEY, JAMES MONTGOMERY (Sept. 25, 1841–Mar. 4, 1894), humorous journalist, "Danbury News Man," may be called the father of the "colyumist," for humor, when he introduced it, was a new feature in journalism. The son of James and Sarah (Magee) Bailey, he was born at Albany, N. Y. His father, a carpenter, died from injuries due to a fall when his son was but two years of age, and three years later (1846) his mother married Daniel Smith, of Rome, N.Y. James received a common-school education, and served an apprenticeship as carpenter, apparently at Albany; in 1860 he went to Danbury, Conn., where he practised this trade for two years. He then enlisted in company C, 17th Connecticut Volunteers, starting for the South shortly before his twenty-first birthday. He remained in the army three years, being captured at Gettysburg and for two months a prisoner on Belle Isle. Already his special talent had manifested itself. An article written in 1860 was accepted by the New York *Sunday Mercury*, which continued to print his efforts for over a year. While a soldier he wrote for a Danbury journal humorous sketches of army life.

The war over, Bailey with Timothy Donovan, a printer and fellow soldier, purchased the *Danbury Times* (1865), conducting it as a Democratic organ. In 1870 they consolidated with it the *Jeffersonian*, a Republican paper, thus initiating the *Danbury News*, "an eight-page journal containing statements almost TOO GOOD TO BE TRUE"; and Bailey now assumed the name "The Danbury News Man." This weekly newspaper soon launched on a career unique in journalistic history. Its circulation of 1,920 in January 1873, leaped to 30,000 in September of the same year. It was read and quoted with delight the country over, and even abroad, for years thereafter. The cause was Bailey, who had a faculty for injecting humor into commonplace events or inventing ridiculous situations, and portraying them, sometimes with side-splitting effect, and again with sly humor less hilarious but equally satisfying. Undoubtedly he lightened care in thousands of homes. This was not through the *News* alone, but through his books, whereby he gave new life to the products of his pen. *Life in Danbury* and the *Danbury News Man's Almanac* (both 1873) were followed by *They All Do It* (1877), *England from a Back Window* (1878), *Mr. Phillips' Goneness* (1879), and *The Danbury Boom* (1880). The popularity of these publications may be inferred from the fact that 33,000 copies of his first book sold within eleven weeks. His *History of Danbury*, Conn., appeared after his death.

In 1873 he visited California and in 1874 Europe. As usual he saw the merry side of everything—witness his *England*. In 1876 he appeared as a truly *popular* lecturer. Two years later Donovan withdrew from partnership with Bailey, who, thenceforth sole editor and proprietor of the *News*, added a daily, the *Danbury Evening*

News, in 1883. Realizing that his humorous efforts sometimes faltered, he gradually withdrew from this field, building up a strong local newspaper. In appearance he was tall, dignified, and athletic, with handsome face, dark hair and mustache, and mirthful eyes. One of his traits was a liking for dogs; another his aversion to wearing a necktie. His humor was always natural and kindly. He was a close observer of men and things, and wisdom mingled with his drollery. The English amused him, but he admired their real worth. His writings and speech alike abounded with wit. Yet he was a man of mercurial nature, passing suddenly from sunny moods to fits of depression. Although at its zenith his income attained $40,000, he died comparatively poor, for, while he lived plainly, he gave lavishly, even when he knew he was imposed upon. His interests were not solely journalistic. He became president of the Danbury Board of Trade, was a founder and president of the Danbury Hospital, and president of the Danbury Relief Society. He supported liberally the Children's Home and was active in the Baptist Church. He was married (1866) to Catharine Douglass Stewart of Danbury, who survived him.

[The best available account of Bailey is a sketch in the opening pages of his *Hist. of Danbury,* completed by Susan Benedict Hill (1896). A chapter is devoted to Bailey in Robert Ford's *Am. Humorists* (1897), pp. 193–212. He is the subject of an article "A Yankee Humorist," by G. W. Hallock, in *Munsey's Mag.,* XI, 238–41. His obituary appeared in the *Danbury News* of Mar. 5, 1894. A later issue of the *News* contained an address on Bailey by the Rev. Andrew C. Hubbard.]

R. S. B.

BAILEY, JOSEPH (May 6, 1825–Mar. 21, 1867), Union soldier, engineer, was born in Pennsville, Ohio, and journeyed with his parents, while still a boy, to Illinois. Here he studied civil engineering, married Mary Spaulding in 1846, and the following year, moved to Kilbourn City, Wis., where he successfully engaged in lumbering and in engineering construction. At the outbreak of the Civil War he raised a company in the 4th Wisconsin Regiment. Of this company he was appointed captain and was mustered into federal service, July 2, 1861. With his regiment, he was sent immediately to Maryland, and, in the following spring, to New Orleans with Gen. Benjamin Butler's expedition. The remainder of his war service was along the Gulf. He was promoted major of his regiment, May 30, 1863; lieutenant-colonel, July 15, 1863; and colonel, May 3, 1864. During much of this time he was on detached service and, owing to his engineering skill, was successively engineer 2nd division, 19th corps, distinguishing himself at Port Hudson in July 1863, chief engineer defenses of New Orleans, and military engineer 19th corps. It was in 1864, on Gen. Banks's Red River expedition, that Bailey rendered his outstanding service. The army marched overland accompanied on the river by a fleet of light-draft gunboats and transports which, aided by high water, passed upstream without difficulty. When, however, the retiring army reached Alexandria on Apr. 26, the water had subsided and the fleet could not pass over the falls. In this emergency, Bailey, then engineer 19th corps, recommended construction of wing dams to raise the water in the river high enough to permit the boats to pass over the falls. He executed this task with such skill and energy that in twelve days the entire fleet, thirty-three vessels all told, had cleared the obstruction. More than $2,000,000 had been saved to the government. For this act Bailey was granted the thanks of Congress, was brevetted brigadier-general June 7, 1864, and was presented by Admiral Porter with a sword. Participating later, with distinction, in the reduction of Mobile, he was appointed, on Nov. 10, 1864, brigadier-general of volunteers and on Mar. 13, 1865, major-general by brevet for gallant and meritorious services in the campaign of Mobile. Resigning on July 7, 1865, he settled in Vernon County, Mo. In the fall of 1866 he was elected sheriff, and on Mar. 21, 1867, was murdered, near Nevada, by two bushwackers whom he had arrested and who, while returning to the county seat, shot him in the back of the head.

[M. M. Quaife, *Wis.; Its Hist. and Its People*(1924), I; *Hist. of Columbia County, Wis.* (1914), ed. by J. E. Jones, I; F. B. Heitman, *Hist. Reg.* (1890), p. 101; *Official Records,* see Index; Muster Rolls, 4th Wis. Inf. Records, A. G. O.]

C. A. B.

BAILEY, LYDIA R. (Feb. 1, 1779–Feb. 21, 1869), was for sixty years connected with the printing industry in Philadelphia, being one of the first women printers in that city. She was nineteen years of age when she married Robert Bailey, a printer (son of Francis Bailey [*q.v.*]) of the Quaker City, in the autumn of the year 1798. At that time an epidemic of yellow fever in Philadelphia caused a general stoppage of business and an exodus of many of the inhabitants, which may account for the fact that no record of her marriage has been found. Robert Bailey died in March 1808, and left his widow impoverished, in debt, and with four children, the youngest only four months old. But she was a practical printer, and proceeded to carry on such business as she had. Philip Freneau, the poet of the Revolution, some of whose works had been printed by Francis Bailey, learned of the widow's plight, and gave her the publication of a new edition of his *Poems,* marked "Third Edition" on the title, which was issued in two volumes in 1809. In a few years, through her care as a printer, and the influence of her husband's family, Mrs. Bailey prospered. "During the old Whig Administration she had a rich and valuable patronage from Councils and the departments" (*Sunday Dispatch,* Philadelphia, Feb. 28, 1869). For a long period—from about 1830 to 1850—she was designated the City Printer for Philadelphia. Her specialty was book work, in which she was assisted by her son, Robert William, when he became old enough to stand at a case. In her later years she depended considerably upon her son, and when he died, in 1861, she realized that she was unequal to the task of continuing the business, and retired. "Steam presses were fatal to her courage and she surrendered to an instrumentality she could neither comprehend nor compete with" (*North American,* Feb. 24, 1869). She died in 1869, three weeks after reaching her ninetieth birthday, and was buried in the Bailey vault in the burial ground of the Third Presbyterian Church, Philadelphia, to which congregation she made the initial gift for an endowment fund. Mrs. Bailey's printing office had the distinction of having produced a number of men who became leaders in the trade in Philadelphia. At the time of her death the *North American* spoke of her as "one who enjoyed woman's rights to the full, though living before a formal exposition of that doctrine, and who as a practical printer had considerable deserved local fame."

[Records of the Third Presbyt. (Old Pine Street) Church, Phila., and the obituary notices in the newspapers of that city, are the main sources of information. The date of Mrs. Bailey's birth is derived from the inscription on her tombstone. See also H. O. Gibbons, *A Hist. of Old Pine Street* [Church] (1905).]

J. J.

BAILEY, RUFUS WILLIAM (Apr. 13, 1793–Apr. 25, 1863), Congregational clergyman, college president, was born at North Yarmouth, Me., the son of Lebbeus and Sarah (Myrick) Bailey. After graduating from Dartmouth College in 1813, he taught for a short time in academies at Salisbury, N. H., and Blue Hill, Me., and then studied law in the office of Daniel Webster. After a year of this study, however, he decided to go into the ministry, and went to Andover Theological Seminary to prepare himself. He spent one year at Andover and then finished his preparation with Francis Brown, president of Dartmouth College. During the year 1817–18 he was employed as a tutor at Dartmouth, after which he was ordained pastor of the Congregational Church at Norwich, Vt. Later he held a pastoral charge at Pittsfield, Mass., but gave it up in 1827 for reasons of health, moving to the South where he engaged in a long and active career of teaching and preaching in South Carolina, North Carolina, and Virginia. In 1854, he became professor of languages at Austin College, Tex. He was made president of that institution in 1858 and held this office up to the time of his death. He was twice married: in 1820 to Lucy Hatch, the daughter of Reuben Hatch of Norwich, Vt., and after her death to Mrs. Mariette (Perry) Lloyd, of Waterbury, Conn.

Bailey was a prolific writer. To the *Patriarch,* of which he became editor in 1841, he made numerous contributions. A number of his letters written to newspapers on the subject of slavery were later collected and published in a volume called *The Issue* (1837). Many of his sermons were published, a number of them in a little book, entitled *The Family Preacher* (1837). But he was perhaps best known in his own day and later for his text-books on spelling and grammar which were widely used in the South. Over half a million copies of his *Scholar's Companion* (1830) had been sold before the time of his death; and it continued to sell long afterward. In his writings the moral-religious purpose was almost always, if not always present. In the introduction to the 1863 edition of his *Scholar's Companion,* he says of his book: "Beyond mere orthography and correct pronunciation, it is designed to introduce the young mind into the inner life of words, and thus into the inner life of the soul. It is a spelling-book, but that is not all. It teaches correct pronunciation, but that is not all. It is a defining Dictionary,—but still more, it discriminates the nicest shades of difference in words, in thought, and contributes eminently to form the mind to truth, and the character to uprightness, and the soul for its immortal destiny." This sublime confidence in the power of precept seems to have animated Bailey's other writings and very probably his whole career.

[G. T. Chapman, *Sketches of the Alumni of Dartmouth Coll.* (1867), p. 163; *Barnard's Am. Jour. of Ed.,* XIII, 215; *The Patriarch, or Family Library Mag.,* vols. I and II, 1841–42.]

J. F. S.

BAILEY, THEODORUS (Apr. 12, 1805–Feb. 10, 1877), naval officer, was born at Chateaugay, in the north-eastern part of New York, and received his early education at the academy in

Plattsburg, less than thirty-five miles distant. Thus he breathed the very air of Macdonough's operations on Lake Champlain in the War of 1812, resulting in the famous victory of September 1814. This had its influence, and three years later, Jan. 1, 1818, the boy secured an appointment as midshipman. There were advantages in being the son of Judge William Bailey and Phœbe Platt and the nephew of Gen. Theodorus Bailey (the latter holding at different times several offices of distinction in both the State and city of New York), but he did not find that family connections made naval life easy or promotion rapid. His first two years of service were spent off the coast of Africa in the frigate *Cyane*. Then he was transferred to the ship of the line *Franklin,* ordered to the Pacific. His advancement to the lieutenant's grade came Mar. 3, 1827; and, assigned to the *Vincennes,* he sailed about the Pacific, to China, and then home by way of the Cape of Good Hope, the cruise lasting three years and two months. On June 23, 1830, he married his cousin, Sarah Ann Platt. In 1846, he was given his first independent command, the store-ship *Lexington.*

In the Mexican War, Bailey rendered efficient service. Embarking company F, 3rd Artillery, with three officers later to become famous, Sherman, Halleck, and Ord, he sailed from New York, around the Horn, to Monterey, the voyage taking 198 days (for a detailed account of the voyage, see Sherman's *Memoirs*). During the latter part of the Mexican War he conducted troops to Lower California and blockaded San Blas, which he captured. He was promoted to commander Mar. 6, 1849, and to captain, Dec. 15, 1855. From 1853 to 1856 he commanded the *St. Mary's,* visiting the Marquesas, Society, Samoan, and Fiji Islands, and improving the relations between the natives and American citizens in the last two places. On his return, arriving opportunely at Panama during an uprising in April 1856, Bailey was "of great assistance to our commerce and citizens," affording "protection to the persons and property of the thousands of our countrymen crossing the Isthmus, from the violence of an ungoverned population" (*Annual Report of the Secretary of the Navy,* 1856, p. 408).

Shortly after the breaking out of the Civil War, Bailey was ordered to command the large steam frigate *Colorado,* engaged in the blockade of Pensacola. There he matured the plan and attended to the details of fitting out the expedition that destroyed the privateer *Judah,* Sept. 14, 1861 (*Official Records,* XVI, 670). His greatest service was with Farragut in the attack on New Orleans, where he was second in command. Since the *Colorado* was too large to be taken over the bar into the Mississippi, he transferred his flag to the little gunboat *Cayuga.* Though a medical survey reported that his health was such that it would be dangerous for him to take part in the fight, he ignored this except to protest indignantly to Farragut, "I'll lead your fleet up the river, if I burst my boiler" (Headley, p. 236). On Apr. 24, 1862, he led the way past Forts Jackson and St. Philip, fought (for a while unsupported) the Confederate river defense fleet, captured the Chalmette Regiment, and attacked the Chalmette batteries (Alden, pp. 117, ff.). Bailey characterized the fight "as a contest between iron hearts in wooden vessels and ironclads with iron beaks—and the iron hearts won" (Report to Secretary of the Navy, May 7, 1862). When the fleet had arrived at New Orleans he was sent into the city, and attended only by Lieut. George H. Perkins as his aid, without a guard and without arms, he passed through an excited and hostile mob. "Through the gates of death those two men walked to the City Hall to demand the town's surrender. It was one of the bravest deeds I ever saw done" (George W. Cable, in *Battles and Leaders of the Civil War,* II, 21). Still suffering from ill health, Bailey was sent north and was honored by being the bearer of dispatches and reports of the victory to Washington. After a brief tour of duty at Sacketts Harbor he had sufficiently recovered to be ordered, Nov. 4, 1862, to relieve Rear Admiral Lardner in the command of the East Gulf blockading squadron. Here again he showed efficiency, and in eighteen months his force captured 150 blockade runners. In the spring of 1864, learning that Farragut was preparing an attack on Mobile, he volunteered to join forces, but yellow fever, breaking out at Key West, and spreading through the East Gulf blockading squadron, thwarted the plan. Shortly after, Bailey, showing evidence of wear from his long service in an enervating climate, was relieved and ordered to command the Portsmouth Navy Yard, Sept. 30, 1864. He was promoted to the rank of rear admiral July 25, 1866, and was retired Oct. 10 of the same year. His last years were spent in Washington, D. C.

[The best sketch of Bailey's career is to be found in J. T. Headley, *Farragut and Our Naval Commanders* (1867), ch. 10; a briefer article is by Katharine Mimmack, in *Biog. Sketches of the Bailey-Myers-Mason Families* (1908); an obituary appeared in the *Army and Navy Jour.,* Feb. 17, 1877. His letters and reports are included in the *Official Records* (1894–1917). For an account of Bailey and the *Cayuga* at New Orleans, see C. S. Alden, *George Hamilton Perkins* (1914).]

C. S. A.

BAILLY, JOSEPH ALEXIS (Jan. 21, 1825–June 15, 1883), sculptor, was born in Paris, the son of Joseph Philidor Bailly, a manufacturer of cabinet furniture. He studied for a time under Baron Bozio in the French Institute, worked in his father's factory, was a conscript in the Garde Mobile and during the Revolution of 1848 shot at his captain, escaped to New Orleans, and, after sojourns in New York, Philadelphia, and Buenos Ayres, settled in Philadelphia. In 1850 he married Louisa, daughter of Louis David of Brie, France. He at first devoted himself to wood-carving and the cutting of portraits in cameo but soon took up sculpture, turning out numerous portraits—busts, medallions, and statues. He was an indefatigable and rather facile worker. The Pennsylvania Academy of Fine Arts possesses two examples of his portraits—a bust of his wife and a plaster medallion of William Emlen Cresson. For the grave of the latter in Laurel Hill Cemetery he did a seated bronze effigy (1869) and near-by a similar seated figure of William F. Hughes (1870). Both have the characteristic realism of the latter nineteenth century, and the statue of Cresson the added characteristic of an accumulation of accessories on the base. Busts of Gen. Grant and Gen. Meade are likewise recorded. Bailly's work, however, was not confined to private commissions, for Philadelphia possesses several public monuments by his hand. One of the earliest was a standing figure of Franklin cut from Brunswick stone and placed on the corner of the Public Ledger Building in 1866. This work was removed when the present edifice was built. In 1869 he made a marble statue of Washington, which was placed in front of the rear façade of Independence Hall. For better preservation it was later removed from its open-air pedestal to a position on the second floor of the City Hall, in a window overlooking the central courtyard, a position it still occupies. Its place near Independence Hall was taken by a bronze replica. Of all the effigies of Washington it is perhaps the most vacuous. The bronze statue of Witherspoon, erected in Fairmount Park in 1876, possesses a certain graceful dignity which makes it somewhat more pleasing than the earlier statues. Though most of his work was for Philadelphia, Bailly made for Washington, D. C., a statue of Gen. John A. Rawlins (1874), which was cast from Confederate cannon captured by Grant's armies. When the Centennial Exposition was held in Philadelphia in 1876, Bailly exhibited an equestrian statue of President Guzman Blanco of Venezuela, which is now in Caracas, where is also another statue of Blanco by him. At the Exposition, likewise, was a statue of "Spring," which has since disappeared. Of the same order of idealized subject as this last statue are two marble groups in the Pennsylvania Academy, "The Expulsion" and "The First Prayer." These works, in treatment and execution, recall the work of mid-nineteenth century French sculptors such as Perraud and Crauk. Bailly evidently attained to considerable reputation in Philadelphia, for he was made an Academician in 1856 and was an instructor at the Pennsylvania Academy from 1876 to 1877. He died of heart disease and was buried in Mount Peace Cemetery, where there is no longer even a headstone to mark his grave.

[Article in *Biog. Encyc. of Pa. of the 19th Cent.* (1874), possibly by Bailly himself; brief notices in C. E. Clement and L. Hutton, *Artists of the 19th Cent.* (ed. of 1885); L. Taft, *Hist. of Am. Sculpture* (new ed., 1924), p. 505; brief obituary in Phila. *Public Ledger,* June 19, 1883.] E. G. N.

BAIN, GEORGE LUKE SCOBIE (May 5, 1836–Oct. 22, 1891), merchant-miller, the son of Robert Scobie Bain and Charlotte Murdoch Brown, natives of the central lowlands of Scotland, was born at Stirling, where he received his early education. Despite the fond hopes of his mother, who desired her son to become a minister of the Free Church of Scotland, he ran away from home at the age of fifteen and obtained employment as a cabin-boy on a ship whose destination was Montreal, Canada. When young Bain arrived in that city, he decided to remain, and was soon at work in an accountant's office. Three years later he removed to Portland, Me., where he obtained his first knowledge of the flour business while employed by the commission house of Mackintosh & Company. In 1856 he succumbed to the lure of the West and removed to the growing young city of Chicago, where he secured a position in the flour department of a prominent commission house. The following year, at the age of twenty-one, he made his début in the business world by organizing a commission house under the name of Bain & Clarke. After a varied business career in Chicago, he moved to St. Louis in 1865, and there shortly afterward established the commission house of George Bain & Co. This firm did a successful business in flour, grain, and other products. But in 1871 Bain severed his connection with the commission house, and purchased a half interest in the Atlantic Mills, then one of the largest establishments in St. Louis. During the next twenty years he was actively engaged as a manufacturer and shipper of flour, contributing in no small degree toward making St. Louis one of the greatest milling centers in the United States. He was the pioneer in developing the direct exportation of flour from St. Louis to foreign countries. He was one of the organizers of the millers in Missouri and throughout the country. In 1874 the Missouri Millers' Association elected him its first president, and in the same year the Millers' National Association chose him its first vice-president. In 1875 he was elected president of the latter body, and held that position for eight consecutive years. While he took a prominent part in the business life of St. Louis, he was also active in politics, fraternal circles, and philanthropic work. Possessed of great energy and initiative, Bain had, according to a eulogy delivered in 1891, "positive views on all questions that had two sides, and hesitated not to express them, regardless of numbers or consequences." On Nov. 5, 1857, he married Clara C. Mather at Chicago, Ill.

[Geneal. of the Bain Family (MS. in the Mo. Hist. Soc. Lib., St. Louis); Robt. E. M. Bain, Statement, Oct. 14, 1927, St. Louis; *Northwestern Miller,* Oct. 30, 1891; L. U. Reavis, *Saint Louis, the Future Great City of the World* (1882), pp. 231–33; *Encyc. of the Hist. of St. Louis* (ed. by Wm. Hyde and Howard Conard (1899), I, 101–02; E. D. Kargau, *Mercantile, Industrial, and Professional Saint Louis* (1902), pp, 101–02, 109.

R. P. Bi—r.

BAINBRIDGE, WILLIAM (May 7, 1774–July 27, 1833), naval officer, was born at Princeton, N. J., fourth son of Absolom Bainbridge, a physician of eminence who shortly afterward moved to New York. Dr. Bainbridge, descended from a good English family prominent in New Jersey since the middle of the seventeenth century, had married the daughter of John Taylor of Monmouth County, N. J., who, at his own request, was entrusted with the education of his grandson. This education appears to have been an excellent one and was continued until the lad's fifteenth year, at which age his family, yielding to his pleadings, and sensible that his sturdy physique and adventurous nature fitted him for an active life, allowed him to go to sea, placing him under the care and patronage of a sea captain of reputation who commanded a Philadelphia merchantman.

His progress in seamanship and his development of the qualities of command were steady and swift, and these, added to his vigorous personality, a fair education and influential family connections, led to rapid advancement in his profession. Within three years he was made an officer and at the age of eighteen chief mate, in which capacity, during a voyage to Holland, he recovered his ship from the hands of mutineers by a display of sheer fearlessness and dash, and was rewarded with the command of the ship when not yet twenty. From this time until 1798 he commanded vessels in the European trade, which was carried on at the height of the excitement of the hostilities following the French Revolution. Occasions were not lacking, even for merchant captains, that required much tact and determination. In 1796, his ship lying in the Garonne, Bainbridge was entreated by a brother American captain to help quell a serious mutiny, which he succeeded in doing by prompt and vigorous action though at the expense of a painful injury. Shortly after this, his ship the *Hope,* armed only with four nine-pounders and with a crew of eleven, was attacked near the West Indies by a small British privateer of double his force, which began the action without displaying her colors. Upon receiving a broadside from the *Hope,* she ran up the British ensign, which, however, not only failed to intimidate the American skipper, but caused him to attack so furiously that the Englishman struck his flag. Bainbridge's crew were eager to take possession of the prize, but this could not be permitted, since the armament of the *Hope* was legally for defense only. Instead, Bainbridge contented himself with hailing the English captain, ordering him to go about his business and to report to his masters that, if they wanted his ship, they would have to send a bigger vessel or a better commander. On the voyage home a sailor was taken out of his ship, under the pretense that he was a deserter, by the powerful English cruiser *Indefatigable.* The protest of the American commander being derided, he declared that he would take a man out of the next British ship of his own strength he fell in with, as compensation, and within a week he made good his threat by seizing a sailor on board a British merchantman of greater force than the *Hope.*

In 1798, when the aggressions of France and the depredations of the Barbary States called into being the new American navy, Bainbridge received command of the *Retaliation,* 14 guns, with the rank of lieutenant commandant. In September of that year, while cruising in the West Indies, the consorts of his ship having made sail to the eastward in chase of three vessels supposed to be British, Bainbridge was left alone to cope with three other craft approaching from the west, two of which proved to be the French frigates *L'Insurgente* and *Volontier,* forming an overwhelming force, to which the mortified but powerless young commander was obliged to strike his flag. Taken aboard the *Volontier* a prisoner, he was able, by his quickness of wit, to save from capture his two consorts, the *Montezuma* and *Norfolk,* with which the faster French frigate, *L'Insurgente,* was about to close, being much more than a match for both. Of this latter fact, however, the captain of the *Volontier,* the French superior officer, was unaware, and, to assure himself on the point, turned to Bainbridge, standing at his side, and inquired as to the armament of the American vessels. Bainbridge's ready answer that the ship carried 28 long twelves and the brig 20 long nines, in reality double the actual force of the American vessels, so impressed the French commander that he recalled his consort by signal, and the *Montezuma* and *Norfolk* made good their escape. Taken a prisoner to Guadaloupe, Bainbridge was subjected to the equivocal machinations of the French governor, who, by alternately ill-treating the American prisoners and making flattering promises, endeavored to persuade the young commander to make certain political concessions which far exceeded his authority and which were promptly refused, as was also the suggestion that he should return in command of his ship to the United States, but refrain from all acts of hostility toward French shipping. The diplomatic tact and firmness displayed under these difficult circumstances were appreciated by the Government, and Bainbridge, on his return home, was promoted to be master commandant and given command of the *Norfolk,* 18 guns, one of the vessels which his presence of mind had saved for his country. It is likely that Bainbridge's account of the cruelty and indignities suffered by the Americans at Guadaloupe was partly responsible for the prompt passing by Congress of the Retaliation Act, a direct consequence of the unjust decrees of the French Republic; Vice-President Jefferson wrote at the time, "Within an hour after this [Bainbridge's arrival] was known to the Senate, they passed the retaliation act" (Harris, p. 33).

Joining Commodore Truxtun's squadron, Bainbridge took the *Norfolk* into the harbor of St. Kitts to renew her topmasts lost in a desperate attempt to overhaul a large schooner, and was directed to assemble a convoy of over a hundred sail and escort them to the United States. Falling in with an enemy frigate, he signaled the convoy to disperse, and so occupied the frigate by inducing her to chase that every one of the vessels under his protection escaped, while he himself, under cover of night, gave his enemy the slip and rejoined his convoy at the appointed rendezvous, a feat highly praised by naval experts. After numerous successes in the West Indies he was ordered to cruise off Havana with two other vessels under his command, and rendered such excellent service in convoying and in blockading enemy privateers, that on May 2, 1800, he was promoted to be captain, at that time the highest rank in the navy, still wanting six days of being twenty-six years of age.

The same month he was given command of the *George Washington,* a small converted merchantman rated as a frigate, carrying 24 guns, and received orders, with what grace may be imagined, to bear his country's tribute to the Dey of Algiers. At this time the Barbary States claimed jurisdiction in the Mediterranean and adjacent waters, the methods employed in the execution of which were little short of piratical. No concerted, energetic attempt had ever been made by the Christian nations to put a stop to a system under which they paid blackmail euphemistically termed tribute, for the protection of their maritime commerce. The United States had presented the Dey of Algiers with a handsome new frigate in 1798 and two schooners in 1799 in partial payment of our dues, which the Republic was too poor to honor in full. Bainbridge was not spared even a deeper humiliation than that felt by his fellow officers of the Navy. Having delivered the tribute of his country to the Dey, and while preparing for his return voyage, he was astonished and confounded to receive from the Dey, who was a vassal of the Sultan of Turkey, a request, tantamount to a command, to proceed in the *George Washington,* manned by her American complement but under the Ottoman flag, to Constantinople with a special embassy from the Dey to the Sultan. After repeated desperate attempts on the part of Bainbridge and the American agent, Mr. O'Brien, firstly to avoid the mission altogether and then at least to sail with the American flag at the main, the American commander was in the end forced to accede to all the demands of the Dey. Bainbridge himself wrote to a friend concerning this incident: "The unpleasant situation in which I am placed must convince you that I have no alternative left but compliance, or a renewal of hostilities against our commerce. The loss of the frigate and the fear of slavery for myself and crew were the least circumstances to be apprehended, but I knew our valuable commerce in these seas would fall a sacrifice to the corsairs of this power, as we have here no cruisers to protect it . . . I hope I may never again be sent to Algiers with *tribute,* unless I am authorized to deliver it from the mouth of our cannon" (*Ibid.,* p. 45). The voyage to Constantinople and the sojourn there of several weeks were uneventful, but resulted in creating an excellent impression in Turkey of the young American republic, of which the port authorities there had never heard. Upon his return to Algiers, Bainbridge was met with another request to carry an embassy to the Sultan, and his refusal led to a show of fury on the part of the Dey which was only quieted by the production of a special letter of protection which the powerful Capudan Pasha had given the American commander. Americans were thereafter no longer molested; Bainbridge even succeeded in rescuing from slavery a number of French citizens, though his own country was practically at war with France, and landing them at Alicante; his humanity and chivalry drawing from Napoleon, then First Consul, a letter of "acknowledgment and thanks."

On his return to the United States, Bainbridge had the satisfaction of learning, not only that his conduct under the trying circumstances of his European mission had received the full approval of the government, but that, although he stood only twenty-seventh on the list of twenty-eight captains in the Navy, he had been selected as one of the nine allowed by the new reduction law to be retained. Given command of the *Essex,* 32 guns, he proceeded to the Mediterranean with the squadron of Commodore Dale, whose orders were to put a stop to the depredations of the Bashaw of Tripoli; but upon his reporting that his ship was in unseaworthy condition, Bainbridge was directed to take her home in the summer of 1802, when she was laid up for repairs. After a visit to his family in Philadelphia and various shore duties which occupied him until May 21, 1803, he received on that day the command of the frigate *Philadelphia,* 44 guns, with orders to join the Mediterranean squadron of Commodore Preble, operating against Tripoli. Arriving at Gibraltar the last of August, he was successful in capturing several Barbary corsairs in which he found a number of American prisoners, and then proceeded to the harbor of Tripoli; but at its very entrance occurred another of those mischances to which Bainbridge, entirely without fault of his own, was subjected in the course of his career. On Oct. 31, 1803, while chasing a Moorish craft into the harbor, the *Philadelphia,* though provided with the best maps and making repeated soundings, ran fast aground on an uncharted reef several miles from the city of Tripoli. Desperate efforts were made to lighten and float her, even to throwing overboard all save the stern gun, but in vain. The helpless frigate was soon surrounded by numerous Tripolitan gunboats, and finally Bainbridge, after rendering his ship as unseaworthy as possible under the circumstances, was obliged to surrender with his crew, numbering 315 persons. The captives were humanely treated by the Bashaw, but remained prisoners until the end of the war. The *Philadelphia* was soon afterward floated, taken into the harbor, and was in process of being fitted out as a Tripolitan cruiser, when Stephen Decatur [*q.v.*], acting upon a suggestion contained in a letter from Bainbridge to Commodore Preble, succeeded in the brilliant exploit of cutting out and burning to the water's edge the captured vessel during the night of Feb. 15, 1804. The chagrined Bashaw retaliated upon Bainbridge and the other American captives by removing them to the dungeons of the castle, whence they witnessed the several bombardments of Tripoli by the American squadron. In the spring of 1805 negotiations were begun between the American consul-general to the Barbary States and the Bashaw, and, several obstacles arising, Bainbridge was, by common consent, chosen to discuss these with the American representatives. Leaving his own son, a naval officer, in the hands of the Bashaw as a hostage, he went aboard the American flagship, the *Constitution,* and in the end was not a little responsible for the peace which followed in early June 1805. A naval court of inquiry, consisting of Captains J. Barron, H. G. Campbell, and Stephen Decatur, which convened at Syracuse on June 29, completely exonerated Bainbridge from all blame in connection with the loss of the *Philadelphia,* a result which was made a foregone conclusion by a letter to Bainbridge signed by the entire complement of his vessel, praising his caution, courage, and resourcefulness on the occasion. One of his first acts upon returning to the United States, where he encountered only sympathy and admiration, was to initiate negotiations through the Secretary of the Navy which led to a resolution of thanks by Congress to the Danish consul at Tripoli, N. C. Nissen, whose friendly offices had rendered less distressful the captivity of the American seamen.

Bainbridge was assigned to the navy-yard at New York, but finding his financial situation somewhat embarrassed on account of his long captivity, he obtained a furlough and entered the merchant service as captain and part owner. An incident at this period nearly terminated his career on account of his inability to swim, an odd circumstance in the life of a sailor and athlete. Falling into the sea while boarding his vessel from a small boat, he was only rescued, after sinking three times, by the efforts of his colored servant. He continued in the merchant service with success until March 1808, when he was ordered to Portland, and soon after received command of the fine frigate *President,* 44 guns, with jurisdiction over the southern half of the coast, flying his broad pennant of commodore for the first time.

In 1810 he once more returned to the merchant service, in the European trade. While entering the Baltic on a voyage to St. Petersburg, his ship was stopped by a Danish cruiser and taken into Copenhagen. His plight, however, was soon ended by the mediation of his friend, Nissen, and his vessel released. Soon after this, the affair between his old ship, the *President,* and the *Little Belt,* coming to his ears, he hurried home, reaching Washington in February 1812, and placed his services at his country's disposal. To his mortification, however, he learned that it was seriously contemplated to lay up all the vessels of the Navy, lest they might fall into the hands of the powerful fleets of Great Britain. In dismay and indignation he allied himself with another officer of spirit, Commodore Charles Stewart [*q.v.*], and the two drew up and sent to Congress through the Secretary of the Navy, a protest couched in such insistent yet logical terms, that the Government refrained from further action, and a design which would have rendered the United States defenseless on the seas at the outbreak of the second war with Great Britain was frustrated. It is related that later, when the news arrived of the third signal victory of an American frigate over a British rival within a few months, the Secretary of the Navy remarked to Commodore Stewart, "We are indebted to Bainbridge and yourself for these flags and victories. Had it not been for your strong remonstrance, not a vessel of war belonging to the government would have left its anchorage" (Harris, p. 136).

At the outbreak of the war, June 18, 1812, Bainbridge was commandant of the navy-yard at Charlestown (Boston), and when Isaac Hull [*q.v.*], after his victory over the *Guerrière,* applied for leave of absence, Bainbridge asked for and obtained command of the victorious *Constitution,* the frigate *Essex* and the sloop of war *Hornet* completing his squadron, which was to operate in the Southern Atlantic. On Dec. 29, while cruising without his consorts in the neighborhood of Bahia, Brazil, he fell in with a large British frigate and at once attacked. A spirited action ensued, both ships maneuvering to rake and to avoid being raked. Early in the fight Bainbridge received a musket-ball in the hip, and a few minutes later a second injury, but continued to direct the battle from the quarter-deck. The second wound was received when the steering wheel of the *Constitution* was knocked into splinters by an enemy shot, making it necessary to steer the ship by means of two tackles below decks, a serious handicap in a battle between two sailing vessels. The outcome of the furious encounter was decided by the superior gunnery of the American frigate. The British ship had on board the British governor of Bombay and other passengers, and Bainbridge's humane treatment of his prisoners and of the wounded earned him the praise of his enemies.

Returning to Boston in February 1813, he remained there for the rest of the war, superintending the construction of the *Independence,* a line-of-battle ship of 74 guns, the command of which he took, joining the squadron of Commodore Decatur in the Mediterranean. He arrived, however, after the latter had brought the war against the Dey of Algiers to a successful close. Remaining in European waters, Decatur's successor as commander-in-chief, Bainbridge arranged several difficulties with the Barbary powers, and on returning to the United States spent some years at Boston and Newport, flying his pennant on the *Independence.* In the spring of 1820 he proceeded for the fifth time in his life to the Mediterranean, flying his flag on the new and powerful line-of-battle ship *Columbus,* 80 guns, and remaining abroad about a year, for the purpose of impressing the several predatory nations with the present power of the United States. This was Commodore Bainbridge's last service afloat. He died of pneumonia at Philadelphia on July 27, 1833, leaving a son and four daughters by his wife, a lady of the West Indies named Susan Hyleger (the date of his death is usually given as July 28 on the authority of his tombstone, but the correct date is found in military and naval announcements of July 27). He was of handsome and commanding presence, ardent and sanguine in temperament, and though excitable, was calm in moments of danger. His bravery, chivalry, and generosity were proverbial in the Navy.

[Thos. Harris, *Life and Services of Commodore Wm. Bainbridge* (1837); Jas. Fenimore Cooper, *Lives of Distinguished Am. Naval Officers* (1846), I, and *Hist. of the Navy* (2nd ed., 1846); Livingston Hunt, "Bainbridge under the Turkish Flag," in *U. S. Naval Institute Proc.,* June 1926; G. W. Allen, *Our Navy and the Barbary Corsairs* (1905); Stanley Lane-Poole, *Story of the Barbary Corsairs* (1890); MSS. in the Office of Naval Records and Lib. at Washington.]

E. B.

BAIRD, ABSALOM (Aug. 20, 1824–June 14, 1905), Union soldier, was born at Washington, Pa., the son of William and Nancy (Mitchell) Baird. His father was a distinguished member of the Pennsylvania bar and his grandfather, Dr. Absalom Baird, a surgeon in the Revolutionary army. His great-grandfather, Lieut. John Baird, participated in the Forbes expedition against the French and Indians at Fort Duquesne in 1758. Upon graduation from Washington College, Absalom Baird studied law but the threatened rupture between the United States and Mexico induced him to seek admission to the United States Military Academy in 1845, in order to prepare himself for the war that was impending. He was graduated in 1849 and assigned to the artillery. Three years campaigning against the Seminole

Indians were succeeded by six years as instructor at West Point and these by duty in Texas, a frontier then distinctly unfriendly.

Shortly after the outbreak of the Civil War, Baird was appointed captain and assistant adjutant-general, and when McDowell's army marched into Virginia accompanied it as adjutant-general of Tyler's division, participating in the engagement at Blackburn's Ford and in the battle of Bull Run. Returning to the War Department he was promoted, Nov. 12, 1861, to major and assistant inspector-general and during the winter gained an understanding of volunteers that later proved invaluable. When, in the spring of 1862, McClellan's army moved to the Peninsula, Baird forsook his desk for the remainder of the war. As inspector-general and chief of staff, 4th corps, he took an active part in the operations at Yorktown and Williamsburg. For his services he was appointed brigadier-general of volunteers, Apr. 28, 1862, and ordered to Kentucky, where he participated with his brigade in the capture of Cumberland Gap in June and later was directed to organize a division in Gen. Gordon Granger's Army of Kentucky. This organization he pushed with restless energy and, in a month, the division moved to central Kentucky, to guard that section against Confederate cavalry raids until January 1863. As part of Rosecrans's army during the eight months following, Baird's division engaged in minor operations near Franklin and Shelbyville, Tenn. At the request of Gen. George H. Thomas, commanding the 14th corps, Baird was transferred to that corps in August 1863.

At this time, which marks the beginning of his distinguished military service, Baird was in the prime of life, active, energetic, ambitious; a just commander, a strict disciplinarian, and an aggressive fighter. With the 1st division he crossed the Tennessee River and the mountains and gained contact with Bragg's army on Sept. 11. On Sept. 19, the first day of the battle of Chickamauga, his division was heavily engaged and suffered severe losses. On Sept. 20, it was on the left of Thomas's corps and of the Union army. To obtain possession of the roads to Chattanooga, in the rear of the Union army, the Confederates during the forenoon launched three powerful attacks against Baird's division, all of which were repulsed, the last largely through his personal exertions. The fighting continued ceaselessly throughout the afternoon, and when Thomas, at nightfall, retired to Rossville Gap, Baird's division was the last to leave the field, having suffered greater losses than any other division engaged except Brannan's. For his gallantry and steadfast courage Baird was brevetted lieutenant-colonel in the regular army, and both Rosecrans and Thomas recommended his promotion to major-general of volunteers. In the battle of Chattanooga which followed, his division, on Nov. 25, as part of Thomas's corps, stormed Missionary Ridge in superb style. For this he was brevetted colonel in the regular army and again recommended for promotion to major-general by Grant and Thomas. A winter spent in outpost duty and skirmishing with the enemy was followed by participation in Sherman's Atlanta campaign, during which Baird's division was under fire nearly every day from May to August 1864. At the battle of Jonesboro he personally conducted a successful charge by one of his brigades against the enemy's entrenchments. For this he was awarded a medal of honor and for services rendered in the campaign Sherman recommended his promotion to major-general. He accompanied Sherman on his march to Savannah, where he received his brevet as major-general of volunteers, Sept. 1, 1864, and again through the Carolinas until Johnston surrendered.

After the war Baird served as assistant commissioner in the Freedman's Bureau until September 1866, when he was discharged from the volunteer service and reverted to his permanent grade of major and assistant inspector-general. Shortly thereafter he received his brevets as brigadier-general and major-general in the regular army. He was promoted successively lieutenant-colonel and, in September 1885, brigadier-general and inspector-general. About the War Department the impressive dignity of his manner, his long white mustache, and the high beaver hat he favored, made him a notable figure. In 1887 he attended the maneuvers of the French army and received from the French Government the decoration of commander of the Legion of Honor. Retired for age on Aug. 20, 1888, he died near Relay, Md., June 14, 1905, and was buried at Arlington National Cemetery.

[Old Files Section, A.-G. O.; *Official Records*, see Index; G. W. Cullum, *Biog. Reg.*, vol. II; Files Hist. Section, Army War College.]

C. A. B.

BAIRD, CHARLES WASHINGTON (Aug. 28, 1828–Feb. 10, 1887), Presbyterian clergyman, historian, the second son of Robert Baird [*q.v.*] and Fermine (Du Buisson) Baird, was born in Princeton, N. J. He was educated abroad and at the University of the City of New York, from which he graduated in 1848. In the spring of 1852 he graduated from Union Theological Seminary and immediately went abroad to become chaplain of the American Chapel in Rome under the care of the American and Foreign

Christian Union. Returning to America in 1854, he found himself prevented by ill health from taking a parish and devoted himself instead to liturgical studies. In 1855 he published his *Eutaxia or the Presbyterian Liturgies; Historical Sketches by a Minister of the Presbyterian Church,* and in 1856, *A Book of Public Prayer, Compiled from the Authorized Formularies of Worship of the Presbyterian Church, as Prepared by the Reformers, Calvin, Knox, and Others.* In 1859 he became pastor of the Reformed Dutch Church of Bergen Hill in South Brooklyn, N. Y. In 1861, he accepted a call to the Presbyterian Church of Rye, Westchester County, N. Y., in whose service he remained until his death twenty-six years later. Soon after accepting this call he was married to Margaret Eliza Strang, a young lady of Huguenot descent.

A man of handsome appearance and refined manners, he displayed as pastor a tact and sympathy which made him beloved. His scholarly tastes found expression not only in addresses like that delivered before the Phi Beta Kappa Society of the University of the City of New York (1886) on "The Scholar's Duty and Opportunity," but in two very solid historical works, both based on prolonged and careful study of original sources. The first of these grew out of a Thanksgiving Day sermon, elaborated in six years of labor into *The Chronicle of a Border Town: A History of Rye, 1660–1870* (1871). The subject of the second, *The History of the Huguenot Emigration to America,* 2 vols. (1885), was undoubtedly suggested to him by his long residence abroad in boyhood, and by the fact that his mother and his wife were both of Huguenot descent. It is a careful and scholarly production of some 800 pages, based as far as possible upon original sources. He himself had conducted researches in London at the State Paper Office, the British Museum, the Library of Lambeth Palace, etc., and correspondents had explored for him archives at Paris, Leyden, and La Rochelle. The work was unfortunately left incomplete at his death; it does not describe the Huguenot settlements in the Southern and Middle States, or conclude with the general discussion of Huguenot character and the Huguenot element in the population of this country, as promised in the preface.

[*Memorials of the Rev. Charles W. Baird* (1888); sketch in *N. Y. Geneal. and Biog. Rec.*, Oct. 1890; obituaries in *N. Y. Tribune, N. Y. Herald,* Feb. 11, 1887.]

P. V–D.

BAIRD, HENRY CAREY (Sept. 10, 1825–Dec. 30, 1912), publisher, economic writer, the son of Eliza Carey and Capt. Thomas J. Baird, a West Point graduate, was born at the United States Arsenal, Bridesburg, Pa., where his father was in command. His grandfathers, Henry Baird and Mathew Carey [*q.v.*], were both Irish political refugees to America, and the Celtic love of contest and vigor in debate were prominent characteristics through his long life. He was educated in private schools until the age of sixteen, when he entered the publishing house of Carey & Hart in Philadelphia, which had been founded by his grandfather and was carried on by his uncles. Soon the old firm was dissolved, and Baird established a new enterprise under the style Henry Carey Baird & Company, which in 1849 became the first publishing house in America to make a specialty of books on technical and industrial subjects. In September 1850 he married Elizabeth Davis Pennington of Philadelphia. The principal interest in Baird is as an expositor and popularizer of the economic teachings of his uncle Henry C. Carey [*q.v.*], and in a wider sense of the "Pennsylvania school" of "national economists," which had received its original impulse from Mathew Carey. Baird was not an original thinker, rarely departing from the conclusions of his preceptors. He was, however, thoroughly convinced of the revolutionary importance of the doctrines which he inherited, and made himself an ideal disciple. The happenings of the time confirmed him in his views, and afforded a stage on which he could play an active part. His writings were controversial rather than systematic, consisting chiefly of a large number of newspaper and periodical articles. He preferred the bayonet rather than long-range artillery. His whole appearance and manner were alert and forceful, his reasoning was quick and bold, and he had an unusual aptitude for turning an occasion to his uses.

To Baird it seemed that the old teachers of political economy had seriously erred in extending their doctrines and making them applicable to the dealings of the whole world, for in so doing the fact was lost sight of that the nation, as the unit of economic activity, interposed itself between the individual and the universe of people, modifying most of the principles which had been laid down. He held that association is the central requirement in producing wealth and utilizing resources. This association, being by national units, naturally leads to the encouragement of a diversity of employments within every country, and this in turn calls for protective tariffs and a denial of free trade as a hurtful fetish. He contended that money (which he held to be a standard of payment rather than of value) should be a thing of a country, not of the whole world, and that the currency of a nation "should in no wise be based upon the precious metals," which were liable to export beyond the control of the authorities of a state. He thus advocated permitting the circulating medium to be regulated in amount by the business demands of the community. Particularly he was eager to break industrial and financial tyrannies by a liberal issue of notes as opposed to bank loans which open the way to concentration of economic power. In common with all the members of his school, Baird was an optimist. He was not impressed with the importance of conserving wealth in goods and gold, but pleaded for the augmenting of economic capacity in the people and in their instruments of production and means of enjoyment. A free-flowing circulation of money, he held, had a fructifying influence on this capacity.

At first a Whig, he became a Republican, but left that party after the Civil War and was one of the organizers (1874–76) of the Greenback party. By this party he was nominated for treasurer of Pennsylvania (which nomination he declined) and for mayor of Philadelphia. In 1876 before the Committee on Ways and Means of the House he successfully argued against the issue of $500,000,000 of 30-year 4½ per cent gold bonds, and in the same year gave testimony before the United States Monetary Commission supporting the remonetization of silver. Two years later, before the House Committee on Banking and Currency, he opposed the resumption of specie payments. In 1884 he supported Blaine as a protectionist but had no political affiliations thereafter. In his last years, illness compelled him to give up active attention to his business. He died at his home at Wayne, Pa.

Most of Baird's two score of papers, the vast majority of them on economic subjects, were published or republished by his firm; among them may be mentioned, as typical, *Protection of Home Labor* (1860); "Money and Its Substitutes," in *Atlantic Monthly*, March 1876; *The Necessary Foundations of Individual and National Well-Being* (1883); "Of Money, the Instrument of Association," in *National Review*, May 10, 1890; *Money and Bank Credit in the United States, France and Great Britain* (1891); and "Carey and Two of His Recent Critics," in *Proceedings of the American Philosophical Society*, 1891, vol. XXIX. Baird contributed three articles—"Bank," "Money," and "Political Economy"—to the *American Cyclopedia;* these are less partisan than his other writings, and the last is particularly detailed and informing.

[*Who's Who in America*, 1899–1912; F. B. Catchings, *Baird and Beard Families* (1918), p. 128; "Docs. Accompanying the Rept. of the U. S. Monetary Commission," *Senate Rept. 703, pt. 2*, 44 Cong., 2 Sess.; *Publisher's Weekly*, LXXXIII, 18–19.] B. M.

BAIRD, HENRY MARTYN (Jan. 17, 1832–Nov. 11, 1906), Presbyterian clergyman, historian, son of Robert Baird [*q.v.*] and Fermine (Du Buisson) Baird, and brother of Charles Baird [*q.v.*], was born in Philadelphia. A large part of his boyhood was spent with his parents in Geneva and Paris; he graduated from the University of the City of New York in 1850. His bent for linguistic and historical study was already declared. He spent a year in historical studies at home in New York, a year in Athens, and a year in Rome. He then studied theology for two years at Union Theological Seminary in New York, but graduated from the Seminary at Princeton in 1856. He served, 1855, as a tutor in classics at Princeton College, pursuing at the same time graduate studies in the Seminary. At the end of that period he accepted a call to the chair of Greek language and literature in New York University. Soon after this, he was married, Aug. 15, 1860, to Susan Elizabeth Baldwin, who, together with four children, survived him. He continued in the service of New York University until in 1902 increasing age inclined him to seek relief from the regular duties of teaching. Four years later he died in Yonkers, N. Y., of apoplexy, in his seventy-fifth year.

In addition to the labor of teaching, Baird wrote very widely. He produced many addresses and articles like "The Diplomatic Services of Benjamin Franklin," an address before the American Philosophical Society, Apr. 17, 1890 (*Proceedings*, XXVIII, 209–25), and "Hotman and the Franco-Gallia," *American Historical Review*, July 1896. He also published nine volumes. These were not in the field of Greek language or literature, with the single exception of a book of travel entitled *Modern Greece* (1856), which devotes fifty pages to the modern Greek language and modern Greek literature.

Besides *The Life of the Rev. Robert Baird* (1866) and *Theodore Beza, the Counsellor of the French Reformation* (1899), his most important works were six volumes on the Huguenots: *The History of the Rise of the Huguenots of France* (1879) in two volumes; *The Huguenots and Henry of Navarre* (1886) in two volumes; *The Huguenots and the Revocation of the Edict of Nantes* (1895) in two volumes. This series, on which the writer spent more than thirty years, deserves a permanent place among the monuments, all too scanty, of American historical writing upon European subjects. It is based to a great extent upon original contemporary sources, which are freely cited by extract and reference upon practically every page. For manuscript research the author had little opportunity, but he knew the printed original sources thoroughly. To be sure, his enthusiasm for the Huguenots occasionally suspended the full operation of his critical faculties. For example, he writes of the abjuration of Henry of Navarre, which brought peace to France and to Europe, that he shall be obliged "to trace the decadence which led to an act as disastrous to public morality as disgraceful to the King himself." But his treatment is straightforward and free from all taint of casuistry, and no observant reader has any trouble in eliminating the personal equation of the investigator. His deep and broad scholarship, his candor, and the vivacity of his narrative atone for his inability to maintain always a judicial attitude.

[*Necrological Report, Princeton Theol. Sem.* (1907), pp. 460–61; sketch by Samuel M. Jackson in *Book Buyer,* Sept. 1895; obituaries in *N. Y. Tribune, N. Y. Times,* Nov. 12, 1906.]

P. V–D.

BAIRD, MATTHEW (1817–May 19, 1877), locomotive builder, was of Scotch-Irish stock and was born near Londonderry, Ireland. The father, a coppersmith, brought his family to America in 1821, settling in Philadelphia. The boy attended school until he was about fifteen; he then went to work in a brick-yard and was later for a time employed as assistant to a professor of chemistry in the University of Pennsylvania. At the age of seventeen, he entered as an apprentice the copper and sheet-iron works of the New Castle (Del.) Manufacturing Company, where he remained two or three years. For a time following he was superintendent of the New Castle railroad shops. In June 1838 he was made foreman of the sheet-iron and boiler department of Baldwin's locomotive works at Philadelphia. Twelve years later he left this employment and with his brother John went into the marble business. In 1854 he bought from Matthias W. Baldwin [*q.v.*] an interest in the Baldwin works, the firm becoming a partnership under the name of "M. W. Baldwin & Company." On Baldwin's death (Sept. 7, 1866), Baird became sole proprietor. The next year he reorganized the firm, taking as partners George Burnham and Charles T. Parry and changing the name to "The Baldwin Locomotive Works, M. Baird & Company, proprietors." In April 1873 he retired from the firm, closing out his interest for $1,660,000. For a time he was inactive, but the jewelry firm in which one of his sons was a partner having failed, Baird bought the son's interest (1876) and assumed management of the business, which he conducted until his death. He was married three times, and a large family survived him. His fortune, despite the great shrinkage of values following the panic of 1873, was estimated at $2,000,000.

Baird was a skilled mechanic, with a turn for experimentation. He has been sometimes represented as a notable inventor, but his gift in mechanics seems rather to have been a talent for making practical the inventions of others. The first spark-arrester, with which his name is associated, may have been quite as much the invention of Richard French as his own; but the substitution of a deflector of fire-brick for the plate of destructible metal first employed is credited to him alone. To this knack of improving technical processes was added great executive ability. *The Iron Age,* on his decease, spoke of him as one who had "won distinction and fortune by honest and intelligent application," combined with natural mechanical gifts, and said that the success of the Baldwin works was "largely due to [his] energy, skill and honesty." He had wide business interests outside of his special line, having been a director of several railroad and manufacturing companies as well as a director of the Central National Bank and an incorporator of the American Steamship Company. He was a kindly, generous man and made many gifts to welfare organizations.

[J. T. Scharf and T. Westcott, *Hist. of Phila.* (1884); *The Iron Age* (editorial), May 24, 1877; obituaries in the *Inquirer,* the *Press,* and the *Public Ledger* of Phila., May 21, 1877.]

W. J. G.

BAIRD, ROBERT (Oct. 6, 1798–Mar. 15, 1863), Presbyterian clergyman, was born on a Pennsylvania farm not far from Pittsburgh, of a Scotch family which had reached America by way of Northern Ireland. His father, Robert Baird, a soldier in the army of Washington, had, at the conclusion of the Revolution, bought several hundred acres of virgin forest, settled upon it with his wife, Elizabeth (Reeves) Baird, and by assiduous toil subdued it to fertility. At the age of fifteen Robert was sent, clothed in homespun, to the Academy of Uniontown, where he had the good fortune to fall into the hands of a teacher who read his New Testament in Greek and nearly wore out his copies of Horace, Virgil, and Cicero. He next attended Washington and Jefferson Colleges (then separate institutions), studied theology at Princeton Seminary, graduating in 1822, and spent five years as principal of the Princeton Academy. On Aug. 24, 1824, he was married to Fermine Du Buisson, a young lady of Huguenot descent. Becoming intensely interested in the establishment of a proper school system in the state, he wrote a series of letters on education "To the People of New Jersey," which were published in the principal newspapers of the state, and he also devoted himself to lobbying in the legislature. In the judgment of a competent observer, President MacLean of Princeton, he did more than any other man "to direct the public attention to this subject and to induce the Legislature to pass the requisite laws for the establishment and maintenance of a system of common schools" (Baird, p. 60).

He then became interested in Sunday-schools and in 1829 was appointed general agent of the American Sunday School Union. During five years spent in this service he traveled all over the settled parts of the United States and founded thousands of schools, many of them in places where no churches existed. He wrote reports, addresses, and communications to the religious periodical press, and in addition published *A View of the Mississippi Valley* (1832) and *A Memoir of Anna Jane Linnard* (1835).

In 1834 the French Association, composed of people who desired to aid the Protestant Church of France, was formed in New York, and Baird was sent abroad as their agent to reside in Paris and "make himself acquainted with the religious condition and prospects of France and other countries of the continent." During his stay at Paris he became interested in the prospects of beginning a movement in Europe similar to that of the American Temperance Society and its affiliated organizations. At the suggestion of the American ambassador at the court of France, he wrote his *Histoire des Sociétés de Temperance des États Unis d'Amérique* (Paris, 1836), which was translated into German and Swedish. In the interests of prohibition, he made three tours of the countries of Northern Europe, which carried him from Brussels to Moscow. When the French Association developed into the Foreign Evangelical Society, and later into the American and Foreign Christian Union, Baird remained in its service and he subsequently became an ardent advocate of the Evangelical Alliance for the Protestant world. In the service of these organizations he crossed the ocean nine times and traveled more than 300,000 miles. Besides the works mentioned above, he wrote: *L'Union de l'Église et de l'État dans la Nouvelle Angleterre considerée dans ses effets sur la Religion aux États Unis* (Paris, 1837); *Memoir of the Rev. Joseph Sanford, A.M., Pastor of the Second Presbyterian Church of Philadelphia* (1836); *Visit to Northern Europe or Sketches, Descriptive, Historical, Political and Moral of Denmark, Norway, Sweden, and Finland, and the Free Cities of Hamburg and Lübeck* (1841); *Religion in the United States of America* (1843); *Sketches of Protestantism in Italy Past and Present, Including a Notice of the Origin, History and Present State of the Waldenses* (1845, 2nd ed., 1847), *The Christian Retrospect and Register: A Summary of the Scientific, Moral and Religious Progress of the First Half of the 19th Century* (1851).

[Henry Martyn Baird, *Life of the Rev. Robert Baird* (1866); John F. Hageman, *Hist. of Princeton and Its Institutions* (1879); John MacLean, *Hist. of the Coll. of New Jersey* (1877), II.]

P. V–D.

BAIRD, SAMUEL JOHN (Sept. 17, 1817–Apr. 10, 1893), Presbyterian clergyman and author, son of Rev. Thomas Dickson Baird, by his second wife, Esther (Thompson) Baird, was born at Newark, Ohio. His early years were spent at Pittsburgh, where he helped his father in the publication of *The Christian Herald.* He began his collegiate education at Jefferson College, Pa., but on account of ill health was obliged to suspend it, and after a brief rest he took charge in 1839 of a school near Abbeville, S. C. Subsequently he opened a Female Seminary at Jeffersonville, La. Resuming his studies, he prepared himself for the Presbyterian ministry by finishing his college course at Centre College, Danville, Ky., and his theological training at the Indiana Theological Seminary, New Albany, Ind., where he graduated in 1843. In 1840 he was married to Jane Jemima Wilson. On the completion of his theological studies he preached as a licentiate, first in Baltimore, Md., and later in Kentucky and the Southwest. In 1854 he was ordained by the Presbytery of Cedar [later Cedar Rapids] and became the pastor of the Presbyterian church at Muscatine, Ia. Here he served until 1857. From 1857 to 1865 he was the pastor of the church at Woodbury, N. J. He left this field in order to promote the work of the American Bible Society with which the Virginia Bible Society coöperated in the state of Virginia. This position he occupied for ten years, surrendering it in 1875 in order to assume the pastorate of the Third Presbyterian Church in that city. His next field of service was in the church of Ronceverte, W. Va. This he held from 1884 to 1888, with his residence at Fort Spring in the same state. From 1888 to 1891 he lived in retirement at Blacksburg, Va., and removed the next year to Staunton. He died at the residence of his son, Robert W. Baird, in West Clifton Forge, Va. Baird made a special study of the Presbyterian form of church government, and of its practical workings. What the Presbyterian Church most needed in the first half of the nineteenth century was an adequate codified collection of the decisions made by its governing body, the General Assembly. Before the year 1821, nothing but brief excerpts of the deliverances of this body were available. At various intervals between 1821 and 1854 efforts had been made to supply the need, but their success was only partial. Baird undertook single handed the work of producing his *Collection of the Acts, Deliverances, and Testimonies of the Supreme Judicatory of the Presbyterian Church to the Present Time* (1854). This work was revised and reissued in a second edition (1856) and was commonly called "The Assembly's Digest." The General Assembly of 1856 (o. s.) gave the work such recognition as raised it to the rank of a semi-official statute book. Baird's other works in the same field are: *The Church of Christ, Its Constitution and Order* (1864); *A History of the Early Polity of the Presbyterian Church in the Training of Ministers;* and *A History of the New School and the Questions Involved in the Disruption* (1868). He also published books of more general theological interest, among them, *The Socinian Apostacy of the English Presbyterian Churches* (1857); *The First Adam and the Second: the Elohim Revealed in the Creation and Redemption of Man* (1860); and *The Great Baptiser; a Bible History of Baptism* (1882). He was a man of scholarly instincts and intuitions, careful and accurate in research, and exhaustive in treatment. His powers as a public speaker were not above the average, and his general temper was that of the conservative rather than the aggressive thinker.

[*The Presbyt. Encyc.* (1884), to which Baird himself gave a brief sketch of his life; the *Gen. Biog. Cat. of McCormick Theol. Sem.* (1912), p. 5; the *Minutes of the Gen. Ass. of the Presbyt. Ch., 1854–92;* Fermine Baird Catchings, *Baird and Beard Families* (1918), pp. 57, 109, 111–12, 115–16.]

A. C. Z.

BAIRD, SPENCER FULLERTON (Feb. 3, 1823–Aug. 19, 1887), zoologist, son of Samuel Baird and Lydia McFunn Biddle, was born in Reading, Pa., the third of seven children, all of whom reached maturity with a degree of personal distinction. Back of them on both sides lay an ancestry of God-fearing, intelligent, energetic forebears, almost entirely of English and Scotch blood. Spencer's father was a man of culture and ability, a lawyer by profession. After his death in 1833, Mrs. Samuel Baird made her home in Carlisle, Cumberland County, Pa., where at the age of thirteen young Spencer entered the local Dickinson College, in which his brother William, his closest associate for many years, was already a senior. In the physical surroundings of Carlisle the two boys, both possessed by a passion for natural history, found abundant satisfaction. Fields, woods, streams, and ponds offered a peculiarly rich nature fauna, while the regional limestone carried many interesting fossils. From extended rambles over the countryside the lads would return laden with specimens of birds and beasts to be preserved and studied. Together they undertook to secure a complete series of the birds of Cumberland County. A new species of fly-catcher thus obtained in 1840 led to a warm friendship between young Spencer and Audubon, the ornithologist, the first of a succession of scientists whom the youth modestly laid under tribute to his insatiable thirst for knowledge of natural history. Vacations he devoted largely to collecting excursions, to visiting all zoological workers and museums within reach, or to copying zoological descriptions and plates from books he could not himself own. The growing list of scientific acquaintances recorded even in his early diaries reads a little like a catalogue of recognized authorities of the day. In some of their homes, especially in that of Audubon, the engaging youth was a welcome guest.

In 1840 Spencer took his A.B. degree at Dickinson College; and in 1843 the institution conferred upon him the degree of Master of Arts. During this period he began and abandoned the study of medicine, finding it unsuited to his tastes; but meanwhile he greatly enlarged his scientific connections of all sorts and read extensively. At the same time he was studying both French and German as a means of acquainting himself at first hand with foreign researches in natural history. Ultimately he also acquired at least a working knowledge of Italian, Spanish, and Danish. Drawing, mathematics, mineralogy, iron metallurgy, and chemistry he pursued with enthusiasm. Tutoring occupied him to some extent. The home collection of bird skins and other material grew at an embarrassing rate, especially after he instituted a series of exchanges both in this country and abroad; by the summer of 1845, a special workshop had to be provided. All this rather to the scandal of certain relatives who thought he should be preparing "seriously" for a life work!

In the fall of 1846 Baird entered the faculty of Dickinson College as professor of natural history, having shortly before married Mary Helen Churchill (1821–91), a well-educated, highly intelligent young woman, daughter of Col. Sylvester Churchill, inspector-general during the Mexican War. The union was most happy. Mrs. Baird's charm and devotion to her husband's welfare made his home continuously a center of delightful hospitality. Unfortunately she suffered much from ill health, but so far as possible she forwarded his activities, and was of especial help in his literary work. Their daughter, Lucy Hunter Baird, shared her father's interests to a marked degree, even in childhood, and cared tenderly for her mother's declining years.

At Dickinson the handsome young professor became very popular, inaugurating independently in America the method of field study of botany and zoology so successfully used already by Agassiz at Neuchâtel and, later, in this country. Baird's first meeting with Agassiz took place in the fall of 1847. Their future relations were friendly and mutually helpful; and only Agassiz's multifarious activities prevented the coöperation of these two outstanding naturalists of the day in a contemplated monograph on American fishes. Most of Baird's students were but little younger than himself, then only twenty-three. In several members of the group he inspired a permanent love of natural history. Two of them (Dr. Caleb B. R. Kennerly and John B. Clark) later became valuable aids as collectors for the National Museum. Baird now augmented his former scientific repertory by elaborate studies of fish and reptilian forms. "Forty live snakes in a barrel" he boasts of having, in one of his many letters to his brother Will. He was making the college museum (which had already received the bird-collection) "look quite smart with the additions." Afterwards, the relative tractability of harmless reptiles as household pets seems to have commended them to the family; and little Miss Lucy had for a "favorite playmate" at one time a black snake six or seven feet long—at least when the creature rode around with her on her father's shoulder, "its tail touched the floor." In 1848 the chair of chemistry was added to that of natural history at Dickinson, a fact which brings to mind Baird's surprising knowledge, in after years, of general science, as to the progress of which he kept well informed. His early study of foreign language was, of course, of great assistance here. In March 1849 he undertook the contributing editorship of *The Iconographic Encyclopedia,* published by Charles Rudolph Garrigne in 1852, and later accepted several other similar assignments, notably *The Annual Record of Science and Industry* put out by the Harpers from 1871 to 1877.

In 1850 Baird went to the Smithsonian Institution at Washington as assistant secretary to the venerable head, Joseph Henry, the physicist, upon whose death, in 1878, he was unanimously elected to the secretaryship. Among his original duties as "Keeper of the Cabinet" was "to take charge of the making of collections for the Smithsonian Museum and to request of officers of the Army and Navy . . . and of other persons such assistance as might be necessary for the accomplishment of the intended object." Construing these instructions literally and building upon a multitude of personal connections already laid, Baird developed a huge network of agencies, both private and governmental, by means of which a steady stream of material flowed into the Smithsonian from practically all over the world. In 1879, Congress authorized a building to house these collections. It is now one of the great museums of the world, a center of important work in ethnology and related fields as well as in zoology and botany.

For nearly twenty years Baird was a most prolific writer on birds. In his efforts to clear up tangled and useless synonymy and ensure accuracy in the recognition of species, he departed widely from the loose and general type of description hitherto current. He always began with a particular individual and then indicated with precision any deviations due to age, sex, geographical separation or other influences which other specimens might exhibit. Such minute exactness made the definition of local subspecies possible, and went far toward establishing the theory that, whatever other factors may occur in evolution, changes due to separating barriers constitute a main element in the differentiation of forms. Baird was not a theorist and did not worry much over the origin of forms; much of his work in fact antedated Darwin's illuminations. He described what he saw, and in such fashion that no subsequent observer had any doubt as to what he meant. This persistence in accuracy is the foundation of the "Baird School" in ornithology, so ably represented by Elliott Coues, Joel A. Allen, Robert Ridgway, John Cassin, Thomas M. Brewer, and the American ornithologists of to-day. Among Baird's extensive publications may be cited: *Catalogue of North American Birds* (1858); *Review of American Birds* (1864–66); *A History of North American Birds* (1874), in collaboration with T. M. Brewer and R. Ridgway; *North American Reptiles* (1853), in collaboration with Charles Girard; and *Catalogue of North American Mammals* (1857). His other publications, including official reports, bring the number of his titles up to 1,068, according to the bibliography prepared by his assistant, Dr. G. Brown Goode.

The third stage in Baird's career dates from the organization in 1871 of the United States Commission of Fish and Fisheries. In addition to already heavy duties, he was now asked by President Grant to assume the headship of the new Commission. For this position he was the logical selection, having actively interested himself in the study and collection of fishes for many years previous to this date. As the original plans did not seem to involve excessive or long-continued investigations, "only the summer months of one or two years, requiring comparatively little trouble and responsibility," he felt willing to undertake the additional duty—without pay, however, in order to keep the office out of politics. In the end its increasing usefulness, with manifold connections, made great inroads not only on Prof. Baird's time and strength, but on his purse and private residence as well. In view of these facts, and in recognition of his extraordinary volunteer service, Congress appropriated after his death a considerable sum for the support of his wife and daughter. It also made the office of commissioner a salaried one for the future.

The position of Fish Commissioner brought Baird's knowledge and influence into the direct service of the government, while the effort further constituted a most effective move for the preservation of wild life. It also gave him a vastly increased opportunity to assist young naturalists and to develop in the aggregate more research than he could personally have accomplished had he refrained from executive burdens. Thorough studies of the life and life histories of American fishes, including those of Mexico and Canada, were instituted; by means of the steamer *Albatross,* the deep waters of the Atlantic and Pacific were explored; numerous fish hatcheries increased the abundance of local fishes and the extension of the range of trout and other valuable forms, besides carrying out the introduction and acclimatization of several foreign species. In brief, the work of the new Commission comprised all possible forms of ichthyological knowledge and fish-protection. The principal headquarters for investigation were at Wood's Hole, Mass., where the rough buildings contained tables for a few summer students invited by Baird to work on the abundant material daily brought in. Alongside of this informal beginning grew the present great marine laboratory of Wood's Hole, regarded as "the lineal descendant" of Agassiz's famous school at Penikese.

One of Baird's most cherished ideals was that of coöperating bureaus of science, that is, he would have the various workers supported or aided by the government join together as associates and friends, not as rivals, in the increase and diffusion of knowledge, This meant the development of a special morale based on high principles which would give government service a dignity rare in other quarters of the capital. He would weed out all those who, in Cassin's words, "look on science as a milch cow, rather than as a transcendent goddess." To a large extent he was successful in these aims; and it is not too much to say that in the seventies and eighties government science reached a degree of dignity and effectiveness it had not before possessed.

In person, Baird was slightly over six feet in height and of robust build. Keen, kindly, clear-grey eyes looked out from under a fine forehead. In later years he always wore a beard. His general appearance carried the impression of a self-reliant man of affairs. It would seem that he attended church with some regularity, though with a considerable degree of denominational tolerance. He had only one "vice"—that of over-work. Indefatigable labors from youth up resulted in dangerously recurring attacks of heart-trouble from which he died on Aug. 19, 1887, at Wood's Hole, whither he had gone to await the end. Shortly before his death, he asked to be wheeled all around the Commission station and through the laboratory for a final contact with the work of his hands. He is buried at Oak Hill Cemetery, Washington, but at Wood's Hole a granite boulder bears a bronze tablet placed there in his memory in 1902 by the American Fisheries Society.

It has been wisely observed that no man was more typical of our nation at its best than Spencer Fullerton Baird. In the front rank of American naturalists, one of the ablest teachers of natural history, a great administrator of great affairs, with personal character above reproach, he lived in the open, and spent himself in the service of humanity.

[Wm. H. Dall, *Spencer Fullerton Baird* (1915), a masterly biog. by a lifelong associate; G. B. Goode, "Biog. Sketch of Spencer Fullerton Baird," *Bull. U.S. Natl. Museum,* vol. XX (1883), containing an elaborate bibliography; J. S. Billings, *Memoir of Spencer Fullerton Baird* (1895); C. F. Holder, *Spencer Fullerton Baird* (1910); David Starr Jordan, "Spencer Fullerton Baird and the U.S. Fish Commission," *Sci. Mo.,* Aug. 1923.]

D. S. J.
J. K. J.

BAKER, BENJAMIN A. (Apr. 4, 1818–Sept. 6, 1890), playwright, actor, manager, was born in New York City. After escaping from the trade of harness-maker to which he had been apprenticed, he made his stage début in Natchez, Miss., Feb. 14, 1837, as one of the soldiers, McStuart, in *Rob Roy.* For a season he followed the fortunes of this traveling company, sharing its hardships and gaining experience as a "walking gentleman," playing among other parts Brabantio to the elder Booth's Othello. In 1839 he went to New York, continuing to support Booth at times, and, after a period at the New Chatham Theatre he was engaged as prompter and actor by Mitchell, who was about to open the Olympic Theatre. Baker began his playwriting with burlesques such as *Amy Lee,* suggested by the then popular *Amelie,* but his best-known play brought into being almost a new dramatic variety. It was produced at the Olympic Theatre, Feb. 15, 1848. According to the rules, each member of the company could choose the play to be presented at his benefit and Baker wrote for his own a sketch descriptive of the seamy side of New York life, called *A Glance at New York in 1848.* It was built around the character of Mose, the New York volunteer fireman, the part being created for Frank Chanfrau [*q.v.*]. At first Mitchell refused to allow the play to be put on, because of what he considered its vulgarity, but Baker insisted, and when Chanfrau appeared, dressed in the red shirt and surmounted by the plug hat and soap locks of the "Bowery boys," the house rose to him. The realism with which Baker had portrayed one of the city's institutions, and the skill with which Chanfrau acted the part, made them both celebrities. Baker wrote a companion play, *New York As It Is,* produced at the Chatham Theatre, Apr. 17, 1848, Chanfrau acting in both plays on the same evening. Other playwrights imitated the character of Mose in New York, Philadelphia, and other cities, and a species of play in which local conditions were made the background of vivid melodrama arose, to continue till the present day. Baker himself contributed *Three Years After* (National Theatre, June 4, 1849) and *Mose in China* at the same theatre, June 24, 1850. None of these has been printed except *A Glance at New York* (New York, n. d.).

In 1851 he managed jointly with W. B. English the Howard Athenæum, in 1852 conducted the National Theatre in Washington, D. C., and then went to San Francisco, where he managed the Metropolitan Theatre for Mrs. Sinclair after her divorce from Edwin Forrest. An engagement to manage Edwin Booth's Company brought him back to the East in 1856, where he continued to act as manager and theatrical agent either in New York City or elsewhere. In 1885 he became assistant secretary of the Actors' Fund in New York and remained in that office until his death. He was known in theatrical circles as "Uncle Ben Baker" and was widely known and beloved.

[The chief sources of information are G. O. Seilhamer, *An Interviewer's Album* (1881), pp. 97–104; T. A. Brown, *Hist. of the Am. Stage* (1870), p. 17; and the New York newspapers, especially the *N.Y. Herald,* Sept. 7, 11, 1890. For the plays see T. A. Brown, *Hist. of the N.Y. Stage* (1903), I, 282–85; J. N. Ireland, *Records of the N.Y. Stage* (1867), II, 507–10, 533–35, 539; A. H. Quinn, *Hist. of the Am. Drama from the Beginning to the Civil War* (1923), pp. 304–7.]

A. H. Q.

BAKER, BENJAMIN FRANKLIN (July 10, 1811–Mar. 11, 1889), musician, teacher, composer, son of John and Sally Baker, was born in Wenham, Mass. The family removed to Salem in 1822, where at the age of fourteen he took up the study of music and sang in the Howard Street Presbyterian Church. In 1831 he began to teach singing. From 1828 to 1833 he lived in Boston, studying, teaching, and singing in churches. In 1833 he traveled with a concert company, after which he went to Bangor, Me., where he spent several years, combining business and music. He did not decide to make music-teaching his profession until 1837, when he returned to Boston to reside permanently. He studied with John Paddon and sang in the choir of the Chauncy Place Church. In 1839 he took charge of the music in Dr. William Ellery Channing's church, which position he retained until 1847. In 1841 he held the first of a series of musical conventions which were very popular from 1841 to 1848. In 1841 he was elected successor to Lowell Mason as teacher of music in the public schools of Boston. He held this position until 1850, personally instructing about 8,000 students weekly. He also introduced music into the schools of neighboring cities, Lowell and Lawrence. He was president of the Boston Musical Education Society for seven years and vice-president of the Handel and Haydn Society for six years, appearing as soloist in many of the concerts of the latter organization. In 1847 he began preliminary efforts toward establishing a music school, with the aim of placing the finest instruction in all branches of music within the reach of all. There was no such institution in the United States at that time. It did not materialize, however, until 1857, when the Boston Music School was opened, with all departments fully organized with capable teachers, Baker being principal of the school and instructor in voice. The opening of this school was an epochal event for American music, and it flourished unrivalled until 1868, when Baker retired from active work and closed the school. He had given liberally of his time to the development of a desire for music in other cities, as well as in Boston, yet he found time for contributing to periodicals and for composition. For several years he edited the *Boston Musical Journal.* His earliest publication was a book of songs which he edited in collaboration with Isaac B. Woodbury in 1838. This was followed by the *Boston Musical Education Society's Collections* (1842), *Choral* (1845), both of these also with Woodbury; *Haydn Col-*

lection of Church Music (1850), with L. H. Southard; *Melodia Sacra* (1852), with Johnson and Osgood. Among his own compositions are the following: *Death of Osceola,* a vocal quartet (1846); *Stars of the Summer Night,* vocal quartet (1865); and three cantatas, *The Storm King* (1856), *The Burning Ship,* and *Camillus the Roman Conqueror,* the two latter published in 1865. He was also the author of the text-books *Theory of Harmony* (1847) and *Theoretical and Practical Harmony* (1870). In all he published some thirty books including selections of church music and glees. He was married on Nov. 21, 1841, to Sabra L. Heywood of Grafton, Mass.

[*Cyc. of Music and Musicians* (1888), ed. by J. D. Champlin and W. F. Apthorp, p. 111; Theodore Baker, *Biog. Dict. of Musicians* (3rd ed., 1919), p. 44; *Grove's Dict. of Music and Musicians, Am. Supp.; Boston Post* and *Boston Evening Transcript,* Mar. 12, 1889.]

F. L. G. C.

BAKER, DANIEL (Aug. 17, 1791–Dec. 10, 1857), Presbyterian clergyman, educator, was descended from members of a Puritan congregation which settled at Dorchester, Mass., in 1630. In 1695 a group of descendants of this congregation formed a church which removed to the Ashley River just above Charleston, S. C. In 1752 came another removal to Midway, Ga., in what is now Liberty County. Here Daniel Baker was born. Left an orphan while still a child, he went to Savannah when fourteen years old and worked for the next six years in various commercial establishments. But the deeply religious atmosphere in which his early years were spent had left a deep impress upon the mind of the sensitive boy and he determined to be a preacher. Fully aware of the need of an education, in 1811 he took advantage of an opportunity to go to Hampden-Sidney College in Virginia. Here he spent two years in hard study and then went to Princeton where he graduated in 1815. While in Princeton his religious zeal manifested itself in organizing prayer meetings among his fellow students. He then studied theology for a year under a Presbyterian minister in Winchester, Va. In 1816 he married a Virginia girl, Elizabeth McRobert. After this he held various Presbyterian pastorates—at Harrisonburg, Va., Washington, D. C., Savannah, Ga., and Tuscaloosa, Ala. His growing reputation for persuasive eloquence drew him into much evangelistic work.

In 1840 he was sent to the Republic of Texas as an evangelistic missionary. He participated in the organization of the first presbytery of his church in Texas and proposed the establishment of a church college for young men. He remained in the Republic but a short time, soon accepting a pastorate at Holly Springs, Miss. But his interest continually turned to Texas and in 1848 he was recalled there. He found that the establishment of a college had been agreed upon by the presbyteries but that little had been done on the project. He threw himself into the work with characteristic energy, selected Huntsville as the site, was made "general agent," and began soliciting subscriptions. In November 1849 the legislature granted a charter to Austin College, so named in honor of Stephen F. Austin. In spite of the poverty of Texas at that time and the small membership of his own church, Baker was markedly successful in obtaining funds both for its maintenance and endowment. In 1853 he became president as well as general agent. He repeatedly made extensive tours over both Texas and the United States as a whole in search of funds and equipment. For several years he endeavored to obtain grants from the state legislature in the form of endowed scholarships, but state policy was against grants of public money to denominational schools and he never succeeded. His advocacy of a general public-school system, however, probably had much to do with the passage of the act of 1854 to provide a system of public schools. As the college grew the problem of obtaining support became heavier, and in January 1857 he resigned the presidency in order to devote his whole time to the work of the agency. But his work was nearly over, for he died suddenly at the home of his son, W. M. Baker, in Austin. His name has been perpetuated in Daniel Baker College, established at Brownwood, Tex., in 1889.

[*The Life and Labors of Daniel Baker* (1858), by his son William Mumford Baker, based largely upon a manuscript autobiography, is the only extensive biog. A good brief sketch is in Henry A. White, *Southern Presbyterian Leaders* (1911). Considerable material on Baker's work in Texas may be found in contemporary Texas newspapers, in the *Texas Presbyterian,* in the records of Austin Coll. (which was removed to Sherman in 1878), and in an unpublished thesis in the Lib. of the Univ. of Texas, "The Hist. of Austin Coll.," by P. E. Wallace.]

C. W. R.

BAKER, EDWARD DICKINSON (Feb. 24, 1811–Oct. 22, 1861), soldier, senator, was born in London, England, the son of a school teacher, and was brought with the family to Philadelphia in 1815. He lived in the latter city until 1825. For a time he was apprenticed to a weaver. The family moved to New Harmony, Ind., in 1825, for a year or more, and then went to Illinois, settling at Belleville, St. Clair County. As a boy Edward gave evidence of promising intellectual gifts and was an avid reader, but had little systematic education. Studying law in the office of Judge Caverly of Carrollton, he was admitted to the bar at the age of nineteen. On Apr. 27, 1831, he was married to Mary A. Lee, a widow with two children. He was a private soldier in the brief Black Hawk War. In 1835 he moved to Springfield for the serious practise of his profession, becoming one of a brilliant circle who won fame both in the law and in politics, among them Lincoln, Douglas, Browning, Yates, and Trumbull. Already he was acquiring reputation as an orator, and this naturally took him into politics. From 1837 to 1840 he represented Sangamon County in the General Assembly, and was state senator from 1840 to 1844. Lincoln and Baker were rival Whig candidates for congressional nomination, but Baker won and was elected, the only Whig chosen in Illinois for the Twenty-ninth Congress. Although out of harmony with his party, he supported the policy of President Polk on the Oregon question. When the Mexican War began he promptly went to Illinois, raised a regiment of volunteers, and led them to join Gen. Taylor. In December 1846 he was back in Washington as bearer of dispatches. Being still a member of the House and speaking in uniform, he advocated with telling effect better measures for the equipment of the soldiers. Then he resigned his seat, went to the front, and served with distinction at Cerro Gordo. The command of a brigade devolved upon him when Gen. Shields was wounded. Soon thereafter, his regiment not reënlisting, he resigned his commission and returned to the practise of law.

In 1848 he moved into the Galena district, announced himself an Independent Whig candidate for Congress, and won a personal triumph in that Democratic district—this after a residence of only three weeks. He was also one of the unsuccessful Taylor presidential electors. Lincoln and other Whigs in Illinois, Iowa, and Wisconsin urged his appointment to a cabinet position, and Baker was grievously disappointed in not being chosen. There was little save for certain displays of oratorical eloquence to distinguish his service in the Thirty-first Congress. In 1851 he carried out a contract to grade a section of the Panama railway, but was obliged to return home to recover from fever. In 1852 he was attracted to California, where he at once became prominent as a lawyer and public speaker. California was Democratic, but he was active as a Whig and then as a Republican in the face of discouragements. Public disfavor fell upon him when he followed his sense of duty in defending the notorious Cora, opposing the Vigilance Committee of 1856. Yet he was in demand as an orator, his most notable speech being the funeral oration on Senator Broderick, on Sept. 18, 1859. Shortly thereafter the Republican organization of Oregon sent a committee to invite him to go to that state to give popular leadership, with the understanding that he would be the preferred candidate of the party for United States senator. He embraced the opportunity to realize a life-long ambition, moved to Oregon in February 1860, and was elected senator in October by a combination of Republicans and Douglas Democrats. This was a famous victory over the regular Democrats led by the redoubtable Joseph Lane, and contributed materially to the choice of Lincoln electors. Starting promptly for Washington, Baker was given a reception in San Francisco which was utilized for the national campaign with great and perhaps decisive effect in the close contest to win California for Lincoln. Baker entered on his duties Dec. 5, 1860, the only Republican from the Pacific Coast sent to support the new administration. This circumstance, coupled with his reputation as an orator and his known intimacy with Lincoln, gave him immediate prominence. Lincoln invited him to Springfield for a personal conference, which was held in the latter part of December, and continued to rely greatly on his advice about checkmating secession movements in the Pacific states. The first of two remarkable replies to Senator Judah P. Benjamin was delivered on Jan. 2, 1861 (*Congressional Globe,* 36 Cong., 2 Sess., pp. 224–29, 238–43). Of this effort Sumner said: "That speech passed at once into the permanent literature of the country, while it gave to its author an assured position in this body" (*Ibid.,* 37 Cong., 2 Sess., p. 54). In New York on Apr. 19 Baker was one of the speakers at an enormous mass meeting in Union Square, delivering an oration of great popular effect. His famous reply to Senator Breckinridge was delivered in the Senate on Aug. 1, 1861 (*Ibid.,* 37 Cong., 1 Sess., pp. 377–79), when he came in uniform directly from training the troops he was commanding. On the 21st of April he had accepted an invitation to help raise and to be the colonel of a "California regiment" to be enlisted in New York and Pennsylvania. The effort was so successful that Baker was given charge of a brigade. He declined successive offers of appointments as brigadier-general and major-general, because acceptance would require resignation as senator from Oregon. He was killed in action at the unfortunate affair of Ball's Bluff on Oct. 22, 1861.

[Jos. Wallace, *Sketch of the Life and Pub. Services of Edward D. Baker* (1870); John D. Baltz, *Hon. Edward D. Baker* (1888); Elijah R. Kennedy, *The Contest for*

California in 1861 (1912); *Biog. Cong. Dir.* (1913), p. 452; Wm. D. Fenton, "Edward Dickinson Baker," *Quart. Ore. Hist. Soc.*, Mar. 1908, pp. 1–23; *California and Californians*, ed. by R. L. Hunt (1926), II, 578, V, 143–44.]

C. A. D—y.

BAKER, FRANK (Aug. 22, 1841–Sept. 30, 1918), anatomist and historian, was born at Pulaski, N. Y., the son of Thomas and Sybil (Weed) Baker. His ancestors, who came from Gloucestershire, England, settled in New England and fought in the Revolutionary War. In 1861, Baker enlisted in the 37th New York Volunteers, serving until 1863; he then entered the government service at Washington, D. C. He was graduated with the degree of M.D. from Columbian (now George Washington) University in 1880. After some years of practise in Washington, he became, in 1883, professor of anatomy in the Georgetown University School of Medicine, holding this chair continuously for thirty-five years until his death. During this entire period he contributed many papers on anatomy and allied subjects to scientific societies. He also reported frequently on various phases of medical history, a subject in which he took the greatest interest.

His anatomical papers dealt especially with the teaching of anatomy. He visualized anatomy as a living subject and used his knowledge of anthropology and embryology to emphasize its dynamic character. He founded the biological and anthropological societies of Washington, D. C., served as president of the Association of American Anatomists, 1897, secretary of the Washington Academy of Science from 1890 to 1911, and edited the *American Anthropologist* from 1891 to 1898. He collaborated with Dr. John S. Billings in the *Medical Dictionary* (1890), and contributed the section on medical and anatomical terms in the *Standard Dictionary* (1890), as well as the anatomical article in Buck's *Reference Handbook of the Medical Sciences.* In 1889, he was appointed superintendent of the United States Life Saving Service and from 1890 to 1916 served as superintendent of the National Zoological Park, D. C. He read a number of papers on medical history before the Johns Hopkins Medical Society and was one of the founders of the Medical History Club of Washington. His "History of Anatomy" in Stedman's *Reference Handbook of the Medical Sciences* (1913), I, 323–45, is one of the best accounts of the subject ever written. He collected a valuable library on anatomy, which was divided after his death between the library of the Surgeon-General's Office, Washington, and the medical library of McGill University.

Baker's fine presence and his lively sense of humor made him a most popular teacher. His lectures to art schools were largely attended. He was a life-long friend of Walt Whitman and John Burroughs, all three having been in the government service together. By his confrères he was considered as "probably the most erudite physician in Washington." On Sept. 13, 1873, he married Mary E. Cole of Sedgwick, Me. His death occurred in Washington, Sept. 30, 1918, and his widow and six children survived him.

[The chief biog. reference is Dr. Fielding H. Garrison's obituary in the *N. Y. Medic. Jour*, 1918, CVIII, 859 (bibliography). Baker's most important anatomical papers will be found in the *Medic. Rec.*, 1884, XXV, 421–25, and in the *N. Y. Medic. Jour.*, 1887, XLVI, 451–57. An important hist. paper, on "The Two Sylviuses," appeared in the *Bull. of the Johns Hopkins Hospital*, 1909, XX, 329–39.]

H. R. V.

BAKER, GEORGE AUGUSTUS (March 1821–Apr. 2, 1880), portrait painter in oils and miniature, was born in New York, the son of a miniature painter, George Augustus Baker, who was born at Strassburg, France, and settled in New York City. From his father he received his first instructions in art and at the age of sixteen he started on his professional career as a miniature painter. He was so successful at painting portraits on ivory that his work was in constant demand and during his first year he painted 150 miniatures at five dollars apiece. For seven years he continued the profession of miniature painting, studying all the while at the National Academy of Design to equip himself as a portrait painter in oils. He then sailed for Europe, where he studied from 1844 to 1846, returning in the latter year to New York City, where he became as popular a painter of portraits in oils as he had been a miniature painter. In 1851 he was elected National Academician. He excelled in his portraits of women and children, and his portrait of one of the children of A. M. Cozzens was exhibited at the Paris Exposition in 1867. After 1866 he lived in Darien, Conn. Although a life-long sufferer from neuralgia and afflicted with serious eye-trouble, he produced a great many portraits and had orders for two years in advance. His work is highly finished and carefully drawn and he confined himself almost entirely to painting portraits. "Love at First Sight," "Wild Flowers," "Faith," and "The May Queen" are the titles of some of his compositions. His portrait of the artist John F. Kensett is owned by the Metropolitan Museum of Art, New York. Many of his paintings were bought by G. M. Vanderbilt for his collection.

[H. C. Tuckerman, *Bk. of the Artists* (1867); H. W. French, *Art and Artists in Conn.* (1879); T. Bolton, *Early Am. Portr. Painters in Miniature* (1921); *N. Y. Tribune*, Apr. 3, 1880; Clement and Hutton, *Artists of the Nineteenth Cent.* (1879).]

T. B.

BAKER, HARVEY HUMPHREY (Apr. 11, 1869–Apr. 10, 1915), first judge of the juvenile court of Boston, was the son of James Baker, a merchant from Cape Cod, and Harriet M. (Humphrey) Baker, whose father owned a farm in Brookline, Mass. He was born in the old farmhouse in Newton St., and there he lived until his death, the day before his forty-sixth birthday. He prepared for college at the Roxbury Latin School; graduated from Harvard in 1891, with membership in Phi Beta Kappa, and from the Harvard Law School in 1894, receiving the degree of Master of Arts at the same time. He began immediately the practise of law, and soon became a member of the firm known later as Hayes, Williams, Baker & Hersey, keeping this connection until his death. In the town meetings and other affairs of Brookline he took an active part, serving as clerk of the police court for a year and as a special justice from 1895 to 1906. When the Boston juvenile court was established in 1906, Governor Curtis Guild selected him to be the first judge. The appointment did not escape criticism. Baker's life had been free from financial care, sheltered from temptations and even from much contact with such problems as confront the boys and girls who would come into the court. Though his intimate friends knew him as the best of story-tellers, the joyous companion of country walks, to the casual acquaintance his premature grayness, a pronounced stoop, and the habitual seriousness of his expression gave an impression of reserve and austerity. He was not even married. How could he be expected to understand the wayward children of the city? On his own side, when he accepted the appointment, after visiting many of the existing juvenile courts and institutions for delinquent children in the country, it was not only with a modest sense of duty but also in a spirit of adventure. In the nine years that remained before his early death he established the Boston juvenile court in a position of leadership in the country; and for himself he found increasing satisfaction in the work, which demanded the full exercise of every faculty.

His success as judge of the juvenile court was due to the simplicity and sincerity of his character; to the quality of his intelligence and knowledge; and to his unsparing use of mind and time and energy on the problems which came before him. Fairness, patience, tact, ability to see many conflicting points of view, firmness when necessary, were characteristic of his dealings. The atmosphere of his court was serious, almost solemn. There were no distracting decorations in the room. Few persons were present: sometimes no one but the judge and the child; frequently only the probation officer in addition. He liked to think of the court as a dispensary and of the officials as physicians, concerned not to treat symptoms, represented by the offense which brings the child into court, but to study the child's conduct as a whole, and give a prescription that will cure whatever is wrong in the situation.

In finding the right prescription and in seeking to understand his cases, he developed a high degree of coöperation between the juvenile court and the various social agencies of the city. But with the best use of existing facilities he was increasingly oppressed with the conviction that "juvenile courts and all other agencies are dealing with children without sufficient knowledge of what is really the matter." In his review of the first five years of the court (cited below) he urged the creation of a "clinic for the intensive study of baffling cases." When after his death his friends and associates established a memorial of him and his work it took the appropriate form of an endowment for such a clinic, organized in April 1917, and named the Judge Baker Foundation.

[*Harvey Humphrey Baker, Upbuilder of the Juvenile Court,* published by the Judge Baker Foundation, Boston, 1920 (133 pp.), contains a sketch of his life, by Roy M. Cushman, secretary of the Foundation, who had been associated with him as probation officer; Judge Baker's "Review of the First Five Years of the Boston Juvenile Court," and an article by Judge Baker on "The Procedure of the Boston Juvenile Court," reprinted from the *Survey* of Feb. 5, 1910; short articles by C. C. Carstens and Charles F. Dole in the *Survey* of Apr. 24, 1915.]

L. B.

BAKER, JAMES (Dec. 19, 1818–May 15, 1898), trapper, guide, pioneer settler, was born at Belleville, Ill. His parents are said to have been of Scotch-Irish stock and to have come from South Carolina. He early learned the use of firearms, but had little schooling. At nineteen he started west, and in St. Louis met James Bridger, then recruiting a company of trappers for the American Fur Company. On May 25, 1839, he left the city with the Bridger party for the annual rendezvous in the mountains. The journey was, according to Baker, a hazardous one, for the Indians along the trail "were as thick as bees" and unusually bellicose. The pacifying genius of Bridger, however, carried the party safely to its destination. Baker spent the next two years in trapping. In the summer of 1840 he returned to St. Louis and also made a brief visit to his boyhood home; but in the spring of 1841 he started again for the mountains. He was in the desperate fight at the junction of Battle Creek and Little Snake River, on the Colorado-

Wyoming line, Aug. 21–22, when thirty-five trappers beat off a large force of Sioux, Cheyennes, and Arapahos, though with the loss of their leader, Henry Fraeb, and three others. In the spring following the famous "cold winter of '45" (which seems actually to have been the winter of 1843–44), when most of the horses and even many of the wild animals in the mountains perished, he took part in a trappers' raid on the horse-herds of the Southern Californians. Though the decline of the fur trade in the early forties drove most of the trappers to abandon the field, Baker stayed on. Little is known of his movements, however, from 1844 to 1855, when he emerged as a chief of scouts for Gen. W. S. Harney at Fort Laramie. In 1857 he guided as far as Fort Bridger a part of the Federal army sent against the Mormons. With Tim Goodale as assistant, he served as guide to Capt. Marcy's expedition which left Fort Bridger on Nov. 24 to cross the Colorado mountains to Fort Massachusetts—an adventure in which both guides lost their way and in which the party narrowly escaped destruction. Returning by the foothills east of the Rockies, and passing by the future site of Denver, where one of the men discovered gold, the expedition reached Fort Bridger on June 9, 1858. Baker remained for a short time in the Green River region, and then returned to the Colorado placers and built a cabin on Clear Creek, near the present Denver. At some time between 1866 and 1869 he returned to Green River. In 1873 he chose for his permanent home a spot in the valley of the Little Snake River, near the scene of the famous battle, erected on it a cabin with a watch tower, and began to raise livestock. Here he died. His grave, which is marked with an inscribed stone, is about a mile from the town of Savery, Wyo.

Baker was six times married—each time to an Indian woman—and had a number of children. He was one of the most picturesque figures of the old frontier. He adopted Indian dress and habits and to a considerable extent was swayed by Indian superstitions. His stalwart form was crowned by a thick shock of chestnut hair which curled in ringlets all over his head, and which was still but slightly grizzled when he reached the age of seventy. All who knew him esteemed him highly. Capt. Marcy wrote of him as "a generous, noble-hearted specimen of the trapper type who would peril his life for a friend at any time or divide his last morsel of food." In 1917 the Wyoming legislature appropriated a sum for the purchase and removal of his cabin to Frontier Park, Cheyenne, and on July 23 of that year, in its new location, it was dedicated with appropriate ceremonies.

[C. G. Coutant, *The Hist. of Wyoming from the Earliest Known Discoveries* (1899); R. B. Marcy, *Thirty Years of Army Life on the Border* (1866); Frank Hall, *Hist. of the State of Colorado*, I (1889); Alice P. Hill, *Tales of the Colorado Pioneers* (1884); J. Cecil Alter, "Jim Baker: Frontiersman," in *The Salt Lake Tribune*, May 13, 1923; Maggie Kilgor, article in *The Wyoming Tribune* (Cheyenne), July 23, 1917.]

W.J.G.

BAKER, JAMES HEATON (May 6, 1829–May 25, 1913), politician, soldier, journalist, was the son of Henry and Hannah (Heaton) Baker, Ohioans of early American stock. When he was an infant the family moved from Monroe, Ohio, his birthplace, to Lebanon. The death of his mother caused him to be sent to his grandfather's home near Middletown, where studies in the local academy prepared him for matriculation at Ohio Wesleyan University in 1847. He was graduated with honors from that institution in 1852, and the following year, after a few months of teaching, he entered the field of journalism by purchasing the *Scioto Gazette* of Chillicothe, Ohio. This newspaper furnished a bridge to politics, for Baker espoused the cause of the new Republican party after its establishment in 1854. In return for his vigorous support of the organization in Ohio he was placed as candidate for secretary of state upon the ticket headed by Salmon P. Chase in 1855, and, with other candidates of the party, he was elected (*History of the Republican Party in Ohio,* 1898, edited by J. P. Smith, I, 37, 40). After the expiration of his term of office, in 1857, he removed to Minnesota Territory, then on the eve of statehood. His marked gifts as a speaker found a ready outlet in the struggle of the Republican party for political control in Minnesota. The party gained an overwhelming victory in 1859 and Baker found himself for the second time a secretary of state. Acceptable service in this position brought him a reëlection. During his second term he resigned to accept the colonelcy of the 10th Minnesota Volunteer Regiment, which was being organized for Civil War service. The Sioux outbreak in the summer of 1862 delayed the departure of his regiment for the South. It was for a time assigned to frontier guard duty and in 1863 formed a part of Gen. Sibley's punitive expedition into Dakota against the fleeing Sioux and gave valiant service in the battle of Stony Lake (*Official Records,* ser. 1, vol. XXII, p. 370). After the return to Minnesota, Baker was ordered to report at St. Louis, where he was placed in command of the post and his regiment assigned to provost guard duty. When the regiment was sent to the front in April 1864 citizens of St. Louis requested that Baker be continued in command of the post, and to his regret he was separated from his regiment. Before the war ended he was made provost marshal general of the military department of Missouri and brevetted brigadier-general.

After the war he spent two years at Booneville, Mo., as register of the land office, and then returned to the farm that he had bought in Blue Earth County shortly after his arrival in Minnesota. In 1871 Grant appointed him United States commissioner of pensions, a position that he held until 1875. In his first report he called attention to the need of consolidating the more than forty laws relating to pensions and his recommendation resulted in the codification act of 1873 (*House Executive Documents,* 42 Cong., 2 Sess., vol. I, pt. 5, p. 379; J. W. Oliver, *History of the Civil War Military Pensions, 1861–85,* ch. 2). For four years after 1875 he held a second federal appointment, that of surveyor general of Minnesota, and did much to arouse popular interest in the state's rich iron deposits. In 1879 he purchased two newspapers in Mankato and consolidated them in the *Mankato Free Press,* which he published for two years. He was elected state railroad commissioner in 1881, and served as chairman of the Railroad and Warehouse Commission created in 1885. He joined the ranks of the Farmers' Alliance, and was placed on its first Minnesota ticket, in 1890, as a candidate for Congress from the second district, but was defeated. The remaining years of his life were spent in comparative retirement, though his interest in politics never waned and he frequently appeared as a public speaker. A taste for history caused him to publish several studies, including a history of transportation in Minnesota (*Minnesota Historical Collections,* IX, 1–34) and a volume entitled "Lives of the Governors of Minnesota" (*Minnesota Historical Collections,* XIII). The chief value of the latter work, a series of slight sketches in journalistic style, lies in the fact that the author had known each of the eighteen governors portrayed. Baker was twice married: in 1852 to Rose L. Thurston of Delaware, Ohio, who died in 1873, and in 1879 to Zulu Bartlett, who survived him.

[Several memorial addresses in Baker's honor appear in *Minn. Hist. Coll.,* XV, 753–57. Sketches of his career are published in W. H. C. Folsom, *Fifty Years in the Northwest* (1888); C. E. Flandrau, *Encyc. of Biog. of Minn.* (1900); Thomas Hughes, *Hist. of Blue Earth County, Minn.* (1909); and *Mankato: Its First Fifty Years* (1903).]

T.C.B.

BAKER, JAMES HUTCHINS (Oct. 13, 1848–Sept. 10, 1925), college president, was born on a farm near Harmony, Me., the son of Wesley and Lucy (Hutchins) Baker, both natives of Maine. A background of stern and rockbound coast, a family English and Revolutionary, childhood and youth passed on a small New England farm, these had implications of ruggedness of body and lankness of limb; of shyness and stubborn aggressiveness; of sound integrity. Twenty weeks a year in the red schoolhouse, a short term in a private academy, the formal clean-cut drill of the Latin school preparatory for college, four years and the B.A. degree in 1873 at Bates College, Lewiston, Me., interspersed with terms of country-school teaching; the result was a New England schoolmaster of the seventies. Two years as principal at Yarmouth, Me., in a public school just evolved from an academy, in the transition stage between the aristocratic Latin school and democracy's high school, sent Baker to his physician, who advised him to go West. Appointed principal of the Denver High School in 1874, he continued there seventeen years. To this pioneer high school in the West he gave a standing in character and scholarship that was recognized by great eastern colleges. January 1892 saw him president of the University of Colorado at Boulder, an institution fifteen years old with sixty-six students. He labored there for twenty-two years, building and reënforcing. In 1914 he retired, his eye undimmed, his natural forces unabated, leaving a university of 1,306 students and an able faculty, with a standing among class A universities.

Baker proposed in the National Education Association the Committee of Ten whose report in 1893 offered the first comprehensive program of secondary education. In 1907 in the same organization he proposed the Committee on Economy of Time in Education. The report of this committee of which he was chairman, delayed till 1913, had no small influence on the nation-wide organization of junior high schools and in the development of the junior college. He published *Elementary Psychology* (1890); *Education and Life* (1900); *American Problems* (1907); *Educational Aims and Civic Needs* (1913); *University Reform and College Progress Relative to School and Society* (1916); *After the War, What?* (1918); *Of Himself and Other Things* (1922). He was president of the National Council of Education in 1892 and of the National Association of State Universities in 1907. At the time of his death in Denver he had just completed plans as editor for the writing of the history of Colorado under the auspices of the State Historical Society as a feature of the semi-centennial anniversary of the state's admission to the Union. A week before his death he remarked, "I anticipate no early taking off, but should anything happen my part of the writing is practically finished." He was married on June 20, 1882, to Jennie Hilton of Denver, who survived him.

[*Who's Who in America*, 1924–25; *Univ. of Colo. Bull.*, 1914; *Colo. Alumnus*, XV; *Rocky Mt. News*, Sept. 11, 1925.]

H. M. B.

BAKER, LA FAYETTE CURRY (Oct. 13, 1826–July 3, 1868), chief of the United States Secret Service, was born at Stafford, N. Y. His father, Remember Baker, was the grandson and namesake of the Vermont border warrior who shared with Ethan Allen the fame or notoriety derived from leadership of the "Green Mountain Boys." La Fayette Baker attained his majority in Michigan, and from 1848 to 1860, as an itinerant mechanic, became a bird of passage, stopping only for brief residences in New York, Philadelphia, and San Francisco. He was in New York at the outbreak of the Civil War, and, having gained some experience, as a San Francisco Vigilante, in the use of high-handed and surreptitious methods of government, he went to Washington seeking employment best suited to his talents. Sent by Gen. Scott on a secret mission to Richmond, Baker succeeded in reaching his objective as a Confederate prisoner, secured the desired information while Jefferson Davis was trying to determine whether he was a spy, then escaped and returned to Washington.

The Richmond episode secured for Baker permanent employment as a detective, and, with later successes, it gained for him a colonel's commission, an appointment as special provost marshal of the War Department in 1862, and the rank of brigadier-general in 1865. Armed with wide powers and unlimited resources he became a veritable Fouché. Due process, warrants for arrest and search, and other constitutional guarantees were disregarded while the chief of detectives ferreted out plotters, traitors, war speculators, bounty-jumpers, and amassed a small fortune for himself. Nevertheless, Baker's ability and service as a detective are unquestionable, as his planning and direction of the expedition that captured John Wilkes Booth and D. C. Herold demonstrated (*Congressional Globe*, 39 Cong., 1 Sess., p. 4187). But his reputation suffered when Congress in distributing the rewards for the capture of the Booth conspirators reduced the Claims Committee's award of $17,500 to Baker, to $3,750, largely because "he was building a big hotel in Lansing" (*Ibid.*, p. 4186; App. p. 423), and when President Johnson dismissed him from office for his insolence in maintaining an espionage system at the White House. His last bid for notoriety was in the rôle of star witness against President Johnson in the impeachment proceedings, where his alleged Adamson letters were to uncrown Cæsar. Curiously, those fabulous documents, like the Canadian letters linking Jefferson Davis with the Booth conspiracy, "eternally eluded the grasp of their pursuers, and the chase ever resulted only in aiding the depletion of the public treasury," with the result that Baker "to his many previous outrages . . . added that of wilful and deliberate perjury" (*House Report No. 7*, 40 Cong., 1 Sess., pp. 110–11). This habitual carelessness in mixing truth and fiction was not overcome in his *History of the United States Secret Service* (1867). He died in Philadelphia, his wife, Jennie C. Curry, to whom he was married Dec. 24, 1852, surviving him.

[B. P. Poore, *The Conspiracy Trial for the Murder of President Lincoln*, 1 (1865), p. 4; R. S. Baker, "The Capture, Death, and Burial of John Wilkes Booth," *McClure's Mag.*, IX, p. 574; *Official Records*, ser. 1, II, III; the *Press* (Phila.), July 4, 1868; D. M. DeWitt, *The Assassination of President Lincoln* (1909), p. 276.]

T. D. M.

BAKER, LAURENCE SIMMONS (May 15, 1830–Apr. 10, 1907), Confederate soldier, was born at Coles Hill, Gates County, N. C., the son of Dr. John Burgess Baker and Mary (Wynn) Baker. (By some clerical error his first name was recorded in the War Department as *Lawrence*, and so spelled, officially, while he was in the army.) He graduated at West Point in 1851, was commissioned in the Mounted Riflemen, and served with his regiment for ten years, chiefly on the frontier. In March 1855 he was married to Elizabeth Earl Henderson of Salisbury, N. C. He was promoted to first-lieutenant in 1859. Although he was opposed to secession, he accepted the decision of his state, resigned his commission (May 10, 1861), and entered the Confederate service. He was appointed lieutenant-colonel of the 1st North Carolina Cavalry, of which another former officer of the regular army (Ransom) was colonel. Under their direction the regiment was at once subjected to a strict discipline and thorough training unusual in newly-raised volunteer regiments. There was bitter feeling at first, among both officers and men, which disappeared as the necessities of military service were realized, and finally changed to pride. In the spring of 1862, Baker was promoted to the colonelcy of the regiment. In June the regiment was ordered to join the Army of Northern Virginia, then engaged in the Peninsular campaign. It arrived on the 28th, after a forced march, and the next day had a spirited engagement with the 3rd Pennsylvania Cavalry, whose colonel—Averell, afterward brigadier-general—had served with Baker in the Mounted Riflemen. For the next year, the regiment, under Baker's command, was actively engaged in all the operations of Lee's army. In the cavalry fight on the last day of the battle of Gettysburg, Wade Hampton, the brigade commander, was wounded, and Baker succeeded him, receiving promotion to the rank of brigadier-general a few days later. His right arm was wounded in a skirmish on the night of July 31–Aug. 1, 1863, and he was sent to the general hospital in Richmond for treatment. The following year he was assigned (June 9) to a territorial command in North Carolina, with headquarters at Goldsboro. Though again wounded in a skirmish on Sept. 22, he soon returned to duty, and late in the year went to South Carolina with a brigade of reserves—boys and exempts brought together by the last desperate effort of the Confederacy—to join the forces which Bragg was assembling to meet Sherman's expected march northward. For a few days he commanded a division, but on Dec. 26 he was relieved and sent back to Goldsboro, disabled on account of intense suffering caused by an old wound—the one received in 1863, apparently, and not the more recent one. He was back in the field again with his brigade for the campaign in the spring of 1865, and was present at the battle of Bentonville. His command was detached, at some distance from the main army, when the news of Lee's surrender reached him. Johnston's army, now the only considerable Confederate organization in existence in the east, evidently needed every available man. Baker's attempt to join it with all his troops was destined to failure, for the roads were almost everywhere blocked by Union soldiers; so, disbanding his force, he tried to make his way across country with some fifty volunteers. On Apr. 20, however, he learned that Johnston was negotiating for surrender, and gave up the struggle. He was paroled at Raleigh on May 8, and began life again as a farmer. In 1878, he became railroad station agent at Suffolk, Va., and continued there until his death.

[G. W. Cullum, *Biog. Reg.*, II, 304; *Bull. Ass. Grads. Mil. Acad.*, 1908, p. 83; *Hists. of the Several Regiments and Battalions from N. C.* (1901); *Confed. Mil. Hist.*, IV, 291–94.]

T. M. S.

BAKER, LORENZO DOW (Mar. 15, 1840–June 21, 1908), sea captain, planter, and merchant, was born at Wellfleet, Mass., the son of David and Thankful (Rich) Baker, of a line of Cape Cod mariners dating from the seventeenth century. Trained by his father from boyhood for a seafaring life, Lorenzo had only the winter months each year in the Wellfleet public school and later a short term in Wilbraham Academy. The elder Baker had been a whaler and the son became a successful fisherman. He was a sailor boy at ten, master of a ship at twenty-one, and was never in his life of nearly seventy years more than two weeks out of sight of the ocean. In 1870, as owner and master of a schooner, he contracted to convey a party of gold-miners, with their machinery and supplies, 300 miles up the Orinoco River in Venezuela. On his return voyage he put into Jamaica, seeking cargo. There his attention was drawn to bunches of bright yellow bananas—a wild fruit that had never been imported to the United States in quantity. He covered the deck of his schooner with the ripe fruit, purchased at twenty-five cents a bunch, and on arrival at Boston was able to dispose of the bulk of the shipment at prices ranging from $2.50 to $3.25 a bunch. This is believed to have been the first cargo of bananas sold at Boston. When the fruit reached the market, most of it was over-ripe and Capt. Baker profited by the experience; thereafter he bought his bananas green, making several voyages a year to Jamaica and back. In 1879 English capital organized the Atlas Line of steamships, and Baker was made the Jamaica agent of the enterprise, receiving five per cent on shipments to American ports. The banana trade had now become important, largely through Baker's energy and business acumen. The sugar industry in Jamaica had ceased to be profitable; the stimulus to banana-growing given by the new American market came at the right time. Baker encouraged both whites and negroes on the island to cultivate the fruit, which had not before been done extensively. Gradually a profitable industry was built up, which brought wealth to Baker and a diffusion of prosperity in Jamaica. A British colonial officer said in 1905, "Capt. Baker has done more for Jamaica than all the Governors and Governments." While he was the Atlas Line representative he continued his heavy shipments of bananas to Boston. He brought about the organization of the Boston Fruit Company in 1885, became its president, and after the formation of the United Fruit Company in 1897, he was managing director of its Jamaica division. Although the latter years of his life were largely passed in Jamaica, Baker was interested in various New England corporations and institutions. A loyal member of the Methodist Episcopal Church, he was for several years a trustee of Boston University. He was married on Dec. 19, 1861, to Martha M. Hopkins, who like himself was a descendant of Stephen Hopkins of the *Mayflower*. There were four children of this marriage.

[Frederick Upham Adams, *Conquest of the Tropics* (1914); Eugene P. Lyle, Jr., "Capt. Baker and Jamaica," *World's Work*, Mar. 1906; Samuel Atkins Eliot, *Biog. Hist. of Mass.* (1913), IV.]

W. B. S.

BAKER, MARCUS (Sept. 23, 1849–Dec. 12, 1903), geographer, the son of John and Chastina (Fobes) Baker, was born in Kalamazoo, Mich. He was educated in the common schools, in Kalamazoo College, and the University of Michigan, graduating from the latter in 1870. He taught mathematics at Albion College, 1870–71, and was instructor in mathematics at the University of Michigan, 1871–73. He was married in 1874 to Sarah Eldred, who died in 1897. In 1899 he was married to Marion Una Strong, who, with two children, survived him. His first conspicuous work was with Dr. W. H. Dall in a survey of little known and difficult Alaskan waters in 1873. He aided in preparing the *Coast Pilot of Alaska* and the bibliography of Alaskan geography. In Los Angeles in 1882 he conducted a magnetic observatory. Beginning with 1886 he was for many years a member of the United States Geological Survey and he contributed much to that creative and fruitful period of the Survey's history. He directed the topographic work of the north-eastern division and thus had much to do with the mapping of southern New England and other regions. For a time he was the editor of topographic maps for the Survey. He contributed to American geography constantly and largely as a member of the Board of Geographic Names, serving much of the time as secretary and editor. In addition to many problems of research in the Survey he prepared for the United States Government an elaborate report on the Venezuelan boundary question and was for a long time employed by Venezuela as an expert in that case. As a member of the Geological Survey he prepared "A Geographic Dictionary of Alaska" (*Survey Bulletin No. 187,* 1902). He had an influential place in scientific societies, notably as a founder and manager, until his death, of the National Geographic Society, and as secretary, editor, and president of the Philosophical Society of Washington. Near the end of his life he became assistant secretary of the Carnegie Institution.

[Sketch by William H. Dall, *Natl. Geographic Mag.*, XV, 40–43; another in *Carnegie Institution Yr. Bk.*, No. 2.]

A. P. B.

BAKER, OSMON CLEANDER (July 30, 1812–Dec. 20, 1871), Methodist bishop, was born at Marlow, N, H., the son of Dr. Isaac Baker, and of Abigail Kidder. At fifteen he entered Wilbraham Academy, in Massachusetts, was converted there, received his license to exhort at the age of seventeen, and in 1830 enrolled in the first class in Wesleyan University, at Middletown, Conn., whose president, Wilbur Fisk, who had also been his principal and teacher at Wilbraham, profoundly influenced him. On account of serious ill health he had to leave college in his senior year. In 1834 he became teacher in the seminary at Newbury, Vt., and in 1838 principal. In the jubilee year of Methodism (1839) the matter of a theological school was agitated by the New England and New Hampshire Conferences, and in 1840–41 Newbury, Vt., was selected as the site. This led Baker to organize in 1840 the theological society of Newbury Seminary for the training of ministers, and in 1841 he and his associates began regular theological classes. In 1843 a portion of the Seminary building was formally dedicated as a theological school. This made Baker the first professor in such a school in Methodism in America, though W. M. Willett had been teaching Hebrew in Wesleyan since 1830. In 1844 Baker resigned to become pastor in the New Hampshire Conference, but had served only two churches, Rochester and Manchester, when in 1847 he was made presiding elder (district superintendent). That same year saw the theological institution (the Methodist General Biblical Institute) reorganized and opened at Concord, N. H., with Baker as professor of homiletics, Methodist discipline, etc. Both in his character and instruction—for he was a born teacher—he left a deep impress upon his students. In 1852, he was elected bishop by the General Conference which met that year in Boston, but Concord remained his home until the end. As bishop he was conscientious, kind, fair, and competent. His unrivalled knowledge of Methodist law comes out in his *Guide Book in the Administration of the Discipline of the Methodist Episcopal Church* (1855, revised ed. 1869). For nearly two generations this was a hand-book for perplexed bishops and pastors, in those years when that mighty little book, *The Doctrines and Discipline of the Methodist Episcopal Church,* was taken seriously. Baker was six feet tall with a smooth, florid, intelligent face. He married Mehitabel Perley, of Leinster, N. H., in 1833. She survived him, dying at Concord May 8, 1890.

[*Christian Advocate* (N.Y.), Dec. 28, 1871, Jan. 4, 1872; *Zion's Herald,* July 24, 1912; Chas. Adams, in *Meth. Quart. Rev.*, Jan. 1878, pp. 111–20; private letters from W. F. Warren, M. D. Buell, and C. S. Nutter, Librarian of the Meth. Hist. Soc. of Boston; O. E. Baker, *The Last Witness* (1853).]

J. A. F.

BAKER, PETER CARPENTER (Mar. 22, 1822–May 19, 1889), printer and publisher, was born in North Hempstead, N.Y., the son of John and Margaret (Boyce) Baker. The father moved to New York while Peter was a child and the latter went to the Harlem Academy to school. When he was but twelve, he exchanged school for business, first in Kasang's printing-office and bookstore on Division St., and later with W. E. Dean, who was an extensive printer and publisher of legal and classical books. Attracted by the mechanical side of these establishments, Baker decided to learn the printer's trade. His apprenticeship completed, he became superintendent for John F. Trow, who was at that time the printer for many large publishers, including D. Appleton & Company and George P. Putnam. The young man derived much satisfaction in supervising the printing of all the volumes of Washington Irving's revised edition of his works. Always keenly interested in the printer's art, he expressed himself publicly in later life thus: "A printer who has no heart in his business, no pride in his calling, who only sees wood and iron and lead about him might better have been born and remained in a junk shop. There must be, if we would give pleasure—and profit may accompany the pleasure—a pride in our profession, a heart in our work, and an ambition to excel" (*Annual Dinner of the Typothetæ, Jan. 17, 1885,* pp. 10–11). In 1850 Baker formed a partnership with Daniel Godwin, and this firm achieved almost a national reputation in the printing business; for an example of their superior workmanship see *Vertoogh van Nieu Nederland* and *Breeden Raedt,* two tracts translated from the Dutch (1854). In 1866 he entered the law publishing field with the firm of Baker, Voorhis & Company. He continued to consider himself primarily a printer, however, and his was a leading part in the organization of the Typothetæ, the purpose of which was stated to be "the general benefit of the trade and the improvement of the typographic art" (*N. Y. Times,* Mar. 22, 1865). Employing printers found such an organization so necessary amidst the chaotic industrial conditions following the war that almost every large city followed the lead of New York and established its Typothetæ.

Baker was much sought as a public speaker, was a strong advocate of the temperance cause, and was also active in charitable enterprises, the Hahnemann Hospital being a particular object of his favor. He was married to Malvina Lockwood, by whom he had three daughters.

[The best source of information is a ten-page sketch by W. W. Pasko in *Old New York,* Dec. 1890, II, 327–38, containing portrait. Obituaries in *Publisher's Weekly,* June 1, 1889, and in *N. Y. Times,* May 21, 1889, are helpful. Baker's personality is portrayed in his addresses, such as *European Recollections, a Speech Before the N. Y. Typographical Soc.* (pamphlet, 1861); *Franklin,* before the same society (pamphlet, 1865); an address at Cooper Union advocating municipal reform, *N. Y. Times,* Sept. 4, 1864.]

A. E. P.

BAKER, REMEMBER (June 1737–August 1775), soldier, the son of Remember and Tamar (Warner) Baker, was born at Woodbury, Conn., in June 1737. He was fifth in descent from Alexander Baker, the emigrant, who arrived in Boston from London in 1635, aged twenty-eight (F. V. Virkus, *Abridged Compendium of American Genealogy,* I, 1925, p. 54). Remember Baker, Jr., was the first cousin of Ethan Allen [*q.v.*], through Allen's mother; and of Col. Seth Warner [*q.v.*], through Warner's father. As a young man in his early twenties Baker took part in the French and Indian War, serving on Lake George and Lake Champlain. It was undoubtedly during this service that he saw the possibilities of the country now known as Vermont, then called the New Hampshire Grants, for he settled at Arlington, with his wife and child in 1764. Together with his cousins, Allen and Warner, he early became prominent in the controversy which raged between the governments of New Hampshire and New York over the jurisdiction of the territory. The cousins sided with those who received their grants from New Hampshire, and persistently fought off the grantees of the New York government. To accomplish this the Green Mountain Boys were organized under the command of Ethan Allen, with Remember Baker in charge of one of the companies. They had made themselves so obnoxious to the government of New York by December 1771 that on the 9th of that month, Gov. Tryon issued a proclamation offering a reward of twenty pounds for the capture of Allen, Baker, and others. To this Allen, Baker, and Robert Cochran replied with a burlesque proclamation, dated at Poultney, Feb. 5, 1772, offering a similar reward for the apprehension of James Duane and John Kempe, two of the New York grantees. As a result, a serious effort was made to capture Baker, who was attacked in his house at Arlington on Mar. 22, 1772, when he was wounded and carried off by Justice John Munro, and his wife and son were injured. A rescue party was formed by some of the New Hampshire grantees, the Munro party captured, and Baker, weak from the loss of blood, brought back in triumph to Bennington (Hiland Hall, *The History of Vermont from Its Discovery to Its Admission into the Union, in 1791,* 1868, pp. 135–37; *Records of the Council of Safety and Governor and Council of the State of Vermont,* I, 1873, pp. 148–50, footnote). The activities of the Green Mountain

Boys continued, and reached such a height that Gov. Tryon issued a second proclamation, Mar. 9, 1774, increasing the amount of the reward for the capture of Baker and Allen to £100.

Baker was with Allen in the Crown Point campaign in the spring of 1775, and the following summer he accompanied Gen. Schuyler on a scouting party up Lake Champlain toward Canada. He was killed in a skirmish with the Indians near St. Johns, in August 1775.

He married, Apr. 3, 1760, Desire, daughter of Consider and Patience (Hawley) Hurlbut, by whom he had an only son, Ozi, who became the grandfather of La Fayette C. Baker [*q.v.*], and the great-grandfather of Ray Stannard Baker, the biographer of Woodrow Wilson. Remember Baker's widow married, secondly, Thomas Butterfield of Colchester, Vt.

[In addition to references cited above, see Wm. Slade, *Vt. State Papers* (1823); Ira Allen, *The Natural and Political Hist. of the State of Vt.* (1798); E. B. O'Callaghan, *Documentary Hist. of the State of N.Y.*, IV (1851). There is a short sketch of his life in A. M. Hemenway's *Vt. Hist. Gazetteer* (1868), I, 765–70.]
G. H. D.

BAKER, WILLIAM MUMFORD (June 5, 1825–Aug. 20, 1883), clergyman, author, was born in Washington, D. C., the son of Daniel and Elizabeth (McRobert) Baker. His father, a native of Georgia, was pastor of the Second Presbyterian Church. William's youth was spent in various parts of the South, where his father, who was becoming known as an evangelist, held many pastorates. He graduated with honor from Princeton College in 1846 and attended Princeton Seminary in 1847–48. He was licensed to preach by the Presbytery of New Brunswick, N. J., Apr. 26, 1848, and was ordained by the Presbytery of Little Rock, Ark., in 1850. He married Susan John Hartman at Raleigh, Tenn., Jan. 5, 1850. After preaching for a short time in Galveston, he reorganized the First Presbyterian Church of Austin, Tex., in May 1850, and remained in this pastorate until 1865. Though devoted to the South and especially to the state of his adoption, he was a firm Unionist and found his position during the Civil War a trying one. During this time he kept a record of his experiences, thinly veiled as fiction, which was published in 1866 under the title of *Inside: A Chronicle of Secession.* Soon after the war he removed to the North and held various pastorates—at Zanesville, Ohio, 1866–72; at Newburyport, Mass., 1872–74; and at South Boston, 1874–76. In the meantime he had published a number of books, and he now resigned his pastorate and for the next four years devoted himself to writing. In 1881 he accepted the pastorate of the South Church in Philadelphia. He continued to write, but his health was bad and after two years he returned to Boston, where he died. Though an effective and even eloquent pulpit orator, Baker is better remembered by his writings. These are marked by a style which, though by no means distinguished, is facile and quietly humorous, shows considerable insight into character, and is penetrated by deep religious feeling. His first book was *The Life and Labors of Daniel Baker* (1858), a memoir of his father. *Inside: A Chronicle of Secession* (1866) was published under the pseudonym of "George F. Harrington." The characters in it are supposed to be drawn from his friends and acquaintances in Austin. Though of slight literary merit, the book has some value to the historical student. After Baker's removal to the North other books appeared with regularity. Most of them reflect his earlier experiences in Texas and other parts of the South. These were: *Oak Mot* (1868); *The New Timothy* (1870), which embodies many of his earlier experiences in Texas; *Mose Evans* (1874); *Carter Quarterman* (1876), which is generally supposed to be the story of his noted father told in a more attractive form than in his earlier book; *The Virginians in Texas* (1878), a story of adventure for boys; *A Year Worth Living* (1878) and *Colonel Dunwoddie, Millionaire* (1878), both of which are descriptive of southern life; *His Majesty, Myself* (1880), descriptive of conditions at Princeton as he saw them when a student there, and published anonymously, as was the book immediately preceding; *Blessed Saint Certainty* (1881); *The Ten Theophanies* (1883), which is probably his chief work of a distinctly religious character; and *The Making of a Man* (1884), which was published posthumously.

[*Princeton Theol. Sem. Necr. Rept.* 1884; *Boston Transcript,* Aug. 21, 1883; personal information from W. S. Red of Austin.]
C. W. R.

BALBACH, EDWARD (July 4, 1839–Dec. 30, 1910), metallurgist, was born in Karlsruhe, Baden, Germany, and came to this country with his father, Edward Balbach, Sr., in 1850. The family is an old and prominent one in Baden, where it has long been associated with the villages of Upper and Lower Balbach and the castles midway between those villages. The elder Balbach was forty-four when he came to America to seek an opportunity for applying his knowledge of chemistry and metallurgy. Having decided on Newark, N. J., the center of extensive jewelry manufacturing, as a favorable location, he returned to Germany and brought his eleven-year-old son over. In 1852 he erected a building and started a business for the treatment of jewelers' sweepings, which formerly had been sent to Europe. After attendance at the Newark public schools, young Balbach at the age of fourteen began to help in the growing business and soon showed that he had inherited his father's technical ability. The business grew, not only in jewelry sweepings but also in the general metallurgy of silver-lead ores, some of which began coming to the Balbach plant from Mexico as early as 1861. The Balbach plant became a leader in lead smelting and refining, and later in copper refining by electrolysis. The Parkes process for the desilverization of lead bullion was first introduced into this country by the Balbachs at the close of the Civil War, and for many years their plant was one of the few sources of refined lead in the United States. The desilverization is accomplished by the addition to the molten bullion of zinc, about sixty per cent of which is recovered by distilling the silver-zinc-lead amalgam in a graphite retort, the zinc vapors being reduced to metal in a condenser attached to the Balbach-Thum desilverizing process. This invention is typical of Balbach's work. It provides an apparatus that is simpler, easier to operate, and more efficient than the rival Moebius process but is somewhat costlier. The older Balbach died in 1890, after which the firm of Edward Balbach & Son was reorganized as the Balbach Smelting & Refining Company, with Edward Balbach, Jr., as president. The company expanded and prospered. The younger Balbach was less German in appearance than his father and more typically an American business man. He was tall and energetic, and had an unusually attractive personality. Although a metallurgist of acknowledged reputation, he never joined the American Institute of Mining Engineers. He was married to Julia Anna Nenninger on Jan. 21, 1869. In later years he maintained a country house at Bernardsville, N. J., and spent his winters at Palm Beach, Fla., where he made valuable investments in property. Balbach's contributions to metallurgy were practical operating methods rather than fundamental changes in theory. He introduced European processes into this country and improved upon them at a time when such processes were kept as secret as possible and when the United States needed such practical methods.

[*Engineering and Mining Jour.*, Jan. 14, 1911; *N. Y. Times*, *N.Y. Tribune*, Jan. 1, 1911.]

P. B. M.

BALCH, GEORGE BEALL (Jan. 3, 1821–Apr. 16, 1908), naval officer, was born at Shelbyville, Tenn., son of George Beall Balch and Martha (Rogers) Balch, first cousins. His parents were of English and Scotch ancestors who settled in Maryland about 1650. His mother died in 1823, and his father, after moving the family to Moulton, Ala., died in 1831. The son was appointed midshipman, Dec. 30, 1837, through his uncle, Gen. Alexander Macomb. His aunt suggested West Point, but he declared that nothing would satisfy him until he felt the deck under his feet (Manuscript Reminiscences by George Beall Balch). In the *Cyane*, Capt. "Mad Jack" Percival, of the Mediterranean squadron under Commodore Hull, he made his first cruise, 1838–41. Of his conduct Percival wrote, "He has escaped the too frequent unprofitable habits of young men in the service at this time" (letter to Mrs. Alexander Macomb, March, 1839). Before the Mexican War, he had served on various ships, been promoted fifth in his class to passed midshipman, July 12, 1843, and spent two years under Maury at the Observatory. Joining the *Princeton*, Apr. 5, 1846, he took part in the unsuccessful expedition against Alvarado, Aug. 7, and the occupation of Tampico, Nov. 10–13; and temporarily served as acting master on the *Falcon* of Tattnall's "Mosquito Fleet" which gallantly covered the landing of Gen. Scott's army at Vera Cruz, Mar. 9, 1847. After the war, in the *Princeton* he made an extensive Mediterranean cruise, 1847–49, visiting particularly Italian ports to protect American interests during the revolutions of 1848. Becoming a lieutenant, Aug. 16, 1850, he joined the *Plymouth*, Capt. Kelly, which afterward became one of Commodore Perry's squadron in the diplomatic expedition to Japan. Balch personally assisted in making surveys in the harbor of Yedo, and around the Lew Chew and Bonin Islands. At Shanghai, Apr. 4, 1854, he was wounded in the hip during a conflict between Chinese rebels and Imperialists.

Further service, as executive officer on various ships and as an instructor in seamanship, naval tactics, and gunnery at the Naval Academy, prepared him for responsible commands in the South Atlantic blockading squadron, during the Civil War. On Nov. 1, 1861, while executive officer of the *Sabine*, he fearlessly assisted in the rescue of some 400 marines and sailors from the sinking transport *Governor*, off Georgetown, S. C. As commander of the *Pocahontas*, Nov. 14, 1861–Sept. 8, 1862, and the *Pawnee*, Oct. 21, 1862–Feb. 28, 1865, he reduced Confederate batteries, occupied islands, and opened inland passages, from Jacksonville, Fla., to Georgetown, S. C.; and in particular coöperated with the army on the Stono River in its operations leading up to the evacuation of Charleston. Especially noteworthy was his engagement July 16, 1863, with the batteries near Grimball's Landing in which the *Pawnee* was hulled thirty-three times but a large body of Gen. Terry's troops saved from capture. Of his services Du Pont wrote, "A more devoted officer our navy does not possess. With the greatest amount of energy and pluck and skill in handling guns, he is always ready, overcomes difficulties, and is ever genial and cheerful" (Rear Admiral Du Pont to Assistant Secretary Fox, Aug. 21, 1862). Dahlgren later declared that he had "always discharged his responsible duties in action and otherwise with alacrity, judgment, and success" (letter of Rear Admiral Dahlgren to Secretary of the Navy Welles, Feb. 27, 1865).

After the war, Balch commanded the *Contoocook* and the *Albany,* flagships of the North Atlantic squadron, was governor of the Naval Asylum in Philadelphia, and sat on important naval boards, meanwhile being promoted captain, July 25, 1866; commodore, Jan. 13, 1873, and rear admiral, June 5, 1878. As superintendent of the Naval Academy, 1879–81, he took steps toward adapting the course of study to the new age of machinery. Having commanded the Pacific fleet for a few months, he was retired, Jan. 3, 1883, after about forty-five years of service in the navy. He resided in Baltimore for twenty-five years after his retirement. He was married twice: to Julia Grace Vinson in 1844, to Mary Ellen Booth in 1865, and had five children by each wife. Dying at the home of one of his daughters at Raleigh, N. C., he was buried in the Naval Academy Cemetery. Of his personal character, Mahan, who was his executive officer on the *Pocahontas,* wrote that he was "a man beloved by all who have known him for his gallantry, benevolence, and piety" (*From Sail to Steam,* 1907, p. 91).

[The chief sources of information about Balch are the official records in the Navy Dept. Lib., some of which have been published in the *Official Records;* letters and papers in the possession of Miss Grace Balch, Concord, N. H.; *Navy Register,* 1839–1909, *Reports Sec. Navy* and *Narr. of the Expedition of an Am. Squadron to the China Seas and Japan, 1852–54, under Command of Commodore M. C. Perry,* vol. II. Biographies of M. C. Perry, S. F. Du Pont, and John A. Dahlgren are important collateral sources. Obituaries in the *Army and Navy Jour.,* Apr. 18 and Apr. 25, 1908.]

C. L. L.

BALCH, THOMAS WILLING (June 13, 1866–June 7, 1927), publicist, was born abroad (Wiesbaden, Germany), where his parents had been living for some six or seven years. His father was Thomas Balch, a Pennsylvania lawyer, who was born at Leesburg, Va., of an old Maryland family. His mother was Emily Swift of an old Philadelphia family. His great-grandfather was Thomas Willing, a prominent Philadelphia merchant of colonial and revolutionary times, who was a member of the First and Second Congresses and president of the Bank of the United States. Balch received his early education in France, but his academic and professional education in the United States. In 1890 he obtained the A.B. degree from Harvard College and five years later the LL.B. degree from the University of Pennsylvania. Although he began the practise of law in 1895, most of his life was devoted to writing and to public-spirited activities. He displayed a penchant for genealogy, publishing *The Brooke Family of Whitchurch, Hampshire, England* (1899), *English Ancestors of the Shippen Family and Edward Shippen, of Philadelphia* (1904), *The Swift Family of Philadelphia* (1906), and the *Balch Genealogica* (1907). His other hobby was international arbitration. Early in the twentieth century he made a trip to Alaska and to St. Petersburg and upon his return wrote and published *The Alasko-Canadian Frontier* (1902) and *The Alaska Frontier* (1903). In 1909 he issued a new edition of *The New Cyneas of Émeric Crucé* (originally published in 1623), and in 1915 a revised edition of *International Courts of Arbitration,* written by his father in 1874 to support his claim that he was "the original recommender of almost precisely the plan of arbitration in the Alabama case, which was finally adopted and carried out to a conclusion at Geneva" (p. 51). The interest of his brother, Edwin Swift Balch, in polar explorations had its counterpart in his own reflections on *The Arctic and Antarctic Regions and the Law of Nations* (1910). He was a member of numerous clubs in Philadelphia and of historical and patriotic societies there and elsewhere, including the Historical Society of Pennsylvania, of which he was one of five vice-presidents. A frequent contributor to the *American Journal of International Law* and the *Revue de droit international et de législation comparée* of Brussels, as well as other scientific, legal, and historical periodicals, he was able, because of his wealth, to indulge his desire for reprints of nearly everything he wrote even to the extent of cloth binding for relatively few pages. On May 26, 1923, he married Dulany Whiting, daughter of Clarence C. Whiting of Roland Park, Baltimore, and a descendant of the Fairfax family of Virginia, who was a little over half his age. Late in 1926 his health began to fail and he went to Atlantic City in the hope that the salt air might speed his recovery. It was there that he died in the following June.

[*Who's Who in America,* 1924–25, gives most of the essential facts. The year of birth is taken from the

Harvard Coll., Class of 1890: Secretary's Report (1915) and is two years earlier than that given by the *Phila. Pub. Ledger*, June 8, 1927, p. 3, col. 3. A rather complete and accurate biog. sketch is given in the *Ledger*, but a number of autobiographical details have been taken from prefaces to his own printed works.] H. F. W.

BALDWIN, ABRAHAM (Nov. 22, 1754–Mar. 4, 1807), statesman, was the son of Michael Baldwin, a blacksmith, who is said to have been a man of powerful, if uncultivated, mind. Born in Guilford, Conn., in 1719, Michael Baldwin was married in 1749 to Lucy, daughter of William and Ruth Strong Dudley, who bore him five children, three of whom survived childhood. Abraham, the third child and second son, was born in North Guilford. His younger sister, Ruth, later married Joel Barlow [*q.v.*]. After the death of his wife, Michael Baldwin married Theodora Wolcot of Coventry, Conn., who bore him seven children. One of these, Henry Baldwin [*q.v.*], later became justice of the United States Supreme Court, and another became prominent in public life in Ohio. The distinction which his children attained was due in considerable part to the ambition and wisdom of the blacksmith father who, in 1775, removed to New Haven to provide more adequate educational opportunities for his already large, and rapidly growing, family. So far as the younger children were concerned, no small share of credit was due to Abraham, for his father's means were not equal to his ambitions. After the death of the latter in 1787, Abraham paid off the debt on the estate, surrendered his own claims, and educated his half-brothers and sisters largely at his own expense.

Abraham, the first of the family to attain distinction, graduated at Yale in 1772. Agreeable to the theological influence of his academic environment, he became a licensed minister in September 1775 and was for four years thereafter a tutor at Yale. Here he won the warm commendation of his colleagues for his learning, piety, modesty, and skilful management of students. In June 1779 he resigned his tutorship to devote himself exclusively to a chaplaincy in the Revolutionary army. From time to time he visited his alma mater, upon one occasion preaching "all day in Chapel," to the satisfaction of President Ezra Stiles, if not of the students. In January 1781 he received a call to return to Yale to assume the professorship of divinity that had been vacated by the death of Napthali Daggett. The unanimous election of one so young was regarded as a great tribute to him, and Stiles anticipated his becoming a learned theologian and a "venerable character." Perhaps his war experiences had modified the young chaplain's point of view and theological ambitions. At any rate, he declined the post, alleging the influence of financial considerations. Stiles thought him influenced also by the prospect of being called "together with a Group or Cluster of Geniuses into a Literary Institution thereafter" (*Literary Diary of Ezra Stiles,* 1901, II, 556). Leaving the army, he returned neither to the ministry nor to education, but entered upon the law, being admitted to the bar in Fairfield County in April 1783. He was destined, however, to contribute very significantly to the educational development of an American state and to carry into public life the conscientiousness, if not the theological emphasis, which was characteristic of New England.

By January 1784, when the General Assembly of Georgia granted his petition to practise in the courts of that state, he had become a resident of the southernmost commonwealth in the young republic. It is uncertain where he first made his home, but in October of this same year he received a grant of land in Wilkes, and in January 1785 he qualified as a member of the House of Assembly from this county. By 1790, when he represented the Middle District in Congress, he was living in Augusta.

The fact that his earliest public activities in his adopted state were connected with an educational project suggests the possibility that his removal to Georgia was made with a view to engaging in some educational work (Henry C. White, *Abraham Baldwin,* 1926, p. 37). At any rate, the General Assembly, a month after his admission to the Georgia bar, set aside a large amount of wild land for the endowment of a college and vested the control of this land in the Governor and seven others, including the newcomer, Baldwin (*Journal of the Georgia Assembly,* Feb. 25, 1784). Although the latter was not a member of this particular Assembly, as has often been said, he probably played a part in the framing of the act. The next Assembly, of which he was a member, adopted a charter, of which he seems unquestionably to have been the author, providing for the organization of a complete educational system in the state (White, *Abraham Baldwin,* p. 157). Authorship of this document entitles him to high rank as an educational pioneer and prophet. He was again appointed a trustee, and shortly afterward elected president, of the yet unestablished university. No funds were available until after the adoption of the constitution of 1798, which required the legislature to make adequate provision for the institution. At length Baldwin, the titular president, now a member of the United States Senate, brought about the organization of the college (called Franklin College) along the lines of Yale but without the latter's theological emphasis, served on the committee which selected the site, and procured the election of Josiah Meigs, whom he had known at Yale, as president. Baldwin served as chairman of the board of trustees until his death, and more than any one else deserves to be called the Father of the University of Georgia, of which Franklin College is the heart.

In the meantime, the former tutor and chaplain had become a prominent figure in Georgia politics. The records of his political activity prior to the Federal Convention are scanty, but we know that he served in the Congress of the Confederation in 1785, and later, and that because of this fact he was entitled to membership in the Georgia House of Assembly. His initial political prominence may have been in part due to his willingness conscientiously to assume tasks with which other men did not care to be bothered, but it was doubtless chiefly due to an almost immediate recognition of his high personal qualifications. His superior training made him an outstanding man in what was then a pioneer state, and at the same time his accommodating temper and his integrity won him friends and inspired confidence in him. At the Federal Convention, he was regarded as the ablest of the three delegates from Georgia. Never aggressive in debate though a good speaker, he was not conspicuous in the discussions, but in the greatest crisis of the Convention he played a significant part. Originally opposed to equal representation of the states in the Senate and favorable to representation on the basis of property, he later changed his vote, brought about a tie between the large and small states, and served on the committee that framed the compromise which was accepted. His decisive action was due to the conviction, doubtless resulting from his personal association with the Connecticut delegation who forced the issue, that the small states would withdraw if not placated. His conciliatory temper thus served to facilitate the fundamental compromise of the Constitution. After the adjournment of the Convention, he manifested patient fidelity by attending the sessions of the moribund Congress of the Confederation until almost its dying day.

Elected to the first House of Representatives under the Constitution, he served continuously in that body until he entered the Senate in 1799, to remain there until his death. Firmly established in the confidence of the Georgia electorate, he loyally identified himself with the interests of his adopted state and showed little sympathy for the Hamiltonian policies which his native section supported. He opposed the assumption of state debts, supported the position of his party on Jay's Treaty, and protested against the enactment of the Alien and Sedition Laws. Throughout his legislative career, he was a consistent, though a moderate, Democratic-Republican. His speeches were generally connected with the reports of committees to which he belonged, or with questions that involved reference to the deliberations of the Federal Convention.

In 1799, he took his seat in the United States Senate. He served as president *pro tempore,* during the first session of the Seventh Congress. As in the House, his speeches were able, moderate, and relatively infrequent, especially during his last years. A consistent supporter of the administration of Jefferson, he made a long speech in favor of the repeal of the Judiciary Act of 1801 (*Annals of Congress,* 6 Cong., 1 Sess., 99–107), and voted for the conviction of Justice Chase on three of the articles of impeachment. Loyal to his constituency, he opposed the receiving of petitions against slavery.

It was characteristic of him to wait until the congressional session was over before he died. His death came Mar. 4, 1807, after a very short illness. Characteristically, also, he talked of public affairs almost to the end. "Take care," he said, "hold the wagon back; there is more danger of its running too fast than of its going too slow" (C. B. Todd, *Life and Letters of Joel Barlow,* 1886, p. 212). He was buried in Washington, beside the remains of his colleague, James Jackson, who had preceded him by only a year. Joel Barlow, alone of his relatives, attended the funeral, but many of his colleagues remained expressly to do him honor. Resolutions of respect were adopted by the Senate when it reassembled in the autumn.

Baldwin was never married, except to his work. Economical and temperate in his habits, he had the means to assist many, outside his own family, to secure an education and become established in business. His name is perpetuated in his adopted state by Baldwin County, established in 1803, and the University of Georgia stands as a monument to his prophetic vision and educational statesmanship. "He may have wanted ambition to make himself brilliant, but he never wanted industry to make himself useful" (*Georgia Historical Quarterly,* III, 171). Serene, benign, good-humored, moderate though firm amid the violence of party strife, he died probably without an enemy.

[Until the appearance of Henry C. White's *Abraham Baldwin* (1926), a fairly extensive but inadequately annotated work, based in part on manuscript materials in Georgia not hitherto utilized, only very brief sketches of Baldwin had appeared in print. The chief contemporary source of all the latter is the article prepared for the press by Joel Barlow immediately after Baldwin's death. This was reproduced, with some additions, in Herring and Longacre, *Natl. Gallery of Distinguished Americans,* IV (1839). See also *Ga. Hist. Quart., III* (1919), 169–73. For information about the family, the authoritative work is C. C. Baldwin, *Baldwin Geneal.* (1881), I. The *Lit. Diary of Ezra Stiles,* ed. by F. B. Dexter (1901), contains considerable information about Baldwin's relations with Yale. For his connections with the University of Georgia, the best works are White's *Abraham Baldwin* (*supra*), C. E. Jones, *Education in Ga.* (1889), and W. B. Stevens, *Hist. of Ga.,* II (1859), though none of these is adequate. For his activities in the Federal Convention and Congress, *Records of the Federal Convention* (1911), ed. by Max Farrand, and the *Annals of Cong.,* 1789–1807, are invaluable. A few letters of his to his sister Ruth and Joel Barlow have been published in C. B. Todd, *The Life and Letters of Joel Barlow* (1886). An etching by Albert Rosenthal (Phila., 1888) is reproduced in Max Farrand, *Fathers of the Constitution* (Chronicles of America), facing p. 160. This is from the original in the Thomas Addis Emmet Collection in the N.Y. Pub. Lib. A painting "after Fulton" in Independence Hall is probably from the same original as Rosenthal's etching.]

D. M.

BALDWIN, ELIHU WHITTLESEY (Dec. 25, 1789–Oct. 15, 1840), Presbyterian clergyman, educator, was the first president of Wabash College, Crawfordsville, Ind., and though he died five years after having assumed that office, his labors helped to assure the permanence of the institution, and his ideas and character did much to shape its spirit and policies. He was born in Durham, Greene County, N. Y., the fourth child and eldest son of Deacon Jonathan Baldwin, and grandson of Abiel and Mehitable (Johnson) Baldwin of Durham, Conn. His mother was Submit, daughter of Deacon Christopher and Patience Lord of Saybrook, Conn. He was a sober-minded boy with little relish for sports but fond of books, and exceedingly careful, it is said, in the selection of his reading. His parents were people of limited means, and he secured his education in the face of many difficulties. He prepared for college under his pastor, Rev. Jesse Townsend, an alumnus of Yale, which college Baldwin entered in 1807. At the opening of his sophomore year he left college to earn money, and spent a year in Bethlehem, Conn., as assistant in the school of Rev. Azel Backus and later took charge of the academy in Fairfield. In 1810 he returned to the next lower class in college, graduating in 1812. After two years more of teaching at Fairfield, he entered Andover Theological Seminary, from which he graduated in 1817. On Sept. 10, of that year, he was ordained as an evangelist at Londonderry, N. H., by the Presbytery of Londonderry. On May 12, 1819, he married Julia, daughter of Elias A. and Elizabeth (Cook) Baldwin of Newark, N. J. He had expected to take up missionary work in western New York and Ohio, but while visiting in New York City he was persuaded to accept the position of city missionary. The field given him was a populous, destitute, and immoral section of the city, and here he labored with self-forgetting zeal for three years. His activities resulted in the establishment of the Seventh Presbyterian Church, over which he was installed pastor on Dec. 25, 1820. During his ministry, in spite of many difficulties, it grew into a church of 600 members. In 1834, a visitor to the city asked him to become president of a Presbyterian college recently founded on the edge of civilization in the upper Wabash country, and in February of the following year he accepted, leaving his church the first of May. Having spent several months in securing funds for the college, he entered on his duties in November, and was inaugurated in July 1836. He was a gentle, simple, practical man, of sound learning, with no unusual gifts save unflagging energy and an extraordinary capacity for heroic fidelity to duty. He gave himself to the upbuilding of the college without reserve, declining two calls to important city churches. He had to face ecclesiastical divisions and collisions, stringent poverty, the reluctance of men of means in the East to extend aid to new colleges in the West, and the general lack of appreciation of the fact that the educated men needed for teaching, preaching, and other professions in the West ought to be educated in the West. To all these he proved himself superior. From the start, the institution was intended to offer liberal culture to all classes, but in order to get a charter from the legislature, "prejudiced against colleges, pianos, and Yankees," it was necessary to name it "Wabash Manual Labor College and Teachers' Seminary." Baldwin endeavored to make it what it was designed to be, saying in his inaugural address: "The term education is of very extensive import. It relates equally to the moral and physical nature of man, and comprises the development and training of all his powers." In 1839 he was given the degree of D.D. by a rival college at Bloomington, Ind., an institution under the control of the Old School branch of the Presbyterian Church, to which he did not belong. After a tedious journey into the northern part of the state in behalf of the college during the summer of 1840, he was taken ill and died in October of that year. A bibliography of his publications, which are chiefly tracts and sermons, may be found in *Biographical Sketches of the Graduates of Yale College* (1912), VI, by F. B. Dexter.

[E. F. Hatfield, *Patient Continuance in Well-Doing: a Memoir of Elihu W. Baldwin* (1843); E. O. Hovey,

"Hist. of Wabash College" in the *Tuttle Miscellany,* a collection of material concerning Wabash College, made by Joseph Farrand Tuttle, third president of the college; E. H. Baldwin, "Inaugural Address," and other addresses and sermons, in the *Tuttle Miscellany;* Wm. B. Sprague, *Annals Am. Pulpit* (1858), vol. IV; Rich. G. Boone, *Hist. of Education in Ind.* (1892); Chas. C. Baldwin, *Baldwin Geneal.* (1881); Jas. H. Smart, *The Schools of Ind.* (1876).] J. H. O.

BALDWIN, FRANK STEPHEN (Apr. 10, 1838–Apr. 8, 1925), inventor, was born in New Hartford, Conn., the son of Stephen Baldwin and Julia (Pardee) Baldwin, both of New England stock. In the summer of 1840 his parents moved to Nunda, Livingston County, N.Y. Here he attended the first free school established by the state. He graduated from the Nunda Institute where he specialized in mathematics, surprising his teachers by memorizing the decimal of Pi to 128 places, which he was still able to repeat up to the time of his death. In 1854 he was enrolled at Union College, Schenectady, N. Y., but was prevented from finishing his course by the illness of his father, the management of whose architectural business he was forced to take over.

The following year Baldwin applied for a patent on an arrowhead self-coupler for railroad cars. Five years later, in 1860, he was instrumental in securing a patent on a corn-planting machine which was a pioneer among machines of this class. In 1869 he went to St. Louis where he worked out a number of inventions. The metal lace latch now found on so many shoes he first devised to aid him in quick dressing. He also invented an anemometer, an instrument for recording the direction of the wind; a registering step for street cars, recording the number of passengers carried, and a street indicator geared from the axle showing the name of each street in succession as the car passed. A little later came the recording lumber-measure—a machine which automatically measured and recorded four different kinds of lumber at the same time. The successful operation of this device led to the conception of a calculating machine of an entirely new type, capable of adding, subtracting, multiplying, and dividing, each with equal facility.

In 1872, Baldwin was married to Mary Denniston and moved to Philadelphia, where a small machine-shop was obtained and he started the development of his calculating machine. He conceived the need of a smaller figuring machine and this led to the conception of an arithmometer which he patented on July 28, 1874. This was one of the first adding machines ever sold in the United States. The calculating machine was placed on exhibition at the Franklin Institute of Philadelphia, and in 1875 was awarded the John Scott medal for the most meritorious invention of the year. Baldwin arranged to have his invention perfected and produced by a Philadelphia machine works, but the concern collapsed in the failure of Jay Cooke and the ensuing panic. In 1876, therefore, he started a small shop in St. Louis, where he brought out a permutation drawer lock, a printing-press counter, a mortar mixer, and a three-speed bicycle. During these years he employed to do model work on his calculating machine William S. Burroughs who about 1880 started work on his own adding machine with a keyboard set up. The Baldwin computing engine was invented in 1890, followed in 1902 by the Baldwin calculator very much like the Monroe calculating machine of to-day. In 1911 Baldwin became acquainted with Jay R. Monroe at that time associated with the legal department of the Western Electric Company of New York. Monroe, after demonstration of the machine, saw its possibilities and the two joined hands to redesign the machine and make it as nearly perfect as possible in its adaptation to modern business. The result was the Monroe Calculating Machine Company which Baldwin happily lived to see filling no small place in the fields of science and business.

[Baldwin's early machines are on exhibition at the National Museum at Washington, D. C., at the Museums of the Peaceful Arts, New York City, and at Orange, N. J. (Monroe Calculating Machine Co.). Obituaries in *Typewriter Topics,* May 1925; *N.Y. Times,* Apr. 9, 1925; personal information.] L. L. L.

BALDWIN, HENRY (Jan. 14, 1780–Apr. 21, 1844), justice of the United States Supreme Court, was born in New Haven, Conn., a son of Michael and Theodora (Wolcott) Baldwin and a half-brother of Abraham Baldwin [*q.v.*]. He graduated from Yale College in 1797 where he was distinguished "for the sturdy energy with which he forced his way in the face of great difficulties to an eminent post at the head of his class" (*Pennsylvania Law Journal,* VI, 1). He studied law with Alexander J. Dallas [*q.v.*], and after completing his legal apprenticeship, set out for Ohio, but stopped in Pittsburgh, was admitted to the bar, and began to practise there and in Meadville, Pa. He was a successful lawyer, and quickly acquired a reputation. Of his habits and mode of life reports are not well authenticated. One story is that he fought a duel with pistols, and that his life was saved by a silver dollar. He was an enthusiastic practical joker, but the few sketches of his career draw a veil over the nature of his pranks. He had one of the finest law libraries in the West, with a particularly rich collection of English reports. His studying was done at night, and he smoked many small black Spanish cigars. "He slept but little, and so thorough was his absorption in his professional studies that for week after week he would study, note, and digest without intermission, and almost without refreshment."

Elected to Congress in 1816, and twice reelected, he served as chairman of the Committee on Domestic Manufactures, and was a strong advocate of protection. His speech in 1820 on the tariff bill was an effective effort, and was widely circulated. He played a serviceable rôle in the Florida treaty negotiations. The southwestern boundary as agreed to by Monroe's cabinet had caused a conflict between Northern and Southern politicians, and Monroe requested Baldwin to act as a mediator. He managed this commission in a firm and prudent manner. In 1822 he had a serious illness, and resigned from the House. Meanwhile, he had been financially affected by the depression of 1820. His service in Washington had resulted in a lack of oversight of his private affairs. In 1828 he was an active and earnest supporter of Jackson, and expected to be secretary of the treasury, but the appointee was Samuel D. Ingham. In 1830 Jackson made him associate justice of the Supreme Court (*vice* Justice Washington). Baldwin was supported by the bench and bar of Western Pennsylvania and by a majority of the legislature. John Bannister Gibson was favored by Calhoun, and Horace Binney was the candidate of the Philadelphia bar. "My friend Baldwin got it," wrote the latter, "and I saw his letter to my friend Chauncey, in which he did me the honour to say that I deserved it, but that he *wanted* it more" (Charles C. Binney, *Life of Horace Binney,* 1903, p. 94). The appointment was confirmed by the Senate with two dissenting votes—Hayne and Smith of South Carolina—whose opposition was due to Baldwin's view of the constitutional aspects of the tariff question.

Baldwin steered an erratic course on constitutional questions. The first important opinion which he handed down was in the Florida Land Case, U. S. *vs.* Arredondo, 6 *Peters* 691 (1832). "Few decisions of the Court at this period," writes Charles Warren, "had a more permanent effect upon the history of the country; for in this case the Court established the public land policy of the Government on the basis of the most scrupulous respect for treaties" (*The Supreme Court in United States History,* 1922, II, 242). At first, Baldwin followed in the path of Marshall, and had a profound reverence for the opinions of that jurist. Later, he refused to belong to the Marshall school of liberal interpretation, and was, on the other hand, unwilling to align himself with the strict constructionists. In 1831 he dissented in seven cases, and his resignation was rumored. In several cases he held the casting vote. His statement of the views of the two schools and his professed adherence to a third theory are expressed in *A General View of the Origin and Nature of the Constitution and Government of the United States* (1837), which is made up in large part of his dissenting opinions.

He is said to have been at his judicial best while on the circuit. In 1833 he decided with great learning the case of McGill *vs.* Brown (F. C. Brightly, *Reports of Cases,* 1896, p. 347), which construed a will making a bequest for pious and charitable purposes. He also sat in the noted trial of John F. Braddel of Uniontown for robbing the mails (1840). He is reputed to have been partly insane during his later years. He had certain peculiar habits, but some of these were not evidence of insanity, *e. g.,* carrying candy in his pockets to dole out to children whom he met, and parading home from a grocery store carrying a ham by the hock. Toward the close of his life, however, he was occasionally "violent and ungovernable in his conduct on the bench" (H. L. Carson, *History of the Supreme Court of the United States,* 1902, I, 281). More than this, he was deeply in debt and regarded his dearest friends with suspicion and distrust. For a time he was unable to perform his judicial duties. He died of paralysis in Philadelphia on Apr. 21, 1844. A subscription among his friends was taken up to pay the expenses of his burial.

[References in addition to those given above: *Cong. Globe,* 30 Cong., 2 Sess., p. 67; *Pa. Law Jour.,* III, 330 (1844); *Allegheny County Bar Ass. Addresses,* 1888, p. 23.]

L. R.

BALDWIN, HENRY PORTER (Feb. 22, 1814–Dec. 31, 1892), business man, governor of Michigan, senator, was born at Coventry, R. I. The son of John Baldwin and Margaret (Williams) Baldwin, daughter of Nehemiah Williams, he was the twelfth child in a family of fifteen. On the maternal side he was descended from Robert Williams, who settled in Roxbury, Mass., in 1638, while the Baldwin family in America originated with Nathaniel Baldwin, who came from Buckinghamshire, England, in 1639, and settled at Milford, Conn. The Rev. Moses Baldwin was one of the early graduates of Princeton, in the class of 1757. His son, a graduate of Dartmouth, was the father of Henry P. Baldwin. Both parents having died before he was twelve years old, the boy was forced to earn his living in a country store. In 1837 he visited Detroit and in 1838 settled there and eventually established a highly successful business as a wholesale dealer in boots and shoes. In 1863 he became president of the Second National Bank (reorganized in 1883 as the Detroit National Bank) and remained president until 1887. On his election to the state Senate in 1861, his business training stood Michigan in good stead in dealing with a treasury emptied by theft and with preparations for sending troops to the Civil War. His health breaking down, Baldwin started for California by way of Panama, but his trip was cut short through the capture of the steamship by Admiral Semmes of the *Alabama.* The prisoners were released at a neutral port. Elected governor of Michigan in 1868, Baldwin gave his attention to securing the resumption of the long dormant geological survey of Michigan, including the copper and iron deposits, and to extending and perfecting the charitable and reformatory institutions of the state. A state public school for dependent children theretofore consigned to county poorhouses; an asylum for insane criminals; an intermediate reformatory for young convicts; and a board of charities and corrections; all, established on his initiative, marked advanced steps in establishing humane relations with and among the classes dependent upon the state. On the death, in 1879, of his political and business associate, Zachariah Chandler, Baldwin was appointed by Gov. Croswell, and afterward elected, to the United States Senate, where he served fifteen months. His monument in Detroit is St. John's Episcopal Church, which exists by reason of his beneficence. He was twice married: in 1835 to Harriet M. Day of Pawtucket, R. I., who died, Jan. 24, 1865; and on Nov. 21, 1866, to Sibyle Lambard of Augusta, Me.

[Chas. Moore, *Hist. of Mich.* (1915), I, 412, 541; Chas. C. Baldwin, *Baldwin Geneal.* (1881); *Compendium of Hist. and Biog. of Detroit and Wayne County* (1909), ed. by C. M. Burton; *Detroit Evening News,* Dec. 31, 1892; H. M. Utley and B. M. Cutcheon, *Mich. as a Province, Terr., and State* (1906), IV, 61; *Rep. Men of Mich.* (1878).]

C. M.

BALDWIN, JOHN (Oct. 13, 1799–Dec. 28, 1884), grindstone manufacturer, university founder, was born at North Branford, Conn., the son of Joseph and Rosanna (Meloy) Baldwin and a descendant of the John Baldwin who came from Buckinghamshire in 1638 and settled in Milford. His father was a blacksmith who had been a captain in the Revolutionary War. His mother, the daughter of an Irish stowaway who had become a prosperous merchant in New Haven, is said to have been well educated for a woman of her day and to have wished to enter Yale. Her son, when a young man, brooding over the exclusion of his mother from that institution, resolved that if ever he attained the means to found a school it should be open to women on the same terms as to men. His parents were poor; he had from an early time to make his own way, and his education was largely self-acquired. His home training was sternly religious and even ascetic. At the age of eighteen he joined the Methodist Church. For a time he attended an academy, where he paid in part for his tuition by chopping wood, building fires and ringing the bell. He picked up enough learning to enable him to teach, his first school being at Fishkill, N. Y., and his next at some place in Maryland. His earnings of several years he invested in a tract of 200 acres of land which he had never seen, at Berea, Ohio. He was married on Jan. 31, 1828, to Mary D. Chappel of New London. The young couple moved to Berea, ending their three weeks' journey to the then mid-western frontier about the first of May. Baldwin erected a grist-mill, a saw-mill, and a carding-mill, all run by water-power, and also the first frame dwelling in the township. A town soon grew up about his settlement. In 1837, with three others, he organized the Lyceum Village and Berea Seminary, which was conducted for five years. About 1842, from a variety of causes, all his enterprises failed and he became bankrupt. Some time afterward he discovered on his land a fragment of sandstone which he used to sharpen a knife. He saw that it was excellent material for grindstones, and he later discovered that a plentiful supply of this rock underlay his land. The incident marked the beginning of the great Berea grindstone industry and the recouping and afterward the immense growth of Baldwin's fortune. He always attributed the discovery to divine response to a special prayer, repeated every day for a month, in which he vowed that if wealth came to him he would devote all but a moderate subsistence for himself and family to God's work.

The ideal of a school open to both sexes and to all races had long possessed him. His first venture toward its realization was made in 1845, when he donated for the purpose thirty acres of land and a brick building at Berea, to the North Ohio Conference of the Methodist Church. The school, known as Berea (sometimes Baldwin) Institute, was opened Apr. 9, 1846. In 1857 it was reorganized as Baldwin University. Baldwin's anti-slavery convictions, which he had held from youth, took him to Kansas in the troublous days of 1858. He carried with him $10,000 in gold. He seems, however, not to have mixed in the border warfare then being waged. Instead he determined upon founding another school. He selected a spot (now Baldwin) in Douglas County, where he erected a university building which he turned over to the local Methodist Conference and which was opened as a school (now Baker University) in September 1859. He returned from Kansas in the same year. Though he was a strong supporter of the Union, no special activities are recorded of his Civil War days. In 1867 he bought 1,700 acres in St. Mary Parish, La., 105 miles west of New Orleans, and established the Baldwin Seminary (now the Baldwin Public School). As local feeling prevented his opening this to both whites and negroes, he accordingly made it a school for whites, but bought more land and established another school to be devoted solely to negroes. The adjoining land was brought to a high state of cultivation and has been for many years a sugar plantation. He and his wife made it their winter home until his death. In 1880 he founded a high school for boys and another for girls in Bangalore, India, and just before his death he donated an additional forty acres to Baldwin (now Baldwin-Wallace) College at Berea. He died at Baldwin, La. His wife, who had been his active partner in all his enterprises, died at Berea, Apr. 17, 1895.

Baldwin was a man of many idiosyncrasies of mind and manner. In business matters he was unmethodical; he kept no books, but from time to time jotted down memoranda on scraps of paper. He was moody; he went about oddly garmented; "He appeared like a humble pilgrim from a far country," writes his biographer, "with a great mission on his mind and heart in the accomplishment of which he must make haste and lose no time."

[A. R. Webber, *Life of John Baldwin, Sr., of Berea* (1925).]

W. J. G.

BALDWIN, JOHN BROWN (Jan. 11, 1820–Sept. 30, 1873), lawyer, politician, was descended from John Baldwin of Bucks, England, one of the earliest settlers in Milford, Conn. Fifth in descent from the emigrant, Briscoe G. Baldwin, judge of the supreme court of appeals of Virginia, married Martha Steele, daughter of Chancellor John Brown of Staunton, Va. John Brown Baldwin, their eldest son, was born at Spring Farm, Staunton. He obtained his early education at the public schools and Staunton Academy and in 1836 entered the University of Virginia, remaining there three years. He then studied law with his father at Staunton, was admitted to the bar in 1841, and commenced practise in his home town. In 1844, he became actively involved in local politics, working and speaking on behalf of the Whig party, and in 1846 he was elected to the House of Delegates. He there championed the "mixed basis" of representation, opposing the preponderant opinion in his district, and consequently was defeated at the ensuing election. In 1859 he was an unsuccessful candidate for the position of judge of the court of appeals. An earnest supporter of the Union, during 1860 he worked indefatigably for peace and was elected to the state convention of 1861 as a Unionist. He voted against the ordinance of secession and was a member of the Union delegation which went to Washington and interviewed President Lincoln, but when secession had been ratified by the people of Virginia he decided that his duty lay with his state. He became inspector-general of the Virginia troops and was appointed colonel of the 52nd Virginia Infantry, August 1861, seeing active service in West Virginia. While at the front he was elected representative from Augusta County to the first Confederate Congress, being reëlected to the second Congress and serving until the conclusion of the war. In October 1865 he was elected to the House of Delegates under the post-war government and was chosen speaker. In this capacity he showed exceptional ability and the rules of procedure which he evolved are still in use, being known as "Baldwin's Rules." He was president of the state conservative convention which met in 1868, but declined to accept the nomination for governor. The same year he was chairman of the Virginia delegation to the National Democratic Convention at New York which nominated Seymour and Blair. Almost his last public service was rendered as a member of the "Committee of Nine" which went to Washington and induced the Federal Government to defer to the wishes of Virginia in regard to the submission of the Underwood constitution to a vote. His health had become seriously impaired and during his last years he took practically no part in public life. He was married on Sept. 20, 1842, to Susan Madison Peyton, daughter of John Howe Peyton, a prominent Staunton lawyer. He was a man of imposing physique and blunt manners, a man of strong opinions, with the ability to clothe them in appropriately forceful language.

[Baldwin's ancestry is traced in L. G. Tyler, *Encyc. of Va. Biog.* (1915), IV, 523–26. An excellent review of his career appeared in J. L. Peyton, *Hist. of Augusta Co., Va.* (1882), p. 379, and shorter notices will be found in J. A. Waddell, *Annals of Augusta Co., Va.* (1902), and in *Am. Ann. Reg.* (1873).]

H. W. H. K.

BALDWIN, JOHN DENISON (Sept. 28, 1809–July 8, 1883), journalist, was descended from a Buckinghamshire county family through the emigrant, John Baldwin, who arrived in Stonington, Conn., in 1664. Five generations later, at North Stonington, John Denison Baldwin was born, eldest son of Daniel and Hannah (Stanton) Baldwin. Daniel Baldwin was a large landowner, who, suffering reverses, removed, when John was seven, to Chenango County, N.Y., at that time a wilderness. Here John toiled on the farm until, after another seven years, the family returned to North Stonington where he was able to attend the village school. At seventeen he was studying at Yale, while supporting himself by public-school teaching. Unable to complete his college course, he began the study of law, then entered Yale Divinity School, from which he graduated in 1834. Ordained in the same year, he became pastor of the Congregational Church at West Woodstock, Conn., until 1837. Later he held pastorates at North Branford and North Killingly. As a preacher he is said to have shown sagacity and public spirit. Eager for further education, he studied French, German, and especially archæology. While at North Branford he published *The Story of Raymond Hill and Other Poems* (1847), which exhibit melancholy beauty and a moral purpose.

From North Killingly he was elected by the Free-Soil party, which he helped to organize in Connecticut, to the legislature, where he sponsored the law establishing the state's first normal school (1850). Reaching the conviction that his services would be more usefully employed in journalism, he abandoned the ministry in 1849 to become owner and editor of the Free-Soil *Charter Oak* at Hartford. Three years later he removed to Boston, becoming editor of the daily and weekly *Commonwealth.* Sumner, Henry Wilson, and Theodore Parker were frequent visitors to his office and became life-long friends. In 1859 he embraced the opportunity to purchase, with his sons, the *Worcester Spy,* which he made one of the leading newspapers of the state. Identifying himself now with the Republican party, he was influential, as a delegate to the convention of 1860, in securing the nomination of Hannibal Hamlin for vice-president. As a party counsellor, Baldwin was always highly valued for his knowledge of men and his political sagacity regarding the effects of measures. He was elected to the Thirty-eighth Congress (1862), and was twice reëlected, becoming a member of committees on expenditures, public buildings, and library. He made notable speeches on state sovereignty and treason, on reconstruction, and in defense of the negro. His efforts—unfortunately premature—for international copyright, won gratitude from authors. Of Baldwin's two works *Prehistoric Nations* (1869) and *Ancient America* (1872), the first sets forth a now wholly discredited theory of the derivation of Western civilization from the Cushites of Arabia, while the second, a popular presentation of American aboriginal peoples, is rated as among the best books of its class then written. Baldwin later published several volumes on his own ancestry, besides contributing to the *Baldwin Genealogy.* His most influential work, however, was through the *Spy.* Here his industry, business capacity, and literary ability had full play and gave the paper wide influence through the state and beyond. Republicans knew it as the "Worcester County Bible," Democrats dubbed it "The Lying Spy." Baldwin's retentive memory afforded wide range of facts, and his direct, forcible, sincere words were always animated by high ideals. A journal's mission, he believed, was the exercise of an influence for right principles and movements; even news was subordinate. Though not a rapid writer, he was a diligent one, making frequent archæological and kindred contributions to magazines. In later years he largely withdrew from active editorial work on the *Spy,* enjoying in retirement his family and books. He was married in 1832 to Lemira Hathaway of Dighton, Mass., by whom he had four children, two daughters who died in early life and two sons, John Stanton and Charles Clinton, who survived him and carried on the *Spy.* He died in Worcester, Mass.

[Sketches of Baldwin's career are given in his own *Record of the Descendants of John Baldwin, of Stonington, Conn.* (1880); *The Baldwin Geneal.* (1881), ed. by C. C. Baldwin; S. E. Staples, *Memorial of John Denison Baldwin* (1884); *Western Reserve Hist. Tract 65* (in vol. II); *Commemorative Biog. Rec. of Tolland and Windham Counties, Conn.* (1903); *Hist. Homes and Institutions and Geneal. and Personal Memoirs of Worcester Co., Mass.* (1907), ed. by E. B. Crane, vol. I; Charles Nutt, *Hist. of Worcester and Its People* (1919), vol. IV; extended obituary in the *Worcester Daily Spy,* July 9, 1883; an unpublished autobiography in the possession of his grandson, Mr. Robert S. Baldwin of Worcester.]

R. S. B.

BALDWIN, JOSEPH (Oct. 31, 1827–Jan. 13, 1899), educator, author, was born in Newcastle, Pa., of Quaker and Scotch-Irish descent, the son of Joseph and Isabel (Cairns) Baldwin. In early childhood he formed the habit of reading books of solid worth. Even when he was plowing upon his father's farm, a useful book was his companion, and from it he would occasionally read a paragraph or two, upon which he would meditate after he resumed his toil. After attending a district school, he was fitted for college at Bartlett Academy in his home town. Desirous of preparing himself for the ministry in the Christian Church, he spent four years in Bethany College, receiving the B.A. degree in 1852. Soon after his graduation he was married to Ella Sophronia Fluhart of Ohio. With the advice and consent of his wife, who believed he was a born teacher, he decided to adopt teaching as his life-work. In the fall of 1852 he removed to Platte City, Mo., and conducted an academy for a year, directing in Savannah, Mo., a boarding school for girls the ensuing three years. In 1856 he assisted in founding the Missouri State Teachers' Association, of which he was chosen vice-president. Returning to Pennsylvania for a year, he was a student in the Millersville Normal School and for a short time was principal of the Lawrence County Normal School. Then, for ten years, he was in Indiana, conducting private normal schools for nine years, and serving in the Union army one year. Being urged by friends in Missouri to return to that state, he founded in 1867 a private normal school in Kirksville. This institution became a state normal in 1870, Baldwin remaining as principal until his resignation eleven years later. For a portion of the summer of 1881 he was employed by the General Agent of the Peabody Fund to deliver lectures to teachers' institutes in Texas. One result of this engagement was his election to the principalship of the Sam Houston Normal Institute, located in Huntsville, Tex. Here he served a decade. In 1891 the regents of the University of Texas selected him as the first professor of pedagogy. He was the author of four professional books, three of which were published in the International Education Series, edited by William T. Harris. The titles, together with the respective dates of publication, are as follows: *The Art of School Management* (1881), *Elementary Psychology and Education* (1887), *Psychology Applied to the Art of Teaching* (1892), and *School Management and School Methods* (1897). In Missouri he is regarded as the founder of her normal school system, and Texas is greatly indebted to him for the growth of her first normal, as well as for the conversion of her people to the doctrine that the professional education of teachers is indispensable.

[Biog. sketch by J. M. Greenwood, *Proc. of the Natl. Educ. Ass.*, pp. 234–35; biog. by E. M. Violette, *Hist. of the First District State Normal of Mo.*, pp. 156–60, details of Baldwin's educ. career in Mo. appearing on other pages; obituaries in the *Austin Statesman* and the *Austin Tribune*, Jan. 14, 1899; personal letters from members of his family to the writer.]

W. S. S.

BALDWIN, JOSEPH GLOVER (January 1815–Sept. 30, 1864), jurist, miscellaneous writer, was born at Friendly Grove Factory, near Winchester, Va. His parents, Joseph Clarke Baldwin and Eliza Baldwin, daughter of Dr. Cornelius Baldwin of Winchester, were distant relatives, descendants (through New England settlers) of a race of gentlemen farmers long prominent in Buckinghamshire, England (*New England Historical and Genealogical Register*, XXVI, 294 ff.; XXXVIII, 160 ff., 289 ff., 372 ff.). The advantage he enjoyed in family and birth, however, was partly counterbalanced by the neglect of his early training. Instead of attending school, he was put to work, serving as clerk in a district court at the age of twelve, and editing a newspaper at seventeen (Bancroft, p. 233); yet by diligent study, later in life, he gained a wide acquaintance with history, an appreciation of both ancient and modern literature and a thorough knowledge of the law. He began early to consider the law as his natural profession, and while still in his teens set about mastering Blackstone's *Commentaries*, under the supervision of his uncle, Briscoe G. Baldwin. Finding Virginia society too orderly for the promise of much profitable litigation, and attracted by opportunities in the newly opened Southwest, in 1836 he packed his belongings in saddlebags, mounted on horseback, and set out for Alabama and Mississippi. In this raw and turbulent region he spent the next eighteen years, some of them years of the "flush times," when on all sides he saw wild speculation, frantic resorting to the law, wholesale political confusion. Settling first at De Kalb, Miss., he made a favorable impression in his first case, the creditable handling of which won him the admiration of an older colleague, Gen. Reuben Davis (*Recollections of Mississippi and Mississippians*, 1889, p. 61). In 1839 he moved to Gainesville, Ala., where there were educated New Englanders and numerous signs of wealth and culture. In the same year he further established himself by marrying Sidney White, daughter of Judge John White of the state. Within a comparatively brief period he became prominent as a lawyer, and entered politics. In 1844 he served as a Whig member of the legislature, but in 1849 was defeated for Congress by the Democratic candidate, Samuel W. Inge. In 1850 he moved to Livingston, and in 1853 to Mobile to become a partner of the noted lawyer, Philip Phillips; but partly out of disappointment over political defeat, and partly in response to the call of a newer country, he now gave up his practise, and in 1854 migrated to California.

For some years before quitting Alabama, Baldwin had followed the custom of writing down, at odd moments, his impressions of the unusual men and scenes around him in court-room, office, tavern. His Virginia training, together with a native shrewdness, enabled him to appreciate the unusualness of the social panorama, while at the same time his own experiences as fortune-seeker led him to sympathize with others who had come hither in quest of wealth or of adventure. As a result, his interpretative volume on backwoods society, *The Flush Times of Alabama and Mississippi* (1853), was entertaining and enjoyed a wide-spread popularity. Encouraged by the reception accorded this, and by praise of an article on Jackson and Clay (in *The Southern Literary Messenger,* September 1853), he published *Party Leaders* (1855), containing sober studies of Jefferson, Hamilton, Jackson, Clay, and Randolph.

His experiences in California were much like those earlier in the Southwest. San Francisco was in the hands of the notorious "Committee of Thirteen," and in the administration of justice all was confusion. As Baldwin himself said, "Law was to be administered almost without a standard" (*Sacramento Union,* May 6, 1863). In helping to establish this standard and so bring order out of chaos, his own labors were noteworthy, and his personal success at the bar was gratifying. On Oct. 2, 1858, he became associate justice of the supreme court, a position he held until Jan. 6, 1862 (*California Blue Book,* 1909, p. 681), when he returned to private practise. His last years, however, were passed under the shadow of misfortune; his six children had all died young, and during the Civil War his aged parents were cooped up in Virginia, beyond his help. At some time in September 1864 he was threatened with lockjaw and underwent an operation, from the effects of which he died.

[The fullest account of Baldwin is by Geo. F. Mellen, in the *Lib. of Southern Lit.,* I (1909), 175–81; Mellen has another account, differing but little from the first, in the *Sewanee Rev.,* II, 171 ff. Still a third commendable sketch is in T. M. Owen's *Hist. of Alabama and Dict. of Alabama Biog.* (1921); III, 80. An excellent appraisal of Baldwin's character, by one of his friends, T. B. Wetmore, appears in *Trans. Alabama Hist. Soc.,* 1897–98, pp. 67–74. Besides those cited in the text, other sources of information are: H. H. Bancroft, *Hist. of Cal.,* VII (1890), 233; *Southern Lit. Messenger,* XXI, 65; W. Brewer, *Alabama: Her Hist., Resources, War Record, and Pub. Men* (1872); Wm. Garrett, *Reminiscences of Pub. Men in Alabama* (1872); *Hist. and Contemp. Rev. of Bench and Bar in Cal.* (1926); autobiographical passages in *The Flush Times;* S. J. Field, *Personal Reminiscences of Early Days in Cal.* (1893).]

J. H. N.

BALDWIN, LOAMMI (Jan. 10, 1744/5–Oct. 20, 1807), civil engineer, soldier, was of the third generation of Baldwins born in Woburn, Mass. The first representative of his family in America was Deacon Henry Baldwin (d. 1698), a native of either Devon or Herts, England, and a founder of Woburn, where he became a freeman in 1652, a selectman in 1681, and a deacon of the church in 1686. He is recorded, also, as a subscriber to the "town orders," drawn at Charlestown, although, on this document, his name is spelled "Bolden," and is not in his handwriting. Deacon Henry's wife was Phœbe, daughter of Ezekiel Richardson. Their son, also Henry (1664–1739), married Abigail, daughter of David Fiske of Lexington, and became the father of James Baldwin (1710–91), a carpenter who, in turn, married Ruth, daughter of Joseph Richardson of Woburn. Their son, Loammi Baldwin, was born at New Bridge, or North Woburn, where he was educated, resided, and died. He was early apprenticed to the trade of cabinet making, and worked at it for several years. That he later became a land surveyor and engineer, and, as recorded, "man of learning," was due to his own ambition and his interest in higher education. With his friend, Benjamin Thompson, famous in afterlife as Count Rumford, he was accustomed to walk several times weekly from Woburn to Cambridge, to attend lectures on mathematics and physics by Prof. John Winthrop of Harvard. On their return home the young men constructed rude apparatus to illustrate the principles expounded.

At the beginning of the Revolution, Baldwin was already established in the practise of civil engineering, but responded to the call to arms by enlisting in the 38th Foot, Col. Samuel Gerrish. Within a few weeks he was commissioned lieutenant-colonel and on Gerrish's retirement succeeded him in command. In the reorganization of the army, the regiment was renamed the 26th, and the number of its companies was increased from eight to ten. Its first year of service was in the vicinity of Boston, but in April 1776 it was transferred to Washington's army and ordered to New York City. There Baldwin commanded the main guard, and was in the retreat to the Delaware River, also in the memorable attack on Trenton, Dec. 25, 1776, when Washington surprised and captured the Hessian commander, Col. Rapp, and 1,000 men. In 1777, because of continued ill health, he was honorably discharged and returned home.

During 1778–79, Baldwin was representative for Woburn in the General Court, being the first to hold the dignity, after the adoption of the state constitution (1779). He was high sheriff of Middlesex County for several years after 1780. The outbreak of Shays's Rebellion, in 1786, found him earnest in his support of the state authority, and one of thirty-seven to protest against Woburn's refusal to help suppress the disorder. He was again a member of the General Court from 1800 to 1804. In the intervals between official engagements, Baldwin probably continued professional practise, although not conspicuously until 1794, when he appeared as a leading projector and chief engineer of the Middlesex Canal. This work, authorized by legislature in 1793, to connect the Charles and Merrimac Rivers, was in process for ten years. During this period Baldwin attained distinction in an entirely new field. While surveying for the canal, near Wilmington, Mass., he encountered a seedling apple-tree, which according to report had been vigorously assaulted by woodpeckers. The fruit, however, proved so excellent that in the following season Baldwin cut scions for grafting on his own trees. The result was the noted "Baldwin" apple, called also "Pecker," "Woodpecker," and "Steele's Red Winter." The hardiness of the trees, the quantity and good average uniformity of their yield, and the firmness of the fruit enabling it to be readily transported and preserved, render this variety "the standard winter apple of Eastern America" (U. P. Hedrick, *Cyclopedia of Hardy Fruits,* 1922, p. 17). One of Baldwin's other interests was the collection of a large and representative library on civil engineering, increased by his sons, Loammi [*q.v.*] and George R. Baldwin, to about 4,000 volumes and presented, some years since, to the town of Woburn. Baldwin was a member of the American Academy of Arts and Sciences, and an honorary graduate of Harvard College (A.M., 1785). He married twice: in 1772 Mary Fowle; and in 1791 Margery Fowle, a cousin of his first wife.

[Chas. C. Baldwin, *Baldwin Geneal., from 1500 to 1881* (1881); Geo. L. Vose, *Sketch of the Life and Work of Loammi Baldwin, Civil Engineer* (1885).]

BALDWIN, LOAMMI (May 16, 1780–June 30, 1838) was a civil engineer, lawyer, and author. His biographer, Prof. George L. Vose, says, "No man so well deserves the name of Father of Civil Engineering in America," and his career shows him to have been the possessor of a well-ordered mind and unusual versatility. Born at North Woburn, Mass., a descendant of Deacon Henry Baldwin, an original settler of that town, he was the third son of Loammi Baldwin [*q.v.*], and his wife, Mary Fowle. After completing his preparatory education in Westford Academy, he proceeded to Harvard College and was duly graduated in 1800. His early predilection for mechanics moved his father to write to his friend, Count Rumford (Benjamin Thompson), inquiring as to the possibility of mastering the trade of instrument-making in two or three years. Discouraged by the reply that the term of apprenticeship was seven years, and that indenture cost several hundred pounds, the son began to read law under the preceptorship of Timothy Bigelow of Groton. There, in 1802, he designed and built the town's first fire-engine, a machine capable of throwing a five-eighths-inch stream to the height of seventy-five feet, which was in continuous use for over eighty years (see files of *Fireman's Standard,* Boston, 1884). The first hose, made in sections, was stitched in a harness shop. After his admission to the bar in 1804, he practised for three years in Cambridge. During this period he produced his pamphlet, *Thoughts on Political Economy* (Cambridge, 1809), a suggestive discussion of population, industry, and currency in the United States, in which he points out the danger of over-immigration impairing "national character," and proposes as a remedy for currency irregularities an extension of the capital of the United States Bank.

In 1807 Baldwin abandoned the law for civil engineering, and in preparation for the duties of this profession visited Europe to inspect public works in England and on the Continent. On his return he opened an office in Charlestown, Mass. In 1814 he began work on building Fort Strong, Noddle's Island, Boston Harbor; in 1819 he succeeded Uriah Cotting as engineer of improvements in Boston city, including the extension of Beacon St. beyond the Common; in the meantime, for three years (1817–20), he was engaged on public works in Virginia. In 1821 he entered on his memorable service as engineer of the Union Canal, one of the outstanding projects of the time, extending seventy-nine miles from Reading to Middletown, Pa., and including a tunnel 739 feet in length on the summit level, three large dams, and an artificial lake of 800 acres. One dam, across a gorge on the Swatara River, exceeded in strength and proportions any previously constructed in America. In spite of the excellence of his plans and the thoroughness of his work, Baldwin became involved in a controversy with the president of the company, Samuel Mifflin, over the proposed width of the canal, resigned, and was succeeded by Canvass White. After completion of the work, the original proportions were found to be correct, and alterations were effected at immense cost.

In 1825, after a year in Europe, Baldwin became associated with the committee on the erection of the Bunker Hill Monument, and was assigned the duty of determining the proportions of the shaft. Taking the committee to the Roxbury Mill-dam, whence Bunker Hill was then visible, he exhibited the effects of various heights by affixing small models to the railing of the sidewalk, so that, at a proper distance away, each would appear to rest upon the hill. Actual proportions were then readily estimated for the accepted model. In the same year, under appointment by the state legislature, he surveyed the route for a proposed canal from Boston Harbor to the Hudson River and the Erie Canal, suggesting a tunnel through the Hoosac Mountain nearly on the line of the present railway tunnel. In 1827 he was again retained to survey for a railroad over the same line, but delegated the work to his brother James. During the next seven years of productive activity he designed and built, simultaneously, large masonry dry docks at the Charlestown (Mass.) and Norfolk (Va.) navy-yards, both completed in 1833. These were works of magnitude at the time, because of the lack of power-driven machinery and the primitive character of many of the appliances used. Pile-drivers were operated by treadmills, a vexation to American spirit, since "reputable workmen" objected to operating them. While on these works Baldwin made surveys for a third naval dry dock in New York Harbor, which was not built until after his death. In 1834 he published an elaborate *Report on the Subject of Introducing Pure Water into the City of Boston,* which listed all neighboring ponds and located all wells in the city as possible sources of supply. He was not destined to complete the work proposed. Another masterly and elaborate work was his *Report on the Brunswick Canal and Railroad, Glynn County, Ga.* (1836), giving details of a proposed inland navigation system, including 900 miles on the Ocmulgee and Oconee Rivers, and opening up an extensive territory. Another project for which he furnished complete plans was a "marine railroad" from Pensacola, Fla. He was a member of the state Executive Committee under Gov. John Davis in 1835, and a presidential elector in 1836.

[Geo. L. Vose, *Sketch of the Life and Works of Loammi Baldwin, Civil Engineer* (1885); *Letters and Documents in Relation to the Dissolution of the Engagement of Loammi Baldwin with the Union Canal Company* (Harrisburg, 1823).]

BALDWIN, MATTHIAS WILLIAM (Nov. 10, 1795–Sept. 7, 1866), manufacturer and philanthropist, was an important figure in the development of the locomotive in America. He was the youngest of five children born to William Baldwin, a carriage maker in Elizabethtown, N. J. The father died when the boy was four years old, the large property which he had accumulated was imprudently lost by his executors, and the family was left to enjoy the doubtful blessings of honorable poverty. Through his mother's efforts, Matthias received a fair schooling, and was then apprenticed to Woolworth Brothers, manufacturing jewelers of Philadelphia, where he eventually became the best workman in their shop. At twenty-four, he set up for himself, but six years later abandoned the jewelry business, deciding that he "could not spend his life making gew-gaws"—especially since the national depression of 1825 made it no longer even financially profitable. He now entered into partnership with one David Mason in a constantly expanding manufacturing business, first producing engravers' and book-makers' tools, next adding hydraulic presses, then copper rolls for printing calico from a steel matrix and forms for new continuous calico color printing; finally in 1827 he constructed a six-horse-power noiseless stationary engine, and the firm began to build engines for sale. At this time, however, Mason became alarmed at these unceasing innovations and withdrew from the business, leaving his more enterprising partner to continue his increasingly successful career alone.

On Apr. 25, 1831, Baldwin exhibited in Peale's Museum a dummy locomotive and two cars, improved from an imported English model and running upon a circular track built for the purpose. He then constructed for the Philadelphia & Germantown Railroad one of the first American locomotives to be actually employed in transportation; he made tools especially designed for the work, and brought his task to completion within six months. The resulting engine, christened "Old Ironsides," was partially of iron and partially of wood, weighed six tons, moved twenty-eight miles an hour, and drew thirty tons. It ran between Philadelphia and Germantown in fair weather—"On rainy days horses will be attached" (advertisement, Poulson's *American Daily Advertiser,* Nov. 26, 1832). During the next ten years, Baldwin constructed many stationary engines and ten more locomotives, introducing continual improvements; after that time he devoted all his energy to locomotives alone. The business prospered, he moved his headquarters from Minor St. to Broad and Hamilton Sts., and successfully weathered several panics, notably that of 1837–40. In 1854 Matthew Baird [*q.v.*] bought an interest in the Baldwin works and became a partner, continuing so until Baldwin's death. A temporary boycott in the South shortly before the war, due to Baldwin's activities on behalf of the colored people, was compensated by the number of engines sold to the Government after hostilities began. Over 1,500 locomotives had been built by his company when Baldwin died in 1866. With remarkable persistence, although suffering great pain, he attended to his business until within a few days of his death.

Baldwin's interests, however, were by no means confined exclusively to business. As early as 1824 he had aided in the foundation of Franklin Institute for the betterment of labor. About 1826 he underwent religious conversion, became a Sunday-school superintendent, and for the next thirty-five years conducted a Bible class (Rev. George Duffield, Jr., *American Presbyterian*, Sept. 27, 1866). In 1827 he married Sarah C. Baldwin (remotely related), by whom he had one son and two daughters. His home life was never extravagant, while he came to devote more than $10,000 a year to charities. In 1835 he founded a school for colored children, and hired the teachers for two years; at about the same time he contributed to the support of the colored evangelist, Pompey Hunt. To the Civil War Christian Commission his company appropriated ten per cent of its yearly income. He donated about $50,000 for seven churches and chapels in Philadelphia. He was for many years county and city prison inspector, attended the state constitutional convention in 1837, and was a member of the legislature in 1854. Fond of music and art, he visited Europe in 1860 to purchase pictures for his beautiful residence in Wissinoming, Frankford, a suburb of Philadelphia. He was a member of the American Philosophical Society, the American Horticultural Society, the Pennsylvania Academy of Fine Arts, and the Music Fund Society. In appearance he was athletic, being an expert archer and enthusiastic horseback rider; the benevolent expression of his face was heightened in later years by his white hair and beard. He practised total abstinence and was reluctant to use the grapes from his country estate even for medicinal wine. His speech was shrewd and concise, his views decided and positive. Doubt was foreign to his nature.

[*Memorial of Matthias W. Baldwin* (1867) with tributes by Rev. Wolcott Calkins, Rev. Daniel S. Miller, Joseph R. Chandler, and Franklin Peale; records of the Franklin Institute, 1832–66, giving detailed accounts of locomotive improvements; address before the Am. Philosophical Soc., Dec. 7, 1866, by Franklin Peale; article by Joseph R. Chandler, *North American U. S. Gazette*, Sept. 14, 1866; brief account of Baldwin's philanthropies, Rev. Llewellyn Pratt, *Am. Presbyterian*, Dec. 22, 1864; press notice of "Old Ironsides," Poulson's *Am. Daily Advertiser*, Nov. 24, 1832; portr., *World's Work*, July 1924.]

F. H. D.
E. S. B.

BALDWIN, ROGER SHERMAN (Jan. 4, 1793–Feb. 19, 1863), lawyer, senator, governor of Connecticut, was the son of Simeon Baldwin [*q.v.*] and Rebecca Sherman, daughter of Roger Sherman [*q.v.*]. He prepared for college first with a teacher in New Canaan, and later at the Hopkins Grammar School in New Haven, under his cousin, Henry Sherman. Even as a boy he was scholarly and had read Virgil to a considerable extent before he was ten. He entered Yale when fourteen years of age and was graduated in 1811. He studied law in New Haven for a time, probably in his father's office, and then entered the Litchfield Law School. When he finished his course Judge Gould wrote to Judge Simeon Baldwin, "I restore your son, somewhat improved, as I hope and believe. At any rate, no student from our office ever passed a better examination." He was admitted to the bar of Connecticut in 1814 and began practise by himself in New Haven. Politically he rose step by step, being successively member of the common council of New Haven, alderman of New Haven, member of the Connecticut Senate, member of the Connecticut General Assembly, and in 1844 and 1845 governor of Connecticut. In 1847 he was appointed by Gov. Bissell to fill the vacancy in the United States Senate caused by the death of Jabez W. Huntington. The following year he was elected by the General Assembly of Connecticut to complete Senator Huntington's unexpired term, which ended in 1851. In 1860 he was one of the electors of the president for the state at large when Lincoln was elected.

In spite of holding high political office, Baldwin's greatest fame was as a lawyer. His name was in every volume of the *Connecticut Reports* for forty-seven years. He was active in the movement for the abolition of slavery, making speeches on the subject at various times. One of his first cases was a writ of *habeas corpus* for the release of a negro seized as a fugitive slave, who had escaped from the service of Henry Clay. Perhaps his most noted case was that of the captives of the *Amistad.* Some negroes captured in Africa were sold to Cubans who started to take them by vessel to Guanaja. They were badly treated and on the second night killed the captain and the cook and attempted to force the Cubans to take them back to Africa. The Cubans managed to bring the boat to the north shore of Long Island, where a government vessel took possession. The negroes were arrested on a charge of murder and piracy. The government vessel libelled the *Amistad,* her cargo and slaves to recover salvage. The Cubans demanded the return of the slaves. A group of persons interested in abolition took up the defense of the slaves. The case went to the United States Supreme Court. Seth P. Staples, Theodore Sedgwick, and John Quincy Adams were associated with Roger Sherman Baldwin for the defense, which was successful. The decision

(United States *vs.* Libellants of the *Amistad,* 1841, 15 *Peters* 518) gave the Africans absolute freedom.

Baldwin was a Whig and helped to organize the Republican party, to which he was loyal but only in so far as he believed in its principles. When he was in the United States Senate he desired reëlection. In the General Assembly was a bare Whig majority, but two or three declined to vote for him because they believed his opinions did not exactly accord with certain party principles as they understood them. A written statement from him would have removed the opposition, but this he refused to give, because he did not wish to be in the position of an office-seeker and believed that members of the Senate should not be bound by pledges of any sort. He was not reëlected. He was eminent in the Senate at a time when Webster, Clay, Benton, Calhoun, and Seward were members. One of his best speeches was on the compromise measures of 1850, especially the Fugitive Slave Law. Another spirited speech was a reply to the Senator from Virginia who compared the Revolutionary history of Connecticut and Virginia in an offensive manner. His last public service was as a delegate from Connecticut to the National Peace Conference at Washington in 1861. He was the state's representative on the Resolutions Committee, which was the most important of the committees. In his later life he resumed practise and had important and lucrative cases. He was frequently in the Federal courts and was often asked for written opinions on difficult questions. He has been considered, by many, the ablest lawyer that Connecticut ever produced. Tall and erect, at sixty-nine he still walked with a firm step. Until the last few years of his life he always wore a full-dress suit of black with the occasional substitution of a blue coat with gilt buttons and buff waistcoat. He was married in 1820 to Emily Perkins, by whom he had six sons and three daughters.

[The most complete accounts of Baldwin's life are found in the article by his son, Simeon Eben Baldwin [*q.v.*], in W. L. Lewis, *Great Am. Lawyers* (1908), III, 493, and in W. S. Dutton, *An Address at the Funeral of Hon. Roger Sherman Baldwin* (1863). Other sketches of his life are in F. B. Dexter, *Yale Biogs. and Annals,* 1805–15, ser. 6 (1912), p. 369; *New Haven Jour.-Courier,* Feb. 21, 1863; Dwight Loomis and J. G. Calhoun, *Judicial and Civil Hist. of Conn.* (1875), p. 252; N. C. Osborn, *Hist. of Conn. in Monographic Form* (1925), III, 230. For other information see *Cat. of the Officers and Grads. of Yale 1701–1924; New Haven Colony Hist. Soc. Papers,* IV; *N. Y. Geneal. and Biog. Rec.,* XLII, 43; B. W. Dwight, *Hist. of the Descendants of John Dwight of Dedham, Mass.* (1874), II, 1108; F. B. Perkins, *Perkins Family of Conn.* (1860), pp. 3, 40, 79, 80; Chas. C. Baldwin, *Baldwin Geneal. from 1500 to 1881* (1881), I, 278, 285; Wm. Prescott, *Prescott Memorial* (1870), pp. 121–23, 172–74; John Quincy Adams, *Memoirs,* ed. by Chas. Francis Adams (1876), X, 287, 358, 360, 395, 401, 429, 430.]

M. E. M.

BALDWIN, SIMEON (Dec. 14, 1761–May 26, 1851), jurist, born at Norwich, Conn., was the youngest of the eight children of Ebenezer Baldwin, farmer and blacksmith, and Bethiah (Barker) Baldwin, grand-daughter of a Massachusetts lawyer. His mother died when he was a few weeks old. His father later married Mrs. Esther (Clark) Backus, to whom Simeon was warmly attached. The boy studied with his brother, Rev. Ebenezer Baldwin, in Danbury, Conn., with Rev. Joseph Huntington of Coventry, Conn., and at "Master Tisdale's School," at Lebanon, Conn. He entered Yale College in 1777, from which he was graduated in 1781, the Revolutionary War having interrupted his education. He was a graduate student at Yale for a year, while teaching in New Haven, and the next year was preceptor of the academy, Albany, N. Y. He then returned to Yale as a tutor for three years. After studying law under Judge Charles Chauncey at New Haven, and under Peter W. Yates at Albany, he was admitted to the bar of New Haven in 1786 and gradually built up an extensive practise. For many years there were always a few men studying law under his direction, and often living in his house. On July 29, 1787 he married Rebecca Sherman, daughter of Roger Sherman [*q.v.*]. They had four children, of whom one was Roger Sherman Baldwin [*q.v.*]. After the death of his wife, Rebecca, Simeon Baldwin married her sister, Mrs. Elizabeth (Sherman) Burr, by whom he had five more children. He was clerk of the United States district and circuit courts for Connecticut from 1789 to 1806, also serving at various times as collector of revenue, city clerk, alderman, and mayor of New Haven. In 1803 he was elected to Congress by the Federalists, where he served well, but not brilliantly, until 1805, when he declined a renomination. He was elected a judge of the superior court of Connecticut in 1806, and became a judge of the supreme court of errors of Connecticut in 1808, and continued in office until 1818, when he was replaced by a Democrat. He held the confidence of the people as a fair-minded judge, having a sound knowledge of law. After his retirement from the bench, his law practise was small, consisting mostly of patent work. His grandson, Simeon Eben Baldwin [*q.v.*], said of him, "In every line of action which he undertook to pursue, he outdistanced mediocrity, but nowhere did he attain the highest rank."

[The chief source of information about Simeon Baldwin is Simeon Eben Baldwin, *The Life and Letters of Simeon Baldwin* (1919). Brief accounts of his life are found in F. B. Dexter, *Yale Biogs. and Annals, 1778–92*, 4th ser. (1907); G. H. Hollister, *Hist. of Conn.* (1855), II, 626; Dwight Loomis and J. G. Calhoun, *Judicial and Civil Hist. of Conn.* (1875); N. G. Osborn, *Hist. of Conn. in Monographic Form* (1925), III, 232. For other information, see C. C. Baldwin, *Baldwin Geneal. from 1500–1881* (1881), I, 273–78; G. S. Hillard, *Memoir, Autobiography and Correspondence of Jeremiah Mason* (1917), pp 15, 17; H. P. Johnston, *Yale in the Am. Revolution* (1888), p. 347; *New Haven Ann. City Reports* (1863), p. 94; Wm. Prescott, *Prescott Memorial* (1870), p. 89.]

M. E. M.

BALDWIN, SIMEON EBEN (Feb. 5, 1840–Jan. 30, 1927), jurist, governor of Connecticut, was the son of Roger Sherman and Emily (Perkins) Baldwin. He married (1865) Susan Winchester of Boston. He was born in New Haven, which continued to be his home throughout his long life; in spite of his participation in activities of national and international importance, he was associated in a peculiar and intimate way with the political, legal, and intellectual life of his native town and state for more than half a century.

As a boy he attended the Hopkins Grammar School in New Haven. Ties of loyalty and interest bound him to this school for the rest of his life. Active in all its alumni work, he was, more specifically, for many years president of its board of trustees; in 1910, on the occasion of the two hundred and fiftieth anniversary of the founding of the school, he delivered a discourse on its history; when shortly before his death it became necessary to house the school in new quarters, he was one of the largest, if not the largest, of the individual donors whose contributions made possible a set of modern buildings for what he was fond of referring to as the fourth oldest institution of learning in the United States.

From the Grammar School he went to Yale, from which he was graduated with the class of 1861. There is scant information as to his four years at college. During that period he kept a diary from which he read extracts on the fifty-fifth reunion of his class, but this diary is not at present available. That the studious traits which he later manifested were not altogether lacking at this time may be inferred from the fact that he was elected a member of Phi Beta Kappa. Such records as we have do not indicate that there was anything unusual about this young student who had among his classroom contemporaries the poet Edward Rowland Sill, and two others who like himself were later to have much to do with the life of the university, his friends Tracy Peck and Franklin Bowditch Dexter.

For the two years following his graduation from college he studied law at Yale, at Harvard, and in his father's office. In 1863 he was admitted to the bar and began the practise of law. His seventeen years of service as an associate justice and chief justice of the supreme court of his state and his four years as governor, coming as they did in the latter part of his life, may have had a tendency to obscure for his later contemporaries the fact that he was at least as much as anything else an eminently successful lawyer. In the practise of the law he won distinction both in his own state and outside, and with it the financial emoluments that usually accompany success at the bar. He was keenly alive to the practical side of the lawyer's work and never lost his zest for it. Till almost the very end of his life he maintained a law office, which he visited daily as long as his health would permit, and kept adding to his law library. As late as 1919 his book *The Young Man and the Law* revealed him still at heart a lawyer. In 1878 he was one of the founders of the American Bar Association of which he later (1890) became the president, and for twelve years (1907–19) he was the director of its bureau of comparative law.

During the middle portion of his life he was actively engaged in teaching law. Here also he showed ability. One who studied law under him and like him became chief justice of the supreme court of errors of Connecticut says that his old pupils regard his work as a teacher "as more distinctive and weightier in influence upon human life than any other portion of his work. Probably in his day not a half dozen teachers of the law in our country could be placed in his class" (*American Bar Association Journal,* February 1927, p. 74). To the same effect may be interpreted the action of the Association of American Law Schools, which in 1902 elected him its president. In 1869 he was appointed to the faculty of the Yale Law School, then in a moribund condition. His active participation in the affairs of that school was to continue for just fifty years, for it was not until 1919 that he retired as professor emeritus. The revival of the law school was largely his work. He increased the size of the faculty, instituted new courses, developed graduate work, and for a long time carried much of the financial responsibility for the school's existence (*Yale Law Journal,* March 1927, p. 680). It was characteristic of him that when shortly before his retirement the method of teaching was changed to the so-called "case system," to which Judge Baldwin, like most of his contemporaries, objected, he never for an instant changed his attitude of loyalty to the school, which some years later was to be most generously remembered in his will.

In addition to his work as lawyer and teacher he took an active part in the public affairs of

New Haven. He served on the Public Parks commission, on the New Haven common council, and on the board of directors of the New Haven Hospital. Deeply interested in religious work, he was president of the New Haven Congregational Club and of the Y. M. C. A. From 1884 until 1896 he was president of the New Haven Colony Historical Association, for which he wrote many papers mostly on subjects of history.

Even more diversified than his activities in local affairs was his participation in those that concerned the state as a whole. Never a politician, and to the end of his days allowing such honors and offices as came to him to come unsought and unfought for, he nevertheless early became identified with the political life of his state. Starting as a Republican, he was nominated for state senator from the fourth district in 1867, but was not elected. In 1884 he was one of the "independents" who refused to support James G. Blaine, and was chosen president of the Republican organization in Connecticut. The greatest of his political honors came to him when he was an old man. Automatically retired from the position of chief justice of the supreme court, Feb. 5, 1910, because he had reached the age limit of seventy years, he that year was nominated for governor on the Democratic ticket and was elected. At the Democratic National Convention in June 1912 he received twenty votes for the presidential nomination. In November of the same year he was elected governor of his state, nominally strongly Republican, for a second term of two years. He was Democratic candidate for United States senator from Connecticut for the term beginning Mar. 4, 1915. Caught in a Republican landslide and defeated, he nevertheless ran ahead of his party ticket by several thousand votes.

It was inevitable that the high regard in which he was held as a lawyer should lead to his being named on various state commissions of reform. In 1872, less than a decade after he began to practise law, the Connecticut legislature elected him one of a commission of five that made the *Revision of 1875, the General Statutes of the State of Connecticut.* In the same year he was a member of a state commission appointed to revise the education laws. Six years later he was named by the governor of Connecticut acting under a resolution of the state legislature one of a commission of five to inquire into the feasibility of simplifying legal procedure. This commission drew up a set of rules and forms which were approved and adopted by the court as the basis of pleading in civil cases. In 1886 a commission was appointed to report on a better system of state taxation. He was a member of that commission and drew the report. Again in 1915–17 he was chairman of a commission established by the State to revise its system of taxation. But his participation in state affairs was not merely political and legal; he was also actively associated with charitable and religious organizations. At one time or another he was a director of the General Hospital Society of Connecticut and a director of the Missionary Society of Connecticut; he served as moderator of the General Conference of Congregational Churches of Connecticut, and he was a delegate of the Congregational Churches to the national council.

His scholarship and his interest in questions of the day led him into affiliations with many of the learned societies. Nor were these affiliations perfunctory only. He regularly attended the society meetings, wrote papers for them, and rose to the highest places in their councils. He was president of the American Social Science Association (1897), International Law Association (1899), American Historical Association (1905), Political Science Association (1910), American Society for the Judicial Settlement of International Disputes (1911), Connecticut Academy of Arts and Sciences, Connecticut Society of the Archæological Institute of America (1914). He was vice-president of the Archæological Institute of America (1898) and of the social and economic science section of the American Association for the Advancement of Science (1903). He was an associate of the Institute of International Law. He was a member also of the National Institute of Arts and Sciences, American Philosophical Society, American Antiquarian Society, and a corresponding member of the Massachusetts Historical Society, Colonial Society of Massachusetts, and L'Institut de Droit Comparé.

His connections with national and international matters touching law and its ramifications were not restricted to membership in learned societies. In 1899 he was appointed by the State Department a delegate from the United States to the Sixth International Prison Congress, which met the next year at Brussels. Again in 1905 he was United States delegate to a similar congress held at Budapest and was made its vice-president. At this congress he presented his report on the question "By what principles and in what manner may convicts be given work in the fields, or other public work in open air?" In 1904, appointed by President Roosevelt one of the delegates to represent the United States, he was elected vice-president of the Universal Congress of Lawyers and Jurists held in connection with the St. Louis Exposition of that year.

His writings cover a number of fields. Among his more pretentious works are: *A Digest of All the Reported Cases . . . of Conn.* (2 vols., 1871, 1882), *Cases on Railroad Law* (1896), *Modern Political Institutions* (1898), *American Railroad Law* (1904), *The American Judiciary* (1905), *The Relations of Education to Citizenship* (1912), *Life and Letters of Simeon Baldwin* (1919), *The Young Man and the Law* (1919). He was a most prolific writer of articles and pamphlets. Some ten years before his death he collected and presented to the Yale Law School nearly a hundred of these in four bound volumes which he entitled in order of numbering: *Law and Law Reform, Studies in History, International and Constitutional Law,* and *Studies in Legal Education and Social Sciences.* While these titles very aptly classify his literary output the volumes themselves do not contain all his miscellaneous publications.

He was not above medium height, somewhat slight of figure and seemingly frail in physique, though this frailty was in appearance only as he was a man of tremendous, tireless energy. Although in no sense athletic, he made some sort of exercise in the open air each day almost a religious duty. At one time this took the form of bicycle rides, though he soon gave these up in favor of walking. His rule was to cover at least four miles a day, rain or shine, and there was no part of the less congested portions of New Haven and its environs over which he had not many times traveled as he walked unhurriedly alone, stooping somewhat, buried in thought, compelled by poor eyesight to keep his gaze fixed upon his path a few feet ahead of him. This methodical exercise he kept up until, in his last years, injuries received as the result of a fall confined him to his home.

His personality, externally at least, was cold, dignified, and grave. Some of those who knew him best say that he was in reality warm-hearted but the characteristics that made an impression on every one were his reserve and his austerity; in general he was an object of respect rather than of affection; he had none of the weaknesses that make men lovable. As deeply religious as any of his Puritan ancestors, he was most broadly tolerant of the beliefs of others. His conception of civic duty was Roman, but he was ever willing to oppose even the State in defending what he regarded as the constitutional and legal rights of the individual. He was frugal to such a degree that on one occasion when traveling as governor with his staff, instead of partaking of a sumptuous dinner in a dining car specially provided for them, he rode in a coach and ate a sandwich which he had brought from home. With this frugality he combined a generosity even more marked. Part of his life was lived in the days of high hats. Such hats, when they became old, were usually donated to the missionaries. To quote from one who for many years served with Judge Baldwin on the committee of a missionary society, "He used to turn in his old high hat at the shop for fifteen cents, but he would give $1,500 to the committee for missions." He was unyielding where a principle was involved; but in matters of mere policy he had the remarkable ability, once he was outvoted, to make the policy of the majority his own even though he had strenuously opposed it. Quiet and unassuming in manner he could be aggressive when he deemed it necessary, as he did in his controversy with Roosevelt when the latter dared to ridicule his ability as a judge. Prompt and unfailing in meeting appointments, unimportant though they might be, he demanded the same consideration from others, even refusing to wait for dinner guests who might be late. Both by nature and training he was conservative, but not reactionary; his mind was open as well as active. If his plea for castration and whipping as generally applicable methods of punishing criminals savors of the archaic (*Yale Law Journal,* June 1899), he was capable also of starting nation-wide comment, as on the radically new ideas embodied in his "The Natural Right to a Natural Death" (*Journal of Social Science,* 1889). In January 1910 he published "The Law of the Airship" (*American Journal of International Law*), and in November "Liability for Accidents in Aerial Navigation" (*Michigan Law Review,* IX, 20). At his suggestion the Connecticut legislature (1911) passed a law regulating the use of flying machines, the first law to be enacted on this subject. France shortly afterward modelled her law on that of Connecticut. In 1911 he had two articles on airship law in foreign journals (*Revue de l'Institut de Droit Comparé* and *Zeitschrift für Völkerrecht und Bundesstaatsrecht*). Notwithstanding his work in many fields, his real interest was always in modern law. He has been called an antiquarian, but his studies in this line did not go beyond colonial history, more particularly Connecticut history. Few men have played a more important part in so many activities that concerned their own community. When he was presented for the degree of LL.D. at the Yale Commencement in

1916 he was called, *inter alia,* "the first citizen of Connecticut." No designation could have fitted him better.

[Good likenesses of Baldwin in his later years in *Am. Bar Ass. Jour.,* Feb. 1927, p. 73 and in *Yale Alumni Weekly,* Feb. 11, 1927, p. 555; for an estimate of the man and his achievements see the articles accompanying these and also *Yale Law Jour.,* Mar. 1927, p. 680; *New Haven Jour.-Courier, Hartford Times, Hartford Courant,* Jan. 31, Feb. 1, 2, 1927; *Who's Who in America,* 1899–1927. There is a complete list of his writings in Yale Univ. Lib.; partial lists, together with considerable biog. material, are given in the records of the class of 1861, Yale College, published by the class secretary, esp. those for the years 1888, 1903, 1907, 1916. His legal bibliography, fairly complete through 1901, was printed in *Yale Law Jour.,* Nov. 1901, pp. 14–16. His opinions and decisions written while he was on the bench will be found in *Conn. Reports,* vols. LXIII–LXXXIII. For the facts in regard to his controversy with Roosevelt, see *Outlook,* vol. XCVII, Jan. 1911, pp. 240–44.] G. E. W.

BALDWIN, THERON (July 21, 1801–Apr. 10, 1870), pioneer Western missionary, educator, the son of Elisha and Clarissa (Judd) Baldwin, was born in Goshen, Conn. He entered college comparatively late, being well over twenty-two when he matriculated as a freshman at Yale. The exacting duties of life on a New England farm and the difficulty of finding a well equipped tutor in the neighborhood, had delayed his preparation but could not quench his ambition. Upon graduation from Yale, he entered the theological department of that institution and became one of the leaders of a small group of students who had banded themselves together as the "Illinois Association," or as it is now known in the history of higher education in the Middle West, the "Yale Band." The members of the Association pledged their lives to the cause of education and religion in the West and, in coöperation with a local group in Illinois led by John M. Ellis, became the founders of Illinois College. Baldwin and his intimate friend, Julian M. Sturtevant, led the way to the West, leaving New England in the fall of 1829, going by way of the Erie Canal, Lake Erie, overland across Ohio, by boat down the Ohio and up the Mississippi to St. Louis and finally overland again to Jacksonville, Ill. While his friend became the first instructor in the pioneer college, Baldwin himself settled as a home-missionary in Vandalia, then the capital of the state. Here he not only preached, but exerted a strong influence upon early movements for the improvement of public education in Illinois and was instrumental in securing from the legislature the charter (1835) under which the three oldest colleges of the state (Illinois, Shurtleff, McKendree) are still operating. In 1831 while on a trip to the East for funds, he married Caroline Wilder of Burlington, Vt. Like other members of the "Yale Band," Baldwin became a trustee of Illinois College, and his advice was frequently sought and followed by Edward Beecher, the first president, and Sturtevant, his successor.

When Benjamin Godfrey, a Cape Cod sailor and merchant of means, who had settled in Illinois, determined to establish a seminary for girls, or "females" as they were usually called in those days, he turned to Baldwin for help. The result was the establishment of Monticello Seminary at Godfrey, Ill., in 1838. Baldwin became the first principal of the school, helping to select its site and determining its course of study and general plan of operation. Before instruction began in the spring of 1838, he made an extensive tour of the East, visiting practically all the "female seminaries" in that section and conferring particularly with Mary Lyon [*q.v.*], who was just then supervising the beginnings of Mount Holyoke at South Hadley.

Baldwin continued as principal of Monticello Seminary until the fall of 1843, when he became the so-called corresponding secretary, or in reality, the executive head of the Society for the Promotion of Collegiate and Theological Education at the West. As secretary of this society, with headquarters in New York City, he performed, perhaps, his most significant service for the cause of higher education in the Middle West. Many of the present strong colleges of that part of the country, such as Western Reserve, Oberlin, Illinois, Wabash, Marietta, Knox, Grinnell, and Beloit, were then in their precarious infancy, and it was due in no small measure to the energy and self-sacrificing work of Baldwin that these institutions survived the financial perils of those years. He remained secretary of the Society until his death, and its twenty-six published annual reports, which he wrote, constitute an interesting record of his labors. He died at his home in Orange, N. J.

[The best biog. sketch is by J. M. Sturtevant, published originally in the *Congreg. Quart.* for April and July, 1875, and reprinted separately the same year. See also the *Autobiography of Julian M. Sturtevant* (1896). For Baldwin's connection with Monticello Seminary, see Theron Baldwin, *Hist. Address,* delivered at Monticello, Ill., June 27, 1855.] C. H. R.

BALDWIN, WILLIAM (Mar. 29, 1779–Aug. 31, 1819), physician, botanist, was born in Newlin, Pa., the son of Thomas Baldwin, a Quaker minister, and Elizabeth (Garretson) Baldwin. At the age of twenty-three he attended one term of medical lectures at the University of Pennsylvania, where he met William Darlington [*q.v.*], with whom he formed what proved to be a lifelong friendship. He later became acquainted with Dr. Moses Marshall, the botanist, and from him acquired an early interest in the biology of plants. He would have liked to continue his botanical studies with Marshall, but his health was poor and he already suspected that he had incipient pulmonary tuberculosis. In 1805, therefore, he enlisted as a ship's surgeon on a merchant ship from Philadelphia to Canton, China. When he returned, he again attended the University of Pennsylvania and was graduated as a doctor of medicine, Apr. 10, 1807. His graduation thesis described his experiences as a physician on the merchant ship (*A Short Practical Narrative of the Diseases which Prevailed among the American Seamen, at Wampoa, in China, in the Year 1805; with some Account of Diseases which Appeared among the Crew of the Ship New Jersey, on the Passage from thence to Philadelphia,* 1807).

He started practise in Wilmington, Del., the next year, and about the same time married Hannah M. Webster. His interest in botany, already stimulated by Marshall, and more especially by Dr. Benjamin Smith Barton, began to show itself. He collected the local flora and started a correspondence with Rev. Henry Muhlenberg of Lancaster, Pa., which lasted until Muhlenberg's death in 1815. In 1811, Baldwin felt that it was necessary to move to a milder climate on account of his health. He therefore went to Georgia, where he made numerous trips on foot into the western part of the state, spending a number of months with the Creek Indians. He was appointed a naval surgeon in 1812 and was stationed at St. Mary's, Ga. Here he spent a number of years doing his duty as a surgeon at the post, but also continually gathering botanical specimens and sending them, or descriptions of them, to his friend, Muhlenberg. Only one observation made at St. Mary's was published by Baldwin (*American Journal of Science,* 1818, I, 355–59). In the winter of 1816–17 he was in East Florida. His descriptions of the flora found there will be found in his letters to his old friend, William Darlington. He went, also, with Rodney, Graham, and Bland, in the frigate *Congress,* to South America in 1817 (H. M. Brackenridge, *Voyage to South America, etc.,* 1819). Although Baldwin's name is rarely mentioned in the official account of the voyage, his botanical experiences are carefully described in his letters.

The next year he returned to Wilmington, where he began to prepare a report on the South American excursion. Only one fragment, however, was published (*Transactions of the American Philosophical Society,* 1825, n. s., II, 167–71). His health by this time was extremely precarious and he therefore requested opportunities for further travel. He was, consequently, chosen to go as botanist on an expedition to the Rocky Mountains commanded by Maj. Stephen H. Long. The expedition left Pittsburgh May 5, 1819, by river steamer. Baldwin was almost too ill to go. He lived on the boat and had botanical specimens, collected by others, brought to him. In spite of the great fatigue caused by any exercise, he proceeded with his work. Maj. Long noted in his journal of July 5 that Baldwin's "devotion to a fascinating pursuit stimulated him to exertions for which the strength of his wasted frame seemed wholly inadequate; and it is not, perhaps, improbable that his efforts may have somewhat hastened the termination of his life" (Edwin James, *Account of an Expedition from Pittsburgh to the Rocky Mountains, etc.,* 1823, I, 83–84). By July 13 the party had reached Franklin, Mo., where Baldwin was taken to the house of Dr. John J. Lowry, in which he died. The best estimate of his character is contained in Darlington's words: "His rare industry and sagacity entitled him to take rank with the most deserving of our pioneers in the field of American botany."

[The chief source of information is the biog. sketch by William Darlington in his *Reliquiæ Baldwinianæ, etc.* (1843). Baldwin's botanical contributions are mostly in books by other writers: Stephen Elliott, *A Sketch of Botany of S. C. and Ga.* (1821); Asa Gray, "A Monograph of the North Am. Species of Rhynchospora," *Annals of the Lyceum of Nat. Hist. of N.Y.,* 1828–36, III, 191–220; John Torrey, "Monograph of North Am. Cyperaceæ," *Ibid.,* III, 239–448. The Baldwin herbarium is now at the Acad. of Natural Sciences, Phila.]

H. R. V.

BALDWIN, WILLIAM HENRY (Feb. 5, 1863–Jan. 3, 1905), railroad executive, was born in Boston, the son of William Henry Baldwin and Mary (Chaffee) Baldwin. The father had given up a successful business to devote himself to the Young Men's Christian Union of Boston, an affiliation which undoubtedly had much to do with his son's interest in social service. The latter received his preparatory training in the Roxbury Latin School, and was graduated from Harvard College with the class of 1885. While not unusual in scholastic achievement, his rank in his senior year was close to distinction, and he won exceptional recognition as a leader in undergraduate activities—as oarsman, editor of the college daily, president of the Dining Association, treasurer of the Coöperative Society, chairman of his class committee, leader of the Glee Club, and a member of five undergraduate clubs. Entering the service of the Union Pacific Railroad in February 1886, he spent a few months in routine training in the accounting and traffic departments in Omaha and was then appointed division freight agent at Butte, Mont. Here was first tested his exceptional ability to get along well with men of all types. In 1888 he returned to Omaha as assistant freight agent but in the following year was transferred to the operating department, first as superintendent of the Leavenworth Division and then as general manager of the Montana Union Railroad. His stay there was short as in 1890 he was promoted to the position of assistant vice-president at Omaha. A year later he left the Union Pacific to become general manager of the Pere Marquette Railroad in Saginaw, Mich., and soon was promoted, being placed virtually in charge of everything except finance, with the title of vice-president. In 1894 he was called to the Southern Railway as vice-president and during the greater part of his two years with that company was in charge of operation and traffic. His last position was as president of the Long Island Railroad from October 1896 until his death.

While engaged in the upbuilding of the Southern Railway system Baldwin became intensely interested in the negro question and then and later took an active part in organized movements to better the condition of colored people. He was a warm supporter of Booker T. Washington and Tuskeegee Institute, of which he was a trustee from 1897. His interest and constructive work in that problem and others of a similar nature, brought about close and sympathetic relations between him and President Roosevelt. Shortly after Baldwin became president of the Long Island he began to be active in advocating measures to combat the major social evils in New York City, notably prostitution, Raines-law hotels, and tenement houses. Largely through his personal efforts the Committee of Fifteen was organized in 1900, with Baldwin as chairman. To its work, he gave unstintingly of his time and strength. The report of the Committee, made after an intensive survey, did much to stimulate public interest and to bring about the passage of remedial laws. Baldwin at that time was in a peculiar position. On the one hand he was the executive head of a public service corporation then undertaking an extension into New York City, and, on the other hand, was the leading spirit of a committee combating an evil strongly intrenched politically. The activities of the committee were distasteful to Tammany Hall, which could seriously embarrass the railroad in its plans for extension. Fearing that his personal activities might injuriously affect the legitimate interests of the company, Baldwin tendered his resignation to President Cassatt of the Pennsylvania Railroad (which had secured control of the Long Island in 1901), but Cassatt refused to accept it. Baldwin was told to go ahead with his committee work and also keep his railroad position.

One criticism of Baldwin was that he was often too impulsive and sometimes too unyielding when compromise would have been wiser. An editorial writer in the *Railroad Gazette,* Jan. 6, 1905, refers to his dogged determination but adds: "He was a man of clear and powerful mind, of quick apprehension, of extraordinary rapidity of decision, and absolutely without fear. He would have been a great soldier." His death on Jan. 3, 1905, followed an illness of several months. He was survived by his wife, whom he had married in 1889, Ruth Standish Bowles, daughter of Samuel Bowles [*q.v.*], and by two children.

[John Graham Brooks, *An Am. Citizen—Life of Wm. Henry Baldwin, Jr.* (1910); editorial references in the files of the *Railroad Gazette; Lives of the Class of 1885,* and an article by a classmate, George R. Nutter, in the *Harvard Grad. Mag.,* March 1905.]

W. J. C.

BALESTIER, CHARLES WOLCOTT (Dec. 13, 1861–Dec. 6, 1891), publisher, author, was born in Rochester, N. Y., the eldest of the four children of Henry Wolcott and Anna (Smith) Balestier. His grandfather, Joseph Nerée Balestier, a journalist and lawyer in New York, who was the son of a French planter in Martinique, married Caroline Starr Wolcott, of Middletown, Conn., grand-daughter of Oliver Wolcott, signer of the Declaration of Independence. His maternal grandfather, Erasmus Peshine Smith, was an educator and international lawyer, and became in 1871 adviser to the Mikado of Japan, for whom he negotiated commercial treaties with the great powers. Balestier's father died when he was nine, and his boyhood was spent in his grandfather's home in Rochester. During Mr. Smith's absence in Japan, the family roved about, and Wolcott attended school in Baltimore, Washington, New York, and Denver, as well as in Brattleboro, Vt., the summer home of the older Balestiers. He was graduated from the Rochester Free Academy in 1880, and entered Cornell in 1881; as a freshman, he was president of his class, and a leader in college pranks. The following year was spent in the South and in Leadville, Colo.; Western life impressed him deeply, and furnished the material for his best literary work. He was in charge of the patent collection of the Astor Library, New York, during most of the year 1884.

When he was seventeen he had begun to send

little tales and essays to the *Atlantic Monthly.* In his academy days he served as reporter on the *Rochester Post-Express.* His first novel, *A Potent Philtre,* a story of Canadian life, appeared in the *New York Tribune* in 1884; his next ventures, the love story *A Fair Device,* and a campaign life of James G. Blaine, were published in the same year, by John W. Lovell. In 1886 appeared his story of Moravian life in Bethlehem, Pa., entitled *A Victorious Defeat.* He had early shown an interest in the drama, and had an amateur company of his own before entering college; in 1884 he dramatized the novel *Gwenn* for Maggie Mitchell, but the play was never produced. The connection with Lovell was to control the rest of Balestier's life. In 1885 he was engaged as editor of *Tid-Bits,* a weekly miscellany; in 1886 this was transformed into *Time,* an illustrated humorous paper, to which Balestier attracted many writers and artists of note. The Lovell business consisted largely in the issue of cheap unauthorized reprints of English books. International copyright was, however, in the air, and in 1888 Balestier was sent to England to secure original manuscripts for the firm. He was an ideal ambassador and soon enlisted the pens of the best writers of England. Arriving unknown, within a few months he had made his rooms in Dean's Yard, Westminster, a literary center unparalleled in the London of that day; he knew everybody. Before long he became managing director of Heinemann & Balestier, a partnership formed with William Heinemann, which launched the "English Library" for publishing English and American books on the continent, in rivalry with the ancient house of Tauchnitz. In 1889 Balestier was joined in London by his mother and sisters. He met Kipling soon after the latter's arrival in England, and shortly added his name to the Lovell list; his sister Caroline became Mrs. Kipling in 1892. In spite of engrossing business, Balestier never ceased to be a writer; his inclination was toward the photographic realism of Howells, his friend and ideal. He took to England the proof-sheets of *Benefits Forgot,* a Colorado novel, and polished away at them constantly; it was published serially in the *Century Magazine* after his death, and later (1894) in book form. He also wrote three short stories, "Captain, My Captain, My Captain!," "A Common Story," and "Reffey," collected in the volume called *The Average Woman* (1892). Association with Kipling was a new spur to his literary ambition, and the two collaborated in *The Naulahka* (1892), to which Balestier contributed the American chapters. After a summer in the Isle of Wight, when he showed alarming signs of overwork, he set out for a business trip to Germany; seized with typhoid, he died on Dec. 6, 1891, in a private hospital in Dresden, where he was buried.

Balestier was a man of slight frame, but of great intensity of mind and body. Edmund Gosse describes him as a carefully dressed young-old man, spare and stooping, with smooth dark hair and whimsically mobile mouth; his complexion was pallid, his dark blue eyes deep set. For sport, for money, he cared nothing; success in the literary business which he had undertaken was his one goal. His short and eager life was a promise rather than an achievement. Though his literary gift was unquestioned, it was as a friend and a business man that he made the deepest impression. His name will be kept alive by Kipling's dedicatory lines "To Wolcott Balestier," prefixed to *Barrack-Room Ballads,* in which he welcomes to his company of "gentlemen unafraid" his brother's spirit: "Sits he with those that praise our God for that they served His world."

[Articles by Edmund Gosse, *Cent. Mag.,* Apr. 1892, pp. 923 ff., and Henry James, *Cosmopolitan,* May 1892, pp. 43 ff. (with portrait); *Annals of Brattleboro, 1681–1895* (Brattleboro, 1922), II, 589 ff., 979 ff.; additional facts supplied by Beatty Balestier, Dummerston, Vt.; by John D. Adams, Memphis, N. Y., and by the N. Y. Pub. Lib. A poem, "Wolcott Balestier," by Richard E. Day, appears in his *Dante: A Sonnet Sequence* (New Haven, 1924).]

F. H. C.

BALL, ALBERT (May 7, 1835–Feb. 7, 1927), engineer, inventor, was born on his father's farm at Boylston, Mass., the youngest child of Manasseh Sawyer and Clarissa (Andrews) Ball. His education began at five years of age when he was sent to the district school and ended in his sixteenth year with one term in high school. He immediately began an apprenticeship in the machinist's trade in Worcester, Mass., serving his time with several organizations, the last being L. W. Pond, a machine-tool manufacturer. Here Ball had charge of making planers, and in 1863 devised his first invention, that of a combined repeating and single-loading rifle. He also perfected a polishing machine capable of polishing flat surfaces. His rifle patent was bought immediately by E. G. Lamson, a manufacturer of Windsor, Vt., who also prevailed upon Ball to go with him. Here he superintended the manufacture of his rifle and also devised and patented the first cartridge-greasing machine which afterward came into general use in American and European arsenals. Ball continued with Lamson until 1868, devoting the last two years privately to devising and patenting a diamond-drill channeling-machine for quarrying stone, especially marble. Upon being reprimanded for this, Ball resigned and went to Claremont, N. H., where he interested James Upham in the manufacture of his new device. As soon as Ball prepared the working drawings, the manufacture was begun in Upham's machine works. The first machine was completed in August 1868, and when tried in the quarries of the Sutherland Falls Marble Company in September proved an immediate success. Five years later Upham and Ball with others organized the Sullivan Machine Company and Ball was made chief mechanical engineer, in which capacity he served for the succeeding fifty years, retiring in 1914. It was during this time that his full power as an inventor was attained, his genius being responsible for the development of many important improvements in mining and quarrying machinery. Among these inventions are diamond core-drills for mineral prospecting; direct-acting steel channeling-machines for quarrying; rock-drills; air-driven coal-picking machines; and continuous cutting-chain coal-mining machines. Ball's diamond core-drill, capable of boring a mile deep, brought him lasting fame, particularly as a result of its initial use in opening up the rich gold-fields of the South African Transvaal. In addition to his mining and quarrying machine inventions, Ball perfected a cloth-measuring machine; wood-pulp grinding machines; corn crackers and crushers; presses for making asphalt paving-blocks; and many other ingenious devices, totaling in the neighborhood of 135 patents. After his retirement he turned his attention to the interesting avocation of violin making and made many instruments of beautiful design and wonderful tone, and developed special machinery for executing unique wood patterns. Ball married Nancy Mary Shaw at Worcester, Mass., on May 7, 1857, to whom were born two sons, one of whom survived him at the time of his death at Claremont at the age of ninety-two.

[Sources of information are *Mine and Quarry,* July 1919; obituary in *Claremont Eagle,* Feb. 8, 1927; W. Kaempffert, *A Popular Hist. of Am. Invention* (1924), II; correspondence with family and with Sullivan Machinery Company.]

C. W. M.

BALL, EPHRAIM (Aug. 12, 1812–Jan. 1, 1872), manufacturer, inventor, was born into a large pioneer family of Lake Township, Stark County, Ohio, and grew up in an atmosphere of frugality to learn at an early age the self-dependence that marked his life. Unable to complete even the meager common education of his day, he was compelled to earn his own living when only fourteen. He chose the trade of carpentry and when in his early manhood he felt equal to the task of supporting a family, he married Lavina Babbs of Stark County. Unfortunately, he had overestimated the earning power of his trade and was forced to find something more remunerative. With his brothers he then engaged to manufacture a thresher. The result being unsatisfactory and the construction of a second equally unprofitable, it was decided to build a foundry for the manufacture of the necessary parts, the unsatisfactory purchase of which had caused the first failures. Ball then (1840) showed his versatility by acting in turn as architect, stone-mason, carpenter, painter, purchasing agent, and financier to the establishment which they built in Greentown, Ohio. Having seen molten iron once in his life, he was the logical choice for foundryman, so with patterns of his own construction he molded and cast the first products. After a year or two of indifferent success he designed his "Blue Plough," which sold so extensively that he was financially able to manufacture the "Hussey Reaper," and later a few threshers. In 1851 Ball's partners sold their interest to C. Aultman and David Fouser, and then George Cook and Lewis Miller were added to the firm which became E. Ball & Company. In the same year Jacob Miller became a partner, the firm name was changed to Ball, Aultman & Company, and the business was moved to Canton, where the manufacture of the "Hussey Reaper" was continued. A series of experiments and tests were made which finally resulted in the first "Ohio Mower." This machine, a two-wheeled mower with flexible finger-bar, was due equally to Ball, Aultman, and Lewis Miller, while the application for the patent revealed a prior machine of similar design by Jonathan Haines of Pekin, Ill. When Aultman and Miller invented and patented several improvements and incorporated them in the "Buckeye Machine," Ball sold his interest and patent rights to the others and in 1859 began the manufacture of the "Ohio Mower" from his own new plant. When this machine was outstripped by the "Buckeye," he began the manufacture of his "New American Harvester," of which he made as many as 10,000 in one year (1865). Later when the great combines were formed Ball stayed out, only to find that he could not compete with them, and finally, in his old age, he was defeated by his own patents which were now owned by others, and knew again the poverty to which he had been born. Ball's principal contribution to the development of agricultural machinery was the "Ohio" or "Ball" mower, described in his patent of Dec. 1, 1857. This was an excellent machine and the first of the two-wheeled flexible or hinged bar mowers to gain a wide reputation as such. Its success and popularity contributed greatly to the change from the single driving-wheel machines to those with double drivers.

[John Danner, *Old Landmarks of Canton and Stark County, Ohio* (1904), p. 902; James L. Bishop, *Hist. of Am. Manufactures from 1608 to 1860* (3rd ed. 1868), pp. 543–44; Robt. L. Ardrey, *Am. Ag. Implements;* U. S. Pat. Recs.]

F. A. T.

BALL, THOMAS (June 3, 1819–Dec. 11, 1911), sculptor, was the son of Thomas Ball and Elizabeth Wyer Hall, who had met at a singing-school—a fact that might be taken as a forecast of the boy's propensities, for his musical ability, often later a means of existence and always a solace to him, declared itself much earlier than his artistic tendencies. His father was a house and sign painter in Charlestown, Mass., when Thomas was born, but the family soon after moved to a house in Leverett Court in Boston. After finishing primary school, Thomas was sent to the Mayhew School for five years. Retiring and shy, he found the school disagreeable and the severity of the masters terrifying. When his father died, he was withdrawn to aid in supporting the fairly numerous family. For many years the father had suffered from lead poisoning and had been able to work but little; so that Thomas's meager help was badly needed. He first worked in a grocery store at one dollar a week, then for a year as errand boy for a tailor. He next secured a place in the New England Museum, an institution somewhat resembling a side-show at a circus. Here he began to copy portraits and to play the violin and sing in the evening for the entertainment of visitors. After three years of such life he apprenticed himself to Abel Bowen, the wood-engraver, still working at the museum in the evenings to support himself. Before his year was up he decided to study painting and began by copying pictures and casts in the studio of the museum superintendent. A position in the choir of St. Paul's Church helped him to earn his expenses. A copy in oils of a print of Lord Byron was successful enough to bring him his first commission—portraits of a family of five, the parents life-size and the children in miniature. He now moved into a small studio of his own, where he executed miniatures at three dollars apiece. After moving into another studio he began painting life-size portraits. A picture of his mother won him a medal at the Exhibition of the Mechanics' Association. He soon moved his studio again, this time to Tremont Row, where he remained for twelve years. Here he painted a number of religious pictures such as the "Holy Family" and "Christ in the Temple." His portrait of Mrs. Richards, editor of the *Transcript,* now in the Boston Museum, also dates from this period. An unfortunate love affair turned him from painting temporarily, and as a diversion he modeled small heads in clay. These were his first attempts at sculpture, which henceforth became his life-work. A small bust of Jenny Lind done from photographs was popular, and he sold many plaster copies of it. Numerous commissions for small portrait-busts now began to pour in. His first life-size bust was of Webster, finished a few days before the statesman's death. He next did a statuette of him, which he sold for five hundred dollars. He had continued his singing and in 1848 sang the title rôle in *Elijah* at its first performance in this country. In one of the church choirs in which he sang he had met Mrs. Wild, in whose home he became a frequent guest, and whose daughter, Ellen Louisa, he married on Oct. 10, 1854. On the following day he and his bride sailed for Italy. They took an apartment and a studio in Florence, which was destined to be Ball's home for the greater part of his creative life. Many American artists were living there at that time, among whom Ball made several friends—Powers, Hart, T. B. Read, and Francis Alexander, whom he had known in Boston. Never having worked from the nude before, he here first began a statue of "Pandora," using a living model. Then came the "Shipwrecked Boy," rather realistic for the fifties. A statuette of Washington Allston and a bust of Napoleon I also date from this time. He likewise did the model for the bas-relief of the "Signing of the Declaration of Independence," copied from Trumbull's painting, for the pedestal of R. S. Greenough's statue of Franklin in front of the City Hall in Boston. This, with the companion piece, the "Signing of the Treaty of Peace in Paris," was his first public commission. The second of these reliefs was made a little later during a stay in Boston, where he occupied a studio on Summer St. Here he modeled also a statuette of Henry Clay and made a bust of Ephraim Peabody for King's Chapel, where it still remains. Other busts of this period were those of President Lord of Dartmouth, Rufus Choate, William H. Prescott, and Henry Ward Beecher.

This stay in Boston was to be marked by the creation of Ball's greatest work, the equestrian statue of Washington in the Public Garden. Some years previously the city had decided to erect a statue of Washington and had designated Crawford as the sculptor, but Crawford had died in 1857. Ball, feeling sure, however, that the project would some time be carried out, modeled a half life-size statue that was so much liked by his brother artists that they attempted, and successfully, to have him commissioned to enlarge it. Funds were raised, in large part by a fair held in the Music Hall, and Ball set to work. A large studio had been constructed for him on the grounds of Chickering & Sons' factory on Tremont St. Here, for more than three years, he labored on the colossal model. He worked alone, for, though he had finally consented to take as a pupil Martin Milmore, who later made the Soldiers' Monument on Boston Common, he would allow no one but himself to put a hand to the statue. He made the model in plaster, for the temperature of the studio often dropped below the freezing point, which would have ruined a work in clay. In 1864 the model was completed. As the foundries were entirely engaged at that time in turning out arms, the plaster statue was cut into sections and stored. It was finally cast in 1869 by the Ames Manufacturing Company at Chicopee and was erected the same year on a pedestal of Quincy granite designed by Hammat Billings, the architect. It has the dignity and restraint, tempered with a certain amount of realism rather advanced for the period, that mark Ball's best work.

The year after the completion of the model, Ball, with his wife and seven-year-old daughter, returned to Florence after having spent nine years in Boston. On his arrival he took an apartment in the Casa Guidi, where for many years the Brownings had resided. He almost immediately set to work on a small model of Lincoln and a kneeling slave, which he called "Emancipation." The group was suggested by the news of Lincoln's assassination, which Ball received in Munich shortly before reaching Italy. For the figure of the slave he himself posed in front of a mirror at the same time that he continued modeling. About this time he began the model of Edwin Forrest in the rôle of Coriolanus for which he had received an order while in America. The model was finished in 1867, the same year that he began "Eve Stepping into Life." Shortly before this he made his first visit to Rome, where he had long desired to go. Here he met Liszt, who promised to sit for his portrait when he went to Florence, but Ball on his return started to make a bust from memory. With the aid of photographs it was finished and put into marble by the time Liszt finally arrived. From this period also dates a small head, "La Petite Pensée," which became very popular. With a considerable number of other works it forms a group contrasting with his monumental works—a group instinct with Victorian sweetness and tenderness. Florence had now become Ball's permanent home, and at Powers's suggestion he bought land adjoining the latter's at Poggio Imperiale and started building a villa. While waiting for it to be completed he made a trip to Boston in 1868, hoping to be present at the unveiling of his "Washington," but that event occurred after his return to Florence. On this visit he entered a competition for the statue of Gov. John A. Andrew and was awarded the commission. On his return to Florence and after his installation in his villa, he began putting this statue into marble. Like most sculptors of his day, he left that process largely to assistants, so that he was soon free to begin the model for the Chickering monument, which represents the Angel of Death lifting a veil from the eyes of Faith. When completed (1872) it was erected in Mount Auburn Cemetery, Cambridge. To the same period belong others of his sentimental group, "Christmas Morning," "St. Valentine's Day," "Love's Memories." Perhaps the best of his imaginative works is the "St. John the Evangelist" (1875), which he made for Aaron D. Williams of Boston, but which now serves as the Oliver Ditson monument in Forest Hills Cemetery. This same year the Lincoln group, modeled ten years before, was erected in Washington, and two years later a replica was given to Boston.

In 1876 Ball visited the Centennial Exposition in Philadelphia, afterward going to Boston, where he received the commission for a statue of Sumner. He also entered the competition for the Washington Monument to be erected in Philadelphia, but the commission was awarded to Siemering, a German sculptor. This same year Ball's colossal statue of Webster, an enlargement of the statuette of many years before, was unveiled in Central Park, New York. A week before this event he returned to Florence, where he received the order for a statue of Josiah Quincy for Boston. This award was made through the influence of the Quincy family, who preferred his model to Story's. The Sumner statue was sent to Barbedienne in Paris to be cast, but the Quincy was sent to Müller of Munich, whom Ball usually employed to cast his bronze figures. The former statue was erected in 1878 in the Public Garden and the latter a year later in front of the City Hall. Ball during these years had had as a pupil Daniel Chester French and later a young Virginian, William Couper. The latter married Ball's daughter Eliza in 1879. After a visit to America in this same year Ball modeled another of his idealized subjects, a group of Christ and a child, which he enlarged the next year. Another of his numerous visits to America was made in 1883, when he modeled busts of Marshall Jewell and

P. T. Barnum. In 1885 he received a commission for another Webster statue, this time for Concord, N. H. It was set up near the State House the following year. He next modeled a David, which was later put into marble, and a colossal statue of Barnum, which was cast in bronze and erected in Bridgeport after Barnum's death in 1891. It had received a first class medal at the Munich International Exhibition in 1888. During another visit to America in 1889 Ball received from E. F. Searles a commission for his statue of Washington begun in the Philadelphia competition. The statue was finished in 1893 and, after being exhibited at the Columbian Exposition, was put up on the Searles estate at Methuen, Mass. The figure of Washington is dignified and majestic, and the four figures around the pedestal are creditable if not inspired work. In 1891 had appeared Ball's autobiography, *My Threescore Years and Ten,* which well shows his gentle and affable nature, his modesty and uprightness. The same could be read in his mild countenance framed in a wealth of hair and beard. In 1897 he finally returned to America, taking up his residence at Montclair, N. J., with his daughter and son-in-law. In his old age he turned again to painting and in 1907 finished a picture of "Mary and Martha," begun some half-century earlier. His death, hastened by injuries received in a fall, occurred after he had passed his ninety-second birthday.

[W. O. Partridge, *New Eng. Mag.,* May 1895; obituary in *Montclair Times,* Dec. 16, 1911; *Who's Who in America,* 1910–11. The main source, however, is Ball's autobiography.]

E. G. N.

BALLARD, BLAND WILLIAMS (Oct. 16, 1759–Sept. 5, 1853), pioneer, Indian fighter, was born near Fredericksburg, Va., the son of Bland and —— (Williams) Ballard, and grandson of the Bland Ballard who died in Spottsylvania County, Va., in 1791. The birthyear given above (instead of 1761, the year generally accepted) is authenticated by a manuscript (8 J, 150) in the Draper collection at Madison, Wis. Early in 1779 young Ballard and his father went to Boonesborough, Ky. One or both of them took part in Col. Bowman's unsuccessful campaign against the Indians at Chillicothe. They returned to Virginia in the fall, but in the following spring young Ballard was again in Kentucky, and it is probable that his father and the rest of the family arrived at the same time. The son's early life was one of toil and hardship and an eager quest for danger. At a time, says his eulogist, Col. Humphrey Marshall, when most Kentuckians were primarily concerned in getting land, young Ballard had devoted himself to the cause of protecting the settlements from Indians. In 1781 he was with Gen. George Rogers Clark in the indecisive attack on the Pickaway towns in Ohio, where he was wounded. In the same year, in the disastrous battle on Long Run (in the present county of Jefferson), Ky., he escaped by killing an Indian and fleeing on his victim's horse. On the following day he was one of a party that renewed the fight and was again a survivor of a defeat. In 1782 he was once more with Clark in an attack on the Pickaway towns, which this time was successful. It was probably in the following winter that he married Elizabeth Williamson, a woman of great courage and the survivor of an Indian massacre at Lynn Station in September 1781, in which her father and one of her brothers were killed. In 1786 he served as a spy with Clark in the expedition against the Indians on the Wabash.

The Ballards with others settled near the present Shelbyville in 1787, and here on Mar. 31 of the following year they were attacked by Indians. The father, stepmother and several children were killed, but Ballard by a heroic defense, in which he was effectively aided by his wife, succeeded in withdrawing the survivors. The next five years seem to have been uneventful, but in 1793 he joined Gen. Wayne, taking part in the campaign which virtually ended with the victory at Fallen Timbers, Aug. 20, 1794. From 1795 until 1811 Ballard lived on his Shelby County farm, during this time serving five terms in the Kentucky legislature. He fought at Tippecanoe, and in the following year, on the declaration of war against England, he organized and was made captain of a company in Col. John Allen's regiment, subsequently attaining the rank of major. In the defeat at Raisin River (Jan. 22, 1813) he was twice wounded and made a prisoner, but escaped the Indian massacre that followed. On his release he returned to his farm. His first wife died Jan. 12, 1827. He then married Diana Matthews, who died Aug. 17, 1835; on Oct. 28, 1841, he married Mrs. Elizabeth Garrett, who survived him. He died at his home, leaving many descendants in Shelby and Henry counties.

Ballard had little education. He was a man of action, and he possessed to an exceptional degree the qualities needful on the frontier—alertness, courage, fortitude, and patient endurance. The regard in which he and his first wife were held by their fellow citizens is attested by the act of the Kentucky legislature in the winter of 1853–54 in providing for the reinterment of their remains in the State Cemetery at Frankfort. On Nov. 8, 1854, the bodies were reburied with imposing ceremonies.

[Eulogy by Col. Humphrey Marshall in the collection, *Obituary Addresses,* etc. (Frankfort, Ky., 1855); MS. notes compiled by R. C. Ballard Thruston, of Louisville, from many scattered references to Ballard.]

W. J. G.

BALLINGER, RICHARD ACHILLES (July 9, 1858–June 6, 1922), lawyer, secretary of the interior, and center of the insurgent fight for the maintenance of the "Roosevelt Policies," was born at Boonesboro, Ia. He came of American stock, his father, Richard H. Ballinger of Kentucky, having read law in the office of Abraham Lincoln and commanded a regiment of colored infantry in the Civil War; and his forebears having served in both the War of 1812 and the American Revolution. His mother was Mary E. Norton of New York. He was graduated at Williams College in 1884, then went into a law office, and was admitted to the bar in 1886. The legal career of Ballinger took him to the Northwest at the moment when the new State of Washington (admitted in 1890) was in process of formation. Living first at Port Townsend, he soon became identified with Seattle. He was superior judge in Jefferson County in 1894, and reform mayor of Seattle in 1904–06. He became an expert in mining law, wrote *A Treatise on the Property Rights of Husband and Wife under the Community or Ganancial System* (1895), codified the statutes of his young state, and carried on a practise which brought him into close contact with every aspect of land law respecting the public domain. In March 1907 he was appointed commissioner of the General Land Office by Garfield, who at the same time became secretary of the interior in the cabinet of President Roosevelt. Ballinger served at this post for only a year, returning in 1908 to his law business; whence he was summoned by President Taft to become secretary of the interior in 1909. There had been many hopes and much talk of continuing J. R. Garfield at this post, since it was here that the battle for conservation was to be fought. The interests of the United States in the lands, minerals, timber, and water-rights still remaining on the public domain, were at stake; and President Roosevelt had formulated a program of conservation, depending at every point upon the advice of Garfield in the Interior Department and Gifford Pinchot, chief of the Bureau of Forestry in the Department of Agriculture. They had interpreted every obscure point of law in the interest of the new policy. The task, difficult at best, was made heavier by the unscientific organization of the government, whereby the Land Office was in one department and the Forestry Service in another; while the Bureau of Mines was not even formed until 1910. It was further complicated because of real doubts as to the legal authority of the United States, in the absence of proper conservation laws.

The failure of President Taft to retain Garfield was irritating to many enthusiastic friends of conservation, who took sides readily when Louis R. Glavis, a field man of the Land Office, complained over the head of his chief to the President, that Secretary Ballinger was impeding the examinations which were likely to show that a group of coal-land claims in Alaska, filed by one Clarence Cunningham and his associates, were fraudulent. The protest of Glavis was dated a week after President Taft had approved the Payne-Aldrich Tariff, incurring thereby the criticism of the insurgent element in the Republican party. It followed also a conference which Glavis had held with Pinchot at a western conservation meeting. On Sept. 13, 1909, President Taft authorized Secretary Ballinger to dismiss Glavis from the service, on the ground of insubordination; and then and later he upheld the character and disinterestedness of Ballinger's service. Glavis, meanwhile, received the encouragement of many conservationists and insurgents, and retorted with "The Whitewashing of Ballinger," in *Collier's Weekly* (Nov. 13, 1909), a crusading journal which had already declared editorially "Ballinger should go" (Aug. 28, 1909). With this beginning the controversy became a public trial of the conservation policies of the Taft administration.

The fight was carried into Congress at its next session, where a joint committee was appointed to investigate the departments under fire. This committee, presided over by Senator Knute Nelson of Minnesota, took much testimony in the spring of 1910, with Glavis represented by Louis D. Brandeis, and Pinchot by George Wharton Pepper. It was charged by the complainants, among other things, that Ballinger was out of sympathy with conservation, and that he interpreted the law in the interest of the claimant wherever possible; it was even charged by the less restrained of the conservationists that he was corruptly guilty of having served the Cunningham claimants in the interval between his terms as commissioner of the General Land Office and as secretary of the interior, and that he would have advanced and allowed the Cunningham claims had it not been for the patriotic intervention of Glavis. The majority of the committee, in its final *Report* (vol. I, p. 90), declared that "Neither any fact proved nor all the facts put together exhibit Mr. Ballinger as being anything but a competent and honorable gentleman, honestly and faithfully performing the duties of his office with a single eye to the public interest." The decision of the committee was unsatisfactory to the critics, who were now set upon preventing the renomination of President Taft in 1912. The controversy continued, bringing the policies of the administration under general attack. The usefulness of Ballinger in the cabinet was destroyed by the clash of opinion, and he resigned in March 1911, being succeeded by Walter L. Fisher, of Chicago.

He returned to his law business in Seattle, where he died June 6, 1922. He was married in 1886 to Julia A. Bradley and was survived by two sons.

[There is no extended sketch of his life, but all the evil that was alleged against him may be traced through *Collier's Weekly,* the *Outlook,* and the newspapers. The Glavis documents are in *Sen. Doc. 248,* 61 Cong., 3 Sess.; while the Nelson Committee testimony and report comprise thirteen volumes, *Sen. Rep. 719,* 61 Cong., 3 Sess.]

F. L. P—n.

BALLOU, ADIN (Apr. 23, 1803–Aug. 5, 1890), Universalist clergyman, reformer, founder of the Hopedale Community, was descended in the sixth generation from Maturin Ballou, American pioneer of an Anglo-Norman family, who shared with Roger Williams in the proprietorship of Providence Plantations in 1646. He was born at Cumberland, R. I., the son of Ariel and Edilda (Tower) Ballou. Seventh of eight children, the boy received an elementary education in Cumberland and near-by schools and a farmer boy's training in hard work. The first excited an irrepressible eagerness for knowledge, the second developed personal responsibility, faithfulness, and self-reliance. Ariel Ballou disapproved his son's earnest desire to enter Brown University, and at seventeen the boy's schooling ceased; but he remained a life-long student. His religious nature asserted itself when he was twelve, and he joined a church of the "Christian Connection" in Cumberland; when eighteen, following what he believed a supernatural call to the ministry, he announced at a religious service his intention to preach at the village church the following Sunday; this he did so acceptably that it led to similar efforts elsewhere, and to his acceptance into fellowship in September 1821. Soon afterward he published an attack on certain Universalist tenets, but further study brought about a change of views and his expulsion from the Christian Church. The Universalists received him gladly, and during 1823 he preached successively in Mendon, Bellingham, Medway, and Boston. In 1824 he was over the Universalist society in Milford, in 1827 over the Prince St. association in New York, and in 1828 back in Milford again. This was a period when the Universalists, although agreed on the central tenet of universal salvation, were much divided on the question whether there is no further punishment or punishment of a limited duration. Ballou, believing strongly that the interests of morality were imperiled by the denial of all future punishment—in this opposing his more celebrated kinsman, Hosea Ballou, editor of the *Universalist Magazine*—and feeling that his coreligionists tended to neglect the practical moral problems of this life, decided to withdraw from the denomination. In 1831 he joined with seven other clergymen to form the "Massachusetts Association of Universal Restorationists," whose doctrines he expounded in the *Independent Messenger* (1831–39). The organization never recruited more than thirty-one ministers and was dissolved in 1841, but Ballou's writings exercised considerable influence on both Universalist and Unitarian thought.

Meanwhile he began to seek a practical outlet for his increasingly radical social views. The outstanding evils of his age, he had come to believe, were war, slavery, and intemperance. The Hopedale Community was his definite protest. This was the first of the Utopian enterprises, such as Brook Farm, Fruitlands, and the Oneida Community, that marked the decade 1840–50. Independently of other movements, Ballou and thirty-one others banded themselves, January 1841, in a joint-stock organization whose object was "to establish an order of human society based on the sublime ideas of the Fatherhood of God and the brotherhood of man, as taught and illustrated in the Gospel of Jesus Christ" (*Hopedale Community,* p. 1). The members bound themselves to abstain from murder, hatred, unchastity, use of liquor as a beverage, and all participation in military or civic activities, including the vote. Each pledged himself "through divine assistance, to promote the holiness and happiness of all mankind."

Hopedale Community, so called from its founders' sanguine expectations, began with a capital of $4,000; 250 acres in the town of Milford were purchased (afterward increased to about 600). Despite some untoward circumstances, the Community prospered for a number of years. All sorts of "queer" persons flocked into it; many withdrew when they found their will could not be law; a few were expelled. With Ballou as president the saner minds held the organization within bounds. Farm work, road-making, building, and various industrial enterprises were carried on. *The Practical Christian,* edited by Ballou, was printed. Religious services were held regularly in the community chapel. A school and a considerable library were established.

In 1852 Ebenezer D. Draper became the second Community president, Ballou desiring to devote himself to the organization of a "Practical Christian Republic" with constituent communities, and to elucidating his principles in *Practical Christian Socialism* (1854). In 1856 Hopedale's membership had reached 110 and the Community joint-stock property $40,000; but discovery that liabilities exceeded resources caused Ebenezer and George Draper, owning three-fourths of the Community stock, to withdraw this from the enterprise. They invested it instead in the Hopedale Manufacturing Company, attained wealth, and gradually transformed the town from a community of idealists into a modern manfacturing center. The Community lingered on as a moral association until 1868, when it was merged with the Hopedale Parish (Unitarian), of which Ballou remained pastor until 1880. Ballou believed the basic cause of Hopedale Community's failure to be moral rather than financial—a lack of whole-souled consecration. The germ of failure lay also in its material ambitions. Individual capacity for industry, after being encouraged, shrank from subjection to community supervision. During the Civil War Ballou maintained his courageous stand of non-resistance. He spent his later years in pastoral and voluminous literary labors; a powerful and persuasive speaker, his writings, though vigorous, were heavy.

Ballou married, 1822, Abigail Sayles of Smithfield, R. I., who died at Milford, 1829; in 1830 he married Lucy Hunt of Milford. His daughter Abigail and her husband, W. S. Heywood, were active in Hopedale Community affairs, as was also his promising son, Adin Augustus, until his untimely death at the age of nineteen. Physically, Ballou is reported to have been a man of commanding bodily presence, with large, well-balanced head and radiant face. A statue of him was erected at Hopedale in 1900. Too independent to be a follower, by his aggressive personality, boldness of thought, and confidence in his own mission, he was destined to be a leader of separatist movements.

The more important of his works are: *Memoir of Adin Augustus Ballou* (1853); *Practical Christian Socialism* (1854); *Primitive Christianity and its Corruptions* (1870); *History of the Town of Milford* (1882); *An Elaborate History and Genealogy of the Ballous in America* (1888); *Autobiography* (1896) and *History of the Hopedale Community* (1897), both edited by his son-in-law, W. S. Heywood.

[G. L. Cary, "Adin Ballou and the Hopedale Community," *New World*, Dec. 1898; L. G. Wilson, "Hopedale and Its Founder," *New Eng. Mag.*, Apr. 1891; obituaries in the *Milford* (Mass.) *Jour.* Aug. 5, 1890, and in the *Boston Jour.* and *Boston Herald*, Aug. 6, 1890; *In Memoriam, Rev. Adin Ballou*, a sermon by C. A. Staples, Aug. 24, 1890 (Boston, 1890); Ballou's correspondence with Tolstoi, *Arena*, Dec. 1890.]

R. S. B.

BALLOU, HOSEA (Apr. 30, 1771–June 7, 1852), Universalist clergyman, belonged to the fourth generation of descendants from Maturin Ballou, probably of Anglo-Norman origin, who came from England to Rhode Island in 1638. The father of Hosea was another Maturin Ballou who had been a Baptist preacher in Rhode Island, but, objecting to a paid ministry, had lived by teaching school and making spinning-wheels. In 1767 he acquired a farm and founded a church in Richmond, N. H., a neighborhood lately settled by Baptists. Hosea, the eleventh child, when two years old lost his mother, Lydia Harris Ballou, of Rhode Island Quaker family. Reared in frontier poverty intensified by the Revolutionary War, a barefoot boy, even in winter snows, he became a tall and powerful man, erect and shapely, of friendly engaging countenance with luminous eyes; and though, far from any school, he learned to write on birch bark with a charred stick and for books had only a Bible and an almanac, he became an accomplished reasoner, master of a diction which was simple, lucid, fluent, impressive, with a singular gift for coining illustrations and parables. Destined to emancipate the Universalist movement from its Calvinistic origins, and to give it a positive theological principle, his views were formed largely in independence of other men or books.

Home instruction made him early familiar with Calvinistic doctrine, and at the age of eighteen, in a season of religious awakening, he joined his father's church (January 1789). Certain neighbors and a distant kinsman, converts to the view of universal salvation as taught by Caleb Rich, a farmer-preacher of Warwick, brought the youth to the necessity of choosing between universal salvation or partiality in the divine favor. This drove him to close study of the Bible and the discovery of texts that implied universal and impartial grace. In the summer of 1789, working on a farm in Hartford, N. Y., he had a discussion with the local Baptist minister which confirmed his tendency to Universalist reading of Scripture. For the next two years he worked on the farm of his older brother David, who had now begun preaching the new doctrine, and in this period also he had some formal education in a meager private school opened in Richmond,

N. H., and one term in an academy in Chesterfield, N. H. By virtue of sleepless toil, this procured for him a certificate of competency as a school-teacher. In 1791 he was excommunicated, solely on doctrinal grounds, from the Baptist Church, and came in contact for the first time with John Murray [*q.v.*] at the New England General Convention of Universalists in Oxford, Mass. (September), and made his first crude and halting efforts to preach. The reading of some deistical writings made him aware of difficulties in orthodox tradition and his wholly independent examination of Scripture led him now to reject the doctrines of the Trinity, total depravity, and the Atonement.

Rapidly developing effectiveness in public speech, he supported himself by a roving teaching career in short-session schools in more than a dozen towns and villages of Rhode Island and Massachusetts, preaching constantly in schoolhouses, homes or barns, and creating new circles of adherents to Universalist doctrine. His great success inspired Elhanan Winchester, when presiding over the New England Convention of Universalists at Oxford, Mass., in September 1794, to summon the young evangelist to the pulpit for an unsolicited ordination. Laying the pulpit Bible to his bosom, he said, "Brother Ballou, I press to your heart the written Jehovah." Married to Ruth Washburn of Williamsburg, Sept. 11, 1796, Ballou established a home in Dana, Mass., as the center of extensive circuit preaching (1796–1803). His itinerant discourses urged that neither Scripture nor reason could support the doctrines of the Trinity, Christ's full deity, human depravity, or eternal punishment. Acting as a substitute for John Murray in the First Universalist Church in Boston (autumn 1797) Ballou's divergence from Murray's views on the first three of the above points created some disturbance, although certain sympathizers invited him to form a second church in Boston. This was declined from an unwillingness to weaken Murray's society. Another six-year period of circuit riding, 1803–09, had for its center Barnard, Vt., with missionary journeys in 1806 and 1807 extending to western New York where Ballou founded a Western Association of Universalists. The famous Universalist confession of faith adopted at Winchester, N. H., in 1803, was of such breadth and simplicity that Ballou's preaching was exempt from dispute. He speedily became an influential author by his *Notes on the Parables* (1804), and by his *Treatise on the Atonement* (1805), which became normative thought for the whole Universalist movement. As a facile writer of verse, without poetic eminence, he contributed 198 hymns to a *Hymn Book* (1808).

In 1809 he began a settled pastorate in Portsmouth, N. H., a period marked by pamphlet controversy with many opponents, the formation of a Ministerial Association in Gloucester, January 1811, and the founding (1811) of the *Gospel Visitant,* the first Universalist periodical, a quarterly serving as organ of the Association. A vigorous sermon (Aug. 20, 1812) justifying the war with Great Britain, led to withdrawals from his church, Portsmouth being intensely Federalist, and he was obliged to add occupation with a private school with his grandnephew, Hosea Ballou, second [*q.v.*], as assistant. In the summer of 1815 he accepted a call to Salem, where again he was involved in pamphlet controversy. But his period of greatest eminence was in Boston in 1818–52. The Calvinist preaching of Murray came to an end in 1815, and his successor, Paul Dean, had modified Murray's doctrine; in the other societies in Massachusetts, Ballou's thought was regnant; hence he now felt justified in accepting the call to a new second church built on School St. Here he preached three times every Sunday without manuscript to crowded audiences, the schism of Unitarian and orthodox Congregationalism having intensified social interest in doctrinal discussion. Ballou was also in constant service at dedications of churches, ordinations, and installations in a rapidly growing denomination, and, in the absence of a theological school, he acted as a teacher of ministerial students. He was studious in repairing the deficiences of his culture by wide reading of history and gained a practical knowledge of Latin, Greek, and Hebrew. He edited a weekly publication, the *Universalist Magazine,* 1819–28, and from July 1830 a more learned bi-monthly, the *Universalist Expositor,* which later under Hosea Ballou, second, became the *Universalist Quarterly.* In these publications he made profuse exposition of Universalist argument. In the winter of 1821–22 he made a protracted visit to Philadelphia where some of his discourses stenographically reported were published as *Eleven Sermons* (1822). Other sermons preached in Philadelphia in November 1834 appeared as *Nine Sermons* (1835). Other book publications were *Select Sermons* (1832), a series of *Lecture Sermons* (1832), and *Examination of the Doctrine of a Future Retribution* (1834).

Ballou's work of most lasting interest is his early *Treatise on the Atonement.* Like all his productions it is controversial in form but calm, dignified, and fair, and it lifts the Universalist idea to the height of positive affirmation, being the first effort to develop a theology from the sole premise of God's universal, impartial, everlasting love. The logic of this determined his interpretation of Bible passages, hence much of his exegesis has been rendered obsolete by modern historical criticism, but nevertheless his exposition of many texts remains unaffected. Its terse style, effortless simplicity, argumentative wit, and concrete illustrations gave the book great influence. Reason and Scripture led Ballou to believe that the life after death would so spiritualize man that the experiences of that life could not be viewed as penal retribution. "If any suffered in the future state, it would be because they would be sinful *in that state*." His final conclusion that the Bible taught no punishment in the future world only became definite through the discussions with Edward Turner in the revised *Gospel Visitant*, 1817.

Ballou was tolerant of divergent views and, desiring union with freedom, refrained from pressing his opinions during the Restorationist Controversy. His elevated character, his noble dignity and patience under attack, his unfailing benevolence and sympathy won for him a reverent devotion. Greatly honored and active to the end, he died June 7, 1852. A statue marks his grave in Mount Auburn Cemetery.

[The chief source on Ballou's early development is an autobiographical fragment contributed to Thomas Whittemore's *Modern Hist. of Universalism* (1830); leading accounts are Maturin Murray Ballou, *Biog. of Hosea Ballou by His Youngest Son* (1853); Thomas Whittemore, *Life of Hosea Ballou*, 4 vols. (1854–55); O. F. Safford, *Hosea Ballou, A Marvelous Life Story* (1889). Estimates are found in J. C. Adams, *Hosea Ballou and the Gospel Renaissance of the Nineteenth Cent.* (1903), which has a print of the splendid portrait painted in 1847; "Hosea Ballou and the Larger Hope," in *Pioneers of Religious Liberty in America* (1903); *The Universalists; The Religious Hist. of New Eng.*, King's Chapel Lectures (1917). Criticism in F. H. Foster, *Hist. of the New Eng. Theology*, ch. XI (1907). Bibliography in Richard Eddy, *Universalism in America*, 2 vols. (1884–86).] F. A. C.

BALLOU, HOSEA (Oct. 18, 1796–May 27, 1861), Universalist clergyman, author, college president, was born in Guilford, Vt. His parents Asahel Ballou, nephew of Hosea Ballou [*q.v.*] and Martha (Starr) Ballou, were early converts to Universalist doctrine. He received his early education in Halifax, Vt., where in 1799 his father settled as a farmer and maker of spinning-wheels and chairs. Notwithstanding marked ability in the district school and under private instruction in Latin from a clergyman in Halifax, he was kept from a college course by the parents' fear of proselyting influences and after three winters of district school-teaching, became assistant at the age of seventeen in the school conducted by his granduncle in Portsmouth, N. H. Having there obtained some theological training, he became a pastor in Stafford, Conn., in 1817, with much itinerant preaching throughout the state. Having married Clarissa Hatch of Halifax, Jan. 26, 1820, he accepted a larger pastorate in the New Universalist Church of Roxbury, Mass., being installed July 26, 1821. Meager salary made it necessary to add the conduct of a private school for boys, a vocation to which he brought genuine scholarship independently acquired. After seventeen years, believing that the church needed another type of ministration, he moved to a pastorate in Medford, Mass., May 1838, where as in Roxbury he was prominent in fostering the public schools. During these pastorates he supervised the theological study of ministerial candidates, attempting a course equal to the full theological curriculum. The most eminent of his pupils were Thomas Starr King, Edwin Hubbell Chapin, Amory Dwight Mayo. He aided in editing the *Universalist Magazine* (1822), the more scholarly *Universalist Expositor* (1830–40), and the *Universalist Quarterly and General Review* (1844–56), contributing to the last two periodicals 121 historical and exegetical articles. In 1829 he published a pioneer American monograph in the field of the history of doctrine, having acquired for the task German, French, and Greek in addition to his command of Latin and Hebrew. This was the *Ancient History of Universalism*, a work which strengthened the confidence of his denomination and ran to four editions. In recognition of his service to scholarship, he was elected to the Board of Overseers of Harvard College, 1843–58. In 1854 he was made a member of the Massachusetts Board of Education.

To his denomination he rendered signal service by efforts to preserve unity in the controversy over future punishment. Although himself believing in retribution beyond death, he resisted the efforts of Rev. Jacob Woods and others to bind the denomination to this view. From the outset also he was urgent for denominational seats of learning and his zeal was rewarded by the incorporation of Tufts College, 1852, over which, after six months' travel in Europe, he was president, 1854–61, combining with that office instruction in history and philosophy. His joy in nature and in friendship and the cheerful humor expressed in his lighter verses are illustrated in the work by Hosea Starr Ballou, *Hosea Ballou, 2nd, D.D., His Origin, Life and Letters* (1896).

[See also Adin Ballou, *An Elaborate Hist. and Geneal. of the Ballous in America* (1888), pp. 293, 755–58;

Hist. of Tufts College, ed. by Alaric B. Start et al. (1896), pp. 15–37; *New Eng. Hist. and Geneal. Reg.,* July 1861.]

F. A. C.

BALLOU, MATURIN MURRAY (Apr. 14, 1820–Mar. 27, 1895), journalist, traveler, author, was the son of Ruth (Washburn) Ballou and Rev. Hosea Ballou [*q.v.*] a distinguished leader among the Universalists; his grandfather was a Baptist clergyman, and four uncles were preachers. He was born in Boston, the youngest son in a family of nine children; was educated at the English High School; and always sought his native city at the end of his many and far travels. At the age of nineteen he became a clerk in the Boston Post Office, and at about the same time began writing for a minor paper known as the *Olive Branch,* continuing to be an inveterate scribbler in the midst of his many other occupations and diversions. He was married on Sept. 15, 1839 to Mary Anne Roberts. Cruises on sea and journeys on land, during which he wrote letters home for publication descriptive of countries and people, much of this periodical material being later embodied in his books, were followed by employment as deputy navy-agent in the Boston Custom House. His chief distinction in American journalism lies in his founding and editorship of *Gleason's Pictorial,* later called *Ballou's Pictorial,* one of the earliest of American illustrated papers. He was the first editor and manager of the *Boston Daily Globe,* from 1872 to 1874, and during his work in journalism he was actively engaged in numerous business and financial enterprises, the most notable of these being the building of the St. James Hotel in the south end of Boston, which is now, under the designation of the Franklin Square House, one of the largest institutions in the country providing comfortable quarters for working women and girls. In 1882 he circumnavigated the globe, and he took many other tours until his death, which occurred in Cairo, Egypt. The many plays he wrote remain unacted, but one or two of them were published. Under the pseudonym "Lieut. Murray" he produced several romances, whose titles are sufficiently indicative of their character: *Red Rupert, the American Buccaneer* (1845); *The Naval Officer; or The Pirate's Cave* (1845); *The Spanish Musketeer* (1847). His books of travel include *Due West; or Round the World in Ten Months* (1884); *Due South; or Cuba Past and Present* (1885); *Under the Southern Cross; or Travels in Australia, Tasmania, New Zealand, Samoa and Other Pacific Islands* (1888). He wrote also *The Biography of Rev. Hosea Ballou* (1852), and *The History of Cuba* (1854). A reviewer in the *Nation* rightly said of him: "Mr. Ballou can tell a fairly interesting story of personal observations and experiences, but he is not a writer to pin one's faith to in matters of solid information." In other words, his literary work was distinctly journalistic and ephemeral. He was a maker of books rather than a literary man, a writer who looked at everything objectively, a traveler who set down his observations first, and his lasting impressions, if he had any, afterward.

[*Boston Globe,* Mar. 29, 1895; O. F. Adams, *Dict. of Am. Authors* (1897), p. 16; Adin Ballou, *Hist. and Geneal. of the Ballous in America* (1888), pp. 131, 332–33; S. A. Allibone, *Critical Dict. of Eng. Lit.* (1859), I, 109.]

E. F. E.

BALTIMORE, CHARLES CALVERT, THIRD LORD. [See CALVERT, CHARLES, 1629–1715.]

BALTIMORE, GEORGE CALVERT, FIRST LORD. [See CALVERT, GEORGE, *c.* 1580–1632.]

BANCROFT, AARON (Nov. 10, 1755–Aug. 19, 1839), clergyman, author, embodied the finest traits of New England Puritanism and was the leader of central Massachusetts churches in the movement through Arminianism to Unitarianism. The son of Lydia (Parker) Bancroft and Samuel Bancroft, a farmer and church deacon in Reading, Mass., who was one of the minority protesting against the dismissal of Jonathan Edwards in the Northampton Council in 1750, he had youthful 'throes' of revolt against the Calvinist theology in which the household was systematically disciplined. During his residence in Harvard College (1774–78) he marched with the Minute Men of Reading to Cambridge after Bunker Hill (*Ancestry of John Davis and Eliza Bancroft,* compiled by Horace Davis, San Francisco, 1897). After his graduation he read theology with the Reading pastor, Thomas Haven, and was licensed to preach. Early in 1780, with permission from the Massachusetts authorities and urged by John Barnard, a Loyalist exile, he sought a career in Nova Scotia where his oldest brother was a prominent jurist. There, however, he found the New England colonists too divided to form permanent churches, and the intolerance and extravagance of itinerant preachers confirmed his leanings to Arminian positions. Returning in July 1783, he spent the autumn as substitute for the invalid pastor of the church in Worcester, and there also a year later, having meantime declined a call to Stoughton and being rejected at East Windsor, Conn., because of his Arminian heresies, he preached as a candidate for the now vacant pulpit (October

1784–January 1785). A majority being firm Calvinists, the town, March 1785, refused to settle Bancroft, or to appoint two ministers of divergent views, or to support two societies. The minority, still subject for some years to taxation for the town church, established a voluntary society which had the unpopularity of being, apart from Boston, the first "poll" parish instead of a territorial organization, the first secession from a Congregational Church on doctrinal grounds, and the first church which in its formulas expressly condemned written creeds and accepted only the Bible as the sufficient rule of faith and practise.

Ordained, Feb. 1, 1788, as an avowed Arminian, Bancroft was shunned by church neighbors and only by taking pupils and boarders could eke out a meager support, but gradually his high character, ability, and public spirit won him a widespread esteem which was heightened by his *Life of Washington* (1807), a popular work often reprinted. His parish, having at first only one professed Unitarian member, followed Bancroft's guidance after the outbreak of the Unitarian controversy in 1815, and in 1822 published his *Sermons on Christian Doctrine,* a systematic formulation which had several editions in England and America. Bancroft contributed discussions to the *Christian Register,* and in 1825, aged seventy, overcame a disinclination to church division and joined the younger liberals in organizing the American Unitarian Association which he served as president with executive talent to 1836. By his marriage with Lucretia, daughter of Judge John and Mary (Church) Chandler he had thirteen children, prominent among whom were the historian George Bancroft [*q.v.*] and Mary, wife of John Davis, governor of Massachusetts. His sermons show an unusual grasp of the history of Christianity, and their formulation of doctrine is the best illustration of the thought of his time and circle, a circle not yet affected by the newer tendencies emergent in Channing. Holding the common view that Scripture must be consistent, he accepted the Arian implications of Pauline and Johannine texts as dominant over the humanitarian view of Christ which he considered a possible inference from the earlier gospels.

[Biog. data are found in Bancroft's published sermons for Apr. 8, 1827 and Jan. 31, 1836. The account in Wm. Lincoln, *Hist. of Worcester* (1836), rests also on Bancroft's oral statements, and Jos. Allen, *Hist. of the Worcester Ass.* (1868), adds quotations from Bancroft's private papers. See also Alonzo Hill in *Am. Unitarian Biog.,* ed. by Wm. Ware (1850); and Elam Smalley, *The Worcester Pulpit, with Notices Biog. and Hist.* (1851). An interesting characterization by Geo. Bancroft is added in W. B. Sprague, *Annals of the Am. Pulpit* (1857), and Samuel A. Eliot's revision of Sprague in *Heralds of the Liberal Faith,* vol. II (1910). Bancroft's publications are listed in Lincoln, Allen, and Eliot. See also Geo. Willis Cooke, *Unitarianism in America* (1902). Manuscript sermons are in the Am. Antiquarian Society, Worcester, and in the N. Y. Pub. Lib.]

F. A. C.

BANCROFT, CECIL FRANKLIN PATCH (Nov. 25, 1839–Oct. 4, 1901), educator, was born in New Ipswich, N. H., the eldest son of James Bancroft and Sarah (Kendall) Bancroft. In securing an education he was helped by Mr. and Mrs. Patch of the neighboring town of Ashby, where he attended the common schools, later completing his college preparation at Appleton Academy, in New Ipswich. At sixteen he entered Dartmouth College, teaching at Groton during the winter in order to support himself through the remainder of the year. He graduated in 1860, the fourth scholar in his class. During the next four years he was principal of Appleton Academy (later McCullom Institute) at Mont Vernon, N. H. In 1864, however, he resigned in order to study for the ministry at Union Theological Seminary, in New York. His course there was interrupted by some months spent with the Christian Commission, assisting wounded soldiers, after which he transferred in 1865 to Andover Theological Seminary, where he graduated in 1867. During his free hours he taught Latin at Phillips Academy thus becoming favorably known to the trustees of that institution. At this time he was recommended to take charge of a school for Southern whites recently established by C. G. Robert, at Lookout Mountain, Tenn. He was ordained on May 1, 1867, was married a week later to Frances A. Kittredge, one of his former pupils at Mont Vernon, and set out immediately with his bride for the South. In spite of his efforts, the new institution met with difficulties and failed after five stormy years. While Bancroft was resuming his studies in the University of Halle, Germany, he received a cable message offering him the principalship of Phillips Academy. He accepted and reached Andover in July 1873. There he remained until his death.

Bancroft found Phillips Academy at a critical moment in its history, when its future was at stake. Its endowment was inadequate; its reputation in scholarship was declining; its students were decreasing in number; and it had fallen out of touch with modern theories of education. During the twenty-eight years of his administration Bancroft transformed the school both materially and scholastically. After surveying the situation, he seized upon the centennial of the academy in 1878 as an opportunity for arousing the interest of the alumni and the general public; and under his supervision an elaborate celebration was held on Andover Hill. He persuaded generous benefactors to form the nucleus of what later became a large permanent fund. Before he died, he had added several modern dormitories, a science building, a gymnasium, and other important improvements to the equipment. One of the dormitories has appropriately been named Bancroft Hall, in his honor.

As Bancroft's reputation grew, the academy became more prosperous. When he took office, there were only 237 students; a quarter of a century later there were more than 400. It is estimated that over 9,600 boys were educated under him at Andover. Meanwhile the faculty was enlarged from four to twenty-two. He had remarkable success in securing and retaining able teachers, who added to the prestige of the school. He liberalized the curriculum without lowering the standard of instruction. He replaced the traditional three-year course by one covering four years; he established a system of written examinations; he discarded many useless subjects; and he eventually accomplished his chief object—"to bring the Academy into perfect harmony and working coöperation with the various colleges and scientific schools and hold it there." His period was marked also by the beginning of organized athletics, the formation of secret societies, the spread of alumni associations, the development of school literary publications, and a somewhat greater individual freedom for the undergraduates.

Bancroft—known familiarly as the "Doctor"—was a broad-minded, versatile, tireless, and patient leader. A shrewd judge of men and motives, he seldom erred in choosing his assistants or in making decisions. His keen and contagious sense of humor was always in evidence. As an executive, he had a rare gift for bringing out the best in others. As a speaker on educational matters he was nationally recognized, and he also threw himself whole-heartedly into all the activities of community life, wearing himself out ultimately with hard work. In personal appearance, he was, in his later days, a man of medium height and slender figure, with kind eyes, gray hair and beard, and native dignity of bearing.

[Claude M. Fuess, *An Old New Eng. School* (1917); the *Phillips Bull.*, the quart. publication of Phillips Acad.; information supplied by many teachers and grads. of Phillips Acad.; obituary in *Boston Transcript*, Oct. 5, 1901.]

C. M. F.

BANCROFT, EDGAR ADDISON (Nov. 20, 1857–July 28, 1925), lawyer, orator, diplomat, was born in Galesburg, Ill., of Scotch-Irish-English stock. His ancestors on both sides came to America during the seventeenth and eighteenth centuries and several of them fought in the Revolution. Edgar was the eldest of the seven children of Addison Newton and Catharine (Blair) Bancroft. He was educated in the public schools of Galesburg, in Knox College, from which he graduated in 1878, and in Columbia University Law School, from which he graduated in 1880. He practised law in Galesburg until 1892, when he moved to Chicago, where he was solicitor for Illinois of the Atchison, Topeka & Santa Fe R. R., 1892–95; vice-president and general solicitor of the Chicago & Western Indiana R. R., and the Belt R. W. Company, 1895–1904, and member of the law firm of Scott, Bancroft, Martin & MacLeish from 1904 to 1924. From 1907 to 1920 he was general counsel to the International Harvester Company, which, with its affiliated companies, he represented in numerous suits in the Federal and state courts. Bancroft early displayed oratorical talent and he made many addresses, patriotic, historical, legal, and memorial. During and after the World War he was often chairman of committees and the orator of the occasion, from the time of Chicago's welcome to Joffre and Viviani, in May 1917 to that of Foch's post-war visit in the autumn of 1921. A volume of his war-time speeches was printed privately in 1927 by his brother under the title of *The Mission of America*, the first speech of the collection. In a memorial pamphlet the America-Japan Society (Imperial Hotel, Tokio) in 1926 published five of his later speeches and addresses in Japan.

A serious race riot began in Chicago on July 27, 1919, and continued for several days. Twenty negroes and fifteen white people were killed and over 500 persons injured before the state militia, assisted by the police, could restore order. On Aug. 20, 1919, Gov. Lowden appointed a Commission on Race Relations, consisting of six representatives of white people, including Bancroft as chairman, and six representatives of the negroes. On Jan. 1, 1921, the Commission submitted an exhaustive report to the Governor, who expressed his appreciation of their services (*The Negro in Chicago; a Study of Race Relations and a Race Riot*, 1922).

In April 1923 the Comité France-Amérique of Paris, an institution organized "to further bonds of sympathy between France and the Nations of America," invited a group of Americans, consisting of Edgar A. Bancroft, George W. Wickersham, former attorney-general of the United States, Prof. William Milligan Sloane of Columbia University, and Samuel Harden Church of the Carnegie Institute of Technology, each with wife or daughter, to visit the French provinces of Morocco and Algiers. The trip occupied six weeks and was the subject of several publications (*Spring in Morocco and Algiers,* by G. W. Wickersham, 1923, and *Greater France in Africa,* by W. M. Sloane, 1924).

In July 1924 Bancroft was summoned to Washington by Secretary of State Charles E. Hughes, and to his surprise was asked to accept the post of Ambassador to Japan. He did so from a sense of duty and with full appreciation of the risk to his health, which for many years had been precarious. Although he arrived in Japan only a few months after the passage of the Exclusion Act, when that nation felt deeply hurt, his pleasing manners, gentle diplomacy, and large experience in friendly relations with persons in all walks of life, soon won him great popularity. His ready eloquence and sympathetic feelings were quickly appreciated and gave him much influence in helping to restore international good-feeling. Eight months of incessant activity were too much for his frail health. He died at Karuizawa, Japan, July 28, 1925. The official honors paid at the funeral service in Japan were only less than those reserved for the Imperial family, and Bancroft's body was transported in a Japanese battle-ship to San Francisco. He was married in April 1896 to Margaret Healy of Brooklyn, N. Y., who died in December 1923. They had no children.

Bancroft was the author of *The Chicago Strike of 1894* (1895); *The Moral Sentiment of the People* (1896); *Destruction or Regulation of Trusts* (1907).

[Juiji G. Kasai, *Foundations of American-Japanese Friendship and a Tribute to Ambassador Edgar Addison Bancroft* (Tokio, 1925); obituaries in *Chicago Daily News,* July 28, 1925, *Chicago Daily Tribune* and *Chicago Herald and Examiner,* July 29, 1925.]

C. H. B.

BANCROFT, EDWARD (Jan. 9, 1744–Sept. 8, 1821), writer and inventor, better known for his double dealing and dishonorable career in the Revolution, was born at Westfield, Mass. Without regular schooling he became in later years well-educated, and studied medicine in England. He had an adventurous early life; a sailor, and then a settler in Dutch Guiana, where he made valuable observations on the manners, customs, and religion of the natives, afterward published. Settling in England he became a writer on American subjects for the *Monthly Review,* published several works, associated with such men as Franklin and Priestley, and in due time was elected to the Royal Society and to the College of Physicians.

His sinister diplomatic career began at the outset of the Revolution. A natural intriguer, he acted as a spy for Franklin in London. When Silas Deane arrived in France as an American commissioner, he received from Franklin a letter of introduction to Bancroft, and the two men were soon on confidential terms. Bancroft commenced furnishing various items of information to Deane in 1776, aided the commissioners in their correspondence, received pay from the government through Deane, and continued to be a trusted agent down to 1783. Franklin and Deane were never undeceived, although the commissioner Arthur Lee and his brother William at times suspected Bancroft. Letters for Deane were even sent in Bancroft's care. He gained the confidence of Paul Jones, and was highly commended in Deane's personal *Narrative* to Congress. To add to the plausibility of his position, he was arrested in 1777 by the English for corresponding with Deane.

Meanwhile Bancroft was pursuing his parallel career as an English spy. In December 1776 he contracted to supply information; for this he received £400—increased later to £1000—per annum. He assumed the name Edwards, and one of his methods was the placing of correspondence in a bottle concealed in the hole of a tree near the Tuileries. He revealed the dealings of Deane with the French Foreign Minister Vergennes; to the British agent Wentworth he sent abstracts of treaties. Nor was he above speculation, though he sometimes suffered losses. He speculated on advance news of Burgoyne's defeat, and on Jan. 27, 1778, he wrote, giving early information of the treaty between France and the United States, with a plan for private gain. His handwriting was identified in the latter instance, as was the case in a letter which he wrote to Ralph Izard, American diplomatist, Oct. 22, 1778. He was commended by the English officials, although at times under suspicion. In his "Memorial" to the Marquis of Carmarthen he claimed credit for furnishing items about supplies, intercourse, and the movements of ships, instancing the sailing of D'Estaing's fleet.

Bancroft made discoveries of dyes for use in the manufacture of textiles, and he received a patent in England for importing yellow oak-bark for dyeing. This right failed of renewal in 1799, in spite of a pamphlet which he addressed to Parliament. He died at Margate, England. He wrote, besides various articles, *Essay on the Natural History of Guiana* (1769); *Remarks on the Review of the Controversy between Great Britain and Her Colonies* (1769); *Charles Wentworth* (1770), a novel assailing Christianity; *Experimental Researches concerning the Philosophy of Permanent Colours* (1794, enlarged edition

1813). Most of his works are in the British Museum.

["The Deane Papers" in *N. Y. Hist. Soc. Colls.* (1886–90); Samuel F. Bemis in *Am. Hist. Rev.*, XXIX, 474, containing at the end Bancroft's "Memorial."]

E. K. A.

BANCROFT, GEORGE (Oct. 3, 1800–Jan. 17, 1891), historian, diplomat, was born in Worcester, Mass., the eighth of thirteen children. His father, Aaron Bancroft [*q.v.*], a Congregational minister, held a pioneer's place in the Unitarian schism of the Massachusetts clergy, became the first president of the American Unitarian Association, and wrote a life of Washington which enjoyed much popularity. In Worcester he was remembered as the last inhabitant to wear small clothes and a three-cornered hat. He came of early New England stock, and so did his wife, Lucretia Chandler, descended from Capt. Benjamin Church [*q.v.*], soldier and historian of King Philip's War, from the Gardiners of Gardiner's Island, opposite New London, and from a succession of John Chandlers in Worcester County, of whom her father, "Tory John," known in England as "the honest refugee," was the third to hold the title of judge. Strangely unlettered, this mother of thirteen possessed great vigor of mind and spirit. Her husband's constant petition at family prayers, "Give us a teachable temper," may be taken to suggest the blended influences to which a boy of the household was subject.

Through George Bancroft's years of school, college, and university he proved himself teachable to a rare degree. After some schooling at Worcester he went at eleven to Phillips Exeter Academy, Exeter, N. H., where in two years he prepared himself to enter Harvard College at the age of thirteen. He had already exhibited the spirit and capacity that marked him, in the class of 1817, as one upon whom the amplest educational opportunities would not be wasted. In college he won the favor, especially, of President Kirkland, Prof. Andrews Norton, and Edward Everett, tutor in Latin during his freshman year. On his graduation, with high but not the first standing, he remained at Cambridge for a year as a student of divinity. At the end of that year, in June 1818, he sailed for Europe, to pursue at Göttingen his studies of theology and philology, his support ensured from scholarship funds of the College and other sources responsive to Kirkland's call. The nickname of "Doctor" bestowed upon him by his fellow students at Exeter and Harvard was to be ratified by the degree of Doctor of Philosophy and Master of Arts, which he received from the University of Göttingen in September 1820.

Bancroft was thus one of the small company of pathfinders in American scholarship who sought in German universities the fulfilment of their formal education. George Ticknor, Joseph Green Cogswell, and Edward Everett had immediately preceded him, and had made so favorable an impression on the scholars they encountered that Bancroft found a cordial welcome awaiting him. Small of stature, with a slenderness retained through life, quickly expressive both in eye and in speech, he carried with him an appeal of youthfulness, enthusiasm, and ability which led to personal relations of a warmth extending beyond the first greetings. His longest single period of study in Europe was at Göttingen, where he remained for more than two years, applying himself chiefly to Oriental languages and biblical learning, and profiting particularly from his contacts with Eichhorn and Heeren, whose teaching in ethnography had its effect upon Bancroft's historical writing in later years. From Göttingen he proceeded to Berlin, and there for several months attended the university courses of Schleiermacher, Hegel, and others. At his departure, in February 1821, he bore with him a letter of introduction from Baron Karl Wilhelm von Humboldt to his brother Alexander in Paris. On the way thither, Bancroft, at Weimar, paid two visits to Goethe, whom he had previously met at Jena, spent several weeks of study at Heidelberg, and added a traveler's impressions of Leipzig and Frankfort to the knowledge of other places in Germany which he had acquired on holiday walking trips from Göttingen. In Paris the letter to Humboldt opened many doors. The great scholar and traveler took the American of twenty-one to a session of the Institut de France, where he listened to Cuvier and others. For about three months in Paris he profited from all his opportunities to meet such figures as Lafayette, Gallatin, then United States minister to France, and Washington Irving. After a flying visit to London, in August 1821, he went on his way, through Switzerland, to Italy, where he visited more than once Napoleon's sister, the Princess Pauline Borghese, at Rome, and at Leghorn enjoyed a meeting and talk with Lord Byron and the Countess Guiccioli. Not only from the arduous studies which he pursued in Germany, but through a social experience quite beyond the natural scope of a Worcester minister's son, with his achievement still ahead, Bancroft turned his four years of Europe to remarkable account.

His letters to friends and family at home record alike his thoughts and the outward happenings of this time. From Göttingen he wrote to Kirkland, "The plan of life, which I have adopted, indicates very clearly that I must become, either an instructor at the University, or a clergyman, or set up a high school" (*Life and Letters,* I, 54). It is significant that he attempted each one of these employments before entering upon politics and the writing of history. In Switzerland and in Italy the ministry was evidently uppermost in his mind (*Ibid.,* I, 122, 136). But soon after his return to America in August 1822, the offer of a tutorship in Greek at Harvard for the ensuing academic year led his feet into the paths of teaching, which he was to follow for nearly ten years.

It was not a satisfying period for him. During the year of his Harvard tutorship he accepted invitations to occupy pulpits in and about Boston. The elder clergy would apparently have been glad to see him justify the reputed promise of his powers. At Worcester he seems to have failed to satisfy either his father or the congregation (*Ibid.,* I, 164 *n.*). If one may judge from the fact that his attempts at preaching lasted only a year, he did not satisfy himself. Nor was his tutorship at Harvard a more rewarding experience. Owing so much as he did to President Kirkland and the Harvard Corporation for his years in Europe, he felt that he must make the requital of at least a year's teaching at Cambridge. But before the year was over he was writing to a friend, "I have found College a sickening and wearisome place. . . . My state has been nothing but trouble, trouble, trouble, and I am heartily glad that the end of the year is coming so soon" (*Ibid.,* I, 163). This feeling must have been shared by the authorities and the students, for the foreign manners and views, educational and social, which Bancroft brought home with him from Europe, served only to produce irritation in Cambridge, and even to estrange some of his best friends. As early as December of 1822 he had decided to undertake school rather than college teaching, and was discussing with J. G. Cogswell the plan which took form in their famous Round Hill School at Northampton.

Bancroft's first published book, a thin volume of *Poems,* appeared in 1823, between his quitting Harvard and establishing himself at Round Hill. It must be included, with his preaching and college teaching, in the list of his early failures, for it lacked any distinctive poetic quality, and is believed to have become, in its author's eyes, one of those youthful indiscretions which may best be forgotten. The Round Hill experiment was a more serious matter, involving eight years of effort, and ending, like Bancroft's previous attempts to find his niche, in failure. The project in which he and Cogswell hopefully united their powers was to establish a boys' school embodying methods of teaching and living which had impressed them in Germany and Switzerland. In theory and on paper, as in the quality of the boys whose parents were attracted by the announcements of the school, it was all that one could wish. In reality the shortcomings and disappointments were many—partly, no doubt, because the institution was too far in advance of its time, and partly by reason of Bancroft's limitations as a teacher. The boys called him "the Critter," and the school paper printed a caricature of him in the semblance of a black devil, horned and tailed (*Proceedings of the Massachusetts Historical Society,* XLVII, p. 222). In 1831, having sold his interest in the school the year before to Cogswell, he brought his teaching to an end—again with a sense of relief. "That was a kind of occupation," he wrote in a letter of 1832, "to which I was not peculiarly adapted, and in which many of inferior abilities and attainments could have succeeded as well" (*Life and Letters,* I, 201).

But the years at Northampton marked, besides the ending of Bancroft's failures, the beginnings of his successes. Of his two fortunate marriages, the first—to Sarah H. Dwight, daughter of Jonathan Dwight, of Springfield, Mass.—occurred Mar. 1, 1827. At about the same time he was taking his first steps in politics and in prose authorship. Both in his politics and his writing—and the two were closely related—he revealed early the qualities which characterized him through life. Passing over some translations of German text-books of Greek, Latin, and history, which Bancroft wished to make available for his and other schools, it should be noted that a Fourth-of-July oration delivered in Springfield in 1826 is the first considerable piece of prose in his long list of writings. Uttered on the day of Jefferson's death, it was animated with the spirit of his political principles as well as with those of the fiftieth anniversary of July 4, 1776. It was the deliverance of a convinced democrat, and so set the note for much of Bancroft's subsequent writing.

Through the later twenties and the early thirties Bancroft's writing, which was abundant, appeared chiefly in periodicals, and largely in the *North American Review,* under several editors. He was at once a valuable and an uncomfortable contributor. His learning enabled him to deal effectively with many new books calling for review. His political views were so positive that when he wrote for the *North American* in 1831 an exhaustive article on the United States Bank, it had an importance which justified the reprinting of it in pamphlet form. It had also an ending, in the magazine, which the editor supplied without the author's knowledge. Bancroft had a valid grievance here, but in other instances (*Smith College Studies in History,* Jan. 1917: "Correspondence of George Bancroft and Jared Sparks, 1823–32") his insistence on his rights as a contributor excites sympathy even for an over-zealous editor. The scope of his articles—financial, political, scholarly—was, however, so broad as to mark their writer as destined to count for something in the intellectual life of his time.

Continuing to live at Northampton after quitting the Round Hill School, he began there the preparation of his *History of the United States,* of which the first of the ten volumes was published in 1834. The second, with a second edition of the first, came in 1837; the third, and last before an intermission of twelve years, in 1840. These three volumes were concerned with the "History of the Colonization of the United States." They were written in a vein which characterized Bancroft's work as a whole, though in diminishing degree as the years went on—the vein of the democrat in politics expressing himself as the democrat in theory. Dr. J. F. Jameson, who finds Bancroft's first volume "redolent of the ideas of the new Jacksonian democracy," has written aptly, "the historian caught, and with sincere and enthusiastic conviction repeated to the American people the things which they were saying and thinking concerning themselves." The warm reception accorded to the book was by no means only from the less thoughtful. An enthusiastic review in the *North American* by Edward Everett was notable not so much as the utterance of a friend of many years as because it came from one whose political views were quite at variance with Bancroft's. In a letter to the author he wrote, "I think you have written a Work which will last while the memory of America lasts" (*Life and Letters,* I, 206). Carlyle, more cautious, wrote after the appearance of the second volume in terms of high praise thus qualified, "I should say . . . that you were too didactic, went too much into the origin of things generally known, into the praise of things only partially praisable, only slightly important" (*Ibid.,* I, 226). It remained for Bancroft's brother-in-law, "Honest John" Davis, to make a plea —when the first volume appeared—which Bancroft, for his final standing, would have done well to heed, "Let me entreat you not to let the partisan creep into the work. Do not imbue it with any present feeling or sentiment of the moment which may give impulse to your mind" (*Ibid.,* I, 211). The three volumes of 1834, 1837, and 1840, open as they were to the charge of setting the key for the continuance of Bancroft's writing—in Dr. Jameson's phrase—"to vote for Jackson," possessed nevertheless a vigor, picturesqueness, and authority, as it was then counted, that gave their author a foremost place, both in popularity and in distinction, among the American writers of his time.

It is evident that one in such a position could be of great use to the Democratic party in Massachusetts at a time when the leaders with a background and training like Bancroft's were chiefly Whigs. His pen and his voice, a less effective implement, were placed freely at the disposal of his party—even to the extent of his writing a Thanksgiving proclamation, in 1837, for Gov. William L. Marcy of the neighboring state of New York. The Whig affiliations of the family to which his first wife belonged restrained him for a time from seeking, or holding, public office as a Democrat. Before her death in June 1837, however, he had run unsuccessfully, in 1834, for election as a representative of Northampton in the Massachusetts General Court. At the end of 1837, Bancroft, a widower with three children, was appointed by President Van Buren, in recognition of party services, Collector of the Port of Boston. In August 1838 Mrs. Elizabeth (Davis) Bliss of Boston, a widow with two sons, became his second wife. Her first husband, Alexander Bliss, had been a junior law-partner of Daniel Webster. Except for the social ostracism to which Massachusetts Democrats of the time were subject, Bancroft's life in Boston, covering seven years, had its agreeable aspects—a good house in Winthrop Place, a growing reputation as a writer, the successful administration of his Federal office, and an effective activity in Democratic politics. As a delegate from Massachusetts he attended the National Democratic Convention of 1844, and bore an important part in the nomination of James K. Polk for the presidency. In the same year he was himself defeated in his campaign for the governorship of Massachusetts.

Again his party services deserved recognition, and it came through his appointment as secretary of the navy in Polk's cabinet. Holding this post only for eighteen months from March 1845, he made his secretaryship memorable, especially by meeting a long-recognized national need, through the establishment of the Naval Academy at Annapolis. He interested himself to good purpose also in the work of the Naval Observatory. In other affairs of the Polk administration he was a faithful supporter of his chief, approving strongly of the President's position in the Oregon Boundary controversy with England, signing, as acting secretary of war in May 1845, the order causing Gen. Zachary Taylor to cross the Texas frontier with his troops, and leading directly to the Mexican War, and, in his own field of the navy, issuing the orders to Commodore Sloat on the Pacific coast which brought about the American occupation of San Francisco and other California towns. Bancroft's identification with an enterprise so unpopular in New England as the Mexican War, and such circumstances as his appearance as the official eulogist of Andrew Jackson soon after his death in June 1845, contributed to the disfavor in which he was held in the dominant circles of Massachusetts—the same circles which looked askance at a later appointee to a cabinet portfolio as one having "merely a national reputation."

Bancroft's national reputation was enhanced in September 1846 by his appointment as United States minister to Great Britain. From the time of Polk's election he would have preferred a foreign post to a seat in the cabinet, for he was bent upon the continuance of his "History," and knew that he could do more, both in research and in writing, as a representative of his country in Europe than as a member of the President's official family at home. While studying in Germany, a young man of twenty, Bancroft had written of himself as "all too American in his ways of thinking." His studies through the intervening years and his experiences in Europe from October 1846 to September 1849, when the work of his English mission came to an end, only confirmed his intense Americanism. In March of 1848, the year of European upheavals, he could write from London, "The world is growing weary of that most costly of all luxuries, hereditary kings," and a fortnight later, "I can only say for myself that my residence in Europe has but quickened and confirmed my love for the rule of the people" (*Ibid.*, II, 31–33). Yet the British liking for the most American of American representatives prevailed in the case of Bancroft, and facilitated the attainment of his diplomatic objects, which were concerned especially with postal and commercial arrangements. He was no less fortunate in his social relations and his historical pursuits. At successive opportunities he went from London to Paris, chiefly in search of the materials of history in the government archives. In England both private and public records were placed at his disposal for transcription. Both there and in France, besides forming personal relations with the holders of the highest political offices, he was much in the society of such historians as Macaulay, Milman, and Hallam in the one country, and Guizot and Thiers in the other. From his three years at the Court of St. James's he returned to the United States enriched for the second time by a rare experience of Europe.

For such a citizen of the world as Bancroft had now become, New York seemed the most appropriate dwelling-place in America, and there he established himself promptly on his return. At about the same time he acquired a summer place at Newport, R. I., which he retained till the end of his life. Here he kept his body and spirit young by the cultivation of roses and by riding. Both in Newport and in New York he took much pleasure, and a distinctive part, in society—a practise which, like his riding, he maintained throughout his days. For eighteen years, from 1849 to 1867, he devoted himself primarily to his "History," and brought out six volumes beyond the three produced before his appointment to London. They were Volume IV (1852), *The American Revolution, Epoch First, The Overthrow of the European Colonial System, 1748–1763;* Volume V (1852), *The American Revolution, Epoch Second, How Great Britain Estranged America, 1763–1774;* Volume VI (1854), *The Crisis*—completing "the history of the American Revolution considered in its causes"; Volume VII (1858) and Volume VIII (1860), *The American Revolution, Epoch Third, America Declares Itself Independent, 1774–1776;* Volume IX (1866), *The American Revolution, Epoch Fourth, The Independence of America Is Acknowledged 1776–1782.* Except that in the seventh volume (1858) Bancroft omitted all footnotes—as if to say that none need question the authority of any statement in his text—these volumes were closely akin, in tone and quality, to those that had preceded them. As a footnote in the second volume, disparaging the accuracy of James Grahame's *History of the Rise and Progress of the United States,* had led to a controversy with President Quincy of Harvard, so the ninth volume, touching frankly on what Bancroft regarded as the shortcomings of several general officers in the Continental Army, involved the historian in what became known as the "War of the Grandfathers" —a conflict of pamphlets between their descendants and the historian. There were valid grounds of objection to some of the statements made by Bancroft. There was some corresponding excess of zeal on the part of the grandsons. If Bancroft gave offense it is clear that certain readers were quick to take it. Orestes A. Brownson [*q.v.*]—for whom, as for Hawthorne, Bancroft, while Collector of the Port in Boston, had found a place in the Custom House—brought a long review of Volume IV to an end with the words, "He would persuade us to condemn our Catholic ancestors and seduce us from allegiance to our Church. We trust no Catholics will suffer themselves to be caught by his insidious flattery" (*Brownson's*

Quarterly Review, October 1852). A New York critic, Gen. John Watts de Peyster declared, "Had Bancroft been born, and reared, and taught in cosmopolitan New York [instead of New England] . . . he would have left a memorial of word-painting such as that of Raphael upon canvas" (*Our Representatives Abroad,* 1874, edited by Augustus C. Rogers, p. 28). Bancroft indeed was so positively himself that differences between him and other positive persons could hardly fail to be violent.

As the Civil War approached, Bancroft took his stand among the Northern Democrats who were opposed to slavery and any dissolution of the Union. Like many Northern Republicans he looked upon Lincoln at first as quite inadequate to the tasks confronting him, but earlier than some of these he realized his misapprehension, and made amends for it by supporting Lincoln and his policies with pen and voice. In the cordial personal relations that came to exist between the two men the President even turned to the historian for counsel on a matter of historical precedent. Lincoln's successor, Andrew Johnson, sought his aid in a more vital matter. Forty years after Johnson delivered his first annual message as President in December 1865, Prof. W. A. Dunning of Columbia made and published the discovery that this message was written by Bancroft (*Proceedings of the Massachusetts Historical Society,* XXXIX, 395). On Feb. 12, 1866, it fell to Bancroft, the Democrat both of practise and of theory, to deliver in the House of Representatives his *Memorial Address on the Life and Character of Abraham Lincoln,* even as twenty-one years before he had made the official eulogy of Andrew Jackson. When Andrew Johnson in May 1867 offered him the post of United States minister to Berlin, it was an act more of personal than of party recognition. Bancroft accepted, and Grant continued him in office until 1874.

These seven years of Bancroft's life, during which his social, political, and intellectual gifts could enjoy abundant expression, were among the happiest of his entire career. His early association with Germany and German scholars gave him a sense of a home-coming, and he was received like a returning son or brother. In his diplomatic work he had the satisfactions of accomplishment in important questions of naturalization, trade-marks, and arbitration on the boundary line between British Columbia and the State of Washington. In his historical studies he caused the Prussian and other European archives to be searched for material of which he made use in his tenth volume, published in 1874, the year of his return to the United States. His political and scholastic interests were closely involved in his social relations. With Bismarck and Moltke, with Mommsen and Ranke—to name but four out of many important figures of the time and place—he found himself on terms of such sympathetic intimacy that during the Franco-Prussian War it was natural for the French to regard him as hostile to their interests (see the lines "Bancroft" in the section "Novembre" of Victor Hugo's *L'Année Terrible*). It was a happy circumstance that his German years included the fiftieth anniversary of his receiving his doctorate at Göttingen, for this event was celebrated by an imposing *jubilæum,* which included the bestowal of the honorary degree of LL.D.—a fitting sequel to the academic honors received while he was minister to England, namely, his election as correspondent of the Institute of France and the honorary degree of D.C.L. from Oxford. In Berlin an honor from which he derived a special pleasure was his election, typifying his identification with the intellectual life of Berlin, as the seventeenth, and only Anglo-Saxon, member of the *Mittwochs-Gesellschaft für Wissenschaftliche Unterhaltung,* a society of sixteen German savants of the highest standing. During his seven years of residence at Berlin he made excursions to Eastern Europe, Greece, and Egypt. Returning to America, and to private life, at the age of seventy-four, he brought with him again ripe fruits of European experience.

Still more a cosmopolite than on his return from England in 1849, Bancroft in 1874 settled in Washington, which became his winter home for the seventeen remaining years of his life. Both there and in Newport he relished greatly the pleasures of society. In voting his admission to the floor of the Senate that body gave but one of many tokens of the unique place he held in the eyes of his contemporaries. With his roses in the summer and his riding throughout the year he kept himself in vigorous condition. Especially through his riding, the small, alert figure, easily identified in Bancroft's later life by the long gray beard he wore, became familiar to many outside his immediate circle. The work he accomplished through these final years called for uncommon activity of both mind and body.

The tenth and final volume of his "History," published in 1874, was designated *The American Revolution, Volume IV.* The main title of the first volume, published forty years before, was *A History of the United States from the Discovery of the American Continent to the Present Time.* In the nine succeeding volumes the words "to the Present Time" were dropped. As the tenth volume dealt with the years 1778–

82, and ended with the peace between the United States and Great Britain, the title of the work in its entirety, even as it stood in the nine volumes following the first, was open to question. When Bancroft, at seventy-four, published his tenth volume, he did not regard his work as finished. In 1876 he brought out, in six volumes, a "thoroughly revised edition" called, on its half-title, the "Centenary Edition." In 1882 he produced, in two volumes, his *History of the Formation of the Constitution of the United States,* and in 1883–85 "The Author's Last Revision" of his "History" as a whole, devoting the sixth and last volume to his *History of the Formation of the Constitution.* In these revisions he sought to correct the mistakes of earlier editions, to profit by newly acquired information, and to reduce the floridity of much of his earlier writing. The complete bibliography of his books and pamphlets (*Life and Letters,* II, 331–41) records the translation of his "History" into several languages, the separate publication of many addresses and controversial papers, and two books which should be named here, *Literary and Historical Miscellanies* (1855) and *Martin Van Buren to the End of His Public Career* (1889).

The extraordinary vitality which enabled Bancroft to perform the labors he accomplished during the ninth decade of his life is illustrated in a letter written by him to Oliver Wendell Holmes in January 1885: "On one of the days in which I wrote my little tribute to your *Life of Emerson,* I was yet strong enough to rise in the night, light my own fire and candles, and labor with close application fully fourteen hours consecutively, that is, from five in the morning till eight in the evening, with but one short hour's interruption for breakfast; and otherwise no repast: not so much as a sip of water" (*Ibid.,* II, 303). Dr. Holmes made the characteristic response, "You must be made of iron and vulcanized india-rubber, or some such compound of resistance and elasticity." (*Ibid.,* II, 305). On the death of Mrs. Bancroft in March 1886, he was companioned for the rest of his life by a daughter of his older son, George, and then by the family of his younger son, John Chandler Bancroft. His own daughters, one of each marriage, had died respectively in 1850 and 1845. In his rounded existence his domestic life was always an important element, and it was a part of his good fortune that only for his last five years was it necessary for him to proceed without the wife of forty-eight years—more than half of his long life. When he passed ninety the inevitable feebleness of old age increased, and on Jan. 17, 1891, he died in Washington. By order of President Harrison the flags of the executive departments at Washington and of the public buildings in cities through which Bancroft's body was to pass on its way to interment at Worcester were placed at half-mast until the burial. The feeling that a truly national figure had departed from the American scene was universal.

The many years of Bancroft's life had wrought some fortunate changes in him. At the end the young scholar who came to grief with patrons and pupils, the young writer who quarreled with editors, the aggressive partisan who appeared to court unpopularity, had given place to the mellowed old man of broadly enlarging social experience and intellectual interests. Though he himself could thus change, his "History," for all its revision, was but the unified completion of what he had begun when only about thirty years of age. Now for many years it has suffered from the applications of the standards of one period to the work of another. Bancroft as a writer was very much a man of the time in which he came to maturity. He wrote with the strong bias of an ardent believer in democratic government. He resented Ranke's telling him that his "History" was "the best book ever written from the democratic point of view," maintaining that the democracy in his book was objective, not subjective (*Ibid.,* II, 183). Yet the spirit of the Fourth-of-July orator of Bancroft's earlier days was continually expressing itself in his pages. His scholarly method was also that of a time that has passed. If he had thought it questionable to present as literal quotations of historic documents, mere paraphrased condensations of them, he would not have exposed himself so freely as he did to detection in this course. His rhetorical and highly ornamental style is another reminder of his belonging to a previous age—an age before the divorce of literature from history was contemplated. "Fine writing" was then a term rather of praise than of reproof. Yet of this writer of history—who used to taste a chapter or two of Gibbon before taking up his own pen (*Memories of a Hundred Years,* 1903, by E. E. Hale, II, 58)—there was reason for the *Harvard Graduates' Magazine,* under the editorship of William Roscoe Thayer, to assert, "His position as Father of American History is as unshaken as that of Herodotus among the Greeks." He produced an "epic of liberty" faithful to the spirit of his time. Though he did not use his manuscript material as later historians would have used it, either directly or indirectly, his collections from original sources, preserved in the New York Public Library, are a monument to his zeal in exploration and an example to younger investigators of history. His work as a whole has been outmoded. Its permanent value may well be found to lie as much in its preservation of the American point of view in the period in which it took form as in its record of an earlier time.

[*The Life and Letters of George Bancroft*, 2 vols. (1908), by M. A. DeWolfe Howe, a biog. based upon Bancroft's personal papers, is the chief source of information about him. The *Century Mag.* published, Jan. 1887, an intimate sketch, "George Bancroft—in Society, in Politics, in Letters," by William M. Sloane, one of his assistants in Berlin. For this paper Bancroft provided material. See also for later critical estimates, the chapter "George Bancroft" in *The Middle Group of Am. Historians* (1917) by John Spencer Bassett, and *The Hist. of Historical Writing in America* (1891) by J. Franklin Jameson, pp. 100–10.]

M. A. DeW. H.

BANCROFT, HUBERT HOWE (May 5, 1832–Mar. 2, 1918), publisher, historian, was descended from John Bancroft, who came to Massachusetts on the ship *James* in 1632. John's grandson Samuel, born at West Springfield, Mass., in 1768 removed to Granville, Mass. Samuel's son, Azariah, in 1814 joined a New England colony at Granville, Ohio. Here was born H. H. Bancroft, the grandson of Azariah and son of Azariah Ashley. His forebears were usually long lived, and his physical endowment was splendid. When in his seventies he is described as straight and of distinguished appearance. He was about six feet in height and had strong, well-marked features, the nose being aquiline. His mother, Lucy D. Howe, was, like his father, the child of an emigrant from the older to the new Granville. The atmosphere of the home was that of strict puritanism, and the family were abolitionists. In his autobiography (*Literary Industries*) he tells that he could read the Bible at the age of three, that he attended the school in his native village, and that he also began a college preparatory course there. But he chose to enter a business life, and at the age of sixteen went to Buffalo, N. Y., to work for a bookseller who was his sister's husband. A. A. Bancroft was attracted to California by the gold-rush. Thither in 1852 followed the son by way of New York and Panama, at first intending to extend his brother-in-law's business on the Pacific Coast. Young Bancroft joined his father in working a mine above Sacramento. In 1853 he found employment at Crescent City and then became a merchant. In 1856 he established himself in San Francisco and in 1858 founded the firm of H. H. Bancroft & Company. This house was a publishing as well as a mercantile concern. In bringing out a handbook in 1859 Bancroft began to collect books dealing with the Pacific Coast. For some years he planned an encyclopedia, and from this project grew his great work, the preparation of a history of the Pacific States. This came to include not only the states and territories of the Pacific Coast and Rocky Mountain area but also British Columbia and Alaska as well as Mexico and Central America. To the history were devoted twenty-eight volumes, and it was preceded in the same series by five on the native races and followed by six volumes of essays. The method of procedure was unique. Bancroft by 1868 had gathered from all parts a good library of works on Pacific Coast history. In that year he installed as librarian Henry L. Oak, who for nineteen years was his assistant in directing the enterprise. A numerous force of assistants was employed to make notes. Spanish archives, particularly those of California, were searched by a force of copyists. Private papers and other historical collections were acquired. To cover the ground more thoroughly, beginning about 1880, reporters were sent out to receive from dictation narratives of prominent pioneers. In the end 60,000 volumes of historical material were brought together. The intention was to found a history of Western America upon original sources. "He who shall come after me," wrote the founder of the plan with true insight, "will scarcely be able to undermine my work by laying another and deeper foundation" (*Literary Industries,* p. 635). The active preparation of manuscript for the press began in 1871 and ended in 1889. The first volume of the *Native Races* appeared in 1875 and the last essay volume of the series in 1890. The work as it stands is by some ten or twelve writers who worked at the Bancroft library in the employ of its proprietor. His original intention was to do most of the writing himself, but the task was too great, even though vastly expedited by library organization and the work of note-takers. He estimated that the first volume which appeared represented labor equivalent to that of one man for ten years (*Native Races,* I, 13). Bancroft's own writing appears in widely scattered parts of the *Native Races* and the *History,* and is said to have aggregated some four and a half volumes. The essay volumes are largely from his own pen. Toward the work of the other writers his relation was that of organizer and general editor. He planned it, with H. L. Oak's assistance allotted parts to different persons, and edited completed manuscripts. Though a man of strong views, he often toned down the personal feeling of those under his direction, and was successful in eliminating some prevalent elements of popular prejudice. The Bancroft house published the work until a subsidiary corporation was organized for the purpose in 1886. Bancroft's attitude toward the enterprise has sometimes been criticized as too much that of the business man. He brought out all the volumes in his own name and never allocated credit for the authorship of the large portion written by those in his employ.

Bancroft continued to write until he was eighty-four. The more prominent of his later works are *Resources of Mexico* (1893), *The New Pacific* (1900), *The Book of Wealth* (1909–10), *Retrospection, Political and Personal* (1910), and *In These Latter Days* (1917). He was married in 1859 to Emily Ketchum and in 1875 to Matilda B. Griffing. His later years were divided between his San Francisco home and his country place at Walnut Creek.

[An autobiographical account of the earlier life of H. H. Bancroft and of his great historical enterprise appears in his *Literary Industries* (1890); of his voyage of 1852 to California in his *Popular Tribunals* (1887). Comment upon his plan of historical work, though not quite accurate in detail, occurs in Langlois and Seignobos, *Introduction to the Study of History* (1898). A statement concerning the authorship of the Bancroft history is made by Henry L. Oak in a pamphlet entitled *Literary Industries in a New Light* (1893). Other statements concerning the matter are presented and conclusions drawn in the *Ore. Hist. Soc. Quart.*, IV, 287–364.] W. A. M.

BANDELIER, ADOLPH FRANCIS ALPHONSE (Aug. 6, 1840–Mar. 18, 1914), historian, anthropologist, explorer, was born in Berne, Switzerland. His father was an officer in the Swiss army, and criminal judge of the Berne district; his mother was a Russian. At the fall of the Patrician Government in 1847, the elder Bandelier left Switzerland and went first to Brazil, whence disgust for slavery drove him to New York and finally to Illinois, where he bought a large tract of land near Highland. He sent for his family in 1848. Adolph had attended the Wengern School in Berne from his fourth year. He was eight when he started with his mother on the journey to America. There being no schools at Highland, he was educated at home. As a boy he was an ardent collector of butterflies, minerals, and botanical specimens. In 1855 he went to Switzerland to study geology at the University of Berne under Prof. Streder. At about this time he gained great inspiration from an interview with Alexander von Humboldt. Returning to America in the late fifties, Bandelier entered a bank founded by his father and other Swiss residents of Highland. It failed during the financial depression following the Civil War. In 1860 he married Josephine Huegy, a girl of Swiss parentage. Beginning in 1877, he published, through the Peabody Museum at Harvard, a series of most scholarly and basically important contributions on the ancient Mexicans (*On the Art of War and Mode of Warfare*, 1877; *On the Distribution and Tenure of Lands*, 1878; *On the Social Organization and Mode of Government*, 1879).

In 1880 he was engaged by the newly organized Archæological Institute of America to conduct researches in New Mexico, where he was extraordinarily active in the field until 1889. He made a brief visit to Mexico in 1881, at which time he became a Catholic. His explorations, which were generally undertaken on foot, and often in the face of great danger from Apache raids, covered nearly the whole of New Mexico and Arizona. He also accomplished much archive work in Santa Fé; and lived with the Pueblos in order to study Indian life and mentality. The results of this decade are recorded in a group of publications which appeared in the early nineties (*Final Report of Investigations among the Indians of the Southwestern United States*, Part I, 1890; Part II, 1892; *Contributions to the History of the Southwestern Portion of the United States*, 1890). The year 1892 brought a radical change in the scene of his work. Under the auspices of Henry Villard of New York he went to South America for archeological and historical investigations. After the death of his wife, at Lima, he undertook extensive explorations along the coast and in the highlands of Peru, lasting until late in 1893, when he returned to Lima and there married Fanny Ritter, a native of Zurich. With her, he spent the next ten years in a series of journeys in Peru and Bolivia, with periods of research in government and church records, and in private libraries in La Paz and other cities. In 1903, at the age of sixty-three, he returned to New York, where he worked in the Natural History Museum, served as lecturer on Spanish-American literature at Columbia, and (1906) joined the staff of the Hispanic Society of America. Symptoms of cataract developed in 1907, and from 1909 to 1911 he was almost totally blind. During that period, he continued with the help of his wife, to write, producing his last book (*The Islands of Titicaca and Koati*) in 1910. In 1911 he received an appointment as Research Associate of the Carnegie Institution of Washington, for archival research in Spain. After a year of preliminary investigations in Mexico, he went to Seville, where he died in 1914.

No American archeologist has depended as did Bandelier upon historical sources; and no American historian has checked his work so fully by a study of archeological materials. He also realized the necessity of collecting from surviving aborigines all possible legendary data, and of imbuing himself with a knowledge of their ways of life and habits of thought. The fields of Bandelier's work—the Southwest, Mexico, South America—were all singularly well-fitted for this type of approach, for in all of them are abundant aboriginal sites; and as to all of them the early Spanish accounts, published and in the archives, are remarkably full. In every case he went directly to original sources, historical or archeological. This, of course, led him to overthrow many generally accepted theories, and resulted in severe controversies with less well-informed or less conscientious writers. His work resulted in the discrediting of the romantic school of American Indian history, and paved the way for scientific, critical research.

[Information from biog. sketch by F. W. Hodge in *Am. Anthropologist,* n. s., XVI, 349–58, 1914 (with bibliography); from friends of Bandelier in Santa Fé; and from letters from Mrs. Bandelier (deposited at Peabody Museum, Harvard). Estimates of Bandelier's work are contained in obituaries by Hiram Bingham, *Nation,* Mar. 26, 1914, and by C. F. Lummis, *El Palacio,* Santa Fé, April, May 1914.]
A. V. K.

BANGS, FRANCIS NEHEMIAH (Feb. 23, 1828–Nov. 30, 1885), lawyer, the son of the Rev. Nathan Bangs [*q.v.*] and Mary (Bolton) Bangs, was born in New York City. He received only an ordinary school education, but in spare hours he earned money by keeping the commercial accounts of his elder brother's firm, and ultimately was enabled to attend the Wesleyan University at Middletown, Conn., and the University of the City of New York, where he graduated in 1845. He then studied for a time at the Yale Law School and was called to the bar of the city of New York in 1850. He commenced practise in that city. At first his progress was slow. His manner was not conciliatory. "At no period of his career, even in its small beginnings, was it possible for him to be obsequious or subservient to any one, however wealthy, influential, or powerful" (E. Randolph Robinson, at meeting of New York City bar, Dec. 12, 1885). Through his early experiences he was equipped with an intimate knowledge of commercial transactions and accounts, and he at first specialized in bankruptcy law. The ability which he displayed when retained on behalf of the assignees of Ketchum, Son & Company, a defaulting firm of New York stock brokers, first brought him into public notice. The various investigations and prosecutions which followed the exposure in 1871 of the operations of the "Tweed Ring" in New York's municipal affairs firmly established his reputation as an able, public-spirited, and fearless advocate. Contemporaneously with the accusations against Tweed and his associates, charges were made reflecting upon the administration of justice in New York City, and Bangs devoted all his energies and ability to the investigation which followed. Owing in great measure to his personal intervention, Judges John H. McCunn of the superior court of New York City, and G. G. Barnard of the supreme court were removed from office, and Judge Albert Cardozo was compelled to resign. Thereafter Bangs was constantly retained as counsel in heavy litigation, more particularly railway and corporation cases. Among the more important suits in which he held briefs were those concerning the Havemeyer and Cesnola estates. From 1873 to the end of his life he enjoyed an increasingly lucrative practise, and was generally recognized as standing at the head of his profession.

One of the secrets of his success was his capacity for concentration and hard work. It was said of him by a distinguished legal contemporary, James C. Carter, that he had on occasions sat down to his work for days for sixteen consecutive hours each day, interrupted only by a hasty meal. Throughout his career he was noted for unremitting toil in the preparation of his cases. Combined with a broad knowledge of law and human nature, unusual acquaintance with commercial and corporation methods, and a rugged yet attractive style of lucid advocacy, his thorough appreciation of every point of his case made him at all times powerful and sometimes irresistible in court. On the other hand his face was not attractive, nor was his manner altogether pleasant. "He was apt to be a little careless as to how he treated people, and at times he might have been regarded as inconsiderate. . . . There were occasions when his impatience and quick temper were somewhat trying" (Theron G. Strong, *post*). Unremitting attention to professional work undoubtedly undermined his health, and he died at Ocala, Fla., at the comparatively early age of fifty-seven. He had few interests outside of his profession, and though a Republican, never aspired to or held public office, "being indifferent to the allurements of pleasure or politics." He was president of the Bar Association of the City of New York 1882–83, and was active in the formation of the Union League Club. He was twice married: on Mar. 12, 1855, to Frances Amelia Bull, who died, Aug. 23, 1868; and, later, to Mary Adams Batcheller.

[His ancestry is set out in detail in *Hist. and Geneal. of the Bangs Family* by Dean Dudley (1896), pp. 9, 233. The best biog. is contained in a pamphlet *In Mem-*

ory of Francis N. Bangs (1885), being a report of a meeting of the bar of the City of New York, held Dec. 12, 1885, on the occasion of his death. Theron G. Strong, in *Landmarks of a Lawyer's Life* (1914), pp. 265–76, surveys the salient features of his career from personal knowledge. A sketch of his life will also be found in *Hist. of the Bench and Bar of N. Y.*, ed. by D. McAdam *et al.* (1897), I, 253–54.]

H. W. H. K.

BANGS, FRANK C. (Oct. 13, 1833–June 12, 1908), actor, son of David Barnwell and Margaret (Cannon) Bangs, was born in Alexandria, Va. His mother educated him strictly, with the idea of his becoming a minister. When only fifteen, he worked on a Washington newspaper, learning typesetting and writing stories; but a performance of the elder Booth as Richard III fired him with a desire to become an actor. Nevertheless, he went to Philadelphia, when eighteen, and began his theological studies. Records state that he was advised by his instructors to give up the ministry. On Sept. 27, 1851, he made his theatrical début at the Washington National, subsequently gaining experience as general-utility actor with Edwin Forrest, Kate and Susan Denin, Charlotte Cushman, Julia Dean, James H. Hackett, and others. He appeared also with the Ravel Troupe (a very popular family of players in the early national period of the American theatre), in *The Miller and His Men,* a pantomime. He then went through the treadmill of experience in Baltimore, Albany, and Washington, as the first walking gentleman and in such so-called juvenile rôles as Romeo, Horatio, and Claude Melnotte. At the Philadelphia Arch Street Theatre, he appeared with Mrs. John Drew and Olive Logan. In 1858–59, through the influence of Joseph Jefferson, he joined the company at Laura Keene's Theatre, making his first New York appearance, Apr. 22, 1858, in J. G. Burnett's *Blanche of Brandywine.* He shared juvenile parts with Lester Wallack, at Wallack's Theatre, N. Y., where he appeared in Boucicault's *Octoroon.*

The war put a stop to his acting for a time; he joined the Confederate army, going into active service with the 3rd Virginia, and was made a prisoner at Hilton's Head. At the close of the war, he returned to the stage, playing in stock at the Washington National. The papers of the time mention that he was unfairly treated by the audiences because of his Southern sympathies. In 1867, however, he met with much success in *After Dark,* at Niblo's Garden, but soon after, owing to a dispute with his managers, Jarrett and Palmer, regarding the casting of *Julius Cæsar,* he retired from the boards, giving most of his time to teaching the art of reading, to coaching amateur dramatic societies, and to lecturing on mental philosophy. In 1870 he was back on the stage, supporting Fechter and Carlotta Leclerq at the Boston Theatre, in *Hamlet* (Feb. 21), *Ruy Blas* (Feb. 28), and *The Lady of Lyons* (Mar. 5). The most notable event in his career was his appearance as Mark Antony opposite Edwin Booth's Brutus and Lawrence Barrett's Cassius, in a revival of *Julius Cæsar* on Dec. 25, 1871. The critic of the *New York Tribune* (Dec. 26, 1871) wrote, "Mr. Bangs achieved good success as Antony. The funeral oration was pronounced with singular discretion and true pathos. A subdued vein of sweetness ran through it, and this set off the fine outburst at the end." Several starring ventures were now attempted, but Bangs was better suited as support than as a star. At various times he appeared in such plays as *The Banker's Daughter, Michael Strogoff, Jim, the Penman,* and *Alabama.* In 1890–91, he was with the Jefferson-Florence company in *The Rivals* and *The Heir-at-law.* In 1892, he revived Boker's *Francesca da Rimini.* Toward the end of his career he was identified with such ephemeral pieces as *The Christian, The Choir Invisible, The Gentleman from Indiana,* and *The Awakening of Helena Ritchie.*

[*Phila. Pub. Ledger,* June 14, 1908; *N. Y. Dram. Mirror,* June 20, 1908; *Green Room Bk.* (Lond., 1908); *N. Y. Clipper,* Apr. 26, 1913; Dean Dudley, *Hist. and Geneal. of the Bangs Family in America* (1896).]

M. J. M.

BANGS, JOHN KENDRICK (May 27, 1862–Jan. 21, 1922), humorist, editor, lecturer, was born in Yonkers, N. Y., the grandson of Nathan Bangs [*q.v.*], and the son of Francis Nehemiah Bangs [*q.v.*] and Frances (Bull) Bangs. In 1883 he graduated from Columbia College. Here he was editor of *Acta Columbiana,* succeeding Nicholas Murray Butler. He married Agnes Lawson Hyde, Mar. 3, 1886, by whom he had four sons. His second wife, Mary Blakeney Gray, he married Apr. 27, 1904. It was in 1884 that as associate editor of *Life* he held his first professional editorial position. He remained in this capacity until 1888, when he was invited by Henry Mills Alden to join the staff of *Harper's Magazine,* and for eleven years he had charge of its humorous department and that of the *Bazaar.* He also wrote the literary notes and many articles, besides contributing to other periodicals. In 1899 he assumed editorship of *Harper's Weekly,* and the same year became the first editor of *Munsey's Weekly,* resigning, however, before the year was up. His earliest book, *The Lorgnette* (with S. W. Van Schaick), was published in 1886. Thereafter, up to 1910, he published over thirty volumes of humor and verse. Perhaps the best known of these are *Tiddledywink Tales* (1891), *Coffee and Repartee* (1893), *The Idiot* (1895), and *A Houseboat on the Styx* (1895). From the middle eighties until 1904 he lived in Yonkers, and during part of that period was vice-president of the board of education. In 1894 he ran for mayor, his defeat enabling him to write one of his most amusing travesties, *Three Weeks in Politics* (1894). In 1901 he went to Cuba and wrote an influential book on Cuban affairs, *Uncle Sam, Trustee* (1902). The financial difficulties of Harper & Brothers led him, in 1903, to become editor of the *New Metropolitan Magazine,* although he continued to write for *Harper's Weekly.* In June 1904, he took editorial charge of *Puck,* and it was during this year that he produced *Lady Teazle,* with Lillian Russell as Lady Teazle. Later he produced a musical fantasy. These two plays were the extent of his dramatic ventures.

Not until 1907 did he really find himself. Early in the nineties he had lectured on *The Evolution of a Humorist,* to which he later added the subtitle, *from Adam to Ade.* Now, breaking away from his editorial moorings, he left Yonkers for Ogunquit, Me., and became a free lance and lecturer. During the next fifteen years, aided by those he called "Salubrities," and his experience as an editor and writer, coupled with a genial personality, he won wide-spread popularity, and was unquestionably one of the best popular humorous lecturers of his generation. His most famous lecture was entitled *Salubrities I Have Met.* He was tall, spare, unaffected, a thorough gentleman in mind and bearing, with a carrying voice, fund of anecdotes and charm of manner, which made him a humorous speaker of rare distinction and taste. He was a man of warm sympathies. During the activities of the American Committee for Devastated France, he lectured and labored without stint in its behalf, and was made a Chevalier of the Legion of Honor.

He was an enormous worker, and at one time wrote under as many as ten assumed names. Early in his career he was in the habit of writing twenty-five jokes a day, just for relaxation. The whimsicalities created by him during his lifetime were of astonishing variety. Although he lacked the severely critical attitude of a higher type of creative artist, he largely made up for this by his singleness of purpose, and his influence on the formative period to which he belongs was considerable.

[Dean Dudley, *Hist. and Geneal. of the Bangs Family in America* (1896), pp. 253–54; *N. Y. Times, N. Y. Tribune, N. Y. Herald,* Jan. 22, 1922; personal information from Francis H. Bangs, son of J. K. Bangs.]

T. L. M.

BANGS, NATHAN (May 2, 1778–May 3, 1862), Methodist clergyman, was born at Stratford, Conn. His first American ancestor, Edward Bangs of Chichester, England, came to Plymouth in the *Anne* in 1623. His father, Lemuel, blacksmith, surveyor, school-teacher, had turned to the Church of England, was severely critical of Methodist preachers as uneducated, and had all his children baptized in the Protestant Episcopal Church. His mother was Rebecca Keeler of Ridgefield, Conn. All but one of the children became members, and four sons ministers in the Methodist denomination. In 1782 the family moved to the town of Fairfield, Conn. Bangs notes as the three most potent influences of his childhood, school with the Bible as text-book, his father's personality and a "resolute mother." He mentions, also, a liberal Puritan parson who encouraged dancing and social games, and an itinerant Methodist preacher. In 1791, the family moved again, to the thinly-settled country near Stamford, N. Y., the boy walking 150 miles. He entered freely into the sports of the primitive community, learned surveying of his father, and picked up enough education to be able to teach in the rural schools. When twenty-one he went to Canada, and took a school in a Dutch community near Niagara. One of the families where he boarded had a small library, and he became familiar with Milton, Bunyan, and Hervey's *Meditations.* An English parson whom he calls "drunken and card-playing," contrasted with James Coleman, a Methodist itinerant, effaced the last trace of his father's anti-Methodism. Bangs joined the Methodist church, discarding "cue" and "ruffles," and soon felt the definite assurance that he was divinely called to preach.

He began opening his school sessions with prayer; and when the Dutch directors objected he gave up his position rather than yield. Licensed to preach in 1801, he entered at once on the laborious service of the early Methodist traveling preachers. For years he rode on horseback through the forests of Upper Canada, sleeping and eating when and where he could find accommodation in a settler's cabin, and preaching when and where he could find a congregation. In 1804 he came into direct contact with Bishop Asbury, "the Apostle of Methodism." He was admitted to Conference, and without the usual two-year delay was made an elder. Assigned to the Province of Quebec, he found his work beset with peculiar difficulties; but is regarded as the founder of Methodism in that district. On Apr. 23, 1806, he married Mary Bolton of Edwardsburg, Upper Canada, daughter of Henry and Margaret (Lateur) Bolton of England. Conditions in

Canada becoming difficult for Americans as the War of 1812 drew near, he returned to the United States; and until 1820 served as pastor and part of the time as presiding elder in the state of New York. His duties taking him into the neighboring parts of Connecticut, he is said to have been influential in the movements which ended the Church and State connection there. In 1820 he was made agent of the Book Concern in New York. He paid the debts of the almost bankrupt institution, and put it on a paying basis. In the years following, he started the system of official church journals, and was himself editor of the *New York Advocate,* the *Methodist Magazine,* and the *Methodist Quarterly Review.* At the same time he had editorial charge of the publications of the Book Concern. Greatly interested in missionary work, he was the founder of the Methodist Missionary Society, for years serving as its secretary without salary. In 1836 he relinquished his connection with the Book Concern in order to give his full time to the Missionary Society. In 1841 he became acting president of Wesleyan University at Middletown, Conn., during the absence on account of illness of President Olin. In the controversy over slavery he took a mediating position, trying in vain to prevent the disruption. Superannuated, according to custom, at the age of seventy-five, he never ceased active participation in church work until his death.

Almost entirely self-educated, Bangs was yet an effective writer. Besides editorials, sermons, and addresses, the list of his published works includes the following: *Christianism* (1809); *Errors of Hopkinsianism* (1815); *Examination of the Doctrine of Predestination* (1817); *The Reformer Reformed* (1818); *Vindication of Methodist Episcopacy* (1820); *Life of Rev. Freeborn Garretson* (1829); *History of Missions* (1832); *Letters to a Young Preacher* (1835); *An Original Church of Christ* (1837); *History of the Methodist Episcopal Church,* in four volumes (1838–40); *Life of James Arminius* (1843); *Present State, Prospects, and Responsibilities of the Methodist Episcopal Church* (1850); *Necessity, Nature, and Fruits of Sanctification* (1851).

[D. Dudley, *Hist. and Geneal. of the Bangs Family in America* (1896); Abel Stevens, *Life and Times of Nathan Bangs* (1863); A. H. Tuttle, *Nathan Bangs* (1909); *Alumni Rec. Wesleyan Univ.* (3rd ed., 1883); *Christian Advocate* (N. Y.), May and June 1862.] C. N.

BANISTER, JOHN (1650–May 1692), botanist, son of John Bannister, was born at Twigworth, Gloucestershire, England. Graduating from Magdalen College, Oxford (B.A. 1671; M.A. 1674), he served several years as clerk and chaplain (J. R. Bloxam, *A Register of St. Mary Magdalen College,* 1853, I, 93); visited the West Indies, presumably as a Church of England missionary; and by 1678 settled in Charles City County, Va., where he devoted himself largely to scientific pursuits. Subsequently he patented land on the Appomattox River and officiated as minister for what was later Bristol Parish. In 1688 he married "a young widow." During his residence in Virginia he studied minutely the plant life of the region; corresponded with such scientists as Ray, Compton, Sloane, Bobart, and Martin Lister, whom he furnished with specimens or drawings of local flora and fauna; and worked at a "Natural History of Virginia," which his premature death terminated. His botanical and entomological articles, some of which appeared posthumously in the *Philosophical Transactions,* include his catalogues of Virginia plants, published in Ray's *Historia Plantarum* and Petiver's *Memoirs; Observations on the Natural Productions of Jamaica; Curiosities of Virginia; Observations on the Musca lupus; On Several Sorts of Snails; The Insects of Virginia;* and *A Description of the Snakeroot, Pistolochia, or Serpentaria Virginiania.* Without being a scientist of major importance, Banister enjoyed considerable reputation with his fellows. The Virginia Council nominated him as an original trustee of William and Mary College; Ray labelled him *"eruditissimus vir et consummatissimus botanicus"*; Lister termed him "a very learned and sagacious naturalist"; the historian Campbell ranks him with John Bartram. Linnæus's Genus 573, a tropical plant of the Malpighia family, is named after him (Bentham and Hooker; *Genera Plantarum,* I, 257). He is commonly stated to have been killed, while on a botanical expedition along the Roanoke River, by falling from a bluff, but it now appears that he was accidentally shot by a companion (*Virginia Magazine of History and Biography,* XI, 163–64). His papers were transmitted to Bishop Compton; his herbarium was left to Sir Hans Sloane, whose collection formed the nucleus of the British Museum.

[There is no full or adequate sketch of Banister extant: material concerning him is fragmentary and contradictory, his letters and manuscripts are not readily accessible, and the early records of the Banister family in America are imperfect. Although John Banister is generally believed to have come to Virginia in 1678, in the *Philosophical Trans.,* XVII, 667–72, are extracts from four letters written from Virginia by him to Dr. Martin Lister, whose dates, from May 5, 1668, to May 12, 1692, indicate twenty-four years' residence in America: it is probable, however, that 1668 here was a misprint for 1678, for Lister comments that Banister "had lived fourteen years at least in Virginia." If the botanist was in America as early as 1668, the ancestry, date of birth, and record of attendance at Oxford given by Goodwin in *The Colonial Ch. in Va.,* p. 248, must be those of a later John Banister—presumably the son of John Banister of Gloucester County, Va. (*Va. Mag. of Hist. and Biog.*, XXVIII, 129).] A. C. G., Jr.

BANISTER, JOHN (Dec. 26, 1734–Sept. 30, 1788), Revolutionary patriot, was born in Bristol Parish, Va., the son of John Banister and Willmuth, Wilmet, or Wilmette Banister, and grandson of John Banister, the naturalist [*q.v.*]. He went to England to study law and was admitted to the Middle Temple on Sept. 27, 1753. His first appearance in history was as a member of the Virginia Convention of 1776. He was in the House of Burgesses of the new state in 1777, and in 1778–79 he was a delegate to the Continental Congress. His position in that body is indicated by the fact that he was one of the framers of the Articles of Confederation; and of course he was a signer of that instrument. In the war he was lieutenant-colonel of cavalry in the Virginia line, during the years 1778–81. That he was highly valued by Washington is shown by an intimate letter which the commander-in-chief wrote to him from Valley Forge (*Writings of George Washington,* edited by Jared Sparks, V, 321–31). In the final campaign of 1781 he aided in repelling the British invasion of his state. He contributed supplies to the cause, and suffered losses of property; his home at Battersea, near Petersburg, was a convenient stopping-place for the British force under Gen. Phillips. Banister was first married to Patsy, daughter of Col. Theodoric Bland, and his letters figure frequently in the extensive correspondence of the *Bland Papers* (1840–43); his second marriage was to Anne, daughter of John Blair of Williamsburg. He was a good writer, well informed on current affairs.

[*Vestry Book and Register of Bristol Parish, Va., 1720–89*(1898); Philip Slaughter, *Hist. of Bristol Parish, Va.* (2nd ed., 1879); E. A. Jones, *Am. Members of the Inns of Court* (1924); Frederick Horner, *Hist. of the Blair, Banister, and Braxton Families*(1898); Chas. Campbell, *Hist. of the Colony & Ancient Dominion of Va.* (1860); *Am. Hist. Rev.*, July 1920; *Va. Mag. of Hist. and Biog.*, XI, 164–65, XX, 283.] E. K. A.

BANISTER, ZILPAH POLLY GRANT (May 30, 1794–Dec. 3, 1874), educator, was born in Norfolk, Conn., the daughter of Joel and Zilpah (Cowles) Grant, of Scotch descent. Both Joel Grant and his wife were sturdy pioneers and stanch Puritans. The rich soil of their farm had only thirty years before been wilderness, and wolves still howled about the one-story house on winter nights. It was in a New England blizzard that Joel Grant lost his life by the fall of his well-sweep, before his daughter was two years old. After learning everything offered in the weather-beaten schoolhouse near by, Zilpah spent several winters at home, sharing the heavy work of the family and reading all available books. Before she was fifteen she had begun her career as a teacher, in the district school of Paug, now East Norfolk, where she taught for two summers. The following two summers she taught at Winchester, and while there went through religious experiences which resulted in her joining the church. For twelve years she taught in the schools of Norfolk and adjacent towns; then came the opportunity to continue her own education. Rev. Ralph Emerson, minister at Norfolk, advised her to use her savings of fifty dollars to go to the seminary at Byfield, Mass., conducted by his brother, Rev. Joseph Emerson. There she became the friend of another student, Mary Lyon [*q.v.*]. After leaving Byfield in 1821 she started a private school at Winsted, but a year later went back as a teacher to Mr. Emerson's school, now removed to Saugus. In 1824 she became principal of the newly endowed Adams Female Academy, at Derry, N. H. She received the school-building without rent but otherwise assumed all responsibility and received all profits. In 1828 she removed her school to Ipswich where she obtained a building on the same terms. Both at Derry and at Ipswich Mary Lyon was her assistant until she left to found Mount Holyoke Seminary, which was modeled after the Ipswich Seminary. In 1839, feeling her health unequal to the work without the help of Miss Lyon, Miss Grant gave up her school.

On Sept. 7, 1841, she was married to William B. Banister, a Dartmouth graduate and former member of the Massachusetts Senate. At her marriage she became the mistress of a Colonial home in Newburyport, where lived also two daughters of her husband by former marriages. The devotion of these step-daughters meant much in her later life, especially after the death of her husband in 1853. A year in France and England, 1860–61, marked the last pronounced activity of her life. The remaining years were quiet, yet full of domestic, religious, and educational interests. A year before her death she visited Mount Holyoke Seminary and spoke before the students. Mrs. Banister's only writings were articles on the education of women. Her chief educational work was as a teacher of girls in days when education for women was not yet formulated. English, the sciences, Bible study, and physical training were stressed in her school, but foreign languages found no place in the curriculum. She was not a learned woman, nor even a wide reader; her wisdom was that of common sense and interest in human beings. As she moved up the aisle to the platform, a tall, erect, figure, with strongly marked features, reflective dark eyes, and dark hair, partly covered by a white head-dress, she represented to the girls assembled a model of womanly refinement and dignity.

[Linda T. Guilford, *The Use of a Life: Memorials of Mrs. Z. P. Grant Banister* (1885); a biog. sketch, with an account of the schools at Derry and Ipswich, by John P. Cowles, in *Barnard's Am. Jour. of Education*, vol. XXX (Sept. 1880); obituary in *Boston Transcript*, Dec. 4, 1874. Mrs. Banister's educational ideals and the course of study in her school are presented in the *Ipswich Seminary Cat.*, 1839.] S. G. B.

BANKHEAD, JOHN HOLLIS (Sept. 13, 1842–Mar. 1, 1920), senator, was born in Moscow, Ala. His father, James Greer Bankhead, was a farmer and Indian-fighter of South Carolina; his mother, Susan (Hollis) Bankhead, was descended from a favorite aide of the Revolutionary general, Marion. The actual settler in Alabama was his grandfather George, who moved from South Carolina to the piney woods of Marion County and built the first mill. John Hollis was brought up on the farm, with little schooling, but this he made up for by diligent reading. He was not twenty-one when the Civil War began, and he emerged from the war a captain. From 1865 to 1868 he was a member of the Alabama legislature. On Nov. 13, 1866 he was married to Tallulah J. Brockman. He was one of Gen. Forrest's Ku Klux, designed to control the unruly freedmen during Congress's military Reconstruction; was again in the legislature (Senate 1876–77, House of Representatives 1880–81); and was warden of the penitentiary (1881–85). He attracted little public notice, however, as Brewer's *Alabama* and Garrett's *Public Men of Alabama*, published about 1872, do not mention him.

In 1886 the sphere of his activities was widened by election to Congress, where he joined in the passage of the anti-trust laws; but his principal work concerned the Post Office Department and the canalization of the Tombigbee River. This stream rises in the coal regions of Alabama and then waters cotton-fields in that state and in Mississippi before joining its sister river, the Alabama. By its improvement it has become one of the most useful water systems of the Union, but it must not be supposed that Bankhead effected this alone, for he was aided if not inspired by interested activities originating from Mobile. In 1906 a singular situation carried Bankhead yet higher. It was so evident that both Morgan and Pettus, long-time senators, were failing from age that the party adopted a succession primary to fill probable vacancies. Bankhead was successful for the first, and on the death of Morgan next year was elected his successor. His principal service, however, was in improving the roads not only of Alabama but of the whole country. He first secured a trial appropriation of $500,000 for demonstration, and this was so beneficial that on July 11, 1916, he procured the passage of an act whereby the United States should aid the states in the construction of rural post-roads. This carried an annual appropriation through 1921 of $5,000,000 to $25,000,000, and was amended, after Bankhead's death, by granting even larger sums. As a memorial a private association in several southern states has planned a Bankhead Highway, starting at Washington and ending on the Pacific, and much of this has been built.

[The chief authority as to Bankhead is the sketch by Thomas M. Owen, his son-in-law, *Hist. of Ala. and Dict. of Ala. Biog.* (1921), III, 88–92. The sources as to his road measures are in the *Statutes at Large*; see also the *U. S. Good Roads Bull.*, Dec. 1920, Jan. 1921. Light on his activities as warden is in Conier *vs.* Bankhead, 70 *Alabama*, pp. 116, 493.] P. J. H.

BANKS, NATHANIEL PRENTISS (Jan. 30, 1816–Sept. 1, 1894), congressman, governor of Massachusetts, Union soldier, was born in Waltham, Mass., the eldest of the seven children of Nathaniel P. and Rebecca (Greenwood) Banks. His father was superintendent of the mill in which is said to have been woven the first cotton cloth manufactured in the United States. After only a few years in the common schools the boy had to go to work in the cotton-mill, from which fact in later years there clung to him the nickname, "the Bobbin Boy of Massachusetts." Keenly ambitious, he set to work to remedy the deficiencies in his own education. By his own efforts he obtained some command of Latin, and diligently studied Spanish, early declaring that America some day would be brought into intimate association with peoples of that tongue. He seized every opportunity for practise in public speaking, lecturing on temperance and taking an active part in a local debating society. He soon became a recognized power in town meeting. For a time he studied to become an actor, and made a successful appearance in Boston as Claude Melnotte in *The Lady of Lyons*, but he soon turned to the law. At twenty-three he was admitted to the bar, but he never practised in the courts. He first entered public service as an inspector in the Boston customs house. For three years he was the proprietor and editor of a local weekly newspaper, the *Middlesex Reporter*. In March 1847 he was married to Mary I. Palmer. Seven times he was a candidate for the lower branch of the Massachusetts legislature before he became a member of that body in 1849. By the "coalition" in 1851 Henry

Wilson as a Free-Soiler was made president of the Senate, and Banks as a Democrat was made speaker of the House, and he was reëlected to that office the following year.

At thirty-seven this self-taught man was chosen president of what has been called "the ablest body that ever met in Massachusetts," the constitutional convention of 1853, over which he presided with rare tact and self-control. Entering Congress in 1853, he served—though not continuously—in ten Congresses, representing five different party alignments. In his first term, though elected as a Democrat, he showed his courage and independence by opposing the Kansas-Nebraska bill. In the Thirty-fourth Congress, to which he had been elected as the candidate of the "Americans" (Know-Nothing party), he was put forward for the speakership in the most stubborn contest in the history of that office. Backed by no caucus, he drew votes from the other Know-Nothing candidates because of his uncompromising record in his first term (H. von Holst, *Constitutional History of the United States,* 1885, V, 204 ff.). As the struggle dragged on, he bluntly declared that the repeal of the Missouri Compromise was an act of dishonor, and that under no circumstances whatever would he, if he should have the power, allow the institution of human slavery to derive benefit from the repeal. He thus came to be regarded as "the very bone and sinew of Free-soilism," and his election (Feb. 2, 1856, on the 133rd ballot, and only after the adoption of a resolution calling for election by plurality vote), was hailed as the first defeat of slavery in a quarter of a century, and was later looked back upon as the first national victory of the Republican party. He held that the speaker's office was not political but executive and parliamentary. To the anti-slavery men he gave a bare majority on the various committees, and made several of his most decided opponents chairmen. Historians of the office rate Banks as one of the ablest and most efficient of speakers (M. P. Follett, *The Speaker of the House of Representatives,* 1902, pp. 36, 58–59; H. B. Fuller, *The Speaker of the House,* 1909, pp. 102–11, 116–17). He showed consideration and consummate tact, and his decisions were prompt and impartial. Though his service was in a period of the bitterest partisanship, not one of his decisions was overruled.

In 1856 Banks declined a nomination for the presidency from the convention of "North Americans," anti-slavery seceders from the "American" convention which had nominated Fillmore. Though he had been the candidate of the "Americans" in his second campaign for Congress and though he had just received this further evidence of their favor, he had already outgrown that nativist association, and in 1857 he cast aside his promising career in Congress to accept the Republican nomination for governor of Massachusetts. To the dismay of conservatives, he adopted the innovation of stumping the state in person, and against the seemingly invincible incumbent of three terms he won the election by a large majority. He held the governorship for three successive years, 1858–60, and proved an effective and progressive executive. He was a pioneer in urging the humane and protective features of modern probation laws, and displayed a great and intelligent interest in all movements for educational progress. His wise forethought as to the militia enabled his successor, Gov. John A. Andrew, to respond at once to Lincoln's call, sending troop after troop of Massachusetts militia, well trained and fully equipped for service.

At the end of his term (January 1861) Banks removed to Chicago, to succeed George B. McClellan as president of the Illinois Central Railroad. But Sumter had hardly fallen when he tendered his services to President Lincoln, and on May 16 he was commissioned major-general of volunteers. His first service was in the Department of Annapolis, where he coöperated in measures to prevent the seemingly imminent secession of Maryland. He was next assigned to the 5th corps in the Department of the Shenandoah. Here the transference of Shields's division to McDowell left Banks isolated with a command diminished to 10,000 to cope with "Stonewall" Jackson's greatly superior forces. The Confederates' capture of Front Royal, May 23, 1862, left no course open to Banks—his force now outnumbered two to one—but precipitate retreat. A race for Winchester, a vigorous battle, in which Banks's command bore itself well, and then a hasty crossing of the Potomac at Harper's Ferry rescued his army, but with a loss of some 200 killed and wounded and more than 3,000 prisoners (J. W. Draper, *History of the American Civil War,* 1868, II, 393). In June, Banks's force was brought into the new consolidation, the Army of Virginia, placed under Gen. Pope. From Culpeper, Aug. 9, 1862, Pope ordered Banks, in case the enemy approached, to "attack him immediately." Acting upon this explicit order, late in the afternoon, Banks's little army, in mood to avenge the humiliations they had suffered in the Shenandoah Valley, charged the enemy with such suddenness and vehemence that the whole of Jackson's left was driven from its position before his reserves could be brought into action. But some lack of tactical skill, the wounding of two of Banks's general officers, and the weight of opposing numbers after the first shock of surprise soon turned the tide of battle, and the Federals were forced into disorderly retreat. Banks was severely blamed for making this attack at Cedar Mountain, and Pope denied that his order authorized the action which Banks took ("Report of the Joint Committee on Conduct of the War," *Senate Report No. 142,* 38 Cong., 2 Sess., pt. III, pp. 44–54). But "it will be hard to prove, if language means anything, that he at all transgressed his [Pope's] orders. Of course the order should not have been given" (William Allan, *The Army of Northern Virginia,* 1892, p. 171, *n.*). For a short time in the fall of 1862 Banks was in charge of the defenses of Washington. In the closing months of the year, at New Orleans he succeeded Gen. B. F. Butler in command of the department. He was assigned the tasks of holding New Orleans and the other parts of the state which had been reduced to submission, and of aiding Grant to open the Mississippi. After placing his garrisons he had hardly 15,000 men left for aggressive action. In April 1863 he succeeded in regaining considerable territory for the Union, and in May he reached Alexandria. His next objective was Port Hudson. On May 25 and 27 he made costly attempts to capture the place by assault, bringing into action negro troops, who, he declared, showed the utmost daring and determination. Repulsed with heavy losses, he began siege. Though hard pressed by famine, the garrison repelled another assault, June 13, but within a week after the fall of Vicksburg it found itself forced to unconditional surrender, July 9, with loss of 6,200 prisoners, a large number of guns, and a great mass of military supplies. The thanks of Congress were tendered to Banks and his troops (Jan. 28, 1864) "for the skill, courage, and endurance which compelled the surrender of Port Hudson, and thus removed the last obstruction to the free navigation of the Mississippi River" (*United States Statutes at Large,* 38 Cong., 1 Sess., Resolution No. 7).

The later movements of the year proved ineffective: although with the coöperation of a naval force Banks had advanced along the coast as far as Brownsville, capturing some works of importance, he found his force inadequate to extend the movement and withdrew to New Orleans. Here in the difficult task of dealing with the civilian population he inherited the unpopularity of his predecessor, and his assassination was attempted. He opposed the admission of Confederate attorneys to practise in the courts. With no legal authority for his action, in January and February 1864, Banks issued orders prescribing the conditions of suffrage and other details as to elections, under which state officers and delegates to a constitutional convention were chosen and a constitution adopted. Although hardly one in seven of the voters of the state voted upon the question of ratifying this constitution, Banks went to Washington, where for months he pressed the recognition of the Louisiana state Government (E. L. Pierce, *Memoir of Charles Sumner,* 1893, IV, 215, 221).

In the opening months of 1864 preparations were made for the ill-starred Red River Expedition. Gen. Grant had strenuously opposed this movement, and later declared that it was "ordered from Washington," and that Banks had opposed the expedition, and was in no way responsible, except for the conduct of it (*Personal Memoirs,* 1886, II, 139–40). The State Department insisted that the flag must be restored to some one point in Texas, as a counter to the movements of the French in Mexico; the President was eager to establish a loyal government in Louisiana; and the agents of the Government and speculators were lured by the great stores of cotton along the river. Starting in the early spring, the only season when the Red River was navigable, Banks advanced with a land force of 27,000 men, Admiral Porter being in command of a supporting fleet of gunboats. When within two days' march of his objective, Shreveport, Banks's army, extending for miles along a single road, encountered the main body of the enemy at Sabine Crossroads, Apr. 8, and was routed. On the following day at Pleasant Hill a fierce battle was fought, in which both parties claimed the victory. Failure of his supplies of ammunition, rations, and water compelled Banks to fall back. Meantime the fleet had been placed in imminent peril by the unprecedentedly early subsidence of the Red River, and was saved only by the brilliant engineering feat of Col. Joseph Bailey in constructing a series of dams that secured enough depth of water to send the gunboats over the shallows (J. W. Draper, *History of the American Civil War,* 1870, III, 235–38). The army followed the naval force down the river, repelling rear attacks. Grant's peremptory recall of 10,000 men left Banks facing a serious crisis. On May 13 he evacuated Alexandria. Though left in nominal command, he was soon virtually superseded by the arrival of Gen. E. R. S. Canby, who had been appointed to the command of all forces west of the Mississippi. A majority of the Committee on the Conduct of the War placed upon Banks a large measure of responsibility for the disasters which befell this expedition, but a minority member, D. W. Gooch, defended him on the ground that the major causes of failure, *i. e.* the unforeseeable difficulties of navigation, and the shortness of the time for which nearly half of the force were "lent" by Sherman, were beyond his control (*Senate Report No. 142,* 38 Cong., 2 Sess., pt. II, pp. 3–401). Although repeatedly in this humiliating expedition Banks showed a lack of military skill, in the main he had to "bear the blame of the blunders of his superiors," who for alleged reasons of state ordered a movement which had little military justification, and doomed it to failure by so organizing it that, while four forces were supposed to coöperate, the commander of no one of them had the right to give an order to another (Asa Mahan, *Critical History of the Late American War,* 1877, p. 407).

Honorably mustered out of military service, Aug. 24, 1865, Banks returned to his native city, and was almost immediately elected as a Republican to fill a vacancy in the House, caused by the death of D. W. Gooch, where he continued to serve from the Thirty-ninth to the Forty-second Congress. During this period he voted for the act stopping further contraction of the currency, and was a member of the committee of five to investigate the *Crédit Mobilier* charges. He was chairman of the Committee on Military Affairs at the time Maximilian was in Mexico and war with France seemed likely to follow. He advised a bold policy in regard to the Alabama Claims, advocated our acquisition of Alaska, and reported a bill asserting the right of every naturalized American citizen to renounce all allegiance to his native land, and authorizing the President, if such right should be denied, in reprisal to suspend trade relations with such a Government, and to arrest and detain any of its citizens. In the campaign of 1872, because of a personal quarrel with President Grant, he supported Greeley's candidacy, and as a consequence was himself defeated for reelection. At the beginning of the short session, the month following this defeat, he tendered his resignation from the Committee on Military Affairs in order that the House might be "represented by some member more unequivocably committed to its policy," but the House by a substantial vote refused to excuse him from such service (Dec. 2, 1872, *Congressional Globe,* p. 10). During the two-year interruption of his congressional career he was elected to the Massachusetts Senate for the session of 1874, but in the following November he was returned to Congress as a Democrat. Two years later he was reëlected as a Republican. At the expiration of this term, he was appointed by President Hayes to the position of United States marshal for Massachusetts, and served from Mar. 11, 1879, to Apr. 23, 1888. In that year he was reelected to Congress as a Republican, defeating Col. Thomas W. Higginson. Before the end of the term his health became seriously impaired; he retired to his home in Waltham, where he died, Sept. 1, 1894. He was survived by a son and two daughters, one of whom, Maude Banks, attained some distinction as an actress. By resolution of the Massachusetts General Court provision was made for the erection of a bronze statue of Gen. Banks upon the grounds of the State House. This statue, by Henry H. Kitson, was unveiled Sept. 16, 1908.

[No general biog. of Banks has been published. The story of his early career is told by William M. Thayer in *The Bobbin Boy* (1860). The main features of his military career are presented in the books and reports above cited; see also *Official Records.* Certain phases are discussed by G. F. R. Henderson, in *Stonewall Jackson and the Am. Civil War* (1898), I, 388 ff., and by Geo. C. Eggleston, in *Hist. of the Confederate War* (1910), I, 208. Frank M. Flynn's *Campaigning with Banks in Louisiana* (1887) contains little of value.]

G. H. H.

BANNER, PETER (fl. 1794–1828), architect, was an Englishman who came to Boston in 1794, according to his grandson, George H. Banner of Washington, N. H. (G. N. Gage and others, *History of Washington, N. H.,* 1886). He appeared in the *New York Directory* as house carpenter and master-builder from 1795 to 1798 inclusive, and in 1806 we find him listed in the *Boston Directory* as architect. He seems to have lived in Boston till at least 1828, the date of the last appearance of his name. No will is on record, and the date and place of his death are uncertain. He may have moved to Worcester, for his grandson, George H. Banner (son of Peter Banner, Jr.) was born in Worcester in 1834, and moved later to Washington, N. H. (*Ibid.,* p. 293). Banner's name appears once in the *Boston Directory* as Baner (1822), and it was also occasionally spelled Bonner. It is so spelled in Ellen S. Bulfinch's *Life and Letters of Charles Bulfinch* (1896), who refers on page 118 to the Park Street Church, built in 1810 "from the design of Peter Bonner, an English architect."

W. W. Wheildon, in the *Memoir of Solomon Willard* (designer of the Bunker Hill Monument), published by the Monument Association of Boston in 1865, states on page 29 that Banner had practised his profession in England before coming to this country. The internal evidence apparently bears this out, for the Eben Crafts House in Roxbury, Mass., attributed to him and built in 1805, shows a developed sense both of composition and technique. The attribution of this design to Banner has been questioned, notably by C. A. Place, in *Charles Bulfinch, Architect and Citizen* (1925), but it appears to be justified. It is made on the basis of Wheildon's statement (*op. cit.*, p. 29), and is followed without question by S. Fiske Kimball (*Domestic Architecture of the American Colonies and of the Early Republic,* 1922). The house is manifestly a work differing from the usual traditional New England mansion of the time; its combination of monumental conception with slimness and extreme refinement of detail seems markedly English; the attribution to Banner is therefore probable.

Banner's great work was the Park Street Church in Boston, in which he was assisted by Daniel Brigham as chief mason, and Solomon Willard (who later himself became an architect) as chief carpenter. The treatment of the front, with high, simple central-entrance motive and the two curved vestibules with a slim colonnade, is unusually fresh, original, beautiful; the whole forms a pleasant foil to the arched windows and severe forms of the church proper. Again, as in the Crafts House, there is a personal note different from the fine New England tradition—a note of finish, monumentality, gracious sophistication. Yet it is the spire which has made the Park Street Church, and Peter Banner with it, famous. Although in one sense it is the final flowering of the tradition of New England spire design, a close examination reveals again and again in the designer a personality and a training different from that of the usual carpenter-architect of the period. The superposed orders are, of course, usual in New England, but the simple way in which the octagonal plan is expressed, and the daring slimness of the columns, with the lightness and delicacy of the detail throughout, reveal a new kind of beauty. Certain critics have found in this steeple the influence of Wren's tower of St. Bride's Church, Fleet St., London (J. Jackson, *The Development of American Architecture, 1783–1830,* 1926, p. 53). Certainly the contrast of plain base and rich spire, and certain tricks in the octagonal plan are the same in each, but nevertheless Banner's interpretation in wood is masterly, and the directness of design and the unassuming expression of the material are even finer than in the Wren example. Of buildings now standing, only the Crafts House at Roxbury and the Park Street Church at Boston can be attributed with any certainty to Banner. It appears, however, that he was the architect of the Old South Parsonage Houses, built in 1809, and long since destroyed. The records of the Old South Church (H. A. Hill, *History of the Old South Church,* 1890, II, 343 ff.) show that Banner won this work over his competitor of the time, Asher Benjamin [*q.v.*]. In fact, after approving the Benjamin plan, the church, at a meeting June 7, 1809, voted to reconsider its former action and to adopt Banner's plan, which was carried into execution, at a total cost of $16,310 (entry of Apr. 11, 1811). In 1819 Banner designed the first building of the American Antiquarian Society at Worcester, Mass., which remained standing until 1910.

[See references in the body of the article.]

T. F. H.

BANNISTER, NATHANIEL HARRINGTON (Jan. 13, 1813–Nov. 2, 1847), playwright, actor, whose birthplace is uncertain, but who was born either in Delaware or Baltimore, Md., made his début in Baltimore at the Front Street Theatre in 1830, as Young Norval. He first appeared in New York at the Chatham Theatre in 1831. He was a popular actor in the South and West, but seems to have been unable to secure a permanent footing in New York. From his many plays he probably made little, although he was one of the most prolific of the early dramatists, and he sold for fifty dollars his most successful piece, *Putnam,* which ran for seventy-eight nights at the Bowery Theatre, New York, where it was first produced, Aug. 5, 1844. It is a vigorous melodrama, in which Washington is a character, but it owed its popularity to the constant danger and thrilling escapes of Israel Putnam, who finally evades Cornwallis by riding down a precipice to the accompaniment of 150 shots. *Putnam* was published in Boston about 1859.

Bannister's other printed plays are *Gaulantus* (1836), produced at the Walnut Street Theatre, Philadelphia, Aug. 31, 1837, a tragedy in rough blank verse dealing with the conquest of Gaul by the Romans; *England's Iron Days* (1837), laid in an indefinite time when Normans and Saxons were at odds, and based on a strife between two brothers; *The Three Brothers* (1840), played at the Chatham Theatre, New York, a more modern but equally illogical melodrama, on Bannister's favorite theme of family quarrels; *The Gentleman of Lyons; or, the Marriage Contract* (1838), played in New Orleans at the Camp Street Theatre in 1837, an obvious imitation of *The Lady of Lyons.* Bannister's unpublished plays as described in contemporary accounts show that he was following the current fashions in playwriting, either by dealing with romantic themes, reproducing historical characters, or putting on the stage contemporary events. His first play, *Rathanemus* (Camp Street Theatre, Mar. 24, 1835) is known, as are most of his works, only by title. *The Destruction of Jerusalem* (Walnut Street Theatre, Nov. 20, 1837) was a spectacular performance, apparently unsuccessful. *Life in Philadelphia; or, The Unfortunate Author* (Walnut Street Theatre, Jan. 15, 1838) may have revealed the playwright's own tragedy. *Caius Silius* (Walnut Street Theatre, Aug. 27, 1838), laid in Rome, had apparently some merit. On Aug. 27, 1838, at the Franklin Theatre, New York, Bannister appeared as Lucinius in his own tragedy of *The Syracusan Brothers,* and on Aug. 31 he played Alvardo in his play of *The Two Spaniards.* For his benefit on Sept. 7, he chose the part of Julian in his *Gentleman of Lyons.* At the same theatre we find him acting Bob Buckeye in his play of *The Maine Question,* which dealt with the dispute between the United States and England over the Northeastern Boundary. Gen. Scott was the leading character. In the cast was Mrs. Bannister, *née* Amelia Greene, whom he had married in 1835 and who was the widow of the playwright John Augustus Stone. After the production of *Robert Emmett* (New Chatham Theatre, New York, Jan. 6, 1840), Bannister devoted himself to the play dealing with American events. *Richmond Hill* (Greenwich Theatre, New York, May 11, 1846) introduced Washington and André. *The Old Waggoner of New Jersey and Virginia* (Arch Street Theatre, Philadelphia, Feb. 10, 1847) dealt with events in the life of Gen. Morgan. *Murrell, the Land Pirate* (Bowery Theatre, Oct. 30, 1847) took the character of Ichabod Crane into the region of the Mississippi. This play was produced in many parts of the country. *Infidelity* was played at the Arch Street Theatre, Feb. 6, 1847, the year of Bannister's death in New York; and *Oua Costa; or, The Lion of the Forest,* laid during the French and Indian War, was put on at the Arch Street Theatre, Nov. 8, 1850. Other productions of Bannister are difficult to identify. Rees states that his *Wandering Jew* was written in fifteen acts and was represented only in part. *Psammetichus; or, The Twelve Tribes of Egypt* was written for Edwin Forrest, but was not produced by him. The passage quoted in Rees is in better verse than that of any of Bannister's published plays.

[There is a fair account of Bannister in James Rees, *The Dramatic Authors of America* (1845), some slight mention of him in T. Allston Brown, *Hist. of the N. Y. Stage* (1903) and *Hist. of the Am. Stage* (1870), in Noah M. Ludlow, *Dramatic Life as I Found It* (1880), in R. F. Roden, *Later Am. Plays* (1900); but the record of his activities has to be pieced together largely from Charles Durang, "The Phila. Stage," printed in *The Phila. Sunday Despatch* (series III); see also J. N. Ireland, *Recs. of the N. Y. Stage* (1866), and A. H. Quinn, *Hist. of the Am. Drama from the Beginning to the Civil War* (1923).]

A. H. Q.

BANVARD, JOHN (Nov. 15, 1815–May 16, 1891), painter, writer, the son of Daniel Banvard, and brother of Joseph Banvard [*q.v.*], was born in New York City. In childhood uncertain health prevented his following outdoor sports, so he amused himself with scientific experiments, verse making, and drawing. His only formal education was received in the New York High School and when he was fifteen he was thrown upon his own resources by the financial failure and death of his father. He went to Louisville, Ky., where he became a drug clerk. When he should have been putting up prescriptions, he was drawing caricatures with chalk upon the walls. Dismissal resulted. Welcoming freedom, he began to paint, but his pictures brought no money and he soon started off with his paint-box after adventure. At New Harmony, Ind., he turned a flatboat into an art gallery and floated down the Wabash River, exhibiting his paintings. A bushel of potatoes, a dozen eggs, or a fowl was an acceptable admission fee to the "show boat." Ignorance of the channel, with its snags and sand-bars, malaria, and scarcity of food made this venture a failure. Pecuniary returns were better when he gave up his boat and painted and exhibited in New Orleans, Natchez, Cincinnati, and Louisville. His ambition was always for size, and he next painted a panorama of Venice, which he had never seen. Having accumulated a small capital, he purchased a museum at St. Louis but lost both capital and museum. Undiscouraged, he peddled goods down the Ohio River to fill his purse. In the spring of 1840, he embarked on the Mississippi River in a skiff, with the project of making drawings for a grand panorama, to be the largest painting in the world. He traveled thousands of miles, exposed to many hardships, drawing incessantly, and sleeping under his skiff with his portfolio for a pillow. With his drawings completed, he erected a building in Louisville and painted the scenes on canvas woven for the purpose at Lowell, Mass. When finished, the "Panorama" was advertised as covering three miles of canvas. The fidelity of the portrayal was testified to by a number of Mississippi River captains and pilots. Its value was geographical; artistic merit it had little or none. It was of the chromo type, and in 1861 Banvard painted the picture, "The Orison," from which the first American chromo was made. "The Panorama of the Mississippi" was exhibited throughout the United States and in London, where it was admired by Queen Victoria. During the Civil War, Banvard furnished to Generals Frémont and Pope information about Island No. 10 in the Mississippi, which assisted in its capture. He later traveled in Europe, Asia, and Africa, and painted scenes in Palestine and a "Panorama of the Nile." His pictures were always rapidly executed and with a certain crude vigor but without technical skill. Banvard was almost as facile a writer as a painter. He wrote about 1,700 poems, some of which appeared in magazines. He also wrote *A Description of the Mississippi River* (1849), *A Pilgrimage to the Holy Land* (1852), *Amasis, or the Last of the Pharaohs* (1864), *The Private Life of a King, Embodying the Suppressed Memoirs of the Prince of Wales, afterwards George IV* (1876), *The Tradition of the Temple,* a poem (1883), *Carrinia* (1875). The dramas *Amasis* and *Carrinia* were performed respectively at the Boston Theatre and the Broadway Theatre, New York. As a writer, Banvard's claim to artistic excellence is probably no stronger than as a painter. But his personality was rugged and original. In his mature years his appearance was like that of many Mississippi River pilots—a thick-set figure, with heavy features, bushy dark hair, and rounded beard. In 1880 he settled in Watertown, S. Dak., where he lived with his children. He died there May 16, 1891.

[One of the chief sources of information is an anonymous biog. pamphlet, *Banvard; or the Adventures of an Artist* (1851). Articles on his life and his "Panorama" appeared in *Howitt's Jour. of Lit. and Pop. Prog.*, II, 145; *Chambers' Edinburgh Jour.*, VII, 2nd ser., 395; and *Littell's Living Age*, XX, 314. Obituary in the *Sioux Falls* (S. Dak.) *Argus-Leader*, May 20, 1891.]

S. G. B.

BANVARD, JOSEPH (May 9, 1810–Sept. 28, 1887), author, Baptist clergyman, was descended from an old French family, the Bon Verds, whose coat of arms later came into his possession. His grandfather escaped from France on account of persecution, first to Amsterdam, then to America. Daniel Banvard, the father of Joseph, and of John [*q.v.*], was involved in a business partnership which failed, his savings were lost, and at his death, soon after, his family was left in poverty. Joseph, born in New York City, was in his early twenties at the time of his father's death and had completed a course at South Reading Academy. He afterward studied at the Newton Theological Institution, from which he was graduated in 1835. He then became pastor of the Second Baptist Church, Salem, Mass., where he remained eleven years. Pastorates of varying lengths followed: in Boston; West Cambridge, Mass.; New York; Pawtucket, R. I.; Worcester, Mass.; Paterson, N. J.; and Neponset, Mass. In 1866 he was elected president of the National Theological Institute, Washington, D. C., a school for colored preachers and teachers, but resigned within a year.

As early as 1850 his interest began to be divided between his clerical duties and the writing of books, particularly history. His most important works are *The Christian Melodist; a Collection of Hymns* (1850), *Novelties of the New World* (1852), *The American Statesman; or Illustrations of the Life and Character of Daniel Webster* (1853), *Priscilla; or Trials for the Truth. An Historic Tale of the Puritans and the Baptists* (1854), *Wisdom, Wit, and Whims of Distinguished Ancient Philosophers* (1855), *Tragic Scenes in the History of Maryland and the Old French War* (1856), *Old Grips and Little Tidd* (1873), *First Explorers of North America* (1874), *Southern Explorers and Colonists* (1874), *Soldiers and Patriots of the Revolution* (1876), and an eight-volume juvenile collection. He had a keen interest in American history, especially that of the colonial era. In his writing of history he showed some knowledge of the use of sources. In one of his prefaces he said, "We have availed ourselves of the most reliable sources of information from the journals and letters of the first Pilgrims down to historians of a recent date." There seems to have been little sifting and weighing of historical material, but the proportion between important and unimportant events was fairly well preserved. He was susceptible to romance in history and obviously enjoyed relating adventures. He had a readable narrative style, enlivened by many details of action and local color. The moral and religious values of history appealed, perhaps disproportionately, to him. In *The American Statesman* he devoted considerable attention to proving Daniel Webster an intrinsically religious man, a devout believer in prayer and the Bible. He died at Neponset, Sept. 28, 1887, and his funeral took place in the Harvard Street Baptist Church, Boston, where he had formerly been pastor.

[Sources of information about Joseph Banvard are an anonymous biog. pamphlet sketch of his brother, John Banvard, entitled *Banvard; or the Adventures of an Artist* (1851), an article on John Banvard in *Howitt's Jour. of Lit. and Pop. Prog.*, II, 145, and obituaries of Joseph Banvard in the *Boston Transcript,* Oct. 1, 1887, and the *Salem Gazette,* Oct. 7, 1887.]

S. G. B.

BAPST, JOHN (Dec. 17, 1815–Nov. 2, 1887), Jesuit missionary, educator, is chiefly noted among his coreligionists for what he suffered in defense of his principles; for it fell to his lot to maintain the Jesuit interests in a hostile environment, for three decades of the nineteenth century (1850–80). He was born at La Roche in Fribourg, Switzerland, a canton noted for its catholicity, at the capital of which Canisius, a celebrated Jesuit of the sixteenth century founded the Collège St. Michel. Here young Bapst was educated, entered upon his novitiate in the order Sept. 30, 1835, and was ordained priest on the last day of 1846. He was destined for missionary work in North America, where about the time he arrived at Baltimore, the Abnaki Indians of Oldtown, Me., were asking for the services of a "Black Robe," in memory of the Jesuits, who had visited them two centuries earlier. Bapst was thereupon sent to these Indians, although then ignorant of their language and also of English. After two years' service among them he found it necessary to supplement his meager stipend by ministering to the Catholics of the nearby towns. In 1850 he was at Eastport, and somewhat later he became priest at Ellsworth, an intensely Protestant town, then seething with the excitement that the "Know-Nothing" party was causing in Maine. Bapst felt called upon to protest against the religious exercises used in the public schools in which the children of his parishioners were required to participate. He went so far as to instigate a lawsuit against the school committee, which so wrought upon the feelings of the town meeting that resolutions were passed for the expulsion and punishment of the priest. Whereupon a mob visited him at his home, tarred and feathered him, and drove him from the place (July 1854). This cruel treatment undermined his health, and it was some time before he recovered sufficiently to carry on his work. In 1858 ground had been broken at Boston for a college, which two years later was assigned to the Jesuits as a training-school. Father Bapst was placed in charge, and maintained the institution for scholastics for about three years; then as Boston College, the school was opened for lay students. As first rector he laid the foundation of this college, and gave it the advantage of his scholarly direction until 1869. After this period he served several New England parishes; and built St. Joseph Church, Providence, in 1877. This was his last parish, as his mind began to fail, due, it was believed, to his afflictions. He retired to the home of his order at Woodstock, Md., where he was cared for in his declining years. He was something of a zealot, learned, pious, and entirely devoted to the traditions of his order and to the upbuilding of the church of his choice.

[On his mission to the Indians, see E. Vetromile, *The Abnakis* (1866), p. 102; John G. Shea, *Cath. Missions among the Indian Tribes of the U. S.* (1854), p. 162. His Ellsworth experience may be inferred from the records of that village, yet extant. His connection with the coll. is told in Rev. W. E. Murphy, "Story of Boston Coll.," in *Cath. Builders of the Nation* (1923), V, 249–53. On his parish at Providence, see R. M. Bayles, *Hist. of Providence County, R. I.* (1891), I, 479. His career is narrated in *Records of the Am. Cath. Hist. Soc. of Phila.* (1889), II, 13, 21.] L. P. K.

BARAGA, FREDERIC (June 29, 1797–Jan. 19, 1868), Roman Catholic missionary, was born in the castle of Malavas, near Döbernig. The assertion that he was of noble birth and renounced a vast heritage to devote himself to the life of a missionary is incorrect, for while his parents, Johann Nepomuc Baraga and Maria Katharin Josefa *née* Jencic, were Slovenians of good family, they were not connected with the aristocracy. When Frederic was nine years old he was sent to be educated by a private tutor at Laibach. There he entered the gymnasium in 1809, and afterward took a law course in the University of Vienna. Upon receiving his degree in 1821, he determined to enter the church. Returning to Laibach, he studied at the seminary there, and was ordained priest Sept. 21, 1823. For seven years he served parishes in his native country, but in 1830, after the founding at Vienna of the Leopoldine Society for foreign missions, he offered himself for service in the United States. In his letter he referred to himself as speaking German, Illyrian, French, Latin, Italian, and English. His services were accepted, and on reaching Cincinnati, early in 1831, he began to add the Ottawa language to his other linguistic accomplishments. In May of the same year, he was sent as missionary to the Ottawa village of Arbre Croche, now Harbor Springs, Mich.

Father Baraga was very enthusiastic about this his first Indian mission, where he was cordially received, and where he baptized and taught many neophytes. In the course of his journeys to various villages of the tribe, he visited the islands in Lake Michigan, and Grand River, where, at the site of the modern Grand Rapids, he began a mission in 1833. At this place, however, he incurred the enmity of the traders for his scathing denunciation of the liquor traffic they carried on with the tribesmen, and in 1835 he was transferred from the Ottawa missions to the far shores of Lake Superior. On July 27, 1835, he arrived at La Pointe, the American Fur Company's station, on Madeline Island, opposite Bayfield, Wis. Here was a village of Chippewa Indians, mingled with many retired French-Canadian voyageurs and half-breeds. The church on the island long shown to tourists as Father Marquette's, was in fact built by Baraga about 1837, after a visit the preceding year to

Europe to obtain funds. His youngest sister, Antonia de Hoeffern, came with him on his return to La Pointe, where her gracious presence was remembered long after the severities of the climate had induced her to return home.

During the long winters of this northern clime, Father Baraga applied himself to the study of the Chippewa language, the universal dialect of all the Northwest. He prepared several religious books in this dialect, some of which were published in Paris, others in Detroit and Cincinnati. But his most useful works, still depended upon by all Chippewa scholars, are his *Theoretical and Practical Grammar of the Otchipwe Language* (Detroit, 1850), and his *Dictionary of the Otchipwe Language* (Cincinnati, 1853). His devotional works are still used in the Catholic missions.

In the course of his ministrations to the members of his scattered flock Father Baraga made long journeys by canoe in summer and snowshoe in winter, encountering many difficulties and enduring many hardships. In this way he visited Grand Portage, Fond du Lac (near Superior, Wis.), and L'Anse at the foot of Keweenaw Bay. At this last place, now the seat of Baraga County, Mich., he began a mission in 1843 to which he soon removed his residence. There he built log houses for his Indian converts, and taught them to live in civilized fashion. While at L'Anse he also ministered to the miners, who about this time were flocking to the newly discovered copper mines in the Northern Peninsula, and by his courtesy and kindliness made friends with both Catholics and Protestants. Heedless of personal comfort, he went wherever need called along the bleak shores of Lake Superior, comforting and admonishing tribesmen, traders, and travelers, counting not his life dear unto himself if by these means he might save others. News of his missions spread, and on Nov. 1, 1853, he was consecrated at Cincinnati bishop of Upper Michigan. The seat of the new bishopric was at Sault Ste. Marie, and from there Bishop Baraga continued his ministrations, often visiting his former missions of Lake Superior. "I have had the pleasure," wrote a traveler of the fifties, "once in my life, of conversing with an absolute gentleman . . . kind, serene, urbane, and utterly sincere. This perfect gentleman was a Roman Catholic bishop who had spent thirty years of his life in the woods near Lake Superior." In 1865 a new bishopric was created called the see of Marquette, and to this embryo town of northern Michigan, Baraga removed his residence. Here he built a cathedral, which two and a half years later became his final resting place. A monument to his memory has been erected in the church at Döbernig, the funds for which were largely contributed by the Slovenians of America.

[Father Chrysostomus Verwyst, *Life and Letters of Rt. Rev. Frederic Baraga, First Bishop of Marquette* (1900); Rev. A. I. Rezek, *Hist. of the Diocese of Sault Ste. Marie and Marquette* (1907), I, 1–215, adds to Verwyst's account new material, esp. several letters of Baraga; see also Rev. J. L. Zaplotnik, "Lecture on Bishop Baraga," in *Acta et Dicta* (1917), pp. 99–100. Baraga's linguistic writings are described in J. C. Pilling, *Bibliography of Algonquian Languages* (1891), pp. 24–30.]

L. P. K.

BARANOV, ALEXANDER ANDREEVICH (1746–Apr. 16/28, 1819), an early Alaska fur-trader, was originally a merchant of Kargopol in eastern Russia. In 1780 he emigrated to Siberia, where he became manager of a glass-factory at Irkutsk and later a successful trader. The return of the Bering party from Alaska in 1742 loaded down with sea otter skins started a rush for the fur-bearing Aleutian Islands. In the course of the next forty years the sea otters were killed or driven off from these islands, and it became necessary to go farther and farther in search of good hunting-grounds. The distant expeditions called for a considerable outlay of money and necessitated the formation of companies. G. I. Shelekhov was one of the ablest of Siberian traders. By 1790 he had formed several companies and had established the American headquarters on Kodiak Island. He offered the place of resident director in America to Baranov, who accepted and started for his post in August 1790. He spent altogether twenty-eight years (1790–1818) in Alaska as head of the Russian American Company (organized in 1799). Until 1808 he directed affairs from Kodiak and after that date from Sitka.

Baranov had enormous difficulties but tremendous will-power. He made a reputation for himself and dividends for his company, but it was done at the expense of the natives of western Alaska, who were practically his slaves. He sent them in their frail skin boats to hunt on the exposed coast between Kodiak and Sitka. Many of the hunters were either swallowed up by the rough sea or killed by the savage natives of those shores. When the otter was driven from the Alaskan coast, Baranov hired out the Aleuts to Yankee traders, who took them to hunt along the California shores. In 1811, 1812, 1813 the company received 270,000 rubles as its share of the California catch. One of Baranov's problems was to get food and supplies in and fur out of Alaska. His fleet was quite untrustworthy. Many of his ships were lost on the way to or from Kodiak to Okhotsk and those that succeeded in making the voyage spent a year or more in the effort. The Russians associated with him were made up in part of incompetent, coarse, brutal half-breeds or criminals of Siberia who could not be trusted. During the first years the colony was undermanned, half starved, down with scurvy or other diseases. Not only was Baranov short of food but also of things to give the natives of south-eastern Alaska in exchange for their fur. In 1800 he began buying supplies from the Yankees, sometimes the ship and cargo. From that time on to the end of his career he was more or less dependent on the American traders. They helped him in various ways. They took cargoes for him to Canton, to Manila, or to Okhotsk. Occasionally they got the best of him, and he clung to them out of necessity rather than choice. He tried to make a deal with Astor's company in the hope of excluding the individual Boston trader, but this agreement was of short duration.

Baranov was a fur-trader rather than an empire builder. He worked for a company that demanded dividends and asked no questions as to means employed. He satisfied the company by exploiting the country and the natives. In this respect he was no worse than the average trader. He was superior to most of them, however, in that he succeeded against such odds. He had to depend on himself, on his fist, and on his brain. This strenuous life began to tell on his health as he grew older. In 1809 he asked to be relieved, but it was not before 1818 that a successor appeared. Toward the end of that year Baranov set out for Russia in the ship *Kutuzov*. It put in for supplies at the Hawaiian Islands, Guam, and Batavia. At the last-named port Baranov was taken ill, and after leaving this place he grew gradually worse. He died on Apr. 28, 1819, and was buried at sea.

[The material for this sketch is taken from K. Khlebnikov's biog. of Baranov, *Zhizneopisanie Alexandra Andreevicha Baranova* (St. Petersburg 1835), P. Tikhmenev's *Istoricheskoe Obozrenie Obrazovaniia Rossisko-Amerikanskoi Kompanii* (Part I, St. Petersburg 1861), and *Materiali dlia Istorii Russkikh Zaselenii* (St. Petersburg 1861). There are numerous references to Baranov in the published journals of traders who visited Alaska during his lifetime.]

F. A. G.

BARBER, AMZI LORENZO (June 22, 1843–Apr. 17, 1909), capitalist, was the first to exploit the so-called pitch lake on the Island of Trinidad, using the asphalt taken from it in the paving of city streets. He was born at Saxton's River, Vt., the son of Amzi D. and Nancy Irene (Bailey) Barber. His father was of Scotch-Irish, his mother of French-English ancestry. His great-grandfather, Thomas Barber, had settled at Townsend, Vt., before the Revolution. His mother's family had migrated to Oneida County, N. Y., where she was born. The elder Amzi Barber, one of the "Lane Seminary rebels," had studied at Oberlin College, Ohio, in the early years of that institution. There the son was graduated in 1867, the family meanwhile having moved from Vermont to Ohio. He was a teacher for four years at Howard University, the school for colored freedmen started after the Civil War at Washington, D. C. Dealing extensively in real estate in the northwest section of Washington, he had his attention directed to the growing importance of asphalt as paving material. In the extensive street improvements made in the District of Columbia, asphalt came into general use for the first time in the United States. In 1878, Barber engaged in the asphalt-paving business, the chief source of supply for the world being the Trinidad deposit to which reference has been made. Ten years later he formed the Trinidad Asphalt Company to take over leases of the deposit, obtaining from the British Government concessions covering the entire "lake" of 114 acres for a term of forty-two years. He was then in a position to supply asphalt to paving companies in the United States and England. After Washington, Buffalo, N. Y., was the first American city to use a large quantity of asphalt for paving, but other municipalities followed. In the first ten years more than 3,500,000 square yards of pavement were laid in the United States. By 1896 there were thirty asphalt-paving companies at work in America and the Barber Company had laid one-half of all the asphalt pavements in the country. The export of asphalt from Trinidad had increased from 23,000 tons in 1880 to 86,000 in 1895. Within the ensuing five years the quantity nearly doubled. This was a period of expansion and of stock-jobbing among the asphalt companies. In the maze of conflicting statements by various interests and in the absence of any authorized responsible publicity, it is difficult, if not impossible, to ascertain the real sequence of developments. In 1899 and 1900 two great combines of asphalt interests were formed—the Asphalt Company of America and the National Asphalt Company. Early in 1901 Barber disposed of his personal holdings and in December of that year both companies were in the hands of receivers. There were charges and recriminations as to the profits made by the transfer of the stocks of various subsidiary companies to the Asphalt Company of America. Barber retired from the asphalt business, although the Barber Asphalt Paving Company continued in existence and after the formation (in 1903) of the "Trust," known as the General Asphalt Company, it was the principal operating branch of the main organization. In 1904 Barber himself organized the A. L. Barber Asphalt Company, an independent concern, for the purpose of marketing the asphalt imported from Venezuela. From 1889 until his death Barber was a member of the Board of Trustees of Oberlin College. He was twice married: in 1867 to Celia M. Brodley of Geneva, Ohio; and in 1871 to Julia Louise Langdon of Washington, D. C.

[*Gen. Cat. of Oberlin Coll. 1833–1908;* article by Jas. R. Severance in the *Oberlin Alumni Mag.,* June 1909, pp. 341–46; Gen. Francis V. Greene, "Asphalt and Its Uses," in *Trans. Am. Institute of Mining Engineers,* XVII, 355–75.] W. B. S.

BARBER, DONN (Oct. 19, 1871–May 29, 1925), architect, son of Charles Gibbs Barber and Georgiana Williams, was born in Washington, D. C., but was brought up in New York City, spending his summers with his grandparents on the Hudson. These early surroundings marked his life, for he remained a New Yorker, first and last, a believer in the greatness of his city, enjoying every phase of its life. He was a member of the class of 1893 in the Sheffield Scientific School at Yale. Here, as a member of the Berzelius Society, he took an active part in the life of the University. His music naturally drew him to the Glee Club, his draftsmanship to the *Record,* with both of which he was closely associated. After graduation he returned to New York, entering the office of Carrère & Hastings, and following a special course at the School of Architecture at Columbia University. During this early period of his professional training he was thus brought into close contact with John Carrère [*q.v.*], in whom he found that inspiration to great effort so valuable to the beginner, while on the other hand Carrère recognized in Barber many of the qualities most essential to the successful practise of architecture, valued the opportunity to help a young man of great promise and, until his own untimely death, kept in close touch with his young friend, exercising always a sane and helpful influence.

In the autumn of 1894 Barber went to Paris to continue his studies. He entered the École National des Beaux Arts in the following spring, and throughout his four years did brilliantly, under the great inspiration of French art. On receiving his *diplôme* in 1898, Barber returned to New York, where he plunged at once into hard work with the enthusiasm that was characteristic of his whole life. In Paris he had met and fallen in love with Elsie Yandell of Louisville, Ky. He wanted to marry but had no means other than what he could earn. His talents and perseverance were such, however, that he was able to marry the following year. He presently bought a place at White Plains, N. Y., where his wife and the four children born to them spent long summers.

Barber worked harder than most men, rarely leaving his office before seven, yet he dined out often, was frequently at the theatre or opera and later at a ball or dance, and was always able to be out again next morning ready for his day's work. His strength was remarkable, but his love of life and of people was even more extraordinary. He kept up his interest in Yale as president of his society's New York club throughout his life. He always had time to help a friend with counsel in his work, or to direct the development of teaching in his art by actively participating in the work of the Beaux Arts Society. His professional position as a foremost American architect of his time is attested by the list of great buildings given below. He accomplished all these in the short space of twenty-seven years, for he died at the age of fifty-four. Professionally he was internationally recognized. He was a member of the Architectural League of New York (president 1925); the National Academy of Design; the Society of Beaux Arts Architects (president 1909, 1910); the National Sculpture Society; the Société des Architectes Diplômés; an honorary corresponding member of the Royal Institute of British Architects, and a fellow of the American Institute of Architects. His buildings include the New York Cotton Exchange, the National Park Bank, the Mutual Bank, the Lotus Club, the Institute of Musical Art, the Central Branch Building of the Young Women's Christian Association, and the Hospital for the Feeble Minded, Randall's Island, all in New York City; in Hartford, Conn., the Travelers Insurance Building, the Ætna Life Insurance Building, the Hartford National Bank, the Connecticut State Library, and the Supreme Court Building; in Washington, D. C., the Department of Justice Building (winner of the Government competition).

Donn Barber's architectural work is marked by unfailing good taste. He was in no sense a strict stylist, although the greater part of his work is Renaissance in feeling, and in much of it the influence of his French training is obvious. The National Park Bank is typical of the academic brilliance of the French idealism; the Connecticut State Library and Supreme Court illustrate his skill in straightforward and monumental planning.

[*Yale Univ. Obituary Rec.* (1925); *Am. Architect,* CXXVII, No. 2474, 537; *Jour. Am. Institute of Archi-*

tects, XIII, No. 7, 274; Thomas Hastings in the *Architectural Rec.*, LVIII, No. 1, 86; *Who's Who in America*, 1925–26.]

C. C. Z.
T. F. H.

BARBER, EDWIN ATLEE (Aug. 13, 1851–Dec. 12, 1916), archeologist, the son of William Edwin and Anne Eliza (Townsend) Barber, was born in Baltimore, Md., and was put to school when old enough at Williston Seminary, East Hampton, Mass. He entered Lafayette College in 1869 but left before completing his course and obtained a position as assistant naturalist with the Hayden Survey (1874–75), in whose ranks many men began a brilliant future. With a *flair* for archeology, Barber gave most of his attention to the collection of prehistoric relics, which, in Colorado, Utah, Arizona, and New Mexico, were rather easy to come at. Archeological work, which was begun by Maj. J. W. Powell in 1869, was still in 1874 in a nascent state, when only preliminary surveys without excavations could be made. Much could be gathered of objects of material culture, as pottery, axes, arrowheads, and the like, weathered out on the sites of ruins. To these objects and especially to the decorated pottery, Barber devoted his attention. The study of ancient Pueblo ceramic art in its infancy was contributed to by him in numerous papers. Not only archeology, but the ethnology of the Indians of the region interested him, and one of his most valuable papers was on the subject of Ute Indian dialects. In ceramic art in its various branches he never lost interest, becoming finally a leading authority. He prepared many short articles which appeared in the *American Naturalist* and which embody most of his work with the Hayden Survey. The demands of education led him to return to Lafayette College, where he obtained the degree of B.S. in 1877. On Feb. 5, 1880, he was married to Nellie Louise Parker. From 1879 to 1895 he was postmaster of West Philadelphia. During a part of this time he was also a graduate student in ethnology and philology at Lafayette College, obtaining the degree of Ph.D. in 1893. The lure of ceramics drew him to the curatorship of this branch in the Pennsylvania Museum and School of Industrial Art in Fairmount Park, Philadelphia, where he became director in 1907. While there his energy was given mostly to the history and classification of modern ceramics by periods, countries, and style of art. He was easily first in this branch of his subject and his numerous books on ceramics are constantly consulted. A fair proportion of his 200 archeological articles were on this topic. None of them stands out as of major importance, although the whole contribution is regarded as of value to science. Most of his work on Western archeology was new and therefore superior by this feature. His leading works on ceramics are: *The Pottery and Porcelain of the United States* (1893); *Hispano-Moresque Pottery* (1915); *Maiolica of Mexico* (1908). Especially interesting was his rediscovery of the Pennsylvania German tulip ware of the nineteenth century, products of a quaint folk art in which tulips and German mottoes were used in the decoration (*Tulip Ware*, 1903).

[*Who's Who in America*, 1916–1917; E. A. Barber, *Geneal. Rec. of the Atlee Family* (1884), pp. 104–5; E. A. Barber, *Genealogy of the Barber Family* (1890), pp. 120–21; J. F. Stonecipher, *Biog. Cat. of Lafayette Coll.* (1913), pp. 184, 655; *Public Ledger* (Phila.), Dec. 13, 1916.]

W. H.

BARBER, FRANCIS (1751–Feb. 11, 1783), Revolutionary soldier, belonged to a family of Irish origin, and was born at Princeton, N. J. He graduated at Princeton in 1767, and a few years later he took charge as rector of the academy at Elizabethtown, which he conducted until the opening of the war. Here among other subjects he taught English, and had for a few months Alexander Hamilton as a pupil.

Barber fought throughout the war, serving in many important campaigns. He is described as "of striking personal appearance"; his tact and ability in discipline are noted; and doubtless it was because of these qualities and his bravery that he won the esteem of Washington, Greene, and Lafayette. He was commissioned major of the 3rd New Jersey Regiment on Jan. 18, 1776, and lieutenant-colonel on Nov. 28, 1776. In the autumn of that year he was at German Flats, N. Y., returning in time to make the Trenton-Princeton campaign. He served at Brandywine, and was wounded at Germantown. When Gen. Steuben undertook the drilling of the army at Valley Forge, Barber was appointed assistant inspector-general. Wounded through the body at the battle of Monmouth, he was able, however, to accompany Gen. Sullivan's punitive expedition against the Indians of western New York; and in the battle of Newtown in 1779 he was again wounded. In the following year when the British from their base at Staten Island advanced to Springfield, N. J., Barber acted as deputy adjutant-general, conducted the pursuit of the enemy from Elizabeth, and received Gen. Greene's especial commendation. He was transferred to the 1st New Jersey Regiment on Jan. 1, 1781, and was immediately entrusted with a delicate mission. Troops of the Pennsylvania and New Jersey line, disheartened and indignant at their long arrears of pay, mutinied, and Barber was assigned by Washington to quell the outbreak. The mutiny occurred at one of the darkest periods of the war, soon after Arnold's treason, when the finances were in confusion, and the outlook most unpromising. The quelling of the mutiny was therefore a vital matter. A few months later came the British invasion of Virginia, and Barber served under Lafayette, commanding at the battle of Green Spring (near Williamsburg) a battalion of Continental light infantry. Lafayette's operations culminated in the siege of Yorktown. In the final assault Barber, fighting under the immediate command of Hamilton, led a battalion, "first in the supporting column"—as Lafayette reported to the commander-in-chief. Following the ending of active warfare the army was stationed at Newburgh, and there Barber was accidentally killed by a falling tree. He was twice married: first, to Mary Ogden, daughter of Robert Ogden; and second, to her cousin, Anne Ogden, daughter of Moses Ogden.

[Ebenezer Elmer, *Elogy on Francis Barber* (1783; reprinted 1917); E. F. Hatfield, *Hist. of Elizabeth* (1868); Charlemagne Tower, *Lafayette* (1895); Barber's Order Book (for the Sullivan expedition) is in the possession of the N. J. Hist. Soc.]

E. K. A.

BARBER, JOHN WARNER (Feb. 2, 1798–June 22, 1885), engraver, historian, was born in East Windsor, Hartford County, Conn., the son of Elijah and Mary (Warner) Barber, and a descendant of Thomas Barber, an Englishman who settled at Windsor with the Stiles party in 1685. In his sixteenth year he was apprenticed to Abner Reed, a bank-note engraver of East Windsor, with whom he remained for seven years, and then opened a business of his own in New Haven, in 1823. His work included both wood and copper-plate engraving, neither of which ever improved beyond the point of mediocrity, his chief concern being not so much the production of engravings as the preaching of the Gospel by means of pictures. When still a young man, he conceived the idea of a history prepared from the personal recollections of participants in the stirring scenes incident to the early settlement of the United States. He drove about the country in a one-horse wagon in order to carry out this historical work, and in 1827 he published his first book, *Historical Scenes in the United States.* He also issued numerous other works on various sections of the country, some of which were illustrated by copper plates "Drawn & Engraved by J. W. Barber, N. Haven." With Henry Howe of New Haven, who accompanied him on his travels, he prepared a series of historical works on New York, New Jersey, and Virginia. *Our Whole Country, or the Past and Present of the United States, Historical and Descriptive* (1861) is his largest work, and required five years to compile. William James Linton, the wood engraver, says that Barber engraved about 400 woodcuts, from original drawings in 1856–61, for this work. Among his other numerous historical works may be mentioned the following: *Past and Present of the United States* (1828); *New England Scenes* (1833); *Connecticut Historical Collections* (1836, 1837, 1846); *Elements of General History* (1844); *Massachusetts Historical Collections* (1839, 1844); *History and Antiquities of New England, New York and New Jersey* (1841, 1856); *History and Antiquities of New Haven* (1831); and *The Loyal West in the Times of the Rebellion* (1865). These exhibit a most painstaking method of gathering minute details, the value of which, as historical data, has largely disappeared with the passing of the generation with which Barber was associated. Taken collectively they are very much in the nature of an immense local history of the country. Several of his emblematic books on religious subjects were combined and issued as a thick octavo volume called *The Bible Looking Glass,* of which 175,000 copies were sold in the United States alone, and of which a revised and a German edition were published as late as 1898.

His religious writings are characterized by faith and enthusiasm. Many of his designs and engravings were allegorical, to which he devoted numerous pages of explanatory text. In these writings he presupposed a great amount of credulity on the part of his readers. His principal works of this type were: *Religious Allegories* (1866); *Religious Emblems* (1866); *The Dance of Death* (1846); *The Book of Similitudes* (1860); and *The Picture Preacher* (1880).

Barber was married twice; first to Harriet Lines, who died in 1826, and second to Ruth Green. By his first wife he had one daughter and by his second, two sons and three daughters. He died in New Haven.

[An accurate biog. of Barber as an engraver is given in *A History of Wood Engraving in America,* by W. J. Linton (1882); brief mention in D. M. Stauffer, *Am. Engravers on Copper and Steel* (1907); and in Wm. Dunlap, *Hist. of the Rise and Progress of the Arts of Design in the U. S.* (1918 ed.); *New Haven Evening Register,* June 22, 1885; H. R. Stiles, *Hist. and Genealogies of Ancient Windsor, Conn.* (1892).]

R. C. S.

BARBER, OHIO COLUMBUS (Apr. 20, 1841–Feb. 4, 1920), manufacturer, was born in Middlebury (now a part of Akron), Ohio, third of the nine children of George Barber, a cooper from Connecticut, and Eliza Smith Barber, of

Dutch descent. Young Barber attended the public schools until his sixteenth year, when he left school to sell matches. In 1847, his father had started a match manufactory in a barn. After the manner of the times, Ohio Columbus traveled by wagon through Indiana, Michigan, and Pennsylvania, distributing his father's product. The business prospered. In 1862, Ohio Columbus, then twenty-one years of age, took entire charge of it. Two years later, the Barber Match Company, a stock company, was formed. In 1881, early in the movement for the consolidation of competing companies, Barber's company combined with a large number of others in the Diamond Match Company. This combination controlled about eighty-five per cent of the trade of the match industry (John Moody, *The Truth About Trusts,* 1904, p. 245; *Barberton News,* Feb. 6, 1920). Besides the numerous plants in the United States, the Diamond Match Company owned controlling interests in factories in England, Peru, Switzerland, Chile, and Germany. Of this large organization Barber was vice-president from 1881 to 1888, president from 1888 to 1913, and chairman of the board of directors from 1913 until his death. While the development of the match industry was the dominant activity of Barber's business career, his other interests were manifold. In 1891, he laid out and developed the city of Barberton, near Akron, and to that place moved the Akron plant of the Diamond Match Company. In order to supply packing-boxes, he went into the manufacture of strawboard. As a result he later became the organizer of the American Strawboard Company. He also established the Diamond Rubber Company which was later absorbed by the B. F. Goodrich Company. He was one of the founders of the First National Bank of Akron and its president. Upon the consolidation of the latter with the Second National, he was again chosen president. He constructed the Akron Barberton Belt Line Railroad, and in other ways had a large part in the industrial development of Akron and the surrounding community. Through the Diamond Match Company his influence was nation-wide. He was also interested in local philanthropies. He built and equipped a hospital at a cost of $200,000 which he presented to the city of Akron. After providing for his family, he left the rest of his estate, amounting to over $500,000, to be used for education along industrial and agricultural lines.

Barber was a tall, erect, well-proportioned man who gave much care to his physical condition. His character was marked by courage, self-confidence, and persistence. He was twice married; in 1866 to Laura L. Brown who died in 1894, and in 1915 to Mary F. Orr.

[S. A. Lane, *Fifty Years of Akron and Summit County* (1892); *Ann. Rept. Western Reserve Hist. Soc.* 1920; O. E. Olin, *Akron and Environs* (1917); G. Frederick Wright, *Representative Citizens of Ohio* (1913). The last is the best account.]

E. J. B.

BARBOUR, JAMES (June 10, 1775–June 7, 1842), statesman, was descended from a Scotch merchant named James Barbour, who in the latter half of the seventeenth century settled in eastern Virginia and there became a prosperous citizen. His son and namesake, dispossessed of his inheritance after his father's death and his mother's second marriage, migrated westward and became, it is said, the first settler in the region between the Blue Ridge and Southwest Mountains, in what was then Culpeper County. His son, Thomas, born near Barboursville village, was for years justice of the peace, served in the House of Burgesses, and was a member of the Virginia conventions of 1774 and 1775. In 1771 he married Mary, daughter of Richard Thomas and Isabella (Pendleton) Thomas. Their third child, James, born at Barboursville, Orange County, Va., was named for his grandfather; their fourth child was named Philip Pendleton [*q.v.*] for his mother's maternal grandfather. The Barbours were one of the chief families of the county, but Thomas Barbour, because of earlier extravagant hospitality and financial reverses, was unable to provide adequately for the education of his two gifted sons. In old age James Barbour stated that he had severely felt the lack of means of obtaining an education. He attended no institution of higher learning, but for a time was the pupil of James Waddel, a blind Presbyterian minister, at the latter's house near Gordonsville. He was admitted to the bar, but attained no such professional distinction as his brother. Chiefly occupied throughout mature life with affairs of state and the management of his plantation, he, like so many other distinguished Virginians of his day, acquired most of his education from his own reading and the political and social life in which he participated.

Entering the Virginia House of Delegates in 1798, he represented Orange County in that body continuously, except for the sessions 1805–7, until 1812. The first moment of his political existence, he said, was that in which he supported the Virginia Resolutions of 1798. In his eloquent speech on this occasion, he showed himself to be a disciple of the Jefferson-Madison school of strict construction and state rights (*The Virginia Report of 1799–1800. . . . Resolutions of Dec. 21, 1798, The Debate and Proceed-*

ings Thereon, 1850, pp. 54–70). Regarding the Alien and Sedition Acts as an usurpation of power by the Federal Government, he asserted the right of the state to declare them unconstitutional. From "absolute consolidated government," he prayed, "Good Lord deliver us!" His prominence in state politics and acceptability to the dominant party are attested by the many marks of preferment he received. Elected speaker of the House of Delegates in February 1809, he continued in this office until his election as governor on Jan. 3, 1812. In 1810 he drew the bill which established the Virginia Literary Fund and laid the foundations for public education in the state (Ruffin's *Farmers' Register,* 1836, III, 688). As governor, his chief activities and recommendations were connected with the prosecution of the War of 1812.

While still governor, he was elected to the United States Senate, following the death of Richard Brent. He took his seat on Jan. 11, 1815, and continued to hold it until appointed to the cabinet in 1825. During part of the first session of the Sixteenth Congress, he was president *pro tem.,* and during his term he served as chairman of the Committees of Military Affairs and Foreign Relations. By supporting the United States Bank and voting for Calhoun's bonus bill, he manifested his sympathy with the nationalistic spirit which immediately resulted from the War of 1812. On the other hand, his advocacy of the indemnification of Matthew Lyon, one of the sufferers under the Sedition Law, was typically Jeffersonian in its characterization of that measure as tyrannical and unconstitutional; and in his conspicuous discussion of the Missouri question, 1820–21, he showed himself to be still an advocate of state rights, though not an apologist for slavery. He proposed in the Senate the linking of Maine and Missouri in one bill (*Annals of Congress,* 16 Cong., 1 Sess., 101–7), consistently opposed the imposition of any conditions upon the admission of Missouri as a state (*Ibid.,* pp. 314–35), and objected at first to any restriction of slavery in the territories. John Quincy Adams stated that, when the conflict was hottest, Barbour informally suggested a convention of states to dissolve the Union (*Memoirs,* V, 13). Ultimately he advocated harmony and mutual concessions, but there can be no question of his loyalty, in this controversy, to state-rights doctrines. His loss of political caste in Virginia was due chiefly to his subsequent association with the nationalistic administration of Adams.

At the beginning of the presidential campaign of 1824, Barbour was one of the warmest champions of a caucus nomination and was accordingly identified with the candidacy of William H. Crawford. At this time, Adams was second only to Crawford in the favor of Virginia. Barbour objected to Jackson, whom he regarded as a mere military man, and his position as chairman of the Senate Committee of Foreign Relations brought him into many contacts with Adams as secretary of state. As the year advanced he came to be regarded as an Adams man, and in due time he was appointed secretary of war by the latter, on the suggestion of Col. R. M. Johnson of Kentucky.

When the attitude of the Adams administration toward the tariff and internal improvements became apparent, the hostility of Virginia, particularly of eastern Virginia, increased. Barbour, however, continued loyal to his chief until 1828 and never indeed broke with him. Already identified with the movement for local internal improvements in Virginia, he stanchly defended the national policy against criticisms emanating from his state. Never a fanatic on the slavery question, he approved of the Panama Congress, which aroused the fears of so many southerners. He conducted the very difficult negotiations with Gov. Troup of Georgia in regard to the Indian question, but seems to have retained the personal esteem of that belligerent advocate of state rights who was so incensed with Adams. The Secretary of War, at first more uncompromising than the President in his attitude toward the defiant state, later consulted frequently with the Georgia delegation in Congress and served as a conciliatory factor. Theories of state rights troubled him little in this controversy, but he manifested on the one hand an appreciation of political considerations and on the other a spirit of benevolence toward the Indians, for whom he finally recommended a territorial government west of the Mississippi. Barbour's identification and sympathy with the administration were so complete that he once thought of becoming a candidate for the vice-presidency with Adams in 1828, but early in that year he expressed the desire to be appointed minister to Great Britain, in succession to Albert Gallatin. Adams felt that his hitherto loyal colleague wanted "to save himself from the wreck" of the administration and rightly thought his retirement from the cabinet would be interpreted as an abandonment of the sinking ship. None the less, he generously made the nomination on May 22, 1828. The appointment came too late to relieve Barbour from political embarrassment and his departure served only to mar somewhat his admirable record of loyalty. Nothing of importance marked his brief diplomatic career, but he was received with great personal favor. He was succeeded early in the summer of 1829 by the Jackson appointee and returned to America in the autumn bearing with him the honorary degree of D.C.L. from Oxford.

Returning to his native county discredited by his association with the late administration, he sought political vindication by offering himself, in May 1830, as a candidate for the House of Delegates. He made a spirited defense of his political conduct and succeeded in gaining the seat temporarily, after a contested election. In February 1831, however, the committee of privileges and elections decided in favor of his obscure opponent. In a valedictory delivered in the House of Delegates, he stated that a "decree of ostracism" had been pronounced against him because of his opinions and that he would not voluntarily again leave his "native mountains." He lived long enough to witness the revival of Whig fortunes. In 1839, he presided over the convention which nominated Harrison and Tyler, and he actively participated in the ensuing campaign. On one occasion, he made a speech of five hours' length, said to have been remarkably able and eloquent. None the less, the Whigs failed to carry Virginia.

After his retirement from politics, Barbour served as president of the Virginia Agricultural Society, and he long advocated agricultural education. In his native county, he was intimately associated with the Orange Humane Society, which educated hundreds of poor children. He was perhaps the first in Virginia to suggest the establishment of a normal and industrial school. He is said to have been a remarkably handsome man, with the grandeur of a Roman senator in his old age. His oratorical powers were generally held in high esteem, but some regarded him as pompous and bombastic. John Randolph, comparing the two Barbour brothers, once said "that Phil could split a hair but that Jim could not hit a barn door" (W. C. Bruce, *Randolph,* II, 202). Barbour was married in 1792 to Lucy, daughter of Benjamin Johnson of Orange County, and had five children. His mansion, "Barboursville," on the edge of the village of that name, was planned in part by Jefferson and is said to have had the finest interior in Virginia. Built in 1822, it now stands amid gigantic box, a splendid ruin.

[The brief account of the life of James Barbour by W. S. Long in the *John P. Branch Hist. Papers* of Randolph-Macon Coll., vol. IV, no. 2 (1914), pp. 34–64, is immature but in general accurate and well-annotated. The James Barbour Papers, in the N. Y. Pub. Lib., consist of 289 letters, mostly to Barbour. Somewhat less than half of these are calendared in the *Bull. N. Y. Pub. Lib.* (1906), VI, 22–34. A collection of letters written to Barbour during the Missouri controversy were published in the *William and Mary Coll. Quart.* ser. I, vol. X (1901), pp. 7–24. The *Jour. of the Va. House of Delegates, 1798–1815,* and the *Annals of Cong.,* 1815–1825, are indispensable for a study of Barbour's legislative and gubernatorial career. The *Memoirs of John Quincy Adams* give much information about Barbour's services as secretary of war. Items of interest and importance may be gleaned from *Niles' Reg.* W. W. Scott, *Hist. of Orange County, Va.* (1907), gives considerable information about the Barbour family. A genealogy, which contains several glaring inaccuracies, may be seen in Philip Slaughter, *Hist. of St Mark's Parish, Culpeper County, Va.* (1877), pp. 118–121.]

D. M.

BARBOUR, JOHN STRODE, JR. (Dec. 29, 1820–May 14, 1892), lawyer, congressman, financier, was born in Culpeper County, Va. On the side of his father, also John Strode Barbour, he belonged to a distinguished family of Scottish descent which had long been prominent in Virginia politics; his mother was Eliza A. Byrne of Petersburg. He received his education in private schools of the community, and at the University of Virginia, where he was granted the B.L. degree in 1842. After four years of practise in his native county, he entered politics as the Democratic candidate for the position of delegate to the legislature from Culpeper, and won against strong Whig opposition. His name appears on the rolls of the House of Delegates for the sessions 1847–48, 1848–49, 1849–50, 1850–51. When the Orange & Alexandria Railroad Company was organized in 1849, the State appointed Barbour to represent its interests on the board of directors. Three years later, the directors elected him president of the company, a position which he held for thirty-three years. Under his management the road of sixty miles (later the Virginia Midland) was extended across the state through Danville, and was enlarged by the addition of several subsidiary lines. There was not a single strike during these years, not even in the lean and troublous decade of the seventies—a fine testimony to his ability and to his justice toward his employees. In consequence of a deadlock in a district convention of his party, he was nominated for Congress, without his knowledge, and was subsequently elected. He remained in Congress from Mar. 4, 1881, to Mar. 3, 1887. He refused renomination in 1886. It was during this period that he made his greatest contribution to the commonwealth. He revived the Democratic party which had ceased to exist as an organization in his state, and conducted the campaign which rescued the state from William Mahone's control. A convention in Lynchburg on July 25, 1883, appointed Barbour chairman of the state executive committee of the reorganized party, a position held by him until 1889 (R. L. Morton, *History of Virginia Since 1861,* 1924, p. 209). His success in defeating Mahone was due to his gift for organization and to the universal confidence and esteem reposed in him. He was a member of the National Democratic Committee from 1884 to 1892. Upon defeating H. H. Riddleberger, Readjuster (Republican), he took his seat in the United States Senate Mar. 4, 1889. Barbour was married in 1865 to Susan Daingerfield of Alexandria, who died in 1886. They left no descendants. Few men in Virginia since the Civil War have enjoyed greater popular confidence and esteem than Senator Barbour, or have been more beloved by their intimate friends and relatives. He was at the day of his death, which came suddenly in his seventy-second year, after a full day's work, a man of fine presence, six feet tall, with sharply cut features, snow-white hair, and dark brown eyes.

[The homesteads of the Barbours were in the path of contending armies during the Civil War, and the family papers were for the most part destroyed. The chief source for the Barbour ancestry is the record written in his family Bible by Gov. James Barbour in 1806. Material from these and other sources may be found in R. T. Green, *Notes on Culpeper County, Va.,* (1900), including a reprint of Slaughter's *Hist. of St. Mark's Parish* (1877), which should be watched for errors in the genealogical notes. See also L. P. duBellet, *Some Prominent Va. Families* (1907), vol. II. Contemporary newspapers, the *Whig,* the *Enquirer,* and the *Dispatch* (all of Richmond), and contemporary legislative journals and debates furnish material. A volume of *Memorial Addresses on the Life and Character of John S. Barbour, Jr.* (1892), contains accounts of his life by Senator John W. Daniel and others, as well as an obituary notice by W. W. Scott, from the *Richmond Dispatch.*]

R. L. M.

BARBOUR, OLIVER LORENZO (July 12, 1811–Dec. 17, 1889), lawyer, author, traced his ancestry to George Barbour, who left England on the *Transport* in 1635, became a freeman in Dedham, Mass., in 1647, and ultimately settled at Medfield; and to William Walworth of London, who came in 1689 to New London, Conn., and located at Groton, Mass. Oliver Lorenzo, youngest son of Oliver and Rosamond (Walworth) Barbour was born in Cambridge, Washington County, N. Y. His early education was received there and at Fredonia Academy from which he graduated in 1827. He took up the study of law, and was called to the New York bar in 1832. On Nov. 19 of the same year he was married to Elizabeth Berry of Whitesboro, N. Y., whose sister, Mrs. Whitcher, was the author of the *Widow Bedott Papers.* He opened an office in Whitesboro, but later moved to Saratoga Springs, N. Y., where his maternal uncle Judge Reuben Hyde Walworth [*q.v.*], chancellor of the state, resided. Entering the Judge's office, he acquired a varied and valuable knowledge of law and practise as his uncle's confidential clerk, eventually relinquishing private practise and devoting himself to legal writing and the work of the chancery office. His first published volume, prepared in collaboration with E. B. Harrington, was an *Analytical Digest of Equity Cases* (1837)—a complete abstract of American, English, and Irish equity reports from Hilary term 1822 to 1836. This was followed by editions of two well-known English treatises, *Collyer on Partnership* (1838) and *Chitty on Bills* (1839), both with American notes by himself. The *Magistrates Criminal Law,* a practical guide to the jurisdiction, duty, and authority in criminal matters of justices of the peace in New York State, and *A Treatise on the Law of Set Off,* appeared in 1841. Barbour began at this time to contribute to the *Saratoga Sentinel* abstracts of the decisions of the chancellor which were published in six volumes (1841–47). Through his contact with the business which passed through the chancellor's hands he had accumulated great stores of practical experiences, which he utilized in the preparation of *A Treatise on the Practise of the Court of Chancery* (1843), immediately recognized by the profession as an authoritative work of great utility. The same year he issued *An Analytical Digest of Equity Cases . . . since . . . 1836.* His next publication was an edition of *Cowen's Civil Jurisdiction of Justices of the Peace* (1844). He now turned to a field in which he was to acquire a more permanent fame. Commencing with the New York court of chancery, abolished by the new state constitution of 1847, he reported the decisions of its last three years in three volumes entitled *Reports of Cases Argued and Determined in the Court of Chancery of the State of New York,* and generally known as "Barbour's Chancery Reports" (1847–49). At the same time he undertook what proved his *magnum opus,* a series of reports of the supreme court of New York, as organized under the 1847 constitution. Commencing in 1848, he continued for thirty years to report its decisions, in a succession of volumes entitled *Reports of Cases in Law and Equity in the Supreme Court of the State of New York,* and generally known as "Barbour's Supreme Court Reports." In all sixty-seven volumes were published (1848–78), embracing the years 1847–77. While engaged in this undertaking he found time to write *A Summary of the Law of Parties to Actions at Law and Suits in Equity* (1864), also preparing a *Condensed Digest of the Decisions of the Court of Appeals and the Commission of Appeals of* *the State of New York* (1877), which is a continuation of Tiffany's well-known work. On relinquishing his duties as reporter in 1878, he prepared a *Digest of Barbour's Reports 1847–77,* which was published in 1880. *A Summary of the Law of Payment* appeared in 1888, and *A Treatise on the Rights of Persons and the Rights of Property* (1890) was published posthumously. He died at his home at Saratoga Springs after a long illness.

Continuously engaged in legal study and writing for over forty-five years, his output was enormous. It has been estimated that his published works amount to nearly 100 volumes, and in addition he left a mass of material practically ready for the press which was never made public. He lived in his work, was very retiring, and never sought public office or preferment. Theron G. Strong says: "My mother used to describe him as one of the most homely and crabbed individuals she ever saw, with little personal attractiveness to make him a successful lawyer, but whose industry was unlimited, and whose personal qualities of heart and of mind were such as to endear him to all who became associated with him" (*Landmarks of a Lawyer's Lifetime,* 1914, p. 32). His brother, John Merrett Barbour, also attained high rank in the legal profession, becoming chief justice of the New York superior court.

["Descendants of Capt. Geo. Barbour of Medfield," comp. by Edmund Dana Barbour, MS. in Lib. of Cong.; C. A. Walworth, *The Walworths of America* (1897); brief sketches in *Green Bag,* II, 46; D. McAdam *et al., Hist. of the Bench and Bar of N. Y.* (1897), I, 254; *Our County and Its People . . . Saratoga County, N. Y.* (1899), ed. by G. B. Anderson.]

H. W. H. K.

BARBOUR, PHILIP PENDLETON (May 25, 1783–Feb. 25, 1841), lawyer, statesman, jurist, was the son of Thomas and Mary (Thomas) Barbour, and the brother of James Barbour [*q.v.*]. Philip was for a time the pupil of Rev. Charles O'Niel, an Episcopal clergyman, the main ingredient of whose pedagogical system is said to have been flogging. The tradition is that the young Barbour showed great aptitude for languages and became versed in classical literature, as one can easily believe from his later speeches. In 1800, after having read a little law, he removed to Kentucky, where he began the practise of the profession in which he was destined to achieve great distinction. In the summer of 1801, he returned to Virginia, borrowed some money, and spent one session at William and Mary College. In 1802, he resumed the practise of law, to which he devoted himself until he entered active political life in 1812.

Elected representative from Orange County to the Virginia House of Delegates in the latter year, he divided his energies during the rest of his life between politics and law. During approximately half of this time he was a member of a legislative body, two years in the House of Delegates and fourteen years in Congress. The other half of his public service was spent, two years in the state, and ten in the Federal, judiciary. There was a legislative interlude within his judicial service, and during most of his career law and politics joined hands. Always he was true to the dominant local tradition of state rights and strict construction, of which he became a conspicuous protagonist.

He entered Congress in September 1814, taking the seat which had been made vacant by the death of John Dawson, and served in that body continuously until 1825, when he accepted an appointment to the general court of Virginia. He held the speakership from 1821 to 1823, when he was defeated by Henry Clay for that office. Unlike his brother James, he was little affected by the nationalistic spirit which marked the first few years after the War of 1812. He was identified rather with the particularistic reaction which soon manifested itself in opposition to the tariff, internal improvements, and the extension of Federal jurisdiction by the Supreme Court under Marshall. He was one of the most prominent of the "new lights" in the Virginia delegation, who combated the policies championed by Clay and Calhoun and sought to restore the fallen prestige of their state by guarding zealously her constitutional rights against alleged Federal encroachments (C. H. Ambler, *Thomas Ritchie,* p. 73). He must be classified, not with the older school of contemporary Virginia statesmen as represented by Monroe and to some extent by his own brother James, but with the new group which centered in Judge Spencer Roane and his own intimate friend, Thomas Ritchie. The former, doubtless more aware of the practical exigencies of government, were relatively tolerant of the growth of national authority, which the latter viewed with an alarm that bordered on hysteria.

The contributions of the younger Barbour to the state-rights reaction were chiefly in the form of constitutional disputation. His speeches in Congress were marked by a predominant constitutional emphasis and a consistent advocacy of strict construction. He opposed the bonus bill for which his brother voted (*Annals of Congress,* 14 Cong., 2 Sess., 893–99). Like him, he denied the right of Congress to impose terms upon the admission of Missouri, but was more inclined to palliate the evils of slavery (*Ibid.,* 16 Cong., 1 Sess., 2054–80). A close reasoner rather than an orator, he was inclined to a "subtility in disquisition" which was not relished by loose constructionists but gratified the sensitive palate of such a constitutional epicure as John Randolph of Roanoke. Serving as counsel for the state in the celebrated case of Cohens *vs.* Virginia, he denied the right of appeal from the decision of a state court to the Federal judiciary, and later he reargued the case in Congress (Charles Warren, *Supreme Court in United States History,* 1926, II, 8, 125n.). During the first half of Adams's administration, with which his brother was loyally associated, he was a member of the judiciary of Virginia, but in 1827, upon the request of many of his former constituents, he resigned and was returned to Congress without opposition, in order to combat the nationalistic tendencies which now seemed ascendant. For the Adams administration he had scant respect. He objected to the large expenditure of public money, particularly for internal improvements, and to the imposition of a tariff (1828) which he termed impolitic, oppressive, and unjust. Convinced that there must be "concession to the remonstrances of a minority," he pinned his hopes on the executive veto after Jackson became president and began to wield this hitherto little-used weapon. He opposed nullification as a method of resistance to the tyranny of the majority, but defended the right of a state to secede in case of hopeless extremity. In order to check the extension of Federal power by judicial construction, he presented a bill in 1829 to require the concurrence of five of the seven judges of the Supreme Court in any decision involving a constitutional question (*Ibid.,* p. 177).

His prominence in state affairs and his alignment in local sectional controversy are clearly indicated by his position and attitude in the Virginia constitutional convention of 1829–30, so fateful in the history of the state. In consequence of the illness of Monroe, president of the convention, Barbour was first appointed president *pro tempore,* and then unanimously elected president (*Virginia Debates,* 1829–30, pp. 608–620). In the chief controversies which marked the convention, he identified himself with the conservative eastern slaveholders against the westerners. He opposed apportionment of representation on the basis of white population exclusively, and favored a "compound ratio," based on white population and property combined (*Ibid.,* pp. 90–98). He regarded some landed interest, though not necessarily a freehold, as a necessary qualification for the suffrage (*Ibid.,* pp. 435–36). Like the majority of his associates in the convention, he erred on the side of immediate rather than ultimate public safety, and he is to be condemned no more nor less than they for his failure adequately to sense the just claims of the westerners, who later in a time of crisis settled their ancient grudge by forming a separate state.

His acceptance of an appointment by Jackson, made in the autumn of 1830 as judge of the United States district court of Eastern Virginia, marked the end of his active political career. Politics, however, he abandoned with reluctance. In a valedictory to the citizens of his congressional district, which the Whigs termed unbecoming, he discussed the political situation and emphasized the necessity for continued insistence upon "restricted construction" of the Constitution. After he became a Federal judge, he presided, in 1831, over a free-trade convention in Philadelphia, and in 1832 he was offered by a group of southern strict constructionists as a candidate for the vice-presidency against Van Buren (A. C. Cole, *Whig Party in the South,* 1913, p. 14). Many of his supporters refused to accept the nomination of Van Buren and organized a Jackson-Barbour movement. Notwithstanding the fact that late in the campaign, after a public statement from Van Buren, Barbour announced his withdrawal to preserve party unity, he received some votes in the national election.

As early as 1831, the possibility of his appointment to the Supreme Court had been suggested and had aroused the fears of nationalists. John Quincy Adams dreaded that if Marshall should retire, "some shallow-pated wild-cat like Philip P. Barbour, fit for nothing but to tear the Union to rags and tatters," would be appointed in his place (*Memoirs,* Feb. 13, 1831). In Virginia there was strong desire for the appointment of Barbour, who was regarded by the dominant group as "eminently fitted to adorn the Bench with his talents and enlighten it with his inflexible and uncompromising State-Rights principles" (*Richmond Enquirer,* Mar. 19, 1836). The reconstitution of the Court, which aroused unwarranted Whig fears and Democratic hopes, did not come until 1836, when Taney became chief justice and Barbour succeeded Duval. Shortly after the new justices took their seats at the opening of the 1837 term, three cases of great constitutional importance, which had been pending for several years, were decided, the Bridge Case, the Miln Case, and the Briscoe Case. In the Miln Case, Justice Barbour delivered the opinion of the Court (II *Peters,* 129–42). Although the change made by the reconstituted Court in the lines of construction laid down by Marshall has been often exaggerated, there was some tendency henceforth to give the benefit of the doubt to the states, and there was greater recognition of economic and social factors. Barbour was a member of the new majority that followed Taney and deserves recognition in connection with this change in emphasis, but his untimely death and relatively short service prevented his exercising his potential influence. His active political life had not been favorable to profound or dispassionate legal scholarship, but he had always retained great interest in his profession. His conscientious study after his appointment to the Supreme Court resulted in the steady increase in his learning and reputation, as Story, who disapproved of the new order, had predicted. His colleagues felt that he would have attained the highest judicial distinction had he lived out his promise of years.

His last association with his fellow justices was in the evening of Feb. 24, 1841, when he attended a conference which lasted until ten o'clock and took part in the deliberations, apparently in good health. The next morning he was found dead in his bed. When the Court assembled that day, the chief justice announced that "Brother Barbour" was dead and that the Court would adjourn. Appropriate resolutions were subsequently adopted by the members and officers of the Court, and a brief sketch of his life, prepared apparently by Story, was incorporated in the records. According to his distinguished colleague, Justice Barbour's "talents were of a high order; but he was distinguished less for brilliancy of effort, than for perspicacious, close, and vigorous reasoning. He sought less to be eloquent than to be accurate" (see 15 *Peters*). Conscientious, upright, and industrious, he was respected by his associates for his talents, virtues, and high sense of duty. Like his brother James, Philip Pendleton Barbour married a daughter of Benjamin Johnson of Orange County. His marriage to Frances Todd Johnson took place in 1804 and had as its fruitage seven children. His mansion, "Frascati," in his native county was built some time before 1830 by workmen who had been engaged in building the University of Virginia, and had a serpentine wall around its garden. Prosperous in his later years, he lived in dignity and comfort as a country gentleman, loyal to the social, as well as the political, traditions of Virginia.

[No adequate account of the life of Philip Pendleton Barbour has yet been published. The sketch by P. P. Cynn in the *John P. Branch Hist. Papers* of Randolph-Macon Coll., IV, no. 1 (1913), pp. 67–77, is much less satisfactory than that of James Barbour in the same publication. The brief accounts of Judge Barbour's life all seem to be based on the obit. notice in Peters's *Supreme Court Reports,* vol. XV, which differs little from the sketch in W. W. Story, *Life and Letters of Joseph Story* (1851), II, 349–50. For his legislative career, the *Annals of Cong.,* continued in the *Reg. of Debates,* are indispensable. The *Va. Debates,* 1829–30 (1831), are valuable, and a considerable amount of source-material, in the form of speeches, etc., is contained in *Niles' Reg.* For his judicial career, see Peters's *Reports,* and for information about the family, see W. W. Scott, *Hist. of Orange County* (1907), and the geneal. in Philip Slaughter, *Hist. of St. Mark's Parish* (1877), pp. 118–21. An engraving of Judge Barbour may be seen in H. L. Corson's *Hist. of the Supreme Court* (1891), I, 295.]

D. M.

BARCLAY, THOMAS (Oct. 12, 1753–Apr. 21, 1830), Loyalist, was born in New York City. His father, Henry Barclay, was rector of Trinity Church; his mother, Mary (Rutgers) Barclay, was the daughter of Anthony Rutgers, a rich brewer. Thomas was educated at King's College (Columbia), and studied law in the office of John Jay. He was married on Oct. 2, 1775, to Susanna De Lancey. As a Loyalist he suffered the loss of his property, estimated at £2,745, and this act is said to have been the first confiscation of Tory property in the state (Flick, pp. 208–9). The Whig committee in charge of operations caused his "hay, forage, stock, and grain, except so much as was necessary to support his family and slaves, to be seized; but it was appraised, sold, and the value deposited in the state treasury until more definite action should be taken" (*Ibid.,* p. 138). Barclay enlisted as captain in the regiment of Loyal Americans in the army of Sir William Howe, was promoted to the rank of major for gallantry at the capture of Forts Clinton and Montgomery, and served until the end of the war. At its close, like so many other Loyalists, he took refuge in Nova Scotia. For over thirty years he held office under the British government. In the colony he was speaker of the Assembly, adjutant-general of militia, and commissary for prisoners. He was consul-general of Great Britain for the northern and eastern states in the decade before the second war with England, and in this important office he exerted his influence toward modifying the harsh measures of the home government (Edward Channing, *Jeffersonian System,* 1906, pp. 182–87). He was also commissioner to carry out the terms of the Jay Treaty (1795), and after the close of the War of 1812 he held a similar position to carry out the provisions of the Treaty of Ghent. His character stood high, and his Loyalist sentiments, as is shown by his correspondence, never wavered. He went to New York as consul-general in 1799 and remained there, with interruptions, until his death in 1830. His *Correspondence* (published in 1894) has thrown light on the strained relations between England and the United States prior to the War of 1812.

[Lorenzo Sabine, *Biog. Sketches of Loyalists of the Am. Rev.* (1864); A. C. Flick, *Loyalism in N. Y.* (1901); *Selections from the Correspondence of Thos. Barclay*, ed. by Geo. L. Rives (1894).]

E. K. A.

BARD, JOHN (Feb. 1, 1716–Mar. 30, 1799), physician, the first in this country to take part in a systematic dissection for the purpose of instruction, the earliest to report a case of extra-uterine pregnancy, and a pioneer sanitarian of New York, was born in Burlington, N. J. The United States was indebted for this able practitioner, and for his more noted son, Samuel [*q.v.*], to the revocation of the edict of Nantes by Louis XIV, in 1685, when some 300,000 Protestant Frenchmen, artisans, men of science and letters, emigrated to the nearby countries of Switzerland, Prussia, Holland, and England, and thence, some of them, to America. Peter, the father of John, went to London and from there was sent by an uncle on a mercantile venture to Delaware. Finding himself unsuited for business he moved to Burlington, N. J., was appointed a judge of the supreme court and a member of the governor's council, and died at an early age, leaving his widow, a daughter of an English physician named Marmion, to bring up a family of seven children on very slender means. John, the third son, was sent to Philadelphia to be educated and was fortunate in being under the instruction of a Scotch gentleman by the name of Annan, an accomplished Latin scholar and a man of polished manners. When the pupil reached the age of fifteen, he was bound apprentice to a Mr. John Kearsly, an English surgeon of the town, talented but of bad temper, who treated his underlings with great severity and subjected them to the most menial tasks. John submitted through fear of disappointing his mother and because of his affection for Mrs. Kearsly, who had shown him great kindness. For seven tedious years he remained with Mr. Kearsly, taking the hours for study from sleep, when the family had gone to bed. He early formed an intimacy with Benjamin Franklin, ten years his senior; they were members of the same social club and corresponded through life.

John Bard settled in practise in Philadelphia, where he married a Miss Valleau, a niece of Mrs. Kearsly, and like himself a descendant of a refugee from France. When he had been there some seven years (1746) he was induced by Franklin to move to New York, to take the place of Dr. Dubois and Dr. Dupie, who had just died of yellow fever. He soon gained a large practise among the better classes; he had sound professional knowledge, considerable conversational ability, and tact coupled with great cheerfulness. He kept the service of the public in mind, and in 1759, upon the arrival in New York Harbor of a Dutch ship containing cases of a malignant ship-fever, he was employed by the town to take quarantine measures. Every nurse and attendant caught the disease, and Bard was impelled to draw up a memorial to the corporation of the town urging the expediency of providing a pest-house against the occurrence of similar epidemics. The result was the purchase of Bedloe's Island with the building upon it and the appointment of Bard as health officer. He held also the position of surgeon and agent for the sick and wounded seamen of the British navy at New York, retaining the office until he retired from practise.

Concerning the first recorded instructional dissection, in which Bard and Peter Middleton were associated, we have this description from the pen of David Hosack, who was in partnership with Bard's son Samuel: "As early, however, as 1750, the body of Hermannus Carrol, executed for murder, was dissected in this city by two of the most eminent physicians of that day, Drs. John Bard and Peter Middleton, and the blood vessels injected for the instruction of the youth then engaged in the study of medicine; this was the first essay made in the United States for the purpose of imparting medical knowledge by the dissection of the human body, of which we have any record" (*American Medical and Philosophical Register*, 1812, II, 228). In a letter to John Fothergill of London, dated Dec. 25, 1759, Bard reported *A Case of Extra-Uterine Fœtus* that was read to "A society of physicians in London," on Mar. 24, 1760, and published subsequently in *Medical Observations and Inquiries*, London, 1763, vol. II. This was a most interesting case, in which Bard, in the presence of an army surgeon named Huck, opened the abdomen of the mother of two children, nine weeks after the delivery of the second, and evacuated a full-time macerated fetus and much pus, the patient subsequently nursing her live baby and making a good recovery. In the numbers of the *American Medical and Philosophical Register* are to be found several papers on yellow fever by John Bard and, after his death, there was published in that periodical (April 1811, I, 409–21) an essay on the nature and cause of malignant pleurisy, which had been "Drawn up at the request of a weekly society of gentlemen in New York, and addressed to them at one of their meetings, January 1749." This is the only and scanty reference to the earliest medical society in New York, which apparently was patterned after the London society of Fothergill.

Soon after the beginning of the Revolution

(1778) Bard retired to a farm he had purchased at Hyde Park, in Dutchess County, on the Hudson. He and his son Samuel, who had joined with his father in practise, held with the mother country to which they were under many obligations. At the peace of 1783 Bard returned to New York and to practise, for his funds were low. On the organization of the Medical Society of the State of New York, in 1788, he was chosen the first president; in 1795, being then in his eightieth year, he gave an address before this society calling attention to the presence of yellow fever in the city and making suggestions as to its treatment. This caused considerable feeling against him in the community, but he persisted in proclaiming the danger until the inhabitants saw that he was right and took proper measures to prevent the spread of the disease. Three years later he gave up practise and retired to Hyde Park, where he had his children about him. There he died of cerebral hemorrhage at the age of eighty-three, full of honors and with the satisfaction of a life of work well done. Up to the end he maintained his charm of conversation, vivacity of manner, and optimism. The engraving of him in the *American Medical and Philosophical Register* shows us a man of middle age, clothed in the custom of his time, and with a wig terminating in a neat braid on his shoulders; the face indicates determination with a background of geniality.

[The chief sources of information about John Bard are Hosack's and Francis's biog. of him in the *Am. Medic. and Phil. Reg.*, 1811; his letters in John M'Vickar, *Life of Samuel Bard* (1822); *Medical Observations and Inquiries* (London, 1762); and biographies, mainly from these sources, in James Thacher, *Am. Medic. Biog.* (1828), and H. A. Kelly and W. L. Burrage, *Am. Medic. Biogs.* (1920).]

W. L. B.

BARD, SAMUEL (Apr. 1, 1742–May 24, 1821), physician, writer on midwifery, was born in Philadelphia, where his father John Bard [*q.v.*] was practising medicine. His mother had been a Miss Valleau, niece of Dr. John Kearsly, an English surgeon of that town. In 1746, John Bard moved to New York, where young Bard was given a grammar school education and entered King's College at the age of fourteen during the presidency of Dr. Samuel Johnson. Destined by his father for the study of medicine, on graduation in 1760 he was sent abroad for that purpose, in spite of the fact that his father's circumstances were not opulent. The ship on which he sailed was captured by a French privateer and taken into Bayonne, where he was thrown into prison. There he stayed five months until released through the good offices of Benjamin Franklin, a friend of his father. He went at once to London and through the intercession of Dr. John Fothergill, another of his father's friends, was admitted as an assistant at St. Thomas's Hospital. From London he went to Edinburgh, then in the zenith of its glory, where he came under the instruction of Cullen, Whytt, the Monroes and Hope, and acquired a reputation as an industrious student and a good classical scholar. When he took his M.D. in 1765, his inaugural essay was entitled *De viribus opii*, said to be a well written and timely article; he was also given a prize for the best herbarium of the indigenous vegetables of Scotland, containing specimens of some 500 plants. Fellow students of Bard in Edinburgh were John Morgan of Philadelphia, Percival, the author of the standard work on medical ethics, and Haygarth, a noted physician of Bath.

On returning to New York, Bard began practise with his father and soon acquired a popularity and a clientage that were quite unusual. He married his cousin, Mary Bard, in 1770, and divided his time between the city and his father's house at Hyde Park, on the Hudson. He did no surgery, preferring to devote himself exclusively to what is called to-day "internal medicine." The question of starting a medical school in New York had been in Bard's mind even before he went abroad. The establishment of the University of Pennsylvania school in Philadelphia by John Morgan, soon after his arrival from foreign studies in 1765, stimulated the New York brethren to renewed attempts to elevate the standard of medicine. Bard took an active part. With Clossy, Jones, Middleton, Smith, and Tennent, the school was opened with Bard professor of the theory and practise of physic; the first degrees being conferred in 1769, Bard delivered an address which was instrumental not only in raising funds for the school, but later in founding the New York Hospital (1791). The school was affiliated with King's College, and Bard was connected with it for forty years, the last twenty as dean of the faculty and trustee.

On the opening of the Revolution, it was not unnatural that Bard's sympathies should be with the mother country since his medical training had been obtained in London and Edinburgh. He deemed it prudent to retire to Shrewsbury, N. J., where he engaged unsuccessfully in the manufacture of salt. When the British took possession of New York, he returned to the city. People mistrusted him for his Loyalist leanings, but the mayor of the city, an old friend of Bard's, called him as his private physician, vouched for him to prominent citizens, and thereby restored him to his former extensive practise. By the end of the war he was in comfortable circumstances.

When the American Government was established in New York, Washington selected Bard as his physician. The New York Hospital was opened in 1791 and Bard began his service as visiting physician, devoting much time to obstetrics; in the following year the medical school was united with Columbia College, and he was continued as professor of theory and practise and was appointed dean of the faculty. He helped found the city library and the New York Dispensary. In 1795 he took Dr. David Hosack into partnership and in 1798 retired to Hyde Park. He returned to New York, however, during the latter year to offer his assistance in the yellow-fever epidemic, caught the disease, and henceforth was definitely obliged to give up active practise. He was elected president of the original College of Physicians and Surgeons in 1811. In Hyde Park he was president of the Agricultural Society of Dutchess County, and a founder of the Protestant Episcopal church there. He lived to the age of seventy-nine, and died from an attack of pleurisy the day after the death of his beloved wife who had had the same disease. Of their ten children but three were alive at the time of their parents' passing, with several grandchildren who had been of great solace to their grandparents in their declining years.

As regards the writings of Samuel Bard, he published an article in 1771 entitled: *An Inquiry into the Nature, Cause and Cure of the Angina Suffocativa, or Sore Throat Distemper, as It Is Commonly Called by the Inhabitants of This City and Colony.* Abraham Jacobi, the noted children's expert, said of this (*Archives of Pediatrics*, N. Y. 1917, vol. XXXIV, nos. 1, 2, 3): "Bard's book is wise and accurate. His style is classical and simple and the description of diphtheria in skin, mucous membrane, and larynx is correct and beautiful." Bard's favorite branch of medicine was midwifery, in which he acquired a high reputation. On retiring into the country he found time to write a text-book on this subject which appeared in 1807, entitled: *A Compendium of the Theory and Practise of Midwifery,* which was intended chiefly for midwives and young practitioners. The work went through three large editions and after it had been enlarged into octavo form, two more. In the year 1811 Bard published *A Guide for Young Shepherds,* said to be the best practical treatise of the time on sheep breeding, the result of many experiments with merino and other brands of sheep which he had introduced into his farm at Hyde Park. He wrote several papers on yellow fever for the *American Medical and Philosophical Register* and for the *Transactions of the College of Physicians of Philadelphia,* besides *A Discourse on Medical Education,* published in New York in 1819.

As a frontispiece to the *Life of Samuel Bard,* by the Rev. John M'Vickar, is an engraving from a portrait of Bard. It shows a thick-set man of about forty; a forceful smooth-shaven face in which the chin is prominent, lower lip thick, the forehead wrinkled with care, and a not too happy expression of countenance.

[H. W. Ducachet, *A Biog. Memoir of Samuel Bard, with a Critique upon His Writings* (1821); John M'Vickar, *A Domestic Narrative of the Life of Samuel Bard* (1822); *Lives of Eminent Am. Physicians and Surgeons of the Nineteenth Cent.*, ed. by Samuel D. Gross (1861).] W. L. B.

BARD, WILLIAM (Apr. 4, 1778–Oct. 17, 1853), pioneer in life insurance, was born in Philadelphia, the grandson of Dr. John and the son of Dr. Samuel Bard. His mother was Mary, the daughter of Peter Bard, and her husband's cousin. William Bard was graduated from Columbia College in 1797, and on Oct. 7, 1802, married Catherine, the daughter of Nicholas Cruger. Of his business career before his entrance into the field of life insurance little is recorded. In 1830 he organized and was made president and actuary of the New York Life Insurance and Trust Company, with a capital stock of $1,000,000. A charter was issued Mar. 9, and business was begun in September. Though several other companies had been chartered to engage, among other activities, in this form of insurance, Bard's company was the first to make it a specialty. Public sentiment was generally either indifferent or hostile, while the other companies neglected it and in some cases discouraged its development. Bard, however, was an enthusiastic advocate and earnestly set himself to the task of converting the opposition. By a judicious use of propaganda and by establishing the agency system he soon brought about a more favorable public attitude. In a booklet published by him in December 1832, which probably was widely circulated, he replied to the current criticisms of life insurance and predicted for it a rapid development. As an evidence of its growth he cited the case of his own company, the New York office of which had had sixty-five policies in force in June and now had 150.

Through his energy and zeal his company prospered. By the end of 1839 it could boast of 694 policies in force, for an amount of $2,451,958. It appears to have been particularly favored, moreover, by the Court of Chancery, which entrusted to it large sums of money. But the competition of other companies—particularly that of the New York Life Insurance Company, organized in 1845—proved hurtful, and though it continued as a trust company, its life insurance business gradually declined. Some time before 1848 Bard retired. He died at his home on Staten Island.

[G. O. Seilhamer, *The Bard Family* (1908); Chas. Kelley Knight, *Hist. of Life Insurance in the U. S. to 1870* (1920); Jas. M. Hudnut, *Semi-Centennial Hist. of the N.Y. Life Insurance Co., 1845–95* (1895); *Hunt's Merchants' Mag.*, II and VIII; Wm. Bard, *A Letter to David E. Evans on Life Insurance* (1832).]

W. J. G.

BARDEEN, CHARLES WILLIAM (Aug. 28, 1847–Aug. 24, 1924), educator, publisher, author, was born of good New England stock in Groton, Mass., a descendant of William Bardeen who landed in Plymouth in 1637. During the Civil War, young Bardeen ran away from school to join the 1st Massachusetts Volunteers as drummer boy. He kept a diary 1862–64, later published under the title of *A Little Fifer's War Diary* (1910), which contains surprisingly mature observations of human nature. On his return from war, he reëntered high school and on a sudden impulse decided to work his way through Yale College. This he did by obtaining scholarships and by tutoring and teaching throughout his college course. At Yale he belonged to four undergraduate organizations, captured three college prizes and was awarded the honor of being appointed to deliver both the junior and senior orations. At the age of twenty-one, he married Ellen Dickerman of New Haven, by whom he had five children. After graduating from Yale he taught as principal of Weston Boarding School, vice-principal of the Connecticut State Normal School, teacher of English in Kalamazoo College, and superintendent of schools in Whitehall, N. Y. In 1873, he had the agency in the state of New York for Clark & Maynard's educational publications with headquarters in Syracuse. He became managing editor in 1874 of the *School Bulletin* and for nearly half a century was its vigorous and versatile editor. He wrote the editorials, collected personal news, and penned trenchant short stories that made it unique among school journals. Under his editorship the *School Bulletin* gained a national reputation. From 1874 to 1880 he had charge of the publishing department of Davis Bardeen & Company. In 1880 he bought it out and carried it on under his own name until it was sold in 1922. He was chosen head of the department of educational publications for the International Congress at Chicago in 1893. For four years he served as director of The National Educational Association. From 1900 to the end of his life he was president of the Educational Press Association of America. He was a member of the Author's Club of London, the Royal Societies of London, president of The Browning Club when it was first formed in Syracuse, member of the National Institute of Social Sciences, president of the Yale Club of Syracuse 1902–12.

The more important of Bardeen's numerous volumes were *Common School Law,* which ran through several editions (4th ed. 1878), *History of Educational Journalism* (1896), *Teaching as a Business* (1897), and *A Dictionary of Educational Biography* (1901). Among the best of his educational short stories were "Roderick Hume," "The Woman Trustee," "The Shattered Halo," "The Yellow Streak," "The Stolen Payroll," and "Castiron Culver."

[Sketches of career in the *Syracuse Post Standard;* the *Syracuse Herald,* Aug. 20, 1924, the *Yale Obit. Rec.,* pp. 1305–07.]

W. H. M.

BARKER, ALBERT SMITH (Mar. 31, 1843–Jan. 29, 1916), naval officer, descendant of an old New England family, was the son of Josiah and Eliza (Cushing) Barker, and was born at Hanson, Mass. Graduating from the Naval Academy in 1862, he was immediately ordered to duty on board the *Mississippi,* and was in her during the bombardment and passage of Forts Jackson and St. Philip below New Orleans, and during the capture of that city in April 1862. When the *Mississippi,* which had been Commodore M. C. Perry's flagship on his expedition to Japan, went aground and was destroyed by her commander, Capt. Melancthon Smith, during an attack on Port Hudson, to prevent her falling into the hands of the enemy (Mar. 14, 1863), Ensign Barker was transferred to the *Monongahela,* and in her took part in the siege and capture of Port Hudson. On Aug. 9, 1863, he was ordered to the *Niagara* on special service. He was promoted to be lieutenant Feb. 22, 1864, lieutenant commander July 25, 1866, commander Mar. 28, 1877, captain May 5, 1892, and rear admiral Oct. 10, 1905. In 1877 he was given command of the *Alert,* in which he explored many islands near New Guinea in search of a shipwrecked crew. During the years 1882–86, in command of the *Enterprize,* he ran a line of deep-sea soundings round the world. In 1886 he was lighthouse inspector; from 1886 to 1891 he was connected with the Bureau of Navigation; in 1891–92 he was in charge of the Washington navy-yard; and in 1892 he was given command of the *Philadelphia.* At the beginning of the war with Spain in 1898 he was a member of the important Board of Strategy of the Navy, and during that war commanded the cruiser *Newark,* participating in the bombardment of Santiago de

Cuba, July 1, 1898. From Aug. 2 of that year to May 29, 1899, he commanded the battle-ship *Oregon* on special service in the Pacific, and succeeded Admiral Dewey in command of the Asiatic Fleet on that date. He afterward held several important commands ashore, and became commander-in-chief of the North Atlantic Fleet in 1903, retiring for age on Mar. 31, 1905. In 1919 the United States destroyer *Barker,* named in his honor, was launched at Philadelphia. He was married on Oct. 16, 1894, to Mrs. Ellen (Blackmar) Maxwell, widow of a missionary to India.

[Data concerning this officer are to be found at the U. S. Navy Dept. in the office of the Naval Records and Library; see also Barker Newhall, *The Barker Family of Plymouth Colony and County* (1900), pp. 45–58.]

E. B.

BARKER, BENJAMIN FORDYCE (May 2, 1818–May 30, 1891), physician, was born in Wilton, Me., the second son of Dr. John Barker, who served in the War of 1812, and Phœbe (Abbott) Barker. His ancestors had come to America about 1640, settling in Massachusetts. He was graduated from Bowdoin College in 1837. From 1838 to 1840 he worked in the office of Dr. Henry I. Bowditch, in Boston. In 1841, he received the degree of M.D. from the Bowdoin Medical College. Because of a tendency toward pulmonary disease, he moved to Norwich, Conn., where he soon became a successful practitioner. While there he also showed an interest in politics and is said to have stumped the state in a presidential election, making a speech in a different town every night for three months. His fondness for music, begun in his college days, continued; he sang in a church choir and composed some melodies. On Sept. 14, 1843, he married Elizabeth Lee Dwight of Harrisburg, Pa., and on Oct. 1 sailed for France to study at the University of Paris. Before his course was finished, however, in the next year, he was called home on account of illness in his family. While he was in Paris he became intimate with Trousseau. Although Barker never returned to France to finish his studies, he was later granted a degree by the University.

After his year in Europe, he became professor of obstetrics in Bowdoin Medical College for a short period, but soon resigned because of his other activities. In 1848, he was made president of the Connecticut Medical Society and delivered an important address on "Some Forms of Disease of the Cervix Uteri." The next year, at the suggestion of Dr. Willard Parker, he moved to New York and incorporated, with others, the New York Medical College, in which he filled the chair of obstetrics. At about this time he developed a partial paralysis of the vocal cords, which remained with him all the rest of his life; at times he was able to speak only in a hoarse whisper. Within the next few years he was appointed obstetrician to many New York hospitals and, in 1861, succeeded in obtaining a charter, with the aid of his friends, for the Bellevue Hospital Medical School, in which he became professor of obstetrics and diseases of women, a position which he held until his death. His practise in New York was very extensive and during his day he was probably the best-known obstetrician in America. He always inspired confidence in his patients by his sanguine temperament, genial manner, and impressive presence; his counsel was wise and tempered by common sense. His practise was limited to non-operative obstetrics and gynecology. It is reported that he introduced the use of the hypodermic syringe into American medicine.

In 1874, he published his book on *Puerperal Diseases,* a treatise which passed through many editions and was translated into French, German, Italian, Spanish, and Russian. It was an excellent book for its time, especially rich in clinical descriptions of diseases. He was connected with numerous medical societies; he founded and was the first president of the American Gynecological Society. For thirty years he traveled to Europe annually and was intimately acquainted with Dickens, Thackeray, and other notable Europeans.

[A very complete biographic notice of Barker will be found in the *Trans. Am. Gyn. Soc.,* 1891, XVI, 551–58, portr., by Dr. James R. Chadwick of Boston, a close associate; an analysis of his social success and character was written soon after his death by Dr. Henry C. Coe (*N. Y. Jour. Gyn. and Obs.,* 1891, I, 112–18); the best account of his early life in Me. and Conn. is by Dr. W. T. Lusk (*Trans. N. Y. Acad. of Med.,* 1892, 2nd ser., VIII, 286–302).]

H. R. V.

BARKER, GEORGE FREDERICK (July 14, 1835–May 24, 1910), chemist and physicist, son of George and Lydia Prince Pollard Barker, was born at Charlestown, Mass. Their comfortable circumstances enabled his parents to give him the advantages of excellent preparatory schooling; at the Classical Academy of Berwick, Me., at Lawrence Academy in Groton, and finally at Yarmouth Academy, Me. At sixteen he began a five-year apprenticeship to a manufacturer of philosophical instruments which further prepared him for the systematic study of the physical sciences. After two years at Yale, where he specialized in chemistry and physics, he was graduated in 1858. As a member of the varsity crew he added physical fitness to his mental preparation for a long and active career. The next seven years were spent in teaching at Yale, Harvard, Wheaton College (Illinois), Albany Medical College, and the Western University of Pittsburgh. He returned to Yale in 1865 with an M.D. from Albany, as demonstrator in the Medical College. Later (1867–73), he was head of the department of physiological chemistry and toxicology at Yale, serving also as lecturer at Williams College. His reputation rests mainly upon his achievements during the twenty-seven years (1873–1900) of his service as professor of physics at the University of Pennsylvania. Barker's active career of forty-two years, though largely academic, included work as consultant, investigator, public lecturer, author, and editor. He was the recipient of many honors. In 1881, as commissioner to the International Electrical Exhibition and delegate to the International Congress of Electricians in Paris, he received from the French Government the decoration of the Legion of Honor with the rank of Commander. By presidential appointment he was a commissioner to the Electrical Exhibition in Philadelphia (1884) and served on the Jury of Awards at the Columbian Exposition. He was president (1879) of the American Association for the Advancement of Science and later (1891) of the American Chemical Society. As an electrician, as a toxicologist, and as a municipal chemist, he was an acknowledged expert. Always conversant with the most recent developments in science, he was the first in America to exhibit radium in radio-active bodies (Edgar F. Smith—personal letter, Nov. 1, 1926). His publications on radioactivity, on the "Conversion of Mechanical Energy into Heat by Dynamo-Electric Machines" (*Proceedings of the American Association for the Advancement of Science,* vol. XXVIII), on metals, auroras, and solar eclipses are all valuable contributions to science. He was the editor or associate editor of a number of scientific periodicals. These honors and achievements bear testimony to his unusual versatility. He was married in August 1861 to Mary M. Treadway of New Haven.

[Edgar F. Smith, "Geo. Frederick Barker," *Am. Jour. of Sci.,* CLXXX, 225–32; Elihu Thomson, "Geo. Frederick Barker," *Am. Philosophical Soc. Proc.,* L; *Pop. Sci. Mo.,* Sept. 1879; *Am. Men of Science* (1906); *Who's Who in America* (1908); *Who's Who in Pa.* (1908); *Public Ledger* (Phila.) May 26, 1910.]

H. C.

BARKER, JACOB (Dec. 17, 1779–Dec. 26, 1871), merchant, financier, lawyer, was born on Swan Island, Kennebec County, Me., where his parents had moved from Nantucket in order to escape the dangers incident to the Revolution. Both parents were distantly related to Benjamin Franklin. The father, Robert, died four months after the boy was born. Sarah (Folger), the mother, was a Friend, and she reared her children in that faith. In April 1785 she brought her family back to Nantucket. Jacob, after attending school for a time at New Bedford, returned home and worked in a store. At sixteen, with $100 saved, determining to become a seaman, he shipped as a green hand on a vessel to New York. His older brother, Abraham, who had preceded him to the metropolis, induced him to give up the sea and to take a clerkship in the commission house of Isaac Hicks. The boy was industrious, shrewd, and ambitious, and while still in the employ of Hicks he acquired a part interest in a fleet of merchant vessels. At the beginning of 1801, having accumulated $5,000, he started a new firm, with two friends as partners. In the same year he married a New Bedford schoolmate, Elizabeth Hazard. Business reverses at this time left him bankrupt, but he immediately began again, and in a few years became wealthy. A Jeffersonian Democrat and one of the founders of Tammany Hall, he yet opposed, in common with the Federalist majority among the merchants of New York City, the party policy making for war with Great Britain. When, however, war was declared (June 18, 1812), he unreservedly supported the administration. Much of his time and effort during the war were expended in raising money for the Government, which was often in desperate straits. His own fortune was wrecked, the British having captured all his ships; his claims against the Government were never fully adjusted; and to cap these disasters, he asserts, he was both discriminated against and calumniated by his Federalist colleagues, who continued to oppose the war and sought to cripple the administration.

Fresh ventures again brought him some measure of success. In 1815 he founded the Exchange Bank, in Wall St., and though it failed in 1819 he continued to extend his operations. The business depression of 1826, however, involved him in various troubles. One of the companies of which he was a director—the Life & Fire Insurance Company—failed, and he and six others were promptly indicted for fraud. A bitter legal contest followed, which was virtually ended, Nov. 14, 1827, by the quashing of the indictment, though a chancery suit dragged on for some months. Barker always maintained that the indictment was the result of a conspiracy on the part of the "moneyed aristocracy" and the Federalists to ruin him; and in numerous letters and articles which from time to time he published during the next thirty-seven years he gave to the world a great mass of details in support of his charge. One result of the trial was his removal from New York. Some of the securities of the bankrupt insurance company consisted of mortgages on plantations in Louisiana, and he was immediately involved in litigation in that state. In 1834, assigning what remained of his New York estate to Fitz-Greene Halleck and two others, he moved to New Orleans, where he studied law and was admitted to the bar. Again he prospered; he became one of the leading capitalists of the South, and was president of the Bank of Commerce when Gen. Butler entered the city. He had opposed secession; but his attitude had apparently not greatly impaired his standing. He came into some prominence again as an opponent of Butler's rigorous rule and, later, of the Congressional measures of reconstruction. In 1869, ill and once more poor, he moved to Philadelphia, to reside with his son Abraham, at whose house he died.

Barker had a stormy and eventful career. One of his chief traits was pugnacity, and circumstances provided him with many opportunities for its exercise. He had an exceptional degree of fortitude; against reverses that would have crushed most men he kept the field, repeatedly making up his losses and regaining his place in the business world. He was proud of his genealogy—particularly that part of it which related him to Franklin—and proud also of his physical resemblance to the great sage. He was not averse to mentioning his own legal and oratorical abilities, or the fact that he had taken part in many historic events and had mixed with many notables. With complacency he records the statement that he had imported the first marine engine used by Robert Fulton and that for twenty years he had had in his employ (before Astor got him) no less a person than Fitz-Greene Halleck. Fate had placed him at the White House in that trying moment after the battle of Bladensburg when Dolly Madison was hastily gathering up her possessions and preparing for flight; and it fell to him and to a New York friend, Robert de Peyster, to carry off and hide, at the behest of Mrs. Madison, the Gilbert Stuart portrait of Washington. Though disavowing any special pride in the act (the honor, as he contended, belonging altogether to Mrs. Madison), he brooked no questioning of his part in it; and when the matter was discussed in the press, thirty-four years afterward, he published long letters about it, proving by the word of Mrs. Madison herself that he and his friend were the actual saviors of the portrait. The fact of which he was most proud was his part in financing the War of 1812, when, he says, he was "the pivot upon which this important nation rested at one of the most important periods of its history." He was an honest man, even though his honesty was often impugned. "As an example of rectitude and upright dealing, carried through the most gigantic operations and disastrous losses," said the *New York Times* on his decease, "there is no brighter page in the merchant annals of our country than his business life."

[Barker Newhall, *The Barker Family of Plymouth Colony and County* (1900); *Incidents in the Life of Jacob Barker of New Orleans, La.* (largely autobiographical, but ostensibly written by a friend, 1855); *The Conspiracy Trials of 1826 and 1827* (also largely autobiographical, but with an introduction by R. D. Turner, 1864); obituaries in *N. Y. Times*, Dec. 27, 1871, and *N. Y. Tribune*, Dec. 28, 1871.] W. J. G.

BARKER, JAMES NELSON (June 17, 1784–Mar. 9, 1858), dramatist and man of affairs, was born in Philadelphia. His versatile career had as its background the personality and life of his father, Gen. John Barker, a soldier and politician of prominence in early Philadelphia, who served as alderman, as major-general of the 1st division of the Pennsylvania militia, and as mayor of Philadelphia in 1808, 1809, and 1812. He resigned as alderman in 1817, when his son was appointed in his place. James Nelson Barker was educated in the Philadelphia schools, trained in the principles of the Democratic party, and given the ideals of a soldier. He possessed the fiery traits of his father's personality with ameliorating polish. He was aided by his father's influence and popularity but had social gifts in his own right which, with his alert, dashing appearance, meant much. His first activities in literature and in politics were nearly simultaneous. He began authorship with an unproduced tragedy, *The Spanish Rover,* in 1804 and, after writing a masque, *America,* that was never printed, reached the stage on Mar. 4, 1807, with *Tears and Smiles,* a deservedly applauded comedy of Philadelphia manners. On Mar. 16, 1808, he confirmed this success with his comic interlude *The Embargo or What News?* upholding the Embargo bills of that and the preceding year. *The Indian Princess, or la Belle Sauvage,* produced Apr. 6, 1808, and advertised as an "operatic melodrama" (*Democratic Press,* Apr. 5, 1808), is important as the first acted play on the Indian by an American, the first on the story of Pocahontas, and the first to be acted in England after a premier production in the United States. Barker's adaptation, at the request of the managers of the Chestnut Street

Theatre, of A. Cherry's *The Travellers, or Music's Fascination,* also won public appreciation. Meanwhile he had become prominent in the political organization of Philadelphia known as "The Democratic Young Men," and in 1809 inaugurated his career as a poet by a song sung at that organization's celebration of the Fourth of July. From Dec. 21, 1809, until the close of March 1810, he was in Washington studying the government, making useful friends, and generally informing himself politically. He was caught up in the gaiety of the capital, entertained by the President, the Secretary of the Treasury, and other officials. In 1811, against the opposition of his father, he married Mary Rogers, who had come to Philadelphia from Connecticut with her brother Edmund, a portrait painter of the day (James Swift Rogers, *James Rogers of New London, Conn. and His Descendants,* 1902, p. 234).

Barker resumed play making in 1812 with *Marmion,* a dramatization of Scott's poem, produced in New York, Apr. 12, as of English origin. On June 1, 1812, he accepted an appointment as captain in the 2nd Artillery and served on the Canadian frontier with a success worthy of his heritage. At the time of his resignation from the army, Apr. 1, 1817, he was assistant adjutant-general with the rank of major (see files, Adjutant-General's Office, Washington). Literature and politics had again claimed his attention in 1816. By July 4 he was active in the "new-school" branch of the Democratic party, composing two poems for the day's ceremonies. On Dec. 18, 1816, he began a series of eleven articles of spirited dramatic criticism in which his attitude toward drama was the same as that which in his plays gives him true significance—"that with a free people and under the liberal care of a government such as ours it might tend to keep alive the spirit of freedom; and to unite conflicting parties in common love of liberty and devotedness to country." (*Democratic Press,* Dec. 18, 1816). He contributed biographies on Jay and Clinton to Delaplaine's one-time much-discussed *Repository;* they are equal to any of the period. Drama, however, was still his favorite literary form; and with *The Armourer's Escape* produced Mar. 21, 1817, and *How to Try a Lover,* written the same year but not then acted, he again illustrated his ability. The slashing eloquence of his political oration of July 4, 1817, aroused much feeling among the Democrats and was widely quoted.

In 1817 Barker became an alderman, in October 1819 he was elected mayor of Philadelphia by the Democratic city council. Always a philanthropist, he used his office on several occasions for charitable purposes, and, through the efficiency of his appointments, stimulated considerable animosity. In the spring of 1820 there were fears of incendiarism in the city; and he, as mayor, organized the citizens for protection. With the split and defeat of his party in the next election he lost the mayoralty but resumed his position as alderman. He made strenuous efforts to harmonize the differences in the ranks of the Democrats, and through 1822 and 1823 was an official of most of the town meetings and a member of every important committee of his party. The finest of his dramas, *Superstition,* was put on at the Chestnut Street Theatre, Mar. 12, 1824. Its theme is taken from New England colonial history and developed with a power that makes it possible to estimate the play as the best drama written in America to that date. Constantly a figure on public occasions in Philadelphia, Barker participated in the reception to Gen. Lafayette in September 1824, and during the parade an ode of his was distributed to the crowds from a press mounted on a wagon (*National Gazette,* Sept. 29, 30, 1824). The annuals of 1825, and for several years following, especially the *Atlantic Souvenir,* contain facile, graceful poetical contributions from his pen deserving a better fate than has been theirs. The most popular were "Little Red Riding Hood" and "The Three Sisters." On Oct. 24, 1825, he delivered an ode, "The Pilgrims of Pennsylvania," before a distinguished audience including John Quincy Adams and the Duke of Saxe-Weimar. His interest in the theatre was continued by way of prologue to Dr. James McHenry's play, *The Usurper,* Dec. 26, 1827, and Richard Penn Smith's *The Eighth of January,* 1829, the second again declaring for American plays by Americans.

Barker was a vigorous participant in Andrew Jackson's campaign for the presidency in 1828, and on Mar. 11, 1829, was appointed collector of the port of Philadelphia, holding that post until 1838. He conducted the custom-house adequately, with attention, at the same time, to political expediency. In 1832 he contributed influential articles to the newspapers on the Bank War, while his oration at the Jackson dinner, Jan. 8, 1835, was an excellent example of aggressive political writing (*Daily Pennsylvanian,* Jan. 16, 1835). His dramatic interests were not entirely submerged by public affairs. On Jan. 13, 1836, he was instrumental in what nearly amounted to a municipal benefit-performance for William B. Wood, Philadelphia actor and manager. On Mar. 26, 1836, his earlier play, *How to Try a Lover,* never before performed, was given at the Arch Street Theatre with enthusiastic approval under the new title, *A Court of Love* (*Ibid.,* Mar. 26, 1836). This was the only play he ever wrote with which he was satisfied. Partly for political reasons, but largely in recognition of Barker's real ability, Van Buren appointed him comptroller of the treasury, Mar. 1, 1838. With his removal to Washington, his name still remained an influence in Philadelphia, appearing prominently among toasts at political gatherings (see files of the *Daily Pennsylvanian*). Following the change in administration, he lost his office in the treasury on Apr. 19, 1841, but with the advent of Tyler was made acting comptroller of the treasury, on Sept. 14 of the same year. Subsequently, he was clerk in the office of the chief clerk of the treasury and long continued to place his valuable experience at the service of the Government. In spite of heavy routine duties his literary production did not altogether cease, as he contributed to periodicals in Washington. The French Revolution of 1848 was the subject of a poem he read before President Polk's cabinet, copies of which were distributed during the procession to celebrate the French success. His letters to his daughter, at this period, reflect an affectionate and domestic temperament of appealing charm. Through the changing administrations he succeeded in retaining his office, and at his death, Mar. 9, 1858, he was still holding his position in the Treasury Department.

[The facts of John Barker's mil. life are to be found in the *Pa. Archives,* 6th ser., vols. I to X, for which there is a complete index. The best analysis of J. N. Barker's plays and position in Am. drama is in A. H. Quinn, *Hist. of the Am. Drama from the Beginning to the Civil War* (1923). The most extended biog. sketch is by Henry Simpson, *The Lives of Eminent Philadelphians* (1859). Wm. Dunlap, *A Hist. of the Am. Stage* (1832), II, 308–16, contains Barker's own story of his plays. His five printed plays are in the Univ. of Pa. Lib. The files of the Phila. *Aurora, Democratic Press, Daily Pennsylvanian,* and *Washington Union* are main sources for biog. facts. Manuscript letters in the Phila. Custom House, Ridgway Lib., and Pa. Hist. Soc. are valuable. Miss Josephine Keys, Barker's grand-daughter, possesses manuscript letters, official commissions, and biog. data.]

P. H. M.

BARKER, JAMES WILLIAM (Dec. 5, 1815–June 26, 1869), merchant, Know-Nothing party candidate for mayor of New York, was born at White Plains, N. Y. He began his business career as a clerk with an extensive mercantile concern in New York City, where he later entered into business for himself, his energy and good management soon making him wealthy. In 1860 he founded a large dry-goods house in Pittsburgh, Pa., one of the first in that city to confine its business exclusively to cloths. He was prostrated by a sunstroke in 1867, and impaired health thereafter obliged him to relinquish active business connections, although the two years of his life that remained found him the president of the Eclectic Life Insurance Company of New York. His chief claim to fame was his activity in New York and national politics. He was an earnest and zealous Whig until the dissolution of that party. In 1854 he was the Know-Nothing party's candidate for mayor of New York City, but was defeated in a closely contested election by Fernando Wood. He always claimed that his defeat was due to an article in the *Tribune,* which claimed that he had set fire to his store for the purpose of cheating the insurance companies (*New York Herald,* June 27, 1869). He brought a libel suit against the *Tribune,* but the case was finally compromised. In 1856, upon the virtual dissolution of the Know-Nothing party and the reëmergence of the anti-slavery agitation (through the repeal of the Missouri Compromise two years before), Barker resumed his political activities, this time as a Republican, and he was a worker in the campaign for Lincoln's election in 1860. Meantime he was a dominant factor in the founding of the "Order of the Star Spangled Banner," a secret organization having for its object the prevention of the political ascendancy of the foreign-born inhabitants of the United States. He became the head of the New York grand council and in 1853 was its principal officer. The resolutions adopted upon his death by the directors of the Eclectic Insurance Company (*New York Times,* June 29, 1869) declared "he left behind an honorable memory for uprightness of character, public spirit, munificence to the poor, liberality to religious enterprises, and diligence in business." He was known for the invariable courtesy of his deportment, and his efficiency and manliness in every place of trust. In heated political campaigns the New York newspapers of his day were not so reliable, and in the eyes of his friends there were no grounds whatsoever for the *Tribune's* charge against him. It was Barker's hatred of litigation and controversy, as well as publicity, that booked largely in the subsequent settlement of the suit. He died while on a visit to Rahway, N. J., and was given a public funeral in New York.

[There are meager accounts of his life in some earlier cyclopedias, but the chief records of him appear in the New York newspapers following his death. All print memorial notices and resolutions in connection with the usual obituaries.]

R. R. R.

BARKER, JEREMIAH (Mar. 31, 1752–Oct. 4, 1835), physician, was the son of Samuel and Patience (Howland) Barker of Scituate, Mass.

He was educated in the common schools and then studied medicine under Dr. Bela Lincoln, a graduate of Aberdeen and Harvard. After an unsuccessful attempt at practising in Gorham, Me., he moved to Barnstable on Cape Cod, where he was at the outbreak of the Revolution. During the war, he served as ship's surgeon, first on a privateer and later in the Penobscot expedition. When this expedition was over, he returned to Gorham and gradually built up a large practise. Later on he practised at Stroudwater but finally retired to Gorham. He was married five times but outlived all of his wives and died at the ripe age of eighty-four.

During his first stay in Gorham, Barker compiled a *Vade Mecum,* containing a digest of current medicine, and *A Book of Anatomy.* He produced a number of well-written papers, on epidemics occurring in Maine, 1790–1810 (published in Mitchill's *Medical Repository*), and planned a history of American epidemics, which apparently was never written. He was a member of the Massachusetts and of the Maine Medical Societies, was an omnivorous reader, and at his death left a medical library of 3,000 volumes.

Barker was a man of many theories. Convinced that much sickness had its origin in inclement weather, he believed that approaching diseases could be predicted from atmospheric conditions. He experimented freely with the use of alkalies as drugs, and supposed that he had found in limewater a universal panacea. More modest than many of his profession, he habitually carried a favorite text-book, *Rush on Fevers,* to the bedside of his patients and consulted it there. He was an indefatigable worker. It is said that during an epidemic of putrid sore-throat he never entered his own house for more than a month, but drove from patient to patient, eating and sleeping anywhere.

[Mitchill's *Medical Repository;* family records.]

J. A. S.

BARKER, JOSIAH (Nov. 16, 1763–Sept. 23, 1847), ship-builder, was born at Marshfield, Mass., the son of Ebenezer Barker, a blacksmith of Pilgrim descent, and of Priscilla (Loring) Barker (Barker Newhall, *Barker Family of Plymouth Colony and County,* 1901, pp. 33, 46). His Revolutionary service began at thirteen. After four short army enlistments spent chiefly in tedious guard duty, he was at sea on the frigate *Hague* during the last year of the war. A veteran at nineteen, he returned to Pembroke, Mass., where he married Penelope, the daughter of Capt. Seth Hatch, on Dec. 9, 1787. In the meantime he had learned to build ships on the North River, whose numerous yards made it a "cradle of New England shipbuilding." The industry was temporarily dull at home, so he built five ships, between 1786 and 1792, in New Brunswick, where vessels enjoyed the advantages of British registry. The Anglo-French war stimulated the New England demand and in 1795 he settled at Charlestown, Mass. His reputation attracted orders from the ship-owners of Boston, and in the next twenty years, the Barker yard turned out nearly forty vessels. In the War of 1812, Barker built on contract the sloop of war *Frolic,* and served as master carpenter on the *Independence,* the first ship of the line in the United States Navy. It has been erroneously stated that he became naval constructor at the Charlestown yard about 1811. He was still building merchantmen in his own yard in 1816, and not until 1826 does his name first appear as naval constructor, at a salary of $2,000, later $2,300. He served in that capacity for twenty years. Among the ships which he constructed were the ships of the line *Vermont* and *Virginia* and the frigate *Cumberland.* In 1834, he rebuilt the *Constitution* in our first naval dry dock. But he does not seem to have been a creative genius in naval architecture; ordinarily, he built along lines received from the chief constructor. His original work was the designing of the sloop *Portsmouth* in 1843, though even there he followed a French model. With his imposing figure, about six feet tall, and his "dignity, urbanity, and hospitality," he was prominent in the comfortable life of the navy-yard and town, but an octogenarian builder of wooden ships was scarcely equal to the new problems arising from steam and iron. In 1843, he was transferred to Portsmouth, and he was finally dismissed from the service on July 9, 1846, at the age of eighty-three (*Navy Register,* 1847, p. 167). He survived this barely a year, dying at Charlestown on Sept. 23, 1847.

[*Memorial of Josiah Barker, of Charlestown,* by Henry H. Edes (1871), reprinted and amplified from his article in the *New Eng. Hist. and Geneal. Reg.,* XXIV, 297–304, based on original family papers; details of Barker's connection with the navy in the *Am. State Papers, Naval Series,* I, 828, 1017, II, 458, III, 272, and in the ann. volumes of the *Navy Reg.,* from 1826 to 1847.]

R. G. A—n.

BARKER, WHARTON (May 1, 1846–Apr. 8, 1921), financier, publicist, the son of Abraham and Sarah (Wharton) Barker, inherited something of the energy and combativeness of his grandfather, Jacob Barker [*q.v.*]. Born in Philadelphia, after attending public schools in that city he entered the University of Pennsylvania. At seventeen he assisted in organizing the 3rd

Regiment (U. S.) of colored troops. In 1866 he graduated from the University with the degree of A.B., and then began work with the banking firm of Barker Brothers & Company, of which two years later he became a member. On Oct. 16, 1867, he was married to Margaret Corlies Baker. In 1878 the Russian Government appointed him its special financial agent in the United States and intrusted him with the building of four cruisers in American shipyards. A year later he was called to Russia to advise on the development of the coal and iron mines north of the Azof, and for his services was knighted by Alexander II. His Russian interests led to his acquirement of interests in the Orient. In 1887 he became associated with Count Mitkiewicz, who professed to have obtained from the Chinese Government, through Li Hung Chang, a $20,000,000 concession, including telegraph, telephone, and banking rights. The project, however, came to naught—according to Barker, because of the antagonism of British capitalists—and resulted in somewhat spectacular litigation between Barker and Mitkiewicz. Barker, while retaining his interest in the family banking firm, organized the Investment Company and also the Finance Company, both of Philadelphia, with a combined capital of $9,000,000. The banking firm was in some difficulty at the time of the Baring failure, but after an assignment in 1890, soon resumed business.

Barker was a student of political, economic, and social questions, and was an active controversialist. To give publicity to his views, he started a weekly periodical, the *American,* which ran from October 1880 to January 1891, was revived in December 1894, and then ran to the end of 1900. Up to 1896 he was nominally a Republican. He had been a leader in the anti-third-term movement against Grant, one of the first to propose the nomination of Garfield, and eight years later an early advocate of the nomination of Harrison. But in 1896 his views on currency reform swung him over to the support of Bryan. He favored what he called an "absolute" money to be issued by the government, and advocated bimetalism only as a temporary makeshift. He later became affiliated with the People's party and supported most of the Populist demands. In 1900, on the same day that the regular Populist convention indorsed Bryan, the "Middle-of-the-Road" Populists chose Barker as their presidential candidate. In the election he received only 50,232 votes. He was not again active in politics. From 1880 till his death he was a trustee of the University of Pennsylvania and was always deeply concerned with its affairs. He was a man of broad social sympathies, was widely informed, and was a voluminous writer of articles and letters on a great range of subjects.

[*Who's Who in America,* 1920–21; obituaries in the *N. Y. Times* and *N. Y. Tribune,* Apr. 9, 1921; *The Great Issues,* a collection of editorials from the *American,* by Wharton Barker (1902).]

W. J. G.

BARKSDALE, WILLIAM (Aug. 21, 1821–July 3, 1863), congressman, Confederate soldier, was born in Rutherford County, Tenn., where his grandfather had settled in 1808, removing from Virginia. The family had been established in the Old Dominion since early in the eighteenth century. He attended the University of Nashville and then studied law at Columbus, Miss. He began the practise of law, but abandoned it to become editor of the *Columbus Democrat,* through which he expressed his strong pro-slavery sentiments. He entered the army in the Mexican War as an enlisted man in the 2nd Mississippi, was appointed captain and assistant-commissary of volunteers in January 1847, and served until August 1848. He was a delegate to the National Democratic Convention of 1852, and a member of Congress from 1853 to 1861. It is sometimes stated that he assisted Preston Brooks in the latter's assault upon Charles Sumner in the Senate chamber, by preventing interference from bystanders; but no witness examined by the congressional committee of investigation makes any mention of his presence (*Report of Select Committee,* 1856). When Mississippi passed the ordinance of secession, an action which he cordially approved, he resigned his seat in Congress (Jan. 12, 1861), and returned home. He was quartermaster-general of the "Mississippi Army" from March 1861 until he entered the Confederate service as colonel of the 13th Mississippi Regiment, which he commanded at the battle of Bull Run. During the months devoted to organization and training, the following autumn and winter, he acquired a reputation as a competent regimental commander, so that in April 1862 his brigade commander (Griffith) recommended his appointment as brigadier-general. The appointment was not made at that time, and it was in charge of his regiment that he went through the greater part of the Peninsular campaign. In July, the division commander (McLaws) again recommended his promotion. Gen. Lee also urged it, referring to his conduct at Malvern Hill—"seizing the colors himself and advancing under a terrific fire of artillery and infantry"—and declaring that he displayed "the highest qualities of the soldier." The appointment was made in August, and he was regularly assigned to the brigade to which his old regiment belonged; he had commanded it by virtue of seniority since the battle of Savage Station (June 29), where Gen. Griffith had been mortally wounded. It now formed a part of McLaws's division of Longstreet's corps. He commanded it in all the battles of the Army of Northern Virginia (except second Bull Run, where it was not present), until the next summer—Antietam, Fredericksburg, Chancellorsville, and Gettysburg. On the second day of the battle of Gettysburg he was mortally wounded in the fighting at the Peach Orchard, falling into the hands of the enemy. He died the next day.

[F. B. Heitman, *Hist. Reg.* (1890), I, 107; *Confed. Mil. Hist.*, VII (Miss.), 239; *Battles and Leaders of the Civil War*, III, 331 ff.; *Official Records*, ser. I, vols. V, XIII, XIV, XXVII, XXXI, XXXIX, XLIII, XLIV; unpublished Confed. records in the War Dept.]

T. M. S.

BARLOW, FRANCIS CHANNING (Oct. 19, 1834–Jan. 11, 1896), Union soldier, was born at Brooklyn, N. Y., the son of the Rev. David Hatch Barlow, rector of the First Unitarian Church of that city. His mother had been Almira Penniman of Brookline, Mass., and when he was two years old the family moved to the mother's home town, where young Barlow was raised. At seventeen he entered Harvard, graduating four years later. Soon after, he went to New York, and in the following year commenced the practise of law, being admitted to the bar in May 1858. In 1859 he formed a law partnership with George Bliss, Jr., with whom he remained until the opening of the Civil War. During this time he wrote occasional law reports and editorials for the *New York Tribune.* On the outbreak of war, Barlow's patriotic spirit led him to abandon his profession on the very eve of his marriage. On Apr. 19, 1861, after declining an appointment as a lieutenant, he enlisted as a private in the 12th New York Infantry. The next day he married Arabella Wharton Griffith of Somerville, N. J., with whom unfortunately he was destined to spend but little time. The day following, he departed with his regiment for Washington. His regiment never got to the front, but served three months in the defenses of the capital. On May 2 Barlow accepted an appointment as first-lieutenant, and served until he was honorably mustered out on Aug. 1 of the same year. He reëntered the military service as lieutenant-colonel of the 61st New York Infantry, on Nov. 9, 1861. With this regiment he returned to Washington, near which, under the direction of Gen. McClellan, the winter was spent in severe preparation for the coming campaigns. Barlow went with his regiment to Fort Monroe, where shortly afterward he was promoted to colonel. He served honorably in the Peninsular campaign, especially at the battle of Fair Oaks. Returning from the vicinity of Richmond, he was placed in command of the 2nd brigade, 2nd division, of Howard's corps. He commanded this brigade during the battle of Antietam. Gallantly leading his men in the Bloody Lane, near the Piper House, Barlow at a critical moment checked an attempt of the enemy to flank the Union line. But he was soon after struck down by artillery fire, which severely wounded him in the groin. For his fine conduct in this and preceding battles, he was appointed brigadier-general Sept. 19, 1862. He was returned to duty in time to take part in the Chancellorsville campaign. Here he commanded the left brigade of the 11th corps, and was involved in its rout, when it was attacked by Jackson. His next duty was at Gettysburg. His command was now part of the advance forces of Meade's army. Still a portion of the 11th (Howard's) corps, Barlow, on July 1, 1863, fought north of Gettysburg to prevent the Confederates from seizing the town and the hills to the south, which were the key positions of that great battlefield. The right of the Federal troops being turned by Early's division, and the men commencing to fall back, exposing the town of Gettysburg to the enemy, Barlow valiantly but vainly attempted to rally his command. He himself was shot through the body by a Minié ball, which passed out close to the spine, paralyzing his legs and arms. Left for dead on the field, he was seen by the Confederate Gen. Gordon, who dismounted from his horse and gave him water, and then had him placed in a building near-by. After the Union victory, the Federal troops found their abandoned general. Under the tender care of his devoted wife, he was eventually brought back to health, but only after some ten months in hospitals.

On rejoining the army he was assigned on Apr. 1, 1864, to the command of the 1st division, 2nd (Hancock's) corps. Barlow served throughout the Wilderness campaign. His division was one of two selected by Hancock to attack the Confederate salient at Spottsylvania on May 12. This attack was launched at dawn, without firing a shot. It became very disorderly but so surprised the enemy that no effectual resistance was offered. It was extremely successful, 4,000 prisoners, including two generals, 30 colors, and 20 guns being captured. It was the greatest blow that Lee's army had received in the campaign, destroying any hope that might have existed of stopping Grant's advance. Barlow took part in further operations during the advance to the James River and in the early battles around Petersburg. But his health broke under the strain of the continued fighting and of the loss of his wife, who died on July 27. He went on an extended trip to Europe, and did not return to duty until Apr. 1 following. During this period he was brevetted major-general "for highly meritorious and distinguished conduct while leading his division in the assault on the enemy's works at Spottsylvania." On Apr. 6, 1865, he was assigned to and assumed command of the 2nd division, 2nd corps. He at once entered into the final fighting of the war. In reserve at Sailor's Creek on Apr. 6, Barlow's division entered line the next day. Near Farmville he seized and held the only bridge to the north side of the Appomattox, which Lee had hoped to destroy to prevent Grant's army from overtaking his retreating troops. The loss of this bridge exposed Lee to simultaneous attacks from front and rear and resulted in his surrender. As a reward for this service, Barlow was appointed major-general on May 25, and assigned to the command of the 2nd corps.

Barlow now entered political life. He accepted the candidacy in New York for secretary of state, and was elected to this office in November 1865. He consequently declined a permanent appointment in the regular army, and resigned his volunteer commission of major-general on Nov. 16. He reëstablished his law partnership with George Bliss, opening offices in New York City in 1866. In 1867 he was married to Ellen Shaw of Boston, who was then living on Staten Island. He was not reëlected as secretary of state. In 1869 President Grant appointed him United States marshal for the southern district of New York. He cleaned out the offices, changing the entire personnel. When called upon for a political contribution assessed on the supposed emoluments of his office, he declined to pay except on the basis of his salary, and carefully eliminated any chances of the receipt by his assistants of any money other than authorized fees. Soon after assuming these new duties, Barlow received from the President command of the combined military, naval, and revenue forces of the Government in the New England states, New York, and New Jersey, under a law of 1818, in order to stop filibustering expeditions against the island of Cuba. He seized a shipload of Cubans, with arms and munitions, and put an end to further movements of this nature.

In 1869, Barlow was again elected secretary of state for New York, and held office during 1870, when he was elected attorney-general of the state, a position he held from 1871 until 1873. His administration was vigorous. In the first year he initiated the prosecution of the infamous "Tweed Ring" and their counsel. About the same time he became one of the founders of the Bar Association. In 1874 he resumed the private practise of law. In 1876 he was appointed to investigate and report upon alleged election irregularities in Florida in connection with the Hayes and Tilden controversy. He made a vigorous report exposing the conditions which had existed before and at the elections. This was his last public service. He continued to practise law until he died at New York, Jan. 11, 1896. He was buried at Brookline, Mass.

Barlow was of medium size, slender, with smooth face, temperamentally enthusiastic and energetic in whatever he undertook. He was not a military genius, but his solid character led to important results in his army career, and these in turn gave him political and business successes. His slight build made him appear younger than he really was, and earned for him in the war the nickname of "boy general." During his life he was greatly respected, and in the important missions which were confided to him he invariably acquitted himself with honor. The State of New York thought so well of him that in 1922 it erected a monument to his memory on the battlefield of Gettysburg.

[E. H. Abbot, "Francis Channing Barlow," in *Harv. Grads. Mag.*, June 1896; *Personal Memoirs of U. S. Grant* (1886), II; F. A. Walker, *Hist. of the Second Army Corps in the Army of the Potomac* (1886); F. B. Heitman, *Hist. Reg.* (1890); *Official Records*, see Index; obituaries in *N. Y. Times*, *N. Y. Tribune*, Jan. 12, 1896; "In Memoriam, Francis Channing Barlow," *N. Y. Monuments Commission* (1923).]

C. H. L—a.

BARLOW, JOEL (Mar. 24, 1754–Dec. 24, 1812), poet, statesman, destined by temperament and circumstance to become one of the most liberal thinkers of his age, was born and reared in the most conservative environment of Federalist Connecticut. His ancestors, of English stock, were in 1653 prosperous farmers in Fairfield; Joel Barlow himself, the fourth child of Samuel and Esther (Hull) Barlow, was born in Redding. Even in his boyhood on the farm, in school in Redding, or under the tutelage, during the years 1772 and 1773, of the Rev. Nathaniel Bartlett, there was evident that energy of thought and action which was to emancipate him from the complacent narrowness of the Hartford circle. After nearly a year at Moor's School, Hanover, N. H., and two months at Dartmouth College, Barlow, never uncertain about his own wishes, became in November 1774 a member of the freshman class of Yale College, together with Oliver Wolcott, Zephaniah Swift, and Noah Webster. Among these distinguished men he was himself quite at ease, studying with his tutors, Timothy Dwight and Joseph Buckminster; writing in 1775 his first poem (not extant); and during his summer vacation of 1776, taking part in the battle of Long Island. On July 23, 1778, he read his first long poem, *The Prospect of Peace,* at the public examination of the senior class, and on Sept. 9, 1778, he received the degree of B.A. at a private commencement of Yale College. Barlow was happily formed by nature for life, and especially for American life of the eighteenth century: he was anxious about his career but he was confident and aggressive. He already had in mind his huge philosophic poem, *The Vision of Columbus,* and despite clouds over his own future and that of his country, he wrote characteristically to Noah Webster in 1779: "You and I are not the first in the world who have broken loose from college without friends and without fortune to push us into public notice. Let us show the world a few more examples of men standing upon their own merit and rising in spite of obstacles." Instead of the despair evident in the writings of some contemporary men of letters, Barlow consistently manifested satisfaction with existing conditions: "The American Republic," he told Webster, "is a fine theatre for the display of merit of every kind. If ever virtue is to be rewarded, it is in America."

This optimism Barlow at once put into practise. Even in these turbulent years (1779–87) the diversity of his activities was amazing. He studied philosophy at Yale; he taught school; he managed a business; he published a journal; he wrote a new version of the Psalms; and he was admitted to the bar (April 1786). Yet such occupations were incidental. His studies were secondary to his gradually growing epic; his connection with the *American Mercury,* which he edited with Elisha Babcock, lasted only from July 12, 1784, to Nov. 14, 1785; and an establishment for stationery and publishing did not hold his interest. He had only a transient satisfaction in his poem, published in 1782, *An Elegy on the Late Honourable Titus Hosmer, Esq.,* and in his curious performance, *Doctor Watts' Imitation of the Psalms of David, Corrected and Enlarged* (1785). Barlow's real interests were in his ambitions as an author and the events of his time. These latter he surveyed from a quasi-military post, having been made, in 1780, through the assistance of Col. David Humphreys and Gen. Greene, chaplain of the 4th Massachusetts brigade. Barlow was a sensitive observer of the thoughts and deeds of men in this struggle for political liberty, and it is probable that some of his later social criticism and theories evolved from what he saw of the American Revolution. His chief concern, however, during the decade after his graduation from college was writing, in accordance with his own special enthusiasms. The traditional meditative mind of the poet was not in him. His prose took form in clear sensible records of what he saw; and his poetry, equally robust, he composed with sound learning and tireless energy. Both prose and poetry he published early, for he was a young man bent on a reputation, but it should be noticed that always in the background of his mind dwelt that indomitable ambition of the larger poem, the vast epic of America. It was known that he was writing this poem, and in 1780 David Humphreys called attention to this "hopeful genius." In the meantime Barlow offered his occasional pieces, and was a contributor in 1786 and 1787 to the famous publication of the "Hartford Wits," *The Anarchiad,* the satire in prose and verse that was appearing in the *New Haven Gazette and Connecticut Magazine.* In the latter year appeared the proof of his boundless, if somewhat absurd, literary dreams, *The Vision of Columbus,* a poem in nine books and more than 5,000 lines. He had written it over a period of eight years, from 1779 to 1787, in leisure stolen from teaching, preaching, publishing, and military service. He had polished and revised, secure in his cheerful egotism that it would be well received. Strangely enough, it was; despite obvious debts to Milton, and stretches of execrable verse, *The Vision of Columbus* won Barlow fame. His contemporaries delighted in the grandiose couplets on the discovery, settlement, and majestic future of America.

Barlow was now thirty-three, and about to embark upon the most romantic period of his career. Personally he was by no means the pompous person who might be pictured from his stately poetry. He had good looks, was agreeable, and was known, on the whole, as the most original of the "Hartford Wits." There was about him a cheerfulness that was both attractive and amusing. In the midst of his busyness he had found time to be in love once or twice. In college days he had been a more or less playful suitor of Elizabeth Whitman, whose pathetic story is described in one of the earliest American novels, Mrs. Hannah Foster's *The Coquette* (1797). The story survives of the meeting of Barlow and Miss Whitman in 1778, at the house of President Ezra Stiles: "Joel and Eliza were ordered to conduct toward each other as man and wife for the whole evening." This they did, "adopting the nine Muses as their children." The incident is interesting as the forerunner of gay letters which show Barlow in a new light, the Barlow who is effectually concealed in all his poetry, save, perhaps, in *Hasty Pudding*. There has survived another series of charming and graceful letters between Barlow and Ruth Baldwin, who in 1781 became his wife, and whom he loved devotedly to the end of his days. During all his intense endeavor, Barlow had an enviable capacity for living happily.

His departure on May 25, 1788 for Europe, where he remained for seventeen years, began the change of the New England Yankee into the Europeanized Democrat. Unsuccessful as a lawyer, he had become in 1787 associated with the Ohio Company which sold in the West many acres to unhappy Frenchmen. Through this connection he became European agent for the Scioto Company, and it was in their behalf that on June 24, 1788 he arrived at Havre. Only his buoyant spirit carried him over his failure to sell shares in France and the collapse of his own organization, La Compagnie du Scioto, formed in 1789. Concerning this episode in Barlow's life has raged a storm of gossip, but the failure of the company was due primarily to lack of assistance from Barlow's American employers, his own inexperience in business, and the dishonesty of several of his associates. The blow was severe, but Barlow's letters of the time are full of delight at the European scene. Puritan orthodoxy dropped from him like a mantle and, like Franklin, he seemed at once to become part of the democratic thought of the age. For most of the time between 1790 and 1792 the Barlows (Mrs. Barlow had joined him in 1790) resided in London, living chiefly by his pen. His zeal and intelligence soon made his name known. He became a prominent member of the London Society for Constitutional Information, and was on friendly terms with Horne Tooke, John Frost, Dr. Priestley, and, especially, Thomas Paine. The angry John Adams considered even Paine "not a more worthless fellow" than Barlow. In this intimacy is the true hint of the intellectual change since the Hartford days. When Paine was imprisoned in Paris, it was Barlow who took charge of the manuscript of *The Age of Reason* and achieved its publication. Nor was he a mere echo of the tumult of radicalism. His own works began to appear, full of fearless thinking and touched with his own warm enthusiasms.

The pioneer of these was his *A Letter to the National Convention of France, on the Defects in the Constitution of 1791 and the Extent of the Amendments which ought to be Applied* (1792). As a reward, the farmer's boy of Redding was made a citizen of France. More significant was the first part (1792) of his *Advice to the Privileged Orders,* a stirring political document which disposes of the critics who label Barlow merely as the grandiloquent versifier. In debt, unquestionably, to Paine's greater work, *The Rights of Man,* it is still unique. It forcibly presents the doctrine of the responsibility of the State, a doctrine as admissibly true to-day as it was then heretical to Barlow's college friends. If these in Hartford denounced, there must have been comfort in Fox's eulogy of the book in the House of Commons. The British Government, in compliment to its vigor, suppressed the volume and proscribed the writer. Barlow sought refuge in Paris, where he calmly wrote the second part of this, his greatest prose work, and also his philippic in verse, *The Conspiracy of Kings* (1792). Among the French he was exceedingly popular. He translated Brissot de Warville's *New Travels in the United States;* he wrote, not without an eye to his French reputation, his *Lettre adressée aux habitants de Piémont, sur les avantages de la Révolution française et la nécessité d'en adopter les principes en Italie* (1793); and he judiciously invested in French government consols. To this capacity for friendliness even more than to his native shrewdness he owed the fact that by 1794 he was a rich man. He was even persuaded by friends to act in the exciting drama of French politics: he went to Savoy and stood for election as its deputy to the Convention. This sally was too much even for the ambitious Barlow. He was defeated, but by one of those paradoxes which make this New Englander's life so whimsical, out of the incident emerged his most delightful poem. This was *Hasty Pudding* (written 1793, published 1796), a witty fusion of homely New England memories and European backgrounds. The successful business man was occasionally homesick and in such a mood one evening, "under the smoky rafters of a Savoyard inn," he found himself facing a steaming dish beloved in Connecticut, hasty pudding. Forgetful for once of the solemnity which usually stifled him in verse composition, he poured forth the merriest of mock pastorals. Here was the Barlow known to intimate friends.

His career now became more and more picturesque. Through the influence of David Humphreys he was appointed in 1795 consul to Algiers. Here and during the remaining years in Europe, from 1797 to 1805, he maintained an amazing mastery of his different interests. He effected treaties with Tunis, Algiers, and Tripoli, and he risked his life to free American prisoners in Africa. He wrote to George Washington, urging him to prevent a war between

England and France, and his letter reveals his entire understanding of a complex situation. He made friends with Robert Fulton, and demonstrated his interest in the latter's "plunging boat" and other scientific ventures by financial assistance. A memorial of the intimacy of the philosopher and the scientist is Fulton's portrait of his friend's serene, intellectual face. Yet, most surprising, through all these stormy years Barlow held fast to his literary passions. It was not significant merely that he gathered material for histories of the French Revolution and of the United States, or that he translated Volney's *Ruins* (1802). It was rather that he still toiled over *The Vision of Columbus,* determined to fulfil that intention of his youth to produce the great philosophic epic. He rewrote and revised, and by 1804 had finished that vast and devastating poem, *The Columbiad.* Early in 1805 he was back in America, obeying at last the injunction of his wife, given many years before, "to go home and be respectable." He meant to enjoy that tranquil life of retirement which he always professed to desire but which he renounced, it seems to the bystander, without great suffering. Now he had come home laden with *The Columbiad* and huge projects. One of these was the establishment of a national institution for research and instruction in the arts and sciences, discussed in his *Prospectus of a National Institution to be Established in the United States* (1805). Finally, in 1807, *The Columbiad* appeared, a colossal affair of writing and bookmaking, with an overwhelming elegance of bindings, steel engravings, and ornament, and with a dedication to Robert Fulton, the patron saint of steam navigation. Since the day in which Barlow thus realized his life-long purpose of an epic appropriate to the size of America, this poem has been transfixed with jests—all of them variations on Hawthorne's laughter at "its ponderosity of leaden verses" (*Mosses from an Old Manse,* 1846, pt. II, p. 132) and Byron's query to George Ticknor, "whether we looked upon Barlow as our Homer" (*Life, Letters and Journals of George Ticknor,* 5th end., I, 59). It was a tough volume, but into its ten books and 3,675 couplets had crept some of the strength of Barlow's mind. He does not now arouse the emotions he desired when Hesper, the guardian angel of the Western Continent, shows Columbus from his Spanish prison the future of America, but there are passages of grandeur, notably those concerning the Prison Ship (bk. VI, ll. 35–122). One amusing postscript to this event was a letter to Barlow from his friend, the former Bishop of Blois, censuring the book as an offense against Christianity. Barlow in his answer declared that he had never renounced Christianity, and added, what seems undeniable, that *The Columbiad* was truly "a moral work."

For five years after his return to America he enacted the rôle of literary and political savant. At his beautiful home near Washington, which he had modestly named Kalorama, he presided with large hospitality over an impressive collection of books, curios, and paintings. His retirement did not prevent his becoming a member of the United States Military Philosophical Society and the American Philosophical Society, or maintaining an active interest in finance as director of the Bank of Washington. His strange career was about to have its proper climax. He was at work, in accordance with a suggestion from Jefferson, on a history of the United States, when President Madison appointed him minister to France. He was to intercede with Napoleon for a more generous treatment of American commerce. In August 1811, he sailed for France with his wife, his nephew, Thomas Barlow, and his niece, Clara Baldwin, on the frigate *Constitution.* On the subject of his mission Barlow found the French officials evasive, but on Oct. 11, 1812, he was informed by Bassano, the minister of foreign affairs, that Napoleon, then engaged in his disastrous invasion of Russia, would meet him at Wilna, Poland, for discussion of a treaty. At the end of October, therefore, Barlow set out, accompanied by his nephew as secretary, on the long, arduous journey to Wilna. Here he remained from Nov. 18 to Dec. 5, hoping to meet the Emperor and to consummate the transaction on which he had labored for more than a year. In the meantime, Napoleon suffered defeat at the Beresina (Nov. 26 to Nov. 28), and Barlow, despairing of his cherished interview, turned back toward Paris. He reached Warsaw safely, after beholding on this journey scenes of great suffering, and being himself imperiled by the hardships. The cold reminded him, he said, of a Connecticut winter. He left Warsaw on Dec. 18 and was soon afterward taken seriously ill. He and his nephew stopped at Zarnowiec, a little village near Cracow, but the exposure and privations of the journey proved fatal. Inflammation of the lungs developed and Barlow died on Dec. 24, 1812. In spite of efforts to restore his body to his birthplace, he still lies in Poland.

[The chief source of information about Joel Barlow is *Life and Letters of Joel Barlow, LL.D.* (1886), by Charles B. Todd. In the unpublished work, "Joel Barlow, His Life and Work to 1790," by Theodore A. Zunder, there is a detailed account of his early life and writings. The best brief sketch of Barlow's life, containing at the end important bibliographical information, was written by Franklin B. Dexter for his

Biog. Sketches of the Grads. of Yale Coll. (1907), IV, 3–16. Interesting facts concerning Barlow were published by Moses Hill in his *Genealogy of the Hill Family from 1632, Including a Biog. Sketch of Joel Barlow* (1879). Contemporary accounts of his life appear in the *Mo. Mag. and British Reg.*, VI, 250–51, and in *Public Characters of 1806*, pp. 152–80. After Barlow's death, P. S. Du Pont (de Nemours) published his "Notice sur la Vie de M. Barlow" in the *Mercure de France*, Apr. 10, 1813, and that same year Konrad E. Oelsner published a longer and better sketch, his *Notice sur la Vie et les Écrits de M. Joel Barlow.* Other sketches of interest can be found in the *Analectic Mag.*, IV, 130–58; in the *Cyc. of Am. Lit.*, I, 391–403; in *The New Englander*, XXXII, 413–37; in Anson P. Stokes, *Memorials of Eminent Yale Men* (1914), I, 126–35. A readable account of Barlow's life, "The Literary Strivings of Mr. Joel Barlow," which was based on Todd's *Life and Letters*, was written by Moses C. Tyler in his *Three Men of Letters* (1895), pp. 131–80. Modern estimates of Barlow's life and work have been given by Vernon P. Squires in "Joel Barlow—Patriot, Democrat, and Man of Letters" in the *Quart. Jour. of the Univ. of N. Dak.*, IX, 299–308, and by Vernon L. Parrington in his "Introduction" to *The Connecticut Wits* (1926), pp. ix-lvii, and in *Main Currents of American Thought* (1927), I, 382–89.]

T. A. Z.
S. T. W.

BARLOW, JOHN WHITNEY (June 26, 1838–Feb. 27, 1914), army engineer, was born in Perry, Wyoming County, N. Y., the son of Nehemiah and Orinda (Steel) Barlow. After attending the public schools and an academy in Wisconsin, he entered the United States Military Academy, from which he was graduated May 6, 1861, as a second-lieutenant of artillery. He fought at Bull Run and throughout the Peninsular campaign, and on May 27, 1862, was brevetted a captain. In July he was transferred to the topographical engineers and in March of the following year to the engineers, four months later reaching the full rank of captain. In 1864 he was transferred to Sherman's army operating against Atlanta, serving temporarily as chief engineer of the 17th army corps. In November he was sent to Nashville, where Thomas placed him in charge of the defenses of the city, and where, for his conduct in the decisive battles of Dec. 15–16, he was brevetted a lieutenant-colonel.

During the first five years after the war he was in charge of various engineering works. In July and August 1871, he commanded the detachment of engineers which, with a party from the Geological Survey under Dr. F. V. Hayden, made the first Government exploration of Yellowstone Park. With the close of this expedition, says Chittenden (*The Yellowstone National Park*), the discovery of the Yellowstone wonderland was made complete; and a result closely following it was the passage of the bill establishing Yellowstone Park, approved Mar. 1, 1872. Though the greater part of his valuable collection of data and photographs was destroyed in the great Chicago fire, Barlow succeeded in finishing an admirable report on the exploration, which was published by the Government in April. In 1879 he was made a major and in 1884 a lieutenant-colonel. In 1886 he was placed in charge of the engineering project at Muscle Shoals, which on Nov. 10, 1890, he completed by the opening of the canal to navigation. In 1892–96 he commanded the party of government engineers which, in coöperation with a similar party from the Mexican Government, placed permanent markers along the whole of the international boundary from El Paso to the Pacific. On May 10, 1895, he was made a colonel, and on May 2, 1901, a brigadier-general and chief of engineers. On the following day, at his own request, he was retired.

Barlow was twice married—on Dec. 26, 1861, to Hessie McNaughton Birnie, of Washington, who died, and on Sept. 17, 1902, to Alice Stanton Turner, of New London. After his retirement he lived in New London. While on a trip with his wife to the Holy Land he fell ill at Jerusalem and died there. The remains were brought to America and after a funeral at Fort Myer, Apr. 20, 1914, were interred at Arlington. Barlow was highly esteemed by those who knew him. Tributes to his memory stressed not merely his gallant record in battle, his many triumphs as an engineer and his exploratory work in Yellowstone Park, but also the modesty and courtesy of his demeanor and the charm of his personality.

[*Who's Who in America*, 1914–15; G. W. Cullum, *Biog. Reg.*; H. M. Chittenden, *The Yellowstone National Park* (1920 edition); obituaries in report of the annual reunion (1915) of the Ass. of Grads. of the U. S. Mil. Acad. and in *Army and Navy Jour.*, Mar. 7, 1914.]

W. J. G.

BARLOW, SAMUEL LATHAM MITCHILL (June 5, 1826–July 10, 1889), lawyer, was born in Granville, Hampden County, Mass. The Barlows were among the earliest colonists in New England, having emigrated from England in 1630. Samuel Bancroft Barlow, a Yale graduate and physician, practising at Granville, married the daughter of Jean Brillot-Savarin, a French *emigré* who had fled from France at the time of the Revolution of '89. Samuel Latham Mitchill Barlow was their eldest son. He received his early education at the common schools of his native town. The family in 1842 moved to New York City, and he obtained a situation in the law office of Willett & Greig at one dollar per week. He was called to the New York bar in 1849, at the same time becoming office manager for the firm. He had already impressed people with his business aptitude, and when, on the death of Greig, he opened an office for himself, he attracted many of the old clientele. A characteristic manifested early in his career was a reluctance to resort to litigation if any other method of achieving the settlement of a claim appeared possible. Consummate tact combined with an almost uncanny knowledge of human nature made him an adept at contriving compromises of dangerous disputes. His first important retainer was on behalf of the claimants under the Mexican Treaty following the War of 1846–47. He soon had more business than he could individually attend to, and in 1852 the firm of Bowdoin, Larocque & Barlow was formed, changed in 1881, when Judge Choate entered the firm to Shipman, Barlow, Larocque & Choate.

Barlow's name became increasingly associated with heavy corporation work involving large financial interests. He made no pretence to being an advocate, and hardly ever appeared in court. His great successes were achieved at the consultation board, where his unerring judgment and a lightning-like capacity of appreciating the crucial point of a problem made him a commanding figure. His skill as a mediator was well exemplified in the Vanderbilt-Aspinwall case. Commodore Vanderbilt and William H. Aspinwall had become bitter enemies over their conflicting Nicaragua and Panama schemes, and were not on speaking terms. Barlow's interest in the dispute was only as representative of a small number of Pacific Mail shares, the pecuniary value being insignificant, but he determined to intervene. He asked the two enemies to dinner at his house, neither having knowledge that the other would be present, and in a tête-à tête discussion, effected a reconciliation. Another instance of his appearance as *deus ex machina* was in connection with the Garrison contract. During the Franco-German War Commodore Garrison and associates held a contract with Gambetta to supply the French Government with arms, the amount involved being $1,000,000. When Gambetta was driven from office his successor, Thiers, repudiated the contract as exorbitant, thus leaving a ship-load of arms in the hands of the American contractors. Bitter dissensions among the latter threatened disastrous litigation, when Barlow, on behalf of a minor member of the syndicate, intervened, arranged a conference, reconciled the malcontents, induced them to entrust their whole interests to him, and within three months had adjusted the matter with the French authorities, and procured payment of the whole amount involved.

The only spectacular event in his career arose in the course of the protracted struggle for control of the Erie Railway, 1872–89. There had been great dissatisfaction with the management of the railway by Jay Gould and James Fisk, Jr., which came to a head after the death of the latter in January 1872. Barlow was retained on behalf of the English Shareholders' Association. Under his advice and with his active participation, the Grand Opera House in New York—headquarters of the company—was forcibly taken possession of, on Mar. 11, 1872, the personnel of the board of directors changed, and Gould ousted, in contempt of an injunction decree obtained by Gould from the court. Barlow also commenced suit against Gould for $9,726,541.26 alleged to have been fraudulently appropriated from the company's funds. The action was compromised, Gould paying $9,000,000 in full settlement, Dec. 18, 1872. On the reconstitution of the Erie Company, Barlow remained the dominant figure in the company's affairs till May 1875 (see E. H. Mott, *Between the Ocean and the Great Lakes: The Story of Erie,* 1899).

Barlow took an active interest in politics. An ardent Democrat, he opposed Tilden and Van Buren and the Free-Soil party in 1848. In 1856 he strongly supported Buchanan, and was the decisive figure in the nomination of Breckinridge as vice-president. Although he opposed the election of Lincoln, he supported the administration whole-heartedly during the war. He was an intimate friend of Gen. McClellan, and assisted his candidature for the presidency in 1864.

An enthusiastic bibliophile and art connoisseur, he assembled a fine library specializing in works on the early history of America. His collection was one of the most valuable in America, since it consisted mainly of original editions and authorities. His collection of paintings and *objets d'art* was equally extensive and more eclectic. The gem of the collection was Van Dyck's "Children of Charles I," purchased by C. P. Huntington for $8,500. In early life he was handsome and fond of dress, but later on became very stout. It is related that he attempted to reduce himself by horseback riding, but after a short trial it was discovered that his horse had lost fifty pounds and he had gained five. Thereafter he allowed nature to take its course. He was very hospitable, a *bon vivant,* and "almost rivalled Sam Ward in his tastes as an epicure." Though he was all his life indefatigable in his attention to business, he reveled in the amenities of his country home, with its gardens and blooded stock. Above all he loved dogs, and for years was a successful exhibitor at the Madison Square Garden dog shows. An expert whist player, he wrote the article on "Whist" in *Appleton's Encyclopædia.* In conjunction with Henry Harrisse he edited *Notes on Columbus* (privately printed 1865), and at his own cost printed for private distribution a number of scarce works on American subjects, dealing chiefly with Columbus. He died suddenly on July 10, 1889, at his country estate, "Elsinore," Glen Cove, L. I. He was married to Mary, daughter of Peter Townsend of Goshen, N. Y.

[*Hist. of the Bench and Bar of N. Y.*, ed. by David McAdam, *et al.* (1897), I, 255; *Mag. of Am. Hist.*, XXII, 315; Theron G. Strong, *Landmarks of a Lawyer's Lifetime* (1914), pp. 443–44; *Critic,* XV, 302, XVI, 56–65; *Am. Annual Cyc. and Reg.*, 1889, p. 618; the *N. Y. Times, Sun,* and *Herald* of July 11, 1889.]

H. W. H. K.

BARLOWE, ARTHUR. [See Amadas, Philip, fl. 1584–85.]

BARNABEE, HENRY CLAY (Nov. 14, 1833–Dec. 16, 1917), actor and singer, was born in Portsmouth, N. H. His father was Willis Barnabee, "a noted whip in those palmy days of the stage coach, his route for many years being between Portland and Boston, *via* Portsmouth" (*Reminiscences,* p. 25). It was he who had brought Lafayette, in 1824, rattling into town. He was also an innkeeper, the old Portsmouth Franklin House being under his care, his wife (1799–1885) and even the lad Henry Clay (bearing a Whig name out of respect for his father's political fervor) helping him run the hostelry. At school the boy took part in *tableaux vivants,* and learned, under the care of a French dancing master, the waltz, polka, mazurka, and quadrille. He had no systematic musical training, and all his life he struggled against his lack of knowledge of musical notation. His high-school teacher was tenor in a local church and fired him with ambition to sing. Amateur performances, where he was required to blacken up as a minstrel, or to dress as a Yankee type, in makeshift halls, constituted his early acting experience. He was definitely inspired to stage work by seeing Junius Brutus Booth in John Howard Payne's *Brutus.* But many years were to pass in mercantile pursuits, in various stores of Boston, before he was to enter the theatre. By 1854, however, while still a clerk, he was recognized as a successful entertainer. His voice was trained by J. Q. Wetherbee, and he sang in various churches, though his livelihood depended on the yardstick. His love for the drama and opera was his dominant taste, and he was an active member of the Boston Handel and Haydn Society. On Dec. 1, 1859, he married Clara George (daughter of Maj. Daniel George, of Warner, N. H.), who was identified with his career as light opera comedian; she died, Dec. 25, 1909.

In 1865, Barnabee left business and entered the lyceum field. On Nov. 9, 1866, he made his professional appearance as Toby Winkle, in *All that Glitters is not Gold,* where he also appeared as Cox opposite the Box of Boston's beloved William Warren. He next organized a touring concert company, and won reputation as a spirited songster, his most famous lyrics being "The Cork Leg" and an encore, "The Patent Arm." The Boston Ideals were founded in 1879, the year that heralded in America the first production of Gilbert and Sullivan's opera, *H. M. S. Pinafore.* Barnabee had seen the London production, first given at the Opéra Comique, May 28, 1878, and he was astute enough to study its stage business at the time. Arrangements were made for the production of *Pinafore* by the Ideals, and it was given a first performance in Boston on Apr. 14, 1879. This proved a substantial start for them, and under Barnabee's guidance they won rapid favor. He was "a born mimic with a mastery of the art of grimacing, and he talked with a decidedly Yankee twang." In 1886, he and his company appeared at Manchester-by-the-Sea, in an outdoor performance of *As You Like It,* one of the earliest open-air theatre attempts in America. After some years of conquest, the Ideals slowly died, with a splendid reputation but a steadily decreasing purse. In order to begin afresh, with a new policy to suit new tastes, Barnabee and W. H. MacDonald organized the Bostonians in 1887. Their most famous production was *Robin Hood* (libretto by Harry B. Smith and music by Reginald De Koven), and in this opera Barnabee found his most famous rôle, the Sheriff of Nottingham, which he claimed to have sung over 1,900 times. "It deserves," wrote H. B. Smith, "a full-length portrait in the theatrical Hall of Fame, beside Jefferson's Rip, Raymond's Colonel Sellers, and Florence's Captain Cuttle" (*Reminiscences,* p. 461).

[The chief source of information about Barnabee is his *Reminiscences* (1913). But other data may be found in *Munsey,* Aug. 1892 and Mar. 1895; the *National Mag.*, Feb. 1918; Mrs. Reginald De Koven, *A Musician and His Wife* (1926).]

M. J. M.

BARNARD, CHARLES (Feb. 13, 1838–Apr. 11, 1920), author, was the son of Rev. Charles F. and Sarah (Holmes) Barnard and the grandson of Charles Barnard, a well-known Boston merchant. He was born in Boston, where he was trained in public and private schools until he was sixteen. Although he looked forward to the ministry and for a time assisted his father at the Warren Street Chapel, he gave up his studies because of ill health. After a brief experience as a florist, he turned to journalism, winning some notice as "Jane Kingsford" by his articles in the *Boston Post* on the Peace Jubilee Concerts. He became assistant editor of the *Boston Journal of Commerce* and editor of *Vox Humana,* Cambridge, Mass. From 1875 to 1884 he conducted the World's Work Department in *Scribner's Monthly* (now the *Century Magazine*), which resulted in his making important contributions on tools and machinery to the *Century Dictionary.* In 1881 he married Mary E. Knight, daughter of Alexander Knight, a New York merchant. Besides serving as superintendent of instruction in the Chautauqua Town and Country Club, he wrote many stories and plays. For several years he lived in New York City, where he became corresponding secretary of the American Dramatists' Club. In 1907 he removed to Darien, Conn., where on a small patch of ground he conducted a Housekeeping Experimental Station. About 1912 he removed to Pasadena, Cal., and spent his declining years in that city.

Barnard's first books, based on his early experiences in intensive agriculture, were *The Strawberry Garden, My Ten-Rod Farm,* and *Farming by Inches.* These were collected (1869) under the title *Gardening for Money* and reprinted (1902) as *$2,000 a Year on Fruits and Flowers.* His other works in this field were *A Simple Flower Garden* (1870) and *My Handkerchief Garden* (1889). As a result of his interest in music he wrote *The Soprano* (1869), *The Tone Masters* (3 vols., 1870–71), and *Camilla, A Tale of a Violin* (1874). Other efforts in fiction were *Legilda Romanief* (1880), *Knights of Today* (1881), *A Dead Town* (1883), and *The Whistling Buoy* (1888). As further evidence of his versatility he produced a book on *Light* (1877) with Alfred M. Mayer; *Coöperation as a Business* (1881); three books (1885–86) on the weather, the soil, and useful plants; *First Steps in Electricity* (1888); and *Graphic Methods in Teaching* (1889). Later he wrote a Bible story-book called *The Door in the Book* (1903) and a technical work on *Tools and Machines* (1903). Throughout his life he engaged in play-writing, producing numerous plays of varying merit. These include *The Triple Wedding* (1883), *The County Fair* (1889), in collaboration with Neil Burgess, who appeared in it with great success for many seasons, and *The Forest Ring* (1901), a fairy drama written with William C. DeMille. His interest in mechanics led to the invention of various labor-saving devices. The clever stage turntable for racing horses perfected for *The County Fair* was in part responsible for the popularity of that play.

[Information furnished chiefly by friends of Barnard or derived from his published works. See, however, *Who's Who in America,* 1916–17, and Oscar Fay Adams, *Dict. of Am. Authors* (1897), p. 19.]

J.L.H.

BARNARD, CHARLES FRANCIS (Apr. 17, 1808–Nov. 8, 1884), Unitarian clergyman, philanthropist, was born on South St., Boston, the eldest son of Charles and Sarah (Bent) Barnard. The boy's delicate health and fondness for open-air sports foreshadowed his largely outdoor career. After studying at the Boston Latin School and under private tutors, he entered Harvard College as a sophomore, graduating in 1828, and then attended the Harvard Divinity School. In 1834 he was ordained as a Unitarian minister at large; William Ellery Channing, delivering the charge, used these words, "The only power to oppose to evil is love, strong, enduring love, a benevolence which no crime or wretchedness can conquer, and which therefore can conquer all." Barnard lived and worked in this spirit. Already he had enlisted in philanthropic work among the poorer classes under the leadership of Dr. Joseph Tuckerman, the pioneer of such service in Boston. It soon appeared that Barnard's talents best adapted him for work among children. In 1832, in the parlors of Dorothea Dix, he gathered a class of three waifs, which rapidly grew. After temporary connection with Hollis Street Church, and inadequate accommodation elsewhere, Barnard, failing to enlist support from the Benevolent Fraternity of Churches (Unitarian) under which he had been serving, appealed to the public for funds for a suitable building. In January 1836 Warren Street Chapel, "the Children's church," was opened, with 730 children in attendance. Here for thirty years Barnard preached and educated children. He was a pioneer in seeking and winning street boys and girls, surrounding them in the chapel with music, pictures, and flowers; giving them outings, establishing evening classes and a free public library. He originated children's Fourth-of-July floral processions, and personally financed a public greenhouse on the Back Bay marshes, where, largely because of his efforts, Boston's Public Garden now blooms. During the Civil War, Warren Street Chapel became under Barnard's superintendence a recruiting center; to it the Union Army owed 500 soldiers. In 1866 the strain of his work affected his mind; thereafter, except for a brief period of service for children at the Harvard Church, Charlestown, Mass., he lived in retirement at West Newton. In 1884 he voluntarily entered the McLean Asylum, Somerville, where he died. In 1889 Warren Street Chapel was renamed Barnard Memorial Chapel. Barnard was twice married: in May 1834 to Adeline M. Russell, who died within a month; and in January 1837 to Sarah Holmes, by whom he had six children.

[Francis Tiffany, *Charles Francis Barnard; A Sketch of His Life and Work* (1895) is the chief source. The *Ann. Reports of Warren Street Chapel,* 1837–64, give Barnard's own record of his work and plans. The 49th (1885) and 54th (1890) *Ann. Reports* contain tributes to him. Obituary in *Boston Transcript,* Nov. 10, 1884. *Harv. Class of 1828 Scrap Book* and *Misc. Recs.* also contain material.]

R. S. B.

BARNARD, DANIEL DEWEY (Sept. 11, 1796–Apr. 24, 1861), lawyer, statesman, was born at East Hartford, Conn. In 1809 his parents, Timothy Barnard of Hartford, Conn., and Phebe Dewey of Sheffield, Mass., removed from the latter place in Berkshire County, to a farm in Mendon, a part of Ontario County, N. Y., which later became Monroe County. Through the influence of his father, who was a county judge, he spent two years in the office of the county clerk at Canandaigua, and then was sent to prepare for college at Lenox Academy, Berkshire County, Mass. In 1818 he graduated from Williams College, a tall, slim, delicate young man, and in 1821 commenced to practise law in Rochester, N. Y. Four years later he was elected prosecuting attorney for Monroe County and in 1827 was sent to Congress, where for one term he participated in the discussions of slavery, the tariff, and the Cumberland Road. Never in robust health, during 1830–31 he spent five months recuperating in Europe, where he studied the Revolution of 1830 and wrote letters for a Rochester newspaper. Changing his residence to Albany in 1832 he took a deep interest in state and national politics. Firm in his convictions and an intense partisan, he was yet in no sense a demagogue. Defeated as a Whig for Congress in 1834, he was elected to the state Assembly in 1837, where he was recognized as an authority on finance, education, and internal improvements. Returned to Congress as a Whig in 1839, he served for six years and in 1845 declined reëlection. His interest centered in such problems as internal improvements, finance, the annexation of Texas, and the tariff, and for four years he was chairman of the judiciary committee. In public life he was trusted by his party friends and respected by his opponents. Upon returning to Albany he devoted himself to the legal profession in which he attained eminence, and to the writing of historical brochures which brought him considerable reputation. From his pen appeared *Lecture on the Character and Services of James Madison* (1837), *Discourse on the Life, Character, and Services of Stephen Van Rensselaer* (1839), *The Colony of Rensselaerwyck* (1839), *The Anti-Rent Movement* (1846), *Treatment of General Scott* (1848), *Discourse on the Life of Ambrose Spencer* (1849), and *Trinity Church* (1857). The crowning honor of his career came in 1850, when President Fillmore sent him as minister to Prussia, a post he filled for three years. While abroad he studied the results of the Revolution of 1848 and wrote a book on the *Political Aspects and Prospects in Europe* (1854). His ablest legal argument was on "The Sovereignty of the States over Their Navigable Waters" in connection with the Albany Bridge Case in 1860. He died at Albany just as the Civil War was breaking out. His acquaintances spoke of him as a man gracious and cultured, attractive in personal intercourse, and of an amiable disposition. He was twice married, first to Sara Livingstone at Rochester in 1825 and secondly to Catherine Walsh at Albany in 1832.

[A brief sketch of Barnard's life, accompanied by a picture in the *Am. Rev.,* VII, 521–32; an appraisal of his life and character in Edward Everett's *Orations and Speeches* (1892), IV, 339–44; letters, letter books, dispatch books, diaries, etc., in the N. Y. State Lib., Albany, N. Y.]

A. C. F.

BARNARD, EDWARD EMERSON (Dec. 16, 1857–Feb. 6, 1923), astronomer, was born in Nashville, Tenn., the posthumous son of Reuben Barnard. His mother, Elizabeth Jane (Haywood) Barnard, was a woman of culture, helpful and inspiring to her sons, whom she was obliged to support. Barnard's early education, with the exception of a few weeks in common school, came from her. At the age of nine he entered the studio of a photographer in Nashville, where he was employed for over sixteen years. This work was undertaken as a mere "job," but the attention to detail, the training in photographic processes and the acquirement of a knowledge of lenses was of great value to him in his pioneer work in astronomical photography. A stray copy of Dr. Thomas Dick's *Practical Astronomer* came into his hands in 1876 and furnished him with his first instruction in astronomy. From this book he learned the names of many of the stars which he already knew by sight. In the same year, a one-inch lens from a broken spy-glass found in the street was fitted in a paper tube to form his first telescope. A little later he and his mother were able to spare enough from his earnings to enable him to buy a real telescope of five-inch aperture. His meeting with Simon Newcomb in 1877 was a turning-point in his career. Newcomb told him that to do real research in astronomy he must be well grounded in mathematics. From then on Barnard devoted what time he could to retrieving the education which he had of necessity missed. In 1881 he married Rhoda Calvert, born in Yorkshire, England, who encouraged and helped him in his education. In May 1881 he discovered his first comet. He observed it again the next night but failed to find it afterward. This discovery was the beginning of his life-long interest in comets. H. H. Warner had offered a prize of two hundred dollars for each unexpected comet discovered by an American observer. The timely winning of five of these prizes made it possible for Barnard to own the little house which he was building. It is still known in Nashville as the "Comet House." Barnard discovered many more comets. His intimate knowledge of the heavens made it easy for him to recognize an intruder.

A serious decision confronted him when he was offered a fellowship in Vanderbilt University, with a stipend of three hundred dollars. He gave up his work in the studio and devoted his whole time to his studies. He received the degree of Bachelor of Science in 1887, at the age of thirty. In the meantime he had become remarkably familiar with the sky, had made a special study of Jupiter and independently discovered the red spot, and had communicated several papers to the astronomical journals. His skill as an observer had become well enough recognized to secure his appointment as an astronomer at the new Lick Observatory with Holden, Burnham, Schaeberle, and Keeler. Here, as junior astronomer, he was assigned to the twelve-inch telescope and the comet-seeker. During this period he made his striking series of observations of the eclipse of the satellite Japetus by the ring-system of Saturn, measuring its changing brightness in the sunlight which filtered through between the separate particles of the crape ring. During the summer of 1889 he began his photography of the Milky Way, securing the first of those beautiful photographs of its intricate structure. After the resignation of Burnham he was allotted one night a week at the thirty-six-inch. It was natural that he should turn to Jupiter, which he had so often observed with lesser instruments. In the search of its neighborhood he saw a tiny point of light which he at once guessed to be a satellite. Subsequent measures verified the discovery of the fifth satellite of Jupiter. This discovery was recognized by the French Academy of Sciences with the award of the Lalande gold medal. It probably also gave added zest to the search for other satellites which resulted in the discoveries of the faint and distant sixth, seventh, eighth, and ninth satellites. At the Lick Observatory, and later at Yerkes, Barnard devoted much time to the measurement of the diameters of planets, and of the larger asteroids, and of both the diameter and positions of satellites. His observations in 1904, 1906, and in 1912–13 of the very faint ninth satellite of Jupiter are apparently the only visual observations ever made of this difficult object.

Barnard never lost an opportunity to photograph comets and during his nights at the big telescopes he measured their positions. It was his delight to study these photographs and trace the history of the changes in the comets' tails. He secured no less than 350 photographs of Comet Morehouse (1908 IV), each one an exciting promise of fresh developments. Forty-two of Barnard's comet plates and ninety-two of his photographs of the Milky Way are beautifully reproduced in Volume XI of the *Publications* of the Lick Observatory. The volume did not appear until nearly twenty years after the photographs were taken, owing to Barnard's dissatisfaction with ordinary means of reproduction—he could not bear to see any of the fine, beautiful details lost. He accepted a position at the Yerkes Observatory in 1895, and in 1897 plunged into observing with the greatest telescope in the world. He began about this time a micrometric triangulation of some of the globular clusters. This work he continued for nearly twenty-five years, hoping to detect motions of the individual stars. His observation of novæ was frequent and minute. He estimated their brightness and examined them carefully. A record of the focus at which the image was sharpest was a record of the change in spectrum. He discovered visually the nebulous ring about Nova Aurigæ in 1892.

The acquisition of the 10-inch Bruce photographic telescope in 1904 was a fresh delight to Barnard in the photography of comets and in the mapping of the Milky Way. His great collection of 1,400 negatives of comets and of nearly 4,000 plates of the Milky Way and other star-fields will be of great value when they can be properly evaluated. Nebulous regions were always of great interest to him, especially the dark markings devoid of stars. Gradually he formed the opinion, now generally held, that these are dark nebulæ, rather than vacancies. No attempt can be made in this article even to mention all the classes of observation to which Barnard's interest led him. His published papers number at least 900. He had two regular observing nights a week with the forty-inch but sometimes worked with it on three or four nights. Many stories are told of his pacing back and forth and of the acuteness of his nervous cough as his night approached with the prospect of clouds. When he was denied the use of the forty-inch he was to be found making long exposures with the Bruce telescope. Frost writes that it was one of his most serious duties as director to keep Barnard from overworking. One of the greatest trials of the latter's life was the refraining from the use of the forty-inch for an entire year on the orders of his doctor.

Barnard had no children and the loss of his wife in 1921 left a great void in his life. His home was always a center of generous hospitality and friendship. Many honors came to him. He was very modest and was often nervous before giving a lecture, but after he was well started and had forgotten himself he was a delightful lecturer. He would take any amount of trouble to be helpful to other astronomers and to laymen interested in astronomy. He was thoroughly beloved by his many friends.

[Edwin B. Frost, "Edward Emerson Barnard" in the *Astrophysical Jour.*, July 1923, pp. 221–35; Robt. G. Aitken, "Edward Emerson Barnard 1857–1923," in *Pub. Astronomical Soc. of the Pacific*, Apr. 1923, pp. 87–94; Philip Fox, "Edward Emerson Barnard," in *Pop. Astronomy*, Mar. 1923, pp. 195–200; obituaries in *Nashville Banner* and *Nashville Tennessean*, Feb. 7, 1923.]

R. S. D.

BARNARD, FREDERICK AUGUSTUS PORTER (May 5, 1809–Apr. 27, 1889), college president, the son of Robert Foster Barnard and Augusta (Porter) Barnard, was born in Sheffield, Mass. His early education was at the village school, at the Saratoga (New York) Academy, and at the academy in the neighboring Stockbridge, where one of his schoolmates was Mark Hopkins [*q.v.*]. Of his subsequent four years at Yale (1824–28), distinguished by high scholarship, Barnard said: "Although I was apparently surrounded by many educational influences, and enjoying, or supposed to enjoy, the instruction of many eminent educators, it was to me a period of almost literal self-education" (Fulton, *Memoirs of Frederick A. P. Barnard*, p. 33). Immediately after graduation, he became a teacher in the Hartford Grammar School, the first of many educational positions. In the next eight years, he was in succession a teacher in the American Institution for the Deaf and Dumb at Hartford (Barnard had become somewhat deaf, an affliction from which he did not recover), a teacher of mathematics at Yale, and also a member of the faculty of the New York Institution for the Deaf and Dumb. In 1837 he was elected to the professorship of mathematics and natural history in the University of Alabama (1837–48), but was later transferred to the chair of chemistry and of natural history (1848–54). On Dec. 27, 1847, he was married to Margaret McMurray of Mississippi. In 1854, he was chosen to the professorship of mathematics and of natural philosophy in the University of Mississippi (1854–56). He became president of the University of Mississippi in 1856 (1856–58), and chancellor in the latter year (1858–61). He was elected president of Columbia College in 1864, a position which he held until his death. This rich, diverse, and unique record was further made notable by many avocations. Among these were his presidency of the American Association for the Advancement of Science, service as astronomer to the Alabama and Florida Boundary Commission, membership in the United States Coast Survey, editorship of Johnson's *Cyclopædia,* much and diverse writing on science and on the administrative problems of the College, and the taking of orders in the Protestant Episcopal Church.

This diverse yet orderly career was, however, divided by a fundamental and unique experience. In the last months of 1860 and the first months of 1861, the causes and conditions long working to make the Civil War came to their head. Of these conditions, as chief executive of the chief university in one of the chief seceding states, Barnard had been an observer. The students of the University of Mississippi, early in 1861, organized themselves into a military company, the University Greys, and asked the governor to muster them into service. The application was accepted. After their departure, the University was broken up. Barnard's situation became difficult. His work of many years was essentially ruined. He loved the Union, loving it far more than he hated slavery. To the institution of slavery he gave little thought in comparison with his loyalty to the Union. The tendering of his resignation, which he speedily made, was declined by the University trustees, under the belief that the war would be a short one. The resignation was withdrawn for a time, but presently, under the active development of the war, was accepted. The University, in fact, became a military school. Barnard was soon offered, by Jefferson Davis, an office as an investigator of the natural resources of the Confederate States, an invitation which he at once refused. He and his wife presently found their way to Virginia, and lived at Norfolk till May 1862. At that time, Norfolk was captured by the Federal troops. Late in 1863, Barnard published his famous *Letter to the President of the United States by a Refugee.* This letter, declamatory in form, fierce and vehement in content, against the Confederate States, was an argument and plea for the support of Lincoln. It created great public interest, and seems to have called special and immediate attention of the trustees of Columbia to his worth and availability as president.

To these various offices and affairs, technical and executive, academic and semi-academic, Barnard brought knowledge, rich and broad, a real affection for students, and a deep appreciation of their needs. He possessed an acute intellect, an alert sense of the worth of general culture, a deep feeling of personal duty, and a genuine understanding of the conditions necessary for making every college and university an integral part of the whole educational system. He was, by nature and training, both a conservative and a progressive, but rather a progressive than a conservative. Having as his specialty mathematics and the allied sciences, he was yet a scholar in Latin and Greek, and knew, in a general way, several modern languages. Above most college presidents, he appreciated the content and relationships of the instruction given by his professorial associates. His intellectual sympathies were warm. He was avaricious of new ideas, both to create and to acquire, to assimilate and to propagate. His spirit was missionary. Born with an instinct for persistent faithfulness, he persevered in the teeth, at times, of strong opposition against his measures. His current portraits indicate a man of dignity, of reserve, and of force, yet of a temperament kindly and sympathetic. He was a prophet, and a prophet to whom was given the privilege of seeing the fulfilment of many of his early teachings and visions.

The educational philosophy, which lay behind his administration of Columbia, and of his other historic, and formative, offices, was at least twofold. First, he held that mental discipline was the primary purpose of the first half of the four-year college course. He also held that the promotion of scholarship should be the primary and formative purpose of the second half. In the changes of academic opinion of his long term, the ideal of mental discipline became less conspicuous, and the idea of culture became more prevailing. This change was also connected with his constantly and urgently held plan for the development of the University in and through Columbia College. In his *Annual Report* of June 1866, he said: "She is the nucleus of what will one day be the great university of the city—possibly of the continent; and it should be an encouragement to all who have any ambition to see our city as preëminent in its literary and scientific character as it is in its population, its commerce, and its wealth, that she is a nucleus so substantial already—so sound and solid at the core, that all future accretions will adhere to her firmly, and constitute the elements of a healthy growth" (*President's Annual Report* for 1866, p. 29. See also, President Butler's *Annual Report,* 1925, p. 11).

Till his death in 1889, Barnard, in report and letter and speech, by arguments formal and informal, urged the development of the university spirit and organization in Columbia. It was an opportune time. Harvard, under Eliot, was promoting a similar growth, and Johns Hopkins, opened in 1876, was developing the first of the great graduate schools. Barnard sought for liberty in the choice of studies, a method which Eliot was introducing and emphasizing. He worked for an inclusive curriculum. He felt that the enlargement of the general field of knowledge, especially of science, should result in an enlargement of the number and subject of collegiate studies. He also did not depreciate the value of the highly specialized courses. He recognized, furthermore, that the change which comes over many students, in the midway period of their course, a change from intellectual boyishness to the beginning of intellectual maturity, should be recognized in the subjects pursued. He also believed in the adjustment of a proper curriculum to public opinion and interpretation, and to the needs of the people.

In his *Annual Report* for 1879, Barnard said: "The principle of elective study is the key which solves the whole difficulty. By limiting the student to a certain number of subjects, sufficient time may be allowed him to perfect himself in each, and sufficient time may be allowed the teacher to do his subject justice. The college may at the same time enlarge the scope of its teaching, and embrace in its general scheme of instruction every subject of literary and scientific interest, without in any degree diminishing the thoroughness with which each branch is taught. And it is only in this way that, in the present age, any college can hope to secure and maintain a really high character as an institution of learning" (Fulton, p. 393).

Barnard's early opinion, however, of the value of the free elective system was in the later years somewhat modified, becoming sympathetic with the judgments of other college presidents. The modification applied to two points: first, he emphasized more fully the duty and the right of the student to seek the counsel of his teachers in making his choice of studies, and secondly, he came to appreciate the value of a certain grouping of studies, or of so-called paralleling or coordinating courses. Through this second method, especially, the peril of intellectual dissipation, he felt, might be largely avoided.

In Barnard's work for the enlargement of Columbia, his two most important services were first, the establishment of the School of Mines, already projected at the time of his election, and at the beginning of his term formally installed, and second, the foundation of collegiate instruction for women which finally resulted in Barnard College. As early as the year 1879, the subject of the education of women by Columbia was first formally brought to the attention of the board of trustees. In the succeeding years, the subject was constantly and urgently discussed. Diverse methods were proposed. In 1882, Barnard almost abandoned hope for the admission of women on an equality with men. But on June 8, 1883, under his constant argument and vigilant appeal, and under a certain degree of public pressure, the trustees voted that a course of collegiate study, equivalent to the course given to young men in Columbia College, should be offered to such women as might desire to avail themselves of it. This course was to be pursued outside the College, but under the direction of the Faculty. Though women were not to be admitted to any of the College classes, they were to be allowed to take the regular examinations, and when they should have successfully passed all examinations during a period of four years, they were to receive the bachelor's degree. During the next five years twenty-eight women were enrolled under these conditions; but the system, if it could be called a system, was a signal failure (*Ibid.*, p. 420).

After five years of this persistent and unavailing effort, in March 1888, "a memorial was presented to the Trustees, proposing the establishment of an institution in connection with the College and on the same general plan as the 'Annex' at Harvard University. The memorial was carefully and favorably considered, and the request of the memorialists was granted, substantially on the following conditions: The students of the Annex were to pursue their collegiate studies in a building, near the College, to be provided by the friends of the movement at their own expense and to be used exclusively for purposes of instruction, not for the boarding or lodging of students" (*Ibid.*, p. 421).

The method thus outlined did not, by any manner of means, meet the full wish of Barnard. Yet an act of incorporation was presently secured. Six months after his death, a college for women, fittingly and gratefully made to bear his name, was opened. Its prosperity for almost forty years is proof and justification of the wisdom of his long-continued and earnest endeavors for the education of women through Columbia University. It is probable that Barnard College constitutes his most significant and distinctive memorial.

Barnard's published writings cover some sixty titles. They are largely pamphlets. The complete collection is found in the Library of Congress and in the Library of Columbia University, each collection supplementing the other. These writings are easily classified in five divisions: educational, economic, scientific, political, sermonic. Of these five the educational is by far the most important. Among its chief titles are: *Improvements Practicable in American Colleges* (1855); *Should Study in College be Confined to a Uniform Curriculum, or Should it be Made to Any Extent Elective?* (1872); *Outline of a Plan for the Instruction of Graduate Classes* (1880); *Should American Colleges be Open to Women as well as to Men?* (1882). Among the economic titles are: *Report on the Principles which should Govern the Tolerance of Deviations from Standard Weight of Coins Weighed in Parcels* (1872); *The Silver Question, & the International Monetary Conference of 1881; The World's Stock of the Precious Metals* (1882). The scientific titles (fewer than one would expect) contain: *On the Pendulum, with a Description of an Electric Block* (1863); *Balance for Determining Specific Gravities by Inspection* (1888). The political writings are represented by one important item: *No Just Cause for a Dissolution of the Union* (Tuscaloosa, Ala., 1851). The sermonic titles include *Gratitude for National Blessings,* delivered at Oxford, Miss., Thanksgiving Day, Nov. 20, 1856 (Memphis, (1857); and *Brevity of Life* (Memphis, 1859).

[*Memoirs of Frederick A. P. Barnard,* by John Fulton (1896); *Hist. of Columbia Univ., 1754–1904; Ann. Report of the President of Columbia Univ.* for 1925; personal letters in the Lib. of Columbia Univ.]

C. F. T.

BARNARD, HENRY (Jan. 24, 1811–July 5, 1900), educationist, shares with Horace Mann [*q.v.*] the distinction of stimulating and directing the revival of popular education which began in this country in the first half of the nineteenth century. Born in Hartford, Conn., the fourth child of Chauncey and Elizabeth (Andrus) Barnard, he embodied the traits of character, regard for learning, and sense of civic responsibility, which characterized the best New England stock. In his boyhood days Hartford was hardly more than a country village, but it was one of the capitals of the state, and its very smallness made it impossible for the townspeople to be unaware of the coming and going of prominent persons and the machinery of legislation operating in their midst, so that young Barnard grew up in the atmosphere of politics and public service. His mother died when he was four years old, but he was fortunate in his father, who had followed the sea, become a farmer, and was a man of some means. Because of this latter fact the son had ample opportunity for schooling and travel, and was able in after years to carry out educational projects which otherwise would have been impossible. More important still, Chauncey Barnard was a man of good sense and tact. One night he heard Henry, then thirteen years old and "the victim of a miserable district school," plotting, with a fellow sufferer, to escape from its tyranny by running away and going to sea. The next morning, without disclosing his knowledge of the plot, he informed the boy that it was time for him to leave the district school, and that he might go to a boarding-school or to sea. Henry chose the former alternative and entered Monson Academy, Monson, Mass. Here he received good instruction, became interested in books and debating, and acquired a love for nature which Wordsworth, whom he visited later, urged him never to lose. Returning to Hartford, he prepared for college at the Hopkins Grammar School, first having been tutored by Rev. Abel Flint, and in 1826 he entered Yale.

Here he attained creditable rank in the required courses, but probably got far more out of his general reading, which was extensive, especially in English literature, and from the literary society, Linonia, to which he belonged, than from the prescribed courses. To the free commingling of the members of the different classes in such societies and to the incentive of their weekly debates, more than to any other source, he once said, he owed his usefulness in public life (*American Journal of Education,* I, 664). Certain it is that while in college he became an excellent writer and a vigorous, resourceful speaker. In his junior and senior years he was librarian of Linonia, and displaying the spirit which characterized his whole life, he used his salary in the purchase of books for the library. Awakened perhaps by his own experience, a lively interest in popular education had already taken possession of him. He had known both the poor teaching and inadequate facilities of the common school, and the excellent training of the select academy. The former institution, he recognized, had one supreme advantage—it was "a school of equal rights, where merit, and not social position, was the acknowledged basis of distinction." It was the school, therefore, in which American boys should be trained, and it should be brought, he felt, to the highest possible degree of excellence. While he was on an enforced visit home due to his participation in the "Bread and Butter Rebellion," a student agitation for better food in the commons, Dr. Eli Todd [*q.v.*], the family physician, awakened in him an interest in Pestalozzi's work. During vacation trips he visited schools in various places, and in 1828 and 1829 published descriptive sketches in the *New England Review.*

He graduated from college in 1830, resolved to give his life to public service, not with any thought of personal aggrandizement, for he seems always to have been extraordinarily indifferent to his own interests, but from an almost apostolic devotion to his country and human welfare. Although he taught for a year in an academy at Wellsboro, Pa., and later made the statement, "So far back as I have any recollection, the cause of true education, of the complete education of every human being without regard to the accidents of birth or fortune, seemed most worthy of the concentration of all my powers, and, if need be, of any sacrifice of time, money, and labor, which I may be called upon to make in its behalf," he appears at first to have had no idea of devoting himself exclusively to the field of education. On the contrary, he turned to the legal profession as likely to afford opportunity for public service, read law with Willis Hall of New York and with William H. Hungerford of Hartford, and in 1833–34 studied in the Yale Law School. In the winter of 1834–35 he was admitted to the bar. He also became active in politics. A strong anti-Jackson man, he was a delegate to the National Whig Convention in 1831, and the following year addressed the state convention and took a prominent part in the presidential campaign. Throughout this period he found time for much general reading and extensive travel. In 1833 he spent two months in Washington, where he met many prominent people, and watched with critical interest the doings of Congress. Later in the year he journeyed through the South, and, the year following, through the West. In 1835–36 he spent nearly a year traveling about Europe. Here he discussed education with Lord Brougham, visited Carlyle, De Quincey, Wordsworth, and Lockhart, conferred with Fellenberg and other Swiss educators, and lived for a time in Paris with Forrest the actor.

The year after his return, the voters of Hartford sent him to the General Assembly as one of their two representatives, and reëlected him in 1838 and 1839. Here he was active in promoting humanitarian legislation. In 1838 he introduced a bill "to provide for the better supervision of the common schools," and supported it in a notable speech. It provided for a state board of commissioners and a secretary chosen by them. Due to his carefully prepared campaign, it was unanimously passed. Naturally, he was one of the commissioners appointed, and when the board organized he secured the election of Dr. T. H. Gallaudet as secretary. The latter declined the position, and Barnard himself was urged to take it. He hesitated, partly because the office had been created through his efforts, and partly because he was not sure he ought to turn from the profession for which he had fitted himself. As a matter of fact, however, he had no great taste for law or politics and in the end he accepted. The work of carrying out the intent of the law and improving the state system of education fell, therefore, largely upon him.

The conditions which he faced would have discouraged a less optimistic and energetic person. There was no centralization or uniformity in the management of the schools. Each was controlled, not by the town, but by an independent school society, which as a rule endeavored to make its allotment from the state school fund suffice to meet its educational needs, and thus avoid taxation. Only the poorer classes availed themselves of free instruction, people of means sending their children to academies. It was estimated that at least 5,000 children did not attend any school. The condition of the schoolhouses was deplorable; there was practically no equipment; the teachers, untrained and inefficient, changed with the seasons. The evils of the situation were not unrecognized, but a general apathy prevailed. It fell to Barnard's lot to wake up the state and start movements which later bore much fruit. In his official capacity he addressed a letter to the people, outlining the plans of the new board; he sent out questionnaires and personally visited schools in all the counties; he presented the facts ascertained in reports to the legislature and addressed public meetings; he started and edited the *Connecticut Common School Journal;* he secured some changes in the school laws; he emphasized the need of trained teachers and started teachers' institutes, which were among the first, if not the first, in the country. After four years of almost incredible activity, he was legislated out of office. Such a campaign as he had waged was bound to awaken some opposition and disturb local politicians. Furthermore, he had formerly been an outspoken Whig. In 1842 the Democrats came into power in the state, and on the alleged ground that the results attained did not warrant further expenditure of funds, direct supervision of schools by the State was abolished.

Barnard's next field of labor was Rhode Island. Here an act had been passed requiring the governor to appoint an "agent" who should collect and disseminate information regarding defects and possible improvements in the school system and elevate the sentiment with respect to public education. Prejudice against it due to the feeling that education like religion did not properly belong to the "civil things" to which government activity should be confined, and that to compel a citizen to support schools was a violation of his freedom, still persisted, and the condition of the schools was even worse than in Connecticut. Appointed agent in 1843, Barnard pursued methods similar to those he had employed in his own state. In a comparatively short time he had revolutionized public sentiment. At his suggestion, early in 1845, the Rhode Island Institute of Instruction was established. The same year he secured the passage of a school act, which, prior to its enactment, Horace Mann declared would give to Rhode Island "one of the best systems of public instruction in the world." When he resigned in 1849 because of ill health, he had put it into successful operation.

By this time he had become widely known, his reports having created a literature of education read abroad as well as in America. He was in demand as a speaker, and had addressed gatherings in all the states then in the Union with the exception of Texas. On a trip West in 1846 he met Josephine Desnoyers of Detroit, whom he married Sept. 6, 1847, and by whom he had five children.

Calls now came to him from different directions. Professorships in at least two colleges were offered him, and he declined school superintendencies in Boston, New York, Cincinnati, and New Orleans, and the presidencies of the Universities of Indiana and of Michigan. Connecticut again sought his leadership. The sentiment in favor of better public schools which he had created there had not died, and with the return of the Whigs to power, legislation was finally effected establishing a normal school at New Britain and stipulating that its principal should also be superintendent of the common schools of the state. Elected Aug. 7, 1849, Barnard undertook the work of this dual position. He planned the work of the normal school, but did no teaching, its immediate management being in the hands of an assistant, leaving him free to give much of his time to the interests of the public schools. During his term of service he drew up a revised code of school legislation which was enacted in 1849, prepared a *History of the Legislation of Connecticut Respecting Common Schools Down to 1838,* which served as his report for 1853, and the next year published in final form his *School Architecture, or Contributions to the Improvement of Schoolhouses in the United States.* In 1852 he took a trip abroad, primarily for his health, though he also gathered much valuable information, and in 1854, the governor commissioned him delegate to the International Exposition of Educational Methods, London, where much respect was shown him. In 1855 he resigned because of ill health, and that he might devote himself to "certain educational undertakings of a national character," the publication of the *American Journal of Education.*

Although this work was to be his major interest for the rest of his life, for brief periods he held three more official positions. From 1858 to 1860 he was Chancellor of the University of Wisconsin and agent of the board of regents of the normal-school fund. Because of poor health and frequent absences his connection with the university was hardly more than a nominal one, and though he did some hard work in the interest of teacher training, he was unable to do for the school system what it had been hoped he might accomplish. For a short time in 1866–67 he was president of St. John's College, Annapolis, Md., resigning to become the first United States Commissioner of Education. Whatever taste for politics he may have had in his youth, he had now lost. His interest, furthermore, had come to be centered in educational literature rather than in administrative work. As a result his experience in Washington was not an altogether happy one. At its close he complained that his office had been changed from place to place without his being consulted; that he had not been able to get authority to print, and that his work had not had adequate support from Congress. In 1868 a bill was passed abolishing the *Department* of Education and creating in its place an *Office* (later changed to *Bureau*) of Education, attached to the Department of the Interior, and reducing the Commissioner's salary from $4,000 to $3,000. Before he relinquished the work of his office, Mar. 15, 1870, he prepared at the call of Congress two reports of especial value, one on the condition and improvement of the public schools in the District of Columbia, a book of 912 pages, printed by the government in 1871; and the other a report on technical education, which was not printed, but appears in a revised form in the *American Journal of Education,* volume XXI.

Barnard's contribution to the furtherance of education in the United States was manifold. Whatever conditions seemed to demand he advocated and worked for with indefatigable energy. His achievements in Connecticut and Rhode Island were of lasting consequence there, and in some degree served as models elsewhere. His counsel and help were given in all parts of the country. He was an effective speaker and his faith and enthusiasm awakened the same wherever he went. His chief service, however, was rendered through the information which he disseminated. From his early years he recognized the great need of enlightening the public and especially those in charge of the schools, and the main purpose of his life was to do this by giving them a complete history of education in all ages and countries. This he did in a remarkable degree in his *American Journal of Education,* a monumental work of thirty-two large octavo volumes of over 800 pages each. It appeared at irregular intervals, the first number in August 1855, the last in 1882. Into its publication he put his whole fortune, thereby impoverishing his later years. It is not a journal of review, as the name might suggest, but a great encyclopedia of educational literature, dealing with every possible phase of its subject. He also published a *Library of Education* in fifty-two volumes, consisting of special treatises taken from the *Journal.*

After leaving Washington in 1870, he made his home in Hartford, living and dying in the house in which he had been born. With his white hair, long, flowing white beard, and benign countenance, he presented in his latter years a patriarchal appearance. He was a man of unostentatious goodness, kindly and generous, unsparing of himself, and willing to give all he had to the cause to which he was devoted. When in 1835 he started out on his western trip, Dr. T. H. Gallaudet urged him to make a public profession of religion. It is not recorded that he did or that he was ever a churchman, but those who knew him intimately gave testimony to his deep religious faith. His wife was a devout French Catholic, but difference in race and belief never disturbed the peace and happiness of their union. Literature and nature were his chief sources of recreation. He was noticeably fond of animals, and in later days it was his habit to spend a part of each morning working in his garden, and the remainder in his study, frequently with two or three kittens playing round him. He was a professional reformer of the better variety with none of the narrowness or intolerance so common to the class. He may have been visionary at times, and some of the projects he recommended were impractical, but the principal things which he advocated have now been incorporated into educational systems. His method was scientific. He first investigated, giving the greatest possible publicity to the facts discovered, and then endeavored, not to revolutionize, but to make such changes and improvements as at the moment seemed expedient. He had a sincere love for humanity and a Jeffersonian faith in the people. He believed that if they were properly informed they could be trusted in the long run to do the right thing, and that in an educated democracy lay the sole hope of a righteous, peaceful, and prosperous world.

[Will S. Monroe has published a *Bibliography of Henry Barnard* (1897); the footnotes in B. C. Steiner's "Life of Henry Barnard" in the U. S. Bur. of Ed. *Bull., 1919, No. 8,* contain many references. For ancestry, see R. R. Hinman, *A Cat. of the Names of the Early Puritan Settlers of the Colony of Conn.* (1852); his educ. work is presented in Noah Porter's "Henry Barnard, His Labors in Conn. and R. I.," reprinted from *Conn. Common School Jour.*, Jan. 1855, in *Amer. Jour. of Ed.*, I (1855–6); A. D. Mayo, "Henry Barnard," *Report of the Commissioner of Ed.*, I, 1896–7; W. S. Monroe, *Educ. Labors of Henry Barnard* (1893); and in memorial addresses in *Addresses and Proc. of the Nat. Ed. Ass.* (1901).]

H. E. S.

BARNARD, JOHN (Nov. 6, 1681–Jan. 24, 1770), Congregational clergyman, was born in Boston, the son of John and Esther Barnard. He was graduated from Harvard College in 1700, resolved to enter the ministry. After six years of study and occasional preaching, in 1707 he was appointed by Gov. Dudley one of the chaplains to the army which was fitted out in Massachusetts to reduce Port Royal and Acadia. This expedition returned within three months without having accomplished anything but the lessening of the reputation of its leaders. Barnard returned to his itinerant preaching, but in 1709 enlisted as chaplain on a large ship sailing for Barbadoes and London. He remained in England for nearly a year, frequently preaching, making many friends, and incidentally taking an active part in the appointment of Jeremiah Dummer as agent for New England. He also interested himself in worldly affairs, recording in his autobiography that he drank a glass of sack with an aged gentlewoman who was surprised that he had learned to speak English in so short a stay; obtained the receipt of some excellent currant wine from the housekeeper of one of his patrons; shared burnt claret with his traveling companions on the way to Litchfield; drank wine with many clergymen, several of whom tried to induce him to find posts for them in New England, and visited Burton, where he found the "best, stoutest and finest ale in England."

Returning to New England in November 1710, he resumed preaching, but because of internal jealousies among the ruling Congregational clergy and his friendship with the unpopular Gov. Dudley, he did not succeed in securing a permanent church. Finally in 1714 he was nominated, with Edward Holyoke [*q.v.*] as candidate for the church at Marblehead, to follow the aged Samuel Cheever as pastor. Since the congregation could not agree upon either candidate, the church finally split, a new meeting-house was erected, and both ministers came to Marblehead. Barnard was ordained in the old church July 18, 1716, having officiated as assistant to Cheever for eight months previous. Here he labored for the remainder of his long life, taking charge of a large and growing congregation and building up a reputation as a fearless and forceful preacher. In 1718 he married Anna Woodbridge of Ipswich. In 1737 he was instrumental in having Edward Holyoke selected as president of Harvard College. For himself, however, he declined all outside honors. In the affairs of the town he took an active interest. From a poor community with no trade and with the people largely dependent upon Boston for their needs and supplies, Marblehead grew to a thriving and prosperous town. Largely through his zeal and suggestion, it improved its natural advantages as a place of commerce, especially in marketing its fish, until by 1766 it had nearly forty vessels engaged in foreign trade, with a resultant increase in wealth and importance.

Barnard died on Jan. 24, 1770. William Whitwell (in his *Funeral Discourse,* Salem, 1770) said: "As a scholar, he was acquainted with the Hebrew, Greek and Latin languages; besides which, in his leisure hours, for mere amusement, he had made great proficiency in the mathematicks. He thoroughly studied the nature of architecture and ship-building and . . . was a master of music in all its parts. . . . As to his person, he was somewhat taller than the common size, and well proportioned. His stature was remarkably erect, and never bent under the infirmities of eighty-eight. His countenance was grand, and his mien majestick, and there was a dignity in his whole deportment." Rev. Charles Chauncy, in a letter written May 6, 1768 (*Massachusetts Historical Society Collections,* ser. I, vol. X, p. 157) said of him: "I esteem him to have been one of our greatest men. Had he turned his studies that way, he would perhaps have been as great a mathematician as any in this country, I had almost said in England itself. He is equalled by few in regard either of readiness of invention, liveliness of imagination, or strength and clearness in reasoning." He printed more than twenty sermons; three volumes of religious doctrine; *Ashton's Memorial, an History of the Strange Adventures and Signal Deliverances of Mr. Philip Ashton* (1725), and *A New Version of the Psalms of David* (1752).

[The chief source of information regarding Barnard's life is the long autobiography written in 1766 and printed in *Mass. Hist. Soc. Colls.*, ser. III, vol. V, pp. 177–245; other references of value are Samuel Dana, *Discourse on the Hist. of the First Christian Church and Society in Marblehead* (1816); W. B. Sprague, *Annals Am. Pulpit,* I, 252; and Joseph Sabin, *Dict. of Books Relating to America* (1868–92), I, 460.] C. S. B.

BARNARD, JOHN GROSS (May 19, 1815–May 14, 1882), Union soldier, son of Robert Foster Barnard and Augusta (Porter) Barnard, and younger brother of Frederick Augustus Porter Barnard [*q.v.*], was born at Sheffield, Mass., in the Berkshire Hills. From one of his relatives, Peter Buel Porter, secretary of war under President John Quincy Adams, he received an appointment to the United States Military Academy at West Point, and entered that institution on July 1, 1829; four years later he graduated second in a class of forty-three. He was assigned as second-lieutenant to the corps of engineers of the army, which was charged with the construction of coast defenses, the improvement of rivers and harbors, and the supervision of the Military Academy. In this corps he served through the various grades to that of colonel, and on his retirement for age in 1881 was president of the Permanent Board of Engineers for Fortifications and River and Harbor Improvements. He was nominated by President Lincoln as chief of his corps in 1864 but at his own request his name was withdrawn, probably to allow an officer of longer service to enjoy that honor. He also served as superintendent of the Military Academy 1855–56.

When he joined the corps of engineers its officers were engaged in the construction of a system of defenses on the Atlantic and Gulf coasts to supplement the few old works constructed immediately after the Revolutionary War. In this work he served as superintending engineer of the fortifications of some of our important ports—Portland and New York on the Atlantic coast, Mobile and the mouth of the Mississippi River on the Gulf coast, and San Francisco on the Pacific coast. All of these works were designed to meet the attacks of wooden vessels armed with muzzle-loading cannon. With the introduction of rifled guns and armored vessels, about the time of the Civil War, the coast defenses had to be modified, and after that war Barnard was charged with the study of this problem. On this work he was sent abroad in 1870 to ascertain the progress made in Europe in the development of iron for defensive purposes. In connection with his work on seacoast defenses he wrote the following: *Dangers and Defences of New York* (1859); "Memoir on National Defences" (in *Proceedings of the Military Association of the State of New York,* 1860, pp. 55–71); *Notes on Seacoast Defence* (1861); *Report on the Fabrication of Iron for Defensive Purposes and its Uses in Modern Fortification especially in Coast Defence,* in collaboration with Lieutenant-Colonel Wright and Capt. Michie of the Corps of Engineers (1871–72).

In the field of river and harbor improvement, Barnard served as superintending engineer on the construction of the Delaware breakwater, the improvement of the Hudson River and New Jersey harbors, and as chairman of boards considering numerous projects. An important service was that in connection with the improvement of the mouth of the Mississippi River. In 1852 Congress appropriated $75,000 for this improvement and a board, of which Barnard was a member, was appointed to recommend the best method of utilizing this sum. In 1871 Congress directed that plans and estimates for further improvement should be prepared by an engineer officer. These plans were completed early in 1873 and a board was convened to report on them. After prolonged controversy, Congress finally accepted Barnard's recommendation that the South Pass be improved by the construction of parallel jetties, and directed that a contract be made with James B. Eads and his associates to carry out this improvement, payment to be conditional on success. Mr. Eads, who had said of Barnard, "His reputation among both civil and military engineers is acknowledged in Europe and America to be equal to that of any other living," appointed him chairman of his board of advisory engineers. Time has confirmed Barnard's views in the matter of improving the mouth of the Mississippi River and the jetty method has since been applied to the wider Southwest Pass. His published works on waterways were: *Outlets and Levees of the Mississippi River* (1859); *Report on the North Sea Canal of Holland* (1872).

In the Mexican War he was assigned the construction of the defenses of the base at Tampico, and later to the survey of the battlefields about the City of Mexico. This last duty probably led to his selection by the Tehuantepec Railroad Company of New Orleans in 1850 as chief engineer to make a preliminary survey for a railway across that isthmus. Such was Barnard's reputation as a military engineer that at the outbreak of the Civil War he was charged with the construction of the defenses of the National Capital. He served as chief engineer of McDowell's army in 1861 and on his reconnaissance the first battle of Bull Run was planned. Of this battle Sherman, who took part in it, says, "It is now generally admitted that it was one of the best planned battles of the war but one of the worst fought." Barnard was chief engineer of the Army of the Potomac in McClellan's Peninsular campaign in which he conducted the siege of Yorktown and directed the engineering operations on the front of Richmond. From the Peninsular campaign until Grant took command of the armies in Virginia he remained in charge of the defenses of Washington and was a member of various defense boards. In June 1864 he was made chief engineer of the armies in the field on the staff of Gen. Grant. Wishing to withdraw one of the corps serving under Gen. Butler south of the James River to reinforce his troops north of the James, Grant sent Barnard to examine Butler's position to see if this could be safely done and on his report the corps was brought across the river. When Sherman's army reached Savannah, Grant sent Barnard there to explain the situation in Virginia and North Carolina so that Sherman could decide on a plan for coöperation. For his military services in time of war Barnard received the brevets of major in the regular army in the Mexican War and of colonel, brigadier-general, and major-general in the Civil War. He was commissioned brigadier-general of volunteers in the Civil War and received the brevet of major-general of volunteers. His contributions to the history of the Civil War were: *The Confederate States of America and the Battle of Bull Run* (1862); *The Peninsular Campaign and its Antecedents . . . as Developed by the Report of Maj. Gen. George B. McClellan and other Published Documents* (1864); *Report of the Engineer and Artillery Operations of the Army of the Potomac from its Organization to the Close of the Peninsular Campaign,* in collaboration with Gen. William F. Barry (1863); *A Report on the Defenses of Washington* (1871).

Notwithstanding his professional occupations Barnard still found time to indulge his love for mathematical and scientific investigation. He was one of the fifty incorporators of the National Academy of Sciences and his published scientific writings indicate a wide field of research: *The Phenomena of the Gyroscope Analytically Examined* (1858); *Problems of Rotary Motion Presented by the Gyroscope, the Precession of the Equinoxes and the Pendulum* (1873); *On the Internal Structure of the Earth Considered as Affecting the Phenomena of Precession and Nutation* (1877); *An Alleged Error in Laplace's Theory of the Tides* (1877); *Some Remarks on the Use and Interpretation of Particular Integrals which "Satisfy" General Differential Equations Expressive of Dynamic Problems in Cases where General Integration is Impossible* (1877). He also wrote for Johnson's *Universal Cyclopedia* (1874–77) some seventy articles on engineering, mathematical, and scientific subjects.

For his personality we have the following from the pen of Gen. Henry L. Abbot of the corps of engineers: "In his personal characteristics Gen. Barnard was a thoughtful, self-contained, and earnest soldier. Under fire he seemed to have no sense of exposure, and in his frequent reconnaissances he was wont to push aside advanced pickets attempting to advise him as to the position of the enemy's sharpshooters, apparently trusting more to his own intuitions than to their local knowledge. His inherited deafness rendered social intercourse somewhat difficult, and to those who did not know him intimately this circumstance perhaps conveyed the idea of coldness and formality; but such was far from his nature. As an aide-de-camp during the Peninsular campaign, I often saw evidences of the warm interest he took in the success of many young officers serving under his orders, and of cordial appreciation of good work done by them. . . . He had a keen sense of humor and a passionate love of music. Indeed he composed many pieces—among others a *Te Deum* that still survives" (*Professional Memoirs, Corps of Engineers,* V, 89).

While stationed in New Orleans, Barnard married Jane Elizabeth Brand, daughter of William Brand and sister of Rev. William F. Brand of Maryland, one of the noted clergymen of that state. She died in 1853, and in 1860 he married Mrs. Anna E. (Hall) Boyd, daughter of Maj. Henry Hall of Harford County, Md.

[H. P. Andrews, *Descendants of John Porter of Windsor, Conn.* (1882); James B. Eads, *Mouth of the Mississippi* (1874); J. J. Williams, *Isthmus of Tehuantepec* (1852); *Report of the Chief of Engineers for 1874,* App. R. 15.]

G. J. F.

BARNES, ALBERT (Dec. 1, 1798–Dec. 24, 1870), Presbyterian clergyman and author, was a prominent figure in the contentions immediately preceding the division between the Old and New Schools of American Presbyterianism in 1837. He was born in Rome, N. Y. His parents, Rufus and Anna Barnes, were connected with the Methodist denomination. Albert was early persuaded by a country schoolmaster, with the reluctant consent of his parents, to leave home for a course of study looking toward the legal profession. After preparatory work at an academy in Fairfield, Conn., he entered Hamilton College. Here his youthful tendency to religious skepticism yielded intellectually to the arguments of Dr. Chalmers in the *Edinburgh Encyclopedia,* and emotionally to the influence of a college friend during a time of special religious interest. He joined the Presbyterian denomination, and decided to make his life-work the ministry instead of the law. After graduating from Hamilton in 1820, he spent the next four years at Princeton Theological Seminary, and then became pastor of the Presbyterian Church at Morristown, N. J.

At this time there was still in operation the so-called "Plan of Union" of 1801 which permitted mixed congregations of Presbyterians and Congregationalists under ministers of either sect. This arrangement had worked to the advantage of the Presbyterians numerically, but at the same time had tended toward decentralization with an accompanying relaxation of dogma, tendencies fiercely resisted by the Old School party in the Presbyterian Church. Barnes, by nature one of the most peaceable of men, now unintentionally became for a time the storm center of this controversy. In a sermon called "The Way of Salvation," delivered Feb. 8, 1839, he denied that the sin of Adam is imputed to his posterity, thus opposing the position of Jonathan Edwards [*q.v.*] and coming into at least verbal disagreement with the Westminster Confession. When he was called soon after, in 1830, to the important First Church in Philadelphia, a minority of the Presbytery, led by Dr. Ashbel Green [*q.v.*], opposed his installation, because of this sermon, and appealed to the Synod, which ordered the Presbytery to make an examination of the offending document. The examiners in due course condemned it as "manifestly, in some of its leading points, opposed to the doctrines of the Confession of Faith" (R. E. Thompson, *History of the Presbyterian Churches in the United States,* 1895, being vol. VI of the American Church History series, p. 106). Summoned to retract, Barnes refused, and laid his case before the Assembly of 1831, which while mildly disapproving of the sermon, upheld Barnes's right to his pastorate.

But Barnes's orthodoxy was now definitely suspect, and on the appearance of his *Notes, Explanatory and Practical on the Epistle to the Romans,* in 1835, Dr. George Junkin [*q.v.*], an Old School leader, at once preferred charges against him. Barnes denied that he held any of the erroneous doctrines of which he was accused, and the Presbytery upheld him, but Junkin appealed to the Synod, which forthwith suspended him from the ministry until he should retract these errors. As Barnes could not well retract views which he had never expressed, he sat quietly for a year, a hearer in his own church, until the Assembly of 1836, in which the New School was predominant, vindicated him and restored him to his position.

In 1837 occurred the formal separation between the Old and New Schools, which divided the Presbyterian Church into two almost equal bodies for thirty-three years. Brethren more pugnacious than Barnes now came into the foreground of controversy while he went a more peaceful way with his work as pastor and writer. He usually rose at four in the morning and devoted the hours until nine to writing. Of this habit he said in later years, "In the recollection now of the past portions of my life, I refer to these morning hours,—to the stillness and quiet of my room in this house of God when I have been permitted to 'prevent the dawning of the morning' in the study of the Bible—I refer, I say, to these scenes as among the happiest portions of my life" (*Life at Three-Score,* 1859, pp. 54–55). Of his eleven volumes of commentaries on the New Testament, Isaiah, and the Psalms, issued as *Notes: Explanatory and Practical* (1832–53), it is said that more than 1,000,000 copies were sold. In them, as well as in his *Scriptural Views of Slavery* (1846) and *The Church and Slavery* (1857), he especially endeavored to prove that the Bible condemned slavery. This was accomplished by a rather free interpretation of scriptural texts. He also wrote numerous other works, mainly on Christian theology and ethics. The *Schaff-Herzog Religious Encyclopedia* (vol. I, 1882, p. 215) credits him with a "directing influence" on four movements: abolition; prohibition; the Sunday-school; New School Presbyterian doctrine. He served as a director of the Union Theological Seminary almost from its beginnings and in 1867 delivered the first course of lectures on the Ely Foundation, afterward published as *Lectures on the Evidences of Christianity* (1868). When the union of the Old and New Schools was broached in 1869, there was a faint revival of old animosities, and Barnes was regarded by some as "an unvenerable relic of an abandoned past" (Thompson, p. 179). To facilitate union, he now withdrew all his publications from the Presbyterian publication committee and transferred them to private publishers. In the year of his death he had the satisfaction to see the first united Assembly of both factions held in his own church, the scene of so many past dissensions. He died suddenly of heart failure, while visiting a bereaved family in his congregation, Dec. 24, 1870. He was survived by his wife, Abby (Smith) Barnes. G. L. Prentiss said of him, "He had a countenance marked in an unusual degree by moral thoughtfulness, benignity, sweetness, refinement, and manly dignity. I never heard him speak in loud or excited tones" (*Fifty Years of Union Theological Seminary,* 1889, p. 169). Shortly before his death Barnes himself wrote, with serene faith, "I shall close my eyes in death with bright and glorious hopes in regard to my native land, to the church, and to the world at large" (*Life at Three-Score and Ten,* 1871, p. 137).

[Autobiographical material in Barnes's *Life at Three-Score* (1859) and *Life at Three-Score and Ten* (1871). E. H. Gillett, *Hist. of the Presbyt. Ch.* (1864); S. J. Baird, *Hist. of the New School* (1868); George Junkin, *The Vindication, Containing a Hist. of the Trial of the Rev. Albert Barnes* (1836); *N. Y. Observer,* 1830–40, containing full reports of proceedings of Assembly, Synod, Presbytery, and statements from both sides in the controversy.] C. N.

BARNES, CHARLES REID (Sept. 7, 1858–Feb. 24, 1910), botanist, came of pioneer stock, from Madison, Jefferson County, Ind. From the first his interest in nature was strong, and his studies, prosecuted with a single-minded thoroughness, took him to Hanover College, from which he was graduated with the degree of A.B. in 1877. During his years at Hanover he was a classmate of Dr. John Merle Coulter, subsequently head of the department of botany at the University of Chicago, and thus began a lifelong friendship between the two. Barnes was principal of the High School at Hanover, 1877–78, principal of the High School at Utica, Ind., 1878–79, and a teacher in the High School at Lafayette, Ind., 1879–80. During the summers of 1879 and 1880 he studied at Harvard under Asa Gray, then the acknowledged leader of American botany, whose work, though largely systematic, was nevertheless original in its day in the stress laid upon the science, then new, of vegetable physiology. Barnes returned to Hanover to gain his degree of M.A. in 1880, and then taught natural science at Purdue University, where he was promoted to a professorship in 1882. In 1887 he took his Ph.D. at Hanover, and immediately thereafter accepted a teaching post at the University of Wisconsin. This he left in 1898 to become plant physiologist with the University of Chicago, then just organizing, where he remained until his death from apoplexy twelve years later.

Barnes's achievements were not in the more spectacular botanical field in which older botanists worked, that of exploration and the description of new species. On the contrary, in his labors the laboratory and its precise equipment, the mechanistic view-point, and the experimental method superseded the observational attitude of the older naturalists. Interest in physiology as the chief aspect of botany was largely created by his text-books and by his great influence over the host of teachers who went forth from the University of Chicago in the first decade of this century. As co-editor, with Dr. Coulter, of the *Botanical Gazette* during its most influential years, Barnes established, by his interest in physiology, his passion for scientific precision, and his love of good English, the high standing of the magazine, and largely imparted to it its physiological and morphological emphasis. In his position as a critic and as a teacher of teachers, he upheld a rigidly high standard and in his thought was relentlessly severe and logical. His earliest work was his "Analytical Key to the Genera of Mosses" (*Purdue University Bulletin,* 1886), followed by other works with similar titles, that were essentially improved editions of the first, in which he for the first time removed the systematic study of mosses from a highly technical sphere, going as far to popularize the Bryophytes as Asa Gray the flowering plants and Eaton the ferns. His most famous papers were on the status of modern botanical research, on the progress of plant physiology, and on the theory of the ascent of water in trees, a problem peculiarly fascinating and one still not completely solved. In collaboration with J. M. Coulter and others he prepared several text-books which have been of great pedagogic influence on the experimental and morphological method of botanical instruction.

[A brief appreciation by H. C. Cowles in *Science,* XXXI, 532–33; sketch in *Gen. Cat. Alumni Hanover Coll.* (1883), p. 46; obituary in *Chicago Daily Tribune,* Feb. 26, 1910.]

D. C. P.

BARNES, CHARLOTTE MARY SANFORD (1818–Apr. 14, 1863), actress and playwright, was the daughter of John and Mary (Greenhill) Barnes, English actors who made their appearance at the Park Theatre, New York, in April 1816. For many years Mrs. Barnes was the leading actress both in tragedy and comedy at the Park Theatre, and her husband was a successful low comedian. On Mar. 22, 1822, Charlotte Barnes, at the age of three, was brought on as the child of her mother who was acting in *The Castle Spectre.* When her own début was made at the Tremont Theatre in Boston, it was as Angela in the same play, and her first appearance on the New York stage, Mar. 29, 1834, was in that part. At Philadelphia in the same year she played Juliet to her mother's Romeo. Charlotte Barnes, however, never succeeded in reaching the position as an actress to which her mother had attained. Ireland tells us that physical defects in eyes, voice, and figure prevented her from ultimate success. Yet her training and ambition led her to attempt tragic rôles like Juliet, and in 1840 she played Thérèse to the Carwin of Edwin Forrest at the Bowery Theatre, New York. In 1842 she visited England, where her performance of Hamlet was well received. She returned in 1846, married Edmon S. Conner, a well-known actor-manager, in 1847, and acted as leading woman in his company. During his managerial career at the Arch Street Theatre in Philadelphia, they raised the standard of production and of behavior in the theatre, being supported by the public press.

Her playwriting began with the tragedy *Octavia Bragaldi; or, The Confession,* performed at the National Theatre, New York, Nov. 8, 1837, Miss Barnes acting in the title rôle. This romantic tragedy in blank verse has a singular interest in dramatic history. It was based on a murder which occurred in Frankfort, Ky., in 1825. Jeroboam O. Beauchamp killed Solomon P. Sharp, solicitor-general of Kentucky, upon discovering that he had seduced his wife before her marriage. T. H. Chivers and Edgar Poe had written closet dramas upon the theme, but Miss Barnes, a girl of eighteen, wrote the first play to be put on the stage, in which she acted with success in the United States and in London (Surrey Theatre, 1863) and Liverpool. In accordance with the literary fashion of the day, she changed the scene to Milan in the fifteenth century and deepened the sympathy of the audience for the heroine by a secret marriage between Octavia Bragaldi and the villain, Count de Castelli. (No marriage had taken place in Kentucky.) Believing Castelli dead, Octavia has married Bragaldi, and, on Castelli's return and repudiation of her, she demands that Bragaldi kill her betrayer. After the murder, Bragaldi kills himself, and Octavia takes poison. Miss Barnes showed some skill in transferring the actual scenes to the new setting, especially in the murder of Castelli, which she surrounded with the glamour of romance in the court-yard of Castelli's palace in the moonlight. (In real life, Beauchamp called Sharp to his own front door and shot him.) The play held the stage as late as 1854, when the author and her husband acted in it at the Bowery Theatre.

Her play of *La Fitte,* a dramatization of the novel of the same name by J. H. Ingraham (Caldwell's New Theatre, New Orleans, 1838), in which she played a young man's part, that of Theodore, seems also to have been a stage success. About the time of her marriage, Miss Barnes attempted a version of the Pocahontas story, which Barker, Custis, and Owen had already put on the stage. *The Forest Princess; or, Two Centuries Ago* was first played at Burton's Arch Street Theatre, Philadelphia, Feb. 16, 1848. Mrs. Barnes had played Pocahontas in Custis's *Pocahontas* in 1830, and possibly her daughter was inspired to write this drama by seeing her in the part. Mrs. Conner's dramatic sense is shown in her statement in the introduction to the printed play, that the defect of the story lies in its division of interest. She endeavored to overcome this by taking Pocahontas to England, where she dies after Rolfe has been accused and cleared of treason. Mrs. Conner also adapted a melodrama, *A Night of Expectations,* from the French. It was played at the Arch Street Theatre, Apr. 9, 1850, where she took the leading part of Madame de Virely, but it may have been performed earlier, as Durang states that she acted in it in England and Ireland with great success. She also adapted *Charlotte Corday* from the French of Dumanoir and Clairville with some assistance from Lamartine's *Histoire des Girondins* (Arch Street Theatre, April 1851). *Octavia Bragaldi* and *The Forest Princess* were published, together with some verse and short stories of a romantic character under the title of *Plays, Prose and Poetry* (Philadelphia, 1848).

[The best accounts of Mrs. Conner are given in Charles Durang, "The Phila. Stage," printed in *The Phila. Sunday Dispatch* (ser. 3, chs. 90, 94, 98, 102), and in J. N. Ireland, *Records of the N. Y. Stage* (1867), II. See also T. Allston Brown, *Hist. of the N. Y. Stage* (1903), I; James Rees, *Dramatic Authors of America* (1845); the introductions to the *Plays, Prose and Poetry;* and A. H. Quinn, *Hist. of the Am. Drama from the Beginning to the Civil War* (1923).] A. H. Q.

BARNES, JAMES (Dec. 28, 1801–Feb. 12, 1869), Union soldier and engineer, was born in Boston, Mass., the son of Jane and Capt. William Barnes. After graduating at the Latin School of Boston he entered commercial life, but, ardently desirous of a military career, gained admission to West Point, from which he graduated in 1829 as number five in a class containing such distinguished men as Robert E. Lee and Joseph E. Johnston. Assigned to the artillery, he served at Fort McHenry and later at West Point. He was promoted first-lieutenant in 1836. Visualizing little prospect of active service he resigned his commission in 1836 and entered the engineering field, where he achieved distinguished success, first as chief engineer and railroad superintendent and later in railroad construction. Between 1852 and 1857 he built six railroads.

With such a record of achievement he was appointed, upon the outbreak of the Civil War, colonel of the 18th Massachusetts Volunteers which, in August 1861, proceeded to Washington for training until March 1862. During McClellan's Peninsular campaign Barnes's regiment formed part of Fitz-John Porter's division, participating in the siege of Yorktown and in the battle of Mechanicsville, June 26, 1862. At the battles of Groveton and Antietam he successfully commanded a brigade in Morell's division of Porter's corps. With this brigade he marched in October and November 1862 to Falmouth, where he received his appointment as brigadier-general of volunteers on Nov. 29. In the Rappahannock campaign which followed, he led his brigade at Fredericksburg, being cited in orders by his division commander and at Chancellorsville, May 2–4, 1863, where, after gallantly participating in the battle, his brigade covered the retirement of the army over the Rappahannock. In May 1863 he was placed in temporary command of the 1st division, 5th corps, which guarded the Rappahannock fords until June 13, when the Union army moved northward paralleling Lee's march into Pennsylvania. Barnes's division arrived at Gettysburg and participated in the fighting of July 2 and 3. On the first day one brigade of his division (Vincent's), by seizing and holding Little Round Top, materially contributed to the Union victory. Barnes has been criticized for his seeming absence from the battlefield in the evening of July 2. Justice to him demands the statement that late in the afternoon of July 2 he was wounded in the left leg by a piece of shell. Unable to move, yet unwilling to leave, he remained on the field, turned over his command on July 3 to Gen. Charles Griffin, the permanent division commander who had returned to duty, and on July 9 was granted sick leave. He returned to his home at Springfield and, after the expiration of a twenty days' extension granted him, rejoined his division Aug. 18, 1863. Thereafter he commanded the defenses of Norfolk and Portsmouth and, in June 1864, the district of St. Mary's and the prisoners' camp at Point Lookout, Md., receiving there his brevet as major-general of volunteers for meritorious services during the Rebellion. He was mustered out Jan. 15, 1866. His health much impaired, he returned to civil life, but did not again take up the duties of his profession. He died in 1869 at Springfield, Mass.

[G. W. Cullum, *Biog. Reg.*, I; Old Files Section, A. G. O.; *Official Records*, vols. XI, XIX, XXI, XXV, XXVII, XL; O. W. Norton, *The Attack and Defence of Little Round Top* (1913); Old Records Div., A. G. O.; S. O. 184, Hdqrs. Army of the Potomac; S. O. 422 War Dept., Sept. 21, 1863; G. O. 148 War Dept., Oct. 14, 1865.]

C. A. B.

BARNES, JOSEPH K. (July 21, 1817–Apr. 5, 1883), surgeon-general, was born in Philadelphia, the son of Judge Joseph Barnes, a native of New England. He received an academic education at Round Hill School at Northampton, Mass., and entered upon a collegiate course at Harvard University. Compelled by ill health to leave college before graduation, he began the study of medicine with Dr. Thomas Harris of the Navy and received his medical degree from the University of Pennsylvania in 1838. He was appointed to the medical corps of the Army in 1840. His first three years of service were with the forces operating against the Seminole Indians in Florida. During the Mexican War, he was with a cavalry column that crossed the Rio Grande with the "Army of Occupation" and later with Gen. Scott's command he participated in every engagement until the capture of the City of Mexico. The outbreak of the Civil War found him at Vancouver Barracks. He was ordered east and served the first year of the war with the forces operating in Missouri. In May 1862 he was detailed as attending surgeon in the city of Washington. Here he fell under the eye of Secretary of War Stanton and when in September 1863 Gen. Hammond was relieved from his position as surgeon-general, Barnes was assigned as acting surgeon-general, and was appointed surgeon-general in August 1864, after the dismissal of Gen. Hammond. As chief of the medical department, Barnes gathered around him a group of brilliant officers and his régime was marked by the production of the voluminous *Medical and Surgical History of the War of the Rebellion* and by the development of the Army Medical Library and Army Medical Museum. It fell to his lot to share in the professional care of two murdered presidents. At the time of the assassination of President Lincoln and the attempted assassination of Secretary Seward, he attended the death-bed of the one and ministered to the successful restoration of the other. During the long illness of President Garfield, he was one of the surgeons who for weeks served in the chamber of the dying president. He reached the age of retirement in 1882 and died the following year. His remains lie in Oak Hill Cemetery, Georgetown, D. C. He was married to Mary Fauntleroy, daughter of Judge Fauntleroy of Winchester, Va.

[*The Surgeon General of the Army,* by James Evelyn Pilcher (Carlisle, Pa., 1905), contains a biog. sketch with portrait. *Am. Medic. Biogs.* (1920), ed. by Kelly and Burrage, also contains a sketch. A fine portrait in oil hangs in the Army Medic. Lib.]

J. M. P.

BARNES, MARY DOWNING SHELDON (Sept. 15, 1850–Aug. 27, 1898), educator, was born at Oswego, N. Y., the daughter of Edward Austin Sheldon and Frances (Stiles) Sheldon. Two years previous to her birth her father had started a "Ragged School" in Oswego and had introduced into it the methods and the spirit of the great Swiss schoolmaster, Pestalozzi. Edward A. Sheldon [*q.v.*] was later principal of the Oswego Normal and Training School. Mary Sheldon was educated in the public schools of Oswego and then in the Oswego Normal School, where she was imbued with her father's enthusiasm for better methods of education. From Oswego she went to the University of Michigan, one of the first women to attend a coeducational institution of higher learning. In a poem written during this period of her life she paid tribute to President Angell as the champion who had opened the gates of knowledge to women. She graduated from the University of Michigan in 1874. During the next two years she taught at the Oswego Normal School, leaving it in 1876 to become professor of history at Wellesley College, then in its infancy. While her work at Wellesley was highly successful, as pupils of hers have enthusiastically testified, she felt the need of broadening her experience and knowledge, and from 1880 to 1882 she traveled and studied in Europe. After her return she again taught at the Oswego Normal School, as instructor in history. In 1884 she married Earl Barnes, professor of history at the University of Indiana, and spent the next seven years of her life in studying, traveling, and writing. In 1891, however, both she and her husband accepted positions at Leland Stanford University, she to teach history, he as professor of education. She was the first woman to be appointed a member of the faculty of Leland Stanford University and her success more than justified the confidence that had been placed in her. In 1897 she left for Europe with her husband, intending to spend two years in study and travel. After more than a year spent in France and Italy, they went to London, where she began to delve among the treasures of the British Museum. Severe illness intervened, however, ending in her death.

In attempting to appraise her work it should be remembered that Mrs. Barnes seems to have placed more emphasis on method than on content. "Her teaching . . ." a former pupil of hers has said, "did not give us enough historical reading, I think, as she had, under the Normal School influences of her rearing, more interest in training the mind to draw right conclusions from data furnished than in enriching our stores of information." It was probably her most important and enduring contribution to the teaching of history that she was one of the first to have her pupils use historical sources and study them critically. She embodied her ideas in several books and many articles. Her *Studies in American History* (1891), written in collaboration with her husband, and her *Sheldon's General History* are filled with extracts from historical sources; and her theories are set forth in detail in her *Studies in General History* (1885) and *Studies in Historical Method* (1896). In appearance she was "small and delicate," according to one of her former pupils, "but agile and graceful, with beautiful, flashing blue eyes. She was in her manner gay and informal." If her success as a teacher was due in part to the inspiration of her father, to her training, travel, study, and experience, it was due also to her buoyant, esthetic personality.

[Katherine Lee Bates, "In Memoriam," *Wellesley Coll. Mag.,* Oct. 1898; Will S. Monroe, *Hist. of the Pestalozzian Movement in the U. S.* (1907), Will S. Monroe, sketch in *Jour. of Ed.,* Sept. 15, 1898; and A. P. Hollis, *The Contribution of the Oswego Normal School to Educ. Progress in the United States* (1898); letters from Miss Katherine L. Bates and Miss Ethel Roberts of Wellesley Coll., from Mr. O. L. Elliott, formerly of Stanford Univ., and from Prof. Teggart of the Univ. of California.]

J. F. S.

BARNEY, JOSHUA (July 6, 1759–Dec. 1, 1818), naval officer, was the seventh of the fourteen children of Frances (Holland) Barney and William Barney, whose father, the first William, came from England to Baltimore County, Md., about 1695. Joshua, with an inborn passion for the sea, was allowed to leave school at the age of ten, but was for three years restrained from following his natural bent, his father compelling him to enter commercial life, the drudgery of which he bore with increasing signs of impatience. Yielding at last to his plainly adventurous nature and his steadfast desire to follow the sea, his father, early in the year 1771, entrusted him to a Baltimore pilot, aboard whose craft he enjoyed a short but useful experience. The next year he was regularly apprenticed to Capt. Thomas Drysdale, his brother-in-law, who commanded a small brig in the Liverpool trade. Here the boy's extraordinary aptitude for his chosen profession became at once apparent. In January 1775, while on a voyage to Nice with a cargo of wheat, the captain died, and, there being no mate, Barney, at the age of fifteen, took command of the vessel, which, in a leaky condition on account of continued storms, he took safely into Gibraltar. Here he successfully negotiated the loan of a large sum for repairs and proceeded to Nice, where he sold his cargo to advantage in spite of the intrigues and extortions of the Sardinian officials. To circumvent these he made the arduous journey across the mountains to appeal personally to the British minister at Milan, who, astonished and delighted at the lad's boldness, interfered effectively in his behalf. On his way back to his native land, Barney took advantage of the opportunity to earn money for his employer by chartering his ship as a transport to the Spanish army, and was a witness of its defeat at Algiers, afterward conveying some of the defeated troops back to Alicante. Then, recrossing the Atlantic in the month of October, he appeared before his astonished employer, who with difficulty believed his romantic story.

In the same month, October 1775, Barney entered the service of the Colonies as sailing-master (master's mate) of the sloop *Hornet,* belonging to Commodore Hopkins's squadron, and so distinguished himself at the capture of New Providence in the West Indies, as well as in an engagement of Hazzlewood's flotilla with two strong British ships, acting on this occasion as a volunteer, that, in June 1776, he was commissioned lieutenant in the regular navy by Robert Morris, president of the Marine Committee of Congress, "in consequence of his good conduct with the flotilla." Serving gallantly in the sloop *Wasp* and afterward in the sloop *Sachem,* he was captured by a British ship while taking a prize into port, but was soon exchanged. In December 1777 he was appointed lieutenant of the frigate *Virginia,* and early in the next year he captured and took into Baltimore a large enemy sloop and a barge, his humane and courteous treatment of his prisoners earning him a letter of thanks, together with a present of English cheese and porter, from the British naval commander in those waters. On Apr. 1 the *Virginia,* in attempting to get to sea, was captured by the British, and Barney, together with a large number of other prisoners, was sent to New York in the *St. Albans,* after a bold and almost successful effort on his part to organize the prisoners and overpower the ship's crew. He was again exchanged in August 1778. As the activities of the American navy at sea were reduced at this time to almost nothing, owing to the complete control of the coasts by the British shipping, Barney accepted the command of several armed merchant vessels, more than once beating off the attacks of enemy privateers of greater tonnage and heavier armament than his own. In March 1780, in his twenty-first year, he married Anne, the daughter of Alderman Gunning Bedford [*q.v.*] of Philadelphia. Soon after he was ordered as first-lieutenant to the *Saratoga,* 16 guns, which, after capturing a number of enemy vessels, herself fell a victim to the British battle-ship *Intrepid.* Taken to England and confined for nearly a year in the Mill Prison near Plymouth, he escaped only to be retaken, but at the second attempt succeeded, through a series of romantic adventures and disguises, in reaching France and, late in December 1781, arrived at Boston, where John Hancock and Samuel Adams "paid him the honor of their special notice and flattering civilities."

The Messrs. Cabot of Beverly, well-known ship-builders, offered him the command of a new privateer of 20 guns, with the privilege of choosing his own cruising ground, but he was loath to make a definite engagement before seeing his family again, and in March 1782 he arrived at Philadelphia, where he found his wife and the little son born during his imprisonment. At this time the State of Pennsylvania, irritated at the annoying depredations of the many British "refugee barges and privateers" along her coast, began to fit out, at her own expense, a number of lightly armed vessels to operate in her own waters. Of one of these, the *Hyder-Ally,* a hastily converted merchantman mounting 16 six-pounders and carrying a crew of only 110 men, Barney was placed in command, with orders to convoy a fleet of merchant ships to the Capes, but on no account to proceed to sea. On Apr. 8, the fleet being anchored off Cape May awaiting a favorable wind, Barney observed the approach, with evidently hostile intent, of three British war-ships, and signaled for the convoy to stand up the Bay, while the *Hyder-Ally* covered the retreat. The fleet obeyed and eventually escaped with the exception of two vessels which ran aground. One of the enemy ships, the privateer *Fair American,* ran down the *Hyder-Ally,* but, as Barney held his position, she sheered off, at the same time firing a broadside, to which Barney did not reply, wishing to reserve himself for the ship astern which was coming up fast, and which afterward proved to be the *General Monk,* 20 guns, commanded by Capt. Rodgers, an officer of reputation. To fight this ship broadside to broadside would have been inviting disaster. Instead, the resourceful Barney, waiting for the enemy to get quite near, threw in his own broadside, righted his helm and kept away. The enemy stood boldly on when Barney, using, it is said, the ruse of shouting false orders to his helmsman who had been informed of the stratagem, placed his vessel in such a position that the jib-boom of the British ship became entangled in the fore-rigging of the *Hyder-Ally,* with the result that the guns of the *General Monk* could not bear and were useless, while those of the *Hyder-Ally* raked the *Monk* fore-and-aft. In twenty-six minutes the British ship, more than twice as powerful in men and metal as her adversary, struck her colors, and Barney, skilfully avoiding the other enemy vessels, took his prize triumphantly into Philadelphia. The American loss was only four killed and eleven wounded, while the loss aboard the *General Monk* was at least three times as heavy. "The action," says Cooper (*History of the Navy,* 1839, I, 237–38), "has been justly deemed one of the most brilliant that ever occurred under the American flag.... The steadiness with which Capt. Barney protected his convoy, the gallantry and conduct with which he engaged, and the perseverance with which he covered the retreat of his prize, all are deserving of high praise. Throughout the whole affair this officer discovered the qualities of a great naval captain; failing in no essential of that distinguished character." For this exploit, so heartening to the Colonial cause just at this time, Barney received the thanks of the State of Pennsylvania, which also presented him with a special sword of honor. Later in the year he was commissioned to bear official dispatches to Dr. Franklin in Paris, where he was made much of by the American Commissioners and by the French officers who had served in America, including Lafayette.

In 1783 came the peace with Great Britain. The navy was practically disbanded and the ships laid up or sold, though Barney continued in service until May 1784, longer than any other officer of the Revolutionary navy. There followed for him ten years of various peaceful activities, including commercial ventures by land and by sea, farming and exploration, in the course of which he visited parts of the South and the frontiers of Kentucky, where he found the rough, adventurous life much to his taste, and where he afterward purchased an estate. In 1787 and 1788 he took an active and influential part as an ardent Federalist, in the debates on the adoption of the Constitution, and had the honor of being for a week Washington's guest at Mt. Vernon. In November 1789 he was appointed Vendue Master by the General Assembly of Maryland, an office of profit which, however, he soon abandoned in order to embark in a commercial undertaking in the West Indies, which, though promising success at first, was eventually ruined by the disorders resultant from the French Revolution and the British "Orders in Council" of June 1793, under which Barney's ship, the *Sampson,* was condemned and confiscated by the Admiralty Court in Jamaica.

In 1794 Barney was named one of the captains to command the six new frigates constructed by Congress in consequence of the depredations of the Barbary corsairs, his name being placed third on the list but after that of Silas Talbot, who was ranked only by John Barry [*q.v.*]. Talbot, though connected with the sea in his youth and commissioned a captain in the navy in 1779, had never served aboard a ship in time of war, and Barney, actuated by a sensitive conception of pride and honor, declined the appointment which he had so hoped to receive, on the ground that he could not serve under an officer who had been junior to him in rank. Though it was pointed out to him that Talbot's rank dated from 1779 and the ranking was technical and implied no slight, Barney persisted in his resolution, though his title of captain was conferred upon him by the State of Pennsylvania and not by the Congress. There can be no question that an injustice was done Barney, who, as Cooper remarks (*Ibid.,* p. 239), "ought to have been presented with the commission of a captain in the American navy for the capture of the *Monk.*" This unfortunate episode, which caused the temporary retirement from his country's naval service of one of her most distinguished officers, was characteristic of the "general irregularities" (*Ibid.,*p. 239) then obtaining in the navy, growing out of the political exigencies of the times.

Returning to the merchant service, Barney took command of the *Cincinnatus,* out of Baltimore, and on July 30 arrived at Havre, having on board as a passenger the new American minister to France, James Monroe. The object of the journey was to recover the value of certain dratts on French officials given Barney in lieu of payment at St. Domingo, and to represent an American firm engaged in shipping flour to France. Accompanying Monroe to Paris, he was paid the compliment of being selected by the Minister to present an American flag to the National Convention, on which occasion he received the ceremonial "fraternal embrace." Soon after this he was offered the command of a 74-gun line-of-battle ship recently taken from the British, but declined, wishing first to carry out his commercial engagements. Bringing these to a close, he held himself at the disposal of the French Minister of Marine, and in the meantime fitted out a small privateer which preyed successfully on British commerce. In 1796 he was appointed captain and *chef de division* (commodore) in the French navy, in which he served with distinction until, after several attempts to resign, he was, in 1802, discharged and placed on the pension list of the Republic. The most brilliant feature of his French service was the manner in which while being watched by a much superior British force at St. Domingo, he succeeded in getting to sea with two frigates. Returning to Baltimore, he soon found his financial situation improved by the payment of certain long-outstanding debts, and, while continuing to engage in business, he permitted himself to be twice nominated for Congress by one of the Democratic factions, being defeated on each occasion. In 1805 he refused the superintendency of the new navy-yard at Washington offered him by President Jefferson. In 1809 he tendered his services to the new president, Madison, being highly indignant at the so-called "Chesapeake incident" (*vide* James Barron), but he does not seem to have reëntered the regular navy even at the breaking out of the war with Great Britain in 1812. Instead he embarked in privateering enterprises on a large scale, numerous and valuable prizes being taken by the armed vessels under his control, and often under his personal command, during the next two years.

Called to Washington by the secretary of the navy in July 1814, for consultation in regard to the protection of that capital, then seriously threatened by a combined sea and land attack, Barney was placed in command of a flotilla of barges carrying heavy guns, together with a few galleys and several schooners, manned by sailors and marines, and for several weeks held the British forces at bay, their repeated attacks being smartly repulsed. On Aug. 16 he reported to the Navy Department that the British were ascending the Patuxent in force, and he was directed to disembark his men and retire to Washington, which, however, he left early on the morning of Aug. 24, proceeding by a forced march to Bladensburg to meet the advance of the British detachment. There his little body of some 500 men were placed at the center of Gen. Winder's position, Barney himself directing the artillery (2 eighteens and 3 twelve-pounder ship's guns mounted on carriages), while Capt. Miller of the marines commanded the rest of Barney's company, seventy marines and 370 seamen armed as infantry. As at Bunker Hill, the two first attacks of the British were bloodily repulsed, chiefly by Barney's guns, but the enemy assaults on the American militia to right and left found such feeble resistance that the little band of sailors and marines was soon flanked and at length forced to abandon the field, leaving both Barney and Miller wounded and in the hands of the enemy, who lost no time in pressing his advance and seizing the national capital. This heroic resistance of the force under Barney alone saved the combat at Bladensburg from being an unqualified disgrace to American arms. He was presented by the city of Washington with a sword of honor, and was afterward appointed Naval Officer at Baltimore, a position which he held for a short time only. He died at Pittsburgh on Dec. 1, 1818, while returning from a visit to his Kentucky estate. "Capt. Barney," says Cooper, "is said to have engaged in twenty-six combats, all of which were against the English, and in nearly all of which he was successful."

[Besides the MSS. in the Office of Naval Records and Lib. at Washington and the several histories of the Am. navy, the following volumes may be consulted: *A Biog. Memoir of the Late Commodore Joshua Barney: from Autobiographical Notes and Journals,* ed. by Mary Barney (1832); *Commodore Joshua Barney* (1912), compiled by W. F. Adams; Ralph D. Paine, *Joshua Barney, a Forgotten Hero of Blue Water* (1924).]

E. B.

BARNUM, FRANCES COURTENAY BAYLOR. [See BAYLOR, FRANCES COURTENAY, 1848–1920.]

BARNUM, HENRY A. (Sept. 24, 1833–Jan. 29, 1892), Union soldier, was born at Jamesville, Onondaga County, N. Y. Descent has been claimed from an English titled family Barnham; the American ancestor was Thomas Barnum (1625–95). Henry's parents were Alanson Levi and Beersheba (Pixley) Barnum. He was educated at Syracuse Institute, and prior to the Civil War was a teacher, studied law and was admitted to the bar, and belonged to the Syracuse militia. He enlisted at the outset of the war, and on May 13, 1861, was chosen captain of company I in the 12th New York Volunteers which he had helped to organize. With this regiment he participated in the first Bull Run campaign, and took part in the preliminary engagement at Blackburn's Ford on July 18, 1861. According to the usual accounts, his company remained firm, and he was particularly commended by Gen. Tyler (according to William Swinton, *Campaigns of the Army of the Potomac,* 1866, p. 48, the 12th New York was completely "disrupted"). He was commissioned major on Nov. 1, 1861, and was a member of Gen. Wadsworth's staff. He fought in various battles of the Peninsular campaign, but his chief distinction came in the concluding one at Malvern Hill on July 1, 1862. At first on the staff of Gen. Butterfield, later in the day he led a charge at the head of his regiment, and was shot through the body. "Surgeons pronounced the wound fatal, and he was left for dead on the field that night, and the official reports of the battle gave his name among the killed" (*New York Tribune,* Jan. 30, 1892). A eulogy on his career was delivered at Syracuse, and the city sent a committee to bring home the body. "Union soldiers built a rough fence around the grave of a buried officer at Harrison's Landing on the James River and set up a headboard with this roughly inscribed legend, 'Major Henry A. Barnum, 12th New York Volunteers. Killed July 1, 1862, at Malvern Hill'" (New York *Sun,* Jan. 30, 1892). In reality, "He was captured by the enemy, and for eight days was in the battlefield hospital, whence he was carried in an old express wagon to Libby Prison. . . . On July 18 he was exchanged" (*New York Tribune,* Jan. 30, 1892). Or, according to another and different account: "Contrary to many reports of this incident, he was not abandoned on the field as dead, but was conveyed by a special detail of his own men to the Malvern House and put under care of surgeons. After the National forces had withdrawn to Harrison's Landing, and while a sufferer at the Malvern House, he, with many others of the wounded under treatment there, was captured by the Confederates and taken to Libby Prison, where he was confined till July 18 following, when he was exchanged" (*Appleton's Annual Cyclopædia,* 1892, p. 533).

Because of his wound Barnum obtained several leaves of absence. Meanwhile he recruited the 149th New York, a cosmopolitan regiment, containing companies of Germans, Irish, and Jews, and was commissioned its colonel on Sept. 17, 1862. He took good care of his men, but his absences were considered unfortunate for the regiment. He fought at Gettysburg, and at Lookout Mountain he was shot in the arm. While on the journey to Washington with the Confederate flags captured in that battle, his old wound reopened, and required heroic treatment. "His wound . . . was considered one of the most remarkable wounds of the war. The government published a history of it, with his portrait, in the surgical and medical history of the war" (*New York Tribune,* Jan. 30, 1892). Recovering, he took part in Sherman's Georgia campaign, was wounded again at Peachtree Creek on July 20, 1864, and commanded the 3rd brigade of the 20th corps in the march to the sea. He led the advance into Savannah, conducting a picked force over the parapets, and guarded the vast stores of cotton from destruction. He was brevetted brigadier-general of volunteers on Jan. 12, 1865, and major-general of volunteers on Mar. 13; he was commissioned brigadier-general of volunteers on May 31, and was for a short time in command of a provisional brigade in the military district of Vermont, New Hampshire, and Massachusetts. Declining a colonelcy in the regular army, he resigned on Jan. 9, 1866.

After the war Barnum practised law in New York City, and held various public offices. In succession he was inspector of prisons in the state, to which position he was elected in 1865; deputy tax commissioner 1869–72; harbor master and port warden from 1888 until his death in New York. He had also served as Republican assemblyman in the legislature. With a high reputation for bravery and patriotism, he was a friend of Grant, Sherman, and other noted men, and was prominent in various military organizations, being Past Commander of the G. A. R. of the Department of New York. He delivered an oration at Detroit before the Society of the Army of the Cumberland on Nov. 15, 1871. From the War Department he received the medal of honor on July 16, 1889, and a gold medal was awarded to him by Congress (*Appleton's Annual Cyclopædia,* 1892). He was twice married: first to Lavina King, and second to Josephine Reynolds.

[Geo. K. Collins, *Memoirs of the 149th Regt. N. Y. Vol. Inf.* (1891); Franklin H. Chase, *Syracuse and Its Environs* (1924); N. Y. newspapers of Jan. 30, 1892; Geo. J. Hagar (?) in *Appleton's Annual Cyc.* (1892); Eben L. and Francis Barnum, *Geneal. Rec. of the Barnum Family* (1912), p. 92.]

E. K. A.

BARNUM, PHINEAS TAYLOR (July 5, 1810–Apr. 7, 1891), "the great American showman," was himself the greatest of his shows, and knew it. When Mme. Tussaud's representative asked him if he was willing to be immortalized in wax for her famous London museum, he replied: "Willing?—Anxious! What's a show without notoriety!" And he sent her an outfit of his clothing from socks to waistcoat. For more than fifty years his name was connected with public entertainment. He openly declared that the public desired to be humbugged, and his hoaxes and impudence were unlimited. He found the American public without easy means of innocent diversion, and left it changed in habit, taught to play, and served with entertainment of complex variety. In this change he played perhaps the leading part.

His ancestors were American, of Yankee stock; his father, Philo F. Barnum, of Bethel, Conn., ran the range of farming, store-keeping, and some of the simpler crafts, without leaving to his son an inheritance of great financial value. His mother was named Irena Taylor. The young Barnum had an aversion to manual labor, and was willing to use his wits to save his muscles; but until he was twenty-five years of age he found no route to prosperity that suited his taste and talent. He kept store and tended bar, ran an abolition newspaper and did odd jobs, sold tickets for a theatre and thus drifted into his career. It was Joice Heth who pointed the way to fortune, and led Barnum to it from the moment of his opening of her receptions in Niblo's Garden, a New York place of entertainment, on Aug. 10, 1835. Joice was a negress, old, wizened, and vituperative, who, when Barnum first learned of her existence, was being exhibited unprofitably in Philadelphia as the nurse of George Washington, 161 years of age. Accompanying her were yellowed papers, including what purported to be an original bill of sale from Augustine Washington, the father of George, dated Feb. 5, 1727, and describing her as then fifty-four years of age. She had been coached to remember all the details of the nursing of the illustrious infant; including with the memories of his youth the famous cherry-tree incident (which, however, she related to a peach-tree). "She has been a member of the Baptist Church for upwards of one hundred years, and seems to take great satisfaction in the conversation of ministers who visit her," wrote Barnum in her advertisement. He bought the rights in her as a curio, and exhibited the woman against a background of patriotic press notices, as long as nature would allow. When she died, too soon for Barnum, and the unkind autopsy showed her age to have been about eighty years, he buried her in his family lot and capitalized her again by running a series of newspaper articles attacking her authenticity and defending his own good faith. Bennett of the *New York Herald* was taken in by the second phase of his hoax, as he had been by the first, and gave much space in his paper to this exposure of the imposture (Sept. 8, 13, 17, 24, 1836). Thus, said Barnum, when age had turned him to reflection, the "least deserving of all my efforts in the show line was the one which introduced me to the business" (*Struggles and Triumphs,* 1874, p. 73).

After Joice Heth there was a period of unprofitable effort in Barnum's life, but there was a persistent drift toward the show business, with acrobatic troupes and a few wild animals on the bill. In 1841 he was in New York dickering with the owners of Scudder's American Museum, who were running a losing race with Peale's Museum. Both concerns had their halls of curios and specimens, and their plaintive advertisements called in vain for public favor. Without gold, but with, as he said, "much brass," Barnum bought first Scudder's and then Peale's, and opened early in 1842 an institution that for a generation was to delight the children of New York and the country visitors. "The American Museum was the ladder by which I rose to fame," he later said. "Keep it before the public," he advertised; " . . . this magnificent establishment has passed into new hands. . . . The place is nightly crowded with the élite of the city. . . . Instruction is blended with amusement." Twice burned down (July 13, 1865, and Mar. 3, 1868), but fully reported each time, the American Museum provided a durable medium for ingenious hoax. There was Niagara Falls, the woolly horse, the Feejee Mermaid, and the bearded lady, whom the skeptics believed to be no lady at all. There was the "Egress," in pursuit of which many an eager patron hurried through the halls, until he found himself outside the Museum. There was a genuinely interesting and diversified collection of museum material, consisting of minerals, fossils, and natural-history specimens. There were playlets on the stage, and freaks on the platforms of the showroom. Above all, there was for many years Gen. Tom Thumb (Charles Sherwood Stratton, 1838–83, *q.v.*), an engaging dwarf whom Barnum found as a lad, and whom he developed into a great celebrity.

With Tom Thumb under his management, Barnum first invaded Europe in 1844, exhibiting his protégé to Victoria and her young family. In Paris he gained the favor of the court, and display space for Tom Thumb and his miniature coach in the imperial enclosure at Longchamps. He was back in England again in 1858, when he lectured at St. James's Hall, Regent St., on "The Science of Money Making, and the Philosophy of Humbug." Since he was a prime exhibit for both, he was a great success, and launched the vogue for American humorists in England, which Mark Twain kept afloat in 1873 with his famous monologue on "Our Fellow Savages of the Sandwich Islands." While in England, Barnum was captivated by the pavilion erected by George IV at Brighton. It was a residence in Indian style, decorated with endless columns and arches, and was novel enough for a showman's home. He had the house copied; and he erected from the drawings a home, "Iranistan," at Bridgeport, Conn., near the field where he maintained an elephant to pull a plow whenever a train passed along the railroad near-by. The housewarming of this curiosity of domestic architecture was another occasion for wide advertising; but its complete destruction by fire

(Dec. 18, 1857) had even greater salvage in the way of publicity.

In the spirit of the impresario, rather than that of the ordinary showman, Barnum brought Jenny Lind to America for a long concert tour in 1850. At the height of her fame in Europe, the Swedish singer had just turned away from opera and its demoralizing influences, to spend the rest of her career on the concert stage. Barnum, with no introduction but his nerve, offered her a profitable contract, which she accepted on a chance. He met her at quarantine, when she arrived in New York, Sept. 1, 1850, and of course had a reporter there to note how he climbed up the ladder "with a choice bouquet carefully stuck in the bosom of his white vest." Bayard Taylor had already written a prize poem for her to sing at her first recital at Castle Garden ten days later. Her tour made Jenny Lind a rich woman, and a sort of "America's sweetheart" two generations ahead of Mary Pickford. It started a long procession of European artists to America.

In the later sixties Barnum sat in the legislature of Connecticut, and even ran for Congress. He determined to retire from the museum business, adjusted his affairs, took a private car of guests over the Union Pacific Railroad, newly opened in 1869; and returned to Connecticut to yearn for the old life and to organize "The Greatest Show on Earth."

With a fully developed circus, which soon had three rings under the main top, he opened this last great speculation in Brooklyn, Apr. 10, 1871; and thereafter for twenty years its opening, generally at Madison Square Garden, marked the official arrival of outdoor spring. "Can a public be satisfied with only eleven camels?" asked the *New York Times,* in a quizzical mood the day after the show began. There was no giraffe in the original menagerie, but the press agent improvised a sad tale of feeding one to the lions to keep them alive on a hard voyage of the animal ship across the Atlantic; and there were four to be burned to death when the menagerie, in connection with the Museum which was still functioning, burned down on Dec. 24, 1872. The papers suggested, quite without foundation it appears, that the numerous fires were only part of the advertising campaign; but Barnum bore it all. He wrote to the editor of the *New York Tribune* in 1877: "I don't care much what the papers say about me, provided they will say something." He had one more fire to reckon with; which on Nov. 20, 1887, destroyed the winter quarters of his circus at Bridgeport.

The first decade of "The Greatest Show on Earth" witnessed the transition of the circus from the wagon show to the railroad show, and the substitution of electricity for the gasoline flares and the calcium lights of the older period. But there was little to be added in the way of organizing skill, or dexterity of the artists. As Barnum grew older, and the competition of the young men who copied his methods became more fierce, he combined forces with the keenest of his rivals, launching the firm of Barnum & Bailey as the result, and opening under the new name in New York, Mar. 28, 1881. To the United States in the following spring he brought Jumbo, who ranked with Tom Thumb and Jenny Lind as the greatest of his exploits in pure showmanship. Jumbo was a huge African elephant, long the pride of the Royal Zoological Society in London. He was sold to Barnum & Bailey in a moment of financial strait, to be regretted instantly when the British press broke out into frantic protest against this American vandalism. Barnum encouraged the protests, but imported the elephant; technically "for breeding purposes," to escape the payment of duty; and he flooded the press with cuts of "The Only Mastodon on Earth," "The Gentle and Historic Lord of Beasts," feeding from third-story windows as he walked along the circus parade. Jumbo earned his cost in his first few weeks in America, and kept up his artistic character to the end, dying a hero's death Sept. 15, 1885, when he was run down by a locomotive. The press agent told how the courageous brute sacrificed himself to save the baby elephant, "Tom Thumb," from destruction. And three days later Barnum was already inquiring of the publishing house of Harper whether they would like to publish an illustrated life of Jumbo for the holidays. Subsequently a female elephant, Alice, was imported from the Royal Zoological Society to take Jumbo's place, was advertised as the widow of Jumbo, and took her station between the stuffed hide of her lord and his articulated skeleton. Later, after she perished in the Bridgeport fire, the remnants of Jumbo were turned over to the natural-history museum of Tufts College, of which Barnum was a benefactor.

In 1889 Barnum rounded out his long career by going to London, where his show exhibited at Olympia and maintained its prestige as an institution. No feature of the circus was more applauded than the circuit of the arena made by Barnum himself in an open carriage; and young Prince George, now George V, was so enthralled that he announced his determination to see the show through "until they sing God Save Grandmother."

Barnum was twice married; in 1829 to Charity Hallett, who died in 1873; and in 1874 to Nancy Fish; but he left no heir to carry on the showman's trade.

[Barnum published his *Life of P. T. Barnum Written by Himself* (1855), as part of his prolific advertising. Thereafter it was often revised, reprinted, and continued to date. It is generally accurate in matters of fact, and can be checked from date to date in the daily press. Many copies he deposited, with autograph letters of gift, in the libraries of the United States. He wrote, or had written, various circus stories for boys. M. R. Werner, *Barnum* (1923) utilized the *Life*, the special collections of Barnum material in the N. Y. Pub Lib. and the Harvard theatrical collection, and the private collections of Leonidas Westervelt and Harry Houdini. See also Joel Benton, *Life of Hon. Phineas T. Barnum* (1891); Chas. J. Finger, *Life of Barnum* (1924); Harvey W. Root, *The Unknown Barnum* (1928).]

F. L. P—n.

BARNUM, ZENUS (Dec. 9, 1810–Apr. 5, 1865), railroad builder, hotel keeper, capitalist, was born near Wilkes-Barre, Pa., the son of Richard and Roseanna (Jemison) Barnum. Of his youth and schooling little is recorded except that he was educated to be a civil engineer. He became a contractor and builder, taking part in the construction of several of the early railroads in Pennsylvania and Maryland. In 1840 he moved to Baltimore to become a partner with his uncle, David Barnum, owner of Barnum's City Hotel, established in 1826. As the associate of David he succeeded, after an interval of some years, his cousin Theron (1803–78) who later became widely known as the owner of Barnum's Hotel in St. Louis. Baltimore was preeminently the convention city of America; the first six National Democratic Conventions (1832–52), the anti-Masonic Convention of 1831, and the Whig Conventions of 1831, 1844, and 1852 met there, and as Barnum's Hotel was the most popular gathering place for the delegates, the fame of uncle and nephew as hospitable Bonifaces was carried to the remotest parts of the nation. On May 10, 1844, David died, and Zenus became sole owner. He was married, Mar. 9, 1848, to Annie B. McLaughlin. About the same time, with two friends, he organized the North American Telegraph Company and contracted with Alexander Bain for the use of his patents in telegraphy on a line to be run from Washington to New York. This line, popularly known as the "Bain Line," was hastily built, reaching New York in December, and under the vigorous presidency of Barnum the company became a strong competitor to the Magnetic Telegraph Company, owned by the group headed by Samuel F. B. Morse. In an infringement suit brought by Morse against Bain the priority of the Morse patents was completely established and on Jan. 1, 1852, the Bain Line was incorporated into the Magnetic Telegraph with Barnum as president. Somewhat later Barnum accepted the presidency of the Baltimore Central Railroad and soon brought it out of a state of insolvency. Another consolidation in the field of telegraphy came on Nov. 1, 1859, when a rapidly growing competitor, the American Telegraph Company, took over the Magnetic properties, Barnum again being chosen as president. His management of Barnum's Hotel had for several years been merely nominal, and in 1857 he had turned over the property to Andrew McLaughlin (probably a brother-in-law). A few years later he seems to have withdrawn from active business, but on McLaughlin's death, Jan. 29, 1863, he resumed the management of the hotel, which he retained until his death. "He was distinguished," said the *Baltimore Sun,* "for his eminently sound judgment and enlarged practical views." In both telegraphy and railroading he was a pioneer, and he came to be known as an organizer and executive of marked ability. He was public-spirited, especially in all that related to the welfare of Baltimore. He was also a "friendly man," of generous disposition and of a winning geniality of manner.

[E. L. and Francis Barnum, *Geneal. Rec. of the Barnum Family* (1912); S. I. Prime, *Life of Samuel F. B. Morse* (1875); J. D. Reid, *The Telegraph in America* (1886); obituaries in the *Sun* and the *Gazette* of Baltimore, Apr. 6, 1865. References to Barnum's City Hotel in Jacob Frey, *Reminiscences of Baltimore* (1893); J. Thos. Scharf, *Hist. of Baltimore City and County* (1881) and *Chronicles of Baltimore* (1874); John C. Gobright, *City Rambles, or Baltimore as It Is* (1857). A sketch of Theron Barnum appears in *Edwards's Great West* (1860), by Richard Edwards and M. Hopewell.]

W. J. G.

BARNWELL, JOHN (*c.* 1671–June 1724), Carolinian officer and colonial agent, was a native of Ireland who emigrated to South Carolina in 1701. By the time of the Tuscarora outbreak he had become a trusted official in the colony of South Carolina, serving as deputy secretary, clerk of the council, and comptroller. He had also taken part as a volunteer against the French and Spaniards in Queen Anne's War. The Tuscaroras in North Carolina, alarmed by the establishment of a Swiss colony at New Bern, had perpetrated an appalling massacre in 1711. Aid was summoned from Virginia and South Carolina, and the latter province responded by sending Col. Barnwell. He conducted a skilful forest march from Charleston to the Neuse River, at the head of a small body of militia and several hundred Indians. He assaulted the palisaded fort in January 1712, and inflicted a considerable blow upon the Tuscaroras. For this service he was thanked by the authorities of North Carolina, though a few months later the government of that colony was dissatisfied with his conduct. The grounds of criticism appear to have been that he made a treaty with the Indians, and then allowed the treaty to be violated. The matter has proved a subject of controversy among local historians. Barnwell was, however, apparently highly esteemed throughout the region for many years after, and was known popularly as "Tuscarora John." In 1715 he was employed in his own colony in warfare with the Yemassee Indians.

In 1720 Barnwell was in London as the agent of the temporary government, since South Carolina had just overthrown the rule of the Proprietors. He coöperated with the other agent Boone in urging action upon the Board of Trade and Plantations, showing the need of protection from natives, Spaniards, and pirates. He was consulted on the preparation of a report on the new form of government, and his advice was asked especially on the establishment of a frontier post. Returning with the new governor, Nicholson, he built in 1721 a post named Fort King George on the Altamaha River, thereby giving offense to the Spaniards. He was regarded as well-informed in military affairs, and commanded the troops in the southern part of the colony. His last public office was as a member of the committee of correspondence to confer with agents on colonial matters. He was married to Anne Berners, according to tradition a sister of an English merchant residing in Charleston.

[Christoph von Graffenried, *Account of the Founding of New Bern,* a contemporary record ed. by Vincent H. Todd (1920); "The Tuscarora Expedition: Letters of Col. John Barnwell" in *S. C. Hist. and Geneal. Mag.* (1908), pp. 28–54; *Ibid.* (1901); Francis L. Hawks, *Hist. of N. C.* (1857), II, 537–42; Edward McCrady, *Hist. of S. C. under the Royal Government* (1899); E. B. Greene, *Provincial America* (1905); also the local histories by R. D. W. Connor, John W. Moore, for North Carolina, and Yates Snowden for South Carolina.] E. K. A.

BARNWELL, ROBERT WOODWARD (Aug. 10, 1801–Nov. 5, 1882), educator, Confederate statesman, was connected by blood with many leading Carolina families. Son of Robert, Revolutionary veteran and member of Congress (1791–93), and Elizabeth Wigg Hayne Barnwell, he was born near Beaufort, center of many Barnwell plantations (Harriette Leiding, *Historic Houses of South Carolina,* 1921, p. 233). After preliminary training in private schools of Beaufort and of Charleston, he entered Harvard, where he graduated in 1821 with highest honors. Having settled in Beaufort, he married on Aug. 9, 1827, Eliza Barnwell, a second cousin. Already he had entered upon a public career, having been chosen a member of the South Carolina House of Representatives in 1826; and in 1829 he was elected, without opposition, to Congress, where he sat until 1833. He signed the Ordinance of Nullification, Nov. 24, 1832. After retiring to his plantation, he was, in 1835, named president of South Carolina College (now the state university), succeeding Thomas Cooper, whose radicalism had damaged the prestige of the school. Barnwell restored public confidence, increased enrolment, added two dormitories, enlarged the library, and materially strengthened the institution.

After 1841, when he retired because of poor health, he lived again upon his plantation until June 4, 1850, when, by special appointment of Gov. Seabrook, he entered the Senate as Calhoun's successor. During his brief term, which expired in December 1850, he was active in defending the Southern position but his spirit was magnanimous. Opposed to the admission of California, for example, he nevertheless presented the credentials of Frémont, first senator from that state. As private citizen again, Barnwell interested himself in the varied efforts to define and enforce the slaveholders' view, though his attitude was moderate rather than extreme. He was in the convention which passed the ordinance of secession, was one of a committee of seven to draw up a "Declaration of Immediate Causes," was one of three commissioners appointed to treat with President Buchanan, and was named a delegate to the Southern Congress in Montgomery, February 1861. He was elected temporary chairman of this body; and he signed the Confederate constitution. Davis, who esteemed Barnwell highly, offered him the portfolio of state but Barnwell's modesty led him to decline. He represented South Carolina in the Confederate Senate.

His property destroyed during the war, Barnwell moved early in 1865 to Greenville, but in December of that year, through the interest of Gov. Perry, he was appointed chairman of the faculty of the University of South Carolina. Removed in 1873 by the mixed board of trustees, he conducted in Columbia a school for girls until 1877, when he was named by Gov. Hampton librarian of the University. He remained in this position until his death.

[For the Barnwell family, see *S. C. Hist. and Geneal. Mag.,* II, 56, 73–74; for Barnwell's career as educator, Maximilian La Borde, *Hist. of the S. C. Coll:* (1859), pp. 236–44, and Edwin L. Green, *Hist. of the Univ. of S. C.* (1916), pp. 45, 49, 105; for his record and speeches as senator, *Cong. Globe,* vol. XXI: for his relation to the secession movement, Yates Snowden, *Hist. of S. C.*, vol. II (1920); for brief biog. sketch and eulogy, B. F. Perry, *Reminiscences of Public Men* (1883).]

F. P. G.

BARR, AMELIA EDITH HUDDLESTON (Mar. 29, 1831–Mar. 10, 1919), author, was born in Ulverston, Lancashire, England, the daughter of the Rev. William Henry Huddleston and his wife Mary. The Huddlestons were of good English stock, and Amelia's father possessed an income in addition to his salary, so that the child had a chance to grow up in an environment favorable to ambition and ideals. She was sent to a dame's school in Shipley, and to private schools in Penrith, Ripon, and elsewhere. When her father lost most of his money through the treachery of a friend, Amelia was forced to prepare to make her own living. She was sent, at the age of sixteen, as a second teacher to a Miss Berner's school; then she went to the Normal School at Glasgow to learn to teach in a general school. Here she met Robert Barr, whom she married, on July 11, 1850, at the age of nineteen. She met Henry Ward Beecher and Harriet Beecher Stowe, on a visit of theirs to England, and they suggested that she come to America, Beecher offering to give her friendly aid if she did so. In 1853, her husband having become bankrupt, she suggested that they leave England and settle in America. They landed in New York Sept. 5, 1853, and at first located in Chicago, where Mrs. Barr opened a school for girls, but because of a political controversy in which her husband became involved, they left hurriedly and started for Texas. On the way they stopped in Memphis, Tenn., where Mrs. Barr was moved by a scene in the slave market. Leaving Memphis suddenly because of an outbreak of yellow fever, they took passage to Texas on a slave ship, where Mrs. Barr's compassion was further aroused. When they arrived at Galveston, they learned that yellow fever was there, too, so they proceeded to Austin. Here she met Sam Houston and other leaders of the new State. Robert Barr was employed as a professional accountant to straighten out the records of the Republic of Texas. Later the Barrs moved to Galveston, where Robert Barr and two sons died in the yellow-fever epidemic of 1867. Just at that time, another child was born to Mrs. Barr, which also died. She and her three daughters continued to make their home in Texas until 1868, when they came to New York and established themselves, with only $5.18 on hand, in rooms in Amity St., once occupied by Poe. Mrs. Barr now took up the profession of authorship, under the encouragement of Henry Ward Beecher, who helped her to find a market for her writings in the *Christian Union* and elsewhere. General recognition came to her with the publication of her *Jan Vedder's Wife* (1885). She wrote in all about eighty books, novels, poetry, miscellanies. Her best-known works, besides *Jan Vedder's Wife*, are *A Bow of Orange Ribbon* (1886), *The Maid of Maiden Lane* (1900), *The Strawberry Handkerchief* (1908), and *The House on Cherry Street* (1909). Mrs. Barr wrote many love stories, tales of married life as well as of young love, but stressed romance rather than the sex element, so that her work could safely be put in the hands of children and young people. She frequently introduced historical material into her fiction, recording various struggles for liberty in European and American history. Her work shows a strong tinge of religion, as she had a good deal of the mystic in her mental make-up. Her books were written too fast to be other than superficial, but they had a wide audience in their day, and some of them are still read.

[Autobiographical writings by Amelia E. Barr: *All the Days of My Life* (1913), and "My Work and Health at 83," in *Ladies' Home Jour.*, XXXII; Hildegarde Hawthorne, "Amelia E. Barr, Some Reminiscences," *Bookman*, LI, 283; H. E. Blake, "Mrs. Barr and Her Story," *Ibid.*, XXXVII, 617; "Amelia E. Barr and the Novice," *Ibid.*, LVIII, 172; articles in the *Dial*, LV, 76; *Nation*, XCVII, 144; *Review of Reviews*, LIX, 548.]

D. S.

BARR, CHARLES (July 11, 1864–Jan. 24, 1911), captain of racing yachts, was born in Scotland at Gourock on the Firth of Clyde. His nautical experience, as was usual in that neighborhood, began early. For a while he was apprenticed to a grocer, and one cold, hard winter he spent on a flounder trawler. What finally made a yachtsman of him was doubtless the success of his brother John, who early became a noted skipper. In 1884 he and John took the forty-foot cutter *Clara* to the United States and sailed her in a number of races. Charles liked America so well that he decided to stay, and in 1889 became a naturalized citizen. For the rest of his life he was in the employment of wealthy yacht owners. His career, unmatched by any other racing skipper, was a series of almost unbroken successes. During his first years in America he was in command of the *Shona, Minerva,* which he brought over from England, *Oweene, Wasp, Gloriana, Navahoe, Vigilant,* and *Colonia.* In 1899 he commanded the *Columbia* in her races with *Shamrock I.* In 1901 he beat *Shamrock II* with the *Columbia,* and in 1903 beat *Shamrock III* with the *Reliance.* Sailing the old schooner *Shamrock* he won the $1,000 Lipton Cup for Frederick Thompson in a race off Cape May. In 1904 he took Morton

F. Plant's *Ingomar* across the Atlantic and won nineteen out of twenty-two races with her in English and German waters. In 1905, with the three-masted schooner yacht *Atlantic,* owned by Wilson Marshall, he won the German Emperor's Cup for a race across the ocean. Barr's time to the Lizard, the finishing point, was twelve days, four hours—3,013 miles at an average speed of 10.31 knots. Thereafter he had charge of two seventy-foot yachts: August Belmont's *Mineola* and Cornelius Vanderbilt's *Rainbow.* In 1910 he took Alexander Smith Cochran's *Westward* to Europe and at Cowes and Kiel made a perfect record. In eleven races of the A class the *Westward* finished first every time. The following winter Barr spent with his wife and family at Southampton, which was Mrs. Barr's native place. He died of heart failure one morning while eating breakfast. In America Barr had lived for the last seven years in New London, Conn. Intelligence, daring, and constant study made Barr the king of racing skippers. "Wee Charlie," as he was sometimes called, was five feet three inches tall. He was dark almost to swarthiness, had keen black eyes and bushy brows, and was habitually taciturn. Watchful of wind, water, and every movement of his opponents, he lost no chance to gain an inch. He took every advantage that a timid rival would give him, and sometimes frightened his crew by the huge spread of sail that he would order on. At first he was unpopular with the American public because of his foreign birth, but his success quieted the murmurers. Among yachtsmen he was universally admired.

[*N. Y. Herald, N. Y. Times, London Times,* Jan. 25, 1911; *Yachting,* Mar. 1911, p. 216; H. L. Stone, *The "America's" Cup Races* (1914); W. M. Thompson and T. W. Lawson, *The Lawson Hist. of the America's Cup* (1902).]

G. H. G.

BARRADALL, EDWARD (1704–June 19, 1743), lawyer, came of good stock as is indicated by the inscription on his tombstone in Burton Church, Williamsburg, which describes him as "armiger," *i.e.,* having a vested right to use coat armor. The place of his birth is not known, nor is the exact date, but it may be confidently assumed that his parents were Henry Barradall and Catherine Blumfield, who were married in England, June 6, 1696. His education was received in England, and he was called to the bar at the Inner Temple. He emigrated to Virginia with his two brothers and two sisters, commenced the practise of law at Williamsburg, and married, Jan. 5, 1735/6, Sarah, daughter of William Fitzhugh of Stafford, Va., and grand-daughter of Col. William Fitzhugh. The early legal reports indicate that he enjoyed a large practise. In 1734 he became legal adviser to Lord Fairfax, Proprietor of the Northern Neck of Virginia, and drafted the act for the quieting of titles to land in the colony, which had been endangered owing to the dubious provisions of the will of Catherine Culpeper, Lady Fairfax (F. Harrison, *Virginia Land Grants,* 1925, pp. 104–8). He was appointed attorney-general of Virginia, Nov. 18, 1737, becoming also judge of the court of vice admiralty, and representative in the General Assembly for William and Mary College. He continued a member of the General Assembly at the sessions of November 1738, May 1740, August 1740, and May 1742, and retained his official position till his death, which occurred at Williamsburg, June 19, 1743. He died childless, neither of his brothers or sisters married, and the family therefore became extinct.

Barradall was the author of "Cases Adjudged in the General Court of Virginia from April 1733 to October 1741." They consist of notes of judicial decisions during the time he was practising law in the colony. It is doubtful if they were assembled with a view to publication, though great care is evinced in the statements of material facts, and the exact points decided. As had theretofore been the custom in the English reports, there are no head notes, and, since the General Court never delivered written opinions, there are almost invariably no stated reasons for the decisions, neither are the arguments dealt with adequately. Despite these defects the reports are very instructive, dealing with construction of wills or deeds relating to land, actions of trespass involving ownership of real estate, actions of detinue relative to ownership of slaves, and occasional suits for slander, thus giving a vivid picture of the course of litigation in the early days of the colony. After Barradall's death his manuscript passed through a number of hands, and the original is lost. The text, taken from a copy in the Virginia State Library, was published in *Virginia Colonial Decisions,* edited by Robert T. Barton.

[All that is known concerning Barradall has been collected by R. T. Barton in *Va. Colonial Decisions* (1909). vol. I, Hist. Intro., p. 243. It has been frequently stated incorrectly that he was the earliest Virginia reporter; both Randolph and Hopkins were prior to him. Other references are *Va. Heraldica* (1908), ed. by W. A. Crozier, and W. Meade, *Old Churches, Ministers and Families of Va.* (1861).]

H. W. H. K.

BARRELL, JOSEPH (Dec. 15, 1869–May 4, 1919), geologist and engineer, was descended from George Barrell, a cooper by trade, who came to Boston in 1637 from Saint Michaels in Suffolk, England, where others of the name still reside. In the early days the family, it is said, were in the main a sea-going people, ship-owners, and merchants. Joseph Barrell was born in New Providence, N. J., the fifth of nine children and the fourth son. His father, Henry Ferdinand Barrell, was born in New York City, but lived the life of a farmer first in Warwick, Orange County, N. Y., and later in New Providence. His mother Elizabeth (Wisner) Barrell was of Swiss descent. Joseph was named after his paternal grandfather, a wealthy resident of Boston, who, thrice-married, became the father of twenty children. That the boy is father of the man was never better exemplified than in the case of Joseph. He early developed a studious turn of mind, but was more interested in the natural sciences, astronomy, and history than in general literature. It is stated that when but a mere lad he would sit for hours wholly wrapped in reading the *Encyclopædia Britannica.* When tired from sitting in one position he would turn around, put his book on the chair, kneeling before it, and continue his reading. When about ten years of age he was given a planisphere and at night with a lantern and a book on astronomy would lie on his back gazing at the stars and learning their names. His studies also early took a geological trend; as a youth plowing on the home farm he would stop his team to examine every peculiar stone that was turned up. Until sixteen years of age he attended public schools in New Providence, where under excellent principals he was fitted for college. The finances of the family not permitting his entering college immediately, he passed a teacher's examination and taught at a small school near his home during the years 1886–87. In the following year he was in attendance at the Stevens Preparatory School at Hoboken, N. J., and also won a scholarship at the Stevens Institute but did not avail himself of it, preferring Lehigh University, which he entered in 1888, graduating four years later. He received the degree of E.M. from the University in 1893, in 1897 that of M.S., and in 1916 the honorary degree of Sc.D.

Barrell's first university position was that of instructor in mining and metallurgy in Lehigh University, a position which he held for four years, teaching mechanical drawing, metallurgy, and design, and practising surveying in the anthracite mines. The years of 1898–1900 were devoted to advanced study in Yale University, his summers being spent in field work with parties from the United States Geological Survey in Montana, where he devoted himself especially to questions relating to mining. He remained teaching geology with biology as a side issue at Lehigh for three years, spending three months of the summer of 1901 in Europe traveling on foot and bicycle or third-class trains, with the object of studying the geology of the land rather than that of seeing the cities. In 1903 he was appointed assistant professor of geology at Yale and in 1908 promoted to a full professorship, one-third of his time to be devoted to teaching geology to undergraduates, one-third to the graduate school, and one-third to research. In this position he remained until his death. How well he improved his opportunity for research is shown by his bibliography.

As a clear scientific thinker Barrell had few equals, and it was a pleasure to listen to his delivery, however abstruse his subject. His words were well chosen, his sentences well balanced. His merit along these lines was early recognized and he was frequently called to the lecture platform of other institutions. His early publications, as a natural result of his training, had to do with mining. From these, however, he soon graduated and we find him dealing with the most profound and complex of geological subjects. He attacked each and every problem confident of solution and his ability to handle it. He had the rare gift of generalizing from the publications of others and the still rarer power of analyzing his own methods of reasoning and thus, in a wholly impersonal manner, determining their value and the reliance to be placed upon them.

As stated, his first studies and publications dealt mainly with subjects relating to mining, but as in the case of his report on the Marysville mining district of Montana his interests led him on to a discussion of the then little-known subject of magmatic stoping which resulted in the production of a paper that has become a classic in the literature relating to igneous intrusions. It very early became evident that mining geology was not his most promising field. He grew with remarkable rapidity, as is shown in his progressive publications dealing with regional geology, geological processes, geological time, isostasy, evolution, and the genesis of the earth. A very considerable portion of his later writings were upon the subject of isostasy—the problem of the relative stability of the earth's crust under the changing conditions of erosion and sedimentation. It was in problems of this nature that his engineering training served him to good purpose and here he displayed to greatest advantage his philosophic trend of mind. Of equal importance and magnitude were his writings on rhythms in geological processes and measurements of geological time, a single paper on which subject covers nearly 160 pages of the *Bulletin of the Geological Society of America.*

He was married in 1902 to Lena Hopper Bailey. He was a fellow of the Geological Society of

America, the American Academy of Arts and Sciences, and the National Academy of Sciences, the last honor coming to him but a few days before his death. In appearance he was rather striking. His height was five feet ten and one-half inches, but his spare build conveyed the impression that he was really considerably taller. His features were fairly large and rugged; with abundant light-brown hair and blue eyes. He impressed one as being a strong man both physically and mentally and with abundance of self-confidence although not in the least egotistical; in fact, modesty was one of his prevailing characteristics. Nevertheless it was over-confidence in his own physical and mental powers that led to his undoing. He prided himself on the longevity of his ancestors and believed that he too would live to great age, discovering only too late that he had overdrawn his resources to a fatal extent.

[Charles Schuchert, *Am. Jour. Science,* ser. 4, vol. XLVIII (1919), whole number CXCVIII, with full bibliography of Barrell's publications, pp. 277–80.]

G. P. M.

BARRETT, BENJAMIN FISKE (June 24, 1808–Aug. 6, 1892), preacher and writer of the New Church, was born in Dresden, Me., where his parents, Oliver and Elizabeth (Carleton) Barrett, supported their family of six boys and three girls by hard work on a farm and by the father's carpentering. Benjamin was eager for education, and as a boy found delight in thoroughly reviewing his school studies. The family was religious, but in no formal way. With difficulty the means were found for Benjamin to attend Bowdoin College, where he graduated in 1832. The first serious consideration of Christian doctrines led him to regard the common idea of three persons in the Godhead as unreasonable, and he found himself in sympathy with Unitarians. He become a student in the Harvard Divinity School, graduated in 1838, and was ordained as a Unitarian minister. The years of study in Cambridge brought association with broad-minded men and encouraged honest research. The instruction, however, did not satisfy Barrett. Toward the close of his course, the teachings of Swedenborg were brought to his attention. He did not accept them immediately, but they became increasingly satisfying to him. A winter was spent in association with the Boston New-Church Society and the students of New-Church teachings which it counted among its members. In the spring of 1840, Barrett accepted an invitation to preach for the New-Church Society in New York City and was ordained as a minister of the New Church. In the same year he married Elizabeth Allen of Bath, Me. A ministry of eight years in New York was followed by two years with the New-Church Society in Cincinnati, Ohio. In 1850 health seemed to require a release from indoor confinement and a change of climate. Opportunity came to engage in a roofing business, and the outdoor life proved useful in restoring health. The year 1854 found Barrett again preaching and writing. In 1864 he became minister of the First New Jerusalem Society of Philadelphia and served that Society until 1871. He was the leading spirit in the formation of the American New-Church Tract and Publication Society and later in forming the Swedenborg Publishing Association. For short periods he edited several periodicals, and in Philadelphia the *New Christianity* was published in the interest of the Swedenborg Publishing Association. Barrett's last years were spent in Germantown, Philadelphia, peacefully active in the work he loved and in the sunshine of his home circle. As a preacher and writer, Barrett was clear and forceful. His style was doctrinal and at times polemic. He opposed the practise of rebaptism in receiving members into the New Church and the disposition to limit the New Church to a religious organization. He encouraged ministers convinced of the truth of New-Church doctrine to continue their usefulness, when allowed to do so, in their existing church connections. Among his more important publications are: *Life of Emanuel Swedenborg* (1841); *Lectures on the New Dispensation* (1842); *Beauty for Ashes* (1855); *The Golden Reed* (1855); *Binding and Loosing* (1857); *Catholicity of the New Church* (1863); *Letters to Beecher on the Divine Trinity* (1860); *Letters to Beecher on the Future Life* (1872); *The Golden City* (1874); *The New Church, Its Nature and Whereabouts* (1877); *The Swedenborg Library,* 12 vols. (1876–81); *Swedenborg and Channing* (1878); *The Question (What Are the Doctrines of the New Church?) Answered* (1883); *The Apocalyptic New Jerusalem* (1883); *Footprints of the New Age* (1884); *Heaven Revealed* (1885); *Ends and Uses* (1887); *The True Catholicism* (1886); *The New View of Hell* (1870); *Autobiography* (1890); *A Cloud of Independent Witnesses* (1891); *Maximus Homo* (1892).

[*Benjamin Fiske Barrett, an Autobiography,* revised and supplemented by his daughter, Gertrude A. Barrett (1890); J. R. Irelan, *From Different Points of View: Benjamin Fiske Barrett, Preacher, Writer, Theologian, and Philosopher: A Study* (1896); W. Barrett, *Geneal. of Some of the Descendants of Thomas Barrett, Sen., of Braintree, Mass., 1635* (1888); list of published writings, *Bowdoin Coll. Lib. Bibliog. Contributions* (1891); *Bowdoin Coll. Lib. Bull.,* I–IV (1891–95), p. 138.]

W. L. W.

BARRETT, GEORGE HORTON (June 9, 1794–Sept. 5, 1860), actor, was born in Exeter, England, of a theatrical family. His father, Giles Leonard Barrett, made his American appearance at the Boston Haymarket Theatre, Dec. 28, 1796; his mother delivered the monody on Washington's death, Jan. 10, 1800, at the Federal Street Theatre, of which Giles soon became manager (W. W. Clapp, *A Record of the Boston Stage,* 1853). Master George about this time (variously stated as 1796, 1798, and definitely by Ireland as Oct. 14, 1799) appeared on the stage of the Federal as Cora's Child in *Pizarro,* though, according to Ireland, at an earlier date, Dec. 10, 1798, at the Park Theatre, New York, he was one of the children in Dunlap's version of Kotzebue's *The Stranger,* in the cast with his father, Mr. Cooper, Mr. Hallam, Jr., Mr. Jefferson, and Mrs. Melmoth. He was thus reared in the oldest tradition of the American Theatre, and continued in it to the end. After his first real essay, as Young Norval, May 5, 1806, for his mother's benefit, Barrett won great applause as a "genteel comedian," his "fine appearance and manly beauty" being best seen in such rôles as Rover, Young Marlow, and Bob Handy. He was popularly known as "Gentleman George." Ireland states that at the New York Park he was Belcour in *The West Indian,* Mar. 5, 1822, and that he also played such rôles as Leon in *Rule a Wife,* Beverly in *The Gamester,* Jeremy Didler (wherein he exhibited delightful vivacity), Charles Surface, and others. He was, asserts Ireland, "indisputably the best light comedian in America."

On June 24, 1825, he married Mrs. Anne Jane Henry (1801–53), who had made her appearance as a dancer in Boston during 1813 and her New York appearance as an actress in the rôle of Letitia Hardy in 1824. Ireland claims that "in the lines of gay, graceful and refined comedy, and the gentler grades of tragedy, the lady has been seldom equaled"; while Fanny Kemble declared her "a faultless piece of mortality in outward loveliness." By a former marriage to W. C. Drummond (1817) she had two children; by Barrett she had a daughter, Georgiana, born in February 1829 (Wemyss, *Chronology*), who for a time acted with her father, but retired on her marriage in 1852 to Phillip Warren, treasurer of the Broadway Theatre. In later years Mrs. Barrett drank to such excess that in 1840 Barrett divorced her.

Meanwhile Barrett's career was a checkered one. In 1828 or 1829, with Gilfert, he ventured as manager of the Bowery Theatre, but, meeting with no success, returned to the stage, from 1830 to 1833 appearing in various capacities. Under Alfred Bunn, at the Drury Lane Theatre, London, he was playing Puff in 1837. At about 1842 (according to William Winter, *The Wallet of Time,* 1913, I, 50) he was keeping a restaurant in St. Louis. In 1847, he was manager of the Broadway Theatre, and thereafter returned to Drury Lane for an engagement. On Dec. 7, 1848 (L. Hutton, *Plays and Players,* 1875) Simpson of the New York Park gave a "star" revival of *The School for Scandal,* Barrett playing Charles Surface to the Sir Peter of Henry Placide and the Sir Oliver of W. E. Burton. He also at this time appeared in a stage version of *Dombey and Son.* In 1852–53, he was stage manager of a theatre in Charleston, S. C., while during the season of 1854–55 he was playing at Burton's Theatre. Soon after this ill health forced him to retire from the stage. At the New York Academy of Music, Nov. 20, 1855, a farewell benefit was tendered him. Part of *The Merchant of Venice* was given, with Wallack, Placide, and Madame Ponisi in the cast. As an apology for accepting the benefit Barrett presented two little girls, offspring of a second marriage with a Miss Mason, then deceased. He delivered a farewell address, and then a scene from *The School for Scandal* closed the program, with Blake, Brougham, Charles Fisher, Lester Wallack, and T. Placide playing. Five years later he died in New York, a teacher of elocution, poor and unknown. Joe Cowell, the pioneer manager of the South, said of him that "as an actor in smart, impudent servants, eccentric parts, bordering on caricature, and light comedy, where the claims to the gentleman do not exceed those required for Corinthian Tom, he is excellent" (*Thirty Years Among the Players,* 1844, p. 74). Laurence Hutton thought even more highly of him: "His manners both on and off the stage were elegant; he had a courtly old-fashioned style about him that was inimitable. . . . He was also a good low comedian, and made some decided hits in low comedy parts, but this was a line of business which he rarely consented to touch, considering it beneath the dignity of so refined and intellectual an artist" (*Plays and Players,* 114).

[*Spirit of the Times,* Sept. 15, 1860; W. D. Adams, *Dict. of the Drama* (1904); J. N. Ireland, *Records of the N. Y. Stage* (1866); F. C. Wemyss, *Chronology of the Stage* (1852).] M.J.M.

BARRETT, KATE WALLER (Jan. 24, 1858–Feb. 23, 1925), philanthropic worker, was born at Clifton, Stafford County, Va., the home of her paternal ancestors for over 200 years; her parents were Withers and Ann Eliza (Stribling) Waller; she was related to Gen. Robert E. Lee. Her general education was received at Arlington Institute, Alexandria, Va. In 1876 she married the Rev. Robert South Barrett of Atlanta, for some years dean of the cathedral there, who sympathized with her desire for further education. With his assistance she was able to complete a course in nursing at the Florence Nightingale Training School and St. Thomas's Hospital, London. In 1892 she received the M.D. degree from the Medical College of Georgia. Her husband died in 1896 and she was left with three sons and three daughters, the youngest only three years old. During his final illness her husband, with her aid, had completed his book *The Reason for the Hope,* which, she said, helped to form her own philosophy of life, "Bread, Beauty, and Brotherhood." Mrs. Barrett identified herself with the National Florence Crittenton Mission for wayward girls, of which she became vice-president and general superintendent in 1897 and president from 1909 until her death. She was also drawn more and more into other philanthropic and sociological work. She held many offices in connection with the Conference for the Care of Delinquent Children (1909), the National and International Councils of Women, the National Congress of Mothers and Parent-Teacher Associations, the Conference of Charities and Corrections, the Daughters of the American Revolution, the Commission on Training Camp Activities during the World War, and other organizations. In 1914 and 1919 she was a representative of the United States Government in Europe in connection with immigration problems. With all her public activities and offices, Mrs. Barrett remained a very human woman, free from the official and institutional attitude. Her book, *Some Practical Suggestions on the Conduct of a Rescue Home* (before 1904) and her chapter in *Fourteen Years' Work among Street Girls as Conducted by the National Florence Crittenton Mission* (1897) show her belief in friendship, work, and religion as the chief influences in rescue homes. She was opposed to separating unmarried mothers from their babies, holding that motherhood is a means of regeneration. A gentle, unaffected, yet forceful woman, she often dispensed good advice to girls in the Crittenton Homes and to mothers who brought them there. Her strong, clear-cut profile, crowned by white hair, was a familiar sight at her desk in the Mission Headquarters in Washington. She died, after a brief illness from acute indigestion, on Feb. 23, 1925, at her home in Alexandria, Va.

[*Who's Who in America,* 1924–25; *Woman's Who's Who of America,* 1914–15; *World's Work,* XLIX; *New International Year Bk.* for 1925; *Evening Star* (Washington), Feb. 24, 1925; *Alexandria Gazette* (Alexandria, Va.), Feb. 24, 1925.]

S.G.B.

BARRETT, LAWRENCE (Apr. 4, 1838–Mar. 20, 1891), actor, won by his energy, persistence, patience, capacity for study and hard work, a place among the leading actors of the nineteenth century. He was born in Paterson, N. J., the son of Thomas Barrett, an Irishman. Practically nothing of his early years is anywhere recorded until a family pilgrimage westward took him to Detroit, where, after a brief experience as an errand boy in a dry-goods store, chance and the necessity of earning his living turned him toward the stage. At the age of fourteen he began an association with the theatre that was continuous until his death. His first engagement was as call boy at the Metropolitan Theatre in Detroit at a salary of $2.50 a week, and his first appearance as an actor was made within a year as Murad in *The French Spy.* Two years as a minor member of a stock company at the Grand Opera House in Pittsburgh followed, and thenceforward his advance was rapid even in a profession of sudden rises to fame. During this period he traveled through the midwestern states in support of various stars, among whom was Julia Dean. He then went to New York, and without the advantage of belonging to a stage family or other influence, he began at once to act leading characters.

His first appearance there was on Jan. 20, 1857, at Burton's Chambers Street Theatre, as Sir Thomas Clifford in *The Hunchback* (a part he had previously acted in the West), in support of an ambitious young woman, Mrs. Dennis McMahon, who was vainly striving to rise out of the amateur into professional ranks. During an engagement of four weeks with her, he also acted the title character in *Fazio,* the Stranger in the play of that name, Armand in *Camille,* Lord Townly in *The Provoked Husband,* Claude Melnotte in *The Lady of Lyons,* and Ingomar, all familiar stage heroes of that time and for many years after. In March of the same year he became leading man with William E. Burton at the Metropolitan, afterward the Winter Garden, making his début there as Matthew Bates in Douglas Jerrold's comedy, *Time Tries All.* While at that theatre he supported Edwin Booth (who had recently returned from California, and was henceforth to be his personal friend and frequent professional associate), Burton himself, James E. Murdoch, Charlotte Cushman, Charles Mathews, James H. Hackett, and Edward L. Davenport. Then he went to Boston, where in the autumn of 1858 he became a member of the Boston Museum Company, opening as Frederick Bramble in *The Poor Gentleman,* with William Warren as Dr. Ollapod, and remaining with that organization two seasons. He was playing at the Howard

Athenæum in Boston, under the management of Edward L. Davenport, when the Civil War broke out, and he responded to an early call for volunteers, becoming captain of company B in the 28th Massachusetts Regiment, and serving from Oct. 8, 1861, to Aug. 8, 1862. Except for brief periods occasioned by illness in his later years, this was the only interruption in his arduous labors as actor and manager during forty years. His style was by that time well formed. He was in no wise magnetic in personality, and he had little in manner, figure, or voice of the romantic stage hero. He was a careful, a painstaking, and a very dependable actor. There was both art and nature in his work, and his art was often unconcealed. By the kind and friendly hand of William Winter he is described as an interpreter of character rather than an impersonator, and especially as an actor who made the elocutionary element in his acting conspicuous and important. He was always a student, and he never left anything to chance.

Immediately after the Civil War ended, his work began to assume a national phase. He acted with Booth and other stars at the Winter Garden Theatre in New York in 1862–63 and 1863–64, and his travels from year to year took him to Philadelphia, to management in New Orleans, back to New York now and then, to Cincinnati, and eventually to San Francisco, where in 1869, in partnership with John McCullough, he gained exceptional popularity. He had visited England in the summer of 1866, but did not act there, returning the next year for a brief engagement in Liverpool. In the season of 1870-71 he played opposite parts to Edwin Booth at Booth's Theatre in New York, and taking over the management of that house in April 1871, he produced *The Winter's Tale,* with himself as Leontes, for a run of six weeks. On many occasions during the ensuing seasons, he played Cassius with Booth and others so often that he became firmly established as the leading representative of that Roman hero on the American stage. His Cassius, in fact, is the Shakespearian part by which he became best known in his own day, and by which he is best remembered. In the seventies and eighties he starred in the principal American cities, and his many tours covered practically the entire country. All the standard plays of that era had become a part of his repertory, and he did his best to enlarge the restricted scope of the American theatre by the production of new works. Among them were *Harebell, or the Man o' Airlie,* adapted by W. G. Wills from the German, in 1871; *Dan'l Druce,* by W. S. Gilbert, in 1876; *A Counterfeit Presentment,* by W. D. Howells, in 1877; *Yorick's Love,* adapted by Howells from the Spanisn, in 1878; *Pendragon,* by William Young, in 1881; a revival of George H. Boker's *Francesca da Rimini,* in 1882; Browning's *A Blot in the 'Scutcheon,* in 1884; an English version of Victor Hugo's *Hernani,* in 1885; *Ganelon,* by William Young, in 1889; and Oscar Wilde's *Guido Ferranti,* in 1891, within a few weeks of his death. It will be noted that all these are poetic plays, far removed in scene and theme from any association with the time of their acting, but in presenting them he was simply following the rule of the American theatre. The time had not come when the stage was to be a reflection of the spirit and life of the moment. During Henry Irving's first visit to this country, Barrett took over that actor's Lyceum Theatre in London for seven weeks in the spring of 1884, and although his engagement there was productive of no finanical success, he was received cordially in professional and artistic circles, and was the recipient of many social attentions, including a banquet given in his honor.

The final stage of his career began in 1886, when he entered into a partnership with Edwin Booth that continued until his death four and a half years later, acting leading parts, and taking the entire burden of business and stage details upon his own shoulders. During their first season, 1886–87, they toured separately, but under Barrett's direction. Their first season together began in Buffalo, Sept. 12, 1887, Booth appearing as Brutus and Barrett as Cassius, and their repertory including *The Merchant of Venice, King Lear, Hamlet, Macbeth, Othello, Katharine and Petruchio, Don Cæsar de Bazan, Richelieu, The King's Pleasure, David Garrick,* and *The Fool's Revenge.* Booth played Shylock, Lear, Hamlet, Macbeth, Petruchio, Don Cæsar, Richelieu, and Bertuccio; Barrett played Bassanio, Edgar, Laertes, Macduff, De Mauprat, Gringoire and Garrick; they alternated Othello and Iago. When the famous testimonial performance of *Hamlet* was given to Lester Wallack in the Metropolitan Opera House, New York, May 21, 1888, Barrett played the Ghost, with Booth as Hamlet, Modjeska as Ophelia, and Joseph Jefferson as the First Gravedigger. While Booth was touring with Modjeska the following season, Barrett sought relief in Europe from a glandular trouble in the throat that had been slowly coming upon him. They acted together during a portion of the winter of 1890–91, and in New York, on March 18, during a performance of "Richelieu," at the Broadway Theatre, he found himself unable to finish acting De Mauprat. Two days later, his chronic disease had so sapped his vitality that he was unable to rally from an attack of pneumonia. He died in his apartment at the Windsor Hotel, and his remains were buried in the cemetery in the little Massachusetts shore town of Cohasset, where he had made his summer home for many years. His determination, his mental and physical vigor, his ability to surmount all obstacles gave him by right a high position in his profession. To see him on the stage was to witness thoroughly efficient visualizations of many of the greatest of dramatic characters. In stature he was above the middle height, his features were of classic mold, his eyes were dark, deeply sunken and alert with mental significance, his bearing was dignified and graceful, his voice was sonorous in its wide range of expression, and both on and off the stage he gave the impression of a man of dominant personality and exceptional intellectual powers.

Among his Shakespearian rôles, in addition to those already noted, were Cardinal Wolsey, Richard III, Romeo, King Lear, Benedick, Hamlet, Shylock, and Macbeth. He also, among many other characters, acted Richelieu, Raphael in *The Marble Heart,* Elliot Grey in *Rosedale,* Lanciotto, Evelyn, the Duke Aranza and Rienzi. His published writings include the biography of Edwin Forrest in the *American Actor Series,* and the sketch of Edwin Booth in the fifth volume of *Actors and Actresses of Great Britain and the United States.* He was married in Boston in 1859 to Mary Mayer, and she with three daughters survived him—Edith, who married Marshall Lewis Perry Williams; Mary Agnes, who became the wife of Baron Hermann von Roder; and Gertrude, who married Joseph Anderson, brother of Mary Anderson. Of his grandchildren, two have followed his profession: Edith, daughter of his daughter Edith; and Lawrence, son of his daughter Gertrude.

[The authorities are Wm. Winter, *Life and Art of Edwin Booth* (1893); Winter's sketch of Barrett and specific criticisms of his acting in *Shadows of the Stage* (3 vols., 1892–95); Elwyn A. Barron, *Lawrence Barrett; a Professional Sketch* (1889); an article by B. E. Woolf in *Famous Am. Actors of Today,* ed. by F. E. McKay and C. E. L. Wingate (1896); an article by W. M. Laffan in the fifth volume of *Actors and Actresses of Gt. Britain and the U. S.,* ed. by Brander Matthews and Laurence Hutton (1886); T. Allston Brown, *Hist. of the N. Y. Stage* (1903); Edwina Booth Grossman, *Edwin Booth, Recollections by His Daughter* (1894); and information from members of the Barrett family.] E. F. E.

BARRINGER, DANIEL MOREAU (July 30, 1806–Sept. 1, 1873), lawyer, congressman, diplomat, eldest son of Gen. Paul Barringer and Elizabeth (Brandon) Barringer, was born at "Poplar Grove," near Concord, N. C. Educated at the University of North Carolina, he graduated in 1826 and remained at the University another year improving his knowledge of Spanish. He then studied law in Hillsboro, N. C., under Chief Justice Thomas Ruffin, and, admitted to the bar in 1829, was immediately successful in practise. Politically ambitious, he also began his public career in 1829 when he was elected to represent Cabarrus County in the House of Commons. He served seven terms by annual election, but was compelled by illness to resign in 1835, in which year he also served as a delegate in the constitutional convention. After some years of ill health, he was again elected to the House and served two terms of two years each. In 1843 he was elected as a Whig to the United States House of Representatives, taking his seat on Dec. 4, 1843, and serving until Mar. 4, 1849, declining reëlection. While in Congress he was active, serving at various times on the Committees on Naval Affairs, Indian Affairs, Revolutionary Pensions, and Revision of the Rules of the House. Though he spoke seldom he was effective on the floor both as a speaker and as a parliamentarian. During Abraham Lincoln's term in the House they shared a desk together and became close friends. In 1849 President Taylor appointed him minister to Spain, and after Taylor's death President Fillmore renewed the appointment. Barringer went to Spain with a keen hope of being instrumental in securing the cession of Cuba to the United States, a thing which he had long favored, but the conditions of his ministry made it impossible, President Fillmore being convinced that the annexation of Cuba would be a fatal mistake. On account of American filibustering expeditions to Cuba, the period was one of rather strained relations between Spain and the United States, and Barringer's post was one of much difficulty. But he established excellent relations with the Spanish court and foreign office, his knowledge of the language stood him in good stead and, poised and tactful, he handled his duties with entire satisfaction to the President and the State Department. When his successor was appointed in 1853, Barringer, after traveling for a time in Europe, returned to North Carolina. In 1854 he was again in the House of Commons for one term. He then temporarily retired from public life, moving to Raleigh and spending most of his time in reading and in social intercourse with his numerous friends. Abundant means made him independent of his profession and he found delight in taking care of his home place. He was strongly opposed to secession. A Union man, he did not approve of it in theory, and, familiar with the economic power of the North, he was convinced that a successful outcome was, at best, highly unlikely. A close friend of Robert E. Lee, he wrote him during the crisis, urging him to use his influence to keep Virginia in the Union, and he himself, in North Carolina, exerted all the influence he possessed in the direction of delay. He was sent by the legislature as a delegate from the state to the Peace Conference in Washington in February 1861. He became convinced at Washington, however, that no compromise would be accepted by the North, and with the call for troops and the secession of North Carolina he yielded, and, as the close, though unofficial, adviser of Gov. Ellis and Gov. Clark, he played a considerable part in public affairs with complete devotion to the Confederate cause. At the close of the war he favored President Johnson's policy and was a delegate to the National Union Convention of 1866. He was a delegate to the National Democratic Convention in 1872, where he advocated the nomination of Horace Greeley, and in the state and national campaigns which followed he was chairman of the state Conservative executive committee. His health failed soon afterward, and he died a year later at White Sulphur Springs, W. Va. He was married to Elizabeth Wethered, daughter of Lewin Wethered of Baltimore, Md.

[The chief sources are the N. C. newspapers of his day, the *Cong. Globe*, 1843–49, and the journals of the N. C. legislature. A brief sketch appears in J. Livingston, *Portraits and Memoirs of Eminent Americans* (1853), p. 51, and a more extended one by Daniel M. Barringer, Jr., is to be found in the *Biog. Hist. of N. C.* (1905), I, 100–110.] J. G. deR. H.

BARRINGER, RUFUS (Dec. 2, 1821–Feb. 3, 1895), Confederate soldier, was the grandson of one Paulus Behringer, who in 1743 came from Würtemberg to Philadelphia, removing after a few years to "Poplar Grove," Cabarrus County, N. C. Paulus Barringer's son, Paul Barringer—the name was promptly Anglicized—was active in politics, and served as a brigadier-general of militia during the War of 1812. Rufus Barringer, son of Paul and his wife Elizabeth Brandon, was born at "Poplar Grove." After graduating from the University of North Carolina in 1842, he studied law, and took up the practise of his profession at Concord, N. C. He was a member of the Assembly in 1848 and 1850, and a presidential elector in 1860. A Whig in politics and a Union man in principle, he opposed secession but accepted the decision of his state and immediately volunteered for military service. He was appointed a captain in the 1st North Carolina Cavalry, and followed its fortunes in the Army of Northern Virginia—the Peninsular campaign, second Bull Run, Antietam, Fredericksburg, and Chancellorsville. He was still a captain at the action at Brandy Station in June 1863, where, as Wade Hampton reported, he "bore himself with marked coolness and good conduct," and was severely wounded in the face; but promotion then came to him rapidly. He was a major in August 1863, and lieutenant-colonel soon after, and in June 1864, was appointed brigadier-general. He was assigned to the command of a brigade in Gen. W. H. F. Lee's cavalry division, and led it until its destruction on Apr. 3, 1865, while covering Lee's withdrawal from Richmond. Barringer himself was captured by scouts serving with the 15th New York Cavalry, which was commanded by Col. John J. Coppinger, afterward a brigadier-general in the regular army, and, during the war with Spain, a major-general of volunteers. Barringer was sent to Fort Delaware for confinement, and released in July, upon taking the oath of allegiance. So ended his military service, during which, it is said, he had fought in seventy-six actions, been three times wounded, and had two horses shot under him. As a soldier, he was "prudent, methodical and cautious," —so wrote an officer who served under him; his courage was shown on many occasions. Returning to North Carolina, he resumed the practise of law at Charlotte. Recognizing the results of the war as fully and ungrudgingly as he had accepted the secession of his state, he favored loyal coöperation with the policies of the national Government, negro suffrage included. Joining the Republican party, whose principles an old Whig could accept more readily than a Democrat, he took an active part in political life. He was a member of the constitutional convention in 1875, and his party's candidate for lieutenant-governor in 1880. He retired from law practise in 1884, and spent the rest of his life on his estate, writing occasional papers on historical subjects, chiefly relating to the Civil War, and taking a keen interest in educational matters. He was married three times: first, in 1854 to Eugenia Morrison, who died in 1858; second to Rosalie Chunn of Asheville, N. C.; third, to Margaret Long of Orange County, N. C.

[*Confed. Mil. Hist.*, IV, 294–98; *Hists. of the Several Regiments and Battalions from N. C.* (1901); *Official Records*, vol. LXVI (pt. 1).] T. M. S.

BARRON, JAMES (1769–Apr. 21, 1851), naval officer, was the younger son of James Barron, a merchant captain who commanded a part of the naval forces of Virginia during the Revolution, and his wife, Jane Cowper. As an apprentice on his father's ship, the younger James saw service during the latter part of that war, proving himself a lad of courage and dash. Following the example of his elder brother, Samuel, he entered the United States Navy as lieutenant, his commission being dated Mar. 9, 1798, and so distinguished himself as an officer of the frigate *United States* under Commodore John Barry, that he was promoted to be captain in 1799. He commanded the frigate *Essex* in the squadron under the broad pennant of his brother, which was sent to the Mediterranean to coöperate with Commodore Preble's fleet; and received the command of the larger frigate *President* when his brother succeeded Preble as commander-in-chief of the forces in European waters. He was actively engaged in operations in the Mediterranean until the year 1805, and was considered an officer of uncommon ability. In 1807, the European tour of duty of the frigate *Constitution* drawing to a close, the *Chesapeake,* 38 guns, then laid up, was chosen to relieve her and was placed under the command of Barron as commodore. The *Chesapeake,* hastily and carelessly equipped, and manned by a new and untrained crew, with Charles Gordon as captain, sailed for her new station on June 22, 1807. A few miles off the coast she was hailed by the British frigate *Leopard,* 50 guns, which sent an officer aboard the *Chesapeake* to demand the surrender of three alleged deserters from the British Navy. This demand being refused by Commodore Barron, the *Leopard* opened a severe fire on the *Chesapeake,* killing three and wounding eighteen men, Barron himself among the latter, besides doing great damage to hull and rigging. Desperate efforts were made by the crew of the American vessel to clear the ship for action, but in a short time Barron, believing that resistance would only subject his crew to massacre and his ship to destruction, hauled down his colors, firing one shot "in honor of the flag." The alleged deserters were then taken off the *Chesapeake,* and the captain of the *Leopard,* having refused to regard the *Chesapeake* as a lawful prize, in spite of her surrender, proceeded on his way, while the *Chesapeake* returned to Hampton Roads to report the occurrence and to repair damages.

This act of unlawful violence was eventually disavowed by the British government. Barron, however, was brought before a court martial in January 1808, largely on the initiative of an address drawn up by Lieut. William Allen [*q.v.*] and signed by six officers of the *Chesapeake,* which requested the arrest of Barron for the disgraceful and premature surrender of his vessel. The court, presided over by Capt. John Rodgers and counting among its members such distinguished officers as Bainbridge and Decatur, while acquitting Barron of cowardice and most of the minor charges, nevertheless, "for neglecting, on the probability of an engagement, to clear his ship for action," sentenced him to suspension from the service without pay for five years. Most of this time he spent abroad as a high officer in the French navy, but on the expiration of his sentence he returned to his native country and reëntered the service. His efforts to obtain active service were, however, systematically blocked by the protests of his brother officers, and he continued on shore duty until his death. In 1820, chafing under what he considered to be the unjust attitude of his colleagues, he sent a challenge to Commodore Stephen Decatur [*q.v.*], whom he charged with being the head of a cabal formed for the purpose of persecuting him. The encounter took place at Bladensburg on Mar. 22, 1820, with Commodores Elliott and Bainbridge as the respective seconds of Barron and Decatur, and resulted in the death of Decatur and the severe wounding of Barron in the thigh. On account of the universal popularity of Decatur, this affair caused all sympathy to be withdrawn from Barron, who was forced to remain on "waiting orders" for the rest of his unhappy life. He died at Norfolk in 1851, the senior officer of the navy at the time.

[Records in the Office of Naval Records and Library, Washington; J. H. Brown, *Am. Naval Heroes* (1899); *The Court-Martial of Commodore James Barron,* pub. by the Navy Dept. (1882); J. F. Cooper, *Hist. of the Navy* (1839).]

E. B.

BARRON, SAMUEL (Nov. 28, 1809–Feb. 26, 1888), Confederate naval officer, was born at Hampton, Va., of distinguished naval ancestry, the son of the commodore of the same name and of Jane Sawyer of Norfolk. Recognition of the service of his father, who died in 1810, doubtless accounts for his admission into the navy at the unparalleled age of a little over two years, his appointment as midshipman dating from Jan. 1, 1812. His first cruise was in his eleventh year, in the Mediterranean, and he was in the frigate *Brandywine* which carried Lafayette to France in 1825. For four years, 1849–53, he commanded the *John Adams* on the African coast; and, with the rank of captain (promoted Sept. 14, 1855), the steam frigate *Wabash,* flagship of Commodore Lavalette, in the Mediterranean, 1858–59. During this cruise his ship remained some time at Constantinople, despite British protests that she was larger than was permitted through the Straits (see narrative of the cruise in the *Auto-*

biography of Admiral Dewey, then a midshipman in the *Wabash*). Just before the Civil War, Barron was assigned to the Mare Island navy-yard, but before going west he was sent to Pensacola to prevent hostilities between naval vessels and shore fortifications occupied by Florida troops. His resignation from the Navy, Apr. 22, 1861, was not accepted, and he is recorded as dismissed. As a captain in the Confederate States Navy he took a leading part in the distribution of ordnance and the organization of naval defense. From April to July 20, 1861, he was chief of the Bureau of Orders and Detail (see his report, June 10, *Official Records of the Union and Confederate Navies,* V, 803), and was then put in charge of the naval defenses of Virginia and North Carolina. He brought up reinforcements during the attack on Hatteras Inlet, Aug. 28–29, 1861, took command of Fort Hatteras, and after its surrender was a prisoner for eleven months until his exchange. On Nov. 3, 1862, he was appointed "to command the naval forces in all the waters of Virginia" (*Ibid.,* VIII, 844). In the summer of 1863 he was sent to England with subordinate officers to bring to America two ironclad rams then under construction at Birkenhead. Upon their seizure in November by the British Government, he went to Paris with his staff, and remained there, as "Flag Officer Commanding Confederate States Naval Forces in Europe," until his resignation from this duty, Feb. 28, 1865. While abroad he was active in fitting out and directing the operations of Confederate commerce destroyers, especially the *Stonewall* and *Georgia.* Of distinguished bearing, courtly, and punctilious, often referred to in Washington as "the navy diplomat," Barron carried the customs and ideals of the old navy into his personal life. After the war his home was at "Malvern," near Loretto, Essex County, Va. He was married, Oct. 31, 1832, to Imogen Wright of Norfolk, and was the father of three sons and three daughters.

[In addition to the references cited above, see J. D. Bulloch, *Secret Service of the Confed. States in Europe* (1884); T. H. S. Hamersly, *Gen. Reg. of the U. S. Navy* (1882); and J. T. Scharf, *Hist. of the Confed. States Navy* (1887). Many of Barron's letters are in the *Official Records;* see especially vols. I–III, on operations of the cruisers. Other material in a manuscript memoir by his son-in-law, Capt. E. R. Baird, Occupacia, Va. Obituary in the *Army and Navy Jour.,* Mar. 3, 1888.]

A. W.

BARROW, WASHINGTON (Oct. 5, 1817–Oct. 19, 1866), editor, congressman, was born in Davidson County, Tenn., the son of a North Carolina emigrant, one of the early settlers of the Middle Tennessee region. After a few years of so-called "classical education" in Davidson Academy, he "read law" as was then the custom and was admitted to the bar. Soon forsaking the practise of law, he turned to politics, in which he was at first a Jacksonian Democrat but later joined the increasing number of Tennesseans who were dissatisfied with the long and rigid domination of Andrew Jackson's followers in Tennessee politics and were then engaged in organizing the Whig party in the state. In 1835 the Whigs gained control of the state and in 1840 a Whig president was elected. Barrow was then rewarded for his political activities by an appointment as American chargé d'affaires at Lisbon, where he served from 1841 to 1844. When he returned to his native state he became editor of the *Republican Banner* of Nashville, the chief newspaper of the opposition party, and in 1847 he was elected and served one term as a Whig member of Congress from the Hermitage, Andrew Jackson's own district. Barrow next appeared in public life as a state senator, and with Gustavus A. Henry and A. O. W. Totten was appointed by Gov. Isham G. Harris to negotiate a "Military League" with the Confederacy. The commissioners agreed with Henry W. Hilliard of Alabama, Confederate agent, upon an arrangement which was ratified on the same day (May 7, 1861) by the legislature (*Acts of Tennessee,* 2nd Extra Session, 1861, p. 21) and Tennessee thus became a virtual member of the Confederacy, a month before the ordinance of secession was adopted by popular vote. Barrow took no further active part in the Civil War but remaining in Nashville as a neutral when it was occupied by the Federal troops, he was placed under arrest by Andrew Johnson, then military governor by President Lincoln's appointment. After a brief detention in the state penitentiary he was released by direction of President Lincoln and later went to St. Louis, where he died soon after the close of the Civil War. A man of great ability, Barrow was apparently destined to an important political career, which was frustrated by the disruption of the Whig party in the fifties and by his own failure to take an active part on one side or the other in the Civil War.

[W. W. Clayton, *Hist. of Davidson County* (1880); Jas. Phelan, *Hist. of Tenn.* (1888), p. 375; *Hist. of Nashville, Tenn.* (1890), ed. by John Wooldridge, pp. 344–45; W. T. Hale and Dixon Merritt, *Hist. of Tenn. and Tennesseans* (1913), II, 512; John T. Moore and Austin P. Foster, *Tenn. the Volunteer State* (1923), I, 471.]

W. L. F—g.

BARROWS, JOHN HENRY (July 11, 1847–June 3, 1902), Congregational clergyman, college president, came of New England ancestry which moved West with the national frontier. His father, John Manning Barrows, was a well-educated preacher and teacher in the new states of Ohio and Michigan. His mother, Bertha Anthony Butler, was a woman of intellectual ability who was one of the early students at Oberlin College, where she became proficient in Greek, Hebrew, and French. Both parents were deeply religious and suffered for their anti-slavery sentiments. John Henry Barrows was born in a log cabin five miles from Medina, Mich. His family traditions as well as his natural abilities made him a good student and at sixteen he entered Olivet College, a newly founded, incomplete, but stimulating institution. After graduating from college he entered Yale Divinity School, where he remained for a year, and in 1868 he entered Union Theological Seminary. The next year he was forced by ill health to give up study, and for something like three years he was a pastor in Kansas. He there gave evidence of his subsequent abilities as a preacher and was called to a temporary pastorate at Springfield, Ill. In 1873 he traveled for a considerable time in Europe and on his return entered Andover Seminary, but left before graduating. On May 6, 1875, he married Sarah Eleanor Mole and became pastor of a Congregational church at Lawrence, Mass. His success in that field led to his becoming pastor of the important First Presbyterian Church of Chicago, a position which he held from 1881 to 1896. During this long pastorate he showed himself an effective preacher, an enemy of religious intolerance, and a pioneer in various undertakings looking toward civic and religious advance.

When Chicago organized the World's Columbian Exposition, he became chairman of its Committee on Religious Congresses. It was under the auspices of this committee that the Parliament of Religions was held. Its purpose was to bring together in conference representatives of all the historic religions for the expression of their similarities and differences, as well as for possible influence upon social, economic, and international life. Much of the immediate success of this remarkable gathering, attended by 150,000 persons, was due to Barrows. Seen in retrospect the World's Parliament of Religions appears less resultful than was foretold. But as an adventure in religious tolerance and an incentive to world brotherhood it was of no small significance. The missionary interests of the time had hardly begun to give justice to non-Christian religions and especially among the more orthodox religious leaders the proposal to bring upon one platform representatives of the great religions of the world aroused anxiety, even suspicion. But the Parliament attracted widespread attention, and Barrows became an outstanding representative of the new interest in the ethnic religions. Whatever else the Parliament may have accomplished, it developed respect for non-Christian religions on the part of intelligent religious persons.

Partly as a result of this new interest, Barrows induced Mrs. Caroline E. Haskell not only to present to the University of Chicago a sum to be used in erecting a building for the study of Oriental history and religion, but also to endow in the University of Chicago the Haskell Lectures of Comparative Religion and the Barrows Lectureship on the relations of Christianity and other religions. The first of these two foundations provided for lectures in the institution itself. The second provided for lectures to be given in India. Barrows was the first lecturer on both of these foundations, giving seven Haskell series, 1895–1901. In 1896 he resigned his pastorate in Chicago and lectured, not only in India but in Japan. His reception was cordial. He went not as a missionary but as a sympathetic expounder of Christianity. His lectures as published do not give the impression of technical scholarship, but are colored by an intelligent interest in all religious faiths. Returning after fifteen months in the Orient, he became president of Oberlin College on Nov. 29, 1898. This institution had long stood for evangelical Christianity and had been a strong influence in the religious life of the Middle West. Barrows brought to his new position the same administrative imagination he had shown in other relations, and immediately undertook the task of giving Oberlin a much wider influence and more complete educational resources. During his brief administration the college added $600,000 to its endowment, erected several new buildings, and gained new prominence in the educational world. His work was brought to an untimely close by his death from pneumonia, after a brief illness, on June 3, 1902. He was the author of *The World's Parliament of Religions* (1893); *Henry Ward Beecher, the Shakespeare of the Pulpit* (1893); *Christianity, the World Religion* (1897); *A World Pilgrimage* (1897); *Spiritual Forces in American History* (1889); *The Christian Conquest of Asia* (1899).

[*John Henry Barrows, A Memoir* (1904) by his daughter, Mary Eleanor Barrows; *Cleveland Plain Dealer,* June 4, 1902; *Congreg. Yr. Bk.,* 1903, pp. 14–15; *Oberlin Coll. Annual Reports,* 1898–1902.]

S. Ma—s.

BARROWS, SAMUEL JUNE (May 26, 1845–Apr. 21, 1909), Unitarian clergyman, editor, reformer, was born in New York, the third son of Richard and Jane (Weekes) Barrows. In early childhood the death of his father left the family in poverty, and Barrows went to work before he was nine years old as errand boy in the printing-press establishment of his cousin, Richard Hoe. He taught himself shorthand and telegraphy, and operated the first private telegraph line in New York. A professional stenographer at eighteen, he became a reporter on the *New York Tribune* three years later. On June 28, 1867, he married Isabel Hayes Chapin. They had one daughter, Mabel Hay, and an adopted son, William Burnet. During 1868 Barrows acted as private secretary to William H. Seward, then secretary of state. In 1871 he entered the Harvard Divinity School, interspersing three years of theological study with summers on the western plains as newspaper correspondent with Stanley and Custer. After a year's further study in Leipzig, he was in 1876 installed as pastor of the First Church in Dorchester, Mass., which he served for four years. From 1880 to 1896 he was editor of the *Christian Register,* the Unitarian national weekly. During these years he traveled widely, both in this country and abroad, and his many-sided interests made him a frequent attendant upon the meetings and a constant contributor to the proceedings of the National Conference of Charities and Correction, the National and International Prison Congresses, the Society for International Law, the Society of Biblical Research, the Lake Mohonk Conferences on the Indian and on International Arbitration, and numerous other organizations. He was one of the earliest friends of Tuskegee Institute, and he had an unfailing interest in the education of the negro and the Indian, in woman suffrage, total abstinence, prison reform, international understanding—in short, every reform that promised better conditions of living anywhere. An indefatigable student of the Greek language and literature, he had the good fortune to be working alongside Dörpfeld at the very time when the actual Homeric Troy was unearthed. In 1896 he was elected to Congress from the tenth district in Boston. During his single term, he interested himself particularly in civil service reform and in parole for Federal prisoners and opposed entrance into the Spanish War up to the very hour of the declaration.

In 1900 he became corresponding secretary of the Prison Association of New York, a position which he held until his death. He made the Association a power for prison reform in New York and throughout the nation, himself drafting and securing the passage of New York's first probation law, and being largely instrumental in the enactment of the Federal parole law. The long series of reports which he wrote and compiled as secretary of the Prison Association and as International Prison Commissioner for the United States, an office to which he was first appointed by President Cleveland in 1895, are among the most valuable documents of American penological literature. During nine years of ceaseless activity, he did an immense amount of work for the improvement of legislation at Albany and Washington, at the same time helping personally hundreds of men at liberty on probation, as well as other needy persons, conducting an enormous correspondence with all parts of the world, carrying on literary and reform activities of the most varied sorts in a dozen different fields. He made repeated trips abroad for the study of prisons and prison methods, coming back in 1907, for example, when a new prison to replace Sing Sing was under contemplation, with detailed plans and descriptions of no less than thirty-six of the best prisons in fourteen different countries. As International Prison Commissioner for the United States, he had much to do with the development of the International Prison Congress, and in 1905 he was elected its president. Always deeply interested in peace, during his term in Congress he was made official American representative on the Interparliamentary Union for International Arbitration, and up to his death he labored zealously in that cause. An accomplished linguist, an enthusiastic worker in copper and brass, a musician of no mean attainments, a public speaker in constant demand, a prolific writer, he was at the same time a man of genial personality, to whom friends and strangers alike turned for personal aid and counsel.

The literary results of his religious and theological studies are to be found chiefly in the files of the *Christian Register* and in magazine articles, and the fruits of his prison studies in his reports and articles (especially "The Criminal Insane in the United States and in Foreign Countries," *Senate Document No. 273,* 55 Cong., 2 Sess.; "The Reformatory System in the United States," *House Document No. 459,* 56 Cong., 1 Sess.; "Prison Systems of the United States," *House Document No. 566,* 56 Cong., 1 Sess.; "Children's Courts in the United States. Their Origin, Development, and Results," *House Document No. 701,* 58 Cong., 2 Sess.). He was also the author of numerous magazine articles on general subjects. In addition, he wrote *The Doom of the Majority* and *A Baptist Meeting House* (1890), two short religious and theological books; *The Shaybacks in Camp* (1887), a description of the life in the Barrows camp on

Lake Memphremagog, written jointly with Mrs. Barrows; and *The Isles and Shrines of Greece* (1898), a product of his long-continued Greek studies.

[The chief source is *A Sunny Life* (1913), a biog. written by his wife, Isabel C. Barrows, which contains an extensive bibliography. See also Guillaume Louis, *Dr. Samuel J. Barrows, Ancien Président de la Commission Pénitentiare Internationale* (Berne, 1909); *Unit. Yr. Bk.*, 1909; *Biog. Cong. Dir.* (1903); *Christian Reg.*, Apr. 21, 29, May 6, 13, 20, 27, 1909; *Survey*, May 29, 1909; *N. Y. Evening Post*, Apr. 22, 1909.] H. R. M.

BARRY, JOHN (1745–Sept. 13, 1803), naval officer, was born at Tacumshane, County Wexford, Ireland, the son of Catherine Barry and John Barry, a clerk in a malt-house. He went to sea in early youth and about the year 1760 settled at Philadelphia, where he became a well-to-do shipmaster and owner. Enthusiastically espousing the cause of the Colonies at the outbreak of the Revolution, he offered his services to the Continental Congress, and was placed in command, independently of Commodore Hopkins's squadron, of the brig *Lexington*, in which, on Apr. 17, 1776, he took the British tender *Edward*, which was the first capture in actual battle of a British war-ship by a regularly commissioned American cruiser. By a resolution passed by the Congress on Oct. 10, 1776, Barry was placed seventh on the list of captains, and was soon after given command of the *Effingham*, 32 guns; but the occupation of Philadelphia by the British in 1777 and the presence of an overwhelming enemy force in the Delaware prevented this vessel from going to sea. This, however, did not condemn the enterprising commander to idleness, and during this year he performed a handsome exploit in the lower Delaware. With four small boats he cut out an armed British schooner without the loss of a man, at the same time capturing a number of transports and a large quantity of supplies destined for the British army, receiving the personal congratulations of Washington on his "gallantry and address" (Jared Sparks, *The Writings of George Washington*, 1834, V, 271). He then volunteered for service with the American army and took part in the Trenton campaign with distinction. In 1778 his vessel, the *Effingham*, against Barry's will, was burnt to prevent her falling into the enemy's hands. He then obtained command of the *Raleigh*, 32 guns, and in her fought a gallant and obstinate battle against superior forces, finally being obliged to beach his ship, but saving most of his crew from capture. In 1781, in command of the *Alliance*, 32 guns, having taken many valuable prizes, he attacked and captured after an obstinate fight the British vessels *Atalanta* and *Trepassy*, being severely wounded in the action. Later in the same year he carried to France the Marquis de Lafayette and the Count de Noailles, and in 1782, while continuing his series of captures of enemy ships, he fought, in the *Alliance*, his last important battle, which he was obliged to break off on the appearance of powerful enemy reinforcements.

In 1794, when the depredations of the Algerine pirates had become insupportable, and Congress ordered the construction of six frigates, Barry was named senior captain and placed in command of the *United States*, 44 guns, being, as Cooper says (*History of the Navy*, 1839, I, 267), "of all the naval captains that remained . . . the one who possessed the greatest reputation for experience, conduct, and skill." During the hostilities with France, after a somewhat unsatisfactory cruise to the West Indies (1798), Barry was placed in command of all the naval forces in those waters, remaining there until the beginning of May 1799. In December of that year he escorted to France the American envoys appointed to treat with the French Republic, and upon his return took command of the Guadaloupe station in the West Indies, which position he retained until 1801. He died two years later at the head of the navy. Cooper, an excellent judge, when mentioning "the naval names that have descended to us, from this war [the Revolution], with the greatest reputation" (*Ibid.*, p. 252), places Barry second only to John Paul Jones, and says, "Commodore Barry, as an officer and a man, ranked very high" (*Ibid.*, p. 374).

He was twice married. The identity of his first wife is uncertain; she was either Mary Burns or Mary Cleary; his second wife was Sarah Austin, whom he married July 7, 1777. Both marriages were childless.

[Records of the Lib. of the Navy Dept.; the Barnes papers in the Lib. of the N. Y. Hist. Soc.; Martin I. J. Griffin, *Commodore John Barry* (1897); John Frost, *Am. Naval Biog.* (1844).] E. B.

BARRY, JOHN STEWART (Jan. 29, 1802–Jan. 14, 1870), governor of Michigan, was born at Amherst, N. H., the son of John and Ellen (Stewart) Barry. His parents early removed to Rockingham, Vt., where he grew to manhood. For two years, beginning in 1824, he conducted an academy at Georgia, Vt., meanwhile studying law, which he afterward practised for several years. In early manhood he married Mary Kidder, of Grafton, Vt., who died in 1869; the union proved childless. He migrated to White Pigeon, Mich., in 1831, and in 1834 removed to Constantine, Mich., which remained his home until his death. He prospered in business and during his later years was regarded as a wealthy man.

Barry was of stern and austere character, wholly lacking in the arts of the politician, and master of but few of the graces of social intercourse. Yet it was his good fortune to come to the front when even his defects were accounted virtues, and he played a notable rôle in the political history of Michigan. His first important public service was as a member of the state constitutional convention of 1835. During the next few years the most extravagant boom Michigan has ever witnessed ensued. It was accompanied by an era of wild-cat banking and a craze for state-constructed internal improvements which could only end in disaster both moral and financial. The bubble burst during the Whig régime of 1840–41, and Barry, who was a Democrat of conservative principles, was elected governor in the latter years, on the wave of a reaction against the policies which had brought the commonwealth to the verge of bankruptcy. It was his task to salvage what might be saved from the general financial wreck, and to restore the state to the pathway of solvency and prosperity. This proved difficult and thankless enough, but the personal qualities of the Governor, reinforced by his substantial business ability, admirably fitted him for its performance. He was reelected in 1843 and during his four years in office (1842–46), the task was substantially accomplished. The state constitution forbade a second successive reëlection to the governorship, but the verdict of the electorate upon Barry's administration was seen in his election to the office for a third term in 1849, a precedent not repeated in Michigan for almost sixty years. Barry was a firm believer in the Jeffersonian principles of constitutional interpretation, and when the sectional dispute progressed to the stage of civil war, his adherence to views which his state had discarded relegated him to political oblivion.

[*Early Hist. of Mich. with Biographies of State Officers, Members of Cong., Judges and Legislators* (Lansing, 1888), pp. 73–74; files of *Detroit Free Press* for 1841, 1843, 1849; obit. notices preserved in the Burton Hist. Coll. of the Detroit Pub. Lib.; Thos. M. Cooley, *Mich.: A Hist. of Governments* (1885), *passim;* Henry M. Utley (and associates), *Mich. as a Province, Territory, and State* (1906), vols. II, III, IV, *passim.*]

M. M. Q.

BARRY, PATRICK (May 24, 1816–June 23, 1890), horticulturist, was the son of a farmer and was born near Belfast, Ireland. He received a liberal education and when eighteen years old became a teacher in the national schools. In 1836 he came to the United States and worked for four years in the Princes' nurseries at Flushing, L. I., where he obtained a thorough knowledge of a large-scale nursery business. He then moved to Rochester, N. Y., and was associated with George Ellwanger in the founding of the Mt. Hope nursery, which became the largest nursery establishment in this country. Many varieties of fruits and other plants were imported from France and Germany, and tested particularly with reference to their adaptability for use in Western New York. Under Barry's guidance fruit-growing was introduced and largely developed in that region. From 1845 to 1853 he was horticultural editor of the *Genesee Farmer,* and later was editor of the *Horticulturist* until 1855. He was also a frequent contributor to the *American Agriculturist* and other journals. In 1851 he published *The Fruit Garden,* an illustrated treatise on the physiology of fruit trees, theory and practise of fruit growing, preserving of fruits, control of diseases and insects, the use of implements. This book was written in a clear and systematic style, with special reference to requirements of small plantations on farms or in villages and towns. With revisions it passed through a number of editions. From 1872 it was called *Barry's Fruit Garden.* He was a secretary of the national convention of fruit growers in 1848, out of which grew the American Pomological Society in 1852. As chairman of a committee he helped prepare the society's classified *Catalogue of Fruits* in 1862, which he revised and enlarged in succeeding years, making it the standard authority on this subject. Under his leadership the Fruit Growers Society of Western New York was organized in 1855 and he was chairman of its executive committee until its name was changed in 1870 to Western New York Horticultural Society. He was also president of the New York State Agricultural Society in 1877 and from 1882 to 1889 member of the first board of control of the New York State Agricultural Experiment Station at Geneva. With increasing wealth he engaged in banking and other commercial activities and was also prominent in the civic life of Rochester. In 1847 he married Harriet Huestis of Richfield, Otsego County, N. Y., by whom he had six sons and two daughters. His son, William C. Barry, succeeded his father in the nursery business and other enterprises.

[*Proc. Western N. Y. Horticultural Soc.* (1891), pp. 6–7; *Proc. Am. Pomological Soc.* (1890); L. R. Doty, *Hist. of Genesee County* (1925), III, 48–53; *Am. Agriculturalist,* Aug. 1890, p. 434; *Garden and Forest,* July 2, 1890, p. 328; *Rochester Morning Herald,* June 24, 1890.]

A. C. T.

BARRY, WILLIAM FARQUHAR (Aug. 18, 1818–July 18, 1879), Union soldier, was born in New York City. His father died while his son was still very young. Under his mother's tutelage the boy grew up, attended the New York High School from 1826 to 1831 and thereafter received from a tutor an unusual knowledge of the classics (Old Files, Adjutant-General's Office). Admitted to the United States Military Academy, he graduated in 1838. His assignment to the 2nd Artillery took him to the Canadian border to enforce our neutrality during the "Patriot War," then in progress in Canada. The headquarters of the regiment were at Buffalo. Here Barry met Kate McNight and married her in 1840 (*Records,* Fort Monroe, Va.). During the Mexican War in 1847, he accompanied his regiment to Tampico, where he became seriously ill. After his recovery he was designated acting assistant adjutant-general of Patterson's division at Vera Cruz and later, on reaching the City of Mexico, aide-de-camp to Gen. Worth, which position he filled until the termination of hostilities (G. W. Cullum, *Biographical Register*). Thereafter, until the beginning of the Civil War, he followed the routine of army duties. Promoted to captain in 1852, he fought the Seminole Indians in Florida; in 1857–58 he was in Kansas attempting, during its troublous *ante bellum* days, to maintain a difficult peace. His outstanding qualifications as an artilleryman were recognized by his detail in 1858–59 on a board to revise the "System of Light Artillery Tactics" (F. F. Rodenbaugh, *The Army of the United States,* 1896).

His services in the Civil War began with the defense of Fort Pickens, Florida, Apr. 19, 1861. On May 14 he was promoted major and, in July, assigned as chief of artillery of the army commanded by his classmate McDowell (*Official Records,* ser. I, vol. V, p. 575). With this army he participated in the battle of Bull Run. Subsequently assigned as chief of artillery of McClellan's Army of the Potomac, he labored tirelessly to increase and improve the artillery, a task which, with the aid of the Ordnance Department, he accomplished. When he took up this work most of the ore for the guns was underground, the lumber for the carriages still growing in the forests, the leather for the harness yet covering the animals, the artillerists a mob of militia. By prodigious exertions the thirty guns on hand in July 1861 had been increased to 520 when McClellan moved in March 1862, the 400 horses to 11,000, the 650 men to 12,500 drilled artillerists, and the whole molded into an artillery organization (*Ibid.,* p. 68). The man who wrought these changes was at this time in the fulness of his powers. Tall, athletic, well-built, with keen eyes, aquiline nose, and rather marked features, he was a noticeable personage. Much of his success may be ascribed to his unusual ability as an organizer, with which he combined a genial, kindly manner and buoyant spirits. By hard work he had accomplished much, yet much remained to be done when the Army of the Potomac took the field, Mar. 14, 1862.

In the Peninsular campaign which followed, Barry, now a brigadier-general of volunteers, took an active part in all the battles and movements of this unfortunate expedition. After the evacuation of the Peninsula he was, at his own request, relieved as chief of artillery, Army of the Potomac, and transferred to Washington as inspector of artillery of the Armies of the United States and chief of artillery of the defenses of Washington. In addition, he served as a member of numerous armament, fortification, and defense boards. In March 1864 he was relieved and appointed chief of artillery, first on the staff of Gen. Grant (*Ibid.,* vol. XXXIII, p. 617) and then, upon the latter's promotion, on the staff of Gen. W. T. Sherman, commanding the Military Division of the Mississippi (*Ibid.,* vol. XXXVIII, pt. 4, p. 23), containing the three armies, of the Cumberland, of the Tennessee, and of Ohio. As Sherman's chief of artillery he engaged in most of the battles of the four-months' advance, which terminated in the capture of Atlanta; in the two-months' operation which had for its object the expulsion of Hood's army from Georgia and northeastern Alabama; in the three-months' campaign from Savannah through the two Carolinas, which terminated in the surrender of Johnston's army at Durham, N. C., on Apr. 26, 1865. He received the brevet rank of major-general of volunteers and colonel in the United States Army, Sept, 1, 1864, for his admirable conduct during the Atlanta campaign, and the brevets of brigadier and major-general in the United States Army, Mar. 13, 1865, for service in the campaign which embraced Sherman's "March to the Sea," and for "gallant and meritorious services in the field throughout the Rebellion" (Old Records Section, Adjutant-General's Office). On Dec. 11, 1865, he was promoted colonel of the 2nd Artillery. Mustered out of the volunteer service in January 1866, Barry was given a special command on the northern frontier during the Fenian troubles of that year. In the fall of 1867 he was selected to organize and conduct the Artillery School at Fort Monroe, Va., where he labored assiduously and successfully for ten years. In 1877, his health then much impaired, he was assigned to the command of Fort McHenry, where he died.

[In addition to the references above, see *Ass. Grads. U. S. Mil. Acad. Ann. Reunion,* 1880, and *Baltimore Sun,* July 19, 1879.]

C. A. B.

BARRY, WILLIAM TAYLOR (Feb. 5, 1785–Aug. 30, 1835), lawyer, statesman, was born in Lunenburg, Va., the son of John and Susannah (Dozier) Barry, and while yet a boy became a part of the great migration of hungry land-seekers and lawyers looking for fortune and fame in Kentucky. Like the Clays and Breckenridges, his family settled in Lexington, the most cultured city west of the mountains. He received his higher education at William and Mary College and his legal training at Transylvania College then entering on a period of remarkable usefulness to the West. Early in the century he began the practise of law in Lexington and in due time became a leader of the Democratic forces in the state. In 1806 he was elected to the Kentucky House of Representatives and again in 1809. As the troubles with England became more exasperating, he took a belligerent stand on the question of war and with his power of oratory stirred up the Kentuckians for the struggle. When the conflict began in 1812, he enlisted, but his only war service of note was in the battle of the Thames, where, as an aide to Gov. Shelby, he won the praise of Gen. Harrison. Barry was more interested in politics than in war, so in 1814 he stood for reëlection to the House and won. His popularity procured for him the next year an election to the United States Senate. The new position seems to have made little appeal to him. He appeared in Washington to take his seat two weeks late (Dec. 18, 1815) and throughout the whole session he did not make a single speech. He attended strictly to his duties of voting, however, and now and then offered a resolution. At the end of the session he resigned and returned to Kentucky.

He entered the state Senate in 1817 and remained there until 1821. By this time the state, having passed through the evanescent and buoyant prosperity following the war, was in the throes of hard times. Forty state banks had been "littered," and had died a speedy death. The state was divided into two bitterly contesting camps, the relief and anti-relief parties. Barry believed in the people and sympathized with them in their troubles. He had no time to study such intricate questions as banks and money while the people were sinking in despair under their heavy debts. He became a leader in the relief party and in 1821 was made their candidate for lieutenant-governor. In the election that followed he defeated W. B. Blackburn, the anti-relief candidate, 33,000 to 22,000. For the next four years he aided Gov. John Adair in putting through relief and replevin laws and in getting more worthless paper money printed. Barry was not a demagogue; he was a true democrat and his interest in the welfare of the people was genuine. One of his most constructive tasks was his effort to supply Kentucky with an effective educational system. As chairman of the committee appointed to investigate this subject he brought before the legislature a comprehensive report of an educational system which bore the approval of Jefferson, John Adams, and Robert Y. Hayne. It was debated but never adopted.

Barry's four years in the state House served to dispel none of Kentucky's distress. Relief measures, it is true, had been passed, but the court of appeals, the state's supreme judicial tribunal, had promptly declared them to be unconstitutional. With this turn to events, the anger of the relief party scarcely knew bounds. Under pressure the legislature voted the court out of existence in 1824, and early the following year it set up a "New Court" with Barry as the chief justice. But the "Old Court" refused to disband, and for two years the state was on the verge of anarchy. In December 1826 the anti-relief party or "Old Court" party, as it was now called, gained control of the state and voted Barry and his associates out of office.

The times were now ripe for the first great national contest in Kentucky. Clay and Jackson were fighting for supremacy. Barry, who had formerly been a close friend of Clay's, deserted him after the Adams alliance and was now seeking to gain Kentucky for Jackson. As part of the plan he ran for governor in 1828 and was defeated by the Clay candidate by only 709 votes out of a total vote of 77,171. In the presidential election he won the state for Jackson by almost 8,000 majority. As a reward for his valuable service Barry was slated for a justiceship in the United States Supreme Court; but because John McLean, the hold-over postmaster general, desired that position, an exchange was made and Barry became postmaster general Mar. 9, 1829. Before two years had passed the Senate was agitating an investigation of the department. A special committee was appointed in December 1830 and in the following March it produced a voluminous report, which was, however, not printed. But Barry was not to be allowed to rest in peace; the agitation, which was continued against him, resulted in 1834–35 in both houses instituting investigations. He was charged with favoritism in making contracts for carrying the mails, with increasing payments to contractors far beyond the published schedules, with sweeping dismissals from office, with illegally borrowing money, and with general looseness in his bookkeeping. Barry successfully refuted the charges which in any way reflected on his own honesty or represented any radical departures from the established customs of the department. He truthfully claimed that the investigations were largely caused by partisan spite, and that it was not only against himself but also against Jackson. Weary of mind and sick of body, he resigned in April 1835, and his steadfast friend President Jackson appointed him minister to Spain. He died in Liverpool on the way to his new mission. Nineteen years later his body was brought back and buried in the Frankfort Cemetery and in 1865 the Kentucky legislature erected a marker over his grave. Barry was twice married: first, to Lucy Overton, and second, to Catherine Mason.

[A sketch may be found in Lewis and Richard H. Collins, *Hist. of Ky.* (1874). Barry's part in the "Old Court" and "New Court" struggle is set forth to a considerable length in W. E. Connelley and E. M. Coulter, *Hist. of Ky.* (1922), II. The following works are also useful: *The Lawyers and Lawmakers of Ky.* (1897), ed. by H. Levin; *Lexington* [Ky.] *Reporter*, Oct. 30, 1813; G. W. Ranck, *Hist. of Lexington, Ky.* (1872); *Encyc. of Va. Biog.* (1915), II, ed. by L. G. Tyler; *Biog. Cong. Dir.* (1903); *Biog. Encyc. of Ky.* (1878).]

E. M. C.

BARRY, WILLIAM TAYLOR SULLIVAN (Dec. 10, 1821–Jan. 29, 1868), Confederate statesman and soldier, was the son of Richard and Mary (Sullivan) Barry, who moved from Virginia and established their home on the Tombigbee River, at the present site of Columbus, Miss., in the latter part of the second decade of the nineteenth century. The son was born in the new home a few months after the Jackson Military Road from Nashville to New Orleans had been completed through Columbus and a post office had been established in the village. After finishing a preparatory course in the home academy, young Barry attended Yale College, where he graduated in 1841. He then returned to Columbus and studied law in the office of Harrison & Harris. After his admission to the bar he formed a partnership with Judge J. S. Bennett. But he soon became "weary of professional monotony," and retired to his farm in Oktibbeha County (1847). Two years later he entered politics, and was twice elected to the lower house of the legislature. Reuben Davis, who knew Barry well, says that he enjoyed the excitement of a political campaign, but "abhorred the labors and responsibilities of office," and "could rarely be induced to work in harness." He was a man of imposing personality and of ability as a stump speaker, though his style was somewhat turgid and sophomoric. The same writer says that as a speaker Barry was in some respects the equal of Jefferson Davis and in others the equal of Sargent S. Prentiss "but in the aggregate inferior to both" (Reuben Davis, *Recollections of Mississippi and Mississippians,* 1889, pp. 97–98, 324–25, 336–37). In 1852 Barry removed to what is now Leflore County, in the Mississippi Delta, and in the following year was elected to the national House of Representatives. In a speech on "Civil and Religious Toleration," which he delivered in Congress, Dec. 18, 1854, he made a strong assault on the policy and principles of the Know-Nothing party. He declined reëlection at the end of his term in Congress, and resumed the practise of law in Columbus.

A few months later he reëntered politics, was elected to the legislature and made speaker of the House. He became a leader in the disunionist wing of the Democratic party in the state, and was among the delegates who withdrew from the Charleston convention in 1860 and nominated Breckenridge and Lane in the Baltimore convention. He was later chosen president of the Mississippi secession convention of 1861. It is said that he never again used the pen with which he signed the ordinance of secession, but carefully preserved it as a family heirloom. He was also chosen as one of the seven Mississippi delegates to the Montgomery convention which organized the Government of the Confederate States, and was then elected a member of the Provisional Congress of the Confederacy. At the inauguration of Jefferson Davis as Provisional President of the Confederacy, Barry made an extempore speech which according to James D. Lynch was "more happily conceived, more eloquently delivered and more highly applauded" than that of any other speaker on that occasion. In 1862 he resigned from the Confederate Congress and organized the 35th Regiment of Mississippi Infantry, of which he became colonel. He served in many engagements in Mississippi from the battle of Corinth to the fall of Vicksburg; also in the Georgia campaign, being wounded at Allatoona. He was finally captured at Mobile, Apr. 9, 1865. After the war he retired to his home, saying to a friend, "My thinking in the past has not been profitable—my hopes for my country have all been blasted, and as far as I can, I will quit thinking and for a while lead a negative existence." His despondency caused a rapid decline of his health, and he died in the house of his sister, Mrs. J. D. Bradford, of Columbus, Miss., Jan. 29, 1868. Shortly before his death he sent the following biographical note to the authorities of Yale College: "Originally a Democrat, then a states rights man, during the war a conscious rebel (so called), and at this time a pardoned reconstructed Johnson man." He then added that he was "Practising law in Columbus, trying to gather from the wreck which the war had made of all our fortunes whatever may be left, and to make a support for my family by my profession. As to religion, by education a Presbyterian; by taste an Episcopalian; in practise, nothing." He was married, Dec. 20, 1851, to Sally Fearn, daughter of Dr. Thomas Fearn, of Huntsville, Ala.

[The principal sources of information on the life of William S. Barry are the newspapers of Mississippi, 1849–68, and the *Cong. Globe* for the 33rd Congress. Biog. sketches will be found in *Biog. and Hist. Memoirs of Miss.* (1891), I, 353–54; James D. Lynch, *Bench and Bar of Miss.* (1881), pp. 295–301; Dunbar Rowland, *Mississippi* (1907), I, 215–16; *Biog. Cong. Dir.* (1903), p. 379.]

F. L. R.

BARRYMORE, GEORGIANA EMMA DREW (1856–July 2, 1893), actress, was a daughter of John Drew [*q.v.*] and Louisa (Lane) Drew [*q.v.*] and member of a theatrical family of English origin (see genealogical table in M. J. Moses, *Famous Actor Families of America,* 1906, and Parker's *Who's Who in the Theatre,* 1925). From her parents she inherited a wit, a fineness, a polish which gave her great appeal. Like most of the Drews, she grew up and was educated in Philadelphia and there entered into her theatrical career under the direction of her mother, beloved of all actresses. This began with a small rôle in Scribe's *The Ladies' Battle* in 1872, at the Philadelphia Arch Street Theatre where she remained for several years. But her brother, John Drew, having, in 1875, joined Augustin Daly, she followed in 1876, making her début as Mary Standish in *Pique* on Apr. 17, taking the place of Jeffreys Lewis. While with Daly, Miss Drew assumed such rôles as Mrs. Torrens in *The Serious Family,* Helen in H. J. Byron's *Weak Women,* Celia in *As You Like It* (to the Rosalind of Fanny Davenport and the Orlando of Charles Coghlan), Louise in *Frou-Frou,* Grace in *Divorce,* Mrs. Gresham in *Life,* Maria in an elaborate revival of *The School for Scandal* (Dec. 4, 1876), and Agnete in *The Princess Royal.* Maurice Barrymore [*q.v.*] was in the company. The two were married, Dec. 31, 1876, the children by this union being Ethel, Lionel, and John—all three with present distinction on the stage. Mrs. Barrymore's natural vivacity and quickness of intellect, her wit and sense of the comic, marked her both on the stage and in society—"a woman with a voice that is thin and that breaks . . . a woman with a fund of animal spirits and *fin de siècle* repartee." She next joined Palmer's stock company; for a while she supported her husband's venture as a star, and at brief periods was in support of Edwin Booth, Lawrence Barrett, and John McCullough. At various times she was also seen in *Diplomacy, The Wages of Sin, Moths, L'Abbé Constantin,* and *Mr. Wilkinson's Widow.* When her husband went to California in support of Madame Modjeska, she and her children joined him there, and it was while living under the sway of Modjeska's charm and devotion that Mrs. Barrymore, whose own family, as well as that of her husband, were Episcopalians, became Catholic. Serious illness cut short her career in 1892, her last Boston appearances being in Bisson's *Settled Out of Court,* Sept. 26, 1892, and Lestocq's *The Sportsman,* Oct. 17, 1892. In May 1893 she journeyed with her daughter Ethel to Santa Barbara, and it was there that she died. Critics of the time drew attention to the contagious humor of her look and gesture, to what they called her *élan.* She had a way, so it was claimed, of saying anything that came into her head. When she supported W. H. Crane in *The Senator,* she was described as being "as handsome as a picture, exquisitely dressed, brimming over with fun and an actress to the tips of her fingers." As to her appeal, the same review declared that "she captured her audience at once and kept them in roars of laughter." Miss Barrymore calls her mother gay and gallant, and designates the association of husband and wife as "a game of battledore and shuttlecock, his amazing brain against her native wit."

[*Ann. Cyc.,* 1893, p. 539; Ethel Barrymore, "Reminiscences," *Delineator,* Sept. 1923; John Barrymore, *Confessions of an Actor* (1926); J. F. Daly, *Life of Augustin Daly* (1917).]

M. J. M.

BARRYMORE, MAURICE (1847–Mar. 26, 1905), actor, whose real name was Herbert Blythe, "was born underground at Fort Agra (India), during those troublous '40's, when the Crown was fighting for control" (Ethel Barrymore, *Delineator,* September 1923). His father was a surveyor for the East India Company. Young Blythe was sent to England to study at Harrow and Oxford, first with the intention of entering the Indian Civil Service and then of becoming a lawyer. But instead the boy became a devotee of boxing and, in 1872, won the Queensberry cup and the amateur championship. In the same year he was induced to go on the stage, much to the consternation of his family. He chose the professional name of Barrymore, for some time retaining Herbert as his middle name. He began his career in a revival of *London Assurance,* and then received an engagement at the London Prince of Wales Theatre in Bulwer Lytton's *Money.* In 1875, with Charles Vandenhoff, he came to America, having previously toured the provinces with that actor.

His début was made in Boston in *Under the Gaslight.* Augustin Daly engaged him for summer stock during 1875, and then for two regular seasons at the New York Fifth Avenue Theatre. There now began a long career of excellent support of famous actors. Barrymore possessed grace of person and keenness of intellect, and these were noticeable as early as 1877, when he supported Jefferson and Fanny Davenport, and was commended by the critics for his Orlando and Orsino. But his many attempts to attain stardom were never successful. In 1878–79, a road company formed by Barrymore included his brother-in-law, John Drew, and his wife. It closed suddenly on Mar. 19, 1879, due to an unfortunate fracas in Texas. A long list of rôles demanded of Barrymore the exercise of his various abilities when he joined Lester Wallack's stock company in such pieces as *Our Girls, Old Heads and Young Hearts, She Stoops to Conquer,* and *The Shaughraun.* In playing parts like George Hastings, or Captain Absolute in *The Rivals,* Barrymore was in his element. In 1881 he went to England. Here, it is said, he offered to the Court Theatre as an original production of his own, a play named *Honour,* which, after acceptance, was discovered to be a mere translation of *L'Honneur de la Maison* by Léon Battu and Maurice Desvignes (*The Theatre,* London, Nov. 1, 1881, p. 301). Barrymore's work was extensively rewritten by dramatists in the employ of the theatre and was produced with proper acknowledgment to the French authors, on Sept. 24. The play was generally stigmatized by the critics as "dreary" and "repulsive," but was immensely successful, enjoying a run of 100 nights. Then began a long association with Madame Modjeska, and for her Barrymore wrote the Polish drama, *Nadjeska,* produced in Baltimore, Feb. 8, 1884. For four seasons he was the ideal Armand, Romeo, and Orlando for Modjeska. And with her, on Apr. 30, 1883, he appeared in *Romeo and Juliet,* the last performance to be given at the famous Booth Theatre in New York. He returned to England in November 1884, appearing at the London Haymarket in such plays as *Diplomacy, Masks and Faces, Engaged,* and *Jim the Penman.* Once more in 1886 he associated himself with Modjeska, ably supporting her in *Mary Stuart* and *Adrienne Lecouvreur.* In rapid succession he supported such players as Mrs. Langtry, Mrs. Bernard Beere, Katharine Clemmons, Olga Nethersole, and Mrs. Fiske, with the latter creating in finished manner the rôle of Rawdon Crawley, in *Becky Sharp* (Fifth Avenue Theatre, Sept. 12, 1898). He was engaged by Belasco for *The Heart of Maryland,* both in New York (Oct. 22, 1895) and in London (Apr. 8, 1898). Interspersed between these various engagements were his associations with A. M. Palmer, with his mother-in-law, Mrs. John Drew, in *The Rivals* (1893), with numberless summer stock companies, and even with vaudeville. It was worry incident upon a theatrical warfare waged between "The White Rats" (a vaudeville organization with which he was identified) and the vaudeville managers that led to a mental breakdown in a New York music hall, during what proved to be his last appearance. From 1901 to the day of his death, he was in confinement in a sanitarium.

Barrymore's personality was attractive, pervasive. He was witty, possessed a rich voice and a magnetic presence. His intellect was keen, though his memory was poor. Augustus Thomas, in several of whose early plays Barrymore appeared, thus describes him (*The Print of My Remembrance,* 1922): "In romantic costume or in evening dress on the stage, he had the grace of a panther. On the street or in the club, or coffee-house, he was negligent and loungy and deplorably indifferent to his attire. In the theatre, a queen could be proud of his graceful attention. Outside, a prize-fighter or a safe-blower was of absorbing interest to him unless some savant was about to discuss classical literature or French romance." During his various London residences, Barrymore was the center of that brilliant coterie which, beginning with Oscar Wilde, included such wits as the Trees, the Asquiths, and Mrs. Langtry. He was twice married: in 1876, to Georgiana Drew [*q.v.*], who died in 1893; and, the year after her death, to Mary Floyd.

[*Dram. Mirror,* Apr. 1, 1905; *Theatre Mag.,* May 1905; J. B. Clapp and E. F. Edgett, *Players of the Present* (1899–1901); *Memories and Impressions of Helena Modjeska* (1910); Joseph F. Daly, *Life of Augustin Daly* (1917); *Famous Am. Actors of Today* (1896), ed. by F. E. McKay and C. E. L. Wingate; John Drew, *My Years on the Stage* (1922).]

M. J. M.

VOLUME I, PART 2

BARSOTTI - BRAZER

(*VOLUME II OF THE ORIGINAL EDITION*)

CROSS REFERENCES FROM THIS VOLUME ARE MADE TO THE VOLUME NUMBERS OF THE ORIGINAL EDITION.

CONTRIBUTORS
VOLUME I, PART 2

Adeline Adams . . . . A. A—s.
James Truslow Adams . . . . J. T. A.
Robert G. Albion . . . . . . R. G. A.
Edmund Kimball Alden . . . E. K. A.
Albert Allemann . . . . . . A. A—n.
Charles Henry Ambler . . . C. H. A.
Katharine H. Amend . . . . K. H. A.
John Clark Archer . . . . . J. C. A.
Raymond Clare Archibald . . R. C. A.
Benjamin Wisner Bacon . . . B. W. B.
Theodore D. Bacon . . . . . T. D. B.
John Bakeless . . . . J. B.
Ray Palmer Baker . . . . . R. P. Ba—r.
Hayes Baker-Crothers . . . H. B-C.
James Curtis Ballagh . . . . J. C. B.
Thomas S. Barclay . . . . . T. S. B.
Charles Russell Bardeen . . C. R. B.
Viola Florence Barnes . . . V. F. B.
Ernest Sutherland Bates . . E. S. B.
William A. Beardsley . . . . W. A. B.
Charles F. D. Belden . . . . C. F. D. B.
Wells Bennett . . . . W. B—t.
John M. Berdan . . . . . . J. M. B.
Francis S. Betten . . . . . . F. S. B.
Ralph Paul Bieber . . . . . R. P. Bi—r.
Theodore C. Blegen . . . . . T. C. B.
G. Alder Blumer . . . . . . G. A. B.
George Blumer . . . . G. B.
Theodore Bolton . . . . . . T. B.
Milledge Louis Bonham . . . M. L. B.
Stephen Bonsal . . . . S. B.
Witt Bowden . . . . W. B—n.
Sarah G. Bowerman . . . . . S. G. B.
Charles N. Boyd . . . . . . C. N. B.
William Kenneth Boyd . . . W. K. B.
Benjamin Brawley . . . . . B. B.
Edward Breck . . . . E. B.
Clarence Saunders Brigham . C. S. B.
Herbert O. Brigham . . . . H. O. B.
Albert Britt . . . . A. B.
Robert Preston Brooks . . . R. P. B—s.
John S. Brubacher . . . . . J. S. B.
Kathleen Bruce . . . . . . K. B.
Philip Alexander Bruce . . P. A. B.
George Sands Bryan. . . . . G. S. B.
Oscar MacMillan Buck . . . O. M. B.
Guy H. Burnham . . . . . . G. H. B.
Walter Lincoln Burrage . . W. L. B.
Pierce Butler. . . . . P. B.
William B. Cairns . . . . . W. B. C.
Charles F. Carey . . . . . . C. F. C.
Harry J. Carman . . . . . . H. J. C.
Clarence Edwin Carter . . . C. E. C.
Hope S. Chamberlain . . . . H. S. C.
Frank H. Chase . . . . F. H. C.
Wayland J. Chase . . . . . . W. J. C.
Francis Albert Christie . . F. A. C.
Allen L. Churchill . . . . . A. L. C.
Dora Mae Clark . . . . . . D. M. C.
Robert Glass Cleland . . . . R. G. C—d.
Oral S. Coad . . . . O. S. C.
Frederick W. Coburn . . . . F. W. C.
James Fairbanks Colby . . . J. F. C.
Fannie L. Gwinner Cole . . . F. L. G. C.
Kenneth Colegrove . . . . . K. C.
Henry C. Conrad . . . . . . H. C. C.
Lane Cooper . . . . L. C.
Edward S. Corwin . . . . . E. S. C.
R. S. Cotterill . . . . R. S. C.
Ellis Merton Coulter. . . . E. M. C.
Isaac Joslin Cox . . . . . . I. J. C.
John Cox, Jr. . . . . J. C.
Verner W. Crane . . . . . V. W. C.
Avery O. Craven . . . . . . A. O. C.
Henry Crew . . . . H. C.
Walter Hill Crockett . . . W. H. C.
Merle E. Curti . . . . M. E. C.
Harrison Clifford Dale . . H. C. D.
Elizabeth Thompson Davison E. T. D.
Ralph Davol . . . . R. D.
Charles De Kay . . . . . . C. De K.
Charles Allen Dinsmore . . C. A. D.
Eleanor Robinette Dobson . E. R. D.
Augustus Waldo Drury . . . A. W. D.
Raymond Smith Dugan . . . R. S. D.
J. H. Easterby . . . . J. H. E—y.
Walter Prichard Eaton . . . W. P. E.
Edwin Francis Edgett . . . E. F. E.
John H. Edmonds . . . . . . J. H. E—s.
Samuel Atkins Eliot. . . . . S. A. E.
Forest Chester Ensign . . . F. C. E.
Charles R. Erdman, Jr. . . . C. R. E.
Logan Esarey . . . . L. E.
Harold Underwood Faulkner H. U. F.
John Alfred Faulkner . . . J. A. F.
Albert Bernhardt Faust . . A. B. F.
Carl Russell Fish . . . . . C. R. F.
Morris Fishbein . . . . . . M. F.
Walter Lynwood Fleming . . W. L. F.
Alexander Clarence Flick . A. C. F.
Blanton Fortson . . . . . . B. F.
Harold North Fowler . . . H. N. F.

Contributors

Early Lee Fox	E. L. F.	Charles Ramsdell Lingley	C. R. L.
Claude Moore Fuess	C. M. F.	Henry Miller Lydenberg	H. M. L.
Kemper Fullerton	K. F.	Thomas Denton McCormick	T. D. M.
John F. Fulton	J. F. F.	Roswell Cheney McCrea	R. C. M.
Clarence M. Gallup	C. M. G.	Philip B. McDonald	P. B. M.
Fielding H. Garrison	F. H. G.	William MacDonald	W. M.
Samuel W. Geiser	S. W. G.	George Tremaine McDowell	G. T. M.
George H. Genzmer	G. H. G.	John H. T. McPherson	J. H. T. M
Beatrice Chandler Gesell	B. C. G.	Harry A. Marmer	H. A. M.
W. J. Ghent	W. J. G.	Thomas M. Marshall	T. M. M.
Colin B. Goodykoontz	C. B. G.	Frederick Herman Martens	F. H. M.
Gladys Graham	G. G—m.	Lawrence Shaw Mayo	L. S. M.
Walter S. Grant	W. S. G.	Leila Mechlin	L. M.
Louis H. Gray	L. H. G.	George Perkins Merrill	G. P. M.
Gilbert Grosvenor	G. G—r.	Roger B. Merriman	R. B. M.
Peter Guilday	P. G.	Edwin Mims	E. M.
Amelia Mott Gummere	A. M. G.	Mary Hewitt Mitchell	M. H. M.
Mary C. Ham	M. C. H.	Carl W. Mitman	C. W. M.
Philip M. Hamer	P. M. H.	Frank Monaghan	F. M.
J. G. de Roulhac Hamilton	J. G. de R. H.	Charles Moore	C. M.
Talbot F. Hamlin	T. F. H.	Thomas F. Moran	T. F. M.
Fairfax Harrison	F. H.	Samuel Eliot Morison	S. E. M.
Benjamin Harrow	B. H.	Richard L. Morton	R. L. M.
Edward Hart	E. H.	Montrose J. Moses	M. J. M.
Louis C. Hatch	L. C. H.	George Fulmer Mull	G. F. M.
Thomas Robson Hay	T. R. H.	Edwin G. Nash	E. G. N.
Stella Herron	S. H.	Allan Nevins	A. N.
Russell Hickman	R. H.	Lyman C. Newell	L. C. N.
John Donald Hicks	J. D. H.	Claude M. Newlin	C. M. N.
Frank L. Hise	F. L. H.	Roy F. Nichols	R. F. N.
Albert A. Hopkins	A. A. H.	A. B. Noble	A. B. N.
Arthur Hornblow	A. H.	Charles Noble	C. N.
Walter Hough	W. H.	Frank M. O'Brien	F. M. O.
Harold Howland	H. H.	John W. Oliver	J. W. O.
Hannah Clothier Hull	H. C. H.	Robert B. Osgood	R. B. O.
William Jackson Humphreys	W. J. H.	Marie B. Owen	M. B. O.
Edith J. R. Isaacs	E. J. R. I.	Francis Randolph Packard	F. R. P.
A. V. Williams Jackson	A. V. W. J.	Victor H. Paltsits	V. H. P.
James Alton James	J. A. J.	Stanley M. Pargellis	S. M. P.
W. L. G. Joerg	W. L. G. J.	Frederic Logan Paxson	F. L. P.
Alfonso Johnson	A—o J.	C. C. Pearson	C. C. P.
Allen Johnson	A—n J.	Henry G. Pearson	H. G. P.
Hope Frances Kane	H. F. K.	Donald Culross Peattie	D. C. P.
Marie A. Kasten	M. A. K.	Frederick Torrel Persons	F. T. P.
Lyman F. Kebler	L. F. K.	A. Everett Peterson	A. E. P.
Herbert A. Kellar	H. A. K.	James M. Phalen	J. M. P.
Louise Phelps Kellogg	L. P. K.	Francis S. Philbrick	F. S. P.
Isoline Rodd Kendall	I. R. K.	David Philipson	D. P.
William Joseph Kerby	W. J. K.	Paul Chrisler Phillips	P. C. P.
Grant C. Knight	G. C. K.	William Whatley Pierson, Jr.	W. W. P.
H. W. Howard Knott	H. W. H. K.	Henry Augustus Pilsbry	H. A. P.
Alois F. Kovarik	A. F. K.	Frank W. Pitman	F. W. P.
William Chauncy Langdon	W. C. L.	John A. Pollard	J. A. P.
Conrad H. Lanza	C. H. L—a.	Herbert Ingram Priestley	H. I. P.
James Melvin Lee	J. M. L.	Richard J. Purcell	R. J. P.
Paul S. Leinbach	P. S. L.	Arthur Hobson Quinn	A. H. Q.
Orin G. Libby	O. G. L.	Charles Henry Rammelkamp	C. H. R.
Charles H. Lincoln	C. H. L—n.	Charles William Ramsdell	C. W. R.

Contributors

Belle Rankin . . . . B. R.
Charles Dudley Rhodes . . C. D. R.
Lyon N. Richardson . . . . . L. N. R.
Irving Berdine Richman . . . I. B. R.
William Alexander Robinson W. A. R.
Lindsay Rogers . . . . L. R.
John J. Rolbiecki . . . . . . J. J. R.
George Rose III . . . . . . G. R.
A. S. W. Rosenbach . . . . . A. S. W. R.
Frank Edward Ross . . . . . F. E. R.
Henry Kalloch Rowe . . . . H. K. R.
Robert R. Rowe . . . . . . R. R. R.
Dunbar Rowland . . . . . . D. R.
Ralph L. Rusk . . . . R. L. R.
Sumner Salter . . . . S. S.
Joseph Schafer . . . . J. S.
Robert Livingston Schuyler R. L. S.
Louis M. Sears . . . . L. M. S.
Benjamin F. Shambaugh . . . B. F. S.
Muriel Shaver . . . . M. S.
William Bristol Shaw . . . . W. B. S.
Hiram H. Shenk . . . . H. H. S.
Clarence A. Skinner . . . . C. A. S.
David Eugene Smith . . . . D. E. S.
Edgar Fahs Smith . . . . . . E. F. S.
W. E. Smith . . . . W. E. S.
James A. Spalding . . . . . . J. A. S.
Thomas Marshall Spaulding T. M. S.
Charles W. Spencer . . . . C. W. S.
Harris Elwood Starr . . . . H. E. S.
Henry P. Stearns . . . . . . H. P. S.
Nathaniel Wright Stephenson N. W. S.
Earl Gregg Swem . . . . . E. G. S.
Edwin Platt Tanner . . . . E. P. T.
Frank A. Taylor . . . . . . F. A T—r.
David Y. Thomas . . . . . . D. Y. T.
Wilbur Fisk Tillett . . . . W. F. T.
Ezra Squier Tipple . . . . . E. S. T.
Francis A. Tondorf . . . . . F. A. T—f.
Alfred M. Tozzer . . . . . . A. M. T.
Alfred Charles True . . . . A. C. T.
William Treat Upton . . . . W. T. U.
Arnold J. F. Van Laer . . . A. J. F. V–L.
Victor C. Vaughan . . . . . V. C. V.
Henry R. Viets . . . . H. R. V.
Jonas Viles . . . . J. V.
Eugene M. Violette . . . . E. M. V.
Dayton Voorhees . . . . . . D. V.
John Donald Wade . . . . . J. D. W.
James Elliott Walmsley . . J. E. W—y.
Frank Weitenkampf . . . . . F. W.
Raynor G. Wellington . . . R. G. W.
Allan Westcott . . . . A. W.
Arthur P. Whitaker . . . . A. P. W.
Walter Lincoln Whittlesey . W. L. W—y.
Robert J. Wickenden . . . . R. J. W.
Jeanne Elizabeth Wier . . . J. E. W—r.
Walter F. Willcox . . . . . W. F. W.
Clarence Russell Williams . C. R. W—s.
Stanley Thomas Williams . . S. T. W.
H. Parker Willis . . . . . . H. P. W.
James A. Woodburn . . . . . J. A. W.
Clinton Rogers Woodruff . . C. R. W—f.
Carter Godwin Woodson . . C. G. W.
Thomas Woody . . . . T. W.
Ernest H. Wright . . . . . . E. H. W.
Helen Wright. . . . . H. W.
Herbert F. Wright . . . . . H. F. W.
Walter L. Wright, Jr. . . . . W. L. W—t.
Mary A. Wyman . . . . . . M. A. W.
Julien C. Yonge . . . . . . J. C. Y.
Edna Yost . . . . E. Y.
Andrew C. Zenos . . . . . . A. C. Z.

DICTIONARY OF

AMERICAN BIOGRAPHY

Barsotti — Brazer

BARSOTTI, CHARLES (Jan 4, 1850–Mar. 30, 1927), editor, publisher, philanthropist, born in Bagni di San Giuliano, near Pisa, doubtless inherited from his father, Giulio, who had achieved success as a country landowner, that executive and managerial ability which enabled him to be successful in his business enterprises. From his mother, Rosa Pannocchia, a native of Santa Maria del Giudice, near Lucca, came his love of music and sculpture. He came to America in 1872, settled in New York City, and in 1880 established, in the old Herald Building, *Il Progresso,* the first Italian daily in the United States. Its success was so remarkable that new quarters had to be secured at 42 Duane St. Continued success made another change necessary, this time to a building owned by the paper itself at 42 Elm St. Subscribers were in a way partners of Barsotti in that they aided him in erecting statues to famous Italians: Giovanni da Verrazano in Battery Park, Giuseppe Garibaldi in Washington Square, Christopher Columbus occupying the pivotal position in Columbus Circle at Fifty-ninth St. and Eighth Avenue, Dante at Broadway and Sixty-third St., and Giuseppe Verdi at Broadway and Seventy-third St. His subscribers also aided him in contributing to the relief of suffering in Italy. In recognition of service in this field Barsotti was decorated by the King of Italy with the Cross of Grand Officer of the Crown of Italy. In his later years he contributed $250,000 toward a tunnel through that mountain, separating Pisa from Lucca, which has been famous ever since Dante's line—*"Per che i Pisan veder Lucca non ponno."* The woman who shared in these enterprises as a life partner was Margaret Heist of Frankfort, Germany, whom Barsotti married in 1875. His last years were spent, not in New York City, but in the little New Jersey town of Coytesville, on the Palisades across the Hudson.

[Long obituary in the *N.Y. Times,* Mar. 31, 1927. In J. Sanford Saltus and Walter E. Tisney, *Statues of New York* (1923), may be found details about the statues erected through Barsotti's efforts.] J.M.L.

BARSTOW, WILLIAM AUGUSTUS (Sept. 13, 1813–Dec. 14, 1865), governor of Wisconsin, was the son of William A. Barstow, one of seven brothers who served in the Revolutionary War. He was born in Connecticut, but settled in Wisconsin in 1839. In April 1844 he married Maria Quarles of Southport, now Kenosha, Wis. He became secretary of state in 1850, and his name never escaped the unkind implication of a phrase used in that year by a Madison editor who was determined to get the contract for state printing even if he had to "buy up Barstow and the balance" of the members of the printing board. He was elected governor, on the Democratic ticket, in 1853. Declared reëlected in 1855, by a slender plurality of 157 votes, he took office for his second term in January 1856; but on the same day his Republican rival in the election, Coles Bashford [*q.v.*], also took the oath of office, and there were two pretending governors in the state. By tacit agreement of the contenders and the legislature, Barstow was left *de facto* governor, pending an examination of the claims of Bashford by the supreme court. The leaders of the Wisconsin bar for the next generation were paraded in this litigation. Barstow denied the right of the court to take jurisdiction over a coördinate branch of the government. He refused to plead when the court assumed jurisdiction, and resigned after testimony had been heard indicating that fraudulent returns had been manufactured in Madison and counted as from precincts which proved to be nonexistent. Bashford was awarded the office by the supreme court, Mar. 24, 1856. Barstow became interested in railroads and their development and in 1855 became president of the St. Croix & Lake Superior Railroad Company. He was also a miller and a banker. During the Civil War he was commissioned colonel on Nov. 9, 1861, raised his own regiment, and in the spring of 1862 was sent as provost-marshal-general to Kansas, where he was defeated and narrowly avoided capture. He served in Arkansas and Missouri (1862–63), after which, because of ill health, most of his military duty was upon courts martial.

[Brief sketches of his life are in *Wis. Hist. Soc. Colls.*, VI, 93–122; see also *The Trial in the Supreme Court . . . of Coles Bashford vs. Wm. A. Barstow* (Madison, 1856).]

F. L. P.

BARTHOLOMEW, EDWARD SHEFFIELD (July 8, 1822–May 1858), sculptor, after spending the first fourteen years of his life at Colchester, Conn., where he attended the Bacon Academy, moved with his parents, Abial Lord and Sarah Gustin, to Hartford. The change made him shy; even in after life he found it difficult to meet strangers. He worked as assistant, first to a bookbinder, then to a dentist, but was dissatisfied and was regarded somewhat as a vagabond by the thrifty people among whom he lived. To escape the uncongenial atmosphere he went to New York, and for a year studied in the "Antique and Life School" of the Academy of Design. On his return to Hartford he became curator of the Wadsworth Gallery and at the same time continued his art work. He soon discovered, however, that he was color-blind. Bitterly disappointed, he turned to sculpture, for even as a boy he had been fond of modeling in clay. He first attempted, with inadequate tools, a medallion of Mrs. Sigourney; then, with better implements, a bust of "Flora." In 1848 he went again to New York to attend a series of anatomical lectures. While there he contracted smallpox, followed by a hip affection which crippled him. Hitherto he had been strong and vigorous, and of prepossessing appearance—tall and dark, but after this calamity he was lame and unwell for the rest of his brief life. Shortly after this an opportunity to go to Italy came and he departed in 1850. Thereafter he made but two visits to America, on one of which he superintended the erection of his monument to Charles Carroll. In Rome he began, with a bas-relief of "Homer led by the Genius of Poetry," the productive period of his life. He studied under Ferrero, working particularly at bas-relief. His first year in Rome was an uphill struggle, but after a four months' journey to Athens and the Near East, he began to win recognition. His most admired work was a statue of "Eve Repentant." Though frequently using biblical subjects ("Paradise Lost"; "Hagar and Ishmael"; "Ruth, Naomi and Orpah"), he more generally resorted to classical themes ("Sappho"; "Calypso"; "Ganymede"; "Diana"; "Belisarius"). He likewise did numerous portraits, such as those of the Colts and their children. True to contemporary American taste and to Italian teaching he was thoroughly neo-classic in the treatment of subject, though fonder of introducing superfluous and picturesque accessories than was Canova or Thorwaldsen. His execution was not always adequate, but this fault he was overcoming when, shortly after his return from his second American trip, he was taken ill. On the advice of his physician he went to Naples, but only to die.

[G. W. Bartholomew, *Record of the Bartholomew Family* (1885); Susan Crane in *Conn. Quart.*, vol. II, no. 3; *Art and Artists in Conn.*, by H. W. French (1879). Articles and notices on Bartholomew are frequently in disagreement as to minor details, *e.g.*, the date of his death which is variously given as the 1st, 2nd, or 3rd of May. A number of his works, either originals or casts, are in the Morgan Memorial Museum at Hartford.]

E. G. N.

BARTHOLOW, ROBERTS (Nov. 28, 1831–May 10, 1904), physician and author, was born at New Windsor, Md. He attended Calvert College (B.A. 1848, M.A. 1854), and in 1852 he graduated from the Medical Department of the University of Maryland. In 1855, he was commissioned assistant surgeon in the United States Army and during the next four or five years saw considerable active service in the West in the troubles with the Mormons and Indians. During the Civil War he was on duty in various military hospitals; wrote *A Manual of Instruction for Enlisting and Discharging Soldiers* (1863), which was the standard authority for many years; and also wrote a book entitled *Qualifications for the Medical Service*. In 1864 he resigned from the army and began the practise of medicine in Cincinnati, receiving the appointment of professor of medical chemistry in the Medical College of Ohio. He soon acquired a large practise but nevertheless found time to establish and edit a medical journal, the *Clinic*. In 1867, he was transferred from the chair of chemistry to that of materia medica. In 1874, he aroused a great sensation by publishing in the *American Journal of the Medical Sciences* the report of a case of malignant tumor of the scalp and skull in which the brain had been exposed by the progress of the disease. With the full consent of the patient, who realized that he was fatally ill, Bartholow applied electric stimulation to various areas of the exposed brain in order to corroborate the results obtained by Hitzig and Ferrier in lower animals. Although his experiments confirmed the observations of these investigators, they resulted in serious damage to the patient, who succumbed a few days later from an extension of the cancer producing a thrombus of the longitudinal sinus. This was candidly admitted by Bartholow in his very full report of the affair ("Experimental Investigations into the Functions of the Human Brain," *American Journal of the Medical Sciences,* April 1874, pp. 305–13). His paper raised a perfect storm of disapprobation and protest, but the consensus of opinion finally turned in his favor. He was appointed professor of the practise of medicine in the Medical College of Ohio, but in 1879 resigned to go to Philadelphia as professor of materia medica and therapeutics in Jefferson Medical College. He resigned this position in 1893 because of failing health and eleven years later died at his home in Philadelphia at the age of seventy-two. Bartholow was a voluminous contributor to periodical medical literature. He wrote no less than four essays which received prizes and after giving up the editorship of the *Clinic* on his removal to Philadelphia he became one of the editors of the *Medical News.* His *Practical Treatise on Materia Medica and Therapeutics* (1876) went through eleven editions, and eight editions were published of his *Treatise on the Practise of Medicine* (1880).

[James W. Holland, "Memoir of Roberts Bartholow," *Trans. Coll. Physicians of Phila.,* ser. 3, vol. XXVI (1904), pp. 43–52; Davina Waterson, sketch in *Am. Medic. Biogs.* (1920), ed. by Kelly and Burrage; *Phila. Pub. Ledger,* May 11, 1904.]

F. R. P.

BARTLET, WILLIAM (Jan. 31, 1748 N.S.–Feb. 8, 1841), merchant, philanthropist, was born in Newburyport, Mass., the son of Edmund and Hannah (Hall) Bartlet and a direct descendant of Richard Bartlet, who settled in Newbury in 1635. At an early age he left school to learn shoemaking. Naturally shrewd and enterprising, he was soon actively engaged in commerce and acquired a considerable fortune. At the close of the Revolution he became the owner of a large fleet of merchant vessels and numerous wharves and warehouses, and was one of the first in New England to undertake textile manufacturing. He served three terms as representative in the Massachusetts General Court, from 1800 to 1802. In 1774 he married Betty (Coombs) Lascomb, widow of Robert Lascomb. As he became increasingly prosperous, he erected in 1798 a large three-story brick mansion on Federal St., in Newburyport, where he lived until his death. An inscription on his monument describes him as "a distinguished merchant and a liberal patron of theological learning." The money which Bartlet accumulated through thrift and wise investments he devoted largely to philanthropic projects, especially to Andover Theological Seminary, opened in 1808. Although he attended public worship regularly, he was not a church member; but Dr. Samuel Spring, a Newburyport clergyman, persuaded him to join with Moses Brown, a fellow townsman, and John Norris of Salem, in supplying the necessary funds for a school in which Calvinistic divinity students could be trained for the ministry. At about the same period a similar plan was formed by Dr. Eliphalet Pearson and a group of his friends living in Andover, Mass., twenty miles from Newburyport, with whom they formed a coalition. To Andover Theological Seminary, Bartlet gave originally $20,000. He later added $15,000 for the endowment of a Bartlet professorship of sacred rhetoric and built two houses for the accommodation of members of the faculty. He provided the money for the erection of Bartlet Chapel (1818) and of Bartlet Hall (1821) for the growing seminary. These structures, when Andover Theological Seminary was transferred to Cambridge in 1908, were purchased by Phillips Academy, Andover, and are to-day occupied by that preparatory school. At his death Bartlet left a bequest of $50,000 to the seminary, and his benefactions to it aggregated more than $160,000. Physically Bartlet was large and powerful, imposing in his bearing, and kept his bodily vigor to extreme old age. His tastes were simple, even crude; he cared nothing for the graces of polite society. In his business dealings he was scrupulously just, paying his debts promptly and insisting that others do the same. He combined frugality in small matters with lavish generosity when his emotions were aroused. Unassuming and modest in his benefactions, he did not wish his name to be mentioned in connection with them and looked upon himself as "the mere steward of a merciful Providence."

[The best account of Bartlet's career is found in the *Hist. of Newburyport, Mass.* (1909), by John J. Currier. *A Memorial of the Semi-Centennial Celebration of the Founding of the Theological Seminary at Andover* (1859) and the *Hist. of the Andover Theological Seminary* (1885), by Leonard Woods, contain additional information. The story of the founding of Andover Theological Seminary is told in *An Old New England School* (1917), by Claude M. Fuess.]

C. M. F.

BARTLETT, ELISHA (Oct. 6, 1804–July 19, 1855), physician, teacher, and author, was born at Smithfield, R. I., the son of Otis and Waite Buffum Bartlett, who were Quakers. His preliminary education was had at a Friends' institution in New York, the details being lacking. We know that he studied medicine with Dr. George Willard of Uxbridge, Dr. John Green and Dr. B. F. Heywood of Worcester, and Dr. Levi Wheaton of Providence; he attended medical lectures in Boston and Providence, entered the medical department of Brown University, and took his degree in 1826, two years before the closing of this branch of the University. In June of that year he sailed for Europe, where he attended the Jardin des Plantes to hear the lectures of Cloquet and Cuvier. In 1827, he settled in Lowell, where he lived for nearly twenty of his remaining twenty-eight years of medical activity. In 1829 he married Elizabeth Slater of Smithfield, R. I. When he had been a citizen for nine years he was elected the first mayor of the new city (1836). From this will be seen that he had an interest in public service. He held his first teaching position in 1832, when not yet twenty-eight years old, as professor of pathological anatomy and materia medica in the Berkshire Medical Institution at Pittsfield, Mass., then a strong school which turned out more graduates in medicine than the Harvard Medical School. A list of Bartlett's teaching positions in the succeeding years is a long one: professor of theory and practise of medicine at Transylvania University, Lexington, Ky., 1841, also 1846; professor of the theory and practise of medicine at the University of Maryland, Baltimore, 1844–46; the same position at the University of Louisville, Ky., 1849–50; professor of the institutes and practise of medicine in New York University, 1850–52; and finally professor of materia medica and medical jurisprudence in the College of Physicians and Surgeons, New York, 1852–55. He had also lectured on the topics of materia medica and obstetrics at the Vermont Medical College in the spring and summer months from 1843 to 1852. It was said of him that he could make the dryest and most barren subject interesting.

Bartlett began his career as a medical writer in the *Monthly Journal of Medical Literature and American Medical Students' Gazette,* only three numbers of which were issued. Then in July 1832 he was associated with Dr. A. L. Pierson and Dr. J. B. Flint in the *Medical Magazine,* which was published monthly in Boston for the succeeding three years. Independently he printed in 1831 a small book entitled *Sketches of the Character and Writings of Eminent Living Surgeons and Physicians of Paris,* translated from the French of J. L. H. Peisse. It contained the lives of nine French physicians and gave an attractive insight into the history of medicine in Paris at the beginning of the nineteenth century. Bartlett's chief work was his treatise on *The Fevers in the United States* (1842), reprinted in 1847, 1852, and 1857, the last after his death. In it he gave a remarkably accurate description of typhoid fever, which in its main outlines cannot be improved to-day. It was one of the most noteworthy contributions to medicine of the first half of the nineteenth century. In his *Essay on the Philosophy of Medicine* (1844), he shows himself to be an acute and thoughtful observer; he applies deductive reasoning to medical problems. It is called by William Osler "a classic in American medical literature" (*American Medical Biographies,* edited by H. A. Kelly and W. L. Burrage, 1920, p. 65). Four years later appeared *An Inquiry into the Degree of Certainty of Medicine, and into the Nature and Extent of Its Power over Disease.* It was a small pamphlet of eighty-four pages that expounded views that were in advance of the times, shocking some of the conservative members of the profession, who preferred to be governed in their ideas by tradition and not by what they saw. Bartlett published, in 1849, *A Discourse on the Life and Labors of Dr. H. Charles Wells, the Discoverer of the Philosophy of Dew,* and the next year a brochure entitled *History, Diagnosis and Treatment of Edematous Laryngitis.* Among his occasional addresses, in which he was at his best, a lecture delivered in 1843, on *The Sense of the Beautiful,* was a plea for the education of the faculty of medicine, and another, *The Head and the Heart, or the Relative Importance of Intellectual and Moral Education,* was an exhortation for a higher tone in social and political morality. One of his last publications was *A Discourse on the Times, Character, and Writings of Hippocrates,* delivered as an introductory address before the trustees, faculty, and students of the College of Physicians and Surgeons, at the opening of the session of 1852–53. This was considered a masterpiece of medical biography, depicting the founder of medicine in the different phases of his life with the utmost clearness and interest.

At the close of the session of the College of Physicians and Surgeons in New York, of 1853–54, a nervous malady from which Bartlett had been suffering, the exact nature of which is not known, became worse. He retired to his birthplace, Smithfield, and after a protracted illness, during which he became paralyzed without impairment of his mental faculties, he died at the comparatively early age of fifty. Bartlett was in his mental outlook and his power of expression far in advance of most of the men of his time.

Most instructors were then everyday practitioners who were content to impart to their students the facts they had gathered, without comment or general application. Bartlett was a man of vision, of wide interests, who saw the relation of medicine to the affairs of the community, and could forecast the trend of doctrines and evaluate them.

[Samuel Henry Dickson, "Memoir of Elisha Bartlett" in S. D. Gross, *Lives of Eminent Am. Physicians and Surgeons* (1861); William Osler, *Elisha Bartlett, a Rhode Island Philosopher* (1900); Elisha Huntington, *An Address on the Life of Elisha Bartlett* (Lowell, 1855).]
W. L. B.

BARTLETT, HOMER NEWTON (Dec. 28, 1845–Apr. 3, 1920), musical composer, was born at Olive, Ulster County, N. Y., and died at Hoboken, N. J. His father, Henry B. Bartlett, claimed descent from Josiah Bartlett [*q.v.*], a signer of the Declaration of Independence, and his mother, Hannah C. Hall, from John Rogers, eighteenth signer of the Mayflower Compact. In his early childhood the family removed to Ellenville, N. Y., where the father kept a general store. At the age of five Bartlett gave signs of musical precocity by playing the violin, holding the instrument cello-fashion between his knees. He played in public at the age of nine and at ten began to compose. His general education, begun at the Ellenville Academy, from which he graduated in 1861, was then continued under private tutors in New York, where he studied piano under Emil Guyon (pupil of Thalberg) and S. B. Mills, organ under Max Braun, and harmony and counterpoint under O. F. Jacobsen. He at once became organist at "Old Spring Street" Church, soon after going to the Marble Collegiate Church, where he remained twelve years, and later to the Madison Avenue Baptist Church, which he served for a period of thirty-one years, when he was retired as organist emeritus in 1912. A man of modest but friendly disposition, he was sympathetic to all progressive tendencies in music and contributed much to the success of the Manuscript Society, the American Guild of Organists, the National Association of Organists, of which he was at one time president, and the Musicians Club of New York. He was an indefatigable worker in his art, one for whom composition was not merely an absorbing interest but virtually a dominant passion. Even when opus numbers had mounted to 269 in the publisher's catalogue and he was near his end, he craved length of days to compose, saying that he had "just begun to know how to write." His music was in general tinged by the suavity which characterized the man. Incapable of giving offense, he gave no intimation of radical tendencies. As he was largely self-taught and a diligent student of the works of his more immediate predecessors, it is not surprising to find in his music numerous instances of imitation. His youthful study of the violin, as also his piano training in the school of Thalberg, somewhat predetermined the marked melodic trend in his compositions, which, while often rich in primary harmonic color and often embellished in florid figuration, show less resource in the use of chromatic tints both in choice and treatment of themes and in infrequent resort to the polyphonic idiom. His Opus 1, "Grand Polka de Concert" (1867), written as a birthday present to the young lady who became his wife, perhaps the most deservedly popular and successful of any Opus 1 by an American composer, is outstanding for its enduring vitality. The list of his published compositions includes about seventy songs, an equal number of piano pieces, and about as many part songs and pieces of church music, besides music for organ and violin.

[For lists of published compositions, see catalogues of G. Schirmer, Inc., and Oliver Ditson Co. Biog. information and critical comment in R. Hughes and A. Elson, *Am. Composers* (revised ed. 1914), pp. 317-23; A. Farwell and W. D. Darby, *The Art of Music* (1915), IV, 383; *Grove's Dict., Am. Supp.* (1920); obituary in *N. Y. Times*, Apr. 4, 1920.]
S. S.

BARTLETT, ICHABOD (July 24, 1786–Oct. 19, 1853), lawyer, politician, was born at Salisbury, N. H., the son of Dr. Joseph and Hannah (Colcord) Bartlett. His father was a trusted and skilful physician with a large practise, and active in the affairs of the community. Ichabod attended the local academy and after graduation at Dartmouth in 1808 studied law. He was admitted to the bar in 1811 and after practising for several years at Durham moved to Portsmouth in 1818, where he resided until his death. He was never married. He began his political career as a Jeffersonian Republican, was clerk of the state Senate in 1817–18, and in the latter year was appointed by Gov. Plumer to study the subject of internal improvements in New Hampshire, preparing an elaborate report on the improvement of roads and waterways which was laid before the legislature of 1819. He represented Portsmouth in the legislature 1819–21, being speaker in the latter year, and again in 1830, 1838, 1851, and 1852 (*New Hampshire Register*). In 1852 he was unsuccessfully supported for the speakership by the Whigs. During his first term in the legislature he supported the Toleration Act in an unusually forceful and eloquent address, one of the few of his speeches which has been preserved (*New Hampshire Patriot*, July 20, 27, 1819). His success at the bar came early, as is evidenced by the fact that in 1817 he appeared before the superior court as counsel for Woodward in the Dartmouth College Case, with which the most eminent lawyers in the state were associated (Timothy Farrar, *Report of the Case of the Trustees of Dartmouth College against William H. Woodward,* Portsmouth, 1819. Bartlett's argument is printed on pp. 116–206). He was solicitor for Rockingham County, 1818–21 (*New Hampshire Register,* 1819–21), and throughout his life appeared in noted civil and criminal cases. In 1822 he was elected to Congress and served three successive terms. He was not prominent in the House, but his sympathies with National Republicanism appear in the few speeches he made in that body. His longest address was a vigorous defense of the administration of President John Quincy Adams, Feb. 6, 1828 (*Register of Debates,* 20 Cong., 1 Sess., 1402–17). He continued more or less active in politics after his retirement from Congress in 1829. In 1831 and 1832 he was National Republican candidate for governor, but was defeated. In 1850 he was a member of the constitutional convention, serving as chairman of the committee on the Bill of Rights. One of the last of his recorded public services occurred in 1852 when, as a member of the judiciary committee of the House, he successfully advocated a bill repealing the "personal liberty law" which had been adopted July 10, 1846. He was recognized as one of the leaders of the bar at a time when New Hampshire possessed a group of lawyers of unusual ability. A contemporary described him as "the Randolph of the North, the brilliant flashes of whose wit, keen sarcasm, and pungent irony, gave life and spirit to the dry juridical discussions, whose logical congruity they were allowed to relieve, but not to impair" (*Eulogy on Levi Woodbury* by Robert Rantoul, Jr., Oct. 16, 1851). He was one of the founders of the New Hampshire Historical Society and its president, 1826–30.

[Sketch by Chas. H. Bell in *The Bench and Bar of N. H.* (1894); another by Henry P. Rolfe, with portrait in John J. Dearborn, the *Hist. of Salisbury, N. H.* (1890). The *Portsmouth Jour.,* Oct. 22, 1853, contains an obituary notice of some length and the issue of Oct. 29 gives, in full, the memorial resolutions of the Rockingham County Bar and addresses by several of Bartlett's associates. Cf. also *Biog. Cong. Dir.* (1913) and L. Bartlett, *Geneal. and Biog. Sketches of the Bartlett Family in England and America* (1876).]

W. A. R.

BARTLETT, JOHN (June 14, 1820–Dec. 3, 1905), editor, publisher, son of William and Susan (Thacher) Bartlett, was born at Plymouth, Mass. His paternal grandfather and his father were both sea-captains, and his maternal grandfather was Dr. James Thacher, a surgeon and historian of the Revolutionary period. His education was that of the Plymouth public schools, and at sixteen he was employed in the University Book Store of Cambridge. This proved for him a college, as he there became a book lover and student. In 1849 he was owner of the store, which grew to be the meeting place for Harvard professors and students who cared for books. "Ask John Bartlett" was the customary advice when any one had difficulty in finding a book or a quotation, and Bartlett was so anxious to deserve his reputation that he began keeping a commonplace-book, which was the embryo of his famous *Familiar Quotations.* During the Civil War he was for a few months a volunteer paymaster in the United States Navy. In 1863 he joined the publishing firm of Little, Brown & Company and in 1878 became senior partner. His work here included personal dealings with authors and he made many warm friends among them, especially those of the Cambridge and Concord group.

In addition to his *Familiar Quotations* (1855), Bartlett was the author of a *New Method of Chess Notation* (1857), *The Shakespeare Phrase Book* (1882), a *Catalogue of Books on Angling, including Ichthyology, Pisciculture, Etc.* (1882), which he presented to Harvard College Library, and a *Complete Concordance to Shakespeare's Dramatic Works and Poems* (1894). He was an ardent fisherman, and his friend James Russell Lowell commemorated a present from him in the poem "To John Bartlett, Who Had Sent Me a Seven Pound Trout." His other favorite recreation was whist; for a quarter of a century he belonged to a whist club of which the other members were Lowell, Charles Choate, and John Holmes, brother of O. W. Holmes; the club was broken up by Lowell's death. In 1851 Bartlett married Hannah Staniford Willard, granddaughter of Joseph Willard, a president of Harvard. They had no children. After her death, a year before his own, he seldom left his home in Brattle St., Cambridge. Before that, in spite of feebleness, he had frequently driven about the streets of Cambridge and the surrounding country, and his face, with its large white mustache, and kindly eyes behind big spectacles, was well known to old residents. He died at the age of eighty-five at his Cambridge home. *Familiar Quotations,* John Bartlett's chief accomplishment, went through nine editions during his life and a tenth edition was revised and enlarged by Nathan Haskell Dole. It contains selections from British and American authors and translations, including the Old and New Testaments. With little formal education, Bartlett yet achieved a measure of scholarship, which was recognized by the conferring upon him of an honorary A.M. degree by Harvard University and by his election to the American Academy of Arts and Sciences.

[The chief source of information is a manuscript book which Bartlett gave to Harvard Coll. Lib. A biographical article based on this appeared in the *Proc. Am. Acad. Arts and Sci.*, vol. XLI. Obituaries in the *Boston Herald*, Dec. 4, 1905, and the *Boston Transcript*, Dec. 4, 1905. Sketch in *Who's Who in America*, 1903–05.]

S. G. B.

BARTLETT, JOHN RUSSELL (Oct. 23, 1805–May 28, 1886), antiquarian, bibliographer, descended from a long line of Rhode Island ancestors, was born at Providence, R. I., the son of Smith and Nancy (Russell) Bartlett. While he was an infant his family moved to Kingston, Ontario, Canada, where he lived until he was eighteen. In the Kingston schools, and later at Lowville Academy in New York and at Montreal, he received his education. In 1824 he returned to Providence, where he became a clerk in the dry-goods store of his uncle William Russell, then took a position as bookkeeper in a bank, and finally in 1831 was chosen cashier of the Globe Bank. During this period his early love of literature and history manifested itself. He became a member of the Franklin Society, which was founded to study the natural sciences, was elected to the Rhode Island Historical Society in 1831, and in the same year was instrumental in the founding of the Providence Athenæum. It was through his connection with the Historical Society that his first antiquarian research was performed. In 1834 Prof. C. C. Rafn, of the Royal Society of Northern Antiquaries of Copenhagen, addressed to the Society certain queries regarding the inscriptions on Dighton Rock, which he hoped to prove were Norse. Bartlett was appointed on a committee to investigate the subject and drew two views of the Rock, with its inscriptions, which are now among the most valuable contributions to this much discussed problem. (*Transactions of the Colonial Society of Massachusetts*, XX, 296).

In 1836 Bartlett moved to New York, where he engaged in mercantile life, but soon became associated with Charles Welford, a bookseller, under the firm name of Bartlett & Welford. Their business consisted largely of the importing of foreign books, and their rooms became a resort for the leading literary and historical scholars of the city. Bartlett was elected corresponding secretary of the New York Historical Society, which brought him into close touch with its president, Albert Gallatin [*q.v.*], with whom he helped to form the American Ethnological Society. He prepared papers to be read before the two societies, aided many scholars, such as E. G. Squier and John L. Stephens, in their historical researches, and began to publish works of his own. His *Progress of Ethnology*, an account of recent researches throughout the world, appeared in 1847, his *Dictionary of Americanisms* in 1848, and the *Reminiscences of Albert Gallatin* in 1849. Of these the *Dictionary* became the best known, passing through four editions, the last in 1878, and being translated into Dutch and German.

In 1850 Bartlett retired from business life and was appointed by President Taylor United States commissioner to run the boundary line between the United States and Mexico, under the Treaty of Guadalupe Hidalgo, in which duty he was employed nearly three years, until February 1853. While on this service he made extensive explorations in Texas, New Mexico, Chihuahua, Sonora, California, and the country now known as Arizona, the particulars of which were published in 1854 in two volumes under the title of *Personal Narrative of Explorations and Incidents Connected with the United States and Mexican Boundary Commission.* He then returned to Rhode Island, where he was elected secretary of state in 1855, which office he continued to hold by annual election for seventeen years. During this period he not only conducted his office efficiently, especially during the troublesome years of the Civil War, but also arranged and classified the great mass of public papers which had accumulated for two hundred years, and had them bound in ninety-two volumes and twenty-eight portfolios. Under authority of the General Assembly, he published in ten volumes the *Records of the Colony of Rhode Island, 1636–1792*, printing in addition to the records many valuable documents from private and institutional collections. He also aided the cause of history in his state by publishing an *Index to the Acts, Resolves and Reports of Rhode Island, from 1758 to 1862*, in twelve volumes (1856–63); *Bibliography of Rhode Island* (1864); *The Literature of the Rebellion* (1866); and *Memoirs of Rhode Island Officers in the Rebellion* (1867).

For the last thirty years of his life Bartlett was closely associated with John Carter Brown in the acquisition and care of the noted collection of books which that scholar had formed at Providence. From 1865 to 1882 he published the *John Carter Brown Catalogue*, a monumental work in four volumes which marked a great advance over all previous attempts to provide a bibliography of early Americana. Its bibliographical descriptions, historical notes, critical valuations, and reproductions of titles and illustrations made this one of the most indispensable works, even to-day, for the student of early American discovery and history.

Bartlett died in Providence on May 28, 1886. He was twice married, first on May 15, 1831, to Eliza Allen Rhodes, by whom he had seven children, and who died Nov. 11, 1853; and second, on Nov. 12, 1863, to Ellen Eddy, who survived him.

[The best biographical sketch is the *Life and Services of John Russell Bartlett,* read before the R. I. Hist. Soc. by Wm. Gammell, 1886. See also long obituary in *Providence Jour.,* May 29, 1886; and sketch by Charles Deane in *Proc. Am. Antiquarian Soc.,* Oct. 1886, p. 179. Bartlett's correspondence and a lengthy autobiography are preserved in the John Carter Brown Lib. at Providence.]

C. S. B.

BARTLETT, JOHN SHERREN (1790–Aug. 23, 1863), physician, journalist, was born in Dorsetshire, England, son of Thomas, a descendant of the Stropham family of Bartletts. He pursued medical studies in London under the direction of Sir Astley Cooper, and was appointed an assistant surgeon in the British navy in 1812. Assigned to the packet *Swallow* bound for Jamaica, he became an American prisoner when that ship was captured by Commodore Rodgers cruising with the frigates *President* and *Congress* in search of the enemy's vessels. Although held as a prisoner in Boston for several months before being exchanged, he experienced much kindness and hospitality there. In turn his was the pleasure, combined with duty, in the latter part of the war, to attend to the wounds of American naval prisoners, including the officers and crew of the *Chesapeake,* at Halifax. The war over, he was satisfied to remain on American soil and set up his physician's sign in friendly Boston. It was as a journalist, however, that Bartlett was to gain his reputation. He conceived the idea of establishing an English newspaper in the United States, a journal which should give to British residents on this continent a true exposition of public affairs, and a general view of the news, politics, and literature of the United Kingdom, and which would aim "to preserve the peace and good understanding between the United States and Great Britain." He thought New York the best center for such a publication and the first issue of the *Albion* appeared there, June 22, 1822. For over a quarter of a century he continued its publication, always contending successfully that "a love for England was not incompatible with respect and regard for this country" (*Albion,* May 6, 1848). At the time when England was claiming her exclusive right to the Oregon territory and the Democrats of the United States were shouting "Fifty-four forty or fight," Bartlett insisted that both parties had rights, and that nothing but a calm and dispassionate examination of them, with a determination mutually to admit these rights, was necessary to a happy issue of the affair. The paper resembled the modern tabloid in its convenient size but in no other respect. It appealed to the reading public because of its reports of naval intelligence from Portsmouth, of police news from Bow St., of the new plays at the London theatres, of the proceedings of Parliament, and of the high literary quality of the contributed articles. To Bartlett must be given credit for introducing Indian corn into England. Besides pointing out in the *Albion* the excellence of the maize as a cheap and wholesome article of diet for the poor, he circulated several pamphlets emphasizing its value and giving directions for preparing and cooking it.

Another publication, the *European,* was begun by Bartlett with the opening of the Cunard Line, in 1840. The paper was printed in Liverpool, containing the latest news from Europe, and forwarded to America at each sailing. The editor's ill health forced him to abandon this enterprise at the end of eighteen months, but it was continued as Willmer's *European Times.* Another breakdown in health caused him to retire from the editorship of the *Albion,* May 6, 1848. In 1847, he was president of the St. George's Society of New York and, ten years later, on the death of the British consul in Baltimore, he was put in charge of the consulate for a time. During his last years he was a resident of New York City and Middletown Point, N. J.

[The best sources of information are the obituary notice in the *Albion,* Aug. 29, 1863, and an article contributed by Bartlett May 6, 1848, on his retirement from the paper. See also editorials in *N. Y. Evening Post,* May 9, 1848, and *N. Y. Jour. of Commerce,* Mar. 25, 1848. The account in *Sketches of the Bartlett Family in England and America* (1876) is faulty in several particulars.]

A. E. P.

BARTLETT, JOSEPH (June 10, 1762–Oct. 20, 1827), adventurer, lawyer, politician, and author, had a spectacular career in New England in the days immediately following the Revolution, and became widely known for his eccentricities, his wit, and his writings. He was born in Plymouth, Mass., the son of Sylvanus and Martha (Wait) Bartlett; graduated at Harvard in 1782, where his scholarship was such that he was one of the three charter members of the Phi Beta Kappa chapter; and then went to Salem to study law. Here he also conducted a school, in connection with which his interest in dramatics appeared, for in *The Holyoke Diaries,* under date of Jan. 21, 1783, is recorded, "We were at a play at the Brick Store." Note: *"The Distracted*

Mother, presented by Mr. Bartlett's school. Music, two fiddles and a drum." An entry of Apr. 29, 1783, mentions another play by "Mr. Bartlett's scholars." With no motive, apparently, but love of adventure, he went to London, where at a play in which American soldiers were ridiculed he arose and shouted, "Hurrah, Great Britain beaten by barbers, tailors, and tinkers." This audacity won him favor with the bloods of the day, and for a time he lived a gay life which ended in the debtors' prison. From this he secured funds for release by writing a play, which he claimed was the first American play presented on the English stage. Unfortunately, the title has not been preserved. Going to Edinburgh, he acted under the stage name of "Mr. Maitland," appearing as Belcour in *The West Indian.* Tiring of this life, he bought a ship-load of merchandise with borrowed money and sailed with it for America. The ship was wrecked on Cape Cod, and Bartlett is said to have shown unseemly haste in saving himself. He resumed the study of law in Boston, and at the time of Shays's Rebellion started for Worcester at the head of a company of volunteers, but news that the insurrection had been put down halted the expedition.

Bartlett was admitted to the bar, and began his legal and political career in Woburn, Mass., where, to attract attention, seemingly, he painted his house black and called it "The Coffin." "As odd as Joe Bartlett" soon became a common expression. His wife, Anna May, daughter of Thomas and Ann Wetherell, whom he married Nov. 15, 1795, was not able long to live with him. He was interested in educational matters and in 1792 was one of a committee of seven "to examine into the government of the schools and recommend some uniform system of instruction." His fellow lawyer, Samuel Lorenzo Knapp, who was too prejudiced to be entirely trustworthy, said that Bartlett's clients were chiefly "harlots, rogues, and knaves of every size and grade." As a political speaker he had the power of setting his audience in a roar, and even sober, thinking men found him irresistible. His political writings had a pungency and satire that made them very effective.

From Woburn, Bartlett removed to Cambridge, without changing his manner of life. He was sufficiently respected, however, to be selected as poet for the Harvard Phi Beta Kappa celebration of 1799. His poem on that occasion, *Physiognomy,* published in 1810, attracted much notice, and even Knapp reluctantly acknowledges that it has "taste and no little splendor, however unjust and satirical it may be." At several sessions, also, Bartlett represented Cambridge in the General Court. By 1803, however, he had moved to Saco, in the present state of Maine, and in 1804 was chosen senator in the Massachusetts legislature from the County of York. He missed an election to Congress by about six votes. In 1805 he was editor of the Saco *Freeman's Friend.* Later he lived in Portsmouth, N. H. A book of more than 400 aphorisms was issued by him in 1810, among which are such sayings as "Conceit more than knowledge influences men to write"; "There never was a party man who acted as cool reason would approve"; and "Men had rather be censured for want of morals than for want of understanding." On the downward road financially and otherwise, he returned to Boston, where he delivered a Fourth-of-July address at the Exchange Coffee-House Hall in 1823, which was published the same year in a pamphlet entitled *The Fourth of July Anticipated,* which also included "The New Vicar of Bray," probably his best known work. He spent his last days in poverty, supported by his friends.

Bartlett is described as "fat, jolly, and infinitely amusing." He was an ardent democrat and a disciple of Thomas Paine. Possessed of exceptional gifts, he lacked sufficient mental and moral balance to use them to the highest advantage. Shortly before his death he wrote his own epitaph:

> "'Tis done! The fatal stroke is given,
> And Bartlett's fled to Hell or Heaven;
> His friends approve it, and his foes applaud,—
> Yet he will have the verdict of his God."

[The dates of Bartlett's birth, graduation from college, and death are variously given. The authorities for those stated are Jas. S. Loring, *The Hundred Boston Orators* (1852); *Harvard Quinquennial Cat.* (1915); and the *Columbian Centinel,* Boston, Oct. 24, 1827. See also Ignatius L. Robertson (Samuel L. Knapp), *Sketches of Public Characters* (1830); Samuel Sewall, *Hist. of Woburn* (1868); Geo. F. Dow, *The Holyoke Diaries* (1911); *The Saco Register,* 1906; W. T. Davis, *Bench and Bar of the Commonwealth of Mass.* (1895), I, 189.]

H. E. S.

BARTLETT, JOSIAH (Nov. 21, 1729–May 19, 1795), physician, Revolutionary patriot, chief justice and governor of New Hampshire, was a son of Stephen and Mary (Webster) Bartlett, and was born in Amesbury, Essex County, Mass. He was educated in the common schools, and after acquiring under private tuition some knowledge of the Greek and Latin languages began, when sixteen years of age, the study of medicine, in his native town, in the office of Dr. Ordway, a distant relative. The large clinical advantages of this office, supplemented by the diligent use of several medical libraries and one large general library, in neighboring towns, qualified him, according to the custom of the times, five years later to enter upon the practise of his profession, which he did in 1750 in the town of Kingston in southern New Hampshire. In this place, which proved to be his permanent home, Bartlett rapidly acquired a large practise as an all-round country physician and early in his career became widely known through his diagnosis of an obscure, malignant, and prevalent disease of the throat and through its successful treatment by the use of Peruvian bark. His experience gradually led him to reject the then accepted pathology and treatment of several other diseases, and relying more and more upon observation of particular cases and experiment in their treatment he introduced many medical reforms. He was married on Jan. 15, 1754, to his cousin, Mary Bartlett of Newton, N. H. They had twelve children, and three of his sons and seven of his grandsons became physicians.

Bartlett's wide intelligence, integrity, and active interest in public affairs led his fellow citizens to choose him as the representative from Kingston to the Provincial Assembly in 1765 and regularly to reëlect him till the outbreak of the Revolution. In 1767 he was appointed by the royal governor, John Wentworth, a justice of the peace and soon after a colonel of a regiment of militia, but when, during the progress of the controversy between Great Britain and the Colonies, he took the side of the people and maintained it with vigor and unfaltering courage, he was summarily dismissed from these offices, in February 1775. Previously, during the critical year 1774 he was recognized as an active patriot by his appointment on the important Committee of Correspondence of the Provincial Assembly and by his election to that Assembly's Revolutionary successor, the first Provincial Congress, which chose him as one of two delegates from New Hampshire to the first Continental Congress. Although he was unable to accept this election, because of the recent destruction of his house by fire, believed to have been set because of his activity in the popular cause, in 1775–76 he was again chosen as a delegate to the Continental Congress, and in the latter year was the first to give his vote in favor of the adoption of the Declaration of Independence, to which his name was duly affixed. Although reëlected to the Continental Congress for 1777 he was unable to serve, because he was worn out by his arduous duties in that body during the previous year, but while at home he was still busy with public affairs.

In 1778–79 he was once more a member of the Continental Congress, and, as the states were called, had the honor of being the first to vote for the proposed Articles of Confederation and Perpetual Union which took effect Mar. 1, 1781. The records of the proceedings of these two Congresses in which he served, as well as his private correspondence, show that he was a member of the most important standing committees in each of these bodies, those of Safety and Secrecy, Munitions, Marines and Privateering, as well as of numerous special committees, such as that on civil government for the United States in 1775 and also on the committee to draft Articles of Confederation in 1778. His constant, painstaking, and arduous service upon these committees made him one of the most influential members of these Congresses in shaping legislation, though he took relatively small part in the debates, of whose too frequent prolixity and futility he was a caustic critic. Physically exhausted by his labors at Philadelphia and New York during 1777–78 and by the difficulties of travel in following the Continental Congress, he declined reëlection and sought a chance to recruit his strength at home, but in 1779 New Hampshire appointed him chief justice of its court of common pleas. In thus elevating a layman to the bench, the State was following an occasional practise due to its social and political conditions in the last quarter of the eighteenth century, but in this case it ran scant risk, since the appointee not only had large knowledge of practical affairs but also was prepared by previous reading of law books, experience as justice of the peace, and fifteen years of almost constant association with lawyers engaged in legislative work.

In 1782 he was promoted to be associate justice of the superior court, and having become chief justice in 1788, ended his service on the bench in 1790. Tradition and his own reported statement make it probable that his decisions, like those of other lay judges of that period, were based upon equity. Some of the ablest lawyers of that time declared that justice was never better administered in New Hampshire than when the judges knew very little law. In 1788, while still upon the bench, Bartlett was a member and temporary chairman of the state convention called to ratify the proposed Constitution of the United States. In this body he was one of the most skilful and resourceful advocates of ratification, and it is doubtful whether, without his personal efforts to allay the opposition of the smaller towns during the three months' interval between the two sessions of the convention, New Hampshire would have had the honor, on June 21, 1788, of being the ninth State to ratify the Constitution, and so establish the Union. In 1790 and each of the two following years he was elected to the highest office in the gift of the State, that of chief executive, then styled president. His popularity appears by the election returns in that year which show that out of a total of 9,854 votes he received 7,385. In June 1793, the newly amended Constitution having changed the title of the chief executive, he was chosen as the first governor of the state. The policy of Bartlett, steadily pursued during the four years of his administration, was expressed in his successive recommendations to the legislature in which he urged: any changes in the laws of the state which might be found necessary to enable it to fulfil its obligations to the recently organized Federal Government; provision for the early payment of the state debt; strict adherence to all engagements, both public and private; economy in public expenditures; the early compilation and revision of all the laws and statutes deemed to be in force, and a better method of selecting certain judicial officers; the promotion of agriculture and manufactures; improvement of roads and possibly the building of canals in some parts of the state, in order to unite the people in a common interest; and the encouragement in every possible way of the rising generation in virtue, morality, and patriotism. At the close of his term of office in 1794, because of ill health he withdrew from politics.

In 1790 Dartmouth College had conferred upon Bartlett, whose keen interest in his profession had not abated during the long period when his preoccupation with public affairs had interrupted his regular practise, the honorary degree of Doctor of Medicine, and in the following year he rendered what was perhaps his greatest service to his profession by securing from the legislature a charter for the New Hampshire Medical Society which, when organized with a constitution and by-laws drafted by his own hand, fittingly elected him as its first president. But he did not long survive his retirement from public life, for he died at his home in Kingston on May 19, 1795. He is described by his contemporaries as a tall man of fine figure, affable but dignified in his manner, and very particular in his dress. He wore his auburn hair in a queue, a white stock at his throat, ruffles at his wrists, short clothes, silk hose, low shoes with silver buckles. His bronze statue, unveiled in 1888, stands in the public square of his native town, Amesbury. His portrait, an oil painting, a copy from the original by Jonathan Trumbull, hangs in the State House in Concord, N. H.

[Levi Bartlett, *Sketches of the Bartlett Family in England and America* (1875–76); Robt. Waln, Jr., *Biog. of the Signers to the Declaration of Independence* (2nd ed., 1828), III, 123; E. C. Burnett, *Letters of Members of the Continental Cong.* (1921–23); J. Farmer and J. B. Moore, "Collections, Hist. and Biog. relating to N. H.," in *N. H. State Papers*, vol. XXII, index; J. B. Walker, *Hist. of N. H. Convention for Ratif. of Fed. Constitution, 1788* (1888), "Presidential Address and Sketch of Josiah Bartlett," by Thomas Luce in *N. H. Medic. Soc. Proc.*, 1926.]

J. F. C.

BARTLETT, PAUL WAYLAND (Jan. 24, 1865–Sept. 20, 1925), sculptor, son of Truman Howe Bartlett and Mary Ann White Bartlett, was born in New Haven, Conn. His father, a sculptor and critic remembered to-day chiefly through his Wells and Clark monuments in Hartford, and his *Art Life of William Rimmer* (1882), was for twenty-three years instructor in modeling at the Massachusetts Institute of Technology, where his vivid and reputedly difficult personality is said to have had a "quickening influence on the artistic life of Boston." The sculptor Herbert Adams, for a brief period a pupil in Truman Bartlett's studio, recalls an emphatic remark: "I would never have a son of mine get his art education in this country!" Paul Bartlett was then already established with his mother in Paris. They had made their home in France since the boy was nine years old. During his most impressionable years he lived in Paris as schoolboy and art student, alert, aggressive, yet thoughtful and sensitive to beauty. Entering the École des Beaux Arts at fifteen, he studied under the sculptor Cavelier, and at about the same time followed the deservedly popular courses in animal sculpture given by Frémiet at the Jardin des Plantes. His animal studies proved immediately rewarding. Early thrown on his own resources, he was able to earn something as "animal specialist" in the studios of sculptors versed merely in the human form and its trappings. Bits of his youthful work are to be found to-day in important sculptural groups abroad. Gardet, the well-known *animaliste*, often employed him as assistant. His skill in the various handicrafts connected with sculpture was not unlike that displayed in youth by Rodin, a master whose influence he later felt.

This early and entire consecration to art gives the key to Bartlett's career. The transplantation from the sober light-and-shade of the New England elms into the gayer arabesques of the Luxembourg Garden, with statues gleaming and fountains playing, had opened his young eyes all the wider to the marvels of art around him. Thanks to his New England inheritance of a persevering spirit and an industrious mind, to say nothing of that desire for expression which was an immediate gift from his father, his education in art was a natural process, liberating and creative from its beginning. At fourteen, he exhibited in the Salon a bust of his grandmother. A few years later his "Bear Tamer," a man standing over two cubs, now a favorite bronze of young visitors at the Metropolitan Museum, received *mention honorable* at the Salon of 1887. With the "Bear Tamer" may be classed the "Dying Lion," as well as the "Ghost Dancer," a lithe savage performing a tribal rite, a figure admired for its anatomy in the Chicago Exposition of 1893, and now in the Pennsylvania Academy of the Fine Arts.

At the Paris Exposition of 1895 was a collection of small bronzes, cast by Bartlett himself, *à la cire perdue*. The subjects were ethnographic whimseys of fishes and serpents, of batrachians, crustaceans, and the like. To the artists who hung over this display, its radiant gemlike colors were even more alluring than its forms. Sculptors who had experimented arduously in alloys and *patines* were the first to acclaim Bartlett's success. His name still brings to many minds a vision of rainbow hues such as they had never before dreamed of associating with the dark stuff they knew as bronze. Jean Carriès declared that Bartlett's *patines* vied with those of the classic Japanese school. These "essays," as the author called them, express his delight in craftsmanship. Even during the last summer of his life, he was eagerly working with pottery and glazes.

In 1895, he received from France the ribbon of the Legion of Honor. But between his native and adoptive countries, his allegiance was never divided. As his position in art became more secure, he visited America more frequently, called home by commissions enthusiastically offered. The Rotunda of the Library of Congress holds twelve heroic bronze statues, two of which, the Columbus and the Michelangelo, are by Bartlett. The architect had naturally given all the sculptors a definite scale for their models. Bartlett remarked, after the placing of his two heroes, "Yes, I made my figures larger than the others. I wanted them to dominate" (personal recollection). A highly unsound principle! His figures not only dominate in spirit, they domineer in size. Aside from this fault, these two romantic portrait-statues are among the best of their kind. The world-map of the great seeker and the leather apron of the great interpreter play their proud parts in dramatic light-and-dark. The Columbus and Michelangelo stand at the portal of Bartlett's great period in his art. He had already acquired the grand style. It now remained for him not to subdue this, but to enhance it by bringing it into noble relationship with architecture.

Later, a more harmonious visualization of sculpture as an element in an architectural ensemble reveals itself in his six decorative figures in marble, for the attic story of the New York Public Library, designed by Carrère and Hastings. The first studies were accepted in 1910. Male figures of "History" and "Philosophy" occupy the end spaces, while between these, and in pairs, are female figures of "Romance" and "Religion," "Poetry" and "Drama." Save only "Drama," with her mask, all might have had other names, since the sculptor has not perturbed them with too much symbolism. They are a happy family of beings from a timeless Golden Age, ample enough to hold something both of Greek beauty and Gothic earnestness. The men are stately, the women gracious, and all their vestments are of that noble nondescript dear to poets but disconcerting to modistes. The marble draperies of the four women suggest music, dancing, flowers.

During one of Bartlett's many visits to his native land, he collaborated (1908–09) with the veteran sculptor Ward in the sculpture for the pediment of the New York Stock Exchange building. The design of the gigantic sculpture, a high relief centering about the "Genius of Integrity," is from the elder master, but we are assured by Lorado Taft that the modeling was Bartlett's. Shortly afterward, this initial experience in pedimental sculpture became of value to Bartlett in his own now untrammeled creation of the sculpture for the pediment of the House wing of the national Capitol. In Roosevelt's administration, the joint committee of the Senate and the House having such matters in charge wrote to the National Sculpture Society asking for ten names of sculptors best fitted to decorate this long-vacant space. As Bartlett's name headed the list, the commission was awarded to him (1909). The plaster models were finished in 1914. The work was carved in marble, in place; it was unveiled in 1916. The problem was to enrich, without disturbing architectural lines, a huge triangle generally seen from below and sidewise. Bartlett's first vision of the work took shape as "Peace Protecting the Arts," with expressive groups leading up to the central figure. His gradually evolved revision created something finer. The central figure, nine feet high, became "Democracy Protecting the Arts of Peace," which are shown on the left by foundryman, printer, textile worker, fisherman; on the right by a Lincoln-like reaper, the husbandman with his ox, the woman in her home, and an idyllic episode of a cherub with a ram. All these groups, each with its special appeal to human sympathy, are bound together in rhythmic unity. The theme is somewhat less magnificent than that chosen by Crawford for the Senate pediment, but it naturally received an ampler treatment than the earlier sculptor could command, out of the meager resources of his time. The two pediments, taken together, are an object lesson in artistic progress during two generations.

Another instance of Bartlett's mature conception of his art as related to the architect's was his so-called "Quadriga of Victory" brilliantly executed to rise above New York's Victory Arch, designed by Thomas Hastings in 1919 to honor Gen. Pershing's troops on their return from the World War. Bartlett's enthusiasm summoned to his Chariot of Victory six horses instead of the customary four. But all who were working for the arch were too busy in that hour of exaltation to be pedantic about the name of this group. It was a work of immense vigor and style, but was not made permanent, the arch itself having been destroyed. At this time Bartlett was chairman of New York's committee on war memorials. As president of the National Sculpture Society (1918), he protested to some purpose against the government's poor designs for military medals and insignia. Throughout the war, he used his gift of literary expression in both French and English, for the comfort and support of France. His war-time messages to that country are models of vigorous prose. Equally fine in literary form is his essay on *American Sculpture and French Influence upon Its Development,* an address which he delivered in Paris under the auspices of the Comité France-Amérique, expounding his theme with brilliant acumen, and with appreciation of his American fellow sculptors. This paper was translated into English, and published in the *New York Times,* Feb. 9, 1913. To academic circles in France, he already spoke with authority. He had been promoted to the grade of Officer in the Legion of Honor in 1908, and elected corresponding member of the Institute of France in 1911, the same year in which he became a member of the American Academy of Arts and Letters. Because he loved America, and desired her progress in the arts, he was always eloquent in pointing out to American students the advantage, indeed, the necessity, of study abroad. Worthy art movements here received his stanch support, while "freak schools," both here and abroad, "studios where they draw with closed eyes" and "cultivate mental aberration" had his vehemently expressed abhorrence. "One has no idea," he writes, "of the swiftness in propagation and the penetrating power of artistic sophisms, when they flatter human fatuity."

Chronologically and artistically, the central work of Bartlett's career is the bronze equestrian statue of Lafayette, in the court of the Louvre. This position in itself would have been a mark of honor to a sculptor of France, a Dubois or a Frémiet. At the turn of the century, a citizen of Chicago had conceived a plan of having American school children contribute a cent or a nickel or a dime each toward an American salute to France in the form of an equestrian statue of Lafayette, to be made by an American sculptor. Karl Bitter was approached; and Bitter, rightly feeling that such an offering ought to be the handiwork of a sculptor with French affiliations, successfully urged the obvious fitness of Bartlett. The opportunity moved Bartlett deeply, and held him long. His first sketches were approved by the architect of the Louvre, in New York, July 4, 1899, the plan being to set up the full size plaster model just a year later, in Paris, in honor of the French Exposition. Bartlett retired to the little French village of St. Leu, where, with a beautiful horse at his command, he worked in solitude and at white heat, returning to Paris to mobilize the various skilled artisans necessary to the conclusion of what was an extraordinary feat. The model when seen in the court of the Louvre was voted a success (1900), but the artist himself was not satisfied. Many months it remained in place, under his criticism. Experience had taught him the value of serene contemplation as well as fierce concentration. Starting anew, he devoted to the work every resource of his art. He made frequent changes, which, as not always happens, were of ultimate advantage. The three-cornered hat of the first study was doffed, the gay coat was exchanged for a severer habit, the action of the hand holding aloft the sword was made more decisive. A different type of horse was used, less flamboyant in movement and in caparison. Every alteration in detail was an improvement in ensemble. With head and sword and spirit uplifted, the young Marquis rides to a victory that will change the world. There is austerity and splendor in the sculpture as in the thought. In 1908, the completed bronze was set up, a signal honor to the soldier, the sculptor, and the two countries they loved. Long studied by the artist, the monument makes an instant appeal to the spectator, whether he views it from the court, or from the Louvre windows. When signing his masterpiece, Bartlett added a tortoise in playful comment. In 1920, the American Knights of Columbus presented to France a bronze replica, which was placed in the city of Metz, where Lafayette was stationed when he dedicated himself to the American cause.

Bartlett's own phrase, "as a fact and as a symbol," used by him to describe his Lafayette, applies fitly to all his statues; to his marble "Puritans" for the Capitol at Hartford, to his Robert

Morris in Philadelphia, his Benjamin Franklin in Waterbury, Conn. As facts and as symbols the citizens of Boston look upon their statues of Alexander Agassiz and of Gen. Joseph Warren. Bartlett's penetrating studies of each subject's psychology were not snap judgments. They resulted from that wise reading which implies constant sifting and choosing. On the whole, he was at his best quite as much in showing real beings whose lives were poetic, or philosophic, or patriotic, as in presenting such abstractions as Poetry, Philosophy, Patriotism. As a fact and as a symbol, therefore, the seated bronze Franklin at Waterbury, completed in 1921, suggests both by its handsome pyramidal composition and its keen characterization the firm basis of common sense from which this apostle of American liberty took his flights into the regions of science and political philosophy. As a fact and as a symbol, Robert Morris, patriot financier of the Revolution, paces his pedestal in front of the Custom House in Philadelphia, studying as of yore the fiscal weather, for which he needs his three-cornered hat, his greatcoat, and his staff. This was the last of Bartlett's statues to be placed in this country (1924).

Reviewing these works, we note that the sculptor was very lucky in one thing, namely, that he was not called upon to celebrate contemporary frock coat and trousers. He appreciated this immunity. His romanticism abhorred the prosaic, and refused to come to grips with it. Yet the poetry of man at his work appealed to him deeply, as his Capitol pediment shows. Aside from a number of portrait busts such as the Elizabeth Cady Stanton of 1887, the Walter Shirlaw owned by the National Academy of Design, and the Walter Griffin of recent date, contemporary subjects did not greatly engage him. His vein led toward the historic. His realm was heroic portraiture, imaginatively conceived, historically documented, and monumentally presented. Yet Taft devotes a page of appreciation to the "logical decorative syntheses" of fishes, sea-horses, and the like, shown in Bartlett's fountain, "The Genius of Man," a feature of the Pan-American Exposition of 1901, at which he received a gold medal. Later, in the Capitol pediment, the ox, ram, lamb, and fish, used in perfect harmony with the draped and partly draped human figures, added much to the appeal of the whole.

Honors too numerous to note followed his path. Wherever his workshop was, there was his home, whether in Washington, New York, or Paris. At the time of his death, he had a beautifully appointed studio in Washington, as well as that celebrated Paris studio and garden where in an earlier generation the French sculptor Bartholdi had created the enormous symbolic "Liberty" now in New York harbor. Bartlett's purchase from France of this studio, and his bequest of it back to France, were in line with his ardor for French-American amity. Welcomed in Belgium, he was made an associate of the Royal Academy, and at the Liège Exposition of 1905, he received first medal. In 1913, he was chosen director of sculpture at the Glasgow School of Art, a position more honorary than arduous. His last important work was the statue of Blackstone, presented by the American Bar Association to the British Bar Association, to be placed in the Royal Law Courts, London. Never had the sculptor developed his teeming ideas with greater zest than in this tribute to British jurisprudence. A successful statue, yet a difficult one, since in less capable hands the subject's greatness might have been smothered under circumstantial wig and robe. Bartlett had also in hand at this time portrait busts of Washington and Franklin for St. Paul's Church in New York. He had just finished his Independence Pilgrimage medal, to be given to those young Americans who having worked best toward making Monticello, Jefferson's home, a shrine, had earned a trip abroad. In the spring of 1925, he came to New York, bringing a copy of the medal. With his customary friendliness, he planned in both countries for the reception, diversion, and enlightenment of those youthful summer pilgrims to France.

In the full tide of a creative power unusual at sixty years, his life was ended by an accident of the everyday kind, in appearance trivial. A misstep in the dark on a steep terrace near a friend's house in the Ardennes, a wrist slightly cut by a jagged rock, that was all. Care was taken in treating the wound, yet within a month, he died of septicæmia, in Paris. He was twice married, each time to an American woman of charm and social prominence. His first marriage took place in Paris. It proved unhappy, and was legally dissolved. In 1913, he was married in Washington to Mrs. Samuel F. Emmons. He had no children.

Fellow artists have well interpreted his personality, Charles Noel Flagg in an oil painting, Charles Grafly in a bronze bust, John Flanagan in a bas-relief. Bartlett's figure was well-knit. He carried himself gallantly, and his years lay lightly on him. His head was striking. He had abundant bright hair, scarcely touched by time; a broad, full brow; brilliant, wide-set blue eyes, with uncommonly large pupils; a ruddy, expressive countenance, the traditional Vandyke mustache and beard, and a strong aquiline nose, a harmonious variant of the type Nature often supplies to her children of genius—witness Saint-Gaudens, Rodin, Anatole France. It was the head of a dreamer, a doer, an enthusiast, a diplomat; a head with a Nordic beginning and a Gallic finish, each noble after its own kind. In short, Paul Bartlett looked what he was, an American citizen whose artistic achievement honors two republics, and is in turn honored by both. The Yankee was born, but the Commandeur was made. Frenchmen speak of him as formed by the *"solide Frémiet,"* the *"illustre Rodin,"* but what he had from these and other masters was fused and transfigured by his own spirit.

[Lorado Taft, *Am. Sculpture* (1903) and *Modern* Tendencies in Sculpture (1917); C. H. Caffin, *Am. Masters of Sculpture* (1903); *Am. Art Annual,* vol. XIV, 1917; Archives Am. Acad. Arts and Letters; Wm. Walton, *Scribner's,* July 1910, and Oct. 1913, C. N. Flagg, *Scribner's,* Mar. 1909; C. V. Wheeler, *Am. Mag. of Art,* Nov. 1925; leading article in *La Peinture,* Paris, Oct. 1923; article in *La Peinture,* 1925. Obituaries and editorials, French and American papers, notably *Le Matin* (Paris), *N. Y. Times, N. Y. Herald Tribune,* on the day following his death.] A. A—s.

BARTLETT, SAMUEL COLCORD (Nov. 25, 1817–Nov. 16, 1898), Congregational clergyman, college president, was born in Salisbury, N. H. His father was also Samuel Colcord Bartlett, a name frequently repeated in the family, whose first American ancestor was Richard Bartlett, who came from England to Newbury, Mass., in 1635; his mother was Eleanor (Pettingill) Bartlett, also of English Puritan stock, her ancestors having come from Yorkshire in 1640. Bartlett's early education was all in the New Hampshire atmosphere. Salisbury Academy, Pinkerton Academy at Derry, and an unnamed private tutor were his teachers. He graduated with high honors at Dartmouth in 1836, and spent the next two years as principal of the Caledonia County Grammar School at Peacham, Vt. After a year as tutor in mathematics at Dartmouth, he entered Andover Theological Seminary. This was the period when Andover was the chief champion of New England Calvinism against Unitarianism; and Bartlett always acknowledged the influence on his thought of Professors Park and Stuart, who were among the most distinguished conservative scholars and theologians of that day. Licensed to preach, Apr. 12, 1843, by the Andover Congregational Association, he was ordained Aug. 2, at Monson, Mass. On Aug. 16, 1843, he was married to Laura Bradlee, of Peacham, Vt., who died Dec. 1 of that year. On May 12, 1846, he married Mary Bacon Learned, daughter of Rev. Erastus Learned and Sophia Bacon Learned, of Canterbury, Conn. In the latter year he became professor of philosophy and rhetoric at Western Reserve College, Hudson, Ohio, an institution which years later, as Adelbert College, became a part of the Western Reserve University, at Cleveland. He continued for five years in this position, and then returned to New England as pastor of the Franklin Street Church in Manchester, N. H. The attraction to the new fields in the West led him in 1857 to accept a call to the New England Congregational Church in Chicago, Ill. When he reached this new field, however, he was at once drafted into the work of establishing a theological institution. In 1858 he was installed as professor of biblical literature and sacred theology in the infant Chicago Theological Seminary. For nineteen years he built his life into the institution, organizing and arranging its first classes, and making his influence strongly felt in all its policies, and generally in educational and religious movements throughout the Middle West.

In 1877, when he was sixty years old, he began the work by which he will be most distinctly remembered. He was elected president of Dartmouth College; and he remained actively connected with the institution for twenty-one years, fifteen as president, and after his resignation at the age of seventy-five, for six years more, as lecturer on "The Bible and its Relations to Science and Religion." His active service as president was a period of continuous growth and progress, but not an untroubled experience. He had decided opinions and policies, and maintained them firmly and persistently. There was much discussion in faculty meetings and with trustees; but never any break. The period of great donations by multi-millionaires had not arrived; but Bartlett's administration saw an addition of $700,000 to the endowments, an increase in the faculty from twenty-one to thirty-four, of endowed chairs from one to six, numerous buildings on the campus, and the development and firm establishment of the scientific department.

Besides numerous sermons, addresses, etc., the list of Bartlett's published volumes includes the following: *The Study of God's Word in the Original Languages* (1858); *Life and Death Eternal* (1866); *Sketches of the Missions of the American Board* (1866); *Historical Sketch of the Hawaiian Mission* (1869); *Future Punishment* (1875); *From Egypt to Palestine through Sinai* (1879); *Sources of History in the Pentateuch* (1883); *Veracity of the Hexateuch* (1897); *Anniversary Addresses* (1893); and *Lectures on Universalism* (undated).

[Gabriel Campbell, "President Bartlett, Reminiseent and Otherwise," *Dartmouth Lit. Mo.,* Mar. 1899; E. J.

Bartlett, *Genealogy of the Descendants of S. C. Bartlett and Eleanor Pettingill* (1915); S. C. Bartlett, "How I was Educated," *Forum*, II, 18–26; J. J. Dearborn, *Hist. of Salisbury, N. H.* (1890); Levi Bartlett, *Genealogy and Biog. Sketches of the Bartlett Family* (1876); obituaries in *People and Patriot* (Concord, N. H.), *Concord Evening Monitor*, and *Manchester Union*, Nov. 17, 1898.]

C. N.

BARTLEY, MORDECAI (Dec. 16, 1783–Oct. 10, 1870), governor of Ohio, was of English descent on both sides of the family. Emigrating from Northumberland County in 1724, his paternal grandfather settled in Loudon County, Va. His father, Elijah Bartley, born in Virginia, married Rachel Pearshall, an English woman, and commenced his family life in Fayette County, Pa. It was in this new home that Mordecai was born. He spent his early years in hard work on his father's farm, obtaining his schooling after the usual fashion of country boys at that time—in the nearest district school during the intervals of farm labor. In 1804 he was married to Miss Welles of Pennsylvania. He was early attracted by the possibilities of the newer country farther west and at the age of twenty-six went to Jefferson County, Ohio, where he settled as a farmer. At the outbreak of the war with Great Britain he raised a company of volunteers, of which he was captain, subsequently serving as adjutant of a regiment under Gen. Harrison. At the close of the war he removed to the almost unbroken wilderness of Richland County, in the interior of the state (1814). Mansfield, then a small settlement, was near-by, but there were no settlers west of the site chosen by Bartley for his new home. Opening a clearing in the forest for his dwelling and first crops, he soon obtained a competence far beyond that of others who followed him. He continued here for twenty years, in the meantime establishing a mercantile house in the town of Mansfield.

Bartley's success as farmer and merchant, coupled with a character that won the confidence of the community, led to his election to the Ohio state Senate (1817). Henceforth he was to spend many years in public life. During his term in the Senate he was appointed by the legislature to the position of register of the Land Office—a position which placed him in charge of the Virginia military district school lands. His keen interest in the advance of public education in Ohio dates from this time. In 1823 he was elected to Congress and was reëlected for three successive terms. At the end of his fourth term he declined again to become a candidate. In Congress he was affiliated with the National Republicans and became a strong supporter of President John Quincy Adams and a warm friend of Henry Clay. One of his few speeches in Congress was in defense of Clay and Adams against the corrupt-bargain charge. Bartley was the first to propose in Congress the conversion of the land grants of Ohio into a permanent fund for the support of the common schools. He secured the earliest Federal appropriations for the improvement of the harbors of Cleveland and other towns on the shore of Lake Erie.

Upon his retirement from Congress (1831) he devoted his entire time to agricultural and mercantile pursuits until his election as governor of Ohio (1844). He was elected by a small majority over David Tod, his Democratic opponent. The gubernatorial succession at this time was a remarkable one: Bartley, elected as a Whig, succeeded his son, Gov. Thomas Bartley, who was a Democrat. The latter had been a candidate for the nomination in the Democratic convention and had lost by one vote. The elder Bartley was sixty-one years old and the younger thirty-two. The Mexican War occurred during Bartley's term as governor, and he was confronted by the difficult task of reconciling his duty as the chief executive of the State with his own personal opposition to the war—an opposition which was shared by almost all the members of the Whig party in the state. When President Polk issued his call for troops Bartley's friends and associates strongly urged him against taking steps to fill Ohio's quota. But he took the high ground that the State was constitutionally bound to respect the requisitions of the national government. His message to the legislature on this point is an able state paper. He therefore adopted prompt measures to raise the necessary volunteers, who were organized under his personal supervision and delivered to the United States authorities. He declined a second nomination, although strongly urged to permit it. After his retirement he abstained entirely from public life. But he remained a stanch and active Whig until the disruption of that party, subsequently joining the Republican party which he supported until his death.

Bartley was a quiet, retiring, undemonstrative man, who enjoyed the respect of his neighbors and constituents, though never arousing their enthusiasm. He was a product of the frontier, but he did not share that section's narrow, provincial outlook. His messages as governor reveal a broad, liberal grasp of affairs. He was unambitious for political power and refused to seek higher honors which were often within his grasp. In his last years he was severely afflicted with paralysis. He died at his home in Mansfield.

[The chief sources are *Register of Debates in Congress*, 1824–33; *Messages, Reports, and other Communications made to the . . . General Assembly of the State of Ohio*, 1845, 1846; and *Documents, including Messages and other Communications made to the Forty-fifth General Assembly of the State of Ohio*, 1847. There are no private letters or memoirs. A short sketch of Bartley's life appears in John S. C. Abbott, *Hist. of the State of Ohio* (1875). An account of the legislative history of Ohio during his administration as governor is found in C. B. Galbreath, *Hist. of Ohio* (1925), vol. II. An obituary appears in the *Dayton Jour.*, Oct. 13, 1870.]

C. E. C.

BARTOL, CYRUS AUGUSTUS (Apr. 30, 1813–Dec. 16, 1900), Unitarian clergyman, was a leader of religious thought and life in the city of Boston in the last half of the nineteenth century. He was born in Freeport, Me., and was educated in the schools of Portland and then at Bowdoin College, where he graduated in 1832. He studied at the Harvard Divinity School, graduating in 1835; preached for a year in Cincinnati and elsewhere; and was then called to the West Church of Boston as associate of the venerable Dr. Charles Lowell, the father of James Russell Lowell. On Mar. 1, 1837, he was ordained as Lowell's successor, and continued as the active pastor until 1889 and as pastor emeritus until his death. On Feb. 7, 1838, he was married to Elizabeth Howard.

The West Church, organized in 1737, had always been the center of liberal religious influences and patriotic enthusiasms. One of its earlier ministers, Jonathan Mayhew, had been a leader among the Revolutionary patriots, and the church had always represented a certain independency in thought and allegiance. It found its fellowship chiefly among the Unitarians, but its free pulpit offered an opportunity for the unhampered development of Bartol's talents. He was neither a controversialist nor a partisan, but he was an inspiring interpreter of life. It was said of him that "his mind was like a mint continually striking off bright coins of thought and speech" (Ames, *post*, pp. 1–2). He was a man of faith and hope and love who worshipped neither antiquity nor novelty but found the presence of God in nature, in history, and in humanity. He was one of the noteworthy circle of self-reliant and independent men and women who more or less identified themselves with the ideas and ideals of Ralph Waldo Emerson, and the Bartol home at 17 Chestnut St., Boston, was for many years the meeting place of the group of transcendental thinkers and writers who in large measure made the fame of literary Boston in the middle of the nineteenth century.

Bartol was a man of slight physique, and his delicate frame, long white hair, and searching eyes gave him a kind of elfish appearance which lent fascination to his personality. His sermons were original and radical in thought and epigrammatic in expression. He sought everywhere the evidences of enlarging truth and enfolding love. With childlike simplicity he saw the best in every man, and the world was to him a temple of the living God in which it was good to dwell. He loved the mystic aspects of religion and indulged in many an airy flight of imagination. There was, too, an unexpectedly practical side to his nature, and in his later years he proved that he could be a shrewd and successful man of business, for he made a comfortable fortune by selling land for summer residences at Manchester-by-the-Sea. He was the author of many articles, addresses, and books, of which the most important were: *Discourses on the Christian Spirit and Life* (1850); *Pictures of Europe Framed in Ideas* (1855); *Radical Problems* (1873); *The Rising Faith* (1874).

[Sketch by C. G. Ames in *Heralds of a Liberal Faith*, ed. by S. A. Eliot, III (1910), 17–22, containing complete bibliography of Bartol's publications; *West Church, Boston, Commemorative Services* (1887); *Harv. Grad. Mag.*, Mar. 1901, p. 421.]

S. A. E.

BARTON, BENJAMIN SMITH (Feb. 10, 1766–Dec. 19, 1815), physician and naturalist, was born in 1766 at Lancaster, Pa., the son of the Episcopalian rector, Thomas Barton, whose avocation was the study of botany and mineralogy. His mother, Esther (Rittenhouse) Barton, was a sister of David Rittenhouse, the astronomer. Both parents died before he was fifteen, leaving him well provided for. As a lad he attended the York Academy, a well-known classical institution, spending his spare time in the woods collecting birds, plants, and insects. After the death of his parents he moved to Philadelphia to live with an older brother, and studied literature, the sciences, and medicine at the College of Philadelphia. As a young man he was one of the survey party which defined the western boundary of Pennsylvania. At this time he met with and became interested in the American Indian and began his collection of native simples. In 1786 he went to Great Britain and studied medicine at Edinburgh and London. He became a member of the Royal Medical Society and won a Harveian prize. In London he came under the influence of the well-known physician, John Coakley Lettsom, and of Sir Joseph Banks, the naturalist. Leaving London, he went to Göttingen where he received his M.D. degree in 1789. Returning immediately to the United States, he settled in Philadelphia, where he practised medicine and taught in the College of Philadelphia, which in 1791 was incorporated with the University. In 1790 he was appointed professor of natural history and botany, later he was transferred to materia medica, and on the death of Benjamin Rush in 1813 he succeeded that worthy in the chair of theory and practise of medicine.

He was never robust and his naturally delicate constitution was impaired by his habits of work. He realized this himself, for he wrote of "the pernicious consequences of his midnight and injurious toils." As an adult he suffered from gout and he finally succumbed to pulmonary tuberculosis in 1815, aged forty-nine. He had married, in 1797, a daughter of Edward Pennington, of Philadelphia, and had two children, one of whom, Thomas Pennant Barton, was a collector of Shakespeariana. There is an excellent picture of Barton in an article by G. F. Butler in the *American Journal of Clinical Medicine,* XVIII, 43. It is a profile and shows clear-cut features said to resemble those of Goethe, with a rather long nose of the Roman type, a well-shaped head, and a firm chin. Barton's chief medical work is his *Collections for an Essay Towards a Materia Medica of the United States* (pt. I, 1798, pt. II, 1804), a systematic treatise on the medicinal plants of the country. It contains lists and descriptions of the various plants, much of the material being based on original investigation. The wide scope of Barton's interests is shown in his non-medical writings, namely, in his *Memoir concerning the Fascinating Faculty which has been ascribed to the Rattlesnake and other American Serpents* (1796), his *New Views of the Origin of the Tribes and Nations of America* (1797), his *Fragments of the Natural History of Pennsylvania* (1799), and his *Elements of Botany* (1803), the first elementary botany written by an American, and in his contributions to the *Transactions of the American Philosophical Society* and to the *Philadelphia Medical and Physical Journal,* which he founded in 1805 and edited until it was abandoned three years later. One finds in this journal articles by him on such diverse subjects as the earthquakes of North America, the anthropology of the Indians, the food of the humming bird, the torpid state of the North American alligator, etc. His writings show that he was more interested in matter than in manner. His style was casual and careless, and it is stated that he was not particularly impressive as a lecturer. He was enthusiastic and perhaps a little over-credulous, particularly as regards the virtues of vegetable remedies. In his articles on natural history, however, he exhibited a proper degree of scientific caution.

[Wm. P. C. Barton, *A Biog. Sketch of Prof. Barton* (1816), containing full bibliography of his writings, and "An Account of the Life of B. S. Barton" in the *Port Folio,* Apr. 1816; Howard A. Kelly, *Some Am. Medic. Botanists* (1914); John W. Harshberger, *The Botanists of Phila. and Their Work* (1899); J. Thacher, *Am. Medic. Biog.,* vol. I (1828); Alex. Harris, *Biog. Hist. of Lancaster County* (1872).] G. B.

BARTON, CLARA (Dec. 25, 1821–Apr. 12, 1912), philanthropist, was named by her parents Clarissa Harlowe. Her father, Stephen, a descendant of Edward Barton who came to Salem, Mass., from England in 1640, was a typical New England farmer, upright and intelligent, hard-working, devoted to his family, able and willing to take his turn as selectman and representative in the legislature. His wife, Sarah Stone, thirteen years younger, and married at seventeen, was the faithful New England housewife and mother, endowed with practical common sense, a strong will, and a quick temper. Their home was in Oxford, Mass., and here their children were born. During the first seven years of their union they had two boys and two girls. No other children came to them until ten years later when Clara was born.

Among the circumstances of her early days which affected her subsequent career was the fact that, owing to her late arrival, she was the only child in the home. Having no playmates, she was left much to her own devices. Her brothers and sisters took her education in hand, and perhaps spoiled her a little. She grew up to be a rather wilful woman, unable to act as a subordinate gracefully or to coöperate easily. Had she received more of the discipline playmates give each other, she might have been saved trouble and humiliation. Her father, who had served in the Indian wars under Mad Anthony Wayne, gave her instruction in army lore, so that when she was thrust into war conditions she was, she declared, far less a stranger there than most women, or even men. For two years her brother David was an invalid. Day and night she was his nurse, leaving him but one half day during that period. Afterward he gave her instruction in handling tools, tying knots, and similar practical accomplishments, which, together with the skill in nursing she had acquired, were of much use to her later. Although super-sensitive, shy, and easily thrown into a panic of fear, she had plenty of courage for such adventuresome undertakings as crossing a river on teetering logs, and riding partly broken colts. Her sensitiveness and shyness so troubled her mother that she consulted Lorenzo N. Fowler, the phrenologist, who was lecturing in Oxford and staying at the Bartons'. "Throw responsibility upon her," was his advice. "As soon as her age will permit, give her a school to teach." This counsel was followed, and at fifteen she began an eighteen-year period of teaching.

In spite of her youth and inexperience, she was successful from the start. Furthermore, she acquired self-confidence and initiative. After conducting several district schools, she went to North Oxford where her brothers had a mill, planned a schoolhouse there, and for ten years superintended the education of the children and operatives. Feeling the need of more education herself, in 1851 she went to Clinton, N. Y., for a course in the Liberal Institute, at the completion of which she accepted an invitation to teach at Bordentown, N. J. Here she did a piece of work in connection with which she displayed the characteristics which determined her whole career—quick and practical response to an immediate need, delight in directing a difficult enterprise, aggressive independence, persistence, courage, and intense nervous energy. Free public schools were rare in New Jersey at that time. In Bordentown the pupils paid fees which constituted the teacher's salary. Disturbed by the large number of children running the streets, Miss Barton offered to serve three months without pay if the town would make the school free to all. In the face of the strongest opposition, she persuaded the committee to try the experiment. It was so successful that soon a more commodious schoolhouse had to be built, and an assistant teacher employed. Presently opposition to a woman's being in charge of so large a school arose, and a male principal was appointed. To be second in command was never to Clara Barton's taste. She resigned, and her career as a teacher closed.

There followed a period of nervous exhaustion and in 1854 she went to Washington to recuperate. Through the influence of the representative from her home district, Col. Alexander De Witt, employment was soon secured for her in the Patent Office, and she made Washington her permanent home. Her war service began in April 1861, with the arrival at the Capital of the Sixth Massachusetts Regiment. It had had to fight its way through Baltimore and many of the men had lost their baggage. Clara Barton was most energetic in supplying their needs. After the battle of Bull Run, she was greatly impressed by the stories she heard regarding the suffering on the field, due in part to lack of supplies. With characteristic independence, she advertised in the *Worcester Spy* for provisions for the wounded. They came pouring in, and she established a distributing agency. Realizing that it was during battles that supplies and ministration were most needed, in July 1862 she succeeded in getting Surgeon-General Hammond's permission "to go upon the sick transports in any direction, for the purpose of distributing comforts for the sick and wounded, and nursing them," and orders from Generals Wadsworth and Pope affording her transportation for supplies and passage through the lines (see copies of official records in W. E. Barton's *Life of Clara Barton,* I, 164–66). During the remainder of the year, with Washington as her base, she rendered heroic service in getting her supplies to the front, distributing them, and ministering personally to the wounded during action. In 1863 she carried on her particular form of work in the operations about Charleston, S. C. The next year after the battle of the Wilderness she was at Fredericksburg, and later with the Army of the James where, under the authority of Surgeon McCormack and Gen. Butler, she acted as superintendent of nurses.

As a war-worker Clara Barton was never associated with the Sanitary Commission, or any other organization. Except possibly for a short time when she was with Gen. Butler's command, she never had any official connection with the army. At the opening of the war she recognized a need, devised a plan for meeting it, and carried it out on her own lines; but it never became anything but her own personal enterprise. Then, as later, she preferred to direct things herself, disliked being under any one's authority, and was by nature incapable of functioning as a related member of a great body. She showed courage, endurance, and resourcefulness on the battlefield, and gave sympathetic aid to many, but in no higher degree probably than did others less known. She was not primarily a hospital nurse. Her particular service was that of securing supplies for the relief of suffering, and getting to a place of great need with them promptly.

For four years after the war, under the authority of the government, Miss Barton superintended a search for missing soldiers. She also delivered lectures on her war experiences. Her health failing, in September 1869 she went abroad for rest. Soon she was in the midst of war again. With the outbreak of the Franco-Prussian conflict, she became associated with the International Red Cross of Geneva, and distributed relief in Strassburg, Paris, Lyons, Belfort, and Montpellier. Characteristically enough, while at Strassburg she devised a plan of her own for aiding destitute women, by which they were to work and be paid for what they did, wrote to Count Bismarck about it, and obtained official recognition of that type of relief. Later, she introduced it at Lyons, and established a workroom, similar to one she had established in Strassburg. In 1873 she returned home, with the Iron Cross of Merit, presented by the Emperor and Empress of Germany, and the Gold Cross of Remembrance, presented by the Grand Duke and Duchess of Baden.

From her experiences abroad resulted the great and chief service of her career, the establishment of the American Red Cross. Due principally to its traditional policy to hold aloof from European alliances, the United States had not been a party to the Geneva Convention, which made the Red Cross possible, when it was drawn up and signed in 1864, although the Government was informally represented at the congress. In 1866, however, Rev. Henry W. Bellows, with others who had been active in the Sanitary Commission, founded the American Association for the Relief of Misery on the Battlefields. It was the first Red Cross organization in this country and its object was to secure the Government's approval of the Geneva treaty, but it was unable to arouse public interest and went out of existence in 1871. It remained for Miss Barton to accomplish what it had failed to do. She had heard of the Red Cross, apparently for the first time in Geneva, where certain of its officials called upon her to inquire why the United States did not enter the compact. This interview led her to study the history of the organization, and later she saw its workings practically exemplified. Upon her return to this country, she was for a long time a nervous invalid, and in 1876 in search of health she went to Dansville, N. Y., which place she made her residence for some years, living first at a sanatorium, and subsequently in a home of her own which she purchased. All the while the need of the Red Cross in this country was on her mind, and in 1877 she wrote to Dr. Louis Appia, one of the Swiss representatives of the society who had called upon her in Geneva, asking if any effort on her part to establish the Red Cross in the United States would be acceptable, and saying that while she was far from desiring the position, if he had no one else in mind, she would be willing to head the enterprise (see correspondence with Dr. Appia printed in Barton's *Life,* II, 121–39). In his reply he said, "I do not see any inconvenience that you should be for America the *head of the Order, the active working head,*" and gave her instructions how to proceed. Monsieur Moynier, president of the International Red Cross Committee, sent her a letter to President Hayes, informing him of Miss Barton's appointment, and requesting that the United States come into the international agreement. As had been her way in previous undertakings, she attempted and carried through this enterprise practically single-handed. She began a campaign of education, personally visiting heads of the State and War Departments, members of the bar, and influential congressmen. In 1878 she published a pamphlet addressed to the people of the United States and the members of Congress on *The Red Cross of the Geneva Convention, What It Is.* She presented Monsieur Moynier's letter to President Hayes, who referred her to the State Department, which took the position that the original decision regarding entering the alliance made in Secretary Seward's day was final. Her efforts with the next administration were more successful, however, and May 20, 1881, Secretary Blaine wrote her a letter, stating that President Garfield would undoubtedly recommend the adoption of the treaty. The following day a meeting was held at which a National Society of the Red Cross was organized, and it was later incorporated. At a subsequent meeting Miss Barton was elected president, though she had tried to get President Garfield to accept that office. The latter was assassinated before he could recommend the adoption of the Geneva Convention, but President Arthur and Secretary Blaine secured its confirmation by the Senate in March 1882. After a four years' struggle an American Red Cross had been established, and it was largely Miss Barton's personal achievement.

For the next twenty-three years she was engaged in directing the activities of the organization, though for a few months in 1883, at the solicitation of Gov. Benjamin Butler who had observed her work in the war, she acted as superintendent of the Woman's Reformatory Prison at Sherborn, Mass. The relief work which the Red Cross carried on during the numerous calamities of this period, she supervised, in most instances personally visiting the fields, even going to Turkey after the Armenian massacres in 1896, and though more than seventy years old, sailing for Cuba with a cargo of supplies for the *reconcentrados* in 1898. At the time of the Galveston flood, when she was seventy-nine, she spent six weeks on the scene. She represented the United States at International Conferences at Geneva in 1884, Carlsruhe (1887), Vienna (1897), and St. Petersburg (1902). At the first of these she caused the introduction of the "American Amendment," which stipulated that when extraordinary calamities occur in times of peace the Red Cross engage in humanitarian work analogous to the duties devolving upon it in periods of war.

While Miss Barton had the abilities which fitted her to bring about the establishment of the Red Cross in this country, she was not so well qualified to direct and develop such an institution.

Her tendency to keep things in her own hands instead of delegating responsibility, her arbitrariness, and her disinclination to seek the best advice available, were not conducive to the most satisfactory management, or to the building up of a great national society. As a result, down to 1905, it had few members and little organization. Furthermore, she seems to have lacked an adequate sense of the society's accountability to the general public, and she failed to devise such a system of accounting as would safeguard herself and preclude the possibility of embarrassing questions. Public confidence in the society therefore weakened, as is evinced by the fact that at the time of the Galveston disaster, only $17,341 of the $1,300,000 contributed for relief was intrusted to the Red Cross. The demand that there should be a reorganization of the financial and business management became insistent, and in 1900 the American Red Cross was reincorporated by act of Congress, the charter requiring that a financial report should be made annually. Dissensions soon arose in the society over Miss Barton's habit of acting in important matters without consulting the executive committee, the fact that in times of disaster a large part of the contributions went to her instead of passing through the hands of the treasurer, and the methods she employed in meetings of the society to achieve her purposes. Finally a minority of the members presented a memorial to Congress, setting forth the unsatisfactory conditions existing in the Red Cross. Miss Barton proceeded to fight to retain her control, and had the "Remonstrants" suspended from the society, though later, for the "harmonizing of existing conditions" she offered to reinstate them. They replied that the real cause of the division in the organization "lay in the method of administration and the personal character of its business management," and suggested a full and thorough investigation. At the annual meeting of the society in 1904, Mr. Richard Olney was asked to appoint a committee to investigate "all matters and differences between the minority and majority members of this corporation," and a committee of three, of which Senator Redfield Proctor was chairman, was named. It held hearings Apr. 12, Apr. 16, and May 2, 1904, and a Treasury expert was employed to audit the books. After the third meeting the investigation was abruptly dropped. The committee never presented a report, and the stenographic records of the testimony introduced by the "Remonstrants" establish nothing more than poor business methods on Miss Barton's part. On June 16, 1904, she resigned, making possible the complete reorganization of the society. She was much embittered by what she considered her ill-treatment, and for a time entertained a wild idea of going to Mexico to organize the Red Cross there, but was dissuaded by her friends from undertaking the enterprise, although she already had packed her things. The remaining years of her life she spent at Glen Echo, just outside of Washington. Here she died in her ninety-first year, and her body was taken back to Oxford for burial.

Clara Barton was a little woman, five feet tall, of slight build, erect carriage, and an air of resolution and strength. She had an expressive face, with prominent nose and large mouth, brown eyes and abundant hair of the same color. Capable of great endurance and hard work under excitement, she was subject during the first half of her life to periods of nervous prostration. She had the New Englander's religious proclivities, and was brought up in the Universalist Church, but was never a church member. For a time she was interested in Christian Science, but she did not adopt it. She had a good mind, kept herself well informed on current affairs, wrote in a clear and interesting style, and was successful as a public speaker. Her early self-consciousness she never wholly overcame, and she was always sensitive to criticism. Unquestionably she enjoyed prominence and leadership. Sincerely patriotic and philanthropic, she was not a reformer in the common acceptance of the term. She did not try to bring conditions into accord with preconceived ideals, but when she saw a practical need, she gave every ounce of her strength to remedying it. Her initiative, inflexible will, tenacity of purpose, and devotion to human welfare, lifted her out of the obscurity of a country farm where she had had few advantages and enabled her to do a great work which gave her a world-wide reputation.

Besides numerous pamphlets she published *History of the Red Cross* (1882); *Report: America's Relief Expedition to Asia Minor under the Red Cross* (1896); *The Red Cross: a History of This Remarkable International Movement in the Interest of Humanity* (1898), subsequently republished as *The Red Cross in Peace and War*; *A Story of the Red Cross* (1904); *Story of My Childhood* (1907).

[This biography is based on documentary material furnished by the American Red Cross including the stenographic records of the 1904 investigation; Miss Barton's *Story of My Childhood;* Wm. E. Barton, *Life of Clara Barton* (1922); P. H. Epler, *Life of Clara Barton* (1915); and Mabel T. Boardman, *Under the Red Cross Flag* (1915).]

H. E. S.

BARTON, JOHN RHEA (April 1794–Jan. 1, 1871), surgeon, was born at Lancaster, Pa., son of Judge William and Elizabeth (Rhea) Barton, nephew of Dr. Benjamin Smith Barton [*q.v.*], and younger brother of Dr. W. P. C. Barton [*q.v.*]. After serving as an apprentice at the Pennsylvania Hospital while attending the Medical School of the University of Pennsylvania, he received his M.D. degree in 1818 at the age of twenty-four. From 1820 to 1822 he acted as surgeon to the Philadelphia Hospital, and in 1823 he was appointed on the surgical staff of the Pennsylvania Hospital. Here he was probably greatly stimulated in his work by the then senior member of the surgical staff, Philip Syng Physick. On Nov. 22, 1826, Barton performed a very remarkable and pioneer operation at this hospital on a case of anchylosis of the hip-joint. By a wedge-shaped incision into the femur he was not only able to straighten a badly placed bone, but also to make an artificial joint at the point of incision which remained useful and in good position for over five years. The operation was done, it is recorded, in seven minutes and "not one blood vessel had to be secured." Barton was assisted by Drs. Hewson and Parrish. In 1837, he reported a similar case, although in his second operation he did not attempt to make an artificial joint. In addition to these two important orthopædic procedures, Barton is also remembered on account of his description of fracture of the lower end of the radius, his bran dressings for fractures of the leg, and for "Barton's bandage," to immobilize fractured jaws. He wired a fractured patella as early as 1834. Only two important papers were published by him: "On the Treatment of Anchylosis, by the Formation of Artificial Joints," *North American Medical and Surgical Journal,* 1827, III, 279–92, and "A New Treatment in a Case of Anchylosis," *American Journal of Medical Science,* 1837, XXI, 332. He retired from practise in 1840 and died in Philadelphia on New Year's Day, 1871, in his seventy-seventh year. His widow, Susan (Ridgway) Barton, as a memorial to her distinguished husband gave $50,000 to the University of Pennsylvania to establish a chair in the principles and practise of surgery in the Medical School.

[*Medical Times,* 1870–71, I, 163; Arthur Keith, *Menders of the Maimed* (1919), p. 173; Alexander Harris, *Biog. Hist. of Lancaster County* (1872), p. 38; *Phila. Pub. Ledger,* Jan. 4, 1871.] H. R. V.

BARTON, ROBERT THOMAS (Nov. 24, 1842–Jan. 17, 1917), lawyer, author, was descended from English ancestors who had settled in Ireland in the seventeenth century. The Rev. Thomas Barton of Monaghan, a Church of England minister and graduate of Trinity College, Dublin, emigrated in 1751 and became rector of St. James's Church, Lancaster, Pa. His grandson, David W. Barton, a lawyer and scholar, married Fannie L. Jones and resided in Winchester, Va., where their son, Robert Thomas Barton, was born. He received a good education, attending Winchester and Bloomfield Academies in Albemarle County, Va., and commenced the study of law, but on the outbreak of the Civil War, he joined the Confederate army, enlisting as a private in Company F, 2nd Virginia Infantry. Five of his brothers also served, three of whom were killed. On the termination of the war he resumed his legal studies and was admitted to the bar in 1865. He opened an office in his home town, Winchester, and practised there for more than fifty years. Inheriting from his father a keen legal instinct, which he fortified with wide study, he soon acquired a substantial practise. He became known as an authority on the practise of the courts, more particularly on the Chancery side, and wrote two manuals, *Law Practice* (1877) and *Chancery Practice* (1881), both of which were received with favor by the profession. In 1883 he was elected a member of the House of Delegates for one term. Although he was more interested in his profession than in politics, he was always to the fore in local and municipal affairs, serving at one time as mayor of Winchester. In 1893 he became president of the Virginia State Bar Association. In 1894 he was nominated for the position of judge of the supreme court of Virginia, but was not elected. His later years were occupied in extensive explorations of the unpublished public papers and records of the colony, as a result of which he prepared *Virginia Colonial Decisions: The Reports by Sir John Randolph and by Edward Barradall of Decisions of the General Court of Virginia 1728–1741,* which was published in two volumes in 1909. These reports of decisions of the highest court of the chief English colony had been preserved only in manuscript form inaccessible to the profession and the public alike. He prefaced the reports with an erudite Introduction, giving a "perspective sketch of the contemporaneous conditions during the times of the decisions, with some account of the writers of them and of the lawyers who practised at the Bar of the General Court of that day." He was also the author of a number of articles and addresses, mostly on historical subjects. He was twice married: on Feb. 19, 1868, to Katie K. Knight of Cecil County, Md.; and on June 10, 1890, to Gertrude W. Baker of Winchester.

[An appreciative sketch of Barton's life will be found in *Va. State Bar Ass. Report,* 1917–18, p. 91. Interesting details appear also in *The Story of Winchester in Va.* (1925), by Oren Frederic Morton.] H. W. H. K.

BARTON, SETH MAXWELL (Sept. 8, 1829–Apr. 11, 1900), Confederate soldier, the son of Thomas Bowerbank Barton, was born at Fredericksburg, Va. Although he was less than sixteen years old when he was admitted as a cadet at West Point, he was more mature mentally than most of his classmates. As often happens, however, his superiority in this respect did not manifest itself in high scholastic standing. As a classmate (Gen. Holabird) tactfully phrases it, "he was fond of reading and gave more attention to the pursuit of general knowledge than to the specific requirements of the course"; and he graduated, in 1849, somewhat below the middle of the class. He was commissioned in the infantry and first assigned to duty at Governors Island, New York Harbor, but went to New Mexico the next year and was at frontier stations during the remainder of his service in the army. In 1853 he was promoted to first liutenant, and in 1857 to captain. He was in action against hostile Comanches in 1857. On June 11, 1861, he resigned his commission, and went from Fort Leavenworth, Kan., to offer his services to his native state. He was appointed a captain of infantry in the regular army of the Confederate States, but in July 1861 was made lieutenant-colonel of the 3rd Arkansas, and joined his regiment. For the next few months he served in West Virginia and the Shenandoah Valley. He was present at the engagements at Cheat Mountain and the Greenbrier River. In the absence of an engineer officer, he designed the defensive works on the Greenbrier, and acted as Jackson's chief engineer in the valley district through the winter. His nomination as brigadier-general was sent to the Confederate Senate in January 1862, withdrawn a few days later, and renewed in March. His brigade was a part of Kirby Smith's command in East Tennessee until December, when he joined the forces at Vicksburg. He took part in the fighting at Chickasaw Bayou, Chickasaw Bluffs, and Champion's Hill, and in the siege of Vicksburg. He was paroled with the other prisoners taken when the city was surrendered, July 4, 1863, and was exchanged a few days later. Assigned to Pickett's division, to command the brigade which had been Armistead's until his death at Gettysburg, Barton joined it in North Carolina, where the division was recruiting and reorganizing. In its operations against Newbern, in January 1864, Pickett alleged want of coöperation on Barton's part. His handling of his brigade was again severely criticized, during the operations south of Richmond in May, and he was summarily relieved from command by his immediate superior, Gen. Ransom. In spite of his earnest request for a court of inquiry, and strong expressions of confidence presented by his regimental commanders in writing, he remained unemployed until the autumn of 1864, when he was assigned to a brigade in the defenses of Richmond. In January 1865 his brigade became a part of G. W. C. Lee's division, with which he served until captured at Sailor's Creek (Apr. 6). A few days later, while confined at Fort Warren, he joined with other eminent prisoners there in indorsement of Gen. Ewell's letter to Gen. Grant, expressing their "feelings of unqualified abhorrence and indignation" at the assassination of President Lincoln (*Official Records,* XLVI, pt. 3, p. 787). With his release from Fort Warren in July 1865, he disappears from history. He died at Washington, and was buried in Arlington Cemetery.

[G. W. Cullum, *Biog. Reg.* (3rd ed. 1891), II, 391; *Confed. Mil. Hist.* (1899), III, 579–81; S. B. Holabird, in *Bull. Ass. Grads. U. S. Mil. Acad.*, 1900, pp. 138–40; *Official Records,* ser. 1, vols. X (pts. 1, 2), XVI (pt. 2), XVII (pt. 1), XXIV (pts. 1, 2, 3), XXIX (pt. 2), XXXIII, XXXVI (pts. 2, 3), XLVI (pt. 2), LI (pt. 2); unpublished Confederate records in the War Department.]

T. M. S.

BARTON, THOMAS PENNANT (1803–Apr. 5, 1869), diplomat, bibliophile, was born in Philadelphia, the only son of Dr. Benjamin Smith Barton [*q.v.*] and Mary Pennington, a daughter of Edward Pennington, of Quaker stock. He was named for the Welsh naturalist, Thomas Pennant, a correspondent of his father, was educated in Philadelphia, and, after the death of his father in 1815, went to France, where he remained for a considerable period. In April 1833 he married Cora Livingston, daughter of the Hon. Edward Livingston [*q.v.*]. When Livingston was sent as minister to France for the purpose of securing a settlement in 1833 of the French Spoliation Claims, Barton accompanied him as secretary of legation. His knowledge of French, and the charm of Mrs. Barton made his life in Paris socially brilliant. Political conditions caused the path of negotiations to be thorny, and in May 1835 Livingston demanded his passports, leaving Barton behind as chargé d'affaires. The Chamber of Deputies finally voted to pay the claims, but attached such conditions, that, acting under instructions, Barton in turn asked for his passports and sailed for home, landing in New York early in January 1836. His duty completed by rendering a report to the government, he retired with his father-in-law to the beautiful family estate, Montgomery Place, near Barrytown on the Hudson.

He devoted himself to forming an arboretum and to collecting the great library which still bears his name and which was his controlling interest for more than thirty years. Most of it was left in his winter house, 8 West Twenty-second St., New York City. He had collected books when a young man, and while in Paris was already devoting special attention to the English drama. He formed close relations with scholarly booksellers in Europe, and became a connoisseur of fine bindings. By 1860 his library already contained 16,000 volumes, and was widely known as one of the great private libraries of the country. Barton was the first important American collector of Shakespeare, of whose works he possessed all the folio editions, and eighteen quartos published before 1623; but his library was also rich in other departments, especially in original editions of Elizabethan authors and in all branches of French literature. Barton was an exact bibliographer, and left elaborate catalogues in his own handwriting, showing the most minute pains in preparation. He loved his books, and no one else was ever permitted to dust them even in his later days when he was a sufferer from gout. He directed that on his death the collection should be kept intact until its sale to some public institution. His widow disposed of the whole to the Public Library of the City of Boston for $34,000; her death occurred two days after the delivery of the books was completed. A catalogue of them was published in 1888. Barton was a man of great refinement, high character, and fastidious taste. A miniature of him, painted in Paris in 1835 by Étienne Bouchardy, shows a young man of marked elegance, mild in expression, with a face framed in handsome brown hair and beard.

[Louise L. Hunt, *Memoir of Mrs. Edward Livingston* (1886); Chas. H. Hunt, *Life of Edward Livingston* (1864); Jas. Wynne, *Private Libraries of N. Y.* (1860), pp. 59–96; *Bull. Boston Pub. Lib.*, July–Sept. 1921 (with portr.); *Ibid.*, Dec. 1927; letters from Miss Julia Barton Hunt, Summit, N.J.]

F. H. C.

BARTON, WILLIAM (May 26, 1748–Oct. 22, 1831), Revolutionary soldier, the son of Benjamin and Lydia Barton, was born at Warren, R. I. When twenty-two years of age he married Rhoda Carver, daughter of Joseph Carver of Bridgewater, Mass. He was a hatter by trade. At the beginning of the Revolutionary War he enlisted, was soon a captain, and on Aug. 19, 1776 became major of Rhode Island troops.

The circumstances under which he sprang into national fame were these: the English commander, Brig.-Gen. Prescott, occupied the island of Rhode Island in December 1776. He held arbitrary rule at Newport, quartered his force largely in farmhouses, laid waste the neighborhood, and exacted contributions. Personally he was ill-tempered, insolent, and contemptuous of Americans. In a previous campaign he had ill-treated Ethan Allen, had been taken prisoner and exchanged for Gen. Sullivan. It occurred to Barton that the recapture of Prescott would serve to procure the release of Gen. Charles Lee, something which seemed very desirable, since Barton shared the prevailing delusion of Lee's loyalty and military importance. Admitting few into his confidence, Barton planned his route and the details of the capture. The men, forty-one in all, were carefully selected, though the entire regiment had volunteered. The force started in boats from Tiverton, on the night of July 4, touched at Bristol, and proceeded thence to Warwick Neck on the mainland. From there, with muffled oars it crossed Narragansett Bay, skirting Prudence Island, and on the night of July 9 landed on the western shore of Rhode Island itself. The house which Prescott occupied with a small body of troops was a mile inland. Barton's party silenced the sentinel, broke into the house, and captured the English general. He was conducted safely to Warwick, sent to the state authorities in Providence, treated apparently with courtesy, and in due time exchanged. He was soon promoted to major-general, but did not escape lampoons and criticisms in the English press, due to the humiliating features of his capture.

Barton returned to Tiverton, and was promoted on Nov. 10, 1777, to the rank of lieutenant-colonel. His achievement, regarded as a most gallant act, had greatly helped morale in a time of especial need. He received a vote of thanks from the Rhode Island General Assembly, and from Congress a resolution of thanks and the gift of a sword. He served through the war, and was wounded in the British retreat from Warren in 1778. In 1787 when his state declined to send delegates to the Federal convention, Barton joined with others in a letter to the convention, pledging support (I. B. Richman, *Rhode Island,* 1905, pp. 250–51). Naturally therefore, he was a member of the state convention in 1790 which adopted the Federal Constitution. In later life he was unfortunate. Having bought (or obtained by grant from Congress) a tract of land in Vermont, he refused to pay a judgment upon it, and was detained as a prisoner for fourteen years, kept in a kind of honorable captivity in the inn at Danville, Vt. On the occasion of Lafayette's famous semi-centennial visit to America in 1824–25 he learned of Barton's plight and paid the claim, thus setting Barton free. The old soldier returned to Rhode Island, and died in Providence.

[Barton's account of his exploit, in MS., is in possession of the R. I. Hist. Soc. See "Life" by Catharine R. Williams in *Biog. of Rev. Heroes* (1839), and especially J. Lewis Diman, *The Capture of Gen. Rich. Prescott by Lt.-Col. Wm. Barton* (1877).] E. K. A.

BARTON, WILLIAM PAUL CRILLON (Nov. 17, 1786–Feb. 29, 1856), botanist, teacher, and naval surgeon, came of a distinguished scientific and professional family. His father, Judge William Barton, was a well-known Pennsylvania lawyer; his mother was Elizabeth (Rhea) Barton, and his uncle was the botanist and physician, Benjamin Smith Barton [*q.v.*], while his grandfather, the Rev. Thomas Barton, had married Esther Rittenhouse, sister of David Rittenhouse [*q.v.*], the celebrated pioneer mathematician and astronomer. W. P. C. Barton grew up in the scholastic atmosphere of what was then the nation's intellectual capital. He received a classical education at Princeton, and his lectures and writings bear the stamp of training in the humanities. Graduating in 1805 with distinction, he studied medicine under his uncle, Dr. B. S. Barton, at the University of Pennsylvania, and upon the recommendation of the celebrated Drs. Physick and Rush, he was in 1809 appointed surgeon in the navy, serving on active duty with the frigates *United States, Essex, Brandywine* and in the naval hospitals, then called marine hospitals, at Philadelphia, Norfolk, and Pensacola. He acquitted himself of his medical duties with unusual distinction; although he was severely criticized for declining sea-duty in wartime (1813), it was Commodore Decatur who urged Barton, then in bad health, not to go on active duty. In 1815 Barton was chosen professor of botany at the University of Pennsylvania, charming many by his light-hearted herborizing expeditions along the Schuykill and by his lectures which were, contrary to the bookish times, demonstrated in his well-stocked conservatories. A court martial faced him in 1818, instigated by rival surgeons of the navy, on charges of conduct unbecoming an officer and a gentleman. Specifically, he was charged with having criticized the marine hospital organization and having intrigued for preferment in his post. The first charge was undeniable, but apparently the court felt that grounds for criticism of the unsanitary hospitals of the day were justified; the second charge was also true in a sense; Barton's correspondence evidences continual remonstrances and petitions to be changed to this or that place or to be excused from this or that duty. President Monroe was cited as a witness for the defense. The court dismissed the case with a mild reproof to Barton.

For three years he was instructor in materia medica at the Jefferson Medical School, an organization which arose from the ashes of an earlier institution which Barton had largely instigated as an insurgent movement against the conservative medical spirit of the day. In 1842 he was ordered by the Navy Department to Washington and became the first of the chiefs of the Bureau of Medicine and Surgery. His tenure of this office was marked by rigid economy and an attempt at radical reforms in the sanitation and temperance of the navy. This won the enmity of many regular navy men and gave rival surgeons an opportunity to attack him, so that in 1844 he resigned the post in the belief that jealousy and intrigue were leagued against him. He was succeeded by his former friend and chief rival, Surgeon Thomas Harris. Barton was retained upon the navy's inactive list, so that in 1852 he was president of the Board of Medical Examiners, and at the time of his death was buried in Philadelphia with full military honors.

As a botanist, Barton was systematic and accurate; for the most part he contented himself with works of limited scope: *Floræ Philadelphicæ Prodromus* (1815); *Compendium Floræ Philadelphicæ* (1824); *Syllabus of Lectures . . . on Vegetable Materia Medica* (1819)—all essentially catalogues and compilations. But his *Vegetable Materia Medica of the United States* (1817–19) is an excellent account of our medicinal plants, while his *Flora of North America* (1821–23), magnificently illustrated by his wife, is, if not as complete as its title might imply, at least a fine piece of popularization of the work of earlier systematists.

Barton's political diatribes, the outgrowth of his controversies in the navy, are marked by a style that appears now as merely quaint classical ornamentation, but was then considered rhetorical grandeur. In 1828 he issued his fruitless *Polemical Remonstrance against the Project of Creating the New Office of Surgeon General to the Navy,* wherein it chiefly appears that Barton was jealous of the new office. His *Hints for Naval Officers Cruising in the West Indies* (1830) contains many literary references and moral admonitions, with remarks on gambling and temperance. Nevertheless, this book and his report on marine hospitals were, according to Pleadwell, the first signs of a modern medical view of sanitation and provision for the sick in the history of the navy. Barton in early life (September 1814) married Esther Sergeant, a granddaughter of his distinguished grand-uncle, David Rittenhouse. He was noted for witty conversation, caustic comment, and a love of the classics and music.

[*William Paul Crillon Barton—A Pioneer in American Naval Medicine,* an extended monograph by Capt. Frank Pleadwell, appeared in the *Mil. Surgeon,* XLVI, 241–81; it is primarily an account of Barton's medical and official work, with extended quotations from his letters and from an unpublished memoir in the possession of the family. For an account of his botanical career see J. W. Harshberger, *Botanists of Philadelphia* (1899).]

D. C. P.

BARTRAM, JOHN (Mar. 23, 1699–Sept. 22, 1777), first native American botanist, was, in the opinion of Linnæus, the greatest contemporary "natural botanist" in the world. His great-grandfather, Richard Bartram, who traced his family to the Norman invaders, lived in Derbyshire, England; his grandfather, John Bartram, left England in 1682 and settled near Darby in Delaware County, Pa., where Bartram's father, William, and his mother, Elizabeth Hunt, continued to live. Bartram's ancestors for three generations belonged to the Society of Friends, and the stamp of the Quaker was evident in his life and character. It is true that toward the latter part of his life his co-religionists "read him out of meeting." The reason for this action was probably merely that as Bartram had learned more of the world and science he had found it difficult to remain as orthodox as his brethren.

He was born at Marple, near Darby, and from the first, in his hardy life as a farm boy, he was struck by the soft charm of the low country south of Philadelphia. There is a pretty story of him, related in a letter from an imaginary Iwan Alexiowitz (*Letters from an American Farmer,* 1782, by St. Jean de Crèvecœur) in which Bartram is made to say that his attention was first attracted to botany when he overturned a daisy with his plow and fell to musing upon the symmetry of its structure. Desirous of learning more about plants, he went, so the story goes, to Philadelphia and purchased such books as he needed, and in this way, despite the persuasions of his wife, who thought he was wasting time, he taught himself the gentle science. The story has been quoted by J. W. Harshberger and by William Darlington. Bartram's son, William, in his sketch of his father says that his father stated that from the age of ten he had had a passion for botany (which is borne out by John Bartram's letters to Collinson), and that being interested also in medicine, his attention turned naturally to healing plants. His systematic study of them was probably first encouraged by James Logan, founder of the Loganian Library, who got him Parkinson's *Herbal,* and it is fairly certain that Bartram went to a tutor in order to acquire the Latin necessary to read Linnæus. He brought to his favorite subject a mind keen to learn yet essentially untutored and never given to bookishness. He had no desire to amass an herbarium or describe new species in formal systematic style. From the outset he was a lover of living plants, a gatherer and distributer of them.

Perhaps to improve his prospects as a husbandman, perhaps in order to found a Botanic Garden, Bartram in 1728 purchased a plot of land at Kingsessing, three miles from Philadelphia, on the banks of the Schuylkill. Here he laid out his Garden and began what were probably the first experiments in hybridizing in America. Here too he erected one of the four stone houses which he built with his own hands, carving over its door a pious inscription in faulty Greek.

Bartram's celebrated correspondence with Peter Collinson, the English plantsman, began at an uncertain date, probably about 1733 (Youmans, p. 27), and forms a delightful chapter in the history of American horticulture. The two Quaker botanists never met, but their letters are marked by an informality and a racy loquacity; the success and failure of every bulb and cutting is discussed, and as the letters were accompanied by a constant interchange of American plants from Bartram and English plants from Collinson, the epistles constitute a very fair historical source book of the first introductions of many plants now famous as exotics in the two countries (for a list of the American plants which England owes to Bartram, see R. H. Fox, *Dr. John Fothergill and His Friends,* 1919, pp. 163–65). Bartram's plants found their way, through Collinson, into the celebrated greenhouses of Dr. Fothergill and Lord Petre, and soon Bartram was illustrious in Europe, corresponding with Linnæus and his patron the Queen of Sweden, with Dillenius of Oxford, Gronovius of Holland, who had published John Clayton's *Flora Virginica* (1762), and with Philip Miller, the great herbalist and gardener of Chelsea. In America, Bartram soon became the admiration of Linnæus's friends and correspondents, John Clayton and John Mitchill of Virginia, Gov. Cadwallader Colden of New York, and Dr. Alexander Garden of Charleston. Benjamin Franklin and George Washington came often to Bartram's garden to rest and philosophize. The fictitious letter from a Russian gentleman, previously alluded to, has value in giving a picturesque thumbnail sketch of the simple farmer who entertained these great men, and others like André Michaux and Peter Kalm, one of Linnæus's favorite students, who made a pilgrimage to his door. Each one he received with the utmost cordiality and simplicity and with no embarrassment either at high estate or learning.

In search of wider and fresher fields, Bartram made many journeys, at his own expense, to the frontiers, traveling generally alone, for he complains that few Americans showed any interest in science or in nature for itself. He traveled usually in autumn in order to gather ripe seeds and roots and bulbs in proper condition for transplanting. His first trip was a brief five weeks' journey to Williamsburg, Va. (1738), and thence up the James and across the Blue Ridge, 1,100 miles in all. In 1751 he published his best journal, *Observations on the Inhabitants, Climate, Soil, etc. . . . made by John Bartram in his travels from Pensilvania to . . . Lake Ontario.* He explored the Catskills with his son, William, in 1755, and in 1760 visited the Carolinas. During his journey to Pittsburgh, then a frontier fort, in 1761 he met with Indians, one of whom snatched the hat from Bartram's head "in a great passion, and chawed it all round . . .," which Bartram took to be a cannibalistic threat, so that in the French and Indian wars of the next years, Friend though he was, he said that the only way to deal with Indians was to "bang them stoutly" (Youmans, p. 34). In 1765, through Collinson's intervention, Bartram was appointed to the post of Botanist to the King (George III), with a stipend of fifty pounds a year. In royal service, then, he immediately set sail for Charleston, whence he journeyed by land through Georgia to St. Augustine and traveled on foot to Picatola, where he obtained a canoe for the exploration of the San Juan (St. John's) River. Nothing missed Bartram's eye—tree, flower, fruit, bird, fish, or mineral, and as he went he prepared a map of the river's course and depths, shoals, and currents. As an example of the value of Bartram's narrative as a source book (*Description of East Florida, with a Journal by John Bartram,* William Stork, London, 1769), there is his description of the royal palm, not known to him by account or by name. Bartram, characteristically, did not publish his discovery as a new species, but contented himself with a delineation of this great tree so unmistakable that no botanist has failed to recognize it. Bartram's discovery of the royal palm where he found it is illustrative of his intuition for unusual discoveries, for that species is not now known except at the extreme southern tip of Florida, the famous outlying colony found by Bartram having been destroyed by a great cold wave in the 1830's.

Bartram gave his attention to other matters besides botany, collecting shells, birds, insects, fishes, and turtles for his English friends, and setting his son to draw them. But a certain tender-heartedness and piety always inhibited his zoological activities.

Geology, too, and the science of the soil fired his imagination, and contrary to the beliefs of his time, he conceived limestones and marbles to have been formed as geologists now believe they were. In a letter to Garden he proposed that extensive borings be made in order to construct a map of the underlying rocks of the country—the first hint of the task later undertaken by the Geological Survey. He seems to have been the first to propose a great western survey trip and suggested this idea to Franklin, who in turn interested Thomas Jefferson in it. Jefferson's instructions to Lewis and Clark bear a strong resemblance to Bartram's suggestions to Franklin.

Bartram's stand against slavery was forthright in an age when abolition was unpopular. He freed his slaves, who remained his paid servants; and like a Saxon lord of old surrounded by his vassals, Bartram always had his negroes at his table, whether alone or entertaining his most distinguished guests.

Bartram was twice married: in January 1723, to Mary Morris, who bore him two sons, and, after her death in 1727, to Ann Mendenhall in September 1729, who gave birth to five boys and four girls. One, William, became in his turn a distinguished botanist. In appearance John Bartram is described by his son as "rather above the middle size, and upright. His visage was long and his countenance expressive of a degree of dignity with a happy mixture of animation and sensibility." No portrait of him exists, the one published in the *Gardener's Monthly* in 1860 being fictitious.

Bartram's Garden was studied by André Michaux, Nuttall, and other celebrated naturalists during its tenancy by his sons John and William. When, much enlarged by William's additions, it passed through mortgage into the Eastwick family it still remained in interested hands, and for a time the well-known editor and botanist, Thomas Meehan, was its caretaker. A period of neglect followed, but it was saved by the efforts of C. S. Sargent of the Arnold Arboretum, and others, and now forms part of Philadelphia's small park system and remains the oldest shrine to botanists in America. Many giant trees known to have been planted by Bartram's hand are still to be seen there.

Bartram's name in science is commemorated by *Bartramia,* a genus of mosses.

[Bartram's life has never been written in detail, despite rich materials; only brief articles have been devoted to him, the best authority being that of his son William, in *Phila. Med. and Phys. Jour.,* Nov. 13, 1804.

The sketch in Wm. Darlington's *Memorials of John Bartram and Humphrey Marshall* (1849) is not wholly accurate, but has immense value as a collection of Bartram's celebrated correspondence with Collinson. Bartram's correspondence with other naturalists might still be assembled but has not yet been. W. J. Youmans's chapter on the two Bartrams in his *Pioneers of Science in America* (1896, pp. 24–39) is more trustworthy than J. W. Harshberger's account of him in *Botanists of Phila. and Their Work* (1899), though the latter contains much of interest about Bartram's houses, gardens, and horticultural remains. A detailed study could best be made from Bartram's own letters and from his various journals and itineraries. Howard Pyle wrote and illustrated a charming article on Bartram's Garden in *Harper's Mag.*, LX, 321–30.]

D. C. P.

BARTRAM, WILLIAM (Feb. 9, 1739–July 22, 1823), traveler and naturalist, was a son of the noted botanist, John Bartram, and his second wife Ann Mendenhall (for ancestry see John Bartram). "Billy," the "Flower-hunter" (Puc-puggy) of the Seminole Indians, was born and reared in the house of stone erected by John with his own hands in his Botanic Garden (the first in North America) at Kingsessing, on the Schuylkill River, now a part of Philadelphia. The boy early displayed great talent for drawing natural objects. Benjamin Franklin offered to teach him printing, and then suggested for him the trade of engraver; but at eighteen William was placed with a Philadelphia merchant named Child. After four years he tried to settle as an independent trader at Cape Fear, N. C. In 1765–66 he accompanied his father in exploring the St. John's River, which they ascended for almost 400 miles (see the father's *Journal,* appended to Wm. Stork's *Description of East Florida,* 3rd ed., 1769). Nothing will now do with "Billy" (1766), "but he will be a planter upon St. John's River"; yet the next year he is again near his birthplace, merely working on a farm. His father's friend, the English naturalist Peter Collinson, had before his death in 1768 shown drawings by William—"elegant performances"—to the Duchess of Portland, and to Dr. John Fothergill, a botanist and a Friend, who soon extended his patronage to the young American. At Fothergill's expense, Bartram spent the years 1773–77 in exploring the southeastern part of the United States. In return, Fothergill was to have seeds, specimens, and drawings; journals and exquisite drawings, some colored, ultimately reached England, but, in that time of war, probably few parcels of seeds or specimens. Bartram made his way back to Pennsylvania in January 1778. In 1782 he was elected professor of botany in the University of Pennsylvania, but declined the position for reasons of health. In 1786 he became a member of the American Philosophical Society, which Franklin had organized as early as 1743, with John Bartram as an original member.

In 1791 Bartram published at Philadelphia his fascinating *Travels through North and South Carolina, Georgia, East and West Florida, the Cherokee Country, the Extensive Territories of the Muscogulges, or Creek Confederacy, and the Country of the Chactaws.* This work was the chief cause of his fame, being republished in London, Philadelphia, and Dublin, and translated into German by Zimmermann, 1793, into Dutch by Pasteur, 1797, and into French by Benoist, 1799. The literary influence of Bartram's *Travels* would furnish meat for a dissertation. The volume fell into the hands of Chateaubriand, Coleridge, Wordsworth, and many another, with happy results to be seen in *Atala, Kubla Khan,* and *Ruth.* Bartram's varied knowledge was at the service of all who applied to him; he corresponded with naturalists abroad, and was honored with membership in foreign learned societies. To B. S. Barton he probably gave the *Observations on the Creek and Cherokee Indians* (1789) which were brought to light by Squier in 1853 (in *Transactions of the American Ethnological Society,* III, 81). His manuscript *Pharmacopœia* of 89 pages (see below) may well have been useful to the same Barton, who repeatedly cites Bartram in *Collections for an Essay towards a Materia Medica of the United States* (part I, 1798, reprinted, 1900). Most of the plates in Barton's *Elements of Botany* (1803) were engraved from drawings by Bartram, and this work is otherwise indebted to his investigations. Barton "loved him for the happiest union of moral integrity with original genius and unaspiring science." William Bartram contributed a biographical sketch of his father to the first volume of Barton's *Philadelphia Medical and Physical Journal,* as well as two articles on birds, "Anecdotes of an American Crow" (in part I, 1805, pp. 89–95; excerpted in William Nicholson's *Journal of Natural Philosophy,* XIII, 1805, pp. 194–98), and "Description of an American Species of Certhia, or Creeper" (in part II, 1805, pp. 103–6). Another of his fugitive writings was an "Account of the Species, Hybrids, and other Varieties of the Vine of North America" (*New York Medical Repository,* I, 1804, 19–24). His list of 215 native species of birds (in the *Travels,* 1791) was the most complete one before that of Alexander Wilson, whom he inspired to the production of the *American Ornithology* (1808–14). "Bartram's Sandpiper" (the upland plover) was so named by Wilson for his benefactor. Portions of a diary he kept at intervals from 1802 to 1822 have been published by

Witmer Stone ("Bird Migration Records of William Bartram," in the *Auk,* XXX, 325–58). He doubtless had a hand in the periodical *Catalogue* of the Botanic Garden, of which an extant copy is dated 1807, but which is said to have been issued annually from 1801 (or earlier).

Bartram was short in stature; his health, never robust, was even; he girt himself from neck to foot in leather when he worked. He was shy but affectionate, his countenance refined and intellectual. He shared his father's enthusiastic Deism, but, unlike him, did not leave the Society of Friends.

His father had died in 1777, and the Botanic Garden passed to William's brother, John, who subsequently took William into partnership with him. After John died in 1812, the Garden belonged to John's daughter, Mrs. Ann Carr, with whom the unmarried William continued to reside until the end. Death came suddenly and kindly to the aged botanist, from a ruptured blood-vessel in the lungs; he had just finished writing the description of a plant, and was stepping out for a stroll in his beloved Garden.

[No adequate biography of William Bartram exists. The chief printed sources of information concerning him are his *Travels,* and Wm. Darlington's *Memorials of John Bartram and Humphrey Marshall* (1849). Research is needed in the Bartram Memorial Lib. at the Univ. of Pa.; in the collection of the Hist. Soc. of Pa., where there are four large manuscript volumes of Bartram papers (see the first volume in particular), two smaller manuscript volumes of portions of his *Travels,* one volume of his letters and papers, 1761–62, his manuscript *Pharmacopœia,* and answers in his handwriting to queries about Indians in J. H. Paine's *Commonplace-book;* in the lib. of the Acad. of Natural Sciences, Phila., where Bartram's manuscript Diary ("Calendar of Natural Hist., Memorable Events, etc.") reposes; and in the archives of the Am. Philosophical Soc., of which at least four of the Bartram family were members before 1787. For the Diary, see W. Stone, as above, and J. H. L. in the *Gardener's Monthly,* May 1869. Two small volumes of Bartram's Journals, in his handwriting, are in the Lib. of the British Museum Herbarium; on this and other points, see R. Hingston Fox, *Dr. John Fothergill and His Friends* (1919), pp. 185–91. Some of his drawings, including several colored ones, are in the botanical collections of the South Kensington Museum, London. There is a good sketch of Bartram's life (with portr.) by G. S. Morris in *Cassinia, Proc. Del. Valley Ornithological Club,* No. 10 (Phila., 1906–7, pp. 1–9). The sketch in J. W. Harshberger's *Botanists of Phila. and Their Work* (1899) is negligible. On the Botanic Garden, see E. O. Abbot, *Bartram's Garden* (illus.), issued by the John Bartram Ass. (1904, reissued 1907, 1915); and John M. Macfarlane in *Univ. Lectures,* by the Univ. of Pa. Faculty, VII, 263–85. For Bartram's relations with Wilson, see *Supp. to the Am. Ornithology,* by Alexander Wilson (1825), containing a life of Wilson by George Ord. For the literary position and influence of Bartram, see E. H. Coleridge in *Trans. Royal Soc. of Lit.,* XXVII (1906), 69–92; Lane Cooper, in *Methods and Aims in the Study of Lit.* (1915), pp. 110–25, and in the *Cambridge Hist. of Am. Lit.,* I (1917), 194–98; J. Bédier, *Études Critiques* (1903), pp. 196–294; G. Chinard, *L'Exotisme Americain dans l'Œuvre de Chateaubriand* (1918) and in *Univ. of Cal. Publications in Modern Philology,* VII, 201–64.] L. C.

BARUCH, SIMON (July 29, 1840–June 3, 1921), physician, the son of Bernard and Teresa (Green) Baruch, was born in Schwersen, which up to 1918 was included in the German Empire and is now part of Poland. His early education was received in the Gymnasium of his native town; but he emigrated to America before completing his studies and continued his professional training in Charleston, S. C., and at the Medical College of Virginia. At the age of twenty-two he received his M.D. degree and immediately joined the Confederate Army with the rank of assistant surgeon. During the next three years he saw much active service. At the close of the war, he settled in Camden, S. C., and there practised medicine until 1881, when he moved to New York. He came prominently before the profession and the public in 1888, when he insisted upon an immediate operation in a case which he had diagnosed as appendicitis. The successful outcome of this operation—said to have been the first of its kind in America—led to a treatment of appendicitis which has saved innumerable lives. Baruch was, however, perhaps best known as the leading exponent of hydrotherapy, a subject largely developed by Winternitz in Vienna. Two of Baruch's books, *The Uses of Water in Modern Medicine* (1892), and *The Principles and Practice of Hydrotherapy* (1898) as well as his introduction into this country of the Brand treatment of typhoid fever by means of full baths, attest his deep interest in and extensive knowledge of the subject. Official recognition of his services to medicine came when he was appointed professor of hydrotherapy at the College of Physicians and Surgeons, Columbia University.

The transition from a physician to a public-spirited citizen and philanthropist was in his case a very natural one; for, being interested in the uses of water in medicine, he turned his attention to the importance of free cleansing baths; and largely through his efforts what is claimed to have been the first public bath in America was opened in Rivington St., New York City, in 1901. Since then more than 100 free municipal bath-houses have been established throughout the country. It was this interest in hydrotherapy which led to Baruch's appointment as a member of the Saratoga Commission, when New York State purchased and restored the Saratoga Mineral Springs. The value of his services may be gauged by the report of the chairman of the Commission, George Foster Peabody: "Without compensation, Dr. Baruch devoted months of his time in making observations at the European Spas and brought to the Commission a complete guide to the building up of Saratoga as a cure."

Baruch was deeply attached to the United States. Even as late as 1917, when this country entered the World War, he wrote: "If I did not stand ready to consecrate heart and soul and all that I possessed to the defense of my adopted country, I would despise myself as a scoundrel and a perjurer and regard myself as an ingrate to the Government that has, for sixty years, enhanced and protected my life, honor and happiness." On Nov. 27, 1867, he married Isabel Wolfe, of Winnsboro, S. C., a descendant of an old American family.

[Irving A. Watson, *Physicians and Surgeons of America* (1896), pp. 534–35; Wm. B. Atkinson, *Physicians and Surgeons of the U. S.* (1878), p. 164; *N.Y. Times*, June 4, 1921; personal information from H. B. Baruch, M.D.]

B.H.

BARZYŃSKI, VINCENT (Sept. 20, 1838–May 2, 1899), Catholic priest, born at Sulisławice near Sandomierz, Poland, was the son of Joseph Barzyński and Mary Sroczyńska. His earlier education was private. He began his studies for the priesthood at the diocesan seminary of Lublin in 1856. He was ordained in 1861. He was engaged in active ministry at Tómaszów when the Polish insurrection broke out in 1863. Owing to his aiding the revolutionists he was obliged to flee after the collapse of the uprising. After a sojourn of more than a year in Austria he went to Paris in 1865. There he met Fathers Semenenko and Kajsiewicz, the founders of the new Congregation of the Resurrection, who invited him to join them. He became a member in Rome. About this time the bishop of Galveston, Tex., was in search of priests for the recent Polish settlements in his diocese. The superior of the Congregation agreed to send him a few priests. Thus Barzyński, in the company of Fathers Bakanowski and Zwiardowski came to Texas in 1866.

Here he labored strenuously, attending the religious needs of the poor Polish farmers, until he was called to Chicago in 1874. He became pastor of the church of St. Stanislaus Kostka, the first Polish congregation in Chicago. He now began the busiest and most constructive period of his career. His work among the ever increasing Polish immigrants in Chicago was beset with many difficulties. He was obliged to contend with the liberal and irreligious elements among the laity as well as with the ill will of many of the Polish clergy. The clergy opposed to him effected his recall by his superiors in Europe. He expressed his willingness to leave, but pleaded to be permitted to extricate his parish from its financial straits. Hence he was allowed to continue his work in Chicago. During his incumbency the large St. Stanislaus Church was erected, and also the largest parochial school in the city. His activities increased with the growing population. It became imperative repeatedly to divide his parish and to organize new ones. He organized more large parishes among the Poles than any other priest in the United States. Despite the founding of new congregations his own grew by leaps and bounds, so that during his lifetime its membership exceeded 50,000.

The labors of Barzyński were not confined to his own parish. He was instrumental in founding an orphanage, establishing Polish newspapers, and introducing and organizing the teaching sisterhoods. He was very active in establishing religious confraternities in his congregation as well as mutual benefit societies. He became the recognized spiritual guide and leader of the Poles in the city of Chicago. Owing to his indomitable energy a writer in a German paper (*Illinois Staatszeitung*, Jan. 20, 1879) compared him to Gregory VII. In January 1899 he suffered an attack of pneumonia. He recovered, but his forces were spent; he fell ill again and died in the Alexian Brothers Hospital. He was buried in St. Adalbert's Polish Cemetery in Chicago.

[Wacław Kruszka, *Historya Polska w Ameryce* (1905); Sanisław Siatka, *Krótkie Wspomnienie o Życiu i Działalności Ks. M. Wincentego Barzyńskiego* (1901), portr.; *Cath. Encyc.*, XVI, 7–8. A brief notice of his death appeared in the *Daily Inter-Ocean*, Chicago, May 4, 1899.]

J.J.R.

BASCOM, HENRY BIDLEMAN (May 27, 1796–Sept. 8, 1850), college president and Methodist bishop, was born at Hancock, N. Y., the son of Alpheus Bascom of French Huguenot stock and Hannah (Houk) Bascom of German ancestry. His parents were very poor, and it was only by the assistance of his mother's brother, after whom he was named, that he was enabled to attend school from his sixth to his twelfth year, at which time his education ended, so far as schools and teachers were concerned. His father moved to Little Valley in western New York in 1808, and it was while residing here that young Henry was converted and joined the Methodist Church at fifteen years of age. In 1812 the family moved to Maysville, Ky., on the southern bank of the Ohio River, but after only a short residence there they moved to the north side of the river and settled permanently in Brown County, Ohio. At an early age Bascom manifested unusual gifts for public speaking and leadership. He was given license to preach when he was only seventeen and the presiding elder immediately appointed him assistant to the pastor of the Brush Creek Circuit in bounds of which the country home of the Bascoms was located. When the Ohio Annual Conference met on Sept. 1, 1813, Bascom was one of the ten young ministers "admitted on trial." The Methodist Circuits of those days embraced as a rule from twenty to thirty preaching places, each of which had preaching once a month. After spending three years on circuits in the Ohio Conference he was transferred to the Tennessee Conference (which at that time had within its bounds a considerable portion of Kentucky) and was appointed two years in succession to Danville, Ky., followed by two years at Louisville. When the Kentucky Annual Conference was organized in 1820, and took over the Kentucky territory then held by the Tennessee Conference, he became a member of the newly established conference, but after preaching for two years on large circuits, he was transferred back to the Ohio Conference and was put in charge for that year of the Brush Creek Circuit where he had begun his ministry nine years before. While pastor at Steubenville, Ohio, in 1823, he was, on the nomination of Henry Clay, elected chaplain to the Congress of the United States. During and following his residence in Washington, 1824–26, he traveled extensively and preached in Maryland, Virginia, and Pennsylvania, making a profound impression by his oratory and drawing vast crowds wherever he went. He was next stationed for a short time at Pittsburgh and later at Uniontown, Pa.; the seat of a newly organized Methodist school called Madison College, of which he was president from 1827 to 1829. He was agent for the American Colonization Society, 1829–31, during which time he traveled far and wide, pleading eloquently for the objects to be accomplished by that society. In 1832 he was elected professor of moral science in Augusta College, Ky., and was thereupon transferred from the Pittsburgh to the Kentucky Conference. Ten years later he was selected for the presidency of Transylvania University at Lexington, Ky., which office he filled from 1842 until 1849, dividing his time after 1846, between duties in this university and his work on the new *Southern Methodist Quarterly Review* to the editorship of which he was elected by the General Conference of 1846.

In the meantime, he had taken an active part in the trying struggle between the Northern and Southern delegates in the General Conference of 1844 over slavery, the outcome of which was the division of the Church. It was he who wrote, at the request of his fellow delegates from the South, the "Protest" of the southern representatives against the action of that Conference with reference to Bishop Andrew of Georgia, excluding him from the exercise of his episcopal office because his wife was a slaveholder. In the "Convention" that met at Louisville, in 1845, to consider and perfect the method and plans for the organization of the Southern Church he wrote the able report of the committee to whom this important matter was referred. These and other state papers showed that he was not only American Methodism's foremost pulpit orator, but one of her greatest ecclesiastical statesmen. In addition to his election as editor of the *Quarterly Review,* the General Conference of 1846 had made him chairman of the commission charged with arranging and settling with representatives of the Methodist Episcopal [Northern] Church all matters relating to, and growing out of, the division of the church. At the meeting of the second General Conference of the Methodist Episcopal Church, South, held in St. Louis in May 1850, when it was decided that only one new bishop was needed, he was elected on the second ballot by a large majority. He lived to preside over only one Annual Conference, the St. Louis, which met at Independence, Mo., on July 10, only six weeks after his ordination as bishop. Returning to his home at Lexington, Ky., he was taken ill in Louisville, where he died.

All his life Bascom was hampered and embarrassed by poverty, having early gone in debt to help support his father and family, who were always in financial straits. During one of the early years of his ministry he traveled 5,000 miles, preached 400 times, and received for the year's service only $12.10! His salary at the institutions which he served as professor or president was inadequate to his necessities. This in part accounts for his postponement of all thought of matrimony until late in life. On Mar. 7, 1839, when he was nearly forty-three years of age, he was married to Miss Van Antwerp of New York City, by whom he had two children.

Bascom possessed the elements that go to make a great orator. Whenever and wherever he preached, he easily and powerfully swayed vast audiences, but his type of oratory, though well suited to impress the typical American of seventy-five or a hundred years ago, would doubtless be accounted too florid, rhetorical, and emotional to impress in an equal degree an audience of the present day. His published works were: *Methodism and Slavery* (1847); two volumes of *Sermons* (1849), of which 20,000 copies were sold; *Works* in four volumes, published posthumously (1855).

[M. M. Henkle, *Life of Bascom* (1856); H. H. Kavanaugh, "Memoir" in Vol. I of the bound copies of *Gen. Minutes of M. E. Ch., South,* pp. 811–15; H. N. Mc-

Tyeire, *Hist. of Methodism* (1884), pp. 655–58; Gross Alexander, *Hist. of the M. E. Ch., South* (1894), pp. 60–61; W. B. Sprague, *Annals of the Am. Pulpit* (1857–69), VII, 534–40; *Southern Meth. Quart. Rev.* for 1850 and 1852.]

W.F.T.

BASCOM, JOHN (May 1, 1827–Oct. 2, 1911), philosopher, college president, was born at Genoa, N. Y., under three unlucky omens. He was "the son of a minister, the youngest child, the only son" (Bascom, *Things Learned by Living,* p. 18). While he was still an infant, his father, the Rev. John Bascom, died; his mother, Laura (Woodbridge) Bascom, was left in straitened circumstances. Both parents were of New England descent and strict Puritanical principles. The shadow of genteel poverty which hung over Bascom's early life was further darkened by what he later called the "perverse theory" of Calvinism, whose intensity of moral idealism nevertheless remained the most striking note of his own character. The energy of an older sister provided for his education as well as that of herself and two other sisters. He attended Williams College, where he distinguished himself in mathematics and not at all in the languages. After graduation in 1849, he taught for a year in Hoosick Falls, N. Y., and then studied law for eight months in a lawyer's office. He was repelled by the conventionality, moral compromises, and personal interests involved in legalism. "My nature called me to crucifixion, but the law would have been to me crucifixion by a rabble of bad boys" (*Ibid.,* p. 52). In search of crucifixion, he entered Auburn Theological Seminary in 1851. There he was profoundly influenced by Laurens Hickok [*q.v.*], professor of theology, and one of the ablest philosophers of his time.

In 1852 he accepted a position as tutor in rhetoric and oratory at Williams, where, according to the custom of the college, the young instructor was badgered by the students and made as unhappy as possible. In the same year he married Abbie Burt, who died two years later. In 1854 he attended Andover Theological Seminary but returned to Williams in 1855 as professor of rhetoric and oratory. In 1856 he married Emma Curtiss. Bascom's vacillation between the careers of clergyman and educator was now over. Yet for the nineteen years during which he remained at Williams his college work was largely distasteful to him. He was not particularly interested in either oratory or rhetoric. He lessened to some extent the drudgery of composition courses, however, by the introduction of æsthetics and English literature, subjects which were then rarely taught. He also solaced himself by the publication of numerous magazine articles and four text-books: *Political Economy* (1859), written before Bascom's faith in technical political economy had been weakened by knowledge of the broader field of sociology; *Æsthetics or the Science of Beauty* (1862), founded on Kames and Campbell; *Philosophy of Rhetoric* (1866), an endeavor to base the rules of rhetoric upon laws of thought; *Principles of Psychology* (1869), revised as *The Science of Mind* (1881), a strict exposition of rational psychology, founded mainly upon Hickok. He also delivered two courses of Lowell Lectures, published as *Science, Philosophy, and Religion* (1871) and *Philosophy of English Literature* (1874).

In 1874 Bascom was offered the presidency of the University of Wisconsin. "As I despaired," he writes, "of a favorable change of work at Williams, and found that my growing freedom of religious thought was making my presence less agreeable to the college, I accepted the invitation" (*Ibid.,* p. 60). The University of Wisconsin was then hardly more than a large academy. There were only 407 students and but eighteen faculty members; there was only one recitation building, with a solitary laboratory stowed away in the basement. Worst of all, there was no definite educational program or subordination of departments. Yet the institution was already on a good foundation; the establishment of a millage tax in 1876 soon assured it a small but steadily increasing income; the faculty was above the average in ability; the students, though rough and undisciplined, were eager. Bascom's incumbency, like that of Angell at Michigan, was notable for internal rather than external improvement. Only a few more buildings were added, the enrolment was increased by only one hundred, but the entire spirit of the place was changed. Bascom left it, at the end of his thirteen years of office, an effective educational institution, organized about the college of liberal arts as its center.

At first he was far from popular. His sharp New England features, challenging eyes, and reserved manner accorded ill with the indiscriminating cordiality of the West. Gradually, however, his underlying kindliness came to be appreciated, while his firmness won him general respect. He assumed direct supervision of disciplinary matters and by a union of reasonableness and determination succeeded in imparting a sense of discipline to the students themselves. All the members of the senior class came under his immediate instruction in philosophy, and for Bascom philosophy was essentially the vision of a rational life. Resisting the vocational appeals of the day, he made the campus a home of liberal culture. He impressed his personality upon both students and faculty, few of whom failed to acknowledge educational indebtedness to him. In his relations with the regents he was less fortunate. In American state universities, then as now, "Rarely, indeed, was any man granted the position of Regent who had any special knowledge of the methods of education, or interest in them" (*Things Learned by Living,* p. 70). The most important figure among the regents at Wisconsin toward the end of Bascom's term was Edwin W. Keyes, the Republican political boss of the state. The friction between this gentleman and Bascom, due to entire difference of outlook, was accentuated by Bascom's advocacy of prohibition which was at that time an unpopular measure in Wisconsin. By 1887, Bascom writes, "I felt it wise to resign rather than to expose myself to those accidents which might make resignation compulsory" (*Ibid.,* p. 74). He returned to Williamstown, and soon was in a condition of poverty, owing to unfortunate financial investments. Hence he accepted a subordinate position as lecturer on sociology at Williams College, where in 1891 he became professor of political science. In 1903 he resigned in order to devote his entire time to writing and public service. He became president of the Williamstown Improvement Society and was active in the establishment of a state reservation and park on Mount Greylock. He died in 1911.

Bascom was a facile and copious writer. The partial bibliography in his *Things Learned by Living* (1913) lists 178 titles, of which twenty refer to books. Of these the most important were *Philosophy of Religion* (1876), *Ethics or Science of Duty* (1879), *Natural Theology* (1880), *Problems in Philosophy* (1885), *The New Theology* (1891), *Historical Interpretation of Philosophy* (1893), *Evolution and Religion* (1897). In these philosophical works he remained to the end essentially a disciple of Laurens Hickok. He adopted the epistemological dualism of Hickok's "Conservative Realism," and like his master he stressed the *a priori* principles of the mind so far as to be on the verge of idealism. At the same time he made more concessions to empirical fact, particularly in the realm of ethics, than Hickok's dogmatic rationalism permitted. He was much interested in harmonizing theology with evolutionary science, and in its main conclusions his philosophy belonged to the most liberal form of Christian apologetics. His writing possessed unusual clarity and stylistic charm. It exercised little influence, however, upon the development of American philosophic thought.

[Bascom's spiritual autobiography, *Things Learned by Living* (1913), is the primary source. For his career at the Univ. of Wis., see *Memorial Service in Honor of John Bascom* (1911), containing addresses by Van Hise, Birge, et al.; J. F. A. Pyre, *Wisconsin* (1920); and R. G. Thwaites, *Hist. of the Univ. of Wis.* (1900). His philosophy is eulogistically expounded by Sanford Robinson, *John Bascom, Prophet* (1922).]

E. S. B.

BASHFORD, COLES (Jan. 24, 1816–Apr. 25, 1878), first Republican governor of Wisconsin, was born of native stock in eastern New York, and emigrated up-state, where he established himself in law and became district attorney of Wayne County in 1847. He moved to Oshkosh shortly after the admission of Wisconsin, entered politics as a Whig, and deserted the Whigs to assist in organizing the Republican party. Nominated for governor in 1855, and apparently defeated by his Democratic opponent, William A. Barstow [*q.v.*], he succeeded, after the latter had assumed office, in proving fraudulent election returns, and was himself awarded the office by the supreme court of the state, Mar. 24, 1856 (*The Trial in the Supreme Court . . . of Coles Bashford vs. Wm. A. Barstow,* 1856). The railroad land grant offered by Congress to Wisconsin in 1856 made necessary a special session of the legislature for its disposition, and occasioned the most spectacular jobbery in the history of the state. The promoters of the La Crosse and Milwaukee Railroad, who lobbied for and won the grant, donated their securities to a majority of the legislature, and rewarded Gov. Bashford with $50,000 (nominal value) of their bonds. In the administration of his successor, a storm of exposure, made more intense by the financial depression of 1857, broke upon the state. Ex-Gov. Bashford removed to Washington, whence he soon departed to the new territory of Arizona, which was created in 1863. Here he filled the offices of attorney-general, councillor and president of the legislative council, territorial delegate, and secretary. He died in Prescott in 1878, survived by his wife, Frances (Foreman) Bashford.

[Material upon the critical point of Bashford's career exists in *Report of the Joint Select Committee, Appointed to Investigate into Alleged Frauds and Corruption in the Disposition of the Land Grant by the Legislature of 1856* (Madison, 1858). P. V. Lawson has a sketch of his life in *Oshkosh Northwestern,* Feb. 8, 1908.]

F. L. P.

BASHFORD, JAMES WHITFORD (May 29, 1849–Mar. 18, 1919), college president, Methodist bishop and missionary, was the son of Samuel Morris Bashford, a physician and Methodist preacher, and Mary Ann McKee, of a distinguished Virginia, Illinois, and Kentucky family. Born at Fayette, Wis., Bashford was prepared for college in a school opened at Fayette by

Parkinson, later professor of mathematics in the University of Wisconsin. He received the degrees of A.B. from that university in 1873, B.D. from the School of Theology of Boston University in 1876, and Ph.D. from the same university in 1881. He was much influenced by the personality and sermons of Phillips Brooks. In 1878 he married Jane M., daughter of W. W. Field of Madison, Wis. His churches were: Harrison Square, Boston, 1875, First, Jamaica Plain, 1878, Auburndale, 1881, Chestnut Street, Portland, Me., 1884, and Delaware Avenue, Buffalo, N. Y., 1887. He was offered the presidency of eleven colleges while pastor at Buffalo and accepted the last, that of Ohio Wesleyan University, where he remained from 1889 to 1904. In May 1904 he was elected a bishop with designation of his field or "area" (not diocese in the usual sense) as China. Here the main work of Bashford's life was done. He brought to it enthusiasm, intelligence, unselfish devotion, and common sense. He became a master in things Chinese; he cultivated friendship with missionaries of other churches, with foreign diplomats, with Chinese statesmen and leaders. He interested himself in China's political development. He personally urged President Taft in 1912 to recognize the Chinese Republic. He was opposed to the adoption of Christianity as a state religion, or even to the official setting apart of Sunday as a day of rest. When Japan presented secretly and with request for immediate acceptance her Twenty-one Demands on China in January 1915, Bashford secured a copy, studied it carefully, and in March wrote two letters, one to Secretary Bryan, the other to President Wilson, in which he sought to arouse the American government to the gravity of the situation (for full text see Grose, *Bashford,* pp. 142–54). In that same spring he was asked by the Board of Missions to return to America. He went immediately to see the Secretary and the President. While his dealings with the Japanese had been always frank, kind, and statesmanlike, Bashford was opposed to the Japanese militaristic policy, as to all militarism. Besides numerous articles in periodicals (see "Prophecy" in the *Methodist Review,* May 1902, and especially "Wesley's Conversion" in the same, September 1903), Bashford published *Wesley and Goethe* (1903), *China and Methodism* (1906), *Christian Missions* (1906), *God's Missionary Plan for the World* (1907), *China: an Interpretation* (1916), *The Oregon Missions* (1918). The last two or three years were spent in much suffering though he worked on with indomitable will. He died in Pasadena, Cal., Mar. 18, 1919.

[In spite of G. R. Grose's admirable brief biog., *James W. Bashford* (1922), the fifty-four volumes of Bashford's notes are still unexplored. For important estimates see the *Christian Advocate* (N. Y.), Mar. 27, 1919, pp. 387 ff.]

J. A. F.

BASKERVILLE, CHARLES (June 18, 1870–Jan. 28, 1922), chemist, was born in Deer Brook, Miss., the son of Charles and Augusta (Johnston) Baskerville. He studied successively at the University of Mississippi, the University of Virginia, Vanderbilt University, and the University of North Carolina (B.S., 1892; Ph.D., 1894). In 1891 he was appointed instructor of chemistry at the University of North Carolina. From then on his promotion at this institution was rapid; and in 1900 he became professor of chemistry in succession to Dr. F. P. Venable, who had been elected to the presidency. In 1904 Baskerville accepted the directorship of the chemical laboratories of the College of the City of New York, in succession to Dr. R. O. Doremus, and here he remained until his death. On Apr. 24, 1895, he had married Mary B. Snow, by whom he had two children.

Baskerville was the author of nearly 200 educational, scientific, and technological papers, in addition to being the author or co-author of a number of books, such as *Qualitative Analysis,* with L. J. Curtman (1910); *Municipal Chemistry,* with other experts (1911); and *Anæsthesia,* with J. T. Gwathmey (1914). His earlier researches dealt with the rare earths (thorium, lanthanum, praseodymium and neodymium) and rare metals (titanium and zirconium). Later, in New York, he turned his attention more to industrial problems: the manufacture and use of several anesthetics employed in surgery; the methods of treating and refining edible vegetable oils; the development of the oil-shale industry; and the recovery of used stock in the pulp and paper industry. Valuable as these contributions may be, Baskerville's name is more particularly memorable for his effectiveness as a teacher of chemistry, and for his activities in connection with the development of the American Chemical Society and its New York branch.

[Obit. notices by W. A. Hamor in *Science,* LV, 693–94 and R. H. Moody in *City Coll. Quart.,* XVIII, 3; additional information furnished by W. H. Pierce, of the Coll. of the City of N. Y.]

B. H.

BASS, EDWARD (Nov. 23, 1726–Sept. 10, 1803), Episcopal bishop, was the great-grandson of Ruth, daughter of John and Priscilla Alden, who married John Bass, the son of Samuel Bass, the first of that family in this country. Edward Bass was born in Dorchester, Mass., and was one of a family of eleven children. His parents were Joseph and Elizabeth (Breck) Bass.

He gained admission to Harvard College at the age of thirteen, graduated in the class of 1744, and for the next three years remained in the college, studying for the M.A. degree, which he received in 1747. He still continued to reside in the college and to carry on his theological studies, but transferred his allegiance from the Congregationalism of his fathers to Episcopacy. This necessitated a trip to England to receive that which he regarded as essential to a valid ministry, but which could not be obtained in this country, ordination at the hands of a bishop. On May 17, 1752, he was made deacon by the Bishop of London, Thomas Sherlock, and a week later was ordained to the priesthood by the same bishop. Upon his return to America, he took charge in the fall of 1752, of St. Paul's Church, in that part of Newbury, Mass., which later became Newburyport.

During the Revolution Bass lukewarmly supported the colonial cause but did not escape altogether from patriot persecutions. At the close of the Revolution the Episcopal Church in America was in a deplorable state, badly shattered, and regarded with disfavor because of its connection with the Church of England. To rehabilitate it and adapt it to the new conditions was a difficult and delicate task. Bishops were chosen in Connecticut, Pennsylvania, New York, Virginia, Maryland, and South Carolina. When Massachusetts was ready to choose its bishop, it turned to Bass, who had been so long in charge of the parish at Newburyport. He was elected June 4, 1789, but his consecration was delayed, and then was indefinitely postponed. His first wife, Sarah Beck, whom he married in 1754, had died May 5, 1789, and within six months he married Mercy Phillips. Such celerity was considered unseemly in a prospective bishop and occasioned much criticism. But on May 24, 1796, he was again elected, and on May 7, 1797, in Christ Church, Philadelphia, he was consecrated the first Bishop of Massachusetts.

The fact that he was now a bishop did not alter his relation to the parish at Newburyport. He continued in charge of that as before. The Episcopal Church in Rhode Island had been under the supervision of Bishop Seabury of Connecticut, but he had died in 1796, and it now placed itself under the charge of Bishop Bass, as did also the Church in New Hampshire. The years covered by the episcopate of Bass were only six, but they were tense years both in church and state. He steered his course through them with honor, aiding by his kindliness and forbearance to put a rein upon bitter party spirit, and to make friends for his church. Not a man of scholarly attainment, he left nothing in print, save one or two sermons in pamphlet form.

[John N. Norton, *Life of Bishop Bass* (1859); Daniel Dulany Addison, *Life and Times of Edward Bass* (1897); *Churchman's Mo. Mag.*, Oct. 1805; *Evergreen*, July 1845, in which is an engraved likeness; Jas. S. Morss, *Brief Hist. of the Episc. Ch. in Newburyport and Vicinity, Being the Substance of Two Discourses Preached in St. Paul's Ch.*, Dec. 31, 1837; W. B. Sprague, *Annals Am. Pulpit*, V (1859); sketch by Wm. S. Bartlett, in appendix to his life of Rev. Jacob Bailey, *Colls. P. E. Hist. Soc.*, II (1853).]

W. A. B.

BASS, SAM (July 21, 1851–July 21, 1878), desperado, was born near Mitchell, Lawrence County, Ind., one of the ten children of Daniel and Elizabeth (Sheeks) Bass. The parents, who were highly respected by their neighbors, were the owners of a small but well-stocked farm. The mother died when the boy was ten. The father, who had married again, died in 1864, whereupon the younger children were placed under the guardianship of a maternal uncle. Sam had no liking for school and it is said did not even learn to read. In the fall of 1869 he left home for St. Louis, going then to Rosedale, Miss., where for nearly a year he worked in a mill. He then went to Denton, Denton County, Tex., and for eighteen months was in the employ of a Mrs. Lacy, who kept a hotel. Later he worked as a cowboy for Col. W. F. Egan, and on the latter's election as sheriff served for a time as one of his deputies. Up to about his eighteenth year he was a well-behaved boy. Before he left home he had become unruly, and had begun to associate with some of the rougher characters of the community. All accounts agree, however, that for his first four years in Texas he was industrious, sober, and honest. The break came in 1875. One of his biographers, moralizing on the transformation, attributes it to his purchase of a racing mare. A period of dissipation, gambling, and dare-deviltry followed, culminating in a horse-stealing raid on the herds of the Choctaws and the Cherokees in the Indian Territory. A desire for new scenes next possessed him, and with Joel Collins, a local cattleman, he assisted in driving a herd of beeves to Kansas, where it was sold. The proceeds, however, most of which belonged to Collins's friends in Texas, were soon squandered. Bass and Collins, with four others, then went to the new town of Deadwood, in the Black Hills, where they shortly began to recoup their losses by robbing stage coaches. Later they moved into Nebraska, and on Sept. 19, 1877, at Big Springs, they held up a Union Pacific train, getting $60,000 in gold from the express car and some $5,000 from the passengers. They fled southward, closely pursued. Collins and a companion were overtaken in Kansas and killed, and a third was killed in Missouri. Bass, however, returned safely to Denton County. Here he organized a new gang, and in the late winter and spring of 1878 held up and robbed four trains in the Dallas-Fort Worth region. Texas Rangers pursued and killed one of the bandits and captured three others. One of the prisoners, Jim Murphy, consented to rejoin Bass and his two remaining companions and give information of their movements. Though suspected by Bass, he was permitted to accompany the gang in a foray southward. An attempt to rob the bank at Round Rock, in the southern part of Williamson County, was frustrated on July 19, through a warning sent by Murphy to the Rangers, and in the ensuing fight Bass was mortally wounded. He died two days later, on his birthday, and was buried at old Round Rock.

Bass was about five feet eight inches tall, somewhat stoop-shouldered, and weighed about 140 pounds. "He would be taken for a good-looking man anywhere," said the *Denton Monitor.* On his tombstone was placed the inscription: "A brave man reposes in death here. Why was he not true?"

[Charles L. Martin, *A Sketch of Sam Bass, the Bandit* (1880); James B. Gillett, *Six Years with the Texas Rangers,* with intro. by M. M. Quaife (1925); Ed. F. Bates, *Hist. and Reminiscences of Denton County* (1918); Owen P. White, *Trigger Fingers* (1926).] W. J. G.

BASS, WILLIAM CAPERS (Jan. 13, 1831–Nov. 15, 1894), college president, youngest of the six children of Henry and Amelia M. (Love) Bass, was born in Augusta and died in Macon, Ga. His father was born in Connecticut, but removed as a child to North Carolina, and later to South Carolina, where he became a Methodist minister. William was sent to the Cokesbury School in South Carolina, and later to Emory College in Georgia, both Methodist institutions. He abandoned his plans to become a lawyer in order to enter the ministry, but as he had borrowed money to maintain himself in school, he determined to teach until he could accumulate enough to pay his debt. He was a pedagogue until he died. His first position was in Greensboro, Ga., where he formed his intimate and enduring friendship with Cosby W. Smith, and where in 1854 he married Octavia Nickelson, daughter of James Blake and Ann Maria (Willy) Nickelson. After one year, Smith left Greensboro to teach at the Methodist Wesleyan Female College in Macon, but Bass continued at Greensboro for two years longer before he became professor of natural science at the Female College in Madison, Ga. A year later he was invited to teach the same subject at Wesleyan, but loyalty to the Madisonians made him decline. The invitation was renewed in 1859, and he accepted. For virtually the remainder of his life he was at Wesleyan—till 1874, as professor of natural science, and afterward as president until his resignation in April 1894. He was not officially connected with the Methodist Conference till 1867, but upon the license of that body he had preached with fair regularity from the beginning of his residence in Greensboro. When his connection at last did become official, his practical activities were not affected—he was merely "appointed" year after year to carry on the work he was already doing. His term of office as executive at Wesleyan covered years of the heaviest financial depression, but he was under the responsibility not only of providing funds for the conduct of the college, but of teaching mental and moral philosophy and of preaching before the young ladies once and sometimes twice every Sunday. He personally attended even to such small matters as purchasing groceries and keeping books for 250 people. And in addition he preached once a month at each of three country churches in the vicinity of his home. He once had as many as sixty students in a senior class, and during the twenty years of his presidency the college graduated far more than half the number of persons it had graduated in the fifty-five years of its existence. From a practical standpoint, the greatest event of his administration was the bestowal upon the college of $125,000 by the philanthropist, George I. Seney. For all his capability in business, he was devout, generous, and affectionate. An estimate of him written when he was an old man said that he was "universally recognized not only as one of the best educators in the South, but as an eloquent preacher and a finished gentleman" (*Biographical Souvenir,* p. 52).

[Sources: *Biog. Souvenir of the States of Ga. and Fla.* (1889); C. E. Jones, *Education in Ga.* (1889); W. J. Scott, *Biog. Etchings of Ministers and Laymen of the Ga. Conferences* (1895); W. J. Northen, ed., *Men of Mark in Ga.* (1911), III, 30–34.] J. D. W.

BASSE, JEREMIAH (d. 1725), colonial governor, was actively connected with the troubles which caused the overthrow of proprietary rule in New Jersey and disturbed the earlier period of royal government. Of his earlier life nothing is known save that he was an Anabaptist minister. In 1692 he was appointed agent of the West Jersey Society, an influential group of Non-Quaker English capitalists who had secured a part of the interest in West Jersey formerly held by the Friend, Edward Byllinge (*New Jersey Archives,* II, 91). In 1697 he was commissioned governor of both East and West Jersey, it being customary for the proprietors of both provinces to name the same person (*Ibid.*, II, 143, 209). But apparently his appointment had been brought about by an active minority. Basse was coolly received by the Friends of West Jersey and his authority denied by Lewis Morris [*q.v.*] and other prominent proprietors of East Jersey on the ground that his commission was not signed by the requisite number of proprietors (*Ibid.*, II, 217). Thus opposed, Basse adopted a policy favorable to the anti-proprietary elements in East Jersey which desired escape from the hated quit-rent. The party strife became in consequence so keen that a revolt led by Morris against Basse was threatened. By showing activity against the pirates, for whom the Jersey shore was a favorite refuge, Basse endeavored to win favor from the Crown. At the same time he tried to show collusion between the pirates and the powerful group of Scotch proprietors at Perth Amboy. But he came into conflict with the royal authorities at New York over the right of East Jersey to have a port of entry (*Ibid.*, II, 157, 218), and was superseded as governor in 1699. But the opposition to the proprietors in East Jersey had gathered such force that the tumultuous "East Jersey Revolution" soon nullified proprietary government.

When royal government was established in New Jersey, Basse secured a royal patent as secretary. Consequently he shared in the ill fame of the corrupt administration of Lord Cornbury [*q.v.*]. He was violently accused of perversions of power (*Ibid.*, III, 127, 152, 253, 254, 325, 429; IV, 71–74, 88, 97). Continuing to act with the anti-proprietary party, he became the ally of Col. Daniel Coxe who was at variance with the Friends in West Jersey (*Ibid.*, IV, 237). Secure in his patent, Basse remained as secretary till the death of Queen Anne. After the opponents of the proprietors had been routed by Gov. Robert Hunter [*q.v.*], Basse made his peace with that crafty Scot. He served with credit in the assembly, being apparently regarded as an authority in finance. In 1719 he was named attorney-general by Hunter himself. Meanwhile he had come under the influence of the Rev. John Talbot [*q.v.*], and joined the group of militant Anglicans at St. Mary's Church in Burlington. Here he officiated as warden and lay reader. From his pen is an interesting history of St. Mary's. From his activities as a whole one gets the impression of an adroit and rather shifty politician of some ability and literary skill. He was denounced in scathing terms by opponents, but allowance must be made for partisanship.

[G. M. Hills, *Hist. of the Ch. in Burlington, N. J.* (1876), gives valuable material, including Basse's will and his own account of St. Mary's; a personal notice is found in Wm. A. Whitehead, *East Jersey under the Proprietary Governments*, pub. in 1846 as *N. J. Hist. Soc. Colls.*, I, and separately in 1875.]

E. P. T.

BASSETT, JAMES (Jan. 31, 1834–Mar. 10, 1906), Presbyterian missionary, was born at Mundus, near Hamilton, Ontario, Canada. He graduated in 1856, at the age of twenty-two, from Wabash College, Indiana, the third of three brothers who took their degrees from this institution. In 1859 he finished his seminary course at Lane. Thereafter he served successively at Yellow Springs, Ohio, and Knoxville, Ill., as pastor of the Presbyterian Church. During 1862–63 he served as chaplain in the Federal army. In 1863 he became pastor of the Presbyterian Church at Neenah, Wis., and during 1869–71 was pastor at Englewood, Ill. On June 19, 1871, he was appointed a missionary of the Presbyterian Church for service in its Persia Mission. Sailing from New York City on Aug. 9, 1871, he arrived in Urumiah, Persia, on Oct. 18. During this year the Urumiah station along with all the Persian work of the American Board was turned over to the care of the Presbyterian Church, and in January 1872 the Urumiah Presbytery was organized for the general administration of the field. Toward the close of the same year Bassett and Mrs. Bassett opened for the Mission a new station at Teheran, the Persian capital. They were welcomed by both Moslems and Armenians who, it may be said, little understood the real nature of this missionary venture. Two French Lazarists and one Gregorian priest were already there. Not long after Bassett's arrival he baptized a "Mohammedan priest" (*i.e.*, a mullah), the first Moslem convert of the Mission.

At Teheran Bassett took up the study of Turkish and Persian, and opened shortly two day schools, one for boys and one for girls. In 1873 he prepared a translation of Christian hymns into Persian. In 1874 he opened a boarding-school for girls. By this time he was preaching regularly in Persian in a school on the east side of town, and in a chapel on the west side. In 1875 he organized a training-school for young men, from which helpers were sent out to work in Hamadan and Resht. Until 1876 the work of the station had been mainly among Armenians, but early in that year a Friday meeting was begun for Moslems. During the year (Mar. 26) the Teheran Presbyterian Church was organized with twelve members, including one former Moslem. In 1878 the membership had grown to twenty-three. At the time there was "considerable activity in the work of distributing the Scriptures."

During 1879–81 the Bassetts were in America on furlough. He wrote for *Leisure Hour* (London) an article, "Out Among the Turcomans" (vol. XXIX, 1880), and prepared a translation of the Gospel of Matthew into Jaghatai Turki (published in London, 1880). In the summer of 1881 he and his wife returned to Persia, where he took charge of all the boys' schools of the Mission, making his home in Teheran. In the next year the Persia Mission was divided, and thereafter Bassett was senior missionary and head of the Eastern Mission. On Christmas Day, 1882, he began in his house services in English for the many English-speaking residents of the capital city. Friction with the government arose over the attendance of Moslems upon mission meetings, and the government prohibited the Mission from allowing Moslem attendance. Bassett, however, persuaded the authorities to place the responsibility upon the Moslems and not upon the Mission, and was enabled to open again the regular chapel services. In 1883 a new chapel building with a seating capacity of 300 was erected on the mission compound, and services were held weekly therein on Sundays and Fridays. The same year saw the appointment of the first United States minister to Persia, effected partly through Bassett's efforts. During 1884 he published from native presses a revised and enlarged edition of the Persian hymnal and his translation of the Westminster Shorter Catechism, and in the *Journal* of the American Oriental Society an article on "The Simnuni Dialects." In the summer of 1884 he resigned from the Mission and returned to America with his family, arriving in October. The rest of his life was spent in pastoral work and in the preparation of two books, *Persia, the Land of the Imams* (1886), frequently cited by later writers on Persia, and *Persia, Eastern Mission* (1890). Relinquishing his last charge in 1905 at Wading River, L. I., he moved to Los Angeles, Cal., where he died. His widow, one son, and four daughters survived him.

[Wabash Coll. Records; contemporary *Annual Reports* of the Board of Foreign Missions of the Presbyt. Ch. in the U. S. A.; data on file in the Board offices.]

J. C. A.

BASSETT, JOHN SPENCER (Sept. 10, 1867–Jan. 27, 1928), historian, was born at Tarboro, N. C., being the second child of Richard Baxter Bassett and Mary Jane (Wilson) Bassett. The Bassett family was of Matthews County, Va., but Richard Bassett, father of Richard Baxter Bassett, located in Williamsburg, where he and his son after him became contractors and architects. Both were strongly opposed to the institution of slavery, but took no part in the anti-slavery agitation. Indeed, Richard Bassett purchased a slave woman at her request, and Richard Baxter Bassett from necessity of his business rather than from choice purchased some negro mechanics. Just prior to the Civil War, Richard Baxter Bassett removed from Virginia to eastern North Carolina, where he became prominent in the construction enterprises of the region. When the war opened he joined Company A (Edgecombe Guards), 1st North Carolina Regiment; but soon after the battle of Big Bethel, he was transferred to the Commissary Department and assigned the duty of manufacturing army supplies.

After preparatory training in the Graded School of Goldsboro, where his father located after the Civil War, and also at the Davis Military School at LaGrange, N. C., John Spencer Bassett in 1886 entered Trinity College (now Duke University), then located in Randolph County, and graduated in 1888. After teaching two years in the Durham Graded School, he returned to Trinity as an instructor, and in February 1890 he organized the 9019, the first scholarship society in the institution. In 1891 he entered the Johns Hopkins University, receiving the doctorate in 1894. He then returned to Trinity, which had been removed to Durham in 1892, as professor of history. The following twelve years marked him as a teacher of ability and resourcefulness. The historical section of the college library was small, but Bassett persuaded the members of a local history club and others to contribute rare books, pamphlets, and manuscripts; such was the beginning of an excellent collection of Southern Americana. Many of the papers read before the club were worthy of publication, and in 1897, through Bassett's initiative, there was established the first publication of the College strictly devoted to scholarship, the *Historical Papers of the Trinity College Historical Society*. His own productivity was notable. *The Constitutional Beginnings of North Carolina* (Johns Hopkins Studies, 1894), his doctoral thesis, was followed by the *Regulators of North Carolina* (American Historical Association, 1895), *Slavery and Servitude in the Colony of North Carolina* (Johns Hopkins Studies, 1896), *Anti-Slavery Leaders in North Carolina* (*Ibid.*, 1898), *Slavery in the State of North Carolina* (*Ibid.*, 1899), *The Writings of Colonel William Byrd* (New York, 1901), *The Federalist System* (New York, 1906), and numerous periodical articles. Yet his interests were not entirely with matters recondite; he was also a social critic, interested in the contemporary cultural and political transformation in the Southern states. As a medium for criticism he persuaded the 9019 to establish the *South Atlantic Quarterly* (1902) of which he was the first editor. In 1903 an editorial article entitled "Stirring up the Fires of Race Antipathy" (vol. II, no. 4), in which a comparison was made of the rise of submerged classes in past ages and the progress of the American negro, so antagonized certain elements of public opinion in North Carolina as to lead to a demand for Bassett's resignation from Trinity. The trustees of the institution, however, refused to yield to this demand and issued a statement in defense of academic liberty ("Trinity College and Academic Liberty," *South Atlantic Quarterly*, vol. III, no. 1). This episode was the last agitation of the race question in North Carolina from that time until the present writing.

In 1906 Bassett was called to Smith College. There he instituted the *Smith College Studies in History*, the first learned publication of that college. His *Life of Andrew Jackson* (2 vols., 1911) was the first well-balanced biography of President Jackson, based to a large degree on manuscript sources. It was followed in 1913 by a *Short History of the United States*; *The Plain Story of American History* (1916); *The Middle Group of American Historians* (1917); *The Lost Fruits of Waterloo* (1918); *Our War with Germany* (1919); *Expansion and Reform* (1926); *The League of Nations, a Chapter in World Politics* (1928); and *Makers of a New Nation* (1928). He was also interested in the collection of the letters of eminent historians and records illustrative of plantation life in the ante-bellum South; hence the *Correspondence of George Bancroft and Jared Sparks* (1917), *The Westover Journal of John Selden, Esq.* (1921), *Major Howell Tatum's Journal* (1922); "Letters of Francis Parkman to Pierre Margry" (1925), which appeared in the *Smith College Studies*, and the *Plantation Overseer as Revealed in His Letters* (Smith College Anniversary Publications, 1925). He was also editor of the *Correspondence of Andrew Jackson*, published by the Carnegie Institution, of which three volumes had appeared at the time of his death, and *Selections from the Federalist* (1921). He contributed an essay on "The Present State of History-Writing" to a symposium, *The Writing of History* (1926), which he also edited, the other contributors being J. J. Jusserand, W. C. Abbott, and C. W. Colby. In 1919 he was elected secretary of the American Historical Association. In the duties of that office he took a peculiar interest, and was one of those responsible for the movement undertaken in 1925 to endow the Association. His death, in Washington, D. C., resulted from an accident which occurred while he was on his way to a meeting of the Council of Learned Societies to represent the American Historical Association. He was married on Aug. 19, 1892, to Jessie Lewellin. Geniality, a certain ruggedness of mind, and an instinct for the practical were his dominating traits. Ever friendly, he was unyielding in matters of principle or conviction. Persistently busy with his pursuits, he always found time to give counsel to others; and he had the faculty of utilizing limited resources for large purposes.

[This sketch is based on a short manuscript memoir by Prof. Bassett and on the writer's personal recollection. His bibliography in *Who's Who in America*, 1926–27, should be supplemented by that in *Herbert B. Adams, Tribute of Friends with a Bibliography* (Johns Hopkins Studies, 1902).] W. K. B.

BASSETT, RICHARD (Apr. 2, 1745–Sept. 15, 1815), Revolutionary statesman, jurist, was born in Cecil County, Md., the son of Michael and Judith Bassett. His father, who was a tavern-keeper at Bohemia Ferry, Md., deserted his wife, and Richard was adopted by a relative named Peter Lawson, from whom he ultimately inherited Bohemia Manor. The active years of Bassett's life were passed in Delaware. In the Revolutionary War he was captain of a troop of Dover Light Horse, and thenceforth for a quarter of a century his career was passed in the politics of his adopted state. Between 1776 and 1786 he was a member of the council of safety and of the state constitutional convention, and served in both branches of the legislature. He was a delegate to the Annapolis Convention, and with the same fellow members from his state represented Delaware in the Federal Convention. Here he was comparatively silent, a far less notable figure than his colleague Bedford. Delaware was the first state to accept the Constitution, and Bassett was a leading member in its ratifying convention. He was one of the first senators from the state, serving in the years 1789–93; on the noteworthy question whether the president should have the power of removal, the vote of Bassett was recorded in the affirmative; on the question of the assumption of state debts, he was recorded in the negative. In the succeeding years, 1793–99, he was chief justice of the court of common pleas; in 1797 as a Federalist presidential elector he voted for Adams. His term as governor, 1799–1801, seems to have been honorable, if not especially important. When President Adams, on Mar. 3, 1801, just prior to his retirement from office, made the famous appointment of "midnight judges" that excited Jefferson's wrath, Gov. Bassett was one of the offending appointees; he was nominated and confirmed judge of the United States circuit court, but his office was soon legislated out of existence. Bassett impressed his contemporaries as a statesman of common sense; in the language of J. T. Scharf, "Few men have served the State in more capacities or with greater efficiency." He had considerable wealth, owned homes in Dover, Wilmington, and Maryland, and, as an enthusiastic Methodist and life-long friend of Bishop Asbury, paid one-half the cost of the First Methodist Church in Dover. He died at his home in Bohemia Manor. His wives were Ann Ennals of Dorchester County, Md., and a Miss Bruff of Talbot County. His daughter Ann married James A. Bayard [*q.v.*], Feb. 11, 1795, and his adopted daughter, Rachel, married Gov. Joshua Clayton [*q.v.*].

[R. E. Pattison, "Life and Character of Richard Bassett" (1900) in *Papers of the Del. Hist. Soc.*, No. 29; H. C. Conrad, *Hist. of Del.* (1908); J. T. Scharf, *Hist. of Del.* (1880); C. P. Mallery, "Ancient Families of Bohemia Manor" (1888) in *Papers of the Del. Hist. Soc.*, No. VII; G. Johnston, *Hist. of Cecil County, Md.* (1881), pp. 170–85; *Biog. Dir. of the Am. Cong. 1774–1927* (in MS).]

E. K. A.

BATCHELDER, JOHN PUTNAM (Aug. 6, 1784–Apr. 8, 1868), physician and surgeon, was born in Wilton, N. H., the only son of Archelaus and Betty (Putnam) Batchelor. He studied medicine with Dr. Fitch and Dr. Matthias Spalding of Greenfield, nearby, and in 1807 obtained a license to practise from the State Medical Society, at the subsequent meetings of which he was prominent as a speaker. He practised first in Charlestown, N. H., but soon wearied of practise in a small village and moved to Pittsfield, Mass., thence to Utica, N. Y., and finally to New York City. During these wandering years he obtained a medical degree at Harvard, with a thesis on *The Disease of the Heart Styled Aneurism.*

Once settled in New York, he became noted as a surgeon and was elected lecturer on anatomy and surgery at Castleton, Vt., and at the Berkshire Institute in Massachusetts. He wrote distinguished medical papers on cholera and paralysis and surgical papers on tracheotomy and fractures. He was a first-rate operator, cutting for stone, and removing cataracts by extraction rather than by couching. In 1825 he gained a wide reputation through ligation of the carotid and subsequent removal of an enormous sarcoma of the lower jaw. He was said to be the first American surgeon to remove the head of the femur; he performed many rhinoplastic operations, and was a specialist in facial surgery. He was clever as an inventor and improver of surgical instruments and his last gift to the profession was a one-handed craniotome in place of the former clumsy instruments used with two. He died in New York City at the age of eighty-three.

[*Med. and Surg. Biogs.* (Phila. 1865), XI, 587–590; H. A. Kelly and W. L. Burrage, *Am. Med. Biogs.* (1920); S. W. Francis, *Biog. Sketches of Distinguished Living N. Y. Surgeons* (1866); F. C. Pierce, *Batchelder, Batcheller Genealogy* (1898).]

J. A. S.

BATCHELDER, SAMUEL (June 8, 1784–Feb. 5, 1879), manufacturer, inventor, son of Samuel and Elisabeth (Woodberry) Batchelder, was born at Jaffrey, N. H. He was reared and educated at New Ipswich, where his father was first postmaster of the town and conducted a tavern and general store. Before his sixteenth year he became manager of his father's store but in 1804 engaged in business for himself at Peterboro, N. H., and in 1806 at Exeter. On his return to New Ipswich, in 1808, he purchased an interest in one of the town's two cotton-mills, which produced 300 pounds of yarn weekly, and gave employment to about 100 home weavers, and before 1812 was its principal owner and manager. As a leading citizen, he filled such offices as selectman, town clerk, postmaster, and, eventually, representative in the legislature, where he was a member of the committee first proposing Daniel Webster for nomination to Congress. In 1810 he married Mary Montgomery, by whom he had six children. His active career, continuing to the advanced age of eighty-six years, included connections with various prominent concerns, notably the Hamilton Manufacturing Company, of which he was manager (1824–31), president (1859–70), and treasurer (1869–71); the Exeter Manufacturing Company, of which he was manager (1855–72); the Everett Mills, of which he was treasurer (1859–70); and the Essex Company, of which he was president (1867–70). He removed, in 1825, to East Chelmsford, Mass., where he was a member of its first board of selectmen; and in 1846, to Cambridge, where he resided until his death, serving on the first board of aldermen, under the new city charter, and as representative in the Massachusetts legislature (1847).

Batchelder invented and introduced many new devices for cotton manufacture, although generally neglecting to seek patent protection. One of his earliest inventions was a machine for winding "cotton balls" for darning and fancy work. Later he produced a loom to weave pillow cases without a seam, providing a hand-controlled movement to close the bottom. In 1832, he invented a stop-motion for the drawing frame, a valuable innovation, since, before its introduction, the slender fleeces of cotton, without twist, had not been strong enough to stand the operation of drawing. A device for dressing yarn for weaving substituted brass steam-cylinders for the usual wood rolls, but was little used because of the small number of power mills then existing. His best known invention is his dynamometer, or "force-measurer," perfected in 1837, for weighing the power of belt-driven machinery, which afforded improved means for determining the power required for driving by water or steam (Julius Weisbach, *Manual of the Mechanics of Engineering,* II, 53–55). He was a constant writer for newspapers and the author of *Responsibility of the North in Relation to Slavery* (1856); *Young Men of America* (1860); *Free Trade and the Tariff* (1861); *Introduction and Early Progress of Cotton Manufacture in the United States* (1836).

[W. R. Bagnall in *Contributions of Old Residents' Hist. Ass. Lowell, Mass.,* III (1887), 187–211; *Samuel Batchelder* (Morning Mail Press, 1885); U. S. Patent Office Records; F. Kidder, *Hist. of New Ipswich* (1852); D. B. Cutter, *Hist. of the Town of Jaffrey, N.H.* (1881).]

BATCHELLER, GEORGE SHERMAN (July 25, 1837–July 2, 1908), Union soldier, statesman, son of Sherman and Mary (Noyes) Batcheller, was a native of Batchellerville, Saratoga County, N. Y. His father was well-known in the county as a citizen and politician, and the family was related to Roger Sherman and to Daniel Webster. He took the degree of LL.B. at the Harvard Law School in 1857, was admitted to the bar the following year, and began at once the practise of law in Saratoga Springs. At the unusually early age of twenty-one he was elected to the Assembly, and in the session of 1859 he was assigned to the important judiciary committee. On Oct. 8, 1860, he was married to Catherine Phillips Cook. Enlisting in the war in the 115th New York Regiment, he rose to the rank of its lieutenant-colonel, having served in several engagements, having been taken prisoner at Harper's Ferry in 1862 and, after his exchange, having been present at the siege of Charleston. During 1863–64 he was deputy provost-marshal-general in the South. After the war he held the office of inspector-general of the New York militia in 1865–68, and in that capacity he reorganized the National Guard of the state. One of his military duties was acting as escort to the funeral cortège as the body of Lincoln was conducted across the state of New York on the way to Illinois. He resumed the practise of law, and also his political activities, being a presidential elector for Grant in 1868, and a member of the Assembly in 1873 and 1874. In the former year he was chairman of the committee on canals and a member of the committee on militia. In the following year he retained his membership on the militia committee, and received the chairmanship of the all-important committee on ways and means. It was undoubtedly his prominence as a politician and lawyer which led President Grant to appoint him as United States judge in the newly created International Tribunal for the legal administration of Egypt. These "Mixed Tribunals," composed of both foreigners and natives, had jurisdiction in cases between foreigners of different nationalities (in certain contingencies also, when foreigners of the same nationality were involved), and in cases between foreigners and natives. They commenced to function in 1876, and Batcheller was soon chosen by his colleagues as the presiding justice. He resigned the position in 1885 and in the year following was again a member of the New York Assembly, serving on the important committees of ways and means, general laws, and military affairs. President Harrison appointed him assistant secretary of the treasury in 1889 and minister to Portugal in 1891. From 1893 he acted as manager of the European interests of various American companies, and in 1897 he was called to preside over the Universal Postal Congress. He was returned to the International Tribunal (his last office) in 1898, at the request of the Egyptian government. President Roosevelt promoted him in 1902 to the Tribunal's court of appeals, and ultimately he became president of that body. His acquaintance with Mohammedan law was evinced in two articles on the subject which he contributed to the *North American Review* for July 1906 and August 1907. The regard in which he was held in Egypt was shown at the time of Mrs. Batcheller's death by unusual courtesies on the part of the Khedive. He was Grand Officer of the Order of The Medjidie, and was decorated with the cross and insignia of the Order of the Crown of Italy. His death occurred in Paris.

[*Albany Evening Jour.,* July 3, 1908; *N.Y. Evening Post, Tribune,* and *Times* of the same date; *Who's Who in America,* 1908–09; F. C. Pierce, *Batchelder, Batcheller Genealogy* (1898). Some of the authorities give the year of his birth as 1836.]

E.K.A.

BATCHELOR, GEORGE (July 3, 1836–June 21, 1923), Unitarian clergyman, was born in Southbury, Conn., the son of George and Mary (Axford) Batchelor. His father, a Baptist minister, while not actually identified with the "Millerite" movement which at that time was active in New England, was among the believers in the speedy end of the world, and Batchelor was reared in an atmosphere of fervent evangelical piety. It was in reaction from the ardors of the Millerites that he became a pronounced liberal, while at the same time retaining a keen interest in religious ideas and principles. He believed it possible to unite an essentially evangelical spirit with progressive and liberal thinking. With this purpose in mind he attended the theological school at Meadville, Pa., graduating in 1863. He was assistant superintendent of the United States Sanitary Commission, 1864–65. On Sept. 18, 1866, he was married to Priscilla Stearns of Cambridge, Mass. He received the degree of A.B. at Harvard in 1866 and that of A.M. in 1870. Meanwhile he became pastor of the Barton Square Church in Salem, Mass., where he had a happy and fruitful ministry. In 1882 he was called to the pastorate of Unity Church, Chicago, and in 1889 he became minister of the First Unitarian Church in Lowell, Mass. Meanwhile he had served as the executive secretary of the National Conference of the Unitarian Churches with such efficiency that in 1893 he was chosen secretary of the American Unitarian Association, the missionary organization of his denomination. He resigned this office in January 1898 to become editor of the *Christian Register* and held that position until his retirement July 3, 1911.

Batchelor was a man of slender frame and slight bodily power but distinguished for sound judgment, thorough thinking, and good administrative capacity. He was a preacher of more than average ability and the author of *Social Equilibrium* (1887), which had a considerable circulation. His influence as editor of the *Christian Register* was wide-spread. As a writer he possessed a lucid and attractive style fortified by a large fund of historical knowledge. While always self-reliant and vigorous in the expression of his own ideas, he was fair and just to those of opposing views. His gifts of mind and heart made him in his generation one of the conspicuous leaders of liberal Christian thought and life in America.

[*Who's Who in America,* 1920–21; *Unitarian Yr. Bk.,* 1924–25; *Boston Transcript,* June 21, 1923.]

S. A. E.

BATE, WILLIAM BRIMAGE (Oct. 7, 1826–Mar. 9, 1905), Confederate soldier, governor of Tennessee, was a descendant of a pioneer family which came to Tennessee in the early days of the Cumberland settlement. He was born at Bledsoe's Lick, one of the Middle Tennessee pioneer settlements, now known as Castalian Springs, in Sumner County. His father, James Henry Bate, the grandson of a Revolutionary soldier, was a farmer. His mother, Amanda (Weathered) Bate, was related to the families of Gen. Sumter of South Carolina and Gen. Coffee of Tennessee. The little formal education he had was gained at a log schoolhouse, later known as the Rural Academy. When he was sixteen years of age, upon his father's death, he left school to become second clerk on the steamboat *Saladin* running on the Cumberland and Mississippi rivers between Nashville and New Orleans. At the outbreak of the war with Mexico, Bate, who was of an ardent temperament, enlisted in New Orleans as a private in a Louisiana company, and is said to have been the first Tennessean to reach Mexican soil. Later he became first lieutenant in Company I of the 3rd Tennessee Volunteer Infantry.

After the Mexican War, Bate established in Gallatin, Tenn., an intensely democratic newspaper called the *Tenth Legion,* and in 1849 he was elected to the state legislature where he served one term. He then decided for the profession of law and studied at the Law School in Lebanon, Tenn., now a part of Cumberland University, where he was graduated after a year's study, in 1852. After a brief practise, he was elected in 1854 as attorney-general of Nashville District, embracing three counties. Notwithstanding his meager knowledge of the law, he appears to have made an efficient attorney-general. In politics he was a strong state-sovereignty man and a supporter of secession, and by 1860 had attained sufficient prominence to be made a presidential elector on the Breckinridge-Lane ticket. In 1856 he was married to Julia Peete of Huntsville, Ala.

Bate went into the Civil War in 1861 as a private in his home company from Gallatin and came out four years later as a major-general. With his command he was distinguished in the fighting at Shiloh, Murfreesboro, Chattanooga, Missionary Ridge, in the Atlanta campaign, and in the fatal Tennessee campaign, which ended in the battles of Franklin and Nashville. His military career closed under Joseph E. Johnston in North Carolina. Bate was a noted fighting general, was wounded three times, and had six horses killed under him in battle. At the end of the battle of Shiloh there were five members of the Bate family lying on the field, dead or wounded. Next to Forrest, he had the most spectacular career of any of the Tennessee generals. In June 1863 he was tendered the nomination for governor of Tennessee, an offer which reached him on the battle-field. His answer became historic, but has reached us in half a dozen different forms. It was probably about as follows: "While an armed foe treads our soil and I can fire a shot or draw a blade, I will take no civic honor. I had rather, amid her misfortunes, be the defender than the Governor of Tennessee" (for another version, see Marshall, *post,* pp. 64–65).

When he came back to his home near Nashville, he found himself disfranchised by the Brownlow régime, and remained so for several years until a more moderate administration came into power in the state. While still disfranchised, he was a delegate to the National Democratic Convention in 1868, and thereafter was for ten years a member of both state and national Democratic executive committees. Gov. Brownlow's hostility to the ex-Confederates was so strong that there was danger of civil war within the state, and on Aug. 1, 1868, Bate, with ten other Confederate generals, among them Gen. Forrest, united in a memorial to the legislature protesting against the hostile policies of the administration. But not until Brownlow left the state, in 1869, were the Confederates restored to political rights. Bate was a presidential elector in 1876 on the Tilden and Hendricks ticket, and in 1882 was elected governor, and later reëlected for a second term. His chief accomplishment while governor was the settlement of the state debt, a problem which had been upsetting the finances of Tennessee since 1865. Bate secured the passing of a plan by the legislature in 1883, which provided that all the old debts about which there was no question should be paid in full, and that those made since the War, particularly those under the Brownlow administration which were tainted with fraud, should be scaled and paid only in part. Bate also secured the passage of an act which established a commission for the regulation of railroads within the state. Notwithstanding strong opposition even within his own party, he became more popular each year and three times came near election as United States senator. Finally in 1886 he was elected by the legislature on the sixty-eighth ballot to succeed Senator Whitthorne. Joining the strong delegation of ex-Confederate leaders who were now, after Reconstruction, coming to Washington to represent the Southern states, he became a useful and influential senator. In 1893 he was the author of the act which repealed all laws then on the statute-book providing for the supervision of local elections by Federal officials, thus removing the last vestige of the Reconstruction legislation. By continued reëlection he was retained in the Senate until his death.

[Park Marshall, *William B. Bate* (1908), a non-critical biography; brief sketches by John Allison in *Notable Men of Tenn.* (1905), and by J. G. Cisco in *Historic Sumner County, Tenn.* (1909); obituaries in the *Nashville Banner*, Mar. 9, 1905, *Chattanooga Daily Times*, Mar. 10, 1905, *Memphis Commercial Appeal*, Mar. 10, 1905. In the Tenn. State Lib. is a collection of undated newspaper clippings, evidently printed about the time of Bate's death. His speeches can be found in the *Cong. Record*, 1887–1905.]

W. L. F.

BATEMAN, KATE JOSEPHINE (Oct. 7, 1843–Apr. 8, 1917), actress, was the eldest daughter of Sidney Frances Cowell Bateman [*q.v.*] and Hezekiah Linthicum Bateman (see *Dictionary of National Biography*), and the granddaughter of Joseph Leathley Cowell (see *Dictionary of National Biography*). With her sister Ellen she made her first appearance at Louisville, Ky., Dec. 11, 1846, in *Children of the Wood*. For several years thereafter the two, known as The Bateman Children, were regarded as prodigies. In 1849, in the New York Broadway Theatre, Kate played Richmond to Ellen's Richard III, Portia to Ellen's Shylock, and Artixaminous to Ellen's Bombasta. Thence they went to the Walnut Street Theatre, Philadelphia, in an engagement beginning on Jan. 7, 1850. Barnum, quick to sense the value of such youthful work, took the girls to London. In 1851 they appeared under the great showman's management at the St. James's Theatre and at the Surrey Theatre. Returning to America in 1852, they toured the United States, going as far west as San Francisco, where they were seen on Apr. 10, 1854.

Kate's father, in 1855, was manager of a St. Louis theatre. Interest in his children's education prompted him to come to New York in 1859, and his daughter temporarily retired from the stage (1856–60). Then she made a second début in her mother's play, *Evangeline*. On Jan. 19, 1863, she appeared at Niblo's Garden, New York, and later on Oct. 1 at the London Adelphi Theatre in *Leah the Forsaken*, a version of Mosenthal's *Deborah*, made for Bateman by young Augustin Daly, then at the outset of his career (J. F. Daly, *Life of Augustin Daly*, 1917; G. W. Curtis, *Harper's Weekly*, Mar. 7, 1863). It was in London during 1865 that she was seen to great advantage as Julia in *The Hunchback*, Bianca in *Fazio*, and Juliet in *Romeo and Juliet* (for critical comment, see Pascoe's *Dramatic List*, 1879). In 1866 she reappeared at Niblo's Garden in such rôles as Pauline and Parthenia. During the year, however, she was married to George Crowe, M.D., one-time editor of the *News* (London), and again retiring from the stage set sail for England. But in 1868, she played at the London Haymarket in a revival of *Leah*, and assumed the new rôle of Pietra in a tragedy by Mosenthal. In June 1869 she was Mary Warner in Tom Taylor's play of that name. Her father became the manager of the London Lyceum Theatre on Sept. 11, 1871. He struggled to make it a success, and it was a young man in his company, Henry Irving, who, by his acting of Mathias in *The Bells* (Nov. 25, 1871), helped him gain financial security. Inasmuch as there was no Ellen Terry at the Lyceum in those days, it was natural that the Bateman daughters should become identified with the early career of Irving. Several years passed, however, before Kate acted with him. She appeared in New York in October 1869 as Leah and Mary Warner, and in 1871 was seen for the first time in the rôle of Beatrice in *Much Ado About Nothing*. In 1872, at the London Lyceum, she once more essayed her favorite part of Leah, and won acclaim as Medea in Wills's adaptation of Legouvé's tragedy, *Medea in Corinth*. It was after Bateman's death, and while Mrs. Bateman was in charge of the Lyceum that Kate was seen with Irving in a revival of *Macbeth* on Sept. 18, 1875. The papers suggested that Irving's Thane was a medieval Mathias and that Miss Bateman's Lady Macbeth displayed too amply the grand manner of acting. Thereafter, with Irving, she was seen on Apr. 18, 1876, as Queen Mary in Tennyson's poetic drama of that name, and on Jan. 29, 1877, as Queen Margaret in *Richard III*. The critics recognized in her work sound judgment, keen intelligence, and power. Irving's prestige was making him ambitious and restless; and he soon announced that he intended leaving the Lyceum. This was the death-knell of Mrs. Bateman. She transferred her energies to Sadler's Wells Theatre, and there she was again aided by her daughters. Kate had been obliged to retire from the stage because of an accident that had marred her personal appearance, but, under her mother's direction, she acted the rôle of Helen Macgregor in *Rob Roy* in October 1879. From this time on, her appearances on the stage were occasional, and added nothing to her fame. Of her acting it was said (London *Times*, Apr. 10, 1917) that she showed "a certain staginess of gait and gesture, and excessive love of the merely picturesque, and the monotony of utterance so often to be found in players whose voices have been exercised in the theatre at an early age." But the general agreement was that she possessed passion and emotion, even though there was a tendency to overaccentuate these.

[T. Allston Brown, *Hist. of the Am. Stage* (1870); Tompkins and Kilby, *Hist. of the Boston Theatre* (1908); Geneal. Table of the Bateman Family in J. Parker, *Who's Who in the Theatre* (1925); Clement Scott and Cecil Howard, *Life and Reminiscences of E. L. Blanchard* (1891); Laurence Hutton, *Curiosities of the Am. Stage* (1891); Wm. Winter, *Brief Chronicles*, Dunlap Society Pubs., 7, 8, 10 (1889–91); Austin Brereton, *Life of Henry Irving* (1908); Bram Stoker, *Personal Reminiscences of Henry Irving* (1906); Percy Fitzgerald, *Sir Henry Irving* (1906); H. B. Baker, *Hist. of the London Stage* (1904); W. D. Adams, *Dict. of the Drama* (1904); J. F. Daly, *Life of Augustin Daly* (1917).]

M. J. M.

BATEMAN, NEWTON (July 27, 1822–Oct. 21, 1897), educator, was born at Fairton, Cumberland County, N. J., the son of Bergen and Ruth (Bower) Bateman. He was of Scotch and English ancestry. When he was eleven years old the family migrated to Illinois. The toilsome, leisureless, moneyless life of the frontier could not cool the boy's eagerness for an education. With $2.50 in cash and only four months of preparation behind him he entered Illinois College, of which the Rev. Edward Beecher, a son of Lyman Beecher, was president. Plain living and high thinking characterized the five professors and rather less than forty students, but young Bateman, in order to stay in college, boarded himself for four years on so narrow a margin that he permanently injured his health. Upon his graduation in 1843 he went to Lane Theological Seminary for one year, but left on account of illness and traveled the country for another year as an agent for a historical chart. After various teaching experiences in St. Louis and in St. Charles, Mo., he became in 1851 principal of the main public school in Jacksonville, Ill. To this position he later added that of county superintendent of schools and in 1857 the principalship of the Jacksonville Female Academy. In 1850 he married Sarah Dayton of Jacksonville. She died in 1857 and in October 1859 he married Annie N. Tyler, who had come to Jacksonville from Massachusetts. She died May 28, 1878. In 1858 the Republican state convention nominated him for state superintendent of public instruction. He was elected and served, 1859–63 and 1865–75, being defeated in the election of 1862. With others he began in 1858 the movement that established the state Normal University. He helped found and for a time edited the *Illinois Teacher*. During his tenure of office the common school system of the state was developed and brought to a high degree of efficiency. His practical sagacity as an administrator and his statesmanlike view of the major aspects of public education are exemplified in seven biennial reports, which were studied with interest all over the United States and even abroad. The moral conviction underlying his work is expressed in the sentence with which he closed the first and the last of these documents: "In the name of the living God it must be proclaimed, that licentiousness shall be the liberty—violence and chicanery shall be the law—superstition and craft shall be the religion—and the self-destructive indulgence of all sensual and unhallowed passions shall be the only happiness of that people who neglect the education of their children." Bateman's head projected only a little above the elbows of his friend Lincoln, who was wont to introduce him as "my little friend, the big schoolmaster of Illinois." He was a member of the committee of three that drafted the bill creating the United States Bureau of Education. He was a member of the state board of health 1877–91, was appointed an assay commissioner by President Hayes in 1878, was president of Knox College 1874–92 and president emeritus from his retirement until his death. His last undertaking was the editing of the *Historical Encyclopedia of Illinois.* He died in Galesburg of angina pectoris.

[N. Bateman and P. Selby, eds., *Hist. Encyc. of Ill.* (Biog. and Mem. ed., 1915) with portr.; *Cat. of Ill. Coll.* (1841, 1855); *Chicago Inter-Ocean,* Oct. 22, 1897; Carl Sandburg, *Abraham Lincoln, the Prairie Years* (1926); information from President C. H. Rammelkamp of Ill. Coll., Apr. 9, 1928.] G. H. G.

BATEMAN, SIDNEY FRANCES COWELL (Mar. 29, 1823–Jan. 13, 1881), playwright, actress, manager, was the daughter of Joseph Cowell, the English actor, whose real name was Witchett. According to his *Thirty Years Passed Among the Players in England and America* (1844), Cowell was in New York City in 1823, but he states that his family was in New Jersey on account of the yellow fever, and the place of Sidney's birth is uncertain. Her mother, Frances Sheppard, died soon after Sidney's birth and the latter's early years were spent in various places as her father's engagements permitted. His association with the theatre brought her upon the stage in New Orleans about 1837. She married, Nov. 10, 1839, Hezekiah Linthicum Bateman, an actor and manager in St. Louis, Mo. Mrs. Bateman was not a great actress, but was a guiding force in the careers of her husband and children, three of whom, Kate, Ellen, and Isabella, became actresses. The Batemans made their first appearance in New York City in 1849 when Kate and Ellen played Richard III and Richmond, at the ages of four and six years.

Mrs. Bateman's comedy, *Self,* was first produced anonymously at Bateman's St. Louis Theatre, June 18, 1856, and was published in the same year. The play is a satire upon social and business life in New York City, and nearly all the characters are conventional stage types. The part of John Unit, a retired banker, the lovable godfather of the heroine, redeemed the play, however, and secured for it a long life. This part was first played by Mark Smith, but when *Self* was repeated at the People's Theatre in St. Louis in April 1857 H. L. Bateman played Unit, and the creation of the part has been incorrectly ascribed to him. In 1859 the Batemans were in New York, where Mrs. Bateman's romantic play, *Geraldine, or Love's Victory,* was produced at Wallack's Theatre on Aug. 22, and ran nightly until Sept. 14, showing unusual vitality for that period. On Mar. 19, 1860, Kate Bateman appeared at the Winter Garden, New York, in a dramatization by her mother of Longfellow's poem *Evangeline,* and at the same theatre on May 21, 1862, in the title rôle of *Rosa Gregorio, or the Corsican Vendetta.* The success of Kate Bateman in Augustin Daly's *Leah the Forsaken,* when her father took her to England in 1863, led to the permanent removal of the family to that country. On June 12, 1865, H. L. Bateman appeared in Mrs. Bateman's play, with the title altered to *Geraldine; or The Master Passion,* at the Adelphi Theatre, London. In 1871, Mr. and Mrs. Bateman undertook the management of the Lyceum Theatre. Here, on Sept. 11, 1871, was produced her adaptation from *Die Grille,* under the title of *Fanchette; or The Will o'-the Wisp,* it having been already tried out at the Edinburgh Theatre Royal on Mar. 6. The great success of the Lyceum, which was partly due to the presence of Henry Irving in the company, led Mrs. Bateman to continue its management after her husband's death in 1875. In 1878 she transferred the lease to Irving and soon after took the Sadler's Wells Theatre, rebuilt it, and during her brief management, restored it to the high position it had held under Samuel Phelps. One of her enterprises was the presentation on Apr. 2, 1880, of the McKee Rankin Company in Joaquin Miller's *The Danites,* claimed by Rankin to be the first instance of a complete American company playing an American play in England. Her death, caused by pneumonia, was the occasion for cordial tributes from the English press. Especial stress was laid upon her extraordinary attention to detail, her versatility, her energy, her courage, and the delicacy and discernment of her taste in theatrical matters.

[Scattered references to Mrs. Bateman's plays are found in J. N. Ireland, *Records of the N. Y. Stage* (1866–67), II, 661, 689, 701. Accurate reports of the first production and of the revival of *Self,* correcting the usual printed statements, are in the *Missouri Republican,* of St. Louis, June 18, 19, 1856, and Apr. 6, 7, 1857. See also London *Times,* Jan. 14, 17, 18, 1881; *Academy,* No. 455, pp. 70–71, which gives an appreciation of her character; and, for collateral items, Laurence Hutton's *Curiosities of the Am. Stage* (1891), pp. 79–80; J. F. Daly's *Life of Augustin Daly* (1917), pp. 48–53. For English performances of her plays, see *"The Stage" Cyclopedia* (1909), ed. by R. Clarence.] A. H. Q.

BATES, ARLO (Dec. 16, 1850–Aug. 24, 1918), author, educator, was born in East Machias, Me., the son of Susan (Thaxter) Bates and Niran Bates, a physician of strong literary tastes. His formal education began with the schools of East Machias, where he graduated from the Washington Academy in 1870. His class in Bowdoin was that of 1876 and it was during his college course that his literary career began. His first payment for writing was a check for three dollars from the *Portland Transcript.* In 1876 he went to Boston, lived in an attic, and wrote copiously; but the greater part of his manuscript was returned, and for a year he had to support himself by teaching and by painting china. In 1878 he was made secretary of a Republican organization and edited a fortnightly political journal called *The Broadside,* and served also as a clerk in the office of "a firm dealing in metals." His work on *The Broadside* may very probably have led to his appointment as editor of the *Boston Sunday Courier,* in 1880, a position which he held till 1893. During this period he produced the larger part of his purely literary work, including nine novels and four volumes of verse. In 1893 he became professor of English in the Massachusetts Institute of Technology. His marriage in 1882 to Harriet L. Vose, daughter of Prof. George L. Vose and Abby Thompson Vose, was a singularly happy union, but was cut short by her untimely death in 1886. She had written for publication under the pseudonym of "Eleanor Putnam"; and the young couple together wrote a fantastic fairy tale, called *Prince Vance,* which had the unusual distinction of being translated and published in Esperanto. His volumes of poetry were all dedicated to her memory. The one entitled *Sonnets in Shadow* is a threnody upon her death. That he carried on his work as teacher of English with enthusiasm and success is clear from the number and quality of his published writings related to that service; particularly, *Talks on Writing English* (1896–1901), *Talks on Teaching Literature* (1906), and *Talks on the Study of Literature* (1895), the last being the Lowell Lectures for 1895. In 1894, at the centennial celebration of the incorporation of Bowdoin College, he read a poem called *The Torch Bearers,* afterward published separately. In 1911, at a meeting of the Phi Beta Kappa Society at Tufts College, he delivered a poem, *The Supreme Gift,* which also was separately published. The later years of his life were spent in Otis Place, Boston, where his life work had been done, and where, after a long illness, he died.

The list of his published writings includes the following: novels—*Patty's Perversities* (1881); "Ties of Blood," serial in the *Boston Courier,* never appearing in book form (1882); *Mr. Jacobs* (1883); *The Pagans* (1884); *A Wheel of Fire* (1885); *A Lad's Love* (1887); *Prince Vance* (1888); *The Philistines* (1889); *The Puritans* (1898); *Albrecht* (1890); *Love in a Cloud* (1900); *The Diary of a Saint* (1902); volumes of short stories—*A Book o' Nine Tales* (1891); *In the Bundle of Time* (1893); *The Intoxicated Ghost* (1908); volumes of poetry—*Sonnets in Shadow* (1887); *Berries of the Brier* (1886); *The Poet and His Self* (1891); *Told in the Gate* (1892); *Under the Beech Tree* (1899); single poems, or odes—*The Torch Bearers* (1894); *The Supreme Gift* (1911); dramatic works—*A Mother's Meeting* (1909); *A Business Meeting, A Gentle Jury, Her Deaf Ear, An Interrupted Proposal*—undated, one-act plays.

[*Who's Who in America,* 1918–19; "Maine in Lit.," *New Eng. Mag.,* Aug. 1900; Interview with Bates, by E. F. Harkins, *Lit. World,* June 1904; *Obit. Record of the Grads. of Bowdoin Coll. for the Year Ending June 1919* (1920).]

C.N.

BATES, BARNABAS (1785–Oct. 11, 1853), pioneer in postal reform, was born in Edmonton, England. His parents brought him to America when he was a child and settled in Rhode Island. He was educated for the ministry, and in May 1814 was chosen pastor of the Baptist church in Bristol. A decided change in his views leading toward Unitarianism brought about, in 1818, a schism in his church, but though he is said to have been deposed from the ministry his faction retained the church edifice. He served a term as collector of the port of Bristol, continuing, however, to preach. On the completion of his term he was again nominated, but according to his statement, through the antagonism of a proslavery senator from his state the nomination was rejected by the Senate. He is said to have become, about this time, a zealous Freemason. Sectarian, anti-Masonic and pro-slavery agitators brought on a riot, in which his life seems to have been endangered and he suffered some loss of property. Because of the schism in his church in Bristol and because of his growing doubt that preaching should be a gainful occupation, he declined, during nearly the whole of the last five years of his pastorate, to accept pay, while out of his own funds he advanced to the church $2,000, only a small part of which was ever returned to him. He left Bristol, probably about the end of 1824, and went to New York, where he opened a bookstore. In January of the following year he started a small weekly journal, *The Christian Inquirer,* "devoted to the support of Free Inquiry, Religious Liberty and Rational Christianity." It was carried on at considerable expense, for though it reached a total of 800 subscribers not many of them, it appears, felt called upon to pay for it. The issue for July 1, 1827, though partly set up, did not appear until Apr. 2, 1828, when notice was given that the paper had been turned over to the *Olive Branch.* Bates had preached in some of the independent pulpits of the city, but in the final issue of his paper announced his retirement from the ministry.

For a time under the Jackson administration he was assistant postmaster of New York. Sir Rowland Hill's famous pamphlet on cheap postage, which appeared in 1837, influenced him greatly, and by 1839 he had become an active advocate of postal reform. His article, "Post-Office Reform—Cheap Postage," in *Hunt's Merchants' Magazine* for March 1840, may well have been, as he asserts, the first argument published in America in behalf of the change. He also arranged the first public meeting in America to advance the cause. This meeting, held in New York, Nov. 24, 1843, petitioned Congress for a flat rate of five cents an ounce, irrespective of distance, and an abolition of the franking privilege. Against great opposition, particularly from the postal authorities, the movement was carried on. A law reducing letter postage to five cents an ounce on distances not exceeding 300 miles, but charging ten cents on greater distances and greatly increasing the already burdensome rates on ocean postage, was signed by President Tyler on the day before he left office, Mar. 3, 1845. It was unsatisfactory to the friends of postal reform, but the results of even the partial reduction of rates were encouraging, and at a meeting in New York on July 1, 1846, demands were made for a uniform rate of two cents an ounce. The New York Cheap Postage Association, with Bates as corresponding secretary, was organized May 26, 1848, following the formation of a similar body in Boston, and renewed efforts were made to bring about further reductions. Bates had lived to see the first authorized issue of postage stamps, Mar. 3, 1847; he was to see (Mar. 3, 1851) the compulsory prepayment of postage and the reduction of rates to three cents a half-ounce for distances under 3,000 miles, but not to see any material reduction in the rates of ocean postage. He died on a visit to Boston, probably in connection with the work of his society.

[Wilfred H. Munro, *The Hist. of Bristol, R. I.: The Story of the Mount Hope Lands* (1880); *Christian Inquirer*, n.s., Jan. 1826–Apr. 1828; Barnabas Bates, *A Brief Statement of the Exertions of the Friends of Cheap Postage in the City of N.Y.* (1848); *N.Y. Tribune*, Oct. 12, 1853.]

W.J.G.

BATES, DANIEL MOORE (Jan. 28, 1821–Mar. 28, 1879), jurist, the son of Jacob and Mary (Jones) Moore and grandson of Elzey Moore, both Methodist clergymen, was born at Laurel, Del. Members of the Moore family had been among the earliest settlers of the state. His parents both died when he was a child and he was adopted by Martin Waltham Bates, a leading Democratic politician, United States senator and lawyer of Dover, Del., who procured an act of the legislature changing the child's name to Daniel Moore Bates. His early education was received at a private school, and he entered Dickinson College in 1835, graduating in 1839. He studied law in Martin W. Bates's office, was admitted to the bar in 1842, and entered into partnership with his adopted father. The firm enjoyed an extensive practise and he soon became generally known as possessing qualities of industry and reliability which marked him out for public employment. In 1847 he was made secretary of state of Delaware, a position which he occupied for four years. In 1849 he removed to Wilmington, and in the same year was by resolution of the General Assembly appointed a commissioner to revise and codify the state statutes, a work which took ultimate shape as the Revised Code of 1852. He was in 1852 appointed United States district attorney for Delaware by President Pierce and held this office till 1861, being reappointed by President Buchanan. In 1861, as one of the five Delaware commissioners, he attended the abortive Peace Conference at Washington, serving on the committee which drafted the scheme of adjustment subsequently submitted to Congress. On Dec. 12, 1865, he was, with the indorsement of the entire state bar, appointed chancellor of Delaware. On his accession to the bench, he addressed himself with great energy to increasing the efficiency of the court, revising the rules and reforming the old practise. In addition, he prepared a manual of Chancery practise and forms for the use of the profession. The General Assembly held in 1871 passed a resolution directing the Chancellor to collect and publish such equity cases as in his judgment should be proper for public information, and he accordingly commenced to assemble the unreported decisions of his predecessors in office. Failing health compelled him, however, to relinquish all work and he resigned Oct. 15, 1873. As a judge he enjoyed the confidence of both the profession and the public. Possessing great patience, an infinite capacity for taking pains, and a logical precision of thought, his decisions carried great weight and always bore evidence of anxious deliberation. Immediately after his resignation, he undertook a long visit to Europe with his family, returning in September 1875 much benefited by the change. He resumed his work on the chancery records and as a result published *Reports of Cases Adjudged and Determined in the Court of Chancery of the State of Delaware*, Volumes I and II, which incorporated all the decisions of utility from 1814 to 1865 (1876, 1878). At the same time he commenced to practise in a small way at Wilmington, but did not attempt any heavy responsibilities. He died rather suddenly at Richmond, Va., while on a business visit. He had married in November 1844 Margaret Handy, daughter of Isaac P. Smith of Snow Hill, Md., an adopted daughter of George Handy of Philadelphia, who predeceased him.

[J. T. Scharf, *Hist. of Del.* (1888), I, 551; *Hist. and Biog. Encyc. of Del.* (1882); *Am. Law Rev.*, XIII, 749; *Daily Republican* (Wilmington), Mar. 29, 1879.]

H. W. H. K.

BATES, EDWARD (Sept. 4, 1793–Mar. 25, 1869), statesman, was the son of Thomas Fleming Bates, a Virginia planter and merchant, who on Aug. 8, 1771, had married Caroline Matilda Woodson. The young couple first lived in Henrico County and there three children were born. About 1776 the family moved to Goochland County, where a home called "Belmont" was established, and where nine more children were born, of whom Edward was the youngest. Thomas F. Bates fought as a volunteer soldier under Lafayette at the siege of Yorktown, but, as a Quaker, paid the price of this patriotic service by being read out of meeting. He also suffered heavy financial losses during the Revolutionary War and died leaving his family in straitened circumstances. Edward was taught to read and write by his father and at the age of ten was placed under the instruction of a cousin, Benjamin Bates of Hanover, Va., and by him was prepared to enter Charlotte Hall Academy in St. Mary's County, Md. He had hoped to attend Princeton, but a serious injury cut short his course at the academy and caused him to give up the idea of a college education. Through the influence of a relative, James Pleasants, a member of Congress, he was then appointed a midshipman in the navy; but because of his mother's objections he declined the appointment. In February 1813 he joined a volunteer militia company which was raised in Goochland County to assist in repelling a threatened attack on Norfolk; and he remained in the army until October, serving successively as private, corporal, and sergeant.

At the suggestion of his brother, Frederick Bates [*q.v.*], then secretary of Missouri Territory, Edward went out to St. Louis in 1814 and began the study of law under Rufus Easton, the foremost lawyer of the territory. In November 1816 he took out a license to practise law, and two years later formed a partnership with Joshua Barton, the brother of David Barton, one of the first United States senators from Missouri. The partnership continued until June 30, 1823, when Barton was killed in a duel. On May 29, 1823, Bates married Julia Davenport Coalter, the daughter of David Coalter, a South Carolinian who had moved to Missouri in 1817. She bore him seventeen children, eight of whom survived him.

Until he was elected to Congress in 1826, Bates held only minor public offices, though he had served acceptably as a member of the state constitutional convention of 1820, as attorney-general, and as a member of the state legislature. In the Twentieth Congress he was the sole representative of Missouri in the lower house, and already the choice of the Whig party for the United States Senate. The followers of Thomas H. Benton, however, had a majority in the state legislature, and Bates was defeated by a few votes. So strong was Jacksonian democracy in Missouri, indeed, that Bates was defeated for reëlection to Congress in 1828. He was still regarded as the leader of his party but he led a forlorn hope. About this time he moved to St. Charles County and located on a farm on Dardenne Prairie. He continued the practise of law, his services being in demand in all of the neighboring counties. There he remained until 1842 when he resumed practise in St. Louis. In 1830 he was elected to the state Senate, where he served for four years, and in 1834 was again elected to the Missouri House of Representatives. The door to more important offices seemed closed to him, but in 1847 his opportunity came. As president of the River and Harbor Improvement Convention which met at Chicago, he made an eloquent speech which attracted the attention of the public and made him a national figure (*Niles' Register,* LXXII, 366–67). In 1850 President Fillmore appointed him secretary of war, but for personal and domestic reasons he declined the appointment.

From this time on his views on social and constitutional questions and on national politics were sought and frequently expressed in speeches and newspaper articles. He opposed the repeal of the Missouri Compromise, a stand which aligned him with the "free labor" party in Missouri, though he still considered himself a Whig and in 1856 acted as president of the Whig national convention which sat at Baltimore. He drew closer to the Republican party when he opposed the admission of Kansas under the Lecompton constitution. His upright and clear-headed course attracted nation-wide attention, and in 1858 Harvard University conferred upon him the honorary degree of LL.D., an unusual honor for a Missourian of that day. Early in 1860 a Bates-for-president movement was launched in Missouri. His supporters contended that a Free-Soil Whig from a border state, if elected on the Republican ticket, would avert secession. The movement received the support of many leaders, particularly in the border states. But the decision of the national Republican committee to hold the convention at Chicago instead of at St. Louis was a serious setback to the Bates supporters and added strength to the candidacy of Lincoln. On the first ballot Bates received only 48 votes; on the second ballot 35; and on the third and deciding ballot only 22.

Soon after the Chicago convention Lincoln decided to offer Bates a cabinet position. Some of Bates's friends had urged, indeed, that he should be appointed secretary of state, but the President felt that the first place in the cabinet should go to Seward. He gave Bates his choice of any other cabinet position and the latter wisely chose that of attorney-general. He was the first cabinet officer to be chosen from the region west of the Mississippi River. For a time he had much influence in the cabinet. It was at his suggestion that the Navy Department began the equipment of a fleet on the Mississippi River. In the *Trent* affair, he urged that the question of legal rights be waived and that every effort be made to avert a war with Great Britain. He differed with Lincoln on the question of the admission of West Virginia to the Union. As attorney-general he filed an elaborate opinion in which he contended that the West Virginia Government represented and governed but a portion of the state of Virginia and that the movement for separate statehood was "a mere abuse, nothing less than attempted secession, hardly veiled under the flimsy forms of law."

From this time Bates's influence in the cabinet gradually waned. He disagreed with many of the military policies. He felt that as the war progressed constitutional rights were giving way before the encroachments of the military authorities. He resented the interference of Seward in matters which belonged to the attorney-general's office. He had little confidence in Stanton, Seward, or Chase, and he felt that Lincoln lacked the will-power to end what Bates considered abuses. In Missouri, moreover, the radical Republicans got control of the state government in 1864, and this meant the end of law in his home state. Weary of a cabinet position in which his views had little weight, and in the belief that he could best serve his country and his state as a private citizen, he tendered his resignation as attorney-general on Nov. 24, 1864.

On Jan. 6, 1865, a radical state constitutional convention assembled in St. Louis and drew up a new state constitution. It also passed an ordinance emancipating the slaves and an ouster ordinance, the intention of which was to place the state judiciary in the hands of the radicals. It also adopted a stringent test oath for voters. Bates fought the radicals by publishing a series of newspaper articles in which he pleaded for a government of law instead of a government of force. By many letters to prominent men all over the North he attempted to arouse them to the dangers of radical rule, insisting that the extreme radicals were nothing less than revolutionists who had seized upon the general zeal for putting down the rebellion and had perverted it into a means of destroying all government by law. This struggle against the Missouri radicals was his last great contest. A few months after his return to Missouri his health began to break. It steadily declined and on Mar. 25, 1869, he died.

In person Edward Bates was small. His early portraits show a strong countenance with clean-cut features, piercing eyes, and a well-formed chin. Until middle life he was clean-shaven, but in his later years he wore a full beard. He was modest and unpretending, but a courageous fighter for law and justice.

[The largest collection of Bates papers, including letters and diary (June 3, 1846–Dec. 25, 1852), is deposited with the Mo. Hist. Soc. in St. Louis. His diary (Apr. 20, 1859–July 30, 1866) is deposited in the MS. Div. of the Lib. of Cong. See Charles Gibson, "Edward Bates," in *Mo. Hist. Soc. Colls.*, II, 52–56 (1900); F. W. Lehman, "Edward Bates and the Test Oath," *Ibid.*, IV, 389–401 (1923); "Letters of Edward Bates and the Blairs," *Mo. Hist. Rev.*, XI, 123–46 (1917); Nicolay and Hay, *Lincoln* (1890); Gideon Welles, *Diary* (1911); Onward Bates, *Bates, et al. of Va. and Mo.* (1914).]

T. M. M.

BATES, FREDERICK (June 23, 1777–Aug. 4, 1825), governor of Missouri, was the eldest son of Thomas Fleming Bates and Caroline Matilda Woodson, and brother of Edward Bates [*q.v.*]. The early death of the father left the family in straitened circumstances and made impossible anything more than a common schooling for the first of the sons. Frederick seems to have supplied the lack of formal instruction by constant reading, for his more famous brother afterward said of him that he was "well-versed in the English classics, not ignorant of French literature and a good historian of all times." At the age of seventeen or eighteen he began the study of law while he served as postmaster and as deputy clerk of the court of Goochland County, Va. Removing to Detroit in 1797, he served in the quartermaster's department of the Army of the Northwest, resigning three years later to become a merchant. He appears to have prospered until June 11, 1805, when his store was burned in the conflagration which destroyed Detroit. Upon the creation of Michigan Territory, he was made an associate judge, and assisted Gov. William Hull and the other judges in drawing up the first territorial code. In November 1806 he was appointed secretary of Louisiana Territory, as well as member of the board of land commissioners and recorder of land titles. His appointment as secretary was due to the fact that the Burr Conspiracy was then developing and Jefferson wanted an official in the trans-Mississippi region on whom he could rely. As secretary Bates succeeded Dr. Joseph Browne, a brother-in-law of Aaron Burr. Until Meriwether Lewis, the new governor, arrived, Bates was acting governor, exhibiting no little initiative and energy. He removed from office dishonest officials, won the support of the French inhabitants, and did much to offset the influence of British traders among the Indians. He was mainly responsible for the revision of the territorial code, and in 1808 published a compilation of the laws of Louisiana Territory, the first book to be printed in what is now the state of Missouri. Three times thereafter he served as acting governor because of the enforced absence or resignation of his chief. He acted as secretary of Louisiana Territory until 1812, and was secretary of Missouri Territory until Missouri was admitted into the Union as a state. Finally in 1824 he became governor in his own right, having defeated no less an opponent than William Henry Ashley. It was during his incumbency that Lafayette visited St. Louis and was lavishly entertained, but the Governor, characteristically, refused to attend the official reception because the legislature had made no appropriation for the occasion. On Mar. 4, 1819, he had married Nancy Opie Ball, daughter of Col. John S. Ball of St. Louis County. After the marriage he and his bride made their home at "Thornhill," an estate of a thousand acres in Bonhomme Township near modern Chesterfield, Mo. There four children were born, and there he died of pleurisy on Aug. 4, 1825. Edward Bates said of his brother, "F[rederick] B[ates] was a man naturally of good parts, far above mediocrity, and by life long practise, methodical and exact in business. . . . He was no public speaker, having never practised, but his powers of conversation were somewhat remarkable—fluent always, sometimes brilliant, and generally, at once, attractive and instructive. He was a very ready writer, using some diversity of style, but generally clear, terse and pungent. His habits were very retired . . . his friends few, but strong and abiding." His portrait shows a refined countenance, a wealth of curly hair, kind but brilliant eyes, a well-formed nose, and firm lips. It is the countenance of a scholarly gentleman of the old school.

[*The Life and Papers of Frederick Bates* (2 vols., 1926), ed. by T. M. Marshall. For the geneal. of the Bates family, see Onward Bates, *Bates, et al. of Va. and Mo.* (printed for private distribution, 1914).]

T. M. M.

BATES, GEORGE HANDY (Nov. 19, 1845–Oct. 31, 1916), lawyer, publicist, son of Judge Daniel Moore Bates [*q.v.*], was born at Dover, Del., and received his primary education in the Wilmington, Del., schools. In 1862 he entered the University of Pennsylvania, but after prosecuting his studies there for two years went West and engaged in business in Michigan. His health, however, became impaired and in 1866 he returned to the East and read law in his father's office at Wilmington. He also attended the Harvard Law School and was admitted to the Kent County (Del.) bar in April 1869. Commencing practise in Wilmington he identified himself actively with the Democratic party and was appointed deputy attorney-general, in this capacity engaging in a number of notable criminal prosecutions, among which was that of the Delaware Bank robbers. Resuming private practise in 1874 he devoted much time to the study of constitutional and international law, and took a prominent part in local politics, being a delegate to the National Democratic Conventions of 1880, 1884, and 1888. He represented New Castle County in the Delaware legislature 1882–83; and was speaker of the House in the latter year. In 1883 he was also appointed a member of the Board of Park Commissioners for the City of Wilmington, an office which he retained till 1894. His political affiliations had brought him into close association with Senator Thomas F. Bayard, and, though never a "practical" politician, he occupied for some years an influential position in the councils of the Democratic party in the state. Retained in much important litigation, his work as special counsel for Delaware in the Delaware-New Jersey boundary dispute was of a high order and exhibited great ability. In 1886 he was, at the instance of Bayard—then secretary of state—appointed by President Cleveland special agent to investigate the condition of affairs in Samoa, concurrently with but independent of similar representatives of Great Britain and Germany. He spent some months in the Islands and his able and exhaustive report, Dec. 10, 1886, reviewed in detail the causes of the difficulties under which the Samoan Government labored and suggested as a solution the formation of a native government but with the real executive power exercised by whites nominated by the three powers, who should mutually guarantee the neutrality and autonomy of the new Government (*House Executive Document No. 238*, 50 Cong., 1 Sess., Appendix A, p. 137). In the futile negotiations which followed he took no part, but he was appointed by President Harrison one of the United States commissioners to the joint conference with Great Britain and Germany on Samoan affairs which met at Berlin April 29, 1889, his colleagues being W. W. Phelps and J. A. Kasson. The treaty which was there concluded between the three powers was a signal triumph for him since its major provisions followed the recommendations embodied in his report to Secretary Bayard. After his return from Berlin he took little part in public affairs, but continued to practise law in Wilmington till 1896, when he removed to Philadelphia. He edited *Delaware Chancery Reports*, Volumes III and IV, and during his later years was associated with Francis Rawle in the second and third revisions of Bouvier's *Law Dictionary*.

He married May 26, 1870, Elizabeth B. Russell, daughter of C. T. Russell, a Boston lawyer, and sister of William E. Russell [*q.v.*], governor of Massachusetts.

[Details of Bates's early career appeared in *Hist. & Biog. Encyc. of Del.* (1882), p. 408. His connection with the Samoan controversy is dealt with in J. M. Callahan, *Am. Relations in the Pacific and the Far East 1784–1900* (1901), pp. 141–43, and Hugh M. Herrick, *Wm. Walter Phelps* (1904), pp. 210–18, which contains a reference to Bates's article "Some Aspects of the Samoan Question," in the *Century Mag.*, Apr. 1889, p. 945. Obituaries in the *N.Y. Times* and *Pub. Ledger* (Phila.), Nov. 1, 1916.]

H. W. H. K.

BATES, JAMES (Sept. 24, 1789–Feb. 25, 1882), physician, congressman, was the eldest son of Solomon and Mary (Macomber) Bates. He was born in Greene, Me., but when he was only seven years of age his father moved to Fayette, Me. There James Bates obtained such education as was possible in the local schools. At twenty-one he entered on the study of medicine with a Fayette physician and with Dr. Ariel Mann of Hallowell. He then took the course given by the Harvard Medical School. In 1813 he joined the medical department of the army and remained there till May 1815, prolonging his service that he might bring the 700 patients under his charge to a condition in which they could make the journey home with safety. After resigning, he was married on July 27, 1815, to Mary Jones of Fayette. For four years he practised at Hallowell, Me., and for twenty-six at Norridgewock, Me. In 1830 he was elected to Congress on the Democratic ticket and served one term. His chief activities were in relation to the tariff and nullification controversy. Bates was a vigorous supporter of the compromise, he moved a postponement of the "force bill," and announced that both he and his constituents were opposed to protection, knowing that it did them more harm as consumers than it did good to them as producers. In 1845 he was made superintendent of the insane asylum at Augusta, Me. In December 1850, part of the asylum was burned with a loss of twenty-eight lives. A coroner's jury found that the fire was due to the faulty construction of an air-chamber planned by Bates. In January 1851, the Governor of Maine appointed him a commissioner to examine the methods of heating and ventilating used in public institutions of other states. He accepted the position and resigned his office of superintendent. His investigations were fruitful and the commissioners for rebuilding the hospital adopted many suggestions made by him (James W. North, *History of Augusta*, 1870, pp. 551 ff.). He then resumed private practise chiefly in Fairfield and North Yarmouth. When about eighty he withdrew from practise but lived twelve years longer, dying in full possession of his faculties at the age of ninety-two. He won great success in his profession and at his death was said on good authority to have been one of the best all-round men in surgery that Maine had produced.

[Sketch in *Trans. Maine Medic. Ass.*, VII, 514; Wm. B. Atkinson, *Physicians and Surgeons of the United States* (1878); Howard A. Kelly, *Cyc. Am. Medic. Biog.*, vol. I (1912).]

L. C. H.

BATES, JOHN COALTER (Aug. 26, 1842–Feb. 4, 1919), soldier, was born in St. Charles County, Mo. His father, Edward Bates [*q.v.*], was attorney-general in Lincoln's cabinet, his mother was Julia Davenport (Coalter) Bates. He was educated at Washington University, St. Louis, and in the opening year of the Civil War he enlisted, and was at the age of nineteen a first lieutenant. He served in the Army of the Potomac until the end, and participated in nearly all its great battles, Antietam, Fredericksburg, Chancellorsville, and Gettysburg. During the last two years he was on the staff of Gen. Meade. He reached the rank of captain in 1863, and was brevetted major and lieutenant-colonel. Continuing in the regular army after the war, he passed about thirty years in the West, largely in northwestern posts and along the Mexican border. In the Spanish-American War of 1898, when the decision was made to invade Cuba, Bates was put at the head of an independent brigade of the 5th Corps. Directly after the landing he was placed in command at Siboney, June 25, and on July 1 he joined Gen. Lawton. He was prominent in the assault on El Caney, and marching to headquarters was active in the fighting of July 2 and

3; his brigade had a record of almost continuous marching and warfare. In the course of the year he was commissioned brigadier-general of volunteers and major-general of volunteers. Like many others among the higher officers he signed the "Round Robin" letter. His Cuban experience has been characterized in these words: "To him as to all of his comrades of rank in Cuba, the Santiago campaign was more of an adventure, with a touch of the romantic in it, than the ordeal of war" (*New York Times,* editorial, Feb. 9, 1919). In 1899 he was ordered to the Philippines, where the insurrection under Aguinaldo had just broken out. In August of that year he negotiated with the Sultan of Sulu a treaty (often called the "Bates Treaty"), by which the Sultan received a monthly subsidy, and acknowledged the sovereignty of the United States. As the treaty recognized the existence of slavery, it did not escape criticism, unwarranted though the criticism may have been. The following year Bates attacked the insurgents in Cavité, and established garrisons on the island of Mindanao. He was commissioned brigadier-general of the United States Army in 1901 and major-general in 1902. At the beginning of 1906 when Gen. Chaffee retired, Bates succeeded as chief of staff and was commissioned lieutenant-general, being one of a comparatively small number in the army to hold this last rank. He retained the office of chief of staff for a few months only, retiring in April 1906. The remainder of his career was uneventful, down to his death at San Diego in 1919.

[F. E. Chadwick, *Relations of the U. S. with Spain* (1911), II; J. H. Latané, *America as a World Power* (1907); H. H. Sargent, *Campaign of Santiago de Cuba* (1907); F. B. Heitman, *Hist. Reg.* (1903); *Who's Who in America,* 1918–19.]

E. K. A.

BATES, JOSHUA (Oct. 10, 1788–Sept. 24, 1864), financier and philanthropist, was born in Weymouth, Mass., the youngest of the three children of Col. Joshua and Tirzah (Pratt) Bates. His ancestors on both sides of the family were among the earliest settlers in New England, their names appearing in the colonial records previous to 1640; his father had been an officer in the Revolution and was a man of some prominence in the community. A boy of delicate health, Joshua received his education partly in the public schools and partly under the tuition of Rev. Jacob Norton, minister of the First Church of Weymouth. A weakness of the eyes, however, which troubled him for many years, prevented a college education. His business career started at the early age of fifteen when he entered the counting house of William R. Gray, eldest son of William Gray, the leading shipping merchant of New England. Here the young man served his apprenticeship, after which he formed a partnership with a Capt. Beckford of Charleston, a former employee of William Gray, but the firm of Beckford & Bates, like hundreds of other concerns, went to smash as a result of the critical commercial years of the War of 1812.

This failure was probably a blessing in disguise. Young Bates during his apprenticeship had so impressed William Gray with his industry, integrity, and ability that the great merchant offered in 1816 to send him to Europe as his general agent. Gray at that time was the largest ship-owner in America, having between thirty and forty square-rigged vessels afloat. Although Bates asserted later that for the first twenty years of his residence abroad he felt like a man with his back to the wall, those were years in which he not only handled with marked success Gray's multitudinous European interests but laid the foundation of a brilliant career as an international banker. A chance acquaintanceship with M. Peter Cæsar Labouchère, related to the Baring family and senior member of the great house of Hope & Company of Amsterdam, resulted in the formation in 1826 of a partnership between John Baring (son of Sir Thomas Baring) and Joshua Bates. This concern, financed by M. Labouchère, specialized in American accounts, and was so successful that it was absorbed two years later by Baring Brothers & Company in which John Baring and Joshua Bates were admitted as partners. This connection Bates maintained until his death, becoming eventually senior partner and building up a large fortune.

During his later years Bates was probably the most influential foreigner in private life in the British Isles. As chief of Baring Brothers & Company, which, with the exception of a short period under Jackson and Van Buren, had been the fiscal agents in England of the United States since the organization of our government, Bates was tied to his native land by economic as well as patriotic interests, and his powerful influence was ever exerted to promote amicable relations between the two nations. In 1854 he acted as umpire (under the convention of 1853) between the British and American commissioners in the disputes over outstanding claims upon which the commissioners could not agree. These claims which ran into several millions had been a matter of controversy between the two nations for nearly thirty years. They were now reduced by the awards to approximately $600,000, and the skill with which Bates, although not a lawyer, decided the delicate questions of international law involved was a matter of satisfaction to both governments.

In 1852 the City of Boston in negotiating with the house of Baring for a water loan submitted numerous city documents, one of which spoke of the project of a public library. The interest of Bates was aroused, and in October of that year he offered $50,000 to the city for the purchase of books if a building be provided and care taken of them, the only conditions being "that the building shall be such as to be an ornament to the city —that there shall be room for 100 to 250 persons to sit at reading-tables—that it shall be perfectly free to all" (*Twelfth Annual Report of the Trustees of the Public Library,* p. 16). The offer was accepted and three years later he announced his intention, in addition to his former donation, "to purchase and present to the city a considerable number of books in trust," a donation which also amounted to $50,000. Upon his death the trustees of the Library "cheerfully" accorded "to him, as its largest benefactor . . . the name and honors of the Founder of the Boston Public Library" and resolved that the large hall of the Library be henceforth known and designated as Bates Hall (*Ibid.,* p. 39).

Joshua Bates is portrayed as a man with round head, broad forehead, prominent nose, firm mouth but small chin—the whole giving an impression of intelligence and kindliness. He was married to Lucretia Augusta Sturgis, by whom he had one son and one daughter.

[Geneal. information can be found in George W. Chamberlain, "Geneal. of Weymouth Families," vol. III of *Hist. of Weymouth, Mass.* (4 vols., 1923). The best account of his life is the *Twelfth Annual Report of the Boston Pub. Lib.* (1864). This is reprinted in *A Memorial of Joshua Bates from the City of Boston* (1865), which likewise contains all of the correspondence relative to the founding of the lib. The story of his benefactions is also told in Horace J. Wadlin, *The Pub. Lib. of the City of Boston* (1911), p. 44 ff. The Boston Pub. Lib. contains a marble bust copied by Noble from one by Wm. Behnes, a portr. in oil by E. U. Eddis, and a daguerreotype.]

H. U. F.

BATES, SAMUEL PENNIMAN (Jan. 29, 1827–July 14, 1902), educator, the son of Laban and Mary (Thayer) Bates, was born at Mendon, Mass. He received his education in the common schools of Massachusetts, at Worcester Academy, and at Brown University. He graduated from the last-named institution in 1851. His intellectual interests were diversified. While in college he was proficient in mathematics and philosophy. The year after his graduation he devoted part of his time to a study of Milton and Shakespeare and for the five years following taught ancient languages in the academy at Meadville, Pa. While at Meadville he gained a local reputation as a lecturer on educational topics at teachers' institutes and served as principal of the academy from 1851 to 1857. He then served as superintendent of the Crawford County schools until his appointment as deputy state-superintendent of public instruction in 1860. He was an active member of the National Teachers' Association and strongly influenced the agitation on the subject of founding a great national university, where professors for colleges and universities might be trained in the science of teaching. His lecture on "Liberal Education" was published in Barnard's *American Journal of Education,* March 1865, pp. 155–76. He was designated by Gov. Curtin to visit the colleges of the state and report upon their condition, and was employed by Edward James of West Chester to prepare a brief exposition of the school laws of Pennsylvania for use in James's volume of *Township and Local Laws.* His thorough acquaintance with the details of the routine of teaching made it possible for him to organize efficiently the details of the work of the Department of Public Instruction. He prepared a series of articles on the subject of physical culture, for the *Pennsylvania School Journal,* after pursuing a thorough course on the subject at the Boston School of Physical Culture. Maj. William C. Armor, feeling that Bates was eminently capable, employed him to write *Lives of the Governors of Pennsylvania* (1873). In 1866 Gov. Curtin appointed him state historian, a position created by the state legislature for the purpose of gathering material and forming complete accounts of the organizations from Pennsylvania that engaged in the Civil War. The results of his efforts were published in the *History of Pennsylvania Volunteers,* in five volumes (1869–70). In 1877 Bates toured Europe and upon his return prepared a series of lectures on "Art Centers of Italy, Naples, Rome, Venice and Florence," which are in the possession of the Meadville Public Library. He married Miss Sarah Josephine Bates of Massachusetts in August 1856, and they were the parents of seven children all of whom were active in the life of the community and state.

[*Meadville Gazette,* 16th year, No. 30; *Meadville Daily Tribune Republican,* XXXVII, No. 5532; Paul Monroe, *Cyc. of Ed.,* I (1911), 332; *Barnard's Am. Jour. of Ed.,* Dec. 1865, p. 682.]

H. H. S.

BATES, WALTER (Mar. 14, 1760–Feb. 11, 1842), Loyalist, the son of John and Sarah (Bostwick) Bates, was born in the eastern part of Stamford, now Darien, Conn. The family was devoted to the Anglican Church, was strongly Loyalist, and at the outbreak of the Revolution was suspected, unjustly, of being in communication with the British. Walter, then a lad of fifteen, was seized and confined in the guard house. What followed may be told in his own words: "I was taken out by an armed mob, conveyed through the field gate one mile from the town to back Creek, then having been stripped my body was exposed to the mosquitoes, my hands and feet being confined to a tree near the Salt Marsh. . . . Twenty stripes was then executed with severity, after which they sent me again to the Guard House" (*Kingston and the Loyalists,* p. 8). Eventually he was released and fled to the mountains; later he joined the Tories in Long Island. In 1783 he made one of the party of 100 New England Loyalists who sailed with their families on the *Union* to Nova Scotia, where each was granted 200 acres of land. He was the first man to be married in the new colony, and rose to a position of some importance, acting for many years as sheriff of King's County. His book, *Kingston and the Loyalists of the "Spring Fleet" of 1783,* left in manuscript and unpublished until 1889, is an important source book on the Connecticut Loyalists. More interesting, extraordinarily readable in fact, is the work which he published in 1816 (second ed. 1817) entitled *The Mysterious Stranger; or Memoirs of Henry More Smith; alias Henry Frederick Moon; alias William Newman: Who Is Now Confined in Simsbury Mines, in Connecticut, for the Crime of Burglary; Containing an Account of His Extraordinary Conduct During His Confinement in the Gaol of King's County, Province of New Brunswick, Where He Was under Sentence of Death: with a Statement of His Succeeding Conduct, Before and Since His Confinement in Newgate.* This apparently authentic tale of the sheriff's experiences with a man who, in addition to other unusual accomplishments, could escape from all chains and who while handcuffed in a dark cell constructed and operated an elaborate marionette show of straw figures, is written with no little literary skill, holding the reader's interest by its command of suspense and its appearance of absolute veracity. If the story is true, Henry More Smith, alias Henry Frederick Moon, etc., was certainly one of the most remarkable criminals on record; if it was fabricated, Walter Bates as a writer of fiction belongs in the class with Daniel Defoe.

[The only known sources are Bates's two volumes and a brief sketch by E. B. Huntington in *Hist. of Stamford, Conn.* (1865). There is a résumé of *The Mysterious Stranger,* by Ernest Sutherland Bates, in "Nor Iron Bars a Cage," *Dalhousie Rev.,* Jan. 1928.]

E. S. B.

BATTERSON, JAMES GOODWIN (Feb. 23, 1823–Sept. 18, 1901), business man, the son of Simeon Seeley and Melissa (Roberts) Batterson, was born in Wintonbury, later Bloomfield, Hartford County, Conn. His early years were passed in New Preston, Conn. He attended a country school and an old-time academy. Having made his way, partly afoot, to Ithaca, N. Y., he there served a three-year apprenticeship in a printing-shop, and after that was associated in business with the elder Batterson, who had set up in Litchfield as a tombstone-cutter. For a year he read law in the office of Origen S. Seymour, afterward chief justice of the state supreme court of errors. In 1851 he was married to Eunice Elizabeth Goodwin. Having removed his business to Hartford, he widened its scope to include contract-work for residences, office buildings, and public structures. By 1875 it had so grown that it was organized into a joint stock company, the New England Granite Works. Batterson introduced labor-saving apparatus and himself invented a turning-lathe for cutting and polishing stone columns. In 1860 he established in New York City large works for supplying interior marbles. One of the numerous important memorials constructed by him is the Soldiers' Monument at Gettysburg. His notable buildings include the State Capitol of Connecticut, which he completed for $13,000 less than the $2,000,000 appropriation. He also furnished the gray Concord granite for the Library of Congress at Washington. Deriving his basic idea from English methods of insurance against railway accidents, he founded the Travelers Insurance Company in 1863 and thus became the pioneer of accident insurance in the United States. The first premium received by the new company was two cents for insuring a Hartford banker from the post office to his house. At first Batterson's venture was opposed and ridiculed; then within two years no less than seventy other companies arose for but a brief existence. The Travelers charter soon was amended to permit business in general accident and life insurance, and subsequently to take in liability insurance also. A lifetime of directed study and wide reading made Batterson uncommonly versatile and well-informed. His researches in geology and mineralogy comprised field-work with James G. Percival in the first geological survey of Connecticut (see Percival's report, 1842), and with Isambard K. Brunel in the Nile Valley during the winter of 1858–59. Deeply interested in sociology and economics, he subsidized the publication of the first complete edition of Walter Bagehot's writings (edited by Forrest Morgan, 5 vols., Hartford, 1889) and wrote *Gold and Silver as Currency in the Light of Experience, Historical,*

Economical, and Practical (Hartford, 1896), a brochure employed as a campaign document. He was a devoted student of the classical languages, and was acquainted with several modern tongues; contributed articles on insurance matters and current topics to the *Travelers Record,* house-organ of the Travelers company; made a number of renderings from the Greek and Latin; and "produced considerable poetry, none of which is so bad as John Quincy Adams's" (New York *Sun,* Sept. 22, 1901).

[*The Travelers Record,* Oct. 1901, pp. 4–5; an article signed "E. D. C." in the *Commemorative Biog. Record of Hartford County* (1901), pp. 23–28; *Jas. G. Batterson,* an address by Wm. F. Henny, delivered at a public memorial service held at Hartford, Sept. 18, 1904, and printed in booklet form; and a biog. in the *Geneal. and Family Hist. of Conn.,* ed. by W. R. Cutter and others (1911), III, 1240–43; *Hartford Times, Hartford Courant,* Sept. 18, 1901.]

G. S. B.

BATTEY, ROBERT (Nov. 26, 1828–Nov. 8, 1895), physician and surgeon, came from English Quaker stock, the American branch of the family having settled in Providence, R. I. His father, Cephas Battey, was born in New York, while his mother, Mary (Magruder) Battey, was a native of Georgia. Born in Augusta, Ga., Robert was educated at the Richmond Academy there and at Phillips Academy, Andover, Mass. (1838–44). He then gave up school and worked in Detroit and in Marshall, Mich., later returning to Rome, Ga., where he became a clerk in a drugstore. By 1849, when he was twenty-one years of age, he had become owner of a drugstore there, which he continued to run until 1855. In 1849 he married Martha B. Smith, by whom he had fourteen children. He studied medicine in Rome under his brother's guidance, and in 1855 entered Prof. James C. Booth's School of Analytical Chemistry, Philadelphia. He also studied at the Philadelphia College of Pharmacy, and subsequently attended two courses of lectures at the Jefferson Medical College and the University of Pennsylvania, receiving his medical degree from the former, Mar. 7, 1857. He then returned to Rome to practise, where his brother was well established. In 1858 an early successful operation for vesico-vaginal fistula brought him local renown; in 1859 he described a simple treatment for congenital club-foot. As a result of this work he was invited to London. Before going abroad, he attended the American Pharmaceutical Association convention in Boston (1859) and presided as vice-president. In Europe, he spoke on vesico-vaginal fistula before the Obstetrical Society of London, on Nov. 2, 1859 (*Transactions of the Obstetrical Society, London, I, 1860*). He performed his operation for fistula successfully at the Dublin Hospital on a case that had been operated five times before. He also visited Scotland, Paris, and Brussels, and was everywhere well received.

He returned home the next year and resumed his practise in Rome, but the Civil War soon interfered. He served throughout the war, first as medical officer in a battalion of artillery, and later as surgeon in the 19th Georgia Volunteers. He saw active service with the Army of Virginia and later under Stonewall Jackson, when he was surgeon to Hampton's and Archer's brigades. After 1862, he was put in charge of various hospitals, first at Atlanta and later at Rome. When he was driven out of Rome by the Northern forces, he took charge of hospitals elsewhere in Georgia and in Mississippi. In 1864 he established a successful hospital in Macon especially for the treatment of soldiers with hernias and fistulas. In April 1865 he was discharged from the army, after a very honorable service. He again returned to Rome, where he resided the rest of his life, except for a few years in Atlanta as professor of obstetrics at the Atlanta Medical College and editor of the *Atlanta Medical and Surgical Journal* (1872–75). He established the Martha Battey Hospital in Rome in honor of his wife, who assisted him at many operations. He was an ardent member of numerous medical societies.

Battey's reputation rests largely on what is known as "Battey's Operation," first performed by him Aug. 17, 1872. He described it as "an operation for the removal of the normal human ovaries, with a view to establish at once the 'change of life,' for the effectual remedy of certain otherwise incurable maladies" (*Atlanta Medical and Surgical Journal,* X, 321). By 1891 he was able to report 300 consecutive cases with a mortality of nine. The reasoning on which his operation was based has long since been recognized as unsound, but his method of procedure by abdominal, and later by vaginal, section opened up an important field of surgery. He also performed other operations, radical in nature for the times, such as perineal cystotomy. In 1877 he introduced iodized phenol as a drug of value in gynecological work. All his work, especially in pelvic surgery, was carefully described in a manner which led even the more conservative members of the profession to study and if necessary operate upon the female reproductive organs. The experience gained by these procedures, plus the advent of asepsis, led to the high standard of abdominal surgery as we know it to-day.

Battey's operative skill, combined with his personal magnetism, drew patients to Rome from a large area. He was in broken health for some years before his death. His son, Dr. Henry H. Battey, continued his practise.

[*Atlanta Medic. and Surgic. Jour.*, ser. 3, I, 496–503; obituaries in *Trans. Am. Gynecologic. Soc.*, XXI, 467–72; *Codex Medicus*, II, 62–63; *Trans. Southern Surgic. and Gynecologic. Ass.*, XV, 415–17; *Atlanta Medic. and Surgic. Jour.*, ser. 3, XII, 489, 613. Battey's principal papers will be found in *Trans. Am. Gynecologic. Soc.*, vols. I to XIII; *Atlanta Medic. and Surgic. Jour.*, vol. X, ff.; and in *A System of Gynecology* (1888), ed. by M. D. Mann, II, 837–49.]

H. R. V.

BATTLE, BURRELL BUNN (July 24, 1838–Dec. 21, 1917), jurist, son of Joseph J. and Nancy (Stricklin) Battle, was born in Hinds County, Miss. He was descended in the sixth generation from John Battle, who came from Yorkshire, England, and settled in 1654 on the Nansemond River in Virginia. His father moved from North Carolina to Mississippi and later to Arkansas, where he settled in Lafayette County and became county judge (J. H. Wheeler, *Historical Sketches of North Carolina,* II, 146). Battle received the A.B. degree at Arkansas College, Fayetteville, in 1856 and the LL.B. at Cumberland University in 1858. He entered upon the practise of law at Lewisville, Ark. In 1861 he enlisted in the Confederate army as a private in the artillery and served until the end of the war. When peace was declared he took up law again at Lewisville, but in 1869 moved to Washington, Ark. He represented Hempstead County in the legislature of 1871 and was one of the leaders in the opposition to Gov. Powell Clayton [*q.v.*] and his successor, O. A. Hadley. When the House voted to impeach Clayton, Battle was appointed a member of the House managers, but the Senate was favorable to the Governor and they could do nothing (J. M. Harrell, *Brooks and Baxter War,* 1893, pp. 98–100; *House Journal,* 1871). In 1879 he moved to Little Rock and there continued the practise of law until his election to the supreme court in 1885. His service on the bench was continuous until 1911, when he declined to stand for reëlection, largely on account of increasing deafness brought about by an injury received in the war. His length of service on the supreme bench, twenty-five years, was the longest in the history of the state up to that time. Battle was considered a remarkable jurist. In the memorial service held at the time of his death Judge W. E. Hemingway said: "His temper was essentially judicial. . . . He deferred a decision until everything that should influence it had been heard." He recognized the established law as "the absolute master of his judicial work" and had no patience with bench-made law. This means that he was conservative. His associates recognized that a bench made up entirely of men of his type would have been wanting in the progressive spirit which is essential to accommodate the law to the changing conditions of society, but considered the presence of one man of his type "a sheet anchor of safety" (*136 Arkansas Reports,* 612–15). During his tenure the laws affecting railroads, carriers, master and servant, and other subjects developed, and "in many instances his opinion constitutes the leading case" (*136 Arkansas Reports,* 618). After retirement he continued to reside in Little Rock until his death. In the opinion of the Little Rock Bar Association "he was a consistent member of the Baptist Church and an ideal Christian gentleman." In 1871 he married Mrs. Josephine A. Witherspoon (*née* Cannon), who died in 1899 without issue.

[The bare facts of Battle's life are found in *Who's Who in America,* IX; his judicial opinions in *Ark. Reports,* XLV–XCVI. The memorial addresses in *136 Ark. Reports* are strong on character, but need to be checked on facts; obit. in *Ark. Democrat* (Little Rock), Dec. 21, 1917.]

D. Y. T.

BATTLE, CULLEN ANDREWS (June 1, 1829–Apr. 8, 1905), politician and soldier, was born at Powelton, Hancock County, Ga., the son of Dr. Cullen Battle, a man of some local prominence, and Jane A. (Lamon) Battle. His brother, Rev. A. J. Battle, was for seventeen years president of Mercer University, Macon, Ga. In 1836 the family removed to Alabama and settled at Eufaula (then called Irwinton). Cullen Battle studied at the University of Alabama, and then read law in the office of John G. Shorter, afterward governor of the state. In 1851 he was married to Georgia F. Williams. He was admitted to the bar in 1852, and soon afterward formed a partnership with William P. Chilton. He acquired considerable reputation as an orator, and began to take some part in politics as an ardent and uncompromising secessionist. In the presidential campaign of 1860 he made, with Senator Yancey, an extensive speaking tour, which not only covered the state but extended to several northern cities, including Boston, New York and Philadelphia. Battle himself was chosen a presidential elector, casting his vote for Breckinridge. After the John Brown raid, he had organized a military company and offered it to Gov. Wise of Virginia, for the defense of that state. The offer was of course declined, but the company was not disbanded, being incorporated with an Alabama regiment of which Battle was appointed lieutenant-colonel. At the beginning of hostilities in 1861 the regiment was called into service to take part in the operations about Pensacola. His state commission being terminated, Battle was appointed major of the 3rd Alabama, a regiment newly organized for Confederate service, and was almost immediately promoted to be its lieutenant-colonel. He served through the Peninsular campaign with it, and when the Colonel (Lomax) was killed at Seven Pines, was promoted to fill his place. He commanded the regiment in the Maryland campaign in 1862, and at Fredericksburg. A few days before the battle of Chancellorsville, he was hurt by his horse's rearing and falling into a ditch. He returned to duty the day before the battle, but wrenched his injured back so severely, in riding, that he was unable to resume command for seven weeks. Rejoining after the army had entered Pennsylvania, he was present at the battle of Gettysburg. In the confusion of the first day's fighting the brigade was broken up, and Battle found his regiment separated from the rest of the command, but adjacent to Gen. Ramseur's brigade. "Attaching his regiment to my command on his own responsibility," wrote Ramseur, "he came in at the right place, at the right time, and in the right way" (*Official Records,* XXVII, pt. 2, p. 587). The brigade was not engaged on the second day. On the third, it was attached to Johnson's division for the attack delivered and repulsed on the Union right, early in the morning. Next month, Battle was appointed brigadier-general, his brigade forming part of Rodes's division of Ewell's corps. He received a vote of thanks from the Confederate Congress (Feb. 6, 1864) when his brigade reënlisted for the war (*Ibid.,* XLIII, 1149). He was present in command through the fighting in the Wilderness and at Spotsylvania, where the brigade lost heavily. At one time when it was driven back in disorder, but rallied, Battle makes the bald report: "I took the colors of the 3rd Alabama in my hand, went forward and asked the men to follow" (*Ibid.,* XXXVI, pt. 1, p. 1084). Later in 1864, while with Early in his Shenandoah Valley campaign, a severe wound received at Cedar Creek ended his active service. He was appointed major-general, and assigned to a division, but the war ended before he had recovered sufficiently to take command. He returned to the practise of law at Tuskegee, Ala., and once more became prominent in politics. Chosen for Congress in 1868, his inability to take the "iron-clad oath" prevented his admission. He was a strong candidate for the Democratic nomination for senator in 1870, but the probability that he could not take his seat if elected caused his name to be eliminated. In 1874 he was a delegate to the Alabama constitutional convention. He removed to Newbern, N. C., in 1880, became editor of the *Newbern Journal,* and was mayor of the city for a time. He died at Greensboro, N. C., and was buried at Petersburg, Va.

[*Confed. Mil. Hist.,* VII (1899), 388–93; unpublished Confed. records in the War Dept.; W. Brewer, *Alabama . . . 1540 to 1872* (1872), pp. 341–42; obituary in the *News and Observer* (Raleigh, N. C.), Apr. 9, 1905.]

T. M. S.

BATTLE, KEMP PLUMMER (Dec. 19, 1831–Feb. 4, 1919), college president, was born in Franklin County, N. C., the third son of William Horn Battle [*q.v.*] and Lucy (Plummer) Battle. Upon his father's coming to live at Raleigh, N. C., in 1839, he was sent to the Raleigh Male Academy. After the removal of his parents to Chapel Hill, he was prepared at the village school for the University of North Carolina, which he entered at the early age of thirteen. At seventeen he graduated, sharing first honor with two others and giving the valedictory. After graduation Battle became tutor, first of Latin, then of mathematics, remaining at the University for four years, during which time he also took his master's degree and a law course. He was then admitted to the bar and practised law in Raleigh with his brother, Richard H. Battle. He also became a director of the State Bank of North Carolina and engaged in various financial and agricultural enterprises. In politics he was, like his father, a Whig. When the Civil War came on he was outspoken as a Union man; but after Lincoln's call for troops he cast his fortune with his state and approved the secession ordinance of 1861. He was active in electing Z. B. Vance governor of North Carolina, and advised and assisted him in withstanding the too great encroachments of the Confederate Government. He was elected state treasurer in 1866, but the Act of Congress of March 1867 deprived him of office. In 1875 he was a leader, as chairman of the reorganized board of trustees, in working for reopening the University of North Carolina, closed since 1868, and in 1876 he was elected president of the revived institution. Battle set to work to raise funds from outside sources because all the endowment of the University had been sunk in Confederate securities. He was successful in collecting enough money for a beginning, and in inducing the legislature to appropriate the first state money ever set apart for the University. His unerring tact, human sympathy, kindly ways, and firm integrity, made him capable of steering the reopened institution to safety through the rocks and shallows of that difficult time. For fifteen years he remained president, was made president emeritus in 1891, accepted the chair of history, and was made professor emeritus in 1907.

During his whole life Battle wrote historical articles for publication, made addresses, and recorded facts such as provide the raw material for history. His short papers have never been collected, but many of them are listed in the Pamphlet Collections of the State Library of North Carolina, and in various periodicals. He wrote a "History of the Supreme Court of North Carolina," published in volume CIII of *North Carolina Reports*. His great work, undertaken in the years of his retirement, was the *History of the University of North Carolina*, in two large volumes (I, 1907; II, 1912), the repository of a mass of facts extending over more than a century of educational development. Battle was a genial man, humorous and humane. He maintained good discipline but by persuasion rather than command. Like his father he was a lifelong Episcopalian and like him a member of the councils of his church. On Nov. 28, 1855, he had married Martha Ann Battle, of Edgecombe County, a distant kinswoman. Their family life was most happy. He survived his wife many years, and lived to a great age, respected and beloved.

[*Biog. Hist. of N. C.*, ed. by S. A. Ashe, VI (1907); letter to Mrs. C. P. Spencer from Battle, giving story of his life, Spencer Papers, II, N. C. State Lib.; *Who's Who in America*, 1899–1919.]

H. S. C.

BATTLE, WILLIAM HORN (Oct. 17, 1802–Mar. 14, 1879), lawyer, jurist, was born in Edgecombe County, N. C., the son of Joel Battle of North Carolina and grandson of Elisha Battle of Virginia. Joel Battle built and operated one of the first cotton-mills in the South. He married Mary P. Johnson of Edgecombe. William H. Battle was the eldest of a large family including six sons. He entered the sophomore class of the University of North Carolina and graduated in two years, as valedictorian, at the age of eighteen. He immediately began the study of law with Chief Justice Henderson of North Carolina, and continued for three years, acting as the amanuensis of his teacher. He was admitted to the bar in 1825, examination being waived by recommendation of Justice Henderson. In this same year he married Lucy M. Plummer of Warrenton, N. C., and settled to practise law in Louisburg, N. C. He was not an orator or impressive as a criminal lawyer, and his success at his profession came slowly. He employed his leisure in intensive study of law, and in editing the *North Carolina Reports from 1789 to 1798*. The older edition of these was exhausted, and the confusion due to new laws conflicting with ancient English statutes was reconciled by Battle's comment in this edition.

In 1833–34, after two previous defeats, he represented his county in the North Carolina House of Commons, although he was in politics a "Henry Clay Whig" and his county was overwhelmingly Democrat. He moved to Raleigh and was a supreme court reporter, 1834–39 inclusive. In 1833 he was appointed with two others to revise the statutes of North Carolina; the revision was published in 1837. In 1839 he was a delegate to the Whig national convention which nominated Harrison. The next year he was appointed judge of the superior court of North Carolina by the Governor. In 1843 he decided to remove to Chapel Hill, N. C., the seat of the University, to educate his sons, and in 1845 he became trustee-professor of law there, serving continuously without compensation until the closing of the institution in 1868. In 1852 he was elected associate justice of the supreme court of North Carolina, which office he filled until 1868 when the state government was overthrown under Act of Congress, March 1867. He left Chapel Hill to return to Raleigh in 1868, where he practised law with two of his sons. The legislature of 1872–73 chose him to revise the statutes of North Carolina a second time. He did this unaided and hurriedly—a great task for any one man. He said that this work was not so well done as he could wish. At this period he was president of the Raleigh National Bank for several years. His wife died in 1874, and returning to Chapel Hill in 1876, he latterly made his home with his son Kemp P. Battle [*q.v.*], then president of the reopened University of North Carolina. He died in 1879 and was buried in Raleigh, N. C.

Battle was a small man in stature, a cheerful and friendly person in disposition. Very modest, laborious, and learned in the law, he was not in any way spectacular, but highly esteemed and respected. He was a life-long Episcopalian, a leading layman of his church, attending its conventions for twenty-five consecutive years. Beside his legal writings, he published in the *University of North Carolina Magazine* before the war short memoirs of early justices of the supreme court of North Carolina—Taylor, Haywood, Gaston, and Henderson—also reminiscences of early days at the University.

[*Raleigh Observer*, Mar. 15, 1879; Mrs. C. P. Spencer, *Churchman*, Apr. 12, 1879; *Obituaries, Funeral and Proc. of Bar in Memory of W. H. Battle* (1879); Proc. in supreme court, *80 N. C. Reports*, 455–64; *Address at Univ. of N. C. Commencement 1879*, by Hon. S. F. Phillips; *Address at Presentation of Portrait to Supreme Court of N. C.*, by Jos. B. Bachelor, in *90 N. C. Reports*, App., Mar. 15, 1892. See also Kemp P. Battle, *Hist. of the Univ. of N. C.*, 2 vols. (1907–12).]

H. S. C.

BAUGHER, HENRY LOUIS (July 18, 1804–Apr. 14, 1868), Lutheran clergyman, college president, was born at Abbottstown in Adams County, Pa., the son of Christian Frederick and Ann Catharine Baugher. His paternal grandfather, John George Bager, who migrated to Lebanon County, Pa., from the Palatinate in 1752, was one of the pioneer German Lutheran clergymen in America. Henry gained his preparatory training at Gettysburg from the Rev. David McConaughty and graduated in 1826 as Latin salutatorian from Dickinson College at Carlisle, Pa. His inclination had been toward the law, and he had already arranged to study under Francis Scott Key, the author of the "Star Spangled Banner," at Georgetown, D. C., but the death of his mother changed the direction of his thoughts, and he decided to enter the ministry. He attended the Princeton Theological Seminary, later transferring to the Lutheran seminary recently established at Gettysburg. In 1828 he was licensed to preach by the West Pennsylvania Synod of the Lutheran Church; in 1829 he became pastor at Boonsboro in Washington County, Md., and on October 29 of that year married Clara Mary Brooks of Carlisle, Pa. In April 1831 he returned to Gettysburg to succeed the late Rev. David Jacobs as a teacher in the gymnasium that had been opened in 1827 as an adjunct to the theological seminary.

The gymnasium prospered and was chartered in 1832 as the Pennsylvania College of Gettysburg. Baugher taught Greek and rhetoric until he succeeded the Rev. Charles Philip Krauth as president in 1850. During Baugher's professorship and presidency, the college remained small, never graduating more than twenty-one students in a single year. Although its resources were meager, the standard of scholarship was high for the time, and the institution exercised an influence wholly beneficial over a great part of the American Lutheran Church. Much of the success of the college was due to the energy, skill, and devotion of its second president, who served it for thirty-six years, performing his duties as teacher and executive until within eight days of his death.

Baugher was of middle height, somewhat stout, with a firm, straight mouth, a delicate, aquiline nose, and remarkably clear eyes. In character he was a slightly irascible saint, but the irascibility softened as age crept upon him, while the saintliness was undiminished. Homer and the Greek Testament were his favorite reading. In theology he was decidedly conservative, finding his masters in the German Lutheran divines of the sixteenth and seventeenth centuries. He was an efficient teacher and administrator, a strict disciplinarian, and the master of a plain, succinct, yet moving pulpit style.

[*Pa. Coll. Bk., 1832–82* (1882), ed. by E. S. Breidenbaugh; *Decennial Report Alumni Ass. Pa. Coll., June 30, 1870* (1871); H. E. Jacobs: *Hist. of the Evangelical Luth. Ch. in the U. S.* (1893), pp. 293, 373, 416, 434; *Am. Luth. Biogs.* (1890), ed. by J. C. Jensson, pp. 63–65; and Baugher's printed baccalaureate sermons for 1855, 1856, 1857, 1858, and 1861; A. R. Wentz, ed., *Hist. of the Gettysburg Theol. Sem.* (1927).]

G. H. G.

BAUM, LYMAN FRANK (May 15, 1856–May 6, 1919), writer, playwright, was born in Chittenango, N. Y., the son of Benjamin Ward and Cynthia (Stanton) Baum. His childhood and early manhood were uneventful. The latter part of his education was received at an academy in Syracuse, N. Y. At twenty-four he began newspaper reporting and 1888–90 was editor of the *Dakota Pioneer,* at Aberdeen, S. D. In 1882 he married Maude Gage of Fayetteville, N. Y. In 1897 he became editor of the *Chicago Show Window,* a periodical for window decorators which he edited until 1902. He had dallied with poetry and prose for some years, and had published a little. In 1899, in collaboration with an artist, W. W. Denslow, he prepared the draft of a book called *Father Goose: His Book.* It was an instant success, selling 90,000 copies in ninety days. This was a great stimulus to Baum, who had been laboring to support a large family on a small income. F. K. Reilly, the publisher, became Baum's friend and adviser; and when Baum read to him the first draft of his *Wizard of Oz,* Reilly immediately suggested that he had the basis of a stage production. The *Wonderful Wizard of Oz* was published in 1900, and in 1901 the play was produced in Chicago, raising Fred Stone and Dave Montgomery, two obscure vaudeville performers, to stardom over night. After the success of the play Baum went abroad for several months, doing much writing in Italy and Sicily. Upon his return he moved to Pasadena, Cal., where he built a home to his liking. One of its interesting features was an enormous birdcage in the flower garden. The cage contained scores of song birds. He liked to write in his garden. He became a grower of dahlias, his varieties taking many prizes in California. Besides several miscellaneous items he published two novels, *The Fate of a Clown* (1905) and *Daughters of Destiny* (1906), issued over the *nom de plume* of "Schuyler Staunton," six books for boys under the pen name of "Floyd Akers," and twenty-four books for girls under the name of "Edith Van Dyne." These books are of no literary value, but were popular for a time, and brought Baum considerable money. The fourteen Wizard of Oz stories will perhaps have a permanent place among children's books. The most typical are *The Wonderful Wizard of Oz, The Woggle-Bug Book,* and *The Tik-Tok Man of Oz.* Eight of Baum's stories were dramatized and produced. He died at his home in Hollywood, Cal.

[Most of the information concerning Baum was obtained from his publisher, Mr. F. K. Reilly of Chicago, who was his close friend; see also *Who's Who in America*, 1912–13; *Chicago Tribune*, May 18, 1919.]
M. S.

BAUSMAN, BENJAMIN (Jan. 28, 1824–May 8, 1909), clergyman of the German Reformed Church, editor, writer, the son of John and Elizabeth (Peters) Bausman, was born on his father's farm near Lancaster, Pa., the youngest of nine children. His ancestry was German, of the Lower Palatinate. What is probably the oldest house now standing in Lancaster bears the inscription, "William Bowsman and Elisabeth Built this House, 1762." Life on the farm was serious. The hard work inured the boy to that habit of tireless industry which was so marked a characteristic of his versatile career. He was six feet in height, lean and lank, of the Lincoln type, with a long, spare countenance and sad brown eyes. He was graduated from Marshall College, Mercersburg, Pa., in 1851, and took one year of professional study in the Theological Seminary at the same place, under the distinguished professors, John W. Nevin and Philip Schaff. In 1853 he was ordained a minister of the German Reformed Church and immediately began the practise of his profession. His most abundant pastoral work was done in Reading, Pa. (1863–1909), where it was virtually concentrated in one congregation, that of St. Paul's, of which he was the founder. He greatly extended the power and influence of his denomination by establishing, at a dozen strategic missionary points in the city, Sunday-schools which afterward developed into flourishing churches. Gifted with a deep and understanding sympathy with the common people he exerted a profound spiritual influence upon the entire community. Bethany Orphans' Home is the most significant memorial of his power of achievement in the field of organized philanthropic endeavor. In the wider sphere of ecclesiastical government he played a large part. He was at one time or another a member of every executive board of the church. He was editor of the *Guardian* (1867–81), a religious and literary magazine for young people. He founded and edited *Der Reformirte Hausfreund* (1866–1903), a bi-weekly paper which, as a moulding force in the religious and social life of the Pennsylvania Germans, was regarded as the most unique of his many undertakings. Appointed delegate to the Evangelical Church Diet at Lübeck, Germany, he seized the opportunity to spend a year of study and leisurely travel in Europe and the Holy Land (1856–57). His observations and impressions are recorded in two books: *Sinai and Zion* (1861), which ran through eleven editions; and *Wayside Gleanings in Europe* (1875). He also edited and published *Harbaugh's Harfe* (1902), a small volume of poems in Pennsylvania-German by Henry Harbaugh, the "poet-preacher" of the Reformed Church—a contribution of distinct value to the study of this peculiar and philologically interesting type of local vernacular. Late in life, Apr. 6, 1875, he was married to Amelia B. Bingaman of Reading, Pa., who survived him. In his theology he was conservative. He accepted the tenets of the Mercersburg school, but no controversial word seems to have come from his lips or pen to feed the flame of theological discontent. "Let us put such theology as we have into harness—get it to work in acts of beneficence, in extending Christ's kingdom," he wrote to a friend. "Witness-bearing for Jesus Christ" was the subject of his last sermon, written four days before his death.

[*Life of Benjamin Bausman*, by H. H. Ranck (1912); *Franklin and Marshall Coll. Obit. Record*, II; *Proc. Alliance of Reformed Churches, Belfast, Ireland, 1884*; "Civil War Reminiscences" in the *Guardian*, 1874; obituaries in the *Ref. Ch. Messenger*, May 13 (portr.), July 15, Aug. 26, 1909.]
G. F. M.

BAXLEY, HENRY WILLIS (June 1803–Mar. 13, 1876), physician and surgeon, son of George and Mary (Merryman) Baxley, was born in Baltimore, where he spent most of his life. He received his collegiate education at St. Mary's College and graduated in medicine at the University of Maryland in 1824. His first public position was that of attending physician to the Baltimore General Dispensary, 1826–29. He subsequently was appointed physician to the Maryland Penitentiary, 1831–32. In the latter year when cholera made its appearance he was sent by the president and directors of that institution to New York to investigate the history and pathology of the disease. His elaborate report was subsequently published in the Baltimore newspapers.

In 1837 Baxley became the occasion, if not the cause, of the temporary disruption of the University of Maryland Medical School. The board of regents of that institution had been abolished by the Maryland legislature in 1825, and a board of trustees created, with the new power of appointing professors regardless of the nomination of the faculty. These trustees were charged by the older professors with extravagance, inefficiency, and financial corruption. Baxley was appointed demonstrator of anatomy in the school in 1834 and allied himself with the trustees. He was unpopular with both students and faculty. Three years later the head of his department, Professor Geddings, resigned, owing, it was thought, to pressure from the trustees. The faculty nominated Dr. William N. Baker to succeed Geddings, but the trustees appointed Baxley. The faculty thereupon resigned in a body and led by Professors Potter and Hall, who had been appointed by the old board of regents, they proceeded to call these regents together, to take possession of some of the buildings, in which they continued their instruction, and to enter suit for the recovery of the other buildings. Meanwhile the trustees, retaining Baxley, appointed new professors to the vacated chairs, and these in their turn gave instruction in the buildings which remained to them. The anomalous situation was ended in 1839 by the court of appeals which declared the act of 1825 unconstitutional and reinstated the regents in control (E. G. Cordell, *Historical Sketch of the University of Maryland School of Medicine,* 1891).

Baxley then joined with Dr. Horace H. Hayden, a pioneer teacher of dentistry, and Dr. Thomas E. Bond, Jr., in the establishment, in 1839, of the first dental college to be formally organized either in this country or abroad, the Baltimore College of Dental Surgery. He became its first professor of anatomy. In 1839 he reported a case of removal of the entire lower jaw of a patient suffering from osteosarcoma. In 1846 he was appointed professor of surgery in the Washington Medical College of Baltimore but resigned in 1847. He was physician to the Baltimore Alms House 1849–50. He is said by Dr. Judson Gilman (*post*) to have been one of the first on record to operate for strabismus. In 1850 he was called to the chair of anatomy in the Medical College of Ohio at Cincinnati and in 1852 was transferred to that of surgery, but remained for only two sessions. During President Buchanan's administration, Baxley visited the west coast of South America and California and the Pacific Islands on a mission to reform hospital work under consular supervision. This mission extended through eighteen months. On his return to America he published a pamphlet entitled *Republican Imperialism, Not American Liberty* and somewhat later his first book, under the title, *What I Saw on the West Coast of South and North America and at the Hawaiian Islands* (1865). He was appointed Government Inspector of Hospitals in 1865. In 1866 failing health caused him to go to Europe where he spent the next nine years mainly in Italy and Spain. During this time he wrote a two-volume book entitled *Spain, Art Remains and Art Realities, Painters, Priests and Princes* (London, 1875).

Baxley was tall, well built, very neat and accurate in all matters, dress included, and in later years had a snow-white beard which reached almost to his waist.

His name is perpetuated in the Baxley Medical Professorship of the Johns Hopkins Medical School. By his will a sum of money amounting to $23,836.52 was received by the trustees of the University to endow any medical professorship that they might think proper. This fund, the first substantial gift received by the University outside of the original endowment, was kept intact and allowed to accumulate until 1901 when it was set apart to endow the professorship of pathology.

[Obituary by Dr. Judson Gilman, *Trans. Medic. and Chirurgical Faculty of Md.,* Apr. 1876; brief biog. by E. F. Cordell in *Am. Med. Biogs.* (1920); additional information from Dr. Henry M. Baxley of Baltimore.]

C. R. B.

BAXTER, ELISHA (Sept. 1, 1827–May 31, 1899), jurist, prominent in Arkansas politics in the Reconstruction period, was born in Rutherford County, N. C., the son of William Baxter, an Irishman, and his second wife, Catherine (Lee) Baxter (*Biographical and Historical Memoirs of North East Arkansas,* 1889, p. 640). In 1849 Elisha Baxter married Harriet Patton of Rutherford County, by whom he had six children. In 1852 he moved to Arkansas where in 1853 he opened a general store at Batesville with his brother Taylor. Two years later they went into bankruptcy, but ultimately paid all their debts. Elisha then worked in a printing office and studied law. He was elected to the legislature in 1854 and 1858, was a Whig and opposed secession, but for a time held the office of prosecuting attorney under the Confederate state government. When Gen. S. R. Curtis entered Batesville, Baxter cast in his lot with the Union but refused to fight against friends (F. Hempstead, *A Pictorial History of Arkansas,* 1890). Forced to leave Batesville, he took his family to Missouri, but was captured and brought to trial at Little Rock on a charge of treason. Escaping from prison, possibly with connivance, he raised the 4th Arkansas Mounted Infantry (Union) and was placed in command at Batesville. Upon the organization of the loyal Murphy state government in 1864, he was elected to the supreme court, but soon resigned on election to the United States Senate. By this time Congress had become wary of Lincoln's plan of reconstruction, and the Wade-Davis Bill was passed in opposition. Several efforts were made to secure the admission of Baxter to the Senate. but all attempts failed, the most favorable vote being 18 to 27. The case was important as setting a precedent for the other Southern states.

In 1868 Baxter became judge of the third circuit under the Reconstruction government. Four years later, in an effort to stem the tide of adverse public sentiment due to the misgovernment of the carpet bag régime, the regular Republicans ("Minstrels"), headed by Powell Clayton [*q.v.*], nominated Baxter for governor on a reform platform. But the "Brindletail" faction refused to accept him and nominated Joseph Brooks on a platform calling a little more forcefully for the removal of political disabilities from the whites. The Democrats endorsed Brooks. The campaign was a heated one, but Baxter was elected by a majority of 2,919. Brooks at once contested the result; the legislature, however, supported Baxter, who was inaugurated Jan. 6, 1873. In his inaugural Baxter promised to carry out reforms, and in a few days the legislature submitted an amendment reënfranchising the whites. Satisfied with this, the Democrats began to lose interest in Brooks, but he did not give up the contest. He tried both the supreme court and a local court, but his case hung fire and many of his Republican friends deserted him. As Baxter continued his program of reform some of the regular Republicans became alarmed and left him for Brooks, but Senators Clayton and Dorsey, the former being the Republican boss, stood by him for another year. Baxter had opposed a bill for the issuance of more bonds for aid to railroads; when in March 1874 he refused to issue any more of those already authorized, because convinced of crookedness in the affair, even Clayton and Dorsey deserted him for Brooks. By a clever move the latter now secured a decision from the supreme court in his favor and seized the executive office. Baxter refused to yield, and both called out the militia. In proportion as the Republicans abandoned Baxter the Democrats rallied to his side. Both parties appealed to Washington. At first President Grant was inclined toward Brooks, but after investigation left the decision to the legislature. The amendment to reenfranchise the whites had been adopted, and special elections to fill vacancies had given the Democrats a majority in the legislature. This body again decided for Baxter, and Brooks was forced to retire. The legislature then called a convention to draw up a constitution, which was adopted by a very large majority. The Democratic nomination was open to Baxter for reëlection, but he declined and retired to his home in Batesville, where he resumed his law practise and engaged in farming until he died.

[John M. Harrell, *The Brooks and Baxter War* (1893) is the best source of information about the chief event in Baxter's life. The text itself, written by an eye-witness, is source material and it gives extensive quotations from the testimony taken by the Poland Committee, *House Report, No. 771,* 43 Cong., 1 Sess. *Appleton's Ann. Cyc.,* 1873, 1874, contains useful information. T. S. Staples, *Reconstruction in Ark.* (1923) is the most recent and scholarly account. The press of the country, especially the *N.Y. Herald, N.Y. World,* and *St. Louis Dispatch* (April–May, 1874), gave considerable space to the contest between Baxter and Brooks. There are good obituaries of Baxter in the *Ark. Democrat,* June 1, 1899, and *Ark. Gazette,* June 2, 1899.]

D.Y.T.

BAXTER, HENRY (Sept. 8, 1821–Dec. 30, 1873), Union soldier, was a native of Sidney Plains, Delaware County, N. Y. His parents were Levi and Lois (Johnson) Baxter. Both grandfathers were veterans of the Revolution. In early life he was associated with his father in the keeping of a store and mill. He made a journey to California at the time of the gold fever. Before the Civil War he organized at his home in Michigan the Jonesville "Light Guards." He entered the war as a captain, was commissioned colonel in 1862 and brigadier-general of volunteers in 1863, and was mustered out of the army in 1865 with the brevet of major-general of volunteers. References to his activities are numerous in the annals of the Army of the Potomac. (Longstreet, *Manassas to Appomattox,* 1896, speaks of Baxter's command composed of volunteers for that act, as crossing the Rappahannock River under fire, shortly before the battle of Fredericksburg, an action which has been characterized as a "brilliant exploit.") At Gettysburg he commanded a brigade in Gen. Robinson's division, belonging to the 1st Corps, then temporarily under Gen. Abner Doubleday. (Doubleday, *Chancellorsville and Gettysburg,* 1882, describes Baxter's brigade as being in the "thickest of the fighting.") In the first day of the battle he captured nearly all of the Confederate brigade commanded by Iverson (*Battles and Leaders of the Civil War,* 1887–88, III, 285). In the final campaigns of 1864–65 under Grant, his brigade formed part of the 5th Army Corps under Gen. Warren. He was desperately wounded at Antietam and again at Fredericksburg, and a third time at the Wilderness, where two horses were shot under him, but recovered in time to serve in the closing battle of Five Forks. His brevet cited his gallantry and services at the Wilderness, Dabney's Mill, and Five Forks. After the war he was register of deeds, and later United States minister to Honduras for three years from 1869 to 1872. His death occurred in his home at Jonesville, Mich. He was married in 1854 to Elvira E. George of Hillsdale County, Mich.

[*Hist. of Hillsdale County* (1879); *Portr. and Biog. Album of Hillsdale County* (1888), pp. 990–91; F. B. Heitman, *Hist. Reg.* (1903).]

E.K.A.

BAXTER, JOHN (Mar. 5, 1819–Apr. 2, 1886), Southern Unionist, was a son of Catherine (Lee) Baxter and William Baxter, an Irish immigrant, who came to Rutherford County in western North Carolina, where he accumulated a modest competence. The only formal education John Baxter received was in the "old field schools." To the last he had little taste for general reading and was markedly a man of slender education except in law. He was first a merchant in a country town, and then after a brief study of law, rose to some prominence at the North Carolina bar. He was several times a member of the North Carolina legislature, and once speaker of the lower house. On June 26, 1842, he married Orra Alexander. In 1844 he was district elector on the Henry Clay presidential ticket. In May 1857 he removed to Knoxville, Tenn., where he soon attained leadership in the law. A Whig in politics, he was a slaveholder with strong sympathies for the Southern position, but was not a secessionist. When the Civil War was drawing near, he advocated in vain a convention of delegates from the Southern states for the purpose of considering means of saving the Union. Against secession he took the stump and made many bitter speeches, but later became more moderate. At a Union convention, held in Greeneville, East Tennessee, on June 17, 1861, it was proposed that a new state be formed which would raise an independent army with Baxter as general, a movement which was not successful on account of the encircling of the region by Confederate forces. For a time it seemed that Baxter might follow the state into the Confederacy, but in 1862 he was publishing a Union newspaper in East Tennessee. The same year he was arrested in Memphis and held in prison for several days as an enemy of the South. When he went back to Knoxville, he openly joined the Unionist sympathizers and was a thorn in the side of the Confederate cause. After the Confederacy failed, Baxter tried in vain, with Thomas A. R. Nelson, to organize a new party, to occupy a middle ground between the Democrats and the Republicans. In the state constitutional convention of 1870 he was one of the few ex-Unionist delegates but in recognition of his learning in the law, he was made chairman of the important judiciary committee, and had much to do in framing the new constitution. At some time between 1872 and 1875 he became a political follower of William G. Brownlow [*q.v.*]. He was now not only a leader of the East Tennessee bar, but was generally considered one of the best lawyers in the state and was engaged in most of the well-known cases which developed in the ten years following the Civil War. He was appointed United States circuit judge by President Hayes in 1877. As judge he made no notable decisions and wrote no notable opinions, but managed to simplify procedure in his court and used drastic measures to clear cases before him of technicalities. He was a man of great native ability, assertive, self-reliant, and of marked individuality. He was fairly learned in the law and based his arguments, even in the more important cases, upon general principles. He was a good speaker with a rather harsh manner, who made bitter enemies and devoted friends.

[W. M. Garrett and A. V. Goodpasture, *Hist. of Tenn.* (1900), pp. 205, 268; W. T. Hale and D. L. Merritt, *Hist. of Tenn. and Tennesseeans* (1913), pp. 1471–72; J. W. Caldwell, *Sketches of the Bench and Bar of Tenn.* (1898); Oliver P. Temple, *Notable Men of Tenn.* (1912); William Rule, *Standard Hist. of Knoxville* (1900); obituaries in *Knoxville Daily Chronicle, Memphis Appeal, Memphis Avalanche, Nashville Daily American*, Apr. 3, 1886.]

W. L. F.

BAXTER, WILLIAM (July 6, 1820–Feb. 11, 1880), clergyman, educator, son of Henry and Mary Baxter, was born in Leeds, Yorkshire, England. In 1828 he came with his parents to Allegheny City, Pa., where he learned the tinner's trade; and also prepared for college. In early life he was a member of the Methodist Protestant Church, but when eighteen years old he joined the "Christian Church," or "Disciples of Christ," with whom he was actively associated for the rest of his life. In 1845 he graduated at Bethany College. After a pastorate in Pittsburgh, Pa., he went south in 1848, serving as pastor at Port Gibson, Miss., and at Baton Rouge, La., conducting evangelistic services in various places, and for three years holding a professorship of belles-lettres at Newton College, Miss. On Mar. 7, 1854, he was married to Mrs. Fidelia (Pico) Vail, widow of a Mississippi planter but born in Massachusetts. In 1860 he became president of Arkansas College, in Fayetteville, Ark. His situation in the little college town was one of peculiar difficulty. Although he had now lived for twelve years in Mississippi and Louisiana, and had, part of the time, held slaves and managed a plantation, his convictions as to Union and anti-slavery were those of the North. He tried to live in peace with his neighbors, while making no secret of his convictions, and to keep his college in operation. It was an effort to do what was impossible; and it ended in 1863, when the college building was burned to the ground, the students were scattered, and he, with his family, was forced to leave the state. His book, *Pea Ridge and Prairie Grove, or Scenes and Incidents of the War in Arkansas* (1864), is important as an authentic record of the experience of a Union man in one of the seceding states, and incidentally reveals its author as a person of character and independence.

For two years after the war Baxter lived in Cincinnati, Ohio, preaching in various places, and active in journalistic and social work. From 1865 to 1875 he was pastor of the Christian Church in Lisbon, Ohio. He died at New Castle, Pa., Feb. 11, 1880. Besides *Pea Ridge and Prairie Grove* he was the author of poems, temperance addresses, and a *Life of Elder Walter Scott* (1874) which is valuable as a record of the early history of the Disciples.

[Alanson Wilcox, *Hist. of the Disciples of Christ in Ohio* (1918); Records of Bethany Coll., 1841–45; Memorabilia of Christian Church, Lisbon, O., through Rev. R. J. Bennett, 1927; letters from sons, William Baxter of Los Angeles, Cal., and R. G. Baxter of E. Baton Rouge, La.]

C. N.

BAYARD, JAMES ASH(E)TON (July 28, 1767–Aug. 6, 1815), statesman, diplomat, was a leader among the Federalists of the United States during the first quarter-century. Of old Huguenot stock, he was descended from Petrus Bayard whose mother Anna, widow of Samuel Bayard and sister of Peter Stuyvesant, came with three children on *The Princess* to New Amsterdam May 11, 1647. Petrus obtained land in New York, Pennsylvania, and Maryland, and his son Samuel in 1698 chose Bohemia Manor, Md., for his home. Here James, of the third generation, brought Mary Ashton, his wife, and here on Aug. 11, 1738, the first James Ashton Bayard was born. He was a surgeon in Philadelphia until his death in Charleston, S. C., Jan. 8, 1770. In 1760 he married Agnes Hodge, who on July 28, 1767, gave him a second son, James Ashton (as the name was originally spelled, although custom has fixed the modern spelling as Asheton).

At the death of his father, James Ashton Bayard was placed under the guardianship of his father's twin brother, John Bayard [*q.v.*] of Philadelphia, which continued until James's graduation from Princeton College, Sept. 29, 1784. During these fourteen years, and especially after the death of his mother in 1774, his immediate surroundings did much to determine the young man's future. His education was essentially conservative, whether at Piqua in Lancaster County from his uncle, at Princeton, or in the circle of Pennsylvania society in which he moved. Upon the completion of his college work he studied law with Joseph Reed and after 1785 with Jared Ingersoll, each of whom strengthened the conservative tone of his earlier training. When, therefore, he was admitted to the New Castle bar in August 1787, and at Philadelphia in September, and began the practise of his profession at Wilmington the same year, he was welcomed as a useful member of the Federalist party. And when on Feb. 11, 1795, he married Ann, daughter of Chief Justice Richard Bassett [*q.v.*] of Delaware, he acquired an important political and social position among the Federalist leaders.

The election of 1796 demonstrated Bayard's vote-getting ability in Delaware, sending him to the House of Representatives, which he entered May 15, 1797. An excellent opportunity to demonstrate his strength came soon after he had taken his seat. On July 3, 1797, Adams sent Congress a message and papers disclosing a plan of certain United States citizens to aid Britain in seizing Spanish territory in Louisiana. Earlier fears of a British attack in this section had been brought to the notice of Timothy Pickering, secretary of state since Dec. 10, 1795, by the Spanish, but such intentions had been denied by the British minister. Now a letter of William Blount [*q.v.*], senator from Tennessee, to James Carey, interpreter to the Cherokee Indians, dated Apr. 21, 1797, had come to light involving the British minister and Blount himself in the plan. The manuscripts were laid before Congress and Blount's guilt seemed plain. No one claimed his innocence, but Gallatin and other Republicans declared that as a senator he was exempt from impeachment. The real criminal, continued Gallatin, was Robert Liston, the British minister, or President Adams, who had had "improper understandings" with him. In this crisis Bayard managed the case against Blount so ably that the latter was expelled from the Senate in July 1797.

Bayard played a decisive part in the disputed presidential election of 1800 when the decision between Jefferson and Burr, both Republicans, was thrown into the House of Representatives. The Federalists, on the principle that any one was preferable to Jefferson, supported Burr for thirty-five inconclusive ballots. Then their leaders decided to shift to Jefferson if they could obtain from him certain assurances as to the future. Bayard's position as the most important Federalist in a border state, as well as his work for Federalist financial measures, 1798–1800, made him the most fitting negotiator for that impartial treatment desired by business interests as well as by office-holders in the National Government. His first approach was through John Nicholas, representative from Virginia and a particular friend of Jefferson. To him Bayard stated that "if certain points of the future administration could be understood and arranged with Mr. Jefferson . . . three states would withdraw from any opposition to his election." They sought only assurance of support for the public credit, the maintenance of the naval system, and security for minor office-holders in their government positions. "I explained," continued Bayard, "that I considered it not only reasonable but necessary, that offices of high discretion and confidence should be filled by men of Mr. Jefferson's choice." In the latter group he placed cabinet officers, and as examples of the former he mentioned collectors at ports of entry. He was assured by Nicholas that the points seemed reasonable, and that Jefferson with the men about him would undoubtedly be of the same opinion. Bayard replied that he "wanted an engagement," and if this were conceded by Jefferson, "the election should be ended." He was unable to obtain a direct promise from Nicholas, but in his deposition of Apr. 3, 1806 (*Bayard Papers,* pp. 128–29), he states that Gen. Samuel Smith took the same three points to the Virginian and was authorized by Jefferson "to say that they corresponded with his views and intentions and that we might confide in him accordingly." Although no Federalist voted for Jefferson, by absence or refusing to vote "the opposition of Vermont, Maryland, South Carolina and Delaware was immediately withdrawn and Mr. Jefferson was made President by the votes of ten states," on the thirty-sixth ballot (Bayard's letter of Feb. 17, 1801, pub. in *Niles' Weekly Register,* Nov. 16, 1822). Shortly afterward, Bayard wrote to President Adams declining the proffered ministry to France as he would have to hold it during Jefferson's term to make it worth while, and if he did so he would be accused of having made an agreement with him.

In the discussions of "the judiciary reform measure" of 1801 and its repeal, Bayard ably defended the Federalist position. The fact that his father-in-law, Richard Bassett, was one of the new judges involved, was unnecessarily invoked to explain his stand. The personal factor may have added vigor to his words, but Bayard's belief in the need for the law and in the increased importance it gave to Delaware (Bayard to Bassett, Jan. 25, 1800) as well as his conviction that the repeal was "a most flagrant violation of the Constitution" and "prostrated the independence of the judicial power," were in all probability quite genuine.

Bayard's work in the Senate began Jan. 15, 1805, and continued until May 3, 1813. Much of his time was occupied with legal business, for while he disagreed thoroughly with the administration which "distinguishes itself only by its weakness and hypocrisy," he was equally certain that "no Federal prescription" would ever be taken to end the "political malady" of the period (to Andrew Bayard Apr. 2, 1805; Jan. 30, 1806; *Bayard Papers,* pp. 164–65). Sane and moderate in his views, Bayard strove to uphold the dignity of his country against Britain or France as readily as he opposed the fitting out of the Miranda Expedition against Spain in 1806. A stanch believer in the superior abilities of an educated leadership, he was willing to subordinate himself if he could thereby be useful. An excellent illustration of Bayard's position was his national service under a hostile administration before and during the War of 1812. In 1808 he was willing to give Gallatin the credit of securing the renewal of the charter of the United States Bank expiring in 1811, or to join in obtaining a charter for a new one. The former was his preference, but during 1810-11 when renewal seemed impossible Bayard willingly served as chairman of the committee to secure a charter for a new institution. Defeated at this time by the vote of Vice-President Clinton, Bayard sought to keep the nation from the war into which she seemed to be drifting. He had little confidence in Napoleon's promises and saw clearly that Britain could not be coerced by commercial regulations (Bayard to Andrew Bayard July 3, 1809; Mar. 5, 1810; to Wells Jan. 12, 1812; *Bayard Papers,* pp. 177, 179, 188). He therefore joined Adams in urging that United States vessels be allowed to defend themselves and was pleased when our war-ships did so in the skirmishes with the Barbary States. He advised Federalist agreement in defensive measures and earnest support for all acts strengthening the army and navy. As late as May 2, 1812, he hoped the fear of additional free states from conquered Canada might induce the South to favor a naval war with Britain rather than land campaigns, a hope which had an unexpected measure of fulfilment in the war which followed. During this war Bayard is said to have "helped with his own hands to build a fort almost on the site of Fort Christina," the old Swedish fortress of 1638. Meanwhile necessity compelled the Republican leaders to abandon many of the methods used by Jefferson to obtain popularity. This brought Bayard and the President more in harmony as to the means of carrying on the war. A careful and judicious man devoted to his nation as well as to family and friends, Bayard was regarded as representing at this time both Federalist and Republican sentiment. The death of his sister Jane, Sept. 30, 1809, after serious mental derangement requiring much care from Bayard, allowed him more time for national service in those trying years, while his wife, who survived him until 1854, helped her husband during the war period by assuming many of the family cares.

With the European crisis of 1813 and the ability of the United States to maintain her rights upon the sea demonstrated, both Britain and the United States wished peace. Adams, Bayard, and Albert Gallatin, from different sections of the country, were appointed by President Madison to represent the United States. Bayard sailed from New Castle, Del., on May 9, 1813. By August 1814 when the representatives of the two nations met at Ghent, Napoleon had been captured, three armies had been sent to America, and Castlereagh, British foreign secretary, was willing to show the contempt he felt for the United States. A description of the negotiations is out of place here. Suffice it to say that eventually a treaty resulted, giving to neither party what it proposed but securing for the United States the control of the Mississippi River, eliminating from discussion certain questions which time alone could settle and others which the war itself had decided. In Bayard's opinion no power in Europe would soon disturb America again (*Papers*, pp. 366–67). On Feb. 27, 1815, Bayard was nominated minister to Russia, but he declined the position as he considered his services at that court unnecessary. His diplomatic ability was recognized in 1814–15, when he was chosen to continue with Adams, Clay, and Gallatin in negotiations for a treaty of commerce with Great Britain. Ill health prevented the completion of this mission, and on June 18, 1815, Bayard sailed from England for Wilmington, where he died six days after his arrival.

[The papers of James A. Bayard, *Am. Hist. Ass. Reports, 1913*, II (1915), ed. by Elizabeth Donnan, and referred to as *Bayard Papers*; Bayard's letters to Cæsar A. Rodney in *Del. Hist. Soc. Papers for 1901* (XXXI); *Mass. Hist. Soc. Proc., Dec. 1914*; J. T. Scharf, *Hist. of Del.* (1888); J. G. Wilson, *Col. John Bayard and the Bayard Family* (1885); *Annals of Cong.*, 1795–1815; *Aurora Gen. Advertiser*, and *Aurora* (Phila., 1795–1815); the more gen. histories of the United States, especially those by Adams, Hildreth, McMaster, and Schouler; *Writings of John Quincy Adams*; *Works of John Adams*; *Complete Works of Benjamin Franklin*; *Works of Alexander Hamilton*; *Writings of Thomas Jefferson*; *Writings of James Madison*.]

C. H. L—n.

BAYARD, JAMES ASHETON (Nov. 15, 1799–June 13, 1880), lawyer, senator, was born at Wilmington, Del. He was the younger son of James A. Bayard [*q.v.*] and Ann (Bassett) Bayard, and brother of Richard Henry Bayard [*q.v.*]. He was educated at Princeton and Union Colleges, graduating at the latter school at the age of nineteen. Although intended for a mercantile career, he turned to the study of law and in the spring of 1822 was admitted to the Delaware bar. A year later on July 8, 1823, he married Ann, daughter of Thomas and Dorothy Willing Francis of Philadelphia, thereby uniting important Pennsylvania families. He won success in his profession, being counsel in many important cases, among them one in which the Chesapeake & Ohio Canal Company was a party, involving about $250,000, and establishing Bayard's reputation. In 1843 he removed to New York City but returned to Wilmington three years later where he assisted in the legal training of his son Thomas Francis Bayard [*q.v.*].

During his early life Bayard had some political experiences, although few victories fell to his share. In the formation of parties 1820–28 he had enlisted with the Democrats and his popularity in Delaware was not increased by Jackson's nomination of him in December 1833 as one of five government directors of the United States Bank for 1834. He was defeated as candidate for the House of Representatives from Delaware in 1828 and 1832, and when the four other nominees of the President had been rejected by a Whig Senate, Bayard refused to serve in the position offered him in 1833. In the Congressional elections of 1834 he was again defeated by John J. Milligan, Whig candidate for reëlection, by 155 votes. In a close contest for the senatorship in 1838 Bayard's campaign failed owing to the refusal of the Whig state Senate to sit in joint session with the Democratic House, preferring that the state should have but one senator rather than lose the opportunity of electing a Whig the following year. Twelve years later, following the agreement of both parties in the state to support the Wilmot proviso, Bayard was elected United States senator (1851–57) upon the sixteenth ballot, being again returned in 1857 and in 1863. Meanwhile as a delegate to the Delaware constitutional convention of 1852–53 he considered his county of Newcastle unfairly treated in the constitutional changes agreed upon. He therefore opposed the work of the convention and helped to defeat it in 1853. The Native Americans carried the state in 1854 so that as a result Delaware waited until 1882 for her new constitution.

Bayard's position in the Senate was not an easy one. From 1851 to 1864, if ever in American history, statesmen were needed. The deaths of Calhoun (1850), Clay and Webster (1852) had deprived the nation of her prominent leaders. Bayard, a friend of the Union as governed by Andrew Jackson, and from a border state as was Jackson, saw his party split by the Dred Scott decision of March 1857. He could join neither Breckinridge nor Douglas, while the personalities of Frémont and Lincoln appealed to him; he, therefore, entered the new Republican party but with his faith in the ideals of Jackson unchanged. The election of 1860 precipitated the crisis, and Bayard supported the new President. His position during the war was bound to prove embarrassing at the best. With Charles Sumner shouting that "nothing against slavery can be unconstitutional" and a growing tendency everywhere to accept the maxim that *inter arma silent leges* as the basis of policy, Senator Bayard adhered to his conservative tradition. He opposed most of the anti-slavery measures enacted between 1861 and 1864. He made a notable speech on Apr. 3, 1862, in opposition to emancipation in the District of Columbia, declaring that it was an outrageous invasion of property rights. It was furthermore, he declared, exceedingly impolitic and likely to cause disloyalty in the border states. If his emphasis on the property aspects of slavery seems anomalous at the present time, his presentation of the race problem which would inevitably accompany emancipation shows that he had a far better appreciation of its magnitude than his Senate contemporaries, and subsequent history has justified many of his predictions. His financial training compelled him to oppose the Legal Tender Act of Feb. 25, 1862, in the Senate and to urge more conciliation and compromise in the Reconstruction policies adopted by the Republicans. On the death of Lincoln the aggressive nature of Thaddeus Stevens repelled him, and he was not at home in the party with which he acted. He opposed the test oath for office-holders, and when the Senate passed the measure, Bayard, although subscribing to it, expressed his dissent by resigning his seat (Jan. 30, 1864). He was succeeded by George Read Riddle, but upon the death of the latter, Mar. 29, 1867, Gov. Gove Saulsbury appointed and the legislature elected Bayard for the remainder of his original term. Like his brother Richard, Senator Bayard gradually returned to the Democratic party and upon the expiration of his term, Mar. 4, 1869, gladly saw his place taken by his son, Thomas Francis Bayard, a Democrat. With this event Bayard's active career ceased, and he passed the remainder of his life in retirement at Wilmington. A conservative in political opinion, Bayard was unfortunate in living in an era which demanded constructive statesmen.

[A few MSS. of James A. Bayard, Jr., are in the Lib. of Cong. and others—originals or copies—are in the Bayard Family collection referred to in *Am. Hist. Ass. Reports, 1913,* II (1915). J. G. Wilson, *Col. John Bayard and the Bayard Family* (1885); J. T. Scharf, *Hist. of Del.* (1888); *Cong. Globe,* 1833–69; *Jour. of the U. S. Senate,* 1851–69; J. B. McMaster, *Hist. of the People of the U. S.*, IV–VII (1895); J. F. Rhodes, *Hist. of the U.S. from the Compromise of 1850,* I–III (1893); Woodrow Wilson, *Hist. of the Am. People* (1918); *Del. Hist. Soc. Papers* (1879), I, No. 7.]

C. H. L—n.

BAYARD, JOHN BUBENHEIM (Aug. 11, 1738–Jan. 7, 1807), merchant and statesman, son of James and Mary (Ashton) Bayard, was born at Bohemia Manor, Md. [for ancestry see James Ashton Bayard]. Educated at Nottingham Institution and by George Duffield, Bayard went to Philadelphia in 1756 and entered the business house of John Rhea. The close of the French War found him a commercial and social leader in the city, a vigorous upholder of provincial rights and a logical signer of the Non-Importation Agreement of 1765. He was no advocate of extreme measures, however, lest they result in a premature break with Great Britain. A member of the Sons of Liberty organized in 1766 and of the Provincial Convention of 1774, Bayard in 1775 urged the appointment of Washington as commander-in-chief of the Continental forces, and by May 1776, when chairman of the Committee of Inspection, he was ready, "at the request of a number of persons," to call a general town-meeting to consider proposals for a convention. This gathering declared "the present government of the province not competent to the exigencies of its affairs." On Oct. 21 Bayard presided over another popular meeting summoned to discuss the new state constitution as announced on Sept. 28. In March 1777 and November 1778, he was chosen speaker of the Assembly to which body he was elected several times, becoming also a member of the Board of War. Bayard's military activities were important. He was major of the second battalion of Philadelphia gentlemen "Associators" which volunteered for service with the Continental forces, and was complimented by Washington for gallantry at Princeton. He became colonel of his battalion in 1777, and later, as a member of the Council of Safety, he visited Washington at Valley Forge. He served one year also on the Supreme Executive Council of the state.

Bayard's principal influence in American affairs resulted from his business and social prestige. In Philadelphia and in New Brunswick, N. J., whither he removed in 1788, his residence was a rallying point for Pennsylvania leaders and for Federalist statesmen throughout the nation. Work for Princeton College and as Whitefield's friend in the Presbyterian Church increased his reputation, as did a good knowledge of the French language. In 1785 he was elected to the Continental Congress from Pennsylvania and was chosen later for various civil and political positions in New Jersey, among them justice of the court of common pleas. Bayard was married three times: his first wife was Margaret Hodge; his second, Mrs. Mary Hodgden or Hodgson; his third, Johannah White, sister or daughter of Gen. Anthony W. White.

[A few manuscripts in the Hist. Soc. of Pa., and others, including those of Bayard's daughter Margaret Bayard Smith, in the Lib. of Cong.; the *Pa. Gazette* and the *Packet*; Thompson Westcott, *Hist. of Phila.* (as published in the *Dispatch* or in the three vol. ed. by Scharf and Westcott, 1884); J. G. Wilson, *Col. John Bayard and the Bayard Family*, with portr. (1885); *N. J. Hist. Soc. Proc.*, ser. 2, vol. V, 139–160; ser. III, vol. II, 100–15.]

C. H. L—n.

BAYARD, NICHOLAS (1644–1707), secretary of the province of New York, was of French descent although born in Alphen, Holland. His grandfather, Balthazar, was at one time pastor of a French church in Antwerp and prior to 1599 was a college professor. Samuel, the father of Nicholas, was a wealthy merchant. Upon his death, he left a family of three sons, a daughter, and his widow Anna, who was a sister of Peter Stuyvesant. She is described as imposing in appearance, highly educated, of good business capacity, and of somewhat imperious temper. When Nicholas was three years of age the family fortunes were transferred to the New World and the little family established itself in New Amsterdam. They were accompanied by a tutor, but he was discharged soon after their arrival and the education of the children was conducted by their mother. This included the teaching of the French, English, and Dutch languages. Association with his uncle, Peter Stuyvesant, director general of the province of New Netherland, and the touch which this gave him with people and affairs of the colony presumably shaped to a considerable extent the life of Nicholas Bayard. At an early age, he began his career as English clerk in the office of the secretary of the province, a position which, after three years of experience, yielded him the equivalent of $5.60 a month. His knowledge of the English language was naturally to his advantage when, in 1664, the English forces secured control of the colony. With the organization of the government, Bayard was assigned to assist the Dutch clerk in translating minutes and other records, and soon succeeded him. He was later appointed surveyor of customs. Under the second short Dutch occupation, he continued as provincial secretary, was commissioned receiver general, was made lieutenant of a newly formed company of militia, and was given power of attorney to collect debts for the Dutch Government.

With the reëstablishment of English control, troubles began for Bayard. With others he presented a petition to Gov. Andros requesting freedom in religion and exemption from bearing arms against the Dutch in case occasion demanded. This was made cause for judgment against him, his "goods and chattels" were forfeited, and he was made a prisoner in the "Hole" in the fort. While awaiting trial, release was obtained only upon giving heavy bonds. But four years later under Gov. Dongan, his star was again in the ascendant. He became a city alderman and a member of the governor's council. In 1685 he was commissioned mayor of New York for two years, continuing to serve at the same time as a member of the governor's council. When Jacob Leisler usurped governmental control, Bayard was one of the especial targets of his attacks. "I was obliged to obscund myselfe upwards the space of five months," he wrote (*New York Colonial Documents*, III, 635). He went to Albany where he was sought in vain by Leisler's forces until his whereabouts were discovered through captured letters and he was seized and imprisoned. Broken in health and spirit, he now petitioned for pardon; Leisler not only refused but, as if to gloat over his downfall, had him carried triumphantly through the fort in a chair in chains. His imprisonment lasted over a year.

At last the long-expected Gov. Sloughter arrived from England and demanded the release of Bayard, who was to be one of his councillors. Leisler in his turn was imprisoned and Bayard's chain was "put on Leisler's legg." In fact, Bayard is said to have been influential in securing the signature of Sloughter (who lodged at the Bayard home) to Leisler's death warrant. In 1697, he was still on the council, but the new governor, Bellomont, soon after his arrival accused his predecessor, Fletcher, of having encouraged and protected pirates with Bayard acting as his broker. Extravagant grants of land made by Fletcher to Bayard and others were declared illegal and finally Bayard was removed from the council. He was later accused of being a leader of sedition and mutiny and of being a Jacobite. A charge of high treason was made against him and he was sentenced to death. While he was in prison awaiting execution of this judgment, Gov. Cornbury arrived. Upon investigation of Bayard's case, the new Governor appealed in his behalf to Queen Anne and after many delays Bayard was ordered reinstated in his honors and property. Aside from his political activities, he was influential in church affairs, holding offices of deacon and elder. He served on a committee to plan the new Dutch church. The clergy of New York testified to his devotion to the "true faith" and that he was a "pious, candid, and modest man." On May 23, 1666, he married Judith Varlet (Varlith) who had in 1662 been imprisoned as a witch by the settlers at Hartford, Conn. They had one son, Samuel Bayard.

[*N. Y. Col. Docs.*, III, IV; *Calendar of N. Y. Hist. MSS., Dutch*; *Records of New Amsterdam*, V; *N. Y. Documentary Hist.*, XI; *N. Y. Hist. Soc. Colls.* (1868). I. N. Phelps Stokes, *Iconography of Manhattan Island* (1922), IV, collates much of the above material in chronological order. J. R. Brodhead, *Hist. of the State of N. Y.* (1853), and Mrs. Schuyler van Rensselaer, *Hist. of the City of N. Y.* (1909), are secondary authorities which adhere closely to the original sources. J. G. Wilson, *Col. John Bayard and the Bayard Family* (1885), furnished geneal. data.] A. E. P.

BAYARD, RICHARD HENRY (Sept. 26, 1796–Mar. 4, 1868), lawyer, senator, son of James A. and Ann Bassett Bayard, was born at Wilmington, Del., shortly before his father entered the national House of Representatives [for ancestry see James Ashton Bayard]. Richard was named for his grandfather Richard Bassett [*q.v.*]. He was educated under Rev. Louis Guillaume Valentin Dubourg of the College of Saint Mary in Baltimore, 1805–10, following which he went to Princeton College, N. J. Upon his graduation he began the study of law. This was temporarily interrupted by military service during the closing period of the War of 1812 in a position secured for him by his mother while his father was absent in Europe. Upon the conclusion of the war he returned to his law studies. On Feb. 28, 1815, he married Mary Sophia, daughter of Charles and Harriet (Chew) Carroll and grand-daughter of Charles Carroll of Carrollton. This connection with the Carroll and Chew families reënforced Bayard's predilection for the law so that he continued heartily in the work after his father's death and was admitted to the New Castle bar in December 1818. For the next decade he pursued his practise seriously and with success. Many of the clients of his late father came to him, and he soon became prominent in the professional and social life of Delaware. His purchase of the John Dickinson mansion at Ninth and Market Sts., Wilmington, which he occupied for years and made a center of social entertainment, increased his popularity in that city. On Oct. 6, 1824, at the time of Delaware's greeting to Lafayette, Bayard was on the committee which extended hospitality to the visitor, and in 1829 he represented one group in the state at the dinner to Louis McLane upon the latter's appointment by President Jackson as minister to Great Britain.

Bayard's participation in politics had begun in 1828 when he was defeated for the national House of Representatives by Kensey Johns, Jr. In January 1830 he was at Washington at the time of the famous Webster-Hayne debate, with manuscripts and other material to aid Senator John M. Clayton in his defense of Bayard's father from the accusations of Jefferson in his memoirs. Returning to Wilmington, he was elected first mayor of the city under the charter of 1832, holding the office for three years. On June 17, 1836, he was chosen to the Senate following the resignation of Arnold Naudain, and served from June 1836 until September 1839. During this period he was among the most resolute opponents of Benton's resolution to expunge from the Senate records the censure of Mar. 28, 1834, passed upon Jackson for his removal of the national deposits in the United States Bank, as Bayard considered such action a "mutilation of the Senate Journal." When the elections of November 1838 gave the newly formed Whig party control of the Delaware Senate, Bayard resigned his national senatorship to become chief justice of his own state. In 1840 he was once more elected to the United States Senate and served until Mar. 3, 1845. He then resumed his law practise until he was appointed chargé d'affaires to Belgium, from Dec. 10, 1850, to Sept. 12, 1853. Upon his return from Europe, he maintained his legal position in Delaware and Pennsylvania for fifteen years but took no active part in politics. After his removal to Philadelphia he lived in retirement until his death.

[The papers of James A. Bayard, *Am. Hist. Ass. Reports, 1913*, II (1915), referred to as *Bayard Papers*; J. G. Wilson, *Col. John Bayard and the Bayard Family* (1885); J. T. Scharf, *Hist. of Del.* (1888); *Cong. Globe*, 1836–45; *Jour. of the U. S. Sen.*, 1836–45; *Jour. of the Executive Proc. of the U. S. Sen.*, 1836–45; J. B. McMaster, *Hist. of the People of the U. S.*, V–VII (1906); J. F. Rhodes, *Hist. of the U. S. from the Compromise of 1850*, I–III (1893); *Del. Gazette*, 1824–36; *Niles' Reg.*, 1836–45; T. H. Benton, *Thirty Years' View* (1854–56).] C. H. L—n.

BAYARD, SAMUEL (Jan. 11, 1767–May 11, 1840), jurist, was born in Philadelphia, fourth son of John Bayard [*q.v.*] and Margaret Hodge [for ancestry see James Ashton Bayard]. He was one of a large family of children brought up in a hospitable home where leading men of the period were entertained. At the time of the Revolutionary War, his father early allied himself with the American cause, and Philadelphia consequently was no longer a safe home for his family. For a few years it was a roving life for the boy Samuel; now at the old manor house in Maryland where aged family slaves were still cared for, now in Philadelphia, and now back again to the farm on the Schuylkill where a cottage was fitted up as a school-room and a teacher secured for the Bayard children and those of a few neighbors. A much interrupted education must have been his but it proved sufficient to permit his graduation from Princeton as valedictorian of his class at the age of seventeen. He studied law with William Bradford and became his law partner, practising law in Philadelphia for seven years. In August 1790 he married Martha Pintard of New Rochelle, N. Y., daughter of Lewis Pintard and Susan (Stockton) Pintard. The following year he was appointed clerk of the United States Supreme Court. When a man was wanted to prosecute United States claims before the British admiralty courts, following the ratification of Jay's treaty with Great Britain, Nov. 19, 1794, Washington chose Bayard to act as the agent of the United States. For four years he with his family was in London in this capacity. The results of his official endeavors indicate the success of his efforts. He with his associates obtained from the British Government, for losses sustained by citizens from illegal and unauthorized captures of their ships on the high seas by English cruisers, the sum of $10,345,000.

When Bayard returned to the United States, he spent several years in New Rochelle and served as presiding judge of Westchester County under appointment of Gov. Jay. In 1803 he removed to New York City and resumed his law practise there. The following year, the New York Historical Society was founded, and Bayard was "a hearty coöperator in establishing this Association." He presented to the society "that remarkable series of MSS., the Journals of the House of Commons during the Protectorate of Cromwell." In 1806 he purchased an estate in Princeton where he lived for nearly forty years. During this time he was widely identified with affairs of community, county, and state. He was a trustee of Princeton College and its treasurer for many years and was one of the founders of Princeton Theological Seminary. For a considerable period he was a presiding judge of the court of common pleas of Somerset County, and he served for several years in the legislature of New Jersey. In 1814 he suffered defeat as a Federalist candidate for Congress. For many years he was a delegate to the General Assembly of the Presbyterian Church; he aided with generous hand St. Clement's Episcopal Church in New York City, of which his eldest son, Rev. Lewis Pintard Bayard, was pastor; and for thirty years he contributed to various religious periodicals. He published a funeral oration on Gen. Washington (1800); *A Digest of American Cases on the Law of Evidence, Intended as Notes to Peake's Compendium* (1810); *An Abstract of the Laws of the United States which Relate to the Duties and Authority of Judges of Inferior State Courts and Justices of the Peace* (1834); *Letters on the Sacrament of the Lord's Supper* (1825).

[J. G. Wilson, *Col. John Bayard and the Bayard Family* (1885); *Judge Bayard of N. J. and His London Diary of 1795–96*, ed. by J. G. Wilson; F. B. Lee, *Geneal. and Memorial Hist. of the State of N. Y.*, IV (1910), 1543.]

A. E. P.

BAYARD, THOMAS FRANCIS (Oct. 29, 1828–Sept. 28, 1898), statesman, diplomat, was the son of James Asheton Bayard, Jr. [*q.v.*] and Ann (Francis) Bayard, and was born in Wilmington, Del., where the family had for several generations been prominent in politics and business. He was educated at a private school in Flushing, N. Y., and never attended college. His father temporarily moved to New York in 1843, where Thomas entered the employ of a mercantile house, and later that of another firm in Philadelphia. When about twenty, however, he began the study of law in Wilmington, was admitted to the bar in 1851, and for the next eighteen years, with the exception of a few years in Philadelphia, practised with great success in that city, becoming a permanent resident in 1858. He had a lucrative practise, serving, in a confidential capacity, in the administration of many estates. In October 1856 he married Louise, daughter of Josiah Lee, a wealthy Baltimore banker. She died Jan. 31, 1886, and on Nov. 7, 1889, he married Mary W., daughter of Dr. George Clymer of the Navy.

In 1869 he was elected as a Democrat to the United States Senate. His only previous experience in public office had been less than a year's service as United States attorney for Delaware in 1853–54. His friends considered his election as a tribute to his professional standing and high reputation for integrity and ability; his opponents, as evidence that the state was a pocket borough of the Bayard family. His service in the Senate, 1869–85, covered a period when the fortunes of his party were, in general, at a low ebb. Throughout most of his congressional career it was in the minority, and had relatively few men of outstanding ability in either house. Bayard acquired a recognized position almost from the start, but being a minority leader, he is naturally remembered rather for his opposition to Republican policies, for his exposure of abuses, for the energy with which he defended unpopular minorities and hopeless causes, than for constructive legislation or the successful solution of great problems. He was to the last a Democrat of the older school, although he lived to see a new generation abandon many of its historic principles for miscellaneous political and economic vagaries. He began by fighting the Reconstruction policies of the Radicals both because he considered them harsh and impolitic, and because they involved an undue centralization of federal power with a corresponding aggrandizement of the Executive branch of that Government. The currency, he declared, could not be "lawfully or safely anything else than a currency of value—The gold and silver coin directed by the Constitution" (*Congressional Record*, 43 Cong., 2 Sess., App., 971 ff.). He hated class legislation of every sort, whether it took the form of ship subsidies, railroad land grants, or tariff protection. Militarism and socialism he considered equally inimical to freedom. Law making, he declared again and again, should be restricted to measures universally accepted as necessary, and administration should above all else be honest and frugal. Admirable as many of these doctrines appear in the abstract, it is hard to believe that he ever grasped the full significance of the changes wrought by the Civil War and the nationalization of economic and social life which followed it.

He was a candidate for the presidential nomination in 1880, and again in 1884, receiving considerable support. The exigencies of party politics, however, made his nomination impossible. He became secretary of state, Mar. 6, 1885, relinquishing his place in the Senate, it was believed, with some reluctance, and largely out of a desire to render President Cleveland any assistance in his power. As secretary, he was confronted with troublesome problems from the beginning of his term. A believer in civil service reforms, and on the whole successful in putting his beliefs into practise (*Nation*, Mar. 7, 1889), he found himself confronted with the demands of party workers whose hunger for patronage had been unsatisfied for twenty-five years. In spite of the fact that foreign governments "had schooled themselves against surprise" at the character of our diplomatic service, wrote one of his critics, some of Bayard's appointments "succeeded in startling more than one of them out of the composure which befits great kings and commonwealths" (Arthur Richmond, in *North American Review*, CXLVIII, 23). Thus Italy and Austria emphatically rejected A. M. Keily as *persona non grata* when appointed successively as minister to those countries, the correspondence thereon achieving the immortality which belongs to "classic cases" in text-books of diplomacy and international law (documentary history of these incidents is found in *Foreign Relations of the United States*, 1885, pp. 28–57, and pp. 549–52). Toward the close of his administration Bayard had the equally unpleasant and famous task of dismissing the British minister for his unfortunate indiscretions during the presidential campaign of 1888 (*Ibid.*, 1888, II, 1667–1729). The three major diplomatic issues of his term he was obliged to pass on unsettled to his successors. The North Atlantic Fisheries question, that perennial source of friction, had suddenly become acute with the expiration of the "fisheries clauses" of the Washington Treaty, July 1, 1885. Complicated by the Canadian desire for tariff concessions, the subject caused a serious clash. Seizure of United States vessels in 1886–87 led to jingoistic talk of reprisals, and even war. The Secretary was apparently better acquainted than many of his critics with certain legal defects in the claims of the United States, and pursued a conciliatory policy which resulted in the Bayard-Chamberlain Treaty of Feb. 15, 1888. Assailed in many quarters as a surrender of United States rights, and considered in the Senate while the presidential campaign was in progress, it was rejected six months later. Fortunately a *modus vivendi* had been arranged to meet such a contingency. The other two issues arose in the Pacific. British protests at the seizure of Canadian sealing vessels in Bering Sea led Bayard to confer with interested Powers regarding the protection of the seal herds by international agreement, but any such agreement was frustrated by Canadian objections, May 16, 1888, apparently in anticipation of the expected defeat of the Fisheries Treaty. Through June and July 1887, another conference with representatives of Germany and Great Britain wrestled unsuccessfully with the problem of adjusting conflicting interests in Samoa. It is also worth noting in view of subsequent developments that Bayard tendered the good offices of the United States (1886) to bring about a settlement of the boundaries dispute between Great Britain and Venezuela. If unsuccessful, his policies were at least consistently on the side of peace and arbitration and the subsequent outcome of the North Atlantic and Bering Sea disputes disproved some of the contentions put forward by opponents who charged him with failure to uphold United States "rights."

Following Cleveland's second inauguration, 1893, he was appointed ambassador to Great Britain, the first time such diplomatic rank had been conferred by the United States. He was in many respects a successful representative, but was probably better appreciated in London than at home. When the Venezuelan flurry of 1895–96 took place, he refused to be stampeded into unfriendly speech or action, and a letter to the President shows that he was perturbed at the prospect of allowing "the interests and welfare of our country to be imperiled or complicated by such a government and people as those of Venezuela" (R. M. McElroy, *Grover Cleveland,* II, 191). He worked quietly, but steadily in the interests of Anglo-American friendship. "He did much to cement cordial relations," says Sir Willoughby Maycock, who had first met him when discussing the Fisheries Treaty some years before. "He entertained on a liberal scale, and was in addition a good sportsman, a keen deer-stalker in the Highlands, while his face was not unfamiliar at Epsom, Ascot and Newmarket Heath" (*With Mr. Chamberlain in the United States and Canada,* 1887–88, p. 37). He was frequently invited to deliver public addresses, a mark of British appreciation which eventually caused him some trouble with his own government. In 1895 several speeches caused unfavorable comment, and when on Nov. 7 in an address on "Individual Freedom," before the Edinburgh Philosophical Institution, he took advantage of the occasion to assail the protective tariff as a form of state socialism responsible for a host of moral, political, and economic evils, the House of Representatives began to rumble with indignation. Threats of impeachment were made, but the offended representatives finally contented themselves with a resolution of censure Mar. 20, 1896 (*Congressional Record,* 54 Cong., 1 Sess., p. 3034. See also *House Document 152,* 54 Cong., 1 Sess.). Bayard's health began to fail while he was abroad and after his return in 1897 he took no part in affairs and seldom appeared in public. He died at Dedham, Mass.

Bayard was a strikingly handsome man, over six feet in height, and of a powerful physique. His contemporaries agree that he had an unusually fine presence, and manners which Maycock describes as "dignified, courteous and prepossessing." He had, however, the convictions of an earlier day as to the responsibilities of political leadership and was never inclined, either politically or socially, to seek popularity with the country at large. He was, therefore, occasionally regarded as austere and even snobbish. As to his integrity there was no difference of opinion. He came unsmirched through a period of legislative service when ethical standards in Congress were at their nadir. John W. Foster, an opponent who severely criticized his conduct of the State Department, declares, "No man of higher ideals or of more exalted patriotism ever occupied the chair of Secretary of State" (*Diplomatic Memoirs,* 1909, II, 265. See also the *Nation,* June 17, 1897).

[The chief sources of information regarding Bayard are speeches made during his career in the Senate, his diplomatic papers found in the *Foreign Relations of the United States* and other pub. records, and a considerable number of political, commemorative, and scholarly addresses, reprinted from time to time and available in larger libraries. Edward Spencer, *An Outline of the Pub. Life and Services of Thomas F. Bayard* (1880), has the common defects of campaign biographies. R. M. McElroy, *Grover Cleveland* (1923), and M. M. Gresham, *Life of Walter Gresham 1832–95* (1919), include interesting references. Files of current journals, especially the *Nation* (N.Y.), contain valuable comments and criticisms on his later career. There is a considerable literature on the Fisheries question, the Bering Sea dispute, Samoa, the Venezuelan boundary, and similar issues which throws light on Bayard's diplomatic activities. An appreciative obituary by G. F. Parker appears in the *Contemp. Rev.,* LXXIV, 675 ff. The *Morning News,* Wilmington, Del., Sept. 29, 30, Oct. 1, has a large amount of obit. material, anecdotes, memorial resolutions, personal reminiscences, etc.]

W. A. R.

BAYARD, WILLIAM (1761–Sept. 18, 1826), merchant, son of Col. William and Catherine (McEvers) Bayard, and descendant of Balthazar Bayard, the Huguenot ancestor of the American family, was born in the village of Greenwich outside New York City. His father, a colonial merchant, extensive landowner, and outspoken Tory, raised a Loyalist regiment and lost his property by confiscation. He sailed for England in 1783, taking all his family except young William, who had just married Elizabeth, the daughter of Samuel Cornell. On Dec. 1, 1786, young Bayard formed a partnership with Herman Le Roy, each investing £2,000. A venture to Teneriffe for liquor was the first step in the development of this firm, which became the leading commercial house of New York during the next forty years. James McEvers, Bayard's cousin, was later taken into partnership, but he and the reserved Le Roy were overshadowed by the personality of Bayard. The commerce of New York was at its lowest ebb when the firm started, but the long wars between England and France brought increased opportunities. Several of their ships were condemned by the belligerents, but the remainder brought in good profits. During the War of 1812, they owned a number of successful privateers. The close of the war found Le Roy, Bayard & McEvers in a commanding position in New York, trading extensively with Europe and the East and West Indies. They had the confidence of the wary Dutch bankers and their London drafts could be used in the place of coin in the East Indian trade. By 1822, they had several ships trading along the South American coast, taking advantage of the revolutions. During the interruption of trade caused by the Embargo the partners had turned to land speculation and the town of Le Roy is still a reminder of their activity in developing Genesee County. Bayard had many other interests. In 1817, he was sounding out the Amsterdam bankers for a loan to finance the Erie Canal. He served as president of the Bank of America, the Chamber of Commerce of the State of New York, the Morris Canal Company, and various other organizations. When merchants assembled at Philadelphia from all the northern states in 1824 to protest against the tariff increase, Bayard was made chairman of the gathering. By that time, his former partners had died and their places were filled by his sons, William, Jr., and Robert. They, rather than their father, were responsible in part for the apparently shameless profiteering of the Bayards and Howlands in building two frigates for the Greeks in 1825. The notoriety caused by this affair undoubtedly hastened the death of the elder Bayard at Greenwich on Sept. 18, 1826, after a long illness. His portrait, by William Dunlap, reveals the face of a statesman rather than a merchant (*Catalogue of Portraits in the Chamber of Commerce,* p. 13). He had a reputation for mildness of temper and charm of manner in addition to the unusual business acumen which made him one of the wealthiest men in the country.

[The principal sources of information are Bayard's extensive commercial and private correspondence in the Bayard, Campbell, Pearsall Papers in the N.Y. Pub. Lib., and his father's lengthy depositions in the Loyalist Transcripts in the same lib. The episode of the Greek frigates is described in his son Wm. Bayard's *Exposition of the Conduct of the Two Houses of G. G. & S. Howland and Le Roy, Bayard & Company in Relation to the Frigates Liberator and Hope* (1826). Notices of Bayard's death appeared in the *Evening Post* and the *Commercial Advertiser* of Sept. 19, 1826.] R. G. A.

BAYLES, JAMES COPPER (July 3, 1845–May 7, 1913), editor, engineer, was born in New York, son of James and Julia Halsey (Day) Bayles. His education in the public schools was terminated by enlistment in the Union army. In 1862, at the age of seventeen, he entered the 22nd Regiment of New York and was soon commissioned an artillery lieutenant. He served eighteen months when his health became impaired. After a year's illness he did some work for the Delamater Iron Works of New York and later was on the engineering staff of the Raritan & Delaware Bay Railroad. In 1865 he formed a connection with Gen. Charles G. Halpin, proprietor of the *New York Citizen,* and during the illness of Halpin he acted as editor of the paper. From 1868 to 1869, Bayles was editor of the *Commercial Bulletin,* from which he resigned to accept the editorship of the *Iron Age.* In 1870 he was married to Ianthe Green, daughter of a New York lumber merchant. For twenty years he remained editor of the *Iron Age;* the position gave him a standing among engineers and business men. In 1874 he assisted the publisher of the *Iron Age,* David Williams, to found another trade-paper called the *Metal Worker* (later changed to the *Sheet Metal Worker*), and he acted as its first editor. He was president of the American Institute of Mining Engineers in 1884 and 1885, although he was not strictly a mining engineer; his actual work in that profession was confined to editorial writings on metals and iron ore and a little research in electro-metallurgy and the microscopic analysis of metals. When the American Society of Mechanical Engineers was founded in 1880 he was a prominent charter member. His sincerest interest in engineering, however, was in sanitation and water supply. He lectured eloquently on these subjects and wrote a text-book on *House Drainage and Water Service* (1878) that passed through several editions. In 1884 he became president of the New Jersey State Sanitary Association. During 1887–88, he was president of the Board of Health of New York City, having been appointed by Mayor Hewitt although he was not a politician. In 1886 he wrote *The Shop Council* to reconcile employers and wage-earners; his advice to workers urged moderation and reason. During the same year he served as non-resident lecturer on labor problems at Sibley Engineering College of Cornell University. Upon his resignation from the *Iron Age* in 1889 when he was forty-four, he engaged in manufacturing ventures but was unsuccessful. He became a member of the editorial staff of the *New York Times* and subsequently engaged in consulting engineering practise in connection with city departments and public utilities. He was a brilliant and versatile editor of the old school, an accomplished speaker, and a refined gentleman. He was not a specialist in the modern industrial sense. In appearance he had the distinguished look of a professional man, with a small pointed beard and mustache. He was an amateur painter. His death, which occurred eight years after that of his wife, was due to pneumonia.

[*Bull. Am. Inst. Mining Engineers,* June 1913; *Iron Age,* May 15, 1913; *N.Y. Times,* May 9, 1913; *Who's Who in America,* 1910–11; *Who's Who in N.Y.,* 1911.] P. B. M.

BAYLEY, JAMES ROOSEVELT (Aug. 23, 1814–Oct. 3, 1877), Roman Catholic bishop, historian, son of Guy Carleton and Grace (Roosevelt) Bayley, was born at Rye, N. Y. On the maternal side, he was the grandson of James Roosevelt, a prominent New York merchant. His paternal grandfather was Dr. Richard Bayley [*q.v.*], professor of anatomy and surgery at Columbia College, New York (1792–1801). He was the nephew of Elizabeth Ann Bayley Seton [*q.v.*], who founded the Daughters of Charity in the United States (1809). Owing to the high position in medical science held by his father and grandfather, he first thought of becoming a physician; but after finishing his secondary studies at Amherst College, he entered Trinity College, Hartford, Conn., to prepare for the Episcopal ministry. After his ordination (1835), he was made rector of St. Peter's Church, Harlem, N. Y. Theological controversy in the Anglican communion over the Tractarian Movement was then reaching a climax; and when Newman's *Tract 90* appeared (February 1841), Bayley decided to give up the ministry in order to go abroad for the purpose of studying the claims of Catholicism. He became a Catholic in Rome on Apr. 28, 1842. He then entered the Seminary of St. Sulpice, Paris, to study for the priesthood. He was recalled by Bishop Hughes of New York and ordained on Mar. 2, 1844. His first post was that of vice-president of St. John's College, Fordham, then the diocesan seminary. Four years later, he became secretary to Bishop Hughes, and on Oct. 30, 1853, was consecrated bishop of the newly created Diocese of Newark, N. J., by Archbishop Bedini, Papal nuncio to Brazil. During his years as secretary to Bishop Hughes (1848–53), he became interested in American Church history. In 1847, Dr. De la Hailandière, who succeeded Bishop Bruté of Vincennes (1834), gave to Bishop Hughes of New York a large collection of original letters and documents on early American Catholic history. These Bayley used for his first volume, *A Brief Sketch of the Early History of the Catholic Church on the Island of New York* (1853, 1874). Out of this valuable material he also published *Memoirs of the Rt. Rev. Simon William Gabriel Bruté, First Bishop of Vincennes* (1855, 1876). At the death of Archbishop Spalding of Baltimore, he was promoted to that archepiscopal see (July 30, 1872). Owing to increasing ill-health, he asked for a coadjutor and Bishop James Gibbons of Richmond was appointed (May 20, 1877).

Bayley's English and Dutch colonial ancestry and his New England training produced in him one of the charming personalities of his day. His bearing was princely, his manner most courteous, but what attracted most in him was a frankness of speech that accentuated his influence far beyond his own communion. He was not a profound scholar, though he read widely, especially in the field of Church history. His busy life of administration left him little leisure for prolonged study. A thorough New Yorker, quick, alert, resourceful and a born leader, he went to Baltimore after thirty years of an uncommonly active life in the North, unfortunately at a time when his energies began to wane. The Roosevelt in him found his Southern flock, priests and people, of a nature different from that of the North and less responsive to his enthusiasm for efficient Church government. Once he had secured the coadjutorship of the future Cardinal Gibbons (1877), his heart naturally turned to his old home in Newark, and here death overtook him. He was buried by his own request at the side of his aunt, Mother Seton, at St. Joseph's Convent, Emmitsburg, Md.

[There is no biog. of Archbishop Bayley, except the sketch in Clark's *Lives of the Deceased Bishops* (1888). His life in New York is treated in J. R. G. Hassard, *Life of Archbishop Hughes* (1866). The years spent as first Bishop of Newark are described in J. M. Flynn, *The Cath. Ch. in N. J.* (1902). James Cardinal Gibbons speaks of him in his *Retrospect of Fifty Years* (1916). See also *The Am. Convent Movement* (1923), by E. I. Mannix and *Cath. Builders of the Nation* (1923), ed. by C. E. McGuire.]

P.G.

BAYLEY, RICHARD (1745–Aug. 17, 1801), physician, came from English and French stock. His mother's family were undoubtedly Huguenots, who settled at New Rochelle, N. Y., about 1688. He was born in Fairfield, Conn., and it is said that he had a good knowledge of French and the Latin classics. About 1766, he went to New York to study with a fashionable English physician, John Charlton, and later he married Charlton's sister. In 1769, Charlton sent him to London, where he remained two years, working under the famous anatomist, William Hunter. On returning to New York, he renewed his connections with Charlton. About this time (1774) his attention was drawn to an epidemic of fatal croup. He carefully examined his patients, making pathological studies of the fatal cases, and clearly differentiated diphtheria from other forms of sore throat. By basing his treatment on his sound knowledge of the pathological process, it is said that he cut the mortality rate of this malignant disease nearly in half. His findings were embodied in a letter to William Hunter (1781).

During the winter of 1775–76 Bayley was again in England, working with Hunter. Returning to America as a surgeon in the English army under Howe, he was stationed at Newport, R. I., where he met Michaelis, the Hessian military surgeon. In 1777, he resigned his army position and returned to New York, where he found his wife in a dying condition. Once again he established himself in New York. In spite of his excellent reputation among physicians, reports soon began to be circulated by the public, no doubt due to Bayley's ardent desire to investigate the pathology of disease, that he had performed cruel experiments upon soldiers in Newport and that he was in the habit of "cutting up" his patients. In 1787, he delivered anatomical lectures in an unoccupied building, using his specimens for demonstration purposes. In this work he was assisted by his son-in-law, Wright Post. Public feeling against him increased; a mob broke into his anatomy room and destroyed all his valuable anatomical and pathological preparations (1788).

In spite of his adversities, Bayley persevered with his studies. In 1792 he was made professor of anatomy, and later of surgery, in the Columbia College medical faculty. His surgery was based upon actual experience and observation. He was the first in this country to amputate an arm at the shoulder-joint. He also was an early promoter of the New York Dispensary. His last contribution to medicine was concerned with yellow fever. This dreaded disease appeared in epidemic form in New York soon after the Revolutionary War. Many fled from the city, but Bayley remained, personally attending his cases and making extensive observations. His views were embodied in a book, published in New York in 1796, entitled, *An Account of the Epidemic Fever Which Prevailed in the City of New York during Part of the Summer and Fall of 1795.* In this volume the disease was clearly described, its seasonal prevalence emphasized, and stress put upon its contagious rather than its infectious nature. About this time Bayley was made health physician to the port of New York and his noteworthy *Letters from the Health Office Submitted to the New York Common Council* dealt with the epidemiology of yellow fever. He assisted in the early formulation of both the federal and the New York state quarantine laws. But he himself died from yellow fever on Aug. 17, 1801.

[The first mention of Bayley's treatment of croup appears in a letter by H. D. Michaelis, published in Richter's *Chirurgische Bibliothek* (1779), V, 734–46. Bayley's letter to Wm. Hunter on the same subject was published by Hugh Gaine, N. Y., 1781. It was reprinted in the *Medic. Repository,* 1809, XII, 331–39, and 1811, XIV, 345–50. Practically all of our knowledge of Bayley is derived from James Thacher, *Am. Medic. Biog.* (1828).]

H. R. V.

BAYLIES, FRANCIS (Oct. 16, 1783–Oct. 28, 1852), scholar, statesman, was descended from the pioneer, Thomas Baylies, who came to Boston from London in 1737. He was a Quaker ironmaster of such uncompromising pacifism that he resigned his position rather than manufacture cannon balls for the Louisburg Expedition (1745). His descendants in the third generation, still making iron from bog ore, overcame their scruples and served with distinction during the American Revolution. Francis, son of Dr. William Baylies, was educated at Bristol Academy, Taunton, Mass.; studied law at Bridgewater with his elder brother William, a member of Congress, and in 1820 was himself elected to Congress, continuing three terms. When the presidential election (1824) was thrown into the House of Representatives, Baylies was the only member from New England to vote against John Quincy Adams, alleging the latter's "moral unfitness." Defeat for reëlection naturally followed. After Jackson became president, friends of Baylies endeavored, unsuccessfully, to secure for him a cabinet portfolio. Later Jackson appointed him acting minister to Buenos Aires with full power to negotiate a treaty. In 1829 the *de facto* governor of the Falkland Islands had issued a proclamation forbidding pelagic fishing thereabout. Fishermen from New England, acting upon long usage, defied the proclamation of a *mare clausum* with the result that four Yankee vessels were seized and held for condemnation. President Jackson sent the sloop of war *Lexington* to disperse the pirates and protect American fishermen's alleged prescriptive rights. The acting governor and his associates were forcibly deported for trial. When Baylies arrived (June 8, 1832) he denied the right of Argentina to prohibit fishing around the Falklands. The government at Buenos Aires declined to negotiate with the United States until apologies and reparations were made for kidnapping Falkland officials. Baylies was unyielding. After suffering personal indignities he requested his passports and sailed (Sept. 8, 1832) with the United States Consul and took with him all archives of the legation in anticipation that war would eventuate. Diplomatic relations were not renewed until 1844. A comprehensive report by Baylies discussing rights of fishermen and titles to subpolar regions was published (1833) in Spanish and English.

Baylies was an indefatigable student and painstaking writer. *An Historical Memoir of the Colony of New Plymouth* (1830), published in four parts, brought literary recognition. Being written before the recovery (1855) of the lost Bradford chronicles, the original edition contains misleading statements based upon hearsay tradition not in harmony with Bradford's contemporaneous record. A second edition (1866), edited by S. G. Drake, contains important corrections. Baylies's other published writings include several pamphlets and fugitive political pasquinades contributed to various newspapers. He prepared a number of lectures for popular lyceums and was occasional orator at Masonic, military, political, and agricultural gatherings. He was married, in his fortieth year, to Mrs. Elizabeth Moulton Deming of Troy, N. Y.

[Private papers in possession of Old Colony Hist. Soc., Taunton, Mass., including Baylies's MSS. for unpublished books on hist., biog. and literary subjects; *Annals of Cong.* and *Reg. of Debates,* 1820–26; archives of State Dept.; biog. sketch by S. G. Drake (who knew Baylies personally) in second edition of *An Hist. Memoir of the Colony of New Plymouth* (1866).]

R. D.

BAYLOR, FRANCES COURTENAY (Jan. 20, 1848–Oct. 19, 1920), author, was born at Fort Smith, Ark., and died in Winchester, Va. Her parents, James L. and Sophie (Baylor) Dawson, maintained only the shifting residence to be expected in the family of an army officer. They lived for a while in San Antonio and New Orleans, but the child's education was conducted by her mother. Toward the close of the Civil War, Mrs. Dawson, having resumed her maiden name both for herself and daughter, came to Virginia, where along with Frances, she took up residence with another daughter, Sophie, married to Gen. J. G. Walker (C. S. A.). Virginia was home to them. There Mrs. Baylor had lived as a girl, a member of an intensely family-conscious group, of a distinguished tradition in colonies as well as state. Soon the entire Walker household went for a long visit in England. Their association here with people of considerable literary importance probably emphasized the habitual bookishness of their surroundings. Frances responded to these surroundings faithfully. Returning to America, she began writing in earnest; first, she gave to the world an anonymous play, *Petruchio Tamed,* and later a series of newspaper articles published in papers from New Orleans to London, and signed with the name of one of her male relatives. In 1885 she published *On Both Sides,* a British-American novel, which had first appeared as two stories in *Lippincott's Magazine*. These stories the author states in her preface, "are now bound together, as I earnestly trust that John Bull and his Cousin Jonathan may be in the future." Other writings followed. Of the novels, *Behind the Blue Ridge* (1887) confined itself to American characters, but all the others—*Juan and Juanita* (1888), *Claudia Hyde* (1894), *Miss Nina Barrow* (1897), *The Ladder of Fortune* (1899) and *A Georgian Bungalow* (1900)—derive much of their interest from the contrast of character between persons of different nationalities. The story-interest of these books is slight, and the character-delineation, while pleasant, is not searching enough to confer permanence. Only one of them, *Juan and Juanita,* a child's book, as were also *Miss Nina Barrow* and *A Georgian Bungalow,* retains its vitality. Dealing with the capture and escape of two Mexican children, it draws too deeply upon the standard devices of suspense to perish readily. It was republished in an elaborate edition in 1926. *A Shocking Example,* a volume of stories collected from the *Atlantic Monthly* and elsewhere, was published in 1889. Her poems were not numerous, but some of them —especially the patriotic ones—were widely popular. In 1896, Miss Baylor was married to George Sherman Barnum of Savannah, Ga. Left a widow after a short time, she took up a brief residence in Lexington, Va., before returning permanently to her old home in Winchester. There, with her mother and her sister and her sister's daughters, she lived placidly, occupied chiefly with projects for a new novel, "The Matrimonial Coolie" (never published), but diverting herself from time to time, after her custom, with music and with pleasant visitors. She died while reading in a public library.

[The chief sources of this article are a letter from Miss Frances A. Walker, the subject's niece; E. A. Alderman and J. C. Harris, *Lib. Southern Lit.* (1908), I; *Book Buyer,* Jan. 1888; *Critic,* Apr. 7, 1888; O. W. and H. B. Baylor, *Baylor's Hist. of the Baylors* (1914); A. C. Gordon, Jr., *Virginian Writers of Fugitive Verse* (1923).]

J. D. W.

BAYLOR, GEORGE (Jan. 12, 1752–March 1784), Revolutionary soldier, was born at Newmarket in the Shenandoah Valley of Virginia, the son of Col. John and Fanny (Walker) Baylor. His wife was named Lucy Page. Early in the Revolutionary War he became one of the military aides of the commander-in-chief, an appointment possibly due to Washington's personal acquaintance with Baylor's father. He served at the battle of Trenton, and directly afterward was sent by Washington to Congress, bearing the news of the victory, and carrying also a captured Hessian standard. In a letter dated Dec. 27, 1776, written by Washington to the president of Congress, Baylor was highly commended. He received the thanks of Congress; John Hancock, its president, wrote to Washington recommending that Baylor be promoted to the rank of colonel and receive the gift of a horse, and these recommendations were promptly carried into effect. When Baylor requested the command of a regiment of cavalry, Washington consented, and wrote to him a letter of advice regarding his selection of officers.

The event with which Baylor's name is chiefly associated occurred in 1778, and is still a matter of debate. After the battle of Monmouth, there were no general engagements by the northern armies, but there were various isolated affairs on a smaller scale. One of these was a British attack on the American forces below the Hudson Highlands, in order to cover operations elsewhere. Part of their force under the Hessian Knyphausen planned to surprise one of the American detachments at New Tappan, but this attempt was detected and failed. The other force under Gen. Grey—"No Flint Grey" of Paoli notoriety in the previous campaign—was directed against Baylor's detachment. This regiment of light horse, the so-called "Mrs. George Washington's Guards," was cantoned at Old Tappan or Harrington near the Hackensack River, about two and a half miles from the main body. It has been stated that Baylor encamped at a distance "to be free, as is supposed, from the control of Wayne" (Washington Irving, *Washington,* 1856–59, III, 472). It is also asserted that there were few precautions against a surprise. Gen. Grey, guided by Tories, on the night of Sept. 27–28 attacked the dragoons who were asleep in barns. The bayonet was freely used. Many were killed or taken prisoners, among the latter being Baylor, who had been bayoneted through the lungs. Out of 104 privates, the loss was sixty-seven (William Gordon, *History of the Rise, Progress, and Establishment of the United States,* 1788, III, 194). Grey was accused of inhumanity, as on the previous occasion at Paoli. His epithet "No Flint Grey" was derived from his order to remove the flints from the soldiers' muskets, in order to preserve silence; the charge was made that his men were commanded to refuse quarter. Baylor on Oct. 19, 1778, wrote a letter to Washington in justification of his action, asserting that his patrols had been cut off, and his communications thereby severed. It does not appear that he was reprimanded by the commander-in-chief. Four years later he was in charge of light troops in the South, and was referred to in a communication by Laurens as a trustworthy officer. He died at Bridgetown, Barbados.

[See Jared Sparks, *Corres. of the Am. Rev.* (1853); Chas. Campbell, *Hist. of Va.* (1860); Wm. Meade, *Old Churches, Ministers and Families of Va.* (1857); O. W. and H. B. Baylor, *Baylor's Hist. of the Baylors* (1914). The older accounts of Tappan in Ramsay, Lossing and Washington Irving emphasize the cruelty of the British. There is a favorable notice of Gen. Grey in the *Dict. of Nat. Biog.*]

E. K. A.

BAYLOR, ROBERT EMMET BLEDSOE (May 10, 1793?–Dec. 30, 1873), jurist, Baptist preacher, was the son of Jane (Bledsoe) Baylor and of Walker Baylor, a soldier in Washington's army, and nephew of George Baylor [*q.v.*], aide-de-camp to Washington. His maternal grandfather, Aaron Bledsoe, was a Baptist preacher in Virginia. R. E. B. Baylor was born in Kentucky, according to one account in Bourbon County, on May 10, 1791, according to another in Lincoln County, May 10, 1793. After being educated in the local schools, he served in the War of 1812, first under Col. Boswell in the fighting at Fort Meigs, later under Gen. Harrison in the campaign against Proctor (autobiographical letter in *Dallas Daily Herald,* Jan. 8, 1874). After the war he studied law in the office of his uncle, Judge Jesse Bledsoe, a noted Kentucky lawyer. In 1819 he was elected to the Kentucky legislature and served one term. In 1820 he moved to Tuscaloosa County, Ala. Here he was elected to the legislature for one term, 1824; and in 1829 he was elected as one of Alabama's three representatives to the Twenty-first Congress. His work in Congress seems to have been undistinguished, and he was defeated for reëlection. In 1833 he moved to Dallas County where he formed a law partnership with G. W. Gayle. He commanded a battalion of volunteers during the Creek Indian troubles in 1836. In the same year he moved again, this time to Mobile. In 1839 he emigrated to the Republic of Texas, settling first in Fayette County and later in Washington, where he resided until his death. Just before leaving Alabama he had joined the Baptist Church and had become a preacher. Though his chief vocation was that of a lawyer, or judge, he continued also as a preacher "without a charge"; and he was from the first a zealous leader in all the affairs of his Church in Texas. He soon achieved prominence in his new home. Within a year after his arrival he took part in the important battle of Plum Creek against the Comanche Indians. On Jan. 7, 1841, he was appointed by the Texas congress judge of the third district of Texas. As the judicial system of the Republic was organized this made him also an associate justice of the supreme court. He held this position until Texas entered the Union; he was then appointed one of the first district judges under the constitution of 1845 and remained on the bench continuously until the Civil War. Although the statement is frequently made that he was a member of the Texas congress, his name does not appear on the rolls of that body. He was a delegate from Fayette County to the constitutional convention of 1845 and served on the committee to report an ordinance accepting the terms of annexation offered by the United States, on the judiciary committee, and on the committee on general provisions of the constitution. He seems to have been highly respected by the other members of the convention. His speeches were few in number, but were always short, clear, and pointed. He favored the exemption of homesteads from forced sale, annual elections, the exclusion of the clergy from the legislature; he opposed the grant of any veto power to the governor (*Journal of Texas Constitutional Convention, 1845,* pp. 8, 15, 136–38, 163, 425–26, 510). Rigidly honest, yet kindly in manner and given to tempering justice with mercy, he enjoyed popularity and even veneration as a judge. Wherever he held court—so great was his religious zeal—he usually followed his work on the bench during the day by preaching or holding other religious services at night. He was always interested in education, and in 1843 was made president of the first Baptist education society in Texas. In 1845 he and W. M. Tryon projected the first Baptist college in Texas. He drew the charter and was chiefly instrumental in procuring its passage through the congress, and despite his protests the college was named for him. Baylor University was first established at Independence, Washington County; in 1886 it was moved to its present site at Waco, and "the female department," Baylor College, was moved to Belton. Judge Baylor made the largest cash contribution to its initial endowment and was for many years chairman of the board of trustees. From 1857 to the Civil War he served as professor of law without pay. For a long time he was moderator of the Texas Baptist Union Association and president of the Baptist State Convention. The last years of his life were spent quietly at his home at Gay Hill. He was never married. He is said to have been a man of impressive appearance, over six feet two inches in height, and of great dignity of face and bearing.

[It is generally stated that Judge Baylor's father was Robert Baylor and that he was an aide-de-camp to Gen. Washington. In the autobiographical letter above referred to, Baylor himself said that his father was Walker Baylor and that the aide-de-camp was his uncle Robert. But in W. C. Ford's *Writings of George Washington,* this man's name is always given as George Baylor. There are four different dates given for Baylor's death, but that adopted is best sustained by contemporary evidence. Apparently Baylor County, Tex., was not named for Judge Baylor, but for a relative, Dr. Henry W. Baylor. In addition to the sources mentioned above, data on the life of Judge Baylor may be found in J. M. Carroll, *Hist. of Tex. Baptists* (1923); Mrs. Georgiana J. Burleson, *Life and Writings of Rufus C. Burleson* (1901); C. W. Raines, *Year Book for Tex.* (1901); Jas. D. Lynch, *The Bench and Bar of Tex.* (1885), and O. W. and H. B. Baylor, *Baylor's Hist. of the Baylors* (1914).]

C. W. R.

BAYLY, THOMAS HENRY (Dec. 11, 1810–June 22, 1856), jurist, congressman, son of Thomas M. and Margaret (Cropper) Bayly, was born at Mount Custis, his father's 675-acre estate about three miles north of Accomac, Va. His father was a graduate of Princeton, a well-to-do and public-spirited planter, who served his state in public office for about forty years, as member of the Virginia Assembly, representative in Congress, colonel of militia during the War of 1812, member of the Virginia convention of 1829–30. Thomas H. Bayly inherited his father's country estate, his political talents, and the good will of his constituency. He went from private schools to the University of Virginia, where he was trained as a lawyer. When only twenty-six years of age, he was elected to the Virginia House of Delegates in which he served from 1836 to 1842. The Assembly appointed him brigadier-general of militia. In 1840, he was chairman of a very important select committee to investigate a controversy between Gov. Gilmer of Virginia and Gov. Seward of New York (*Virginia House Journal and Documents,* 1839–40, Document 57). Sixteen years later, Seward declared in Congress, "I felt his ability and power, while I was compelled also to acknowledge his manliness and dignified bearing" (obituary remarks in Congress, June 27, 1856, in *Congressional Globe,* 34 Cong., 1 Sess., p. 1501). When Judge Upshur entered Tyler's cabinet in 1842, Bayly was appointed in his place as judge of the circuit court of his district. He was elected two years later to the federal House of Representatives to succeed Henry A. Wise (appointed minister to Brazil). In spite of the fact that his party was continually in the minority in his district during the period, Bayly was so well-liked and trusted that he was always reëlected, serving from 1844 until his death in 1856. Though not eloquent, he was a forceful and well-informed speaker. He was a Democrat, a champion of state's rights, but strongly attached to the Union. He was independent, sane, and unusually temperate and free from partisanship during a trying period in national politics (debates in *Congressional Globe;* letters of contemporaries in *Annual Reports of the American Historical Association,* 1899, II, 1032, 1171; 1911, II, 138). A warm friend of Thomas Ritchie, the influential editor of the *Washington Union,* Bayly was sought by the friends of both Calhoun and Clay to enlist Ritchie's influence in their favor. He was instrumental in bringing Ritchie and Clay together; and thus aided materially in carrying through the compromises of 1850 (*Ibid.,* 1899, II, 955–56; C. H. Ambler, *Thomas Ritchie,* 1913, pp. 279 ff). Bayly was an affectionate husband and parent, and a kind master. He was an enthusiastic hunter, and kept a fine pack of foxhounds. He was over six feet tall, fair, and well proportioned. He was married to Evelyn H. May of Petersburg, Va.

[A few printed speeches and reports of Bayly's made in the Virginia Assembly are in the *Bull. Va. State Lib.*, 1917, X. Conway Robinson's *Va. Reports*, I, II (1843–44), contain his judicial decisions. Obituary remarks delivered in Cong. on June 27, 1856, are often inaccurate in details. References in *Ann. Reports, Am. Hist. Ass.* (note Index volume, 1914). Obit. notice in *Richmond Dispatch*, June 27, 1856. L. G. Tyler, *Letters and Times of the Tylers* (1885), I, 589; II, 284. Letter from his daughter, Mrs. Tiffany. Will at Accomac Court House dated July 7, 1853, probated July 28, 1856. The tombs of Judge and Mrs. Bayly are at Mount Custis.]

R. L. M.

BAYMA, JOSEPH (Nov. 9, 1816–Feb. 7, 1892), Jesuit priest, mathematician, physicist, was born at Ciriè, a township twelve miles northwest of Turin. During his childhood his residence was changed by his parents to Turin to insure for him a better education. Having completed his undergraduate studies at the Jesuit College of this city, he matriculated at the Royal Academy of Turin apparently intent on specializing in medicine, the profession of his father. Very shortly, however, he abandoned this project to enter the Jesuit novitiate at Chieti in February 1832. With an unusual combination of scientific and literary talents, at about this time he wrote an epic on Columbus in *ottava rima*, as well as poems in Latin. When his two years of probation, his biennium in philosophy, the prescribed years of professorship in the Jesuit colleges, and his course in theology had been finished, he was ordained to the priesthood in 1847. Thereupon he spent one year in missionary work in Algiers, ministering to the bodily and spiritual welfare of the sick in the Military Hospital. Recalled to Rome by his superiors, for a short period he acted as assistant to the noted astronomer, Fr. Angelo Secchi, then the director of the Osservatorio del Collegio Romano. This position he relinquished to collaborate with Fr. Enrico Vasco in editing the monumental work, *Il Ratio Studiorum adattato ai tempi presenti.* In 1852 he was designated as rector of the Episcopal Seminary of Bertinoro in the Romagna. During the same year he published *De studio religiosæ perfectionis excitando* in three volumes. Transferred to England in 1858, because of the religious intolerance then at its height in Italy, he filled the chair of philosophy at Stonyhurst College for eleven years.

In 1861 he printed for private circulation three volumes entitled *Philosophia Realis.* Until within a few years of his death he persisted in supplementing this work with additions and corrections. The revised copy never reached beyond the manuscript form. His chief work, *Elements of Molecular Mechanics,* appeared in 1866. Prof. Morgan, the mathematican, adjudged this treatise as "being a century before its time" and declared "that not seven of England's scientists were equal to understanding it." Bayma followed the main principles of Ruggiero Boscovich, the parent of modern dynamism, holding that physical matter is reducible to unextended points, materially and mathematically non-continuous. These point-like structures, some attractive, some repulsive, act on each other, and that at a distance, for contact there is none, and so are bound into molecules, and these in turn into bodies. But whereas Boscovich taught that if the distance between these points is infinitesimal, they are repulsive, while, if the distance, remaining always small, is nevertheless slightly increased, the repulsive force is initially decreased, then nullified, then at still greater distances transformed into a force of attraction, Bayma, on the other hand, contended that simple elements cannot be at once attractive at greater and repulsive at lesser distances. If a given element is attractive at any distance, he urged, it will be so at all distances; and if repulsive at any distance, it will be repulsive at all distances. Hence some of the points, he held, must be inherently attractive or repulsive. Objecting to this system of Bayma, metaphysicians urge that he fails to account for the extension and inertia of matter.

In 1869 Bayma was ordered to California to aid with his talents and counsel the newly established mission of California. On his arrival in San Francisco he was installed as president of St. Ignatius College. This position he held for three years, thereafter to become professor of higher mathematics at this same institution of learning. Impaired health forced him to seek rest in the Santa Clara Valley in 1880 and here he launched out, by way of diversion, on a new work on "Cycloidal Functions." Unable to complete these computations, he entrusted them to the Smithsonian Institution at Washington and thereafter they were reconsigned to the then director of Georgetown University Observatory. Apparently they still await publication. At about this same time Bayma brought out several elementary text-books in mathematics. He was taken ill about the middle of January 1892, and his recovery was early despaired of; he died at Santa Clara College on Feb. 7. He was a man of majestic frame and magnificent physique, a profound thinker, but in his personality as simple and guileless as a child.

[*Woodstock Letters,* XXI (privately printed); *De Claris Sodalibus Provinciæ Taurinensis* (Turin 1906);

Cath. Encyc. (1907), articles on "Bayma" and "Dynamism"; documents in archives of Georgetown University.] F. A. T—f.

BAYNHAM, WILLIAM (Dec. 7, 1749–Dec. 8, 1814), physician and surgeon, was the son of Dr. John Baynham of Carolina. After five years of study under Dr. Walker, considered one of the ablest surgeons in America, he went, at the age of twenty, to London. Here he entered St. Thomas's Hospital as a student and so distinguished himself that he soon gained the attention and later the close friendship of Else, the professor of anatomy. In 1772 he was employed, on Else's recommendation, by Charles Collignon, professor of anatomy at Cambridge, to dissect and prepare the subjects for his lectures. He continued in this employment for several winters and in the remaining part of each year was a partner with a surgeon of Margate, named Slater. In 1776 he accepted an offer from Else on the following terms: "He was to superintend the anatomical theatre and dissecting room, prepare bodies for his public demonstrations, make preparations for the museum and to instruct his pupils in the arts of dissecting, injecting, making anatomical preparations, etc., at a salary of eighty and ninety pounds the first two years and one hundred pounds a year for five succeeding years—at the expiration of which (having qualified himself in the interim for the office) Mr. Else was to relinquish to him the professor's chair or to take him as joint professor on equal terms as he might choose." Before the end of this period, however, Else died suddenly, in 1781. Baynham missed by a narrow margin election by the governors of the Hospital to the professorship thus left vacant. Disappointed in his expectations, he became a member of the "Company of Surgeons" and practised surgery for a few years in London and then returned to America, after an absence of sixteen years, and settled in Essex, Va. Here he built up a large practise, becoming especially distinguished in surgery. He performed several operations for stone, cataract, and extra-uterine conception. A detailed account of a case of the latter may be seen by reference to the *New York Medical and Surgical Journal,* I. He is credited with having performed the first successful operation for extra-uterine pregnancy. An alleged discovery by Baynham of a fine vascular membrane on the surface of the cutis immediately under the *rete mucosum* was incorrectly reported by Cruikshank and copied into Wistar's *Anatomy.* Baynham is said to have been slow and not very distinct in the enunciation of his ideas. He generally, on first acquaintance, disappointed those whose expectations had been raised and whose opinions of him had been formed from his reputation. But if not "a ready man," he was a "full and accurate one." He died at the age of sixty-six.

[The chief source of information is the anonymous biographical sketch which appeared in the *Phila. Jour. Medic. and Physic. Sci.,* IV, 1822, pp. 186–203. This sketch is composed of information from three sources and contains in addition a brief paragraph by the editor of the *Journal,* Dr. N. Chapman, who evidently desired to make the account as accurate as possible. The main part of the sketch is by a Virginian who the editor's note states was a friend of Baynham but "not in the profession." This friend supplements his account by extracts from "a Gentleman of high medical reputation both in Europe and America to whom we had applied for information on the subject" and who had been a fellow student of Baynham in London. The editor of the *Journal* in turn supplements the article by extracts from a statement furnished by a "near relative" of Baynham.] C. R. B.

BEACH, ALFRED ELY (Sept. 1, 1826–Jan. 1, 1896), inventor, editor, was born at Springfield, Mass., the son of Nancy (Day) and Moses Yale Beach [*q.v.*], cabinet-maker and inventor. He was six years old when his uncle, Benjamin H. Day [*q.v.*], established *The Sun* (New York), which was eventually purchased by Moses Yale Beach from his brother-in-law. Alfred E. Beach obtained an excellent idea of journalism while working for his father. The *Scientific American* had been founded by Rufus Porter in 1845. Young Beach desired to secure the property, which was unique, and for this purpose formed a partnership (1846) with Orson D. Munn and Salem H. Wales, under the title of Munn & Company—a partnership continued for almost fifty years. The young men purchased the paper, and in time the editorial chair was occupied by Beach. His great service was the technical and legal advice given to inventors. He was prolific in ideas and patented the following: typewriter, 1847; typewriter for the blind, 1857; cable railways, 1864; pneumatic tubes for mail and passengers, 1865; and a tunneling shield. His typewriter had considerable merit and some of its ideas are still used; such as the basket or pot arrangement of the type rods. In his last model the tape was embossed with a male and female die, such as is used in notarial presses. In 1856 the American Institute awarded him a gold medal for this device. He cannot be called the basic inventor of the typewriter, but his contribution was substantial. Though his cable traction system was probably never used, he lived to see the general plan adopted. He likewise invented a pneumatic carrier system. He gave demonstrations of this system in 1867 at the Fair of the American Institute and people rode 107 feet in a tube like those in London and the Hudson Tubes in New York, except that air instead of electricity was used as the motive power. Today the same principle is utilized in mail-tubes and cash-carriers. In 1869 he obtained a charter for a tube to carry mail from Liberty Street, New York, to the Harlem River, with the proviso that the street must not be disturbed. This clause led him to perfect the tunneling shield, which had already been used by Brunel for the Thames Tunnel in 1843. He built a section of an underground road a block long between Warren Street and Murray Street. A 100-horsepower blower was used to propel the car. No profit could be derived under the charter and the idea was finally abandoned, but all may pass through the actual remains of the tunnel which now forms the City Hall station of the Brooklyn-Manhattan Subway. On June 30, 1847, he married Harriet Eliza, daughter of John F. and Harriet (Converse) Holbrook, at Boston, Mass.

[Biog. accounts may be found in H. Ely, *Records of the Descendants of Nathaniel Ely* (1885), p. 386; in *Sci. American*, Jan. 11, 18, 1896; and in *N. Y. Evening Sun*, Sept. 1, 1926. For pneumatic tunnel, see *Sci. American Suppl.*, no. 764, Aug. 23, 1890; for tunneling shield, *Suppl.* no. 574, Jan. 1, 1887; for typewriter, W. Kaempffert, *Pop. Hist. of Am. Invention* (1924), I, 264, 282, 452; II, 366, 372; and E. W. Byrn, *Progress of Invention in the Nineteenth Century* (1900), pp. 174–75, 347.]

A. A. H.

BEACH, FREDERICK CONVERSE (Mar. 27, 1848–June 18, 1918), patent solicitor, publisher, was born on Columbia Heights, Brooklyn, N. Y. His heritage was that of journalism handed down from his grandfather, Moses Yale Beach [*q.v.*]. When he was quite young, his parents, Alfred Ely Beach [*q.v.*] and Harriet Eliza (Holbrook) Beach, moved to Stratford, Conn. A college education was apparently fixed upon for the youth and he received his preparatory education at the public schools in Bridgeport. At the age of seventeen he entered Yale University, graduating in 1868 from Sheffield Scientific School. Two undertakings of his father probably directed young Beach toward invention and the patent business. One of these was his father's typewriter invention and the other his construction of a section of passenger subway, operated by compressed air, beneath Broadway in New York City between Warren and Murray Streets. While still in college Beach, who had become interested in photography, brought to the attention of the United States commissioner of patents the utility and practicability of the photo-lithographic process for patent specifications and suggested a plan of use that was subsequently adopted. Immediately after his graduation from college he represented his father's company, which had started a patent business besides publishing a technical journal, in Washington, D. C. Within a few years he returned to New York for the company and continued in business there. Upon the death of his father in 1896, Beach succeeded him as a director of the Scientific American Company, which office he held to the day of his death. His interest in this business was intense, particularly in those phases pertaining to invention and patents, and in these he showed an unflagging devotion that made him a most valuable business associate. In addition to these several interests he engaged for a time in the manufacture of electrical instruments. He was also vice-president of the Union Waxed and Parchment Paper Company, and was for many years president of the Postal Progress League, which was largely instrumental in bringing about the establishment of the parcel-post system in the United States. Beach's hobby was photography. He was one of the first amateur photographers of note in the United States, his interest leading him to help found the New York Society of Amateur Photographers, now the Camera Club of New York, in 1884. Later, in 1889, with the assistance of several other amateurs, he started a magazine called the *American Amateur Photographer*, later changed to *American Photography*, of which he was editor for many years. In 1902 he became editor-in-chief of the *Encyclopedia Americana*. In 1875 he married Margaret A. Gilbert, of Stratford, Conn.

[*Scientific American*, vol. CXVIII, No. 25; *Am. Photography*, vol. XII, No. 8; *Who's Who in America*, 1916–17.]

C. W. M.

BEACH, MOSES SPERRY (Oct. 5, 1822–July 25, 1892), journalist, inventor, was the second of the eight children of Moses Yale Beach [*q.v.*] and his wife, Nancy Day. He was born at Springfield, Mass., at a time when his father, then only twenty-two years old, was at work on a variety of inventions. When he was twelve years old, his father began his connection with the New York *Sun*, and the boy was well taught by him the craft of the composing and press-rooms. In 1845 Moses Sperry Beach became joint owner, with George Roberts, of the *Boston Daily Times* but in a few months he returned to New York and, on Oct. 2, 1845, with his brother, Alfred Ely Beach [*q.v.*], entered the new firm of Moses Y. Beach & Sons, owners of the *Sun*. During the same year he was married to Chloe Buckingham of Waterbury, Conn. In December 1848 the elder Beach retired, leaving the property to the sons. On Apr. 6, 1852, Alfred Ely Beach withdrew from the *Sun,* and Moses Sperry Beach, then only thirty years old, became sole proprietor of the newspaper. His administration was characterized by the same enterprise and liberality that marked his father's. The *Sun* supported Buchanan in 1856, but was not pro-slavery. It denounced the Dred Scott decision and declared that John Brown belonged in a madhouse rather than on the gallows. Early in 1860, swayed perhaps by his chief editorial writer, John Vance, Beach supported Douglas against Lincoln, although the *Sun* had advised the Democratic party to nominate Sam Houston for president. Before the election, however, Beach turned over the *Sun* (Aug. 6, 1860) to a group of men, headed by the wealthy Archibald M. Morrison, whose intent was to transform this popular daily into a semi-religious newspaper. The price was $100,000 for good will, with a rental to be paid for the building and machinery, Beach retaining all physical ownership. As the new control not only urged the Union generals not to attack on Sunday (*Sun,* July 23, 1861) but refused to accept advertisements on the day of rest, the enterprise failed. On Jan. 1, 1862, Beach announced: "Once more I write myself Editor and sole proprietor of the New York *Sun.* My day dream of rural enjoyment is broken." He set out energetically to recoup the paper's loss of popularity and advertising income. He was able to lower expenses by adopting the stereotyping process and by reducing the number of columns from seven to five. The *Sun* had sold for one cent a copy since its foundation in 1833, but the Civil War sent the price of news-print to twenty-four cents a pound and Beach in 1863 announced with regret, mixed with humor, that thereafter the price of the paper would be "one cent in gold, or two cents in currency." The price remained two cents thereafter for fifty-three years. Beach never pretended to give to the *Sun's* public a news service such as Bennett offered in the *Herald,* profound editorial articles such as Greeley printed in the *Tribune,* or the thorough political news that marked the *Times* under Raymond. The *Sun* was a working man's newspaper and Beach catered to his readers by offering five or six columns of condensed news, one column of editorial, one of jokes and miscellany, one or two of fiction, and nine or ten of advertising. Fiction was one of his specialities and he bought liberally from the authors of the best-sellers of the time, Mary Jane Holmes, Horatio Alger, Jr., H. Warren Trowbridge, and Ann S. Stephens. On the physical side of newspaper production Beach made important contributions, inheriting as he did his father's talent for mechanics. He invented a device for feeding paper to presses from a roll, thus doing away with the use of flat sheets; apparatus for wetting the paper before printing and for cutting after printing; and he is credited with being the first to print both sides of the sheet at once.

His desire for "rural enjoyment" was so deep-seated that in January 1868, when he was only forty-five years old, he sold the *Sun* to a syndicate headed by Charles A. Dana, retaining a small portion of the stock. The price was $175,000. With this and the accumulated profits of previous years he was able to find the leisure he wished. In 1873 he made an extended tour through Norway, Sweden, and Russia. The rest of his life was passed at his large estate at Peekskill, N. Y., where he died at the age of seventy. Beach was a man of dignity, possessor of a pleasing manner and an even temper that reflected itself in his strong, handsome face. He passed almost unruffled through a stormy period of American journalism, perhaps because he was more deeply interested in publishing than in politics. The kindness of his nature is reflected in an incident set down by Mark Twain in *The Innocents Abroad.* Beach was one of the tourists on the immortal voyage of the steamer *Quaker City* in 1867. At Jaffa the Americans were hailed by forty destitute New Englanders—men, women, and children—who had been lured to Palestine by "Prophet" Adams. They begged to be taken at least as far as Alexandria, Egypt—anywhere to get away from Adams and his misguided colony. On reaching Alexandria Beach inquired how much it would cost to send the penniless forty back to Maine by way of Liverpool and, on learning that $1,500 would cover the expense, paid it out of his own pocket—"an unselfish act of benevolence," as Mark Twain called it. Beach, who was a warm admirer and friend of Henry Ward Beecher, brought back from that voyage an olive tree from the Mount of Olives. The wood was made into a pulpit-stand for Plymouth Church, Brooklyn, and still is there.

[Most of the material of this sketch is taken from *The Story of the Sun* by Frank M. O'Brien (1918); cf. also H. Ely, *Records of the Descendants of Nathaniel Ely* (1885), p. 385.]

F. M. O.

BEACH, MOSES YALE (Jan. 15, 1800–July 19, 1868), journalist, inventor, was a descendant of John Beach who came from England about 1635 and settled in the New Haven colony. The father, grandfather, and great-grandfather of Moses Yale Beach all bore the name Moses, the first of them being the son of Thomas, son of John. Each Moses Beach was born on and worked in succession a farm at Wallingford, Conn. (C. H. S. Davis, *History of Wallingford,* 1870). Moses Yale Beach was the son of Moses Sperry Beach and Lucretia Yale, daughter of Capt. Elihu and Lucretia (Stanley) Yale. His mother died when he was four months old and his early years were directed by his stepmother. At the age of ten, according to Dr. Davis, the boy "took charge of considerable of the outdoor work on the farm, besides going a long distance to school" and "from 4 o'clock in the morning until 11 o'clock at night he was generally up and doing, yet found leisure to exercise his mechanical ingenuity in the manufacture of playthings for himself and others." When he was fourteen years old he was bound as an apprentice to Daniel Dewey, a cabinet-maker of Hartford, Conn. The lad's industry was so great that he soon won from his master a contract by which he received two cents an hour for overtime work—a concession which Beach used to describe, in his years of affluence, as the happiest incident of his whole business career. He later bargained with Dewey to buy his freedom at the age of eighteen years for $400; and so diligent was he in extra work at two cents an hour that in 1818 he not only released himself from his apprenticeship but had $100 of business capital. He worked a short time as a journeyman at Northampton and then formed a partnership with another cabinet-maker named Loveland. Their work received a prize from the Franklin Institute. On Nov. 19, 1819, he married Nancy Day of West Springfield, Mass. His next ten years were a struggle for success in the field of mechanics. He invented an engine, the power of which came from explosions of gunpowder. When this failed he turned to steam, then in its early stages, as the motive power for a boat which he intended to run on the Connecticut River from Springfield to Hartford, but his pecuniary resources were too limited to let him make a success of this enterprise. His next invention was a rag-cutting machine for use in paper mills. This would have meant a fortune for him if he had taken out a patent in time, as the process is still used. As it was, his device enabled him to obtain an interest in a paper-mill at Saugerties, N. Y., whither he removed in 1829. This, like his previous ventures, was not a financial success. Five years later Beach went to New York City to join his wife's brother, Benjamin H. Day [*q.v.*], the owner of the *Sun,* as manager of the mechanical department of that newspaper. Day had started the *Sun* on Sept. 3, 1833, and in January 1834 took in his principal reporter, George W. Wisner, as a partner. In 1835 Beach bought Wisner's share for $5,200, and in 1838 Day's interest for $40,000. The *Sun* was then popular, having a circulation of 30,000 copies daily, but its profits, which at one time under Day had reached $20,000 a year, were small. It appeared for a time as if Beach would record another failure. "The first six months after he became entire owner of the paper," says Dr. Davis, "it did not prove as profitable as he had expected and he was ready to sell it out; and he offered it and all the property he then possessed if anyone would take it off his hands and pay his obligations (about $20,000) to Mr. Day; but, not succeeding in effecting a sale he went to work with renewed ardor and before two years had passed the last dollar was paid off." At the age of thirty-eight Beach's unflagging industry was at last rewarded by the beginning of real success.

The following ten years were as busy as any preceding decade of his life. The *Sun,* although first in the field of "penny papers," had to face the competition of the *New York Herald,* which James Gordon Bennett started in 1835. Though enterprising, Beach lacked Bennett's audacity. He established a ship news-service, the *Sun's* own sailing vessels meeting incoming steamships down the bay and there obtaining the freshest news from Europe. Beach used horse expresses to bring important news from Albany "with unparalleled expedition, in spite of wind, hail and rain," as the *Sun* said on Jan. 6, 1841, when it was able to print Gov. Seward's message twenty hours after the Governor presented it to the legislature. Beach ran special trains from Baltimore to New York with the news of the National Democratic Convention of 1844, beating the United States mail train by an hour or more. When Beach bought for the *Sun,* in 1842, the building at the southwest corner of Nassau and Fulton Sts., he built a huge pigeon house which stood for half a century on the roof. There lived the birds that brought to the *Sun* news from the ships at Sandy Hook, from Albany, and even from Washington (*Sun,* Dec. 14, 1843). The craze for speed manifested by Beach and Bennett is supposed to have inspired Edgar Allan Poe to write the "Balloon-Hoax," which he sold to Beach and which appeared in the *Sun* on Apr. 13, 1844. In this fabrication Poe made it appear that the aeronauts Monck Mason and Robert Holland, the novelist Harrison Ainsworth, and five other Englishmen had crossed the Atlantic in a dirigible balloon in three days, landing near Charleston, S. C. The hoax caused as great a sensation as the "Moon Hoax," which the *Sun* had printed eight years before; but in this case Beach made no effort to prolong the delusion, admitting two days after the first publication that Poe had merely tried to satirize the passion for speed.

Most of Beach's energies were directed toward the collection of legitimate news. He had a London correspondent who ran a special horse-express with the news-letters from London to the ships at Bristol. He sent a reporter to cover Webster's speech at the unveiling of the Bunker Hill monument. In the Mexican War, when news was delayed between Mobile, where Mexican tidings arrived by steamer, and Montgomery, he established a special railroad news-service between those Alabama cities. The war showed Beach how the New York newspapers, each acting for itself, were wasting much money. At a conference in his office the *Sun,* the *Herald,* the *Tribune,* the *Courier and Enquirer,* the *Express,* and the *Journal of Commerce* founded the New York Associated Press, designed to coöperate in the gathering of news in Washington, Albany, Boston, Philadelphia, New Orleans, and other news-centers. This conference also formed the Harbor Association, a syndicate through which the New York newspapers were able, with one fleet of news-boats, to do the work in which half a dozen fleets had been employed. Beach is also credited with inventing the syndicated newspaper article, for in 1841, when the *Sun* received by special messenger President Tyler's message to Congress, Beach printed in his office a special message-edition (all alike except the title heads) for twenty other newspapers, which were thus saved the delay and cost of setting up the message. He was the first American publisher to issue a "European edition." This was the *American Sun,* a weekly, issued in 1848, and sold abroad at twelve shillings a year. He also established the *Weekly Sun,* printed every Saturday and circulated among farmers at one dollar a year. Another venture was the *Illustrated Sun and Monthly Literary Journal,* a sixteen-page magazine lavishly illustrated with woodcuts. He personally wrote a brochure entitled *The Wealth of New York: a Table of the Wealth of the Wealthy Citizens of New York City Who Are Estimated to be Worth One Hundred Thousand Dollars or Over, with Brief Biographical Notices.* Several editions of this were published between 1841 and 1856. The price of this early "Who's Who" was twenty-five cents. Copies of it are in the New York Public Library.

Beach devoted himself more to the success of his newspapers than to the political quarrels which marked most journals of his day. His principal adversary was Horace Greeley, who founded the *New York Tribune* in 1841, three years after Beach became owner of the *Sun.* The newsboys of these rival journals fought in the streets, and Greeley's *Tribune* denounced Beach's *Sun* as "the slimy and venomous instrument of Locofocoism, Jesuitical and deadly in politics and grovelling in morals." But the truth was that Beach was an honorable man of business, bent on keeping his *Sun* in its enviable place as the most popular newspaper in the world. On its tenth birthday, Sept. 3, 1843, he was employing eight editors and reporters, twenty compositors, sixteen pressmen and one hundred carriers. The *Sun's* circulation was 38,000. Beach was compelled to buy a new dress of type every three months, for stereotyping had not arrived. In 1848, when Beach turned the newspaper over to his sons, Moses Sperry Beach [*q.v.*] and Alfred Ely Beach [*q.v.*], he anounced that the penny paper, then only fifteen years old, had a circulation of 50,000, "together with the largest cash advertising patronage on this continent." Beach had brought the *Sun* from a tiny three-column paper to one of eight columns, although he never increased the number of pages beyond the original four. Charles A. Dana [*q.v.*], who bought the *Sun* from the Beach family in 1868, wrote of Moses Yale Beach that he was "a business man and a newspaper manager rather than what we now understand as a journalist," but added that "under the stimulus of Mr. Beach's energetic intellect, aided by the cheapness of its price, the *Sun* became in his hands an important and profitable establishment."

In 1846 President Polk commissioned Beach to go to Mexico with a view to arranging terms of peace. The errand was halted by a false report that announced the defeat of Gen. Taylor by Santa Anna. Beach retired from business life in December 1848 because of ill health, and spent his remaining years in his native town of Wallingford, where he died at the age of sixty-eight. He left five sons and three daughters.

[Most of the information not otherwise credited is taken from *The Story of the Sun,* by Frank M. O'Brien (1918); cf. also H. Ely, *Records of the Descendants of Nathaniel Ely* (1885), and *N.Y. Tribune,* July 20, 1868.]

F. M. O.

BEACH, WILLIAM AUGUSTUS (Dec. 9, 1809–June 21, 1884), lawyer, was a descendant of Thomas Beach, the youngest of three brothers who came to New Haven from England in the ship *Elizabeth and Anna* in June 1638 and settled at Milford, Conn. He was the son of Miles and Cynthia (Warren) Beach, and was born at Saratoga Springs, N. Y., where his father had established a mercantile business. His education was received there and at Partridge's Military Institute, Norwich, Vt., after which he entered the office of his uncle, Judge Warren, studying law under the direct supervision of the latter. He was admitted to the bar in August 1833 and opened an office at Saratoga Springs. His father was influential, and the son soon acquired a good connection in the community. Saratoga Springs was then one of the legal centers of the state and Beach became known as a successful advocate and a tireless worker. He was appointed district attorney for Saratoga County, Sept. 11, 1843, and held this office till June 1847, acquiring an intimate knowledge of criminal law and a wide reputation for impressive oratory. In 1851 he moved to Troy, where he obtained a large practise, being particularly effective in jury cases. His fame extended beyond his own county and in 1865 he was retained to defend Col. North before a military commission in Washington on a charge of tampering with the soldiers' votes at the 1864 presidential election. Contrary to all expectations he persuaded the commission that they had no jurisdiction. This was probably the greatest purely forensic feat of his career. He also became associated with the Vanderbilt interests and appeared with C. A. Rapallo on behalf of Commodore Vanderbilt in the Erie Railroad litigation—"the Five Million Dollar Suit"—so impressing his client that, on the elevation of Rapallo to the bench in 1870, Beach was given a general retainer by the Commodore and removed to New York City. For the next fourteen years he appeared as counsel in almost all the *causes célèbres* of the period. In 1872 he was leading counsel for Judge G. G. Barnard, impeached on charges of judicial corruption by the state Assembly before the Senate and court of appeals sitting at Saratoga Springs as a court of impeachment, and though Barnard was convicted, the ability of the defense was universally recognized. One of his few conspicuous failures was in the Tilton-Beecher case, where he was leading counsel for the plaintiff. His final speech here occupied thirteen days whereas "he could have said all that should have been said in a day and with much better effect." He appeared for the defense in most of the notorious murder cases of his period in New York, his particular genius being perhaps more happily exhibited in this class of contest than on the civil side of the courts. Beach excelled as a mere orator. His command of language was wonderful, his sentences exquisitely modeled, his gestures graceful, and his voice musical. He had, however, grave defects, chief of which was a complete lack of humor. Irving Browne said of him that "his side of the case was always a funereal function, conducted with an oppressive and appalling gravity!" His efforts were often marred by outbursts of invective and aggressive displays, symptomatic of his want of tact and control. His intellectual horizon was not extensive, he was a very weak cross-examiner, and his knowledge of the law, though varied, was never profound. He had no interests outside his profession. His own remark that he had always been a wide reader of worthless literature probably accurately expressed the depth of his general culture. In physical appearance he was tall, athletic, and handsome. "He had one of the coldest, most impassive and sphinx-like countenances that I ever beheld. . . . His bearing and dress were impressive. There was a gravity about him, a kind of *noli me tangere* characteristic that forbade anything like familiarity. . . . He invariably wore a double-breasted coat tightly buttoned and there was a sort of military erectness and precision about him which attracted attention and rendered him conspicuous" (Theron G. Strong, p. 285).

[The newspapers of the period are perhaps the best source of information as to Beach's legal achievements. An excellent but somewhat eulogistic review of his life appeared in the *Green Bag,* II, 509, and Irving Browne contributed a very good character sketch to the *Albany Law Jour.,* XLII, 468. Theron G. Strong, in *Landmarks of a Lawyer's Lifetime* (1914), pp. 285–88, has some valuable criticism of his legal career based on personal knowledge. See also E. R. Mann, *The Bench and Bar of Saratoga County* (1876), p. 310; *Central Law Jour.,* III, 36; *Hist. of the Bench and Bar of N. Y.* (1897), ed. by D. McAdam *et al.,* I, 256.]

H. W. H. K.

BEACH, WOOSTER (1794–Jan. 28, 1868), medical agitator, born in Trumbull, Conn., received the usual scanty education of those who then attended the rural schools. Late in his teens he was apprenticed to Dr. Jacob Tidd, a German herb collector and physician of Hunterdon County, N. J., with whom he remained until Tidd's death in 1825. He then moved to New York and matriculated at the College of Physicians and Surgeons, and later, Mar. 7, 1832, was elected member of the New York County Medical Society (*List of Members,* 1806–61, Albany). At the age of thirty-one Beach began to write prolifically in many fields of medical thought, and though not always original he was unusual in his defiance of authority and in the relentless energy with which he urged his views. He opposed blood-letting and purging with mercurials, and preached that most diseases would respond more readily to nature's remedies, such as herbs and roots. In 1833 he published a three-volume work, *The American Practice of Medicine,* which was, as expressed in the subtitle, "A Treatise on the Character, Causes, Symptoms, Morbid Appearances, and Treatment of the Diseases of Men, Women and Children of All Climates, on Vegetable or Botanical Principles; Containing Also a Treatise on Materia Medica and Pharmacy, with an Appendix on Cholera, etc." This text-book had a large circulation and is noteworthy for being the first systematic compendium of medical practise published in America in which pathological changes were correlated with disease processes. Copies of the work were sent to many crowned heads of Europe, and the author received much regal praise, all of which was duly printed in the second edition. There was an abridgment of the treatise in 1846, which passed through at least fourteen editions. The last edition of *The American Practice* (1852) brought heavy losses on the author because of the large number of colored plates illustrating pathological conditions. One may also mention Beach's *Treatise on Pulmonary Consumption, Phthisis Pulmonalis, with Remarks on Bronchitis* (1840), and *An Improved System of Midwifery* (1851). At least a dozen other less important medical works also came from his pen. In addition to Beach's medical activities he for many years published two broadsheets, the *Telescope* and the *Ishmaelite,* and through these channels he had an outlet for many of his novel views and speculations on religion, sociology, and medicine. In the heat of argument a friend once referred to Beach as an "eclectic." He replied quickly, "You have given me the term which I have wanted; I am an Eclectic." So enamoured was he of the epithet that in 1836 he founded an *Eclectic Medical Journal,* and in 1855 became president of the National Eclectic Medical Association. The *Journal* and the Society have had a long record and both are still in existence (1927), but the *Journal* is not recognized by the American Medical Association. Unfortunately Beach's followers attempted to extol him as a prophet and in this way did much to injure his reputation. Beach emphasized early the value of hospital practise for those who would keep abreast of medical progress. In 1828 he opened the United States Infirmary on Eldredge St., New York, where he had a large out-patient clinic. He was the founder of the New York Medical Academy which later became the Reformed Medical Society of the United States. In 1830 he helped to establish a medical department in the new university at Worthington, Ohio. Beach was not unlike Paracelsus: he had brilliant flashes but even his best contributions were marred by a vain boasting and exaggeration. His protests against over-dosing with mercury, though they served a useful purpose, were untruthful in grossly exaggerating the harmful effects of that metal, and this unfortunate tendency is to be found in many of his controversial writings. His logic was often faulty and he allowed himself to be carried away by absurd prejudices. To the end of his life he refused to use a stethoscope (*American Practice,* 1852 ed., I, 529), but he employed direct ear-to-chest auscultation. Though his faults were many he worked unremittingly and wrote with admirable devotion to his subject. Had he possessed a broader cultural background he would undoubtedly have reached greater heights. In 1823 Beach married Eliza de Grove, and had two sons. The drowning of his second son led to a physical and mental break-down and he died shortly thereafter. His oldest son, Wooster Beach, Jr., practised medicine.

[Beach has left biog. material in the introductions to his various works. He frequently gives dates of important events in his life (see esp. *The Family Physician,* 4th ed., 1844, pp. 5–11), and in the 1852 edition of the *Am. Practice* he devotes fifty closely printed pages to a description of his trip to Europe in 1848–49. A. Wilder, follower of the Eclectic school, has written extensively of Beach in his *Hist. of Medicine* (1901), and also in the *Eclectic Medic. Jour.,* 1893, LIII, 113–21, and *Medic. Advocate,* II, 235–37, but these are all injudicious estimates of the man, with fulsome praise; obituary in *N. Y. Herald,* Jan. 30, 1868.]

J. F. F.

BEADLE, WILLIAM HENRY HARRISON (Jan. 1, 1838–Nov. 13, 1915), educator, was born in a log cabin, built by his father, close to the Wabash River in Parke County, Ind. His parents, James Ward Beadle and Elizabeth Bright, had moved after their marriage from Kentucky to the frontier in western Indiana. His early life was typical of the frontier. He learned to use the axe, plow, and rifle, got his education in a log schoolhouse and later in the graded school at the county seat, and enjoyed reading books in the township public library and others which his father brought back from his river trips to New Orleans. His father offered him a farm, but he chose to take instead a thousand dollars for a college education. Entering the University of Michigan in the fall of 1857, he specialized in civil engineering. After his graduation in June 1861 he entered the Union army as first lieutenant of Company A, 31st Indiana Volunteer Infantry. He was repeatedly promoted, and was given the rank of brevet brigadier-general when he was discharged, Mar. 26, 1866. During the war, on May 18, 1863, he had married Ellen S. Chapman at Albion, Mich. Beadle attended the University of Michigan Law School for a year after his discharge and received his LL.B. in March 1867. After practising law in Evansville, Ind., and Boscobel, Wis., he was appointed, March 1869, surveyor general of Dakota territory. As he rode up the broad Missouri Valley to Yankton, the territorial capital, he talked with his predecessor about the natural resources of the state that was to be. "On that journey the school lands were mentioned and I then opened to my companion the theory that these were the great trust of the future commonwealth and should be absolutely secured from waste and cheap sales" ("Memoirs," p. 90). All of Beadle's public services in Dakota territory assisted in the accomplishment of this purpose. In the next four years he became acquainted with the country and early settlers. As secretary of the commission which drew up the code of 1877, he gained valuable experience in clear exposition of complicated ideas. The responsibility for passing the code through the legislature fell largely on Beadle through his chairmanship of the judiciary committee in the House. He accepted the superintendency of public instruction in 1879 with the condition that he "should stand strongly for the principle that no school lands should ever be sold for less than their appraised value, and never for less than ten dollars an acre" (*Ibid.*, p. 169), when statehood was attained. For the next six years Beadle was busily engaged in organizing new schools necessitated by the rapid expansion of settlement, in introducing the township unit of administration, and in holding teachers' institutes. On every occasion, in conversation or on the platform he talked about the protection of the school lands. Many opposed the ten-dollar minimum, as only one state, Colorado, in 1875, had placed a limit as high as $2.50 per acre, and land could be bought in Iowa in the early 80's for $2.50 to $4.00 an acre. But Rev. Joseph Ward, missionary pastor in Yankton since 1868 and founder of Yankton College, gave his whole-hearted support to the movement from the beginning and proved a valuable advocate in the constitutional convention of 1885, where the real test came. To win in the convention it was necessary to get the unanimous indorsement of the committee on school lands. Beadle was not a member of the convention, but was commandeered by the committee to sit with them and give advice. Taking the initiative he drafted an article embodying his main ideas. "It was that formal and complete document, not oral discussions and misunderstandings, that won the case" (*Ibid.*, p. 214). Beadle's careful explanation and Ward's persuasion converted a hostile majority, and the report of the committee was accepted by the convention shortly before adjournment. Thus the matter was settled, as this constitution in 1889 became the state constitution. So strongly was Congress impressed by this movement for the ten-dollar minimum that it required a similar provision for the admission of North Dakota, Montana, and Washington in 1889 and of Idaho and Wyoming in 1890. Beadle continued his educational service by his able and inspiring presidency of the Madison State Normal School from 1889 to 1905 and as professor of history until his retirement in 1912. He died in San Francisco, while on a visit to his daughter. A statue of Beadle, paid for by the contributions of the school children of the state, stands to-day in the capitol building at Pierre with the inscription, "Wm. H. H. Beadle, educator. He saved the school lands."

[The chief source is "Personal Memoirs of Wm. H. H. Beadle," *S. Dak. Hist. Colls.* (1906), III, 85–265; see O. W. Coursey, *A Complete Biog. Sketch of Gen. Wm. Henry Harrison Beadle* (1913); obituary in *Sioux Falls* (S. D.) *Daily Argus Leader*, Nov. 15, 1915. For Beadle's Civil War service, see *Official Records*, ser. I, vol. XXXVII, pt. 2 (1891), and ser. III, vol. V (1900).]

R. G. W.

BEAL, WILLIAM JAMES (Mar. 11, 1833–May 12, 1924), botanist, teacher, was born at Adrian, Mich., the son of a Quaker, William Beal, and of Rachel Comstock. Beal's was the day of homespun clothes, log houses, wooden plows, and this early environment made him through later life economical of time, equipment and energy, and tirelessly industrious. The waste of forests seen in his boyhood made him a conservationist, while his knowledge of the farm boy was invaluable to him in his teaching. He entered the University of Michigan with the class of 1859, and acquired a smattering of zoölogy and botany taught entirely from books. With the degree of A.B. he went to Union Springs, N. Y., in 1859, teaching till 1868. During vacations he studied at Harvard, where Agassiz took him in hand and made a thoroughgoing naturalist of him. Then Beal went to Asa Gray, who led him through systematic botany and what little was then known of the physiology and morphology of plants, converting him easily to the Darwinian theory of evolution. In 1865 he received his S.B. from Harvard, and in 1875 his M.S. from the old University of Chicago, where he went to teach botany in 1868. In 1871 he began teaching at the Michigan Agricultural College, where he continued until his retirement in 1910. Beal is usually considered one of the three pioneers who grew up in the "old botany" and by their efforts helped to usher in the "new botany." He probably did not produce so many botanists as did Bessey and Burrill, but his influence on the raw farm boy was on the side of science. He would drill his students for hours in the Latin names of plants, because he felt that they stood in need of formal training. But he was one with them in his homely use of proverbs and wise saws, the most characteristic of which was his "Keep on squintin'," which he gave to beginning students exasperated with microscopic scrutiny. His publications are said to have numbered more than 1,200; of these, *The New Botany* (1881) had the greatest pedagogic influence. The *Grasses of North America* (2 vols., 1887) in its first edition had to be published at the author's expense, but so great was its popularity among amateurs that it readily found a publisher for subsequent editions. Unfortunately for systematic botany, the book was full of inaccuracies and has thrown much confusion into the tangled nomenclature of the grasses. *Seed Dispersal* (1898) was also immensely popular, and scientifically sound. In *The History of Michigan Agricultural College* (1915), "Pioneer Life in Southern Michigan in the Thirties," chapter IV of *An American Pioneer of Science*, and "Studying the Sciences Fifty Years Ago," in *Michigan Alumnus*, February 1917, he gave historically valuable glimpses of the times. In 1887 he procured legislation creating the Forestry Commission. He founded the college forest preserve in 1875 and in 1906 planted its "Pinetum." To him the college owes its well-stocked botanical garden. He had, it is said, but three antipathies: for alcohol, tobacco, and quack-grass. One might add, as a fourth, hatred of idleness, for after his retirement, when too feeble to walk alone, he would sit and saw up firewood. He died in his sleep, after a paralytic stroke, at the home of his son-in-law, Ray Stannard Baker, at Amherst. His wife was a childhood friend, Hannah Proud, whom he married Sept. 2, 1863.

[R. S. and J. B. Baker, *An Am. Pioneer of Sci.* (privately printed, 1925); *Mich. Alumnus*, May 22, 1924, pp. 946–47; E. A. Bessey, "W. J. Beal" (with portr.) in *Bot. Gazette*, Mar. 1925, pp. 103–06; C. W. McKibbin, "W. J. Beal, Michigan's Pioneer Forester," *Am. Forests and Forest Life*, Apr. 1924, pp. 216–17.]

D. C. P.

BEALE, EDWARD FITZGERALD (Feb. 4, 1822–Apr. 22, 1893), "pioneer in the path of empire," as Bayard Taylor termed him, was born in the District of Columbia. His father was George Beale, a paymaster in the navy, who had won a Congressional Medal for gallantry in the battle on Lake Champlain, Sept. 11, 1814; and his mother was Emily Truxtun, youngest daughter of the famous Commodore. He was a student at Georgetown College when, at the solicitation of his widowed mother, he was appointed by President Jackson to the Naval School, from which, in 1842, he graduated. Early in October 1845, he sailed on the frigate *Congress*, under Commodore Stockton, for California, but twenty days later was sent back with important dispatches. After a long and roundabout voyage, the first of many government missions that were to carry him tens of thousands of miles, he reached Washington in the middle of March 1846. Promoted to the grade of master, he sailed for Panama and overtook the *Congress* at Callao, Peru, in May. Hostilities with Mexico had already begun when the vessel reached Monterey on July 20, and he was at once detached to serve with the land forces. He was with the small body under Lieut. Gillespie that left San Diego and joined Kearny's column just before the disastrous battle of San Pasqual (Dec. 6), and was one of the three men (his Delaware Indian servant and Kit Carson being the other two) who, after the battle, performed the desperately heroic act of creeping through the Mexican lines and carrying the news of Kearny's plight to Stockton.

Two months later (Feb. 9, 1847), still suffering greatly from the effects of that adventure, he was sent east, in the company of Carson and a small guard, with dispatches. He reached Washington about the first of June, and in October was a witness for Frémont in the court martial of "the Pathfinder" instituted by Kearny. As a bearer of dispatches he was now to make, within the short space of two years, six journeys from ocean to ocean. On the second of these (July–September 1848), when he crossed Mexico at imminent danger of his life, he brought the first authentic news of the gold discoveries and a bag of the precious metal. After the fourth journey he was married, June 27, 1849, to Mary, the daughter of Representative Samuel Edwards, of Chester, Pa., but immediately started west again. In December he was back in Washington, where for a time he rested. On Aug. 3, 1850, he was made a lieutenant. In the following May he resigned from the navy and returned to California as a manager for W. H. Aspinwall and Commodore Stockton, who had acquired large properties there. By November 1852 he was again in Washington. President Fillmore appointed him superintendent of Indian affairs for California and Nevada, and Congress, on Mar. 3, 1853, appropriated $250,000 for making effective a project of his for improving the condition of his wards. With his kinsman, Gwinn Harris Heap, and a party of twelve others he left Westport May 6, making on the way a preliminary survey for a railroad, and, traversing southern Colorado and southern Utah, reached Los Angeles on Aug. 22. He held this office until 1856, receiving from the governor of the state the appointment of brigadier-general of militia. In the following year, by appointment of President Buchanan, he commanded an expedition to survey a wagon road from Fort Defiance, N. Mex., to the Colorado River, using for transport a part of the camel herd he had persuaded the Government to import from Tunis. In 1858–59 he surveyed another road to the Colorado River, this time from Fort Smith, Ark. He was appointed, shortly after Lincoln's inauguration, surveyor general of California and Nevada, and, though he asked instead for service in the army, was induced to retain this post until the end of the war. He then retired to the Rancho Tejon, an immense tract that he had bought near the present Bakersfield. Later he bought the Decatur house in Washington, and from about 1870 usually spent half the year in each home. In 1876 President Grant appointed him minister to Austria-Hungary, a post that he held for a year. A Republican, somewhat active in politics, he was strongly but unsuccessfully supported by Grant and others for appointment by President Arthur as secretary of the navy. He died at his Washington home. "A sparkling combination of scholar, gentleman and Indian fighter," Charles Nordhoff described him after a visit to his ranch in 1872 (*California*, 1872, pp. 229–30). Between Carson and himself, each of whom had saved the other's life, existed a bond of the tenderest fellowship. He was the faithful ally of Frémont, and the intimate friend of Bayard Taylor, U. S. Grant, and J. G. Blaine.

[Sources for a study of Beale's life are scattered over a wide field of government documents, Cong. speeches, and chronicles of the frontier. A biog., *Edward Fitzgerald Beale,* by Stephen Bonsal, was published in 1912. Gwinn Harris Heap's jour. of the expedition from Westport to Los Angeles in the summer of 1853 was published in 1854, under the title *Central Route to the Pacific.* The report of the survey from Fort Defiance to the Colorado was published as *House Ex. Doc. 124,* 35 Cong., 1 Sess., and that of the survey from Fort Smith to the Colorado as *House Ex. Doc. 42,* 36 Cong., 1 Sess.]

W. J. G.

BEALE, RICHARD LEE TURBERVILLE (May 22, 1819–Apr. 21, 1893), politician, Confederate soldier, was born at Hickory Hill, Westmoreland County, Va., a descendant of Thomas Beale, who came from England to York County in 1645 and served as a member of Gov. Berkeley's council. His son removed to Westmoreland County, where the family was prominent for the next two hundred years. The Hickory Hill estate was settled by the Turbervilles about 1700, and came into the possession of Robert Beale on his marriage with Martha Felicia, the daughter of George Lee Turberville, an officer in the Revolutionary army and an early member of Phi Beta Kappa. Richard Beale, their son, was educated at Dickinson College and at the University of Virginia, was admitted to the bar in 1839, and took up the practise of law near his birthplace. He was a member of Congress from 1847 to 1849, a delegate to the state constitutional convention in 1851, and a state senator from 1858 to 1860. In May 1861 he was mustered into the Confederate service as a first lieutenant of "Lee's Legion," or "Lee's Light Horse." A month later he saw his first fighting when he commanded a small force which put out in two flatboats from Mathias Point to capture a vessel aground in the Potomac. Lee's Legion was sent to join the army at Bull Run, but arrived the day after the battle, and soon returned to patrol duty along the Potomac. Beale was promoted to captain in July and major in October. Next spring the legion was merged in the 9th Virginia Cavalry, of which Beale was appointed lieutenant-colonel in April and colonel in October. He served with the regiment in all the campaigns of the Army of Northern Virginia, with credit but not with satisfaction. For some reason, which does not appear, he offered his resignation three times, at decent intervals—Nov. 22, 1862, Feb. 8, 1863, and Aug. 25, 1863—but it was not accepted. In his last letter of resignation, he pleaded to be allowed to organize a company of rangers or to enlist as a private. Severely wounded in a skirmish in September 1863, he was unable to resume command for more than three months. Late in 1864 he was given command of a brigade, and his appointment as brigadier-general was recommended. Just at that time, however, a large draft was made upon the adjutant-general's force of clerks, for service in the field, and in the confusion Beale's papers were misplaced. It was not until Feb. 6, 1865, that the appointment was made. After the general surrender he again took up the practise of law at Hague, in his native county, where he lived the rest of his life. He was again a member of Congress from 1879 to 1881.

[R. L. T. Beale, *Hist. of the Ninth Va. Cavalry in the War between the States* (1899); *Confed. Mil. Hist.* (1899), III, 581; *Official Records,* ser. I, vols. XXI, XXV (pt. I), XXXIII.]

T. M. S.

BEALL, JOHN YATES (Jan. 1, 1835–Feb. 24, 1865), Confederate soldier, was born in Jefferson County, Va., in the upper part of the Shenandoah Valley. He came of good family. His mother, a Yates, claimed descent from those English Howards whose ancestor was the "Belted Will" of Scott's poem. His father, George Beall, was the owner of a large farm. John Yates Beall attended the University of Virginia and studied law, but did not take a degree. His intimate friends described him as an earnest and serious young man, of exemplary habits and a marked religious nature. At the beginning of the Civil War he was a private in the "Stonewall

Brigade," but was soon severely wounded and compelled to leave the army. Traveling to relatives in Iowa, he from there proceeded to Canada, and formed schemes for operations against the Federals on inland waters. Returning to the Confederacy, he was appointed by Secretary Mallory acting master in the navy, and was soon at work in Chesapeake Bay. With a band limited in numbers he captured the *Alliance* and other small vessels, cut cables, and performed various exploits until his own capture. Held at first as a pirate, he was released upon threats of retaliation on certain Federals held as hostages. He fought for a short time in front of Richmond, but soon disappeared, and making his way to Canada entered upon the last and noted part of his career. He formed a plan in September 1864 to seize the Federal war-vessel *Michigan* on Lake Erie; and with the aid of helpers on the land, under one Cole, to set free the Confederate prisoners interned on Johnson's Island (entrance to Sandusky Bay). Associated with him was one Burley—known later as a famous English war-correspondent under the name "Bennet Burleigh." The conspirators seized the steamers *Philo Parsons* and *Island Queen* and scuttled the latter. But the plot failed through a "mutiny" of Beall's men and a break-down on Cole's part. The *Parsons* was beached and abandoned, and Beall returned to Canada. On Dec. 16, 1864, he was arrested on the New York side of the frontier at Suspension Bridge, after making several futile attempts to derail trains near Buffalo. His motives are not clear (Shepard, p. 41); perhaps he designed to liberate Confederate prisoners. He was taken to New York, where Gen. Dix was in command, and imprisoned in Fort Lafayette. He was brought to trial on the charges of being a spy, and of "violation of the laws of war." In defense he attempted to show that he was regularly engaged in the Confederate service, but was found guilty and condemned to death. Strenuous efforts were made for a commutation of the sentence by prominent Baltimoreans, by Gen. Roger Pryor, a fellow prisoner, and by such noted men as Thaddeus Stevens and Gov. Andrew of Massachusetts. A petition signed by many congressmen was presented to Lincoln through a personal friend, Orville Browning, but the President declined to interfere, and Beall was executed by hanging on Governors Island. Afterward there appeared a "weird and lurid story" (Markens, p. 10)—thoroughly exploded—that Wilkes Booth, reputed to have been Beall's intimate friend, had a midnight interview with Lincoln; that the President, moved to tears, promised a pardon for Beall but was overruled by Secretary Seward; whereupon Booth, in revenge, formed his plot of assassination.

[F. J. Shepard, "The Johnson's Island Plot" in *Pubs. Buffalo Hist. Soc.* (1906), IX; Daniel B. Lucas (Beall's college room-mate), *Memoir of John Yates Beall* (1865) including Beall's Diary; Isaac Markens, *President Lincoln and the Case of John Yates Beall* (1911); Rev. Jas. H. McNeilley in *Confederate Veteran* (1899), pp. 66–69; W. W. Baker, *Memoirs of Service with John Yates Beall, C. S. N.* (1910); G. A. Foote, *Old Watering Places in Warren County* (1899); and J. H. Crawford in *Southern Hist. Soc. Papers* (1905), XXXIII, 71–78; *Official Records,* ser. I, II, and IV; *Trial of John Y. Beall as a Spy and Guerrillero by Military Commission* (1865).]

E. K. A.

BEALL, SAMUEL WOOTTON (Sept. 26, 1807–Sept 26, 1868), public official, politician, son of Lewis and Eliza Beall, was descended from Ninian Beall, a member of a well-known Scottish family of royalist stock, who came to Maryland and settled in Calvert County shortly after 1650. Samuel was born in Montgomery County, received his education at Union College, Schenectady, and when only a student married Elizabeth Fenimore, daughter of Isaac Cooper of Cooperstown, N. Y., and niece of J. Fenimore Cooper, the novelist. On his graduation in 1827, he was, through the influence of Chief Justice Taney, appointed receiver for the sale of public lands in the northwest, whither he proceeded, establishing the first land office at Green Bay, Wis., and taking an active part in opening up the sparsely settled territory immediately west of Lake Michigan. In 1834 he returned to the East and took up his residence in the vicinity of his wife's relatives at Cooperstown, where his house became the center of a brilliant group of literary notables, including Washington Irving. In 1840 the lure of the wild again drew him to Wisconsin. He first located at Tychora, Marquette County, shortly afterward removing to Taycheedah in Fond du Lac County, where he engaged in farming, and for a short time was Indian agent with the Stockbridge tribe. In 1836 Wisconsin had been detached from Michigan and made a separate territory, and the advisability or otherwise of forming a state government became a subject of much controversy. Beall threw himself with ardor into the fight on behalf of statehood. He was a delegate from Marquette County to the constitutional convention held at Madison, Oct. 5, 1846, was chairman of the committee for the organization of state government, and took a prominent part in the proceedings. When the constitution as then drafted was submitted to the people, Apr. 6, 1847, it was rejected. A second convention was thereupon summoned for Dec. 15 at Madison, which Beall attended as a delegate from Taycheedah, being a member of the committee on general provisions. The constitution then prepared was ratified by the people, Mar. 13, 1848. Beall's activities at these conventions had brought him into considerable prominence, and on Wisconsin's being admitted as a state he was recognized as one of its leading figures. In 1850 he was elected lieutenant-governor, serving in this position for two years, following which he again became Indian agent, in this capacity escorting the tribal chiefs within his district to Washington. Always enamoured of frontier life, in 1859 he was leader of an exploration party to Pike's Peak, Colo., and assisted at the location and founding of Denver. The growth of the new city was such that he was sent specially to Washington to procure the grant of a charter. He returned to Wisconsin in 1861 at the outbreak of the Civil War, and in 1862 was appointed lieutenant-colonel of the 18th Wisconsin Regiment, with which body he took part in much severe fighting. Wounded at both Shiloh and Vicksburg, he was incapacitated for active service during the last stages of the conflict. At the conclusion of the war he returned to Wisconsin for a short time and then moved to Helena, Mont. He was shot and killed in the office of the *Montana Post,* at Helena, Sept. 25, 1868, by George M. Pinney, manager of the *Post,* in the course of an altercation relative to certain articles reflecting on Beall's character which Pinney had published.

Beall was a curious compound of strength and instability. His intellectual endowment was of a high order and his general culture wide. As a man of affairs, he was respected for his invariable courtesy and undoubted integrity. He was a fluent speaker, and the embodiment of dignity when the occasion demanded. Unfortunately he always seemed to act on the impulse of the moment. Of an intensely restless nature, during the last twenty years of his life he was unable to live anywhere but on the fringe of civilization. Many tales are told of his warm-heartedness and generosity. One most characteristic action was on the occasion of the death of his mother who had bequeathed him a small patrimony in Maryland and some thirty slaves: though Beall was not in very good financial circumstances he at once gave the slaves their freedom, at the same time selling the property and devoting the proceeds to their support until they could find employment.

[Beall's forebears are discussed in *Historic Sketches of the Beall and Edwards Families* (1910), by A. S. Edwards. A competent sympathetic sketch of his life appeared in *Memorial Records of the Fathers of Wisconsin* (1880), by H. H. Tenney and D. Atwood. The circumstances of his marriage are narrated in *The Story of Cooperstown,* by R. Birdsall (1917), pp. 191, 195–96. Details of his death, together with extracts from the *Helena Herald* and *Montana Post,* appeared in the *N. Y. Times,* Oct. 13, 1868.]

H. W. H. K.

BEAMAN, CHARLES COTESWORTH (May 7, 1840–Dec. 15, 1900), lawyer, traced his descent from Gamaliel Beaman, probably a native of Bridgnorth, Shropshire, who, emigrating at the age of twelve in 1635, settled in Massachusetts. Sixth in direct line of descent from Gamaliel was Charles Cotesworth Beaman, a New England Congregational minister, who married Mary Ann Stacey of Wiscasset, Me., their eldest son, Charles Cotesworth Beaman, Jr., being born in Houlton, Me. His early education was received at Smithtown Seminary, North Scituate, R. I., whence he proceeded in 1857 to Harvard, graduating in 1861. For the next two years he was principal of the academy at Marblehead, Mass., and then studied law at the Harvard Law School. His Harvard prize essay, "Rights and Duties of Neutrals in Respect to the Armed Vessels of Belligerents," published under a shorter title in the *North American Review,* was read by Senator Sumner, chairman of the Senate Committee on Foreign Relations who thereupon engaged Beaman as private secretary, and after his call to the bar in November 1865, procured his appointment as clerk of the Committee. Beaman occupied this position for three years, during which he laid the foundation for an intimate knowledge of international law. In 1868 he resigned and, going to New York, commenced practise. At this period the controversy between the United States and Great Britain respecting the depredations committed by Confederate cruisers was becoming acute and he made an exhaustive study of the subject. As a result he wrote *The National and Private "Alabama Claims" and their "Final and Amicable Settlement,"* which was published in March 1871. Two months later, by the Treaty of Washington, the Geneva Tribunal of Arbitration was constituted to adjudicate the dispute, and Beaman was appointed solicitor for the United States in the arbitration proceedings. At Geneva his intimate knowledge of all the details proved of inestimable value. He assisted J. C. Bancroft Davis, the United States agent, by arranging the evidence presented with the American case, representing both national and individual claims, and "did his work with admirable fidelity" (Report of Davis, Sept. 21, 1872, *House Executive Document, No. 1, pt. 1,* 42 Cong., 3 Sess.) On his return to New York in 1872 he resumed practise. Following the arbitration award, a Court of Commissioners of Alabama Claims was established at Washington, and he was retained as counsel by a number of the more important claimants. One remarkable case was that of the *Texan Star,* where he successfully maintained a claim for the destruction of that ship by a Confederate cruiser, although it had acquired a British registry in order to avoid capture. In connection with this work he wrote *The Rights of Insurance Companies under the Geneva Award* (1876). During the Geneva proceedings he had come into close contact with W. M. Evarts, whose daughter, Hettie Sherman, he married Aug. 19, 1874, and in 1879 he was offered and accepted a partnership in the firm of Evarts, Southmayd & Choate. He was endowed with exceptionally sound judgment, which, combined with a thorough grasp of legal principles and a wide experience of international matters, gave him unusual prestige professionally. Personally he was much liked, possessing a genial temperament which attracted old and young, and a perfect sincerity of language and demeanor which never left any room for doubt as to his attitude toward any subject under discussion. He was much interested in politics, though the only occasion upon which he aspired for office was in 1894, when he was the unsuccessful Republican and Independent Democratic candidate for the office of judge of the New York supreme court. In 1899 he was appointed a member of the Commission for the Revision of the Charter of the City of New York. He died in New York in December of the following year.

[Details of his ancestry will be found in *The Beaman and Clark Genealogy* by Emily Beaman Wooden (1909). An authoritative review of his life and career, "Memorial of Charles C. Beaman," prepared by Edmund Wetmore, appeared in *Bar of the City of N. Y. Report,* 1901, p. 96. See also *Hist. of the Bench and Bar of N. Y.,* ed. by D. McAdam *et al.* (1897), II, 30, and *Hist. and Digest of the International Arbitrations to which the United States has been a party,* by John Bassett Moore, (1898), I, 495–678; obituary, *N. Y. Times,* Dec. 16, 1900.]

H. W. H. K.

BEAN, TARLETON HOFFMAN (Oct. 8, 1846–Dec. 28, 1916), ichthyologist, the son of George and Mary (Smith) Bean, was born at Bainbridge, Pa., and received his early education at the State Normal School, Millersville, Pa. He obtained a medical degree in 1876 from the Columbian (now the George Washington) University, but, being little disposed to take up the practise of medicine, permitted himself to follow his early zoölogical interests and within a few years became a foremost authority on the fresh-water fish of America and of the northern salt waters. From 1880 to 1895 he was curator of the Department of Fisheries in the United States National Museum, and from 1895 to 1898 director of the New York Aquarium. He acted also as a member of the United States Fish Commission, and from 1906 until his death he was head fish culturist of New York state. Owing to Bean's activities New York became the first state to attempt the preservation of its fish through "green-house" methods of propagation. He was in fact largely responsible for initiating the national movement for preservation of native fish in this country. A profound student of nature, Bean was also a prolific writer, and the bibliography of his books and scientific papers contains 322 titles. His most important contribution was *Oceanic Ichthyology* (1895) written in conjunction with Goode (529 pp., 124 colored plates). His other books were: *Fishes of Pennsylvania* (1893); *Fishes of Long Island* (1901); *Fishes of New York* (1903); *Fishes of Bermuda* (1906). With W. C. Harris he published an important monograph on *The Basses, Fresh-water and Marine* (1905). Bean's scientific attainments were recognized abroad, for he was made Chevalier de la Légion d'Honneur and Officier du Mérite Agricole of France; Knight of the Imperial Order of the Red Eagle, Germany, and of the Order of the Rising Sun, Japan; and honorary member of the Society of Danish Fisheries. In 1908–09 he was president of the American Fisheries Society. His discoveries were noteworthy scientifically, and his studies of the periodic migration of fish proved of great commercial value. For twenty years before his death he was by common consent the most distinguished fish culturist in America, and he had no peers among American ichthyologists. On Jan. 1, 1878, he married Laurette H. van Hook. While in Albany in October 1916 he was injured in an automobile accident, and he died two months later as a result of his injuries.

[Pubs. of the U. S. Fish Commission; *Proc. of U. S. Nat. Museum*; biog. by E. W. Gudger in Kelly and Burrage, *Dict. of Am. Medic. Biog.* (1928); *Jour. Am. Medic. Ass.,* LXVIII, 211; obituary in *Albany Evening Jour.,* Dec. 29, 1916.]

J. F. F.

BEARD, GEORGE MILLER (May 8, 1839–Jan. 23, 1883), physician, son of the Rev. Spencer F. Beard, a Congregational minister, and of Lucy A. Leonard, was born at Montville, Conn. He prepared for college at Phillips Academy, Andover, Mass., and graduated from Yale College in 1862, and from the College of Physicians and Surgeons of New York in 1866. While still a medical student he served as acting assistant surgeon in the West Gulf squadron of the United States Navy. His initial essay in medical literature, to which he soon became a ceaseless contributor, was a paper on "Electricity as a Tonic" (1866). In that year he associated himself with Dr. A. D. Rockwell of New York, with whom, as with a kindred spirit, he conducted researches in electro-therapeutics for a series of years, the results of which were embodied in articles on the *Medical Use of Electricity* and later, in 1871, in *The Medical and Surgical Uses of Electricity.* This latter work was translated into German, had a wide vogue in Europe, and at once gave Beard an international reputation as an investigator. He introduced and popularized the terms "central galvanization" and "general faradization" and gained for them universal acceptance. To the public he early became known by his *Our Home Physician* (1869), *Eating and Drinking* (1871) and *Stimulants and Narcotics* (1871). His literary output, which was continuous and enormous, included: *The Legal Responsibility in Old Age, based on Researches into the Relations of Old Age to Work* (1874); *The Longevity of Brain Workers* (1867); *Hay Fever* (1876); *The Scientific Basis of Delusions* (1877); *Nervous Exhaustion* (1880); *Sea-Sickness* (1880); *American Nervousness* (1881); *Trance and Muscle Reading* (1882); *Psychology of the Salem Witchcraft Excitement of 1692* (1882); *Medical Education and the Medical Profession in Europe and America* (1883); *How to Use the Bromides* (1881); *Current Delusions Relating to Hypnotism* (1882). He founded the *Archives of Electrology and Neurology* (1874–75). In 1868 he became a lecturer on nervous diseases in New York University and later physician to the Demilt Dispensary in the department of electro-therapeutics and nervous diseases. He was several times a delegate to foreign scientific associations, and in 1881 a delegate to the International Medical Congress in London. In neurology he was an American pioneer and made a notable contribution to the study of "neurasthenia," being the first to show clearly and positively that Americans possess a peculiar nervous organization. He maintained that the cause of the greater prevalence of nervous diseases in the United States is dryness of the air and extremes of heat and cold. To him science likewise owes the conception of sea-sickness as a functional neurosis induced mechanically by concussion, and he, too, introduced to the profession and to the public the treatment of sea-sickness by bromides. In psychiatry he was an early champion of reforms, many of which, through his initiative and zeal, became incorporated in subsequent practise, and he was one of the originators of the "National Association for the Protection of the Insane and the Prevention of Insanity." He took strong ground, on the unpopular side, in his published opinions on the trial of Guiteau, the assassin of President Garfield, declaring him insane and irresponsible. Undaunted by the clamor of the people and of many respectable members of his own profession for the death penalty, he prepared a petition to prevent what he regarded as the judicial hanging of a man whose innocence was implicit in his mental disease. His passion for investigation and analysis persisted till the day of his death when, in almost his last words, he said to bystanders at his bed, "Tell the doctors it is impossible for me to record the thoughts of a dying man. It would be interesting to do so, but I cannot. My time has come. I hope others will carry on my work." Dr. A. D. Rockwell, in offering resolutions on Beard's death at a meeting of the Medical Society of the County of New York, on Mar. 26, 1883, said of his associate: "As an investigator he was original and conscientious. As a friend he was generous and steadfast. Exposed by his restless activity to many peculiar attacks, he ever manifested the utmost charity and good humor. Of his worst enemies, he seldom spoke a harsh, and never a vindictive, word." Beard married Dec. 25, 1866, Elizabeth Ann Alden, of Westville, Conn., who survived her husband's death but a few days.

[Kelly and Burrage, *Dict. of Am. Medic. Biog.* (1928); *Jour. of Nervous and Mental Diseases*, X, 130–34 (portr.); *Medic. Record*, Jan. 27, Mar. 3, 1883; *Trans. Medic. Soc. of the State of N. Y.* (1883); R. S. Tracy in *Twenty Years' Record of the Yale Class of 1862* (1884); *Obit. Record Grads. Yale Coll., 1883* (1883).]

G. A. B.

BEARD, JAMES CARTER (June 6, 1837–Nov. 15, 1913), illustrator, author, the son of James Henry Beard [*q.v.*] and Mary Caroline (Carter) Beard, was born at Cincinnati, Ohio. Privately educated, he read law with Rutherford B. Hayes, afterward president of the United States. He was admitted to the bar in 1861, practising long enough to win one case. His brother, Daniel C. Beard, says, "When he got his sheepskin as an attorney and counselor at law, handing it to his father he said, 'I did this for you. I am now going into art for myself.'" During the Civil War he served with the Hundred Days' Men. On Dec. 25, 1862, he married Martha J. Bray of Terre Haute, Ind., the ceremony being performed by Lyman Abbott. For many years he held an editorial position with D. Appleton & Company. He also did a mass of special work for the newspapers, but it is as a writer of illustrated articles on plant and animal life that he is chiefly known. *Harper's Magazine, Saint Nicholas, Century, Outing, Country Life,* and the *Scientific American* were some of the periodicals for which he wrote and drew. He illustrated *Hunting Trip of a Ranchman* (1886), by Theodore Roosevelt, and was the author of *The Adventures of Little Fantasy among the Water*

Devils (published anonymously, 1871); *Little Workers* (1871); *Painting on China* (1882); *Curious Homes and their Tenants* (1897); and *Billy Possum* (1909). For many years he lived in Brooklyn. He moved to New Orleans about the year 1910 and died there Nov. 15, 1913.

[*Who's Who in America*, 1899–1913; information from brother, Daniel C. Beard.] T.B.

BEARD, JAMES HENRY (May 20, 1812–Apr. 4, 1893), artist, was born in Buffalo, N. Y., the son of Capt. James and Harriet (Wolcott) Beard. He was descended on his father's side from Sir James Beard and on his mother's side from Sir Lochlan Maclean. He was the brother of William Holbrook Beard [*q.v.*], who was likewise an artist. Capt. Beard moved his family to a farm near Painesville, Ohio, and died when James was eleven years old. An itinerant portrait painter gave the boy his first thoughts of becoming an artist and when the traveler left town young James started painting portraits on his own account, charging five dollars for a head and fifteen for a portrait including the hand holding a book. At the age of seventeen he ran away from home and worked his way to Pittsburgh. He then worked on the Ohio River, acting as a shipping clerk on a river boat. He lived in Cincinnati about the year 1835. Shortly after that date he made a second visit to Pittsburgh. He now decided to try his fortunes in the South, visiting first Louisville, and then making his way down to New Orleans. He finally returned to Cincinnati, where he married on Aug. 28, 1833, Mary Caroline Carter, the daughter of Col. Thomas Carter, and where he lived for several years. There he made the acquaintance and won the friendship of many prominent men from both North and South who had him paint their portraits. Among the sitters to his brush were Henry Clay, John Quincy Adams, Gen. Harrison, and Gen. Taylor. Harriet Martineau expressed her admiration for Beard in her book of travels in America. In 1846 he went to New York City, where he exhibited his picture entitled "North Carolina Emigrants," for which he received $750. He was a charter member of the Century Club. In 1848 he was made an honorary member of the National Academy. During the Civil War he served in the Union army on the staff of Gen. Lew Wallace, with the rank of captain. In 1870 he returned to New York and in 1872 was elected a National Academician. In 1887 he painted a portrait of Gen. Sherman. During his later years he relinquished portrait painting almost entirely and devoted his attention to painting animals. Whereas his brother, W. H. Beard, showed a fondness for the painting of wild animal life, he himself preferred to paint domestic animals. "The Streets of New York," "The Window," and "There's Many a Slip" are the titles of some of his compositions. He died Apr. 4, 1893, at Flushing, L. I. His four sons, James Carter Beard [*q.v.*], Harry Beard (1841–89), Thomas Francis Beard [*q.v.*], and Daniel Carter Beard (born 1850) all became well-known as artists.

[H. T. Tuckerman, *Book of the Artists* (6th ed., 1882); L. Mead, "Apprenticeship of an Academician," *Am. Mag.*, IX, 192; Ruth Beard, *Geneal. of the Descendants of Widow Martha Beard of Milford, Conn.* (1915); *N.Y. Tribune*, and *N.Y. Herald*, Apr. 6, 1893.] T.B.

BEARD, RICHARD (Nov. 27, 1799–Dec. 2, 1880), Cumberland Presbyterian clergyman, educator, the son of John and Mary (Bartley) Beard, was born in Sumner County, Tenn., and was licensed to preach at the age of twenty-one. After some years of circuit-riding, school-teaching, and study, he entered Cumberland College in Princeton, Ky. Upon graduation he was appointed to the faculty of the college and shortly thereafter, Jan. 21, 1834, married Cynthia Ewing Castleman. In 1838 he took charge of Sharon Academy in Mississippi, but within a few years returned to Cumberland College to become in 1843 its president. Believing in the desirability of a better-educated clergy, he aided in the establishment by his Church of a theological department in Cumberland University, Lebanon, Tenn. To this department, as its first professor of systematic theology, Beard went in 1854, and there he spent the most fruitful years of his life. In the earlier years of this service, inadequately paid, overworked, at times in despair because of the little encouragement given him, he was the only professor in the department and taught almost the whole theological course, including Hebrew, the Greek Testament, evidences of Christianity, and systematic theology. Nevertheless, shortly before the Civil War, he was able to begin putting into printed form his lectures on theology, the "crystallization of Cumberland Presbyterian thought and faith." After the war, in addition to his work in the theological department, he taught for some years as professor of Latin and Greek in the college department. Moreover, he continued publication of his theological lectures and other products of his pen. He served on several occasions as church moderator, and was prominent in committee work, particularly in support of education and of reunion with the Presbyterian Church. His published writings are as follows: *Lectures on Theology* (three volumes, 1860, 186[illegible], 1870); *Wh[illegible] Am I a Cumber-*

land Presbyterian? (1870); *Brief Biographical Sketches of Some of the Early Ministers of the Cumberland Presbyterian Church,* two volumes (1867, 1874); and *Miscellaneous Sermons, Reviews and Essays* (1875).

[*Hist. of the Cumberland Presbyt. Ch.* (1888), by B. W. McDonnold, for many years Beard's colleague in Cumberland Univ.; *Theological Medium,* Oct. 1876; F. B. Catchings, *Baird and Beard Families* (1918); obituary in *Pub. Ledger* (Memphis), Dec. 4, 1880.]
P. M. H.

BEARD, THOMAS FRANCIS (Feb. 6, 1842–Sept. 28, 1905), illustrator, the son of James H. Beard [*q.v.*] and Mary Caroline (Carter) Beard, came of a talented and well-known Cincinnati family. He was educated in the Cincinnati and Painesville, Ohio, schools. His father, his uncle, William H. Beard [*q.v.*], and his brother James Carter Beard [*q.v.*] were painters, and another brother, Dan Beard, a writer, lecturer, and inventor, is still popular for his Boys' Handybooks of Camp-lore, and boys' stories. Known always as Frank Beard, the illustrator started his career early. Before he was twelve he was sending sketches to all the important periodicals, including *Yankee Notions,* one of the earliest American illustrated papers. At the outbreak of the Civil War, though only a boy of eighteen, he was commissioned by *Leslie's Weekly* and *Harper's Weekly* to act as cartoonist for the Army of the Potomac. He served at the same time in the 7th Ohio Regiment. After the war he began lecturing, and at this time originated his "Chalk Talks," popular lectures with rapid chalk illustrating. He was married in 1867 to Helen Augusta Goodwin. From 1881 to 1884 he held the chair of æsthetics and painting at Syracuse University and in 1884, during the Blaine campaign, was editor of *Judge.* A. B. Paine in *Thomas Nast, His Period and His Pictures* (1904) has described the remarkable bitterness of the Cleveland-Blaine campaign. George William Curtis and Thomas Nast were almost equally victims of newspaper attacks. In *Judge,* Frank Beard "never missed an opportunity of presenting him (Curtis) as a saint, a circus performer, or a 'Miss Nancy' . . . usually grinding an organ, while Nast, as a monkey, performed at his command" (Paine, p. 501). Nast's own ideas and illustrations were used against him. As early as 1877, Beard had published *The Blackboard in the Sunday School, A Practical Guide for Superintendents and Teachers,* and he now became more interested in religious publications and in Chautauqua lectures than in social and political reform by means of cartoons. Most of his best-known work was done in connection with Sunday-schools and the Chautauqua movement. About twenty years before his death he began illustrating for the *Ram's Horn,* a religious weekly published in Chicago. In 1890 he became one of the editors and thereafter devoted all of his time to it. The *American Art Annual,* 1905–06, in an obituary notice, states that his cartoons directed against the liquor evil were often extremely effective. He also illustrated a few religious and other books.

[*Who's Who in America,* 1903–05; A. B. Maurice and F. T. Cooper, *Hist. of the Nineteenth Century in Caricature* (1904); *Publisher's Weekly,* Oct. 7, 1905; *Chicago Tribune,* Sept. 29, 1905.]
M. A. K.

BEARD, WILLIAM HOLBROOK (Apr. 13, 1824–Feb. 20, 1900), artist, brother of James Henry Beard [*q.v.*], was born in Painesville, Ohio, the son of James and Harriet (Wolcott) Beard. His mother, left a widow while the boy was still an infant, made every effort to give him an education, for which he showed little inclination. At an early age he became interested in plants and wild life, and showed also great aptitude for swimming, hunting, and wrestling. Following an unsuccessful attempt to earn his living at Painesville, as a portrait painter, he started on a tour of the state as a peripatetic portrait painter. This affording little more than a bare livelihood, he went to New York about 1845, where his brother, James Henry Beard, had established himself. He again specialized in portraits, and then, after several years of travel, moved to Buffalo in 1850 and opened a studio. After a struggle of six years he secured orders sufficient to keep him busy and sailed for Europe in 1856. In Rome he met Gifford, Whittredge, and other American artists, who were later to distinguish themselves. Within two years he was back in Buffalo, where in 1859 he married Flora Johnson, who died a few months after the wedding. On July 7, 1863, he married Carrie, daughter of Thomas Le Clear, the portrait painter. In 1860 he settled in New York. He brought with him a few compositions, humorous story-pictures of animals with such titles as "Grimalkin's Dream" and "Bears and a Bender" and became so popular at this branch of painting that he was condemned to paint animals acting like human beings almost all the rest of his life. He was a member of the National Academy, the Century Club, the Artists' Fund Society, and the Artists' Aid Society. The following are the titles of some of his pictures: "Kittens and Guinea Pig"; "Power of Death"; "Deer in a Wood"; "Spreading the Alarm"; "Flaw in the Title"; "Swan and Owls." He died in New York City.

[H. T. Tuckerman, *Book of the Artists* (1867); L. G. Sellstedt, *Art in Buffalo* (1895), pp. 104–10, and *From*

Forecastle to Academy (1904), p. 282; G. W. Sheldon, *Am. Painters* (1879); obituary in *N.Y. Tribune*, Feb. 21, 1900.]

T. B.

BEARDSHEAR, WILLIAM MILLER (Nov. 7, 1850–Aug. 5, 1902), United Brethren minister, college president, was of Scotch and Welsh descent; his forebears emigrated from Pennsylvania to Dayton, Ohio, about 1796. His parents, John and Elizabeth (Coleman) Beardshear, were pious, industrious farmers of the hardy, pioneer type. Large of frame, the boy at fourteen enlisted in the 184th Ohio Infantry and served till the end of the Civil War. In 1873, when the death of his father interrupted his course at Otterbein University, he married Josephine Mundhenk, also a student there. Returning a year later, he received the B.A. degree in 1876. In 1878 he entered Yale Divinity School, but in the second year broke down from overwork and did not complete the course. He held two pastorates—at Arcanum, Ohio (1876–78), and at the Summit Street Church in Dayton, Ohio (October 1880–July 1881). At thirty his success as a preacher, his striking personality, and the confidence he inspired resulted in a unanimous call to the presidency of Western College, at Toledo, Ia., a position he held for eight years (1881–89). In 1889 he was elected superintendent of the city schools of West Des Moines. In February 1891 he became president of the Iowa State College of Agriculture and Mechanic Arts, a position which he held until his death in 1902. Here he did his chief work (*Proceedings of the National Education Association*, 1903, p. 368). During his presidency the attendance, the number of teachers, and the state appropriation were all more than trebled. New departments were added, new courses organized. To make the work of the college known he gave addresses all over the state—at commencements, teachers' institutes, farmers' clubs. His success was due to a combination of sterling qualities. He had a great-souled enthusiasm, an untiring devotion to his work. "Thank God, I am an enthusiast," he said ("The Geography of Character," in *A Boy Again and Other Prose Poems*, 1904, p. 177). His vision of industrial education was high and exalted, comprehending the harmonious development of the head, the hand, and the heart. He was deeply religious and had the soul of a poet. In his chapel talks he quoted freely from a wide range of authors, mainly the poets and the essayists. "Some books are the livest things in the world," he wrote, "and of such poetry furnishes the largest proportion, for 'poets are the rulers of men's spirits'" ("The Influence of Poetry in Education," *Proceedings and Addresses N. E. A.*, 1900, p. 57).

[*Proc. and Addresses N. E. A.*, 1902, contains "appreciations" by people who knew Beardshear well. The *Iowa Hist. Record* for Oct. 1902 contains about the same "appreciations" with some additions. *Proc. and Addresses N. E. A.*, 1903, pp. 368–69, contains the memorial tribute by Pres. H. H. Seerley. *A Hist. of Western-Leander Clark Coll.*, by Henry W. Ward (Dayton, Ohio, 1911), gives the record of Western College while Dr. Beardshear was president; obituary in *Des Moines Register and Leader*, Aug. 6, 1902.]

A. B. N.

BEARDSLEY, EBEN EDWARDS (Jan. 8, 1808–Dec. 21, 1891), Episcopal clergyman, the son of Elihu and Ruth (Edwards) Beardsley, was descended from William Beardsley, by occupation a mason, who in April 1635 came to America from London in the ship *Planter*. Born in the village of Stepney, town of Monroe, Fairfield County, Conn., Eben worked on the family farm until he was sixteen years old, attending the village school as he had opportunity. Then for a year he went to the Staples Academy, Weston, Conn., and this was followed by a period of teaching in the district school. But the youth's ambition was for an academic education, and to make his final preparation for admission to college he went to the Episcopal Academy in South Norwalk, Conn. He then entered Washington (now Trinity) College, Hartford, graduating with distinction in the class of 1832. After graduation he took charge for a year of a private classical school in Hartford, and then for the next two years served as tutor in his own college. During this time he was preparing himself for holy orders, and on Aug. 11, 1835, was ordained deacon in the Episcopal Church by Bishop Brownell, and by the same bishop was advanced to the priesthood on Oct. 24, 1836. After his ordination to the diaconate he was placed in charge of St. Peter's Church, Cheshire, Conn., where, in addition to his ministerial duties, he undertook the charge of the Episcopal Academy of Connecticut. In April 1848 he was called to the rectorship of the newly organized parish of St. Thomas's Church, New Haven, Conn., a position which he retained until his death. Always deeply interested in the history of the Episcopal Church in this country, and especially in Connecticut, he found time, in the midst of his parochial duties, to gratify his fondness for historical research, and in 1865 published Volume I of *The History of the Episcopal Church in Connecticut*. This was followed by Volume II in 1868. Then came in rapid succession *The Life and Correspondence of Samuel Johnson, D.D.* (1874); *The Life and Times of William Samuel Johnson* (1876); *The Life and Correspondence of the Right Reverend*

Beardsley

Samuel Seabury, D.D. (1881). An abridged edition of the last-mentioned work was published in London in 1884, the year which marked the centenary of Seabury's consecration. In the course of his ministry he preached numerous historical sermons on parish anniversaries. These he had collected and prepared for publication, and in 1892 shortly after his death, they appeared in a volume bearing the title, *Addresses and Discourses.* For half a century Beardsley was one of the conspicuous leaders of his Church. In the diocese of Connecticut, where he lived all his life and did all his work, every distinction was bestowed upon him. He was sent as a deputy from Connecticut to eight general conventions, and twice was elected president of its House of Deputies, the highest honor conferred upon a presbyter. His interest in educational matters was evidenced by his serving as trustee of the Episcopal Academy of Connecticut, of St. Margaret's School for Girls, and of Trinity College. He was active in the formation of the New Haven Colony Historical Society, of which he was president 1873–74. He was married on Oct. 11, 1842, to Jane Margaret Matthews, daughter of Rev. Edmund Matthews of St. Simon's Island, Ga.

[The chief sources of information are manuscript records in the possession of the author of this article and a *Sketch of Wm. Beardsley* (1867), by E. E. Beardsley. A paper on E. E. Beardsley read before the New Haven Colony Hist. Soc., by Rt. Rev. E. S. Lines, D.D., was published in Vol. VII of the Society's *Papers,* and a memorial sermon preached by Rt. Rev. John Williams, D.D., was published in pamphlet form. This has for a frontispiece an engraved likeness by Ritchie.]

W. A. B.

BEARDSLEY, SAMUEL (Feb. 6, 1790–May 6, 1860), congressman, judge, was born at Hoosick, Rensselaer County, N. Y. His parents, Obadiah and Eunice (Moore) Beardsley, removed to a farm at Monticello, Otsego County, while he was an infant. Attending school in the winter and working on the farm in the summer, the lad manifested a love for books and made sufficient progress in learning to become a schoolteacher. Ambitious for a professional career, he first studied medicine with Dr. Joseph White at Cherry Valley and then at the age of eighteen turned to law, entering the office of Judge Hathaway in Rome, whose daughter he married. During this period he supported himself by clerking in the post office and serving as clerk in the county surrogate's court. After admission to the bar, he practised law in Watertown for a year, and then settled in Rome. In 1813 he joined the militia to defend Sackett's Harbor and in 1815 he was made captain. Three years later he was appointed brigade judge advocate, and in 1820 his name appears as major in the Oneida County militia. Meanwhile this military duty did not prevent the young lawyer from serving as town clerk in 1817 and county supervisor in 1818–20. He was appointed district attorney of Oneida County in 1821 and by this time had gained the reputation of being a well-informed and able lawyer. Chosen state senator for the 5th district on the Democratic ticket in 1822, he held that office for but one year because of the determination of tenure by lot. In 1823 he removed to Utica and the same year President Monroe appointed him United States attorney for northern New York, a post he retained for seven years, refusing in 1824 appointment as first judge of Oneida County. Well-known and highly respected in 1830, he was elected to Congress as a Democrat and was subsequently reëlected three times. His speech on the currency question in 1834 attracted national attention for both its eloquence and partisanship. An ardent champion of President Jackson, he became one of the President's confidential advisers and the leader of his party in New York. Fearless and outspoken in his convictions on public questions, he was regarded as a progressive leader and defender of free speech and of the right of petition. Jackson and his friends persuaded him when nominated as circuit judge in 1834 by Gov. Marcy, to remain in Washington. In 1836 he accepted the office of attorney-general of New York, which he filled acceptably for three years. In 1844 Gov. Bouck promoted him to an associate judgeship in the New York supreme court and three years later he became chief justice, the last person to hold the honor in the old supreme court. When the new supreme court was put on an elective basis in 1847, not being among the justices chosen, he resumed the practise of law at Utica. For several years important legal business induced him to reside in New York City. Henceforth his time was devoted almost exclusively to important cases in the court of appeals. He was described by those who knew him best as an ideal judge because of his patient and thorough investigation of every case, his wide legal knowledge, his impartial decisions, his quick perceptions, and his uniform courtesy and dignity. As a lawyer he held high rank, and in terse, vigorous, discerning argument he had few equals, although his manner was constrained and his diction not always graceful. A tall, commanding figure with a large, well-formed head, he was an able leader whose antagonism was felt by his opponents. A weakened vision gave his face the appearance of frowning, but his eyes beamed with kindness and his voice was cordial.

[M. M. Bagg, *Pioneers of Utica* (1877), pp. 559–67; D. E. Wager, *The City of Rome* (1896), pp. 196–98, and *Oneida County* (1896), pp. 235–36; Isaac H. Beardsley,

Geneal. Hist. of the Beardsley-lee Family in America (1902); D. McAdam *et al., Hist. of the Bench and Bar of N.Y.* (1897), I, 258.] A.C.F.

BEASLEY, FREDERICK (1777–Nov. 1, 1845), Episcopal clergyman, philosopher, was born near Edenton, N. C., the son of John Beasley, a planter, and Mary (Blount) Beasley. His early years were spent at home; in 1793 he entered the College of New Jersey, graduating in 1797 with high honors; for the next two years he was a tutor in the college while he studied philosophy and theology under Dr. Samuel Stanhope Smith, its president. He was ordained deacon in 1801, priest in 1802, and in the latter year became rector of St. John's Church, Elizabethtown, N. J. In June 1803 he accepted a call to St. Peter's Church, Albany, where he remained until 1809 when he assumed charge of St. Paul's Church, Baltimore. In July 1813 he accepted the provostship of the University of Pennsylvania, which carried with it the chair of moral philosophy. He resigned in 1828, and was rector of St. Michael's Church, Trenton, N. J., 1829–36, after which he lived in retirement at Elizabethtown. He was twice married: on Aug. 22, 1803, to Susan Dayton by whom he had one child; and on Nov. 27, 1804, to Maria Williamson by whom he had nine children.

Beasley published numerous sermons, pamphlets, and books, of which the most important are: *A Sermon on Duelling* (1811); *American Dialogues of the Dead* (1815); *A Search of Truth in the Science of the Human Mind* (1822); *A Vindication of the Argument a priori in Proof of the Being and Attributes of God, from the Objections of Dr. Waterland* (1825); *A Vindication of the Fundamental Principles of Truth and Order in the Church of Christ, from the Allegations of the Rev. Wm. E. Channing, D.D.* (1830); *An Examination of No. 90 of the Tracts for the Times* (1842). Although in personal relations gentle and confiding to the point of being often victimized, as soon as he took his theological pen in hand Beasley became a polemicist. Proud of his conservatism in thought and dress—still powdering his hair long after the custom had gone out—he was absolutely convinced of absolute truth and his acquaintance with it. The more abstract a proposition, the more violently it seemed to engage his emotions. Although educated by Dr. Smith in the Scottish philosophical tradition, he became convinced that Scottish Realism had been hopelessly contaminated by the empirical idealism of Hume, while John Locke, he believed, was free from all trace of idealism. Thus his most noted work, *A Search of Truth,* was devoted to an elaborate but none too subtle defense of Locke's system, which, he asserted, "never has been and never can be overthrown." The "detestable sophistries" of Berkeley, Hume, Reid, Channing, and Newman drew from Beasley attempted refutations mingled with cries of pain. The spectacle of these sophists so tormented him that his own possession of the truth brought little peace.

[Wm. B. Sprague, *Annals of the Am. Pulpit* (1859), V, 477–84; S. A. Clark, *Hist. of St. John's Ch., Elizabethtown, N. J.* (1857); Joseph Hooper, *Hist. of St. Peter's Ch. in the City of Albany* (1900); Isaac Woodbridge Riley, *Am. Philosophy: the Early Schools* (1907), bk. V, ch. VII.] E. S. B.

BEASLEY, MERCER (Mar. 27, 1815–Feb. 19, 1897), jurist, was born in Philadelphia, the son of Frederick [*q.v.*] and Maria (Williamson) Beasley. His father, an Episcopal minister, was then serving as provost of the University of Pennsylvania. In 1830 the family moved to Trenton, N. J., where Beasley was destined to spend the greater part of his life. After studying with his father he entered in 1833 the junior class of the College of New Jersey (now Princeton University), but remained only a year. In 1834 he was studying law under Senator Samuel V. L. Southard of Trenton, later continuing his studies under his kinsman, former Chancellor Isaac H. Williamson at Elizabeth. He was admitted to the bar in September 1838, and settled in Trenton. For some years thereafter he was more noted as a billiard player and wing shot than for legal acumen. Gradually, the law, especially trial work, absorbed more and more of his interest, and his personal charm and real ability brought him success. His name first appears in the records of the higher state courts in 1849 in a case which he won against the Delaware and Raritan Canal Company (*2 Zabriskie,* 243). Thereafter he acted with increasing frequency as counsel in important cases before the appellate courts. Perhaps his marriage at this period to Frances Higbee of Trenton stimulated his ambition. He interested himself in local politics as a Whig, served on the Common Council of Trenton, and was defeated as a candidate for mayor in 1850. When the Whig Party expired he became a Democrat (*New Jersey Law Journal,* XX). On the death of Chief Justice Whelpley, Gov. Joel Parker appointed Beasley chief justice of New Jersey, Mar. 8, 1864. The term of office was seven years, but he was reappointed four successive times by different governors, some of them of the opposite political party from his own, and thus served continuously until his death, a period just short of thirty-three years. To review his work on the bench would be to outline the development of law in New Jersey for a generation. His decisions in three political cases show his impartiality and courage. In 1866 the Republicans in the legislature passed a bill which put the police of Jersey City under control of a state commission. The city authorities, being Democrats, refused to recognize the act and two mutually hostile police forces preserved disorder in the city. The Chief Justice settled the strife by sustaining the Republican contention in an opinion since followed by the courts of other states because of its clear legal reasoning (Pangbourn *vs.* Young, *32 New Jersey Law Reports,* 29). A few years later he upheld the State's claim to its riparian lands against strong pressure from railroads and land speculators (Stevens *vs.* P. & N. Railroad Company, *34 New Jersey,* 532). In 1890 New Jersey was afflicted with two Senates. A quorum of Democratic "hold overs" had organized against the newly elected Republican senators, who thereupon went into separate session. Violence was imminent when the aged Chief Justice, again deciding against his own party, restored the reign of law. In appearance he was strikingly handsome with bold, clear-cut features and a mobile mouth. His second wife, whom he married Oct. 16, 1854, was Catherine Ann, daughter of Charles Haven of Trenton. He remained in office with his mental powers unimpaired until his death from pneumonia, Feb. 19, 1897.

[J. W. McGeehan, "Mercer Beasley" in *N. J. Law Review,* I (1915–16), 71–85; J. Whitehead, "The Supreme Court of N. J.," in the *Green Bag,* Nov. 1891, p. 457; W. S. Sackett, *Modern Battles of Trenton* (1895); M. D. Ogden, ed., *Memorial Cyc. of N. J.* (1917), p. 231; *Newark Daily Advertiser,* Feb. 19, 1897; *Daily True American* (Trenton), Feb. 20, 24, 1897.]

D.V.

BEATTIE, FRANCIS ROBERT (Mar. 31, 1848–Sept. 3, 1906), Presbyterian clergyman, was born at Guelph, Ont., Canada, the son of a Scotch emigrant, Robert Beattie, and of Janet McKinley. He was reared in the Presbyterian faith, although apparently with no thought of his later ministry. From his father's farm he went to the University of Toronto where he graduated in 1875, receiving the M.A. degree one year later. In 1878 he graduated from Knox Theological College and entered immediately on a ministry which ended only with his death. For ten years he served as pastor in Canadian churches, five of the ten being spent in Brantford, Ont. During this Canadian pastorate he wrote and published two books which attracted attention among clergymen—*The Utilitarian Theory of Morals* (1884) and *Methods of Theism* (1887). Because of the first-mentioned book, Illinois Wesleyan College conferred on him the Ph.D. degree in 1884, and the Columbia Seminary (South Carolina) elected him to the chair of apologetics in succession to Dr. Woodrow. Five years at Columbia gave him a reputation as educator and minister that resulted in his election in 1893 to the professorship of apologetics and systematic theology in the newly founded Presbyterian Theological Seminary at Louisville, Ky. In this position he remained until his death. At Louisville Dr. Beattie continued to add to his reputation. *Radical Criticism* appeared in 1896, *Presbyterian Standards* in 1898, *Apologetics* in 1903, and *Christianity and Modern Revolution* in 1906. The *Apologetics* was his most ambitious work, being designed for three volumes. Only one volume was completed and this has been widely used as a text in theological schools. Dr. Beattie was associate editor of the *Christian Observer* after 1893, and associate editor of the *Presbyterian Quarterly Review* after 1895.

He was twice married. His first wife, Jean G. Galbraith of Toronto, whom he married in 1879, died in 1897; his second wife was Lily R. Satterwhite, who survived him. He was by all accounts a vigorous and inspiring teacher, but his work in this field necessarily brought little recognition. He was an outstanding figure among the Louisville ministers and was well-known throughout the South for his work as a harmonizer. His chief claim to distinction lay in his writings. His books were scholarly and not without interest, though their appeal was limited.

[*Who's Who in America,* 1906–07; files of the *Louisville Courier-Jour.* and of the *Christian Observer;* information from Dean C. R. Hemphill of the Presbyt. Theological Seminary at Louisville. There are obituaries in the *Louisville Herald, Courier-Jour.,* and *Evening Post* of Sept. 4, the *Globe* (Toronto) of Sept. 5, and the *Christian Observer* of Sept. 12, 1906.]

R. S. C.

BEATTY, ADAM (May 10, 1777–June 9, 1858), lawyer, agricultural writer, the son of an Englishman, William Beatty, and of Mary Grosh, daughter of a New York family of German extraction, was born at Hagerstown, Md., and in 1800 moved to Lexington, Ky. He studied law there with James Brown, brother-in-law of Henry Clay. In 1802 he began the practise of law at Washington, Mason County, Ky., in 1804 married Sally Green, daughter of Capt. John Green of Mason County, and in 1811 was appointed circuit judge by Gov. Charles Scott, serving in that office until November 1823. He became a member of the Kentucky legislature in 1809 and was reëlected several times. From 1836 to 1839 he was a state senator. In 1840 he served as a presidential elector, voting for Harrison. He was an unsuccessful candidate for Congress in 1829 and in 1831. From 1823 on he made farming his principal business, and after the organization of the Kentucky State Agricultural Society in 1838 he was active in its affairs and became vice-president. He was greatly interested in the improvement of agriculture, studied the available American and foreign literature on the subject, and imported purebred live stock. He was early a contributor to the agricultural press and for many years wrote often for the *Kentucky Farmer* and other papers. He was the author of many essays and letters on agricultural subjects, and for some of them received prizes from the Kentucky Society. A considerable number of these essays and letters were assembled in a book first published in 1843 as *Southern Agriculture,* and in a revised edition as *Essays on Practical Agriculture* in 1844. This work includes a general article on the agriculture of Kentucky and special articles on corn, hemp, tobacco, a system of agriculture best adapted to Kentucky, rotation of crops, advantages of manufactures to agriculture, breeding horses for agricultural purposes, grass in woodlots, feeding cattle and sheep, wheat in rich vegetable soils, etc. It also contains letters to Thomas B. Stephenson on soils and grasses, and to Edmund Ruffin on soils. Beatty died at the age of eighty-one on his farm in Mason County.

[H. Levin, *The Lawyers and Lawmakers of Ky.* (1897); L. Collins, *Hist. of Ky.* (rev. and enlarged by R. H. Collins, 1874), vol. II; J. L. Coulter in *Cyc. of Am. Ag.,* ed. by L. H. Bailey (1909), vol. IV; Vital Statistic Records in possession of Ky. State Hist. Soc.]

A. C. T.

BEATTY, CHARLES CLINTON (*c.* 1715–Aug. 13, 1772), Presbyterian clergyman, was born in County Antrim, Ireland, the son of John Beatty, an officer in the British army, and of Christiana Clinton, who was an aunt of George Clinton [*q.v.*]. The father died while Charles was young, and his mother came to America in 1729 with her brother Charles, father of George Clinton. Beatty had received a classical and religious education in Ireland but on reaching America, because of his poverty, he became a pedler. He stopped at the Log College, Neshaminy, Pa., where William Tennent, the head master, persuaded him to enroll as a student and prepare for the ministry. In 1742 he was licensed to preach at Nottingham. The next year he was assigned to William Tennent's church at Neshaminy and upon Tennent's retirement succeeded him in the pastorate, being formally ordained and installed in December 1743. The church was disrupted by discordant factions, but Beatty met the situation with prudence and dignity. He was interested in all missionary experiments and sympathized with David Brainerd in his efforts to convert the Indians. Brainerd visited Beatty's house and took part in a communion service at his church, which he mentions in his journal. In 1764 Beatty was chosen moderator of the synod. He was married, June 24, 1746, to Anne Reading, whose father was president of the Council of New Jersey and later governor of the province. He was appointed to take a missionary trip to Virginia and North Carolina in 1754. In the next year he became chaplain to the Pennsylvania troops who were sent under William Franklin to defend the northwestern borders of the state after the massacre of the Moravian missionaries near Lehighton. In 1758 the two synods of New Brunswick which had differed on matters of doctrine were united, and Beatty was appointed on a committee to establish a fund for the relief of poor Presbyterian ministers, ministers' widows, and their children. Two years later he was sent to England by the synod to solicit funds for the committee. He was successful and received a donation from George III. Three years later he was sent with Duffield to investigate the condition of the Indian tribes. In the next year Beatty went again to England because of his wife's health, but she died shortly after their arrival. Since 1763 he had been a trustee of the College of New Jersey, and in 1772 because it was greatly in need of funds he agreed to visit the West Indies and solicit money. He died of yellow fever, soon after reaching the island of Barbados. One of the most popular preachers of his day, he published only one sermon, *Double Honour Due to the Laborious Gospel Minister* (1756), preached at the ordination of the Rev. William Ramsay. His other publications include the *Journal of a Two Months' Tour Among the Frontier Inhabitants of Pennsylvania* (1768), a *Letter to the Rev. John Erskine,* in which the hypothesis that the Indians are the descendants of the Ten Tribes is maintained by a variety of arguments, and *Further Remarks Respecting Indian Affairs,* an account of what had been done for the Indians in America.

[W. B. Sprague, *Annals Am. Pulpit,* III (1858), 119; A. Alexander, *The Log College* (1851); *Presbyt. Mag.* (1852), pp. 412–19; J. Smith, *Old Redstone, Hist. Sketches of Western Presbyterianism* (1854), pp. 119–27; T. Murphy, *The Presbytery of the Log College* (1889), pp. 113–17.]

M. A. K.

BEATTY, JOHN (Dec. 19, 1749–Apr. 30, 1826), Revolutionary soldier and politician of New Jersey, was born in Neshaminy, Pa., the eldest son of the Rev. Charles Clinton Beatty [*q.v.*] and Anne (Reading) Beatty. There were ten children in the family; all four of the brothers who volunteered in 1776 became Continental officers. Graduating at Princeton in 1769, Beatty studied medicine with Benjamin Rush, and in 1772 began to practise at Hartsville, Bucks County, Pa. He married Mary, daughter of Richard Longstreet of Princeton, Mar. 22, 1774. Enlisting in the war, he was commissioned captain in the Pennsylvania Battalion on Jan. 5, 1776, and major of the 6th Pennsylvania the same year. In the disastrous battle and surrender of Fort Washington, Nov. 16, 1776, Beatty was one of the captives. He was severely treated and was not exchanged until May 8, 1778. Perhaps in consequence of this experience, he was appointed in 1778 commissary general of prisoners with the rank of colonel. In this capacity he received from Washington explicit instructions, in 1779, with regard to prisoners on parole, and with reference to exchanges. Arrested and tried on the charge of trading with the enemy, he resigned from the army on Mar. 10, 1780, after receiving a severe reprimand in general orders from headquarters. He passed the remainder of his life in New Jersey, at his home near Princeton, occupied with the practise of medicine, with state politics, business, and church affairs. He was a member of the New Jersey legislature, a delegate to the Continental Congress 1784–85, a member of the state convention that in 1787 ratified the Federal Constitution, and a member of the Third Congress, 1793–95. On the expiration of his term in Congress he became secretary of state of New Jersey, and held that office until 1805. His first wife dying in 1815, in 1818 he married Mrs. Kitty Lalor of Trenton. In his later years he was president of the Trenton Banking Company and of the Delaware Bridge Company.

[*Biog. Encyc. of N. J.* (1877), p. 271; *Biog. Cong. Dir. 1774–1911* (1913); *Pa. Archives*, ser. 2, vol. X, pp. 142–43; F. B. Lee, *Geneal. and Personal Memorial of Mercer County, N. J.* (1807); J. M. Beatty, "Letters of the Four Beatty Brothers of the Continental Army, 1774–94" in *Pa. Mag. of Hist. and Biog.*, XLIV, 193.]

E. K. A.

BEATTY, JOHN (Dec. 16, 1828–Dec. 21, 1914), soldier, legislator, banker, writer, was born near Sandusky, Ohio, the son of James and Elizabeth (Williams) Beatty. His grandfather, John Beatty, born in Ireland, located in Norwich, Conn., in 1796, later moving to New London. In 1815 he led a group from Connecticut into the Western Reserve, settling near the present site of Sandusky, Ohio. Young John received a fair education in the common schools and then engaged in the banking business. Shortly after his marriage to Lucy Tupper of Cleveland, in 1854, he moved to Cardington, where he and his brother William opened Beatty Brothers' Bank, conducting the business under that name until 1863, when it was incorporated as the First National Bank. Beatty took an active interest in public affairs, but though more or less identified with local politics, did not hold office until 1860. From his grandfather, who was an Ohio leader of the ante bellum schism in the Methodist Church and a staunch anti-slavery man of the James G. Birney school, young Beatty acquired his first political tenets and adhered to them through life. In 1852 he supported John P. Hale for the presidency; in 1856 he cast his vote for John C. Frémont. In 1860 he was the Republican presidential elector for the 13th (Ohio) congressional district.

In April 1861 he organized a company, led it to Camp Dennison at Columbus, and when it was incorporated in the 3rd Ohio Volunteer Infantry became its captain. On Apr. 27, 1861, he was appointed lieutenant-colonel of the regiment. After a short period of training he accompanied his command to western Virginia where he served in the forces under Gen. McClellan. In November 1861, Beatty, with his regiment, was transferred to Kentucky and on Feb. 12, 1862, was made colonel. In the spring of 1862 the regiment became a part of the command of Gen. O. M. Mitchell and participated in an extended raid into Tennessee and northern Alabama. When Bragg began his movement through Kentucky in the summer of 1862, Beatty's regiment marched with Buell's pursuing army and in October participated in the bloody battle of Perryville. On Dec. 26, 1862, Beatty was assigned to a brigade command and was engaged in the four-day battle at Murfreesboro, Dec. 29, 1862–Jan. 2, 1863, during which he had two horses shot under him. On Mar. 12, 1863, he was promoted to brigadier-general, to rank from Nov. 29, 1862, in recognition of his gallant conduct at Murfreesboro. Leading his brigade during the Tullahoma, Chickamauga, and Chattanooga campaigns, he commanded the first of Thomas's corps to cross Lookout Mountain. Following Grant's defeat of Bragg at Missionary Ridge, Beatty's command accompanied Sherman on his march to Knoxville, Tenn., for the relief of Burnside's besieged command (Whitelaw Reid, *Ohio in the War*, 1868, I, 924–25; J. W. Keifer, *Slavery and Four Years of War*, 1900, I, 180 ff., 211 ff., 233, 241, 264 ff., 279, 300 ff.; *Memorial, Military Order of the Loyal Legion*, Feb. 3, 1915, pp. 3–4).

On Jan. 28, 1864, Beatty resigned from the army and returned to his banking business in Cardington so as to allow his brother William to enter the army. He continued in the banking business and in the management of his large farm until in 1868 he was elected to the Fortieth Congress from the 8th Ohio district in place of Cornelius S. Hamilton, deceased. He took his seat on Feb. 5, 1868; was reëlected to the Forty-first and Forty-second Congresses; and served until Mar. 13, 1873. He was first a member of the committee on invalid pensions, then chairman of the committee on public buildings and grounds, and finally chairman of the committee on public printing. At the close of his second full term, though strongly solicited to be again a candidate for reëlection, he declined. Some of his army friends in Columbus had urged him to come there and open a bank. This he did, organizing the Citizens' Saving Bank, which opened for business July 1, 1873. Beatty was elected president and served until July 1, 1903, when his bank was consolidated with the Citizens' Trust and Savings Bank. He retired from active business to devote his time to writing, but did not lose contact with public affairs. In 1884 he was an unsuccessful Republican candidate for the nomination for governor against J. B. Foraker (Foraker, *Notes of a Busy Life,* 1916, I, 175–90) and later was one of the Republican presidential electors-at-large for Ohio; in 1886–87 he served as Republican member of the state board of charities; and from 1891 to 1895 was president of the Ohio Chickamauga and Chattanooga Military Park Commission (W. H. Perrin and J. H. Battle, *History of Morrow County, Ohio,* 1880; *Biographical Congressional Directory,* 1911; letter from F. R. Shinn of Columbus, Ohio, Feb. 23, 1927).

During his war service Beatty had kept a diary which he published in 1879 under the title *The Citizen Soldier.* Emboldened by its success, and following a natural inclination, he wrote *The Belle o' Becket's Lane* (1883), the scene of which is laid near his birthplace, and *McLean, A Romance of the War* (1904), both of them historical novels. In 1902 appeared *The Acolhuans,* a prehistoric novel dealing with the mound builders of Ohio. In 1894 *High or Low Tariff, Which?* was printed and in 1896, during the silver controversy, Beatty published his *Answer to "Coin's Financial School."* He was also the author of a number of miscellaneous papers (Randall and Ryan, *History of Ohio,* 1912, V, 64; *Ohio Archæological and Historical Publications,* XII, 104 ff.).

[In addition to references above, see O. C. Hooper, *Hist. of the City of Columbus, Ohio;* Chas. Robson, *Biog. Encyc. of Ohio* (1876), p. 641; A. J. Bauchman and R. F. Bartlett, *Hist. of Morrow County, Ohio* (1911); H. L. Peeke, *Centennial Hist. of Erie County, Ohio* (1925); obituary in the *Ohio State Jour.* (Columbus), Dec. 22, 1914; *Who's Who in America,* 1914–15.]

T. R. H.

BEATTY, WILLIAM HENRY (Feb. 18, 1838–Aug. 4, 1914), jurist, was born at Monclova, Lucas County, Ohio. His parents (Henry Oscar and Margaret Boone Beatty) were Kentuckians and soon after William Henry's birth went back to Kentucky where they remained until the boy was fifteen. They then joined the movement to California and, journeying by way of the Isthmus, reached Sacramento in 1853. Some years later Beatty returned to the East to enter a preparatory school and afterward matriculated at the University of Virginia. In 1858 he returned to California to join his father, whose career had been his source of inspiration, in his practise of law. In 1863, the silver excitement drew him to Nevada, where he was appointed the first city attorney of Austin. Less than a year later, upon the admission of Nevada, he became judge of the district court of Lander County. This office he held in Lander and White Pine Counties until 1875, when he became associate justice of the supreme court of Nevada. Three years later he was made chief justice and served in this capacity for two years. He then returned to Sacramento to resume his private practise. In 1888, because of his recognized ability and experience, he was called upon to assume the position of chief justice of the State of California, left vacant by the death of Chief Justice Morrison. At the close of this term, in 1890, he was elected chief justice for the full term of twelve years and in 1902 was reëlected for a second term but did not live to serve out the entire time. He died at his home in San Francisco on Aug. 4, 1914. During his long years of service as chief justice he had won for himself an outstanding place in the development of California jurisprudence, not only because of the clarity and soundness of his decisions, but also because of his high ideals of justice and his unswerving loyalty to the best traditions of his office. "For more than a quarter of a century he presided over the Supreme Court of California with dignity and rare ability. . . . Throughout his long life he knew but one fear, and that was the fear of doing an injustice to his fellow man" (Memorial of the California State Bar Association, *168 California Reports,* 802–03). The more personal records of his life show him to have been a man of extremely lovable disposition and irreproachable character. He was married in 1874 to Elizabeth M., daughter of Robert Carter Love of Salisbury, N. C.

[A memorial prepared by the Cal. State Bar Ass. in *168 Cal. Reports,* 799–803, gives the most complete account of Beatty's life. Additional material is given in O. T. Schuck, *Hist. of the Bench and Bar of Cal.* (1901). Beatty's decisions as chief justice of Cal. are found in *77–166 Cal. Reports.*]

R. G. C—d.

BEAUCHAMP, WILLIAM (Apr. 26, 1772–Oct. 7, 1824), Methodist clergyman, was born in

Kent County, Del., the son of a Methodist clergyman, William Beauchamp. He was sent to a good school where he was taught English grammar and Latin. At sixteen he joined the Methodist Episcopal church. At eighteen he taught in a neighborhood school at Monongahela, Pa. It was his desire, however, to enter the ministry and he gave his time to systematic and regular classical reading and study and became proficient in Latin, Greek, and mathematics, and later in Hebrew. At nineteen he began to preach, two years later he left home to travel with the presiding elder, and in 1794 became an itinerant preacher on trial on the Alleghany Circuit. In 1796 he was admitted into full connection on the Pittsburgh Circuit and at twenty-five was an elder. The next years saw him in Pittsburgh, New York, Boston, and Provincetown, Mass., and in 1800 he was on Nantucket Island. Because of ill health he asked to be allowed to remain there and was not transferred for seven years. He married Mrs. Frances (Rand) Russell, June 7, 1801. From 1807 until 1815 he lived in his father's neighborhood in Wood County, Va., as local preacher and here he did his first writing, *Essays on the Truth of the Christian Religion* (1811) which established his reputation. He edited the *Western Christian Monitor,* the only paper of its kind in the Methodist Church in 1816, in Chillicothe, Ohio. While he lived in this region there was a great revival of religion, which was attributed to his eloquence as a preacher. In 1817 with Thomas S. Hinde and William McDowell, both Methodist preachers, he established the town of Mount Carmel, Ill. He surveyed the town, helped draw up a rigid code of puritanical laws, and built up a congregation. In 1821 because of ill health he lived quietly for some time on his farm near Mount Carmel, but the next year saw him a member of the Missouri Conference stationed at St. Louis. In 1823 when he was a delegate to the Methodist General Conference in Baltimore he was nominated for bishop, but lost the election by a few votes. The next year, which was his last, he was appointed presiding elder of the Indiana District. He was considered one of the ablest men of his profession. Though he had not had great advantages in formal education, he was a formidable opponent in controversy and his attainments were varied and extensive. In addition to his classical knowledge, he was acquainted with medicine and often made use of it in his pioneer surroundings. His reputation as a writer was considerable. Besides his work as editor of the *Western Christian Monitor* and his early *Essays on the Truth of the Christian Religion,* he published in 1849 *Letters on the Call and Qualifications of Ministers* and *Letters on the Eternal Sonship of Christ.* He died in Paoli, Orange County, Ind.

[W. B. Sprague, *Annals of the Am. Pulpit,* VII (1865); *Minutes of the Ann. Conferences of the M. E. Ch. for 1733–1828,* I, 1840; Theophilus Arminius, "Memoir of the Rev. W. Beauchamp" in the *Meth. Mag.,* Jan., Feb., Mar., 1825.]

M. A. K.

BEAUCHAMP, WILLIAM MARTIN (Mar. 25, 1830–Dec. 13, 1925), archeologist, historian, was born in Coldenham, Orange County, N. Y., the son of William Millett Beauchamp and Mary (Jay) Beauchamp. His father had come from Somerset, England, in 1829, and in 1831, taking his family and possessions in two white-covered wagons, removed to Skaneateles, Onondaga County, where in 1840 he founded the *Skaneateles Democrat.* In his father's printing office William learned to love printing and writing. He decided, however, to enter the Episcopal ministry. Educated at the Skaneateles Academy and the Delancey Divinity School at Geneva, N. Y., he was ordained priest in 1863. As rector of Grace Church, Baldwinsville, N. Y., he served from July 1, 1865, to Oct. 1, 1900, when he retired from the active ministry. After 1900 he resided at Syracuse and, though often preaching, devoted himself mainly to research and writing (*Syracuse Post-Standard,* Dec. 14, 1925). Though deeply versed in local history, his dominating interest was in the past of the Six Nations and other aborigines. He became, among white men, the greatest authority on the history and institutions of the Iroquois. In a sense he was the successor of Lewis Morgan in this field. His interest in the Indians began in childhood, and was increased by his friendship with Albert Cusick, an Onondaga in orders in the Episcopal Church. From him he received much valuable information. In 1904 he was himself adopted into the Eel Clan of the Onondagas as Wah-Kat-yu-ten, the "Beautiful Rainbow." He was the author of many books and papers, among them: *The Iroquois Trail* (1892); *Indian Names in New York* (1893); *History of the New York Iroquois* (1905); *Past and Present of Syracuse and Onondaga County* (1908); *Revolutionary Soldiers Resident or Dying in Onondaga County, N. Y.* (1913); *Moravian Journals Relating to Central New York, 1745–66* (1916); *Iroquois Folk-lore* (1922); and *The Life of Conrad Weiser* (1925). Especially noteworthy was his work as archeologist of the New York State Museum. Preparing thirteen bulletins for the Museum, he threw much new light on the past of the aborigines. He possessed unusual skill in sketching Indian relics. From these sketches his bulletins were often illustrated. He was one of the first (1897–1902) to discover Eskimo influence and culture in New York State dating from a very early period (*Bulletin of the New York State Museum, no. 16,* p. 11, *no. 22,* p. 75, *no. 50,* pp. 328–30). He was active in promoting the Onondaga Historical Association of Syracuse and was a member of many learned societies. He was very short of stature, but deep in chest and powerful. "His ruddy cheeks, snow-white beard, and twinkling eyes made him beloved by all who knew him" (*Syracuse Journal,* Dec. 14, 1925). Of genial disposition, he was possessed of a quaint and whimsical humor. Always an out-door man, he roamed with keen eye the hills and woods of central New York and knew their flora and geology as well as their archeology. He became notable for extreme age and as a nonogenarian retained in a remarkable degree his strength and mental power. His best work was done after three score and ten. He was married to Sarah Carter of Ravenna, Ohio, Nov. 26, 1857.

[Beauchamp left ten large manuscript volumes entitled "Antiquities of Onondaga," and numerous notebooks. These are in possession of his family. A brief memoir by R. D. Burns appears in *Researches and Trans. of the N. Y. State Archæol. Ass.,* vol. III, no. 1. A similar sketch is prefixed to W. M. Beauchamp's "Notes of Other Days in Skaneateles" in *Ann. Vol. of the Onondaga Hist. Ass. for 1914* (1915).]

E. P. T.

BEAUMONT, JOHN COLT (Aug. 27, 1821–Aug. 2, 1882), naval officer, was born at Wilkes-Barre, Pa., of New England stock, third of the ten children of Andrew and Julia (Colt) Beaumont. Through the influence of his father, who was a member of Congress (1833–37) and a friend of President Jackson, he secured an appointment as midshipman, Mar. 1, 1838. Two years later he sailed in the *Constellation* on a long cruise to the East Indies and around the world. In the Mexican War he served on the *Ohio* at the fall of Vera Cruz, and later in the Pacific. Sea service was varied by tours of duty at the Naval Observatory, Washington, in 1848 and 1852–54. As a passed midshipman (promoted May 20, 1844) he visited Mediterranean ports on the *Independence,* 1849–52; and as a lieutenant (promoted Aug. 29, 1852) he was in the *Hartford* in the East Indies at the opening of the Civil War. His war service was entirely as a ship commander on the Virginia rivers and Atlantic coast. He was in the gunboat *Aroostook* in attacks on Confederate batteries in the James River and at Fort Darling in May 1862, and in the *Sebago,* in the South Atlantic Blockading Squadron, 1862–63. Transferred to the monitor *Nantucket,* he took a leading part in the capture of Fort Wagner in July 1863, and was engaged in other attacks on the defenses of Charleston. In the first bombardment of Fort Fisher, Dec. 24–25, 1864, he declined to withdraw, though the boiler of his ship, the *Mackinaw,* was pierced by a shell and ten of his crew were wounded. In the *Mackinaw* he was also in the second attack on Fort Fisher, and in subsequent operations on the Cape Fear River. Of a jovial, social disposition, with a host of friends, and with a reputation as a skilful officer experienced in ironclads, he was selected to command the new monitor *Miantonomoh,* in the squadron which took Assistant Secretary of the Navy Fox to Russia in the summer of 1866 to express American appreciation of Russia's friendly attitude during the war. The first monitor to cross the Atlantic, the *Miantonomoh* was a "show ship," visited by thousands during her tour of the chief ports from Kronstadt to Lisbon. In July 1867, Beaumont was promoted to captain, but complaints of no very serious nature regarding the reception of visitors on the *Miantonomoh* led to his temporary retirement. He was restored to the active list by Act of Congress, June 10, 1872; was chief signal officer, 1874–79; and was commandant of the Portsmouth Navy Yard at the time of his retirement as rear admiral, Feb. 3, 1882. He died of heart disease at Durham, N.H., and was buried in the National Cemetery at Arlington. He was twice married: on Oct. 27, 1852, to Fanny Dorrance, who died in 1855; and again, in 1874 to Fannie S. King of Washington, D. C.

[Numerous letters, reports, etc., relating to Beaumont appear in the *Official Records* (see index, esp. of vols. VII–XIV). His service record is available in *Navy Registers, Reports of the Secretary of the Navy,* and in T. H. S. Hamersly's *Gen. Reg. of the U. S. Navy* (1882). Information regarding his personal life has been drawn from the *Hist. of Luzerne County, Pa.* (1893) and from papers in the possession of his son, Lieut.-Col. John C. Beaumont, U. S. Marine Corps.]

A. W.

BEAUMONT, WILLIAM (Nov. 21, 1785–Apr. 25, 1853), surgeon, was descended from William Beaumont, who in 1635 sailed on the *Eliza de Lond* for Massachusetts, where he tarried long enough to marry Lydia Danforth at Cambridge, and then sought a more permanent residence in Connecticut. In the sixth American generation, William Beaumont, the son of Samuel and Lucretia (Abel) Beaumont, was born. He was the third child and the second son in a family of nine, four brothers and five sisters. The father, following the English custom, bequeathed all his land to his oldest son, Samuel. The War of Independence, in which William's father and uncles had served, had recently closed, and the financial condition of the Connecticut farmer required the closest economy in family expenses. There was much bitterness along party lines between neighbors, Jeffersonian democrats and Hamiltonian federalists, the Beaumonts adhering to the former. Even religious discourses took second place at town meetings and other assemblies. The family attended the Congregational Church but feeling as to creed seems to have been devoid of extravagant expression. William Beaumont never affiliated with any church. In his maturity, replying to a letter from one of his sisters, he wrote: "Though I am not a professor or even a convert to any particular religious sect, yet I am a strict believer in the great good effects of moral and virtuous examples."

There is no evidence that young Beaumont had more than a common school education, but that he attained proficiency in the English language and some knowledge of Latin is shown by his subsequent writings. In early manhood he began a diary which he continued through life and this was fortunately preserved by one of his daughters and later was turned over to Dr. Jesse S. Myer, who wisely used these records in his *Life and Letters of Dr. William Beaumont* (1912). This diary contains not only records of his professional experiences but his observations and comments in his extensive travels, and notes on the books he read. He early showed the possession of three essential qualifications to success: intelligence, industry, and integrity. In 1806 with a horse and cutter and $100 of hard-earned money he drove to Champlain, a village in New York, near the Canadian border. Here he taught school and read medicine for three years. Dr. Pomeroy of Burlington, Vt., supplied him with books and directed his reading. In 1810 Beaumont became an apprentice to Dr. Benjamin Chandler of St. Albans, Vt. In this capacity he swept the office, kept up the fires, learned to fill prescriptions, rode with his preceptor long distances through the forests, studied the symptoms of patients, assisted in surgical operations, and made autopsies in fatal cases. Of all these the student made notes which even now are well worth reading. Between preceptor and apprentice there appears to have been only one rift. The doctor was a violent Federalist and when his apprentice differed from him, he would threaten to turn him out of doors and have nothing more to do with him. In this connection there are interesting points in the letters. Beaumont's father heard that Dr. Chandler had converted the young man to Federalism and wrote a chiding letter. The son replied as follows: "Yes, dear Sir, erase and let any impression be obliterated from every mind of my ever being made a convert to the present system of Federalism. Sooner might they remove the everlasting hills than bribe my integrity, make my faith waver, shake my belief or break my course from the pole star of Republicanism while reason holds her empire over the province of my intellect."

When the lad had finished his apprenticeship the doctor gave him a most hearty indorsement and on the second Tuesday in June 1812 Beaumont was licensed by the Third Medical Society of Vermont to practise medicine. On Sept. 13, 1812, the young doctor was commissioned by President Madison as surgeon's mate to the 6th Infantry at Plattsburg, N. Y. Beaumont has left a graphic description of the battle of York (Toronto) where the retreating English exploded a magazine of 300 barrels of powder under the feet of the advancing Americans. Three hundred were wounded and sixty killed. "A most distressing scene ensues in the hospital—nothing but the groans of the wounded and the agonies of the dying are to be heard." The young surgeon operated for forty-eight consecutive hours and it may be mentioned that this was done without anesthetics. At the close of the war (1815) the strength of the army was reduced to 10,000 and the officers carefully culled. In this process Beaumont was retained while many older men were discharged. Seeing no career in the army in peace, however, he resigned and began private practise in Plattsburg. During his army service his work came under the observation and won the admiration of Joseph Lovell, who, in 1818, became the first surgeon-general. He offered Beaumont a position in his office which was first accepted and then declined. But private practise in Plattsburg did not prove lucrative or stimulating, and in 1820 Beaumont again enlisted, was given the rank of post surgeon, and was ordered to Fort Mackinac. In the travel journal from Plattsburg to Mackinac may be found much of the young man's philosophy. At that time the Fort was occupied by five or six companies, while the village had a population of about 500, swelled in summer-time to about 5,000 by the incoming of the employees of the fur company, consisting largely of drunken Indians and half-breeds. Among these were many brawls and broken heads. Beaumont was the only doctor within a radius of 300 miles and had abundant surgical material. In 1821 he married Mrs. Deborah Platt of Plattsburg, who proved in every way a fit companion for the army surgeon. Although a Quaker, she was devoted to Shakespeare and devised amateur theatricals in various posts to which her husband was assigned. Many officers both of the line and of the staff testified in their letters to the wholesome hospitality and good cheer found in her home. Immediately after the marriage she accompanied her husband to Fort Mackinac where their first child, a daughter, was born.

On June 6, 1822, occurred the accident to Alexis St. Martin, which was to make him and his surgeon immortal. Beaumont records the case in his diary as follows: "St. Martin, a Canadian lad, about nineteen years old, hardy, robust and healthy, was accidentally shot by the unlucky discharge of a gun on the 6th of June, 1822. The whole charge, consisting of powder and duck shot, was received in the left side at not more than two or three feet distance from the muzzle of the piece, in a posterior direction, obliquely forward and outward, carrying away by its force the integuments more than the size of the palm of a man's hand; blowing off and fracturing the sixth rib from about the middle anteriorly, fracturing the fifth, rupturing the lower portion of the left lobe of the lung and lacerating the stomach by a spicule of the rib that was blown through its coat; landing the charge, wadding, fire in among the fractured ribs and lacerated muscles and integuments and burning the clothing and flesh to a crisp. I was called to him immediately after the accident. Found a portion of the lung as large as a turkey's egg protruding through the external wound, lacerated and burnt, and below this another protrusion resembling a portion of the stomach, what at first view I could not believe possible to be that organ in that situation with the subject surviving, but on closer observation, I found it to be actually the stomach with a puncture in the protruding portion large enough to receive my forefinger, and through which a portion of the food he had taken for breakfast had come out and lodged among his apparel. In this dilemma I considered any attempt to save his life entirely useless. But as I had ever considered it a duty to use every means in my power to preserve life when called to administer relief, I proceeded to cleanse the wound, give it a superficial dressing, not believing it possible for him to survive twenty minutes. On attempting to reduce the protruding portions, I found that the lung was prevented from returning by the sharp point of the fractured rib, over which its membrane had caught fast, but by raising up the lung with the forefinger of my left hand I clipped off, with my penknife in my right hand, the sharp point of the rib, which enabled me to return the lung into the cavity of the thorax, but could not retain it there on the least effort of the patient to cough, which was frequent."

The patient was placed in the military hospital where Beaumont dressed the wound once and often twice a day for quite a year. Fortunately the stomach adhered to the intercostal muscles and did not drop back into the abdominal cavity. For a long time food could be kept in the stomach only by the daily application of a pad of lint held in place by adhesive straps. Ultimately a flap of the inner coat of the stomach formed a valve closing the orifice, but easily pushed back exposing the interior of the organ. Beaumont made every possible effort to close the orifice but fortunately for science was unable to do so. About the end of the first year, St. Martin was adjudged a pauper and was ordered to be transported to Lower Canada, a distance of nearly 2,000 miles as one had to go at that time, in an open boat. Beaumont, seeing that this could only end in great suffering and death, made an earnest plea in which he indulged in sarcastic words about "Charity." The authorities were deaf to appeals and the doctor took his patient to his own home, continued to dress his wounds, and clothed and fed the injured man. How he did this when his salary was only $40 a month, with himself and family to support, is a question which only the charitable can solve. The idea of making scientific studies in digestion on his patient apparently did not occur until early in 1825. By this time St. Martin had become quite a lusty man, capable of doing heavy service, such as chopping wood and keeping the house fires going. Late in 1824 Beaumont reported the case to the surgeon-general, but by a strange irony of fate, the report appeared in the *Medical Recorder* as "A Case of Wounded Stomach, by Joseph Lovell, S.G., U. S.A." This mistake was not intentional on the part of Lovell and was soon corrected. In March 1825 the Medical Society of Michigan Territory at a meeting in Detroit made Beaumont an honorary member. This was the first recognition he received from the profession.

With his experiments only fairly begun, Beaumont was ordered to Fort Niagara with two months leave of absence. He took St. Martin to Plattsburg via Burlington and settled down quite satisfied with the prospect of a few weeks of uninterrupted study, when he awoke one morning to find that his patient had stolen away and had probably gone to his home in Lower Canada. Beaumont put his experiments in shape and the article appeared in the *Medical Recorder*. In this series he had studied the temperature of the stomach in digestion, the movements of the walls, the relative digestibility of certain foods, and had shown that the gastric juice, when removed from the stomach and placed in bottles, digests food in the same way but more slowly than under natural conditions. These findings were sufficient to overthrow many of the prevalent theories as to stomachic digestion. Some had held that the stomach is only a reservoir for food and has no digestive action; others, that it is only a grinding or triturating organ; others still, that the stomach is only a fermentation vat.

An incident occurred at Fort Niagara which illuminates the character of Beaumont. A Lieut. Griswold presented himself at sick report. Beaumont admitted him to the hospital and after making a thorough study of the case came to the conclusion that he was a malingerer. The doctor prepared a potion containing some twenty grains of calomel and five or six of tartar emetic. After informing the lieutenant of the composition of this powder he told him that he could take it or report for duty. The lieutenant chose duty. The result was a court martial in which Beaumont was the chief witness, and the lieutenant was pronounced guilty and it was recommended that he be dismissed from the service. The President of the United States reversed this finding and in doing so criticized the doctor severely, whereupon Beaumont issued a circular containing the following passage: "Whether the plan adopted, either in a moral or professional point of view, be justifiable or not I leave for medical men and candid judges to decide; it was salutary and had the intended effect of returning Lieut. Griswold to his duty without prejudice to his health or constitution; neither is it of very great moment with me whether a successful experiment be of *less* or *more* than doubtful propriety, that speedily returns a soldier from *sick report* to the effective service of the government, be he *private, non-commissioned* or *commissioned officer;* neither do I think it of very great consequence whether it be done *secundum artem, secundum naturam* or *terrorem,* provided it be *well done.*" The circular runs through many pages in like tone. It is to the credit of President John Quincy Adams that there is no record of a second court martial. It is to the further credit of President Adams that he commissioned Beaumont surgeon on Nov. 28, 1826.

In May 1826 Beaumont was transferred to Fort Howard on Green Bay and in 1828 to Fort Crawford on the upper Mississippi. During these years he kept up a correspondence with the officers of the fur company in his search for St. Martin. Finally the truant was located in Lower Canada, where he had married and become the father of two children. At Beaumont's expense the whole family was transferred to the far-distant post and in August 1829, after an interruption of four years, the experiments were again begun and continued until the spring of 1831, when St. Martin and his family, increased by two, were allowed to go home with the promise to return when requested. It is worthy of note that this journey was made in a canoe down the Mississippi, up the Ohio, across to Lake Erie and thence to Montreal. Beaumont had long been desirous of enlisting the interest of some competent chemist in the study of the gastric juice. With this in view he asked for a year's leave of absence with permission to carry St. Martin to Europe. This was granted in May 1831 but was subsequently withdrawn. The reason for this change on the part of the Secretary of War was the outbreak of the Black Hawk War and the simultaneous appearance of Asiatic cholera for the first time in this country. One of the early cases developed in a soldier on a transport on Lake Erie. At Detroit, and a few days later at Chicago, a panic ensued; soldiers deserted and the disease was carried to remote posts. Beaumont saw more of this disease than he did of battle and has left a fanciful theory of its nature. As it turned out, it is just as well that he did not get to Europe, as will be seen later.

On Aug. 22, 1832, Col. Zachary Taylor, commanding officer at Fort Crawford, issued an order granting Beaumont six months' furlough, and on the next day the latter left with the intention of taking St. Martin to Europe. The Canadian kept his promise, reported to the doctor in October at Plattsburg, and signed a document binding himself to serve for one year. A like contract has probably never been written. Alexis pledged himself to submit to all experiments and William agreed to pay all expenses, furnish Alexis with good sustenance, suitable housing, wearing apparel, washing, and $150. Beaumont wisely concluded that his furlough of six months was not sufficient to justify the journey to Europe. Both took residence in Washington and the experiments were continued from November 1832 to March 1834. In December 1832, Alexis was enlisted as sergeant at $12 a month, $2.50 a month for clothing, and 10 cents a day for subsistence. In his enlistment papers his age is given as twenty-eight; his birthplace as Berthier, Lower Canada; and his occupation as a laborer.

These were the golden days of the experimentation, and the facilities enjoyed by the investigator were largely due to the intelligent appreciation of the work by Surgeon-General Lovell, supported by the Secretary of War, Lewis Cass. Foreign books were secured and the literature on gastric digestion was thoroughly studied. Giving up hope of taking Alexis to Europe, Beaumont sought aid in this country. He was fortunate in securing the interest of Prof. Robley Dunglison of the University of Virginia, recently established along scientific lines through the efforts of Thomas Jefferson. Dunglison had written a voluminous compend on physiology, in which he discussed the multitudinous theories of digestion. He wrote to Beaumont, suggested lines of experimentation, and made a visit to Washington to see for himself. Beaumont supplied Dunglison with samples of the juice, and the latter, with the aid of his colleague, Prof. Emmet, made an analysis and pronounced the acid to be free hydrochloric. Prout, in 1824, had come to the same conclusion, but his evidence was not altogether convincing and the scientific world was slow to believe that a mineral acid could be formed in the body. Even after Beaumont's publication, Lehmann in Germany wrote a paper showing, to his own satisfaction at least, that it could not be true.

On the expiration of his furlough Beaumont was assigned to duty in New York City, but after six weeks, he wrote the Surgeon-General: "I expect to leave the city in a few days to visit my family at the North . . . I doubt not this measure will meet your approbation. I have not been able to complete the series I had on hand when I left Washington, but I am determined to do it soon even if I have to shut myself up with Alexis in a convent, or retire to some seclusion in the country. My official duties are very light and would not interfere at all with my experiments could I avoid the vexatious social intercourse to which I am perpetually exposed in this city. It is an unfavorable place for the pursuit of physiological inquiries and experiments." While in New York, Beaumont, with bottles of the gastric juice, visited Prof. Silliman of Yale, but this distinguished chemist, although deeply interested and inclined to be helpful, could only advise Beaumont to send the fluid to Prof. Berzelius of Stockholm. This was done, but the great chemist of his time acknowledged his inability to make the analysis. Indeed, the only help Beaumont received from any chemist was the information given by Dunglison, who determined the nature of the free acid and suggested the presence of a second digestive factor which later research proved to be pepsin.

Beaumont wished to publish his studies in book form, but found that he could do so only at his own expense. The first edition of 1,000 copies, bearing the title: *Experiments and Observations on the Gastric Juice and the Physiology of Digestion,* was published at Plattsburg in 1833. The paper was poor; the illustrations were crude; typographical errors were many; but the contents constituted the greatest contribution ever made to the knowledge of gastric digestion. Beaumont had made such an exact study of the physical and chemical properties of the gastric juice that with the exception of the discovery of pepsin, the closest research of modern times has added but little to the work done by him. Both the medical and lay press gave most complimentary reviews, some of which would prove amusing to present-day readers. Prominent members of Congress and other public men to whom complimentary copies were sent thanked the author most profusely, but when a bill was presented to Congress to appropriate $10,000 for further prosecution of the work it failed by a vote of 56 to 129. Financially the publication was a failure. Lilly, Wait & Company, booksellers of Boston, took 500 copies, but in Beaumont's papers he instructs a cousin to sue the company for unpaid dues, and there is no record that any part was collected. A German translation and an English edition appeared within a few years, and since that time no writer on gastric digestion has failed to utilize Beaumont's work. In 1847 Chauncey Goodrich of Burlington published a second edition of 1,500 copies. The agreement was that the author was to receive 200 copies and should have the exclusive sale in Missouri and in all states south and west thereof. Beaumont did receive a few copies but otherwise the agreement was not observed.

The book detailed 238 experiments. These were followed by a table showing the relative digestibility of many articles of diet and the results stated have been but little modified by subsequent studies. There are fifty-one conclusions, most of which are still accepted. The presence of a second digestive factor in the gastric juice (which the discovery of pepsin has since proved) was surmised. Our knowledge of alimentary digestion has been greatly widened since Beaumont's time. The peptic glands, their innervation, the *modus operandi* by which free acid is formed, pancreatic and intestinal digestion, were unknown to him. Nevertheless, no other man, with the possible exception of Claude Bernard, has made so important a contribution to the physiology of digestion. An American physician studying in Paris wrote Beaumont in 1850: "The publication of your observations exposing so clearly and analytically the physiology of the stomach was the commencement of a new era in the study of this important organ and those associated with it. Your experiments are constantly imitated here upon animals by a large number of investigating physiologists among whom M. Bernard probably stands first. His discoveries, of which you have doubtless heard, have rendered the functions of the pancreas, liver, etc., as clear as yours do those of the stomach, but his observations have necessarily been limited to animals, and in the absence of yours upon man, would lose much of their value, since no other evidence exists of the identity of the process of digestion in man and the lower animals. . . . He feels some interest in knowing the subsequent history of Martin and requested me to write you inquiring whether you have kept sight of him, what is the nature of his occupation, his health, etc., if he is still living, with such other information concerning him not contained in your publication as you may think fit to communicate."

Early in 1834, the patient "with a lid on his stomach" returned to Canada and although Beaumont succeeded in locating him and made many attempts to have him returned, once sending his son for him, he failed. St. Martin lived twenty years longer than his doctor and died at St. Thomas de Jolliette at the age of eighty-three. His family refused an autopsy and buried him eight feet below the surface in order to make difficult attempts at resurrection.

In 1834 Beaumont was ordered to Jefferson Barracks, twelve miles below St. Louis, and later was transferred to the St. Louis Arsenal where he was permitted to live in the city and engage in private practise, which soon became large and lucrative. In 1836 Beaumont's good angel, Surgeon-General Lovell, died and was succeeded by Thomas Lawson, who continued in this position until 1861. No more favors could be obtained and Beaumont's first request was granted only under unjust conditions and in derogatory terms. It was soon rumored that Beaumont was to be transferred to Jefferson Barracks where it would be impossible for him to do private practise. But he had many stanch friends among the line officers stationed in the central west, among whom were Maj. Ethan Allen Hitchcock and Robert E. Lee and, besides, his work was highly appreciated by the Missouri senators, Thomas H. Benton and Lewis F. Linn, the latter having previously served with Beaumont as an army surgeon. Through the intercession of these and other friends the blow was delayed. It must be admitted that Beaumont's letter to the Surgeon-General on receipt of the denial of his request for a furlough was not tactful. Indeed, he was never tactful. He possessed an excess of *fortiter in re* and was deficient in *suaviter in modo*. He did not hesitate to use forceful language even when addressing the President of the United States or the Surgeon-General. It is evident, however, from the Washington letters to Beaumont from Hitchcock and Lee that Lawson was seeking an opportunity to humiliate his subordinate. It came in General Order 48, dated Sept. 18, 1839. This assigned Beaumont to a board to convene at Fort Brook, Fla., on Nov. 15 following. It was met by Beaumont's resignation, conditional on the withdrawal of the order. Lawson attempted further humiliation by declining to accept the resignation until the order had been complied with. The resignation was accepted, however, on Jan. 20, 1840, to take effect as of date of Dec. 31, 1839. Thus the second Surgeon-General drove from the corps the man who, up to that time, had most highly honored it and to whose work under adverse conditions every member of the corps now points with pride. But Beaumont at this point committed a great indiscretion. He sought reinstatement, memorialized President Van Buren and characterized the Surgeon-General as one whose capacity was at zero. His friends, Hitchcock and Lee, did the best they could for him, but the request was undignified and the language vitriolic.

The subsequent history of Beaumont is that of a private physician in St. Louis. He had all the professional work he could do, acquired ample means, bought a forty-acre tract, then in the country, now bounded by Jefferson Avenue and Beaumont St. In the profession he had his warm friends and bitter enemies and was involved in two malpractise suits in both of which his reputation was sustained by the courts. In one of these he had trephined a broken skull and there were colleagues who testified that death was due to the operation and that Beaumont wanted to see what was going on within the brain as he had done with St. Martin's stomach. In the cholera epidemic of 1849 he rendered heroic service to both poor and rich. In March 1853 he fell upon ice-covered stone steps and developed a carbuncle on his neck; he died on Apr. 25. He and his wife, who lived until Jan. 23, 1870, now lie in Bellefontaine Cemetery. They left one son and two daughters.

St. Martin was not the first man with a gastric fistula. The record of a round dozen or more may be found in medical literature. Some of these were housed for long periods in great hospitals and seen by the most eminent physicians of the time, but nothing came from these opportunities. In this instance the man met the opportunity. "Every physician who prescribes for digestive disorders and every patient who is benefited by such a prescription owes gratitude to the memory of William Beaumont for the benefit of mankind."

[Jesse S. Myer, *Life and Letters of Dr. Wm. Beaumont* (1912); Wm. Osler, "Wm. Beaumont; A Pioneer

Am. Physiologist," *Physician and Surgeon,* Dec. 1902; Thos. Reyburn, "Memoirs of the Late Dr. Beaumont," *St. Louis Medic. and Surgic. Jour.,* 1854; John Goltra, "Wm. Beaumont as a Scientist," *Physician and Surgeon,* Dec. 1902; Victor C. Vaughan, "Wm. Beaumont and His Work," *Trans. Mich. State Medic. Soc.,* 1896; *Physician and Surgeon,* Dec. 1902.]

V. C. V.

BEAUPRÉ, ARTHUR MATTHIAS (July 29, 1853–Sept. 13, 1919), diplomat, was born in Oswego township, Kendall County, Ill., his father, Matthias Beaupré, a French Canadian, having migrated in 1838 from Canada to Joliet, Ill., where he married Sarah J. Patrick, a native of Ontario, subsequently moving to Oswego. Arthur's youth was spent in Kendall County and his education was procured in the public schools at Oswego and De Kalb, to which latter place the family moved in 1865. On leaving school in 1869 he entered the office of the *De Kalb County News,* learning the printing business and supplementing his education by individual study. A Republican, he became interested in politics at an early age, and on his removal to Aurora in 1874 was elected city clerk and commenced to study law. Shortly afterward he was appointed deputy clerk of Kane County and having been admitted to the Illinois bar commenced practise in Aurora. He was married, on Oct. 20, 1880, to Mary F., daughter of C. W. Marsh of De Kalb, the inventor of the "Marsh harvester." In 1886 he received the Republican nomination for clerk of Kane County and, being elected by a large majority, retained the position for eight years. Both as lawyer and official he showed marked ability and his prominence in local and state politics induced President McKinley to appoint him consul general and secretary of the United States legation to Guatemala and Honduras, Oct. 7, 1897. In this position he met with unqualified success, his urbane, dignified manners and courtly demeanor making a deep impression on the temperamental Guatemalans. He also attracted the confidence of his foreign colleagues to such an extent that in March 1899 he was invited by Great Britain and Honduras to act as sole arbitrator in the dispute respecting the detention of the British schooner *Lottie May* and the arrest and imprisonment of her captain by the government of Honduras in 1892 (*Foreign Relations of the United States,* 1899, pp. 371–72). Beaupré was transferred to Bogota as consul general and secretary of the legation to Colombia, Oct. 27, 1899. At that period the question of a trans-isthmian canal was being vehemently debated, and the conclusion of the Hay-Pauncefote Treaty in 1901 left the United States free to negotiate with Colombia relative to the cession of rights over territory in Panama. Though Beaupré was only in a subordinate position at Bogota, he enjoyed the confidence of President Roosevelt, and on Feb. 12, 1903, three weeks after the signing of the Hay-Herren Treaty the President appointed him minister to Colombia and entrusted to him the delicate task of inspiring the ratification of the treaty by the Colombian Congress. His promotion from consul to minister was almost unprecedented, the records of the State Department affording but one other instance of such an appointment. Deceived at first as to the good faith of the Colombian government, he later realized its intention to extort better financial terms, and in striking dispatches he kept Secretary Hay *au fait* with the tortuous policy pursued by President Marroquin, which ultimately resulted in the rejection of the treaty. The revolution which immediately followed in Panama, and the prompt recognition by President Roosevelt of the new government produced intense excitement in Bogota. Enraged mobs menaced the United States legation, and Beaupré was threatened with personal violence. His position had been a difficult one and this was accentuated by the cutting of the cables, thus severing his communications with Washington. His conduct throughout, however, met with the cordial approval of the President and Secretary of State (*Foreign Relations of the United States,* 1903, pp. 132–230). In 1904 he was appointed minister to the Argentine Republic, remaining at Buenos Aires four years, and becoming minister to the Netherlands and Luxemburg in 1908. While at The Hague President Taft appointed him a member of the administrative council of the Permanent Court of Arbitration and he was also a delegate to the International Exchange Conference. In August 1911 he was appointed minister to the Republic of Cuba and held this position till June 1913. The last months of his residence in Havana were signalized by scurrilous attacks upon him and Hugh S. Gibson, secretary of legation, in the newspaper *Cuba,* wherein they were accused of enriching themselves by blackmail and graft. The author of the libels was ultimately forced to make a complete retraction (*Foreign Relations of the United States,* 1913, p. 412). Beaupré's last diplomatic appointment was as chief of the special mission to represent President Wilson at the inauguration of Menocal as President of Cuba, May 14, 1913. Six weeks later he retired from the service, his diplomatic career having extended over a period of sixteen years. On returning to the United States he took up his residence in Chicago. Stricken with paralysis in June 1915, he was a confirmed invalid during the last four years of his life.

[Details of his family and early life appeared in *Commemorative Portr. and Biog. Record of Kane and Kendall Counties, Ill.* (1888), p. 657. See also R. W. Joslyn and Frank W. Joslyn, *Hist. of Kane County, Ill.* (1908), II, 75; *Who's Who in America*, 1918–19; obit. notices in Chicago *Herald and Examiner* and *Chicago Daily Tribune*, Sept. 15, 1919.]
H. W. H. K.

BEAUREGARD, PIERRE GUSTAVE TOUTANT (May 28, 1818–Feb. 20, 1893), Confederate soldier, was of French ancestry. About the year 1600 the Chevalier de Beauregard, scion of an ancient and honorable family, married the daughter of one Toutant, a French gentleman of Welsh ancestry, and their son assumed the surname of Toutant de Beauregard. Later generations contracted this to Toutant-Beauregard, and eventually the hyphen was dropped. Jacques Toutant-Beauregard, after visiting the colony of Louisiana in the service of Louis XIV, finally settled there. His grandson, also named Jacques, married Hélène Judith de Reggio, of a family which traced descent from the house of Este. Their son Gustave (he did not use the name of Pierre) was born in the parish of St. Bernard, near New Orleans, and received his early education in that city and in New York. He graduated at West Point in 1838, second in a class of which Irvin McDowell, his opponent at Bull Run twenty-three years later, was also a member. As second lieutenant and first lieutenant of engineers he was employed on fortification work chiefly in Louisiana, until 1846, when he went to Mexico as an engineer on the staff of Gen. Scott. He was present at the siege of Vera Cruz and the battles of Cerro Gordo and Contreras, and received a brevet Aug. 20, 1847, for gallant conduct in the latter engagement. Whether or not he originally suggested attacking the City of Mexico by way of Chapultepec, it is certain that he advocated it in opposition to nearly all the general officers and engineers, and that his views finally prevailed (Justin H. Smith, *War with Mexico*, 1919, II, 149). He was twice wounded at the taking of the city and received another brevet on Sept. 13, 1847. After the war he was engaged in engineering in his native state almost continuously until the Civil War, being chief engineer in charge of draining the site of New Orleans, 1858–61. He was promoted captain Mar. 3, 1853. In 1860 he was selected as superintendent of West Point, but his openly expressed intention of going with his state if it should pass an ordinance of secession made the expediency of his appointment more than doubtful, and he had hardly arrived at West Point, in January 1861, when the Secretary of War directed his transfer. He was superintendent of the Academy for just five days. On Feb. 20 his resignation from the army was accepted.

He was at once appointed brigadier-general in the Confederate army and was sent to take command of the forces around Charleston. Acting on instructions from the Confederate government, he demanded the surrender of Fort Sumter, and upon Maj. Anderson's refusal ordered the bombardment that compelled the evacuation of the fort and began four years of civil war. His high reputation as a soldier and his popularity on account of the taking of Sumter dictated his assignment to an important field command. On June 1, near Manassas, Va., he took charge of one of the two Confederate armies which were being assembled near the Potomac, and which were later merged to form the historic Army of Northern Virginia. Gen. Joseph E. Johnston, with the other, was in the Shenandoah Valley, but when Gen. McDowell advanced toward Manassas, he evaded the forces which had been directed to detain him, and joined his army with Beauregard's on the eve of the battle of Bull Run. Johnston, being the senior, commanded the combined force, but as he was unfamiliar with the ground and the disposition of the troops, the preliminary orders for the battle were drawn up by Beauregard. The disastrous defeat of the Union army of July 21, however, was not due to any control of the action by general headquarters. During the day Beauregard was in personal charge of the Confederate left, bore himself bravely, and had a horse killed under him. His popular reputation was greater than ever, and his government recognized his services by promotion to the full rank of general. In the spring of 1862 he was sent to the western theatre of operations, and was second in command, under Gen. A. S. Johnston, of the army which attacked Grant at Shiloh on Apr. 6. Beauregard succeeded to the command when Johnston was killed, pressed the attack, and ended the day with an apparent victory; but the arrival of Buell's army turned the scale against him and he was forced to retreat after the second day's fighting. He fell back to Corinth, Miss., fortified it for a siege, and delayed the advance of the Union army as long as possible, finally evacuating the town. In June sickness compelled him to turn his command over to Gen. Bragg. Upon his recovery he was charged with the defense of the South Carolina and Georgia coasts, particularly of Charleston, which the United States government made vigorous efforts to capture. Although repeated attacks were made in 1863 by land and water, and Fort Sumter reduced to ruins, the city remained in Confederate possession. In the spring of 1864

Beauregard was again in the field. Grant's plan of operations contemplated an advance toward Richmond from the southeast by Butler's Army of the James, while Meade's Army of the Potomac, which Grant himself accompanied, engaged Lee in front. Beauregard, however, defeated Butler at Drewry's Bluff, "bottled him up" at Bermuda Hundred, and removed him from the board for all practical purposes. When the Army of the Potomac shifted to the south of Richmond and began the siege of Petersburg, June 15, it fell to Beauregard to hold back the enemy until Lee could come to his assistance. His command was now merged with Lee's. In September he returned to the west in administrative command. The closing months of the war found him once more second in command, as at Bull Run, to Gen. J. E. Johnston, with whom he served through the campaign of the Carolinas until the surrender. After the war, he was for five years president of the New Orleans, Jackson & Mississippi Railway, declining offers of the command of the army of Roumania in 1866 and of that of Egypt in 1869 and again in 1870. He then became manager of the Louisiana lottery, a lucrative position, but one in which he was naturally subjected to much criticism. In 1888 he became commissioner of public works of the City of New Orleans. He was for many years adjutant-general of Louisiana. He wrote *Principles and Maxims of the Art of War* (1863), *Report of the Defense of Charleston* (1864), *A Commentary on the Campaign and Battle of Manassas* (1891), and numerous papers on Civil War subjects. He is described as a small man, of typically French appearance, soldierly in bearing, animated and agreeable in manner. "As a general, Beauregard was strong in fortification, and of unquenchable courage, but weak in strategy and wanting in coolness, insight, and method on the battlefield. His dispatches lack clearness, and at times candor; while rhetoric is a pitfall he rarely resists" (Johnston, p. 35). In September 1841 he married Laure, daughter of Jules Villère, a sugar planter of Plaquemines Parish. In 1860 he married Caroline, daughter of André Deslonde, a sugar planter of St. James's Parish. She died in the spring of 1864.

[Alfred Roman's *Mil. Operations of Gen. Beauregard* (1884) covers its subject in great detail, quotes many documents in full, and was personally approved by Beauregard, but its tone is one of uncritical admiration throughout. Articles (including several by himself) in vols. I (1887) and IV (1888) of *Battles and Leaders of the Civil War* give a full hist. of his campaigns. For Bull Run, see also R. M. Johnston's *Bull Run—Its Strategy and Tactics* (1913); for Drewry's Bluff and Petersburg, an article by Johnson Hagood in vol. XXVIII (1900) of the *Southern Hist. Soc. Papers*, pp. 318–36. Other references are G. W. Cullum, *Biog. Reg.* (3rd ed., 1891), I, 697–98 and *Official Records*, ser. 1, vols. I, II, X (pts. 1, 2), XXV (pts. 1, 2), XXXVI (pts. 2, 3).]

T. M. S.

BEAVER, JAMES ADDAMS (Oct. 21, 1837–Jan. 31, 1914), Union soldier, governor of Pennsylvania, traced his ancestry to George Beaver, an Alsatian Huguenot, who came from Rotterdam on the *Friendship*, reached Philadelphia, Nov. 2, 1744, and settled in Chester County, Pa. From George Beaver was descended Jacob, a country storekeeper who married Ann Eliza, daughter of Abraham Addams. James Addams Beaver, born in Millerstown, Perry County, was the third of their four children. The early death of his father and Beaver's poor health left the education of this son until 1852 to his grandfathers and his stepfather, Rev. S. H. McDonald. When James was thirteen years old his mother moved to Belleville in Mifflin County. Two years later he entered Pine Grove Academy (in Center County) and in 1854 became a junior at Jefferson College, Canonsburg, receiving his A.B. in 1856 at the age of nineteen. Upon leaving college he began the study of law under Hugh Nelson McAllister at Bellefonte, and was admitted to the Center County bar in January 1859. The Lincoln campaign of 1860 made Beaver expect war, and he joined the Bellefonte Fencibles, a military company under Andrew G. Curtin, the later war governor. The next year he tendered the services of this company to Gov. Curtin and became its first lieutenant on Apr. 21, 1861, when it enlisted for three months as Company H of the 2nd Pennsylvania Volunteer Infantry. The company saw service in the Shenandoah Valley under Sheridan. At the expiration of three months Beaver was honorably mustered out, only to become lieutenant-colonel of the 45th Pennsylvania Infantry, stationed in South Carolina. He remained in the South until Sept. 4, 1862, when he resigned to accept the colonelcy of the 148th Pennsylvania Regiment, recruited near his home for three years. With these men he joined the Army of the Potomac after Fredericksburg (Dec. 13, 1862), was wounded at Chancellorsville (May 3, 1863) and was taken to a Washington hospital. Before complete recovery he took charge (June 18, 1863) of Camp Curtin, a recruiting station in Pennsylvania under Major-General Darius N. Crouch. Here, by June 30, he had organized three emergency regiments which fought at Gettysburg. Relieved from duty at Camp Curtin on July 15, 1863, Beaver rejoined the main army July 31 with little active service before the Wilderness campaign (May 5–7, 1864) and the march against Petersburg. His gallant work at Cold Harbor (June 3) and distinguished conduct until his leg was shot through at Ream's Station (Aug. 25) justified his appointment as brevet brigadier-general of volunteers Nov. 10, to rank from Aug. 1, 1864.

Incapacitated for active service, Beaver was honorably discharged from the Union forces Dec. 22, 1864, and resumed the responsibilities of civil life. On Dec. 26, 1865, he was married to Mary Allison McAllister, the daughter of his former partner, at Bellefonte. He acquired a lucrative practise at the Center County bar. Defeated for governor by Robert E. Pattison in 1882 (by 40,-202 votes) he established the Bellefonte Nail Works in 1883, and three years later was elected governor (by a plurality of 42,651 votes) over Chauncey F. Black for the four years beginning Jan. 18, 1887. As governor he won advances for temperance, industrial education, good roads, and waterways throughout the state. He presided at the Forestry Congress in Atlanta, Dec. 7, 1888, and in 1889 he urged adequate forest reserves in his own state to prevent the recurrence of such distress as was caused by the Johnstown flood in the Conemaugh Valley. Retiring from office in 1891, he resumed his law practise and was also president of the Blubacker Coal Company of Cambria County. On July 1, 1895, his appointment of June 28 as judge of the Pennsylvania superior court became effective. This commission was renewed by election for ten years on Dec. 19, 1895, and again for an equal period Dec. 19, 1905, his work as a jurist ending only with his death.

[A campaign life of Beaver by Frank A. Burr was published at Phila. in 1882. Short biog. sketches are in John B. Linn's *Hist. of Centre and Clinton Counties* (1883), and in the Pennsylvania press at the time of Beaver's death, *e.g.* the *Pub. Ledger*, Feb. 1, 1914. Certain family items are in the *U.S. Census of 1790* (1908). The best records of Beaver's military life during the Civil War are in the *Official Records*; ser. 1, vol. XIV, covers his service in S.C.; vol. XXV, pts. 1 and 2 relate to the Chancellorsville campaign; vol. XXVII, pts. 2 and 3, and vol. XXXVI, pts. 1, 2, and 3 cover the period of his later service in the Army of the Potomac.]

C. H. L—a.

BECK, CARL (Apr. 4, 1856–June 9, 1911), surgeon, son of Wilhelm and Sophia (Hoehler) Beck, was born at Neckargemünd, near Heidelberg, Germany. He was a grandson of Carl Hoehler, a surgeon in the army of Napoleon I. He was educated at the home of his grand-uncle, August Hoehler, a Lutheran minister of Freiburg, and at the universities of Heidelberg, Berlin, and Jena, obtaining the degree of M.D. at the latter university in 1879. In 1881 he was married to Hedwig Loeser, youngest daughter of Heinrich Loeser, president of the supreme court of Saxony. During the same year he came to America and settled in New York where he soon attracted attention as a bold and skilful surgeon. He was appointed professor of surgery at the New York Postgraduate School and was president of St. Mark's Hospital for twenty-five years. He devised a new method for extensive excision of ribs, a method of operating in hypospadias, and a new suture in hare-lip operations. When Roentgen, in 1895, discovered the X-ray, Beck was one of the first to study its application to medicine and surgery and to develop its diagnostic and therapeutic possibilities.

He was a very active man and a prolific writer. Among his medical works may be mentioned: *Fractures, with an Appendix on the Practical Use of the Roentgen Ray* (1899); *Principles of Surgical Pathology* (1905); *Surgical Diseases of the Chest* (1907); *Roentgen Ray Diagnosis and Therapy* (1909). He was also a frequent contributor to American and German medical journals. Being a man of an idealistic turn of mind, he did not lose himself in his professional work, but amid the cares of his professional life found time to devote himself also to literature. In his *Heidelberg und Studententhum* he described the gay and carefree life of his student days, while in his novel *Der Schwabenkonrad* he related the adventures of one of his forebears in the Thirty Years' War. During the last years of his life the heavy work began to tell on him. He died in Pelham, near New York.

[*Boston Med. and Surgic. Jour.*, 1911, CLXIV, 869; *Deutsche Med. Presse* (Berlin), 1911, XV, 112; *Med. Wochenschrift* (München), 1911, LVIII, 1105; *Surgery, Gynecology, and Obstetrics* (Chicago), V, 683 (portr.).]

A. A—n.

BECK, CHARLES (Aug. 19, 1798–Mar. 19, 1866), classical scholar, was born at Heidelberg, in Baden. His father, a merchant, died when Charles was a boy, and his mother married Dr. De Wette, a well-known theologian, Biblical critic and interpreter, who was at that time professor at Heidelberg and later at Berlin. He was a gentle, kind, learned, and wise step-father, and Charles had excellent advantages. As a student in the University of Berlin he devoted himself chiefly to the classics, then he studied theology and was ordained at Heidelberg, July 7, 1822. He obtained the degree of Ph.D. at Tübingen in 1823, and expected to enter the ministry, but was prevented by the political conditions of the time. In 1819 a young German fanatic, named Sand, had murdered the poet and dramatist Kotzebue as a traitor, spy, and mercenary tool of Russia. De Wette wrote a letter to the mother of Sand after her son's execution, and this was construed against him, as implying, in one passage, extenuation of the crime. De Wette was removed from his professorship and went with his family to Basel, where he was given a professorship in the university. Here Beck, after finishing his theological studies, was employed as docent in the university. Meanwhile Dr. Follen, an older friend of Beck, became an object of political suspicion, was compelled to leave Germany, and went to Switzerland, where he taught first in a school at Chur, then at the university of Basel, until, in 1824, the government at Basel yielded to the pressure exerted by the Allied Sovereigns and exiled him. He went to America, and Beck, feeling that there was no hope for the friends of freedom in Germany, or even personal safety in Switzerland, went with him. They sailed from Havre Nov. 5, 1824, and reached New York Dec. 19.

Beck soon became connected with the Round Hill School at Northampton, Mass. (at that time under J. G. Cogswell), and then, in 1830, with two others, opened a school at Philipstown on the Hudson, opposite West Point. In 1832 he was elected professor of Latin at Harvard College. After serving in that capacity for eighteen years with eminent success, he retired in 1850. As professor he was distinguished for his unvarying fidelity to his work, for the conscientious strictness and fulness of his instruction, and for his gentlemanly courtesy and dignity. He became a member of the American Oriental Society in 1843, and a member of the American Academy of Arts and Sciences in 1845. In 1865 he was appointed by the governor and council of Massachusetts a trustee of the Massachusetts School for Idiotic and Feeble-minded Youth. He was for two years a representative of Cambridge in the state legislature. He married in 1827 Louisa A. Henshaw, of Northampton, Mass., who died in 1830; in the following year he married her sister, Mrs. Teresa H. Phillips, who died in 1863. Beck was a man of large views, high public spirit, and consistent moral and religious principle. He had a deep sense of his civic and political duties, and was a loyal and patriotic citizen of his adopted country. As a scholar he was careful, conscientious, and independent, though he lacked something of the constructive imagination which the truly great scholar must possess. He was one of those who introduced into the United States the scholarship of Germany, which made the teaching of the classics more alive and worth while, and he must be included among those whose influence led the ambitious young American scholars of the two following generations to study in German universities.

Beck's published works include, in addition to articles in American and foreign periodicals, a Latin monograph entitled *Statius: Ad Calpurnium Pisonem Poemation auctori vindicavit et adnotatione instruxit Carolus Beck* (1835); an *Introduction to the Metres of Horace* (1835); a *Latin Syntax,* chiefly from the German of Zumpt (1838); a translation of Munk's treatise on metres (1844); editions of Cicero's *Brutus* (1837), Seneca's *Medea* (1834), and Seneca's *Hercules Furens* (1845); and a collation and description of the manuscripts of the *Satyricon* of Petronius Arbiter (1863). This last is perhaps his most important work. A monograph *On the Consolidation of the Worcester and Western Railroads* (1864) shows his interest in the affairs of his own time.

[*The Christian Citizen: A Discourse Occasioned by the Death of Chas. Beck,* delivered Mar. 25, 1866, before the First Parish Church in Cambridge, by Wm. Newell (1866); Andrew P. Peabody, *Harvard Reminiscences* (1888); J. L. Chamberlain, *Harvard Univ.* (1900).]

H.N.F.

BECK, JOHANN HEINRICH (Sept. 12, 1856–May 25, 1924), conductor, composer, violinist, teacher, was the son of Charles and Rebecca Butler Beck of Cleveland. On June 19, 1890, he married Blandina Fellar of Tiffin, Ohio. Beck was born in Cleveland and except for the period of his study abroad, spent his whole life there. He was educated in the Cleveland schools; at the age of twenty-three he went to Leipzig where he studied for three years, specializing in stringed instruments and composition. His teachers in the latter were Richter, Reinecke, and Jadassohn, while his violin study was under Schradieck and Herman. He also studied the history of music with Oscar Paul. He made his début as both violinist and composer in the Gewandhaus, Leipzig, May 17, 1882, appearing in his own "String Quartette in C Minor." In referring to this quartette, the *Leipziger Tageblatt* called attention to the originality of the themes, and the natural and unconstrained flow of the different parts. The first *allegro* and the *scherzo* were particularly praised (Mathews, *A Hundred Years of Music in America,* p. 666). Soon afterward he returned to Cleveland. Shortly after his return he organized the Schubert String Quartette, which did valuable pioneer work in making known the best class of chamber music. Some years later he undertook a long and arduous term as orchestral conductor, spending one season as director of the Detroit Symphony Orchestra (1889–90) and the period from 1901 to 1912 as director of the Cleveland "Pop" Orchestra, the immediate predecessor of the present Cleveland Symphony Orchestra. In these semi-popular programs the fine discrimination and high ideals of the conductor were always in evidence,

Along with this regular work, he conducted the Pilgrim Orchestral Club (1904–10) and the Elyria Orchestra (1905–07). During these busy years of directing and teaching he found time also for composition; but little or none of it has been published. He appeared as guest-conductor frequently in the presentation of his own works, as for instance, the Overtures, "Romeo and Juliet" and "Lara," Boston Symphony Orchestra, Chicago, 1886; "Skirnismal," 1887; "Moorish Serenade," Philadelphia, 1889; "Scherzo in A Major," Thomas Orchestra in Detroit, 1890; "Der Freudekuss," Cleveland Orchestra, 1900, and at the request of the music committee, St. Louis Exposition, 1904; a "Scherzo in F," Thomas Orchestra, Cleveland; also a string sextette, Indianapolis, 1888. He also wrote a tone poem for orchestra, "Aus meinem Leben"; "The Sea at Evening" and "Wie schön bist Du" for voice and orchestra; a cantata, "Deukalion" (Bayard Taylor). There is also a string quartette in D Minor beside songs and violin pieces. The "Scherzo in A," mentioned above, was later taken to Europe by F. X. Arens and played in Vienna, Dresden, Leipzig, and Hamburg. The "Sextette in D Minor" has been played in New York, Boston, Cincinnati, Philadelphia, Detroit, Indianapolis, and other cities.

On the occasion of Beck's sixty-seventh birthday, the Cleveland Public Library paid notable tribute to the respect in which he was held by his fellow townsmen, by placing on exhibition original manuscripts of his compositions, programs from the days when he directed Cleveland's first "Pop" orchestra, and books containing allusions to his reputation as a scholar and composer. Death came suddenly to him as he was returning with some friends from an orchestral concert, and just as he had been remarking the death of his good friend, Victor Herbert, which had occurred that afternoon.

His influence on the musical life about him was always wholesome. As a composer, primarily for the orchestra, he showed that he had not spent his formative years in Leipzig for nothing; he was sincerely fearful of anything savoring of the decadent in his art; yet he was not unduly conservative, and observed with real sympathy the ever increasing richness and power of modern orchestral technique and did not hesitate to take his own share in it.

[The most detailed study of Beck's work is found in Rupert Hughes and Arthur Elson, *Am. Composers* (new revised ed., 1914), pp. 406–11. Other sources of information are the *Times* (Cleveland), and *Topics* (Cleveland), May 31, 1924; *Who's Who in America, 1924–25*; C. Saerchinger, *Who's Who in Music* (1918); *Grove's Dict. of Music and Musicians, Am. Supp.* (1920).]

W. T. U.

BECK, JOHN BRODHEAD (Sept. 18, 1794–Apr. 9, 1851), physician, expert in medical jurisprudence, was born in Schenectady, N. Y. He was the third son of Caleb Beck, who had married Catherine, only daughter of the Rev. Derick Romeyn, a founder of Union College. Dr. Theodric Romeyn Beck [*q.v.*], distinguished in American medical jurisprudence, was an older brother. A younger brother was Lewis Caleb Beck [*q.v.*], naturalist and sometime professor of chemistry at Albany Medical College. Early left fatherless, John went to live at Rhinebeck, N. Y., with his uncle, the Rev. John B. Romeyn, who guided the boy's education. In 1804 Dr. Romeyn took his nephew to New York. Beck entered Columbia College at the age of fifteen, and four years later graduated with highest honors. Immediately thereafter he went abroad with his uncle and patron, applying himself assiduously, while in London, to the study of Hebrew. On his return to America he took up the study of medicine with Dr. David Hosack of New York. In 1817 he graduated at the College of Physicians and Surgeons of New York, having submitted a thesis on Infanticide, which afterward, with additions, was incorporated into the great treatise of his brother, T. Romeyn Beck of Albany, on Medical Jurisprudence, a medical classic in which John Brodhead collaborated. For many years he was looked upon as the standard authority on the medicolegal aspects of infanticide, both in this country and England. In 1820 he made to the New York Board of Health a "Report Concerning the Nature and Origin of Malignant Fever (Yellow Fever) in Middletown, N. Y.," which subsequently was published in the *New York Medical and Physical Journal,* of which (in 1822) he was one of the founders and editors. To that publication he also contributed, among other articles, one entitled, "An Examination of the Medicolegal Question whether in cases of Infanticide the floating of the lungs in water can be depended on as a certain test of the child's having been born alive"—an exhaustive inquiry into the subject which enhanced the author's renown. In 1826 he became professor of materia medica and botany in the College of Physicians and Surgeons of New York, which chair was subsequently exchanged for that of medical jurisprudence. He was married in 1831 to Anne, daughter of Fanning C. Tucker. In 1835 he was appointed one of the physicians of the New York Hospital, in which position he developed marked skill in the clinical investigation of disease. In 1843 he published *Medical Essays;* in 1849 his work on *Infantile Therapeutics* appeared, and in the following year he wrote a *Historical Sketch of the State* *of Medicine in the Colonies,* being his inaugural address as president of the State Medical Society.

Although for many years Beck was an invalid and a martyr to pain, he had untiring energy as practitioner, teacher, and writer. He was an able controversialist, for he possessed a logical mind, with clearness of apprehension and scholarly diction. In the moral sphere of conduct he never sacrificed principle to expediency. He died of malignant disease of the bowel, after long suffering. His chief biographer, Dr. C. R. Gilman, relates that his friend told him, some months before his death, that for five years he had not been free from pain for one single half-hour.

[*N. Y. Jour. of Med.*, Sept. 1851 ; H. A. Kelly and W. L. Burrage, *Am. Medic. Biogs.* (1920) ; S. D. Gross, *Lives of Eminent Am. Physicians and Surgeons of the 19th Cent.* (1861), pp. 605 ff.]

G. A. B.

BECK, LEWIS CALEB (Oct. 4, 1798–Apr. 20, 1853), physician, chemist, son of Caleb and Catherine (Romeyn) Beck, and brother of John Brodhead Beck [*q.v.*] and Theodric Romeyn Beck [*q.v.*], was born at Schenectady, N. Y., a few months after the death of his father. His early education was acquired in the grammar schools of his native city. In 1817 he received the A.B. degree from Union College. He immediately began the study of medicine with Dr. Thomas Dunlop; studied in the College of Physicians and Surgeons, New York, 1816; and was licensed to practise medicine in February 1818. In the autumn of 1819 he entered into active practise in his home city. On the solicitation of his brother Abram, an attorney, he went to St. Louis to establish a practise, but found no opening to his liking. Instead, he conceived the idea of collecting information for a gazetteer. A year later found him back in New York State. The death of his brother again took him to St. Louis but after a brief sojourn he returned to Albany, N. Y., where he began the practise of medicine. These journeys, mostly on horseback, proved of great value to the young observer. During his travels he made notes on botany, geology, mineralogy, climate, and the habits of the people; these, having already served him for articles in St. Louis and Albany newspapers, 1820–21, formed the basis of the *Gazetteer of the States of Illinois and Missouri* (1823), completed in 1822. The same year he published some observations on milk sickness, a serious disease, the cause of which is still unknown ("Facts Relative to a Disease, generally known by the name of Sick Stomach, or Milk Sickness," in the *New York Medical and Physical Journal,* 1822).

Notwithstanding the fact that he engaged in the practise of his profession early in life and gained eminence therein, Beck's energies were directed mainly along educational and investigational lines. He began his public life in 1824 as teacher of botany in Berkshire Medical Institution and during the same year became junior professor of botany, mineralogy, and zoölogy in Rensselaer Polytechnic Institute in Troy, N. Y. On Oct. 17, 1825, he was married to Hannah Maria, daughter of Maj. Israel Smith. In 1826 he accepted the chair of botany and chemistry in the Vermont Academy of Medicine. Four years later he was professor of chemistry and natural history in Rutgers. He was professor in New York University in 1836 and accepted the professorship of chemistry and pharmacy in the Albany Medical College in 1840. He held his Albany and Rutgers positions simultaneously for many years. His lectures were continued at Albany up to the time of his death. He made numerous contributions to medicine, chemistry, botany, mineralogy, and the purity of foods and drugs. In 1831 there appeared his *Manual of Chemistry Containing a Condensed View of the Present State of the Science.* Two years later the *Botany of the Northern and Middle States* was published. His manual, *Adulterations of Various Substances Used in Medicine and the Arts, with the Means of Detecting Them* was made available in 1846. A committee of the New York state legislature selected him to make an investigation of the purity, character, and manufacture of potash. The results were published as a state document in 1836. The same year the New York state officials decided to make a geological survey. Beck was employed as mineralogist, and published a *Mineralogy of New York* in 1842. The United States Congress in 1848 made the first appropriation for chemical examinations of foodstuffs. Beck was selected for the task and the results of his investigations, dealing primarily with breadstuffs, were published in Appendix I to the "Report of the Commissioner of Patents for the Year 1848" (*House Executive Document 59,* 30 Cong., 2 Sess.) and in Part II of the "Report of the Commissioner of Patents for the Year 1849" (*House Executive Document 20,* and *Senate Executive Document 15,* 31 Cong., 1 Sess.).

[J. V. P. Quackenbush, sketch of Beck in *Trans. N. Y. Medic. Soc.*, 1854, p. 63 ; A. March, "Lewis C. Beck," in S. D. Gross, *Lives of Eminent Am. Physicians and Surgeons of the 19th Century* (1861) ; sketch by Mrs. C. E. Van Cortlandt in *Annals Medic. Soc., County of Albany* (1864) ; L. F. Kebler, "A Pioneer in Pure Foods and Drugs : Lewis C. Beck," in *Industrial and Engineering Chemistry,* Sept. 1, 1924.]

L. F. K.

BECK, THEODRIC ROMEYN (Aug. 11, 1791–Nov. 19, 1855), physician, was the eldest of five brothers, three of whom, John Brodhead Beck [*q.v.*], Lewis C. Beck [*q.v.*], and himself, attained distinction in medicine. Of mixed English and Dutch descent, he was born in Schenectady, N. Y. His father, Caleb Beck, a lawyer, dying while Theodric was quite young, his early training fell to his mother, Catherine Theresa Romeyn, a well-educated, well-balanced woman. She instilled into her sons the importance of system. Her father, the Rev. Derick Romeyn, a professor of theology in the Dutch Reformed Church and a founder of Union College, doubtless counseled her. Beck received his formal education in the Schenectady Grammar School and in Union College, from which he graduated at sixteen. Soon thereafter he entered on the study of medicine under Doctors Low and McClelland of Albany, the former a man of talent, a classical scholar and a lover of books, the latter a practical Scot. A year later Beck moved to New York City and studied at the College of Physicians and Surgeons under David Hosack's preceptorship. He graduated in 1811, aged twenty. In the same year he began practise in Albany and continued until 1817. While well fitted for the work, he probably did not enjoy the arduous life of a general practitioner. His strength was unequal to the task, and the inevitable scenes of suffering wore on him. No doubt, too, his literary trend was a factor in his decision to abandon practise. An unsolicited appointment as principal of the Albany Academy came to him in 1817. He held this position until 1853. Under his administration the Academy attained and held high rank. In 1815 he had been appointed professor of the institutes of medicine and lecturer on medical jurisprudence in the Western College of Physicians and Surgeons in Fairfield, Herkimer County, N. Y. The title of his chair was changed in 1826 to professor of medical jurisprudence and in 1836 to professor of materia medica. In 1840 the school was given up. From 1840 to 1843 Beck was professor of materia medica in the Albany Medical College. He was president of the State Medical Society for three successive terms, was secretary of the New York State Board of Regents from 1841 almost to the time of his death, and had much to do with the foundation and policy of the New York State Library and the State Cabinet of Natural History. On the establishment of the State Lunatic Asylum at Utica in 1842, he was made a member of the board of managers, and was president of the board in 1854. His interest in this work was very great, and, on the death of the first superintendent, Amariah Brigham, he undertook the editorship of the *American Journal of Insanity* which he continued for four years. The philanthropic side of his character is shown by his interest in the deaf and dumb. He was a friend of Gallaudet and collected statistics of the deaf and dumb in New York State to call attention to their needs. He was also interested in all aspects of natural science. In 1813, as a counselor of the Society for the Promotion of Useful Arts, he delivered an address urging a survey and development of the mineral resources of the United States. His biographer, Frank Hamilton, says: "To that elaborate and timely paper, the American manufacturer is, to-day, in no small degree indebted for his wealth and prosperity" (*Lives of Eminent American Physicians and Surgeons of the Nineteenth Century,* edited by S. D. Gross, 1861, pp. 776–95). Beck's fame as a writer mainly rests, however, upon his *Elements of Medical Jurisprudence.* The first edition was published in 1823, after ten years' preparation; numerous American and foreign editions followed. It was the first authoritative book on medical jurisprudence published in the United States and was extensive in scope, well planned, clearly and logically written.

Beck always had excellent health except for a brief period in his early professional career when he became apprehensive and perhaps a trifle neurasthenic. His portrait shows regular, strongly marked features, a broad brow, rather widely set eyes with somewhat puffy lower lids, heavy eyebrows, a large Roman nose, a long upper lip, a firm, well-shaped mouth, and a good chin with a slight median cleft. He had a mane of dark, shaggy hair in artistic confusion. He was married, in 1814 at Caldwell, Warren County, N. Y., to Harriet, the daughter of James Caldwell. She died in 1823, at the age of thirty-one, leaving two daughters.

[E. H. Van Deusen, *Am. Jour. of Insanity,* 1855, XII, 105; *N. Y. Jour. of Medicine,* Jan. 1856, p. 2; *Albany Evening Jour.,* Nov. 19, 1855; *Albany Evening Atlas,* Nov. 19, 20, 1855.]

G. B.

BECKER, GEORGE FERDINAND (Jan. 5, 1847–Apr. 20, 1919), geologist, mathematician, and physicist, was born in New York City. His father was Alexander Christian Becker of a Danish family settled in Archangel, Russia, where Samuel Becker, the head of the house, held for a time the office of Danish consul. He was a man of wealth and given to lavish entertainment, but lost his property through his absorption in science, particularly chemistry. Because of financial troubles Alexander Becker emigrated, and settled in New York. His first venture was in mercantile life. Finding this distasteful, he studied medicine and entered upon the practise of his profession, but died when his son George was only two years of age. The latter's mother was Sarah Cary Tuckerman, a daughter of the Rev. Joseph Tuckerman [*q.v.*] known in Boston as a philanthropist and the first "Minister at Large." He was a graduate of Harvard and an overseer and intimate friend of William Channing, Joseph Story, and other prominent men of his day. With a view to the education of the two children, Alexander Rudolph and George F., it was natural therefore that the family should move to Cambridge where the mother's circle of friends and acquaintances included such men as Benjamin Gould, Louis Agassiz, Benjamin Pierce, Jeffries Wyman, Asa Gray, H. W. Longfellow, and J. R. Lowell. It was a stimulating atmosphere for a young, studious, and growing boy, and one by which George profited, particularly through the friendly interest of Agassiz, Pierce, and Wyman. There is abundant evidence of a strong attachment between mother and son, and it is told that when he was four years old he quietly listened the evening through while she read the history of the Commonwealth of Massachusetts. After he had been put to bed and sleep had come to him, his lonely mother, overcome with memories, kneeled at his bedside and as he turned to her, said, "O my child, whom do you love?" and the little fellow sleepily responded, "Any one who will do good to the Commonwealth of Massachusetts."

Becker showed early a leaning toward the natural sciences. Games and sports interested him but little. He preferred roaming the fields and woods, collecting and studying plant and animal life, and came to know all the New England birds and many of the batrachians and other reptilia. In this work he received direct encouragement from men like Wyman and Pierce. He was fitted for college in Latin and Greek under the tutelage of Prof. William B. Atkinson and entered Harvard in 1864. He wrote that he had no difficulty in keeping up with his class and had plenty of leisure for his field studies. Along toward the middle of his college course his interest in natural history became secondary to that in mathematics and chemistry. Immediately after graduation, he went to Germany where he received the degree of Ph.D. (*summa cum laude*) from the University of Heidelberg in 1869. At the outbreak of the Franco-Prussian War he obtained a position on the Crown Prince's staff as a reporter for the *New York Herald.* He was at the battle of Werth, Aug. 6, 1870, and was under fire at Strasbourg, but soon after the fall of that city on Sept. 28, 1870, he went to Berlin to resume his studies. He was graduated with high honors from the Royal Academy of Mines in 1871. Determination to master certain of the problems in the metallurgy of iron and steel caused him to undertake, while in Germany, the somewhat unusual task of a puddler in the Royal Iron Works. His success was such as to win him a certificate as practical worker. Returning to America, he was employed during 1872–73 as a construction engineer in steel works at Joliet, Ill., and while here he is stated to have invented, but not to have patented, an improved puddling process which was in use in both Joliet and Youngstown for many years. Shortly after this, he went to California, partly it is stated on account of his health, though it seems probable that the field was the most promising to one of his profession. Here he remained during 1874–79 as lecturer and instructor in mining and metallurgy in the state university at Berkeley. While here he came under the influence of Clarence King who was then engaged with the 40th Parallel survey. In 1879, when King became director of the consolidated geological surveys, Becker was among the first to receive an appointment, and it was here that his career as a geologist and physicist may well be said to have begun.

Soon after his appointment, Becker made a reconnaissance survey of the San Francisco, Utah, Eureka, Nev., and Bodin, Cal., mining districts, with a view of planning future work rather than of making exhaustive studies in any single district. Owing to a change in plans by the director this work was never carried out in detail. Early in 1880 Becker was instructed by the director of the Survey to undertake, in addition to his Survey duties, those of a special agent of the 10th Census and to assist in the compilation of statistics and technical information relative to the precious-metal industries of the country. The work was carried on in collaboration with S. F. Emmons [*q.v.*], and the results were published in Volume XIII of the Census Reports, entitled *Statistics and Technology of the Precious Metals* (1885). It contained chapters on the geology of the western states and territories, statistics of production, and information on most of the important features of hydraulic mining. In March of 1880, Becker had been also instructed on the part of the Survey to make a reëxamination of the Comstock Lode. This work, which was carried on at the same time with the Census investigation, was completed in two years, the report, *Geology of the Comstock Lode and the Washoe District,* forming Monograph III (1882) of the Survey series. While many of the ideas which Becker put forward in this report have been the subject of controversy, it may safely be said to mark a new era in geological investigations in America. No previous investigations, by any survey, had been undertaken on so broad a basis. No known and available means of discovery were left untried. The appearance of this monograph placed Becker in the front rank among American geological investigators.

His next field of work comprised, under the administration of J. W. Powell, a study of the quicksilver deposits of the Pacific Coast. This proved a somewhat prolonged investigation and for its satisfactory completion necessitated a study of deposits of similar nature in Italy and Spain. Though under government authority he was obliged to carry on this portion of the work at his own expense. The results of these studies appeared in 1888, as Monograph XIII of the Survey series, under the caption, *Geology of the Quicksilver Deposits of the Pacific Slope.* In 1896, under the auspices of an English company and at the instance of John Hays Hammond, he visited the Witwatersrand of South Africa, for the purpose of studying the gold fields. It was while employed in this work that he became conversant in some detail with matters relating to the Jameson raid and the Boer War, and prepared an article on "The Witwatersrand and the Revolt of the Uitlanders," published in the *National Geographic Magazine,* November 1896. In this he set forth in a dispassionate and impartial way the prevailing conditions as they appeared to an outsider. In accordance with an arrangement made with the War Department, Becker, under orders of July 8, 1898, visited the Philippines for the purpose of investigating and reporting on the mineral resources of these islands. He here became involved in a number of military reconnaissances and engagements, and even exposure to gun fire; and was twice cited for bravery. Later he was one of a committee of five called by President Roosevelt to report upon a plan for a scientific survey of the islands. He was also a member of the committee of the National Academy of Sciences appointed in 1915 by President Wilson to report upon the possibility of controlling the slides in the Panama Canal, which then seriously threatened to interfere with its usefulness, but he was prevented by ill health from visiting the Canal in person.

The most original, outstanding, and valuable of Becker's work was not along the lines of descriptive geology. His interests lay largely in the more abstruse chemico-physical problems concerning which he had almost from the start taken advanced grounds, not merely in relation to the problems to be solved, but as well in regard to the methods of their solution. Along these lines he was a pioneer and it is not too much to claim that the present Carnegie Geophysical Laboratory is the outgrowth of his work more than of that of any other one man. With all his close attention to detail in matters of science, he was by no means oblivious of his duties as a citizen. Convinced of the soundness of his own views on any subject, he did not hesitate to make them known wherever he felt it necessary or advisable. A striking feature of his career was his versatility which he seems to have cultivated rather than restrained. This is illustrated in a lecture prepared by him in 1904 entitled: *How Small an Army We Need,* which was favorably reviewed even by military authorities. He enjoyed a wide range of acquaintances both among the scientific fraternity in America and abroad and in what is commonly spoken of as "society," particularly that of the higher circles of political life. Around his hospitable table there gathered members not only of the congressional delegations but of the cabinet, Supreme Court, and foreign legations as well. He was an original fellow of the Geological Society of America and was president of the same in 1914. He was a member of the National Academy of Sciences, the Washington Academy of Sciences, the Geological Society of Washington, the American Institute of Mining Engineers, and an honorary member of the Geological Society of South Africa. He was married first to Sarah M. Barnes from whom he was legally separated in 1879, and on June 17 of the same year to Alice Theodora Watson who died early in the year following; then on Feb. 11, 1902, he was married to Florence Serpell Deakins. During the later years of his life, he suffered severely from asthma and its complications, but retained active interest in his work until the last. He died at his home in Washington at the age of seventy-two years.

[Geo. P. Merrill, "Biog. Memoir of Geo. Ferdinand Becker," *Memoirs Nat. Acad. Sci.*, XXI, to which is appended a full bibliography of Becker's publications; *Harvard College Class of 1868, Fortieth Anniversary, Secretary's Report No. 8, 1868–1908.*] G. P. M.

BECKNELL, WILLIAM (*c.* 1790–*c.* 1832), explorer and trader, was possibly a native of Kentucky but was early domiciled in Missouri. His claim to recognition rests on his pioneer achievements in the Santa Fé trade. Until the arrival of Pike's expedition, which entered the country without authorization, the Spanish government of New Mexico seems not to have been hostile toward the occasional Americans who settled within its jurisdiction. After 1810, however, a number of Americans ventured into New Mexico, many of whom were either imprisoned or deported. The overthrow of Spanish power in 1821 seemed again to open up possibilities for better relations, and a number of expeditions, including one under Becknell, left immediately. Setting out with a pack outfit, like the others he followed the old route to the upper waters of the Arkansas and thence south to Taos and Santa Fé where he sold at a distinct profit the supply of goods he had transported from the states. The entire expedition consumed only five months. Encouraged by his first success, Becknell set out again in 1822, this time with wagons and a larger company who apparently had answered his alluring advertisement in the *Missouri Intelligencer* for men "to go westward for the purpose of trading for horses and mules and catching wild animals of every description." It is this expedition that gives Becknell his fame as the founder of the Santa Fé trail, for instead of crossing from the Missouri to the Arkansas and following the latter to its upper waters, he left the Arkansas near Dodge City, crossed to the Cimarron which, according to Gregg, he reached after great suffering from heat and thirst, followed up the South Fork and over the divide to the forks of the Canadian and across the mountain pass to San Miguel. Thus was traced the famous Santa Fé trail soon to be the accepted route for the substantial commerce of the prairies. Caravan followed caravan in the next decade, and hundreds of thousands of dollars worth of Yankee merchandise was conveyed over this famous trail and profitably disposed of in Santa Fé and the other settlements of the southwest. Becknell made at least one more journey to New Mexico whence he proceeded on a trapping expedition to Green River (Colorado) in 1824. His later life is quite obscured though it is possible that he died in 1832.

[The best account of Becknell's historic expedition to Santa Fé is his jour. of the expedition published in the *Missouri Intelligencer*, Apr. 22, 1823, and reprinted in *Mo. Hist. Soc. Colls.*, July 1906. He published an account of his 1824 trip in the same jour., June 25, 1825. See also Letter of Alphonso Wetmore to John Scott, Aug. 19, 1824, in *House Doc. No. 79*, 18 Cong., 2 Sess., and *The Jour. of Jacob Fowler* (1898), ed. by Elliott Coues, pp. 167–68. The principal secondary materials are Josiah Gregg, *Commerce of the Prairies* (1884), and Hiram M. Chittenden, *The Am. Fur Trade of the Far West* (1902).]

H. C. D.

BECKWITH, JAMES CARROLL (Sept. 23, 1852–Oct. 24, 1917), painter, was the son of Charles and Martha (Owen) Beckwith, who had moved from the Eastern States to Hannibal, Mo., where James Carroll was born. His father later became a prominent wholesale grocer in Chicago, and James's boyhood was spent in that city. His tendencies toward art manifested themselves early and were encouraged by his mother who possessed much personal taste and charm. He began his studies at the Chicago Academy of Design in 1868 under Walter Shirlaw, but these were cut short by the great Chicago fire of 1871. This event altered the family fortunes. His father, who up to this time had frowned upon an artistic career, now gave his consent, and Beckwith went to New York. Entering the classes of the National Academy of Design under Prof. L. E. Wilmarth, he worked there for two years. In October 1873 he sailed for Paris. Here he entered the National School of Fine Arts, studying in its various classes and especially in the *Cours Yvon*. Adolphe Yvon had been a favorite artist under the Second Empire, having painted the Prince Imperial's and other portraits, and especially battle scenes from the Crimean and Italian campaigns, to be seen at Versailles. As a master of drawing he was unrivaled. At this time in the Paris art world also appeared the painter Carolus Duran (whose real name was Charles Durand), who opened a studio where a chosen group of the younger men sought his instruction. Among them were John Singer Sargent and Beckwith, who became fast friends. Taking a studio at 73 rue Notre Dame des Champs, they lived and worked together during the four succeeding years. Carolus Duran associated them with himself in the decoration of a ceiling at the Luxembourg Palace, of which the subject was "The Glory of Marie de Medicis," introducing their portraits, with his own, in the work. Beckwith exhibited at the Salon of 1877 the "Head of an Old Man," and to the Paris Universal Exhibition of 1878 sent "The Falconer," afterward exhibited in America.

Returning to Chicago in 1878, he set up his easel in that city, so as to be near his family, and began to paint portraits. After the intense art life of Paris, Chicago had a most depressing effect on the enthusiastic young painter and as he wrote in 1882, "I determined to come on to New York, sink or swim, survive or perish, rather than rot in the miserable mediocrity of a Western Studio" (letter to the writer). He came to New York in 1879, and, his uncle Mr. Sherwood having erected the Sherwood Studios at the corner of Sixth Ave. and West Fifty-seventh St., he took a studio and worked there during the thirty succeeding years. At this time, a number of the younger artists had returned from foreign schools, and, meeting with a rather cool welcome from the conservative elements of the old Academy of Design, formed the Society of American Artists, a rallying point for the advanced elements. Beckwith was one of its most active members. A corresponding means of education, the Art Student's League of New York, was organized, the most efficient of the younger men becoming instructors. Beckwith at first had charge of the antique classes and later of the life classes. The effect of his teaching was evidenced in the success of many who worked there under his instruction during the last two decades of the century. It gave nothing to be unlearned, whether students proceeded to European art centers or remained to develop their art in this country. At the same time Beckwith became one of New York's most efficient and popular portrait painters. At the National Academy Exhibition of 1879, he had shown a portrait of Mrs. R. H. McCurdy which was much remarked, as were succeeding contributions to the Academy and to the Society of American Artists' Exhibitions. Several summers were spent in Europe studying and making some remarkable copies of Velasquez, Van Dyck, Rubens, and the Venetians. Among prominent New Yorkers whom he painted was LeGrand B. Canon, who had been useful in financial crises of the Government during the Civil War (1861–65). This portrait is now at the Century Association and a replica is at the Union League Club. A series of the captains of Company K, 7th Regiment, included the portrait of Capt. Joseph Lentilhon, in service uniform, with drawn sword passed under his folded left arm. That of John Murray Mitchell in crimson tunic and white gauntlet was painted for the New York Fencing Club, of which Beckwith was president for some time. Another is that of William Walton, the artist and writer, exhibited in New York, Paris, and other cities and now at the Century Association. Other sitters were Theodore Roosevelt, Mark Twain, Thomas P. Janvier, Paul du Chaillu the African explorer, and William M. Chase the painter. In "Mr. Isaacson," the portrait of a man of many languages who had been translator for the Hirsch Fund, the subject stands smiling benignly with hands clasped in front, full of Hebrew good humor. Beckwith used the same model in "The Diamond Broker." His portraits of women showed a delicate perception and sympathetic appreciation of feminine beauty and character, whether in the flush of youth or in the gentler phases of later years. He was married on June 1, 1887, to Bertha Hall, daughter of a prominent New York merchant, and her full-length portrait was shown in the Paris Exposition of 1900. Another of Luisita Leland, exhibited at Knoedler's in 1909, is of the utmost brilliance in light, color, and refined design. Pictorial quality was united to careful likeness in "The Authoress." Genre was united to portraiture in "A Baptism at Onteora." In the mess hall at West Point is "1806," an old soldier with quizzical expression, wearing the high shako and close-buttoned tunic of the date indicated. Beckwith's skill in decorative design was exemplified in a number of paintings and pastels for which the draped and undraped figure furnished motives. Such was "La Cigale" from La Fontaine's fable, a blonde girlish type shivering under the first snowflakes. "The Awakening," "Danse Antique," and "The Nautilus" gave opportunities for expressing an almost Greek sense of beauty. At the Chicago Exhibition of 1893, Beckwith decorated one of the domes of the Liberal Arts Building, typifying Electricity as a sprightly genius at the apex, throwing forked flashes to female figures in the pendentives, representing the Dynamo, the Arc-light, the Telegraph, and the Telephone. The wrecker's axe destroyed the originals with other similar works after the Exhibition, though the preparatory studies may remain. At the village of Onteora in the Catskills, where Beckwith had a summer home and studio, he painted "The Blacksmith," purchased for the National Gallery in Washington.

In all that could advance the interests of art and artists in New York and throughout the country, Beckwith's activity was unbounded. He was among the earliest promoters of the Art Guild of New York and president of the Free Art League, as a result of whose efforts examples of original works from abroad now come and go without restraint for the better education of artists and public. In the Artist's Fund Society of New York, he worked for the benefit of needy artists and their families, leaving a generous bequest for this purpose. He was an active member of the Century Association of New York, and of the National Institute of Arts and Letters. He was elected a National Academician in 1894, and was a member of the American Water Color Society and of a number of other art clubs throughout the country. In 1910, he and his wife went to Europe, visiting France, Belgium, and Italy, and bringing back a series of fresh figure and landscape subjects. Historic monuments and the Châteaux fountains and statues, especially of Versailles, were portrayed with a freshness which vividly recalled their ancient splendors. By taste, education, and practise Beckwith believed in precise design and had no sympathy with careless, bizarre, or slovenly work that invoked originality as its excuse. As a member of the New York Metropolitan Museum of Art and as chairman of the Ways and Means Committee of the National Academy of Design, he sought to increase their educational usefulness. After 1911 he lived and had his studio at the Hotel Schuyler, 59 West Forty-fifth St., New York. Slight in figure, he was quick and elegant in his movements. His features were finely modeled, with a broad brow and ample coronal development. Deep-set gray eyes looked out with penetrating kindliness. A small mustache and a touch of pointed beard aided a certain resemblance to De Champaigne's portrait of Richelieu, while Van Dyck's portrait of Van der Gheest, sometimes called Gevartius, in the National Gallery at London, looks strangely like him. His diction was precise, clear, and musically resonant; with the distinction of manner characteristic of a seventeenth-century cavalier, he was more genially occupied with the activities and life of his own day. At the time of his association with John Sargent under Carolus Duran, there was little room for choice between the brilliancy of their studies. As Samuel Isham remarks (*History of American Painting,* 1905, p. 526), "Beckwith has kept the quality of his master's handling better than almost any other of his pupils. It does not change his personality; it does not make him a copyist, but it enables him to say what he has to say easily and rather sumptuously with heavy impasto, rich shadows and broad strong handling." Sargent remained in Europe amid more helpful conditions to achieve unequaled success as a portraitist. Beckwith returned to America and sacrificed a large part of his time and talent for its art education and general advancement. The honors he received were scarcely commensurate with his merits or the benefits he bestowed: awards at the Paris Salon, and at the Paris Expositions of 1889 and 1900, medals at the Atlanta and St. Louis Expositions, and a gold medal at Charleston in 1902. He exhibited in the Royal Academy at London in 1892, at the Chicago World's Fair, and at other American and European Expositions. He worked unceasingly, though his health was never robust. Less than three months before he died, he published a letter, "Right Art Training," in the *New York Times* (Aug. 5, 1917), deploring the extravagancies encouraged in various schools. These were its closing words: "Do not imagine that there is any short road to mastery of this most difficult profession, but look at the methods and example of our ally France, from whom the American people are just beginning to realize how much they can learn." He died from a sudden heart attack in New York, Oct. 24, 1917, and his funeral at St. Thomas's Church was attended by the leaders in New York's art, literary, and social life, with which he had so actively associated for nearly forty years. "A Romance in the Life of Van Dyck," by Carroll and Bertha Beckwith, was published in *Scribner's Magazine,* July 1, 1918.

[*Who's Who in America,* 1916–17; "The Portraits of Carroll Beckwith" by Robt. J. Wickenden, *Scribner's Mag.,* Apr. 1910; obituaries in the *N. Y. Times,* Oct. 25 and Oct. 29, 1917.]

R. J. W.

BECKWOURTH, JAMES P. (Apr. 26, 1798–*c.* 1867), hunter, squaw-man, raconteur, was born in Virginia, the son of a mulatto mother and a white father, and closely resembled an Indian in figure and physique. Having removed with his father to St. Louis, he joined the fur-trading expedition organized by William H. Ashley and Andrew Henry in 1823, apparently as a groom. He appears to have performed his duties with sufficient faithfulness to have warranted Ashley in taking him along as a sort of body-servant and horse-wrangler on his expedition to the Rocky Mountains in the winter of 1824–25. He continued in the employ of Ashley's successors, married a series of Blackfoot, Snake, and Crow maidens, finally abandoning the whites for about six years to live among the Crows upon whom, if we are to believe his account, he made as great an impression for strength and skill as he had upon the whites. By 1833 he had abandoned his Indian associates and resumed civilized life. In 1844 he was in California where he joined Kearny's force, but following the Mexican War returned to California. Removing to Missouri he joined the stampede to Colorado in 1859, took part in the Cheyenne War of 1864, and settled near Denver where he died about 1867. There is little to differentiate Beckwourth's exploits from those of a number of his contemporaries save that he was fortunate in finding a biographical editor, T. D. Bonner, whose *Life and Adventures of James P. Beckwourth, Mountaineer, Scout, and Pioneer and Chief of the Crow Nation of Indians,* "written from his own dictation," appeared in 1856. In 1892, Charles G. Leland ("Hans Breitmann") reëdited the *Life* with a brief introduction. The inflated style and high-sounding phrases of the biography, whether they be Beckwourth's own words or Bonner's, reflect the bombast and egotism of the narrator.

[Ashley's narrative of his expedition (H. C. Dale, *Ashley-Smith Explorations,* 1918) furnishes practically the only test by which to gauge the truth of any considerable portion of Beckwourth's self-glorifying autobiography. For the main incidents in which he participated Beckwourth is shown to be, aside from his patent egotism, singularly reliable. His last years are covered in L. R. Hafen, "The Last Years of Jas. P. Beckwourth" in the *Colo. Mag.,* Aug. 1928.]

H. C. D.

BEDFORD, GUNNING (Apr. 7, 1742–September 1797), Revolutionary soldier and politician, has been constantly confused by historians with his namesake and cousin, the delegate to the Federal Convention, who styled himself Gunning Bedford, Jr. [*q.v.*]. The confusion is heightened by the fact that their careers were almost precisely contemporary and that both held high office in Delaware and in the nation. The subject of this article is often alluded to as Col. Bedford, or Gov. Bedford; in the records he is sometimes mentioned as Gunning Bedford, Sr. The family came from New Jersey or Pennsylvania and settled in New Castle Hundred, Del. Gunning's father, William Bedford, was a farmer. He himself first appears in history as a major in the Revolutionary War. He was deputy quartermaster-general, lieutenant-colonel of a Delaware regiment Jan. 19, 1776, and muster-master-general June 18, 1776. His regiment took part in the battle of Long Island, but he was detained that day in New York, serving on a court martial. Soon after, he fought at the battle of White Plains and was wounded. The list of political offices which he held is an extended one. He became a prothonotary in 1779; was a representative in the Delaware legislature 1784–86, and a member of the state Senate 1788; he was elected to the privy council in 1783 and 1790. In 1788 he was appointed register of wills, and in the following year a justice of the peace. Meanwhile he was a delegate to the Continental Congress 1783–85, and to the state convention which met in 1787 to ratify the Federal Constitution. As presidential elector he voted for Washington in the first election. The culmination of his political career was his term as governor of the state, an office which he held from January 1796 until his death. His wife, Mary, was the sister of the Delaware statesman George Read, a signer of the Declaration of Independence.

[H. C. Conrad, *Papers of the Del. Hist. Soc.*, vol. III, no. 26 (1900); and the same writer in his *Hist. of Del.* (1908).]

E.K.A.

BEDFORD, GUNNING (1747–Mar. 30, 1812), Revolutionary statesman, came from a family that settled originally in Jamestown, Va. His parents were Gunning and Susannah (Jacquett) Bedford. He was born in Philadelphia, and graduated at Princeton in 1771 in the class with James Madison. He styled himself Gunning Bedford, Jr., and is frequently confused with his cousin Gov. Gunning Bedford (called also Col. Gunning Bedford in military allusions). In Philadelphia he studied law with Joseph Read, and was admitted to the bar. At about this time he was married to Jane Ballareau Parker. He soon settled in Dover, Del., removing thence to Wilmington, Del., and—much later—to a farm called "Lombardy" on the Brandywine. That he served in the war as aide to Washington cannot be confirmed in the records, though it is so stated by his daughter in her will. His active life was closely associated with the history of his adopted state. He was a member of the legislature, of the state council, delegate to the Continental Congress, 1785–86, to the Annapolis Convention, 1786, to the Federal Convention, 1787, and to the Delaware Convention which ratified the United States Constitution in December of that year. During part of this period he was attorney-general of the state, having been appointed in 1784, and serving until 1789. He played a considerable part in the Federal Convention. Delaware, in commissioning its delegates, restrained them from assenting to any change in the "rule of suffrage"—that is, one vote for each state—and Bedford was a champion of the small states in general and of Delaware in particular. He was a fluent speaker, debated often and with emphasis, and was "impetuous" and "irrepressible." At first he supported the project of amending the Articles. Later, he favored equal representation of the states, and removal of the president on request of the state legislatures; he favored a short term of three years for the president, who was to be reëligible only after nine years. He opposed a strong central government and opposed every check upon the legislative branch. When the debates reached their most dangerous point, he made the "most intemperate speech uttered in the Convention"; he "challenged the large States to do their worst," and hinted that the small states might seek foreign alliances. He was a member of the grand committee to consider representation. On July 17, he moved to confer on Congress the power "to legislate in all cases for the general interests of the Union, and also in those in which the States are severally incompetent . . ." (*Madison Papers,* II). After this he apparently took little part in the Convention. In his last year as attorney-general, the draft of the new judiciary bill was sent to him for criticism. Washington appointed him a judge for the Delaware district in 1789, and he held this office until his death. He was a presidential elector in 1789 and in 1793, and president of the trustees of Wilmington Academy and of the college which developed from the Academy. Personally he has been described as tall and stout, handsome, and sociable.

[Henry C. Conrad, in *Papers of Del. Hist. Soc.*, vol. III, no. 26 (1900); John P. Nields, *Paper, Nov. 18, 1897, on presentation of a portr. of Bedford to the U. S. Courts at Wilmington*; *Records of the Federal Convention*, ed. by M. Farrand (1911); W. T. Read, *Life and Correspondence of Geo. Read* (1870).]

E.K.A.

BEDINGER, GEORGE MICHAEL (Dec. 10, 1756–Dec. 8, 1843), soldier, pioneer, congressman, was born in York County, Pa., the third child of Henry and Magdalene (von Schlegel) Bedinger, but soon afterward was taken to Shepherdstown, Va. (now West Va.). His grandfather, Adam Büdinger, was a German emigrant from Alsace. As a boy George attracted attention as a ballad singer, and on the outbreak of the Revolution joined Washington's command at Cambridge. He reënlisted at various times for short terms until the spring of 1779, when he made a trip to Boonesborough, Ky. At this time the Kentucky settlements were hard-pressed by the Indians from the north of the Ohio. Col. John Bowman organized an expedition against the Indian villages around Chillicothe and selected Bedinger as his adjutant and quartermaster, who rendered valuable aid. On their retreat they were followed by the Indians and attacked in the most distressing circumstances. Bedinger was one of the leaders in a counter charge by a cavalry detachment that prevented any further pursuit. After seven months in Kentucky Bedinger returned to eastern Virginia and in 1780 went with a wagon train to South Carolina. The next year he rejoined Washington's army and was present at the siege of Yorktown, leaving, however, before Cornwallis surrendered. About the time hostilities with England ended he formed a partnership in the milling business with James Rumsey [*q.v.*]. In 1784 he journeyed down the Ohio again to Louisville. For the next few years he visited back and forth a number of times between Shepherdstown and the Kentucky country. His love of adventure and excitement led him to join the St. Clair expedition against the Indians in 1791. Although taking no part in the contentions and turmoils preceding Kentucky's admission into the Union, he immediately thereafter entered politics and was honored with both state and national offices. In 1792 and 1794 he represented Bourbon County in the legislature and from 1803 to 1807 served in the lower house of Congress. One of the earliest and most bitter opponents of slavery in Kentucky, he tried while a congressman to circumscribe the institution as much as possible. He also opposed paying the claims arising out of the Georgia Yazoo Fund. Bedinger was married twice: first to Nancy Keene, who died at the birth of her first child in 1787, and then to Henrietta Clay, who bore him nine children. One son, Henry, became a congressman from Virginia and later served as minister to Denmark. Bedinger died on his farm near Blue Licks and was buried in the family cemetery on the banks of the Licking River.

[The Bedinger MSS., consisting mostly of reminiscences of contemporaries concerning him, are in the Draper Collection, in the Wis. His. Soc. Lib. Other sources are, Mrs. Danske, *Geo. Michael Bedinger* (1909); Lewis and Richard H. Collins, *Hist. of Ky.* (1882); *Louisville Weekly Jour.*, Jan. 19, 1844; W. H. Perrin, et al., *Kentucky: a Hist. of the State* (1886), pp. 167 ff.; L. F. Bittinger, *Bittinger and Bedinger Families: Descendants of Adam Büdinger* (1904).]

E. M. C.

BEE, BARNARD ELLIOTT (February or March 1824–July 22, 1861), Confederate soldier, was born at Charleston, S. C., the son of Barnard E. Bee, who in 1835 removed to Texas, and later became secretary of state of the short-lived Republic. Although the father had thus expatriated himself, the son was appointed a cadet "at large" at West Point, entered in 1841, and graduated in 1845. He was commissioned in the 3rd Infantry and at once returned to his adopted state with Gen. Taylor's army of occupation. He served with this army in the early part of the Mexican War, being engaged in the battles of Palo Alto and Resaca de la Palma. After a brief period of recruiting duty, he returned to the front with Gen. Scott's army, went through the entire campaign against the City of Mexico, was wounded at Cerro Gordo, and received brevets for gallant and meritorious conduct there and at Chapultepec. In 1854 his native state presented him with a sword of honor for "patriotic and meritorious conduct" in the war. The rest of his service in the army was on the frontier. He was promoted to first lieutenant in 1851, and upon the organization of the 10th Infantry in 1855 was appointed captain in the new regiment. Resigning on Mar. 3, 1861, he was commissioned a major of infantry in the Confederate army, and on June 17, 1861, was appointed brigadier-general and assigned to a brigade in Gen. Johnston's army. His brigade was one of those that bore the brunt of the first attack at Bull Run on July 21. It suffered heavily, and finally broke up, but had held back the Union advance long enough for the defense to be organized in the rear. Pointing to Jackson's brigade, "standing like a stone wall," he reformed the remnant of his command in line with it, and held his ground. To hold the raw and undisciplined troops up to their work required desperate exertions and reckless exposure on the part of the officers. Having lost nearly all of his field officers, Bee himself at last fell mortally wounded. He died the next day. As a general officer who lost his life in a heroic and successful fight, he naturally became a popular hero in the South. He is chiefly remembered now as the man who gave Stonewall Jackson the name by which he is known in history. These accidental titles to fame have rather obscured his real merit. He showed a capacity for command that was not usual in the early days of the war, and it is fair to suppose that he would have risen high if he had lived.

[G. W. Cullum, *Biog. Reg.* (3rd ed., 1891); *Confed. Mil. Hist.*, vol. V (1899), pp. 375–77; *Official Records*, ser. I, vol. II; R. M. Johnston, *Bull Run, Its Strategy and Tactics* (1913), pp. 202–03.] T.M.S.

BEE, HAMILTON PRIOLEAU (July 22, 1822–Oct. 2, 1897), Confederate soldier, was born in Charleston, S. C. His grandfather, Thomas Bee, had been a federal judge. His father, Barnard E. Bee the elder, removed to Texas in 1835, took a leading part in the establishment of the Republic, and was its secretary of state under President Lamar. His family joined him in 1837. Hamilton Bee was secretary of the commission for determining the boundary between the United States and Texas in 1839, and secretary of the senate of Texas in 1846. Enlisting as a private in the Mexican War, he became a lieutenant in the Texas Rangers and afterward in Bell's regiment of Texas Volunteers, seeing service under Taylor in northern Mexico. After the war he was a member of the legislature, serving a term as speaker of the House of Representatives. In 1861, he was elected brigadier-general of militia, but did not long remain satisfied with an inactive position. The blockade was shutting off commerce through southern ports and stimulating traffic through Mexico, and Bee applied for command at Brownsville. "I am not much of a military man," he wrote, Dec. 12, 1861, "but was under fire at Monterey and did not run"; and pointed out that the commander on the border should be one "who speaks the language and understands the Mexican people." He was appointed brigadier-general in the Confederate army in March 1862 and was assigned to the post he desired. His most important duties were to facilitate the importation of munitions from Europe through Mexico and the exportation of the cotton which paid for them. Military operations in his district were on a small scale. His services to the Confederacy in this administrative position were great, but he had no opportunity to acquire the military experience which he lacked, and which other volunteer generals, no better qualified than he, were slowly and painfully gaining. Accordingly, when called into the field in command of a cavalry brigade to resist Banks's advance up the Red River in the spring of 1864, his handling of troops was severely criticized. It was alleged that the Confederate victory at Sabine Cross Roads (or Mansfield) might have been decisive if he had acted more aggressively, and Gen. Taylor censured his defense at Monett's Ferry, though Kirby Smith declared that in this engagement his "defense of the position was that of a brave and gallant soldier." Gen. J. G. Walker wrote: "His courage, honor, and integrity are universally conceded,—but I would regard it as a public calamity to know of his being assigned to an important command." Bee continued on duty in the field, but there were no further operations of importance west of the Mississippi. In February 1865 he was assigned to command a division in Wharton's cavalry corps, and later he had a brigade in Maxey's infantry division. He surrendered along with the rest of the trans-Mississippi troops, and was paroled at Columbus, Tex., June 26, 1865, being then designated as a major-general. He had never been legally appointed to this rank, but Kirby Smith, cut off from his government as he was, assumed the right to make promotions in his army on his own authority. Bee withdrew to Mexico, but returned to Texas in 1876, and spent the rest of his life in San Antonio. In 1854 he married Mildred Tarver of Alabama.

[F. B. Heitman: *Hist. Reg.* (1903), II, 44; *Confed. Mil. Hist.* (1899), XI (Tex.), 225–26; *Official Records*, ser. I, vols. IV, IX, XV, XXVI (pts. 1, 2), XXXIV (pts. 1, 2), XLI (pt. 2), XLVIII (pts. 1, 2), LIII; unpublished Confederate records in the War Department.]

T. M. S.

BEECHER, CATHARINE ESTHER (Sept. 6, 1800–May 12, 1878), educator, reformer, was the eldest of the nine children of Rev. Lyman and Roxana (Foote) Beecher; she was born at East Hampton, Long Island, where her father was pastor of the Congregational Church. Henry Ward Beecher [*q.v.*] and Edward Beecher [*q.v.*] were her brothers and Harriet Beecher Stowe [*q.v.*] her sister. The large family was brought up in great measure under her care. Trained to industry by her mother, who, as her daughter wrote, "was remarkable not only for intelligence and culture, but for a natural taste and skill in domestic handicraft," she obtained her early education principally at home. When she was ten years of age her father removed to Litchfield, Conn. There she attended a private school at which what was taught was typical of the educational opportunity for girls of that period—the primary branches and drawing, painting, and music. When she was sixteen her mother died and for two years thereafter, till her father married again, she shared with her aunt the care of the home. At nearly twenty she again took up the study of the piano and of drawing, and about a year and a half later began teaching in a private school for young ladies in New London, Conn. Largely by independent study she had gained a knowledge of mathematics, Latin, and philosophy. In 1823 by the sudden death of her affianced lover, Prof. Alexander Metcalf Fisher of Yale College, both her plans for married life were shattered and her religious faith deeply shaken. Eventually determining, as she said, "to find happiness in living to do good," she began in 1824 at Hartford, Conn., a small private school for young ladies. Success at once attended this venture which came to be a school of more than 150 pupils, famous for its advanced curriculum and its excellence of teaching in a day when school opportunities for women in the higher branches of learning were very few. In 1832 when her father accepted the presidency of Lane Theological Seminary in Cincinnati, Ohio, she disposed of her interests in the Hartford school and went west with him. In Cincinnati she organized "The Western Female Institute" on the model of her Hartford school. This enterprise flourished till 1837, when because of failing health and the financial stringency of that period of panic, she gave it up.

Having secured some restoration to vigor through rest and travel, she directed her energies to the promotion of several enterprises she had originated. One of these was, as she said, "the securing professional advantages of education for my sex equal to those bestowed on men." And another, the finding in the East capable and devoted women teachers for the new and isolated communities of the South and West. In the interest of these movements she helped to organize in Boston "The Ladies' Society for Promoting Education at the West," and secured the founding of "female colleges" at Burlington, Ia., Quincy, Ill., and Milwaukee, Wis. Having had experience of the almost insuperable task of promoting higher education without endowment, she sought to develop a public opinion that would provide for "American women a liberal education . . . by means of endowed institutions on the college plan of organization . . . to include all that is gained by normal schools, and also to train women to be healthful, intelligent, and successful wives, mothers and housekeepers" (*Educational Reminiscences*, pp. 154–55). Thus she was one of the early forces which created in this country the opportunity for the higher education of women, promoting it by her career as a teacher, by her writings and her lectures and by the schools she helped to establish. Her works on domestic science, also, and her public advocacy of this branch of knowledge helped to create a public opinion favorable to its entrance into the curriculum of the schools. With both voice and pen she was a determined opponent of woman suffrage and came to be one of the leaders of the early anti-suffragists. In appearance she strongly resembled her brother, Henry Ward Beecher, as the portrait of her that has come down to us shows: endowed with great force of character and of personality, she possessed both charm and sparkling wit. She did not marry. The following are her chief writings: *A Treatise on Domestic Economy for the Use of Young Ladies at Home and at School* (1841); *Miss Beecher's Domestic Receipt Book* (1846); *Physiology and Calisthenics for Schools and Families* (1856); *The Duty of American Women to their Country* (1845); *An Essay on Slavery and Abolitionism, with Reference to the Duty of American Females* (1837); *The Evils Suffered by American Women and American Children: the Causes and the Remedy* (1846); *Woman Suffrage and Woman's Profession* (1871).

[The chief source of information about Miss Beecher is her *Educational Reminiscences and Suggestions* (1874), reprinted in abbreviated form in Henry Barnard, *Am. Jour. of Education*, XXVIII, 65–94. See also Lyman Beecher's *Autobiography* (1864) and Charles E. Stowe's *Life of Harriet Beecher Stowe* (1889).]

W. J. C.

BEECHER, CHARLES (Oct. 7, 1815–Apr. 21, 1900), Congregational clergyman, was born in Litchfield, Conn., the last of the nine children of Lyman Beecher by his first wife, Roxana Foote. Almost forty years later he prefaced his *Redeemer and Redeemed* with the words: "To her who gave me birth; consecrated me to the ministry; died before I knew her; whom, next to my Redeemer, I most desire to meet in the Resurrection, to Roxana Beecher, I dedicate this work, for the execution of which I am chiefly glad to have lived; in the hope that she will not, on account of it, be sorry for having borne me." For some years it seemed as if the mother's hope for her last-born would not be fulfilled, for after being prepared for college at the Boston Latin School, and Lawrence Academy, Groton, Mass., graduating from Bowdoin College (1834), and studying theology under his father at Lane Seminary, he lost practically all faith in the Christian doctrines in which he had been schooled. He taught music, for which he had much aptitude, in Cincinnati, and later was a shipping clerk in New Orleans. Settling in Indianapolis while his brother, Henry Ward, was pastor there, he took charge of the music in the latter's church, and finally, Nov. 9, 1844, having become more settled in his views, he was ordained pastor of the Second Presbyterian Church, Fort Wayne, Ind. Two sermons preached there he published in 1846 under the title, *The Bible a Sufficient Creed.* On July 23, 1840, he had been married to Sarah, daughter of Nathaniel and Mary (Porter) Coffin of Jacksonville, Ill.

His career was a varied one. In 1851 he became pastor of the Free Presbyterian, later the First Congregational Church, Newark, N. J., where his anti-slavery views separated him and his church from the fellowship of the other churches of the city. Here he published in 1851 *The Duty of Disobedience to Wicked Laws, a Sermon on the Fugitive Slave Law.* For a short time he was professor of rhetoric in Knox College, Ill. From Nov. 19, 1857, to May 4, 1881, he was pastor of the First Congregational Church, Georgetown, Mass. In 1863 he was convicted of heresy by the Essex North Conference because of his belief in the preëxistence of souls, but his church sustained its pastor, and later the Conference rescinded its action. In 1864 he represented the town in the Massachusetts legislature. He made his home in Florida from 1870 to 1877, and was superintendent of public instruction in that state (1871–73). From 1885 to 1893 he was acting pastor of the church in Wysox, Pa., and he spent his closing years in Georgetown, Mass.

He was a man of wide learning and of musical as well as literary ability. In 1851 he published in collaboration with John Zundel, organist of his brother Henry's church in Brooklyn, *The Metronome or Music Teacher's Assistant, a New Manual of Sacred Song.* He also wrote several hymns, and selected the music for the *Plymouth Collection* (1855). In 1849 he published *The Incarnation, or Pictures of the Virgin and Her Son,* which portrays Gospel narratives in the aspects which they present to an imaginative mind, with the appliances of geographical, historical, and critical knowledge. He wrote two books on spiritualism, *A Review of the "Spiritual Manifestations"* (1853), and *Spiritual Manifestations* (1879), in which he states his view of the spirit world, and expounds a kind of "Christian spiritualism." Based in part on ingenious and sometimes fantastic symbolic interpretations of portions of the Bible, he evolved a theology, or cosmology, which is presented in the last mentioned work and in *Redeemer and Redeemed* (1864), *The Eden Tableau* (1880), and *Patmos, or the Unveiling* (1896). He also edited the *Autobiography, Correspondence, etc., of Lyman Beecher, D.D.* (1864).

[*Congreg. Yr. Bk.*, 1901; *Obit. Record Grads. Bowdoin Coll.* (1911); *Outlook,* LXIV, 943.] H. E. S.

BEECHER, CHARLES EMERSON (Oct. 9, 1856–Feb. 14, 1904), paleontologist, the son of Moses and Emily (Downer) Beecher, was born in Dunkirk, N. Y. He was fitted for college at the high school in Warren, Pa., whither his parents moved shortly after his birth, and was graduated from the University of Michigan with the degree of B.S. in 1878. For the first ten years immediately succeeding his graduation he served as an assistant to the eminent paleontologist, James Hall [*q.v.*], in Albany, N. Y. In 1888, having been given charge of invertebrate fossils in the Peabody Museum, he removed to New Haven where he remained the rest of his life. In 1891–92 he took charge of Prof. J. D. Dana's classes in Yale University, and showed such capacity for teaching that in the last named year he was appointed assistant professor of historical geology in the Sheffield School. In 1897 he was appointed to full professorship and became a member of the governing board of the School. Two years later (1899) he succeeded Prof. O. C. Marsh as curator of the geological collections and became a member of and secretary to the board of trustees of the Museum. In 1902 his title was again changed, this time to that of University Professor of paleontology.

Beecher was a born naturalist with leanings toward paleontology, and was, moreover, skilful in the manipulation of tools and materials. Some of his most interesting discoveries, as for instance that in 1893 of limbs and antennæ on trilobites, were rendered possible by his skill in cleaning and uncovering these most delicate portions of the fossil remains. It is stated that he began collecting shells and fossils when not more than twelve years of age, and at twenty, while a student in college, he published his first paper—a list of the fresh-water shells in the region of Ann Arbor, Mich. His first paleontological paper, dealing with new genera and species of Devonian fossils, was published by the Geological Survey of Pennsylvania in 1884. As a collector he was unexcelled and on his appointment to the position of curator of the geological collections at Yale he presented without restrictions his entire personal collection of upward of 100,000 specimens to the Museum.

Of a kindly and enthusiastic disposition, he was eminently successful as a teacher in both graduate and undergraduate schools. As an investigator he was of a philosophic turn of mind, caring little for the mere description of species, his most monumental writings dealing with the ontogenetic stages in fossil species and their genetic sequence through the geological formations. His writings on the origin and significance of species may also be mentioned in this connection. In 1899 he was elected to the National Academy of Sciences. He was also a fellow of the Geological Society of America, the Geological Society of Washington, the Boston Society of Natural History, the American Association of Conchologists, the Connecticut Academy of Arts and Sciences, and the Malacological Society of London. Personally he was of a quiet and unassuming nature, industrious in the extreme, loyal and trustworthy. He was married on Sept. 12, 1894, to Mary Salome Galligan of Warren, Pa., by whom he had two daughters. His death through heart failure was sudden and wholly unexpected. He was "one whom science could ill afford to lose, and to whom, humanly speaking, there should have remained many years of industry and fruitful research" (W. H. Dall, *Science*, Mar. 18, 1904).

[C. Schuchert, in *Am. Jour. Sci.*, June 1904, gives a full bibliography of Beecher's publications, pp. 421–22. W. H. Dall, in *Biog. Memoirs, Nat. Acad. Sci.*, vol. VI (1909).]

G. P. M.

BEECHER, EDWARD (Aug. 27, 1803–July 28, 1895), Congregational clergyman, college president, the third child of Rev. Lyman and Roxana (Foote) Beecher, was born at East Hampton, Long Island. He was the brother of Catharine Beecher [*q.v.*], Henry Ward Beecher [*q.v.*], and Harriet Beecher Stowe [*q.v.*]. After graduating from Yale in the class of 1822, teaching at Hartford, Conn., for a year, studying for a short time at Andover Seminary and tutoring at Yale for another year, he became in 1826 pastor of the Park Street Church, Boston. Four years later, on the recommendation of President Day of Yale, he became the first president of Illinois College at Jacksonville. (See Theron Baldwin, and J. M. Sturtevant.) That he should have been willing to give up the pastorate of a prominent church on Boston Common to become president of a college that could boast only one small brick building, located on the outskirts of a little log-cabin village on the western prairies, showed that he had in him the qualities of a true pioneer missionary. He served as president of Illinois College for nearly fourteen years, gathering about him a faculty of able young men who in time won real distinction for this western college. A new and commodious dormitory for students and faculty was added to the college plant in less than two years after he came to his post. He was frequently in the East trying to raise additional funds for the enterprise and met with a measure of success, but the panic of 1837 gave the college a financial blow from which it never recovered during his administration.

It was hardly to be expected that a member of the Beecher family could remain passive when the clouds of the slavery controversy cast their shadow over the community. A large majority of the settlers in that part of the state were from the South and the president, realizing that the fortunes of the college might be seriously jeopardized by radical utterances, hesitated at first to take a determined stand, but when, as he himself remarked, the principles of free speech and a free press became involved in the issue, he could remain "silent no longer." He fearlessly stood by Elijah P. Lovejoy, helping him to guard his press in the warehouse at Alton the night before Lovejoy was shot. He took an active part in helping to organize the first state anti-slavery society of Illinois. Some of his students were indicted by a local grand jury for harboring runaway slaves, and personal violence was threatened against some of his colleagues on the faculty. Religious controversies also disturbed the peace of the campus, but Beecher and his colleagues courageously stood their ground against local bigotry.

In 1842, when college finances were at a low ebb, he again went East to see if he could retrieve the failing fortunes of the institution. Begging for money, however, was a task which he did not enjoy, for he was primarily a preacher and a scholar. He never returned to his post as president, resigning in 1844 to accept the pastorate of the Salem Street Church in Boston. He became one of the founders of the *Congregationalist* and served as its editor-in-chief from 1849 to 1853. In 1855, he returned to the West as first pastor of the First Congregational Church of Galesburg, Ill., where he served until 1871, when he removed to Brooklyn, apparently to be with his distinguished brother. He remained henceforth without any regular pastoral charge except for a few years when he served a small Congregational church at Parkville, near Brooklyn. He died at the ripe age of nearly ninety-two years. His wife, Isabella P. Jones of Wiscasset, Me., who had borne him eleven children, survived him a few months.

He was a somewhat prolific writer on theological subjects, among his more important books being: *Baptism, Imports and Modes* (1841); *The Conflict of Ages* (1853); *The Papal Conspiracy Exposed* (1855); *The Concord of Ages* (1860). He also wrote a *Narrative of the Alton Riots*—an important contemporary account of that episode in the slavery controversy.

[Material on Edward Beecher is scant. See his *Alton Riots* (1838); Bateman and Selby's *Hist. Encyc. Ill.* (1906); *Congreg. Yr. Bk.* for 1896; J. M. Sturtevant, *Autobiography* (1896); *Summary of the Record of the Class of 1822, Yale College, to the Close of 1879* (1879); *Record of the Meetings of the Class of 1822, Yale College, etc.* (1869).]

C. H. R.

BEECHER, HENRY WARD (June 24, 1813–Mar. 8, 1887), clergyman, one of the most conspicuous figures in the public life of his time, was born in Litchfield, Conn., and lived there until he was thirteen years old. Outdoor life in this New England hill town, where, he once said, "it almost required medical help to get sick," developed the physical robustness he inherited through his father, and the love of nature and appreciation of beauty which he derived from his mother. The Beecher line, English with a slight admixture of Scotch and Welsh, went back to the company of Puritans who came over to Boston with John Davenport in 1637, and the next year founded New Haven. It was a succession of hardy Connecticut farmers and blacksmiths, noted for their Samson-like feats of strength. They were much given to marrying; Henry's grandfather had five wives and twelve children, and his father Lyman [*q.v.*], three wives and thirteen children. The latter, pastor of the church in Litchfield, was one of the leaders of New England Congregationalism, a man of keen mind, quick wit, and fertile imagination, but averse to hard study. Revivals and doctrinal combat afforded him his keenest delights. He was restless, impulsive, and of unstable nervous organization, bursting into tears at the slightest provocation. Preaching excited him to a high degree, and a thunderstorm stirred him almost to frenzy. Moods of hilarious cheerfulness took possession of him, in which he was capable of horseplay and rather crude practical jokes. He was erratic, disorderly in his habits, and a careless spender. On the other hand, Henry's mother, Roxana Foote, was a shy, sensitive, self-abnegating woman, who loved flowers and all beautiful things, sang, played the guitar, did fine embroidery, and painted on ivory. With all her artistic temperament, however, she had far more poise and sound judgment than her husband. Her ancestry went back to Nathaniel Foote, one of the original settlers of Wethersfield, Conn., and still farther, to James Foote, a cavalier who, according to tradition, helped King Charles II conceal himself in the royal oak. Her father and mother, Eli and Roxana (Ward) Foote, were Episcopalians and Loyalists. After bearing Lyman Beecher nine children she died of consumption when Henry was about three years old. Not long after her death, her place was taken by Harriet Porter, a beautiful, aristocratic person of elegant manners and exquisite sense of rectitude and propriety, who awakened in the Beecher children awe rather than warm affection.

For a boy of Henry Ward's nature and needs, life in the Litchfield parsonage was both favorable and unfavorable. There was an atmosphere of intellectual virility there, but an unwholesome amount of theological discussion, and as he became older he had agonizing periods of concern over the unsaved condition of his soul. A spirit of cheerfulness and even hilarity pervaded the household, however. Lyman Beecher romped with the children and went fishing with them. Strict discipline was enforced and independence and resourcefulness were developed. "I was brought up to put my hand to anything," Henry once declared, and boasted that he could go into an abandoned blacksmith's shop, start a fire and put a shoe on his horse. He also learned to knit mittens and suspenders, an accomplishment for which he professed to be thankful. Nevertheless the Beecher household was too busy and crowded for a younger child to receive much personal attention and affection, and Henry needed both. In spite of the fact that he was robust, fun-loving, and full of animal spirits, he was a shy, backward lad, so thick of speech that he could hardly be understood. Undreamed of emotional possibilities were stored up within him. In the fields and woods where he loved to be by himself, these were stirred, but not at home. Unquestionably, as a youth, he was lonely, self-centered, and suppressed.

It was his "misfortune," he said in after years, "to go to a district school." "I have not a single pleasant recollection of my schoolboy days." Diffidence and a defect in verbal memory, which he never overcame, caused him to be regarded as unusually stupid. So backward was he that when he was ten years old, his father sent him to a school in Bethlehem, Conn., conducted by a Rev. Mr. Langdon. Here he was home-sick and studied little, spending as much time as he could in the woods. He was next sent to the school which his sister Catharine was teaching in Hartford, where he was the only boy among some forty girls. When in 1826 Lyman Beecher became pastor of Hanover Church, Boston, Henry was at the age of inner turbulence and longing for romantic adventure. He wanted to go to sea. His shrewd old father told him that if he was to follow the sea he ought to learn navigation. Henry swallowed the bait and was landed in the Mount Pleasant Classical Institute, Amherst, Mass. Here for the first time he had the advantage of contact with boys of varying types from different parts of the country. He became popular with them and a leader in their sports. William P. N. Fitzgerald, an ex-cadet at West Point, instructor in mathematics, taught him how to study; and John E. Lovell, with persistent, interested coöperation on Beecher's part, made something of an orator out of him. Here, too, for the first time, his fervid emotional nature had some expression and human response, partly through his practise in declamation, but more particularly through one or two intimate friendships.

In 1830 he entered Amherst College, graduating four years later. He stood low in his classes, for he had his father's averseness to hard study, and was never disposed to subject himself to a fixed régime. As his moods dictated, however, he read widely in the English classics. He also acquired a considerable knowledge of phrenology, which he always felt was a great help to him in appraising men's powers and tendencies. In public speaking he attracted some attention, and he made frequent contributions to the *Shrine,* one of the college papers. During the long winter vacations he taught school, and on occasions lectured or preached. He was a lusty youth, active in such athletics as were then common, popular with his fellows, noted for his skill in storytelling and mimicry, his quickness in repartee, his hilarity, and practical jokes.

Thus far young Beecher had had no satisfying religious experience. During a revival at Mount Pleasant Academy he had gone through a brief period of religious excitation which he hoped was conversion, and his father had hustled him into the church. He had no firm ground to stand upon, however, and in college suffered much from uncertainty and doubt. He knew that his mother on her death-bed had dedicated him to the ministry, and that his father expected all his sons to become preachers. Upon graduating from college, therefore, following the course of least resistance possibly, he entered Lane Theological Seminary, Cincinnati, of which his father had become the head. Here his exuberant vitality and his interest in what was going on about him, led him to give as much time to extra-curriculum activities as to his studies. He continued his general reading, lectured, preached, wrote articles for the *Daily Evening Post* of Cincinnati, and for a few months, acted as editor of the *Cincinnati Journal,* a Presbyterian weekly. During the excitement which followed the destruction of James G. Birney's printing office by a pro-slavery mob, he was sworn in as special constable. His doubts about entering the ministry continued. For systematic theology he had no appetite then or thereafter, and scant intellectual capacity for dealing with its problems. Calvinism, which had overshadowed him from infancy, with its emphasis upon the sovereignty of God, its rigidity and sternness, was repellent to a nature like his, rebellious to all restraint, extraordinarily sensitive to the beauty and joyousness of life, and craving love and companionship. He was determined to preach the Gospel, if at all, as it was revealed to him and not as it was taught in the schools. Religious certitude finally came to him through an ecstatic personal experience. One beautiful May morning in the Ohio woods there entered his soul an intoxicating sense of God as one who loves "a man in his sins for the sake of helping him out of them," not "out of compliment to Christ, or to a law, or to a plan of salvation, but from the fulness of His great heart"; and of Christ as one whose nature it is to lift man "out of everything that is low and debasing to superiority." Later there came a realization of Christ as ever near him, a companion and friend to uphold and sustain him. Here was a conception opening up possibilities of a highly emotional religious life, and a field for preaching exactly suited to Beecher's temperament and gifts.

After this May morning experience he had no more doubts as to his life work. In 1837 he was licensed to preach by the Cincinnati Presbytery, and accepted a call to a church of twenty members in Lawrenceburg, Ind. He went back East in the summer of that year and, on Aug. 3, married Eunice White Bullard of West Sutton, Mass., to whom he had become engaged while he was a student at Amherst. The young couple had no capital and began housekeeping in two rooms over a warehouse, the scanty furnishings being provided through the sale of some of their personal belongings, and gifts from their parishioners. The salary was meager and Beecher was not too proud to wear the cast-off clothing of others. It did not always fit, but he was never particular about his personal appearance. A child was soon born to them, the first of ten. Beecher applied for ordination to the Miami Presbytery, a decidedly Old School body, the Scotch-Irish members of which suspected his orthodoxy because he was Lyman Beecher's son. With more cleverness than candor apparently, he answered their questions satisfactorily. A resolution was passed, however, to the effect that the Presbytery would ordain only those who would give adhesion to the Old School Presbyterian General Assembly. With this condition Beecher refused to comply, and he returned to Lawrenceburg unordained. His church supported him and became an independent Presbyterian body. Later, Nov. 9, 1838, he was ordained by the New School Presbytery of Cincinnati. Beecher remained in Lawrenceburg until July 1839, when he became pastor of the Second Presbyterian Church of Indianapolis, a New School congregation which had withdrawn from the First Church. Here he remained eight years.

During the first decade of his ministry, Beecher was feeling his way, getting command of himself and learning how to use his endowment. He began his career with a considerable fund of varied information derived from wide reading; a passionate fondness for outdoor life; a liking for people whatever their station which sometimes made him dangerously careless in his choice of associates; an ambition to be an effective preacher; and beneath all, a powerful and sincere moral earnestness. He was disposed to be a law unto himself, not only theologically, but in all things. In a lesser degree he had his father's emotional instability, and the latter's zest for action, disorderly habits, strain of coarseness, and financial ineptitude. Neither in the pulpit nor out of it did he pay much attention to the conventionalities. There was little in his dress or his demeanor to suggest his profession. He went hunting and fishing, romped with the young, played copenhagen at Sunday-school picnics, painted his house, pushed a wheelbarrow through the streets, went to fires and held the hose, with the same indifference to appearances with which in after years he would walk the streets of New York munching peanuts, and leaving a trail of shucks behind him. His high spirits, genial disposition, interest in all aspects of human life, and his freedom from any ostentatious piety made him popular generally. For a long time his preaching did not satisfy him. Finally through a study of Jonathan Edwards and the methods employed by the apostles as revealed in the book of Acts, he grasped the idea that the secret of successful preaching lies in its singleness of aim—that of effecting a moral change in the hearers; and that a sermon is good only as it has power on the heart. Upon this principle, therefore, he shaped all his preaching. People flocked to hear him; he assisted in revival services about the state; and with increasing frequency was called to give lectures and addresses for special occasions.

He also began that association with periodicals through which his influence was to have a reach which the pulpit alone could never have afforded. The *Indiana Journal* introduced into its columns an agricultural department, the contents of which were published every month in magazine form under the title, *Indiana Farmer and Gardener,* later changed to *Western Farmer and Gardener,* and of this Beecher was made the editor. His knowledge of agriculture was not extensive, although he was an enthusiastic experimental gardener; but with the remarkable capacity for assimilating and putting to practical use the results of other people's labors, which was a life-long characteristic, he perused Loudon's encyclopedias of horticulture and agriculture, together with works on botany, and wrote for the *Farmer,* according to an associate, "all the articles in it that were good for anything." Many of them were later published under the title *Plain and Pleasant Talk About Fruits, Flowers and Farming* (1859). They are written in a direct, pithy style, with touches of humor and imagination, contain a goodly amount of worldly wisdom, and besides imparting agricultural information, advocate cleanliness, temperance, better public schools, more education for farmers, and attention to beauty as well as to utility.

A Beecher could hardly help being a reformer. Henry Ward's early efforts to improve social conditions were directed chiefly against the vices which commonly exist in a frontier community. While in Indianapolis he delivered a series of addresses which included such subjects as "Industry and Idleness," "Twelve Causes of Dishonesty," "Gamblers and Gambling," "The Strange Woman," "Popular Amusements." They attracted much attention at the time, and, published in 1844 under the title *Seven Lectures to Young Men,* were widely read in this country and abroad. They are remarkable for their shrewd analysis of human motives, their graphic descriptions, and picturesqueness of language, their realism, and their trenchant style. He was criticized at the time, and has been condemned since, for seeming to side-step the slavery question in a community where abolitionists were not popular. His comparative silence on this subject could not have been due to lack of courage, for Beecher always displayed a boldness, not to say rashness, in doing what he wanted to do. The Beechers were all opposed to slavery, but Henry shared his father's antipathy to the extreme abolitionists, "he-goat men," the latter called them, "who think they do God service by butting everything in their line of march which does not fall in or get out of their way." Not only did he distrust their methods, but their anger, malice, and evil-speaking were foreign to his genial, kindly disposition. The probability is that he was unwilling to do anything which might interfere with the main purpose of his life—preaching the Gospel with power to all sorts and conditions of men. Running through his intensely emotional nature, there was a strain of hard, practical common sense, exhibited in the advice he gave to his brother Charles: "Preach little doctrine, except what is of mouldy orthodoxy, keep all your improved breeds, your short-horned Durhams, your Berkshires, etc., way off to pasture. They will get fatter, and nobody will be scared. . . . I do not ask you to change yourself; but, for a time, while captious critics are lurking, adapt your mode so as to insure that you shall be rightly understood." In line with this advice, with respect to slavery, in his early days he permitted himself to be governed by expediency rather than by a heroism of questionable wisdom. In his later years he affirmed that he had often touched upon this subject indirectly, but it was not until his Presbytery recommended that all Presbyterians preach upon it at least once annually that he made it the theme of a sermon.

By 1847 Beecher's fame had gone abroad. That year he received calls to the Park Street Church, Boston, and to the Old South Church of the same city. These he declined. He liked the West, and wanted to stay there; but his wife did not, and her health was poor. Accordingly when invited to take charge of the newly organized Plymouth Church of Brooklyn, Congregational in polity, he accepted. Here, Oct. 10, 1847, he began a public career which for conspicuousness and influence has probably not been equaled by that of any other American clergyman. People came to hear him in increasing numbers. His unconventionality, his audacity, wit and humor, his theological latitude, his dramatic ability and picturesqueness of language, his friendly intimacy and naturalness, fascinated them. At first they came out of curiosity, but they kept coming, and from other motives. His sympathetic understanding of the human heart, and his appreciation and varied application of fundamental spiritual truths met their religious needs. In January 1849 the church building which the society had acquired burned, and a larger one, with a semi-circular auditorium, especially designed to give the audience opportunity to see and hear Beecher, and Beecher freedom to exercise his powers, was erected. Thereafter his weekly congregation averaged about 2,500 persons. Visitors to New York from all over the country and from abroad made it a point to hear him. His sermons, taken down stenographically, for they were never written out, were printed each week in pamphlet form and widely circulated. Entering the lecture field, he was soon one of the most popular of public speakers. He early became a regular contributor to the *Independent,* and his connection with it did much to make it widely read. From 1861 to 1864 he was editor, and from 1870 to 1881, editor of the *Christian Union.* For these papers he wrote some of the "strongest editorials in the American press" (*Cambridge History of American Literature,* 1921, III, 325). He was also for a time a contributor to the *New York Ledger.* The effect of his personality and gifts was extraordinary. "He has had the misfortune of a popularity which is perfectly phenomenal," his sister, Harriet Beecher Stowe, wrote to George Eliot. . . . "I remember being in his house one evening in the time of early flowers, and in that one evening came a box of flowers from Maine, another from New Jersey, another from Connecticut—all from people with whom he had no personal acquaintance, who had read something of his and wanted to send him some token" (Charles E. Stowe, *Life of Harriet Beecher Stowe,* 1889, p. 478).

From the beginning he used his pulpit, or platform, for he would have no pulpit in his church, for the discussion of public questions and the advocacy of reforms. His pronouncements therefrom and through the press made him a recognized leader of the anti-slavery forces. While not always consistent or well advised, on the whole his views and policies stand the test of time. He believed that slavery is fundamentally wrong, but held that under the Constitution there could be no interference with it in the slave states. He insisted, however, that it should be rigidly confined therein, and thus circumscribed, he felt, it would die. He opposed the compromise measures of 1850, on the ground that liberty and slavery are irreconcilable elements in our political system. He counseled disobedience to the Fugitive Slave Law, declaring that the requirements of humanity are above those of the Constitution. He urged Northerners to emigrate to Kansas, and use force to make it free soil. While expressing sympathy for John Brown, he deprecated his raid at Harper's Ferry as the act of a crazy old man, and denied the right of Northerners to attempt to breed discontent among the bondsmen, or to stir up bitterness against the South. He campaigned for Frémont, and in 1860 for Lincoln. After the war broke out, he urged its vigorous prosecution by the North, criticizing Lincoln severely for his delay in issuing an emancipation proclamation. In 1863 he visited England, and in the face of violent opposition supported the North in a number of speeches, which, while their influence in determining English opinion may have been exaggerated, were extraordinary platform accomplishments. After the war, although solicitous for the rights of the freedmen and advocating that they be given the franchise, he was in sympathy with President Johnson in the latter's desire that the seceding states be promptly admitted to the privileges of statehood in the Union, and military government in the South be discontinued as soon as possible. A letter expressing these sentiments written to a convention of soldiers and sailors held in Cleveland, Ohio, known as the "Cleveland Letter," was interpreted as a repudiation of the Republican party, and brought down upon him much criticism and abuse.

Neither in political nor in religious matters did Beecher display any particular originality. He broke no paths into new realms of truth; he started no new movements. He was not an investigator, a close reasoner, or even a student in the common acceptance of the term. He had little capacity for dealing with abstruse subjects, and seldom discerned the subtler elements in matters spiritual or temporal. The more or less obvious and practical were always his forte. Nevertheless, he had unusual intellectual vitality and fertility. He exploited every field of human interest, and was able to grasp fundamental principles, perceive essential facts, and with rare expository ability set them forth clearly and persuasively. Quickness of wit and resourcefulness enabled him always to take command of a situation. His type of mind, however, was preëminently that of the poet. He thought in images and analogies. Never when speaking, he affirmed, was he at a loss for a word or a figure; his embarrassment was in choosing from the number which rose up before him.

The physical and emotional, in fact, were the dominant elements in Beecher's nature. These gave to his career both its strength and its weakness. In personal appearance he is said to have been one of the most striking figures in New York. He was of medium height and large girth, with broad shoulders upon which rested a lionesque head. His hair, gray in his later years, hung down in flowing locks over his coat collar. He was full-blooded, and his face, always clean-shaven, was ruddy in hue. His grayish-blue eyes were full of changing expression. He had a rich, sympathetic, flexible voice, responsive to every shade of emotion. His physical resources seemed inexhaustible. He exuded vitality and with it exuberant good humor. His senses were unusually acute. He had the artist's eye for colors, and took a sensuous delight in them. He deliberately turned to beautiful objects for their intoxicating effect, carrying precious stones in his pocket to be brought forth and gazed at when he felt so disposed. Some of them soothed him; others, he confessed, produced much the same effect as champagne. He craved an emotional atmosphere for his preaching, always had flowers in the church, and insisted upon hearty congregational singing. He displayed great charm and tact in meeting people, and a freedom with his friends, including women, which was unconventional, but so spontaneous and natural as to be inoffensive. There was nothing mean or petty in his constitution, but an overflowing good-will toward all. Free from race or sectarian prejudices, he was a Congregationalist because of the freedom that denomination afforded, but he appreciated the good in other churches, though he opposed all efforts to bring about organic church unity, convinced that the differing beliefs, tastes, and needs of men will forever make it impossible. When all is said, however, he was essentially a man of moods and impulses. He never thoroughly disciplined himself, or held himself to a fixed routine. He did what he felt like doing, and lacking a fine sense of propriety he frequently did and said what was in bad taste and unworthy of him. If he liked a thing he wanted it, an art dealer once commented, and no one could convince him that something else was more beautiful or better. Similarly he gave his approval to men and measures, because something in them appealed to him strongly, often to the chagrin of his friends and to his own later embarrassment.

His attitude on matters great as well as small was likewise determined by his emotional reactions. Just as the theological conceptions which came to him in the Ohio woods were precisely those which satisfied his inner cravings, so, throughout his career, his beliefs and activities were determined, not by critical, intellectual tests, but by the fact that they coincided with his feelings, predispositions, and intuitions. His intense love of freedom was due in no small part to his rebellion against the repressing influences and restraining Calvinism under which he grew up; his hatred of theological controversy and his tolerance, to the same cause. He believed in a personal God, but God had little reality to him except as personified in Christ. It was the latter to whom he prayed, and in whom his passionate nature found that for which it hungered. "Shall I twine about him every affection," he said, . . . "feed upon him as my bread, my wine, my water of life; . . . in his strength vanquish sin, draw from him my hope and inspiration; . . . die in his arms, awake with eager upspring to find him whom my soul loveth, only to be put away with the announcement that he is not the recipient of worship!" (*Sermons,* Harper's ed., 1868, I, 85). "I accept without analysis," he elsewhere says, "the tri-personality of God. I accept the Trinity; perhaps because I was educated in it. No matter why, I accept it" (Theological Statement, given in Lyman Abbott, *Henry Ward Beecher,* 1903, p. 432). He preached the love of God and the joy and glory of the Christian life, but put comparatively little emphasis upon God's righteousness and the importance of self-discipline, sacrifice, and the sterner virtues. Similarly, his activities in behalf of reform were determined by his dominant feelings. The condition of the slaves stirred his sympathies, and slavery itself was opposed to his love of freedom and his religious sentiments. He supported the woman suffrage movement, because he felt that the franchise is a natural right, and rebelled against interference with the exercise of it. He was a free-trader, because he believed protection to be socialistic in principle, and his individualism revolted against the militaristic aspects of that system. In his later years he embraced the theory of evolution gladly, because, as he interpreted it, it fitted in with his optimistic confidence in the possibilities of human nature, and his conviction that man had never fallen, but had ever been ascending. At the same time, he clung to his belief in miracles and special providences.

It is a mooted question whether Beecher's intensely emotional and sensuous nature, his lack of rigorous self-discipline, his rather unstable religious convictions, and his tendency to be a law unto himself, resulted in his being guilty of immoral acts; or whether he was the victim of false accusations. Theodore Tilton, a brilliant literary and newspaper man, and a radical reformer, was in his early years one of Beecher's admirers and protegés. Both Mr. and Mrs. Tilton were members of Plymouth Church and its pastor was a frequent caller at their home. Through Beecher's influence Tilton had been made assistant editor of the *Independent,* and upon the former's retirement from that office had become editor-in-chief. His criticism of the "Cleveland Letter" had caused Beecher to sever all connection with that paper. Tilton's unconventional views on marriage and religion became offensive to many of the subscribers, and that fact, together with the popularity of the *Christian Union* under Beecher's charge, reduced its circulation. Henry C. Bowen, its proprietor, relieved Tilton from the editorship, retaining him as a regular contributor, and made him editor of the *Brooklyn Union.* Late in 1870, partly through his influence, Beecher affirmed, Bowen summarily severed Tilton's connection with both papers. Rumors of gross immoralities on Tilton's part were afloat, and Beecher, on the advice of Mrs. Beecher, had counseled Mrs. Tilton to separate from him.

Scandalous stories affecting Beecher's character seem also to have had a clandestine existence for some years. In an interview on Dec. 30, 1870, Tilton accused Beecher of improper relations with his wife, on the basis of a written confession made by her, which, after a call from Beecher, she retracted, saying it had been obtained under duress. A policy of silence was adopted by all concerned, but the story leaked out. On Nov. 2, 1872, Victoria Woodhull published in *Woodhull and Claflin's Weekly* a highly colored account of "the character and conduct of Rev. Henry Ward Beecher in his relation with the family of Theodore Tilton." Not until June 30, 1873, however, did Beecher make public denial of the stories and rumors concerning him. In June 1874, Tilton published a statement in which he charged Beecher with an "offense against him which he forebore to name." Beecher then asked a committee of six from his church and society to investigate. After examining thirty-six witnesses, including Tilton, who made a partial statement and then refused to be questioned further, the committee reported that it "found nothing whatever in the evidence that should impair the perfect confidence of Plymouth Church or the world in the Christian character and integrity of Henry Ward Beecher." On Aug. 20, 1874, Tilton filed a complaint against Beecher, charging him with adultery with Mrs. Tilton, and demanding damages of $100,000. The trial lasted six months, and was discussed all over the country. Public opinion was sharply divided. After nine days' deliberation, the jury failed to agree on a verdict, the final vote being nine to three in favor of the defendant. A year and a half later, a council of Congregational churches, made up of 244 representatives, convened at Plymouth Church, and, after an examination, declared: "We hold the pastor of this church, as we and all others are bound to hold him, innocent of the charges reported against him, until substantiated by proof." A committee of five was appointed to receive any charges and proof that might be offered, but none was forthcoming.

A review of the evidence presented at the trial, by an impartial body of people, would probably result in a difference of opinion such as existed in the jury. One cannot escape the conviction, however, that Beecher spoke truly when, as alleged, he told two of his attorneys who apologized for coming to consult with him on a Sunday afternoon: "We have it on good authority that it is lawful to pull an ass out of the pit on the Sabbath day. Well, there never was a bigger ass, or a deeper pit." Even his friends would probably have admitted a measure of truth in this statement from a newspaper review of the case: "Sensible men throughout the country will in their hearts be compelled to acknowledge that Mr. Beecher's management of his private friendships and affairs has been entirely unworthy of his name, position, and sacred calling" (*New York Times,* July 3, 1875).

The remainder of Beecher's career was somewhat shadowed by this scandal. His popularity, however, was not destroyed. The trial had cost him $118,000, and although for years his income had been large, he was always poor. To rehabilitate himself financially he lectured throughout the country. His voice was still heard on public matters. He attacked the corrupt judges of New York, advocated President Arthur's renomination, opposed Blaine, and actively supported Cleveland for the presidency. He also worked on his *Life of Jesus the Christ,* the first volume of which had appeared in 1871. He did not live to finish the task, but it was completed by his sons and published in 1891. Beecher's purely literary attempts were not particularly successful. In 1867 he had published a novel, *Norwood, or Village Life in New England,* a series of descriptive sketches rather than a story. Just before his trial he had delivered the first three courses of the Lyman Beecher Lectures at Yale (*Yale Lectures on Preaching,* 1872–74). They still rank high among the many given in this series, and contain a wealth of homiletical wisdom. His disbelief in a literal Hell, and his acceptance of the evolutionary hypothesis, subjected him to much criticism, and on Oct. 10, 1882, he withdrew, against its protest, from the Association of Congregational Ministers to which he belonged, that his brethren might not "bear the burden of responsibility of being supposed to tolerate the views" he had held and taught. In 1885 his *Evolution and Religion* appeared. For four months in 1886 he was in England where he preached and lectured. He conducted the services in Plymouth Church with his usual vigor on Feb. 27, 1887, but on the following Sunday was at the point of death from cerebral hemorrhage, the end coming two days later. Forty thousand people viewed his body as it lay in the church before being taken for burial to Greenwood Cemetery.

[Much autobiographical material may be found in Beecher's sermons and addresses. For the former, see *Plymouth Pulpit,* vols. I–X (1868–73), new series, vols. I–VII (1873–84), and *Sermons by Henry Ward Beecher* (2 vols., 1868). *Lecture Room Talks* (1870, 1872) is also illuminating. *Star Papers, or Experiences of Art and Nature* (1855) and *New Star Papers, or Views and Experiences of Religious Subjects* (1859) contain contributions to the *Independent; Eyes and Ears* (1862), contributions to the *N. Y. Ledger. Freedom and War* (1863) is a collection of discourses on topics of the times. See also *Patriotic Addresses* (1887) ed. by John R. Howard, and *Lectures and Orations by Henry Ward Beecher* (1913) ed. by N. D. Hillis. Many compilations of his utterances have been made. There are a number of lives of Beecher, no one of which is altogether satisfactory. The latest, Paxton Hibben's *Henry Ward Beecher, An American Portrait* (1927), while bringing to light some new material and valuable for the social background it sketches and its list of sources, is decidedly unfriendly and fails to give a well-rounded portrayal. Earlier biographies are for the most part laudatory and uncritical. Among them are Lyman Abbott and S. B. Halliday, *Henry Ward Beecher* (1887); Thos. W. Knox, *Life and Work of Henry Ward Beecher* (1887); Jos. Howard, Jr., *Life of Henry Ward Beecher* (1887); Frank S. Child, *The Boyhood of Henry Ward Beecher* (1887); Wm. C. Beecher and Sam. Scoville, *A Biog. of Rev. Henry Ward Beecher* (1888); John R. Howard, *Henry Ward Beecher, a Study* (1891); J. H. Barrows, *Henry Ward Beecher* (1893). Lyman Abbott, *Henry Ward Beecher* (1903), is an interpretation of Beecher's life and views, which while eulogistic is not without discrimination and contains a bibliography of Beecher publications prepared by W. E. Davenport. An analysis of Beecher's qualities as a preacher may be found in L. O. Brastow, *Representative Modern Preachers* (1904). For report of the Tilton–Beecher Case see, *Theodore Tilton vs. Henry Ward Beecher, Action for Crim. Con. . . . Verbatim Report by the Official Stenographer,* pub. by McDivitt, Campbell & Co., New York (3 vols., 1875), and Austin Abbott, *Official Report of the Trial of Henry Ward Beecher* (2 vols., 1875).]

H. E. S.

BEECHER, LYMAN (Oct. 12, 1775–Jan. 10, 1863), Presbyterian clergyman, was born in New Haven, Conn., the son of David Beecher by his third wife, Esther (Lyman) Beecher. His father and grandfather were blacksmiths. His mother died of consumption two days after he was born, and he was brought up by an uncle and aunt on their farm in Guilford, Conn. Entering Yale when he was eighteen years of age, he was profoundly influenced by Timothy Dwight [*q.v.*], who became president of the college at the end of Beecher's sophomore year. After graduation he remained as a student of divinity under Dwight, who was also the professor of theology. In 1799 he was ordained over the Presbyterian Church at East Hampton, L. I., and on Sept. 19, 1799, he was married to Roxana Foote of Guilford, Conn. In East Hampton he preached with ever increasing power and reputation for ten years. His salary, at first $300 and fire-wood, was raised to $400, but a growing family made a change desirable. A published sermon of his so impressed Judge Reeve, founder of the Litchfield Law School, that he was called to the church in that town. Litchfield was then famous in New England for its distinguished men and for the wealth and culture of its leading families. Hither Beecher removed his household in 1810. Belonging to the new school of Calvinism which laid unremitting stress on the freedom of the human will, he aimed, according to the custom of those days, at a continuous revival. Preaching twice on Sunday, holding services during the week in school-houses and private homes, he soon made a deep impression on the town, and the meeting-house was crowded. At that time enforcement of the liquor laws was lax, and sentiment was apathetic to the evils of excessive drinking, even at the formal meetings of the ministers. Beecher was deeply concerned and preached in 1825 six successive sermons on the evil of intemperance; these had great effect and, when published, passed through many editions in this country and in England and were translated into several foreign languages. Largely through Beecher's efficient leadership the General Association of Connecticut adopted drastic recommendations regarding temperance. Beecher took a prominent part in the formation of a Domestic Missionary Society for the education of young men for the ministry, as well as in establishing the American Bible Society, and he was a founder and constant contributor to the *Connecticut Observer*. In 1826 a wave of reaction against Unitarianism was so evident that the orthodox churches of Boston considered the time ripe for the establishment of a new church, which was organized in Hanover Street with thirty-seven members. Lyman Beecher was called as the minister most capable of expounding and enforcing evangelical doctrines. Astonishing results came from his six and a half years of intense activity. Leonard Bacon in his memorial address declared "that no such religious movement had been known in Boston since the period of the Great Awakening eighty years before." The revival unfortunately also had its less attractive side. In 1831 Beecher delivered a series of fiery and intolerant lectures and sermons against the Catholics and thus became indirectly responsible for the sacking of a convent of Ursuline nuns at Charlestown by the Boston mob (James Truslow Adams, *New England in the Republic 1776–1856,* 1926, pp. 334–36). Meanwhile, for the training of ministers in the West, Lane Theological Seminary had been started in Cincinnati; and Lyman Beecher was chosen as its first president and professor of theology, with a pledged endowment of $60,000 dependent upon his acceptance. This opportunity for influencing the religious life of the West made a strong appeal to Beecher. In 1832 he removed to Cincinnati to be the head of the new seminary and also pastor of the Second Presbyterian Church of that city. Almost immediately he was plunged into a violent theological controversy. The conservative Presbyterians assailed him bitterly with formal charges of heresy, slander, and hypocrisy: of heresy because his interpretation of the Westminster Confession differed from theirs, of slander because he maintained that his views were those of a large body of evangelical Christians, of hypocrisy because he pretended that his doctrines squared with the Scriptures and the Confession. He was acquitted by the local presbytery and then by the synod. His opponents appealed to the General Assembly, but after three years of litigation were persuaded to withdraw the case. This debate had a disastrous effect on Presbyterianism in the West and was one of the causes which led to the division of 1837–38. Himself a discreet abolitionist, Beecher opposed the rules issued by the trustees in his absence in August 1834, which forbade all discussion of slavery by the students. He obtained a revision of these rules, but the seminary lost most of its students to Oberlin College, where a more liberal attitude prevailed. After eighteen years of service Beecher resigned in 1850, and the last years of his life were spent in the home of his son, Henry Ward Beecher, in Brooklyn, where he died. His first wife bore him five sons and four daughters, and died of consumption Sept. 24, 1816. He married Harriet Porter of Portland, Me., in November 1817; after bearing him three sons and one daughter, she died July 7, 1835; his third wife was Mrs. Lydia (Beals) Jackson of Boston.

[For general characterization of Lyman Beecher see sketch of Henry Ward Beecher. The chief sources for Lyman Beecher's biography are: F. B. Dexter, *Biog. Sketches Grads. Yale Coll.*, vol. V (1911); *Autobiog., Correspondence, etc., of Lyman Beecher* (1864); L. Beecher, *Works* (3 vols., 1852–53); C. E. Beecher, "Sketches and Recollections of Dr. Lyman Beecher" in *Congreg. Quart.*, July 1864; *Obit. Record Grads. Yale Coll.*, 1863; D. H. Allen, *Life and Services of Rev. Lyman Beecher* (1863); J. C. White, *Personal Recollections of Lyman Beecher* (1882); E. T. Hayward, *Lyman Beecher* (1904); C. M. Rourke, *Trumpets of Jubilee* (1927); G. C. Woodruff, *Geneal. Reg. of the Inhabitants of the Town of Litchfield, Conn.* (1900); N. Goodwin, *The Foote Family: or the Descendants of Nathaniel Foote* (1849); Paxton Hibben, *Henry Ward Beecher* (1927).]

C. A. D.

BEECHER, THOMAS KINNICUT (Feb. 10, 1824–Mar. 14, 1900), Congregational clergyman, was born in Litchfield, Conn., the twelfth of Lyman Beecher's thirteen children. His mother was Harriet (Porter) Beecher. He was educated chiefly in the West, where, after a pastorate of some years in Boston, his father went to take charge of Lane Theological Seminary, when Thomas was about eight years old. He graduated from Illinois College, of which his brother Edward was president, in 1843; and later studied theology under his father. Like the rest of the Beecher children he found himself unable to accept the Calvinistic doctrines which had overshadowed his youth, and instead of immediately entering the ministry he turned to teaching. He was principal of the North East Grammar School, Philadelphia, and later of the high school in Hartford, Conn. The urge to preach finally mastered him, however, and he was ordained in September 1851 at Williamsburg, N. Y., where he organized a Congregational church. In June 1854 he became pastor of the Independent Congregational Church, Elmira, N. Y., of which he continued as pastor and pastor emeritus until his death. On Sept. 24, 1851, he married Olivia Day, daughter of President Day of Yale College. She died in August 1853, and on Jan. 21, 1857, he married Julia, daughter of Rev. Henry and Eliza (Webster) Jones, a grand-daughter of Noah Webster. In 1863 he was chosen chaplain of the 141st New York Volunteers and served four months with the Army of the Potomac.

During his long residence in Elmira he became one of its most picturesque and best known citizens. A striking figure with his waving white hair, always shabbily dressed, for he impoverished himself by his generosity, highly unconventional according to ministerial standards of the days, he was popular with all classes. To his parishioners he was affectionately known as "Father Tom." Having a liking for mechanics, he long kept the town clock in order, and on his trips to New York, it is said, frequently ran the locomotive of the train on which he traveled. For years he edited a weekly "Miscellany," first in the *Elmira Advertiser,* and later in the *Gazette,* in which he expressed independent, if not always defensible, views, some of which attracted wide attention. He was the candidate of various parties for political offices, but was never elected. He also became known as a pioneer in the "institutional church" movement. He built a new edifice, one of the first of its kind, equipped with gymnasium, library, lecture rooms, and other provisions for social work, which Mark Twain described under the title "A New Beecher Church" in *A Curious Dream* (1872). He took an advanced position regarding Sunday-school methods, grading his school and requiring serious, systematic work on the part of teachers and pupils. Although essentially orthodox, he was broad in his sympathies and in 1870 published *Our Seven Churches,* in which he set forth the admirable characteristics of the various denominations represented in Elmira, and in the last chapter, his own conception of the "Church of Christ." He also published a considerable number of short pamphlets on various subjects, and after his death appeared *In Tune with the Stars* (1902), stories for children.

[*Congreg. Yr. Bk.*, 1901; *Who's Who in America,* 1899–1900; *N. Y. Times,* Mar. 15, 1900; *Appleton's Ann. Cyc., 1900* (1901); W. S. B. Matthews, "A Remarkable Personality," *Outlook,* LXXXII, 555.]

H. E. S.

BEER, GEORGE LOUIS (July 26, 1872–Mar. 15, 1920), historian, publicist, the second son of Sophia (Walter) and of Julius Beer, a member of the Jewish community of Hamburg who had come to the United States in early life and had established himself in business as an importer of tobacco, was born on Staten Island and received his early education, which was of the best, in New York schools. At the age of sixteen he entered Columbia College, where he came in contact with the group of scholars—Burgess, Osgood, Seligman, and others—who were building the reputation of the Columbia Faculty of Political Science. After graduation in 1892, he returned to Columbia for further study. His master's essay, *The Commercial Policy of England toward the American Colonies* (1893), which was published in the Columbia Studies in History, Economics and Public Law, shows that the youthful author was already possessed of mature judgment and is marked by the same historical-mindedness and freedom from distorting patriotic bias that are evident in his later historical writings. For the next ten years Beer was engaged in the tobacco business, in which he was very successful, but historical scholarship never lost its attraction for him, though as a lecturer at Columbia, 1893–97, he showed no great interest in teaching. In order to devote himself to the more exhaustive study of the subject which he had sketched in his master's essay he retired from business in 1903. Accompanied by his wife, Edith C. Hellman of New York, a niece of Prof. Seligman, he went to London, where he remained for more than a year, spending most of his time in examining unpublished documents in the Public Record Office.

Beer's reputation as an historian rests upon three books that he wrote as instalments of a projected work on the economic aspects of British colonial policy in the seventeenth and eighteenth centuries. The first of these to appear was *British Colonial Policy, 1754–65* (1907). Based largely upon official documents, it did full justice to the British official point of view during a critical period in the history of the empire and served as a much-needed corrective of interpretations of British policy inspired by American patriotism. In *The Origins of the British Colonial System, 1578–1660* (1908), Beer placed the early English colonial movement in its historical setting and described the beginnings of the imperial economic system. Following further research in England, he brought out in two volumes *The Old Colonial System, Part I* (1912), the most thorough and authoritative work that has been writen on English colonial policy and practise with respect to imperial trade and defense during the period 1660–88. Beer had accumulated a great mass of material for the volumes that he had planned on the history of the colonial system from 1689 to 1754, but the outbreak of the World War turned him to enterprises of a different nature. His historical work, though unfinished, ranks as one of the major contributions to knowledge made by American historical scholarship in the present century.

During the war Beer devoted much time and energy to the promotion of sympathetic understanding between the United States and the British Empire. As American correspondent of the *Round Table* he made regular contributions to that journal from 1915 to 1918, in which he surveyed for its readers in England and the British dominions the development of American public opinion concerning the war; and during the same years articles from his pen on the British Empire, American foreign policy, and other subjects relating to the war appeared in American periodicals. In 1917 he published the most widely read of all his books, *The English-Speaking Peoples,* in which he urged the formation of an intimate, coöperative alliance between the United States and the British Empire as the best hope for a better world order in the future. In the autumn of 1917 he became a member of the group of investigators, popularly known as "The Inquiry," formed by Col. House at President Wilson's request, to study questions that were likely to come before the peace conference. As colonial expert Beer prepared a number of reports, the more important of which were published after his death in *African Questions at the Paris Peace Conference* (1923). He believed that the guiding principle of colonial administration should be the welfare of the native peoples, and in a report on Mesopotamia, which he completed in January 1918, occurs what is probably the earliest use of the term "mandate" in its present meaning. He was chief of the colonial division of the American delegation at the Paris Peace Conference and sat on a number of its important commissions. As a member of the Mandates Commission he had much to do with drafting the mandates for the administration of the former German colonies, and there is no doubt that his views counted heavily in the colonial settlement for which the Treaty provided. The extent and accuracy of his knowledge on many subjects that came before the conference and the sanity of his judgment made a deep impression, and his views were often sought on other than colonial questions. When the secretariat of the League of Nations was organized Beer was appointed head of the Mandates Division, but the failure of the United States to join the League prevented him from entering upon the duties of this office. Until almost the end of his life he cherished the hope of returning to his historical labors, but the progress of a fatal disease, probably hastened by the strain of his work at Paris, made this impossible.

[*George Louis Beer: A Tribute to His Life and Work in the Making of History and the Moulding of Public Opinion* (1924) contains a series of biog. sketches, including an estimate of his work as an historian by Prof. Chas. M. Andrews and an account of his activities at the Peace Conference by Prof. James T. Shotwell, together with a number of shorter appreciations by prominent men who had been brought into personal contact with him; his work on the commissions of the Peace Conference is described by Prof. Louis Herbert Grey in his introduction to Beer's *African Questions at the Paris Peace Conference;* an unsigned appreciation appeared in *Pubs. Am. Jewish Hist. Soc.,* Nov. 28, 1922.]

R. L. S.

BEER, WILLIAM (May 1, 1849–Feb. 1, 1927), librarian, son of Gabriel and Harriet (Ferguson) Beer, was born at Plymouth, England. He early developed an interest in libraries, acting as one of the directors of the Cottonian Library at Plymouth, 1869–71. He was also secretary of the Devon and Cornwall Natural History Society, and, with his friend, J. Burt, discovered a Lake village at Dossmire Pool in Cornwall. From 1871 to 1877 he was in Paris, where he studied medicine, modern languages, and art, and formed associations with the students in the studios of Gerôme and Duran. He returned to England in 1877, and accepted, at Newcastle-on-Tyne, a position in a glass manufacturing company, learning many valuable secrets of the art of stained-glass window making. Here, for two years, at the College of Physical Science, he studied mining engineering under Alexander Herschel. He became a member of the Newcastle Antiquarian Society, and investigated such subjects as the Roman occupation of Britain, and more especially the Roman wall, in which research he was associated with D. Brun and John Clay of the Chesters. He worked also in the public library of Newcastle, and formed an excellent collection of the literature of Northumberland. In 1884 he went to Canada, but soon after settled in the United States and practised mining engineering in Michigan, Montana, and Wyoming. In 1889 he withdrew from this profession to become librarian of the free public library of Topeka, Kan. He also organized here a series of extension lectures. Two years later he was made librarian of the Howard Memorial Library of New Orleans, then newly organized by Miss Annie Howard (Mrs. Parrott). In 1896 he was also appointed librarian of the New Orleans Free Public Library, then newly formed by consolidating the Fisk Free Library and the Lyceum Library.

Beers

After organizing this institution, he resigned in 1906 to devote himself exclusively to the Howard Library, which he developed on a broad basis as a reference library, giving particular attention to material connected with Louisiana. At his death, the library contained over 80,000 volumes, and many valuable manuscripts and maps. Beer, who never married, was a prominent figure in the social and literary life of New Orleans for many years. He was an intimate friend of George W. Cable, Ruth McEnery Stuart, and Grace King. Until his death he was a member of the Advisory Board of Editors of the *Louisiana Historical Quarterly,* and contributed frequently to its pages.

[This sketch is based on material furnished by Beer himself and on the recollections of his friends in New Orleans. There is an appreciation of Beer by Henry P. Dart in the *La. Hist. Quart.,* Apr. 1927. See also *Who's Who in America,* 1926–27; *Times-Picayune* (New Orleans), Feb. 2, 1927; J. S. Kendall, *Hist. of New Orleans* (1922), III, 1184; Edward Laroque Tinker, "Wm. Beer, 1849–1927," in *La. Hist. Quart.,* Jan. 1928, containing bibliography of Beer's writings.] I. R. K.

BEERS, ETHEL LYNN (Jan. 13, 1827–Oct. 11, 1879), poet, was born at Goshen, N. Y., the daughter of Horace William Eliot and Keziah (Westcott) Eliot. On the side of her father, who was a soldier in the War of 1812, druggist, justice of the peace, and postmaster, she was a descendant, in the seventh generation, of John Eliot, the apostle to the Indians. Her mother was a daughter of David N. Westcott, colonel of state militia, member of the state legislature, and member of the state constitutional convention. The girl, baptized Ethelinda, early began to contribute to the magazines under the name of Ethel Lynn. At the age of nineteen she was married, on Mar. 5, 1846, to William H. Beers, son of Cyrenius Beers of New York, and henceforth wrote under the name of Ethel Lynn Beers. On Nov. 30, 1861, there appeared in *Harper's Magazine* her poem "The Picket Guard," better known from its opening words "All Quiet Along the Potomac"—a poem suggested by seeing that oft-repeated caption in a newspaper, followed by the notice "A Picket Shot." The verses pay a tender tribute to the unknown soldier and, while a little sentimental for modern taste, achieve a genuine pathos. Over a year later the poem was reprinted anonymously in a Southern paper with the statement that it had been found on the dead body of a soldier. The authorship was generally ascribed in the South either to Lamar Fontaine or Thaddeus Oliver, both Southerners, and the former repeatedly urged his claim but without being able to support it by any satisfactory evidence. Alone of the three, Mrs. Beers produced other poems of some merit, the three most popular being entitled "Weighing the Baby," "Baby Looking Out for Me," and "Which Shall It Be?" She was a frequent contributor to the *New York Ledger* and in 1863 she published *General Frankie: a Story for Little Folks.* Although a woman of cheerful personality, she had a premonition that she should die immediately after the appearance of her collected poems. *All Quiet Along the Potomac, and Other Poems* was published on Oct. 10, 1879, and she died on the following day.

[*Geneal. of the Descendants of John Eliot 1598–1905* (1905); *N. Y. Times,* Oct. 13, 1879, p. 5; *N. Y. Evening Post,* Oct. 14, 1879, p. 3; *N. Y. Ledger,* Nov. 8, 15, 1879. On the authorship of "All Quiet Along the Potomac" see James Wood Davidson, *The Living Writers of the South* (1869), pp. 194–201.] E. S. B.

BEERS, HENRY AUGUSTIN (Jan. 2, 1847–Sept. 7, 1926), author and educator, was born in Buffalo, N. Y., where his parents, Connecticut people, were spending the winter on a visit. On his paternal side he was descended from James Beers, who came from England in 1634 and settled in Fairfield, Conn., in 1659. His grandfather, Seth Preston Beers, was the leading lawyer of Litchfield County, and a prominent member of the Connecticut legislature. His father, George Webster Beers (1816–63; B.A. Trinity College, Hartford, 1839), lived in Litchfield. There Beers gained his intimate knowledge of New England nature and in his grandfather's library his intimate knowledge of New England literature. His mother was Elizabeth Victoria Clerc. On the maternal side his inheritance was entertainingly different. Both grandparents were deaf-mutes. His grandfather, Laurent Clerc, had been one of the favorite pupils of the Abbé Sicard in the national institution for deaf-mute instruction at Paris, and had come to this country to assist Thomas Gallaudet in founding the asylum for deaf-mutes at Hartford, where he taught many years. The family occupied the Lydia Sigourney house, the former home of the "Swan of Hartford" so that in Hartford also his associations were literary.

From the Hartford High School Beers passed his examinations for Yale College in 1864, when he was slightly over seventeen years of age. Partly on account of his youth and partly on account of his health he was kept out of college for a year and entered Yale as a member of the class of '69. The composition of this class was exceptional in that there were enrolled in it a number of men who had fought through the Civil War. They were both older than the normal Yale undergraduate and less amenable to discipline. The resulting humorous situations later found in Beers a chronicler (*The Ways of Yale in the Consulship of Plancus,* 1895). In the class was Maj. Edward Heaton, who married Beers's only sister Charlotte, and whose sister, Mary, Beers himself married in Covington, Ky., July 7, 1873. Beers was an able student. He won first prize in English composition and the prize for an original English poem in his sophomore year; a Philosophical Oration appointment in his junior year; and a High Oration appointment in his senior year. Yet he was far from being merely a student. He participated in the various extra-curriculum activities of his day. In the debating society, Brothers in Unity, he won the first prize in its junior debate; he was a member of Kappa Sigma Epsilon, Alpha Delta Phi, and Skull and Bones; a member of the Varuna Boat Club, the Red Letter Literary Club, and a contributor to the *Yale Literary Magazine.* Such diverse interest reflected the breadth of his nature, and his college course was successful in the three directions, study, books, friends.

On leaving college he studied law in the office of Pierrepont, Stanley, Langdell & Brown, and was admitted to the bar in May 1870. His practise was not so lucrative but that he was willing to resign it to accept the position of tutor in Yale College. There his life followed the usual routine of appointment: tutor, 1871–74; assistant professor, 1875–80; professor, 1880–1916; professor emeritus, 1916–26. The only breaks in this succession were in the summer and autumn of 1876 when he studied in Europe, chiefly at Heidelberg with Kuno Fischer, where, with characteristic modesty he remarks, "I attended a few lectures," and some weeks in 1877 when he attended Bronson Alcott's School of Philosophy at Concord, where he had the opportunity of knowing Lowell and Emerson. For forty continuous years he taught at Yale where his slight figure was a familiar and greatly beloved sight on the campus. In spite of his dislike of publicity, his great knowledge of English literature and his keen critical judgment won him admirers, but he refused all honorary degrees; "empty honors" he called them. Two of his students, however, in 1923 founded in Yale College the Henry A. Beers Prize in American Literature as a memorial to him. Toward the end of his life he became a personified Yale tradition, one who embodied the past in himself and stood for the best in old Yale.

Beers's published work may be divided into three classes: his poetry; his creative prose; his scholarly prose. His poetry varied from *vers de société* to dramatic monologue, from burlesque to intimate studies of New England landscape. The sonnet, "The Singer of One Song," and the dramatic monologue, "The Dying Pantheist," are both well known. The preference of the author was, however, for the poems dealing with scenery around New Haven, such as "The Upland," "The Pasture Bars," or "Beaver Pond Meadow." His creative prose consisted for the most part of short stories contributed to various magazines. They show his interest in the subtleties of everyday life. He aimed to present only those moments when the soul is at the cross-roads and a slight impetus may change the course of life. His scholarly work is best represented by his volumes on the history of romanticism in England. Here he was the first to trace the development of this movement in English literature from its slow beginnings in the first quarter of the eighteenth century to its culmination in the age of Walter Scott (*History of English Romanticism in the Eighteenth Century,* 1899) and then to its decline in the Victorian period (*History of English Romanticism in the Nineteenth Century,* 1901).

[Family knowledge and personal reminiscence; Records in the Dean's Office, Yale Coll., Secretary's Office and Treasurer's Office, Yale Univ.; class books of the class of '69; *Men of Mark in Conn.,* ed by N. G. Osborn, I (1906), 120.]

J. M. B.

BEHAN, WILLIAM JAMES (Sept. 25, 1840–May 4, 1928), sugar planter, political leader, was born in New Orleans, the son of John Holland and Katherine (Walker) Behan. He attended the University of Louisiana—now Tulane—and the Western Military Institute in Nashville. At the beginning of the Civil War he enlisted with the New Orleans Washington Artillery, and being soon promoted to commissioned rank, served with the Army of Northern Virginia from Bull Run to Appomattox. After the war he returned to New Orleans and became a wholesale grocer, and there in June 1866 he was married to Katie Walker. A determined opponent of carpet-bag government, he took an important part in organizing the Crescent City White League, and in September 1874 he was one of the two men in command of the League forces in their battle against the Federal forces then in New Orleans —the Battle of the Custom House. In 1874–82 he was major-general of the Louisiana National Guard, in 1882–84 mayor of New Orleans, in 1888–92 a member of the state Senate, in 1889–91 major-general of the state Confederate Veterans Association, and from 1905 for many years Commander of the Washington Artillery Veterans Association. During his administration as mayor he manifested his accustomed great vigor and integrity, and, exerting himself particularly to thwart ring politics, he was on that issue defeated for a second term. The conviction among his followers that his defeat was fraudulent was so intense as to tempt them to protest the election by violence, but plans in that direction were at length abandoned. In the early 1890's he removed from New Orleans to his extensive and efficiently conducted sugar-plantation at White Castle, La., and at about this time, along with a number of other planters, in protest against the Democratic scheme for reducing the tariff on sugar, he went over to the Republican party. From 1896 he was a regular delegate at Republican national conventions, in 1900–12 he was a member of the Republican Executive Committee of Louisiana, and in 1904 he was Republican candidate for governor. In 1902 he returned to live in New Orleans. His wife, herself a person of large public usefulness, died in 1918. During the World War he was one of a commission appointed to visit France. His death occurred suddenly in New Orleans.

[J. S. Kendall, *Hist. of New Orleans* (1922), vols. I and II, esp. the articles on Behan and his wife, II, 784–88, *Who's Who in America,* 1924–25; *New Orleans Item,* May 4, 1928.]

J. D. W.

BEHRENDS, ADOLPHUS JULIUS FREDERICK (Dec. 18, 1839–May 22, 1900), clergyman, was born in Nymwegen, Holland, the son of Martina Everdina (Jacobs) Behrends and Charles Augustus Behrends, a Lutheran minister. When he was but five years old the family emigrated to Ohio. He graduated from Denison University in 1862, and from the Rochester Theological Seminary in 1865. In the latter year he became pastor of the Warburton Avenue Baptist Church at Yonkers, N. Y., and remained in that position till the fall of 1873, when he accepted a call to the First Baptist Church in Cleveland. There his opposition to the Baptist custom of restricted or "close" communion was expressed in a sermon that provoked criticism and led to his resignation in January 1876. This was a turning point in his life. He said, shortly before his death, that when he cut loose from the Baptists he stood ready for an open door and determined to accept the first call that came, whether it was Methodist, Presbyterian, or Congregational. It came from the Union Congregational Church of Providence, R. I.; and here he remained till 1883, when he was invited to the pulpit of the Central Congregational Church of Brooklyn, N. Y. This congregation had not attained the commanding position that it reached under Behrends and his successor, Cadman; but it was already one of the prominent churches of the denomination, and its pastor had to stand comparison with Henry Ward Beecher, Richard S. Storrs, and T. DeWitt Talmage. How Behrends met the test may be judged from an editorial in the *Outlook,* June 2, 1900, which characterized him as "one of the not large number of truly great preachers." Behrends was popular not only as a preacher; his services were in request for lectures. In 1886 he gave a course on "Socialism and Christianity" at the Hartford Theological Seminary; in 1890 he delivered the Lyman Beecher Lectures on Preaching at Yale University, his topic being "The Philosophy of Preaching"; and in 1896 he gave a series of addresses at Syracuse University on missions. He was twice married: first on Aug. 24, 1865, to Harriet E. Hatch of Rochester, N. Y., who died Jan. 27, 1882, leaving him with six children; and second on June 6, 1885, to Mrs. Frances Rouse Otis of Cleveland, who bore him one child and survived him. His published writings include: *Counting the Cost* (1881), a sermon; *The World for Christ* (1896); *The Old Testament Under Fire* (1897); *Sursum Corda, a Book of Praise* (1898). In 1904 William Herries edited a number of writings by Dr. Behrends, and issued them with a biographical introduction under the title, *The Christ of Nineteen Centuries.*

[*Congreg. Yr. Bk.,* 1901; *Brooklyn Daily Eagle,* May 22, 23, 1900; information from Mrs. Geo. H. Olney, Behrends's daughter.]

C. N.

BEHRENS, HENRY (Dec. 10, 1815–Oct. 17, 1895), priest of the Society of Jesus, was born at Munstadt, Hanover. Nothing is known about his parents and childhood. He entered the Society of Jesus Dec. 27, 1832, at Stäffis (Estavayer), Switzerland, and spent the next ten years in the ascetical and scientific training customary in his order. His first position as educator in the College of Freiburg, which disclosed an uncommon ability, was terminated in 1847 by the political troubles in Switzerland. The city had joined the Sonderbund. It was conquered by the troops of the opposition who were bent on killing the Jesuits. After all the other Jesuits had fled from the college, Behrens alone remained in disguise, and by his courage and presence of mind prevented the destruction of the building and saved much of its property. Later a hasty flight with a number of hairbreadth escapes saved his life. Some forty of the exiled Jesuits were sent to found an institution in America, with Behrens as superior. Among them were Father Anthony Anderleddy, later Superior General of the order, and Father Miege, who eventually became Vicar Apostolic of Kansas. The journey from Antwerp to New York, made in a frail sailing vessel under a rather inexperienced captain and a less experienced crew, lasted forty-two days, and ended in a great disappointment. At New York the exiles learned that the institution they intended to found had become impossible by the death of the bishop who had invited them to America. So Behrens returned home, after providing for his charges as best he could. The Jesuits, now exiled from Switzerland, began to work in Germany. Behrens may be said to have been one of the pillars of the new German province. He always held responsible positions. Nearly all the time he was master of novices and local superior. For three years he governed the province as Provincial. During the Franco-Prussian War he acted as superior of the Jesuits who labored in the German army as chaplains and nurses. He soon brought it about that the Jesuits and other religious, including the Sisters, became the preferred workers in the hospitals, though at first they had been merely tolerated. In spite of these unselfish services to the country, the Jesuits, two years later, were expelled from Germany. For a second time Behrens was a man without a country.

The German Jesuits at that time had in America what was called the Buffalo Mission, that is, several houses which were in many ways independent of the American Jesuit authorities. (It was dissolved in 1907.) The Buffalo Mission became the field of Behrens's activity for the rest of his life. He arrived at Buffalo, in 1872, and at once became superior of the Mission. He held this office 1872–78, and again 1886–92. His first care was to learn the language of the country, a task to which the man of nearly sixty devoted himself with the alacrity of a studious boy. His administration was marked by that vigor combined with paternal kindness which had always distinguished him. He wanted his men to be earnest workers, inspired by the noblest motives, and untiring in their various occupations. In 1886 he established St. Ignatius College (now John Carroll University) at Cleveland. His zeal extended to the Indians of South Dakota, where the mission stations of St. Francis and Holy Rosary arose through his efforts. While not engaged in the duties of superior he labored humbly as one of the rank and file. What perhaps made him especially popular among the people of Buffalo was his work in the confessional, to which he remained attached all the years of his life. He also acted as chaplain in the hospitals of the city, and was indefatigable in caring for the inmates of the Good Shepherd Home. The Golden Jubilee of his priesthood, in 1892, was an almost citywide celebration. All who had come within the radius of his kind, if somewhat stern, influence were his devoted friends.

[*P. Heinrich Behrens, Eine Skizze seines Lebens und Wirkens* (Buffalo, 1896); unprinted documents in the archives of the houses of the former Buffalo Mission; recollections gathered from those who knew Behrens personally.]

F. S. B.

BEISSEL, JOHANN CONRAD (April 1690–July 6, 1768), hymn-writer and founder of the Solitary Brethren of the Community of Seventh Day Baptists at Ephrata, was born in Eberbach, Germany. A posthumous child, born two months after the death of his drunken father, who was a baker, Beissel also lost his mother when he was only a boy of eight. Early apprenticed to a baker, who was a musician and taught the boy to play the violin, he displayed extraordinary natural gifts, learning much by reflection without any instruction. He was small and insignificant in body. His conversion took place in his twenty-seventh year. He early revealed a pietistic trend, accepting celibacy as a primary requirement for a man who intends to devote himself to the service of God. Before his death, he named the many blessings which he had received and placed high in the list that God had "preserved him from the allurements of the female sex." He worked as a journeyman baker at various places, but because of his views he was soon banished from the Palatinate. Persuaded by his friends, Stiefel and Stuntz, he started with them for America in 1720, arriving that autumn in Boston. He went first to Germantown, in Pennsylvania, where for a year he studied the weaver's trade, under Peter Becker, a Baptist and organizer of the Church of the Brethren. In 1721 Beissel and Stuntz erected a "Solitary" residence in Muehlbach (Mill Creek, Lebanon County). Here Stiefel came, declaring that henceforth he would work on Sunday, observing Saturday as the Sabbath; but Beissel was too much of an ascetic for Stiefel, and the latter left for Bethlehem. One after another who had joined themselves to Beissel forsook him, Stuntz finally selling the dwelling-house to reimburse himself for the traveling expenses he had loaned to Beissel. After much fasting and prayer, Beissel came to the decision to submit to apostolic baptism at the hands of his friend, Peter Becker. He now assumed the name "Friedsam Gottrecht." Seven years after his baptism, he founded the "Economy" at Ephrata, located in Lancaster County. In 1732 he was joined by some of the Solitary Brethren (unmarried men), Sisters (devoted to virginity), and married couples, who on joining the settlement were pledged to continence, being convinced by Beissel that "the married state had originated in sin, and would therefore have to come to an end." At first the Order of Spiritual Virgins and the Solitary Brethren were quartered in the same building. This gave rise to much suspicion and bitter persecution. Nevertheless, some persons of wealth and prominence were attracted by the zeal and strict regimen of the sect, notably Conrad Weiser, an elder of the Lutheran Church, who for a time was regarded as a follower of Beissel. Pastor Peter Miller of Philadelphia, a graduate of Heidelberg and a scholarly theologian, also became a follower of Beissel, and ultimately his successor as head of the Order. The wife of Christopher Sauer, the well-known printer and publisher, deserted her husband to win spiritual regeneration among the mystics of Ephrata, and later became the Prioress. The Community gradually grew, until about the middle of the eighteenth century it contained several hundred members. The men then lived in a large communal dwelling or monastery, and the women in another house of the same sort. The largest chapel in Pennsylvania at that time was provided for their joint use. The meeting-house for divine worship also contained large halls for holding Agapae (Love-Feasts), as well as cells for the Solitary, after the manner of the old Greek churches. The Sisters were veiled, and both sexes were garbed with unattractive hoods with cowls, like the Capuchin, so designed that but little was visible of "that humiliating image revealed by sin." All members of the settlement were required to give Beissel weekly written confessions of their spiritual condition. These confessional papers (called Lectiones) were read by Beissel to the congregation, and several hundred of these were later published. The colony excelled in the printing of books and in the making of illuminated manuscripts. In the year 1747 appeared the *Turtel Taube* ("Turtle Dove"), the hymnal of the Ephrata Kloster (Cloister), with both words and tunes largely from the pen of Beissel. He is said to have composed over 1,000 hymns, of which 441 were printed. Although he had no sense of meter or of rhythm, he evolved a distinctive system of harmony, a unique musical notation, and a series of quaint melodies which exerted considerable influence on American hymnology. He often led the Sisters and Brothers of the cloister on a midnight tour of the grounds, singing hymns. Schism and frequent quarrels marked the brief history of the colony, but despite the rigors of their experience Beissel had no difficulty in holding a considerable part of his band of followers together. The decline of the colony began with his death, although its customs were continued well into the nineteenth century, particularly at Snowhill Monastery in Franklin County, Pa. The influence of the little order, which disbanded long ago, is still traceable, and perhaps its chief legacy is the "Paradisiacal Wonder Music," which Beissel and his followers composed and which remains as proof of the native genius of this self-instructed baker, who might have gained eminent distinction as a composer, if he had been properly trained in the art of composition.

[*Chronicon Ephratense*, compiled by Brothers Lamech and Agrippa, translated from the original German by Dr. J. Max Hark (1889); *The German Sectarians of Pa. 1708–1800* (1899–1900) by Julius F. Sachse; *Hist. of the Ch. of the Brethren of the Eastern District of Pa.* (1915), pp. 32–43; *Pa. German Soc. Proc. and Addresses*, XXI; *Phila. Bulletin*, Mar. 9, 1927.]

P. S. L.

BELCHER, JONATHAN (Jan. 8, 1681/2–Aug. 31, 1757), merchant and colonial governor, was descended from Andrew Belcher, the first of his family to emigrate from England to Massachusetts, son of Thomas Belcher of London, clothworker, and grandson of Robert Belcher of Kingswood, Wiltshire, weaver. The date of Andrew's arrival in New England is unknown but we find him keeping a tavern in Cambridge from 1654 to 1673. He married a sister of Deputy-Governor Danforth, and his second son by this marriage, another Andrew, lived at various times at Hartford, Cambridge, Charlestown, and Boston. Through his marriage to Sarah Gilbert of Hartford he eventually inherited a large property at Meriden which passed to his son Jonathan, the subject of this sketch (W. H. Whitmore, "Record of the Descendants of Andrew Belcher," in *New England Historical and Genealogical Register,* 1873). The future governor's background was thus intercolonial from his earliest connections, so that Gov. Talcott of Connecticut later wrote to him that "our Assembly look upon you to be at least half a Connecticut man by birth."

Jonathan's father became a prosperous merchant and was a member of the Massachusetts Council from 1702 until his death, Nov. 6, 1717. His second daughter Elizabeth married Daniel Oliver and became the mother of Lieutenant-Governor Andrew Oliver and of Chief Justice Peter Oliver. Her sister Mary married George Vaughan of Portsmouth, afterward lieutenant-governor. With such a setting, the career of Jonathan as merchant and politician was obviously a natural one. He was born at Cambridge and went to Harvard, where he graduated in 1699. He then went to Europe, traveling somewhat extensively on the continent as well as in England, for a number of years. Returning to Boston, he established himself as a merchant and accumulated a considerable fortune. On Jan. 8,

1705, he married Mary, daughter of Lieutenant-Governor William Partridge of Portsmouth, N. H.; she died on Oct. 6, 1736, and on Sept. 9, 1748, he married Mary Louisa Emilia Teal in Burlington, N. J., who survived him.

Belcher's political career began with his election to the Massachusetts Council in 1718. He was reëlected in 1719, 1720, 1722, 1723, 1726, 1727, and 1729, but his last election was negatived by Gov. Burnet. The perennial question of the executive's salary as a dispute between governor and Assembly was in especial evidence during Burnet's term, and in 1728 Belcher was appointed by the House to represent its side of the case in England as a colleague of the colony's regular agent, Francis Wilks. Two months earlier Belcher had also been appointed by the Connecticut Assembly to attempt to secure a reversal in England of the decision in the important case of Winthrop *vs.* Lechmere, which was threatening the validity of all land titles in the colony. He arrived in London early in 1729, and, soon after, word was received of the death of Gov. Burnet. Belcher, with the advantage of being on the spot at the critical moment, secured the post for himself, the government being probably partly influenced by the facts that he was colonial born and at the same time a "prerogative man," and so presumably pleasing to parties on both sides of the water. His commission was dated Jan. 8, 1729/30, and he landed in Boston on Aug. 10 as governor of Massachusetts and New Hampshire.

From the nature of its duties, the position of royal governor in energetic, liberty-loving colonies was one in which it was impossible to please all. The difficulties were rather enhanced than diminished when the governor was a son of the colony. Belcher's term offered no exception. There was the inevitable and interminable quarrel over the salary question, but in Belcher's case there were other factors which led to his eventual downfall. He was fond of office, and as governor tried to compromise by maintaining the royal prerogative sufficiently to retain his post, and by advancing colonial interests, at the expense of the Crown, to maintain his popularity at home. The colonials had by this time thoroughly awakened to the value of their natural resources, and the larger business men were striving to "utilize them through commerce." One sphere of speculation was the eastern territory of Maine, and there Belcher came into conflict with royal authority which was trying to retain control of the timber. Moreover, a rapidly expanding commerce had created currency difficulties, and when an unsound scheme was set on foot to found a "Land Bank" to issue notes, Belcher promptly took sides with the more conservative business elements. The object was good but the methods of reducing the opposition indulged in by the governor and the conservatives were high-handed and drastic. Belcher's temper was irascible and his language vituperative. His words as well as his acts constantly created enemies for him. A boundary dispute between Massachusetts and New Hampshire brought about much ill-feeling. In this case Belcher was accused, unjustly apparently, of accepting a bribe. Finally, a group of enemies brought charges against him in England, some of which were signed with forged names, and he was dismissed from both governorships May 7, 1741.

A few years later, he went to England, rehabilitated himself in the opinion of the English government, and in July 1746 was appointed governor of New Jersey, the commission being dated the following February and he himself arriving in his new province in August. Although serious riots occurred over the land question, his term there was much more tranquil than in New England and, on the whole, satisfactory. He was greatly interested in the founding of the College of New Jersey (Princeton), and on his death bequeathed his library of 374 volumes to that institution. It had been proposed to give to the present Nassau Hall the name "Belcher Hall," but he had declined the honor and suggested the name now in use. His character appears clearly in the large mass of correspondence left by him. With wealth, literary tastes, and unusual advantages in travel, he yet remained an uncultured man of small views. He was sanctimonious yet showered abusive epithets on all who differed from him. Aggressive where he felt he had the power, no one could fawn lower to secure advantages for himself and his family. He was vain and self-seeking but as an official was by no means below the average of the day, and in such matters as his opposition to unsound currency in Massachusetts and in the founding of Princeton he rendered genuine service.

[The chief sources of information are the volumes of his published letters. The most important of these are the "Belcher Papers," *Mass. Hist. Soc. Colls.*, ser. 6, vols. VI, VII. There are also many letters in the "Talcott Papers," *Conn. Hist. Soc. Colls.*, IV, V. The letters relating to his N. J. period are printed in *N. J. Archives*, VII, VIII. The *N. H. Provincial Papers*, IV, contain much documentary material relating to his administration of that colony. There is an almost contemporary, and very fair, account of his term in Massachusetts in Thomas Hutchinson's *Hist. of the Province of Mass. Bay* (1764–1828), vol. II. His commission as governor of Mass. and N. H. may be found in *Col. Soc. of Mass. Pubs.*, II, 119 ff.; see also H. L. Osgood, *Am. Colonies in the Eighteenth Cent.* (1924), vol. III, ch., XVI.]

J. T. A.

BELCOURT, GEORGE ANTOINE (Apr. 22, 1803–May 31, 1874), Catholic missionary, was born at Bay du Febvre, Province of Quebec, Canada. His parents were Antoine Belcourt and Josephte (Lemire) Belcourt. He was educated at the college of Nicolet and was ordained as a priest Mar. 18, 1827. In 1831 he was selected for the mission field of western Canada to work among the Saulteux, or Chippewas. After some months of study of the Algonquin language, he set out for his mission field, arriving at St. Boniface (Winnipeg) on the Red River June 17, 1831, after a canoe voyage of over 2,000 miles. In 1834 he established his permanent mission at Baie St. Paul on the Assiniboine River, thirty-five miles west of the present city of Winnipeg. Here he spent thirteen years of arduous labor, receiving but $500 annually for the support of his work. In 1845 at the request of the leaders, he accompanied the annual buffalo hunt of half-breeds and Indians into what is now North Dakota. They spent six weeks in the region between Devil's Lake and the Missouri River, bringing back their year's supply of meat, hides, and pemmican for the inhabitants of the lower Red River Valley. The priest held a daily religious service, took an active part in the hunting of the buffaloes, and left an interesting and accurate eye-witness account of the entire hunt. As an historical document this narrative is of considerable importance as furnishing a picture of what had come to be a regular frontier institution of over sixty years' standing. The next year he again accompanied the buffalo hunt, but on this occasion his services as a physician were most in demand. He had to combat an epidemic of dysentery and measles that raged among the families on the expedition during the entire hunt. When his supply of medicine was exhausted, he traveled from the camp, west of Dog Den Butte, to the Fort Berthold village of the Mandans and Gros Ventres on the Missouri River where the white traders gave him the much-needed medicine. By request he preached in this Indian village, which numbered 2,000 souls, and after the service he was asked to return and establish a mission there. In 1846 a bitter contest broke out between the half-breeds and merchants of Fort Garry and the officials of the Hudson's Bay Company, the latter being opposed to permitting free trade with Pembina and Fort Snelling on the American side of the line. Father Belcourt, by his great influence with the half-breeds, prevented them from resorting to violence. Later he persuaded them to conform to the English custom and to petition the Crown for redress of their trading grievances. Chief-Factor Christie and other officers of the Hudson's Bay Company were so angered at the part played by Father Belcourt that he felt obliged, in the interest of harmony, to resign his position in 1847. He was immediately appointed as missionary at Pembina on the Red River, a short distance south of the Canadian line. He traveled to this station from Quebec by way of Chicago and St. Paul, arriving in July 1849. He built himself a bark cabin and spent the winter in traveling on snowshoes over an area 900 miles in breadth, going as far west as Turtle Mountain. For the next two years he had as his assistant a missionary who afterward became well known as Father Lacombe of the Edmonton district. In 1850 he abandoned Pembina on account of the flood that spring and established a new mission at St. Joseph, now Walhalla. In pursuance of the policy of encouraging the Indians to adopt a more settled life, he set up the first saw-mill and grist-mill in this part of the northwest. Gov. Ramsay of Minnesota Territory was a great admirer of Father Belcourt and aided him in his work wherever possible. In 1858 the latter resigned his position and returned to Quebec. He held a pastorate at Rustico, Prince Edward Island, for ten years, and died at Shediac, New Brunswick. He was known throughout the northwest as one of the greatest of the pioneer missionaries of his time. His unflagging zeal for the cause of his mission field was equaled only by his tireless researches in the language of the Saulteux. His *Principes de la Langue des Sauvages appelés Saulteux* was published in Quebec in 1839.

[G. A. Belcourt, "Mon itinéraire du lac des Deux-Montagnes à la Rivière Rouge," *La Revue Canadienne* (1913); *Proc. Royal Soc. of Canada*, 1920, XIV, 23; *Colls. State Hist. Soc. of N. Dak.*, V, 134 ff.; *Minn. Hist. Soc. Colls.*, I, 193 ff.; *House Ex. Doc. No. 51*, 31 Cong., 1 Sess., pp. 44 ff.]

O. G. L.

BELDEN, JOSIAH (May 4, 1815–Apr. 23, 1892), California pioneer, was born in Cromwell, Conn., the son of Josiah and Ruth (McKee) Belden and a descendant of Richard Bayldon, who came to that state from England in 1645. His mother died when he was four years old. He attended the common schools until he was fifteen, when his father died, and he was then apprenticed to a jeweler in Albany. In 1836 he moved to Philadelphia and later to Vicksburg, continuing in the jewelry business. At Independence, Mo., in May 1841, he joined the Bartleson-Bidwell party, which was to make the first emigrant wagon-train journey from the Missouri to the Pacific. With about half of the original company, though without the wagons, which had been abandoned east of the Sierras, Belden arrived at the

Marsh ranch, near Mount Diablo, Nov. 4. At Monterey, Oct. 20, 1842, when Commodore Jones, in the belief that war had been declared, compelled the surrender of the town, Belden raised the American flag. He also, a few days later, after serving in the interim as the town's *alcalde,* pulled the flag down. For two years he ran a branch store at Santa Cruz for Thomas O. Larkin, the American consul. In 1844 he became a Mexican citizen and was awarded a tract of land in the Sacramento Valley. Here he established a ranch, though he gave most of his time to business ventures in Monterey and San Francisco. He seems to have borne only a minor, if any, part in the contest of 1846. At the time of the gold discovery he was in San José in charge of a branch store for Mellus & Howard, the largest firm on the coast. He left for the mines, but soon came back and resumed his business, which now, due to the influx of gold and the eagerness of the Mexicans to buy everything offered for sale, became exceedingly prosperous. In 1849 he married Sarah M. Jones, a pioneer of 1846. In the same year he closed his business and invested heavily in San Francisco real estate. On the incorporation of San José as a city, in 1850, he was elected its first mayor, and he later served on its council. He supported the Union party in the campaigns of 1860–61 and during the Civil War he took a special interest in the Sanitary Fund, to which he made large contributions. In 1876 he was a delegate to the Republican National Convention. About 1881 he moved from San José to New York. In his later years he spent much time in foreign travel. At the time of his death, which occurred in his New York home, he was a member of the Union League Club and a director of the Erie Railroad.

Belden is described as domestic in his tastes, unassuming and democratic in manner, and punctiliously honest in his dealings. Bancroft speaks of him as "clear headed" and praises a chronicle of his California experiences which at the request of the historian he wrote in 1878. The considerable fortune which he built up had its beginnings in the friendship and confidence which he inspired among his Mexican fellow-citizens of San José, who not only bought his goods with great prodigality but entrusted to him, on his mere word of honor, large quantities of gold. From his profits he bought real estate, of which at the time of his death he was a large holder.

[Jessie Perry Van Zile Belden, *Concerning Some of the Ancestors and Descendants of Royal Denison Belden and Olive Caldwell Belden* (1898); H. H. Bancroft, *Hist. of Cal.* (1885), II, 715; T. H. Hittell, *Hist. of Cal.* (1885), II, 331; Zoeth Skinner Eldredge (ed.), *Hist. of Cal.* (1915), III, 362; obituaries in the *N. Y. Tribune,* Apr. 25, 1892, and *N. Y. Sun,* Apr. 26, 1892. An account of the historic journey to the coast is given by Gen. John Bidwell in the *Century Mag.,* Nov. 1890.]

W. J. G.

BELKNAP, GEORGE EUGENE (Jan. 22, 1832–Apr. 7, 1903), naval officer, the son of Sawyer B. and Martha (Aiken) Belknap, was born at Newport, N. H. He was appointed midshipman in 1847 and was promoted to be passed midshipman in 1853, master in 1855, and lieutenant in September of the same year. From 1847 to 1850 he served on the brig *Porpoise* off the coast of Africa, and later (1856–57), serving on the sloop *Portsmouth* of the East India Squadron, he was commended for gallant behavior during the naval attack on the Barrier Forts at Canton, China. In April 1863 he served as executive officer of the *New Ironsides,* flagship of Admiral Du Pont, in the attack on the forts in Charleston Harbor, and was especially commended for the state of efficiency to which he had brought his ship, as well as for his conduct in action. He commanded the monitor *Canonicus* in the attacks on Fort Fisher in December 1864 and January 1865, after which he returned to duty off Charleston, his ship firing the last gun before the surrender of that city. Belknap was promoted to be commander in 1866, commanding the *Hartford* on the Asiatic Station, and directing, among other activities, the expedition against Formosa. In the *Tuscarora,* in 1873 and 1874, he made extensive deep-sea surveys for submarine cable routes, developing the use of piano wire for sounding. He became captain in 1875, and commanded the Navy Yard at Pensacola and then the cruiser *Alaska* in the Pacific. After a tour of service at the Norfolk Navy Yard he served as superintendent of the Naval Observatory, and as commandant of the Mare Island Navy Yard, California. He was promoted to be commodore in 1885. He then became commander-in-chief of the Asiatic Station for three years, and was president of the Board of Inspection and Survey until his retirement in 1894, having been made rear admiral Feb. 12, 1889. After retirement he was appointed chairman of the Board of Commissioners of the Massachusetts Nautical Training School and during the war with Spain was appointed chairman of a board on naval coaling stations. He died at Key West while again on special duty. He was greatly respected as an officer of high character and uncommon ability, his wide experience, especially in foreign relations, giving much weight to his influence and opinion. He was married twice: to Ellen D. Reed in Newport, N. H., in 1861, and to Frances G. Prescott in Calcutta, India, in 1866.

[Navy Registers, 1848–1903; *Report of the Secretary of the Navy,* 1863–65; obituary in *Army and Navy Jour.,* Apr. 11, 1903; *Who's Who in America,* 1901–02.]

E. B.

BELKNAP, JEREMY (June 4, 1744–June 20, 1798), Congregational clergyman, was born in Boston, Mass. He was christened Jeremiah by his parents, Joseph and Sarah (Byles) Belknap, but later adopted the abbreviated form of his first name. His father was a leather-dresser and furrier; his mother was a niece of Rev. Mather Byles. Jeremy prepared for college at Mr. Lovell's school, and entered Harvard before he was fifteen years old. Upon graduating from Harvard in 1762 he taught school at Milton, Mass., for a year or two, and afterward at Portsmouth and Greenland, N. H. While thus engaged, he was studying for the ministry, and in 1766 he went to Dover, N. H., where he was installed as pastor of the Congregational church. In the following year he married Ruth Eliot, daughter of Samuel Eliot, a bookseller in Cornhill, Boston. Although the relations between Belknap and Gov. John Wentworth were distinctly cordial, the former favored the American cause in the approaching Revolution, especially after the passage of the Boston Port Bill. Soon after hostilities began he was appointed chaplain to the New Hampshire troops at Cambridge, but his health and other considerations prevented him from accepting the office (*New Hampshire State Papers,* VII, 562). After the war, in 1786, he resigned from his parish at Dover, and after preaching at various places in New Hampshire and Massachusetts he accepted, early in 1787, a call to the Federal Street Church in Boston. He continued as minister of that society during the remainder of his life.

Belknap's reputation rests chiefly on his *History of New Hampshire,* a work in three volumes which is remarkable for its research, impartiality, and literary merit. The author began it soon after establishing himself at Dover and he completed it more than twenty years later. The first volume appeared in 1784; the others followed in 1791 and 1792. In many ways Belknap's *New Hampshire* is the counterpart of Hutchinson's *History of Massachusetts-Bay,* but it has the additional merit of being a complete study to 1789, including a valuable treatise on the natural history of New Hampshire. About 1787 Belknap amused himself by writing *The Foresters,* a humorous allegory describing the origin and rise of the British colonies in North America. It appeared serially in the *Columbian Magazine,* and later (1792) the chapters were collected and put forth as a small book. Belknap's next production was his *American Biography,* two volumes containing sketches of the lives of the more famous early explorers and colonial leaders. The first volume was published in 1794; the second, just after his death in 1798.

In Boston, Belknap discovered other gentlemen who were interested in the writing of history and in the preservation of historical papers and memorabilia. Conspicuous among these were William Tudor, the Rev. John Eliot, the Rev. Peter Thacher, and James Winthrop. In the summer of 1790 Belknap formulated a plan for an "Antiquarian Society," and in January of the following year he and his four friends mentioned above held their first meeting. This was the beginning of the Massachusetts Historical Society, which was incorporated in 1794. Its first president was James Sullivan, who later became governor of Massachusetts; Belknap was elected corresponding secretary. This society was the first of its kind in the United States, and Belknap endeavored to promote the formation of similar institutions in the other states. Besides his historical works he wrote a biography of Isaac Watts, which appeared anonymously in 1793 in the same volume with a life of Dr. Doddridge by Andrew Kippis. In 1795 he published *Dissertations on the Character, Death, and Resurrection of Jesus Christ, and the Evidence of his Gospel;* in the same year he issued a collection of psalms and hymns, which was widely used by the Congregational churches of New England for many years. Other significant publications were a *Sermon on Military Duty* (1773), a *Discourse intended to Commemorate the Discovery of America by Christopher Columbus* (1792), and a *Sermon delivered before the Convention of the Clergy of Massachusetts* (1796). A portrait of Belknap by Henry Sargent in the possession of the Massachusetts Historical Society shows a thick-set, perhaps corpulent man, with an intelligent and benevolent countenance. His health appears never to have been robust, but he seldom spared himself on that account either in his ministry or in his literary pursuits.

[There is a good brief biography of Belknap by his grand-daughter, Jane Belknap Marcou (1847). Several volumes of his correspondence are preserved in the library of the Mass. Hist. Soc. Many of these papers have been printed in the Society's *Collections,* ser. 5, vols. II, III, and ser. 6, vol. IV. His "Journal of a Tour from Boston to Oneida, June, 1796," is printed in the *Mass. Hist. Soc. Proc.,* XIX, 396–423. A number of interleaved almanacs containing notes made by Belknap are also preserved in the Society's library.]

L. S. M.

BELKNAP, WILLIAM WORTH (Sept. 22, 1829–Oct. 13, 1890), secretary of war, was born in Newburgh, N. Y., the son of Gen. William Goldsmith Belknap, who later gained prominence in the Mexican War, and Ann Clark Belknap. The younger Belknap attended Princeton College, studied law at Georgetown, D. C., was admitted to the bar in 1851, began practise in Keokuk, Ia., and sat in the Iowa legislature as a Douglas Democrat, 1857–58. At the opening of the Civil War Belknap received a commission as major of the 15th Iowa Infantry, and served with distinction at Shiloh. Of this engagement, Col. H. T. Reid reported: "Major Belknap was always in the right place at the right time, directing and encouraging officers and men as coolly as a veteran" (*Official Records,* ser. I, vol. X, p. 289). He was mentioned for "conspicuous gallantry" at Corinth, was in command of the 15th Iowa at the siege of Vicksburg and during the Meridian expedition under Sherman in the early months of 1864. On July 30, 1864, he was commissioned brigadier-general on Sherman's recommendation, and placed in command of the 4th Division of the 17th Corps, of which the 15th Iowa was a part. Until the close of the war, he was in command of the 4th Division through Sherman's campaign in Georgia and northward across the Carolinas. The opinion of Belknap's work which was held by his superiors is typified in the report of Col. William Hall, referring to an engagement before Atlanta on July 22, 1864: Belknap displayed "at all times the highest qualities of a soldier, cheering his men by his voice, and encouraging them by his personal disregard of danger" (*Ibid.,* vol. XXXVIII, pt. 3, p. 595). He was mustered out on July 27, 1865. Upon his return to civil life, Belknap became a collector of internal revenue in Iowa, and in 1869 secretary of war in the cabinet of President Grant. On Mar. 2, 1876, the chairman of the committee on expenditures in the War Department reported to the House of Representatives that he had found "unquestioned evidence of the malfeasance in office by General William W. Belknap." The evidence was read and the Secretary impeached by a unanimous vote. Meanwhile Belknap resigned, and Grant accepted his resignation. The gravamen of the charges was that Belknap had received $24,450 during 1870–76 for appointing a certain John S. Evans to the post-tradership at Fort Sill. In the resulting trial before the Senate, thirty-five voted "guilty" and twenty-five "not guilty," short of the necessary two-thirds for conviction; of the twenty-five, however, twenty-two declared that Belknap's resignation took him outside the jurisdiction of the Senate (cf. Constitution, article II, sec. 4). The fact of the payments by Evans for his immunity from removal seems to have been admitted on both sides of the controversy. It is impossible to be sure, however, whether Belknap was aware of the bargain, or whether his wife made the arrangement and received the money without his knowledge. After his retirement from public office, Belknap lived for a long time in Philadelphia, but later practised law in Washington. Belknap was three times married. His first wife was Cora Le Roy, of Vincennes, Ind., and his second, Carrie Tomlinson of Kentucky, who died in 1870. He then married Mrs. John Bower, the sister of his second wife. His death occurred in Washington.

[Jesse R. Grant, *In the Days of My Father General Grant* (1925); the military record is best followed in the *Official Records;* official records of the impeachment are found in: *Reports of Committees of the House of Representatives,* 44 Cong., 1 Sess., *No. 186,* "Malfeasance of W. W. Belknap, Late Secretary of War," *No. 345,* "Impeachment of William W. Belknap," and *No. 791,* "Report of the House Managers on the Impeachment of W. W. Belknap, Late Secretary of War"; the best account of the trial is in the *Cong. Record,* vol. IV, pt. 7, 44 Cong., 1 Sess., "Trial of W. W. Belknap"; *Iowa Hist. Record,* July 1885; *Ibid.,* Jan. 1891; obituaries in the *Evening Star* (Washington, D. C.), Oct. 13, 1890; *Washington Post,* Oct. 14, 1890; *Hist. of Lee County, Ia.* (1879), p. 683; E. M. Ruttenber, *Hist. of the County of Orange, N. Y.* (1875), pp. 360 ff.; *Hist. of the 15th Reg., Ia. Veteran Volunteer Inf.* (1887), ed. by W. W. Belknap; L. D. Ingersoll, *Hist. of the War Dept of the U. S.* (1879); H. White, *Life of Lyman Trumbull* (1913).]

C. R. L.

BELL, ALEXANDER GRAHAM (Mar. 3, 1847–Aug. 2, 1922), inventor of the telephone and the outstanding figure of his generation in the education of the deaf, was born in Edinburgh, the second of the three sons of Alexander Melville Bell [*q.v.*], a scientist and author in the field of vocal physiology and elocution, and of Eliza Grace Symonds (1809–97), the daughter of a surgeon in the Royal Navy. His grandfather, Alexander Bell (1790–1865), was a professor of elocution in London. From both sides of the family he inherited a scientific tendency and an instinct for applying knowledge to practise. During his earlier years he was taught at home, by his mother, a woman of admirable character who was also unusually gifted, a musician and painter of ability. From her Bell obtained his accuracy and sensitiveness of hearing and his love for music. When he was ten years old he went to McLauren's Academy in Edinburgh, and then to the Royal High School, from which he graduated at the age of thirteen. A visit to his grandfather in London extended to more than a year, and brought him many educational and cultural advantages. At the age of sixteen he secured a position as a pupil-teacher of elocution and music in Weston House Academy, at Elgin in Morayshire. The next year he spent at the University of Edinburgh, and then returned to Elgin for two years, thereafter spending a year (1866–67) as an instructor in Somersetshire College at Bath in England.

The distinctive achievement of his father, Alexander Melville Bell, was the invention of Visible Speech, a system of symbols by which the position of the vocal organs in speech was indicated. When the grandfather died in 1865, Alexander Melville Bell moved to London to take up his father's work there, and about two years later Alexander Graham Bell became his father's professional assistant in London. At this time he matriculated at University College, London, taking courses in anatomy and physiology for three years, 1868–70. While his father was absent in America on a lecture tour in 1868, Alexander Graham Bell took entire charge of his father's professional duties. The next year Alexander Melville Bell took his son into full partnership with him, an arrangement which continued until the family sailed for America, arriving in Quebec on Aug. 1, 1870.

Alexander Graham Bell early showed an aptness for systematic investigation and promise of inventive ability, which his father encouraged. The former's first piece of original scientific work was set forth in a letter to his father, from Elgin, Nov. 24, 1865, on the resonance pitches of the mouth cavities during the utterance of vowel sounds. His father suggested to him that he send this study to Alexander J. Ellis, an eminent phonetician and friend in London. Ellis called his attention to the work of Helmholtz on vowel sounds. This resulted in Bell's beginning the study of electricity as applied in telegraphy. At this time he conceived his first idea for the electrical transmission of speech. His work for the deaf, also, grew out of his position as his father's assistant. One of his father's pupils, Miss Susanna E. Hull, had a school for deaf children in Kensington. At her request in May 1868, Alexander Melville Bell sent his son, then twenty-one years old, to her school to adapt Visible Speech and its teaching to the work for the deaf, and during the same year in an influential lecture at the Lowell Institute, Boston, he told of the use of Visible Speech in the London School. As a result, in the following year through the efforts of the Rev. Dexter King a special day school for the deaf, the first of its kind anywhere, was started by the Boston School Board with Miss Sarah Fuller as principal. She had heard Alexander Melville Bell's lecture and persuaded the School Board to engage his son to come and train her teachers in the use of Visible Speech. Bell began his work at Miss Fuller's school on Apr. 10, 1871. He added to Visible Speech a system of notation that improved it for use with the deaf. This is still the basis of the method used in teaching the deaf to talk.

After three months of Miss Fuller's school, Bell visited the Clarke Institution for the Deaf at Northampton, Mass., and the American Asylum for the Deaf at Hartford, Conn. As a demand for his services resulted, in October 1872 he opened a private normal class in Boston to which institutions could send teachers for training in the use of Visible Speech. Early in 1873 he was appointed professor of vocal physiology and the mechanics of speech in the School of Oratory of Boston University. There also he started a normal class for the training of teachers of the deaf. Bell's lectures at Boston University attracted wide attention and the University of Oxford invited him to deliver a course there. This he did with notable success in 1878. His normal work became still more extensive through a series of conventions of teachers of speech to the deaf, which he started and led. His work also became more intensive, as he took a number of private pupils. One of these was the five-year-old son of Thomas Sanders of Haverhill, Mass., who was born deaf. Bell had charge of the child's entire education for more than three years, 1873–76, living with him at the home of the grandmother in Salem. Believing that the principle of Froebel's kindergarten method would be useful in the teaching of the deaf, he used both playing and working as direct means of instruction.

Bell's inventive activities were not suspended by these interests, though invention was always subordinate in his own mind to his main purpose to devote his life to the welfare of the deaf. His approach to his inventive work through the science of acoustics and his work for the deaf was particularly favorable to the success later of his telephonic experiments. Further, so remarkable was his teaching of the little Sanders boy that Thomas Sanders in generous gratitude offered to meet all the expenses of his experimenting and of securing patents for his inventions. A little later Gardiner G. Hubbard, a man of notable public spirit and an active friend of the education of the deaf, also became interested in Bell and gave most important and effective assistance in the commercial management of his inventions. During the years 1873–76, Bell was experimenting along three related lines—to invent a phonautograph; a multiple telegraph; and an electric speaking telegraph or telephone. He hoped in his phonautograph to invent an instrument with which he could explain to his deaf pupils how to make their tone-vibrations correctly by comparing visual records of the sounds they made with standard records. For this Dr. Clarence J. Blake, an aurist, suggested that he use an actual human ear in studying the question, and prepared one for him. Bell never brought his phonautograph to such a stage as to be of practical use for his purpose, but it was of value to him in his telephone experiments; from it he took the conception of the membrane element in the telephone.

His experiments in telegraphy Bell had begun at Elgin when only eighteen. At that time telegraphy constituted the whole art of electrical communication. Before leaving London for America in 1870, Bell had secured a copy in French of Helmholtz's book, *The Sensations of Tone*. His study of this book was an important help in gaining a correct knowledge of the physical principles underlying the theory of sound. Thereafter he advanced with a firmer step in all his researches. After coming to America, what time he could spare from his work for the deaf he gave to telegraphy, hoping to invent a device that would send two or more telegraph messages over a wire at the same time. In his multiple harmonic telegraph he utilized the fact that a tuned reed will vibrate when its own note is sounded near it. A number of reed transmitters were attached by leads to the one wire; at the other end of the wire a similar number of leads ran to receivers in which the reeds were attuned accurately to their corresponding transmitters. Each receiver would in operation vibrate in response only to its own transmitter. These experiments resulted in two patents. The first was No. 161,739, Apr. 6, 1875, for an Improvement in Transmitters and Receivers for Electrical Telegraphs; the other was No. 178,399, June 6, 1876, for Telephonic Telegraph Receivers. From his arduous study and experimentation in telegraphy Bell gained invaluable advantage in the mastery of the principles of electrical wave transmission.

But the speaking telephone was always in Bell's mind the most important invention. In the summer of 1874, following his usual custom, he had gone to his father's home at Brantford, Ontario, to spend his vacation. While there, on July 26, 1874, Bell tells us, he formed clearly in his mind the theory of the telephone that ultimately proved to be correct. How to realize this theory in practise was a problem which presented many difficulties. Bell had learned at the Massachusetts Institute of Technology that some of the points he had discovered concerning the application of acoustics to telegraphy had already been discovered by Joseph Henry [*q.v.*]. In order to learn which of his own discoveries were new and which were old he called upon Prof. Henry at the Smithsonian Institution. The aged scientist treated him with genuine interest and gracious respect, even asking permission to verify Bell's experiments and publish them through the Smithsonian Institution, giving Bell full credit for them. Much encouraged, Bell told Joseph Henry about his telephone idea and asked Henry whether he ought to publish it at its present stage and allow others to work it out or try to finish it himself. Henry declared it to be the "germ of a great invention" and told him to go ahead himself. Bell then said that he lacked the electrical knowledge that was necessary. Henry emphatically replied, "Get it!" This sympathetic and unhesitating confidence in him by Joseph Henry led Bell to persevere. Whatever observations he made, whatever experiments he was conducting, his mind henceforth was always alert to note anything which might throw light on his telephone problem. At length on June 2, 1875, in the shop at 109 Court St., Boston, while preparing the apparatus used in his harmonic telegraph for an experiment, Bell observed an effect, the significance of which he alone was competent to appreciate. He was tuning the receiver reeds and his assistant, Thomas A. Watson, was plucking the transmitting reeds to give him the pitch over the wire. In one transmitter the contact point was screwed down too far and Bell's sensitively accurate ear heard not only the pitch or tone of the reed but also the overtones. He knew at once that he had found what he had been seeking, that any condition of apparatus that would reproduce the tone and overtones of a steel spring could be made to reproduce the tone and overtones of the human voice. After repeatedly verifying the fact he had observed, Bell gave Watson directions for making the first telephone. When tested the next morning Watson could recognize Bell's voice, and could almost understand some of the words. Experimenting to improve the quality of the transmission followed. On Mar. 10, 1876, the telephone transmitted its first complete intelligible sentence, "Mr. Watson, come here; I want you." Bell's subsequent development of the telephone in quality and distance of transmission was rapid, until in about a year, Apr. 3, 1877, he was able to conduct a telephone conversation between Boston and New York with some degree of success. In September and October 1875, Bell had written the specifications for his application for a patent. The historic first Telephone Patent, No. 174,465, had been allowed on Bell's twenty-ninth birthday, Mar. 3, and had been issued to him on Mar. 7, 1876. On Jan. 30, 1877, another patent was issued to him, No. 186,787, for the substitution of an iron or steel diaphragm for the membrane and armature in the telephone of the first patent. Many claimants now came forward to contest Bell's rights, but after the most prolonged and important litigation in the history of American patent law, including about 600 cases, the United States Supreme Court upheld all of Bell's claims, declaring that he was the discoverer of the only way that speech could be transmitted electrically (*126 United States Reports*). His first announcement and demonstration of the telephone to the scientific world was in an address before the American Academy of Arts and Sciences in Boston on May 10, 1876. On June 25, 1876, at the International Centennial Exhibition at Philadelphia, through the interest of Dom Pedro II, the Emperor of Brazil, who was present as a guest of honor, and to whom a few months before Bell had shown the school for the deaf in Boston, Bell had an opportunity to explain his telephone to the judges, among whom were Sir William Thomson, Joseph Henry, and other prominent scientists. This demonstration was in itself an important introduction of the telephone to the scientific world. Lectures before scientific societies led to a demand for lectures for the general public. At Salem on Feb. 12, 1877, the telephone was used for the first time to send a report to a newspaper. With the spring of 1877 the commercial development of the invention came to the front. The first telephone organization was effected on July 9, 1877, in the form of a trusteeship called the Bell Telephone Company with Gardiner G. Hubbard as trustee and Thomas Sanders as treasurer.

On July 11, 1877, Bell married Mabel G. Hubbard, the daughter of Gardiner G. Hubbard. This girl of eighteen, who was to be an exceptional help-meet for him the rest of his life, was entirely deaf from early childhood. There was, therefore, a keen personal element in his sympathy for the deaf and in his work for them. Early in August he sailed with his bride for Europe to introduce the telephone into England and France. A prospectus which he wrote for a group of capitalists in London contains a remarkable prediction of the development of telephone service, describing in detail its uses fifty years later. While he was in England he also gave considerable attention to the education of the deaf, and took part in the inception of a day school for the deaf at Greenock in Scotland. He returned to America in the fall of 1878, and that winter moved to Washington, D. C. His inventive work now followed related lines rather than the development of the telephone itself. In 1880 the French Government awarded him the Volta Prize of 50,000 francs, for the invention of the electric speaking telephone. He devoted this money to the promotion of research and invention and to the work for the deaf by financing the Volta Laboratory, in which he associated with him his cousin, Chichester A. Bell, and Sumner Tainter. Each had his own special work, and all three coöperated on some undertaking of common interest and probable profit whereby the laboratory might be maintained. Bell continued in the Volta Laboratory an investigation, which he had started in 1878, into the causes and conditions of congenital deafness in New England. He prepared a memoir on *The Formation of a Deaf Variety of the Human Race* (1884) and a study of the results of the marriage of the deaf. He also initiated a movement for certain fundamental improvements in the taking of the Census of 1890 with respect to the deaf. During these years of the Volta Laboratory he invented the photophone, an apparatus for transmitting speech over a ray of light by means of the variable electric resistance of selenium to light and shade. He also invented the induction balance for locating metallic objects in the human body, first used on President Garfield, and the telephone probe which he developed from the former invention. These he did not patent but gave to the world. He further invented an audiometer, thus bringing his inventive work a step nearer to his service to the deaf.

Bell was interested in Edison's invention for recording sound, the phonograph. But Edison's tinfoil records left much to be desired. Accordingly the members of the Volta Laboratory Association invented an improved recorder, a flat wax record, a wax cylinder record, and an improved reproducer, and jointly received patents for these improvements on May 4, 1886. When these patents were sold to the American Graphophone Company, the Laboratory was converted into a Volta Bureau for the Increase and Diffusion of Knowledge Relating to the Deaf. This Bureau worked in close coöperation with the American Association for the Promotion of the Teaching of Speech to the Deaf, organized in 1890, of which Bell was elected president and to which he gave altogether more than $300,000.

Through his study of marriage among the deaf, Bell was led to give attention to the whole field of longevity and eugenics. An important contribution to this subject was his *Duration of Life and Condition Associated with Longevity* (1918). In this connection he made an excursion into the breeding of multi-nippled and twin-bearing sheep at his summer home on Cape Breton Island. This broad interest in eugenics and his optimistic attitude toward its problems was recognized by his election as honorary president of the Second International Congress of Eugenics.

During the last twenty-five years of Bell's life

aviation was his predominant interest. He was one of the first to consider aerial locomotion practicable, and in 1891 encouraged and financially coöperated with Samuel P. Langley, the secretary of the Smithsonian Institution, in the study of aviation. His own experiments followed the line of kite development and resulted in his invention of the tetrahedral kite and the application of that principle of construction to various uses. In 1907 Bell founded the Aerial Experiment Association, of which he was president and to which he gave $50,000. The first public flight of a heavier-than-air machine was made under the auspices of this organization in 1908. He and his associates also solved the problem of the stability of balance in a flying machine, using rigid instead of flexible supporting surfaces and providing ailerons for the wings and the rudders. During the war Bell invented a motor boat which attained a speed of seventy-one miles an hour. In 1883 with the coöperation of Gardiner G. Hubbard, he established *Science,* now the organ of the American Association for the Advancement of Science, and maintained it for several years. From 1896 to 1904 he was president of the National Geographic Society and did much to forward the development of the society and its magazine. In 1898 he was appointed a regent of the Smithsonian Institution, serving continuously until his death. In 1891 he had started by a generous gift the Astrophysical Observatory of the Smithsonian, and in 1904 he brought the body of James Smithson from Genoa to Washington. The honors, medals, and degrees that were received by him were numerous. In these marks of recognition from Harvard, Oxford, Heidelberg, Edinburgh, and other institutions, Bell's work for the deaf, his inventions for the hearing, and his other services and attainments were alike honored. In 1915 he opened the first transcontinental telephone line from New York to San Francisco. In 1917, at Brantford, Ontario, the Duke of Devonshire, as governor general of Canada, unveiled the Bell Telephone Memorial in honor of the inventor of the electric speaking telephone and dedicated the old home at Tutelo Heights as a public park. In 1920, the home of his childhood, Edinburgh, Scotland, conferred upon him the freedom of the city and elected him a burgess and guild brother of the city. He had taken out his first papers for citizenship in the United States at Lawrence, as early as Oct. 27, 1874, and he received his final papers from the supreme court of the District of Columbia at Washington, Nov. 10, 1882, but he never lost his love for his native Scotland and had a large estate in the new Scotland (Nova Scotia), on the Bras d'Or Lakes of Cape Breton Island. There he spent his summers, and there he died. He was buried on top of a mountain in a tomb cut in the rock, while every telephone on the continent of North America remained silent.

In appearance, during his earlier years, he was a tall, spare young man, with pale complexion, piercing black eyes and bushy, jet black hair and side whiskers, quick of motion, serious and grave. In his later years he was conspicuous for his majestic presence and his radiant manner. His hair and beard had become pure white but his keen black eyes still dominated the situation. The gravity of his youth had given way to a sympathy and joviality which won both old and young.

[Papers in possession of the Bell family and of the Am. Telephone and Telegraph Company; *The Deposition of Alexander Graham Bell* (1908); Fred De Land, *Dumb No Longer* (1908); Thomas A. Watson, *Exploring Life* (1926).]

W. C. L.

BELL, ALEXANDER MELVILLE (Mar. 1, 1819–Aug. 7, 1905), educator, the younger son of Alexander Bell, professor of elocution in London, was born in Edinburgh and mainly educated at home. Like his elder brother who had already settled in Dublin, he followed the family profession and in 1843 established himself in Edinburgh. The father and two sons were the leading teachers of the science of correct speech at the three capitals of England, Ireland, and Scotland for the ensuing twenty-two years. At that time teachers of elocution, especially those who undertook to cure stammering and other defects of utterance, made a great mystery of their art. Bell, with the candor and truthfulness that were a marked feature of his family, declared that there was no mystery about it except such as arose from the little attention that had been paid to the science of speech. At the outset he published his methods. He early conceived the idea of a physiological alphabet which would furnish to the eye a complete guide to the production of any oral sound. This idea he carefully worked out during the next twenty-three years and gave to the world in his *Visible Speech: the Science of Universal Alphabetics* (1867). In his physiological or pictorial alphabet "each symbol means a definite position of the organs of speech, which, if correctly assumed, produces a definite result. Every sound possible for the human voice can be represented by these symbols. There is, therefore, no language or variation of language in dialect, or even individual idiosyncrasy of utterance, which cannot be represented by Visible Speech and reproduced vocally by any one knowing the system." Some of its more important practical uses are in the recording of unwritten languages and disappearing dialects, the correction of defects of vocal utterance, and the training of oral teachers of the deaf. It is upon this universal alphabet that Alexander Melville Bell's claim to lasting remembrance chiefly rests. Fourteen of his forty-nine published works relate to this subject. His books on elocution remain the standard authority, more than 250 editions of *The Principles of Elocution* and *The Standard Elocutionist* having been printed.

After the death of his father Bell moved to London, where he lived for five years, lecturing on elocution in University College and giving public readings from Shakespeare and Dickens. In 1868 he visited America to give a course of lectures before the Lowell Institute of Boston and in other cities of the United States and Canada. Two years later he returned to deliver a second course of twelve lectures before the Lowell Institute, and the following year had the honor of presenting a third and similar course. He settled in Brantford, Ontario, Canada, in 1870 and later held the professorship of elocution in Queens College, Kingston. When his distinguished son, Alexander Graham Bell [*q.v.*], permanently located in Washington, D. C., the father was persuaded to move to the same city (1881), and at the age of seventy-eight he was admitted to American citizenship, Jan. 12, 1897. He was twice married: to Eliza Grace Symonds in 1844, and to Mrs. Harriet Guess Shibley in 1898.

[S. S. Curry, *Alexander Melville Bell* (1906); John Hitz, "Alexander Melville Bell" in the *Ass. Rev.*, VII, 421 ff.; the *Washington Post*, Aug. 8, 1905. For further information consult the Volta Bureau of the Am. Ass. to Promote the Teaching of Speech to the Deaf, 1601 Thirty-fifth St., Washington, D. C.]
G. G—r.

BELL, CHARLES HENRY (Nov. 18, 1823–Nov. 11, 1893), lawyer, politician, author, son of John and Persis (Thom) Bell, and nephew of Samuel Bell [*q.v.*], was born at Chester, N. H., in a neighborhood where the family had been prominent for a century or more. Both his father and uncle held numerous public offices, including the governorship. Charles Bell enjoyed the best educational opportunities available in the state, attending Pembroke and Phillips Exeter Academies and graduating from Dartmouth in 1844. He entered the legal profession and practised at Chester, Somersworth, and Exeter. He settled at the latter town in 1854 and there resided for the rest of his life. He was twice married: on May 6, 1847, to Sarah Gilman of Exeter, who died Aug. 22, 1850; and on June 3, 1857, to Mary (Gray) Gilman, widow of Joseph Gilman of Exeter. He was a successful lawyer and Chief Justice Charles Doe once remarked of him, "A mind more capable of grasping, mastering, and presenting legal questions quickly, clearly and thoroughly, I have never known." In 1868, however, he gave up active practise, although still handling occasional cases of special importance. In 1856 he had begun a period of ten years' service as solicitor for Rockingham County. He represented Exeter in the lower house 1858–60, being speaker in the latter year, and again in 1872 and 1873. He was a member of the Senate 1863–64, serving as president in his second term. In 1879 he was appointed to fill a vacancy in the United States Senate, serving for a few months pending the meeting of the legislature. The legality of his appointment was contested in the Senate, but he was finally seated (*Congressional Record,* 46 Cong., 1 Sess., p. 355). He was governor, 1881–83, and in 1889 was president of the seventh constitutional convention.

He is, however, chiefly remembered as a student and writer of New Hampshire history, and a collector of miscellaneous Americana. He was active in the New Hampshire Historical Society, the Prince Society, and similar organizations. His most important works were *John Wheelwright* (1876), a monograph showing research and critical ability, *History of the Town of Exeter, New Hampshire* (1888), and *The Bench and Bar of New Hampshire* (1894), which was in the hands of the printer at the time of Bell's death. The latter is his most important work and contains biographical sketches of 871 New Hampshire jurists and lawyers. It shows laborious research and great skill in presentation. His work throughout is characterized by clearness and simplicity of style. In addition to the above, he was the author of numerous shorter studies, and many of his addresses and commemorative orations were reprinted.

[A brief account of the life and services of Chas. H. Bell, by Jeremiah Smith, is included in the former's *The Bench and Bar of New Hampshire.* This sketch, which pays special attention to Bell's legal career, was privately printed in 1894, together with a character sketch by Mellen Chamberlain. It contains, p. 19, a list of Bell's published works and addresses. In Jan. 1895 there appeared "A Memoir of Chas. H. Bell," by Edmund F. Slafter in the *New Eng. Hist. and Geneal. Reg.*]
W. A. R.

BELL, CLARK (Mar. 12, 1832–Feb. 22, 1918), lawyer, the son of Philander F. and Sylvia (Jones) Bell, was born at Whitesville, Jefferson County, N. Y. He was educated at Franklin Academy, and after leaving school assisted his father in the blacksmith business. He studied law in his leisure hours and was admitted to the bar at Rochester in 1853. Opening an office at Hammondsport, N. Y., he continued in practise there till 1861, when he removed to Bath, and acted as assistant district attorney for Steuben

County, 1861–62. Shortly thereafter he became associated with the promoters of the Union Pacific Railroad and Telegraph Company which, organized under Acts of Congress in 1862, found itself unable to proceed with construction, partly owing to the depression caused by the war. He was appointed attorney to the company, assisted in its reorganization in October 1863, and the same year moved his office to New York City. He drafted the act which was passed by Congress and approved July 2, 1864, radically changing the constitution of the company and the terms under which federal aid was extended, and he continued to act as the company's attorney during the whole period of construction (1864–69). He was later retained by the Pacific Mail Steamship Company and the Rock Island Railroad, and, so long as he remained in active practise, was associated with important corporation and industrial enterprises. In 1870 he was elected a member of the Medico-Legal Society of New York, and two years later became its president, devoting a large part of his time to its business and taking a prominent part in all its discussions. He soon became recognized as a leading New York expert in medical jurisprudence, and contributed valuable papers on that subject to the proceedings of the Medico-Legal Society. In 1872 he was counsel for George Francis Train, against whom lunacy proceedings had been commenced under somewhat extraordinary circumstances. The trial before Chief Justice Daly and a jury was lengthy, lasting from Apr. 9 to May 6, 1873. Bell had for some years prior to this studied the subject of mental diseases extensively and his successful contest with the professional mental experts in this case brought him into great prominence. In 1884 he was active in establishing the *Medico-Legal Journal* and became its editor. Thenceforth he was a constant contributor to its columns on matters of common interest to the legal and medical professions. In 1885 he represented the United States at the Paris Congress of Medical Jurisprudence. His *Judicial History of the Supreme Court of the United States and Provinces of North America* was published in 1895. He founded the American Congress on Tuberculosis in 1900, editing the *Bulletin* of its proceedings in four volumes. He was appointed United States delegate to the International Medical Congresses held in Paris in 1900 and Lisbon in 1906, taking an important part in the discussions. He also wrote *Spiritism, Telepathy and Hypnotism* (1902), which attracted much attention and passed through several editions. The first of his *Medico-Legal Studies* had appeared in 1889, and they had reached eleven volumes when advancing years compelled him to retire from his activities. In addition to his writings he edited the *Bulletins of the Medico-Legal Congresses,* 1889 and 1895, and *Medico-Legal Papers* in three volumes. He died very suddenly in New York on Feb. 22, 1918. He was married in 1858 to Helene S. Taylor. He had always evinced a love for country life, and much of his leisure was devoted to the study of agricultural problems. He was known in New York quite as much as a breeder of trotting horses as he was in the capacity of medico-legal expert.

[The various volumes of the *Medico-Legal Jour.* contain elaborate notices of his activities in the field of medic. jurisprudence. An article in *The Lawyer and Banker,* V, 336, gives details of his career, but must be used with caution since on several points it is inaccurate. A good appreciative obituary appeared in the *N.Y. Times,* Feb. 23, 1918. For particulars of the reorganization of the Union Pacific Railway see N. Frohman, *Hist. of the Union Pacific* (1923) and J. P. Davis, *Union Pacific Railway* (1894). Bell's speech to the jury in the Train case was printed verbatim in pamphlet form in 1873 accompanied by an excellent report of the whole case itself.]

H. W. H. K.

BELL, HENRY HAYWOOD (Apr. 13, 1808–Jan. 11, 1868), naval officer, born in North Carolina, was appointed a midshipman in the United States Navy Aug. 4, 1823, and was promoted to be lieutenant Mar. 3, 1831, commander Aug. 12, 1854, and commodore Aug. 21, 1862. In 1828–29 he was in the *Grampus,* clearing the Cuban coast of pirates, and in 1856 he commanded the *San Jacinto,* flagship of the East India Squadron, taking a prominent part in the capture and destruction of four barrier forts near Canton, China, in November of that year. He was on that occasion in command of one wing of a landing party from the fleet which stormed the first fort, and held it until the following day, when the fleet shelled the remaining forts into submission. At the outbreak of the Civil War, Bell, a Southerner by birth and married to a Virginia lady, was compelled to make the distressing decision between devotion to his native state and loyalty to his flag, under which he had served long and honorably. This decision, however, appears to have caused him little effort, his sense of duty triumphing over all other considerations. His friend, Edward A. Pollard, writes (*Galaxy,* November 1868) that, though he expected him to go with his state, when the subject was broached, shortly after President Lincoln's proclamation of war, Bell cut the conversation short with the emphatic declaration, "I have made up my mind; I shall stand by the flag."

His most conspicuous service in the Civil War was as fleet-captain of the West Gulf Squadron under Farragut, whose chief-of-staff he was during the actions leading to the opening of the Mississippi River in 1862. In the battle between the fleet and Forts Jackson and St. Philip he commanded one of the three naval divisions, consisting of six vessels. When the fleet lay before New Orleans, Bell was chosen by Farragut to carry out the hazardous task of hoisting the flag of the United States over the custom house and hauling down the flag of the State of Louisiana which floated over the city hall, and which the mayor of New Orleans had declined to remove. With a party of sailors and marines, at the risk of his life, he marched through the hostile streets and directed from the roofs of the custom house and the city hall the raising of the one flag and the lowering of the other. The landing party returned to its boats taunted with cries of "Hurrah for Beauregard! Hurrah for Jeff Davis!" (*Official Records,* ser. I, vol. XVIII, p. 698). In 1863 he was for a time in command of the West Gulf Squadron, and in 1865 was ordered to command the East India Squadron, in which capacity he was active in subduing the pirates infesting the China seas. On July 25, 1866, he became rear admiral; he was placed on the retired list in 1867; but, while awaiting his relief, he was drowned by the capsizing of his barge on a bar in the river near the city of Osaka, Japan, as he was about to pay a visit to the United States minister. He was buried at Hiogo, Japan, the American and British squadrons taking part in the funeral ceremonies. Bell was distinguished by high technical skill in his profession, and an almost fanatical devotion to duty, tempered by great kindliness and a quiet sense of humor.

[Navy Registers, 1824–68; *Report of the Secretary of the Navy,* for 1857, 1864, 1866, 1868; *Official Records of the Union and Confederate Navies,* ser. I, vol. XVIII; L. Farragut, *Life of Wm. Glasgow Farragut.*]

E. B.

BELL, ISAAC (Nov. 6, 1846–Jan. 20, 1889), cotton merchant, politician, was the son of Isaac Bell, for many years commissioner of Charities and Corrections of the State of New York. He was educated in private schools in New York City. Starting his business career in a clerkship with Brown Brothers & Company in New York, he became interested in the cotton business which in those years (from 1870 on) was assuming an extraordinary speculative activity. He determined to establish a brokerage house in the cotton region itself and went to Savannah, Ga., where he successfully conducted his own office. An attractive offer from the firm of Arthur Barnwell & Company led him to move to Charleston, S. C., there becoming a member of that firm, and repeating the success already gained in Savannah. As his knowledge of the cotton business increased, he determined to carry out what appears to have been his original design, that of uniting actual operations in the cotton region with the speculative market of the North, a familiar method to-day, but representing a plan then relatively little known in practise. Accordingly he established two houses of his own, one in New Orleans, the other in New York City, under the firm name of Isaac Bell, Jr., & Company. The venture was profitable, and with the money he had accumulated and inherited he retired from business in 1877 and removed to Newport, R. I. In the year 1878 Bell married Jeannette Gordon Bennett (the sister of James Gordon Bennett [*q.v.*]) and affiliated himself with the social and literary circles in which the Bennett family was conspicuous. Bell now took up politics as an avocation and began to play a considerable part as a Democrat in the local public affairs of Rhode Island. He was, however, rather too much of an aristocrat to catch the popular fancy, besides running counter to the traditional prejudices of the region, and a campaign for election to the United States Senate on the Democratic ticket proved a complete failure. President Cleveland, nevertheless, in his effort to consolidate the Democratic support of the Eastern seaboard communities and especially to recognize the wealthier element among the Democrats of New York and the adjacent states, named him minister to the Netherlands. His career in that position (March 1885–May 1888) was of no special note. Returning from Europe he became a delegate to the St. Louis convention of 1888 and shared actively in the campaign of that year, but the defeat of President Cleveland for a second term naturally resulted in his retirement from politics; and a decline in health shortly set in which developed into the illness (pyæmia) which caused his death.

[The principal sources of information concerning Bell's activities are to be found in current newspaper discussion during the period of his greatest activity in the cotton market, 1870–77, and during his political campaign in R. I. Incomplete and unsatisfactory newspaper biographies were generally published by the N. Y. newspapers at the time of his death. See *N. Y. Herald, Times, Tribune,* Jan. 21, 1889.]

H. P. W.

BELL, JACOB (Dec. 17, 1792–July 21, 1852), ship-builder, the son of John and Deborah Clock Bell, was born at Middlesex (now Darien), Conn., where his ancestor, Francis Bell, had been one of the first settlers in 1641. Jacob Bell entered into partnership with David Brown about 1820 and they took over the shipyard formerly run by Adam and Noah Brown on the East River at the foot of Houston St., New York City. In 1821 they launched their first ships, the *William Tell* and *Orbit.* The firm was known as Brown & Bell until the former's death about 1848, when Bell conducted it in his own name until his death. Their yard held its own with the principal local rivals, William H. Brown and William H. Webb. They seem to have been equally successful in turning out fast sailing vessels and in keeping up with the latest developments in steamships. The firm was in close relation with Edward K. Collins [*q.v.*]. In 1834 they joined with him in starting the New York Marine Dry Dock Company, and, shortly afterward, built the *Garrick, Roscius, Sheridan,* and *Siddons* for his transatlantic Dramatic Line of sailing packets. They are credited with building in 1840 the first ocean steamships launched in New York, the *Lion* and the *Eagle,* which became Spanish war-ships. A year later they built the fast little schooner *Angola* for the opium trade. Their clippers were surpassed only by the products of their former pupil, Donald McKay. The partners built the *Houqua* (1844) and *Samuel Russell* (1847). Among the best clippers built by Bell alone were the *Oriental* (1849), *White Squall* (1850), *Trade Wind* (1851), the largest clipper yet built, and *Messenger,* launched three months before his death. The *Jacob Bell,* named for himself, was completed four months after he died by his son Abraham. Even more conspicuous products of the Bell yard were the steamships *Pacific* and *Baltic* for the Collins Line. Bell was married on May 10, 1821, to Mary Clock of Darien, Conn.

[Frequent references to Bell's shipbuilding will be found in J. H. Morrison, *Hist. of the N. Y. Shipyards* (1909) and A. H. Clark, *The Clipper Ship Era* (1910). Complete details of the principal clippers are given in O. T. Howe and F. C. Matthews, *Am. Clipper Ships* (2 vols., 1926, 1927). Statistics of the output of the various New York yards will be found in contemporary issues of *Hunt's Merchant's Mag.* Genealogical details are given in the *N. Y. Geneal. and Biog. Reg.,* XXVIII, 153, XXIX, 63. Biographical details are given in E. F. Hatfield, *Riches in Death: a Discourse Occasioned by the Decease of Mr. Jacob Bell* (1852); a short obituary appeared in the *N. Y. Jour. of Commerce,* July 22, 1852.]

R. G. A.

BELL, JAMES MADISON (Apr. 3, 1826–1902), negro poet and lecturer, was born at Gallipolis, Ohio. Here he lived until 1842, when he removed to Cincinnati, where he lived with his brother-in-law, George Knight, and learned the plasterer's trade. Meanwhile his radical feeling against slavery was encouraged by the persecution that he saw visited upon some persons of missionary spirit who taught negroes. In his twenty-second year he married Louisiana Sanderline, who became the mother of several children. In August 1854 he removed with his family to Canada, where he lived until 1860. He became a personal friend of John Brown and assisted in getting men to go on the raid of 1859. In 1860 he went to California, where he worked earnestly against the disabilities that the negroes suffered and where he wrote some of his poems. In 1865 he removed to Toledo, Ohio, bringing his family from Canada. After the Civil War he traveled much in the Eastern states, encouraging the freedmen to make the most of their new opportunities and instructing them in their civic duties. In 1868 he was elected delegate from Lucas County to the state convention and then delegate at large from Ohio to the national Republican convention that nominated Grant for a second term, and he later appeared on the public platform in behalf of Grant's candidacy. Bell was an able speaker and was also well known as a reader of his own poems. "The Day and the War" was inscribed to the memory of John Brown, and "The Progress of Liberty" is suggestive of Byron; but in general the verse is without any distinctive literary quality.

[*The Poetical Works of James Madison Bell* (1901) with a biog. sketch by Bishop B. W. Arnett, is practically the sole authority. For year of death see *Ohio Centennial Anniversary Celebration . . . Complete Proceedings* (1903), p. 639.]

B. B.

BELL, JAMES STROUD (June 30, 1847–Apr. 5, 1915), merchant miller, the son of Samuel and Elizabeth (Faust) Bell, was born in Philadelphia. After graduating from the Central High School in that city at the age of sixteen, he began work in his father's milling and flour brokerage establishment. He received a thorough training in every department of the business. Five years later he was admitted to the firm (which now became Samuel Bell & Sons) as a partner, and here he remained for twenty years. The firm was a sales agent for Washburn, Crosby & Company, operating by lease the mills of the C. C. Washburn Flouring Mills Company in Minneapolis, and through the connection Bell came to be well known to the officers of this company. The year 1888 was a critical one for the milling industry. Speculators had forced up the price of flour beyond an export basis, and the millers—particularly the Minneapolis company, which in 1887 had sold forty per cent of its product abroad—faced the necessity of making an intensive cultivation of the home market. Bell was asked to become a partner in the firm, and on his acceptance it was reorganized (September 1888), as Washburn, Martin & Company. He at once took a leading part in its direction, and when, a year later, it was changed to a corporation, under the name of the Washburn-Crosby Company, he was chosen president. He had been a miller and a broker of mill products; he was now to become a merchant miller—perhaps, as the press termed him at the time of his death, "the greatest merchant miller of the world." In methods of reaching the public, both with his product and with the arguments for buying it, he was an originator; he placed on the market a wide range of cereal preparations in attractively labeled cartons, and by effective advertising made them known throughout the country. Under his control the corporation steadily expanded. In 1899 the leased mills were bought and the capital stock was increased to $1,200,000. A branch mill was built at Buffalo in 1903, another in the following year at Louisville, and others later at Great Falls and at Kalispell, Mont. Further increases in the capital stock were made in 1903 and 1907 and again in 1909, when it was placed at $6,000,000. At the time of his death the productive capacity of the mills, which had been 8,000 barrels a day when he joined the company, had risen to 27,700 barrels. He had wide commercial and financial interests; for many years he was vice-president of the Minneapolis Trust Company as well as of three other companies and a director of the Northwestern National Bank.

The obituaries of Bell give him a commanding position in the trade; no other man, said the *Northwestern Miller,* in so short a time made so great an impress on the milling industry. They stress, among his personal qualities, his helpful kindness to young men, many of whom, by his encouragement, he set on the pathway to material success. Though a strict disciplinarian, he was not an autocrat; his democracy and humaneness were shown, said one, by the fact that men could take orders from him and still love him. His business standards were of the highest; his word was his bond, and though hesitant in making promises he was faithful in keeping them. He was twice married—on Jan. 8, 1873, to Sallie Montgomery Ford, who died, and on Sept. 28, 1912, to Mabel Sargent, who survived him.

[*Who's Who in America,* 1914–15; W. C. Edgar, *The Medal of Gold* (1925); obituaries in the *Minneapolis Tribune* and the *St. Paul Pioneer Press,* Apr. 6, 1915, and the *Northwestern Miller,* Apr. 7, 1915.]

W. J. G.

BELL, JOHN (Feb. 15, 1797–Sept. 10, 1869), Southern statesman, was the son of Samuel Bell and Margaret Edmiston Bell, pioneer settlers of Tennessee. He was born on his father's farm near Nashville a few months after Tennessee had come into existence as a state. He was a precocious youth. In 1814, at the age of seventeen, he graduated from Cumberland College, an institution that later became the University of Nashville. Before he was twenty-one he had been admitted to the bar, had begun practise at Franklin, Tenn., and had served as senator in one session of the state legislature. Declining reëlection, he moved to Nashville where for some years he devoted himself to the practise of his profession and became one of the most eminent of the members of the Nashville bar. He was twice married: first, early in life, to Sally Dickinson, and after her death to Jane Erwin Yeatman, wealthy widow of Thomas Yeatman. In 1827 he began the first of fourteen successive years in the lower house of Congress. In his first campaign he defeated by a considerable majority Felix Grundy, who had the support of the popular idol of his state, Andrew Jackson. Yet Bell was a supporter of "Old Hickory" for the presidency and in his address to the voters in 1826 he had denounced the Henry Clay-John Quincy Adams combination and had urged upon the voters the support of Jackson as the instrument for their destruction. For some years in Congress he was a member of the Jackson party and supported the chief measures of the Jackson administration. He could never be, however, the unquestioning follower of any man, and in time there developed a breach between Jackson and Bell that ultimately made the latter the leader of the Whig party in Tennessee. In Jackson's war against the national bank Bell refused to follow the President despite the latter's threat that if he should "not come out clearly and distinctly against all national banks he" would be "politically destroyed" (Jackson to Van Buren, Aug. 16, 1834, Van Buren Papers, Library of Congress). In 1834 Bell was the opponent of a fellow Tennessean, James K. Polk, for the speakership of the House, and with the support of anti-Jackson members he won this coveted office. For more than a decade these two men were both political and personal enemies, and not until after Polk had become president were they even on speaking terms. Jackson preferred Polk, who was always a loyal follower. A complete break with Jackson occurred when Bell became the leading advocate of the presidential candidacy of Hugh Lawson White in opposition to Jackson's selection, Martin Van Buren. Bell still professed allegiance to the principles of the Democratic party; he declared White to be a better Jackson man than was Van Buren; yet Jackson declared that Bell had "turned a good Whig" (*John Bell; his "Past History connected with the Public Service,"* 1860, p. 7). This Bell finally admitted on the politician's plea that this new party was pledged to support the policies of the original Jackson party. The Whig party now became and continued for two decades to be the dominant party in Tennessee and Bell was its acknowledged leader. Despite Jackson's continued efforts, Bell's constituents returned him to Congress until in 1841 he entered the cabinet of President Harrison as secretary of war. He held this position only a few weeks, however, for after Harrison's death his successor, Tyler, rejected the legislative program of the Whigs, and Bell and other cabinet members resigned.

For the next six years Bell remained in retirement, but in 1847 he was elected to the United States Senate and he continued in this office till 1859. During this period of twelve years, characterized by the development of an increasingly bitter sectional spirit, Bell distinguished himself as one of the most consistently conservative and nationally-minded Southerners. He was a large slave owner; he had no love for the abolitionists; yet he never entered the camp of the apostles of slavery. Temperate in his emotions, judicial always in the formation of his opinions, yet on occasion powerful in attack upon his enemies, he had no sympathy for extremists North or South. As a member of the lower house of Congress he had voted with John Quincy Adams in defense of the right of petition against those who sought to prevent the reception or the consideration of anti-slavery petitions. In the Senate, when the controversy over the question of slavery in the territories that had been acquired from Mexico threatened a dissolution of the Union, Bell affirmed the constitutionality of congressional prohibition of slavery in the territories, though he opposed the use of this power on grounds of policy. He was the outstanding supporter of President Taylor's plan of avoiding the direct issue by admitting the territories to statehood even though the exclusion of slavery should be the result of this. He also offered a plan of compromise. He objected to certain features of Henry Clay's compromise measures of 1850, but after their passage he gave them his support. In 1854 he parted reluctantly from his Southern colleagues and opposed the reopening of the bitter controversy over slavery by the passage of the Kansas-Nebraska Act. The well-known results of this act were as he had predicted. Four years later he defied instructions from the Tennessee legislature to support the admission of Kansas under the Lecompton constitution and spoke and voted against that attempt to force slavery upon an unwilling people. For his attitude in the slavery controversy he was most bitterly denounced by increasing numbers in the South, but gained commendation in the North.

The Whig party was now dead. Bell gave support to the short-lived Americans and even considered the possibility of a uniting of moderate Republicans and former Southern Whigs. To many a Southerner he was "harloting" with the hated Black Republicans. The possibility of such a union passed, however, and secession and civil war drew on apace. In the momentous presidential campaign of 1860 moderate men, most of them former Whigs, nominated John Bell for the presidency and Edward Everett for the vice-presidency. Their party they called the Constitutional Union Party and their platform was "The Constitution of the country, the Union of the states, and the enforcement of the laws." But the time for moderation had passed; the slavery question could not be settled by ignoring it; and Bell secured the electoral votes of only three states, Tennessee, Kentucky, and Virginia. His campaign had been a plea for the preservation of the Union, and for some months after Lincoln's election and while states of the lower South seceded he and his followers opposed secession, and Tennessee remained within the Union. When Lincoln's administration began Bell was in Washington and sought there to promote a compromising spirit and the adoption of a temperate policy that would, he hoped, prevent civil war. But when Maj. Anderson's small garrison at Fort Sumter was fired upon and Lincoln called for troops, Bell was compelled to make what was probably the most momentous decision of his many years in public life. Disapproving secession "both as a constitutional right, and as a remedy for existing evils," he urged that if the federal government should attempt the coercion of the "seceded States," Tennessee should enter into "alliance" with them and resist suppression of the "Revolution" "at all hazards, at any cost, *and by arms . . .*" (*Nashville Patriot*, Apr. 19, May 10, 1861). Tennessee did as Bell advised. His own career was ended. When the state was invaded by troops of the United States he left for the lower South. Family tradition tells of an old man, heartbroken, who paced the floor lamenting the war and what war brought to the South and to the nation. When the war ended he returned to Tennessee; his health failed; and in Stewart County, near Bear Spring Furnace, he died.

[A small but valuable group of Bell's letters was edited by St. George L. Sioussat in *Tenn. Hist. Mag.*, III, 196–227. Information regarding his life can be secured from the newspapers and the congressional debates. See also brief campaign document, *The Public Record and Past History of John Bell* (1860); A. V. Goodpasture, "John Bell's Political Revolt and his Vauxhall Garden Speech," *Tenn. Hist. Mag.*, II, 254–63; article by O. Z. Bond in the *Nashville Banner*, Mar. 19, 1910. The most satisfactory sketch of Bell's life is by Joshua W. Caldwell in *Am. Hist. Rev.*, IV, 652–64. The best discussion of his break with Jackson and Polk is in Eugene I. McCormac, *Jas. K. Polk* (1922), *passim*.]

P. M. H.

BELL, LOUIS (Dec. 5, 1864–June 14, 1923), physicist, engineer, was descended from John Bell, a staunch Scotch-Irishman who in 1719 left County Antrim, Ireland, to join, in 1720, the small colony of his countrymen already settled at Londonderry in the southeastern corner of New Hampshire. Here the family prospered and became prominent in the public affairs of county and state. The grandfather of Louis Bell was Samuel Bell [*q.v.*], twice elected senator from New Hampshire and Daniel Webster's intimate friend, while his father was Col. Louis Bell, educated at Brown University, a man of commanding physique, clear head, and scientific tastes. In the final charge by which the Union troops captured Fort Fisher, N. C., on Jan. 15, 1865, Col. Bell took part, and died of wounds received in action on that day. It is little wonder that the son, then only six weeks old, always regarded his father as a hero. His broken-hearted mother, Mary Ann Persis (Bouton) Bell, died a few months later; the boy Louis and his sister, four years older, grew up in the home of their grandmother, the widow of Gov. Samuel Bell, at Chester, N. H. Twelve years in this quiet, remote village where he was in close contact with nature and enjoyed the privileges of a well-stocked library, breathing the atmosphere of a family acquainted with men of large affairs, turned the child into a lad with a mind which was as clear and alert as his body was strong and vigorous.

At Phillips Exeter Academy he prepared for Dartmouth College, where he matriculated in 1880 and graduated in 1884. It is easy to see that Bell's later life and qualities were foreshadowed in his college career. Here we find him exhibiting that keen literary taste which never deserted him and a remarkable accuracy in the bending of words to give precisely the meaning which he intended. Poet at the freshman class dinner, associate editor of the *Dartmouth*, he won honorable mention in English, and final honors in physics. An innate sense of humor led him to take the initiative in certain gibes and pranks; for one of these he was rusticated during a period of three months, a time of exile spent mostly at the Astor Library in New York City where he lived with an uncle. A year of graduate work at Dartmouth preceded three years of residence at Johns Hopkins University. In Baltimore, he began serious work in physics and chemistry, taking an active part in the Journal Club, investigating the absorption spectrum of nitrogen peroxide (*American Journal of Chemistry*, 1885–86), the ultra-violet spectrum of cadmium (*American Journal of Science*, 1886), and other similar problems. His most important work at Baltimore was his determination of the wave-length of the D_1 line in the spectrum of sodium. Rowland had just completed (1887) his atlas of the solar spectrum and had spent several of the best years of his life in measuring relative wave-lengths throughout this spectrum. It was clear that the value of this work would be greatly enhanced if these relative wave-lengths were all referred to one standard line whose length was known with high precision. Bell spent two years of skilful and careful work, with four of Rowland's finest gratings, in an attempt to arrive at just such a value for the D_1 line. To his result, Rowland gave a weight equivalent to that of all four of the best previous observers and used this mean as the base of his justly celebrated Preliminary Table of Solar Spectrum Wavelengths. The accuracy of Bell's value at the time of its publication (1888) was estimated to be of the order of one part in 100,000. Within three or four years, however, the interferometer method was employed by Michelson—also by Perot and Fabry—for the same purpose. The fact then emerged that the grating method used by Bell was inevitably, if not inherently, affected with an error of at least one part in 30,000.

On leaving Johns Hopkins University in 1888, Bell spent two years in finding himself, one of these at Purdue University in charge of the recently initiated course in electrical engineering. Two years later he accepted the editorship of the *Electrical World*. In 1893, he was married to Sarah G. Hemenway of Somerville, Mass. In the same year he was appointed chief engineer in the Power Transmission department of the General Electric Company. Polyphase transmission which at this time was just coming into practise challenged and fascinated Bell's admiration; he made himself an authority on the subject and installed at Redlands, Cal., the earliest three-phase transmission plant for general service. After 1895, however, he maintained a private office, as consulting engineer, in Boston. Here, as he once remarked, a large part of his business was "to diagnose sick electric railways." Along with his engineering practise he found time to join O. T. Crosby in the authorship of *The Electric Railway* (1892). In 1896, appeared his *Power Transmission for Electric Railroads*, which was almost immediately followed by his *Electric Power Transmission*. His text-book on *The Art of Illumination* first appeared in 1902. The two articles contributed to the eleventh edition of the *Encyclopædia Britannica*, "Motors,

Electric" and "Power Transmission, Electric," illustrate Bell's scientific style at its best; excellent analysis, clarity, and precision of language, together with emphasis, not on defunct apparatus, but upon general principles. Within the last year of his life Bell published *The Telescope* (1922), giving the history of the instrument and the principles which underlie its numerous and diverse modern forms. This volume is the work of an amateur in the high and literal sense of that word.

Bell's first love and his ruling passion was the subject of light. Naturally therefore he was an active member of the Illuminating Engineering Society (which came into existence in the same year with the tungsten lamp) and of the American Academy of Arts and Sciences, and was a frequent contributor to the proceedings of each. The former of these societies elected him to its presidency. A large number of patents—more than forty—bear witness to his originality. In any group he was a striking figure; a tall blond, with a rather high-pitched voice, socially inclined, seeing a humorous side to every question, penetrating in his judgments, tenacious in his beliefs, but not to the point of allowing prejudice to produce blindness. His fascinating mastery of English and his sense of fairness made him the best of company.

[J. P. Houston, *Hist. of the Class of 1884, Dartmouth;* Louis Bell, *John Bell of Londonderry and his Scottish Ancestry,* a privately printed pamphlet of twenty pages; A. E. Kennelly, *Proc. Am. Acad. Arts and Sciences,* 1925, LIX, 633–39; Edward S. King, *Popular Astronomy,* 1923, XXXI, 635–40; editorial in *Electrical World,* June 1923.] H. C.

BELL, LUTHER VOSE (Dec. 20, 1806–Feb. 11, 1862), physician, politician, was descended from Robert Le Bel, a Norman, who migrated to Scotland in the eleventh century. A descendant, Matthew Bell, born about 1650, moved to Londonderry, Ireland. His son, John, emigrated to Londonderry (now Derry), N. H., in 1720. The latter's son, John Bell, senator, and his grandson, Samuel [*q.v.*], chief justice, governor, and senator, were both New Hampshire products. Luther Vose, fifth child of Samuel's first wife, Mehitable (Dana) Bell, was born in Francestown, N. H. He went to school at local institutions, and entered Bowdoin College at twelve. Graduating in 1823 he immediately began the study of medicine in New York City under his elder brother, Dr. John Bell. Soon he moved to Hanover and in 1826 he received his M.D. from Dartmouth. Too young to practise, he spent a year in a "Commercial Emporium," where he doubtless picked up some knowledge of men and affairs. Starting practise in Chester, N. H., he led the strenuous life of a country doctor and became deeply interested in the needs of the insane. In 1835 and 1836 he was elected representative and persuaded the state legislature to establish an institution for their proper care. He was called in 1836 to be physician and superintendent of the McLean Hospital for the Insane at Charlestown, Mass. Here he took a lively interest in medical and administrative problems. His annual reports are models, and in them he discusses and illuminates various psychiatric subjects. He resigned on account of ill health after twenty years of admirable service.

Bell early showed literary aptitude. In 1835 he wrote a Boylston Prize Essay on New England diet in which he sagely remarks "the Yankee Citizen . . . encounters his dinner as he would any other necessary work that has to be accomplished." In 1848 he wrote *On a Form of Disease Resembling Some Advanced Stages of Mania and Fever.* Hereafter this type of insanity was recognized as Bell's Disease or Bell's Mania. After his retirement from hospital work he was often called upon as a medico-legal expert. As a witness he was concise and practical and carried great weight with judge and jury. During his active years he frequently appeared as a lyceum lecturer. His talks, usually on mechanical problems, "showed a bent of mind adapted to the conveyance of profitable instruction in a lively way." He was always an adherent of the Whig party. In 1850 he was an executive councillor to Gov. Briggs of Massachusetts. As a delegate to the Whig national convention of 1852 he advocated the candidacy of Daniel Webster. At the outbreak of the Civil War, in spite of poor health, he at once enlisted. He was appointed surgeon to the 11th Massachusetts Regiment but was soon promoted and became Hooker's brigade surgeon. In February 1862, at Budd's Ferry, Maryland, he died, probably from some complication of pulmonary tuberculosis. He was married to Frances Pinkerton, daughter of James Pinkerton, of Derry, N. H., in 1834.

[Isaac Ray, in *Am. Jour. of Insanity,* Oct. 1854; G. Alder Blumer, in *Albany Medic. Annals,* June 1908; Andrew McFarland, *Am. Jour. of Insanity,* Jan. 1878; Geo. E. Ellis, *Proc. Mass. Hist. Soc.,* ser. 1, vol. VII, p. 27; John Carroll Chase, *Hist. of Chester, N. H.* (1926).] G. B.

BELL, PETER HANSBOROUGH (Mar. 11, 1808–Mar. 8, 1898), soldier, governor of Texas, congressman, was born in Culpeper County, near Fredericksburg, Va., the son of James Madison Bell, of Scotch-Irish stock, and Elizabeth (Hansborough) Bell. Such education as he received was probably in the local schools.

When news of the Texas Revolution came early in 1836 he hastened to take part. He arrived just in time to join Sam Houston's little army before the decisive battle of San Jacinto in which he participated as a private in Karnes's cavalry company. He remained in the army where he soon attracted favorable notice. In May 1837 he was appointed by President Houston assistant adjutant-general; in 1839–40 he served as assistant adjutant and inspector general. In 1842 he went with Gen. Somervell as aide-de-camp on his fruitless expedition to the Rio Grande. In 1845 he was commissioned a captain of rangers and was in this service when the war with Mexico began. He then became lieutenant-colonel of rangers under the celebrated Col. Jack Hays and with a portion of the regiment kept guard over the Rio Grande frontier. After the close of the war he was placed in command of the ranging companies maintained by the state on the Indian frontier. He had acquired great popularity, and when he became a candidate for governor in 1849 against the incumbent, George T. Wood, he defeated him by means of the western vote. When he assumed office in December 1849 the country was in the midst of the great political crisis which had been precipitated by the Wilmot Proviso; but in Texas public interest centered upon the dispute which had arisen between the state and the United States authorities concerning jurisdiction over the Santa Fé region. The situation was really dangerous, for President Taylor was immovable and Gov. Bell stood stiffly upon the rights of Texas and threatened to call out volunteers to maintain her claims by force. Even after this controversy had been settled amicably, Bell had many difficult problems to deal with; the settlement of the heavy public debt; the defense of the frontier against the Indians; the improvement of transportation facilities; and the establishment of a public school system. Though none of these was settled during his administration, his conduct of his office met popular approval and he was reëlected in 1851. Just before the close of his second term he was chosen as congressman from the western district to succeed Volney E. Howard, an able man who had held the place for four years. In Congress Bell voted with the state rights and pro-slavery men. His only speech of consequence was on the Texas debt bill, Feb. 5, 1855; but he voted for the Kansas-Nebraska bill and he was reëlected over a strong Know-Nothing opponent, Judge John Hancock. In 1857 he married Mrs. Ella Eaton Dickens of North Carolina, removed to that state, and thereafter lived quietly on her plantation in Warren County. Despite his former political attitude, he seems to have been opposed to secession in 1861—probably on the ground of expediency—and he refused a commission as colonel proffered him by Jefferson Davis. His fortune swept away by the war, he lived thereafter in retirement, his heart in the past "with his adopted state, Texas." In his prime, he was a man of strong physique, soldierly bearing, and kindly manner. He lies buried in Littleton, N. C.

[The biographical sketch of Bell in the *Tex. State Hist. Ass. Quart.*, III, 49, has been much discredited by other evidence adduced, *Ibid.*, XIII, 325. There is no adequate account of his whole career in Texas, but some information may be had in the following: *Southwestern Hist. Quart.*, vols. XXIII, XXVIII; W. C. Binkley, "The Expansionist Movement in Tex.," *Univ. of Cal. Pubs. in Hist.*, vol. XIII, the best account of the Santa Fé controversy; D. G. Wooten, *A Comprehensive Hist. of Tex.* (1898), vol. II; and contemporary Texas newspapers, esp. the *Daily Express* (San Antonio), Mar. 12, 1898.]

C. W. R.

BELL, ROBERT (*c.* 1732–Sept. 23, 1784), publisher, bookseller, and book-auctioneer, was a native of Glasgow, Scotland, and served his apprenticeship there as a bookbinder. Later he went to work at this trade for Samuel Taylor at Berwick-upon-Tweed, and from there moved to Dublin where he set up a bookselling and bookbinding business for himself. This venture did not prove successful, and he came to America (*c.* 1766). His employer and other acquaintances in Berwick had come to Philadelphia, so it was natural for him to locate in that city. In the spring of 1768 his advertisements as "Bookseller and Auctioneer" begin to appear in the Philadelphia newspapers. He offers to buy "Libraries or parcels of books," or owners "may have them exhibited with a regular catalogue by auction . . . where the intrinsic merit and excellence of each book shall be rationally expatiated upon with truth and propriety" (*Pennsylvania Journal,* Apr. 7, 1768). One such library "consisting of Law, History and Entertainment" he announces he will begin to sell "by Auction," on June 13, "From four o'clock to seven each evening" (*Ibid.,* June 9, 1768). As an auctioneer this "stout, chunky man" appears to have been very successful, his drollery attracting buyers. "It was as good as a play," one writer says, "to attend his sales at auction. There were few authors of whom he could not tell some anecdote which would get the audience in a roar. He sometimes had a can of beer aside him and would drink comical healths." (William McCulloch, "Additions to Thomas's History of Printing," *American Antiquarian Society Proceedings,* n. s., XXXI, 232).

Not only in Philadelphia but in other large towns and cities along the Atlantic seaboard Bell plied his vocation, sending a supply of books ahead of him; he thus became "well known for diffusing of literature" (*Pennsylvania Gazette,* Oct. 6, 1784). He liked to call himself "Provedore to the Sentimentalists in America" (*Illumination for Legislators and for Sentimentalists,* 1784, title page). When the British were occupying Philadelphia in the Revolutionary War Bell kept a circulating library and was patronized extensively by the officers; his rule was a deposit of a guinea for each book, the money to be returned with a sum deducted for the loan when the book was returned. After the Revolution when the State of Pennsylvania was contemplating legislation that would provide for the office of book-auctioneer for the city of Philadelphia, Bell issued a pamphlet entitled *Memorial on the Free Sale of Books,* arguing that no one should be "restricted and fettered in a Free-State in the Propagation of Literature" (p. 6). He would object to being appointed to the "Office of Book Auctioneer" himself, he says (p. 6), and he aims to strengthen his cause by reprinting John Dickinson's *Sentiments on What is Freedom, and What is Slavery,* Raynal's *Sentiments on Liberty,* and Rousseau's *Sentiments on Government, Law, Arbitrary Power, Liberty, and Social Institutions.* Nevertheless the Pennsylvania Assembly passed (May 4, 1784) what Bell called "a tyrannical embargo" on his selling books "By Auction," which impelled him to issue *Bell's Address to Every Free-Man,* in the course of which the Commonwealth is portrayed saying to him (p. 5).

"Pray stop, Master Bell, with your selling of Books,
Your smart witty Sayings, and cunning arch Looks:
By Auction, I mean—'tis a shocking Offence
To sell Wit or Humor, or e'en common Sense,
Unsanction'd by Law, on any Pretence."

The expression "common Sense" which he brought into his versification had more than the ordinary meaning to his readers because it was Bell who, in 1776, had brought out the first edition of Paine's *Common Sense.* Previously (1770) Bell had published in three volumes the first American edition of Robertson's *The History of the Reign of Charles the Fifth, Emperor of Germany,* and this was followed by an American edition of Blackstone's *Commentaries.* Publishing appeared to increase rather than diminish Bell's zeal as a seller of books, and he was on the way to Charleston, S. C., for one of his auction sales when he was taken ill and died in Richmond, Va., where also he was interred. He married in Dublin and left his wife and two children (son and daughter) there when he came to America. The son joined his father later in Philadelphia but went back after his death. Another daughter (illegitimate) survived him in Philadelphia.

[There is a brief sketch in Isaiah Thomas, *Hist. of Printing in America* (1810), II, 68–69. Bell's individuality appears in his *Memorial on the Free Sale of Books* (1784), his *Address to Every Free-Man* (1784), and his many advertisements in the columns of the *Pa. Gazette* and the *Pa. Jour.*]

A. E. P.

BELL, SAMUEL (Feb. 8, 1770–Dec. 23, 1850), lawyer, governor of New Hampshire, senator, was the son of John and Mary Ann (Gilmore) Bell, and a grandson of John Bell, a Scotch-Irishman who settled in Londonderry, N. H., in 1720. He was born and brought up in Londonderry, working on his father's farm and attending the district school in the winter months. Later he studied at New Ipswich Academy, taught school, and graduated from Dartmouth in 1793. He was admitted to the bar in 1796 and began practise at Francestown, later removing to Amherst, and finally about 1812 to Chester where he maintained a residence henceforth. He was twice married: on Nov. 26, 1797, to Mehitable Dana of Amherst, who died in 1810, and on July 4, 1828, to Lucy Smith, also of Amherst. He was successful in his law practise from the outset and rapidly acquired a competence, although meeting severe losses in the failure of the Hillsborough Bank in 1809. His presidency of this ill-fated institution was afterward used against him as a Federalist campaign argument (*New Hampshire Gazette,* Feb. 3, Mar. 2, 1819). As a Jeffersonian Republican, he represented Francestown in the legislature 1804–06, being speaker in the last two years. He was president of the state Senate 1807–08 and member of the Executive Council in 1809 (*New Hampshire Register,* 1805–10). After several years' retirement from public affairs, due to ill health, he was appointed associate justice of the superior court in 1816, where he served for three years. In 1819 he was chosen governor. The Federalist party was now moribund, and his election was welcomed by its leading organ as a "harbinger of peaceful times" (*Portsmouth Oracle,* Mar. 13, 1819). He was reëlected in the three succeeding years with only scattering opposition. The most important enactment during his administration was the Toleration Act of 1819, which ended the power of the towns to tax for the support of clergymen. He advocated and secured the enactment in 1821 of an important statute conferring chancery powers on the superior court in matters affecting the trusteeship of charitable and other foundations. He was a pioneer in calling attention to the evils of intemperance and demanding a stricter licensing system. In the emphasis laid in his annual messages on the need of developing manufactures and diversifying the economic life of New Hampshire, it is easy to perceive the principles which later made him an ardent supporter of the tariff. He expressed disapproval of internal improvements by the national government, however, and in 1822 the legislature memorialized Congress against the practise. Beginning in 1823 he served two successive terms in the United States Senate. His career in that body was undistinguished, although he appears to have had the respect and confidence of his associates, including Webster. He spoke infrequently, but his speeches against the abolition of imprisonment for debt (*Register of Debates in Congress,* 20 Cong., 1 Sess., cols. 85–87), against a bill settling the claims of Revolutionary officers (*Ibid.,* cols. 436–40), against the preëmption and graduation of the prices of public lands (*Ibid.,* 21 Cong., 1 Sess., pp. 8, 416 ff.), and his stalwart opposition to President Jackson's bank policy (*Ibid.,* 23 Cong., 1 Sess., cols. 566–69, 1538–41), throw considerable light on his principles and show that he possessed some of the characteristics of the Ulster Scot. His longest congressional speeches were on tariff subjects, including one in support of the compromise measure of 1833 (*Ibid.,* 22 Cong., 2 Sess., cols. 742–45). By 1834 the tide of Jacksonian Democracy was running strongly in New Hampshire, and the legislature of that year passed resolutions which declared that he was misrepresenting the state and demanded his resignation (*Ibid.,* 23 Cong., 1 Sess., cols. 2064, 2067). At the expiration of his term the following March, he retired to his farm in Chester where he spent the remainder of his life.

[Chas. H. Bell, *Bench and Bar of N. H.* (1894); Wm. Cogswell, in the *N. H. Repository* (1846), I, 264; Benj. Chase, *Hist. of Old Chester* (1869).]

W. A. R.

BELLAMY, EDWARD (Mar. 26, 1850–May 22, 1898), author, was born at Chicopee Falls, Mass., the third son of Rufus King Bellamy and Maria Louisa (Putnam) Bellamy. His father had served as Baptist minister at Chicopee Falls uninterruptedly for thirty-five years. A preference for a settled habitat and home sights also appeared in Edward Bellamy, who spent practically all his life in Massachusetts—most of it in Chicopee Falls, his residence there being broken only by short periods in Boston, New York, and Colorado—and who chose American villages as the setting for most of his earlier fiction. He was educated almost wholly in the local schools, though he was for a short time at Union College with an older brother, pursuing a special course of study in literature, largely self-selected. At eighteen he went abroad for a year, spending most of the time in Germany. The reticence that characterized him as a man was already evident in college, and during his European travels appears for the first time that interest in the relief of social ills which was to mark the rest of his life. "It was in the great cities of Europe and among the hovels of the peasantry," he wrote later, "that my eyes were first fully opened to the extent and consequences of 'Man's inhumanity to man.'" On his return he studied law and was admitted to the bar, later joining the editorial staff of the *Springfield Union,* and working for a few months on the New York *Evening Post.* In 1880, with his brother Charles, he founded the Springfield *Daily News;* but his heart was never in journalism and he took little part in the editorial direction of the paper. In 1879 he began publication in a country paper of his unfinished historical novel, *The Duke of Stockbridge,* which was eventually completed by another hand and appeared as a book only after Bellamy's death. His choice of subject, Shays's Rebellion, plainly foreshadowed the social interests which produced *Looking Backward.* He had already begun to contribute to the magazines the short stories which were collected and published after his death as *The Blind Man's World and Other Stories* (1898). When his *Dr. Heidenhoff's Process* appeared, in 1880, he was acclaimed as the lineal descendant of Hawthorne, and Howells described the book as "one of the finest feats in the region of romance." This work, like the "romance of immortality," *Mrs. Ludington's Sister* (1884) which followed, made use of Bellamy's study of psychic phenomena, a subject in which he always had a lively, though in no sense morbid, interest.

A purely literary career, above all others that which appealed to Bellamy most strongly, now opened before him. In 1882 he had been married to Emma Sanderson, of Chicopee Falls, and a few years after his marriage he began to concern himself seriously with social questions. "According to my best recollection," he writes, "it was in the fall or winter of 1886 that I sat down to my desk with the definite purpose of trying to reason out a method of economic organization by which the republic might guarantee the livelihood and material welfare of its citizens on a basis of equality corresponding to and supplanting their political equality." Two years later, *Looking Backward* was published.

In spite of the undeniable charm of his earlier stories, Bellamy's permanent reputation rests on this utopian romance, and perhaps in less degree upon its sequel, *Equality*. When he wrote the book which was speedily to bring him national—and even international—fame, the fiction he had already published had won scant attention, and he deliberately made up his mind to undertake a new genre. The mild form of utopian socialism expounded in *Looking Backward* was by no means new to the American public. Numerous editorial writers had paved the way, there was a small socialist literature, and there had already been at least one socialistic novel, now forgotten. The sensation created by *Looking Backward* was due to its intrinsic qualities, to a charming style, and to an adroit fashion of presenting its socialist—or "nationalist," since it advocated nationalization —doctrine as after all no more than "an enlightened self-interest or wholesale common sense." The book achieved a popularity which endured for several years, sold a million copies, and has been fairly steadily in print ever since. Bellamy Clubs were organized to discuss the social implications of the romance, which became a kind of Bible to many people. As William Dean Howells later wrote (Preface to *A Hazard of New Fortunes*), "the solution of the riddle of the painful earth through the dreams of Henry George, through the dreams of Edward Bellamy, through the dreams of all the generous visionaries of the past, seemed not impossibly far off." The success of *Looking Backward* wrought a singular change in its author. He, whose most marked characteristic had been his modesty and a reticence which had been his from boyhood, now took a vigorous and enthusiastic share in the propaganda for nationalism, being firmly convinced that the conversion of a capitalistic society to his own utopianism was possible, by the method of peaceful persuasion, in the immediate future. In 1891 he founded in Boston the *New Nation,* a weekly supported almost wholly by the owner-editor's income from his sucessful book, then in its three hundred and seventy-first thousand. The *New Nation* continued publication for a few years only, after which Bellamy, whose health had suffered from his exertions, went into retreat, publishing little except a few magazine articles, but working steadily upon his second utopian romance, *Equality,* which was published in 1897. During the years in which he worked to complete this book his health was steadily failing, but he absolutely refused to leave his home in Chicopee Falls until it was finished. His journey to Colorado, in a vain effort to resist tuberculosis, was too long delayed, and when it was obvious that his life could not be saved, he was brought back to Chicopee Falls, where he died.

[No biography of Edward Bellamy has ever been published. His cousin, Francis Bellamy, contributed a short sketch as an introduction to the posthumous edition of *The Duke of Stockbridge* (1900). Henry Austin wrote an obituary article "Edward Bellamy," for the *National Magazine,* Oct. 1898, which contains some personal reminiscences and a portrait. Another portrait and further biographical facts are included in the 1910 edition of *Equality.* William Dean Howells wrote a prefatory sketch for *The Blind Man's World* (1898)and Sylvester Baxter an introduction for the memorial edition of *Looking Backward* (1917). The most vivid account is Caroline Ticknor's in her *Glimpses of Authors* (1922). There is a short critical discussion of Bellamy's ideas in Rudolf Blueher's *Modern Utopien* (1920). The controversial literature is, of course, voluminous.]

J. B.

BELLAMY, ELIZABETH WHITFIELD CROOM (Apr. 17, 1837–Apr. 13, 1900), author, was born near Quincy, Fla., the daughter of William Whitfield and Julia Stephens Croom. Her education in Philadelphia and New York gave her a life-long interest in music and literature. She was married in 1858 to her cousin, Charles E. Bellamy, who was a native of North Carolina. They had two children, neither of whom survived infancy. Dr. Bellamy died in 1863 while acting as a surgeon in the Confederate Army. Mrs. Bellamy, left destitute, began teaching in Mobile, Ala., and continued there, so occupied all her life. In 1870, calling herself "Kamba Thorpe," but permitting herself before long to be referred to in advertisements as "a Southern lady," she published a novel, *Four Oaks.* This was followed in 1876 by *The Little Joanna.* Both of these are romantic stories of the South, vaguely localized. The realistic impulse so far mastered her in 1888 that her *Old Man Gilbert,* published in that year, disclosed not only the real name of its author but the definite scene and time of its action, Tallahassee, Fla., 1857. The central character, Gilbert, is a typically humorous negro, domineering but indulgent and unexpectedly capable. *Penny Lancaster* (1889), the story of a Georgia farm, turns still faithfully upon affairs of the heart, but is freighted with different implication —it tells, in fact, how a woman without sacrificing any of her charm and virtue—and the consequence of those qualities, a satisfactory husband—may none the less at need be a thorough-going person of affairs, turning events to her own will. The writing of these four novels and stories which appeared in the better magazines of the country, together with her teaching, did not suffice to fill Mrs. Bellamy's time during the many years which she spent at the home of her brother. She was an enthusiastic student of Shakespeare, about whom she regularly gave courses of private lectures. The newspapers at the time of her death referred to her as a "typical Southern woman," who would leave a very gracious memory.

[T. McA. Owen, *Hist. of Ala. and Dict. of Ala. Biog.* (1921); *Mobile Reg.*, Apr. 14, 15, 1900; *Who's Who in America*, 1899–1900.] J. D. W.

BELLAMY, JOSEPH (Feb. 20, 1719–Mar. 6, 1790), theologian, was born in Cheshire, then part of Wallingford, Conn., the fifth child and fourth son, of Matthew and Sarah (Wood) Bellamy. They were of English stock, though the name would indicate a French ancestor further back. A remarkably bright farmer's boy, he went to Yale, a few miles away, where he graduated in 1735 when he was but sixteen. After two years' study of theology, partly with Jonathan Edwards, whose ardent disciple he became, he was licensed to preach, though even yet only a few months over eighteen. After preaching in various churches he went in November 1738 to supply the pulpit in the newly organized parish of Bethlehem, Conn., then part of the town of Woodbury on the northwestern outskirts of the colony. A church was organized, of which he was pastor until his death over fifty years later. He married on Apr. 27, 1744, Frances Sherman of New Haven, who died in 1785; in 1786 he married, as his second wife, a lady already twice widowed, whose maiden name was Abiah Burbank. He was full of enthusiasm for the Great Awakening, and for the New Light theology, inaugurated by Jonathan Edwards, which had been the occasion of the revival, since it enabled the preacher to call men to repentance, as the older Calvinism had not. In this vein he preached with fervor, cogency, and success, first to his own parish, and from 1742 on, from place to place in and around Connecticut for a part of the year, during several years. He was a man of commanding presence with a fine voice and a keen mind and was regarded as even more powerful as a preacher than he was later as a writer. He was, however, domineering and censorious of any that stood in his way, with a biting wit, although he mellowed somewhat as he grew older.

Settling down at the close of the revival he began writing in defense of this new theology, his first notable work being *True Religion Delineated* (1750). Its important points were first, his definition of religion, in accordance with Edwards's theory of virtue, as love to God; second, his clarifying of the distinction between natural and moral inability which was the foundation of the New Light theology; third, a more humane theory of the atonement, developed from Grotius, which made it universal instead of being limited to the elect, and based it on the moral government of God rather than on the satisfaction of his offended dignity as a sovereign. This work brought him into prominence. Young men came to him to study for the ministry, and a sort of theological seminary grew up in this tiny backwoods settlement. In 1758 appeared his work on *The Wisdom of God in the Permission of Sin.* God, he argued, did not ordain, but only permitted sin, and that because he foresaw it to be the means to the greatest good. This work also attracted attention and aroused controversy. His last important theological work was a series of pamphlets from 1762 to 1770 in opposition to that curious anomaly, the Halfway Covenant, which the New Light theology had made superfluous. He was a striking example of bold, independent thinking in early New England. His published writings consist of the two mentioned (the treatise on Sin being part of a volume entitled *Sermons . . . on The Divinity of Christ. The Millenium. The Wisdom of God in the Permission of Sin,* 1758), together with sermons and controversial pamphlets.

[A complete list of Bellamy's publications with a sketch of his life and a list of authorities may be found in F. B. Dexter, *Biog. Sketches Grads. Yale Coll., 1701–1745* (1885), pp. 523 ff. See also Frank Hugh Foster, *A Genetic Hist. of the New Eng. Theology* (1907).]

T. D. B.

BELLEW, FRANK HENRY TEMPLE (Apr. 18, 1828–June 29, 1888), caricaturist, illustrator, was born in Cawnpore, Hindustan, the son, it is said, of an English officer. He spent some years in France and England, and in 1850 came to the United States, where he was active in New York City for over thirty-five years. He brought into our comic journalism a bit of the flavor of *Punch,* to which he contributed some small drawings in 1860, when he revisited England. In various attempts to found an American comic paper there appeared drawings signed by his familiar triangle which was sometimes blank, sometimes enclosed the name Bellew or the initials F. B. Such publications were the *Lantern,* his full-page political cartoons in which were quite in the *Punch* manner; *Yankee Notions; New York Picayune; Nick-Nax; Vanity Fair* (New York); *Punchinello; Wild Oats; Texas Siftings.* He has been credited with having had a hand in the founding of some of these journals. Last-page "comics" in *Harper's Weekly* and *Scribner's Monthly* also bore his signature, and for the *Fifth Avenue Journal* (1872) he drew a series of *portraits-chargés,* as the French call them—"slightly tinged with the tincture of caricature," that *Journal* had it—somewhat like those in the London *Vanity Fair,* or the "Puckographs" in *Puck* (New York). He even wrote and illustrated a volume on *The Art of Amusing* (1866), containing suggestions for parlor amusements of a somewhat elementary order. "His forte," we are told, "was writing and sketching stories for children." As an illustrator he appeared in *Harper's Magazine,* T. W. Strong's *Illustrated American News* (1851), the first noteworthy publication of its kind here—and in books such as T. B. Gunn's *Physiology of the New York Boarding-House* (1857), Stephen C. Massett's *Two Logs, by Jeemes Piper* (1864), and John T. Irving's *The Attorney* (1853). The last was a not highly successful attempt to illustrate by etching, in the manner of the plates by Phiz and others in the Dickens-Ainsworth period in England. Bellew, it was said, had an inexhaustible fund of ideas. His son Frank P. W. (1862–94), better known as "Chip," likewise had a "limitless invention," to which John Ames Mitchell paid tribute. The son drew many droll designs for *Life* and other publications, a number being republished in volumes such as *Chip's Dogs* (1895). The work of both father and son provided amusement without slapstick vulgarity.

[Material on Bellew is somewhat contradictory in statement. Perhaps the best biog. sketch is that in *Appleton's Ann. Cyc.* for 1888. *Wild Oats* published a humorous account, accompanied by a clever caricature portr. of Bellew by Livingston Hopkins. See also obituaries in *N.Y. Times* and *N.Y. Tribune* for June 30, 1888, and F. Weitenkampf's *Am. Graphic Art* (1924). Tom Masson wrote of the son in *Munsey's Mag.,* XXXIII, 601–7.]

F.W.

BELLINGHAM, RICHARD (*c.* 1592–Dec. 7, 1672), colonial governor of Massachusetts, son of Frances (Amcotts) Bellingham and William Bellingham of Manton and Brombye ("Lincolnshire Pedigrees," *Publications of the Harleian Society,* L, 118), was born at Boston, Lincolnshire, England, probably in 1592. Trained as a lawyer, he was made a freeman in 1625 (*New England Historical and Genealogical Register,* XXVIII, 14) and served as recorder of the borough from 1625 to 1633 (Pishey Thompson, *History and Antiquities of Boston,* 1856, p. 428). He was also a member of Parliament for Boston in 1628 (*Accounts and Papers, Members of Parliament, Part I, Parliaments of England, 1213–1702, Commons Return No. 69, 1878,* p. 476), and in the following year became one of the patentees of the Massachusetts Bay Charter. Together with his first wife (Elizabeth, daughter of Samuel Backhouse) and his son, Samuel, who was to be a graduate of Harvard's first class (1642), he came to New England in 1634 and settled at Boston, where he was elected deputy governor in 1635. The General Court seems to have appreciated his legal knowledge, for on more than one occasion he was ordered to examine and criticize the laws of the colony. He served as assistant, 1636–40, 1642–53; as treasurer, 1637–40; as deputy governor, 1635, 1640, 1653, 1655–65; as governor, 1641, 1654, 1665 until his death in 1672 (W. H. Whitmore, *Massachusetts Civil List* (1870). Contemporary writers agree on his honesty and marked legal ability, but consider him of slow and difficult speech. Bellingham's espousal of the popular cause, which brought him into conflict with Gov. Winthrop, probably dates from the "Stoughton affair" in 1635 (*Massachusetts Historical Society Proceedings,* LVIII, 450). By the time of the trial of Nicholas Trerice in 1639 there had developed an open breach, and in the election of 1641 Bellingham was chosen governor by a majority of six votes over Winthrop. His administration was marked by disputes with the other magistrates, and it is significant that the annual allowance of £100 to the governor was withdrawn by the Court. In the same year he further irritated the magistrates and clergy by his unique marriage to Penelope Pelham, in which he not only violated the law by neglecting the previous publication of his intentions, but performed the ceremony himself. As governor, he refused to leave the bench to stand trial, and the perplexed magistrates dropped the case. During the confusion following the Restoration, Bellingham rendered valuable service to the colony. He had succeeded Endicott as governor upon the latter's death in 1665, and was in office during the visit of the Royal Commission to Boston in that year. With others he was appointed to receive the Charter for safe keeping, and under his leadership the General Court denied the authority of the Commission, on the grounds that the Charter did not require the recognition of that body. As a result, Bellingham with several others was summoned to England in 1666 to explain his action, but the tactful present of a shipload of masts to the Royal Navy enabled him to ignore the order. He died on Dec. 7, 1672, and his peculiar will, which provided for the eventual entrusting of his large estate to the care of the clergy, produced litigation lasting over 100 years (*Collections of the Massachusetts Historical Society,* ser. 5, vol. VI, p. 197; *New England Historical and Genealogical Register,* XIV, 237).

[For Bellingham's political life see the *Records of the Governor and Company of Mass. Bay* (1853). Winthrop's *Hist. of New Eng.* (esp. Savage's edition of

1853) shows Bellingham in an unfavorable light. A favorable impression of him is gained from Wm. Hubbard's *Gen. Hist. of New Eng.* (pub. in 1815 as *Mass. Hist. Soc. Colls.*, ser. 2, vols. V, VI, and separately in 1848), while Edward Johnson in his *Wonder-Working Providence* (1654) is decidedly eulogistic. There is a short biog. by E. H. Goss in the *Mag. of Am. Hist.*, XIII, 262.]

H. P. S.

BELLOMONT, Earl of. [See COOTE, RICHARD, 1636–1701.]

BELLOWS, ALBERT FITCH (Nov. 29, 1829–Nov. 24, 1883), landscape painter, etcher, born in Milford, Mass., was the only son of Dr. Albert J. and Pamela (Fitch) Bellows, and was descended from John Bellows who emigrated to Massachusetts on the *Hopewell* in 1635. At an early age he was placed in a boot and shoe store, but at the age of sixteen he moved to Boston, with the consent of his parents, and entered the architectural office of A. B. Young. In 1849 he went into partnership with an architect named J. B. Toule, but abandoned architecture for painting at the end of a year. On Aug. 5, 1851, he married Candace J. Brown of Fall River. He was the principal of the New England School of Design in Boston, 1850–56. Upon his resignation from this position, he visited Paris during the Exposition and then lived in Antwerp where, after studying at the Royal Academy, he was elected an honorary member of the Royal Society of Painters of Belgium in 1858. Upon his return he lived in New York City and was elected a member of the National Academy in 1861. In 1865 he began painting in water-colors. In 1867 he returned to Europe, painting in England, France, and Belgium, and being elected an honorary member of the Royal Belgian Society of Painters in Water Colors in 1868. Moving to Boston shortly after, he remained in that city until the great fire of 1872, in which his studio and with it much of his work was destroyed. He then settled in New York City. He was one of the early members of the American Society of Painters in Water Color. This association published his book entitled *Water Color Painting; Some Facts and Authorities in Relation to Its Durability* (1868). The subjects of his paintings in this country were rural scenes, painted with homely fidelity, in the vicinity of New York, Boston, and Windsor, Conn. His technique both in oils and water-colors was of the early painstaking type. Some of his later oil paintings were carried out with the palette knife instead of a brush. Besides displaying at the National Academy, he showed his work in 1876 at the Philadelphia Centennial, and in 1878 at the Paris Exposition. "The First Pair of Boots," "A New England Village," "The Notch at Lancaster" are some of the titles of his paintings. Toward the end of his career he devoted much time to etching, and was one of the first in this country to attempt large etched plates. Of some fifteen etchings the most important were "The Inlet," "The River-side Inn," and "The Mill-stream." He was a member of the New York Etching Club, the Philadelphia Society of Etchers, and the Society of Painter-Etchers of London.

[Thos. Bellows Peck, *The Bellows Geneal.* (1898); H. T. Tuckerman, *Book of the Artists* (1867); H. W. French, *Art and Artists in Conn.* (1879); G. W. Sheldon, *Am. Painters* (1879); W. Montgomery, *Am. Art* (1889).]

T. B.

BELLOWS, GEORGE WESLEY (Aug. 12, 1882–Jan. 8, 1925), painter, lithographer, illustrator, was the son of George and Anna (Smith) Bellows, and traced his descent to Benjamin Bellows who founded the town of Walpole, Vt., during the eighteenth century. His grandfather was a seafaring man, a whaler who lived at the Montauk end of Long Island. His father was a builder and something of an architect in Columbus, Ohio. Bellows once wrote of the "two Sunday freedoms" of his boyhood, the freedom to read and the freedom to draw, and he went on to describe the Sundays when he created ambitious compositions with his pencil while his mother read to him. At school he was received with "a certain deference" because of his talent and was called "the artist." After graduation from the Ohio State University in 1903 he went to New York in 1904 and began the study of oil painting under Robert Henri. He also studied with Kenneth Hayes Miller and H. G. Maratta. Later he became fascinated with the idea of dynamic symmetry. "Ever since I met Mr. Hambidge," he said of the man who developed the theory, "and studied with him, I have painted few pictures without at the same time working on his theory." Henri helped him to develop his artistic personality. From Maratta he learned the importance of setting his palette. From Hambidge he took what he needed to help him in his composition. For the rest, he studied the paintings and prints of Goya and Daumier; and constantly experimented on his own account. But the study of the manifestations of life itself held more interest for him than the study of art. He liked to watch crowds of every-day people, he liked to draw the children in the streets, he liked to attend the prize fights at Tom Sharkey's who was once a boxer and staged encounters after he was too old to "stay in the ring." This life Bellows presently began to depict. One of the first of his paintings to win recognition was called "Forty-Two Kids" (1907), an animated canvas representing boys bathing along the New York river front. "Rain on the River" (1908), "Sharkey's" (1909), "Warships on the Hudson" (1909), and "Polo Game at Lakewood, New Jersey" (1910) are the titles of paintings that followed this first success. In 1908, five years after he began his studies, he exhibited a landscape that won a prize at the National Academy of Design. The next year he was elected an associate member of the National Academy. He was the youngest man ever to receive such recognition, being twenty-seven at the time. He now began to be taken more seriously by the older men. The late John W. Alexander predicted that he would become the foremost artist of the younger generation. In 1910 he became one of the teachers at the Art Students League, teaching there again in 1918 and 1919. He also taught at the Art Institute in Chicago during 1919. Although he never left the United States, he frequently exhibited his work abroad, in Buenos Aires, Munich, Venice, Berlin, Paris, and London. In 1910 he married Emma Louise Story of Upper Montclair, N. J., and made his home at 146 East Nineteenth St., New York City. Here he remained the rest of his life except for summers spent at Monhegan and Ogunquit, Me.; Newport, R. I.; Camden, Me.; Carmel, Cal.; Santa Fé, N. Mex.; and Woodstock, N. Y. Of his studio in New York City he made a splendid painting during the winter of 1919. The picture represents the artist working at a portrait of his wife while his two small daughters, Anne and Jean, play about on the floor; his mother-in-law and the maid stand by the telephone; and a printer bends over a lithographic press on the floor above. He painted a great variety of themes. The Brooklyn water front is the subject of "Men of the Docks" (1912); a dancer on horseback viewed by a Goya-like crowd is the subject of "The Circus" (1912); while "The Cliff Dwellers" (1913) is a picture of several layers of humanity on an East Side street in New York. As time went on, he felt more and more drawn from the city and by 1915 he was painting during the summer at Ogunquit, Me. But humanity he always painted, figures almost invariably playing an important part in his landscapes even along the Maine coast. "The Sand Team" (1917) was painted in California; "Fishermen's Huts" (1918) was painted at Newport. He then painted two large canvases with the horrors of war as the subject. One called "Edith Cavell" (1918), possibly his greatest work, received the sharp criticism of Joseph Pennell. The other, called "The Return of the Useless" (1918), represents a train load of French peasants returned by Germany as unfit for work.

In 1916 he made his first experiments in lithography in which he became more and more absorbed. Sometimes he made lithographic replicas of his paintings; but most of his lithographs are original scenes—in the men's gymnasium, at a prayer meeting, a shipwreck, or a prize fight—or studies of the nude figure; in short, as was the case in his paintings, he drew every-day scenes and plain houses by preference. "I am sick," he once said, "of American buildings like Greek temples and of rich men building Italian homes." In 1921 he induced his friend, Bolton Brown, to undertake the printing of his lithographs, an association lasting four years. He also undertook book illustrations, among them a series of drawings for "The Wind Bloweth" by Donn Byrne, which appeared in the *Century Magazine* from November 1921 to October 1922. Another series, appearing in *Hearst's International Magazine* from November 1922 to June 1923, illustrated a novel by H. G. Wells entitled "Men Like Gods." Several of these illustrations he redrew on the lithographic stone. A huge painting of "The Crucifixion" (1923), which caused a great stir when it was shown at first, was the subject of a drawing, then a lithograph. It was painted at Woodstock, N. Y. The next year he painted a vigorous picture of Jack Dempsey being knocked through the ropes in his fight with the Argentine boxer, Firpo. "Ringside Seats," "The Pic-nic," "River Front," and finally "Two Women," the latter a new treatment of Titian's "Sacred and Profane Love," were all painted the last year of his life. Prizes of one sort or another were awarded to his paintings at the National Academy of Design (1908, 1913, 1915, 1917); the Pennsylvania Academy (1913, 1917, 1921); the Carnegie Institute, Pittsburgh (1913, 1914, 1922); the National Arts Club (1921); the Corcoran Gallery of Art (1923); the International Exposition, Buenos Aires (1918); the Panama Pacific Exposition (1915); the Chicago Art Institute (1915, 1921, 1923); Newport Art Association (1918). Every important American museum owns examples of his work. He died of appendicitis at the Post Graduate Hospital, New York City, survived by his wife and two daughters, Anne and Jean. "In appearance," writes Frank Crowninshield, "he was tall, shambling and a little ungainly. By nature he was of a firm and elevated character; determined, enthusiastic and honest to the point of bluntness. He liked inordinately, baseball, music and reading."

Technically the earliest work of George Bellows shows a restricted color scheme in which blacks, whites, grays, with reds and yellows, predominate, as witness his portrait "The Cross-Eyed Boy" (1906), where the influence of Goya and Hals are obvious. Seven years later he painted his splendid full-length portrait of Dr. Thompson, which ranks with the full-length portraits of Whistler, Velasquez and Henri. As time went on, the Goya influence became fused with that of Daumier; and, finally, with Greco and Renoir; and there was likewise a noticeable improvement in color. His picture of "The Pic-nic" (1924) is an exquisite harmony of form, color, and composition. But the foregoing is a tabulation of influences merely. Everything that Bellows painted was stamped with his own personality. His work ranks with the most significant art of his epoch.

[*Metropolitan Museum of Art, Memorial Exhibition of the Work of Geo. Bellows* (1925); *N.Y. Times,* Jan. 9, 1925; *Am. Mag. of Art,* Dec. 1925; *Arts and Decoration,* Aug. 1914; *Century Mag.,* Oct. 1923; *N.Y. Times Mag.,* Jan. 25, 1925; *Am. Architect,* Dec. 29, 1920; *Internatl. Studio,* May 1925; *Scribner's Mag.,* May 1928; *Geo. W. Bellows: His Lithographs* (1927), comp. by Emma S. Bellows, with a biog. sketch by Thos. Beer.]

T. B.

BELLOWS, HENRY WHITNEY (June 11, 1814–Jan. 30, 1882), Unitarian clergyman, was born in Boston, the son of John and Betsey (Eames) Bellows. The family home was at Walpole, N. H. He attended the Round Hill School at Northampton, where George Bancroft the historian was one of the principals, entered Harvard College at fourteen, and graduated in 1832. During his college career his father suffered financial reverses, and upon graduation Bellows at once began to teach, first at Cooperstown, N. Y., later as a private tutor in a wealthy family in Louisiana. He graduated from the Harvard Divinity School in 1837. His first preaching was at Mobile, Ala., but in 1839 he was invited to take charge of the First Unitarian Church in New York City. This was a severe task for a man of twenty-four, but Bellows was equal to it and soon won a conspicuous place in the civic, social, and religious life of New York. He was one of the founders of the Century, Union League, and Harvard Clubs of New York, and was often found at these and other clubs, always the center of a group that admired his brilliant conversation. His church grew rapidly in numbers and influence and soon had to find new quarters, building the Church of All Souls on Fourth Avenue. In his preaching he was always springing some surprise on the community, sometimes a bold theological heresy, sometimes the advocacy of an unpopular reform, sometimes the championship of a misunderstood class. He was often called upon to deliver occasional addresses. In 1847 he began publication of the *Christian Inquirer,* which he continued to edit until it was merged with the *Christian Register* of Boston. He also gave freely of his time, thought, and devotion to establishing Antioch College at Yellow Springs, Ohio. The Civil War afforded him opportunity for the exercise of his varied gifts. He was the originator, founder, and president of the United States Sanitary Commission, the great national organization which cared for the sick and wounded. By his personal appeal he raised in the North millions of dollars for this work and directed it with great skill and unflagging zeal. The end of the war found him with a fund of unspent energy at his disposal. He applied his powers first to the reorganization of his own religious fellowship, founding the National Conference of Unitarian Churches in 1865, the Ministers' Institute in 1866, and then a series of state and local conferences. If the church to which he belonged had proved more plastic to his shaping hand, it might well have grown into one of the large Christian bodies. He was editor of the *Christian Examiner,* 1866–77. Then he threw himself into the work of Civil Service Reform, attacking the spoils system in every shape and on every hand and organizing state and national associations. He naturally found himself frequently in conflict not only with a misled public opinion, but also with vigorous personalities, and in these encounters proved himself a stalwart fighter.

Bellows was not technically a scholar but he was a man of wide reading, quick insight, and great power of interpretation. He published numerous books, sermons, and articles, of which the best known are: *The Treatment of Social Diseases* (1857), *Restatements of Christian Doctrine* (1860), *The Old World in Its New Face* (1868–69), and *Twenty-four Sermons* (1886). Conservative in feeling, he was often radical in thought. He did his most effective work as an inspirer of men in common purposes and aims. With exceptional talents for public action and for social and religious organization, he had, too, a genius for friendship and domesticity. His first wife, whom he married Aug. 13, 1839, was Eliza Nevins Townsend of New York. She died Aug. 27, 1869, and on June 30, 1874, he married Anna Huidekoper Peabody of Boston. He died at his home in New York, Jan. 30, 1882.

[J. W. Chadwick, *Henry W. Bellows: His Life and Character* (1882); *Bellows Geneal.* (1898), ed. by J. B. Peck; articles in *Unitarian Rev.,* Mar. 1882, and in *Christian Reg.,* Feb. 2, 9, 16, 23, 1882; C. J. Stillé, *Hist. of the U. S. Sanitary Com.* (1866); *U. S. Sanitary Com. Bull.* (3 vols., 1866); W. E. Barton, *Life of Clara Barton* (1921).]

S. A. E.

BELMONT, AUGUST (Dec. 8, 1816–Nov. 24, 1890), banker, diplomat, patron of art, sportsman, of Jewish descent, the son of Simon and Frederika (Elsaas) Belmont, was born in the small town of Alzei, in the Rhenish Palatinate. His father, a wealthy landed proprietor, was able to permit his son to choose his own career. In this choice there was no hesitancy, and at the age of fourteen the youth entered, without pay, the office of the Rothschilds, at Frankfurt-am-Main, to learn the business. His first duty was to sweep the offices, but his industry and his remarkable talent for finance won quick promotion, and after three years' service at Frankfurt he was sent to the branch office at Naples. Here he gave continued proof of his unusual capacity, and, among other accomplishments, carried on successful negotiations with the Papal Court. In Naples much of his leisure was spent in the galleries, where he laid the foundation for an appreciation of art that was to make him one of the foremost collectors of his generation. His duties in Naples completed, he was sent by his employers to Havana, Cuba. While he was at sea the financial panic of 1837 began in the United States. Belmont was quick to sense the possibilities in the financial chaos then prevailing. Having executed his commissions in Havana, he notified the Rothschilds that he was entering business on his own account and sailed for New York on the first available ship. He rented a small office on Wall St., and there established, practically without capital, the foundations of the great banking house of August Belmont & Company. His only tangible asset—that, indeed, a great one—was the agency in the United States for the Rothschilds. Belmont's success was immediate and undisturbed; within a few years he was one of the leading bankers of the country. In August 1841 he fought a duel at Elkton, Ind., with William Hayward of South Carolina and as a result carried a wound with him throughout life. Securely established in business, he became, as speedily as possible, a citizen. Joining the Democratic party, he cast his first vote, in 1844, for Dallas and Polk. In the same year he was appointed consul-general for Austria in the United States. This post he held until 1850, when he resigned as a protest against the severe treatment of Hungary, and especially of the patriot Louis Kossuth, by the Austrian Government. This official position, combined with the charm of his personality, and his great wealth, which he spent freely, made him a conspicuous figure in the social life of New York. In 1849 he added to his prestige by marrying Caroline Slidell Perry, daughter of Commodore Matthew Calbraith Perry, who "opened" Japan to the Western nations. Belmont's political services and influence were rewarded in 1853 by his appointment by President Pierce as minister to the Netherlands. This post he held with conspicuous success until the expiration of Pierce's term in 1857. He was now recognized as one of the most influential of the younger leaders of the Democratic party. He was opposed to slavery as an institution, but supported the policies of Stephen A. Douglas rather than those of the abolitionists. Following the split in the Democratic party at Charleston in 1860, he took an active part in the Baltimore convention of the same year. Although he strongly opposed the nomination and election of Lincoln, there was no faltering in his devotion to the Union. "I prefer," he said in a letter to John Forsyth of Mobile, Ala., in 1860, "to leave to my children, instead of the gilded prospects of New York merchant princes, the more enviable title of American citizen, and as long as God spares my life I shall not falter in my efforts to procure them that heritage" (*Letters, Speeches and Addresses,* 1890, p. 39). With the outbreak of war, he supported the Government with the greatest vigor. He aided in raising and equipping the first German regiment sent from New York City. In other ways he aided the Union cause, but his most valuable service, perhaps, was a constant correspondence with influential friends in Europe, the Rothschilds and others, in which he set forth forcibly the Northern side in the great conflict. He visited London in 1861 and Paris in 1863. In England he urged upon Palmerston and others the ethical and political claims of the North, and from Paris wrote to Seward that the Emperor Napoleon was the real center of French sympathy for the South. His influence upon public opinion in financial and political circles, both in England and throughout continental Europe, was of value to Lincoln and his advisers. Belmont continued to be a power in his party until 1872, when, the Democrats having accepted Horace Greeley as their nominee, he retired from active political life. His interest in party politics never ceased and he was a constant attendant at state and national conventions as a delegate, and often as presiding officer. Belmont was an eager and intelligent collector of paintings, porcelains, and other objects of art. His collections were sold by auction after his death. He was also a lover of horses and of horse racing, and was, for many years, president of the American Jockey Club.

[*N.Y. Sun,* Nov. 25, 1890; R. J. H. Gottheil, *The Belmont-Belmonte Family* (1917); A. Belmont, *A Few Letters and Speeches of the Late Civil War* (1870).]

A. L. C.

BELO, ALFRED HORATIO (May 27, 1839–Apr. 19, 1901), Confederate soldier, Texas journalist, was born at Salem, N. C., the son of Edward and Amanda (Fries) Belo. He opposed secession by separate state action, but when North Carolina withdrew from the Union he volunteered in the Confederate Army, raised the 1st Company Forsythe Riflemen and became its captain. His company was made part of the 55th Carolina Regiment under Col. J. Connally and Belo became quartermaster. He was promoted to major and then was made colonel when Col. Connally became brigadier-general. He was wounded twice at Gettysburg and again when Grant attacked Cold Harbor, but remained with the colors until Lee surrendered. After the war he rode horseback from North Carolina to Texas, where he joined the *Galveston News*, in September 1865, as bookkeeper. In March 1866 he became one of the owners in the firm of W. Richardson & Company. He was married to Nettie Ennis of Galveston on June 30, 1868. In 1875 he bought out Richardson's interest in the publishing firm and changed its name to A. H. Belo & Company, incorporating under that name in 1881. Until his death he was president of the corporation. Stern and austere, a quiet, conscientious worker, Belo used his military training in forming rules and methods of discipline on his publications, adopting an unrelenting and vigorous stand against the old style of personal journalism and entangling alliances. Believing in the future of his adopted state, he regarded it as the mission of the *News* "to furnish people with news and labor for the development of Texas." With his associates he contracted in 1883 with the Galveston, Houston & Henderson Railroad to run a special mail car every day in the year to carry papers out into the state. This is said to have been the first daily newspaper service of its kind in the world. Also in 1883 Belo built what is reported to have been the first modern exclusive newspaper plant in the United States, which was also the first fireproof building in Texas. He conceived the new and bold idea of duplicating the *Galveston News* simultaneously at Dallas to facilitate early delivery in all sections of Texas. The *Dallas News* was started Oct. 1, 1885, and the venture proved successful beyond expectation, setting a precedent in journalism. The *Dallas News* was the third paper of consequence in America to own its own home devoted exclusively to the publication of a newspaper. Belo was one of the incorporators of the Associated Press and served two terms as vice-president.

[The chief sources of information are the files of bound volumes of the *Dallas News* at the time of his death and newspaper clippings from the scrap-book of G. B. Dealey, now president of the A. H. Belo Corporation.]

A—o J.

BEMAN, NATHAN SIDNEY SMITH (Nov. 26, 1785–Aug. 6, 1871), Presbyterian clergyman, college president, was born at New Lebanon, N. Y., the son of Samuel and Silence (Douglass) Beman, of German and Scotch ancestry, from whom he acquired a taste for learning and an interest in theology. Matriculating at Williams College in 1803, he withdrew at the end of the second term and entered Middlebury College a year later. During the interim he taught at Fairhaven, Vt.; upon graduation, in 1807, he became preceptor at Lincoln Academy, Newcastle, Me. In 1809 he accepted a tutorship at Middlebury. He was pastor of the First Presbyterian Church, Portland, Me., during 1810–12. He then established a school at Mount Zion, Ga., where, with the exception of a year (1818) which he spent as president of Franklin College, he remained until he was called to Troy, N. Y., in 1823, as minister of the First Presbyterian Church. There he became associated with Rensselaer Polytechnic Institute. In 1842 he was elected vice-president and, in 1845, president, a position which he held until 1865. Although he was professor of philosophy until his retirement, and although he served as director during 1859–60, succeeding Benjamin Franklin Greene, he does not appear to have aided him in the reorganization linked with his name. In the city, however, he was a power during the forty years of his ministry. His first independent publication, reprinted in England, consisted of *Four Sermons on the Doctrine of the Atonement* (1825). Although he published other addresses, his influence was due primarily to his impressiveness in the pulpit. Reserved and even arrogant, he nevertheless held his congregations by an eloquence wrought of emotion as well as intellect. Many of his discourses—especially his Thanksgiving orations—were pugnaciously controversial. He assailed relentlessly the doctrine of the apostolic succession maintained by the Protestant Episcopal Church. Even more biting were his attacks on the claims of the Roman Catholic hierarchy, which he challenged in his *Letters to Rev. John Hughes* (1851). His chief battlefield, however, was the Presbyterian Church. In 1826 he initiated a series of revivals which aroused the antagonism of conservative clergymen. Although he was rebuked by a convention summoned in the same year, he was chosen moderator of the General Assembly in 1831. By 1837, however, he had become head of the New School movement; and, as such, he was largely responsible for the disruption of 1838. Without slighting his parochial duties, he acquired a reputation as a publicist that was more than local. In his advocacy of abolition, especially, he incurred the enmity which is the lot of every reformer.

[Beman's career as an educator is reflected in the minutes of the Board of Trustees of Rensselaer Polytechnic Institute and in the catalogues and registers, 1842–65. Palmer C. Ricketts, *Hist. of Rensselaer Polytechnic Institute* (1895) contains a note of his services. A fuller sketch occurs in Henry B. Nason's *Biog. Record of the Officers and Grads. of the Rensselaer Polytechnic Institute* (1887). Beman's ministry in Troy is treated in the *Proc. Centennial Anniv. First Presbyt. Ch., Troy* (1891). His conduct is criticized severely in Josephus Brockway's *Delineations of the Characteristic Features of a Revival in Troy* (1827). Although equally biased, Marvin R. Vincent's *Memorial Sermon* (1872) and the addresses and notices printed with it contain much valuable information.]

R. P. Ba—r.

BEMENT, CALEB N. (1790–Dec. 22, 1868), agriculturist, inventor, publicist, was for many years a resident of northern New York state. It is well authenticated that the Bements, who were of English, Dutch, and French extraction, honorably assisted in the early settlement of New York, but it is uncertain to which branch of the family Caleb belonged. Prior to 1834 he is known to have been a printer by trade and also to have engaged in the hotel business. In April of that year, he purchased his subsequently celebrated "Three Hills Farm" near Albany, and thereafter for a number of years intelligently devoted himself to agricultural theory and practise. Quickly becoming dissatisfied with the crude farm apparatus of the day, before the end of 1835 he invented, and shortly afterward offered to the public, two implements, designated as Bement's Expanding Corn Cultivator and Bement's Turnip Drill. These machines, which he manufactured himself and placed on sale in Albany and New York, were improved from time to time in the next half-decade, and came into considerable use among farmers. Simultaneously with these inventive and manufacturing efforts, Bement began to display his long-continued interest in improved live stock, by importing, breeding, and distributing through sale, blooded Berkshire and China hogs, Southdown and Leicester sheep, Hereford, Devon, Ayrshire and Shorthorn Durham cattle, and poultry. After 1834 he frequently exhibited his animals at the annual fairs of the New York State Agricultural Society and won numerous prizes. Not content with these enterprises, Bement at the same time commenced offering his opinions and ideas upon farming to the agricultural press. These original contributions not only presented the results of his own careful and extended experiments at "Three Hills," but frequently added, by way of preface, informing historical summaries gained from a wide reading of ancient and contemporary agricultural writers in Europe and America. In this period and later Bement also showed a notable generosity of spirit, as well as vision, by publicly calling attention to every new machine, improvement in livestock, or agricultural practise, which came within range of his inquiring mind. Bement's pioneer activities along these and similar lines did much to encourage the introduction of better machinery and improved breeds of live stock in New York and other states.

Having tasted of the fruits of authorship through his published correspondence, Bement in January 1844 became one of the editors of the *Central New York Farmer,* but because of the competition with other agricultural papers the *Central Farmer* perished of financial atrophy at the end of the year. In the meanwhile in July 1844 he gave further proof of his diverse abilities. Turning over "Three Hills," which by now had become a show place, to a manager, who continued to breed and sell improved live stock under his supervision, he reëntered the tavern business by leasing the American Hotel in Albany for a number of years. This hostelry, under his guidance, soon became the rendezvous of all the agricultural notables who came that way. Bement's table, supplied from his farm, was justly famed, and many pleasant agricultural gatherings took place under his hospitable roof. One of the most valuable of Bement's activities consisted of the completion and publication of his *American Poulterer's Companion* in 1844. This book was proclaimed by the editor of the *Cultivator* as the most complete and practical treatise on the subject of poultry which had appeared up to that time, and was long regarded as a classic by agriculturists. Engaged with his hotel and his farm, Bement did not undertake any new enterprise until the beginning of the year 1848, at which time he purchased the *American Quarterly Journal of Agriculture and Science,* announced himself as editor, and offered it to the public. This second attempt at editorship, like the first, ended in disaster, the publication discontinuing for lack of financial support at the end of 1848. In the following year, possibly due to financial losses, Bement advertised his livestock at "Three Hills" at public auction. In 1853 he appeared before the public as the proprietor of the Albany Steam Mills, where he manufactured and sold Bement's Compound, a substitute for yeast. In 1855 he added *The Rabbit Fancier* to his *Poulterer's Companion,* a work which increased his reputation as an author. Shortly afterward, he left Albany and took up his residence at Springside in Dutchess County, N. Y. Here he farmed again and continued his writings for the agricultural press, devoting much of his attention to poultry. In 1867 he moved to Poughkeepsie, and died in that city the next year.

As indicated by his career, Bement was a man of unusual intelligence, wide interests, and varied talents, accompanied by great industry. Lacking in humor, he atoned for this fault by an equanimity of temperament which enabled him to face the vicissitudes of a long life with unfailing courage. His numerous articles and his books are simply and clearly written but lack distinction of style. Frequently derived from his own extended researches they contain much detailed and valuable information. The practical tone which characterizes the writings of his early years is mellowed with a philosophic attitude in the later period. Bement's chief claim to be remembered proceeds from his vision and breadth of spirit as a pioneer agriculturist in a changing period of American farming, from his influence in encouraging his contemporaries to improve their agriculture, and from the very considerable addition which he made to our knowledge of live stock, including poultry.

[Among the chief sources are the *Cultivator,* 1835–47; *Central N. Y. Farmer,* 1844; *Am. Agriculturist,* 1843–47, 1859; *Genesee Farmer,* 1846–47, 1859–60, 1862; *Am. Quart. Jour. of Ag. and Sci.,* 1848; *Am. Farmer,* 1847–48, 1853; *Southern Planter,* 1845–46, 1859; *Pa. Farm Jour.,* 1853; *Valley Farmer,* 1857, 1859; *Prairie Farmer,* 1847, 1849–50; *Country Gentleman,* 1857, 1859–60, 1864–67, 1869; *Rural Annual,* 1862; *Trans. N. Y. State Ag. Soc.,* 1842, 1847, 1853; *Poughkeepsie Daily Eagle,* Dec. 24, 1868.] H. A. K.

BEMENT, CLARENCE SWEET (Apr. 11, 1843–Jan. 27, 1923), collector, born in Mishawaka, Ind., was descended from John Bement who was settled in Massachusetts in 1635; another of his ancestors was the *Mayflower* passenger, Francis Cooke. Clarence Sweet Bement was the son of Emily (Russell) Bement and of William Barnes Bement, the celebrated manufacturer and inventor of machine tools and patron of fine arts. Early in life he identified himself with his father's business in Philadelphia, and in 1870 he entered the firm which then became William B. Bement & Son. On Dec. 19, 1871, in Philadelphia, he was married to Martha Shreve Ridgway, by whom he had four children. Seventeen years later, the retirement of his father made him the senior partner in the firm and he held that position until August 1899, when the firm of Bement, Miles & Company was merged into the Niles-Bement-Pond Company. Primarily a business man for many years, Bement nevertheless had diversified tastes and pursuits. He was prominent among a small group of Americans who found relaxation from their occupations in the pursuit of some branch of art or science. It was to minerals that he devoted the most of his leisure and the greatest care, his interest in this subject beginning when he was still a lad in school. His collection of minerals became the foremost of its class in America, being rated "the finest ever made by a private individual," and a medal of appreciation was conferred on its owner by the University of Munich. It was purchased by the late Mr. J. Pierpont Morgan for the American Museum of Natural History, New York City. Among its more than 12,000 treasures, the four hundred specimens of meteorites stand out prominently. Another pursuit, perhaps the second to find expression, was Bement's search for rare books, which resulted in the formation of one of the most noted private libraries in the country. A portion of this library passed into the hands of Harry Elkins Widener, forming the nucleus of the Widener Library at Harvard University. Bement's interest was not merely acquisitive however, and he was one of the original founders of, and a silent partner in the Rosenbach Company of Philadelphia and New York, dealers in rare books. During the latter years of his life he became interested in numismatics. At first this interest extended to both ancient and modern coins, including the American series and paper money. He concentrated later on Greek and Roman coins, of which his collection in time became one of the finest in America. It was sold in Lausanne, Switzerland, in January 1924. The extreme diversity of Bement's artistic and other interests can be judged by the societies of which he was a member. These included the American Philosophical Society, the Academy of Natural Sciences, the Numismatic and Antiquarian Society, the Pennsylvania Academy of the Fine Arts, the Philobiblon Club, the Franklin Institute, the Historical Society of Pennsylvania, the Colonial Society, and the Pennsylvania Society of the Sons of the Revolution.

[MSS. of the late J. Granville Leach; *A Descriptive Cat. of Greek Coins from the Bement Coll.* (Am. Numismatic Soc., 1921); A. S. W. Rosenbach, *Books and Bidders* (1927); *Phila. Inquirer* and *Public Ledger* (Phila.), Jan. 28, 1923; *Col. Soc. of Pa., Charter, Constitution,* etc. (1914), p. 38.] A. S. W. R.

BEMIS, GEORGE (Oct. 13, 1816–Jan. 5, 1878), lawyer, publicist, was a member of a well-known Massachusetts family. Joseph Bemis, the original immigrant, had come from England and settled at Watertown in 1640, his descendants for 150 years continuing to live there. Seth Bemis, a Watertown manufacturer and Harvard graduate, married Sarah Wheeler of Concord and moved to Waltham, Mass., where their youngest child, George, was born. Having been fitted for college at the school of the Rev. Samuel Ripley in Waltham, he proceeded to Harvard where he graduated with distinction in 1835. Entering the Harvard Law School he obtained the degree of LL.B. in 1839, and on being admitted to the Boston bar in the same year, commenced practise in that city. While at the Law School he had been a Sunday-school teacher at the State Prison at Charlestown, and had become keenly interested in the subject of crime, punishment and reform. On becoming a lawyer one of his first steps was to attack the system of cumulative punishment of offenders which then prevailed in Massachusetts. As a result of his efforts the whole system of punishment in the state was radically changed. In the meanwhile he was becoming known as an expert in the more difficult phases of criminal law. The case which established his reputation was that of the Commonwealth *vs.* Rogers, a convict who was tried in 1844 for murder of the warden of the prison in which he was confined. Involving the law of insanity and uncontrollable impulse as an excuse for homicide, it attracted wide attention and his defense was considered masterly (*7 Metcalf,* 500). In 1850 he was associate counsel with the attorney-general for the prosecution in the trial of Dr. Webster for the murder of Dr. Parkman, most of the heavy detail work being undertaken by him. After the trial he published a complete report of the proceedings. In 1858 he was compelled to retire from active practise owing to a severe hemorrhage of the lungs, and thereafter his health continued so impaired that he spent the remainder of his life abroad. He never married. Financially independent, he turned his attention to public international law and rendered valuable assistance to the United States Government in connection with the *Alabama* claims. He also contributed to the public discussion of the rights and duties of neutrals in the following pamphlets: *Precedents of American Neutrality, in Reply to the Speech of Sir Roundell Palmer in the British House of Commons* (1864); *Hasty Recognition of Rebel Belligerency and Our Right to Complain of It* (1865); *American Neutrality, Its Honorable Past, Its Expedient Future* (1866); and *Mr. Reverdy Johnson: The Alabama Negotiations, Their Just Repudiation by the Senate of the United States* (1869). Though necessarily controversial in character these writings were distinguished for their uniformly high level of thought and an absence of prejudice which stamped their author as a publicist of outstanding merit. He died at Nice, France, Jan. 5, 1878. Under a bequest in his will, the present Bemis Professorship of International Law at Harvard was established and endowed.

[Details respecting the Bemis family are contained in T. W. Draper, *The Bemis Hist. and Genealogy* (1900) and Henry Bond, *Genealogies and Hist. of Watertown, Mass.* (1860). The only article which does justice to the main currents of his life appeared in the *Am. Law Rev.,* XII, 599.]

H. W. H. K.

BENAVIDES, ALONZO DE (fl. 1600–1664), Franciscan friar, was the son of Pedro Alonzo Nieto and Antonia Murato de Benavides. His birthplace was the Island of San Miguel (probably São Miguel of the Azores). He made his vows in the Franciscan convent in the City of Mexico in 1603 and was afterward made Master of Novices in the monastery of Puebla. In 1621 New Mexico was erected into the "Custodia de la Conversion de San Pablo" and Benavides was appointed Father Custodian. He arrived in New Mexico in the following year taking with him at royal expense twenty-six or twenty-seven friars. Their work was among the Apaches of the Upper Gila in what is now the southwestern part of New Mexico. Shortly after his arrival in Santa Fé, Benavides began to build a suitable convent and church for the chief town of the province. Before he had presented his now famous *Memorial* he had initiated mission or convent buildings in no less than ten places. One was at Picuries, among the Tiwas where the natives were at first unfriendly. Another was the mission of San Gerónimo at Taos, among the same people. At Ácoma the Queres submitted to indoctrination in 1629 and accepted a missionary. Among the fourteen Pira towns Benavides established missions in 1626 at Pilabo, Senecú, and Sevilleta. In addition to this, and efforts to indoctrinate the Moquis, Benavides, while at Senecú, made a convert of Sanaba, a chief of the Gila Apaches, a circumstance which opened opportunity for missions in the river country. Among the Tiwas he founded on Sept. 17, 1629, a convent and church at Santa Clara de Capoo, a Tiwa town on the edge of the Apache country; it became the center of work in teaching and converting the powerful and warlike Navajo Apaches. The New Mexico missions are believed to have had more than 16,000 converts. In 1629, it seems, Benavides was relieved of his custodianship and returned to Mexico and in 1630, to Spain, where his *Memorial* was presented to the king. It is this document that has done the most to keep the name of Benavides alive. It shows him to have been a zealous religious propagandist, of an enthusiastic personality, and of considerable courage and fortitude. The *Memorial* is entitled, "Memorial which Fray Juan de Santander of the Order of Saint Francis, Commissary-General of the Indies, presents to His Catholic Majesty, the King, Philip IV, Our Lord, made by the Father

Fray Alonso de Benavides, Commissary of the Holy Office and Custodian that was of the Provinces and Conversions of New Mexico. In It are Treated the Treasures spiritual and temporal, which the Divine Majesty hath manifested in those Conversions and New Discoveries by means of the Priests of this Seraphic Order." Its object was to persuade the king to send more missionaries to New Mexico and to erect more churches, and in this it succeeded. The *Memorial* won great favor, as is evidenced by the translations that were made within the three following years into four languages—French, Dutch, Latin, and German. In 1634 Benavides wrote, at the request of Pope Urban VIII, a revision of the *Memorial,* a copy of which in his own handwriting and bearing his signature is in the Propaganda Archives in Rome. This revision, having as its object the granting of more extensive privileges and being to an even greater extent than the original *Memorial* a work of propaganda and promotion, emphasizes the difficulties of the labors and the sufferings of the missionaries, which Benavides with characteristic modesty and self-abnegation had almost ignored in the original *Memorial.* It is a more interesting work, giving the history of the missions and making the descriptions of the physical aspects of the country incidental to the story of what the missionaries were doing. In 1631 Benavides had written to the Fathers in New Mexico expressing the hope "to go back there to finish my days if He will allow me to do so in the company and service of your Reverences." Acording to Figueroa in his *Bezerro General,* Benavides returned to Mexico in 1632, and went to New Mexico again in 1633 or 1634. He states that there is a record of the Mexican province having sent him 100 pesos while there in 1634. Probably in the spring of 1634 Benavides was appointed assistant to the Archbishop of Goa in Portuguese India, and on the death of the latter he succeeded to the office.

[The chief sources of information about Benavides are his *Memorial* of 1630, tr. into English by Mrs. E. E. Ayer, with annotation by Frederick W. Hodge and Chas. F. Lummis (1916); his manuscript *Memorial* of 1634, discovered by the Rev. Peter Guilday in the Propaganda Archives at Rome after the publication of the Ayer edition of the 1630 *Memorial*—a photographic reproduction of the former together with several collateral documents, being in the Am. Hist. Dept. of the Cath. Univ. at Washington; the "Bibliography of Fray Alonso de Benavides," by F. W. Hodge, pub. in vol. III of *Indian Notes and Monographs* (1919); Lyman P. Powell, *Historic Towns of the Western States* (1901), pp. 453–54; Francisco Palou, *Life of Junipero Serra,* tr. by C. Scott Williams, with notes by Geo. Wharton James (Pasadena, 1913), containing Benavides's letter, "Tanto que se sacó . . . ," p. 327; J. G. Shea, *Hist. of the Cath. Ch. in the U. S.* (1892).]

H. I. P.

BENBRIDGE, HENRY (May 20, 1744–February 1812), early American portrait painter, was born in Philadelphia, the only child of James and Mary (Clark) Benbridge. When he was seven years old, his mother, who had been left a widow, was married to Thomas Gordon, a wealthy Scotchman. The boy's artistic talent was encouraged. He made for his stepfather's drawing-room decorative designs which were much admired. When he was fourteen years old he may have watched John Wollaston [*q.v.*] paint Mr. Gordon's portrait. It has been plausibly urged (Charles Henry Hart, "The Gordon Family, painted by Henry Benbridge," *Art in America,* VI, 191–200), that young Benbridge had instruction from Wollaston, since his earliest known portrait, that of his half-sister Rebecca Gordon, "seems to hark back to Wollaston." In his twenty-first year Benbridge was sent to Italy where he studied with Batoni and Raphael Mengs. In 1769, on order from James Boswell, biographer of Dr. Samuel Johnson, he made in Corsica a portrait of Pascal Paoli which he took to London. It was exhibited (1769) at the Free Society of Artists, and from it three mezzotints were scraped and published with the artist's name signed "Bembridge." Like other young Americans he was encouraged by Benjamin West. He wrote, Dec. 7, 1769, to his stepfather: "Upon my arrival I waited upon Mr. West who received me with a sort of brotherly affection, as did my cousin, Mrs. West." Impelled, apparently, by a longing to rejoin his family, he left England in 1770, bearing from West the following note of recommendation to Francis Hopkinson: "By Mr. Benbridge you will receive these few lines. You will find him an Ingenous artist and an agreeable Companion. His merit in the art must procure him great incouragement and much esteem. I deare say it will give you great pleasure to have an ingenous artist resident amongst you."

At Philadelphia Benbridge married a Miss Sage and was admitted Jan. 18, 1771, to membership in the American Philosophical Society, of which Franklin was a founder. He painted the large portrait of the Gordon family, with six figures, one of his masterpieces. Suffering, however, from asthma, he sought a more congenial climate and removed to Charleston where he succeeded Jeremiah Theus (d. May 18, 1774) as the popular portrait painter of South Carolina. He there made many likenesses of southern men and women, several of which have been popularly attributed to John Singleton Copley, an artist who never painted in the South and who left America in 1774. About 1800 Benbridge settled at Norfolk, Va., whence he made frequent visits to his native city. At Norfolk he gave to Thomas Sully [*q.v.*] his first lessons in oil painting. He had previously instructed Thomas Coram, of Charleston. Sully (as quoted by Dunlap, *History of the Arts of Design,* I, 167) describes his master as "a portly man of good address—gentlemanly in his deportment." Benbridge's health is said by Hart to have declined in middle age. Dunlap's assertion that his last years were passed "in obscurity and poverty" has been disputed.

As a technician Benbridge drew well and painted solidly, exhibiting many characteristics of the late Italian masters. His contemporary Charles Fraser (quoted by Dunlap) said that "his shadows were dark and opaque and more suitable to the historical style." Hart says "Benbridge was impregnated by the brownish sameness of Batoni's palette and his shadows were too opaque, and although later he was somewhat emancipated from these errors, all his work belongs to the late Italian school." His paintings, nevertheless, were notably good in respect of their black-and-white values and some of his miniatures are exquisite. His Italianate mode was much appreciated in the Middle and Southern states during his lifetime.

[The detailed but somewhat unreliable acount of Benbridge given by Wm. Dunlap in his *Hist. of the Rise and Progress of the Arts of Design in the U. S.* (1834) is corrected by F. W. Bayley and C. E. Goodspeed in a footnote in their revised edition (1918), I, 164. A brief notice of Benbridge, his self-portr. and his painting of Mrs. Thomas Hartley and Family was given by F. W. Bayley in his undated pamphlet *Little Known Early Am. Portr. Painters, No. 4.* Chas. Henry Hart, whose researches disclosed many heretofore unknown data concerning Benbridge, contributed to his cat. of the Herbert L. Pratt collection a succinct account which was amplified in his article, cited above (*Art in America,* VI, 191–200), in which he supplemented and corrected meager information concerning "An Early American Artist: Henry Bembridge," by William Roberts, of London (*Art in America,* VI, 96 ff.).] F. W. C.

BENEDICT, DAVID (Oct. 10, 1779–Dec. 5, 1874), Baptist clergyman, historian, was born in Norwalk, Conn., the eldest child of Thomas Benedict, a farmer, and of Martha Scudder. He joined the Baptist Church in Stamford, Conn., in 1799, was a shoemaker's apprentice, and went to school at Mt. Pleasant (now Ossining), N. Y. Here he met expenses by tutoring younger pupils, among whom was Francis Wayland, later president of Brown University. After two years Benedict himself entered Brown and graduated in 1806, delivering an earnest oration on "Ecclesiastical History." He issued his first publication, anonymously, while he was still in college—a pamphlet entitled *The Watery War, or a Poetical Description of the Controversy on the Subjects and Mode of Baptism, by John of Enon.* It was widely circulated, and was reprinted in 1843. After graduation, he accepted his first and only pastorate, at a salary of $400 a year, with the newly organized First Baptist Church of Pawtucket, to whose people he had preached when he was a student. He led them effectively for twenty-three years. On May 5, 1808, he married Margaret Hubbel Gano, daughter of Stephen Gano [*q.v.*], who was pastor of the First Baptist Church of Providence. They lived together sixty years and had twelve children.

Deeply engaged in the study of Baptist history, which he deemed his real vocation, Benedict ultimately gave up his pastorate. In a day of heavy postage he wrote hundreds of letters of inquiry and traveled nearly 4,000 miles on horseback throughout New England and as far west as the Mississippi. He rightly claimed a wider acquaintance with Baptist men and affairs than any one else then living. His chief works were: *A General History of the Baptist Denomination in America and Other Parts of the World* (2 vols., 1813), not free from defects or infelicities, but a pioneer work, widely used; *Abridgment of Robinson's History of Baptism* (1817); *History of All Religions* (1824); *A General History of the Baptist Denomination in America and Other Parts of the World* (1848), a different work from the previous one bearing the same title; *Fifty Years among the Baptists* (1860), his last personal publication. As a nonagenarian, with good health and eyesight, he still worked assiduously, and before his death had practically completed a "Compendium of Ecclesiastical History" for popular use, and a *History of the Donatists* which was published posthumously. In his pastorate he wrote and collected hymns for church use, publishing them in editions reaching 20,000 copies. He pioneered in founding Sunday-schools throughout the Blackstone Valley, with paid teachers in various churches. Elected a trustee of Brown University in 1818, from 1858 he was senior member of the Corporation, and, until his last year, was absent from but one meeting in fifty-five years. He was sometime postmaster of Pawtucket. Though hale to the last, he survived but a few days the deaths of his oldest daughter and of a beloved sister in the same week late in 1874.

[H. C. Graves, "Sketch of the Life and Work of Dr. Benedict" in *Hist. of the Donatists* (1875); H. M. Benedict, *Genealogy of the Benedicts in America* (1870); *Proc. R. I. Hist. Soc.,* 1874–75, pp. 89–90; *Baptist Encyc.* (1881); *Providence Jour.,* Dec. 7, 1874.] C. M. G.

BENEDICT, ERASTUS CORNELIUS (Mar. 19, 1800–Oct. 22, 1880), lawyer, educationist, was a descendant of Thomas Benedict of Nottinghamshire who emigrated to New England in 1638, remaining for a time in Massachusetts and finally settling in Norwalk, Conn., with which place his descendants were long associated. Erastus Cornelius was the son of Joel Taylor Benedict, a clergyman, and of Currance, daughter of Deacon Adin Wheeler of Southbury, Conn. He was born at Branford, Conn., but the family moved to New York State in 1803, residing successively at New Windsor, Franklin, and Chatham, where young Benedict received his early education in the district schools. In 1816 he became a teacher, and in September 1818 entered Williams College, graduating in 1821 with high honors. He then became in turn principal of the Johnstown and Newburgh Academies, later joining the teaching staff at Williams College, and studying law in his leisure hours. He was admitted to the New York bar in 1824 and removing to New York City, obtained a position as deputy clerk in the United States district court of southern New York. In this office he acquired an intimate knowledge of admiralty law, which later induced him to resign his appointment, and enter into practise, devoting his attention to admiralty cases. He quickly became known as a specialist, and built up an extensive connection, gradually acquiring a reputation as one of the foremost admiralty lawyers of his day. On May 7, 1833, he was married to Caroline Margaret, daughter of Moses Bloodgood. In 1840 he was elected a member of the city common council, and in 1842 he was appointed a school trustee. For nearly forty years thereafter he was a prime factor in the development of education both in the city and state. In 1848 he became for one term a member of the state legislature. In 1850 he was elected a member of the board of education of the City of New York of which he became president. During the thirteen years for which he remained a member of the board he initiated and carried through reforms which resulted in the public schools of the city being consolidated into a harmonious and flexible system of high efficiency. In the course of this work he was mainly instrumental in establishing the Free Academy, which subsequently developed into the College of the City of New York. In 1855 he had been appointed by the state legislature to the board of regents of the state university. He resigned from the board of education in 1863, and in the following year was again elected a member of the Assembly, serving one term. In 1872 as a reform candidate he was elected to the state Senate, and was nominated a member of the court of impeachment before whom the charges against the members of the New York judiciary which arose out of the exposure of the "Tweed Ring" were heard. In 1878 he was selected as chancellor of the state university, continuing to hold that position till his death, which occurred in New York City, Oct. 22, 1880. Despite his absorption in educational problems, he had continued the active practise of his profession, and in 1850 had published a treatise, *American Admiralty,* which was for years recognized as the standard work on the subject in the United States, passing through a number of editions. He also wrote *A Run Through Europe* (1860), being an account of a holiday trip which he had taken in 1854. The most striking testimony to the versatility of his culture is, however, found in his metrical translations from the French, German, and Latin, *The Hymn of Hildebert and Other Mediæval Hymns* (1861) attracting wide attention. In one of his translations of "*Dies Irae*" he used only words of Gotho-English derivation. He was the author of numerous addresses on historical and educational subjects.

[H. M. Benedict, *The Genealogy of the Benedicts in America* (1870) contains full details of the family history, in addition to a sketch of Benedict's career. Information will also be found in *Hist. of the Bench and Bar of N. Y.*, ed. by D. A. McAdam et al. (1897), I, 259, and *Am. Annual Cyc. and Reg.*, 1880, p. 56; long obituaries in *N. Y. Times* and *N. Y. Tribune,* Oct. 23, 1880.]

H. W. H. K.

BENEZET, ANTHONY (Jan. 31, 1713–May 3, 1784), philanthropist, author, was born in San Quentin, in Picardy, France, the son of Jean Étienne Benezet. The family were Huguenots. Increasing persecution, following the revocation of the Edict of Nantes, caused the parents in 1715 to take refuge in Rotterdam, soon leaving Holland, however, for London, where they remained sixteen years. Here the young Anthony received a liberal education, served an apprenticeship in a mercantile house, and coming under Quaker influence, joined that sect at the early age of fourteen. In 1731 the family removed to Philadelphia, bringing with them the lad of eighteen, "well recommended by divers Friends." For a brief time, Anthony appears to have been in business with his brothers, John, Philip, and Daniel, who later were successful importers of goods from London, Philip Benezet's advertisements being frequent in the *Pennsylvania Gazette* about 1759–60. In May 1736 Anthony Benezet married Joyce, daughter of Samuel and Mary Marriott of Burlington, N. J., and began a happy married life of forty-eight years. Dislike for the merchant's life to which he had been brought up, after a brief experience as a manufacturer in Wilmington, Del., determined him to follow his inclination to teach. Going first to the Germantown Academy, in 1742 he became a teacher in the Friends' English Public School in Philadelphia, now the William Penn Charter School, where he remained for the next twelve years. In this profession, to which the rest of his life was devoted, Benezet found congenial occupation, and an outlet for the energies of his active and altruistic mind. Finding female education defective, he established a girls' school in 1755.

At this time Benezet, always an omnivorous reader, began to be greatly interested in the amelioration of conditions among the slaves, and the reports of travelers and agents in the West Indies and in Africa aroused his pity and indignation. John Woolman of New Jersey, although seven years younger than himself, had completed his first tour among the slaveholders of the South, and their life-long intimacy resulted in Benezet's carrying on the remarkable pioneer work of Woolman, after the death of the younger man. He began to publish articles in almanacs and the papers of the day, and issued pamphlets, usually gratuitously distributed, on the subject of slavery. His knowledge of French led to a voluminous correspondence abroad with such men as the Abbé Raynal in France, and Granville Sharp, Wilberforce, and Clarkson in England. He also corresponded with Benjamin Franklin while the latter was abroad. He wrote Frederick the Great on the unlawfulness of war, and sent letters acceptably to the queens of England, France, and Portugal.

In 1766, finding himself absorbed in too many activities to carry out his philosophy of the simple life of studious leisure, and in frail health, he retired to Burlington, N. J., the early home of his wife, and sought a quieter existence. But the urge toward alleviation of at least some of the sufferings of his fellow-beings was too great to be resisted, and at the end of less than two years he was again in Philadelphia, teaching, and writing voluminously. It was probably while in Burlington that he wrote what is perhaps his most important work—*A Caution and Warning to Great Britain and Her Colonies on the Calamitous State of the Enslaved Negroes* (1766). This was examined and approved by the Yearly Meeting of Philadelphia in 1766, and many copies were distributed in England. It was shortly followed by his *Historical Account of Guinea; Its Situation, Produce and the General Disposition of Its Inhabitants* (1771), a publication which gave to Thomas Clarkson his first facts on the slave trade, and was the source of the impulse to begin his long and active protest against it.

It was natural, when the French in 1756 were expelled from Acadia, that the 500 who made their way to Philadelphia should find in Anthony Benezet their chief friend. The whole Quaker body joined him for their relief, together with the French residents, and in Philadelphia many of the Acadians found a permanent home. Benezet established and taught for the last two or three years of his life, a school for the "Blacks," which, after the death of his wife, he left his slender fortune to endow. The Overseers of the Friends' Public Schools were made the trustees. This school has been fostered ever since by the Quakers, and, merged with other and similar charities, is now (1927) the "Benezet House" of 918 Locust St., Philadelphia. In 1774 Benezet published his essay on the immoderate use of liquor, *The Mighty Destroyer Displayed,* which suggested to his friend, Dr. Benjamin Rush, the latter's pamphlet in 1776, *Sermons to Gentlemen on Temperance and Exercise.* In 1780 appeared Benezet's *Short Account of the People Called Quakers; Their Rise, Religious Principles and Settlement in America.* Just before his death the Indians, for whom he had long labored, and their injustices under the new Government, were engaging Benezet's attention, and he wrote *Some Observations on the Situation, Disposition, and Character of the Indian Natives of This Continent* (published anonymously, 1784). This is thought to have been intended as a prelude to a more extended work on the subject.

[Roberts Vaux, *Memoirs of the Life of Anthony Benezet* (1817); Wilson Armistead, *Select Miscellanies* (1851), I, 119, 133, 148 ff.; Marquis de Chastellux, *Travels in North-America* (London, 1787), pp. 278 ff.]

A. M. G.

BENHAM, HENRY WASHINGTON (Apr. 8, 1813–June 1, 1884), engineer, soldier, was born in Quebec, Canada. His mother, Rebecca Hill, born in Quebec in 1783, was the daughter of Lieut. Joseph Hill of the British army. His father was Jared Benham, the son of Darius Benham of Meriden, Conn., and a descendant in the seventh generation of Joseph Benham, one of the first settlers of Wallingford, and probably the son of John Benham, who is believed to have come over in the *Mary and John* in 1630 (*New England Historical and Genealogical Register,* XXXIX, 92). Jared Benham died while his son Henry was young, and his widow then married Liberty Perkins of Meriden, Conn. Henry's attempts to acquire a schooling met with opposition from his stepfather. Hidden in a garret, and helped by his loyal and devoted mother, he surreptitiously acquired sufficient education to enter Yale in 1832. Disliking the menial duties by which he attempted to defray his expenses at college, he sought and obtained an appointment to West Point. Entering on July 1, 1833, he graduated first in his class, and on July 1, 1837, was commissioned brevet second lieutenant of engineers. Until 1847 he was engaged in engineering duties, principally in connection with coast defenses. Promoted first lieutenant of engineers on July 7, 1838, he entered the Mexican War with that rank. He took part in the battle of Buena Vista, Feb. 22–23, 1847, being employed in making reconnaissances, and in carrying information and orders. Slightly wounded, he was highly commended by Gen. Wool, and was brevetted captain for gallant and meritorious conduct. Promoted captain of engineers on May 24, 1848, he was in charge, from 1848 to 1853, of the repairs of the defenses of New York Harbor, of sea-wall construction in Boston Harbor, of building the Buffalo Lighthouse, and of the Washington Navy Yard. From Mar. 29, 1853, to Nov. 1, 1856, he was assistant in charge of the United States Coast Survey Office at Washington, his duties calling him to Europe. From 1856 to 1861 he was in charge of engineering work connected with the defenses of Boston Harbor, New Bedford Harbor, Newport Harbor, and Sandy Hook, and in charge of the building of the Potomac Aqueduct.

On May 14, 1861, he was appointed chief engineer of the Department of the Ohio. In McClellan's West Virginia campaign he commanded the advance guard of Gen. T. A. Morris's column which pursued the Confederates under Gen. R. S. Garnett from Laurel Hill, defeating them at Carrick's Ford on July 13, 1861. This campaign won for him a brevet as colonel, high praise from Morris and McClellan, a commission as brigadier-general of volunteers, and the command of a brigade in West Virginia (*Official Records,* ser. I, vol. II: reports of Gen. Morris, p. 68; Gen. McClellan, p. 207; Capt. Benham, pp. 222–23. *Battles and Leaders of the Civil War,* vol. I, pt. I: "McClellan in West Virginia," by Major-General J. D. Cox, p. 126). The aggressiveness and energy which gained this advancement brought reverses when injudiciously exercised. On Sept. 10, 1861, he incurred the displeasure of Gen. Rosecrans by too rapidly developing the engagement at Carnifex Ferry, W. Va. Rosecrans also held him responsible for the failure to capture Floyd's Confederate forces after their demonstration at Gauley Bridge on Nov. 1, 1861, and charged him with disregarding orders (*Ibid.,* ser. I, vol. V: reports of Gen. Rosecrans, pp. 129 and 253; Gen. Benham, pp. 133 and 278). Gen. Hunter claimed that Benham's unsuccessful attack on Secessionville, James Island, S. C., on June 16, 1862, was in violation of orders, and relieved Benham of his command. On Aug. 7, 1862, his appointment as brigadier-general of volunteers was revoked; and on Sept. 8 he was placed in charge of coast defense work at Portsmouth Harbor, N. H. (*Ibid.,* ser. I, vol. XIV: reports of Gen. Hunter, Gen. Benham, etc., pp. 41 ff. and see also Appendix).

An appeal to President Lincoln resulted in the cancellation, on Feb. 6, 1863, of the revocation of his appointment, and his detail, in the spring of 1863, to command the engineer brigade of the Army of the Potomac. Until June 8, 1865, excepting about ten months passed in command of the Ponton Depot at Washington, D. C., he rendered valuable service with that brigade, particularly in the construction of ponton bridges for the army, and in the construction and command of the defenses of City Point, Va. He had been commissioned major of engineers on Aug. 6, 1861, and lieutenant-colonel on Mar. 3, 1863. His gallant, meritorious, and faithful services during the Civil War were rewarded by the brevets of brigadier-general United States Army, major-general United States Volunteers, and major-general United States Army. On Jan. 15, 1866, he was mustered out of the volunteer service; and on Mar. 7, 1867, was commissioned a colonel, corps of engineers. From June 17, 1865, until his retirement from active service, June 30, 1882, he was in charge of the construction of the defenses of Boston Harbor and New York Harbor. He had married on Oct. 3, 1843, Elizabeth Ann McNeil of New Hampshire; and she, two daughters, and a son, survived him.

[G. W. Cullum, *Biog. Reg.* (3rd ed., 1891) contains a succinct account of Benham's military record. Interesting details can be found in "Recollections of Mexico and the Battle of Buena Vista" and "Recollections of West Virginia Campaign," written by himself, published in the monthly magazine, *Old and New,* June, July 1871, June 1873, respectively, and reprinted as pamphlets. Obituaries may be found in the *N. Y. Tribune, N. Y. Herald* and *N. Y. Times.*]

W. S. G.

BENJAMIN, ASHER (June 15, 1773–July 26, 1845), architect, author, was born in Greenfield, Mass., June 15, 1773, and twice married; first to Achsah Hitchcock, Nov. 30, 1797, and second to Nancy Bryant, on July 24, 1805. It is likely that Greenfield was his home during his early professional life, as much of his work was in places easily accessible from there, and as his first book, *The Country Builder's Assistant* (1797), was published near-by in Deerfield. A second edition, enlarged, was printed in Boston, but sold especially by Alexander Thomas, in Worcester, in 1798, which may indicate a residence there as well. It is certain that Benjamin lived for some time in Windsor, Vt., as records show that he owned a house there for two years, and designed at least two houses, the Hatch and Jones houses, as well as (probably) the Old South Congregational Meeting House, which resembles much of the work published in his various books. He also evidently worked in various places in the Connecticut Valley prior to 1803, when he appears in the Boston directory. During this period we find him striving for another outlet for his desire to popularize architecture in America, for several times in 1802 there appeared in the Windsor local paper an advertisement by Benjamin proposing the start of a school of architecture (A. J. Wardner, *Old South Meeting House, Windsor, Vt.*). In Boston he appears to have prospered, as he owned two houses at the time of his death and left one to each of his daughters, Sarah Smith Benjamin and Elizabeth Augusta Bliss (Alexander J. Wall, *Books on Architecture Printed in America 1775–1830,* 1925, p. 6). There is evidence that he fulfilled at least to some extent his ambition to teach architecture, for Robert Henry Eddy of Boston writing in 1872 for the Historical and Genealogical Society states that he "studied architecture with the late Asher Benjamin, architect" (*New England Historical and Genealogical Register,* XLII, 214). This was probably prior to 1833. Benjamin died in Springfield, Mass., on July 26, 1845 (*Boston Daily Evening Transcript,* July 30, 1845).

Besides the buildings mentioned above, Benjamin has been credited with the design of the Carew House, Springfield; the Hollister House, Greenfield; the Alexander House, Springfield; the Colton House, Agawam (1806); the West Church, Boston; the First Congregational Church, Bennington, Vt. (1806), similar to plate 33 of *The Country Builder's Assistant;* the First Parish Church, Bedford, Mass., exactly like plate 39 of *The American Builder's Companion;* and the old Congregational Church of Northampton, burned many years ago, but shown on a Bartlett drawing published in 1839, and illustrated by figure 212 in *The American Spirit in Architecture,* by Talbot Faulkner Hamlin, being volume XIII, 1926, of *The Pageant of America.*

It was, however, even more as author than as architect that Benjamin was important. Through his books "late colonial" details and designs were broadcast throughout New England, as English ideas had been broadcast by English books in colonial times, and there is scarcely a village which in moulding profiles, cornice details, church spire, or farm-house does not reflect his influence. How much of the designs he published were original with him is not known; certainly he copied widely and eagerly. Aymar Embury, who published in 1917 a reprint of some of his work, notes a cornice type (plate 12, *The American Builder's Companion*) common in Litchfield, Conn., long before the date of the book, and Fiske Kimball states that Benjamin "codified Bulfinch's innovations" (*Domestic Architecture of the American Colonies and of the Early Republic,* 1922). Yet original or not, Benjamin's plates formed a collection harmonious and almost always in perfect taste.

The series of his books serves, too, as an excellent criterion of popular taste, which they both recognized and stimulated; the earlier works, up to 1814, contain only the refined delicacies of the typical New England "late colonial"; but in *The Rudiments of Architecture* (1814) Greek orders appear, and in *The Practical House Carpenter* (1830) he remarks, "Since my last publication, the Roman School of Architecture has been entirely changed for the Grecian." His influence was thus great in popularizing the Greek Revival. His publications include *The Country Builder's Assistant,* with thirty plates (Deerfield, 1797); *The Country Builder's Assistant,* with thirty-seven plates (Boston, 1798); *The American Builder's Companion,* with forty-four plates, by Asher Benjamin and Daniel Reynard (1806), of which a second edition, revised and enlarged, with fifty-nine plates, was published in 1811 and a third in 1816, while fourth, fifth and sixth "revised and enlarged" editions, the fourth with sixty-one plates, the fifth with sixty-three, and the sixth with seventy, appeared in 1820, 1826, and 1827; *The Rudiments of Architecture* (1814, and a second edition 1820); *The Practical House Carpenter* (1830, frequently republished). A portrait of Asher Benjamin exists in the possession of a great-grand-daughter, Mrs. Chester W. Bliss of New London, Conn.; it shows a strikingly handsome man of about fifty, smooth shaven, with a long slender face.

[In addition to the references above, see Thos. E. O'Donnell, "Asher Benjamin," in *Architecture,* Dec. 1926, pp. 375 ff.; Howard Major, *The Domestic Arch. of the Early Am. Republic* (1926); John Bullock, *The Am. Cottage Builder* (1854); Jos. E. Chandler, *The Colonial House* (2nd ed., 1924); Chas. A. Place, *Chas. Bulfinch: Architect and Citizen* (1925); Harold D. Eberlein, *The Architecture of Colonial America* (1915); *House Beautiful,* Sept. 1912, p. 114.]

T. F. H.

BENJAMIN, GEORGE HILLARD (Dec. 25, 1852–Nov. 10, 1927), lawyer, engineer, and patent expert, was born in New York City, one of the sons of Park Benjamin [*q.v.*] and Mary Brower (Western) Benjamin. His descent was from John Benjamin, who migrated from England to Watertown, Mass., in 1632. His father was a well-known poet and editor who had been associated with Horace Greeley on the *New Yorker* (before the founding of the *Tribune*).

The boy was fitted for college at Phillips Andover Academy and entered Union College, Schenectady, N. Y., in 1868; but left before the graduation of his class to begin his professional studies at the Albany Medical College. He was keenly interested in branches of science and technology outside his profession; to familiarize himself with advanced work in those fields he studied at the University of Freiburg, Germany, later receiving his doctorate in philosophy from that institution. For four years (1876–80) he practised medicine at Albany, N. Y.; but in 1880, at the age of twenty-eight, he removed to New York City, joining the staff of *Appleton's Cyclopædia of Applied Mechanics,* of which his brother, Park Benjamin II [*q.v.*], was editor. In his editorial work the legal aspects of engineering commanded more and more of his attention. Thus he was led to study patent law and in 1884 he was admitted to practise. Still he always had far more than a merely legalistic interest in engineering and technical problems. His counsel was sought in the organization of large corporations, notably the Western Electric Company, the General Railway Signal Corporation, and United States Steel. As a technical engineer, Benjamin long represented the German firm of Siemens and Halske. He frequently appeared as an expert witness in important patent litigation and other suits in which the Government was interested. He was a contributor to the technical journals and at times to the daily newspapers. His mind was unusually versatile in technical directions and so keen that the mere suggestion of an idea could be converted by him into a patentable invention literally over night. He was the patentee of a great many devices as well as the joint assignee of many of his clients' inventions. The same year that he was admitted to practise patent law he devised and patented an underground electric conduit; the following year a glass-melting furnace; the next year he was assignee with a Swiss client of a dynamo-electric machine; and the following year secured three patents on pipe couplings and expansion joints. A tin-plate manufacturing process was patented by him in 1892, and in 1893 he patented and assigned to his client, the Siemens Halske Company, Berlin, Germany, an incandescent electric lamp and an electric street-railway trolley. Benjamin's inventive work extended over the chemical and metallurgical fields as well. He devised a process of manufacture of diethyl ether in 1900; secured four patents for a metallurgical furnace in 1905; one for a regenerative gas furnace in 1910; for a by-product coke oven in 1920; for a metal casting furnace as late as 1923; and during the last ten years of his life was much interested in and invented processes for curing, preserving, and drying tobacco, beet sugars, and fruits. The United States Government employed him as an expert on high explosives. During the World War he served as chairman of the executive committee of the Mayor's Committee on National Defense in New York City. He was interested in the perfection of sound-detecting devices on American war-ships to detect approaching submarines. For many years he gave attention to problems in the detection and prevention of crime. He was thoroughly conversant with the Bertillon system of measurements and its application. He was consulted by Scotland Yard in difficult cases of crime detection, particularly such as involved chemistry. His reputation in this field, as well as in technical engineering, was international. Benjamin married, first, Jane Seymour of Ogdensburg, N. Y., in 1875; second, Mrs. Grace (Smith) Tremaine of Buffalo, N. Y., in 1901.

[Benjamin wrote little outside of professional reports and briefs, cyclopedia articles, and short contributions to the technical journals. Obituaries were published in the New York newspapers of Nov. 11, 1927. See also *Who's Who in America,* 1926–27.]

W. B. S.
C. W. M.

BENJAMIN, JUDAH PHILIP (Aug. 6, 1811–May 6, 1884), lawyer and statesman, was born in the island of St. Thomas, British West Indies. His parents (Philip Benjamin, an English Jew, and Rebecca de Mendes, of a family of Portuguese Jews) removed to Charleston, S. C., when their son was a mere lad. He was sent later to the Fayetteville Academy, Fayetteville, N. C., and thence to Yale. He entered college in 1825, but left without taking a degree in 1827. The next year he found a position with a commercial house in New Orleans. He was poor but resolute, with a cheerful and attractive personality which enabled him to make friends rapidly. In French New Orleans he eked out his slender resources by giving lessons in English. There is a tradition that one cautious gentleman refused to employ him as tutor for his daughter for fear the girl would fall in love with him. This was what happened in the case of a pupil of his, Mademoiselle Natalie St. Martin, whom he married in 1833. Meanwhile he had prepared himself for the legal profession through hard work in the office of a notary by whom he had been employed as clerk. A considerable reputation as a lawyer was promptly attained, and in 1834 it was greatly enhanced when he issued in coöperation with Thomas Slidell a *Digest of the Reported Decisions of the Superior Court of the Late Territory* *of Orleans and of the Supreme Court of Louisiana* (2nd ed., 1840). His reputation became national through his participation in the celebrated case of the brig *Creole,* involving delicate questions of international law. His brief in this case, a review of the status of slavery under international law and the United States domestic law, was printed as a pamphlet and widely circulated. So rapid was his rise at the bar that he soon became wealthy, purchased a sugar plantation, and for a time was even more concerned in his activities as a planter than as a lawyer. His eager and acute mind was applied with energy to the problems of sugar chemistry; he had Rillieux, inventor of a new process, install it at his plantation, and in 1846 and 1848 he wrote for *De Bow's Review* a series of articles setting forth the new theories and methods in the industry. The failure of a friend whose note for $60,000 he had indorsed cost him his plantation and threw him back upon his law practise. Thereafter until the end of his life, his devotion to the law, in which he attained the highest eminence, was tempered only by his interest in politics.

Being naturally a conservative he had joined the Whig party; in 1842 he had been elected to the state legislature; in 1844–45 he was a delegate to the constitutional convention; in 1848 he was a presidential elector on the Whig ticket; in 1852 he was elected by the Whigs to the United States Senate; and in the summer of that year was the leading spirit in the convention which drew up the constitution of 1852. At this time Benjamin had great dreams about the future development of American commerce. He was one of the foremost organizers of the Jackson Railroad, now the Illinois Central, and projected the great Tehuantepec Company to build a railroad and ultimately a canal across the Isthmus of Tehuantepec. "What have we before us?" he wrote, "The Eastern World . . . Its commerce makes empires of the countries to which it flows, and when they are deprived of it they are as empty bags, useless, valueless. That commerce will belong to New Orleans" (*Picayune,* Jan. 7, 1852, in Butler, p. 126).

This vision of Southern greatness with Asia as its source, following close upon the Southern attempt in 1850 to get an outlet to the Pacific, gives the keynote of Benjamin as a politician during the fifties. He shared the general Southern belief that foreign expansion of some sort was the one way to repair the defeat of the South through the upsetting of the sectional balance in the Compromise of 1850. Gradually he reached the conclusion accepted by many Southern Whigs that the new conditions had put the South on the defensive and that a confessed "Southern party" ought to be formed. This chain of reasoning formed the intermediary through which he passed from the Whig to the Democratic party. On May 2, 1856, he made a speech in the Senate on the Kansas Bill and confessed himself a Democrat. He became an ardent partisan of Buchanan, that year, and on the expiration of his term in the Senate was returned for a new term by his new friends.

During the stormy events of the late fifties Benjamin took a leading but hardly a commanding part as a Southern advocate. He was one of the earliest of the Southern senators to advise secession, following the election of Lincoln. On Dec. 8, 1860, he advocated separate secession by Louisiana; on Dec. 14, he signed the famous address of Southern members of Congress "To Our Constituents." This was followed by a very able defense of the right of secession and of the Southern policy (speech in the Senate, Dec. 31, 1860, *Congressional Globe,* 36 Cong., 2 Sess., pp. 212–17), which further enlarged his reputation as a defender of Southern rights. Shortly after the secession of Louisiana he made his brilliant last speech to the Senate (Feb. 4, 1861, *Ibid.,* pp. 721–22), and withdrew.

Three weeks later Jefferson Davis appointed him attorney-general of the Confederacy. Politically the appointment was eminently appropriate. No other Southern leader could rival Benjamin as a lawyer. It is probable, however, that personal reasons of a sort peculiarly effective with Davis contributed to direct his choice. The nature of the Confederate President was intensely susceptible to ideas of honor. At one time during the heat of debate he had used words about Benjamin to which the latter had replied by a note demanding a duel. Davis, his anger having passed, was deeply sensitive to the wrong he had committed, declined the duel as not justifiable, and made a public recantation. Both men, in this quarrel, bore themselves so scrupulously according to the code which both accepted, that the incident proved to be the beginning of intimacy. Davis trusted far his estimates of men. Through the troubles which they now had to meet in common Davis and Benjamin developed close personal affection which no opposition was able to break.

Until his entrance into the Confederate cabinet Benjamin had enjoyed popularity. The tenor of his story now with singular rapidity changes. His brief tenure of the attorney-generalship afforded him no opportunity to display his legal powers. But it appears to have cemented his friendship with Davis. In these days, J. A. Jones set down in his *Diary,* "Mr. Benjamin is a frequent visitor at the [War] department and is very sociable; some intimations have been thrown out that he aspires to become, some day, Secretary of War. Benjamin unquestionably will have great influence with the President, for he has studied his character most carefully. He will be familiar not only with his likes, but especially with his 'dislikes'" (*A Rebel War Clerk's Diary,* 1866, I, 71). Without taking too seriously Jones's innuendo it is plain that Benjamin was just the man to be a consolation to the nervous and excitable Davis. It is also plain that he understood how to get on subtly with individuals. At the same time he appears to have lacked that instinct for men in the mass—at least for Americans in the mass—without which it was predestined that he should fail as a leader of the Confederacy. It is possible that his preoccupation during formative years with the legal and social genius of a Latin community, Louisiana, may have made it hard for him to sense the typically Anglo-Saxon community which formed the greater part of the South.

It was part of Benjamin's ironic fate to enter upon great offices under conditions that made it impossible to succeed in them. When Davis translated him to the War Department, Sept. 17, 1861, the tragedy of his life began. The first main division of Confederate history was nearing its end. The central, but secret, event of that period had been the competition of Southern and Northern agents in Europe in attempting to corner the munitions market. Benjamin's predecessor, Leroy P. Walker [*q.v.*], had failed lamentably to equip the Southern armies through purchases abroad; the financial credit of the Confederacy was not equal to its needs; and the shipment of such arms as were purchased had been ruinously interrupted by the Federal blockade. So inadequate were the supplies of the Confederate army that Davis, at a conference of generals in July, had refused to authorize a movement northward to follow up the victory of the First Manassas.

The real condition of the War Department was not generally known when Benjamin became secretary. The government would not take the people into its confidence and rested its defense of inaction on the avowed theory that the war should be entirely defensive so as not to estrange through invasion those Northerners who, it was believed, were at heart for secession. The result of this lack of candor was a furious tension in which many people sought nervously for some point of attack upon the government. They found it in what seemed to be a blunder of the Secretary of War. There appears, now, to be little if any ground for holding him directly responsible for the loss of Roanoke Island early in 1862, almost coincident with the loss of Forts Henry and Donelson. These disasters were the match in the magazine, and there was an explosion of popular rage. Roanoke Island in particular became the shibboleth. Its defenders, was the cry, had been unable to hold their ground through the incompetence of the Secretary of War who had failed to equip them adequately, and had disregarded urgent appeals for more ammunition. A motion was introduced in the House of Representatives asserting that Benjamin had "not the confidence of the people of the Confederate States, nor of the Army" and requesting his retirement from the War Office.

By this time the relations between Davis and Benjamin had become very close. The attack upon the Secretary moved the President to indignation. Furthermore, he construed the criticism of the War Office as a criticism of the Administration. To his haughty and sensitive spirit both personal and public obligation made it necessary for him to stand firm against the popular clamor. The course which he took was perhaps Benjamin's greatest misfortune. It made permanent his estrangement from the Southern people.

The Secretary of State, R. M. T. Hunter [*q.v.*], had recently resigned. While a committee of Congress was investigating the affair of Roanoke Island and it was practically certain that the result would be an indictment of Benjamin, Davis appointed him secretary of state. Congress, cheated of its prey, could do nothing but delight in the report of the committee, which held "the late Secretary of War" largely responsible for the defeat at Roanoke Island.

Why Benjamin, who generally was astute, should have allowed himself as secretary of state to be put in such a false position before the Southern people is a mystery. He never revealed his inner life. He may truly be called the sphinx of the Confederacy. The only plausible explanation is that his point of view was irreconcilable with those of the people surrounding him. Apparently he had an innate attitude toward government, and toward all phases of public policy, which in certain respects, the planter type with its romantic mixture of individualism, class consciousness, and idealistic patriotism, found bewildering. Despite a surface geniality his mind was coldly realistic. It could not understand sentimental glamour, and it was firmly bureaucratic. This led to small errors of judgment that had large result, as when he scoffed at the emotionality inspired by barefoot soldiers, saying that they had doubtless traded their shoes for whiskey. He did not perceive how certain it was that a storm was going to break upon him as a result of Davis's rashness and his own lack of insight.

It broke in the midsummer of 1862 when Edward A. Pollard [*q.v.*] published *The First Year of the War*. This was a stinging attack upon the administration, especially the War Office. Pollard furiously denounced the elevation of Benjamin to secretary of state as an "ungracious and reckless defiance of popular sentiment." Powerful newspaper connections were behind Pollard, and from this time forward Benjamin's situation leads Prof. Dodd to speak of him as "the hated Jew" whom Davis kept in office despite the thousand and one protests of the Southern people. This unpopularity made no impression upon Benjamin's exterior. He was always the same calm, amused, smiling person whose equanimity in the dark days of the latter part of the war gave offense to many ardent natures. He was the very opposite of the over-strained and over-sensitive Davis, and seems to have been the chief mainstay, among men, of his afflicted chief.

There can be little doubt that no other Southern leader saw the problems of the desperate Confederate government with the same objectivity, the same relentless detachment, that Benjamin did. Probably he was the first to face the fact that the war could not be won on the basis on which it had been commenced. The vision of pure state rights together with the patriarchal system of slaveholding would have to go. Doubtless, he did not care if it did. State rights had not for him the sanctity they had for the born Southerner. They were mechanism only. Slavery, too, was for him a mere social device that was being made over by the crisis through which the South was passing. It is scarcely fanciful to suspect that the crisis was bringing out in him the Latin element assimilated in his youth and stripping him of certain Anglo-Saxon views acquired in middle life. At any rate, it was still early in the war that the idea of using the negro as a weapon, and at the same time facing toward a new relation of the black and white races in the South, found a place in his thoughts. It was first expressed in connection with the imperative problem of the reinforcement of the armies. That Benjamin was adroitly feeling the pulse of the hour may be inferred from his letters, such as one written late in 1864 (*Official Records,* ser. IV, vol. III, p. 959) urging the enrolment of slaves as soldiers, advising a campaign of education in the newspapers, and adding to all this a startling new suggestion. Very delicately he intimated that a dictatorship on the Roman model might be the Confederacy's only salvation. There can be no doubt that he had Davis in mind.

During the winter of 1864–65 Benjamin kept himself in the background. His plan for arming the slaves was on every tongue. It aroused widespread terror. The President, at first, held off from committing himself and then rather suddenly and quite unwisely became an advocate. Despite the natural prejudice of the slaveholding community against such a measure, the peril of the Southern armies compelled its serious consideration. Bills were introduced into Congress providing in one way or another for black soldiers. At last Benjamin decided that it was time for him to come to the front. On Feb. 9, 1865, he made a public address, destined to be his last. His purpose was to fill his audience with a sense of the desperate situation of Lee's army (Benjamin to Lee, *Official Records,* ser. I, vol. XLVI, pt. 2, p. 1229), and after this impressive picture to pass triumphantly to the conclusion that the only way to relieve the situation was to enrol as soldiers those slaves "who might volunteer to fight for their freedom."

But even then, ignoring the desperation of the hour, a movement was forming to resist at all cost the proposal to enrol black soldiers. Benjamin's phraseology in his last speech drew the lines sharp. He assumed that emancipation would follow military service. That was the crux. The bills in Congress while they permitted black enrolment held out no promise of emancipation. A variety of reasons lay back of this attitude, ranging all the way from questions purely constitutional to the blunt exclamation of Senator Hunter, "If we didn't go to war to save our slaves what did we go to war for?" The constitutional enemies of black enrolment and the uncompromising devotees of slavery now drew together in a party of opposition that fixed upon Benjamin as its chief enemy. At this critical moment he was unable to restrain his tongue. There was quick reaction in both houses of Congress. On Feb. 13, 1865, the Senate divided evenly on a resolution declaring that "J. P. Benjamin is not a wise and prudent Secretary of State, and has not the confidence of the country" (*Journals,* IV, 550, 552, 553); on the fifteenth a third of the House sustained a similar resolution of censure (*Journals,* VII, 582). Though Benjamin enlisted Lee in the cause of enrolment with emancipation, and though Davis and others accepted the idea as inescapable, the only bill which Congress passed was a virtual defeat for Benjamin. It provided for slave soldiers but did not provide for emancipation (*Journals*, VII, 611–12, 729).

Benjamin was now entirely possessed by his idea, and so was Davis. As a last stroke, in January 1865 they sent Duncan F. Kenner [*q.v.*] to London with a proposal to effect general emancipation as the price of British intervention and the raising of the blockade. Kenner was told that he came too late (see J. M. Callahan, *The Diplomatic History of the Southern Confederacy*, 1901).

It is evident that Benjamin had hopes of the Hampton Roads Conference, but what connection he had with it is uncertain. It is also uncertain just what share he had in rejecting the indirect overtures made to the Confederate government through semi-official agents earlier in the winter. Considering his activity for black enrolment and his international policy, it seems fair to conclude that like Davis he continued hopeful almost to the moment when Richmond fell. He probably agreed with Davis in refusing to make concessions.

The tremendous energy of the Northern armies in January and February 1865 shattered all his hopes. He left Richmond in the President's party and was present in the council of the fugitive cabinet, at Greensboro, Apr. 12, when he approved the granting of permission to J. E. Johnston [*q.v.*] to open negotiations with Sherman. Continuing with the President in his flight southward, Benjamin's last official act was his advice given in writing during the short stay of the party at Charlotte where the cabinet discussed the terms of Johnston's surrender. Very characteristic was his cool and resolute acceptance of the accomplished fact. A few days later he left the presidential party and struck off for the coast, thus escaping capture along with Davis when the latter was overtaken by Federal cavalry at Irwinsville.

Benjamin made good his escape, reaching the West Indies and passing thence to England, having decided to attempt a career at the English bar. With this object in view he entered as a student at Lincoln's Inn, Jan. 13, 1866. His circumstances were such as to cause him much uneasiness, for he had lost practically all his fortune. It was customary with all aspirants to the bar to read with some eminent counsel and he had been fortunate in being received into Charles Pollock's chambers, but this fact only increased his financial responsibilities. He was driven to newspaper work in order to eke out his depleted exchequer, and the editor of the London *Daily Telegraph* employed him as a leader writer, particularly on international subjects. Then followed a unique recognition of his standing in the legal world, *viz.*, the action of the Benchers of his Inn of Court in dispensing with the three-year rule and calling him to the bar June 6, 1866, after less than five months as a student. The selection of his circuit became a matter of vital importance. The choice was decided by his Southern affiliations. Liverpool was the market whither the major portion of the pre-war cotton crop of the Southern states had been exported and sold, and its merchants and lawyers were in close touch with the leaders of the shipping industry of New Orleans and New York and presumably aware of Benjamin's high standing in his profession. He accordingly joined the northern circuit which at the time included that town. As anticipated his first retainers were from Liverpool solicitors, but progress was slow, and in the year of his call to the bar he lost the remnant of his private fortune in the failure of his bankers. Meantime he had been engaged on the preparation of a *Treatise on the Law of Sale of Personal Property*, which was published in 1868. This work, ostensibly based upon Blackburn's treatise of an earlier date, was so much wider in scope, and displayed such profound familiarity with the authorities in both English and Civil law that it at once became standard, being accepted "whenever cited, without the usual objection that it was the work of a living author" (*Law Times*, Feb. 17, 1883). From the day of its appearance, retainers poured in upon him. In 1869 he became a "Palatine silk," being made a Queen's Counsel for the County Palatine of Lancaster, and, though for some unexplained reason his name was not included among those who were created Q. C. in January 1872, his argument in Rankin *vs.* Potter (*Law Reports, E. & I. App. Cas.*, VI, 83)—his first reported case in the House of Lords—so impressed the Lord Chancellor, Lord Hatherley, that the latter directed a patent of precedence to be issued to Benjamin, who was thus placed in a position equivalent to that which he would have occupied if the dignity had been actually conferred. Practising in all the courts of common law and equity, in an incredibly short time he established himself as without a superior in appeal cases, and such was the volume of work which came to his chambers that he was at length compelled to confine himself to the court in banc, court of chancery, and appeal courts, declining *nisi prius* retainers. Even then he was unable to accept all the briefs which were proffered him and ultimately he went "special," declining to appear before any court other than the House of Lords or the Judicial Committee of the Privy Council, unless he received a special fee of 100 guineas. Between June 1872 and December 1882, he appeared as counsel in no less than 136 reported cases heard before the two last-named tribunals of last resort—every one of which involved questions of great legal significance or affecting momentous financial interests. He was seen at his best perhaps in Privy Council appeals, whose infinite variety enabled him to exhibit his wide familiarity with different systems of law. His briefs dealt with appeals from such diverse courts as the Supreme Courts of Canada and New Zealand, the High Court of Griqualand West, the Consular Courts of Constantinople and the Court of Appeals of Malta, and involved, *inter alia,* difficult points of French law in Quebec, native African law and custom, Scots law, and the constitutional law applicable to almost every British dependency (see *Law Reports, E. & I. App. Cas.,* vols. VI–VII; *Law Reports, H. L. Scotch Ap.,* vol. II; *Law Reports, App. Cas.,* vols. I–VIII). Among the more important cases involving legal principles in which he was counsel were: Ashbury Railway Carriage and Iron Company *vs.* Riche, deciding that a company created a corporation under the Companies Act of 1862 is not thereby created a corporation with inherent common law rights (*Law Reports, E. & I. App. Cas.,* VII, 653); Debenham *vs.* Mellon, defining the circumstances under which a wife has authority to pledge her husband's credit for necessaries (*Law Reports, App. Cas.,* VI, 24); Lord Advocate *vs.* Lord Lovat, dealing with a salmon fishery on a Scotch river as purtenant to barony land and title (*Law Reports, App. Cas.,* V, 273); Charles Russell *vs.* The Queen, the "local option" case, deciding that the Canada Temperance Act of 1878 was within the legislative competence of the Dominion Parliament (*Law Reports, App. Cas.,* VII, 829). Benjamin also held briefs for the Liquidators of the City of Glasgow Bank throughout the prolonged litigation arising from the collapse of that institution. Perhaps his greatest triumph was achieved in The Queen *vs.* Keyn—the Franconia Case—where, appearing for the defense, he obtained an acquittal on the ground that the British courts had no criminal jurisdiction over a foreigner for acts committed on foreign ships within British territorial waters—two members of the Court of Crown Cases Reserved expressly adopting Benjamin's major contention (*Law Reports, Exchequer Div.,* II, 63). This case and that of Thomas Castro *vs.* The Queen (*Law Reports, App. Cas.,* VI, 229), where he was leading counsel for the Tichborne claimant in the latter's fruitless appeal to the House of Lords against his conviction, were among the few criminal cases with which Benjamin was associated in his English career. His life during these years was divided between Paris, where from even before the Civil War he had maintained a home for his wife and daughter, and London, which during term claimed him for five days in the week. In May 1880, stepping off a moving streetcar in Paris, he was thrown to the ground, his right arm torn from its socket, his shoulder-blade broken, and the left side of his forehead fractured. Contrary to the orders of his physician, upon partial recovery he resumed his practise, but early in 1883 the state of his health compelled him finally to retire. This was the occasion of an unprecedented "collective farewell" which the Bar of England took of him at a public banquet in his honor given in the Inner Temple Hall, June 30, 1883. He died ten months later in Paris.

As a lawyer his preëminence was displayed in many specialized fields. It has been claimed that he was not successful before a jury or in the handling of witnesses, yet the fact remains that a large proportion of his early cases were of this character. Undoubtedly his chief sources of strength, apart from his profound acquaintance with the principles of law, were his capacity for logical analysis and the extraordinary facility with which he expressed his arguments in impressive convincing sequence and form. No superfluous words obscured the clarity of his contentions, his language was choice, his manner was deferential yet confident, and confidence carried with it conviction. He was particularly effective before the Judicial Committee and the House of Lords, where the gravity of the issues and the exceptional intellectual strength of the tribunal appeared to call forth all that was in him of mental endowment and argumentative power.

[The only biography is *Judah P. Benjamin* (1907) by Pierce Butler, good but partisan. There is a useful article in the *Jewish Encyc.,* and one in the *Dict. of Nat. Biog.* Benjamin figures, of course, in all the political literature of the Confederacy, as in Davis, *Rise and Fall of the Confederate Government* (1881), but has had no such consideration as he deserves. The *Cong. Globe* and the *Jour. of the Cong. of the Confederate States* (1904–05) are important as sources; also Jas. D. Richardson, *Messages and Papers of the Confederacy* (1905); *Official Records of the Union and Confederate Armies*; Dunbar Rowland, *Jefferson Davis, Constitutionalist* (10 vols., 1923). See also *Times* (London), Mar. 9, 1884; Chas. Pollock, "Reminiscences of Judah Philip Benjamin," *Fortnightly Rev.,* Mar. 1898; "Judah P. Benjamin: a Bibliography" in *Menorah,* Nov. 1902; Gustavus H. Wald, "Judah P. Benjamin," in *Harvard Grads. Mag.,* June 1928.]

N. W. S.
H. W. H. K.

BENJAMIN, NATHAN (Dec. 14, 1811–Jan. 27, 1855), missionary, the son of Nathan Benjamin, a Revolutionary soldier of distinction, and of Ruth (Seymour) Benjamin, was born in Catskill, N. Y. The father dying when the son was two years of age, the family moved to Williamstown, Mass., which now became their home. Nathan attended the old Academy at Bennington, Vt., but his college preparation was chiefly under Prof. Ebenezer Kellogg of Williams College. He graduated at Williams in 1831, studied theology two years at Auburn, and graduated at Andover in 1834. During the latter year, after a severe struggle at the prospect of sundering home ties, he accepted an appointment as a foreign missionary. After spending one winter in New Haven and another in New York in the study of medicine, and a few months in Vermont as an agent of the American Board of Commissioners for Foreign Missions, he was ordained at Williamstown, Apr. 21, 1836, and sailed at once for Greece. After eighteen months at Argos, he removed to Athens, where he remained till 1845. He was then transferred to the Armenian mission at Trebizond, but eighteen months later returned to America on account of his wife's health. On the improvement of the latter he returned to the Armenian mission and was at Smyrna from 1847 to 1852, when he removed to Constantinople, where he died of typhus fever three years later. He was wonderfully successful as a preaching and teaching missionary. He preached in both Greek and English and exerted a marked influence on educated Greeks through his Bible classes and through personal contact. But his chief work was that of an editor and translator engaged in supplying the country through the mission press with the Bible and evangelical literature in the vernacular. On his return from America he took up the same work for Armenia, acquiring a new language after he was thirty-five. He possessed remarkable executive ability and had large financial and administrative responsibilities in connection with the missions. During his last two years in Athens he was acting American consul, and he founded the *Morning Star*, the first Armenian newspaper. On Apr. 25, 1836, he was married to Mary G. Wheeler of New York City.

[The *Missionary Herald*, May 1855, contains a full account of Benjamin, by Rev. H. G. O. Dwight, a fellow missionary. Another excellent article is found in Hewlitt's *Williams Coll. and Foreign Missions* (1914). The facts of his life in briefer form are given in Calvin Durfee's *Biog. Annals of Williams Coll.* (1871).]

F. T. P.

BENJAMIN, PARK (Aug. 14, 1809–Sept. 12, 1864), editor, poet, was the son of Parke Benjamin, a sea-captain and trader of old New England stock who had extensive interests in Norwich, Conn., and Demerara, British Guiana. His mother, Mary Judith Gall, was a native of Barbados. He was born in Demerara, and remained there until the age of four, when he was sent to Norwich to receive treatment for an affliction which, nevertheless, left him permanently lame, with shrunken limbs. The rest of his life was spent in the United States. His early schooling was received at Colchester, Conn., and Jamaica Plain, Mass. In 1825 he entered Harvard, but two years later, in accordance with his father's wish, he transferred to Washington, now Trinity, College, at Hartford. After his graduation in 1829 he founded the *Norwich Spectator*, which survived but ten issues—the first of a long list of editorial and publishing ventures. In 1830 he entered the Harvard Law School but with characteristic restlessness removed to the Yale Law School in 1832. For a time he lived in Boston, nominally practising law, on friendly terms with the literary set. He had already written much verse. *The Harbinger*, published in 1833 in aid of a charitable fair, was made up of poems which Benjamin, his former Harvard classmate O. W. Holmes, and John O. Sargent had previously contributed to magazines. In 1834 he was employed by Joseph T. Buckingham on the *New England Magazine*, and in 1835 he became editor and owner. At the close of the year the magazine was discontinued and merged with the *American Monthly Magazine* in New York, and Benjamin became associated with Charles Fenno Hoffman in the editorship. After various vicissitudes this periodical came to an end in 1838. For a short period Benjamin was literary editor of Horace Greeley's *New Yorker*. By this time he had come to be known as a caustic literary critic. After a brief connection with the *Evening Tattler*, a one-cent daily, and the *Brother Jonathan*, a literary weekly, he withdrew to found in 1839 journals of his own on the same plan—the *Evening Signal* and the *New World*. R. W. Griswold was at first associated with the *New World*, but Benjamin frequently had difficulties with his colleagues, and Griswold remained for only five issues. The *New World*, the most important and the longest-lived of Park Benjamin's publishing experiments, was one of the fairly profitable but much censured journals which throve by reprinting British writings without remuneration to the authors. Besides the material in the regular numbers Benjamin issued "extras" containing novels and other longer works. Under the lax postal laws these could be mailed at the periodical rate; a revision of the law that conferred this privilege hastened the downfall of the *New World*. Besides British books the extras included a few American writings of no value, the one famous one being Walt Whitman's temperance novel, *Franklin Evans*. In both the editorial conduct and the selling methods of the *New World* and the *Evening Signal*

Benjamin adopted the sensational devices of personal journalism. He was especially noted for his vituperative abuse of rival editors and conspicuous authors, the *Signal* winning a place in the list of papers that were successfully sued for libel by James Fenimore Cooper. After the suspension of the *New World* in 1845 Benjamin planned a number of undertakings, literary and other, some of which were never begun and none of which were of long continuance. One of his many publishing ventures was a literary weekly in Baltimore. An example of his methods of attracting attention is afforded by a special Fourth-of-July issue of the *Constellation*, "The most gigantic paper the world has seen," printed on a single sheet 72 by 100 inches. For some time he conducted a literary agency; and he went on the lyceum platform, sometimes lecturing, more frequently reading didactic and mostly satiric treatises in heroic couplet composed for the purpose. In 1848 he married Mary Brower Western of Dosoris Island, L. I., and spent the remainder of his life rather quietly in New York.

Benjamin wrote much verse, and held a prominent place in earlier American anthologies. His poems are as yet uncollected, and few survive now even as fugitive pieces. His literary criticisms and comments on public affairs are often biting; in estimating them allowance must be made for the slashing editorial manners of the time. An apparent acerbity of temper, which showed itself not only in his writings but in his frequent quarrels with associates, has been ascribed by some to sensitiveness over his physical deformity. It should be remembered, also, that he had warm personal friends. His importance in American literary history comes more from his relationship with others than from the permanent value of anything he wrote.

[A biography prepared by Merle M. Hoover of Columbia University after access to the Benjamin family papers is in manuscript and, through the courtesy of Mr. Hoover, has been available for the preparation of this article.]

W. B. C.

BENJAMIN, PARK (May 11, 1849–Aug. 21, 1922), author, patent lawyer, was born in New York City, the son of Park Benjamin [*q.v.*] and Mary (Western) Benjamin, and brother of George Hillard Benjamin [*q.v.*]. He was graduated from the United States Naval Academy in 1867, and in the same year brought out his first book, *Shakings: Etchings from the Naval Academy*. After several cruises with Admiral Farragut he resigned from the Navy to take up the study of law. He was admitted to the bar in 1870 after a year's study at the Albany Law School. It was as a patent solicitor that he spent most of the time which he devoted to his practise. Due to an unusual knowledge of both technical and legal matters, and to a large store of information on scientific subjects, he was most valuable as an expert witness or technical adviser on matters relating to patents. For many years he served a large and wealthy clientele in this capacity and his testimony as an expert witness is written into many cases involving patent rights and patent infringements. His legal work was done in New York City, but he possessed a summer home in Stamford, Conn. He was thrice married—to Helen Campbell, to Isabel Torrans, and to Ida Crane, his daughter by whom, Dorothy, became the wife of Enrico Caruso. He was associate editor of the *Scientific American*, 1872–78, and took charge of the production of *Appleton's Cyclopædia of Applied Mechanics*, 1881–92, as its editor-in-chief. Many articles from his pen on technical or scientific subjects appeared in the *Scientific American* and other technical publications. During his connection with the *Scientific American* he published his *Wrinkles and Recipes* (1873), compiled from the magazine. This was probably the best seller of all his books. Other works written by him include *The Age of Electricity* (1886); a history of electricity called *The Intellectual Rise in Electricity* (1895); *The United States Naval Academy* (1900); and *The Voltaic Cell* (1893). Until the very time of his death, he was also a frequent contributor to non-technical periodicals, particularly the *Independent*. Scores of articles from his pen, for the most part on subjects pertaining to our own or foreign navies and naval affairs, appeared in this magazine. He believed that the American navy was inadequate and in 1881 launched out into the realm of highly imaginative fiction to help get this idea into public consciousness. His short story, "The End of New York," picturing vividly the destruction of that city as a result of inadequate naval defenses, made a great impression at the time of its publication and is included in Volume V of *Stories by American Authors* published by Scribners in 1884. During the World War the *Independent* still held its columns open to Benjamin's discussions of naval policies. In conjunction with R. M. Thompson and E. J. Berwind, he collected a valuable library of books, particularly on scientific subjects, which he presented to the library of the United States Naval Academy at Annapolis.

[Material for this biographical sketch has been gathered from various sources in the N. Y. Pub. Lib., such as newspaper and magazine files, and verified by Mr. Walter Benjamin, a brother of Park Benjamin, and by contemporaries of Benjamin in the field of patent law, particularly Mr. A. Parker-Smith.]

E. Y.

BENJAMIN, SAMUEL GREENE WHEELER (Feb. 13, 1837–July 19, 1914), author, painter, diplomat, called himself a free-lance. Routine and a fixed abode did in fact make him ill. Accustomed to hardship on land and water, able to face undaunted a winter storm on a mere chip of a boat and to pass untouched through epidemics of typhus and cholera, he broke down completely when immured for a few years (1861–64) as an assistant in the New York State Library at Albany. He had no capacity for self-discipline. Quick, energetic, versatile, romantic, not without conceit, he tried his hand at many things, saw much of men and manners, climates, governments, enjoyed them all hugely, and left behind him a small residue of lasting achievement.

Born at Argos, Greece, the son of an exceptionally able and cultured missionary, Nathan Benjamin [*q.v.*], and of Mary Gladding Wheeler, he passed his first eighteen years in Greece and the Levant, chiefly in Athens, Smyrna, Trebizond, and Constantinople. He reveled in the picturesque, occasionally dangerous, life around him, picked up several languages, attended school in Smyrna and learned Latin from his father, got his lifelong passion for the sea and for sailing ships during a voyage to the United States in the winter of 1847–48, acquired the elements of drawing from various teachers—German, Dutch, Armenian, and Italian, and made sufficient progress in it to send acceptable pictures to the *Illustrated London News* during the Crimean War in 1854. When the elder Benjamin died of typhus, Jan. 27, 1855, the family returned to the United States. Benjamin graduated from Williams College in 1859, taught school for a while, married Clara Stowell of Brookfield, Mass., Oct. 20, 1863, was an assistant librarian in Albany for several years, made a trip to Europe to regain his health, and until 1882 lived in succession in Brookfield, Salem, Boston, and New York. About 1870 he established himself in Boston as a marine painter. In this work he aimed, he says, at boldness and force rather than refinement; his pictures sold at prices ranging from $60 to $600. While an undergraduate at Williams he had begun writing for the magazines; although such tasks irked him he turned out numerous articles, chiefly on art and travel. As an author he was conscientious in gathering his materials but sometimes careless in composition. One book *The Multitudinous Seas* (1879) he wrote in four days; sometimes he would dictate an article while painting. His first book had appeared in 1860: *Constantinople, The Isle of Pearls, and Other Poems.* Other characteristic volumes are: *Ode on the Death of Abraham Lincoln* (1865); *The Turk and the Greek* (1867); *The Choice of Paris: a Romance of the Troad* (1870), which he considered his best book; *Contemporary Art in Europe* (1877); *Art in America* (1879); *The World's Paradises* (1879); *Troy: Its Legend, History, and Literature* (1880); and *The Cruise of the Alice May* (1884). Much of his time was spent at sea; of his forty-five voyages across the Atlantic the majority were made in sailing ships. Even in the roughest weather he was never seasick; he set great store by his use of whiskey and tobacco, and drank water rarely, sometimes not for months. Generally sociable, he was particularly fond of mariners and Turks, and distrusted missionaries. His first wife having died, he married Fannie Nichols Weed in November 1882. He was the first American minister to Persia, 1883–85. He made a wily, pertinacious diplomat, quite capable of taking care of himself and of the missionaries whose tactics furnished the principal subject of his negotiations. The Persians liked him. He drafted the diplomatic code used by the American legation in Persia. On his return to the United States at the close of President Arthur's administration he published *Persia and the Persians* (1886) and *The Story of Persia* (1887), both of which are still useful to English readers. The rest of his life was comparatively uneventful. He made his home first on Staten Island, later in Washington, D. C., and finally in Burlington, Vt.

[The chief source is Benjamin's autobiography *The Life and Adventures of a Free Lance* (1914), posthumously published, badly edited; see also *Who's Who in America*, 1914–15.]

G. H. G.

BENNER, PHILIP (May 19, 1762–July 27, 1832), merchant and ironmaster, was born in Chester County, Pa., the son of Henry and Dinah (Thomas) Benner. His father, an ardent Whig, was imprisoned by the British during the Revolution, and Philip, a youth in his early teens, enlisted as a private under his neighbor and relative, Gen. Anthony Wayne, and served through the war. At the conclusion of the conflict he engaged in the iron business at Coventry in the northern part of Chester County and at the same time conducted a store in Vincent township. Believing that there was a brighter future toward the west he purchased in 1792 the Rock Forge lands on Spring Creek, Centre County, and in the following year commenced his improvements by erecting a house and saw-mill. In 1794 he set up what was probably the first forge in Centre County, in 1799 he erected a slitting-mill, and in 1800 a second forge and a nail-mill. These early enterprises were carried on under great difficulty, for it was necessary to transport from Chester

County not only his workmen but also the provisions to maintain them. From the time of his arrival at Spring Creek, however, until his death forty years later, Benner was the leading iron manufacturer of that region, greatly extending his operations and building up a large fortune. His first iron had been shipped to the East, but impressed with the rising importance of the West, he struck out in a new channel by opening up an iron trade with Pittsburgh. As a result of this he engaged without competition for many years in the transportation of "Juniata iron" to Pittsburgh and the Western country.

Benner was a man of many interests. Not only did he manufacture and transport iron by his own teams, but he maintained stores in Ferguson township and at Bellefonte. Like most wealthy men of the time he speculated heavily in real estate and accumulated a large amount. In 1824 he commenced operating the Logan's Branch Woolen Factory. As the leading shipper of Centre County he was naturally interested in transportation facilities, and among the foremost in the movement for their development. He was the first president (1821) of the Centre and Kishacoquillas Turnpike Company and with two others represented Centre County as commissioner of the Bellefonte, Aaronsburg and Youngstown Turnpike Company, created by a law of Apr. 11, 1825. One of the founders of Bellefonte, he contributed largely to the construction of the waterworks in 1808 and erected a number of the best houses in the village, his own residence being among those still standing (1927). Interested in politics, he established in 1827 the *Centre Democrat* to promote the Jacksonian democracy but he did not personally edit this newspaper, and sold it in 1831 to John Bigler, later governor of California. A man of great industry, alert mind, and indomitable will, Benner represented the type of frontiersman who, already in possession of some capital, moved westward to enlarge his fortune and contribute prominently to the upbuilding of a community. He married Ruth Roberts (1765–1825) by whom he had a large family, eight of the children surviving him. His religious affiliations were with the Quakers.

[John Blair Linn, *Hist. of Centre and Clinton Counties, Pa.* (1883) contains the fullest account. See also Sherman Day, *Hist. Colls. of the State of Pa.* (1843). There is an incomplete file of the *Centre Democrat* in the office of that paper at Bellefonte.]

H. U. F.

BENNET, SANFORD FILLMORE (June 21, 1836–June 11, 1898), physician and song writer, was born in Eden, N. Y., the son of Robert and Sally (Kent) Bennet. The family moved to Lake County, Ill., when the boy was six years old, living first in Plainfield, and three years later moving to a farm near Lake Zurich. His family was distinguished by more than ordinary ability. Two brothers became physicians and the father served as assessor, town trustee, school director, and for eight years as a justice of the peace. Young Bennet, who had been attending district school, was sent to the Academy at Waukegan, Ill., at sixteen, and in two years was teaching school at Wauconda. He entered the University of Michigan in 1858 but left before graduation to take charge of the public schools at Richmond, Ill. Two years later he was married to Gertrude Crosby Johonnatt and they moved to Elkhorn, Wis., where he became joint owner and editor with Frank Leland of the *Elkhorn Independent.* But toward the end of the Civil War he sold his interest to serve a three months' term as second lieutenant in the 40th Regiment of Infantry, Wisconsin Volunteers (May 25–Sept. 16, 1864). Returning to Elkhorn he opened a drug-store and took up the study of medicine. It was during this period that the verses which he had been writing in a desultory fashion most of his life began to acquire a vogue. Most of them were set to music, and "The Sweet By and By," his most popular hymn, for which J. P. Webster wrote the music, has been translated into many languages, including Chinese. In 1871, with Webster, who was a gifted musician, he published *The Signet Ring,* an anthology of hymns, of which the 100 or more from his own pen formed a substantial portion. At thirty-eight he received a degree from Rush Medical College in Chicago and moved to Richmond, Ill., where he established a flourishing practise. He was a frequent contributor to the *Richmond Gazette,* and for a time was one of its editors and publishers. In the year of his death he published *The Pioneer, an Idyll of the Middle West,* which tells of frontier experiences during the thirties and forties, especially in Lake and McHenry counties, Ill.

[H. A. Kelly and W. L. Burrage, *Am. Medic. Biogs.* 1920; *Wis. Hist. Soc., Newspaper Cat.,* 1911; *Wis. State Jour.* (Madison), June 14, 1898.]

M. A. K.

BENNETT, CALEB PREW (Nov. 11, 1758–May 9, 1836), Revolutionary soldier, governor of Delaware, was born in Kennett township, Chester County, Pa. His father was Joseph Bennett, a respectable Chester County farmer who came from English stock, and his mother was Elizabeth Prew Wiley, a widow, who was the daughter of Caleb Prew, for whom the son was named. When young Caleb was three years of age, the father moved to Wilmington and engaged in sailing vessels to and from the Bahamas. The education of the son was limited, as at fifteen years of age, at the breaking out of the Revolutionary War, he enlisted as a private. Near the close of his life he wrote an interesting account of the Delaware Regiment, in which he served. Presumably owing to his youth, he reached the rank of first lieutenant only. He was at Brandywine and at Germantown and rendered heroic service in the disastrous Southern campaign in the 1780's under Generals Greene and Gates when the Delaware Regiment was so badly cut to pieces and lost so many of its officers that Bennett was next in rank to the commanding officer, at the close of the battle of the Cowpens. The story of the war, "all of which he saw and part of which he was" is modestly told, but is convincing of the fact that, youth as he was, he served with bravery and efficiency. At the surrender at Yorktown, he was in command of one of the batteries, and in close touch with Washington.

At the close of the struggle the Delaware Regiment was disbanded and Bennett was honorably discharged and resumed his residence in the city of Wilmington, Del. He was then but twenty-three years of age. For some years he conducted the public ferry that crossed the Christiana River, in that city, on the Kings Road, leading from Philadelphia to New Castle, and engaged with his father in the shipping trade. On Apr. 5, 1792, he was married at Tinicum Island, near Philadelphia, to Catherine Britton, daughter of Richard Britton of Delaware County, Pa. Taking his bride to Wilmington he continued to reside there, for ten years or more, and then moved to New Castle, Del., and for a time was an inn-keeper at that place. He was an active member of the Delaware Society of the Cincinnati. In 1813 he was appointed major of artillery in the Delaware militia and during the War of 1812 was in command of the port of New Castle. In 1807 he was elected, by the Levy Court, treasurer of New Castle County, Del., and by successive elections, from year to year, continued in that office for a period of twenty-six years. In the state campaign of 1832, he was the nominee of the Jackson Democrats for the office of governor. His opponent was Arnold Naudain. Bennett received a total vote of 4,220, Naudain a total of 4,166—giving a majority of 54 votes to Bennett. The latter was the first Democrat elected governor of the state. His administration started under happy auspices. His inaugural address showed his loyalty to Andrew Jackson, emphatically announcing unflinching adherence to the Union and the Constitution and strongly condemning the nullification doctrine at that time rife in South Carolina. Unfortunately his administration was of short duration. He was inaugurated governor on Jan. 15, 1833, and died at his home in Wilmington on May 9, 1836. He was interred in the graveyard adjoining the Friends Meeting House at the corner of Fourth and West Sts., in Wilmington.

[Records of births, marriages, and deaths, from the family Bible of Caleb P. Bennett, in possession of the Pub. Archives Commission of Del. For Bennett's "Brief Account of the Del. Regiment in the Revolution," see *Pa. Mag. of Hist. and Biog.*, vol. IX, no. IV (1885).]

H. C. C.

BENNETT, CHARLES EDWIN (Apr. 6, 1858–May 2, 1921), classical scholar, was born at Providence, R. I., the son of James and Lucia (Dyer) Bennett. He was graduated from Brown University in 1878, after which he taught for a year in a school at Milton, Fla., and for two years at Sing Sing, N. Y. He then studied for a year (1881–82) at Harvard University and for two years in Germany (Leipzig, 1882–83; Berlin, 1883–84; Heidelberg, 1884). He was principal of the preparatory department of the University of Nebraska for five years, after which he was professor of Latin in the University of Wisconsin (1889–91) and professor of classical philology at Brown University (1891–92) before his election, in 1892, to the professorship of Latin in Cornell University, which he held to the end of his life. He married, June 29, 1886, Margaret Gale Hitchcock, of Lincoln, Nebr. He was president of the American Philological Association, 1907–8, and was a member of the American Philosophical Society. From 1892 until his death he was editor of the *Cornell Studies in Classical Philology* and from 1895 to 1905 of the *College Latin Series* published by Allyn and Bacon. In addition to a very considerable number of articles in periodicals his published writings comprise: *A Latin Grammar* (1895, with many later editions), *Appendix to Bennett's Latin Grammar* (1895), *A Latin Composition* (1896), *The Foundations of Latin* (1898), *The Quantitative Reading of Latin Poetry* (1899), *The Teaching of Latin and Greek in Secondary Schools* (1900, with George P. Bristol), *Latin Lessons* (1901), *Preparatory Latin Writer* (1905), *The Latin Language* (1907), *First Year Latin* (1909), *Syntax of Early Latin* (vol. I, 1910, vol. II, 1914), and *New Latin Composition* (1912), besides annotated editions of *Cæsar's Gallic War,* books I–IV (1903), *Cicero, Selected Orations* (1904), *Virgil, Æneid,* books I–IV (1905), and also translations of *The Characters of Theophrastus* (1902, with William A. Hammond), *Horace, Odes and Epodes* (1914, Loeb Classical Library), and *Frontinus, The Stratagems and the Aqueducts of Rome* (1925, Loeb Classical Library). Most of these books are text-books for the use of pupils in secondary schools, but Bennett's scholarship was such that even in text-books he embodied the results of original thought and research, making those books of value to professional scholars, as well as to teachers and pupils. His contributions to knowledge in the fields of Latin syntax (chiefly in his *Syntax of Early Latin*) and metric (chiefly in articles) gained him an international reputation among scholars, his text-books made him favorably known to great numbers of his countrymen, and men of letters honor him for his translations. He was one of the outstanding classical scholars of his time.

There was nothing spectacular in Bennett's quiet and studious career. He was primarily interested in enlarging human knowledge concerning the Latin language and literature, but he was also of marked ability as a teacher, especially of mature and competent students. His standards were high and exacting. He had a quick and versatile mind and was an entertaining talker, greatly interested in the arts, especially in ecclesiastical architecture, as well as in music, literature, and the culture of flowers. He was also an enthusiastic fisherman. He had in him a strong mystic vein, a reverent and religious spirit. During the great war he was active in relief work and was chairman of the Belgian Relief Committee of Tompkins County. His death was caused by heart failure and came suddenly, almost without warning.

[*Who's Who in America,* 1920–21; obituaries in the *Ithaca Jour.-News,* May 2, 1921, the *Cornell Daily Sun* and the *N. Y. Times,* May 3, 1921, the *Am. Jour. of Philol.,* XLIII, 189, *Classical Philol.,* XVII, 279, *Classical Jour.,* XVIII, 23, and the *Circuit,* the advertising medium of Allyn & Bacon, Aug., Sept. 1926.]

H. N. F.

BENNETT, DE ROBIGNE MORTIMER (Dec. 23, 1818–Dec. 6, 1882), freethinker, was born on a farm on the east shore of Otsego Lake in New York. As a boy of fourteen, while returning from a visit to an uncle in the Berkshires, he fell in with two members of the Shaker society at New Lebanon, N. Y., and after enjoying their kindness and good victuals for almost two weeks confessed such sins as he had on hand, was received into the sect, and wrote to his Methodist mother and sister to come and join him. At New Lebanon he worked in the seed gardens, learned the primitive pharmacy of roots, barks, and herbs, and rose to be the physician of the community; but on Sept. 12, 1846, together with his sister and several others, he left the Shakers and on Oct. 12 of that year married Mary Wicks, who had also been one of the seceders. For the next twenty-seven years he lived in various places, usually as nurseryman, druggist, or both, prospering at times but in the end coming invariably to grief. In Cincinnati, for several years, he made as much as $10,000 annually as purveyor of "Dr. Bennett's Quick Cure, Golden Liniment, Worm Lozenges, and Root and Plant Pills." Meanwhile he had absorbed Paine's *Age of Reason,* had been converted to freethinking, and was nursing an ambition to write. Finally, at Paris, Ill., on Sept. 1, 1873, he launched his periodical, the *Truthseeker,* sending 12,000 copies broadcast over the country. In December he moved to New York, taking his new enterprise with him. The *Truthseeker,* devoted to a kind of inverted Fundamentalism, was written in a plebeian style, copious and clear, never elegant, and not always correct. At first it led a hand-to-mouth existence, but ultimately as the organ of village infidels scattered far and wide it enjoyed a mild efflorescence. Bennett thriftily republished much of the contents of the paper in the form of tracts and books and also dealt in freethinking and liberal publications of all kinds. At best his propaganda would have been galling to the orthodox, but the jocose indecorum and irony that he permitted himself in discussing the delinquencies of clergymen and the less edifying portions of the Biblical narrative proved unbearable, and Anthony Comstock undertook to dispose of him. The first two attempts failed, the cases not even coming to trial, but on June 5, 1879, before a judge friendly to Comstock, Bennett was convicted of sending indecent matter through the mails and was sentenced to serve thirteen months in the penitentiary and to pay a fine of $300. (The "indecent matter" was E. H. Heywood's pamphlet, *Cupid's Yokes.*) All efforts to get him off, including a petition to President Hayes, were unavailing, and Bennett, now over sixty years old, was sent to prison. On his release, Apr. 29, 1880, his friends gave him a reception in New York and sent him to Brussels as a delegate to a congress of freethinkers, but his health had been undermined. On July 30, 1881, he started from New York on a trip around the world and reached home on that day a year later. On Dec. 6, after a short illness, he died. He was an amalgam of quack, crank, and idealist. The quack and crank are somewhat excused by the hard conditions of his early life; the idealist, in spite of faults of taste and mistakes of judgment, was for almost a decade an effective popular spokesman for liberal ideas in religion and ethics.

[All accounts of Bennett derive from the autobiographical sketch in *The World's Sages, Infidels and Thinkers* (1876), which should be supplemented by the material in *A Truth Seeker Around the World* (4 vols., 1882) and by the files of the *Truthseeker.* See also S. P.

Putnam, *400 Years of Freethought* (1894) and Heywood Broun and Margaret Leech, *Anthony Comstock, Roundsman of the Lord* (1927).]

G. H. G.

BENNETT, EDMUND HATCH (Apr. 6, 1824–Jan. 2, 1898), jurist, legal writer, the son of Adaline (Hatch) Bennett and of Miles Lyman Bennett of Sharon, Conn., a judge of the supreme court of Vermont for a number of years, was born at Manchester, Bennington County, Vt. He received his early education at Manchester and Burlington Academies, proceeding thence to the University of Vermont where he graduated in 1843. After teaching for a time at a private school in Virginia, he returned to Vermont and commenced the study of law in his father's office at Burlington. He was admitted to the Vermont bar in 1847, but shortly afterward moved to Massachusetts and was admitted to the Suffolk County bar, July 3, 1848. He commenced practise at Taunton, and took an active part in the public life of the community. Politically he was an adherent of the Whig party. In May 1858 he was appointed judge of probate and insolvency for Bristol County and he continued to hold this office for twenty-five years. In 1864 when Taunton was incorporated as a city he was unanimously elected its first mayor, taking office Jan. 2, 1865, and being reëlected in 1866 and 1867. In 1870, 1871, and 1872 he lectured at the Dane School of Law at Harvard. In the latter year he was offered the position of dean of the Law School which had been established in connection with Boston University, but was unable to accept, joining the faculty, however, as a lecturer. In 1876 the offer was renewed and this time was accepted. Bennett now opened a branch law office in Boston. Developing great powers of organization, he administered the Boston Law School in a remarkably successful manner. As a lecturer he developed unsuspected strength. Some of his colleagues surpassed him in erudition and knowledge of the science of law, but his great command of language and ability to impart his knowledge to others combined with an innate courtesy to make him an effective teacher and source of inspiration to students. In 1883 he resigned from the judiciary. In 1891 he was appointed chairman of the Board of Commissioners for the Promotion of Uniformity of Legislation in the United States, and in 1896 he became chairman of the state commission on revision of the public statutes.

Throughout his life he was an incessant writer and the list of his published works amounts to over one hundred volumes. He prepared a *Selection of Leading Cases in Criminal Law* (vol. I, 1856) in conjunction with F. F. Heard; *Massachusetts Digest, 1804–57* (1862), with F. F. Heard; *Massachusetts Digest, 1857–69* (1872), with H. W. Holland; *Fire Insurance Cases, being a Collection of All Reported Cases in England, Ireland, Scotland and America to Date* (1872–77); *Farm Law* (1880), a lecture on the legal rights of farmers; and *Massachusetts Digest, 1869–79* (1881), with R. Grey and H. W. Swift. He also edited many of Joseph Story's works. He was associated with the *American Law Register* of Philadelphia, and contributed a large number of articles to law periodicals. He had great literary ability, but little that he wrote was destined to be of any permanent value. He never concentrated his efforts, his labors were dissipated over an extent of subject-matter prohibitive of other than superficial results, and he will be remembered as a teacher, when his books are forgotten. He was married to Sally, daughter of Samuel L. Crocker of Taunton. His second son, Samuel C., succeeded him as dean of the Boston Law School.

[An excellent detailed review of his career will be found in *The Judiciary and the Bar of New Eng.* (1900), by Conrad Reno, I, 9. An appreciative sketch appeared in the *New Eng. Mag.*, IV, 225. See also *Green Bag*, I, 62; and *Hist. of Taunton, Mass.* (1893), by S. H. Emery.]

H. W. H. K.

BENNETT, EMERSON (Mar. 16, 1822–May 11, 1905), poet, novelist, who produced more than fifty novels and serials and some hundreds of short stories, was born at Monson, Mass., and was educated in the district schools and Monson Academy. At seventeen he set out to see the world, and was soon drawn to New York, where he began his literary career in 1840. He was still in that city as late as October 1842 and about this time published there his first book, *The Brigand*, which was justly ridiculed as a "little 'poeticle pamphlick'" (*Knickerbocker*, December 1842). In 1843 he was in Philadelphia, and his first brief novel, *The Unknown Countess*, was written in competition for a prize offered by a newspaper there; but he soon continued his migration westward, this time by way of Baltimore and Pittsburgh to Cincinnati, where he arrived in the spring of 1844. Soon he was busy contributing to newspapers and magazines, and in 1846 conducted a quarto weekly, the *Casket*. In the same year he made substantial contributions to all of the four issues of the *Quarterly Journal and Review*, whose editor described him as a writer of power, and commended his poems for their purity, but warned him that in his prose he made his readers too familiar with desperate characters. In 1847 he married Eliza G. Daly of Philadelphia.

He seems to have remained at Cincinnati as late as September 1850; in December of that year, however, he was back at Monson, Mass., and soon afterward he must have established himself at Philadelphia, where he spent the apparently uneventful remainder of his life. During the early fifties the Jameses at Cincinnati and T. B. Peterson at Philadelphia were kept busy publishing his novels. Some of them, before appearing in book form, were printed as serials in the *Saturday Evening Post,* and were reputed to have swelled the circulation of that periodical; but perhaps the best proof of popular success was the announcement by Robert Bonner in 1856 (*New York Ledger,* Sept. 6) that Bennett was now engaged to write exclusively for his paper, which then claimed the largest circulation in America. Here the romancer appeared in the congenial company of such writers as Sylvanus Cobb and Mary Gibson. For years Bennett continued to produce a great quantity of fiction; but he lived to be an old man, and eventually found himself forgotten by the reading public. In 1901 he entered the Masonic Home in Philadelphia, where he died after a long illness (*Telegraph,* Philadelphia, May 12, and *Press,* Philadelphia, May 13, 1905).

The evolution of Bennett as a writer of fiction seems comparatively simple. *The League of the Miami,* published in its first form in 1845 (*The League of the Miami,* n. d., preface of 1850 and p. 116), though still, like *The Brigand* and *The Unknown Countess,* concerned with intrigue for the possession of an inheritance—a theme which long remained attractive to Bennett—and employing too the device of concealed identity, is unlike the earlier poem and novel in its western setting, which from this time was so commonly used by Bennett that he came to be known almost entirely as a romancer of frontier life. *The Bandits of the Osage* (1847) and *Mike Fink* (1848) are quite in the style of *The League of the Miami,* but carry the reader still farther westward. *The Prairie Flower* (first published in 1849) and its sequel, *Leni Leoti,* perhaps the two most popular novels of Bennett to be printed in book form —no less than 100,000 copies of each are said to have been sold—exemplified a third stage: adventures among the Indians were now his staple materials. Henceforth, though a few of his novels, like *Ellen Norbury* and *The Orphan's Trials,* deal with city life and social problems, possibly under the influence of Dickens, Bennett generally combined the tradition of Cooper, who was just at this time ending his career, with the artless tradition of the tale of Indian captivity, known throughout America since the time of Mary Rowlandson. He dealt with the pioneer Virginia of Nathaniel Bacon's day, and he followed the changing frontier thence westward step by step to the Pacific. He sent his characters to Oregon and to California and into Texas when men were eager to hear of those places. But in spite of his professed devotion to realism and to history, his appeal was undoubtedly due chiefly to his inexhaustible flow of crude, melodramatic incident and to his frankly sentimental plots and obvious moralizing. The flimsy fictions which he wrote had not the vitality to keep them alive to the end of the author's lifetime. But they were a landmark in that era in which the dime novel was the dominant sub-literary type.

[The best available accounts are those in W. H. Venable's *Beginnings of Literary Culture in the Ohio Valley* (1891); *Who's Who in America,* 1903–05; and Bennett's *Villeta Linden* (1874). All these are based, partly at least, upon information derived directly from Bennett himself. The most important sources are the newspapers and magazines of Bennett's own day and the prefaces of his books.]

R. L. R.

BENNETT, FLOYD (Oct. 25, 1890–Apr. 25, 1928), aviator, was born near Warrensburg, N. Y., the son of Wallace and Henrietta Bennett. Quitting school at seventeen, he worked for a year in a lumber camp and then took a course in automobile engineering at Schenectady. He found employment in the People's Garage at Ticonderoga and out of his earnings bought a half interest in the business. In the war year of 1917 he grew restless, sold his share in the garage, and after some months of indecision enlisted for aviation duty in the Navy. While in the service he was married in February 1918 to Cora Lillian Orkins of Ticonderoga. In 1925, during his second enlistment, he was among the men assigned to Richard Evelyn Byrd on the Donald B. MacMillan expedition to northwestern Greenland. "It was in this group," Byrd wrote, "that I discovered Floyd Bennett. . . . Up to the time of the Greenland expedition he had been an obscure aviation mechanic aboard a man-of-war, not even specially well known on his ship. Once he had his chance, he showed that he was a good pilot and one of the finest practical men in the Navy for handling an airplane's temperamental mechanisms, and above that a real man, fearless and true —one in a million." Almost immediately Bennett became his commander's trusted friend and adviser. Together they made a series of remarkable flights, from Etah over Ellesmere Island. Once during a flight the oil in the tank heated up and threatened to kill them both by exploding, but Bennett crawled out on the wing of the plane in the Arctic gale and unscrewed the cap on the tank, thereby relieving the pressure. When their ship turned southward at the end of August, the two discussed the possibility of a flight to the North Pole. Next summer they realized their plan. On May 9, 1926, with Bennett as pilot and Byrd as navigator, the three-engine Fokker monoplane, *Josephine Ford,* flew 1,360 miles from King's Bay, Spitzbergen, to the Pole and back in fifteen and one-half hours. Bennett also took a leading part in the incredibly difficult and hazardous preliminary work of landing the plane from the ship at King's Bay and of building a suitable runway for the take-off. For his share in the achievement he received the Congressional Medal of Honor and a gold medal from the National Geographic Society and was promoted by an act of Congress, Jan. 5, 1927, to warrant machinist. Under the auspices of the United States Department of Commerce and the Guggenheim Foundation he took the *Josephine Ford* on a tour of forty-four cities without missing a single engagement. Byrd and Bennett had begun to plan a trans-Atlantic flight the very hour they hoisted anchor at Spitzbergen. Bennett was to be the pilot. Their plane, the *America,* was of the same type as their previous one, but larger and equipped with some new devices, including a switch designed by Bennett for cutting out all three engines simultaneously. On her first flight, over Hasbrouck Heights, N. J., Apr. 20, 1927, the *America* proved nose-heavy and crashed on landing. Bennett's switch probably saved Fokker, Byrd, Noville, and Bennett from the fate that a short time before had befallen René Fonck's two men. Bennett, with a thigh, a shoulder, and a rib broken, was near death for a week and was unable to participate in the trans-Atlantic flight, but Byrd saw to it that the public realized how much Bennett had done to make the exploit possible. Bennett's pride in his chief and devotion to him were matched by Byrd's admiration and affection for Bennett. Second-in-command of Byrd's expedition to the South Pole, Bennett was in charge of all details relating to transportation when death cut short his career. In April 1928 a newspaper syndicate engaged him and Bernt Balchen to fly a plane from Detroit to Greenly Island, in the Strait of Belle Isle, where Köhl, von Hühnefeld, and Fitzmaurice had landed from their flight from Ireland. Bennett and Balchen left Detroit Apr. 20, both men suffering from heavy colds. When they reached Lake Ste. Agnes, Bennett was too ill to proceed and was rushed to the Jeffrey Hale Hospital at Quebec. His wife and his friend were with him when he died. Mourned everywhere in America, he was buried in the Arlington National Cemetery. He was regarded by experts as one of the most skilful, courageous, and intelligent of American air pilots, and his sterling personal qualities made him a popular hero.

[R. E. Byrd, *Skyward* (1928); Navy Records; newspapers—see *N. Y. Times Index.*]

G. H. G.

BENNETT, JAMES GORDON (1795–June 1, 1872), editor, was born in Keith, Banffshire, Scotland. The year of his birth is frequently misstated; the name-plate placed on his coffin by his family gave it as 1795, but the month was unknown. Bennett himself declared that his paternal line was traceable to the Norman invasion, and was identified with the family of the Earls of Tankerville. He was named after the Rev. James Gordon, pastor of a church at Strathbogie (Pray, *post,* p. 31). His family being Catholic, after attending school at Keith he was sent to a Catholic seminary at Aberdeen for several years to be trained for the priesthood. From his own statements late in life it may be inferred that as a youth he was not devotionally inclined, but was warmly interested in literature. Among the books which impressed his boyish imagination were Byron's poems, Franklin's autobiography, and the Waverley novels, then just appearing. *Rob Roy* led him to visit Glasgow, and he declared long after that "I remember to this hour every nook and corner of that enchanting place so beautifully described by Walter Scott" (*Ibid.,* p. 33). In the spring of 1819, upon a sudden impulse, he left Aberdeen and emigrated to Halifax, Nova Scotia, where he earned his living by teaching. He shortly made his way to Portland, Me., and thence to Boston. Without friends, money, or work, he suffered for food, and was at one time rescued from two days of starvation by finding a shilling on the ground.

His first important employment was solicited of Henry W. Dutton, foreman of the publishing office of Wells & Lillie in Boston; Bennett stated that he was not a printer, but wished to be about the office to enjoy its facilities for mental improvement (*Boston Transcript,* June 3, 1872). He was given a position as copyholder, and by his diligence soon won promotion to a clerkship in the firm's bookstore in Court St. He was a constant attendant at the sermons of the best Boston ministers and missed no opportunity for self-improvement. In 1822 he went to New York, and made a slender living by writing for the press (Pray, *post,* p. 46). The following year A. S. Willington, proprietor of the Charleston (S. C.) *Courier* was attracted by him and took him to Charleston for miscellaneous work, including translating from Spanish-American newspapers. Here he saw slavery in practise, and formed impressions which always made him sympathetic with the Southern point of view. Returning to New York in October 1823, he advertised the opening of a "permanent commercial school" in Ann St., where he would teach elocution, algebra, geometry, history, political economy, English composition, commercial law, bookkeeping, and other subjects; the school to be conducted "according to the inductive method of instruction" (*Ibid.*, p. 50). Dr. J. S. Bartlett, long editor of an English journal in New York called the *Albion,* was named as reference. This school, however, seems never to have been opened, Bennett lacking the necessary capital. He continued to make a living by desultory newspaper writing, and delivered a course of lectures on political economy in the vestry of the Old Dutch Church.

Little by little Bennett advanced to responsible posts in New York journalism. He was employed for a time in 1825 at a low salary upon a Sunday journal called the *New York Courier,* owned by John Tryon. Bennett purchased this paper upon credit, but failing to make it pay restored it to Tryon. During 1826 he became a regular contributor to Thomas Snowden's *National Advocate* and to the *Mercantile Advertiser.* Here and in the *Courier* he attracted attention by a series of attacks upon speculators and sharpers in the mercantile community, and by his informative reports of the trials of some of them, notably Jacob Barker and Henry Eckford. His exposure of the excesses of the joint-stock fever of the time aroused much resentment. At the same time he affiliated himself with Tammany Hall, and gave support in politics to Martin Van Buren. An opportunity for promotion came when in November 1826 the associate editor of the *New York Enquirer,* W. W. Graham, fell in a duel, and the editor and owner, the eccentric and versatile Mordecai M. Noah, found it necessary to replace him. Bennett was forthwith employed, and spent the years 1827–28 on the staff of that newspaper, partly in New York and partly in Washington.

As Washington correspondent of the *Enquirer,* Bennett soon won a national reputation by a series of articles, modeled in style upon Horace Walpole's letters, in which he pungently and boldly sketched the leading figures in Washington politics and society. Abounding in personalities, they were much attacked but eagerly read. He was assiduous in attending Congressional debates, and by his application to work even injured his eyesight. In New York and Washington he dealt with a multitude of subjects: the tariff, the Federal bankruptcy bill, the Greek rebellion, the theatrical appearances of Macready and Forrest, the French, English, and Italian opera companies, and the new books. With the approach of the presidential election of 1828 he devoted himself to the support of Andrew Jackson's candidacy. His description of the inauguration of Jackson in March 1829 was in a vein of rapturous enthusiasm. On returning from Washington he sought James Watson Webb, the chief proprietor of the *Courier,* and suggested that Webb should purchase the *Enquirer* and make the combined journals the leading Eastern newspaper. This purchase was effected, the first issue of the *Morning Courier and New York Enquirer* appearing May 25, 1829. When Democratic politicians showed doubt of Webb's loyalty, Bennett visited Saratoga Springs and Washington to secure the support of such leaders as Silas Wright, Edwin Crosswell, Jesse Hoyt, and Van Buren. The result was an arrangement by which the *Courier and Enquirer* was made a staunch Jacksonian organ, and Bennett was installed in the fall of 1829 as associate editor. Since Webb was a vain, irascible, unstable man, the shrewd and enterprising Bennett was the paper's real head.

From the autumn of 1829 till the autumn of 1832, three years, Bennett gave the *Courier and Enquirer* vitality as a newspaper and power as a party organ. His report of the famous trial of the Crowninshields at Salem, Mass., for the murder of Capt. Joseph White, added materially to his reputation. Bennett maintained against Attorney-General Percy Morton the right of the press to report the trial without permission of the court, and vindicated his contention that the newspapers are "the living jury of the nation." During 1830 he engaged fiercely in the United States Bank controversy, supporting President Jackson throughout. In April 1831, however, a share was bought in the *Courier and Enquirer* by M. M. Noah, representing United States Bank interests, and Bennett's articles against that institution ceased to appear. He continued to deal with political subjects. At the beginning of 1832 he was responsible for the *Courier and Enquirer's* proposal that Martin Van Buren be nominated for the vice-presidency with Jackson, while he warmly supported William L. Marcy for nomination as governor of New York. During the summer the newspaper carried the names of Jackson, Van Buren, and Marcy at the head of its editorial columns. On Aug. 18, 1832, however, Noah left the firm, Webb assumed full control, and the *Courier and Enquirer* was suddenly made a Whig organ. The result was the immediate resignation of Bennett.

Thirty-seven years old, possessing a little capital and a remarkably varied experience of journalism, Bennett now resolved to set up an independent establishment. On Oct. 29, 1832, he issued the first number of the New York *Globe,* a two-cent morning newspaper which endured for only one month. He then went to Philadelphia, and purchasing a small share in a newspaper called the *Pennsylvanian,* became its editor. Needing a loan of $2,500 to obtain complete control, he applied to his old political associates—Jesse Hoyt, Martin Van Buren, and others—but they closed their purses. The party leaders had marked his growing independence and feared he would prove unreliable. Bennett's bitterness was great; he wrote Hoyt that Van Buren could aid him as easily as he could drink a glass of Saratoga water, and yet treated him as if he were "a boy—a child—cold, heartless, careless, and God knows what." For lack of funds, Bennett retired from the *Pennsylvanian* in December 1833, but he was still undaunted.

Meanwhile there had occurred, in September 1833, the establishment of the penny press of New York City, in the emergence of the astonishingly successful *Sun,* founded by Benjamin H. Day and sold for one cent a copy (Frank M. O'Brien, *The Story of the Sun,* 1918, p. 25). Bennett was impressed by the sudden rise of the *Sun* to a circulation, in the spring of 1834, of 8,000. He applied during the summer of 1834 for a position in association with Day but was refused. Thereupon he began laying plans for a journal of his own. Arranging a business connection with two printers of 34 Ann St., Messrs. Anderson and Smith, he began the publication, May 6, 1835, of the *New York Herald,* a four-page newspaper, four columns to the page, which sold for $3 a year or one cent a copy. His publishing office was in the cellar of 20 Wall St., where a plank across two flour-barrels served as business and editorial desk. Possessing but $500 in capital, and no party support, his poverty compelled him to serve as editor, reporter, proof-reader, folder, and cashier. It was in truth "one poor man in a cellar against the world" (James Parton, *Famous Americans of Recent Times,* 1867, p. 277).

Yet a combination of reasons gave the *Herald* immediate success. Most important of these was the fact that it redeemed Bennett's promise to "give a picture of the world," its local news being comprehensive, piquant, and bold, and covering many neglected subjects. Its editorials were brief, pungent, independent, and lighted up by a vein of Mephistophelian mockery. Bennett disclaimed all political ties, saying that "We shall support no party, be the organ of no faction or coterie, and care nothing for any election or any candidate, from President down to constable. We shall endeavor to record facts on every public and proper subject, stripped of verbiage and coloring, with comments, when suitable, just, independent, fearless, and good tempered." The *Herald's* boldness in laughing at churches, politicians, and pompous public characters, and exposing financial rogues, appealed to all. In its second issue, delayed till May 11, it printed the first money-market report, and three days later ran a table of sales on the Stock Exchange. It printed also the first reports of religious conventions. By rejecting the credit system, and demanding cash, Bennett kept his financial independence. Working fifteen or sixteen hours a day, at the end of three months he made the *Herald* profitable, and was able to engage a cheap police reporter. When the great fire of December 1835 occurred, Bennett again showed his enterprise by giving the city the fullest reports, and published a picture of the burning Exchange and a map of the devastated district.

His labors continued arduous and his career stormy. During 1836 he closed a lucrative advertising contract with Dr. Benjamin Brandreth, the pill-maker; and in the fifteenth month of the *Herald* he felt able to raise its price to two cents. He was then able to boast a circulation of 30,000 to 40,000 daily. His flings at the financial operations of James Watson Webb and Nicholas Biddle aroused Webb's ire, and twice during the year, in January and May, Webb assaulted him in the street. Bennett published full accounts of these affairs, and in reply to editorial attacks declared that he would not be daunted: "I am building up a newspaper establishment that will take the lead of all others that ever appeared in the world in virtue, in morals, in science, in knowledge, in industry, in taste, in power, in influence" (*N. Y. Herald,* Oct. 29, 1836). He was viciously attacked by other journals for the flippancy, impudence, and sensationalism of his columns. His treatment of the murder of Helen Jewett (April 1836) and the trial of Richard P. Robinson for the crime, the *Herald* propounding a theory to show Robinson's possible innocence, even set afloat a story that his columns had been bought. This charge was frequently repeated (see Bennett's editorial, *Herald,* Feb. 25, 1855). Meanwhile, the editor's labors continued incessant. He rose at five, wrote his leading editorials, squibs, and sketches before breakfast, spent the hours from nine to one reading newspapers and editing copy, wrote a column of news, received callers, went to Wall St. and wrote his money article, dined at four, read his proofs, took in cash and advertisements, and went to bed at ten o'clock. But he gradually assembled an adequate staff, and after a few years could give himself more leisure.

On May 1, 1838, he sailed for a combined pleasure and business trip to Europe, and returning to New Mill, Scotland, found his mother and sister alive, but his father and brother dead. Visiting Paris and the principal British cities, he established six European correspondents for the *Herald.* During his five months' absence he wrote a series of letters to the paper. Early the next year he made a tour of the South, perfecting the *Herald's* news and business arrangements. Already he was opposing the renomination of President Van Buren, and during the campaign of 1840 he combated both Van Buren and Gov. W. H. Seward. The year 1840 was marked also by Bennett's marriage in St. Peter's Church in Barclay St. to Henrietta Agnes Crean, a descendant of the Crean Lynch family of Ireland, who had come to America with her family in 1838. She was a linguist and composer of some ability, and Bennett published an editorial of astounding vulgarity upon her virtues. On their return from their wedding trip to Niagara Falls they found that Bennett's enemies had unsuccessfully tried to induce Charles Stetson, manager of the Astor House, to bar his doors against them. During 1840–41 the press campaign against Bennett, partly inspired by the Van Burenites, reached new heights. Park Benjamin [*q.v.*] called him an "obscene foreign vagabond, a pestilential scoundrel, ass, rogue, habitual liar, loathsome and leprous slanderer and libeller" (C. H. Levermore, p. 463).

Yet the *Herald* was increasingly prosperous. In 1841 Bennett, attending Harrison's inauguration in Washington, organized a corps of reporters, at a cost of almost $200 a week, and commenced a fight, ultimately successful, to obtain their entry at will to the galleries of Congress. The newspaper boasted (Oct. 20, 1841) an annual revenue of $130,000; its weekly edition circulated 1,550 copies in Boston, 500 in New Orleans, and 450 in Pittsburgh. The following May it removed to a new building at Fulton and Nassau Sts., with facilities for printing 50,000 to 60,000 copies daily. Bennett's organization was now excellent, his chief lieutenant being Frederic Hudson, whom the elder Bowles called the best newspaper manager in America. In 1843 Bennett and his family made a tour of the British Isles and France. While in Dublin he clashed violently with Daniel O'Connell, who had been given a prejudice against him through some misstatements by the lecturer, James Silk Buckingham; and Bennett set forth the facts in a dignified letter to the London *Times* of Aug. 28, 1843. He returned to London on Oct. 21, announcing that he found himself "fresh, vigorous, renovated." His quarrel with O'Connell now gave fresh intensity to an old feud with Bishop John Hughes of the Catholic Church in New York, whom he accused of meddling with party politics and of hostility toward the public schools. As a result, Bennett treated with great cordiality the new Native American or Know-Nothing party (John Hughes, *A Letter on the Moral Causes That Have Produced the Evil Spirit of the Time,* 1844); but in the presidential election of 1844 he and the *Herald* supported James K. Polk.

For the next twenty years Bennett's life was comparatively uneventful, being identified with the steady rise of the *Herald* to preëminence as a news-gathering sheet. His corps of correspondents, European and American, was unrivaled. He kept a fleet of dispatch boats cruising outside Sandy Hook, at a distance of from 50 to 250 miles, to intercept steamers from Europe and hasten their news to shore (Pray, p. 375). The *Herald* was the first newspaper to make lavish use of the telegraph. On Dec. 26, 1844, it announced an overland express service from New Orleans to carry the Texas news, and upon the outbreak of war in 1846 this service was made weekly or oftener. The New York news of the *Herald* was the fullest to be had; and particularly valuable, as the slavery question grew prominent, was its comprehensive Southern intelligence.

Editorially, the *Herald* was for the most part on the Democratic side. In the campaign of 1848 it supported Gen. Taylor, whom Bennett had proposed for the presidency as early as 1846. Four years later it advocated the election of Franklin Pierce. Already Bennett was charged with being under the influence of Southern leaders. In 1856, however, he surprised his readers by aligning the *Herald* with the new Republican party for John C. Frémont. Four years later, alarmed by the prospect of civil war, and influenced by the sentiment of the commercial community in New York, he supported Douglas against Lincoln. The course which Bennett gave the *Herald* just before the outbreak of the Civil War excited much indignation among patriotic men. He was frankly in favor of letting the seceding states go, and even proposed a reorganization of the Union under the new Southern constitution, with the New England states left out. With the actual firing on Fort Sumter, however, Bennett grasped the demands of public opinion, and began to make the *Herald* a newspaper of acceptable loyalty, though sometimes copperhead in tone. After some hesitation, it gave Lincoln warm support for reëlection in 1864. During the war the *Herald* reached the height of its fame as an enterprising and exhaustive purveyor of the news. Its average week-day circulation in December 1860 was about 77,000; this rose steadily, and of one issue in 1864 more than 132,000 copies were sold. The newspaper employed sixty-three war correspondents in different theatres, and spent a total of $525,000 in gathering war news (Allan Nevins, *The Evening Post: A Century of Journalism,* 1922, pp. 267–83). Its dispatches from the front were rivaled only by those of the *Tribune,* and its European dispatches were unequaled. Lincoln constantly read it, and but for the fact that its editorials maintained what John Bright called "a reckless tone," its repute would have been high.

Bennett spent much time during the late forties and the fifties traveling in Europe, the United States, and the West Indies, and was presented (January 1847) at the court of Louis Philippe. Despite frequent absences, his supervision over the *Herald* was constant until 1867, when he retired; and he not merely directed its policy but wrote steadily for its columns. Its circulation when he resigned it to his son was 90,000 daily; its advertising revenue was surpassed only by that of the London *Times,* and its annual profits approached $400,000. Honors outside journalism had no appeal to him, and in 1864 he refused the offer of appointment as minister to France, made by Lincoln. He lived with increasing luxury, owning a country residence at Washington Heights, with ample grounds, a town house at the corner of Fifth Ave. and Thirty-eighth St., and a yacht which at the outbreak of the Civil War he gave to the Government. Even after he quitted active control of the *Herald* he gave the newspaper much attention. Gradually becoming feebler, on May 25, 1872, he was attacked by a convulsive seizure, with epileptic symptoms. On June 1, after receiving the last sacrament from Archbishop McCloskey, he died. The softening of the old ill-feeling against him was indicated by the list of pall-bearers at the funeral (June 12), which included Horace Greeley, George Jones of the *New York Times,* Charles A. Dana, D. M. Stone, Robert Bonner, and George Childs of the Philadelphia *Public Ledger.* He was buried in Greenwood Cemetery, Brooklyn. It was realized that, with all his errors, he had been perhaps the chief figure in a great and democratic revolution in journalism, a natural and beneficial concomitant of the rise of Jacksonian democracy. In person he was more than six feet tall, broad-shouldered, florid of complexion, with hair at first sandy and later silver, with eyes of grayish blue, and an air of command. His modesty of bearing in private was in strong contrast with the audacious vanity and even vulgarity with which he had been wont to parade his affairs in the *Herald.*

[The fullest source of information upon Bennett's life is the files of the *Herald,* in which he wrote frankly and at times boastfully of his successes, reverses, and ambitions. Isaac Pray's *Memoirs of Jas. Gordon Bennett and His Times, by a Journalist* (1855) contains many inaccuracies which might have been corrected but for the author's resolve not to consult Bennett or any one connected with him. It is, however, the best single volume for the period covered. An illuminating interpretation, with some information, is furnished by C. H. Levermore in "The Rise of Metropolitan Journalism," *Am. Hist. Rev.,* VI, 446–65. There is a chapter upon "The Jas. Gordon Bennetts and Their Newspaper" in Oswald Garrison Villard's *Some Newspapers and Newspapermen* (1923); there is a sketch with some facts not easily available elsewhere in Jas. Melvin Lee, *Hist. of Am. Journalism* (1917), pp. 193–200, and Don C. Seitz has written a somewhat journalistic volume in *The Jas. Gordon Bennetts* (1928). A collection of obituaries appeared in the *N. Y. Herald,* June 2–14, 1872.]

A. N.

BENNETT, JAMES GORDON (May 10, 1841–May 14, 1918), editor, capitalist, was born in New York City, the son of James Gordon Bennett [*q.v.*] and Henrietta Agnes Crean, who two years previous to her marriage had arrived with her family from Ireland. The first of three children, he was born in Chambers St., then a fashionable place of residence. He was educated under the supervision of his mother, chiefly in Europe, to escape the atmosphere of calumny surrounding his father (Isaac Pray, *Memoirs of James Gordon Bennett,* 1855, p. 281); following a course with private tutors, he attended the École Polytechnique in Paris. In 1861 the outbreak of war brought him back to the United States, and to emphasize the loyalty of the Bennett family, he entered the navy, receiving a commission as lieutenant. From this service arose his lifelong interest in nautical affairs, which made the *Herald* long unrivaled in its attention to ship, naval, and military news. With the close of the war Bennett began a thorough training in the more important departments of the *Herald.* On the retirement of Frederic Hudson in 1866 he became managing editor, and the following year, when his father ceased to give the paper constant attention, he became its chief executive officer (*Literary Digest,* June 1, 1918). He combined a busy social life, moving in the faster set of young New York bachelors, with an erratic but energetic attention to the newspaper. Its achievements in reporting the Civil War had lifted the *Herald* to the height of its fame. The younger Bennett was responsible for several news exploits of importance. In 1867 he dispatched Henry M. Stanley, whose reports of Gen. W. S. Hancock's expedition against the Indians had attracted attention, to be *Herald* correspondent with the British army against the Emperor Theodore of Abyssinia. Stanley's success in sending back the first news of the capture of Magdala secured Bennett's special favor, and Bennett gave him a roving commission. In 1869 he met Stanley in Paris, and informed him that he was to go to Africa to search for David Livingstone. An expedition was outfitted from Zanzibar, and the result was a journalistic feat of the first importance, Stanley finding Livingstone at Ujiji on Nov. 10, 1871 (*The Autobiography of Sir Henry Morton Stanley,* 1909). This achievement was set forth in detail in the *Herald.*

Meanwhile, under Bennett's management of the *Herald,* Aloysius MacGahan had made his remarkable reputation as a reporter of the Franco-Prussian War and the Commune. Bennett, always ready to pay lavishly for unusual news, sent him to the Crimea, to Geneva for the sitting of the Alabama Claims Arbitration Commission, and with the Russian expedition of 1873 against Khiva; and MacGahan's heroic exploits in Central Asia were recounted in full in the *Herald* (J. Aloysius MacGahan, *Campaigning on the Oxus,* 1874). In 1875 Bennett, joining hands with Capt. Allen Young and Lady Franklin, financed an expedition in the bark *Pandora* under Capt. Young to search for the Northwest Passage. It was a failure, but MacGahan, who accompanied it, wrote some excellent letters to the *Herald* (MacGahan, *Under the Northern Lights,* 1876). During the panic year 1873–74, Bennett and the *Herald* opened kitchens for the poor in the slum districts of New York, where Delmonico's served soup and other food. The newspaper was at this time active in other charitable enterprises. Its most important benevolence was the Herald Relief Fund for Irish sufferers, established in 1882 at the time of the agrarian outrages. Bennett, always impulsively generous, headed the subscription list with a gift of $100,000 and thus earned the enduring gratitude of Irish-Americans.

In these early years he showed a capacity for gathering about him men of unusual ability. His staff included Charles Nordhoff, who in the early seventies became Washington correspondent, John Habberton, Ivory Chamberlain, John Russell Young, and George W. Hosmer. Unfortunately, Bennett, always eccentric, temperamental, and irascible, developed a jealousy of the men who gained great prominence on the *Herald,* and this led to the departure of Stanley and an open rupture with MacGahan (F. L. Bullard, *Famous War Correspondents,* 1914, p. 140). Bennett early made two ventures in the establishment of fresh journals. In 1867, with his father's support, he founded the *Evening Telegram,* which adopted a light and sensational tone, and for years showed a heavy deficit; at one time, in the fall of 1897, Bennett resolved to discontinue it and published a notice to that effect, but repented and kept it alive. More important was his establishment in 1887 of the Paris edition of the *New York Herald.* Always a warm lover of France, Bennett found that nation misunderstood and disliked in the United States following the Franco-Prussian War. He designed his Paris edition not as a business enterprise but as an institution for fostering friendship between the two nations. It was seldom profitable financially; it was badly edited, presenting little news except scrappy cablegrams and social gossip; but it attained a circulation before the World War of almost 25,000 and as a gesture of amity it was greatly appreciated by the French public.

The year 1877 marked a sharp turning point in Bennett's life, witnessing his virtual expatriation. The cause lay in a scandal which made America repugnant to him. He had become engaged to be married to Edith May, of a prominent Washington family; the engagement was abruptly broken off by the May family under mysterious circumstances; his fiancée's brother, Fred May, attacked Bennett with a horsewhip on Jan. 3, 1877, as the latter was emerging from the Union Club on Fifth Avenue; and a duel followed immediately on the Delaware-Maryland border-line, shots being exchanged harmlessly. The stories circulated about the affair made New York unbearable to Bennett, and he took up his residence abroad. He maintained three homes in America: the old Bennett homestead on Washington Heights, Manhattan, a house at 37 West Forty-seventh St., and a villa at Newport. But except for flying visits he spent his entire time in his Paris home, his shooting lodge at Versailles, his villa at Beaulieu, or on his yacht. His management of the *Herald* and *Telegram* was by cable, and became more explosive, erratic, and domineering than ever.

Under these circumstances he did less and less to maintain the *Herald's* reputation for news enterprise. His last great effort to create "exclusive" news was his expenditure, 1879–81, of large sums in supporting the expedition of George Washington De Long to the Arctic. De Long had proposed this trip as early as 1873. His ship, the *Jeannette,* was caught in the polar pack, crushed, and sunk, and most of the crew, including the commander, perished (George W. Melville, *In the Lena Delta,* 1884). In 1883 Bennett and John W. Mackay established the Commercial Cable Company, which laid a line across the Atlantic and broke the grip of the existing cable monopoly. This undertaking proved very profitable, the association of the *Herald* and the cable company being of mutual benefit, and it supported for some years the *Herald's* reputation for preëminence in foreign news, but in the nineties this was gradually lost. In 1893 Bennett moved the paper from its old home at Broadway and Ann St. to a beautiful new structure at "Herald Square" (Broadway and Sixth Ave.), a stroke which did much to sustain the prestige of the journal.

In his ambition to remain editor of the *Herald* and *Telegram* in fact as well as name, Bennett refused to delegate adequate authority to the home staff. The city editor, who was actually managing editor, had certain powers, but was always subject to unexpected orders. The chief incumbent of this office was William C. Reick, through whom in the Spanish-American War Bennett spent $300,000 for news service. Bennett hired, promoted, demoted, and discharged men with lightning rapidity and frequently without reason. On a sudden whim he once made the first reporter to meet him coming up New York Bay the city editor. He issued eccentric orders with regard to editorial and news policies. These erratic acts did both the morale of the staff and the *Herald's* reputation for reliability great damage. The circulation of the paper was also badly injured in 1884 by a disastrous war with the news-dealers (Don C. Seitz, *Joseph Pulitzer,* 1924, p. 146); while the rise of the *World* under Pulitzer, the reinvigoration of the *Times* under Adolph S. Ochs, and the emergence of "yellow" journalism under William Randolph Hearst, all struck it heavy blows. By 1900 the *Herald* had declined seriously in circulation, revenue, news-enterprise, and prestige. In 1907 Hearst instigated the indictment of Bennett, with his advertising manager and the *Herald* corporation, on the ground that the personal column of advertisements was used for immoral purposes and violated the postal laws. Bennett pleaded guilty and paid fines aggregating $31,000—a humiliating episode. By the outbreak of the World War the newspaper's position was so precarious that only the sudden prosperity of the *Telegram* enabled the joint establishment to pay its way.

Bennett remained a prominent figure in European society and in the world of sports. He had introduced polo to Newport in the seventies, had been an ardent yachtsman from youth, and a leader in coach-driving. In 1870 he sent his yacht *Dauntless* to England and raced her against the British yacht *Cambria* to America, losing by the narrowest of margins. He was for a time commodore of the New York Yacht Club. His steam yacht *Lysistrata,* the largest ever built on the Clyde (1900), carried a crew of 100 men and was long famous. When the automobile was still in process of early development, he offered the James Gordon Bennett cup to be competed for by the best international types. This was followed by the gift of cups for balloon-racing (1906) and aeroplane-racing (1908). One of his ambitions was to stimulate an interest in sports among the French, and for this purpose he offered numerous trophies; it is not too much to say that his name became the most prominent in France of those identified with sports. It has been estimated that during his long ownership of the *Herald* he drew from it and spent $30,000,000.

In every sense Bennett was a man of the world. He entertained lavishly, his circle of friends becoming more and more European as his connections with America grew weaker. His point of view became European rather than American, a fact which injured the *Herald.* He made little effort to escape scandal. Much attention was at one time attracted by a series of unsuccessful suits brought by Mlle. Juliette Schettler, daughter of a French actress, Mlle. Camille Clermont, to prove that he was her father and should support her. Many stories were told during his lifetime of his personal peculiarities—his lavish tips; his intense hatred for a few men, notably Jay Gould and William Randolph Hearst; his love for owls; his fondness for dogs, which made him devote the *Herald* to a long campaign against vivisection; and his strange mixture of canniness and naïveté. He became one of the most picturesque figures of two continents.

Apparently a confirmed bachelor, Bennett used to remark: "I suppose no woman who ever lived could get along with me as wife." But on Sept. 10, 1914, he was married in Paris to the Baroness de Reuter, widow of Baron George de Reuter; at the same time becoming a member of the Protestant Episcopal Church. His wife had been Maud Potter of Philadelphia. During the next four years he was preoccupied with the war. His newspapers, which he now governed through a series of committees, were vigorous partisans of the Allies. At his death, which was caused at Beaulieu by heart disease, he left the greater part of his fortune to found the James Gordon Bennett Memorial Home for New York journalists; a shelter, in memory of his father, for indigent newspaper men who had been connected for at least ten years with some daily published in Manhattan. His estate was found to be much reduced and heavily involved, and the number of annuities provided for various persons prevented the prompt establishment of this home.

[The only volume devoted to Jas. Gordon Bennett, Jr., is Albert Stevens Crockett's *When Jas. Gordon Bennett Was Caliph of Bagdad* (1926), a sketchy book of reminiscences by an associate and employee. A chapter is given to the two Bennetts in Oswald Garrison Villard's *Some Newspapers and Newspapermen* (1923). Reminiscences by James B. Townsend were published in the *N. Y. Times* of May 19, 1918; by "Spillane" in the *N. Y. Evening Mail,* May 14, 1918; and by Arthur H. Warner in the *Evening Post* of July 6, 1918. Six chapters are devoted to him in Don C. Seitz's *The Jas. Gordon Bennetts* (1928).]

A.N.

BENNETT, NATHANIEL (June 27, 1818–Apr. 20, 1886), lawyer, jurist, was born at Clinton, Oneida County, N. Y., and passed his youth on his father's farm. In 1832, having spent two years at Partridge's Military School, Buffalo, he entered Canandaigua Academy, where one of his schoolmates was Stephen A. Douglas, passing from there to Hamilton College, and completing his education at Yale University, where, however, he did not graduate. He then studied law at Buffalo, and having been admitted as an attorney in 1840 and a counsellor in 1843, practised there for eight years, at the same time actively interesting himself in politics. He became an ardent supporter of the "Barnburners" cause, and was a member of the convention at Buffalo in 1848 which nominated Van Buren for the presidency. His health had never been strong, necessitating periodical vacations during which he had sought relief in extensive travel, and on the discovery of gold in California in 1849 he determined to settle on the Pacific Coast. Journeying by way of Panama, he landed in San Francisco June 30, 1849, and proceeded to the mining camps. Locating on the Tuolumne River, he made a lucky strike and in three months had realized a considerable fortune. He thereupon returned to San Francisco in October, and opened a law office in partnership with John Satterlee who subsequently became a judge. California had just adopted a constitution preparatory to admission as a state, and at the ensuing elections Bennett was returned as a senator for San Francisco. The first matter to come before the new legislature was the basic law of the new state, as a strong feeling had been manifested in favor of the Louisiana Civil Code in preference to the English Common Law. A Senate judiciary committee, on which Bennett served, was appointed to investigate, and it reported, Feb. 27, 1850, recommending that the courts be governed in their adjudications by the English Common Law as received and modified in the United States. This report—able and exhaustive—in the preparation of which Bennett exercised a weighty influence, was accepted and acted upon. In the meantime he had been elected by the legislature as associate justice of the new supreme court of California. At the request of his colleagues he assumed the task of reporting the decisions of the court and in 1852 published *Reports of Cases Determined in the Supreme Court of California,* vol. I, embracing all decisions of the court from its organization in March 1850 to the end of June term, 1851. His preface contains an authoritative account of the conditions in California previous to the organization of the state government. He retained his position but a short time, resigning Oct. 3, 1851, and paying an extended visit to the East. On his return to San Francisco in 1853 he resumed practise and acquired an extensive clientele, chiefly associated with "big" business. Affiliating himself with the Republican party, he officiated as chairman of the first Republican state convention at Sacramento, and was nominated in 1857 for judge of the supreme court on the party ticket but met with defeat. Thenceforth he devoted himself to his profession, being for some years prior to his death admittedly the leader of the state bar. He became very prominent in connection with the notorious litigation known as the "Bonanza Suits." In May 1878, action was brought against John W. Mackay, James G. Fair, and others, alleging misappropriation of funds of the Consolidated Virginia Mining Company, and other suits followed involving approximately $36,000,000. He acted as attorney for the plaintiff in some of these actions, which were ultimately compromised on terms which were never divulged. He died in San Francisco, Apr. 20, 1886. Somewhat paradoxically, though "a slow deliberate pertinacious man," he was a brilliant speaker, frequently called upon on great public occasions. As a lawyer he acquired a wide reputation, enjoying the confidence of leading financial and industrial institutions. In a pioneer community his scholarship and general culture were considered remarkable.

[The only adequate biography is in *Hist. of the Bench and Bar of Cal.,* ed. by Oscar T. Shuck (1901), p. 445, which work also describes the genesis of the judicial system of the state. See also *Cal. Supreme Court Reports,* vol. I, preface and notes; files of the *Alta California, San Francisco Chronicle,* and *Evening Bull.*]

H.W.H.K.

BENNING, HENRY LEWIS (Apr. 2, 1814–July 10, 1875), jurist, statesman, soldier, was born on a plantation in Columbia County, Ga., the son of Pleasant Moon and Matilda Meriwether (White) Benning, the third of eleven children. He attended Franklin College (University of Georgia), where he graduated with first honors at the age of twenty. Upon his graduation he moved to Columbus and there made his home for the rest of his life. At twenty-one he was admitted to the bar, and two years later was appointed solicitor-general for his judicial circuit. He afterward served a term in the General Assembly. On Sept. 12, 1839, he married Mary Howard Jones of Columbus, by whom he had ten children, of whom five daughters survived him. His only son died of wounds received in the Civil War. Able, logical, industrious, and of the highest integrity, he had not a few of the qualities of Calhoun. He was convinced that to free the negroes would create such social chaos in the South as to make civilization impossible and life for the whites unendurable. He believed emancipation, and the subsequent enfranchisement of the slaves, inevitable if the South remained in the Union. He therefore became an ardent secessionist. But while he felt secession necessary he considered it by no means the solution of the problem. He feared some of the northernmost slave states might, from economic reasons, develop a sentiment against the institution, and he would protect the lower South from the chaos of emancipation by the formation of a "consolidated" Southern Republic, with strong centralized powers, so that slavery could be put "under the control of those most interested in it" (letter to Howell Cobb, "Toombs, Stephens and Cobb Correspondence," *American Historical Association Annual Report,* 1911, II, 171).

In the crisis of 1850 he was for immediate withdrawal from the Union, and became an enthusiastic supporter of the movement to hold a Southern conference at Nashville. In the election held in Georgia to name delegates to this conference he was successful, but most of the other secessionist candidates were overwhelmingly defeated, and the small number of votes cast showed that the vast majority of the people were not aroused. Indeed, the fact that Georgia, generally regarded as a pivotal state, had thus decisively repudiated the "Southern-rights" movement, foredoomed the convention to failure. But Benning was persistent and resourceful. Ostensibly in an effort at compromise, he introduced at Nashville a resolution to the effect that nothing less than the Missouri line could be accepted by the South as a settlement of the territorial problem. He believed the South could be persuaded to demand this as an ultimatum; that the North would promptly reject it; and that secession would then be the only alternative. The resolution was duly passed, but the result was not what he had hoped it would be. Meeting in December, the Georgia Convention, instead of ratifying the action of Nashville, accepted Clay's compromise measure, "being impelled thereto" (in the language of the resolution) "by an earnest desire to save the American Union." In 1851 Benning accepted the nomination of the Southern-rights Democrats as one of their candidates for Congress and, although he ran ahead of his party, was defeated in the Constitutional Union "landslide" of that year. In 1853 he was elected by the General Assembly as an associate justice of the Georgia supreme court, where he delivered, in the case of Padleford *vs.* Savannah (14 *Georgia,* 438), an exhaustive opinion in support of the principle that a state supreme court is not bound by the decisions of the Supreme Court of the United States on constitutional questions. The two courts he held to be "coördinate and co-equal." This remarkable decision, comprising eighty pages, is perhaps the most vigorous and elaborate exposition of the doctrine of "strict construction" ever set forth in a judicial pronouncement. At the expiration of his term in 1859 the General Assembly failed to reëlect him, largely because of the activities of an influential and disgruntled litigant.

Benning is generally regarded as having acted always with the Southern extremists, but in 1860 he refused to follow Yancey out of the Democratic party upon the disruption of the Charleston Convention; on the contrary he was vice-president of the adjourned convention of the "regulars" which met at Baltimore and nominated Stephen A. Douglas for the presidency. But in 1861 he took an active part in the Georgia Convention which adopted the Ordinance of Secession, and was sent by that body as its commissioner to the Virginia Convention. There he delivered a carefully prepared address on the race problem and secession.

Thomas R. R. Cobb said (*American Historical Association Annual Report,* II, 544) that Benning was seriously considered for a cabinet position in the newly established Confederacy, but he volunteered in the army, and was made colonel of a regiment which he organized in Columbus. His record as a field officer and as brigadier-general was distinguished. His steadfastness in critical situations earned for him the sobriquet "Old Rock." At Sharpsburg his defense of a bridge over Antietam Creek was heroic. At Chickamauga he had two horses shot from under him; cutting a third from an army wagon, he rode bareback into the fight at the head of his brigade. He went through the heavy fighting on Little Round Top at Gettysburg unscathed, but was severely wounded in the Wilderness. At Petersburg, during a fierce Federal assault, his brigade for hours withstood the whole attack alone. Throughout the varying fortunes of war he seems never to have lost hope that the South would win, and when a courier notified him at Appomattox that Gen. Lee was going to offer terms of surrender, it is said that he was heart-broken.

Returning home he found his houses burned, his goods and money vanished, and his dependents increased by the widow and children of his wife's brother, who had fallen in the war, and by his sister's orphans. He resumed the practise of law. On July 8, 1875, having spent the preceding night upon a case in which he was interested, he was stricken with apoplexy on his way to the court, and the next day he died.

[R. H. Shryock, *Ga. and the Union in 1850* (1926); A. R. Lawton, "Judicial Controversies on Appellate Jurisdiction," in *Report of the 38th Ann. Sess. of the Ga. Bar Ass.* (1921); a short biography of Benning by his daughter in *Men of Mark in Ga.*, vol. III (1911). Benning's judicial opinions are to be found in volumes XIV to XXIX, inclusive, of the *Ga. Reports*. See also *Atlanta Constitution*, July 11, 1875.] B.F.

BENSON, EGBERT (June 21, 1746–Aug. 24, 1833), Revolutionary leader, was the son of Robert Benson and Catherine Van Borsum. He was graduated from King's College in 1765, read law in the office of John Morin Scott, and was admitted to the bar in the January term of the New York supreme court, 1769. Commencing the practise of his profession at Red Hook in Dutchess County in 1772, he soon became prominent in that region in promoting activities for the patriot cause, organizing revolutionary proceedings there and in the province generally, and taking a leading part in launching and maintaining the new state government. He was a member of the Provincial Congress, 1776, and of the Council of Safety, 1777–78, attorney-general 1777–87, and a member of the first legislative assembly, elected in 1777, wherein, according to Chancellor Kent, he "drafted much of the legislation passed by that body and was the most confidential and efficient adviser of the elder Clinton." He was active in the political development of the American union, being a delegate to the Congress of the Confederation, 1781–84, and serving on commissions for managing the embarkation of Loyalists for Nova Scotia, for adjusting boundary disputes betwen the states, and for promoting the power of the union government. With Hamilton, he was a delegate from New York to the Annapolis Convention in 1786, and was a zealous advocate of the adoption by his state of the draft from the Philadelphia Convention. As a representative from New York in the first two Congresses under the Constitution, he was a strong and conspicuous supporter of the Administration, being especially identified with Hamilton's measures for the public credit, and with the framing of the fundamental statutes organizing the Executive Department. In 1794 he was appointed a justice of the supreme court of New York, and is described by Chancellor Kent as having in his seven years' tenure of that position done more to reform the practise of that court than was ever done before or since. His service here was terminated in 1801 by the "midnight appointment" from President Adams as chief judge of the second United States circuit court. Owing to the repeal shortly thereafter of the law establishing this court, Benson retired from public life, except for a service of a few months in 1813 as representative from New York in the United States Congress. His reputation for legal learning was second only to that of Hamilton. He received the degree of Doctor of Laws from Union, 1779, from Harvard, 1808, and from Dartmouth, 1811. He was a regent of the University of the State of New York, 1787–1802, and a trustee of Columbia College, 1804–15. He was one of the founders of the New York Historical Society in 1804, and was its first president from 1805 to 1815. He never married. In his later years he lived at Jamaica, N. Y., where he died. He was the author of *Cases and Queries Submitted to Every Citizen of the United States* (1809), *A Vindication of the Captors of Major André* (1817), and *A Memoir on Dutch Names and Places* (published posthumously, 1835).

[Jas. G. Wilson, *Memorial Hist. of N.Y. City* (1892); B. F. Thompson, *Hist. of Long Island, N. Y.* (1918), IV, 249 ff.; *Memoirs and Letters of Jas. Kent* (1898), pp. 20–23.] C.W.S.

BENSON, EUGENE (Nov. 1, 1839–Feb. 28, 1908), painter, was born at Hyde Park, N. Y., the youngest son of Benjamin P. Benson. When he began his study of art he was poor, but increased his small income by contributing to several New York dailies and to various periodicals, signing the name "Proteus" to his articles in the New York *Evening Post*. In 1856 he was studying at the National Academy of Design, at the same time taking up portrait work in the studio of J. H. Wright. He moved to New Haven in 1869 and remained four years, residing near East Rock. In 1873 he went abroad to study in France and Italy. He established a studio in Florence, spent a number of years in Rome, and moved to Venice in 1888, where he continued to live until his death. His paintings were chiefly of story-telling and symbolic subjects, though his portraits were successful. His modeling and color were effective. He exhibited frequently at the Royal Academy in London, and at the National Academy in New York, of which he was elected an associate in 1862. He contributed to the Centennial Exposition at Philadelphia in 1876, to the Paris Exposition in 1878 and to the Mechanic's Fair in Boston. His "Strayed Maskers" at the Royal Academy in 1873, his "Bazaar at Cairo," exhibited in the National Academy, and his "Slaves Tower" were especially noted at the time of their exhibition, and were afterward purchased by private collectors. He was the author of two books—*Gaspara Stampa, the Story of Her Life* (1881) and *Art and Nature in Italy* (1882). He married Mrs. Henriette (Malan) Fletcher, a daughter of Dr. César Henri Malan of Geneva, Switzerland. Her daughter was Julia Constance Fletcher, the novelist, author of *Kismet.*

[Clara E. Clement and Laurence Hutton, *Artists of the 19th Cent.* (1916); H. W. French, *Art and Artists in Conn.* (1879); E. Benezit, *Dictionnaire Critique et Documentaire des Peintres et Sculpteurs,* vol. I (Paris, 1911); obituary in *Il Secolo, Gazzetta di Milano,* Mar. 11, 1908.]

H. W.

BENT, CHARLES (Nov. 11, 1799–Jan. 19, 1847), the eldest of four brothers whose activities fill a large space in the annals of the Colorado-New Mexico frontier, was born at Charleston, Va. (now W. Va.). His father was Silas and his mother Martha (Kerr) Bent. In 1788 the family moved to western Virginia, where Silas became a judge of the court of common pleas, and in 1805 to Marietta, Ohio. Appointed principal deputy surveyor of the new Territory of Louisiana, Silas moved with his family to St. Louis, arriving there Sept. 17, 1806. Both Charles and his brother William [*q.v.*], ten years his junior, became interested in the fur trade, and it is probable that both of them were in the Sioux country, as employees of the American Fur Company, as early as 1823. In the following year the brothers, with Ceran St. Vrain, who for many years was to be their associate, visited the upper Arkansas on a fur-trapping expedition and built a stockade in the vicinity of the present Pueblo. Charles was probably a member of the expedition, led by St. Vrain, which in June or July 1826 visited Santa Fé and trapped the New Mexican streams. In 1828 the three associates, now organized as Bent & St. Vrain, began the building of what was to become the most famous of the old trading posts, Bent's Fort, at a point on the Arkansas near the present La Junta. In 1829 and again in 1832 and 1833 Charles captained a trading caravan to Santa Fé from the American settlements.

The fort was completed in 1832, and thereafter Charles and St. Vrain made their permanent homes in New Mexico and gave most of their time to the New Mexican business of the company, leaving to William and to the two younger brothers, George (1814–46) and Robert (1816–41), the management of the fort. In 1835, at San Fernando de Taos, Charles married Maria Ignacia Jaramillo (whose younger sister, Josefa, subsequently married Kit Carson) and fixed his residence there. Gen. Kearny, after his bloodless conquest of New Mexico, appointed Charles civil governor (Sept. 22, 1846) and left for California. The departure of the troops gave occasion for an attempt by Mexicans and Indians in certain localities to overthrow the American rule. In the uprising at Taos, Jan. 19, 1847, Charles and several others were killed. He was everywhere loved and admired for his sterling character, and the tragedy of his death was deeply felt throughout the frontier. Kit Carson, linking his name with that of St. Vrain, in a statement dictated in 1857, regretted that he could not pay an adequate tribute to them for their kindness. "I can say only," he continued, "that their equals were never in the mountains."

[Sources: Geo. B. Grinnell, "Bent's Old Fort and Its Builders," *Kansas State Hist. Soc. Colls.,* vol. XV (1923); Blanche C. Grant (ed.), *Kit Carson's Own Story of His Life* (Taos, 1926); Edwin L. Sabin, *Kit Carson Days* (1914); Stella M. Drumm (ed.), *Down the Santa Fe Trail and into Mexico,* the Diary of Susan Shelby Magoffin, 1846–47 (1926); Allen H. Bent, *The Bent Family in America* (1900).]

W. J. G.

BENT, JOSIAH (Apr. 26, 1771–Apr. 26, 1836), manufacturer, was born at Milton, Mass., the son of John (1746–1817) and Hannah (Coller) Bent (1746–1816). The father, a Revolutionary soldier, had been among those who responded to the Lexington alarm and had taken part in the siege of Boston. Josiah, the eldest of eight children, was a Milton farmer until the age of thirty, but like many Yankees of his generation was little interested in agriculture and sought to escape into manufacturing. His name is associated with the manufacture of water-crackers which appear to have been "made first in this country" by him (A. K. Teele, *History of Milton*). Beginning with the Dutch oven of his own home in 1801 and peddling the crackers himself, he continued with a constantly increasing output until he retired in 1830. These crackers, made simply of flour and water, without salt or shortening, and baked in Dutch ovens by the heat of hard wood fagots, became almost a household necessity in New England and attained an international reputation. Almost a century later they were still made by hand, and by essentially the same process. Concerning the founder of the industry little is known. He was evidently a man of persistence, energy, and ability. While his neighbor manufacturers were turning to textile manufacturing he continued to bake crackers. After his retirement in 1830 he served as representative in the state legislature for one term, 1832–33. He married, Mar. 28, 1794, Susanna (1776–1857), daughter of Samuel Tucker, Jr., of Milton, by whom he had eight children.

[A. H. Bent, *The Bent Family in America* (1900), pp. 105–06; W. R. Cutter, ed., *New Eng. Families: Geneal. and Memorial* (1913), II, 845; A. K. Teele, ed., *Hist. of Milton, Mass., 1640 to 1887* (1887), 386–87.]

H. U. F.

BENT, SILAS (Oct. 10, 1820–Aug. 26, 1887), naval officer, oceanographer, was born in South St. Louis, the eleventh child of Judge Silas Bent and Martha (Kerr) Bent, and brother of Charles and William Bent [*q.q.v.*]. Appointed a midshipman in the navy at the age of sixteen, he spent the following twenty-five years in that service, rising to the grade of lieutenant. During these years he served in various waters and became familiar with the oceanography of the seven seas, rounding Cape Horn four times and the Cape of Good Hope once, and crossing the Atlantic five times and the Pacific twice. In 1849 he was with Commander James Glynn when the latter sailed the U. S. Brig *Preble* into the harbor of Nagasaki and in the face of hostile demonstrations demanded and succeeded in securing the release of eighteen American sailors who had been shipwrecked and had been imprisoned by the Japanese authorities. As flag lieutenant aboard the *Mississippi,* which carried Commodore Matthew C. Perry on his well-known Japan Expedition, between the years 1852 and 1854 he made hydrographic surveys in Japanese waters, the results being incorporated in a publication issued by the government entitled *Sailing Directions and Nautical Remarks: by Officers of the Late U. S. Naval Expedition to Japan* (1857). In connection with these oceanographic labors he carried out a study of the great Pacific current known as the Kuro Siwo, which was printed in Perry's official report of the Japan Expedition ("Report on the Kuro-Siwo or Gulf Stream of the North Pacific Ocean" by Lieut. Silas Bent, in Narrative of the Expedition of an American Squadron to the China Seas and Japan, 1856, *House Executive Document 97,* 33 Cong., 2 Sess.).

In 1860 Bent was detailed to the Hydrographic Division of the Coast Survey, but on Apr. 25 of the following year he resigned his commission because "his sympathies were with his native state" (Allen H. Bent, *The Bent Family,* 1900, p. 129). In 1857 he had married Ann Eliza Tyler of Louisville, Ky., and on resigning his commission he returned to St. Louis and assumed the management of the Tyler estate. Oceanography still claimed his interest, as evidenced by an address before the St. Louis Historical Society in 1868 on "The Thermometric Gateways to the Pole" which was printed in St. Louis the following year. In this and in a later publication (1872) he maintained that the Gulf Stream from the Atlantic and the Kuro Siwo from the Pacific maintained an open sea about the North Pole. At this time considerable interest in North Polar exploration was manifested both in Europe and in America and while Bent's conclusions with regard to an open Polar Sea were not accepted by the leading authorities, his thesis encouraged discussion of the problems of polar exploration. He died on Aug. 26, 1887, at Shelter Island, L. I., and was buried in Louisville, Ky.

[Allen H. Bent, *The Bent Family* (1900), pp. 128–29, which contains also an excellent photograph; Silas Bent, *Gateways to the Pole* (1872); the official records of the Navy Dept.]

H. A. M.

BENT, WILLIAM (May 23, 1809–May 19, 1869), the son of Silas and Martha (Kerr) Bent and brother of Charles Bent [*q.v.*], was born in St. Louis. In his fifteenth year he appears to have been with a trapping expedition on the upper Missouri. From 1824, when with his brother and Ceran St. Vrain he trapped the upper Arkansas, the Colorado frontier was his home. Though the planning of Bent's Fort was predominantly the work of Charles, its building (1828–32) was mainly under his own direction. Owing to the long absences of the other partners he had most to do, moreover, with its management, and it was often, in his honor, called Fort William. He was the general director of the company, the vast business of which included the gathering of robes and peltries, the trading of goods to the Indians, the raising of horses and mules, and often the transportation of government supplies. He became the sole owner by the retirement of St. Vrain at about the end of 1848. By this time, however, the fort had become associated in his mind with many distressing memories. The death of his brothers—Robert, who was killed by the Comanches in 1841; George, who died of consumption in 1846, and Charles, who was killed in the Taos uprising in 1847—with the death in the same year of his wife, Owl Woman, a Cheyenne, whom he had married in 1835 and who had borne him four children—preyed upon his mind and decided him to remove to other scenes. He offered to sell the fort to the government, but in the negotiations that followed the price offered was so low that he indignantly rejected it. He thereupon (summer of 1849) packed up all his possessions, and after his new wife—Yellow Woman, the sister of Owl Woman—his children, his employees, and his stock had all been safely removed, he blew up the structure with gunpowder.

Thirty-eight miles downstream he built a new trading post. In 1859 he leased it to the government, whereupon it became the first Fort Lyon. In the same year he built a stockade at the mouth of the Purgatoire (Las Animas), took up land and began ranching, though serving also for the year as an Indian agent. After the death of Yellow Woman, he married at Westport, in 1867, Adalina, the daughter of Alexander Harvey and a Blackfoot woman, and returned with her to the Purgatoire. To the neighborhood, beginning with the fall of 1867, other settlers came, Kit Carson among them (for the last few months of his life), and the town of Boggsville, named for a nephew of Bent's, was born. Here, in the frequent company of men whom he had known for many years, he spent his last days. According to Sabin (*Kit Carson Days,* 1914, p. 635) he died at the home of Judge R. M. Moore, his son-in-law.

William Bent—he was usually "Col." Bent after August 1846, when he guided Kearny's column from the fort to Santa Fé—was the first permanent white settler in Colorado and in later days came to be regarded as its most prominent citizen. Perhaps no frontiersman of the trans-Mississippi West was more widely known. His reputation for probity and fair dealing equaled that of his two partners and could hardly have been greater. The tributes of respect paid to these three men have generally not discriminated among them: what has been given to one has been given to all. Yet it seems likely that William was regarded as the special friend and helper of the trapper and hunter, and it is certain that he held the confidence of the Indians to a degree unshared by any other trader.

[See bibliography following sketch of Charles Bent.]

W. J. G.

BENTLEY, WILLIAM (June 22, 1759–Dec. 29, 1819), Unitarian clergyman, author, was born in Boston, Mass., the son of Joshua and Elizabeth (Paine) Bentley. Through the generosity of his maternal grandfather he was educated at Harvard, graduating in 1777. After graduation he taught school for three years, and then returned to the college as a tutor in Latin and Greek, holding this position until his ordination over the East Church at Salem in September 1783. Here he remained until his death thirty-six years later. He was never married. Distinctly a liberal in theology and politics, he became a pioneer in Unitarianism, at a time when New England was still Calvinistic. While the educated clergy were almost wholly Federalist he was a Jeffersonian Republican. His church was a notable center of liberalism, to be attributed both to the leadership of its pastor and to the presence in its membership of many merchants and shipmasters, freed from New England parochialism by the broadening influence of foreign commerce and travel. Bentley was naturally in a somewhat isolated position, and this, combined with personal limitations, prevented his exercising a greater influence on the thought of the day. He was, however, an important factor in New England affairs, not only in the pulpit but through his regular contributions to the *Salem Register,* which entitle him to a recognized place in the history of American journalism. He delivered occasional public addresses and anniversary orations, the style of which appears somewhat turgid and bombastic to a later age. He was an active worker in Freemasonry. He also conducted an extensive correspondence with scientists, writers, and men of affairs in both Europe and America. In his insatiable fondness for books, in his interest in all kinds of natural phenomena and scientific experimentation, and in his taste for philosophical discussion, he had qualities in common with Thomas Jefferson, with whom he regularly corresponded, and who unsuccessfully tried to lure him from New England with an offer of the presidency of the projected University of Virginia. Bentley was one of the few great linguists in America, speaking fluently the chief languages of Europe, and having a reading knowledge of many others, including Arabic and Persian. He was a member of the Massachusetts Historical Society, and began a history of Salem, part of which was published in its collections. The historical and natural curiosities which he collected he afterward bequeathed to the American Antiquarian Society and other institutions. His library, remarkable considering his scanty resources, was left to Allegheny College, Meadville, Pa.

Bentley will, however, be longest remembered through his voluminous diary covering the period from Apr. 30, 1784, to Dec. 29, 1819, which, after lying in the custody of the American Antiquarian Society for many years, was finally published by the Essex Institute, 1905–14. The four bulky volumes with their accumulation of parish gossip, shipping news, vital statistics, and petty miscellany, are a joy to the local antiquarian and genealogist. Scattered through the mass of trivialities there is real history, and in the aggregate the diary constitutes a unique and invaluable picture of a New England seaport in the formative years of the new republic. It also reveals the sturdy qualities of mind and character, the manifold interests, and the numerous eccentricities of the author.

[The *Diary of William Bentley,* vol. I, contains a sketch by Jos. D. Waters, originally written in 1868, a list of Bentley's MSS. and miscellaneous papers in possession of the Am. Antiquarian Soc., and a bibliography. The essay on "Ecclesiastical Origins of Unitarianism in Salem," included in *Social Equilibriums and Other Problems Ethical and Religious* (1887), by Geo. Batchelor, discusses Bentley's influence. J. T. Buckingham in *Specimens of Newspaper Literature: with Personal Memoirs, Anecdotes and Reminiscences* (1850), II, 341–50, has an excellent sketch.]

W. A. R.

BENTON, ALLEN RICHARDSON (Oct. 1, 1822–Jan. 1, 1914), college president, was born in Ira, Cayuga County, N. Y., and was the son of Allen Benton of the vicinity of Albany. His mother was Deborah Willey of East Haddam, Conn. His early training was on the farm. He had his primary education in the common schools of his home; his secondary at Elbridge Academy in Onondaga County and Fulton Academy in Oswego County; his collegiate at Bethany College, Va., graduating in 1847. He taught five terms in the common schools of his home community and after graduating opened a private school in Cincinnati. While on a visit to Rush County, Ind., in 1848, he met Elder Henry R. Pritchard of the Christian Church, through whom he was appointed principal of Fairview Academy (*History of Rush County,* 1888, p. 814). After serving as principal here for six years he was called to Indianapolis in 1855 where he conducted a select school for a few months while rooms were being prepared for the opening of the Northwestern Christian University (*Indianapolis Daily Journal,* July 25, Nov. 2, 1855). He taught here from 1855 till 1861 as professor of ancient languages. In the latter year he became president of the institution, serving till 1868, continuing also to teach the ancient languages. From 1868 to 1871 he taught Latin in Alliance College, Ohio, being president the last two years. In 1871 he was called to Lincoln to organize the new University of Nebraska. After serving five years as chancellor of the University he returned in 1876 to North Western Christian (since 1877, Butler) University as professor of philosophy and Biblical literature. In 1886 he again became president of Butler, serving till 1891, after which he resumed his professorship till 1900. At the death of his wife in 1900 he withdrew from active teaching and engaged in church work. In 1909 he went to Lincoln, Nebr., and made his home with his daughter, Mrs. J. S. Dales, until his death. His life and influence were positive but quiet. Although his life had been spent in the service of the classical tradition, he did not seriously oppose the elective system which encroached upon it. Personally Benton would have passed among strangers as a prosperous business man, or a lawyer. He preached and taught and smoked his pipe with equal ease and dignity. There seem to have been no rough corners to his character, and no sharp turns in his life. He wrote nothing for publication, took no prominent part in politics, and belonged to no organization other than the Christian Church. He was married in 1851 to Silence Howard of Oswego, N. Y., a cousin of W. C. Bryant.

[*Butler Alumni Quart.,* vol. III; *Pictorial and Biog. Memoirs of Indianapolis* (1893), p. 91; *Indianapolis News,* Jan. 2, 1914; *Indianapolis Star,* May 6, 1906, Jan. 2, 1914; *Indiana School Jour.,* 1856–1900, *passim.*]

L. E.

BENTON, JAMES GILCHRIST (Sept. 15, 1820–Aug. 23, 1881), ordnance expert, was born in Lebanon, N. H., the son of Calvin and Mary (Gilchrist) Benton. His father was postmaster of Lebanon for many years, a wool merchant, and the first to introduce merino sheep into New England. Benton graduated from the United States Military Academy at West Point, July 1, 1842, was promoted to brevet second lieutenant in the Ordnance Corps, and assigned to Watervliet Arsenal, Troy, N. Y. He was promoted to second lieutenant, Mar. 3, 1847. The following year he was promoted to first lieutenant and assigned to duty in the Ordnance Office at Washington, and assisted in the preparation of *A System of Artillery for the Land Service* and the *Ordnance Manual.* From 1849 to 1857 he served at various arsenals and at Washington, where he was engaged in making experiments to determine the model of a new rifled musket to replace the smooth-bore then in use, and from 1857 to 1861 he was an instructor in ordnance and gunnery at the United States Military Academy. While there he published *A Course of Instruction in Ordnance and Gunnery, for the Use of Cadets at the United States Military Academy,* and he also designed for the Seacoast Service a wrought-iron gun-carriage that was adopted by the government. He was promoted captain, July 1, 1856, after fourteen years' continuous service. He was assigned, Apr. 28, 1861, to duty as principal assistant to the Chief of Ordnance, and retained this position until Sept. 15, 1863, when he was promoted to major, and assigned to the command of the Washington Arsenal, where he remained until June 1866. Soon after he assumed command, an explosion took place in one of the storerooms. He entered the building, and, with the assistance of a single man, extinguished the flames. In July 1864, on the occasion of another explosion, he entered a magazine, stripped off his coat, threw it over an open barrel of powder that was dangerously close to the flames, and carried the barrel in his arms to a place of safety. He was assigned to the command of the National Armory at Springfield, Mass., in 1866, where he remained until his death. The various improvements in the Springfield rifle, in the models known as the 1866, 1868, 1873, and 1879, were made under his direction and were largely due to his inventive skill. Among his inventions were the electro-ballistic machine or "chronograph" for determining the velocity of projectiles, an improved caliper for inspecting shells, a velocimeter, a spring-dynamometer, a cap-filling machine, a reinforcing cap for cartridge cases, and the electro-ballistic pendulum. He also devised a system for loading and maneuvering barbette guns under cover from the enemy's fire, by depressing the muzzle of the piece and using a jointed rammer. He never took out a patent on his inventions, holding that the government that had educated him was entitled to benefit in every way by his time and talents. He was brevetted lieutenant-colonel and colonel, Mar. 13, 1865, for "faithful and meritorious services in the Ordnance Department" during the Civil War. He received his promotion to lieutenant-colonel, June 23, 1874, and to colonel, May 29, 1875.

Benton served on many special details, among which were the boards on ordnance; on seacoast rifles, cannon, carriages, projectiles, etc.; to examine ordnance officers for promotion; to consider the Protocol of the International Military Commission relative to the use of certain projectiles in war; on superintending the arming of certain seacoast fortifications; to determine the proper caliber of small arms; on the manufacture of Rodman's 15-inch guns; to examine ordnance and ordnance stores in various countries in Europe; on army revolvers; on selection of a magazine gun for the United States Service. He was married, Aug. 17, 1859, to Catherine L., daughter of Gen. J. Watson Webb. Benton was a man of dignified deportment, frank, genial, of unassuming manners, kind, and sympathetic.

[G. W. Cullum, *Biog. Reg.* (3rd ed., 1891); *Reports of the Chief of Ordnance, U. S. Army*; records in the Adjutant-General's Office, Washington, D. C.; obituary by Gen. Benét in *Army and Navy Jour.*, Aug. 27, 1881; obituary in *Springfield* (Mass.) *Republican*, Aug. 24, 1881.]

C. F. C.

BENTON, JOEL (May 29, 1832–Sept. 15, 1911), journalist, poet, was the son of Simeon Blackman and Deborah (Hallock) Benton. Almost all of his ancestors were members of a group which emigrated from England in 1639, and after landing at New Haven settled the town of Guilford, Conn. The Bentons lived in Guilford for five generations; in 1794 Caleb Benton, Jr., with his family, moved to Amenia, N. Y. Here Joel, great-grandson of Caleb, was born, and was educated in the local Amenia Seminary. On leaving school at the age of nineteen he was placed in charge of the weekly *Amenia Times*, which started publication in that year, and is still published under the name of the *Harlem Valley Times*. In 1856 he laid down his irksome editorial duties, and spent the next fifteen years in farming and miscellaneous literary work, including some lecturing. He acted as principal of the Academy, was town supervisor and a delegate to Democratic conventions; as candidate for the state Assembly he was defeated. He took special satisfaction in the conduct of a notable lyceum course, in which he enrolled the leading lecturers of the day. He was a natural hero-worshipper, and his happiest hours were spent in association with his literary acquaintances. His admiration for Horace Greeley led him back in 1872 to the editor's chair, in support of Greeley's presidential campaign; he was also in constant demand as a speaker at rallies. His father's death in 1883 left him burdened with debt, which he strove manfully to pay off. He spent two years in Minnesota, where he wrote for papers in Chicago and St. Paul. Returning east in 1885, he made his home for the rest of his life in Poughkeepsie as a professional writer. He died in the Vassar Brothers Hospital at Poughkeepsie, and was buried in the Poughkeepsie Cemetery.

Launched on a journalistic career at an early age, Benton always wrote with ease. His work is marked by keen observation, a pleasant humor, and a gift of phrase; his style is allusive, and tends to be over-literary. His spirit—except in political discussion, when he could be caustic—was gentle, and he was at his best in writing of out-of-door life or of the great men whom he had known. His verse is pleasing and expressive of his love for nature, but it is on the whole conventional and lacking in power. He was apparently susceptible to feminine charm, but he never married, and his poetry is marked by sentiment rather than emotion. His life and his work belonged to the Hudson River School, but he was always in a backwater, a local rather than a national figure. In addition to magazine articles and much verse, some of which has been included in the anthologies, he published the following books: *Emerson as a Poet* (1883); *The Truth about Protection* (1892); *Greeley on Lincoln* (1893); *In the Poe Circle* (1899); *Life of*

P. T. Barnum (1902); *Persons and Places* (1905); *Memories of the Twilight Club* (1909). He also edited the volume entitled *Amenia Seminary Reunion* (1907). He was a man of medium height, with luxuriant black hair and beard and expressive black eyes; he had a natural distinction of carriage and was fastidious in dress. In his later years he cultivated a resemblance to the poet Tennyson, in which he took great satisfaction.

[*Daily Eagle* (Poughkeepsie), Sept. 16, 1911; Chas. E. Benton, *Caleb Benton and Sarah Bishop, Their Ancestors and Descendants* (1906); Chas. E. Benton, *Troutbeck, a Dutchess County Homestead* (1916); letters from Chas. E. Benton, Rochester, N. Y., Joel E. Spingarn, Amenia, N. Y., and A. S. Frissell, New York City.]

F. H. C.

BENTON, JOSIAH HENRY (Aug. 4, 1843–Feb. 6, 1917), lawyer, a descendant of Andrew Benton who came from England about 1630 and settled in Milford, Conn., was the son of Josiah Henry and Martha (Danforth) Benton. He was born in Addison, Vt., and was educated in the common schools and at Bradford (Vt.) Academy, and at the New London (N. H.) Literary and Scientific Institute. When nineteen he became a private in Company H of the 12th Vermont Volunteers, serving from August 1862 to July 1863 in the Civil War. He graduated from the Albany Law School in 1866, and was admitted to the New Hampshire bar on May 5 of the same year. On May 19, 1866, he married Josephine Emery Aldrich, who died on Apr. 8, 1872, and on Sept. 2, 1875, he married Mary Elizabeth Abbott. From 1866 to 1872 he carried on a successful law practise in Lancaster, N. H. He was assistant clerk of the New Hampshire House of Representatives in 1868, and clerk of that body in 1870 and 1872; in 1869 he was private secretary to the governor of New Hampshire.

He settled in Boston in 1872, and was actively identified from that time with the development of the city. He served as counsel for the Old Colony Railroad and allied companies (1878), until the lease of those properties to the New York, New Haven & Hartford Railroad Company (1893), when he became the Massachusetts counsel for that corporation. In 1879 he became a director of the Northern Railroad of New Hampshire. He lectured on corporations and railroad law at the Law School of Boston University for twenty years. In 1894 he became a member of the board of trustees of the Boston Public Library, giving conspicuous service as president of the board during the last nine years of his life. From 1909 to 1913 he was chairman of the board of trustees of the Massachusetts State Library. From 1910 to 1917 he was a trustee of Boston University. Throughout his life he collected editions of the English Prayer Book and related material to show its origin and growth. At his death this unique and valuable collection of six hundred and twenty-one items was bequeathed to the Boston Public Library. Besides numerous pamphlets Benton was the author of *Samuel Slade Benton; His Ancestors and Descendants* (1901); *The Story of the Old Boston Town House, 1658–1711* (1908); *Voting in the Field; a Forgotten Chapter of the Civil War* (1915).

[*Sixty-sixth Ann. Report Trustees Boston Pub. Lib.*, 1917–18, pp. 2–7; unpublished notes for an autobiographical sketch; *Boston Transcript, Post, Jour., Globe, Herald*, Feb. 7, 1917; *New Eng. Hist. and Geneal. Reg., Supplement to Apr. 1918.*]

C. F. D. B.

BENTON, THOMAS HART (Mar. 14, 1782–Apr. 10, 1858), statesman, was born at Hillsboro, N. C. He was the son of Jesse Benton, a Loyalist, who had been secretary to Gov. Tryon, and of Ann (Gooch) Benton, of excellent Virginia stock. Upon the death of his father, Thomas became at the age of eight the head of the family. After some preliminary study with a friend of his father, a short term in grammar school, and a partial course at the University of North Carolina, he undertook the supervision of the "Widow Benton's Settlement," a farm of 3,000 acres with a claim to some 40,000 acres near Nashville, Tenn. He was in 1809 a state senator in Tennessee, and took much interest in land tenure, and the rights of slaves in capital trials. He was admitted to the bar in 1811. Five of his seven brothers and sisters succumbed to tuberculosis, and Benton himself was in the incipient stages when the régime of camp life in the War of 1812 rebuilt his vigor, though all his life undue exertion of his throat would induce a hemorrhage. Benton at this time won the permanent friendship of Sam Houston, and the temporary enmity of Andrew Jackson. The trouble with the latter grew out of a tavern brawl in which Thomas supported his brother Jesse in a mêlée of knives, pistols, and clubs. Jackson long carried a bullet fired by Jesse or perhaps by Thomas. Notwithstanding his excellent prospects in Tennessee at the close of the war, Benton removed in 1815 to St. Louis, where, as editor of the *Missouri Enquirer* and in the enjoyment of a lucrative law practise, he speedily identified himself with his adopted state. The most regrettable incident of his career occurred on Sept. 27, 1817, when, in the second of two duels with Charles Lucas, a young United States district attorney, he shot down and killed his opponent. The record in the case is not favorable to Benton who, contrary to the wishes of the seconds and in violation of the accepted duelling code, after he had already wounded his antagonist, by whom he had been challenged, in turn forced a later meeting in which, as the inferior marksman, Lucas was almost certain to be killed (see *Switzler's Illustrated History of Missouri,* 1879, pp. 481–86).

Nominated by the son of Daniel Boone, and with the support of David Barton, his co-senator, Benton was first elected to the United States Senate in 1820, and took his seat in 1821. Also at this time he married Elizabeth McDowell, of a prominent Virginia family. In the Senate he became involved almost immediately in his lifelong legislative interest, the defense of sound money. He favored settlers and discouraged land speculators. He deplored the sacrifice of Texas in 1819, and lauded to an uncomprehending public the significance of Oregon. He brought salt within the reach of western farmers, and in the interest of Missourians, defended a tariff upon lead. He promoted the navigation of the Mississippi, and advocated a national highway to New Mexico. In the election of 1824, Benton originally favored Henry Clay. He afterward opposed John Quincy Adams, though he did not believe in the "corrupt bargain" with Clay. Long estranged from Jackson, he now renewed his friendship with him. In the debate on the Panama Congress, he held that the Monroe Doctrine applied solely to the defense of our own territories. In the duel between Clay and Randolph growing out of the Panama debate, he acted as a friend of both parties, though more attached to Randolph. Meanwhile he was working steadily for Jackson in the approaching campaign of 1828. Success achieved, he became the administration spokesman in the Senate. His views on slavery now materially changed. While in 1820 he had opposed all slavery restriction in Missouri, by 1828 he had come to favor gradual abolition. Slavery was apparently hindering settlement—which to a westerner and expansionist was a serious indictment. Even when a discussion on Foot's resolution restricting land sales widened into the celebrated Webster-Hayne debate, Benton did not immediately perceive the issue between Union and Disunion. To defeat the Foot Resolution, he attacked the Webster speech in words he afterward regretted. Convinced at last of Calhoun's secession plans, he henceforth fought for Jackson and the Union. On the rejection by the Senate of Van Buren's nomination as minister to England, Benton actively championed the former secretary, and urged him to stand for nomination as vice-president on the Jackson ticket in 1832. In the nullification crisis, he favored a repeal of the offensive tariffs of 1828 and 1832, but disliked the compromise tariff of 1833, desiring to keep the issue more clearcut between nullification and submission.

Benton was the Senate floor leader in the war upon the National Bank. Always a "hard money" man, he favored a gold and silver coinage, but no bank of issue with its paper currency. In February 1831 he introduced a resolution opposing the re-charter five years later of the National Bank. His anti-Bank speeches, then and later, won a popular support which enabled Jackson finally to veto the re-charter. Benton thoroughly indorsed removal of the government deposits, prior even to the expiration of the charter. When hard times followed, he insisted that they were artificially created by the Bank. A resolution of censure against Jackson he capitalized into a contest for expunging. Just before the administration closed, he won his point, Jan. 16, 1837 (Rogers, *Benton,* p. 159). His method of holding his followers together by culinary and bibulous inducements has often been described. Excitement ran so high that it was feared his life was in danger from toughs who were said to have been hired by the Bank. Jackson's debt to Benton was immense, and the influence of the latter was now at its maximum.

In his attack upon the Bank, Benton was destructive; in championing "hard money," he worked creatively. His first move was to change the ratio between gold and silver from 15 to 1, as established by Jefferson, to the more accurate 16 to 1. Gold coins, dubbed "Benton's mint drops," returned to circulation. Further impetus was lent by the "specie circular" of Jackson, stipulating that public lands be paid for in hard money, an action sponsored by Benton and carried through by Jackson against the unanimous opposition of his cabinet. The most constructive financial legislation of that generation grew out of Benton's struggle for "hard money." On this issue the Democratic party divided into "Hards" and "Softs," and Benton was nicknamed in derision "Old Bullion," a name which stuck, and gave him satisfaction. Such profound changes in the financial structure nevertheless hastened the panic of 1837, which Benton attributed to the machinations of the Bank, a malicious explanation unworthy of his better judgment. Meanwhile, the country marched steadily toward a specie basis along the line of Benton's policy (*Ibid.,* 184).

Another economic issue on which Benton held strong views was the distribution of the public lands, a vital concern in the days when the Government was doing a "land office" business. On this question, as on that of the Bank, Benton's position was democratic. He favored reduction in the cash price for land, and advocated the grant of free homesteads of 160 acres based on five years' settlement and improvement. "He was," says Rogers, "the father of the cheap land system," thus anticipating Abraham Lincoln in one respect at least.

As a Democrat, Benton was naturally a Van Buren man in 1840. Again as a Democrat, he instinctively took sides with Tyler in the latter's conflict with the Whigs. But when his ancient enemy, Calhoun, received the State portfolio, and the acquisition of Texas became an avowed policy, Benton was opposed. He seems honestly to have felt that the time for Texan annexation had been in 1819, and that the Spanish treaty of that year sacrificed the interests of the West. But having done so, it was, in Benton's estimation, a fact accomplished, and he viewed the absorption of Texas at this late date as an unwarranted affront to Mexico. In 1845, annexation being finally determined by joint resolution, Benton sought to conciliate Mexico by treating the boundary as still a subject for negotiation. He was angered when Tyler anticipated the Polk Administration by sending a single commissioner to adjust the issue, without regard to varying shades of opinion within the United States.

Benton's attitude toward Oregon, the exploration of which owed much to Frémont, his own son-in-law, paralleled his attitude toward Texas. Always a Westerner, and one of the first to call his countrymen's attention to the territory, when the issue reached a climax he preferred compromise to war. In 1842 he criticized the Webster-Ashburton Treaty for its failure to include a settlement as to Oregon. But in 1844 he had no fondness for the campaign slogan, "54° 40′ or fight," and he counseled Polk against adhering to it afterward. The 49th parallel was the boundary he wished, and the boundary secured. Never was Benton more bitterly assailed. His pioneering to arouse opinion, and then refusing to follow that opinion into extremes, seemed utterly inconsistent to the frontier mind, in other words, to Benton's own constituents in Missouri.

Yet when the Texan issue really led to war, Benton not only upheld the Government, but even sought a high command. Polk was willing to name him general, a sort of chief of staff to determine military policy, but Buchanan and other Democrats opposed. Though Benton finally declined a major-generalship, his military ambitions were achieved vicariously through the work of Frémont in taking California previously to the actual declaration of war.

This intellectual detachment of Benton's, curious in a man personally so dynamic, dictated his attitude toward slavery. Here again, as has been noted in connection with his earlier legislative attitudes, Benton was essentially a moderate. As abolitionism gained converts in the North, and as Calhounism threatened secession in the South, Benton's moderate position grew increasingly difficult of maintenance. But moderate he was, and moderate he remained. Extension and agitation he equally opposed; abolitionists he scorned. His cry was peace, peace, when there was no peace. Notwithstanding abolitionists and their wiles, Benton's belief in the essential fairness of the North was confirmed by his success in gaining an extension of Missouri on the northwest by an area equal to Delaware, wrested from free territory without any Northern protest. But whatever good-will Benton may have felt for slavery was entirely subordinate to his loyalty to the Union. In 1847, notwithstanding specific instructions from the Missouri legislature, he refused to uphold the Calhoun Resolutions in the Senate, because he regarded them as subversive of the Union. In the great debates on the Compromise of 1850, he maintained consistently his opposition to what he deemed too generous a concession to secessionists. He desired the admission of California as a free state. He objected to the scheme of Calhoun's followers to divide California by the Missouri Compromise line extended. He believed that secessionists could not be satisfied with any solution short of complete control of the Government, and hence he deemed the Compromise a hollow sham. During the debate, Senator Foote of Mississippi drew a pistol on Benton—the greatest indignity the Senate had ever suffered. Throughout the session Benton found himself in active opposition to his colleague, Atchison.

His opposition to the Compromise was his last important act as senator. In the breach within the Democratic ranks in 1848, caused by the decision of Van Buren to run as an independent against Lewis Cass, the party's nominee, he had avoided taking sides—a fatal error. Henceforth he was a man without a party, and his political career was doomed. When in 1850 he opposed the Compromise, he offended his constituents past all forgiveness. Notwithstanding his championship of essential Western interests, such as the pony express, the telegraph, and the railroad, of which latter Benton was an early and influential spokesman, advocating federal aid by means of land grants for a transcontinental line with its terminus at St. Louis, Missourians could not forgive their senator's defection on the major issue, slavery. In 1850 a Whig senator was chosen from Missouri. Undiscouraged, Benton secured election to the House of Representatives, where he vainly fought the Missouri Compromise repeal. He now lost his seat in Congress, and in 1856 failed of election as governor. Though his political career was over, a test of party allegiance remained in his support in 1856 of Buchanan as against Frémont. Indeed on this as on other issues, Benton displayed remarkable consistency.

To quit the forum he so long had graced was a heavy blow. Indeed, his death from cancer in 1858 was probably hastened by his political dethronement; possibly, also, by the burning of his house and papers while he was in the midst of preparing his memoirs. For in his retirement, Benton composed at top speed, made possible by his remarkable memory, the elaborate *Thirty Years' View* (1854–56), in which he surveyed the whole course of politics as he had seen it intimately from 1820 to 1850—one of the outstanding autobiographies of politics. Side by side with this book, he completed another monumental work, *Abridgement of the Debates of Congress from 1789 to 1856* (1857–61).

[Theodore Roosevelt, *Thos. Hart Benton* (1886); Wm. M. Meigs, *Life of Thos. Hart Benton* (1904); Jos. M. Rogers, *Thos. H. Benton* (1905); sketch by Benton's daughter, Mrs. Frémont, in John C. Frémont, *Memoirs of My Life*, vol. I (1887); Clarence Henry McClure, "Early Opposition to Thos. Hart Benton," *Mo. Hist. Rev.*, X, 151–96.]

L. M. S.

BENTON, THOMAS HART (Sept. 5, 1816–Apr. 10, 1879), educator, was of English-Scotch ancestry, his grandfather being Jesse Benton, who in 1765 came from England to North Carolina as private secretary to William Tryon. Of Jesse's four sons, the eldest, Thomas Hart Benton [*q.v.*], uncle of the subject of this sketch, became a distinguished statesman. Samuel, father of Thomas, Jr., was also a man of more than ordinary ability, well educated for his time, a leader among his fellows, active in the Texas Revolution, and a member of congress in that republic. Young Thomas was born in Williamson County, Tenn. First instructed by his father, he later attended an academy at Huntington, Tenn., and then Marion College in Missouri, attaining proficiency in the classics. He went into the Iowa country in 1837 while it was yet a part of Wisconsin, and settled in Dubuque, a frontier town of 1,200 inhabitants. Here in 1838–39 he conducted what was probably the first classical school in Iowa. On the organization of the State of Iowa, 1846, he was elected to the Senate, serving as chairman of the committee on schools, and securing the legislation upon which has been built the public-school system of the state. In 1848 he was elected to the office of state superintendent of public instruction. He served for two terms, six years, declined reëlection, and entered the banking business in Council Bluffs and Omaha. He married, 1851, Susan Culbertson of Boalsburg, Pa. In 1857 Iowa adopted a new constitution, in which public education was organized under a state board with an executive secretary. To this secretaryship Benton was called in 1858, a position which he filled until 1862, when he was commissioned colonel of the 29th Iowa Infantry. He served throughout the Civil War and was mustered out in 1865 with a brevet title of brigadier-general. He immediately accepted nomination for the governorship of Iowa on a soldiers' platform, opposed to negro suffrage, and though defeated by the Republican candidate, received a large vote. In 1866 he moved to Marshalltown as collector of United States revenue in the sixth congressional district, serving during the administration of President Johnson. For several years after the death of his wife, 1869, he lived in Cedar Rapids, as auditor of a railroad. He died at the home of his sister in St. Louis, Mo., and was buried with Masonic honors at Marshalltown, Ia.

[T. S. Parvin, "Thos. Hart Benton, Jr.," *Ia. Hist. Record*, vol. XVI (1900); Benj. F. Gue, *Hist. of Ia.*, vol. IV (1903); Clarence R. Aurner, *Hist. of Ed. in Ia.*, vols. I, II, III, IV (1914); educational reports of Thos. Hart Benton as superintendent of public instruction in *Jour. of Ia. House and Senate*, 1850–54, and his reports as secretary of state board of education, in *Ia. Legislative Docs.*, 1860–64.]

F. C. E.

BERG, JOSEPH FREDERIC (June 3, 1812–July 20, 1871), Dutch Reformed clergyman, was the son of Rev. Christian Frederic Berg, a native of Jutland, Denmark, and his wife Hannah Robinson Tempest, an Englishwoman, who were Moravian missionaries at Grace Bay on the island of Antigua, B. W. I. He was the first white child born on the island. At the age of four he was placed in a Moravian school at Fulneck, England, and in 1825 he came to the Moravian Academy at Nazareth, Pa., where he studied theology and was licensed to preach at nineteen. On Oct. 2, 1835, he was ordained and installed pastor of the German Reformed Church at Harrisburg, Pa. Two years later he went to the Race Street Church, Philadelphia. After a notable pastorate of fifteen years he withdrew from the German Reformed Church because of his opposition to what he considered the latitudinarian and Romanizing tendencies of the Mercersburg theology, and went to the Second Dutch Reformed Church of Philadelphia, taking a large part of his congregation with him. In June 1861 he was elected to the chair of didactic and polemic theology in the Theological Seminary at New Brunswick, N. J.; he was also professor of the evidences of Christianity in Rutgers College from 1862 to 1867.

He was master of many languages and his general information was encyclopedic. While a student at Nazareth, at the age of seventeen, he taught chemistry. During his Harrisburg pastorate he taught the classics at Mercersburg and declined a permanent professorship there. While at Race Street he obtained the degree of M.D. at the Jefferson Medical College. His preaching was not characterized by display, but he used his learning in a telling manner, with a wealth of well-chosen illustration. He engaged in much controversy with the Roman Catholics, edited an anti-Papal magazine, *The Evangelical Quarterly,* and wrote several books against Rome, such as *Lectures on Romanism* (1840); *Papal Rome* (1841), and *The Inquisition; Church and State; or, Rome's Influence upon the Civil and Religious Institutions of our Country* (1851). He was also a prolific contributor to periodicals and newspapers and wrote a number of story-books for children. His portrait in oil is the property of the Theological Seminary at New Brunswick. On Feb. 4, 1835, he married Eleonora Pomp of Easton, Pa.

[E. T. Corwin, *Manual of the Reformed Ch. in America* (3rd ed., 1879); *Centennial of the Theol. Sem. of the Reformed Ch. in America* (1885); *Reformed Ch. Messenger,* July 26, 1871. The writer is also indebted to Dr. Berg's daughter for much personal information.]

F. T. P.

BERGER, DANIEL (Feb. 14, 1832–Sept. 12, 1920), United Brethren clergyman, was born near Reading, Pa., the son of Daniel and Esther Boda Berger. His great-grandparents on both sides were emigrants from Germany. When Daniel was six years old, his parents, impelled like their ancestors to seek larger freedom and opportunity, sold their property and fell into line with the stream of immigration westward. A four weeks' journey by wagon brought them to Springfield, Ohio, where Daniel's father bought a farm on which was a log cabin. This the family occupied until a more comfortable home could be built. The two sons and daughters attended the district school, the boys spending their summers in hard work upon the farm. At the age of eighteen, Daniel entered the Ohio Methodist Conference high school, where he remained for two years, when he was made assistant principal of an academy at New Carlisle, Ohio. After serving here for three years he was appointed principal of one of the two large district schools in Springfield, and later, principal of the newly established high school. On July 28, 1853, he married Mary Frances Merry, a cousin of Cardinal Merry del Val. Brought up a devout Catholic, she had already become a Protestant, and later wrote a good-tempered booklet, entitled *In and Out of Catholicism.* During the six years Berger had been teaching, he had been preparing himself privately for the ministry, and in 1854 had been licensed by the Miami Conference of the Church of the United Brethren in Christ. He served in the pastorate from 1858 to 1864, at which time he was chosen editor of the *Religious Telescope,* the chief periodical of the United Brethren Church, published at Dayton, Ohio. This office he filled until 1869, when he became editor of the Sunday-school literature of his denomination. His work in this capacity covered a period of twenty-six years, and was marked by careful scholarship and lucid presentation. Beginning with a single children's paper, the publications came to include a complete line of literature for pupils, teachers, and officers. He also served for twelve years as a member of the International Sunday School Lesson Committee. He was a contributor to the *Schaff-Herzog Encyclopædia* and to the American Church History series, and was the author of a *History of the Church of the United Brethren in Christ,* published in 1897.

[Articles in the *Religious Telescope* for Oct. 2, 1920, and A. W. Drury's *Hist. of the United Brethren in Christ* (1924).]

A. W. D.

BERGH, CHRISTIAN (Apr. 30, 1763–June 24, 1843), shipbuilder, the third of his line in America to bear his name, was a son of Christian II, and Catrina (Van Benschoten) Bergh. He was born in Dutchess County, N. Y., near Rhinebeck, where his family had lived since the beginning of the eighteenth century. As a thirteen-year-old lad he experienced some of the harsh realities of civil war; for at the outbreak of the Revolution his father was penalized for Loyalist leanings by confiscation of his farm and homestead. The family took refuge within the British lines at New York City and at the end of the war migrated with thousands of other Loyalists to the Canadian provinces. The Berghs were among those who joined the new settlement at Shelburne, Nova Scotia, a community made up almost entirely of immigrants from the United States and numbering within three years after its founding, in 1783, about 10,000 persons. Fishing and shipbuilding were leading industries in the new town almost from the first and young Bergh, who was nearing his majority, had a good opportunity to master the ship-wright's trade. After a few years, when Shelburne's first prosperity had declined and the Berghs returned to

New York, he opened a shipyard on the East River and began to build merchant vessels. Through the first third of the nineteenth century he continued that industry with marked success. The United States frigate *President,* one of the men-of-war that achieved fame in the War of 1812, was a product of the Bergh yards. When she was badly crippled in a sea fight with four British ships and compelled to surrender, her captors considered her a model of naval architecture and recommended the method of her construction to British shipbuilders (James Barnes, *Naval Actions of the War of 1812,* 1896, p. 227). Bergh's only absence from New York was the period from 1812 to 1815, during which he was engaged in building war vessels for the United States on Lake Ontario. During those years work at the New York yards was suspended, but was resumed after peace, when many packet ships were built there and one war vessel, the *Hellas,* for the Greek government. Until 1837, when Bergh retired, the sailing ships built at his yards were unsurpassed in design or construction and won wide repute. One of his London packets made the Atlantic passage to England in fourteen days and ten hours, leading the *Great Western* (which was under steam) to Cape Clear. The "close rudder" was early a feature of the Bergh ships. Some of the swiftest of pilot boats used in that period were products of the Bergh yards. Bergh was six feet four inches in height and in his latter years was a well-known figure in the Corlears Hook section of New York, where his yards were located. He sometimes presided at political rallies in Tammany Hall. In politics he was a Jackson Democrat; his patriotism was never questioned. Somewhat late in life he married Elizabeth Ivers of Connecticut. He had two sons, one of whom, Henry [*q.v.*], was the founder of the American Society for the Prevention of Cruelty to Animals.

[A brief sketch of Christian Bergh, written by his son, Henry Bergh, *N. Y. Times,* Mar. 18, 1888; "The Berghs of New York," by Rev. Beverley R. Betts, *N. Y. Geneal. and Biog. Record,* XIX, 122; *Concerning the Van Bunschoten or Van Benschoten Family in America,* by Wm. Henry Van Benschoten (1907).]

W. B. S.

BERGH, HENRY (Aug. 29, 1811–Mar. 12, 1888), was America's outstanding pioneer and propagandist in work for the humane treatment of animals. The early history of the anti-cruelty movement in this country is his biography. His father, Christian Bergh [*q.v.*], was a prominent New York shipbuilder. His mother, Elizabeth Ivers, was of old Connecticut stock, with Knickerbocker affiliations. Henry received his formal education in New York City, studying at Columbia College, from which, however, he did not graduate. In his twenty-fifth year he was married to Catherine Matilda Taylor, daughter of a wealthy English architect and builder residing in New York. Shortly after, in 1837, he and his brother Edwin undertook the management of their father's shipyard, which they continued until after the death of Christian Bergh in 1843. Having received a comfortable fortune under his father's will, Bergh and his wife spent the next years traveling in Europe and the East. While in Europe in 1863 he was appointed secretary of legation at St. Petersburg, an office he was obliged to resign in 1864 owing to Mrs. Bergh's inability to endure the severe winter climate of Russia. While in St. Petersburg he became interested in the prevention of cruelty to animals, which was strikingly prevalent. On occasion he intervened in behalf of suffering horses in ways which would have been violently resented but for his official connection. His interest in anti-cruelty work was stimulated through acquaintance with the Earl of Harrowby, president of the Royal Society for the Prevention of Cruelty to Animals. He returned to New York following the Civil War, and after a brief rest began to mature plans for an American organization modeled upon the English one. At the start he met with sneers and rebuffs. He persisted, however, and from time to time interested prominent citizens in his efforts. He lost no opportunity to make a popular appeal, often calling for help from bystanders in cases of cruel treatment of horses on the streets of the city. Many a street sermon was thus preached, and in this way his presence and mission became familiar to a widening circle. On the night of Feb. 8, 1866, he delivered a lecture in Clinton Hall on statistics relating to the cruelties practised on animals, with a view toward founding a society for their prevention. Offers of assistance were freely made to him after the lecture. As a result of ensuing efforts the state legislature, on Apr. 10, 1866, granted a charter of incorporation to the American Society for the Prevention of Cruelty to Animals. This act legalized a body, independent of existing constituted authorities, to enforce local laws for animal protection. Bergh was elected its president, and during the next two decades he gave his energies to the building up of the society and to the extending of statutory provision against a long array of animal abuses. In 1875 he was instrumental with Elbridge T. Gerry and others in forming a Society for the Prevention of Cruelty to Children, thus inaugurating a movement which in its growth has far outstripped its parent. The latter, however, always commanded

Bergh's main interest, and when he died in 1888 he left the animal protective movement a matured and vigorous one. Countless cruelties had been suppressed or minimized, the idea had spread to other cities, states, and countries, and hundreds of auxiliaries had sprung up in all parts of the world.

Bergh's figure was, of course, a very familiar one about the city. His appearance was striking, lending itself easily to caricature. He was tall and spare, but of vigorous muscular development. His face was long and thin, resembling pictures of Don Quixote, with sunken eyes and prominent cheek bones. His attire was always faultlessly neat.

Aside from his activities as an anti-cruelty propagandist, he found time to indulge literary and artistic inclinations. He wrote several plays, as well as a volume of tales and sketches entitled *The Streets of New York*. In middle life he wrote some verses designed to show the folly of scheming mothers with marriageable daughters (*"Married Off," A Satirical Poem*, London, 1860). As literary achievements none of these efforts deserve particular notice. Bergh's fame rests on his work as a friend of dumb beasts.

[The above data were obtained largely from former officials of the American Society for the Prevention of Cruelty to Animals, who knew Bergh during the period of his greatest activity. Extensive obituaries were published in the *N. Y. Herald, N. Y. Times*, and *N. Y. Tribune* of Mar. 13, 1888; the *N. Y. Times* of Mar. 18, 1888, contains J. H. Tooker's reminiscences of Henry and Christian Bergh. See also R. C. McCrea, *The Humane Movement* (1910); "Henry Bergh and His Work," in *Scribner's Mo.*, Apr. 1879; and Clara Morris, "The Riddle of the Nineteenth Century: Mr. Henry Bergh," in *McClure's Mag.*, Mar. 1902. Most accounts give the year of his birth as 1823; the date given above is from Wm. H. Van Benschoten, *Concerning the Van Bunschoten* or *Van Benschoten Family in America* (1907), pp. 669–76.] R. C. M.

BERGMANN, CARL (Apr. 11, 1821–Aug. 10, 1876), orchestral conductor, was born at Ebersbach in Saxony. His parents later removed to Breslau, where he studied under A. Hesse. Between 1842 and 1848 he was an orchestral leader in Vienna, Budapest, Warsaw, and Venice. Implicated in the Revolution of 1848 he was obliged to leave Germany and in the autumn of 1849 came to New York. There he joined the Germania Orchestra, originally made up of twenty-four German musicians, which had set a new high standard of orchestral playing in this country. Bergmann started in as violoncellist, but soon became conductor. From 1852 to 1854 he conducted the Handel and Haydn Society in Boston, but in the latter year he returned to New York as conductor of the Männergesangverein Arion. In 1858 he became for a year conductor of the New York Philharmonic Society. In 1858–59 he was again conductor, from 1859 to 1865 alternate conductor with Theodore Eisfeld, and from 1865 to 1876 sole conductor of the Society. In this period he introduced to this country many works by Wagner, Liszt, Rubinstein, Berlioz, Brahms, and other composers of the romantic school. "It was in fact Bergmann . . . who created an interest for the works of those masters. He did not play these works with the intention merely of bringing forward novelties, but from a conviction that he was promoting the new art-aspirations as engendered by our modern art-spirit" (F. L. Ritter, *Music in America*, 1883, p. 350).

In the field of opera Bergmann conducted apparently the first complete performances in German in this country of Beethoven's *Fidelio* (New York, Dec. 29, 1856), and Wagner's *Tannhäuser* (New York, Aug. 27, 1859). He had previously performed the *Tannhäuser* overture, first with the Germania Orchestra on Dec. 3, 1853, and with the Philharmonic Society in April 1855. The *Lohengrin* prelude and *Rienzi* overture had also appeared on Germania Orchestra programmes prior to 1854, doubtless for the first time in this country. In addition to his activity in conducting orchestral concerts and opera, Bergmann conducted the New York Harmonic Society (choral), and its successor the Mendelssohn Union. He was associated as 'cellist with William Mason, Theodore Thomas, and others in chamber music performances in 1855–60. After the death of his wife in 1875 mental depression made him so morose, moody, and at times childish, that he was finally in February 1876 obliged to resign his position with the Philharmonic Society, and a few months later he died. His compositions, few in number and now forgotten, were for orchestra. Theodore Thomas said of him: "Bergmann gave the impression that he never worked much, or cared to do so. He lacked most of the qualities of a first-rank conductor, but he had one great redeeming quality for those days which soon brought him into prominence. He possessed an artistic nature, and was in sympathy with the so-called 'Zukunftmusik'" (George P. Upton, *Theodore Thomas*, 1905, I, 36). According to F. L. Ritter, Bergmann was "at the height of his American career, the most respected and admired musical leader in the country" (*Music in America*, p. 349).

[Cesar Saerchinger, "Musical Landmarks in N. Y.," *Musical Quart.*, Apr. 1920; Wm. Mason, *Memories of a Musical Life* (1901); H. E. Krehbiel, *The Philharmonic Soc. of N. Y.* (1892); *Grove's Dict. of Music and Musicians* (1904), I, 308–09; good obituaries in the *N. Y. Staats-Zeitung*, Aug. 13, 1876; *N. Y. Times*, Aug. 13, 1876; *N. Y. Tribune*, Aug. 14, 1876.] C. N. B.

BERKELEY, JOHN (d. Mar. 22, 1622), English ironmaster, was the hereditary owner of Beverstone Castle, Gloucestershire. He was married to Mary, daughter of John Snell, Esquire, had ten children, and undoubtedly suffered economic pressure. In 1597 he sold his ancestral castle, possibly to enter the iron industry, for the man recommended in 1621 to erect and conduct ironworks on the Virginia frontier could have been no industrial novice. The Society of Southampton Hundred, holding patents under the Virginia Company of London and obliged by it to employ an anonymous gift of £550 in educating Indian children as Christians, determined to augment the sum and use it in erecting "an ironwork" in Virginia, promising for Indian education the returns *pro rata* on the gift. By 1621, £4,000 was ventured and Capt. Bluett was sent with eighty workmen to Virginia. Bluett died shortly after reaching Jamestown, and the authorities, accepting Berkeley's terms, gave him Bluett's privileges with means to hire twenty additional mechanics and to transport them, himself, his son, and three personal servants from the Isle of Wight before August. Berkeley was appointed to the Virginian Council; he built ironworks on the west side of Falling Creek, south of James River, seven miles below Richmond, and early in 1622 sent word to England that he expected to make iron by Whitsuntide. But when the Londoners voted to meet his expenditures, Berkeley and his workmen lay dead in Virginia surrounded by ruined machinery. On Mar. 22, under crafty Opechancanough the Indians massacred 347 white persons in Virginia. Maurice, John's son, survived, and the company, powerless to provide funds to recreate the works, granted his petition to release him from their service and give him the 800 acres formerly promised him and his father for their service in the ironworks. John Berkeley ended tragically and his work perished with him. But he built for himself a home in men's minds. The Virginia Historical Society preserves slag from his furnace; and though Virginian ironmaking was not rooted until after 1710, Berkeley's furnace constitutes him the first American ironmaster and Virginia the seat of the first iron smelted in America.

[The chief sources of information in America about John Berkeley are *The Berkeley MSS.*, by John Smyth of Nibley, ed. by Sir John Maclean (3 vols., 1883–85), and *The Records of the Va. Co. of London . . . from the MS. in the Lib. of Cong.* (2 vols., 1906), ed. by Susan Myra Kingsbury. Similar information but no new material of significance is in the *Va. Hist. Soc. Colls.*, n. s., vols. VII and VIII (1888–89); Edward D. Neill, *Hist. of the Va. Co. of London* (1869); Alexander Brown, *The First Republic in America* (1898); *Va. Mag. of Hist.*, vols. I–XXXIV (1893–1926); and the *William and Mary Coll. Quart.*, 1st ser., vols. I–XXVII (1892–1919), 2nd ser., vols. I–VI (1921–26). The material in the last two publications does not always tally with that of the two chief sources cited above.] K. B.

BERKELEY, NORBORNE. [See BOTETOURT, NORBORNE BERKELEY, BARON DE, *c.* 1718–1770.]

BERKELEY, Sir WILLIAM (1606–July 9, 1677), colonial governor of Virginia, the son of Maurice Berkeley of Bruton, Somerset, and the brother of John, first Lord Berkeley of Stratton, was a member of a celebrated family which during several centuries had enjoyed great influence at the English Court. He matriculated at Queen's College, Oxford, Feb. 14, 1623, and received the degree of B.A. from St. Edmund Hall, July 10, 1624, and that of M.A. from Merton College, July 10, 1629 (Joseph Foster, *Alumni Oxonienses,* 1892, p. 114). While still young, he had a seat in the Privy Chamber; was known at Whitehall as a polished courtier; and in London at large, as a playwright of merit. He was knighted by King Charles I at Berwick, July 27, 1639. His first colonial office was a commissionership of Canadian affairs (*Calendar of State Papers, Colonial Series, America and West Indies, 1574–1660,* 1860, p. 9), but its powers were exercised in England. It was not until 1642 that he went out to Virginia to take over its government; and there he remained, with the exception of a rare visit to England, down to the year 1677. He found the colony on his arrival torn by factions; but he soon quieted these by his unwearied promotion of the best interests of the community. His disinterestedness was illustrated in his offering no objection to the grant to the General Assembly of the right to act as a final court of appeal in Virginia, even from the decisions of the General Court, over which he himself presided. To encourage diversification of crops, he cultivated flax, cotton, and rice, on his own lands. He also experimented with silk production; and, during one year, was able to send 300 pounds of silk to the King as a gift (*Ibid., 1661–68,* 1880, No. 1805, pp. 594–95). He encouraged the manufacture of cloth by using his own looms to provide his family and his slaves with material for garments. He built his own mansion of brick, and urged others to follow his example. He sent a band of explorers to discover the easiest route to the country beyond the mountains; and, on one occasion, was prevented only by heavy rains from leading a large party of gentlemen in person into the wilderness for the same purpose. Naturally bold and resolute, he mustered a small army in 1644, the year of the second great massacre of the whites by the Indians, and, marching at its head to the frontier, completely crushed the savages lurking in the forest, and wrested a peace from them that lasted for a generation. His courageous spirit was even more conspicuously exhibited in the war with the Dutch in 1665. When hostilities began in European waters, he placed the colony in an attitude of defense by strengthening the forts, and arming and drilling every person available for military service. When the Dutch war-vessels arrived off the Virginia capes, they found the merchant ships fully manned, and equipped, and concentrated in a single fleet (*Ibid., 1661–68,* 1880, No. 1193, p. 380). It was not Berkeley's fault that some of these ships were captured. The defense on land, which was under his immediate eye, was so firm that the invasion stopped at the water's edge.

His administration, during its early years, was characterized by only two serious defects: he was relentless in persecuting the Quakers and the Puritans (*Hening's Statutes,* II, Acts of 1661–62), and he showed little appreciation of learning. He actually thanked God that there was neither a printing-press nor a free school in Virginia—a groundless assertion, in the latter case, as there were two excellent free schools in the colony, which still survive. He had always been animated by a spirit of almost preposterous loyalty to the throne. When the Civil War began in England, he expressed himself with violence in opposition to the movement, and influenced the General Assembly to condemn it in language equally embittered (*Ibid.,* I, 335). He encouraged the Cavaliers to come over in large numbers, and gave an asylum to the persecuted clergy of England. The King's execution aroused him to a fury of hatred and resistance. Parliament called upon him to submit to the Commonwealth, but he defiantly refused to do so; and when the Parliamentary fleet arrived in Virginia, it found the colony fully armed to meet it. Surrender took place only after a compromise had been effected (*Calendar of State Papers, Colonial Series, America and West Indies, 1574–1660,* 1860, No. 46, p. 376). The deposed Governor remained quietly on his plantation until the Restoration, when he was promptly put back in office.

From this time, his conduct was not at all consistent with the spirit of his earlier administration. It is true that he protested personally against the damage which the Navigation Act inflicted on the colony; and he also urged the adoption of a temporary cessation of tobacco culture as a means of raising the price of that staple; but he was too much inclined to repeat in Virginia the irregular policies that had been introduced in England under the reactionary influences then prevailing. Thus he established a Long Parliament of his own, which became a mere tool of his will. The former independent vestries and county courts fell under his thumb. So did the Council. And so did the General Court. The people had little share in the administration, even of their local affairs. There were other grave causes for popular discontent, and the whole number combined culminated in the insurrection of 1676. The spark that started this conflagration was an Indian invasion, accompanied as usual by murders and robberies. The leader in the uprising against the Governor was the younger Nathaniel Bacon [*q.v.*] to whom Berkeley had declined to give a commission. Without the commission Bacon marched against the Indians and destroyed their stronghold; but on his return to Jamestown, he was arrested by Berkeley and compelled to submit. While engaged in enlisting troops to carry out a second expedition, he was proclaimed an outlaw; but advancing on Jamestown in force, he compelled Berkeley to give him a commission. Later, Berkeley sought safety in flight across the Bay; but having captured a large vessel in Bacon's possession, he returned to Jamestown, only to be driven out again after a pitched battle. It was not until Bacon's death that Berkeley found a permanent foothold at Jamestown. He then entered upon a course of execution and confiscation too violent to be approved by the English Government, and a commission was sent out to Virginia to report upon the conditions that prevailed there. Berkeley declined to yield his place to his newly appointed successor, and withdrew only when his health had become shattered. He died in England a short time afterward, without having been able to talk with the King. But perhaps little would have been gained had he done so, for Charles is reported to have remarked, "The old fool has killed more people in that naked country than I have done for the murder of my father."

[A full account of the English Berkeley family will be found under the head "Berkeley" in the *Dict. Nat. Biog.* Indices of British Colonial Papers from 1642 to 1677 reveal a long series of reports relating to his administration. Many of these papers have been reprinted in the *Va. Mag. of Hist. and Biog.* and *Wm. and Mary Coll. Quart. Mag.* For the executions and confiscations, see *Hening's Statutes,* II, 547–50. See also John D. Burk's *Hist. of Va.* (1805), II, 250–53, 259–64.]

P. A. B.

BERKENMEYER, WILHELM CHRISTOPH (1686–1751), Lutheran clergyman, was living in Hamburg in May 1724 when the Lutheran Consistorium of Amsterdam inquired whether he would receive ordination and go to New York to succeed the late Justus Falckner as pastor of the Lutherans on Manhattan Island and in its vicinity. At first he demurred; but falling dangerously ill he resolved that if his life were spared he would go. On May 24, 1725, he was ordained at Amsterdam and proceeded to England to take ship for America. Of his earlier life little is known. He had been born at Bodenteich in the then Duchy of Lüneburg, the son of Jürgen Berckenmeyer, and had studied at the University of Altdorf under a Dr. Christoph Sonntag whose principal maxim, *Quo proprior Luthero eo melior Theologus,* Berkenmeyer took with him to New York. Toil and trouble were the customary lot of the colonial Lutheran ministers; in Berkenmeyer's case the trouble began ahead of time while he was still at Cowes in the Isle of Wight. There a letter was forwarded to him from the church council in New York, stating that they had already chosen a "God-fearing and able man" as pastor. Berkenmeyer, however, did not turn back. On his arrival, Sept. 22, 1725, he called together the council, presented his credentials, made a brief speech, and was thereafter master of the situation. The interloper, Dieren (Düren, Dören) by name, was a Pietistically inclined tailor with an uncontrolled impulse to clamber into unoccupied pulpits. He was unordained, uneducated, and theologically so ambidextrous that he could be either Lutheran or Reformed as the situation required. To a man like Berkenmeyer, with his solid learning, staunch orthodoxy, and high conception of the ministerial office, no one could have been more offensive, but he was by no means rid of him. Berkenmeyer had to minister to several congregations in New Jersey, to others scattered along the Hudson Valley as far north as Albany, and even to one or two along the Mohawk. Opportunities for an agile wolf to intrude into the fold were numerous, and Dieren availed himself of them whenever he got a chance. On Oct. 25, 1727, Berkenmeyer married Benigna Sibylla, eldest daughter of the late Josua von Kocherthal. On June 29, 1729, he consecrated a new church, Trinity, in New York. In 1731 he divided his immense parish in two and, leaving the southern half to Michael Christian Knoll, made his home thereafter at Loonenburg, now Athens, N. Y., whence he made regular visits to congregations at other points. On Aug. 20, 1735, at Raritan, N. J., he presided over a special meeting of three clergymen and nine laymen; this meeting has been described, though erroneously, as the first Lutheran synod in America (H. E. Jacobs, *A History of the Evangelical Lutheran Church in the United States,* 1893, pp. 125–26). Until 1743 he was the only regularly called and ordained Lutheran minister in upper New York. He preached in Dutch, German, and English, and corresponded in Latin with the Swedish clergymen on the Delaware. He was a bitter opponent of Calvinism without and of Pietism within the Lutheran Church. He was consequently openly hostile toward Johann Christoph Hartwig, writing several pamphlets against him as he did against Dieren, and somewhat aloof in his attitude toward Mühlenberg, who called on him in New York once in 1750 and was courteously received. With his own congregations he was popular in spite of a certain gruffness of manner. Like his parishioners he kept negro slaves, but he gave conscientious attention to their spiritual welfare. We last hear of him on Aug. 25, 1751, when he baptized two children, although himself sick unto death. He is buried at Athens, N. Y.; his widow was still living in 1775.

[W. J. Mann, B. M. Schmucker, W. Germann, eds., *Nachrichten von den vereinigten Deutschen Evangelisch-Lutherischen Gemeinden in Nord-America,* Erster Band (Allentown, Pa., 1886), usually cited as the *"Hallesche Nachrichten"*; E. B. O'Callaghan, ed., *Doc. Hist. of N. Y.*, vol. III (1850); *Eccl. Records State of N. Y.*, see index volume (1916); A. L. Gräbner, *Geschichte der Lutherischen Kirche in America* (St. Louis, 1892); for MSS. see Gräbner's "Vorwort."]

G. H. G.

BERKOWITZ, HENRY (Mar. 18, 1857–Feb. 7, 1924), rabbi, son of Louis and Henrietta Berkowitz, was a native of Pittsburgh, Pa. He received his elementary and secondary education in the public schools of that city, graduating from the Central High School in 1872. Then he attended Cornell University for one year. In 1876 he entered the Hebrew Union College of Cincinnati, the theological seminary of liberal Judaism, and at the same time matriculated at the University of Cincinnati. He graduated from the latter institution with the degree of B.A. in 1881 and was a member of the first class of rabbis, four in number, to be ordained in the United States, which event took place July 14, 1883. During the latter year he was married to Flora Brunn of Coshocton, Ohio. He assumed charge of the congregation Sha'are Shomayim of Mobile, Ala., where he remained until 1888 when he was called to the pulpit of the B'nai Jehuda congregation of Kansas City, Mo. He made the third and last change of pulpits in 1892 when he accepted the call to the historic Rodeph Sholem congregation of Philadelphia, Pa., serving as rabbi for thirty years until ill health compelled his retirement two years before his death. A man of fine sensibilities, he was active while in Mobile in the organization of a humane society for the prevention of cruelty to children and animals, and in Kansas

City he was chiefly instrumental in the creation of its first bureau of charities. In recognition of this service the governor of the commonwealth appointed him to represent the state at meetings of the National Conference of Charities and Corrections. When a Vice Commission was appointed in Philadelphia in 1912, the mayor of the city named him a member of the commission; his contribution to the work consisted of a personal investigation of vice conditions and their solutions in European cities, whereof he made an able report to the municipal executive. He served his city also as a member of the Board of Recreation and as a vice-president of the Universal Peace Union and Social Purity Alliance.

Deeply impressed by the work of the Chautauqua Assembly, he instituted a movement along similar lines in Jewish circles when he founded the Jewish Chautauqua Society in 1893. This effort to stimulate popular education constitutes Berkowitz's chief contribution to Jewish institutional and educational activity in the United States. He served as chancellor of the society from the date of its foundation. In his own special rabbinical field he stood among the leaders. When the Central Conference of American Rabbis was organized at Detroit, Mich., in 1889, Berkowitz was a charter member and served as secretary of the meeting for organization. He functioned as chairman of the committee to draft a formula for the reception of proselytes and the committee on arbitration to adjust differences between congregations and rabbis. He was also a member of the Conference committee on a "Union Prayer Book." The Conference publications, "Prayers for Private Devotion" and "The Union Hagadah," were made possible by his guidance. His career as author began during his student days at the Hebrew Union College when, in collaboration with his classmate Joseph Krauskopf, he published in 1883 three text-books for Jewish religious schools, namely, *Bible Ethics, First Union Hebrew Reader,* and *Second Hebrew Reader.* His other published works were *Judaism on the Social Question* (1888); *The Open Bible* (1896); *Kiddush, or Sabbath Sentiment in the Home* (1898); *The New Education in Religion* (1913), and *Intimate Glimpses of the Rabbi's Career* (1921). This last-named book reveals the man himself and makes clear the reason why Berkowitz was acclaimed during his lifetime the best-loved rabbi in the United States.

[The *Am. Jewish Yr. Bk.,* XXVI, 448–58; *Yr. Bk. Central Conference of Am. Rabbis,* XXXIV, 174–77; obituaries in the Phila. newspapers of Feb. 8, 1924.]
D. P.

BERMUDEZ, EDOUARD EDMOND (Jan. 19, 1832–Aug. 22, 1892), lawyer, jurist, was the son of Judge Joachim Bermudez of New Orleans and his wife, Emma Troxler. The family, of French and Spanish blood, had wide connections in Latin America, in France, and in Spain. The father became a noted citizen, as judge of the probate court, and the son was familiar from his youth with several languages, French, Spanish, German, in addition to English. His formal education was received in Spring Hill College near Mobile (B.A. 1851) and in the office of Justice Thomas B. Monroe of Kentucky, with whom, after the custom of those days, he read law. Returning to New Orleans after his course with Justice Monroe, he passed his examinations creditably and received his degree in law from the University of Louisiana (now Tulane) in 1852. Though not yet of legal age to practise, he was presented for the bar by Judah P. Benjamin. In January 1853 he married Amanda Elizabeth Maupassant.

A well-established practise of his profession was interrupted by the political disturbances preceding the Civil War. Bermudez was a member of the Convention of 1860, and was one of the minority who opposed the secession of Louisiana from the Union. When the war began, however, he entered the Confederate army as a lieutenant in the 1st Louisiana Infantry. He became judge-advocate of the brigade; served as adjutant, provost-marshal-general, and post commandant at Mobile; and after the cessation of hostilities held the position of assistant city attorney of New Orleans. He was removed from office (1867) as "an impediment to reconstruction," by order of Gen. Sheridan. Resuming the private practise of law, he became very successful, and his office was the training school for such men as Charles T. Soniat, C. F. Claiborne, Edward Douglass White. With the gradual passing of the evil days of "radical" rule, the people of Louisiana set about the reorganization of the government. Gov. Wiltz made a fortunate and wise selection of Edouard Bermudez to fill a place on the bench of the supreme court of the state. He was appointed (April 1880) for a term expiring in 1892. A man of great vigor, of most scholarly tastes, he was favorably known to both the French and English elements in the state. He was of high temper, but patient, clear-headed, and firm on the bench. During the very bitter conflict regarding the Louisiana lottery, it was characteristic of him that he held firmly to the principle that he was a jurist and not a politician, and that he would not as chief justice take an active part in the controversy, but would decide points of law according to the law when cases were brought before him. It was always understood that Bermudez was a lottery man, but it was perfectly clear that the more sinister elements in the lottery camp could not make use of him. The severe strain told upon his health, however; with unflinching courage and devotion he was able barely to complete his term upon the bench. He died in New Orleans, Aug. 22, 1892.

[The only printed sources of information are the notices in the press (*Times-Democrat, Picayune,* etc.) of New Orleans, Aug. 23, 1892, and the memorial tribute in the *Louisiana Annual* for 1892.] P.B.

BERNARD, BAYLE. [See BERNARD, WILLIAM BAYLE, 1807–1875.]

BERNARD, Sir FRANCIS (July ?, 1712–June 16, 1779), colonial governor, the only child of the Rev. Francis Bernard and his wife, Margery Winlowe, came of an old and well-connected English county family. The date of his birth is unknown, but as he was baptized July 12, 1712, and as baptism usually took place a few days after birth, he probably was born in that month. He became a scholar of St. Peter's College, Westminster, in 1725, proceeding thence to Christ Church, Oxford. In 1733 he became a member of the Middle Temple, was called to the bar in 1737, and soon after settled at Lincoln as a provincial counsel. In 1740 he was appointed commissioner of bails for Lincoln, York, Nottingham, etc., and in 1741 married Amelia Offley, daughter of Stephen Offley of Norton Hall, Derbyshire. The marriage ended the first phase of his career. His aristocratic tastes and a rapidly growing family made an increased income essential. His wife was a niece of the first Viscount Barrington and of Col. Shute, formerly governor of Massachusetts. Bernard soon became intimate with her cousin, the second Lord Barrington, who thenceforward was to be his political sponsor in England. Through Barrington's influence he was appointed governor of New Jersey, arriving there on June 14, 1758. His short term of office was successful and uneventful and was ended by his transfer to Massachusetts. His commission as governor of that colony was dated Jan. 14, 1760, and he arrived in Boston the 2nd of the following August.

The nine years which he spent there were among the most turbulent in the history of the colony. The problems with which he had to grapple were beyond the power of English statesmen to solve and well beyond that of Bernard. On his arrival he wrote that he found the political parties so equally divided that it would be "madness for me to have put myself at the head of either." On account of the necessity of exercising his appointing power he was at once, however, drawn into the arena, and in the steadily growing bitterness of the disputes with the mother country it was inevitable that the representative of the Crown should incur the resentment of the colonial patriots. To indicate the delicacy of Bernard's task it is only needful to point out that his years of office covered the attempted enforcement of the new Sugar Act, the issuance of the hated Writs of Assistance, the Stamp Act, and the quartering of troops in Boston. Had his lot fallen on less troublous times he might have made a good record. He was by no means devoid of ability, and more open than many governors to the colonial point of view. In the trying months of 1763 and 1764 he showed wisdom and a liberal tendency. He realized as few did that the old triangular problem of New England, Old England, and the West Indies, which had taken legislative shape a generation earlier in the Molasses Act, was in reality more of a dispute between England and the island planters than between England and the American continental merchants. He strove hard by sensible arguments sent to his superiors to procure a lowering or abolition of the duties under the Sugar Act, and he regarded the Stamp Act as most inexpedient. As representative of the home Government, however, he was forced to carry out their policies. He did not always do so judiciously and as the turmoil became greater he lost what balance of judgment he may have possessed. He misread the signs of the times and did not understand the people he governed. Innocently but disastrously, he misrepresented conditions to the Government in England, and began to flounder in his own local policies. In October 1768, Commodore Hood, writing to Grenville, said of the Governor, "his doubles and turnings have been so many, that he has altogether lost his road, and brought himself into great contempt." Bernard's ideas on colonial trade were for the most part sound and favorable to the colonists, but his political ideas were fantastically opposed to the wishes and instincts of the people. For example, his scheme for dividing New England into new governments, one of which should embrace Massachusetts, New Hampshire, Rhode Island, and half of Connecticut, showed a doctrinaire obliviousness to colonial psychology. In 1769 a number of letters from him to officials at home were published in Boston and completed his unpopularity. The Assembly sent charges against him to England and he was removed from his post, sailing from Boston Aug. 1, 1769, amid somewhat ungenerous exhibitions of popular rejoicing. The accusations against him of underhand dealings do not bear examination and the English Government finally rejected the Assembly's complaint as "groundless, vexatious, and scandalous." Meanwhile, he had been made a baronet, becoming Sir Francis Bernard of Nettleham, Lincolnshire, by patent dated Apr. 5, 1769. His later years were spent in England and marred by disappointments. A promised pension of £1,000 a year was not paid, though he seems to have received £500 annually, and was appointed commissioner of customs for Ireland. He never resided there and resigned the post in 1774. A pleasant recognition came on July 2, 1772, when he was made an honorary D.C.L. by Oxford but his closing years were spent in almost complete retirement at his place at Aylesbury, where he died June 16, 1779, leaving eight children.

[The first two volumes of *The Bernards of Abington and Nether Winchendon* (1903), by Mrs. Napier Higgins, form practically a biography of the Governor. The letters which did so much to bring his career to an end were published at Boston, 1769, as *Letters to the Right Honourable the Earl of Hillsborough from Gov. Bernard, Gen. Gage, and the Honourable his Majesty's Council for the Province of Massachusetts Bay.* His *Select Letters on the Trade and Government of America* were published in two editions in London in 1774. His commission as governor of New Jersey is given in *N. J. Arch.*, ser. I, vol. IX, pp. 23 ff.; that for Massachusetts in *Pubs. Col. Soc. Mass.*, II, 146 ff. There are thirteen volumes of his correspondence in manuscript in the Harv. Coll. Lib. from which a selection of letters was published by the University Press at Cambridge in 1912 as *The Barrington-Bernard Correspondence.* Alden Bradford's *Speeches of the Governors of Mass. from 1765 to 1775 and the Answers of the House of Representatives* (1818), should also be consulted as well as Hutchinson's *Hist. of Mass. Bay,* vol. III (London, 1828).]

J. T. A.

BERNARD, JOHN (1756–Nov. 29, 1828), actor, theatrical manager, the son of John Bernard, an Irish lieutenant in the British navy, and of Ann Bernard, the daughter of a post captain (J. H. Bernard, *The Bernards of Kerry,* 1922), was born at the naval station at Portsmouth, England. As a boy of ten he began attending the local theatre, where London actors sometimes appeared. At the Latin Academy near Chichester, to which he was sent, he displayed great zeal for acting, and his success as Hamlet at the age of sixteen fired him with determination to make the stage his career. Accordingly he found employment with a strolling company until his mother broke up a performance and marched him back home. All efforts to direct him into the naval or the legal profession proving fruitless, his parents finally allowed him to follow his desire. He was soon engaged as a light comedian by the able Norwich company. At the age of nineteen he married Mrs. Cooper, a fellow player six years his senior. Subsequently he saw service in various provincial companies, including a season at the famous Bath Theatre, until in 1782 he and his wife made a professional visit to Ireland. Two years of Irish hospitality proving too much for his constitution, he accepted another engagement at Bath. Thence he was summoned in 1787 to Covent Garden, the *Ultima Thule* of his dreams, where he played second to Lee Lewis, one of the leading comedians of his day. Experiments with a summer theatre in the provinces led Bernard to form a theatrical circuit in 1791, with playhouses at Plymouth, Dover, and the Isle of Guernsey. This undertaking eventually entailed considerable financial loss, while membership in various convivial clubs, including the celebrated Beefsteak Club, further depleted his resources. Consequently an offer from Wignell, the Philadelphia manager, to come to America at a salary of £1,000 for the first year proved irresistible.

He arrived in the summer of 1797 accompanied by the second Mrs. Bernard, formerly Miss Fisher of the Guernsey company. After making his American début in New York on Aug. 25, as Goldfinch in *The Road to Ruin,* he established himself at Philadelphia, where he remained for six years, playing comedy parts and occasionally more serious rôles, such as Shylock and Hotspur. In 1803 he signed for Boston, and in 1806 he became joint manager of the Federal Street Theatre there. He visited England in the latter year to secure additional players, and, being again a widower, married a Miss Wright as his third wife. After five seasons of unprofitable management at Boston, he withdrew in 1811. A tour of Canada was followed by some performances at the Thespian Hotel at Albany. In January 1813 Albany's first regular playhouse was opened under Bernard's management. Retiring from this position in 1816, he renewed his connection with the Boston theatre and there made his final American appearance, Apr. 19, 1819, in *The Soldier's Daughter.* He then returned to England, where he died in poverty nine years later.

Although Bernard was in error in looking upon himself as one of the founders of the American stage, he was, nevertheless, the most finished comedian this country had yet seen. The Prince of Wales (later George IV) said of him that he could make one laugh heartily without feeling that one had got into low company. His figure, countenance, and manner were marked by a light neatness admirably adapted to the rôles in which he specialized (John Genest, *Some Account of the English Stage from the Restoration in 1660 to 1830,* 1832, VII, 274). America regarded him with general approval. Dunlap called him "a great comedian" (*A History of the*

American Theatre, 1832, p. 183). Other commentators bore testimony to the distinction of his acting and the excellence of his character (William B. Wood, *Personal Recollections of the Stage,* 1855, pp. 46, 72, 88; W. W. Clapp, *A Record of the Boston Stage,* 1853, p. 80; H. P. Phelps, *Players of a Century—a Record of the Albany Stage,* 1880, pp. 44, 45, 51; J. N. Ireland, *Records of the New York Stage,* 1866, I, 160). Socially he achieved a success here, largely because he honestly liked the Americans and showed no trace of condescension toward them.

[Aside from two or three dramatic trifles Bernard's writing consisted of an extensive autobiography, three volumes of selections from which were printed after his death: *Retrospections of the Stage* (2 vols., 1830), ed. by his son [Wm.] Bayle Bernard; and "Early Days of the Am. Stage," ed. by Bayle Bernard, published in *Tallis's Dramatic Mag.,* 1850–51, and republished, with additions from manuscripts prepared by Mrs. Bayle Bernard, as *Retrospections of America* (1887), ed. with an introduction by Brander Matthews and Laurence Hutton. These works, which are the chief source of information about his life, are full of amusing stage anecdotes; they make it clear that Bernard took pleasure in his profession and keenly enjoyed life.]

O. S. C.

BERNARD, SIMON (Apr. 22, 1779–Nov. 5, 1839), French military engineer, was born at Dôle, in the Department of Jura, France. His boyhood was spent in extreme poverty. Graduating at the École Polytechnique, he was appointed lieutenant of engineers in 1797, served in the Army of the Rhine and then in Northern Italy, and was made captain in 1800. He was brought to the personal attention of Napoleon through his success in a secret mission through South Germany and Austria in 1805, collecting information for the campaign which culminated in the battle of Austerlitz. On Mar. 10, 1809, he was married to Marie de Lerchenfeld. From 1810 to 1812, having acquired a high reputation as a military engineer, he was charged with the design and construction of the fortifications of Antwerp. In 1813 he was appointed colonel and aide-de-camp to the Emperor, with whom he served the greater part of the time until the abdication. He distinguished himself by his defense of Torgau during the siege of 1813. Remaining in the army of the Restoration, he was appointed *maréchal de camp* (brigadier-general) in 1814, but rejoined Napoleon on his return from Elba and remained with him till the end. According to Barras, he was the "last officer whom Napoleon had seen by his side at Waterloo" (*Memoirs,* English translation, 1896, IV, 363–64). He then sought and received employment in the United States, on Lafayette's recommendation, a resolution of Congress authorizing the President "to employ a skillful assistant" for the corps of engineers. Bernard was given the pay and the courtesy title of brigadier-general, and placed on the board for planning the coast defenses. Although nominally only an assistant, he was actually allowed such independence that the chief of engineers, Col. Joseph G. Swift, finally found his situation intolerable and resigned from the army in 1818, and was followed a few months later by the senior officer of the board, Lieut.-Col. William McRee (a fort in Pensacola harbor, projected by Bernard, was afterward named Fort McRee). Thereafter the board consisted of Gen. Bernard and Maj. Joseph G. Totten, with other officers temporarily assigned. The two permanent members, both great engineers, preserved harmony by working independently of each other as a rule, and gradually worked out a complete system of defense, including not only plans for modern forts on the coast, but also a project for extensive development of interior communication by roads and canals. The fortifications were largely completed sooner or later. The work of the board also served as the basis on which several canals were constructed, before the railroad era rendered the comprehensive plan of communications obsolete. Upon the accession of Louis Philippe, Bernard gave up his position and returned to France. His work in the United States had been of incalculable value, though it is unfortunate that he was employed in such a way as to force out of the army two of its ablest engineers. His chief monument is Fort Monroe, in Virginia—the greatest fortress in the country when planned, and still preserved in all its perfection. Restored to the army in France, he was appointed lieutenant-general in 1831, and served as aide-de-camp to the King and then as inspector-general of engineers. He was minister of war for a short time in 1834, and again from 1836 to 1839. He was created baron shortly before his death.

[Article by Gen. W. H. Carter in *Jour. of the Mil. Service Institution* (1912), LI, 147–55, republished (1913) in *Professional Memoirs, Corps of Engineers,* V, 306–14; L. A. F. de Bourrienne, *Life of Napoleon Bonaparte* (English translation, 1831), II, 380–82; G. W. Cullum, *Biog. Reg.* (3rd ed., 1891), I, 55, 61, 65, for mention of Bernard's relations with Swift, McRee, and Totten.]

T. M. S.

BERNARD, WILLIAM BAYLE (Nov. 27, 1807–Aug. 5, 1875), dramatist, biographer, a son of the English actor John Bernard [*q.v.*], was born in Boston. His mother had been a Miss Wright, whom his father had married as his third wife shortly before leaving London and who had previously been the governess of his motherless children. The entire family returned to England in 1819, and that country was thenceforth Bayle Bernard's home. Many years later, in his biography of Samuel Lover with whom he had been "intimate for several years from the period of his first arrival in London," he refers to his native country in these words: "Born in America—where I had traveled in my youth—I was able to enlarge from my own memory many of his necessarily hasty jottings upon western scenery and cities." Later on in the same book he recalls the "look of Boston" as "unequivocally English." In addition to this life of Lover, which was declared by the *Spectator* to "fill an undeniable blank in biographical literature," he prepared from manuscript papers his father's *Retrospections of the Stage, by the late John Bernard, Manager of the American Theatre and formerly Secretary of the Beefsteak Club,* which was published in two volumes in London in 1830, and two years afterward in Boston. From other manuscripts he compiled and edited "Early Days of the American Stage," which appeared serially in *Tallis's Dramatic Magazine* in 1850 and 1851. A portion of these papers, with additions from manuscripts prepared by his widow, appeared in book form in 1887 under title of *Retrospections of America (1797–1811)*, edited with an introduction by Brander Matthews and Laurence Hutton. His association with the stage as an actor was brief, but he was all his life a constant and successful writer of popular plays which he had begun to produce while serving as a clerk in the Army Accounts Office from 1826 to 1830. During that period he also wrote a novel entitled *The Freebooter's Bride*. He made one of the early dramatic versions of *Rip Van Winkle* (1832) which was acted by James H. Hackett both in England and in this country (its first performance was at the Park Theatre in New York, Sept. 4, 1833). The same actor also played the leading part in another of his comedies, *The Kentuckian*. He wrote plays for Yankee Hill, Josh Silsbee, and other American actors, and may therefore be considered the popularizer, if not the inventor, of the eccentric rural American on the stage. Many of his plays were farces, among them *His Last Legs* (1839), one of the most popular pieces of its kind both in England and in America, in which Hackett, John Brougham, and other famous actors for many years played the once familiar comic character of O'Callaghan. Bernard made a stage version of *Faust,* produced with Spohr's music at Drury Lane in London with Samuel Phelps as Mephistopheles and Mrs. Hermann Vezin as Marguerite. This play was acted many times by Lewis Morrison on the American stage after Sir Henry Irving's production of W. G. Wills's version of *Faust* had re-created a theatrical interest in the old story. Among Bernard's more than one hundred plays are *The Dumb Belle* (acted at the Olympic Theatre in 1831 with Madame Vestris in the title rôle), *The Tide of Time, The Nervous Man, The Old Style and the New, The Evil Genius, The Middy Ashore,* and *The Man with Two Lives.* He was an active participant in the literary, theatrical, and bohemian life of London for nearly half a century, and there is scarcely a book of theatrical reminiscences of his period in which he is not frequently mentioned. His biographical works about his father make him a valuable contributor to the annals of the early American stage.

[*Retrospections of the Stage* (1830) and *Retrospections of America* (1887) furnish important information about Bayle Bernard, as does also *The Life and Times of Edward Leman Blanchard* (London, 1891), by Clement Scott and Cecil Howard. A valuable article in the *Era* (London) Dec. 2, 1899, contains material about Bayle Bernard's version of *Rip Van Winkle*; further information upon the same subject is given by William Winter in *The Jeffersons* (1881). In Bernard's *Life of Samuel Lover* (1874) are scattered autobiographical bits.]

E. F. E.

BERNAYS, AUGUSTUS CHARLES (Oct. 13, 1854–May 22, 1907), surgeon, was born at Highland, Ill., the son of Dr. George Bernays and Minna Döring, German Jews from Hesse-Darmstadt. His father later locating in St. Louis, the young Augustus obtained his primary education in public and private schools there. He received the degree of B.A. from McKendree College, Lebanon, Ill., in 1872 and his medical degree from Heidelberg in 1876. Following special courses under Von Langenbeck in Berlin and Billroth in Vienna he qualified for membership in the Royal College of Surgeons of London in 1877. Returning to St. Louis he took up the practise of medicine with his father. His is credited with being the first in that city to devote himself exclusively to surgical practise. From an association with Lister in London he became a pioneer in antiseptic and later in aseptic surgery. A daring operator, confident and resourceful, he excelled in the difficult field of plastic surgery. He successively occupied the chairs of surgery at the St. Louis College of Physicians and Surgeons and at Marion Sims College; his undoubted popularity as a teacher lay in his mastery of the basic medical sciences and in his enthusiastic earnestness. His writings were mainly case reports in medical periodicals, illustrating special pathology, surgical anatomy, or surgical technique. In his *Golden Rules of Surgery* (1906) he summarized his earlier observations on the science and art of his craft. In 1903 he suffered a stroke of apoplexy, after which he practised little, devoting his time to travels and writing. He died suddenly at the age of fifty-two from rupture of a cardiac aneurism.

Bernays was of the romantic temperament, emotional, impulsive, lacking in tact, and given to forceful and extravagant language. He was an outspoken and aggressive agnostic. In his early career these traits, together with questions of ethics, brought him into controversy with the St. Louis Medical Society. The gambling spirit was inherent in him. His diversions were attending horse races, betting on them, keeping a stable, and training the horses. His portraits show an aggressive face of Oriental cast, high, broad forehead, prominent eyes, and full lips. He never married but always made his home with a sister, to whom he was devotedly attached.

[A detailed biography with bibliography of Bernays's writings is contained in *Augustus Charles Bernays; a Memoir,* by Thekla Bernays (1912). This work contains portraits at different times of life. The various biographical sketches written at the time of Bernays's death add nothing to the data contained in his sister's book.]

J. M. P.

BERRIEN, JOHN MACPHERSON (Aug. 23, 1781–Jan. 1, 1856), congressman, was a native of New Jersey. His forebears were men of some prominence, his grandfather, John Berrien, having been a judge of the supreme court of New Jersey, and his father, also named John, a major in the American Revolution. The family was of Huguenot descent. His mother, Margaret MacPherson, of Scotch lineage, was the sister of John MacPherson, who, as aide-de-camp to Montgomery, was killed in the battle of Quebec. His parents removed to Georgia in 1782. After preparatory schooling in New York, Berrien matriculated at Princeton and was graduated in 1796. Returning to Savannah he studied law in the office of Joseph Clay, a federal judge; was admitted to practise in 1799; elected solicitor of the eastern circuit (1809); a year later became judge of the same circuit and held office until 1821; served one term (1822–23) in the state Senate; and, in 1824, was elected United States senator. He was an adherent of the Jackson faction of the Democratic-Republican party. In his speeches he advocated the current Georgia views in the controversy over the final Creek land cession. He opposed the Tariff of 1828, presenting a protest of the Georgia legislature against it. In 1829 he resigned to take office as attorney-general in Jackson's first cabinet, but, becoming estranged from the President on account of the Eaton affair, resigned on June 22, 1831. After ten years in private life he was returned to the Senate in 1841 as a Whig and served until May 28, 1852.

The period of his second session in the Senate was a momentous one in American history, and Berrien, then in the prime of his intellectual powers, became an outstanding leader in his party. He was a man of commanding personal appearance, a learned and skilful advocate, and an orator of unusual power. He supported the Whig positions on the Bank question, protective tariffs, territorial extension, and compromise of the slavery issue. Thus he at first opposed the annexation of Texas (*Congressional Globe,* 28 Cong., 2 Sess., pp. 383–87), alleging unconstitutionality in the attempted mode of admission. But in the next session, after the joint resolution of Congress had been passed committing the United States to the admission of Texas on certain conditions, and after these conditions had been met, he felt obliged to sustain the pledge of the country. Furthermore, he was then able to discover good reasons why Texas should be admitted, and so voted. He opposed the Mexican War, speaking against the bill declaring war and refusing, though present, to cast a vote on the final passage of the bill (T. H. Benton, *Abridgment of the Debates of Congress from 1789 to 1856,* XV, 505, 510). On the bill to provide $3,000,000 to be used in effecting a peace with Mexico, Berrien introduced an amendment (*Congressional Globe,* 29 Cong., 2 Sess., pp. 325–330) against taking any territory from Mexico, basing his opposition on the ground that the free states, by reason of their numerical superiority, would exclude slavery and thus deny to the South equal participation in the benefits of such acquisition of territory. He appealed to senators to exclude "this direful question" (slavery) from the national councils. When it began to look as if all factions in the anti-slavery North would combine to adopt the Wilmot Proviso, excluding slavery from the new territories, Calhoun called a caucus of Southern representatives and senators, Democrats and Whigs, and sought to form a Southern party (December 1848). Calhoun's *Address* was adopted, the Whigs voting against it. Berrien also issued an *Address to the People of the United States* (February 1849) in which he pleaded for a compromise of the slavery problem. The next year, however, he altered his position. He came out against Clay's Compromise, abandoning his long-sustained position of moderation and shifting over to a strong pro-Southern attitude. On the final passage of the various component parts of the Omnibus Bill he voted against the admission of California and the abolition of the slave trade in the District of Columbia, and for the organization of territorial government in New Mexico and Utah and the new Fugitive Slave Law. Convinced that the Whig party could no longer be relied on to protect Southern interests, he withdrew from the party in 1850. He strongly advocated "Non-Intercourse" in a business way as a form of resistance against Northern encroachment on Southern rights. He rejected secession, but believed resistance within the Union a necessity. In the stirring gubernatorial campaign in Georgia in 1851, in which the "finality" of the Compromise of 1850 was the issue, Berrien, in a half-hearted manner, accepted the "Georgia Platform," on which the Union candidate, Howell Cobb, ran, but took no active part in the campaign. A few weeks after the election it became incumbent upon the legislature to elect a United States senator, Berrien's term approaching a close. Berrien at first declined to become a candidate for reëlection, but later on announced that he would accept, if elected. The Union Democrats and Whigs combined to defeat him and elected Robert Toombs in his place (Nov. 10, 1851). Berrien thereupon resigned his senatorship. When the American or Know-Nothing party was organized, he joined it; and his last political activity was to preside over a state convention of the new party held at the Capital in December 1855. Shortly after this meeting, he died on Jan. 1, 1856. Thus passed from the stage one of the last of the elder statesmen, for many years regarded as the ablest constitutional lawyer in the Senate.

[U. B. Phillips, *Ga. and State Rights* (1902), and R. H. Shryock, *Ga. and the Union in 1850* (1926), discuss briefly Berrien's positions on political questions. Chas. C. Jones's address delivered before the Ga. Bar Ass. (*Report,* 1891) is devoted largely to an account of Berrien's personal traits and his career as a lawyer. There is a contemporary sketch of considerable importance in S. F. Miller, *Bench and Bar of Ga.* (1858), vol. I, ch. 3.]

R. P. B–s.

BERRY, HIRAM GREGORY (Aug. 27, 1824–May 3, 1863), Union soldier, was a native of Thomaston (now a part of the city of Rockland), Me. His parents were Jeremiah and Frances (Gregory) Berry. He came of fighting stock, as his grandfather was a soldier of the Revolution, and his father a veteran of the War of 1812. He began life as a carpenter, but rose to be a builder and a business man, and president of a bank. He was a Democrat in politics, a member of the legislature, and one of the early mayors in the new city of Rockland. Having been a captain of militia before the Civil War, at its beginning he was chosen colonel of the 4th Maine. He led this regiment, and afterward a brigade, and finally a division in the Army of the Potomac, and served from the first battle of Bull Run until his death. He was commissioned brigadier-general of volunteers Mar. 17, 1862, and commanded a brigade in Gen. Kearny's division during the Peninsula campaign. He was particularly distinguished at the battles of Williamsburg (May 5) and Fair Oaks (May 31–June 1, 1862), and was commended by the division commanders Kearny and Hooker, by the corps commander Heintzelman, and by McClellan. Suffering from injury and ill health he was on furlough at Rockland, but returned in time for the battle of Fredericksburg, having been commissioned major-general of volunteers Nov. 29, 1862. A picturesque incident is related in regard to this battle: the Confederate general, A. P. Hill, is said to have presented his compliments to Berry, with the remark that his command was the "best behaved brigade that he ever saw under fire" (Gould, p. 221).

In February 1863, after Hooker had succeeded Burnside in command of the Army of the Potomac, Berry was promoted to a division (formerly Hooker's division) in the 3rd Corps. As general of this division he had an important part in the battle of Chancellorsville, May 2 and 3, and was killed in the crisis of the struggle. "The damage incurred in the rout of the Eleventh Corps, great as it was, had been almost repaired before the morning of the 3rd by the readiness and energy of Pleasonton, Sickles, and Hiram G. Berry . . . " (Nicolay and Hay, *Abraham Lincoln, A History,* 1890, VII, 104). According to a fellow-officer, "He was a plain, straightforward man, tall and broad-shouldered. His blue flannel blouse and his whole dress gave him very little of a military air. But whoever judged him from his appearance would have judged badly . . . he was not the less a good officer, as faithful to his duty as he was devoted to his soldiers. . . . In him the moral energy strove against physical weakness" (Regis Trobriand, *Four Years with the Army of the Potomac,* 1889, p. 370). Berry's gallantry and bearing under fire—as at the battle of Fredericksburg—and his personal relations with his men, are illustrated by a variety of anecdotes.

[Edward K. Gould, *Major-General Hiram G. Berry* (1899); Nathaniel Butler, *Discourse at the Funeral of Major-General H. G. Berry* (1863); Alexander Webb, *The Peninsula: McClellan's Campaign of 1862* (1881); F. B. Heitman, *Hist. Reg.* (1903).]

E. K. A.

BERRY, JAMES HENDERSON (May 15, 1841–Jan. 30, 1913), governor of Arkansas, senator, was born in Jackson County, Ala., son of James M. and Isabella Jane (Orr) Berry. His mother was a descendant of John Orr, who settled in Pennsylvania early in the eighteenth century. James was the fourth of ten children. When he was seven years old his father moved to Carrollton, Carroll County, Ark. His educational advantages were very meager, the best being one year at the Berryville academy. He enlisted in the Confederate army in 1861 and was elected second lieutenant in Company E, 16th Arkansas Infantry. He fought at Pea Ridge (Elk Horn), Iuka, and Corinth, losing a leg at the last-named place. On his recovery he went to Texas and remained there until the war closed. In returning home he stopped at Ozark, taught school a while, read law, and married Lizzie Quaile. Going back to Carrollton, he was elected to the legislature in 1866, being the youngest member of that body. As soon as the legislature adjourned he took up the practise of law at Carrollton, but moved to Bentonville in 1869 and formed a partnership with Sam W. Peel. His political career began in 1872, when he was elected to the legislature as a Democrat. A bitter struggle was on in the effort to recover the state from carpet-bag rule. At first the legislature had a Republican majority, but several resigned to accept appointments and enough Democrats were elected to give them control. When the Republican speaker, C. W. Tankersly, sided with Brooks at the called session of 1874 in the Brooks-Baxter war, he was deposed and Berry was elected in his place (Dallas T. Herndon, *Centennial History of Arkansas,* 1922, I, 312–13). In 1878 he was elected judge of the circuit court of the fourth district, serving for three years. In 1882 he was nominated by the Democratic convention as candidate for governor and was elected by a considerable majority. A leading plank in the Democratic platform was the demand for the re-submission of the Fishback amendment repudiating the bonds issued by the carpet-bag government to aid in building railroads and levees and the "Holford" bonds ($500,000) issued in 1838 to the Real Estate Bank. This had failed to get the necessary majority in 1880. Berry now championed the amendment and in his inaugural address advocated re-submission. The amendment was re-submitted and this time was carried by a large majority (Fay Hempstead, *Pictorial History of Arkansas,* 1890, pp. 281–83). The Holford bonds had been disposed of in violation of law, but all really due on them except $67,967.33 had been paid by this time (W. C. Evans, "History of the Public Debt of Arkansas," a master's thesis in manuscript, Library of the University of Arkansas). Berry's administration also marked the beginning of labor legislation in the state.

In 1885 he was elected to the United States Senate and served continuously until 1907, when he was defeated by Jeff Davis. While senator, he supported Senator Beck's bill to prohibit members of Congress from serving as attorneys for any government-aided railroad, was on the committee on public lands, and was chairman when the Democrats had a majority. In this position he sought to protect the public interests, especially against fraudulent entries and timber thieves. He took a lively interest in Indian affairs and introduced a bill creating the Territory of Indianola for the region occupied by the Indians with a view to allotting the lands in severalty. His bill failed, but later some of his ideas were incorporated in the bill providing for the Dawes Commission. In October 1910 Berry was appointed, at the request of President Taft, to mark the graves of Confederate soldiers who had died in Northern prisons, and he carried the work to completion in 1912.

[Berry's *Autobiography* (1913) is undoubtedly the most reliable source for the bare facts of his life. See *Cong. Record,* 1885–1907, for his career in Congress. A portrait of him appears in John Hallum's *Biog. and Critical Hist. of Ark.,* vol. I (1887).] D. Y. T.

BERRY, NATHANIEL SPRINGER (Sept. 1, 1796–Apr. 27, 1894), governor of New Hampshire, son of Abner and Betsey (Springer) Berry, was born at Bath, Me. The accidental death of his father, a ship-builder, when Nathaniel was six years old, meant a boyhood of hard work and meager educational opportunity. When about fourteen he moved to Lisbon, N. H., and soon afterward to Bath, in the same state. He served an apprenticeship in the tannery business, afterward settling in 1818 at Bristol, N. H., where he established a tannery which he operated for many years. He had personally investigated improved methods and equipment used in tanneries in the state of New York and was reported to be the first tanner in New England to use hot liquids, a method which greatly reduced the time required for the treatment of hides. He was henceforth identified with many activities, business, political and religious, in the town of Bristol, and in its records his name constantly appears on committees, directorates, and programs. He was twice married: on Jan. 26, 1821, to Ruth Smith, who died in 1857; and in January 1860 to Mrs. Louise Farley.

Berry represented Bristol in the legislature 1828, 1833, 1834, and 1837, and the neighboring town of Hebron in 1854. He was senator from the 11th district in 1835 and 1836. Beginning with 1841, he was associate justice of the court of common pleas and in 1856 began five years' service as probate judge of Grafton County. He was a Democrat in his earlier years and a delegate to the Baltimore Convention of 1840, but with the rise of the slavery issue he became increasingly dissatisfied with the Democratic attitude toward that question and by 1844 had definitely severed his connection with the party. In 1846 he was supported for the governorship by the Liberty party and a group of independent Democrats. The question of the annexation of Texas was disrupting the existing parties, and Berry received enough popular votes to force the decision into the legislature where, however, he failed of election. In the following years he devoted himself to the organization of the Free-Soil movement and was unsuccessfully supported for the governorship by the new party and sundry coalitions in 1847, 1848, 1849, and 1850.

He was generally regarded as an extremist and too closely allied with the abolitionist wing of the Anti-Slavery movement. In 1861, when nominated for the governorship by the Republican party into which he had naturally gravitated, he was denounced by the leading Democratic organ as "one of the fossils of the old abolition party who has been scarcely heard of for ten years past ... a man who had been regarded as too ultra and fanatical even for the radical tone of their party during the last six years. . . . To vote for Berry is to vote to aggravate present difficulties, to oppose all concessions for the preservation of the Union, to invite and hasten the untold woes which must attend the fratricidal strife, the bloody civil war, which their policy is sure to precipitate upon the country" (*New Hampshire Patriot and State Gazette,* Jan. 16, 1861). Elected nevertheless, Berry in his inaugural message, June 4, 1861, made a spirited call for men and money to meet the crisis, declaring his confident expectation that "the principles upon which the republic was founded will be vindicated and made permanent; the Constitution will be sustained; the Constitutional rights of all American citizens, in all the States, will receive new guaranties; the freedom of speech and of the press everywhere in our land will be effectually secured; and the Government will come forth purified and strengthened" (*New Hampshire Statesman,* June 8, 1861). He threw himself into the difficult task of getting the state on a war footing, and proved an energetic and inspiring executive, ranking high among the "war governors." From the first he strongly advocated emancipation. In September 1862 he attended the conference of loyal governors at Altoona, and his name appears on the formal address which the conference presented to President Lincoln. After his retirement from the governorship in 1863, he moved in the following year to Massachusetts, where he resided for some time with members of his family at Andover and Worcester; later, for several years, he resided with a daughter in Milwaukee, Wis. His last years were spent at the home of a son in Bristol, N. H. Although some had considered his age a disqualification for the strenuous duties of the governorship in 1861, he survived his retirement from that office for more than thirty years, dying at the age of ninety-seven.

[A brief biography, with portrait, in *Hist. of the Town of Bristol* (1904), by R. W. Musgrove; obituary in the *Concord Evening Monitor,* Apr. 27, 1894.]

W. A. R.

BERTRAM, JOHN (Feb. 11, 1796–Mar. 22, 1882), sea-captain, merchant, was born in the parish of Saint Sauveur in the island of Jersey, the son of John and Mary (Perchard) Bertram. In 1807 the family moved to America, settling by chance at Salem where young John continued the education commenced in Jersey and in England. Late in 1812 he went to sea as cabin-boy in the merchantman *Hazard* at five dollars a month, and then served in two privateers, the *Monkey* and the *Herald,* the latter being captured by the British. Returning from prison at the close of the war, he continued at sea, sailing to various parts of the world. By 1821, he had risen to mate, and his first command was the schooner *General Brewer,* which he chartered for a profitable venture to St. Helena. His eyes were constantly open for trading opportunities, and his fortune began to rise after two successful years of gathering hides on the coast of Patagonia. His last voyage as captain was to Zanzibar in the *Black Warrior* in 1830. He was able to buy from the sultan a cargo of gum copal. This was much in demand by the varnish makers at home and was the beginning of a very lucrative trade. Upon his return in 1832, Bertram stayed ashore as shipowner and merchant, continuing the Zanzibar trade and later developing a lively commerce with Para. The first ship sent to California from the United States at the time of the gold rush was the brig *Eliza* which he dispatched in December 1848. At the same time he and his associates gave rush orders for the construction of a large clipper ship which bore his name. This, with several other clippers, brought him large profits from the Pacific trade. During the fifties, he foresaw the decline in American shipping and gradually restricted his scope of commerce to Zanzibar. By 1856 he was becoming interested in western railways and subscribed heavily to several lines. During his later years, he was much interested in philanthropy. "I want to live so long as I can do good, no longer," he once said. The Bertram

Home for Aged Men and the Salem Fuel Fund were among his special benevolences, but he gave generously to dozens of others. He was the last of the merchants of the old type, holding a position similar to that of Derby, Crowninshield, and Peabody at the beginning of the century. His portrait shows a keen but kindly face with much white hair and white whiskers. He was married three times: in 1823 to Mary G. Smith, in 1838 to Mrs. Clarissa Millett, and in 1848 to Mary Ann Ropes.

[The best account of Bertram's life is the detailed memorial in the *Essex Institute Hist. Colls.*, XXI, 81–96. There is a shorter sketch in the same series, XV, 308, with a portrait, and scattered references to his ships will be found throughout the collections. An excellent portrait, with a short account, is in R. D. Paine's *Ships and Sailors of Old Salem* (rev. ed., 1923), pp. 440–45.] R. G. A.

BESSEY, CHARLES EDWIN (May 21, 1845–Feb. 25, 1915), botanist, was born in a log house on a farm in Wayne County, Ohio. His father's family was of Huguenot extraction, the name having originally been Bessé. The family is supposed to have fled from Alsace in the seventeenth century, first to England, then to Pennsylvania. His father, Adnah, taught school in Ohio, and married Margaret Ellenberger, one of his pupils. Charles Bessey received his early training from his father; he entered an academy at Seville, Ohio, in his seventeenth year, but the death of his father caused him to take a teaching position at Wadsworth. He soon reëntered the academy, only to be a spectator of its dissolution. At last, largely self-taught, he entered the Michigan Agricultural College in 1866, graduating in 1869 with the degree of B.S. He intended to prepare himself for a career of civil engineering, but his noticeable love of plant life caused President Abbott and Prof. Prentiss to persuade him to become a botanist. After graduation he accepted an instructorship in botany and horticulture at Iowa State College of Agriculture. He was active the following year in the famous meetings of the Farmers' Institute held in Iowa, and in 1875 and for several years after was president of this organization. In 1872 he met Asa Gray at the meeting of the American Association for the Advancement of Science at Dubuque, and in the winter of 1872–73 he studied under Gray. He returned to Harvard for another period of study under him in 1875–76. The strict and formal training imparted by the leader of American botany was a lasting influence in Bessey's career, balancing his strong practical inclinations with a grounding in the theory of botany.

In 1884 he accepted the invitation of the University of Nebraska to take the chair of botany, but only after he had made a visit, had found the institution without plans or equipment for botanical courses, and had, by a tentative refusal, inaugurated favorable changes in the new institution. From then on till his death his name was associated with that of agriculture and botanical science in Nebraska. He threw himself at once into the work of agricultural organization, and into the investigation of the state's vegetation. The popularity of his teaching methods, untechnical and well illustrated, was immediate, and when he received his crowning honor, in his election as president of the American Association for the Advancement of Science in 1910, his return from the meeting was celebrated by an ovation from the entire body of the University. In the closing years of his life he assumed heavy administrative duties as dean and chancellor.

During the years 1883–1914 he issued seven text-books of botany; and the number of his miscellaneous articles is well above a hundred, of which the most suggestive are those dealing with the reconstruction of the evolutionary tree of the plant phyla and families. (See his "Evolution and Classification," in *Proceedings of the American Association for the Advancement of Science,* vol. XLII; "The Phyletic Idea in Taxonomy," in *Science,* n. s., vol. XXIX, 1900; and "The Phylogenetic Taxonomy of Flowering Plants," in *Annals of the Missouri Botanical Garden,* vol. II, 1915). Whatever the limitations of Bessey's view-point, he set the mind of the botanical fraternity in motion, after it had lain too passive on the vital subject of classification, and his influence ultimately reached European circles. One of his last and most philosophic addresses was his prophetic "Some of the Next Steps in Botanical Science," in *Science,* n. s., XXXVII, 1–13 (1913).

[R. J. Pool, *Am. Jour. Bot.,* II, 505–18, with portrait and bibliography.] D. C. P.

BETHUNE, GEORGE WASHINGTON (Mar. 18, 1805–Apr. 28, 1862), Dutch Reformed clergyman. was born in New York, the son of Divie (afterward Richard) Bethune, of Huguenot extraction, and his wife, Joanna Graham, both being natives of Scotland. The boy was reared in a home of wealth and piety, was instructed by private tutors and at the academy at Salem, N. Y., and entered Columbia in 1819. After three years there he went to Dickinson College, Carlisle, Pa., where he graduated in 1823. After studying theology at Princeton, he was ordained by the Second Presbytery of New York, Nov. 10, 1827, and immediately entered the Dutch Reformed Church, where he remained throughout his life. His pastorates were: Rhinebeck, N. Y., 1827–30; Utica, 1830–34; the First and Third churches in Philadelphia, 1834–49; Brooklyn Heights, 1850–59; and the Twenty-first Street Church, New York City, 1859–62. He made several extended trips to Europe, and died of apoplexy at Florence, Italy, where he had gone for the recovery of his health.

At various times in his life the way was opened to him to become chaplain and professor of moral science at West Point, chancellor of New York University, and provost of the University of Pennsylvania. But he preferred to remain in the pastorate. While in Brooklyn he was for a time lecturer on pulpit oratory in the Theological Seminary at New Brunswick. His pulpit work was distinguished for its oratorical power and its devotional qualities. He was an exact student, a musician, a poet, the author of several well-known hymns and many publications on religious themes. He published a volume of his own poems, entitled *Lays of Love and Faith* (1848), and edited *The British Female Poets, with Biographical and Critical Notices* (1848). In 1846 he issued the first American edition of Walton's Complete Angler, in which the volume of the work itself was nearly equaled by that of the editor's introduction and appendix containing ballads, music, and papers on American fishing, with the most complete catalogue of books on angling ever printed. Owing to the public feeling against the propriety of such a book by a clergyman, it was published anonymously. An untiring fisherman, Bethune also collected about 700 works on angling and kindred subjects. In politics he was a staunch Democrat, was opposed alike to slavery and Abolitionism and was a prominent member of the Colonization Society. He was the author of a letter to President Buchanan urging him to suppress the pro-slavery propaganda of the South, and when the Confederacy was formed he stood firmly for the Union. On Nov. 4, 1825, he married Mary Williams, to whom he was deeply devoted. Mrs. Bethune, who survived her husband, was an invalid for most of her life, and there were no children.

[*A Memoir* (1867) of Dr. Bethune was written by Dr. A. R. Van Nest, his colleague in his last pastorate. Briefer accounts are found in Henry Fowler's *Am. Pulpit* (1856) and Edward T. Corwin's *Manual of the Reformed Ch. in America* (3rd ed., 1879). All the foregoing have portraits, and in the last there is a full bibliography of Bethune's published works.]

F. T. P.

BETTENDORF, WILLIAM PETER (July 1, 1857–June 3, 1910), inventor, manufacturer, was born in Mendota, Ill., the eldest of the four children of Michael and Catherine (Reck) Bettendorf. His meager schooling was acquired in the common schools of Missouri and Kansas, where his parents made their home, and at St. Mary's Mission School, an Indian school in Kansas. When about fifteen he began work as a machinist with the Peru Plow Company (Peru, Ill.), later being employed with the Moline Plow Company (Moline, Ill.), and with the Partin & Orendorff Company (Canton, Ohio); in 1882 he returned to the Peru Plow Company as superintendent and remained with them until 1886. In 1879 he married Mary Wortman, who died in 1901; and in 1908 he married Mrs. Elizabeth Staby. His career as an inventor began in 1878 with the invention of the first power-lift sulky plow. A few years later he invented the Bettendorf Metal Wheel (for wagons and farm implements) and the machinery for its manufacture. In 1886, in conjunction with his brother, J. W. Bettendorf, he undertook the manufacture of this wheel at Davenport, Ia., and was successful. The further use of steel for farm implements intrigued his imagination, and in 1892 he developed a steel gear for farm wagons. New machinery for its manufacture had to be designed and built, and he gave all his time to the task. In 1905 this machinery was sold to the International Harvester Company, but his own company at Davenport, which was manufacturing steel gears in addition to the metal wheels, continued the manufacture of gears under contract. The next step conceived in Bettendorf's fertile brain was to enter the railroad field, where steel was fast being substituted for wood. His Davenport plant was large and in many ways adapted to this kind of manufacturing; so he soon began to add railway-car parts to its production. A new car bolster designed and patented by him, using two commercial I-beams shaped and joined together with a few small parts, had an immediate sale and is found today under railway cars all over the country. After this came a new cast-steel side-frame truck and then the Bettendorf integral journal-box. Eventually he was manufacturing complete railway cars. His aim was always toward simplification—fewer parts, less weight, greater strength. At the time of his death he was working on a complete steel freight car. With success in the manufacture and sale of railway car parts assured, a new plant was built three miles from Davenport in a town called Gilbert. The name of this town was changed to Bettendorf, and he took an active interest in the development and welfare of this community. His success was due not only to his inventive ability but to the confidence which he justly inspired and to the business ability which, combined with that of his brother, made it possible for him to weather the competition which was so keen a part of the manufacturing life of his day.

[Material for this sketch has been obtained from the *Railway Age Gazette,* XLVIII, No. 23; *Farm Machinery,* June 7, 1910; *Farm Implement News,* June 9, 1910; and from Mr. Henry Bellinghausen, attorney for the Bettendorf Co.]

E.Y.

BETTS, SAMUEL ROSSITER (June 8, 1786–Nov. 3, 1868), jurist, son of Uriah and Sarah (Rossiter) Betts, was born at Richmond, Berkshire County, Mass. He was first educated in the rural school, then tutored for college at Lenox Academy, Lenox, Mass. In 1806, after four years of study, he graduated from Williams College. Removing to Hudson, N. Y., he began to study law and was admitted to the bar in 1809, opening a law office in Monticello in the newly organized Sullivan County. His legal practise was disrupted by the War of 1812 when he enlisted in the army and served in the defense of New York Harbor until appointed by Gov. Tompkins as division judge-advocate in that vicinity (Daniel D. Tompkins, *Public Papers . . . Military,* I, 720). After the war he was elected to Congress in 1815 from Sullivan and Orange counties but declined reëlection in 1817 and resumed the practise of law at Newburgh. While a congressman, on Nov. 4, 1816, he married Caroline A. Dewey of Northampton, Mass. For two years he served as district attorney of Orange County. His genial disposition, industry, and ability brought him into prominence, and led to his appointment in 1823 as a circuit judge of the supreme court of New York. Three years later in 1826 he was elevated by President John Quincy Adams to the United States district court for the southern district of New York—a position he filled till 1867, more than forty years, with urbanity, kindness, wisdom, and legal erudition. When he moved to New York City in 1827 the admiralty court had few cases but under Judge Betts its work was quadrupled. He is generally credited with an authoritative restatement of American admiralty law, and his decisions in numerous cases of maritime law gave him such a high standing as a judge in that branch of law that for a score of years none of his rulings were appealed. With the outbreak of the Civil War such problems as slavery, neutrality, blockade, prize, and contraband, involving both national and international law, came before him as new questions and were settled on cogent reasoning and fundamental legal principles. In addition to these cases in admiralty law, violations of the national criminal law and cases of patents and bankruptcy were presented to him for adjustment. His decisions were characterized by learned research, clarity, and logical statement. Many of his opinions, accepted as fundamental statements of the law, were written after the age of seventy-five.

[The best biography of Betts has been written by two of his descendants in a privately published pamphlet, *Thos. Betts and His Descendants* (1888). An appreciation of his life and work by his legal colleagues is given in Benedict, *Reports,* vol. II, App., pp. 559–62. In 1838 Betts published an authoritative work on *Admiralty Practice.* His legal opinions are published in Blatchford and Howland, *Reports,* vol. I (covering the period 1827–37); Olcott, *Reports* (covering the period 1843–47); Abbott, *Reports of Cases in Admiralty* (covering the period 1847–50) and Blatchford, *Prize Cases* (covering the period 1861–65). See also Blatchford, *Reports* (covering the period 1845–67), and Benedict, *Reports* (Eastern District N. Y., 1845–67). *The Civil List* of N. Y. contains data on his political service.]

A. C. F.

BEVERIDGE, ALBERT JEREMIAH (Oct. 6, 1862–Apr. 27, 1927), senator, historian, was born on a small farm in Highland County, Ohio, the son of Thomas H. and Frances (Parkinson) Beveridge. In 1865 the father, after the loss of his property, moved the family to a farm in Illinois. Young Beveridge's early life was one of privation and hardship. He was a plowboy at twelve, a railroad hand with a section gang at fourteen, a logger and teamster at fifteen. Before he was sixteen, however, he managed to enter a high school. His yearning for knowledge led him to determine to go to college, and with a loan of $50 from a friend, in the fall of 1881 he entered Asbury College, now DePauw University, at Greencastle, Ind. During his college course he won the inter-state oratorical honors and prizes sufficient to provide for two of his college years. He graduated in 1885. He was twice married: in 1887 to Katherine Langsdale of Greencastle, Ind., who died June 18, 1900; in 1907 to Catherine Eddy of Chicago. Admitted to the bar in 1887, for twelve years Beveridge practised law in Indianapolis. Meanwhile he had become well known in his state as a political orator. In every campaign for fifteen years, beginning while yet a college boy, as early as the Blaine campaign of 1884, he had stumped the state from end to end. In a deadlock among the leading senatorial candidates in 1899 the Republican legislative caucus turned to him as a compromise candidate, and he was elected to the United States Senate at the age of thirty-six, being among the youngest members ever to sit in that body. In 1905 he was reëlected without opposition within his party, but in 1911, chiefly because of party schism, he was defeated for a third term, after which he never again held public office. The twelve years of his senatorial service were a period of agitation, of party revolt and insurgency, leading to the rise of the Progressive party. Beveridge was one of the Senate "insurgents," one of the original Progressive Republicans. He supported the Roosevelt policies, such as equal industrial opportunities, prevention of trust abuses, government regulation of public service corporations, a strong navy, the meat inspection law (which he drafted), conservation of national resources, and extension of nominating primaries. He was outstanding and effective in his opposition to injurious child labor, proposing an amendment (to a pending bill on child labor in the District of Columbia) prohibiting inter-state commerce in the product of factories and mines where children under fourteen years of age were employed. His speech on this amendment, occupying parts of three days (Jan. 23, 28, 29, 1907), was a notable contribution to the controversy (*Congressional Record,* 59 Cong., 2 Sess., pp. 1552–57). He favored a tariff commission, to be conducted on non-partisan lines, in the hope of taking the tariff out of politics and thus sparing the country from the business uncertainty resulting from frequent revisions. It was on the Payne-Aldrich Tariff Act, in the first year of President Taft's administration (1909), that the disruption in the Republican party occurred. Beveridge was in the forefront of the insurgent senators in opposition to this party bill. He believed that the "Old Guard" leaders cared nothing for the well-being of the masses but were working constantly for the protection of selfish interests, and that the Aldrich tariff was a "revision upward" and was, therefore, a betrayal of party pledges. Because of his independence of his party, the "stand-pat" Republicans in Indiana helped the Democrats to defeat him for the Senate in 1911.

With this senatorial experience and his democratic disposition it was easy and natural for him to go with Roosevelt into the Progressive party in 1912. In the Progressive National Convention in Chicago in that year it was Beveridge, as temporary chairman, who sounded the "keynote" in a campaign address, entitled "Pass Prosperity Around." During the same year he was nominated by the Progressive party of Indiana as its candidate for governor. He received 10,000 more votes than the Republican candidate, but was defeated by the Democratic candidate, Samuel M. Ralston. In 1914, after the adoption of the Seventeenth Amendment, the Indiana Progressives nominated Beveridge as their candidate for the United States Senate, but Progressive support had fallen away, and he came in third in the popular vote. In 1916, together with Roosevelt, he rejoined the Republican party, and supported Charles E. Hughes for the presidency. In 1922 he was nominated for the United States Senate by the Republicans of Indiana in a state-wide popular primary, defeating Harry S. New, the sitting senator, but in the ensuing election he was again defeated by Samuel M. Ralston, the Democratic nominee. This closed his political career.

He was a pronounced nationalist, suspicious of foreign countries, with some anti-British feeling, a stout opponent of America's having anything to do with the League of Nations; at times disposed toward jingoism in speech, declaring himself for "America first! Not only America first, but America only!" He was somewhat temperamental, but his finer qualities greatly overtopped his minor defects. He had a rare political aptitude, and no man ever questioned his public integrity or his political courage.

But he was even more distinguished as a historical writer than as a politician. In his early service in the Senate he already showed an overwhelming desire to get information at first hand, even traveling to the Philippines in order to make a personal investigation of the Philippine problem. During the Japanese and Russian struggle in order to satisfy himself as to the situation he took a trip to Siberia and Russia, the outcome of which was *The Russian Advance,* published in 1903. In 1905 he brought out *The Young Man and the World,* in 1906 *The Bible as Good Reading,* in 1907 *Meaning of the Times,* in 1908 *Work and Habits* and *Americans of Today and Tomorrow,* —volumes intended especially for young men and women. In 1915, while spending a year as a war correspondent in Germany he produced his *What Is Back of the War,* which was regarded in America as distinctly pro-German, and brought the author some unpopularity. Beveridge's greatest work, however, was his biography of Chief Justice John Marshall, designed as an historical and political interpretation of the Supreme Court and of Marshall's part in giving that court its place in American history. This task he accomplished in a way that gained the universal approval of scholars and critics. As a biographer Beveridge showed his characteristic industry in gathering his materials, a discriminating mind in sifting and evaluating, a painstaking care in revising and rewriting until the facts took on their right relations and proportionate importance, and "the picture stood out as an historic and artistic whole." Bringing to his task sympathy for his subject, the art of eloquent and effective writing, and an undimmed historical imagination, he produced an outstanding historical biography. The first two volumes of *The Life of John Marshall* appeared in 1916, the second two in 1919. Beveridge then turned his attention to what he considered a harder and more important task, a similar biography of Lincoln in four volumes. At the time of his death two of these volumes had been substantially completed. He brought to this task the same qualities that had been applied to his *Marshall.* He had a horror of mistakes and his completed chapters had been read in manuscript by many historical scholars and were carefully revised and rewritten, some of them as many as fifteen times. His death was regretted on many accounts, but above all because of the loss to the world of his uncompleted Lincoln.

[*Pearson's Mag.*, Oct. 1910; *Am. Mag.*, Oct. 1910; *Saturday Evening Post*, Apr. 2, 1910; *Our Day*, July 1899; *Outlook*, July 18, 1917; *Am. Rev. of Revs.*, June 1927; *N. Y. Times*, Apr. 28, 1927; the *Indianapolis Star*, and *News*, same date.]

J. A. W.

BEVERLEY, ROBERT (*c.* 1673–1722), historian of Virginia, was the second son of that Robert Beverley (*c.* 1641–1687), representative of a "cavalier" family of the minor gentry of Yorkshire, who had emigrated to Virginia in 1663, and there played a conspicuous part in quelling Bacon's Rebellion. His mother, probably daughter of a Hull merchant, is recorded prior to her Beverley marriage in 1666 as the widow of George Keeble, a Virginia planter and magistrate. The future historian was born on his father's dwelling plantation in Middlesex County, and was sent thence, for education, to England. On his return to Virginia after his father's death he enrolled himself a volunteer scrivener in the provincial secretary's office, where his parts soon recommended him for service as clerk of a legislative committee; and by 1696 he had achieved the important posts of clerk of the General Court, clerk of the Council, and clerk of the General Assembly. As an incident to this employment at the statehouse he had become a freeholder in Jamestown, and on that footing sat as the burgess for the capital in the Assemblies of 1699, 1700–2 and 1705–6. In June 1703 he went to England to protect his interest in a litigation there pending before the Privy Council, and was detained for eighteen months. Being invited by a bookseller to criticize the MS. of Oldmixon's *British Empire in America,* he found the account of Virginia so jejune that he was moved then and there to put together his own *History and Present State of Virginia* (1705); a little book which has survived for two centuries by reason of its tonic originality, shrewd observation, and humorous commentaries upon the foibles of the Southern planter. Racy of the soil of Virginia, it is distinguished from other early American books by its freedom from any effort to ape a literary Oxford manner. During this sojourn in England, Beverley sent home several indiscreet letters on public affairs, one of which persuaded the Assembly to formulate an Address to the Crown, preferring what proved to be frivolous charges against Robert Quarry, the surveyor general of customs. The reply to this Address, a mortifying rebuke to the Assembly, ended Beverley's political career within a year after his return to Virginia. He now retired to Beverley Park, an estate on the upper waters of the Mattapony in King and Queen County, and there lived the remainder of his life, presiding in the county court, experimenting with viticulture, and speculating boldly in frontier lands. A call for a new printing of his *History* induced him to revise the book, though he did not improve it; and with the new edition he published also *The Abridgement of the Public Laws of Virginia* (1722), which he had compiled for his own use as a working magistrate. He died shortly after and was buried at Beverley Park, leaving one of the largest landed estates in contemporary Virginia. He was married to Ursula, second daughter of the first William Byrd of Westover, who died after a year of marriage in her seventeenth year, leaving a son, William (1698–1756), who built the notable house, "Blandfield," on the Rappahannock, where his descendants persist to this day.

[The sources for Beverley's life, now available, are his own prefaces and the public documents of the colony, principally the contemporary journals of the Council and the House of Burgesses, pieced out by scraps of county and other local records. His family, interesting for its sustained public service throughout the colonial period and for its alliances, is fortunate in having its generations recorded and fully documented by Dr. W. G. Stanard, in *Va. Mag.*, vols. II, III, XX, XXI, XXII.]

F. H.

BEWLEY, ANTHONY (May 22, 1804–Sept. 13, 1860), Methodist clergyman, was born in Tennessee, the son of a local Methodist preacher. He was a member of the Tennessee Conference 1829–37 and then moved with his wife and children to southwestern Missouri. He joined the Missouri Conference in 1843 but declined to go with it into the Methodist Episcopal Church South in 1845. With a few others of like convictions he maintained a loose association and preached to a handful of sympathizers until 1848, when the group was reorganized as the Missouri Conference of the Northern Church and Bewley was assigned to the Washington Mission in Arkansas. There for ten years he worked amid social ostracism and petty persecution, his children excluded from the schools and his sisters so intimidated that they did not dare attend his preaching. In 1858, as a reward for this devotion to his Church and its principles, he was sent on missionary work to Johnson County, Tex., just south of Fort Worth, in territory dangerous for an abolitionist or a supposed abolitionist to enter. For two years he held his ground, and then Bishop Ames, as if bent on making a martyr, reassigned him to the same post. Bewley made a visit to his old friends in Missouri and then returned reluctantly to Texas. Serious trouble arose immediately through the publication of a letter, dated July 3, 1860, purporting to be addressed to Bewley by a W. H. Bailey at Benton Creek. The letter gave a long list of "fellow workers," and discussed the certain election of Lincoln, the underground railroad, combustible material for firing buildings, plans for destroying towns and mills, and methods of coöperating with "our colored friends." The letter contained nothing that could have been news to Bewley if he had been implicated in such a plot, but it sounded every note calculated to excite mob fury. Church as well as secular papers republished the letter. With his wife and children, Bewley fled north through Indian Territory to Arkansas and on across the Missouri line. Meanwhile rewards totaling $1,000 had been offered for his capture, and a posse led by A. G. Brayman and Joe Johnson of Fort Worth was in pursuit. On Sept. 3, 1860, he was overtaken near Cassville, Mo. He was not allowed to say good-by to his wife, but a bundle of clothes which she sent after him was given to him, and at Fayetteville, Ark., where he was held Sept. 4–7, he was allowed to write her a farewell letter. From Fayetteville he was taken to Fort Worth, where a mob hanged him to a tree that had been used on similar occasions. His murder terminated the activities of the Methodist Episcopal Church in Texas.

[C. Elliott, "Martyrdom of Bewley" in *Meth. Quart. Rev.*, Oct. 1863; M. Phelan, *A Hist. of Early Methodism in Texas 1817–66* (1924); L. C. Matlack, *The Antislavery Struggle and Triumph in the M. E. Ch.* (1881).]

G. H. G.

BIARD, PIERRE (*c.* 1567–Nov. 17, 1622), Jesuit missionary, was born at Grenoble, France. He entered the Society of Jesus, June 5, 1583, and in 1608, while professor of theology and Hebrew at Lyons, was named by the Royal Confessor head of the Acadia Mission founded in 1603 by the Huguenot, De Monts. In spite of Calvinist opposition, two Jesuits, Biard and Massé, sailed on Jan. 26, 1611, with the expedition financed largely by the Marquise de Guercheville, and after violent storms, graphically described in Biard's Letter, reached Port Royal on May 22. Here, with only scanty supplies, they held religious services and instructed the Indians. With difficulty they learned the language and endeavored to convey some general spiritual concepts to a people whose ideas were solely of sensible objects. By means of the material helps of the Church and by aiding the Indians in illness, Biard won their confidence. He visited the French trade-posts of the St. John and the St. Croix and also the later Castine where he saw the Penobscots, "the finest assemblage of savages." On a trip along the coast from Port Royal to Kinnibéqui (Kennebec) to see the English fort, as he entered the Great Bay of the "very beautiful river Pentegoet" (Penobscot) he was in grave danger of attack; yet soon he was performing a cure on a sick native.

In 1613 with La Saussaye he helped found a settlement at St. Sauveur, now Bar Harbor, which was soon plundered by the English under Samuel Argall [*q.v.*], later governor of Virginia. The carrying off of Biard and another priest to Virginia, their escape from hanging, their forced return to witness the destruction of Port Royal, their second storm-tossed voyage with their captors, the drifting to the Azores and to Wales, and the final landing in France all make a thrilling tale. Lescarbot, the parliamentary advocate and historian, differs, however, from Biard in his account of the sacking of the settlements, and intimates that dissensions had arisen between Biard and Saint-Just, the head of the colony, which provoked Biard in resentment to tell the Governor of Virginia that colonists had captured an English vessel and were about to fortify the post with thirty cannon (See Marc Lescarbot, *Histoire de la Nouvelle France,* 1617; an English translation of the fifth book, relating to Acadia, in *Forerunners and Competitors of the Pilgrims,* 1912, pp. 523–62). Yet Lescarbot calls Biard "a very learned man—highly spoken of." In his own account Biard appears as a keen observer of new lands; a single-minded worker for the Faith: a writer direct and vivid in pictures of Indian ceremonies and fighting; a sympathetic analyst of Indian nature; a healer claiming no personal merit for "cures" wrought by prayer; and finally the courageous voyager forgiving his piratical captain and even rescuing him from death on the hazardous journey homeward. On his arrival in France, Biard was accused of having been in league with the marauders who destroyed the settlements (*Factum du Procès, Entre Messire Jean de Biencourt . . . et Pierre Biard,* 1614), and set to work upon his *Relation* which constitutes his defense (see Pierre Biard, *Relation de la Nouvelle France,* 1616; translated in *The Jesuit Relations,* ed. by R. G. Thwaites, 1897, vols. III, IV). Upon its publication he returned to his work as professor of theology; later, he served as spiritual adviser in an army campaign and, as a result of its privations, died at Avignon while resting among simple novices of the order.

[In addition to references given above see H. P. Biggar, *The Early Trading Companies of New France* (1901); *Cath. Encyc.*; Street's *Hist. of Mt. Desert*, ed. by S. A. Eliot (1905). There is uncertainty as to the exact dates of Biard's birth and death; those given in *Jesuit Relations* are the ones followed in this sketch.]

M. C. H.

BIBB, GEORGE MORTIMER (Oct. 30, 1776–Apr. 14, 1859), lawyer, senator, the son of Richard and Lucy (Booker) Bibb, was born in Prince Edward County, Va. He early went to college, graduating from both Hampden-Sidney and William and Mary, and in his old age held the sentimental distinction of being the oldest living graduate from each. Not caring for the ministry, he made the very natural choice of the law and soon began its study under Richard Venable. After beginning his practise in Virginia, in 1798 he took up his residence in Lexington, Ky. His profound and exact legal ability, together with a courtly manner, won him when only thirty-two years old (1808) an appointment to the bench of the court of appeals, the highest court in the state. The next year he was elevated to the chief justiceship, but resigned in 1810. In 1811 he was elected to the United States Senate. Here, as one of the "War Hawks," he took a prominent part in forcing war against Great Britain and in loyally upholding President Madison in carrying it on. But his Kentucky law practise and associations had greater attractions for him than being a senator in the muddy village of Washington, so in 1814 he resigned, and took up his residence in Frankfort. For the next ten years and more he was closely associated with state politics and party maneuvers. In 1816 Gov. George Madison died and the lieutenant-governor, Gabriel Slaughter, became governor. Immediately the question arose on the interpretation of the constitution concerning the succession: whether the lieutenant-governor should serve out the unexpired term of his predecessor or a special election should be held. The peace of the state was soon upset, and Bibb, becoming a member of the lower house of the legislature in 1817, did all within his power to unseat Slaughter and to question the validity of his acts. The movement to oust Slaughter, however, failed. In 1822 Bibb and Henry Clay were appointed commissioners to Virginia to plead before the legislature there for an agreement which would straighten out the complicated land claims which had become more confounded by certain occupying-claimant laws passed by Kentucky, which the United States Supreme Court had declared unconstitutional in the case of Green *vs.* Biddle. Clay and Bibb visited Virginia and addressed the legislature but to no effect. The next year both were appointed to uphold Kentucky before the Supreme Court in a re-hearing. They argued the case in Washington but failed to win the decision. In the devastating fight between the Relief and Anti-Relief parties, Bibb stood behind the radicalism of the latter group, and when violent hands were laid on the court of appeals, resulting in setting up a new court, Bibb supported the latter and practised before it. In his attempt to compose the judicial squabble, Gov. Joseph Desha appointed Bibb chief justice in 1827. Bibb resigned the next year to become again a United States senator, serving this time the full six years. In national politics he was at first a supporter of Andrew Jackson. In 1824 he had opposed Clay on the ground that he could not be elected president, and when he reached the Senate he stood behind President Jackson in opposing the Maysville Road Bill. A few years of close association with Jackson convinced him, however, that the President was a tyrant who refused other people the right to an opinion. He especially disagreed with Jackson on the bank question. When his term as senator had expired in 1835 he returned to Kentucky and became chancellor of the Louisville court of chancery, holding this position until 1844 when President Tyler appointed him secretary of the treasury. Bibb went out of office with Tyler on Mar. 4, 1845. He remained in Washington and Georgetown for the rest of his life, practising before the District courts and serving as chief clerk in the attorney-general's office. He was a typical "gentleman of the old school," ever refusing to discard knee-breeches for pantaloons. Twice married, he was the father of seventeen children.

[Mrs. Chapman Coleman, *The Life of John J. Crittenden* (1871); T. M. Green, *The Spanish Conspiracy: A Review of Early Spanish Movements in the South-West* (1891); Lewis Collins, *Hist. of Ky.* (1874), II, 277; *Reg. of Ky. State Hist. Soc.* (1903), I, 43; *Louisville Daily Courier*, Apr. 19, 1859.]

E. M. C.

BIBB, WILLIAM WYATT (Oct. 2, 1781–July 10, 1820), governor of Alabama, was born in Amelia County, Ga. His grandfather was one John Bibb, a Huguenot from Wales who located in Hanover County, Va.; his father was William Bibb, a captain in the Revolutionary Army. His mother, Sally Wyatt, a descendant of Gov. Francis Wyatt of Virginia, was the daughter of William and Sallie Wyatt, and a relative of Martha Custis Washington. William Wyatt Bibb was educated at the University of Pennsylvania, graduating in medicine in 1801, and went at once to Petersburg, Ga., where he practised his profession. He served in both the House and Senate of the state legislature, and, elected as a Democrat to the United States Congress, he continued there from Jan. 26, 1805, to Nov. 6, 1813, when he resigned. He was then elected to fill the vacancy in the Senate caused by the resignation of William H. Crawford and served for three years, when he again resigned before the expiration of his term. His second resignation was due to a nation-wide disapproval of the congressional measure fixing the salaries of congressmen and senators at $1,800 a year, the services of these officials prior to that time having been paid *per diem* during the sittings of the Congress. President Monroe appointed Bibb, in April 1817, governor of the newly formed Territory of Alabama. He entered upon his duties at St. Stephens, and when the territory was admitted to the Union as a state his administration was indorsed by a popular vote which continued him as governor. The power of the Creek Indians having been broken by the army led by Andrew Jackson, following the massacre of Fort Mims, the administration of Bibb was pacific. His experience in public life was regarded as of great value in the formative period of the state's political history and especially in the framing of the constitution. He was married in 1803 to Mary Freeman, known as "the beauty of Broad River," daughter of Col. Holman Freeman of Wilkes County, Ga., a Revolutionary hero and Whig leader under Gov. Elijah Clark. Bibb died in Autauga County, Ala., from the effects of a fall from a horse frightened by a violent thunder storm. He was succeeded as governor by his brother, Thomas Bibb, who was at the time serving as president of the Alabama Senate.

[A. J. Pickett, *Hist. of Ala.* (1851); G. R. Gilmer, *Sketches of Some of the First Families of Upper Ga.* (1859); C. E. Jones, "Gov. William Wyatt Bibb," *Pubs. Ala. Hist. Soc.*, III, 1899; *Pubs. Ala. Hist. Soc. Misc. Coll.*, I, 1901; L. L. Knight, *Standard Hist. of Ga. and Georgians*, VI (1917); T. M. Owen, *Hist. of Ala. and Dict. of Ala. Biog.*, III (1921).] M. B. O.

BICKEL, LUKE WASHINGTON (Sept. 21, 1866–May 11, 1917), mariner-missionary, eighteen years captain of the ship *Fukuin Maru*, planned and developed under the auspices of the American Baptist Missionary Society a notable work of evangelization and education on the islands of the Inland Sea of Japan. He was of German descent, his father, Philipp, one of the young revolutionists of 1848, having fled to this country, married Katherine, daughter of Rev. Samuel R. Clarke, become a Baptist minister, and served in the Civil War. At the time of Luke's birth, he was publishing German Christian literature in Cincinnati, Ohio; but when the former was about twelve years old he returned to Germany with his family to carry on publishing work for the Baptists there. The son graduated from the Reformed Church Academy, Hamburg, in 1880, took three years' collegiate work at Soest, and then spent a year at Wandsbeck Gymnasium.

Although interested in religious activities, he was passionately fond of the sea, and at eighteen he was apprenticed for a term of four years on an English merchant sailing ship. By the time he was twenty-eight, he had become a captain, holding, though an American, a British Board of Trade certificate as master mariner. In 1893 he married Annie Burgess, a native of Norwich, England, and established a home in London. Soon, yielding to his wife's persuasions, he gave up the sea, and assumed control of the business of the London Baptist Publishing Society. The American Baptist Missionary Society, having been offered means to build a vessel for work among the Inland Sea islanders, asked him to captain the ship and the work. He consented, took a brief course at Spurgeon's College, and started for Japan, arriving in May 1898. The *Fukuin Maru* was built for him and dedicated Sept. 13, 1899. On this vessel and its successor, of the same name, built some fourteen years later, he traveled among the islands, establishing and directing missions for the rest of his life. He was a man of large proportions, great strength and courage, and as capable in mind as in body. His physical ability, nautical knowledge, and unselfish services, won the respect and confidence of the people. Selecting a strategic center in each group of islands, he made that a nucleus, arranging that from that center work should be carried on in every village in the group. Weakened by his strenuous life and a siege of typhoid fever, he failed to rally from a minor surgical operation and died at the age of fifty-one, but so well had his plan and work succeeded, that at his death there were sixty-two regular preaching places, fifty-two Sunday-schools with 3,500 pupils, and 400 villages in which services were occasionally held; while all denominations regarded his achievement as among the most notable in the missionary annals of the Japanese Empire.

["The Mission Ship 'Fukuin Maru'," ch. X in *The Christian Movement in Japan*, 1908, was written by Bickel. See also Chas. K. Harrington, *Captain Bickel of the Inland Sea* (1919); J. A. Foote, "Luke W. Bickel: An Appreciation," *The Standard*, June 30, 1917; F. C. Briggs, "Luke W. Bickel," *The Christian Movement in the Japanese Empire*, 1918; C. K. Harrington, "A Missionary Captain and His Gospel Ship," *Missionary Review of the World*, Sept. 1917; *Ann. Report of Am. Bapt. Foreign Missionary Soc.*, 1917.] H. E. S.

BICKERDYKE, MARY ANN BALL (July 19, 1817–Nov. 8, 1901), "Mother Bickerdyke," one of the most capable and beloved of the women who ministered to the sick and wounded during the Civil War, was born in Knox County, Ohio, near what is now Mount Vernon. She was the daughter of Hiram and Anna (Rodgers) Ball, and came of rugged, fighting stock. David Ball, her first American ancestor on the paternal side, emigrated to this country from England some time before 1700 and settled at Newark, N. J. Three of his sons were in the War of the Revolution. Mary's grandfather, David, had gone to Ohio the year it was admitted as a state, and become a well-to-do citizen. On her mother's side she was descended from Thomas Rodgers who came over in the *Mayflower*. John Rodgers, her grandfather, as a lad of sixteen had gone into the battle of Bunker Hill and fought through the seven years of the war. In his household her early years were spent, for her mother died when she was seventeen months old. Later she lived with her uncle, Henry Rodgers. Brought up on a farm and fond of outdoor life, she developed physical hardiness, and became a frugal, competent housekeeper. At the age of sixteen she entered Oberlin College and spent four years there. An epidemic caused her to leave before graduating, and the removal of her uncle's family to Cincinnati prevented her return. Here she took a course of training for nurses under Dr. Reuben D. Mussey [*q.v.*], and became familiar with hospital work. On Apr. 27, 1847, she married a mechanic, Robert Bickerdyke, who was a widower with children. Several children were born to her. In 1856 the family moved to Galesburg, Ill., where her husband died two years later. In 1861 she was listed in the Galesburg directory as a "botanic physician."

When the war broke out, the patriotic women of her town, recognizing her peculiar fitness, urged her to attach herself to the army. With $500 worth of supplies which were put at her disposal she began work in the regimental hospitals at Cairo, Ill., and continued her service until Mar. 20, 1865. She was in nineteen hard-fought battles in the departments of the Ohio, Tennessee, and Cumberland armies. Whether ministering to men on the field, assisting at the operating table, running diet kitchens where she generally did the cooking herself, superintending hospitals, or foraging for supplies, she was equally efficient. A surgeon of the 22nd Illinois Infantry, Dr. Woodward, describes her as "a large, heavy woman of forty-five years, strong as a man; muscles of iron; nerves of steel; sensitive but self-reliant; kind and tender; seeking all for others, nothing for herself" (Julia A. Chase, *Mary A. Bickerdyke,* 1896, p. 11). She made the enlisted men her special care, and fought for their rights like a tigress, and they loved her as a mother. She was a terror to incompetent and dissipated officers, and invariably effected their discharge. She cut through red tape ruthlessly and sometimes violated army procedure, but though called to account by subordinate officials she was always sustained by their superiors. She was an especial favorite of Gen. Grant and Gen. Sherman; the former gave her a pass to and from any point in his military division with free transportation at all times, and after the battle of Vicksburg she became a special attaché of Sherman's corps. The Sanitary Commission made her its agent and had implicit confidence in her management. Her executive ability was of a high order, and her native economy saved the Commission and the Government an incalculable amount. One of her achievements was the establishment of army laundries. Previously the clothing and bedding of wounded soldiers had been destroyed. She procured washing machines, portable kitchens, and mangles, and with the aid of contrabands, who were devoted to her, she cleansed and prepared for redistribution what formerly had been a total loss. She also made her contrabands salvage accoutrements left on the battlefield. Innumerable stories are told of her resourcefulness in overcoming obstacles. Because of the uniqueness of her character and work, she was one of the most picturesque as well as efficient women of the army.

Her career after the war was a varied one. She became a legally admitted pension attorney and helped nurses and veterans secure pensions. Gen. Logan voiced a general feeling when he wrote to the chairman of the pension commission, "I desire to introduce Mother Bickerdyke. What she wants is right, and what she says will be the truth." For a year she was housekeeper in the Chicago Home for the Friendless. In 1867 she initiated a movement to get ex-soldiers to go West and through her influence some 300 families migrated to Kansas. She herself settled in Salina, and opened a hotel under the patronage of the Kansas Pacific Railroad. For four years she did missionary work in New York, under the direction of the Board of City Missions. In 1874 she returned to Kansas to live with her two sons, and at the time of the locust plague went to Illinois and secured relief for the sufferers. Later she was in California, working in the United States Mint. Congress in 1886 granted her a pension of twenty-five dollars a month. She died at the home of her son at Bunker Hill, Kan., and was buried in Galesburg, Ill., where by means of an appropriation of $5,000 made by the State in 1903 a monument has been erected to her memory.

[Mary A. Livermore, *My Story of the War* (1888); L. P. Brockett and May C. Vaughn, *Woman's Work in the Civil War* (1867); Mary A. G. Holland, *Our Army Nurses* (1895); Florence S. Kellogg, *Mother Bickerdyke* (1907); "Diary of Mrs. E. C. Porter," *U. S. Sanitary Commission Bull.*, Sept. 1, 1864.] H. E. S.

BICKETT, THOMAS WALTER (Feb. 28, 1869–Dec. 28, 1921), governor of North Carolina, was born in Monroe, N. C., the son of Thomas Winchester and Mary (Covington) Bickett. Receiving his preparatory education in the public schools, he entered Wake Forest College in 1886 and received the bachelor's degree in 1890. He taught for two years, first at Marion and then at Winston-Salem, reading law at the same time, and in 1892 entered the law school of the University of North Carolina. He was admitted to the bar in February 1893 and practised for a time in Monroe and later in Danbury, but in 1895 moved to Louisburg. There, on Nov. 29, 1898, he married Fannie N. Yarborough. At the bar Bickett was quickly successful and won a great though local reputation, not only for professional ability, but for the satisfying human qualities which distinguished him through life. Inheriting a full share of Irish wit, he was a gifted teller of anecdotes which were racy of the soil and full of good humor which made him widely popular. But he had at the same time convictions which were passionately held and sternly followed. In his sympathy for the unfortunate and the oppressed was to be found the key-note of his real nature.

He took no active part in politics until 1906 when he was elected to the lower house of the state legislature, serving one term and taking a rather prominent part, for a new member, in the advocacy of legal reforms, an enlarged educational program, and more adequate care of the unfortunate. The next year he so distinguished himself in the Democratic state convention by a speech nominating an unsuccessful candidate for governor that he was nominated for attorney-general, a position which he filled for eight years. During this time he represented the state in five cases before the Supreme Court of the United States, the most notable being the Tennessee boundary dispute, and won all of them. In great demand always as a speaker he became widely known during these eight years and in 1916 he was nominated for governor in the first state-wide primary and was elected by a large majority over Frank A. Linney, the Republican candidate.

He proved himself, in spite of small executive powers, capable of vigorous and highly successful executive leadership. During his four-year term he recommended to the legislature forty-eight measures, forty of which were enacted into law. Among these were statutes providing for a six-months school term with increased salaries for teachers, for broader agricultural education, for more liberal support of the state's institutions, both educational and charitable, for an improved system of state highways, for more humane prison administration, and for tax reform. He believed that it was the major function of government to improve the economic and social condition of the mass of the people, and throughout his term he sought to improve the lot of the tenant-farmer class, to encourage home ownership, to elevate the negro, and to better the relations of capital and labor. During the war Bickett threw himself passionately into the task of leading the state to the exertion of its utmost power. Every agency of the state was brought into action and by proclamations and public addresses, in which were combined wit, sentiment, idealism, and deep conviction, he interpreted the struggle as he conceived it in terms that all could understand.

Bickett was short of stature and of thick-set frame. His ruddy face was frequently lighted by a smile of compelling charm and his blue eyes furnished a clear index to his quick turns of feeling. He died suddenly of apoplexy less than a year after his retirement from office, and was survived by his wife and one son.

[*Pub. Letters and Papers of Thos. Walter Bickett* (1923), comp. by Santford Martin and ed. by R. B. House; memorial sketch by Jas. S. Manning in *Proc. of the N. C. Bar Ass.*, 1922; *Who's Who in America*, 1920–21. The N. C. newspapers about the dates of his nomination for governor and of his death contain much material relating to him.] J. G. de R. H.

BICKMORE, ALBERT SMITH (Mar. 1, 1839–Aug. 12, 1914), educator, was born in Tenant's Harbor, Me., the son of John and Jane (Seavey) Bickmore. The great event of his childhood was a voyage with his father, a sea-captain and ship-builder, to Bordeaux. Prepared for college at the New London (N. H.) Academy, he was graduated from Dartmouth in 1860. His bent toward natural history then led him to the Lawrence Scientific School of Harvard University to study under Agassiz. Soon appointed an assistant in the Museum of Comparative Zoology, in 1862 he accompanied an expedition of P. T. Barnum's to Bermuda, where he made an extensive collection of marine animals for the museum. In 1862–63 he served with the 44th Massachusetts Volunteers, a nine-months regiment, and upon being mustered out returned to Cambridge with "a very fine collection" which he had made upon the North Carolina coast while detached from his regiment upon special hospital duty (*Annual Report of the Trustees of the Museum of Comparative Zoology,* 1862, 1863). Having received his B.S. from Harvard in 1864, in January 1865, financed in part by "friends of science in Boston and Cambridge," he embarked upon a voyage to the East. He traveled through the Malay Archipelago and the Dutch East Indies collecting shells and bird-skins, penetrated into a part of China unexplored by "foreigners" (see "Sketch of a Journey from Canton to Hankow," *Journal of the Royal Geographical Society,* XXXVIII, 1868, and *American Journal of Science,* July 1868), and visited the little-known Ainos of Japan. Returning to Boston in December 1867, during the following months he published several papers: "A Description of the Banda Islands" (*Proceedings of the Royal Geographical Society* 1867–68, pp. 324 ff.), "Some Remarks on the Recent Geological Changes in China and Japan" (*American Journal of Science,* March 1868), "The Ainos, or Hairy Men of Yesso" and "The Ainos, or Hairy Men of Saghalien and the Kurile Islands" (*Ibid.,* May 1868), and completed his *Travels in the East Indian Archipelago* (London 1868; New York 1869; Jena 1869). In 1868–69 he served as professor of natural history in Madison (now Colgate) University.

Meanwhile, for several years Bickmore had been elaborating a plan, conceived while he was a student under Agassiz, for a great natural-history museum, to be located in New York. Upon Bickmore's return from the East William E. Dodge 2nd, with whom he had been in correspondence, introduced him to Theodore Roosevelt (father of the President), who immediately took an active interest in the project. Under Roosevelt's leadership a series of informal conferences in the fall of 1868 led to a meeting of prominent citizens at the home of Benjamin H. Field in January 1869, at which the first board of trustees of what was to become the American Museum of Natural History was elected. Bickmore contributed the title of the institution—national in scope, the definition of its relations with the municipality, the plan adopted for its financing, and not least, the enthusiastic arguments which won the support of Tweed and Tilden and secured from the legislature, without amendment, the charter as it had been drawn by Joseph Choate. Appointed superintendent in 1869 he served in that capacity till 1884, when he resigned to become curator of the Museum's Department of Public Instruction. The education of the public had been one of the ideals of the founders, and under Bickmore's curatorship the schools of both city and state were brought into organized relation with the Museum, and Bickmore's lectures, illustrated by stereopticon slides from collections made by himself, became an increasingly important annual institution. In 1904, incapacitated for active service by chronic rheumatism which confined him to a chair, he was made curator emeritus of his department, but he continued in the office of trustee, which he had held since 1885. He died in August 1914 at his summer home in Nonquitt, Mass. A colleague has referred to Bickmore's "unflagging industry, his unshakable resolution" which were "supported by an almost sublime optimism." During his lifetime a division of the new building was named in his honor, and since his death he has been acclaimed "Father of the Museum."

Bickmore was married in 1873 to Charlotte A. Bruce of New York.

[*Am. Museum Jour.,* 1900–01, Nov. 1911, Apr. 1914, Feb. 1915, May 1917; *Forty-sixth Annual Report Am. Mus. Nat. Hist.,* pp. 15, 95; *Fifty-eighth Annual Report,* p. 1; *Watchman-Examiner,* Aug. 27, 1914; George H. Sherwood, *Free Education by the Am. Mus. of Nat. Hist.* (1918); *Bull. Geol. Soc. of America,* Mar. 1915; *Who's Who in America,* 1914–15; *Who's Who in N. Y.,* 1914; *N. Y. Times,* Aug. 14, 1914.]

E. R. D.

BIDDLE, CLEMENT (May 10, 1740–July 14, 1814), Revolutionary soldier, merchant, was descended from William Biddle, a shoemaker and colonel in Cromwell's army, who came to America in 1681 and by purchase from William Penn established himself as one of the proprietors in West New Jersey. His grandson, John, removed to Philadelphia in 1730 and six years later married Sarah Owen. Five children were born of this marriage, of whom Clement was the second. While still a boy he entered his father's shipping and importing business, and in 1771 his name appears as a partner in the firm. His commercial life was soon interrupted by the approach of the Revolutionary War. With his older brother, Owen, he signed the non-importation agreement of 1765, and for the next ten years was active in the patriotic cause in Philadelphia. In 1775 he helped to raise in Philadelphia a company of volunteers, the "Quaker Blues," and on July 8, 1776, was appointed by Congress deputy quartermaster-general for the militia of Pennsylvania and New Jersey with the rank of colonel. He took part in the battle of Trenton and was delegated by Washington to receive the swords of the surrendering Hessian officers. He also participated in the battles of Brandywine, Germantown, and Monmouth. In November 1776 Gen. Greene made him his aide-de-camp, and in

July 1777 appointed him commissary-general of forage. In this position he served until June 1780, when he resigned in order to give attention to his business affairs. In September 1781, at the urgent request of Greene, the supreme executive council of Pennsylvania appointed him quartermaster-general of the state militia with the rank of colonel. After the Revolution Biddle continued in his business as a merchant and importer in Philadelphia and came to hold many positions of honor and trust under both state and federal governments. He was in continual correspondence with Washington, whose factor he was in Philadelphia and with whom he was on terms of friendship. In 1788 he became a justice of the court of common pleas and in 1789 Washington appointed him United States marshal of Pennsylvania, in which office he continued until 1793. Biddle was twice married. His first wife was Mary Richardson, who died in 1773 without surviving children. In 1774 he married Rebekah Cornell, whose father at the time of his death in 1765 was lieutenant-governor and chief justice of Rhode Island. Of this marriage there were born thirteen children, of whom five died before reaching maturity.

[The chief source of information about Biddle is the manuscript "Washington Correspondence with Clement Biddle" in the Pa. Hist. Soc. Lib. in Philadelphia. See also *Pa. Mag. of Hist. and Biog.*, vols. XLII, XLIII. The genealogy of the Biddle family is given in "Col. Clement Biddle with a genealogy of the Biddle Family" in *Boogher's Repository* (1883), I, 101. Other sources are "A Sketch of William Biddle and Thomas Biddle" in *Pa. Mag. of Hist. and Biog.*, vol. XIV; "Owen Biddle," *Ibid.*, XVI; and Henry D. Biddle, *Notes on the Genealogy of the Biddle Family* (1895).]

R. S. C.

BIDDLE, HORACE P. (Mar. 24, 1811–May 13, 1900), jurist, writer, was born in what is now Hocking County, Ohio, the son of Benjamin and Abigail Converse Biddle. His parents came to Ohio from Connecticut and built a home in what was then Fairfield County on the Hocking River. Here Horace Biddle was born and reared on a backwoods farm. Like most boys of the time, he attended the country school for a few weeks during the winter months and worked on the farm during the summer. His school days were numbered but he read everything that came his way. He scorned the mere form but cherished the content of an education. Looking upon honors, titles and degrees as "burdens rather than buoys," he used to say that a man's name should float him without prefixes or suffixes. He finally determined to study law and entered the office of Hocking H. Hunter, a successful lawyer and striking personality of Lancaster. Admitted to the Ohio Bar in 1839, in October of the same year he began to practise in Logansport, Ind. It was here that he spent the major part of his active life and built up his legal reputation. He dabbled in politics somewhat but was in no sense a politician. He was a useful and influential member of the convention which drafted the Indiana constitution of 1851. In 1846 he was elected president judge of the eighth Indiana district, and in 1857 he was elected to the supreme bench but was denied his commission as it was decided that no vacancy existed at the time. At a later time (1874) he was again chosen to the supreme court of Indiana, this time by an unprecedented majority. In 1881 he returned to private life to devote himself to literary pursuits. His home was on "Biddle's Island" in the Wabash River. Here, an adept in woodcraft and an expert fisherman, he spent many happy days communing with nature and reading the books of his splendid library—said to be the largest private library in Indiana at that time. He had a decided bent for language. He made translations from French and German poets and was a regular contributor to leading periodicals. He could also translate from the Portuguese, Spanish, and Italian. He was familiar with Latin and had some knowledge of Oriental languages. He published several volumes of poems, among them *American Boyhood* (1876) which a reviewer in the *Nation* (XIII, 15) pronounced an original and interesting book which would have been vastly better in prose. His most ambitious book was *The Musical Scale* (1860), in which he sought to explain the law governing the arrangement of the musical scale. With his long white beard and patriarchal appearance, he was a striking figure in Indiana for many decades. He was individual and not without his eccentricities. When he was elected to the supreme court he disposed of his law books so that, as he said, the lawyers could not borrow them and forget to bring them back. He remained a student of philosophy, science, literature and music throughout his entire life.

[Eva Peters Reynolds, *Horace P. Biddle* (1890); Jacob P. Dunn, *Indiana and Indianians* (1919), III, 1220; *Encyc. of Biog. of Ind.*, ed. by Geo. I. Reed (1899), II, 170; *Hist. of Cass, Miami, Howard, and Tipton Counties* (1898), I, 1–4; *Biog. Hist. of Eminent and Self-Made Men of Ind.* (1880), II (10th Dist.), 4.]

T. F. M.

BIDDLE, JAMES (Feb. 18, 1783–Oct. 1, 1848), naval officer, was born in Philadelphia, the son of Charles and Hannah (Shepard) Biddle, the family, of the Quaker faith, having been one of prominence since early colonial times. After finishing a course of study at the University of Pennsylvania, where he showed particular interest in literature, he and his younger brother, Edward, in the year 1800 received warrants as midshipmen in the navy, and were attached to the frigate *President,* which sailed for the West Indies in September of that year, upon a cruise during which the younger brother died of fever. On the termination of our misunderstanding with France, James Biddle, as one of the few who escaped the effect of the radical reduction of the navy, was retained as midshipman. During 1802 he served aboard the *Constellation,* in the squadron engaged in the protection of American shipping in the Mediterranean against Tripolitan vessels. On returning home in the spring of 1803, he was transferred to the *Philadelphia,* under the command of Capt. William Bainbridge [*q.v.*], and in her shared in the disaster of her grounding near Tripoli on Oct. 31, 1803, and her surrender to the enemy, as well as in the subsequent imprisonment of the ship's company for nineteen months. Upon the conclusion of peace with Tripoli, Biddle returned to the United States with Capt. Bainbridge, and was given command, with the rank of lieutenant, of a gunboat engaged in protecting the South Atlantic Coast against marauding privateers. In 1807, obtaining leave of absence, he made a voyage to China as first officer of a merchant ship, and upon his return he was detailed to the Delaware flotilla employed in enforcing the embargo. In 1809 he became second lieutenant of the *President* under his old commander, Bainbridge, and in 1810 obtained his first independent command, that of the sloop-of-war *Syren.* He subsequently served for short periods in the *Constitution* and again in the *President,* and in 1811 was bearer of dispatches from the American Government to its minister to France, remaining nearly four months in Paris.

On the breaking out of the second war against Great Britain, Biddle was appointed first lieutenant of the sloop-of-war *Wasp,* commanded by Capt. Jacob Jones [*q.v.*], and took part in the desperate close-quarters fight which ended in the boarding and capture of the British brig *Frolic,* the boarding party being led by Biddle, who sprang into the rigging and tore down the British ensign with his own hands. He was left in charge of the prize with orders to make his way to Charleston, but the appearance of the powerful British ship-of-the-line *Poictiers,* 74 guns, resulted in the capture of both vessels, the American officers and crew being taken to Bermuda and paroled in March 1813. Both Jones and Biddle were promoted for the capture of the *Frolic,* Biddle to the rank of master-commandant. Given command of the sloop-of-war *Hornet,* he started to accompany the *Peacock,* the *Tom Bowline,* and the ill-fated *President,* to the rendezvous designated by Commodore Stephen Decatur [*q.v.*], at Tristan d'Acunha. Becoming separated from his consorts, he fell in with the British brig *Penguin,* of more than the *Hornet's* armament and crew, and a severe engagement ensued terminated by the *Penguin's* surrender. Capt. Biddle, who had been promoted to this rank before taking the *Penguin,* was destined, in what proved to be the last regular naval action of the war, to bring his actual warlike experience to a close by a dramatic escape from a British line-of-battle ship which appeared and was approached unawares by the *Hornet,* Apr. 27, 1815. Discovering his mistake at 9 p. m., Biddle changed his course away from the enemy, and a long chase began, lasting until the next evening, the Briton occasionally getting within firing distance. By dint of throwing overboard stores, extra boats, spars, ammunition, sheet-anchor, and at last every gun save one, the determined American captain had the satisfaction of saving his ship, which he brought into New York in July 1815, after peace had been signed.

Continuing in active duty after the war, Biddle was sent on the sloop-of-war *Ontario* to the Columbia River in 1817 to take possession of the Oregon territory. In 1822 he commanded the *Macedonian* on the West India station as commodore, and from 1826 to 1832 he cruised in South American waters and in the Mediterranean. His services in protecting American shipping in South America, at a time when revolutionary disorders particularly menaced it, earned him the gratitude of American merchants. From 1838 to 1842 he was at the head of the Naval Asylum at Philadelphia, and as commodore of the East Indian Squadron, he negotiated, in 1846, the first treaty between the United States and China. His last command was on the Pacific Coast during the war with Mexico. He died in Philadelphia.

[Jas. Fenimore Cooper, *Hist. of the Navy of the U. S.* (1839); J. H. Brown, *Am. Naval Heroes* (1899); Chas. Biddle, *Autobiography* (1883); *Cumming's Evening Telegraphic Bull.,* Oct. 2, 1848; Navy Registers, 1816–48; A. T. Mahan, *Sea Power in Its Relations to the War of 1812* (1905); T. Roosevelt, *The Naval War of 1812* (1882).]

E. B.

BIDDLE, NICHOLAS (Sept. 10, 1750–Mar. 7, 1778), naval officer, was the sixth son of William Biddle, a member of an old, originally Quaker family of New Jersey, and his wife, Mary Scull, daughter of Nicholas Scull, for many years surveyor general of Pennsylvania. Nicholas was born in Philadelphia some years after his father had moved to that city, and was bred to the sea, his first voyage being made to Quebec at the age of thirteen. After a short but eventful career in the merchant service, in which he experienced his full share of hardship and even shipwreck, showing on several occasions uncommon determination and pluck, he decided to enter the British Navy. Proceeding to London with letters of recommendation from Thomas Willing of Philadelphia, president of the Bank of North America, to Willing's brother-in-law, Captain, afterward Admiral, Sterling, R. N., Nicholas served for some time as midshipman in the latter's sloop-of-war *Portland* in 1772. In the autumn of that year, his cruise having come to an end, he asked to be transferred to one of the ships which the Royal Geographical Society sent out in 1773 under Capt. Phipps, afterward Lord Mulgrave, to discover the polar limits of navigation; but, his application being refused, he abandoned his career in the navy, and shipped before the mast on board one of the vessels of the polar expedition. Here he found himself in the company of young Horatio Nelson, afterward England's greatest naval hero, who, like himself, had made the sacrifice of his rank in order to indulge his spirit of adventure. Both were eventually appointed coxswains, in spite of their youth. The expedition penetrated as far north as 81° 39′, and experienced the usual hardships and vicissitudes of an Arctic voyage. Upon his return to England, Biddle, owing to the strained relations between England and her American colonies, resigned his commission, returned to Philadelphia, and offered his services to the Continental Congress.

He was given charge of the *Franklin,* a "Provincial Armed Boat" or galley, fitted out by the Pennsylvania Committee of Safety for the defense of the Delaware, on Aug. 1, 1775, but in December of the same year he was placed in command of the brig *Andrea Doria* (14 guns and 130 men) with the rank of captain, and ordered to join the squadron of Esek Hopkins, commander-in-chief of the naval forces of the United Colonies, with which he took part in the expedition against New Providence. During and for some time after this service the efficiency of his vessel was greatly reduced by a violent epidemic of smallpox, to which many of his crew fell victims. On the breaking up of the fleet he cruised in the North Atlantic and took a large number of prizes laden with arms and ammunition, which thus fell into the hands of Washington, then at Cambridge, instead of those of the British forces. Off the coast of Newfoundland he was fortunate enough to capture two armed transports with 400 Highlanders destined for the British army at Boston. J. F. Cooper (*History of the Navy,* 1839, I, 114) thus refers to this period of Biddle's career:

"This vessel, a little brig, carrying 14 fours, actually took two armed transports filled with soldiers, and made prizes of so many merchantmen, that, it is affirmed on plausible authority, when she got back into the Delaware, but five of the common men who composed her original crew were in her; the rest having been put in the prizes, and their places supplied by volunteers from among the prisoners. Captain Biddle gained much credit for this cruise, and on his return, he was appointed to the command of the *Randolph* 32, then recently launched."

Ordered by the Marine Committee to Martinique (February 1777), the *Randolph* encountered a violent storm after leaving the Delaware capes, and lost her masts, which, as appears in a letter from Biddle to his brother, were made of rotten timber, for he writes from Charleston, "A person of credit declares to me that he knew those spars our masts were made of to have lain these eighteen years in the water at the mast yard." Repairs being quickly made, Biddle undertook a successful cruise to West Indian waters, capturing among other prizes the English ship *True Briton,* 20 guns, which, with three merchantmen that she was convoying, he carried into Charleston harbor, occasioning great satisfaction throughout the South. During the remainder of the season the *Randolph* was blockaded in Charleston by a superior British force, but in late February, 1778, in company with four small war-vessels fitted out by the State of South Carolina and placed under Biddle's command, he put to sea in quest of several British ships which had been cruising off Charleston for some time. About three o'clock on Mar. 7 a sail was made out to windward, whereupon the squadron hauled on the wind and stood for her. Unfortunately she proved to be the "two-decker" *Yarmouth,* carrying 64 guns. Awaiting the approach of the American vessels, Captain N. Vincent of the *Yarmouth* ranged up on the weather quarter of the largest, the *Randolph,* which, upon the British demand to show her colors, hoisted the American ensign and poured in a broadside. There is no authoritative report from an American source on the scene which followed, but we have the report of the British captain, dated Mar. 17, 1778, in which he says: "A smart action now commenced and was maintained with vigor for twenty minutes, when the stranger blew up. The two ships were so near each other at the time that many fragments of the wreck struck the *Yarmouth.* . . . Early in the engagement Commodore Biddle was wounded, but, ordering a chair, was placed in it on the quarter-deck, and continued to direct the battle and encourage the crew. His fire was constant and well directed. . . . Just then while a surgeon was examining his wound, the *Randolph* was blown up and the commander, with 311 of her 315 officers and men perished" (*Ibid.,* I, 146). Such was the heroic end of a man of whom Cooper wrote (*Ibid.,* I, 148) : "His death occurred at the early age of twenty-seven, and he died unmarried, though engaged, at the time, to a lady in Charleston. There is little question that Nicholas Biddle would have risen to high rank and great consideration, had his life been spared. Ardent, ambitious, fearless, intelligent, and persevering, he had all the qualities of a great naval captain, and, though possessing some local family influence perhaps, he rose to the station he filled at so early an age, by personal merit. For so short a career, scarcely any other had been so brilliant; for though no victories over regular cruisers accompanied his exertions, he had ever been successful until the fatal moment when he so gloriously fell." In personal appearance Biddle was of athletic frame and strikingly handsome, while his manner was animated and entertaining. His brother Charles pays tribute to his temperate mode of life in these words, "I believe he never drank a quart of liquor in his life" (Charles Biddle, *Autobiography,* 1883, p. 108).

[S. P. Waldo, *Biog. Sketches of Am. Naval Heroes* (1823) ; Edward Biddle, "Capt. Nicholas Biddle," *Proc. U. S. Naval Institute,* Sept. 1917 ; G. W. Allen, *A Naval Hist. of the Am. Rev.* (2 vols., 1913).]

E. B.

BIDDLE, NICHOLAS (Jan. 8, 1786–Feb. 27, 1844), litterateur, scholar, statesman, financier, was born and died in Philadelphia. He came of an old Quaker family of some wealth that followed William Penn into West Jersey early in 1681. William Biddle of the third generation in West Jersey married Mary, the daughter of the Pennsylvania surveyor, Nicholas Scull, and became a resident of the newer colony across the Delaware. It was a son of this marriage, Charles Biddle, a vice-president of Pennsylvania under the constitution of 1776, who gave the name of Nicholas to his own son, born of Hannah Shepard of Beaufort, N. C. At the age of ten years, Nicholas Biddle entered the University of Pennsylvania and was ready to graduate when he was thirteen, but was not allowed to receive his degree because of his youth. He immediately entered the College of New Jersey at Princeton in 1799, where he took advanced work, especially in the classics, and graduated in 1801 as valedictorian, dividing honors for first place with another student. It was during this year that Joseph Dennie established in Philadelphia the *Port Folio,* the first periodical avowedly devoted to making an American literature, and young Biddle was among the young men who caught Dennie's outlook and enthusiasm. Though he was devoted to the study of the classics and French literature, he selected the law as his profession. He seems to have studied the latter under his elder brother, William S. Biddle, and the well-known jurist William Lewis, both of whom recognized his ability as a scholar of unusual grasp and as a writer. Indeed his family expected him to become a writer rather than a lawyer.

When Gen. John Armstrong was sent as minister to France in 1804, he took Biddle as his secretary. They sailed for France in August and were present on Dec. 2 at the self-coronation of Napoleon at Notre Dame. Among the tasks which fell to the legation was the settlement of the claims of those who had been despoiled by French privateers in the Napoleonic wars. Although but eighteen years old, Biddle was intrusted with the auditing and payment of these spoliation claims, allowed by the French Government, which were to be met out of the Louisiana purchase fund. He began the study of French law and continued his study of European languages and history, winning notable French friendships that continued throughout his life. Late in 1805 he began to travel in Switzerland and Southern France, and in 1806 proceeded through Italy and Sicily to Greece. In August he retraced his steps, with more travel in France, Germany, and Holland, and, having been chosen by Minister James Monroe to be secretary of legation at London, he was soon established in that diplomat's family, and so remained until August 1807, when he returned to Washington and Philadelphia. Monroe used to tell with delight of a visit to Cambridge University when Biddle conversed with the dons on the difference between classic and modern Greek. All were impressed with the young man's knowledge, and the friendship of minister and secretary was destined to have an important influence on the latter's future career.

On his return from abroad Biddle resumed his legal studies with his elder brother; but he was not admitted to the bar until Dec. 11, 1809. He was still primarily the student, caring little for the practise of law. Early in 1809 he became a member of the "Tuesday Club" established by Joseph Dennie to encourage contributions to the *Port Folio,* and some notable articles on the fine arts were among his earliest papers, although he had written for it as early as 1806—had become indeed Dennie's favorite coadjutor. From his entry into the "Tuesday Club," for the next five years, he led the life of a man of letters, interrupted only by a short service in the House of

Representatives of Pennsylvania in the winter of 1810–11, and by his marriage, Oct. 4, 1811, to Jane, the daughter of John Craig of "Andalusia" on the Delaware—if either of these events could be called an interruption. As early as February 1810, Gen. William Clark, after the death of Capt. Meriwether Lewis, had asked Biddle to write the narrative of their expedition into the Louisiana country. He consented and with the aid of Clark's oral statements undertook to weave the mass of notes and journals into a coherent narrative. This he did with a high degree of success. During the year or more of his work on this narrative (March 1810–July 1812), he was increasingly active in the editorial management of the *Port Folio,* partly because of the illness of Dennie during most of 1811; and upon the latter's death, at the beginning of 1812, Biddle became editor of what was then the leading literary periodical in America. His election to the legislature, however, forced him to give up this post and to turn over the work of carrying through the press his *History of the Expedition of Captains Lewis and Clark* (1814) to Paul Allen, a journalist of Philadelphia. As a writer Biddle was quite as skilful in verse as in prose, with a lightness of touch and mixture of wit, humor, and sentiment worthy of more publication than his modesty and more serious purposes permitted. His brilliant bit of humor, entitled *Ode to Bogle,* dedicated to his little daughter "with a mint stick," an account of a "colorless colored man" who had local fame as both a caterer and undertaker, was published in his own day (1829) and republished long after his death.

From this scholarly life so much to his taste, Biddle was drawn by the predicament of his old friend, James Monroe, then secretary of war, and of his country, paralyzed by lack of funds to carry on the war. He not only aided in getting loans for the War Department, but entered the state Senate in 1814 and initiated measures for the protection of Philadelphia. He was in thorough sympathy with Secretary Monroe and President Madison in securing the re-charter of the second Bank of the United States in 1816, even though his own father was a director of a powerful rival bank. The most notable feature of his four years' service in the state Senate, however, was his remarkable report on the Hartford Convention of January 1814, which had proposed seven amendments to the Constitution. This report, published on Mar. 7, 1815, was a cogent reply to the New England proposals and an able defense of the Constitution as it was.

Near the close of Biddle's service in the state Senate President Monroe asked him to prepare a digest of international exchange, which was issued in 1819, entitled *Commercial Regulations.* The President also invited him to become one of the five government directors of the Bank of the United States. Biddle had hoped to resume his studies, and had refused to become a director for the majority stockholders; but looking upon the call of President Monroe as the summons of his commander-in-chief to public service, he accepted the appointment. With characteristic energy, he threw himself into the study of banking and soon became one of the best informed and most efficient members of the board. It was a crucial period in the history of the Bank. The conservative policy of President Cheeves, however prudent for the stockholders of the institution, had only accentuated the hostility of state banks and bankers in the South and West. Yet with all its embarrassments, as Biddle wrote in 1822, it had sustained the national currency and rescued the country from the domination of irresponsible banks and their depreciated currency. In this year Cheeves retired from the presidency and Biddle was elected in his place. He promptly stated what he considered the true policy of the Bank in a letter to Robert Lenox (R. C. McGrane, *Correspondence of Nicholas Biddle,* 1919, p. 31): "We have had enough & more than enough of banking in the interior. We have been crippled & almost destroyed by it. It is time to concenter our business—to bank where there is some use & some profit in it, and therefore (while anxious to do business in the interior the moment there is clear prospect of doing it usefully & safely) to make at present the large commercial Cities the principal scene of our operations." It is generally admitted that Biddle's management of the Bank for the next five years was wise. It did a successful business, extending its own operations conservatively, and it did much to establish itself in public confidence by furnishing a stable currency and by restraining state banks which were inclined to do unsound business. Yet the Bank always had its enemies. Some, holding to a strict construction of the Constitution, denied the power of Congress to charter such an institution; others, like Martin Van Buren, aided those who desired to make New York the financial capital of the country, and were bent upon breaking the power of "Chestnut Street"; still others strove to make political capital out of this rivalry. Although Biddle had made it an absolute rule that the Bank of the United States should be neutral in politics, he had become, through accident, a stockholders' director, with proxies among their four-fifths (the government had one-fifth), so that he not only represented their capital rather than that of the government, but had the power to protect their interests against the government. When, then, President Jackson declared in his inaugural address that not only the constitutionality and expediency but also the success of the Bank in creating a sound and uniform currency were open to question, Biddle, as leader of the vast number of those who regarded the Bank as a necessity, was instantly alert to the menace, as was the whole financial world. President Biddle, the financier, became at once Mr. Biddle, the editor, and almost every prominent friend of the Bank offered his services on his staff; for they believed as their editor-financier believed, that only a lack of knowledge of currency, finance, and economics could be the basis of a real antagonism to the system. Probably the best article was that written by Albert Gallatin, at Biddle's suggestion, which appeared in the *American Quarterly Review* in December 1830, and which the Bank republished and distributed widely.

The decision to apply to Congress for a new charter in 1832, four years before the expiration of the old, was probably Biddle's. He had been warned that this course would project the Bank as an issue into the presidential campaign of 1832, but he thought this hazard offset by others. This now seems to have been an error of judgment. But on the failure of the Bank to secure a new charter, it did what the Bank of North America had done when its right to a national charter was questioned, namely, secured a state charter; and on the expiration of the old national charter on Mar. 1, 1836, it became "The Bank of the United States of Pennsylvania" and continued its operations almost uninterruptedly, functioning very much as the old Bank had done and as the Bank of North America had done under similar conditions.

In March 1839 Biddle resigned, and retired to "Andalusia," his country seat on the Delaware. "Andalusia" became the scene of an intellectual and social life which was not then common in the United States. Distinguished European exiles were often his guests, and records of their conversations on great events abroad were preserved by him. His interest and aid in all branches of internal development did not diminish his love for classic Greece and her freedom. His active mind not only determined the character of education in Girard College, of whose board he was president, but its architecture. Both the college and the Bank of the United States, as well as his remodeled seat at "Andalusia" followed classic Greek lines. His later papers and addresses were notable for their peculiarly modern tone, one of them advocating shorter hours and higher wages for workmen as sound economic truth. With his death at the age of fifty-eight, there passed a great gentleman and scholar.

[The only sketch of Nicholas Biddle is an excellent one by R. T. Conrad in Jas. Herring's *Nat. Portrait Gallery* (1854), reproduced in the *Autobiography of Chas. Biddle* in 1883. See also *The Second Bank of the U. S.* by Ralph C. H. Catterall (1903); and the Biddle Papers, Lib. of Cong.]

BIDLACK, BENJAMIN ALDEN (Sept. 8, 1804–Feb. 6, 1849), diplomat, was born at Paris, Oneida County, N. Y. His father, Benjamin Bidlack, was the great-grandson of Christopher Bidlack, who settled at Windham, Conn., in the late seventeenth century. His mother's name was Lydia Alden. His parents were among those Connecticut pioneers who settled in the Wyoming Valley north of Philadelphia, a great many of whom were martyrs to their patriotism in the massacre during the Revolution—an event which Bidlack vividly portrayed in an address delivered on Washington's birthday, 1839, at Wilkes-Barre (published in 1842). He received his early education at Wilkes-Barre and read law in the office of Garrick Mallery. An early marriage with Fanny, daughter of James Stewart, proved of short duration, and on Sept. 8, 1829, he married Margaret, daughter of William Wallace. Shortly after his admission to the bar, he was appointed deputy attorney for Luzerne County. In 1833 he participated in the purchase of the newspaper *Republican Farmer,* upon the subsequent sale of which he established and edited the *Northern Eagle,* the first paper published in Pike County. A brief period (1835–36) in the Pennsylvania legislature as the representative of Luzerne County gave him a taste for legislation which eventuated in two terms in the federal Congress (1841–45) as a Democrat. Failing to be reëlected in 1844, he secured, through the influence of a fellow Pennsylvanian, the new secretary of state, Buchanan, an appointment as chargé d'affaires in New Granada, one of three republics formed by the splitting up of the United States of Colombia. It is significant that the principal pending business of the mission consisted of the claims of American citizens, including Simeon Toby, president of the Insurance Company of the State of Pennsylvania, who was interested in the *Brig Josephine* claim. Leaving his wife and the rest of his family, Bidlack arrived at his post in company with one son on Dec. 1, 1845. He immediately set to work upon the settlement of the claims with remarkable success. Six months later in the course of negotiations looking toward the abolition of differential duties the question of interoceanic communication came to the fore. British and French interests were active in their attempts to secure rights for the construction of a macadamized road or a railroad. Bidlack repeatedly wrote the State Department for instructions, but through the impossibility of rapid communication with the Department and the latter's distraction to more pressing affairs nearer home in Mexico, he was forced to proceed with the negotiation of a treaty concerning trans-isthmian communication or let the matter go by default to one of the other countries. He chose the former alternative and on Dec. 2, he concluded and signed a general treaty of peace, friendship, commerce, and navigation between the United States and New Granada, including the abolition of differential duties—a concession which had unsuccessfully been urged for twenty years—and the right of way across the Isthmus of Panama by any mode of communication in return for a guarantee of neutrality and of Granada's sovereignty over the Isthmus. This did not reach the Department until Jan. 28. Meanwhile (Jan. 2), the Department had authorized Bidlack to negotiate a treaty about the differential duties only. Consequently President Polk was surprised and at first inclined to consider the treaty an "entangling alliance," but eventually (June 10, 1848) it was ratified. Buchanan, in notifying Bidlack of this action, congratulated the latter "upon the association of your name with this instrument. It has been most favorably received by the public, and, I doubt not, will be of great and lasting advantage to both countries" (MSS. Department of State, Instr., Col., XV, 117). Repeated requests for leave of absence to visit his wife and family having been denied or ignored, Bidlack died at his post in the following February. The American residents of Bogota erected a monument to his memory, but a far more lasting monument he erected in his own memory when he negotiated, without power or instructions, the Treaty of 1846.

[A few of the more important official letters to Bidlack are printed in the *Works of Jas. Buchanan*, collected and edited by John Bassett Moore (12 vols., 1908–11). Most of the details of Bidlack's life, especially while chargé d'affaires, have been taken from manuscript dispatches in the Department of State. There is a good sketch in G. B. Kulp, *Families of the Wyoming Valley*, III (1890), pp. 1134–38.]

H. F. W.

BIDWELL, BARNABAS (Aug. 23, 1763–July 27, 1833), writer, lawyer, the son of Rev. Adonijah Bidwell and Jemimah Devotion Bidwell, was born in Tyringham (now Monterey), Mass. He graduated from Yale in the class of 1785. During his senior year he wrote and published a tragedy, *The Mercenary Match*, which was acted by his college mates. Immediately after graduation he began teaching in a young ladies' school at New Haven, and in October 1787 he was appointed to a tutorship at Yale, a position from which he resigned in September 1790. He then took up the study of law and began to practise at Stockbridge, Mass. He was appointed treasurer of Berkshire County in September 1791. After serving as state senator from 1801 to 1805, he was elected to Congress, but here he disappointed those who expected leadership from him. President Jefferson, however, found him useful as a member of committees by which he aimed to carry out his plans, especially those having to do with the purchase of Florida from Spain. In this connection Bidwell, "timid indeed, but cunning, supple, and sly," as one historian describes him, incurred the contempt of John Randolph, who branded him and his kind as Jefferson's "back stairs favorites" and "pages of the presidential water-closet." When the abolition of the slave trade came up for discussion in the House in 1806, Bidwell strongly opposed a bill that would substantially make the government a dealer in slaves (Richard Hildreth, *History of the United States of America*, 1851, V, 566–71, 630).

In 1807 he accepted an appointment as attorney-general of Massachusetts in place of returning to Congress. Three years later, at a time when President Madison was considering him for the Supreme Court of the United States, an investigation of his accounts as county treasurer, an office he had held for nineteen years, put an end to all further political aspirations by disclosing a shortage of about $10,000. In order to avoid trial Bidwell absconded to Canada and settled with his family on the north shore of Lake Ontario. Being an alien, he was barred from practising in the Canadian courts, and for the same reason he was not permitted to serve in the legislature, although elected to that body. In his last years he was described as "a profound jurist, a man of great culture and attainments outside the law as well as in it." Before his disgrace his abilities had won for him the honorary degrees of master of arts from Yale and Williams and of doctor of laws from Brown. He was married in 1793 to Mary Gray, a native of Stockbridge.

To-day Bidwell is known chiefly as the author of an undergraduate tragedy. *The Mercenary Match* is a not unimportant specimen of early American drama. Designed, like other school plays of the time, to display the oratorical powers of the performers, it is filled with long, declamatory speeches as artificial as the improbable plot. It is distinguished, however, by the general smoothness of the blank verse and the occasional felicity of the phrasing—qualities seldom found in eighteenth-century American plays. Aside from this drama Bidwell's published writings consist of a few orations and political speeches. He is also said to have contributed eleven sketches to Robert Gourlay's *Statistical Account of Upper Canada* (1822).

[Edwin M. Bidwell, *Genealogy to the Seventh Generation of the Bidwell Family in America* (1884); *Reminiscences of the Rev. Geo. Allen* (1883); *The Lit. Diary of Ezra Stiles* (1901), ed. by Franklin B. Dexter; John F. Schroeder, *Life and Character of Mrs. Mary Anna Boardman* (1849); Franklin B. Dexter, *Biog. Sketches of the Grads. of Yale Coll.*, IV (1907), 387 ff.]

O. S. C.

BIDWELL, JOHN (Aug. 5, 1819–Apr. 4, 1900), California pioneer, politician, was born in Chautauqua County, N. Y., the son of Abram and Clarissa (Griggs) Bidwell. In 1829 the family moved to Erie County, Pa., and two years later to Ohio, stopping first in Ashtabula County and in 1834 going to Darke County. In the fall or early winter of 1836 young Bidwell, determined upon getting an education, walked 300 miles to Ashtabula in order to enter Kingsville Academy. Here he made such rapid progress in his studies that in the following year he was elected principal of the institution. In 1838 he returned home and spent the winter teaching, but in the following spring decided to seek his fortune in the West. After some wandering he took up a land claim near Weston, Mo., in the vicinity of Fort Leavenworth, and for something more than a year supported himself by teaching. Losing his land to a claim-jumper because he was still a minor, and hearing of the wonders of the Pacific slope from one of the noted Robidou brothers, he now resolved to make his way to California. In May 1841, at Independence, Mo., he started with Bartleson's party of sixty-nine persons, including Josiah Belden [*q.v.*]. At Fort Hall the party divided, about half going to Oregon. The California contingent, thirty-two strong, after suffering great hardships, including the loss of their wagons, reached the foot of Mt. Diablo Nov. 4, the first emigrant train to make the journey from the Missouri.

Bidwell found work with Sutter at Fort Sutter and remained with him for several years. In 1844 he was naturalized and received a grant of land. On the outbreak of the revolt of Alvarado and Castro against Micheltorena, in December 1844, Bidwell and Sutter took the field in defense of the Governor, and after his defeat at Cahuenga, Feb. 22, 1845, both were for a time imprisoned, but soon made their peace with the victors. The Bear Flag revolt of the following June (1846) found Bidwell reluctant to join, but on July 4 he served as one of the committee that drew up the resolution of independence from Mexico. He accompanied Frémont to Monterey, where he was made a second lieutenant of the California Battalion, and then to the south. After the surrender of Los Angeles he was appointed magistrate of the San Luis Rey district. On the revolt of the Californians he fled to San Diego, later serving under Stockton as a quartermaster, with the rank of major, in the reconquest of Los Angeles. On the conclusion of peace he returned to Sutter's Fort. Following Marshall's discovery of gold, he prospected for a time and was the first to find gold on Feather River. In 1849 he acquired the extensive Rancho Chico, of 22,000 acres, north of Sacramento, and for the remainder of his life he was a cultivator of the soil, bringing his ranch to a high state of development and becoming the most noted agriculturist of the state. He maintained, however, a keen interest in public affairs and for many years was active in politics. In the same year that he took over the ranch he was chosen a member of the constitutional convention (though he learned of the fact too late to serve) and was also elected to the state Senate. In the following year he was one of the commission to carry to Washington a block of gold-bearing quartz as California's contribution to the Washington Monument. In 1854 and again in 1860 he was one of the vice-presidents of the Democratic state convention, and in the latter year he was also a delegate to the Charleston convention, where he supported Douglas. He was a strong defender of the Union and after 1861 affiliated with the Union party. In 1863 Gov. Stanford appointed him a brigadier-general of militia, doubtless in recognition of his services in thwarting the secessionists of the state. In the following year he was a delegate to the Baltimore convention, at which Lincoln was nominated; and was also elected to the House of Representatives. He declined a renomination in 1866, and in the following year was an unsuccessful candidate for governor on the Republican ticket. Later he became an independent, running for governor as an anti-monopolist in 1875. He was the candidate of the Prohibition party for governor in 1890 and two years later its candidate for president. He did not again engage actively in political affairs, but spent his remaining days in the supervision of his ranch. He was one of the early regents of the University of California, and in 1888 he donated the land on which a State Normal School was subsequently built. He was a constant advocate of internal improvements and was one of the first proponents of a transcontinental railway. To the Indians, many of whom he had in his employ, he was a friend, helper, and teacher. He died suddenly of heart failure following over-exertion in cutting down a tree.

Bidwell was married in Washington in 1868 to Annie, daughter of J. C. G. Kennedy, superintendent of the Census of 1850 and of 1860. She was a woman of many accomplishments and an efficient partner in all her husband's activities. Bidwell Park, a tract of 1,900 acres, said to be one of the most beautiful natural parks of California, given by the widow to the city of Chico, commemorates his life and career.

[E. M. Bidwell, *Genealogy to the Seventh Generation of the Bidwell Family in America* (1884), p. 92; H. H. Bancroft, *Hist. of Cal.*, II (1885); C. C. Royce, *John Bidwell* (1906); Marcus Benjamin, *John Bidwell, Pioneer* (1907); John Bidwell, "The First Emigrant Train to Cal.," *Century Mag.*, Nov. 1890; *A Journey to Cal.* (pamphlet, published probably in Weston, Mo., about 1843, from a MS. sent from California by Bidwell). Most of his writings, which are largely autobiographical, are collected in the Royce volume. A smaller collection appears in a pamphlet, *Echoes of the Past About Cal.* (Chico, probably 1900); *San Francisco Chronicle*, Apr. 5, 1900.]

W. J. G.

BIDWELL, MARSHALL SPRING (Feb. 16, 1799–Oct. 24, 1872), lawyer, politician, was descended from Richard Bidwell, a pioneer settler of Windsor, Conn., in 1630, and was the son of Barnabas Bidwell [*q.v.*], and Mary (Gray) Bidwell. Born at Stockbridge, Mass., he obtained his early education there and, after his father's flight to Canada, at Bath, Ont., where his father established a school. On the family's subsequently removing to Kingston, he studied law there and was admitted to the bar of Upper Canada in April 1820, opening an office in Kingston and later in Toronto. He was married to Clara Willcox of Bath. In 1821 his father, elected that year as Reform member of the House of Assembly for the united counties of Lennox and Addington in the legislature of Upper Canada, was, as an alien, not permitted to serve. Marshall Bidwell thereupon became a candidate for his father's seat. Canadian politics had become exceedingly bitter and he was strongly opposed by the "Family Compact" or Government party. He contested the constituency three times and was ultimately elected in 1824, the Reform party having meanwhile procured the passing of an act relaxing the conditions under which persons who had resided in or taken an oath of allegiance to a foreign state could be excluded. Bidwell at once became a prominent figure in the political arena, having early developed strength as a forceful debater with an intimate knowledge of constitutional law and precedent. His reputation as an able attorney was materially assisted by his success as chief counsel for the plaintiff in the celebrated suit of McKenzie *vs.* Jarvis *et al.*, "the type-riot case." In 1828 he was reelected member for Lennox and Addington, and was chosen speaker of the House in 1829, being now one of the acknowledged leaders of the Reform party whose head was William Lyon Mackenzie. The following year the legislature was dissolved and Bidwell's party suffered defeat in the general election, but he was again returned. Growing discontent at the arbitrary actions of the Government party had been manifest for some time, and at length culminated in a victory for the Reform party at the elections of 1834, Bidwell becoming speaker of the House in 1835 for the second time. Another general election took place in 1836 and he lost his seat, having represented Lennox and Addington for eleven years. Political feeling in Upper Canada had now reached such a pitch that its repercussions had aroused the British Government to the necessity of conciliating the extreme factions, and the lieutenant-governor, Sir Francis B. Head, was instructed to appoint Bidwell to the first vacant judgeship of the Court of King's Bench. This Head deliberately refused to do, and in the meantime what is known as "the Upper Canada Rebellion" broke out under the auspices of William Lyon Mackenzie. Bidwell, a republican in principle, took no part in the rising and was not implicated in it. He refused to be a member of the proposed provincial convention, and announced his withdrawal from public life. The authorities became, however, suspicious of his good faith, and Sir Francis Head determined to compel him to leave the country. The circumstances under which this was brought about have been a matter of great controversy. The truth appears to be that Bidwell was led to believe that a charge of treason would probably be made against him upon which, in the disturbed condition of the province, he would not get a fair trial. In any event he wrote, Dec. 8, 1837, to Head that he had determined to leave the province forever, and he departed two days later. He went at once to New York City and was admitted by courtesy to the New York bar, where he speedily acquired a good practise. A case which brought him into prominence there was the libel suit by Fenimore Cooper against W. L. Stone, editor of the *New York Commercial Advertiser*, relative to the conduct of Commander Perry at the battle of Lake Erie in September 1813. Bidwell specialized in the law of real property, trusts, and construction of wills and in his later years appeared almost exclusively in the higher trial and appellate courts. In New York he became very popular, socially and professionally, being a man of great personal charm and equable temperament, and interesting himself actively in religious and charitable institutions. It was gradually realized in Canada that Sir Francis Head's action in procuring Bidwell's practical expulsion had been inexcusable, and, after the constitutional troubles of Upper Canada had been adjusted, vain efforts were from time to time made to induce him to return. Bidwell died in New York City.

[Edwin M. Bidwell, *Genealogy to the Seventh Generation of the Bidwell Family in America* (1884); H. J. Morgan, *Sketches of Celebrated Canadians* (1862); J. C. Dent, *The Canadian Portrait Gallery* (1880), II, 108; E. F. De Lancey, "Marshall S. Bidwell," *N. Y. Geneal. and Biog. Record* (1890), XXI, 1; *In Memoriam, Marshall S. Bidwell* (N. Y. Bar, 1872); J. C. Dent, *The Upper Canada Rebellion* (1885), containing an extended account of Bidwell's political career; *Hist. of the Bench and Bar of N. Y.*, ed. by D. McAdam *et al.* (1897), I, 261.]

H. W. H. K.

BIDWELL, WALTER HILLIARD (June 21, 1798–Sept. 11, 1881), editor, publisher, was the son of William Bidwell of Farmington, Conn., and his wife, Mary Pelton. The family ancestry had mingled strains of English, Scotch, and French blood. He lived the usual life of the son of a Connecticut farmer till he was twenty-one, when he prepared for Yale, entering as a sophomore and graduating in 1827. In 1833 he graduated from the Yale Divinity School, having meanwhile married Susan M. Duryea of New York, and his course having been interrupted by a year spent in Europe for his wife's health. On Sept. 19, 1833, he was ordained and installed pastor of the Congregational Church at Medfield, Mass., but on account of the failure of his voice he retired from the ministry four years later. Moving to Philadelphia, he became in 1841 editor and proprietor of the *National Preacher and Village Pulpit*, which he continued for nineteen years, publishing sermons from about 500 preachers of all evangelical denominations. In 1843 he also became editor and proprietor of the *New York Evangelist*, which he conducted for nearly twelve years. From 1846 to 1849 he was proprietor and editor of the *Biblical Repository and Classical Review* and also of the *Eclectic Magazine; Foreign Literature*. He edited the latter till 1868 and owned it till his death, or for a period of about thirty-five years. In 1860 he became publisher and proprietor of the *American Theological Review*, whose editor was Prof. Henry B. Smith of Union Theological Seminary. Two years later it passed into other hands and was merged with the *Presbyterian Quarterly Review*. At one time Bidwell was the owner of five periodicals. Between 1848 and 1854 he published a series of seven missionary maps, of which his brother O. B. Bidwell was the maker. In 1864–65 he suffered a serious breakdown due to the mental strain of overwork, and spent two years abroad in the recovery of his health. After this, his sole editorial work was in connection with the *Eclectic Magazine* till 1868, when he retired from all active duties. He made six extensive tours in foreign countries partly for reasons of health, but mainly in the interests of the *Eclectic Magazine*. In 1867 he was appointed by Secretary Seward a special commissioner of the United States to various countries of Western Asia, and in this connection he made an extensive tour through Egypt, Greece, and the Levant. After his retirement he made several additional trips abroad, but the home of his latter years was mainly at Oberlin, Ohio, where he found the religious atmosphere congenial. He spent the last year of his life in Chicago, but died at Saratoga Springs, N. Y. His life was one of great activity and usefulness, and he had a very extensive acquaintance in America and abroad, especially with Protestant ministers of all denominations.

[*Obit. Record Grads. of Yale Univ.* (1890), p. 78; *Eclectic Mag.*, LXIII, and a fuller account in the latter publication for Nov. 1881. There is a briefer notice and estimate in the *Evangelist*, Sept. 20, 1881. Portraits are to be found in the *Eclectic Mag.*, XLII, LXIII.]

F. T. P.

BIEN, JULIUS (Sept. 27, 1826–Dec. 21, 1909), lithographer and map engraver, was born in Naumburg near Cassel, Germany, the son of Emanuel M. Bien, lecturer and lithographer. He attended the Academy of Fine Arts at Cassel and the Städel Art Institute at Frankfurt-am-Main, where he studied painting and specialized in the graphic arts. Having participated in the revolutionary movement of 1848, he came to the United States in the following year, settling in New York City. There he began business on a small scale with one lithographic hand press. Some of his early major commissions were to prepare the illustrations for the report on European railways by Zerah Colburn and A. L. Holley (*The Permanent Way and Coal-Burning Locomotive Boilers of European Railways*, 1858), and to produce a chromo-lithographic edition, by transfer from the original copper plates, of Audubon's *Birds of America*. The latter undertaking had to be abandoned soon after its inception because of the Civil War.

Having observed and reflected on the generally low standard of maps being produced in the country of his adoption, Bien saw in this deficiency an opportunity to apply his knowledge. He sought an interview with President Pierce, who referred him to the Secretary of War, Jefferson Davis, who was at the time the responsible head of the Pacific Railroad surveys. The reports were being published, and the engraving of a number of the maps was entrusted to Bien. Outstanding among these was the general map of the territory between the Mississippi and the Pacific on the scale of 1 : 3,000,000 (accompanying Lieut. G. K. Warren's memoir in Volume XI), which first adequately represented the relief of this vast area, in its various editions successively incorporated new explorations, and remained the standard map of the West for more than twenty-five years.

From then on to the end of the century there was scarcely a major geographical or geological publication issued by the Government for which maps were not engraved and printed by Bien. Nor were these merely translations on stone of author's drawings; often it was due alone to the method of representation devised by Bien that the geographical significance of the facts they portrayed became fully apparent. This is especially true of the maps and atlases accompanying the decennial census reports, of which Bien engraved those for the Ninth to the Twelfth Census (1870–1900). Noteworthy among these was a series of maps in the text volumes of the Tenth Census showing population density in the different sections of the country on larger scales than have ever been attempted since. Other outstanding cartographic productions by Bien were: the *Geological and Geographical Atlas of Colorado* (1877), by F. V. Hayden; the *Geological and Topographical Atlas Accompanying the Report of the Geological Exploration of the Fortieth Parallel* (1876), by Clarence King; the numerous map sheets on the scale of four or eight miles to the inch issued by the United States Geographical Surveys West of the One Hundredth Meridian under G. M. Wheeler (the representation of relief by hachures or shading on the topographic sheets of this series represented a degree of technical excellence in that domain not surpassed in this country before or since); and the atlases accompanying the following United States Geological Survey reports: C. E. Dutton's *Tertiary History of the Grand Canyon District* (1882) with W. H. Holmes's masterly drawings; G. F. Becker's *Geology of the Comstock Lode* (1882); S. F. Emmons's *Geology and Mining Industry of Leadville, Colorado* (1883–86); and *Geology of the Yellowstone National Park* (1899) by Arnold Hague and others. The monumental *Atlas to Accompany the Official Records of the Union and Confederate Armies* (War Department, 1891–95) contains no less than 175 plates consisting of plans of battles and other military operations. It also includes a useful general map of the eastern half of the country on an exceptionally large scale (ten miles to the inch). During the Civil War itself Bien had made an active contribution by equipping a field map printing outfit for Sherman on his march to the sea. Many maps were also engraved and printed for state geological surveys, including the "Hand Atlas" for the *Second Geological Survey of Pennsylvania* (1884–85) by J. P. Lesley and the atlas for the *Geology of New Hampshire* (1878) by C. H. Hitchcock. Of a number of atlases Bien was publisher in his own name, *viz.*, Westchester County, N. Y. (1893), New York State (1895), Pennsylvania (1900), and the excellent topographic *Atlas of the Metropolitan District Around New York City* (1891). The total production of the Bien establishment amounts literally to thousands of different maps. During his long career Bien did more than any other to create and establish scientific standards in American cartography.

On the personal side the outstanding traits of Bien's character were breadth of view, tolerance, and love of his fellow man. Kindly and modest in personal relations, his life was characterized by many deeds of unobtrusive philanthropy. In 1863 he married Almira M. Brown of Philadelphia, who survived him until 1918.

[On Bien's life printed sources are practically limited to entries in *Who's Who in America* (last in volume for 1908–09, the *Jewish Encyc.*, III (1902), and an obituary in the *National Lithographer*, Jan. 1910. In addition this sketch is based on his son Julius's personal recollections.]
W. L. G. J.

BIENVILLE, JEAN BAPTISTE LE MOYNE, Sieur de (Feb. 23, 1680–Mar. 7, 1767), governor of Louisiana, founder of Mobile and New Orleans, was the eighth son of Charles le Moyne, Canadian pioneer, ennobled by the King in 1676 for his great services, and granted the seigneury of Longueuil. There Jean Baptiste was born; his mother was Catherine Tierry, called Primot from an adoptive father. Both parents dying while the boy was young, his elder brother Charles, Baron de Longueuil, gave him a father's care. When in 1691 his brother François, Sieur de Bienville, was killed in the Iroquois wars, the title was bestowed upon Jean. Of all the Le Moynes, Pierre, Sieur d'Iberville [*q.v.*], nineteen years older than Jean, was most illustrious; the boy longed to follow in his elder's footsteps, and at the age of twelve became *garde-marine* in the royal navy, and entered service on his brother's vessel. In the naval battles in the North Atlantic and Hudson Bay from 1695 to

1698 Bienville took his part, and was seriously wounded, Sept. 5, 1697, while serving a battery on the frigate *Pélican.*

King William's War having closed with the peace of Ryswick in 1697, the French government sent Iberville to re-discover the mouth of the Mississippi, attempted formerly by La Salle, and there to form a French colony. Bienville accompanied the expedition which left Brest on Oct. 24, 1698, in two small vessels, and six weeks later landed on an island in the Gulf of Mexico, off what is now Biloxi. He was very useful to the exploring party, because of his aptitude for learning Indian languages, and his ability in conciliating the tribesmen. Exploring a great stream near their landfall, he secured from a chief a letter, written some years before by Henry de Tonty, La Salle's faithful friend, which assured the adventurers that they had found the Mississippi.

The first settlement was made on the coast at Old Biloxi, where Iberville, May 24, 1699, left his infant colony to the care of Sauvole, with Bienville second in command. Twice in 1699 the latter explored the lower reaches of the Mississippi, and in October boarded and ordered off a British vessel, which had come to found a colony, saying that this river was appropriated to Louis XIV. (Alvord and Carter, "The New Regime," *Illinois Historical Collections,* XI, 417–19, gives the log of the English captain. Bond.) Early in 1700 the colony of Biloxi was cheered by the arrival of Tonty, who came from Illinois to cast in his lot with the Canadians on this southern shore. This same year, March to May, Bienville explored the Red River as far as Natchitoches, making alliances with the Indians of that region. In 1701 Sauvole died, leaving Bienville in command; Iberville, visiting his colony, brought his young brother a commission as king's lieutenant. The next year Bienville determined to remove headquarters to a better site, and on Mobile Bay built Fort Louis. which was in 1710 removed to the present site of Mobile. He was much engaged in Indian negotiations, when Queen Anne's War made it necessary to carry help to the Spanish settlements in the Gulf of Mexico. From them he imported into his colony the dread scourge of yellow fever, from which Tonty died in 1704 and Iberville in 1706.

After Iberville's death the colony declined, and Bienville had to contend with enemies within and without. Supporting the Jesuits, he was attacked by the Seminary priests and by Nicolas de la Salle, the commissary, who made such serious charges against him that a new governor was sent to replace him. This successor having died en route, Bienville remained in office and was later exonerated and restored. The colony, however, lacked workers and Bienville suggested that Indian prisoners brought by his allies be exchanged in the West Indies for negro slaves. In 1712 the King granted Louisiana to a company founded by Antoine Crozat, who displaced Bienville as governor and sent Cadillac to supplant him. The former governor was left as second in command, during Cadillac's administration (1713–16). He at first contemplated marrying a daughter of the new governor (see his letter in King, *Sieur de Bienville,* 198–205). The relations of the two officials soon became strained, however, and Bienville never married. In 1716 Cadillac sent him against the Natchez Indians, whom he reduced to obedience by stratagems of doubtful utility. When Cadillac was recalled, Bienville hoped to succeed him, but was disappointed, for Crozat sent another governor, who remained but a year, when Crozat's company was dissolved. Louisiana in 1717 passed into the hands of the colonization company founded by the financier, John Law, and became the object of wild speculation. Law restored Bienville to the command of the province, and secured for him the cross of the Order of St. Louis. Large accessions of colonists now began to be poured into Louisiana. Bienville had to furnish provisions for all of these, and to aid in the settlement of the great concessions granted to noblemen by the company. He saw the importance of changing the colony's base to the Mississippi, and in 1718 had New Orleans laid out; it did not, however, become the capital until 1722. In 1719 when Spain and France went to war, Bienville twice captured Pensacola. Soon after this Law's "Mississippi bubble" burst and its promoter fled from France. The Company of the Indies, however, continued to govern Louisiana until 1731. After removing his capital to New Orleans, Bienville promulgated the "Black Code," a series of regulations for the negroes, for which he has been blamed by a more humane age.

Louisiana's difficulties with the Natchez, with whom a second war was fought in 1723, and the lack of support by the Company brought ruin upon Bienville. In 1724 he was accused before the court; and the next year was summoned to France, with his brother and nephew. For the first time since its inception Louisiana was without any of the Le Moyne family. In Paris Bienville made a notable defense of his administration, and in a state paper of great force exposed the difficulties of the colonial life. Nevertheless he was degraded and deprived of all his offices. He dwelt quietly in Paris until 1732 when, Louisiana having been brought to the verge of ruin by the inadequacy of the governor and the rebellion of the Natchez, Bienville was implored to return. Upon his arrival in 1733 as royal governor he was received "with a joy and satisfaction without parallel."

The final decade of his governorship was disturbed by Indian wars. The Natchez had fled to the Chickasaw, who refused to give them up, and went to the English to trade. In 1736 Bienville ordered an expedition against these Indians, the Illinois contingent of which was overwhelmed by the tribesmen, and its commander, chaplain, and twenty other Frenchmen were burned at the stake. Bienville, then advancing from Mobile, was forced to retreat. To avenge this catastrophe another expedition took place in 1739–40, when a Canadian contingent met Bienville's near Memphis, and forced a peace, which in the end proved undecisive. Worn with these and other troubles, the governor asked for release from his heavy responsibilities. His request was granted, and on May 10, 1743, he left Louisiana never to return. His declining years were spent in Paris, where he lived on his pension and maintained his interest in his former colony. When in 1766 Jean Milhet came as envoy from the Louisianians to protest the cession to Spain, Bienville accompanied him in his futile audience with the minister. He himself suffered the pain of seeing France cede the colony he had striven to build.

Bienville has been extravagantly praised and unjustly blamed. His was a difficult, at times almost a hopeless, task; his resources were meager and his support poor. That he succeeded at all is proof of his ability. Not a man of the highest qualities, he was none the less loyal to his King and to his kinsfolk; and without him French Louisiana could hardly have been maintained.

[The sources for Bienville's career are numerous and full. Official and other documents are in Pierre Margry, *Découvertes et Établissements des Français dans l'Amérique Septentrionale* (Paris, 1880–86), IV, V, VI; Le Page du Pratz, *Histoire de la Louisiane* (Paris, 1758); Bernard de la Harpe, *Journal Historique de l'Établissement des Français à la Louisiane* (New Orleans, 1831); Dumont de Montigny, *Mémoires Historiques sur la Louisiane* (Paris, 1753): all written by travelers or colonists of Bienville's time. For modern works see Chas. Gayarré, *Hist. of La.* (4th ed. 1903), I; Grace King, *Jean Baptiste le Moyne, Sieur de Bienville* (Makers of America series, 1892); Alcée Fortier, *Hist. of La.* (1904), I; Frédéric de Kastner, *Héros de la Nouvelle France*, 1st ser. (1902), and *Le Moyne de Bienville et l'Etablissement de la Louisiane* (Quebec, n. d.); Pierre Heinrich, *La Louisiane sous la Compagnie des Indes* (Paris, 1908); Marc de Villiers, "Hist. of the Foundation of New Orleans," translated for *La. Hist. Quart.*, Apr. 1920; Peter J. Hamilton, "The Private Life of Jean Baptiste le Moyne, Sieur de Bienville," *Papers of the Iberville Hist. Soc.*, No. 1.] L. P. K.

BIERCE, AMBROSE GWINETT (June 24, 1842–1914?), journalist, author, youngest of the numerous children of Marcus Aurelius and Laura (Sherwood) Bierce, was born in a log cabin on Horse Cave Creek, Meigs County, Ohio, whither the family had migrated from Connecticut. His parents were farmers—poor, obscure, and eccentric. Bierce was reticent concerning his humble origins, and of his childhood little is known. He received no general education beyond that afforded by his father's small library. At the outbreak of the Civil War he joined the 9th Indiana Infantry and served with distinction through many of the most difficult campaigns of the western armies. He twice risked his life in rescuing fallen companions from the battlefield and at Kenesaw Mountain was himself severely wounded. The war over, he became custodian of "captured and abandoned property" at Selma, Ala., resigning in 1866 to accompany Gen. W. B. Hazen on an inspection tour of the northwestern army posts. This completed, Bierce, discouraged with his prospects for advancement, joined his brother Albert in San Francisco, and while working with him in the Mint contributed paragraphs to the weeklies, especially the *Argonaut* and the *News Letter.* In a period of very bitter personal journalism his caustic wit and courage quickly brought him recognition and with it the editorship of the *News Letter.* The *Overland Monthly* published his first short story, "The Haunted Valley," in 1871. On Christmas Day of that year he married Mary Day of San Francisco and several months later they went to England.

During the next four years Bierce was on the staff of *Fun;* he edited for the Empress Eugénie the two numbers of the *Lantern* and contributed articles to *Figaro* and *Hood's Comic Annual.* He found stimulating associates in a bohemian group that included George Augustus Sala, W. S. Gilbert, and Tom Hood the younger. In 1872 he published, under the pseudonym of "Dod Grile" and in confessed collaboration with Satan, *The Fiend's Delight,* a "cold collation of diabolisms," and *Nuggets and Dust Panned Out in California.* Both books were collections of mordantly humorous sketches he had contributed to various California journals, while two years later a third volume, *Cobwebs from an Empty Skull,* containing many articles that first appeared in *Fun,* established the reputation of "Bitter Bierce" as a vitriolic wit.

Returning to San Francisco in 1876, he wrote

for the *Wasp* and the *Argonaut* until William Randolph Hearst took over the *Examiner* in 1887. From March of that year until he went East Bierce conducted a column of "Prattle" on the editorial page of the Sunday *Examiner*. This was the most active and fruitful period of his life. He became the literary dictator of the Pacific Coast; his keen wit and fearless satire

"Exposed the fool and lash'd the knave."

Although journalism gave him freedom of expression and a livelihood it was "frankly low and rotten" and was hateful to him. In his art he found a refuge from the newspapers and in the midst of much potboiling wrote a little for posterity. His first volume of short stories, *Tales of Soldiers and Civilians,* "denied existence by the chief publishing houses of the country," was published by a merchant friend, E. L. G. Steele, in 1891. These grim and vivid stories, without humor and without sentiment, attracted little attention and were soon forgotten. In 1892 Bierce revised and rewrote G. A. Danziger's *The Monk and the Hangman's Daughter,* a medieval romance. This, his longest piece of sustained narrative, fully reveals his deep feeling for beauty and his power of subjective analysis. As a world of rogues and fools provoked his bitter satire and at length wearied him, so a spirit world of masques and shadows fascinated him and brought forth his best art. *Can Such Things Be?* (1893), weird stories of the supernatural, rousing terror and pity, mark the perfection of his power and style.

Sent by Hearst to Washington in 1896, Bierce was instrumental in defeating Huntingdon's proposed refunding bill. The next year he returned East and became Washington correspondent of the New York *American.* His *Devil's Dictionary* (1906), sardonic comments on a world he knew too well, addressed to "enlightened souls who prefer dry wines to sweet, sense to sentiment, wit to humor, and clean English to slang," was a collection of earlier work. He continued writing but the creative period was over: his satire was milder and his stories less effective. In his *Collected Works* (1909–12) he achieved the success of one of his own characters who "sought obscurity in the writing and publishing of books." Those twelve volumes did little to promote his own reputation and perhaps much to hasten the financial disaster which now, as usually, soon overtook his publishers.

At length, in 1913, lonely and weary of the world, he asked a few friends to "forgive him in not 'perishing' where he was," and having settled his affairs, disappeared into warring Mexico. "Goodbye," he wrote, "if you hear of my being stood up against a Mexican stone wall and shot to rags please know that I think it a pretty good way to depart this life. It beats old age, disease, or falling down the cellar stairs. To be a Gringo in Mexico—ah, that is euthanasia!" (*Letters,* pp. 196–97). Many and weird are the stories concerning his fate, but all agree that at last he found "the good, kind darkness" that he sought.

Bierce was not a disciple of Poe, but evolved his own type of the short story: brilliant, witty, and climactic. His situations often unusual and abnormal, with cruel and ironic motifs, he wrote some of the most terrifying and hauntingly suggestive stories in our literature. Bierce learned much from Poe and Bret Harte and, in his turn, influenced Stephen Crane and O. Henry. That "soul" and sentiment notably absent in his stories did find expression in his life and its rich friendships. His many social criticisms were independent and aggressive. Fiercely individualistic, he fought socialists as well as "mobocrats" and while greatly admiring Jesus as "a lightning moral calculator" hurled his sharpest shafts at priests and theologians.

[*Letters of Ambrose Bierce, ed. by Bertha Clark Pope, with a memoir by Geo. Sterling* (1922); "Bits of Autobiography" in vol. I of *Collected Words*; Vincent Starrett, *Ambrose Bierce* (1920), repr. in *Buried Cæsars* (1923); Percy Boynton, *More Contemporary Americans* (1927); Geo. Sterling, "Shadow Maker" in the *Am. Mercury,* Sept. 1925, and his introduction to *In the Midst of Life* (Modern Lib., 1927); Percival Pollard, *Their Day in Court* (1909); Paul Jordan Smith, *On Strange Altars* (1924); Van Wyck Brooks, *Emerson and Others* (1927); Vincent Starrett, *Bibliography of Ambrose Bierce* (Centaur Press, 1928); Fred Lewis Pattee, *The Development of the Am. Short Story* (1923); introduction by Herman George Scheffauer to the translation of a selection of Bierce's short stories, *Physiognomien des Todes* (Munich, 1922); private information.]

F. M.

BIERSTADT, ALBERT (Jan. 7, 1830–Feb. 18, 1902), landscape painter, was born of German parents, Henry and Christiana M. Bierstadt, at Solingen near Düsseldorf on the Rhine. His parents brought him to the United States as a child in arms. Educated in the schools of New Bedford, Mass., he turned to art and when twenty-one determined to start as a painter. When twenty-three he visited the land of his birth. He studied in Düsseldorf four years under Achenbach and Lessing; thence he departed for Rome which at that time was sought by American painters and sculptors as well as German, British, and French. In 1857 he was back in the United States and the following year joined a surveying expedition for an overland wagon route under Gen. F. W. Lander. The grandeur of landscape in the Far West did not daunt him; with sketches he laid the foundation of a score of big canvases painted in following years. In 1861 he exhibited "Laramie Peak," now in the Buffalo Academy of Fine Arts; in 1863 "Lander's Peak, Rocky Mountains"; in 1864 "North Fork of the Platte," bought by Judge Henry Hilton of New York City for his private gallery, and in 1865 "Looking down Yosemite Valley," bought by W. H. Crosby. In 1866 Lucius Tuckerman bought "El Capitan, Merced River" and the Lenox Library, "Valley of the Yosemite," now in the New York Public Library. For his private collection the senior August Belmont purchased "Burning Ship." The Boston Athenæum has an early painting, "Arch of Octavian, Italy."

Bierstadt made visits to Europe in 1867, 1878, and 1883. In France he was made a member of the Legion of Honor (1867) and in Austria of the Order of St. Stanislas (1869), while Prussia, Bavaria, and Belgium granted him medals. In 1870 Mrs. A. T. Stewart bought "Emerald Pool, Mount Whitney." Other large landscapes are: "In the Rocky Mountains" (1871); "Great Trees of California" (1874); "Valley of Kern's River, California" (1875), bought for the Hermitage, St. Petersburg, Russia. In 1877 Lewis Roberts bought "Mount Whitney, Sierra Nevada," and the Earl of Dunraven, "Estes Park, California." In 1878 the Corcoran Gallery, Washington, D. C., purchased "Mountain Lake, Mount Corcoran, Sierra Nevada." A large studio which Bierstadt had at Irvington-on-the-Hudson was burned down in 1882; he then opened a studio in New York City. In 1883 he painted "Geysers" and in 1884 "Storm on the Matterhorn, Switzerland" and "View on Kern River." For the Capitol at Washington he painted "The Discovery of the Hudson River" and "Entrance into Monterey." Not content with all these big landscapes he began in 1885 the painting of wild animals of North America, following in the footsteps of Audubon, James E. de Kay, Wilson, and others.

Bierstadt was a handsome man of polished manners and distinguished bearing. In 1886 he married Rosalie Osborne who died in 1893. In 1894 he married the widow of David Stewart. The great size of most of his canvases did not fit them for rooms of ordinary wall space. Düsseldorf pictures of moderate dimensions at moderate prices sold far and wide in the United States, so that Bierstadt found a receptive atmosphere, though his pictures have the same defects as theirs—lack of warmth and little technical cleverness. It was not till his later years, however, that amateurs deserted him for landscapists gifted with deeper mentality and equipped with stronger technique. The formal dignity of Bierstadt, the size of the canvases he covered, the convincing quality of his personal address gave him for a long time advantage over his contemporaries. The present fashion finds his huge canvases singularly dull and monotonous, wanting in personal charm like stage painting, without dramatic vigor or imagination.

[*Zeitschrift für Bildende Kunst*, vol. V (1870), pp. 65–74; H. T. Tuckerman, *Book of the Artists* (1867); Samuel Isham, *Hist. of American Painting* (1905); *Current Lit.*, Apr. 1902; *Outlook*, Mar. 1, 1902; Chas. E. Fairman, *Art and Artists of the Capitol* (1927).]

C. De K.

BIGELOW, ERASTUS BRIGHAM (Apr. 2, 1814–Dec. 6, 1879), inventor and economist, was born in the town of West Boylston, Mass., the second son of Ephraim and Polly (Brigham) Bigelow. His father had a small farm and also plied the trades of wheelwright and chairmaker, but the family resources were scanty, and the son was soon faced with the problem of earning his own living. Between the ages of ten and twenty he found many different kinds of employment. He worked on a neighboring farm; he played the violin in the orchestra of the Lancaster Orthodox Church, and also at country dances; he was a clerk in S. F. Morse's retail dry-goods store in Boston; he taught penmanship at Newark, and wrote a small pamphlet of twenty-five pages called *The Self-Taught Stenographer* (1832); having sold copies to the value of $75 in Boston within ten days, he had a larger edition printed and attempted to distribute it throughout New England and the Middle States, but emerged from this venture $400 in debt and with a large portion of the edition still unsold. During these early years he gave constant proofs of his ardent longing for an education. At the age of eight he had mastered the early stages of arithmetic without the aid of his teacher, who stoutly maintained that he was still too young; he passed a winter at Leicester Academy in preparation for the study of medicine; he had visions of entering Harvard. But his ambitions for a literary or professional life were never to be realized; before he had reached his twenty-fifth year it had become evident that he was destined to be an inventor.

His first considerable invention came in 1837, in the shape of a power loom for the production of coach lace; this machine contained most of the essential features subsequently developed in the more permanently important carpet looms which were to follow. Its immediate success brought him promptly to the fore. A company was formed for the building and operating of the new looms, and was incorporated by act of the legislature on Mar. 8, 1838; it was named by the inventor "The Clinton Company," apparently because of his fondness for the Clinton House in New York, at which he was in the habit of staying; and "Factory Village" near Lancaster, the home of the new plant, soon came to be called "Clintonville," and finally "Clinton." During the next twenty years the number and importance of Bigelow's mechanical discoveries multiplied apace. He will always be principally remembered as the inventor of power looms for the production of Brussels, Wilton, tapestry, and velvet carpetings, and has been justly described as the originator of every fundamental device of a distinctive character which appears in these machines; but he also greatly improved the methods of manufacturing ingrain carpets, and invented looms for the making of counterpanes and ginghams, silk brocatel, pile fabrics, and wire cloth. Many of the plants for the production of these articles were set up at Lowell, and a few at Humphreysville (now no longer extant) near Derby, Conn., but Clinton continued to be the principal center of the various "Bigelow mills." The importance of his inventions was widely recognized before the middle of the nineteenth century, not only in the United States but also in Europe, which he visited frequently, beginning in the year 1841; six large volumes of his English patents between 1837 and 1868 are preserved with the original drawings in the Massachusetts Historical Society.

Bigelow's reputation does not rest solely on his mechanical inventions; he also deserves an honorable place on the roll of American economists. In *The Tariff Question Considered in Regard to the Policy of England and the Interests of the United States,* a large quarto volume with careful statistical tables, which was published in 1862, and in the smaller monograph, *The Tariff Policy of England and the United States Contrasted* (1877), he maintained "that there is no ultimate principle of universal application involved either in free trade or protection; they are questions of policy"; and gave reasons why it would be unsafe at that time for the United States to abandon its import duties. In 1860 he was nominated as candidate for Congress by the Democrats of the Fourth Massachusetts (Suffolk) district, but was defeated, after a close contest. In his later years he was much interested in the progress of scientific education, and was a leading member of a committee of twenty-one, appointed Jan. 11, 1861, to carry into effect proposals which led to the foundation of the Massachusetts Institute of Technology (*Memorial History of Boston,* edited by Justin Winsor, IV, 274 n.).

Bigelow was of medium stature, with a tendency to stoop in later years; his complexion fair, his eyes gray, with massive overhanging brows, his forehead broad and high. His chief mental trait was an intense power of concentration. It is a curious fact that he was almost totally unable to make anything with his own hands, and had the greatest difficulty in drawing even the simplest sketches of the different parts of his machines; he was consequently always obliged to employ a draftsman in preparing the plans of his inventions. His character was marked by uprightness, conservatism, generosity, and kindliness; he was a most genial host, "and never seemed so happy as when he had guests at his table," both at his country estate in the White Mountains, and in his house in Boston, where he died. He was twice married, first, to Susan W. King, who died in 1841, and second, to Eliza Frances Means.

[Genealogical details may be found in Gilman Bigelow Howe's complete but often inaccurate *Genealogy of the Bigelow Family of America* (1890). The fullest and most sympathetic account of Bigelow's early and middle life is that of his intimate friend and kinsman Nehemiah Cleaveland, in *Hunt's Merchants' Mag.,* Feb. 1854, pp. 162–76. Andrew D. Ford's *Hist. of the Origin of the Town of Clinton, Mass.* (1896), pp. 192 ff. and references there, is the best authority on his later years, and his relations to Clinton. A memoir by Delano A. Goddard is printed in *Proc. Mass. Hist. Soc.,* XIX, 429–37. *A Century of Carpet and Rug Making in America,* published by the Hartford-Bigelow Carpet Co. (1925), also contains much useful information. The most recent account of Bigelow's whole career was printed in the *Clinton Item,* Apr. 12, 1927, by Francis H. Sawyer of Clinton, who is probably better informed than anyone else now living, in regard to the origin and development of the Bigelow mills in that town.] R. B. M.

BIGELOW, FRANK HAGAR (Aug. 28, 1851–Mar. 2, 1924), meteorologist, was the only son of Francis Edwin and Ann Hagar Bigelow and seventh in descent from a John Bigua, or Biglo, whose marriage was recorded in Watertown, Mass., in 1642. He attended both the primary and the high school of Concord, Mass., his birthplace, and also, for three years, a Latin school in Boston. His mother was interested in astronomy and had a small telescope, a circumstance that helped to arouse in her son his lifelong interest in astronomical problems. After graduating from Harvard College in 1873, Bigelow took a position as assistant astronomer at the Cordoba Observatory, Argentina. There he remained three years, returning to the United States in 1876 to study for the ministry. Receiving his degree of B.D. from the Episcopal Theological School at Cambridge, he became for a short while, 1880–81, rector of St. Paul's Church, Natick, Mass. His lungs soon became affected, however, and he had to give up active ministerial work. He then returned to his former place in Argentina, 1881-83. After this he held many posts, notably that of chief of the climatological division in the United States Weather Bureau (1906–10), that of editor of the *Monthly Weather Review* (1909–10), and lastly that of professor of meteorology, Oficina Meteorologica, Cordoba, Argentina (1910–21). He also was professor of solar physics at George Washington University (1894–1910) and served as assistant rector of St. John's Church. He had an active part in the United States Eclipse Expedition to West Africa, 1889; to Newberry, S. C., 1900; and to Spain, 1905. Naturally, too, he was a member of several scientific societies. After retiring at the age of seventy due to failing eyesight incident to diabetes, he went first to Marseilles, then to London, and, finally, to Vienna where he died. His wife, Mary E. Spalding, whom he married in 1881, survived him only a few days.

His voluminous writings cover a wide range in the fields of climatology, meteorology, and kindred subjects. Among the best are two ponderous volumes, *Report on the International Cloud Observations,* based on records made throughout the United States in 1896–97, and *Report on the Barometry of the United States, Canada, and the West Indies,* published as Reports of Chief of Weather Bureau for 1898–99, and 1900–01, respectively. He demonstrated the fact that the centers of extra-tropical cyclones are neither all warm nor all cold, but occur on a line of separation between adjacent warm and cold masses of air. This discovery attracted very little attention until years afterward when it was elaborated by others, explained, and made a powerful aid in foretelling the coming weather. In 1904 Bigelow elaborated and urged a plan for the study of atmospheric electricity and terrestrial magnetism and their relation to solar conditions. As his wishes in this matter could not be closely followed he became discouraged, and being quite reserved, was soon seeing too much of himself and too little of others. Presently he felt an urge to rewrite meteorology, an urge that resulted in many papers, two books, and five supplements, the last appearing shortly before his death and bearing the title *The New Must Replace the Old, Delenda est Carthago, Atmospheric Physics as Applied to a Reformed Meteorology.* But all this reforming effort produced little or no effect. His real contributions to meteorology had long been made.

[*Monthly Weather Review,* Mar. 1924; *Who's Who in America,* 1922–23; G. B. Howe, *Genealogy of the Bigelow Family* (1890).]

W. J. H.

BIGELOW, HENRY JACOB (Mar. 11, 1818–Oct. 30, 1890), surgeon, the oldest son of Jacob Bigelow [*q.v.*], an eminent physician of Boston, and of Mary Scollay, is noted for important contributions to surgery and for having published the first account of the use of ether in a surgical operation. He was born and spent his youth in the stimulating atmosphere of his father's house on Summer St. in Boston, and received his early education at Chauncey Hall. He was prepared for college at the Boston Latin School, entered Harvard at the age of fifteen, and was graduated with the class of 1837. After leaving college he studied with his father as preceptor, and attended lectures at the medical schools of Harvard and Dartmouth. In 1838–39 he was house surgeon at the Massachusetts General Hospital (Boston). Owing, however, to pulmonary symptoms which had threatened him from time to time for several years, he passed the winter of 1839–40 in Cuba, and in the spring went from there to Europe where he remained, except for a short visit home in 1841 (when he took his degree from the Harvard Medical School), until 1844. During these years Bigelow came under the influence of Louis in Paris, who was then at the height of his powers, and under his instruction laid an excellent foundation for work in surgical pathology and in clinical medicine. On returning to Boston he soon acquired a large practise, but to broaden his experience established a charitable out-patient clinic in the basement of the First Church on Chauncey Place, an action which unfortunately made him the object of much ridicule.

An important event in Bigelow's career was his association with the discovery of surgical anæsthesia. During the summer of 1846 W. T. G. Morton [*q.v.*], a Boston dentist, studied the effects upon animals of the inhalation of sulphuric ether, and on Sept. 30, 1846, after learning that Prof. Charles T. Jackson [*q.v.*] had inhaled it without subsequent ill-effect, Morton employed ether successfully on a human being during the extraction of a tooth. On Oct. 16, 1846, Morton, probably through Bigelow's influence (Hodges, p. 139), was permitted to give ether to a patient at the Massachusetts General Hospital who was to have a tumor removed from his neck by Dr. John Collins Warren. Ether anæsthesia proved successful with this and other cases. Bigelow read a preliminary communication concerning Morton's results to the American Academy of Sciences on Nov. 3, 1846. The first printed account appeared on Nov. 18, 1846, in the *Boston Medical and Surgical Journal* under the title: "Insensibility during Surgical Operations, Produced by Inhalation."

Bigelow also made important surgical contributions. Through his Boylston Prize Essay, *Manual of Orthopedic Surgery* (1844), he directed attention to a field of surgical endeavor then neglected in this country. According to Garrison (*History of Medicine,* 1913, p. 538) he was the first in America to excise the hip joint (*American Journal of the Medical Sciences,* 1852, XXIV, 90). In 1869 he described the iliofemoral (Y–) ligament and its mechanism, and demonstrated the importance of the structure in reducing dislocation of the hip by the flexion method (*The Mechanism of Dislocation and Fracture of the Hip,* 1869). William W. Reid [*q.v.*] had clearly described the flexion method of reducing dislocation of the hip in 1851 but, though his results were published in the *Boston Medical and Surgical Journal* Bigelow gave him no credit. Bigelow also improved an instrument (lithotrite) for crushing stones of the bladder and perfected an evacuator of large caliber to secure immediate removal of the fragments. He designated the operation "litholapaxy" (*American Journal of the Medical Sciences,* 1878, LXXV, 117–34). In 1871 he published his *Medical Education in America,* a work which reflected little credit upon his reputation.

In forming an estimate of Bigelow one cannot forget that he was unscrupulous at times and became, especially in later life, something of a martinet. In his dealings with students he gained the reputation of being something of a poseur, but as he was exceptionally skilful, quick, and resourceful, there were few who did not admire him. For nearly forty years he was the dominating figure in New England surgery and stood on an equal footing with S. D. Gross [*q.v.*] of Philadelphia. As a lecturer he was terse and epigrammatic, and being ambidextrous and an exceptional draftsman, he had no difficulty in holding the attention of his students. He left the stamp of his striking personality upon all of his younger associates many of whom have recalled his exacting ways with a feeling of gratitude. "In personal appearance he was tall and rather slight, his elastic step betraying a nervous organization. He had well-moulded features which were unobscured even by a full beard, and his agreeable voice and manner always attracted attention." He was married on May 8, 1847, to Susan Sturgis, daughter of William Sturgis. She died in 1853 leaving one child, William Sturgis Bigelow [*q.v.*]. An excellent full-length portrait of Bigelow hangs in the Boston Medical Library.

[The chief source of information is *A Memoir of Henry Jacob Bigelow* prepared anonymously in 1900 by his son, William Sturgis Bigelow, as a fourth volume in a collected edition of his works. The memoir of Bigelow by Oliver Wendell Holmes in the *Proc. Am. Acad. of Arts and Sci.,* 1890, vol. XVI, is particularly happy in its estimate of his character. A later notice by G. H. Monks is to be found in *Surg. Gyn. and Obstet.,* July 1924, pp. 112–16. All of the Bigelow letters and manuscripts have been deposited in the Boston Medical Library. The best account of the ether episode is probably that of R. M. Hodges, *A Narrative of Events Connected with the Introduction of Sulphuric Ether into Surgical Use* (1891). The extensive literature on the introduction of anæsthesia is listed with copious annotations in the *Bibliotheca Osleriana,* ed. by W. W, Francis (1928).]

J.F.F.

BIGELOW, JACOB (Feb. 27, 1787–Jan. 10, 1879), botanist and physician, was of Massachusetts ancestry, the son of Jacob Bigelow, a Congregational minister, and of Elizabeth (Wells) Bigelow (*Vital Records of Sudbury, Mass.,* 1903; *Genealogy*). He entered Harvard at the age of sixteen and graduated in 1806. In 1809 he matriculated in the medical department of the University of Pennsylvania, studying under Dr. B. S. Barton [*q.v.*], botanist and physician, whose work on the medicinal plants of the United States exerted a strong influence on Bigelow's subsequent career. He received his M.D. from Pennsylvania in 1810. On returning to Boston (1811) he formed an association with Dr. James Jackson [*q.v.*] whose successor he ultimately became. Whilst building up his medical practise, Bigelow had not forgotten his botanical interests, and in 1812 gave, in conjunction with a Dr. Peck, a series of botanical lectures at Harvard. He was the first native botanist to collect and to systematize the knowledge of the New England flora in a thorough-going way. In connection with his botanical lectures and in the preparation of drugs for his medical practise, he commenced the intensive study of the flora of the Boston region, and in 1814 published a modest book, *Florula Bostoniensis.* The first edition of this work dealt only with the flora within a ten-mile radius, but by 1824 Bigelow had, with Dr. Francis Booth, explored the mountains of New Hampshire and Vermont, so that he was able to reprint his book, retaining its unassuming title, but now enlarged, corrected, popularized, and in a general way made useful for all New England. The *Florula Bostoniensis* remained the standard manual of New England botany till the appearance of Gray's *Manual* (1848). Bigelow's most important botanical contribution, the *American Medical Botany,* in three volumes, began to appear in 1817; the second volume was published in 1818, and the last in 1820. This work contained sixty plates colored by a special process of the author's own invention. Bigelow also took an important part in preparing the first *American Pharmacopœia,* which appeared in 1820. He departed from Continental usage in insisting upon the utmost simplicity in nomenclature. In 1822 was issued his *Treatise on the Materia Medica,* which was intended as a sequel to the *Pharmacopœia.*

In 1815 Bigelow had been made professor of materia medica in the Harvard Medical School, a post which he continued to hold until 1855. During these years his medical fame was increasing, for not only was his position at the Massachusetts General Hospital and the Harvard Medical School conspicuous, but his lectures, delivered before various medical organizations, were often revolutionary and always of enduring influence. It was he who made the first effective protest in America against ill-chosen drugs and large doses, and against excessive blood-letting. He embodied in his *Discourse on Self-limited Diseases* (1835) the idea that many disorders if left to the natural recuperative powers of the patient would disappear more rapidly than from excessive medical treatment. Of this lecture Dr. Oliver Wendell Holmes (*Proceedings of the American Academy of Arts and Sciences,* 1879, p. 16) said that it exerted more influence upon medical practise in America than any work that had ever been published in this country. In his *Address on the Limits of Education* (1865) Bigelow attacked classical education, denying that the dead languages were the indispensable preliminaries to all useful training. He was the more entitled to do this because he was himself a classical scholar of brilliant attainments.

In 1832 he was sent to New York with a committee to study the newly arrived Asiatic cholera. Upon his return his native state refused to readmit the committee, so great was the terror of Boston, but Bigelow eluded the quarantine and hastened back to his patients. For some years (1816–27), beside all his other duties, he had been holding the chair of application of science to the useful arts, established by Count Rumford, and in connection with his teaching of mechanics, for which he had a passion, he invented the term "technology." In 1829 he published his Rumford lectures under the title *Elements of Technology,* and they were again expanded in 1840 in a work *The Useful Arts.* From 1847 to 1863 he was president of the American Academy of Arts and Sciences, of which he was a member for sixty-seven years.

One of the many acts of his vigorous life was the foundation of Mt. Auburn Cemetery (1831), in Cambridge, Mass., in an effort to protect the health of the community which was then often imperiled by injudicious interment. He is often asserted to have been the first to conceive that cemeteries might receive the attention which is ordinarily devoted to private gardens. An act of doubtful æsthetic value, but well intended, was his erection of a great stone sphinx in the cemetery, to commemorate the dead of the Civil War. His dominant personality caused its erection in spite of opposition, but in the blindness (cataract) that came upon him he could not see the monument he had raised, and had to be lifted to trace with his fingers the enigmatic countenance. Before his death, which occurred in Boston, his intellectual faculties became somewhat impaired. But even in his mental uncertainties a sort of playful genius exhibited itself in the clever doggerel by which he translated Mother Goose into Latin under the title of *Chenodia.* His early metrical reflections in English and the classic tongues had been privately and anonymously printed. In addition to the works already mentioned, he wrote: *Nature in Disease* (1854); *Eolopœsis, American Rejected Addresses* (1855); *Brief Expositions of Rational Medicine* (1858); and *Modern Inquiries* (1867). He was married in 1817 to Mary Scollay, daughter of Col. William Scollay.

[The most comprehensive authority is G. E. Ellis's *Memoir of Jacob Bigelow* (1880), with portrait, but it is inaccurate, poorly arranged and unattractively written. Asa Gray evaluated Bigelow's botanical work in *Am. Jour. Sci.,* Apr. 1879, pp. 263–66. L. H. Bailey's memorial in *Bot. Gazette,* May 1883, pp. 217–222, is based upon Gray's, but contains some incidents not mentioned by the older botanist. For a colorful popular account see H. A. Kelly, *Some Am. Medic. Botanists* (1914). Oliver Wendell Holmes's obituary of Bigelow in the *Proc. Am. Acad. Arts and Sci.,* 1879, is a classic in this kind of writing. See also J. G. Mumford, "Jacob Bigelow: A Sketch," reprinted from the *Johns Hopkins Hospital Bull.* (1902) in his *Surgical Memoirs* (1908), and G. B. Howe, *Genealogy of the Bigelow Family of America* (1890). All of the Bigelow manuscripts, including the original plates of the botanical works, were deposited in the Boston Medic. Lib., Jan. 1927, by the executors of William Sturgis Bigelow, grandson of Jacob Bigelow.]

D. C. P.
J. F. F.

BIGELOW, JOHN (Nov. 25, 1817–Dec. 19, 1911), editor, diplomatist, author, was born at Bristol, now Malden, N. Y., the son of Asa Bigelow and Lucy Isham, both natives of Connecticut. He attended Washington, now Trinity, College, at Hartford, Conn., but left in his junior year with a slight opinion of his teachers, and graduated at Union College, Schenectady, N. Y., in 1835. Three years later he was admitted to the New York bar. His first public office was that of an inspector of Sing Sing prison. In 1844, apparently through the influence of Samuel J. Tilden, he joined the Free-Soil Democrats. In 1848 he was invited by William Cullen Bryant to share in owning and editing the New York *Evening Post,* a connection that continued until 1861, when the paper was sold to Parke Godwin. On the questions of anti-slavery and free trade, to both of which the paper was devoted, his editorial attitude was outspoken and uncompromising. A visit to Jamaica afforded material for a series of newspaper letters later published (1851) as *Jamaica in 1850.* The same year (1850) saw his marriage to Jane Poultney of New York, formerly of Baltimore. In 1853–54 he visited Haiti to study "the African as he had developed in freedom," a later by-product of the visit being his *Wit and Wisdom of the Haytians* (1877), a collection of proverbial sayings. Incidentally the journey introduced him to the writings of Swedenborg, whose doctrines he presently accepted. Two of his later writings, *Molinos the Quietist* (1882) and *The Mystery of Sleep* (1897), reflect indirectly his interest in Swedenborg's philosophy. A campaign *Memoir of the Life and Public Services of John Charles Frémont* (1856) is still of some value for its California documents. A visit to Europe in 1858 won him the friendship of Sainte-Beuve, Cobden, Bright, Thackeray, and many others, and paved the way for his later success as a diplomatist.

Returning to the United States in 1860, he was appointed in 1861 consul-general at Paris, and in April 1865, was made minister to France, a post he held until September 1866. He established close personal relations with the French, German, and Austrian press, then mainly dependent upon London for American news and inclined to sympathize with the Confederacy, and exposed and defeated plans intended to secure effective French support for it. A summary sketch of American history bearing his name was published at Milan in 1863 under the title *Gli Stati Uniti d'America nel 1863.* Letters and papers of Slidell and others that he purchased at this time, supplemented by the Slidell-Benjamin correspondence found in the Confederate archives, form the documentary basis of *France and the Confederate Navy, 1862–68: An International Episode* (1888), one of the most valuable of his writings, but his charge, later elaborated in *Lest We Forget* (1905) and the *Retrospections,* that Gladstone subscribed to the Confederate cotton loan appears to have been unfounded (E. D. Adams, *Great Britain and the American Civil War,* 1925, II, 163). Bigelow skilfully warned Napoleon III of the folly of supporting an imperial program in Mexico, at the same time successfully urging a waiting policy upon the Administration at Washington. In the American diplomacy of the Civil War his work ranks second in importance only to that of Charles Francis Adams at London. Following his return to the United States, in 1867, he held no public office until 1875, when Gov. Tilden placed him on the commission which broke up the New York canal ring. The same year he was elected secretary of state for New York, where he served one term.

The remainder of his long life was devoted to writing and editing, although he was United States commissioner to the Brussels Exposition in 1888 and a delegate to the New York constitutional convention in 1893. His special interest in France had already produced *Some Recollections of Antoine Pierre Berryer* (1869), *Beaumarchais the Merchant* (1870), and *France and Hereditary Monarchy* (1871), and to these he added *Some Recollections of the late Edouard Laboulaye* (1889). His *Life of Benjamin Franklin* (1874; 2nd ed., revised and corrected, 1879) reproduced the famous *Autobiography,* the manuscript of which he had discovered and correctly printed for the first time (1868). *The Complete Works of Benjamin Franklin* (10 vols., 1887–88), although incomplete, displaced all previous editions in its chronological arrangement and exact reproduction of the original texts. Bigelow's abilities as an editor and his limitations as a biographer appear in sharply contrasted light in his *Writings and Speeches of Samuel J. Tilden* (1885; supplemented by *Letters and Literary Memorials,* 1908), and the later *Life of Samuel J. Tilden* (1895). The *Writings* are carefully edited, but the *Life,* while of primary importance, is marred by numerous errors apparently due to hasty writing or lax revision, and by biased judgments of many of Tilden's contemporaries, notably Grover Cleveland. A report to the New York Chamber of Commerce on the Panama Canal (1886); a life of Bryant in the American Men of Letters series (1890); *The Supreme Court and the Electoral Commission* (1903), an open letter to Joseph H. Choate; *Our Ex-Presidents: What shall we do for them? What shall they do for us?* (privately printed, 1906); *Peace Given as the World Giveth—or, The Portsmouth Treaty and its First Year's Fruits* (1907); *A Substitute for the Tariff upon Imports* (1908), an open letter to Charles E. Hughes; *The Panama Canal and the Daughters of Danaus* (1908); and occasional articles in periodicals, showed the wide range of his intellectual activity. *Toleration, and Other Essays and Studies,* a posthumous collection, appeared in 1926.

[The chief authority to 1879 is Bigelow's *Retrospections of an Active Life* (5 vols., 1909–13), of which vols. IV and V were prepared by his son, John Bigelow. The work, often exceedingly discursive, contains many letters and documents. A sketch by Henry Van Dyke is to be found in a collection of *Memorial Addresses* delivered before the Century Association, New York, Mar. 9, 1912. Obituaries were published in the N. Y. papers, Dec. 19, 20, 1911.] W. M.

BIGELOW, MELVILLE MADISON (Aug. 2, 1846–May 4, 1921), educator, legal writer, was descended from Mary Warren and John Biglo of Watertown, Mass., who were married on Aug. 30, 1642. The son of William Enos Bigelow of Michigan, a Methodist clergyman, and Daphne F. Madison of New York, he was born near Eaton Rapids, Mich. His early education was received in the public schools wherever his father happened to be stationed within the territory embraced by the Detroit Conference, much of which was sparsely populated frontier country. Inheriting many of the characteristics of his mother, a remarkable woman, he was able to overcome the somewhat crude educational facilities of Milford, Port Huron, and Ypsilanti. Proceeding to the University of Michigan at Ann Arbor, he graduated A.B. in 1866, and LL.B two years later. He studied law at Pontiac for a short time, and went from there to Memphis, where his uncle, Joseph Enos Bigelow, was practising. In March 1868 he was admitted to the Tennessee bar. He had become interested in the historical development of the law and now determined to undertake research work in that line in preference to the actual practise of his profession. With this end in view he removed to Boston in 1870, and was admitted a member of the Boston bar. At that time the trustees of Boston University were considering the advisability of establishing a law school in the University and Bigelow was in 1871 appointed a member of a committee to investigate and report. The report, which he himself prepared, was favorable, and in September 1872 the Boston University Law School was opened, Bigelow being appointed a member of the faculty (*Green Bag*, I, 54). Thus commenced a connection which was maintained throughout fifty years as lecturer, professor, and dean. He was now engaged in a work for which by the nature of his previous studies he was admirably fitted, which coincided with his own inclinations and yielded the opportunity to indulge in research which was his chief delight. "Bigelow was not fit for a practising lawyer. He had not the litigious instinct, nor had he the instinct for business, nor for money. He was a scholar, if ever a pure scholar was born on earth, and he was an instructor and not a denizen of courts" (Brooks Adams, in *Boston University Law Review*, I, 169). At the outset, in addition to his lecturing duties, he undertook a post-graduate course at Harvard, receiving the degree of Ph.D. in 1879.

His initial publication was the first volume of *Reports of all the Published Life and Accident Insurance Cases, American Courts* (1871), the series being continued in four subsequent volumes, the last of which appeared in 1877. His next work, *The Law of Estoppel and its Application in Practice* (1872), at once attracted attention by its masterly handling of an extremely technical and difficult branch of the law, as well as by its attractive style. It established Bigelow's reputation as a legal writer and passed through many editions. Then followed *An Index of Cases overruled, reversed . . . by the Courts of America, England, and Ireland* (1873), a supplement to which was issued in 1887, a scientific selection of *Leading Cases on the Law of Torts* (1875), and a text-book, *The Law of Fraud and the Procedure pertaining to the Redress thereof* (1877), both of the latter being in the nature of preparatory work for two treatises which were to come from his pen later. Next to appear was his *Elements of the Law of Torts* (1878), a work intended for students, covering a field which had hitherto been greatly neglected. It became the standard text-book in all American law schools, and its inclusion by the University of Cambridge, England, in the list of works recommended for study, led ultimately to the preparation by Bigelow of an English edition which was published by the Cambridge University Press in 1889. This was the first instance of such an honor being accorded to an American text-book and indicated the high academic standard which Bigelow had attained. He had not confined his labors, however, to the law as it existed, but, pursuing a line of research which always had for him a particular fascination, read deeply in the ancient English records, the early results of which were embodied in his *Placita Anglo-Normannica: Law Cases from William I to Richard I preserved in Historical Records*, published in London in 1879, and republished in Boston two years later. His cases "are gleaned almost without exception from monkish chronicles, from diplomata, from Domesday Book, from anything in fact except what would be called a law book at the present day" (P. H. Winfield, *The Chief Sources of English Legal History*, 1925, p. 146). It was a bold experiment on Bigelow's part but the result justified the risk. In undertaking this work he entered a field—the study of legal history—which had been considerably neglected. Then came *Elements of Equity* (1879) and the *Law of Bills, Notes and Cheques illustrated by leading cases* (1880)—both students' books—which were followed by *History of Procedure in England from the Norman Conquest: the Norman Period 1066–1204* (1880), another excursion into legal antiquities, which confirmed previous estimates of the depth of his scholarship and the ability of his pen. This work also met with a hearty reception in English university circles. The succeeding eight years were devoted to assiduous work at the Law School and to the preparation of a monumental treatise on the *Law of Fraud on its Civil Side* which appeared in two volumes in 1888–90, and immediately became recognized as the most valuable work on that subject which had been produced in America. Bigelow subsequently published *Elements of the Law of Bills, Notes and Cheques and the English Bills of Exchange Act* (1893), *Cases on the Law of Bills, Notes and Cheques* (1894), and a treatise on *The Law of Wills* (1898), the latter exhibiting all the qualities which had made his *Estoppel* and *Torts* so conspicuously successful. In 1903 he wrote articles on "The Declaration of Independence" and "The Constitution," for *The Cambridge Modern History,* vol. VII. He contributed to and wrote a preface for a collection of essays entitled *Centralization and the Law* (1906). Other later works of his were *A False Equation—The Problem of the Great Trust* (1911), and *Papers on the Legal History of Government; difficulties fundamental and artificial* (1920). In addition, he contributed many articles on legal and kindred subjects to current periodicals, including the *Law Quarterly Review.* He died in Boston after a long illness, being the last survivor of the original faculty of the Boston Law School. He was three times married: (1) in 1869 to Elizabeth Chamberlin, daughter of Alfred Bragg of Milford, Mass., who died in 1881; (2) in 1883 to Cornelia Frothingham Read, who died in 1892; (3) in 1898 to Alice Bradford Woodman, who survived him.

[Particulars of Bigelow's ancestry are to be found in *Genealogy of the Bigelow Family of America* (1890), by Gilman Bigelow Howe, and in *Memoirs of the Judiciary and Bar of New Eng.* (1901), by Conrad Reno, II, 635, which also contains a sketch of his life. The best accounts of his activities are in *Boston Univ. Law Rev.,* I, 153, "Memorial of Melville Madison Bigelow," and II, 17, "Melville M. Bigelow and the Legal Profession"—the latter being a brilliant characterization study by Chas. W. Eliot.]

H. W. H. K.

BIGELOW, WILLIAM STURGIS (Apr. 4, 1850–Oct. 6, 1926), physician, orientalist, was the son of Henry Jacob Bigelow [*q.v.*], and grandson of Jacob Bigelow [*q.v.,*], eminent physicians of Boston. An only child, he was left solitary by the early death of his mother, Susan Sturgis, whose loss he felt severely, and he grew to manhood shy and retiring. He passed through Harvard College (class of 1871) without special distinction, and then took up the study of medicine. In the course of his work he developed a keen interest in the purely scientific aspects of medicine, the more practical phases of a practitioner's routine being distasteful to him. After graduating from the Harvard Medical School in 1874, he went abroad for five years He studied first in the clinics at Vienna in company with Frederick C. Shattuck of Boston. He spent a year or more with Pasteur, acquiring an intimate knowledge of bacteriological technique. He was much influenced by Ranvier, the professor of histology, and also by Waldeyer, with whom he passed the summer of 1878 in Strassburg. He returned to Boston in 1879 with great enthusiasm for bacteriology, and set up a private laboratory in Pemberton Square. His father, however, gave him no encouragement in his investigations and prevailed upon him to take the post of surgeon to out-patients at the Massachusetts General Hospital, and as this gave him little opportunity for developing bacteriological interests his laboratory had to be discontinued. Few men could have had less taste for surgery than the sensitive Bigelow, and it was not long before he gave up entirely all thoughts of practise. In 1882 he left for Japan in order to divert his mind, and there spent seven years without break, collecting works of art, and studying the language, philosophy, and religion of a race which was then little known in the western world. Largely as a result of his activities in collecting, the Boston Art Museum now possesses the richest collection of Japanese works of art to be found anywhere in the world, not excepting Japan. While in the East, he also became interested in Northern Buddhism and devoted himself to a study of its philosophy. In 1908 he delivered his Ingersoll Lecture on *Buddhism and Immortality,* which helped to bring to the western world an understanding of Buddhistic philosophy. In recognition of his attainments, the Japanese Government made him a Commander of the Imperial Order of the Rising Sun. He never married. Bigelow published two scientific papers: "Notiz über den Theilungsvorgang bei Knorpelzellen, sowie über den Bau des Hyalinknorpels" (*Archiv für mikroskopische Anatomie,* 1879, XVI, 457–63), after his association with Waldeyer, and "The Study of Bacteria and their Relation to Disease" (*Boston Medical and Surgical Journal,* 1882, CVI, 248–50), published during his service at the Massachusetts General Hospital. Short discussions by him are also to be found in the *Boston Medical and Surgical Journal,* 1879, CI, 23 and 1881, CV, 233.

[An appreciation by Dr. Frederick C. Shattuck is to be found in the *Proc. Mass. Hist. Soc.,* Nov. 1926. The *Boston Evening Transcript* contained notices on Oct. 6, Oct. 8, Oct. 9, Oct. 11, 1926. Further information has been supplied by Dr. Frederick C. Shattuck and Dr. Harvey Cushing.]

J. F. F.

BIGGS, ASA (Feb. 4, 1811–Mar. 6, 1878), North Carolina jurist and politician, was born at Williamston, Martin County, N. C., the son of Joseph Biggs, merchant and elder of the Primitive Baptist Church, and Chloe Daniel, his third wife. His parents were poor and uncultured but strong in moral and religious qualities. Growing rapidly in mind and body, the boy at fifteen quit the Williamston Academy, clerked in neighboring stores, and, having read law privately, began its practise in 1831. Next year he attended a party convention, traveled to New York, and married Martha Elizabeth Andrews, who brought him some slaves and eventually bore him ten children. Until 1845, and intermittently thereafter until 1858, he was primarily a lawyer, painstaking, honest and financially successful. It was politics, however, that brought him into public notice. He had espoused the cause of Andrew Jackson early, and was sent to the state constitutional convention of 1835. Here he said nothing, learned much, and voted as planter interests and sectional jealousies required. Then he went to the House of Commons for two terms and to the Senate for one (1840–45). A single term in Congress immediately followed. These honors, far from being thrust upon him, were won by hard-fought campaigns in which he made a reputation by refusing either to "treat" or to trim on public issues. In the Democratic state convention of 1850 he attracted state-wide attention by attempting to commit the party against state internal improvements. Desisting, however, in the interest of party harmony, he was the next year appointed joint codifier of the state's laws by Gov. Ellis, whom the convention of 1850 had nominated. There followed four years of quiet, dignified and congenial labor, only slightly seasoned with politics, after which he returned to the Senate, saw Moore and Biggs's *Code* safely adopted, and was elected, along with Gov. Ellis, to the federal Senate. Here, because of his stand for economy in government, place was made for him on the Finance Committee. But the tall, black-haired and somber-faced North Carolinian was not happy in Congress: his political reading was inadequate; his health became impaired by severe labor without exercise; the Government was corrupt and growing worse; his domestic affairs and religious life—he had had a remarkable religious experience in 1851—were upset. Accordingly he resigned to become district judge of North Carolina (1858–61). Decidedly pro-Southern in his views, he was active in the Secession Convention until called to the duties of Confederate district judge (December 1861–April 1865); and he supported the Confederacy whole-heartedly and prayerfully to the end. His fortune swept away by war and his law practise handicapped by the hostility of the state supreme court (to which, characteristically, he refused to apologize for signing a certain famous "Solemn Protest"), he began life anew in 1868 in Norfolk, Va.; and there he died ten years later.

[Biggs's *Autobiography*, ed. by R. D. W. Connor in *Pubs. N. C. Hist. Commission, Bull. No. 19*, 1915, was written for his children in Mar. 1865, with a short conclusion on July 1, 1865. Bound with it is his *Journal of a Trip from Williamston to N. Y. and Back in 1852*. His constitutional views may be found in *Cong. Globe*, 34 Cong., 1 Sess., p. 1962, and in appendices to his *Autobiography*. F. S. Spruill, *Address on Presentation of Portrait of Hon. Asa Biggs, Jan. 18, 1915*, is thoughtful, suggestive, eulogistic. Samuel A. Ashe in his *Hist. of N. C.*, vol. II (1925), and J. G. de Roulhac Hamilton in his *Reconstruction in N. C.* (1914) furnish background. An obituary is in the *News and Observer* (Raleigh), Mar. 7, 1878. A portrait hangs in the federal court-room at Raleigh.]

C. C. P.

BIGGS, HERMANN MICHAEL (Sept. 29, 1859–June 28, 1923), one of the pioneers of preventive medicine, was born in Trumansburg, N. Y., the son of Joseph Hunt and Melissa (Pratt) Biggs. The family was of English stock tracing its descent from a George Biggs who had come to America in 1690. Hermann Biggs received his elementary education at Ithaca, N. Y., graduated from Cornell University in 1882, and in the next year received his M.D. degree from Bellevue Hospital Medical College—an achievement which although it testifies to his brilliance also indicates the lax state of medical education at that time. After a year as interne at Bellevue Hospital, Biggs went to Germany for post-graduate work and spent the next two years in Berlin and Greifswald. Upon his return, he was put in charge of the newly opened Carnegie Laboratory of the Bellevue Hospital Medical College. From then on promotion at the college was rapid: he was lecturer on pathology, 1886; professor of pathology, 1889; professor of materia medica and therapeutics, 1892; professor of therapeutics, 1898; professor of the practise of medicine, 1912. On Aug. 18, 1898, he married Frances M. Richardson of Hornellsville, N. Y.

He began the practise of medicine at the time when the "germ theory" was rapidly developing into what has since become the science of bacteriology. One cannot realize Biggs's service to public health unless one is familiar with the unsatisfactory state of things at the time he began. Little progress had been made for fifty years. Matters changed rapidly after 1892, when Biggs organized the department of pathology and bacteriology of the New York City Health Department and became pathologist and director of the laboratories. These laboratories are said to have been the first municipal bacteriological laboratories in the world, and the methods inaugurated there have been widely followed. He introduced the use of bacteriological methods in the sanitary surveillance of infectious disease. In 1894 he introduced the use of diphtheria antitoxin in this country, and he obtained the necessary legislation and appropriations which enabled the department to produce, use, and sell biological products. The formulation and direction of the work in New York City for the prevention of tuberculosis was another notable achievement. Biggs successively established the notification of tuberculosis, the examination of sputum, the visitation of cases by nurses, the disinfection of premises, the compulsory segregation of careless cases, tuberculosis clinics, the Otisville Sanatorium for incipient cases, and the Riverside Hospital for advanced cases. Throughout his twenty-two years of service, his knowledge, sincerity, and tact enabled him in spite of all the vicissitudes and turmoils of New York politics to carry out his plans unhindered.

Early in 1914 he was appointed state commissioner of health and chairman of the public health council of the State of New York, a body recently created by the legislature and clothed with broad powers of sanitary control. As commissioner he reorganized the work for children, and very soon developed an efficient state-wide division of infant and maternity welfare. At the time of his death it was one of the most effective ministers to the public health. Among his other activities, Biggs wrote works dealing with Pasteur's prophylactic treatment of rabies, the outbreak of cholera in New York in 1893, the treatment of tuberculosis, and the use of antitoxin in the treatment of diphtheria, and other subjects, and contributed frequently to periodical literature.

[*Monthly Bull. N. Y. State Dept. of Health,* July 1923; *Science,* Nov. 23, 1923, p. 413; *Am. Medicine,* July 1923, p. 530.] B.H.

BIGLER, JOHN (Jan. 8, 1805–Nov. 29, 1871), governor of California, was born near Carlisle, Pa. The son of Susan (Dock) Bigler and Jacob Bigler, a farmer, he came of a German family which had been in America for over a hundred years and had been represented by both paternal and maternal grandfathers in the Revolutionary War. His education was interrupted after his entrance into Dickinson College (at Carlisle) by the removal of the family to Mercer County, where his father apprenticed him to a printer. This training led him at the close of his apprenticeship in 1827 to undertake the editorship of the *Centre County Democrat,* located at Bellefonte, where he remained for the next five years. He then took up the study of law and after having been admitted to the bar, removed some years later to Mount Sterling, Ill., where he continued his practise. Caught by the spirit of the Gold Rush in the spring of 1849, he set out with an overland company bound for California. With him he took his wife, a woman none too strong for the severe undertaking, and his infant daughter. The journey, made by ox-team and covered wagon, ended at Sacramento on Aug. 31. To Mrs. Bigler belonged the honor of being the first white woman to make her home in Sacramento. Bigler found no opportunity in the small, disorganized community to practise his profession; and, as he was without funds with which to maintain his family, he turned his hand to whatever came along. He found employment with an auctioneer for a time; later he cut wood in the adjoining country, bringing it into town for sale; he unloaded river steamers; and finally secured a contract with a Sacramento merchant to make up a number of calico comforters, for which he received in partial remuneration calico for dresses for his wife and daughter.

Bigler's position in the community appears not to have suffered because of his humble pursuits, and in November 1849 he was elected to the Assembly of the first state legislature. This body convened at San José on Dec. 16, 1849, and proceeded to complete the organization of the state government. Bigler served as assemblyman for two terms and was twice chosen speaker of that body. In 1851 he was elected governor on the Democratic ticket and two years later was reëlected. He ran for a third time, but was defeated. President Buchanan, shortly after his inauguration, appointed Bigler United States minister to Chile. This post Bigler held for four years, during which he was instrumental in effecting the settlement of a number of long-standing and troublesome questions. In 1861 he returned to California and resumed the practise of law. A year later, he was persuaded to run on the Democratic ticket for Congress but was defeated. He never again held public office but remained active in the affairs of his party and served three times as delegate to the national Democratic convention. His death occurred on Nov. 29, 1871. During his lifetime he had commanded general respect. His sympathetic understanding of the needs of the new settlers had made him also much beloved; and his achievements in the field of politics had added materially to the success of the party to which he gave his loyalty.

[A very full account of the life of Bigler is to be found in *Representative and Leading Men of the Pacific* (1870), ed. by Oscar Shuck. Some additional material is to be found in the *Pubs. Hist. Soc. of Southern Cal.* (1903), in H. H. Bancroft, *Hist. of Cal.* (1890), vols. VI, VII, and in the *Sacramento Daily Union,* Nov. 30, 1871.]

R. G. C—d.

BIGLER, WILLIAM (Jan. 1, 1814–Aug. 9, 1880), governor of Pennsylvania, senator, was born at Shermansburg, Cumberland County, Pa. His parents Jacob and Susan (Dock) Bigler, Pennsylvania Germans, decided soon after his birth to attempt to lift the burden of poverty from their shoulders, purchased a large tract of wilderness land in Mercer County, and migrated thither. But misfortune pursued them: the title to the tract was bad, and they lost their investment. For a few years Jacob Bigler attempted to support his family on a small farm, but discouragement and labor were too much, and he died when William was small. Hard work and little schooling were the lot of the latter, and at fourteen he entered the printing office of his brother John [*q.v.*] at Bellefonte, Center County. In 1833 he decided to set out for himself; so, acquiring a second-hand printing outfit and borrowing twenty dollars, he moved to Clearfield, where he established the *Clearfield Democrat,* "an eight by ten Jackson paper intended to counteract the influence of the seven by nine Whig (*sic*) paper." On Mar. 23, 1836, he married Maria J. Reed, daughter of a local magnate, and soon thereafter sold his paper and entered a partnership with his father-in-law, in which he amassed a fortune as a lumberman. In 1841 he was elected to the state Senate, where he served six years, twice as speaker. In the legislature he was mainly concerned in keeping the state solvent and in providing adequate railroad transportation to the westward counties. His political influence reached its high point in 1851 when he was nominated and elected governor. As executive he pursued a course in opposition to wholesale chartering of banks, in one message vetoing eleven bank charters. He also was successful in his fight against "omnibus" bills, the legislature passing a law which provided that each bill should deal with only one subject. He was renominated in 1854 but the Know-Nothing enthusiasm made his reëlection impossible. He was immediately made president of the Philadelphia & Erie Railroad Company, and a year later he was elected to the United States Senate, Jan. 14, 1856, as a vindication which he demanded for his sorry defeat in 1854. He promoted the nomination of Buchanan, who had become estranged from him during the governorship largely because Bigler saw fit to recognize Buchanan's enemies and to remain inactive in 1852 when the latter was endeavoring to obtain the presidential nomination. In the Senate he was more active in committee than on the floor. He favored Buchanan's Lecompton policy after a visit to the Territory of Kansas in the summer of 1857. He was active in behalf of a Panama canal and a Pacific railroad and was opposed to the tariff of 1857. In the trying days of 1860–61 he protested against secession and favored the Crittenden compromise, serving as one of the committee of thirteen appointed in the Senate. His retirement in 1861 was of course inevitable. He remained a Democrat as long as he lived, made one campaign for Congress, attended most of the national conventions, and was one of the visiting statesmen who went to Louisiana after the election in 1876 to look after Tilden's interest. He was also prominent in the state constitutional convention of 1872–73 and active in the promotion of the Centennial in 1876. Most of the last twenty years of his life however were spent as a railroad promoter and capitalist in Clearfield. His stature was commanding and his face full and genial; he has been characterized as wise rather than brilliant, a politician destroyed by the disaster of 1861 which he had so long labored to prevent.

[Wm. C. Armor, *Lives of the Governors of Pa., 1609–1872* (1872); L. C. Aldrich, *Hist. of Clearfield County, Pa.* (1887); obituaries in *Phila. Press* and *Record,* Aug. 10, 1880. A number of Bigler's letters are in the possession of the Pa. Hist. Soc.]

R. F. N.

BILLINGS, CHARLES ETHAN (Dec. 5, 1835–June 5, 1920), manufacturer, tool-maker, was born in Wethersfield, Vt., son of Ethan Ferdinand and Clarissa (Marsh) Billings. His great-grandfather, Joseph Billings, had settled in Windsor, Vt., in 1793. Shortly after the birth of Charles Billings, the family moved to Windsor where he received a brief education in the public schools. At the age of seventeen he was engaged as an apprentice in the gun department of the old Robbins & Lawrence shop in Windsor, which made guns and machine tools and which markedly influenced American shop practise by training men destined to distinction. After serving three years, he became a journeyman machinist and a year later, when he was twenty-one, having gained a fundamental knowledge of machine-shop practise, he went to Springfield, Mass. A few months later he moved to Hartford, Conn., where for six years he was employed at the pistol factory of Samuel Colt, serving as tool-maker and die-sinker and for three years as foreman of the die-sinking department. While at Colt's he became an expert in drop-forging—a process for forging between dies by a drop-hammer. This process, which was coming into popularity as a means of manufacturing tools and machine parts, was a step in the replacing of hand work by standardized quantity production. In 1862 he was engaged by E. Remington & Sons of Ilion, N. Y., and, despite the criticism of conservative associates, he developed a process of treating drop-forgings that caused extraordinary saving of labor in manufacturing pistols. A single adaptation of drop-forging to the shaping of pistol frames by machinery saved this company many thousands of dollars in labor. As these improvements in firearms came at the time of the Civil War, they were particularly important. In 1865, at the close of the war, Billings returned to Hartford, and for three years was superintendent of manufacturing for the Weed Sewing Machine Company, which had taken over the old Sharps rifle works built by Robbins & Lawrence. While there he devised a method for making sewing-machine shuttles by drop-forging—a decided improvement over the old method of brazing the parts together. This was patented in 1867. In 1868 he became president and superintendent of the Roper Sporting Arms Company at Amherst, Mass., in association with C. M. Spencer. During the next year the business was moved to Hartford and reorganized as the Billings & Spencer Company. The sale of Roper sporting arms suffered a severe setback and in 1870 the firm took up the manufacture of drop-forgings in general, including machinist's small tools. The business prospered and grew, largely because of the inventive ability of Billings, the president. Among the outstanding inventions was the Billings commutator-bar for electric dynamos, made from drop-forged copper and invented in 1886. Other inventions included drills, chucks, pocket-knives, wrenches, etc., all made by machinery instead of by the old slow hand methods. Billings served as president of the American Society of Mechanical Engineers in 1895, as alderman and city councilman at Hartford, as president for twelve years of the board of fire commissioners, as high dignitary in the masons, as a bank trustee, etc. He was twice married; first to Frances M. Heywood on Jan. 5, 1857; second to Evalina Case Holt on Sept. 9, 1874.

[An excellent source on the general development of modern machine-shop practise and the men who influenced it is *English and American Tool Builders* (1916), by Joseph W. Roe. An interesting obituary of Billings is to be found in the *Trans. Am. Soc. Mech. Engineers* (1920), vol. XLII.]

P. B. M.

BILLINGS, FREDERICK (Sept. 27, 1823–Sept. 30, 1890), lawyer, railroad president, philanthropist, was born at Royalton, Vt., the fourth child of Oel and Sophia (Wetherbe) Billings, both of whom were of New England descent (Dana, *History of Woodstock*, pp. 594–97). In 1835 young Frederick moved with his parents to Woodstock, Vt., and a few years later entered the state university at Burlington, graduating in 1844. He then read law, and for two years, 1846–48, held a minor appointive state office. In 1848 he caught the gold fever from a seafaring relative, and early in 1849 went via the Isthmus to California. Here he had the good judgment to open a law office rather than to dig for gold, and reaped a rich harvest when the inevitable demand for legal talent set in. A partnership which he early formed with another lawyer grew rapidly into the leading law firm of San Francisco. Billings soon acquired wealth, prominence, and political influence. The latter he used in 1861 to prevent the loss of California to the Union. He was for a time attorney-general of the state, and could doubtless have had a political career. As attorney for Gen. Frémont in the matter of the Mariposa estate, Billings went to England in 1861. Returning to the United States, he was married on Mar. 31, 1862 to Julia, daughter of Dr. Eleazer Parmly, of New York City, and attempted to resume his law practise in San Francisco. Ill health prevented and in 1864 he went back to his old home in Woodstock, where a few years later he purchased the famous Marsh estate. This he enlarged and improved until, according to the local historian, "his home on the hill has come to resemble one of the baronial estates of the old world."

Billings's interest in the Northern Pacific railway was aroused by a trip to the Far Northwest in 1866. He bought one of the original twelfth interests in the company, and for many years its affairs claimed his chief attention. He organized its land department, and, knowing that the grant of lands received from Congress must be made to yield settlers rather than profits, kept the price of land low and inaugurated an extensive campaign of advertising. The results were highly gratifying, and the Northwest boomed until the panic of 1873 brought things to a standstill. Billings devised a plan of reorganization by which the prostrate Northern Pacific might be set on its feet, persuaded the directors to accept his plan, secured court assent to it, and put it into effect. In May 1879 he became president of the reorganized company. With the hard times at an end, he found money to begin construction westward from Bismarck, Dakota Territory, where the terminal had been since 1873, and eastward from the navigable waters of the Columbia River. The earnings of the company grew, its credit rose, and finally, in 1880, Billings persuaded a syndicate of bankers to purchase $40,000,000 of its first mortgage bonds, enough to secure the completion of the road. This was regarded at the time as a financial triumph, and the Northern Pacific was described by a high authority as "the most important enterprise before the country, prosecuted by a single corporation, with a distinct purpose, and independent of entangling alliances" (*Commercial and Financial Chronicle,* XXX, 650; XXXI, 560, 579, 589; XXXII, 335–36). "Entangling alliances," however, were not easily avoided. Henry Villard, president of the O. R. & N., which operated a road along the southern bank of the Columbia River, feared the competition of the advancing Northern Pacific, and sought an agreement with it. Finding Billings "lukewarm and hard to satisfy," Villard determined to secure for himself a voice in Northern Pacific affairs. The result was his famous "blind pool," through which he was able to buy a large block of Northern Pacific stock. Villard now expected representation on a revised directorate, but this Billings sought to forestall. A struggle ensued, Billings at last capitulated, and an agreement was reached. In September 1881 the presidency was turned over to Villard, and Billings, although continuing as a director, ceased to take an active part in the company's management. The road was completed under Villard's leadership, but the credit for making its completion possible belongs chiefly to Billings (Villard, *Memoirs,* II, 291–300; *Commercial and Financial Chronicle,* XXXII, 313, 368, 421).

In spite of Billings's ill health, his fortune, now materially increased, commanded his attention. He was one of the active promoters of the Nicaraguan canal project. He devoted himself to philanthrophy, finding an outlet for his religious zeal in constructing a chapel for the Congregational Church of Woodstock, and in rebuilding its church and parsonage. He built a church, also, in Billings, Mont., a town named for him. He purchased for the University of Vermont the valuable George P. Marsh collection of 12,000 volumes, and built and endowed at a cost of $250,000 a library building for the same institution. His numerous other benefactions included generous gifts to Amherst College and to Moody's School at Northfield, Mass. Billings's active business life did not prevent him from cultivating a fine appreciation of art and literature. He was devoted to the cause of public education, and was once considered for the presidency of the University of California. He was a forceful public speaker. His success in business came from an admirable compound of ability to plan and of ability to act. Commanding in appearance, gifted with the social graces, he won friends for himself and for his projects. For a long time he conquered his own ill health as he conquered other obstacles, but in 1890 death overtook him.

[Obituaries in *N. Y. Times* and *N. Y. Tribune,* Oct. 1, 1890, in *Univ. of Vt. Obit. Record,* No. I, 1895, and in *Appleton's Ann. Cyc. for 1890,* p. 634; longer sketches are by H. A. Hazen, in the *New Eng. Hist. and Geneal. Reg.,* XLV, 259–65, and by J. W. Buckham, in *Sunset,* XVI, 487–91. H. S. Dana's *Hist. of Woodstock, Vt.* (1889) contains some useful material. Billings's railway achievements are set forth in his address *The Northern Pacific R. R.: Its Hist. and Equitable Rights* (1880), and in E. V. Smalley, *Hist. of the Northern Pacific R. R.* (1883). *The Memoirs of Henry Villard* (1904), II, give a good account of the Billings-Villard controversy, and an article by J. B. Hedges, "The Colonization Work of the Northern Pacific R. R.," in the *Miss. Valley Hist. Rev.,* XIII, 311–42, tells of the activities of the land department under Billings.]

J. D. H.

BILLINGS, JOHN SHAW (Apr. 12, 1838–Mar. 11, 1913), librarian, surgeon, was descended from William Billings of Somersetshire who migrated to New England about the middle of the seventeenth century. In the course of six generations the family removed through New York State to Switzerland County in southeastern Indiana, where John was born to James Billings and his wife, Abby (Shaw) Billings, the latter descended from one of the *Mayflower* Pilgrims.

As a boy John read voraciously, learned Latin with a little aid from a clergyman of the neighborhood, and later made an agreement with his father to waive all claim to an inheritance in favor of the other child, a sister, if the father would help him through college. He prepared himself, and at the age of fourteen entered the sub-freshman class of Miami University at Oxford, Ohio, some fifty miles from his home. Five years later he received the degree of B.A. with honors and in the fall of the following year began his professional studies at the Medical College of Ohio. In the spring of 1860 he obtained his M.D. and in the fall was appointed demonstrator of anatomy in the medical college at which he had studied. A year later he went before the medical examining board of the regular army, then being rapidly enlarged to meet the demands at the opening of the war, and passed at the top of the list. He received his commission the following spring and was put in charge of a hospital. At the end of the summer he became executive officer of a Philadelphia hospital filled with thousands of sick and wounded, and at that post developed a facility in disposing of official business by which he was ever after characterized. In April 1864 he was assigned to duty with the medical director of the Army of the Potomac and during the Wilderness campaign was a medical inspector in fact if not in title for that army. He wrote: "I am to be what you might call the Medical Statistician of the Army of the Potomac. I am to collect and consolidate all sorts of reports—and when a battle comes off I am to wander round from Hospital to Hospital collecting records—overseeing the surgery in an unofficial way— . . . the sort of work just suits me" (Garrison, p. 76). In July he was invalided back to Washington and in December he was transferred to the surgeon-general's office where he remained until his retirement from active duty thirty years later. During the first few years of this period his time was occupied largely with routine departmental duties in connection with the closing of many great army hospitals and the discharge of civilian physicians and surgeons.

During his student years in the Medical College Billings had been aroused to the need of a great medical library in the United States. His graduating thesis had been on "The Surgical Treatment of Epilepsy." The six months which he spent in writing it, ransacking the while the libraries of Cincinnati and of eastern cities for material, showed him that there were more than 100,000 printed volumes of medical books and journals to search, that no medical library in the United States possessed the majority of these books, that under the circumstances it was an immense task to collect the information he needed, and that the burden of work was greatly increased by the fact that many of the volumes were not indexed or were badly indexed. This experience led him after peace came "to try to establish for the use of American physicians a fairly complete medical library and in connection with this to prepare a comprehensive catalogue and index."

Soon after beginning his Washington life Billings was put in charge of the Surgeon-General's Library and much of his time thereafter was devoted to fostering its growth. A sum of $80,000, turned in from the army hospitals after the war, was made available, and, energetically using this opportunity, he increased the library from 600 entries in the catalogue of 1865 to more than 50,000 entries in that of 1873. After he had seen the Surgeon-General's Library thus grow under his hands, he printed in 1876 a Specimen Fasciculus of a Catalogue and submitted it to the medical profession for suggestions. It was well received and four years later Congress provided for printing Billings's monumental work, the *Index Catalogue,* in the preparation of which he was ably assisted by Dr. Robert Fletcher. The first volume appeared in 1880. The reception it had from those professionally qualified to pass judgment is indicated by a contemporary estimate. "The prospective labour still before the compilers of this valuable work is so gigantic and the standard of those who have undertaken it so high that the accomplishment seems almost unattainable" (*Lancet*). One volume of the *Index Catalogue* including about one thousand pages royal octavo appeared each year thereafter until 1895 when the sixteen volumes had been printed and Billings, retiring from the service, left his successors to produce a second series, 1896–1916, even more voluminous, and to begin upon a third. In 1879 the *Index Medicus,* planned by Billings and Fletcher as a monthly guide to current medical literature and a companion publication to the *Index Catalogue,* began to appear, and it was continued without a break until after the retirement of Billings in 1895. By these two great works physicians and surgeons throughout the world were afforded a guide to the literature of their profession past and current far superior to the guides available to the members of any other profession. The *Index Catalogue* is probably the most important contribution yet made to American medicine (Welch) and the work which constitutes Billings's "float through posterity" (Osler). The Surgeon-General's Library is now without a serious rival since it comprises nearly one million books and pamphlets and the largest collection of medical periodicals in the world.

As Billings in 1873 was beginning his work at cataloguing and indexing the Surgeon-General's Library, Johns Hopkins of Baltimore died, leaving a generous endowment for a great hospital. The trustees asked five experts in hospital construction to submit sketch plans for the construction, heating, ventilation, and administration of the proposed group of buildings. The plans of Billings were accepted, the architects' plans were adapted to them, and Billings, with the consent of the Surgeon-General, was appointed medical adviser to the trustees. In this capacity he presented a series of reports upon hospital construction and organization, and the relation of hospitals to the training of nurses and medical men, which have become classical. In one of them he wrote: "A sick man enters the Hospital to have his pain relieved—his disease cured. To this end the mental influences brought to bear upon him are always important, sometimes more so than the physical. He needs sympathy and encouragement as much as medicine. He is not to have his feelings hurt by being, against his will, brought before a large class of unsympathetic, noisy students, to be lectured over as if he were a curious sort of beetle. . . . In this Hospital I propose that he shall have nothing of the sort to fear" (Garrison, p. 185). With these words, says his biographer, Billings swept away the old-fashioned clinical lecture and showed how to overcome the well-founded horror of hospitals existing at that day among nearly all classes. The plans for which he was so largely responsible "influenced hospitals in a way unparalleled in the history of hospital construction" and gave "a tremendous impetus to better hospitals" (H. M. Hurd in *Johns Hopkins Hospital Bulletin,* August 1914, p. 245). The new hospital was to be an integral part of the Medical School which Hopkins also endowed and both were to aim at raising the level of medical training in the United States. That Billings selected first William H. Welch, whom he met as a student in Germany, and later William Osler for the staff of the medical school illustrates his power of judging not merely performance but promise in younger men.

Perhaps the greatest change in medicine during the present generation has been a shift in emphasis from curative to preventive medicine, from caring for the individual patient to caring for community health; in this change Billings was a pioneer. He was one of the original members of the American Public Health Association which was formed in 1872 and to that organization he gave much time and energy. In 1878 a report which it received about the recent alarming epidemics of yellow fever was referred to a committee of which he was chairman, and the report urged that the work be broadened so as to include a search for the cause of yellow fever, a search which could best be prosecuted in Havana. It was more than twenty years before this hint was followed, with results now known to the world. A few months later the wide alarm over the ravages of yellow fever resulted in the creation of a National Board of Health mainly to aid localities menaced or decimated by that pestilence. Billings was made its vice-chairman and proved most efficient first in confining the disease to Memphis where it had gained headway and then in crushing it at that focal point. This victory was a main cause of his election the following year to the presidency of the American Public Health Association.

However it may be with curative medicine, for preventive medicine vital statistics is an indispensable foundation. Billings's first publication used the statistical method and in later years whatever the theme upon which he was writing he was likely to try the same method upon it. He was in charge of the vital statistics of the federal censuses of 1880 and 1890 and although the imperfections of his material prevented him from making in those reports any contributions of the first importance, the soundness of judgment, professional knowledge, and statistical acumen there displayed contributed much to rescue American work in this field from well-deserved reproach and to point out the one open path toward improvement, voluntary collaboration between the federal government and the states, a path which has been trodden with success now for half a century. Billings was informed about the best current European work in vital statistics and applied the approved methods so far as they could be adapted to the refractory American material. He introduced corrected death rates and life tables for unselected populations wherever the American figures were accurate enough to justify those refinements; he was the first to suggest the possibility of the mechanical methods of tabulation which were successfully employed in the United States census of 1890 and which since then have spread through the civilized world.

Five years before the date upon which Billings was to retire from active duty in the army the University of Pennsylvania with the permission of the Surgeon-General appointed him director of its University Hospital and professor of hygiene; after his retirement he removed to Philadelphia to give himself more fully to these duties. One year later, however, after securing the reluctant consent of the University authorities he resigned to accept a greater and more congenial task in New York City where the remaining seventeen years of his life were spent. Three libraries and library endowments in that city, the Astor, Lenox, and Tilden foundations, were consolidated in 1895 by common agreement and with the hope that a library worthy to be compared with the best in Europe might result from the union. The many problems involved in the execution of the plan required a director of energy and expert knowledge, and it was natural that Billings should be chosen. The city gave land in a central location and constructed upon it a library building following the plan which Billings originally sketched. While it was being erected, Billings supervised the reclassification and recataloguing of the books in the three libraries and the consolidation of New York's numerous free circulating libraries into branches of this central library. He also persuaded Carnegie to provide the $5,000,000 needed for building these branches, now more than forty in number, on condition that the city would furnish the necessary land, which was done. Of the New York Public Library as it stands to-day he was "in a very real sense the creator." It now contains more than 3,000,000 books and pamphlets.

In his last eleven years Billings was active in the organization and guidance of the Carnegie Institution of Washington, designed to encourage research, especially in the fields of pure and applied science. For most of that time he was chairman of the board of trustees and member of the executive committee and "he gave a surprisingly large amount of time and attention to the affairs of the Institution" and "rendered invaluable services during this formative period" (President Woodward in *Carnegie Institution of Washington Year Book*, 1913, pp. 8–10).

Billings was high-spirited and imperious in temper and in his later years the recurrent physical pain of which he never spoke added at times an edge to his words. His absorption in matters of large moment interfered with his enduring fools gladly; his army training developed an innate self-reliance and domination which to some were repellent; his achievements were not such as to split the ears of the groundlings; and his humor, at times somewhat grim, was not always understood by little men. During his lifetime his work won perhaps more honor abroad than at home because medical knowledge and skill in many countries of Western Europe then stood higher than they did in the United States. At the seventh meeting of the International Medical Congress in London he was invited as a representative of American medicine to give one of the four general addresses, the others being by selected representatives of France, Germany, and England. This was the first time American medicine had been so recognized and his address on "Our Medical Literature" was his best public effort. It was received with great enthusiasm. The *Lancet* spoke of it as "remarkable even among all those of the past week (*sc.* by Virchow, Pasteur, Huxley, Paget, *et al.*) for its great ability, practical value and wit." "Tall and largely built, he was . . . a commanding presence, with flow of wholesome English, ready wit and humor. . . . The figure of athletic build, the large blue eyes, a certain happy sense of easy competence, won regard and held the respectful attention" (Mitchell, p. 382). Billings was married on Sept. 3, 1862, at Georgetown, D. C., to Katharine Mary Stevens, daughter of Hestor L. Stevens who had been a representative in Congress from Michigan, 1853–55, and had settled in Washington after his term in Congress was ended. Of this marriage six children were born of whom a son and four daughters survived.

[The main source of information is Fielding H. Garrison's *John Shaw Billings: A Memoir* (1915), which contains a good bibliography, omitting, however, one important article, "The Diminishing Birth Rate in the U. S.," in *Forum*, XV (1893), pp. 466–77. Other sources are H. M. Lydenberg's *John Shaw Billings* (1924), S. Weir Mitchell's "Memoir" and F. H. Garrison's "Scientific Work of John Shaw Billings" in the *Nat. Acad. of Sci. Biog. Memoirs*, vol. VIII (1919), and W. F. Willcox, "John Shaw Billings and Federal Vital Statistics" in *Am. Statistical Ass. Jour.*, XXI (1926), pp. 257–66.] W. F. W.

BILLINGS, JOSH. [See SHAW, HENRY WHEELER, 1818–1885.]

BILLINGS, WILLIAM (Oct. 7, 1746–Sept. 26, 1800), early singing-master and composer of hymn tunes, was born in Boston, the son of William and Elizabeth (Clark) Billings. He was a tanner by trade and wholly untutored in music, except for a very limited knowledge of reading notes, which he probably acquired in one of the singing-schools of his period. He may also have gained some information through reading the *Introduction to Singing* in the English hymn-tune collections or perhaps in Tansur's *Musical Grammar,* though his style shows no resemblance to that pedantic work. His schooling was equally meager, but he was a music enthusiast, zealous in self-praise and possessing some musical talent on which he relied to such an extent that he had no hesitancy in entering the field of composition. He appeared at a time when church music was in an utterly crude though transitional state. Singing by rote ("lining-out") had lost its hold and had been largely superseded by psalm-tune books (psalms were the only texts permitted in the church music of New England), but the only available books were small compilations made by foreign-trained ministers who had some knowledge of harmony. The number of tunes was very limited and the choirs, weary of the monotonous repetition of the old music, were eager for something new. Billings, who was himself an ardent choir-singer, was keenly alive to this situation. In writing his first tunes he merely imitated those that pleased him and in the absence of paper chalked them on the board walls of the tannery and on sides of leather. In attempting to gain a hearing for his music he had every disadvantage, for he was not only eccentric, but deformed; one leg was shorter than the other and one arm withered, he was blind in one eye, his appearance was slovenly, and his voice loud and rasping. But his earnestness and enthusiasm attracted the attention of Gov. Samuel Adams and Rev. Dr. Pierce of Brookline, both music-lovers, who encouraged his efforts and sang beside him in the choir, though they well knew that his voice easily drowned their own. He soon abandoned his trade in order to enter upon a musical career, becoming a singing teacher and the trainer of the choirs of some of the important churches in Boston, notably the Brattle Street Church and the Old South Church. In this field his influence was deep and far-reaching. He did much to improve the rhythmic singing of the choirs and insisted on more exact pitch. Instruments were not as yet used in the churches, and the "striking-up" of the tune was a very uncertain and hazardous matter, often resulting in distressing and disastrous efforts to find the correct pitch. To remedy this situation he was the first to introduce the pitch-pipe. For the purpose of maintaining the pitch he also introduced the "viol" (violoncello). During his early years in music he had written many tunes that were sung by the choirs and had caught the popular fancy. His first published book, which he affectionately called his "Reuben" (being his first-born) appeared in 1770, engraved on copper by Paul Revere and bearing the following title-page: *The New England Psalm-Singer: or American Chorister. Containing a number of Psalm-tunes, Anthems and Canons. In four or five Parts. (Never before published.) Composed by William Billings, a Native of Boston in New England. Matt. XXI, 16. "Out of the Mouth of Babes and Sucklings hast thou perfected Praise." James V, 13. "Is any merry? Let him sing Psalms."*

O praise the Lord with one consent.
And in this grand design
Let Britain and the Colonies
Unanimously jine! [join].

Boston, New England. Printed by Eades and Gill.

Billings had been much impressed by the contrapuntal style of some of the English music, though he knew nothing of the rules of counterpoint. Notwithstanding this, he made bold efforts at "fuguing" and, crude and discordant though they were, they met with approbation, possibly because of their originality and greater melodic freedom. Billings says of this "fuguing" that "it has more than twenty times the power of the old slow tunes, each part straining for mastery, the audience entertained, their minds surpassingly agitated and extremely fluctuated, sometimes declaring for one part, and sometimes for another . . . O ecstatic! Rush on ye sons of harmony!" In 1778 his second book, *The Singing Master's Assistant or Key to Practical Music*, was published, disclosing that in the intervening eight years he had learned much. This book, which was really an abridgment of his first book, had sixty tunes, some of which were new; some had words adapted from the Psalms by Watts and others, and some were by Billings himself, although he knew as little about poetry as he did about music. But this book was a great improvement over the first and was known as "Billings' Best." A second edition appeared in 1779 and a third in 1780. On the outbreak of the Revolution he became an ardent patriot and several of his patriotic songs, besides being sung in the homes, followed the Continental soldiers to camp. His "Chester" was the most popular of these and was played by the army fifers. The following is the first stanza:

"Let tyrants shake their iron rod,
And Slavery clank her galling chains;
We fear them not, we trust in God;
New England's God forever reigns."

Other books of his were: *Music in Miniature* (1779), *The Psalm Singer's Amusement* (1781), *The Suffolk Harmony* (1786), and *The Continental Harmony* (1794). His influence was not confined to Boston but extended beyond its borders. He started a singing-school of forty-eight members in Stoughton in 1774, and from this was developed the oldest musical organization in America. On Nov. 7, 1786, it was merged into the Stoughton Musical Society, which is still in existence. Important among the members of the original singing-school and heading the singers of "the treble" was Lucy Swan, daughter of Major Robert Swan, who became the second wife of Billings on July 26, 1774. His first wife had been Mary Leonard, whom he had married on Dec. 13, 1764. Crude and grotesque as was much of his music and poetry, his great sincerity as well as the fewness of musicians gave him temporarily a large influence. He was close enough to the comprehension of his generation to be appreciated, where a finer creative genius might have failed. He died, however, poor and neglected.

Some of his tunes survived for a time, but were gradually replaced by better ones.

[Frank J. Metcalf, *Am. Writers and Compilers of Sacred Music* (1925), pp. 51–64; Louis C. Elson, *Hist. of Am. Music* (rev. ed., 1915), pp. 12, 26; Louis C. Elson, *Nat. Music of America* (rev. ed., 1924), p. 67; Frederic L. Ritter, *Music in America* (1883), p. 58; *Grove's Dict. of Music and Musicians, Am. Supp.* (1920), p. 386 under "Tune-Books."] F. L. G. C.

BILLY THE KID (Nov. 23, 1859–July 15, 1881), desperado, born in New York City, was William H. Bonney, the son of William H. and Kathleen Bonney. In 1862 the family moved to Coffeyville, Kan., where the father died. The mother, with her two children, moved to Colorado, where she married a man named Antrim. About 1865 the family moved to Santa Fé and in 1868 to Silver City, N. Mex. The boy had some schooling, but by the time he was twelve had become a frequenter of saloons and gambling places and an adept at cards. It was at this age that he is said to have stabbed to death a man who had insulted his mother. At sixteen he and a partner, near Fort Bowie, Ariz., killed three peaceful Indians for the furs they were transporting. After various spectacular adventures on both sides of the border, with a supposed record of twelve killings, he appeared in the Pecos Valley in the fall of 1877 and became an employee of J. H. Tunstall, a cattleman. On Feb. 12, 1878, he witnessed from a distance the opening scene in the Lincoln County cattle war, when his employer was killed by a posse of the Murphy faction. He became the fighting leader of the McSween faction, took part in several savage combats, was one of the party of six that on Apr. 1 killed Sheriff James A. Brady and a deputy, and in July figured conspicuously in the battle at Lincoln. With the arrival in August of Gen. Lew Wallace, whom Hayes appointed governor under instructions to end the war, a tacit truce began. Wallace issued a provisional amnesty to those not under indictment for crime, and in a conference with the Kid urged him to surrender, promising him a pardon in case he were convicted. The Kid, declaring that he should be murdered the moment he laid down his arms, refused the terms; and later, with a band of twelve companions, started on a career of wholesale cattle stealing with incidental killings. In 1880 a number of cattlemen, headed by John S. Chisum [*q.v.*], a former friend of the Kid, induced Pat Garrett, also a former friend, to accept the nomination for sheriff. Garrett was elected, and at once began a campaign to break up the Kid's band. In a fight at Fort Sumner, on Christmas Eve, 1880, one of the band was killed. The others fled, but a few days later the Kid, with three companions, was compelled to surrender. At Mesilla, in March, he was convicted of killing Sheriff Brady and was sentenced to be hanged at Lincoln on May 13. Conveyed to Lincoln, he was kept in confinement until Apr. 28, when, though shackled with handcuffs and leg irons, he contrived to kill the two deputies who guarded him and escaped. Two months and a half later he was trapped at the home of Pete Maxwell, in Fort Sumner, and shot and killed by Garrett.

Billy the Kid was the most famous outlaw of the Southwest. He had a score of twenty-one killings and is said to have expressed a wish to add two more to the list. He was about five feet eight in height, slender and well proportioned. His hair was light brown, and his eyes were gray. His face was long, and except for its thick coat of tan, colorless. His front teeth were large and slightly protrusive. He was left-handed. His manner was quiet and unassuming, and he had an unstudied grace of movement. On the range he dressed roughly, but he was something of a dandy in town. He danced well, was a frequenter of balls and fandangoes and was a notable favorite among women. His mood was cheerful and carefree, even in the greatest stress of danger. He had many friends, most of whom found excuses for his outlawry, and a certain glamour invests his career. He was, nevertheless, a cold-blooded killer who as a rule shot down his victims without shadow of provocation and who probably never felt a twinge of remorse.

[Pat F. Garrett, *The Authentic Life of Billy the Kid* (1882); G. B. Anderson, *Hist. of New Mexico* (1907); C. A. Siringo, *Hist. of "Billy the Kid"* (1920); W. N. Burns, *The Saga of Billy the Kid* (1926).] W. J. G.

BIMELER, JOSEPH MICHAEL (*c.* 1778–Aug. 27, 1853), founder of the Separatist Society of Zoar in Ohio, was born in Germany, presumably in Wurttemberg, where for some ten years he labored as a teacher among a persecuted sect of Pietists, living meekly and changing his abode from time to time in order to avoid the eye of the government. He was of lowly origin, had been a weaver, was lame in one leg, and was disfigured by an enlarged, protruding eye, but he had educated himself rather successfully, and his intelligence, energy, and character were those of a superior man. In addition he had the spiritual power of a genuine religious leader. In 1817 he joined a company of about 300 Separatists from Wurttemberg, Bavaria, and Baden, who sailed from Hamburg to find a home in America. A woman mystic named Barbara Grubermann had been their moving spirit, but she died before they left Germany. On the voyage Bimeler—or Bäumler, to give him his original name—doctored the sick, cheered the downhearted, imparted religious and secular instruction, and by sheer force of character made himself their indispensable leader. Thereafter his career was the history of the company. They landed in Philadelphia on Aug. 14, 1817, and were hospitably received and cared for by members of the Society of Friends, who also enabled them, through Bimeler as their agent, to buy 5,500 acres of wooded upland in Tuscarawas County, Ohio. Bimeler with a few others preceded the main party, cleared ground for crops, built a cabin, and laid out the village of Zoar, named for the little city to which Lot had fled from Sodom and Gomorrah. Drastic measures were necessary to preserve the life of the colony. In order to pay for their land they agreed that no one was to marry and that husbands were to live apart from their wives. Community of goods was also adopted, although against Bimeler's own judgment. Under his benign autocracy the colony slowly got on its feet and finally reached prosperity. When the land was paid for marriage was reintroduced, Bimeler himself taking a wife. The brewery, flour mill, woolen and linen manufactory, and other communal enterprises throve; ironworks failed to pay, but Bimeler kept the plant in operation for several years so that outsiders employed in it would not lose their livelihood. Meanwhile he showed himself as successful in guiding the religious life of the community as he was in developing its material resources. No member of the Society was ever convicted of crime; the village jail was used exclusively by visitors. No one begrudged Bimeler the mansion which he lived in or the extra comforts that he allowed himself, with the exception of a few malcontents, whose suit to have the property partitioned ultimately reached the United States Supreme Court. The Court in its decision upheld the Society, vindicated Bimeler's administration as "not only not fraudulent but above reproach," and described him as "a man of great energy and high capacity for business." Toward visitors to the community Bimeler showed himself affable and remarkably open-minded; toward his own people his position compelled him to be somewhat reserved and decisive. After his death he was venerated as one of the saints, and written versions of his discourses took on an almost sacred character; but without his intelligence and driving power the Society stagnated and finally disintegrated.

[E. O. Randall, *Hist. of the Zoar Soc.* (2nd ed., Columbus, Ohio, 1900); C. Nordhoff, *The Communistic Societies of the U. S.* (1875); W. A. Hinds, *Am. Communities and Co-Operative Colonies* (2nd revision, 1908); G. B. Landis, "The Soc. of Separatists of Zoar" in *Annual Report of the Am. Hist. Ass. for 1898* (1899); *Penny Mag.*, VI, 411–12 (London, 1837); Henry Howe, *Hist. Colls. of Ohio*, III, 387–89 (1891); J. B. Mansfield, *Hist. of Tuscarawas County, Ohio* (1884). Bimeler's addresses fill three massive volumes: *Die Wahre Separation, oder die Wiedergeburt, Dargestellet in Geistreichen und Erbaulichen Versammlungs-Reden und Betrachtungen* (Zoar, Ohio, 4 pts. in 2 vols., 1856–60); *Etwas fürs Herz! oder Geistliche Brosamen von des Herrn Tisch Gefallen* (Zoar, Ohio, 2 pts., 1860–61).]

G. H. G.

BINGHAM, AMELIA (Mar. 20, 1869–Sept. 1, 1927), actress, was born at Hicksville, Ohio, the daughter of John B. and Marie (Hoffman) Smiley. Her father kept the local hotel. In 1890, while at home for the summer from Ohio Wesleyan University, she took part in amateur theatricals, and a guest of the hotel conceived a good opinion of her acting. He was Lloyd Bingham, manager of a theatrical road company. At his persuasion she went on the stage, toured the Pacific Coast as a member of McKee Rankin's company, and on Dec. 18, 1893, made her New York début in *The Struggle for Life* at the People's Theatre. Meanwhile she had married her discoverer. During the following years she acted in a series of melodramas: *The Power of Gold, The Shaughraun, The Colleen Bawn, The Village Postmaster, The Mummy, Captain Impudence,* and *Nature.* In 1897, under the management of Charles Frohman, she starred in *The White Heather* and was later seen in *The Pink Dominos, On and Off, The Proper Caper, At the White Horse Tavern, The Cuckoo, His Excellency the Governor,* and *Hearts are Trumps.* Her road tours took her in time into every state in the Union, and with her statuesque beauty and vibrant voice she became one of the most popular of American actresses. Year after year she and her husband returned for their vacation to Hicksville, where she gradually overcame the prejudices of her Methodist relatives and friends, the final proof of her uprightness coming when she lent money to a fellow-townsman in distress. In the summer of 1900 she went to Europe for rest and change. On her return she found herself without an engagement and, taking her cue from several English actresses, decided to become her own producer. She took over the Bijou Theatre in New York, accepted Clyde Fitch's *Climbers* after every important manager in the city had declined it, assembled an excellent company, and produced the play, Jan. 15, 1901, with great success. She herself took the part of Mrs. Sterling. In 1902 she produced *Lady Margaret* and *The Modern Magdalen* and in 1903 *The Frisky Mrs. Johnson,* another conspicuous success. Later she acted in *Olympe, Mlle. Marni,* and *The Lilac Room.* At various times she was a member of stock companies, including engagements in St. Louis in 1907, 1909, 1910, and 1911. Later plays in which she appeared were: *One of Our Girls, A Contented Woman, The Eternal City, A Modern Lady Godiva, My Wife's Husbands, Her Other Self, The New Henrietta,* a revival of *The Climbers* (Academy of Music, May 1914), *Mama's Affairs,* the 1925 revival of *Trelawney of the Wells,* and *The Pearl of Great Price,* to her part in which she objected because, as she said "for years I have played decent women on the stage." In 1909 she fulfilled a vaudeville engagement in London, appearing in an act called *Great Moments from Great Plays.* Her husband, who had been her manager, died at sea while a member of the Ford Peace Party Dec. 22, 1915. Her home in later years, 103 Riverside Drive, was a veritable museum of mirrors, armor, statuary, coins, bric-a-brac, antiques, and thirteen striking clocks, some collected by her husband, others the gifts of admirers. It was there that she died of heart disease aggravated by a touch of pneumonia.

[*Who's Who on the Stage,* 1908; J. Parker, ed., *Who's Who in the Theatre* (5th ed., London, 1925); L. C. Strang, *Famous Actresses of the Day in America,* Second Series (1902); *N. Y. Times,* Dec. 23, 1915; *N. Y. Times,* and *Herald Tribune,* Sept. 2, 4, 1927; M. J. Moses and V. Gerson, *Clyde Fitch and His Letters* (1924); F. W. Faxon, ed., *The Dramatic Index 1910–27* (1911 ff.).]

G.H.G.

BINGHAM, ANNE WILLING (Aug. 1, 1764–May 11, 1801), Federalist society leader, was one of the thirteen children born to Thomas Willing and Anne (McCall) Willing of Philadelphia. Her inheritance on both sides was enviable and was undoubtedly an important factor in her later success. Thomas Willing was a wealthy merchant of English descent and education, who had become a power in colonial politics and who is said to have resembled his friend Washington in character. Mrs. Willing, whose beauty was not eclipsed even by that of her daughter, belonged to the influential McCall family of Philadelphia. Already an acclaimed beauty in a city famous for its beautiful women, Anne Willing at the age of sixteen was married (Oct. 26, 1780) to William Bingham [*q.v.*], one of the wealthiest men in the American Colonies. In 1783 Mr. and Mrs. Bingham sailed for Europe, where the appearance, charm, and wit of the twenty-year-old wife became the subject of flattering attention. Mrs. Bingham was presented at the court of Louis XVI, and, writing of her at this time, Miss Abigail Adams said, "Mrs. Bingham gains my love and admiration more and more every time I see her; she is possessed of greater ease and politeness in her behavior than any person I have seen." After five brilliant years in Paris, London, and The Hague, Mrs. Bingham returned home admirably prepared to reign over the "Republican Court" in Philadelphia. During the decade when her salon was at its height no single character of political importance but came to some extent under the influence of her personality. There was nothing of the democrat and nothing of the Puritan about Mrs. Bingham. Her vocabulary and taste in anecdote are reported to have been those of her contemporary the Duchess of Devonshire, and the extravagance of her entertainments surprised, and, in the case of Brissot de Warville at least, shocked European visitors. "Mansion House," built by the Binghams on their return from Europe, was modeled on the residence of the Duke of Manchester, "the dimensions of the original being somewhat enlarged in the copy." If Harrison Gray Otis was pained to find Mrs. Bingham's daughter clad only in her dress and chemise on a January day in Philadelphia; if there was amusement at a long line of Bingham servants, hurtling the names of arriving guests across the sidewalks, up the stairs, and along the corridors; if it leaked out that Mrs. Bingham had a protracted quarrel with a theatre manager over the owning of a box; these were but shallow ripples on a deep stream of admiration that flowed steadily in the conversation, letters, and diaries of the period. While it was probably her wealth and beauty that brought important personages to Mrs. Bingham, it was certainly her intelligence, sagacious wit, and a flair for analysis that made them listen to her. Shortly after the birth of her only son, in her thirty-seventh year, she insisted upon attending a sleighing party, and the resultant exposure caused an attack of lung fever which rapidly grew so serious that her physicians advised a milder climate. Carried from her luxurious home upon a palanquin which drew the eyes of hundreds, she was placed aboard her husband's elaborately appointed yacht and taken to the Bermuda Islands. There after a few weeks the lovely Anne Bingham died in unaccustomed exile.

[Thos. Willing Balch, *Willing Letters and Papers* (1922); Rufus W. Griswold, *The Republican Court* (1864); Samuel E. Morison, *Life and Letters of Harrison Gray Otis* (1913), I, 135–39; Henry Wansey, *An Excursion to the United States* (1798), p. 136 (description of the "Mansion House"); Jean Brissot de Warville, *New Travels in the United States* (Bowling Green, Ohio, 1919), p. 190; Claude Bowers, *Jefferson and Hamilton* (1926).]

G. G—m.

BINGHAM, CALEB (Apr. 15, 1757–Apr. 6, 1817), pioneer writer of text-books, was born in Salisbury, Conn., of Daniel Bingham and his wife, Hannah Conant. After attending district school he was prepared for college by the local minister and entered Dartmouth in 1779. At graduation in 1782 he had the honor of the valedictory address (in Latin). In that year he became master of Moor's Indian Charity School which President Wheelock of Dartmouth had founded in 1754 and maintained as an appendage to the college. After several years he moved to Boston, where he was, according to the city records of 1784, "approbated by the selectmen to keep a private school for the instruction of young ladies in the useful branches of reading, writing, etc." He published his first text-book primarily for use in this school, under the title, *The Young Lady's Accidence or a Short and Easy Introduction to English Grammar: Designed Principally for the Use of Young Learners, more especially of the Fair Sex, though Proper for Either* (1785). This was the second English Grammar published in the United States, that of Noah Webster having preceded it by one year. It was but a little book of sixty pages characterized by simplicity and clearness, and was long and widely used in the schools. In 1789 a reorganization of Boston's public schools was made, and Bingham had an important part in effecting the innovations then started. Appointed to be master of one of the three new Reading Schools he gave up his private school and served the city for seven years. Then he set up as a bookseller and occasional publisher at 44 Cornhill, remaining there for twenty-one years. "His bookstore was the favorite resort of all the Boston teachers, and education was continually discussed there" (*American Journal of Education,* X, 597). It was here that agitation for free primary schools centered, Bingham being prominent in advocating them, though they were not fully established till after his death. His store was also the headquarters of the local Jeffersonian Republicanism of which he was a disciple. Several times he ran unsuccessfully for the state Senate. During the governorship of Elbridge Gerry he was appointed director of the state prison and served for several years. In 1794 he first published a "Selection of Lessons for Reading and Speaking" entitled *The American Preceptor.* Three years later he brought out *The Columbian Orator* "designed for a Second Part of the American Preceptor." Few, if any, of the selections which these books comprise are from his pen; many of them are of a deeply religious sort, reflecting truly the spirit of their times, for until the appearance of these readers and those of Webster, the Bible and the psalm-book had been the principal school reading-books. Others of the selections are strongly patriotic, and were both expressions and developers of the growing enthusiasm for the young American republic. For a quarter of a century, especially in the district schools, these readers surpassed in popularity all their competitors and made their author nationally known. Other text-books of his were: *The Child's Companion, being an Easy and Concise Reading and Spelling Book, for the Use of Young Children* (1792); *Juvenile Letters, being a Correspondence between Children, from Eight to Fifteen Years of Age,* a joint production of Bingham and one of his daughters, and designed to introduce children to English composition. His *Astronomical and Geographical Catechism* (1803) was based on the *School Geography* of Jedidiah Morse and comprised a set of questions and answers, both of which, according to the practise of those days, were to be committed to memory and recited verbatim. In 1796 he published for teachers of writing the first set of copy-slips printed in this country. He was a good French scholar and published his own translation of Chateaubriand's *Atala* (1802). On his native town he bestowed a generous gift of books to be the beginning of its public library and he was active in promoting town libraries in many other places. In religion he was a conservative Congregationalist, adhering to the older form of this faith when the churches of Boston became Unitarian. Of attractive appearance, nearly six feet in height and well proportioned, he impressed his contemporaries with his dignity, geniality, and integrity. He was fond of music and a member of the choir of the churches with which he was connected. At his death, in Boston, he was survived by his wife, Hannah (Kemble) Bingham, and by two daughters.

[The chief source of information is a biographical sketch by Wm. B. Fowle, Bingham's employee and successor, in Henry Barnard's *Am. Jour. of Ed.,* V, 325; in a biographical sketch of Fowle, *Ibid.,* X, 597, additional material is to be found. Bingham's text-books are best described in Clifton Johnson, *Old-Time Schools and School-Books* (1904); Geo. E. Littlefield, *Early Schools and School-Books of New England* (1904); Justin Winsor, *Memorial History of Boston* (1880–81).]

W. J. C.

BINGHAM, GEORGE CALEB (Mar. 20, 1811–July 7, 1879), portrait and genre painter, was born on a plantation in Augusta County, Va., the son of Henry Vest and Mary (Amend) Bingham. He was of mixed stock, chiefly Scotch and German. In 1819 the family emigrated to Franklin, Mo., then on the frontier, and in Missouri Bingham spent most of his life. He began early to copy engravings and to paint with home-made pigments, learned to roll cigars, worked as a cabinet-maker's apprentice, read law and theology, but was encouraged by Chester Harding [*q.v.*] to persist with his painting, and by 1834 had definitely made art his vocation. About 1837 he studied for a short time at the Pennsylvania Academy of Fine Arts. He lived in Washington, D. C., 1840–44, was in Europe, with his headquarters at Düsseldorf, 1856–58, returned to Germany for a few months in 1859, and made numerous short trips to various parts of the United States, but Missouri was his home. At different times he set up his studio in Arrow Rock, Columbia, Jefferson City, St. Louis, and Kansas City, where he died. His first genre painting to receive much attention was "Jolly Flatboatmen," which was selected by the American Art Union in 1846 for its annual engraving. His other noteworthy pictures include "Raftsmen Playing Cards" (by 1847), "Canvassing for a Vote" (by 1851), "Emigration of Daniel Boone" (1851), "County Election" (1851–52), "Stump Speaking" (1853–54), "Verdict of the People" (1854), "Gen. Lyon and Gen. Blair Starting for Camp Jackson" (about 1862), "Major Dean in Jail" (1866), "Order No. 11" (about 1868), and "The Puzzled Witness" (1874). His portraits, which vary noticeably in execution with his interest in the sitter, were once a standard article of furniture in prosperous Missouri homes. As the list of his genre pictures indicates, Bingham's avocation was politics. In 1846 he was elected to the legislature as a Whig by a margin of three votes; his opponent, one Sappington, contested the election and was sustained by the Democratic majority in the House. In 1848 Bingham declined the nomination at first but accepted it when he heard that Sappington would run against him; this time he beat him by twenty-six votes. He was a conspicuously honest and efficient state treasurer 1862–65, and was made adjutant-general of Missouri in 1875. He married Elizabeth Hutchison of Boonville in 1836, Eliza K. Thomas of Columbia in 1847, and Mrs. Mattie Lykins of Kansas City in 1878. He was small and delicate in appearance and, having lost all his hair from a severe attack of measles when he was nineteen, always wore a wig. In his genre work, although his coloring is never satisfactory and his drawing sometimes faulty, he has preserved, with realism and humor, certain characteristic scenes in old-time Missouri life.

[F. H. Rusk, *George Caleb Bingham, the Missouri Artist* (Jefferson City, Mo., 1917) is detailed, discriminating, and carefully documented.]

G. H. G.

BINGHAM, HARRY (Mar. 30, 1821–Sept. 12, 1900), lawyer, politician, traced his descent from Thomas Bingham of England, one of the landed proprietors of Norwich, Conn., in 1659. The son of Warner Bingham, a prosperous farmer, state senator, and judge of Essex County, Vt., and of Lucy (Wheeler) Bingham, he was born in Concord, Vt. His early education having been obtained at the common schools, he entered the Lyndon Academy in 1838, proceeding thence in 1839 to Dartmouth College, where he graduated in 1843. He had taught school in vacations, and this he continued to do, on commencing the study of law. He passed a short time in law offices at Concord and Lyndon, but completed his studies at Bath, N. H., being admitted to the New Hampshire bar at Lancaster in May Term 1846. The same year he opened an office in Littleton, N. H., and practised there all his life. He was an ardent Democrat, and, being the only lawyer of that persuasion in the town, quickly obtained the nucleus of a thriving practise, which ultimately became one of the largest in the state. In 1861 he was elected to represent Littleton in the New Hampshire House of Representatives, and became Democratic leader in the legislature. Although a strong partisan he did not countenance machine politics, and he was able—apart from purely party measures—to exercise an influence in the House disparate to the numerical strength of his political following. He was reëlected no less than seventeen times between 1861 and 1891, in addition to being state senator for Grafton District 1883–87. When in the House he was always a member of the judiciary committee, being its chairman in 1871 and 1874. In 1865 and 1867 he was Democratic nominee for Congress, and was candidate for the United States Senate on seven occasions. He was a delegate to the national Democratic conventions at New York in 1868, Baltimore in 1872, Cincinnati in 1880, and Chicago in 1884 and 1890. An unswerving Gold Democrat, he declined to follow Bryan, and from the first refused to support the Chicago platform. He attended the Philadelphia peace convention of 1866, and took a conspicuous part in the proceedings of the state constitutional convention of 1876, being chairman of the committee on the legislative department.

The only office he ever held was that of United States treasury agent, to which he was appointed by President Johnson in 1867. He was nominated by Gov. Weston in 1874 chief justice of the superior court of judicature, but the appointment failed of confirmation by the Council. Retained in most of the heavy local litigation of his time, he was not an outstanding advocate, but his briefs were always prepared with the utmost attention to detail, and his manner of presenting his cases in clear, unpretentious style before judge or jury, his manifest sincerity and his scrupulous accuracy, were very attractive and had no small share in the attainment of many notable successes. For thirty years he was an acknowledged leader of the New Hampshire bar, and in 1893 was elected president of the Grafton and Coos Bar Association. He was unmarried.

[A detailed acount of his career by H. H. Metcalf appeared in the *Granite Mo.*, V, 277. Other information is contained in the *Judiciary and the Bar of New England*, ed. by Conrad Reno (1901), II, 41; *Green Bag*, XIII, 105; *Am. Law Rev.*, XXXV, 434, and *Dartmouth Coll. Ass. Alumni, Memorials of Judges* (1881), pp. 25–30. See also obituary in *Manchester* (N. H.) *Union*, Sept. 13, 1900.]

H. W. H. K.

BINGHAM, HIRAM (Oct. 30, 1789–Nov. 11, 1869), missionary, translator, was the seventh of thirteen children of Calvin and Lydia (Denton) Bingham, of Bennington, Vt. His father was a farmer. The son's early education was received in the local schools. In his twenty-third year he entered Middlebury College, and graduated in 1816. With the Christian ministry in mind, he went to Andover Theological Seminary and while there decided to offer himself for foreign-mission service in the Sandwich Islands. He graduated from Andover in 1819, and in the fall (Sept. 29) of that year was ordained at Goshen, Conn., for the work abroad under the American Board of Boston. At the ordination service he met Sybil Moseley, of Westfield, Mass., whom he married on Oct. 11, 1819, at Hartford. They joined a large company which sailed on the brig *Thaddeus* out of Boston harbor on Oct. 23, 1819, bound for the Sandwich Islands and the establishment of mission work. Admitted by the king "for a year," the party divided itself by royal permission and arrangement between Kailua on Hawaii and Honolulu on Oahu. Mr. and Mrs. Bingham were among those who disembarked at Honolulu on Apr. 19, 1820. For many months they lived in a native hut, until he erected in February 1821 a frame house which was sent out from America. Bingham and the others addressed themselves at once to the acquisition of the language, and to its reduction to writing. An alphabet of twelve letters was soon devised, and the missionaries set themselves the task of teaching a people to read, a task much simplified by the king's suggestion that his people learn. In 1822 Bingham issued his *Elementary Lessons in Hawaiian*, and thereafter came a steady output of works composed by various members of the mission. In October 1825 Bingham began the translation of the New Testament into Hawaiian, and by 1839 the entire Bible had been done by him and his associates, he himself contributing Luke, Colossians, Hebrews, Leviticus, Psalms 1–75, and Ezekiel. In 1828 the Gospel of Matthew, translated by himself and Thurston, was published, and in 1829 his own Luke. In 1831 he issued his *First Book for Children* and his *Scripture Catechism*. The services were first held in the open under immense hau (*hibiscus Titiaceus*) trees. In August 1821 a church was erected. Slowly the mission became fully organized. In February 1823, Bingham, Thurston, and Ellis, the ordained men, signed an article of incorporation of the Hawaiian Clerical Association which continued in power until 1863, when the Hawaiian Evangelical Association was formed. During 1826 Bingham made a one-hundred-mile preaching tour of the island in company with Kaahumanu, wife of the first great king, and chief pupil of the Binghams, who herself occupied the throne from 1823 to 1832. She had become Christian early in 1825 and was now urging the new faith upon her subjects. On June 1, 1840, the Mission "reluctantly, yet on the whole cheerfully, recommended that Brother and Sister Bingham make a visit to the United States," on account of Mrs. Bingham's health. Accordingly the parents and their small children left Honolulu Aug. 3, 1840, for New York. Mrs. Bingham's health continued poor and she died at Easthampton, Mass., on Feb. 27, 1848. Since the American Board thought it unwise for Bingham to return, he occupied himself in America with preaching and writing. For a time he served in New Haven as pastor of an African Church. On Aug. 24, 1854, he married Naomi Emma Morse. His voluminous and generally reliable *Residence of Twenty-one Years in the Sandwich Islands; or The Civil, Religious, and Political History of Those Islands* was published in 1847. In 1863 certain friends put an annuity at his disposal. Shortly after passing his eightieth birthday he died in New Haven.

[Wm. Ellis, *Jour. of a Tour Around Hawaii* (1826); Sheldon Dibble, *Hist. of the Sandwich Islands* (1843); R. Anderson, *Hist. of the Sandwich Islands Mission* (1870); O. H. Gulick, *Pilgrims of Hawaii* (1918); *Hawaiian Mission Centennial Book* (1820); E. C. Hawley, *Introduction of Christianity into the Hawaiian Islands* (1922); *Missionary Herald*, 1820–41.]

J. C. A.

BINGHAM, HIRAM (Aug. 16, 1831–Oct. 25, 1908), missionary to Micronesia, was the sixth child of Hiram Bingham [*q.v.*] and Sybil (Moseley) Bingham. He was born in Honolulu, where his elementary education was obtained in the Honolulu school for missionary children. A fortnight before his ninth birthday he started for America with his parents and two sisters. Some time after his arrival he entered Williston Academy, Easthampton, Mass. From there he went to Yale, where he graduated in 1853. For one year he served as principal of the Northampton

(Mass.) High School. The next he spent abroad as a private tutor. Then with his mind turned toward a missionary career he entered Andover Seminary, but ill health compelled him to leave in the spring of 1856. On Nov. 9, 1856, he was ordained in New Haven, on Nov. 18 he was married to Minerva Clarissa Brewster of Northampton, and on Dec. 2 he and Mrs. Bingham sailed from Boston on the brig *Morning Star,* the first of several missionary vessels of that name, bound for Honolulu and Micronesia. They arrived at Ponape, Gilbert Islands, Sept. 23, and established a missionary station at Apaiang. The Gilbert Islands lie along the equator and were then as now almost unendurable to white men. Proper food was scarce, epidemics of disease frequently broke out amongst the islanders, and unscrupulous traders were bitter in their opposition to mission work. Yet Bingham remained seven years. His work was destined to be mainly with the language. (Up to 1870 scarcely fifty good converts were numbered by the mission.) He put in his seven years to good advantage, and when ill health compelled his withdrawal he was equipped to proceed with the creation of a Gilbertese literature. He visited the United States in 1865 and on Nov. 12, 1866, sailed from Boston in command of the second *Morning Star,* a small two-masted schooner. As commander of this vessel he visited the Marquesas Islands mission of the native Hawaiian churches and made the tour of Micronesia, returning to Honolulu Dec. 16, 1868. Taking up his residence in the Hawaiian capital, he gave his time to work on the Gilbertese Bible. On Friday evening, Apr. 11, 1873, at "a joyful gathering at Honolulu" Bingham announced the completion of the translation of the entire New Testament, and had copies for distribution. Sharing the honor of the occasion was Moses Kaure, a Gilbert Islander who assisted Bingham in his translations.

On June 9, 1873, Mr. and Mrs. Bingham sailed again for the Gilbert Islands and resumed their residence at Apaiang. He preached at least once every week in the church, taught in the school, and began work on a Gilbertese dictionary. New schools and churches were organized in inland regions, and many new members were received into the Apaiang Church. Early in April 1875, however, Bingham's health gave way again and he had to leave the Islands. Receiving some medical aid en route Mrs. Bingham was able to get her feeble husband back to Honolulu in November by way of Samoa and Australia. He did not venture again to Apaiang and Micronesia, but remained in Honolulu except for several trips to the United States (1887, 1892–93, 1908), on behalf of the printing of translation materials. By 1890 Bingham had finished the Gilbertese translation of the entire Bible, and before his death had seen seven editions of it. His Gilbertese dictionary was published in 1908. Bingham was also the author of a Gilbertese hymn and tune book (1880), and of commentaries on the Gospels and the book of Acts, and of a *Gilbert Islands Bible Dictionary* (1895). Mrs. Bingham published a book of *Bible Stories in the Gilbertese* (1875). No small result of their literary work was the amplification to 12,000 words of a poverty-stricken language of 4,000. Bingham's end came suddenly at the Johns Hopkins Hospital in Baltimore, where he had gone for an operation, Oct. 25, 1908.

[*Obit. Record Grads. Yale Univ. . . . for 1909* (1909); T. A. Bingham, *Genealogy of the Bingham Family in the U. S.* (1898), pp. 94, 138; O. H. Gulick, *Pilgrims of Hawaii* (1918); R. Anderson, *Hist. of the Sandwich Islands Mission* (1870); *Missionary Herald,* Dec. 1908.]

J. C. A.

BINGHAM, JOHN ARMOR (Jan. 21, 1815–Mar. 19, 1900), lawyer, Ohio politician, was born in Mercer, Pa., the son of Hugh Bingham, a carpenter. After securing such elementary education as his neighborhood offered, he spent two years in a printing office, a like period at Franklin College, then studied law, was admitted to the bar, and began practise at Cadiz, Ohio, in 1840. He soon became prominent as a stump speaker in Harrison's "log cabin, hard cider" campaign. In 1854 he was elected to Congress, and served continuously until 1873, except for the Thirty-eighth Congress, when, failing of reëlection, he was appointed judge-advocate in January 1864, and solicitor of the court of claims the following August. When political fortunes failed him again in 1873 he was solaced by the appointment as minister to Japan, a position he held for twelve uneventful years.

Bingham was a clever and forceful speaker, overflowing with invective, rhetorical phrases, and historical allusions of varying degrees of accuracy. In two of the most dramatic episodes of the immediate post-war period—the trial of the assassins of Lincoln, and the impeachment of Andrew Johnson—he played a leading rôle. In the conspiracy trial his part as special judge-advocate was to bully the defense witnesses and to assert in his summary of the evidence that the rebellion was "simply a criminal conspiracy and a gigantic assassination" in which "Jefferson Davis is as clearly proven guilty . . . as is John Wilkes Booth, by whose hand Jefferson Davis inflicted the mortal wound upon Abraham Lincoln" (Benn Pitman, *Assassination of President*

Lincoln . . ., 1865, pp. 351, 380). In defending the legality of the military court set up by President Johnson, he argued that the executive could exercise all sorts of extra-constitutional powers, even to "string up the culprits without any court"—an argument which was somewhat embarrassing when he was selected by the House as one of seven managers to conduct the impeachment of President Johnson. He had voted against the first attempt at impeachment and had opposed the second, holding the President guilty of no impeachable offense (D. M. DeWitt, *Impeachment*, p. 506), but he finally yielded to party pressure and voted for impeachment after the Senate had declared the President's removal of Secretary Stanton illegal. It fell to him to make the closing speech at the trial. For three days (May 4–6) he rang the changes on the plea of the defense that the President might suspend the laws and test them in the courts—"the monstrous plea interposed for the first time in our history" (*Trial of Andrew Johnson*, II, 389 ff.). His confident manner carried conviction to the galleries, who pronounced it one of his greatest speeches.

In the work of reconstruction, Bingham's chief contribution was the framing of that part of the first section of the Fourteenth Amendment which forbade any state by law to abridge the privileges or immunities of citizens of the United States, or to deprive any person of life, liberty, or property without due process of law or to deny the equal protection of the laws (Kendrick, *Journal*, p. 106).

Bingham was married to Amanda Bingham, a cousin, by whom he had three children. He died at his home in Cadiz, Ohio. He did not introduce the resolution at the Whig national convention of 1848 containing the spirited anti-slavery apothegm carved on his monument at Cadiz, the resolution ascribed to him having been introduced by Lewis D. Campbell. Stenographic reports fail to show that Bingham ever spoke on the floor of the convention (*North American and United States Gazette*, and *Public Ledger*, both Philadelphia, for June 8, 9, 10, 1848).

[B. B. Kendrick, *Jour. of the Comm. of Fifteen on Reconstruction* (1914); *Trial of Andrew Johnson*, pub. by order of the Senate as a supplement to *Cong. Globe* (1868); *Cong. Globe*, 1854–73, *passim*; *Ohio Arch. and Hist. Pub.*, X, 331–52; D. M. DeWitt, *The Judicial Murder of Mrs. Surratt* (1895) and *The Impeachment and Trial of Andrew Johnson* (1903); *Evening Star* (Washington), Mar. 19, 1900; *Cadiz Democrat Sentinal*, Mar. 22, 1900.]

T. D. M.

BINGHAM, WILLIAM (Apr. 8, 1752–Feb. 6, 1804), banker, legislator, son of William and Mary (Stamper) Bingham, was born in Philadelphia. The family had been prominent in England. James (great-grandfather of William), who died in December 1714, was the first Pennsylvania representative. William's father served in the French wars 1748–62 and was a vestryman at St. Peter's church until his death in 1769. The son graduated from the University of Pennsylvania in 1768 and in 1770 was appointed British consul at St. Pierre, Martinique. He continued until 1776, after which he served four years as Continental agent in the West Indies. This experience determined Bingham's future. Joint ownership of privateers and constant trade gave him unusual wealth for that period. Upon his return to Philadelphia he married Anne, daughter of Thomas and Anne (McCall) Willing on Oct. 26, 1780, the bride being described by Anna Rawle, her neighbor, as one who "might set for the Queen of Beauty." Certainly she was a leader in Philadelphia society and the Bingham mansion became at once an important political and social center of the national capital [see Anne Willing Bingham]. Washington writes frequently in his diary of having tea at this house, and later of promising Mrs. Bingham to sit for his portrait to Gilbert Stuart. She died in Bermuda, May 11, 1801. In 1780 Bingham enlisted in the Philadelphia "Associators," later becoming captain in the city cavalry, but his effective national service was as a founder and director of the Pennsylvania Bank under President Willing. Incorporated May 26, 1781, and chartered Dec. 31 as the Bank of North America, it was the first bank in the country and gave increased stability to American finance. During 1784–86 Bingham was in Europe. Here his *Letter from an American . . . to a Member of Parliament*, in reply to Lord Sheffield (London and Philadelphia, 1784), and his friendship with Lord Shelburne strengthened Adams and Franklin in their contest for American commercial rights. On his return to Pennsylvania Bingham served in the Continental Congress 1786–89, the Pennsylvania Assembly 1790–95 and the United States Senate 1795–1801. His real-estate interests made him an advocate of internal improvements. The founder of Binghamton, N. Y., and the owner of considerable oil lands in Pennsylvania, he was the first president of the Philadelphia and Lancaster Turnpike Corporation, which built the earliest and for years the best turnpike in the United States. His two million acres of timberland in New England, pictured in his *Description of Certain Tracts . . . in the District of Maine* (1793), and his West Indian experience made him see the importance of American shipping. He was vice-president of the Society for Political Inquiries until the death of Franklin in 1790, a trustee of the University of Pennsylvania, and a frequent host to Presidents Washington and Adams, as to other American and foreign statesmen. One of his daughters married (1) Comte de Tilly and (2) Henry Baring; another daughter married Alexander Baring, Baron Ashburton, who obtained Bingham's fine collection of American pamphlets published between 1755 and 1782.

[Bingham MSS. and papers in the Hist. Soc. of Pa.; the Robert Morris MSS., the Naval MSS. of the Revolution, and the Washington MSS. in the Lib. of Cong.; T. A. Bingham, *Genealogy of the Bingham Family in the U. S.* (1898); J. T. Scharf and J. Westcott, *Hist. of Phila. 1609–1884* (1884), I, II; *Pa. Mag. of Hist. and Biog.*, vol. XLII, no. 3, vol. XLVII, nos. 2, 4; T. Westcott, *Historic Mansions and Buildings of Phila.* (1877), pp. 337–49.] C.H.L—n.

BINGHAM, WILLIAM (July 7, 1835–Feb. 18, 1873), educator, was the fourth child of William James and Eliza (Norwood) Bingham. His grandfather, the Rev. William Bingham, was a Scotch-Irish Protestant who came from Ireland after being involved in the plots which culminated later in Emmet's Rebellion. He taught at Wilmington, N. C., from 1789 until 1793, when he established at Pittsboro a school of his own which he removed, after serving for a time as professor of Latin in the University of North Carolina, first to Hillsboro and later to Mount Repose. He died at the age of seventy-two years after gaining an enviable reputation as scholar and teacher. His eldest son, William James Bingham, the second headmaster of the Bingham School, was also a successful teacher. Before the Civil War he was interested in plans for the emancipation of the negroes and for returning them to Africa, but when the War broke out he gave his whole heart to the Southern Confederacy. His son, the subject of this sketch, entered the University of North Carolina in 1853 and was graduated with highest honors in 1856. In December 1856, he married Owen White of Raleigh, N. C., and almost immediately joined his father as a partner in the school. His father being in delicate health and his brother Robert being only eighteen years of age, William became at once the controlling member of the partnership, and under his control the school grew in size, efficiency, and reputation. During the war he served the Confederacy untiringly, though prevented from joining the army. At the same time he carried on the work of the school, which was incorporated as a military academy in 1864, the principal receiving the rank of colonel. In December of that year Bingham moved the school to a place near Mebane in Orange County, and made it a boarding school in which the pupils lived entirely under his own care. In 1865 he bought out the interest of his brother-in-law and his cousin and became the sole proprietor of the school, the reputation and influence of which was increased by his extraordinary teaching power and the merit of his books. He published *A Grammar of the Latin Language* (1863), *Cæsar's Commentaries on the Gallic War* (1864), *A Grammar of the English Language* (1868), *A Latin Reader* (1869), and when seized with his final illness was busy with a text-book on Latin composition.

[*Biog. Hist. of N. C.*, ed. by Samuel A. Ashe, vol. VI (1907), esp. pp. 74–82 by Mrs. Preston Lewis Gray; Walter P. Williamson, "The Bingham School" in *Our Living and Our Dead*, May 1875; *N. C. Presbyterian*, Dec. 24, 1896; Chas. L. Roper, *The Church and Private Schools of N. C.* (1898).] H.N.F.

BINNEY, AMOS (Oct. 18, 1803–Feb. 18, 1847), zoologist, was born in Boston, the second child of Col. Amos Binney and Hannah (Dolliver) Binney, and came of a family traceable to John and Mercy Binney of Hull, Mass., who came from England in 1678 or 1679. Many members of this family were prominent in shipping, commerce, the professions and public affairs of New England. Binney was educated at Brown University, graduating in 1821. During his college years he became interested in the natural sciences. Like most young naturalists he collected birds' eggs, afterward taking up the collection and study of land shells and other mollusks. After beginning the study of medicine, ill health led him to a horseback trip to Cincinnati, followed by a year in Europe, where natural-history museums and art galleries were his favorite haunts. Restored to health he turned homeward, resumed his studies, and received the degree of M.D. from Harvard in 1826. This course of study was undertaken chiefly for the sake of scientific training, in those times not offered in college courses. He had no desire to practise medicine, preferring to become associated with his father in real estate and other business ventures. His leisure was always devoted to scientific studies. After his father's death he carried on the business with marked success until 1842.

In 1830 Binney, Augustus A. Gould, and several others founded the Boston Society of Natural History. From the outset Binney contributed freely to the resources of the Society, both scientific and financial. He gave papers on zoological and paleontological subjects, and was president of the Society from 1843 until his death. Elected to the state legislature in 1836, he was instrumental in obtaining state support for geological, zoological, and botanical surveys, resulting in the classical *Massachusetts Reports* by Gould, Harris, and others, useful far beyond the borders of the state. About 1835 Binney began the studies for his chief work, *The Terrestrial Air-Breathing Mollusks of the United States and the Adjacent Territories of North America.* Practically completed at the time of his death, it was published posthumously (1851) under the editorship of Dr. A. A. Gould, with an anatomical chapter by Dr. Joseph Leidy of Philadelphia. The illustrations were copperplates mostly engraved by Alexander Lawson. They have perhaps never been surpassed for scientific fidelity combined with artistic excellence. This scholarly and beautiful work gave Binney an international reputation in the scientific world of the time. It is generally recognized that the clarity and the high standard set by this work of Binney, and later by that of his son, served to preserve the literature of land mollusks from the confusion which is so apparent in American work on other molluscan groups of the middle decades of the last century.

Binney was a handsome man of dignified presence, over medium height, with dark eyes and black hair. A somewhat formal and reticent manner concealed a generous and friendly nature. "He possessed the art of writing amusing and descriptive letters to perfection." He was fond of pictures and a generous patron of art. In 1827 he married a cousin, Mary Ann Binney. Of their five children the third, William Greene Binney, continued and extended his father's scientific work with ability, succeeding him as the chief authority on American land mollusks.

[A. A. Gould, "Memoir of Dr. Amos Binney," in vol. I (1851) of Binney's *Terrestrial Air-Breathing Mollusks;* C. J. F. Binney, *Genealogy of the Binney Family in the U. S.* (1886).]

H. A. P.

BINNEY, HORACE (Jan. 4, 1780–Aug. 12, 1875), lawyer, son of Dr. Barnabas and Mary (Woodrow) Binney, was descended from Capt. John Binney, who came to Hull, Mass., about 1678. Horace was born in the Northern Liberties, Philadelphia, where his early education was obtained at the Friends Almshouse School and the Grammar School of the University of Pennsylvania. In 1788 he went to a classical school at Bordentown, N. J., but his father had died in 1787 and on his mother's subsequent marriage to Dr. Marshall Spring, the family removed to Watertown, Mass. After a short period of private tuition Binney entered Harvard College in July 1793, graduating in 1797 with high honors. At first he meditated taking up medicine but his stepfather dissuaded him, and going to Philadelphia, he endeavored to enter a mercantile office, but found no vacancy. He thereupon studied law in the office of Jared Ingersoll, working steadily and eschewing social attractions though he could "play pretty well on the flute and sing an agreeable song." He was admitted to the Philadelphia bar in March 1800, and started practise in that city, but for the first five years made little progress. Politics had no attraction for him, but he was persuaded in 1806 to be a candidate for the legislature on a fusion ticket of Federalists and Independent Democrats, and headed the poll. His record in the legislature was undistinguished, but he was brought into contact with influential underwriters and merchants, and his legal ability was speedily recognized. At this period marine-insurance litigation was particularly heavy in Philadelphia, the maritime measures adopted by Great Britain and France against each other's trade during the Napoleonic War seriously affecting United States commerce, and continually raising new points in insurance law. The first important retainer Binney received was in Gibson *vs.* Philadelphia Insurance Company (1 *Binney,* 415) in 1808, involving the correct mode of adjusting a particular average under a clause in a respondentia bond, and the ability he displayed was such that he soon had all the business he could attend to. In 1809 appeared the first volume of his *Reports of Cases Adjudged in the Supreme Court of Pennsylvania,* undertaken at the suggestion of Chief Justice Tilghman. Ultimately extending to six volumes, covering all important cases down to September 1814, these reports have always been considered very valuable, their accuracy never having been challenged. Binney had in January 1808 been elected a director of the first United States Bank, and his first case in the Supreme Court of the United States—which he won—was United States Bank *vs.* De Veaux (5 *Cranch,* 6), respecting the right of a corporation composed of citizens of one state to sue a citizen of another state in the federal courts. In 1810 he was elected to the common council of Philadelphia, and reëlected in 1811, being appointed president of that body each term. A Federalist in politics, he attended as a delegate from Pennsylvania the convention at New York in June 1812 and unsuccessfully opposed the proposition of alliance with the Clinton Democrats. Four years later he was induced to return to the municipal arena, and was a member of the Philadelphia select council during the years 1816–19; but steadfastly declined to be a candidate for Congress. He was now recognized as one of the leaders of the Philadelphia bar, and his reputation extended beyond the limits of his state. In 1823 he argued the case of Lyle *vs.* Richards (9 *Sergeant & Rawle,* 322), one of the two great cases upon which his reputation as a lawyer rests. It dealt with the construction of a devise with contingent remainders in tail and the validity of a common recovery, involving an intricate discussion of the application of the common law to real property in the state, and his contention was upheld by the court. In 1827 the bar of Philadelphia almost unanimously recommended his appointment to the chief justiceship of Pennsylvania, and in 1829 President Jackson was urged to appoint him to the Supreme Court of the United States. Both movements were unsuccessful, but he had not been consulted on either occasion, and he had no inclination to take a seat on the bench, as was evidenced by his declining in 1830 an offer from Gov. Wolf, of a position on the supreme court of Pennsylvania.

He was now commencing to feel the continuous strain of court work, most of it involving heavy responsibilities, and he contemplated an early retirement. But powerful influences were brought to bear which induced him to become a candidate for Congress on the anti-Jackson ticket in 1832. He consented on the understanding that he would not be required to support a protective tariff, that a vote for him should only be considered a vote against Jackson, and that if elected he should not be bound to any party. After a stirring campaign he was elected and took his seat in Congress Dec. 2, 1833. In the House he was an outstanding figure, but he could effect nothing in the face of the majority which the President commanded. His bitter disappointment was expressed in the statement that "the spirit of party is a more deadly foe to free institutions than the spirit of despotism." As a debater he showed himself second to none in the House, and his speeches reached an unusually high level, but he disliked his environment, and declined a renomination. In May 1836 he undertook a European tour with his daughter and niece, visiting Great Britain, France, Holland, Belgium, Switzerland, and Italy, being away over a year. On his return in 1837 he definitely retired from court work, confining himself to giving opinions, particularly with regard to land titles, in reference to which he was, and still is, regarded as almost infallible. He was vehemently opposed to the amendment proposed in the Pennsylvania consitutional convention of 1837–38 making the tenure of judges for a term of years only instead of during good behavior, and he published an eloquent address to the people appealing to them to vote against it, but in vain.

In 1844 he emerged from his semi-retirement and appeared in the Supreme Court of the United States at the imperative call of the City of Philadelphia in connection with the case of Vidal *et al. vs.* Philadelphia *et al.* (2 *Howard,* 127), involving the validity of a bequest by Stephen Girard of large properties to the city upon trust to establish a college for poor white male orphans. Relatives of the deceased claimed, *inter alia,* that the City could not hold a trust and that the objects were too vague. The question was of momentous importance to the City inasmuch as it had large commitments, having sold part of the property and undertaken the erection of expensive buildings in connection with the gift. An appeal had been taken by Girard's heirs from a decision of the United States circuit court in favor of the trust, and after the argument in the Supreme Court a re-argument had been directed, for which purpose the appellants had retained Daniel Webster. Binney's argument, remarkable for its erudition and power, was perhaps the most brilliant that has ever been addressed to the Supreme Court, and carried the day. This was his last appearance in court and undeniably his greatest triumph. That same year the anti-Catholic riots occurred in Philadelphia—the worst disturbances ever experienced by that city—and the civic authorities through incompetence or timidity failing to rise to the occasion, Binney stepped in and by his bold advice and resolute action restored order and confidence. In 1846 he evidenced his indifference to public opinion and the complete detachment with which he could scrutinize a legal problem, when he advised the City of Philadelphia that it could not legally subscribe for shares in the Pennsylvania Railroad Company. In 1850 he began to experience trouble with his eyes, and decided to withdraw completely from practise. His temperament, however, was such that he could not remain unemployed. Earlier in his career he had, by his *Eulogium upon . . . William Tilghman, C. J. of Pennsylvania* (1827) and *Eulogy on the Life and Character of John Marshall* (1835), shown the possession of literary ability of high quality. He now turned to his pen again. His first publication was *The Alienigenæ of the U. S. under the Present Naturalization Laws* (1853), addressed to the question of citizenship of children born outside the United States. This was followed by an obituary, *Horace Binney Wallace* (1853); *Bushrod Washington* (1858); *The Leaders of the Old Bar of Philadelphia* (1859); and *An Enquiry into the Formation of Washington's Farewell Address* (1859). The outbreak of the Civil War found him ranged with the administration, though he did not approve all its acts. It however gave occasion for the first of his series of

"Habeas Corpus Pamphlets," *The Privileges of the Writ of Habeas Corpus under the Constitution* (1862), wherein he upheld the legality of the President's action in suspending the writ. Two subsequent pamphlets elaborate his argument, and the three together compose a very valuable constitutional treatise.

As a lawyer preëminent, he was for nearly thirty years the acknowledged leader of the Pennsylvania bar, and it is doubtful whether there was during that time his superior in the country. His devotion to principle, his sincerity, and his fearlessness in the discharge of what he conceived to be his duty, combined to give him a prestige and influence in Philadelphia which during the latter part of his life were unique. A convinced Federalist as long as that party was in existence, he later refrained from any party affiliations. He was married to Elizabeth, youngest daughter of Col. John Cox of Bloomsbury Court, Trenton, N. J., and he died at Philadelphia Aug. 12, 1875.

[His ancestry is traced in *Geneal. of the Binney Family in the U. S.*, by C. J. F. Binney (1886). The standard authority for particulars of his life and career is *The Life of Horace Binney, with Selections from his Letters* (1903) by his son, Chas. Chauncey Binney. See also, *In Memoriam H. Binney,* extract from minutes of Philadelphia contributorship for Insurance of Houses (1875); "A Discourse illustrative of the Life and Character of Horace Binney" by Wm. Strong, in *Proc. Am. Phil. Soc.*, XVI, 1–51; *Memorial Biogs. of the New Eng. Historic Geneal. Soc.*, VII, 163; *A Sketch of Horace Binney* (1907), by Hampton L. Carson.]

H. W. H. K.

BINNS, JOHN (Dec. 22, 1772–June 16, 1860), journalist, politician, author, was born in Dublin, Ireland. His father, John Binns, a prosperous hardware dealer, died in 1774. Mary (Pemberton) Binns, his mother, remarrying within a short time, did not provide her three children with the decencies justified by their inheritance, but she was lavish of her counsel regarding morality and social deportment. This regimen, together with a little schooling and much indiscriminate reading, constituted John's education. By 1794 he was in London, associated with William Godwin and other agitators. He joined and became president of the London Corresponding Society, the avowed object of which was the reform of Parliament on a basis of universal suffrage, but the suspected object of which was the establishment of a British republic. Identified by the officials with political principles then dominant in France, Binns was imprisoned several times before 1801, when there was a general release of political prisoners in England. He then emigrated to America, arriving in September 1801, and proceeding directly to Northumberland, Pa., at that time "capital" of the projected community of free spirits—Coleridge and Southey among them—who talked of coming hither from Europe. Joseph Priestley and Thomas Cooper were already on the ground, but their thought was not so advanced as to prevent Binns, soon after his arrival, from engaging in a duel, or from marrying Mary Anne Boyster, with whom he joined the Church of the United Brethren, and by whom, in time, he had ten children. So much advanced thought did not prevent, either, his pride in certain physical characteristics—animation and grace, a fine person, a pleasing voice, all as nicely disciplined as one could wish. On July 4, 1802, Binns addressed his community on the glory of America, a subject which he further expatiated upon, from a Republican view-point, in a letter to the Federalist *Northumberland Gazette.* From 1802 to 1807, after a method considered perhaps too direct and personal even for those direct, personal times, he published the *Northumberland Republican Argus.* He suspended this activity and changed his residence in order to establish in Philadelphia the *Democratic Press,* a paper published from 1807 till 1829, always direct and personal, always one of the leading organs of its party in the state, but, at the outset, because of its name, *Democratic,* held even by its friends to be almost too daringly radical. Governed largely by his belief that Andrew Jackson was a "tyrant," Binns opposed his election to the presidency in 1828, and in spite of his Irishman's consistent antipathy for England, found himself supporting John Quincy Adams. As part of his campaign against Jackson he published and distributed everywhere pictures of eight imaginary coffins bearing inscriptions relative to the martyrdom of their all too real inmates, soldiers, who, retiring from service at the expiration of their enlistment, though before the military emergency was past, had been, at Jackson's command, executed. This shift of allegiance brought disaster to Binns. His home was attacked by a mob, and financial difficulties necessitated the discontinuance of his paper. In 1819 he published an elaborate engraving of the Declaration of Independence, "far surpassing anything that the pencil and the burin have hitherto accomplished in this country" (*Port Folio,* January 1819). The attendant circumstances included angry charges and counter-charges that involved plagiarism of the idea, at least, of making such an engraving, and charges also to the effect (not new to him) that Binns, being no native American, was unworthy of popular confidence. It is likely that the noise did not trouble him, for by now he doubtless thought controversy quite normal. He was an alderman of Philadelphia from 1822 till 1844, and he was for many years a ready orator for all occasions. It was said that no one could comprehend the phrase "Irish eloquence" without having heard him. He boasted that never till he was almost sixty did he write out a speech in advance—till then the inspiration of the moment had always been enough. In 1840 he published *Binns's Justice*, a manual of Pennsylvania law. The book passed through as many as six editions before his death. The last edition, the eleventh, was published in 1912. *Recollections of the Life of John Binns Written by Himself* was published in 1854. It is the discursive chatter of a forgotten old man.

[The chief sources of this article in addition to those already mentioned are J. Binns, *Monumental Inscriptions* (1828), *Oration* (1810); B. O. Tyler, *Declaration of Independence* (1818); D. P. Brown, *First Speech* (1818). Notices appear also in H. C. Bell (ed.), *Hist. of Northumberland County, Pa.* (1891); J. T. Scharf and T. Westcott, *Hist. of Phila.* (1884); E. P. Oberholtzer, *Phila.; a Hist. of the City and Its People* (n. d.).]

J. D. W.

BINNS, JOHN ALEXANDER (*c.* 1761–1813), Virginia farmer, was born in Loudoun County, Va., probably in the year 1761, the son of Charles and Ann (Alexander) Binns. His father was evidently a man of means, for in 1782 he presented his son with a farm of 220 acres upon which to begin his career. Agriculture at that time in Virginia and Maryland labored under serious difficulties. The separation from England had closed valuable markets, and "soil exhaustion" (the fruit of long-continued tobacco planting and poor methods) threatened to force the abandonment of large portions of the older sections. If agriculture was to be maintained and disaster avoided, fundamental changes were necessary. To this task young Binns set himself. His first step toward improvement, he tells us, was taken in 1784 when he purchased a small quantity of gypsum from a ship captain at Alexandria and applied it as a fertilizer to his crops. It was not the first time in America that this had been done, but it was the first trial by a common farmer and the first to give wide practical results. Enlarged yields encouraged further trials and in the years that followed Binns experimented with gypsum on clover, grass, and grains (sometimes applied to the soil, sometimes to the seed before planting, and sometimes to the growing plant) recording his findings with such care and detail as to warrant their acceptance even today, "as legitimate fertilizer experiments" (Rodney H. True, "John Binns of Loudoun," *William and Mary College Quarterly*, January 1922, pp. 20–39). The results which Binns obtained were startling. His timothy and corn crops doubled, his oats yielded twice as much as his neighbor's, and fields once as barren "as the main roads" were by 1803 producing forty bushels of corn to the acre. In the course of time, doubters were convinced and before long the granaries of the county were glutted and threshing was being delayed because of heavy yields of grain. Soon "meadows [once] infested with sedge and broom grass," were "well-set with white and red clover" and "old fields" had become fruitful again. All this just at the time when the Napoleonic Wars were opening markets for grain in Europe and in the West Indies (A. O. Craven, "Soil Exhaustion as a Factor in the Agricultural History of Virginia and Maryland, 1606–1860," being vol. XIII, no. 1 of *University of Illinois Studies in the Social Sciences*, 1926). In 1803 Binns incorporated his ideas on agricultural improvement through gypsum, clover, deep plowing, etc., in a pamphlet called *A Treatise on Practical Farming*. In this way the "Loudoun System" became widely known and practised in Virginia and Maryland. Thomas Jefferson sent copies to his English friends, Sir John Sinclair and William Strickland, recommending them as the means whereby lands once "exhausted and wasted" had become the most productive in the state. As Jefferson said, "These facts speak more strongly . . . than . . . polished phrases."

[The chief source of information about John Binns is his own pamphlet, *A Treatise on Practical Farming*, a copy of which is in the Jefferson Collection, Lib. of Cong. Mention is made of his work in letters in the Jefferson Papers, Lib. of Cong. The exact date of his death is uncertain, but his will, dated Jan. 11, 1813, was offered for probate in November of the same year.]

A. O. C.

BIRCH, THOMAS (July 26, 1779–Jan. 14, 1851), pioneer landscape and marine painter, was the son of William Russell Birch [*q.v.*], miniaturist and engraver. English by birth, he had his professional training at and near Philadelphia. William Dunlap states that young Birch "from infancy (to use his own expression) 'could sketch a little,'" and intimates that the youth preferred, to his father's discipline, "the instruction of nature, and studied on the banks of the Schuylkill." His companions on sketching tours were John Wesley Jarvis, afterward a distinguished portrait painter, and Samuel Seymour, who became an engraver and who served as draftsman with Capt. Long's expedition to the Yellowstone River. Birch was married on June 1, 1802, to Ann Goodwin. He was presumably responsible for many of the views of country seats published by W. Birch & Son. His portrayals of architecture are praised by Anne Hollingsworth Wharton (*Heirlooms in Miniature*, 1898, I, 143); she writes: "To him [Thomas Birch] the present generation is indebted for the many paintings in water color which he made of old country seats and historic buildings in the middle and southern colonies, and especially in and around Philadelphia." Birch likewise painted snow scenes, and in 1807 he visited the Capes of Delaware and began to do marine views. He was an exhibitor, in 1811, at the first annual exhibition of the Society of Artists, held at the Pennsylvania Academy of Fine Arts (Helen W. Henderson, *The Pennsylvania Academy of Fine Arts,* 1911).

The War of 1812 turned Birch's attention to the artistic possibilities of the sea fight. "His first regular essays in this department," says Dunlap, "were made at the commencement of the late war between his adopted and his native country. England was known as his country, but he felt as an American. The desperate fights which could lower the flag and the pride of the boasted mistress of the ocean were his chosen subjects." Birch's first picture in this genre was his "Engagement of the Constitution and the Guerrière," made for James Webster, a Philadelphia publisher. It is now at the Naval Academy, Annapolis. Subsequently Nicholas Biddle, afterward president of the United States Bank, commissioned Birch to do "The Wasp and the Frolic." Then came "The United States and the Macedonian," portrayals of Perry's victory on Lake Erie and McDonough's on Lake Champlain, and a succession of similar subjects which, as Dunlap wrote, "furnished employment to his pencil in the path he had chosen, and in which he stands unrivaled in our country." Some of the best of the historical pictures of the *Naval Monument* (Boston, 1816), to which Michele Felice Corné was a principal contributor, were after designs by Thomas Birch. He also designed several coins for the United States Mint (*American Art News,* Feb. 22, 1808).

[Wm. Dunlap, *Hist. of the Rise and Progress of the Arts of Design in the U. S.,* with supplementary footnote by the editors, Frank W. Bayley and Chas. E. Goodspeed (1918 ed.); Clara Erskine Clement and Lawrence Hutton, *Artists of the Nineteenth Century and their Works* (1879). Birch's portrait by John Neagle was reproduced in the *International Studio,* Oct. 1924.]

F. W. C.

BIRCH, WILLIAM RUSSELL (Apr. 9, 1755–Aug. 7, 1834), painter and engraver, was born in Warwickshire and professionally educated at Bristol and London. He showed in 1775 (Thieme and Becker, *Allgemeines Lexicon der Bildenden Künstler,* 1910, IV) two miniatures, "Head of Psyche" and "Jupiter and Io" at the Society of Artists. In 1781 he exhibited an enamel miniature, "Mother and Child," at the Royal Academy (according to Samuel Redgrave, *Artists of the English School,* 1874) and in 1782 he was represented at the Academy by a "Portrait of a Child Going to Bed." J. J. Foster (*Dictionary of Painters of Miniatures,* 1926) writes admiringly of Birch's enamel portrait of the first Earl of Mansfield, after Sir Joshua Reynolds, now in the Bentinck-Hawkins collection in the Ashmolean, Oxford. The *Dictionary of National Biography* notes that in 1785 Birch was awarded a medal of the Society of Arts for excellence in his art and improvements in its processes. His one work published in England was the *Délices de la Grande Bretagne* (1789), a portfolio depicting ancient buildings and scenery (copy in the Boston Public Library). Its stippled plates are beautifully rendered, with good feeling for romantic and dramatic effects. In 1794 he came to America bringing with him his seven-year-old son Thomas Birch [*q.v.*]. He engraved a series of twenty-eight *Views of Philadelphia* (1798–1800), and a smaller series, published in 1808, of plates depicting American country seats. He also designed a famous New York City view (1803) with white horse in the foreground (described by Frank Weitenkampf in *Print Connoisseur,* January 1924). Some of his prints are inscribed as "drawn, engraved and published by W. Birch, Springland, near Bristol, Pennsylvania"; others as "drawn and engraved by W. Birch & Son, Philadelphia." His miniatures on enamel, of which he made at least sixty in America, gave him his chief reputation. Justly celebrated is his miniature portrait of George Washington, which was among the historic relics inherited and collected by William Lanier Washington and dispersed after exhibition at the Anderson Galleries, New York, in 1917. Of this work Elizabeth Bryant Johnson, author of *Original Portraits of Washington,* is quoted in the exhibition catalogue as writing: "It is said in outline to be precisely like the first Stuart, though the unpleasant impression arising from the false teeth is happily avoided." This miniature, according to W. S. Baker (*Engraved Portraits of Washington,* 1880), was painted in 1796 from life by request of Mr. Van Staphorst of Holland, a friend of American independence. Birch's contemporary, William Dunlap, wrote of it, "I remember seeing a miniature of Washington, executed by him in enamel; which I thought very beautiful, and very like Trott's copy from Stuart's original picture. My impression is that it was copied from Trott. Birch could design." This brief estimate of Birch's ability coincides with twentieth-century opinion.

[Wm. Dunlap, *Hist. of the Rise and Progress of the Arts of Design in the U. S.* with supplementary note by the editors, Frank W. Bayley and Chas. E. Goodspeed (1918 ed.); J. J. Foster, *Miniature Painters, British and Foreign* (1903); Anne Hollingsworth Wharton, *Heirlooms in Miniature* (1898), which mentions an unpublished autobiographical sketch. A technical description of several of Birch's American plates is printed in *A Descriptive Catalogue of an Exhibition of Early Engraving in America,* Dec. 12, 1904–Feb. 5, 1905, Museum of Fine Arts, Boston.] F.W.C.

BIRD, ARTHUR (July 23, 1856–Dec. 22, 1923), composer, belongs to that small but interesting group of American musicians who, for one reason or another, have elected to spend their mature life abroad rather than at home in America; so that, while in Europe they have been looked upon as Americans, in America they have been almost regarded as Europeans. In fact, Bird's works have been so uniformly published and performed abroad that to most Americans he is practically unknown. He was born at Cambridge, Mass., the son of Horace and Elizabeth (Homer) Bird; and even as a child showed great interest in music, being unusually gifted in improvisation. When nineteen years old he went to Europe and spent two years under Haupt, Loeschhorn, and Rohde in the study of theory and piano. In 1877 he returned to America and took up his residence in Halifax, Nova Scotia, where he served as organist and choirmaster in the Kirk and as head teacher of piano in the Young Ladies' Academy and the Mount St. Vincent Academy of that city. Here he remained until 1881, when he again repaired to Berlin for further study, this time with Heinrich Urban in composition and orchestration. He also spent a year or so in close social and musical contact with Liszt during the memorable last years at Weimar, where Liszt paid the young American composer the honor of having many of his compositions performed. In 1886 Bird gave his first Berlin concert with excellent success, the Berlin papers giving him high praise. Even more successful, however, was a later concert at Sondershausen, where the Allgemeine Deutsche Musik Verein, under the personal auspices of Liszt, played his "Carnival Scene" for full orchestra. Also in 1886 at the invitation of the committee of the North American Sängerbund in Milwaukee, Bird visited America and officiated as director of the Milwaukee Musical Festival of that year. Returning to Germany from this visit he spent the entire remainder of his life in and about Berlin, taking an interested part in all its musical activities. On Feb. 29, 1888, he married Wilhelmine Waldmann at Peterboro, England. He was a prolific composer in almost all forms, from symphony and opera down. Not least in importance among his numerous interests was his valuable service as Berlin correspondent for the *Musical Leader,* Chicago, and as writer on various musical topics for the *Etude, Musician,* and other musical magazines. In 1901, with his serenade for wind instruments, *opus 40,* he achieved the Paderewski prize, founded by the famous Polish pianist to encourage American musical composition. This serenade was first performed in America by the Longy Club, Mar. 31, 1902; later, in Berlin, Feb. 6, 1908. On the latter occasion the musical critic of the *Berliner Börsen Courier* wrote of it as "distinguished for the freshness and spontaneity of its invention, as well as the clever craftsmanship and the clear and compact disposition of its different parts." This might very well be taken as a summing up of Bird's style in general. Arthur Farwell (*Art of Music,* IV, 402) wrote, "Bird is a musician of German training and French sympathies and calls himself a 'conditional modernist.'" It is quite evident both from Bird's writings and from his compositions that these conditions loomed large. In fact, his work is characterized rather by a certain attractive and facile lyricism than by any great depth, and he seems to have been but slightly influenced by the modern trends of musical composition. A strange development of the last years of his compositional activity was a frequent writing for the harmonium.

Of Bird's numerous compositions the following are perhaps best known: for orchestra, "Symphony in A," *opus 8* (1886); "Carnival Scene," *opus 5* (1887); for piano, two hands, three "Waltzes," *opus 12* (1886); "Eight Sketches," *opus 15* (1887); "Puppentänze," four pieces, *opus 19* (1887); and two early suites, *opus 4* and *opus 6;* for piano, four hands, three characteristic "Marches," *opus 11* (1886); ballet music, *opus 13* (1886); introduction and fugue, *opus 16;* "Zwei Poesien," *opus 25;* two pieces for violin and piano, *opus 9;* numerous songs, of which perhaps the five songs, *opus 36* (1896), are the best; for organ, three "Oriental Sketches" (1903) and a "Concert Fantasia" (1905); a ballet, "Rübezahl"; the comic opera, *Daphne,* produced at one of Mr. Bagby's *Musicales* at the Hotel Waldorf-Astoria, New York, in 1897; and numerous compositions for the harmonium.

[*Musical Courier,* Dec. 7, 1898; *Musical America,* Feb. 9, 1924; *Musical Leader,* Mar. 2, 1922, Jan. 31, 1924.] W.T.U.

BIRD, FREDERIC MAYER (June 28, 1838–Apr. 2, 1908), Lutheran and Episcopal clergyman, hymnologist, editor, was born in Philadelphia, the son of Robert Montgomery Bird [*q.v.*] and of Mary Mayer, whose father, Philip Mayer, was for fifty-two years pastor of St. John's Lutheran Church on Race St. Probably the influence of the grandfather accounts for the fact that after graduating from the University of Pennsylvania in 1857 Bird entered Hartwick Lutheran Theological Seminary at Hartwick, N. Y., but, as the scanty records of his life show, he had little genius for remaining long in one place. After one year at Hartwick 1858–59 he transferred to Union Theological Seminary in New York, graduated in 1860, was ordained to the Lutheran ministry Sept. 3, 1861, was pastor at Rhinebeck, N. Y., 1860–62, was chaplain in the United States Army 1862–63, was pastor at West Philadelphia 1865–66 and at Valatie, N. Y., 1866–68, was ordained a deacon of the Episcopal Church Oct. 25, 1868, and priest June 18, 1869, was rector at Spotswood, N. J., 1870–74, and in Indianapolis 1874, was temporary supply at Hightstown, N. J., 1875–76, was rector at Iowa City, Ia., 1877–78, and at Waterloo, Ia., 1879–81, and was chaplain and professor of psychology, Christian evidences, and rhetoric in Lehigh University 1881–86. In 1877 he married Frances Snowhill of Spotswood, N. J. He published *Charles Wesley Seen in His Finer and Less Familiar Poems* in 1867, with Beale Melancthon Schmucker [*q.v.*] did most of the work on *Hymns for the Use of the Evangelical Lutheran Church* (1865), which has had a wide and wholesome influence on American Lutheran hymnody, collaborated with Bishop Odenheimer on *Hymns of the Spirit* (1871) and contributed hymnological articles to the *Schaff-Herzog Encyclopedia,* to Jackson's *Concise Dictionary of Religious Knowledge,* and to Julian's *Dictionary of Hymnology.* His hymnological library included about 3,000 volumes and was said to be the largest in the United States; it was presented by Henry Day, Esq., to Union Theological Seminary in 1888. He also did much miscellaneous work for various encyclopedias, was interested in numismatics and philately, published two novels, *A Pessimist in Theory and Practice* (1888) and *An Alien from the Commonwealth* (1889)—the latter an agreeable study in local color—under the name of "Robert Timsol," was editor of *Lippincott's Magazine* 1893–98 and wrote for it various articles, including some breezy disquisitions on the art of fiction, and in 1893 brought out *The Story of Our Christianity.* During his latter years he made his home in South Bethlehem, Pa., where he died.

[*Who's Who in America,* 1908–09; *Union Theol. Sem. Gen. Cat. 1836–1918* (1919); *Gen. Alumni Cat. of the Univ. of Pa.* (1917); C. E. Foust, *Life and Dramatic Works of R. M. Bird* (1919).]

G. H. G.

BIRD, ROBERT MONTGOMERY (Feb. 5, 1806–Jan. 23, 1854), playwright, novelist, editor, physician, was descended on his father's side from Thomas Bird, an Englishman who settled in New Castle County, Del., about 1700, while his mother, Elizabeth von Leuvenigh, came from early Dutch settlers of the same period. He represented a stock which had been for a century substantial citizens and cultivated people. His father, John Bird, was a member of the state Senate and filled other public offices until his sudden death in 1810 left his family in straitened circumstances. Montgomery Bird, as he was called by his family, had been born in New Castle. After his father's death he was brought up by his uncle, Hon. Nicholas van Dyke, who had been president of the State of Delaware, and was one of its leading citizens. Bird's early schooling, either at Newcastle or Philadelphia, made little impression upon him, but his reading was wide, especially in romance. Fortunately, he came under the influence of an inspiring teacher, Walter Johnson, at Germantown Academy in Philadelphia, and here he prepared for entrance to the Medical School of the University of Pennsylvania in 1824. In April 1827 he took the degree of M.D., having studied with such men as Robert Hare, Philip Syng Physick, and John Redman Coxe. But his study of medicine was due rather to the belief of his family that he should enter a profession, than to any real ability as a physician. He practised medicine for about a year, in Philadelphia, but as he disliked taking fees, his career was brief. His interest in science remained keen, however, and when the Pennsylvania Medical College was established in 1841, Bird became professor of the institutes of medicine and materia medica. His notebooks, filled with references to his reading in chemistry, botany, and agriculture, as well as in history and literature, ancient and modern, reveal him as one who responded instinctively to intellectual stimulation. His comments show, too, that he studied creatively, and his knowledge of Latin, Greek, Spanish, French, and Italian was active and not merely a polite accomplishment.

With an unusual equipment, and a desire to create, Bird entered upon a career as a writer with two handicaps. He had the artist's disregard of financial returns, and he faced the conditions which at that time in America made the lot of an author who depended exclusively upon his writing almost hopeless. His first manuscript of any length, *'Twas All for the Best,* is dated May 1827, but fortunately he turned from this imitation of British comedy to romance, in which his forte lay. *The Cowled Lover* and *Caridorf,* romantic tragedies, and *The City Looking Glass* and *News of the Night,* comedies of life in Philadelphia, remain in manuscript. The first two reveal an imaginative power and *The City*

Looking Glass is an early example of the play of low life. But his first drama of significance was *Pelopidas,* a tragedy based upon the revolt of Thebes against her Spartan oppressors. Though not written for Edwin Forrest, it was purchased by him, with a promise of the payment of one thousand dollars. Forrest's comments upon the manuscript show why he never produced it. While the character of Pelopidas is well drawn, it is really surpassed in interest by that of others, notably Philidas, the Theban patriot who plays the dangerous game of the apparent traitor, and Sibylla, the wife of Pelopidas. So, probably by mutual agreement, Bird substituted *The Gladiator* for *Pelopidas.* In the character of Spartacus, the Thracian captive of Rome, forced into the arena as the price of reunion with his wife and child, Bird provided a part exactly suited to Forrest. It proved to be one of the most vital creations of the stage. The motives of self-preservation, of family love, and of personal honor are made concrete in one heroic character, which Forrest acted as long as he lived and which held the stage in other hands as late as 1893. *The Gladiator* was first performed Sept. 26, 1831, at the Park Theatre, New York, and scored an instant success. Contemporary criticism records the effect upon the audience in Philadelphia who "rose and cheered in their seats" (Durang). The British actor, Wemyss, states that "The effect at the closing of the second act, I do not believe was ever surpassed in any theatre in the world." Forrest chose *The Gladiator* for his opening bill when he played at Drury Lane, Oct. 17, 1836. Notwithstanding the severe test, for Forrest was playing the work of a young man in a repertoire composed almost exclusively of Shakespeare, Bird's merit was generally recognized, and he was elected an honorary member of the English Dramatic Authors' Society. *The Gladiator* brought him another distinction, for when in 1853 it was played for the thousandth time, it was the first play written in English to be given so often during the lifetime of the author.

Encouraged by the success of *The Gladiator,* Bird wrote the tragedy of *Oralloossa,* laid at the time of the assassination of Pizarro and the revolt of Diego de Almagro. He created the character of Oralloossa, the heir of the Incas, for Forrest, who produced the play at the Arch Street Theatre, Philadelphia, Oct. 10, 1832. While it has its fine moments, it has not the force of *The Gladiator,* and Forrest withdrew it from his repertoire after the second season. Bird was intensely interested in Mexico and South America, and in 1833 he and Forrest started for a tour of those countries. Owing to a cholera epidemic, their expedition only reached New Orleans, but it gave Bird an opportunity to see many of the Southern cities, and to explore the Mammoth Cave of Kentucky. His best play, *The Broker of Bogota,* was produced by Forrest at the Bowery Theatre, New York, Feb. 12, 1834. It is a domestic tragedy, laid in Santa Fé de Bogota, in South America, in the eighteenth century. The character of Febro, the money-lender, whose heart is broken by the treachery of his oldest and best-loved son, is the product of even a finer art than that which created Spartacus. Febro is all the more heroic because he struggles and suffers without losing his middle-class character and meets the blows of fate with dignity. *The Broker of Bogota* was a stage success and was played by Forrest until the last years of his career. Among the Bird manuscripts, a letter from Forrest, written on the night of its first performance, prophesies that "it will live when our vile trunks are rotten." The last work Bird did for Forrest was the revision of *Metamora,* John A. Stone's Indian play. Then came a break between the friends, due to Forrest's refusal to keep his financial agreements, made orally to Bird, who trusted him without any written contract. Bird had sold *The Gladiator* to Forrest for one thousand dollars, with the understanding that two thousand more was to be paid if the play was successful, and he also believed that the same agreement held good for the later plays. He received, however, only one thousand dollars each for *The Gladiator, Oralloossa* and *The Broker of Bogota,* and nothing for *Metamora* or *Pelopidas,* while from *The Gladiator* alone, Forrest made a fortune.

Discouraged by these circumstances, Bird turned to novel writing. In 1834 he published *Calavar; or The Knight of the Conquest,* a romance of the expedition of Cortez in 1520, following this in 1835 with *The Infidel; or The Fall of Mexico,* which deals with events a year later. These novels are based on wide reading and have the virtues and faults of the romantic school. Before *Calavar* appeared, Bird paid a visit to England, where he found his hopes of securing any return for his work futile. In 1835 appeared *The Hawks of Hawk Hollow,* a novel laid in and near the Water Gap of Pennsylvania, toward the close of the Revolution. Bird's picture of the decaying fortunes of a once prominent family, and his establishment of a sense of impending doom hanging over a race that has proved disloyal to its native country, make it one of the best of his novels. It was not, however, the most popular. After an anonymous story, *Sheppard Lee* (1836), a curious study of metempsychosis, he wrote *Nick of the Woods, or The Jibbenainosay, A Tale of*

Kentucky (1837), which had a pronounced success, was reprinted at least ten times in London by 1900, and four times in Germany. In the character of "Bloody Nathan," the Quaker who takes his revenge upon the Indians for the murder of his family, he created a striking figure, and his picture of the Indians, drawn without the idealization of Cooper, but rather as cruel, savage, and treacherous, was based, at least, upon personal observation. *Peter Pilgrim; or a Rambler's Recollections* (1838) is a collection of sketches, including a realistic picture of a Mississippi River steamboat, and a detailed description of the Mammoth Cave. *The Adventures of Robin Day* (1839) is a picaresque novel, laid in Philadelphia, in the Southwest, in Florida, and upon the sea.

The intensity of Bird's mental labors, spurred on by necessity and inadequate recompense, led to a breakdown in health and his retirement to a farm on the Eastern Shore of Maryland in 1840, where his health was for a time restored. In 1841–42–43, he delivered courses in materia medica at the Pennsylvania Medical College, and, on account of his friendship for John M. Clayton, he became active in politics, declining proposals to be himself a candidate for office, but acting as Clayton's representative in the Whig convention at Baltimore in 1844. At Clayton's suggestion he purchased in 1847 a share in the Philadelphia *North American,* and became literary editor. After the retirement of George R. Graham in 1848 the paper continued to be published by the firm of McMichael and Bird, but the incessant labors attending the production of a daily newspaper, upon which he did more than his share, again undermined Bird's health. Anxiety, too, as to the conduct of the paper, in which his authority was not equal to his responsibility, brought on what was then called "suffusion of the brain." He died in Philadelphia and was buried in Laurel Hill Cemetery. He had married in 1837 Mary Mayer, daughter of Rev. Philip F. Mayer, rector of St. John's Lutheran Church, Philadelphia. He had one son, Rev. Frederic Mayer Bird [*q.v.*], who was editor of *Lippincott's Magazine,* 1893–98, and who completed and published in that journal in 1889 his father's unfinished manuscript of "Ipsico Poe," under the title of "A Belated Revenge."

Robert Montgomery Bird was tall, fair, and of a commanding presence. In his journals, his correspondence, his editorials, he reveals the most uncompromising integrity, and an almost quixotic sense of right. Driven by unfortunate conditions from dramatic authorship at the height of his success, his plays were kept from publication by the selfishness of Forrest, who, even as late as 1869, refused Frederic Bird permission to print them. Forrest's refusal was all the more churlish since an examination of the copyright records in 1916 failed to reveal any copyright taken out by him. The fact that Bird's plays remained unpublished until 1917 (see Bibliography) has prevented his sterling work from receiving its proper place in our literary history.

[The MSS. of the plays, poems, and biographical material were presented by Robert Montgomery Bird, grandson of the playwright, to the Lib. of the Univ. of Pa. Among these is a manuscript life of Bird, by his wife, which is the main source for his biography. In 1917, the present writer published for the first time *The Broker of Bogota,* in his *Representative Am. Plays,* and in 1919 Dr. Clement E. Foust issued his *Life and Dramatic Works of Robert Montgomery Bird,* which contains *Pelopidas, The Gladiator, The Broker of Bogota,* and *Oralloossa.* For discussion of the plays, see Jas. Rees, *The Dramatic Authors of America* (1845); F. C. Wemyss, *Twenty-six Years of the Life of an Actor and Manager* (1847); W. R. Alger, *The Life of Edwin Forrest* (1877), vol. I; A. H. Quinn, *A Hist. of the Am. Drama from the Beginning to the Civil War* (1923), ch. XI. For general bibliography, see Dr. Foust's *Life* and *The Cambridge Hist. of Am. Lit.* (1917), I, 493–94, 525–26.]

A. H. Q.

BIRD WOMAN. [See SACAGAWEA, *c.* 1787–1812.]

BIRGE, HENRY WARNER (Aug. 25, 1825–June 1, 1888), Union soldier, was born at Hartford, Conn., where the Birge family had been established as early as 1640. At the outbreak of the Civil War he was a merchant in Norwich, Conn. Appointed major of the 4th Connecticut Infantry, May 23, 1861, he served with it in Maryland, without contact with the enemy, until Nov. 13, 1861, when he resigned in order to take command of a new regiment being organized in his state. On Feb. 18, 1862, he reëntered the service as colonel of the 13th Connecticut. The regiment was at once assigned to the expedition which was being organized to take New Orleans, arrived at Ship Island on Apr. 13, and entered the city when it was occupied by Gen. Butler a few days later. For the next few months it was engaged in minor operations in Louisiana. Upon the reorganization of Gen. Banks's command (19th Army Corps), in preparation for the Port Hudson campaign, Birge was assigned to the command of the 3rd Brigade, 4th Division, to which his own regiment belonged. The investment of Port Hudson was completed on May 26, 1863. An assault the next day being repulsed with heavy loss, regular siege operations were begun. A second assault on June 14 also failing disastrously, the besieging army suffering terribly with sickness and heat, and a Confederate army threatening New Orleans in the rear, it became evident that the city must be taken quickly if at all. The siege works were pressed vigorously forward, and meanwhile an "élite storming party" was organized, in order to penetrate the defense at all costs. Birge was selected to command. The party was made up of carefully chosen volunteers, mostly from the 13th Connecticut, organized into two battalions of eight companies each, and daily trained for its undertaking. On June 28, Birge reported 67 officers and 826 enlisted men present for duty. On July 7, all preparations were made for springing two mines, to precede the assault, when word was received of the surrender of Vicksburg, which put an end to the garrison's hopes of holding out at Port Hudson. Articles of capitulation were signed on July 8, Birge being one of the commissioners on behalf of Gen. Banks. He was appointed brigadier-general of volunteers on Sept. 19, 1863. He commanded a brigade, and at times a division, in the Red River campaign in the spring of 1864. Gen. Banks, in his report of the campaign, wrote that "Gen. Birge, as in all actions in which he has been engaged, deserved and received the highest commendation." Soon after, a part of the 19th Army Corps, including his brigade, was moved to Virginia, arriving on the James River late in July. Immediately afterward, it was moved to Savannah. There it remained in garrison until March, when it became a division of the 10th Army Corps, with Birge as its commander, and joined Schofield's army in North Carolina. On the surrender of the Confederate forces, Birge was assigned to the command of the district of Savannah. He resigned on Oct. 18, 1865, and returned to civil life. After the war he engaged in cotton planting and in the lumber business in Georgia, and later engaged in various enterprises in Texas and the West. His last years were spent in New York City, where he died.

[F. B. Heitman, *Hist. Reg.* (1903), I, 219; *Official Records,* ser. 1, vols. XV, XXVI (pt. 1), XXXIV (pts. 1, 3, 4), XL (pts. 1, 3), XLIII (pt. 1), XLVII (pt. 3); Homer B. Sprague, *Hist. of the 13th Infantry Regiment of Conn. Volunteers* (1867); Richard B. Irwin, *Hist. of the Nineteenth Army Corps* (1892); *N. Y. Times, N. Y. Tribune, Hartford Courant,* June 2, 1888.]

T. M. S.

BIRKBECK, MORRIS (Jan. 23, 1764–June 4, 1825), Illinois pioneer, publicist, was born at Settle, England, the son of an influential Quaker, Morris Birkbeck, and of Hannah Bradford. By 1794, as leaseholder, he was farming an estate of 1,500 acres at Wanborough in Surrey, where he was the first man to raise merino sheep in England, and was master of the hamlet. On Apr. 24, 1794, he married Prudence, daughter of Richard and Prudence Bush of Wandsworth, Surrey, who died Oct. 25, 1804, leaving him with seven children. In 1814, accompanied by his friend George Flower [*q.v.*], he traveled in France; his *Notes on a Journey through France* (1814) reveals a good-tempered, fair-minded observer, well grounded in science and the humanities. A liberal in politics and religion, he found it increasingly irksome to be taxed by a government that denied him a vote and tithed by a church whose doctrines he disapproved, and in 1817, with a party consisting chiefly of his children, he emigrated to the United States, where George Flower, who had gone before, now joined him. During 1817–18 Birkbeck either for himself or others entered 26,400 acres of public land in Edwards County, Ill., while Flower was raising more money and colonists in England. Birkbeck's *Notes on a Journey in America from the Coast of Virginia to the Territory of Illinois* (1817) was published in Philadelphia, London, Dublin, and Cork, ran through eleven editions in English in two years, and appeared in German at Jena (1818). His *Letters from Illinois* (1818), published in Boston, Philadelphia, and London, went through seven editions in English besides being translated in 1819 into French and German. In directing settlers to the prairie lands of the west these two books exercised a widespread influence, and incidentally brought down on their author the hearty vituperation of William Cobbett, who was in the pay of eastern land speculators. In 1818 he laid out the town of Wanborough, which has since vanished. That same year he and Flower parted and were never reconciled; the cause of the feud, which did irreparable injury to their colonization scheme, remains conjectural. A little later he became president of the first agricultural society in Illinois and gave a great impetus to the raising of cattle and to the scientific tilling of the soil. In 1823, by cogent articles contributed to newspapers under the name of "Jonathan Freeman," he helped to consolidate the anti-slavery forces in Illinois and to save the state for freedom. In 1824 an old London acquaintance, Edward Coles, now governor of Illinois, appointed him secretary of state; for three months he served with conspicuous ability, and then was turned out by the pro-slavery element in the state Senate, who refused to confirm the appointment. On June 4, 1825, returning from a visit to Robert Owen at Harmony, Ind., he was drowned while swimming his horse across the Fox River. In person he was below middle stature, spare, muscular, and wiry, his face bronzed and lined by exposure to the weather. He was one of the ablest, most cultured, and most public-spirited men on the frontier. His services to his adopted country were ill requited and soon forgotten.

[R. Birkbeck, *The Birkbecks of Westmorland and Their Descendants* (London, privately printed, 1900); G. Flower, *Hist. of the English Settlements in Edwards Co., Ill.* (1882); *The English Settlement in the Illinois: Reprints of Three Rare Tracts on the Illinois Country* (1907), ed. by E. E. Sparks; J. Woods, *Two Years' Residence in the Illinois Country* (1822); W. Faux, *Memorable Days in America 1819–20*, being vol. XI (1905) of *Early Western Travels 1748–1846*, ed. by R. G. Thwaites; S. J. Buck, *Travel and Description 1765–1865*, being vol. IX of *Ill. State Hist. Lib. Colls.; Bibliographical Series*, II, (1914); S. J. Buck, *Illinois in 1818*, being the Introductory Volume (1917) of *Ill. Centennial Publications*; T. C. Pease, *The Frontier State 1818–48*, being vol. II (1918) of the *Centennial Hist. of Illinois*.]

G. H. G.

BIRNEY, DAVID BELL (May 29, 1825–Oct. 18, 1864), Union soldier, was the son of James G. Birney [*q.v.*], who was a native of Kentucky and a graduate of Princeton, but who later moved to Huntsville, Ala., where he became a successful planter as well as one of the leaders of the Alabama bar. Here it was that David Bell Birney was born. In the year 1838 the Birney family moved to Cincinnati—after the father had freed his own slaves and had actively identified himself with the emancipation movement. In 1844 James G. Birney became the national presidential candidate of the Anti-Slavery party. With such family influences, it was natural that the son should take an active part in the war between the states. Young Birney received his education at Andover, and after graduation, went into business, first in Cincinnati and later in Upper Saginaw, Mich., where he studied law and was admitted to the bar. But in the year 1848 he moved to Philadelphia and became a clerk in a mercantile agency, which position he held until 1856, when he engaged in law practise. The year preceding the Civil War found him a successful practitioner with many influential friends. He foresaw the outbreak of war, and late in the year 1860, entered upon an intensive study of military subjects. For some years he had been a member of the historic 1st Troop of Philadelphia City Cavalry, and in February 1860 he secured appointment as lieutenant-colonel of a regiment of Pennsylvania militia. The young civilian was better prepared for a military career than most of the inexperienced field-officers, hastily mustered into the United States service in the spring of 1861. Although it never assembled or paraded, his militia regiment formed the basis of the 23rd Regiment of Pennsylvania Volunteers, upon the President's call for volunteers; and, as such, performed guard duty north of the Susquehanna, and during the summer of 1861 engaged in minor operations along the upper Potomac. Birney received his baptism of fire at Falling Waters, West Va., and later his regiment occupied Winchester. The term of enlistment of the three-months volunteers expiring, a new regiment was formed from the old through consolidation and reënlistments; and within a few days after Aug. 17, 1861, due to his energy and leadership, the regimental commander was able to parade a new 23rd Regiment through the streets of Washington, its soldiers sworn in for three years' service. Then began a long period of drill and training, and such was the favorable impression created by Birney's capacity for command and proper ideas of discipline, that early in 1862 he was appointed a brigadier-general of volunteers. His first assignment was to a brigade of Gen. Kearny's division. As a brigade commander, he participated in the early operations of the Army of the Potomac, including Centreville and Manassas, and later in 1862 engaged with his brigade in the sanguinary battles of the Peninsular campaign—Yorktown, Williamsburg, Fair Oaks, Malvern Hill. At Fair Oaks, he was unjustly charged with having "halted his command a mile from the enemy," and was brought before a court martial. After careful consideration of the evidence, the court, composed in the main of regular officers, honorably acquitted him. Transported back to Alexandria, Va., Birney's brigade was pushed forward to the support of troops engaged in Pope's campaign, and on Aug. 31, 1862, took an active part in the Union victory at Chantilly, Va., where Birney's warm friend and military superior, Gen. Phil Kearny, lost his life. He succeeded Kearny as division commander, and led his division through the battles of the Army of the Potomac, until the middle of July 1864. At Fredericksburg, his division was in support of Meade; and although it was charged that Birney failed to comply with urgent instructions, careful investigation at the time failed to substantiate such charges, and Gen. Stoneman reported that Birney's division "probably saved the entire left wing from disaster." For his able leadership at Chancellorsville, Birney was promoted, May 5, 1863, to be major-general of volunteers. At Gettysburg, he commanded the 3rd Army Corps after Gen. Sickles was wounded, and was struck twice by enemy's bullets, but was only slightly injured (*New York Herald*, July 6, 1863). Thereafter, Birney's division followed Grant through his first campaign against Richmond until July 23, 1864, when Grant selected Birney to command the 10th Army Corps. After these major operations in which for months his system had been weakened by exposure and fatigue, Birney became seriously ill with malarial fever of an especially virulent type; and against his wishes to remain in the field, was ordered home for recuperation. He reached Philadelphia on Oct. 11, 1864, where, after acute suffering, he died on Oct. 18, in the thirty-ninth year of his age. His last words in delirium were, "Boys! Keep your eyes on that flag!" Resolutions of the Philadelphia Board of Trade characterized him as "an honest citizen, a gallant soldier, and a pure, chivalric, self-sacrificing patriot." So great was the esteem in which Birney's life and services were held, that during the fall of 1864 and the spring of 1865 a group of Philadelphia friends raised a trust fund of nearly thirty thousand dollars by popular subscription, which was wisely invested by trustees for the benefit of Birney's widow and six small children.

[Oliver W. Davis, *Life of David Bell Birney* (pub. anonymously, 1867) is the principal source; see also *Official Records, Army and Navy Jour.*, Oct. 22, 29, Nov. 19, 1864, and "Report of the Joint Committee on the Conduct of the War," *Senate Report No. 142*, 38 Cong., 2 Sess. The honorable acquittal of Birney by court martial is in General Order No. 135, Headquarters Army of the Potomac, June 19, 1862 (War Department files).] C.D.R.

BIRNEY, JAMES (June 7, 1817–May 8, 1888), lawyer and diplomatist, the eldest son of James G. Birney [*q.v.*] and brother of David Bell Birney [*q.v.*] and of William Birney [*q.v.*], was born at Danville, Ky. His academic education was obtained at Centre College, Danville, and at Miami University, Oxford, Ohio, from which latter institution he graduated in 1836. In 1837–38 he taught in the Grammar School of Miami University; then he studied law at Yale for two years and began to practise at Cincinnati. He became a trustee of the Saginaw Bay Company, and in 1857 removed to Lower Saginaw (now Bay City), Mich., where he made his home until his death. In 1859 he was elected to the state Senate as a Republican, and successfully opposed the transfer to the state school fund of the proceeds of the sales of swamp lands given to the state by the federal government in aid of the construction of roads. From Jan. 1 to Apr. 3, 1861, he was lieutenant-governor, resigning that office to accept an appointment as judge of the eighteenth judicial circuit to fill a vacancy. Although his standing as a lawyer was high, he appears to have been somewhat wanting in judicial temperament, and at the end of four years, notwithstanding that he had been nominated to succeed himself, he failed of election. In the state constitutional convention of 1867, of which he was a member, he was made chairman of a select committee on procedure, and of a committee which reported the provisions for the executive department. In 1871 he established the Bay City *Chronicle,* changing the paper from a weekly to a daily in 1873. In 1876 he was a commissioner from Michigan to the Centennial Exposition at Philadelphia. Toward the end of that year he was appointed by President Grant minister resident at The Hague, a post which he retained until 1882, when he resigned. At the time of his death he was president of the Bay City board of education. He married, June 1, 1841, Amanda S., daughter of John and Sophia Moulton of New Haven, Conn., and cousin of Commodore Isaac Hull.

[There is a summary sketch of Birney's life in *Mich. Biogs.* (1924), I, 84; and there is a brief account by A. C. Maxwell in the *Mich. Pioneer and Hist. Colls.*, XXII, 227–30 (1893). See also the *Jour. of the Mich. Constitutional Convention of 1867.*] W.M.

BIRNEY, JAMES GILLESPIE (Feb. 4, 1792–Nov. 25, 1857), anti-slavery leader, was the son of James Birney, an Irish expatriate who migrated to America in 1783 and in 1788 removed to Kentucky, where he eventually became one of the richest men in the state. Although a slaveholder, the elder Birney advocated a free state constitution for Kentucky and favored emancipation. He married about 1790 a daughter of John Read, also an Irish exile; she died in 1795. James Gillespie, the only son of the marriage, was born at Danville. He was educated at Transylvania University, Lexington, Ky., and at the College of New Jersey (now Princeton), where he graduated in 1810. He read law in the office of Alexander J. Dallas [*q.v.*] at Philadelphia, was admitted to the bar in 1814, and began what presently became an important practise at Danville. On Feb. 1, 1816, he married Agatha, daughter of William McDowell, United States district judge, and niece of Gov. George McDowell of Kentucky. The marriage brought him some slaves. In August 1816 he was elected to the lower house of the legislature. Two years later he removed to Madison County, Ala. He was not a member of the Alabama constitutional convention, but he seems to have been largely responsible for the inclusion in the state constitution, in amended form, of certain provisions of the Kentucky constitution permitting the legislature to emancipate slaves and prohibiting the introduction of slaves into the state for sale. In October 1819 he took his seat as a representative in the first General Assembly of Alabama, but his opposition to a resolution indorsing the candidacy of Andrew Jackson for president was unpopular, and he was not reëlected. He had already attained marked prominence as a lawyer, but by 1820 neglect of his plantation, together with gambling, brought financial embarrassment, and in January 1823 he removed to Huntsville, later selling his plantation with its slaves. At Huntsville his legal practise shortly recouped his finances, and thereafter, for most of his life, he was comparatively wealthy. For several years he acted as counsel for the Cherokee Nation. He had been brought up an Episcopalian, but in 1826, mainly through the influence of his wife, he became a Presbyterian. From about this time dated his interest in the colonization movement and the restriction of slavery and the domestic slave trade. A bill which he drafted to give effect to the provision of the Alabama constitution prohibiting the importation of slaves for sale, although passed by the General Assembly in January 1827, was repealed in 1829, following the election of Jackson. He was nominated a presidential elector on the Adams ticket in 1828, but Birney strongly disapproved of the policy of attacking Jackson personally, and urged the Northern element of the party to direct their opposition to the annexation of Texas and the issue of nullification. A visit to New York and New England in the fall of 1829 impressed him with the superiority of free institutions, economic and social, to those of the slave states, but he was not yet an abolitionist, and his growing reputation as an anti-slavery supporter rested upon his repugnance to slavery in general and his advocacy of gradual emancipation. For reasons not divulged he parted company politically with Henry Clay, one of his father's intimate friends, in October 1830. Another anti-slavery bill, the passage of which in Alabama he secured in January 1832, was repealed in December. In August of that year he accepted a commission as agent of the American Colonization Society, and for some months traveled and lectured in the South in behalf of that organization. An idea that Kentucky was "the best site in our whole country for taking a stand against slavery" (letter to Gerrit Smith, in W. Birney, *Life and Times of James G. Birney,* p. 131) led him in November to return to Danville. Several of his occasional writings, among them two letters on slavery and colonization addressed to Rev. R. R. Gurley (1832), essays on slavery and colonization contributed to the Huntsville *Advocate* (1833), and two letters to the Presbyterian Church (1834), belong to this period. The emancipation of his six slaves in 1834 was later described in detail in a letter (1836) to Col. Stone, editor of the New York *Spectator* (Birney, *op. cit.,* Appendix D). Convinced that colonization would increase the interstate slave-trade, and unable to reconcile it with his views of religion and justice, he resigned in 1834 the vice-presidency of the Kentucky Colonization Society, stating his reasons in a *Letter on Colonization* (first published in the Lexington *Western Luminary* and later reprinted in several editions), which added to his reputation and definitely allied him with the more aggressive anti-slavery forces. March 1835 saw him active in forming the Kentucky Anti-Slavery Society, but the membership of the American Anti-Slavery Society, whose meeting at Cincinnati he attended, did not seem to him effective. In a speech at the New York meeting of the Society in May 1835 he forcibly urged united action by all opponents of slavery. A second visit to New England, after the New York meeting, was interrupted by news of outspoken hostility to the publication in Kentucky of an anti-slavery weekly, the first number of which he had planned to issue on Aug. 1. An attempt to mob him on his return was defeated, but the publication of the paper was delayed and his mail was repeatedly rifled. The continuance of opposition determined him to remove to Ohio, and at the beginning of January 1836 he issued at New Richmond, near Cincinnati, the first number of the *Philanthropist,* continuing the publication, with the editorial assistance of Gamaliel Bailey, until September 1837, when he removed to New York. In the *Philanthropist* Birney not only attacked both Democrats and Whigs for their attitude toward slavery, but also urged upon the abolitionists the necessity of political action. On July 30 another plan to assault him at a public meeting was frustrated; his *Narrative of the Late Riotous Proceedings,* published soon after, described the episode, and was followed in October by a letter *To the Slaveholders of the South.* On several occasions later he was exposed to personal danger, meetings at which he spoke were interrupted, and his paper suffered; his son and biographer, however, is authority for the statement that "no man ever laid an unfriendly hand upon him during his public career" (Birney, *op. cit.,* p. 252). The convention of the New England Anti-Slavery Society at Boston, May 30–June 2, 1837, which he attended, found him an open dissenter from the "no government" or political abstention views of Garrison's followers, and a champion of organized political action and voting. For harboring in his home an escaped slave, Matilda, who was subsequently claimed and returned as a fugitive, he was indicted in Cincinnati, was acquitted after pleading his own case, and presently published his argument. In September, having been elected executive secretary of the American Anti-Slavery Society, he removed to New York, and spent the winter of 1837–38 in visiting such of the state legislatures as were in session. A published letter to Representative F. H. Elmore of South Carolina, in response to a request for information regarding anti-slavery organizations, separated him still farther from the Garrisonians by establishing his position as an upholder of the Federal Constitution. A *Letter on the Political Obligations of Abolitionists,* prepared as a "report on the duty of political action" for the executive committee of the American Anti-Slavery Society in May 1839 (published in the Boston *Emancipator* May 2; replied to at much length by Garrison May 31; the two reprinted as a pamphlet), was an incisive criticism of the constitution of the Society and of the Garrisonian policy, and brought appreciably nearer the ultimate breach in the abolition ranks. For the next few years Birney was the most conspicuous representative and the ablest spokesman of those who sought to get rid of slavery by political means as well as by moral suasion. On Nov. 13, 1839, a state convention at Warsaw, N. Y., unanimously nominated him for president, but the nomination was declined, partly because the convention was not national in character, and partly because he thought it inexpedient to make an independent nomination until the candidate of the Whigs had been selected. In April 1840, the Whigs having nominated William Henry Harrison, Birney was again nominated at Albany, N. Y., by an anti-slavery convention representing six states. The new party, generally known as the Liberty party, had at first no name and adopted no platform. The popular vote polled was 7,069, drawn from the six New England states, New York, New Jersey, Pennsylvania, Ohio, Illinois, and Michigan (Edward Stanwood, *History of the Presidency,* I, 203). In the same year Birney went to England, where he was one of the vice-presidents of the World's Anti-Slavery Convention. His best-known work, *The American Churches the Bulwarks of American Slavery,* was written and published in England (1840; 2nd, and first American, edition, "By an American," 1842; 3rd ed., 1885). He had already, in 1839, emancipated twenty-one slaves, a part of his father's estate, at a cost of $20,000 in the form of compensation for the interest of a co-heir. His wife died in 1839, and in 1841 he married Miss Fitzhugh, sister-in-law of Gerrit Smith. The next year he removed to Bay City, Mich. In August 1843 he was again nominated for president, this time by a convention at Buffalo, N. Y., comprising 148 delegates from twelve states. The platform, by far the longest that any party had yet adopted, added to its denunciation of slavery an announcement of the purpose of the abolitionists, "whether as private citizens or as public functionaries sworn to support the Constitution of the United States, to regard and to treat the third clause of the fourth article of that instrument, whenever applied to the case of a fugitive slave, as utterly null and void, and consequently as forming no part of the Constitution of the United States, whenever we are called upon or sworn to support it." No electoral votes were won, but the popular vote of the Liberty party, drawn from the same states that voted for Birney in 1840, with the addition of Indiana, was 62,300. The "Garland Letter," issued on the eve of the election and purporting to solicit for Birney a Democratic nomination for the Michigan legislature and stating his intention to defeat Clay, was a forgery. Horace Greeley's charge in the *New York Tribune* that Birney had sought a Democratic nomination in New York and tried to catch the Democratic vote was widely believed at the time but appears improbable (Stanwood, *op. cit.,* I, 224). In the summer of 1845 a fall from a horse, resulting in partial paralysis, made Birney an invalid and brought his public career to a close. His *Examination of the Decision of the Supreme Court of the United States in the case of Strader et al. v. Graham, concluding with an Address to the Free Colored People, advising them to remove to Liberia* (1852), was written in 1850: the decision in question was one much relied upon by Chief Justice Taney in the Dred Scott case (1857). About 1853 Birney removed from Michigan to Eagleswood, near Perth Amboy, N. J., and died there Nov. 25, 1857. In the history of the American anti-slavery movement he occupies a peculiar position. Never a supporter of slavery in principle, notwithstanding that he owned slaves, he accepted the institution for a time as he found it and worked earnestly to ameliorate its conditions. He early manifested an almost insuperable repugnance to selling slaves, and was at pains to explain and defend his course in disposing of the few that he held. Acquaintance with the North convinced him that the overthrow of slavery was as necessary for the whites as for the negroes, and he passed gradually, but on the whole rapidly, from advocacy of gradual emancipation, reinforced by colonization in Africa, to a conviction that abolition must be secured by constitutional political means. He was too reasonable, and perhaps too good a lawyer, to follow Garrison in the latter's denunciation of the Constitution, but he was nevertheless willing at last, as the party platform on which he stood in 1844 showed, to nullify so much of the Constitution as gave countenance to fugitive slave legislation or identified the federal government with the support or extension of slavery. The assertion of his biographer that he "voted Free Soil or Republican tickets, state and national, except Van Buren, as long as he lived," helps to explain the distrust with which Garrison and other radical abolitionists regarded him, although the statement could hardly have applied to the elections of 1840 and 1844.

[The chief authority, except for the presidential campaigns of 1840 and 1844, is *Jas. G. Birney and His Times* (1890), by his son, Wm. Birney. The book was inspired by what the writer believed to be the misrepresentations of W. P. and F. J. Garrison's *William Lloyd Garrison* (1885–89), with which its statements and comments should be compared; it is extremely hostile to Garrison and to much of the view of the abolition movement which Garrison's biographers present. The latter, in turn, are persistently hostile to Birney. A review of Wm. Birney's book in the *Nation* (New York), L, 206, is informing. An earlier life by Beriah Green, *Sketches of the Life and Writings of Jas. Gillespie Birney* (1844), written as a campaign document and laudatory, contains many extracts from Birney's writings; see especially pp. 100–04, a summary of Birney's letter of acceptance in 1840, and pp. 105–15, virtually the whole of the letter of acceptance in 1843, dissecting the claims of John Quincy Adams to the support of abolitionists. See also the anonymous *Tribute to Jas. G. Birney* (Detroit, Mich., n. d., *c.* 1865). References in the voluminous literature of the anti-slavery movement are many, but usually brief. Most of Birney's writings appeared first as contributions to newspapers or magazines, subsequently in pamphlets; to those already mentioned are to be added *Vindication of the Abolitionists* (1835), a reply to resolutions of an Alabama committee proposing drastic dealings with abolition agitators; *Addresses and Speeches* (1835); various articles in the *Quarterly Anti-Slavery Magazine* and the *Emancipator* (1837–44), and *Speeches in England* (1840).]

W. M.

BIRNEY, WILLIAM (May 28, 1819–Aug. 14, 1907), Union soldier, author, was born in Madison County, Ala., the son of James G. Birney [*q.v.*] and Agatha McDowell. At some time prior to 1845 he was practising law in Cincinnati, Ohio. In February 1848, being a member of a Republican student organization in Paris, he commanded at a barricade in the Rue St. Jacques during the revolutionary outbreak. In the same year he won in a competitive examination an appointment as professor of English literature at the Lycée at Bourges, where he remained for two years. During his five years' residence abroad he wrote for English and American papers, among other things reporting the first World's Fair at London (1851). He appears also to have paid some attention to the history of art and current activities in art education (see his *Art and Education,* a lecture before the Washington Art Club, Feb. 6, 1878). Upon his return to the United States he established the daily *Register* at Philadelphia (1853) and edited it for two years. At the outbreak of the Civil War he raised a volunteer company in New Jersey, and became in succession captain of the 1st New Jersey Infantry and major and colonel of the 4th New Jersey Infantry. In 1863 he was appointed one of the superintendents of the enlistment of colored troops, in which capacity he organized seven regiments. On May 22, 1863, he was made brigadier-general of volunteers. While in command of colored troops he freed the inmates of the slave prisons at Baltimore. He took part in a number of important engagements, and after the battle of Olustee, Fla. (Feb. 20, 1864), aided in recovering the state from the Confederates. During the last two years of the war he commanded a division. On Mar. 13, 1865, he was made brevet major-general of volunteers "for gallant and meritorious service during the war," and on Aug. 24 was mustered out. After a residence of four years in Florida he removed to Washington, where he practised law, wrote fortnightly letters to the New York *Examiner,* and served for a time as United States attorney for the District of Columbia. His best-known writing, *James G. Birney and His Times,* appeared in 1890. In his later years he interested himself in religious controversy, publishing *Functions of the Church and State Distinguished: A Plea for Civil and Religious Liberty* (1897); *Revelation and the Plan of Salvation* (1903); *Creeds not for Secularists* (1906); *Hell and Hades* (Truth Seeker Tracts, New Series, No. 51, New York, n. d.), and *How Christianity Began (Ibid.,* No. 54, n. d.). He was twice married: in 1845 to Catherine Hoffman, and in 1891 to Mattie Ashby.

[*Who's Who in America,* 1899–1907; F. B. Heitman, *Hist. Reg.* (1903); *Official Records,* see Index; *Washington Post,* and *Evening Star,* Aug. 15, 1907.]

W. M.

BISHOP, ABRAHAM (Feb. 5, 1763–Apr. 28, 1844), politician, was born in New Haven, the son of Samuel and Mehetabel (Bassett) Bishop. His father was a respected and well-to-do citizen who exemplified the steady habits of his native state by more than fifty years' service as town clerk and representative in the Assembly, besides holding at different times several other local offices, including, late in life, that of mayor. Abraham graduated at Yale in 1778. Inasmuch as he was less than sixteen years of age at graduation it is not surprising that he led an unsettled life for some years following. In 1785 he was admitted to the bar but never attained any professional distinction, not even practising with any regularity. In 1787–88 he visited Europe and, like his classmate Joel Barlow, was profoundly influenced by its intellectual unrest and the political and religious skepticism of the revolutionary era. He returned, as President Stiles of Yale sourly remarked, "full of Improvm^t^ and Vanity," but more likely merely impressed with the unprogressive and static character of Federalist Connecticut.

For several years he taught school, lectured, and engaged in miscellaneous activities. William Bentley records him in 1792 as "Alias J. Martin, schoolmaster, actor, excentric writer, traveler" (*Diary*, 1905, I, 391). Making all due allowance for political detraction such as that of the *Connecticut Courant*, Aug. 16, 1802, which described him as a man "whose life is but another name for deformity," he appears in his early life to have been somewhat dissipated. On Mar. 11, 1792, he married Nancy, daughter of the notorious Timothy Dexter of Newburyport. His eccentric and semi-illiterate father-in-law described him as the "two leged Conekett boull—short Neck, boull head, thik hare, big sholders, black Corlley hare," with comments on his character as unflattering as those on his appearance (J. P. Marquand, *Lord Timothy Dexter of Newburyport, Mass.*, 1925, pp. 363 ff.). This connection soon ended in a squalid family quarrel and the divorce of his wife. In 1802 he married Betsey Law of Cheshire, Conn., who died Sept. 11, 1817, and on Jan. 3, 1819, he married Mrs. Elizabeth (Nicoll) Lynde of New Haven, who survived him.

Soon after his marriage in 1792 he returned to New Haven, where he lived for the remainder of his life. He taught school and was in 1795 made clerk of the county court, in 1796 of the probate court, and in 1798 of the superior court. He became an ardent supporter of Jefferson, which in a Federalist community like Connecticut was the equivalent of moral and political treason, and by 1801 accordingly, he had been ousted from the last of these local offices. In 1801 President Jefferson removed the Federalist collector of the port and assigned the place to Samuel Bishop. As his father was in feeble health it was generally considered that the appointment was in effect that of Abraham himself, and indisputably a reward for political services. The protest of the New Haven merchants thereat, and President Jefferson's reply will always appear as landmarks in the history of American civil service (see C. R. Fish, *The Civil Service and the Patronage*, 1905, pp. 32–38). In 1803, on the death of his father, Bishop was formally appointed collector and held the place until removed by President Jackson in 1829. His official career thus coincided with a distinct epoch in the history of Federal patronage and he was first a beneficiary and then a victim of two great exponents of democratic administration. One of his contemporaries noticed the fact that the possession of a lucrative office quieted his radical tendencies and that his political activity quickly subsided after 1804 (S. G. Goodrich, *Recollections of a Lifetime*, 1856, I, 125). He spent the rest of his life acquiring respectability, a belief in the protective tariff, and a fortune, apparently with marked success in each endeavor.

Bishop's political activity was largely concentrated in a period of six or seven years around the opening of the century and he unquestionably exercised an important influence both within his own state and in New England at large. He delivered a series of noteworthy addresses which were in several instances enlarged and printed for general reading. They were widely circulated and quoted. He had a command of simple, forcible English, a distinct satirical bent, and some sense of humor, a combination which made him a dreaded and hated opponent of that conservative, religious, legal, and propertied alliance which completely dominated Connecticut prior to 1818. The most noteworthy of these productions were *An Oration on the Extent and Power of Political Delusion* (1800); *An Oration delivered in Wallingford* (1801); *Proofs of a Conspiracy, Against Christianity, and the Government of the United States* (1802); *Oration in honor of the Election of President Jefferson and the Peaceable Acquisition of Louisiana* (1804). "Have mercy upon us! ye well-fed, well-dressed, chariot-rolling, caucus-keeping, levee-revelling federalists; for we are poor, and wretched, and ignorant and miserable" is the demagogic theme running through many of his pamphlets. Nevertheless, he performed a valuable service when he assailed the alliance of church and state, the clannishness produced by family alliances in business and politics and the exaggerated respect for wisdom of ancestors who as he said "fought, quarreled, sinned and punished, as often in proportion to their numbers as their posterity." Conservative Federalism also needed to be continually reminded that "everything valuable in our world has been at one time, innovation, illuminatism, modern philosophy or atheism" to those disturbed by it.

[Bishop's pamphlets are found in many of the older New England libraries. The best summary of his life is that by F. B. Dexter in *Biog. Sketches Grads. Yale Coll., IV*, (1907), pp. 17–24, which includes a list of his publications and a bibliography. Another brief sketch by the same author appears in *Mass. Hist. Soc. Proc.*, ser. II, vol. XIX, pp. 190–99. The studies by R. J. Purcell, *Conn. in Transition, 1775–1818* (1918); and M. L. Greene, *The Development of Religious Liberty in Conn.* (1905), show the political and social background of Bishop's career and contain considerable direct information. There are numerous references to Bishop in the *Lit. Diary of Ezra Stiles*, ed. by F. B. Dexter (1901), vols. II, III.]

W. A. R.

BISHOP, JOEL PRENTISS (Mar. 10, 1814–Nov. 4, 1901), lawyer, was born in Volney, Oswego County, N. Y., being a descendant in the direct male line from John Bishop, who, coming from England, settled at Guilford, Conn., in 1639. His father, Amos Bishop, a farmer of small means, son of Deacon David Bishop of Guilford, married Fanny Prentiss, of Paris, Oneida County, N. Y., and shortly after his birth the family moved to Paris. His youth was spent working on the farm, and his early education was obtained by intermittent attendance at Whitestone Seminary, Oneida Institute, and Stockbridge Academy. In 1830 he became a public school teacher, thus earning enough to continue his studies in his spare time. In 1835 he became associated with the New York Anti-Slavery Society, and for a time was its general business manager, assisting also to edit *The Friend of Man.* He removed to Boston in 1842, entered a law office, supporting himself by literary work outside office hours, and was admitted to the bar Apr. 9, 1844. Commencing practise in Boston, he slowly built up a connection, devoting his leisure to the collection of material for a treatise on the law of domestic relations. His *Commentaries on the Law of Marriage and Divorce, and Evidence in Matrimonial Suits* was published in 1852 and immediately attracted attention by its independent standpoint and freshness of treatment. Encouraged by its reception, and urged thereto by the profession, he thenceforward devoted himself to legal authorship, relinquishing active practise. His next work, *Commentaries on the Criminal Law,* in two volumes (1856–58), placed him in the front rank of contemporary legal authors, being distinguished for clarity of style, scrupulous accuracy and originality of thought. Additional editions of both these early books were quickly called for, and they continued in demand until long after his death. His subsequent publications included *Commentaries on the Law of Criminal Procedure; or, Pleading, Evidence and Practice in Criminal Cases* (1866); *First Book of the Law* (1868), an introduction to legal science, study, and practise; *The Law of Statutory Crimes* (1873); *Commentaries on the Law of Married Women* (2 vols., 1873–75); *Doctrines of the Law of Contracts in their principal outlines,* a small elementary work (1875); *Commentaries on the Written Law and their Interpretation* (1882); *Prosecution and Defence* (1885), a book of forms and practise; *Commentaries on the Law of Contracts* (1887), designed to supersede his smaller work on this subject; *Commentaries on the Non-contract Law . . . or the Everyday Rights and Torts* (1889); *New Commentaries on Marriage, Divorce and Separation* (2 vols., 1891), and *New Criminal Procedure* (2 vols., 1895–96). Occasionally he ventured into lay fields, with articles and pamphlets on current topics, the more noticeable of these being *Thoughts for the Times* (1863); *Secession and Slavery* (1863), *Look and Think: Strikes and their related Questions* (1886), and *Common Law and Codification* (1888). His life was uneventful. He never aspired to public office of any kind, and early in his career refused the appointment of chief justice of the Hawaiian Islands offered him by King Kamehameha III. He died at Cambridge, Mass.

Though Bishop's books varied greatly in merit, they maintained, considering the large and constant output, a surprisingly high standard of excellence, combining extreme accuracy and clear style with effective exposition. He always worked entirely independently of previous writers on the subjects he treated. His *Commentaries on Marriage, Divorce and Separation* and his *Criminal Law* have become classics. His early years were one long indomitable struggle in an environment of poverty, and his after life was characterized by incessant industry in his chosen vocation. An unfortunate peculiarity of an otherwise admirable personality was his inordinate self-esteem. A leading law periodical, criticizing one of his prefaces in his lifetime, did not hesitate to say that it was "characterized by the most enormous vanity, a quality in which this author surpassed every other man of distinction since the death of Cicero" (*American Law Review,* XXVII, 939).

[Bishop by request contributed to the *Central Law Jour.,* XX, 321, a brief resumé of the first forty years of his life—valuable as the only record of that period, but he gave no particular phases of his work and character; in *Am. Law Rev.* XXXVI, 1 is an article intimate and appreciative, which fills up the gaps in his autobiographical sketch.]

H. W. H. K.

BISHOP, NATHAN (Aug. 12, 1808–Aug. 7, 1880), educator, philanthropist, was born in Vernon, N. Y., and died in Saratoga Springs, N. Y. He was the eldest son of Elnathan and Statira (Sperry) Bishop, both of New England stock. His education was secured by dint of great personal effort. When eighteen, as a student in the academy at Hamilton, he found time to teach the lower classes. In 1832 he entered Brown University, but, owing to school-keeping, private tutoring, acting as bell-ringer, milking the president's cows, and other activities, he did not graduate until 1837. The next year he served as tutor in mathematics; in 1842 he became a member of the board of trustees; in 1849–50 he coöperated with Dr. Wayland in plans for reorganization and served as solicitor of the $125,000 subscription sought; and in 1854–61 he was made a member of the Board of Fellows. In 1838 the public school system of Providence was reorganized, provision being made for a superintendent of public schools. To this Bishop was chosen, and from 1839 to 1851 he served so acceptably that it was said that the Providence schools ranked with the first in the country. His success gained recognition beyond the state; in 1851 he was appointed superintendent of public schools in Boston, where he served six years. Good judgment, scholarship, business ability, and kindliness contributed to his success in education and philanthropy. His *Reports* during his superintendency show the outstanding character of his work and were responsible for extending his educational influence beyond the confines of the state. By fortunate investment of his limited income from teaching he became independent. In 1857 he gave up teaching and moved to New York, where in 1858 he married Caroline (Cauldwell) Bleecker, widow of Garrat Noel Bleecker. Because of the financial stringency of the times, he did not enter the publishing business, as he had planned, but devoted his remaining years to denominational, educational, and philanthropic work. Several engagements of this nature came now in quick succession; during the Civil War he was chairman of the executive committee of the United States Christian Commission; in 1867 he was appointed a member of the Board of State Commissioners of Public Charities; he was one of the first trustees named by Matthew Vassar for Vassar College; and in 1865 he was elected to the board of managers of the American Bible Society. He took a leading part in the work of the New York Sabbath Committee (1859); the American Branch of the Evangelical Alliance (1866)—in the interests of which he was sent to Russia in 1870; the American Revision Committee—both as contributor and chairman of the finance committee; and the American Baptist Home Mission Society, to which he rendered conspicuous service. Being named by President Grant to the Board of United States Indian Commissioners in 1869, he went with others to visit certain tribes in the Southwest. While thus engaged, he contracted malaria, from which he never fully recovered.

[The best sources are: *A Layman's Ministry* (n.d.); *Baptist Home Missions in North America: 1832–82* (1883); the Necrology in the *Providence Daily Jour.*, June 15, 1881; and official records of Providence and Boston public schools, 1839–51 and 1852–57. Long obituaries appeared in the *N. Y. Eve. Post*, Aug. 7, 1880, *N. Y. Tribune*, Aug. 8, 1880. There are also sketches and appreciations in the *Baptist Weekly*, Aug. 12, 1880, and the *Examiner and Chronicle*, Aug. 12, Aug. 26, Sept. 9, 1880.]

T. W.

BISHOP, ROBERT ROBERTS (Mar. 30, 1834–Oct. 7, 1909), lawyer and jurist, was born in Medfield, Mass., the son of Jonathan Parker and Eliza (Harding) Bishop. The father was a country lawyer who lived on a farm and had sat in the state legislature. At the age of sixteen the boy entered Phillips Academy, Andover, working his way through school and learning the meaning of scholarship under a great teacher, Samuel H. Taylor. Graduating in 1854, he studied law with the firm of Brooks and Ball, in Boston, simultaneously pursuing the regular course at Harvard Law School, from which he took a degree in 1857. He married, Dec. 24, 1857, in Holliston, Mass., Mary Helen Bullard. In 1861 he moved to Newton, Mass., where he spent the remainder of his life.

For a brief period, while establishing himself in his profession, he was a law reporter for the *Boston Daily Advertiser*. In 1861 he associated himself with Thornton K. Lothrop in the firm of Lothrop & Bishop, which conducted many important litigations before its dissolution in 1879. Bishop entered public life as a Republican in 1874, through an election to the Massachusetts House of Representatives, but he declined a second term because of his duties as a member of the Newton Water Board, which was then completing a system of water-works for that city. He became a state senator in 1878 and was reëlected for three successive years, being the president of the Senate for 1880, 1881, and 1882. During his term of office he published *The Senate of Massachusetts: an Historical Sketch* (1882), which is the authoritative book on the subject.

In 1882, after a contest in the Republican convention at Worcester, Bishop received the nomination of his party for governor. The Democratic candidate was the aggressive Benjamin F. Butler, who, in an acrimonious campaign, defeated Bishop, 133,946 to 119,997. Various factors, including the prevailing discontent and a desire for a change of party at any cost, affected the result. On Mar. 7, 1888, Bishop was appointed associate justice of the Massachusetts Superior Court, a position which was most congenial to him. On the bench he was distinguished by his unfailing courtesy, his careful consideration of cases, his patience and open-mindedness, his dignity, and his complete impartiality. While still on the bench, he died in his seventy-sixth year, after a brief illness from pneumonia. He was a deliberate and thoughtful man, of conservative tendencies, who once said of himself, "I am not much for speed, but I think I have staying qualities." The *Boston Evening Transcript* said of him editorially, "In a judiciary justly renowned for integrity and acquirement he held deserved prominence."

[The *Green Bag* for Jan. 1911 (vol. XXIII, no. 1) has an excellent article on Bishop, written by Jos. T. Bishop. The *Proceedings of the Suffolk Bar and Superior Court in Memory of Judge Bishop,* Dec. 18, 1909, were printed and published in 1911. The *Boston Evening Transcript* for Oct. 8, 1909, has a full obituary.]

C.M.F.

BISHOP, SETH SCOTT (Feb. 7, 1852–Sept. 6, 1923), Chicago laryngologist, the son of Lyman Bishop by his wife, Maria Probart, was born at Fond du Lac, Wis., and obtained his early education at the Pooler Institute of his native town. He attended Beloit Academy (1872–73) and passed two academic years at Beloit College (1873–75), but was forced to leave college "on account of his eyes" and did not obtain an academic degree. Despite his eyes he evidently made rapid progress in medical work, for he obtained his M.D. from Northwestern University in 1876. He also studied medicine for a short time at New York University, and supported himself during his early years of practise by learning the printer's trade. Though at first a general practitioner, he later limited his work to the diseases of the ear, nose, and throat. In 1887 he was awarded first prize by the United States Hay-fever Association for an essay upon the etiology and treatment of hay-fever (*Journal of the American Medical Association,* July 23, 1887). He was later appointed to the chair of otology, rhinology, and laryngology at Loyola University School of Medicine, and he held a similar position at the Chicago Post-Graduate Medical School. He became surgeon to the Jefferson Park Hospital, the Illinois Charitable Eye and Ear Infirmary, and consulting surgeon to several other religious institutions. From 1912 until his death, Bishop was a member of the board of contributing editors of the New York *Medical Times.* He was also an early editor of the *Illinois Medical Bulletin,* which ran from 1902 to 1908. His chief contributions to medicine were his two well-illustrated text-books, *Diseases of the Ear, Nose and Throat and Their Accessory Cavities; a Condensed Textbook* (1897), the third edition of which appeared in 1904, and *The Ear and Its Diseases, a Textbook for Students and Physicians* (1906). In the preface of the latter work he refers to the unprecedented sale of his first text-book and states that both were based upon the case records of an active practise extending over twenty-five years. Though his works were well illustrated, his style of writing was not always lucid. On page 415 (Fig. 199) of his second text-book is a photograph of the author. He was married Mar. 23, 1885, to Jessie A. Button.

[*Medic. Times,* N. Y., LI, 243; *Jour. Am. Medic. Ass.,* Chicago, LXXXI, 945; *Ill. Medic. Jour.,* XLIV, 304; *Who's Who in America,* 1922–23; private information.]

J.F.F.

BISHOP, WILLIAM DARIUS (Sept. 14, 1827–Feb. 4, 1904), railway official, was the son of Alfred and Mary (Ferris) Bishop, and was born in Bloomfield, Essex County, N. J. Having been graduated from Yale in 1849, he shortly became a director of the Naugatuck Railroad, which Alfred Bishop, who was a railway contractor, had built through the Naugatuck Valley of Connecticut from Bridgeport to Winsted. W. D. Bishop was first made superintendent of this road and then in 1855 was chosen to its presidency. In 1850 he had married Julia A. Tomlinson of Bridgeport. He was elected in 1857 a Democratic member of the Thirty-fifth Congress; and when he failed of reëlection was appointed United States commissioner of patents by President Buchanan. During his brief term as commissioner (1859–60), he is said to have done good service, especially in putting in order the Patent Office records and in systematizing the work of his subordinates. In May 1866 he left the presidency of the Naugatuck to take up that of the New York & New Haven. Under his régime, the New York & New Haven acquired both the Hartford & Connecticut Valley and the Harlem & Port Chester, and leased the Shore Line. With this consolidation, the road became increasingly powerful. So late as 1885 there were as many as twenty-two railroads in Connecticut; and it must be said that from the earliest days of railway building in the state the influence of the numerous separate companies, as they contended or united with one another in order to control legislation and obtain special privileges, had been far from beneficial in public affairs. During Bishop's administration, the New York & New Haven system gained an ascendancy it never lost. While he was executive head of this system, Bishop was admitted to the Fairfield County bar (1870), represented Bridgeport in the General Assembly (1872), was a state senator, 1866, 1877, 1878, and had a conspicuous part in general railway legislation. Extensive and thoroughgoing improvements were made by him in local railroad conveniences at Bridgeport. He was a director of the Bridgeport Steamboat Company, operating between Bridgeport and New York; and also of the Housatonic Railroad, extending from Bridgeport to Pittsfield, Mass. In March 1879 he retired from the presidency of the New York & New Haven, but until his death he remained upon the board of directors. In 1883 he was once more called to be president of the Naugatuck, and he held this office until his retirement in October 1903. Although in over a half-century of busy life he engaged in many activities, yet primarily he was a railroad man, and it was in problems of railway construction and management that he found his chief interest. His formal practise of the law was largely confined to a few patent cases of more or less importance.

[The sources of information regarding Bishop are mainly: Lewis and Calhoun, *The Judicial and Civil Hist. of Conn.* (1895); N. G. Osborn, *Men of Mark in Conn.* (1906); *Geneal. and Family Hist. of the State of Conn.* (ed. by W. R. Cutter and others, 1911); *Obit. Record Grads. Yale Univ.* (1910).]

G. S. B.

BISPHAM, DAVID SCULL (Jan. 5, 1857–Oct. 2, 1921), baritone, was the son of William D. Bispham of old Jersey Revolutionary stock, and of Jane Scull, daughter of a Philadelphia Quaker family, who would not allow a piano in her home. David Bispham was born in the latter city, and one of his earliest recollections was "seeing men armed with shotguns jump on the Market Street horse-cars to take the first train to Gettysburg during Lee's invasion of Pennsylvania." An eight months' tour of Europe at the age of twenty-one fanned to flame the repressed musical leanings of his childhood, and in 1880 he began to appear as a singer in amateur stage performances and in the choirs of St. Mark's and Holy Trinity churches in Philadelphia. Returning to Europe, definitely committed to a musical career, he studied from 1886 to 1890 in Florence under Vannuccini and Lamperti, and in London under Shakespeare and Randegger. He made his début on Nov. 3, 1891, at the Royal English Opera House, London, as the Duc de Longueville in Messager's comic opera *La Basoche.* On June 25, 1892—he had continued to sing in comic opera in the meantime—he made his first appearance as a dramatic baritone in serious opera as Kurwenal in *Parsifal,* at the Drury Lane Theatre. This at once established his reputation as a "singing actor"; he continued to sing in opera in London, and from 1896 to 1909 divided his time between Covent Garden and the Metropolitan Opera House in New York. At the same time he achieved a reputation as a singer in oratorio and on the concert stage (the Christ in Bach's *The Passion According to St. Matthew,* and the baritone solos in the Perosi oratorios may be mentioned in the former connection); while his recitals in London and New York were so successful that, in a measure, they overshadowed his operatic achievement so that after 1909 he gave up the opera stage to devote himself almost exclusively to recital work. He had studied and sung in Bayreuth, however, and was considered one of the best Wagnerian baritones of his day: aside from Beckmesser, Wolfram, Alberich, Wotan, and Hunding, his forty-odd rôles included Verdi's Falstaff, Boito's Mefisto, Mascagni's Alfio, and Humperdinck's Peter. In the United States he created the part of Chillingworth in Walter Damrosch's *Scarlet Letter.* Endowed with a personality of much charm, a thorough artist in every sense, and a man of the highest culture, Bispham's real histrionic gifts and command of a notably flexible and sonorous vocal organ were paired with an intense musical temperament. After 1918 he devoted most of his time to teaching, and published two volumes of "Bispham Songs." The singer's married life was not happy: and in 1908 he separated from his wife, Caroline Russell, daughter of the late Gen. Charles Russell, whom he had married on April 28, 1885. Though he wrote no "method," his autobiography, *A Quaker Singer's Recollections,* contains much information regarding his ideals and their development; and practical hints for the vocal student are contained in a series of three articles by Herbert Wilber Greene entitled "Quotations from a Conversation with David Bispham" in the *Musical Observer,* February, March, April, 1919. Bispham's service in establishing high standards in the American song recital field is beyond question. He gave recitals of Beethoven, Schubert, Schumann, and the best older and modern French and Italian songs in English (being the first to sing Brahms' *Four Serious Songs* in the United States). In the moot question as to whether foreign songs should be sung in their original tongues in the United States and Great Britain he advocated the use of English, writing "Ever since the production of 'The Vicar of Wakefield' in London (1906) . . . I have been more than ever addicted to the use of our own language in my concerts. . . . To all American singers I say, sing your songs in well-chosen English, if singing to an English-speaking audience, and sing them so that every one understands your words. . . . Get away from this foreign language fad and you will find yourself nearer the heart of the audience" (*A Quaker Singer's Recollections,* p. 342). Bispham's undeviating stand at a time when the artistic pros and cons of the question were hotly debated was influential in encouraging the employ of the vernacular in American song recital.

[The principal source is Bispham's enjoyable and humorous autobiography, *A Quaker Singer's Recollections* (1920). The articles in *Grove's Encyc. of Music and Musicians* (1904), I, 333, and *Am. Supp.* (1920), p. 133, are full and reliable, and the notice in Theodore Baker's *Biog. Dict. of Musicians* (3rd rev. ed., 1919) also calls for mention. A readable sketch of Bispham's life appeared in *Musical America,* Oct. 8, 1921, and his name frequently occurs in the memoirs of contemporaries: Hermann Klein, *Music and Mummers* (1925);

Walter Damrosch, *My Musical Life* (1923); James M. Glover, *Jimmy Glover, His Book* (3rd ed., 1911).]

F. H. M.

BISSELL, EDWIN CONE (Mar. 2, 1832–Apr. 10, 1894), Congregational clergyman, the son of George C. and Elizabeth (White) Bissell, was born in Schoharie, N. Y. He prepared for college at Monson Academy, graduated from Amherst in 1855, for one year taught at Williston Seminary, Easthampton, Mass., and then began his theological studies at Hartford Theological Seminary, finishing them at Union Theological Seminary, N. Y., in 1859. During the latter year he married Emily Pomeroy, daughter of Col. Oren Pomeroy of Somers, Conn. In September 1859 he was ordained to the ministry in West Hampton, Mass., where he remained as pastor of the Congregational church until 1864. During this pastorate he organized Company K of the 52nd Massachusetts Volunteers and for the year 1862–63 served as their captain at the front. In 1864 he became pastor of the Green Street Congregational Church in San Francisco, remaining until 1869 and serving also two years as editor of *The Pacific*. For a year after this (1869–70) he served as pastor of the Fort Street Church in Honolulu, H. I., but was called thence to the Congregational Church in Winchester, Mass., where he remained until 1873. His varied experience in the pastorate was then still further diversified by five years' service under the A.B.C.F.M. as missionary in Austria, working among the Bohemians of Gratz. He returned to America in 1878 and spent two years of special study at Boston and then spent a year or two more in Germany at the University of Leipzig. This diversion of his activities toward a teaching career may perhaps be ascribed to his having published during his pastorate at Winchester a small volume entitled *The Historic Origin of the Bible* (1873), which won for him in 1874 the honorary degree of D.D. from his alma mater, an honor later duplicated by Lake Forest University. In 1880 he published a revised translation with introduction and notes of *The Apocrypha of the Old Testament*, being Volume XV of the American edition of Lange's Commentaries and in the following year was made Nettleton professor of Hebrew language and literature in Hartford Theological Seminary. This position he held until 1892, when he resigned to become professor of Hebrew in McCormick Presbyterian Theological Seminary in Chicago, where he served until his death. He was a patient and painstaking teacher, interesting himself in the questions of historical criticism and documentary analysis which were then beginning to agitate the American church, and devoting to them a large number of contributions to reviews and periodicals. His chief work, *The Pentateuch, Its Origin and Structure*, appeared in 1885, to be followed in 1888 by *Biblical Antiquities*, in 1891 by a text-book on Hebrew Grammar, and in 1892 by the Book of Genesis printed in colors. In all these works he defended the traditional view, applying his linguistic knowledge against the now dominant theory of the Graf-Wellhausen school.

[*Biog. Record Alumni Amherst Coll.* (1883); *Obit. Record Grads. Amherst Coll.* (1894); C. D. Hartranft, *Memorial Address* (1894); *Springfield Republican* and *Hartford Times*, Apr. 11, 1894.]

B. W. B.

BISSELL, GEORGE EDWIN (Feb. 16, 1839–Aug. 30, 1920), sculptor, was descended from Huguenot ancestors who came to America in 1632 and settled at Windsor, Conn. George was born at New Preston, Conn., to Hiram Bissell, a quarryman, and his wife, Isabella Jones. About 1853 the family moved to Waterbury, where George became a clerk in a store. His education was received partly at the Northville Academy and partly at the Gunnery, Washington, Conn. The latter school he entered when he came of age, intending to prepare for college. The Civil War, however, changed his plans, for, after teaching in a district school for a few months, he enlisted as a private in the 23rd Regiment of the Connecticut Volunteers, in which he served 1862–63. When his company was mustered out he became a paymaster in the United States Navy (1863–65). After the war he married, on Aug. 16, 1865, Mary E. Welton of Waterbury, and soon after joined his father and brother in the marble business in Poughkeepsie, N. Y. Without any previous training he took to making designs and models for monuments. His first commission (1871) was a life-size marble figure of a fireman for the Fire Department of Poughkeepsie. In 1875 he went to Europe, studying in Paris, Florence, and Rome. At Paris, either at this time or later, he worked under Aimé Millet and Tabar. In 1876 he was a pupil at the English Academy in Rome. On his return to Poughkeepsie he did a number of portrait busts. From 1878 dates the colossal granite figure for the John C. Booth family monument. From 1883 to 1896 his time was largely divided between Paris and Poughkeepsie. Among his works dating from this period are: "Soldiers' Monument" (1883–84) and "Col. John L. Chatfield" (1887), both in Waterbury; "Gen. Gates" on the Saratoga Battle Monument at Schuylerville, N. Y.; "Lincoln" (1893), Edinburgh, Scotland; "Standard Bearer," Winsted, Conn.; "Union," Salisbury, Conn.; "Chancellor John Watts," Trinity

Churchyard, N. Y.; "James Kent," in the Congressional Library. All these works show his realistic tendency, though in non-portrait figures, such as those on the Waterbury monument, his realism is somewhat tempered. In 1896 he settled in Mt. Vernon, N. Y., and in the same year did the "Abraham de Peyster" for New York City, a much reduced variant of which is in the Metropolitan Museum, where also is a marble bust of Mary Justina de Peyster. Though continuing to live at Mt. Vernon until his death, he kept a studio in Florence from 1903 to 1905 and from 1907 to 1909. In 1898 he made the "President Arthur," in New York; in 1899 the navy group on the colonnade of the arch temporarily erected on the occasion of Admiral Dewey's return; and in 1900 "Lycurgus" on the Appellate Court building. For the Pan-American Exposition he made "Hospitality," and for the Louisiana Purchase Exposition "Science" and "Music." At this latter exposition he received a silver medal. The Elton Memorial Vase in Waterbury at the entrance of Riverside Cemetery, where are a number of other monuments by him, was made in 1905. Among his remaining works many are widely scattered: "Lincoln" at Clermont, Ia.; "Burns and Highland Mary" (a relief) at Ayr, Scotland; a colossal bust of Admiral Dahlgren on the Civil War Memorial in Philadelphia; "Samuel Sloan" in Hoboken, N. J.; and "John Starin" in Fultonville, N. Y. Though he turned to sculpture somewhat late, his output, during his long life, was considerable. His works show a seeking for realism, often tempered, however, by a certain amount of idealization. In his best works there is dignity and restraint. He was a charter member of the National Sculpture Society. A genial, kindly person, in temperament and appearance, he was affectionately termed "Père Bissell" by the younger sculptors who knew him, and in his family the same traits made him beloved.

[*The Town and City of Waterbury,* ed. by Jos. Anderson (1896), III, 1037; *Who's Who in America,* 1920–21; *N. Y. Times,* Aug. 31, 1920; *Hartford Times,* Aug. 31, 1920; Lorado Taft, *Hist. of Am. Sculpture* (rev. ed., 1924, pp. 245–47; *Am. Art Annual,* ed. by F. N. Levy, XIV; *Internat. Studio,* vol. XXVIII (Apr. 1906), p. xliii.]

E. G. N.

BISSELL, GEORGE HENRY (Nov. 8, 1821–Nov. 19, 1884), promoter of the petroleum industry, was born at Hanover, N. H., the son of Isaac and Nina (Wempe) Bissell, of Norman and Belgian descent, respectively. He attended the military school at Norwich, Vt., the Kimball Union Academy at Meriden, N. H., and Dartmouth College, where he was graduated in 1845. For a short time he was professor of languages at the University of Norwich but soon resigned to go to Washington, D. C., as correspondent for the Richmond *Whig.* He then spent a short time in Cuba before going to New Orleans, where he was on the editorial staff of the New Orleans *Delta.* In 1846 he was elected first principal of the new high school and later became superintendent of the New Orleans schools. During this period he also studied law and graduated LL.B. from Jefferson College. Because of ill health he was compelled to return north, going to New York City, where he was admitted to the bar (1853) and began the practise of law in partnership with J. G. Eveleth. In 1855 he was married to Ophie Griffin of New York City. While on a visit to Dartmouth College his attention was drawn to a sample of petroleum from the Oil Creek region, Pennsylvania, which so interested him that he sent his partner to investigate the source. Finding a ready demand for petroleum, the bulk of which was then used for medicinal purposes, Bissell and Eveleth bought and leased 200 acres of oil lands for $5,000 and in 1854 organized "The Pennsylvania Rock Oil Company," the first oil company in the United States, with a nominal capital of $500,000. The company proceeded to develop the land by digging wells and trenching—the crude method then used—to collect the surface oil. Since the return from the sale proved insufficient to pay expenses, a sample of the petroleum was sent to Prof. Silliman of Yale for analysis in the hope that more valuable use for the oil would suggest itself. Prof. Silliman's report gave information concerning the fractional distillation of the crude and concluded with the belief that "the company have in their possession a raw material from which by simple and inexpensive processes they may manufacture very valuable products." When this report was published the company was reorganized with Prof. Silliman as president, and the work of trenching and digging continued until 1858. The next development was that of boring for oil in the manner of artesian wells, as is done to-day. There is no doubt that Bissell was the first to suggest this important innovation but the story of how it occurred to him has many versions. It is most probable that the salt wells in the oil district suggested oil wells of the same type. When the first drilled well had been sunk by the Seneca Oil Company, lessees of the Pennsylvania Rock Oil Company (1859), Bissell moved to Franklin, Pa., and with Eveleth invested more than $300,000 in oil lands. Returning to New York (1863), he devoted the rest of his life to the promotion of enterprises connected with the petroleum industry.

[*Hist. of Venango County, Pa.* (1879), ed. by J. H. Newton; *A Pop. Hist. of Am. Invention* (1924), ed. by W. B. Kaempffert; Ida M. Tarbell, *Hist. of the Standard Oil Co.* (1904); obituary in *N. Y. Herald*, Nov. 20, 1884.]

F. A. T—r.

BISSELL, WILLIAM HENRY (Apr. 25, 1811–Mar. 18, 1860), congressman, governor of Illinois, came of poor parents living in Yates County, N. Y., but he secured a fair common school education, graduated from Jefferson Medical School, Philadelphia, in 1834, and took up the practise of medicine in Monroe County, Ill. Known for his ability as a public speaker, he was induced to become a candidate on the Democratic ticket, for a seat in the lower house of the state legislature, and although the county was considered a Whig stronghold he was elected. The experience of two years proving agreeable, he then attended a law school in Lexington, Ky., in preparation for a political career. Meantime (1839) he married Emily James, who died the following year, and in 1841 he married Elizabeth Kane. As a lawyer at Belleville, Ill., he quickly took rank among the best in that circuit and was elected prosecuting attorney. It was said to be a hopeless task "to defend where he was prosecuting." Though modest and courteous in manner, he was capable of arousing the passions by his choice language, his keen humor, and his cutting satire. His legal career was interrupted by the Mexican War. Enlisting as a private, he was elected captain and then colonel of the 2nd Illinois, a regiment which was highly rated for its service at the battle of Buena Vista on Feb. 23, 1847. On his return Bissell was elected a representative in Congress, without opposition, in 1848 and again in 1850. Because of a speech during his first term he gained a national reputation. In reply to a Virginia member who claimed that it was a Mississippi regiment which saved the day at Buena Vista, Bissell declared that at the critical moment this regiment was not within a mile and a half of the scene of action (*Congressional Globe*, 31 Cong. 1 Sess., vol. XXII, pt. I, App. p. 228). For this assertion he was challenged to a duel by Jefferson Davis, colonel of the Mississippi regiment. The challenge was accepted, but President Zachary Taylor brought about an adjustment. In opposition to the Southern leadership of the national Democratic party, Bissell announced himself as an independent candidate for Congress in 1852 and was elected. Unable to take part in debate because of illness due to exposure in the army and a partial paralytic stroke, which forced him to go on crutches for the remainder of his life, he was now about to abandon politics. But in the first Republican convention at Bloomington, Ill. (May 29, 1856), wherein were Abraham Lincoln, John M. Palmer, Gustav Koerner, and other well-known representatives from the several political parties, Bissell was the unanimous choice for governor. In the election, he led the state ticket to victory, receiving a plurality of 4,729 votes over the Democratic nominee. The Democrats, however, were in control in both houses of the legislature and united in their opposition to any policy proposed by the Governor. He was bitterly attacked at the opening of the session by John A. Logan on the ground that as a challenger or one who had accepted a challenge to a duel he had sworn falsely in taking the oath of office. In reply, Bissell stated that whatever occurred was outside the jurisdiction of the State of Illinois and therefore did not interfere with his taking the oath. Governor and legislature came to grips over his demand for a law providing for the redistricting of the state based on the census of 1855. The Democrats determined to keep their ascendancy by a bill which gerrymandered the state. Having passed both houses, the measure was sent to Bissell, who refused to sign it. Numbers of Republicans having withdrawn, the bill could not be passed over his veto, and the legislature was forced to adjourn without action on a large number of appropriation measures and on several hundred bills. Some ten months before the expiration of his term of office, Bissell's death occurred, due to an attack of pneumonia, and thus "it was not granted him to see the cause victorious for which he had so nobly fought" (*Memoirs of Gustav Koerner*, 1909, II, 80).

[Jos. Gillespie, *Recollections of Early Illinois*, Fergus Hist. Series 11–15; *Pubs. Illinois Hist. Lib.*, no. 9 (1904), no. 10 (1905); John M. Palmer, *Bench and Bar of Illinois* (1899); Arthur C. Cole, *Era of the Civil War* (1919).]

J. A. J.

BISSELL, WILSON SHANNON (Dec. 31, 1847–Oct. 6, 1903), lawyer, was born in Oneida County, N. Y., of Scotch-Irish stock, and at the age of five was taken to Buffalo by his parents, John and Isabella Jeannette (Hally) Bissell. Destined for the law, he was sent to school in New Haven, Conn., and he was graduated at Yale in 1869. Two years later he was admitted to the bar, and soon became associated with the firm of lawyers to which Grover Cleveland belonged,—in the same office from which Millard Fillmore had gone to the vice-presidency of the United States in 1849. Bissell's friendship with Cleveland, who was ten years his senior, lasted for the rest of his life. He accompanied Cleveland to Albany when the latter was inaugurated as governor of New York in 1883. He appears to have declined a position in the first cabinet that Cleveland formed, in 1885; but he accepted the post office in the second cabinet in 1893. His two years as postmaster general were not productive of novel results in administration, or of happiness to himself. After two years of a prosaic and honorable business administration, disliking the burdens of patronage and the publicity of office, he resigned and returned to his law practise. His permanent satisfactions came from his work as counsel for railroad and other corporations, and from his association with the non-political activities of Buffalo. The Buffalo Historical Society found in him an active, though non-producing member, and owes him much for his services in procuring the notable building that houses its collections. He was a friend to the struggling University of Buffalo, which had been no more than a group of professional schools until, about 1900, it prepared to launch a college of liberal arts. Bissell became chancellor of the University in 1902, holding a position which had generally been ornamental since the day when Millard Fillmore held it. He died in the second year of his office, and was survived by his widow, Louisa Fowler (Sturges) Bissell, whom he had married in 1889.

[*Obit. Record Grads. Yale Univ.* (1910); *Sixth Biog. Record Class of 'Sixty-Nine, Yale Coll.* (1895); H. W. Hill, *Municipality of Buffalo* (1923), II, 904; *Pubs. Buffalo Hist. Soc.*, VII, 488; *Buffalo Express*, Oct. 7, 1903.]

F. L. P.

BITTER, KARL THEODORE FRANCIS (Dec. 6, 1867–Apr. 10, 1915), sculptor, of sound burgher stock, arrived in New York in his twenty-first year, without money, without friends, without English. To offset these lacks, he had health, intelligence, energy, and a passion for art. He had also a valuable though brief experience in decorative modeling, gained at a time when his native Vienna was undergoing great changes, morally and intellectually, the historic city wall having been razed to make way for the famous Ring, with its façades blooming with sculpture. What Bitter brought with him made the foundation of his success. For, working obscurely with his mates to adorn Vienna, he had already formed ideals of coöperation, of leadership, of civic pride, of the importance of beauty in a city's life.

His father, Carl Bitter, was a Protestant who, with his journeyman's kit on his back, had come from Baden in South Germany to seek his fortune in Vienna, where later he became a chemist. He married Henriette Reitter, a Catholic, by whom he had three sons. Karl Theodore Francis, or as he called himself, Karl, was the second of these, and grew up a headstrong, beauty-loving child, with his father's independence, his mother's idealism, and a keen mind of his own. After a period at the Volksschule, he went to the Gymnasium. Here, when he was ten years of age, his encounters with the all-important Latin grammar were markedly unsuccessful. In explanation to his parents, he declared, as an ingenious defense, that the Latin teacher was so ugly to look at that one simply could not learn. As Karl had the gift of eloquence and an interest in affairs, his father had planned for him a career in law, while his mother, a devout woman, had dreamed of the priesthood. But without Latin, what hope in either field? The boy was not sorry. Near his home was a stoneyard, where he had spent magical hours watching the workmen, until at length he was allowed to try his hand. He thereupon became an apprentice, of sorts, in his spare moments. When his anxious parents found it out, they concluded that it was better to let nature, which in Karl's case was art, take its course. He was entered at the Kunstgewerbeschule, the imperial school for applied arts, from which, when old enough, he passed to the Kunstakademie. Attending these schools from 1882 to 1887, he was eager, tireless, filled with delight in his work, and often an arrogant leader of rebellion against the less progressive instructors. When he was twenty, his studies, together with his labors as an obscure assistant in Vienna's adornment, were interrupted by his call to military service. Most of his comrades were regarded as professional students, and therefore were to serve but one year. Bitter, however, had left the Gymnasium too early to have the required certificate, and so was drafted for three years. This injustice he felt keenly. After serving faithfully one year, he took matters into his own hands, renounced his allegiance, and fled to Germany, where he picked up a living as best he might, en route for America. In Berlin he found a friend in a former comrade, Rudolph Schwartz, who aided him with money for his passage, and for his immediate needs in a strange land.

The day after he reached New York, Bitter found work at the first door at which he knocked. He had stumbled on a firm of architectural modelers. Having no English, he let his drawings and photographs speak for him. He was shown some clay, with a crude indication of an angel within it, and was motioned to go to work. He obeyed to such purpose that at the end of a week he received to his amazement a pay envelope of $48. His modeling in this shop met the kindly eye of Richard M. Hunt, the famous architect.

Hunt urged him to set up for himself, promising him considerable interior sculpture for the C. P. Huntington house, then under way. Bitter's talent and training made him just the sculptor Hunt had long been looking for, namely, a facile, imaginative modeler, versed in ornament. That Bitter's gift had also its serious side appears from the fact that in 1891, sixteen months after his arrival in New York, he won the competition for the most important of the three bronze gates of Trinity Church, provided for by the John Jacob Astor bequest, the subject of the competitive panel being "The Expulsion from Paradise." Then came the Chicago Exposition. As Hunt's protégé, Bitter distinguished himself in the elaborate scheme of sculptural decoration for Hunt's Administration Building at the head of the Court of Honor, a scheme in which battalions of forms at once decorative and functional embossed the whole structure with their impassioned story of "The Elements, Controlled and Uncontrolled" (1893). "The zest which he put into these themes," says Taft, "revealed a temperament of singular power and intrepidity, if not a mature taste." The public admired, the architects admired, and thereafter Bitter had no lack of orders for such work. A fifty-foot pediment in terra cotta over the main entrance to the Pennsylvania Railroad Station in Philadelphia, a thirty-foot panel in the waiting-room, and ten panels celebrating the cities along the line had an undisciplined grace that took the public eye (1894). His next achievement was a host of interior and exterior sculptures, of fluent technique and admirable variety, in relief and in the round, in stone, wood, bronze, and polished steel, created to adorn "Biltmore," the Vanderbilt villa in North Carolina (1895). During the following year he completed three colossal stone atlantes, representing the White, Negro, and Malay races, for the façade of the St. Paul Building, in New York, and three years later he undertook the four figures, Architecture, Sculpture, Painting, and Music, for the front of the Metropolitan Museum. In 1899 he made his contribution, a spirited naval group, to that extraordinary sculptural improvisation, the Dewey Arch.

In his bronze statue of Dr. William Pepper, provost of the University of Pennsylvania, a meditative seated figure in academic gown, Bitter expressed himself with a deeper significance than ever before (1898). But the architects were still clamoring for his decorative work, and his gift of leadership still kept him at the head of a group of assistants profitably turning out an amazing amount of architect's fodder, even while he himself longed to make some nobler use of his power. In 1896 he gave up his New York establishment for a romantic site at Weehawken, building there in due season, house, studio, stable. He was not only the maker of equestrian groups, such as the dashing "Standard Bearers" of the Buffalo Exposition (1901), called by Saint-Gaudens the finest of the Exposition sculptures, and the noble presentment of Gen. Sigel on Riverside Drive, New York (1907), he was also a lover of the horse; and his horseback exercise doubtless contributed to his soldierly erectness of bearing. Tall, slender, dark-haired, dark-eyed, dark-bearded, Bitter had nothing of the Teuton in his aspect. Perhaps his military experience was a help to him in his able leadership of the workers associated with him while he was director of sculpture at the Pan-American Exposition (1899–1901), at the St. Louis World's Fair (1902-04), and even at the Panama-Pacific Exposition, where his directorship was generally advisory rather than personal (1912–15). He was twice chosen president of the National Sculpture Society (1906, 1914), and was a member of the New York Municipal Art Commission from 1912 until his death.

On the happy conclusion of his task at the Buffalo Exposition, he was married (1901) to Marie A. Schevill of Cincinnati, Ohio, a lady of marked musical talent and of sensitive artistic appreciation. The pair went abroad for the ensuing summer, but as it was not until 1909 that Bitter received his amnesty from Franz Josef, he was obliged to meet relatives and friends outside the Austrian border. In 1910, however, he revisited his native city, and with great satisfaction renewed old ties, only to realize more fully than ever how dear to him was his American citizenship, which he had obtained as early as possible after his arrival in New York. His marriage was an ideal one. At the turn of the century, when he brought his bride to Weehawken, his first step was to reorganize his studio, "a flourishing decorative establishment," writes his biographer, Dr. Schevill, "fairly flooded with orders, and often with the appearance more of an industrial battlefield than of a retreat of an artist. One after another the helpers were dismissed, and further decorative orders, especially if they carried the unsavory odor of commercialism, rigorously refused." For Bitter, this meant temporary financial loss, and permanent spiritual gain. His draped "Thanatos," in his Hubbard Memorial at Montpelier, Vt. (1903), has often been compared with Saint-Gaudens's celebrated Rock Creek figure, but only as a lyric may be compared with an epic. In his marble Villard Memorial at Sleepy Hollow (1904) a more austere note is sounded by means of a handsome and unique architectural ensemble, the central feature of which is the undraped seated figure of a smith resting beside carved bay trees. These and other memorials reveal Bitter's valiant attempt at a farewell to the commercial element in his art. Happily he still retained the lessons learned in properly relating sculpture to architecture. He had not yet finished with expositional sculpture, however. As director of sculpture at the St. Louis Fair, he succeeded notably in evoking plastic unity of design from an assemblage of models from many hands. His own contribution is a great shaft swarming with history-telling figures. Of this work, one feature has been preserved in bronze for the Jefferson Memorial Building in St. Louis. It is a large relief in eighteenth-century vein, showing Livingston, Monroe, and Marbois signing the Purchase Treaty. The historical studies Bitter then made led him to an intense interest in early American heroes, especially Jefferson; a decade later, during the last three years of his life, he created in addition to other important works, no less than three bronze statues of Jefferson. The first was for the Jefferson Memorial Building; the second, a seated figure of heroic size, and flanked by a Hamilton, also from Bitter's hand, was placed in front of the Court House at Cleveland; the third, commissioned by his friend, Charles R. Crane, was unveiled on the grounds of the University of Virginia three days after Bitter's death. These three bronzes differ suitably in design. The first reveals Jefferson as pioneer, the last as patriarch, while the second chooses middle ground. Bitter's enormous productivity is shown by the host of works created by him and his assistants during the interval between the St. Louis Fair and the San Francisco Fair. Included are two important pediments and four heroic groups for the Wisconsin State Capitol at Madison (1908–12), four Chinese figures for the façade of the Brooklyn Museum (1909), statues of Lords Somers and Mansfield for the Court House at Cleveland (1910), and many portraits in relief or in the round. By frequent trips abroad, Bitter, master of many materials, kept himself abreast of all the new movements in art. In the granite panels for his finely conceived and nobly placed Schurz monument in New York (1913), as in the perforated marble screen behind his statue of Thomas Lowry, a leading citizen of Minneapolis (1915), and the sternly cut granite figures for the First National Bank Building in Cleveland (1908), he showed himself an adept in modern simplicity; while on the other hand, in his memorials to Dr. Angell and to Dr. Tappan at Ann Arbor, Mich. (1910, 1913), he made a sober return to a generally useful realism of manner, not untouched by poetic idealism. The frieze of little children in his Prehn Memorial at Passaic, the graceful kneeling figure in the Kasson Memorial at Utica, the Goose Girl fountain at Pocantico Hills, and the unfinished studies for the Depew fountain for Indianapolis finely express their opposed emotions of joy and sorrow. In his relief portrait of Dr. Angell for Ann Arbor and in his bronze statue of President White of Cornell University (1915), Bitter enjoyed the opportunity, rare for sculptors, of studying his subjects from life rather than afterward.

Thus far, Bitter's gifts to his adopted country were: first, a swarm of decorative sculptures in the Viennese manner; next, a successful management of the sculptural elements in three World's Fairs, to be followed by a more permanent civic service, valuable in many directions; and last, his solid achievements as a many-sided sculptor of increasingly high ideals. He had received golden honors, including the Architectural League Medal of Honor in Sculpture (1914). Fond of music and reading, he took special pleasure in the study of history, of philosophy, of comparative religion. The headstrong youth had matured into the thoughtful, kindly man who had learned to persuade instead of to domineer. His last work, not yet put into bronze at the time of his tragic death, but faithfully completed by his friend Isidor Konti, is a calm and happy figure of "Abundance" crowning the great fountain in New York's Plaza. In a spirit of elation on the evening of the very day when he had put the last touches to his full-sized model, he and his wife attended the opera. The performance over, they started across Broadway, when suddenly an automobile out of control swept them down. Mrs. Bitter escaped with minor injuries, her husband lived but a few hours. His life was cut short before he had reached the fullness of his powers. In his latest work, every element attested and prophesied still further growth, still higher ideals.

[The most reliable information concerning Karl Bitter is found in the biography written by his brother-in-law, Dr. Ferdinand Schevill, and issued under the auspices of the National Sculpture Society in 1917. From 1891 until after Bitter's death, numerous articles in the press and in magazines chronicled his activities. See esp. *Sketch Book,* VI, 1; *Brush and Pencil,* XIII, 199, 466; *Am. Art News,* XIII, 4; *Am. Arch.,* CVII, 274; *Art and Progress,* VI, 285, 295; *Arch. Record,* XLII, 280. Bitter's work is described in Lorado Taft's *Hist. of Am. Sculpture* (1903), and in the same author's *Modern Tendencies in Sculpture* (1921).] A. A—s.

BIXBY, HORACE EZRA (May 8, 1826–Aug. 1, 1912), Mississippi pilot, was born in Geneseo,

N. Y., the son of Sylvanus Bixby and his wife, Hannah Barnes, who had been the widow of Benjamin Kneeland. In his early teens he ran away from home and wandered as far as Cincinnati, where he found work in a tailor's shop. At eighteen he became a "mud clerk" on the river steamboat *Olivia* and two years later was made her pilot. The rest of his long life was passed on the Mississippi and her great tributaries. He soon was known as a "lightning pilot"—one whose courage, judgment, and knowledge of the uncharted, unmarked, ever changing river were equal to any emergency, and his services were usually required on the large boats plying between St. Louis and New Orleans. But in April 1857 he happened to be taking an "ancient tub" from Cincinnati to New Orleans when one morning a young printer, Samuel Clemens by name, invited himself into the pilot house, struck up an acquaintance, and did much of the steering for the remainder of the trip, while Bixby sat at his ease and nursed a sore foot. The rest of the episode has been recorded, though not with complete historical accuracy, in some of the most vivid pages of American prose. When Clemens received his pilot's license, Sept. 9, 1858, Bixby took him for a while as a partner, and the two friends met again long after in 1882 and 1902. In the years just before the Civil War Bixby was frequently engaged in the lucrative Missouri River trade, sometimes making almost $1,800 a month. So retentive was his memory that he learned the Missouri in an incredibly short time: for his trained intelligence it was enough to see each section of the river once in daylight and once by night. In 1860 he married Susan Weibling of New Orleans. She died in 1867, and on Jan. 2, 1868, he married Mary, daughter of Capt. Edwin A. Sheble of St. Louis, who outlived him. During the Civil War he was pilot on the gunboat *Benton* and rose to be chief of the Union River Service. For two or three years he was captain and owner of a boat that made trips to Fort Benton, Mont. Occasionally, in the upper reaches of the Missouri, the boat had to stop while a herd of buffalo swam the river; at other times there were meetings, more or less exciting, with Sioux Indians. Later he was one of the owners of the Anchor Line, which operated a fleet of palatial river steamers between St. Louis and New Orleans. He himself was captain of the *City of Baton Rouge*. At first the line prospered; later it lost many of its boats and finally disappeared from the river. Bixby, of small physique but wiry and tremendouslv energetic, stayed on the Mississippi long after the glory of its commerce had disappeared. He entered the government service and at the age of eighty-six was commander of the snagboat *Wright*. At last, however, he decided that he was growing too old for active service, and two days after his decision he died suddenly at his suburban home in Maplewood, Mo.

[Letter to writer from Bixby's daughter Edwina (Mrs. Louis Tousard Pim) June 25, 1928; *St. Louis Globe-Democrat*, Aug. 2, 3, 1912; S. F. Kneeland, *Seven Centuries in the Kneeland Family* (1897), p. 345; A. B. Paine, *Mark Twain* (1912); Mark Twain, *Life on the Mississippi* (1883); *Official Records U. and C. Navies*, ser. I, vol. XXIII.]

G. H. G.

BIXBY, JAMES THOMPSON (July 30, 1843–Dec. 26, 1921), Unitarian clergyman, author, was born in Barre, Mass., the third child of Clark Smith Bixby, a merchant, and of Elizabeth (Clark) Bixby, daughter of Abijah and Elizabeth (Heald) Clark of Hubbardston, Mass. The family leaving Barre, the son prepared for college in the Cambridge High School and graduated from Harvard in 1864. After employment for three years in New York as a private tutor, he received the degree of A.M. from Harvard and entered the Harvard Divinity School, being the first to receive (1870) the degree of B.D. from that school. On Sept. 1, 1870, he was married to Emma Gibson of Boston. Ordained Sept. 20, 1870, he was pastor of the First Parish, Watertown, Mass., until April 1874, and from November 1874 to 1878 was pastor of the Independent Congregational (Unitarian) Church of Belfast, Me. He then became professor of religious philosophy and ethnic religions in the Meadville Theological School, serving also as pastor of the Unitarian Church of Meadville, Pa. From July 1883 to June 1885 he was in Europe, studying in the universities of Heidelberg, Jena, and Leipzig, and obtaining the degree of Ph.D. in Leipzig in March 1885. For a year after his return he supplied the Unitarian Church of Ann Arbor, Mich., and then was settled over the Unitarian Church in Yonkers, N. Y., from January 1887 until he retired in December 1903. During this pastorate he was prominent in New York in the activities of the Reform Club, the Authors Club, and the Liberal Ministers' Association, being chairman of the latter organization for twelve years (1891–1903). In such circles his genial disposition, his magnanimous judgments, and his unusual fluency of expression won him high favor. His preaching, though often too burdened with learning, was marked by deep spirituality and sensitive comprehension of human suffering. His first wife having died on Mar. 20, 1902, he was married on Feb. 24, 1906, to Clara Webster Parker of Yonkers, and continued to reside in Yonkers until his death.

In his earlier pastorates Bixby published in the *Unitarian Review* many vigorous discussions of the problems created for religion and ethics by the evolutionary science of Spencer, Darwin, and Huxley. In this connection he argued (1874) that science, to be complete as science, must apply its methods of observation, induction, and verification to the indisputable facts of religion in human experience. He was heralding a new "scientific theology." Other articles (1876, 1877) advocated a Theistic Monism on the basis of evolutionary science. Bixby won distinction also as an early expositor of the philosophy of Lotze and of the physiological psychology of Fechner and Wundt (1877). A second stage in his career was marked by his interest in comparative religion, which bore fruit in many articles in the *Unitarian Review* (1880–90) and the *New World* (1892–1900) and in lectures before the Meadville Theological School (1887–1899) and the Greenacre Summer School. The most widely influential of his books was *The Crisis in Morals* (1891) which reappeared in larger revision as *The Ethics of Evolution* (1900), a searching criticism of the Hedonism of Spencer's *Data of Ethics,* followed by a constructive argument that the source of moral principles is found in the fundamental unity of life with its pressure to larger and higher existence. His other books were *Similarities of Physical and Religious Knowledge* (1876); *Religion and Science as Allies* (1889); *The New World and the New Thought* (1902); *The Open Secret; A Study of Life's Deeper Forces* (1912). In his last years, afflicted with blindness, he dealt with the question of immortality (*Bibliotheca Sacra,* October 1916; *Biblical World,* September 1920).

[W. G. Bixby, *Bixby Family Record,* pt. 3, p. 584; *Report of the Class of 1864, Harvard Coll.* (1919); F. A. Christie, *The Makers of the Meadville Theological School* (1927).]

F. A. C.

BJERREGAARD, CARL HENRIK ANDREAS (May 24, 1845–Jan. 28, 1922), mystical philosopher and librarian, born in Fredericia, Denmark, where his father was principal of the local Latin school or gymnasium, was the son of Janus Bagge Friis and Louise (Nielsen) Bjerregaard. He studied at his father's school, but did not graduate there or at the University (letter, Apr. 21, 1927, from Konst, Universitetsinspøkter, København); served as a volunteer spy in the Schleswig-Holstein war, tried various occupations, went to St. Petersburg and other parts of Europe as a teacher in the household of the Danish minister to Russia, entered the Danish military service as a candidate for officer (in the reserve not the regular service) on July 2, 1866, reached the rank of second lieutenant, and was dropped from the army rolls on Jan. 1, 1894. His actual connection with the army ceased many years earlier, however, for he left the service and the country without permission in the summer of 1873, on the eve of a police investigation into an alleged offense against the civil criminal code. The offense could scarcely have been of gravest character, as he was permitted to return on a visit in 1904, and on Sept. 11, 1920, the King made him a Knight of Danebrog. He explained his departure by saying he anticipated an assignment to garrison duty in the Danish West Indies, or by saying he had been seen with socialists while in uniform.

In August 1873, he landed in New York, penniless and friendless. A linoleum factory in Salem, N. J., gave him work for a month at starvation wages, but left him stranded when the panic of September 1873 closed its doors. Six years of distress and privation followed. He managed to bring over in the summer of 1874 his wife and the two children then born to them. In October 1879, the struggle for existence was lessened somewhat by his appointment to the staff of the Astor Library. He remained with that institution and its successor, the New York Public Library, until his death. He had been a reader and student wherever he found himself, and his connection with the library gave a welcome chance to work with books and to follow his scholarly instincts. Increasing command of English brought opportunities for self-expression on the lecture platform, and as his name became better known there came increased demand for his writings on philosophy and related topics. His books include *Lectures on Mysticism and Talks on Kindred Subjects* (1896); *Lectures on Mysticism and Nature Worship, Second Series* (1897); *Sufi Interpretations of the Quatrains of Omar Khayyam and Fitzgerald* (1902); *The Inner Life and the Tao-Teh-King* (1912); *The Great Mother: a Gospel of the Eternally Feminine* (1913). Lesser known sides of the man were his love of nature and his sense of artistic expression. He frequently took friends and fellow spirits on Sunday walks for combined exposition of flowers, mysticism, botany, oriental philosophy. Shortly before his death he took to painting in oil as another form of expression, and though he certainly was not a great artist his work was vibrant with a note of individuality.

He was married on Sept. 30, 1868, to Mathilde Georgina Thomsen by whom he had seven children.

[Dahl og Engelstoft, *Dansk Biografisk Haandleksikon,* I; *Illustreret Familie-Journal* (Minneapolis), July

1905; *Norden* (Racine, Wis.), Sept. 1905; *Am.-Scandinavian Rev.*, June 1921; *N. Y. Evening Post*, Apr. 11, 1914, Jan. 8, 1921; *Sun* (N. Y.), Oct. 30, 1920; *N. Y. World*, Oct. 23, 1921; *N. Y. Herald*, May 24, 1915; *Bull. N. Y. Pub. Lib.*, Feb. 1922.] H. M. L.

BLACK, FRANK SWETT (Mar. 8, 1853–Mar. 22, 1913), lawyer, governor of New York, the son of Jacob and Charlotte (Swett) Black, was born on a farm at Limington, York County, Me. He obtained such education as the rural community afforded, and upon the removal of his parents to Alfred, Me., where his father was keeper of the county jail, he prepared for college at Limerick and Lebanon academies, meanwhile working and teaching school to earn expenses. At eighteen, a slender young man six feet three inches in height, he entered Dartmouth College. Although forced by circumstances to earn his way, he graduated in 1875 as an honor man, having married in his senior year Lois B. Hamlin of Provincetown, Mass. Declining several school principalships, he accepted the editorship of the *Journal* at Johnstown, N. Y., devoting himself meanwhile to the study of law. Severing his connection with the *Journal* because of a difference of opinion with the owner over the Blaine-Conkling controversy, he located in Troy, N. Y., continued his legal studies, and supported himself and family meanwhile with newspaper and clerical work. Admitted to the bar in 1879, he joined the firm of Smith, Wellington & Black for a year and then set up his own office. Native ability, hard work, and the mastery of every case, quickly won for him a wide legal practise and a reputation as one of the leading attorneys in his section of the state. By 1888 his wit and eloquence as a public speaker brought him into prominence as a campaign orator for the Republican party of which he was an ardent member. As chairman of the Republican committee for Rensselaer County in 1893 his successful efforts to clean up certain election frauds resulted in his election to Congress in 1894 and in his reëlection two years later. Meanwhile as a delegate to the Republican National Convention he helped to nominate McKinley for the presidency and was active in his election. The Republican State Convention held at Saratoga Springs in 1896, captivated by his address as temporary chairman, nominated him for governor. After a spectacular campaign, he was elected by the largest plurality ever given in the state to a gubernatorial candidate. Serving but one term, from 1897 to 1899, he urged the completion of the capitol at Albany, the preservation of the forests, biennial sessions of the legislature, a sensible civil service code, reform in the election laws, and the improvement of roads. Most of his recommendations were enacted into law. During his administration the Spanish-American War broke out and it was largely due to his efforts that New York responded so quickly with men and money. Upon retiring to private life he resumed the practise of law in New York City, where his services were in much demand by litigants with important cases. He was generally regarded as an able lawyer, a fearless and incorruptible statesman, and a man of charming manner.

[No complete biography of Frank Swett Black has been written. Brief sketches of his life are given in E. L. Murlin, *N. Y. Red Book* (1897), pp. 91–104; Chas. E. Fitch, *Official N. Y. from Cleveland to Hughes* (1911), I, 149–63; Rutherford Hayner, *Troy and Rensselaer Counties* (1925), II, 482; *Albany Jour.*, Mar. 22, 1913. His messages as governor are in Chas. Z. Lincoln, *State of N. Y., Messages from the Governors* (1909), IX, 738–886.] A. C. F.

BLACK, GREENE VARDIMAN (Aug. 3, 1836–Aug. 31, 1915), dentist, was born on a farm near Winchester, Ill., a son of William and Mary S. (Vaughn) Black. When he was eight years old, the family removed to another farm near Virginia, Ill., where they made with their own hands the brick out of which their house was constructed. The little lad helped as his puny strength permitted. At seventeen he took up the study of medicine with an elder brother, Dr. Thomas G. Black of Clayton, Ill. Three years later he entered the office of Dr. J. C. Speer, Mt. Sterling, Ill., as a student of dentistry; in 1857 he began practise in Winchester, Ill., and in 1860 he married Jane L. Coughennower. In 1862 he enlisted in the 129th Illinois Volunteer Infantry, serving as sergeant, mostly on scout duty, until disabled by an injury to the knee, which led to his discharge in 1863. In 1864 he resumed the practise of dentistry, in Jacksonville, Ill., and in 1865, his first wife having died two years earlier, he married Elizabeth Akers Davenport. Shortly after he began practise in Jacksonville, he formed a class in chemistry among the school teachers and others which he continued for several years. From 1870 to 1880 he lectured in Missouri Dental College on pathology, histology, and operative dentistry. He was professor of dental pathology in Chicago College of Dental Surgery 1883–89, introducing the teaching of dental technics in 1887; professor of dental pathology and bacteriology in the University of Iowa 1890–91; and professor of dental pathology and bacteriology in Northwestern University Dental School from 1891 until his death, becoming in 1897 dean of the school and professor of operative dentistry in addition to his other professorships. Black's first important paper (*Missouri Dental Journal,* July 1869) reported his investigation into the cause of the loss of workability by cohesive gold when stored in the dental cabinet. Its demonstration of the cause, the remedy, and means of prevention has remained unquestioned, the successful rule of practise by dentists. Black's views on "Diseases of the Peridental Membrane," presented in a chapter contributed to the *American System of Dentistry* (1886), were sharply criticized at first but finally accepted. His next important dental investigation was reported in a series of papers (*Dental Cosmos*, January, February, May, June, July, 1891) entitled "Management of Enamel Margins," setting forth the doctrine of "Extension for Prevention," *i. e.*, the extension of the cavity in order to prevent further decay. The idea was bitterly assailed in some quarters, but is now the basis of the accepted method of preparing cavities for filling. In 1895 Black presented in the *Dental Cosmos* (May-September) "An Investigation of the Physical Characters of the Human Teeth in Relation to Their Diseases and to Practical Dental Operations, together with the Physical Characters of Filling Materials." In this he definitely destroyed two myths that had been everywhere accepted as true. The first was that some teeth were soft and prone to caries, while others were hard and practically immune. Black showed that neither the density of the tooth nor the percentage of lime-salts it contains has anything to do with its liability to caries. The second had to do with the idea expressed in the common saying, "for every child a tooth." Black showed that, contrary to the common belief even among dentists at that time, the teeth of women during pregnancy are not leached of their lime-salts. As a third result of this investigation, Black evolved a method of making alloys for amalgam that assured their stability. This method he taught to all who cared to learn. To-day practically all dental amalgam alloys are made by the Black method, and amalgam, then a despised outcast, has come to be valued second only to gold as a filling for tooth cavities. Dr. Black was a voluminous writer. Besides the reports of his investigations, of which only a few of the more important have been mentioned, he wrote several books and numerous papers. At a banquet tendered to him five years before his death by the Chicago Odontographic Society, and attended by several hundred dentists from this country and abroad, a pamphlet—admittedly incomplete—was distributed containing more than five hundred titles of books, reports, papers, and major discussions. His style was singularly clear and simple, a clean-cut statement of facts and of the logical deductions from them, with a notable lack of technical terms. He wrote for the understanding of the many, with an unusual faculty of making his ideas available for practical application. His first book, *The Formation of Poisons by Micro-Organisms* (1884), is still looked upon as an authoritative statement of the subject as then developed. In 1887 came *A Study of the Histological Characters of the Periosteum and Peridental Membrane.* In 1891 he produced his *Dental Anatomy,* a minute study of the macroscopical structure of the human teeth, the recognized text-book of the dental colleges to-day. In 1893, as chairman of the committee on nomenclature of the Columbian Dental Congress, his comprehensive report laid the foundation for a scientific dental nomenclature. In 1908 his *Operative Dentistry* appeared in two volumes: Volume I—*Pathology of the Hard Tissues of the Teeth;* Volume II—*Technical Procedures in Filling Teeth.* In 1915 appeared a third volume to be grouped with the two just mentioned, entitled *Diseases and Treatment of the Investing Tissues of the Teeth and the Dental Pulp,* his final presentation of this subject. He was also an inventor. In 1871 he designed one of the first cord dental engines. Much of his experimental work took him into unknown fields and he was compelled to devise, in some cases to personally make, much of the apparatus he used. In 1904 he supplied the patterns for 102 "cutting instruments" for carrying out the exact measures he regarded as necessary to the proper excavation of cavities. He made the drawings for many of the illustrations in his books and papers, played several instruments with more than the touch of an amateur, and had a fine singing voice. His varied activities continued till within a few weeks of his death. The last article from his pen, a study in collaboration with Dr. Frederick S. McKay of "Mottled Teeth, an Endemic Developmental Imperfection of the Enamel," theretofore unknown in dental literature, appeared in July 1915. Physically, Black was tall though never robust in build, but capable of almost unlimited endurance, as was necessary in the strenuous life he led. Always he wore a full beard, its dark, almost black color bleaching with advancing years. Of a simple, unaffected personality, willing to learn from others, never failing in his willingness to help others, he had the respect and affectionate regard of all who came in contact with him. He steadily refused to commercialize his work, devoting his energies mainly to the elucidation of problems for the benefit of his colleagues, though he engaged in many scientific investigations outside of dental matters. He was accorded numerous honors, including the presidency of the National Dental Association in 1901, the first International Miller Prize in 1910, and honorary degrees from five institutions. The character of the man was not one whit below the level of his achievements. One of his biographers voiced the feeling of his profession in these words: "He was great in achievements, great also in his simplicity and sincerity. He climbed the heights, but he took his fellows with him every step of the way."

[The facts for this sketch of Dr. Black were gained from files of the dental magazines, transactions of dental societies, and from correspondence with his son, Dr. Arthur D. Black. There is a sketch by A. W. Harris in *Science*, n. s., XLII, 496–97.]

F. L. H.

BLACK, JAMES (Sept. 23, 1823–Dec. 16, 1893), lawyer, founder of the National Prohibition Party and its first candidate for president (1872), was born in Lewisburg, Pa., the son of John and Jane (Egbert) Black. His father, an engineer and contractor, had a leading part in building the Grand Trunk Railroad, and the first Croton (N. Y.) Dam. His grandfather, John Black, came to America in 1790 from Scotland, and settled in Union County, Pa., where the family lived for two generations. James Black moved with his parents to Lancaster in 1836, and there married (1845) Eliza Murray, daughter of William Murray. His formal schooling ended in 1843, after he had spent three years in Lewisburg Academy. Upon leaving the academy he read law and was admitted to the Lancaster County bar in 1846, at the time when Thaddeus Stevens and James Buchanan were the leading local attorneys. At sixteen he became a convert to the cause of temperance. According to the story that he and other temperance writers used to tell, he was forced on one occasion, when employed as a mule-driver on the Pennsylvania and Union Canal, to join the older men in a drinking orgy. Upon recovering from the effects and realizing what had occurred, he made a vow forever after to abstain from the use of intoxicating liquors. This marked a turning-point in his life. In 1840 he was one of the first in Lancaster to join the local branch of the "Washington Association." This association had recently been organized in Baltimore by members of a drinking club, who, after listening to a lecture on temperance, Apr. 6, 1840, decided to reform, and changed their name to the "Washington Temperance Society." In 1846 Black helped to organize the Conestoga Division of the Sons of Temperance in Lancaster. In 1855, because of his leadership, the Prohibition Party in Lancaster County elected two members to the Pennsylvania state legislature. In 1857 he was instrumental in organizing the Lancaster Lodge of Good Templars, of which in 1864 he was elected Right Worthy Grand Councillor. It was at the request of the Grand Lodge that he prepared his celebrated "Cider Tract," which resulted in barring cider drinkers from the order. Following the Civil War, he worked more ardently than ever for prohibition. He early sensed the need for an extensive educational campaign, and at the National Temperance Convention in Saratoga, 1865, he presented a plan and had it approved, of establishing a National Publication House. He was responsible for the first state prohibition convention in Pennsylvania, held in Harrisburg in February 1867, and served as its chairman. In 1872 the National Prohibition Party decided to nominate a national ticket. At the convention in Columbus, Ohio, Feb. 22, six names were presented for the presidential nomination: Ben F. Butler, David Davis, Samuel P. Chase, J. D. Cox, Horace Greeley, and James Black. A majority of the committee on nominations voted for Black, and he was made the unanimous choice. In the election he polled 5,608 votes (Smull, *Legislative Handbook of Pennsylvania,* 1872, p. 393). From this time until his death, Black had a voice in virtually every platform, resolution, and official document written by the Prohibition Party. He was a member of the Lancaster Methodist Episcopal Church, and in 1869, he with twenty-seven other individuals organized the Ocean Grove (N. J.) Association. He was a life-long collector of books and pamphlets on temperance, and at the time of his death (1893) had probably the most complete temperance library in existence.

[The Hon. David F. Magee of Lancaster, an intimate friend and associate of Black, and now Secretary of the Lancaster County Historical Society, assisted in obtaining many of the facts used in this sketch. Black's son, William Murray Black, Major-General, U. S. A., retired, supplied the facts and dates regarding the family's genealogy. The story of Black's sudden decision to take up the cause of prohibition appears in numerous temperance publications; the earliest printed account is found in the *Daily New Era* (Lancaster, Pa.), Dec. 16, 1893, and was probably written by the late Hon. John H. Landis, a life-long associate and friend. Black himself was the author of three small volumes,—*Is There a Necessity for a Prohibition Party?* (1878); *Brief Hist. of Prohibition* (1880); and *Hist. of the Prohibition Party* (1885).]

J. W. O.

BLACK, JEREMIAH SULLIVAN (Jan. 10, 1810–Aug. 19, 1883), attorney-general, of Scotch-Irish, Irish, and German descent, the son of Henry and Mary (Sullivan) Black, was born near Stony Creek, Pa. He grew up in this pioneer agricultural community a quick-witted, homely, nervous boy. As his appearance made him a tempting object of ridicule, he early learned the utility of hard-hitting and tongue-lashing and gained skill in the art of self-defense; controversy became second nature. He went to various schools irregularly kept in the locality at Stoystown, Berlin, and Somerset, and "finished" at the academy in Bridgeport, Pa. But much of his preparation came from his own enterprise; his restlessness ever required something for his mind to feed upon. He had imagination and a feeling for rhythm; Horace, the Bible, and Shakespeare he read with a retentive memory, and throughout the remainder of his life he could startle or thrill with a variety of apt quotations. His inclination was toward medicine, but his father had other plans and at seventeen sent him to Somerset to study in the office of Chauncey Forward, leader of the bar and prominent politician.

Black's law apprenticeship had all the advantages arising from the patronage of a prominent man. Forward pushed him, and within three years he was admitted to the bar, Dec. 3, 1830. Thereupon his teacher went to Congress leaving him in charge of his extensive practise. Very shortly he was appointed deputy attorney-general for the county and in this manner found himself on one side or the other of nearly every case before the county court. It was a responsibility which weighed heavily upon Black because self-confidence came slowly and with difficulty, but in the constant matching of wits with the elder lawyers he learned to use effectively his mental agility and telling speech. Politics was of course inevitable to most lawyers in those days, and in the exciting 'thirties he marched with his teacher in the Jacksonian ranks. His relations with Forward were perhaps the greatest influence in his life. Besides following him in law and politics he married Forward's daughter, Mary, in 1836 and after his preceptor's death embraced his religious views, becoming an ardent Campbellite after a deep religious experience. In 1842 Gov. Porter solved a patronage tangle by using Black as a compromise appointee and placing him upon the bench as president judge of the court of common pleas for the sixteenth judicial district (Franklin, Bedford, and Somerset counties). After nine years' experience he was elected to the supreme bench of the state and was reëlected in 1854; by lot he served the first three years as chief justice. As lawyer and judge, Black does not seem to have studied widely, but rather to have reduced the law to a number of fundamental principles and to have based his arguments and his decisions on strikingly clear and convincing statements of these maxims. As judge his principal contribution is said to have been his clarity of reasoning and statement in defining the meaning of corporation charters when that problem first arose.

Black had been an active supporter of Buchanan for twenty years and in 1857 the latter appointed him attorney-general at the last moment as a compromise between Pennsylvania factions. So at forty-seven, Black went to Washington to begin his national career. Though not yet as eccentric as he was later to become, he was quite a "character." He was tall, rather slouching, and loose-jointed, given to quick and erratic movements. His clothes and his wig never seemed to fit, but his keen gray eyes and infectious laugh made him singularly attractive in some moods. He was temperamental and proverbially absent-minded; he could lose himself in a task completely and become perfectly oblivious of surroundings. His ability to love and hate was marked, and his usually sound judgment could be much distorted by his emotions; stubbornness in holding to his opinion was not the least apparent of his numerous decided characteristics. Thus equipped Black started on a very trying four years. His most important problem was connected with California land titles. The policy of Congress in forcing every one to prove his title in that region had caused innumerable suits. As many of the actions involved government titles and depended upon the widely dispersed Spanish archives, Black sent Edwin M. Stanton to California to collect the records and investigate. With local aid the latter uncovered a system of fraud which when presented to the Supreme Court caused it to reverse many decisions sent up from the district court. Black considered this the great achievement of his régime; H. H. Bancroft after his investigations is not so confident (*History of California,* 1888, VI, 573–74). The other important legal problem which confronted the attorney-general was that of enforcing federal laws locally unpopular. There were three classes of cases of this type, dealing with the slave trade, filibustering expeditions, and return of fugitive slaves. In directing these, Black sought to enforce the law both in the North and the South but without much success, for though to him law was law, this fact was not so potent among the laity.

An incomplete picture of his life in Washington would be presented, however, if consideration were given only to his legal duties. As a member of Buchanan's cabinet he had to be politician and minister as well as lawyer. As politician he must aid Buchanan in keeping the Democratic party solid. In this capacity his greatest task was his controversy with Douglas when the latter attacked the administration policy. He entered into a pamphlet war with the Illinois senator and ably attacked squatter sovereignty, basing his argument upon the ground that territorial legislatures could never make laws violating the fifth amendment. As cabinet minister, Black did his share in shaping the administration's Kansas policy, upholding the Lecompton Constitution as legally adopted, in the vain hope that statehood would bring to an end the turmoil. But the greatest problem was secession. Lincoln's election causing the administration to realize the imminence of secession, Black was called upon to give advice as to the proper course to pursue in the event of such action. The Attorney-General prepared an opinion wherein he argued that while the Executive might not coerce a seceding state, he was in duty bound to enforce the laws and protect federal property. Black urged that proper garrisons be placed in the federal forts in the South as precautionary measures; but these measures Buchanan would not take. For this reason, ostensibly, Cass resigned as secretary of state, and Buchanan chose Black to fill his place, commissioning him on Dec. 17, 1860. His brief tenure of this office witnessed little of note in our foreign relations, an abortive negotiation with Great Britain over the northwest boundary being the only action attempted; but the domestic difficulties were a continuous nightmare. How to maintain the authority of the federal government and yet not take any steps that would cause secession; this was the difficult problem which Buchanan and his advisers faced.

Almost the day Black entered the State Department, South Carolina seceded and immediately attempted to negotiate for the control of federal property within state limits. Buchanan refused to recognize South Carolina's pretensions, but in the course of correspondence with her commissioners the President made some statements which Black thought insufficiently explicit in denying South Carolina's contentions. He threatened to resign; Buchanan, however, accepted some of his suggestions and at length when the tone of the commissioners became too overbearing broke off correspondence with them and sent the *Star of the West* with supplies to aid Major Anderson in Charleston Harbor. Black was somewhat relieved at this outcome, but when the *Star of the West* was forced to return his hopes failed. He did what he could to urge further reinforcements and the mobilization of troops to protect Washington, but Buchanan was pinning his hopes upon the Peace Convention. With this disappointment came another: the Senate refused to confirm Black's appointment to the Supreme Court made by Buchanan Feb. 5, 1861; Republicans, Douglas Democrats, and the Southern sympathizers were all hostile to Black. On Feb. 28, the Secretary sent a circular letter to our foreign ministers urging them to do what they could to prevent any recognition of the Confederacy by foreign powers and upon Mar. 4 he retired.

In the weeks and months following Lincoln's inauguration Black reached the lowest point of his career. He was not in good health; several times during his service in the cabinet he had been forced to leave his duties to conserve his strength. He had lost his savings, entrusted to a relative for investment. He was, besides, a member of a defeated and discredited party and the impending conflict was paralyzing normal business activity; there seemed nothing in the future. Black suffered as only a temperamental person can. He retired to York, Pa., in which vicinity he was to live the remainder of his days, and there his material fortunes began to mend. He was appointed United States Supreme Court reporter in December 1861 and prepared *Black's Reports,* vols. I and II. But his greatest good fortune was his knowledge of the California land cases. There was to be litigation for the next decade and his expert services proved generally successful to the side retaining them; hence enormous fees came his way and even his carelessness could not return him to poverty. During the war he was a sharp opponent of the administration's "unconstitutional" program of disregarding civil rights and confiscating Southern property. He continued his protest against secession, however, and paid lip service at least to the successful prosecution of the war. He supported McClellan in 1864 and undertook an unofficial mission to see Jacob Thompson in Canada on behalf of peace, a commission which Stanton afterwards repudiated. The close of the war found him deep in the Milligan and McCardle cases which gave him free rein for powerful forensic condemnations of the war despotism. He aided and advised Andrew Johnson in his constitutional law and was to be one of his counsel before the impeachment court but withdrew in a fit of pique because Johnson would not overrule Seward for one of his clients. During this period, in 1869, Black met with a serious acident which deprived him of the use of his right arm. Nothing daunted, he learned to use his left. Fame was his, pleasant surroundings, fortune; he had reached about as high a plane of freedom as one can attain; oblivious of any unconquerable situation, he lived a curiously egocentric, mentally active life that made him a renowned "character," the hero of many a comic anecdote, and a great controversialist. He defended Christianity, he defended Buchanan, he defended Tilden before the Electoral Commission, he participated in magazine-article wars, he championed unpopular causes, he helped revise the Pennsylvania constitution of

1873 where his chief activity was directed toward controlling and regulating railroads and corporations. He reveled in righteousness and expression. So his life increased in its satisfactions and its independence until he died in August 1883, his great mental energy unflagging to the end. For more than a quarter of a century he had played a dynamic and dramatic rôle upon the national stage as a defender of the Constitution, the Union, and the Ten Commandments.

[There is no life of Black. His son, Chauncey F. Black, edited his *Essays and Speeches* (1885), prefaced by a biographical memoir, while his daughter, Mary Black Clayton, was the author of *Reminiscences of Jeremiah Sullivan Black* (1887); both of these, however, are appreciations. Articles upon his career and its various phases are, Henry C. Niles, "Jeremiah S. Black and His Influence on the Law of Pennsylvania" in *Ninth Annual Report of the Pa. Bar Ass.* (1903); Margaret C. Klingelsmith, "Jeremiah S. Black" in *Great Am. Lawyers*, ed. by Wm. Draper Lewis (1909), VI, 1–75; Francis Newton Thorpe, "Jeremiah S. Black," in *Pa. Mag. of Hist. and Biog.*, L, 117–33, 273–86; Roy F. Nichols, "Jeremiah S. Black" in *Am. Secretaries of State and Their Diplomacy* (1928), VI. The papers of Jeremiah S. Black are in the Manuscript Division of the Lib. of Cong. and a number of his letters are in the Buchanan MSS. in the Hist. Soc. of Pa. His reminiscences were published by Frank A. Burr in the *Phila. Press*, Aug. 7, 14, 21, 28, 1881.]
R. F. N.

BLACK, JOHN CHARLES (Jan. 27, 1839–Aug. 17, 1915), lawyer, soldier, was the son of John C. Black, a Presbyterian minister, and of Josephine (Culbertson) Black, both originally of western Pennsylvania. He was born in Lexington, Miss., but his parents later moved to Midway, Ky., and then returned to western Pennsylvania. After the death of the father in 1844, the family of four, consisting of two boys and two girls, John being the oldest, were taken by their mother to Danville, Ill., where her brother resided. At the opening of the Civil War, John was a junior in Wabash College. He enlisted immediately after the fall of Fort Sumter, serving in a company of Zouaves which was organized and commanded by Lew Wallace. For three months after this company became a part of the 11th Indiana Regiment he served as sergeant-major of the regiment. Then returning to Danville, he recruited a company for the 37th Illinois Infantry and was made major. With this regiment, he took part in thirteen battles and was severely wounded, losing, permanently, the full use of his right arm at the battle of Prairie Grove, Ark., Dec. 7, 1862. Shortly after, he was made a colonel and for gallantry in action at the storming of Fort Blakely, Ala. (Apr. 9, 1865), he was brevetted brigadier-general. After studying law and being admitted to the bar, he began the practise of law at Danville, Ill., but soon moved to Champaign, Ill., where he attained prominence in his profession. In 1867 he married Adaline L. Griggs. He is described as a man of medium height, fair complexion, handsome features and of graceful movements (*Memoirs of Gustave Koerner*, II, 563). Because of his ability as a public speaker, he was in demand on patriotic occasions and in the conventions of the Democratic party of which he was a member. In 1866, 1880, and 1884, he was a candidate of that party for membership in the House of Representatives and in 1879 opposed John A. Logan for a seat in the Senate. Meantime, in 1872, on a fusion of the Liberal Republicans with the Democratic party Gustave Koerner and John C. Black were the nominees of their respective parties for governor of Illinois and lieutenant-governor. But they were defeated by Richard J. Oglesby and John L. Beveridge representing the regular Republican party. Beginning in 1885, Black served for four years as commissioner of pensions, having been appointed by President Grover Cleveland. On retiring, he took up the practise of law in Chicago. While serving as congressman at large from Illinois, having been elected in 1892, he was once more rewarded by President Cleveland with appointment to office. Resigning his seat as a representative, he became United States attorney for the northern district of Illinois (1895–98). For ten years, beginning with 1903, he was a member of the United States Civil Service Commission, serving nine years of the period as president of the Commission. In 1913, he retired from public life, but continued to devote much time to the interests of the Grand Army of the Republic, of which he had served as commander-in-chief, 1903–04.

[Much of the information about the career of Gen. Black was secured in conversation with his son John D. Black. The chief sources of printed information are: *Memoirs of Gustave Koerner, 1809–1896* (2 vols., 1909), ed. by Thos. J. McCormack; *Bench and Bar of Illinois*, ed. by John M. Palmer (1899); obituaries in *Chicago Tribune* and *Chicago Record Herald*, Aug. 18, 1915.]
J. A. J.

BLACK HAWK (1767–Oct. 3, 1838), Sauk war chief, named Ma-ka-tai-me-she-kia-kiak (Black Sparrow Hawk), was born in the great Sauk village on Rock River, Illinois, two miles above the outlet of that stream into the Mississippi, near the present city of Rock Island. During the period of actual Spanish rule on the Mississippi (1769–1804) the Sauks, Foxes, and other Indian tribes were accustomed to take furs to St. Louis, there to trade them for supplies, and it was at St. Louis that Black Hawk heard of the Americans, for whom, as dispossessors of the Spanish, he conceived a hearty dislike. In 1804, William Henry Harrison, on behalf of the United States, negotiated a treaty with a band of Sauks at St. Louis, under Quashquame and two other chiefs

—one a Fox—whereby the Sauk and Fox nations ceded to the government the whole of their country east of the Mississippi. Of this treaty Black Hawk in particular never recognized the validity, claiming that it was entered into without tribal warrant, by chiefs who had gone to St. Louis for quite other ends, and who were badly intoxicated. This contention modern scholarship is on the whole disposed to accept (T. C. Pease, "The Frontier State," 1918, *Centennial History of Illinois,* II, 153, citing Annie H. Abel, *Annual Report of the American Historical Association,* 1906, I, 267). The War of 1812 broke forth and Black Hawk joined the British as a leader under Tecumseh. He fought at Frenchtown, Fort Meigs, and Fort Stephenson, but whether or not he was at the battle of the Thames, where Tecumseh fell, is not altogether certain. Brooding over the injustice of the Treaty of 1804—a treaty which he himself (wittingly or unwittingly) was in 1816 brought to confirm—Black Hawk, between 1816 and 1829, sought to enlist support from the British in Canada. He formed relations with a Winnebago prophet (medicine man), Waubesheik or White Cloud, and the twain plotted a great Indian confederacy against American encroachment. In June 1831, with Black Hawk clinging defiantly to the village of the Sauks, Gen. Edmund P. Gaines, in response to an urgent request by the governor of Illinois (John Reynolds), was sent to Fort Armstrong on the island of Rock Island, and Black Hawk withdrew beyond the Mississippi to the mouth of the river Iowa. But in April 1832, encouraged by what he believed to be assurance of help from Canada, he recrossed the Mississippi, with perhaps two hundred warriors with their women and children, and set out for Rock River. Winnebagoes, Potawatomi, and Mascoutins had promised to join him, and this some of them now did. But before Black Hawk could repossess himself of his ancestral seat, now largely in the hands of white settlers, Gen. Henry Atkinson with a force of United States troops landed in Illinois, below Rock River. With the coming of Gen. Atkinson, the Black Hawk-White Cloud confederacy (so far as in existence) fell rapidly to pieces. "I concluded," says Black Hawk, "to tell my people that if White Beaver (Gen. Atkinson) came after us, we would go back. . . . I discovered that the Winnebagoes and Potawatomi were not disposed to render us any assistance." The Black Hawk War (so called) was precipitated through an assault by a body of Illinois volunteers on a flag of truce sent out by Black Hawk for a parley—two of the Indians being killed. The conflict lasted till Aug. 2, 1832, when at the mouth of the Bad Axe River in Wisconsin, he and his warriors, with their families, were overwhelmed by Gen. Atkinson and the Illinois volunteers. Black Hawk himself, along with his two sons, the prophet White Cloud, and the prophet's follower Neapope, was made prisoner and taken to Prairie du Chien, whence, under charge of Lieut. Jefferson Davis, he was transferred to Fort Armstrong, now in the hands of Gen. Winfield Scott. In the spring of 1833, by order of the President (Andrew Jackson) the fallen chief and his party were carried East, met the President, and after a short confinement at Fortress Monroe were returned to their own country—Iowa. Here, under the supervision of the Sauk Chief Keokuk, Black Hawk spent the remainder of his days. On his trip to Washington, Black Hawk was shown marked attention, and the experience quite changed his attitude toward the Americans. He wished to set forth to them the reasons for his conduct, and his story, dictated to the United States interpreter at Fort Armstrong, Antoine Le Claire, was prepared for publication by an Illinois journalist, J. B. Patterson, and in 1833, "tenth moon," duly given forth. The book has become an American classic. On Oct. 3, 1838, Black Hawk, not long after a second visit to the East, died at his lodge on the river Des Moines. He was laid away, Sauk fashion, in a reclining posture, beneath a wooden shelter, and by his side were placed the many gifts,—swords, cane, and medals,—which had been made to him. Death, be it said, did not bring him rest. In 1839 his sepulchre was invaded, his head severed from the body, and, together with other parts of the skeleton, carried away to be put on exhibition. Ultimately the bones were recovered, but were consumed in the burning of the Historical Society Building in Burlington, Iowa, where, by consent of his family, they had been placed.

[*Autobiography of Black Hawk* (Rock Island, Ill., 1833; new ed., 1882, with *A Hist. of the Black Hawk War,* by J. B. Patterson; annotated ed., 1916, by Milo M. Quaife); Benj. Drake, *Life and Adventures of Black Hawk, with Sketches of Keokuk,* etc. (1839); Perry A Armstrong, *The Sauks and the Black Hawk War* (1887); Frank E. Stevens, *The Black Hawk War* (1903); Jacob Van der Zee, "The Black Hawk War and the Treaty of 1832," *Iowa Jour. of Hist. and Politics,* XIII, 416; I. B. Richman, "Black Hawk, Keokuk and their Village," *John Brown Among the Quakers and other Sketches* (3rd ed., Hist. Dept. of Iowa); *Bull. 30, Bureau of Am. Ethnology.*]

I. B. R.

BLACKBURN, GIDEON (Aug. 27, 1772–Aug. 23, 1838), Presbyterian clergyman, missionary to the Indians, was born in Augusta County, Va., the son of Robert Blackburn. In his boyhood his family moved to eastern Tennessee where he attended Martin Academy and studied for the ministry under Dr. Robert Henderson.

In 1792 he was licensed to preach by the Abingdon Presbytery and began his ministry by holding services for some soldiers whom he had accompanied on an expedition against the Indians. Soon he established the New Providence Church and was given charge of another ten miles distant. On Oct. 3, 1793, he married Grizzel Blackburn, a distant cousin, by whom he had eleven children. His most notable work was the establishment of a mission to the Cherokee Indians. When he was unable to interest his own presbytery in the subject, he took his plea to the General Assembly, which, in 1803, voted $200 for the support of the work. Blackburn collected additional funds on the outside and having secured the approval of President Adams and the Secretary of War, opened a school for the Cherokee children in 1804. A teacher was employed, and Blackburn had general supervision in addition to his regular church services. This work he continued until 1810, by which time the hardships of the frontier had so undermined his health and the demands of the mission work so strained his finances that he felt compelled to resign. During the next twenty-three years he continued his teaching and preaching, was president of Harpeth Academy, and of Centre College, served as pastor of churches in Louisville and Versailles, Ky., and did much itinerant preaching. He is described as "the best type of backwoods eloquence," a commanding figure, above average height, with strongly marked features and flowing black locks.

Because of his success as a money raiser he was invited, in 1833, to go to Illinois by some persons interested in education in that region, and in 1835 was given the task of raising funds for Illinois College. Later he conceived a unique plan for raising an endowment for a school at Carlinville, Ill. The government was placing large tracts of land on the market and Blackburn offered to enter lands for friends of the cause at the rate of two dollars an acre. After paying the $1.25 per acre to the government, twenty-five cents was to go to him for his services and fifty cents for lands for the school. In this way he raised funds to enter a little over 16,656 acres for the institution. In the following year, 1838, he died. The institution he planned for was not opened until 1857. Beginning as a primary school, it later became Blackburn Theological Seminary and, when the theological courses were discontinued, Blackburn College.

[Sketches in W. B. Sprague's *Annals of the Am. Pulpit*, vol. IV (1858), and E. H. Gillett's *Hist. of the Presbyt. Ch. in the U. S.* (1864). In the *Panoplist*, June, July, and Dec. 1807 and Feb., Mar., May, and Dec. 1808, are letters from Blackburn describing his mission work. For endowment plan see *Blackburn Coll. Bull.*, 1915.]

B. R.

BLACKBURN, JOSEPH (fl. 1753–63), colonial portrait painter, is represented in art museums and private collections by distinguished and beautiful canvases, but left almost no other record of himself. His name in several publications and on museum labels has been given as "Jonathan B." Blackburn, but since 1919 it has been generally accepted that he was Joseph Blackburn, resident at Boston and Portsmouth, N. H., and perhaps elsewhere in the colonies. His paintings were usually signed "I (or J) Blackburn" with the date appended. Several writers, apparently accepting without scrutiny H. W. French's statement to that effect, have said that the artist signed himself "J. B. Blackburn." Examination of more than eighty canvases attributed to Blackburn has disclosed no such signature. One signature "Jos Blackburn" has been found. William Dunlap, in his *History of the Arts of Design in the United States* (1834), wrote: "All we know is that he [Blackburn] was nearly contemporary with Smibert, and painted very respectable portraits in Boston." Augustus T. Perkins, contributing to *Proceedings of the Massachusetts Historical Society* (1878) his list of portraits attributed to Blackburn, admitted that his own, and others', investigations had not shown "whence Jonathan B. Blackburn came and where he went on leaving Boston." Perkins conjectured that Blackburn taught Copley and that chagrined by his pupil's superiority he went away. Neither of these assumptions is probable. In *Art and Artists in Connecticut* (1879) French stated that Christopher B. Blackburn, an itinerant painter and jack-of-all-trades who worked in several towns, had a son, J. B., possibly born in Wethersfield, probably about the year 1700. This conjecture has frequently, and uncritically, been reprinted as if it were fact. Frank W. Bayley (1917) noted in a Portsmouth newspaper the name of Joseph Blackburn as that of one for whom posted letters were held. The same name was found in a Boston list. Following this clew Lawrence Park examined Blackburn signatures and (1918) discovered at Brooklyn a portrait signed "Jos Blackburn 1755." Soon after this John Hill Morgan came upon a receipted bill for the Mrs. Nathaniel Barrell portrait signed by Joseph Blackburn at Portsmouth, 12 July, 1762. These discoveries were published in the *Boston Sunday Herald,* in September 1919, and subsequently in several other publications. Research since 1919 has revealed few additional data concerning Blackburn. His name, as "Mr. Blackburn," occurs in two letters written, 1757, by Mrs. Richard Russell and now at the American Antiquarian Society, Worcester. The three Tucker family portraits, owned in Baltimore, appear to have been painted at Bermuda, 1753, indicating that Blackburn may have come thence to America. No Blackburn portrait dated later than 1763 has been found. Mr. Morgan reasonably conjectures that the painter went to Jamaica with his sitter, Sir Alexander Grant, who in 1764 became governor of that colony. Blackburn evidently came to America with a well-formed style, painted industriously among wealthy colonial families and, apparently, had no purpose to remain. His manner somewhat resembles that of the English painters Thomas Hudson (1701–79) and Joseph Highmore (1692–1780). No record of his British connections has been disclosed. One writer has assumed, without supporting evidence, that he traveled under an assumed name. As a painter Blackburn had admirable feeling for graceful gesture and sumptuous textures. He was perhaps inferior as an artist to Robert Feke, but was a better draftsman than Smibert or Badger. Among notable portraits attributed to him are those of Jeffery Amherst, Theodore Atkinson, Sr., Theodore Atkinson, Jr., Joshua Babcock, Mrs. Joshua Babcock, Mrs. Nathaniel Barrell, Mrs. John Bours, Rev. Peter Bours, Mrs. Thomas Bulfinch, Mrs. Wiseman Claggett, Mary Holyoke Cutts, Samuel Cutts, Mrs. Thomas Deering, Mary Faneuil, Mary Brown Greenleaf, Mrs. Thomas Hancock, Daniel Henchman, William B. Johnson, Lady Pepperell and Sister, James Otis, Joshua Warner, Joshua Winslow.

[Lawrence Park, "Joseph Blackburn, a Colonial Portrait Painter," *Proc. Am. Antiquarian Soc.*, n. s. XXXII, 1922; John Hill Morgan, "Notes on the Portrait of Lettice Mitchell," *Brooklyn Museum Quart.*, 1919; Lawrence Park, "Two Portraits by Blackburn," *Art in America*, Feb. 1919.]

F. W. C.

BLACKBURN, JOSEPH CLAY STYLES (Oct. 1, 1838–Sept. 12, 1918), Confederate soldier, senator from Kentucky, belonged to a family that had been prominent in the political history of Kentucky from the formation of the state. Several members served in the legislature; his father, Edward Blackburn, was a prosperous and well-known planter of considerable local influence; and a half-brother, Luke P. Blackburn [*q.v.*], was governor 1879–83. J. C. S. Blackburn was born near Spring Station in Woodford County and was educated at Centre College, from which he graduated in 1857. He read law in a private office and was admitted to the bar in 1858. For the next two years he practised in Chicago but returned to Kentucky in 1860 in order to work for the election of Breckinridge. For Blackburn the Civil War interrupted a legal career not over-rich in promise. He joined the Confederate army and fought throughout the war with valor but without distinction. For a year he served on the staff of Brigadier-General Preston as volunteer aide-de-camp with the rank of captain and received special mention by that officer for good conduct at Chickamauga. Later he served as a lieutenant under Polk and in March 1864 was authorized to raise a cavalry company for special service along the Mississippi. His company was virtually independent, and its activities were such as to make it equally obnoxious to friend and foe (*Official Records,* ser. I, vol. XLIX, pt. I, p. 1010). After the war, Blackburn lived for a few years in Arkansas but returned to Kentucky in 1868. Family influence and the enthusiasm for Confederate veterans in the general reaction against military interference in Kentucky soon carried him into public life, sending him to the legislature in 1871 and again in 1873. This was followed by ten years 1875–85, in the national House of Representatives and twelve, 1885–97, in the Senate. He failed of reelection in 1896 because of his ardent advocacy of free silver and his support of Bryan, but was elected for the third time in 1901. Beaten in 1907, he retired to private life and held no more offices except by appointment. Roosevelt appointed him governor of the Canal Zone, but he resigned after two years. In 1914 Wilson appointed him resident commissioner of the Lincoln Memorial and this position he held till his death. For twenty years "Joe" Blackburn was probably the most popular man in Kentucky. This was due to his genial disposition, his perfervid oratory, his war record, and his astonishingly retentive memory, which enabled him, it is said, to call by name the majority of the voters of his state. As a legislator he cannot be placed in the first rank and his name is not connected with any great measure. He was a vigorous debater, whose powers of vituperation often provoked his opponents to physical violence. In the House he gained notoriety for his filibuster against accepting the decision of the electoral commission in 1877 and by his activity in unearthing the scandals of Grant's administration. In the Senate his debating powers and continued service combined to make him of considerable influence. He was twice married; in 1858 to Therese Graham of Danville, who died in 1899; in 1901 to Mrs. Mary E. Blackburn of Washington, D. C.

[Blackburn's career in Congress may be followed in the *Cong. Record.* The *Official Records of the Union and Confederate Armies* make only meager mention of him and it is possible that in some instances they confuse him with his numerous relatives. O. O. Stealey, *130 Pen Pictures of Live Men* (1910) contains a character sketch of him by a reporter who was perhaps not unbiased. The *Biog. Cyc. of Ky.* (1896) gives the outstanding facts of his life, while all histories of Kentucky devote some attention to his career. Cf. also *Who's Who in America*, 1899–1918; O. O. Stealey, *Twenty Years in the Press Gallery* (1906); W. E. Connelley and E. M. Coulter, *Hist. of Ky.* (1922), vol. II; *Louisville Evening Post*, Sept. 12, 1918.] R. S. C.

BLACKBURN, LUKE PRYOR (June 16, 1816–Sept. 14, 1887), physician, surgeon, governor, the son of Edward M. and Lavina (Bell) Blackburn, was born in Fayette County, Ky., although his parents' home was in Woodford County. His grandfather George Blackburn moved to Kentucky about 1780 from Culpeper County, Va., and settled in Woodford County, calling his estate "Blackburn's Post." His father was prepared for the law but chose rather to engage in farming and breeding thoroughbred horses, for both of which he became well-known. Luke P. Blackburn, determining on the study of medicine, took advantage of Transylvania University to prepare himself. He graduated in 1834 with the M.D. degree and immediately began his practise in Lexington, Ky. The next year he married Ella Guest Boswell, and before the year was over, cholera having broken out in Versailles, Ky., he offered his services free to a people almost completely deprived, by death or desertion, of medical attention. Here he developed characteristics and interests that were to constitute his chief claim to distinction: generosity with his medical skill and services, and a profound knowledge of epidemics and their control. So grateful were the people of Versailles that they prevailed upon him to settle in their town. Here Blackburn attempted to supplement his income by a venture into the manufacture of rope and bagging, but in 1839 he failed with considerable financial losses. Though not greatly interested in politics at the time, he represented Woodford County in the legislature in 1843. Three years later flush times in Mississippi drew him to Natchez, where he soon began a work destined to tax his capacities and to make him known to the whole nation. He assumed general control of the yellow fever epidemics which broke out in the lower Mississippi Valley in 1848 and 1854, and became so much interested in the welfare of the rivermen that at his own expense he set up a marine hospital in Natchez. Later he induced Congress to take charge and to erect others. In his efforts to control yellow fever, he held that a quarantine station on the Mississippi below New Orleans would be of inestimable value. To aid him in carrying out this plan Mississippi commissioned him a representative to Louisiana to induce her to erect such a station, and while on this visit he addressed both the Louisiana House and Senate and secured favorable action. He later induced the federal government to assume control. In 1856 while he was on a visit to New York, yellow fever broke out on Long Island and at the request of the mayor he assumed control, refusing to make any charges for his services. In 1857 he visited the principal hospitals of England, Scotland, Germany, and France, and while in Paris met Julia M. Churchill of Louisville, Ky., whom he married on his return, his first wife having died in 1855. He made his home in New Orleans until the Civil War broke out. Being a strong secessionist, he offered his services to the Confederacy. He was attached as a surgeon to the staff of Gen. Sterling Price, with $50,000 given by Mississippi to be used in caring for the sick troops of that state. To secure medical supplies for the Confederacy he visited Canada and was prevailed upon by the governor-general to go to the Bermuda Islands to relieve distress there. In 1867 he moved to Arkansas to live on a plantation but returned to Kentucky in 1873 and made his home in Louisville. Two years later he assumed control of the yellow fever situation around Memphis and in 1878 gave free his services to Hickman, Ky., suffering under a like epidemic. He had long held an ambition to be governor of his native state and in 1879 secured the Democratic nomination and election. His administration was conspicuous for the large number of pardons which he granted in order to relieve bad prison conditions. He died in Frankfort, Ky.

[For a physician's account and estimate of Blackburn see *Ky. Medic. Jour.*, vol. XV, no. 11 (1880). Other sources of information are, Appleton's *Annual Cyc.*, 1887; L. and R. H. Collins, *Hist. of Ky.* (1874), vol. I; *Lexington Morning Transcript*, Sept. 15, 1887; *Biog. Cyc. of the Commonwealth of Ky.* (1896); *Louisville Courier-Journal*, Sept. 15, 1887; H. A. Kelly and W. L. Burrage, *Am. Medic. Biogs.* (1920).] E. M. C.

BLACKBURN, WILLIAM MAXWELL (Dec. 30, 1828–Dec. 29, 1898), Presbyterian clergyman, son of Alexander and Delilah (Polk) Blackburn, was born at Carlisle, Ind. He was educated in the Academy of La Porte, Ind., and later at Hanover College, graduating in 1850. After spending a year in teaching he entered Princeton Theological Seminary. Here he spent four years, pursuing theological studies, but not graduating. He was licensed to preach by the Presbytery of New Brunswick in April 1853, and was ordained by the Presbytery of Lake on Sept. 28, 1854. His first charge as a minister was the church at Three Rivers, Mich., where he preached from 1854 to 1856. From this work he was called to Erie, Pa., to take charge of the newly organized Park Presbyterian Church. The following year he was installed as pastor of this church and continued as such until 1863. When he left this field it was in order to supply the pulpit, and then become the pastor, of the Fourth Presbyterian Church of Trenton, N. J. On Aug. 16, 1864, he was married to Elizabeth Powell. In 1868 he was called to the professorship of Biblical and ecclesiastical history in the Seminary of the Northwest (later McCormick Theological Seminary), Chicago. This position he occupied until 1881. Meantime in addition to his labors as professor in the seminary he served as acting pastor of the Fullerton Avenue Presbyterian Church of Chicago (1869–71). In 1881 he accepted a call to the Central Presbyterian Church of Cincinnati, Ohio, which he served until 1884. From this pastorate he was called to the presidency of the Territorial University of North Dakota. He served in this position, however, only until the next year, when he was transferred to the presidency of Pierre University in South Dakota (removed in 1898 to Huron, S. Dak., and renamed Huron College). From 1885 to the day of his death Blackburn was not only president of the University, but also professor of mental, moral, and political science, and from 1886 to 1890, and again from 1892 to 1894 he had charge of the local Presbyterian Church at East Pierre, S. Dak.

Blackburn early developed aptitude for and facility in writing. His first effort, a translation of Gerhard's *Sacred Meditations,* was followed by *The Holy Child* (1859), a story for use in Sunday-schools, which proved successful and was republished in England. This was followed by a series of six juvenile tales under the general title of the "Uncle Alick Stories." In the same popular vein but of wider interest, Blackburn produced a large number of historical and biographical works designed to disseminate knowledge concerning the important personalities and events of the world's religious life, especially those of the Reformation period. He also published a comprehensive treatise on church history under the title: *History of the Christian Church from its Origin to the Present Time* (1879), which received wide recognition, and was used as a text-book in the study of the subject, though recent advances in this field of knowledge have practically superseded it. Great energy characterized all his numerous activities: his writing, his labors as pastor, teacher, and college president, his work on committees of Presbytery and Synod. In personal appearance and bearing he was dignified and even courtly, producing the impression of one who was a forceful thinker but was indisposed to impose his thoughts upon others.

[*Princeton Theol. Sem. Alumni Cat.* (1909); *McCormick Theol. Sem. Gen. Cat.* (1912); Le Roy J. Halsey, *Hist. of the McCormick Theol. Sem.* (1893); the *Minutes of the Gen. Assembly of the Presbyt. Ch. and of the Synod of S. Dak.* (1886–98); Thos. L. Riggs, "Wm. Maxwell Blackburn," *S. Dak. Hist. Colls.,* I, 25–36.]

A. C. Z.

BLACKFORD, CHARLES MINOR (Oct. 17, 1833–Mar. 10, 1903), lawyer, came of a family of which there is no American record prior to Benjamin Blackford who was born in New Jersey Oct. 31, 1767, and went to Virginia in 1789. His son, William Matthews Blackford, editor and part owner of the *Lynchburg Virginian,* married Mary Berkeley Minor, daughter of Gen. John Minor, and their second son, Charles Minor Blackford, was born at Fredericksburg, Va. He obtained an excellent education from his father, who was a noted scholar, and at private schools at Fredericksburg and Lynchburg. Entering the University of Virginia Oct. 1, 1850, he passed to the Law School, graduating LL.B. in 1855. The same year he commenced practise in Lynchburg. "My success," he wrote later, "was not particularly brilliant but it was sure and steady." He married Susan Leigh, daughter of Thomas M. Colston of Fauquier County, Va., Feb. 19, 1856. On the outbreak of the Civil War he was commissioned first lieutenant in the 2nd Virginia Cavalry, the first mounted regiment organized in Virginia, and took part in the battles of Manassas, Slaughter's Mountain, and Fredericksburg. During the winter of 1863 he was appointed judge advocate of the 1st Army Corps under Longstreet and was present at Gettysburg, Chickamauga, and the Wilderness. On the conclusion of the war he resumed practise at Lynchburg, being "the only lawyer in town who kept his office open, for there were no courts and no business." In 1866 he entered into partnership with Col. T. J. Kirkpatrick and the firm gradually acquired the most extensive legal connection in Virginia, being engaged in much heavy corporation litigation, including Gilbert *vs.* Washington City Virginia Midland Electric Railway Company (*33 Grattan,* 586, 645), which involved the powers and duties of a court of equity in dealing with foreclosure and receivership where there was a plurality of mortgages on different parts of a railway—the largest case up to that time tried in a Virginia court. His cases were always elaborately prepared and in court he was strong and aggressive, though ever courteous to his opponents and deferential to the bench. In his early years a Whig and later a Democrat, he never aspired to office; and the adoption of the free silver plank at the Chicago convention caused him to vote for McKinley at the ensuing presidential election. He always took a keen interest in local administration, occupying the position of city solicitor from 1869 to 1881 and being for a time a member of the city council and school board. He was also an influential and active supporter of the Protestant Episcopal Church. An original charter member of the Virginia State Bar Association, he was elected its president in 1894. He died at Lynchburg, Mar. 10, 1903.

Of pronounced literary tastes, possessing exceptional culture, and widely read, he was the author of *Memoirs of the Army in Virginia* (1894–96); *Legal History of the Virginia Midland Railway Company* (1881); *Campaign and Battle of Lynchburg* (1900); *Historical Sketch of the Book of Common Prayer*; and a number of articles and addresses, including a masterly "Trials and Trial of Jefferson Davis," read before the Virginia State Bar Association, 1900. All his writings were distinguished for their attractive style and effective handling of material.

[The chief authority for the more important features of his life is his own autobiographic sketch in his war memoirs. See also *Va. State Bar Ass. Report,* 1903, p. 67.] H. W. H. K.

BLACKSTONE, WILLIAM (1595–May 26? o. s., 1675), New England colonist, was descended from a family of some distinction near Salisbury, England. Attending Emmanuel College, Cambridge, he took the degrees of B.A. in 1617 and M.A. in 1621, and took orders in the Church of England. About 1623 he came to Massachusetts and was the first settler to live on the land where Boston now stands. He continued there after the Puritan immigration but in April 1633 the new settlers limited him to fifty acres. Neither he nor the Puritans liked each other. It was enough for them that he was a Church of England man, and his own most famous remark is that he left England because he did not like the lord-bishops and would not now be under the lord-brethren. In 1634 he decided to remove, sold his property, except six acres, and settled at Study Hill, as he called his place, in what is now Cumberland, about three miles from Pawtucket. In 1659 he married Sarah, widow of John Stevenson of Boston, Endicott performing the ceremony. By her he had a son John. She died in June 1673 and Blackstone himself was buried May 28, 1675. He was a man who has perhaps gained in interest from a certain mystery attaching to him. He lived the life of a recluse, was cultured and devoted to his library of 186 volumes, and at the same time was thoroughly at home with the Indians, whom he much preferred to the Bostonians. He planted the first orchards in Massachusetts and seems to have had some property. In King Philip's War, soon after his death, his house and library were burned. His son, who was no credit to him, married, and the family is still extant.

[L. Bliss in his *Hist. of Rehoboth* (1836), is the best source of information, with references to all contemporary sources. L. H. Tilton in *Hist. of Rehoboth* (1918) gives a few additional facts as to descendants. S. C. Newman's letter in S. G. Arnold, *Hist. of R. I.* (1860), II, 568–70 should be consulted. There is a good brief account by C. F. Adams, *Three Episodes in Mass. Hist.* (1892), I, 322–38. See also L. M. Sargent, *The Blackstone Family* (1857), and J. W. Blackstone, *Lineage and Hist. of Wm. Blackstone* (1907).] J. T. A.

BLACKWELL, ANTOINETTE LOUISA BROWN (May 20, 1825–Nov. 5, 1921), reformer, was born in Henrietta, Monroe County, N. Y., the daughter of Joseph and Abby (Morse) Brown, both of New England descent. At the age of nine she joined the Congregational Church and soon was speaking publicly in meetings; at sixteen she was teaching school; later she attended Oberlin College, completing the literary course in 1847 and the theological course in 1850. Refused a ministerial license, because of her sex, she preached wherever churches, of any creed, would receive her until in 1852 she became the regular pastor of the Congregational Church in South Butler, N. Y. She had already joined the movements for abolition, prohibition, and woman's rights—three reforms which, however illogically, usually drew the same supporters. Her efforts at first were devoted mainly to harmonizing these reforms with the teachings of the Bible, but theological difficulties grew upon her until she resigned her pastorate in 1854 and, eventually, became a Unitarian. In the summer of 1853 she came into national prominence when although a regularly authorized delegate to the World's Temperance Convention in New York City she was refused permission to speak; her "unwomanly conduct" in striving quietly for three hours to be heard, amid a tumultous group of angry, shouting men, was severely criticized by many newspapers, although Horace Greeley in the *New York Tribune* succinctly characterized the convention's achievements toward temperance as consisting in "First Day—Crowding a woman off the platform; Second Day—Gagging her; Third Day—Voting that she shall stay gagged" (*New York Daily Tribune,* Sept. 9, 1853).

Miss Brown was married on Jan. 24, 1856, to Dr. Samuel C. Blackwell, brother of Elizabeth Blackwell and Henry Brown Blackwell [*qq.v.*]. She became the mother of six children. During the early years of the Civil War she was prominent in the movement for the immediate emancipation of the slaves and until the end of her life remained active in the causes of woman suffrage and prohibition. A very effective speaker, she habitually devoted her eloquence to the presentation and support of particular resolutions rather than to mere general inspiration. Although far from unemotional, her appeal was mainly to the reason, and to considerations of practise. The same qualities appeared in her numerous books: *Shadows of Our Social System* (1855); *Studies in General Science* (1869); *A Market Woman* (1870); *The Island Neighbors* (1871); *The Sexes Throughout Nature* (1875); *The Physical Basis of Immortality* (1876); *The Philosophy of Individuality* (1893); *Sea Drift; or Tribute to the Ocean* (1902); *The Making of the Universe* (1914); *The Social Side of Mind and Action* (1915).

[*Who's Who in America*, 1899–1921; Frances E. Willard and Mary A. Livermore, *A Woman of the Century* (1893), later included in their *Portraits and Biogs. of Prominent Am. Women* (1901); *Hist. of Woman Suffrage*, ed. by Elizabeth Cady Stanton, Susan B. Anthony, and Matilda Joslyn Gage, I (1881), 119, 152, 186, 449 (portrait), 473, 524, 553, 624, 723, 862; II (1882), 723, 862; obituary in *Newark Evening News*, Nov. 5, 1921.]

E. S. B.

BLACKWELL, ELIZABETH (Feb. 3, 1821–May 31, 1910), the first woman doctor of medicine of modern times, was born in Bristol, England, one of nine children of Samuel Blackwell, a sugar refiner, and his wife, Hannah Lane. Henry Brown Blackwell [*q.v.*] was her younger brother; another brother, Samuel, was to become the husband of Antoinette Louisa (Brown) Blackwell [*q.v.*]. At the age of twelve (August 1832), she sailed with her family in the merchant ship *Cosmos* from Bristol to New York, where the family remained for six years and then moved to Cincinnati, Ohio. Elizabeth had attended local schools at Bristol and New York, but her formal education was cut short by the death of her father (1838) a few months after reaching Ohio. This calamity left the family unprovided for, and consequently when twenty-one (1842) Elizabeth began to teach school, her first position being in Henderson, Ky., but her ardent antipathy to slavery caused her after a year to seek another post. In 1844 she first thought of studying medicine, and during the next year, while supporting herself by teaching at Asheville, N. C., she began to read medical works, and in 1847 continued her medical studies under the guidance of Dr. Samuel H. Dickson, professor at Charleston Medical College. The problem of securing entry into a medical school proved difficult; she was refused at Philadelphia and New York, but in October 1847 the Geneva Medical School of Western New York accepted her application. Through tact and dignity she succeeded in overcoming the prejudice of undergraduates and instructors, but in the world at large she was regarded "as either mad or bad." She received her M.D. in 1849, which led to much comment in the public press both in America and abroad (see *Punch*, XVI, 226, 1849). After graduation she sailed immediately for England and was courteously received, but she regarded the opportunities on the Continent as more favorable and accordingly went to Paris, where, on June 30, 1849, she entered La Maternité and had six months of obstetrical experience in that institution. A purulent ophthalmia contracted at the end of her service there caused her to lose the sight of one eye, which put an end to the surgical aspirations which she had previously entertained. She then studied at St. Bartholomew's Hospital in London and was permitted to practise in all branches of medicine except, ironically enough, gynecology and pediatrics. At this time she received congratulations from Florence Nightingale, Lady Byron, the Herschels, Faraday, and others of note. She returned to New York in 1850 to practise, and, on encountering prejudice, opened a private dispensary of her own which later (May 1857) became incorporated into the New York Infirmary and College for Women, a hospital entirely conducted by women. In this venture she was joined by her sister, Emily, who had also become qualified in medicine, and by Marie Zakrzewska, and they were supported by the Quakers of New York. During the Civil War, Dr. Blackwell was active in the organization of a unit of field nurses which did much to win sympathy for the feministic movement in medicine. In 1869 she decided to settle permanently in England where, as in America, she aimed to secure free and equal entrance of women into the medical profession. Later (1875) she became professor of gynecology in the London School of Medicine for Women which had just been established, and continued her activities there until 1907 when she became enfeebled following an accident in Scotland. She had taken a house in Hastings where she died, May 31, 1910. She was buried at Kilmun, Argyllshire. An excellent portrait of her hangs in the London School of Medicine for Women.

Dr. Blackwell was an active writer and her works had a wide circulation. The *Laws of Life* (New York, 1852) was reissued in London in 1859 and again in 1871. She was active in public health, and several of her popular lectures—"How to Keep a Household in Health" (1870),

The Laws of Life with Special Reference to the Physical Education of Girls (1852), *The Religion of Health* (1871), and *Counsel to Parents* (1879)—did much to arouse popular interest in the subject. She wrote extensively also on problems of sex and moral education of the young. Her other writings are listed in the *Index Catalogue of the Surgeon-General's Library* and in the *Dictionary of National Biography.*

[Elizabeth Blackwell, *Pioneer Work in Opening the Medical Profession to Women; Autobiographical Sketches* (London, 1895); *The Times* (London), June 2, 1910; *N. Y. Evening Post,* June 1, 1910; Mesnard, *Miss E. Blackwell et les femmes médecins* (Paris, 1889); Frances Hays, *Women of the Day* (London, 1885); *Brit. Medic. Jour.,* 1910, I, 1523; *Del. State Medic. Jour.,* 1916, VII, 3–24; *Lancet* (London, 1910), I, 1657; *Medic. Mag.* (London), IX, 117–25; *Medic. Record* (N. Y.), LXXVII, 1016; *Woman's Medic. Jour.* (Cincinnati), XX, 155, 174, 188, 208.]

J. F. F.

BLACKWELL, HENRY BROWN (May 4, 1825–Sept. 7, 1909), editor, one of the earliest advocates in America of woman suffrage, was born in Bristol, England, the son of Samuel and Hannah (Lane) Blackwell and brother of Elizabeth Blackwell [*q.v.*]. Samuel Blackwell was an advanced Liberal and a great admirer of American institutions. In 1832 the family came to New York City where the father engaged in sugar refining. The Blackwells took an active interest in the anti-slavery movement and their Long Island home was soon a refuge for persecuted abolitionists. In 1838 they moved to Cincinnati, Ohio. A short time after, Samuel Blackwell died and left his widow with nine children to support. Henry became an office boy, later drifting into milling and then into the hardware business. In 1853 he made his first speech for woman suffrage at a convention in Cleveland, Ohio. During the same year he attended a legislative hearing in Massachusetts at which Lucy Stone spoke in support of a woman suffrage petition. This meeting was the beginning of his courtship of Lucy Stone. After promising to devote himself to the work of advancing woman suffrage, he obtained Miss Stone's consent to marriage. On the day of their marriage, May 1, 1855, they published a joint protest against the inequalities in the marriage law. This protest was widely distributed and attracted much attention (*Woman's Journal,* Sept. 11, 1909). Soon after his marriage Blackwell moved with his wife to New Jersey where he engaged in book-selling, sugar refining, and real estate, making money in each venture. With the exception of one year at Kemper College in St. Louis he obtained most of his education through reading. In 1858 while in the book business, he introduced many agricultural libraries into the Illinois schools. In 1867 he wrote a message to the Southern legislatures proposing the extension of woman suffrage in the South as a counterbalance to negro suffrage (*What the South Can Do,* 1867). When the American Woman Suffrage Association was organized in 1869, Blackwell was financially able to devote most of his time to it. In 1870, when the *Woman's Journal* was founded in Boston, he contributed a substantial sum of money. Later when an editor was needed who would work without salary, he consented to fill the place and remained editor of the *Journal* until his death, which occurred in Dorchester, Mass. He was interested not only in woman suffrage, but in other liberal movements such as activity against the deportation of political refugees, the Armenian massacres of 1895, and the Russian pogroms. His interest in economic affairs was shown by his activity in favor of reciprocity with Canada (*Reciprocity, a Republican Issue,* 1904). He was a kindly, sympathetic person, always willing to aid humanitarian causes.

[Most of Henry Blackwell's writing, aside from the pamphlets mentioned above, appears in the form of signed editorials in the *Woman's Journal* from 1870 to 1909. Obituaries appeared in the *Woman's Journal,* Sept. 11, 1909, and in the *Boston Transcript, Boston Post,* and *Boston Daily Globe,* Sept. 8, 1909.]

M. S.

BLACKWELL, LUCY STONE. [See STONE, LUCY.]

BLADEN, WILLIAM (Feb. 27, 1673–August 1718), publisher, was born at Hemsworth, Yorkshire, England, the son of Nathaniel Bladen and his wife Isabella, daughter of Sir William Fairfax, a general of Cromwell's time. Bladen came to Maryland in 1690, and soon became active in public affairs. In 1692 the Archives of Maryland record an allowance of 4,000 pounds of tobacco to Bladen for transcribing the laws. In 1695 he was recompensed for "fair Copy of the Laws sent for England, 2 Journalls, 2 Copyes of the Court house act" (*Archives of Maryland,* XIX, 198), and in 1696 the records again reveal his clerical activities. Meanwhile (*c.* 1695), he was made clerk of the House of Assembly, and in 1696 he proposed to the Assembly the advantages of a printing-press for printing the laws and offered to send for press and appurtenances if the governor would give his permission for their use. Upon receiving the sanction of assembly, council, and governor, Bladen, "at Great Charge and Trouble," as he informed the officials on May 4, 1700, finally procured "printing press Letters papers Inck printer &c." (*Ibid.,* XXIV, 22). For his assistance an ordinance was passed making obligatory the use of legal papers printed by Bladen and fixing the price thereof. The printing of the "body of Laws . . . soe that every person might easily have them in their houses without being troubled to goe to the County Court house to have recourse thereto" was arranged for, and it was also ordered that "every County be Oblidged to take one faire Coppy endorsed and Titled to be bound up handsomly" (*Ibid.*, XXIV, 83) for which Bladen was to receive from each county 2,000 lbs. of tobacco. Evidently an inefficient printer had been obtained, as the committee that compared the printed laws with the original found many errata, and Bladen was required to have these printed and sent to the several counties. In 1698 he became clerk of the governor's council and Gov. Nicholson paid him tribute in a letter to the Board of Trade. Apologizing for his delay in forwarding journals, etc., Nicholson says: "Another Reason is the great scarcity of good Clarks; (so that I am allmost forced to make according to the proverb Bricks without straw) only Mr. Wm. Blaiden whome I have found the most capable in all Respects, I have removed from being Clark of the House of Delegates, to that of the Council" (*Ibid.*, XXIII, 489). Collector of port and district of Annapolis, surveyor of port, register of court of admiralty, clerk of the free school, attorney-general of Maryland at a salary of £100 a year, and clerk of council of state at a fee of 12,000 lbs. of tobacco, are titles indicating some of the other offices in which Bladen served his generation. He married Anne Van Swearingen in 1696; a son, Thomas, became proprietary governor of Maryland. The exact date of Bladen's death is uncertain, but he was buried on Aug. 9, 1718.

[The *Archives of Maryland,* particularly Vols. VIII, XIX, XXIII, XXIV, and XXV, are the primary source; among secondary sources may be mentioned J. T. Scharf, *Hist. of Md.* (1879), I, 362, L. C. Wroth, *Hist. of Printing in Colonial Md.* (1922), and Christopher Johnston, "Bladen Family," *Md. Hist. Mag.*, Sept. 1910.]

A. E. P.

BLAIKIE, WILLIAM (May 24, 1843–Dec. 6, 1904), lawyer, athlete, and promoter of physical training, was born in New York City, the son of Rev. Alexander and Nancy (King) Blaikie. He prepared for college at the Boston Latin School, graduated from Harvard in 1866, and from the Harvard Law School in 1868, being one of the two honor men of his class. After serving as pardon clerk in the United States Attorney-General's office (1869–70) and as assistant in the office of the United States district attorney, New York (1870–72), he established himself in practise in that city. He was twice married, first, to Isabella Stuart Briggs of Harrisburg, Pa., July 3, 1872; and second, to Rebecca Wynne Scott of Elk Horn, Ky., Oct. 6, 1891.

From boyhood he was an all-round athlete. When seventeen years old and weighing 133 pounds, he lifted a weight of 1,019 pounds. He was captain of a winning football team at the Boston Latin School, and in 1866 stroked Harvard's victorious crew. For ten years he held the amateur long distance walking record, having covered the 225 miles between Boston and New York in four and one-half days. Throughout his life his interest in physical education remained strong, and by lecturing and writing he added impetus to the rapid development in that field which took place in the eighties and nineties. In 1879 he published *How to Get Strong and How to Stay So,* the last edition of which appeared in 1902, a book of nearly 300 pages, interesting, untechnical, and not without charm of style. It had wide popularity in this country and in Europe. In 1883 he issued a manual entitled *Sound Bodies for Our Boys and Girls,* which in the form of safe and simple exercises embodies some of the suggestions in his earlier work. Its clarity and illustrations made it a book suitable for schools or private use. As has been the case with many athletes, Blaikie did not attain old age, but died suddenly of apoplexy in his sixty-second year.

[*Who's Who in America,* 1903–05; *Boston Evening Transcript,* Dec. 7, 1904; *N. Y. Tribune,* Dec. 7, 1904; *Harvard Grads. Mag.*, Mar. 1905.]

H. E. S.

BLAINE, JAMES GILLESPIE (Jan. 31, 1830–Jan. 27, 1893), statesman, was born at West Brownsville, Pa. He was the son of Maria Louise Gillespie and Ephraim Lyon Blaine, and fifth in descent from the first James Blaine who emigrated from Londonderry in 1745. His paternal ancestors were for the most part Scotch-Irish and Scotch Presbyterians. The Gillespies were Roman Catholics of Celtic Irish stock. In America the Blaines settled about Lancaster and Carlisle, Pa., were active in business, and played a prominent part in the Revolution. After the Revolution they crossed the Alleghanies and settled in the vicinity of Pittsburgh. In 1842 Ephraim Blaine was elected prothonotary of Washington County and thereupon moved to the county seat. At the age of thirteen James entered Washington College which his father and many other relatives had attended. His age at graduation is an indication of the limited nature of the college course. He secured, however, a sound grounding in the classics, in English, and in mathematics. He began at once to teach in the Western Military Institute, at Georgetown, Ky. He did not like the South, and was ambitious to study law. From 1852 to 1854 he taught in the Pennsylvania Institute for the

Blind, at Philadelphia, where he could study law at the same time.

On June 30, 1850, he secretly married Harriet Stanwood, at that time teaching in Kentucky, but belonging to an old Massachusetts family, one branch of which settled in 1822 at Augusta, Me. As the legality of this marriage was in doubt, they were remarried on Mar. 29, 1851, at Pittsburgh, Pa. Through this connection came, in 1854, an opportunity to enter journalism at Augusta. Through the financial assistance of Mrs. Blaine's brothers he was able to purchase an interest in the *Kennebec Journal.* For several years he also served on the editorial staff of the *Portland Advertiser.* Although he left journalism in 1860, it was, aside from politics, his profession, and he may be said to have been the most prominent of American statesmen to receive their training from that calling. He settled in Augusta, joined the Congregational church, and from 1854 was identified with Maine, illustrating a migration unusual in American history. Augusta remained his home, and here he raised a family of seven children, of whom four survived him. Much of his time, however, was spent at Washington, and in his later years, his summers at Bar Harbor.

Blaine was of a stalwart, well-proportioned physique, with a large, fine head; distinctly a commanding figure. His eyes were particularly brilliant; his voice effective and attractive. His manner had much of the dignity of his generation of statesmen. Much more striking, however, was his magnetic quality, which gave charm to his social intercourse, and which made his oratory perhaps the most thrilling of his day. It was probably the exhaustion coming after demonstrations of such power, which caused his complaints of ill health, which often puzzled his friends. Undoubtedly he had much of what is called temperament. It followed that he was at his best with a crowd or audience. He was not a club man, and had more followers than intimates.

His mental characteristics were decidedly those connected with mathematical talent. His speeches were carefully prepared and contained much exact information. One of his greatest political assets was his ability to remember names and faces. He was an expert in the interpretation of election returns. He had in addition an intuitive talent for political leadership. It was this talent, combined with an imagination which gained in power as he gained confidence in himself, which distinguished his foreign policy; but by the time he put this forward, when fifty, he had, perhaps, lost his earlier zest for the exact study upon which he based his domestic policies. His humor, which must have been native, was slow to develop and was assiduously cultivated. Developed by the repartee of debate, it became one of his effective political weapons.

Blaine came to his leading political ideas by nature and by inheritance. His family were Whigs. Thomas Ewing of Ohio was a cousin of his mother. He was a great admirer of Henry Clay, on whose famous Lexington speech of 1847 he took notes. To advocate measures of a nationalizing character was, therefore, natural to him. His interest in the question of slavery was equally keen. In 1854, his first year of editorship, he abandoned the name Whig, and was instrumental in causing those Maine voters, who, under many political titles, were opposed to the Kansas-Nebraska bill, to adopt the new Western cognomen of Republican; thus giving that name currency in the East. In 1856 he was a delegate to the first national Republican convention, and one of its secretaries. He was, therefore, one of the genuine founders of that party, which he expected to carry on Whig measures as well as to oppose slavery.

While Maine was located so far to one side of the country as to miss that strategic importance of a central position which has counted for so much in American politics, nevertheless Blaine found there two advantages. The Maine elections were, during most of his career, held a month earlier than those elsewhere, and were consequently watched eagerly all over the country. More important was the fact that the number of men of exceptional ability in the politics of the state was particularly large. The editor of the rival newspaper at Augusta was Melville W. Fuller, later chief justice of the United States. The strength of the Maine politicians helped him not only by rivalry, but also by support. He was always surrounded by a strong group of local supporters, such as William Pierce Frye, Thomas Brackett Reed, and Nelson Dingley. The Maine habit of keeping such men long in office made them an increasingly powerful group. In a new party young men have an exceptional opportunity. In 1859 he was made chairman of the Republican state committee. He kept this post until 1881, and made himself the accepted and acceptable dictator of his party in the state.

In 1858 he was elected to the state legislature and was twice reëlected. During the last two terms he was Speaker of the House of Representatives. This success was won by his editorial skill and ability in political management and in legislative business. It was not until 1860 that he began his career as a public speaker. He entered Congress in 1863, serving in the national House of Representatives until July 10, 1876. In 1869 he was elected speaker, serving until the Democratic House of 1875 took office; after which he became leader of the Republican opposition. On July 10, 1876, he became senator, holding that office until Mar. 5, 1881.

During these years Blaine rose to be a national figure. He exhibited an unusual level-headedness, and changed his views less often than most men during the trying period of Civil War and Reconstruction. These views were sufficiently direct and clear-cut to arouse enthusiasm, but did not share the radicalism and vindictiveness of the extremists. He was firmly a Lincoln man, although in 1860 most of his Maine associates preferred Seward. Before he entered Congress he helped to win a victory in the state election of 1863 on Lincoln's program of Unionism, dropping in that election the designation of Republican, and doing much to organize the large Union majorities of that year, so necessary to offset the Democratic gains of 1862.

Early in the Reconstruction period he came out for negro suffrage, but accepted the lead of neither Thaddeus Stevens nor Charles Sumner. Rather he began to make connections with certain Western leaders, like Bingham and Garfield. He first attracted wide notice by joining with Bingham in adding as an amendment to Stevens's bill for the military government of the South, a provision for reconstruction. This amendment was characterized by the extreme Radicals as "making universal suffrage and universal amnesty" the basis of reconstruction (J. F. Rhodes, *History of the United States,* 1906, VI, 19). After a severe fight the amendment was attached to the bill, though its amnesty feature was modified.

This was a notable victory for a youngster over the venerable Republican floor leader. Stevens's death Blaine regarded as "an emancipation for the Republican party." Asked who could take his place, Blaine replied, "There are three young men coming forward." He pointed to Allison of Iowa, Garfield of Ohio, and, looking up into the dome of the Capitol, said, "I don't see the third" (G. F. Hoar, *Autobiography,* 1903, I, 239). He remained opposed to the extreme coercive measures of the Grant administration, helping to defeat a new Force Bill. On the other hand, in 1875, when the Democrats had gained control of the House, he opposed a general amnesty bill, making a violent attack on Jefferson Davis which left no doubt of his genuine Unionism. On the whole he came well through this trying period with the reputation of a liberal who could nevertheless be trusted even by the Grand Army.

During these years he built up also a strong popularity in the West. His associates were Garfield and Allison. He assisted in 1872 in a reduction of the tariff (Horace White, *The Life of Lyman Trumbull,* 1913, pp. 354–55). His position on the currency was that of a moderate, with tendencies toward sound money. He was regarded as loyal to the principles and practises of his party, but was not an extremist. As important as the friendships which he made was one lasting enmity. This was with the brilliant representative from New York, Roscoe Conkling. In April 1866 they became engaged in a violent personal encounter, when Blaine was presenting a report from the committee on military affairs. Words ran very high, and Blaine accused Conkling of editing his remarks for the *Congressional Globe* in a way to place Blaine's rejoinders in a false light. This break was never healed. Conkling became one of the leading supporters of Grant, and Blaine became the head of opposition within the party. Gradually there formed two Republican factions, the Stalwarts, or Grant men, and the Half-Breeds, among whom Blaine was most conspicuous—a rivalry kept before the country by the wit of Conkling and the dramatic instinct of Blaine. The probable retirement of Gen. Grant from the presidency in 1876 left the field open to many candidates. Circumstances seemed to have made Blaine the leading candidate for the Republican nomination when a dramatic episode occurred which probably barred the door of the presidency to him forever, as the cry of "Bargain and Corruption" had barred it to his hero Clay. The Democratic committee investigating the charges of railroad graft brought charges of corruption against Blaine. The proof of their truth or falsity was supposed to rest in a collection known as the "Mulligan Letters." These letters Blaine secured. He refused to hand them over to the committee of "southern brigadiers," but he himself read from them to the House in a brilliant and dramatic speech.

The facts seem to be that a decision of Speaker Blaine saved a land grant for the Little Rock and Fort Smith Railroad in 1869. Blaine, thereupon, on the basis of this favor, asked the favor of the railroad managers. He received the privilege of selling bonds on a commission that was secret and certainly generous. He claimed that he lost money on the transaction, as the bonds fell, and he felt under obligation to reimburse his friends. This loyalty to his friends and disregard for the public interest was characteristic of the time.

The fact that he conferred the favor before, and not after, receiving the return favor, differentiated him from many public men. It was, nevertheless, true that Blaine became wealthy without visible means of income, and that he resisted all attempts "to expose his private business." His standards were not below those of many public men of his time, but they rendered him anathema to those who were endeavoring to raise the public standards, particularly to the group headed by Carl Schurz, whose independence of party rendered them so powerful in politics from 1868 to 1895. (The best statement of the charges against Blaine is in Carl Schurz, *Speeches, Correspondence, and Political Papers,* 1913, IV, 239–48; the most considered historical judgment is F. L. Paxson, *Recent History of the United States,* 1921, pp. 90–91.)

It was under such circumstances that Blaine was first a candidate for the presidency. As always with him the striking accidental combined with the well-earned weight of facts to influence the result. Five days before the convention he was prostrated by the heat of Washington, and the uncertainty of his recovery became a factor in the voting. His name was presented by Robert G. Ingersoll in a speech which has generally been considered the most brilliant nomination in the history of our conventions, and which designated Blaine as the "Plumed Knight," a title which always clung to him. In this convention he had the strongest initial vote, 285, to 125 for his nearest rival, Oliver P. Morton of Indiana who was among those favored by Grant. In addition the anti-Grant forces were in a majority in the whole convention. It was felt, however, that the feeling of the administration against Blaine was so strong that the support of powerful men would be lacking in the campaign should he be nominated, and that the Schurz group would turn to the Democrats. The vote of Rutherford B. Hayes, governor of Ohio, grew steadily, and when New York transferred its vote from Conkling to Hayes, Blaine telegraphed Hayes his congratulations, although Hayes was not nominated until the seventh ballot. It was by such impulsive and generous gestures that Blaine won the widespread affection which was his great political asset.

During the Hayes administration Blaine, now senator from Maine, was preparing for the next campaign. He supported the administration against the attacks of Conkling, their brilliant exchanges keeping both constantly in the public eye. It was a contest for tactical advantage but Blaine strengthened his reputation for moderation and for consideration of the West.

President Hayes was not a candidate for renomination. The Stalwarts concentrated their attention upon again nominating Grant himself, securing a solid block of over three hundred delegates who never wavered. Blaine was again the leading candidate in opposition, with an initial 284 delegates. The others were divided among other Half-Breed leaders, the most important being Senator John Sherman of Ohio and Senator George F. Edmunds of Vermont. Again Conkling's extreme bitterness against Blaine was feared as a factor in the subsequent campaign, and on the thirty-sixth ballot, Gen. James A. Garfield, a friend of Blaine, was nominated. Again Blaine took the result with good nature and worked in the closest intimacy with Garfield in the subsequent campaign. To assuage the disgruntled Stalwarts, Chester A. Arthur of New York was nominated for the vice-presidency.

Garfield appointed Blaine as secretary of state and the administration might almost be called that of Garfield-Blaine. Among its lesser political measures were a series of appointments which violently angered the Stalwarts. After Garfield was shot and died, and Arthur, the friend of Conkling, succeeded, Blaine's influence in the administration was gone, and he tendered his resignation, Sept. 22, 1881. At the request of President Arthur, however, he continued to serve as secretary until Dec. 19, 1881.

The division in the Republican party still remained, but on the whole the Half-Breeds gained. However much Blaine was a politician, it seems to be the fact that from 1876 he was the choice of the majority, or of the largest faction of Republicans, who believed that he had been kept from nomination by political expedients and who felt that his time had now come. Remaining in Washington, he wrote the first part of his *Twenty Years of Congress* (Volume I published 1884) and articles setting forth his position. He was also in daily touch with his political associates. As the presidential year approached President Arthur received the support of the Stalwarts for renomination, but that faction was steadily losing power. In the convention of 1884 Blaine was nominated for the presidency on the first ballot, and Gen. John A. Logan of Illinois was chosen as candidate for vice-president.

His Democratic opponent was Grover Cleveland, who as governor of New York had attracted the favor of those particularly interested in certain reforms, as that of the civil service. This fact, combined with the suspicion clinging to Blaine as a result of the affair of the Mulligan Letters, caused the group led by Carl Schurz, which had up to this time coöperated with the Republicans, to shift to the support of Cleveland. Their numbers were not large and some associated with them, as Theodore Roosevelt and Henry Cabot Lodge, refused to change. Nevertheless they were men of prominence and their desertion weakened the Republican hope of success. Popularly they were designated as Mugwumps.

The foreign policy which Blaine had developed while secretary of state, moreover, seems to have caused more apprehension than enthusiasm. His tilts with Great Britain, however, were popular with the Irish-Americans, and it was hoped that he could divide that vote. At the very end of the campaign, in a speech at the Fifth Avenue Hotel in New York, a supporter of Blaine, the Rev. S. D. Burchard [*q.v.*], referred to him as fighting the Democratic party as "the party whose antecedents are rum, Romanism, and rebellion." This expression, coming too late to be explained away, undoubtedly alienated many Irish Catholics, and in view of the closeness of the vote in New York, the key state, where a change of 600 votes would have turned the election, may well have meant the defeat of Blaine. He lost Connecticut, New York, New Jersey, and Indiana, and the election.

Blaine now resumed the writing of his *Twenty Years in Congress,* publishing the second volume in 1886. In the following year he published a collection of his speeches with the title *Political Discussions: Legislative, Diplomatic, and Popular.* He still remained the most powerful Republican, and expectation was general that he would be nominated again in 1888. Before the convention he went for a long trip to Europe. On Jan. 25, 1888, he wrote home from Florence stating that he was not a candidate, and that he could not accept unless he were to be chosen by an unanimity which was impossible. This decision was confirmed by other letters, and finally convinced his friends, although votes were still cast for him in the convention. He was, however, though still away, a powerful factor, and was instrumental, if not the chief influence, in causing the selection of Benjamin Harrison of Indiana, as candidate.

It was taken for granted, upon the election of Harrison, that the chief post in the cabinet would be offered to Blaine. The offer was made and accepted and Blaine entered upon the most fruitful part of his career. These were, however, unhappy years for Blaine. In 1890 he lost two children. His relations with the President became strained, and his health was not good. As the presidential year approached, again he announced that he would not be a candidate, which left the President the leading aspirant, but not a popular one. When the convention met, the President had almost, but not quite, a majority of pledged delegates. On June 4, three days before the convention, Blaine resigned in a curt letter, and his resignation was as curtly accepted. Such action can hardly be interpreted otherwise than that Blaine hoped for a miracle, for a demonstration of that enthusiasm which he still inspired so convincing as to sweep the convention off its feet. He received 182 $\frac{5}{6}$ votes, but Harrison was nominated on the first ballot. With that generosity which always characterized him, Blaine returned to Washington, was reconciled with the President, and took what little part in the campaign his health allowed. His health, however, rapidly declined, and on Jan. 27, 1893, at the age of sixty-two, he died. In spite of this early death, Blaine seemed to have well rounded out a career. New times were calling for men of different training. He impresses one, moreover, as having lived at the height of his powers in the years between 1865 and 1885, and to have died an old man.

The permanent influence of Blaine on American life has been through his foreign policy. On Mar. 7, 1881, he first entered upon his duties as secretary of state. This position in American government has taken on a double significance; the secretary is, under the president, the leader of the administration, and is also the foreign minister. The general expectation was that in an unusual degree Blaine would emphasize the political aspects of the office. Intimate friend of the President, he was in the public eye a more considerable figure. This political reputation, moreover, had been built up on the basis of his leadership in domestic problems. It was not, therefore, supposed that he would do more than follow the routine policies of the country, perhaps with some tincture of his customary dash.

It is too little to say that this expectation was shattered. From the time he took office, Blaine made foreign affairs his leading interest. He made them the outstanding point in the appeal to the people for the presidency to which he constantly aspired. Nor does this seem to have been merely an intellectually contrived project for political advancement. Almost alone among the public men of his period, he saw in American foreign relations not merely a series of episodes, to be dealt with according to the fixed rules of the Monroe Doctrine and of international law, but a general situation calling for a constructive policy, to be adjusted to changing conditions. His rising interest in diplomatic problems may well have been due to native instinct. He had the qualities of a diplomat, and his personal conduct of such affairs was his strongest asset; though his personal feeling was perhaps too strong, as is evinced by his refusal while in London to meet Lord Salisbury, because of their acrimonious exchanges.

Blaine's generation in the United States was almost totally without the basic training for diplomatic thought or practise. It was the nadir of American diplomacy. This defect Blaine at fifty was not prepared to make good by study. His years of strenuous application had passed. He remained, therefore, lamentably ignorant of international law and of diplomatic history. In addition his major interest in politics often caused him to be careless in the selection of his agents in critical situations. These defects seriously affected his reputation. That they marred his success is more doubtful; he was a forerunner of American world interests, and so far in advance of the public that even perfect achievement would scarcely have won popular support in his time.

Blaine's first term as secretary lasted only from Mar. 7, 1881, to Dec. 19, 1881. On Mar. 7, 1889, however, he again entered the office, serving until June 4, 1892. In the interval, neither the Republican administration of President Arthur and Secretary Frelinghuysen, nor the Democratic administration of President Cleveland and Secretary Bayard, was in harmony with his views. Blaine, however, during this period, made his chief residence in Washington, with summers at Bar Harbor, and one visit to Europe. He was always in the closest touch with his group of Republican leaders in Congress, and his influence was very powerful. He remained thus constantly a force in determining United States policy, and this period of his life is distinctly a unit.

There were several closely interknit problems to which he devoted his attention. Ever since the Civil War the relations between the Latin-American countries and Great Britain had been growing more intimate at the expense of the United States. This was due in large measure to the supplanting of the latter's merchant marine by the British. Furthermore the competition of South American nations, particularly of Argentina, was encroaching upon the command of the European food trade by the United States, at the same time that the latter's manufactures, which were Blaine's chief concern, were reaching the point where foreign markets were deemed necessary. Lastly, the question of an inter-oceanic canal had assumed a new importance in the light of the successful forcing of the isthmus of Suez.

From these factors Blaine evolved a policy well coördinated and appealing. In form, this was much influenced by his admiration for Henry Clay. Like Clay he was not satisfied with the negative features of the Monroe Doctrine. He would unite the nations of America into a real system, with the United States as "elder sister." He would maintain peace among them by the use of the good offices of the United States and by arbitration. For constructive purposes he would call them all in joint conference to plan measures of mutual advantage. He would rally them to an extension of Clay's American system, "America for the Americans." That this policy might bring some occasion for dispute with Great Britain was politically an advantage, for any baiting of the British lion was pleasing to the Irish vote which was large and strategically placed. The traditional division of the world into two hemispheres, set forth in the Monroe Doctrine, would be maintained.

When Blaine took office in 1881 a concession for the building of a canal across the isthmus of Panama had already been obtained from the Republic of Colombia by a French company headed by the famous De Lesseps, the constructor of that at Suez. Both Secretary Evarts and President Hayes of the preceding administration had strongly taken a stand refusing to join in an international guarantee of the neutrality of such a canal, and insisting that such a canal must be built under the auspices and sole protection of the United States and the country through which it was constructed. Blaine promptly endorsed this policy, sending instructions to the American ministers in Europe, that the "guarantee given by the United States of America does not require re-enforcement, or accession, or assent from any other power." He stated that the passage of hostile troops through such a canal when either the United States or Colombia was at war was "no more admissible than . . . over the railroad lines joining the Atlantic and Pacific shores of the United States."

This was in fact a change in policy on the part of the United States, which had until the time of Evarts stood for an international control of such a canal. It was, in addition, in direct contravention of the Clayton-Bulwer treaty of 1850 with Great Britain, which had agreed to a canal under a joint international guarantee and had invited others to join in a guarantee of neutrality. On Nov. 1, 1881, Blaine took up this treaty. He argued that the treaty was void because of changed conditions, and contrary to the established policy of the United States. A lively interchange of notes, however, between the governments of the United States and Great Britain, failed to eliminate the treaty, nor was there any peaceful method of voiding the Colombian concession to the French company. Blaine, therefore, used his influence to promote the project of a United States canal through the nearby isthmus of Nicaragua. His canal policy was continued by Frelinghuysen, but negotiations with Nicaragua were brought to an end by President Cleveland, who reverted to the earlier United States policy, that such a canal "must be for the world benefit, a trust for mankind, to be removed from chance of domination by any single power." This matter continued as a subject of political and international controversy for twenty years. Ultimately the policy of Blaine was accepted by the United States. The plan for a Nicaragua Canal was not dropped until President Roosevelt succeeded in so modifying the Clayton-Bulwer treaty as to allow the canal at Panama to become a United States property, fortified by the United States.

A similar question confronted Blaine when he became secretary a second time, in 1889; that of the protection of the seal herds which bred on the Pribilof Islands of Alaska. The question of their destruction by Canadians and other deep-sea fishers had reached an acute stage under President Cleveland. Blaine at once took the stand that Bering Sea was a closed sea and part of the territorial waters of the United States. This position was historically unsound and was out of harmony with the previous policy of the United States as it had been evolved in the case of the northeastern fisheries. He negotiated, however, with the British minister in the United States, Sir Julian Pauncefote, a rather remarkable treaty by which legal rights were submitted to arbitration, and, in case the United States were to lose, for a scientific enquiry to be made to determine measures necessary to protect seal herds. Pending the arbitration they were placed under the protection of a *modus vivendi*. The United States lost its case but Blaine had raised the question of the protection of such animal life as migrates from country to country and uses the high seas. Since his day much has been done in this direction, by treaties between various countries interested.

The main constructive portion of Blaine's foreign policy had to do with South America. This had been foreshadowed before he became secretary by his support of subsidies to revive the United States's shipping connections with that continent (Blaine, *Political Discussions*, pp. 186–93). As secretary one of his first acts was to stand between Latin-American countries and Europe. To prevent the seizure of Venezuelan custom-houses by the French for payment of a claim, he urged Venezuela to pay through the agent of the United States and threatened that should no payment be made within three months, the United States would herself seize the custom-houses and collect the money. He protested June 25, 1881, in a letter to Lucius Fairchild, minister to Spain, against the proposal of Colombia and Costa Rica, to submit a boundary dispute to Spain for arbitration. This was not a denial of right, but an expression of his hope, that the United States might become sole arbitrator in such disputes (see C. R. Fish, *American Diplomacy*, 1915, pp. 384–85).

He devoted much attention to keeping the peace in America by active mediation. Convinced that Guatemala was right in a dispute with Mexico, he wrote the latter: "This country will continue its policy of peace even if it cannot have the great aid which the coöperation of Mexico would assure; and it will hope at no distant day to see such concord and coöperation between all nations of America as will render war impossible." His greatest interest was in the war actually in progress between Chile and Peru, over the Tacna-Arica territory. His first agents to the two countries were diplomatically incompetent, but finally he sent William H. Trescot of South Carolina, an accomplished diplomat. Trescot was to warn Chile against an unwarrantable use of her victories, and to threaten her with intervention, not by the United States alone but by joint action of the American powers (*Ibid.*, p. 386). Already Blaine was making preparations to secure such American coöperation, by developing the idea of Pan-Americanism, which had been so dead since Clay's fiasco with the Congress of Panama. On Nov. 29, 1881, he asked all the independent nations of America to discuss arbitration, and inaugurate an era of good will. This invitation was withdrawn when, after the assassination of Garfield, Blaine was succeeded by Frelinghuysen. In fact his whole Latin-American policy was promptly dropped. It did not, however, cease to be discussed. It was attacked as partial and blustering and apt to bring hostility between Europe and America. Its errors of detail were severely arraigned. It seems to have served Blaine little politically, as the country was uninterested in foreign affairs. Blaine defended his policy in magazine articles, and urged it through his friends in Congress. In 1888 Congress passed a bill calling a Pan-American congress, which President Cleveland allowed to become a law without his signature (M. Romero, "The Pan-American Conference," *North American Review*, September, October, 1890). On Oct. 2, 1889, this Congress met at Washington, with a long program including arbitration and the facilitating of commercial intercourse; but avoidance of all exciting questions. While without power, it drew up, under the personal influence of Blaine, many desirable recommendations, and in particular laid the foundation of the Bureau of American Republics at Washington, which has proved a permanent contribution. The vitality of this coöperation was in Blaine's mind to rest upon increased commercial intercourse, which he planned to promote by reciprocity treaties authorized in 1884. The new McKinley tariff bill, then under discussion in Congress, put on the free list most of the agricultural products of Latin America, thus depriving the United States of any *quid pro quo* in bargaining. Blaine, on July 11, 1890, wrote Senator Frye of Maine: "There is not a section or a line in the entire bill that will open the market for another bushel of (American) wheat or another barrel of pork." His views received much support from the West, and were offered in an amendment, fixing a duty upon sugar and such commodities, but allowing the President power to remove such duties in the case of "all products of any nation of the American hemisphere upon which no export duties are imposed" in case the agreed products of the United States should be admitted free of duty. This amendment was not passed, but a "reciprocity" clause was introduced, which left the products in question on the free list, but allowed the President to impose a tax in case the duties imposed by any nation on articles from the United States appeared to him "unequal and unreasonable." This ignored Blaine's intention of specially cementing relations with American powers; nevertheless he concluded under it a number of treaties, which were in operation too short a time to demonstrate their possible effect.

As had been customary since the days of Webster, Blaine considered the Hawaiian Islands as part of the American hemisphere. He found them a kingdom closely bound to the United States by a reciprocity treaty, but with a government which he believed was strongly susceptible to foreign influences, especially that of Great Britain. In 1881 he wrote the American minister there that should the native population continue to decline, the United States would be obliged to take over the islands. On becoming secretary again in 1889, he sent as minister John L. Stevens, one of his closest friends and business associates. On Feb. 8, 1892, Stevens wrote Blaine that "annexation must be the future remedy or else Great Britain will be furnished with circumstances and opportunity to get a hold on these islands which will cause future serious embarrassment to the United States." After Blaine's retirement a revolution broke out, which was sympathetically supported by Minister Stevens and which could hardly have been beyond Blaine's vision of the possible.

While pursuing his policy of America for the Americans, Blaine did not stand apart from movements to improve general international organization. He negotiated an important treaty on extradition with Great Britain, joined in a general act for the suppression of the African slave trade, and made the United States's first treaties on international copyright.

Blaine is conspicuous as the only outstanding public figure between Seward and Hay who was really interested in foreign affairs. His contributions, the Pan-American Union and reciprocity, are of less importance than the fact that he attracted public attention to international problems, and in particular to certain lines of policy relating to America, which were followed out by Roosevelt, and are still (1927) developing.

[Blaine was not careful of his correspondence; letters of his, however, are found in the Lib. of Cong., in the McCulloch, W. T. Sherman, Staunton, and Israel Washburn MSS. Aside from official records, the chief source of information is his own *Twenty Years of Congress, from Lincoln to Garfield* (2 vols., 1884–86), which stands high in character among works of its kind. He also published: *Political Discussions, Legislative, Diplomatic, and Popular* (1856–86); an article on "The Foreign Policy of the Garfield Administration," *Chicago Weekly Magazine*, Sept. 16, 1882, and many other articles and editorials. Gail Hamilton, *Biog. of Jas. G. Blaine* (1895), p. 722, gives an account of his ancestry and intimate life. The biography by Edward Stanwood, *Jas. Gillespie Blaine* (1905) is the most complete account of his political career. The Mulligan Letters are discussed by J. F. Rhodes, *Hist. of the U. S.*, VII (1906), 193–206, and by F. L. Paxson, *Recent Hist.* (1921), pp. 90–91. In 1884 nearly a score of campaign biographies were published, containing many extracts of speeches and letters; perhaps the best is that of J. C. Ridpath, *Life and Work of Jas. G. Blaine* (1893). *Letters of Mrs. Jas. G. Blaine*, ed. by Harriet S. Blaine Beale, appeared in two volumes in 1908. See also Alice Felt Tyler, *The Foreign Policy of Jas. G. Blaine* (1927).]

C. R. F.

BLAIR, AUSTIN (Feb. 8, 1818–Aug. 6, 1894), governor of Michigan, was born at Caroline, Tompkins County, N. Y. His great-great-grandfather came from Scotland in 1756 and settled on land now covered by Worcester, Mass. In 1809, his father, George Blair, built the first log cabin in Tompkins County, N. Y. Blair's mother was Rhoda (Blackman) Mann, widow of Sabin Mann. Ardent advocates of the abolition of slavery, the parents lived to see their hopes realized, and their son an instrument in the accomplishment. Austin Blair was educated at Cazenovia Seminary and Hamilton and Union Colleges, graduating from the latter in 1837. He was admitted to the Tioga County bar in 1841, and removed to Jackson, Mich., where he became a Whig and an active supporter of Henry Clay. From 1845 to 1849 he was a member of the state legislature, where he incurred the hostility of leaders of his party by advocating the granting of the ballot to colored citizens, and of the clergy by aiding to secure the abolition of capital punishment. Cutting loose from the Whigs, Blair in 1848 was a member of the Buffalo convention of Free-Soilers that nominated Van Buren and Adams for president and vice-president. As a member of the mass convention of Whigs, Democrats, and Free-Soilers, held "under the oaks at Jackson," July 6, 1854, he participated in the formation of the Republican party. Republican leader in the state Senate from 1855, he led the Michigan delegation at the Chicago convention that nominated Abraham Lincoln. Michigan supported Seward, and Blair was one of the trio (William M. Evarts and Carl Schurz being the others) to whom the Seward cause was intrusted on the floor of the convention. An unsuccessful candidate for the United States Senate in 1857, when Zachariah Chandler displaced Lewis Cass, Blair was elected governor in 1860, and on Jan. 3, 1861, he declared in his inaugural address that "the Federal Government has the power to defend itself, and I do not doubt that that power will be exercised to the utmost. It is a question of war that the seceding states have to look in the face" (*Detroit Free Press,* Jan. 4, 1861). The news of the bombardment of Fort Sumter reached Detroit Saturday, Apr. 13; on Sunday the state sprang to arms; $100,000 was raised by subscription to equip troops, the treasury having been emptied by theft. On May 15, a week earlier than was required, the Michigan regiment was the first to reach Washington from the West. This initial energy continued unabated to the end; and by his energy, steadfastness, and good judgment Austin Blair came to be numbered with Andrew of Massachusetts, Morgan of New York, Curtin of Pennsylvania, Dennison of Ohio, Morton of Indiana, Yates of Illinois, and Kirkwood of Iowa in the illustrious band of "War Governors" who staunchly upheld President Lincoln. When Blair retired from the governorship in 1865, the end of the war was in sight. A year later he was elected to Congress, where he served from 1867 to 1873. In 1871, he was supported by the soldiers and the Republican newspapers in his candidacy for the Senate, but after a bitter contest the choice of the legislature was Thomas W. Ferry, with whom Blair had made an unsuccessful combination against Senator Chandler in 1869. Feeling that his public services had entitled him to election to the Senate, and chagrined over defeat as the result of (as he believed) political trickery characteristic of his party, Blair joined the Independent Republican movement in 1872. He took the stump for Horace Greeley, and allowed himself to run for governor of Michigan on a fusion ticket. He was overwhelmingly defeated. Finding his new political bedfellows uncongenial, he was welcomed back to the Republican party, and in 1885 was nominated for justice of the Michigan supreme court on the ticket with Justice Thomas M. Cooley; but both were defeated by reason of venomous newspaper attacks on decisions of the court alleged to favor railroads. From 1882 to 1890 Blair served by election two terms as a regent of the University of Michigan. The controversies in which he had been engaged from boyhood had burned themselves out, and the latter days of his life were spent in the practise of his profession. He was married in February 1849 to Sarah L. Ford, and his son, Charles A. Blair, was a justice of the Michigan supreme court from 1904 until his death in 1912.

[H. M. Utley and B. M. Cutcheon, *Mich. as a Province, Territory and State* (1906), vols. III, IV; J. F. Rhodes, *Hist. of the U. S.*, vols. II (1894), VI (1906); Chas. Moore, *Hist. of Mich.*, vol. I (1915); E. W. Leavitt, *The Blair Family in New Eng.* (1900); *Evening News* (Detroit), Aug. 4, 1894.]

C. M.

BLAIR, FRANCIS PRESTON (Apr. 12, 1791–Oct. 18, 1876), journalist, politician, was descended from John Blair, a Scotch-Irish immigrant to America in the early eighteenth century, who settled in Bucks County, Pa., and held the first chair of theology in Princeton College. John's son, James, a Virginia lawyer, early moved to Kentucky where he served as attorney-general of the state (1796–1816). Francis Preston, born at Abingdon, Va., was one of the sons of James Blair. He was a sickly lad with a consumptive tendency which he later outgrew. Educated at Transylvania University, he graduated with honors (1811), studied law, was admitted to the bar (1817), but owing to a vocal defect never practised. In 1812 he volunteered for service against Great Britain to act as aide to his uncle George Madison, then governor of Kentucky. At Vincennes he was seized with a hemorrhage from his lungs which forced him to return to Frankfort. To improve his health he tried to farm but his liking for politics led him to make farming an avocation and politics his profession. This he did when Kentucky was agitated over relief measures, mainly financial and judicial, and convulsed with the New Court *vs.* Old Court struggles. Blair joined the relief party and became clerk of the new court of appeals. He, Maj. W. T. Barry, and Amos Kendall were bosom friends and political allies. He assisted Kendall, who edited in Frankfort, Ky., the *Argus of Western America* and the *Patriot,* and his editorials and pamphlets were pungent condemnations of the Old Court party. He finally emerged from this singularly bitter political controversy as clerk of the state circuit court, editorial contributor to the *Argus of Western America,* and president of the Commonwealth Bank. He assisted his father in the preparation of the argument for the right of a state to tax the Bank of the United States (1811) and opposed its recharter.

In spite of their divergent views Blair in 1824 wanted Clay for president of the United States, and even after the election of Adams he remained hopeful until late in 1825 that Clay would mould the Administra 'on's policy in the interests of the West. The publication of the first presidential message to Congress, however, definitely alienated him from the Administration. He joined the ranks of Jackson where he served whole-heartedly as a member of the Jackson committee at Frankfort. He advocated direct election of the president by the people, legislative control of judicial decisions, cheap lands for settlers, and the abolition of imprisonment for debt. His articles in the *Argus of Western America,* after the election of 1828, attacking the Bank of the United States and nullification, received considerable notice. He answered, editorially, Cheves and McDuffie of South Carolina on the tariff and nullification. Blair maintained that Congress had the power to levy a tariff, and that the tariff should be regulated downward, and that the country was fortunate in having a president who said: "The Union must be preserved." At the same time he was arguing that the Bank of the United States was trying to ruin the democratic Commonwealth Bank of Kentucky, of which he was president. When Maj. W. T. Barry and Amos Kendall were established in offices at Washington, they, upon President Jackson's request for advice, suggested Blair for the editor of the proposed Administration organ to replace Duff Green's *Telegraph.* Jackson called Blair to Washington where he established the *Globe* in 1830.

Blair adopted the significant slogan: "The World is governed too much." He received the patronage of the Administration and with the able John C. Rives as a business manager the *Globe* was made a financial success. Nullification, the United States Bank, and Clay's "American System," were viciously and effectively attacked while he warmly advocated Jacksonian measures and championed the cause of Jackson and Van Buren in their respective campaigns. Few men exerted a political power more potent than Blair through the *Globe* during 1832–41. Being eager to supply their readers with daily proceedings in Congress, Blair and Rives also published the *Congressional Globe.* Blair became a confidential member of the Kitchen Cabinet. He accompanied President Jackson on vacation trips, talked with him about public policies before he had breakfasted, and then hurried to the *Globe* office to pursue his adopted policy of "shooting the deserters" and to give the cue to the Administration papers throughout the country. He constantly used his vitriolic pen against men who opposed "the democracy." His editorials were so skilfully written that he often goaded the opposition to madness. Blair believed that a political party existed primarily to carry out the will of the people, that every man should be a defender of the sacred Constitution of the United States. "The Constitution" and "the Union" were his watchwords. When the question of the annexation of Texas became a campaign issue he joined the Benton-Van Buren wing of his party, thereby alienating a majority of the annexationists. Even though he supported Polk after the Baltimore Convention (1844), and offered to conduct the *Globe* as strongly for Polk's administration as he had for Jackson and Van Buren, Polk felt that he must have a new editor. He forced Blair to sell his interests in the *Globe* to Thomas Ritchie of the Richmond *Enquirer* (1845), offering Blair the Spanish mission as a sop. Blair refused the post.

Silver Spring, Blair's country estate, near Washington, D. C., became a political shrine when he retired from the *Globe.* He had expected to live a quiet life but reëntered politics in 1848 when he joined Van Buren in advocating Free-Soilism. In 1852 he supported Pierce, believing that Jacksonian Democracy would be revived. Pierce made overtures to Blair early in 1853, but Blair thought Pierce broke his promises in his cabinet appointments and failed to adopt the methods of Jackson and "the [true] democracy." Finding himself bitterly disillusioned, he denounced the Kansas-Nebraska Act as a violation of the Missouri Compromise. Still hoping to see a revival of "the Democracy" he became one of the principal organizers of the Republican party, and used his influence to effect the nomination of Frémont. By 1858 he was rejoicing over Buchanan's accusation that he was in rebellion against the Democratic party. He wanted a Democrat of the old faith to resist the Southern influences but, caught in the political drift, he joined his sons in the campaign for Lincoln, and was an active member of the Chicago convention in 1860. After 1861 his advice was offered to the President and welcomed by him. Blair's love for Southern friends, desire for peace, and concern for the Union, caused him to go unofficially to Richmond to confer with Jefferson Davis in 1864. He proposed peace on the basis of a joint effort to be made by the North and South to expel Maximilian from Mexico. The Hampton Roads Conference (1865) was the result. Blair fully embraced Lincoln's plan of reconstruction, and after the President was assassinated, the Radicals drove him back into the Democratic party. He wanted Grant to head the Democratic party in 1867; he supported Seymour in 1868, and Greeley in 1872. He died believing that he had been a true Jacksonian Democrat and a disciple of Lincoln. He was married to Eliza Violet Gist, daughter of Nathaniel Gist and grand-daughter of Sir Christopher Gist; his sons, Montgomery [*q.v.*] and Francis Preston [*q.v.*], were both prominent in politics.

[The chief sources of information are found in the Blair Papers (unpublished); Jackson Papers (in process of publication); Van Buren Papers (unpublished); and in various newspapers. The *Globe* (Washington, D. C., 1831–45); *Argus of Western America* (Frankfort, Ky., 1827–30); *Nat. Intelligencer* (Washington, D. C., 1830–45); *Spectator* (Washington, D. C., 1844); *Kentuckian* (Frankfort, Ky., 1828) are especially good for information during the years indicated. "Annals of Silver Spring" by Gist Blair in *Records of the Columbia Hist. Soc.*, XXI (1918), contains a vivid description of Silver Spring. *Thirty Years' View* (1858) by Thos. Hart Benton has an interesting account of the establishment and disestablishment of the *Globe*. Glimpses of Blair's impressions of Washington and men in 1830 may be had in Thos. M. Clay's article, "Two Years with Old Hickory," in *Atlantic Mo.*, LX, 187–99. It is now certain that Blair was the author of the *Life and Public Services of Gen. Wm. O. Butler* (1848), a work generally ascribed to his son, Francis Preston Blair, Jr. Blair wrote a number of political pamphlets, among which are: *Gen. Jackson and Jas. Buchanan* (1856); *A Voice from the Grave of Jackson* (1856); *To My Neighbors* (1856); and *To the Working Men* (1869). An obituary notice appears in the *N. Y. Herald*, Oct. 19, 1876.]

W. E. S.

BLAIR, FRANCIS PRESTON (Feb. 19, 1821–July 9, 1875), Union soldier, statesman, was born at Lexington, Ky., the third and youngest son of Francis Preston Blair [*q.v.*]. While a child he was taken to Washington, D. C., by his father and there he attended a select school. As a young man he contributed to the editorial columns of the *Globe*, edited by his father, who took great pride in educating his son for a political career. Blair graduated at Princeton (1841) and then entered the law school at Transylvania University. After graduating there, and upon admission to the bar at Lexington, Ky., he went to practise with his brother, Montgomery [*q.v.*] in St. Louis (1842). Three years of intense study and practise of law injured his health. While he was seeking rest and recreation in the Rocky Mountains the Mexican War broke out; consequently, he joined a company of Americans which was commanded by George Bent. When Gen. Kearny took New Mexico Blair was appointed attorney-general for the territory.

Upon returning from the West Blair was married on Sept. 8, 1847, to Appoline Alexander of Woodford County, Ky., and resumed his law practise in St. Louis. Having pronounced views on the extension of slavery he established a Free-Soil paper, the *Barnburner*, to further the interests of the cause in Missouri. He organized and led the Free-Soil party in that state and voted for Van Buren in 1848. Henry Clay found supporters in him, his father, and Montgomery, for his Compromise of 1850. Though a slave owner, Blair denounced the Kansas-Nebraska Act as a violation of the Missouri Compromise, and his views on slavery, so clearly and forcefully expressed, marked him as a character dangerous to slave interests. Two terms in the Missouri legislature (1852–56) gave him opportunity to express his Free-Soilism and prepare himself for Congress. He was like Thomas Hart Benton in his methods, although in 1856 he refused Benton's request to retract some of his public statements on slavery. Benton was defeated for governor of Missouri in that year, while Blair, who voted for Frémont, was the only Free-Soiler elected to Congress from a slave state. In his first speech in Congress he warned the South that slavery was bound to die. He urged the South to adopt the policy of gradual emancipation by deportation and colonization. He was defeated for reëlection to Congress (1858). In 1859 he published an argumentative "address" on colonization, entitled, *The Destiny of the Races on This Continent*.

The years 1858 to 1861 were eventful years for Blair. He opposed the extension of slavery on the basis that it was an economic hindrance to the development of the West, as well as socially and morally wrong. His family connections, his brilliance, his ability as an extemporaneous speaker, and his courageous frank manner, made him one of the popular orators of the day. As a speaker he was in demand in Minnesota and Vermont where he campaigned for the Republicans, in Illinois where he hoped to ruin the political fortunes of Douglas, and in Missouri where he battled against the "Nullificationists" and Benton's old enemies, especially the "Fayette Clique." He organized the Union party in Missouri and largely transformed it into the Republican party; in the latter he became the "leading spirit and chief adviser" in his own state. Like his father, he was a constitutionalist and an unyielding unionist. He was a Democrat-Republican who used parties merely as a means to an end.

The speeches and letters of Blair indicate that he feared a coming catastrophe long before the Civil War. The spectre of "Nullification" haunted him. He tried in vain to convert Northern men to his scheme of colonization. He supported Edward Bates for the presidential nomination through fear of secession early in the campaign of 1860, but he turned to Lincoln on the third ballot in the Chicago convention. After the convention few men labored as faithfully as he in the campaign. Consequently, he was ready to act quickly and decisively when civil war loomed. He organized the "Wide Awakes" in St. Louis, had men secretly drilled, secured ammunition and arms, kept himself informed of movements at Washington, and as a friend and supporter stood well in Lincoln's favor.

Blair was elected to Congress in 1860. In the spring of 1861 he determined to save Missouri for the Union. After much political maneuvering and "Home Guards" organizing, he and Gen. Lyon marshalled their forces sufficiently to compel the surrender of Camp Jackson, a camp of state militia sympathetic with the Confederacy. It was a play of Blair and his Unconditional Unionists against Gov. Jackson and his confederates, who desired to carry Missouri into the Confederacy. The capture of Camp Jackson drove thousands of Missourians into the Confederate cause, but the issue was now sharply drawn in the state; the United States arsenal at St. Louis was saved, and the state remained Unionist. Blair was offered a brigadier-generalship but refused in order to avoid political complications in Missouri.

In the Thirty-seventh Congress, as chairman of the Committee on Military Defense, Blair's policy was to crush the rebellion as quickly as men and money could do it. His policy included the acceptance of all volunteer troops for service, government control of railroads and telegraph lines, and the construction of a ship canal from Lake Michigan to the Illinois River for commercial and military purposes. He caused Frémont to be sent to Missouri to command the forces in that region but soon became disgusted with Frémont's policy, criticized him, and was, in turn, arrested and imprisoned by him. Blair's father and brother attempted unsuccessfully to stop the quarrel. For this and other reasons Lincoln removed Frémont. Blair's enemies in Missouri increased in number, particularly while he was in the army. In 1862, when the Union cause looked dark, an appeal was made to Blair to raise troops and lead them to the front. He immediately raised seven regiments, received the appointment of brigadier-general, and saw his first hard fighting at Vicksburg where he showed bravery and leadership. He was in many engagements, was raised to the rank of major-general, and completed his military career with Sherman on the march through the South. As commander of the 15th and 17th Corps, respectively, he received the praises of Generals Sherman and Grant. Blair was considerate of his officers and men and was popular among them. While in the army he made his own opinions and the wishes of Gen. Sherman known to his brother, the Postmaster General, who in turn communicated the information to the President. In 1864 Blair was recalled from the battlefield to help organize Congress and to defend Lincoln's plan of reconstruction. On Feb. 5 and 27, 1864, he made two provocative speeches: one defending the President's policy; the other, against Secretary Chase and the Radicals whom he derisively called Jacobins. A storm of condemnation from the Radicals fell on his head. Chase threatened to resign, and Blair returned to his command.

When the war closed Blair was financially ruined as he had spent much of his private means in support of the Union. His attempt to retrieve his lost fortune on a cotton plantation in Mississippi failed. He then turned his attention to politics in Missouri where a set of Radical Republicans had gained control within the party. He opposed the registry laws, test oaths, the policy of sending carpet-baggers to the South, and the disfranchisement of the whites and the enfranchisement of the negroes. He wished to allow the states to return to the Union to work out their own problems if they recognized abolition as an accomplished fact and swore allegiance to the Constitution. President Johnson nominated Blair for collector of internal revenue at St. Louis, and then to the Austrian mission, only to see the Senate refuse to confirm his appointment in each case. Blair was then appointed as commissioner on the Pacific Railroad but Grant removed him as soon as he became president. The Radicals in Missouri caused Blair to defend the conservatives and ex-Confederates. He began his work of reorganization of the Democratic party in 1865, supported Johnson in 1866, and received the nomination for vice-president with Seymour in 1868. In the latter year his public utterances and his notorious

"Broadhead Letter," addressed to J. O. Broadhead, declaring that it would be the duty of the Democratic candidate if elected to abolish the Reconstruction governments, gave the opposition an opportunity to distort Blair's meaning when he advanced his plan of reconstruction. He maintained that the Constitution had been perverted. To restore it, he would have the people, by their mandate expressed at the polls, declare the acts of the Radical Congress "null and void"; compel the army to undo its usurpations of power in the South; disperse the carpet-bag governments; allow the whites to reorganize their own governments and elect senators and representatives. After the Democratic defeat in 1868 he coöperated with the Liberal Republicans, secured election as representative to the Missouri legislature; and was, by that body, chosen United States senator. He helped to secure the nomination of Horace Greeley for president (1872), and through coöperation with the Liberal Republicans saw the Radicals ousted from power in Missouri. He was defeated for reëlection to the United States Senate in 1873. During the same year Blair was stricken with paralysis, never to recover. He was generous to a fault, cordial, and seldom held a personal grudge against a political enemy. His scathing denunciations of his political opponents antagonized them but his faculty for remembering names and his sociability endeared him to many people. He was nominally state superintendent of insurance when he died. His friends erected a fitting monument to his memory in Forrest Park (St. Louis) and Missouri placed his statue in the United States Capitol.

[The chief sources are the Blair Papers (unpublished). Two biographies of a political and biased nature are: Jas. Dabney McCabe (Edward Martin), *The Life and Public Services of Horatio Seymour Together with a Complete and Authentic Life of Francis P. Blair, Jr.* (1868); David Goodman Croly, *Seymour and Blair: Their Lives and Services* (1868). A manuscript copy of a sketch of the life of Blair, presumably written by Montgomery Blair, is in the Blair Papers. Short sketches exist by: Wm. Van Ness Bay, in *Reminiscences of the Bench and Bar of Mo.* (1878); Augustus C. Rogers, *Sketches of Representative Men North and South* (1874); Chas. P. Johnson, "Personal Recollections of Missouri's Statesmen" in *Proc. Mo. Hist. Soc.*, Jan. 22, 1903; and John Fiske, *The Mississippi Valley in the Civil War* (1900). The best account of Blair's services in Missouri during the early part of the Civil War is found in *Gen. Nathaniel Lyon and Missouri in 1861* (1866) by Jas. Peckham.]

W. E. S.

BLAIR, HENRY WILLIAM (Dec. 6, 1834–Mar. 14, 1920), congressman, the son of William Henry and Lois (Baker) Blair, of Scotch-Irish descent, was born at Campton, N. H. When he was only two years old his father died as the result of an accident, and his mother being unable to provide for the entire family, several children, including Henry, were brought up by neighbors. His mother died in 1846. Until the age of seventeen he lived with a neighboring farmer, attending school in the seasons when farm work permitted. He studied several terms at Plymouth Academy and New Hampshire Conference Seminary, his attendance being irregular because of the necessity of self-support. The strain on his health proved so severe that he was unable to enter college. In 1856 he began the study of law in the office of William Leverett of Plymouth, was admitted to the bar in 1859, and in the following year was appointed solicitor for Grafton County. He was married on Dec. 20, 1859, to Eliza Ann Nelson. On the outbreak of the Civil War he promptly offered his services but was twice rejected as physically unfit, and it was not until the following year that he was accepted. Going to the front as captain in the 15th New Hampshire Volunteers he rose to the rank of lieutenant-colonel, but was invalided home after being severely wounded at Port Hudson. He resumed practise but was handicapped by bad health for a number of years as a result of his army experience. He represented Plymouth in the lower house in 1866, and in the two succeeding years was chosen senator from the 11th district. Entering the Forty-fourth Congress in 1875, he was for the next twenty years a prominent figure in national affairs. He was a member of the House in the Forty-fourth, Forty-fifth, and Fifty-third Congresses, and senator from 1879 to 1891. Declining an appointment to the federal bench on his retirement from the Senate, he accepted President Harrison's offer of the post of minister to China. He was recalled while on his way to the Pacific Coast, however, on representations from the Chinese Government that his attitude on the immigration question had rendered him *persona non grata* (*Congressional Record,* 52 Cong., 1 Sess., 3151 ff.). On his retirement from active politics in 1895, he settled in Washington, D. C., where he resumed the practise of law.

Blair had the orthodox Republican faith in sound money, the tariff, and the pension system, and his arguments on these subjects were frequently printed in quantity for circulation as campaign documents. He also had, however, a strong humanitarian bent, firm religious convictions, and an enthusiasm, sometimes almost visionary, which frequently put his views far ahead of those of his contemporaries. In 1876, he introduced in the House a joint resolution amending the Constitution by prohibiting the manufacture, importation and sale of distilled liquors after Jan. 1, 1900, a plan which he claimed would have some of the merits of the slave-trade clause of 1787, permitting time for the necessary educational work and the adjustment of property rights. He asked "the considerate attention of all men now, for the time is coming when it will be forced upon them" (*Ibid.,* 44 Cong., 2 Sess., App., p. 16). He was a pioneer in the effort to interest the National Government in public education and in 1876 introduced a bill for the purpose of applying the proceeds of public land sales to education (*Ibid.,* 44 Cong., 1 Sess., App., pp. 235 ff.). As chairman of the Committee on Education and Labor in the Senate he gave earnest support to the project of national aid to the public schools. In 1881 he introduced in the Senate a bill proposing to "extend and vitalize" the common school system of the country by distributing among the states, on the basis of illiteracy, the sum total of $120,000,000 in annual instalments covering a period of ten years. This measure, or a substantially similar one, passed the Senate on three different occasions, only to die in committees of the House. Blair also introduced a constitutional amendment requiring the states to maintain free non-sectarian schools, and prohibiting religious establishments (*Ibid.,* 50 Cong., 1 Sess., p. 4615). In 1890 he introduced in the Senate a resolution requesting the President to summon an international conference to deal with the suppression of the slave-trade, the traffic in alcohol and weapons with backward peoples in Africa and Asia, and more important, to consider the problem of reduction and disbandment of existing military and naval establishments and the creation of tribunals for the peaceful settlement of controversies. An ardent supporter of woman suffrage, he repeatedly championed a constitutional amendment. He was concerned at the growing importance of labor problems and his activity in this field eventually resulted in the creation of the Department of Labor. More than once he demanded that the people of the District of Columbia be enfranchised and granted representation in Congress. Sabbath observance, the interests of the colored race, pension legislation, the prevention of railroad monopoly, the proper utilization of the public lands, were also topics in which he was deeply interested.

[A sketch of Henry W. Blair appears in Ezra S. Stearns, *Hist. of Plymouth, N. H.* (1906) ; another, with portrait, in David L. Perkins, *Manchester Up to Date* (1896) ; another in Emily W. Leavitt, *The Blair Family of New England* (1900).]

W. A. R.

BLAIR, JAMES (1655–Apr. 18, 1743), founder and first president of William and Mary College, was born in Scotland. The names of his parents are not known. He attended the University of Edinburgh, receiving the degree of Master of Arts in 1673. He was ordained in the Church of England and for several years preceding the year 1682 was rector of the parish of Cranston in the diocese of Edinburgh, serving with "exemplary diligence, care and gravity." Due to the disfavor of the Church of England in Scotland, he left his native land for England. We have no record that he continued his connection with the Church in England after his removal. For part of the three years preceding his departure for Virginia, he was employed in the office of the Master of the Rolls in London where he became acquainted with Dr. Henry Compton, Bishop of London, who prevailed upon him to go as a missionary to Virginia. He reached Virginia in 1685, and accepted the rectorship of the parish known as Varina at that time, but after 1720 always referred to as Henrico. The Bishop of London, whose diocese included Virginia, had no representative, with official title, in Virginia until Dec. 15, 1689, when he appointed Blair his commissary or deputy, with authority to supervise the clergy in a general way, but without the power of ordination or confirmation. As commissary, Blair began the custom of calling the clergy of the colony together occasionally in conventions. In the first convention, which met in 1690, he urged that the clergy take the initiative in the establishment of a college. Although there were other prominent men in the colony, who supported the project of a college, the chief burden of its promotion fell upon Blair. He well deserves, therefore, the title of founder of the College of William and Mary. In the spring of 1691 the General Assembly considered the establishment of a college, and Blair was selected May 20, 1691, to proceed to England and to present a memorial in behalf of the projected college to their Majesties King William and Queen Mary. The Assembly had previously asked him to assist a committee in drawing up the memorial. He reached London Sept. 1, 1691. Dr. Henry Compton, Bishop of London, Dr. Edward Stillingfleet, Bishop of Worcester, and Dr. John Tillotson, Archbishop of Canterbury, were all exceedingly interested in the college, and befriended Blair to the utmost. On Nov. 12, 1691, introduced by the Archbishop, he presented his memorial to the King, by whom it was graciously received and referred to proper officials for further consideration. Blair had to wait patiently for months while the charter was passing through the routine of the different offices. In the meantime, he was busy in the solicitation of funds. On Feb. 27, 1692, he wrote home that the Bishop of Salisbury had succeeded in getting two hundred pounds from the Boyle bequest for the college. Through his own direct efforts he assisted in obtaining an order in council that certain seized property of former pirates should be returned to them if they would give 300 pounds to the college. The charter was finally granted on Feb. 8, 1693, and in this document Blair is named as the first president "during his natural life." This clause of the charter carried out the wish of the General Assembly in its memorial which had named James Blair "as a fit person to be president." He was also named in the charter as rector of the board of visitors for the first year. He laid the charter before the Virginia Assembly on Oct. 20, 1693. By request of the board of visitors, he resigned his living in Henrico, and became minister of the Jamestown church in 1694. As Middle Plantation, later Williamsburg, the site selected for the college, was only seven miles from Jamestown, he was near enough to watch the construction of the college building, and to supervise the early instruction. He retained the charge at Jamestown until 1710, when he was appointed rector of Bruton parish in Williamsburg. This parish he retained until his death in 1743. He was appointed by the King to the council in the spring of 1694. The executive journal of the council shows that he was first present on July 18, 1694. His position as commissary therefore did not seat him *ex officio* in the council. He remained a member of the council until his death, though he was suspended by Andros for purely personal reasons from Apr. 19, 1695, to Aug. 12, 1696. On the latter date by order of the King he was again seated in the council. There were some opponents to the college, and Sir Edmund Andros, the governor, becoming the leader of the opposition, hindered the erection of the building and annoyed Blair in many ways. There was a hearing in London before the Archbishop of Canterbury and the Bishop of London upon charges brought against Andros, Dec. 27, 1697, when Blair himself was present. Blair was sustained, and Andros was recalled. The succeeding governor, Francis Nicholson, though at one time most friendly to Blair and the college, was no better than Andros. He used every means to obstruct the work of Blair both as commissary and president. With five other members of the council on May 20, 1703, Blair petitioned the Queen to remove Nicholson. This petition was sustained and Nicholson was recalled in 1705. Blair lived in harmony with the other governors, Nott, Spotswood, Drysdale, and Gooch, except in the later years of Spotswood's administration, when a quarrel arose over the rights of the governor and the commissary in regard to the appointment of ministers. Due not only to Blair's unfriendliness, but to other causes, Spotswood was removed in 1722. In 1726 Blair was again in England attending to college business. On Feb. 27, 1729, the transfer of the property of the college from the trustees was made to the faculty. After overcoming the determined opposition of two governors, the indifference of some of the prominent and wealthy in the colony, and the supreme misfortune of a disastrous fire in 1705 which destroyed the main building, Blair at last saw the college well established. At the time of his death it had three substantial buildings. From December 1740 to July 1741, Blair, as president of the council, was acting governor of the colony in the absence of the governor. His death occurred Apr. 18, 1743. A determined independence and firm assertion of his personal and official rights were his characteristics. He was somewhat inclined to be pugnacious, but justly so. He represented the church and the college in the midst of self-seeking politicians, and was therefore somewhat suspicious and impatient. He had many bitter enemies. The charges against him are variations of these two: first, that, being a Scotchman, he befriended his countrymen in church preferment; second, that he was particular in expecting payment of his salary as president and commissary. The careers of Andros and Nicholson, both before and after they came to Virginia, sustain Blair's charges against them. M. C. Tyler in his *History of American Literature* speaks of Blair as "the creator of the healthiest, and the most extensive intellectual influence that was felt in the southern group of Colonies before the Revolution." He married June 2, 1687, Sarah Harrison, the daughter of Col. Benjamin and Mrs. Hannah Harrison, of Wakefield, Surry County. He left an estate of about £10,000 to the family of John Blair [1687–1771, *q.v.*], his nephew and he left his library and £500 to the college. Blair was joint author with Henry Hartwell and Edward Chilton of *The Present State of Virginia and the College . . . to Which is Added the Charter,* originally written for the Board of Trade in 1697 but not published at that time. It was printed in London by J. Wyat in 1727 and has been reprinted in the *Calendar of State Papers, Colonial, 1696–97,* pp. 641–66, and in the *Massachusetts Historical Collections,* ser. 1, vol. V, pp. 144–60. Blair's sermons upon *Our Savior's Divine Sermon on the Mount* were published in five volumes in London in 1722. Copies of this edition may still be seen in some of the older houses in Virginia. A second edition in four volumes, with a prefatory note by Dr. Daniel Waterland, highly complimentary to Blair, was published in London in 1740. A Danish edition of the sermons translated by Dideric de Thurah was issued in Copenhagen in 1761, in four volumes.

[The only life of Blair is D. E. Motley's "Life of Commissary Jas. Blair" (*Johns Hopkins Univ. Studies in Hist. and Polit. Sci.*, XIX, no. 10, 1901). The author drew extensively upon the documents in Bishop W. S. Perry's *Papers Relating to the Hist. of the Ch. in Va., 1660–1776* (1870). These documents were copied from the archives at Lambeth and Fulham, and from the letter books of the Society for the Propagation of the Gospel in Foreign Parts. Bishop Perry's *Hist. of the Am. Epis. Ch., 1587–1883* (1885) also should be consulted; see in this work, I, 113–28, "The College at Williamsburg and President Blair," with illustrative and critical notes. The following works also are useful: J. S. M. Anderson, *Hist. of the Ch. of Eng. in the Colonies and Foreign Dependencies of the Brit. Empire* (1856); W. Meade, *Old Churches, Ministers and Families of Va.* (1856); L. G. Tyler, *Williamsburg, the Old Colonial Capital* (1907), *The Cradle of the Republic* (1900), and *The College of William and Mary* (1907); Frederick Horner, *Hist. of the Blair, Banister, and Braxton Families* (1898).]

E. G. S.

BLAIR, JOHN (1687–1771), **acting governor** of Virginia, the son of Archibald Blair, brother of James Blair [*q.v.*], was probably born in Virginia. His father was a student at the University of Edinburgh in 1685; he married three times, and John Blair was the son of the first wife, whose name is unknown. John received his education at the College of William and Mary, and as early as 1713 held the position of deputy auditor-general *pro tem.* His uncle and father were both prominent in the political affairs of the colony, and he doubtless owed much to their influence. His father was a member of the House of Burgesses, 1718–34. On Feb. 5, 1727, John Blair was appointed naval officer for the upper district of James River, and on Aug. 15, 1728, he took oath as deputy auditor-general, which position he filled until his death in 1771. From 1734 to 1740 he was a member of the House of Burgesses. According to Gooch, Blair was in narrow circumstances until he and his children received about £10,000 by the will of his uncle James Blair, who died in 1743. On Feb. 26, 1745, Gooch recommended John Blair for appointment to the Council and this recommendation was approved by the board of trade. Among Blair's activities was an interest in lands in the western part of the colony. As early as Nov. 4, 1745, a grant to him and his associates of 100,000 acres west of the Fairfax line was voted by the council. In addition to his services as councillor, Blair was appointed in 1746 on the committee to revise the laws, and was one of the committee of correspondence with the colonial agent Montague in England. As president of the Council he was twice called upon to act as governor, from January 1758, the time of Dinwiddie's departure, until the arrival of Fauquier, June 7, 1758; and again from Fauquier's death, Mar. 3, 1768, to the arrival of Botetourt in October 1768. As governor, he seems to have been agreeable to all political factions. His letter to the King's attorney of Spotsylvania County, July 16, 1768, in regard to the treatment of Baptists, gives us a most favorable view of his character. Instead of countenancing persecution of this sect, he advocated a liberal and sympathetic policy. In the Two Penny Act controversy he took the popular view and supported the act by his vote in council. He fully approved of the doctrine expressed by the General Assembly Mar. 31, 1768, that only the Assembly could make laws regarding the colony's internal policy of taxation. When Gov. Botetourt died Oct. 15, 1770, the duties of governor would again have devolved upon Blair but in order to avoid this, he resigned his seat in the Council. His death occurred in his eighty-fifth year. He was married to Mary Monro, daughter of Rev. John and Christian Monro, of St. Johns Parish, King William County, by whom he had ten children. Aside from his official papers as governor, we have nothing remaining of a literary nature, except his diary for the year 1751. This reveals him as a typical Virginia public man of that day, interested in the minor affairs of the town and colony, conscientious in his official duties, and not averse to the pleasures and amusements of the time.

[Blair's official career as burgess and councillor may be traced in the *Jours. of the House of Burgesses* and in the *Legislative Jours. of the Council of Colonial Va.* Transcripts of his letters as president of the council to the secretary of state and to the board of trade are in the Force Transcripts in the Lib. of Cong. For his letters to Washington, see S. M. Hamilton, *Letters to Washington*, vol. V. His diary for 1751 is printed in full in the *William and Mary Quart.*, VII, 134–53, and VIII, 1–17, accompanied by valuable notes of the editor, Lyon G. Tyler. Frederick Horner's *Hist. of the Blair, Banister and Braxton Families* (1898) has a chapter entitled "John Blair, Sr." which adds little to our information about him, but the letters of his children printed therein tell us much of their family life and of the general social conditions in Williamsburg in the eighteenth century. In this chapter may be found Blair's well-known letter to the King's attorney of Spotsylvania County.]

E. G. S.

BLAIR, JOHN (1732–Aug. 31, 1800), **jurist**, was born in Williamsburg, Va., son of John Blair [*q.v.*] and Mary Monro, daughter of Rev. John and Christian Monro of King William County. He attended William and Mary College, and later studied law at the Middle Temple in London in 1755. He entered the House of Burgesses in 1766, being elected to represent the College of William and Mary. His service began while his father was president of the Council. He continued to represent the College through the session of 1770. He probably became clerk of the Council after the close of the legislative session, June 28, 1770, for we find Washington in a letter of Oct. 5, 1770, referring to him as clerk. He retained this position as late as June 24, 1775. He signed the association entered into by the gentlemen of the House of Burgesses and the body of merchants, June 22, 1770, in which the signers agreed not to import certain specified goods from Great Britain until the Act of Parliament which imposed a duty on tea, paper, glass, and painters' colors was totally repealed. He was also a signer of the association of May 27, 1774. He probably succeeded his father as deputy auditor. In the convention of May 6, 1776, which met at Williamsburg for the purpose of drawing up a constitution for the new commonwealth of Virginia, John Blair was a representative, elected by the College of William and Mary. He was a member of the committee of twenty-eight which framed a declaration of rights and a plan of government. On June 30, 1776, he was elected a member of the Privy Council of the new state and was reëlected on May 29, 1777. On Jan. 23, 1778, he was elected one of the judges of the general court, by joint ballot of the Assembly. His successor in the Council was not elected till May 29, 1778. He may have served therefore on both Council and court for a time. He later became chief justice of this court. In 1780 upon the death of Robert Carter Nicholas he was elected a judge of the high court of chancery, and by virtue of both positions became judge of the first court of appeals of Virginia. In the important case of Commonwealth of Virginia *vs.* Caton *et al.*, in November 1782, which brought up the respective rights of the judicial and legislative branches of the government, Blair with the rest of the judges was of the opinion that the court could declare any act or resolution of the legislature unconstitutional. On Dec. 4, 1786, he was selected by the General Assembly one of the delegates to the convention in Philadelphia for framing a constitution, and he was one of the three from Virginia who voted for the acceptance of the document. He was returned from the county of York to the convention which met in Richmond in 1788 for the consideration of the proposed constitution. In this convention he was a firm supporter of the new constitution. On Sept. 30, 1789, he was appointed by President Washington an associate justice of the Supreme Court. On Jan. 27, 1796, he resigned. He was "blameless of disposition, pious, and possessed of great benevolence and goodness of heart." His wife, who was Jean Balfour, died Nov. 22, 1792. After his resignation from the Supreme Court he returned to Williamsburg and lived there until his death on Aug. 31, 1800. "He was about five feet ten inches in height, of erect and imposing stature, with a noble forehead, blue eyes, a well formed nose, and hair inclining to be red" (Robert Bolling, *Memoir of a Portion of the Bolling Family in England and Virginia,* 1868, pp. 33–34). He was a sincere and consistent patriot in the American Revolution. In his judicial career he was a conservative. His support of Madison and Washington in the struggle to frame and adopt a constitution showed him to be a firm believer in a strong federal government. No speeches of Blair have been preserved.

[*The Jours. of the House of Burgesses,* 1766–1770, and the *Jour. of the Convention of 1776* give us Blair's record in the Revolutionary cause and the Minutes of the Council, in manuscript, in the Va. State Lib., his career as a councillor. The most noted cases in which he took part on the Supreme Bench were Hayburn's Case, *2 Dallas 409;* State of Georgia *vs. Brailsford 2 Dallas 415;* Chisholm *vs.* Georgia, *2 Dallas 419;* Penhallow *vs.* Doane's admr., *3 Dallas 54.* The sketch of Blair in Hugh Blair Grigsby's *Convention of 1776* (1853) is useful. In Frederick Horner's *Hist. of the Blair, Banister, and Braxton Families* (1898) there is a chapter on Judge Blair, in which there are printed some interesting letters from him to his sister, Mrs. Braxton.]

E. G. S.

BLAIR, JOHN INSLEY (Aug. 22, 1802–Dec. 2, 1899), capitalist, philanthropist, the son of James and Rachel (Insley) Blair, was born on a farm on the banks of the Delaware, two miles below Belvidere, N. J. His school instruction, obtained during a few brief months in the winters, ceased when he was eleven years old, and he went to work in a country store. It is said that when ten years of age, he exclaimed to his mother, "I have seven brothers and three sisters. That's enough in the family to be educated. I am going to get rich." At eighteen he was his own master and owner of a store. At twenty-seven he had a chain of five general stores in the northern part of New Jersey and ran four flouring-mills. He married, Sept. 20, 1828, Ann Locke of Frelinghuysen, N. J., grand-daughter of a Revolutionary captain. In 1833 he became interested with Col. George W. Scranton and Seldon T. Scranton in tne mines at Oxford Furnace. Success in this enterprise led in 1846 to his participation in the founding of the Lackawanna Coal & Iron Company. Mining led to railroad promotion, and it was in this enterprise that he amassed the greater part of his fortune and reputation. In 1852 the Delaware, Lackawanna & Western Railroad, so named at Blair's suggestion, was organized. He became one of the largest stockholders and served as a director from the organization of the road until his death.

He was always keenly interested in politics, state and national. He attended every national convention of the Republican party from its founding till 1892. In 1868 he was the unanimous choice of the New Jersey state Republican convention for governor, but lost the election to Gov. Randolph. The campaign cost Blair over $90,000 personally. In 1860, when attending the convention at Chicago, Ill., which nominated Abraham Lincoln, Blair's attention was attracted to the great possibilities of Western development through the extension of railroads. He joined with Oakes Ames and others in getting the charter of the Union Pacific Railroad, and personally built the first one hundred miles west from Omaha, having been responsible for the adoption of that route. His operations in the West extended in succeeding years to Iowa, Wisconsin, Kansas, Nebraska, Dakota, Missouri, and Texas. He was at one time president of sixteen different railroads, and is said to have been the individual owner of more miles of railroad property than any other man in the world. He laid out sites for more than eighty towns, and owned lands equal to half the area of his native state. He was a man of unusual energy and possessed a remarkable physique. He told friends that it had been his custom to travel about 40,000 miles a year and that he reduced this to 20,000 only when he reached the age of eighty-five. When ninety-two years old, he would often be at his desk at 5:30 a. m., and business would then claim his attention during the greater part of the day. His habits were always simple, and his acquisition of millions made little change in his mode of living. He continued to reside in New Jersey in his beloved Blairstown, his enormous enterprises being directed from this inaccessible little village. One of the institutions which claimed his special favor and attention was the Blair Presbyterian Academy at Blairstown. Blair Hall at Princeton University, of which institution he was made a trustee in 1886, is another monument to his liberality. Grinnell and Lafayette Colleges were also special recipients of his benevolences. He was a most liberal benefactor of the Presbyterian Church, of which he was a life-long member. In the eighty towns in the West, whose sites he was instrumental in selecting, he helped erect, by gifts of land and money, more than one hundred churches. The value of his estate was roughly estimated at the time of his death at $70,000,000 and he was said to have given away over $5,000,000.

[*N. J. Hist. Soc. Proc.*, 3rd ser., vols. III and IV; the *Sun* (N.Y.), *N.Y. Herald, Times, Tribune*, Dec. 3, 1899; C. M. Knapp, *N. J. Politics during the Period of the Civil War and Reconstruction* (1924); letters of J. I. Blair in Princeton Univ. Library.]

C. R. E.

BLAIR, MONTGOMERY (May 10, 1813–July 27, 1883), lawyer, statesman, eldest son of Francis Preston Blair, Sr. [*q.v.*], was reared in Franklin County, Ky., amidst the scenes of political strife between "relief" and "anti-relief" and "Old" and "New Court" factions. The schools of Kentucky gave him his early education. He was appointed by President Jackson to West Point in 1831; after his graduation in 1835 he received a lieutenancy in the army in time to serve in the Seminole War. The next year he resigned his commission in order to study law in Transylvania University. He settled in St. Louis in 1837 as the protégé of Thomas Hart Benton. After practising law two years he was appointed United States district attorney for Missouri, only to be removed for political reasons by President Tyler. He served in St. Louis as mayor (1842–43) and as judge of the court of common pleas (1845–49). In 1849 he resigned to resume his law practise. In 1853 he moved to Maryland where he practised law chiefly before the Supreme Court of the United States. President Pierce made him the first solicitor for the court of claims of the United States (1855) but President Buchanan dismissed him because of his pronounced views on slavery. He was a Free-Soiler in principle, believed slavery could be peaceably settled, generally held the political views of border statesmen, and had sympathy with the interests of the West. After joining the American party he left it because of its silence on slavery and became a Democratic-Republican in the Republican party. His prestige was greatly increased among anti-slavery people when he became counsel for Dred Scott. His sense of fairness led him to help secure a defense attorney for John Brown after the Harper's Ferry incident. He was a delegate to the Democratic national conventions in 1844, 1848, and 1852. In 1860 he presided at the state Republican convention at Baltimore and attended the Chicago national convention as a delegate from Maryland. Because of his services to the Republican party, his family connections, and his political views and experiences he was made postmaster general in Lincoln's cabinet, where he belonged to the Bates-Welles-Blair group. He strongly urged the reënforcement of Southern forts, particularly Fort Sumter, which he believed could be held against the Confederates, and threatened to resign if that fort were not reenforced. Without being obsequious he was a staunch supporter of Lincoln. He strongly opposed Secretary Chase's views, befriended Mc-

Clellan, and insisted from the beginning of the incident that the seizure of Mason and Slidell was illegal. In his own department he organized the postal system for the army, introduced compulsory payment of postage and free delivery in cities, improved the registry system, established the railway post-office, organized the postal draft plan which his successor put into operation, stopped the franking privileges of postmasters, and was instrumental in bringing about the Postal Union Convention at Paris (1863). In the Union national convention (1864) the Radicals succeeded in passing a resolution which virtually demanded the dismissal of Blair from the cabinet. The President, after a fair assurance of victory at the polls, bowed to political expediency and requested Blair's resignation, which was cheerfully given. Blair continued, however, to work loyally for Lincoln. After the assassination of Lincoln, Blair advised Johnson to dismiss the old and appoint a new cabinet. He sought moderation for the South, asserting and believing that Lincoln's plan of reconstruction was just and best. He decried the disfranchisement of the Southern whites and enfranchisement of the negroes. His views brought him into conflict with those held by the radical reconstructionists. He drifted back to the Democratic party, where he supported Seymour in 1868 and Greeley in 1872, and championed Tilden's cause in 1876. With the financial aid of W. W. Corcoran he established a newspaper, the *Union* (Washington, D. C.), to uphold Tilden's claims to the Presidency. As Tilden's counsel he appeared before the Electoral Commission. He declared Tilden represented "the one issue"—reform. Being elected to the Maryland House of Delegates (1878) and immediately made chairman of the judiciary committee, Blair proposed the resolution which denied the right of President Hayes to office. Though honest in his belief that Hayes was illegally chosen president, he aroused the intense enmity of many people by his method of agitating the question. He unsuccessfully ran for Congress in 1882. Blair was tall and spare, clean-shaven, with light hair and bluish-grey eyes. His speech was slow, his voice calm. Few men were more courteous and genial than he, but he was temperamentally combative and obstinate when he thought he was right. Though deeply religious he held anti-ritualistic sentiments. As a lawyer he used persuasive argument which was the result of research and logical reasoning. While he had strong prejudices, he was shrewd, frank, and thoroughly honest. He was twice married: to a Miss Buckner of Virginia, who died in 1844, and to a daughter of Judge Levi Woodbury of New Hampshire. He was an inveterate worker and died while engaged in writing a life of Andrew Jackson.

[The Blair Papers (unpublished); Levi Woodbury Papers (unpublished); "Montgomery Blair" in *Maryland in National Politics* (1915) by Jesse Frederick Essary; "Montgomery Blair" in *Sketches of Representative Men North and South* (1872), ed. by Augustus C. Rogers; "The Public Career of Montgomery Blair, Particularly with Reference to His Services as Postmaster General of the United States" by Madison Davis in the *Records of the Columbia Hist. Soc.*, XIII (1910), 126–61; *Diary of Gideon Welles* (1911); J. G. Nicolay and John Hay, *Abraham Lincoln* (10 vols., 1890).]

W. E. S.

BLAIR, SAMUEL (June 14, 1712–July 5, 1751), Presbyterian clergyman, was born in Ulster, Ireland, the son of William Blair. He came to America in early youth and was drawn into the movement headed by William Tennent for a broader and more aggressive evangelicalism in the young Presbyterian Church. With Tennent's four sons and a few other young men of talent and devotion he entered the academy at Neshaminy, near Philadelphia, founded by Tennent for the education of ministers and nicknamed by his critics the "Log College" because of its crude domicile and equipment. Blair was licensed to preach by the presbytery of Philadelphia at the early age of twenty-one, Nov. 9, 1733, and in the following year was settled as pastor of the double charge consisting of the churches at Middletown and Shrewsbury, N. J. While occupying these pulpits he joined with some others in the organization of the Presbytery of New Brunswick (1738). His success as a preacher called attention to him and he was invited to the leadership of the more important work at New Londonderry, Chester County, Pa. (known also as Fagg's Manor). He began his labors here in 1739 and was installed in 1740. During his ministry of twelve years in this field, he threw himself into a number of enterprises of importance. First of all, in addition to his pastoral labors he conducted a rudimentary theological seminary. Among his pupils some came to prominence and leadership in the church, notably Samuel Davies, successor to Jonathan Edwards in the presidency of the College of New Jersey (Princeton), and John Rodgers, first moderator of the General Assembly of the Presbyterian Church. In 1740 the evangelistic fervor aroused by George Whitefield's visit and preaching in America reached Blair's parish and found him ready to place himself in the forefront of the movement. His gifts as a preacher made his pulpit one of the conspicuous centers of the revival. When Whitefield's manner became the subject of criticism and controversy, Blair was called upon to take part in the defense of the movement. In this work he had the coöperation of his old fellow-student, Gilbert Tennent. The struggle became acute and from the mere defense of the revival Tennent and Blair assumed an aggressive attitude, bringing before the Synod of 1740 charges against the ministry of negligence in the performance of their duties and of lack of interest in their spiritual functions. On being challenged to produce their evidence they were obliged to confess that they had not based their charges upon adequate investigations. In the division of the Presbyterian Church which resulted from this controversy, Blair, like all the other followers of Tennent, went with the "New Side" (Synod of New York), became its chief spokesman, and wrote its declaration of principles. He is described as "grave and solemn, yet cheerful, pleasant, and witty."

[*The Works of the Rev. Samuel Blair, Late Minister of the Gospel at Fagg's Manor, in Chester County, Pa. Containing a Collection of Sermons on Various Subjects: together with several Treatises, in a Vindication of the Brethren etc., the Doctrine of Predestination, etc., a Sermon on his death by Rev. Mr. Finley* (1754), ed. by John Blair; A. Alexander, *Biog. Sketches of the Founder and Principal Alumni of the Log College* (1851); E. H. Gillet, *Hist. of the Presbyterian Ch. in the U. S.* (1864); J. S. Futhey and Gilbert Cope, *Hist. of Chester County, Pa.* (1881).]

A. C. Z.

BLAKE, ELI WHITNEY (Jan. 27, 1795–Aug. 18, 1886), inventor, manufacturer, son of Elihu and Elizabeth (Whitney) Blake, was born in Westborough, a small village in Massachusetts sixteen miles east of Worcester. In Westborough lived his famous uncle, Eli Whitney, and also his maternal grandfather, the latter, in good Yankee fashion, being both farmer and mechanic, and having not only a complete kit of cabinet-making tools but a turning-lathe as well. In this environment Blake was reared. His life differed, however, from that of the average youth of his day and was more like that of a young man of the twentieth century in that his parents apparently were fully resolved from his birth to enable him to be well educated. His mother probably had not had time to forget the firm opposition of both her father and stepmother to her brother's ambition to obtain a college education. At all events, young Blake was prepared for Yale at Litchfield Academy, entered college at the age of seventeen, and graduated with the class of 1816. After spending the year succeeding graduation in the Litchfield Law School, at the request of his uncle, Eli Whitney, he abandoned a professional career and entered his uncle's employ in the manufacture of firearms at Whitneyville, a suburb of New Haven. Upon the death of Whitney in 1825, Blake with one of his brothers carried on the armory business at the same place until 1836. During this time he made several important inventions having to do with the manufacture of arms, which were immediately adopted in armories throughout the country. In 1836 the armory was given up, and with two brothers, Blake established in Westville, another suburb of New Haven, a manufactory of domestic hardware, which was the pioneer establishment in this field in the United States. He continued as the directing head of this establishment for thirty-five years and then retired at the age of sixty-six. While assistant to his uncle in the armory, Blake married Eliza Maria O'Brien of New Haven, on July 8, 1822. They had twelve children, ten of whom lived to maturity. Each of their six sons attended Yale and five graduated, the sixth being prevented from completing his course by ill health. Among the patents granted by the United States Patent Office to the Blake brothers, Philos, Eli, and John, for inventions made during the period of their hardware manufacturing business, were a door lock and escutcheon (Dec. 31, 1833), thumb latch (July 21, 1840), castors for bedsteads (June 30, 1838), button, plate, and turn for fastening cupboard and other doors (Mar. 21, 1843). In 1855 Blake served on a committee of townsmen who had charge of the macadamizing of one of the principal streets of New Haven. His attention was drawn to the need of a machine to perform the labor of crushing the various sizes of stone used in this type of paving. He apparently devoted all of his energies and inventive genius to the solution of the problem, and on June 15, 1858, United States patent No. 20,542 was granted him for a stone crusher. It is for this invention that Blake is best known. For originality, simplicity, and effectiveness the Blake type of crusher has not been surpassed for general use and is still employed the world over. All of his life Blake was a profound student of mathematics and physics, and in his later years, particularly after his retirement from active business, found his happiness in studying problems of aerodynamics. He was one of the founders and several times president of the Connecticut Academy of Sciences, and wrote many valuable papers for the *American Journal of Science* and other scientific periodicals. Just four years before his death he gathered together a number of these papers and published them in a single volume, under the title *Original Solutions of Several Problems in Aerodynamics* (1882), which was probably his most valuable contribution. After an old age of honored retirement, he died at his home in New Haven, Conn., in his ninety-second year.

[W. H. Doolittle, *Inventions in the Century* (1902), being vol. XVI of the Nineteenth Century Series; *Biog. Sketches of the Members of the Class of 1816, Yale Coll.* (1867); *Obit. Record Grads. Yale Univ.* (1887); obituaries in *New Haven Evening Reg.*, Aug. 18, 1886, and in *New Haven Morning Jour.*, Aug. 19, 1886; Records of the U. S. Patent Office.] C. W. M.

BLAKE, FRANCIS (Dec. 25, 1850–Jan. 19, 1913), inventor, physicist, was born in Needham, Mass., a descendant of William and Agnes Blake, who came to America in 1630 from Somersetshire, England, and settled in Dorchester, Mass. They were leaders in colonial affairs. Francis Blake was of the eighth generation. His father, also Francis Blake, was a business man and for many years United States appraiser at Boston. His mother was Caroline Burling, daughter of George Augustus Trumbull. Blake attended the public schools until he was sixteen years old, when he left Brookline High School to accept a position as draftsman in the United States Coast and Geodetic Survey in Washington, the position having been secured for him by an uncle, Commodore George Smith Blake. It was in this service for thirteen consecutive years that he acquired the scientific education which led to his later successes in civil life. During this time he assisted in many of the most important scientific achievements of the Survey, including hydrographic surveys of the Susquehanna River, the west coast of Florida, and the north coast of Cuba. He assisted in the determination of the transcontinental longitude between the observatory of Harvard College and San Francisco. A metallic circuit of 7,000 miles with thirteen repeaters was employed and the experiment resulted in a signal being sent from Harvard Observatory to San Francisco and back again in eight-tenths of a second. In 1870 he was temporarily detached from the Survey to serve as astronomer of the Darien Exploring Expedition, under Commander Selfridge. This expedition was undertaken primarily to determine routes for a ship canal across the Isthmus of Darien. His final work with the Survey was in the determination of differences in longitude between the observatories at Greenwich, England; Paris; Cambridge, Mass.; and Washington. Upon the completion of this work he retired to his home in Weston, Mass. His work with the Survey developed his interest in physics and electrical communication, and at an early period he began devoting his leisure moments to experimental physics, building up at the same time a well-equipped laboratory in his home. Within a month of his retiring in 1875, he began experimental work on a telephone transmitting instrument, and in 1878 received a United States patent for a transmitter the mechanical features of which made practical the fundamental principles of the Berliner microphone. This patent was purchased in November 1878 by the Bell Telephone Company, and Blake was immediately employed to perfect it. It was the adoption of the Blake transmitter that enabled the Bell Telephone Company to succeed in an intensely competitive field. Blake continued his laboratory work, particularly in electrical communication, and between 1878 and 1890 received twenty patents. He married Elizabeth L. Hubbard on June 24, 1873, in Weston, Mass. He was a Fellow of the American Association for the Advancement of Science, a member of the American Institute of Electrical Engineers, of the corporation of the Massachusetts Institute of Technology, and also of several historical societies.

[D. H. Hurd, *Hist. of Middlesex County, Mass.*, vol. I (1890); E. W. Byrn, *The Progress of Invention in the Nineteenth Century* (1900); *Who's Who in America*, 1912–13; *Report of the Supt. of the U. S. Coast Survey 1867–74;* Records of the U. S. Patent Office; F. W. Wile, *Emile Berliner, Maker of the Microphone* (1926); *Boston Transcript* and *Daily Globe*, Jan. 20, 1913.] C. W. M.

BLAKE, HOMER CRANE (Feb. 1, 1822–Jan. 21, 1880), naval officer, son of Elisha and Marilla (Crane) Blake, was born in Dutchess County, N. Y., but the next year his parents removed to Hancock County, Ohio. After serving as acting midshipman on board the frigate *Constellation* for some time, he was warranted as midshipman on Aug. 20, 1842, in accordance with the recommendations of his commanding officers. He saw service on several war-ships and in many seas, and enjoyed one year, 1845–46, at the Naval School, Annapolis. He became passed midshipman, 1846, lieutenant, 1855, and lieutenant commander, 1862, commanding the steamer *Hatteras* in the Western Gulf Blockading Squadron. On Jan. 11, 1863, he was ordered by signal to chase a sail to the southeastward, which, when approached and hailed, at first pretended to be a British war-ship. Before a boat could be lowered the suspicious stranger hailed in her turn, announcing that she was the Confederate ship *Alabama.* A broadside immediately followed, to which the *Hatteras* replied. Commander Blake endeavored immediately to close with the enemy, which was of greatly superior power, in order to take her by boarding. This intention was frustrated by the *Alabama's* captain, and, after a sharp fight in which several shells exploded in the *Hatteras,* depriving Blake of the power of maneuvering his vessel or working the pumps to quench the fire which broke out, he was no longer able to continue the unequal battle, and surrendered his ship, which sank ten minutes after her crew had been taken off by the *Alabama*. After being exchanged, Blake was exonerated and commended by the Navy Department, and received command of the gunboat *Eutaw* in the North Atlantic Squadron, taking part in several actions in the Virginia rivers. An interesting letter is extant in the Navy Department from representatives of the crew of the *Hatteras,* petitioning the Secretary of the Navy to place their "brave and excellent commander" in command of a "fast and well-armed steamer, and that in company with him we may seek out and capture our former foe," a request which it was impossible to fulfil, as measures had already been taken which eventually resulted in the destruction of the *Alabama.* Blake was commissioned commander Mar. 3, 1866, captain May 25, 1871, and commodore in 1879. He was married to Mary Flanagan, by whom he had two children.

[Sketch and portrait in Ellery Bicknell Crane, *Genealogy of the Crane Family,* II (1900), 151–54; obituary in *Army and Navy Jour.,* Jan. 24, 1880; *Official Records,* ser. 1, vol. XIX; Navy Registers, 1823–80.]

E. B.

BLAKE, JOHN LAURIS (Dec. 21, 1788–July 6, 1857), Episcopal clergyman, author, was born in Northwood, N. H., the son of Jonathan and Mary (Dow) Blake. He worked on his father's farm in summer and went to the district school in winter, attended Phillips Exeter Academy, and graduated in 1812 from Brown University. He was licensed as a Congregational minister in 1813, but soon turned to the Episcopal Church. He married Louisa Gray Richmond June 25, 1814, who died Jan. 3, 1816; on Dec. 6 of the same year he married Mary Howe. Upon his ordination as an Episcopal deacon in 1815 he organized St. Paul's parish in Pawtucket, R. I., and was its rector until 1820. He then took charge of parishes in Concord and Hopkinton, N. H., and at Concord started a girls' school that succeeded so well that in 1822 he moved it to Boston, where he continued to maintain it until 1830. In Boston he was also rector of St. Matthew's 1824–32 and editor of the *Gospel Advocate,* which in January 1827 was merged with the *Episcopal Watchman.* The rest of his life was given chiefly to literary work of one sort or another. He made his home in New York for a time and about 1846 moved to Orange, N. J., where he died. He seems to have been an amiable, dutiful man, a diligent though decidedly uncritical student and writer. As cleric and schoolmaster he had acquired a varied stock of information, which he purveyed at first in small packages as text-books and later in whole tomes as one-volume encyclopedias. He wrote in all more than forty books, most of them texts of geography, the natural sciences, and Christian evidences, together with various reading books and other miscellaneous productions. The farmer being especially dear to his heart, he endeavored to further scientific agriculture and rural education in general with *A Family Text-Book for the Country, or the Farmer at Home, Being a Cyclopædia of the More Important Topics in Modern Agriculture* (1853), an alphabetization of definitions, anecdotes, homilies, and tidbits of information not altogether trustworthy. The same characteristics reappeared in his larger work, *A Family Encyclopedia of Useful Knowledge* (1852). Somewhat better was the book by which he was most widely known, his *General Biographical Dictionary* (1835, 13th ed., rev. and enlarged, 1856), which enjoyed for almost a generation a good reputation and a useful career as a reference book.

[*Hist. Cat. of Brown Univ. 1764–1904* (1905); E. C. Cogswell, *Hist. of Nottingham, Deerfield, and Northwood, N. H.* (1878), pp. 645–47; *Church Rev. and Ecclesiastical Reg.,* Oct. 1857.]

G. H. G.

BLAKE, LILLIE DEVEREUX (Aug. 12, 1835–Dec. 30, 1913), author, reformer, was descended on both sides of the family from Jonathan Edwards. George P. Devereux, her father, was a wealthy gentleman of Raleigh, N. C., where Lillie was born; her mother, Sarah Elizabeth Johnson, of an old New York and New England family, was descended from the Hon. William Samuel Johnson. Her mother moved to New Haven on the death of her husband when Lillie was two years old, and the child attended Miss Apthorp's school for girls and later was tutored in college subjects by Yale professors. At twenty she married Frank G. Q. Umsted, Philadelphia attorney. They had two children. She now began to write, but without the definite social and political bias which characterized her later work. A short story was published in the *Atlantic Monthly* and there was a novel, *Southwold* (1859). Four years after their marriage her husband died, leaving her with a depleted fortune and two small children to support. She wrote feverishly during this period, completing a book of stories, and two novels in the *New York Mercury,* "The Orphan or The Mystery of Maple Cottage" and "Ireton Standish or the False Kinsman." During the first year of the Civil War she was Washington correspondent of the *New York Evening Post.* She published *Rockford, or Sunshine and Storm* in 1863. Under various *noms de plume,* one of which was Tiger Lily, she also contributed to the *Galaxy* which was later merged with the *Atlantic Monthly.* She was married again, in 1866, to Grenfill Blake, a merchant of New York City, where she lived from that time. Her interest in the rights of women crystallized a few years later and she became active in agitation for enfranchisement and economic reforms for women. She arranged conventions, addressed committees, presided at public meetings, and made extensive lecture tours. In her spare time she wrote articles for newspapers and periodicals, and fiction which carried her message. The best known of her novels is *Fettered for Life, or Lord and Master* (1874, republished in 1885), "designed to illustrate the subject condition of women" (*Testimonial to Mrs. Blake, National Pageant and Dramatic Events in the History of New York,* Union Square Theatre, Nov. 25, 1889). She was one of the delegation from the National Woman's Suffrage Association which presented the Declaration of Rights at Independence Hall, Philadelphia, on July 4, 1876; she was president of the New York State Woman's Suffrage Association for eleven years; and in 1900 she founded the National Legislative League. She championed measures which established matrons in police stations, women census takers, seats for saleswomen, and women physicians in insane asylums admitting women patients. One of her most important activities was in behalf of the school suffrage laws for women in New York State, in the passage of which in 1880 she was largely instrumental. In reply to Dr. Morgan Dix's *Lectures on the Calling of a Christian Woman* (1883) she herself gave a series of lectures, published as *Woman's Place Today* (1883), which created a sensation in the current press and did much to waken women and convert them into active workers. She was president of the New York City Suffrage League from 1886 until 1900. A woman of unusual beauty and charm, she was not an easy prey for the cartoonists who amused themselves at the expense of the early suffragists.

[*Who's Who in America,* 1899–1912; *N. Y. Times,* Dec. 29, 31, 1913; *N. Y. Tribune,* Dec. 31, 1913; *Sun,* Dec. 31, 1913; manuscript letter from Mrs. Blake's daughter, Miss Katherine D. Blake.]

M. A. K.

BLAKE, LYMAN REED (Aug. 24, 1835–Oct. 5, 1883), inventor, was born at South Abington, Mass., the son of Susannah Bates and Samuel Blake, directly descended from William and Agnes Blake who came to Dorchester, Mass., from Plymouth, England, in 1630. Lyman, the youngest of ten children, eight of whom were girls, received the usual district school education of the period. During his school vacations he worked for the shoemakers of Abington and at sixteen was regularly employed by his older brother Samuel, who was manufacturing shoes in a small way. From Samuel's "factory" the cut-out parts of shoes were given to the shoemakers, who worked on them at home and then returned the finished shoes. Lyman's duties at the factory were to give out the stock, receive the finished shoes, and keep account of these. Following this he worked with Edmund Shaw, agent for the Singer Sewing Machine Company at Abington, setting up sewing machines in the shoe factories and teaching operators their use. By 1856 he had saved money enough to purchase an interest in the shoemaking firm of Gurney & Mears, which became Gurney, Mears & Blake. Here he immediately organized a stitching room, put in machines, and taught the operators in what was probably the first such room to be run on the "contract" system. At that time the machines were able to sew only the seams of the uppers which were then hand-sewed or pegged to the sole. Blake entertained the idea of a machine capable of sewing the soles of shoes to the uppers. His partners thought this a bit visionary and suggested that any work on the machine should be done on his own time. Blake went ahead at night and first designed a shoe that could be sewed. This shoe is essentially the present-day shoe and is considered by many as Blake's most important invention. It is described in Patent No. 29,561. He then whittled a wooden model of a machine that would, in his opinion, sew such a shoe. He had the parts made for a metal machine, put them together, and found that it worked. He immediately patented the machine (Patent No. 20,775, July 6, 1858) and through his patent attorney met Gordon McKay (1859), who was able and willing to promote it. McKay paid Blake $70,000 for this patent, $8,000 in cash, and $62,000 from the profits of the company. Because of poor health Blake then moved to Staunton, Va., where with the $8,000 he was able to open a retail shoe store, though the Civil War very soon forced him to leave his store and return to the North. In 1861 he rejoined McKay and to promote the introduction of his machine, did all in his power to improve it. With McKay he worked out the details of the factory system which made the machine available and traveled over New England introducing the machine and instructing manufacturers in its use. Blake's machine, when finally perfected, came into almost universal use, as is indicated by Blake's own statement that in fifteen years (1861–76) over 177,000,000 pairs of shoes had been sewed on the McKay machines at a saving of $14,000,000. Today, with many refinements, it is an important link in the series of machines that allows the shoe to be completely machine made. Unfortunately for the fame of Blake the machine has always been known in this country as the McKay machine, although in Europe, where his patents were handled so carelessly that he received very little from them, he did have the satisfaction of having it known as the Blake machine. The product and process patents on the shoe were reissued to Blake in 1874 and reassigned by him to the McKay Association, for which he received a large sum of money. He then retired from active business and spent most of his remaining years in travel. He was married on Nov. 27, 1855, to Susie V. Hollis of Abington.

[B. Hobart, *Hist. of the Town of Abington, Plymouth County, Mass.* (1866); *Vital Records of Abington, Mass., to the Year 1850*, vol. I (1912); B. E. Hazard, *Organization of the Boot and Shoe Industry in Mass. before 1875* (1921); F. A. Gannon, *Short Hist. of Am. Shoemaking* (1912); *Supt. and Foreman*, Oct. 27, 1896; obituary in *Boston Evening Transcript*, Oct. 6, 1883; *Shoe and Leather Reporter*, Mar. 13, 1884; A. Getchel, *In the Matter of the Application of Lyman Blake for Extensions of Letters Patent No. 29,561* (1874).]

F. A. T—r.

BLAKE, MARY ELIZABETH McGRATH (Sept. 1, 1840–Feb. 26, 1907), author, daughter of Patrick and Mary (Murphy) McGrath, was born in Dungarven, Ireland, and died in Boston. Her father came to Massachusetts about 1850 and settled in Quincy. There, prospering as a worker in marble, he was able to send his children to the best schools and to devote much of his own time to reading. Mary completed her formal education at Emerson's Private School in Boston (1859–61) and at the Academy of the Sacred Heart, Manhattanville (1861–63). In 1865 she was married to John G. Blake, a Boston physician who had known her first through the poems which she had already begun publishing in the newspapers. She was the mother of eleven children, to whom she was thoroughly attentive, but her maternal duties did not check either the steady flow of verse which "welled from her heart spontaneously" (Conway, "M. E. Blake," p. xiii), or the "Rambling Talks" which she contributed regularly for many years to the *Boston Journal.* A devout Catholic, she wrote many articles for the *Catholic World,* but she published also in *Scribner's* and even in *The Congregationalist.* From time to time she published collections of her poetry. Her *Poems* (1882) contains matter written as early as 1863. *Verses along the Way* appeared in 1890, and *In the Harbour of Hope,* 1907. She wrote also two books of poems for children, *The Merry Months All* (1885), and *Youth in Twelve Centuries* (1886). Her writing was so esteemed in the Boston of her time that she was invited by the city to prepare memorials for Wendell Phillips and other celebrities. But the artistic value of her work is not commensurate with her reputation. She published in prose three volumes of travel, *On the Wing* (1883)—dealing with the western United States; *Mexico* (1888)—in collaboration with Margaret F. Sullivan; and *A Summer Holiday in Europe* (1890). "She had visited Europe," it is reported, "five times; thrice on walking trips of educative purpose with her three younger children; and in every land she could make herself at home with its people" (Conway, "M. E. Blake," p. xvi). She opposed militarism, and in 1887 denounced it in her pamphlet, *The Coming Reform.* Of her six children who reached maturity, she sent five sons to Harvard and one daughter to Radcliffe.

[K. E. Conway, "Mary Elizabeth Blake," in M. E. Blake, *In the Harbour of Hope* (1907); J. B. Cullen, *Story of the Irish in Boston* (rev. ed., 1893); *Who's Who in America,* 1906–07; *Publishers Weekly,* Mar. 9, 1907; *Boston Globe,* Feb. 27, 1907.]

J. D. W.

BLAKE, WILLIAM PHIPPS (June 21, 1825–May 22, 1910), geologist and mining engineer, was born in New York City, the son of Adeline (Mix) Blake and of Elihu Blake, a prominent surgeon dentist and lineal descendant of William Blake who settled in the Massachusetts Bay colony about 1630. W. P. Blake was fitted for college at private schools in New York and entered the Sheffield Scientific School to graduate in the course in chemistry in 1852. He then became chemist and mineralogist of the New Jersey Zinc Company and chemist of the chemical works at Baltimore, Md. In 1854–56 he was one of the geologists of the Pacific Railroad surveys. On Dec. 25, 1855, he was married to Charlotte Haven Lord Hayes. From 1856 to 1859 he was engaged in investigating the mineral resources of North Carolina and adjacent regions and in the last-named year became editor and proprietor of the *Mining Magazine,* the name of which he subsequently changed to the *Mining Magazine and Journal of Geology, Mineralogy and Metallurgy, Chemistry and the Arts.* The venture did not prove a success, in part owing to the approach of the Civil War, and the publication was suspended in 1860. In 1861–63 Blake was employed as mining engineer by the Japanese government and in company with Raphael Pumpelly he organized the first school of science in Japan and taught there both chemistry and geology. In 1863 he returned to the United States by way of Alaska and explored the Stickeen River region, discovering and describing the Stickeen glacier. Returning to California he resumed his profession of mining engineer, making special studies of the Comstock Lode, and in 1864 he was appointed mineralogist of the state board of agriculture, and also professor of mineralogy and geology in the College of California (afterwards the University of California at Berkeley). In 1867 he was appointed commissioner for California to the Paris Exposition and was editor of the six volumes of reports of the United States Commissioners. In 1871 he was chief of the scientific corps of the United States to Santo Domingo, and in 1873 he was commissioner of the United States to the Vienna International Exposition. His manifest efficiency in this capacity led to his appointment by the Smithsonian Institution to collect and install the government exhibit, illustrating the mineral resources of the United States, at the Philadelphia Centennial Exposition of 1876. His work in the preparation of this exhibit was enormous but highly successful. These collections, in connection with those of several foreign governments turned over at the close of the exposition, formed the basis of the New National Museum's collections begun in 1879–80. To Blake also fell the somewhat onerous task of editing the notes and describing the fossils collected long before by the French-American geologist, Jules Marcou, who, through a falling out with the then secretary of state, had relinquished his work, leaving his collections in confusion, and had returned to France. Blake was for some fifteen years engaged in sundry economic surveys in the West, and in 1895, although already in his seventieth year, he became professor of geology and mining, and director of the School of Mines at the University of Arizona at Tucson. This position he resigned in 1905, but retained until his death the honorary and nonsalaried appointment of territorial mineralogist and geologist, to which he had been appointed in 1898. Blake stood all of six feet in height and with his strong features and abundant growth of beard and snow-white hair made a very striking appearance. He is stated to have been an ideal teacher, a strong, aggressive fighter, fair and above board in all things. He died from pneumonia brought on by exposure when receiving the degree of LL.D. at Berkeley in 1910.

[R. W. Raymond, biographical sketch in *Trans. Am. Inst. Mining Engineers* (1910), containing full bibliography of Blake's publications; G. P. Merrill, *First 100 Years of American Geology* (1924).]

G. P. M.

BLAKE, WILLIAM RUFUS (1805–Apr. 22, 1863), actor, was born in Halifax, N. S., of Irish parentage, his father being a descendant of the Blakes of Galway. Early attracted to the stage, he made his first appearance with a company of strolling players in Halifax as the Prince of Wales in *Richard III*. He was first seen in this country in 1824 when as a light comedian he appeared on July 12 at the old Chatham Theatre, New York, as Frederick Bramble in *Poor Gentleman* and as The Three Singles in *Three and Deuce, or Which Is He?* He remained several seasons at this house, appearing in *Pizarro, Speed the Plough, The Rivals, Damon and Pythias,* and *Three and Deuce*. On Aug. 26, 1826, he married Mrs. Caroline (Placide) Waring, a member of the famous Placide family of actors. The following year he went into theatrical management, assuming successively the direction of the Tremont Theatre, Boston, 1827; of the Walnut Street Theatre, Philadelphia, 1829; and, with H. E. Willard, of Mitchell's Olympic Theatre, New York, which he opened in 1837. In 1839 he went to England, appearing at the Haymarket Theatre in *Three and Deuce*. Returning to America, he was for a time stage manager of the Walnut Street Theatre, Philadelphia, and in 1848 he accepted a like position at the Broadway Theatre (Wallack's), New York. Afterwards he was a member of the stock companies at Burton's, Laura Keene's, and Wallack's, with which last theatre he was chiefly identified, "receiving, as we have heard, the heaviest salary of any actor on the stock list" (J. N. Ireland, *Records of the New York Stage,* 1866, I, 448). His last appearance in New York was on Apr. 16, 1863, as Geoffrey Dale in *The Last Man* and he was seen for the last time on any stage Apr. 21, 1863, at the Boston Theatre as Sir Peter Teazle.

T. Allston Brown says of him: "In his early days he was a really handsome man. He excelled in the old comedies, and his performance of Young Dornton in *The Road to Ruin* was considered one of the best ever known to the stage. As his bulk increased with his years, he was compelled to abandon light-comedy parts and adopt the portraiture of the old comedy uncles and fathers, and also some parts purely sentimental. In the former he was undoubtedly one of the most mirth-provoking of actors, and his Lord Duberly in *The Heir at Law* always attracted large audiences to Wallack's, Burton's, and at Laura Keene's, where he played the most brilliant engagements of his life" (*A History of the New York Stage,* 1903, I, 280). William Winter speaks of the "richly humorous Blake, so noble in his dignity, so firm and fine and easy in his method, so copious in his natural humour" (*Shadows of the Stage,* 1892). J. N. Ireland says of him: "In certain characters he surpassed all who had attempted them. His Jesse Rural, Geoffrey Dale, Hardcastle, Old Dornton, Admiral Kingston, Sir Peter Teazle, Sir Willoughby Worrett, Sir Anthony Absolute, Governor Heartall, etc., were examples of perfection.

. . . In the line of 'old men' we doubt if he has ever been excelled on the New York boards." Ireland also refers to "the immense rotundity which, independent of other causes, ultimately placed him among the greatest of modern comedians. He experienced the usual vicissitudes of an actor's lot—at one time enjoying the greatest popularity, and at another visited with undeserved neglect" (*Records of the New York Stage,* I, 447). According to T. Allston Brown, he was the first actor ever called before the curtain in America—an incident which occurred at Boston in 1827.

[In addition to the references given above see obituaries in *Boston Evening Transcript,* and *Evening Post,* Apr. 23, 1863.] A. H.

BLAKELOCK, RALPH ALBERT (Oct. 15, 1847–Aug. 9, 1919), landscape painter, the son of R. A. Blakelock, a homeopathic physician, was born in New York City. His father desired him to study medicine, but he turned to music and the fine arts and entered the school of Cooper Union (F. W. Morton, "Work of R. A. Blakelock," *Brush and Pencil, post*). He attended classes there for a time but soon took his own course. The rich color schemes and enamel-like technique of Albert Pinkham Ryder fixed his attention. Ryder had sometimes used Indian figures and groups imaginatively as vehicles for moods. Blakelock followed suit on somewhat larger canvases, with a special liking for trees in silhouette against rather irrelevant skies, afterward widening his scope to woodland dreams and moonlights. Colors of rich deep timbre fascinated him; he used them like themes in music. At the Metropolitan Museum, New York, his "Pipe Dance" shows umbers and reds in a late afternoon effect with tree masses somber against a yellowish cloudy sky. "Indian Encampment" in the same museum is lighter in tone but with the strong impasto of A. P. Ryder; an effect of pale sunlight in early autumn. The St. Louis Museum has a foreign theme: "From St. Ives to Lelant." Blakelock's devotion to landscapes with groups of Indians has suggested that he made an early trip to the West, but probably this is an unsafe inference; his Western landscapes belong to a later date. Realism was not his aim. Similar tones with strong impasto are seen in paintings by George Bogert and Julian Rix. In 1892 Blakelock received an Honorable Mention at the exhibition of the Pennsylvania Academy, and in 1899 in New York he took the first Hallgarten Prize at the National Academy of Design. It was just then, when beginning to appeal to a wider circle of amateurs, that he experienced a mental breakdown. While in an asylum at Bennington, N. Y., he was elected associate of the National Academy in 1913 and three years later academician. Partly owing to his unhappy condition, which precluded further output, partly to the publicity consequent thereon, Blakelock's paintings, which hitherto had found little favor among the dealers, began to grow scarce and rise in value. At auctions they were competed for; a group of collectors, including the late Senator W. A. Clark of Montana and New York, bid them up, a large "Moonlight" with foliage etched on a dark sky fetching $20,000. These honors reacted to a very limited extent on the painter who had found it difficult in the eighties and nineties to dispose of his work. But in 1916 his health improved so distinctly that he left the asylum and came to New York where his return created much interest, not only owing to the signal appreciation of his pictures shown by high prices but because of sympathy for a man with an attractive personality who had been overtaken by disaster at the high tide of his career. Unfortunately the improvement did not persist. He tried to paint but the results were inadequate. Perhaps realization of his plight preyed on his mind, already shattered by his infirmity. In 1918 he had to return to the asylum, and in the following year he died at a camp in the Adirondacks.

There is something childlike and winning in Blakelock's moods; they recall many of the colorful dreamy pictures by eighteenth-century Hollanders and English landscapists influenced by Rembrandt. Rich mellow tones that salute the eyes as organ tones appeal to the ears may leave the intellectual votary of art cold, but to the sensuous they are a joy. Blakelock's gift was not wide. His was not a nature to formulate themes of tragedy, nor did he lean toward the religious or sublime. Though born in a great city his affections were rustic, not urban, as if the spirit of Barker of Bath or Old Crome had returned to earth and sought a painter like in tastes, simplicity, and unpretence. The names given his pictures signify little, for he was not telling a story, he was expressing a mood or a dream or a memory. Among his notable works are: "Shooting the Arrow"; "Bannock Wigwam in Peaceful Dale"; "Autumn" bought by Mrs. Kurtz; "Moonlight," 1886, bought by Catholina Lambert for his collection in "The Castle," Paterson, N. J.; "Sunset, Nevarra Range" bought by Wm. T. Evans; "Colorado Plains" in the Corcoran Gallery, Washington, D. C.; "October Sunshine" in the Art Museum of Worcester, Mass.; "The Capture" in the Brooklyn Art Institute; "Canoe Builders," "Sunset," and "Moonrise" in the National Gallery of Art at Washington.

[Elliott Daingerfield, *Ralph Albert Blakelock* (privately printed, 1914); Frederick Fairchild Sherman, *Landscape and Figure Painters of America* (privately printed, 1917), pp. 23–30; Frederick W. Morton, "Work of Ralph A. Blakelock," *Brush and Pencil*, IX, 257–69; N. N. (E. Pennell), "Blakelock," *Nation*, Aug. 23, 1919.]

C. De K.

BLAKELY, JOHNSTON (October 1781–October 1814), naval officer, was born near the village of Seaford in the County of Down, Ireland, whence, when he was two years old, his father, John Blakely, emigrated with his family to America, settling at Wilmington, N. C. Johnston was prepared for college at a school in Flatbush, L. I. He attended the University of North Carolina in 1797, and about this time his father died, leaving Edward Jones, an eminent lawyer of Wilmington, guardian of his son. A few years later Johnston lost his patrimony and was forced to suspend his education. On Feb. 5, 1800, he accepted the appointment of midshipman in the Navy. Serving in the Mediterranean squadron on the *President, John Adams,* and *Congress,* he took part in the operations of the squadron before Tripoli. On Feb. 10, 1807, he became a lieutenant. In 1811–13 he commanded the brig *Enterprise,* in which he cruised off the coast of the United States, capturing the armed schooner *Fly.* On July 24, 1813, he was commissioned master commandant and given command of the sloop-of-war *Wasp.* In December he married Jane Ann Hoope (or Hooper), daughter of a New York merchant. On May 1, 1814, he sailed from Portsmouth, N. H., on the *Wasp,* and after capturing a number of enemy vessels, fell in with the British brig *Reindeer* on June 28 in the English Channel. In the ensuing close-quarters battle, the *Reindeer,* gallantly fought by her commander, Capt. William Manners, and his crew, was badly worsted by the superior gun power of the *Wasp,* and hauled down her flag when her captain was shot dead in a vain attempt to board the American vessel. The *Reindeer* was burnt, and Blakely proceeded to L'Orient, France, in order to land his numerous prisoners and to refit. Here he remained seven weeks, resuming his cruise on Aug. 27, and taking three more enemy vessels by Sept. 1, one of which was cut out from a convoy and burnt under the eyes of the convoying 74-gun ship. In the late afternoon of Sept. 1, he fell in with four sails, one of which proved to be the British brig *Avon,* slightly inferior in force to the *Wasp.* Blakely at once attacked, even surrendering the weather position in order to force the enemy to fight before her consorts could close. After an hour's combat the *Avon* answered Blakely's hail with the announcement that she had struck, but, before possession of the prize could be taken, a second enemy brig was observed approaching with two more coming up in the offing, and Blakely was obliged to abandon his prize. In this fight the *Wasp* was much damaged in sails and rigging, while the *Avon* sank two hours after the engagement. "The course of the *Wasp* after this event," says Mahan (*post,* II, 257), "is traced by her captures. The meeting with the *Avon* was within a hundred miles of that with the *Reindeer.* On Sept. 12 and 14, having run south three hundred and sixty miles, she took two vessels; being then about two hundred and fifty miles west from Lisbon. On the 21st, having made four degrees more southing, she seized the British brig *Atalanta,* a hundred miles east of Madeira. This prize being of exceptional value, Blakely decided to send her in, and she arrived safely at Savannah on Nov. 4, in charge of Midshipman David Geisinger, who lived to become a captain in the navy. She brought with her Blakely's official despatches, including the report of the affair with the *Avon.*" Three weeks after the capture of the *Atalanta,* the *Wasp* is known to have been nine hundred miles farther south but nothing more was ever heard of her. Blakely was commissioned captain on Nov. 24, 1814, before the loss of the *Wasp* was known and was also tendered the thanks of Congress and a gold medal for his victory over the *Reindeer.* A sword awarded him by the General Assembly of North Carolina was presented to his widow, accompanied by a resolution "That Capt. Blakely's child be educated at the expense of this State; and that Mrs. Blakely be requested to draw on the Treasurer of this State, from time to time, for such sums of money as shall be required for the education of the said child."

[John H. Wheeler, *Hist. Sketches of N. C.* (1851); Wm. Johnson, "Biog. Sketch of Capt. Johnston Blakely," *N. C. Univ. Mag.*, Feb. 1854; K. P. Battle, "A N. C. Naval Hero and his Daughter," *N. C. Booklet,* Jan. 10, 1902; John Frost, *Am. Naval Biog.* (1844); Jas. Fenimore Cooper, *Hist. of the Navy,* II (1839); Theodore Roosevelt, *The Naval War of 1812* (1882); A. T. Mahan, *Sea Power in its Relations to the War of 1812* (1905).]

E. B.

BLAKESLEE, ERASTUS (Sept. 2, 1838–July 12, 1908), Congregational clergyman, was the son of Joel and Sarah Maria (Mansfield) Blakeslee, and was born in Plymouth, Conn. In his boyhood he attended the district school and worked on his father's farm and in his carriage shop. Deciding to enter the ministry, he prepared for college at Williston Seminary, Easthampton, Mass., and entered Yale in the class of 1863. On Oct. 9, 1861, he joined Company A, 1st Connecticut Cavalry, and received rapid promotion for bravery and distinguished service. In 1864 he obtained his degree at Yale and was enrolled with his class. On Mar. 13, 1865, he was commissioned brevet brigadier-general "for gallant conduct at Ashland, Va., June 1, 1864." He was the only brigadier-general from Connecticut who had enlisted as a private and had held every rank from second lieutenant up. From 1865 to 1876 he engaged in business in New Haven and in Boston. In the fall of 1876 he entered Andover Seminary and graduated in 1879. While a graduate student at Andover, he was called to the Second Congregational Church in Greenfield, Mass., and was ordained there, Feb. 11, 1880. In July 1883 he became pastor of the Second Church, Fair Haven, Conn. (now the Pilgrim Church, New Haven). In the fall of 1887 he declined the presidency of Atlanta University, but accepted a call to the First Congregational Church of Spencer, Mass. As a business man he was successful, and patented a number of valuable inventions. As a pastor he was far-seeing and resourceful. At Greenfield he organized the Connecticut Valley Congregational Club. In New Haven he became a prominent promoter of the Christian Endeavor movement, then in its infancy, was the first president of the New Haven Union, and wrote the Christian Endeavor constitution of Connecticut. Realizing the inadequacy of the Sunday-school "helps" of the time, he devised for his own school in Spencer, in 1888, a system of lessons designed to impart a more comprehensive knowledge of the Bible, and graded to meet the needs of pupils of various ages. These lessons were so successful that in 1891 he began their publication for wider use, and in 1892 resigned at Spencer and organized in Boston the Bible Study Publishing Company. He formed also the Bible Study Union, composed of prominent religious educators, as a sort of advisory board, so that his publications became known as the *Bible Study Union Lessons.* During his lifetime about 170 volumes of these lessons, for all grades, were published. They have been widely used and translated into many languages, doing much to bring biblical instruction in the Protestant Churches into harmony with pedagogical principles. Blakeslee was a member of the Council of the Religious Education Association, of the Society of Biblical Literature and Exegesis, and of the Victoria Institute of London. He wrote a history of his regiment, and originated the scheme of the *Harmony of the Gospels,* later worked out by Stevens and Burton (Dr. Frank K. Sanders in *Sunday School Times,* Aug. 23, 1908). He was an able speaker, a strong and positive character, and a gentle and lovable personality. He was married on Mar. 30, 1865, to Mary Goodrich North of New Haven. From 1892 until his death he made his home at Brookline, Mass.

[Shortly after Blakeslee's death, a pamphlet, *In Memoriam,* was issued, containing much biographical material. Cf. also *Congreg. Yr. Bk.,* 1909; *Congregationalist,* July 23, 1908; *Obit. Record Grads. Yale Univ.*; *Boston Evening Transcript,* July 13, 1908; *Triennial Meeting and Biog. Record of the Class of '63 in Yale Coll.* (1869); *Official Records,* ser. I.]

F. T. P.

BLALOCK, NELSON GALES (Feb. 17, 1836–Mar. 14, 1913), physician, agriculturist, at the time of his death was recognized as the foremost citizen of the State of Washington. This, no doubt, was due to the fact that his career was far more than that of the physician who confines himself exclusively to medical practise. After working his way through academy and college in Mitchell County, N. C., the place where he was born, young Blalock moved to Philadelphia and secured his medical education in Jefferson Medical College of that city, graduating in March 1861. He then took up the practise of medicine in Decatur, Ill., but soon joined the 115th Illinois Volunteers as a surgeon and served with ability during the Civil War. He returned to Decatur after the war and practised his profession successfully for twelve years until 1873, when he went West with a wagon train and settled in Walla Walla, Wash. He at once established a remunerative and important practise, performing on an average a surgical operation each day and delivering during the course of his career some five thousand babies. He was of the old-time practitioner type, seldom keeping his books in good condition, so that when he died he had over $40,000 in outstanding bills unpaid. Nevertheless he was the first practitioner in Walla Walla to establish modern electric equipment in his office, including X-ray. Blalock was also widely known for his interest in civic and educational affairs, serving for many years as a member of the board of trustees and later as president of the board of trustees of Whitman College. He was a member of the board of trustees of the public schools and for a number of terms mayor of his city. He aided in calling the constitutional convention of Washington in 1889, and was instrumental in framing the constitution. In the development of the agricultural factors of Washington state he aided much by inaugurating the fluming of lumber from the mountains, raising wheat in the uplands, and establishing a large orchard for the raising of fruit and vegetables which is still known as the Blalock orchard. From his first marriage, to Panthea A. Durham who died in 1864, there was a son who succeeded his father as a physician in Walla Walla. From a second marriage, to Marie G. Greenfield, there were two daughters. The death of Blalock at the age of seventy-seven closed a long career of service to his community and to the state.

[*Memorial Address, Joint Session of Senate and House, 14th Legislature of the State of Washington,* 1915, pp. 45–50; *Post Intelligencer* (Seattle), Mar. 15, 1913; *Spokesman-Review* (Spokane), Mar. 15, 1913; Wm. D. Lyman, *Lyman's Hist. of Old Walla Walla County* (1918), II, 5–8.] M. F.

BLANC, ANTOINE (Oct. 11, 1792–June 20, 1860), Catholic archbishop, a native of Sury near Lyons, France, was among the first ecclesiastical students raised to the priesthood after the religious restoration in France. Bishop Du Bourg of New Orleans who had come to France for the purpose of securing priests for the missions of the Mississippi Valley ordained him on July 22, 1816. With several young seminarians Blanc landed at Annapolis in 1817 and after being entertained by Charles Carroll of Carrollton was sent to the Mississippi Valley where for nearly fifteen years he labored in the missions. In 1831 Bishop de Neckère of New Orleans appointed him vicar-general, and when the Bishop died in 1833 Blanc was named administrator and on Nov. 22, 1835, was consecrated bishop of the diocese, which included the states of Louisiana, Mississippi, and, in 1838, Texas. In 1842 the question of the authority of the Bishop to appoint the rector of the Cathedral brought Bishop Blanc into conflict with the trustees of the church. When the latter refused to accept the rector appointed by the Bishop the church was for a few months placed under the ban of the interdict. Finally the trustees took the matter to court asking $20,000 damages. They were represented among others by Pierre Soulé and Christian Roselius. The court dismissed the petition and the decision was sustained by the Supreme Court. During this same period the Bishop with a number of prominent Catholic laity worked strenuously to counteract the influence of the Know-Nothing party. In 1850 Pius IX established the Archdiocese of New Orleans, and Bishop Blanc was raised to archepiscopal dignity in 1851. His principal services were in building new churches to meet the demands of the growing population, in the establishment of schools and orphan asylums, and in the systematizing of church affairs in general. In order to provide priests for the diocese he invited the Jesuits and the Lazarists to establish seminaries. To care for the free colored orphans and the aged he founded the Sisters of the Holy Family, the first colored sisterhood in the United States. When Bishop Blanc took charge of the diocese the only churches in New Orleans were the Cathedral, St. Patrick's, and the chapel attached to the old Ursuline convent. In 1854 there were eighteen churches. The Archbishop was one of the American delegates to Rome in 1855 when the dogma of the Immaculate Conception was proclaimed. In January 1860 he was taken seriously ill but rallied and apparently regained his usual health. He died suddenly June 20, 1860, and was buried in the St. Louis Cathedral. According to contemporary accounts, he was a man calculated to win the esteem and affection of all who made his acquaintance. He was remarkably gentle and mild in his manners and affable with all (*New Orleans Daily Crescent,* June 22, 1860).

[Alcée Fortier, *Louisiana* (1909), vol. I; *Daily Picayune* (New Orleans), Jan. 9, 14, 1844, Apr. 17, 1850, June 22, 1860, and other New Orleans papers of June 21, June 22, 1860; Archives of the St. Louis Cathedral, New Orleans.] S. H.

BLANCHARD, JONATHAN (Jan. 19, 1811–May 14, 1892), Presbyterian clergyman, college president, the son of Jonathan and Mary (Lovel) Blanchard, was born in the little town of Rockingham, Vt., of pure English ancestry. His early education was obtained in the common schools of the town and from private instructors. He was a school-teacher at the age of fourteen and entered Middlebury College at the age of seventeen, graduating in 1832, when he was twenty-one years old. For two years he taught at Plattsburg Academy and afterwards studied at Andover and at Lane Theological Seminary in Cincinnati. In the latter city he was ordained pastor of the Sixth Presbyterian Church in September 1838. From the beginning Blanchard was a strong temperance advocate and in 1834, at the age of twenty-three, he became a violent abolitionist. In 1843 he attended the World's Anti-Slavery Convention in London and was elected American vice-president of that body. On his return from England he delivered a series of spirited lectures on the wrongs of Ireland. In spite of the fact that Cincinnati was almost as strongly pro-slavery as any southern community, he never hesitated to attack that institution in sermons, in articles, and in private conversation (see *A Debate on Slavery . . . Between the Rev. J. Blanchard and N. L. Rice,* 1846). Almost as violent was his hatred of secret societies and especially of the Masonic order. This, too, he attacked in every way and at every opportunity. As the Civil War approached he more and more coupled Masonry and slavery and declared that the Masonic order was concerned in the attempt at disunion. During his Cincinnati pastorate he founded and edited a church paper later known as the *Herald and Presbyter.*

In 1845 he was elected president of Knox College, at Galesburg, Ill., and held that position until 1857. Under his administration the financial condition of the college was greatly improved and the number of students practically doubled. Blanchard's outspoken attitude on many subjects, however, brought him into frequent controversies, and the later years of his administration were full of strife and difficulty. After resigning the presidency he served for a year as acting president and teacher, at the same time conducting the *Christian Era* which he had founded. In 1860 he took the presidency of Wheaton College, at Wheaton, Ill. While there he published *Freemasonry Illustrated* (1879) and founded and edited the *Christian Cynosure*. He became president emeritus in 1882 and died on May 14, 1892. He was married in 1838 to Mary Avery Bent, by whom he had twelve children, five sons and seven daughters. One son, Charles Albert, succeeded his father as president of Wheaton College, and died on Dec. 20, 1925.

[J. W. Bailey, *Knox College* (1860); Rufus Blanchard, *Hist. of Du Page County, Ill.* (1882), pp. 174 ff.; T. S. Pearson, *Cat. of Grads. of Middlebury Coll.*; *Chicago Tribune*, May 15, 1892.]

A. B.

BLANCHARD, NEWTON CRAIN (Jan. 29, 1849–June 22, 1922), lawyer, governor of Louisiana, the son of Carey H. and Frances Amelia (Crain) Blanchard, was born in Rapides Parish, La. He was reared on his father's cotton plantation in that parish and was educated in private schools and the Louisiana State Seminary of Learning (now the Louisiana State University). He was granted the LL.B. degree by the University of Louisiana (now Tulane) in 1870 and in the next year began the practise of law at Shreveport, La. He soon entered politics, and through a period of over forty years he achieved considerable success in that field. He first became prominent for the part that he took in resisting the reconstruction policy of the national government in Louisiana and, with a number of other men in his parish (Caddo Parish), he was arraigned before the federal authorities in New Orleans on the charge of intimidating the negroes from voting. Popular sentiment, however, was with them and they were acquitted. In 1879 he was elected as the representative of Caddo Parish to the Louisiana state constitutional convention and served on many of its more important committees. In 1880 he was chosen to represent the fourth Louisiana district in the Forty-seventh Congress and was reëlected to the five succeeding congresses (1881–93). He was chairman of the Rivers and Harbors Committee of the lower house under Speaker Crisp and was active in securing legislation for the improvement of the Mississippi levees. In 1893 he was appointed by the governor of Louisiana, and in 1894 he was elected by the Louisiana state legislature, to the United States Senate to fill out the unexpired term of Edward Douglas White who had been appointed to the United States Supreme Court by President Cleveland. As senator he was especially interested in getting such tariff legislation as would benefit Louisiana's agricultural interests. On the expiration of his term in the Senate, he was appointed associate justice of the supreme court of Louisiana and served in that capacity from 1897 to 1904. From this position he was elevated in 1904 by the vote of the people of the state to the governorship of Louisiana for a term of four years. His administration as governor was marked by the creation of several state boards and departments, including a board of charities and corrections, a board of equalization, and a reform school; by the revision of the system of taxation so as to lay a heavier burden upon the corporate interests in the state; by the encouragement of education; by making elective by popular vote a large number of state and local officers heretofore appointed by the governor, such as the supreme court justices, the register of the state land office, the parish assessors, the members of the parish school boards and the state tax collector of New Orleans; and by providing for state-wide primaries for all state and national offices. At the close of his term as governor, he resumed the practise of law at Shreveport. That did not bring his public career to an end, however. In 1913 he was elected to the Louisiana state constitutional convention which had been called primarily to fund the public debt of the state, and he was chosen by that body as its president. In this position he did much to shape the work of the convention. He was a delegate-at-large to several Democratic national conventions and also served several times as national Democratic committeeman for Louisiana. He was twice married, first, on Dec. 16, 1873, to Emily Barret of Shreveport, who died on July 27, 1907, and second, on Jan. 29, 1909, to Charlotte Tracy of Baton Rouge. He was a man of large physique and presented a rather striking and somewhat pompous appearance. His state papers, especially his judicial decisions, were marked for their clarity of expression and intelligent comprehension of the subject in hand.

[Brief biographical sketches may be found in the daily newspapers of New Orleans and Shreveport, La., for June 23, 1922, and also in Alcée Fortier, *Louisiana* (1909), I, 100–106.]

E. M. V.

BLANCHARD, THOMAS (June 24, 1788–Apr. 16, 1864), inventor, son of Samuel and Susanna (Tenney) Blanchard, was born in Sutton, Worcester County, Mass. He came of very old New England stock, and his father was a farmer. Early in life he evinced a fondness for mechanical subjects, his tools being limited to a knife and a gimlet. At the age of thirteen he invented an apple-parer which made him a favorite at the "paring bees" of the neighborhood. When quite young he went to reside with an elder brother who made tacks by hand. The youthful Thomas invented a counter with a bell for keeping tally on production. He worked on a tack-making machine which could turn out 500 tacks a minute—one of the first automatic machines. The perfecting of this device required several years' labor. He sold his patent rights for this invention for $5,000—a large sum for that period. Next he turned his attention to the turning of gun barrels. He devised a lathe which not only turned the barrel externally but, when the breech was reached, by means of a special mechanism cut both the flat and oval portions. Here we have an important step—one machine performing two dissimilar operations. Blanchard now entered the employ of the great Springfield Arsenal, for which he invented a machine which would not only cut in a straight line but would bore and mortise so neatly that when the operation was complete the lock would fit closely to the stock. While puzzling over the problem of how to turn a gun-stock, the whole principle of turning irregular forms from a pattern burst upon Blanchard's mind. Models were constructed which worked so well that a shoe last, a gun-stock, spokes of wheels, hat-blocks, or other articles of irregular shape could be produced at will. The invention consisted of a friction-wheel which touched the pattern and a cutting-wheel secured to the same shaft. A large driving drum allowed the belt which turned the two wheels to slide up and down so that power was supplied irrespective of the position of the cutting-wheel to the wood being shaped. The friction-wheel followed the contour of the pattern and pushed the cutting-wheel in and out of contact with the wood being machined. The machine not only duplicated but made articles longer or shorter, larger or smaller, and right and left. The importance of this invention can hardly be overestimated and many machine tools, as well as woodworking machinery, depend on this principle; even dies for medals employ the same idea.

Blanchard worked for the Government for five years and in the meantime his invention was extensively pirated. He received a royalty of "nine cents" on each musket produced at Harper's Ferry and Springfield. When his patent expired in 1833 he petitioned Congress for a renewal which was granted on the ground that this was an original machine, standing among the "*first* American inventions." The renewal was granted in 1834. This patent contained mistakes which well-nigh caused Blanchard to lose all his rights; but Congress finally rectified the mistakes and Blanchard was upheld in the courts. He also invented machines for cutting and folding envelopes. In 1825 he built a steam carriage and secured a patent on it, and in 1826 he tried to promote a company to build railroads. The legislature of Massachusetts approved the plan, but capitalists considered it visionary. Blanchard went to New York and tried to get Gov. Clinton interested, proposing to build a railroad from Albany to Schenectady; but Clinton was of the opinion that it was too soon after the completion of the Erie Canal. Finding himself ahead of the times, Blanchard abandoned the project, and devoted his attention to steam navigation of rivers where there were shoal rapids. He constructed a boat with a stern wheel placed far astern where the greatest eddy is found; this boat made trips between Hartford and Springfield. Blanchard also designed and built several kinds of shallow-draft steamers which were introduced on western rivers, making the upstream trip possible,—a type of boat which later came into universal use.

[E. W. Byrn, *Progress of Invention in the Nineteenth Century* (1900), pp. 368–69; Henry Howe, *Memoirs of the Most Eminent Am. Mechanics* (1844); W. Kaempffert, *A Pop. Hist. of Am. Invention* (1924), I, 136; II, 412, 413, 416; J. W. Roe, *Eng. and Am. Tool Builders* (1926), pp. 6, 140, 142, 219, 220–221; Asa H. Waters, *Biog. Sketch of Thos. Blanchard and His Inventions* (1878); *Boston Evening Transcript*, Apr. 18, 1864.]

A. A. H.

BLANCHET, FRANÇOIS NORBERT (Sept. 3, 1795–June 18, 1883), Catholic missionary and first archbishop of Oregon City, was the son of Pierre and Rosalie Blanchet, Canadian land owners, who traced descent from the earliest adventurers of New France. Well connected with the best families, the Blanchets had given a number of sons and daughters to the Church and one of them had founded the *Canadien*, an influential journal. Educated at the parish school of St. Pierre, Rivière du Sud, Quebec, and at the Sulpician petit seminary of Quebec, Blanchet in 1816 entered the major seminary where he won distinction in theological studies. Ordained in 1819, Abbé Blanchet was assigned to the Cathedral for a year. He was then sent as a missionary to the Acadians and Micmac Indians of New Brunswick, where in addition to the native dialect he learned English in order to serve a group of Irish immigrants. For seven years, Blanchet labored zealously in this vast, wild region where he built three churches and made visitations by horse, snow-shoes, canoe, and dog-sledges, according to seasonal demands. With regret he left this perilous work and his primitive communicants for the rectorship of a well-established parish at the Cedars near Montreal. During the cholera (1832), the abbé was presented with loving cups by non-Catholics in admiration of his courageous service which knew neither creed nor race. It was here that he came into contact with the fur-traders and learned of the need for priests among the trappers, traders, and Catholic Iroquois in the Oregon region. The French petition for a priest through Dr. McLoughlin, chief factor of the Hudson's Bay Company, was heard by the bishops of the Red River Valley and of Quebec. Blanchet was ready and was thereupon appointed vicar-general to Archbishop Signay of Quebec with jurisdiction over the whole Oregon region though cautioned to establish his missions north of the Columbia River. Accompanying the annual Hudson's Bay Express, he preached at all posts on the route and at the Red River was joined by Abbé Modeste Demers, a newly ordained priest. The French and half-breeds at Vancouver and in the settlement of St. Paul's in Willamette Valley welcomed the missionaries for whose reception they had built a log church. From the first these missionaries were successful, aided as they were by Catholic half-breeds and Iroquois from whom they learned the various native dialects and who popularized their work among the pagan redmen. Demers with his chapel at Fort Nesqually as a center labored among the northern tribesmen as far as Alaska, and Blanchet served missions at St. Paul's, Astoria, Walla Walla, Vancouver, Cowlitz, and the Cascades. Their work was made easier with the conversion of Judge Peter Burnett, and the American official Secretary Long.

All this success aroused bitterness. Methodists circulated the "disclosures of Maria Monk," which Blanchet answered by citing the American Protestant exposé. Religious, political, racial, and fur trading rivalries combined to separate the Catholic and Protestant missionaries. Blanchet had little interest in Oregon politics, but he did not discourage the projected if extra-legal settlers' government. Later charges that Catholics inspired the Indian uprising which resulted in the murder of Marcus Whitman's party have been disproven. The Indians were actually aroused by the loss of hunting lands, stories of rival traders, absurd belief that Methodist settlers had poisoned the game and brought smallpox, by the murder of a chief by an American, and the whipping of Indians for thefts from the Methodist mission. The younger Blanchet and Abbé Brouillet visited the Indians assembled in Walla Walla to aid the factor in quieting them and in obtaining the release of prisoners (1847). They also consoled the survivors, and risked death by burying the dead. Blanchet, however, did not hesitate to attend the five Indians who were executed for supposed complicity in the Whitman murder after a dubious trial (1849).

In the meantime Blanchet, who in 1843 had been made vicar apostolic and titular bishop at the joint suggestion of the archbishops of Quebec and Baltimore, learned on the way to Paris of his elevation to the archbishopric of the newly established see of Oregon City (1846) with his brother Augustine as bishop of Walla Walla and his faithful friend Demers as bishop of Vancouver, a recognized part of Canada. Blanchet visited Rome, France, and the German states in the interest of his archdiocese and obtained the services of several priests and Notre Dame nuns. While abroad, he was received in audiences by the courts of Belgium, Bavaria, Austria, and France and was presented with a purse by Louis Philippe and the Leopoldine Society. On his return he consecrated Bishop Demers and held a provincial council. At his invitation, the Oblate Fathers soon sent a mission band (1848). The diocese faced bad years with the seizure of McLoughlin's estate in Oregon City, the withdrawal of communicants for the California mines, and Cayuse and Rogue Rivers Indian Wars of which the Whitman massacre was a prelude; yet the bishop was of good heart at the First Plenary Council of Baltimore. In 1855 he visited Peru, Bolivia, and Chile where he collected enough money to meet the diocesan debts, because of the enthusiasm aroused by his Spanish publication of the story of Oregon. Four years later he was in Canada seeking aid and enlisting thirty-one priests and nuns, including the Sisters of Holy Names of Jesus and Mary, for service in Oregon. By 1862 when the bishop moved his see to Portland, conditions had become normal as the Civil War had little effect on the Coast. In time he built a cathedral, St. Michael's College (1871), and a hospital under the Sisters of Providence (1875).

Bishop Blanchet representing the Catholic hierarchy protested against the unfairness of Secretary Delano of the Interior in applying Grant's Indian policy of assigning the Indian agencies to "such religious denominations as had hitherto established missions among the Indians." Of thirty-eight reservations only four were assigned to Catholics, although on the basis of Indian desires and the number of active stations fully two-thirds might have been allotted with justice. The Yahima tribesmen seem to have been assigned to Methodists who showed marked hostility to Catholic priests, though Methodist missions were inactive and regarded as unsuccessful by Indians and candid observers. At any rate, Blanchet's heated correspondence with Delano aroused the Catholic hierarchy to establish a permanent Catholic Indian Commission at Washington to deal with the Commissioner of Indian Affairs and assume general supervision over Catholic missions.

Soon after celebrating his golden jubilee, Blanchet journeyed over the new transcontinental railroad from San Francisco and accompanied Bishop John Ireland to the Ecumenical Council in Rome (1870) where he was appointed an orator and warmly supported the formal declaration of infallibility. Worn by age, he obtained the Alaskan missionary Charles Seghers as coadjutor bishop (1879). Two years later he resigned and as titular archbishop of Amida retired to the hospital which he had founded. Here he lived two years, rounding out sixty-four years as a priest and forty-five as a missionary apostle on the Pacific Coast.

His writings include: *Fiftieth Jubilee Sermon* (1869); *Letters on Catholic Indian Missions together with Reply of Secretary of Interior* (1871); *Chinook Dictionary and Catechism* composed (1838) by M. Demers and revised (1867) by F. N. Blanchet with corrections by Rev. L. N. St. Onge (1871); *Historical Sketches of the Catholic Church in Oregon* (1878, 1910); and *Historical Notes and Reminiscences* (1883).

[Archbishop C. Seghers, *Life and Labors of F. N. Blanchet* (1883); R. H. Clarke, *Lives of Deceased Bishops of Cath. Ch. in U. S.* (1872), III, 438–502; E. V. O'Hara, *Pioneer Cath. Hist. of Ore.,* based on manuscript journals and letters in Portland Cathedral archives (1911); F. V. Holman, *Dr. John McLoughlin, Father of Ore.* (1907); H. M. Chittenden and A. T. Richardson, *Life, Letters and Travels of Pierre-Jean De Smet, S. J.* (1905); Katherine Hughes, *Father Lacombe, the Black-Robe Voyageur* (1911); M. de Baets, *Mgr. Seghers, Lapôtre d'Alaska* (Paris, 1896); C. A. Snowden, *Hist. of Washington* (1909), II, 159–72; J. G. Shea, *Hist. of the Cath. Ch. in U. S.* (1892), IV; Peter Burnett, *Recollections and Opinions of an Old Pioneer* (1880).]

R. J. P.

BLAND, RICHARD (May 6, 1710–Oct. 26, 1776), statesman, was the son of Richard Bland of Berkeley and Jordan's Point, Va., and his second wife, Elizabeth, daughter of William Randolph I of Turkey Island. His paternal grandfather, Theodorick Bland of Westover, was the immigrant ancestor of the family in Virginia. Both father and grandfather were successful planters, and influential in the government of the colony. Richard Bland was educated at William and Mary College. It is sometimes stated that he also attended the University of Edinburgh, but of this we have no proof. In 1742 he first took his seat from Prince George County in the House of Burgesses, and served continuously from that time until 1775. As early as 1753, in his discussion of the pistole fee demanded by the governor, he became the champion of public rights. It is likely that he was the author of both the "Two Penny" bills. In the controversy which raged after the passage of the bills, he opposed the clergy most vigorously. In *A Letter to the Clergy of Virginia* (1760) and in *The Colonel Dismounted* (1764) he supported the right of the General Assembly to enact this legislation, which was in effect a reduction of the salaries of the clergy. He was a member of the committee of the House of Burgesses, in the October 1764 session of the Assembly, to draw up an address to the king, a memorial to the lords, and a remonstrance to the House of Commons respecting taxation imposed on Virginia by any other power than its own legislature. In 1766 he printed in Williamsburg *An Inquiry into the Rights of the British Colonies,* the earliest published defense of the colonial attitude in regard to taxation. This was reprinted in the *Political Register,* London, 1769. He was a sincere advocate of colonial rights, but wished to avoid a break with the mother country, until every effort had been made for conciliation. In 1765 he opposed Henry's resolutions against the Stamp Act, and in March 1775 was not in favor of Henry's plan of immediately arming the colony. Though he was somewhat conservative at this critical time he was sent by his constituents to the revolutionary conventions of March 1775, July 1775, and May 1776. After the adoption of the state constitution, he was a member of the first House of Delegates, and served until his death. In his legislative career, he was a member of leading committees, and was always in demand for drawing up memorials. Due to his careful study of the ancient records of the colony, he was considered the best authority of the time on its history. When the non-importation agreement was drawn up in 1769, he was one of the first to sign. On Mar. 12, 1773, he was appointed by the House a member of the committee of correspondence with the sister colonies. He was placed on the committee of safety by the convention of July 1775. Elected as a delegate to the First Continental Congress, he was present throughout the session. He was elected to the Second Congress, but was present a few days only. Upon his third election on Aug. 11, 1775, he declined to serve. Jefferson refers to him as "the most learned and logical man of those who took prominent lead in public affairs, profound in constitutional lore, a most ungraceful speaker," and again he speaks of him as "one of the oldest, ablest and most respected members." He was "staunch and tough as whitleather," writes Roger Atkinson, "he has something the look of old parchments, which he handleth and studieth much." To Bland's industry in collecting old records, we are indebted for the preservation of valuable historical documents. He was thrice married: first to Anne, daughter of Col. Peter Poythress, by whom he had twelve children; second to Martha Macon, widow of William Massie; third to Elizabeth Blair, widow of John Bolling, and daughter of John Blair, president of the Council. His writings include: *A Fragment on the Pistole Fee, Claimed by the Governor of Virginia, 1753* (edited by W. C. Ford, 1891); *A Letter to the Clergy of Virginia* (1760); *The Colonel Dismounted, or the Rector Vindicated* (1764); *Inquiry into the Rights of the British Colonies* (1766; a new edition, edited by E. G. Swem, 1922); *A Treatise on Water Baptism against the Quakers* (title mentioned by Atkinson, but no copy known); *On the Tenure of Land in Virginia* (no copy known).

[The sketch of Bland by Hugh Blair Grigsby in his *Convention of 1776* (1855), pp. 57–67, is the best we have. The reader should also consult the preface to the reprinted edition, 1922, of *Bland's Inquiry into the Rights of the British Colonies*, ed. by E. G. Swem. In the *William and Mary Quarterly*, XIX, 31–41, Dr. L. G. Tyler discusses "Bland's constitutional argument in *The Colonel Dismounted*." For the controversy between Rev. Samuel Shield and Bland see Dixon and Hunter's *Va. Gazette*, July 8, July 22, and Aug. 5, 1775.]

E. G. S.

BLAND, RICHARD PARKS (Aug. 19, 1835–June 15, 1899), congressman, known to both friends and opponents as "Silver Dick," was throughout the last quarter of the nineteenth century the leader of the group in Congress favoring the bimetallic standard of currency or "Free Silver," a leadership for which his earlier life and environment were peculiarly appropriate. Born near Hartford, Ky., the son of Stoughten Edward and Margaret Parks (Nall) Bland, he was self-supporting as a mere boy. After a year at Hartford Academy he taught school in Kentucky, and after his removal to Missouri in 1855, in Wayne County on the Ozark border. The next year he went to California and for ten years lived in the mining camps of California, Colorado, and Nevada, prospecting, working as a miner, teaching school, and, after his admission to the bar, serving as treasurer of Carson County, then in Utah Territory. He returned to Missouri in 1866, and in 1869 opened his office at Lebanon, a little Ozark town, his home until his death. Though the boundaries of his Congressional district were repeatedly changed, they always included much of the Ozark country. Thus he was intimately acquainted with the problems of the silver miners and of the more primitive frontier farmers, the two economic groups most devoted to Free Silver.

He prospered as a lawyer, making many friends by his gratuitous aid to Democrats disenfranchised under the test oath, and in 1872 he was nominated for Congress without much effort on his part, and was elected with the help of the Liberal Republicans; save for one Congress, 1895 to 1897, he served continuously until his death. His first term in Congress was only normally eventful, but in the Democratic House of 1875–77 he was appointed chairman of the Committee on Mines and Mining and began his life-long fight against the "Crime of '73" and the demonetization of silver. Bland's bill for the free coinage of silver passed the House in the second session but was smothered in the Senate. His leadership in the fight was recognized by his appointment to the congressional "Silver Commission" of 1876–77. In 1879 he became a member of the Committee on Coinage, Weights and Measures, and its chairman in 1883, serving in that capacity whenever the Democrats controlled the House. He became a national figure with the passage over Hayes's veto in 1878 of the compromise Bland-Allison Act remonetizing silver and providing for a limited coinage. The Bland Bill as it had passed the House provided for free coinage. He succeeded in defeating the repeal of the Bland-Allison Act in 1886, but again failed to secure a free coinage act. In 1890 he bitterly opposed the Sherman Silver Purchase Act as a travesty on bi-metallism and again fought in vain to secure a free coinage act. The climax of his fight for free coinage came in his leadership of the unsuccessful opposition in 1893 to the repeal of the Sherman Act unless accompanied by the passage of a free coinage bill. In his famous "Parting of the Ways" speech of Aug. 11, 1893, he served notice that the western Democrats would put Free Silver above party loyalty. Defeated for the first time in 1894 (by 70 votes) because of Democratic disgust with Cleveland and the presence of a separate Populist candidate, he preached Free Silver from the lecture platform and in 1895 was the leader of the Pertle Springs convention where the Free Silver wing secured control of the Missouri Democracy. The similar control of the national party at Chicago made him admittedly the logical candidate for president in 1896. But his long career and a certain lack of appeal to the public imagination and to the crusading zeal of the Free-Silverites were fatal handicaps. After leading on the first three ballots, Bland withdrew his name when the set toward Bryan was unmistakable. He emphatically negatived the movement to nominate him as vice-president and later just as decidedly the proposal of nomination for governor; instead he was triumphantly reëlected to Congress in 1896.

While Bland's views on the currency were quite unorthodox, his speeches and debates show wide reading and a real, if frankly one-sided, study. Unlike many of the free-silver inflationists he recognized the evils of a fiat paper money inflation. He also saw the desirability of an international agreement on bi-metallism; he believed however that an independent adoption by the United States would soon force the other nations into line, though this would involve, he admitted, a considerable temporary wrench to the bankers and investors. Throughout he urged the advantages of Free Silver to the "producing classes" in general rather than primarily to the agrarian group. This real interest in the common people was also clearly reflected in his denunciation of monopolies and his arguments against the protective tariff; he vigorously supported the Mills Bill and took the lead in opposing the McKinley tariff. At the very end of his career he was ân extreme anti-imperialist. Not a brilliant speaker or debater, he was effective through his mastery of his data, his clear-headedness and self-control, and a certain blunt honesty and sincerity. In a period of rather low standards in public life he was unusually sensitive as to personal and official honesty, withdrawing from the practise of law when first elected, refusing a silver service presented by the miners, and actually persisting in his refusal of his back pay under the "Salary Grab" act and of his mileage for a few days' recess between sessions. In 1873 he married Virginia Elizabeth Mitchell of Rolla. Both at Washington and on his farm near Lebanon he lived very simply on his salary, and died probably poorer than when he entered public life. In his virtues and even in his failings, he suggests the better type of ante-bellum Jacksonian Democrat.

[W. V. Byars, *An American Commoner* (1900); W. R. Hollister and H. Norman, *Five Famous Missourians* (1900), pp. 95–172; *Cong. Record,* 56 Cong., 1 Sess., pp. 3894 ff.; *Globe-Democrat* (St. Louis), June 16, 1899.] J. V.

BLAND, THEODORICK (Mar. 21, 1742–June 1, 1790), Revolutionary soldier, was born in Prince George County, Va., the son of Theodorick Bland of Cawsons on Appomattox River and Frances Bolling, only daughter and heir of Drury Bolling. Through his mother he was a descendant of Pocahontas. At the age of eleven he was sent to school in Wakefield, Yorkshire, England, where he remained until 1758. In 1759 he was in Liverpool, attending an infirmary as a student of physic. He entered the University of Edinburgh in 1761, and received the degree of M.D. in 1763. After graduating he spent some time in London, and probably also in Leyden and Paris. He was back in Virginia in 1764, and began the practise of his profession in his native county. He continued in active practise until 1771, when he retired and became a planter, his health having suffered from the exposure incident to a country practise. In the conflict between England and the Colonies, he took a determined stand against the mother country. On June 24, 1775, he was one of a party of twenty-four gentlemen who removed the arms from the governor's palace in Williamsburg to the powder magazine. Toward the end of this year he wrote some bitter letters in the *Virginia Gazette* against Lord Dunmore under the signature of "Cassius." He was ambitious to help his country in the field, and on June 13, 1776, was appointed captain of the 1st Troop of Virginia Cavalry, and on Mar. 31, 1779, was made colonel of the 1st Continental Dragoons. He was with the main army in New Jersey and Pennsylvania in 1777, and was present at the battle of Brandywine on Sept. 11. In referring to Bland's services at this battle, Gen. Henry Lee says "Col. Bland was noble, sensible, honorable, and amiable, but never intended for the department of military intelligence." On Nov. 5, 1778, Washington ordered Bland to assume command of an escort to conduct the Convention troops (the Saratoga prisoners) from Connecticut to Albemarle County, Va. He was placed in command of the post at Charlottesville which guarded these prisoners, but in November 1779 he received permission to retire from this station. In 1780, the General Assembly of Virginia elected him a delegate to Congress, a position which he filled with honor for three years. At the conclusion of his term, he returned to his plantation, Farmingdale or Kippax, in Prince George County, which had been plundered by the enemy. He was in the House of Delegates in the sessions of 1786–87, 1787–88, and 1788. In the Assembly of 1786 he was an unsuccessful candidate for governor, against Edmund Randolph. He was a member of the Virginia convention of 1788 for the consideration of the proposed Federal Constitution, and voted against its adoption. He was elected a member of the first House of Representatives and served until his death. He was married to Martha Dangerfield, probably a sister of Col. William Dangerfield of Belvidera near Fredericksburg. Chastellux speaks of him as a "tall, handsome man." Campbell remarks that he was a man of most agreeable manners, and strict integrity of conduct. He was not "distinguished for extraordinary exhibitions of genius, but for plain, practical qualifications."

[*The Bland Papers,* ed. by Chas. Campbell, and published in two volumes in 1840, with a memoir by Campbell prefixed, is the principal source of information. Selections from the Chas. Campbell papers, now in the Va. Hist. Soc., have been printed in the *Va. Mag. of Hist.,* IX, 59–77, 162–92, 298–306, and constitute important documents. Bland's will is published in the *Va. Mag. of Hist.,* III, 315. His thesis at Edinburgh was entitled *De Concoctione Alimentorum in Ventriculo.* There are two letters of Bland in R. H. Lee's *Life of Arthur Lee* (1829). There are some interesting references to Bland's career in the Continental Congress in Hunt's edition of Madison's works, vol. I.]

E. G. S.

BLAND, THOMAS (Oct. 4, 1809–Aug. 20, 1885), naturalist, was born at Newark, Nottinghamshire, England, the son of Dr. Thomas Bland. His mother was a Shepard, niece of Richard Shepard, the conchologist. He was educated at the Charterhouse School, London, where he was a classmate of Thackeray. He then studied law, and after practising in London for a time, emigrated to Barbadoes (1842) and later to Jamaica, where he became interested in the *Mollusca* through a visit of Prof. Charles B. Adams of Amherst (1848–49) and plunged at once into a study of the rich fauna of the West Indies. In 1850 he became superintendent of a gold mine at Marmato, New Granada (now Colombia), where he continued his study of shells. He settled in New York in 1852 and becoming acquainted with William G. Binney, who was just starting to complete the work of his father, Amos Binney, on *The Terrestrial Air-Breathing Mollusks of the United States,* etc. (1851–78), the two collaborated in a number of papers on terrestrial mollusks, the most important of which was Part I of "Land and Fresh-Water Shells of North America," published in the *Smithsonian Miscellaneous Collections,* vol. VIII (1869). "It systematized, expanded and put in manual form the knowledge of the land shells of this continent and placed this information within the reach of students everywhere. For many years it was the chief authority in its particular field, and even at this late date it must still be consulted by all who study this fauna" (letter of William B. Marshall, Conchologist of the United States National Museum). During his scientific career Bland produced seventy-two papers on the *Mollusca* of the United States and region of the Antilles, most of which were published in the *Annals of the Lyceum of Natural History of New York* and in the *American Journal of Conchology.* They dealt not only with description of species, but anatomy, classification, geographic distribution, and the development of the *Mollusca* as well.

Bland was a fellow of the Royal Geological Society of London, a member of the American Philosophical Society, and of a number of other societies devoted to natural history.

[A complete bibliography of Bland's scientific works was compiled by Arthur F. Gray and published in 1884; see also biographical sketches in *Science,* Nov. 13, 1885, and in the *Am. Jour. of Sci.,* Nov. 1885.]

F. E. R.

BLANKENBURG, RUDOLPH (Feb. 16, 1843–Apr. 12, 1918), mayor of Philadelphia, was born in Barntrup, Germany, the son of the Rev. Ludwig and Sophie (Goede) Blankenburg. He spent his early years in Hillentrup, where his father's church was, and it was there that he was educated under private tutors and at the Real Gymnasium. He preferred business to the ministry and went to an uncle in Lipstadt where he received the basis of what was to prove an uniquely successful business career. What he had heard of America, and especially his reading of *Uncle Tom's Cabin,* gave him an interest in this country which could only be satisfied by making it his home, which he did in 1865, seeking naturalization at the earliest possible day. On arriving in Philadelphia he secured a position with an importer and manufacturer of yarns and notions. Then he became successively a traveling salesman and European buyer for the concern. He was married on Apr. 18, 1867, to Lucretia, daughter of Dr. Hannah Longshore of Philadelphia. In 1875 he established the firm of R. Blankenburg & Company, at the head of which he remained until it was incorporated in 1905. After that he continued as a member of the board of directors. Blankenburg achieved fame,—city, state, and national, as an impassioned tribune. He was a champion of the rights and privileges of the people rather than a reformer, although he possessed a large measure of reforming zeal. He early manifested an interest in public affairs, an interest that was increased and fashioned by his association with the Society of Friends shortly after his arrival in the United States. His voice was early heard in behalf of the downtrodden and oppressed, and this led him to oppose those forces in public life which he believed to be responsible for their condition. In 1881 he was one of the leaders in the formation of the famous "Committee of 100" in Philadelphia, from which however he promptly resigned when it endorsed the sitting mayor (William D. Stokley) for another term. Within a month he was invited to return to the Committee, which reconsidered its endorsement of Stokley and nominated Samuel G. King, a Democrat, who was elected. This action established Blankenburg as a leader among the reform forces. He had a ready wit, a fearless courage, a commanding presence and personality and an imagination that added fire and color, if not always accuracy, to his addresses. So picturesque was he as a crusader that he was popularly known by the sobriquet "The Old War Horse of Reform." He was an accomplished phrase-maker and his designation of his opponents as "the powers that prey" has become a part of the language of politics.

A Republican in national affairs, he was in almost constant opposition to the dominant Republican organization in Philadelphia and Pennsylvania. His most picturesque fight was his organized attack on Quay in 1897 and 1898. Quay supported Boies Penrose and Blankenburg supported John Wanamaker in his unsuccessful attempt to win the election to the United States Senate. In 1906 he was compelled, against his wishes and vigorous opposition, to accept the Independent nomination for county commissioner. He and his colleagues were elected over the regular Republican candidates, he leading the ticket by a majority of over 50,000. In 1911 he was persuaded to become an Independent candidate for mayor and was elected over the regular Republican candidate by the narrow margin of 5,000 votes. During his four years of office he earned for himself the title of the "Old Dutch Cleanser." Public administration, however, did not appeal to him for he was essentially an advocate and was more at home in arousing interest than in organizing and directing it. Nevertheless, his administration was characterized by many improvements especially in the department of public works presided over by Morris L. Cooke to whom he gave hearty support. Another phase of public activity to which Blankenburg made a large contribution was in the realm of public charity. He it was who organized the Citizens' Permanent Relief Committee which contributed largely to affording relief in disasters like the Charleston earthquake, the Russian famine, and the Johnstown flood. He was the animating leader of the warfare on the "loan sharks," recovering many thousands of dollars for those who would otherwise have been helpless. He also organized a philanthropic pawn shop. A big, dominating man glowing with health, with a rich, powerful voice, he was a jovial companion who played as hard as he worked.

[*Who's Who in America,* 1916–17; Geo. E. Mapes, "An Uncompromising Fighter," *Outlook,* LXXXIII, 220; *Am. Mag.,* LXXVI, 58; *Yr. Bk. of the Pa. Soc.* (1919), p. 172; *Phila. Inquirer* and *Public Ledger,* Apr. 13, 1918; personal knowledge.]

C. R. W—f.

BLASDEL, HENRY GOODE (Jan. 20, 1825–July 26, 1900), governor of Nevada, the son of Jacob and Elizabeth Blasdel, was born in Dearborn County, Ind. His mother was of German descent, a native of Virginia. His father's ancestors came from Scotland to New England in the early seventeenth century and two hundred years later his grandfather went with the westward tide of emigration to the Old Northwest, settling at the site of the present Cincinnati in 1804. A large amount of land was acquired a short distance to the west in Dearborn County, Ind. There the grandfather and father engaged in farming and to this occupation Henry Goode was born and bred. At the age of seventeen, while as yet possessed of only a common school education, the death of his father took from him the opportunity for further study in the schools, but he read such law books as were accessible. On Dec. 9, 1845, he married Sarah Jane Cox, of Southern parentage, and eighteen months later they removed to Aurora, Ind., where Blasdel as a produce merchant shipped goods to New Orleans and later entered the steamboat business. In January 1852 he went as a prospector to Yankee Bar on the American River in California, then shortly tried farming in Santa Cruz County, and soon afterward entered the mercantile produce business in San Francisco. Here his family joined him. Here also he became financially prosperous but the crisis of 1860 deprived him of his fortune and he went with the rush of miners to Virginia City, Utah Territory. There he built the Empire and the Hoosier State Mills, which were respectively the second and the third mills. He was the first superintendent of the Potosi mine and later was in charge of the Hale and Norcross. He also was associated with ex-Governor Colcord in mining operations in Aurora. So long as he supervised a property it was closed on Sunday and at one time, although in especial need of money, he left a quartz mill of which he was manager because he was required to keep it running on the first day of the week.

In politics he was an Old Line Whig until in 1860 he joined the Republican party. In 1864 when on a visit to the old home in Indiana he attended the convention that nominated Abraham Lincoln for a second term and was an unofficial representative of Nevada in the convention of the National Union League as well as a member of that body's committee which informed President Lincoln of his nomination by the

League. In the fall of 1864, upon his return from the East, he was drafted by the National Union League of Nevada as a candidate for governor of this new-born state. He was elected by a large majority and was reëlected in 1866, serving until 1870, after which he turned again to the business of mining. He was six feet, five inches in height; he had keen intelligent eyes, handsome features, and a smile that won all hearts. Until old age he retained his youthful appearance. In character he was unswerving. At one time he failed in a wheat deal for $80,000 but he later paid all his debts, even to the extent of forcing money upon his creditors when it was not collectible in law. His creditors then presented him with a watch which he carried till his death. Inside the cover was engraved: "Presented by a few friends, who can appreciate integrity." He was buried in Mountain View Cemetery in Oakland.

[Files of the *Gold Hill News*, 1864, 1866, and of the *Reno Evening Gazette*, 1900; Alonzo Phelps, *Contemporary Biog. of Cal.'s Representative Men* (1881), II, 122–24; *Hist. of Nev.* (1881), ed. by Myron Angel, pp. 87, 89, 679; H. H. Bancroft, *Hist. of Nev., Colo., and Wyo.* (1890), p. 184; *Statutes of Nev.*, 1864, 1866, 1868; *Jour. of the Nev. Assembly*, 1864–65, 1866.]

J. E. W—r.

BLATCHFORD, RICHARD MILFORD (Apr. 23, 1798–Sept. 4, 1875), lawyer, was the ninth of the seventeen children of Samuel Blatchford, a Nonconformist minister from Plymouth Dock, Devon, England, who came with his wife Alicia (Windeatt) to the United States in 1795. Born at Stratford, Conn., Richard attended the common schools, and completed his education at Union College, Schenectady, where he graduated in 1815. He then became a school teacher at Jamaica, L. I., studying law in his spare time. On his admission to the New York bar in 1820, he commenced practise in New York City, devoting himself more particularly to mercantile law and finance. In 1826 he was appointed counsel and financial agent of the Bank of England in the United States and shortly afterwards was retained in a similar capacity by the Bank of the United States. When the charter of the Bank of the United States expired in 1836, to him was confided the adjustment of all outstanding matters between it and the Bank of England. His services were also requisitioned on occasion by the Bank Commissioner of the State of New York. In politics he was a prominent adherent of the Whig party of that time, was an intimate friend of W. H. Seward, and in 1855 was elected a member of the state Assembly, serving one term. When the war broke out in 1861 Blatchford was indefatigable in organization work in the New York area, and President Lincoln appointed him one of the Committee of Three to superintend the disbursement of the public monies appropriated to the purpose of raising troops for the Union. In 1862 he was appointed United States minister to the States of the Church at Rome. Though he held this post only until the following year, his conduct of his delicate diplomatic duties at a critical period earned unstinted praise from the Administration.

Blatchford always manifested an intense interest in the public park system of the City of New York. In 1859 he had been appointed commissioner of Central Park, continuing as such until the new city charter came into operation in April 1870. In December 1872 he became commissioner of public parks of the city, but impaired health shortly compelled him to retire. He died at Newport, R. I., after a long illness. He was married three times: first on May 17, 1819, to Julia Ann, daughter of J. P. Munford of New York City, who died in 1857; second, on Nov. 8, 1860, to Angelica, daughter of James A. Hamilton of Nevis, Westchester County, N. Y., who died in 1868; third, on Jan. 18, 1870, to Katherine, daughter of Philip Hone. His son by his first marriage, Samuel, became successively United States district judge of the southern district of New York, United States circuit judge of New York, and finally associate justice of the Supreme Court of the United States. A man of spotless integrity, high ideals and single-hearted devotion to public service, Richard Blatchford enjoyed unreservedly the respect and confidence of his fellow citizens.

[A brief account of his immediate antecedents will be found in *Abridged Compendium of Am. Genealogy*, ed. by F. A. Vickers (1925). Various incidents of his life are recounted in *Blatchford Memorial II, A Geneal. Record of the Family of Rev. Samuel Blatchford*, by E. W. Blatchford (1912). Obituaries appeared in the *N. Y. Times*, *N. Y. Tribune*, *N. Y. Herald*, Sept. 5, 1875.]

H. W. H. K.

BLATCHFORD, SAMUEL (Mar. 9, 1820–July 7, 1893), lawyer and jurist, was the grandson of a dissenting minister who had come to the United States in 1795 from Devonshire and after trying several different localities had settled in Lansingburg, N. Y. His father, Richard Milford Blatchford, was born in Stratford, Conn., graduated from Union College, was admitted to the bar of New York, was counsel for the Bank of England and the Bank of the United States, and served in the New York legislature. His mother, Julia Ann, daughter of John P. Mumford, a well-known publicist, was a noted belle. Samuel was born in New York City. His first education was received at Pittsfield, Mass., at the school of William Forrest; later he attended an academy in New York City and the grammar school of Columbia College. He learned rapidly and showed a marked studious bent, although his devotion to books did not keep him from spending some time on outdoor sports. At thirteen he was ready to matriculate at Columbia College. He graduated in 1837 and then became private secretary to William H. Seward, a post which he held until he reached his majority. Association with Seward was in itself not inadequate legal training. Blatchford was admitted to the bar in 1842, and the next year began to practise with his father. He married Caroline, daughter of Eben Appleton of Lowell, Mass., Dec. 17, 1844. Meanwhile he served as military secretary on Gov. Seward's staff and in November 1845 went to Auburn as a partner of Seward and Christopher Morgan. When this firm was dissolved in 1854 he returned to New York and formed his own firm of Blatchford, Seward & Griswold, Seward being an adopted son and nephew of the ex-Governor. The firm prospered. Blatchford became particularly expert in international and maritime law and had many notable successes at the bar. He remained a consultant of the firm until 1862 (David McAdam and others, *History of the Bench and Bar of New York,* vol. I, 1897).

On May 3, 1867, President Grant appointed him a district judge of the southern district of New York. Here he was confronted by a number of international and admiralty matters that arose as a result of the Civil War. Five years later he was made a circuit judge for the second judicial district. Here though he specialized in patent law, his opinions on bankruptcy, copyright, libel, and maritime torts gave him a great reputation for learning. Many of his opinions, published in the reports which he himself edited, are extremely learned discussions of the points involved. His decisions were rarely reversed. He was appointed to the Supreme Court of the United States by President Arthur and was confirmed by the Senate, Mar. 2, 1882, taking the place of Judge Hunt who had been incapacitated for five years. On the Supreme Court bench Blatchford was one of the hardest working judges, rivaled only by Justice Miller. He gave opinions in 430 cases. During his ten years on the Supreme Court his most elaborate decision was probably Pennsylvania Railroad *vs.* Miller (132 *United States Reports,* 75). This case held that a corporation was bound by a new constitutional provision imposing burdens not contemplated by the corporation's charter. He also decided the famous case of Terry *vs.* Sharon (131 *United States Reports,* 40) and spoke for the majority of justices in the much more important case of Cunningham *vs.* Neagle (135 *United States Reports,* 1)—a case which contributed materially to the supremacy of federal authority. (See W. H. Taft, *Our Chief Magistrate and His Powers,* 1916, chap. 4). In several important cases (Dobson *vs.* Hartford Carpet Company, 114 *United States Reports,* 439, and Dobson *vs.* Dornan, 118 *United States Reports,* 10) Blatchford announced the status of design patents and laid down rules for infringement of design. These decisions were influential in determining the nature of the statute that Congress later passed (Act of Feb. 4, 1887; 24 *United States Statutes at Large,* 387), to afford special remedies for the infringement of design patents. Of somewhat austere personality and of studious temperament, Blatchford was one of the most respected justices on the bench. If his judicial style sometimes lacked concision and suffered from dullness, of his learning there was no question. If was difficult to be interesting in discussing patents and trademarks. As Chief Justice Fuller said of him, Blatchford "was at home in every branch of the jurisdiction of the courts in which he sat. It may be justly said that he displayed uncommon aptitude in the administration of maritime law and of the law of patents, his grasp upon the original principles of the one, and his mastery of details in the other aiding him in largely contributing in the development of both." His death occurred at Newport, after a short illness.

[H. L. Carson, *The Supreme Court of the U. S.* (1892); A. Oakey Hall, "Justice Samuel Blatchford," in the *Green Bag,* Nov. 1893; Chas. Warren, *The Supreme Court in U. S. Hist.* (1922); *Minnesota Law Jour.,* July 1893; *Am. Law Reg.,* Sept. 1893; *Albany Law Jour.,* Nov. 18, 1893; *N. Y. Tribune,* July 8, 1893; David McAdam *et al., Hist. of the Bench and Bar of N. Y.,* I (1897); *Am. Law Rev.,* Nov.–Dec. 1893; "The Supreme Court of the U. S. Memorial for Samuel Blatchford," in *150 U. S. Reports,* p. 707; S. Blatchford, *The Blatchford Memorial* (1871); E. W. Blatchford, *The Blatchford Memorial,* vol. II (1912).]

L. R.

BLAUSTEIN, DAVID (May 5, 1866–Aug. 26, 1912), rabbi, educator, social worker, was born in Lida, Province of Vilna, Russian Poland, the youngest son of Isaiah and Sarah Natzkovsky Blaustein. He received his early education in the Hebrew school of his native town, but, longing for larger opportunities, he ran away from home at the age of seventeen, and, crossing the Prussian frontier, entered the Hebrew academy at Memel. After a brief sojourn in this border town he settled in Schwerin, the capital of Mecklenburg-Schwerin, where he attended a teachers' preparatory school. His stay here terminated in 1886 when Bismarck promulgated the decree forbidding Russian Jews to live in Germany. He emigrated to the United States and landed at

Boston. His career as an educator began shortly after his arrival when he established a German and Hebrew school. He matriculated at Harvard College in 1889 and graduated with the degree of B.A. in 1893. While attending Harvard, he founded the Sheltering Home for Immigrants, his earliest service to the immigrant Jews, to whose welfare he devoted much thought and time throughout his life. In 1892 he was elected rabbi of the congregation of Sons of Israel and David at Providence, R. I., and for a number of years taught at Brown University as assistant professor of Semitic languages. He received the degree of M.A. from Brown in 1898, in which year he resigned as rabbi to accept the superintendency of the Educational Alliance of New York City. This proved the beginning of his real work. The Educational Alliance was the educational and social center of New York's East Side Ghetto. His selection for the post was unwelcome to many of the East Side leaders, and to allay their fears he determined to institute no definite policy until he had studied the situation. As the first step toward this end he undertook a survey of the neighborhood and with it as a guide set himself to fit the activities of the Alliance to the needs of the people. He strove to bring the opposing leaders and factions into harmony, and to make the building a common educational and social center for all groups. Thus the Educational Alliance became a true community house and set an example for Jewish settlements in other cities. The Americanization of the immigrant had been the chief purpose of the founders of the Alliance, but other problems, serious and complicated, enlisted the attention of the superintendent, among them the constantly widening breach between the older and the younger generation. He was unable to satisfy the ultra-radical group who in 1901 founded a new institution, known as the Educational League, with an absolutely free platform, as a protest against what this group considered Blaustein's reactionary policy. Largely because of this dissension Blaustein resigned his position in 1907. A year later he went to Chicago to assume the superintendency of the Chicago Hebrew Institute. Here too he fell into disfavor with the radical element, who boycotted the institution when he refused to let Emma Goldman speak in its hall. After he resigned the superintendency in 1910 he devoted the remaining two years of his life to social studies. On Sept. 18, 1911, he married Miriam Umstadter of Norfolk, Va. During a five-months tour of the country, from October 1911 to February 1912, he made studies of the immigrant Jewish problem and the Jewish situation generally. He may be considered the first in the line of trained Jewish social workers. Original in thought and method he left a deep impression on the development of social thought and endeavor in Jewish communal activity.

[Miriam Blaustein, *Memoirs of David Blaustein* (1913); Boris D. Bogen, *Jewish Philanthropy* (1917), pp. 39, 231 ff., 240, 286; *N. Y. Times, Sun* (N. Y.), Aug. 28, 1912; *Secretary's Fifth* and *Sixth Report, Harvard Coll., Class of 1893* (1913, 1918); *Reform Advocate,* Aug. 31, 1912.] D. P.

BLAVATSKY, HELENA PETROVNA HAHN (July 30, 1831–May 8, 1891), founder of the Theosophical movement, was born at Ekaterinoslav in Southern Russia. She was the daughter of Col. Peter Hahn and grand-daughter of Gen. Alexis Hahn von Rottenstern Hahn of old Mecklenburg stock. Her mother, Helena Pavlovna Fadeev, a distinguished novelist writing under the pseudonym of "Zinaida R-va," was an aunt of the celebrated Count Witte and a daughter of Privy-Councillor Andrey Fadeev and Princess Helena Dolgoruki. Further back, her ancestors were allied with the royal family. She passed an undisciplined childhood, at one time with her father in an army camp, and then, after the death of her mother, with her maternal grandparents. Their old country mansion at Saratov, much like a feudal castle, in the midst of parks and forests, fed the high-spirited girl's naturally romantic disposition. Hysterical and subject to hallucinations, she lived in a world of her own fancy when she was not quarrelling with her various governesses. "The slightest contradiction brought on an outburst of passion, often a fit of convulsions" (her aunt, Nadejda Fadeev, quoted in Sinnett, *post,* p. 27). In 1844 her father took her to Paris and London where she received some instruction in music, in which she showed remarkable talent, but he soon found his thirteen-year-old daughter too much for him and returned her to her grandparents. She grew up as reckless, self-willed, and erratic a young person as was to be found in all Russia. On July 7, 1848, she was married to Gen. Nikifor Vasilevich Blavatsky, at one time vice-governor of Erivan, who according to her statements was then seventy-three years old, although forty-five years later he was said to be still alive. She soon deserted her husband and returned to her grandfather who immediately shipped her to her father, but on the way she escaped and got to Constantinople. Here she seems to have formed a liaison with the Hungarian revolutionist and opera-singer Metrovich (or Mitrovich) which was followed by another with an unknown Englishman (S. Y. Witte, *Memoirs,* 1921, pp. 5–6). Then ensued a long period of wanderings about European capitals and gambling-places, in the

Near East, in Egypt, and possibly even to America (1851, 1853) and India (1853, 1856, 1869). No accurate record of these years can be pieced together from her own utterly unreliable and contradictory statements. Thus, in her first interview in America in 1874 (*New York Graphic,* Nov. 13) she made no mention of having been to India but claimed to have made a fortune by selling ostrich feathers in Africa and, on another occasion, to have penetrated into the Sudan and lived for four months without seeing a white face, while incidentally translating Darwin and Buckle into Russian! Later, in the information which she gave A. P. Sinnett for his *Incidents in the Life of Mme. Blavatsky* (1886), the ostrich feathers, Darwin, and Buckle were forgotten, but three trips to India and a residence in Tibet were substituted. In 1858 she was, according to her own statement, "converted to spiritualism" by the celebrated medium, Daniel D. Home, in Paris. In 1860 she was again in Russia, seeking reconciliation with her family and, at Pskov and Tiflis, creating a local sensation by her exhibitions of spirit-rapping. The arrival of Metrovich in Tiflis led to a renewal of their former relations and a new scandal. The two hastily went to Kiev whence they were ejected for pasquinades by Mme. Blavatsky against the Governor-General (Witte, *op. cit.,* pp. 7–8). Her statement that she was with Garibaldi in the battle of Mentana, Nov. 3, 1867, seems to have been without other foundation than her romantic imagination. She was in Odessa at some time between 1867 and 1871, still with Metrovich whom she supported by making and selling artificial flowers. In 1870 she was ship-wrecked off Spezzia. The next year she was investigating and practising spiritualism in Cairo. In 1872 she was back in Russia, in 1873 again in Paris, and in July of the latter year she crossed to New York by steerage and settled in one of the poorer quarters of the city. Her once attractive appearance was now a thing of the past: she had grown enormously corpulent, was slovenly in dress, gorged herself on fat meat, smoked incessantly, and swore like a trooper. Her personal duplicity and profound contempt for humanity were, however, concealed beneath an engaging frankness of manner. Her unconventionalities attracted the unconventional. Above all, her large mystical blue eyes magnetized and fascinated. She was about to start a new religious movement.

In the summer of 1874 the alleged spiritualistic phenomena of the Eddy brothers at Chittenden, Vt., received great publicity through the favorable articles of Henry Steel Olcott [*q.v.*] in the *New York Graphic.* Mme. Blavatsky visited Chittenden, met the receptive Olcott, and soon convinced him of her own psychic powers. During the ensuing year they became very intimate and wrote numerous articles in defense of spiritualism. But in the winter the disastrous exposure of the medium, Mrs. Nelson Holmes, in Philadelphia, caused public interest in spiritualism to wane. Mme. Blavatsky, up to this time under the "control" of the famous spook, "John King," shifted her allegiance, announced that she was in touch with certain Egyptian masters, "the Brothers of Luxor," and strove to found a society for the study of Egyptian occultism. This took form eventually in the Theosophical Society, started on Sept. 7, 1875, with sixteen members, Olcott as president, and herself as corresponding secretary. The aims of the Society were later enlarged to embrace the promotion of the brotherhood of man, the study of comparative religion, and the study of occultism in general. In the autumn of 1877 Mme. Blavatsky published in New York her celebrated *Isis Unveiled,* a two-volume work on occultism, largely made up of unacknowledged quotations. In this she denounced spiritualism as bitterly as she had formerly denounced its opponents. In 1878 a branch of the Theosophical Society was formed in London. Meanwhile, and very incidentally, claiming to be a widow, Mme. Blavatsky had been again married, to a Russian named M. C. Betanelly, from whom she was divorced on May 25, 1878.

The parent society in New York failing to prosper, Olcott and Mme. Blavatsky now decided to try their fortunes in India. They sailed on Dec. 18, 1878, and arrived in Bombay, Feb. 16, 1879. Even before this they had affiliated with the Arya Samaj, a group headed by a Hindu mystic, Dayananda Saraswati, but within a short time they and the venerable Hindu were denouncing each other as "humbugs." Mme. Blavatsky supported herself and Olcott by writing, under the pseudonym of Radda-Bai, for the *Russky Vyestnik,* a series of exceedingly able travel sketches (translated into English under title *From the Caves and Jungles of Hindostan,* 1892). Meanwhile her production of "psychic phenomena" converted A. P. Sinnett, editor of the leading Anglo-Indian paper, the *Allahabad Pioneer,* in whose pages the Theosophical movement was widely advertised. The two founders established their own magazine, the *Theosophist,* and began to gain adherents throughout India; in 1880 they carried the movement to Ceylon; in 1882 they fixed the permanent headquarters of the Society at Adyar, a suburb of Madras, in a bungalow fitted up with an "occult room" and a "shrine." By means of these, Mme. Blavatsky received over the astral telegraph mysterious letters from her latest masters, two Tibetan Mahatmas named "Morya" and "Koot Hoomi." In 1883, however, it was brought out that one of Koot Hoomi's letters, published in Sinnett's *Occult World* (1881), was taken verbatim from a spiritualistic address delivered by a certain Mr. Kiddle in America. This discovery led to numerous resignations from the London branch, and the situation became so serious that early in 1884 Olcott and Mme. Blavatsky paid a trip to Europe. Hardly had they departed before her secretary, Mme. Emma Coulomb, together with her husband, both residents in the Theosophical bungalow, began to circulate stories of wholesale trickery on Mme. Blavatsky's part. These were published in the *Christian College Magazine* at Madras in the fall, and the much-harassed Theosophical leaders now hurried back to India, closely followed by Richard Hodgson, come to make an investigation on behalf of the British Society for Psychical Research. This investigation was carried on for three months; when it became known that the investigator's report would corroborate the Coulomb charges, Mme. Blavatsky resigned her position as corresponding secretary of the Society and sailed once more for Europe.

In April 1885 she arrived at Naples, desperately ill, impoverished, and all but universally discredited. But her spirit was indomitable. She settled down to an obscure life in Würzburg, Germany, where as soon as her health was a little better she devoted herself to her most important piece of writing, *The Secret Doctrine* (1888), in two large volumes, an elaborate exposition of the basic ideas of Theosophy. Toward exposures of her past she adopted the attitude of a religious martyr persecuted by unbelievers, and this rôle gradually gained her more followers than she had lost. In the spring of 1886 she moved to Ostend and in the summer of 1887 to London. There in September 1887 she organized the Blavatsky Lodge; in October 1888 she established the Esoteric Section of the Theosophical Society with herself as head; in August 1890 authority over the entire European Theosophical organization was given to her. During all this time she was suffering from a variety of diseases any one of which, in the opinion of her physician, would have sufficed to kill an ordinary person. Nevertheless, in these years, besides her other activities, she edited a monthly Theosophical magazine, *Lucifer* (1887–91) and wrote the *Voice of the Silence* (1889), a Theosophical rhapsody; *The Key to Theosophy* (1889); a *Glossary of Theosophical Terms* (1891); and *Nightmare Tales* (published posthumously, 1892), a collection of semi-mystical short stories. At the time of her death, on May 8, 1891, she was once more the recognized head of a great religious movement. Although unquestionably a charlatan, with a superficial knowledge of the Oriental philosophy which she advocated and a character the reverse of her own teachings, she made a deep appeal to the childish love of mystery and magic still latent in most human beings. She possessed the rare power of temporarily believing whatever she wanted to believe. Thus she hypnotized others, having first hypnotized herself, and, although one of the most unspiritual of women, she gained from her followers a veneration amounting almost to idolatry.

[There are several biographies of Mme. Blavatsky but none satisfactory. A good sketch in Russian by Zinaida Vengerova will be found in the *Kritico-biograficheskii slovar russkikh pisatelsi i uchenikh* (St. Petersburg, 1889–1904, vol. III), on which the sketches in other Russian encyclopedias are mainly based. The best account in English of her early life is in A. P. Sinnett, *Incidents in the Life of Mme. Blavatsky* (1886), ch. I–VI, based largely on a narrative in Russian by her sister, Mme. Vera Jelihovsky. For a discussion of her travels see Arthur Lillie, *Mme. Blavatsky and Her "Theosophy"* (1895), ch. II, III; for her residence in America: H. S. Olcott, *Old Diary Leaves, First Series*, published first and in fuller form in the *Theosophist*, 1891; for her residence in India: the Hodgson report in *Proc. British Soc. for Psychical Research*, vol. III (1885); Mme. E. Coulomb, *Some Account of My Intercourse with Mme. Blavatsky from 1872 to 1884* (Lond. 1885); Franz Hartmann, *Observations during a Nine Months Stay at the Headquarters of the Theosophical Society* (Madras, 1884); *Mahatma Letters to A. P. Sinnett* (1923); John N. Farquhar, *Modern Religious Movements in India* (1915); for her later life: V. S. Solovyoff, *A Modern Priestess of Isis* (1895); *Letters of H. P. Blavatsky to A. P. Sinnett* (1924); A. P. Sinnett, *Early Days of Theosophy in Europe* (1923); Countess Constance Wachtmeister, *Reminiscences of H. P. Blavatsky and "the Secret Doctrine"* (1893); Alice L. Cleather, *H. P. Blavatsky: Her Life and Work for Humanity* (Calcutta, 1922); *The Theosophical Movement 1875–1925* (1925). The recent *Life of Madame Blavatsky* (1927) by Baseden Butt is negligible. A good brief account of the teachings of Theosophy is that by A. P. Warrington, *Encyc. Americana* (1925), XXVI, 517–22.]

E. S. B.

BLECKLEY, LOGAN EDWIN (July 3, 1827–Mar. 6, 1907), jurist, the son of James and Catherine (Lutes) Bleckley, was born in Rabun County, Ga., shortly after that mountainous region had been quitted by the Cherokee Indians. His father, a native of North Carolina, was a man of influence in the community, being successively sheriff, clerk, ordinary, and county judge. His mother was of German ancestry and through her Bleckley is supposed to have inherited his love for the abstruse. He was a frail lad, but studious, and from the age of eleven, when he became a sort of clerical assistant in his father's office, his youth was largely spent in reading such law books and legal documents as he could lay hands upon. In this manner he prepared himself for the bar to which he was admitted shortly before he was nineteen. When twenty-one he moved to Atlanta where, at the age of twenty-six, he was elected solicitor general (prosecuting attorney) for the judicial circuit. At the outbreak of the Civil War he became a Confederate soldier, but his service in the field was cut short by ill health and he was transferred to the law department of the army where he remained until 1864. He then was made reporter for the Supreme Court of Georgia, resigning in 1867 to resume active practise. In 1875 he was appointed an associate justice of the State Supreme Court and thus, in his forty-ninth year, began the career which was to make him distinguished. Overwork forced his retirement in 1880, but he went back upon the bench in 1887 when appointed chief justice and remained for seven years, after which failing strength again compelled him to resign. He was married twice; first in 1857 to Clara Caroline Haralson; again, in 1893, to Chloe Herring. Five children were born of each marriage.

During all of his life he was a student,—of law, philosophy, metaphysics, mathematics. His general reading and intellectual interests were extensive. But save for a few years' meager instruction in early youth and a short course in higher mathematics at the University of Georgia in his old age, he had no schooling. He wrote many essays of a philosophical nature and not a few poems. One of his poems, "In the Matter of Rest," he read from the bench upon the occasion of his first retirement. In 1892 the University of the South conferred upon him the degree of D.C.L. Few of his decisions established novel principles. No great political or constitutional question was presented to the court while he was a member. But owing to his profound knowledge of the law, his sound reasoning, his faculty for making the complex simple, and his delightful literary style,—which abounds in quaint phrases, pertinent witticisms, and humorous allusions,—his opinions have taken high rank, and have been widely quoted in the United States, in Canada, and, to less extent, in Great Britain. He captured the imagination of his contemporaries no more by the unusual quality of his judicial decisions than by his engaging and unconventional personality. His dress was of Quaker-like simplicity; his manners were gentle; his countenance was serene. Well over six feet in height, spare, but of large frame, with flowing beard and long white hair, he had in his latter years the appearance of a patriarch.

[The chief source is the *Memorial of Logan E. Bleckley* (1907), containing sketches by Jos. R. Lamar, Walter B. Hill and others, a brief autobiography, several of Bleckley's essays, a number of his poems, and an article by Alfred H. Russell entitled "Wit and Wisdom of Chief Justice L. E. Bleckley in the Georgia Reports." See also *128 Ga. Reports*, 849; *Men of Mark in Ga.*, IV (1908), 80–88; *Green Bag*, IV, 49, 72, X, 530, XV, 555; *Atlanta Georgian*, Mar. 6, 1907; *Augusta Chronicle*, Mar. 7, 1907. Bleckley's personal appearance is described from memory.]

B. F.

BLEDSOE, ALBERT TAYLOR (Nov. 9, 1809–Dec. 8, 1877), Confederate official, editor, author, was the grandson of Rev. William Bledsoe, who, because of the persecution of the Baptists in Virginia by the then established church, removed from Orange County into the wilds of Kentucky in the later years of the eighteenth century. William's son, Moses Ousley Bledsoe, in 1816 founded and edited in Frankfort, Ky., the *Commonwealth*. He married Sophia Childress Taylor, who was related to President Taylor. Of their union Albert Taylor Bledsoe was the first-born. He graduated in 1830 at West Point Military Academy, where he was a fellow student of Jefferson Davis and Robert E. Lee. For a while he was stationed at the Indian forts in the West, but returned east to study law, theology, and philosophy in Kenyon College, Ohio. He was adjunct professor of mathematics and teacher of French in Kenyon College, 1833–34, and was professor of mathematics in Miami University, 1835–36. In the latter year he married Harriet Coxe of Burlington, N. J., and in 1838 moved to Springfield, where for ten years he practised law in the same courts with Lincoln and Douglas. His continued interest in theology led to the writing of an *Examination of President Edwards' "Inquiry into the Freedom of the Will"* (1845). From 1848 till 1854 he was professor of mathematics at the University of Mississippi and from 1854 to 1861 he held the same chair at the University of Virginia. The results of his studies during those years are found in *A Theodicy: or Vindication of the Divine Glory* (1853) and the *Essay on Liberty and Slavery* (1856). On account of his training at West Point he entered the Confederate army as colonel in 1861 and then became assistant secretary of war. Believing that Bledsoe's brain could be of more service than his arm, President Davis sent him to London to investigate certain historical problems involved in the issues between the North and the South and perhaps to influence English public opinion. When he returned in February 1865, he had collected the material which he soon used in his volume, *Is Davis a Traitor?, or Was Secession a Constitutional Right Previous to the War of 1861?* (1866). In this book, which proved to be a mine of material for the lawyers who were defending Davis, Bledsoe restated with real clearness and force the position of Calhoun and other Southern leaders and laid the basis for much of his future writing. In 1867 he became the founder and editor of the *Southern Review,* published in Baltimore. For ten years he was the fiery protagonist of the Lost Cause. The magazine was dedicated to "the despised, disfranchised, and down-trodden people of the South." "Shall we bury in the grave of the grandest cause that has ever perished on earth," asks the editor, "all the little stores of history and philosophy which a not altogether idle life has enabled us to amass, and so leave the just cause merely because it is fallen to go without our humble advocacy? We would rather die." In a later volume he writes: "To abandon the *Review* would be like the pang of death to me. It is the child of my affection. Money is not my object. I am willing to be a slave for the South." In this spirit he toiled unceasingly, writing nearly always three to five articles for each number, and for one number of 250 pages all but one article. But so poverty-stricken were the Southern people and so seemingly indifferent to his efforts to plead their cause that he received but little compensation and was dependent for the support of his family on the salaries of his daughters, who were school-teachers.

The historical significance of Bledsoe's writings, now buried in the files of the old *Review,* is that they represent the attitude of the unreconstructed Southerner in the ten years after the Civil War. Although he often quoted the words of Gen. Lee to him, "You have a great work to do; we all look to you for our vindication," his spirit was exactly opposite to that of the man who moved out of the shadows of Appomattox into the dawn of a new day, and who urged all Southerners to become Americans, and to "unite in the restoration of reason, the allayment of passion, and the dissipation of prejudice." Bledsoe interpreted the war as a conflict between principle and brute force. He justified secession as a constitutional right and slavery as a moral right sanctioned by the Bible. He seemed like a Titan fighting against all the tendencies of modern life and thought. Democracy, he contended, is an impossible form of government because it enthrones the tyranny of the mob; it is the result of the infidel doctrinaires of the eighteenth century, including Jefferson, whom he bitterly denounced as the source of the South's woes; instead of being the last hope of the world, it is the last madness of a self-idolizing nation. Industrialism is the enemy of chivalry and beauty, and science is the enemy of faith. The new doctrine of Evolution destroys the story of the Fall of Man, which is the corner-stone of theology. German philosophy and higher criticism are responsible for the reign of rationalism, which can only be overthrown by the religious faith of the South. Because "we can no longer trust the mental and moral training of our sons and daughters to teachers and books imported from abroad," Bledsoe advocated a series of text-books to be written for the most part by professors in the University of Virginia. The South must maintain its higher education against the whole tendency toward the uniformity and standardization of the infidel and utilitarian public school system. All along the line there must be "a renewal of the old fortifications," "a return to the old paths." Ever a fighter, Bledsoe was engaged in continuous controversy, not only with other editors and authors, but, in his later years, with various denominational leaders in the South over such questions as infant baptism, predestination, the mode of baptism, etc. It is little wonder that he gave way under the strain of financial burdens, excessive work, and bitter disputation. He died at Alexandria, Va., Dec. 8, 1877. His daughter, Sophia Bledsoe Herrick, who had helped him with his editorial duties, later became one of the editors of *Scribner's Magazine.*

[Sketch by Sophia Bledsoe Herrick in the *Lib. of Southern Lit.,* vol. I (1907); Jas. W. Davidson, *Living Writers of the South* (1869); Edwin Mims, "Southern Mags." in *The South in the Building of the Nation,* vol. VII (1909).]

E. M.

BLEECKER, ANN ELIZA (October 1752–Nov. 23, 1783), poet, was born in New York City, the posthumous daughter of Brandt Schuyler and Margareta (Van Wyck) Schuyler. Belonging on her father's side to one of the most aristocratic families in the colony, she came into the world an heiress of considerable fortune. With her one brother and two sisters she was brought up in an atmosphere of comfort and culture, and while still very young began to write creditable verse. She was married, Mar. 29, 1769, to John J. Bleecker, a gentleman of good family in New Rochelle. They first went to Poughkeepsie for two years and then removed to Tomhanick, near Schaghticoke, N. Y., a frontier village where Bleecker possessed some landed property. Here he "built him an house on a little eminence, which commanded a pleasing prospect" of orchard, meadow, stream, and hill. Although Mrs. Bleecker sometimes became a little weary of her rustic neighbors and compared herself to Orpheus

Impatient trees, to hear his strain
  Rent from the ground their roots:—
Such is my fate, as his was then,
  Surrounded here—by brutes

she really had many friends of her own class, and

her familiar verse of this period is full of glee. When misfortunes came, however, they came fast. In the summer of 1777 the approach of Burgoyne's army counseled withdrawal to a safe community and Bleecker went to Albany to arrange for accommodations there. During his absence, Mrs. Bleecker, alarmed at the breakfast table by news that hostile Indians were within two miles of the village, rushed impetuously from the house, carrying a young baby on her arm and leading a four-year-old daughter. Joining a stream of refugees, she was able to secure a place in a wagon for the children, but was obliged to walk, herself, all the way to the nearest settlement of Stony-Arabia. This town proved itself to deserve its name by refusing shelter to the fugitives, but finally one of its richest citizens did permit Mrs. Bleecker to spend the night on the bare floor of an attic. The next morning her husband found her and they proceeded to Albany and thence down the Hudson to Red Hook where her mother was awaiting them. On the journey, however, her baby sickened and died; it was buried on the riverbank in a coffin hastily prepared from a dining-table. A few days later, her mother also died, and within a few weeks her only surviving sister.

After Burgoyne's surrender, the Bleeckers returned to Albany where prudence would have bade them remain. But Albany, in Mrs. Bleecker's words "that unsociable, illiterate, stupid town," proved insupportable, and in spite of danger they went back to their beloved Tomhanick. From this time until the end of the war Bleecker, like his fellow-townsmen, was away much of the time on militia duty, and although the adjacent forest swarmed with Indians and Tories the village was often left without a single male defender. Mrs. Bleecker consoled herself as best she might during these years of loneliness and terror by the reading of Homer, Virgil, Theocritus, Ariosto, and Tasso. During the winter of 1779 she was again obliged to save her life by flight, this time to the settlement of Coeymans, but in the ensuing spring returned once more to Tomhanick. In 1781 her husband was captured by Tories and for six days she was in doubt as to his fate; at the end of that time he reappeared, having been unexpectedly rescued by a party of Vermonters, but the emotional reaction was too great for Mrs. Bleecker's health, worn out by constant nervous strain; a severe illness followed from which she never really recovered. After peace was declared, her husband took her on a visit to New York, hoping that old scenes would revive her waning interest in life, but the city had been devastated, family and friends were gone, and she returned to Tomhanick to die. "My days have been few and evil," she had written in 1780, and in 1783 she wrote "I die of a broken heart." She died on Nov. 23 in the latter year.

Mrs. Bleecker's poems, published in the *New York Magazine* but not collected in book form until after her death, show much variety of subject-matter and some technical proficiency; although her emotion is too unrestrained for modern taste, she does at time invest the meters of Pope with lyrical quality. Her letters reveal a personality of much charm and grace, with a lightly satirical wit and gayety until overclouded by her later melancholy.

[*The Posthumous Works of Ann Eliza Bleecker,* containing her letters and a memoir by her daughter, Margaretta V. Faugeres (1793); Geo. W. Schuyler, *Colonial N. Y.,* II (1885); J. Munsell, *Annals of Albany,* vol. VI (1855), containing inscription on Mrs. Bleecker's tombstone.]

E. S. B.

BLENK, JAMES HUBERT (July 28, 1856–Apr. 20, 1917), Catholic archbishop, the youngest of the sixteen children of James Blenk and Catherine Wigman, was born in Neustadt, Bavaria. His parents were Protestants and died in that faith. The family came to America when he was a baby. Environmental influences were responsible for his conversion to Catholicism. He attended services at the Cathedral with his Catholic playmates and the ritual of the Church appealed to him so strongly that he was baptized at the age of twelve. His early education was received in New Orleans and later he attended a Franciscan school in New York. Ill health interfered with his desire to join the Redemptorist order. He secured a position as teacher of mathematics at Jefferson College, Convent, La. The college was under the control of the Marists and when his health improved he applied for admission to that order. His ecclesiastical training was received in France and Ireland. On Aug. 16, 1885 he was ordained. His first assignment was to Jefferson College, of which he became president in 1891. Under his leadership the college progressed rapidly and in order to better utilize his talents the general of the Marists sent him to visit the various houses and missions of the order in France, England, and Ireland. Upon his return to New Orleans in 1897 he was put in charge of the Holy Name Church in Algiers. Archbishop Janssens appointed him on the board of consultors of the diocese. When after the Spanish-American War Archbishop Chapelle of New Orleans was appointed apostolic delegate to Cuba and Porto Rico to adjust matters pertaining to the church, Father Blenk was selected as auditor and secretary of the delegation. As a result of his excellent work, he was named first bishop of Porto Rico in January 1899. In Porto Rico he Americanized the Catholics, provided for education, and adjusted the affairs of church and state very satisfactorily. He became archbishop of New Orleans on July 2, 1906, and devoted his energies to systematizing and unifying the activities of the church. A common system of parochial schools with uniform text-books and teaching was organized. Catholic high schools were established and the Jesuits were aided in organizing Marquette University. Provision was made for the training of priests. The Fathers of the Congregation of the Holy Ghost and the Josephites were invited to come to the diocese in order to establish churches and schools for the negroes, and through his influence Mother Catherine Drexel established a school for their higher education. When priests and nuns were driven out of Mexico, Archbishop Blenk gave them shelter. His last work was when he accompanied Dr. Kelly of the Church Extension Society to Cuba and to New York in the interests of the Mexican refugees. The diocese gained both spiritually and materially under the leadership of Archbishop Blenk, due not only to his executive ability but to his untiring energy and the fact that he was—"approachable, companionable and democratic" (*Times-Picayune,* New Orleans, Apr. 21, 1917).

[Archives of the St. Louis Cathedral, New Orleans; *Daily Picayune* (New Orleans), July 2, 3, 7, 10, 1899, Apr. 25, 1907; *Daily States* (New Orleans), Apr. 21, 1917; *Morning Star* (New Orleans), Apr. 21, 1917.]

S. H.

BLENNERHASSETT, HARMAN (Oct. 8, 1765–Feb. 2, 1831), associate of Aaron Burr, son of Conway Blennerhassett, an Irishman, was born in Hampshire, England, where his mother, a daughter of Thomas Lacy, was temporarily visiting. Educated at Trinity College, Dublin, he was admitted to the Irish bar in 1790. Afterward he spent several years in travel on the continent, being in Paris at the first anniversary of the taking of the Bastille and at the Festival of Confederation in the Champ de Mars. Influenced by his reading of Voltaire and Rousseau, he became an ardent republican. He was a cultured man with some talent for music and a flair for science, and was gifted, according to contemporary report, with "all sorts of sense except common sense." In 1796 he married Margaret Agnew and brought his bride to America. Two years later they settled on an island in the Ohio River near Parkersburg, then in the state of Virginia. In undertaking to make this a sylvan retreat he sunk a large part of his patrimony. "Foreign frescoes colored the ceilings,—the walls were hung with costly pictures, and the furniture, imported from Paris and London, was rich, costly, and tasteful. Splendid mirrors, gay colored carpets, and elegant curtains embellished their apartments. Massive silver plate stood on the sideboard. The drawing-room resembled the richest Parisian *salon* in the heyday of Louis XIV" (E. O. Randall, *Ohio Archæological and Historical Society Quarterly,* I, 132).

Blennerhassett's reputation rests upon his connection with Aaron Burr. This began in May 1805, when he may have casually met Burr at Marietta. In that year the latter twice visited the island establishment. Blennerhassett's apparent means, his enthusiasm, and his desire to escape from his wilderness home commended him to one who hoped to profit from the disturbed conditions of the southern frontier. On his own part Blennerhassett eagerly responded to Burr's vague proposals. In the following year when Burr journeyed westward the second time, Blennerhassett's island became a center for his activities. In a measure the master of the island proved too enthusiastic a recruit. To him are attributed a series of articles, published in the *Ohio Gazette,* under the pseudonym "Querist," which discussed the probability of a separation of the western states from the Union. One fails to see how they could have helped Burr's main plan, which was to prepare the West for an invasion of Mexico, unless he intended through the publication to deceive the Spanish authorities as to his real purpose.

Blennerhassett supervised operations on the island and on the nearby Muskingum, contributed liberally of his means, and also assisted in making the first payment on the Bastrop Purchase which Burr proposed to colonize. He interviewed John Graham, the agent of the federal government sent to watch Burr, and assured him that their plans were not illegal. Later such recruits as assembled on the upper Ohio made the island their headquarters. These preparations, coupled with the enmity that Blennerhassett had already excited among his neighbors, led the militia of Wood County, Va., to make a descent on the island, Dec. 11, 1806. Blennerhassett and Comfort Tyler, another prospective colonist, had hurriedly left the island the night before. The militia thereupon looted the mansion and outbuildings. The fugitives succeeded in passing the various militia groups stationed along the river and ultimately joined Burr at the mouth of the Cumberland. In company with Burr and other leaders Blennerhassett was detained by the authorities of Mississippi Territory, but after a hearing before the district judge, he was released. He was arrested again in Kentucky and brought to Richmond for trial. When the government failed to convict his principal, either for treason or for misdemeanor, the court entered a *nolle prosequi* also against Blennerhassett's indictment. His appearance at the trial elicited from Wirt a famous oratorical gem. His island residence was ruined, and in a few years fire and the floods swept away what the militia had spared. For a time he became cotton planter in Mississippi and spent three years, 1819–22, as a lawyer in Montreal. Then he returned to Europe and died on the island of Guernsey. His wife, a prepossessing woman of considerable talent, attempted to recover from Congress the value of the property but died shortly after she came to this country for the purpose.

[Wm. H. Safford, *Life of Harman Blennerhassett* (1853); Wm. H. Safford, ed., *The Blennerhassett Papers* (1864); *Century Mag.*, July 1901.]

I. J. C.

BLINN, HOLBROOK (Jan. 23, 1872–June 24, 1928), actor, was born in San Francisco, the son of Col. Charles H. and Nellie (Holbrook) Blinn. His father was a surveyor, his mother an actress. The boy caught his first glimpse of theatrical life in 1878, when he appeared as a child in *The Streets of New York*. The year 1891–92 he spent not too successfully at Leland Stanford Jr. University and then went on the stage, playing Corporal Ferry in *The New South* at Stockwell's Theatre, San Francisco, Sept. 12, 1892, under the management of William A. Brady. He made his New York début in the same play at the Broadway Theatre, Jan. 2, 1893, and continued to act in it for two seasons. Later he returned to California, got together a company of his own, and took it to Alaska. One member of the troupe was Ruth Benson, whom he married. She was the daughter of Maj. Henry McKinley Benson, U. S. A., appeared with her husband in several plays, and outlived him. Blinn made his London début as Wing Shee in *The Cat and the Cherub* at the Lyric Theatre, Oct. 30, 1897. He was popular in London and until 1903 had more engagements in England than in the United States. He was a life governor of Charing Cross Hospital. In 1900, in New York, he acted with Maurice Barrymore in *The Battle of the Strong*. In 1907–08, under the management of Arnold Daly [*q.v.*] he acted in *The Shirkers, How He Lied to Her Husband, The Van Dyck, After the Opera, The Hour Glass,* and *Candida;* later he was to be seen with Daly in *The Regeneration*. For three seasons 1908–11 he was leading man with Mrs. Minnie Maddern Fiske in *Salvation Nell, The Pillars of Society, Hannele, The Green Cockatoo, Becky Sharpe,* and *Mrs. Bumpstead-Leigh*. In 1913 he organized the Princess Theatre, New York, and produced thirty one-act plays, with which he later went on tour. Always a competent player, he enjoyed steady employment; yet, except while with Daly and Mrs. Fiske, he acted in few plays of distinction. His best work was done in the last decade of his life, but he remained a popular and superficially brilliant, rather than a distinguished, actor. In 1919 he starred as Henry Winthrop in *The Challenge;* in 1920 he was Jeffrey Fair in *The Famous Mrs. Fair* and joint star with Mary Nash in *Man and Woman;* for three seasons 1920–23 he played Pancho Lopez in *The Bad Man* with gorgeous comic verve; he starred in *The Dove* 1925–26 and produced and starred in Molnar's *The Play's the Thing* 1926–28. His home was at Croton-on-Hudson. There, while riding a new horse, he was thrown June 16, 1928, and badly bruised. Infection set in, and he died after a week's illness. He was buried in the old Sleepy Hollow Cemetery, in Scarborough, N. Y.

[*Who's Who in America*, 1928–29; J. Parker, ed., *Who's Who in the Theatre* (5th ed., London, 1925); *Leland Stanford Jr., Univ. Alumni Dir., 1891–1910* (1910); *N. Y. Times*, June 25, 26, 28, 1928. See also *N. Y. Times Index* under *Blinn* and *Plays; San Francisco Chronicle*, Sept. 12, 1892; F. W. Faxon, ed., *The Dramatic Index 1910–28* (1911 ff.).]

G. H. G.

BLISS, AARON THOMAS (May 22, 1837–Sept. 16, 1906), governor of Michigan, was born at Peterboro, Madison County, N. Y. He was the seventh child of Lyman Bliss, who traced his ancestry back to Thomas Bliss, a settler in Hartford, Conn., in 1636. His mother was Ann (Chaffie) Bliss. From his dry-goods store at Bouckville Aaron T. Bliss enlisted, Oct. 1, 1861, in the 10th New York Volunteer Cavalry, and went to the front as a first lieutenant, becoming captain a year later. Wounded while stubbornly defending the retreat of Wilson's Raiders, he was captured and suffered imprisonment in Salisbury, Andersonville, Macon, Charleston, and Columbia prisons, escaping from the latter in November 1864. Broken health caused his resignation three months later. In 1865 he went to Saginaw, Mich., and in the pine forests began a career that took him from a driver of logging teams to the head of one of the successful lumber firms of the Saginaw Valley. A paying farm of a thousand acres afforded recreation. His wife, Allaseba, daughter of Ambrose Phelps of Madison County, N. Y., shared both early privations and later success, and in philanthropy had a life all her own. Taking a leading part in the Michigan department of the Grand Army of the Republic, Bliss was elected first to the state Senate in 1882, and next as a member of the Fifty-first Congress, 1889–91. He was defeated for reëlection to Congress; but in 1900 he wrested from six other candidates the Republican nomination for governor. He succeeded the spectacular H. S. Pingree, and was reëlected in 1902. His name is linked with the establishment of the Indian School at Mt. Pleasant and the Michigan Soldiers' Home at Grand Rapids. He was a good administrator, and during his service as governor the educational and charitable interests of the state advanced steadily. He stood for the equal taxation of railway properties, and without being a reformer was a sound progressive. His gifts to Saginaw and to the Methodist Episcopal Church were extensive.

[J. H. Bliss, *Geneal. of the Bliss Family in America* (1881); H. M. Utley and B. M. Cutcheon, *Mich. as a Province, Territory and State* (1906), IV, 252; *Mich. Biogs.* (1924), ed. by the Mich. Hist. Commission; J. C. Mills, *Hist. of Saginaw County, Mich.*, II (1918), 24–28.]
C. M.

BLISS, CORNELIUS NEWTON (Jan. 26, 1833–Oct. 9, 1911), merchant, politician, was the son of Asahel Newton Bliss and of Irene Borden (Luther) Bliss. He was born in Fall River, where his father died at the age of twenty-six when the son was still very young. His mother, re-marrying, removed to New Orleans with her husband, Edward S. Keep, and the boy was left in the competent care of his grandmother. He attended the public schools of Fall River, and Fisher's Academy, working at odd jobs in his spare time. At the age of fourteen he joined his mother in New Orleans, and for a short time was clerk in the dry-goods store of his stepfather. Seeing little opportunity for a business career in the South, he returned to New England, and in Boston sought employment from James M. Beebe, then the leading dry-goods merchant of New England. He was given a beginner's place, from which he steadily rose until he became a member of the firm. There was in the employ of J. M. Beebe & Company during these years another young man, who was destined to large things in business and politics. This was Levi P. Morton, and the friendship between him and Bliss lasted as long as they both lived. In 1866 Bliss became convinced that manufacturing offered greater opportunities than wholesaling, and, severing his connection with J. M. Beebe & Company, he became the New York partner in the house of J. S. & E. Wright of Boston, operators of large textile mills. Soon the New York branch outstripped the mother house in volume of business, and the firm of Wright, Bliss & Fabyan became one of the most important in its line in the United States. On the death of the Wrights, the firm took the name of Bliss, Fabyan & Company, and Bliss remained its head until his death. On becoming a citizen of New York he took an immediate and intelligent interest in the civic and political affairs of the city. He was a Republican of the conservative type, but he frequently opposed with vigor the policies and performances of Thomas C. Platt, then the Republican leader of the state. In 1884 he supported Chester A. Arthur for the presidency, and in 1887 served as chairman of the Republican state committee. He began in 1892 his long service as treasurer of the Republican national committee. In this capacity he served with great ability in the presidential campaigns of 1892, 1896, 1900, and 1904. In the last year Alton B. Parker, Democratic candidate for the presidency, charged that Bliss, as treasurer of the Republican national committee, had procured excessively large contributions from corporations, and especially from those benefited by a high protective tariff. To these charges Bliss made no reply, and refused in any way to be drawn into the controversy. He declined, however, to serve longer as treasurer. In 1896 he was urged by McKinley to accept the Treasury portfolio, but refused. He agreed, however, in order to relieve the President in an awkward political complication, to become secretary of the interior. This office he filled most competently for two years. He had, however, little liking for the routine of political office, and resigned in 1898 to return to the management of his business. President McKinley urged him in 1900 to accept the nomination for the vice-presidency, but he declined. Had his decision been otherwise, he, and not Theodore Roosevelt, would have become president in 1901. Bliss refused repeatedly to be a candidate for state and municipal offices, including those of mayor of the city and governor of the state. Nevertheless, he gave his services freely as a member of civic and political committees. He was a consistent advocate of a high protective tariff, and was for many years president of the Protective Tariff League. He was an official in many large financial and industrial organizations, and served for a short time as president of the Fourth National Bank. He was married, on Mar. 30, 1859, to Elizabeth Mary Plummer of Boston.

[J. H. Bliss, *Geneal. of the Bliss Family in America* (1881); *Who's Who in America*, 1910–11; *Tribute of the Chamber of Commerce of the State of N. Y. to the Memory of Hon. Cornelius Newton Bliss* (1911); obituaries in *N. Y. Times, N. Y. Tribune, N. Y. Herald*, and *Sun* (N. Y.), Oct. 10, 1911.]
A. L. C.

BLISS, DANIEL (Aug. 17, 1823–July 27, 1916), missionary educator, founder and first president of Syrian Protestant College (now the

American University) of Beirut, was born in the village of Georgia, Vt. He was one of the seven children of Loomis and Susanna (Farwell) Bliss. His early lot was cast on various farms in his native state and in Ohio. His devout and loving mother died when he was nine years old. He spent his youth in the neighborhood of Painesville and Kingsville, Ohio, living with relatives and others, and supporting himself from the age of sixteen by farming, tanning, and tree-grafting. He attended the district schools and in 1846 entered the Kingsville Academy, studying and teaching therein until graduation in 1848. On Nov. 7, 1848, he arrived at Amherst College, Mass., in the middle of the fall term and was admitted upon examination to the freshman class. He was strong-minded, robust in physique, and a liberal in religion,—testifying, however, years afterward that he "never opposed what he believed to be true Christianity." What modest debts he accumulated in making his way through Amherst he cleared from the proceeds of a private school which he conducted in Shrewsbury, Mass., during the summer of 1852. He graduated from Amherst in the latter year and during 1852–55 attended Andover Seminary in preparation for the ministry and foreign missions. On Oct. 17, he was ordained at Amherst, and in November was married to Abby Maria Wood, of Westminster, Mass. Receiving appointment by the American Board and being assigned to Syria, Mr. and Mrs. Bliss sailed from Boston on Dec. 12, 1855, for Malta, Smyrna, and Beirut. After a short stay in Beirut they left on Apr. 15 for Abeih, a Lebanon village 2,500 ft. above the sea, where they worked for two and one-half years among the few hundred Christian and Druse villagers. This was Bliss's apprenticeship, and under his hand the school which Dr. Van Dyck had opened in 1843 grew rapidly into an academy of importance. The Syrian work at the time was almost exclusively amongst non-Moslems, for while Turkey was tolerant of Christian missionaries, she did not guarantee immunity to Moslem converts to Christianity. For four years from Oct. 16, 1858, the Blisses were in charge of the Girls' Boarding School in Suq al-Gharb, five miles above Abeih. It was there he preached his first Arabic sermon on Dec. 12, 1858, and displayed further his fitness for educational work. When the Syrian Mission voted on Jan. 27, 1862, to recommend the founding of a "Literary Institution," Bliss was assigned the task and privilege of organizing and presiding over it. He and Mrs. Bliss came at once to America, where he took the first steps in the new assignment. Syrian Protestant College was chartered in 1864 by New York State, and began an independent career under its own trustees with Bliss as president. Enough endowment was raised to enable the Institution to open in Beirut on Dec. 3, 1866, the aim being to serve "all conditions and classes of men without regard to colour, nationality, race, or religion." Arabic was the medium of instruction for the first seventeen years; thereafter, English. After existence in various quarters until 1873 the present site was occupied, where the corner-stone of the main building had been laid on Dec. 7, 1871. Bliss acted also as professor of Bible and ethics, and as treasurer. He was the active head of the College for thirty-six years and saw its enrolment grow from sixteen to over six hundred students. In 1902 he resigned, being succeeded by his second son, Dr. Howard Sweetser Bliss [*q.v.*], but after his retirement he still continued his daily classes, attended faculty meetings, and preached an occasional sermon. A hall of the Beirut institution bears his name, and his memory is preserved by Arabic text-books of his own composition in moral and in natural philosophy.

[*Reminiscences of Daniel Bliss* (1920), ed. by his eldest son, F. J. Bliss; C. A. Hoppin, *The Bliss Book* (1913); J. H. Bliss, *Geneal. of the Bliss Family in America* (1881); contemporary numbers of the *Missionary Herald.*]

J. C. A.

BLISS, EDWIN ELISHA (Apr. 12, 1817–Dec. 20, 1892), missionary, was born in Putney, Vt., the son of Henry and Abigail (Grout) Bliss. He was one of eight children, and one of three who became missionaries. A sister, Emma (Mrs. Van Lennep) went to Turkey, and a brother, Isaac Grout, to Turkey and Egypt. Edwin's early education was finished at the High School in Springfield, Mass., where his parents then dwelt. Thence he went to Amherst College, graduating in 1837. For two years following graduation he taught in Amherst Academy, and then entered Andover Seminary, from which he received his diploma in 1842. On Feb. 26, 1843 he married Isabella Holmes Porter, of Portland, Me. His ordination had taken place on Feb. 8, 1843, and on Mar. 1 he and Mrs. Bliss sailed from Boston on the bark *Emma Isadora* with a notable company bound for Smyrna.

After arrival in the East the Blisses proceeded to Trebizond instead of to Kurdistan and the Nestorian Mission, for they learned of trouble in the Kurdish mountains and could secure from the government (Turkey) only permissive passports and not protective *firmans*. They never, in fact, went into Kurdistan. Instead, they were "permanently connected with the Mission to the Armenians," and labored from 1843 to 1851 at Trebizond and from 1851 to 1856 at a new station opened by Bliss at Marsovan. At both stations the evangelical work suffered severe persecution at the hands of the orthodox Armenians. In February 1856 Bliss was transferred from Marsovan to Constantinople to give his time to literary work, and for thirty-six years he labored quietly and effectively in the department of publication. He edited the *Avedaper* (*"Messenger"*) from 1865 to 1892, a newspaper which had become in 1855 a weekly issued in three forms: Turkish in Armenian characters, Turkish in Greek characters, and Armenian in Armenian. It had 1,500 subscribers and some ten thousand readers throughout Turkey, and was a fruitful agent of inspiration to Christian workers, and of social and religious reformation. Its editor declared one of its important offices to be the exposure of "the shameless misstatements" made in other papers about the work of the American Board. Bliss edited, also, a monthly children's paper issued in the three forms mentioned above. In addition to this editorial work he wrote pamphlets and tracts, "helps in Bible study, narratives of Christian life and experience." He was the author of a *Bible Handbook* (in Armenian), and frequent articles in the *Missionary Herald.* He visited the United States four times on various errands, including the quest of health. While located at Marsovan he had contracted malaria from which he was never thereafter free. Before his death he had been for some time in feeble health and unable to work.

[Geo. Washburn, "Rev. Edwin E. Bliss," *Missionary Herald,* Feb. 1893; *Congreg. Yr. Bk.,* 1893; *Andover Theol. Sem. Necrology,* 1892–93; J. H. Bliss, *Geneal. of the Bliss Family in America* (1881).] J. C. A.

BLISS, EDWIN MUNSELL (Sept. 12, 1848–Aug. 6, 1919), missionary, editor, was born at Erzerum, Turkey, the son of Isaac Grout and Eunice (Day) Bliss, and nephew of Edwin Elisha Bliss [*q.v.*]. His father was agent of the American Bible Society for the Levant and missionary of the American Board. Edwin's early years were spent in Constantinople where his education was begun as one of the first students of Robert College under Cyrus Hamlin. In 1866, after four years in the College, he entered the Springfield, Mass., High School. After two years there he entered Amherst College from which he graduated in 1871 as valedictorian of his class. He spent the year 1871–72 in the Yale Divinity School and had begun his second year when called back to Constantinople because of his father's failing health. During the next three years he served as an assistant agent of the Bible Society, traveling extensively in Turkey, Egypt, Persia, and the Holy Land. In 1875 he resumed his studies at Yale and received in 1877 the B.D. degree. He was ordained in New Haven on May 18 of his senior year. Returning to the Levant, he served again as assistant agent of the Bible Society. He was married in Urumia, Persia, on June 5, 1885, to Marie Louise Henderson of New York City, and for two years thereafter resided in Constantinople as assistant agent of the Society. The health of Mrs. Bliss failed and in 1887, together with her daughter, Elizabeth Labaree, she returned to America, where she died on Dec. 12 of that year. Because of this loss Bliss resigned his post in 1888 to the great regret of the Bible Agency, and took up his residence at home.

From 1889 until 1891, the year of publication, Bliss was editor of the *Encyclopædia of Missions,* and filled the office with distinction. It was for this work in particular that his alma mater bestowed upon him in 1896 the honorary degree of D.D. From 1891 to 1901 he was associate editor of the *Independent,* New York City, serving also during one year (1898–99) as lecturer on foreign missions in the Yale Divinity School, and one year (1900) as editorial writer for the *New York Times,* and *Harper's Weekly.* He was chairman of the Press Committee and the Committee on Publication of the Ecumenical Foreign Missions Conference, New York City, 1900. On Nov. 8, 1900, he married his second wife, Theodora Crosby of Georgetown, Mass. During 1902–04 he was field agent for New England of the American Tract Society, in 1904 joint editor of a second edition of the *Encyclopædia,* and in 1905 general secretary of the Foreign Missions Industrial Association. In 1907 he was called to Washington for special work in the Bureau of Census—as expert on religious bodies—and remained at this post until his death at the age of seventy-one.

Bliss was the author of *The Turk in Armenia, Crete, and Greece* (1896); *Turkey and the Armenian Atrocities* (1896); *Concise History of Missions* (1897); *The Missionary Enterprise* (1908), and a series of historical sketches of the sects of Christendom for the World Conference on Faith and Order (1920), in addition to miscellaneous writings and his work in the Bureau of Census (see especially *Religious Bodies,* 2 vols., 1916). He was a rapid writer, quick in thought, and of a nervous temperament. While never very robust he was seldom ill. He was impulsive and generous.

[*Who's Who in America,* 1918–19; *Amherst Coll. Biog. Record,* 1821–1921; *Reports of the Am. Bible Soc.*; files of the *Missionary Herald*; information from Bliss's widow, Mrs. T. C. Bliss.] J. C. A.

BLISS, ELIPHALET WILLIAMS (Apr. 12, 1836–July 21, 1903), manufacturer, was one of the six children of John Stebbins Bliss, a physician and farmer whose ancestors had settled in Springfield, Mass., and of Ruby Ann (Williams) Bliss. He was born at Fly Creek, Otsego County, N. Y. Educated in the public schools and at Fort Plain Seminary, the boy spent his life on a farm. A pronounced mechanical bent, however, led him to an apprenticeship in a machine shop in Otsego County, where he remained until the age of twenty-one. Seeking wider mechanical opportunities he moved to New England and obtained work in the Parker gun factory in Meriden, Conn., where he was soon advanced to the position of foreman which he held for seven years. During the Civil War he served as a corporal in Company I of the 3rd Connecticut Volunteers. An older brother, Lucien Wood Williams Bliss, was a major in the Confederate army. Following the war Bliss returned to Fly Creek, N. Y., married Anna Elizabeth Metcalf on June 19, 1865, and in the following year located permanently in Brooklyn, N. Y., where he was employed for a short time with the Campbell Printing Press Company. In 1867 he founded the machine shops which through his ingenuity and perseverance were to grow into the E. W. Bliss Company and the United States Projectile Company, concerns which at his death employed 1,300 men. Bliss's mechanical interests developed along two lines: the manufacture of tools, presses, and dies for use in sheet metal work, and the manufacture of shells and projectiles. For the former numerous patents were taken out, either his own inventions or patents assigned to him. Under his own name are machines for manufacturing and soldering metal cans and for shaping and casting sheet metal. One of the important orders which the company obtained was for part of the material used in the Brooklyn Bridge. From the time when Bliss had worked in the Parker gun factory, he had been interested in projectiles, and with the development of his machine shops he naturally turned to this phase. The E. W. Bliss Company obtained control of the patents for the manufacture of the Whitehead torpedo in use in the navy, while the United States Projectile Company during his later life manufactured most of the shells in use in the large guns in the navy. In addition to his machine shops Bliss was deeply interested in the development of Brooklyn. He invested heavily in real estate, was vice-president of the Brooklyn Heights Railroad and of the Brooklyn Gas Fixture Company, and was a director of the Kings County Trust Company. His residence, "Owl's Head," located on the heights of Bay Ridge, contained an observatory which swept the harbor and was long one of the "show estates" of Brooklyn. In his later years Bliss devoted much of his time to club activities. He was an active member of the leading New York and Brooklyn social and athletic organizations, particularly the latter, maintaining a membership in five important yacht clubs. The bulk of his large estate went to his widow, with some provisions for the Episcopal Church of Bay Ridge, of which he was a member, and for the maintenance of the E. W. Bliss Kindergarten which he had supported during his life.

[*Who's Who in America,* 1903; J. H. Bliss, *Geneal. of the Bliss Family in America* (1881); *N. Y. Tribune,* July 22, 1903, Aug. 14, 1903; *Sun* (N. Y.), July 22, 1903; *Brooklyn Daily Eagle,* July 22, 1903.]

H. U. F.

BLISS, GEORGE (Apr. 21, 1816–Feb. 2, 1896), merchant, banker, was a descendant of Thomas Bliss, who was driven from England by religious persecution and settled at Braintree, Mass., in 1635. The son of William and Martha (Parsons) Bliss, George Bliss was born at Northampton, Mass. The straitened means of his parents compelled him in his eighth year to leave school in order to aid in the farm work. His education thereafter was sporadic and broken. At sixteen, he took a clerkship in the dry-goods store of Harvey Sanford, in New Haven, and soon became a trusted agent of the owner. At eighteen years, he was the purchasing representative of the shop and was admitted into partnership in 1837, when only twenty-one years old. Three years later he married Catherine Sanford, the daughter of his partner. In 1844, having accumulated some small savings, he removed to New York and there joined John J. Phelps and S. B. Chittenden, forming the firm of Phelps, Chittenden & Bliss, at No. 12 Wall St., and engaging in the wholesale dry-goods trade. In 1853, upon the retirement of Chittenden, Bliss himself became the head of the firm, being joined by James H. Dunham and others, as George Bliss & Company, with headquarters at No. 340 Broadway. In spite of difficulties in the panic of 1857 and later, the firm was able to maintain itself. At the opening of the Civil War, Bliss recognized that the issue of irredeemable paper would result in advance of prices. He greatly extended his purchases, taking on long lines of goods which became immensely enhanced in selling value. He was also able to foresee the close of the war and sold heavily. Thus he laid a substantial foundation for his large fortune of later years. His first wife having died on Mar. 13, 1862, he married Augusta H. Smith of New Haven on July 22, 1868. The second phase of his career opened in 1869, when he retired from the dry-goods trade and joined Levi P. Morton in the banking business under the firm name of Morton, Bliss & Company. The new enterprise did a large and profitable business up to the panic of 1873, then suffered some moderate reverses but recovered its prosperity during the extensive government refunding operations between 1875 and 1879 in which it had an important part. Bliss was one of the comparatively few business men who believed that specie payments should and could be inaugurated at an early date. In April 1878, he personally advised the House Banking and Currency Committee to that effect. He correctly foresaw the great improvement in business conditions which would follow resumption and was able to take advantage of it in his regular routine of banking transactions. He was a Republican but by no means a mere partisan. He regarded the tariff bill of 1890 as a blunder and severely criticized the attitude of the Republican politicians on the silver question. During his later years, he made many public benefactions, including the stone church on Blackwell's Island and similar buildings elsewhere.

[The most complete source of information is a memoir written for private circulation by the late James Cross who was associated with Bliss in business; this is now in possession of the Bliss family. There is a good sketch in H. Hall, *America's Successful Men of Affairs*, vol. I (1895), and there are good obituaries in the *N. Y. Times*, *N. Y. Tribune*, and *Sun* (N. Y.), Feb. 3, 1896.]

H. P. W.

BLISS, GEORGE (May 3, 1830–Sept. 2, 1897), lawyer, was descended from Thomas Bliss, a farmer of Belstone, Devonshire, England, who left Plymouth for Boston in 1635 and settled at Braintree, Mass. Seventh in direct line of descent from Thomas, George Bliss of Springfield, Mass., was a leading lawyer, speaker of the lower house and president of the Senate of the state legislature, subsequently becoming prominent in western railway circles. He married Mary Shepherd Dwight, and their only son, George Bliss, Jr., was born at Springfield. He received his early education at home, and in May 1846 went to Europe, spending eighteen months in travel. In 1848 he entered Harvard College, graduating in 1851. While there he assisted David A. Wells in the preparation of two volumes of *The Annual of Scientific Discovery*. In 1851 he again went to Europe, remaining there two years, traveling extensively and studying at Paris and the University of Berlin. In 1853 he commenced the study of law at Springfield, and after a year at the Harvard Law School (LL.B. 1856) completed his course in New York City, being admitted to the New York bar in 1857. A strong Republican, he took an active interest in politics. In January 1859, he became private secretary to E. D. Morgan, the governor of New York, and at the outbreak of war in April 1861 joined the latter's staff. In 1862 he was appointed paymaster of the state with the rank of colonel. In that year he was also commissioned captain in the 4th New York Heavy Artillery. With the authority of the Secretary of War he, on behalf of the Union League Club, organized the 20th, 26th, and 31st Regiments of New York colored troops. At the close of the war he returned to law practise and, in 1866, was appointed attorney for the newly constituted Metropolitan Board of Excise and Board of Health. In this capacity he carried to a successful conclusion the heavy litigation involving the constitutionality of the legislation which created the boards, the New York court of appeals finally holding that the Acts were valid. In December 1872 Bliss was appointed United States attorney for the southern district of New York, retaining the position till Jan. 24, 1877. During his tenure of office he conducted the prosecutions which followed the disclosure of serious frauds in the customs service involving a loss to the government of over $1,000,000. He drafted, on behalf of the Republican general committee, the New York city charter of 1873, and remained closely in touch with all subsequent amendments, being also the promoter and draftsman of the original Tenement-House Act for the city. In 1879 he was appointed by the state legislature a member of the commission which, in that and the succeeding year, compiled *The Special and Local Laws Affecting Public Interests in the City of New York*. This was followed by *The New York City Consolidation Act* of which he was the draftsman. In 1882 he was retained by the federal government as special prosecutor to assist the Attorney-General in the celebrated "Star Route" postal conspiracy cases against Senator Stephen W. Dorsey, ex-Assistant Postmaster-General Brady, and others. In 1884, in association with F. R. Coudert, he represented the Roman Catholics of the state of New York before the constitutional convention in opposition to a proposed amendment forbidding state aid to religious and charitable institutions. In recognition of this and other services rendered to the Catholic Church, to which he had become a convert, Pope Leo XIII in 1895 conferred upon him the title of "Commendatore of the Order of St. Gregory the Great." He withdrew from active participation in politics toward the end of 1893. An intimate friend of President Arthur, and one time supporter of Roscoe Conkling, he had always refused, except during the stress of civil war, to be a candidate for or hold public office. Nevertheless, he occupied a dominant position in the Republican party counsels both federal and state. He died at Wakefield, R. I., Sept. 2, 1897.

As a lawyer in a broad sense he was always adequate, painstaking, and reliable, safe rather than brilliant. From the overthrow of the Tweed Ring down to the day of his death, he was intimately associated with all legislation affecting the interests of New York City, and his skill as a legislative draftsman was demonstrated in his work upon the city charter and as a codifier. He was the author of *The Law of Life Insurance* (1872); *The New York Code of Civil Procedure* (1877), of which there were several editions; and *The General Rules of Practice of all the Courts of Record of the State of New York* (1881). He was an occasional contributor to the *North American Review* and wrote much for the *New York Times* and *New York Tribune*. He was twice married: on Oct. 22, 1856, to Catherine Van Rennselaer Dwight of Springfield, who died in 1884; and on May 25, 1887, to Anais Casey, who survived him.

[His ancestry is traced in *Genealogy of the Bliss Family in America* (1881), by J. H. Bliss. A sketch of his life is contained in *Hist. of the Bench and Bar of N. Y.*, ed. by D. McAdam *et al.*, II, (1899), 44–46. Obituaries appeared in the *N. Y. Times, N. Y. Tribune, N. Y. Herald*, and *Sun* (N. Y.), Sept. 3, 1897.]

H.W.H.K.

BLISS, HOWARD SWEETSER (Dec. 6, 1860–May 2, 1920), missionary educator, was born at Suq al Gharb, Syria, the second son of Rev. Daniel Bliss [*q.v.*], and Abby (Wood) Bliss. Soon after his birth the family moved to Beirut in connection with the founding (1862–66) of Syrian Protestant College (now the American University of Beirut) under the father's presidency. In the cosmopolitan atmosphere of city and college Howard obtained his early education from his parents and from mission schools. He continued his studies in America in the Amherst (Mass.) High School, and in 1878 passed into Amherst College, from which he graduated in 1882 with honors. He served as instructor in Latin in Washburn College, Kansas, 1882–84 and then entered Union Theological Seminary, New York City. He graduated from the seminary in 1887 with the award of a traveling fellowship which enabled him to continue his studies in Mansfield College, Oxford, 1887–88, and in Göttingen and Berlin Universities, 1888–89. Returning to America in the fall of 1889, he was married on Nov. 7 to Amy, daughter of Eliphalet W. Blatchford of Chicago, Ill. In January 1890 he was ordained and then served with Dr. Lyman Abbott as assistant pastor of Plymouth Church, Brooklyn, until 1894. Thereafter until 1902 he was pastor of Union Congregational Church, Upper Montclair, N. J. In 1902 the trustees of Syrian Protestant College selected him to succeed his father in the presidency of that institution. He was formally inducted in May 1903. During his administration the campus area was considerably extended, the number of buildings doubled, the enrolment increased to about one thousand, and the teaching and adminstrative force increased to about eighty. Students were drawn from many lands—as widely separated as Russian Tartary and Newfoundland—and from the ranks of many different religious bodies. Bliss maintained the predominantly Christian character of the institution, but so liberal was his policy that toward the close of his administration non-Christian students were slightly in the majority. His tact, fearlessness, and perfect frankness in dealing with the Turkish Government during the World War enabled the college to continue its work with honor and dignity and almost without interruption. The four and one-half year strain, however, told severely upon Bliss's health. In 1919, while in Paris appearing before the Peace Conference on behalf of Syrian and Near Eastern affairs, he contracted his last illness. A short stay in his American home in Jaffrey, N. H., renewed his strength for a time and he went about filling public engagements until stricken with hemorrhage in Bridgeport, Conn. He died at Saranac Lake, N. Y., and was buried at his own request in Jaffrey, under the shadow of Mt. Monadnock. He was a man of fine personal presence and distinguished bearing, fearless yet patient, firm yet tactful. His Christian statesmanship is best seen in his remarkable paper on "The Modern Missionary," in the *Atlantic Monthly*, May 1920.

[J. H. Bliss, *Geneal. of the Bliss Family in America* (1881); *Who's Who in America*, 1919–20; Frederick J. Bliss, *Reminiscences of Daniel Bliss* (1920); *Amherst Coll. Biog. Record* (1921); annual reports of Syrian Protestant Coll.]

J. C. A.

BLISS, JONATHAN (Oct. 1, 1742–Oct. 1, 1822), jurist, was born in Springfield, Mass. Descended from Thomas Bliss of Belstone, Devon, he was the son of Capt. Luke and Mercy (Ely) Bliss. His parents were well-to-do, and he received a good education, entering Harvard College where he graduated in 1763. He then read law in the office of Lieutenant-Governor Hutchinson, where he was a fellow student of Sampson Salter Blowers [*q.v.*], and on his admission to the provincial bar, commenced practise in Boston. He acquired a good connection and quickly came to the front. In 1768 he was elected to the General Court of Massachusetts from Springfield, and was one of the minority of seventeen who were in favor of acceding to a demand of the home Government that a certain obnoxious vote should be rescinded—hence the reproachful term "rescinder." He was a consistent supporter of the British Government throughout the pre-revolutionary troubles. At the outbreak of hostilities in April 1775, he accompanied Earl Percy on his march to Concord following the skirmish at Lexington. Later in the same year he removed to England and resided there for nine years, joining the New England Club of Loyalists in London. His name appeared in the Massachusetts Proscription Act, 1778, as an enemy of the State, and as such he was forbidden to return thither. In 1785 he was appointed by the Crown attorney-general of the newly formed province of New Brunswick, and leaving England, took up his residence at St. John, N. B., where he practised for twenty-four years. The year of his arrival he was elected member for St. John in the House of Assembly, and was intimately associated with all the legislation of New Brunswick's formative period. His legal ability gave him a leading position at the bar, and he appeared as counsel in most of the important causes of his time. He was retained in 1790 by Benedict Arnold in the suit for slander which the latter brought against Manson Hart. In a test case on the subject of slavery heard in 1800 before the full bench, he appeared for the master. His speech "was divided into thirty-two heads" (J. W. Lawrence, *post*), despite which the court was divided in opinion. In 1809 he was appointed chief justice of New Brunswick and retained this position till his death at Frederickton, N. B. He married a daughter of Hon. John Worthington of Springfield, Mass. As a lawyer he ranked high in the estimation of his contemporaries, and in his public career he consistently adhered to the principles of loyalty to the Crown which he had imbibed in his youth. As attorney-general and chief justice he enjoyed the unreserved confidence and respect of the people of New Brunswick.

[His ancestry is fully detailed in *Genealogy of the Bliss Family in America* (1881), by J. H. Bliss, which also contains a short sketch of his life, p. 75. See also *The Judges of N. B. and Their Times* (1907), ed. by A. A. Stockton, p. 155; *The Am. Loyalists* (1847), by Lorenzo Sabine, I, 233; *1783–1883 Footprints, or Incidents in Early Hist. of N. B.* (1883), by J. W. Lawrence; and *Jour. and Letters of the late Samuel Curwen* (1842), ed. by G. A. Ward, p. 508; "Extracts from the Jour. of Edward Oxnard," *New Eng. Hist. and Geneal. Reg.*, XXVI (1872).]

H. W. H. K.

BLISS, PHILEMON (July 28, 1814–Aug. 24, 1889), congressman, jurist, was born in North Canton, Conn., of early Puritan stock through both parents, Asahel and Lydia (Griswold) Bliss. The family moved to Whitestown, N. Y., in 1821, where Philemon attended the local academy and Oneida Institute, but lack of funds compelled him to withdraw from Hamilton College in his sophomore year, and ill health cut short his training in a local law office. He began the active practise of law at Elyria, Ohio, in 1841, and two years later married Martha W. Sharp. His public career began in 1849 with his election by the Ohio legislature as judge of the 14th judicial district where he served until 1852. Of Federalist and Whig antecedents, he had campaigned actively for Clay in 1844, but his pronounced anti-slavery views carried him into the Free-Soil party in 1848 and later into the Republican. In 1854 he was elected to Congress from a formerly Democratic district and was re-elected in 1856. His dislike of controversy and his weak voice—he struggled all his life against bronchial and pulmonary weakness—unfitted him for debate, but his set speeches are able statements of the advanced anti-slavery, anti-state-sovereignty views. In 1861 he accepted an appointment as chief justice of Dakota Territory, hoping that the drier climate would relieve his throat trouble. Two years later he resigned, and coming to Missouri with improved health, in 1864, he brought his family to St. Joseph. Here he served as probate judge and as a member of the county court of Buchanan County; in 1867 he was appointed a curator of the state university, serving until 1872 and taking an active part in its reorganization. In 1868 he was elected to the state supreme court for a four-year term on the Radical or Republican ticket, and won the respect and confidence of all parties in a time of great political bitterness. The dominance of the Democratic party after 1872 ended his political career. In that year the curators of the university appointed him first dean of the newly created department of law, which position he held until his death in 1889. He died at St. Paul, Minn., whither he had gone for his health, and he was buried at Columbia, Mo.

While a man of decided convictions and unquestioned intellectual courage—he was a lifelong Republican in a state and community intensely Democratic—he had an essentially judicial and peaceful temperament. In spite of his lifelong struggle against physical weakness and his retiring disposition, he gave a great and well recognized service in the training of the post-bellum generation of lawyers, and in the restoration and advancement of the standards of the legal profession in Missouri. His sound legal knowledge is evidenced by his *Treatise upon the Law of Pleading under the Codes of Civil Procedure*

(1870), a text nationally used and frequently revised until superseded by the modern case method.

[J. H. Bliss, *Geneal. of the Bliss Family in America* (1881); *The Bench and Bar of St. Louis* (1884), pp. 376–79; W. F. Switzler, "Hist. of the Univ. of Mo." (MSS.).] J. V.

BLISS, PHILIP PAUL (July 9, 1838–Dec. 29, 1876), singing evangelist, was the writer of gospel songs which have had extraordinary popularity. They appeared as an adjunct to the organized revivalistic enterprises of the last half of the nineteenth century, furnishing the emotional atmosphere which contributed much to the success of Moody and other evangelists, and breathing the breath of life into the social meetings of the churches. Judged by standards of art they are decidedly inferior, but the masses could understand and sing them, and their melody, martial note, joyousness, and hope produced the religious exhilaration desired.

Philip Bliss was a tall, well-framed man, with clustering black hair, full beard, easy manners, buoyant spirit, and gifted with a rich baritone voice of wide range. Grandfather and great-grandfather had been Seventh Day Adventist preachers. The most of his youth was spent in Pennsylvania, where in a log house in Clearfield County he was born to Isaac and Lydia (Doolittle) Bliss. Until he was sixteen he worked on farm and in lumber camp, but got enough learning here and there to enable him to teach in schools in New York and Pennsylvania. At J. G. Towner's singing school in Towanda, Pa., and at the normal academy of music in Geneseo, N. Y., he received a little training in music. On June 1, 1859, he married Lucy J. Young, one of a family of singers.

He began his professional career by teaching music in Bradford County, Pa., at two dollars an evening and his board. Acquaintance with the composer and publisher, George F. Root [*q.v.*], led to his association with the firm of Root and Cady of Chicago sometime about 1865, and for nearly ten years he traveled over Illinois conducting musical conventions and giving concerts. He became chorister of the First Congregational Church, Chicago, superintendent of its Sunday-school, and a frequent singer at religious gatherings. His song book, *The Charm* (1871), made him popular as a composer of Sunday-school music. This was followed by *The Song Tree* (1872), *The Sunshine* (1873), *The Joy* (1873). Dwight L. Moody and Maj. D. W. Whittle persuaded him to take up evangelistic work, and during 1874–75–76 he traveled through the West and South with the latter. In 1874, with Ira Sankey, he brought out *Gospel Songs*, which contained "Hold the Fort," "Only an Armor Bearer," "Let the Lower Lights Be Burning," "Pull for the Shore," and other songs long unexcelled in popularity. Of the $60,000 profits he gave his share to charitable and evangelistic projects. The Ashtabula train disaster ended his career. Getting free from the wreck himself, he returned to his wife who was pinned down, and both were burned to death.

[J. H. Bliss, *Geneal. of the Bliss Family in Amer.* (1881); D. W. Whittle, *Memoirs of Philip P. Bliss* (1877); W. H. Daniels, *D. L. Moody and his Work* (1875); J. W. Hanson, *The Wonderful Life and Works of Dwight L. Moody* (1900).] H. E. S.

BLISS, PORTER CORNELIUS (Dec. 28, 1838–Feb. 2, 1885), journalist, was the son of the Rev. Asher Bliss, for many years a missionary to the Indians, and of Cassandra (Hooker) Bliss. Born on the Cattaraugus Reservation of Senecas in New York, his chief interest in childhood was in observing the habits and life of the Indians. When a young man, he studied for a year at Yale and received the degree of B.A. at Hamilton. In 1860 he began his travels by a tour through Maine, New Brunswick, and Nova Scotia, in the service of several Boston societies, to investigate the condition of Indian tribes in that region. After fulfilling this commission in 1861, he went to Washington, hoping to secure a position in the Interior Department which would give him the opportunity to continue his studies of the Indians beyond the Mississippi. He failed to obtain more than a clerkship, but when Gen. James Watson Webb was made minister to Brazil in 1861, Bliss was appointed his private secretary. Gen. Webb surrendered his office in 1862. Bliss, instead of returning to the States, made a trip to Buenos Aires. Almost immediately he was commissioned by the Argentine Republic to explore the country known as the Grand Chaco, an immense desert inhabited by Indian tribes. He spent eight months in this service, acquainting himself with various Indian dialects and studying the antiquities of the country and the habits of the natives. The results of his explorations were published by the Argentine government and are standard works on the Indian tribes of the Grand Chaco. Then for a short time Bliss edited a monthly periodical in Buenos Aires called the *River Plate Magazine*. In 1866 he went to Paraguay and became private secretary to Charles A. Washburn, who was serving as United States minister. The same year President Lopez appointed Bliss to write a history of Paraguay. While this work was in progress, Lopez declared war against Brazil, Uruguay, and the Argentine Republic, and from this event the trouble of the young historian began. Knowing that he had come from Brazil the Paraguayans suspected him of hostility to Lopez. Soon the archives of the government were closed to him and he was told that his contract was ended and that he would not be paid for his work. At about this time, Washburn resigned his position as minister and with Bliss prepared to sail for the States. On their way to the boat, Bliss was seized by the police and thrown into prison. For three months he was subjected to severe torture in efforts to force him to admit a conspiracy against Lopez. He was finally released at the demand of the United States Government and returned to Washington, where he was made translator to the State Department. At his request, the committee on foreign affairs of the House investigated the charges made against him in Paraguay and declared them unfounded. In 1870 President Grant appointed Bliss secretary of the legation to Mexico, which position he held for four years. While there he found time to study and write on the history, geography, and condition of Mexico and on American enterprises in that republic. He became an active member of the Mexican Geographical and Statistical Society and was chairman of its committee on archeological explorations. Reports of the latter were published in the bulletin of the society. In 1874 Bliss went to New York City and became one of the editors of *Johnson's New Universal Cyclopædia,* taking charge of the biographical department. He contributed over 1,500 biographies to that publication. He also wrote for it articles on Sanskrit and Portuguese literature. When the *Cyclopædia* was completed in 1877, Bliss became editor of a literary periodical called the *Library Table,* which venture soon failed. In 1878 he wrote in collaboration with Dr. L. P. Brockett, a history of the Russo-Turkish War, entitled *The Conquest of Turkey.* It is a very detailed and carefully written history, including the causes of the war, and the principals that took part in it. During the same year Bliss became one of the editors of the *New York Herald* and in 1879 he again visited South America as correspondent for the *Herald.* The material he sent back to his paper contained many bits of forgotten lore and many pieces of quaint erudition. He was perhaps the best informed man of his time concerning the political situation of the South American countries. He returned to the United States and in 1881 went to Mexico on a gold-hunting expedition on his own responsibility and in behalf of some friends. After this trip he failed rapidly in health and except for a few months, when he edited the *New Haven Morning News,* did no more active work. At the age of forty-seven he died, in New York City.

[The *N. Y. Herald,* Feb. 3, 1885, contains an obituary of Bliss. An interesting article dealing with his life and travels is found in the *N. Y. Times,* Jan. 5, 1885. *House Report No. 65,* 41 Cong., 2 Sess., gives a detailed account of his work and imprisonment in Paraguay; see also *Senate Exec. Doc. 5, Pt. 3,* 40 Cong., 3 Sess.]

M. S.

BLISS, WILLIAM DWIGHT PORTER (Aug. 20, 1856–Oct. 8, 1926), Christian Socialist, was the son of the missionaries, Edwin Elisha Bliss [*q.v.*] and Isabella Holmes (Porter) Bliss and was born in Constantinople, Turkey. He was educated in Robert College, Constantinople; Phillips Academy and Amherst College, Massachusetts, and the Hartford Theological Seminary, from the last-named of which he graduated in 1882. On June 30, 1884, he married Mary Pangalo, of Constantinople. As a Congregationalist he was for a time pastor of a church in Denver and later in South Natick, Mass. In 1886 he joined the Protestant Episcopal Church and for the years 1887–90 was the rector of Grace Church, South Boston. About this time he became deeply influenced by the Christian Socialist doctrines of Maurice and Kingsley, of which he continued an active exponent for the remainder of his life. In 1889 he organized the first Christian Socialist Society in the United States, and in the same year started a propagandist periodical, *The Dawn* (discontinued in 1896). In 1890 he founded the Church of the Carpenter, in Boston, of which for four years he was the rector. Other pastorates were at San Gabriel, Cal., 1898; Amityville, L. I., 1902–06, and West Orange, N. J., 1910–14.

His activities in social service covered a broad range. His lecture trips carried him to almost every state of the union. In 1887 he was the Labor party candidate for lieutenant-governor of Massachusetts; in 1894 national lecturer for the Christian Socialist Union and in 1899 president of the National Social Reform Union. From 1907 to 1909 he was an investigator for the United States Bureau of Labor and from 1909 to 1914 he was connected with Dr. Josiah Strong's American Institute of Social Service. His labors as writer, compiler, and editor were, when considered in the light of his other activities, prodigious. In 1891 he published collections of the social writings of Ruskin and Mill under the titles *The Communism of John Ruskin* and *Socialism, by John Stuart Mill,* and also an abridgment of Thorold Rogers's *Six Centuries of Work and Wages.* In 1895 he produced the

Handbook of Socialism, in 1897 the *Encyclopedia of Social Reform,* in 1906 (with W. H. Tolman) the third volume of *Social Progress, a Year Book,* and in 1908 a revised and greatly enlarged edition of the *Encyclopedia.* In collaboration with Dr. Strong he also produced *Studies in the Gospel of the Kingdom* and for a year (1895–96) edited a monthly periodical, *The American Fabian.* During the World War he was in charge of educational work among interned French and Belgian soldiers in Switzerland. From 1921 to 1925 he was rector of St. Martha's Church in New York City. Toward the end of his pastorate his health failed. He died, after a lingering illness, in St. Luke's Hospital, and his funeral was held in the Cathedral of St. John the Divine.

Bliss was an omnivorous reader and a tireless propagandist. Much of his editorial work, however, was too hurried to take first rank in scholarship. He was impatient to get things done; if the product was honest and a contribution to human welfare, it would do. He is best remembered for his moral force, his passion for justice, his crystalline sincerity and perfect disinterestedness. He believed what he professed; he was a missionary who carried his religion into the workaday world. Unaggressive, but persistent, he preached his gospel of social salvation to all who would listen or read, and did it with a sheer disregard of personal consequences. He died a poor man.

[*Who's Who in America,* 1926–27; obituaries in the *N. Y. Times* and the *N. Y. Herald Tribune,* Oct. 9, 1926; personal recollections of the writer.] W. J. G.

BLITZ, ANTONIO (June 21, 1810–Jan. 28, 1877), magician, is said to have been born in Kent, England, though his autobiographical *Fifty Years in the Magic Circle* (1871) mentions his seeing "white cliffs across the water" and his traveling to England from his birthplace. In this same work he tells of picking up tricks from passing gypsies, and of astonishing the countryside with them to such an extent that his father sent him out with a servant to make a fortune with his entertainment when he was thirteen years old. His first professional appearance was in Hamburg in 1823 and he was exhibited in central and western Europe for two years. Shortly after his return his mother died and he left home thereafter alone. His performances were often viewed with alarm by the superstitious country people, particularly as he was fond of playing practical jokes on the people wherever he happened to be. He had become a ventriloquist by this time and the ignorant were quite sure that the devil accompanied him. He married a Breton woman, whose first name was Marie, and in the following year the first of their several children was born. In 1834 he came to New York, appearing at the Masonic Hall and at Niblo's Garden with much success. He toured the States, the West Indies, Canada, and finally had a long engagement in Philadelphia, where he resided thenceforward. He was a genial little man with a fringe of whiskers, and not at all the type of the traditional magician, but he was very popular as is proved by the fact that he had thirteen imitators who even took his name with little alteration. He was also a bird-trainer and his combination of sleight-of-hand, ventriloquism, and bird tricks gave a program that was varied enough to avoid monotony. He appeared for a long time in Philadelphia at one of the museums established in imitation of Barnum's. Having made a moderate fortune he gave much time to performances for charity. His autobiography is devoted entirely to personal anecdotes and is of no literary value.

[Antonio Blitz, *Fifty Years in the Magic Circle* (1871); H. R. Evans, *The Old and the New Magic* (1906)—somewhat inaccurate; J. W. Forney, "Anecdotes of Public Men" in *Washington Sunday Chronicle,* Jan. 19, 1873, reprinted in the *Press* (Phila.), Jan. 20, 1873; obituary in *Phila. Inquirer,* Jan. 29, 1877.]

K. H. A.

BLOCK, ADRIAEN (fl. 1610–1624), Dutch mariner and explorer, first emerges from complete obscurity about 1610, when he made a voyage to the Hudson River, in company with Hendrick Christiaensen. In the spring of 1614 he was placed in command of one of a fleet of five sail sent out by the merchants of Amsterdam and Hoorn. The fleet ascended the Hudson River, where Block's vessel was accidentally burned. probably near the site of Albany. He then constructed the *Onrust,* a yacht forty-four and one-half feet long, in which he explored the region to the east of New York Bay. He sailed through the "Hellegat," so named by him, into Long Island Sound, explored "Roodeberg" (New Haven Harbor), and the "Versche Rivier" (the Connecticut), as far as an Indian village near the site of Windsor, Conn. He explored the island which bears his name, calling it "Adrianbloxeyland," although it was probably discovered in 1524 by Verrazano, who compared a "triangular shaped island" in this region to the Isle of Rhodes. Proceeding across Buzzards Bay and around Cape Cod, which he named Cape Bevechier, Block then explored "Wyck" (Massachusetts Bay) as far north as "Pye Bay," 42° 30′, which corresponds to Nahant Bay. Having exchanged vessels with Christiaensen he returned to Holland. The first detailed map of the southern New England coast, the "Figurative Map" of 1616, which became the basis of trading privileges to "New Netherland," was drawn as far as Cape Ann from data furnished by Block (thence northward being probably modeled after Champlain's map of 1607, or a common original). Block probably did not return to America. Early in 1615, in command of a whaling fleet, he sailed for Spitzbergen, and in December 1624 was still engaged in that industry.

[Our knowledge of Block's voyages is largely derived from Johan de Laet's *Nieuwe Wereldt* (1625) and N. J. van Wassenaer's *Historisch Verhael* (1624–1625). Translations of the pertinent parts of these works will be found in *N. Y. Hist. Soc. Coll.*, 2 ser., vols. I, II; E. B. O'Callaghan, *Doc. Hist. of the State of N. Y.*, vol. III (1850); and J. Franklin Jameson, *Narratives of New Netherlands* (1909). J. R. Brodhead, *Hist. of the State of N. Y.*, vol. I (1853), is the principal secondary authority. The Figurative Map is reproduced in Brodhead, *Docs. Rel. to the Col. Hist. of the State of N. Y.*, vol. I. A model of the *Onrust* may be seen in Congress Hall, Philadelphia.] R. H.

BLODGET, LORIN (May 25, 1823–Mar. 24, 1901), statistician, climatologist, publicist, was descended from Thomas Blodget, merchant, of London, England, who was one of the first sworn as freemen at the founding of Boston, 1632. His grandfather was a soldier in the Revolutionary War (American side), and his father served in the War of 1812. His parents, Arba Blodget (1789–1838) and Bebe (Bullock) Blodget, lived on a farm near Jamestown, N. Y. He was educated at the Jamestown, N. Y., Academy and at Geneva (now Hobart) College, but did not graduate, having to leave college because of his father's death. When a youth of but seventeen, he taught a country school in Chautauqua County, N. Y. He early developed an active interest in politics and in 1848 took the stump as a Whig against the nomination of Taylor for president, and was a delegate to the convention that nominated Van Buren. When about twenty years of age he became one of the voluntary meteorological observers of the Smithsonian Institution; and in 1851 was appointed "assistant professor" at the Institution, in charge of researches on climatology. In this capacity he prepared, and in 1857 published, his *Climatology of the United States,* a quarto of 536 pages, in which there are full comparisons of the climate of this country with those of Europe and Asia at the same latitudes. It was based on all the appropriate meteorological data that he could obtain; *viz.,* those which for years had accumulated in the Surgeon General's Office, those gathered by the Smithsonian Institution, and many furnished by individuals in various parts of the country. This first work of importance on the climatology of any portion of America was so carefully and thoroughly done that the subsequent myriads of observations have essentially but confirmed Blodget's major conclusions.

During 1852–56 he was employed on the Pacific Railroad survey for the War Department, and directed the determinations of altitudes and gradients by the use of the barometer. The latter portion of this time he was in the War Office to which he had been transferred. From 1857 to 1864 he was associate editor of the *North American* of Philadelphia, and wrote for it numerous editorials; and from 1858 to 1865 secretary of the Philadelphia Board of Trade. He originated the Bounty Fund of Philadelphia during the Civil War, raised $530,000, and was secretary of the Fund. In 1863 he was placed in charge of the financial and statistical reports of the United States Treasury; and in the following year published his *Commercial and Financial Resources of the United States.* From 1865 to 1877 he was United States appraiser of merchandise, appointed by Lincoln, and residing in Philadelphia. He prepared tariff acts and bills, and wrote reports on finance, revenue, industrial progress, and censuses of industry, which fill some 150 volumes and 350 pamphlets. In addition to his other and varied interests, he took an active part in the meetings and deliberations of several scientific societies, especially the American Association for the Advancement of Science and the American Philosophical Society, of which he was a member. In 1856 he married Mary Elizabeth Gibbs of Alexandria, Va.

[*Who's Who in America,* 1899–1900; *Phila. Inquirer,* Mar. 24, 25, 1901; *Public Ledger* (Phila.), Mar. 25, 1901; information from Mrs. John Molitor, Germantown, Philadelphia, Pa.] W. J. H.

BLODGET, SAMUEL (Apr. 1, 1724–Sept. 1, 1807), merchant, manufacturer, canal builder, was born in Woburn, Mass., the son of Caleb and Sarah (Weyman) Blodget. Caleb was an innholder, moderator of "proprietor's meetings," and the promoter of the first stage line between Haverhill and Boston. Very little is known of the early life of Samuel though his subsequent attainments indicate that he received the limit of the education then available. He served in the French and Indian Wars and was at Louisburg in 1745. He then bought and worked a farm in Goffstown for a short time before returning to the army as sutler to the New Hampshire Regiment, seeing action at Fort William Henry (1757). Shortly after this he successfully engaged in general merchandising in Boston, later manufacturing potash and pearl-ash. which part of his business he extended to Hempstead, Goffstown, New Boston, and other places, with his main establishment at Haverhill (1760).

In these places he continuously expanded his activities, establishing stores for his employees, purchasing lands and timber, and erecting sawmills. His lumber was sold in Haverhill and Newbury and his potash and furs in London where he had profitable business arrangements with Sir William Baker. In 1769 he moved with his family from Boston to Goffstown to be more conveniently located for business. Here he was prominent in the community and was given the first appointment of justice of the inferior court for the County of Hillsborough. About this time he began to consider the construction of a canal around the Amoskeag Falls of the Merrimac, to more conveniently connect his timber lands with the markets. But then the Revolutionary cause attracted him and in 1775 he joined Gen. Sullivan's Brigade as a sutler, remaining with it until the army left Boston when he returned to his farm. During the latter part of the war he developed a device for raising sunken ships, in the operation of which he spent four years in Europe with very little success. Returning to Amoskeag and his plans for the canal, he commenced actual construction on May 2, 1794. The work progressed rapidly to the point of the building of the locks, for which Blodget had an original design, but here he met repeated failure and in 1780 an unusually high freshet carried off the locks and ruined the work of five years, with a personal loss to Blodget of $20,000. In 1798 he had obtained a charter and now after agreeing to adopt a proven type of lock he was able to sell stock to raise funds. He then appealed to the legislature of New Hampshire and was authorized to raise $9,000 by lottery, but after expending $12,000 and failing to complete the canal he received another lottery grant of $12,000, with the managers of which he became involved in such a legal tangle that the project would have failed had not the Massachusetts legislature now aided him with lottery grants in that state. The locks were completed in December 1806, and the canal was officially opened on "May Day," 1807, to render valuable service to the community until supplanted by the railroad many years later (1842). Blodget married Hannah White of Haverhill in 1748. He died Sept. 1, 1807, at Derryfield, Mass.

[Isaac D. Blodgett, *Asahel Blodgett, his Am. Ancestors and his Descendants* (1906); G. W. Chase, *Hist. of Haverhill, Mass.* (1861); C. E. Potter, *Hist. of Manchester, N. H.* (1856); *Manchester Hist. Soc. Colls.*, I, 121–76.]

F. A. T—r.

BLODGET, SAMUEL (Aug. 28, 1757–Apr. 11, 1814), merchant, economist, architect, was born in Goffstown, N. H., the son of Samuel [*q.v.*] and Hannah (White) Blodget. The character of his father, a man of long business experience and much imagination, seems to have been reflected in that of the son. The latter served in the Revolution, as a captain of New Hampshire militia, resigning Dec. 22, 1777. He then engaged in business in Exeter, N. H., and, this proving unsuccessful, went into the East India trade in Boston, acquiring a fortune. In 1789 he removed to Philadelphia where in 1792 he became one of the directors of the Insurance Company of North America. This same year he married Rebecca Smith, the daughter of the Rev. William Smith, provost of the University of Pennsylvania. She was a notable beauty and wit, whose irrepressible remarks on her husband's "comical look" are borne out by his portrait in the office of the Superintendent of the Capitol at Washington.

Although not a professional architect, he designed the building of the first Bank of the United States in Philadelphia, still standing after having been occupied for a century by Girard's Bank. It was the first important building in America to be executed in marble, and was occupied in 1794. The design was taken from that of the Exchange in Dublin, a work of Thomas Cooley. Blodget may have known this through Malton's engraving, which had just appeared, or he may have seen the original, since he had more than once visited Europe. Of the Bank of the United States, B. H. Latrobe, though criticizing both the prototype and the execution of Blodget's design, admits that the columns have a very beautiful appearance (*Journal of Latrobe*, p. 84), and commends it as "a bold proof of the spirit of the citizens who erected it, and of the tendency of the community to *force* rather than *retard* the advancement of the arts" (*Anniversary Oration before the Society of Artists in Philadelphia,* May 8, 1811).

In 1792 Blodget began to be interested in the new Federal City. He commenced to buy Washington real estate in 1792 and from that date became very actively engaged in the promotion of its realty developments, the erection of public buildings, and the founding of a national university at the new capital, which he was the first to suggest. His time was completely engrossed in the interests of Washington. During a visit to Boston for the purpose of floating a loan to secure money for the erection of federal buildings Blodget prepared a competitive design for the Capitol, with a tall dome and four Corinthian porticoes modeled on those of the Maison Carrée. This was sent to the Commissioners of the Federal City in Philadelphia on July 1, 1792 (War

Department, Office of Public Buildings and Grounds, *Letters to Commissioners,* II, III). Although it arrived after July 15, the date of the closing of the competition, the design was considered at the Commissioners' meeting of August 27. In presenting this plan Blodget asked that it be considered only as a study. The Commissioners invited him to submit complete drawings, sending for his use a statement of some changes in requirements. Blodget seems, however, not to have availed himself of this opportunity for there is no mention of a second design. No example of his draughtsmanship remains, his first study having doubtless been returned to him. Another design for the city of Washington was that for a bridge over the Eastern Branch submitted to the Commissioners Nov. 27, 1795 (Department of State, *District of Columbia Papers,* II, 107). The record of its reception makes no comment on the features of the plan nor is there any further mention to show whether or not it was the one executed in 1804 (W. B. Bryan, *A History of the National Capital,* 1914, I, 427). On February 10, 1797, Blodget wrote the Commissioners of his success in executing an amphitheatre 249 feet in circumference on the scheme of the Halle aux Blés in Paris, and undertook to submit a model, with a view to the construction of the proposed dome for the Conference Room of the Capitol (Office of Public Buildings and Grounds, *Letters Received,* II, 1060). His efforts in design and his endeavors to erect numerous houses and a hotel were all a part of Blodget's sustained effort toward the development of Washington. In the year 1793 he held official position as "Superintendent of the Buildings," the active representative of the Commissioners. The office, however, was allowed to expire with the end of Blodget's term of one year.

In promoting the sale of Washington real estate Blodget's resort to lotteries, though they were at first sanctioned by the authorities, finally brought him into discredit. Moreover, the failure of both lotteries brought Blodget's financial ruin, since he had put up his property as security for the payment of the prizes. It is of interest to note that the principal prize of the first lottery was to be a hotel to cost $50,000. The plans for this building, known as Blodget's Hotel, were prepared by James Hoban, the architect of the President's House, and the structure was in part completed by Blodget. The prizes for the second lottery were houses to be erected in the city, the best one to cost $30,000. It was further proposed that such funds as were left after the payment of these prizes should go toward the founding of the national university. Although Blodget's schemes were economically unsound and impractical there is no evidence that he acted in bad faith, and the fact of his complete financial downfall attests the sincerity of his belief in the lotteries and other ventures. Even while imprisoned for debt he solicited funds for the national university, and upon his release after a short period this project seems to have been his principal interest. At his death he left a fund of $7,000 collected for this purpose. A general likeness is apparent between the fate of Blodget and that of Robert Morris and other too sanguine investors of the time. So completely did he finally drop out of public affairs that his death in a Baltimore hospital in 1814 received no notice in the Washington papers.

[The principal events of Blodget's career are documented in W. B. Bryan's *Hist. of the National Capital,* I (1914). His connection with the Bank of the United States is traced by J. T. Scharf and T. Westcott, *Hist. of Phila.* (1884), II, 1068; with the Capitol, by F. Kimball and W. Bennett in the *Jour. of the Am. Institute of Architects,* Jan., Mar. 1919, as well as by G. Brown, *Hist. of the U. S. Capitol* (1900). Some letters regarding him are printed in *Records of the Columbia Hist. Soc.,* XVII (1914). Details of his land speculations may be gleaned from the *Pa. Archives,* ser. III, vols. XXIV–XXV. His own published writings include two volumes on economics, *Thoughts on the Increasing Wealth and National Economy of the U. S.* (1801) and *Economica: a Statistical Manual for the U. S.* (1806), the latter including personal reminiscences and apologetics.]

W. B—t.

BLODGETT, BENJAMIN COLMAN (Mar. 12, 1838–Sept. 22, 1925), pianist, organist, music-teacher, composer, was born in Boston, Mass., the son of Henry and Louise (Allen) Blodgett. His first musical instruction was received from James Hooton, pianist, and W. R. Babcock, organist. At the age of twelve he became organist of the Essex Street Congregational Church, and three years later of the Eliot Church in Newton. In 1858 he went to Leipzig, where three years were spent in study with Moscheles, Plaidy, Richter, and Hauptmann. Then he returned to Boston, became organist of the Park Street Church, and was active as a teacher and concert pianist. He was married on Mar. 5, 1862, to Alethea E. Pulsifer of Newton, Mass. His work from 1865 as teacher of music at Maplewood Institute, Pittsfield, Mass., led to the organization of a separate music school in 1870, under Blodgett's direction. He became director of music and teacher of piano playing at Smith College, Northampton, Mass., in 1878, and two years later assumed the direction of the School of Music affiliated with the College. He remained in this position for twenty-five years until 1903. In 1904 he went to Leland Stanford University, Palo Alto, Cal., as organist and director of the choir, with a daily organ recital in the chapel as a part of his duties. The destruction of the chapel by the earthquake of April

1906 interrupted this series, and shortly afterward Blodgett retired from active musical work. His last years were spent with his family in Seattle, Wash.

The educational work done by Blodgett at Northampton was advanced and noteworthy. He gave frequent lecture-recitals, displaying marked powers as a pianist and ability in speaking. His organ playing was distinguished by an unusual talent for improvisation. A personal friend of Wagner, Blodgett attended the first performance at Bayreuth in 1876, and the first performance of *Parsifal* in 1882. His published compositions include études for the piano, church music, and a cantata, "The Prodigal Son" (1895). The unpublished works are headed by an oratorio on the Book of Job, written for women's voices for the Smith College commencement of 1889, and revised the following year (both versions with full orchestra).

[Sketch compiled chiefly from information supplied by friends and associates of Blodgett. Some personal reminiscences appeared in *Musical America,* June 2, 1917, and a short obituary was published in *Music and Musicians* (1925).]

C. N. B.

BLODGETT, HENRY WILLIAMS (July 21, 1821–Feb. 9, 1905), lawyer, was of English ancestry, the paternal family having been founded in Massachusetts in 1630. He was born at Amherst, Mass. His father, Israel Porter Blodgett, was a blacksmith; his mother, Avis (Dodge) Blodgett, is said to have been a woman of exceptional qualities and education. In 1831 the family removed to Illinois. His father was an abolitionist, whose house was a station on the underground railroad for escaped slaves. Many of his father's patrons were Indians, and many of his own early playmates were Indian boys. He was educated in the common schools, spending also one year in Amherst Academy. Thereafter he taught school, and finally in 1842 began the study of law. After his admission to the bar in 1844 he removed to Waukegan, Ill., which thenceforth remained his home. He was a delegate in 1848 to the Free-Soil Democratic convention which nominated Martin Van Buren; was the Free-Soil candidate for Congress from his district in 1850; was elected in 1852 as an anti-slavery man (the first ever so elected) to the Illinois state legislature; and helped to organize the Republican Party in the state. He remained a member of it from its beginning. From 1852 to 1854 he was a member of the Illinois House of Representatives, and from 1859 to 1863 a member of the state Senate. To him was largely due legislation giving married women independence in the control of their property. He was constantly in the front line of anti-slavery agitation in the decade before the Civil War. In 1860 he was a delegate to the Republican national convention that nominated Lincoln. After this early dip into politics the law absorbed all his interest. He was associated, in particular, with the legal departments of several railroads, and of one, which became the important Chicago & Northwestern, he was the main promoter, attorney, director, and president. In 1869 he was appointed United States district judge for the northern district of Illinois, and in 1891 was chosen as one member of the newly established circuit court of appeals, seventh circuit. It seems probable that the allowance of priority to receivers' certificates over a railroad first mortgage originated with him (being derived from admiralty doctrine), though it was a fellow judge who first so held. Among the famous cases that came before him as a federal judge were the Whiskey Ring cases of 1876. He resigned his judicial offices in 1892 to act as one of the counsel for this country in the Bering Sea arbitration, an appointment amply justified by his great reputation as an admiralty lawyer. One unfortunate episode marked his judicial career. In 1877, upon the initiative of certain individual members of the Chicago Bar Association, inquiries were made by a Congressional committee in contemplation of his impeachment. They found that the Judge had borrowed money from his referees (though not out of the funds of bankrupt estates in their hands) but had repaid it all with interest; other charges were found unsupported. The committee acquitted him of dishonest intent and did not impeach him (*House Report No. 142* and *House Miscellaneous Document No.22,* 45 Cong., 3 Sess.).

Blodgett was a truly distinguished lawyer. In common law, equity, criminal, patent, bankruptcy, and admiralty law he was equally a master. He had a keen logical, acutely analytical mind, great experience in large business problems, unusual insight into men, sound judgment in both law and practical affairs. To these ideal judicial qualities he added patient industry in research and an encyclopedic memory. His face was strong and commanding. An injury to one of his legs gave him a peculiar and ungainly gait; possibly owing to the same injury he was irascible, and sometimes impatient with tyros. He was also characterized by some prejudices—including a dislike of stenographers. He took very voluminous notes of cases in his court, made up his record according to them and his memory, regardless of the records of these "nimble-fingered gentry," and by his notes determined bills of exceptions and certificates of evidence. Such faults were compensated for by his ability, learning, conscientiousness in studying his cases, and abhorrence of subterfuges and delays in procedure. On the whole he was a unique personality and a very great judge. In his home surroundings he was a charming companion, in whom humor and a natural dignity, unconscious and never assertive, were strong characteristics. He married (Apr. 29, 1850) Althea Crocker of Hamilton, N. Y., by whom he had five children, of whom three daughters lived to maturity. In religious views he was first a Congregationalist, and finally a Unitarian.

[John M. Palmer, *Bench and Bar of Illinois* (1899), I, 245; *Portrait and Biog. Album of Lake County, Ill.* (1891); *Chicago Legal News*, Feb. 11, 1905.]

F. S. P.

BLOEDE, GERTRUDE (Aug. 10, 1845–Aug. 14, 1905), poet, was born in Dresden, Germany, the daughter of Dr. Gustavus Bloede, a German Liberal, and his wife Marie, half-sister of the Silesian poet Friedrich von Sallet. Dr. Bloede, after imprisonment in Dresden during the Revolution of 1848, escaped to America with his family and settled in Brooklyn, N. Y., where he was for years editor of the *New-Yorker Demokrat*, a Republican daily. Gertrude was privately educated, was a natural student, and became a musician and a linguist of ability. She spoke English, French, and German fluently and read Latin, Italian, and Dutch without difficulty. The Bloede home was a center for literary gatherings, frequented by such men as Stoddard, Stedman, Aldrich, and Bayard Taylor. With these associations, Gertrude Bloede early began to try her hand at writing. Her first published work was in the form of verses contributed to magazines under the pseudonym Stuart Sterne. A volume of *Poems* appeared in 1875 and was favorably reviewed by Richard Grant White, critic of the *New York Times*, who also helped to find a publisher for the narrative poem *Angelo* (1878). Three other volumes of verse followed; *Giorgio* (1881), *Beyond the Shadow and Other Poems* (1888), and *Piero da Castiglione* (1890). A novel, *The Story of Two Lives* (1891), was Miss Bloede's only sustained prose writing. She lived at the time of her death with her sister, Mrs. Susan T. King of Greene Ave., Brooklyn. She died while on a summer sojourn at Baldwin, L. I. Her small, large-eyed, serious face showed her tense, nervous temperament. She shunned general society and steadily refused membership in women's clubs and participation in other women's activities of Brooklyn. She cared for the companionship only of intimate friends whose pursuits were, like her own, intellectual. She loved city life, not for its diversions, but because she could find in it greater retirement than in the country. Her poetry shows much feeling but little inspiration; the form is stiff, lacking in musical quality, and often inadequate to the thought. Her narrative poems are introspective and emotional, but undramatic. *Angelo* has for its subject the friendship of Michelangelo and Vittoria Colonna and ends with the death of Vittoria. *Giorgio* tells the story of the painter Giorgione and his unhappy love. *Piero da Castiglione*, her most facile long poem, is a story of struggle between love and priestly vocation during the time of Savonarola. Her shorter poems are subjective reactions to beauty in the outside world, common human experiences, and religious theories, and are perhaps more adequate in form than the longer poems. Her novel, *The Story of Two Lives*, written chiefly in the form of a journal, is slow in action, devoid of characterization, and conventional in phrasing.

[The chief sources of information about Gertrude Bloede are *Who's Who in America*, 1903–05, and her own works, including the prefaces, which reveal much of her personality. A sketch of her life appeared in *Am. Women* (1897), ed. by Frances Willard and Mary A. Livermore. An obituary notice was published in the *Brooklyn Daily Eagle*, Aug. 16, 1905.]

S. G. B.

BLOOD, BENJAMIN PAUL (Nov. 21, 1832–Jan. 15, 1919), philosopher, mystic, and poet, was descended on his father's side from Jeremiah Blood, an Irish emigrant of the middle of the eighteenth century. Jeremiah's son Robert was a thrifty farmer who acquired large holdings in Schenectady and Montgomery counties, N. Y.; he married Mary Simons (Simmons), by whom he had nineteen children, one of whom, John, was the father, by Mary Stanton, of Benjamin Paul Blood. On his mother's side the latter was descended from John Howland, the *Mayflower* Pilgrim. He was born and brought up in the town of Amsterdam, N. Y.; he attended the local schools of Amsterdam, Amsterdam Academy, and, for a time, Union College; in due course he inherited a farm which had been in the family for one hundred and thirty years. He was twice married: first to Mary E. Sayles, who died in 1873; and second to Harriet A. Lefferts. His long life, passed in and near his birth-place, was almost devoid of outward incident. Too self-sufficient to feel the need of travel, incurious as to the details of the world, he found in his inner life and in his reading of poetry and philosophy material for sufficiently rich experience. His career as an author began early. Before he was twenty-one he had completed *The Bride of the Iconoclast* (not published until 1854), a long Shelleyesque poem in Spenserian stanzas, and *The Philosophy of Justice* (1851), the writing of which converted him, temporarily, from atheism to a very unorthodox Christianity. These works show an astonishingly precocious subtlety of thought and mastery of style in both prose and verse. Blood had already elaborated a definite theory as to the relation of sound to sense, somewhat similar to the theories of Plato, Swedenborg, and Burns (see his valuable "Suggestions Towards the Mechanical Art of Poetry" in *The Bride of the Iconoclast,* partially reprinted in *Pluriverse* as a supplementary essay on "The Poetical Alphabet"). Some unknown cause now intervened, however, to inhibit Blood's productivity. At long intervals there appeared from his pen, *Optimism* (1860), an attempted theodicy, and *The Colonnades* (1868), a philosophical epic in blank verse. For the rest he contributed when the mood took him an occasional letter to "such far-from reverberant organs of publicity as the *Gazette* or the *Recorder* of his native Amsterdam, or the *Utica Herald* or the *Albany Times*" (William James, "A Pluralistic Mystic," *Hibbert Journal,* VIII, 738). Had it not been for his personal experience with anæsthetics (nitrous oxide), an experience first obtained prosaically in a dentist's chair and then repeated poetically and voluntarily during a period of twenty-seven years, Blood might have remained all his life in contented obscurity. Impressed by the quasi-mystical state of philosophic certainty and peace induced by anæsthetics, seemingly an attainment of consciousness of pure being, he printed in 1874 *The Anæsthetic Revelation and the Gist of Philosophy,* which he mailed to numerous authors in this country and in Europe. As a result there ensued a remarkably fruitful correspondence, notably with Hutchison Stirling, Alfred Tennyson, and William James. In 1889 several of Blood's earlier letters to newspapers appeared in a revised form as quasi-Hegelian "Philosophic Reveries" in the *Journal of Speculative Philosophy,* XX, 1–53. He steadily moved, however, toward a more dynamic and pluralistic philosophy which found its final expression in his intransigeant *Pluriverse* (published posthumously in 1920). Horace Meyer Kallen, who knew Blood personally, writes (letter to author), "At heart he was, I think, a monist always." In that case, Blood's intellect triumphed strikingly over his emotions, for his critique of monism in *Pluriverse* was ruthless. He was a keener reasoner than either James or Bergson, and, if he entered late into the ranks of the pragmatists, he brought to them a much-needed dialectical ability. Poetry seems to have tempted him less in later years, although he contributed from time to time a number of short poems to *Scribner's Magazine* (December 1888, July 1899, March 1900, December 1901, January 1903, March 1915, January 1919). His last acknowledged prose was an Introduction to the anonymous *A Capitalist's View of Socialism* (1916). Old age did not break his serenity of spirit and he could write "I am thankful at having seen the show; and although, after eighty-five years, the stars are flickering slightly, and the winds are something worn, I am still clear and confident in that religion of courage and content which cherishes neither regrets nor anticipations" (*Pluriverse,* p. 245).

[The biographical material is singularly scanty. The present sketch is chiefly based upon Horace Meyer Kallen's introduction to *Pluriverse* and upon information supplied by Mr. Kallen and by Blood's daughter, Miss Anna W. Blood of Amsterdam, N. Y.] E. S. B.

BLOODWORTH, TIMOTHY (1736–Aug. 24, 1814), politician, was born in New Hanover County, N. C., and died in Washington, N. C. He had few social or educational advantages. James and Thomas Bloodworth, politicians, are mentioned as his brothers, but there is no further record of his domestic relationships. He is reported to have adorned eight or ten occupations, ranging, by way of the ministry, from cobbler and wheelwright to United States Senator and philanthropist at large. In January 1775 he was a member of the New Hanover County Committee of Safety, and two years later he was one of the eleven justices present at that county's first non-royal court. As a state legislator, 1779–84, he supported a relentless policy against all who had remained loyal to England. In 1784 he was elected to represent North Carolina in the Continental Congress in New York, but was given no money for his expenses. This oversight did not delay him, since at other times he had advanced the state money out of his own pocket. He resigned from the Congress in August 1787 and returned to North Carolina to help dissuade the state from ratifying the proposed Federal Constitution. His view was the popular one, but circumstances outside the state proved strong enough to compel ratification. Locally he honored no such compulsion. As lieutenant-colonel of the militia in the Wilmington district, he refused in 1793 to execute orders enforcing Washington's proclamation of neutrality in the war between France and England. He was intensely radical, almost, said a North Carolina historian writing of him in the 1870's, "a red Republican in his views, and intolerant of opposition." At the time, this attitude carried him to the United States Senate, a haven which in 1789 he had sought vainly. He was in the Senate Dec. 7, 1795–Mar. 3, 1801, but he evidently left no great impression. That fervor, in fact, which was his chief political merit, had never been conspicuously operative in affairs of more than sectional interest. When he resigned his office in 1807 he had achieved something like venerableness, and he was settled off as collector of customs for the port of Wilmington. This place he filled placidly until he died. Almost all his life he stood against the main trend of history, and sixty years after his death even a newspaper editor in the North Carolina state capital was obliged to admit that he had never heard of him.

[The sources of this sketch are W. E. Dodd, "Timothy Bloodworth" in S. A. Ashe, *Biog. Hist. of N. C.* (1905); *Biog. Cong. Dir.* (1903); James Sprunt, *Chronicles of the Cape Fear River* (1916); A. M. Waddell, *Hist. of New Hanover County* (1909); J. H. Wheeler, *Reminiscences and Memoirs of N. C.* (1884).]
J. D. W.

BLOOMER, AMELIA JENKS (May 27, 1818–Dec. 30, 1894), reformer, was born in Homer, Cortland County, N. Y., the daughter of Augustus Jenks who was killed at the battle of Gettysburg. Her education was limited to a few terms at the district school. At seventeen she herself taught a short term. She then lived for several years with a married sister in Waterloo, N. Y. In 1837 she was governess and tutor of three small children in the family of Oren Chamberlain near Waterloo. Three years later she was married to Dexter C. Bloomer, a young Quaker. Through the influence and encouragement of her husband who was much interested in current events, as editor and part owner of the weekly Whig newspaper, the *Seneca County Courier,* Mrs. Bloomer began to write unsigned articles for newspapers on the social, moral, and political questions of the time. At the first public meeting on woman's rights in 1848 in Seneca Falls, in which Lucretia Mott and Mrs. Stanton were active, she was an interested spectator. She took no part in it, however, and did not sign the resolutions or the declaration of independence. Her earliest activity as a reformer was in the temperance movement. In January 1849 she started the *Lily,* one of the first papers of its kind published by a woman. For six years she continued its publication, writing vigorous articles on education, on unjust marriage laws, and, later, on woman's suffrage. She was therefore one of the actual pioneers in the woman's rights movement. Mrs. Stanton became an early contributor, writing over the name of "Sunflower." The subscribers increased in number from two or three hundred for the first issue to over 4,000 twice a month by 1853. From 1849 to 1853 Mrs. Bloomer entered a new field for women by becoming deputy to her husband who was postmaster of Seneca Falls. In 1850 the heading of her paper "published by a committee of ladies" was dropped and Mrs. Bloomer's name appeared alone as publisher and editor and a new heading "devoted to the interests of women" was substituted. But although throughout her life she devoted her efforts to temperance and woman's rights her name through newspaper publicity and ridicule is associated in the public mind with dress reform, which was actually first suggested by a conservative rival paper. This was merely an episode in her life, though perhaps an important one. After the ridicule began she continued to carry out the idea in practise until after a period of six or eight years the matter was dropped by the papers. The circulation of the *Lily* was much increased by the notoriety given her. Because of the dress she wore—an ordinary bodice, short skirt, and full trousers, later called "bloomers"—large crowds came out to hear her speak in New York City and other towns in New York State where she talked in 1853, together with Susan B. Anthony, the Rev. Antoinette L. Brown, and other leaders in the woman's movement. Horace Greeley sat on the platform at one of her talks and she was favorably reported in the *Tribune.* In this year, the Bloomers left Seneca Falls for Mt. Vernon, Ohio, where they lived for a year while Mr. Bloomer edited and was part owner of the *Western Home Visitor.* A year later they moved to Council Bluffs, Ia., which was their home until Mrs. Bloomer's death. The *Lily* was now sold, as Council Bluffs was too far from a railroad to make mailing it practicable, but Mrs. Bloomer kept up her interest throughout her life in the various questions it had advocated. She wrote and lectured and her home was always open to all friends of reform.

[D. C. Bloomer, *Life and Writings of Amelia Bloomer* (1895); Elizabeth Cady Stanton, *et al., Hist. of Woman Suffrage,* vol. I (1881), vol. II (1887); *Bloomerism, or the New Female Costume of 1851* (1851); *Ia. State Reg.* (Des Moines), Jan. 1, 1895.]
M. A. K.

BLOOMFIELD, JOSEPH (Oct. 18, 1753–Oct. 3, 1823), lawyer, soldier, was descended from Thomas Bloomfield, major in Cromwell's army, who emigrated from Woodbridge, on the river Deben in Suffolk, by way of Massachusetts to Woodbridge on Woodbridge Creek, Middlesex County, N. J. His descendants were noted for public spirit and in 1796 certain rural settlements in Essex County, N. J., were named "Bloomfield" (now an apartment-house suburb of Newark) after his great-great-grandson (J. W. Dally, *Woodbridge and Vicinity,* 1873, p. 1). The latter was born in Woodbridge, his father being Dr. Moses Bloomfield, a founder of the New Jersey Medical Society and a member of the colonial assembly and of the provincial congress, who freed fourteen slaves on July 4, 1783, to prove his belief in the Declaration of Independence. Joseph's mother was Sarah (Ogden) Bloomfield. He was educated at the Rev. Enoch Green's Classical Academy in Deerfield Street, Cumberland County, whence he went to study law in the home and office of Cortlandt Skinner, the Colony's royalist attorney-general, at Perth Amboy. Admitted to the New Jersey bar Nov. 12, 1774, he prepared to practise law at Bridgeton but in 1775 was commissioned captain in Col. Elias Dayton's Regiment (later the 3rd New Jersey) and took part in the Quebec expedition but got no further than the Mohawk Valley. As Gen. Schuyler's guard officer he brought the Declaration of Independence to Fort Stanwix, he became major and judge advocate of the northern army, and he fought at Monmouth and at Brandywine where "he was wounded in the bridle arm." Resigning in 1778, he married on Dec. 17, Mary, daughter of Dr. William McIlvaine of Burlington and Philadelphia. She died in 1818 but his second wife, Isabella (family name unknown), survived him. There were no children.

Settling in Burlington, the old capital of West Jersey, in 1794 Bloomfield commanded an infantry brigade of New Jersey militia and took an active part in suppressing the Whiskey Rebellion without bloodshed. He was mayor of the town, 1795–1800, clerk of the state assembly for several years, register of the court of admiralty, and attorney-general of New Jersey, elected in 1783, reelected in 1788, resigning in 1792 when he served as a presidential elector, opposing John Adams. Changing his politics to Jeffersonism, he was elected governor by the New Jersey legislature, 1801, over Richard Stockton. In 1802 a tie vote emptied the governor's chair, but Stockton withdrew after defeats in 1803 and 1804 so Bloomfield was returned unopposed until 1812. As governor he signed, 1804, the gradual emancipation act, amended 1846, which reduced the slave population of New Jersey from six per cent of the total in 1800 to eighteen individuals by 1860. He was a leader in the work of legal and gradual emancipation. The Bloomfield Compilation of New Jersey Laws, 1811, was named in his honor. As governor he was *ex officio* chancellor, but no record was made of his decisions though a few of his opinions were published much later. "A particular friend of Burr's," Bloomfield, as governor, requested the prosecutor of Bergen County to enter a *nolle prosequi* to the indictment of Aaron Burr for shooting Hamilton in their duel at Weehawken. This was done, as urged by leading Republicans, and Burr thus left free to preside at the impeachment trial of Justice Samuel Chase of the United States Supreme Court. In 1812 President Madison appointed Bloomfield brigadier-general in the United States Army. He commanded the 3rd Military District, headquarters at New York, organized and trained new troops, marched to Plattsburgh with eight thousand men, and, later, put Philadelphia "in a complete state of defence," largely by his own energy and money (*True American,* Trenton, Oct. 11, 1823). He was twice elected to Congress, sitting from Mar. 4, 1817, to Mar. 4, 1821.

In manner Bloomfield was of the old school, wearing always the ruffles, powdered hair and cue of Washington's day. Neither war nor politics ruffled his benevolent, courteous, and sensible good nature. His portrait in major-general's uniform, by W. H. Griffin, in the governor's office at Trenton, is a pleasing contrast to the dourness of other New Jersey patriots. Accounts describe him as housed and served "in the style of a gentleman of fortune," but he disliked his official title "Your Excellency." Bruised by the upset of his gig while viewing lands near Cincinnati, Ohio, in 1823, he was badly bled by local doctors and died on reaching home.

[There is a good sketch of Bloomfield by L. Q. C. Elmer, son of his friend and subaltern officer Jonathan Elmer, in his "Reminiscences," *N. J. Hist. Soc. Colls.,* VII, 114–37; also interesting notes by Wm. Nelson, *Ibid.,* IX, 36–40.] W. L. W—y.

BLOOMFIELD-ZEISLER, FANNIE. [See ZEISLER, FANNIE BLOOMFIELD, 1863–1927.]

BLOOMFIELD, MAURICE (Feb. 23, 1855–June 13, 1928), Orientalist and philologist, son of Solomon and Bertha (Jaeger) Bloomfield, was born in Bielitz, Austria, whence his parents came to the United States when he was four years old. They made their home first in Milwaukee and then in Chicago, where the boy's early schooling was received. At sixteen he entered the University of Chicago, remaining there for three years (1871–74), and finished his collegiate education at Furman University, Greenville, S. C. (1876–77), obtaining the degree of M.A. It appears that during these Greenville days the young man was influenced by the well-known Biblical scholar Crawford H. Toy to turn his attention to Oriental studies, and he became a graduate student at Yale University for the academic year 1877–78, specializing in Sanskrit and comparative philology under the renowned William Dwight Whitney. On completing this year of advanced work he was awarded a fellowship in the newly opened Johns Hopkins University at Baltimore, where Charles Rockwell Lanman, five years his senior and afterward distinguished as professor of Sanskrit at Harvard, became his preceptor. He received from Johns Hopkins the degree of Ph.D. in 1879, the title of his dissertation being "Noun-formation in the Rig-Veda." After two fruitful years in Germany (1879–81), where he studied at the universities of Berlin and Leipzig under the acknowledged masters of his day in the field of Indology and Indo-European philology, he was called back to the Johns Hopkins University, in 1881, as professor of Sanskrit and comparative philology, and entered upon his long scholarly career, rendered famous by his teaching, researches, and publications.

Bloomfield was not only eminently successful as a teacher but the number likewise of his published writings, always recognized for their excellence and originality, was particularly large. The combined list (referred to in the bibliography below) comprises nearly two-hundred entries of articles and reviews contributed to learned journals on subjects relating to the languages, literature, history, and religion of ancient India, as well as on comparative and historical grammar. His chief fame rests on his important volumes concerned with editing, translating, or interpreting the sacred texts of the Vedas. His great *Vedic Concordance* (1906), which was crowned by the Royal Academy of Bavaria with the Hardy Prize, will ever remain a standard work, and of like value and usefulness are the two volumes of *Rig-Veda Repetitions,* published in 1916. A compact and very suggestive book, entitled *The Religion of the Veda* (1908), presents in admirable form a series of lectures which he delivered that year in the course of American Lectures on the History of Religion. While constantly engaged in the study and interpretation of the Rig-Veda, he devoted himself likewise to the exposition of the Atharva-Veda, on which he became the foremost authority, editing the *Kauçika-Sutra of the Atharva-Veda* (1890), followed by a translation of "Hymns of the Atharva-Veda" (1897, in the *Sacred Books of the East,* vol. XLII) and by an elaborate monograph "The Atharva-Veda" (1899, in the *Grundriss der indo-arischen Philologie und Altertumskunde,* vol. II, part 1 B). In 1901 there appeared the chromo-photographic reproduction in three volumes of the unique Tübingen manuscript of the *Kashmirian Atharva-Veda,* which he edited in collaboration with the German scholar Richard Garbe. He also published, in the latter part of his life, a number of valuable monographs on the subject of Hindu fiction, particularly his book on the *Life and Stories of the Jaina Savior, Parçvanatha* (1919). As a philologist, moreover, Bloomfield was particularly attracted by comparative grammar, one of his many suggestive monographs being "On Adaptation of Suffixes in Congeneric Classes of Substantives" (published in the *Journal of American Philology,* 1891, XII, 1–29). He took a lively linguistic interest in the discoveries, made at the beginning of this century, of manuscript fragments among sand-buried ruins in Turkestan, Central Asia, which brought to light languages that were hitherto practically unknown, and later in the problem of the "Hittite" languages, evoked by remarkable finds of cuneiform tablets in Asia Minor, which captivated his fancy and inspired his pen. The high quality of his work throughout was recognized by universities at home and abroad through the bestowal of honorary degrees. He was a member of many learned societies and academies both in Europe and America, and was especially active in the American Oriental Society, serving as a director 1884–1928, a vice-president in 1906 and again later, and president 1910–11. He was a foundation member of the Linguistic Society of America in 1925, and its second president (1926), though ill health prevented him from taking the chair.

Bloomfield never lost his youthful enthusiasm, which he imparted to a large number of students, many of whom have since won distinction. His style of lecturing, like his writing, was clear and precise, and his manner of expression, which was unique in its way, was lightened by a subtle sense of humor that was sometimes tinged with a touch of irony. His capacity for work was remarkable, but he knew also how to play, finding recreation in social intercourse, music, novels, and walking. He was a distinctly human scholar and was very devoted in his home life. He was twice married, his first wife being Rosa Zeisler, of Vienna, whom he married on June 20, 1885, and who died on June 20, 1920, leaving a son and a daughter. On July 9, 1921, he married Helen Townsend Scott of Baltimore, who had been one of his graduate students in Sanskrit, and who survives him. His sister Fannie Bloomfield Zeisler [*q.v.*], a celebrated pianist, two years his junior, died in 1927. He himself retired from active service at the University in 1926 and became professor emeritus, having suffered from heart trouble during the preceding year. In 1927 he moved to San Francisco, where his son, Dr. Arthur Bloomfield, was head of the Leland Stanford Hospital. In that city he continued to lead quietly his normal life, keeping up research work, enjoying the theatre and social diversion, interested in new acquaintances and in all that the city offered. His death occurred, after a brief illness, on June 13, 1928.

[A biographical sketch, with a bibliography of his writings up to 1920, is prefixed to a volume of *Studies in Honor of Maurice Bloomfield by a Group of his Pupils, New Haven* (1920); consult later the obituary article in *Language,* IV, 214–17, and that by F. Edgerton in *Jour. of the Am. Oriental Soc.,* XLVIII, 193–99; compare also *Who's Who in America,* 1926–27. Some data were kindly furnished by Mrs. Bloomfield, supplemented by the present writer's memory of a long and cherished friendship with Bloomfield.] A. V. W. J.

BLOOMGARDEN, SOLOMON (Mar. 1870–Jan. 10, 1927), writer, who was to enrich New York's East Side with his personality, his writings, and his philosophy, under his pen-name of Yehoash, was born in the town of Wertzblowo in Lithuania. He was the son of Caleb Bloomgarden, a Talmudic scholar, and his wife, Dobre-Chave. The poetry and scholarship of the Talmud which his father taught him to read and interpret were exactly the right basis for the development of his literary talent. Whatever else his mind needed of the world's intellectual wealth he chose himself and became not only a deep student of the literature of Jewish life and history, but a master of the great literature of the world and of languages as separate as Arabic, Russian, German, and English. In 1890 he came to America where he was obliged to end a brief business career and to retire to Denver on account of illness. But soon he was back in New York. From his earliest youth he wrote poetry and to the last day of his life he was an indefatigable, even a feverish, worker at varied forms of literary expression. Poems, essays, special articles, poured from his pen. For a short time, as a young man, he wrote in Hebrew and even in English, but the great portion of his work, all that best represents him, is in Yiddish. Besides his verse and his essays it includes translations of such works as *The Song of Hiawatha* from the English (1910), the *Sayings of the Fathers* (*Pirke Aboth*) from the Hebrew (1912), and the compilation of the *Yiddish Dictionary Containing all the Hebrew and Chaldaic Elements of the Yiddish Language* (1911), in collaboration with Dr. Charles D. Spivak. His greatest work was the translation of the Jewish Bible into Yiddish. A large part of this was published serially in a New York journal (the *Day*), to which he was a frequent contributor. Since his death the task has been completed and the Bible is being published in its entirety and with Bloomgarden's valuable commentaries by the Yehoash Publishing Company, New York. Only a few stray works of Bloomgarden's are available in English, *The Feet of the Messenger,* a translation by Isaac Goldberg (published by the Jewish Publication Society, 1923) of the book which Yehoash made as a record of his stay in Palestine, cut short by the war; also "The Shunamite," translated by Henry T. Schnittkind and published (1925) in Frank Shay's collection, *Twenty-Five Short Plays, International.*

In August 1904 Bloomgarden married Flora Smirnow. They had one daughter, Evelyn.

[All of the Jewish newspapers published interesting accounts of Yehoash and his work at the time of his death. One of the best accounts in English is "The Passing of Yehoash," by Elbert Aidline Trommer, in the *Jewish Tribune* of Jan. 14, 1927. There is an extended criticism and appreciation by Charles Madison in *Poet Lore,* XXXVII, 537–50.] E. J. R. I.

BLOUNT, JAMES HENDERSON (Sept. 12, 1837–Mar. 8, 1903), lawyer, congressman, diplomatic envoy, will be remembered chiefly as that special commissioner of President Cleveland to Hawaii, whose report largely determined the policy against annexation. Born in Jones County, Ga., the son of Thomas and Mary (Ricketts) Blount, he was graduated from the University of Georgia in 1857, studied law, and was admitted to the Macon bar. During the Civil War he served in the Confederate army as a private in the Floyd Rifles until he was invalided home. On partial recovery he organized a company known as Blount's Cavalry, of which he was made colonel, but soon came the news of Appomattox. During the troubled period of Reconstruction he took an active part in maintaining order, and his powers of persuasion or command were often called upon to control the passions of threatening mobs. In 1872 he was elected to the federal House of Representatives from the sixth congressional district, and retained his seat by successive elections until 1893, when he declined further nomination. He had served prominently on the Appropriations and the Ways and Means committees, and as chairman of the Committee on Post Office and Post Roads and the Committee on Foreign Affairs. His experience and competence in the field of foreign relations led to his appointment in March 1893, shortly after his last term had expired, as a special commissioner to Hawaii with paramount authority to represent the United States Government and to investigate the details of the crisis in the affairs of the islands. This episode proved the most conspicuous distinction of Blount's career.

Since early in the century a large majority of the white residents of the islands had been of American birth, and had largely influenced or controlled the native government. As early as 1853 and 1854 and again in 1866 suggestions of annexation to the United States had been favorably entertained by the native rulers. In 1891 however Queen Liliuokalani ascended the throne and soon inaugurated a policy tending to strengthen native rule and increase the power of the crown. Opposition fostered by the American element finally led to the setting up of a provisional government, which on Jan. 17, 1893, declared the queen deposed. Sanford B. Dole, the Hawaiian-born son of American missionaries, was head of the provisional government. The American minister to Hawaii was John L. Stevens. John W. Foster had just succeeded James G. Blaine as secretary of state. On Jan. 16 at the request of Minister Stevens the captain of the United States cruiser *Boston,* which by chance or design had anchored at Honolulu shortly before, landed 300 marines. It is a matter of dispute whether Minister Stevens and the marines aided the provisional government in overpowering or overawing the unhappy queen. Secretary Foster elaborately says they did not (perhaps protesting too much). Blount, Cleveland, and Gresham more than imply they did. At any rate the queen under protest yielded to *force majeure* and appealed to the United States Government for justice. Dole despatched five commissioners to negotiate a treaty of annexation. They reached Washington on Feb. 3; the treaty was drafted and sent to the president on Feb. 14, and submitted to the Senate on Feb. 15, with an urgent recommendation of "prompt action" (Message of Feb. 15). Mar. 4 however found it still unratified, and Cleveland's first official act was to withdraw it and send Blount out to investigate. Meanwhile at the request of the provisional government Stevens had accepted the islands as a protectorate of the United States, and raised the American flag over the Government House.

Commissioner Blount promptly arrived at Honolulu and, convinced by his early investigations of the complicity of American interests in the revolution, he ordered the flag lowered and the marines withdrawn, putting an end to the protectorate. Stevens resigned and was recalled in May, and Blount was appointed minister in his place, remaining in Hawaii until August. On his return the report of his investigations was accepted by the President as decisive. On Dec. 18 Cleveland sent to Congress a message which contained the words:

"By an act of war, committed with the participation of a diplomatic representative of the United States, and without the authority of Congress, the government of a feeble but friendly and confiding people has been overthrown. A substantial wrong has been done, which . . . we should endeavor to repair . . . "

The report and the President's action were received by the country at large with conflicting sentiments, and not a little excited opposition was expressed. The high motives of the commissioner, however, remain unimpeached. His outstanding characteristic seems to have been unswerving integrity and devotion to duty. This was recognized in the remarkable tributes paid him by his colleagues of the House on the occasion of his retirement (*Congressional Record,* 52 Cong., 2 Sess., 1207–08).

In appearance Blount is described by his daughter as "of medium stature, florid complexion, a penetrating steel-gray eye before which falsehood or deceit trembled. His fine head of hair became snowy white very early in life, giving him distinction among the members of the House." He spent the last decade of his life in the practise of law in Macon and in the care of his country estate. He was married to Eugenia Wiley, daughter of Dr. Jack Barnett Wiley and Ann Clapton Wiley.

[The chief sources of information about the public life of Blount are the *Cong. Record,* 1873–93; Sec. Foster's letter to President Harrison, Feb. 15, 1893, *Sen. Ex. Doc. 76,* 52 Cong., 2 Sess.; Sec. Gresham's Report, *House Ex. Doc. 47,* 53 Cong., 2 Sess.; Blount's Hawaiian Reports, *House Ex. Docs. 47, 48, 76, Sen. Ex. Docs. 13, 46,* 53 Cong., 2 Sess. Personal information from his daughter, Mrs. Walter D. Lamar.]

J. H. T. M.

BLOUNT, THOMAS (May 10, 1759–Feb. 7, 1812), Revolutionary soldier, merchant, politician, was born in Edgecombe County, N. C., the son of Jacob and Barbara (Gray) Blount. At the age of seventeen he enlisted in the 5th Regiment, and added his name to the Revolutionary annals of North Carolina that already included his father and two brothers, Reading and William [*q.v.*]. Late in 1777 he was taken prisoner by the British, carried to England, and held until the close of the war (J. K. Turner and J. L. Bridgers, *History of Edgecombe County, N. C.,* 1920, p. 106). Returning to his native state he joined his brother, John Gray, who was engaged in foreign trade, and opened a branch store at Tarboro, Edgecombe County. In 1786 they were agents and trustees for the state in the Martinique debt settlement. A republican in politics, Thomas participated in the second North Carolina convention called to consider the ratification of the national Constitution, opposed James Iredell's federalist amendments, but voted for ratification without amendment. Elected to the lower house of the state legislature in 1789, he served on the commission to locate and plan the state capital, gave his name to Blount St., Raleigh, and in general made himself so useful that he was rewarded with a seat in Congress in 1793. From then until the time of his death in 1812 he served continuously, except for the intervals of the Sixth, Seventh, and Eleventh Congresses. His achievements as a national legislator were not conspicuous. He was an adroit politician of the old Revolutionary school, who "wined and dined" for political support, discussed horse-racing more than political issues, and defended his loyalty by answering George Thatcher's charge of Francophil sympathies with a challenge to a duel. He married Jacky Sullivan Sumner, daughter of the Revolutionary general, Jethro Sumner.

[*N. C. State Records,* XVII–XXIV; *The Harris Letters,* ed. by H. M. Wagstaff (Jas. Sprunt Hist. Pub., vol. XIV, 1916); J. H. Wheeler, *Reminiscences and Memoirs of N. C.* (1884), pp. 130–131; *National Intelligencer* (Washington, D. C.), Feb. 11, 1812.]

T. D. M.

BLOUNT, WILLIAM (Mar. 26, 1749–Mar. 21, 1800), territorial governor of Tennessee, senator, was descended from Thomas Blount, son of Sir Walter Blount, who came to Virginia shortly after the restoration of Charles II and settled on Pamlico Sound in North Carolina. Jacob Blount, grandson of Thomas, married Barbara Gray in 1748, and the first born of their eight children was William. Of the latter's youth we know little save that, as his letters of a later period witness, he received a good education for that day. On Feb. 12, 1778, he married Mary Grainger, daughter of Col. Caleb Grainger of Wilmington, N. C. (Family records). In 1776 he entered the service of revolutionary North Carolina, was paymaster of various units of North Carolina's troops during the Revolution, and thereafter, for the remainder of his life, was almost continually in public office. Between 1780 and 1789 he was four times member, and once speaker, of the state's House of Commons, and twice a member of its Senate. In 1782–83 and again in 1786 and 1787 he served as a delegate to the Congress of the United States. He was also a member of the Convention of 1787 that framed the United States Constitution. In this convention, aged thirty-eight, he thus impressed one of his colleagues: "Mr. Blount is a character strongly marked for integrity and honor . . . He is no Speaker, nor does he possess any of those talents that make Men shine;—he is plain, honest, and sincere." He took no part in the debates in the Convention, and he signed his name to the completed constitution, not to signify his approval of it, but to "attest the fact that the plan was the unanimous act of the States in Convention" (Farrand, *Records of the Federal Convention,* III, 95; II, 645–46). Nevertheless, in the North Carolina convention of 1789 he voted for ratification of the Constitution. Ambitious for further political advancement, he desired election to the United States Senate, but failed to secure it. He then turned to the trans-Alleghany region, with which for some years he had been familiar as a speculator in Western lands and as a representative of North Carolina in dealings with the Indians. In 1789 North Carolina had ceded to the United States her claims to trans-mountain lands, and in 1790 Congress provided a territorial government for this cession. Blount now actively sought the governorship of this territory, and in June of 1790 he secured the appointment from President Washington. With the governorship went also the office of Superintendent of Indian Affairs for the Southern Department. When he crossed the mountains to begin his administration of affairs Blount found the inhabitants divided into hostile factions and a clash threatened between frontier interests and the pacific Indian policy of the United States government. Blount handled the affairs of his dual office with tact and firmness, with a conscientious regard for the orders of his superiors and yet with sympathy for the frontier settlers, with an eye also to his own advancement, and with a considerable measure of political adroitness. He was on friendly terms with the leading men of the territory, and he sought and secured a personal popularity with the generality of settlers. He was president of the convention which met in January 1796 and proclaimed the transformation of the territory into the State of Tennessee, and by the first legislature of the new state he was elected to the United States Senate. His service in that body, however, was brief. As territorial governor, he had continued his dealings in Western lands. He now became involved in financial difficulties and entered into a plan to launch an attack, by Indians and frontiersmen in coöperation with a British fleet, upon Spanish Florida and Louisiana for the purpose of transferring the control of those provinces to Great Britain. Unfortunately for Blount a letter that he wrote to an interpreter in the Cherokee Nation, speaking in veiled language of the plan and of his desire to have the Indians put into a frame of mind to aid him, came into the hands of President Adams, who sent it on July 3, 1797, to Congress. This letter, wrote Blount, made "a damnable fuss" in Philadelphia, but he hoped the Westerners would "see nothing but good in it, for so [he] intended it" (*Wisconsin Historical Collections,* X, 411). The senators saw it otherwise and expelled him from their body, July 8, by a vote of twenty-five to one. In the House of Representatives impeachment proceedings were begun at once, but did not come before the Senate for final decision until January

1799, when the impeachment was dismissed for lack of jurisdiction. Blount, meanwhile, had returned to Tennessee. That he had lost nothing of the confidence of the people of that community was evidenced by his election, in 1798, to the state Senate and his elevation by that body to its speakership. Further political preferment, perhaps, he might have had but for his death in 1800.

[Information, including many of Blount's letters, may be found printed in the *State Records of N. C.* (16 vols., 1895–1905), in *Am. State Papers, Indian Affairs,* I (1832), in H. M. Wagstaff (ed.), *The Papers of John Steele* (2 vols., 1924), in M. J. Wright, *Wm. Blount* (1884), and in the *Am. Hist. Mag.* (Nashville), I–IV, VI, *passim.* Some unpublished letters are in the Manuscript Div. of the Lib. of Cong., in the Draper Papers at Madison, Wis., in the collections of the Tennessee Hist. Soc., and in the McClung Collection (Knoxville) of photostats from the Spanish Archives. His journal as territorial governor is printed in the *Am. Hist. Mag.,* II, 213–277. Frederick J. Turner has edited "Documents on the Blount Conspiracy, 1795–1797," with a detailed bibliographical note, in the *Am. Hist. Rev.,* X, 274, 574–606.] P. M. H.

BLOUNT, WILLIE (Apr. 18, 1768–Sept. 10, 1835), jurist, governor of Tennessee, belonged to a family prominent in eighteenth-century North Carolina. Of the third generation in that colony was Jacob Blount who was three times married and the father of thirteen children. Willie, pronounced Wiley, was born of the second marriage, to Hannah Baker, née Salter, widow of William Baker. His father was a man of wealth and Willie received an education at the institutions that are to-day Princeton and Columbia Universities. When his older and more accomplished half-brother William Blount [*q.v.*] was appointed governor of the Southwest Territory, Willie followed him to that frontier community, served him as private secretary, and was by him licensed to practise law in the territorial courts. When the territory became the State of Tennessee in 1796, Willie Blount was elected by the first legislature one of the three judges of the superior courts of law and equity, a position, however, which he shortly resigned. Some time after 1802 he removed from Knoxville, where he had made his home, to Montgomery County and married Lucinda Baker. In 1809, after one term of service in the legislature, he was elected governor of the state, defeating William Cocke by a majority of about 3,000 votes (*Wilson's Knoxville Gazette,* Sept. 9, 1809). In 1811 and 1813 he was reëlected for the constitutional maximum of three successive terms. As governor, he pointed out the need of extinguishing Indian titles to land in Tennessee, of securing for the state improved facilities of communication and transportation, and of devoting the energies of the people to the development of the wealth of the state. "Attention in us in these things," he asserted to the legislature in 1811, is more "important to the future growth of our infant state, than time devoted to the idle whimsies of foreign relations . . ." Yet the last two of his three administrations fell largely within the period of the second war between the United States and Great Britain, including with it the war with the Creek Indians. To this war and to Gen. Andrew Jackson, Blount gave energetic support, and enjoyed a considerable measure of popularity as Tennessee's war governor. In 1815 he retired from office to assume the more leisurely duties of a planter in Montgomery County. One may assume that he did this with a sigh of relief, for earlier he had written, ". . . the trade of governing does not suit my genius as well as retirement; I am tired of it." In truth, as Blount himself realized and as many who knew him have testified, he was a man of only ordinary abilities. One cannot, perhaps, better estimate his mental worth than to quote the comment of a contemporary that "in writing, he would labor a great deal, and say but little" (Draper Papers, 3xx18). Yet he was patriotic and honest. Agreeable, even affectionate, and at heart a democrat, he had many personal friends and few, if any, enemies. Twice after 1815 he came from retirement. In 1827 he was a candidate for governor in opposition to Sam Houston and Newton Cannon and was overwhelmingly defeated (*Knoxville Enquirer,* Aug. 15, 22, 29, 1827). In 1834, the year before his death, he served actively in the Tennessee constitutional convention, sponsoring in particular the provision of the new constitution that directed the legislature to encourage internal improvements.

[Blount's official papers, together with most of his private papers, including a history of Tennessee in manuscript, appear to have been destroyed. Some letters from him and some extracts from his writings are in the Draper Papers in Madison, Wis. A few letters, relating mainly to his religious opinions, are owned by the Tenn. Hist. Soc., a few are in the Robertson Correspondence (*Am. Hist. Mag.,* V), and a number to Andrew Jackson have been printed in *Correspondence of Andrew Jackson,* I, II (1926–27), ed. by J. S. Bassett. A brief pamphlet by Blount, *A Catechetical Exposition of the Constitution of the State of Tenn.: intended principally for the use of Schools,* was printed in Knoxville (1803).] P. M. H.

BLOW, HENRY TAYLOR (July 15, 1817–Sept. 11, 1875), capitalist, diplomat, congressman, was the son of Peter and Elizabeth (Taylor) Blow. When he was thirteen, his father, a Virginia planter of moderate circumstances, migrated to the West and settled in St. Louis. Henry enjoyed the best educational advantages of the time and locality and graduated with distinction from St. Louis University. He commenced the study of law but abandoned it in order to enter business with his brother-in-law. In the economic transformation of St. Louis from a frontier town to an industrial and commercial center, Blow was an important figure. He was a pioneer in the lead and lead-products business and was instrumental in the opening and development of the large lead mines of southwestern Missouri. He was also president of the Iron Mountain Railroad. The educational and cultural interests of St. Louis came soon to realize that in Blow they had a devoted friend and generous supporter; that he was, in every sense, a public-spirited citizen. In common with many of the leading business men of the city, he was a Whig. In 1854 he was persuaded to become a candidate for the state Senate and was easily elected. Here he became one of the party leaders in the turbulent sessions of the following four years when factionalism was at its height. As chairman of the important committee on banks and corporations, Blow represented adequately and effectively the commercial and financial interests of St. Louis, which were conservative. He had opposed since 1854 the extension of slavery and with the final disappearance of the Whig party, he became, successively, an American and a "black" Republican. Together with Blair, Brown, and others of similar views, Blow supported the Free-Soil movement and helped to organize the Republican party in Missouri. He was a delegate to the national convention of 1860. Laboring tirelessly to keep Missouri in the Union, in the early and critical months of the war he was active in the raising and equipping of troops for the support of the government. Lincoln appointed him minister to Venezuela in 1861 but he returned in 1862 to become a Republican candidate for Congress as a "charcoal," that is, a Republican who favored the immediate and uncompensated emancipation of the slaves in Missouri. He was elected, and was reelected in 1864. His congressional career was marked by close application to committee work and to conferences; he rarely spoke on the floor of the House and took little part in the acrimonious debates which marked the early days of reconstruction. As a member of the joint committee on reconstruction, he supported the policies of Stevens during the first session of Congress in 1866, but during the second he was a follower of the more conservative John A. Bingham. He was singularly free from those bitter personal and political animosities which were dominant during the reconstruction period, especially in the border states. As a business man he was concerned with the restoration and rehabilitation of St. Louis and her markets. He retired from public life in 1867 and devoted himself to the development of his mining properties. Because of his thorough knowledge of the important interests involved, Blow was prevailed upon to accept in 1869 the appointment as minister to Brazil, a position which he held for two years and in which he did much to further closer relations between the two countries, before returning to St. Louis to his numerous business interests. With the reorganization of the District of Columbia government in 1874, Blow reluctantly accepted an appointment on the new board of commissioners and assisted in the reconstruction of the District. He announced his definite retirement from politics in 1875, and died suddenly on Sept. 15 of that year. He was married to Minerva, daughter of Col. Thornton Grimsley of St. Louis.

[The chief facts concerning Blow's political career can be found in the files of the *Mo. Republican*, the *Mo. Democrat*, and the *Mo. Statesman* during the years he was in public life. The *Cong. Record* for the 39th and 40th Congresses is useful for the years 1863–67. Blow's work on the joint committee on reconstruction is appraised in B. B. Kendrick, *Jour. of the Joint Committee of Fifteen on Reconstruction* (1914). There are general accounts of his life in W. B. Stevens, "Lincoln and Mo.," *Mo. Hist. Rev.*, X, 63 ff., and S. B. Harding, "Mo. Party Struggles in the Civil War Period," *Annual Report, Am. Hist. Ass.*, 1900; H. L. Conard, *Encyc. of the Hist. of Mo.* (1901), I, 305–06.] T. S. B.

BLOW, SUSAN ELIZABETH (June 7, 1843–Mar. 26, 1916), kindergartner, the daughter of Henry Taylor Blow [*q.v.*] and of Minerva (Grimsley) Blow, was born in St. Louis, Mo. Her childhood was passed in a cultivated home, and the deeply religious character of her early training quickened a serious and reverent attitude toward life which led her very early to consecrate herself to education. A complete surrender to the mysticism and symbolism of Froebel's philosophy was the natural outcome of a prolonged study of Hegel, Schelling, Fichte, and Kant, a close association with the transcendental philosophy of the Concord School, and the influence and support of Dr. William T. Harris [*q.v.*], superintendent of schools in St. Louis and an able exponent of German idealism. After some acquaintance with the kindergarten methods of Germany, Miss Blow conceived the idea of opening a kindergarten in St. Louis. Dr. Harris received the suggestion with favor, and Miss Blow, in order to fit herself for this responsibility, went to New York to study for a year with Mme. Maria Kraus-Boelte, called the spiritual daughter of Froebel. Mme. Kraus-Boelte had established a class for mothers and kindergartners in that city in 1871. Miss Blow became the first kindergartner in America trained by Mme. Boelte and upon her return to St. Louis in 1873 opened the first public kindergarten in the Des Pères School in Carondelet, a suburb of St. Louis, and in 1874 opened a training school which played a significant part in the history of education in her time.

When Miss Blow began her teaching, no translation of Froebel's *Mother Play* had been made. Miss Blow assumed this task and translated these songs and plays from week to week for use in the kindergarten. The work was done, however, with an untroubled orthodoxy that did not take into account the theory of evolution which gave a new interpretation to the laws of growth and necessitated a revision of the plays and games of the kindergarten. When a more liberal group of students began such a revision in 1887, Miss Blow did not lend her support to the movement. The social significance of her work must not be underestimated, however, for her belief in the *Gliedganzes* or member-whole of Froebel's philosophy found expression in many pragmatic, correlated educational activities of social significance. She gave hearty support and direction to mothers' meetings, home visitation, school gardens, and nature study. She was an instinctive leader with strong personal power. The training which she offered was built upon a broad cultural background, awakening in her students an intellectual curiosity and a recognition of fundamental spiritual values which gave permanence and direction to the kindergarten as an educational institution. Ill health forced her to retire from active work during a period of about ten years. In 1895 she began to lecture again in Boston, conducting study classes in the Bible, Homer, Dante, Goethe, and Shakespeare. The last years of her life were spent in New York, where she was connected with the graduate department of the New York Kindergarten Association. A list of her publications includes: *Symbolic Education* (1894); *The Mottoes and Commentaries of Froebel's Mother Play* (1895); *The Songs and Music of Froebel's Mother Play* (1895); *Letters to a Mother on the Philosophy of Froebel* (1899); *Educational Issues in the Kindergarten* (1908); *Kindergarten Education* (1900).

[*Pioneers of the Kindergarten in America* (1924); G. Stanley Hall, *Educational Problems* (1911); Ilse Forest, *Preschool Education* (1927); *Kindergarten Mag.*, Oct. 1895; *Elementary School Teacher*, Dec. 1906; Nina C. Vandewalker, *The Kindergarten in Am. Education* (1908); Denton J. Snider, *The St. Louis Movement* (1920); David H. Harris, ed., *The Early St. Louis Movement* (1921).]

B. C. G.

BLOWERS, SAMPSON SALTER (Mar. 10, 1742–Oct. 25, 1842), jurist, was born in Boston, the son of Lieut. John and Sarah (Salter) Blowers. He was a descendant of Pyam Blowers—the name being indifferently spelled Blower or Blores—who settled at Cambridge, Mass., toward the end of the seventeenth century. Educated at the grammar school, Boston, and at Harvard College where he graduated in 1763, Sampson Blowers studied law with Lieut. Gov. Hutchinson, was admitted to the bar at Boston in 1766, and commenced practise in that city. In 1770 the so-called "Boston massacre" occurred, in which a party of British soldiers under Capt. Preston fired on a mob in the streets, killing and wounding a number of citizens. The soldiers were subsequently tried for murder. Blowers was retained for the defense, in association with John Adams and Josiah Quincy, and an acquittal was secured in all but two cases wherein verdicts of manslaughter were returned. Thus brought into public notice, Blowers was thereafter known as a strong supporter of the royal administration and incurred the active enmity of the local patriots. In 1774 he went to England, becoming in 1776 a member of the New England Club of Loyalists which was formed in London during that year. Returning to Boston in 1778, he found that his name was in the Proscription Act as an enemy of the new state. He was arrested and imprisoned for a short time, and on his release went to Halifax, Nova Scotia, whither a large number of Loyalists had preceded him, and commenced the practise of law there. From Halifax he returned to Newport in April 1779; and was there appointed judge of the Rhode Island court of vice-admiralty. On the evacuation of Newport by the British, in October 1779, he sailed for England to seek compensation for his financial losses. The next year he came back to America, this time with the appointment of solicitor-general for New York. Early in September 1783 he sailed for Halifax with his wife and her sister (A. W. H. Eaton, article in *Americana*, XI, 52–53). In September 1784 the province of New Brunswick was formed by dividing Nova Scotia, and on Dec. 24, 1784, Blowers was appointed attorney-general of Nova Scotia as reconstituted. He was also elected from Halifax County to the new House of Representatives in the following year, and when the Assembly met at Halifax, Dec. 5, 1785, he was elected speaker, continuing as such till his appointment, Jan. 3, 1788, as a member of the legislative council, when he vacated his seat in the House and the speakership. In the council he was distinguished for the broad-minded nonpartisan manner in which he discussed all matters which came up for consideration, and his varied experience and robust patriotism combined to give him great influence. He was appointed chief justice of Nova Scotia and president of the council, Sept. 9, 1797, and occupied this position for thirty-six years. He was an excellent, conscientious judge, and performed his duties "with great assiduity" (letter of Wentworth to Secretary of State, see B. Murdock, *History of Nova Scotia or Acadie,* 1865–67, II, 214). The Lieutenant-Governor, Sir George Prevost, reported that "the Chief Justice is most deservedly and universally esteemed" (*Ibid.,* II, 286). At the same time he had a proper appreciation of the dignity of his office, as was evidenced by his abstention from attendance at Council during the absence of Sir George Prevost on the expedition to Martinique in 1808–9, his reason being that he was senior to the Hon. A. Croke who had been appointed *ad interim* president of the province during the Lieutenant-Governor's absence. He retired in 1833; and died at Halifax, Oct. 25, 1842, having thus passed the century by more than five months. He married in 1774 Sarah, daughter of Benjamin Kent of Boston, who was himself a Loyalist and refugee, and she survived him, dying in 1845 at an advanced age.

[Brief details of Blowers's ancestry will be found in Jas. Savage, *Geneal. Dict. of the First Settlers of New Eng.* (1860), I, 206, and Lucius R. Paige, *Hist. of Cambridge, Mass.* (1877), p. 489. A short sketch of his life appeared in Lorenzo Sabine, *Loyalists of the Am. Rev.* (1864), I, 233. There is a laudatory reference to him in the *Diary and Letters of Thos. Hutchinson* (1883), I, 341–42.]

H. W. H. K.

BLOXHAM, WILLIAM DUNNINGTON (July 9, 1835–Mar. 15, 1911), governor of Florida, was born almost within sight of the state capitol. His father, William, of English ancestry, was a native of Alexandria, Va., and moved with his wife, Martha Williams, to Leon County, Fla., in 1825. He became a planter, served in the Seminole War, and died in Tallahassee in 1862. The son, William, was educated for the bar at William and Mary College where he was graduated in 1856, but the state of his health forced him also to become a planter. An early and lively interest in politics led to his election to the Florida House of Representatives where he served in the important session of November–December 1861. In the following February he was elected captain of a newly organized infantry company which was at once mustered into Confederate service for three years; but, his health again becoming impaired, he did not complete this service and returned to his planting. After the war he took part from the beginning in the resistance of the Conservatives to the radical and negro government of the state; became a candidate for presidential elector on that ticket in 1868 and supported it actively on the stump; and was elected lieutenant-governor in 1870, in a period of continual radical victories, but only after a noteworthy campaign in which, notwithstanding the lack of railroads, he spoke in almost every county. Again leading the party in the same fight in 1872 he was defeated for the office of governor; but, still a leader, he had a large share in the overthrow of the foreign and negro element in 1876, was appointed secretary of state, and was finally elected governor in 1880. The success of his administration (1881–85) was without precedent in the state. By 1883, for the first time in the state's history, there was no floating debt and no deficit; funds were in the treasury for current expenses, and the reduction of the large debt contracted by the radical government had begun. Hence, he recommended to the legislature a reduction in taxation from a levy of nine mills to five mills, and this was reduced by an additional mill the next year. His most serious and pressing problem was the relief of the Internal Improvement Fund which was overwhelmed by debt and litigation. By effecting a sale to Hamilton Disston, on June 1, 1881, of 4,000,000 acres of lands held under the Fund, at twenty-five cents per acre, nearly all in cash, the Board of Trustees, of which he was chairman, rescued the Fund from insolvency and prevented a forced sale by its creditors (*Message,* Jan. 2, 1883; Caroline M. Brevard, *A History of Florida,* 1924–25, II, 182–86).

After the close of his term as governor, Bloxham declined appointment as United States minister to Bolivia, but accepted that of United States surveyor-general of Florida, in which office he served four years, to 1889, when he was appointed state comptroller. Elected to that office the next year, he was reëlected in 1892 for the four-year term. His service as comptroller left its mark upon the financial history of Florida; his recommendations for reforms, dealing mainly with the cost of criminal prosecutions, the equalization of assessments, and payment of interest on state deposits in banks, were carried out by the administration, the legislature, and the people through constitutional amendment. In January 1897 Bloxham was again inaugurated as governor, the first to be elected to that office for the second time. During this term (1897–1901) occurred the Spanish-American War, when Florida became the principal theatre of encampment and embarkation of the army. Bloxham's public service had now covered a period of forty years and he had been all but continuously in office for twenty-five years. In 1857 he had married Mary C. Davis, who died in 1904. In 1907 he married Mrs. G. Moss Norvell, who survived him. He was above medium height, with erect carriage, a high, broad forehead, small bright eyes, and thin compressed lips. Though aggressive he was conservative, was uncommonly effective as an orator, and "a thoroughly likable man" (W. W. Davis, *The Civil War and Reconstruction in Florida,* 1913, p. 620).

[R. H. Rerick, *Memoirs of Florida* (1902), vol. I; and *Makers of America* (Fla. ed. 1911), I, 104–28.]

J. C. Y.

BLUE, VICTOR (Dec. 6, 1865–Jan. 22, 1928), naval officer, born in Richmond County, North Carolina, came of distinguished Scotch, Welsh, and Huguenot ancestry settled in the Carolinas before the Revolution. His father, John Gilchrist Blue, was a lieutenant-colonel in the Confederate army. His mother was Annie M. Evans, daughter of Williams Evans, a brigadier-general of South Carolina militia in the nullification trouble of 1833. A younger brother, Rupert Blue, was Surgeon-General, United States Public Health Service. After boyhood on his father's plantation, "Bluefields," Marion, S. C., and high-school work at Laurinburg, N. C., Victor was appointed to the Naval Academy, graduating in 1887 in the engineering branch of the service, from which five years later he was transferred to the line. In the Spanish War he was a lieutenant in the converted yacht *Suwanee.* Having had previous experience ashore in Cuba, May 31–June 1, 1898, in an effort to land munitions for the insurgents, Blue volunteered for two highly difficult scouting expeditions through the Spanish lines at Santiago. By the first, June 11–13, he established definitely that all Cervera's squadron was in the harbor, thus giving assurance for the transport of troops from Tampa. By the second, June 25–27, he identified and accurately located each enemy vessel for purposes of a projected torpedo attack. Accompanied only by insurgent guides, he traveled on each trip over sixty miles on mule-back, penetrating two miles or more within the Spanish lines to hills overlooking the harbor. On Admiral Sampson's recommendation he was promoted five numbers for "extraordinary heroism." In addition to other routine assignments, he served on the staff of Rear Admiral Cooper, in command of the Asiatic Fleet, 1903–04; as executive officer of the *North Carolina,* 1909; as commander of the *Yorktown* and later as chief of staff in the Pacific Fleet, 1910. On Mar. 26, 1913, while still in the grade of commander, he was appointed by Secretary Daniels chief of the Bureau of Navigation, with the temporary rank of rear admiral; and in this important office, controlling all matters relating to personnel, he worked harmoniously with the secretary in the expansion of the navy which preceded American entry into the World War. On Aug. 10, 1916, he left the bureau to command the battleship *Texas.* For the grounding of his ship on Block Island in the next year he was reduced ten numbers. The *Texas,* in January 1918, joined Admiral Rodman's squadron with the British Grand Fleet in the North Sea, and in this trying service Blue remained in her command until the close of the War. For a brief period, from December 1918 until his retirement, he was again chief of the Bureau of Navigation. He was made permanent rear admiral in April 1919, and was retired in the following July, owing to heart trouble. His later life was spent chiefly at Fort George, Fla., where he had extensive real estate interests. He died of heart failure on a train while going from Fort George to Washington for treatment. Blue was married, Oct. 17, 1899, to Eleanor Foote Stuart, a grandchild of Gen. David Stuart of Detroit. Of his two sons, John Stuart and Victor, the elder, John, became an officer in the navy. In addition to the bold spirit displayed in the Spanish War, Blue had the sound judgment and qualities of coöperation required for the important administrative duties of his later years. He was of dark complexion and large build, fond of social life, "a generous-hearted, lovable man," as a classmate and fellow officer describes him, "with a fund of quiet merriment which was a distinguishing characteristic."

[Sketch is based chiefly on information from family and naval sources, and from Navy Department records. See especially "Naval Operations of the War with Spain," *House Doc. No. 3,* 55 Cong., 3 Sess. Obituaries appeared in the *N. Y. Times,* Jan. 23, 1928, and *Army and Navy Record,* Jan. 28, 1928.]

A. W.

BLUM, ROBERT FREDERICK (July 9, 1857–June 8, 1903), painter, was the son of Frederick and Mary (Haller) Blum. His father was a native of Germany, born at Rohrbach, in the Rhine Palatinate of Bavaria, whence he emigrated in the early "fifties," coming in a sailing ship to New Orleans and up the Mississippi and Ohio rivers to Cincinnati, where at the time of Blum's birth he was occupied as a designer of insurance charts. Here Blum was born, his mother being also of German extraction. His school days began in 1864 while the Civil War was in progress. After passing through the various grades he entered high school in 1873. Chafing at its restraints he left it in 1874 to enter Gibson & Sons' Lithographic Establishment on Elm Street, Cincinnati, as an apprentice. In addition to his daily practise, he studied drawing in the evenings at the Mechanics' Institute and in 1875 entered the

McMicken School of Design where Alfred Brennan and Kenyon Cox were fellow pupils, sketching from the nude in pencil and pen and ink. As early as 1872 his eye had been attracted by some Japanese fans, which were being hawked in connection with the holding of a "Sänger-fest" in Cincinnati. He bought several of the best for study. He was also interested in reproductions of the Spanish painter Fortuny and others of that school. When he visited the Centennial Exhibition of 1876 at Philadelphia, in company with Kenyon Cox, he was able to study original works by masters of the Hispano-Roman School and the marvels of art in the Japanese section. He then resolved to visit Europe and Japan—ambitions which were afterward realized. He remained in Philadelphia with Cox to study nine months in the life classes of the Pennsylvania Academy of Fine Arts. Brennan soon joined them, a loft in Elbow Lane serving the three as a studio. In 1877 Blum returned to Cincinnati, but notwithstanding parental advice to stick to lithography, he returned to Philadelphia and soon after, in 1878, went on to New York, where he first lived at 91 Clinton Place (East Eighth St). After four months of struggle and privations, his clever sketches caught the eye of A. W. Drake, the art editor of *Scribner's Monthly* and *St. Nicholas,* who gave him commissions. An excursion to Alexandria and Yorktown, Va. (November 1879), in company with Lungren, and O'Donovan the sculptor, resulted in a series of clever sketches of old Colonial life in which the eighteenth-century costumes and poses recalled those preferred by Fortuny, whose works, light in subject but profoundly skilful in technique, strongly influenced Blum's manner at this time.

Working in a studio at 21 East Fifteenth St. in 1879 Blum saved enough money by spring to permit a four months' visit to Europe. Sailing from New York in company with A. W. Drake on the *Arizona,* he visited London, Paris, Genoa, and Rome, afterward going to Venice. Here he found Whistler occupied with his now famous etchings and pastels, living with Blum's fellow townsman, Duveneck, in the Riva Schiavoni, where he joined them. Martin Rico, the Spanish painter, was also in Venice, and these combined influences must have been invaluable to the young artist. Returning to New York in September 1880, Blum took a studio at the Sherwood Building, recently erected at 58 West Fifty-seventh St. A number of pen and ink studies of Joe Jefferson as "Bob Acres" and "Rip Van Winkle," as well as of other actors and actresses, appeared about this time in *Scribner's* and the *Century* magazines as evidences of his astounding skill, and have been classed as *chef-d'œuvres* by Joseph Pennell in his *Pen Drawing and Pen Draughtsmen.* Decorations for Mr. Roberts's residence on the northwest corner of Washington Square and University Place were completed during April and May, 1881, and in June we find Blum again in Venice occupying rooms with his friend Baer. In 1882, he joined the jolly party of artists, including William Chase, Carroll Beckwith, Lungren, Quartley, A. A. Anderson, and F. P. Vinton, who passed the time in decorating the captain's cabin of the *Belgenland,* about which event Clarence Buel, of the *Century,* also on board, wrote an article, "Log of an Ocean Studio," five of the illustrations being by Blum. In July we find Blum at Madrid, where he made a copy of Velazquez's "Mœnippus." In 1883 he visited Long Meadows, Mass., with Durand, and passed August and September with Turcas at Ellenville, N. Y. A visit to Vinton was coïncident with a trip to Boston for the Century Company. The completion of another large decoration was the prelude to his sailing for Antwerp in July 1884, where he met Chase, Ulrich, and Baer, with whom he visited Brussels, proceeding to Haarlem and Zandvoort in Holland, where he remained at work for some time. The annual pilgrimage to Europe was repeated in 1885 with visits to Venice, Paris, and London, and on his return to New York in September, he took the studio lately vacated by Alden Weir at the Benedict Building, Washington Square, which he retained till 1893. In the meantime an opportunity came, in 1889, to make the long-deferred visit to Japan, with a commission to illustrate Sir Edwin Arnold's "Japonica," published serially in *Scribner's Magazine* (1890–91), and afterward in book form. Here he remained over two years, sending back a series of drawings of unequalled fidelity and beauty. He recorded his impressions in "An Artist in Japan," a series of papers published in *Scribner's Magazine* (1893). While engaged on the illustrations for "Japonica," he painted and sketched unceasingly, his most important work in oil colors being "The Ameya" or "Candy Blower," exhibited at the National Academy of Design (1892), and now at the Metropolitan Museum of Art, New York.

Soon after the return from Japan, Blum moved to 90 Grove St., where with his friend, Baer, he had renovated a house, arranging for convenient studios and living quarters, and thus they became the pioneers in the "Greenwich Village" migration of New York artists. It was here he designed and carried out the decorations for the Mendelssohn Glee Club Hall, which occupied almost five years to complete. This has been termed a "personal message of joyous freshness and sensitive rhythms." On one wall he painted "Moods of Music"—a frieze twelve feet high and fifty feet long,—a series of dancing figures, in light tones and colors, representing musical movements from the stately *andante* to the lively *allegro.* The costumes are of Grecian simplicity, and before painting the composition he modeled each figure separately in the nude and arranged the groups on an architectural background, with innumerable sketches in crayon and pastel. When this first frieze was completed, he took up the execution of "The Vintage Festival" on the opposite wall. Profiting by his first experience, he made this more positive in color and divided it into contrasting groups upon an architectural background of white marble. When the building for which they were painted was demolished some years ago, these decorations were happily preserved and they have found a fitting home on the side walls of the sculpture hall of the Brooklyn Museum of Art, having been generously donated by the heirs of Alfred Corning Clark who had been Blum's "perfect patron" in carrying out the work. Another important decoration for the Proscenium of the New Amsterdam Theatre, undertaken in collaboration with the artist A. B. Wenzell, was in progress at the time of Blum's death.

One is impressed by his versatile use of various mediums. Perhaps the early experiences with lithographic crayon led to his skilful use of pastels later on. Oscar Wilde happening into his studio one day said, in commenting on their delicacy, "Your pastels give me the feeling of eating yellow satin." Blum was one of the founders of the Society of Painters in Pastel, and became its president. Among the eleven etchings shown at the Memorial Exhibition at Knoedler's Galleries, New York, in April 1904, were "The Hag," a masterly character sketch of an old woman smoking a pipe, dated 1879; "The Etcher," showing William Chase at work in his Tenth Street studio; and a keenly characterized profile portrait of the artist himself, besides others, done at Venice and in Holland. Water-color he always found a particularly sympathethic medium; its fluid transparency and telling accents served in numerous studies at Venice, in Holland, and later in Japan. Although he seems to have found oil colors less pliable, even designating them at first as "a nasty medium," yet his "Lace Makers," which gained him a gold medal in New York and another in bronze at the Paris Universal Exhibition of 1889, gave no evidence of technical difficulties. The exhibition of his "Bead Stringers" resulted in election as an associate of the National Academy of Design and gained a diploma at Philadelphia. "The Ameya" or "Candy Blower," which he classed as "the one important picture of my Japan trip," resulted in his election to full membership in the National Academy. He was also a member of the Society of American Artists and of the Water Color Society. In twenty-five years of unremitting toil, he had achieved a distinguished position. Honored with the friendship of some of the most notable artists of his time, both in America and abroad, he was singularly happy in intimate relations established with Whistler, Chase, Duveneck, Martin Rico, Carroll Beckwith, Bacher, Cox, and his lifelong friend, afterward the executor of his estate, William J. Baer. At the relatively early age of forty-six, an attack of pneumonia carried him off in five days at New York. He was buried at Cincinnati, and, appropriately, by the devoted efforts of his sister, Mrs. Haller, and of his friend, William J. Baer, a collection of his works which includes one hundred and forty originals and forty reproductions, has been placed in a special gallery at the Cincinnati Art Museum, with a bronze portrait bust by the sculptor, C. H. Niehaus.

[R. Bridges, *Lamp,* July 1903; Mrs. C. M. Fairbanks, *Metropolitan Mag.,* July 1904; Royal Cortissoz, *N. Y. Tribune,* June 30, 1895, *N. Y. Times,* Feb. 2, 1913, *N. Y. Herald Tribune,* Apr. 25, 1926; Clarence Cook, *Studio,* Dec. 5, 1891; Jos. Pennell, *Pen Drawing and Pen Draughtsmen* (1889, rev. ed. 1920); personal recollections, supplemented by information furnished by Mr. Wm. J. Baer.]

R. J. W.

BLUNT, EDMUND MARCH (June 20, 1770–Jan. 4, 1862), hydrographer, was born in Portsmouth, N. H., the son of William and Elizabeth (March) Blunt. His boyhood and early manhood were spent in his native city and in Newburyport, Mass., where he had many contacts with the life of the sea as both places enjoyed at that time a rather prosperous commerce. It was in Newburyport that he embarked on a business career, beginning in 1793, with Howard S. Robinson, the publication of the *Impartial Herald.* In the same year he married Sally Ross of Newbury. For three years he carried on newspaper publishing along with his bookstore which stood just a few doors below the Wolfe Tavern. This feature of his business had a steady growth until in 1802 there were 3,000 volumes available for circulation. The step which without doubt was the most important in his career was his decision in 1796 to publish the *American Coast Pilot,* compiled by Capt. L. Furlong. This book, which contained "directions for principal harbors, capes, and headlands of the coast of North and part of South America" (19th ed., title-page), filled a long felt need and found a ready sale not only in America but also in Europe where it was translated into the more important languages. The first edition was soon exhausted and others were called for. These Blunt personally sponsored and edited. Between the editions of the *Coast Pilot,* Blunt found time to publish in 1799 a *New Practical Navigator* which in turn was followed in 1801 by the publication of *Bowditch's New American Practical Navigator.*

These books together with nautical charts made Blunt's workshop the center of American nautical publications. An incident which arose in connection with the publication of the charts gives considerable insight into Blunt's character. In 1805 James Akin was engaged in engraving maps and charts for Blunt when the latter became infuriated in a dispute over some details of the work and seizing a heavy iron skillet threw it at Akin. In revenge Akin published a caricature called "Infuriated Despondency" representing Blunt in the act of throwing the skillet. This engraving he sent to England with instructions to have it reproduced on crockery. A large number of household utensils bearing the caricature were imported and sold in Newburyport but most of them were purchased by Blunt's friends and broken up. In July 1805 Blunt sued Akin for libel. A decision was rendered in favor of the defendant after a long and bitter contest. Shortly after the quarrel Blunt moved to New York City, where he continued to carry on his nautical publications, at first alone, and later with his sons E. and G. W. Blunt [*q.v.*]. A notable work of this period was his *Stranger's Guide to the City of New York* which appeared in 1817. His death, at Sing Sing (now Ossining), N. Y., was mourned by large numbers of his intimates among the old school of American shipmasters.

[The chief source of information is John J. Currier's *Hist. of Newburyport,* vol. I (1906), vol. II (1909). Much information regarding the character of Blunt's work and publications can be had from the prefaces of the various editions of the *Coast Pilot.* A notice of his death appeared in the *N. Y. Times,* Jan. 6, 1862.]

G. H. B.

BLUNT, GEORGE WILLIAM (Mar. 11, 1802–Apr. 19, 1878), hydrographer, was born in Newburyport, Mass., the son of Edmund March Blunt [*q.v.*] and Sally (Ross) Blunt. He inherited his father's love of the sea and left school at the age of fourteen to serve five years before the mast. On his return in 1821 he married Martha Garsett and settled in New York City, where he established with his brother, Edmund, a publishing house making a specialty of nautical works. He immediately began marine surveys of the Bahama Banks and of New York Harbor for the purpose of revising existing charts. In 1833 he was appointed first assistant of the United States Coast Survey—a position which he held until the time of his death. He was the moving spirit of his publishing house, which was kept constantly busy printing nautical books and charts. He himself edited *The Young Sea Officer's Sheet Anchor* (1843), *Memoir of the Dangers and Ice of the North Atlantic Ocean* (1845), *The Way to Avoid the Center of our Violent Gales* (1868), *Pilot Laws, Harbor and Quarantine Regulations of New York* (1869). *Bowditch's Navigator* and *Blunt's Coast Pilot,* both of which were originally published by his father, continued to run into large and numerous editions. The chart business of the firm also grew rapidly; new charts were constantly added to the list and older ones were revised so that by 1863 the Blunts were publishing "charts of all the navigable world, from the best authorities" (preface to the nineteenth edition of *Blunt's Coast Pilot*). As a side line they handled all types of nautical instruments of American manufacture and by means of a dividing engine which was perfected "after a labor of over five years [were] enabled to divide astronomical and nautical instruments to a degree of precision which they [guaranteed] to be equal to the best of foreign make" (*Ibid.*). That Blunt's work was basic in the organization of the United States Hydrographic Office is borne out by the fact that, "The first important accessions to the stock of chart-plates came through purchase from the firm of E. & G. W. Blunt, nautical publishers, of New York City, under authority conferred upon the Secretary of the Navy by the Act of Congress establishing the Hydrographic Office. Twenty-four copperplate charts, relating mainly to the coast of America, were thus added to the list of issues; and besides these, the copyrights of *Bowditch's American Practical Navigator,* and a few volumes of *Coast Pilots and Sailing Directions* were also acquired by purchase" (Pamphlet dated Jan. 1, 1910 issued by the Bureau of Equipment, Navy Department). Even in the midst of his busy publishing career Blunt never lost his interest in the practical side of navigation. He served for thirty-two years on the Board of Pilot Commissioners; he and his brother constantly forwarded to Washington complaints of captains about the lighthouse service; and it was largely through their efforts that reforms in that bureau were instituted (Arnold B. Johnson, *The Modern Lighthouse Service,* 1889, p. 15). He found time to help organize the pilotage system in New York

Bay and from 1845 up to the time of his death except for a six months' period served as pilot commissioner. He was for a time a harbor commissioner and a trustee of the Seamen's Retreat. In 1852–54 he served as a commissioner of immigration. With his death which occurred in New York City, the American sailor lost an interested and devoted friend.

[In addition to the references given above, see J. J. Currier, *Hist. of Newburyport*, vol. I (1906), vol. II (1909), and an excellent obituary in the *N. Y. Times*, Apr. 20, 1878. Much information regarding the character of Blunt's work and publications can also be gleaned from the prefaces to the various editions of the *Coast Pilot*.] G. H. B.

BLUNT, JAMES GILLPATRICK (July 21, 1826–July 25, 1881), physician, soldier, politician, was born in Trenton, Hancock County, Me., and after passing his earlier years in the little town of Ellsworth, yielded to his love of travel and adventure and went to sea. From his fifteenth to his twentieth year he was a sailor. Subsequently he decided to study medicine, and in the year 1849 graduated from the Starling Medical College, Columbus, Ohio. He practised his profession in New Madison, Ohio, where he married Nancy Carson Putnam, daughter of Ernestus and Elizabeth Putnam. In 1856 he moved to Kansas, where he settled at Greeley and continued the practise of medicine, but soon became actively interested in politics and took an active part in the anti-slavery movement. He was closely associated with John Brown, and his strong antipathy toward slavery took practical form in aiding Brown in secretly removing slaves from the United States into Canada. A member from Anderson County, of the now historic constitutional convention, which met at Wyandotte, July 5, 1859, and which framed the constitution of Kansas, Blunt was made chairman of the committee on militia,—an appointment which probably influenced his future military career. On July 24, 1861, he was mustered into the Union army as lieutenant-colonel of the 3rd Kansas Volunteers, and later was placed in command of cavalry attached to the brigade of Gen. James H. Lane. On Apr. 8, 1862, he was promoted brigadier-general, and placed in command of the military department of Kansas. He first distinguished himself with his brigade of Kansans and Cherokees, Oct. 22, 1862, in what is known as the battle of Old Fort Wayne, near the southwest corner of Missouri. Here he encountered the enemy, some 3,000 to 5,000 Indians under Col. Douglas H. Cooper, concentrated near Maysville and on their way north to invade Kansas. The Confederates were severely punished and gave up their northward march, and on Nov. 20, 1862, Gen. Schofield turned over to Blunt command of what was known as the Army of the Frontier (*Battles and Leaders of the Civil War*, III, 446–47). Continuing his active operations against the Confederates, Blunt attacked Gen. Marmaduke, Nov. 28, 1862, at Cane Hill, and signally defeated him. These successful operations were recognized by the Federal government by Blunt's promotion to major-general, Nov. 29, 1862. Still on the aggressive, Blunt again attacked the enemy under Gen. Hindman on Dec. 7, at Prairie Grove, and, with the coöperation of Gen. Herron, caused Hindman to fall back fifty miles to the Arkansas River and to abandon his objective of occupying Missouri. Following up his advantage, Blunt captured Van Buren on the Arkansas, Dec. 28, again defeated the Confederate forces, and destroyed four of their gunboats. In June 1863, having been relieved of command of the Department of Kansas. he took the field with the Army of the Frontier, and on July 16 defeated Gen. Cooper at Honey Springs, and opposed with his division the threatened invasion of Missouri by Gen. Sterling Price. At Newtonia, Mo., Oct. 28, 1864, he defeated Price, and in combination with Gen. Sanborn, engaged in a final skirmish with Shelby's cavalry. This ended what is known in history as the disastrous "Price Raid." Viewed in the light of a subsequent study of conditions obtaining at that period, it seems quite certain that had not Blunt and his veteran soldiers thrown themselves across Price's advance, he would undoubtedly have captured Kansas City and occupied southeastern Kansas. After Price's defeat, the latter crossed the Arkansas River above Fort Smith with a few pieces of artillery, and with his army reduced by captures and dispersion to some 5,000 demoralized men. Most of the noted guerrilla bands followed Price from the state (*Ibid.*, IV, 374–77). At the close of the Civil War, Blunt was honorably mustered out of the service, July 29, 1865, and settled in Leavenworth, Kan., where he resumed the practise of his profession. About the year 1869, he removed to Washington, D. C., where for twelve years he practised before the Federal departments as a solicitor of claims. On Apr. 9, 1873, Blunt and others were charged by the Department of Justice with conspiracy to defraud the government and a body of Cherokee Indians in North Carolina, but about two years later he was discharged by the United States Court in North Carolina, hearing the case (D. W. Wilder, *The Annals of Kansas*, 1875, pp. 609, 680). His health gradually giving way, Blunt was, on Feb. 12, 1879, admitted as a patient to St. Elizabeth's, the government hospital for the insane, where he finally died. His remains were sent to Kansas for interment.

[Besides the references cited above, see F. B. Heitman, *Hist. Reg.* (1903); Wm. E. Connolly, *Standard Hist. of Kan.*, II (1918); *Kan. State Hist. Colls.*, I, II; *Evening Star* (Washington, D. C.), July 28, 1881.]

C. D. R.

BLYTHE, HERBERT. [See BARRYMORE, MAURICE, 1847–1905.]

BOARDMAN, THOMAS DANFORTH (Jan. 21, 1784–Sept. 10, 1873), pewterer, was born in Litchfield, Conn., the son of Oliver and Sarah (Danforth) Boardman. Oliver Boardman had served in the campaign against Burgoyne and at that time kept a diary now available in printed form in *Collections of the Connecticut Historical Society*, VII, 221–37. He removed from Litchfield to Hartford, where presumably Thomas was apprenticed. There, at all events, the latter began work in the ranks of craftsmen pewterers—possibly as early as 1807, though the date is not definitely known. On May 28, 1812, he was married to Elizabeth Bidwell Lewis of Glastonbury, who died in 1869. It is stated (Charlotte Goldthwaite, *Boardman Genealogy*, 1895, p. 448) that "Mr. Thomas D. Boardman and his family were all useful members of Dr. (Horace) Bushnell's church"— *i.e.*, the North Congregational, of which Bushnell was pastor from 1833 to 1859. During this period Boardman's shop was at 59 Main St., and his output included basins, ladles, porringers, and plates (ranging from six-inch through larger sizes). J. B. Kerfoot's *American Pewter* (1924, p. 58) has a picture of a T. D. Boardman communion flagon, thirteen and one-half inches in height. The recorded touch-marks employed by Thomas Boardman in his first period were: TDB in a rectangle; T. D. BOARDMAN in a rectangle; a spread-eagle with TDB; a spread-eagle surrounded by THOMAS D. BOARDMAN. He also occasionally used an X to indicate fine quality—this being uncommon with American makers, though standard practise in England. According to Kerfoot, Boardman stands out as the last pure representative of ancient traditions in pewter-making. A few specimens of his craftsmanship are in the Morgan collection of the Wadsworth Atheneum (*Bulletin of the Wadsworth Atheneum*, I, No. 2).

During Boardman's second period, he and his brother Sherman were in partnership, under the style of T. D. & S. Boardman, with an establishment on Main St., near Morgan. Pioneers in this country in the manufacture of britannia-ware and block-tin, they "carried on a successful business . . . for more than fifty years" (Goldthwaite). The old principles of craftsmanship were being affected by the rising tendency toward quantity production. The firm of Boardman brothers would seem to have led the way, and to have done much to set the patterns for new designs. It has been stated that the two Boardmans and William Calder of Providence, R. I., "are, between them, responsible for the great majority of the surviving porringers of early American origin" (Kerfoot, p. 44). "Offshoots" (Goldthwaite, p. 448)—affiliated concerns—appeared in New York and Philadelphia. The precise relation of these "offshoots" to the original firm has been considerably mooted. One view regards them as agencies for the sale of wares from the Hartford workshops, which thus found new outlets. The firm's own touch-mark was TD & SB in a rectangle.

[In addition to sources given above, see E. T. Freedley, *Leading Pursuits and Leading Men* (1856), p. 404.]

G. S. B.

BOAS, EMIL LEOPOLD (Nov. 15, 1854–May 3, 1912), was for thirty years the general manager for the United States of the Hamburg-American Steamship Line and for about five years its sole American director. He was born in Goerlitz, Germany, the son of Louis and Minna Boas. After attending the local schools he was sent to the Royal Frederick William Gymnasium, in Breslau, and then to the Sophia Gymnasium, in Berlin. He graduated at the unusually early age of eighteen and at once began work as a clerk in the banking office of C. B. Richard & Boas, of which an uncle of his was a member. In the following year (1873) he was transferred to the New York office of the firm, which was then the American representative of the Hamburg-American Steamship Company. By his close application to the interests of the company he attracted the attention of its heads and was promoted. He was married, Mar. 20, 1888, to Harriet B. Sternfeld, who afterward became prominent in various women's organizations. In 1892, when the steamship company established a separate office in New York, he was made one of the three directors and also the general manager. In 1907 he became the sole director, or "resident manager." For his services in the development of their commerce and in safeguarding the welfare of their subjects he was many times decorated by European rulers.

Boas witnessed the evolution of the ocean-going steamship from the packet type of the seventies to the huge liner of the present day. As a clerk in the Richard & Boas office he had made shipping his particular study and had become a master of technical detail. He took a leading part in building up the New York agency until it became the center and controlling pivot for a vast network of steamship routes, and he was energetic in all movements looking toward the improvement of commercial and traffic facilities. Following the *Titanic* disaster he was the first steamship manager to announce an intention of providing an adequate number of life-boats for passengers and crew. He also began an investigation of safety devices, but his study was stopped by his death, less than a month later, at his summer home in Greenwich, Conn.

Boas was one of the foremost business men of the metropolis. He was an incredibly active man, and the strain of work is said to have worn him down. His activities, however, extended far beyond his business. His range of interests was wide, and the number of organizations to which he belonged was exceptionally large. An advocate of Germanic culture, he was a leading figure in the German societies. He was also a music lover and a cultivator of rare flowers. Above all, he was a life-long student, and to his acquaintances he gave the impression of being a scholar rather than a business man.

[*Who's Who in America,* 1912–13; obituaries in the *Times, Sun, Tribune,* and *Herald* of New York, May 4, 1912.] W. J. G.

BÔCHER, MAXIME (Aug. 28, 1867–Sept. 12, 1918), mathematician, born in Boston, was fortunate in his parentage. His father, Ferdinand Bôcher, born in New York City of Normandy parents, was one of the best-known teachers in the country, being for many years professor of French at Harvard, a man of all-round culture, and a great collector of books in the field of French literature, art, and history; his mother, Caroline Little, belonged to one of the oldest New England families, tracing her ancestry back to Richard Warren of the *Mayflower* company and maintaining the best of the intellectual and moral traditions of Boston and the East. Passing from the Cambridge Latin School to Harvard, where he graduated in 1888, Bôcher's education at home and in the schools was built upon a more secure foundation than came to the lot of most men in his day. In college he took a broad course but found his chief interest in mathematics; while he received the bachelor's degree *summa cum laude,* he at the same time had the distinction of highest honors in his chosen subject, his thesis being "On three systems of parabolic coördinates."

It was characteristic of the catholicity of view of his father and himself that his doctor's degree was taken at Göttingen. Family reasons might have suggested Paris, but scientific reasons in the late eighties pointed clearly to Germany, and notably to Klein, who was then lecturing on the potential function and studying especially the series and integrals employed in the theory. It was in this domain that Bôcher began his most serious work. His paper, "Ueber die Reihenentwickelungen der Potential-theorie" (Göttingen, 1891) not only served as his doctor's dissertation but secured for him a prize offered by the University and hence bore upon the title-page the words "Gekrönte Preisschrift und Dissertation." Far from narrowing his interests, as is so often the case, his investigation broadened them, extending his work into the fields of theoretical physics, pure geometry, and higher analysis. His later work, however, was not so much in the field of pure geometry as in that of differential equations, series, and higher algebra. In September 1891 he became instructor in mathematics at Harvard, in September 1894 assistant professor, and in 1904 professor. As a teacher, he was unusually successful. He was clear in his lectures and stimulating in the suggestiveness of his assignments. His great influence on mathematics in America was exerted in the seminar where he did much to train some of the later leaders in mathematical research in this country. In the year 1913–14 he was exchange professor at Paris. His most important publications consisted of nearly a hundred memoirs and reviews in his field of interest, and an algebra (1907) which gave a new view of the higher domain of this important branch of mathematics. Less significant as mathematical contributions but very stimulating in the more elementary courses were his works on trigonometry (with Mr. Gaylord) and analytic geometry. On the completion of his course at Göttingen he had married Marie Niemann of that city, and she, with three children, survived him. His health began to fail at about the time of his lectures in Paris, and his closing years were a period of trial for one upon whose strength so many demands were made and who felt himself unable to give to his students the degree of assistance that had characterized his earlier days. His loss to American scholarship was severely felt, not alone in this country, but by the entire mathematical world.

[For the biography of Bôcher consult "The Life and Services of Maxime Bôcher" in the *Bull. Am. Mathematical Soc.,* XXV, 337–50, by his colleague Prof. Wm. F. Osgood. For a summary of his contributions consult "The Scientific Work of Maxime Bôcher," *Ibid.,* pp. 197–215, by Prof. Geo. D. Birkhoff. In the latter article will be found a complete list of Bôcher's publications chronologically arranged. The Minute on his life and services, placed upon the records of the faculty of arts and sciences of Harvard University, was printed in *Science,* Nov. 29, 1918.] D. E. S.

BOCOCK, THOMAS STANLEY (May 18, 1815–Aug. 5, 1891), congressman, was born in that part of Buckingham County, Va., which later became a part of Appomattox County. He was one of the twelve children of John Thomas and Mary (Flood) Bocock. Receiving his preparatory work, as well as his later law course, from a brother, Willis P. Bocock, later attorney-general of Virginia, he ranked first among the B.A. graduates of Hampden-Sidney, in 1838. Elected to the General Assembly at the age of twenty-seven he remained until 1845, when he became county commonwealth's attorney. In 1847 he went to the United States House of Representatives, where he was appointed to the naval committee and was for a decade its chairman. His vote on the compromise measures of 1850 is not recorded, but he favored the Kansas-Nebraska bill and the Lecompton constitution. He developed great skill in what Congressman S. S. Cox called "parliamentary skirmishing" (Cox, *Union-Disunion-Reunion: Three Decades of Federal Legislation,* 1885, p. 74), and was the Democratic candidate for the speakership against John Sherman and fourteen lesser candidates. On the first ballot he received eighty-six votes—twenty more than Sherman, but still less than a majority. The balloting went on from Dec. 5, 1859, until Feb. 1, 1860, when, Bocock and Sherman both having withdrawn, Pennington was elected on the forty-fourth ballot. The story used to be told that after the war older members of the House sometimes absent-mindedly voted "Bocock" or "Sherman" instead of "Yes" or "No."

Following Virginia's passage of the secession resolution, Bocock, on May 7, 1861, entered the Provisional Congress of the Confederate States as a delegate from Virginia. He became, by unanimous vote, speaker of the Confederate House of Representatives in both the First and Second Congresses, and headed the delegation that presented to President Davis what the latter called "a warning if not a threat" that the House was in a mood to pass a vote of want of confidence in the President's cabinet (N. W. Stephenson, *The Day of the Confederacy,* 1919, p. 156). After the war Bocock entered the General Assembly, 1869–70, as a moderate Conservative; was a delegate to the Democratic national conventions of 1868, 1876, and 1880; and in the *post-bellum* contest between Virginia's "readjusters" and those who advocated the payment of the war debt, dollar for dollar, he came forward as a compromiser in the Bocock-Fowler bill which failed of passage (C. C. Pearson, *The Readjuster Movement in Virginia,* 1917, p. 79). He became attorney for two or three railroads, held high rank as a practising attorney, and rendered great service to Hampden-Sidney College in its post-war financial difficulties (*Richmond Dispatch,* Aug. 7, 1891).

Bocock was a skilful parliamentarian, as is very evident from a perusal of the *Congressional Globe.* He was in great demand as presiding officer of conventions in Virginia. This is accounted for by his ability to preserve order, and by suggestion to call forth motions suited to the parliamentary situation. He was also in demand as a speaker. A lover of books, he collected one of the largest private libraries in Virginia. On Aug. 5, 1891, he died at "Wildway," six miles from Appomattox Court House. He was twice married, first to Sarah P. Flood, and, second, to Annie Faulkner.

[*Jours. of the General Assembly of Va.*; *Cong. Globe,* for the years 1847–61; *Jours. of the Confed. Cong*; *Sen. Doc. 654,* 61 Cong., 2 Sess.; Thos. Cary Johnson, *Thos. S. Bocock*; *Political Pamphlets,* vols. XXVIII, XXXI (Va. State Lib.).] E. L. F.

BOEHLER, PETER (Dec. 31, 1712–Apr. 27, 1775), was a bishop in the *Unitas Fratrum,* commonly called the Moravian Church. The *Unitas Fratrum* of the eighteenth century was a revival of the old church organization in Bohemia and Moravia, dating from the time of John Hus. Refugees from Moravia found religious freedom on the lands of Count Zinzendorf in Herrnhut, Saxony, and developed there a community which became the center of a great spiritual awakening. Peter Boehler early felt the influence of the Moravian Brethren, and carried that influence to England and America as religious teacher and as organizer of other communities on the order of Herrnhut. He was born in Frankfurt-am-Main, son of John Conrad Boehler and his wife, Antonetta Elizabetha Hanf. The father was a worthy burgher, innkeeper and brewer, and at one time comptroller at the Corn Office (Lockwood, *Memorials,* p. 52). The child Peter began school at the age of four, started Latin at eight, and was ready for the Gymnasium in Frankfurt at ten. On the advice of his instructors he prepared for the study of theology instead of medicine as he had planned. In 1731 he went to the University of Jena where he yielded to the influences of the pietists, especially the lecturer Spangenberg. When Zinzendorf visited the University in 1732, Boehler made a sacred agreement with him to carry on the work of Christ. Boehler became Magister Legens in 1736 with the right to lecture as junior professor. Two years later he entered upon the missionary endeavors which occupied most of his life. According to a project arranged by Zinzendorf and the English Society for the

Propagation of the Gospel, Boehler was to organize missions among the negro slaves of South Carolina in the vicinity of Purysburg. At the same time he was to act as pastor to a group of Moravians in Savannah. Boehler spent several weeks in England on his way to America,—weeks significant for his contact with the founders of Methodism, the spread of Moravian doctrines, and the organization of classes. He preached frequently to groups in London, and visited Oxford twice in the company of the Wesleys, addressing both citizens and students. His success as an evangelist was due both to his personality and the clarity of his argument. A frank and open countenance with clear, fearless eyes gained the trust of his listeners, whether in public addresses or in private conversations. His discussions of the cardinal points in the doctrine of the *Unitas Fratrum* influenced the Wesleys at a time when they were still uncertain of their faith. When Boehler left England John Wesley exclaimed, "O what a work hath God begun since his coming into England."

The American mission of Boehler and his companion, Georg Schulius, began in September 1738. The possibilities for success were not promising, for the company of Moravians in Savannah had dwindled to nine, and there were practically no negro slaves around Purysburg. Boehler suffered a severe illness, and Schulius died. In the meantime the Moravians in Georgia were troubled by the warfare with the Spaniards, and decided to migrate to Pennsylvania. Boehler became their leader. At that time began his connection with George Whitefield when the Moravians took passage for Philadelphia in Whitefield's sloop. With some difficulty Boehler managed to hold his small group together after they reached Pennsylvania, for they were without funds. Whitefield had purchased land at the forks of the Delaware, and there the Moravians agreed to build a stone school-house for his use. The obstacles which the Brethren had to face that year in the wilderness tested the ability of their leader. The work was barely begun when winter set in, and doctrinal differences which had developed between Whitefield and the Moravians made him question the desirability of having the Brethren on his land. They stayed during the winter, however; then moved to the site of Bethlehem. They were later able to purchase the land at the forks from Whitefield. Before the permanent settlement was made Nitschmann had succeeded Boehler, and the latter had sailed for Europe in January 1741. While in England he preached for a while in Yorkshire, assisting Ingham. After a visit to his family in Frankfurt he returned to England to organize a new company of emigrants to America, the "Sea Congregation." His wife, Elizabeth Hobson, whom he married in London on Feb. 20, 1742, accompanied him on this second expedition.

Boehler's varied experiences during his stay in America included a trip through the Indian country west of Bethlehem, and expulsion from New York in 1743 under a colonial law which forbade the teachings of papists and Moravians. For over a year he was in charge of the community at Bethlehem, and Syndic of the Pennsylvania Synod. Relieved of responsibility by the arrival of Spangenberg, he returned to Europe. Although his ship was captured by a French privateer, he was released in France and found his way into Germany through Holland. Six of the eight years which intervened before his next visit to America were spent in England where he acted as superintendent of the Moravian Church. He was consecrated bishop on Jan. 10, 1748. His genius for financial management saved the English branch of the Church from bankruptcy and placed it on a firm basis. Another opportunity to exercise his financial ability presented itself when he returned to Bethlehem in 1753 and rescued the mortgaged lands from threatened foreclosure. A period of eleven years of service in America ensued, during which time he was absent only six months when attending a General Synod in Germany. For eight of these years he was vice-superintendent of the American Province. The new community of Bethabara in North Carolina was organized during this time. Boehler's later years were filled with the duties of a member of the Directory, and then of the new board called the Unity's Elders' Conference. Official business often called him to England, and on one of these visits he was stricken with paralysis. He died on Apr. 27, 1775, and was buried in the Moravian cemetery in Chelsea.

[The two best accounts of the life of Peter Boehler are the ones included in Edmund de Schweinitz, *Some Fathers of the Am. Moravian Ch.* (Bethlehem, 1881) and *Memorials of the Life of Peter Boehler* by J. P. Lockwood (London, 1868). The relations of Boehler with the Wesleys may best be studied from the *Jour. of John Wesley* (Standard Ed. of his works, N. Y., 1909). A contemporary history of the Unitas Fratrum, *Alte und Neue Brueder-Historie oder kurz gefasste Geschichte der Evangelischen Brueder Unitaet in den aeltern Zeiten und insonderheit in dem gegenwaertigen Jahrhundert* by David Cranz (Barby, 1771) is invaluable for background and for many of the most important facts of Boehler's life. There is an English translation by Benj. La Trobe (London, 1780).] D. M. C.

BOEHM, HENRY (June 8, 1775–Dec. 28, 1875), Methodist itinerant preacher, was born in Lancaster County, Pa., the son of Martin [*q.v.*] and Eve (Steiner) Boehm. His father was expelled from the Mennonites for his "too evangelical opinions" (Abel Stevens, *A Compendious History of American Methodism,* 1867, p. 352), and became a bishop of the United Brethren Church, the members of which were largely German Methodists. His home at Conestoga sheltered many of the itinerant preachers of the pioneer period of Methodism and in "Boehm's Chapel," built in 1791, their voices were heard. Henry Boehm's boyhood was passed under frontier conditions and amid these religious influences. He was a vigorous, daring, self-trained young man of twenty-five when he himself became an itinerant preacher, traveling circuits in Maryland, Virginia, and the regions beyond. Later he labored in Pennsylvania, introducing Methodism into Reading and Harrisburg. His success was augmented by his ability to preach fluently both in English and German. Before 1810 he had preached in German in fourteen different states. At Bishop Asbury's request he superintended the translation of the Methodist Discipline into the German language, thus giving material aid to the progress of the Methodist Episcopal Church among the Germans of the United States. As traveling companion of Bishop Asbury for five years he visited annually not only all the states along the Atlantic coast, but all the frontier settlements and many of the isolated homes. After he ceased to travel with Bishop Asbury he was appointed to various important districts of the rapidly growing denomination needing skilled leadership, and then to pulpits of commanding influence in Pennsylvania and New Jersey until old age compelled him to ask release from regular ministerial duties. After his one hundredth birthday he preached several times, and only a few days before his death gave an effective formal address.

[Boehm's *Reminiscences, Historical and Biographical, of Sixty-four Years in the Ministry,* ed. by Dr. John B. Wakeley (1865; republished with additional chapters in 1875 under title, *The Patriarch of One Hundred Years*); sketch by J. B. Good in Alex. Harris, *Biog. Hist. of Lancaster County* (1872), pp. 49–62; *Jour. of the Rev. Francis Asbury* (1832), vols. II, III; *Minutes of the Annual Conferences of the M. E. Ch. for 1876*; J. M. Buckley, *Constitutional and Parliamentary Hist. of the M. E. Ch.* (1912); J. G. Hurst, *Hist. of Methodism* (1902–04); Wm. H. Daniels, *Illus. Hist. of Methodism* (1880); the Wakeley Collection of MSS. in Drew Theological Seminary, Madison, N. J.]

E. S. T.

BOEHM, JOHN PHILIP (1683–Apr. 29, 1749), German Reformed clergyman, was born at Hochstadt, near Frankfurt-am-Main, Germany, the son of the local Reformed pastor, Philip Ludwig Boehm, and his wife Maria, and was baptized Nov. 25, 1683. He was schoolmaster of the Reformed congregation at Worms Mar. 11, 1708–Nov. 22, 1715, and at Lambsheim, a short distance southwest of Worms, from then till 1720, when he emigrated with his family to Pennsylvania. Before moving to Worms he had been married to Anna Maria Stehler; his second wife was Anna Maria Scherer of Lambsheim. He settled as a farmer in Whitpain Township, Philadelphia (later Montgomery) County, and, being devoted to the Reformed Church, gathered his German neighbors together and conducted services for them. This beginning led to work that made him the founder of the German Reformed Church in Pennsylvania. At the earnest entreaty of friends who urged that he could not justify his refusal before God, he finally, with some misgiving, assumed the pastoral office. The territory that he covered in his ministerial visits extended from the Delaware to the Susquehanna and from Philadelphia to the Blue Mountains; every month, he wrote in a letter of July 9, 1744, he traveled over 100 miles preaching the gospel and administering the sacraments. He served the congregations of Falkner Swamp, Skippack, and Whitemarsh (1725); Conestoga, the older Tulpehocken congregation, and Philadelphia (1727); Egypt, probably (1734); Cocalico (1735); Oley (1736); the second Tulpehocken congregation (1738); Providence (1742); Coventry (1746); and Whitpain (1747); but he was not allowed to carry on this work in peace. In 1727 the Rev. George Michael Weiss, university educated and regularly ordained, appeared on the scene, denounced Boehm as a mere farmer unfit for the duties of the ministry, and attempted, with some success, to wrest his congregations from him. Boehm and his friends, recognizing that his position was irregular, appealed to the Classis of Amsterdam, which ruled that Boehm's call to the ministry was lawful and his acts valid but stipulated that he should receive ordination. He was accordingly ordained in New York on Nov. 23, 1729, by the Dutch Reformed clergymen, Henricus Boel and Gualtherus Du Bois. Weiss thereupon professed to be reconciled but later resumed his poaching on Boehm's preserves. Trouble of another sort came with Count Zinzendorf's visit to Pennsylvania (Nov. 29, 1741–Dec. 31, 1742). An honest sectarian, Boehm saw the results of his long, body-breaking labors melting away before the Count's unionistic movement and resisted furiously. His *Getreuer Warnungsbrief an die Hochteutsche Evangelisch Reformirten Gemeinden und alle deren Glieder in Pensylvanien* (Phila., A. Bradford, 1742) was part of his counter-propaganda. As old age came upon him, he found his duties increasingly onerous and begged the Dutch

Church authorities for aid. This came at last in the person of Michael Schlatter [*q.v.*], who visited Boehm, Sept. 7, 1746, the day after his arrival in Philadelphia. On Sept. 29, 1747, the Coetus of Pennsylvania was formed; at its second meeting the next year Boehm was elected president. By this time he had given up all his congregations except the one Schlatter had organized for him in Whitpain Township. Seven months later he died unexpectedly at his son's home at Hellertown. His funeral sermon, it would have chagrined him to know, was preached by a Mennonite. He was buried in the church now named for him in front of the pulpit under the altar. As a successful farmer, he left a respectable estate.

[W. J. Hinke, *Life and Letters of the Rev. John Philip Boehm* (1916); J. I. Good, *Hist. of the Ref. Ch. in the U. S. in the Nineteenth Century* (1911); J. I. Good and W. J. Hinke, eds., *Minutes and Letters of the Coetus of the German Ref. Congregations in Pa., 1747–92* (1903).] G. H. G.

BOEHM, MARTIN (Nov. 30, 1725–Mar. 23, 1812), Mennonite bishop, United Brethren bishop, was the son of Jacob Boehm, one of the Mennonites from the Palatinate, who settled in Conestoga Township, Lancaster County, Pa., in the early eighteenth century (I. Daniel Rupp, *A Collection of Upwards of Thirty Thousand Names of German, Swiss, Dutch, French, and other Immigrants in Pennsylvania, 1727–76*, 1876, Appendix III, p. 436). Jacob married into the Kendig family, early settlers in the county, became a deacon in the Mennonite Church, and prospered as farmer and blacksmith. Martin Boehm received his early education at home. He knew both German and English. Though the former was his mother tongue and the language which he used in preaching, he possessed a library of English works which according to his son Henry [*q.v.*], he read "with great pleasure and profit; among others, Wesley's *Sermons* and Fletcher's *Checks*" (Henry Boehm, *Reminiscences, Historical and Biographical, of Sixty-four Years in the Ministry*, 1865, p. 383). His mind was strong and stored with learning, according to his friend, Bishop Asbury. Like his father, Martin Boehm was a farmer; but religion early became the main interest of his life. He inherited the paternal estate which he cared for until his own son Jacob was old enough to manage it. In 1753 he married Eve Steiner, a woman of Swiss ancestry. About three years later he was chosen by lot as a preacher for the Mennonites (Minton Thrift, *Memoir of the Rev. Jesse Lee with Extracts from his Journals*, 1823, p. 253). In 1759 he became a bishop. Because formalism characterized the Mennonite Church, as it did many of the religions of the day, his task as preacher proved difficult. After experiencing a spiritual conversion he gradually broke away from the orthodox manner of worship, and was influenced to preach a more vital faith. During a preaching tour in the Shenandoah Valley he heard of the teaching of George Whitefield. Later, preachers of the "new light" movement found their way into Lancaster County where they were welcome in Boehm's home.

Of great significance in his later life was his connection with William Otterbein. The two preachers met sometime between 1766 and 1768 (A. W. Drury, *History of the Church of the United Brethren in Christ*, 1924, p. 88). Boehm was addressing an overflow congregation in an orchard not far from Lancaster. Otterbein was among the listeners, and at the close of the service he is said to have clasped Boehm in his arms, exclaiming, "We are brethren." Otterbein and Boehm were chosen at the first annual conference in 1800 as the first bishops of the Church of the United Brethren in Christ. Long before 1800, however, Boehm's connection with the Mennonites had been broken. The Mennonites had censured him for his doctrine and his method of preaching because they thought he was lacking in respect for the ordinances of the church, and because he associated with men of other denominations (John F. Funk, *The Mennonite Church and Her Accusers*, 1878, pp. 42 ff.). Reproofs failed to bring Boehm back into the narrow ways of the sect. Bishops, ministers, and deacons, in conference, therefore, decided to exclude him and his followers from communion and the counsel of the brotherhood. He continued his itinerant preaching, nevertheless, and became more and more successful. He still wore the long beard and plain costume of the Mennonites, and maintained also their simplicity of manner. These characteristics marked his appearance in the pulpit, but more impressive were the sweetness of his character and a quality common to successful revivalists, a peculiar magnetic force. He traveled widely through southern Pennsylvania, Maryland, and Virginia, holding service in barns when the regular meeting places failed to accommodate the crowds of Lutherans, Reformed, Mennonites, and Dunkards who flocked to hear him. Boehm often united in services with other preachers who laid emphasis upon the things of the spirit. He was present at the conference in Baltimore where the Church of the United Brethren in Christ was first organized. He also attended the second conference in 1791, the first annual conference in 1800, and every succeeding conference, with the exception of those in 1806 and 1808, until two years before his death (Drury, *op. cit.*, p. 208; and *Religious Telescope,* June 5, 1926). While thus playing an important part in the Church of the United Brethren, Boehm also formed a connection with the Methodists. A "class" was formed at his house in 1775, and Methodist ministers frequently preached in his father's home until the Methodists built a chapel on land which had belonged to the Boehms. In 1802 Boehm allowed his name to be placed on the class book to comply with Methodist rules of attendance, but evidence that he ever left the Church of the United Brethren is lacking. Boehm's liberality, which had caused his break with the Mennonites, made the dual connection with Methodists and United Brethren possible. In referring to his membership in the Methodist class he said, "For myself, I felt my heart more greatly enlarged towards all religious persons and to all denominations of Christians" (Francis Hollingsworth, *Methodist Magazine,* June 1823, VI, 212). Thus affiliated with two churches, he continued to serve in the ministry, preaching occasionally, though growing more and more feeble, till his death, Mar. 23, 1812.

[References given above.] D. M. C.

BOELEN, JACOB (*c.* 1654–1729), silversmith, was born in the Netherlands and brought to America about 1659. The name of his master has not yet been discovered. He was married on May 21, 1679, to Catharina Klock. His brother Henricus (b. 1661) was associated with him in his work and later his son Henricus (b. 1697) carried on his business in the shop on lower Broadway. Judged by the excellence of his general workmanship and the skill of his engraving, he ranks as one of the best of the early silverworkers of New York City. He was admitted a freeman in 1698 but before that time had begun his public services, having been an assessor for the North Ward 1685–94, having been appointed "brant-master" in 1689, and being alderman from the North Ward 1695–97–98–1701. His name was signed to a petition for the restoration of the bolting monopoly to New York. His will was proved Mar. 23, 1729.

[E. Alfred Jones, *The Old Silver of Am. Churches* (1913); F. H. Bigelow, *Historic Silver of the Colonies and its Makers* (1917); Robt. Ensko, *Makers of Early Am. Silver* (1915); Stephen Ensko, *Am. Silversmiths and their Marks* (1927); Metropolitan Museum of Art Catalogues of Silver Exhibitions,—namely, the Clearwater Collection, the Hudson-Fulton Celebration Exhibition, and the 1911 Exhibition of Silver used in New York, New Jersey and the South.] K. H. A.

BOGARDUS, EVERARDUS (1607–Sept. 27, 1647), second minister of New Netherland, was born at Woerden, Netherlands, the son of Willem Bogardus. He matriculated in Leyden University, July 17, 1627, as a student of letters, but on Sept. 9, 1630, before he had finished his studies, he was sent by the Consistory of Amsterdam as a comforter of the sick to Guinea, whence he returned in 1632, with good testimonials. After having been examined and ordained for the ministry, he was, on July 15, 1632, accepted for service in New Netherland, as successor to Rev. Jonas Michaëlius, the first minister. He sailed the same month with Wouter van Twiller, the newly appointed director general, in the ship *Soutberg,* which arrived at New Amsterdam in April 1633. His advent in New Netherland marks the erection of the first church edifice at New Amsterdam, a plain wooden building, on the site of the present 39 Pearl Street, which took the place of the mill loft used by Michaëlius. Bogardus soon came into conflict with Van Twiller, whom he threatened to denounce openly from the pulpit. He was also antagonistic to Lubbert van Dincklagen, the public prosecutor, who on his return to Holland, in 1636, laid charges against Bogardus before the Classis of Amsterdam. On July 8, 1638, Bogardus petitioned the director and council of New Netherland for leave to go to Holland to defend himself, but it was felt that he could not be spared. Van Dincklagen renewed his accusations and, in 1640, requested the Classis to be relieved from the excommunication which had been passed upon him through the machinations of Bogardus. After some correspondence with the Consistory of New Amsterdam, the Classis, in 1644, resolved to postpone action until Bogardus could be heard. Meanwhile, in 1638, Bogardus married Anneke Jans, the widow of Roeloff Jansen van Masterland, an early settler of Rensselaerswyck. Through this marriage Bogardus came into possession of a farm of sixty-two acres on Manhattan Island, which in 1636 had been granted to Roeloff Jansen and which afterward became known as the "Domine's Bouwery." In 1642, at the wedding of Bogardus's eldest stepdaughter, Sara Roeloff, to Dr. Hans Kierstede, Director General Kieft secured subscriptions for a new church. From the pulpit in this church, Bogardus afterward severely criticized the director's Indian policy and made uncomplimentary allusions to his person. Kieft at first sent him a "Christian admonition," which Bogardus refused to receive, and then, on Jan. 2, 1646, in the name of the council, sent him a formal communication, in which among other things he accused him of having appeared in the pulpit while drunk and in which he threatened to prosecute him in a court of justice for stirring up the people to mutiny and rebellion. Bogardus admitted some facts, but demanded proof of others and denied that Kieft and his council had jurisdiction to try his case. The director and council offered to submit the matter to impartial judges. Bogardus, however, preferred to defend himself before the Classis of Amsterdam and requested that another minister be sent over in his place. On Aug. 17, 1647, he and Kieft and many other passengers sailed on board the ship *de Princesse* from New Amsterdam. The captain having missed his reckoning, the ship was wrecked during a violent September gale near Swansea, on the southern coast of Wales. Out of about one hundred persons on board, eighty-one perished, among them Kieft and Bogardus.

[Manuscript minutes of the Consistory and of the Classis at Amsterdam, the New York Colonial MSS. in the N. Y. State Lib. at Albany, and the letters and documents in the Sage Lib. at New Brunswick, N. J.; J. R. Brodhead and E. B. O'Callaghan, *Docs. Relating to the Colonial Hist. of the State of N. Y.*, I (1855), 206, 299, 345, 417, and XIV (1883), 12, 16, 59, 69–73, 82–87; *Ecclesiastical Records of the State of N. Y.*, I (1901), 81, 87, 126–27, 181, and VII (1916); *Van Rensselaer Bowier MSS.* (1908), pp. 77, 352, 404, 423, 431, 615, 648; J. R. Brodhead, *Hist. of the State of N. Y.*, I (1853); J. F. Jameson, *Narratives of New Netherland* (1909); E. T. Corwin, *Manual of the Reformed Ch. in America* (4th ed. 1902).]

A. J. F. V-L.

BOGARDUS, JAMES (Mar. 14, 1800–Apr. 13, 1874), inventor, was born in Catskill, N. Y., the son of James and Martha (Spencer) Bogardus. After attending school at irregular intervals until he was fourteen years old, Bogardus became an apprentice to a watchmaker, specializing from the very beginning in engraving and die-sinking. After completing his apprenticeship he left Catskill and went to New York City where he lived and worked for the rest of his life. The earliest record of Bogardus's inventive powers and mechanical skill is the award to him of the gold medal of the American Institute of New York at its first Fair in 1828, for an eight-day, three-wheeled chronometer clock. Two years later on Mar. 2, 1830, he received a patent for a clock which was a most complicated timepiece. The same year he perfected his first generally useful invention, patented May 25, 1830. It was a "ring flyer" and was largely used for fifty years or more thereafter in cotton-spinning machinery. This was followed the next year by another successful invention, namely, an eccentric sugar-grinding mill. From these two inventions Bogardus received sufficient remuneration to permit him to resume work in die-sinking and engraving and in 1831 he made an engraving machine capable of turning imitation filigree work, rays radiating from a common point, and figures in relief, all in one operation. Its special use was for making engraved metal watch dials. About this time, too, he perfected a so-called transfer machine with which he introduced the production of bank-note plates from separate dies. Again on May 18, 1832, he received a patent for an improvement in the striking parts of clocks. By this time Bogardus was being recognized as an unusual technician, and besides his own work he was often called upon to develop the ideas of others. Thus on Mar. 19, 1833, Miles Berry received a patent for a dry gas meter which was devised by Bogardus. The latter improved the meter during the next two years and was again awarded the gold medal of the American Institute in 1835. On Sept. 17, 1833, he received a patent for a metal-cased pencil, the lead of which was "forever pointed." In 1836 Bogardus went to England and almost immediately accepted a public challenge to construct an engraving machine. This machine made not only an accurate facsimile of the head of Ariadne on a medal but from the medal engraved comic facial expressions. With the machine Bogardus, at her own request, engraved a portrait of Queen Victoria. In 1839 he won the award of $2,000 offered by the English Government for the best engraving machine and plan for making postage stamps. Upon returning to New York in 1840, Bogardus continued his inventive work and during the next seven years perfected a number of devices. These included a white lead paint grinding-mill, a rice grinder, a new eccentric mill, a dynamometer, and a portable horse power. Probably his greatest contribution was his introduction of the use of cast-iron for the frames, floors, and all supports of buildings. His first construction of this sort was his own five-story factory building erected in 1850. This is said to have been the first complete cast-iron building in the world. He patented his method and in the years following erected many other iron buildings throughout the United States and in Cuba. Amongst these were the office building of the Baltimore *Sun*, the Adams Express Building in Washington, the Birch Building in Chicago, and the Public Ledger Building in Philadelphia. Of his last inventions the more important were a machine for pressing glass, a machine for cutting India rubber threads for the production of shirred goods, a pyrometer of great accuracy, and a deep-sea sounding device. Bogardus married Margaret Maclay, the eldest daughter of Rev. Archibald Maclay, D.D., of New York, on Feb. 12, 1831. None of their children having lived to maturity, they adopted a niece, Harriet Hogg, who survived them.

[Sources of information on James Bogardus are *Scientific American,* May 2, 1874; Records Am. Inst., N. Y.; the *New York Herald,* Apr. 14, 1874; *Hist. of Greene County, N. Y.* (1884); U. S. Pat. Office Records; *Centenary Celebration of the First Commercial Gas Co.:* account published by Am. Gas Institute, 1912.]

C. W. M.

BOGART, JOHN (Feb. 8, 1836–Apr. 25, 1920), engineer, was descended from Dutch ancestors who settled in 1641 at Albany, N. Y., where he was born, the son of John Henry and Eliza (Hermans) Bogart. His formal education was received at the Albany Academy and at Rutgers College, from which he was graduated in 1853 with the degree of A.B. He commenced the study of law but, due to ill health, forsook it for the active exercise of engineering. His first position was a temporary one with the New York Central Railroad. He served as an engineer during the Civil War. In 1870 he was married to Emma Cherrington Jefferis of West Chester, Pa. His engineering life was remarkable for the diversity of its accomplishments. Probably he was best known for his work in connection with public park planning and improvement in New York City and many other American cities, and for his contribution to hydro-electric development in the United States and Canada. As consulting engineer for the Cataract Construction Company (later the Niagara Falls Power Company) he traveled all over Europe, studying existing methods of power generation and transmission, and at Domène, opposite the Grand Chartreuse in the Dauphiné Alps, where the power for a paper-mill was drawn from a glacial stream in the mountains four miles away, he found the precedent which had great influence in the final decision as to the system to be adopted at Niagara. Possibly his main contribution to hydro-electric development was in his work as chief engineer of the Chattanooga and Tennessee River Power Company on a 60,000 horse-power plant in the Tennessee River near Chattanooga. "This work was particularly difficult on account of the great variation in head on the turbines and the difficult foundations for the dam. It was found necessary to resort to reinforced concrete pneumatic caissons in making the excavation and afterward to incorporate these as part of the dam. As far as known, this was the first instance where pneumatic caissons had been used for this purpose" (*Transactions of the American Society of Civil Engineers,* LXVIII, 1349).

As advisory engineer for the original Rapid Transit Commission of New York, Bogart prepared plans and contracts for the first subway system. He prepared plans for tunnels under the Hudson to Jersey City and Hoboken, and for the subway now operating between New York and Queens. He was delegated by the president to represent the United States at the international Navigation Congresses held in Düsseldorf, Germany, in 1902; in Milan, Italy, in 1905; and at St. Petersburg, Russia, in 1908. His technical work covered the field of engineering from railroads, canals, water-works, tunnels, parks, and bridges to hydro-electric development, dams, inland-waterway and irrigation projects. He earnestly believed that the great engineer was the man who, rather than specializing too deeply on any one phase of engineering, is capable of combining all essentials into a harmonious whole, and his varied work throughout a life of eighty-four years was a successful effort to realize this conviction.

[Files of the Am. Soc. of Civil Engineers, of which Bogart was, for years, secretary, especially biographical material prepared by Chas. A. Pohl, his partner, and by Herbert Spencer; article in the *Engineering News-Record,* vol. LXXXIV.]

E. Y.

BOGGS, CHARLES STUART (Jan. 28, 1811–Apr. 22, 1888), naval officer, was born at New Brunswick, N. J., the son of Robert Morris Boggs and his wife, Mary, a sister of the heroic Capt. James Lawrence, of "Don't give up the ship" fame. He was a descendant of Ezekiel Boggs who came from Ireland to Delaware about 1741. After several years in the well-known military school of Capt. Partridge at Middletown, Conn., young Charles was appointed a midshipman on Nov. 1, 1826, and was ordered to the sloop-of-war *Warren,* attached to the United States Squadron in the Mediterranean, at that time engaged in protecting American commerce against the Greek and North African pirates. Having served a short time on the ship-of-the-line *Delaware* in the same squadron, he was, in 1830, ordered to the schooner *Porpoise* of the West India Squadron, where he spent two years. On Apr. 28, 1832, having become passed-midshipman, he was attached to the receiving-ship at New York, and spent the next four years mostly on land duty. In 1836 he was appointed master of the ship-of-the-line *North Carolina,* and shortly afterward, as acting lieutenant, to the *Enterprise.* On Sept. 6, 1837, he was promoted to lieutenant, and, after returning home in the *North Carolina,* did notable service in the training of naval apprentices until 1842, when he joined the sloop *Saratoga* and took part in the hostilities against certain African slave ports. In 1846–47 he served on board the steamer *Princeton,* taking part in the bombardment of the castle of San Juan de Ulloa and the capture of Vera Cruz. The United States brig *Truxtun,* having been wrecked on a bar near that city and having fallen into the hands of the Mexicans, Boggs, in charge of a hazardous boat expedition, with great gallantry cut out and retook the ship. He was promoted commander Sept. 14, 1855. For the next three years, having received a furlough, he commanded the mail steamer *Illinois* in the service of the California Steamship Company. At the outbreak of the Civil War he was placed again on active service at his own request, and was given command of the steamer *Varuna,* which, as a unit of Farragut's fleet below New Orleans, was the first vessel to force its way past the batteries. Once beyond the fire of the forts, Boggs succeeded in doing great damage to the Confederate gunboats and auxiliaries. At dawn the next morning (Apr. 25, 1862) the *Varuna* was attacked by two powerful rams and run down by one of them, the *Stonewall Jackson.* Boggs was able, however, to beach the *Varuna,* and in a disabled and sinking condition she continued to fire, practically destroying her two adversaries, until her guns actually sank below the surface of the river. For his signal gallantry in this action Boggs was promoted to be captain, and given command of the *Sacramento* of the blockading squadron off Cape Fear; but, in consequence of overwork and exposure, he was obliged to return to shore duty, and during the rest of the war was in New York, superintending the building and fitting out of vessels for the navy. In 1866 he resumed sea duty as commander of the steamer *Connecticut,* and on a special cruise to the West Indies caused an international incident by demanding the surrender of the Confederate ironclad *Albemarle* in the harbor of Havana, an act resented by the Spanish government. In 1867–68 Boggs commanded the schooner *De Soto.* He was promoted to rear admiral on July 1, 1870, and placed in charge of the third lighthouse district. He commanded the European Fleet in 1871–72, and retired in 1872. He was married twice: on Dec. 4, 1834 to Sophia Dore, who died on Nov. 10, 1872; and on Apr. 8, 1875 to Henrietta Eugenie (Molt) Bull, a widow.

[*Official Records,* ser. I; David D. Porter, *The Naval Hist. of the Civil War* (1886); Wm. E. Boggs, *The Geneal. Record of the Boggs Family* (1916); Navy Registers, 1820–88; obituary in *Army and Navy Jour.,* XXV, 799–800.]

E. B.

BOGGS, LILLBURN W. (Dec. 14, 1792–Mar. 14, 1860), governor of Missouri, was born in Lexington, Ky., the eldest son of John M. and Martha (Oliver) Boggs. In 1816 he came to St. Louis and soon married Julia, daughter of Judge Silas Bent, thus identifying himself with the fur trading group. [See sketches of Charles and William Bent.] He served as first cashier of their bank, the Bank of Missouri. Always drawn toward the frontier, after an unsuccessful venture at store-keeping at Old Franklin in 1818–19, he spent several years as deputy factor and Indian trader under George C. Sibley at Fort Osage and New Harmony Mission, finally again opening a general store at the new town of Independence. He married as his second wife in 1823 Panthea Grant Boone, grand-daughter of Daniel Boone. His public life began with his election to the state Senate in 1826. He was reelected in 1830, elected lieutenant-governor in 1832, and governor in 1836, defeating the popular W. H. Ashley. As governor he showed independence verging on unconventionality in his appointments. His policy on two other problems aroused widespread opposition and criticism—the "Mormon War" and the construction of the new capitol. When the Mormons, after their expulsion from Jackson and Clay counties, refused to be bound by the attempt to segregate them in a county of their own, and the people of the adjacent counties appealed to the governor for aid, he called out a formidable force of militia and expelled the Mormons from the state. He was bitterly criticized for the expense of the expedition and for his famous order that the Mormons must be exterminated or driven from the state if necessary for the public good. As originally authorized the new capitol was to cost $75,000; by 1840 $200,000 had been spent and the building was still unfinished. Moreover the panic had made the sale of bonds impossible and the governor had secured the funds on short term loans from the new state bank. Searching legislative investigation revealed no trace of fraud or mismanagement. The governor had simply decided (and wisely) on the type of building needed and had gone straight to his goal. During his administration and on his urgent advice and support, the Bank of the State of Missouri was chartered, a conservative and highly successful state bank. Boggs was also largely instrumental in the establishment of the state university and the passage of the first (if ineffective) public-school law. The panic effectually blocked his plans for railroads and public improvements. Shortly after his retirement as governor he was the victim of a murderous assault universally believed to have been instigated by the Mormons. He served in the state Senate from 1842 to 1846, where he was one of the few Democrats who voted against Benton in 1844. This closed his political career in Missouri.

Always attracted to the Far West, having (*c.* 1829) once engaged in the Santa Fé trade, and now with two sons in the Rocky Mountain fur trade, in 1846 he moved with his family to Napa Valley, Cal. With the breakdown of the Mexican régime he was appointed at once by the American military authorities *alcalde* of all California north of the Sacramento and was the sole civil authority there until the inauguration of the state government. At Sonoma the ex-Governor engaged once more in trade, and for the first time successfully, being just in time to profit by the gold rush. After paying his numerous debts and acquiring a competency he retired to his farm in Napa Valley, where he died.

["Lillburn W. Boggs," by his son (W. M. Boggs) *Mo. Hist. Rev.*, IV, 106–10; biographical sketch by Wm. Southern, Jr., in *Messages and Proclamations of the Governors of Mo.*, I, 303–6 (portrait); biographical sketch (probably by W. M. Boggs) in *Hist. of Napa and Lake Counties, Cal.* (1881), pp. 373–86; J. R. Cable, "The Bank of the State of Mo.," *Columbia Univ. Studies*, CII, No. 2; Jonas Viles, "Capitals and Capitols of Mo.," *Mo. Hist. Rev.*, XIII, 135, 232.] J. V.

BOGUE, VIRGIL GAY (July 20, 1846–Oct. 14, 1916), civil engineer, the son of George C. and Mary (Perry) Bogue, was born at Norfolk, N. Y. He received his preparatory school education at Russell's Military School, New Haven, Conn., and then attended the Rensselaer Polytechnic Institute from which he was graduated with a degree in civil engineering in 1868. On Mar. 2, 1872 he married Sybil Estelle Russell of San Francisco. His death occurred on board the steamship *Esperanza* en route from Mexico to New York City.

Bogue's chief work was in connection with railroads, in both North and South America. As a young man, just a year out of college, he went to Peru where he had his first railroad experience. Part of that time was spent as assistant engineer (1869–77) on the construction of the Oroya Railway which, in crossing the Andes, reaches the highest altitude of any railway in the world. During his last years in Peru (1877–79) he was manager of the Trajilo Railway. While assistant engineer for the Northern Pacific Railroad (1880–86), in locating a line across the Cascade Mountains in Washington, he discovered and named Stampede Pass through which he drove a two-mile tunnel. At the completion of this work he became chief engineer for the Union Pacific System, serving in this capacity for five years; then, in 1891, he established himself as a consulting engineer with offices in New York City. Transportation problems very largely occupied his time during the twenty-five years he was engaged in private practise. He was a member of the commission appointed by President Harrison to investigate methods for improving the navigation of the Columbia River, and of the commission appointed by Mayor Strong to determine the feasibility of operating surface cars on Brooklyn Bridge. For three years he was consulting engineer for the governor of New Zealand on a route for a proposed railway across the South Island. From 1905 to 1909, the four years during which the Western Pacific Railway was constructed, he acted as both its vice-president and its chief engineer. The capacity which made him so valuable in railroad work was his combination of a practical constructive talent with a fine sense of the economic aspects of railway operation. Some of his most important work included economic studies of railroad problems. He investigated and made a report for the Canadian Pacific on the economies of the line that existed from Calgary to Vancouver, B. C., as compared with a proposed revised line and other routes. Another of his reports was on the costs of revisions and improvements of the Tehuantepec National Railway in Mexico, and of its port facilities. Water transportation problems also interested him and he made the plans for extensive water-front improvements at both Seattle and Tacoma. Another notable work was his report on the economics of the Denver, Western & Pacific Railway.

[Material for this sketch has been obtained from the *Railway Age Gazette*, Oct. 20, 1916, and the *Engineering News*, Oct. 19, 1916. There are obituaries in the *N. Y. Times, N. Y. Herald,* and *Sun* (N. Y.) for Oct. 16, 1916.] E. Y.

BOGY, LEWIS VITAL (Apr. 9, 1813–Sept. 20, 1877), lawyer, senator, was the son of Joseph Bogy, a native of Kaskaskia, Ill., and a member of an early French pioneer family. Joseph Bogy was one of the secretaries of Gov. Morales during the Spanish occupation of the Louisiana Territory, and after the purchase, he removed to Sainte Genevieve, Mo., where he became a leading figure in the economic and political life of southeastern Missouri. Here he married Marie Beauvais, and several years later his son, Lewis Vital, was born. Because of limited facilities and ill health, the early education of the boy was seriously hampered. After much difficulty, he commenced the study of law and was graduated in 1835 from Transylvania University,—his studies being interrupted by service in the Black Hawk War. He removed to St. Louis in 1836 and within a decade had built up an extensive and lucrative practise. His attention and energy were largely occupied with the development of railroads and of iron mines. He suffered heavy financial losses in both ventures. From the first, he participated in Democratic politics, being elected in 1840 a member of the legislature from St. Louis. Returning in 1849 to Sainte Genevieve, he again became candidate for the legislature, representing the anti-Benton faction, but was defeated by a combination of Whigs and Benton Democrats. Two years later, he opposed Benton for Congress in a bitter and protracted contest but was unsuccessful (*Missouri Statesman*, May–August 1854). Dogged perseverance, a marked characteristic of Bogy, served him well during these campaigns, and he was elected in 1854 to the legislature. Here he became a leader of the anti-Benton forces and a supporter of D. R. Atchison for senator. Upon the outbreak of the Civil War, Bogy espoused the Southern cause, although he had no direct part in the spectacular events in Missouri during the spring and summer of 1861, which resulted in the military defeat and political elimination of the disloyalists. "During the war he kept very quiet," although it was well known that his sympathies were with the South. He did not subscribe to the oath of loyalty required of attorneys and abandoned his legal practise. In 1862, he became the Democratic, or "snowflake," candidate for Congress but was defeated by Francis Preston Blair, Jr., an ardent supporter of the Lincoln administration. The election district was under martial law and was administered by provost marshals. At the close of the war, he became a determined and relentless opponent of the Missouri Radicals and was a leader in the reconstruction of the Democratic party. He advocated the Liberal Republican movement in 1870 as a temporary expedient for the benefit of the Democratic party. In 1872 the Democrats gained complete control of the state and Bogy became a candidate for senator, as the successor to Blair. His chief support came from those pro-slavery Democrats who had remained at home during the war. He received the nomination after a spirited contest in the party caucus and was elected. Grave charges of bribery and of other irregularities were made subsequent to the election, but after a somewhat perfunctory investigation, Bogy was fully exonerated (*Missouri Statesman,* Feb. 28, 1873; *Senate Document, No. 186,* 49 Cong., 2 Sess.). He entered the Senate when the grave conditions in financial affairs and in the South were the foremost issues. His views of public questions were essentially Western and he strongly advocated the inflation bill of 1874. He was a severe critic of the policy of the Grant administration in Louisiana during the troubles of 1874–75. In the deliberations of the Senate concerning the disputed election of 1876, he was one of the chief critics of the Louisiana Returning Board and of Packard. In his views both on the financial situation and on the election of 1876, he was supported by his constituents in Missouri. Neither an interesting speaker nor an effective debater, he stood in suggestive contrast to his colleague, Carl Schurz, with whom he was in complete disagreement on most political questions. Following a prolonged illness, he died during the fifth year of his term. He was married to Pelagie, daughter of Bernard Pratte, a member of one of the pioneer families of St. Louis.

[The public career of Bogy can be traced in the files of the *Mo. Republican* and the *Mo. Statesman.* The *Jefferson City Tribune* gives complete information concerning his election to the Senate. The *Cong. Record,* 43, 44, and 45 Cong., is useful for his senatorial career. Sketches of his life appear in W. V. N. Bay, *Reminiscences of the Bench and Bar of Mo.* (1878), and in L. U. Reavis, *St. Louis: The Future Great City of the World* (1870).]
T. S. B.

BOHM, MAX (Jan. 21, 1861–Sept. 19, 1923), painter, son of Henry Justus Edmond and Emilie (Stuhr) Bohm, was born at Cleveland, Ohio, where his father was a successful lumber merchant. His grandfather, Karl Christian Bernard Bohm, an eminent jurist, author, and a friend of Goethe and Schiller, left Saxony because of his political views and, coming to America in the middle of the nineteenth century, settled near Cleveland. Max Bohm in his early youth displayed a talent for painting and at the age of eleven was studying at the Cleveland Art School. In 1887 an artist aunt took him to Europe and for some years he worked at the Louvre and the Académie Julien and studied under Jean Paul Laurens, Lefebvre, and Benjamin Constant. His early work was marine canvases in which he depicted the vast salty sweep of the sea, sailors, fisherfolk, and their boats. He painted with a large, bold gesture; his conceptions were rugged and lofty. At the age of twenty-one his first picture was accepted by the Salon. His first notable success came about six years later with "En Mer," which was given a place of honor in the Paris Salon, and "Crossing the Bar." For twelve years Bohm taught and lectured in London and Paris. In 1898 he married Zella Newcomb of London. Herself an artist and a remarkable personality she did much to mould his life and his art. His "Golden Hours" and "The Family" attracted wide attention when exhibited in 1911; the following year the French government purchased "The Family," a group portrait of his wife and two children and one of the most successful of his paintings, for the Luxembourg Museum. Bohm executed the mural decoration in the Court House at Cleveland. A more notable achievement is the music room murals in the home of Mrs. Mary Longyear in Brookline, Mass. His paintings are included in the collections of the Metropolitan Museum, the National Gallery at Washington, the Boston, Detroit, and Minneapolis Museums, and in many private collections. While at work on important commissions he died suddenly of heart failure at his summer home in Provincetown, Mass.

Bohm's life was reflected to an extraordinary degree in his art. He conceived the world to be filled with active and joyous life, honest toil, and simple pleasures, the whole enhanced by sentiment and love, and filled with a lofty purpose. He eschewed realism and sought to portray ideas rather than the mere facts of nature. He possessed a deep reverence for what appealed to him as the beautiful and noble in life and these he symbolized in an art that was essentially romantic and idealistic. He believed in emotional painting only and maintained that if a man did not have "a deep urge to paint a great thought there was no use in trying to 'carry on' by the mere exercise of paint and brushes." He had a profound faith in the future of American art and constantly urged less reliance on European traditions and opinions and a greater confidence in native ideals.

[*N. Y. Morning Telegraph*, Sept. 30, 1923; *Art News*, Nov. 1, 1924; *Internat. Studio*, May 1924; Samuel Isham and Royal Cortissoz, *Hist. of Am. Painting* (1927); private information.] F. M.

BOHUNE, LAWRENCE (d. Mar. 19, 1621), is notable as the first physician general of the London Company in Virginia, but the little that is known of him relates almost entirely to his interest in colonization. Contemporary accounts testify that he was "a worthy Valiant Gentleman, a long time brought up amongst the most learned Surgeons and Physitions in Netherlands" (Smith, II, 548). It cannot be said when he first came to America, but he was appointed on Dec. 13, 1620, to be physician general for the company, a position he had occupied before. He was concerned with the importation of fruit trees and of seed; and in connection with one James Smith he transported 300 colonists. The court of Virginia on recognizing him as one of its functionaries awarded him, for the prosecution of some plans of his, 500 acres of land and twenty laborers—this project had apparently been explained to the court most vaguely, but it seemed "to promise much benefit." Somehow he was in England in the winter of 1620–21, and in the beginning of February he set out on his second journey to America. In the West Indies, the ship on which he had taken passage was attacked by a superior force of Spaniards. In the ensuing fight he took part valiantly, but was killed before the enemy was beaten off.

[Capt. John Smith, *Travels and Works* (1910), ed. by Ed. Arber; Caleb C. Magruder, *Interstate Medic. Jour.* (St. Louis), June 1910, reprinted in H. A. Kelly, *Cyc. of Am. Medic. Biog.* (1912); *Records of the Va. Co. of London* (ed. by S. M. Kingsbury, 1906).] J. D. W.

BOIES, HENRY MARTYN (Aug. 18, 1837–Dec. 12, 1903), capitalist, of Puritan and Huguenot descent, the son of Joseph Milton Boies and Electa Caroline (Laflin) Boies, was born in Lee, Berkshire County, Mass. He graduated in 1859 from Yale, and two years later married Emma Brainerd, who died in 1868. During the six years after his graduation from college he undertook a number of business ventures, most of which were futile quests of fortune,—as sales agent in Chicago for a powder company, partner in a Hudson River transportation company, Wall Street speculator, newspaper writer, clerk, oil promoter in West Virginia. In 1865 he located at Scranton, Pa., as a member of a powder manufacturing firm, of which he later became president. In 1870 he married Elizabeth Linen Dickson, daughter of Thomas Dickson of Scranton, a noted manufacturer. Boies made extensive scientific studies of explosives, and invented a widely used device for enabling miners to use blasting powder more safely and effectively, together with machinery for its manufacture. He took the lead in the expansion and reorganization of his firm, and continued his connection with its business after the firm was merged with the Du Pont interests and after other enterprises demanded a large share of his attention. In 1872 he became one of the organizers and directors of the Third National Bank of Scranton. Ten years later he became president of the Dickson Manufacturing Company, and inaugurated a policy of expansion which gave the company an international position in the manufacture of engines and machinery. It was during his presidency of this company that he made a second important invention—a steel car wheel designed to meet the constantly increasing demands of weight and speed. He also devised machinery, organized a company, and built a plant for its manufacture (*Railway Gazette*, XXX, 338).

When he left college and went to Chicago in 1859 Boies became a member of the Ellsworth Zouaves, a prominent military organization. Although he was not a member of the combatant forces during the Civil War, his interest in military affairs continued throughout his life. In 1877, during the coal strikes and the national railway strike, he took the lead in the formation of the Scranton City Guard. Fear of public disturbances led to a public meeting presided over by Boies, and to the organization of a battalion of which he was chosen major. As might be inferred from his business connections, he was extremely hostile to the miners and the railway workers and he believed that military means should be available for the repression of industrial disturbances. When the battalion became the 13th Regiment of the National Guard of Pennsylvania, Boies became colonel of the regiment. He instituted the first rifle range, established the office of inspector of rifle practise, created a regimental school for officers, wrote articles on military subjects, and in other ways promoted efficiency in the military organization of the state and nation. His appointment in 1887 as a member of the Pennsylvania Board of Public Charities led to his principal ventures in the field of authorship, notably his *Prisoners and Paupers* (1893) and *Science of Penology* (1901), in which he took relatively advanced positions with respect to the humanitarian treatment and reformation of offenders. The book was used as a college text and was one of the pioneer attempts at a scientific treatment of a grave social problem. Boies traveled widely, read extensively, wrote and made public addresses on varied subjects, and had active connections with an unusually large number of business, civic, religious, social, and learned organizations.

[J. H. Odell (ed.), *Henry Martyn Boies* (1904); F. L. Hitchcock, *Hist. of Scranton and Its People* (1914); H. E. Hayden (ed.), *Geneal. and Family Hist. of the Wyoming and Lackawanna Valleys* (1906).]

W. B—n.

BOIES, HORACE (Dec. 7, 1827–Apr. 4, 1923), governor of Iowa, was born in a log cabin on a farm in Erie County, N. Y., and was educated in the country schools. His father, Eber Boies, who served in the War of 1812, was of French ancestry; his mother, Esther Henshaw, was the daughter of a soldier of the American Revolution who was of English ancestry. At the age of sixteen Horace Boies, carrying some clothes and other belongings in a red bandana handkerchief and one dollar in his pocket, boarded a lake boat at Buffalo, N. Y., bound for Wisconsin Territory. There he worked as a farm hand helping to put in crops, harvest the grain, and break the prairie sod. Late in the fall of 1844 the serious illness of his mother compelled his return to New York. But the lure of the frontier soon recalled him to the West—to Illinois and to Wisconsin Territory. Here he worked in the fields during the summer and gave some attention to schools during the winter. At the age of twenty-one he was back in Erie County, where he married Adella King, and at her suggestion entered upon the study of law in the office of a village attorney. In 1849 he passed the examinations and was admitted to bar. For fifteen years he practised law in the vicinity of Buffalo. His first wife having died in 1855, in 1858 he married Versalia M. Barber. Removing to Waterloo, Ia., in 1867 he entered into a law partnership with H. B. Allen. Like many another lawyer, Boies was drawn into politics. He was first a Whig, then a Republican, and finally a Democrat. In 1857 he had been elected by the Republicans to a seat in the lower house of the New York legislature, where he served for one term. When the Republicans of Iowa committed their party to prohibition by constitutional amendment, Boies left the party and voted with the Democrats. He opposed the amendment on the grounds that it would deprive individuals of property without compensation and would violate the fundamental principle of "the largest possible liberty of the individual consistent with the welfare of the whole." He denounced "as merciless in their severity many of the penalties inflicted by the prohibitory statutes of the State." On this issue he was elected governor of Iowa in 1889 and was reëlected in 1891. In his second campaign for governor he denounced the protective tariff as "unjustly burdensome to the agricultural interests of the country." Largely because the Republican party had modified its attitude on prohibition, he was defeated in his candidacy for a third term in 1893. Election and reëlection to the office of governor in a state in which the Republican party had never before been defeated since its organization in 1856 attracted to Boies nation-wide attention. Thus in 1892 he had a considerable following for the Democratic presidential nomination. At the convention in 1896 he was the second in the balloting with a good prospect of winning the nomination when Bryan captivated the delegates with his "cross of gold" speech. In 1893 Cleveland offered Boies the portfolio of secretary of agriculture. "This I declined," wrote Boies, "for the double reason that its acceptance would compel my resignation as governor of the state, and for the further reason that I did not believe myself qualified to discharge the duties of that office." He spent the later years of his life partly in Iowa and partly in southern California. Although he had given up the practise of law he retained an interest in farming. He owned thousands of acres of land in Iowa, Nebraska, and Canada.

A man of medium size, Boies walked erect to the end of his long life: he possessed the sturdiness of the pioneers. The dominant expression of his unseamed face was one of human sympathy. Free from ostentation in speech and manner, he was inclined to reticence. While moderate in his opinions, he was courageous in the expression of his convictions. In politics he was not a good mixer, and he shunned publicity. He lived simply and without pretense. He was a member of no church and belonged to no secret order. In view of his stand on the constitutional and statutory regulation of the manufacture and sale of intoxicating liquors it is an interesting fact that he was a member of the Good Templars, a world-wide fraternal society for the promotion of total abstinence.

[Unpublished autobiographical letters addressed to Benj. F. Shambaugh; autobiographical sketch dictated in 1914 upon the request of Edw. H. Stiles and published by him in *Recollections and Sketches of Notable Lawyers and Public Men of Early Ia.* (1916); autobiographical sketch published in the *Waterloo Tribune,* Apr. 6, 1923; Shambaugh's *Messages and Proclamations of the Governors of Ia.,* VI, 269–429.] B. F. S.

BOISE, REUBEN PATRICK (June 9, 1819–Apr. 10, 1907), jurist, lawmaker, was the son of Reuben Boies (not Boise) Jr., and Sarah (Putnam) Boies. Born at Blandford, Hampden County, Mass., he was educated partly in the public schools of that place and graduated from Williams College in 1843. At Westfield, Mass., an uncle, Patrick Boies, practised law, and under his tuition young Boise was initiated into his future profession, being admitted to the bar in 1847. Previously he had spent one year in Missouri as a teacher. After practising several years in Chicopee, in 1850 he went to Portland, Ore., where he began his distinguished career as a lawyer. Beginning in 1851 as prosecuting attorney under the territorial legislature, he became code commissioner in 1853 and with two associates prepared the first Oregon code. In the constitutional convention, 1857, he was one of half a dozen leaders who were chiefly responsible for the character of the new state constitution. He was chairman of the committee on the legislative department and reported the article constituting it of fifteen senators and thirty representatives, with the power to double the respective numbers as population increased. The sessions were technically not restricted to a definite period of time; but members were to receive pay for only sixty days, which constituted an effective practical limitation. This article still remains in force. Boise took an active part in the discussion of every important feature of the constitution. He favored the policy of rigidly limiting the powers of corporations, which was good democratic doctrine in that day. He was concerned to make the cost of government for the new and impecunious commonwealth as light as possible. For that reason he voted to make the governor *ex officio* state treasurer. His influence upon the new constitution can be described as neither conservative nor radical. He was eminently practical, seeking a sound, workable system adapted to the conditions of the people. In 1857 he was appointed, by President Buchanan, a member of the Oregon territorial supreme court. After statehood he was elected to the supreme bench of the state, where he served with distinction for twelve consecutive years, being chief justice during two periods of two years each, and after an intermission of four years, he was again on the supreme bench for four years, till 1880. Thereafter he was judge of the third judicial district over whose court he presided for eighteen years, though not continuously. He practised law at Salem from 1892 to 1898 when he was once more elected to the judgeship in his eightieth year, serving the full term of six years, the oldest judge in Oregon.

He owned 640 acres of Willamette Valley land near Dallas which he developed into a valuable estate. He was always deeply interested in farming, in scientific training for agriculture, and in the development of social life among farmers. He was a frequent contributor to agricultural journals, was a member of the governing board of the Oregon Agricultural College (as well as of other educational institutions) and was chosen master of the state Grange during a succession of years. He also attended meetings of the national Grange. He was twice married: in 1851, to Ellen F. Lyon, who died in 1865; and, in 1867, to Emily A. Pratt.

Boise was a man of soldierly bearing, erect, and dignified. His eyes were hazel, his hair black and curly, and he wore a full close-cropped beard. He had a large head with very high forehead, and prominent Roman nose. In speaking and writing he was solid rather than brilliant. He was deliberate, definite, impressive, intent on facts and arguments, but little given to embellishment. His opinions delivered from the bench were marked by clearness, cogency, and brevity. In private he was chary of words but sympathetic and interested. The same spirit characterized his relations with his fellow-men in the mass. Generous views, a steady concern for the welfare of the people, and admirable judgment enabled him in a long active life to do much for the development of Oregon from a primitive western community to a modern commonwealth.

[*Ore. Reports,* vols. I–XLVII, for cases decided by Boise; *Ibid.,* XLIX, 23–29, "In Memoriam, Hon. Reuben P. Boise"; *Morning Oregonian,* Apr. 11, 12, 1907; short sketch in *Ore. Hist. Quart.,* VIII, 201–4; personal letter of Reuben P. Boise, Jr., Apr. 4, 1927.] J. S.

BOISSEVAIN, INEZ MILHOLLAND (Aug. 6, 1886–Nov. 25, 1916), reformer, was born in New York City, the daughter of John W. and Jean (Torrey) Milholland. Her father was a newspaper man. She received her early education at the Comstock school in New York, the Kensington High School, London, and the Willard School in Berlin, and obtained the B.A. degree at Vassar in 1909. As a student she was known as an active radical. She started the suffrage movement at Vassar, enrolled two-thirds of the students, and taught them the principles of socialism. With the radical group she had gathered about her, she attended socialist meetings in Poughkeepsie which were under the ban of the faculty. She was also devoted to athletics and held records in basket ball. After graduation she tried for admission at both Oxford and Cambridge with the purpose of studying law, but without success. She also failed to gain admission to the Harvard Law School, but was finally matriculated at the New York University Law School, from which she took her LL.B. degree. She was interested in every way in the working conditions and rights of women and took a prominent part in the shirtwaist strike in New York in 1912. She was a member of the Political Equality League, the Woman's Trade Union League, the Women's Political Union, the National Child Labor Committee, the Fabian Society, and the Women's Social and Political Union of England. On July 14, 1913, she was married in London to F. E. Boissevain, son of Charles Boissevain of Amsterdam. In December 1915 she joined the Ford Peace Party which, however, she left at Stockholm because she considered its methods undemocratic. Her most prominent work was done in connection with the movement for woman's suffrage. After the suffrage convention in Philadelphia in 1912 she organized a picturesque demonstration in Washington in which, mounted on a white horse, she led a parade of women down Pennsylvania Avenue. She was then called the American Joan of Arc. At the head of a department for women in *McClure's Magazine* which began in 1913, she wrote a number of articles on woman's rights. Her mind was full of ideas and she expressed herself well. Aligned with the radical wing which early in 1916 took the name of National Woman's Party, she took an active part in the presidential campaign of that year. She traveled through the twelve western states which at that time had given women the vote and appealed for help for the Republican party which had pledged itself to support an amendment granting woman suffrage. Unsparing of her strength, she collapsed in Los Angeles during a speech and after ten weeks died of anemia brought on by her over-exertions. The National Woman's Party held a beautiful and striking memorial service for her on Christmas Day 1916 in Statuary Hall in the Capitol at Washington.

[*Who's Who in America*, 1914–15; *World Today*, Mar. 1910; *McClure's*, July 1912, Jan., Feb., Mar., 1913; *Harper's Weekly*, May 30, 1914; *Photo Era*, Dec. 1916; *Good Housekeeping*, Aug. 1918; I. H. Irwin, *The Story of the Woman's Party* (1921); *Los Angeles Times*, Nov. 26, 1916; *N. Y. Times*, Nov. 26, 1916.]

M. A. K.

BOKER, GEORGE HENRY (Oct. 6, 1823–Jan. 2, 1890), was playwright, poet, patriot, diplomat. The ancestry and environment which shaped Boker's character were typical of the America which built a patrician caste upon the foundations of commercial success. He was descended from a Quaker family of Nottinghamshire, which had come to England, by way of Holland, from the French town of Nîmes, where the name had originally been Bocher. Charles Boker, father of the playwright, was a banker, who restored the Girard Bank to solvency after the panic of 1837. George Boker grew up among cultivated surroundings, in the Philadelphia which still preserved the Colonial tradition, social and architectural. From his boyhood, he was a reader of romance, and his philosophy of composition was expressed by his advice to R. H. Stoddard, "Get out of your age as far as you can."

Boker graduated from the College of New Jersey, as Princeton was then called, in 1842. His contributions to the *Nassau Monthly*, of which he was one of the founders, show an unusual maturity of thought, of which one sentence "if there is one offence in a nation which we should willingly forgive, it is the undue pride and admiration of its great men" is typical. After his marriage to Julia Mandeville Riggs of Georgetown, D. C., in 1844, and a foreign tour, he gave up his study of law and devoted himself to writing. His first volume of lyric and narrative verse, *A Lesson of Life* (1848), was only promising, but in *Calaynos*, published in the same year, he showed his power as a playwright. It is a blank verse tragedy, laid in Spain in medieval times, and based upon the Spanish horror of any taint of Moorish blood. Although *Calaynos* was written for the stage, Boker had to wait for foreign approval before he could secure a hearing from his own countrymen. Samuel Phelps produced *Calaynos* at the Sadler's Wells Theatre, in London, May 10, 1849, without the formality of asking Boker's consent. Encouraged by reports of the play's success, James E. Murdoch produced it at the Walnut Street Theatre, Philadelphia, Jan.

20, 1851, and it was later revived. But although Boker received overtures for his next play from managers here and abroad, *Anne Boleyn* (1850) never saw the stage. It was not as lofty in conception as *Calaynos,* or as charming as his romantic comedy, *The Betrothal,* which was first performed at the Walnut Street Theatre, Philadelphia, Sept. 25, 1850, with "as brilliant success as ever greeted any production within the walls of this edifice" (Durang, *The Philadelphia Stage,* ser. III, ch. 112). A love story of medieval Italy, the characters were better drawn than is usual in romantic drama, and the verse showed Boker's usual distinction. It was produced at Drury Lane, Sept. 19, 1853. Boker next attempted a social satire, laid in England in 1851, in *The World a Mask,* which was put on at the Walnut Street Theatre, Philadelphia, Apr. 21, 1851. This play, which still remains in manuscript, was well received, but the mingled prose and verse have not the dignity of Boker's poetic drama. *The Widow's Marriage,* a comedy in blank verse, of the days of George II, was a much better play, but the inability of Marshall, the manager of the Walnut Street Theatre, to find an actress capable of portraying the leading character of Lady Goldstraw, prevented its performance.

Boker was widely read in the history of Spain and he found in the career of Leonor de Guzman, the mistress of Alphonso XII, a fine subject for an heroic tragedy. In *Leonor de Guzman,* which was written for Julia Dean, and first produced at the Walnut Street Theatre, Oct. 3, 1853, he portrayed a striking contrast between the characters of Leonor and of Queen Maria, the two women who had loved the dead King, and he preserved the sympathy of the audience for both of them. Second only to his next play, *Leonor* is a powerful study of human passions of an exalted kind. The climax of Boker's achievement was his tragedy of *Francesca da Rimini,* first produced by E. L. Davenport at the Broadway Theatre, New York, Sept. 26, 1855. Taking the historic story of Francesca and Paolo, wife and brother of Prince Lanciotto of Rimini, who loved each other and who died by his hand, Boker created the character of the medieval prince who, misshapen and misunderstood, is yet "the noblest heart in Rimini." For the first time in literature, the husband became the most appealing figure, and so skilfully did Boker blend history and tradition, so powerful was his interpretation of the Italian spirit of the thirteenth century in terms of passion, pride, and brotherly affection, that he produced the greatest piece of dramatic poetry written in the English language and presented on the professional stage during the nineteenth century. Compared with Boker's characters, vitally human either in love or hate, the creations of later writers in English seem pale and ineffective. Due to Davenport's mechanical interpretation, *Francesca da Rimini* was only moderately successful upon its first production. But when revived by Lawrence Barrett, who acted Lanciotto in 1882, with Otis Skinner as Paolo, and Marie Wainwright as Francesca, it made a profound impression, and provided Barrett with one of his best parts. In 1901 Otis Skinner again revived *Francesca,* taking the part of Lanciotto, Aubrey Boucicault playing Paolo and Marcia von Dresser, Francesca. This superb production proved, once more, the perennial appeal of this drama, truly "not of an age but for all time."

But the lack of recognition in 1855 of his real ability discouraged Boker, and when *The Bankrupt* was produced at the Broadway Theatre, Dec. 3, 1855, he did not allow his name to be attached to it. Perhaps it was a recognition on his part that the play, a prose melodrama, in which a much injured hero returns to Philadelphia in 1850 to revenge himself upon his persecutors, is the poorest of his dramas. Boker could not trifle and was primarily a poet.

In 1856 he collected his lyric and narrative verses and published them, together with *Calaynos, Anne Boleyn, Leonor de Guzman, Francesca da Rimini,* and *The Widow's Marriage,* in two volumes, entitled *Plays and Poems,* which have been five times reprinted. Among his lyrics, his sonnets are the most outstanding. He had a gift for the sonnet on public affairs, and those addressed to England, at the time of the Crimean War, were often reprinted during the World War as representative of his discriminating sympathy with Great Britain. His love sonnets, with their haunting beauty of phrase, gave him rank among American sonneteers second only to Longfellow. Seventy-seven sonnets were included in the *Plays and Poems,* but Boker wrote altogether three hundred and fourteen. Some of these have only recently been brought to light (see E. S. Bradley's *A Newly Discovered American Sonnet Sequence, Publications of the Modern Language Association of America,* vol. XL, 1925, pp. 910–20).

During the years immediately following his father's death in 1857, Boker's attention was turned from poetry through his brave and successful legal fight to rescue Charles Boker's name from calumny and his property from seizure. It was not until 1873 that a final judgment was rendered, which established the fact that his father had saved, not wrecked, the Girard Bank. Boker paid his respects to the vilifiers of his father's memory in his *Book of the Dead,* written between 1858 and 1860 but not published until 1882.

Both as a poet and a citizen, Boker rendered sterling service to his country during the Civil War. Like all war poetry, his is uneven, varying from the ill-considered attack on McClellan, "Tardy George," which he omitted when his *Poems of the War* were published in 1864, to his stirring "Black Regiment," his touching "Dirge for a Soldier," in memory of Gen. Philip Kearny, and his noble "Ode to America," written in March 1862, when the cause of the Union seemed dark. These were published in 1864 and on July 20, 1865, Boker read before the Phi Beta Kappa Society at Harvard College his "Our Heroic Themes," in which he paid one of the earliest and most discriminating tributes to Abraham Lincoln. It was the Philadelphia patrician who first spoke of Lincoln as "Lord of himself, an inborn gentleman."

Boker had been a Democrat, but when Fort Sumter fell, he recognized that there could be no question of divided allegiance. Knowing how close and intricate were the social and economic relations between Philadelphia and the South, he took an active part, in November 1862, in the foundation of the Union Club, which became on Dec. 27 the "Union League of Philadelphia," the first in the country. Boker was its first secretary and devoted a large share of his time to the organization of its activities. The services of the Union League in raising money, in encouraging enlistment and in combating the more subtle social influences which disturbed Philadelphia during the earlier days of the Civil War, were directed by Boker, and he remained secretary until 1871. During the years 1865 to 1871 he was quietly helping other poets who were not so securely established. Through him, Charles Godfrey Leland became managing editor of the Philadelphia *Press,* and Richard Henry Stoddard, William Gilmore Simms and Paul Hamilton Hayne were introduced to the pages of *Lippincott's Magazine* with which Boker was endeavoring to restore the lost primacy of Philadelphia in the magazine world.

In 1869 Boker published *Königsmark, The Legend of the Hounds, and Other Poems,* the first being a verse drama, written about 1857, dealing with the love of Queen Sophia of Hanover for a colonel of the guards. "The Legend of the Hounds," a stirring narrative, was based upon a tradition that an owner of a smelting furnace in the Lebanon Valley of Pennsylvania cast into the flames a dog who had displeased him. Boker's skill in transferring this incident to an English setting and his establishment of the supernatural, in the terrible effect upon a human being of the ghostly pack of hounds which hunt him to his doom, make this poem noteworthy. Among his other narrative poems, "The Ivory Carver," a celebration of faith, and "The Countess Laura," are the best.

Boker was appointed minister to Turkey, Nov. 3, 1871. By his dignity, his prompt courage and his tact, he reëstablished our diplomatic relations with the Porte. Two treaties were negotiated by him, one securing for the first time recognition by the Ottoman Government that Turkish subjects, when naturalized according to American law, became American citizens, and the other referring to the extradition of criminals. Hearing that his son George, who was military attaché to the Legation, had been insulted by Turkish soldiers in the Pera, or foreigners' quarter of Constantinople, Boker drove instantly to the Porte and protested so effectively that the foreign quarter was thereafter forbidden ground to the Turkish soldiery. With a capacity for detail, Boker also recognized the importance of dealing in a large way with the problems of diplomacy. When the Khedive of Egypt sought his aid in the establishment of judicial freedom from Turkish interference, Boker advised the United States Government at once to take a broad view of the request, but had the mortification of seeing his constant representations disregarded, while one by one the chief European nations took the proper steps. Boker's informal letters to Bayard Taylor reveal his sympathy with any nation that sought to respect itself, and his disappointment at being unsupported in his efforts to help Turkey in her desire to control her internal affairs without dictation from the powers of Europe embittered his stay in Constantinople. He disliked also the constant wrangles with the Turkish Government in which, however, he seems to have been unvaryingly successful. He welcomed, therefore, the promotion implied in his appointment as Envoy Extraordinary and Minister Plenipotentiary to Russia, leaving Constantinople on May 4, 1875, and presenting his credentials to Alexander II in St. Petersburg on July 24. There was something regal in Boker's nature, which had won him the regard of the Sultan and the Khedive and which established a personal friendship with the Czar. The immediate result was the change of attitude toward the Centennial Exposition, in which Russia had hesitated to participate. The account of the dinner given in his honor by the Commission on the Russian section of the Exposition reveals him in that happy attitude and tactful expression which won friends everywhere for him and for his country

(*Journal de St. Petersbourg,* LIII (1877), 68). But the administration of Hayes was unfriendly to Boker and despite the intimation from Alexander II that his continuance in office would be most agreeable to the Czar, Boker was recalled in January 1878. His return was a signal for Philadelphia to bestow such honors upon him as the presidency of the Union League and of the Philadelphia Club. In 1886 he became president of the Fairmount Park Commission and devoted his attention to the beautifying of the park system, remaining in the office until his death.

The impulse to write, which had been checked by the lack of appreciation of his work, was renewed by the success of the revival of *Francesca da Rimini* by Lawrence Barrett in 1882. He first revised *Calaynos,* but a disagreement with Barrett concerning the royalties on *Francesca da Rimini* prevented its production. In the meantime Boker had written *Nydia* in 1885 for Barrett, a blank verse tragedy which owes its central situation to Bulwer's *Last Days of Pompeii,* but which is entirely original in language and in feeling. The play was not produced, and Boker rewrote it under the title *Glaucus* in 1886, probably to give Barrett a more definitely leading part. These plays, still unpublished, contain some of his loftiest poetry. *Nydia,* especially, in its depiction of the passion of the blind girl for Glaucus, is one of the finest conceptions in our dramatic literature. It is evident from the manuscripts that Boker was preparing a revised edition of his works, but illness prevented his completion of the project. His death on Jan. 2, 1890, at his home in Philadelphia, from disease of the heart, brought forth renewed interest in his poetry and led to the publication of the fifth edition of his *Poems and Plays* and the reprinting of his *Poems of the War.*

The very qualities which made Boker so preeminently a patrician, defeat the attempt to draw any adequate portrait of him. He was tall, and long enjoyed the reputation of being "the handsomest man in Philadelphia." But, from his early days at college until his death, he guarded the privacy of his own emotions so well that his personality cannot be transferred to the printed page. It is only in the unguarded letters to Taylor that we discover the disappointment of the high-minded gentleman, who longed to devote his life to poetry, which his countrymen did not appreciate, or to playwriting, which the circumstances of the American Theatre made hazardous, or to the service of his country, to which the sordid politics of the day put an end. To the Philadelphia that would give him any honors except the one he craved, he presented the smiling unconcern which never betrayed how deeply the iron had entered into his soul.

[The best and only biography is *Geo. Henry Boker, Poet and Patriot* (1927), by Edward Scully Bradley. This contains a complete bibliography. The present account is based also on the inspection of the manuscripts now at Princeton University and, until her death, in the possession of the daughter-in-law of the poet, Mrs. Geo. Boker, who furnished many of the details. From the personal side, interesting pictures are given by R. H. Stoddard, "Geo. Henry Boker," *Lippincott's Mag.,* June 1890; C. G. Leland, "Reminiscences of Geo. Henry Boker," *American* (Phila.), Mar. 1, 1890; an anonymous "Some Recollections of Boker," *Atlantic Mo.,* Mar. 1890; and Jas. Barnes, "Geo. H. Boker," *Nassau Lit. Mag.,* XLVI (1891), 90. Contemporary criticism of his plays is to be found in C. G. Leland, "Boker's Plays," *Sartain's Mag.,* June 1851; in Wm. Winter, *Wallet of Time,* I (1913), 312–22; and more recent studies in A. H. Quinn, "The Dramas of Geo. Henry Boker," *Pub. Mod. Lang. Ass.,* XXXII (June 1917), 233–66; J. W. Krutch, 'A Little Known Am. Dramatist," *Sewanee Rev.,* Oct. 1917; A. H. Quinn, "Geo. Henry Boker, Playwright and Patriot," *Scribner's Mag.,* June 1923; Boker's services to the Union are treated in the *Reception Tendered by the Members of the Union League of Philadelphia to Geo. H. Boker, Dec. 22, 1871* (1872), and in *The League for the Union* (1888). An interesting foreign view of Boker is given in "Biographie du très honorable, Geo. H. Boker, Ministre des États Unis d'Amérique" in *L'Orient Illustré,* Constantinople, June 13, Aug. 22, 1874. Boker's works are now out of print, except *Francesca da Rimini,* included by A. H. Quinn in *Representative Am. Plays* (1917).]

A. H. Q.

BOLDT, GEORGE C. (Apr. 25, 1851–Dec. 5, 1916), hotelman, was born in the Island of Rugen, in the Baltic Sea. The son of a merchant, and educated in the common schools, he came alone to the United States at the age of thirteen, and went to work in a hotel in New York City. With his savings he started a chicken farm and sheep-ranch in Texas. This venture proving unsuccessful, he returned to the hotel service at Cornwall-on-Hudson, N. Y., afterwards taking a position in Parker's Restaurant, Broadway, New York City, where he advanced through successive stages from general-utility man to steward. His next post was as steward of the famous Clover Club in Philadelphia, where influential members helped him convert a large private residence on Broad St. into a hotel, called the Bellevue. His policy was to charge high prices for good things, which at the same time preserved its exclusiveness. Meanwhile, he turned a favor for William Waldorf Astor, and won his gratitude. When Astor decided to abandon his residence at Fifth Ave. and Thirty-fourth St., New York, Boldt was instrumental in persuading him to build on the site the Waldorf Hotel, then the most magnificent in the world, of which he was named manager. When it opened, in 1893, there were but thirty-two guests, and other hotelmen smiled at its apparent failure. But the public which demanded the best found that they could get it at the Waldorf. Within a few years it was too small for the great business Boldt had built up, and by 1898 the Astoria was completed, forming the Waldorf-Astoria, which Boldt made famous the world over as the acme of what a good hotel should be. By actual count some 20,000 people a day entered the Waldorf-Astoria, which had some 1,800 employees. While continuing as president of the Waldorf-Astoria Hotel Company, he again turned to Philadelphia, bought the old Stratford, adjoining the Bellevue, and on its site erected the new Bellevue-Stratford Hotel. He was president or a director of a number of insurance companies and other corporations; was president of the Holland Library, Alexandria Bay, N. Y., and of the Thousand Islands Country Club; a trustee of the Saturday and Sunday Hospital Association, and active head of the trustees of Cornell University, to which he gave $100,000, and for which he planned its comprehensive system of dormitories. He rode frequently in Central Park, and was a good judge of a saddle horse. Married to Louise, daughter of William Kehrer of Philadelphia, he had a winter home at Santa Barbara, Cal., and a summer estate of 1,000 acres on the St. Lawrence River. In 1909 Tammany Hall considered him as a possible candidate for mayor of New York. More than any other man he was responsible for the modern American hotel. He was a lovable, simple person, and when he died the flags on almost every New York hotel were placed at half-staff. Simeon Ford, dean of New York hotelmen, said of him: "George Boldt invented the theory that the public was right. . . . He trained his employes to give the patron something he would like, and he never let a man leave his doors unsatisfied." His place in the hotel business was peculiar to himself, there was none to dispute his preëminence, none who attended to the multifarious duties of the hotel proprietor with the same unflagging enthusiasm, or who did more to raise it from the dull routine of a business to something approaching a profession.

[The chief source is Simeon Ford's *Recollections*; see also the obituaries in the *N. Y. Times, Herald,* and *Evening Post,* Dec. 6, 1916. Trade journals such as the *Hotel Reporter* and the *Hotel Gazette* give technical and statistical information about the Waldorf-Astoria under the Boldt régime.] R. R. R.

BOLL, JACOB (May 29, 1828–Sept. 29, 1880), Swiss-American geologist and naturalist, son of Henry and Magdalena (Peier) Boll, was born in Bremgarten, Canton Aargau, Switzerland. After two years at the University of Jena (which he left without a degree) he returned to his native town, married Henriette Humbel (1854), and settled down to a long career as apothecary in his own pharmacy in Bremgarten. His interest in natural history had been awakened during his *gymnasium* days in Switzerland, and had been fostered at Jena. His persistent study of the natural history of his canton bore fruit in a number of now little-known papers, and in a thin book on the flora of Canton Aargau, published in 1869. In this year he visited Texas (whither his family had preceded him), and during 1870 collected so well in Texas for Louis Agassiz at Harvard that there are said to be Boll specimens in pretty nearly every department of the Harvard Museum. The winter of 1870 Boll spent with Agassiz at Harvard, returning to Switzerland in the spring. He remained in Switzerland until after the death of his wife, which occurred in August 1873. He then decided to accept the repeated invitations of Agassiz to become a staff-member of the Museum of Comparative Zoology at Cambridge, and came to America for the second time in January 1874. On reaching Cambridge, he first learned of the death of Agassiz on Dec. 14, 1873. At once he returned to Texas, and during the years 1874–80 he investigated the geology and natural history of that state. During the four seasons of 1877–80 he collected fossils and reptiles, chiefly in northern and northwestern Texas for Edward D. Cope [*q.v.*]. He died in the field while collecting fossils in Wilbarger County.

Boll first intelligibly identified the Permian rocks of northwest Texas (*American Naturalist,* XIV, 684–86). He discovered many new species of fossil plants and animals which were described by Cope in a series of contributions on the Permian vertebrates of Texas (1878–83). Many Boll specimens of recent Texas reptiles, batrachia, and fishes are referred to by Cope in his book entitled, *On the Zoological Position of Texas* (1880). Boll's large collection of microlepidoptera, embracing species from the entire world, passed at his death into the hands of B. Neumoegen and Dr. C. V. Riley, with whom he had worked on the United States Entomological Commission for the study of the Rocky Mountain locust (1877–80). He was an indefatigable collector in all groups of insects, and most of the European museums have specimens of his collecting. He was commissioned by European silk-growers to investigate American species of silkworms, with an eye to the introduction into Europe of hardy species. His cantonal government commissioned him (1874) to make extensive collections of the Colorado potato beetle (just then becoming a pest in America), as well as to collect (1871) the seeds of woody plants, and the fresh-water and marine mollusks of Texas. During the last two years of his life he printed in the

American Naturalist (June 1879; September 1880) two papers that "were only the introduction to what promised to be valuable original contributions to the geology of Texas" (R. T. Hill, "Present Condition of Knowledge of the Geology of Texas," in *Bulletin XLV of the United States Geological Survey,* 1887).

[*Galveston News,* Oct. 10, 21, 1880; *Dallas Daily Herald,* Oct. 7, 19, 1880; *Dallas Morning News,* Oct. 21, 1928; a documented appraisal of Boll's contributions to the biology of the Southwest, to appear shortly in *Am. Midland Naturalist.*] S. W. G.

BOLLAN, WILLIAM (*c.* 1710–*c.* 1776), lawyer, agent of Massachusetts, was born in England, probably about 1710. He came to America while young, studied law in Massachusetts with Robert Auchmuty, and became an able lawyer. As early as 1732 he was "Counsellour at Law" for Harvard College (*Harvard College Records,* II, 606, 619, 623), and the next year was retained by King's Chapel on behalf of "the suffering members of the Church of England" (Henry Wilder Foote, *Annals of King's Chapel,* vol. I, 1882, p. 462). As a prominent Anglican he was associated with John Checkley [*q.v.*]. He acquired land in both Massachusetts and Rhode Island. On Sept. 18, 1736, he made a motion before the court at Bristol in the case of Frost *vs.* Leighton, the motion being renewed at York on June 22 following. This interesting colonial case, arising from an incident connected with the King's rights to timber in New England, resembled in some respects the celebrated case of Marbury *vs.* Madison in the United States Supreme Court (*Publications of the Colonial Society of Massachusetts,* III, 254 ff.). In 1743 Bollan had become advocate general and on Sept. 8 he married Frances, the daughter of the governor, William Shirley. His wife died in childbirth and was buried Feb. 18, 1744/5 leaving a daughter, Frances Shirley Bollan. In 1745 he was sent as colonial agent to London to endeavor to obtain repayment to Massachusetts of £183,649 spent by that colony for the Louisburg expedition. In this he was successful, after three years' negotiating, the British government finally sending £200,000 in silver to Massachusetts. Bollan continued in England as agent and stood stoutly for the interests of the colony, opposing, for example, the attempts against the charters in 1749, resisting the order against erecting slitting mills in 1750, and the legislation forbidding paper money in 1751. In spite of this he does not seem to have been popular with the more radical patriots of the lower house, perhaps in part from his being a Churchman and in part from his too close connection with the governor, who was succeeded by Pownall in 1757 (cf. James Otis's unfair opinion, *Massachusetts Historical Society Collections,* LXXIV, 76). In 1762 Bollan was rather curtly dismissed as agent of the colony although he continued to act as agent for the Council. In 1769, £300 allowed him for so doing was disallowed by the governor. In the same year he gained popularity with the Assembly by obtaining and sending to them thirty-three letters of Bernard and Gage, for which act he was denounced by Lord North. He wrote several pamphlets, published in London, in favor of the colonies and was for conciliatory measures in 1775. He was a man of property and at one time was lending nearly £5,000 to the colony (*Ibid.,* p. 37) where he had real estate at the time he died. He was a man of ability and loyal to his trust as agent. John Adams called him "a faithful friend to America" and Hancock spoke of the colony's great debt to him. The colony, however, delayed eight years before paying the salary due him to his daughter.

[There is neither biography nor extended notice of Bollan. A number of letters to and from him are given in the volume of the *Mass. Hist. Soc. Colls.,* cited above (separate title, *Jasper Mauduit*). There is also a short letter in *Col. Soc. Mass. Pubs.,* VII, 212–13. Official communications may also be found in the manuscript records of the two houses of the General Court. His work in England for Gov. Bernard in connection with the Mt. Desert Grant is noticed in *Col. Soc. Mass. Pubs.,* XXIV, 204 ff. A rather detailed account of his services in obtaining reimbursement for the colony's expenditures in the Louisburg expedition is given in Geo. A. Wood, *Wm. Shirley,* vol. I (1920), esp. pp. 399–407, 409–10.] J. T. A.

BOLLER, ALFRED PANCOAST (Feb. 23, 1840–Dec. 9, 1912), civil engineer, was born in Philadelphia, the son of Henry J. and Anna M. (Pancoast) Boller. After a preparatory education at the Episcopal Academy, he entered the University of Pennsylvania and was graduated in 1858 with the A.B. degree. Three years later he received his C.E. from the Rensselaer Polytechnic Institute and then spent several years in bridge and aqueduct construction work for railroads. He was married on Apr. 28, 1864, to Katherine Newbold of Philadelphia. From 1866 to 1870 he was associated with Samuel Millikin as an agent for the Phœnix Iron Company. From 1871 to 1873 he was vice-president and engineer for the Phillipsburg Manufacturing Company, and in 1874 he opened an independent office in New York City where he soon acquired an important professional practise. A partnership was formed in 1898 with Henry M. Hodge. Later Howard C. Baird became a member of the firm. Boller was consulting engineer for various projects and improvements of the Lake Superior Company at Sault Ste. Marie in Canada and Michigan. He was an expert, too, in the matter of foundations and acted as consulting engineer on a number of deep and difficult foundations in New York City. Among the remarkable bridge designs made by him and his partners is the draw-span of the Thames River Bridge at New London, Conn. This span, 503 feet in length and weighing 1,200 tons, was the longest ever attempted up to that time. The Central Bridge over the Harlem River at 155th St., New York City, 4,500 feet long, costing over two million dollars, and having a draw-span weighing 2,400 tons, was said at the time of its construction to be the heaviest movable mass in the world. Other bridges designed and built by Boller and his partners include the bridge over the Monongahela River for the Wabash Railroad at Pittsburgh; the Municipal Bridge over the Mississippi at St. Louis; and the State Bridge over the Connecticut River at Saybrook, Conn. His firm acted as consulting engineers for the steel framework of the Singer Building and the Metropolitan Life Insurance Building in New York City. Boller was the author of a *Practical Treatise on the Construction of Iron Highway Bridges, for the Use of Town Committees* (1876). He was an expert in bridge engineering and stood in the front rank of structural engineers of his day. With sound judgment, he designed his structures skilfully and with great daring, and as much as any man of his day was responsible for the great progress during the latter half of the nineteenth century in the art of bridge design and building. Intuitively he was artistic. In his spare hours he used to do landscapes in water colors. This fondness for the artistic and an appreciation for architectural symmetry had a marked influence on his work. The 155th Street Bridge in New York City exemplifies his ability to combine technical principles and practical utility with beauty of outline.

[*Trans. Am. Soc. Civil Engineers,* LXXXV, 1653; *Engineering News,* Dec. 19, 1912.] E. Y.

BOLLES, FRANK (Oct. 31, 1856–Jan. 10, 1894), nature writer, secretary of Harvard University, was born at Winchester, Mass., the son of John A. Bolles and his wife, Catherine Dix, a sister of John Adams Dix [*q.v.*]. His love of nature and of writing showed itself early. When his father was appointed solicitor of the navy in 1866, the family moved to Baltimore and the next year to Washington. Bolles studied law in Washington, spent the summer of 1879 in Europe, and entered the Harvard Law School, from which he graduated in 1882. While studying at Harvard, he founded and was first president of the Harvard Coöperative Society, compiled a genealogy of his mother's family, won the Bowdoin prize for an essay on international arbitration, and with two other Harvard Law students brought out *A Collection of Important English Statutes* (1880). Two later, enlarged editions were entirely his own work. In October 1884 he married Elizabeth Quincy Swan, of Cambridge, Mass., by whom he had four daughters. After some journalistic and editorial experience on the *Boston Advertiser,* he became in 1886 a secretary to President Eliot of Harvard and in 1887 secretary of the University. The latter post, which up till then had been that of a glorified bookkeeper, Bolles made into an office of wide influence. He was kind, candid, and approachable, concerned for everything affecting the welfare of the University, and unremitting in his endeavor to make Harvard equally hospitable to the unknown poor boy and to the son of the affluent and influential alumnus. He built up a remarkably efficient employment bureau, helped to found the *Harvard Graduates Magazine,* and arranged for numerous loans to needy students. His memory retained names, faces, and personal histories beyond the capacity of the most elaborate filing system; his industry was unflagging, his resources of ideas and enthusiasm apparently inexhaustible. The tall, rugged man with bearded face and friendly eyes became one of the most popular men in the Yard.

As passionate as his devotion to Harvard and Harvard's sons was his love of nature. His official duties were confining, but on afternoons and holidays he would make short excursions on foot or by train to the open country and write up his notes on birds and flowers while returning at night on the cars. His summers were given to an abandoned farm at the base of Mt. Chocorua, in New Hampshire, where he could lie motionless behind a bush all day, when he chose, studying the habits of sparrow, wren, owl, and woodpecker. Encouraged by James Russell Lowell, he published a collection of sketches, *The Land of the Lingering Snow,* in 1891. He followed it with a similar volume, *At the North of Bearcamp Water,* in 1893. Early in January 1894, an attack of grippe developed into the pneumonia from which he died on Jan. 10. *From Blomidon to Smoky, and Other Papers* (1894) and *Chocorua's Tenants* (1895), in verse, were issued posthumously. Bolles's English is limpid, his attitude toward nature impersonal and yet sympathetic.

[W. R. Thayer, "Frank Bolles," in *Harvard Grads. Mag.,* VI (1893–94), 366–72; *Boston Advertiser, Jour.,* and *Transcript,* Jan. 11, 1894; *Harvard Coll., Report of President and Treasurer, 1893–94.*] G. H. G.

BOLLMAN, JUSTUS ERICH (1769–Dec. 9, 1821), agent of Aaron Burr, was born in Hoya,

Hanover, studied medicine at Göttingen, and practised for a time in Carlsruhe and Paris. From the latter city in 1792 he fled to London and later went to Vienna for the purpose of locating and freeing Lafayette, who was then confined at Olmütz. He was assisted by F. K. Huger, a young American from South Carolina. Lafayette escaped but was recaptured and Bollman himself spent several months in prison. He was released on condition that he leave Austria. In 1796 he came to America where his attempted rescue of Lafayette assured him a cordial reception, and when after some years he failed in business, Jefferson, of whose friendship he seemed disposed to take advantage, offered him in succession the consulate at Rotterdam, the commercial agency at Santo Domingo, and the Indian agency at Natchitoches, La. (*Jefferson Papers 131, 132, 144, 153, 154*). The tender of the last-named position occurred in the latter part of 1805. Shortly afterward Bollman became a confidential agent of Burr and as such attempted to interest prospective settlers in the settling of the Bastrop land grant. He was entrusted with a copy of Burr's famous cipher letter, which, in December 1806, he delivered to Gen. Wilkinson at New Orleans. Shortly afterward he was arrested by military authority along with his fellow messenger, Samuel Swartwout, and hurried off by sea to Washington, where they were brought before the district court and, on the evidence afforded by Wilkinson's version of the cipher letter and Eaton's deposition, were remanded to prison. On a writ of *habeas corpus* they were brought before the Supreme Court. Chief Justice Marshall, in reviewing their case, laid down some of the principles that afterward guided him in defining "treason" at the Burr trial. The hearing attracted wide attention and influenced the discussion then going on in Congress over the proposal to suspend the writ of *habeas corpus.* The prisoners were released and were then and later recipients of many attentions from those who did not favor the arbitrary policy of the administration. On Jan. 23, 1807, Bollman secured a personal interview with Jefferson, at which Madison was present, and gave in detail the plans of Burr, which he claimed were in no way directed against the interests of the United States. Later at the request of the president and on the latter's assurance that this testimony should be kept inviolate, he committed his statements to writing. This document was given to George Hay, the district attorney who conducted the prosecution against Burr, and was produced in the court room at Richmond, together with a pardon for Bollman, when the latter was called as a witness. Bollman refused the pardon which would have been a virtual admission of guilt and his testimony was not unfavorable to Burr (A. J. Beveridge, *Life of John Marshall,* 1916–19, III, 450–453). The collapse of the case against the latter saved Bollman from any serious consequences. Later he was the author of some pamphlets dealing with the banking system of the United States between 1810 and 1816. After that date he resided for some years in London where he likewise wrote on the banking system of England and engaged in an extended discussion of Ricardo's theories. He died in Jamaica.

[Casual references to Bollman occur in the manuscript collection of the Jefferson Papers, vols. CXXXI–CLXIV. The last contains his statement of Burr's plans. For a general account of his connection with the conspiracy, see the references in the article on Burr, particularly those to the works of Beveridge and of McCaleb. Among Bollman's pamphlets may be mentioned, *Paragraphs on Banks* (1810), *Plan of an Improved System of the Money Concerns of the Union* (1816), *A Letter to Thos. Brand* (1819), and *A Second Letter to the Hon. Thos. Brand* (1819).] I. J. C.

BOLTON, HENRY CARRINGTON (Jan. 28, 1843–Nov. 19, 1903), chemist and bibliographer, was descended from good English stock on his father's side, after whom Bolton Abbey, Priory, Woods, etc., were named. He was the only child of Dr. Jackson Bolton and Anna Hinman (North) Bolton, the daughter of Dr. Elisha North, one of the first American physicians to practise vaccination. He was born in New York City, and was educated at Columbia University, graduating in 1862; his studies in chemistry were continued under Wurtz and Dumas in Paris, Bunsen at Heidelberg, Hofmann at Berlin, and Wöhler at Göttingen where he took his doctor's degree in 1866, his thesis being on The Fluorine Compounds of Uranium. In connection with this work he isolated and preserved a material which was kept in phials. After his death these were found to give off radioactive rays, due to the presence in the material of radium, so that he very nearly anticipated the work of the Curies. After graduating at Göttingen he returned to New York and opened a private laboratory. In 1872 he became an assistant at Columbia, and in 1875 professor of chemistry in the Woman's Medical College. In 1877 he accepted the chair of chemistry at Trinity College, where he remained for ten years. He then retired and, having sufficient means, devoted his time to literary and scientific pursuits. In 1882 a visit to the "Singing Beach" at Manchester, Mass., interested him in this subject; he wrote several papers and with his wife traveled many thousand miles to investigate similar occurrences elsewhere. While at Columbia he published papers on the action of organic acids on minerals. He was interested in folk-lore, was one of the founders of the American Folk-Lore Society, contributed to the *Journal of American Folk-Lore,* and published *The Counting Out Rhymes of Children* (1888) and other similar works. He was also interested in alchemy and the history of chemistry and wrote *The Follies of Science at the Court of Rudolph II, 1576–1612* (1904), and the *Evolution of the Thermometer, 1592–1743* (1900). In 1874 he proposed and carried out a pilgrimage to the grave of Priestley at Northumberland, Pa. Here an acquaintance with Priestley's descendants enabled him to edit the *Scientific Correspondence of Joseph Priestley* (1892), an account of the Lunar Society, and an inventory of the contents of Priestley's laboratory destroyed by the rioters in 1791. In connection with his own work on uranium he published in the *Annals of the New York Lyceum of Natural History* (1870), an index of the literature on the subject; this was the beginning of an interest in bibliography which he cultivated with zeal and great success for the rest of his life. In 1885 he published a *Catalogue of Scientific and Technical Periodicals, 1865–82* (1885), and in 1893 the first part of his *Select Bibliography of Chemistry* which was continued in several volumes. He was chairman of a committee on the bibliography of chemistry of the American Chemical Society and wrote many annual reports. He married Henrietta Irving, a great-niece of Washington Irving, in 1893; died in Washington, D. C.; and is buried in the Irving plot at Tarrytown-on-the-Hudson. He was a man of medium height and rather stocky build, with blue eyes. His disposition was kindly and amiable and he was deeply religious, a great traveler, full of anecdote, and fond of funny stories. He had met most of the noted chemists of his generation, with whom he was a general favorite.

[Sketch by F. W. Clarke, in the *Proc. Am. Chemical Soc.,* 1904, p. 6; sketch in the *Pop. Sci. Mo.,* XLIII, 688 ff.; obituary in the *N. Y. Tribune,* Nov. 20, 1903; personal information.] E. H.

BOLTON, SARAH KNOWLES (Sept. 15, 1841–Feb. 21, 1916), author and reformer, came of distinguished New England stock. Her father, John Segar Knowles of Connecticut, was descended, through his mother, Mary Carpenter, from Elizabeth Jenckes, sister of Joseph Jenckes, governor of Rhode Island 1727–32, and through his father from Henry Knowles, one of the earliest settlers of Portsmouth, R. I.; her mother, Elizabeth (Miller) Knowles, had among her ancestors, Nathaniel Stanley, treasurer of Connecticut Colony; Col. John Allyn, secretary of the colony and historian of the Pequot War; and Col. William Pynchon, one of the incorporators of Massachusetts Bay Colony. On the Knowles side the family had been Quakers for generations. Born at Farmington, Conn., Sarah Knowles passed her childhood in the country, where her fondness for pets, particularly hens, laid the foundation for her later interest in animal welfare. Losing her father when she was eleven, she and her mother went to live with an uncle, Samuel Miller, and later she resided with another uncle, Col. H. L. Miller, an able lawyer of Hartford, Conn. Here she became acquainted with Lydia Sigourney and Harriet Beecher Stowe. Her pen was early busy; she wrote verses, publishing some of them at the age of fifteen, and she had a passion for biographical writing. After graduating from the Hartford Female Seminary in 1860, she went with a Prof. Tenney to teach school in Natchez, Miss. Forced to return by the outbreak of the Civil War, she taught for a time in Meriden, Conn. At the age of twenty-three she brought out a volume, *Orlean Lamar and Other Poems* (1864), of which one reviewer said "Very well to have written but a great mistake to have published." She next produced "Wellesley," a novel on the insurrection of Kossuth, which was published in the *Literary Recorder* in 1865. In the following year (Oct. 16, 1866) she married Charles Edward Bolton of Cleveland, Ohio, a man of congenial humanitarian interests. They were drawn more and more into the temperance movement, and in 1874 they took a prominent part in tthe Woman's Temperance Crusade in Ohio. Mrs. Bolton also wrote for the cause a book called *The Present Problem* (1874), but only 250 copies were sold. During 1878–81 she was on the editorial staff of the *Congregationalist* in Boston. The next two years she spent in Europe, making a study of higher education for women and of the methods used by employers to better the condition of their employees. On her return she read an influential paper on the latter subject before the American Social Science Association at Saratoga. Secretary of the Woman's Christian Association and assistant corresponding secretary to Frances E. Willard in the Woman's Christian Temperance Union, Mrs. Bolton nevertheless found time for voluminous writing. In addition to two more volumes of didactic, sentimental poetry, *From Heart and Nature* (in collaboration with her son, Charles Knowles Bolton, 1887), and *The Inevitable and Other Poems* (1895), she published several works of fiction, and a long series of books designed to assist in popular education, their character indicated by titles such as *Poor Boys Who Became Famous* (1885), *Girls Who Became Famous* (1886), *Famous American Statesmen* (1888), *Famous Men of Science* (1889). Written with enthusiasm and a vigorous narrative power, these biographical works perhaps merited the large sale which they obtained. A reformer to the last, Mrs. Bolton rounded out her life by devoting herself to the welfare of the animals she had loved in youth. She was chiefly responsible for the Ohio law stopping the sport of pigeon-shooting and on several occasions she deterred the Cleveland city council from waging war on the faithful dog.

[*Sarah K. Bolton, Pages from an Intimate Autobiography* (1923), ed. by Chas. Knowles Bolton; *The Boltons in Old and New England* (1890), by Chas. Knowles Bolton; *Who's Who in America,* 1914–15.]

E. S. B.

BOLTON, SARAH TITTLE BARRETT (Dec. 18, 1814–Aug. 4, 1893), poet, born in Newport, Ky., was the daughter of Jonathan Belcher and Esther (Pendleton) Barrett, pioneer settlers of Indiana. Her grandfather, Lemuel Barrett, was an Englishman who emigrated to New Jersey some time before 1754, and her mother's father, a cousin of James Madison. Her early days were spent in the wilderness, about six miles from Vernon, Ind., where her father had staked a farm. Of this period her poems entitled "Our Pioneers" and "A Pioneer Grandmother" are reminiscent. When she was nine, her father sold his farm and moved to Madison. Here she got some knowledge in the schools, and as much outside. Before she was fourteen, verses from her pen had been published in the Madison *Banner,* and she soon became a regular contributor to the newspapers of her home town and Cincinnati. In her seventeenth year, October 1831, she married Nathaniel Bolton, a young newspaper man, and went to live in Indianapolis. Thereafter her life was shaped by her husband's fortunes until his death in 1858. He was first editor of the *Indiana Democrat;* then proprietor of a farm outside the city, his house there a tavern which became a stopping place for distinguished men and something of a social center, Mrs. Bolton acting as housekeeper and cook, besides running a large dairy. Later he was state librarian, then clerk of a United States Senate committee, and finally consul at Geneva, which appointment gave Mrs. Bolton opportunity for extensive travel. Two children were born to her. About five years after his death, she married, Sept. 15, 1863, at Keokuk, Iowa, Judge Addison Reese, and for the next two years lived with him at his home in Canton, Mo. The climate there was not favorable to her health, and she returned to Indianapolis, where she made her home until her death, though she spent two or three years abroad. She was always known as Sarah T. Bolton, and used the name "Reese" only for business purposes.

Her writings and participation in public affairs made her a prominent figure in Indiana. She was interested in various reforms, and was an active aid to Robert Dale Owen [*q.v.*] in his effort to secure property rights for women in the constitutional convention of 1850. She was a true child of the rising West, an ardent democrat and champion of freedom, full of fiery patriotism and faith in the country's future. These characteristics are reflected in many of her poems. As a whole these are of no great literary merit, but have the melody, sentimentality, and moral and religious flavor relished by the fireside magazine readers of their day. *Paddle Your Own Canoe* and a few others had wide popularity. *Poems* appeared in 1865, and a collection of her writings with a sketch of her career was published in 1880 under the title, *The Life and Poems of Sarah T. Bolton.* A volume of selections, *Songs of a Life Time,* edited by John Clark Ridpath, was published in 1892. It contains an introduction by Lew Wallace and a proem by James Whitcomb Riley.

[*Ladies' Repository,* Feb. 1852, pp. 69–73; Wm. W. Woollen, *Biog. and Hist. Sketches of Early Indiana* (1883); J. P. Dunn, *Greater Indianapolis* (1910); obituary in *Indianapolis Sentinel,* Aug. 5, 1893; and information furnished by Mrs. Adah Bolton Mann.] H. E. S.

BOLTWOOD, BERTRAM BORDEN (July 27, 1870–Aug. 15, 1927), chemist, and physicist, was born in Amherst, Mass. His father was Thomas Kast Boltwood, a lawyer; his grandfather, Lucius Boltwood of English descent, was active in the founding of Amherst College, was secretary of its corporation (1828-64), and was also the first candidate of the Liberty Party for governor of Massachusetts, in 1841; the ancestors of his mother, Mathilda (Van Hoesen) Boltwood, were among the first Dutch settlers in Rensselaer County, N. Y. His boyhood was spent in Amherst, Castleton on Hudson, and Albany, N. Y. He prepared for Yale at the Albany Academy and entered Sheffield Scientific School of Yale University in 1889. As a freshman at Yale he received the first-rank prize in physics and as a senior he took the highest rank in chemistry, reading a dissertation at the commencement ceremonies. After graduation in 1892 he studied two years in Munich under Professor Krüss, giving special attention to rare earths and analytical methods; he spent part of 1896 in Leipzig in Ostwald's laboratory. At Yale he was assistant in chemistry, 1894–96; received the Ph.D. degree in 1897; and was instructor in analytical, later in physical, chemistry 1896–1900. During 1900–06, he conducted a private laboratory in New Haven and during this period he started the important work in radioactivity which he continued when he accepted an assistant professorship in physics in Yale College (1906–10). From 1910 to 1927 he was professor of radio chemistry. With the late Prof. H. A. Bumstead he devoted much time and energy to the building of the new Sloane Physics Laboratory (1912) of which he was, in 1913–14, the acting director in the absence of Prof. Bumstead. As the representative of the chemistry department it was also his lot to plan the construction and equipment of the Sterling Chemical Laboratory (1921). The work in connection with this undertaking proved so severe that his health broke down under the strain. He had two or three periods of nervous depression from which he apparently recovered; but there was a recurrence of this to some degree in the summer of 1927, when he ended his own life in Maine whither he had gone to recuperate.

While Boltwood contributed to laboratory technique and arts, his prominence was primarily in actual scientific contributions of the first magnitude in the realm of radioactivity. To him are due the following fundamentally important contributions: (1) The proof that radium is a disintegration product of uranium. (2) The discovery of a radioactive element, ionium, the parent substance of radium. (3) The experimental work showing the inseparability by chemical means of ionium and thorium, a fact which aroused interest among chemists and physicists the world over and is the basis from which the branch of science called isotopy has arisen. (4) The contribution of the experimental evidence that the "lead" found in uranium minerals must be the final product of disintegration in the uranium-radium series, a fact amply verified by others. (5) The statement of a theory and invention of a method for the calculation of the age of uranium minerals from their lead and uranium content—a method which, with some important modifications, constitutes our best method in determining the age of a geological formation. (6) The experimental evidence that actinium is also a genetic descendant of uranium but not in the same line as radium. Besides these important investigations, to Boltwood was due the first investigation in this country of the radioactivity of natural waters (Hot Springs Reservation) and the giving to the measurements obtained a quantitative significance in terms of uranium, there being at that time no radium standard. He also investigated the production of helium in minerals; as product of alpha-ray emission from radium; and from ionium. Pointing out (1905) the significance of lead and helium and perhaps other elements as the disintegration products of one form or another, he raised the question about the origin of elements. In regard to his scientific work he was amazingly modest as is exemplified by his statement in *Who's Who,* where the only words bearing on his work are that he was a "contributor to chemical journals." He was unmarried; possessed great personal charm; and had a wide acquaintance with matters outside of his science.

[*Who's Who in America,* 1924–25; *Am. Men of Sci.* (3rd ed., 1921); scientific notebooks and personal papers left in Boltwood's estate to his heir, Lansing V. Hammond; scientific publications in *Am. Jour. of Sci.,* 3rd ser. L, 4th ser. XXVI (1895 to 1908) and 4th ser. L (1920); *Philosophical Mag.* (London), IX (1905) and XXII (1911); *Nature,* LXX (1904) and LXXV, LXXVI (1907), C (1918); *Physikalische Zeitschrift,* VII and VIII (1906–7); *Proc. Royal Soc.,* LXXXV (1911); *Science,* XLII (1917); *Yale Alumni Weekly,* Apr. 19, 1918; *Industrial and Engineering Chemistry,* XV (1923); Records, Yale University Secretary's office, and longer biographical sketches from these sources prepared for the *Yale Scientific Mag.,* II (1927), and for the *Am. Jour. of Sci.,* 5th ser., XV (1928); also personal acquaintance.] A.F.K.

BOLTZIUS, JOHANN MARTIN (Dec. 15, 1703–Nov. 19, 1765), Lutheran clergyman, was twenty-nine years old and held the post of inspector-vicar in the Latin School connected with the Lutheran Orphanage at Halle, Germany, when he was called as pastor of a company of about one hundred Salzburgers who had agreed to emigrate to the English colony of Georgia. He had grown to manhood in the Orphanage, had studied at the University of Halle, and was imbued with the Pietism that emanated from those two institutions. He accepted the call, was ordained at Wernigerode Nov. 11, 1733, and proceeded to Amsterdam, where his congregation was ready to embark. With him went Israel Christian Gronau, a teacher in the School, who was ordained at the same time. The emigrants landed at Savannah on Mar. 12, 1734, and were welcomed with a salute of cannon and a gala dinner. Gen. Oglethorpe himself helped to select a site for their town of Ebenezer.

For the next thirty years Boltzius was the religious and business leader of the little colony. His charges were among the thousands of Protestants who had been driven from the archiepiscopal duchy of Salzburg because of their religion. They were simple folk, pious, industrious, uneducated, impoverished by confiscation and exile, and bewildered by their situation on the Georgia frontier. In spite of an excessively high death rate, the handicap of having to move their town in 1736 to a more wholesome locality, and the hardships incident to pioneer life, the Salzburgers ultimately attained a mild prosperity and were noted for their neatness, order, and industry. The religious life, after the manner of the Pietists, was cultivated assiduously, and perhaps to excess. There was no crime. Differences were settled by a committee of arbitration appointed by the chief pastor. As money was scarce tokens signed by Boltzius took the place of small coins and passed at their face value. The two pastors became brothers-in-law by marrying the daughters of a woman named Kroher. In 1737 John Wesley, on his visit to Georgia, became Boltzius' friend. Wesley, however, because of his High Church principles, refused to admit Boltzius to the Lord's Supper, and years later set down in his journal the appropriate comment on his own folly. Another visitor was George Whitefield, who took the Ebenezer orphanage as a model for his own, and was generous in his gifts of money, ironware, and church bells. In October 1742 Henry Melchior Muhlenberg, on his way to Pennsylvania, visited Boltzius, who accompanied him as far as Charleston, where, mindful of his frail wife and two sick daughters, he turned back. A son Boltzius sent home to Halle to be educated. To the Rev. Samuel Urlsperger of Augsburg, who collected the funds out of which the salaries of the ministers were paid, he wrote voluminous reports on all phases of the colony's life. In his last years he was ill a great deal, but he had able assistants in Hermann Heinrich Lemke and Christian Rabenhorst. After much suffering patiently borne he finally succumbed to dropsy.

[*Aüsfuhrliche Nachrichten von der Königlich-grossbrittannischen Colonie Saltzburgischer Emigranten in America* (19 pts. in 3 vols., Halle, 1741 [1735]–1752); *Americanisches Ackerwerk Gottes,* etc. (5 vols. in 3, Augsburg, 1754–67); *Zuverlässiges Sendschreiben von den geist-und-leiblichen Umständen der Saltzburgischen Emigranten,* (Halle, 1736); *Ausführliche Nachrichten von den Saltzburgischen Emigranten, etc.* (Halle, 1744). The foregoing were compiled from Boltzius' letters, diaries, etc., by Samuel Urlsperger of Augsburg and are usually cited as the *"Urlsperger Nachrichten."* Cf. also *An Extract from the Journals of Mr. Commissary Von Reck . . . and of the Rev. Mr. Bolzius,* etc. (London, for the S. P. C. K., 1734, repr. in Peter Force, *Tracts,* Washington, 1836–46, vol. IV, 1846, No. 5); N. Curnock, ed., *The Jour. of the Rev. John Wesley, A.M.* (Standard Ed., London, n. d.). Good secondary accounts are P. A. Strobel, *The Salzburgers and Their Descendants* (Baltimore, 1855); C. C. Jones, Jr., *The Dead Towns of Georgia* (Savannah, 1878); A. Prinziger, art. in *Mitteilungen der Gesellschaft für Salzburger Landeskunde,* vol. XXII (Salzburg, 1882); A. L. Gräbner, *Geschichte der Lutherischen Kirche in America* (St. Louis, 1892).] G. H. G.

BOMBERGER, JOHN HENRY AUGUSTUS (Jan. 13, 1817–Aug. 19, 1890), clergyman of the German Reformed Church, college president, the son of George and Mary (Hoffmeier) Bomberger, was born in Lancaster, Pa. His ancestors on both sides were German. His father was a merchant but his mother's father and two of her brothers were ministers and he himself was early destined for the ministry. He was educated at Marshall College (Mercersburg, Pa.) and was the only member of its first graduating class in 1837. He spent one year of theological study under Dr. Frederick A. Rauch, the first president of Marshall College and a professor in the Theological Seminary of the Reformed Church. On Dec. 27, 1838, he was ordained a minister of the (German) Reformed Church and immediately entered upon pastoral work at Lewistown, Pa., at a salary of "from $400.00 to $500.-00." His longest and most fruitful pastorate was that of the Old Race Street Church in Philadelphia (1854–70), which included a parochial school. Three congregations branched off from this church, and a tremendous impetus was given to church extension in Philadelphia. During the Civil War Bomberger was a radical abolitionist and an ardent supporter of the Union. Active in the Christian Commission he was a potent force in organizing patriotic impulse into forms of service. He was a dominant figure in the judicatories of the Church and served on most of its executive boards and important committees. He was president of the Board of Home Missions for many years, and represented his denomination in the Alliance of Reformed Churches at Belfast, Ireland (1884). He was a working member of the American Tract Society, the American Bible Society, and the American Sunday School Union. He was twice married: first, in 1839, to Marian Elizabeth Huston of Mercersburg, Pa., who died in 1855; and second, in 1863, to Julia Aymer Wight of Philadelphia, who died in 1889. His published works include *Kurtz's Text-Book of Church History* (2 vols., 1860–62), pronounced by Dr. John W. Nevin "among the most important contributions yet made to the theological literature of the country"; and *The Protestant Theological and Ecclesiastical Encyclopedia* (1858–60)—a condensed translation, with additions from other sources, of the first six volumes of *Herzog's Real Encyklopädia* then in course of serial publication. He was the founder and editor of the *Reformed Church Monthly* (1868–76). As the recognized leader of the so-called antiliturgical party, he was foremost in the movement that led to the establishment of Ursinus College and became its first president (1869–90), filling at the same time the chair of moral and mental philosophy and evidences of Christianity. The publications that best reveal his theological views are his articles in the *Mercersburg Review* and his articles in the *Reformed Church Monthly* and the *Christian World* (1861–90). He was a skilled controversialist and an able speaker. Even though at times his arguments appear to have been more personal than logical his sincerity need not be questioned. He had an engaging personality, great social talents, and a mind tempered with imagination and sentiment.

[*Franklin and Marshall Coll. Obit. Record,* vol. I; *John H. A. Bomberger* (Ursinus College, 1917); *New Schaff-Herzog Encyc. of Religious Knowledge* (1910); *Reformed Ch. Mess.*, Aug. 28, 1890.] G. F. M.

BOMFORD, GEORGE (1782–Mar. 25, 1848), soldier, was born in the city of New York. His father was an officer of the Continental army in the Revolution. He was appointed a cadet in the army on Oct. 24, 1804, commissioned as second lieutenant of engineers, July 1, 1805, and for the next seven years was engaged upon fortification work in New York Harbor and Chesapeake Bay. He was promoted first lieutenant in 1806, captain in 1808, and major in 1812. Upon the outbreak of the war with Great Britain he was assigned to ordnance duty, for which he proved to have a special talent. Knowledge of the manufacture of ordnance was rare in this country, and his exceptional abilities made him indispensable. The howitzer or shell gun named the Columbiad, from Joel Barlow's epic poem, was Bomford's invention. He was appointed lieutenant-colonel of ordnance in 1815, and in 1832 was made colonel and chief of ordnance of the army. Upon the death of Mrs. Barlow, whose sister he had married, he bought the famous estate of Kalorama, which lay just outside the limits of the city of Washington as then constituted, between the present location of Florida Avenue and Rock Creek. It is commonly associated with Joel Barlow, who owned it, however, for only five years, during part of which time he was absent on a diplomatic mission in France, while it was Bomford's for nearly thirty. During his occupancy it was famous as the resort of statesmen and diplomats. The trees and plants collected there from all parts of the world, under Mrs. Bomford's judicious direction, made it one of the most notable botanical gardens in the country. The failure of a large cotton mill which Bomford had established on Rock Creek crippled his fortunes, already impaired by unfortunate investments in Washington real estate, and late in life he was obliged to sell Kalorama to settle his liabilities. He died at Boston, where he had gone to witness the casting of some heavy guns. Bomford was the greatest ordnance expert of his time in the United States, an inventor of note, and an able organizer and administrator. A good writer and speaker, his opinions carried great weight both in the executive departments and in Congress. "His official papers in particular were models of reserve force, lucid argument, and fluent style" (Dutton). He was a public-spirited citizen, interested in religious, philanthropic, and artistic activities in the District of Columbia, notably in the movement which led to the building of the Washington Monument.

[G. W. Cullum, *Biog. Reg.* (3rd ed., 1891), I, 58–59; article by C. E. Dutton in *The Army of the United States* (1896), ed. by T. R. Rodenbough and W. L. Haskin; Corra Bacon-Foster, "The Story of Kalorama," in *Columbia Hist. Soc. Records,* XIII, 98–118.] T. M. S.

BONAPARTE, CHARLES JOSEPH (June 9, 1851–June 28, 1921), lawyer, municipal and civil service reformer, attorney-general, was the son of Jerome Bonaparte and Susan May Williams. His grandfather was that Jerome, King of Westphalia, who married Elizabeth Patterson of Baltimore [*q.v.*], and subsequently separated from her, at the command of his august brother, the Emperor Napoleon. Any pride of French ancestry that Charles Joseph might have paraded was inhibited by the good sense of his mother who came of New England stock and was intensely American. He was educated first in a French school near Baltimore, his birthplace, and then under private tutors. He was regarded as a brilliant scholar, a reputation which he seems to have sustained at Harvard College. Graduating in 1872, he at once entered the Harvard Law School where he took a keen interest in current politics as they were discussed in the debating society. Two years later he graduated from the Law School, was admitted to the bar, and began to practise in Baltimore. Possessed of ample wealth, he experienced none of the initial hardships of a young lawyer; and from the outset he put his legal talents at the service of litigants who, or whose causes, appealed to his ardent desire for justice. His fellow practitioners regarded him as a skillful and resourceful attorney. It was public causes, however, which appealed most strongly to him. He identified himself with the reform party which was trying to purge Baltimore of its corrupt ring; he was one of the founders of the Baltimore Reform League and became its chairman; he helped to found and support *The Civil Service Reformer,* the organ of the Maryland Civil Service League; and he was also one of the founders of the National Civil Service Reform League. His interest in civil service reform brought him into contact with Theodore Roosevelt, then civil service commissioner, who later as president repeatedly sought his services, first as member of the board of Indian commissioners charged with the investigation of conditions in the Indian Territory, and then as special counsel to prosecute alleged frauds in the postal service.

In 1905 he was invited to enter President Roosevelt's cabinet as secretary of the navy, with the expectation of succeeding to the attorney-generalship on the retirement of William H. Moody. The appointment stirred more than ordinary public interest. Even the Republican press indulged in good-natured raillery at the thought of the grand-nephew of the Little Corporal becoming head of the United States navy. He afterward described his manifold administrative duties in an article contributed to the *Century Magazine* (March 1910), which revealed not only his high ideal of public service but his unfailing good-humor in the discharge of duty. In December 1906 he was appointed attorney-general and transferred his abundant energies to the more congenial duties of the Department of Justice at a time when President Roosevelt needed a hard-hitter in his fight with "bad trusts." During his term of office he appeared personally before the Supreme Court in more than fifty cases. Aside from the prosecutions begun by his predecessors, he instituted twenty suits under the anti-trust laws, of which eight were eventually decided in favor of the government. His most notable achievement was the dissolution of the American Tobacco Company, though the decree was not issued until after he had left office.

Bonaparte went out of office with President Roosevelt in March 1909 and returned to his somewhat desultory law practise in Baltimore. His dominant interest was still good government. He was one of the founders of the National Municipal League and later its president. An effective public speaker, he was much in demand wherever the cause of civic reform needed a fearless champion. He was, in short, as Senator Gorman once contemptuously called him, a "professional reformer." Nominally a Republican, he did not hesitate to act as an independent in politics. He had attacked the war policy of President McKinley; he followed Roosevelt in the Progressive party of 1912; but he labored to prevent a rupture in the Republican party in 1916 when he believed that a united party was necessary to defeat the Wilson administration. Bonaparte bore little resemblance to his famous ancestor. He was taller, of sturdier build, with large strong neck and massive head. "A vast, round, rugged head," observed one of the newspaper correspondents who delighted to interview him, "with curious rises over the temples. . . . Beneath the forehead lurks the Bonaparte smile. It is there all the time" (*Baltimore Sun*, June 29, 1921). On Sept. 1, 1875, he had married Ellen Channing Day of Hartford, Conn., and a few years later he established a country estate at "Bella Vista," not far from Baltimore. There, after a lingering illness, he died as he had lived, a devout and loyal communicant of the Catholic Church.

[J. B. Bishop, *Chas. Jos. Bonaparte. His Life and Public Services* (1922) is a laudatory biography but gives the main facts of his career. There is an informing obituary in the *Baltimore Sun*, June 29, 1921, as well as an editorial comment. See also the *Baltimore American*, June 29, 1921, and the *Baltimore News*, June 28, 1921. The trust prosecutions are listed in *Administration of the Sherman Anti-Trust Law* (1926).]

BONAPARTE, ELIZABETH PATTERSON (Feb. 6, 1785–Apr. 4, 1879), wife of Jerome the brother of the Emperor Napoleon, was born in Baltimore, the daughter of William and Dorcas (Spear) Patterson. Her father emigrated to that city from County Donegal, Ireland, in 1766, dealt shrewdly in arms and munitions during the Revolution, and as merchant, banker, and land-owner became one of the wealthiest men in Maryland. His daughter was early famous for her beauty, and was ambitious and headstrong as well as beautiful. She made a conquest of the nineteen-year-old Jerome Bonaparte when he visited Baltimore; and on Christmas Eve, 1803, with the reluctant consent of her father, she married him. Expecting trouble, her father tried to protect her by a special marriage contract and, though himself a Presbyterian, had the ceremony performed by the ranking Catholic ecclesiastic in the United States. The father's foreboding was justified; Napoleon, refusing to recognize the marriage, ordered his brother to return to France alone. When the truant finally did return in 1805, it was on a ship of his father-in-law's and accompanied by his wife. At Lisbon they parted, Jerome hastening to Paris to negotiate a reconciliation, while Elizabeth, forbidden to land on European soil, proceeded ultimately to England, where her son, Jerome Napoleon Bonaparte, was born at Camberwell, July 7, 1805. In his brother's presence Jerome's resolution melted. Pope Pius VII declined to annul the marriage, but a French council of state was more pliable, and Jerome as the last reward of his compliance was married to the Princess Catharine of Württemberg and was made king of Westphalia. To his first wife, who wasted no pity on herself, Napoleon gave an annual pension of 60,000 francs, on condition that she stay in America and renounce the Bonaparte name. She vegetated in Baltimore until the Napoleonic fabric crashed in 1815. Then she secured a divorce from Jerome by a special act of the Maryland legislature and set out for Europe, where she spent most of her time until 1840, was made much of in society, and found an appreciative audience for her extraordinary beauty, caustic wit, and brummagem royalty. She spent lavishly to educate her son and to clothe herself, but was otherwise parsimonious. The second Jerome finally disappointed her by failing to make a brilliant European match and by condescending to marry a girl from Baltimore, Susan May Williams. With the Bonapartes her relations were prevailingly cordial; Napoleon himself she admired as a man after her own heart. The legitimacy of her son was recognized by Napoleon III but his right to succession disallowed. The last eighteen years of Madame Bonaparte's life were passed in Baltimore. She lived obscurely in a boarding house and by pinching economy and strict attention to her real estate was able to leave a fortune of approximately $1,500,000 to her two grandsons.

[All accounts of Mme. Bonaparte derive from E. L. Didier, *Life and Letters of Mme. Bonaparte* (1879).]

G. H. G.

BONAPARTE, JEROME NAPOLEON (Nov. 5, 1830–Sept. 3, 1893), soldier, was born at Baltimore of Susan (Williams) Bonaparte and the elder Jerome Napoleon Bonaparte, son of Jerome, King of Westphalia. He was educated in private schools, and for a short time was a student at Harvard, withdrawing upon his appointment to a cadetship at the Military Academy. He graduated at West Point in 1852, a classmate of Slocum, Crook, and Stanley, and was commissioned in the Mounted Riflemen (now the 3rd Cavalry). For the next two years he served in the United States army, and then, upon the invasion of the Crimea, resigned his commission, went to France, and was appointed a second lieutenant of dragoons in the army of his imperial cousin. He was assigned to duty as an aide to Gen. Morris, who commanded a cavalry division, and under him he served with credit throughout the war, seeing plenty of hard fighting at Balaklava and Inkermann, and during the siege. He received British and Turkish decorations, as well as the award of the Legion of Honor. At the end of the war, he did not return to his native country, but settled himself to the permanent career of a French army officer, probably not without some calculations as to what the turn of events might some day bring to a Bonaparte of recognized military achievement. He had been promoted to first lieutenant in 1855; he was a captain in 1859, a major in 1865, and a lieutenant-colonel in 1870. During this time his service was active and varied, including a campaign in Algeria, and field service in the Austrian war, in which his conduct at Montebello and Solferino gained him a decoration from the King of Sardinia. The death of his father in 1870 recalled him to America for a brief period, but the declaration of war against Prussia brought him back to France almost immediately. Moving to the front in August, in command of his regiment, he was turned back by the news of the surrender at Sedan. Accompanying the Ex-Empress until she was placed in safety in England, he returned to Paris and served through the siege. But he was an imperialist rather than a Frenchman. The fall of the empire had put an end to any hopes he may have cherished, and he offered his resignation from the army which was no longer the Emperor's. Before he could leave Paris, the city was in the hands of the Commune, and as a Bonaparte he was of course proscribed. Barely escaping with his life, he returned to Baltimore. Thereafter he lived chiefly in Washington and Newport, with extended trips to Europe. He was married to Caroline Le Roy (Appleton) Edgar, widow of Newbold Edgar of New York. He died at Pride's Crossing, Mass.

[G. W. Cullum: *Biog. Reg.* (3rd ed. 1891), II 480–81; *Bull. Ass. Grads. Mil. Acad.* (1894), pp. 53–55.]

T. M. S.

BONARD, LOUIS (1809–Feb. 21, 1871), early benefactor of the American Society for the Prevention of Cruelty to Animals, was born in Rouen, France. About 1849 he left that country and after successful trading operations in South America and California, settled in New York City where he invested his gains in real estate. He was an eccentric individual, something of a genius in a mechanical way, parsimonius, but known to a few to be kind of heart. In the cellar of one of his tenement houses in Mulberry Street he had a workshop, equipped for doing the odd jobs necessary to keep his property in repair. Here, too, he worked on his inventions, which included a circular loom for weaving hats, a brick-making machine, and a machine for casting iron, all of which he patented. The newspaper report, which appeared after his death and has been perpetuated, that he was a miser, living in squalor in a single room, was unfounded. His apartment was in a large modern brick house in Wooster Street, and was clean, though modestly furnished (letter by Henry Bergh, *American Society for the Prevention of Cruelty to Animals, Fifth Annual Report,* 1871). He had a religion of his own, he confessed, "based upon justice and humanity." His agent declared that he was generous to un-

Bond

fortunate tenants, and fond of animals, his indignation being aroused by any act of cruelty toward them (*New York Times,* May 11, 1871). Having watched with admiration the activities of Henry Bergh [*q.v.*], founder of the American Society for the Prevention of Cruelty to Animals, Bonard, at his death, left all his property, amounting to about $150,000, to that society. The will was contested by alleged heirs in France, and by two persons claiming as legatees under a previous will, one of the grounds being that the testator entertained an insane illusion that upon his decease his soul would enter into the body of some animal, and that, influenced by this delusion, he executed the will with a view to the better security of his future existence. The case attained some celebrity (Austin Abbott, *Reports of Practice Cases Determined in the Courts of the State of New York,* new series, XVI, 1876). Ultimately the property went to the society, which erected a monument to his memory in Greenwood Cemetery, New York City, where he was buried.

[In addition to references above, see annual reports of Am. S. P. C. A. 1871–72; C. C. Buel, "Henry Bergh and His Work," *Scribner's Mo.,* April 1879; *N. Y. Times,* Feb. 28, 1871, Sept. 13, 1871.] H. E. S.

BOND, ELIZABETH POWELL (Jan. 25, 1841–Mar. 29, 1926), educator, author, was a descendant of John Howland, the *Mayflower* Pilgrim, and of other New England ancestors. She was one of the four children of Townsend and Catherine (Macy) Powell. Born in Dutchess County, N. Y., when she was four years of age the family moved to Ghent, N. Y., where she attended a small country school until she was sixteen years old, after which she had one year at the State Normal School in Albany. Brought up in a Quaker environment, she passed a quiet childhood, the chief incidents of which were the frequent visits of anti-slavery advocates to her parents' home. From the age of fifteen she made visits to Boston where association with the families of the leading abolitionists and men of letters enriched her young life with interests and ideals which were, as she herself expressed it, "in some measure equivalent to the broadening influence of modern college life." In Boston she also attended Dr. Dio Lewis's school for physical culture. This training led to her appointment as "Instructor in Calisthenics" at Vassar College, 1866–70. On May 23, 1872, she married Henry Herrick Bond, a lawyer of Northampton, Mass. Her husband died in 1881, leaving her with one child, Edwin Powell Bond. Five years later, her abiding interest in higher education led her to accept a call to Swarthmore College, where she became dean in 1890. Her special task was to preside over the students' social life, and she succeeded to an extraordinary degree in placing the college life in a home setting. Coeducation was still on trial in the East, and Dean Bond raised it from the stage of doubt and experiment to an assured success. She was the author of two volumes, entitled *Words by the Way* (first series, 1895; second series, 1901), which are collections of addresses made to the students of Swarthmore, to whom they are dedicated. She was also a frequent contributor in both prose and verse to current periodicals. In 1906, she retired from active service with the title of "Dean Emeritus," and resided for the remainder of her life in Germantown, Philadelphia. She continued her interest in education, and aided as she could such movements as the advancement of women, international peace, and especially the promotion of the negro race, whose problems had stirred her heart in youth and had not been wholly solved, she believed, by freedom from slavery. She lectured frequently, to school, club, and college audiences, on all of these topics. One of her favorite and most popular lectures was upon the reminiscences of her personal friendship with Emerson and Garrison, their families, and the literary and anti-slavery circles of which they were the center. She was a life-long member of the Society of Friends (Liberal Branch) and frequently shared in the ministry in its meetings for worship. Her simplicity and graciousness of demeanor, her dignity of bearing, her characteristic manner of dress, her gentleness of spirit, her delicacy of feeling, her culture and appreciation of the beautiful, her gifts of mind and heart, and her implicit obedience to the demands of an unusually sensitive Puritan-Quaker conscience, combined to create in her a personality whose impress left a permanent influence upon the ideals of her time.

[The chief sources of information about Elizabeth Powell Bond have been her own manuscripts, letters, and diaries. The manuscript of "Dean Bond of Swarthmore, A Quaker Humanist," by Emily Cooper Johnson, in process of publication, was also consulted, as were obituary notices in the *N. Y. Times,* and Philadelphia *Public Ledger,* Swarthmore *Phœnix, Friends' Intelligencer,* and accounts of a memorial meeting to Dean Bond, held in Swarthmore College on June 5, 1926.] H. C. H.

BOND, GEORGE PHILLIPS (May 20, 1825–Feb. 17, 1865), astronomer, was the son of William Cranch Bond [*q.v.*], director of the Harvard College Observatory, and of Selina (Cranch) Bond. He graduated from Harvard in 1845 and was immediately appointed assistant observer. He himself said, in speaking of his brother William, "His natural bias toward astronomy was far stronger than mine. While I was in a manner pressed into the service, he entered of free choice." His strongest inclination was toward ornithology but he had a strong passion for all the beauties of nature, and he was very happy in his ability to make other people, especially children, see these beauties. He and his father worked together on many investigations. The method of determining parallax by measurements of right ascension, east and west of the meridian, was independently proposed by the Bonds and applied to Mars in 1849–50. On the death of his father in 1859 George Bond succeeded him as director of the Harvard College Observatory. He had no private resources at his disposal and the funds of the institution were wholly inadequate to its needs. The war broke out and further pinching economies became necessary. In spite of all these difficulties the work of the observatory was continued at the same high standard.

George Bond is usually credited with the discovery of Hyperion, the eighth satellite of Saturn, and of the crape ring. In the years 1847–56 a vast quantity of drawings and measurements of Saturn were accumulated. The observation of new divisions and of the transparency of the crape ring called for a revision of the theory of a solid structure of the rings. The facts were reviewed and the hypothesis of a fluid state of the rings advanced by George Bond in 1851. No memoir on comets approaches in completeness that of the Donati comet of 1858 by George Bond in the *Annals of the Harvard College Observatory,* vol. III (1862). Every phenomenon of the great comet was described, the text illustrated with a remarkable series of drawings, and many important conclusions drawn. George Bond should be regarded as the true founder of photographic astronomy. He quickly recognized and put to the test its possibilities in mapping the sky, in measuring double-stars, in determining stellar parallax, and in measuring the brightness of the stars. He saw clearly what certainly would be finally accomplished by the new process and fretted only at the necessary delay in discovering the means of increasing the sensitiveness of the plates. His researches in photometry were most suggestive. His photographs showed that the reflecting power of Jupiter is much greater than that of the moon; with his ingenious device of reflection from a silvered glass globe he determined the variation of the brightness of the moon with phase and compared the brightness of the moon with that of Venus, Jupiter, and the sun. At the time of his death he was at work on the discussion of the drawings and measurements of the Orion Nebula which he had undertaken as a vindication of his father's work.

Bond was deeply religious, conscientious, and untiring. In appearance he was rather tall and slender, becoming in later years painfully thin. While modest and unassuming, he had a strong sense of justice and a due estimate of his own worth. The loss of his wife, Harriet Gardner Harris, of his youngest child, and of his father, all within a few months, and the contraction of the disease (tuberculosis) which destroyed him at the age of forty combined to make his path hard. Though repeatedly warned that the only remedy was rest, he could not leave his work.

[Edward S. Holden, *Memorials of Wm. Cranch Bond and of his Son, Geo. Phillips Bond* (1897); *Am. Jour. of Sci. and Arts,* Mar. 1865; *Proc. Am. Acad. of Arts and Sci.,* VI, 499–500; *Memoirs of the Am. Acad. of Arts and Sci.,* containing Bond's numerous scientific papers.] R. S. D.

BOND, HUGH LENNOX (Dec. 16, 1828–Oct. 24, 1893), jurist, was born in Baltimore, the son of Christina (Birckhead) Bond and Dr. Thomas E. Bond, a physician and clergyman, one of the founders of the city's first medical school, and at one time editor of the *Christian Advocate.* In early childhood Hugh Bond was taken to New York, where he lived until he graduated from the University of the City of New York in 1848. He returned to Baltimore to read law, and was admitted to the bar in 1851. He married in 1853 Anne Griffith Penniman of Baltimore. In 1860 he was appointed by Gov. Thomas H. Hicks as judge of the criminal court, in 1861 he was elected to the same position. He was a valuable addition to the American Party in the conservative state of Maryland. Less radical than Henry Winter Davis, he was no less loyal to the Union. The attack of Apr. 19, 1861, on the 6th Massachusetts Regiment on its way through Baltimore gave him the first opportunity to exercise a fearless sense of right which was characteristic. According to his charge to the grand jury, those who took part in the riot had been guilty of murder. Other decisions during the war were his release on *habeas corpus* writs of seventy-five Unionists who had been arrested for displaying flags; his committal to jail of police commissioners appointed by Gov. Swann; his charge to the grand jury to indict military commissioners appointed by the national government who tried citizens for offenses against the United States when Maryland was not under military law; his release on *habeas corpus* writs of children of free colored people apprenticed to slaveholders under an old law.

At the same time he had active political and humanitarian interests. He was a supporter of Davis and when the latter's election to Congress was in doubt in October 1863, he wrote Secretary Stanton about the possibility of postponing the draft until the canvas of votes could be completed (B. C. Steiner, *Life of Henry Winter Davis,* 1916, citing the *Official Records,* ser. 3, vol. III). His protest gave an impetus to the support of emancipation by the non-slaveholding whites in Maryland through the resulting levy of slaves which released the whites. Impelled by a warm interest in the negro, he started and later helped support an educational plan (nicknamed "Timbuctoo") which developed into the "Association for the Improvement of Colored People." In 1868 schools for colored children were established in Baltimore through the efforts of this organization.

Rearrangement of the courts by the new state constitution of 1867 automatically retired Judge Bond from the criminal court bench and he took up private practise. In 1870 President Grant appointed him judge of the newly created fourth United States circuit court, including Maryland, Virginia, West Virginia, and the Carolinas. The Senate confirmed his appointment by a majority of four votes. Almost immediately he was called upon to hear the Ku Klux cases of South Carolina. His independence of judgment was conspicuous here. Fines and imprisonment which he imposed broke the reign of terror that had held nine counties of the state helpless. Five years later Bond gave the famous decision which made Hayes President of the United States when he released on *habeas corpus* writs the members of the state board of canvassers of South Carolina who had been illegally imprisoned by order of the South Carolina supreme court in the effort to force the electoral vote of the state for Tilden. For almost twenty-five years more he was an active and valuable judge in the fourth United States circuit. Many important civil and criminal cases were heard by him, among which the Virginia Coupon cases of 1886 (*Federal Reporter,* vol. XXIX), the receivership and sale of the Atlantic, Mississippi & Ohio Railroad, and the Navassa Island murder case were conspicuous.

[*Sun* (Baltimore), Oct. 26, 1893; *Weekly Sun* (Baltimore), Oct. 28, 1893; *Baltimore American,* Oct. 25, 26, 27, 1893; B. C. Steiner, *Life of Reverdy Johnson*; *Proc. in the Ku Klux Trials at Columbia, S. C., in the U. S. Circuit Court, Nov. Term, 1871* (1872).]

M. A. K.

BOND, SHADRACH (*c.* 1773–Apr. 13, 1832), governor of Illinois, belonged to a prosperous farm-owning Episcopalian family of Baltimore County, Md. His father, Nicodemus Bond, a man of marked piety, became a Methodist, and on his death bed in 1804, manumitted his four slaves (*Baltimore Wills,* VII, 315). His mother, Rachel, was the daughter of a plantation-owner by the name of Richard King Stevenson. She bore her husband ten children, of whom Shadrach was the sixth. He retained the piety of his father but was captivated by the lure of adventure in the West. An uncle, also bearing the name of Shadrach Bond, had been a member of the gallant little band under George Rogers Clark which opened up the Illinois country in 1779; after roving the prairies several years he settled in the fertile American Bottom along the Mississippi below Kaskaskia. Here he was joined by his nephew about the year 1791. With avuncular aid the latter secured a number of land grants (*American State Papers: Public Lands,* II, 123, 132, 135, 204). His fondness for hunting was not allowed to interfere with prosperous farming and public service. In 1806, he became adjutant of the militia in St. Clair County and two years later, lieutenant-colonel. Having been elected in 1806 to his uncle's former seat in the territorial legislature, in 1807 he succeeded his uncle in the council. In 1808 he again succeeded his uncle as presiding judge of the court of common pleas for St. Clair County. In 1812 he was elected as first delegate to Congress from the territory of Illinois. His principal achievement at Washington was the preëmption law of 1813. Thousands of settlers had trespassed upon the public lands before these were offered for sale, and their great concern was to insure themselves against having their lands sold at a higher figure than the minimum of one dollar and a quarter per acre at the public auction or acquired by the holders of unlocated military grants. With the help of Jeremiah Morrow, of Ohio, Bond secured the passage of an act somewhat more generous than the preceding acts, granting preëmption of 160 acres up to two weeks before the public sale. He also increased his popularity at home by securing the passage of an act raising ten companies of rangers from the Western frontier and by his strenuous efforts to secure payment for the Illinois militia in the War of 1812.

Resigning in 1814 to accept the appointment of receiver of public moneys at Kaskaskia, Bond spent four years settling claims to lands in southern Illinois with fairness to his neighbors and loyalty to the federal government. He shrewdly avoided taking sides in the factional dispute between the Edwards group and the Thomas group which divided Illinois politics for two decades. Thus, although a man of no great ability, and a constant seeker after public office, his popularity was such that in 1818, when Illinois with a population of 35,000 reached statehood, he was elected governor. Although the possessor of fourteen slaves (Census of 1820) he had remained silent during the controversy over slavery which agitated the constitutional convention of 1818, and he now straddled the question during the struggle which culminated in the defeat of the pro-slavery attempt for a new constitution in 1824. He appears, however, to have been considerably under the influence of Elias Kent Kane, whom he appointed as secretary of state, and who became the leader of the pro-slavery movement. His administration was simple and honest. In his message to the first general assembly he had the foresight to recommend the construction of a canal connecting Lake Michigan and the Illinois River. Although bitterly criticized for his personal interest in the wildcat bank established by the legislature (*Illinois Emigrant,* Shawneetown, Apr. 3, 1819, p. 1), his financial record appears to have been sound (J. C. Pease, *The Frontier State,* 1918, II, 52–69). At the expiration of his four-year term, he resumed his occupation of farming. He continued his interest in politics, campaigning for Jackson and running for Congress in 1824, but being defeated. He supported internal improvements, being one of the incorporators of the Illinois & Michigan Canal Company in 1825 (*Illinois Intelligencer,* Springfield, Mar. 25, 1825). In 1825 he was appointed register of the land office at Kaskaskia and held this position at his death.

Bond prided himself on his generous hospitality. On his farm near Kaskaskia he built a large two-story brick house with broad verandas in Southern fashion, and received many guests. In 1810, he married a distant cousin, Achsah Bond, of Nashville, a woman of considerable character and charm, who accompanied him on his arduous journeys to Washington as delegate to Congress, and who shared his delight in sociability. A German writer who visited the frontier in 1819 has left a pleasing picture of the distinguished company and the courtesy that he found in the home of Gov. Bond (Ferdinand Ernst, *Reise durch das Innere der Vereinigten Staaten,* p. 32). One of his contemporaries describes Bond as of military bearing, six feet in height, erect and compact, with black hair and commanding appearance, a description comporting with his portrait which is in the possession of the Chicago Historical Society. The bad grammar of his letters as delegate to Congress bears witness of the limitations of his early education. He was a man of business but not of original ideas. His state papers while governor were supposed to have been drafted by Kane.

[J. C. Smith, *Freemasonry in Illinois* (1903); John Reynolds, *Pioneer Hist. of Illinois* (1852), not always trustworthy; W. H. Brown, *Early Hist.* (1840); Henry Brown, *Hist. of Illinois* (1844); Thos. Ford, *Hist. of Illinois* (1854); E. B. Washburne, *Edwards Papers* (1884); E. B. Greene and C. W. Alvord, *Governor's Letter-Books* (1909).]
K. C.

BOND, THOMAS (1712–Mar. 26, 1784), physician, the son of Richard and Elizabeth (Chew) Bond, was born in Calvert County, Md. After studying medicine with Dr. Alexander Hamilton, of Annapolis, Md., he completed his medical education in Europe, chiefly at Paris. About 1734 he began practising medicine in Philadelphia where he was joined a few years later by his brother Phineas. "He was of delicate constitution," according to Thacher, "and disposed to pulmonary consumption, for which he went on a voyage when a young man, to the island of Barbadoes. By unremitted care of his health, the strictest attention to diet and to guard against the changes of temperature, and also by frequently losing blood when he found his lungs affected, he lived to an age which the greater part of mankind never reach." Although Bond's chief interest lay in medicine, especially in its application to hygiene and epidemiology, he was an excellent surgeon, performing amputations and operating for stone in the bladder with much success. His name is still applied to the splint he devised for use in fractures of the lower extremity of the radius. Benjamin Rush ascribed to Bond the credit for the introduction and general use of mercury in the practise of Philadelphia physicians. Bond was also a great believer in the efficacy of various forms of baths, hot, cold, and vapor, in the treatment of disease.

The best account of Bond's connection with the founding of the Pennsylvania Hospital, the oldest hospital in the United States intended solely for the reception of the sick, injured, and insane, and unconnected in any way with the idea of a poorhouse or almshouse, is given by Benjamin Franklin in his *Autobiography.* With great generosity Franklin disclaims the credit frequently ascribed to him of being the founder of the Hospital, and tells how Bond had conceived the idea and sought to obtain subscriptions for the project with but little success, largely because he was generally asked "Have you consulted Franklin on this business?" Bond had not heretofore spoken to Franklin on the subject because he felt it was one in which he might not be interested. When he finally in 1751 approached him Franklin entered into the plan with the greatest enthusiasm and with the aid of his shrewd advice and great influence the Hospital was soon launched on its beneficent career and was open for the reception of patients in February 1752. Bond was a member of the first staff and served as physician to the Hospital until his death. One of the objections raised to the establishment of the Hospital had been the expense incident to paying for the services of physicians. This was overcome when Bond, his brother Phineas, and Dr. Lloyd Zachary offered to give their services for nothing. In 1766 Bond began the delivery at the Hospital of the first course of clinical lectures to be given in the United States. He had previously secured the consent of the Managers of the Hospital to such a course by asking them to meet at his house where he read them an address in which he showed the value of such a course in connection with the newly projected plans of Dr. John Morgan and Dr. William Shippen, Jr., for a medical school in Philadelphia. The Managers not only permitted Bond to give his lectures but thought so highly of his remarks that they ordered them copied into the minutes. Bond was a member of the original board of trustees of the College of Philadelphia, as the University of Pennsylvania was then called, and took a great interest in the establishment of its Medical School in 1765. He was also one of the founders of the American Philosophical Society in 1768. Although sixty-four years old, he volunteered his services to the Committee of Safety in 1776 and did considerable service in the organization of the army. He was president of the Humane Society of Philadelphia which was founded in 1780 and took much interest in its affairs. Thacher gives the following as his contributions to medical literature: "An Account of a Worm bred in the Liver," *Medical Observations and Inquiries by a Society of Physicians in London,* May 1, 1754; "A letter to Doctor Fothergill on the use of the Peruvian Bark in Scrofula," *Ibid.,* vol. II. Bond's "Essay on the Utility of Clinical Lectures" is printed in T. G. Morton's *History of the Pennsylvania Hospital* (1895). He was married to Sarah Roberts by whom he had seven children, two of whom became physicians.

[Jas. Thacher, *Am. Medic. Biog.* (1828); G. W. Norris, *Early Hist. of Medicine in Phila.* (1886); manuscript ledgers and letters in the Lib. of the Coll. of Physicians of Phila.]

F. R. P.

BOND, WILLIAM CRANCH (Sept. 9, 1789–Jan. 29, 1859), astronomer, was born in Falmouth (now Portland), Me., where his father, William Bond, had settled in 1786 and engaged in the export of lumber. His mother was Hannah Cranch. The venture in the lumber business proving unsuccessful, William Bond moved to Boston and returned to his trades of silversmith and clockmaker. There followed years of struggle with poverty. It was necessary for young Bond to leave public school at an early age and share in the support of the family. His brother describes him as the best-tempered boy he knew and says that he was the best of the boys at making traps and snares. He soon became an admirable workman. At the age of fifteen he made a ship's chronometer and at about the same time, a quadrant. For many years preceding the War of 1812 the chronometers of most of the ships sailing out of Boston were rated by his instruments. He was entirely self-taught, at a time when astronomy was just starting in America. His brother describes the first transit instrument in the house at Dorchester—"a strip of brass nailed to the east end of the Champney house, with a hole in it to see a fixed star and note its transit." His mother shared his plans and sympathized with his high aspirations. His independent discovery of the comet of 1811 shows him to have been a constant observer at that time, though no one knew of his discovery until several months later. With what instruments he could make or procure he watched and recorded the positions of the heavenly bodies with no other apparent motive than a love of the occupation. In 1815 when preparing for a trip to Europe he was commissioned by Harvard College to visit the English observatories and gather data concerning instruments and mountings. While the building of an observatory in Cambridge had to be delayed for many years, Bond's report was satisfactory in every way and his contact with European astronomers was of great value to him. In 1819 he married his cousin, Selina Cranch, in Kingsbridge, Devonshire. She was the mother of his six children. After her death, in 1831, he married her elder sister, Mary Roope Cranch. Household expenses were willingly cut down to save money for the purchase of costly instruments and books. The only parlor in the house at Dorchester was sacrificed to science—a huge granite block rose in the middle of the room and the ceiling was intersected by an opening in the meridian. During this period Bond did pioneer work on the rates of chronometers and in meteorology and magnetism. The children were impressed into service as assistants and recorders. William Cranch Bond, Jr., a lad of great promise, was an especially devoted assistant until his death in 1841.

After thirty years of unremitting observation in Dorchester and at a time when he was beginning to be able to enjoy more leisure for astronomy, Bond consented in 1839 to move to Cambridge and take charge of what was then little more than a plan for an observatory. No salary was attached to the office until 1846. The last observation in Dorchester was made on Dec. 25, 1839. The first at Cambridge is dated Dec. 31. By the generosity of the citizens of Boston and the vicinity it finally became possible to order a 15-inch telescope, matching the one newly put into operation at Pulkovo. During the last twelve years of Bond's directorship this instrument was in constant use by him and his son George. It is difficult, and perhaps not important, to weigh the credit which should be given to each. During the administration of the elder Bond elaborate studies were made of the Orion and Andromeda nebulæ and of the planets. The photographic process, invented by Daguerre in 1839, was here first put to practical astronomical use. The regulating device which made the chronograph an instrument of precision is also to be attributed to the Bonds. In his later years William Bond was very frail in health. He is remembered in his last years as a gentle, kindly old man, serene and placid. He was deeply religious, modest, and retiring.

[Edward S. Holden, *Memorials of William Cranch Bond and of His Son, George Phillips Bond* (1897); *Annals of the Harvard Coll. Observatory*, vol. I, pt. 1, vol. II, pt. 1, vol. VII.] R. S. D.

BONER, JOHN HENRY (Jan. 31, 1845–Mar. 6, 1903), editor, poet, the son of Thomas Jacob and Phœbe Elizabeth Boner, was born in Salem, N. C. After an academic education varied by rambles along the Yadkin River and prentice work at versifying, the youth was put to learn the printer's trade. At twenty-two he ventured to establish the *Salem Observer* but met with failure; in the same year he edited the *Asheville Pioneer*. Moved by Whig influence and anti-slavery sentiment among his Moravian ancestors, Boner early cast his lot with the Republican party. He was recognized by appointment as secretary of the constitutional convention (1868) and as clerk of the House of Representatives of North Carolina (1869, 1870). Feeling assured of his future, Boner now married Lottie Smith of Raleigh. But in the following year the Carpet-Baggers were routed at the polls, and Boner, refusing to modify his politics, found all doors closed to him in his own state. He had been worsted in his first encounter with partisan government. Removing to Washington, he entered the Government Printing Office as typesetter. His first publication, *Sparrows in the Snow* (1877), was negligible; but *Whispering Pines* (1883) won the poet recognition in New York, and friendship from Edmund Clarence Stedman. Although Boner's lyrics of this period were entirely conventional, his sketches of life among Moravians and negroes were sincere and appealing. At this juncture, the Democratic party gained control of national affairs; Boner's activities in North Carolina were recalled; and he was dismissed from his position as proof-reader because of "offensive partisanship." For the second time the vagaries of politics had frustrated the poet.

Brought to New York by Stedman, Boner soon established himself as an editor, serving on *The Century Dictionary* (1887–91), *A Library of American Literature* (1888–90), the New York *World* (1891–92), and *The Standard Dictionary* (1892–94). His associates found him dignified and reserved: only his wife and a few intimates knew his gentle humanity. His lyrics were now surer in execution, deeper and wider in emotional range; but sentimentalism defeated his attempt at interpreting the metropolis in verse. Elated by appointment in 1894 as an editor on the *Literary Digest*, he began building a home for his old age, "Cricket Lodge" on Staten Island. But in the following year he disagreed violently with his editor and characteristically resigned rather than yield to his superior. Weakened in health, he struggled to support himself by hack-writing, particularly for *Appleton's Annual Cyclopædia* (1896–99). Out of disaster came his finest lyrics—his chief claim to more than local reputation. Such work, however, did not maintain the payments on "Cricket Lodge": his home was lost. Thus the poet, unable to concede or to conciliate, was finally broken by the discipline of journalism.

Ill and destitute, Boner was in 1900 reinstated in his former position in Washington, through the intervention of friends. His health did not allow him to remain at the desk: on the proceeds of *Some New Poems* (1901) he recuperated in North Carolina. In January 1903 he returned to Washington, where he died. Sensitive and high-spirited, kindly yet unyielding, Boner, like the three poets whom he most highly revered—Spenser, Keats, and Poe—had failed to adjust himself to the realities of a commercial civilization. His last volume, *Poems* (1903), was published by his widow. The Boner Memorial Association in 1904 removed his remains from the Congressional Cemetery in Washington to the Moravian burying-ground in his beloved Salem. Participation in this ceremony by the governor of the state indicated that the foremost poet of North Carolina was no longer an alien among his own people.

[The foregoing sketch is based primarily on the publications and records of the concerns with which Boner was associated and on a manuscript letter from Mr.

Frank Vizetelly. Scattered biographical data appear in the *South Atlantic Quart.*, Apr. 1904; *Memorial of John Henry Boner* (1905); *Charlotte Observer*, Jan. 6, 1906; *Lib. of Southern Lit.*, I, 415; *Who's Who in America*, 1901–2.] G. T. M.

BONHAM, MILLEDGE LUKE (Dec. 25, 1813–Aug. 27, 1890), Confederate soldier and congressman, was descended from Nicholas Bonham, who was living in Barnstable, Mass., in 1659 when he was married to Hannah Fuller, grand-daughter of a *Mayflower* Pilgrim. James Bonham, fifth in the line of descent from Nicholas, moved to South Carolina after the close of the Revolution and married Sophie Smith. Their eighth child, Milledge Luke, was born at Red Bank, Edgefield District. His father died when he was two years old and under the care of his mother he was educated in the "old field" schools of Edgefield District, the academies of Edgefield and Abbeville, and the South Carolina College, graduating in 1834 under the presidency of the famous Dr. Thomas Cooper. He successfully practised law in the intervals of his public and military life. He was in command of the South Carolina Brigade in the Seminole War and was always interested in the militia, holding the office of major-general of militia for several years. He served in the state legislature from 1840 to 1844 representing Edgefield District. He was married Nov. 13, 1845, to Ann Patience Griffin. When war was declared with Mexico in 1846 he was appointed by President Polk lieutenant-colonel of the 12th Infantry. His adjutant was Capt. Winfield Scott Hancock, afterward major-general in the United States Army, and his brigade commander was Gen. Franklin Pierce, afterward president. He was an original member of the Aztec Club, was cited by Gen. Pierce for conspicuous service, and for a year served as governor of one of the conquered provinces. Upon his return to Edgefield he resumed his law practise and was elected in 1848 solicitor of the southern district in South Carolina, serving till 1857 when he was elected as States Rights Democrat to fill the unexpired congressional term of his cousin, Hon. Preston S. Brooks. He remained in Congress till the secession of South Carolina in 1860. Appointed commander-in-chief of the South Carolina troops around Charleston, at the request of Gov. Pickens he waived his rank and served under Gen. Beauregard of the newly created Confederate Army. In April 1861 he was appointed brigadier-general in the Confederate Army, and was in command of the first troops arriving in Virginia for the defense of Richmond. He led his brigade in the fighting around Fairfax, Centerville, Vienna, and First Manassas. He was one of the many officers who protested against President Davis's interpretation of the ranking of officers who had served in the "old army," and in 1862 he resigned his commission in the army and was at once elected to the Confederate Congress. Later in the same year he was elected governor of South Carolina and served with marked success in a period of internal difficulties. In February 1865 he was reappointed brigadier-general of cavalry and served under Joseph E. Johnston until he surrendered with Johnston's army. After the end of the Civil War he resumed his law practise, served in the legislature in the early days of Reconstruction, was a delegate to the national Democratic convention in 1868, but kept out of active politics till the "Red Shirt Campaign" of 1876, when he took an active and enthusiastic part in restoring white supremacy in the state government. He was appointed by Gov. Wade Hampton in 1878 as railroad commissioner and served in this capacity during the difficult days of building up the wrecked transportation system of the state until his death, which occurred suddenly on Aug. 27, 1890, from the bursting of a blood vessel.

[Bonham's personal papers and a manuscript sketch of the Bonham family, written by Judge M. L. Bonham, are now in the possession of Dr. M. L. Bonham of Hamilton College. There are other sources in the Pickens-Bonham manuscripts and the Hammond Papers in the Lib. of Cong. A life of Bonham is in preparation by his grandson, Dr. M. L. Bonham.] J. E. W—y.

BONNER, JOHN (*c.* 1643–Jan. 30, 1725/26), mariner and mapmaker, born possibly in London, came to Boston about 1670. He began his career there in that year by purchasing the *Recovery*, in which his first extended venture was in 1671–72 from Boston to Virginia, Barbados, England, Ireland, and back to Boston, a charter-party with Henry Ashton and others. He became owner or master of many other vessels, including the *Amity, Speedwell, Crown, Mary* (in Phips's Canada Expedition of 1690), *Two Brothers, Three Friends,* and the brigantine *Hope* (a flag of truce to Quebec in 1706) in which he brought home the Rev. John Williams of Deerfield [*q.v.*], author of *The Redeemed Captive* (1707). He was a member of a committee on building the Province Galley in 1693 and of a committee on repairing a later Province Galley in 1709; chief pilot of Admiral Walker's disastrous expedition, 1711; maker of a draught of the entrance of Boston Harbor, 1716; and member of a committee to inspect another draught of the same and report on the necessity of a second lighthouse, 1718. He made a chart of Canada River before 1711, a plan of the Boston waterfront in 1714, and published "A Curious ingraven map of the town of Boston" during 1722. Only two copies of the original exist: one in possession of I. N. Phelps Stokes of New York, and the other at the Massachusetts Historical Society, Boston. A contemporaneous opinion of him from the *Boston Newsletter* of Feb. 3, 1726 (*i. e.*, 1725/26), reads as follows: "He was a Gentleman very Skillful and Ingenious in many Arts and Sciences; especially in Navigation, Drawing, Moulding of Ships, &c. One of the best acquainted with the Coasts of North America, of any of his time; of great Knowledge and Judgement in Marine Affairs; was very much consulted, improved and relyed upon by the Government as a Principal Pilate [*sic*], in our Marine Expeditions; and with diligent Care and Faithfulness discharged his Trust. In short, He was brave, hardy, healthy, sober, industrious, honest, good natur'd, as well as Religious; and much belov'd by all that knew him." He was married four times: (1) to Rebecca Greene; (2) to Mary Clark, who died Apr. 20, 1697; (3) to Persis Wanton, on Sept. 28, 1699; (4) to Susannah Stilson, on June 2, 1709, who died in January 1710/11.

[The principal sources of information are the *Boston Newsletter*, 1704–26; *Boston Gazette*, 1719–26; *New Eng. Courant*, 1721–26; *Reports of the Record Commissioners of the City of Boston* (1876–1909); *Calendar of State Papers, America and West Indies*, 1603–1714; *Vital Records of Cambridge, Mass.* (1914); *Pubs. Colonial Soc. of Mass.*; *Acts and Resolves, Public and Private, of the Province of the Mass. Bay*, vols. I, II, VII–XI; *Records of the Governor and Company of the Mass. Bay in New Eng.* (1853–54); *Records of the Court of Assistants of the Colony of the Mass. Bay* (1901–28); *Proc. and Colls. of the Mass. Hist. Soc.*; *New Eng. Hist. and Geneal. Reg.*, Apr. 1851, July 1860, July 1889; manuscript records in the Massachusetts Archives.]

J. H. E—s.

BONNER, ROBERT (Apr. 28, 1824–July 6, 1899), newspaper publisher and famous turfman, born near Londonderry, Ireland, came to America in 1839. Learning the printer's trade on the *Hartford Courant* in Connecticut, he became a remarkably fast compositor and early showed a fondness for fast horses. While still a typesetter for the *Courant*, he was constantly swapping horses to get one that had more speed. Believing that New York City offered greater opportunities for a practical printer than Hartford, he went in 1844 to the metropolis where in 1851 he purchased from the profits of his printing plant the *Merchant's Ledger*, a commercial sheet published in the interest of the dry-goods trade. Promptly shortening the name, he excluded all news of that business and turned the paper into a family newspaper by substituting popular fiction for quotations on stock for merchants. To secure circulation he became a lavish purchaser of advertising space in newspapers though he refused all advertisements submitted for publication in the *Ledger*. He originated freak advertising and what is known to-day as "teaser copy." For example, he would purchase a whole newspaper page and then put in each column, "Read *The New York Ledger*," repeated over and over again until the jumble filled all the space. When in 1860 his press room was "gutted" by fire he distributed the printing of his *Ledger* among a dozen other plants and advertised in the leading daily papers throughout the country, "Unless we are burned out more than once a week, *The New York Ledger* will be ready Monday mornings on all newsstands of the United States, the Sandwich Islands and New Jersey." Even in his personal advertising he was also spectacular. He once offered for sale his summer home from which he wanted to get away as fast as one of his famous horses could carry him because all his family and servants had the ague and fever. Cash was demanded because "any security would get the fever and ague and become shaky" (see advertisements in New York newspapers, September 1867). He advertised his stable by getting occupants of the White House to ride behind his horses. To the public he sold the *Ledger* as cheaply as possible, three dollars a year, but to authors—he had a mania for "big names"—he paid startling sums. To Mrs. James Parton, who, writing under the *nom de plume* of "Fanny Fern," was one of the "best sellers" of the day, he paid $100 a column and to Edward Everett, for a series of short articles, he gave $10,000. Obtaining contributions from Raymond of the *New York Times*, Greeley of the *New York Tribune*, and Bennett of the *New York Herald*, he put all three articles in one issue of the *Ledger*. Always he was seeking some new thing or an old thing that could be done in a new way. Even in producing his periodical he sought profits in a novel way for the time—from circulation alone (see editorial in the New York *Sun*, Mar. 13, 1875). He achieved his ambition and saw the weekly sales reach nearly the half-million mark. The profits from the *Ledger* went in part to establish racing records. For fast horses, which he never allowed to run again for money prizes, Bonner spent more than $500,000. Cornelius Vanderbilt had about everything he wanted except Bonner's Dexter, a great trotter. The end for both Bonner and his *Ledger* came at about the same time. An attraction at the 1926 National Horse Show in New York City was a racing sulky over which was this placard, "Once pulled by Maud S., owned by Robert Bonner."

[The files of the *N. Y. Ledger* constitute the best biography of Robt. Bonner. His influence on later periodicals of the family type is discussed by S. N. D. North in the eighth volume of the quarto series comprising the final report on the *Tenth Census* (1884), p. 119. His spectacular advertising campaigns are treated by Frederic Hudson in *Journalism in the U. S.* (1873), pp. 646 ff., but too much emphasis is put upon those inserted in the *N. Y. Herald* with which Hudson was connected. Briefer but more accurate is the mention made of Bonner by Augustus Maverick in *Henry Raymond and the N. Y. Press* (1870), p. 346. A letter about Bonner from "an old friend," printed in the N. Y. *Sun,* July 8, 1899, sets forth Bonner's views on horse racing and an editorial in the *N. Y. Times* for the same date reviews his career as a publisher.] J. M. L.

BONNEVILLE, BENJAMIN LOUIS EULALIE DE (Apr. 14, 1796–June 12, 1878), soldier, was born in or near Paris, France, the son of Nicholas and Margaret (Brazier) de Bonneville. His father was a learned philosophical radical, an editor and pamphleteer, and an intimate friend of Lafayette, Condorcet, and Thomas Paine. His mother was educated and talented. Paine was for a time a dweller in their home and was godfather to one of the sons who was named for him. When he left Paris for America in the fall of 1802 it was agreed that the Bonnevilles should follow him. Mme. Bonneville and the children arrived in August of the next year, but Bonneville, who had incurred the wrath of Bonaparte, was kept under close surveillance and could not leave France until after the Corsican's downfall. Mme. Bonneville gave her children careful training. Benjamin entered West Point on his seventeenth birthday and graduated Dec. 11, 1815. He served in some of the New England garrisons and in recruiting service until 1820 and was then transferred to a force constructing a military road through Mississippi. His connection with the frontier, which was to continue throughout the greater part of his life, began with his assignment to Fort Smith, Ark., in 1821. After four years at this post and at Fort Gibson, Okla., he was detached (1825) to serve as aide to the nation's guest, Lafayette, and on the completion of the visit accompanied the Marquis to France. On Oct. 4 of that year he reached the rank of captain. In November 1826, he was back at Fort Gibson, where, except for some months at St. Louis, he remained four years.

The fur trade had long fascinated him, and he now resolved to reap some of the rewards it offered in fortune, fame, and adventure. In the fall of 1830 he took an eight months' leave of absence in New York, where he interested several capitalists, including Alfred Seton, a onetime Astorian, in a project for a thorough exploitation of the fur country. Astor, too, though the project involved certain competition with the American Fur Company, was friendly. Provided with funds, Bonneville asked for a two years' leave of absence for the purpose of exploration and the gathering of information. Leave was granted and on May 1, 1832, with an imposing force of 110 men, he left Fort Osage, Mo., for Green River. He spent more than three years in the mountains, sending detachments of trappers and hunters in every direction, but the result was negative. He could not successfully compete with men who knew the field. Early in July 1835 he gave up the struggle and with a part of his force started for the settlements. Reaching Independence on Aug. 22, he learned that he had been dropped from the army on May 31, 1834, for overstaying his leave of absence. He hastened to report to Astor in New York and then went to Washington to begin a campaign for reinstatement. Against the protests of many of his fellow officers, President Jackson, on Apr. 22, 1836, restored him to his captaincy. He was again sent to Fort Gibson, but finding the social atmosphere uncongenial was soon detached for service at other posts. A major in 1845, he served with distinction in the Mexican War, winning a lieutenant-colonelcy for gallantry at Contreras and Churubusco. On Feb. 3, 1855, he was made a colonel. He was retired, Sept. 9, 1861, for disability caused by sickness and exposure in the line of duty, but immediately became active again in various services, continuing till after the close of the war. On Mar. 13, 1865, he was brevetted brigadier-general for long and faithful services. On Oct. 15, 1866, his connection with the army closed, and he moved to Fort Smith to spend his remaining days. He had married, early in his young manhood, Ann Lewis, who, with an infant daughter, had died in St. Louis. At Fort Smith, in 1870, he married Susan Neis, who survived him. He died at his home.

It is impossible to reconcile the familiar picture of Bonneville drawn by Irving with that drawn by Chittenden. To the engaging social qualities given his subject Irving further adds the moral quality of disinterestedness and the merit of high achievement as an explorer. Chittenden, on the other hand, regards Bonneville as "a history-made man," unentitled to the fame Irving brought to him; he was not a man of honor or he would not have pretended to the government that his purely commercial venture was an attempt at exploration, and he was not an explorer, since he gave to the world little that was new. Certain merits the historian allows him: he was a skilful commander, for he lost not a single life in any case where the men were under his personal control, and he showed an exceptional humaneness in dealing with the Indians.

[G. W. Cullum: *Biog. Reg.* (3rd ed., 1891); H. M. Chittenden, *The Am. Fur Trade of the Far West* (1902); Moncure D. Conway, *Life of Thos. Paine* (1892); Washington Irving, *The Adventures of Capt. Bonneville* (1837); Grant Foreman, *Pioneer Days in the Southwest* (1926).] W. J. G.

BONNEY, CHARLES CARROLL (Sept. 4, 1831–Aug. 23, 1903), lawyer, educationist, reformer, son of Jethro May Bonney and Jane Charity Lawton, was descended from Thomas Bonney or Boney, a shoemaker of Sandwich, who came to New England in 1634 on the ship *Hercules.* He was named after the last surviving signer of the Declaration of Independence. Born at Hamilton, N. Y., he was brought up on his father's farm, attending the district school and Hamilton Academy. In 1847 he became a school teacher and intermittently attended Madison (now Colgate) University, studying law in leisure moments. In 1850 he removed to Peoria, Ill., and opened a school called the Peoria Institute. Continuing his law studies he was admitted to the Illinois bar Sept. 23, 1852, and commenced practise there. During 1852–53 he was public lecturer on education for Peoria County and later vice-president of the Illinois State Teachers Association, being also instrumental in the calling of the first state educational convention and contributing on scholastic matters to the press. On Aug. 16, 1855, he married Lydia A. Pratt of Troy, N. Y. He was a persistent advocate of legal and constitutional reforms, and a prominent speaker and writer on behalf of the Democratic party until the year 1860, when he relinquished active participation in politics. Having become well-known in the state through these activities, he moved in 1860 to Chicago, where he soon acquired an extensive legal connection as a general practitioner. His interests were wide, his energy unbounded, and his mind fertile in projects for the advancement of his fellows. During his early years in Chicago he wrote two law books: *Rules of Law for the Carriage and Delivery of Persons and Property by Railway* (1864), and *Summary of the Law of Marine, Fire and Life Insurance* (1865), primarily intended for the general public and not pretending to be exhaustive treatises. When the Civil War broke out he supported the Government in all its war measures, at the same time remaining, as he always had been, a convinced state's rights supporter. After the termination of the war, an important constitutional question arose as to the right of Congress to impose a tax on processes of states' courts, and he was successful in establishing the doctrine that Congress cannot destroy the agencies of the states through the exercise of its taxing power, and that similarly state legislatures cannot destroy or impair agencies of the federal government. In 1872–73 he lectured on medical jurisprudence at Hahnemann Medical College, Chicago. In 1882 he was president of the Illinois State Bar Association. He had been one of the founders of the Citizens' Law and Order League of the United States and at its first national convention at Boston in 1883 he was elected president. Subsequently under the name of the International Law and Order League the organization held seven consecutive annual conventions in different centers, at each of which he officiated as president, contributing addresses of great value on various subjects of national importance. In 1887 he was prominently mentioned for a vacancy as associate justice of the United States Supreme Court, but political and other exigencies did not admit of the appointment. In 1889 he attracted great attention by his advocacy of the establishment of a permanent international court of justice, thus laying the foundation stone of the Arbitration Court at The Hague. When the project of holding the Columbian Exposition at Chicago in 1893 was launched, he conceived the idea of holding auxiliary congresses in conjunction with the larger undertaking, and it was mainly due to his initiative and organizing force that the project was carried out. As president of the Auxiliary, he was completely successful in maturing plans by which representatives of many nations were brought together for discussion of matters of common interest at the World's Fair, the most conspicuous success of which was the Parliament of Religions. The addresses he delivered to the latter and the religious denominational congresses were subsequently published under the title *World's Congress Addresses* (1900). The energy with which he devoted himself to this work and his untiring exertions at the congresses themselves undermined his health, ultimately bringing on paralysis, and compelling him to relinquish all his manifold activities. He died in Chicago Aug. 23, 1903.

Throughout his life he was distinguished for remarkable activity of mind and body, combined with methodical precision of work and great courtesy. He was "never known to be too busy to give a person a civil answer or to treat him otherwise than as a gentleman" (Judge J. B. Bradwell). His activities were spread over a wide field, though they could be summed up in a single phrase, the diffusion of knowledge. Practically self-educated, he was a pioneer in the fields of education and social reform. A ready and impressive speaker, he was much in request on anniversary and similar occasions, and many of his addresses and papers were published. He also edited a volume of the poems of Judge A .W. Arrington (1869).

[Bonney's ancestry is traced in Chas. L. Bonney, *The Bonney Family* (1898). Biographical details will be found in F. B. Wilkie, *Sketches and Notes of the Chicago Bar* (1871) and *The Bench and Bar of Chicago*

(1883), and appreciative notices appeared in the *Am. Bar Ass. Report,* 1903, p, 708, and *Proc. Ill. State Bar Ass.,* 1908, pt. 11, p. 125. The article in the *Am. Law Rev.,* XXXVII, 745, is discriminating and well-balanced.]
H. W. H. K.

BONNEY, WILLIAM H. (1859–1881). [See BILLY THE KID.]

BONWILL, WILLIAM GIBSON ARLINGTON (Oct. 4, 1833–Sept. 24, 1899), dentist, inventor, was the eldest son of Dr. William Moore Bonwill, descendant of an old Huguenot family of Camden, Del., and of his wife, Louisa Mason (Baggs) Bonwill. He attended an academy in Middletown, Del., "clerked" in a grocery store, and taught school, previous to taking, in his twentieth year, private instruction in dentistry with Dr. Samuel W. Neall of Camden, N. J. This was supplemented by studies under Dr. Chapin A. Harris and Dr. A. A. Blandy of Baltimore. In October 1854 he began the practise of dentistry in Dover, Del., and on June 13, 1861, he married Abigail E. Warren of Dover. He received the degree of D.D.S. from the Pennsylvania College of Dental Surgery in 1866, and later the M.D. from Jefferson Medical College. While he was on a visit to Philadelphia, Feb. 28, 1867, his attention was attracted by the tapping of a telegraph sounder in the old Continental Hotel. Then and there the idea of the electro-magnetic mallet was born. This, when perfected, became an important factor in the development of "contour" filling operations. In his earlier years Bonwill had been attracted by Dr. Arthur's idea of "permanent separations" for the prevention of tooth decay, and he invented the diamond drill for forming the separations without disfiguring the teeth. With the introduction of the electro-magnetic mallet his views changed. It was patented in 1873 and in 1875 the Franklin Institute of Philadelphia awarded him the "Cresson" gold medal of the first class for its invention.

His regard for contour work became even more decided after he brought out his automatic engine-mallet. Thereupon he became as bitter an opponent of the old non-cohesive gold filling as he had before been its ardent advocate. The engine-mallet he esteemed more highly than the electro-magnetic, a preference probably due in some degree to bitterness engendered by the need for modification of the earlier appliance. He could conceive a stupendous, epoch-making mechanical idea and develop it to the point of practicality in his hands, but almost invariably his inventions had to be carried to their final perfection by others. His teeming brain would be busy with a new idea long before the mechanical details of an invention could be worked out. He was a wonderful operator. It is doubtful if the combination of speed and skill with which he habitually worked has ever been surpassed. When at the height of his career as a gold operator he was attracted to amalgam work. After many experiments he devised an alloy which satisfied his requirements, and in its use he became as skilled as with gold. He originated the use of Japanese bibulous paper in the introduction of amalgam fillings; invented a double-disk device for reducing and pointing root-canal broaches, vulcanite and carborundum disks, a cervical matrix, and numerous attachments for the dental and surgical engines, several of which are still largely used. He invented two forms of dental engines, the last of which, of the cord type, became the progenitor of the Bonwill Surgical Engine.

He was equally distinguished as a prosthetic dentist. His method of selecting porcelain teeth for artificial dentures was original. Instead of choosing them by the set he picked them individually, sometimes breaking up several sets in order to get what he wanted. It cannot be denied that the sets so selected, as mounted by him, were remarkably artistic. He was the first to break away from the "barn-door hinge" articulator with which dentists had worked up to that time; the first to devise an anatomical articulator, with which to imitate the various movements of the mandible in mastication. This was founded on his belief in the geometrical construction of the human mandible. This postulate of geometrical construction, he believed, contained a basal truth, which, carried to its logical sequence, demonstrated the negation of the doctrine of organic evolution; and he wrote several papers in support of his idea. Outside of the dental field he made a number of inventions: improvements in grain reapers, kerosene lamps, shoe fasteners; was at work on an aerial trolley car; and claimed to have invented the "Giffard" injector four years before it was brought out in France.

Physically he was slightly above average height, and very slender, apparently unable to cope with the tremendous tasks he set for himself; but he was a tireless worker. It was his habit to place pad, pencil, and a night light near his bed that he might not lose any inspiration that came to him during the night. Kindly, generous, ready at all times to give of his best in knowledge or demonstration, to any one who asked it, he could not brook opposition. His faith in his ideas allowed no question, and he demanded unfaltering belief from others. As a teacher he was interesting and instructive, welcoming freely all who sought his help. As a writer, he was discursive. His bubbling thoughts ran away with him, often leading him into new paths before the old was cleared of the jungle. This oftentimes obscured his ideas to those who had not the patience to dig out their meaning. Notwithstanding his idiosyncrasies, his great abilities were honored at home and abroad. Russian, Dutch, German, Spanish, and French dental societies bestowed honors and decorations upon him. Some of his most notable papers were as follows: "The Electro-Magnetic Mallet" (1874), *Pennsylvania Journal of Dental Science,* I, 257; "The Air as an Anesthetic" (1875), *Ibid.,* III, 57; "The Salvation of the Human Teeth" (1881), *Transactions of the Odontological Society of Pennsylvania,* 1881, p. 107; "Plastic Gold Alloys" (1882), *Ibid.,* 1882, p. 143; "Geometrical and Mechanical Laws of Articulation" (1885), *Ibid.,* 1885, p. 119; "Regulators and Methods of Correcting Irregularities" (1887), *Ibid.,* 1887, p. 281; "New Method of Clasped Plates *vs.* Movable or Unmovable Bridge-Work" (1890), *International Dental Journal,* XIV, 86; "What Has Dentistry to Demonstrate Against the Hypothesis of Organic Evolution?" (read before the World's Columbian Dental Congress, Aug. 15, 1893), *Transactions,* I, 226.

[C. Newlin Pierce, "Memoir of Dr. Wm. G. A. Bonwill" in *Proc. Am. Phil. Soc.,* I, 206–09; *Dental Cosmos,* Oct., Nov., 1899; *Pub. Ledger* (Phila.), Sept. 25, 1899; B. W. Weinberger, *Orthodontics: an Hist. Rev. of Its Origin and Evolution* (1926); *Dental Digest,* Oct. 1899.]

F. L. H.

BONZANO, ADOLPHUS (Dec. 5, 1830–May 5, 1913), engineer, inventor, was born at Ehingen, Würtemberg, Germany. He received his education at the gymnasia in Ehingen, Blönsdorf, and Stuttgart, although his father and other members of his family had emigrated to Texas. In 1850 he came to Philadelphia for two years of further study, particularly aimed at the mastery of English. Recognizing the possibilities offered by the iron industry in the development of this country, he apprenticed himself to the Reynolds Machine Works in Springfield, Mass., in order to supplement his academic studies with practical shop experience. He became one of the skilled mechanical superintendents of his day. On July 2, 1857, he was married to Laura J. Goodell of Detroit. In 1865 he engaged himself with the Detroit Bridge and Iron Works and from that day until his retirement (1898) he was an influential factor in the bridge industry. "In the work of the pioneer and formative period of American bridge construction, Mr. Bonzano had no peer" (*Transactions of the American Society of Civil Engineers,* LXXVII, 1846). In 1868 he became a partner and chief engineer in Clark, Reeves & Company at Phœnixville, Pa. This firm dissolved in 1884 to be succeeded by the Phœnix Bridge Company which Bonzano served as chief engineer until 1893. His last five years of active professional practise were spent as a consulting engineer in New York City. Some of the bridges resulting from his professional activities are the Pecos Aqueduct which carries the Southern Pacific Railroad over the Pecos River; the Red Rock Cantilever Bridge over the Colorado River Canyon on the Atchison, Topeka & Santa Fé; the Chesapeake & Ohio Railroad Bridge over the Ohio River at Cincinnati; the Susquehanna River Bridge at Sunbury, Pa., and the Columbia Bridge in Fairmount Park, Philadelphia. Bonzano had a large share in the development of the modern draw-span. The construction of the turntable in the 274-foot double-track draw of the New York Central & Hudson River Railroad at Albany, built in 1870, embodied original features which he designed and which were later accepted as standard practise. He was one of the first engineers to recognize the merits of the Phœnix column and used it in the Sixth and Ninth Avenue Elevated structures in New York City. Bonzano gave many inventions to the world, chief of which is the rail joint which bears his name. In draw-span construction he was the first to use the locking roller with a pair of links at the draw end, and soon after modified this by the knuckle joint. The use of a vertical screw for operating the locking mechanism was also original with him. In addition to his accomplishments in mechanical lines he was a talented musician—an able pianist, organist, and choir master. He was a familiar figure at the opera, and a man of whom it was said, "he never had an enemy."

[*Trans. Am. Soc. Civil Engineers,* LXXVII, 1846; *Engineering News,* May 15, 1913; J. S. Futhey and Gilbert Cope, *Hist. of Chester County, Pa.* (1881), p. 484.]

E. Y.

BOONE, DANIEL (Nov. 2, n.s., 1734–Sept. 26, 1820), pioneer, Indian fighter, was born about eleven miles from Reading, Pa., the son of Squire and Sarah Morgan Boone. The family were Quakers. Daniel's grandfather, George, a weaver and small farmer, had come to America with his family from near Exeter, England, arriving in Philadelphia Oct. 10, 1717. To his father's vocations Squire Boone added blacksmithing and stock-raising, and Daniel from his early days was a general helper. At twelve, with a rifle which his father had given him, he became a hunter of game and furs. He probably had no regular schooling. In the spring of 1750 most of the Boones, Daniel among them, started for North Carolina, and after tarrying for perhaps a year in the Shenandoah Valley arrived at Buffalo Lick, on the north fork of the Yadkin, in 1751. For several years the youth continued to work for his father. In 1755, as a teamster and blacksmith, he accompanied a North Carolina contingent in the Braddock campaign. Here he met John Finley, a hunter, who told him stories of the Kentucky wilderness that fired him with the determination to see the land for himself. He was in the disastrous battle of July 9 and escaped on one of his horses. Returning to North Carolina, he resumed work on his father's farm. On Aug. 14 of the following year he married Rebeccah Bryan, the seventeen-year-old daughter of a neighbor. In 1765, following a visit to Florida, he resolved to settle in Pensacola, but on his wife's objection the project was given up.

His thoughts again turned to Kentucky, and in the fall of 1767, with a companion or two, he started westward, reaching a point in the present Floyd County, from which he returned in the spring. Finley, in the rôle of a peddler, wandered into the neighborhood the following winter, and the Kentucky venture was planned anew. On May 1, 1769, a party consisting of Boone, his brother-in-law John Stuart, Finley, and three others, started out and after traversing Cumberland Gap entered the present Estill County and set up their camp at Station Camp Creek. After many adventures Boone and his brother, who had joined the party late in 1769, returned to their homes in the spring of 1771. As an agent of Col. Richard Henderson, of the Transylvania Company, who had planned a great colony in Kentucky, he set out in March 1775 with the first division of settlers. On Apr. 1 he reached what was to become Boonesborough, where he at once began the erection of a fort. In the early fall he returned to North Carolina and brought back his family and twenty young men. Hunting, surveying, and Indian fighting occupied his time for the next two years. On the organization of Kentucky as a county of Virginia in the fall of 1776, he was made a captain of the militia, later becoming a major. In February 1778 he was captured by the Shawnees, but escaped in June, and in September rendered important service in the defense of Boonesborough. He spent a year in the east, but in October 1779 returned with a new party of settlers. The repudiation by Virginia of Henderson's land titles sent him east again in the following spring with $20,000 collected from the settlers for the purchase of land warrants, but on the way he was robbed of the entire amount. Returning to his home, he moved to Boone's Station. On the division of Kentucky the same year into three counties, he was made lieutenant-colonel of Fayette County, and in April of the following year was chosen a delegate to the legislature. In 1782 he was made sheriff and county lieutenant and served also as a deputy surveyor. He moved to Maysville in the spring of 1786, and in the fall of the following year was elected to the legislature. He had taken up many tracts of land, but all of them had been improperly entered, and in 1785 the first of a series of ejectment suits by which he was to lose all his holdings was begun. In the fall of 1788 he abandoned Kentucky, moving to Point Pleasant, at the mouth of the Great Kanawha, in what is now West Virginia. A year later he was appointed lieutenant-colonel of Kanawha County and in 1791 was chosen its legislative delegate.

At some time in 1798 or 1799, with his last Kentucky holding lost, he moved to the present Missouri, where his son Daniel Morgan had preceded him, and obtained a land grant at the mouth of the Femme Osage Creek. On July 11, 1800, he was appointed magistrate of the district, a post he held until the cession of the territory to the United States. His land title was voided by the United States land commissioners, but after many delays was confirmed by Congress on Feb. 8, 1814. He journeyed to Kentucky, probably in 1810, to pay off his debts, an action that gave him one of the greatest satisfactions of his life, but left him, according to tradition, with a surplus of only fifty cents. His wife died Mar. 18, 1813, and his remaining years he spent mostly at the home of his son Nathan, where he died.

Boone's appearance has often been described, but with an unfortunate lack of agreement. To Audubon his stature "appeared gigantic," to the editor of the *Missouri Gazette* "common," to the Rev. J. E. Welch "rather low." Daniel Bryan, a relative by marriage, records it as "about five feet, eight or nine inches." His head was large, his eyes were blue (light according to some, dark according to others), and his look was sharp and alert. Originally his hair was light and his eyebrows were yellow. He had a wide mouth, thin lips, and a nose somewhat of the Roman type. The portrait of him painted by Chester Harding a short time before his death is probably the only authentic representation of him ever made. In his prime he was a man of great strength, lithe and quick in movement, and a fast runner.

Modern criticism has dealt destructively with the Boone legend. Boone first came into general notice by means of John Filson's *The Discovery, Settlement, and Present State of Kentucke* (1784), purporting to be told by Boone himself, but given in words that Boone could not possibly have used. It gained wide circulation in England through its inclusion in the second and third editions (1793, 1797) of Gilbert Imlay's *A Topo-*

graphical Description of the Western Territory of North America. The seven stanzas that Lord Byron devoted to him in the eighth canto of *Don Juan* (1823) made him a world-wide celebrity, and he gradually became the one overshadowing figure of the frontier. He was acclaimed the discoverer of Kentucky, its first explorer, its first settler, its chief military protector, and even, as the title of a reprint (1847) of Timothy Flint's biography hailed him, "The First White Man of the West." None of these distinctions belonged to him; nor did his services to the community, meritorious though they were, equal in importance those of certain other men. He had, however, his own ample titles to fame and the regard of posterity. In every duty he bore his part manfully. He had the qualities most needed on the frontier—courage in a rare degree, great fortitude, an iron endurance, a mastery of woodcraft, and signal expertness with the rifle. Though his letters reveal him as close to the border line of illiteracy, he had strong native intelligence; and though not a man of affairs, his counsels were always eagerly welcomed. He was loyal in friendship, honest, truthful, and modest. One of his prime characteristics was serenity of mind. He never seemed irritated or excited, and though often wronged he never harbored rancor. He was one of the most respected and beloved of the nation's heroes.

[The earlier biographies and sketches of Boone are all, in varying degrees, untrustworthy. *Daniel Boone* (1902), by Reuben Gold Thwaites, is based on the great mass of source material in the Draper collection, at Madison, Wis. Much valuable information is given in *The Boone Family* (1922), by Hazel Atterbury Spraker, which includes a sketch of Boone by Jesse Procter Crump; and other information, less critically examined, in *A History of the Pioneer Families of Missouri* (1876), by W. S. Bryan and Robert Rose. Stewart Edward White's *Daniel Boone, Wilderness Scout* (1922), though written for boys and deficient in detail, gives a clearer presentation of Boone and his environment than most of the lives written for adults. A searching examination of "the Boone Myth," by Clarence Walworth Alvord, is given in the *Jour. of the Ill. State Hist. Soc.,* Apr.–July 1926. Incidental references to early accounts of Boone are given in Ralph Leslie Rusk, *The Literature of the Middle Western Frontier* (1925).] W. J. G.

BOORMAN, JAMES (1783–Jan. 24, 1866), merchant, railroad president, son of John and Mary (Colgate) Boorman, was born in the county of Kent, England, of Scotch ancestry. He came with his parents to New York in 1795; was apprenticed to Divie Bethune, and entered into partnership with him in 1805. In March 1813 he joined with a fellow Scot, John Johnston, in forming the New York mercantile house of Boorman & Johnston, which became successively, Boorman, Johnston & Company, and Boorman, Johnston, Ayres & Company. Adam Norrie became a partner in 1828. A subsequent department of the business was conducted as Boorman & Clark. At first Boorman sold Scotch cloths from Dundee, and Virginia tobacco, handling virtually all of the latter that came from the Richmond market. Later the firm did an enormous business in iron from Sweden and England. From South St. the house moved to Greenwich St. The business became so large that the partners had to relinquish a part of it. They were the largest importers of Madeira wines, and they received large consignments from Italy. Their counting-room was over the Bank of the Republic. "A more remarkable man than James Boorman never lived" (Scoville, I, 157). In 1835 he received from Sweden a consignment of immense iron pillars, and the entire trade was much amused by Boorman's valiant effort to sell what no one wanted. Undaunted, he tore out the front of his store, put the pillars under the front wall, and with this increased support added several stories to the building. Aside from his own business he was made chief of every corporation with which he connected himself. He was the originator of the Hudson River Railroad, and as a director he led the board in bringing about the removal of Hon. Azariah C. Flagg as president of that road (*Communications from J. Boorman,* W. C. Bryant & Company, 1849, reprinted in the *Evening Post*). He himself succeeded Flagg. At this time he wrote to the directors: "It will, I hope, not be deemed impertinent for me to add that my services to you as president are gratuitous. . . ." He was chairman of a committee of the road that awarded a contract to Peter Cooper for rails to extend his road to Albany, was a large owner in the Troy & Schenectady Railroad, and was a founder of the Bank of Commerce. He retired in 1855. No New York merchant was more liberal in benevolence. He gave with great liberality to the Institution for the Blind, the Protestant Half-Orphan Asylum, the Southern Aid Society, the Union Theological Seminary, and Trinity Church, of which latter he was long an officer. His town house was at Waverley Place and Washington Square. He also owned No. 1 Fifth Ave., the fine home that was later the residence of the Duncans, and he possessed a country estate at Hyde Park, Dutchess County, N. Y. He married Mary Wells Davenport on Nov. 10, 1810, and they later adopted a daughter. He was inclined to be headstrong, he had little patience with incompetency, and none at all with shams; his integrity was of that rare sort that is never questioned.

[Boorman is mentioned prominently in J. A. Scoville, *The Old Merchants of New York City* (1863).

The lengthy pamphlet entitled *Communications from Jas. Boorman to the Stockholders of the Hudson River Railroad Co., in Reply to Mr. A. C. Flagg, late President of that Co.,* contains much valuable information. He gives some facts of his financial dealings in his *Statement of the Administration of the Estate of Jas. R. Smith* (1865). His will, made in 1862, is on file in the N. Y. Pub. Lib. Obituaries were published in the *N. Y. Times* and *N. Y. Daily Tribune,* Jan. 26, 1866.]

R. R. R.

BOOTH, AGNES (Oct. 4, 1846–Jan. 2, 1910), actress, was born Marian Agnes Land Rookes, daughter of Capt. Land and Sara Rookes, in Sydney, Australia. Her father was a British officer quartered there. She was early apprenticed to the stage as a child dancer, and in that capacity, at the age of twelve, appeared with Mrs. Wood's company in San Francisco, in 1858, under the name of Agnes Land. A little later she appeared with the company of the famous and much-married Ada Isaac Menken. Like so many young dancers of that day, her aim was the dramatic stage, and she began to act at Maguire's Opera House, in San Francisco, where she remained till 1865. During this period, in 1861, she married Harry Perry, a popular actor, who died in 1863. Joseph Jefferson wrote of him, "Youth, vivacity and a ringing laugh made him altogether one of the most captivating fellows in his line. . . . On the occasion I speak of he was quite intoxicated with happiness, being in the height of a honeymoon. His bride was Miss Agnes Land—a young lady who had lately arrived from Australia, and whose talents and beauty combined with his own made them valuable members of the theatrical profession" (*Autobiography,* 1890, p. 230). In 1865 Agnes Land—the name by which she was still known—heard the call of Broadway, and crossed the continent to appear at Booth's Theatre. She was then only nineteen. A little later she supported Edwin Forrest in *Richelieu,* and attracted so much attention that from that time on her services were in constant demand. In 1867 she married Junius Brutus Booth the younger (elder brother of Edwin), and thereafter always appeared as Agnes Booth. The marriage was a happy one. There were two sons—Junius Brutus Booth, III, and Sydney Barton Booth. Mr. and Mrs. Booth acted frequently together, but Mrs. Booth also appeared in support of other male stars, notably her brother-in-law Edwin Booth, McCullough, Wallack, Barrett, and E. A. Sothern. She also served, at different times, as leading woman of the Union Square and Madison Square Theatres, both under the management of A. M. Palmer, and as the star of *The Sporting Duchess* during its tour of the country in 1895–96. Booth died in 1883, and on Feb. 4, 1885, Mrs. Booth married John B. Schoeffel, owner of the Tremont Theatre in Boston. After this marriage, she was under no necessity to act, but continued to do so for a dozen years, her connection as leading woman with Palmer's company at the Madison Square Theatre following the new alliance. She was leading woman of this company in 1890, when the youthful Augustus Thomas, then a newspaper reporter in St. Louis, sent a one-act sketch to Maurice Barrymore, also a member of the company, which was used as a curtain raiser and led to Mr. Thomas's engagement to become dramatist to the theatre (at a salary of $50 a week). In his book, *The Print of My Remembrance* (1922, pp. 288 ff.), he tells how he wrote *A Constitutional Point* for Mrs. Booth—a one-act play twenty years later to become the third act of his noted drama *The Witching Hour.* A. M. Palmer, the manager, considered that the public would not understand this sketch, so he put it away, and wrote another, *Afterthoughts,* which Mrs. Booth acted. That she herself may not have been eager to do the more modern sketch is indicated by the fact, recorded by Mr. Thomas, that when his play, *Alabama,* a pioneer of the new American drama, was read to the company, in 1891, Mrs. Booth paused at the stage manager's desk as she was leaving the house and whispered, "Rotten, thank you." In fact, she at first refused her part of May Brookyn, but later reclaimed it, after the play was a sensational success. In 1892, she appeared in a sketch also written for her by Mr. Thomas, in which he supported her. Her last appearance of any moment was as Rose in *L'Arlésienne* at the Broadway Theatre, New York, Mar. 22, 1897. She retired from the stage to her home in Brookline, a suburb of Boston, and devoted the remaining years of her life to social activities.

Mrs. Booth as actress belonged to an earlier generation in training and style. She had no "line," but played all sorts of parts. Indeed, her versatility was exceptional. She was best liked, perhaps, in rôles calling for a mingling of light comedy and sentiment, but she was competent in tragedy and melodrama. Her style, however, was robust and had little in common with the naturalistic methods which in her later years were conquering the stage.

[*Who's Who in America,* 1910–11; J. B. Clapp and E. G. Edgett, *Players of the Present* (1899), pp. 43–47; L. C. Strong, "Agnes Booth," in *Famous Am. Actors of Today* (1896), ed. by F. E. McKay and Chas. E. L. Wingate; *Boston Evening Transcript,* Jan. 3, 1910.]

W. P. E.

BOOTH, EDWIN THOMAS (Nov. 13, 1833–June 7, 1893), actor, the fourth son of Junius Brutus Booth [*q.v.*] and Mary Anne (Holmes) Booth, was born on his father's farm near Bel

Air, Md. He was named after the actors Edwin Forrest and Thomas Flynn, but dropped the "Thomas" in later life. His formal education, such as it was, was obtained at various small private schools in the neighborhood, kept by a Miss Susan Hyde, by a Frenchman, M. Louis Dugas, and by a Mr. Kearney. Far more important for his development were the long theatrical journeys on which he early began to accompany his father. To see to it that that erratic genius did not break his engagements, murder some one, or commit suicide during his times of intoxication and half-insanity was a heavy responsibility for the fragile youth and made him grave, serious, and melancholy beyond his years. His wayward father loved him deeply and would yield to the lad's suasion when deaf to the entreaties of all others. But having derived more fame than happiness from his own theatrical career, he at first resisted his son's desire to go on the stage, although the extent of that resistance seems to have been much over-emphasized by the latter's biographers. Edwin Booth's first appearance, in the minor part of Tressel in *Richard III* on Sept. 10, 1849, at the Boston Museum, was featured on the program, and during the next two years he played occasionally with his father in such juvenile parts as Wilford in Colman's *The Iron Chest* and Titus in Payne's *Brutus* until in 1851 at the National Theatre, New York, the elder Booth one night without warning forced his son to appear in his stead as Richard III. Following these sporadic performances the younger Booth obtained an engagement, at a salary of six dollars a week, with Theodore Barton of Baltimore, but here he was a complete failure. He had not yet learned to overcome his smallness of stature, was awkward and ill at ease, and gave no indications of his future greatness.

In July 1852 he accompanied his father to California, where, under the management of his brother, Junius Brutus Booth, Jr., they had a profitable engagement at the Jenny Lind Theatre, San Francisco, and a very unprofitable one in Sacramento. At the latter place for his benefit Edwin Booth played Jaffier in *Venice Preserved* to his father's Pierre. California then suffering one of its intermittent states of financial depression, the elder Booth decided to return home but died during the long journey. Meanwhile Edwin together with the actor D. W. Waller attempted the theatrical conquest of Nevada County; the venture was not successful, their party was snowed in, barely escaping starvation, and Edwin returned to San Francisco in a penniless condition. Here he was again employed by his brother, in varying capacities ranging from utility man to star, occasionally appearing in such rôles as Petruchio (never one of his best), Richard III, Macbeth, Hamlet, Sir Giles Overreach, Sir Edwin Mortimer; later he joined Mrs. Catherine Forrest Sinclair, who had newly opened the Metropolitan Theatre; and still later he played with James E. Murdoch [*q.v.*] and Laura Keene [*q.v.*], the latter attributing her failure to "Edwin Booth's bad acting." During most of this time Booth lived with another actor, D. C. Anderson, in a small shack on a tiny plot of ground which they jestingly named "the Ranch." In 1854, despite mutual dislike, Booth and Miss Keene, accompanied by Anderson, made a professional trip to Australia, during which, in Sydney, Booth appeared for the first time as Shylock, a character whom, contrary to his custom, he refused to idealize and presented, then and always, as a purely malevolent villain. At Melbourne the business alliance with Miss Keene ended in financial disaster; and Booth and Anderson returned to America, stopping on the way for two months at Honolulu, where, among other performances, they produced *Richard III* before King Kamehameha IV.

On his arrival in San Francisco, Booth was offered an engagement by Mrs. Sinclair at the Metropolitan and for a short time played Benedick to her Beatrice in *Much Ado;* then came a brief engagement at the American Theatre in the same city; and then, in August 1855, he was again in Sacramento, playing juvenile parts in comedies and melodramas at the Sacramento Theatre. During the fall he joined a company of strolling actors under one Moulton to visit the mining towns in the neighborhood, but each appearance was, by a curious coincidence, so uniformly followed by a fire after they left town that Booth became known as "the Fiery Star" and eventually the community rose against the dangerous intruders, who ignominiously dispersed and sought safety in the valley. Back in Sacramento, Booth obtained a brief engagement at the Forrest Theatre in November, but was soon dismissed for reasons of economy. He was once more saved from imminent starvation by Mrs. Sinclair, who opportunely started at the Sacramento Theatre a joint stock company which he joined as leading man. On Dec. 10 they produced for the first time in America *The Marble Heart or the Sculptor's Dream,* in which Booth created the part of Raphael. In February the company took over the Forrest Theatre where Booth continued to act, after the departure of Mrs. Sinclair for the East, until the end of April. By that time his popularity had become such that on Apr. 19 he received a "Grand Complimentary

Testimonial tendered by the Members of both Houses of the Legislature and the Citizens of Sacramento," on which occasion he presented *The Iron Chest,* repeating the performance on Apr. 22 by request of members of the legislature unable to attend the previous production. Then followed a week at the Sacramento Theatre, a two weeks' successful engagement in San Francisco, another run at the Sacramento Theatre, May 15–June 7, and a final farewell appearance in San Francisco, in *King Lear*—in the Nahum Tate version, which he later abandoned—prior to his departure for the East. (The above paragraph, which differs materially from the accounts given by William Winter and Asia Booth Clarke, is based largely upon the Sacramento play-bills of the period.)

He had left the East a callow youth hardly started in his profession; he returned to it an accomplished actor. His style was inevitably moulded by that of his father and by the whole Kean tradition but it was marked by an intellectuality and a sustained power which the elder Booth never achieved. Not super-eminent as a comedian, in tragedy the younger Booth was soon to reach the level of Kean himself. On his arrival in the East he played at the Front Street Theatre in Baltimore and then toured the South in preparation for a momentous engagement in Boston, the city which was still considered the arbiter of American taste. He made a triumphant appearance there as Sir Giles Overreach on Apr. 20, 1857, and immediately repeated the triumph in numerous rôles at Burton's Metropolitan Theatre, New York. Subsequent tours in the West and South maintained his newly-established position at the very top of his profession in America. On July 7, 1860, he was married to Mary Devlin, a young actress of great charm who had played Juliet to the Romeo of Charlotte Cushman but who now after her marriage retired from the stage. In September of the following year he appeared at the Haymarket, London, in the rôles of Shylock, Sir Giles, and Richelieu, but aroused intense enthusiasm only in the last-named part, which was probably his greatest rôle. There followed relatively unsuccessful engagements at Liverpool and with a stock company at Manchester of which the youthful Henry Irving was a member. In 1862 and 1863 Booth was seen at the Winter Garden, New York, the latter engagement being interrupted by the sudden death of his passionately loved wife on Feb. 21 at their home in Dorchester Mass., leaving him with the care of a daughter, Edwina, then only two years old. After a temporary retirement, Booth undertook the management of the Winter Garden, also purchasing in conjunction with his brother-in-law, John S. Clarke [*q.v.*], the Walnut Street Theatre, Philadelphia. On Mar. 28, 1864, he scored a notable success at Niblo's Theatre, New York, in the rôle of Bertuccio in Tom Taylor's *The Fool's Revenge,* an adaptation of Hugo's *Le Roi S'Amuse.* The next season saw his famous run of one hundred nights as Hamlet, a rôle particularly well adapted to his own melancholy, intellectual, and lofty temperament. The assassination of Lincoln by Booth's younger brother, John Wilkes Booth [*q.v.*], on Apr. 14, 1865, sent the actor into a long retirement. But he himself had been entirely loyal to the Northern cause and when he returned to the stage on Jan. 3, 1866, at the Winter Garden, although threats had been made against his life, he found that his audience was equally loyal to him. He now put on a series of the most lavishly staged performances which had yet been seen in America, terminated on Mar. 23, 1867, by the disastrous burning of the Winter Garden in which his scenery and costumes, his library, and a valuable gallery of theatrical portraits were completely destroyed. Booth almost at once started plans for a new theatre to be the most beautiful in America, and the building, known as Booth's Theatre, at the corner of Twenty-third St. and Sixth Ave., was opened on Feb. 3, 1869, with a performance of *Romeo and Juliet.* On June 7, 1869, Booth was married to his leading woman, Mary McVicker, an actress of more ambition than ability; she left the stage after her marriage, but her restless energy fed upon itself until she became insane, dying on Nov. 13, 1881. Meanwhile in the midst of increasing domestic and financial misfortune, Booth reached his high-water mark as an actor. The seasons 1869–74 at Booth's Theatre were an epoch in the history of the American stage. Booth's most notable performances in his own theatre were as Romeo (a study in adolescence), as Othello (emphasizing the poetic aspect of the character), as Benedick (for the first time in New York, Mar. 6, 1871), as Macbeth (Charlotte Cushman objecting to his idealistic interpretation because "Macbeth was the great ancestor of all the Bowery ruffians"), as Hamlet, as Richelieu, and at various times as Brutus, Cassius, and Mark Antony. Other players at Booth's Theatre were Joseph Jefferson, John S. Clarke, Edwin L. Davenport, John McCullough, John E. Owens, Lawrence Barrett, Mrs. Emma Waller, Charlotte Cushman, and Kate Bateman. But Booth had no head for pecuniary details, his business associations were unfortunate, and the most artistic theatre in America met financial disaster during the panic of 1873–74. Booth withdrew from it in 1873 and the next year he went into bankruptcy. The theatre itself continued to function until Apr. 30, 1883, when it was closed and a little later was torn down.

Booth soon paid off his debts but his career henceforth was that of a traveling actor without a permanent theatrical home. After the age of forty his powers slowly began to decline. His health, possibly injured by excessive drinking in early manhood and by excessive smoking at all times, was gradually undermined by the strain of an actor's life augmented by his long series of personal disappointments. In his acting he often seemed tired; his voice, always his weakest point, tended to become monotonous; his gestures became more formal. Yet he carried on gallantly for almost twenty years, and even to the very end he remained one of the greatest actors of his day. In 1877 he arranged for publication the text of fifteen of his usual plays, which were brought out in 1878 as *Edwin Booth's Prompt Book* under the editorship of William Winter. This work, invaluable for students of the acting drama, includes *Richard II, Richard III, Henry VIII, Hamlet, Macbeth, Othello, Lear, Merchant of Venice, Much Ado, Katherine and Petruchio, Richelieu, The Fool's Revenge, Brutus, Ruy Blas,* and *Don Cæsar de Bazan.* Booth's courage and his dramatic sincerity were well shown by his not stepping out of his rôle when twice fired at by a lunatic during a performance of *Richard II* at McVicker's Theatre, Chicago, on Sept. 23, 1879. (Wags said that the attempted assassination was due to anger at Booth's temerity in reviving so poor a play.) In the season of 1880–81 he had a brilliant repertoire engagement of 119 nights at the Princess's Theatre, London, shortly followed by an engagement in *Othello* at the Lyceum with Henry Irving, the two alternately playing Othello and Iago. In 1882 Booth reappeared at the Princess's, toured the British Isles, and gave extraordinarily successful performances at Berlin, Hamburg, Hanover, Leipsic, and Vienna. After his return to America, when not traveling he made his home at No. 29 Chestnut St., Boston, until his retirement from the stage, after which he lived in the building at 16 Gramercy Park, New York, which he had presented to the Players' Club founded by him in 1888. In the years just prior to his retirement Booth played continuously with Lawrence Barrett, from 1887 until the latter's death in March 1891, with the exception of a single season, 1889–90, with Mme. Helena Modjeska. His last performance was in *Hamlet* at the Academy of Music, Brooklyn, on Apr. 4, 1891. A slight stroke of paralysis two years earlier had left his health permanently enfeebled, and he now sank steadily until his death on June 7, 1893.

"Booth was marked out by fortune for honour and despite. He felt the strangeness of his lot, and reflected much upon the mysteries of life and death. Helped by his religion, a kind of stoical Christianity, he came to some definite conclusions in the face of all the mysteries. 'All my life,' he wrote to Mr. Winter, in 1886, 'has been passed on picket duty, as it were. I have been on guard, on the lookout for disasters—for which, when they come, I am prepared. . . . Why do not you look at this miserable little life, with all its ups and downs, as I do? At the very worst, 'tis but a scratch, a temporary ill, to be soon cured, by that dear old doctor, Death—who gives us a life more healthful and enduring than all the physicians, temporal or spiritual, can give' " (Copeland, pp. 149–50). Booth expressed his brave, beauty-loving personality almost as fully with the pen as on the stage; he was among the best of American letter-writers. Unfortunately the largest collection of his letters, those addressed to William Winter, was sold at auction after the latter's death and hopelessly scattered. The much-needed edition of Booth's letters will probably never appear.

[Wm. Winter's tedious but usually accurate *Life and Art of Edwin Booth* (1893, rev. ed., 1894) is the chief source. See also Asia Booth Clarke, *The Elder and the Younger Booth* (1882); Laurence Hutton, *Edwin Booth* (1893); Lawrence Barrett, "Mr. Edwin Booth" in *Actors and Actresses of Gt. Brit. and the U. S.* (1886), ed. by Brander Matthews and Laurence Hutton; Edward Robins, *Twelve Great Actors* (1900), pp. 279–311; Lyman Abbott, *Silhouettes of My Contemporaries* (1921), pp. 16–27; Edwina Booth Grossman, *Edwin Booth, Recollections by His Daughter* (1894); Ella V. Mahoney, *Sketches of Tudor Hall and the Booth Family* (Bel Air, Md., 1925); Henry A. Clapp, "Edwin Booth," *Atlantic Mo.*, Sept. 1893; Wm. Bispham, "Memories and Letters of Edwin Booth," *Century Mag.*, Nov., Dec. 1893; Mrs. Thos. Bailey Aldrich, *Crowding Memories* (1920), *passim.* For Booth's interpretation of Shakespearian rôles see his notes contributed to *Othello* and *The Merchant of Venice* in H. H. Furness's Variorum Edition, and also Chas. Townsend Copeland's excellent *Edwin Booth* (1901).]

E. S. B.

BOOTH, JAMES CURTIS (July 28, 1810–Mar. 21, 1888), chemist, was born in Philadelphia, the son of George and Ann (Bolton) Booth. His early education was obtained in the public schools of his native city and in Hartsville (Pa.) Seminary. Entering the University of Pennsylvania in 1825, he studied chemistry with Hare and Keating. Upon receiving the A.B. degree in 1829 he continued to study chemistry for a year or more at the Rensselaer Polytechnic Institute, Troy, N. Y., taught chemistry in Flushing, L. I., in the winter of 1831–32, and then went to Germany, where he studied analytical chemistry with

Wöhler in Hesse-Cassel and with Magnus in Berlin. He also attended lectures in Vienna and visited chemical plants on the continent and in England. On his return to Philadelphia in 1836, he started a student-laboratory where men could obtain practical training in chemistry—especially analytical chemistry—by personal instruction. With him were associated successively Martin H. Boyé [*q.v.*], Thomas H. Garrett, and Andrew A. Blair. In 1878 the firm became Booth, Garrett & Blair. Many men of this period received their technical education in this unique training school, and several became distinguished chemists. From 1836 to 1845 Booth was professor of chemistry applied to the arts in the Franklin Institute, from 1842 to 1845 he taught chemistry in the Philadelphia Central High School, and from 1851 to 1855 he was professor of chemistry applied to the arts in the University of Pennsylvania. While teaching in the Central High School he analyzed sugar and molasses with the polariscope—probably the first chemist in America to use the polariscope for this purpose. Owing to his knowledge of chemistry, mineralogy, and geology he was made a member of the first geological survey of Pennsylvania. Later he became state geologist of Delaware. Although he subsequently abandoned geology he retained his interest in mining and metals, especially iron. In 1849 he was appointed melter and refiner at the Philadelphia mint, and for thirty-nine years he devoted his skill and energy to the exacting duties of this position. Meanwhile he found time to prepare the reports of the Franklin Institute Committee on Science and Arts, a report on *Our Recent Improvements in the Chemical Arts* (1851), and numerous papers for scientific periodicals. In conjunction with Martin H. Boyé, Campbell Morfit, and R. S. McCulloh he wrote an *Encyclopædia of Chemistry, Practical and Theoretical* (1850). Two years later he edited T. R. Belton's translation of Regnault's *Elements of Chemistry*. In 1860 he tried to interest iron manufacturers in a system of control analysis of iron ores, and although unsuccessful he and his business associates (Garrett and Blair) continued to study iron ores and ultimately one of them (Blair) wrote the *Chemical Analysis of Iron*, which has gone through many editions and is authoritative to-day in its field. Booth was an active member of the following organizations: the American Philosophical Society, the Academy of Natural Sciences, the Maryland Institute for the Promotion of Mechanic Arts, the Philadelphia Society for the Promotion of Agriculture, the Historical Society of Pennsylvania, and the American Chemical Society (president in 1883 and 1884). He was married, on Nov. 17, 1853, to Margaret M. Cardoza. As an analyist he was skilful and accurate, and as a consulting chemist he was indefatigable and resourceful, especially in metallurgical processes. As a teacher of practical chemistry he was unsurpassed by his contemporaries; a course in his laboratory was considered indispensable to the chemists of his day.

[The chief source of information is a brochure, *Jas. Curtis Booth*, by Edgar F. Smith, presented at a meeting of the Am. Chem. Soc., Sept. 9, 1922: see also "Jas. Curtis Booth," by Paterson Du Bois, in *Proc. Am. Phil. Soc.*, XXV, 204, and obituary in the *Press* (Phila.), Mar. 22, 1888.] L. C. N.

BOOTH, JOHN WILKES (1838–Apr. 26, 1865), actor, assassin of President Lincoln, was the brother of Edwin Booth [*q.v.*] and the son of Junius Brutus Booth [*q.v.*] and Mary Ann (Holmes) Booth. He was named after the celebrated English agitator, a distant relative of his grandfather. Born and brought up on his father's farm near Bel Air, Md., he received an irregular schooling in neighboring academies. The taint of his father's insanity perhaps appeared in his unbalanced disposition. As a boy he would charge through the woods on horseback, holding an old lance, and shouting battle-cries; more than once he ran away from home and school to mingle with the oyster fishermen on Chesapeake Bay; on one occasion in order to win a bet he drove a sleigh in July across the dirt roads to Bel Air and back. Aside from a detestation of cats which led him to violate his father's benevolent principles by exterminating all those on the farm, his character was marked by great kindliness. In a large family of brothers and sisters he was always his mother's favorite. His courtesy, gayety, care-free generosity, and extraordinary beauty—black eyes, black hair, and a face which resembled Poe's but was far handsomer—fascinated his acquaintances. It is said that he had the physical defect of markedly bowed legs but was accustomed to conceal it by wearing a long cloak. Although of less than medium height, he was athletic, a skilful horseman and fencer, and a crack pistol-shot. Early attracted to the stage, he made his début at the age of seventeen in the rôle of Richmond at the St. Charles Theatre, Baltimore. During the season of 1857–58 he played subordinate rôles at the Arch Street Theatre, Philadelphia, then under the management of his brother-in-law, John Sleeper Clarke [*q.v.*]. Here he was frequently hissed for his neglect to learn his parts adequately. He developed rapidly, however, into an actor of distinction; in the next year he played leading Shakespearian rôles in a stock company at Richmond, Va.; and in 1860 he began a meteoric career as star. After his opening appearance at Columbus, Ga., in September of that year, he toured the South and Southwest and then successfully invaded the North. Women proved particularly vulnerable to his charm, on and off the stage, and he was reputed to be the hero of numerous amours. In May 1861 at Madison, Ind., an actress, Henrietta Irving, attacked him with a dirk, and then stabbed herself almost fatally (*Courier*, Madison, May 10, 1861). In 1862 and 1863 he was enthusiastically welcomed at the Boston Museum (which then possessed the most critical audience in America) ; his performance of Romeo was declared by the *Chronicle* (Washington, D. C.) to have been the best ever rendered in that city; his contemporaries, Edwin Booth and Joe Jefferson, declare that he was one of the most promising actors of the day, and the veteran manager Ellsler even asserted that "John has more of the old man's power in one performance than Edwin can show in a year" (Clara Morris, *Life on the Stage,* 1901, p. 103). His acting was marked by inspiration rather than finish, and he was given to daring innovations, rendering the death of Richard III, for example, in a realistic manner that astounded his contemporaries. Although careless in his enunciation and prone to slur minor passages in his haste to reach the big scenes, his fire and passion more than atoned for these defects. His repertoire included *Richard III, Romeo and Juliet, Hamlet, Macbeth, Othello, The Merchant of Venice, Katharine and Petruchio, The Lady of Lyons, Money, The Robbers, The Marble Heart, The Apostate, The Stranger,* and *The Corsican Brothers.* Had his temperament permitted whole-souled attention to his art, he would probably have become one of the leading figures in American theatrical history. But in 1863 a slight bronchial trouble led to his temporary retirement from the stage, and the investment of a part of his theatrical earnings in oil speculations; and in 1864–65 his notable appearance at the Winter Garden, New York, on Nov. 25, in *Julius Cæsar* in which he played Antony to Edwin Booth's Brutus and J. B. Booth, Jr.'s Cassius, and his equally notable last performance, on Mar. 18, at Ford's Theatre, Washington, in the part of Pescara in *The Apostate* at John McCullough's benefit were, both of them, mere interludes in the great political conspiracy which the young actor now had in hand.

From even before the beginning of the Civil War Wilkes Booth's sympathies, unlike those of the rest of his family, had been with the South. Slavery he sincerely regarded as "one of the greatest blessings (both for themselves [the slaves] and us) that God ever bestowed upon a favoured nation. Witness heretofore our wealth and power, witness their elevation and enlightenment above their race elsewhere" (letter of Booth in Clara E. Laughlin, *The Death of Lincoln,* 1909, p. 21). In 1859 he had been a member of a Virginia militia company, which took part in the arrest and execution of John Brown. He had not enlisted in the Confederate army—ostensibly because of a promise to his mother, more probably because of an unwillingness to serve in a subordinate capacity—but as the war proceeded he came to see it more and more violently as a simple struggle between tyranny and freedom. "That he was insane on that one point, no one who knew him well can doubt" (Edwin Booth to Nahum Capen, in Ella V. Mahoney, *Sketches of Tudor Hall and the Booth Family,* 1925, p. 38). As early as the fall of 1864 he formed a daring project to abduct President Lincoln and carry him to Richmond, thereby, as he hoped, either to end the war or at least to secure an exchange of Southern prisoners. In September he enrolled his first recruits, two former schoolmates named Samuel Arnold and Michael O'Laughlin, both ex-Confederate soldiers, who after two years of service had returned to their native Maryland and were living in Baltimore. Booth shortly thereafter divested himself of his oil holdings and proceeded to Montreal in order to put his valuable theatrical wardrobe in safe custody and to place between seven and eight hundred dollars in a Canadian bank. The efforts made by the prosecution in the conspiracy trial to show that he was at this time in communication with the so-called "Canadian Cabinet" of the Confederacy rested entirely on the later discredited testimony of the spies, Sanford Conover and Richard Montgomery. In reality Booth was the last man to have sought orders from above, and throughout gloried in the fact that he was acting on his own responsibility. During November and December he was much in Washington, engaged in exploring the roads in lower Maryland. On Dec. 23 he made the important acquaintance of John H. Surratt, son of a widow, Mary E. Surratt, who had kept a tavern in Surrattsville, Md. John Surratt in 1862 had left St. Charles's College, where he was being educated for the Catholic priesthood, and had become a secret dispatch-rider for the Confederacy, carrying messages between Richmond and the North. His mother had meanwhile sold her tavern and moved into Washington where she kept a boarding-house. Surratt entered with eagerness into Booth's plot and soon gained two other adherents, David E. Herold, a feeble-minded youth of nineteen, and George A. Atzerodt, a middle-aged coach-maker at Port Tobacco on the Potomac, who was secretly engaged in ferrying Confederate sympathizers back and forth across the river. Arnold and O'Laughlin moved into Washington in February. On Mar. 1, Booth added the last and most noted conspirator to his band, Lewis Thornton Powell, calling himself Payne, son of a Baptist minister in Florida, Confederate soldier at the age of sixteen, wounded at Gettysburg, captured and escaped, now adrift in the North, penniless and half-mad. The band, thus constituted, lay in wait, on the afternoon of Mar. 20, to seize the President while driving near the Soldiers' Home in the outskirts of the city but their plans were frustrated by his not appearing. Learning that their plot was suspected, the conspirators separated, Arnold and O'Laughlin returning to Baltimore, and Surratt going first to Richmond and then to Canada. During the next few weeks the capture of Richmond and the surrender of Lee ended all possibility of Lincoln's abduction. Booth's six months of plotting had come to naught.

Just when he decided upon the assassination cannot be absolutely determined but it was probably after Lincoln's speech from the White House window on Apr. 11, in which the President advocated limited negro suffrage. Not until noon of Apr. 14, when Booth learned that Lincoln was to attend Laura Keene's performance of *Our American Cousin* at Ford's Theatre that night, were the details definitely arranged. Of his remaining accomplices, Atzerodt was deputed to murder Vice-President Johnson in his room at the Kirkwood Hotel; Payne, guided by Herold, to assassinate Secretary Seward in his home; while Booth reserved to himself the more difficult and spectacular task of killing the President. Atzerodt, however, lost his courage and did nothing. Payne, a young gladiator, fulfilled his part of the agreement to the extent of seriously wounding Seward and three others who sought to capture him, but being deserted by the frightened Herold, fled to the woods north-east of the city, whence he returned three nights later to be arrested at Mrs. Surratt's. Meanwhile Booth, having prepared the President's box in the afternoon so that its door could be barred to prevent pursuit, during the performance, at a little after ten o'clock entered the theatre, coolly surveyed the audience, and made his way to the box. Coming in noiselessly, he shot the President through the head, wounded with his dagger Major Henry R. Rathbone, who strove to seize him, and leaped to the stage, shouting *"Sic semper tyrannis!* The South is avenged!" But his spur, caught in the folds of the flag that draped the box, caused him to fall, breaking his left leg. He managed, nevertheless, to limp swiftly across the stage and down the stairs to the rear of the theatre, where he mounted a horse kept in readiness and fled through the night. After crossing the Navy Yard Bridge he was joined by Herold; toward morning the pain from his leg became so intense, the splintered bone "tearing the flesh at every jump" (Booth's Diary), that the two turned eight miles out of the way to go to the house of Dr. Samuel A. Mudd, a Confederate sympathizer, who set Booth's leg and gave him rest and refreshment. Precious time, however, had been lost, and after leaving Mudd's the two wandered all night in the marshes, only reaching their goal, the Potomac, on the morning of Apr. 16, twelve hours behind schedule. Here they were secreted for six days and five nights in a pine thicket, virtually surrounded by pursuing Union troops, but secretly supplied with food and newspapers by Thomas A. Jones, a farmer and Confederate underground-mail carrier, who waited the chance to put them across the river. This man risked his life, when he might instead have obtained the $100,000 reward offered for the criminals, not so much, as he testifies, through loyalty to the Confederacy as through sympathy for Booth, who even in his agony and despair retained his old power of fascination (Thomas A. Jones, *J. Wilkes Booth,* 1893). Finally the two fugitives on Apr. 23 succeeded in crossing the Potomac, and the next day crossed the Rappahannock, proceeding three miles farther on to the residence of Richard H. Garrett, who took them in under the guise of Confederate soldiers. Here, in Garrett's barn, in the early morning hours of Apr. 26 they were surrounded by a band of soldiers and detectives from Washington who had traced them beyond the Rappahannock. Owing to the fact that the three officers in charge, Lieut. Edward P. Doherty (Regular Army), Lieut.-Col. Everton J. Conger (Secret Service), and Lieut. Luther B. Baker (Secret Service), gave conflicting testimony in a subsequent unsavory squabble over the rewards, it is difficult to make out in every detail just what happened, although the main outline is clear. Summoned to surrender, Herold soon came out and gave himself up, but Booth maintained an undaunted attitude. Theatrical to the end, he called out in the darkness, "Captain, give a lame man a chance. Draw up your men before the door and I'll come out and fight the whole command." This being refused, his voice was again heard, "Well, my brave boys, you can prepare a stretcher for me." The barn was set on fire, Booth was dimly seen for a moment in the blaze erect on his crutch, then fell just as a shot was heard. His captors were divided as to whether he shot himself or was struck by a bullet fired just at that moment by Sergeant Boston Corbett, a religious monomaniac who justified himself in disobeying the order not to fire by saying, "Providence directed me." As Corbett stood some thirty feet from the barn and fired through a mere crack, unless Providence also directed the bullet, the probability is that Booth shot himself. The dying man was pulled out from the barn and carried to the porch of the house where he lingered until about seven o'clock, having recovered consciousness sufficiently to murmur, "Tell Mother—tell Mother—I died for my country," words which she was destined first to receive through that day's newspaper.

That the man who was slain in this encounter was indeed Booth was rendered reasonably certain by his words and actions and by the diary and a Canadian bill of exchange found in his pocket. The body was taken on board the monitor *Montauk,* where it was identified by Dr. John F. May, who had operated for a tumor upon Booth's neck in the previous year (John F. May, "The Mark of the Scalpel," *Columbia Historical Society Records,* XIII, 51). It was then secretly buried under the floor of one of the warehouses in the Arsenal Grounds on Greenleaf's Point where at that time it was customary for felons to be buried.

The other victims of Booth's mad act, his various accomplices, met an even more hapless fate than his own. They were all soon captured and imprisoned, together with Mrs. Surratt, Dr. Mudd, and Edward Spangler, a scene-shifter at Ford's Theatre who was accused of preparing the President's box for the assassination and of assisting Booth to escape. With the possible exception of Mrs. Surratt, all were loaded with irons and their heads covered with flannel bags devised by the ingenuity of Secretary Stanton. The trial, which lasted from May 10 to June 29, was before a military commission headed by Major-General David Hunter. Joseph Holt [*q.v.*], the judge-advocate general of the army, led the prosecution, assisted by Hon. John A. Bingham [*q.v.*] and Col. Henry L. Burnett [*q.v.*]. All the prisoners were accused of conspiring with Jefferson Davis and Confederate officials in Canada to murder the President of the United States, and the death penalty was demanded for all. The determination to implicate the Confederacy in the assassination governed the proceedings of one of the most irregular trials known to history. All manner of irrelevant testimony was introduced; the counsel for the defense, Hon. Reverdy Johnson [*q.v.*] and Gen. Thomas Ewing [*q.v.*] were bullyragged and insulted; witnesses were intimidated; and evidence in the possession of the Government was deliberately suppressed, notably Booth's diary, which would have overthrown the theory of a general plot to assassinate. (See *The Assassination of Abraham Lincoln,* 1909, by David Miller DeWitt, and *The Judicial Murder of Mary E. Surratt,* 1895, by the same author. The full account of the proceedings in *The Conspiracy Trial,* 3 vols., 1865–66, edited by Benjamin Perley Poore, should be compared with the officially expurgated *Assassination of Lincoln,* 1865, compiled by Benn Pitman. Cf. also the lame defense of the Military Commission in *The Assassination of Lincoln,* 1892, by Gen. T. M. Harris, a member of the Commission). The authority of the tribunal was unsuccessfully attacked by Reverdy Johnson on grounds identical with those later upheld by the Supreme Court in the Milligan case (Bernard C. Steiner, *The Life of Reverdy Johnson,* 1914, pp. 115–16). All of those accused, with the exception of Spangler, were adjudged guilty "of combining, confederating, and conspiring with . . . Jefferson Davis . . . to kill and murder . . . Abraham Lincoln," at the very time when the Government was preparing to abandon the case against Davis (Roy F. Nichols, "United States *vs.* Jefferson Davis," *American Historical Review,* January 1926). In the rendering of the sentences, however, a half-hearted and capricious effort was made to recognize varying degrees of guilt among the prisoners. Spangler, convicted only of abetting Booth's escape, was given six years' imprisonment, while Dr. Mudd, actually proven guilty only of the same crime, was condemned to life imprisonment, as were also Arnold and O'Laughlin, actually guilty of the attempt at abduction but innocent of any complicity in the murder. (All of these were pardoned by President Johnson by Mar. 4, 1869, with the exception of O'Laughlin who died of yellow fever, Sept. 23, 1867, at Fort Jefferson, Dry Tortugas Island, Fla.) Herold, Payne, and Atzerodt, who were clearly the most guilty, were condemned to be executed together with Mrs. Surratt, against whom the evidence was the weakest of all, it not even being absolutely proven that she knew of the abduction plot. To be sure the same tribunal that sentenced Mrs. Surratt signed a petition to President Johnson to commute the sentence to life imprisonment, but, according to the

President, Judge Advocate Holt never showed him this petition, and all mention of it was carefully excluded from the official Pitman report. Mrs. Surratt was hanged with the others on July 7, 1865. All this time her son, John H. Surratt, probably ignorant of the events of the trial, was kept in hiding by a Roman Catholic priest at St. Liboire, Canada. He later went to Europe, became a member of the Papal Zouaves in Rome, was apprehended, made a daring escape, was again apprehended, and was finally returned to America in December 1866. The Government, holding that he had been a ringleader in the conspiracy to assassinate, made every effort to obtain his conviction, but at the end of his trial, before a civil court and lasting from June 10 to Aug. 10, 1867, the jury stood eight to four for acquittal. Surratt was kept in prison until June 22, 1868, when he was released on bail, and three months later the indictment against him was nolle-prossed. During the trial the Government promised to place in evidence Booth's manuscript diary but it again failed to do so. The existence of the diary had become known through an indiscreet remark in La Fayette C. Baker's *History of the United States Secret Service* (1867), and in May 1867, during the impeachment proceedings, Johnson ordered Stanton to produce it. Its publication (*Daily Morning Chronicle,* Washington, May 22, 1867) led Gen. Butler on the floor of the House to charge John A. Bingham with having deliberately perverted justice in the case of Mrs. Surratt, a charge to which Bingham made a very weak reply. The tragic diary, consisting of a few pages jotted down in physical and mental agony at hurried moments during Booth's flight, gives convincing evidence that his fevered mind, seeing the world through an emotional cloud, envisaged his act as that of a Brutus or William Tell; that he was amazed at the public reception of the crime; that his insane deed, productive of nothing but woe to himself, his friends, and the whole South, was initiated solely by his own gallant but disordered spirit.

In February 1869 the bodies of the conspirators, who had been buried beside Booth, were restored to their families; that of Booth himself was reinterred, on Feb. 20, in an unmarked grave in the Booth lot in Greenmount Cemetery, Baltimore, a number of his fellow-actors serving as pall-bearers (see "Lincoln Obsequies," a volume of newspaper clippings in the Library of Congress). While in the undertaker's shop in Baltimore the body had again been identified, in various ways, by Mrs. Rogers, an old Bel Air friend; by Col. William M. Pegram, Henry C. Wagner, and other acquaintances; and by a dentist who recognized his filling in one of the teeth (Mahoney, p. 48). Despite all this positive identification, humanity was loth to part with so picturesque a character as Booth, and a widespread legend arose that he had escaped capture and was still alive. Report had it that he was seen in London, Paris, and India, and was even masquerading as a minister in Atlanta, Ga. Many believed that John St. Helen, an erratic personage moving about Mexico, Texas, and Oklahoma in the years after the war, finally committing suicide in 1903 at Enid, Oklahoma, under the name of David E. George, was in reality the escaped John Wilkes Booth. (For St. Helen's claims, see Finis L. Bates, *The Escape and Suicide of John Wilkes Booth,* 1908; W. P. Campbell, *The Escape and Wanderings of J. Wilkes Booth,* 1922, and documents in the possession of Mr. Clarence True Wilson, Washington, D. C.; for a refutation of these claims see William G. Shepherd, "Shattering the Myth of John Wilkes Booth," *Harper's Magazine,* November 1924.) St. Helen's mummified body was exhibited in Chicago, Memphis, and elsewhere, and those who so desire may still examine it at Venice, Cal.

[In addition to the references cited above, see, for Booth's acting, theatrical criticisms in the Boston newspapers, May 12–24, 1862, and Jan. 19–Feb. 14, 1863. Booth's diary, the boot taken from his broken leg by Dr. Mudd, and other personal articles are in the possession of the War Dept., Washington, D. C.]

E. S. B.

BOOTH, JUNIUS BRUTUS (May 1, 1796–Nov. 30, 1852), English actor, of Jewish descent (see below), was born in London, the son of Richard Booth, a lawyer, and the grandson of John Booth, a silversmith. His mother had been a Miss Game or Gam. The Booths were related to the Wilkes family and shared the radical views of John Wilkes. In his youth Richard Booth ran away from home to join the American Revolutionists although he only got as far as Paris; in his later years he is said to have kept in his drawing-room a picture of George Washington before which he insisted that all visitors should bow in reverence. Junius Brutus Booth early showed an embarrassing multiplicity of talents, especially for painting, poetry, sculpture, and female seduction. After learning the art of printing, studying a little law, and contemplating the career of a midshipman, he finally, when seventeen years old, and much against his father's will, went on the stage. His first appearance was with an amateur company in a temporary theatre in Tottenham Court Road in the part of Frank Rochdale in Colman's

John Bull, but he soon obtained regular employment with a company of comedians under Penley and Jonas at Peckham and later at Deptford. His début with them was in the rôle of Campillo, a minor character in *The Honeymoon,* on Dec. 13, 1813. During the next year, after a severe illness, he accompanied the same company on a tour of some months in Holland and Belgium. On May 8, 1815 he was married, in London, to Marie Christine Adelaide Delancy, with whom he had eloped from Brussels; later, he deserted her after she had borne him a son, Richard Junius, who served in the Confederate army, and a daughter, who died in infancy. In the summer of 1815 he filled an engagement with the Worthing and Brighton Theatres, in the ensuing season played unimportant parts at Covent Garden, and then filled another engagement at Worthing and Brighton. His appearances as Fitzharding in the comedy of *Smiles and Tears,* as Bertram in *Bertram,* and as Sir Giles Overreach, all aroused favorable comment so that he was engaged to appear at Covent Garden in the rôle of Richard III on Feb. 12, 1817. His striking similarity in appearance and manner to Edmund Kean challenged comparison with the most famous actor of the day, and a furious discussion arose in the public press between the "Boothites" and the "Keanites." There seems to have been no just ground for the charge of imitation which was brought against Booth: both actors belonged to the realistic school of Cooke, but Booth gave his lines differently from Kean and his emphasis was more intelligent (for examples see *The Actor,* 1846, pp. 36–37). After a successful repetition of the performance of Richard III, Booth not unnaturally asked for an increase of salary at Covent Garden; this being refused, he was persuaded by Kean to join the latter at Drury Lane on a three years' contract, but after a single notable performance of Iago to Kean's Othello, he became convinced on good grounds that he was going to be kept subordinate to Kean; forthwith he promptly returned to Covent Garden and signed a three years' contract with that house. This unprecedented struggle between the two leading theatres of England for the services of an actor of twenty-one, together with Booth's carelessness in regard to legal ties, made him the temporary center of English theatrical history. His reappearance at Covent Garden was the signal for a riot in the theatre, and the play was given entirely in pantomime, as no words could be heard above the storm of cat-calls, hissings, and applause. His subsequent appearances were marked by similar scenes but with decreasing vehemence; gradually the excitement subsided, and Booth now paid the penalty for his previous notoriety by having to play to smaller houses; nevertheless he ended the season with an established reputation as one of the leading actors on the English stage.

In the following year he toured the provinces and in the autumn returned to Covent Garden where he repeatedly appeared as Richard III and as Iago and also added the innovation of playing Shylock in Jewish dialect. In 1820 his most important activities were an engagement as King Lear (Nahum Tate's version) at Covent Garden, a long run at the Cobourg Theatre in *The Lear of Private Life* and another in *Horatii and Curiatii,* an engagement at Drury Lane where he played Iago to Kean's Othello, Edgar to his Lear, and Pierre to his Jaffier and a particularly noteworthy performance of *Julius Cæsar* at Drury Lane in which Booth played Cassius to the Brutus of James W. Wallack and the Antony of John Cooper.

On Jan. 13, 1821, Booth was married to Mary Anne Holmes, and shortly afterward the couple visited France and Madeira and then in April sailed on the ship *Two Brothers* for America. Landing at Norfolk, Va., Booth immediately obtained an engagement at Richmond, followed by one in the Park Theatre, New York, and others in Boston, Philadelphia, and the leading Southern cities. In the following summer he purchased a large farm in a beautiful secluded tract of woodland near Bel Air, Harford County, Md., twenty-three miles from Baltimore. Here in a comfortable log cabin, with his vegetable garden, orchard, and vineyard, his fish-pond and herd of sheep, the actor spent as much time each year as he could steal from his profession. Here his father soon joined him and here were born his children, Junius Brutus, Edwin [*q.v.*], Asia Frigga, and John Wilkes [*q.v.*], besides several others who died in childhood. The most important events in Booth's long stage career in America were his performance of Pescara, a part expressly written for him, in Sheil's *Apostate* at the Park Theatre in June 1827; his stage management of the Camp Street Theatre, New Orleans, in 1828, when he also appeared at the Théâtre d'Orléans as Oreste in Racine's *Andromaque* in French (Booth being a remarkable linguist familiar also with German, Dutch, and Hebrew); his management in 1831 of the Adelphi Theatre in Baltimore when he first introduced Charles Kean to an American audience, in *Hamlet,* he himself gracefully taking the minor part of the Second Grave Digger; and his playing of Pierre to Edwin Forrest's

Jaffier and of Othello to Forrest's Iago in September 1831 at the Park Theatre. He made tours of England in 1825–26 and in 1836–37, the first unsuccessful because of the hard times, and the second saddened by the death of a favorite son. Booth now became increasingly subject to temporary fits of insanity; in one of these during a trip to the South in 1838 he attempted to drown himself and also one night attacked his manager, Thomas Flynn, with an andiron, receiving in the encounter a broken nose which permanently marred his handsome countenance and somewhat nasalized his melodious voice. From this time he appeared in the theatre less frequently, although he played every year in Boston and New Orleans where he was an especial favorite. In the spring of 1852 he and Edwin Booth, who had now been on the stage for several years, joined the younger Junius Brutus Booth, also an actor, in California; after some weeks of fairly successful performances in San Francisco and Sacramento, the elder Booth decided to return home. He stopped on the way at New Orleans, where he played for the last time, in a series of six performances at the St. Charles Theatre. Having overtaxed his strength, he caught a severe cold and died alone in his cabin on the steamboat *J. S. Chenoweth* on the way to Cincinnati. His funeral in Cincinnati was attended by great crowds of people, including throngs of negroes. The body was later removed to Greenmount Cemetery, Baltimore.

Owing to his attacks of madness, his intemperance, and his general irresponsibility, Booth broke his theatrical engagements with reckless frequency, and on more than one occasion, when irritated, came forward to the footlights and expressed his contempt of the audience. But the public always forgave him because of his unquestioned ability. He was easily the foremost tragedian of his day in America. Although short in stature, he dominated the stage by the passion and fire of his performance. His best rôles were those of villains and semi-villains; Richard III, Iago, Shylock, Sir Giles Overreach, Pescara, Luke in *Riches* (an adaptation of Massinger's *City Madam*) and Sir Edward Mortimer in Colman's *The Iron Chest*,—to which somber list should be added, curiously enough, the comic rôle of Jerry Sneak in Foote's farce, *The Mayor of Garratt*. He was essentially an emotional rather than intellectual actor, depicting best of all the passions of ambition, jealousy, hatred, fear, and revenge. His own blank verse tragedy of *Ugolino*, piously produced by John Wilkes Booth at the Boston Museum in 1863 (published in French's *American Drama*, No. CXX), is a mediocre work. An amateur student of the Koran, Catholic theology, and occultism, he believed in the transmigration of souls and the equality of man. He was a vegetarian both in theory and practise, on his farm he refused to permit even the most noxious animals to be killed, and at least on one occasion he went to the length of arranging an elaborate funeral for some of his dumb friends (James Freeman Clarke, "My Odd Adventure with Junius Brutus Booth," *Atlantic Monthly*, VIII, 296–301, who also states that Booth told him he was of Jewish ancestry). Equally noteworthy, despite Booth's irascibility and moodiness, was his erratic kindness toward every type of human being.

[The standard biography, *The Elder and the Younger Booth* (1882), by Asia Booth Clarke, is largely based upon an anonymous but generally accurate work, *The Actor: Passages in the Lives of Booth and Some of His Contemporaries* (1846). See also Oxberry's *Dramatic Biog.*, IV (1826). For an elaborate but somewhat amateurish study of Booth's acting see *The Tragedian* (1868), by Thos. R. Gould. The sketch by Jos. Knight in the *Dict. of Nat. Biog.* (1921–22), based mainly on Oxberry, is unfair to Booth in several particulars.] E. S. B.

BOOTH, MARY LOUISE (Apr. 19, 1831–Mar. 5, 1889), author, translator, editor, was the daughter of William Chatfield Booth, descendant of Ensign John Booth, who came to this country from England in 1649. Her mother was a grand-daughter of one of the exiles driven from home by the French Revolution. From her father she inherited a high measure of single-mindedness and integrity, and an enthusiasm for books; while her mother endowed her with the brilliancy and vivacity of the old French émigrés. She was born at Yaphank, on Long Island, N. Y. Mentally precocious, she learned English and French simultaneously, reading the Bible and Plutarch at the age of five, Racine at seven, Hume and Gibbon before she was ten. At fourteen she became a teacher in a school established by her father in Brooklyn, but she did not pursue the vocation. She devoted herself instead to study, acquiring a thorough knowledge and fluent use of German, Italian, and Spanish, in addition to French which had been one of her two mother tongues. Her translations from the French of *The Marble-Workers' Manual* (1856) and the *New and Complete Clock and Watch-Makers' Manual* (1860) were long recognized as valuable works of reference in their respective fields. In 1859 she published a *History of the City of New York*, which was the first complete work upon the subject. It sold for many years and was revised and enlarged by her in 1880. The outbreak of the Civil War gave her an opportunity for the use of her talents which she eagerly seized. In a single week she translated Count Agénor de Gasparin's *The Uprising of a Great People* (1861), working almost twenty-four hours a day. The appearance of the book met with a remarkable outburst of enthusiasm. Charles Sumner wrote to her: "It is worth a whole phalanx in the cause of human freedom," and he said of her translations of Augustin Cochin's *Results of Slavery* (1863) and *Results of Emancipation* (1863) that they were "of more value to the North than the Numidian cavalry to Hannibal." President Lincoln sent her a letter of thanks for her achievement in stimulating and encouraging the people of the Union. She gave herself to this work with ardor and energy, producing other translations, corresponding with friends of the Union cause in France, and publishing their replies in the press and in pamphlets. In later years she said that "all hours have since seemed thin and poor beside those of that glowing and stormy epoch." During this period of her life she produced about twenty volumes of translations. In 1867 Harper & Brothers invited her to become the editor of *Harper's Bazar,* which they were just establishing. She edited it with conspicuous success for twenty-one years, attracting to its pages many of the most prominent novelists, story writers, and essayists of England and America. She prized lofty standards of womanhood and lent her influence to the cause of higher education for women, but the activities of the so-called woman's movement were distasteful to her and in spite of the urging of many of her friends, she remained unconvinced of the desirability of woman suffrage. Though not conventionally beautiful, she was possessed of a majestic bearing, large and soft dark brown eyes, a luminous smile and "hands as exquisite as if carved in ivory." She was described by an intimate associate as "a sagacious and energetic woman, with as cool judgment as brilliant foresight . . . full of both critical power and of imagination, of the love of nature and of beauty in every form."

[Obituary by Harriet Prescott Spofford in *Harper's Bazar,* Mar. 30, 1889; other obituaries in *N. Y. Times* and *N. Y. Tribune,* Mar. 6, 1889.] H. H.

BOOTH, NEWTON (Dec. 30, 1825–July 14, 1892), governor of California, senator, the son of Beebe and Hannah (Pitts) Booth, was born in Salem, Washington County, Ind. Little is known of his life up to the time of his graduation from Asbury (now DePauw) University in 1846. He entered upon the study of law and was admitted to the Indiana bar three years later. The lure of the West, however, was strong and 1850 found Booth answering its call and moving westward with the pioneers who sought gold and opportunity on new horizons. He settled in Sacramento where he engaged in a mercantile and grocery business. In 1856 he returned to Indiana, but 1860 saw him again in Sacramento. His interest in literature and history, and his extensive reading on those subjects, now brought him increasingly into demand as a lecturer and writer. As early as 1862 he began to contribute to the *Sacramento Union,* a paper wielding a remarkable influence in California during the years 1850–75. His strong support of the Union cause at the time of the Civil War, together with his ardent devotion to the Republican party, led him into political life, and resulted in his election in 1863 as state senator from Sacramento, an office which he held for one term. In the years immediately succeeding, he threw himself whole-heartedly into the cause of his party, and helped to carry the state for Grant in the presidential election of 1868. In 1871 he became the eleventh governor of California. He went into office on a platform whose chief feature was opposition to the granting of subsidies to the railroad. This issue was then the source of bitter controversy, but it died down to some extent following the election. Booth's administration was notable for a genuine attempt at economy in public affairs and also by a successful revision of the statute law. The resignation of Eugene Casserly as senator from California in 1873 led Booth, while still governor, to seek appointment at the hands of the legislature for the unexpired term. In this move he was unsuccessful. His defeat, however, was only temporary; for at the next election the legislature returned him to the United States Senate for the full term of six years. In March 1875 he accordingly resigned the governorship, a position which he had retained even in the face of criticism while he was seeking election, and took up his duties in the national capital. There, during his single term, he was active in accomplishing the adoption of the silver certificate and the redemption of the subsidiary coins, secured the passage of a bill for the settlement of land titles in California, and was a member of the committees on Public Lands, Patents, Manufactures, and Appropriations. It is generally agreed that he was a man of exceptional ability and unquestioned integrity. His strong partisanship, together with his eloquence and literary talent, made him a leader in the political life of California from the days of early statehood almost up to the time of his death. This occurred at Sacramento on July 14, 1892, when he was sixty-seven years of age. He was married on Feb. 29, 1892, to Mrs. J. T. Glover.

[The most complete record of the life of Newton Booth is to be found in the *Hist. of Cal.* (1898), by Theodore H. Hittell. Additional material appears in *Cal. and Californians* (1926), ed. by Rockwell D. Hunt, and in an excellent obituary in the *Sacramento Record-Union,* July 15, 1892.] R. G. C—d.

BOOTH-TUCKER, EMMA MOSS (Jan. 8, 1860–Oct. 28, 1903), Consul of the Salvation Army, at the age of ten converted a little Jewish playmate to Christianity and thus inaugurated an extensive career of salvation. She was born in Gateshead, England, a daughter of William and Catherine (Mumford) Booth. There were six children in the family, of which Harold Begbie says in his *Life of General William Booth* (1920) that outside the pages of Dickens it was probable that no other such household ever existed. William Booth had begun night street-preaching at seventeen, and a year after Emma's birth resigned from the New Connection Methodist Church in order to devote himself entirely to evangelical preaching. Unlike her brothers and sisters, Emma, who was a nervous, delicate child, made no attempt at public speaking for some time, contenting herself with conducting a children's Bible class where she had "frequently a row of weeping penitents" to her credit (F. St. G. de L. Booth-Tucker, *The Consul,* 1903). But at sixteen she spoke before a meeting at St. Leonard's and five souls sought salvation; after this experience she became a frequent speaker. Booth founded the Salvation Army two years later, as a means to his complete independence, and in 1880 Emma was made Mother of a training home to prepare women cadets for officership. The organization flourished under her administration, for she had a winning personality and a capacity for hard work. She spent much time with individual cadets, praying with them and advising them, and when they left each carried an inscribed photograph of her. When the campaign of the Army in India expanded under the impetus of a $25,000 donation she met Frederick St. George de Lautour Tucker, who was summoned from India to head the fifty officers to be sent there. Emma selected the group and helped him organize them. They became engaged, but Tucker departed without her, to return a year later for their wedding, which was celebrated before five thousand spectators in Clapton Congress Hall in London. A second collection of $25,000 was raised on this occasion and fifty more officers ("The Wedding Fifty") set out for Bombay, this time under the joint command of Tucker and his bride, who was given the title of Consul. The Consul assumed native costume and manners, and was soon embarked on a career of lectures which took her to inland villages in Southern India, and to Ceylon. The illness of her mother recalled her to England after a few years, but on Mrs. Booth's death in 1890 she returned to India only to find her own health failing. With her husband she went to England once more and in 1896 Tucker was made Commander in charge of the work in America. An assembly of four thousand received them at Carnegie Hall in New York. They settled in Mt. Vernon, a suburb of New York, with their children, of whom there were seven at the time of Mrs. Booth-Tucker's death. The work in America took a more practical turn, perhaps because of the criticism with which Gen. Booth's book *In Darkest England* (1890) had been met. Much of the Consul's time was spent in organizing industrial homes providing temporary employment, rescue homes for women, workingmen's hotels, orphanages, and country homes for city poor; much of it also was spent in the care of the Salvation Army's three farm colonies. But she continued her speaking: her most famous lecture, "Love and Sorrow," describing the activities of the Army, was delivered for two years in fifty cities. She liked to lead marches through the slums at midnight to "stir things up" and gather the "roughs" about her for prayer. In the midst of her duties she visited the sick, wrote innumerable letters of exhortation and encouragement, and articles for the official publication, the *War Cry.* She was on a speaking tour when her train was wrecked near Dean Lake, Mo., and she and Col. Thos. C. Holland, in charge of the Colorado farm colony, were fatally injured. Thousands crowded Carnegie Hall for her funeral services. Her published work is *The League of Love, Being the Assistant Rescue Branch of the Salvation Army* (1896).

[In addition to references given above, see Commander F. St. G. de L. Booth-Tucker, "Farm Colonies of the Salvation Army," *Bull. U. S. Bureau of Labor,* No. 48; Albert Shaw, "A Successful Farm Colony in the Irrigation Country," *Rev. of Revs.,* Nov. 1902; "Commander Booth-Tucker and His Work in America" (editorial), *Rev. of Revs.,* Nov. 1904; *St. Louis Globe-Democrat,* Oct. 30, 1903.] M. A. K.

BOOTT, KIRK (Oct. 20, 1790–Apr. 11, 1837), manufacturer, was a son of Kirk Boott, an English merchant, originally of Derbyshire, who settled at Boston after the American Revolution, and of Mary (Love) Boott. He studied at Rugby Academy, England, whence he entered Harvard College in the class of 1809. There he "sowed an abundance of wild oats but never graduated" (Charles Cowley, *A Handbook of Business in Lowell, with a History of the City,* 1856, p. 72). Being militarily inclined he was sent to England where a commission had been procured for him. He served in the Peninsular War under Wellington, commanding a detachment at the siege of San Sebastian. His regiment was ordered in 1813 to New Orleans, but Boott, unwilling to join an expedition against his native land, secured a detail to a military academy for more instruction (*History of Middlesex County, Mass.*, edited by S. A. Drake, 1880, II, 74). He married, at about this time, Ann Haden of Derby. In 1817 Boott's father died, and soon after this the son, who had been dependent on a subaltern's meager salary (*Reply to a Pamphlet recently Circulated by Mr. Edward Brooks*, p. 49), entered his father's firm in Boston expecting a good living from it. In this he was disappointed. The business was in such shape that he found himself practically without employment. In 1821, while passing a day at Nahant with Patrick Tracy Jackson [*q.v.*], he applied for a position as manager of an enterprise then projected by several Boston capitalists at East Chelmsford, afterward Lowell. When, later, negotiations for control of the holdings of the Proprietors of Locks and Canals on Merrimack River were completed, young Boott was engaged as agent of the newly incorporated Merrimack Manufacturing Company. Boott did not originate the cotton manufacture (as is explained in a letter written by his associate Nathan Appleton to John A. Lowell and quoted in Drake's *History*, II, 58–62), but after the enterprise was under way he became its dictator. He enlarged the Pawtucket Canal, which had been opened Oct. 18, 1796, for conveying logs around Pawtucket Falls, and he dug a lateral canal to bring power to the Merrimack Company's first unit. Other canals followed, and on them other cotton factories. Boott inaugurated a machine-shop which, with Maj. George Washington Whistler as superintendent, began the making of locomotives in America. He brought to his mill village much of the best mechanical talent of his time. Brick boarding-houses were built for the operatives, most of them young women from the nearby farms, and elaborate rules and regulations for their conduct were adopted. St. Anne's Church, Episcopal, was erected after the design of an English parish church, and all operatives were at first taxed for its support. Boott built for himself a mansion,—still standing in upper Merrimack St., and used as a corporation hospital. In these and many other undertakings he proved himself an indefatigable worker. "He gave his whole zeal and strength to promote the prosperity of the new village. He watched its growth with a personal interest, resolving here to live and die" (Henry A. Miles, *Lowell as it Was and as it Is*, 1845, p. 87). To the new place, when in 1826 it was about to be set off from Chelmsford as a separate township, Boott wished to give the name of Derby, after his English ancestral home, but he was overruled by his directors, who chose the name of Lowell in honor of Francis Cabot Lowell [*q.v.*]. Boott's surname is still perpetuated in one of its chief manufacturing corporations; his Christian name in a down-town street (Frederick W. Coburn, *History of Lowell and its People*, 1920, I, 149).

Boott carried more burdens than one man should. To his friend, Edward Brooks, he wrote, Sept. 29, 1830 (*Correspondence between Edward Brooks and John A. Lowell, with Remarks by Edward Brooks*, p. 15): "I am almost worried out. Committee after committee keep coming up in relation to the increase of the Appleton works, or a new concern, for all of which many calculations are required, taking all my time and, since this unhappy disclosure [of his brother's mismanagement of the family property] I get neither rest nor sleep." His nerves tense, Boott quarreled with his chosen director, Rev. Theodore Edson, D.D., over a difference of opinion regarding the public school system (Charles C. Chase, "Lowell," in D. H. Hurd's *History of Middlesex County, Mass.*, 1890, II, 116). When the town meeting voted to sustain Dr. Edson and built two modern school-houses, Kirk Boott withdrew from St. Anne's and for a time attended the Unitarian Church. Before his death, however, he returned to his pew in the Episcopal Church whose forms he loved. He died while driving his chaise in Merrimack St., on Apr. 11, 1837.

Boott's personality, projected upon the town and city of Lowell, considerably determined the character of many American industrial communities. He was a pioneer of industrial feudalism, a benevolent despot, a driver of men and women, an emotional, opinionated, and well-meaning man who was endowed with constructive imagination and ability to organize.

[In addition to the references given above, see *Proc. in the City of Lowell at the Semi Centennial Celebration* (1876); Frank P. Hill, *Lowell Illustrated, a Chronological Record of Events* (1884); Wilson Waters and Henry Spaulding Perham, *Hist. of Chelmsford, Mass.* (1917); the various and numerous publications of the Old Residents' Hist. Ass. and its successor, the Lowell Hist. Soc.]

F. W. C.

BORDEN, GAIL (Nov. 9, 1801–Jan. 11, 1874), surveyor, inventor, the eldest son of Gail and Philadelphia (Wheeler) Borden, was born on his father's farm at Norwich, N. Y. He was of the seventh generation descended from Richard Borden who settled at Pocasset (now Portsmouth), R. I., in 1638. His mother was the great-great-grand-daughter of Roger Williams.

His youth was that of a farmer's son of the times, with the additional interest of surveying taught him by his father. When he was fourteen his parents moved to what is now Covington, Ky., and within a year, they moved again, into the Territory of Indiana. Here Borden obtained his only schooling, totaling one and one-half years. During this time he farmed, practised surveying, became an expert rifleman, and captained a company of militiamen. Almost as soon as he stopped being a pupil he began teaching school and from nineteen to twenty-one taught in the backwoods schools of the territory. Because of poor health he left home in 1822 and proceeded further south, settling shortly thereafter in Amite County, Miss. Here he taught school and was county and United States deputy surveyor for six or seven years, after which he went with his bride of less than a year to join his parents in Stephen A. Austin's colony in Texas. Borden's first employment here was farming and stock raising. He was subsequently appointed by Gen. Austin to superintend the official surveys of the colonies. He represented his district at the convention held in 1833 at San Felipe to seek separation from Mexico and during the war he and his brother published the only newspaper issued in the territory. When the republic was founded Borden compiled the first topographical map and made the surveys for and laid out the city of Galveston, and was made collector of customs there. From 1839 to 1851 he was agent for the Galveston City Company, a corporation owning large areas of land on which the city was built. At an age when many men are desirous of reducing the number of their activities, Borden, who for fifty years had led the varied and rugged life of a pioneer, began the most important work of his life. His greatest pleasure lay in doing something for his fellow-man and it was this characteristic that led to his new and wholly different work. One of the greatest hardships of the pioneer was that of securing and carrying sufficient food on his migrations, and Borden set to work with the fixed idea of preparing food in concentrated form. He first developed a meat biscuit. Its value was quickly recognized, and Borden invested all that he had in a plant for its manufacture. A strong and influential competition of Army food contractors, however, resulted in the failure of the undertaking and Borden lost everything. He had an exhibit of his meat biscuit at the London Fair in 1851 and received "the great council medal" and was elected an honorary member of the London Society of Arts. It is said that on his way back from Europe he was impressed by the plight of the immigrant children on board ship because of the impossibility of giving them wholesome milk. So, when his meat biscuits failed he thought of concentrating milk. He left Texas and went north to New Lebanon, N. Y., where he had friends in the Shaker Colony. He began at once experimenting in their laboratory and condensing milk, using, particularly, a vacuum pan of the type used in making sugar. He applied for a patent in May 1853 "on a process of evaporating milk in vacuum." For three years the process was questioned by the Patent Office until Borden's contention that the important function of the vacuum was to protect the milk from air and to keep it clean while it was being condensed was scientifically proven. On Aug. 19, 1856, Borden received Patent No. 15,553 for "the concentration of milk." He endeavored to go into production immediately after the issuance of his patent but until he met Jeremiah Milbank, he failed to secure enough money to build a plant. Manufacture was started in 1858 and the first big condensary was opened in 1861 at Wassaic, N. Y. But for the Civil War it might have taken years to introduce this new product. It was found, however, to be a very valuable food for soldiers, nourishing and easily carried, and the public learned from the soldiers. After the business was established on a firm basis Borden returned to Texas and in the town of Borden he turned his attention to the concentration of other foods, including fruit juices, tea, coffee, and cocoa. On July 22, 1862, the Patent Office granted him Patent No. 35,919, "for concentrating cider and other juices and fruits." He continued his experimental work thereafter until the end of his life. Borden's first wife was Penelope Mercer of Amite County, Miss., whom he married in 1828. She was the mother of all his children and died in 1844. He later married Mrs. A. F. Stearns, and some time after her death he married in 1860 Mrs. Emeline Eunice (Eno) Church. He died at his home in Texas at the age of seventy-three.

[*Hist. and Geneal. Record of the Descendants . . . of Richard and Joan Borden* (1899), compiled by Hattie Borden Weld; Records of the Borden Co., N. Y.; U. S. Pat. Office Records; obituary in *N. Y. Tribune,* Jan. 14, 1874.]

C. W. M.

BORDEN, RICHARD (Apr. 12, 1795–Feb. 25, 1874), manufacturer and executive, was descended from the Quaker, Richard Borden, who settled at Pocasset (now Portsmouth), R. I., in 1638. He was born in Freetown, Mass., the ninth child of Thomas and Mary (Hathaway) Borden. His scholastic training was obtained during the winter terms of the district school, while strenuous work on his father's farm and in his father's grist and saw-mills contributed to the sturdy physique with which he was endowed. As manager, between the ages of eighteen and twenty-five, of his father's grist-mill, he was accustomed to sail down the river in the sloop *Irene and Betsey* and collect the grain to be milled. These voyages suggested to Richard Borden and a shipbuilder, Maj. Bradford Durfee, the possibility of enlarging the operations, and under their supervision several vessels were constructed for the river trade. The making of nails and other metal accessories for sloops resulted in the formation in 1821 of the Fall River Iron Works, destined to a leading place among Fall River industries. Its original capital was $18,000; without a single outside dollar added to the original investment it had attained in 1845 a capitalization of $960,000 with a plant valued at half a million. Richard Borden took an active part in the formation of this company, "was appointed treasurer and agent, a position which he filled ably and satisfactorily up to the day of his final withdrawal from business, a period of over fifty years" (F. M. Peck and H. H. Earl, *Fall River and Its Industries,* 1877, p. 48).

Borden's connection with cotton milling originated from his position in the Fall River Iron Works. The immense success of the enterprise led the company into schemes for the development of water power and cotton milling. In this way the iron works company became an owner in the Watuppe Reservoir Company, in the Troy Cotton and Woolen Manufactory, in the Fall River Manufactory, in the Annawan Mill built by it in 1825, in the American Print Works built by it in 1834, in the Metacomet Mill built in 1846, and in various transportation enterprises. In most of these concerns, which were pioneers in the cotton industry, Borden took a prominent part, as well as in others. He was president and director of the American Print Works, the American Linen Company, the Troy Cotton and Woolen Manufactory, the Richard Borden Mill Company, and the Mount Hope Mill Company, and was a director of the Annawan and Metacomet Mill Companies. He was also president of the Fall River National Bank and of the Watuppe Reservoir Company. Not only was Borden a leading entrepreneur and magnate in the development of Fall River cotton, but to him must be given credit for breaking the geographical isolation of that city and achieving direct connections with Boston and New York. Borden's interest in transportation never died after his early experience, and we find the Fall River Iron Works under his inspiration inaugurating a regular line of steamers in 1827 between Fall River and Providence. In 1846 mainly through his personal efforts a railroad line from Fall River to Myricks was constructed to connect with the New Bedford & Taunton Railroad and thence by the Providence Railroad to Boston. Subsequently he built to South Braintree, striking the Old Colony Railroad at that point. He also projected the Cape Cod Railway Company, of which he was president, and which built from Middleborough down the Cape. Simultaneously with the railroad enterprises Richard and his brother Jefferson organized (1847) a steamship line between Fall River and New York which was enormously successful from the start. In 1864 Borden planned a better rail connection with Boston and secured a charter for a railroad. The opposition, however, of the Old Colony Railroad, and Borden's advanced age led him to sell both his charter and the steamship company to that railroad. He was a man of strong physique, of handsome and commanding presence, and of generous disposition. In private life he is described as a "sincere outspoken Christian," as "one of the leaders in the Central Congregational Church," and as an active worker in Sabbath School Missions (*Ibid.,* p. 52). He was married, on Feb. 22, 1828, to Abbey Walker Durfee by whom he had seven children.

[The best sketch of Borden's life is in the *Biog. Encyc. of Mass.* (1883), II, 89–96. See also Hattie Borden Weld, *Hist. and Geneal. Record of the Descendants . . . of Richard and Joan Borden* (1899), pp. 166–69, and the obituary in the *Boston Morning Jour.,* Feb. 26, 1874.]

H. U. F.

BORDEN, SIMEON (Jan. 29, 1798–Oct. 28, 1856), skilled mechanic and civil engineer, was the oldest son of Simeon and Amy (Briggs) Borden and was of the fourth generation born on the Borden estate established by his great-grandfather, Joseph, at Fall River, Mass. When Simeon was eight his family moved to Tiverton, R. I., to take over the farm left to his mother, and it was here that the boy acquired a rudimentary education in the country schools. When he was thirteen his father died, whereupon he stopped school to assist his mother in the management of her farm. Within six years his mother also died, and Borden at nineteen had thrust upon him the full responsibility of the estates of both parents. He was successful in this, settling and dividing the estates after some years. From the time he stopped school he studied applied mathematics at home as best he could, and also mastered the metal and wood-working crafts. His interests lay in the latter direction, so when freed of the farm responsibilities he entered a machine shop, becoming superintendent in two years when he was thirty years old.

When the legislature of Massachusetts in 1830 passed a law requiring Boston and the several towns of the state to make accurate maps by trigonometrical survey Borden was engaged to construct the base bar for the measurement of the base line. This he completed in the winter of 1830. It was fifty feet in length, was inclosed in a metal tube, and was so compensated as to remain constant in length at all temperatures. Four compound microscopes were employed with it for taking constant readings. This instrument was, at the time it was constructed, the most accurate of its kind in the United States and brought Borden much recognition. He had nothing to guide him in its construction and it was entirely through his own resources and by repeated experiments that he succeeded so admirably. Borden assisted in the survey for the season of 1831, particularly in the measurement of the base line, and again in 1832, after which he continued with it until its completion in 1841, having full responsibility following the resignation of the chief surveyor in 1834. He prepared and read an account of the survey at a meeting of the American Philosophical Society in 1841 which was subsequently published (*Transactions of the American Philosophical Society,* n. s., IX). During the succeeding ten years Borden served as engineer and surveyor for several railroads in New Hampshire, Maine, Massachusetts, and Connecticut. He also made the survey of the line between Rhode Island and Massachusetts which was used in the United States Supreme Court case of Rhode Island *vs.* Massachusetts in 1844. In 1851 he published his computations and methods for running curves for railroads under the title, *A System of Useful Formulæ.* This was based upon a paper read before the Boston Society of Civil Engineers in December 1849. His natural ability and acquired knowledge of the principles of mechanics brought him into prominence in the closing years of his life when he was often called upon to testify as an expert in the courts. Besides his other duties he represented Fall River in the state legislature in 1832–33, 1844–45, and 1849. He never married, and died at the age of fifty-eight at the home of his brother, Congressman Nathaniel B. Borden.

[Hattie B. Weld, *Hist. and Geneal. Record of the Descendants . . . of Richard and Joan Borden* (1899); *Proc. Am. Phil. Soc.,* vol. II (1841–43).] C. W. M.

BORDLEY, JOHN BEALE (Feb. 11, 1727–Jan. 26, 1804), lawyer, agriculturist, was the posthumous son of Thomas Bordley, by his second wife, Mrs. Ariana Vanderheyden Frisby. His father came from Yorkshire, England, in 1694, settled in Maryland, and was attorney-general there in 1712. John Bordley was born at Annapolis, and after his mother's death was brought up by Col. Hynson at Chestertown, Md. He studied law under his eldest brother, Stephen, and also did much general reading of history, philosophy, science, and arts. In 1750 he married Margaret Chew, who died Nov. 11, 1773. Their joint property included several farms, on one of which, near Joppa, Md., they resided twelve years. In 1753 Bordley was appointed prothonotary of Baltimore County, and after resigning this office and moving to Baltimore, he was appointed a judge of the Maryland Provincial Court in 1766, and the following year also judge of the Admiralty. In 1768 he was one of the commissioners to determine the boundary between Maryland and Delaware, and was also member of the Governor's Council during the administrations of Governors Sharpe and Eden. In 1770 he came into possession of 1,600 acres on an island at the mouth of Wye River, and resided there. He also purchased Pool's Island, near Joppa. From this time he farmed on a large scale and endeavored to improve practises with the aid of imported machinery, seeds, and treatises on husbandry. He rotated crops and grew wheat, as a substitute for tobacco, together with hemp, flax, cotton, and many kinds of vegetables and fruits. He made bricks, salt, and beer, the last, as better than whiskey, for his farm people. He was on the side of the colonists in their contest with Great Britain and helped to supply the American army with food. On Oct. 8, 1776, he married Mrs. Sarah Fishbourne Mifflin, of Philadelphia, and moved to that city in 1791. Believing that agriculture might be advanced by a society of "well informed men of liberal minds" he brought about the formation of the Philadelphia Society for Promoting Agriculture in 1785, and was its vice-president and active in its affairs until his death. He was of large frame, is characterized as "beneficent, vigorous and original," was interested in painting and music, and was a member of the Protestant Episcopal Church.

Results of his farm operations and studies were published at first on written cards, and then on handbills and as essays. Among these are: *A Summary View of the Courses of Crops, in the Husbandry of England and Maryland* (1784), and *Sketches on Rotations of Crops and other Rural Matters* (1797). His *Essays and Notes on Husbandry and Rural Affairs,* published in 1799, and with additions in 1801, is a book of 566 pages describing a system of farming based on rotation of crops and deals with the several kinds of crops, fruits, and animals grown on English and Maryland farms (particularly his own), manures, farm buildings, dairy products, food and diet for farm people, etc. American and foreign practises are compared and results of experiments are given. The style is clear and practical, an effort evidently being made to give such data as would enable the intelligent farmer to make use of the information thus conveyed. Bordley also published an essay on *Money, Coins, Weights and Measures* in 1789 and a supplement to this in 1790.

[Mrs. Elizabeth Bordley Gibson, *Biog. Sketches of the Bordley Family of Md.* (1865); the *Minutes of the Phila. Soc. for the Promotion of Agriculture, 1785–1810* (1854); Robt. Wilson, "Wye Island," in *Lippincott's Mag.*, Apr. 1877.] A. C. T.

BORÉ, JEAN ÉTIENNE (Dec. 27, 1741–Feb. 2, 1820), sugar planter, is generally credited with having established the sugar industry in Louisiana. The family belonged to the old Norman nobility and some of its members had risen high in the service of the French kings. One Michel de Boré had been a *conseiller de roi* as well as a postal official under Louis XIII, and Robert Louis de Boré, the great-grandfather of Étienne, had performed like services for Louis XIV. For some reason not explained, Étienne's father had turned from the life at court and had sought his fortunes in the far-off French possessions in America. There he married one Céleste Thérèse Carrière, and there his son was born. The stay in America, however, was short, and, at the age of four years, the boy was taken to France to be educated, and, when his age permitted, to take his place as a member of the *Mousquétaires du Roi,* the king's own household troops in which the private held the rank of captain. For ten years he remained in the service, then accepted the command of a company of cavalry, only to resign and turn his face westward toward the land of his birth,—prompted, no doubt, by his recent marriage to Marguerite Marie Destrehans, daughter of the former royal treasurer in Louisiana who had large possessions in that province. Establishing himself upon a plantation situated six miles above the city of New Orleans he shared the hopes and disappointments of the native planters in the search for a profitable staple and at length, like the others, turned his major attention to the cultivation of indigo. For a time all went well but in the early seventeen-nineties insects ravaged the crops with disheartening regularity and slaves used in the work sickened and died. In despair the planters were forced back into the old search for a staple ("Memoir of the Present State of Louisiana by Chevalier de Champigny," in B. F. French, *Historical Memoirs of Louisiana,* 1852, V, 145). Under such conditions Étienne Boré resolved upon a new attempt at the hitherto unsuccessful making of sugar. Purchasing cane from the planters Solis and Mendez, who raised it for syrup and tafia, he planted his fields, built a sugar house, and in 1795 was ready for a trial. Amid intense excitement the time for the strike was awaited, and the cry of the sugar maker, "It granulates," was carried far and wide as the announcement of a new day for the province. Louisiana had at last found a staple. From this time on Boré's fame and fortune expanded. Profits took the place of losses; his fields widened and his negroes, under semi-military discipline, grew in numbers and contentment. His great house with its moat and ramparts, reminiscent of old France, opened its doors with equal hospitality to the exiled brothers of Louis XVI or to the American generals who were serving with Andrew Jackson. Throughout the province he was honored and revered as the great benefactor of agriculture. When Louisiana was transferred from Spain to France in 1803 Boré was appointed mayor of the city of New Orleans and continued to serve on into the American period. He was then appointed a member of the first Legislative Council under the new government, but, consistent with his opposition to the form of government imposed, he refused to serve, and returned to his rural life. He died at the age of seventy-nine years, requesting that his funeral be conducted with the greatest simplicity, so that the money saved thereby might be given to the Charity Hospital of New Orleans. The wish was characteristic of the man.

[Chas. Gayarre, *Hist. of La.* (1854); Grace King, *Creole Families of New Orleans* (1921); *De Bow's Rev.*, XXII, 615–19; G. H. V. Collot, *Voyage Dans L'Amérique Septentrionale* (1826); obituary in *Courrier de la Louisiane,* Feb. 4, 1820.] A. O. C.

BOREMAN, ARTHUR INGRAM (July 24, 1823–Apr. 19, 1896), governor of West Virginia, senator, was the grandson of John Boreman, a native of Manchester, England, who became a merchant in Philadelphia and assistant paymaster of the Revolutionary army. John Boreman's son, Kenner Seaton Boreman, was a successful merchant in Waynesburg, Pa., and married Sarah Ingram by whom he had seven children, among them Arthur Ingram. The latter prepared for law by a course of reading and observation largely under the direction of his brother William, a distinguished lawyer and member of the Virginia legislature. He was admitted to the bar in 1845 and removed the following year to Parkersburg, where he became prominent in the practise of his profession. In

Borglum

1855–61 he represented Wood County in the Virginia House of Delegates, being a member of the famous extra session of 1861 which called a convention, without popular referendum, to consider the subject of secession. Boreman had opposed secession in all its phases and especially that by Virginia under the existing circumstances. When the Virginia convention voted to secede, Apr. 17, 1861, he became active in efforts to hold western Virginia in the Union. He was president of a convention that met in Wheeling, June 11, 1861, and reorganized the government of Virginia with a complete set of loyal officials, including United States Senators. Soon after he became a judge of a circuit court of the reorganized government, which office he held for two years. Meanwhile political events in western Virginia moved rapidly. The reorganized government consented to the dismemberment of Virginia, and West Virginia was admitted to the Union. Officers of the former moved to Alexandria, giving place to those of the new state, among them Boreman, the unanimous choice for governor. He was reëlected in 1864 and again in 1866, but before his third term expired, he resigned to accept a seat in the United States Senate, which he occupied from Mar. 4, 1869, to Mar. 4, 1875. In the Senate he served with ability as a member of the committees on Manufactures and Claims and as chairman, in turn, of the committee on Political Disabilities and Territories. The national political upheavals of the seventies carried West Virginia into the Democratic column and retired Boreman to private life. He resumed the practise of law, and devoted himself to home and church, having married in 1864 Mrs. Laurane Bullock, daughter of Dr. James Tanner of Wheeling. In 1888 he was reëlected to the judgeship which he filled years before and which he continued to hold until his death.

[G. W. Atkinson and A. F. Gibbons, *Prominent Men of W. Va.* (1890); T. C. Miller and H. Maxwell, *W. Va. and Its People*, vol. III (1913); *Jours. of W. Va. Leg.*, 1863–69; *Wheeling Daily Intelligencer*, Apr. 20, 1896.]

C. H. A.

BORGLUM, SOLON HANNIBAL (Dec. 22, 1868–Jan. 31, 1922), sculptor, fourth child of Dr. James de la Mothe Borglum and Ida (Michelson) Borglum, was born in Ogden, Utah. There were six sons and three daughters. The father and mother were Danes, who came to this country in the early sixties, settling for a time in Ogden. From them Solon derived many of the sturdy traits characteristic of the North Danish stock. His feeling for form and his instinct for anatomical structure were a two-fold inheritance from his father, who, arriving here as a wood-carver, later became a physician, practising at Fremont, Nebr. Since his work carried him far and wide into the country, Dr. Borglum had many horses, and these young Solon loved better than his school-books. The boy spent some not too happy years in the public schools of Fremont and Omaha, and in Creighton College, but at sixteen he was sent to western Nebraska as cowboy on his father's 6,000-acre ranch. Afterward, he took charge of a larger outfit. During many years of close, sympathetic watching of animals he developed an extraordinary sense of animal form and movement. His vision and memory were swift, fine, true. Often he spent his leisure jotting down on stray bits of paper his visual impressions of man and beast in action, in repose, in transition. His artist brother, Gutzon, returning from study abroad, was amazed by the vitality and truth of these rude sketches, and urged the ranchman to turn artist.

Solon, like his father before him, had the courage to make a complete change in his way of life. He was then twenty-six, and without any knowledge whatever of art as taught in schools. He joined his brother in the Sierra Madre mountains, studying under him for some months, passing then to Los Angeles, and later to Santa Ana, where he rented a so-called "studio" at two dollars a month. The confinement irked him. He therefore set on his door a sign, "In Studio Saturdays Only." The rest of the week he spent roaming the mountains, living among the lawless, meeting with the disinherited, and eating with the uncivilized,—Indians, half-breeds, white men, types noble or ignoble. Being spiritually-minded, he was strengthened, not coarsened, by contact with the wild free life he loved and studied. A sound instinct had told him that "Saturdays Only" would appeal to clients who might be indifferent to unrestricted privileges of visit. Promptly appeared a manly sitter, an Eastern school teacher, whose portrait he painted for five dollars. Acquaintance ripened into friendship, interest was aroused, other clients came. Ladies took lessons at a dollar apiece. Encouraged by friends, he exhibited his work, made sixty-five dollars, and with this, fortified by a railroad pass received from a brother, he went to Cincinnati to study at the Art Academy, joining both day and evening classes.

In his narrow rented room he knew the loneliness of cities. But not too far away were the United States Mail stables, lit all night, and these he frequented in the early morning hours, to study the horses. He learned from veterinaries, he worked at dissections. Experimenting in clay, he modeled a sketch of a horse pawing its dead mate, and showed it to Mr. Rebisso, director of sculpture at the Academy. Rebisso recognized the young man's gift, invited him to work in his (Rebisso's) own studio, and made it possible for him to go to Paris. At last, after obstacles that would have daunted a man of less intrepid mind, Borglum had found in sculpture his true lifework. "All this," writes Mrs. Borglum, "with no money, and at the cost of much suffering. At the Art School he won a scholarship so small that it was not expected to be used abroad; still, Solon went to Paris with it. A horse which he had modeled with Rebisso was cast, and copies were sold, mostly to students, thus giving him enough money for his steamer ticket. Later the school bought another horse, which allowed him to remain another year; they also prolonged the scholarship. Then Theodore B. Starr began taking up his work, and life became more easy."

Borglum's stay in Paris gave him larger advantages for special study and a wider horizon of general culture. At "l'Académie Julien" he studied six months under Denys Puech, then one of the new forces in French sculpture. Frémiet, veteran master of animal form, was his constant adviser, correcting the ardent young American's work out of his own inexhaustible lore. "Mon ami," said M. Frémiet, "you're lucky! You lived, you had something to say before you studied art." And Solon Borglum, wherever he went, had the advantage of a rare personal charm springing chiefly from native goodness, from his quick and abounding sympathy toward all life. To his first Salon he sent two spirited groups, both well received, especially his "Lassoing Wild Horses." The next year, 1899, he won honorable mention at the Salon, for his "Stampede of Wild Horses," and in 1900 a silver medal at the Paris Exposition. On Dec. 10, 1898, in Paris, he married Emma Vignal, daughter of a French Protestant clergyman. The couple spent the following summer in Crow Creek Reservation, among the Sioux Indians.

After one more year in Paris, they remained near New York, making at Silvermine, Conn., their studio home, Rocky Ranch. Here during a period of seventeen years Borglum's art found natural and varied expression in works ranging from busts to equestrians, from small bronzes such as the "Bulls Fighting" and the "Border of White Man's Land" in the Metropolitan Museum to the four large groups modeled for the St. Louis Exposition, 1904, and the "Pioneer Group," Court of Honor, San Francisco Exposition, 1915. Made a member of the National Sculpture Society in 1901, he received a silver medal at Buffalo, 1901, a gold medal at St. Louis, 1904, and a silver medal at Buenos Aires, 1910, becoming an associate member of the National Academy of Design the same year. His sculpture is impressionistic, deeply felt, soundly constructed. He is at his best in frontier themes such as "Burial on the Plains," "Pioneer in a Storm," "Snow Drift," "The Blizzard," "The Intelligent Bronco," "The Rough Rider," "Cowboy at Rest." Among his works are two fine equestrians, the "Bucky O'Neill," Prescott, Ariz., the "Gen. John B. Gordon," Atlanta, Ga. Other works of note are "Soldiers and Sailors Monument," Danbury, Conn., the "Hurley Monument," Topeka, Kan., the "Washington, 1753," owned in Canada, the austere "Schieren Memorial," Greenwood Cemetery.

"Solon never lost the spirit he put into a sketch," wrote Gutzon Borglum, justly extolling as a rare creative gift the power to retain in a long-considered heroic group all the vitality and charm of the first swift rendering. Nor was Solon Borglum one of those sculptors whose labors end with the completion of a clay model turned over to the practitioners. He could, and when advisable did, carve in marble and in wood, with a hand not enfeebled by super-civilization. A photograph which shows him carving his marble group, the "Command of God," indicates well this sculptor's aspect; his frame, not tall, but powerful, his intellectual head, his eager, friendly countenance.

On the entrance of the United States into the World War, Borglum, by reason of age refused as a soldier, went to France with the "Y." His service abroad was of indomitable heroism. Frequently under fire, escaping when a shell blew up his canteen, gassed twice, continuing in the saddle before complete recovery, he won the hearts of the French officers with whom he worked shoulder to shoulder in the Foyer du Soldat. "He was the first American to enter Rheims when the German Army fell back," declared Raymond V. Ingersoll in a personal tribute (*New York Times,* Feb. 13, 1922). "He and a French co-worker were there with a small donkey to carry the materials for hot drinks." The citation for his Croix de Guerre honors him for what the French commandant calls his *"âme d'apôtre."* George S. Hellman, Lloyd Warren, and Ernest Peixotto (*Sun,* New York, Feb. 19, 1922) laud his work as director of sculpture at the A. E. F. art training center at Bellevue.

After his return home, he founded a school of sculpture based on principles set forth in his *Sound Construction* (copyright 1923), a book of six hundred drawings, the fruit of his life's observations in comparative anatomy, and in the basic forms of all nature as seen in all great art.

He was an inspiring teacher of fundamental truths. One of his last works of sculpture is the "Little Lady of the Dew," a kneeling figure in marble. Here, as in his two standing figures of the same period, "Aspiration" and "Inspiration," the ideal theme is a departure from his usual choice. It would seem that a new chapter in his artistic life was opening when he died, a few days after an operation for acute appendicitis.

The main body of his work, depicting as it does a vanishing phase in American life, has a unique historic value. More than any other of our artists, he himself was part of all he tells. His frontier groups form an epic,—an epic sculptured in free verse. They reveal clearly their open-air origin; often they are enveloped in the elements (see the "Burial on the Plains," the "Mare and Foal in a Snow Drift"). Subtleties of modeling, academic nobility in composition, the grand style of past ages, were outside Borglum's purposes and powers. His passion in sculpture was to impart the very essence of things seen and felt; hence, and not because of Rodin's influence, he became a master of elimination. Surely no man knew better than he every strap and buckle horse or rider might wear; but he was an artist and not a harness-maker in shaping his bronze and marble tales. In its own large, unacademic way, his sculpture has saved for our contemplation certain swiftly-passing moments in the march of American frontier life.

[Chas. H. Caffin, *Am. Masters of Sculpture* (1903); Lorado Taft, *Hist. of Am. Sculpture* (1903); Arthur Goodrich, "The Frontier in Sculpture," *World's Work*, III, 1857; Louise Eberle, "In Recognition of an American Sculptor," *Scribner's Mag.*, Sept. 1922; Gutzon Borglum, letter in *N. Y. Times*, Mar. 5, 1922, reprinted, with illustrations, in the *Am. Mag. of Art*, Nov. 1922.]

A. A—s.

BORIE, ADOLPH EDWARD (Nov. 25, 1809–Feb. 5, 1880), merchant, financier, was the eldest of the twelve children of John Joseph Borie, a Frenchman who established himself early in the nineteenth century as a merchant and manufacturer at Philadelphia and of Sophia Beauveau, a refugee from Haiti. He graduated from the University of Pennsylvania in 1825, and studied and traveled in Europe. In 1839 he married Elizabeth Dundas McKean. Upon his return from Europe in 1828, he entered his father's mercantile business. His firm carried on trade with Mexico, the West Indies, and the Far East, engaging particularly in the silk and tea trade. His mercantile career extended over a period of about thirty years, during the epoch of the clipper ships, when Philadelphia's foreign trade was in its prime. The magnitude of his operations is indicated by his complaints of property damages amounting to $100,000 in China during the disturbances of 1857–58. He was a pioneer in seeking the diplomatic and naval support of the government for safeguarding his interests abroad. Gradually he became interested in financial and railroad enterprises, serving from 1848 to 1860 as president of the Bank of Commerce, and becoming director in several leading business institutions of Philadelphia. Before the Civil War, his connection with political affairs was slight. In 1843 he was consul to Belgium. He was a champion of Whig policies, particularly protection. He supported Lincoln in 1860, and upon the outbreak of the Civil War became an ardent Unionist. His activities in this connection were mainly as an organizer and vice-president of the Union League, which assumed national importance because of its influence in promoting similar organizations in other cities. He was the moving spirit in the recruiting and equipping of a number of regiments, as well as in promoting Unionist sentiment. His war-time acquaintance with Gen. Grant developed into an intimacy, and led to the appointment of Borie in 1869 as secretary of the navy. With no experience and little interest in public life, with varied business connections and fragile health, his tenure of office was largely nominal, and he resigned June 25 of the same year. According to one of his colleagues in the cabinet, "he often said, 'The department is managed by Admiral Porter, I am only a figure head'" (G. S. Boutwell, *Reminiscences of Sixty Years in Public Affairs*, 1902, II, 212). He held no other important public office.

Borie was a noted patron of art and learning. His collection of paintings received considerable recognition (*Lippincott's Magazine*, X, 221–26). His philanthropies were varied and extensive. His continued intimacy with Grant resulted in his being invited to join the Ex-President's party which toured the world in 1878–79. Shortly before the conclusion of the tour his age and ill health caused him to withdraw from the party, and early the next year he died in the city of his birth.

[Obituaries were published in the *Press*, the *Inquirer*, the *Public Ledger*, the *Bulletin*, and other Philadelphia journals, and in some other newspapers, notably the *N. Y. Times* of Feb. 6, 1880. An extensive biographical sketch of Borie's family by F. W. Leach appeared in the *North American* (Phila.), Jan. 5, 1913. The record of his connection with the Union League is available in *Chronicle of the Union League* (1902), and in the archives of the League's Library. For anecdotal accounts and reflections, see J. R. Young, *Around the World with Gen. Grant* (1879). Some of his correspondence is preserved in the manuscript collections of the Pa. Hist. Soc.]

W. B—n.

BORLAND, SOLON (Sept. 21, 1808–Jan. 1 or 31, 1864), senator, diplomat, Confederate soldier, was born near Suffolk, Va., received an elementary education in North Carolina, studied medicine, and then located in Little Rock, Ark. When the Mexican War opened he volunteered and served until the capture of the City of Mexico. On Apr. 24, 1848, he took his seat in the United States Senate by appointment in the room of A. H. Sevier, resigned. Later he was elected for the regular term beginning in 1849. At first he seems to have played no conspicuous part in the proceedings of the Senate, taking very little part in the debate on such important matters as the compromise measures of 1850, but later he took considerable interest in foreign affairs. On Apr. 3, 1853, he resigned from the Senate and fifteen days later was appointed minister to Nicaragua and the other Central American states, vice John Slidell, declined. By this act Honduras was recognized as an independent state (J. B. Moore, *Digest of International Law,* 1898, I, 92). Borland entered upon his official duties on Sept. 14, 1853. In a little over six months he started home, coming to Punta Arenas on the Accessory Transit Company's steamer *Routh.* At this time the Transit Company (Cornelius Vanderbilt) was engaged in a controversy with the authorities at Greytown. While Borland was waiting for transportation home the authorities of Greytown came to arrest Capt. Smith, of the *Routh,* on the charge of having murdered a native boatman, but Borland told them that the United States did not recognize their right to arrest an American citizen and ordered them to leave. This produced great excitement and later in the day, when he went to visit the American consul, a crowd attempted to arrest him. In the fracas some one threw a broken bottle and struck him in the face. On reaching Washington Borland reported the matter to President Pierce, who sent the U. S. S. *Cyane,* Capt. Hollis, to the scene of trouble. The captain demanded $24,000 damages for the Transit Company and an apology for the indignity to our minister. Satisfaction not being forthcoming he completely destroyed the town next day (July 13, 1854) by bombardment and fire, although there had been a complete change in the city government and the offenders could not be found. His actions met with protest from Great Britain, but were approved by President Pierce (Moore, II, 414–416; VII, 112–14; W. O. Scroggs, *Filibusters and Financiers,* 1916, pp. 75–76). On July 13, Borland was offered the governorship of New Mexico, but declined and resumed his practise in Little Rock. While the secession convention was in session, but before it took final action, Borland raised a company of militia and with the approval of Gov. Rector proceeded by steamer to Fort Smith to demand the surrender of the fort, but Capt. S. D. Sturgis learned of his approach and abandoned the fort shortly before his arrival. Borland raised the Third Arkansas Cavalry, of which he was made colonel. He participated in several battles east of the Mississippi River and was involved in the disaster at Port Hudson. He rose to the rank of brigadier-general, but was forced to give up service on account of his health and died in or near Houston, Tex. He was thrice married: to Mrs. Huldah Wright of Suffolk, who bore him two sons; to Mrs. Hunt of Tennessee, no issue; and to Mary J. Melbourne of Little Rock, who bore him one son (died in 1862) and two daughters.

[In addition to references above, see Fay Hempstead, *A Pictorial Hist. of Ark.* (1898).] D.Y.T.

BOSS, LEWIS (Oct. 26, 1846–Oct. 5, 1912), astronomer, was born in Providence, R. I., the son of Samuel P. and Lucinda (Joslin) Boss. He studied at Dartmouth, graduating in 1870 with the A.B. degree. After graduation he held a position in the government Land Office and was often at the Naval Observatory. In 1871 he was married to Helen Hutchinson of Washington. From 1872 to 1876 he was assistant astronomer with the survey party of the United States-Canada boundary. The need of more precise places of stars for his latitude work led him, during his evenings in camp, to an investigation of the systematic errors of star catalogues; to a discussion of instrumental errors and methods of reduction; and finally to the construction of a new homogeneous declination system. The discussion of nearly one hundred star catalogues, which this involved, showed clearly the attention to detail and the critical handling of observational material which made him the foremost American authority on star positions. It told severely upon his health and eyesight and the resulting catalogue of five hundred standard stars was not completed until after his appointment in 1876 as director of the Dudley Observatory in Albany (Lewis Boss, *Report on the Declination of the Stars Employed in Latitude Work with the Zenith Telescope . . . and a Catalogue of Five Hundred Stars for the Mean Epoch 1875,* 1878). The catalogue finished, he undertook the observation of one of the zones of the Astronomische Gesellschaft program of star positions on which another observatory had defaulted. He made all the observations himself and minutely investigated the graduation errors and his magnitude equation. Begun ten years after some of the other zones were started, his zone was the first completed for publication. The catalogue also contained the proper motions of the stars, compiled from a comparison with older catalogues, and a valuable discussion of the sun's motion. Boss observed the solar eclipse of 1878, and in 1882 was chief of a government expedition to Chile to observe the transit of Venus. Later he became the editor and manager of an Albany newspaper, and entered actively into civic matters and into the presidential campaign of 1884. He was state superintendent of weights and measures of New York from 1883 to 1906. Meanwhile he was maturing his plans for a great catalogue to contain standard positions and proper motions of about twenty-six thousand stars, involving re-observation with a single instrument and a critical discussion of all catalogue positions. Observations were begun at Albany and carried nearly to completion for the northern stars, while the arduous labor of reduction and discussion went on. A grant from the Carnegie Institution in 1904 made it possible for Boss to secure much needed clerical aid, and to transfer the meridian circle to Chile for the observation of the southern stars. This monumental work is being carried to completion under the direction of his son, Benjamin Boss. *The Preliminary General Catalogue of 6188 Stars for the Epoch 1900* was published by Lewis Boss in 1910 as Carnegie Institution of Washington Publication No. 115. In discussing the proper motions of these stars, he detected the community of motion of the Taurus cluster and thus opened the way to a powerful method of measuring distance; he made a determination of precession and of the sun's motion; he studied the average proper motions of stars of various spectral types and the average motion of stars in various galactic latitudes.

[Benj. Boss in *Nat. Acad. of Sci. Biog. Memoirs,* vol. IX (1920); R. H. Tucker in *Astron. Nachrichten,* CXCIII, 29–32; *Pubs. Astron. Soc. of the Pacific,* XXIV, 256–60, and *Pop. Astron.,* Nov. 1922; *Astron. Jour.,* Nov. 13, 1912; *Jour. Brit. Astron. Ass.,* Oct. 1912.] R. S. D.

BOSWORTH, EDWARD INCREASE (Jan. 10, 1861–July 1, 1927), Congregational clergyman, educator, the son of Franklin S. and Sarah (Hunt) Bosworth, was born in Elgin, Ill. The first ancestor in this country on his father's side was Benjamin Bosworth, a major in the Revolutionary War. Edward Bosworth was a student at Oberlin College, 1879–1881, but graduated at Yale in 1883. In the same year he returned to Oberlin to enter the Theological Seminary, on graduating from which in 1886 he was ordained to the Congregational ministry and served for a year as pastor of the Mt. Vernon Congregational Church. He was then elected professor of English Bible in the Oberlin Theological Seminary (1887), a title changed to professor of New Testament Language and Literature in 1892. He was the dean of the Seminary, 1903–23, and acting president of the College in the difficult war year, 1918–19. His career was diversified by several years abroad: he was a student in the University of Leipzig, 1890–91; spent the winter of 1891–92 in Athens; lectured in Japan in 1907, in Turkey in 1911, and in Athens in 1927. He was married to Bertha McClure of Elgin, Ill., on Oct. 1, 1891.

It was the influence which Dr. Bosworth exerted upon Oberlin College and through it upon the religious life of his time that imparts to his career its larger significance. Working in closest harmony with his life-long friend, President King, he shaped the ideals and determined the fortunes of Oberlin for almost half a century. Under these two men the institution rapidly and healthfully expanded into one of the strongest colleges in the country. Dr. Bosworth was a sound and accurate scholar, but his real power lay in the classroom. He had that best gift of a teacher, the ability at once to stir curiosity and to check undisciplined speculation. His life-work fell at a time of transition in theological thinking and when the process of secularization and materialization in our colleges was going on at a rapid rate. His own religion was intellectually well fortified, salted with shrewd common sense, but in its essence mystical. He became one of the chief influences which enabled Oberlin College to effect a change from the older to the more modern points of view in theology without loss of a vital interest in religion. His books which have had a world-wide circulation have contributed to the same end. Among them are: *Studies in the Acts and Epistles* (1898); *Studies in the Teachings of Jesus and His Apostles* (1901); *Studies in the Life of Jesus Christ* (1904); *New Studies in Acts* (1908); *Christ in Everyday Life* (1910); *Thirty Studies about Jesus* (1917); *Commentary on Romans* (1919); *What It Means to Be a Christian* (1922); *The Life and Teaching of Jesus* (1924).

[*Who's Who in America,* 1926–27; *Oberlin Alumni Mag.,* July, Oct., 1927; personal recollections.] K. F.

BOSWORTH, FRANCKE HUNTINGTON (Jan. 25, 1843–Oct. 17, 1925), laryngologist, the son of Daniel P. Bosworth, merchant, and Deborah Wells, both of New England ancestry for many generations, was born in Marietta, Ohio. His primary education was received in the schools of his native town and from 1858 to 1860 he attended Marietta College. In 1860 he entered the junior class at Yale, graduating in 1862. During the Civil War he was in active service in West Virginia under Gen. Rosecrans and was also sent to the Peninsula where he joined in opposing the raids of Gen. Morgan. After the war he settled in New York and graduated in 1868 from Bellevue Hospital and Medical College as valedictorian of his class. In 1873, after his internship at Bellevue, he was appointed lecturer on diseases of the upper air tract and in 1881 was made full professor, a position which he retained after Bellevue became united with New York University and until his final retirement from active work. He issued a *Handbook upon Diseases of the Throat for the Use of Students* (1879), and in 1881 he published the first edition of his celebrated *Manual of the Diseases of the Throat and Nose*. In 1878 J. Solis-Cohen [*q.v.*] of Philadelphia had published his monograph on laryngology, and later Sir Morell MacKenzie issued another work on the same subject (1882). The contributions of these three men may be said to have created the science of laryngology. Bosworth's most extensive work, *A Treatise on Diseases of the Nose and Throat,* appeared in two volumes in 1889 and 1892 and it is to be noted that during his ten years of active practise he changed his emphasis from the throat to the nose by reversing their order in the title of his later publication. His shorter text-book of the *Diseases of the Nose and Throat* was brought out in 1896 and enjoyed great popularity for nearly a generation. Bosworth wrote easily and his text-books and scientific papers were always eagerly awaited by those engaged in his specialty. He presented original ideas and was responsible for many contributions to the physiology and the pathology of the sinuses and nasal obstruction. Soon after the introduction of cocaine he devised a nasal saw by means of which septal spurs and other obstructions could be readily removed. His studies were promptly recognized in this country and abroad, and in consequence he was elected honorary fellow of the British, French, and German Laryngological Societies. He was also one of the founders (1873) of the New York Laryngological Society. It has been well said that Bosworth "more than anyone who had gone before, gathered the disjointed and scattered fragments of laryngological knowledge, developed the science of rhinology and, welding all into a perfectly coördinated form, established them as definite and distinguished departments of medical science." He was a man of wide interests and literary tastes. He was well known among dramatists and actors of note and was fond of horses and racing. For many years he studied art and acquired more than an amateur's knowledge of painting. On Sept. 12, 1871, he married Mary Hildreth Putnam, and two children survived their father: a son, F. H. Bosworth, Jr., dean of the School of Architecture at Cornell, and a daughter, wife of Hon. Walter R. Herrick of New York.

[*The Twenty Years' Record of the Yale Class of 1862* (1884); *Yale Univ. Obit. Record of Grads. Deceased during the Year Ending July 1, 1926;* Dr. D. Bryson Delavan, obituaries in the *Medic. Jour. and Record,* 1926, CXXIII, 125–126 (with portrait), and in the *Laryngoscope,* 1925, XXXV, 950–60; obituary in the *N. Y. Herald Tribune,* Oct. 18, 1925.] J. F. F.

BOTELER, ALEXANDER ROBINSON (May 16, 1815–May 8, 1892), congressman, Confederate soldier, was the son of Dr. Henry Boteler, a graduate of Dr. Rush's medical school, Philadelphia, and of Priscilla (Robinson) Boteler, whose father was a successful Baltimore ship owner and merchant and whose mother was a daughter of the artist Charles William Peale. Boteler's mother having died when he was four years old, he lived with his grandmother in Baltimore. At eighteen he entered Princeton and roomed with the poet-novelist Philip Pendleton Cooke [*q.v.*]. Graduating in 1835, in the following year he married Helen Macomb Stockton of Princeton and they went to live at his father's estate, "Fountain Rock," in Shepherdstown, Va. (now W. Va.). In addition to his agricultural interests Boteler entered politics, as a Whig, and as a presidential elector voted for Winfield Scott in 1852. In 1859 he was elected to the United States House of Representatives, succeeding Charles J. Faulkner who was appointed minister to France. During the sectional struggle in Congress, in 1860, Boteler sought to avoid disunion and secured the passage of a resolution creating a committee of one from each state to consider the "perilous condition of the country" (*Congressional Globe,* 36 Cong., 2 Sess., p. 6). He made an appeal for the Union so effectively that a fellow member, S. S. Cox, considered it "the most eloquent speech, next to that of Sergeant S. S. Prentiss in his own case, ever delivered in Congress" (see S. S. Cox, *Union-Disunion-Reunion, Three Decades of Federal Legislation,* 1885, p. 93; *Congressional Globe,* 36 Cong., 1 Sess., p. 583.) With Virginia's passage of the secession resolution Boteler left Congress and was elected to the General Assembly of Virginia; but in the meantime his district elected him as its delegate to the Confederate Provisional Congress, which he entered on Nov. 27, 1861. He was also a member of the first Confederate Congress, presenting a design for the flag and being influential in the selection of the seal. In the summer of 1862 he was serving as volunteer aide on the staff of his friend, Stonewall Jackson, who upon more than one occasion appealed, through Boteler, to the Congress.

After Jackson's death, he became aide to J. E. B. Stuart (*Official Records,* ser. IV, vol. II, p. 718). Later he was aide to Governors Smith and Letcher. He was West Virginia's commissioner at the Philadelphia Exposition 1871–76; he was appointed by Arthur as a member of the Tariff Commission in 1881; he was assistant attorney in the United States Department of Justice in 1882 and 1883; he was clerk of pardons in the same department, 1884–89.

Boteler was the author of a number of pamphlets and articles. His description of John Brown's Raid (which occurred near his home and to part of which he was an eye-witness) appeared in the *Century Magazine,* July 1883. He wrote "My Ride to a Barbecue," and presented in writing the claims of James Rumsey as the inventor of the steamboat. He probably had much to do with the placing of the memorial to Rumsey on the Potomac near Shepherdstown. He was also an artist. In 1887 the Military Historical Society of Massachusetts purchased "The Boteler Collection" composed of oil sketches of Robert E. Lee, Longstreet, Jefferson Davis, Wade Hampton, Pickett, and John H. Morgan, and a pencil sketch of John Brown.

[A sketch of Col. Boteler's life was written by his grand-daughter, Miss Helen B. Pendleton, for the *Shepherdstown Register,* Aug. 14, 1924. References to the friendship of Stonewall Jackson and Boteler are found in R. L. Dabney, *Life and Campaigns of Lieutenant-General Thos. J. Jackson* (1866), John Esten Cooke, *Stonewall Jackson* (1863) and H. A. White, *Stonewall Jackson* (1909). His legislative career can be followed in the *Cong. Globe,* 36 Cong., and in the "Jours. of the Cong. of the Confederate States," *Senate Doc. No. 234,* 58 Cong., 2 Sess.] E. L. F.

BOTETOURT, NORBORNE BERKELEY, Baron de (*c.* 1718–Oct. 15, 1770), colonial governor of Virginia, was sprung from the family which, in Sir William Berkeley, had already furnished the colony of Virginia with one governor. He was the son of John Symes Berkeley. It was not until 1764 that he acquired his title. He had already served as colonel of the Gloucestershire militia and as a member of Parliament. He was appointed governor of Virginia in 1768, and unlike his predecessors subsequent to Howard, he went out to the colony in person, instead of sending a deputy to perform his duties. He brought over with him, for gala occasions, a resplendent coach and a team of cream-white Hanoverian horses, a present to him from the Duke of Cumberland (*William and Mary College Quarterly Magazine,* XIII, 87). Disembarking at Hampton, he journeyed to Williamsburg overland, and was received on its outskirts by a concourse of citizens; the town at night was illuminated; and a grand banquet in his honor was given. A eulogistic ode was also composed and published in the *Gazette.*

Botetourt promptly summoned the General Assembly, and, dressed in a light red coat, decorated with gold braiding, drove to the Capitol in his glittering coach, drawn by his Hanoverian horses in their silver mounted harness,—the whole a counterpart of King George's equipage at the opening of Parliament. And it was also observed that the Governor, in delivering the address, imitated the mannerisms of his royal master when reading his speech from the throne. But the burgesses were not so awed by all this state as to refrain from passing resolutions upholding the colonists' rights, which had recently been grossly violated by the transportation of Americans oversea to be tried by English juries. So frankly did they express themselves that Botetourt summoned them to the council chamber, and having rebuked them for their boldness, dissolved them as a body. But most of the burgesses reassembled in the Raleigh Tavern, and adopted a resolution, offered by Washington, but really drafted by Mason, that they would neither import nor buy any article that was subject to a parliamentary tax. When the general tax was repealed by Parliament, the tax on tea was retained. The merchants of the colony, in concert with the burgesses, at a meeting at Williamsburg formed an association which bound its members to purchase no tea, no British manufactures, and no slaves, imported into the colony in British vessels, until all the regulations subjecting colonial imports to a tax had been revoked. It is said that Botetourt was so much mortified by his inability to restore good feeling between the colony and the mother country, after these causes of difference arose, that he sank into a fever and died. The people of Virginia made allowance for the difficulties of his position, and remembered only his good intentions in their favor. His administration was, on the whole, so beneficent that, after his death, a marble statue was erected in his honor. This still stands in the quadrangle of the College of William and Mary.

[L. G. Tyler, *Williamsburg the Old Capital* (1907); Indices of *Brit. Col. Papers,* 1768–70; *Minutes of Virginia Council* and *Minutes of House of Burgesses,* 1768–70.] P. A. B.

BOTSFORD, GEORGE WILLIS (May 9, 1862–Dec. 13, 1917), historian, was descended from Henry and Elizabeth Botsford who came from Leicestershire, England, and settled in Milford, Conn., in 1636. He was the son of William Hiram and Margaret (Johnson) Botsford, who were living in West Union, Ia., when he was born. He received his early education in public schools and was graduated as bachelor of arts at the University of Nebraska in 1884. The same university conferred upon him the degree of A.M. in 1889. After a short period of teaching and a brief sojourn at Johns Hopkins University he entered Cornell University as a graduate student, where he attained the degree of Ph.D. in 1891. Meanwhile he had been professor of Greek at Kalamazoo College, 1886–90. He married Lillie M. Shaw, of Kalamazoo, Mich., Aug. 30, 1891. He was professor of Greek in Bethany College, 1891–95; then was appointed instructor in the history of Greece and Rome at Harvard University, where he remained six years, until 1901. He was appointed lecturer on ancient history at Columbia University in 1902, instructor in 1903, adjunct professor in 1905, and professor in 1910, and was thus one of the few professors of ancient history in the United States. In the year 1909–10, and again in 1913, he was engaged in historical research in Italy. He was a member of the American Philological Association and the American Historical Association and at the time of his death was a member of the board of editors of the *Political Science Quarterly.*

Botsford was a scholar of unusual ability, extraordinary industry, and great singleness of purpose. His original contributions to historical knowledge were made, for the most part, in articles published in periodicals, but his books, even when they were designed primarily as textbooks for schools, not only contained the generally known and accepted facts, but also embodied the results of serious original research. The titles of his books are as follows: *The Development of the Athenian Constitution* (1893); *A History of Greece for High Schools and Academies* (1899); *A History of Rome for High Schools and Academies* (1901); *An Ancient History* (1902); *The Story of Rome as Greeks and Romans tell it* (1903; with Lillie S. Botsford; an elementary source-book); *Ancient History for Beginners* (1904); *The Roman Assemblies* (1909); *History of the Ancient World* (1911); *A Source-book of Ancient History* (1912; with Lillie S. Botsford); *Hellenic Civilization* (1915; with E. G. Sihler); and, published after his death, *Hellenic History* (1922). Most of these books have been widely used in schools and colleges, and the reputation of their author is deservedly great.

Botsford was powerfully built and perhaps of somewhat less than the average height. Apart from the intellectual quality of his face, there was nothing especially striking in his appearance. He was rather shy and not greatly interested in general society. Indeed he was so devoted to his work as to be almost a recluse. He was very highly esteemed and admired by his colleagues on account of his scholarly achievements, but had comparatively little social intercourse with them. On the last day of his life he came from his home at Mt. Vernon to take up his appointed work at the University, and immediately upon his arrival complained of feeling unwell. He was escorted to his study where, before a physician could reach him, he died of acute indigestion. Death came upon him in the midst of his activity as a teacher and while his capacity for productive scholarship was at its height.

[*Who's Who in America,* 1916–17, and *Who's Who in New York,* 1918; obituaries in N. Y. papers, Dec. 14, 1917.] H. N. F.

BOTTA, ANNE CHARLOTTE LYNCH (Nov. 11, 1815–Mar. 23, 1891), author, hostess to literati of New York, was the daughter of Patrick Lynch, who, having been imprisoned in England for taking part in the Irish Rebellion of 1798, refused allegiance to the British Government, and, in the first decade of the nineteenth century, came, an exile, to America. In Bennington, Vt., he carried on a dry-goods business, and married, in 1812, Charlotte Gray, daughter of Lieut.-Col. Gray, an officer in the Revolution. Anne Charlotte Lynch inherited from her father, who died when she was not yet four, an ardent, poetic temperament and keen perceptions; from her mother, energy and good judgment. What success she had in her career she attributed to learning early her own limitations. Diligent in her studies and artistic in her tastes, she found her power to do creative work less than her ability to stimulate others. People, she confessed, were the main passion of her life. As soon as she was able to make a home for her mother, after graduating from the Albany Female Academy in 1834, teaching for a time there and in a private family on Shelter Island, N. Y., she settled in Providence, R. I. Here, in her own household, she continued to educate young women, and her home became a gathering-place for the more cultured people of the community. After the year 1845, when Miss Lynch moved to New York, taking a position as teacher of English composition in the Brooklyn Academy for Women, her home in Waverley Place was a center for the most brilliant intellectual and artistic life of the city. Her personal charm, intuitive sympathies, and skill at repartee attracted to her modest drawing rooms, among others, Bryant, Horace Greeley, Margaret Fuller, Willis, and Poe; and hither came Bayard Taylor and R. H. Stoddard for their introduction to the literati of New York. In 1851 Miss Lynch spent a season in Washington while occupied in seeking through Congress delayed payment for her grandfather's military services. The paying of this debt by the Government brought easier circumstances to her and to her mother; and during 1853 she traveled abroad, giving some time to the study of art, particularly sculpture. In 1855 she married Prof. Vincenzo Botta [*q.v.*]. Guests from home and abroad were entertained at their residence at 25 West Thirty-seventh St., which Emerson called "the house of the expanding doors."

Anne C. Lynch Botta's literary work was for the most part poetic, elevated in theme, simple and direct in style, as in the sonnets, "The Ideal," "The Ideal Found," and "Vita Nuova." Her personal charm is more evident, perhaps, in occasional verse, such as "To Juliette's Twins." During her residence in Providence and later she contributed poetry to various magazines, particularly to the *Democratic Review*. Her collected poems, first published in 1849, went through three editions, but it could hardly be said that Mrs. Botta stood out with distinction from the host of sister poets composing verse in the same period. In 1860, however, she published *A Handbook of Universal Literature,* which has gone through many editions, and was a notable achievement for a woman of her time. She was modest in character, devoted to family and friends, and, according to Willis, "equally beloved of man and woman" (*Memoirs of Anne C. L. Botta,* p. 321). Slender, with dark hair and eyes, she bore herself with a certain grace and freedom of movement in harmony with a spirit of perpetual youth. A hostess, presiding with tact and simplicity over the first important salon in the history of American letters, she is a figure to be remembered in the social and literary life of the mid-nineteenth century.

[The chief source of information is *Memoirs of Anne C. L. Botta with Selections from her Correspondence and from her Writings in Prose and Poetry,* ed. by Vincenzo Botta (1893). A description of Mrs. Botta's salon may be found in Hervey Allen, *Israfel, The Life and Times of Edgar Allan Poe* (1926), pp. 677–80, and an appraisal of her literary work in Poe's *Works,* ed. by Stedman and Woodberry (1894–96), VIII, 124–26. Obituaries appeared in the *N. Y. Times* and *N. Y. Tribune,* Mar. 24, 1891.] M. A. W.

BOTTA, VINCENZO (Nov. 11, 1818–Oct. 5, 1894), scholar, was born at Cavallermaggiore, Piedmont, Italy. Destined for the Church, he gave up all thought of the priesthood shortly after he entered upon his ecclesiastical studies. Graduating from the University of Turin, he taught philosophy at his *Alma Mater,* at Cuneo, and then at Turin. From this university he received the degree of doctor of philosophy. In 1849 he was elected to the Sardinian Parliament where he rendered important service in the cause of Italian unity. In conjunction with Dr. Parola he was appointed in 1850 by the government to examine into the educational system of Germany. His report was printed by the State. In 1853 he came to the United States to study our public school methods and was so attracted by the country and the opportunities offered here that he settled in New York City and became a naturalized citizen. He was called to teach Italian language and literature in the University of the City of New York, a position he held until a few years before his death. In 1855 he was married to Miss Anne C. Lynch, brilliant daughter of an Irish exile. Possessing ample means they entertained generously and their "evenings" became widely known for the distinction and wit of the people assembled. During the Civil War Botta championed in the Italian press the cause of the Union. As 1865 approached when Italy and the world were to celebrate the six hundredth anniversary of the birth of Dante, he wrote as his contribution a book entitled *Dante as a Philosopher, Patriot and Poet* (1867), republished as *Introduction to the Study of Dante* (1886). The first portion of the volume is an excellent interpretation of the character and peculiar genius of the great Italian, and the latter part an analysis of the Divine Comedy, based upon Cary's translation. In 1871 Victor Emmanuel made Botta a Commander of the Order of the Crown of Italy, and in 1879 King Humbert sent him a gold medal struck in honor of his services to Italy in the United States. On the night of Oct. 3, 1894, in his seventy-sixth year, Botta fell from the window of his bedroom in the third story of his house and died two days after from his injuries. In his will he left his library and his own bust in marble to the University of the City of New York, and his works of art to the National Academy. His published works include *Public Instruction in Sardinia* (1858); *Discourse on the Life of Count Cavour* (1862); "An Historical Account of Modern Philosophy in Italy" in F. Ueberweg, *History of Philosophy* (1874); *Memoirs of Anne C. L. Botta* (1894).

[Obituaries at the time of Botta's death in the *N. Y. Tribune* and *N. Y. Times*; article by Ernest G. Sihler in *N. Y. Univ.* (1901).] C. A. D.

BOTTINEAU, PIERRE (*c.* 1817–July 26, 1895), Chippewa half-breed, has been called the Kit Carson of the Northwest. He was born about 1817 in the Red River country near Bear Point at the mouth of the Turtle River, the son of Joseph Bottineau, a fur-trader of French ancestry, and Clear Sky, a Chippewa woman. He early gained experience as a guide on overland expeditions in the north country. In the winter of 1837 he conducted three members of the abortive James Dickson filibuster from the Selkirk settlement to Fort Snelling, a hazardous trip in the course of which two members of the party perished in a blizzard. At Fort Snelling Bottineau was employed by Henry H. Sibley, agent of the American Fur Company. In 1841 he settled on a claim in what is now the heart of St. Paul; five years later he bought a tract of land near the Falls of St. Anthony, later a part of Minneapolis.

From 1850 to 1870 Bottineau guided many civil and military expeditions into the West. These trips took him to the Red River Valley, to the mining country of Montana, to the Frazer River in British Columbia, and to other regions. In 1853 he served as guide for the Pacific Railroad expedition of Gov. Stevens, leading the party across the prairies, then swarming with buffaloes, as far as Fort Benton; and sixteen years later he led the directors of the Northern Pacific on a re-survey of this route. In 1862 he guided the James L. Fisk expedition to the Montana mining country; and the next year he was a trusted scout on Gen. Sibley's military expedition to the Missouri River in pursuit of hostile Sioux. During an attack on Fort Abercrombie he slipped out through the Sioux lines as a messenger to secure aid for the fort.

Bottineau lived until 1895, a quarter of a century after he retired from the active life of the frontier, most of this time at Red Lake in northwestern Minnesota. In addition to French and English, he spoke Chippewa and Sioux and is said to have had some knowledge of Mandan, Winnebago, Cree, and other dialects. He knew the wilderness, was a straight shooter and skilled hunter, and won wide fame for his daring exploits. Gov. Stevens said that he surpassed "all his class in truthfulness and great intelligence," had the "broadness of view of an engineer," and was "the great guide and voyageur of Minnesota" (Hazard Stevens, *The Life of Isaac Ingalls Stevens,* 1900, I, 310).

[Information on Bottineau may be found in diaries and other accounts of the various expeditions which he accompanied, as, for example, Isaac I. Stevens, "Narrative and Final Report of Explorations for a Route for a Pacific Railroad," *House Ex. Docs., No. 56,* 36 Cong., 1 Sess.; the Martin McLeod Diary and the Samuel R. Bond Journal, in the manuscript division of the Minn. Hist. Soc.; and Daniel S. B. Johnston, "A Red River Townsite Speculation in 1857," in *Minn. Hist. Colls.,* XV, 411–34. An unpublished paper on Bottineau by Margareth Jorgensen is in the manuscript division of the Minn. Hist. Soc.]

T. C. B.

BOTTOME, MARGARET McDONALD (Dec. 29, 1827–Nov. 14, 1906), writer, organizer of the International Order of the King's Daughters and Sons, was the daughter of William and Mary (Willis) McDonald. Born in New York City, she spent her childhood in Brooklyn and was educated at Prof. Greenleaf's school, Brooklyn Heights. After her marriage to the Rev. Frank Bottome, a Methodist Episcopal clergyman, her interest in religious questions crystallized. For twenty-five years she gave informal talks on Bible subjects, and was an associate editor of the *Ladies' Home Journal.* Her most important work germinated from a gathering of nine women at her house on Jan. 13, 1886, met to talk over means of coöperation "for their own greater advancement in true Christian living and usefulness in practical good works." This small group became the nucleus of the King's Daughters, which subsequently added men to its membership and altered its name accordingly. Each of the original ten women organized another group and each member of each succeeding group did the same until in 1907 the membership was conservatively estimated at 500,000 in twenty-six states and five Canadian provinces. Men and boys were admitted in 1887, in 1889 the order was incorporated under the laws of New York state and in 1891 the term "International" was added to the name. For sixteen years the founder of the order conducted a department in the *Ladies' Home Journal* called "Mrs. Bottome's Heart to Heart Talks with the King's Daughters." The organization devoted itself chiefly to the development of character and training for Christian service. No sectarian lines were drawn. Groups of ten met to read and pray once a month. The work, which progressed quietly and without newspaper notice, included a variety of philanthropic undertakings, including work for the aged, for seamen, home and foreign missions, outings and vacations for women and children. Some notable institutions were established in the United States, among them the Frank Bottome Memorial Settlement in New York, the Day Nursery of Los Angeles, the National Junior Republic in Washington, D. C., the Gordon Rest for working women and girls in New England. University Extension work was done without a fee, professors and others giving their services. Mrs. Bottome herself was constantly writing for the *Silver Cross,* the monthly magazine of the order, which was first published in October 1888. In 1896 she was elected president of the Medical Missionary Society. She published *A Sunshine Trip: Glimpses of the Orient* in 1897, and from time to time other little books of a definite religious bent. *Heart to Heart Letters, being Extracts from the Letters of Margaret Bottome to a Son* (1909) was published after her death.

[*Who's Who in America,* 1906–07; "The Story of the King's Daughters," by Herbert O. McCrillis, *New Eng. Mag.,* Jan. 1907; *Silver Cross,* esp. Jan. 1907; obituaries in N. Y. papers, Nov. 15, 16, 1906.]
M. A. K.

BOTTS, CHARLES TYLER (1809–1884), editor, was born in Virginia (either at Dumfries or Fredericksburg) in the year 1809, the fourth son of Benjamin and Jane (Tyler) Botts. His father was a lawyer of some importance, being conspicuous in the trial of Aaron Burr, and had just moved to Richmond when both he and his wife perished in the great theatre fire of Dec. 26, 1811. Two of the sons thus left to the care of relatives were trained for the law, Charles Tyler and his older brother John Minor [*q.v.*], but both early abandoned it for the pursuit of agriculture. The older brother became a gentleman farmer mainly interested in politics, while Charles Tyler was more practical and cast his lot with that group who were struggling to restore "the exhausted fields of old Virginia." He took an active part in the work of the Henrico County agricultural society and showed a keen understanding of the problems faced. His interests were ever practical and the invention of an improved straw-cutting machine indicates the trend of his efforts (*American Agriculturist,* III, 309; *Cultivator,* X, 93). In 1841 he decided to establish a journal to help forward the new agriculture. Virginia's first agricultural paper, the *Virginia Planter,* had long ago ceased to exist and Edmund Ruffin's *Farmer's Register,* by refusing to accept advertising, had kept its price beyond the reach of common men. Botts now proposed "a plan . . . of publishing an agricultural paper at so small a price as to bring it within the reach of all . . . " and to present his materials "in simple and condensed style" which all could understand. The *Southern Planter* was a success from the beginning. Its suggestions, like its editor, were practical. Crop rotation and diversification, improved stock, the use of better machinery, together with the application of manure and other fertilizers, were advocated in and out of season. So sound were its policies that it alone of all the papers established in this period has survived, to boast to-day of being "the oldest agricultural journal in America."

In December 1846 Botts sold his paper to P. D. Bernard, remaining for a period as a contributor, but in 1848 catching the California fever and going to Monterey as keeper of United States naval stores. He soon drifted to the mines and, after experiencing the lawless interregnum, was sent to the constitutional convention of 1849. Here he took a prominent part, opposing Gwinn, King, and others in their effort to extend the boundaries of California to include all the lands acquired from Mexico in an attempt to solve the entire question of slavery extension. To Botts this was but to entangle California's affairs with an insolvable national problem and thus destroy the hope of permanent local government. His wisdom is apparent to-day. Failing by one vote of being elected attorney-general in 1849, he became a member of a San Francisco law firm and in the years following was conspicuous in many important cases in the new state. He served as judge for a time in the Sacramento district and then returned to editorial work as publisher of the *Standard* at Sacramento. In 1861 he was appointed state printer. After the Civil War he returned to the South but was soon back in California practising law. His last years were spent in Oakland where he died in 1884. He was married to Margaret Marshal of Fredericksburg, Va.

[*Southern Planter,* Richmond, Va., 1841–46; Geo. A. Goode, *Va. Cousins* (1887); *Tyler's Quart. Hist. Mag.,* V, 252; H. W. Bancroft, *Works,* XIX, 725–26; XXIII, 271, 288; T. H. Hittell, *Hist. of Cal.,* II (1885), 769, 771, 789, 811.]
A. O. C.

BOTTS, JOHN MINOR (Sept. 16, 1802–Jan. 7, 1869), congressman, lawyer, author, the son of Jane (Tyler) Botts and Benjamin A. Botts, well-known Virginia lawyer, one of Aaron Burr's counsel, was born at Dumfries, Prince William County, Va. He lived for a short time at Fredericksburg, and was living in Richmond when both his parents perished in the Richmond Theatre fire in 1811. His education was confined to Latin, Greek, and mathematics, as taught in the private schools of the day. At eighteen, with six weeks' private study, he was admitted to the bar, and practised law with fair success for six years. He married Mary Whiting Blair and soon became a successful farmer. In 1831 he entered politics as a Whig candidate for the legislature, was elected in 1833, serving till 1839, when he entered Congress as a member from the Richmond district. He served till 1843, and again in the session 1847–49. Powerful in build, aggressive, often violent in speech, distrusting and denouncing the Democrats as a party of disunion led by John C. Calhoun, he was an outstanding opponent of every measure advocated by Democrats, standing with them only in opposition to Northern abolitionists. He ably supported John Quincy Adams in his fight against the "Gag Law" of 1836. He considered President Tyler guilty of treachery to the Whig party in his bank veto and ever after opposed him unrelentingly. Botts was a member of a select committee which criticized Tyler's veto of the Whig Tariff, declaring that his reasons were "feeble, inconsistent, and unsatisfactory" (*Congressional Globe,* Aug. 16, 1842). He opposed strenuously the annexation of Texas and the Mexican War, but as chairman of the Committee on Military Affairs, did his part in bringing the war to a successful conclusion. He was a member of the Virginia constitutional convention of 1850 which struggled with the question of a mixed basis of representation in proportion to the number of white inhabitants and also to the taxes raised. He advocated a division of the state at the Blue Ridge Mountains with equal representation in both houses of the legislature (*Journal of the Constitutional Convention 1850–51,* Appendix). Called to Washington by Henry Clay to aid in the compromise measures of 1850 he played a vital part in their passage. In 1852 he resumed his law practise in Richmond, making it a matter of principle to take only cases in which he was satisfied with the justice of his position. He was a member of the Whig convention of 1852, at Baltimore, casting the only vote from the South for Scott on the first ballot. After the collapse of the Whig party he was an unsuccessful candidate for Congress on the Know-Nothing ticket in 1854.

From this time he gave himself to opposing what he believed to be a conspiracy of certain "Democratic bosses" to bring on secession rather than yield control, and from this time his hostility to Jefferson Davis grew more intense. He was especially violent in his characterization of Gov. Wise, of Virginia, "The Unwise Henry A.," asserting that the John Brown affair was deliberately used to further the secession conspiracy. As a member of the reorganization movement of 1859, against the Democrats, he supported Goggin against Letcher for governor of Virginia, and was considered as a presidential nominee of the "Opposition" in 1860. He claimed, in what was one of his greatest speeches, at Lynchburg, October 1860, that the Democratic party deliberately split in order to make inevitable the election of Lincoln and the success of the secession plot (*Political Pamphlets, IV, No. 48,* Virginia State Library). Nominated for the convention called in Virginia to decide on secession, and defeated, as he claimed, by fraud, he did what he considered his greatest piece of work in trying to prevent the secession of Virginia. There followed the most disputed act of his life when he said on the basis of personal knowledge that President Lincoln offered through J. B. Baldwin to stop the fleet which was about to sail for Charleston if the Virginia convention would adjourn *sine die.* This offer was not reported to the convention and in his testimony before the Reconstruction Committee, Feb. 10, 1866, Baldwin testified that no such offer had been made (Botts, *Great Rebellion,* pp. 194–202). After the passage of the Ordinance of Secession, Botts, believing that secession was now inevitable, wrote a series of letters to Attorney-General Edward Bates, at Washington, proposing a constitutional amendment in accordance with which the Southern States could withdraw peacefully. With the ratification of the action of the convention by the people, Botts withdrew from public life to his farm near Richmond, and rarely left his premises, though he talked freely. On Mar. 1, 1862, President Davis proclaimed martial law in and near Richmond, and before daybreak next morning Botts was arrested and confined for eight weeks in a negro jail. After the transfer of Benjamin, secretary of war, whom Botts cordially hated, to the State Department, Randolph, the new secretary of war, had him released on parole. In January 1863 he purchased a farm and located in Culpeper County, entertaining officers of both armies and suffering from depredations of soldiers of both armies. He was offered the nomination for United States Senator by the "Restored Government" in 1864, but refused. In 1866 he proposed a plan of reconstruction which was rejected. He presided over the organization meeting of the "Union Republican Party of Virginia" at Alexandria, in May 1866, and opposed manhood suffrage strongly, but finally accepted it. He led the Virginia delegation to the "Convention of Southern Loyalists" at Philadelphia in 1866. Representing the conservative element of the Unionists, remembered as one of those who had signed Jefferson Davis's bail bond, he lost control of the party to the radicals. Afterward to the disappointment of his older friends he accepted the radical position, was defeated for the constitutional convention by a conservative from his own county, and for the last two years of his life took no active part in politics.

[The chief source of authority for John Minor Botts is his *Great Rebellion,* autobiographical to an extent, started in 1861, and published with a voluminous appendix of speeches and letters in 1866. A short sketch by Clyde C. Webster was published in the *Richmond Coll. Hist. Papers,* I, No. 1, June 1915. A sketch written by his son-in-law, D. S. Lewis, and published in the *Spirit of the Valley* (Harrisonburg, Va.), is out of print. The collected Political Pamphlets in the Va. State Lib. contain his outstanding speeches. The files of the Richmond *Whig,* which in general supported his politics, are also in the State Lib.]

J. E. W—y.

BOUCHER, JONATHAN (Mar. 12, 1737/8–Apr. 27, 1804), Loyalist, Anglican clergyman, was born in the village of Blencogo in the county of Cumberland, England, the third child of James and Ann Barnes Boucher, who kept an alehouse. In after years he recalled rather bitterly the penury and hardships of his boyhood; but the father, though a ne'er-do-well, had native ability and some education, and eked out a livelihood as village schoolmaster. From him Boucher learned to read and spell, so that he could go to school and begin the study of Latin at the age of six. Both parents desired to make a scholar out of the lad. He was first sent to a little free-school at Bromfield and then to a school at Wigton where at sixteen he himself did some teaching in a night school. Having found his *métier,* he became two years later an usher in a school at Saint Bees kept by the Rev. John James. This kindly and generous master did much for the further education of his usher and finally procured for him a position as tutor to a gentleman's sons at Port Royal, in Virginia. Thither Boucher sailed in April 1759.

He was at first somewhat disdainful of his new surroundings, finding the manners and conversation of the Virginians "almost in everything the very opposite to my taste" (Letter to Rev. James in *Maryland Historical Magazine,* VIII, 4). That he never did find himself wholly at one with his associates in the colonies was, in a large measure, the cause of his later misfortunes. He was soon living beyond his means, beginning an indebtedness to Mr. James which was not discharged for many years. To better his fortunes, he returned to England in 1762 to take orders, having been assured of the vacant rectory in Hanover Parish. He was ordained without any further preparation and returned the following summer. Subsequently he removed to the rectory of St. Mary's in Caroline County, where he bought a small plantation and took nearly thirty boys as pupils, "most of them the sons of persons of the first condition in the colony" (*Reminiscences,* p. 41). Among these boys was "Jacky" Custis, the son of Mrs. Martha Washington, for whose proper training his step-father, Col. George Washington, was much concerned (*Writings of Washington,* Ford edition, II, 257). Thus began an acquaintanceship which Boucher improved to the utmost. In 1770 he was appointed to the rectory of Saint Anne's in Annapolis, which he had solicited for several years. Thither he removed with some of his slaves and two of his pupils, one of whom was Master John Parke Custis.

Annapolis was then, in Boucher's opinion, "the genteelest town in North America." He took an active part in its social life; patronized the local theatre; "wrote some verses on one of the actresses and a prologue or two"; became the first president of the Homony Club, a literary organization; and enjoyed an intimacy with Gov. Eden and his family. As chaplain of the lower house of the Assembly, he had no little influence in shaping legislation, according to his own account (*Reminiscences,* p. 92); but he was unable to prevent a reduction in the stipend of the clergy. His efforts in their behalf, however, and his persistent advocacy of the establishment of an American Episcopacy, were rewarded by King's College of New York with the degree of Master of Arts. When the desirable rectory of Queen Anne's Parish in Prince George's County fell vacant, it was bestowed "unsolicited" upon him by Gov. Eden. Shortly after, he married a Miss Eleanor Addison who brought him a comfortable dowry. He bought a plantation on the Potomac and prepared to settle down to a comfortable existence, when he became involved in the controversy of the colonies with the mother country.

Ever a firm supporter of established authority, Boucher regarded as seditious all the various extra-legal organizations, which the colonists devised to resist the acts of Parliament. When the provincial convention proclaimed a solemn fast-day by way of protest, he announced his intention of preaching against active resistance, but was forbidden to enter his pulpit by a body of armed men. From this time on, believing his life in danger, he never preached without a pair of loaded pistols lying on the cushion (*Ibid.,* p. 113). He was under constant surveillance by the local committee of safety; grew more and more unpopular; and was burned in effigy. Finally, fearing the worst, he and his wife abandoned their home and property and departed for England in September 1775.

Boucher never returned. Friends procured for him the curacy of Paddington and a pension from the government, while he added to his income by tutoring and writing for journals. During the last nineteen years of his life he was vicar of Epsom. He never recovered his property in Maryland, but he shared in the compensation which the royal government allotted to loyalists. In 1797 he published thirteen discourses preached in America, with a lengthy preface under the title *A View of the Causes and Consequences of the American Revolution*—a book of considerable historical interest. He spent the latter part of his life making a glossary of obsolete and provincial words, a part of which was published after his death as *A Supplement to Dr. Johnson's Dictionary of the English Language* (1807). Another edition with the title

Boucher's Glossary (1832–33) contains a discursive introduction on philology.

[Boucher's autobiography was published in 1925 by his grandson Jonathan Bouchier under the title *Reminiscences of an Am. Loyalist 1738–1789.* It should be supplemented by "Letters of Rev. Jonathan Boucher" printed in vols. VI–IX of the *Md. Hist. Mag.*, and by *Letters of Jonathan Boucher to Geo. Washington* (1889), ed. by W. C. Ford.] A—n. J.

BOUCICAULT, DION (Dec. 26, 1820–Sept. 18, 1890), dramatist, actor, was born in Dublin. His mother was Anne Darley Boursiquot, sister of George Darley, poet, who went from Dublin to London and was admired by Carlyle. She married Samuel Smith Boursiquot, a Dublin merchant of French ancestry, but was divorced from him in 1819. Dion was apparently the natural son of Dionysius Lardner, then boarding at her house, whom Dion in later life physically resembled. Lardner wrote popular science articles and was a man of some ability. He supervised and paid for Dion's education, and the boy was named after him "Dionysius Lardner" Boursiquot. Dion went to school in England and entered London University, but experience in school plays had given him such a passion for the theatre that in 1837 he got jobs acting in provincial theatres, under the name of Lee Moreton, and in 1840 came back to London determined to shine as author and actor. The first play he submitted to Charles Mathews and Madame Vestris at Covent Garden was rejected, but a second was accepted. This was *London Assurance,* based in part, at least, on a suggestion from John Brougham [*q.v.*]. Produced Mar. 4, 1841, it was a striking success, Mrs. Nisbet as Lady Gay Spanker being particularly popular. It is said Boucicault wrote the part in for her after the original MS. had been completed. The play was burlesqued by Thackeray (*Sketches and Travels*) but coming in an age of inflated rhetorical drama it seemed to have a freshness and high spirits very welcome to the people, and it foreshadowed to some slight extent the modern drama. But Boucicault was not a conscious reformer, and his next plays were either imitations of eighteenth-century English styles still persisting on the stage or adaptations from the French. He turned them out in rapid succession. Lack of international copyright made it cheaper for managers to put on French adaptations than to pay for original plays, and Boucicault, to live in the style he had adopted, had to do a vast amount of hack work. From 1844 to 1848 he was in France, where he married a French woman who died while they were on a tour of the Alps. Boucicault said she fell over a precipice. In 1848 he returned to London and became an assistant to Charles Kean at the Princess's Theatre, for whom he adapted *Pauline* (1851) and *The Corsican Brothers* (1852) from Dumas, and *Louis XI* (1853) from Delavigne. He also made other adaptations, now quite forgotten.

In September 1853 he sailed for New York where many of his plays were already familiar. On a different boat sailed Agnes Robertson (born in Edinburgh, 1833), an actress and singer also from Kean's company. It was generally assumed that she had married Boucicault. She made her début at Burton's Theatre, N. Y., Oct. 22, 1853, in *The Young Actress,* a musical interlude adapted by Boucicault, and was immediately a sensational success. In Boston the following January crowds trailed her through the streets and she played for nine weeks to capacity business. A tour followed, Boucicault acting with her. In 1856 they were back in New York. Pleased with America, and quick to adapt himself to new conditions, Boucicault turned out *The Poor of New York,* "a superficial but graphic picture" of the panic of 1857, and it had a long run at Wallack's. The next year he wrote *Jessie Brown, or the Relief of Lucknow,* with his wife as Jessie and himself as the Sepoy villain. Again a great success. The same year (1858) he opened a theatre in Washington, in partnership with William Stuart, and the next year, with Stuart, directed the Winter Garden in New York, for which he "adapted from the French" a play that turned out to be simply a dramatization of Dickens's *Cricket on the Hearth.* He called this play *Dot,* and assigned the rôle of Caleb Plummer to Joseph Jefferson, who records in his *Autobiography* (p. 209) how much Boucicault helped him to act it. Presently he made a stage version of *Nicholas Nickleby,* and then followed (1859) one of his greatest successes, and something of a milestone in the American theatre—*The Octoroon,* a problem play about slavery. The subject was gunpowder, of course, but Boucicault escaped offending either side (see Jefferson's *Autobiography,* pp. 213–15). Possibly that is not the highest merit in a problem play. Boucicault next formed an alliance with Laura Keene, and produced in 1860 a stage version of Gerald Griffin's Irish novel, *The Collegians.* This play, *The Colleen Bawn,* was the first of a long series of Irish comedy dramas. He had tapped a new vein, and one in which he worked with more sincerity than in any other. On this play, perhaps, and on *Arrah-na-Pogue* (1864), *The O'Dowd* (1873), and *The Shaughraun* (1874) his fame as a dramatist now largely rests.

Boucicault returned to London in 1862 and in

1865 made the version of *Rip Van Winkle* used by Jefferson. He remained in London for ten years, then returned to the United States and continued to write, act and produce plays here till his death in 1890. But after *The Shaughraun* either his powers declined or public taste changed, and his fortunes steadily sank. In 1885 he went to Australia and there married Louise Thorndyke. Miss Robertson at once sued for and obtained a divorce. At the time of his death he was teaching in a school of acting in New York for $50 a week. Boucicault's talent was that of a stage manager and dramatic technician rather than that of a sincere creative artist. He had a fatal facility. He wrote or adapted 132 plays, an average of much more than two a year, seeking always immediate popularity. He also originated the system of casting a play entirely in New York and taking the whole company around the country, thus inaugurating the so-called "long run" system, and sounding the knell of the older stock companies. Fond of good living, a gay, careless spender, his money went as fast as it came. He had a broad, bald forehead, a delicate, white skin, a Celtic wit, and as actor excelled in parts, especially Irish parts, calling for high spirits, dash, and a flavor of romantic tenderness. It may justly be said that more than any other one man he kept the American drama lively and popular during the mid-nineteenth century, while waiting the birth of a realism he was not quite artist enough to bring about.

[Townsend Walsh, *The Career of Dion Boucicault* (1915); Geo. Wm. Curtis, remarks on Boucicault's Irish drama in the "Easy Chair," *Harper's Mag.*, July, 1875; *North Am. Rev.*, Sept. 1877, and scattered issues during the next twelve years, containing Boucicault's own articles on the art of playwriting; Wm. Winter, *Other Days* (1908); Montrose J. Moses, *Famous Actor-Families in America* (1906), pp. 115–40.] W. P. E.

BOUCK, WILLIAM C. (Jan. 7, 1786–Apr. 19, 1859), governor of New York, was of German ancestry, his great-grandfather having been one of the first of a company of German Palatines to settle in the Schoharie Valley beyond the Helderbergs. William Bouck, William C.'s grandfather, was the first male child born of white parents in the valley, and it was he who established the old Bouck farm in Schoharie County on which the future governor was born. The latter's father was Christian Bouck and his mother before her marriage was Margaret Borst who, like her husband, was a descendant of one of the first settlers of the Schoharie district. Bouck's father, a man of abundant means, planned to give him an extensive schooling but the demands of the farm, the scarcity of labor, and the habit of frugality so characteristic of the German pioneer frustrated this plan and the boy did not get beyond the district school. "Until I was twenty-two years of age," he wrote, "no common laborer on my father's farm did more work than myself either in clearing land or in the harvest field. Often have I gone to the plough before daylight, and from it after dark." In 1807 he was married to Catherine, daughter of Jacob Lawyer, by whom he had eleven children. He early became interested in politics and, like the majority of farmers of his day, was an ardent and zealous adherent to the principles expounded by Thomas Jefferson. During his lifetime he was an undeviating Democrat and a loyal party-man. Before his election as governor he held several offices including town-clerk, supervisor, sheriff, and state assemblyman. His opposition to De Witt Clinton and his lack of confidence in Clinton's views on internal improvements were perhaps the chief reasons why Bouck was at first skeptical about the wisdom of building the Erie and Champlain canals. He was one of the first of the unconvinced, however, to change his mind and to give the Clintonian proposal whole-hearted support. In 1821 he was named as canal commissioner and assigned to superintend construction of the most difficult section of the Erie Canal—that from Brockport to its western terminus. He was also selected to take charge of the work on the Cayuga & Seneca, the Crooked Lake, the Chemung, and the Chenango canals. After serving nineteen years as canal commissioner he was removed by the Whig legislature in 1840 for political reasons.

His removal, if anything, increased his popularity with the people of the state, and in the autumn of 1840 he was unanimously nominated as the Democratic candidate for governor, but was defeated by Gov. Seward by a small majority of about 5,000 votes. His party became seriously split into two factions—the conservatives or Hunkers and the radicals or Barnburners—largely over the allied questions of internal improvements and state finances. Bouck, a leader of the former faction, was again unanimously nominated for the governorship in 1842 and was elected by a majority of about 22,000. From the outset, his administration was a stormy one despite his efforts to conciliate and harmonize the conflicting party factions. Toward its close he was obliged to call out the militia to protect Columbia County from the riots incited by the "Anti-Renters" (Smith, *post,* II, 311). Failing of renomination, he returned to Schoharie County where he was chosen as a delegate to the constitutional convention of 1846. While the convention was in session he was appointed by President Polk federal assistant treasurer in the City of New

York. He discharged the duties of this office until removed by President Taylor in May 1849. Once again he retired to his Schoharie farm where he died at the age of seventy-three. He was regular and frugal in his habits and was blessed through life with good health. The official honors bestowed upon him he owed not so much to the backing of powerful friends as to his native talent and strength of character.

[John S. Jenkins, *Lives of the Governors of the State of N. Y.* (1851), pp. 689–721; Ray B. Smith, ed., *Hist. of the State of N. Y., Political and Governmental* (1922), vol. II, ch. XVII; Chas. Z. Lincoln, "The Governors of New York," *Proc. N. Y. Hist. Ass.*, IX, 87; Jeptha R. Simms, *Hist. of Schoharie County and Border Wars of N. Y.* (1845); *N. Y. Times*, Apr. 21, 1859.]
H. J. C.

BOUDINOT, ELIAS (May 2, 1740–Oct. 24, 1821), Revolutionary statesman, was the fourth of the same name in direct descent, and has been often confused with his younger brother, Elisha (1749–1819), and with this brother's son, Elias E. (1791–1863). Driven out of Marans, Rochelle, France, by the revocation of the Edict of Nantes (1685), Elias Boudinot the first, a prosperous merchant, elder in the Reformed Church, Seigneur de Cressy, went to London, thence to New York about 1687, joined in protest against Leisler's maladministration, bought extensive lands in Bergen County, N. J., and died in New York in 1702. Elias the second (1674–1719) married Marie Catherine Carrée, and through their daughters was built up a remarkable matrimonial network of the Boudinot family with the Ricketts, Chetwood, Chandler, Clayton, Vergereau, Tennent, and other families noted in colonial law, church, and business affairs. Elias the third (1706–70), postmaster and silversmith of Princeton, married Catherine Williams of Antigua, British West Indies; their daughter, Annis, married Richard Stockton, signer of the Declaration of Independence, father-in-law of Benjamin Rush and grandfather of Richard Rush. Elias the fourth, born in Philadelphia, married, Apr. 21, 1762, the signer's sister, Hannah Stockton (July 21, 1736–Oct. 28, 1808), whom he had long courted, and urged to "press forward toward a heavenly goal." Their courting names "Eugenia" and "Narcissus" were in use thirty years later. Neither a classical academy education, baptism by George Whitefield, nor early and arduous study of law, could mar the serenity of Elias's temper or the poise of his good sense. Licensed counsellor and attorney-at-law, 1760, sergeant-at-law, 1770, he became a leader in his profession (hon. LL.D. Yale, 1790) and a trustee of Princeton (1772–1821). Two fellowships founded by him are extant there. He is described as tall, handsome, "every way prepossessing," elegant, eloquent and emotional. He could use tears to good effect but his advice to his only child, Susan Vergereau (1764–1854), married to William Bradford, attorney-general (1794–5), was: "take the world as you find it" and convert even prejudices to usefulness.

Supporting gentry rule, legal government, and property rights, he was a conservative Whig in politics but followed the liberal trend of his Colony and his connections, and entered on revolution chiefly by opposing Gov. William Franklin. On June 11, 1774, he became a member of the Committee of Correspondence for Essex County, N. J., but felt a "firm dependence in the mother country essential." In March 1775, with William Livingston, he hurried the New Jersey Assembly into approving the proceedings of the first Continental Congress at Philadelphia (*New Jersey Archives*, ser. 1, vol. X, p. 575). In August 1775 he, then a member of the New Jersey Provincial Congress, procured from Elizabethtown eight or ten half-casks of powder for Washington's army at Cambridge, the forces there being down to eight rounds per man. In April 1776 at New Brunswick he quashed Dr. John Witherspoon's queer attempt to rush New Jersey into declaring for independence. On June 6, 1777, by commission dated May 15, Congress appointed him commissary-general of prisoners, with the pay and rations of a colonel, five deputies, and full power even to altering the directions of the board of war. Thus he was drawn into "the boisterous noisy, fatiguing unnatural and disrelishing state of War and slaughter" (to his wife July 22, 1777). This he did, not only to "be of some service to the Prisoners" but also "to watch the Military and to preserve the Civil Rights of my Fellow Citizens" (*Journal*, p. 67). He organized the care of the American prisoners despite great difficulties, and put in $30,000 of his own money to do it. On William Duer's insistence he recovered most of this despite New England opposition. Washington offered to stand half the loss, corrected Boudinot's judgment as to treason and military tactics, and relied on him to reconcile Steuben to other officers and for certain secret service information. Their relations were close and, on Boudinot's part, extremely reverential.

On Nov. 20, 1777, he was elected delegate to Congress, and wrote of Philadelphia, "This City is enough to kill a horse" (to his wife July 9, 1778). He did not attend Congress until July 7, 1778, and then only on Washington's insistence that it was his only chance to be reimbursed in "hard money," *i.e.*, out of the cash captured from Burgoyne (*Journal*, p. 69). Rechosen to Congress until 1784, president Nov. 4, 1782, acting also as secretary of foreign affairs from June 16, 1783, he served on over thirty committees and usually as chairman, while his social grace and legal acumen were invaluable in dealing with representatives of other countries. He signed the treaties of peace with Great Britain and of alliance with the French king, the proclamations for cessation of hostilities, thanksgiving, discharging the army, and removing the Congress to Princeton, and presided at that session in Nassau Hall when Washington was thanked for his services "in establishing the freedom and independence of your country." His benevolent good sense went far to neutralize the acidities of our peace commissioners abroad.

As a strong Federalist he helped ratify the Constitution in New Jersey and conducted Washington into New York for the first inauguration. Elected to the House of Representatives in the first, second and third Congresses, he fathered many essential measures and took part in practically all important debates. In the great assault of February 1793 on Hamilton's conduct of the federal Treasury, Boudinot led the defense. In 1795 he succeeded David Rittenhouse as director of the United States Mint and reorganized the enterprise with "great industry as well as ability" (J. R. Snowden, *A Description of the Medals of Washington,* 1861, p. 185). Some of his rules are still in force. His technical skill and his care for the employees are shown by his letters to Jefferson of June 16, 1801, and Apr. 17, 1802. He resigned July 1, 1805, to study the Bible at his home in Burlington, N. J. His religious works, *The Age of Revelation* (1801), *Memoirs of the Life of the Rev. William Tennent* (1807), *The Second Advent* (1815), *A Star in the West* (1816), may be read by those curious to do so. His guiding thought was "I am satisfied that the grace of God is not confined to Sect or Party." He was the first counsellor named by the United States Supreme Court (Feb. 5, 1790) and seems never to have lost either his taste for the practise of his profession or his acute and sensible interest in public affairs. Save when absent on duty, he spent his entire life in New Jersey, living successively at Princeton, Elizabethtown, and Burlington. His will, July 3, 1821, disposed of a large property, including several tracts of wild land in Pennsylvania, to innumerable dear ones and good causes. He seems to have had few quarrels, and no enemies.

[Boudinot's letters and papers have not been published. His *Journal* (1894) deals only with selected "American Events during the Revolutionary War" but affords interesting side-lights on the man. *The Life, Public Services, Addresses and Letters of Elias Boudinot* (1896) by a collateral descendant, Jane J. Boudinot, includes much material but the selection and arrangement are not impressive. This is the chief source. His public activities are reflected in the *Journals of the Continental Congress,* the *Annals* of the first, second, and third Congresses, and in the published letters of leading men of the period.]

W. L. W—y.

BOUDINOT, ELIAS (*c.* 1803–June 22, 1839), Indian editor, was born in Georgia among his people, the Cherokees, who, due to contact with the whites, were rapidly becoming civilized. His Indian name was Galagina (pronounced Kill-ke-nah). In 1818 he, with two other young Cherokees, was sent by the missionaries to the mission school at Cornwall, Conn. While there he took the name of the benefactor of the school, Elias Boudinot [*q.v.*]. Meanwhile George Guess (Sikwaji, or Sequoyah), a young man of Cherokee-German blood, who could not read, invented a Cherokee syllabary of eighty-six characters. This was immediately followed by a great increase of interest in Indian education and in 1824 the National Council decided to establish a newspaper, the *Cherokee Phœnix,* and employed young Boudinot as editor at $300 a year. The greater part of the paper was printed in English, but a fourth or more was in Cherokee and it was very popular among the natives. In his editorial work Boudinot was assisted by the Rev. Samuel A. Worcester, a medical missionary. The paper appeared weekly, except for occasional omissions, from Feb. 21, 1828, until October 1835, when it was suppressed by the Georgia authorities for unfavorable remarks about the attitude of the state (Rachel C. Eaton, *John Ross and the Cherokee Indians,* 1921, pp. 33, 37, 57). In 1833 the United Brethren's Missionary Society published in Cherokee characters at New Echota a book by Boudinot called *Poor Sarah or the Indian Woman.* From 1823 until his death Boudinot collaborated with Worcester in translating several books of the New Testament into Cherokee. In 1831 the Council elected John Ross, who was bitterly opposed to removal to the West, chief executive for an indefinite term. This seemed to John Ridge, cousin to Boudinot, a death blow to his own political ambitions and he gradually, under pressure and persuasion from government agents, became an advocate of removal. In 1835 Boudinot joined him and a few others in signing, without any authority, a treaty for removal, and on June 22, 1839, after arrival in the Indian Territory, Boudinot was treacherously murdered in revenge for his part in the transaction. He was twice married: in 1826 to Harriet Ruggles Gold, who bore him six children, and, after her death in 1836, to Delight Sargent, who died without issue.

[*Bureau of Am. Ethnology, Bull. 30,* I, pp. 162–63; Wilson Lumpkin, *The Removal of the Cherokee Indians from Ga.* (1907); L. L. Knight, *Georgia and Georgians* (1917) and *Georgia's Landmarks, Memorials, and Legends* (1913), vol. I. Incomplete files of the *Cherokee Phœnix* may be found in the N. Y. State Lib., another more nearly complete in the British Museum.] D. Y. T.

BOUDINOT, ELIAS CORNELIUS (Aug. 1, 1835–Sept. 27, 1890), Indian lawyer, was born in the Cherokee Nation, near the site of Rome, Ga. He was the son of Elias Boudinot [*q.v.*] 1803–39 and Harriet Ruggles Gold, whom Elias had married at Cornwall, Conn. On the assassination of his father (1839) all the children were sent to Cornwall and distributed among Harriet Gold's sisters, Elias Cornelius going to Manchester, Vt. He first tried engineering and spent one year with a railroad in Ohio, but gave that up and settled in Fayetteville, Ark. Here he studied law under A. M. Wilson and was admitted to the bar in 1856. While practising law he gave a part of his time to editorial work on the *Arkansian.* In 1860 he was made chairman of the Democratic state central committee and went to Little Rock, where he became chief editorial writer for the *True Democrat.* In 1861 he was elected secretary of the secession convention. After the state seceded he went to the Indian Territory, where he helped Stand Waitie raise an Indian regiment, in which he rose to the rank of lieutenant-colonel. In 1863 he was elected delegate for the territory to the Confederate Congress and served until the end of the war. After the war he took part in restoring peaceful relations between the Cherokees and the United States. Soon after this he started a tobacco factory in the Territory, but in 1868 it was seized by the government under an act of that year. Boudinot then spent many years in Washington, trying to recover his property and working for the good of the Indians. The court of claims finally allowed a part of his claim. He was an ardent advocate of education for the Indians, of breaking up the tribal relations, and of allotting the lands in severalty. For this he incurred the enmity of his tribe, but lived to see his policy put partially into effect and to regain the good will of his people. He was a man of striking appearance, a very forceful speaker, a good writer, and an amateur musician of no mean attainments. In Washington he became acquainted with many distinguished men. There he married Clara Minear, and brought her to Fort Smith in 1885. He practised law, gave entertainments, and farmed in the Territory until his death.

[E. C. Starr, *Hist. of Cornwall, Conn.* (1926), pp. 156, 378; S. W. Harman, *Hell on the Border* (1898); *Ark. Gazette* (Little Rock), Sept. 28, 1890. A portrait of him appears in *In Memoriam: Elias Cornelius Boudinot* (n. p., n. d.).] D. Y. T.

BOULIGNY, DOMINIQUE (*c.* 1771–Mar. 5, 1833), legislator, born in New Orleans, La., was the son of Francisco Bouligny and Marie Louise le Senechal d'Auverville. The family was of Italian origin and was founded in Milan in the fourteenth century by Mateo Atendolo, the first count of Bolognini. The family name was changed in its spelling from Bolognini to Bouligny in the early seventeenth century when a member of the family, then in the service of the Spanish king, was captured by the French and taken to Marseilles. In the early eighteenth century, Joseph Bouligny, the progenitor of the Louisiana Bouligny family, settled in Alicante, Spain. His son, Francisco, the father of Dominique, was born there in 1736 and came to Louisiana in 1769 with O'Reilly, the first Spanish governor of Louisiana. Dominique Bouligny attained considerable political prominence in Louisiana in the first three decades of the nineteenth century. He was elected to the first legislature of the Territory of Orleans in 1805 as one of the ten representatives of the parish of Orleans. In 1813 he was one of a number of New Orleans citizens who subscribed $10,000 to secure the safety of the state during the war that was then going on between the United States and England. In the following year he was chosen by the people of New Orleans as one of a committee of nine to counteract the effects of an appeal which an English army officer by the name of Col. Nicholls had issued from Pensacola, calling upon the people of Louisiana who were of Spanish, French, Italian, and British descent to rebel against the "usurpation" of the Americans in their country. The committee issued a stirring address to the people, urging them to remain loyal to the American government. Bouligny was elected to the United States Senate in 1824 to succeed Henry Johnson who had been elected governor of Louisiana, and he served in that body until 1829. He married Arthemise Le Blanc, and on his death in New Orleans he left six sons and six daughters. Many of his descendants are still living in New Orleans.

[Grace King, *Creole Families of New Orleans* (1921), ch. XVIII, deals with the Bouligny family and is the best source of information concerning its history. There are scattered references in Chas. Gayarré, *Hist. of La.,* vol. IV (1866), and Alcée Fortier, *Hist. of La.,* vol. III (1904).] E. M. V.

BOUNETHEAU, HENRY BRINTNELL (Dec. 14, 1797–Jan. 31, 1877), miniature painter, was born in Charleston, S. C., son of Peter Bounetheau, an officer of Huguenot descent who fought in the American Revolution. Little is known of his life except that he devoted his entire time to art for a period only and remained to the end a business man who spent a portion of each day painting excellent miniatures. He managed to produce a considerable amount of work and although his likenesses never went above a high respectable average, he will be remembered as a competent craftsman who carried on the tradition of his fellow townsman, Charles Fraser. At a first glance, indeed, his miniatures might be taken easily for those painted by Fraser during his later years. The miniatures of both men are generally rectangular in shape. Both men posed the sitter in about the same position. Both frequently introduced a conventional column in the background. Fraser's work, however, became more vigorous and he painted with dashing, straight strokes as he grew older, while Bounetheau from beginning to end generally used an effective method of stippling.

Bounetheau had the advantage of Fraser in his early training. Fraser while still a boy was condemned to the study of law whereas Bounetheau studied art early in life. About the age of sixteen, he went into business and worked for the firm of Dart & Spear. His reliability, accuracy, and general personal integrity were recognized by his fellow citizens and he later became an officer in the Bank of Charleston. After leaving the firm of Dart & Spear, he went into business for himself, becoming a partner in the firm of Hamilton, Son & Company. It is not known for what reason, but it is a matter of fact that the partnership was dissolved at the end of two years. Bounetheau then took "to miniature painting for support, and displayed so much skill that his pictures soon became the rage," according to a newspaper obituary. He finally became the chief accountant for the C. N. Hubert Company, holding this position for the rest of his life. He was married to Julia Clarkson Dupré, and died in Charleston, S. C. Their son, Henry Dupré Bounetheau, lost his life in the great fire at Jacksonville, Fla., 1901, in which, also, many miniatures by his father were burned.

But in spite of this disaster there still remain numerous miniatures by Bounetheau. Among the portraits which he painted, two, those of Charles C. Pinckney and Nathaniel Greene, were engraved, the first being engraved by Longacre and the second by A. B. Durand. Other portraits by Bounetheau are those of Charles Austin Pringle, Dr. T. L. Ogier, Henry Heyward Manigault, William Ravenel, and the Hon. James R. Pringle.

[The principal source of information concerning Bounetheau is the extended obituary notice in the *News and Courier* (Charleston, S. C.), Feb. 1, 1877. A summary of this account is given in Theodore Bolton, *Early Am. Portrait Painters in Miniature* (1921), where seventeen of Bounetheau's miniatures are listed and one of these, the portrait of Henry H. Manigault, is reproduced. The engravings after Bounetheau's portraits mentioned in the text above appeared in Jas. Herring and Jas. B. Longacre, *The Natl. Portrait Gallery of Distinguished Americans* (1834–39).] T. B.

BOUQUET, HENRY (1719–Sept. 2, 1765), British officer, was born of a good French Protestant family at Rolle, Canton Vaud, Switzerland. In 1736 he entered the service of the States General of Holland as a cadet in the regiment of Constant, and two years later was commissioned as lieutenant. During the war of the Austrian Succession he served the King of Sardinia, and displayed such coolness and resourcefulness in action that the Prince of Orange engaged him as captain-commandant, with the rank of lieutenant-colonel, in a newly-formed regiment of Swiss Guards. In 1748 he accompanied the officers who received from the French the evacuated forts in the Low Countries, and shortly after traveled through France and Italy with Lord Middleton, from whom he acquired the foundations of his excellent knowledge of English, which he wrote with grace and precision. On his return he devoted himself to a thorough study of his chosen profession of arms, especially in the mathematical branches, and throughout his career continued to enjoy scientific discussion.

In the fall of 1755 James Prevost, supported by the urging of Joseph Yorke, British minister at The Hague, succeeded in gaining Bouquet's consent to take the lieutenant-colonelcy of the first battalion in the newly-planned Royal American Regiment (later the King's Royal Rifle Corps), and in the spring of 1756 Bouquet left for North America, where he contributed to the remarkable recruiting success the regiment enjoyed in 1756 among the Germans of Pennsylvania, and had his first experiences of the unwarlike but obstinate temper of the Quakers, which he never ceased to impugn. The center of the quartering dispute in Philadelphia in the winter of 1756, he met greater resistance in quartering regulars in 1757 in Charleston, S. C., where he commanded a small force of provincials, Royal Americans, and, later, Montgomery's Highlanders. This was the only independent command assigned him by a commander-in-chief during the war.

Promoted to be colonel in America only in January 1758, he served as second under Brigadier John Forbes in the weary expedition against Fort Duquesne, and his rare patience and tact were largely responsible for overcoming the delays of provincials and the uncertainties of transportation, for building new forts, and for cutting through western Pennsylvania the great highway known as "Forbes' Road," which resulted in the evacuation of Fort Duquesne by the French. His foreign birth prevented Amherst from giving him the command in the west at Forbes's death (*Northcliffe Collection,* Ottawa, 1926, p. 114), and he served for the remainder of the war under Stanwix and Monckton, occupied chiefly in the supervision and strengthening of the western forts, Pitt, Venango, and Presqu'isle. He was commissioned colonel by brevet in 1762, and was naturalized by Maryland and by the Supreme Court of Pennsylvania. Neither the attractions of domestic life upon his estate at Long Meadow, Md., nor the importunities of his many warm American friends could lure him from the army during the war (*Pennsylvania Magazine of History and Biography,* III, 121–143), and leave of absence was denied him in 1761. He continued, therefore, to exploit to the full his long experience on the frontier, by adapting the discipline of European armies to the exigencies of wilderness warfare, and by drilling his own first battalion in the principles of open-order combat and extreme mobility of action.

In Pontiac's conspiracy he proved the worth of his methods. In 1763 he marched a small army of Royal Americans and Highlanders towards Fort Pitt, and at Edgehill, within a short distance of Braddock's fatal field, repulsed a considerable number of Delawares and Shawnees. The following day, Aug. 6, the Indians again attacked at Bushy Run, and Bouquet, drawing up his troops in circle to protect his convoy, lured them from cover by the feigned retreat of one segment, and crushed them by a bayonet charge when they rushed into the gap. Henceforth the Indians respected him, perceiving, as not many contemporaries did, that he was the most brilliant leader of light infantry the war produced, and incomparably in advance of the military practise of the day. The following year he commanded the southern of the two expeditions sent to pacify the Indians, led a small force of provincials and regulars to the forks of the Muskingum, and, by an admirable mixture of firmness and justice, forced the surrender of all prisoners in Indian hands and concluded a general peace. Publicly thanked by the king in general orders, and by the assemblies of the southern provinces, he received the unexpected rank of brigadier in 1765, and the command of the southern district. At Pensacola, the same year, fever carried him away prematurely.

[The sole authority for Bouquet's European career is C. G. F. Dumas's biographical preface to the French edition (1769) of Wm. Smith's *Hist. Account of the Expedition against the Ohio Indians in 1764* (1765) reprinted in *Ohio Valley Hist. Ser., No. 1* (1868). The chief sources for his American career are the thirty manuscript volumes in the British Museum, transcribed for the Canadian archives, and calendared in Douglas Brymner's *Report on Canadian Arch.* (1889), as the Bouquet Collection. Some letters are printed in full in Mary C. Darlington, *Hist. of Col. Henry Bouquet and the Western Frontiers of Pa.* (1920) and in *Mich. Pioneer and Hist. Colls.,* XIX, 27–295. Bouquet's military abilities are appraised in Sir Edward Hutton, *Henry Bouquet* (1911); Lewis Butler, *Annals of the King's Royal Rifle Corps,* vol. I (1913); and Col. Jas. F. C. Fuller, *British Light Infantry in the Eighteenth Century* (1925). American appreciations are Cyrus Cort, *Col. Henry Bouquet and his Campaigns* (1883) and J. C. Reeve, "Henry Bouquet," in *Ohio. Arch. and Hist. Quart.,* XXVI, 489–506. Parkman's *Conspiracy of Pontiac* (1851) is the charming and classic account.]

S. M. P.

BOUQUILLON, THOMAS JOSEPH (May 16, 1840–Nov. 5, 1902), Catholic theologian, was born at Warneton, Belgium. He was the second of five children. The family had owned land in the vicinity of Ypres and Warneton for 200 years. Search made at the time of his death failed to bring to the surface any records that might have a bearing on the hereditary background of his life. Bouquillon entered the College of St. Louis at Menin in 1854. He studied philosophy and related sciences at the Preparatory Seminary at Roulers where his ability attracted much attention. He entered the Theological Seminary at Bruges in 1861. Two years later he went to the Gregorian University at Rome where he completed his theological studies. While there he formed an intimate and enduring friendship with Rampolla del Tindaro who later as cardinal became secretary of state for Pope Leo XIII. Bouquillon was ordained to the Catholic priesthood at Rome in 1865. He then took up graduate studies in theology and received the degree of D.D. in 1867. He was at once appointed professor of moral theology in the Seminary at Bruges where he remained in that capacity until 1877. During that period he developed a plan of extension courses for laymen interested in theological studies. In August 1877 he accepted appointment to the chair of theology in the Catholic University of Lille in France. Eight years later he gave up active work as professor and retired to the Benedictine Monastery at Maredsous, Belgium, where he devoted himself entirely to theological and historical research. In 1889 he was asked to take the chair of moral theology in the newly founded Catholic University at Washington, D. C. After some hesitation he accepted the position and entered upon his duties as graduate professor in the same year. He taught there until his death at Brussels in 1902 following a surgical operation. He was buried at Croix, Nord, France.

Bouquillon's chief service to Catholic thought lies in his effort to restore to moral theology the scientific and historical prestige with which Saint Thomas and other early theologians had invested it. In the *Summa Theologica* of the former the theological sciences appear as related aspects of the body of revealed truth, and contemporaneous natural and social sciences are woven into one complete system with it. Bouquillon brought to the task of restoring moral theology to its historical and scientific prestige, unusual command of the whole field of theological literature, a well-balanced knowledge of ecclesiastical and secular history, a philosophical temperament, untiring research, and a gift of balanced exposition. His *Theologia Moralis Fundamentalis* (3rd edition, Bruges, 1903) is the finished product of his gifts and industry. It did much to rehabilitate moral theology in harmony with his great ideal. His special treatises, *De Virtutibus Theologicis* (2nd edition, Bruges, 1890) and *De Virtute Religionis* (Bruges, 1880), displayed the same scholarship and breadth of treatment in their respective fields. Bouquillon exerted far-reaching influence upon the development of the Catholic University at Washington. Shortly after he began to teach there he published a series of lectures in which he discussed the theoretical principles that govern the relations of church, state, and family in the field of education (*Education, to Whom Does It Belong,* Baltimore, 1891). He took the position that "education belongs to men taken individually and collectively in legitimate association, to the family, to the state, to the Church, to all four together and not to any one of these four factors separately." It was his purpose to show "that the doctrine of the Church is not opposed to a reasonable liberty or to the just prerogatives of the state in matters of education" (*Education, a Rejoinder to Critics,* Baltimore, 1892). His views were opposed by some Catholic leaders and a controversy resulted in 1891 and 1892. Against him it was argued that no one "has the right to educate the children of anybody unless the parents give him the power" (Holaind, *The Parent First,* 1891). The issue that arose resulted from differences of approach to the problem. Bouquillon maintained his original position without modification: a purely abstract exposition of principles independent of circumstances of time and country. In the course of the controversy he published a third pamphlet, *Education, A Rejoinder to the Civilta Cattolica* (Baltimore, 1892). All of these pamphlets appeared simultaneously in French. (See also "The Catholic Controversy about Education" in the *Educational Review,* April 1892.) Aside from the original works mentioned Bouquillon edited and annotated numerous Latin and French works, and contributed twenty-one articles in Latin and in French to the *Revue des Sciences Ecclésiastiques,* and fifteen to the *American Catholic Quarterly Review* and the *Catholic University Bulletin.*

[A short account of Bouquillon's life is contained in *Thos. Bouquillon, Notice Bio-Bibliographique par le Chanoine H. Rommel* (Bruxelles, 1903). Some of the material contained there will be found in the *Cath. Univ. Bull.,* Jan. 1903. There is also a biographical sketch by Wm. J. Kerby in the *Cath. Encyc.,* vol. II (1907).]

W. J. K.

BOURGMONT, ETIENNE VENYARD, Sieur de (*c.* 1680–*c.* 1730), French explorer, was the son of Charles de Venyard, Sieur de Vergié, a Norman physician. Of an undisciplined and adventurous nature, Étienne early sought New France, where he was at first merely a *voyageur.* Having obtained the rank of ensign in the army, he was stationed at Detroit and in 1705 he was temporarily in command upon the retirement of Alphonse de Tonty. As commandant he became embroiled in an Indian revolt in 1706, and the next year deserted, probably because of a love affair with Madame Tichenet, called "La Chenette," who followed him to an island in Lake Erie. There with other deserters he lived a dissolute life, until a detachment was sent to arrest the band. Bourgmont, who was befriended by Cadillac, was allowed to escape, and fled to Louisiana, where he lived for a decade among the Indians of the Missouri River. The extent of his explorations is not certain; in 1717, however, he wrote an article called *La Description* detailing the courses of the Missouri as far as the Arikara villages in the later Dakota. For his services as an explorer and pacifier of Indians, Gov. Bienville asked for him a captaincy and sent him to France in 1719 to report his discoveries. The Company of the Indies granted him permission to build a fort on the Missouri, and to make peace with the Padouka (now the Comanche) Indians on the borders of Spanish territory. Bourgmont came back to Louisiana in 1723 and late in that year built the post called Fort Orléans on the Missouri just above Grand River. Thence in 1724 he undertook an expedition westward in which he penetrated to the western border of the present state of Kansas, held a council with the Padouka, and formed an alliance. After his return he persuaded a number of chiefs to accompany him to Paris, among whom was the Michigami named Chicagou. They were received with great éclat, and entertained by royalty. Bourgmont did not return to Louisiana with them; he is said to have married a rich widow and to have remained in France. The date or place of his death is not known.

[The most recent account of Bourgmont, founded on documentary sources, is that of Baron Marc de Villiers, *La Découverte du Missouri et l'Histoire du Fort d'Orléans* (Paris, 1925). Brief but excellent sketches are in *Mich. Pioneer and Hist. Colls.*, XXXIV, 306–7; Louis Houck, *Hist. of Mo.* (1905), I, 258. Pierre Margry, *Découvertes et Établissements des Français dans l'Amérique Septentrionale* (Paris, 1876), VI, 388–448, gives several documents concerning Bourgmont and the journal of his western expedition. For its route see *Kan. Hist. Trans.*, IX, 255–57, and *Kan. Hist. Colls.*, XIV, 450–55. The account in Le Page du Pratz, *Histoire de la Louisiane* (Paris, 1758) is believed to be apocryphal.] L. P. K.

BOURKE, JOHN GREGORY (June 23, 1846–June 8, 1896), soldier, ethnologist, was the son of Edward and Anna (Morton) Bourke, natives of Galway, Ireland, and is said to have been descended from the Norman De Bourgh family and from Godfrey de Bouillon. His birthplace was Philadelphia. His family had great ambitions for his education, putting him at eight years of age to studying Latin, Greek, and Gaelic with a Jesuit priest. At sixteen, pretending he was eighteen, he ran away from home in 1862 and joined the 15th Pennsylvania Cavalry with which he served during the rest of the Civil War. He then obtained an appointment to the United States Military Academy, where he graduated in 1869. For the next fourteen years he served under Gen. George Crook in the Southwest with the 3rd United States Cavalry, with which he remained for the rest of his life. Becoming interested in the study of the Indian, he observed the habits and customs of many tribes, hostile and peaceful, and methodically reduced what he heard or saw to careful notes. Primarily necessary in campaigning and in diplomacy with the Indians, these data formed the basis of his scientific and historical writings, often accomplished in the field. He first wrote *The Snake Dance of the Moquis of Arizona* (1884), the pioneer publication on the subject, containing much of interest to ethnologists. Detailed to Washington to work up his notes, he wrote ten ethnological papers for the *American Anthropologist* and completed *The Medicine Men of the Apache* (1892), a major paper published by the Bureau of American Ethnology. Meanwhile he had also produced *An Apache Campaign* (1886), *Mackenzie's Last Fight with the Cheyennes* (1890), *On the Border with Crook* (1891), and *Scatalogic Rites of all Nations* (1892). Bourke's historical writings are unusually vivid, as he was a good story teller and had a generous fund of wit and humor, while his scientific writings, compiled from his notes and unmarred by immature generalizations, will always be storehouses upon which workers may draw with profit. Bourke had deep-set gray eyes under bushy eyebrows, a prominent nose, well-formed chin, and the heavy mustache of the period. Of average height, his frame well-muscled, he gave the impression of endurance. This ensemble was informed by a lively, kind, shrewd, and attractive spirit.

[G. W. Cullum, *Biog. Reg.* (3rd ed., 1891); F. W. Hodge, "John Gregory Bourke," *Am. Anthropologist*, IX, 245–48; information from Bourke's daughter, Mrs. Sara Bourke James; personal recollections of the writer.] W. H.

BOURNE, BENJAMIN (Dec. 9, 1755–Sept. 17, 1808), soldier and jurist, was born in Bristol, R. I., the son of Shearjashub and Ruth (Bosworth) Church Bourne. He was graduated from Harvard College in 1775. In January 1776 he was appointed quartermaster of the second regiment of the Colony Brigade under command of Col. Henry Babcock, who was later succeeded by Col. Christopher Lippitt. He was later appointed ensign in Capt. Arnold's company and under date of Dec. 4, 1776, volunteered to cross the North River. He received his final pay at Chatham, N. Y., and returned to King's County, R. I., on Jan. 18, 1777. In February 1780 he was elected a deputy or representative in the legislature from Bristol. At the following session in May he was a deputy and also clerk of the General Assembly and in the same month he became a member of the Council of War. He retained the position of clerk until May 1786, and then became a deputy from Providence, serving from May 1787 to May 1790. During his term of office he became deeply interested in the ratification of the Federal Constitution on the part of Rhode Island and was a member of the General Assembly when a petition was received from the town of Providence requesting that the General Assembly call a convention to consider the acceptance of the Constitution of the United States. The General Assembly refused the request of the petitioners, but as in the interval the new government had been recognized in New York the situation in Rhode Island was far from satisfactory, and again the town of Providence chose a committee, of which Bourne was a member, to draft a petition to Congress asking for due consideration to Rhode Island in the emergency. This petition was transmitted to Congress by the hands of President Manning of Rhode Island College, and Bourne. In November 1789 Rhode Island was the only state remaining outside of the Union and at the January session in the following year Bourne renewed his motion for the calling of a convention and it was carried in the lower house by a strong majority. It afterward was passed by the state Senate with a very close vote. Bourne was sent as a delegate to the convention for the ratification of the Constitution, which occurred on May 29, 1790, in the town of Newport. In August of the same year President Washington visited Providence, and Bourne served as a member of the committee to receive him. Doubtless on account of his activity in connection with the Constitution, the State chose him as her first representative to the Congress of the United States and he served in the First, Second, Third, and Fourth Congresses. In September 1801 he became judge of the United States district court for the district of Rhode Island. He was married to Mrs. Hope (Child) Diman, widow of Capt. Benjamin Diman of Bristol.

[W. H. Munro, *Hist. of Bristol, R. I.* (1880); W. R. Staples, *Annals of the Town of Providence* (1843); *Biog. Cong. Dir.* (1911); manuscript records, State Record Commissioner's Office.] H. O. B.

BOURNE, EDWARD GAYLORD (June 24, 1860–Feb. 24, 1908), historian, educator, the son of Rev. James Russell and Isabella Graham (Staples) Bourne, was born in Strykersville, Wyoming County, N. Y. His father, a Congregational pastor, was descended from Richard Bourne who settled in Plymouth Colony about 1626, the family homestead being at Bourne, formerly in the town of Sandwich. His mother's mother was a Sears whose family was of Mayflower stock. His early life was spent mainly in New England rural parishes. A long illness in boyhood left him permanently lame. He prepared for college at Norwich Free Academy, ranking first in his class. In both school and college his love of books had no rival and he read widely in excess of all requirements. At Yale, where he graduated with the degree of B.A. in 1883, he distinguished himself in the classics until senior year when his interest was aroused in economics by Sumner and he won the Cobden medal. Declining a scholarship for classical study at Athens, he remained a graduate student of economics and history for five years, holding a Foote fellowship, being instructor in medieval history (1885–87) and lecturer on political science from 1886 to 1888. He then became instructor in history and economics in Adelbert College (1888–90) and professor of history there during the following five years. In 1892 he received the degree of Ph.D. from Yale, and in 1895 returned to New Haven as professor of history. In 1895, also, he was married to Annie Thomson Nettleton, daughter of William A. and Eliza Lyman (Thomson) Nettleton of Stockbridge, Mass. For the first two years of his professorship he taught European history, thereafter mainly American history. Preëminently a master of historical criticism, Bourne in his articles, reviews, and books revealed rare keenness in the application of its principles to problems of authorship and veracity, and to detection of plagiarism and legend. He tried for the Porter prize and his essay, suggested by Sumner, was developed into his first book, *The Surplus Revenue of 1837* (1885), the standard monograph on the subject. In Cleveland began a long friendship with J. F. Rhodes for whose history he collected materials and rendered valuable advice, services acknowledged by Rhodes in a grateful tribute (Rhodes, *Historical Essays,* 1909, pp. 191–200). From student days he contributed constantly to various periodicals. Thirteen of his more important articles appeared as his second book: *Essays in Historical Criticism* (1901). Here his critical sense was skilfully revealed in "The Legend of Marcus Whitman," wherein he distinguished between fact and myth, a revelation which evoked much protest from devotees of legend (see Myron Eells, *Reply to Professor Bourne's "The Whitman Legend,"* 1902; also, favorably to Bourne, W. I. Marshall, *History vs. The Whitman Saved Oregon Story . . . ,* 1904). Bourne's conclusions, however, "impressed scientific scholars as conclusive" (J. F. Jameson, *American Historical Review,* VII, 745–7). The period of discoveries and Spanish Colonization enlisted Bourne's chief interest in later years. His historical introduction to Blair and Robertson's *Philippine Islands* appeared in 1903. His third and best-known volume was *Spain in America* (1904; Spanish translation, 1906) wherein he gave an appreciative recognition of the work and purposes of Spain. The narrative was interwoven with shrewd criticism and original conclusions. If the book created too favorable an impression of Spanish institutions and culture (see M. Oppenheim, *American Historical Review,* XI, 394–97), that may have been owing to excessive reliance upon official documents and laws. Bourne edited Woolley's *Journal* (1902), Fournier's *Napoleon* (1903), Roscher's *Spanish Colonial System* (1904), and narrative sources for *De Soto* (1904), *The Northmen, Columbus, and Cabot* (1906), and *Champlain* (translated by Mrs. Bourne, 1906). As an early and energetic member of the American Historical Association, he was chairman (1901–8) of its historical manuscripts commission which published the diary and part of the correspondence of Chief Justice Chase (1903). For the New England History Teachers' Association, of which he was president in 1901, he served on the committee of five who prepared *Historical Sources in Schools* (1902). In recognition of rare editorial ability he was considered for editor of the Massachusetts Historical Society and his appointment was prevented only by declining health (Rhodes, *Historical Essays*, p. 199). His last undertaking was a life of Motley which he did not live to complete. Suffering nearly two years from hip-joint disease, he died in New Haven, in his forty-eighth year.

[Correspondence and materials for a life of Bourne possessed by his brother, Henry Eldridge Bourne; appreciations by A. B. Hart, A. G. Keller, and others, including a bibliography of Bourne, in *Yale Alumni Weekly,* Mar. 25, 1908 (*Yale Reprints,* No. 2); F. H. Herrick in *Western Reserve Univ. Bull.*, XI, 96–103.]

F.W.P.

BOURNE, GEORGE (June 13, 1780–Nov. 20, 1845), Presbyterian and Dutch Reformed clergyman, abolitionist, was born in Westbury, England, and was educated at Homerton Seminary in London. From there he came to Virginia and Maryland. He was pastor of a Presbyterian church in South River, Va., in 1814. As a result of his strong reaction to his direct contact with the institution of slavery, he was one of the first in the United States to advocate immediate emancipation (*The Book and Slavery Irreconcilable,* 1816). He was bitterly persecuted by the advocates of slavery and called before a Presbyterian council where he was condemned on a charge of heresy for his anti-slavery views. He was finally compelled to leave the Southern states. For a while he lived in Germantown, Pa. (*Manual of the Reformed Church*), a little later in Sing Sing, N. Y., where he was principal of an academy as well as pastor of a Presbyterian church. In Quebec from 1825 to 1828, he had two Presbyterian churches, and here he became a strong opponent of Catholicism. Two years later he was back in New York, but without a church. Presbyterian records list him as an editor in 1831 and in 1832 Garrison writes of him as publishing "a spirited journal, entitled, *The Protestant.*" The following year saw him a member of the Dutch Reformed Church, which had perhaps the greatest tolerance for his extreme anti-slavery principles. He supplied the Houston Street Chapel and vacant churches, and at the same time contributed to periodicals and the press, and was the author of a number of works which expressed his views. Garrison said of him, "Bourne thunders and lightens," and he frequently recognized his courage and the vigor and strength of his mind. He was among the fifty or sixty delegates present at the Philadelphia convention for the formation of the Anti-Slavery Society in 1833 (*Garrison*). At an anniversary meeting in 1837, he offered a resolution censuring clergymen who during the past year had defended slavery and opposed the enlightening of their congregations "without the advice and consent of the pastors and regular ecclesiastical bodies" (*Ibid.*). He was opposed to "woman's rights," and felt certain that no woman would be allowed a seat in the world anti-slavery convention, although Lucretia Mott had been appointed as a delegate by the American society. Naturally belligerent, he had no patience with the policy of non-resistance. He wrote Garrison in 1838 that he anticipated no peace from his "non-resistance oppugnation" but foresaw in it only mischief to the anti-slavery cause. He lived at West Farms from 1839 to 1842, and at the time of his death in 1845 was employed on the *Christian Intelligencer* in New York. His published works are: *The History of Napoleon Bonaparte* (1806); *The Spirit of the Public Journals; or, Beauties of the American Newspapers for 1805* (1806); *The Book and Slavery Irreconcilable* (1816); *The Picture of Quebec* (1829); *An Address to the Presbyterian Church, Enforcing the Duty of Excluding All Slave-holders from the "Communion of Saints"* (1833); *Lorette, The History of Louise, Daughter of a Canadian Nun, Exhibiting the Interior of Female Convents* (1834); *Man-Stealing and Slavery Denounced by the Presbyterian and Methodist Churches* (1834); *Picture of Slavery in the United States of America* (1834); *Slavery Illustrated in Its Effects upon Woman and Domestic Society* (1837); *A Condensed Anti-Slavery Bible Argument* (1845).

[*Minutes of General Assembly of the Presbyt. Ch.*, vols. III, V, VI, VII; *Manual of the Reformed Ch. in America* (1879); *Liberator,* vols. I, II; *Wm. Lloyd Garrison, Told by His Children* (1885–89); *N. Y. Herald,* Nov. 22, 1845; *N. Y. Tribune,* Nov. 21, 1845.]

M.A.K.

BOURNE, NEHEMIAH (*c.* 1611–1691), ship builder, British rear admiral, was born in London, the son of Robert and Mary Bourne. His father, a Wapping shipwright, desired in his will that Nehemiah become a scholar and be brought up at Cambridge University, but the son cared more for the father's trade than for the father's wishes. He married young and in 1638 migrated to Massachusetts, where he was a shipbuilder and merchant first at Charlestown, later at Dorchester, and finally at Boston. He had the distinction of building Gov. Winthrop's ship, the *Trial,* the first vessel of any size to be laid down at Boston. The *Trial* was of between 160 and 200 tons burden, was ready in June 1641, but had to wait another year until her rigging arrived from London. The subsequent career of her builder, though not known in detail, is full of interest.

He was a major in the Parliamentary army, returned to Massachusetts to take back his family, and in 1650 became commander of the frigate *Speaker* in the Parliamentary navy. In this ship he brought to London the Scottish records, insignia, and regalia taken at Stirling Castle, for which he received a gold medal worth £60. As commander of a squadron near the mouth of the Thames, he notified Admiral Blake on May 18, 1652, that Van Tromp with forty sail was off Southend-on-Sea. In the battle of the following day he and his squadron played a prominent part. On that same day he was appointed "Rear Admiral of the Fleet of the Commonwealth of England and Captain of the ship (*St. Andrew*) of 60 guns." In less than a year he was made Commissioner of the Navy charged with refitting, victualing, and manning ships sent to Harwich and Yarmouth from the main fleet. At the same time he appears to have engaged in mercantile pursuits, probably in a way that legitimately combined public service with private profits. At the Restoration he decamped to the continent, was later pardoned, and spent his last years in England. He was buried in Bunhill Fields beside his beloved wife, Hanna, by whom he had four sons and a daughter. His will, dated Feb. 11, 1690/91 and probated May 15, 1691, shows that the doughty old merchant, sea fighter, and Puritan died in comfortable circumstances.

[I. J. Greenwood, "Rear Admiral Nehemiah Bourne," *New Eng. Hist. and Geneal. Reg.*, Jan. 1873, pp. 26–36; article "Nehemiah Bourne" in *Dict. of Nat. Biog.*, vol. VI (1886).] G. H. G.

BOURNE, RANDOLPH SILLIMAN (May 30, 1886–Dec. 22, 1918), essayist, was born in Bloomfield, N. J., the son of Charles and Sara (Randolph) Bourne. Owing to a fall in infancy, he was deformed,—hunchbacked, with a stunted body, large head, and heavy features; only those who recognized the keenness of his mind and the beauty of his spirit could forget his physical appearance or write of it like Van Wyck Brooks, "I shall never forget . . . that odd little apparition with his vibrant eyes, his quick bird-like steps"; less appreciative observers could see only a painful outward ugliness. Bourne attended the public schools of Bloomfield, earned his living for a time as an assistant to a manufacturer of automatic piano music, and in 1909 entered Columbia University where he graduated in 1913. In 1913 also he published *Youth and Life,* a book of radiantly idealistic essays inspired by the thought of an approaching "youth movement" in America. Enabled by a Gilder Fellowship to spend a year in European travel and study, on his return he submitted to Columbia a remarkably incisive report on European cultural conditions, modestly entitled "Impressions of Europe 1913–14." Profoundly influenced by the educational theories of John Dewey, he produced, somewhat in their vein, *The Gary Schools* (1916) and *Education and Living* (1917), but the failure of liberal pragmatism to meet the issues raised by the World War gradually drove him to a more radical philosophy. He became a pronounced pacifist and in the *Masses* and the *Seven Arts* vigorously attacked America's entrance into the war. With the suspension of the *Seven Arts* in September 1917 his chief organ of expression was gone; in extreme poverty he held on his lonely way; and at the time of his death he was engaged in a work upon the State the published fragments of which present a close analysis and scathing indictment of that institution. He died in the influenza epidemic of 1918. Of his two posthumously published works, *Untimely Papers* (1919), edited by James Oppenheim, and *The History of a Literary Radical* (1920), edited by Van Wyck Brooks, the former constitutes the most trenchant expression which we have of the attitude of the suppressed minority during the World War. In his early death America lost a writer of great promise, a critic at home in philosophy, education, politics, and literature but homeless in his contemporary world.

[Introductions by Brooks and Oppenheim to the volumes mentioned above; *Who's Who in America,* 1918–19; personal acquaintance.] E. S. B.

BOUTELL, HENRY SHERMAN (Mar. 14, 1856–Mar. 11, 1926), lawyer, diplomat, was born at Boston, Mass., the son of Lewis Henry and Anna (Greene) Boutell. A colonial ancestry entitled him to membership in the Sons of the American Revolution and in the Society of Colonial Wars. His college education was secured at Northwestern (A.B. 1874, M.A. 1879) and Harvard (A.B. 1876, A.M. 1877). After studying law in an office, in 1879 he was admitted to the bar and began practise in Chicago. Although both able and prominent as an attorney (representing, for example, the Baltimore & Ohio Railroad in securing a right of way into Chicago, and in the erection of its terminal therein), his tastes from the beginning ran to public life, and he was soon both active and useful as a worker in the Republican party. In 1884 he was a member of the lower house of the state legislature, and from 1897 to 1911 a representative of Chicago districts in Congress. There he was a member of the committees on Rules, and on Ways and Means, and was chairman of the Committee on Expenditures of the Navy. He was an effective speaker and of considerable influence, but his tariff views were unacceptable to business interests in Chicago, which forced his retirement. President Taft then appointed him to the post of envoy extraordinary and minister plenipotentiary to Portugal, on Mar. 2, 1911. He never assumed its duties, and on Apr. 24, 1911, he was given a similar appointment to Switzerland. In this post he served from May 17, 1911, to July 31, 1913. He did not find the diplomatic service to his liking, and resigned. Before he did so he had declined the chief-justiceship of the United States court of claims tendered him by President Taft (January 1913). With this his public career ended, except for service (November 1913) as chairman of a board of arbitration which settled an important dispute between the operatives and officers of the Chicago, Burlington & Quincy Railway. From 1914 to 1923 he taught constitutional law and international law in Georgetown University, in Washington, D. C. He was short of stature, very erect and dignified of carriage, alert in movement. Distinctly of the scholarly type, he was very widely read, and active, so long as he resided in Chicago, in the Literary Club of that city. His speeches, which reflected his reading, were always graceful and sometimes eloquent. In his political opinions he was fairly liberal, but in the regulation of purely personal affairs and conduct he was notably conservative. He was a rare combination of force and urbanity. Although unfailingly careful to avoid giving offense to anybody with whom he came in contact, invariably gracious, and charming in manner, his opinions were not lacking in definiteness, and he was not in any way colorless. These qualities should have won him great distinction either in law or diplomacy, but in politics they left him merely a staunch and dependable "party" man, whose mental independence and natural talents were hampered by party platforms. He did not win in public life the renown of which his abilities and early professional success gave promise. On Dec. 29, 1880, he was married to Euphemia Lucia Clara Gates of Providence, R. I. He died at San Remo, Italy. Several children survived him.

[The chronology of Boutell's life is given, inadequately, in *Who's Who in America*, 1908–09; and in the *Biog. Cong. Dir. 1774–1911*; see also obituaries, Mar. 13, 1926, in the *Chicago Daily Tribune* and the *Washington Post*, as well as the sketch in *Harvard Coll. Class of 1876, Tenth Report* (1926).] F. S. P.

BOUTELLE, CHARLES ADDISON (Feb. 9, 1839–May 21, 1901), naval officer, journalist, congressman, was the son of Charles and Lucy Ann (Curtis) Boutelle. He was born in Damariscotta, Me. When he was nine years old his parents moved to Brunswick. There he received a common school and academic education. His parents wished him to go through college but he had a strong craving for a seafaring life and preferred to accompany his father on his voyages. On returning from a voyage in 1862 he found the country in the midst of the Civil War and promptly enlisted in the navy and took part with credit in various operations. In 1863 he was acting master on board the U. S. S. *Sassacus*. On May 5 he showed great coolness and courage in a desperate conflict of the *Sassacus* with the Confederate iron-clad *Albemarle* and for his gallant conduct was made an acting volunteer lieutenant, the highest position attainable by a volunteer. In the winter of 1864–65 he took an active part in the operations at Mobile. In 1866 he was discharged from the service at his own request. Boutelle received high praise from his superiors. One said, "I regarded him as one of the best of the volunteer appointments, officer-like in his bearing, intelligent and exhibiting an interest in his professional improvement, gunnery and small arms, unusual in one not bred to the service." Another officer in reply to a request for a recommendation for a special appointment wrote: "He is brave to a fault; he is intelligent and possesses the adornments of a cultivated gentleman." After leaving the service Boutelle fitted out and commanded a steamer plying between New York City and Wilmington, N. C., and later he engaged with the shipping commission firm of Walsh & Carver in New York City. From boyhood Boutelle had been interested in journalism, he had already contributed to political journals, and in 1870 he became managing editor of an old and influential paper, the *Whig and Courier* in Bangor, Me. In 1874 he became principal owner. In 1880 he was nominated on the Republican ticket for Congress, made a whirlwind campaign, and greatly cut down the majority of the Democratic sitting member at the previous election, but failed of success. He then took an active part in the national campaign in Ohio and New York. He was renominated for Congress in 1882, was elected, and was reëlected for nine successive terms. As editor and politician as well as soldier Boutelle was a hard though clean fighter and a foe to compromise. He was an intense Republican of the reconstruction school, an ardent protectionist, always ready to do battle for the legal rights of the negroes, for a high tariff, and for liberal pensions. He vigorously opposed the conciliation policy of Hayes, the reinstatement of Fitz-John Porter, and the removal of the disabilities of Jefferson Davis. But as the years passed he softened and at the close of his career he was highly regarded by his political opponents. A strong sound-money man, he opposed the war with Spain, fearing that it would be used to drive the country to a silver basis. His most individual work was his championship of a modern and stronger navy in the period between the Civil and the Spanish wars when the public took little interest in the question of sea power. He was an ardent admirer of James G. Blaine and his constant and unflinching supporter for the presidency. As editor, Boutelle kept his paper free from yellow journalism; late in life it was sold, first to a friendly syndicate and then to a journalistic and political rival. In 1899 Boutelle had an attack of congestion of the brain from which he never recovered. He was, however, reëlected to Congress but resigned and died in 1901. His Maine colleagues in the House placed in the Central Church of Bangor a stained glass window as a memorial in his honor. Boutelle was married to Elizabeth Hodsdon, daughter of Adjutant-General Hodsdon of Augusta, who predeceased him.

[*Hist. of Penobscot County, Me.* (1882), pp. 766, 915; *Biog. Encyc. of Me.* (1885), ed. by H. C. Williams, p. 308; *Bangor Daily News,* May 22, 1901; *Daily Eastern Argus,* May 22, 1901.] L. C. H.

BOUTON, JOHN BELL (Mar. 15, 1830–Nov. 18, 1902), author, was born in Concord, N. H., where for more than forty years his father, Rev. Nathaniel Bouton [*q.v.*], was pastor of the First Congregational Church. He was of French descent through Jean Bouton, who came to this country from England in 1635 and settled in Connecticut. His mother, Mary Anne Persis Bell, daughter of Gov. John Bell of New Hampshire, was of Norman origin, though after the Conquest the Bells settled in the south of Scotland and later in the north of Ireland, from which country John Bell emigrated to New Hampshire in 1720. John Bell Bouton grew up in a home where interest in public service and literary pursuits was fostered. He graduated from Dartmouth College in 1849, having taken high rank as a scholar. He studied law, but in 1851 became editor of the *Cleveland Plain-Dealer.* In 1857 he removed to New York, and was for many years one of the editors and owners of the *New York Journal of Commerce.* For about ten years he was also an editor of *Appleton's Annual Cyclopedia.* On Dec. 4, 1873, he married his cousin Eliza, daughter of John and Eliza (Bell) Nesmith of Lowell, Mass. Severing his business connections in 1889, he made his home in Cambridge, Mass., and spent his time in travel and writing. His publications include a volume of essays, *Loved and Lost* (1857); *Round the Block, an American Novel* (1864) which, though long and tedious, portrays rather well some of the manners of the time in New York, and reveals skill in character portrayal; *A Memoir of General Louis Bell* (1865); *Roundabout to Moscow, an Epicurean Journey* (1887), a good-humored and entertaining narrative of travels in Europe; *The Enchanted, an Authentic Account of the Strange Origin of the New Psychical Club* (1891); *Uncle Sam's Church: His Creed, Bible and Hymn-book* (1895), a plea for the development of a patriotic cult. He also edited the *Autobiography of Nathaniel Bouton* (1879).

[*Dartmouth Coll. Cat.* (1910); obituaries in *Boston Evening Transcript,* Nov. 18, 1902, and information supplied by Hollis R. Bailey, Esq.] H. E. S.

BOUTON, NATHANIEL (June 29, 1799–June 6, 1878), Congregational minister, historian, was a descendant in the sixth generation of Jean Bouton, a French Huguenot, who came from England to New England in 1635, and in 1651 became one of the founders of Norwalk, Conn. Nathaniel was born in Norwalk, the fourteenth and youngest child of William and Sarah (Benedict) Bouton. His father was a farmer who could provide no more than a common school education for his children; but Nathaniel aspired to something more, and succeeded at fourteen in becoming an apprentice to a printer who was also the editor of a weekly paper at Bridgeport, a few miles away. The boy was bright, conscientious and affectionate, though somewhat quick-tempered and fond of disputation. Beside learning his trade, he occasionally wrote contributions for the paper. At a time of special religious interest, when he was sixteen, his own religious nature was aroused and he became active and successful in evangelistic work among those of his own age. This turned his thoughts to the ministry and, with the help of those whose interest had been aroused by his activity, he procured his release from his apprenticeship, prepared himself for college, and made his way through Yale (where he graduated in 1821) and through Andover Seminary (graduating in 1824). He was called almost immediately to the First Congregational Church of Concord, N. H., then the only church in the place. He spent the rest of his life in Concord, for forty-two years as a notably successful pastor, and for ten years thereafter as state historian. He was thrice married; first, on June 11, 1825, to Harriet Sherman; second, on June 8, 1829, to Mary Ann Persis Bell; and third, on Feb. 18, 1840, to Elizabeth Ann Cilley. He is described by his son John B. Bouton [*q.v.*] as "a medium-sized man, spare and sinewy, with a clean-shaven face, regular features, piercing, gray-blue eyes and shaggy eyebrows."

Incidentally to his pastoral work he became a student of New Hampshire history and a zealous member of the state historical society, editing in 1850 Volumes VII and VIII of its *Collections.* In 1856 he published his *History of Concord, N. H.,* and in 1861 he brought out an annotated edition of *Lovewell's Great Fight at Pigwacket, 1725.* After his resignation of his pastorate the office of state historian was created for him in order that he might edit and publish the entire documentary history of New Hampshire, from the beginning of the settlement in 1623 to the adoption of the constitution in 1784. This he did in ten volumes averaging over 850 pages apiece, which appeared annually from 1867 to 1877. It was an arduous task, four-fifths of the manuscript being written out in his own hand. Though not his chief interest, which was the ministry, this labor of his old age is his chief claim to remembrance, and his enduring monument. He contributed also to religious journals and published a number of sermons, and addresses, largely biographical and historical. Though not a man of great originality, he was kindly and lovable, and an indefatigable worker, who well served his day and generation.

[The chief sources are Bouton's *Autobiography* (1879), ed. by John Bell Bouton, and the latter's *Sketch of the Character and Life-Work of Rev. Nathaniel Bouton* (1902); see also obituary in the *Concord Daily Monitor,* June 7, 1878.] B.W.B.

BOUTWELL, GEORGE SEWALL (Jan. 28, 1818–Feb. 27, 1905), politician, born in Brookline, Mass., was the son of Sewall and Rebecca (Marshall) Boutwell, both of old Massachusetts stock. His boyhood was passed in Lunenburg, Mass., where from the age of thirteen to seventeen he was employed in a small store with the privilege of attending school during the winter months. When he was seventeen he became clerk in a store in Groton, Mass. He devoted much of his time to self-education in the hope of becoming a lawyer, and at an early age began to write articles for the newspapers on political topics, and to make addresses. In 1841 he was married to Sarah Adelia Thayer. He was an active Democrat, and during seven sessions between 1842 and 1850 represented Groton in the lower house of the state legislature. Through his useful work there he became one of the leaders of the younger element of the party, whose anti-slavery leanings made possible the coalition with the Free-Soilers which in 1850 defeated the Whigs. As a result of this coalition, Boutwell was elected by the legislature governor for the year 1851, and Charles Sumner, representing the Free-Soilers, was elected senator; the same political combination effected Boutwell's reëlection for 1852. After the expiration of his term he pursued legal studies with the purpose of becoming a patent lawyer; from 1855 to 1861 he was secretary of the state board of education. In January 1862 he was admitted to the Suffolk bar.

The important part of Boutwell's career lies in the field of national politics. He had been one of the organizers of the Republican party in Massachusetts in 1855, and he consistently represented its radical wing,—more, however, on the side of practical politics than in its idealistic aspect. From July 17, 1862, to Mar. 3, 1863, he was commissioner of internal revenue, and in that short period did effective work in organizing this new branch of the government. His activities as a radical Republican were most conspicuous during his terms of service as representative in Congress from 1863 to 1869 in connection with the problems of reconstruction. As a member of the Joint Committee on Reconstruction he helped in framing the Fourteenth Amendment; his belief in the necessity of full suffrage for the negro led to his advocacy of the Fifteenth Amendment. His support of the congressional plan of Reconstruction involved persistent, vigorous, and even fanatical opposition to President Johnson and his policies. In the movement for the impeachment of the President he was among the leaders, being chosen by the House of Representatives as one of its seven managers to conduct the impeachment. His suggestion that a suitable punishment for Johnson, the "enemy of two races of men," would be his projection into a "hole in the sky" near the Southern Cross, drew the ridicule of William M. Evarts, counsel for the defense. Boutwell's efforts on behalf of the radical Republicans were rewarded by a place in Grant's cabinet as secretary of the treasury. To this position he brought qualifications chiefly of a political nature, and he was not a supporter of civil service reform; but he labored diligently in improving the organization of the department and in reducing the national debt. Before the end of his four years as secretary he had effected the redemption of 200 millions of six per cent bonds and sold an equal amount bearing interest at five per cent (*Report of the Secretary of the Treasury,* December 1872, iii). Early in his administration occurred the famous "Black Friday," on which day an attempted corner in gold was broken by his release of Treasury gold.

From March 1873 to March 1877, he served a four-year term as senator from Massachusetts. On his failure to be reëlected by his party he was appointed commissioner to revise the statutes of the United States. In 1880 he became counsel and agent of the United States before a board of international arbitrators for the settlement of claims of French citizens against the government of this country, and of American citizens against the government of France. In his practise as a lawyer, which he resumed after his retirement from the Senate, he handled numerous cases involving questions of international law. The independence of spirit which at various times in his career he had manifested,—in marked contrast to his general disposition for party regularity—showed itself in his last years in his opposition to the policy of the Republican party on the Philippine question, and led to his withdrawal from the party; he was president of the Anti-Imperialist League from its organization in November 1898 until his death in 1905. He was the author of *Thoughts on Educational Topics and Institutions* (1859); *A Manual of the Direct and Excise Tax System of the United States* (1863); *Speeches Relating to the Rebellion and the Overthrow of Slavery* (1867); *The Constitution of the United States at the End of the First Century* (1895); *The Crisis of the Republic* (1900).

[Boutwell's *Reminiscences of Sixty Years in Public Affairs* (1902) contains interesting though guarded accounts of the public men of his time; to it is prefixed a biographical sketch which appeared in the *Memoirs of the Judiciary and the Bar of New Eng.*, Jan. 1901. For his connection with the impeachment of Johnson see D. M. DeWitt, *The Impeachment and Trial of Andrew Johnson* (1903); E. P. Oberholtzer, *Jay Cooke* (1907) has numerous references to Boutwell as secretary of the treasury.] H. G. P.

BOUVET, MARIE MARGUERITE (Feb. 14, 1865–May 27, 1915), linguist, writer of books for young people, was born in the French city of New Orleans, of French parents. Her father, Jean François Bouvet, was a descendant of François, Comte de Bouvet d'Asti in Piedmont. Her mother, Adelphine Bertrand Bouvet, daughter of a cavalry officer of Charles X, attended the Convent of the Sacred Heart, Paris, and took a degree at the Sorbonne. The parents were married in New Orleans and there the father died in 1870, after having suffered loss of fortune in the Civil War. In early childhood Marguerite spent seven years with her father's parents in their home near Lyons, France, and memories of this period are embodied in several of her books. She attended Loquet-Leroy Female Institute, New Orleans, in which her mother was a teacher, and was graduated from St. Mary's College, Knoxville, Ill., in 1885. After graduation she became a teacher of French and compiled a book of French quotations, *Fleurs des Poètes et des Prosateurs Français* (1900). Soon her interest in teaching was shared, if not overshadowed, by the interest of authorship. She wrote books for young people, with quiet narratives, simply but not childishly told, so that many older people have found them interesting. Most of the settings are European and quaint foreign characters and customs are well described. *Sweet William* (1890), which is located at Mont St. Michel, in Normandy, and introduces the character of William the Conqueror, is the one of her books which best meets the approval of children's librarians. *Little Marjorie's Love Story* (1891), *Prince Tip Top* (1892), *My Lady* (1894), and *Pierrette* (1896) are less successful. *A Child of Tuscany* (1895) is a story of child life in Florence. *A Little House in Pimlico* (1897) has a London child for its central figure. *Tales of an Old Château* (1899) recounts incidents of the French Revolution, told to Marguerite Bouvet during her childhoood in France. *Bernardo and Laurette* (1901) has good atmosphere of the Savoy Mountains and the Rhone Valley. *Clotilde* (1908) is a story of child life in New Orleans. *The Smile of the Sphinx* (1911), with setting divided between Baltimore and France, is artificial. According to later standards, sentimentality is the chief fault of all Marguerite Bouvet's work. Two extended visits in Europe, after she had begun to write, enabled her to make her European stories realistic. For some years before her death she and a friend of St. Mary's College days made their home together in Reading, Pa. She was a member of the Woman's Club there and her adaptability, gracious manner, and Gallic vivacity won her many friends.

[*Who's Who in America*, 1914–15; *Woman's Who's Who of America*, 1914–15; *Men and Women of America* (1910); private information.] S. G. B.

BOUVIER, JOHN (1787–Nov. 18, 1851), judge, legal writer, was born at Condognan, Department of Gard, in France, of French-Quaker parentage. At the age of fourteen he emigrated from France with his parents, John and Marie (Benezet) Bouvier, to Philadelphia, where members of his mother's distinguished family already lived. The following year his father died. A friend of his family, Benjamin Johnson, who was a printer and bookseller, took him into business. When he became twenty-one his friends set him up in the printing business in Philadelphia, whence he moved to West Philadelphia, later to Brownsville where he edited and published a weekly newspaper, the *American Telegraph,* and still later to Uniontown where he published the *Genius of Liberty,* also continuing the *American Telegraph.* In 1818, he was admitted to the bar in Uniontown, and in 1822, was admitted to practise before the supreme court of Pennsylvania. In the following year he returned to Philadelphia. While studying law he made an abridgment of *Blackstone's Commentaries.* During his years of study he had discovered the handicap under which the student and lawyer labored at that time due to the lack of a dictionary containing legal information logically and conveniently compiled. He began work on a great dictionary and indefatigably applied himself to it, in spite of increasing duties. In 1836 he was elected recorder of Philadelphia, and on the abolition of the mayor's court in 1838, he was made associate judge of the court of criminal sessions. Nevertheless, in 1839, he was able to give his completed dictionary to fill the need of the profession. It was entitled, *A Law Dictionary Adapted to the Constitution and Laws of the United States and the Several States of the American Union.* He sought to cover all legal subjects and terms arising under such a title, giving citations from federal and state courts. Eminent jurists such as Kent and Story, to the latter of whom the work was dedicated, attested its value and importance, and received it with unqualified commendation, stating that it would receive a response from the bar all over the United States. The dictionary passed through three editions during the twelve years following, and Bouvier was preparing a fourth at the time of his death. In these subsequent editions he not only rewrote many of the earlier articles, but added copiously to them, covering omissions and new developments. By the year 1886, when it was first revised, there had been fifteen editions. Since that revision there have been two others, with many editions. In 1841–45 Bouvier issued a new edition of *Matthew Bacon's Abridgment of the Law* in ten volumes, making its first index. In 1851 he published the *Institutes of American Law* in four volumes, which was a compendium of American law based upon the system of Pothier, which he greatly admired. Of this work there was a second edition in 1870.

[*North Am. Rev.*, July 1861; *Law Reporter,* XIV, 466; *Legal Intelligencer,* XXIV, 373; Henry Simpson, *The Lives of Eminent Philadelphians* (1859), pp. 111–23.] G. R.

BOWDEN, JOHN (Jan. 7, 1751–July 31, 1817), Anglican clergyman, educator, the son of Thomas Bowden, an officer in the British army, was born in Ireland where his father was serving at the time. He came to America in the care of a Church of England clergyman, following his father who had come here with his regiment, and for two years he was a student at the College of New Jersey (afterward Princeton). When his father's regiment was ordered home young Bowden returned with him. But in 1770 he came back to America to carry on his studies. This time he entered King's (afterward Columbia) College, and graduated in the class of 1772. He then studied for holy orders, and in 1774 was ordered deacon by the Rt. Rev. Frederick Keppel, Bishop of Exeter, and advanced to the priesthood the same year by the Rt. Rev. Richard Terrick, Bishop of London. In the fall of this year he returned to New York, and accepted an invitation to serve as an assistant minister in Trinity Church. During the troublous times of the Revolution he resigned his position and remained without a parish until the close of the war when, in December 1784, he became rector of St. Paul's Church, Norwalk, Conn. Here he remained until the fall of 1789, when the condition of his health made it imperative that he should seek a change of climate, and he accepted an invitation to take charge of the church in St. Croix in the West Indies. He did not obtain the benefit which he had anticipated, and after a stay of about two years he returned to this country and made his home in Stratford, Conn., where he established a small school. Among the Connecticut Episcopalians, who were now forging ahead under the vigorous leadership of Bishop Seabury, a movement was inaugurated as early as 1792, looking to the founding of an institution of learning within the bounds of the Diocese of Connecticut, which should be under Episcopal control, but not narrowly sectarian. The result was the Episcopal Academy of Connecticut located at Cheshire, which opened its doors for the admission of pupils in June 1796. The constitution provided that "female education may be attended to under this institution," and that was the policy of the school until 1836, when it became exclusively a boys' school. For the first principal of this academy Bowden was unanimously chosen. He accepted and took with him most of the pupils who were under his charge at Stratford. He administered the affairs of the Academy with marked distinction and success until April 1802, when he resigned to become professor of moral philosophy, belles lettres, and logic in Columbia College, which position he held until his death. When the Diocese of Connecticut was called upon to choose a successor to Bishop Seabury, who died Feb. 25, 1796, Bowden was unanimously elected to that office, Oct. 19, 1796. He requested that he might delay his answer until the annual convention in the following June. At that time he signified his unwillingness to accept, the condition of his health being not the least of the reasons which governed him in making his decision. The testimony of Bowden's contemporaries is that he was a man of fine scholarship, an effective teacher, a true gentleman. He lived in times of ecclesiastical controversy, when to give and take in the form of pamphlets was the recognized and orthodox mode of warfare. In the defense and exposition of his cherished principles of church doctrine and government, he struck vigorous blows. These controversial pamphlets constitute, for the most part, his literary production. Among the more important are: *A Letter to Ezra Stiles* [*on*] *Church Government* (1788); *An Address from John Bowden, A.M., to the Members of the Episcopal Church in Stratford* (1792); *Two Letters to the Editor of the Christian's Magazine* (1807); *A Full Length Portrait of Calvinism* (1809). He was married to Mary Jervis, and one of his three sons graduated from Columbia in the class of 1813, and became a clergyman in the Episcopal Church. He died at Ballston Spa, N. Y., and was buried there.

[*Christian Jour.*, Jan. 1818; Rev. John McVicar, *Address before the Alumni of Columbia Coll.* (1837); Rev. Wm. Berrian, *Sketch of Trinity Ch. N. Y.* (1847); W. B. Sprague, *Annals of the Am. Pulpit*, vol. V (1859).]

W. A. B.

BOWDITCH, CHARLES PICKERING (Sept. 30, 1842–June 1, 1921), archæologist, was the son of Jonathan Ingersoll Bowditch and Lucy O. Nichols, and the grandson of Nathaniel Bowditch [*q.v.*]. He received the A.B. degree from Harvard College in 1863 and the A.M. degree three years later. He served in the Civil War as second lieutenant, first lieutenant, and captain of the 55th Massachusetts Volunteer Infantry and as captain of the 5th Massachusetts Volunteer Cavalry. On June 7, 1866, he was married to Cornelia L. Rockwell. His broad interests are shown in his membership in learned societies connected with the fields of art, science, archæology, anthropology, geography, history, and genealogy and in many of these he held the highest offices. He was treasurer of the American Academy of Arts and Sciences from 1905 to 1915 and president from 1917 to 1919. As trustee of the Hopkins Fund and as member of the faculty of the Peabody Museum his affiliation with Harvard University was a very close one. He was the greatest benefactor the Museum ever had. Two large exhibition halls are filled to a great extent with the results of frequent expeditions to Yucatan and Central America, planned and financed by him. By his own individual studies he occupied at the time of his death a commanding position in American archæology. He was the greatest scholar of Maya hieroglyphic writing and no one working in this field can disregard his pioneer work. Special mention should be made of his book, *The Numeration, Calendar Systems and Astronomical Knowledge of the Mayas* (1910). This work was a landmark in the study of the Central American writing and served to focus attention on the subject as no other book had done. His mental agility in working out the dates of the inscriptions and his feats of rapid calculation were received with wonder and admiration by his friends and colleagues. He collected and presented to the Peabody Museum one of the best working libraries in Maya studies and he was responsible for the publication of several ancient documents in facsimile. He also gave the Museum over fifty thousand pages of photographic reproductions of manuscripts and rare books dealing with the languages of Mexico and Central America. This collection comprises practically everything in manuscript form now extant on the languages of these regions. His benefactions included the founding of fellowships and instructorships in Central American archæology. There is perhaps no other instance in American anthropology where an effort in one field of interest was so long sustained, so intense, and so productive of results. Following in the footsteps of his illustrious grandfather who translated Laplace's monumental *Mécanique céleste*, he translated numerous Spanish works the most important of which were Landa's *Relación de las Cosas de Yucatán* and Avendaño's *Relación*. His mind was an analytical one; he was a worthy foe of speculative theories and his studies and deductions in the Maya field were based on sound mathematical calculations. He was of striking appearance with a commanding figure. He had a very strong personality, trying to carry out the letter of the law and expecting others to do so. He was forceful yet full of modesty, always with opinions but willing to reason, wrathful before underhandedness but just to all.

[*Am. Anthropologist*, n.s., XXIII, 353–59 (portr.); *Proc. Am. Acad. of Arts and Sci.*, LVII, 476–78; *Report of the Class of 1863 Harvard Coll.* (1903, 1913); *Who's Who in America*, 1920–21.]

A. M. T.

BOWDITCH, HENRY INGERSOLL (Aug. 9, 1808–Jan. 14, 1892), physician and abolitionist, third son of Nathaniel Bowditch [*q.v.*] and Mary (Ingersoll) Bowditch, was born in Salem, Mass., where he resided until 1823 when his family moved to Boston. He received his early education at the Salem Private Grammar School, but when fifteen he entered the Boston Public Latin School. As a boy he exhibited no evidence of precocity, though at fourteen he won a diploma for Latin. He entered Harvard College in 1825, graduating in 1828, but did not distinguish himself as an undergraduate; his diary (*Life*, I, 12) at that period, however, shows a serious-minded young man, deeply religious and conscientious. With some misgivings he entered the Harvard Medical School (M.D., 1832), and went from there to the Massachusetts General Hospital (Boston) where he served during 1831–32 as a house-officer under James Jackson [*q.v.*]. He went to Paris in 1832, and his father's international reputation brought him at once into contact with many of the best minds of France. For two years Bowditch studied under Louis and followed him in his wards at *La Pitié*, from time to time in company with other young Boston physicians. He became deeply attached to Louis and looked upon him as the greatest leader of that day in medical science. When Bowditch went to England the contrast between Louis and the English physicians whom he met seemed so great that he left London in disgust (*Life*, I, 55) and returned to Paris for an extra year. While in England he attended and was deeply moved by the funeral of Wilberforce, whose writings had stirred him and were largely responsible for stimulating his desire for freedom of the slaves. His letters from Europe (*Life*, I, 32) are those of an alert and discerning fellow with much tact and a broad understanding of human nature. His religious turn of mind, however, always showed itself in his letters, and they exhibited little humor. In 1834 he returned to Boston where he soon acquired a moderate practise. At that time William Lloyd Garrison was thundering his denunciations of slavery. Bowditch listened and became at once an ardent follower. He severed his connection with Warren Street Chapel because the "pillars" of this institution refused to listen to abolitionist sermons. In 1842 Massachusetts opinion was acutely aroused by the arrest in Boston of George Latimer, a runaway slave. William F. Channing, Frederick S. Cabot, and Bowditch formed themselves into a "Latimer Committee" and edited the *Latimer Journal and North Star*, a tri-weekly publication issued from Nov. 11, 1842, until May 10, 1843. Bowditch's ardor in the cause of Latimer threatened to unbalance his mind. Later he assisted other runaway slaves, and no one did more than he to foster anti-slavery feeling in the North. Consequently this pious Christian did much to bring about the Civil War into which he entered with the spirit of a crusader of old. When his son, Nathaniel, was killed (1863) he said, "This summoned me like the notes of a bugle to a charging soldier" (*Ibid.*, II, 16). It led him to write *A Brief Plea for an Ambulance System for the Army of the United States; as drawn from the Extra Sufferings of the Late Lieut. Bowditch and a Wounded Comrade* (1863). The feeling created by this pamphlet eventually caused the government to establish an ambulance unit of men trained to care for the wounded,—one of the great services rendered to the Northern armies.

Bowditch's other medical contributions were numerous and important. His training with Louis had aroused his interest in the diseases of the chest, and in 1846 he published *The Young Stethoscopist*, a work used by medical students for fifty years. Puncturing of the chest (paracentesis thoracis) for removal of pleural effusions was advocated by Bowditch in 1851 in a paper read (Oct. 20) to the Boston Society for Medical Observation (*American Journal of Medical Science*, April 1852). The use of the trocar and suction pump for this operation had been suggested by Dr. Morrill Wyman of Cambridge, Mass., but the world is indebted to Bowditch for bringing the procedure to the attention of physicians and, through repeated efforts, convincing them of its value. The operation was not new, having been employed spasmodically since the time of Hippocrates, but substitution of a hollow needle for a lancet made the procedure safe and simple. As a student of tuberculosis, also, Bowditch became distinguished. In 1836 appeared (in Boston) his English editions of Louis's two monographs on *Fever* [typhoid] and on *Phthisis*. The latter work greatly amplified Laennec's classical treatise (1819) on the pathology of tuberculosis. For many years Bowditch collected evidence concerning the influence of damp soil upon the spread of tuberculosis, which was carefully tabulated case by case and analyzed after the numerical method of Louis, but he did not publish his conclusions until 1862 (*Consumption in New England; or Locality One of Its Chief Causes*). Tuberculosis was a subject which occupied his mind until his death, his last published work being on the open-air treatment of the disease (*Transactions of the American Climatological Association*, VI, reprinted, XXVIII). In this paper one finds the modern conception of tuberculosis therapy clearly enunciated.

Bowditch's greatest service lay in the public health measures which were instituted through his efforts, and with the lapse of time his work in this field assumes ever-increasing significance. In 1869 was established the first Massachusetts State Board of Health (*Life*, II, 217–39) on which Bowditch served until 1879 preparing reports upon general questions relating to public health. The Massachusetts Board was the second in this country, the first having been established in Louisiana (1855). Bowditch's most important contribution in the field was his book, *Public Hygiene in America* (1877), in which is given a history of preventive medicine and a summary of sanitary law in various parts of the world. Bowditch's influence in stimulating the public health movement in the country was probably greater than that of any other man of his time. From 1859 to 1867 he was Jackson Professor of Clinical Medicine at the Harvard Medical School. He was a Fellow of the American Academy, an active member of the Massachusetts Medical Society (in which he held secretarial offices from 1849 to 1854), and was associated with the Massachusetts General Hospital from May 6, 1838, until the end of his life. He was also instrumental in founding the Boston Medical Library. In 1838 he married Olivia Yardley, an English girl of great charm whom he had met six years before at his lodgings in Paris. She died in December 1890, and he in January 1892 at the age of eighty-three.

[The numerous letters and diaries of Bowditch have been collected by his son, Vincent Yardley Bowditch, in a two-volume work, *Life and Correspondence of Henry Ingersoll Bowditch* (1902). A bibliography of his scientific works is to be found in the *Index Catalogue of the Surgeon General's Library,* ser. 1, 2, and 3. See also *Boston Medic. and Surgic. Jour.,* CLXVII, 603–07. All of Bowditch's numerous case-books have been deposited in the Boston Medic. Lib.] J.F.F.

BOWDITCH, HENRY PICKERING (Apr. 4, 1840–Mar. 13, 1911), physiologist, came of Massachusetts families remarkable for scientific ability. His father, Jonathan Ingersoll Bowditch, a Boston merchant, who wrote on navigation and published nautical tables, was the son of the famous Nathaniel Bowditch [*q.v.*], the translator of Laplace and author of the *New American Practical Navigator* (1802). His mother, Lucy Orne Nichols, a grand-daughter of Col. Timothy Pickering (Washington's secretary of state), was related to John Pickering, an authority on Indian languages; to the astronomers, Edward and William Pickering; and to the mathematician, Benjamin Pierce;—a group of intellectuals who might have found a place in Francis Galton's "Noteworthy Families." Born in Boston, young Henry Bowditch was raised in the austere fashion of the place and period, but like other boys played on the Common and skated on the Frog Pond, and after the removal of his family to an estate at West Roxbury (1853) became expert in swimming, diving, sailing, and boat-building, through the attractions of Jamaica Pond nearby. He was prepared for college at the school of Epes S. Dixwell and entered Harvard in 1857, having already evinced an aptitude for medicine by setting up a complete articulated skeleton from the cadaver of one of his father's horses. Upon his graduation (1861), he entered the Lawrence Scientific School (Cambridge), where his studies in chemistry and natural history were interrupted by the Civil War. In November 1861 he was commissioned second lieutenant in Company G, 2nd Battalion, 1st Massachusetts Cavalry. He participated in a number of raids and engagements, was wounded in the right forearm while leading a charge at New Hope Church (Nov. 27, 1863), entered Richmond with Weitzel (Apr. 3, 1865) as a major of the 5th Massachusetts Cavalry, and was honorably discharged from his command on June 3, 1865. At this period, he was described by Maj. H. L. Higginson as handsome, refined, homegrown, "with a fondness for keeping face clean and clothing neat when those attributes were a rarity," reserved and unbending in manner, of unequivocal loyalty and courage, yet with no particular liking for army life. Directly upon leaving the army, he resumed his studies at the Lawrence School, this time under the stimulating influence of the eminent comparative anatomist, Jeffries Wyman. While pursuing this course, he fulfilled the requirements of the Harvard Medical School, from which he was graduated M.D. in 1868. In the late summer of the same year, he proceeded to Paris, to follow physiology under Claude Bernard, histology under Ranvier, and neurology under Charcot. A chance meeting with the physiologist, Willy Kühne, in March 1869, led Bowditch to enter the laboratory of Carl Ludwig (Leipsig) in September. Ludwig was the greatest trainer of physiologists who ever lived, in Heidenhain's view, "the only physiologist who ever did anything." Under such a leader, Bowditch acquired the formative and directive stimuli which were to determine his subsequent career. Upon entering the Leipsig laboratory he delighted the old master by promptly inventing an automatic contrivance for registering the time relations of the blood-pressure tracings made on the revolving smoked drum attached to Ludwig's kymograph (1869). Under Ludwig, Bowditch made two investigations which are now classical. The first (1871) demonstrated the *Treppe* or step-wise increase of contraction of cardiac muscle under successive uniform stimuli, and the fact that, independently of the strength of stimulus, it will either contract to the maximal limit or not at all ("All or None" law). The second demonstrated that delphine will make the apex of an isolated heart beat rhythmically (1871), a discovery ten years in advance of the introduction of Ringer's solution (1880). A third paper, on the effect of variations of arterial blood-pressure upon the accelerator and inhibitory nerves of the heart, followed in 1872. Meanwhile, Charles W. Eliot, the new president of Harvard, had proposed that Bowditch give a course of university lectures on physiology in the second Harvard term (1871). This proposition Bowditch declined, as interrupting his studies, but Eliot's subsequent invitation "to take part in the good work of reforming medical education," with the offer of an assistant professorship of physiology (April 1871), was accepted, and Bowditch took ship from Liverpool on Sept. 14. Five days before sailing, he was married to Selma Knauth, the daughter of a hospitable Leipsig banker.

Bowditch came to his Harvard chair with a complete outfit of novel apparatus, purchased abroad at his own expense, but could only get the use of two small attic rooms in the old Medical School building on North Grove Street. Here, however, the first physiological laboratory in our country was started (1871), and Bowditch soon made it a going concern, imbued with the spirit of his great teacher. He invented new apparatus and gathered around him, as pupils, some of the best experimenters of his time, notably: C. S. Minot, W. P. Lombard, J. J. Putnam, William James (physiology), Isaac Ott and R. W. Lovett (experimental pharmacology), Stanley Hall and E. E. Southard (psychology), J. W. Warren (experimental pathology) and O. K. Newall (experimental surgery). With Minot, he showed the superiority of chloroform over ether in depressing vaso-motor reflexes (1874); with G. M. Garland, the effect of respiratory movements on the pulmonary circulation (1879–80); with Southard, the relative accuracy of sight and touch in estimating spatial relations (1880–82); with Stanley Hall, various optical illusions relative to moving objects (1880–82); with Warren, the effect of varying stimuli upon contraction and relaxation of blood-vessels (1883–86), and the effect of voluntary effort and external stimuli in reënforcing and depressing the knee-jerk (1890). In 1885 Bowditch made an investigation of the utmost practical importance, *viz.*, his conclusive proof that nerve fibre cannot be tired out. Bernstein (1877) had concluded that the nerve in a nerve-muscle preparation can be tetanized (exhausted) by 5–15 minutes' stimulation, but Wedensky (1884) and Maschek (1887) had gotten response after 1–9 hours' stimulation by blocking the nerve by means of a galvanic current applied between the point of stimulation and the muscle (Wedensky) or by etherizing the same area (Maschek). Bowditch completed the proof by producing a functional nerve-block with curare and got muscular twitchings after 1–4 hours' stimulation in warm-blooded animals. He concluded that a nerve is like a telegraph wire and the passage of a nerve-current analogous to that of light or electricity. This method of proof was the rationale of the conduction anæsthesia (nerve-blocking) subsequently introduced into surgery by Halsted, Cushing, and Crile. A minor experiment of 1876 illustrates Bowditch's originality of approach, namely his proof that ciliated epithelial cells can move weights up an inclined plane in one minute (unit) time with a force equal to the amount of work required to lift their own weight 4.25 metres. Of a piece with his skill in devising experiments was his talent for mechanical invention. He was the inventor of the Bowditch clock, the comfortable "Bowditch chair," a new induction coil, a new plethysmograph and many other ingenious devices used in the Harvard Laboratory. He was a pioneer in composite photography, to which he contributed a memorable early paper (*McClure's Magazine*) in 1894. Perhaps his most important work, apart from physiological experimentation, was his study of the rate of growth in school children (1872–91). In anthropometry, a Chinese invention, Bowditch was a pioneer. His measurements showed, in opposition to Quetelet's findings, that up to 11–12, boys are heavier and taller than girls, girls larger at 13–14, after which boys are again larger up to manhood; that large children begin to grow earlier than small children, that growth is more dependent upon environment (optimum nutrition) than upon race; and that loss of weight in growing children is a warning signal of approaching illness or decline in health. These data, in which Galton's percentile grades were utilized, are but little known apart from school hygiene, in which they are of paramount importance. With Bowditch's appointment to the Harvard chair, physiological teaching came into its own, and ceased to be a subordinated subject in the medical curriculum. Five years before, the few lectures given were delivered by the Parkman professor (O. W. Holmes), as part of his anatomical course. Five years later, Newell Martin brought the methods of Huxley and Michael Foster to Johns Hopkins University (1876). Bowditch taught the subject for thirty-five years, was appointed full professor in 1876 and George Higginson professor in 1903, and resigned this chair in 1906. Although a pioneer in laboratory instruction, he held fast to the didactic lecture and declared that "a good teacher with a bad method is more effective than a bad teacher with a good method." As early as 1900, he saw clearly that, apart from base-line instruction in the fundamental disciplines, elective courses would become a necessity in the crowded medical curriculum of the future. During the decade 1883–93, he was dean of the Harvard Medical Faculty, introduced a four-year course and a chair of bacteriology (H. C. Ernst), was a prime mover in the planning of the new school in Boylston St. (1881) and of the splendid later units which he lived to see completed in 1906. In 1896, he filed a strong brief against the anti-vivisectionists and did important public service through his reports on the alcohol problem in 1872, 1894, and 1903 (Committee of Fifty). He was a founder of the American Physiological Society (1887), succeeded Weir Mitchell as its second president (1888), and was reëlected during 1891–95. In 1877, he became a coeditor of Sir Michael Foster's *Journal of Physiology,* in which the investigations of the Harvard Laboratory were published up to 1898, when the *American Journal of Physiology* was established and financed by Bowditch's assistant, W. T. Porter. Bowditch was elected to membership in most of the leading scientific societies and received honorary doctorate degrees from the Universities of Cambridge (1898), Edinburgh (1898), Pennsylvania (1904), and Harvard (1906). Before his resignation from his chair (1906), he had become afflicted with a hopeless form of paralysis agitans. He quietly passed away on Mar. 13, 1911.

In his particular period, Bowditch was unquestionably the foremost American physiologist after Beaumont. His findings on the *Treppe,* the "All or None" principle, and the indefatigability of nerve are truly classical. Such features of conduction anæsthesia as shockless surgery or auto-surgery (operating upon oneself before a mirror) really derive from his nerve-blocking experiment of 1890. The rationale of school lunches and of the "Watch me grow" cards of school inspectors is to be found in his acute reasoning from the data of juvenile anthropometry. His mechanical ability ranged from prompt insight into the workings of complex apparatus, to such modes of handicraft as glass-blowing, turning the lathe, kite-flying, photography, and the making and repairing of furniture. In person, he was a sturdy, gallant, well-set-up figure of medium height, with aquiline features, pointed beard, cavalry mustache and shrewd, penetrating, humorous glance; serious and austere *au fond* rather than witty, yet full of fun and fond of a hearty laugh. The athletic habits of his boyhood were maintained and at his summer camp in the Adirondacks, where he entertained the leading physiologists of Europe for twenty years, he knew how to play. He was happy in his married life, and left a family of two sons, five daughters, and ten grandchildren. Recalling his visits to the Surgeon General's Library with his charming wife, it was a pleasure to see him enter an office room. He seemed to light up the musty atmosphere, as Osler may be said to have warmed it. His blithe, buoyant personality radiated joy of life and good will toward his fellow men.

[The authoritative biography of Bowditch is that of his Harvard successor, Prof. W. B. Cannon (*Memoirs Nat. Acad. Sci.,* XVII, 183–96). Appreciative memorials in *Science,* Apr. 21, 1911, p. 598, and *Boston Medic. and Surgic. Jour.,* Mar. 23, 1911, p. 438, cover much the same ground.]

F. H. G.

BOWDITCH, NATHANIEL (Mar. 26, 1773–Mar. 17, 1838), astronomer and mathematician, born in Salem, Mass., was the fourth of seven children of the shipmaster and cooper, Habakkuk Bowditch, by his wife Mary Ingersoll. His Bowditch ancestors were residents of Thorncombe, Dorsetshire, England, for at least one hundred and fifty years before the American founder of his family, a clothier, arrived at Salem, Mass., in 1671. So straitened were the family's circumstances that Nathaniel left school shortly after his tenth birthday to assist in his father's cooper shop. At about the age of twelve he became a clerk or apprentice in a ship-chandlery, an occupation which he continued until his first voyage in 1795. During these years he was constantly reading and studying. With a very retentive memory (except for people and their names) he acquired a vast fund of general information by reading every article in the four folio volumes of *Chambers' Cyclopædia* and *Supplement.* He began the study of algebra when fourteen years of age, constructed an almanac for 1790 when he was fifteen, studied French, and Euclid's *Elements,* and commenced at seventeen the acquisition of Latin in order to read Newton's *Principia,* which with volumes of the *Transactions of the Royal Society of London,* and many other scientific works was for him a source of constant inspiration and delight. During this period he also made a sun-dial and assisted in making a survey of Salem. Between Jan. 11, 1795, and Dec. 25, 1803, he made five voyages, the first in the capacity of clerk, the next three as supercargo, and the last as master and supercargo. In this way, being a keen observer, he became somewhat acquainted with many peoples in such places as Lisbon, Cadiz, Madeira, Réunion, Sumatra, Batavia, and Manila, and his journals of the voyages contain many interesting passages. Although every spare moment was devoted to study, he was popular with the crews and always ready to talk to them about the subjects engrossing his attention. He improved his knowledge of languages, especially Spanish, continued mathematical reading, and, on the suggestion of a publisher at Newburyport,

Mass., checked up the accuracy of the popular English work of J. H. Moore, *The Practical Navigator* (1st ed., London, 1772; 20th, 1828). From the thirteenth English edition of this work was prepared, in 1799, the first American edition "improved . . . revised and corrected by a skilful mathematician and navigator" (no name). This was Bowditch's first publication (in which his brother William collaborated). A second edition appeared in 1800. After preparing copy for a third edition, the additions to the original work were so numerous that it was decided to issue the volume under a different title, *The New American Practical Navigator,* as if Nathaniel Bowditch alone were the author; the book was mostly printed, but not published, in 1801. The printed copy was sold for 200 guineas to the English publishers of Moore's work on condition that the American and English editions should appear simultaneously in June 1802. The English edition was edited by Thomas Kirby (2nd ed., 1806; 3rd ed., 1809). A thirty-six page appendix to the first American edition was published in 1804. Nine other editions appeared during Bowditch's life, the last being the tenth in 1837. At least fifty-six further editions or reprints have since appeared under various auspices and editing. A few sections were translated into German by A. Hirsch (Giessen, 1863). In 1844 *Bowditch's Useful Tables* were reprinted from the work and of these there have been at least seventeen editions or reprints. During the first third of the nineteenth century the Bowditch-Moore work was the best of its kind in the English language. Bowditch's practical knowledge of this subject, acquaintance with various tables published, and his gift of clear exposition, accuracy in computation, and thoroughness, contributed notably to this result. After his third voyage, in 1799, Bowditch was elected a Fellow of the American Academy of Arts and Sciences of which he was afterwards to be president for the last nine years of his life. In 1802, shortly before he started on his fifth voyage, Harvard University conferred on him the honorary degree of Master of Arts, greatly to his surprise and gratification. It was about this time that he won the ardent admiration of a prominent Salem captain by translating a Spanish business document; this resulted in 1804 in his appointment as president of the Essex Fire and Marine Insurance Company, an office which he conducted with great sagacity and success till his removal to Boston in 1823 to become (at more than three times his previous salary) actuary of the Massachusetts Hospital Life Insurance Company, a position which he held till his death.

To the period of Bowditch's residence in Salem belongs practically all of his scientific activity. Apart from the work already mentioned, and a dozen problems proposed and solved in the five numbers of Adrain's *Analyst* (1808 and 1814), he made an admirable chart of the harbors of Salem, Beverly, and Manchester from a survey taken during 1804–06 (published 1806; second ed. 1834). But much more important were the twenty-three papers published (1804–20) in the *Memoirs of the American Academy of Arts and Sciences,* and the preparation of the translation, with much of the commentary, of the first four volumes (Paris, 1799–1805) of Laplace's *Mécanique céleste.* Indeed this latter work was done before 1818, although publication did not take place till 1829–39. The delay was caused by the fact that in wishing to preserve his entire independence Bowditch declined both the suggestion to publish his work by subscription, and the offer of the American Academy of Arts and Sciences to publish it at its own expense, and had to arrange his finances so as to have $12,000 available for publication expenses. So elaborate were the notes, in elucidation and in attempting to bring the subjects up to date, that the completed work contained nearly four thousand quarto pages and was considerably more than double the size of the original. This was Bowditch's most notable piece of scientific work and "made an epoch in American science by bringing the great work of Laplace down to the reach of the best American students of his time" (Newcomb, *Side-Lights on Astronomy,* 1906, p. 282). Most of Bowditch's twenty-three papers mentioned above dealt with astronomical and nautical matters. Those on the orbits of the comets of 1807, 1811, and 1819 were based on an enormous mass of calculations still preserved. Perhaps the most popular of his papers was the one in which he brought together various observations regarding the meteor that exploded over Weston, Conn., in 1807. This was reprinted in full in England, and abstracts appeared in both Germany and France. Bowditch's paper on the motion of a pendulum suspended from two points is notable because he there discussed mathematically for the first time what were many years later to become famous, in connection with certain acoustical phenomena, as Lissajous curves (Loria, *Spezielle algebraische und transscendente ebene Kurven,* I, 1902, 482). Bowditch was not a genius or discoverer, but rather a singularly sagacious critic, of the Delambre type, with an exceptionally endowed mind. That he won such a prominent place among early American intellectuals, and accomplished so much of a scientific nature, while most of his time was devoted to other affairs, was mainly due to his methodical habits, mental alertness, and indefatigable energy. He was married first on Mar. 25, 1798, to Elizabeth, daughter of Francis Boardman, but she died about six months later. On Oct. 28, 1800, he married his cousin Mary, only daughter of Jonathan Ingersoll, by whom he had six sons (two of whom attained to positions of eminence) and two daughters. The union proved to be extraordinarily felicitous. Inflexible integrity, loftiness of purpose, warmth of heart, simplicity of bearing, and entire absence of selfish ambition, were personal characteristics of Bowditch to offset occasional lapses in good judgment and unwise impetuosity of speech. In appearance he was slight of stature, "with high forehead, bright and penetrating eye, open and intelligent countenance." The best portrait of him is the one by Gilbert Stuart, his last work (1828). It is unfinished, only the head being painted and that not entirely completed. The hair is gray and the eyes grayish brown (L. Park, *Gilbert Stuart,* 1926).

[Exact information regarding Bowditch's early American and English ancestry, back to the first part of the sixteenth century, has been only recently discovered: *New Eng. Hist. and Geneal. Reg.,* LXXII (1918), LVIII (1924). The most valuable printed source of general information concerning Bowditch is the *Memoir* by his eldest son, Nathaniel Ingersoll, which appeared in the posthumous fourth volume (1839) of the *Mécanique Céleste.* Since only 500 copies of this work were printed the biography was reprinted in 1840, with four pages of supplementary material which is still further developed in *Remarks concerning the Late Dr. Bowditch by the Rev. Dr. Palfrey with the Replies of Dr. Bowditch's Children* (1840). A third edition with further additions and illustrations by Bowditch's third son, Henry I., was published in 1884. There was a supplement entitled *Christmas Day, Dec. 25, 1886* issued with two broadsides entitled respectively Bowditch Ancestry and Ingersoll Ancestry. The bibliography of the writings of Nathaniel Bowditch in the *Memoir* was reprinted in Runkle's *Mathematical Mo.,* vol. II, 1860. Henry I. was also the author of an excellent anonymous *Memoir* of his father (1841, 1870), for the young, the first edition of which (practically the same as what appeared in Horace Mann's *Common School Jour.,* vol. II, 1840) was a little volume for the Warren Street Chapel; he published further: *Sketch of the Life and Character of Nathaniel Bowditch . . . made at the dedication of the Bowditch School* (1863). There is material of value in *Life and Correspondence of Henry Ingersoll Bowditch by his son V. Y. Bowditch* (1902). In the Boston Pub. Lib. are thirty-one volumes of Bowditch's manuscripts which include the journals of his five voyages 1795–1803; (the Essex Institute has Bowditch copies of the journals of the second and fifth voyages). There are also three volumes of correspondence, mainly connected with his translation, of which the four manuscript volumes were willed to Harvard College but by vote of the President and Fellows, in 1884, were deposited in the Boston Pub. Lib. There are also two volumes of valuable manuscript biographical material prepared by N. I. Bowditch. In the library of the American Academy of Arts and Sciences there is some Bowditch correspondence. Interesting facts are given in H. S. Tapley's *Salem Imprints 1768–1825* (1927).] R. C. A.

BOWDOIN, JAMES (Aug. 7, 1726–Nov. 6, 1790), merchant, Revolutionary statesman, the son of James and Hannah (Pordage) Bowdoin, was born in Boston. The family was of French origin, his grandfather, Pierre Baudouin, a Huguenot refugee, having settled in New England in 1687, first in Maine, and three years later, during the Indian wars, at Boston. The first James Bowdoin became one of the leading merchants of America and at the time of his death in 1747 had accumulated what was probably the largest estate in New England. A final accounting to the Suffolk probate court in 1757 showed a total valuation of £82,875 sterling, a huge sum for that period. The second James Bowdoin graduated from Harvard in 1745 and became a merchant like his father. He married, Sept. 15, 1748, Elizabeth, daughter of John Erving, another prosperous Boston merchant. While not as active in business as his father had been, he was a successful man of affairs and made profitable use of his share of the estate. He met serious losses from time to time in the troublous years of revolutionary disturbance, but on Jan. 26, 1779, Samuel Dexter, writing him as to the havoc wrought to creditor interests by paper money, remarks, "The sum you had out on loan was vastly greater than mine; your loss, consequently, if your debtors have been as cruelly unjust as mine, is proportionally greater. But your real estates will, after all, leave you a gentleman of an ample fortune" (*Proceedings of the Massachusetts Historical Society,* ser. 1, vol. VI, p. 360). In addition to important properties in Boston, Bowdoin was a large holder of Maine lands. His familiarity with problems of commerce, industry, money, exchange, and related matters is apparent in his writings and public activities during the prolonged disputes with the mother country and in the domestic disturbances which followed the establishment of American independence. It was natural that British trade restriction should be opposed by merchants like Bowdoin, Hancock, Gerry, Quincy, and others, whose interests were adversely affected, but their property holdings also made their position especially dangerous should resistance prove unsuccessful.

Bowdoin's political career began in 1753 when he was elected to the General Court, and continued with brief intermissions, due in most cases to ill health, until Massachusetts had ratified the Federal Constitution thirty-five years later. He lacked a robust physique and contemporaries describe him as consumptive, facts which undoubtedly prevented him on several occasions from attaining greater distinction in public affairs. He served in the lower house for three terms, and in 1757 was chosen a member of the Council. His appearance in the latter body was of the utmost importance. The Council had, in general, been more inclined to support the imperial viewpoint than the popular branch, and with the rise of troublesome issues after the close of the French and Indian War, its attitude was likely to be decisive in developing Massachusetts policies. A divided Assembly would have been of great advantage to the British authorities. It was Bowdoin's influence that aligned the Council with the colonial interests (Thomas Hutchinson, *History of Massachusetts Bay,* III, 1828, p. 156). He was in close touch with Sam Adams, John Hancock, James Otis, and other popular leaders, and Hutchinson in one of his letters describes him as "talking their jargon, where government is the subject." Bowdoin was the author of many of the documents since published in the *Massachusetts State Papers,* protests, petitions, addresses to the British governors and similar statements on current issues. As might be expected from a man thoroughly conversant with colonial trade conditions, he continually stresses the economic aspects of the dispute, although some able constitutional arguments are offered as well. His letters to friends in England, especially those to former Gov. Thomas Pownall, with whom he was on cordial terms, show the same emphasis on the desirability of freer trade relations (*Massachusetts Historical Society Collections,* ser. 6, vol. IX, p. 142).

In 1774 Bowdoin's service under the Province Government was terminated when Gen. Gage negatived his election to the Council. He had served in that body for sixteen out of seventeen preceding years, covering the entire pre-Revolutionary agitation. A few days before the final disintegration of British authority the General Court elected him as delegate to the Continental Congress. At this point the failure of his own health and the serious illness of his wife led him to decline the new post and John Hancock was chosen to fill his place. Inability to accept this election was unfortunate. It deprived the Congress of a potential leader of temperate statesmanlike qualities and it later subjected Bowdoin himself to charges of luke-warmness in the cause of revolution. The letters of contemporaries and the fact that he retained the confidence and friendship of the other Massachusetts patriots are a sufficient refutation of charges of malingering or indifference. In August 1775 the Provincial Congress appointed him first member of the executive council of twenty-eight which handled much of the public business in the years preceding the establishment of regular government under the constitution of 1780. Still complaining of physical weakness, he felt obliged to resign in 1777. He was unable, in fact, to do much work between the outbreak of the war and the meeting of the constitutional convention, Sept. 1, 1779.

Bowdoin's election to the latter body marks the beginning of the great period in his career. In the next ten years Massachusetts was transformed from a loosely organized revolutionary community into a stable, well-governed commonwealth. It passed from the inflation and demoralization of war conditions through a slough of economic depression and bankruptcy to economic stability, restored credit, and commercial revival. In this period Bowdoin was an outstanding figure and his services at the most critical moment made him "the great governor" of that long interval between the departure of Gen. Gage and the inauguration of John A. Andrew. Bowdoin was elected president of the constitutional convention and chairman of the subcommittee which was charged with the actual drafting of the instrument. John Adams was the author of the greater part of the constitution which finally appeared, but John Lowell, himself a member, states that Bowdoin was frequently consulted and exercised considerable influence. Hancock was chosen governor at the first election, Bowdoin declining the lieutenant-governorship and also a place in the Senate. He served, however, with a committee of jurists which was engaged in the important task of revising and adjusting the old laws to meet the new conditions of statehood. With the restoration of peace a serious situation arose. Massachusetts like the rest of the country suffered from the stoppage of foreign trade, a staggering burden of public and private debt, and all the other social and economic evils which follow a protracted war. When Hancock announced his retirement from the governorship in January 1785, it was apparent that serious trouble impended. Party lines were not yet drawn, but Bowdoin was put forward as the candidate of the conservative mercantile interests and in this contest can be clearly traced the beginnings of the great division which eventually resulted in the Federalist and Republican alignments. The contest between Bowdoin and Thomas Cushing, the latter regarded as the "popular" candidate, was close and bitter. Bowdoin now had to face charges of luke-warmness in Revolutionary days and pro-British leanings, the second being rendered plausible by the fact that his only daughter had married John Temple, a former surveyor-gen-

Bowdoin

eral of customs who later inherited a baronetcy. Through lack of a popular majority the election was thrown into the legislature. Here the Senate, where commercial and property interests were disproportionately strong, insisted on the selection of Bowdoin and the lower chamber at length receded from its preference for his opponent. On May 26, 1785, his election as governor was formally announced.

Bowdoin's administration, and particularly his handling of the crisis of 1786–87, were long the theme of unqualified eulogy. That he performed great services for the state, and incidentally, for the country at large, is undeniable. Whether a higher quality of statesmanship could not have averted actual insurrection is another question. The legislature, as such bodies frequently do, wasted time on irrelevant matters and showed no disposition to attack the difficult problems demanding solution. The Governor can hardly be said to have shown the ablest type of leadership at this juncture. His formal address of May 31, 1785, was a clear and accurate summary of existing conditions. Time, he stated, was needed to remedy the situation. Retrenchment, strict economy, payment of interest when due, and a general adherence to "principles of honor and strict honesty" would bring eventual cure. As a diagnosis and statement of a wholesome regimen for the future it was admirable, but a patient suffering as acutely as Massachusetts was in 1785 needed immediate relief. In one matter, however, the Governor displayed the vision of a real statesman, in a plea for an enlargement of the powers of Congress which would permit adequate control of commerce, without which stable conditions were likely to prove impossible. Resolutions supporting this idea and recommending a convention of delegates from all the states to act on the problem were voted by the legislature and transmitted by the Governor to the delegates in Congress and the other state executives. Bowdoin therefore deserves an honorable place among those who took an early and influential part in the movement which eventually produced the Federal Constitution. At his suggestion the legislature passed an act intended to impose retaliatory restrictions on British shipping, the effects of which were promptly nullified by the selfish action of Connecticut in opening her ports, an action which at least confirmed Bowdoin's contentions as to the need of national control. His messages at subsequent sessions during the year show the same interest in and grasp of commercial principles displayed in the dispute with the mother country. His suggestions as to the need of developing American manufactures, especially in woolens, are in line with those urged by the advocates of "the American system" several decades later. One manufacture, that of gunpowder, he declared might prove essential for the safety of the Commonwealth itself. He was reëlected without difficulty in 1786. Internal conditions were going from bad to worse and by the summer of 1786, the situation in Massachusetts was rapidly getting out of hand. County conventions were meeting and threatening to stop the operations of the courts. Foreclosure proceedings, inevitable under the existing depression, were stirring the debtor classes to actual resistance. In September several instances of armed interference with judicial processes actually occurred. The Governor met the situation with promptness and vigor. The legislature was summoned in special session, militia were ordered out to protect the courts and the Governor announced that the authority of the government would be exercised to maintain order and enforce the laws. Compared with the dilatory actions of the legislature at this period the Governor's conduct stood out in bold contrast. Funds were gathered from various voluntary subscribers, Bowdoin himself, it is said, contributing generously. Beginning in January 1787, Gen. Benjamin Lincoln's militiamen by a few vigorous blows dispersed the insurgents and ended the danger. "Vigour, decision, energy, will soon terminate this unnatural, this unprovoked insurrection, and prevent the effusion of blood," said Bowdoin to the February session of the legislature, "but the contrary may involve the Commonwealth in a civil war, & all its dreadful consequences; which may extend to the whole confederacy, & finally destroy the fair temple of American liberty, in the erecting of which, besides the vast expence of it, many thousands of valuable citizens have been sacrificed." There is abundant evidence that this view was shared in official circles throughout the confederation, that steps were being taken to meet possible developments, and that Bowdoin's Napoleonic methods were widely approved beyond New England and that their success greatly increased his prestige. In Massachusetts, however, his standing had suffered. There was an undercurrent of sympathy, not wholly unjustifiable, for the insurgents, and a feeling that needed reforms had been too slow in forthcoming. In a retrenchment movement the legislature had reduced the Governor's salary, an act which Bowdoin promptly vetoed on constitutional grounds, to his own political hurt. In the spring elections Hancock was again chosen governor by a decisive majority. Bowdoin retired Apr. 26, 1787, with a graceful acknowledgment of the fact that the public desires coincided with his own.

One more public service remained. The Massachusetts situation had furnished a powerful impetus to the movement toward effective union of the states. On Jan. 9, 1788, the Massachusetts convention met to pass on the adoption of the Federal Constitution. Bowdoin was a delegate from Boston and his son represented Dorchester. He spoke but twice in the course of debate, defending the principle of delegated powers under which he said, "the whole Constitution is a declaration of rights" and urging adoption as the only preventive of financial collapse and general anarchy. Ratification was voted by a narrow majority, and on Aug. 12 Bowdoin wrote to a relative in England his confident expectation that the states "from choice as well as necessity," and in view of past experiences would loyally support the new plan "and will be very happy under it" (*Proceedings of the Massachusetts Historical Society*, ser. 2, vol. XI, p. 178).

His death took place on Nov. 6, 1790. He had renewed in 1788 a long-standing correspondence on scientific matters with Benjamin Franklin, whose death preceded his own by a few months. Like Franklin, he had found time in the midst of public affairs and business activity to develop an interest in science and literature. He was especially interested in physics and astronomy and wrote a number of papers for the *Transactions of the American Academy of Arts and Sciences* (founded in 1780) of which he was the first president, and to which he bequeathed a valuable library. Amid the political disturbances of 1769 it is interesting to find him discussing with Gen. Gage the organization of an expedition to Lake Superior to observe the transit of Venus. He was a member of several learned societies, American and foreign, and the holder of honorary degrees from Harvard and Edinburgh. With such a combination of interests in life, it was eminently fitting that his chief memorial should have been the college chartered four years after his death and named in his honor, which in 1802 on the edge of the Maine wilderness began the work of developing in a new generation something of the same interest in letters, science, and public service.

Lacking the qualities which made Sam Adams a great popular leader, or the training and cast of thought which enabled John Adams, Thomas Jefferson, or Alexander Hamilton to exert such profound influence on the political theory of the day, and unlike Franklin or Robert Morris debarred from a wider field of service in diplomacy or administration, Bowdoin has, nevertheless, a secure place among the founders of the republic. Massachusetts occupied a strategic position. A leader who contributed so largely to its conquest by the forces of independence and who rendered equally important service in consolidating that position amid the confusion and turmoil which followed the victory is entitled to national recognition.

[The chief sources of information regarding James Bowdoin are the Bowdoin and Temple Papers published in the *Mass. Hist. Soc. Colls.*, ser. 6, vol. IX and ser. 7, vol. VI. The preface in the former volume contains a list of scattered papers published from time to time in earlier volumes of the *Proceedings* of the same society. The collection of documents, *Speeches of the Governors of Mass. from 1765 to 1775; and the Answers of the House of Representatives to the Same* (1818), ed. by A. Bradford, includes many items drafted by committees of which Bowdoin was a member. His messages and other papers issued while governor are to be found in *Laws and Resolves of Mass. 1786–87* (1863, reprinted 1893). An account of Bowdoin's life and services is given by R. C. Winthrop in *Washington, Bowdoin and Franklin* (1876). Daniel Goodwin in *Provincial Pictures* (1886) has a brief sketch. Casual letters and references occur in the papers of the Adamses and other contemporaries, and Temple Prime in *Some Account of the Bowdoin Family* (1887) has genealogical data. There is a considerable monograph literature on Massachusetts history during the period of Bowdoin's public life, especially the later stages, among which the following will be found useful: A. E. Morse, *The Federalist Party in Mass. to the Year 1800* (1909); J. P. Warren, "The Confederation and the Shays Rebellion," *Am. Hist. Rev.*, XI, 42–67; H. A. Cushing, *Hist. of the Transition from Provincial to Commonwealth Government in Mass.* (1896); S. B. Harding, *The Contest over the Ratification of the Federal Constitution in the State of Mass.* (1896); and S. E. Morison, "The Struggle over the Adoption of the Constitution of Mass. (1780)," *Mass. Hist. Soc. Proc.*, L, 353–411.] W. A. R.

BOWDOIN, JAMES (Sept. 22, 1752–Oct. 11, 1811), merchant, diplomat, was the only son of Gov. James Bowdoin [*q.v.*]. He was third in succession to bear the name, and the last of the Boston branch of the family in the male line. He was born in Boston, graduated at Harvard in 1771, studied at Christ Church, Oxford, traveled in Europe, and returned to Massachusetts shortly after the outbreak of the Revolution. Unable to enter military service because of bad health, which handicapped him throughout life, he engaged in mercantile business for several years. He married on May 18, 1781, his cousin Sarah, daughter of his father's half-brother, William Bowdoin. Like the other members of the family he seems to have been a successful business man but his property had now reached the stage where undoubtedly he could apply to his own affairs the rules he suggested "as a friend who had had a little experience upon this subject" to George W. Erving: "Avoid all speculations with a view to accumulation. You will find the legal interest of money upon good securities, or investments in the public stocks of the U. S. for your productive capital, and the lands of the U. S.

from their gradual increase in value will be the best plan of appropriating such sums as you may not require for your immediate support. . . . A man who is not and cannot be at the beginning and end of active commercial concerns ought never to be engaged in them . . ." (*Massachusetts Historical Society Collections,* ser. 7, vol. VI, p. 306). He was five times elected to the General Court as representative of Dorchester, 1786–90, was a member of the state Senate in 1794 and 1801, and of the Governor's Council in 1796. He was also a member of the convention of 1788, where he spoke and voted for the ratification of the Federal Constitution. In 1796 he moved from Dorchester to Boston. Since he was a Jeffersonian Republican, in spite of connections social and otherwise which might have been expected to draw him into the opposite party, strong Federalist predominance in the Boston district after 1801 ended any chance of political advancement in the region. In 1797 he published anonymously *Opinions Respecting the Commercial Intercourse Between the United States of America, and the Dominions of Great Britain, Including Observations upon the Necessity of an American Navigation Act,* which in its strictures on British trade regulations, its keen analysis of commercial principles, and its vigorous demand for a retaliatory policy, is reminiscent of some of his father's pronouncements thirty years before.

In November 1804 he was appointed minister to Spain by President Jefferson and sailed for his post the following spring, his health in the meantime having become so seriously impaired that he dared not risk a journey to Washington for a farewell interview with the President. The Administration was then engaged in devious negotiations with Spain regarding the possible acquisition of West Florida, the western boundaries of the Louisiana Purchase, and sundry spoliation claims. On reaching the Spanish coast in the summer of 1805 he learned that his predecessor had been successful in negotiating a treaty and that relations with Spain were so unsatisfactory that he deemed it inadvisable to proceed to Madrid, a decision which met the approval of the President and Secretary of State. He spent some time in England and then in Paris. On Mar. 17, 1806, negotiations were transferred to Paris, where he was empowered, together with Gen. Armstrong, minister to France, to conduct new negotiations respecting Florida. This, of course, meant that all transactions would be dominated by Napoleon whom Bowdoin described as "the wonder, the dread, the admiration of Europe." Spain, he had already discovered, was "so completely under control of this government that it has but the semblance of independence, and it may be considered as little more than a department of France with the Prince of Peace its prefect" (letter to President Jefferson, Mar. 1, 1806). His experience during the next two years was unfortunate. He failed to maintain working relations with his colleague, and his letters disclose frequent annoyances and rebuffs. Negotiations failed, Napoleon's ruthlessness, foresight, and deceit completely baffling the American diplomats who were as unsuited for such a contest as Massachusetts militia officers would have been for Austerlitz or Wagram. He returned to America in 1808, receiving, however, friendly assurances of confidence and esteem from the President.

The remainder of his life was given to study and the improvement of his agricultural property, especially the estate at Nashawn Island, Buzzard's Bay, where his death occurred three years later. One of his last activities was the translation of Louis Daubenton's *Instruction pour les bergers et pour les propriétaires de troupeaux* (1810), an edition of which he printed at his own expense in the interest of the growing woolen industry. He is reported to have been increasingly active in various philanthropic activities during his last years. He had already donated land and money to the college which had been named in honor of his father and he made additional bequests in his will, including a collection of paintings and drawings made while abroad, his library and scientific apparatus. Dying without issue, he made the college residuary legatee and following the death of his nephew, James Temple Bowdoin, a reversionary interest in the estate brought a further notable increase to its resources in 1844, although not without troublesome litigation.

[A brief biographical notice of the younger Bowdoin is prefixed to the "Bowdoin and Temple Papers," *Mass. Hist. Soc. Colls.*, ser. 6, vol. IV. A considerable body of correspondence, especially letters written from abroad, is found in *Ibid.*, ser. 7, vol. VI, pp. 199–456. An obituary notice of some merit appears in the *Independent Chronicle,* Boston, Oct. 21, 1811.] W. A. R.

BOWEN, ABEL (Dec. 3, 1790–Mar. 11, 1850), wood engraver, publisher, one of twelve children of Abel Bowen and Delia Mason, was born in Sand Lake Village, Greenbush, N. Y. In 1811 he moved to Boston and soon established himself as a printer. He then began a varied activity, characteristic of a period when Americans apparently regarded themselves as capable jacks-of-all-trades. A wood engraver, he turned also to copper engraving. Stauffer lists portraits and views by him, some from his own drawings, somewhat dry and colorless. In 1821 he was associated with Alexander McKenzie, copperplate printer. He drew on stone the illustrations for an American edition of Sir Astley Paston Cooper's lectures. Of his work on wood, his copies of English cuts for an American edition of *The Young Ladies' Book* (1830) were "very remarkable for their fidelity to the original," writes W. J. Linton. The combination "engraver, publisher" describes his activity. Described by W. H. Whitmore as "one in the chain of local antiquaries," Bowen early began to publish or plan volumes illustrated with copperplates or wood engravings or both, many of them by himself. There were the *Naval Monument* (1816), Caleb H. Snow's *History of Boston* (1825), in which Abel's brother Henry appears as printer, and *Picture of Boston* (1828). In 1834 appeared the first number of the *American Magazine of Useful and Entertaining Knowledge*, in Boston, published by John L. Sibley and James B. Dow, and copyrighted by the Boston Bewick Company. This company was a group of wood engravers (Bowen, Alonzo Hartwell, John H. Hall, Wm. Croome, John C. Crosman, and others), associated "for the purpose of employing, improving, and extending the art of engraving. . . ." The Introduction to the magazine promises that "the engravings will be of the first order," and in volume one there is an article on Thomas Bewick, "our patron saint." At the end of the second volume the editor, in an adieu to his duties, states that the embellishments were selected chiefly by the engravers, and suggests that "the interests of the work might have been promoted by allowing the editor the privilege of a veto, at least." One is inclined to agree with him. The third volume was issued in 1837 without the name of the Bewick Company. Whitmore quotes "one of the artists of the last generation" thus: "Bowen was the real founder of the art of wood engraving here [*i. e.,* in Boston], not so much by his own productions as by the stimulus he gave to the subject." As to his influence, Linton names Croome, Devereux, Mallory, Kilburn, Childs, George Loring Brown, and Hammatt Billings among his pupils, for which list no confirmation has been found. Of Bowen's private life little has been recorded. We are told that he was married to Eliza Healy, had ten children, and struggled on, year after year, in the face of reverses, poverty, and long continued illness, and that he died after two years of illness, patiently borne.

[The principal source of information is W. H. Whitmore's "Abel Bowen: a Sketch," in *Bostonian Soc. Colls.*, vol. I (1887), containing impressions of a number of copperplates and woodblocks engraved by Bowen. D. M. Stauffer's *Am. Engravers upon Copper and Steel* (1907), with Fielding's *Supplement* (1917), lists his work on copper. W. J. Linton's *Hist. of Wood-Engraving in America* (1882) deals with his engravings on wood.]

F.W.

BOWEN, FRANCIS (Sept. 8, 1811–Jan. 21, 1890), philosopher, was born in Charlestown, Mass., the son of Dijah and Elizabeth (Flint) Bowen. One of a large family, he was early obliged to support himself, at least in part, by clerking in a publishing house and by teaching. He was educated in the Mayhew School, Boston, in Phillips Exeter Academy (one term), and in Harvard College (three years), graduating from the latter with highest honors in 1833. His Bachelor's oration, we are assured, was "a sober, chaste performance" (*Proceedings of the Massachusetts Historical Society,* January 1890). He taught mathematics for two years at Exeter, after which he returned to Harvard as tutor in intellectual philosophy and political economy. In 1839 he went to Europe for a year of study and travel. In 1843 he succeeded Dr. Palfrey as proprietor and editor of the *North American Review,* a position which he held for a little over a decade. During the visit to America of Louis Kossuth, in 1851, the cause which the Hungarian revolutionist represented was sharply attacked by Bowen (*Hungary, The Rebellion of the Slavonic, Wallachian, and German Hungarians against the Magyars*). The imperialist paid for this temerity in offending popular American sentiment by losing an appointment to which he had been nominated as McLean professor of history in Harvard. In 1853, however, he was appointed Alvord professor of natural religion, moral philosophy, and civil polity in the same institution. This position he held for thirty-six years. He came into national prominence once again in November 1888. Long known as a protectionist in principle, he was then appealed to by the Republican national chairman for a public indorsement of the party's tariff platform, to which he replied by a stinging denunciation of the current tariff as a tyranny, crushing native industries and taxing the necessities of life (*Nation,* Nov. 8, 1888). At the age of seventy-four he resigned his position in Harvard, and died shortly thereafter. He was married to Arabella, daughter of Col. and Eliza (Austin) Stuart.

As a philosopher Bowen was chiefly interested in harmonizing philosophy with Christianity. His type of thought might be characterized as natural realism modified by Kantian elements. His most important work, *Modern Philosophy, from Descartes to Schopenhauer and Hartmann* (1877), is of value for its power of critical exposition and illustration and its terse, lucid, and animated style. Its analysis and discussion of

Kant's thought is particularly able and interesting. In his polemics Bowen was somewhat prone to bend logic to meet the demands of argument, as in his vigorous attack upon the theory of evolution. He too frequently confounded the appeal to reason with the appeal to the emotions. He also spread his energy over too many fields to attain supremacy in any of them. Besides numerous magazine articles, he was the author of: *Life of Sir William Phips* (1837); *Life of Baron Steuben* (1838); *Critical Essays on a Few Subjects Connected with the History and Present Condition of Speculative Philosophy* (1842); *Life of James Otis* (1844); *Life of Benjamin Lincoln* (1847); *Lowell Lectures on the Application of Metaphysical and Ethical Science to the Evidences of Religion* (1849); *Documents of the Constitution of England and America to 1789 compiled and edited* (1854); *Principles of Political Economy* (1856); *Virgil, with English Notes* (1860); *Treatise on Logic* (1864); *American Political Economy* (1870); *Modern Philosophy, from Descartes to Schopenhauer and Hartmann* (1877); *Gleanings from a Literary Life* (1880); *A Layman's Study of the English Bible* (1885).

[Sketch in *Old Charlestown* (1902), by Timothy T. Sawyer; Chas. W. Eliot, *Harvard Memories* (1923), p. 73; *Memorials of the Class of 1833 of Harvard Coll.* (1883); *Harv. Univ. Quinquennial Cat.*, 1915; *Boston Evening Transcript*, Jan. 22, 1890; *Boston Herald*, Jan. 22, 23, 1890; *Critic*, Feb. 1, 1890.] E. S. B.

BOWEN, GEORGE (Apr. 30, 1816–Feb. 5, 1888), missionary, was born in Middlebury, Vt. His father, a New York merchant and man of means, spent his money in building up a library in his home, rather than in the education of his children. He took George from school at the age of twelve to train him to take over the business. George loathed the business and took refuge in the library, where he read omnivorously. At the age of sixteen he decided on a literary career combined with music. His love of operatic music set him to studying German, French, Italian, and Spanish. These he further mastered by four years of extensive travel in Europe (1836–40). A chapter in Gibbon's *Decline and Fall of the Roman Empire* had turned him in 1833 into a sceptic and bitter critic of all religion. During the years in Europe he built up his defenses against Christianity. The death of his fiancée in quiet Christian trust changed him. On returning home one evening he discovered that a librarian's error had placed in his hands Paley's *Natural Theology*. This work drove him to a rereading of the Bible and a fresh search. The result was a "conversion" that completely transformed his life (April 1844). Within four weeks he had offered himself to the American Board of Commissioners for Foreign Missions, and after three years at Union Theological Seminary, New York (1844–47), he sailed for India. He arrived in Bombay Jan. 19, 1848, and to this city he gave the remaining forty years of his life. He never married, he took no furlough, he went to no hills for his health. Slight of build and not robust, he remained at his post. Sensing keenly the social chasm between the native and the European he tried to bridge it by living in the simplicity of the poor, in a little room of an old pensioner's mud-walled house, on less than $200 a year. He withdrew from the American Board and earned his living by tutoring, and later, by editing and publishing the *Bombay Guardian* (associate editor, 1851–54; editor, 1854–88). His conduct pained his friends and stirred up the European community, which felt itself disgraced by this erratic missionary. Yet he was no ascetic, for he went wherever he was invited, and ate what was set before him. He later confessed that the chasm was more than social and the experiment not altogether successful, though he did not regret his step. He preached daily in the streets of the city in the Marathi and Hindustani languages, and served, without pay, as the editor of the Marathi publications of the Bombay Book and Tract Society, and agent of the Tract Depot, to which he transferred his living quarters. In 1871 he associated himself with the work begun by William Taylor, the traveling Methodist evangelist, for the Europeans and English-speaking Indians of Bombay. This relationship resulted in his joining the Methodists (1873). He became a charter member of the South India Conference, was three years presiding elder in Bombay, and twice, in the absence of the bishop, the president of the Conference. His editorials in the *Bombay Guardian*, "sharply pungent or sweetly fragrant," attracted attention and were published in Scotland (Edinburgh) and the United States (Presbyterian Board of Publications, Philadelphia) in three volumes: *Daily Meditations, The Amens of Christ*, and *Love Revealed*. They have been widely influential as books of devotion. His death, by pneumonia, revealed strikingly the hold he had gained upon the affections of the city of his life-service. He was known as "the white saint of India."

[The chief sources of information are the files of the *Bombay Guardian* (1851–88); the *Annual Reports* of the Missionary Soc. of the M. E. Ch.; the *Annual Reports* of the South India Conference of the M. E. Ch.; the introduction to Bowen's *Daily Meditations* (1865); Wm. Taylor, *Four Years' Campaign in India* (1876); and the many testimonials at the time of Bowen's death, particularly "In Memoriam, Geo. Bowen," *Christian Advocate* (N. Y.), 1888, pp. 120 ff.; see also E. M. Bliss, *Encyc. of Missions* (1891).] O. M. B.

BOWEN, HENRY CHANDLER (Sept. 11, 1813–Feb. 24, 1896), merchant, publisher, editor, was descended from Lieut. Henry Bowen, one of the first settlers of Woodstock, Conn., who had come from Wales with his father, Griffith, in 1638. George Bowen, descendant in the fifth generation from Henry, kept the country store and tavern at Woodstock, and there Henry Chandler was born. His mother was Lydia Wolcott Eaton. He was educated at Woodstock and Dudley Academies. After four years as clerk in his father's store, he went to New York to work in a silk house. In 1838 he established the firm of Bowen & McNamee, which later became Bowen & Holmes. In 1850 Bowen & McNamee were attacked, especially by the *Journal of Commerce*, because of their refusal to sign a call, prepared by a large group of prominent merchants, for a meeting to indorse the fugitive slave law. They published a card in which they informed the public that while they were silk merchants, as individuals they entertained their own views "on the various religious, moral and political questions of the day." They then added, "We wish it distinctly understood that our goods, and not our principles, are on the market." In 1848 Bowen joined in founding the *Independent*, a weekly journal of Congregationalism with strong anti-slavery principles. Later he became its publisher and finally its sole proprietor. He promptly brought the paper from a losing to a paying condition. Henry Ward Beecher and Theodore Tilton became successive editors of the *Independent* and Bowen was drawn by his intimacy with them into the mazes of the famous legal action of Tilton *vs.* Beecher for alienation of affections. On Dec. 26, 1870, he carried from Tilton to Beecher a letter demanding that the latter, "for reasons which you explicitly understand," immediately resign his pastorship of Plymouth Church and leave Brooklyn. A few days later he abruptly terminated the contract which he had with Tilton as a special contributor to the *Independent* and as editor of the *Brooklyn Union*, which he also owned. In April 1872, as the result of an arbitration by friends of the three men, a tripartite agreement was signed by Bowen, Tilton, and Beecher in which Bowen declared that "having given credit . . . to tales and innuendoes affecting" Beecher and having repeated them, he now felt that he had done Beecher wrong. He expressly withdrew all "the charges, imputations and innuendoes" and promised that he would never by word or deed "recur to, repeat or allude" to them again. At the same time he paid Tilton $7,000 in satisfaction of the broken contracts and published in the *Independent* a card in which he recognized Tilton's "honest purposes, and his chivalrous defense of what he believes to be true, as well as those qualities of heart which make him dear to those who know him best." Beecher reprinted with his cordial approval this "honorable testimony from Mr. Bowen" in the *Christian Union*, which he was then editing. In December 1873, charges were brought against Bowen before Plymouth Church of "uttering slanders affecting the good name" of its pastor, but the recommendation of the Examining Committee, that they be dismissed on the ground that he had agreed to keep to the letter and the spirit of the "tripartite agreement," was adopted. Shortly afterward he published a card protesting against the action because he had never seen a copy of the charges and because the committee had not put its recommendation "on the only pertinent basis that there was no evidence to sustain the charges." He expressed amazement that the "tripartite agreement" had been made public, "all the parties to which were solemnly pledged not to reveal it." Bowen was active in the development of Congregational interests in New York and Brooklyn, and was instrumental in the raising in 1852 of the Albany Fund for the erection of Congregational churches throughout the country, to which he made a substantial contribution. He participated in the organization of the Congregational Union, from which developed the Congregational Church Building Society. He was a generous benefactor of his native town, and subscribed liberally to rebuild and endow Woodstock Academy, to pay the town's Civil War debt, and to support the Woodstock Agricultural Society. He established a public park in Woodstock and held there for many years, on the Fourth of July, celebrations at which many eminent public men were speakers. He was married on June 6, 1844, to Lucy Maria, daughter of Lewis and Susanna (Aspinwall) Tappan of Brooklyn, and on Dec. 25, 1865, to Ellen, daughter of Dr. Hiram and Marian (Chandler) Holt of Woodstock. He had seven sons and three daughters by his first wife and one son by his second. He died in Brooklyn, Feb. 24, 1896.

[Obituaries of Bowen were published in the *Independent*, Feb. 27, Mar. 5, 1896, and in various New York and Brooklyn papers, Feb. 25, 1896. His ancestry is set forth in Edward Augustus Bowen, *The Lineage of the Bowens of Woodstock, Conn.* (1897) and in the *New Eng. Hist. and Geneal. Reg.*, L, 364–65. Frequent references to him will be found in Clarence Winthrop Bowen, *Hist. of Woodstock, Conn.* (1926). See also Paxton Hibben, *Henry Ward Beecher* (1927).] H. H.

BOWEN, HERBERT WOLCOTT (Feb. 29, 1856–May 29, 1927), writer, diplomat, was born in Brooklyn, N. Y., the second son of Henry Chandler Bowen [*q.v.*] and Lucy M. (Tappan) Bowen. The elder Bowen was long the editor and owner of the *Independent* and was prominent in the anti-slavery campaigns and in his support of Henry Ward Beecher in many of the controversies in which he was involved. The younger Bowen was educated at the Brooklyn Polytechnic and later abroad and graduated from Yale in the class of 1878. He and W. H. Taft, later United States president, were final contestants for the class championship in wrestling;—it has always been a matter of dispute as to which won the title. After studying law at Columbia University, Bowen was admitted to the bar and practised in New York until he was, in 1890, appointed consul in Barcelona. Here he served with distinction for nine years. In 1895 his post was made a consulate-generalship and he was promoted so that he might become the first occupant. Bowen's stay in Spain was ended by the outbreak of the Spanish-American War. During the period of hostilities he was frequently called to Washington and his familiarity with Spanish conditions was of service to the Departments of State and of War. In 1899 he was appointed minister-resident and consul general in Persia where he served acceptably for two years. Toward the end of 1901 he was sent to Venezuela as envoy extraordinary and minister plenipotentiary. When he arrived in Caracas, he found in the archives of the legation documents which he considered highly compromising to the good name of the United States and involving the personal integrity of one of his predecessors. These he forwarded to Washington with an explanatory letter, which was acknowledged in a perfunctory manner. A more insistent letter from Bowen drew from Secretary of State Hay a personal reply which in paternal language advised him not to add to the number of his enemies. Meantime, the seizure of the Venezuelan naval vessels and the blockade of Venezuelan ports by a combined German, British, and Italian squadron to enforce the claims of their nations long ignored, created a crisis. The Dictator, Castro, was at this time (December 1902) facing an internal revolt and believed the naval demonstration designed to aid the cause of his rival. He at once had hundreds of Germans, English, and Italian residents herded in the city jail. Bowen remonstrated with the Dictator and by his transparent frankness secured a complete ascendancy over him. On setting out to meet the revolutionists, Castro would have left complete powers in Bowen's hands. Bowen declined to accept unlimited powers, but he secured the liberation of all foreigners. When Castro returned in triumph after crushing the revolt, Bowen returned to the United States with a commission authorizing him to effect a settlement of foreign claims or to provide for their submission to arbitration. Bowen found President Roosevelt desirous himself to act as arbitrator, but he insisted on carrying the matter to The Hague Tribunal. During the negotiations that followed, the relations between the President and the envoy were tense and led to mutual recriminations. While Bowen was still in Europe, articles appeared in newspapers alluding to the incriminating documents which he had found in Caracas and submitted to the Department of State. Though Bowen was in no way responsible for these articles, President Roosevelt preferred charges against him and selected Secretary of War W. H. Taft to pass upon them. As a result, Bowen was dismissed from the diplomatic service with a reprimand in June 1905. He retired to a farm near Woodstock, Conn., where he wrote his memoirs, published a few months before his death. He had published several books of verse and a brief digest of International Law (1896). He was twice married: on Feb. 26, 1895, to Augusta F. Vingert, and on Jan. 25, 1902, to Carolyn Mae Clegg.

[*Who's Who in America*, 1926–27; *Quarter-Centenary Record, Class of 1878, Yale Coll.* (1905); *In the Matter of the Charges of Mr. Herbert W. Bowen . . . against Mr. Francis B. Loomis . . . and the Counter Charges of Mr. Loomis against Mr. Bowen* (Govt. Printing Office, 1905); *Venezuelan Arbitrations of 1903 . . . with App. Containing . . . Bowen Pamphlet Entitled "Venezuelan Protocols"* (Govt. Printing Office, 1904); *Hartford Times*, May 30, 1927; personal information.] S.B.

BOWEN, THOMAS MEADE (Oct. 26, 1835–Dec. 30, 1906), miner, lawyer, politician, was born near Burlington, Ia., was educated at an academy in the neighboring town of Mt. Pleasant, and was elected to the Iowa House of Representatives in 1856 from Wayne County. In 1858 he moved to Kansas where he engaged in the practise of law until the outbreak of the Civil War. During the war he was advanced from captain of the 1st Regiment of Nebraska Volunteers to colonel of the 13th Kansas Infantry and to the rank of brigadier-general by brevet. When the Confederacy collapsed he was stationed in Arkansas, and there he remained to take an active part in the reorganization of the state government; he was president of the constitutional convention held under the Reconstruction Act of 1867, and for four years served as a judge of the state supreme court. In 1871 he was appointed governor of Idaho Territory, but after about a week in Boise he resigned, the work and environment not being to his liking. Again he busied himself in Arkansas reconstruction politics, only to be defeated in 1873 by Stephen W. Dorsey in an attempt to win a seat in the United States Senate. In 1875 Bowen moved to Colorado; after a few months in Denver he went to Del Norte, a new town in the San Luis Valley, where he established a law office and became interested in mining ventures. So poor was he at this time that he is said to have walked over half the distance between Denver and Del Norte. He made friends easily, and in 1876, shortly after the organization of the new state government, was elected judge of the fourth judicial district of Colorado. As judge he was fearless, but lacking in any sense of judicial dignity either on or off the bench. The most famous case that came before him was one that grew out of the rivalry between the Denver & Rio Grande and the Santa Fé railways for the control of the Royal Gorge. The struggle, legal and physical, had been in progress fully a year when attorneys for the Denver & Rio Grande appeared in Judge Bowen's court in the little Mexican village of San Luis and asked for an injunction restraining the Santa Fé from transacting business in Colorado on the ground that it was a foreign corporation. In spite of charges made in open court by the attorneys for the Santa Fé that the judge was biased, Bowen refused a change of venue and granted the injunction; a few days later his decision was set aside by Judge Moses Hallett in Denver (see files of *Denver Tribune,* June 1879), although the courts later, in effect, sustained Bowen's action. For several years he had been investing his money in mines; about 1880 his faith was abundantly rewarded by a rich strike in the Summittville (Colorado) district. He resigned his judgeship, was elected to the lower house of the Colorado legislature in 1882 and in the following year, after a prolonged fight in the Republican caucus, was elected to the United States Senate. He served the full term of six years (1883–89) without distinction. When he retired from the Senate he was practically penniless; again he engaged in mining, and again he found a fortune. His last years were spent in Pueblo, Colo.; at his death he was survived by his wife (Margaretta Thurston) to whom he was married while a resident of Arkansas. He was tall and slender, slovenly in dress, breezy in manner, open-handed, loyal to his friends, a boon companion. He had a ready tongue and a nimble wit. His knowledge of the law was not profound, but he was shrewd and clever if not always impartial. In the words of one of his successors in the Senate (Charles S. Thomas), "Bowen achieved some distinctions but ignored or despised their responsibilities."

[Frank Hall, *Hist. of Colo.* (1895), IV, 298; H. J. French, *Hist. of Idaho* (1914), I, 78; the files of the *Denver Tribune* and the *Rocky Mountain News* for 1879 and the years following; obituaries in the *Pueblo Chieftain, Denver Republican,* and the *Rocky Mountain News,* Dec. 31, 1906.] C. B. G.

BOWERS, ELIZABETH CROCKER (Mar. 12, 1830–Nov. 6, 1895), actress, was born at Ridgefield, Conn. Her father, the Rev. William Crocker, was a Methodist clergyman. She made her first appearance on the stage as Amanthis in the *Child of Nature,* Dec. 3, 1846. On Mar. 4, 1847, she married David P. Bowers, a well-known Philadelphia actor. Her first appearance on the stage as Mrs. D. P. Bowers was at the Walnut Street Theatre, Philadelphia, as Donna Victoria in *A Bold Stroke for a Husband,* Mar. 11, 1847. The following year she acted at the Arch Street Theatre and in 1853 became a member of the stock company at that house, remaining several seasons and becoming an immense favorite. On the death of her husband in 1857, she retired temporarily from the stage, but on Dec. 19, 1857, became lessee of the Walnut Street Theatre, opening it as the People's Theatre with *London Assurance* and remaining its manager until January 1859. A few months later she leased the Academy of Music, Philadelphia, for a short season and during this time married Dr. Brown, a chemist of Baltimore, who died in 1867. In 1861 she went to England, making her appearance at Sadler's Wells as Julia in *The Hunchback* and creating a very favorable impression. In 1863 she returned to this country and was seen at the Winter Garden, New York, playing the title rôle in *Lady Audley's Secret,* and Julia in *The Hunchback* to Lawrence Barrett's Sir Thomas Clifford. A starring tour followed, after which she reappeared at the Winter Garden, Oct. 15, 1866, in *Lady Audley's Secret.* On Nov. 23 of the same year, she acted Romeo to the Juliet of her sister, Mrs. F. B. Conway. On Dec. 16, 1867, she was seen at the Broadway Theatre (Wallack's) as Dora. After more starring tours she again appeared in New York, at Booth's Theatre as Lady Macbeth to Booth's Macbeth. During this engagement she also acted Beatrice in *Much Ado About Nothing,* Portia in *The Merchant of Venice* and Margaret in *Richard III.* On Jan. 20, 1883, she married James C. McCollum, and for the next few years retired from the stage, devoting her time to teaching elocution. Early in 1892 she took a benefit at Palmer's Theatre, New York, and on Feb. 3 was seen at that house as Mme. d'Arcay in the first performance of *The Broken Seal.* The following year, on Feb. 5, she played the Duchess of Berwick in the first New York performance of Oscar Wilde's comedy *Lady Windermere's Fan.* On Oct. 24 of the same year she appeared at the Em-

Bowers

pire Theatre, New York, as Mrs. Kirkland in David Belasco's play *The Younger Son,* and on Dec. 11 played Lady Carolina in support of Rose Coghlan in Oscar Wilde's *A Woman of No Importance.* She was again seen at Palmer's on Oct. 8, 1894, as Mrs. Woodville in A. W. Gattie's drama *The Transgressor,* the occasion being the American début of Olga Nethersole. On Nov. 12 she played Lady Wargrave in the first American performance of Sidney Grundy's *The New Woman.* This was the last part she played in New York. "An actress of great distinction, she had beauty as well as talent," says a contemporary critic, "a voice of fascinating sweetness, a refined manner and a cultivated mind." She died in Washington Nov. 6, 1895.

[T. A. Brown, *Hist. of the Am. Stage* (1870) and *Hist. of the N. Y. Stage* (1903); Alan Dale (A. J. Cohen), *Familiar Chats with Queens of the Stage* (1890); *N. Y. Dram. Mirror,* XXXIV, 15; *Washington Post,* Nov. 7, 1895.] A.H.

BOWERS, LLOYD WHEATON (Mar. 9, 1859–Sept. 9, 1910), lawyer, was born at Springfield, Mass., the son of Samuel Dwight and Martha Wheaton (Dowd) Bowers. On both sides his ancestors were Puritans who had settled in New England more than two centuries before his birth. His family removed in his infancy to Brooklyn, N. Y., and later to Elizabeth, N. J., and there he was prepared for college by a private tutor. Entering Yale in 1875, he was graduated as valedictorian of his class in 1879. His standing had been but once equalled. For one year he remained as a graduate student, then traveled in Europe, and, despite a tempting offer of a teaching position at Yale, turned to the profession of the law. He was graduated from the Columbia Law School, admitted to the New York bar, and received a clerkship in a leading firm of New York City in 1882. Such were his abilities that in one year he became managing clerk, and in January 1884 a member of the firm. Ill health, however, compelled him to rest, and as a result of a summer's travel in the Northwest he moved in October 1884 to Winona, Minn., where he formed a partnership with Thomas Wilson, former chief justice of the state supreme court. Here he practised until 1893. He then became the general counsel of the Chicago & North Western Railway Company, one of the great railway systems of the country, and in this office he served until 1909, when he was appointed by President Taft, an intimate friend since college days, solicitor-general of the United States. Little more than a year was given him to occupy this position of honor and responsibility.

The years of his work with the North Western were a period of extraordinary industrial development. Incidentally to this development litigation arose—involving federal control of the railroads under the Interstate Commerce Act of 1887, the powers of the states to control intrastate commerce, and to tax corporations, and the application of the Sherman Anti-Trust Act of 1890—which involved social and political issues of vast importance. In this litigation Bowers played a conspicuous part. His success in winning cases for the government during his brief service as solicitor-general was phenomenal. He was regarded by his railroad associates, at least, as no mere partisan, but on the contrary as mindful of the railroads' duties as quasi-public corporations; and according to an intimate associate he found especial happiness, as solicitor-general, in the fact that he could act solely as lawyer, rather than counsel, and for the whole country rather than for a special interest. Contrary criticism has been made, however, by men of other economic outlook, of the government's policy—for which he at least shared responsibility—in the cases decreeing the "dissolutions" of the Standard Oil and Tobacco trusts in 1910 (221 *United States Reports,* 1, 106). It is well known that only his death prevented his nomination by President Taft for appointment to the Supreme Court of the United States.

Although he published nothing, and was in that sense wholly absorbed in the law, he retained throughout life a catholicity of intellectual interests, particularly in literature. Art and music, in his later years, also shared his interest. Of sturdy frame, with dark seamed face and brilliant eyes under beetling brows, he was a striking figure. In forensic argument he was not of the calm and calculating type, though resourceful, but impetuous and masterful in manner. With juries he was far from successful; but he was exceedingly strong in his grasp of the legal factors in a case and was effective with a court. Notwithstanding some reserve, his charm of manner, marked by kindly sympathy, easily won friends, whom he held by the attractions of a broad and generous nature. He married twice; first (on Sept. 7, 1887) Louisa Bennett Wilson of Winona, Minn., who died on Dec. 20, 1897; and second (in 1906) Charlotte Josephine Lewis of Detroit, who survived him.

[*Memorials of the Chicago Bar Ass.,* 1910–11; *Hist. of the Class of '79, Yale Coll. 1875–1905,* pp. 111–12; *Who's Who in America,* 1910–11; *Chicago Daily Tribune,* Sept. 10, 1910.] F.S.P.

BOWERS, THEODORE SHELTON (Oct. 10, 1832–Mar. 6, 1866), Union soldier, was born in Hummelstown, Dauphin County, Pa., the son of George and Ann Maria Bowers. His early life was spent in extreme poverty. As a boy he removed to Mt. Carmel, Ill., learned the printer's trade, and eventually became editor of the local newspaper, the *Register*. He entered the volunteer army in October 1861 as a private in the 48th Illinois Infantry. In January 1862, shortly before the advance against Forts Henry and Donelson, he was detailed as a clerk at Gen. Grant's headquarters, where he soon came to the favorable notice of the commanding general. He was appointed a first lieutenant in March, and soon after was regularly assigned as an aide to Gen. Grant. Faithful and efficient in the performance of his duties, and attached to his chief with a semi-feudal devotion, Bowers became one of that little official family which the great commander kept with him in all his campaigns, east or west. He was promoted to captain in November 1862, and major in February 1863. He was captured in Van Dorn's raid on Holly Springs, Miss., in December 1862, but made his escape in a few hours. Soon after the taking of Vicksburg, he succeeded Rawlins as Grant's adjutant-general, and was made a lieutenant-colonel (Aug. 30, 1863). In that capacity he served through the Virginia campaigns of 1864 and 1865, and was present at the surrender at Appomattox. After Grant's assignment to the command of all the armies, he obtained Bowers's appointment as a captain in the quartermaster department of the regular army (July 29, 1864). This insured that he would be retained in the service after the volunteer forces should be mustered out, but he never actually served under this commission, nor under a later regular-army appointment as major in the adjutant-general's department (Jan. 6, 1865), for he died before his discharge from his volunteer commission as lieutenant-colonel. His death occurred at Garrison, N. Y., as he was returning, with Gen. Grant, from a visit to West Point. Bowers left the train to attend to baggage, and in trying to board it again fell under the wheels. He was buried at West Point. "Gallant little Bowers," Charles King calls him, and a better description of him would be hard to find. His career was determined in the first place by the accident of his attracting Grant's attention, and later by his own merits and the mutual loyalty of his chief and himself. His services were recognized by the award of no less than four brevets, the last being as brigadier-general. The G. A. R. post at Mt. Carmel was named for him.

[F. B. Heitman, *Biog. Reg.* (1903), I, 234; article by Theodore G. Risley in *Jour. Ill. State Hist. Soc.*, XII, 407–11. The extensive correspondence indexed under Bowers's name in the *Official Records* consists of the letters received and sent by his office, and tells little of his personal history. Obituary in the *United Service Mag.*, V (N. Y., 1866), pp. 360–63.] T. M. S.

BOWIE, JAMES (1796–Mar. 6, 1836), Texas soldier, was born in Burke County, Ga., the son of Rezin (probably James Rezin) Bowie. His mother's name is recorded in Spanish documents as Alvina (also Elvy) Jones, but the surname may be only a blundering attempt to write the word "Jane." The year of his birth has been variously given; some writers place it as late as 1805, but the date is inconsistent with the generally accepted statement that his parents moved to Catahoula Parish, La., in 1802. He had four brothers—David, Rezin P., John J., and Stephen—all of whom appear in the early chronicles. Of his youth little is known. Tradition makes him a participant in a desperate encounter on the banks of the Mississippi, Sept. 19, 1827, in which, after being badly wounded by a bullet, he killed his opponent with a knife. It has been many times asserted (see Eugene C. Barker, *Quarterly of the Texas Historical Association,* VI, 148) that with two of his brothers, Rezin P. and John J., he made large sums of money through the sale of negro slaves smuggled into Louisiana and Texas by Lafitte the pirate. The story is, however, denied by the family of Rezin P. Bowie. About 1828 he came to Texas, making San Antonio his home and prospecting the San Saba region for a lost mine. On Oct. 5, 1830, he became a Mexican citizen and at once began to acquire extensive tracts of land, largely through the device of inducing Mexicans to apply for grants and then buying them, when obtained, at merely nominal prices (*Ibid.*, X, 77).

Bowie was married, Apr. 25, 1831, to Ursula, the daughter of Vice-Governor Juan Martin de Veramendi of San Antonio. The growing tension between the Americans and the Mexican Government found him usually with the element favoring resistance. As a captain he was in the fight at Nacogdoches in August 1832, and after the surrender of Piedras's command conveyed the prisoners to San Antonio. During the comparative quiet of the next twenty months he was busy with his own affairs, but on the revival of the movement against the central government he at once took a leading part. He was chosen a member of the first committee of safety, organized at Mina (now Bastrop), May 17, 1835. With the outbreak of hostilities shortly afterward his qualities of energy, daring, and resourcefulness came into full play. As a colonel of the revolutionary forces, though never in command of more than a handful of men, he was an important factor in the campaign which by Dec. 15 had cleared Texas of the Mexican army. When at the beginning of 1836 the army, with Santa Anna at its head, returned, Bowie was located with Col. William Barret Travis, and about 150 men (the number later increased to 188), at San Antonio. Retreating across the river and making their stand at the abandoned Alamo mission, they were overwhelmed after a desperate resistance, and all of them including Bowie, who was lying ill on a cot, were killed.

Bowie was six feet tall, well proportioned, with erect carriage, fair complexion, and small blue eyes. He was quiet and unobtrusive in demeanor. Of his courage, strength, and agility many stories are told; it has been said of him that he "was known to rope and ride alligators." One of his titles to fame is the reputed invention of the bowie knife. The accounts, however, are conflicting, some attributing it to his brother Rezin; but a correspondent, Gid L. Sowell, of Rosedale, Okla., in *Frontier,* August 1925, repeats a family tradition that James Bowie had injured himself in an Indian fight by letting his hand slip from the hilt to the blade of his butcher knife; that he thereupon suggested to John Sowell, the blacksmith of Gonzalez, the addition of a guard, and that Sowell, from a model cut in wood by Bowie, made the first weapon and gave it the name it has since borne. It is certain that the weapon became widely popular. As early as 1840, occasionally known as the "Arkansas toothpick," it was being made in large quantities by a firm in Sheffield, England, for the Texas trade.

[Louis J. Wortham, *Hist. of Texas* (1924); Dudley G. Wooten, *Comprehensive Hist. of Texas* (1898), founded upon H. Yoakum, *Hist. of Texas* (1855); Homer S. Thrall, *Pictorial Hist. of Texas* (1879); Evelyn Brogan, *Jas. Bowie, a Hero of the Alamo* (1922).]

W. J. G.

BOWIE, ODEN (Nov. 10, 1826–Dec. 4, 1894), governor of Maryland, the eldest son of William D. and Mary Eliza (Oden) Bowie, was born and spent most of his life on his father's estate "Fairview" in Prince Georges County, Md. His first instruction was received at home under a tutor, but upon his mother's death, when he was only nine, he was sent to the preparatory school attached to old St. John's College, Annapolis. After three years there he entered St. Mary's College, Baltimore, from which he graduated in 1845. Shortly after leaving college he enlisted as a private in the Baltimore and Washington Battalion and left for the Mexican border. At the battle of Monterey, Bowie's commander, Lieutenant-Colonel Watson, was mortally wounded. In imminent peril of his life, young Bowie stayed with the dying colonel until he received from him important messages and papers. Almost surrounded by the enemy, he mounted his horse and made a desperate and successful dash for safety. For this gallant action he was promoted to a lieutenancy and later commissioned a captain in the Voltigeur Regiment. The Maryland legislature passed a set of complimentary resolutions expressing "The thanks of his native State for distinguished gallantry displayed during the three days' siege of Monterey" (Resolution 43, Act of 1847). Illness, due to the climate of Mexico, compelled him to return to Maryland before the close of the war.

From his father, who had served in both houses of the legislature, Bowie inherited a keen interest in politics. Almost immediately after his return from Mexico he became a candidate for the legislature. He was under age at the time, but would have arrived at his majority before the legislature convened, a fact, however, which was not generally known. His opponents, who talked much of his youth, succeeded in raising a doubt as to his elegibility and Bowie was defeated by ten votes. In 1849 he was again a candidate for the House of Delegates, and had the honor of being the only Democrat elected that year in his county. A few years later he was elected state senator, but in 1861, when a candidate for the same office, he was defeated by Federal military interference at the polls. In 1860 he was chosen president of the Baltimore & Potomac Railroad, then but recently organized, and filled that office until his death. It was largely due to his management and unflagging perseverance that the railroad finally achieved success. Bowie's sympathies were with the South, although he did not approve of the radical course of the secessionists. He used every effort to preserve the organization of the Democratic party and it was largely due to him that that party regained control of the state. He was chairman of the state central committee during the war, and in 1864 was sent as a delegate to the Chicago convention which nominated Gen. McClellan for the presidency. The Democratic nominee for lieutenant-governor in 1864, he was defeated by the Union candidate, Cox; but in 1867 he was elected governor of Maryland by the largest majority ever given by the state to any candidate. He did not become governor *de facto* until Jan. 13, 1869, and remained in office until Jan. 10, 1872. The settlement of the dispute with Virginia regarding oyster-beds, the collection of arrears from the Baltimore & Ohio Railroad due the state, and the collection from the United States government of money loaned by Maryland for war purposes were among the many questions settled during his able administration.

Bowie was active in the organization of the Maryland Jockey Club and was long its president. He owned many famous race horses, and it was a keen grief to him when in 1890, on account of failing health, he was compelled to part with them. Four years later he died at "Fairview" and was buried in the family graveyard a short distance from his home. He was married in 1851 to Alice, daughter of Charles H. and Rosalie Eugenia (Calvert) Carter.

[Heinrich E. Buchholz, *Governors of Md.* (1908); Walter Worthington Bowie, *The Bowies and their Kindred* (1899); *Baltimore Sun*, Dec. 5, 1894.] E. T. D.

BOWIE, RICHARD JOHNS (June 23, 1807–Mar. 12, 1881), politician, was born in Georgetown, D. C., the son of Col. Washington Bowie and Margaret (Johns) Bowie. He received a classical education under Dr. Carnahan and was a student at the university in Georgetown. He studied law under Clement Cox and was admitted to the bar of the District of Columbia when but nineteen. At the age of twenty-two he was admitted to practise before the United States Supreme Court. In the same year he moved to Rockville, Montgomery County, Md., where he immediately took an active interest in public affairs and rose to prominence in his profession.

Politically he was a Whig. A man of brilliant intellect, combined with much legal learning, he soon became a leader in his party. In 1835–36–37 he was elected to the Maryland Senate. In 1845 he became prosecuting attorney for Montgomery County and held that office for four years. From 1849 to 1853 he was a representative in Congress. He was an ardent admirer of Henry Clay and it is claimed by his friends that he made the first public speech in the House of Representatives in favor of the compromise measures of 1850. He was an eloquent, forcible, and convincing speaker and always actively interested in any important measure brought before Congress during his four years in the House. In 1854 the Whigs nominated him for governor of Maryland. The Whig party had split asunder over the slavery question and that year was practically destroyed. The Democratic candidate was elected and Bowie suffered his first political defeat. He was a staunch Unionist, and with the unswerving honesty and moral courage that marked the man, he opposed secession and tried to avert the war which he feared was inevitable. At the election of 1861 he was chosen to succeed Judge LeGrand as chief justice of the court of appeals. During the four years of civil war, when citizens were illegally arrested, civil courts often disregarded, and martial law held sway, the court over which he presided remained above suspicion or reproach. He remained on the bench of that court until his death, with the exception of a slight interval after the adoption of the constitution of 1867, when the judicial system of the state was again changed. In 1871 occurred the next general election and Judge Bowie was restored to the judicial seat by popular vote. In 1876, as he was approaching the age limit of seventy years, the legislature extended his term until the expiration of the period for which he had been elected. This great tribute was paid to a Republican judge by a Democratic legislature with only three dissenting votes. His private life was as irreproachable as his public career. He died at his residence "Glenview" after a few days of illness, and was buried in Rockville cemetery. He was married in 1833 to Catherine L. Williams, of Hagerstown, Md.

[*The Green Bag*, VI, 274; Walter Worthington Bowie, *The Bowies and Their Kindred* (1899); *Baltimore Sun*, Mar. 14, 1881.] E. T. D.

BOWIE, ROBERT (March 1750–Jan. 8, 1818), governor of Maryland, was born at "Mattaponi," near Nottingham, Prince Georges County, Md., the third son of Capt. William and Margaret (Sprigg) Bowie. He received his education at the schools of the Rev. John Eversfield, near Croom, and the Rev. Mr. Craddock, near Baltimore. In 1770 he eloped with Priscilla, the daughter of Gen. James John Mackall, of Calvert County. Though he was barely twenty, and the bride not yet fifteen, the marriage proved a happy one. His father gave him a house in Nottingham and a farm nearby. Upon the death of his father he inherited "Mattaponi," which thenceforth was his summer residence.

At a meeting of "Freeholders and citizens" held in Upper Marlborough in November 1774, young Bowie was appointed a member of a committee to see that the resolutions of the American Continental Congress were carried into effect. This was the beginning of his leadership in county and state affairs. In September 1775 a Committee of Observation was formed, and he, with several others, was instructed to enrol a company of "Minute Men." He was commissioned first lieutenant in a company of militia formed in Nottingham in 1776. In June of the same year, he was commissioned captain of the 2nd Battalion, Maryland Flying Artillery, and with this battalion he joined Washington in his campaign near New York. In the several important battles of the Revolution in which Bowie took part he showed courage and good judgment, though he won no special distinction.

After the close of the war he returned to his

native county, and became keenly interested in politics. From 1785 to 1790 he was a member of the House of Delegates, having been elected for six consecutive terms. While in the legislature he strongly advocated a measure for establishing St. John's College, Annapolis. Three years after retiring from the House of Delegates he was appointed a major of the militia and justice of the peace in Prince Georges County. In 1801–02–03 he was again a member of the legislature. At this time the people of Maryland were clamoring for a more radical democrat than Gov. Mercer to fill the executive chair. Bowie was the logical man, and on Nov. 17, 1803, the General Assembly cast the majority of votes in his favor. The following day he resigned from the House of Delegates to become governor of Maryland. He was reëlected in 1804 and again in 1805, which made his first administration cover the full three years for which he was eligible. After leaving the executive chair in 1807 he was again appointed a justice of the peace.

In 1811, when America was about to enter on her second war with England, Bowie came forward as a champion of the Republican party, which, almost to a man, advocated a declaration of war. In November 1811 the Republicans predominated in the legislature, and Bowie was again elected governor of Maryland. In June 1812, when war was finally declared, the delighted Governor "proceeded through the streets bare-headed to the State House, where he congratulated the leaders upon the welcome news" (*Annapolis Gazette,* June 12, 1812). Unfortunately, in August 1812 an article appeared in a Baltimore paper which maddened the Republicans against whom it was directed. An infuriated mob attacked a house where a number of Federalist leaders were being entertained, killing several and beating several more. Indignation meetings were held throughout the state and the Governor was urged to make an investigation and punish the instigators of the riot. Bowie, failing to apprehend the criminals, was accused of shielding them. Whether he was guilty or blameless, the unfortunate event terminated his public career, though he fought hard until his death to recover the gubernatorial seat. He was an implacable enemy, but a most loyal friend, and those who knew him in private life loved him well for his generosity and kindly spirit. He died at his home in Nottingham, and was buried in the family graveyard at "Mattaponi."

[Heinrich E. Buchholz, *Governors of Md.* (1908); Walter Worthington Bowie, *The Bowies and Their Kindred* (1899).] E. T. D.

BOWLER, METCALF (1726–Sept. 24, 1789) judge, was born in London. When about seventeen years of age he accompanied his father, Charles Bowler, to Boston, where the latter purchased land in the vicinity of the Common and Beacon Hill, later moving to Newport, R. I., and serving as collector of His Majesty's revenues. Business man, adventurer, genial host, and patriot, Metcalf Bowler lived prosperously through the days of Newport's commercial supremacy. His marriage to Anne, daughter of Bathsheba (Palmer) Fairchild and Maj. Fairchild, a business associate, founded a large family of eleven children. His commercial prosperity permitted him to maintain them in considerable state in what was later known as the Vernon House on Mary and Clarke Street. During the French and Indian War, both as an investment and an adventure, he fitted out four privateers, the *Prince Frederick,* the *New Concert,* the *Diana,* and the *Defence.* While these brought him large profits, lengthy litigation in prize suits, often with appeals to England, brought him equally great losses. Representative in the Rhode Island General Assembly, and speaker of the House of Representatives, 1767–76, he led the opposition to the Stamp Act, representing the colony, in 1765, at the New York Congress. Appreciation of his services resulted in his choice, the following year, as the one to present to the King a message of thanks for the act's repeal. The people's confidence in him was further evidenced by his election, in 1768, as assistant judge of the supreme court, and, in 1776, as chief justice. Service with the Committee of Correspondence in 1773, his signature upon the Rhode Island Declaration of Independence, and the marriage of his daughter, Bathsheba, to the Marquis Langfroi are but a few of the indications of his close association with the colonial cause. The accounts of the fame of his choice fruits and rare flowers and his *Treatise on Agriculture and Practical Husbandry* (1786) show him to have been a skilful horticulturist. Virtually ruined by the Revolution, he opened a small shop at Providence, and, in 1787, the "Queen's Head" tavern. Two golden eagles, devices derived from the Bowler coat of arms, which originally ornamented the gateposts of his Portsmouth farm, to-day face each other on Thames St., Newport. The wood-work and paneling of one of the rooms of his Portsmouth house may be seen in the American wing of the Metropolitan Museum.

[N. P. Bowler, *Record of the Descendants of Chas. Bowler* (1905); G. C. Mason's *Annals of Trinity Church, Newport* (1890–94); W. P. Sheffield, *Priva teers and Privateersmen of Newport* (1883); E. M. Stone, *Our French Allies* (1884).] H. F. K.

BOWLES, SAMUEL (June 8, 1797–Sept. 8, 1851), newspaper editor, was born in Hartford, Conn. He was the son of a pewterer of Boston whose business had been ruined by the Revolution and who had removed to the former city in 1798, opening first a bakery and later a grocery. The father became a cripple and his means were slender; dying in 1813, he left Bowles as his only inheritance a watch and the family Bible. The boy, who had finished his common school education and gone into the grocery shop at fifteen, was now apprenticed to a printer. During this apprenticeship he joined with a dozen other youths in forming a literary and debating club, which gave him a taste for intellectual pursuits. This connection, he wrote later, "I consider an important era in my life—a sort of redeeming season, saving me from dangerous tendencies. It gave a good direction to my habits, strengthening my mind to resist temptation, and led me to prefer mental to sensual pleasure" (*Springfield Daily Republican,* Sept. 10, 1851). His first employment as printer was with the New Haven *Register,* where he rose to be foreman. In 1819 he formed a partnership with John Francis of Wethersfield in publishing the *Hartford Times,* an unsuccessful weekly sheet. His associate was intemperate and incompetent, he fell into debts which it took him many years to discharge, and constant overwork impaired his health. An attack of typhus which prostrated him for the greater part of a year also left him subject to recurrent attacks of dysentery throughout life. On Feb. 12, 1822, he married Huldah Deming of Wethersfield, a descendant of Miles Standish, who matched his hard sense, frugality, and industry with similar qualities of her own. More than two years later, in 1824, the *Hartford Times* having failed, he loaded his wife, his baby daughter, a hand printing press which he had hired, and some household goods upon a flatboat, and ascended the Connecticut River to establish a new weekly in Springfield, Mass.

Bowles took this step at the invitation of some Springfield Anti-Federalists, who helped him obtain loans aggregating $400 for the purchase of type and other equipment. The first issue of the *Springfield Republican* appeared on Sept. 8, 1824, with about 250 subscribers at $2 a year. Bowles was proprietor, publisher, reporter, editor, compositor, pressman, and business manager; and as his son's biographer says, "it must be owned by one who reads the first numbers that one man might have produced it all without any dangerous strain on his powers" (Merriam, I, 4). In the next fifteen years the weekly *Republican* grew steadily but slowly. At one time it had as many as five rivals, while it also had to meet the competition of New York and Boston papers. But it crushed or absorbed the other local weeklies, while its thorough system of local intelligence gradually made it indispensable to readers of western Massachusetts. Bowles in 1824 supported William H. Crawford for the presidency and opposed John Quincy Adams. Four years later, however, distrusting Jackson for his autocratic temper, he stood behind Adams for reelection. Throughout Jackson's administration Bowles kept the *Republican* in the opposition, advocating the election of Clay in 1832 and being identified with the Whig party from the moment of its birth. His position upon slavery was that of most Massachusetts Whigs; he deplored the agitation of the question and assailed the Abolitionists, but opposed the spread of the institution and attacked the annexation of Texas and the Mexican War. But in these years the editorial vigor and the influence of the *Republican* were slight.

By the beginning of the forties the *Republican* had 1,200 subscribers, printed fourteen or fifteen columns of news weekly, and was ready for expansion. After the completion of the Boston & Albany Railroad in 1839 Springfield grew rapidly as a manufacturing and railway center. In 1842 Bowles publicly proposed the establishment of a daily edition, but was dissuaded by business friends from this risky undertaking as there was then no daily paper in Massachusetts outside Boston, and but one in Connecticut. But the elder of Bowles's surviving sons, Samuel Bowles, Jr., urged his father not to abandon the plan, and promised to assume the main responsibility. The first issue of the daily *Republican* appeared Mar. 27, 1844, an evening paper of four small pages. At the end of two years it had only two hundred subscribers, and not until after its transformation, in December 1845, into a morning paper, did it gain an air of permanency. The basis of its prosperity, and of the future power of the *Republican,* was the organization by the two Bowleses of a local correspondence which thoroughly covered every town and hamlet of the upper Connecticut valley.

Till his death from his dysenteric affection in 1851, Bowles remained identified with the weekly *Republican,* his son taking charge of the daily. He represented the best type of country editor of the period: slow, cautious, thrifty, measurably far-sighted though provincial in outlook, and shrewd though limited in education. He insisted upon complete editorial independence, and late in life boasted that he had rejected "with scorn" several alluring offers of financial aid if he would permit others to use his journal. Bowles's great service was in firmly establishing the organ which the energy and brilliance of his son made nationally famous.

[Samuel Bowles himself left one printed production, a pamphlet called *Geneal. and Hist. Notes of the Bowles Family* (Springfield, 1851), which sheds some light upon his early life. Thomas M. Farquhar's *Hist. of the Bowles Family* (1907) deals fully with his ancestry. The first chapters of George S. Merriam's *Life and Times of Samuel Bowles* (1885) furnish the best connected account of his career. This is supplemented by the history of the *Republican,* Richard Hooker's *Story of an Independent Newspaper* (1924). See also Willard G. Bleyer, *Main Currents in the Hist. of Am. Journalism* (1927), pp. 252 ff.] A.N.

BOWLES, SAMUEL (Feb. 9, 1826–Jan. 16, 1878), editor, was the son of Samuel and Huldah Bowles. Born a year and a half after the founding of the *Springfield Republican,* the younger Bowles was reared in a frugal household, sharing his room with three of his father's apprentices. He attended the public schools, carried the weekly *Republican* to a round of subscribers, and early showed a preference for books over outdoor pursuits. When about thirteen he was sent to a private school and gained some knowledge of the Latin classics; but although he wished to go to college, his father, who desired him to be trained as a printer, disapproved. In later life he spoke of the want of a college education with deep regret, but in large measure he atoned for it by reading. The newspapers and magazines in his father's office engaged the boy so that "you might speak to him half a dozen times and he would never know it" (Merriam, I, 19). At seventeen he entered this office as a general helper—running errands, doing mechanical jobs, and writing local items. The youth's enterprising spirit was proved within a year by his insistence upon the establishment of a daily edition, and his agreement to assume most of the extra labor. Little capital was required, an associate contracting to print both the daily and weekly for one year for $1,450 (Hooker, p. 38). The issue began without a single subscriber or advertiser, and the prospectus announced that if the loss after a half-year or year proved too great, "we shall stop" (*Springfield Republican,* Mar. 27, 1844). To add to the difficulties, the younger Bowles's health broke down so seriously that in the winter of 1844–45 he went to Louisiana to recuperate, and could give no help beyond a series of fifteen news-letters. When he returned, however, he threw himself into the work with such energy that on Apr. 1, 1846, the owners could announce that "The *Republican* is now placed on a permanent basis." The staff was small and upon him fell the task of laboring till two or three o'clock in the morning to gather and write the late news, while he gave earnest attention to the editorial page.

In his early twenties Bowles's characteristic traits all asserted themselves—his impetuosity, his driving vigor, which sometimes kept him working forty hours at a stretch, his intensity, his nervousness, his exuberant over-activity, his erratic changes of mind, his combativeness. At the outset a newspaper war with the *Springfield Gazette* helped the *Republican* to strike its gait. "That aroused my ire and I determined that we would not be beaten," he wrote later. "After a year my opponents came to me and wanted a truce, but I said, 'No, you began the fight and now you shall have it.' And they did, till they were driven from the field." In 1848 the *Republican* absorbed the *Gazette,* and established its supremacy in western Massachusetts. The following year it was joined by the versatile and fluent Josiah Gilbert Holland. He and two other men already on the paper, William B. Calhoun, who as a leader-writer surpassed even his chief, and George Ashmun, known later as a Republican politician and a friend of Lincoln, made up an able editorial corps. Dr. Holland, after two years' service, bought a quarter interest in the *Republican* for $3,500. Bowles did much reporting: "News," he held, "is the distinctive object of the *Republican,* to which all other things must bend." He kept his ear constantly open; hearing local gossip, talking to politicians, pumping his wide acquaintance, and condensing the result for the paper. Telegraphic news was rapidly developed. A number of features were instituted: a daily column of "Local Items" maintained with distinctive enterprise, a weekly column of "Religious Intelligence," then new in secular journalism, a chapter of "Sunday Thoughts," by Dr. Holland, and agricultural advice. On the editorial page Bowles more and more displaced the long articles with pithy and pungent editorials. His father's death in 1851 found him able to take control of the paper in every department (Merriam, pp. 64 ff.).

Politically the course taken by Bowles showed as yet neither the independence nor the steadiness which later characterized it. During Polk's administration he supported the Wilmot Proviso and in 1848 declared emphatically: "Congress is the battleground of slavery and freedom . . . Our motto is NO COMPROMISE, NO MORE SLAVE TERRITORY." But the paper wavered from this position in 1850, when it gave grudging support to Daniel Webster in his advocacy of Clay's compromise plan, and applauded the 7th of March speech as "broad, patriotic, and honest." At the beginning of 1851 Bowles announced that the *Republican* was still devotedly Whig, though the Whig party was clearly moribund. In the early fifties the *Republican* attacked the Abolitionists, urged citizens of Springfield to stay away from their meetings, and declared that the fugitive slave act must be sustained in the Northern courts. Bowles's attitude toward slavery, in brief, was still conservative. But the beginnings of the Kansas-Nebraska struggle gave him a new decision and aggressiveness. He declared of the Kansas-Nebraska bill that "it is a monstrous proposition," "a huge stride backward," a piece of legislation "against the spirit of republicanism" (*Republican,* Feb. 8, 1854). Thereafter the *Republican* was a leader in the struggle for the constitutional defeat of slavery. When Judge Loring issued a warrant for the arrest of the slave Anthony Burns, it demanded his removal from the bench; it vehemently supported the Emigrant Aid Society; and Bowles was one of the first men in the East to call for the organization of a new anti-slavery party.

By the beginning of 1854 the editor had definitely repudiated his old Whig allegiance. For the pretensions which the Native American Party briefly made in 1854–55 to be the real opposition to the Democrats he had nothing but scorn. The editor struck a telling blow at this party, whose anti-alien principles he cordially disliked, when he attended its national convention in Philadelphia in June 1855. Its sessions were supposedly secret and none but delegates were admitted to the floor. But Bowles's close contacts with Henry Wilson and other Massachusetts delegates enabled him to send daily letters to the *New York Tribune, Boston Atlas,* and *Springfield Republican,* packed with information, and slashing in their denunciation of the convention majority as "weak tools of political gamblers and slavery propagandists." He characteristically believed that the right of the public to obtain the facts rose superior to the oath of secrecy binding his friends. His exposure of the subserviency of the Know-Nothings to slavery did much to hasten the disintegration of the party the following year. Meanwhile Bowles was persistently urging the formation of a new party of freedom which should be "able to win in the great contest to be fought in '56 with the slave-power of the country." Both in the *Republican* and by personal efforts, using his tact and magnetism effectively, he labored with New England politicians for this end. In August 1855 he presided in Boston over a conference of influential men, the callers of which included Charles Francis Adams, R. H. Dana, Jr., George Boutwell, and H. L. Dawes, which was intended to bring about a fusion of Know-Nothings, Free-Soilers, and independent Whigs upon a Republican ticket; and though this effort proved a failure, he helped give the Republican party a strong state organization.

Perhaps partly because of his friendship with N. P. Banks, Bowles was one of the earliest editors to advocate the nomination of John C. Frémont by the Republican party (letter of Apr. 19, 1856; Merriam, I, 171). He was present at Cincinnati when the Democrats nominated Buchanan, and at Philadelphia when the Republicans chose Frémont; he had an exuberant confidence in Republican success, and labored with indefatigable energy, working two days and two nights without sleep in election week. With its espousal of the new party the *Springfield Republican* entered upon the flood-tide of its success. It rose rapidly to a circulation of more than 5,000 for the daily and more than 10,000 for the weekly, and the *New York Tribune* shortly hailed it as "the best and ablest country journal ever published on this continent." Its staff was small, numbering but three men beside Bowles, but all were accustomed to work twelve or more hours daily. Its Boston and Washington correspondence ranked with the best; its telegraphic news was painstakingly handled and condensed; and its editorial interpretation and leadership were unexcelled. At all times the local correspondence from Connecticut Valley towns and villages was admirably complete. The demand of the North and West for just such strong free-soil opinion as it furnished, and the desire of the flood of emigrant New Englanders for a weekly journal of home intelligence, gave the *Republican* a circulation and influence throughout all the free states and territories.

It is difficult to excuse Bowles for yielding at this moment of success to a step which came near proving irreparably disastrous. Already he had refused a position on the *New York Tribune* as editorial writer and head of its Washington bureau, while he had shown scant enthusiasm when Charles A. Dana at the close of 1856 undertook fruitless negotiations with a group of Philadelphians to establish a new daily, with a capital of $100,000, of which Bowles was to be editor. His place was as the master of provincial journalism. Yet early in 1857 he resigned the editorship of the *Republican* and assumed that of a new Boston newspaper, the *Traveller.* This represented an amalgamation of the old, weak, semi-religious journal of the same name; the *Atlas,* which had once been the leading Whig paper of New England but had lost ground, and the *Telegraph and*

Chronicle, a worthless anti-prohibition journal. Bowles, investing $10,000 in the enterprise, was given a salary of $3,000 a year and a bonus of one-tenth of the capital stock. The daily was to be Republican, independent, and progressive, to have a large staff, and to take the leadership among Boston journals; but it was unfortunately by no means so strong as it looked. The owners and officers were not united in any common policy; Bowles found his best efforts thwarted and misunderstood; while the capital was insufficient to ensure a vigorous start. After four months he resigned. The verdict of his friends was that "Sam Bowles and Boston did not suit each other" (Merriam, I, 183). Fortunately he had retained his controlling ownership of the *Republican,* and had kept his wife and family in Springfield. Following a short vacation in the West he returned to Springfield and Dr. Holland relinquished the editorship to him. Thereafter he was content to make his provincial environment yield, by hard work, the rewards of power which might have come more easily in one of the large cities.

In the heated years up till 1861 Bowles steadily increased the influence of the *Republican.* The basis of this influence was the vogue of the weekly newspaper, which dealt in national rather than local intelligence, and could be as well published from a small city as a metropolis. By 1860 the weekly *Republican* had a circulation of 11,280 copies (as against 5,700 for the daily), and was read everywhere in the Mississippi Valley. Its power was far from reaching that of the weekly *New York Tribune,* but it equaled that of the weekly *Evening Post.* Bowles gave it intense and unwearying personal supervision. As a subordinate wrote, "he knew everything, saw everything, dictated everything, and his dictation dictated every time" (Merriam, I, 104). Electric, incisive, eager, a bundle of nerves, he drove himself and drove his small staff incessantly. News was rewritten with a thoroughness unknown elsewhere; everything that came over the telegraph was freshened and invigorated; the correspondents were held to a high standard; and the editorials were pungent, authoritative, and forcible. Two nights in the week Bowles snatched only a few hours' sleep in the office; other nights he brought a bottle of cold tea and labored till one or two o'clock. "The sparkle, the vivacity, the drive, the power of the *Republican,*" wrote Dr. Holland later, "cost life. We did not know when we tasted it and found it so charged with zest that we were tasting heart's blood, but that was the priceless element that commended it to our appetites. A pale man, weary and nervous, crept home at midnight, or at one, two, or three o'clock in the morning, and while all nature was fresh and the birds were singing and thousands of eyes were bending eagerly over the results of his night's labor, he was tossing and trying to sleep."

As one of the "Black Republican" leaders, Bowles denounced the execution of John Brown, supported Lincoln warmly, and when secession began declared sternly for "the defense of the Union and the enforcement of the laws" (*Republican,* Jan. 9, 1861). Unlike Greeley and Bryant, the editor after the beginning of the war did not join the ranks of the "radicals" who urged the President to hasten emancipation, prosecute the war without regard for the feelings of the border states, and adopt harsh measures with all rebels. When Lincoln modified Frémont's emancipation order, Bowles supported him; he defended the President against the Massachusetts Republican Convention of 1862; and he argued for his financial policy when he came into collision with Congress upon the further issue of legal-tender notes. At times he criticized Lincoln severely for his infringements upon civil rights and his interferences with military operations, while in 1863 he regarded his chances of reëlection as poor. But he loyally supported the President for renomination without any of the hesitancy which marked the radical editors just named, and declared that "his way of saving the country is recognized as the only way." Later the editor advocated the mild and magnanimous policies of reconstruction outlined by Lincoln, condemned the measures of Congress, and attacked the carpet-bag régime. In spite of this, he was in favor of the impeachment of Andrew Johnson.

The political and financial corruption of the seventies found in Bowles an assailant who did not hesitate at personal risk. His denunciation of James Fisk, and especially of his financial coup of 1868, of which the *Republican* said that "nothing so audacious, nothing more gigantic in the way of real swindling has ever been perpetrated in this country," provoked Fisk to institute a libel suit for $50,000. The suit was not pressed, but when Bowles next visited New York (December 1868) he was suddenly seized at his hotel upon a writ issued by the notorious Judge McCunn, and hurried off to Ludlow Street jail for the night. A little later Bowles's attacks upon the Erie Railroad looters brought him into collision with David Dudley Field, the counsel for Fisk, Gould, and Tweed. There ensued a sharp exchange of letters, later published in pamphlet form, in which Bowles showed how far

Field had overstepped the line proper to an honorable lawyer. In Massachusetts the editor marshalled his staff to an assault upon the corrupt railroad lobby at the State House which had battened upon the Hoosac Tunnel appropriations. But Bowles's zeal as a reformer was best manifested in the Liberal Republican movement of 1872. Shocked by the Crédit Mobilier and other scandals, he joined hands with Horace White, Murat Halstead, Carl Schurz, and other rebels in promoting the Cincinnati Convention, and when it met labored on the spot for the nomination of Charles Francis Adams. Keenly disappointed when Greeley was named instead, he wired the *Republican* to accept the ticket but "not to gush." He admitted that Greeley would give the country a "political hurly-burly and party interregnum," but till the end he argued for his election (*Republican,* July 26 *et seq.*). Greeley's indorsement by the South, he said, "means that *the war is really over.*"

The last twenty years of Bowles's life were marked by ill health caused by overwork and manifesting itself in insomnia, neuralgia, and dyspepsia. The prosperity of the *Republican* fortunately made possible the enlargement of its staff by men of ability, including Francis A. Walker, Frank B. Sanborn, and Charles G. Whiting, and enabled Bowles to take frequent vacations. He was in Europe for seven months in 1862, made a tour to California in company with Schuyler Colfax and A. D. Richardson in 1865, returned as far as Colorado in 1868, and was in Europe again in the summer of 1871. Newspaper letters written during his first western tour were reprinted in *Across the Continent: A Summer's Journey to the Rocky Mountains, the Mormons, and the Pacific States with Speaker Colfax* (1865), which reveals a keen observation and graphic, incisive style. His second Western trip gave him the material for *The Switzerland of America: A Summer Vacation in the Parks and Mountains of Colorado,* and the same year it appeared (1869) he combined the two under the title of *Our New West: Records of Travel Between the Mississippi River and the Pacific Ocean.* They have some permanent value as a study, descriptive but not analytic, of social conditions. When in the office Bowles continued to work, and to make his men work, at reckless speed. His look, said a friend, was never of repose; it "was always 'fire or tire.'" He himself wrote that "my will has carried me for years beyond my mental and physical power: that has been the offending rock" (Merriam, I, 398). His discipline was sharp, and he kept his force in a state of tension. His short, stinging reproof, his irritable intolerance of shirking or blundering, his curt, generous praise of good work, his alternation of black and friendly moods, made him feared, obeyed, and admired.

Bowles had married Mary S. D. Schermerhorn of Geneva, N. Y., on Sept. 6, 1848, and the union was one of singular happiness and devotion; his letters reveal the constancy and depth of his feeling for his wife and their ten children. Mrs. Bowles made it her chief object to give him quiet and rest, and while tense and self-centered at his desk, at his home he was gracious, kindly, and delightful. His pleasure in domestic life did not interfere with social life outside, and even in ill health his acquaintance with politicians and others grew steadily larger and more intimate. His tall, slightly stooping figure, his keen eye and powerful personality, were well known in Washington and New York. At all gatherings his charm was marked. "I never knew a man who knew him," wrote Henry L. Dawes, "who wouldn't rather have him at his table than any other man in the world." He particularly liked association with women, "to chaff with and to rub your mind out of its morbidity." But his devotion to the *Republican* above all other interests and his irritable intensity made him enemies as well as friends. Even his laudatory biographer admits that he "overdid the part of censor," and he alienated many men by unreserved criticism (Merriam, II, 360–62). He was, as Wendell Phillips Garrison wrote, "a great gossip and by no means a safe confidant" (*Nation,* XLI, 553). Priding himself upon his independence of friends, local prejudices, and church or partisan allegiance, and declaring that "the *Republican* is one thing, Sam Bowles another," he was ruthlessly slashing at times. In 1874 he opposed the candidacy of his brother-in-law, Henry Alexander, Jr., for Congress, causing a permanent family estrangement. A year later came a rupture with his younger brother, Benjamin Franklin Bowles. The latter for many years had been in charge of the counting room, but his methods seemed to Bowles inadequate to meet new requirements, and Bowles dismissed him by letter. The younger brother, deeply wounded, went abroad and died (1876) in Paris. When Bowles decided in 1872 to dissolve his partnership with Clark W. Bryan and several associates who held minor shares in the *Republican,* giving them full control of the job-printing and book-binding business, he did so with a tactlessness which alienated Bryan, and caused him to purchase the *Springfield Union* and to make it a formidable rival of the *Republican.*

The editor's health, despite a trip to California

with Mrs. Bowles in 1873 and a tour to Europe the next year, steadily declined, and in 1876 he suffered an attack resembling paralysis. He supported Hayes for the presidency, but believed that Tilden had been legally elected, and was disgusted by the methods which were used to procure Republican victory. The new president's policies, however, filled him with exultation. Hayes's plans for reconciliation and reform were precisely those for which the *Republican* had striven for a decade. Bowles was also pleased that, following a financial slump in the first shock of the panic of 1873, the *Republican* had risen to an unprecedented prosperity (Merriam, II, 416). In December 1877, occurred another stroke of apoplexy, and six weeks later he died. A memorial service at the Springfield Unitarian Church, Jan. 23, 1878, was the occasion for an expression of admiration for the man from many of the most eminent national leaders.

The principal achievements of Bowles were two: he was a pioneer in the establishment of independent journalism, and he gave the country its first powerful demonstration of what might be done with a newspaper in a provincial city. Beginning with his declaration of complete independence in the year of the Kansas-Nebraska debate (*Republican,* May 31, 1854), he consistently placed public welfare above party success, and was able in 1872 to boast that in the emergence of the "Higher Journalism" which obeyed only its own elevated conscience, "the *Springfield Republican* may honorably claim to have been both a leader and a prophet" (*Weekly Republican,* Dec. 20, 1872). In asserting this independence he labored under the handicap of publishing in a small inland town, overwhelmingly and narrowly Republican in views. He succeeded because he made the *Republican* a model newspaper, which could find its patronage among intelligent readers all over the nation; it was model in the pithy condensation and the intelligence of its news, in its dignity, in its elevated moral tone, in its clarity, pungency, and sparkle, and in the force of its editorial opinions. As an editorial writer Bowles had marked limitations. Profound analysis was beyond him, he was incapable of elaborate or subtle thinking upon abstract topics, and his knowledge showed the deficiencies of a man who had never studied systematically and had read few books. He wrote for the crowd, not for the cultured few. Moreover, he was erratic and impulsive, and himself said that he had a "fine and vagrant head" (Bradford, p. 282). His judgment of men was poor. He wrote of Lincoln that he was "a simple Susan," and of John A. Andrew that he was "conceited, dogmatic, and lacks breadth and tact for government," while he greatly overpraised Banks, Dawes, Colfax, and others. He scorned consistency, declaring that as a journalist he could not "live to be as old as Methuselah, and brood in silence over a thing till, just before I die, I think I have it right." But he was a master of the vivid, penetrating phrase, and he kindled all he wrote with the fire of his restless, emotional personality. As an administrator his nervousness, headlong energy, and imperious temper made him a hard master, but he had a faculty of extracting enormous quantities of high-grade work from his subordinates. He burned himself out too fast, but for a quarter-century he was one of the real leaders of American opinion. As Henry Watterson said, he became more than a journalist—he became one of the real statesmen of his time.

[The second Bowles was fortunate in his biographer. George S. Merriam's *Life and Times of Samuel Bowles* (2 vols., 1885), though at times somewhat unguarded in its laudation, gives a well-rounded impression of the editor and his work, and its full selection of letters affords an interesting insight into his personality. The review of this volume in the *Nation,* XLI, 553, probably by W. P. Garrison, offers a critical corrective of some of its judgments. Gamaliel Bradford, in *Union Portraits* (1916), pp. 263 ff., has ably analyzed Bowles's character. Richard Hooker gives a careful sketch of the *Republican* under his guidance in *The Story of an Independent Newspaper* (1924), and additional material is furnished by Willard G. Bleyer in *Main Currents in the Hist. of Am. Journalism* (1927), pp. 252 ff., and in George H. Payne's *Hist. of Journalism in the U. S.* (1920), pp. 323 ff. His place in the life of Springfield is somewhat inadequately indicated in M. A. Green, *Springfield 1636–1886* (1888), pp. 542 ff.] A. N.

BOWLES, SAMUEL (Oct. 15, 1851–Mar. 14, 1915), editor, was the fourth of the name in direct succession and the third known as a journalist. As the eldest son, he was early trained by his father to take charge of the *Springfield Republican.* He attended the public schools of Springfield and entered Yale, but being of delicate health remained only two years and took special studies instead of the regular course. He traveled in Europe 1869–71, spending most of his time in Germany, and contributing some correspondence to the *Republican.* In 1873 he was placed upon the staff as editorial assistant under his father's exacting discipline, and after some experience in writing editorials and gathering news, undertook in 1875 the business management. The growth of the newspaper, the withdrawal of his uncle B. F. Bowles from the counting room, and the failing health of his father threw an increasing responsibility upon him, so that the death of the elder Bowles found him ready to assume full charge. Thereafter he performed for nearly four decades the duties of editor, publisher, and treasurer.

With the exception of his marriage on June 12, 1884, to Elizabeth Hoar of Concord, Mass., daughter of Rockwood Hoar, all the important events in the life of the third Bowles were connected with the *Republican.* He never became a public figure like his father; he traveled little, mingled little with political leaders, and wrote no books and few signed articles. But he held decisive control of the character of the *Republican,* and maintained it at the highest level of American journalism. He seldom contributed to its pages, saying that he could not write but could "tell others how and what they ought to write" (Hooker, p. 156). But while he placed his desk in the business department, he directed all the important editorial utterances, was in close touch with the news-gathering, and daily read and sternly criticized every column. Conservative in taste, he insisted upon a standard of old-fashioned dignity. Not until late in life did he remove from the front page the advertisements which gave the *Republican* an English look. His one important innovation was the founding (Sept. 15, 1878) of the *Sunday Republican,* which as a summary of the news of the week and a repository of special features largely took the place of the weekly *Republican.*

The third Bowles continued his father's policy of aggressive editorial independence. In 1884 he joined the mugwumps in attacking Blaine and supporting Cleveland, whose reëlection he advocated in 1888 and 1892. He opposed Bryan and free silver in 1896, but four years later accepted imperialism as "the paramount issue," and waged one of the greatest campaigns of the *Republican* in assailing the annexation of the Philippines. The same issue, raised by the seizure of Panama, helped Bowles decide in 1904 to stand with Parker against Roosevelt; but four years later he advocated the election of Taft. Two of his abiding editorial tenets were tariff reduction and international conciliation, and the *Republican* denounced all forms of jingoism—particularly what it called Henry Cabot Lodge's "aristocratic demagogism"—unsparingly. Both in the editorial and news departments Bowles was fortunate in the assistants he found and developed. The staff when he assumed charge included W. L. Warren as chief editorial writer, Charles G. Whiting, and Solomon B. Griffin, who for more than forty years was managing editor. With their aid Bowles made the *Republican* famous as a school for journalists, and among other pupils trained Talcott Williams, George Harvey, Robert H. Lyman, George Kibbe Turner, and Louis A. Coolidge. The talent which the *Republican* attracted gave it a high literary quality, and helped it overcome in its presentation of news the handicap of meager financial resources. By economy and conservative guidance Bowles kept it moderately prosperous, and was able to set conscience above revenue by excluding in 1914 all liquor advertisements.

The third Bowles, like his father, believed office holding incompatible with editorial independence, and repeatedly refused opportunities to enter public life. He was active in the Springfield Board of Trade, and was responsible for the leading position which Springfield took in the national movement for a safe and sane Fourth. He was always prominent at gatherings of journalists, was a member of the advisory board of the Pulitzer School of Journalism, and in 1913 became a director of the Associated Press. Despite his ill health, the finer side of social life appealed to him and he adorned it (Griffin, p. 36). Many of his subordinates found him, because of inherited dyspepsia and other ailments, irritable and sharp-tongued, but all admired his fine ability and sensitive conscience. He repeatedly said that "I realize I came after a great man; I have never expected personal fame," but his death was the occasion for many tributes to the devotion and skill with which he had maintained and enlarged the heritage from his father. Another recognition came in honorary degrees given him by Amherst College and Olivet College. He left two sons, of whom Sherman Hoar Bowles remained the controlling force in the *Republican* office.

[The fullest record of the career of the third Bowles is in the obituary notice of the *Springfield Republican,* Mar. 16, 1915. This is supplemented by the full and accurate obituary in the N. Y. *Evening Post,* Mar. 16, 1915, probably prepared by his former colleague, E. P. Clark. Richard Hooker, *The Story of an Independent Newspaper* (1924) outlines the history of the *Republican* under his control, and Solomon B. Griffin, *People and Politics as Observed by a Massachusetts Editor* (1923) adds many personal touches.] A. N.

BOWLES, WILLIAM AUGUSTUS (Oct. 22, 1763–Dec. 23, 1805), adventurer, son of Thomas and Eleanor Bowles, was born in Frederick County, Md. At the age of thirteen he joined the British forces, and in 1778 was made an ensign in the Maryland Loyalist Corps. Shortly after the arrival of the corps at Pensacola (December 1778) he was cashiered. With this event began his life-long, though intermittent, connection with the Creek Indians, with whom he now took refuge. Reinstated in his commission in 1781, he was put on half-pay in 1783. After several years' wandering in the Southern states and the Bahamas he returned to the primitive life of the Creek country, partly, no doubt, because of his maladjustment to civilized society. While on the Island of Providence he had formed a connection with the governor, Lord Dunmore (formerly of Virginia) and a wealthy merchant, John Miller, which shaped his course for the rest of his life. Desiring to supplant Panton, Leslie & Company in the profitable trade with the Creek Indians, and nursing war-time grievances against Spain, these men made Bowles their instrument. With such backing he thrice attempted to drive Panton and the Spaniards out of the Floridas. According to his own statement, Bowles had a larger purpose, namely, to establish an independent Muscogean state trading with all nations. At other times he seems to have regarded himself as a second Robert Clive (*American Historical Review,* VII, 729), with Dunmore and Miller playing the part of the East India Company and the Creek warriors that of sepoys, and with the reincorporation of the Floridas in the British empire as his objective. Although he failed in every attempt, he alarmed the governments of Spain and the United States, caused Panton's company heavy losses, and destroyed Alexander McGillivray's ascendance over the Creek Indians.

Bowles first appeared in Florida in 1788, but soon retired, and in December 1790, at the end of the Nootka crisis, we find him in England with a party of Indians. In July 1791 he was again in Providence, and about Aug. 19 he appeared at St. Mark's, Fla., in his second and most formidable attempt to gain control of the Creek country. This time he made a determined effort to conciliate the Spanish officials, but one of his renegade followers later testified that, together with William Blount and John Sevier, Bowles was concerting a plan to drive Spain out of the Floridas and Louisiana. At any rate, after he had plundered Panton's store at St. Mark's, Gov. Carondelet procured his arrest through an unsavory stratagem (Feb. 26, 1792). Although much impressed by his striking personality, Carondelet sent him to Havana, whence, after a brief interval, he was taken to Spain. Kept in confinement at Madrid from September 1792 toJanuary 1794, he was then sent to the Philippines. As he was being brought back to Spain he escaped from the ship and made his way to Sierra Leone, where the British governor showed him every courtesy (*Archivo de Indias, Papeles de Cuba, Leg. 2371,* Bowles to Grenville, June 5, 1798, draft, signed). Thence in 1798 he returned to England, where he prepared for his third filibustering expedition to Florida, obtaining for a time the backing of the Missionary Society. In September 1799, he was once more in Florida. Early the following year he and his followers, who were mostly Lower Creeks, again plundered Panton's store and even captured the Spanish fort at St. Mark's. The fort was very shortly retaken by the Spaniards, but for nearly three years Bowles continued to live at Miccosukee with about sixty followers, who, said Benjamin Hawkins, were "more attentive to frolicking than fighting" (*Letters of Benjamin Hawkins,* 1916, p. 418). In 1802 Gov. Folch of Pensacola offered a reward of $4,500 for his capture, and in 1803 he was seized while at a feast at Tuskegee and was turned over to the Spanish officials (A. J. Pickett, *Alabama,* 1851, I, 191–92). Sent to Havana and imprisoned in the Morro Castle, he died on Dec. 23, 1805. He was married to a daughter of a Creek chieftain and left a number of descendants, among them Chief Bowles, the friend of Gen. Sam Houston.

[Most of the reliable information about Bowles is still buried in MSS. The chief printed sources are: *The Authentic Memoirs of Wm. Augustus Bowles* (1791), reprinted, with portrait, in the *Mag. of Hist.,* Extra 46 (Tarrytown, 1916); E. Alfred Jones, "The Real Author of the 'Authentic Memoirs of Wm. Augustus Bowles,'" *Md. Hist. Mag.,* XVIII, 300–308, showing that the *Memoirs* were written by Capt. Benjamin Baynton; Le Clerc Milfort, *Mémoire ou coup-d'œil rapide sur mes différents Voyages et mon Séjour dans la Nation Crëck* (Paris, 1802), pp. 116–28; *The Jour. of Andrew Ellicott* (1814), pp. 226–32; *Am. Hist. Rev.,* VII, 706–35; T. M. Farquhar, *Hist. of the Bowles Family* (1907).]

A. P. W.

BOWMAN, JOHN BRYAN (Oct. 16, 1824–Sept. 29, 1891), founder of Kentucky University, was of German stock that entered Kentucky by way of Virginia, his grandfather, Abram Bowman, having been colonel of the 8th Virginia German Regiment in the Revolutionary Army. John's father, also a John Bowman, married Mary Mitchum and settled in Mercer County. He was one of the incorporators and trustees of Bacon College, Harrodsburg (Robert Peter, *Transylvania University,* 1896, p. 20), so that his son had an early opportunity for observing the technique of academic organization and for developing an enthusiasm for higher education. At the age of fifteen the son united with the Christian church, an affiliation he retained until his death. After graduating from the newly-founded Bacon College in 1842 he studied law but did not practise; instead, having married Mary Dorcas Williams in 1845, he occupied himself with the management of "Old Forest Farm," his inherited estate in what was then called the Cane Run section of Mercer County. For ten years he lived there the life of a country gentleman and then, stirred by the collapse of his alma mater and concerned over the prospect of collegiate training in Kentucky, he attracted state-wide attention by a bold challenge to his church to erect a university on the ruins of the failing college. He was then only thirty, and he set to work with all the energy and hope of youth to achieve this ambition. For the projected university Mercer County contributed $30,000; then Bowman set out, driving and riding through the most favorable counties, exerting argument and personality, and astonishing even his friends by taking subscriptions to the amount of $150,000 in 150 days (*Report of Board of Curators of Kentucky University,* 1866). In 1858 the legislature granted the institution a charter naming it Kentucky University. Popular clamor forced it to open prematurely in Harrodsburg as Taylor Academy in that year; in 1859 the College of Arts and Sciences opened with nearly 200 students. During the Civil War, Bowman, a slaveholder, held to the Union, and as regent managed the affairs of the university so adroitly that, surrounded by armed forces as it often was, not a dollar was lost nor did classes suspend for more than a week. Accidental fire destroyed the buildings in 1864 and the university subsequently languished. A fortunate event, however, gave great encouragement to Bowman's plans. Accepting the provisions of the Morrill Act of 1862, the Kentucky Assembly had appointed a committee to receive bids for the location of an Agricultural and Mechanical College, and this committee suggested to Bowman the union of this new college with Kentucky University. Lexington having made the most favorable bid, it was decided to consolidate Transylvania University, Kentucky University, and the A. & M. College there, the whole being called Kentucky University. This institution opened in October 1865, with Bowman as regent. For nine years he directed the policies for the University, accepting no salary but having free residence in "Ashland," former home of Henry Clay, which the university had purchased and to which Bowman gave added fame by his hospitality. But dissensions presently arose, chiefly owing to the rival claims of church and state in regulating an institution under joint control. In June 1874 Bowman resigned his office and in 1878 the legislature provided for the separation of Kentucky University from the A. & M. College, thus preparing the way for the latter to become the present State University (A. F. Lewis, *History of Higher Education in Kentucky,* 1899, p. 91). Besides bringing the university to the point where in 1870 it was among the largest in the country, Bowman had busied himself with many other affairs: he had had a share in founding Hocker (now Hamilton) College, the Commercial College, and the College of the Bible, all in Lexington; he had helped establish the street-railway system in the same city; he had argued in Washington for irrigation in New Mexico. President Grant offered him the appointment of minister to Ecuador, but he declined in order that he might devote himself to his educational programs. Pictures of Bowman reveal a face expressing considerable determination, and those who knew him agree that to much charm of bearing he added the force of an aggressive and tenacious character.

[W. H. English, *Conquest of the Country Northwest of the Ohio River 1778–83* (1896), containing genealogical material collected by Bowman himself, who contemplated writing a history of his family; Mabel H. Pollitt, *A Biography of J. K. Paterson* (1925), which gives a clear account of the union of the colleges; *Biog. Encyc. of Ky.* (1874), p. 627; personal information from Mrs. Nannie Bowman Moore of Harrodsburg and from Mrs. W. F. Lafferty of Lexington.]

G. C. K.

BOWMAN, THOMAS (July 15, 1817–Mar. 3, 1914), Methodist Episcopal bishop, educator, was born in Berwick, Pa., the son of John, a successful business man, and Sarah (Brittain) Bowman. He came of stock which had a decidedly religious strain, Scotch Presbyterian on his mother's side, but Methodist on the paternal ever since his grandfather, after whom he was named, was converted and later ordained by Francis Asbury, becoming a pioneer preacher of that denomination throughout eastern Pennsylvania. Thomas had sufficient mental ability to enter the junior class of Dickinson College at the age of eighteen, after one year's preparation at Wilbraham Academy, Mass., and three at Cazenovia Academy, N. Y. He graduated, valedictorian, in 1837. His first inclination was toward the law, which he studied for a year under Judge John Reed, noted Pennsylvania jurist, but turning to the ministry, he entered the Baltimore Conference in 1839. From 1840 to 1843, he taught in the Dickinson Grammar School. Owing to poor health and the circumstances of his aged parents, for five years he ran a farm and small flour mill in his native town. In 1842 he married Matilda Hartman, by whom he had eleven children. From 1848 to 1858 he was principal of Dickinson Seminary, Williamsport, Pa., from 1858 to 1872 president of Indiana Asbury (later DePauw) University; and in 1872 he was elected bishop.

Possessing a keen analytical mind and the gift of exposition he was an unusually successful teacher. Although much engaged in other labors, he preached continually, acquiring a wide popularity, and in 1864–65 serving as chaplain of the United States Senate. Through his executive talent, he contributed much to the educational and administrative activities of his church. When he took charge of Dickinson Seminary, it was practically without funds or prospects. He left it on a sound foundation with about four hundred students. He was an important factor in the development of Asbury University, not only serving as president for fourteen years, but also acting as trustee, 1875–95, president of the board, 1887–95, and chancellor, 1884–99. He is credited with having been the main agent in securing Washington DePauw's donations to the institution. As bishop he was indefatigable in superintending the work of the denomination in this country, and visited all the Conferences in Europe, China, Japan, India, and Mexico. A lecture by him "Romanism Enslaves, Degrades, Corrupts" was published in *Popular Lectures on the Errors of the Roman Catholic Church* (1878), but his activities left little time for authorship.

[The *Christian Advocate,* Mar. 12, 1914, contains portrait. See also the same paper for Mar. 26, Apr. 16, May 14, 1914; *First Fifty Years of Cazenovia Seminary* (1877); *Who's Who in America,* 1912–13.]

H. E. S.

BOWNE, BORDEN PARKER (Jan. 14, 1847–Apr. 1, 1910), philosopher, of Puritan descent, was the son of Margaret (Parker) Bowne and of Joseph Bowne, farmer, justice of the peace, and local preacher of his religious faith, well known as an opponent of slavery and of liquor. The boy grew up sensitive to his environment, shy in disposition, and attracted to books. His mind was alert and capable of deep impressions. He attended Pennington Seminary, and then by his own effort prepared himself to enter the sophomore class of the University of the City of New York. He made a brilliant reputation,—second to none in the history of the University, and was graduated valedictorian of his class in 1871. He taught school for a year, and then was pastor of a Methodist church in Whitestone, N. Y., in 1873. There followed a period of study in Europe at Halle and Göttingen, and he returned to America in 1875 to become for a year assistant professor of modern languages in the University of the City of New York. During the same time he was religious editor of the New York *Independent.* His interest in philosophy had developed strongly in college. He had written a discriminating criticism of the philosophy of Herbert Spencer, which was published in the *New Englander* without signature and was popularly ascribed to a much older man. In 1876 Boston University, of his own Methodist denomination, invited him to head its department of philosophy, and he accepted. His service for nearly thirty-five years as head of the department of philosophy and as dean of the graduate school brought fame to the University. More than once he was invited to join other faculties, but he was loyal to the institution to which he had given himself. In 1905–06 he made a tour around the world, receiving a specially cordial reception in Japan. He gained a new respect for the Oriental peoples, especially China. At home he was always occupied with teaching or writing, so that he had little leisure for the enjoyment of nature or the cultivation of wide friendships, though he prized both. He took an interest in mechanical things, and found recreation in walking, but his favorite relaxation was gardening. He took special pride in his rose garden at Longwood. He was happy in his home life, simple in his tastes, but appreciative of artistic furnishings. To him personality was the secret of reality, life the expression of thought and the test of truth. He lectured in crisp, breezy fashion, with an original way of expression and with touches of humor. He clarified the subject by his lucid thought and language and by copious illustration, then left it to the student to think for himself. A written quiz was the usual test of attainment. A pupil could absent himself when he chose; when present he must be alert and responsive. The lecturer had little patience with laziness or uncertain grasp of intellect or faith.

His philosophical ideas were matured early in life, but he did not hesitate to change his terminology for the sake of clearness or emphasis. His early philosophy was an objective idealism, which resembled the thinking of Lotze, but Bowne was no man's understudy. Lotze was a monist in philosophy, but not so Bowne. Lotze cared for religion incidentally, Bowne made it central. His faith colored all his thought. As the years passed he stressed more and more the reality of the self back of all categories and laws, free from bondage to inanimate nature, learning empirically, and expressing itself in moral conduct. He called this doctrine transcendental empiricism, because man's experience is not limited to the senses. At a time when a mechanistic determinism was popular he rejected every argument against the freedom of personality. He insisted that no sound theory of knowledge was possible on any necessitarian basis. He never tired of maintaining the freedom of the self and its relation to the Unseen that was behind the universe. He anticipated the modern notion of relativity in insisting that time and space are only relative terms, not by any means to be thought of as controlling factors. He found values in the intuitional, the intellectual, the utilitarian, balancing them in the fashioning of his ethics. He brought all philosophy and religion to the pragmatic test of life. So insistent was he upon the central importance of personality that he came to believe that no other term so well defined his thought as Personalism, and by that name his philosophy has come to be known. After 1905, when he felt that he had established his philosophical position, he turned his attention to theology. He was of service to his fellow Methodists in clearing away obstructions to modern thinking. Rather conservative, as, for example, in his christology and in his attitude toward evolution, when so many men were captivated by the idea of that principle as an active agent in creation, he stood for the right of criticism and the duty of an open mind towards all investigation. His strength of conviction and outspoken opinions aroused the opposition of certain defenders of orthodoxy, and he was tried for heresy before his own New York East Conference, but he was in no danger of conviction. He took part in the defense of the accused in a similar trial of his colleague, Prof. Mitchell, an experience that embittered him against theological obscurantists. Religion was to him the sanction of ethics, as ethics was the expression of religion. His books covered the whole field of philosophy, and made valuable contributions to theology. They include: *The Philosophy of Herbert Spencer* (1874), *Studies in Theism* (1879), *Metaphysics* (1882), *The Theory of Thought and Knowledge* (1897), *Introduction to Psychological Theory* (1886), *Principles of Ethics* (1892), *The Christian Revelation* (1898), *The Immanence of God* (1905), *Personalism* (1908), *Studies in Christianity* (1909). After his death in 1910 Mrs. Bowne edited a series of sermons under the title *The Essence of Religion*, which revealed Bowne's religious experience. In 1912 his lectures were published on *Kant and Spencer: a Critical Exposition.*

[*The Meth. Rev.*, May–June, 1922, was a Bowne memorial number. Other valuable sources of information and estimate are the *Personalist*, I, 5–14; *Zion's Herald*, Dec. 18, 1912; *Am. Jour. of Theology*, July 1910; C. B. Pyle, *The Philosophy of B. P. Bowne* (1910).] H. K. R.

BOWNE, JOHN (*c.* Mar. 1, 1627/28–Oct. 10, 1695), Quaker leader, was born at Matlock, Derbyshire, England, the son of Thomas, and grandson of Anthony Bowne, of the Lime Tree Farm, Matlock. He came to Boston in 1649, returned to England in 1650, and again came to Boston in 1651. He then removed to Flushing, L. I., purchasing a home lot in 1653, and marrying in 1656 Hannah Feake, daughter of Lieut. Robert Feake of New England. In 1662 he was arrested on a complaint that a meeting "of the abominable sect called Quakers" was held every Sunday at his house. He was taken from his sick wife and child to New Amsterdam, where, refusing to pay a fine, he was imprisoned, first in the dungeon, then in the prison room of the Stadt Huys. After four months' imprisonment, during which his door was occasionally left open in hope that he would escape, he was banished. Being the most prominent leader of the Quakers, if he could be scared away or deported the disturbing sect might be scattered. The directors of the West India Company, on receipt of Stuyvesant's report of Bowne's banishment, issued on Apr. 16, 1663, N.S., their famous order establishing religious liberty in New Netherland, on the ground that "people's consciences should not be forced, but every one left free in his belief." Meanwhile Bowne landed in Ireland, crossed Ireland and England, visiting Quakers, and reached Amsterdam on May 9, 1663, N.S. The next day he appeared before the directors. They had lost the noble impulse of Apr. 16, and it took them a month to agree that Bowne should have his chest (left on board off Ireland), and a passport. He reached home a year and seven months after his arrest. He was thereafter a large land-holder and farmer. He married, second, Hannah Bickerstaff, and, third, Mary Cock. In 1683 he was county treasurer, and in 1691 was elected representative from Queens County to the General Assembly, but not seated, as he would not take the prescribed oaths, although willing to sign the Test and to engage to perform the tenor of the oaths under penalty of perjury. The Quaker record states that "John Bowne dyed the 20 day of the 10 month in the yeare 1695 And was buryed ye 23 day of the same being about 68 yeares of age. He did Freely Expose him selfe his house and Esteate to ye service of Truth And had a constant Meeting In his house neare About forty yeares. Hee allso suffered very much for ye truths seak."

[The manuscript of Bowne's *Journal*, giving a complete account of his imprisonment and banishment, is lost, but a copy is in the N. Y. Pub. Lib. Geo. Bishop's *New England Judged* (2nd ed. 1703) erroneously related the story of Bowne's banishment, and Jos. Besse's *Collection of the Sufferings of the people call'd Quakers* (1753) increased the errors. "John Bowne: Pioneer of Freedom," by John Cox, Jr. (not yet published) is the first careful study of the man, in relation to the background of time and conditions.] J. C.

BOYCE, JAMES PETIGRU (Jan. 11, 1827–Dec. 28, 1888), Baptist minister, educator, of Scotch-Irish ancestry, the son of Ker and Amanda Jane Caroline (Johnston) Boyce, was born near tidewater at Charleston, S. C. His grandfather was a soldier in the Revolution, his father a wealthy cotton merchant in Charleston.

The boy early showed an inclination for books, was fitted for college before he was old enough to enter Charleston College, and later revealed his intellectual abilities there and at Brown University, where he graduated in 1847. A religious conversion turned his thoughts to the ministry as a profession, and he was licensed to preach. He spent two years at Princeton Theological Seminary, acquiring an enviable knowledge of theological literature, and specializing in the department of theology. In 1851 he settled as pastor of the Baptist Church in Columbia, S. C. In 1855 when only twenty-eight years old he was elected professor of theology in the theological department of the new Furman University at Greenville, S. C. On Dec. 20, 1858, he was married to Lizzie Llewellyn Ficklen.

Theological instruction in preparation for the Baptist ministry had hitherto been limited to personal guidance in the homes of leading ministers, and later to instruction in theological departments of academies and country colleges, such as Furman. Boyce was among the first to see that there was need of a theological seminary on an independent, well-endowed foundation, and he soon gave up the regular work of instruction at Furman, and became the spokesman for the new enterprise. The matter was agitated for several years before it took definite form. Boyce became a familiar figure on the plantations as he drove about soliciting support. He possessed an extensive tract of land near Greenville which brought him in large agricultural profits, and his father, also, assisted him financially so that he was able to live without salary. In 1859 the Southern Baptist Theological Seminary, with Boyce at its head, was organized at Greenville where it took over the theological department and library of Furman. The outbreak of the Civil War scattered its students, sent Boyce as a chaplain to a South Carolina regiment, and stopped any further receipt of funds. The recovery of educational institutions after the war was necessarily slow, and the Seminary had no buildings and little endowment. Out of his reduced fortune Boyce paid necessary bills to keep the school open, and it slowly recovered, ultimately moving to Louisville, Ky., where it became a credit to the denomination. Boyce shaped the curriculum on the elective principle, which he had learned from his president at Brown, Francis Wayland. As a theologian he maintained staunchly the conservative opinions that were characteristic of the Southern churches. He was highly regarded for his executive ability, for a number of years was president of the Southern Baptist Convention, and once was vainly urged to become president of the South Carolina Railroad Company at a salary of $10,000. His last years brought him ill health, which sent him to California, Alaska, and Europe. He died at Pau, France.

[John A. Broadus, *Memoir of Jas. Petigru Boyce* (1893); John R. Sampey, *Southern Baptist Theol. Sem.* (1890); *Necrological Report Alumni Ass. Princeton Theol. Sem., May 7, 1889; News and Courier* (Charleston, S. C.), May 6, 8, 1875; *Courier-Jour.* (Louisville, Ky.), Dec. 27, 28, 29, 1888.] H. K. R.

BOYD, BELLE (May 9, 1843–June 11, 1900), Confederate spy, was born in Martinsburg, Va., and from twelve to sixteen attended Mount Washington College. She was seventeen at the outbreak of the Civil War. The story of her achievements for the South rests mainly on her own none too trustworthy account in *Belle Boyd in Camp and Prison* (2 vols., London, 1865). It seems that during the early part of the war in conversation with Union officers quartered in Martinsburg, she picked up important military intelligence which she communicated to Southern officers, sometimes at the risk of her life. One of her notes was intercepted and she became a suspect. After the second capture of Martinsburg by the Union troops she went to Front Royal, where she found Gen. Shields occupying her aunt's house. While a council of war went on in the dining-room, Belle was lying in the closet above, her ear to a hole in the floor. The conference over, she saddled her horse, and with her passes, rode fifteen miles, returning undiscovered before dawn. But her most important service to the Confederate cause was a communication to Gen. Jackson's forces that by advancing rapidly they could save the bridges which the Federals were planning to destroy and keep open the road for an advance on Gen. Banks. Running over open fields, where her blue dress with its white apron was a target for picket shots and shells, she waved her bonnet at the first line of Confederates as a sign to advance, which they did. Jackson thanked her in the following terms: "I thank you, for myself and for the army, for the immense service that you have rendered your country today." After the retaking of Front Royal by the North, she was arrested in July 1862 and ordered to the Old Capitol prison in Washington, but was released a month later for lack of evidence against her. At this time, according to her own statement she received a commission as "captain and honorary aide-de-camp" to Gen. Jackson. In August 1863 she was arrested once more and kept in Carroll prison until Dec. 1. The following spring she sailed for England with letters from Jefferson Davis, was captured on her way but again released and continued on her trip. In August of the same year she married the man who had been her captor, Lieut. Sam Wylde Hardinge. Upon his death she went on the English stage, making her début as Pauline in the *Lady of Lyons* at the Theatre Royal, Manchester, in the latter part of 1866. A successful experience encouraged her to try the same career in America. Her first appearance was at Ben De Bar's Theatre, St. Louis. Then followed a starring tour of the South and Southwest. In January 1868 she appeared in New York in *The Honeymoon.* Later in the same year she joined the Miles and Bates stock company at Cincinnati but was soon engaged by the Greenwalls for their stock houses in Houston and Galveston. She married John Hammond, a former officer in the British army, in 1869, and Nathaniel High of Toledo in 1885. On Feb. 22, 1886, she presented a dramatic narrative of her own exploits as Confederate spy, at the People's Theatre, Toledo, Ohio. This type of lecture she continued until her sudden death from a heart attack, in Kilbourne, Wis., whither she had gone to speak. Dion Boucicault's play *Belle Lamar* is said to have been based on her experiences during the Civil War.

[Belle Boyd, *Belle Boyd in Camp and Prison* (1865); B. J. Lossing, *The Pictorial Field Book of the Civil War* (1874); T. A. Brown, *Hist. of the N. Y. Stage* (1903); *Milwaukee Jour.*, June 12, 1900; *N. Y. Times*, June 13, 1900.]

M. A. K.

BOYD, DAVID FRENCH (Oct. 5, 1834–May 27, 1899), educator, the son of Thomas Jefferson and Minerva Anne (French) Boyd, was born at Wytheville, Va. His father's family had been established in America by John Boyd who emigrated from Ayrshire, Scotland, and settled in Maryland in the late seventeenth century. David Boyd was educated in the famous Pike Powers classical school at Staunton, Va., and at the University of Virginia, graduating in 1856. He taught school in his native town for one year and then in the fall of 1857 went to Sherman, Tex., to assist in the construction of a railroad in that part of the state. But on his arrival he found that the project had been abandoned and he turned back to school teaching. After three years at Homer, and Rocky Mount, both in Louisiana, he was elected professor of ancient languages and English literature in the Louisiana State Seminary of Learning which opened its doors on Jan. 2, 1860, at Pineville, near Alexandria, with William Tecumseh Sherman as superintendent. In June 1861 he resigned his position in the seminary and entered the service of the Confederacy as a private in Company B, 9th Louisiana Infantry, which was shortly sent to Virginia for duty. He quickly rose in the ranks until by May 1862 he was major and brigade commissary in Richard Taylor's brigade of Stonewall Jackson's corps, and took part in the famous Valley campaign of Jackson that terminated in the latter's death. When Taylor was transferred to the Trans-Mississippi department, he accompanied him as captain of engineers. In the latter part of 1863 he constructed Fort De Russy on the Red River below Alexandria. He was captured by the "Jayhawkers" in February 1864 near Black River, La., and was confined in Federal prisons at Natchez, Miss., and at New Orleans. Through the intercession of Gen. Sherman, he was exchanged in the following July for two Federal officers of the same rank. In December 1864 he became major and adjutant-general in Brent's cavalry brigade which guarded Kirby Smith's front from Arkansas to the Gulf of Mexico during the last stages of the war. He surrendered at New Orleans in June 1865.

Elected superintendent of the Louisiana State Seminary, Boyd reopened it in October 1865. He was immediately confronted with the difficult problems of how to obtain financial support from state legislatures that were controlled largely by the carpet-baggers and negroes, and how to preserve the institution for the exclusive use of the young white men of Louisiana. Coupled with these problems was the broader one concerning the public schools of the state. According to the Louisiana state constitution of 1868 there were to be no separate public schools for the white and the colored children of Louisiana. Boyd joined hands with other prominent men in the state in securing the passage of a law in 1869 and a supplementary law in 1870, providing that in every parish in the state there should be one or more public schools, with the understanding that one should be for white children and the other for negroes. Before these troublesome questions could be fully decided, the building in which the seminary had been housed from the beginning was burned to the ground on Oct. 15, 1869. For the moment the situation was very serious. Boyd secured accommodations for the seminary in a part of the building for the Louisiana State School for the Deaf and Dumb in the southern part of Baton Rouge, and in two weeks after the fire the students resumed their work. In 1870 the seminary was renamed by the state legislature the Louisiana State University and the title of its head was changed from superintendent to president. In 1876, largely through Boyd's efforts, the Louisiana Agricultural and Mechanical College, which had been chartered in 1870 and opened at Chalmette, near New Orleans, in 1874, was merged with the university. By that time Boyd had, by his aggressive policy, incurred the enmity of some of the leading politicians in Louisiana. Opposition to him grew with each succeeding session of the state legislature and even appeared in the state constitutional convention in 1879. As a result he was removed from the presidency of the university in 1880 by the new board of supervisors, appointed by Gov. Nicholls under the constitution of 1879, on the charge of mismanagement of funds. This charge was thoroughly investigated by a special committee appointed by the state legislature in 1882 and was found to be without the slightest foundation. In 1884 the board that had dismissed him recalled Boyd unanimously to the presidency of the university. During the first three of the four years intervening between his dismissal and recall, he was engaged in conducting private military academies in Virginia, one at Locust Dale and another at Greenwood, and in 1883–84 he served as president of the Polytechnic Institute at Auburn, Ala. His second administration in the Louisiana State University saw the removal of the university from the building of the State School for the Deaf and Dumb to the buildings and grounds of an abandoned United States army post in the northern part of Baton Rouge. He had since 1870 had this change of quarters in mind, as he realized that it would be quite impossible for the university to grow and develop without a home of its own. He acted, however, without waiting for the authorization of the board of supervisors of the university, was in consequence severely censured by the board, and shortly after resigned. He remained with the university, however, for two years as professor of mathematics (1886–88). In 1888–93 he served as superintendent of the Kentucky Military Institute at Farmdale, Ky.; in 1893–94 he was a professor in the Ohio Military Academy at Germantown, Ohio; and in 1894–97 he was a professor in the Michigan Military Academy at Orchard Lake, Mich. In January 1897 he returned to Baton Rouge as professor of philosophy and civics in the Louisiana State University, which position he retained until his death in Baton Rouge in 1899. He was married on Oct. 5, 1865, to Esther Gertrude Wright, daughter of Dr. Jesse D. Wright, formerly of Saybrook, Conn.; to them were born seven sons and one daughter. Boyd was a man of slight stature, and in his later years was somewhat stooped, which fact, together with his sloping shoulders, made him appear even smaller. He possessed, however, boundless energy and great physical endurance. He was quick to take action and assume entire responsibility, when he thought something needed to be done. Had he been more cautious, he would have saved himself much trouble and embarrassment but his educational achievements in Louisiana would probably have been less.

[*W. T. Sherman as a Coll. President* (1912), ed. by W. E. Fleming, contains many letters that passed between Sherman and Boyd during 1859–61 while they were connected with the La. State Seminary of Learning. The same subject is covered by Boyd himself in the *Am. Coll.*, vol. II, no. 1, Apr. 1910, reprinted in the *Univ. Bull., La. State Univ.*, n. s., no. 10, Oct. 1910. "The Life and Services of D. F. Boyd" by A. A. Gunby in the *Univ. Bull., La. State Univ.*, ser. II, no. 2, June 1904, is an address delivered at the laying of the corner stone of the Alumni Memorial Hall at the La. State Univ., May 31, 1904. A sketch of Boyd by his son, Leroy S. Boyd, appears in T. M. Owens, *Hist. of Alabama* (1921), III, 187–89).]

E. M. V.

BOYD, JOHN PARKER (Dec. 21, 1764–Oct. 4, 1830), soldier of fortune, was born in Newburyport, Mass., the son of James and Susanna Boyd. The year following the end of the Revolution he obtained a commission as ensign, and rose to the rank of lieutenant. About 1789 he arrived in India, in quest of fortune. The conditions in that country favored a military adventurer. The British East India company and the French were in almost constant opposition, and the native Hindu and Mohammedan princes were frequently involved in warfare. Boyd, like the Italian condottieri, and other adventurers, sold his services, now to one prince, now to another. At one time the Nizam of Haidarabad, acting on British suggestions, engaged Boyd, who owned a body of troops, "a ready formed and experienced corps of 1800 men" (Compton, p. 340). Again, he entered the employ of the Peshwa of Poona at a salary of 3000 rupees a month, placed a new Peshwa on the throne, and commanded a brigade in the army of that native prince. "Riding into the very heart of Tippoo's dominions, he would strike a series of paralyzing blows, burn a dozen towns, exact a huge indemnity" (Powell, p. 10). "Military history presents no more fantastic picture than that of this Yankee adventurer spurring across an Indian countryside with a brigade of beturbaned lancers, and a score or so of lumbering elephants, the muzzles of field-guns frowning from their howdahs, tearing along behind him" (*Ibid.*, p. 14).

After nearly a score of years in India, Boyd returned to the United States, and in 1808 he reentered the army as colonel of the 4th Infantry. At the head of this regiment he fought under Harrison at the battle of Tippecanoe in 1811. At the opening of the War of 1812 he was commissioned brigadier-general, and served on the Canadian border. He led a brigade at the capture of Fort

George May 27, 1813, and at the battle of Chrystler's Farm on the following Nov. 11, he was in command. In this engagement, the climax of Wilkinson's disastrous campaign, about 2000 Americans were defeated by 800 of the enemy, and the battle—in the words of the historian Adams—"was ill-fought both by the generals and the men," and "had no redeeming incident." Boyd was discharged from the army in 1815, and toward the end of his life was naval officer for the port of Boston. His character was thus described by a fellow officer in the War of 1812: "A compound of ignorance, vanity, and petulance, with nothing to recommend him but that species of bravery in the field which is vaporing, boisterous, stifling reflection, blinding observation . . ." (Morgan Lewis, quoted in Adams, VII, p. 162). Adams adds that Boyd was competent only for the command of a regiment, and that he lacked the confidence of the army. "Brown was said to have threatened to resign rather than serve under him, and Winfield Scott . . . described Boyd as amiable and respectable in a subordinate position, but 'vacillating and imbecile beyond all endurance as a chief under high responsibilities'" (Adams, VII, 188).

[J. P. Boyd, *Documents and Facts Relative to Military Events* (1816), an attempted justification of his military conduct; Herbert Compton, *Military Adventurers of Hindustan* (1893); E. A. Powell, *Gentlemen Rovers* (1913); Henry Adams, *Hist. of the U. S.* (1889), VI, VII,; F. B. Heitman, *Hist. Reg.* (1890); *Vital Records of Newburyport, Mass.* (1911).]

E. K. A.

BOYD, LYNN (Nov. 22, 1800–Dec. 17, 1859), lawyer, congressman, was of Scotch descent, his ancestors settling early in Virginia. His grandfather, James Boyd, moved to South Carolina, served in the Revolution there and lost heavily at the hands of the British troops. His father, Abraham Boyd, who also fought in the Revolution, fell in early with the migration to Tennessee, crossing the mountains in company with Andrew Jackson, and settling at Nashville, where Lynn was born. In 1803 he removed to a farm in Christian County, Ky., where Lynn grew up as an ordinary laborer, working hard and getting little schooling. When only nineteen years old the youth was appointed to assist in securing from the Chickasaw Indians the Kentucky lands west of the Tennessee River, thereafter known as the Jackson Purchase on account of Andrew Jackson's connection with the mission. In 1826 he moved into the Purchase, settled on a farm in Calloway County, and the next year secured an election to the legislature to represent the four counties constituting the Purchase at that time. He always maintained a keen interest in this particular part of Kentucky and was looked upon by the people there as a special patron. In 1828 and 1829 he was returned from Calloway County as a representative at Frankfort at the same time that his father was representing Trigg County, and in 1831 Lynn, having returned to Trigg County, was elected as its representative.

Boyd had a degree of ambition which did not let him rest contented with merely state honors. In 1833 he ran for Congress from the first district and was defeated by his Whig opponent, but in 1835 he won, only to lose again in 1837. Determined to be in Congress he ran again in 1839, was elected, and continuously thereafter until 1855 he represented the first district at Washington, so strongly entrenching himself in the affections of the people that at times he was elected without opposition. He was a staunch supporter of Andrew Jackson and always remained a loyal Democrat. He stood squarely behind Jackson in opposition to the United States Bank. In return for this loyalty and out of sentiment for Boyd's father, Jackson steadily lent his influence to the advancement of the son. Boyd was much interested in the annexation of Texas and played a prominent part in the maneuvers leading up to the joint resolution of annexation. During the Mexican War he held the important chairmanship of the committee on military affairs, and later he became chairman of the committee on territories, where he was confronted with the task of trying to solve the difficult question of territorial organization necessitated by the Mexican conquest. He had a passion for the preservation of the Union, and when the compromise measures came before the House in 1850 he led the fight for their passage. Being now one of the most prominent figures in Washington he developed aspirations for the presidency, but his boom never went far. In 1856, however, he was Kentucky's favorite son for the vice-presidency. During the last four years of his congressional career (1851–55) he was speaker of the House. In 1855 he returned to Kentucky, but soon developed a desire to enter the United States Senate. As a step in this direction he sought the governorship in 1859. He received nothing better than the lieutenant-governorship, which he accepted but which he did not live to fill. He was the popular idol of western Kentucky; traditions of his manly vigor and handsome figure are still handed down. He was married twice, first in 1832 to Alice C. Bennett of Trigg County, and then in 1850 to Mrs. Anna L. Dixon of Pennsylvania, a relative of President Fillmore.

[G. W. Thompson, *Biog. Sketch of Hon. Lynn Boyd* (1852); *Ky. Statesman*, Dec. 20, 23, 1859; Richard H.

and Lewis Collins, *Hist. of Ky.*, vol. II (1874); H. Levin, ed., *Lawyers and Lawmakers of Ky.* (1897); R. F. Nichols, *The Democratic Machine, 1850–54* (1923).]
E. M. C.

BOYD, RICHARD HENRY (Mar. 15, 1843–Aug. 23, 1922), negro clergyman, was the son of Indiana Dixon, a slave of B. A. Gray, a planter in Noxubee County, Miss. Named Dick Gray by his master, he went by this name until 1867 or 1868 when he changed it himself to R. H. Boyd. When he was six years old, the Grays moved to Washington County, Tex., where they lived on a large plantation until the outbreak of the Civil War. Boyd accompanied his master as a servant in one of the Confederate armies fighting around Chattanooga. Upon the death of his master and three of his sons, the slave returned to take charge of the plantation. In the capacity of manager, he served efficiently, not only in the production of cotton but in selling it at points across the border in Mexico. Upon the break-up of this family a few years later, he became first a Texas cowboy and then a laborer at a sawmill in Montgomery County. In 1869 he was married to Hattie Moore. A turning point in his life came in 1870 or 1871 when he professed religion and entered the Baptist ministry. He was ordained in the latter part of the same year. Although inspired to preach, he was handicapped in that he had had no literary training. He had never attended a public school, and it was only after 1865 that he was even taught the alphabet. Having, however, a desire to learn, he secured the assistance of white people who taught him to read and to spell. After he was ordained to the ministry, he spent two years in what is now known as Bishop College at Marshall, Tex., a school founded and operated by the Home Missionary Society of New York. Entering seriously upon his task as a minister, Boyd not only served an influential church himself, but organized with six other churches the first negro Baptist Association in Texas about 1872. He built churches at Waverly, Old Danville, Navasota, Crockett, Palestine, and San Antonio. He was named secretary of the negro Baptist Convention of Texas and elected superintendent of missions in that state. Serving in these positions, he conceived the idea of publishing literature for negro Baptist Sunday Schools. He brought out his first religious pamphlets for the years of 1894 and 1895. He later published several useful works, among which should be mentioned the *Pastor's Guide*, the *Church Directory*, and *Jubilee and Plantation Songs*. An opportunity for the furtherance of his plans came in 1896, when, while attending the national Baptist convention at St. Louis, he was elected secretary of the home mission board to do mission work among the negroes of the United States. He soon gained sufficient impetus to organize, in January 1897, the National Baptist Publishing Board which issued the first series of negro Baptist literature ever published. His task was a difficult one, for neither he nor his denomination had any money. He had courage, however, and soon won the support of influential friends among the whites who were seriously impressed with the importance of this work. The publishing project rapidly developed into the source of supply of religious literature for the negro Baptists throughout the world. Unfortunately, however, in 1915, because of certain questions as to the management of its affairs, there came a split which resulted in two factions of the negro Baptists of the country, one adhering to the leadership of Boyd and the other to that of the president of the Baptist convention, Dr. E. C. Morris. The latter faction has since then established another large publishing house known as the Sunday School Publishing Board.

[*A Memorial Program*, published in pamphlet form by the National Baptist Publishing Board in March 1927, contains a brief sketch of Boyd. The *Nashville Tennesseean* and *Nashville Banner* contain long obituaries, Aug. 24, 1922. Additional information in detailed form may be obtained from *A Story of the National Baptist Publishing Board*.]
C. G. W.

BOYDEN, SETH (Nov. 17, 1788–Mar. 31, 1870), inventor, manufacturer, is called by Thomas A. Edison "one of America's greatest inventors." He was born in Foxborough, Mass., the son of Seth and Susanna (Atherton) Boyden and the brother of Uriah Atherton Boyden [*q.v.*]. His father was the inventor of a leather-splitting machine, the recipient of numerous awards for improvements in agriculture, and the proprietor of a small forge and machine shop. His grandfather, Uriah Atherton (who is said to have cast the first cannon made in America), was still operating his foundry at Foxborough during Seth Boyden's early life. With this background, a scanty education proved no serious handicap, and at the age of fifteen we find Seth enjoying a local reputation as a skilful mechanic and repairer of watches, clocks, and guns. At twenty-one he had constructed machines for manufacturing nails and cutting files, and at twenty-five he took an improved leather-splitting machine to Newark, N. J., to supply the trade with split sheepskins and leather for bookbinding. This seems to have been the most important move of his life, for the many industries of Newark afforded the opportunities that enabled him to maintain his continuous output of inventions. In 1819 he successfully duplicated the lacquer of a piece of European ornamental leather and established the first factory for the production of varnished or "patent" leather, founding an important American industry. With this enterprise barely established, he turned his attention to malleable cast-iron, the secret of which was also a jealously guarded European one. Here he applied himself to experiment for six years, succeeding in running off his first cast of malleable iron on July 4, 1826. In 1828 the Franklin Institute awarded him a premium for his malleable castings, and in 1831 he was granted the first patent issued for this material. That year he sold his "patent leather" factory to concentrate his efforts on the commercial production of malleable iron, and in 1837 sold the malleable iron business to engage in the construction of locomotives. He built three, and then turned to the manufacture of stationary steam engines, in which connection he made the first application of "cut-off" governing, a method effecting a more economical steam consumption. In connection with his engine works he was making a furnace grate bar in 1847 which he adapted to the manufacture of oxide of zinc, the same grate (the Wetherill) that is used in the "American Process" to-day. In 1849 he made an unsuccessful trip to the California gold fields. Returning the next year he then developed an inexpensive process for manufacturing "Russia" sheet-iron; achieved a reputation for his development of the famous Hilton strawberry; invented an important hat-forming machine; made a gold-like alloy "oroide"; and published a treatise on atmospheric electricity (1868). Incidentally, he is credited with having made the first daguerreotype in this country, and with extending important aid to Morse. He died in Hilton, N. J.

[Jos. Atkinson, *Hist. of Newark, N. J.* (1878); J. L. Bishop, *Hist. of Am. Manufacturers* (1861); Angus Sinclair, *Development of the Locomotive Engine* (1907); *Foxborough's Official Centennial Record* (1879); Records of the N. J. Zinc Co., N. Y.; E. C. Kreutzberg in *Iron Trade Rev.*, Feb. 11, 1926; *Brass World*, Mar. 1926; Patent Office records.] F. A. T—r.

BOYDEN, URIAH ATHERTON (Feb. 17, 1804–Oct. 17, 1879), engineer, inventor. He was born at Foxborough, Norfolk County, Mass., son of Seth and Susanna (Atherton) Boyden. After attending country school, he assisted his father in farming and blacksmithing. At the age of twenty-one he went to Newark, N. J., to work for his oldest brother, Seth Boyden [*q.v.*], who was a manufacturer and inventor of note. He returned to New England and took part under James Hayward in the first survey for the Boston and Providence Railroad. Later he worked at the dry-dock in the Charlestown navy-yard under Col. L. Baldwin, and still later at Lowell in the construction of the Suffolk, Tremont, and Lawrence mills, and the Boston and Lowell Railroad. This was an era of industrial expansion for New England and of pioneer experiment in engineering—particularly railroading and hydraulic development. Boyden had little formal education but his Yankee ingenuity and initiative enabled him to pick up quickly the main principles of applied science and technique. At the age of twenty-nine he opened an office in Boston as an engineer. From 1836 to 1838 he supervised the construction of the Nashua and Lowell Railroad. But it was not in railroading that he was to make his mark. He became engineer for the Amoskeag Manufacturing Company and designed hydraulic works at Manchester, N. H. In 1844, when he was forty, he devised a turbine water-wheel for the Appleton cotton-mills at Lowell. This was based on a design of Fourneyron, a Frenchman and the inventor of the outward-flow turbine, but Boyden's improvements made a more efficient design. Tests showed that his turbine, which was for seventy-five horsepower, delivered seventy-eight per cent of the power expended. Two years later he designed for the same company three turbines of 190 horse-power each. His compensation was to depend in a sliding scale upon the performance of the turbines. Tests, which Boyden also improved and systematized, showed an efficiency of eighty-two per cent, so that he was paid $5,500. Among the improvements was a well-designed scroll penstock, a suspended top bearing, and a diffuser showing the principles of the modern flaring draft-tube. He was the inventor of the hook-gauge, which with his other inventions he patented and which thereby contributed to his ample income. The principle with which his name is most commonly associated is the spiral approach, which has the advantage of admitting water to the turbine at a uniform velocity. The Boyden water-wheel soon became well known throughout the country and was adopted in many mills and power-plants; he has been called the father of American mixed-flow hydraulic turbine design but this title probably is not deserved —although Boyden might have liked to appropriate it. The science of hydraulics had not advanced much beyond the empirical stage, and as most of the formulas were known to Boyden, his work was along sound engineering lines. In his later years he retired from active practise and devoted his time to the study of pure science—an unusual procedure for a practical, "uneducated" engineer. In particular he investigated the velocity of light, the compressibility of water, and the subject of "caloric" or heat.

One elaborate experiment consisted of tests to determine the velocity of sounds traveling through the conduit pipes of the Charlestown and Chelsea water-works. It is interesting to note that as early as 1826, when he was twenty-two years old, the *New Jersey Eagle* published an article by him entitled "An Attempt to Explain the Cause of the Warmth at the Poles of the Earth." In 1874 he deposited $1,000 with the Franklin Institute, to be awarded to any resident of North America who should determine whether light and other physical rays travel at the same rate—a rather naïve proposal. He gave $1,000 to the town of Foxborough, which was later used to finance a small library called the Boyden Public Library. At his death most of his fortune, more than a quarter of a million dollars, was left to a Board of Trustees to be used for establishing observatories on mountain tops. Boyden never joined the American Society of Civil Engineers and never married, but lived frugally at a hotel in Boston—an old-fashioned figure of a man with fringe whiskers.

[*Lowell Hydraulic Experiments* by Jas. B. Francis (2d. ed., 1868); an article on "The American Mixed-Flow Turbine and its Setting" by Arthur T. Safford and Edward Pierce Hamilton in the *Trans. Am. Soc. Civil Engineers*, LXXXV (1922); *Thos. Boyden and his Descendants* by W. C. Boyden *et al.* (privately printed, Boston, 1901); *Boston Evening Transcript*, Oct. 17, 1879; *Boston Morning Jour.*, Oct. 18, 1879.]

P. B. M.

BOYÉ, MARTIN HANS (Dec. 6, 1812–Mar. 5, 1909), chemist, physicist, geologist, was born in Copenhagen, where his father, Mark Boyé, a chemist, superintended the Royal Porcelain Manufactory. Martin received his educational and scientific training in Copenhagen, graduating from the University of Copenhagen in 1832 and from the Polytechnic School in 1835. In 1836 he arrived in New York, "his object in coming to America being the desire to obtain an open field for research along his chosen line." In 1837 he became a student and assistant cf Robert Hare. The next year he was closely associated with Henry D. Rogers in the geological survey of the State of Pennsylvania—occupying himself chiefly with the chemical analysis of rocks and minerals, as well as in the study of certain interesting and new derivatives of platinum. Simultaneously, in the laboratory of Robert Hare he discovered and studied ethyl perchlorate, an exceedingly unstable ether, and also methyl perchlorate, which was not so treacherous. In 1844 he graduated as an M.D. from the Medical School of the University of Pennsylvania and was also accorded the A.M. degree *causa honoris* in recognition of numerous literary contributions of great merit. He was a member of the American Philosophical Society; and was one of the twenty scientists who met in Philadelphia in 1840 and organized the American Association of Geologists which later passed into the American Association for the Advancement of Science; and was for seventy-two years a member of the Franklin Institute. He carried out many scientific studies of merit in association with James Curtis Booth [*q.v.*] (Booth & Boyé, Chemists, 27 N. 7th St.—as says an old City Directory), and was much occupied with the study of minerals and ores of Pennsylvania, in one of which—iron pyrites from Gap Mine, Lancaster County—he found four and one-half per cent of nickel (the mine being later worked for nickel, long used in our coins). In 1845 he became professor in the Central High School of Philadelphia, where he is said to have been an earnest, enthusiastic, and successful teacher. While thus engaged he wrote *A Treatise on Pneumatics: being the Physics of Gases, including Vapors* (1855) and *Chemistry, or the Physics of Atoms* (1857). Both books were vigorous presentations of their topics. He was also associated with James Curtis Booth in the preparation of the first part of the *Encyclopædia of Chemistry* (1850). The article on "Analysis" by Boyé was extended into an independent volume of exceptional merit. In 1845 he refined the oily product from cotton-seed, getting a bland, colorless oil, adapted for cooking and salad dressing, as well as for the making of a soap surpassing even the best Castile. A sample of the oil made in 1848 was preserved until 1876 when it gained the first premium at the Centennial Exposition in Philadelphia. In his later years he traveled extensively. He closed his career at Coopersburg, Pa., where he pursued "the most noble and useful avocation of man—agriculture."

[Edgar F. Smith, *Martin Hans Boyé—Chemist* (1924); sketch in C. R. Roberts, *Hist. of Lehigh County, Pa.* (1914), vol. II; *Who's Who in America*, 1908–09; *Science*, Mar. 19, 1909; *Press* (Phila.), Mar. 6, 1909.]

E. F. S.

BOYESEN, HJALMAR HJORTH (Sept. 23, 1848–Oct. 4, 1895), author, educator, was born at Frederiksvärn, a fishing village on the southern coast of Norway. His father was a teacher of mathematics at the naval academy there located. A considerable part of the son's childhood was passed in the home of a maternal grandfather who was a judge at Systrand on the Sogne-fjord, where the boy imbibed, with the wild beauty of the scene, a great deal of balladry and folk-lore from the servants of the house. He was educated in the Latin School at Drammen and the gymnasium at Christiania; later at the University of Leipsig and the University of

Christiania, where he received the degree of Ph.D. in 1868. From a residence in America his father had formed so great an admiration for the country that he exacted from each of his sons a promise to spend at least a year in the United States, and it was in fulfilment of this vow that Hjalmar and his brother sailed for this country early in 1869.

After several months of travel, Boyesen settled in Chicago as editor of a Norwegian weekly called the *Fremad,* in which he continuously opposed the denominational schools then flourishing among the Scandinavian settlers in the Middle West. His progress in English was unusually rapid, but he soon realized that in order to secure a mastery of the tongue sufficient for literary work he must associate chiefly with persons to whom it was native. He therefore left the *Fremad* and went as tutor in Greek and Latin to Urbana University, a Swedenborgian institution in Ohio. Acute homesickness during his residence there inspired what is probably his best novel, a story of Norwegian life called *Gunnar.* Through an accidental meeting between the author and Prof. Child of Harvard, the story came to the attention of William Dean Howells, then editor of the *Atlantic,* and was issued serially in that magazine in 1873. Its acceptance by Howells was a decisive incident in the life of Boyesen, persuading him to continue in America and in academic life, and the enduring friendship that ensued with Howells was of great influence in his career. To prepare himself more fully as a teacher, he spent the year 1873 in philosophical and linguistic studies at Leipsig and returned the next year to an appointment in the German department at Cornell. While there he married Elizabeth Keen of New York. In 1880 he came to New York as a literary free lance, but accepted a post in the German department of Columbia in the year following, and succeeded to the Gebhard Professorship of German there in 1882; eight years later he was given the chair of Germanic Languages and Literatures, which he continued to hold till death.

He was gifted with unusual versatility. An alert and stimulating teacher, he was more capable in communicating literary enthusiasm than in training pupils to rigorous scholarly method. Yet his scholarship, if relatively unoriginal, was fully competent, and his work on *Goethe and Schiller* (1879) embodied in its time the best treatment of *Faust* in the language. As a writer of criticism he sometimes missed the finer discriminations, owing to a warmth of temperament that occasionally betrayed him into controversial ardor or tempted him to paradox and overstatement; but his opinions were forceful and illuminative, and his *Essays on Scandinavian Literature* (1895) contain much sound and valuable matter. The *Essays on German Literature* (1892) and the *Commentary on the Writing of Henrik Ibsen* (1894) are somewhat less substantial; as is also the collection of *Literary and Social Silhouettes* (1894). He wrote the history of his native land in the *Story of Norway* (1886). His chief aspiration was to make a name in poetry, but he was not primarily a poet in temperament and he was more heavily handicapped in verse than in prose by the use of an adopted tongue; his *Idyls of Norway* (1882) are therefore somewhat mediocre in conception and rough in execution.

He was at his best in books for boys and in fiction. His juvenile books comprise *The Modern Vikings* (1887) and *Boyhood in Norway* (1892), both of them skilfully executed. The list of his novels demonstrates unusual industry and fertility. Themes from Norway furnished his best material, as in *Gunnar* (1874) and in many of the shorter stories that followed, but he has also admirable pictures of the Scandinavian settlements in the Middle West. *Falconberg* (1879) makes capital out of his experience in journalism, and *The Mammon of Unrighteousness* (1891) draws from the life at Urbana a good deal of satirical comment on the American faith in the power of education. His bent for satire is further illustrated in the *Social Strugglers* (1893) where he is especially interested in religious hypocrisy as a ladder for social ambition.

The main literary debt of his novels is to Tolstoy, Björnson, and Turgenev, though there is also a noticeable influence from Howells. The earlier romanticism of a work like *Gunnar* was discarded in favor of an ardent realism in the later novels. With this came an abundance of satire, sometimes a little heavy-fingered, and of humor that is always vigorous and occasionally even boisterous, rather than urbane. And though he gained a remarkable command of his adopted language, he occasionally betrayed his foreign birth, not only in negligible slips of idiom but also in missing certain of the nicer distinctions of social values in American life. But he was a sturdily convinced American; so much so that toward the close of his life he preferred not to speak his native tongue. And always a man of strong public spirit, he could be counted on for ardent defense of every cause that stirred his faith.

Among his other works of fiction are: *A Norseman's Pilgrimage* (1875), *Tales from Two*

Hemispheres (1876), *Queen Titania* (1881), *Ilka on the Hill-top* (1881), *A Daughter of the Philistines* (1883), *The Light of Her Countenance* (1889), *Vagabond Tales* (1889), *Against Heavy Odds* (1890), *A Fearless Trio* (1890), *A Golden Calf* (1892), and *Norseland Tales* (1894). These were accompanied by a very large number of stories and articles in the magazines; and *Ilka on the Hill-top* was successfully dramatized on the New York stage in 1884. His works were variously translated into German, Norwegian, Swedish, Russian, French, Italian, Spanish, and modern Greek.

[The best account is by B. W. Wells in the *Sewanee Review,* May 1896; there are articles by Theodore Stanton in the *Open Court,* Feb. 13, 1896, by G. M. Hyde in the *Dial,* Dec. 1, 1895, by W. H. Carpenter in the *Columbia Bulletin,* Dec. 1895, and anonymously in the *Critic,* Oct. 12, 1895. See also accounts of interviews with Boyesen in the *Sunday News-Tribune* (Detroit), Apr. 8, 1894, and in the *Book Buyer,* Oct. 1886.]

E. H. W.

BOYLE, JEREMIAH TILFORD (May 22, 1818–July 28, 1871), Union soldier, was the fourth son of Elizabeth (Tilford) and John Boyle, chief justice of the Kentucky court of appeals (1810–26) and one of the most noted of early western jurists. After the orthodox classical education at Centre and Princeton, Jeremiah studied law in the office of Gov. Owsley and at Transylvania and upon the completion of his work entered upon the practise of his profession at Danville, Ky. Here he remained in apparent content until the outbreak of the Civil War. He was a slaveholder and like most slave owners in Kentucky, a Whig. Not suspecting the coming of emancipation he determined his attitude toward secession more by his political affiliations than by his economic interests and became one of the most active of Union men during the short-lived effort for neutrality. In November 1861 his zeal in recruiting for the Union army gained for him a commission as brigadier-general of volunteers. His ensuing military career was distinguished more by activity than by success although he fought with "conspicuous gallantry" at Shiloh (*Official Records,* ser. 1, vol. X, pt. 1, p. 355). Shortly after this battle Secretary Stanton appointed him military commander of Kentucky, the appointment apparently being due to the pressing solicitations of the Kentucky delegation in Congress. Boyle remained military commander until Jan. 12, 1864, and his conduct during the period has been a subject of acrimonious controversy until this day. It cannot be said that he proved himself very efficient against his armed enemies. John Morgan raided the state almost at will, guerrillas ravaged the country, and Louisville itself (Boyle's headquarters) was saved from Bragg only by the dilatoriness of Bragg himself. In fact, Boyle was finally removed from his position because of his military ineptitude (*Official Records,* ser. 1, vol. XXXII, pt. 2, p. 10). Against non-combatants, however, he displayed considerable ability although Kentucky historians are inclined to question the wisdom of his measures. His arrests of people suspected of sympathizing with the Confederacy, his use of troops to control elections, and his domination of the judiciary made open enemies of many people who had hitherto been neutral. His policy of assessing upon "disloyal" people of the neighborhood the damages caused by guerrillas alienated the more moderate of the Union men. Whatever the merits of these measures he succeeded in keeping the support of the active Union leaders of Kentucky (*Louisville Daily Journal,* Jan. 9, 1864). By his policy he forced the resignation of Gov. Magoffin and undoubtedly increased the bitterness between factions throughout the state. For the most part he acted on his own initiative and on occasion his zeal seemed to outrun that of Stanton himself. He retained, throughout, the respect of both friend and enemy for his personal integrity and after his removal whatever feeling existed against him was soon forgotten in the general execration of his successors. Upon retiring from the army, he helped organize the Louisville City Railway Company, of which he soon became president. In 1866 he became president of the moribund Evansville, Henderson & Nashville Railroad and made it a successful enterprise. He came to have large interests in railway and land properties in the West and amassed a large fortune before his death. From his marriage (1842) with Elizabeth Owsley Anderson were born twelve children, four of whom survived him.

[For the life of Boyle prior to the Civil War one must depend on brief sketches in encyclopedias and Kentucky history. For his military career an abundance of source material is scattered through the *Official Records* and through the files of contemporary newspapers, particularly the *Louisville Daily Jour.* and the *Louisville Daily Democrat.* E. M. Coulter, *Civil War and Readjustment in Ky.* (1926) has a good treatment of his conduct as military commander although the most detailed account is given by Manning in his (unpublished) "Reconstruction in Ky.," a thesis submitted to the Faculty of the University of Louisville in part fulfilment of the master's degree, 1926.]

R. S. C.

BOYLE, JOHN (Oct. 28, 1774–Jan. 28, 1835), judge, the son of John Boyle, was born on the Clinch River near Tazewell in Botetourt County, Va. His parents, inconspicuous in the history of their times, moved to Kentucky in 1779 and settled at Whitley's Station not far from Boonesborough. They later removed to Garrard County where they remained until death. Young Boyle had no educational advantages beyond the instruction he received in Latin, Greek, and in a few other subjects from Samuel Finley, a Presbyterian minister. Having a strong inclination for the law he began the study of that subject under Thomas Davis, who later represented Kentucky in Congress, and whom Boyle succeeded in that position in 1803. Boyle took little part in speech-making in the House of Representatives but by a close attention to his duties and by a strict adherence to the principles of Jefferson, won the admiration and good opinion of the President. He was elected for three successive terms, refusing further service in this capacity, due to his desire to return to his home life in Kentucky. In 1809, just before leaving Washington, he was offered by James Madison, the incoming President, the governorship of the Illinois Territory. After reaching Kentucky he rejected the honor and thereby made the vacancy which Ninian Edwards filled, who in turn by resigning his position on the bench of the Kentucky court of appeals left a justice-ship vacant which Boyle accepted. The next year (1810) Boyle was appointed chief justice to succeed George M. Bibb, who had resigned, and it was in this capacity that he did the work upon which his reputation chiefly rests. His decisions were logical, sound, and conservative, setting a great store on precedent.

He was a great power in the state in heading off the replevin laws, and other relief measures during the early twenties. When summoned before the legislature for his adherence to conservative principles, he ably defended the position of the court, and when the legislature sought to abolish the court after it had failed to unseat Boyle and the other justices, he continued the fight for the supremacy of the old court. In 1826 after the struggle was over and the old court had been reëstablished, he resigned and was immediately appointed by President Adams district judge for Kentucky. Twice he might have received an appointment to the United States Supreme Court had he desired it. Honored in his day as a great jurist, he died near Danville. He was married in 1797 to Elizabeth Tilford, who died in 1833, a victim of the cholera.

[Facts relating to the life and character of Boyle may be found in Richard H. and Lewis Collins, *Hist. of Ky.* (1874); *Biog. Encyc. of Ky.* (1877); H. Levin, ed., *Lawyers and Lawmakers of Ky.* (1897); Z. F. Smith, *Hist. of Ky.* (1886); Mrs. Chapman Coleman, *Life of John J. Crittenden* (1871), vol. I. His decisions in the Ky. court of appeals are published in Bibb's (4 vols.), Marshall's (3 vols.), Littell's (5 vols.), and Monroe's (7 vols.) *Reports.*]

E. M. C.

BOYLE, JOHN J. (Jan. 12, 1851–Feb. 10, 1917), sculptor, was the son of Samuel and Catherine (McAuley) Boyle, both of whom were of North of Ireland stock. On the father's side were generations of stone-cutters; the mother's father was a village blacksmith. J. J. Boyle was born in New York; but in 1851 his father moved to Philadelphia where two of his brothers lived. In early life he had little book-learning, save what he got from the public schools of his boyhood. On account of his father's early death, the need to earn came to him young. He worked first as iron-moulder, then as stone-cutter, next as stone-carver. Meanwhile he carried on studies with Eakins at the Pennsylvania Academy of Fine Arts. Then, having saved money enough, he went to Paris (1877) and entered the École des Beaux Arts where he remained three years.

During his course at the Beaux Arts, the summer of 1878 brought him decorative work on a London leather exchange building,—five panels and some caryatids. The next year he made two portraits, and exhibited a bronze bust at the Paris Salon. His true vein was to declare itself later. The opportunity came in 1880, when he received from Martin Ryerson the commission for "An Indian Family," a handsomely mounted bronze group now in Lincoln Park, Chicago. Before beginning this work, he spent two months among the Indians to be commemorated. In the treatment of the dominant male Indian, surrounded by squaw, papoose, and watchful dog, the composition prefigures the sturdy quality of Boyle's art. With a characteristic forthrightness far removed from complacency, the sculptor states that when "An Indian Family" was shown in Philadelphia, "its excellence impressed many." In fact, the Fairmount Park Art Association of that city promptly gave him a commission for an heroic group in similar vein, "The Stone Age," in which a vigilant aboriginal mother holding a stone hatchet clasps one papoose, while another crouches at her feet, not too near the slain bear cub with which the hatchet has just dealt. The work shows Boyle's characteristic massiveness of design, his deep emotion, untainted by sentimentality. It was executed in Paris,—clay, plaster, and bronze; the plaster model received honorable mention at the Salon of 1886; the bronze was set up in Fairmount Park in 1888.

In 1882, he was married, very happily, to a helpmeet with charm and understanding, Elizabeth Carroll of Philadelphia. After the completion of "The Stone Age," the couple enjoyed a period of travel and study, which included a tour in Switzerland, and eight months in Italy. In 1891–92 Boyle did "effective if ephemeral" work on the sculptural decorations for the Transportation Building at the Columbian Exposition. An intimate bronze group of mother and two children, "Tired Out," won applause and a medal at this exposition. At Buffalo in 1901 his two great groups, "The Savage Age," "East and West," were among the finest of the expositional decorations; their excellence entitled them to a permanency which circumstances denied them. Toward the close of 1893 he went to Philadelphia, where during the next two years he made for the Library of Congress in Washington the bronze statues of Plato and Lord Bacon, neither work remarkable except for entire competence from an architectural point of view. These indoor figures have not the vividness and color of his open-air sculptures. Perhaps the super-civilized subjects enticed him not. To this period belong also three heroic busts (in the University of Pennsylvania, Bryn Mawr College, First Unitarian Church, Philadelphia), as well as portraits for Hahnemann Hospital and for the Penn Charter School.

It has been noted that in general his genius is happiest in themes that are elemental rather than elegant. He is successful also in his delineations of vigorous, manly characters; himself an individualist, he delighted in strongly marked types. His heroic seated bronze statue of Franklin, presented by J. C. Strawbridge to the City of Philadelphia in 1900, gives the beholder a deep sense of the greatness of heart and brain in this our "first civilized American." The sculptor's enthusiasm has re-created "Poor Richard" in terms at once monumental and intimate.

In 1902, Boyle removed from the city of his boyhood to the city of his birth. His art was well known throughout the country; he had received many medals and honors. He was a charter member of the National Sculpture Society. From Jan. 1, 1906, to Dec. 31, 1908, he served as sculptor member of the Art Commission of the City of New York. In the midst of architectural decorations and portrait work, he turned with special zest to the statue of Commodore John Barry, for which Congress had appropriated $50,000 in 1906. This work, unveiled in Washington May 16, 1914, President Wilson making an address, consists of an heroic bronze figure of the Commodore, standing gallantly on a high, richly-wrought, widely-based stone pedestal. It remains the most important of the sculptor's later achievements. Within three years, after a long illness ending in pneumonia, he died in New York, his wife surviving him.

[C. H. Caffin, *Am. Masters of Sculpture* (1903); Lorado Taft, *Hist. of Am. Sculpture* (1903); *Fairmount Park Art Ass., an Account of its Origin and Activities* (1921); obituaries in *Public Ledger* (Phila.), *Phila. Inquirer*, *N. Y. Herald*, Feb. 11, 1917. Numerous press notices detailed Boyle's activities from 1880 until the year preceding his death.] A. A—s.

BOYLE, THOMAS (June 29, 1776?–Oct. 12, 1825?), sea captain, was one of the outstanding privateersmen in the War of 1812. Aside from that, little is known of his life. It is said that he was born at Marblehead, Mass., was commanding a ship at sixteen, and was married in 1794 at Baltimore which was thereafter his home. In July 1812, he took command of the 14-gun privateer schooner *Comet*. The first cruise of four months netted prizes valued at about half a million dollars. In December 1812, he dodged the Chesapeake blockading squadron and made for Pernambuco, where he took three armed British merchantmen after fighting off their convoy, a Portuguese warship. Altogether, he captured twenty-seven prizes in the *Comet*. In 1814 he changed to an even faster vessel, the 16-gun brig *Chasseur,* known as "The Pride of Baltimore." A cruise in the English Channel and West Indies resulted in eighteen prizes. At one time, he was nearly surrounded by four British warships, but he outmaneuvered them all. His most unique exploit was his proclamation in 1814, declaring the British Isles in "a state of strict and rigorous blockade." He stated that he considered his force "adequate to maintain strictly, vigorously and effectually, the said blockade." This was a direct burlesque of the "paper blockades" of the American coast pompously proclaimed by Admirals Cochrane and Warren. Boyle dispatched it in a released cartel, requesting that it be posted in Lloyd's Coffee House. On his final cruise, he captured the British naval schooner *St. Lawrence* in a fifteen-minute fight off Cuba on Feb. 26, 1815. During the war, he captured some eighty prizes, valued at considerably more than a million. This compares favorably with the record of the *America* under Chever and others. Boyle was described as a quiet, unassuming man with a strong sense of humor and "superb audacity." Coggeshall, the contemporary privateersman-historian, said that Boyle combined "the impetuous bravery of a Murat with the prudence of a Wellington." Boyle took particular delight in tantalizing the stronger but slower British warships with his own fast craft. He returned to the merchant service after the war. In 1824, he beat off a pirate attack in the brig *Panopea* (*Niles' Weekly Register,* XXVI, p. 328). He is said to have died at sea a year later.

[Chapters are devoted to Boyle's exploits in E. S. Maclay, *Hist. of the Am. Privateers* (1889), pp. 279–99; and E. P. Statham, *Privateers and Privateering* (1910), pp. 307–16. There is a contemporary account in Geo. Coggeshall, *Hist. of the Am. Privateers* (2nd ed. 1856), pp. 132–39, 358–69. *Niles' Weekly Reg.*, IV,

71 (1813) quotes extracts from the *Comet's* log, and VII, 290 (1815) quotes the proclamation. Part of the *Chasseur's* log is quoted in the *Md. Hist. Mag.*, I, 168 ff., 218 ff. Dates of birth, marriage, and death are given in J. T. Sharf, *Hist. of Md.* (3 vols., 1879), III, 135n., but these could not be confirmed in local records.]

R. G. A.

BOYLSTON, ZABDIEL (Mar. 9, 1679–Mar. 1, 1766), physician, the first to introduce the practise of inoculation for smallpox into America, was the grandson of Thomas Boylston, Esq., who migrated from England to Watertown, Mass., in 1635, and the son of Mary Gardner and Dr. Thomas Boylston, the earliest physician of Muddy River (now Brookline, Mass.). Though he never obtained a medical degree, he received medical instruction from his father and from a Dr. Cutter of Boston. In a comparatively short time he acquired a good reputation and considerable wealth, and it has been said that "he was remarkable for his skill, his humanity, and close attention to his patients." However, one hears little of Boylston in the colony until June 1721. On Apr. 15, 1721, smallpox made its appearance in Boston, brought by a ship from the Tortugas (*Boston News-Letter,* Apr. 13–17, 17–24, 1721, nos. 893–94). By the middle of May the disease was rife in the colony. Boylston began to inoculate on June 26, and the circumstances which led him to employ this procedure demand consideration. Cotton Mather on Dec. 13, 1707, had been presented by his parishioners with a slave named Onesimus who later informed Mather that he had been inoculated in Africa, and that it was common among the Guramantese tribes so to protect themselves (Klebs, p. 70). On June 6, 1721, Mather circulated in manuscript an "Address to the Physicians of Boston" exhorting them to inoculate. The "Address" consisted chiefly of an abstract of the Timonius and Pylarinus papers (1714 and 1716) upon inoculation in Constantinople which had appeared in Volume XXIX of the *Philosophical Transactions of the Royal Society.* On June 24 Mather wrote a letter to Boylston in which he said, referring to inoculation, "If upon mature deliberation, you should think it advisiable [*sic*] to be proceeded in, it may save many lives that we set a great value on" (Fitz, p. 318). The result was decisive. Two days later Boylston inoculated his own son Thomas, and two negro slaves. He did not inoculate himself since he had had the disease in 1702. Later he inoculated his son John, and on July 21 seven patients received the pustule. There is no evidence to warrant the belief that Boylston yet knew of the inoculations carried out the preceding April in London at Lady Mary Wortley Montagu's instigation. The uproar created by the practise placed Boylston's and Mather's lives in danger. Their houses were attacked by enraged mobs and a hand grenade was thrown into Mather's study. Abusive attacks were launched against them in the *Boston News-Letter* and a war of pamphlets began in which Benjamin Colman [*q.v.*], William Douglass, William Cooper, Increase Mather [*q.v.*], Isaac Greenwood [*q.v.*], and many anonymous writers participated. Three times Boylston was called before the selectmen of Boston to account for his actions and the feeling finally became so intense that Boylston and Mather were forced to prepare a joint pamphlet in their own defense which appeared about Sept. 1, 1721 (*Some account of what is said of Inoculating or Transplanting the Small Pox By the Learned Dr. Emanuel Timonius, and Jacobus Pylarinus . . . Answer to the scruples of many about the Lawfulness of this Method*). Parts I and III of this work were by Mather, Part II chiefly by Boylston. There also appeared during these months a series of letters and pamphlets reporting the progress of Boylston's inoculations. Kittredge has pointed out that probably all were draughted by Mather, but they are to be looked upon as joint contributions since Boylston supplied the chief data. We may list them as follows: (1) "The Little Treatise on the Smallpox," June 29, 1721 (published in Mather's *The Angel of Bethesda,* 1722–23, pp. 112–41); (2) the so-called "Dummer Letter," *An Account of the Method and Success of Inoculating the Small-Pox, in Boston in New England,* dated Sept. 7, 1721 (published anonymously London, 1722); (3) "A Faithful Account of what has occur'd under the late Experiments of the Small-Pox . . . Published, partly to put a stop unto that unaccountable way of Lying . . . and partly for the Information & Satisfaction of our Friends in other Places," *Boston Gazette,* Oct. 30, 1721 (anonymous); (4) *Sentiments on the Small Pox Inoculated* (folio broad-sheet, Boston, Nov. 23, 1721); (5) "The way of Proceeding in the Small Pox inoculated in New England," *Philosophical Transactions,* no. 370, dated Nov. 30, 1721 (anonymous); (6) "Curiosa Variolarum," Mar. 10, 1721/22, an unpublished letter to J. Jurin of the Royal Society; (7) "The Case of the Small-Pox Inoculated; further Cleared," May 4, 1823 (unpublished, and also to Jurin, Original MS. in American Antiquarian Society Library). By the end of February 1721/22, Boylston had inoculated 241 persons of whom only six died after inoculation, and of these at least four had contracted the disease before inoculation. He did not publish his results under his own name until 1726, when he issued in London *An Historical*

Account of the Small-pox inoculated in New England dedicated to Princess Caroline. A second edition was brought out in Boston in 1730. Meanwhile, Boylston, at Sir Hans Sloane's invitation, had spent some two years in London in 1724–26 during which time he prepared his book and lectured to the Royal College of Physicians and to the Royal Society of which in July 1726 he was elected Fellow. However, he did not inoculate while in England. Boylston's *Historical Account* showed that he kept careful records of everything he did. The results are logically set forth and clearly tabulated, and the work is in every way a masterly clinical presentation,—the first of its kind from an American physician.

On returning to Boston, Boylston, having accomplished his great work, settled down quietly to a comfortable practise, inoculating from time to time when an epidemic threatened. He corresponded with his friends in London (see Sloane MSS. 4055) but his only published communication was the "Ambergris in Whales" which appeared in 1726 in the *Philosophical Transactions,* XXXIII, 193. He retired from practise in the forties and spent his declining years on his farm in Brookline raising highly-bred horses. At the age of eighty-four he was seen breaking a colt. He died on Mar. 1, 1766, after many years of pulmonary trouble (mentioned in his letter of Dec. 19, 1737, to Sir Hans Sloane), and was buried in the old cemetery at Brookline. Boylston was married on Jan. 18, 1705, to Jerusha Minot of Boston by whom he had eight children. The Boylston academic foundations in Harvard University were left by Ward Nicolas Boylston, grandnephew of Zabdiel Boylston. Those at the Medical School were left in honor of the inoculator.

[There is an excellent paper by Reginald H. Fitz, "Zabdiel Boylston, Inoculator, and the epidemic of smallpox in Boston in 1721," in *Bull. Johns Hopkins Hospital,* 1911, XXII, 315–27. The perplexing question of Boylston's relation to Cotton Mather in the authorship of the earlier anonymous inoculation pamphlets has been dealt with extensively by G. L. Kittredge in his "Lost Works of Cotton Mather," *Proc. Mass. Hist. Soc.,* Feb. 1912, pp. 418–79. For Boylston's relation to Douglass, Geo. H. Weaver's paper on Douglass (*Bull. Soc. Medical Hist. of Chicago,* 1921, XI, 229–59) may be consulted. The place of Boylston in the history of variolation is discussed by A. C. Klebs in his "Historic Evolution of Variolation," *Bull. Johns Hopkins Hospital,* 1913, XXIV, 69–83. The account of Boylston's life in Jas. Thacher's *Am. Medical Dict.* (1828) is the most extensive of the early accounts, but is inaccurate in many details. Photostats of Boylston letters and manuscripts were furnished the present writer by the authorities of the British Museum, the Royal Society, and the Mass. Hist. Soc.]

J. F. F.

BOYNTON, CHARLES BRANDON (June 12, 1806–Apr. 27, 1883), Presbyterian and Congregational clergyman, author, was born in West Stockbridge, Mass. The Boyntons were among the early settlers of the township. The names of his parents are not recorded, but they may have been Henry and Mary (Meacham) Boynton (J. F. and C. H. Boynton, pp. 234, 285; and H. Child, *Gazetteer of Berkshire County, Mass., 1725–1885,* 1885, p. 389). After attending the Stockbridge Academy he became a member of the class of 1827 at Williams College, but on account of ill health left in the senior year without taking his degree. Thereafter he engaged in business, was president of the first railroad in Berkshire County, studied and practised law, was a justice of the Berkshire County court and a member of the Massachusetts House of Representatives. On Nov. 5, 1834, he married Maria Van Buskirk of Troy, N. Y., by whom he had seven children. Having studied theology privately with the Rev. Mr. Woodbridge of Spencertown, N. Y., he was ordained by the Columbia Presbytery in October 1840. He held charges at Housatonic, Mass., 1840–45, and at Lansingburg, N. Y., 1845–46, and then went to Cincinnati to the Vine Street Church, at that time the Sixth Presbyterian, where he remained till March 1856. While in the West, Boynton became actively interested in the anti-slavery movement. In the autumn of 1854 he was one of a party sent to explore and report upon the climate, soil, productions, general resources, and promise of the territory of Kansas. His report, *A Journey Through Kansas* (1855), is an interesting account of the country before the trouble over slavery had grown acute. From 1856 to 1857 he was in his native Berkshires again as pastor of the South Church in Pittsfield. He then returned to the Vine Street Church in Cincinnati, only to leave it to be chaplain of the House of Representatives from 1865 to 1869. While in Washington he was pastor of several churches and a teacher in the United States Naval Academy. Meanwhile he was busy writing. In 1856 he had published anonymously *The Russian Empire: its Resources, Government, and Policy.* In 1864 appeared *English and French Neutrality and the Anglo-French Alliance, in their Relations to the United States and Russia.* Some chapters from this work were republished in 1865 as *The Navies of England, France, America, and Russia,* and the whole book, considerably revised, was reissued in 1866 as *The Four Great Powers: England, France, Russia, and America: their Policy, Resources, and Probable Future.* In these books Boynton advocated a strong navy and an alliance, formal or informal, with Russia to offset the encroachments of England and France, but his understanding of world politics was not equal to his earnestness and patriotism. In 1867–68 he brought out in two ponderous, stodgy volumes a *History of the Navy during the Rebellion*, a semi-official work, for which he had access to the archives of the Navy Department. He was pastor of the Vine Street Church in Cincinnati for the third time from 1873 to 1877, and died at the home of a daughter in Cincinnati on Apr. 27, 1883.

[*Congreg. Yearbook for 1884*, p. 20; *Cincinnati Enquirer*, Apr. 28, 1883; *Gen. Cat. of the Officers and Grads. of Williams Coll. 1795–1910* (1910); J. F. and C. H. Boynton, *The Boynton Family* (1897), p. 234. Several of Boynton's sermons have been published as pamphlets.]

G. H. G.

BOYNTON, EDWARD CARLISLE (Feb. 1, 1824–May 13, 1893), soldier, a descendant of John Boynton, who came from England to Salem, Mass., in 1638, was the son of Thomas Boynton, who served as an officer in the War of 1812, and of Sophia (Cabot) Boynton. He was born at Windsor, Vt., was appointed a cadet at the Military Academy in 1841, and graduated in 1846 in the class of McClellan and Stonewall Jackson. He was commissioned in the artillery, and served with Duncan's battery in the latter part of Gen. Taylor's campaign in Mexico. Joining the army of Gen. Scott, he was present at the siege of Vera Cruz, the battles of Cerro Gordo, Contreras, and Churubusco, and several minor actions, being severely wounded at Churubusco. After the Mexican War, he was assigned to duty at West Point, and remained there for seven and a half years, following this with a few months' service with the expedition against the Seminoles in Florida. While teaching at West Point he had acquired considerable reputation as a scientist, which led to the offer of professorships at the University of Mississippi and at the New York State Normal School. Accepting the former, he resigned his commission as first lieutenant (Feb. 16, 1856), and took up his duties as professor of chemistry, mineralogy, and geology. The outbreak of the Civil War created a situation intolerable for a Unionist professor in a seceding state. Although Boynton declined the colonelcy of a Vermont regiment, offered him in May 1861, relations continued strained, and finally (Sept. 6, 1861) he was dismissed from the institution for "evincing a want of attachment to the Government of the Confederate States." As an enemy of the existing order of things, his presence was not desired in Mississippi, nor could he wish to remain there, but with war flagrant the authorities were not inclined to put the services of an ex-officer of the army at the disposal of the United States. As a condition of his being allowed to depart, they wisely exacted a pledge from him that he would not serve in the field against the Confederacy. For this reason he declined the colonelcy of another Vermont regiment, which was at once offered him. His abilities were utilized without breach of faith on his part, however, by his appointment as a captain in the 11th Infantry, and assignment to duty as adjutant and quartermaster of the Military Academy. His case may offer infinite opportunity for the casuist to exercise his ingenuity. At least once in 1864 the War Department grew restive, or perhaps forgetful, and considered ordering him to join his regiment in the field, but the idea was abandoned—fortunately, one must think. After all, the position he occupied was an important one, and had to be filled by some one, in war or peace. He continued on duty as adjutant at West Point until 1871, though he was relieved from the additional labor of the quartermaster's office as soon as the war ended. In 1872 he resigned from the army, and spent the remainder of his life at Newburgh, N. Y. For eight years he was superintendent of the water-works, and afterward was for some time secretary of the local board of trade. During his career as a teacher he had published several papers on chemical subjects. His long residence at West Point, with its revolutionary associations, turned his interest to historical matters, and led to the publication of a *History of West Point, and its Military Importance during the American Revolution; and the Origin and Progress of the United States Military Academy*, a large part of which is devoted to a minute study of the topography of the neighborhood, from a military viewpoint, to the system of defenses erected during the Revolution, and to the administration of the fortress during that period. Soon after his removal to Newburgh, he became a member of the board of trustees of Washington's headquarters there, and for several years was president of the Historical Society of Newburgh Bay and the Highlands. He compiled and published a collection of Washington's orders, issued at Newburgh. He also wrote some minor historical papers, and was part author of Webster's *Army and Navy Dictionary*, published in 1864. He married Mary J. Hubbard.

[Obituaries in the *Newburgh Daily Jour.*, May 13, 1893; *Bull. Ass. Grads. U. S. Mil. Acad.*, 1893, pp. 138–42; G. W. Cullum, *Biog. Reg.* (3rd ed., 1891), II, 265–66; unpublished War Department Records.]

T. M. S.

BOZEMAN, JOHN M. (1835–Apr. 20, 1867), trail-maker, was a native of Georgia, where he left a wife and two children, to try his luck at placer mining near Cripple Creek, Colo., in 1861.

Learning of rich gravels in Montana he set out with eleven companions, arriving in Virginia City in June 1862. The bonanzas of Idaho and of Alder Gulch, Bannack, and Virginia City were bringing thousands into Montana. The Mullan Road from Walla Walla to Fort Benton, opened in 1861, provided an approach from the west, but gold seekers from the east only reached the diggings by boat to the head of navigation of the Missouri and thence by road, or else by an equally circuitous route over the Oregon trail to Fort Hall and north to Virginia City. It was to discover a more direct route east that Bozeman and his partner, John M. Jacobs, left Bannack in the winter of 1862–63. Venturing along the old trail into the territory east of the Big Horn Mountains reserved by treaty to the Indians, and apparently quite insensible of danger, they were attacked by a party of marauding Sioux, robbed of horses, guns, and ammunition, and turned adrift on foot, finally reaching the Platte after severe hardships. Untaught by experience, Bozeman returned the following spring at the head of a party of freighters and emigrants, but, when about a hundred miles north of Fort Laramie, the party was induced by an Indian attack to follow the safer route west of the Big Horn Mountains via Bridger Pass into Virginia City. The determined Bozeman, however, again venturing across the Indian country, and traveling chiefly by night, finally crossed the divide (Bozeman Pass) between the Yellowstone and the Gallatin and reached Virginia City. In 1864 he conducted one of many caravans over his "road." The Indians had become increasingly menacing as their treaty lands were invaded, and in 1865–66 the government undertook to police the Bozeman road by successive Powder River expeditions and the erection of Forts Reno, Phil Kearny, and C. F. Smith. The Fetterman massacre of December 1866 reëstablished by force of arms the Indian claim, and led to the abandonment of the Bozeman road south and east of Fort C. F. Smith. Still blind to the Indian danger, Bozeman and a companion left Virginia City, on Apr. 16, 1867. Four days later, at the crossing of the Yellowstone, five Indians approached their noon camp. Assuming them to be friendly Crows, Bozeman welcomed them only to discover too late that they were Blackfeet. He was instantly shot, while his wounded companion escaped. He thus at last paid the penalty of ineptitude and lack of judgment in dealing with the hazards of the country.

[G. R. Hebard and E. A. Brininstool, *The Bozeman Trail* (1922); *Mont. Hist. Soc. Trans.*, vol. I, 1895; *Montana Post*, May 4, 1867.] H. C. D.

BOZEMAN, NATHAN (Mar. 25, 1825–Dec. 16, 1905), physician, the son of Nathan and Harriet (Knotts) Bozeman, was of Dutch descent. He was born in Butler County, Ala., studied medicine at the University of Louisville, graduating in 1848, and began practise in Montgomery, Ala., where he became intimately acquainted with Marion Sims and his work. It was at that time that Sims first succeeded in curing vesico-vaginal fistula, a problem on which the gynecologists of Europe and America had worked for years without arriving at a solution. Bozeman took great interest in this question. He improved Sims's method by substituting the "button" or "shot" suture for Sims's clamp suture; this was a great advance as the new suture practically eliminated failures. In 1859 Bozeman for the first time performed kolpokleisis as a means of treating vesico-vaginal fistula. In the same year he made a trip to Europe demonstrating his methods. On his return he settled in New Orleans but soon the Civil War broke out and Bozeman served during the whole four years as a surgeon in the Confederate Army. After the war he settled in New York, where he established a private hospital for women. In 1868 he was attacked by Prof. Simon of Heidelberg on a question of priority concerning the operation of kolpokleisis. He at once crossed the Atlantic to defend his position by demonstrating his own method before the medical faculty of Heidelberg. In 1878 he was appointed surgeon to the New York State Women's Hospital. The work being too heavy, he resigned this position in 1888 and established a private sanitarium. He was a masterful surgeon, most skilful in adapting established methods to individual cases. He was remarkably successful in operations for vesical and fæcal fistulæ in women, particularly one complication of pyelitis, which he treated by catheterizing the ureter through a vesico-vaginal opening (1887–88). He invented a self-retaining vaginal speculum and an operating chair for the knee-chest position. His most important writings are: *Remarks on Vesico-Vaginal Fistula with an Account of a New Mode of Suture* (1856); *Application of the Button Suture to the Treatment of Varicose Dilatation of Veins* (1860); *The Gradual Preparatory Treatment of the Complications of Urinary and Fæcal Fistulæ in Women* (1887); *Chronic Pyelitis Successfully Treated by Kolpo-Uretero-Cystotomy* (1888). He was twice married: first, to Fannie Lamar of Macon, Ga., and, second, to Mrs. Amelia (Lamar) Ralston of the same city. He died of apoplexy, Dec. 16, 1905.

[Sketch of Bozeman by his son, Nathan Bozeman, in H. A. Kelly, *Cyc. of Am. Medic. Biog.* (1912), vol.

I; sketch in *Physicians and Surgeons of the U. S.* (1878), ed. by Wm. B. Atkinson; *Album, Am. Gynecol. Soc.*, 1918, p. 68. A complete list of Bozeman's writings is contained in the *Cat. of the Surgeon-General's Lib.*, ser. 1, vol. II, and ser. 2, vol. II.] A. A—n.

BOZMAN, JOHN LEEDS (Aug. 25, 1757–Apr. 20, 1823), lawyer, historian, the son of John and Lucretia (Leeds) Bozman, belonged to an old Maryland family and was born on an estate later named "Belleville" in Oxford Neck, Talbot County, Md. When he was ten years old, his father died, and his education was then guided by his grandfather, William Leeds. The youth attended Back Creek Academy, afterwards Washington Academy, Somerset County, and later entered Pennsylvania College (the University of Pennsylvania). After his graduation he became a lawyer's apprentice to Judge Robert Greensborough in 1777. His interest in law and his natural ambition caused him to go to England in 1784 for further study at the Middle Temple, London. On his return to Maryland he was admitted to the bar. He was a Federalist with perhaps Tory leanings imbibed from his grandfather. In 1794 he ran for a seat in the lower house of Maryland but was defeated, his record of public office-holding being limited to the appointive office of deputy attorney-general under Luther Martin, 1789–1807. When he abandoned the practise of law and retired to his farm is not known, but from that time he devoted himself to the accumulation of a library and literary pursuits (Bozman Papers, in the Library of Congress). He intended to write a series of "Law tracts or Essays on Several subjects arising under the Laws of Maryland," but prepared only one, under the title *Observations on the Statute of 21 Jac. I. Ch. 16 in application to Estates tail* (1794). He was also interested in the American Colonization Society. In support of the society's plan to transport the whole negro race to Africa he published an essay in 1820 entitled, *An Essay on the Late Institution of the American Society for Colonizing the Free People of Color of the United States.* His chief literary production was a history of Maryland on which he began working about 1805 but which he left uncompleted when he learned that another man had undertaken the same task. In 1811, however, he published what he had already written, under the title *A Sketch of the History of Maryland during the Three First Years after its Settlement.* Later, when the other author died, Bozman resumed his own work with the intention of writing a history of Maryland from its earliest settlement to the Confederation, but illness intervened, making him again discontinue his studies a few years before his death in 1823. The manuscript at the time of his death was complete to 1660 and practically ready for printing. His nephew, John Leeds Kerr, offered it to the Maryland legislature for publication. It was accepted and published in two volumes in 1837, under the title *The History of Maryland, from its First Settlement . . . to the Restoration.* The first volume is merely introductory, and the history itself is contained in the second. It is based on a study of the records at Annapolis and of printed works, but though accurate and detailed is not final, for much material has since been uncovered. The account is prejudiced against the Puritans, and this is in part responsible for the biased treatment of the Claiborne episode. It is not a finished history but is valuable as material for history (Justin Winsor, *Narrative and Critical History of the United States,* III, 560).

[The chief source is *A Memoir of John Leeds Bozman* by Samuel A. Harrison, Fund Pubs. No. 26 (1888). There is also a sketch of Bozman in a *Hist. of Talbot County, Md., 1661–1861* (1915) by Oswald Tilghman, but the account practically duplicates that of Harrison.] H. B–C.

BRACE, CHARLES LORING (June 19, 1826–Aug. 11, 1890), philanthropist, born in Litchfield, Conn., came on both sides of old and distinguished New England stock. His father, John Brace [*q.v.*], was the grandson of Capt. Abel Brace, a Revolutionary officer, and was descended from Stephen Brace (or Bracy) who came from England to Hartford in 1660; his mother, Lucy Porter of Maine, was related to the Beechers and was a descendant of Rufus King. Charles, efficiently guided in his studies, and in trout-fishing, by his father, was ready for college at the age of fourteen but delayed two years, entering Yale in 1842 and graduating in 1846. He then taught country schools (Ellington and Winchendon, Conn.) for a year, returning to New Haven in 1847 to study theology in Yale Divinity School. The course there bred more doubts than convictions, and two ensuing years in New York turned his attention away from theology to thoughts of work among the delinquent classes of the metropolis. In the fall of 1850 he took brief walking trips in Ireland, England, and the Rhine country with two life-long Connecticut friends, John and Frederick Olmstead [*q.v.*], then lingered on through the winter in Berlin, and in the spring ventured into Hungary, where he was imprisoned for a month as a Kossuth sympathizer, being released through the efforts of the United States minister, only after thirteen trials by court martial. Upon his return to America he published *Hungary in 1851* (1852) and *Home Life in Germany* (1853). In 1854 he made a flying trip to the British Isles to bring back as his bride Letitia Neill whom he had met upon his previous visit. Meanwhile he had definitely entered upon his life-work. In 1853 he was influential in founding in New York City the Children's Aid Society, an organization which, under his direction, worked mainly among the foreign immigrants, establishing cheap lodging houses, industrial schools, night schools, summer camps, and sanitariums. It also, in the course of years, found homes and employment in the country for more than 100,000 city waifs. Brace was a pioneer in modern philanthropic methods, grounding all his efforts on the principle of self-help, and opposing every charitable enterprise which tended toward pauperization. During his years of work in the slum districts he showed himself brave, resourceful, and tolerant, inspired by a belief in the infinite worth of every human soul as having that within it "which shall live when the old world has passed by." His remarkable success brought him an international reputation, and he had a large circle of distinguished friends on both sides of the Atlantic, including Emerson, Theodore Parker, Asa Gray, Henry Ward Beecher, Darwin, John Morley, and John Stuart Mill. Of several later trips to Europe, the last, taken in quest of health, ended at Campfer in the Engadine, where he died on Aug. 11, 1890. In addition to his earlier books, Brace was the author of: *The Norse Folk; or, a Visit to the Homes of Norway and Sweden* (1857); *The Best Method of Disposing of our Pauper and Vagrant Children* (1859); *The Races of the Old World: a Manual of Ethnology* (1863); *Short Sermons to Newsboys* (1866); *The New West; or, California in 1867–68* (1869); *The Dangerous Classes of New York, And Twenty Years' Work Among Them* (1872); *Gesta Christi; or, a History of Humane Progress under Christianity* (1882); *The Unknown God; or, Inspiration Among Pre-Christian Races* (1890).

[The chief source is *The Life of Chas. Loring Brace, largely told in his own letters* (1894), edited by his daughter, Emma Brace. The N. Y. press contained obituaries at the time of his death.] E. S. B.

BRACE, DEWITT BRISTOL (Jan. 5, 1859–Oct. 2, 1905), physicist, son of Lusk and Emily (Bristol) Brace, was born at Wilson, N. Y., received his preparatory education at Lockport, and graduated from Boston University in 1881. Then followed two years' graduate study at Johns Hopkins University, and two years more at the University of Berlin (Ph.D. 1885) to which he was attracted by the fame of Helmholtz and Kirchhoff. After a year as acting assistant professor of physics at the University of Michigan, he became instructor in the department of chemistry and physics at the University of Nebraska. In 1888 he became head of the newly established department of physics, a position held until his death. In 1901 he married Elizabeth Russell Wing, a former graduate of the University of Nebraska.

His first decade at Nebraska was concerned with the cares incident to building up a department of physics and starting what later became the department of electrical engineering. Having very meager funds at his disposal, he converted a university carpenter into an instrument maker who constructed most of the institution's first real laboratory equipment. Later, he developed an electrician's helper into a most efficient lecture demonstrator and manipulator with whose help he eventually worked up an unexcelled series of lecture experiments. Little evidence exists, outside the memory of his students, of any research activity in that period. The university authorities, frowning for policy's sake upon such a misuse of public funds, cleared away, under trivial excuse, the key part of a set-up he had made, with borrowed apparatus, for remeasuring the velocity of light. He was by no means inactive, however, for during this time an interesting electric generator and also a rectifier were designed, constructed, and patented. Ill luck attended him here, too, for both became obsolete before they could be promoted. With scientific instruments he was more successful; among several, the Brace spectrophotometer (described in 1899) and the Brace Half Shade Elliptic Polarizer and Compensator (described in 1904) are of recognized merit.

The second decade was one of constantly accelerated scientific production. It was initiated in 1896 by a change occurring in his staff which led to the appointment of two young instructors actively interested in research and two teaching graduate students who formed the nucleus of a graduate organization. This called for research problems, research equipment, and graduate courses in theoretical physics. To create an atmosphere of research, he deemed it necessary that all should be busy with it. By shouldering the lion's share of both undergraduate and graduate instruction, he allowed his associates a generous part of their time for the purpose and at the same time impressed them with the importance of this phase of their duties.

His own chosen field was optics, and here he was primarily concerned with the fundamental principles affecting the velocity of propagation of light. In his doctor's thesis, he had described (G. M. Wiedermann, *Annalen der Physik und*

Chemie, Neue Folge, XXVI, 1885, p. 576) not entirely conclusive attempts to prove that a clockwise circular vibration travels along a magnetic field in a material medium with a velocity different from that of a counter clockwise vibration. Sixteen years later, he proved by a very ingenious device that the refractive index of such a medium differed for the two vibrations to an extent that permitted observable separation of a plane polarized incident beam into two beams circularly polarized in opposite directions. Likewise, either he or his students were engaged for some years in studying the effects of an electric field, static and kinetic mechanical stresses, and "æther drift" on the velocity of propagation of light through matter. These investigations were uniformly distinguished by the sensitiveness of the methods used for detecting or measuring the effects.

Although fifteen contributions under his own name and about an equal number by his students complete the list of publications for which he was primarily responsible, these dealt largely with the fundamental problems of the day and were as crucial as the method of attack could possibly be made. The more important of them are to be found in the *London, Edinburgh, and Dublin Philosophical Magazine,* October 1897, November 1899, April 1901, February 1903, April 1904, July 1905, September 1905, November 1905; and in the *Physical Review,* January 1904, November 1905. Brace also translated and edited *The Laws of Radiation and Absorption* (1901), consisting of memoirs by Prévost, Kirchhoff, and others.

[*Who's Who in America,* 1903–05; Ellery W. Davis, sketch in *Science,* Oct. 27, 1905; *Neb. State Jour.,* Oct. 3, 1905.] C. A. S.

BRACE, JOHN PIERCE (Feb. 10, 1793–Oct. 18, 1872), educator, author, editor, was born in Litchfield, Conn., son of Susan (Pierce) and James Brace, writing-master in Miss Sarah Pierce's school. His aunt (Sarah) superintended his education, sending him to Williams College, where he was graduated in 1812. He made some preparation for the ministry, sudied medicine, and spent two years in the Litchfield Law School. But he was born for one profession, and in 1814 became head teacher for Miss Pierce, later becoming associate principal and gradually taking the real leadership. He widened the course of study, adding botany, astronomy, and chemistry to the curriculum. When the school was incorporated in 1827 he was also made secretary of the board of trustees. During these years the school was a leader in the education of women. The establishment of other schools and changed conditions lessening its prosperity, Brace resigned in 1832 to become head of the Hartford Female Seminary. The fifteen years he was principal made this school equally notable. He later taught at the academy in New Milford for two or three years. In 1849 he entered upon a new work, the editorship of the *Hartford Courant,* then a small paper which could be prepared for publication by one person. His office, a dingy little sanctum, was filled with books, many of them valuable. Traces of his earlier profession appear occasionally in his editorials, one entitled "Criticisms" attacking common mistakes in English. At the age of seventy (1863), he retired to the old family home in Litchfield. A relative bequeathed him a "handsome competence," and although he was confined by rheumatism to a wheeled chair, and sometimes even bedridden, he spent his days not unhappily, practically living in his library among his books. He died in Litchfield, and was buried in Hartford.

He was twice married: first, to Lucy Porter of Portland, Me., descendant of Rufus King, and sister of Mrs. Lyman Beecher; and, second, to Louisa Moreau of Hartford. Contemporaries emphasized his "vast and multifarious acquirements," his "reputation as one of the most cultured men of his time," and his passion for imparting knowledge. His interests seemed all-embracing, including subjects like heraldry and astrology. He collected minerals, a valuable herbarium, and, as the girls reported, "bugs . . . and a plenty of butterflies and spiders." He found time to correspond with foreign scientists, and exchanged specimens. Besides his "exquisite feeling for nature," he was a famous fisherman and "gardened furiously." He left a few poems—Indian ballads and descriptions of local scenery—written for the school and for a literary coterie in Litchfield; some scientific articles; and two novels, *Tales of the Devils* (1847), and *The Fawn of the Pale Faces or, Two Centuries Ago* (1853), a story of early Connecticut, "elegantly written" in the prevailing fashion.

[Emily Noyes Vanderpoel, *Chronicles of a Pioneer School* (1903); Emma Brace (ed.), *Life of Chas. Loring Brace* (1894); Samuel Orcutt, *Hist. of the Towns of New Milford and Bridgewater, Conn.* (1882); P. K. Kilbourne, *Sketches and Chronicles of the Town of Litchfield, Conn.* (1859); A. C. White (ed.), *Hist. of the Town of Litchfield, Conn.* (1920).] M. H. M.

BRACHVOGEL, UDO (Sept. 26, 1835–Jan. 30, 1913), author, the son of Ferdinand Brachvogel, was born at Herrengrebin near Danzig. He received a classical education, and studied law at the universities of Jena and Breslau. After passing his first state examination in 1858, he visited Vienna, where he counted among his friends the poet Friedrich Halm (Baron Münch-Bellinghausen), and the tragedienne Juli Rettich. There he published his first volume of poems, under the title *Jugendgedichte* (1860). He did not establish himself as a lawyer, but during the next six years, 1860–66, lived in Hungary as clerk or agent of a private company. When the latter dissolved Brachvogel emigrated to the United States. In 1867 he was in St. Louis on the editorial staff of the German newspaper *Die Westliche Post,* and in 1875 he removed to New York in answer to a call to the editorship of the *Belletristisches Journal,* for many years a leading German literary journal published weekly. He was married on Jan. 12, 1878, to Käthe Müller of Oldenburg, Germany, whom he met at the home of his friend, Carl Schurz. In 1886 he resided in Omaha, Neb., where at first he edited a German political daily, but soon became the agent of the Germania Life Insurance Company of New York. As general agent of the same company he was subsequently transferred to Chicago, but the last years of his life he spent in New York City as correspondent of various journals in America and abroad. A second volume of his poems appeared shortly before his death, in 1912, entitled *Gedichte* (Leipzig and New York), with a dedication to his wife, and a very good portrait of the author. Upon this volume of German verse, an excellent collection of the best of his many scattered ballads and metrical translations, Brachvogel's reputation as an author will mainly depend. His prose style, especially in his late period, does not satisfy high standards. In his poetical work the influence of Ferdinand Freiligrath is apparent both in form and spirit. We find the same devotion to the theme of personal and political freedom, and the fondness for the descriptive historical ballad. Noteworthy examples of the latter type are the poems: "Capua," "Römische Nacht," "Jacobus de Benedictis," "Persepolis," "Canossa," "Hängende-Gärten Mythe," "Commœdia divina und Tragœdia humana." In the group "Americana" there are two pieces which take rank with the best produced by German verse-writers in America, *viz.*: "Ne-ah-ga-rah (Donner der Wasser)," and "Indianer-Sommer"; there are also occasional poems above the level of daily journalistic effort, as: "La Cuba Libre," "Die Maine," "Titanic-Requiem." Some of the earlier poems as: "Pour la Gloire," "Die Spinnerin," "Eine Ungenannte" show flashes of poetic inspiration arising from deep human sympathy; the selections from American poets, Longfellow, Bret Harte, Joaquin Miller, Poe, Whittier, and others, exhibit the author's artistic skill as a translator. The most ambitious among Brachvogel's prose translations was his rendering of Bret Harte's *Gabriel Conroy,* published in 1876 (Stuttgart), a year after the appearance of the original. An appreciative essay on Bret Harte appeared shortly after (in *Deutsche Bücherei XIV,* 1882). Brachvogel similarly introduced Bayard Taylor to German readers and translated Hawthorne's *Scarlet Letter* for Walter Damrosch's opera on that theme (1894). Others of his published essays were: "Die deutsche Presse in den Vereinigten Staaten" (in Armin Tenner's *Amerika,* Berlin and New York, 1884) and *Das Theissland und sein Dichter* (New York, 1881). The latter is reminiscent of Brachvogel's early residence in Hungary, and euolgizes Hungary's greatest lyrical poet Sandor Petöfy, a martyr to the cause of political freedom in the Hungarian revolution of 1849. The chief value of the essay consists in the author's artistic rendering into German of some of the choicest lyrics of the Hungarian poet-patriot.

Brachvogel was born into an age of old world culture when literature and journalism were not yet distinct callings, and when lyrical composition was the pastime of most persons of education and refinement. He was too young to take part in the revolutionary struggle of 1848–49, as did Hecker, Schurz, Sigel, Brentano, Ottendorfer and many others who became journalists in the United States and continued there the fight for liberty and union with pen and sword. Brachvogel arrived in the United States after the Civil War was over, nor was he of the aggressive disposition of his contemporary Joseph Pulitzer, associated with him in 1868 on the staff of the *Westliche Post* in St. Louis. At the latter's death Brachvogel corrected some of the legends that had grown up about the meteoric career of his much admired friend. (Cf. *Die Pulitzer Legende,* and *Aus Pulitzers Jugendjahren,* in *Rundschau zweier Welten,* ed. by G. S. Viereck, December 1911, and January 1912). Guided by a peaceful star, Udo Brachvogel was not a fighter, a leader, or man of action; he was an observer, a thinker, a contemplative poet.

[Alexander J. Schem, *Deutsch-amerikanisches Conversations-Lexicon* (New York, 1869–74); G. A. Zimmermann, *Deutsch in Amerika* (Chicago, 1892); G. A. Neef, *Vom Lande des Sternenbanners* (Heidelberg, 1905); *Jahrbuch des Verbands deutscher Schriftsteller in Amerika* (New York, 1911). G. S. Viereck in his article: "Udo Brachvogel, Deutsch-Amerikas grösster Balladendichter" (see *Das Buch der Deutschen in Amerika,* Philadelphia 1909, pp. 397–98), mentions a novel by Brachvogel, *King Corn* and several short stories, none of which have appeared in book form. It is probable that these and many other writings in prose and verse will be found among Udo Brachvogel's papers, which have been presented to the N. Y. Pub.

Lib. (see Descriptive Bulletin written by Mabel C. Weeks), by the surviving children of the author, Miss Claire Brachvogel and John K. Brachvogel (lawyer), both of New York City. The manuscript collection is unusually rich in letters of distinguished contemporaries in literary, artistic, and political careers.] A. B. F.

BRACKENRIDGE, HENRY MARIE (May 11, 1786–Jan. 18, 1871), lawyer, author, son of Hugh Henry Brackenridge [*q.v.*] and his first wife, was born in the frontier village of Pittsburgh. His mother died in 1788 and the early years of his life were spent in the homes of various friends and relatives in and near Pittsburgh. The elder Brackenridge began his son's education by setting him to the horn-book at the age of two. From this time lessons were his daily regimen. At the age of seven he was sent by flatboat on a rough and dangerous voyage to the village of St. Genevieve in upper Louisiana to learn French. After returning to Pittsburgh three years later, he studied English and the classics chiefly under his father's guidance, although he spent a short time at the Pittsburgh Academy. He derived from his father a love of reading, a wide range of interests, and a liberal political philosophy. His wit, too, was an inheritance; he was known as "the comical son of a comical father" (*Niles' Register,* Oct. 6, 1832, p. 96). He studied law in Pittsburgh and was there admitted to the bar in 1806. Then, after a few months with his father in Carlisle, he went to Baltimore, where, for over a year, he studied admiralty law and found solace in the social life of the city, and particularly in its bookstores and libraries, while he waited for the practise which never developed. From Baltimore he went to Somerset, Pa., but the western territory soon lured him with its promise of greater opportunities. The years 1810–14 were spent in Missouri and Louisiana in the practise of law, and in the pursuit of various studies suggested by his new environment. The Spanish language, which he learned in St. Louis, was of great value in his later career, while his researches in natural history, geography, and Indian antiquities found expression in articles for the *Missouri Gazette* which attracted the notice of Thomas Jefferson. In 1811 he made a voyage up the Missouri with Manuel Lisa of the Missouri Fur Company, keeping a journal which was later used by Irving as a source for his *Astoria* (1836).

In November 1811 Brackenridge left St. Louis for New Orleans. There he studied Spanish law, thus laying the foundation for his later participation in Spanish American affairs, and continued his research on subjects of territorial interest. Chapters on Louisiana were added to his articles on Missouri and his journal of the Missouri River voyage to form his first book, *Views of Louisiana* (Pittsburgh, 1814. Reviewed in *Edinburgh Review,* July 1819. German translation, Weimar, 1818). Until the War of 1812 Brackenridge was also very busy with legal work. He assisted in framing the legislative act for the judiciary system of Louisiana, and served as deputy attorney-general and as district judge. During the war he sent information to the government regarding British preparations for invading Louisiana (*Recollections,* p. 280). This correspondence led President Madison to suggest the possibility of his appointment to the diplomatic service. Tempted by the hope of a diplomatic career, Brackenridge went to Washington, but his appointment was not secured until 1817, and he spent the interim practising law in Baltimore, and as a member of the Maryland legislature. Also, he wrote, in six weeks, a spirited but rather rhetorical *History of the Late War* (Baltimore, 1816; revised edition, 1817. French translations, 1820, 1822. Italian translation, 1824). His earlier studies in New Orleans were utilized in an article on the boundaries of Louisiana for Walsh's *American Register* (1817).

In 1817, when the question of recognizing the South American nations was the great political issue, Brackenridge published a pamphlet, *South America, A Letter on the Present State of that Country to James Monroe.* He urged recognition, recommending an American foreign policy such as was later defined in the Monroe Doctrine. In England the pamphlet was viewed as being "in some degree official" (*The Pamphleteer,* XIII, 37), and the Spanish minister employed an English writer to answer it (*Recollections,* p. 286). In France it was translated by the Abbé de Pradt, Bishop of Malines and diplomat, who commented on the brilliant talents of its author (*Ibid.,* p. 287). In connection with this issue Brackenridge found his opportunity for diplomatic service. He was made secretary of the commission sent to study the political situation in South America. The character of his views and their weight with the ranking commissioner are indicated by a note in Adams's Diary: "Rodney, the President hinted, is under the influence of Brackenridge, a mere enthusiast" (J. Q. Adams, *Memoirs,* IV, 155). The *Voyage to South America* (1819), a study of the political, social, economic, and intellectual status of the country, shows, however, that although Brackenridge was an enthusiast, he recognized the weaknesses of the Spanish American republics.

After his return from South America, Brackenridge continued his service in the Maryland legislature where he supported such liberal measures as the bill designed to admit Jews to public office (Speech of Jan. 20, 1819, in *Speeches on the Jew Bill,* Philadelphia, 1829). In 1821 his knowledge of Spanish affairs secured for him service under Andrew Jackson, then governor of Florida. First as secretary and translator, then as judge, he remained in Florida until 1832, when Jackson removed him from office. In presenting his case in *Letters to the Public* (1832), he attacked Jackson bitterly. After this time Brackenridge took little part in public affairs save for a brief reëntry into politics in 1840–41 as congressman (*Congressional Globe,* 26 Cong., 2 Sess., pp. 14, 141), and as a member of the commission provided for in the Mexican Treaty of Apr. 11, 1839. His later years, spent in the town of Tarentum which he established on the large estate near Pittsburgh acquired through his marriage to Caroline Marie (1827), were devoted to private business and to literature. In 1834 he published his *Recollections of Persons and Places in the West,* a valuable source for the early social history of the West, as well as for the personal history of his own early years. His "Biographical Notice of H. H. Brackenridge" (*Southern Literary Messenger,* January 1842), and his *History of the Western Insurrection in Western Pennsylvania* (1859) are largely concerned with a defense of his father's part in the Whiskey Rebellion. Most of his minor writings of this period deal with political and legal subjects. When he died in 1871, his career had spanned almost the whole of the nation's history. He had, without attaining positions of the highest eminence, been an intelligent and liberal participant in public affairs and an enlightened commentator on them.

[The sources for Brackenridge's biography are his own writings, particularly *Recollections of Persons and Places in the West* (1834; enlarged and revised edition, 1868); *Views of Louisiana; together with a Journal of a Voyage up the Missouri River, in 1811* (1814); *A Voyage to South America* (2 vols., 1819); and *Letters to the Public* (1832). The most complete list of his writings is in Joseph Sabin's *Dictionary of Books Relating to America,* vol. II (1869). An obituary appeared in the *Pittsburgh Daily Gazette,* Jan. 19, 1871.]

C. M. N.

BRACKENRIDGE, HUGH HENRY (1748–June 25, 1816), jurist, author, belonged to a family which came from near Campbeltown, Scotland, to a farm in York County, Pa., in 1753. Their economic status was such that they were able to complete the journey only by selling their surplus clothing. Hugh Henry, who was five years old at the time of the migration, early showed great zeal and capacity for learning. Encouraged by his mother, a woman of ability and intellectual ideals, he began the study of the classics with the help of a neighbouring clergyman, and by the time he was thirteen years of age he had made notable progress, although his opportunities to secure reading matter were so limited that he often walked thirty miles to borrow books and newspapers. When he was fifteen years old he took charge of a school in Maryland in order to earn money for a higher education. About 1768 he entered Princeton, then under Dr. Witherspoon, where he served as master in the grammar school while he pursued his studies. He found congenial classmates in Philip Freneau and James Madison (Madison, *Writings,* 1900, I, 20, 22), who were, like himself, devoted to literature and attentive to political issues. In politics they were ardent Whigs. The Commencement poem, *The Rising Glory of America,* written by Brackenridge and Freneau in 1771 (published in 1772), is an expression of the growing national feeling. After his graduation Brackenridge, while head of an academy in Maryland, studied divinity. He took his master's degree at Princeton in 1774, writing *A Poem on Divine Revelation* for Commencement.

During the Revolution, Brackenridge contributed patriotic writings to the cause and served as chaplain. The first of his literary productions of this period were two plays, *The Battle of Bunker's Hill* (1776) and *The Death of General Montgomery* (1777). *The Battle of Bunker's Hill* was, according to Brackenridge's statement, written to be performed by the pupils in his academy. The theme of the drama, the superior fighting spirit of the American troops as compared with the British, was especially pointed by the device of putting praise of American valor into the mouths of the British officers, Howe and Gage. In the second play, *The Death of General Montgomery,* Brackenridge expressed bitter resentment against the instigation of Indian atrocities by the British. The Ghost of General Wolfe appears as a dramatic character to castigate the English government and to foretell the future greatness of the American Union. Both these dramas are written in dignified, if somewhat stilted, blank verse and are cast in the neo-classical mold, due attention being given to the dramatic unities. In style and structure they are superior to the other American plays of the time. Brackenridge, however, disavowed any ambitious dramatic intention in the compositions, insisting that they were designed only for academic and private performance. Evidence that they were used as the author intended is found in a list of plays performed by Harvard students at the time, which includes the titles of Brackenridge's pieces (Claude C. Robin, *New Travels through North America . . . in 1781,* English translation, Boston, 1784). His published sermons, *Six Political Discourses* (1788), were fiery exhortations to fight. During 1799 he edited the patriotic and literary *United States Magazine* in Philadelphia. Having given up the ministry on account of difficulties with the creed, he studied law with Samuel Chase in Annapolis, removing thence to the frontier village of Pittsburgh in 1781.

Pittsburgh was the scene of his most important work. He helped to stimulate the dawning cultural life of the community by assisting in the establishment of the first newspaper (*Pittsburgh Gazette,* 1786), the first bookstore (1789), and the Pittsburgh Academy (1787). He also had an active political career. In 1786–87 he was a member of the state assembly. In 1787–88 he was the foremost champion in the western country of the Federal Constitution, satirizing its opponents in contributions to the *Gazette;* and he was an unsuccessful candidate for the state constitutional convention. In the Whiskey Rebellion of 1793–94, Brackenridge, interested in the development of both the federal government and the western country, played a part which, though unsatisfactory to the insurrectionists, led federal officials to suspect him of disloyalty. He was, however, completely exonerated by Alexander Hamilton, who investigated his conduct (*Incidents of the Insurrection in the Western Parts of Pennsylvania,* 1795, II, 75–78).

His political experiences of this period found expression in many contributions to the local paper in ironical Hudibrastic verse and in prose. It was on the basis of these experiences, also, that he wrote his most important work, *Modern Chivalry,* a satirical picaresque novel which appeared in various parts from 1792 to 1815. *Modern Chivalry* was the first literary work of the West, and one of the most important American satires of its period. Written under the influence of Lucian, Swift, Samuel Butler, and Cervantes, it satirizes the various follies of the time, especially the social and political ambitions of the uneducated and the incapable. Although Brackenridge was a democrat, he did not accept the current romantic conception of "the people," having observed that the democratic fiat often made statesmen of illiterate persons.

Nevertheless, he was a leader of the Republican party in the West, and, as a reward for his exertions, he was appointed justice of the supreme court of Pennsylvania by Gov. McKean on Dec. 17, 1799. In 1801 he removed from Pittsburgh to Carlisle, where he resided until his death in 1816. His legal studies were the chief product of these years in Carlisle. He collaborated with the other members of the supreme court in a study of the English laws in force in Pennsylvania (1808). His chief contribution to legal literature was *Law Miscellanies* (1814). Brackenridge's political writings at this time included a campaign pamphlet for Gov. McKean (*The Standard of Liberty,* 1804) and informative newspaper articles on current affairs. His purely literary work of this later period showed deterioration. Additions to *Modern Chivalry* published in 1804–05 and 1815 are of interest chiefly for their criticism of new popular follies, such as the attack on the judiciary and the opposition to learning.

Brackenridge was married twice. The date of his first marriage and the name of his first wife, the mother of H. M. Brackenridge [*q.v.*], are unknown. In 1790, two years after her death, he married Sabina Wolfe, a farmer's daughter, for whose hand, in typically eccentric fashion, he proposed on their first meeting (John Pope, *A Tour through the Southern and Western Territories,* 1792, pp. 14–17). Although successful as a jurist, Brackenridge did his most important work as a writer of Revolutionary propaganda, and as a satirist of abuses in the new democracy. While his political activities, his eccentricity, and his caustic wit made for him many enemies, his ability and honesty won for him the respect of friends and enemies alike. He was, as portrayed by Gilbert Stuart, and as described by his own son, "a gentleman of the old school."

[H. M. Brackenridge's "Memoir of H. H. Brackenridge," *Southern Lit. Messenger,* Jan. 1842 (reprinted in *Modern Chivalry,* editions of 1846 and 1856), and *Recollections of Persons and Places in the West* (1834, revised edition 1868) are the chief sources. H. H. Brackenridge's *Incidents of the Insurrection in the Western Parts of Pa.* (1795) and *Gazette Publications* (1806) contain autobiographical material. Contemporary files of the *Pittsburgh Gazette* and *The Tree of Liberty* contain much material. C. F. Heartman's *Bibliography of the Writings of Hugh Henry Brackenridge* (1917) is indispensable. Brackenridge's professional career is surveyed in "Hugh Henry Brackenridge, Lawyer," by Myrl I. Eakin (*Western Pa. Hist. Mag.,* July 1927), and "Hugh Henry Brackenridge as a Judge of the State Supreme Court, 1799–1816," by Mildred Williams (*Ibid.,* Oct. 1927). C. M. Newlin's "The Writings of Hugh Henry Brackenridge" (*Ibid.,* Oct. 1927) is a study of his literary work. An article by D. P. Brown in the *Forum,* I, 396 ff., contains many colorful personal anecdotes.] C. M. N.

BRACKENRIDGE, WILLIAM D. (June 10, 1810–Feb. 3, 1893), botanist, gained his position in science by the exceptional opportunities offered in the celebrated expedition under the command of Capt. Wilkes. Born in Ayr, Scotland, he began life as a gardener's boy and rose to be head gardener of Dr. Patrick Neill's grounds at Edinburgh. Several years were spent on the Continent, especially in Poland and as a student under Friedrich Otto, the garden director at Berlin. Brackenridge came to America about 1837 in the employ of Robert Buist, the Philadelphia nurseryman, and in the following year he seized the incomparable opportunity offered by the fitting out of the expedition that was to explore the Pacific for the United States Government. The places left open for botanists on this trip were naturally coveted. Nuttall, by his previous travels in the Pacific, was preëminently fitted for the position, Rafinesque hinted that he had desired it, and Asa Gray was actually slated to fill the chief berth. But Gray resigned in order to work with Torrey in the publication of a flora of North America, and Brackenridge, then comparatively obscure, was appointed assistant botanist to the eminent Dr. Pickering, chief naturalist of the party. The six sailing vessels left Hampton Roads, Va., on Aug. 19, 1838. Briefly, the itinerary was from Virginia to Madeira, thence to Rio de Janeiro, around the Horn to Chile and Peru, with inland trips, as to Lima in the Andean highlands, and thence among the islands of the Pacific to Tahiti, Samoa, the Fiji Islands, New Caledonia, and Sydney, Australia. Inland trips were made in New South Wales, and thence the party proceeded to New Zealand, the Fijis, the Hawaiian Islands, and back to the North American continent where Washington, Oregon, and the Mt. Shasta country of California were explored. The party continued past the Hawaiian Islands once more, through the Ladrones to Manila, where interior Philippine trips were made, and then through the Sulu Archipelago to Singapore, the Cape of Good Hope, and St. Helena, till New York was reached on June 9, 1842, after nearly four years of sailing and scientific collecting. Species of plants to the number of 10,000, representing about 40,000 specimens, had been collected, besides about a hundred living plants and many seeds. The botanical gleanings of the trip formed the nucleus of the National Herbarium.

In Washington Brackenridge was given a small greenhouse and was entrusted with the growing of the living plants, in addition to the preparation of the report on the ferns of the expedition. He remained in competent charge of the rare living plants even after their removal to the new Botanical Garden, in 1850, at the foot of the Capitol, where to this day many may be seen. But though a good field botanist, Brackenridge lacked training in systematic botany, and the difficulties of making a scientific report on the ferns, with descriptions in both Latin and English, were embarrassing. In this Asa Gray was of assistance, intimating, indeed, in his letter to Engelmann of Dec. 7, 1853, that most of the valuable work was his own, a claim which overstresses Latinity and nomenclature. Certainly the *Filices, Including Lycopodiaceæ and Hydropterides,* volume XVI (1854) was Brackenridge's, and his scientific masterpiece. Unhappily, the quarto volume of text and the magnificent folio of plates were practically all destroyed by fire in 1856, so that they are the scarcest of the reports of the expedition, and indeed among the rarest of all modern botanical monographs of value. In 1855 Brackenridge purchased thirty acres near Baltimore, Md., and there spent the rest of his life. For some years he was horticultural editor of the *American Farmer,* but he spent most of his energies as a nurseryman and landscape architect, so that his influence may be traced in many of the older estates around Baltimore, in which city he died.

[An excellent bit of historical reconstruction by Dr. J. H. Barnhart in *Jour. N. Y. Bot. Garden,* XX, 117–24 is the most extensive and valuable contribution to the meager knowledge about Brackenridge. There is also a brief notice of him in the *Gardener's Mo.,* XXVI, 375–76.]

D. C. P.

BRACKETT, ANNA CALLENDER (May 21, 1836–Mar. 9, 1911), educator, was the eldest of the five children of Samuel E. and Caroline S. Brackett. She received an education at both public and private schools in and about Boston, among others at Mr. Abbott's noted academy for girls. This training she capped with a course at the state normal school at Framingham, Mass., which she completed in 1856. She first exercised her teaching abilities in East Brookfield, Mass. From there she went as an assistant to the high school at Cambridge, Mass. So highly, however, did the Framingham State Normal School rate its own product that Miss Brackett was called back there for two years as assistant principal. In 1860 she went to Charleston, S. C., to become vice-principal of a normal school there, but was forced to retire from the city after the bombardment of Fort Sumter. She then became principal of the normal school at St. Louis—the first woman to head a normal school in the United States. Hearing that New York City was much in need of a private school for girls she came East again in 1870 and with Ida M. Eliot, her assistant in St. Louis, established a school on West Thirty-ninth St. It was in the education of American girls that she found her major interest for the next twenty-five years. Her books, *The Education of American Girls* and *Woman and the Higher Education,* published in 1874 and 1893 respectively, set forth a program based on a high respect for woman's mental vigor. Her own school maintained very high standards, so high, in fact, that some of her pupils were admitted to advanced standing at institutions such as Vassar. She was greatly influenced by the German philosopher Rosenkranz in his treatment of general educational philosophy. Her command of this author in his native tongue enabled her to contribute a translation of his philosophy of education as the first volume of the International Education Series, edited by William T. Harris. She was thus enabled to fill what seemed to her, during her normal school work, a regrettable lack of any such thoroughgoing exposition of the fundamental principles of education as was available abroad. This philosophical interest of Miss Brackett was also manifest in a deeply religious nature. She was a thorough student of the Bible and for many years, even after her retirement from active teaching in 1895, continued her Bible classes. She was a very popular editor of a page in *Harper's Bazar* on passing thoughts, where in 1892 appeared her informal essay on "The Technique of Rest." This proved so popular that more articles of a similar nature were called for which were finally collected into a volume by that name. For the use of her school she made a collection of poetry in collaboration with Miss Eliot. So well was this received that a later edition was undertaken for family use. Miss Brackett herself left about 150 poems of which some are quite charming. As her health failed, she came to spend more and more time at her home at Stowe in the Green Mountains of Vermont. There she kept open house, especially for those needing rest.

[The best source of biographical material on Anna Callender Brackett is Miss Edith Kendall's *In Memoriam*, undertaken to raise a scholarship fund in her honor. Her name also appears in *Who's Who in America* up to her death. Her activities in the National Education Association are reported in the bulletins of that association for 1871 and 1872.] J. S. B.

BRACKETT, EDWARD AUGUSTUS (Oct. 1, 1818–Mar. 15, 1908), sculptor, was born in Vassalboro, Me., a descendant of Richard Brackett who settled in Braintree, Mass., in 1629, and a son of Reuben Brackett and Eliza (Starkey) Brackett. His parents were natives of Vassalboro, and members of the Society of Friends. His father was a farmer, clock-maker, and nurseryman. He was educated in the common schools of Vassalboro and at the Friends' School in Providence, R. I. His father moved to Lynn, Mass., and thence to Cincinnati in 1835. There Edward cut blocks for printing and began the study of art. In 1839, two years after his mother's death, he went to New York City, and a few months later to Washington, D. C., where he modeled a bust of Senator Tallmage. Returning to his Cincinnati home he was commissioned to make a bust of William Henry Harrison. In 1841 he bought a tract of wooded land at Winchester, then part of South Woburn, Mass., and there built a house after his own plans. A studio in Boston was opened in the same year. In 1842 he married Amanda, daughter of Zaccheus Folger of Cincinnati, who died in 1871, leaving him two sons and two daughters. In the following year he married Elizabeth F., daughter of James B. Bellville, of Mount Washington, Ohio, by whom he had one daughter. He made his reputation and is best remembered by his portrait busts of Bryant, Longfellow, Allston, Sumner, Choate, Benjamin F. Butler, John Brown, Garrison, Wendell Phillips, and others. His bust of Brown, in private ownership, was highly praised by Jarvis. The Worcester Art Museum owns his most ambitious work, "The Ship-Wrecked Mother and Child." He is represented by portrait busts in the Metropolitan Museum of Art and the Boston Athenæum. As a sculptor he was entirely self-taught. He did not limit his activities, however, to this field, but is said to have always had some outside interest, such as the rearing of bees or the cultivation of winter grapes in hothouses. He served for one year in the Civil War as first lieutenant and battalion quartermaster of the 1st Massachusetts Cavalry. Shortly after the war he became interested in the habits of fish and their increase by artificial propagation, which interest brought him to the attention of the newly appointed Fish Commission of Massachusetts. In 1869 he was appointed one of the commissioners on Land Fisheries and in 1873 he abandoned his other activities to devote his attention to the science of pisciculture. He was chairman of the commission for twenty-seven years during which time he made annual reports. He was the inventor of the hatching trap that is now in universal use, and of a fish way which has been successful even over the highest dams. He also experimented in raising Mongolian pheasants, quail, and grouse for the purpose of stocking the state of Massachusetts. His interests further included spiritualism and poetry. He wrote: *Materialized Apparitions; if not Beings from Another Life What are They?* (1886), and three volumes of verse, *Twilight Hours: or Leisure Moments of an Artist* (1845); *The World We Live In* (1902); and *My House: Chips the Builder Threw Away* (1904).

[Herbert I. Brackett, *Brackett Genealogy* (1907); H. T. Tuckerman, *Book of the Artists* (1867); *Artists' Year Book* (1903); Lorado Taft, *Hist. of Am. Sculpture* (1903); *New Eng. Hist. and Geneal. Reg.*, LXII, 313; *Boston Daily Globe*, Mar. 16, 1908.] L. M.

BRADBURY, JAMES WARE (June 10, 1802–Jan. 6, 1901), lawyer, senator, was born at

Parsonsfield, Me., the son of James Bradbury, a successful physician, and of Ann (Moulton) Bradbury. His great-grandfather was an active Whig of Revolutionary times, and among his ancestors was Robert Pike, the opponent of the persecution of the Quakers and of the witchcraft delusion. Bradbury fitted for college at Gorham Academy under Rev. Reuben Nasson and entered Bowdoin College as a sophomore in 1822. Among his classmates were Longfellow and Hawthorne and among other fellow students were William Pitt Fessenden and Franklin Pierce. On completing his course Bradbury ranked third in his class, standing just above Longfellow. After graduation he served as preceptor of Hallowell Academy for a year and studied law with two prominent Maine Democrats. After being admitted to the bar he took up his residence in Augusta. On Nov. 25, 1834, he was married to Eliza Ann Smith of that city. By unremitting industry, sound judgment as a counsellor, ability as an advocate, and strict integrity he won a high position at the bar. Among his clients were some of the principal railroads of the state and he appeared as counsel before courts and legislative committees. He drew many bills and was the author and champion of an important act protecting the rights of the smaller bondholders when a mortgage was foreclosed.

On coming to Augusta, in order to become acquainted with the people, he edited for a year the *Maine Patriot,* a Democratic paper. He usually avoided public office and stump speaking but he engaged actively in party management in the county and the state and was especially useful in maintaining harmony. In 1846 he was elected to the United States Senate as a compromise candidate. The Hamlin men and the conservatives had been deadlocked and rather than have the election fail Hamlin advised his friends to vote for Bradbury who though a conservative was a moderate one. Bradbury's action in the Senate justified the description. He strongly favored the compromise measures of 1850, and though these came to be regarded by many of New England's best men as a truckling to the South he never changed his opinion. Bradbury did not forget that his duty as a good Democrat was to smite the Whigs. His principal effort was the introduction of a resolution requesting information concerning President Taylor's removals from office and the delivery thereon of a very partisan speech. His most important individual constructive work was the preparing and championing a bill creating a Board of Accounts to pass on claims against the government. The bill did not become a law but the act establishing the Court of Claims, passed a few years later, closely resembled his bill. Bradbury gave much attention to bills public and private in which his constitutents were interested. One of his principal speeches was in behalf of the French Spoliation claimants, many of whom were Maine citizens. His chief opponent on this occasion was his college mate Senator Felch of Michigan. On the expiration of his term Bradbury declined being a candidate for reëlection and resumed the practise of law, which he continued with marked success until his retirement in 1876. He retained his interest in politics, however, was a delegate to the Democratic national convention of 1852, and is said to have taken an important part in securing the nomination of Franklin Pierce. When the Civil War broke out, Bradbury immediately took his stand in favor of maintaining the Union by force if need be, and in August 1861, when the Democratic state convention denounced the war, Bradbury instantly led a secession of nearly half the members. He regarded this as one of the most important acts of his life, believing that if the whole Democratic party in Maine had been represented as opposed to the war this evidence of division in the North would have encouraged England and France to recognize the Confederacy. The last years of his life, though uneventful, were characterized by quiet service to the community. He was president of the Maine Historical Society, 1873–89, overseer (elected 1850), and later trustee, of Bowdoin College, and chairman of the trustees' committee on finance for more than thirty years.

[Bradbury wrote two articles of an autobiographical nature, "Railroad Reminiscences" in the *Me. Hist. Soc. Colls.,* ser. 2, vol. VII, and "The First Democratic Convention in Me. during the Rebellion" in *Me. Hist. Soc. Colls.,* ser. 3, vol. II. The best account of his life is a sketch in the *Bradbury Memorial* (1890) by Wm. Barry Lapham. There is a good obituary in the *Daily Kennebec Jour.* (Augusta, Me.), Jan. 7, 1901. See also *Obit. Record Grads. Bowdoin Coll. for the Decade ending 1 June 1909.*]

L. C. H.

BRADBURY, THEOPHILUS (Nov. 13, 1739–Sept. 6, 1803), jurist, a descendant of Thomas Bradbury who settled at Salisbury, Mass., in 1638, and the son of Theophilus and Ann (Woodman) Bradbury, was born at Newbury, Mass. He attended the public schools there, proceeding in due course to Harvard College where he graduated in 1757. He then went to Falmouth (now Portland) and taught in the grammar school, at the same time studying law. On his admission to practise before the court of common pleas in May term 1762, he opened an office in Falmouth, being the first resident lawyer in that part of the country. In 1763 he was appointed collector of excise, and in 1765 was admitted to the bar of the superior court. For eleven years he and David Wyer, who had followed him a year later, were the only lawyers in the district, and between them monopolized all the legal business. A good lawyer, grave and dignified in manner and an excellent special pleader, Bradbury had great influence with both court and jury and enjoyed a lucrative practise. In 1777 he was appointed state attorney, but the destruction of Falmouth by the British in 1775 had prostrated all business, and in 1779 he resigned, went to Newburyport, Mass., and commenced practise anew in that town. Assisted by his family associations, he quickly acquired a prominent place in public life, representing his district in both branches of the General Court. In 1795 he was elected to the Fourth Congress as representative from Massachusetts, and was reëlected to the Fifth Congress in 1796. He was counsel for Newburyport in the suit which was brought against that town by the proprietors of the common land in the town of Newbury alleging that the respondents had in 1771 taken possession of certain of the common land, called "the middle ship yard," and had never made compensation. The case, which was of intense local interest, was heard at the April term of the court of general sessions at Salem 1797, and terminated in favor of Bradbury's clients. The same year he was appointed a justice of the supreme judicial court of Massachusetts. Upon the bench he displayed those qualities of courtesy and dignity combined with extensive knowledge of law and procedure which had distinguished his career as a practitioner. In February 1802 he had a paralytic stroke, which rendered him incapable of performing his judicial duties. It appearing that there was no reasonable ground to hope that he would ever be able to resume his seat on the bench, he was in July 1803 removed from office on address of the two branches of the General Court—the sole constitutional method available for meeting such a contingency. He only survived two months, dying at Newburyport, Sept. 6 following. He was married in 1762 to Sarah, daughter of Ephraim Jones of Falmouth.

[Wm. Willis, *Hist. of the Law, the Courts and the Lawyers of Me.* (1863), pp. 93, 123, and *The Hist. of Portland* (1831); W. T. Davis, *Hist. of the Judiciary of Mass.* (1900), p. 303; E. Vale Smith, *Hist. of Newburyport* (1854), p. 345; J. J. Currier, *Ould Newbury* (1896), p. 617.] H. W. H. K.

BRADBURY, WILLIAM BATCHELDER (Oct. 6, 1816–Jan. 7, 1868), music teacher, piano manufacturer, was born in York, Me., and died in Montclair, N. J. He was the son of David and Sophia (Chase) Bradbury, and a descendant in the sixth generation from Thomas Bradbury who came from Derbyshire, England, to Agamenticus, now York, in 1634. The inheritance of a taste for music from his parents both of whom were "excellent singers," the father being the leader of a choir, and the fact that he readily mastered any musical instrument that came to his hand, though he never saw a piano or organ until he went to Boston at the age of seventeen, is about the extent of the record of Bradbury's boyhood. In Boston he entered the family of Sumner Hill, from whom he received his first lessons in harmony. Later, having come under the influence of Lowell Mason, he became his pupil in Boston and a close follower of his methods, so that in 1836 he was sent to Machias, Me., and later to St. John's, N. B., to conduct singing classes. In 1840 he went to a Brooklyn church as organist and the next year to the First Baptist Church in New York. There and in other churches he instituted free singing classes similar to those of Lowell Mason in Boston, which in both instances led to the introduction of music in the public schools. At annual festivals held in the Tabernacle the singers, all children, at times numbered 1,000. For use in these classes, festivals, and conventions he compiled many singing books adapted to the primitive needs of the time. In the first one, *The Young Choir* (1841), and in four later ones of more importance, *The Psalmodist* (1844), *Choralist* (1847), *Mendelssohn Collection* (1849), and *Psalmista* (1851), he was assisted by Thomas Hastings (1787–1872), pioneer in church choral singing and psalmody. *The Shawm* (1853), perhaps the most extensively used of any of the earlier books, included the sacred cantata "Daniel," music by George F. Root and Bradbury, words by C. M. Cady and Fannie J. Crosby. *The Jubilee* (1858) had a sale of over 200,000 copies; *Fresh Laurels* (1867), 1,200,000; *The Golden Chain*, about 2,000,000. *Esther* (cantata, 1856) was a favorite production of money-making choirs throughout the country for many years. Altogether over fifty different books were published. They all followed much the same pattern, consisting of the rudiments of notation and sight-reading, exercises in part singing, short easy glees, hymn-tunes, chants and anthems, aiming to afford adequate training to young aspirants for the church choir. In spite of the many critical sneers at "sugared American psalmody" and the belittling of its æsthetic value, it must be admitted that this music met the need of the time and fed the infantile musical life the country over as no other music could. While few of Bradbury's tunes are still in use, several have a strong hold on popular favor, *e.g.*, "Just as I am" and "He leadeth me," which are worthy examples of a sincere and simple musical expression of the sentiment of the text.

The years 1847–49 were spent abroad, mostly in study under Wenzel, Boehme, and Hauptmann at Leipsig, whence Bradbury sent letters to the *New York Observer* and other religious papers. In 1854, assisted by his brother, Edward G., and a German piano maker, he established the firm of Lighte, Newton & Bradbury, which soon became very successful as the Bradbury Piano Company, the instrument being endorsed by Theodore Thomas, William Mason, and many others. The business, later under the control of F. G. Smith, was finally absorbed by the Knabe Piano Company.

[The *N. Y. Musical Gazette* has a series of articles on Bradbury, running from Dec. 1867 to June 1868, the material for which was furnished by Bradbury himself. See also *Grove's Dict. of Music and Musicians, Am. Supp.* (1920), article "Tune-books"; Francis Oakley Jones, *Jones's Handbook of Music and Musicians* (1887); W. S. B. Mathews, *A Hundred Years of Music in America* (1889); articles by F. J. Metcalf and L. B. Starkweather, in the *Choir Herald* (Dayton, Ohio), vol. XIX, no. 7, Apr. 1916, pp. 122 ff., 145 ff.] S.S.

BRADDOCK, EDWARD (1695–July 13, 1755), British general, entered the army in 1710 as ensign in the Coldstream Guards, the regiment of his father, Major-General Edward Braddock. In that regiment he rose rapidly, becoming lieutenant of the grenadier company in 1716, captain-lieutenant with the army rank of lieutenant-colonel in 1734, captain in 1736, second major with the army rank of colonel in 1743, first major in 1745, and lieutenant-colonel of the regiment in 1745. He was probably not present either at Dettingen or Fontenoy, but accompanied the second battalion of the Coldstreams to Ostend in July 1745. Later in the year he served under Cumberland in the suppression of the Jacobite rebellion of 1745–46 (Daniel L. MacKinnon, *Origin and Services of the Coldstream Guards,* 1833, I, 381). In 1747 he commanded the second battalion in Lestock's and St. Clair's abortive attempt on Port l'Orient, was subsequently employed under the Prince of Orange at Bergen-op-Zoom, and was later quartered in Bois-le-Duc. Forty-three years' continuous service in one of the haughtiest regiments in the British army produced a man who was the sternest of disciplinarians, often brutal in dealing with civilians, and poor in purse, the butt of Fielding's satire and Walpole's wit. Appointed colonel of the 14th Regiment in 1753, he joined his men at Gibraltar, where he won their confidence and adoration (*Letters of Horace Walpole,* 1840, III, 145). Major-general in 1754, he was selected by Cumberland to proceed to North America as commander-in-chief of all His Majesty's forces raised or to be raised there (T. W. Riker, "The Politics behind Braddock's Expedition," *American Historical Review,* XIII, 742–52). He sailed in December with two regiments of British foot and landed at Hampton, Va., in February 1755.

By the words of his instructions Braddock theoretically wielded greater military power than any man had ever enjoyed before in America, and his meeting in April with five colonial governors at Alexandria marked the nearest approach to the colonial unity which the Board of Trade had advocated for more than fifty years. But the British ministry had under-estimated the difficulties of campaigning in the wilderness of the new world. Braddock's own disdain of provincial troops complicated his task, and he found himself hampered by lack of money, provisions, transportation, and laborers. Dinwiddie, Washington, and Franklin contributed materially, and Braddock gratefully acknowledged their aid, but the inadequacy of preparations in England, and the prevailing jealousy of the colonies toward one another, constituted a problem not to be solved by a man of his training. In accordance with his orders to attack Fort Duquesne, he began the task of cutting a road westward from Fort Cumberland, with 1,400 British regulars, some 700 provincials from Virginia, Maryland, North Carolina, and South Carolina, and a detachment of sailors from the fleet. The first road across the Alleghanies, it became later a highway of western expansion and the foundation of the National Road. Its slow building through the thick and mysterious forests sapped the strength and spirits of the men.

At Little Meadows, for want of transportation (*English Historical Review,* January 1886, I, 150–52) the army divided, and Braddock, with 1,400 men, pushed on toward the fords of the Monongahela, throwing out flankers and advance pickets. But the absence of Indian allies, with whom he could not deal sympathetically, prevented adequate dispositions against surprise (*Correspondence of William Shirley,* 1912, II, 313), and on July 9, eight miles from Fort Duquesne, the advanced guard received a withering fire from some 900 French, Canadians, and Indians, stationed on either side of a heavily-wooded ravine. It fell back in confusion upon the van, under Lieutenant-Colonel Gage, marching too closely upon its heels, and out of the ensuing disorder it proved impossible to form the troops. Ten minutes later Braddock came up with the main body, but either because the order to form line-of-battle was not given or because the men were too confused to obey, the army preserved its column formation and was thus flanked on both sides by the enemy. Without knowledge of open fighting, Braddock refused to order his men to the shelter of the trees, as the provincials urged him to do. For three hours the redcoats presented the best of targets to their invisible foes. Sixty-three of the eighty-nine officers, and over half the army, were killed and wounded, and when Braddock, who had had four horses shot under him, was wounded in the arm and lungs, the remainder retreated in headlong rout to the camp of the second detachment. Braddock was borne back in a litter, and died four days later near Great Meadows, murmuring, according to tradition, "We shall better know how to deal with them another time."

[Winthrop Sargent, *The Hist. of an Expedition against Fort Duquesne* (1855) being vol. XV of the *Memoirs Pa. Hist. Soc.*, is the best and fullest account, and contains Orme's journal, the Morris journal, and Braddock's instructions. Braddock's orderly-book is printed as an appendix to W. H. Lowdermilk's *Hist. of Cumberland* (1878). Other documents are printed in *Pa. Arch.; The Official Records of Robert Dinwiddie* (2 vols., 1883–84), ed. by R. A. Brock; Sharpe Corres. in *Arch. of Md.*, vol. VI (1888); *Docs. Relative to the Col. Hist. of the State of N. Y.*, vol. VI (1855); and Jacob Nicolas Moreau, *The Conduct of the Late Ministry, or a Memorial Containing a Summary of Facts* (1757), a translation from the royally-authorized *Mémoire contenant le Précis des Faits . . .* (1756), and reprinted in N. B. Craig's *Olden Time*, vol. II (1847). The *Mo. Bull. of the Carnegie Lib. of Pittsburgh*, Nov. 1906, contains a list of references on Braddock's expedition. For a general account see H. Baker-Crothers, *Virginia and the French and Indian War* (1928).] S. M. P.

BRADFORD, ALDEN (Nov. 19, 1765–Oct. 26, 1843), author, was a descendant of Gov. Bradford of Plymouth and also of John Alden and was the son of Col. Gamaliel and Sarah (Alden) Bradford of Duxbury, Mass. His father was a ship-owner, magistrate, and a person of considerable importance in an inconsiderable place. Young Alden was the first of the line to go to college, graduating from Harvard in 1786, after which he taught school for a year at Milton. After studying for the ministry under Samuel West, a leading liberal of his day, Bradford obtained a license to preach in 1790 but then accepted a tutorship in Greek at Harvard. He resigned this position three years later and became pastor of the Congregational Church at Wiscasset, Me. In 1795 he married Margaret Stevenson of Boston. Wiscasset was then a brisk little town but much given to tuberculosis, which Bradford attributed to the drinking of tea and spirits until he was himself attacked. He promptly gave up the ministry and was at once cured. He continued to reside at Wiscasset and was soon appointed clerk of the court for Lincoln County, an office which he retained until with his fellow Federalists he was swept from office in 1811. He next established himself in a book-selling business in Boston but the firm was unsuccessful and it took him many years to clear off the debts. In 1812 he was appointed secretary of the Commonwealth of Massachusetts, which post he retained for twelve years. In 1824 he was again removed by the defeat of the Federalists, the excuse in Bradford's case being charges which were wholly unsubstantiated and which were later entirely refuted. He then became editor of the *Boston Gazette,* continuing a somewhat unprofitable interest in politics, although he obtained a minor appointment as justice of the peace at New Bedford. He seems to have taken up with several of the "isms" of the day, being known as a strong "anti-Masonry" man, a temperance advocate, and a Unitarian, or, as he called himself, a "Berean." Bradford was a prolific writer, the bibliography of his works containing over forty items. None of these have any living interest to-day except the few in which he printed original historical documents. His *History of Massachusetts to 1820* (1822–29) had a contemporaneous but not a permanent value, which may be said of other original historical works. His *Speeches of the Governors of Massachusetts 1763–75* (1815), usually cited as *Massachusetts State Papers,* is valuable for the original material printed in it. It is the printing of original letters and other papers which also gives value to his *Life of Jonathan Mayhew* (1838). He was a man of strong, upright character, of public spirit, of cultivated tastes,—of large use to his own generation and of some slight use to this.

[The only scholarly account of Bradford's life is the seven-page article, with bibliography, by S. E. Morison, in *Mass. Hist. Soc. Proc.*, LV, 153–64.] J. T. A.

BRADFORD, ALEXANDER WARFIELD (Feb. 23, 1815–Nov. 5, 1867), lawyer, the son of Rev. John M. and Mary (Lush) Bradford, was born in Albany, N. Y. His primary education was received at the Albany Academy, whence he proceeded to Union College, Schenectady, where he graduated in 1832. On leaving Union he went to New York City, took up the study of law, and was admitted to the bar in 1837. Commencing practise, he also became active in political circles, being a staunch adherent of the old Whig party of that day. His progress in his profession was slow and he devoted a portion of his time to literary pursuits. In 1841 he published his *American Antiquities and Researches into the Origin and History of the Red Race,* a work which attracted much notice, as a pioneer venture in the ethnological field of the American Indian.

In 1843, he became corporation counsel to the City of New York, and in 1848 was elected surrogate for the city and county of New York, a position to which he was twice reëlected. As surrogate he was a conspicuous success. During his tenure of office he "contributed to build up almost a complete system of jurisprudence in the Surrogate Court," his thorough acquaintance with the law of wills and intestate property and the inter-relation of civil and canon law, giving his decisions a weight which extended beyond the confines of his own jurisdiction. He prepared *Reports of Cases Argued and Determined in the Surrogate's Court of the County of New York* (4 vols., 1851–57), covering the cases between 1849 and 1857. These reports have always been considered very valuable by the profession. He retired from the bench in 1858, being the same year elected a member of the state assembly, in which he served for one term. On his resumption of private practise he quickly acquired a lucrative legal connection, particularly in his special department of civil or ecclesiastical law. He was a member of the commission appointed in 1857 by the New York State legislature to reduce the law of the state to a systematic code. In 1865 they reported a civil code, "the first real code in good and correct sense of the term prepared in this country" (Charles Warren, *History of the American Bar,* 1911, p. 533). It failed, however, of adoption. His health gradually broke under the pressure of continuous application to professional duties, and he died in New York City Nov. 5, 1867.

He combined a singularly equable temperament with an unobtrusiveness which made him friends among all classes. His learning and general scholarship were universally recognized, and in his special sphere of law he had no peer in this country. He occasionally contributed to historical and other periodicals. For some years he was associated with Dr. Anthon in editing *The Protestant Churchman.* The *Catalogue of the Private Library of the Late A. W. Bradford, Esq.* (1868), prepared for the sale which took place after his death, discloses 920 items, covering a wide range of subjects, including a copy of John Eliot's Indian Bible, the first book printed in America.

[The *Testimonial of Respect of the Bar of N. Y. to the Memory of Alexander W. Bradford* (1868) contains an authoritative review of his life. An extended report of the meeting of the N. Y. bar on the occasion of his death appeared in the *N. Y. Times,* Nov. 8, 1867. A brief notice of his career occurs in *Hist. of the Bench and Bar of N. Y.,* ed. by D. McAdam *et al.* (1897), I, 266. The New York press of Nov. 7, 1867, contains obituaries, that in the *N. Y. Times* being contributed by an intimate acquaintance.] H. W. H. K.

BRADFORD, AMORY HOWE (Apr. 14, 1846–Feb. 18, 1911), Congregational minister, the son of Rev. Benjamin Franklin Bradford and Mary A. Howe, was eighth in descent from Gov. William Bradford of the Plymouth Colony. He was born in Granby, N. Y., graduated from Hamilton College in 1867, and was married to Julia S. Stevens of Little Falls, N. Y., in 1870. In the latter year he entered on a life-long pastorate at Montclair, N. J. His church became, some years before his death, one of the strongest in the denomination. In 1884 he studied at Oxford University and his sermons were much appreciated in English pulpits. In 1888 he published his first book, *Spirit and Life.* It was followed by *Old Wine, New Bottles* (1892); *The Pilgrim in Old England* (1893); *Heredity and Christian Problems* (1895); *The Growing Revelation* (1897); *The Sistine Madonna* (1897); *The Holy Family* (1899); *The Return to Christ* (1900); *The Age of Faith* (1900); *Spiritual Lessons from the Brownings* (1900); *Messages of the Masters* (1902); *The Ascent of the Soul* (1902); *The Inward Light* (1905); *My Brother* (1910); and *Preludes and Interludes* (1911), edited by his son. These books were largely made up from his sermons and addresses, though considerable material was added. As may be inferred from their titles, their chief purpose was the promotion of progressive orthodoxy, that is the maintenance of all that was of value in the earlier orthodoxy, while restating it in terms that were in accord with the progress of historical and other scientific research. "Old Wine in New Bottles" was the name he gave to this procedure. From 1892 to 1899 he was an associate editor of the *Outlook,* then actively engaged in the same effort. Such studies inevitably lead to questions of philosophy, in which Bradford took an active interest, and in 1892 he was made president of the American Institute of Christian Philosophy. In the same year he delivered the Southworth Lectures at Andover Seminary. In 1895 he was sent to Japan, as one of a delegation to inspect the missions there; and from 1901 to 1903 he was moderator of the National Council, the foremost position in the Congregational fellowship. In 1904 he was made president of the American Missionary Association.

[The chief source is an obituary by John R. Howard, formerly of Montclair, prepared for the family. Obituaries were also published in the *Outlook,* Mar. 4, 1911, the *Congregationalist,* Mar. 4, 1911, the *Newark Sun,* Feb. 20, 1911, and the *Sun* (N. Y.), Feb. 19, 1911.] T. D. B.

BRADFORD, ANDREW (1686–Nov. 24, 1742), pioneer printer and magazine publisher, was the son of William Bradford [*q.v.*], the pioneer printer of the middle colonies, and of Elizabeth Sowle, daughter of Andrew Sowle, a London printer and publisher. When seven years of age he went with his father to New York City where the latter had been appointed "printer to the Crown." Most of his education he doubtless obtained as he learned the printing trade in his father's shop. Leaving New York City in 1712, he still continued for some time a sort of partnership with his father after he had taken up his residence in Philadelphia, where in 1714 he issued from his own press *The Laws of the Province of Pennsylvania.* Later appointed the official "printer to the Province," he became an importer of books published in England. Selling these in his shop, he exerted no mean influence upon the culture of Philadelphia. On Dec. 22, 1719, he began the *American Weekly Mercury*—the first newspaper in Pennsylvania and the third in the United States. In 1721 he was bold enough to express the hope that the General Assembly might find "some effectual remedy to revive the dying credit of this province" (*Weekly Mercury,* Jan. 2, 1721). For his criticism, brief as it was, he was summoned before the Provincial Council but suffered neither imprisonment nor fine, though he was warned not to publish in the future anything concerning the affairs of the government without the permission of the governor or secretary. He did not escape, however, so easily, a few years later when he published a series of essays about provincial matters—a series started by Benjamin Franklin but continued by other authors. For printing these contributions, especially the one on the tendency of power to perpetuate itself, he was again summoned before the Council (*Minutes of the Provincial Assembly,* III, 392), and later sent to prison. But he continued his newspaper without interruption. Whatever may have been the official decision in the case, he found so much favor with his fellow citizens that he was shortly afterward elected a councilman of the city. In supporting his case he set forth those principles that later enabled Andrew Hamilton, in New York City, to free John Peter Zenger in the most famous case for press freedom in colonial days. Benjamin Franklin has left a record of criticism of the *American Mercury* for its poor typographical appearance. But Isaiah Thomas (*History of Printing,* 1810, II, 326) asserts that the typography of the *American Mercury* was "equal to that of *Franklin's Gazette.*" Franklin and Bradford were not only competing publishers for many years in the newspaper field, but for a short time were competitors in the magazine field. In January 1741 Bradford issued the first copy of the *American Magazine.* Three days later Franklin followed with a rival, the *General Magazine* (A. H. Smyth, *The Philadelphia Magazines,* 1892, p. 26). Neither magazine lasted longer than six months. Bradford was twice married, first to a woman named Dorcas and next to Cornelia Smith of New York City, a relative of his father's second wife. He adopted William 3rd, a son of his brother, William 2nd. His adopted son became the famous "patriot-printer" of the Revolution and his widow, Cornelia, was one of the first women to edit a newspaper in America. While Andrew Bradford led a less spectacular life than that of his father or that of his adopted son, he held official positions from both city and church. He was postmaster at Philadelphia during the decade 1728–38. Elected a vestryman of Christ's Church in 1726, he was reëlected for eleven years and in all probability for other terms, though official confirmation is lacking. He derived considerable wealth from successful real estate investments in Philadelphia.

[The most detailed biographical sketch of Bradford may be found in the *Address,* delivered in 1869 by Horatio G. Jones before the Hist. Soc. of Phila. See also "Bradford Family of Printers," by Henry Lewis Bullen, in the *Am. Bull.,* Apr., July, 1913; and Henry Darrach, *Bradford Family* (1906). Bradford's connection with the *Am. Mercury* is told in detail by Jas. Melvin Lee in *Hist. of Am. Journalism* (1917), pp. 31 ff.] J. M. L.

BRADFORD, AUGUSTUS WILLIAMSON (Jan. 9, 1806–Mar. 1, 1881), governor of Maryland, was born at Bel Air, Harford County, Md., in the year 1806, the son of Samuel and Jane (Bond) Bradford. He was of British descent, both his paternal and maternal ancestors having come to this country before the Revolution. He received his elementary education at Bel Air Academy under the Rev. Reuben H. Davis, who was a noted teacher in his day. In 1822 he entered St. Mary's College, Baltimore, from which institution he graduated at the head of his class in 1824, when in his eighteenth year. He returned to Bel Air to take up the study of law in the office of the then well-known lawyer, Otho Scott. In 1827 he was admitted to the bar and practised law in his native town until 1831. In that year he decided to make his home in Baltimore, feeling that in that city there would be a wider field for him in his profession than in the village of Bel Air. During the outbreak of the cholera epidemic in 1832 he returned to Bel Air, where he lived for the following six years. In 1838 he again took up his residence in Baltimore to stay for the remainder of his life. He soon became a prominent member of the Whig party, and for a number of years devoted much of his time to its political organization. He was an ardent admirer and supporter of Henry Clay, and in 1844 was an elector on the Clay ticket. The defeat of Clay was such a bitter blow to him that for some years thereafter he would neither go upon the stump nor attend any political meetings. During this period of political inactivity he devoted himself to law, and acquired a good practise, although he never rose to any great distinction in his chosen profession. In 1835 he was happily married to Elizabeth Kell, the youngest daughter of Judge Kell of Baltimore. There were twelve children by this union, seven of whom were living at the time of his death. In 1845 he was appointed by Gov. Pratt clerk of the Baltimore county court and filled that office faithfully and efficiently until the close of the year 1851. For the next ten years he took very little part in public affairs.

In 1861 the people of America were much concerned lest the differences between the North and the South should lead to civil war. Peace conferences were held in various parts of the country and in the spring of 1861 Gov. Hicks sent Bradford as a representative of Maryland to the conference held in Washington. He there made a strong speech in favor of the Union, and in the following summer, when the Union party was formed in Maryland, Bradford was named its candidate for governor. Gen. Benjamin C. Howard was nominated by the Democrats. On Sept. 11 President Lincoln's secretary of war, Simon Cameron, wrote that "the passage of any act of secession by the legislature of Maryland must be prevented." The members of the legislature not strongly in favor of the Republican administration were arrested, and Maryland consequently, so far at least as her government was concerned, was definitely on the side of the Union. Bradford was elected by a majority of 31,000, but it is beyond question that this great majority was due in part to intimidation and unlawful use of the soldiery. The federal administration and its Maryland representatives seemed to feel that they were justified in using rather questionable methods to prevent the people of Maryland from voting for any one who was not a candidate on the Union ticket. The military officers were given authority to suspend the habeas corpus and to arrest any suspicious persons and keep them confined until after the election. No one knowing Bradford's high sense of duty and honor could believe that he had any direct share in the way in which his gubernatorial campaign was managed, but it is to be regretted that that military interference with the voters against which he fought so courageously during his administration should have helped to carry him into office. In his inaugural address (January 1862) Bradford stood strongly in favor of the Union. From the beginning of his administration he endeavored unceasingly to have Maryland support the federal government, but at the same time he opposed any unlawful use of the soldiery. When Gen. Lee's army invaded Maryland in 1862 Bradford issued a proclamation calling upon the citizens to enrol themselves in military organizations, promising them they would not be required to join the federal army without their full consent. Organizations and volunteers immediately responded to the proclamation. Again in 1863, upon the second invasion of the state, Bradford called for 10,000 volunteers, and in June of that year he decided to equip them and organize them into companies without waiting for regimental organization. Many men too old to be drafted offered their services for home defense, and were accepted by the governor. On June 21, 1863, he issued his third appeal for volunteers, and this was answered by the formation of three other regiments. In November 1863 he came into serious conflict with the federal authorities. Major-General Schenck had issued an order for military officers to be present at the polls on the day of election to carry out certain restrictions upon the voters and to arrest any suspicious persons. Bradford wrote to President Lincoln assuring him of the state's loyalty and begging him to prevent any such interference by the soldiery. The President's reply was not satisfactory, and in November 1863 Bradford issued a proclamation declaring that whatever power the state possessed was to be used to support the proper officials in the discharge of their duties. Schenck immediately issued an order forbidding the newspapers to publish the proclamation, which did not appear in the Baltimore papers until the morning of the election, too late for circulation in the rural parts of the state. As a result there was the same military interference at the polls as in 1861.

Bradford was opposed to slavery both on moral and economic grounds, but he also opposed federal interference with the slaves in Maryland and exerted his efforts to have the practise of carrying off the slaves at night discontinued. The question of negro emancipation was discussed at the legislative session of 1864, and Bradford called a state convention to meet in Annapolis that year with a view to abolishing slavery. At that convention was adopted the constitution which abolished slavery in Maryland and disfranchised all who fought for or aided the Confederacy. In the summer of 1864 the Confederate forces invaded Maryland, camping near Reisterstown. A squad of them, detailed for the purpose, visited Bradford's residence, about four miles from Baltimore, and burned it to the ground, destroying his furniture, private papers, and entire library. The Governor was absent from home at the time, but the Confederates left a note telling him that the house had been burned in retaliation for the burning of the home of Gov. Leitcher of Virginia by Gen. Hunter. Under the constitution of 1864 Thomas Swann was elected governor of Maryland and on Jan. 10, 1866, Bradford retired. His speech at the induction of Gov. Swann into office was exceptionally eloquent. In 1867 he was appointed by President Johnson surveyor of the port of Baltimore, and held that office until Gen. Grant removed him in April 1869. In 1874, without his knowledge or consent, he was nominated by Grant to the office of appraiser-general in the Baltimore custom house, but immediately declined the position on the ground that he was not fitted by training for an office which required an experienced and judicious merchant. After his retirement as surveyor of the port of Baltimore he held no public office, but devoted the remainder of his life to his legal practise and his well-loved family. His last appearance in public life was as presidential elector on the Greeley ticket in 1872. The following story aptly illustrates his high sense of duty. His eldest son, a youth of twenty, had entered the Confederate army and been made an officer on the staff of a distinguished general. In 1864 he was found entering Washington in a wagon, was arrested as a spy and placed in the Capitol Prison. To the adjutant-general of the state fell the difficult task of telling Bradford of his son's arrest. After many minutes of silently pacing the floor the chief executive said, "Berry, I have made up my mind; if William has come within our lines as a spy he must take the consequences. My duty to my official position will not permit me to take any action." Happily it was proved that the young officer was not a spy, but an ill man trying to get to his home. "After a life full of years and of honor" Bradford died at his home in Baltimore, in his seventy-sixth year.

[H. E. Buchholz, *Governors of Md.* (1908); J. T. Scharf, *Hist. of Md.* (1879); *Sun* (Baltimore), Mar. 2, 1881; *Baltimore American and Commercial Advertiser*, Mar. 2, 1881; papers loaned by Bradford's son, Samuel Bradford.] E. T. D.

BRADFORD, EDWARD GREEN (July 17, 1819–Jan. 16, 1884), jurist, born at Bohemia Manor, Cecil County, Md., a descendant of William Bradford, governor of Plymouth Colony, was the son of Moses and Phœbe (George) Bradford. His father was editor for several years of the *Delaware Gazette*, a Federalist paper; his mother was of a wealthy Irish family. They moved to Wilmington, Del., soon after his birth. He was educated in the Wilmington schools, Bristol College, Philadelphia, and at Delaware College. He graduated in 1839 and studied law under Chief Justice Gilpin, then attorney-general. He was admitted to the bar in 1842 and appointed deputy attorney-general immediately. He held this position for eight years. He had shown an interest in politics while still a law student and took an active part in the Harrison-Tyler campaign of 1840. In 1849 he represented New Castle County in the state legislature and was offered the Whig nomination for Congress but did not accept it. President Lincoln, in 1861, appointed him United States district attorney for Delaware and President Johnson reappointed him in July 1865. A man of courageous opinions, he resigned his office the following year because of disapproval of Johnson's policies. For some years he practised law successfully and in 1871 was appointed by President Grant as United States district court judge for Delaware. At various times in his life he took a decided stand in politics. He was active in the organization of the Republican party in Delaware, at the outbreak of the Civil War he was a declared Union man and during the reconstruction period took an advanced position on suffrage. His career as judge was rather uneventful, although many important cases came before him. Other offices held by him were city solicitor of Wilmington, director for thirty years of the Wilmington Farmers' Bank, and vestryman of Trinity Church for a long period. At the time of his death the Wilmington *Daily Republican*, in an editorial which spoke highly of his abilities, stated that he would have been a worthy successor of John Middleton Clayton as United States senator, an office which he had all his life greatly desired. The weakness of the Republican party in the state was given as the only reason for his non-election.

[J. T. Scharf, *Hist. of Del.* (1888), I, 560; *Daily Republican* (Wilmington), Jan. 17, 1884.] M. A. K.

BRADFORD, EDWARD HICKLING (June 9, 1848–May 7, 1926), orthopædic surgeon, educator, and public servant, descendant of William Bradford, governor of Plymouth Colony, was the son of Charles F. Bradford, a Boston merchant, by his wife Eliza E. Hickling. He was born in Roxbury, Mass., and prepared for college at the Roxbury Latin School. Entering Harvard, he received his A.B. in 1869, and after a brief trial of business, matriculated at the Harvard Medical School, won an M.A. in 1872, and was graduated as M.D. in 1873, while serving as a surgical house pupil (1872–73) at the Massachusetts General Hospital. In 1873–75 he pursued his medical studies overseas in the clinics of Vienna, Paris, Berlin, Strassburg, and London. In 1875 he began general practise in Boston and was made a member of the staff of the Boston Dispensary in 1876, and of the Boston Children's Hospital in 1878. He also served as surgeon to out-patients at the Boston City Hospital and was appointed to the visiting staff in 1885. As the years went by, his broad view of medicine focused more and more sharply upon the cripple. He finally resigned from all his important hospital positions except that at the Children's Hospital, and eventually was appointed chief of its orthopædic staff. He became a member of the teaching force in the department of surgery in the Harvard Medical School in 1881, and as a result of brilliant work in his chosen field, was made assistant professor of orthopædic surgery in 1889. A new chair was created for him in 1903. He was the first full professor of orthopædic surgery. This chair he occupied until 1912. During these years he was an alert, resourceful, constructive, persuasive member of the Faculty of Medicine. In 1887, conscious of the need of some national association to foster the growth and raise the standards of this fast developing specialty, he was influential in founding the American Orthopædic Association and was elected its president in 1888. Bradford and Lovett's text-book on *Orthopædic Surgery,* published in 1890, was the standard for many years and ran through numerous editions. Bradford founded in 1893 the Boston Industrial School for Crippled and Deformed Children, the first of its kind in America. This school still remains a model. It was Bradford who persuaded the State of Massachusetts, in 1904, to establish its unique Hospital School at Canton. Until his death, as chairman of the trustees, he guided the academic and vocational training of the physically handicapped minor wards of the state. In 1912 when he gave up his active hospital duties and was made emeritus professor, he accepted the appointment of dean of the Harvard Medical School. Through the trying war years he increased the usefulness of the institution and did important work on the supervising committee of the selective service commission of the State of Massachusetts. In 1918, he relinquished the duties of deanship and in 1919 was made a member of the board of overseers of Harvard College and chairman of its medical committee. He was married to Edith Fiske of Boston on June 20, 1900. In his personality were combined humor, generosity, urbanity, patience, and humility. His open mind sought and found truth which he shared with others. He was a man of deep religious faith. To serve his fellow men with intelligence and kindness was the activating motive of his life.

[Robt. B. Osgood, "Edward Hickling Bradford," *Jour. of Bone and Joint Surgery,* July 1926; *Boston Medic. and Surgic. Jour.,* May 27, 1926; *Eleventh Report of the Class of 1869, Harvard Coll.* (1919); *Boston Evening Transcript,* May 8, 1926; Records of the Harvard Medical School, Boston City Hospital, Boston Dispensary, Boston Children's Hospital; information from Mrs. E. H. Bradford.] R. B. O.

BRADFORD, GAMALIEL (Jan. 15, 1831–Aug. 20, 1911), banker, publicist, was born in Boston, the son of Gamaliel and Sophia Blake (Rice) Bradford, and the seventh in descent from Gov. William Bradford of Plymouth Colony. His father, who was superintendent of the Massachusetts General Hospital, died Oct. 22, 1839, leaving his family comparatively poor. In 1849 Bradford graduated sixth in his class at Harvard and for the next year or two was in the employ of the *Nautical Almanac* at Cambridge. During this period he made two trips to Europe and acquired an abiding enthusiasm for music, riding, and German. At the invitation of his cousin, George Baty Blake, he became a clerk in the banking house of Blake, Howe & Company, displayed great aptitude for the business, was made a partner in 1858, and retired with an ample competence in 1868. After spending a year in Washington he returned to Boston and devoted the rest of his long life to the study of government and to the advocacy of certain reforms. In April 1878 he was elected to the Massachusetts Historical Society, and until increasing deafness cut him off from general conversation he did his full share to enliven the Society's meetings. On a good many topics he held strong convictions, and all who knew him became acquainted with them. Early in life he had been, like his father, an abolitionist; during the Civil War he was a mordant critic of Secretary Chase's currency measures; later he advocated civil service reform and city charters, waged and won almost single-handed a campaign to retain the yearly election in Masachusetts, joined the Mugwumps when Blaine was nominated by the Republicans in 1884, and thereafter opposed the Republican policies of centralization, high tariffs, and imperialism. His pet theory was that the executive—mayor, governor, or president—should normally have the power to initiate legislation, and to that end he urged that members of the cabinet have seats in the legislature. This is the principal theme of his one book, a substantial two-volume treatise on *The Lesson of Popular Government* (1899). [See the review in the *Nation,* LXVIII, 335–36, 359–61.] The purely theoretical character of his studies is brought out in the fact that he failed to recognize the extent to which a strong executive can influence legislation unofficially. The only office that he ever held was member of the Wellesley School Committee, although three times he offered himself as a candidate for governor and once polled some three thousand votes. Such influence as he had was exerted largely through his letters to the papers; he contributed several thousand, over a period of forty years, to the Boston *Advertiser* and *Transcript,* the Springfield *Republican,* the New York *Times, Tribune, Evening Post,* and *Nation,* and the *Bankers' Magazine.* Into these casual communications he poured an amazing wealth of information, shrewdness, and literary power. He lived during the winter in apartments overlooking the Charles River at Harvard Bridge; his summer home was at Wellesley Hills. When returning one Sunday evening from a call on his son he was knocked down by a trolley car and died a few hours afterward. He was buried in Mount Auburn Cemetery.

On Oct. 30, 1861, Bradford married Clara Crowninshield Kinsman of Newburyport, Mass., who died June 9, 1866. Of their three children the only one to reach maturity was Gamaliel Bradford, the biographical essayist.

[*Proc. Mass. Hist. Soc.,* vols. XLV (1912), XLVII (1914); *Who's Who in America,* 1910–11; *Harvard Quinquennial Cat. 1636–1915* (1915); H. S. Bradford, *One Branch of the Bradford Family* (privately printed, 1898); *Nation,* XCIII, 156 (Aug. 24, 1911); obituary and editorial in *Boston Evening Transcript,* Aug. 21, 1911. The Mass. Hist. Soc. has six folio scrapbooks containing his letters and miscellaneous writings, with editorials and cartoons against him.] G. H. G.

BRADFORD, JOHN (June 6, 1749–Mar. 20, 1830), pioneer printer of Kentucky, was born in Prince William (later Fauquier) County, Va., the son of Daniel and Alice Bradford. His father was the eldest son of John Bradford and his wife Mary. His grandfather of the same name is said to have been born about the year 1680 and to have married in 1710. Beyond this his lineage is uncertain. It may be added, however, that he was not related to the Bradfords of Massachusetts unless very remotely. After his marriage in 1771 to Eliza James, a daughter of Capt. Benjamin James of Fauquier County, he evidently went to Kentucky in 1779, but the rest of his family did not join him there until six years later. Before the arrival of his wife, there is evidence that he served in Bowman's campaign against the Indians and as a deputy surveyor under George May, the chief surveyor of what was then Kentucky County, Va. He first settled on Cane Run, but in or about the year 1787 he moved with his family to Lexington where he thereafter made his home. At the third —sometimes called the fourth—convention which assembled at Danville on Sept. 4, 1786, to discuss the separation from the State of Virginia and the establishment of a new state, a committee appointed to induce a printer to settle in the territory finally selected Bradford, even though he was without practical experience. The first number of his paper, the *Kentucke Gazette* (spelling changed to "Kentucky" in March 1789), came from his log cabin print shop on Aug. 11, 1787. Associated with him in the enterprise was his brother Fielding—a partnership which lasted until June 7, 1788. Greatly handicapped in getting paper, ink, etc., Bradford produced a newspaper that compared very favorably with the precursors of the press in other territories. From his shop in 1788, he sent forth the *Kentucke Almanac,* the pioneer pamphlet of the West. In connection with his duties as Printer of the Territory he published in 1792, the acts of the first session of the Kentucky legislature, the first book printed in Kentucky. In addition to his printing, he continued at times his work as a civil engineer and served as a deputy under Col. Thomas Marshall, first chief surveyor of Fayette County and father of Chief Justice John Marshall. The epithet, "the Kentucky Franklin," was sometimes applied to Bradford, for he was both a printer and a philosopher, and was also interested in mathematics and astronomy. Like Franklin he did much to promote education. He was in turn clerk of the board of Transylvania Seminary, a member of the board, and then chairman. Resigning the chairmanship in 1795, he became, with the founding of Transylvania University in 1799, the first chairman of the board. Resigning again in 1811, he became chairman again in September 1823 and held that office until November 1828. He was instrumental in founding the Lexington Library which he often served as one of its trustees. He held numerous offices connected with the county of Fayette and represented that county in the House of Representatives of Kentucky in 1797 and again in 1802. In his early newspaper days he was somewhat litigious, as were most pioneer printers, but in later years he became more charitable in his views, and in his respect for the rights of others. In politics he was a Jeffersonian Republican and was a member of the Democratic Society of Lexington which was modeled after the Jacobin Society of Philadelphia. He was never so partisan, however, but that he was willing to admit to the columns of his paper the contributions of those who were opposed to him in political matters. Through the pamphlets which came from his press he did much to promote public discussion of political affairs. On Aug.

25, 1826, he began the publication of his "Notes of Kentucky" in the *Kentucky Gazette* which in 1802 he had transferred to his son Daniel, but which in 1809 had been sold to Thomas Smith who in turn in 1814 had returned the paper to Fielding Bradford, Jr. In this series John Bradford contributed sixty-two papers, the last of which appeared in January 1829. Because he had been so closely associated with the Kentucky pioneers, he knew intimately about the struggling days of Kentucky and could therefore write with authority. At the time of his death he was high sheriff of Fayette County.

[Clarence S. Brigham in the *Proc. Am. Antiquarian Soc.*, vol. XXIV, pt. 2 (1914), pp. 380 ff., in tracing the history of the *Ky. Gazette,* shows the connection of Bradford and his descendants with that newspaper. Jas. Melvin Lee in *Hist. of Am. Journalism* (1917), ch. XI, outlines the conditions under which Bradford started his paper. Valuable material will be found in *Biog. Encyc. of Ky.* (1878), p. 415; Lewis and R. H. Collins, *Hist. of Ky.* (1874), II, 170 ff.; W. H. Perrin, *Pioneer Press of Ky.* (1888), pp. 14 ff.; *Ky. State Hist. Soc. Reg.*, XVII; *Mag. of Am. Hist.*, XVIII, 125; *Niles' Weekly Reg.*, XXXVIII, 174.] J. M. L.

BRADFORD, JOSEPH (Oct. 24, 1843–Apr. 13, 1886), actor, journalist, poet, and playwright, born near Nashville, Tenn., was christened William Randolph Hunter. His father, being one of the wealthiest slave owners in the South, was able to rear the son in luxury and to surround him with books which furnished a background for his later literary career. At sixteen young Hunter matriculated on Sept. 29, 1860, in the United States Naval Academy at Annapolis. His standing in his class at the end of the first year was high, but the official record also recorded 120 demerits. He was dismissed on Apr. 14, 1862. On July 9 he enlisted as an acting master's mate and served successfully in the North Atlantic Blockading Squadron on the U. S. S. *Minnesota* and on the U. S. S. *Putnam.* His service in the navy, under his real name, caused a break in the family ties. Under the assumed name of Joseph Bradford he then went on the stage in Baltimore. (His father's wealth went to the next of kin, but the memory of his mother was recalled in the adoption of her maiden name.) Later he played in light comedies with several stock companies in various cities along the Atlantic Coast. A road tour took him to Boston, where he decided to write plays rather than to act in them. Here he also wrote numerous poems often based on topics of the day. Of these the most extensively quoted in the press was the one on the death of Gen. Grant. In addition to his work as a playwright, he wrote for Boston newspapers. His best journalistic work was possibly done for the *Boston Courier* over the signature of "Jay Bee." Of his more important plays, mention may be made of the following: *New German* (1872), a play in five acts, written in collaboration with F. Stinson; *Law in New York* (1873), with Stinson; *20,000 Leagues Under the Sea* (1874), libretto by Bradford; music by G. Operti; *The Conditional Pardon* (1875), a play in five acts, with Stinson; *Fritz's Brother* (1875), with J. K. Emmet; *Out of Bondage* (1876), a play in four acts; *In and Out of Bondage* (1877), a musical drama; *Our Bachelors* (1877), a comedy in four acts; *A. A. 1900* (1879), a comedy in four acts; *John Mishler* (1882), a play in three acts and a prologue; *One of the Finest* (1883); *A Wonderful Woman* (1883); *Cherubs* (1885); *Rose and Coe* (1886), a comedy in three acts.

[Biographical material about Jos. Bradford is scant and jejune. The most important source of information is the *Naval Acad. Reg.*, 1860, p. 15. His work as a playwright is recorded in various items preserved in the Theatre Collection of the Harvard Coll. Lib. Obituaries published in Boston and New York papers paid a fine tribute to his contributions to lighter drama and comedy, but were incomplete as to details of his life.] J. M. L.

BRADFORD, THOMAS (May 4, 1745–May 7, 1838), printer and publisher, was the eldest son of William Bradford [*q.v.*], the "patriot-printer." His mother, Rachel, was the daughter of Thomas Budd who with George Keith opposed in 1692 Lieutenant-Governor Lloyd in the Quaker wrangle that resulted in the withdrawal of William Bradford [*q.v.*], the first printer of that name, from Philadelphia to New York. For several years Thomas Bradford attended what is now the University of Pennsylvania, but in 1762 he went to work for his father on the *Pennsylvania Journal and Weekly Advertiser,* a paper that first bore the joint imprint of father and son on Sept. 4, 1766. He took an active part in resisting the Stamp Act and was one of the principal promoters of the movement among the merchants of Pennsylvania and its sister state of Delaware to have no commercial transactions with England until the obnoxious act was repealed. The partnership with his father lasted until the occupation of Philadelphia by the British troops in 1777, when publication was temporarily suspended. After the evacuation of that city by the British, the *Journal* resumed publication with the name of only the son in its imprint. During the Revolutionary War Bradford also served as captain of a militia company and later as deputy commissary-general of prisoners in the American army where he had the rank of lieutenant-colonel. The business rather than the editorial side of newspaper publishing was always the more interesting to him and doubtless had much to do with his decision to start a daily paper that specialized in the news of the business world. This paper, started by him in 1797, was called the *Merchants' Daily Advertiser*. After the death of his younger brother, the Hon. William Bradford [*q.v.*], attorney-general of the United States, he came into possession of the larger part of the estate. The pressure of outside business interests practically forced him to turn over the management of the *Merchants' Daily Advertiser* to his son Samuel. The latter, being more interested in politics, changed the name of the paper in 1798 to the *True American* which was the pioneer paper to have a literary supplement. The son, however, lacked the executive ability of his father who had to resume active management of the paper in 1801. In spite of the fact that Bradford had cherished since the days of the Stamp Act a hatred of England, he was perfectly willing to publish the political pamphlets of William Cobbett who was attacking everything that was French and was stoutly defending England. Fearful of the windows of his print shop, Bradford insisted that the pamphlets should appear anonymously. In fact, he insisted upon such high rates of payment that he practically forced Cobbett to become a publisher—something that Bradford later regretted because of the extensive sale of Cobbett's pamphlets. After the death in 1805 of his wife, Mary Fisher, whom he had married in 1768, Bradford took even a more energetic interest in civic affairs. He was especially active in the American Philosophical Society of which he was a charter member. In spite of close application to business, he retained remarkable health. When seventy-five years old he made a trip from Philadelphia to Pittsburgh on horseback in order to inspect several tracts of land scattered over several counties in western Pennsylvania. He seems to have suffered no physical inconvenience from the trip, since immediately upon his return to Philadelphia he resumed active control of his affairs which in his absence had been managed by his second son, William Bradford, who later became a bookseller in Philadelphia. Meanwhile his elder son, Samuel, had become a publisher in New York. One other son, Thomas, became a member of the Philadelphia bar. In addition to these three sons, he had three daughters. He did not leave as direct an imprint upon the journalism of his day as did the other editorial members of the Bradford family, because he was chiefly interested in the commercial side, yet the financial page and the book page of the modern metropolitan journal go back in their evolution to innovations made by him. His remarkable health continued until about six months before his death when he suddenly lost the use of his eyes. Accustomed to activity, he chafed under this affliction until his death in his ninety-fourth year.

[Brief biographies of Bradford's children may be found in *Bradford Family—1660–1906* (1906) by Henry Darrach. His newspaper activities are recorded in a bibliographical way by Clarence S. Brigham in the *Proc. Am. Antiquarian Soc.*, vol. XXXII (1922). His business relations with Cobbett are taken up in *The Life and Letters of William Cobbett in England and America* (1912) by Lewis Melville. An appreciation of his life appears in *Hist. of Phila.* (1884) by J. T. Sharf and T. Westcott. There is an editorial tribute to his services in the *Public Ledger* (Phila.), May 9, 1838.]

J. M. L.

BRADFORD, WILLIAM (1589/90–May 9/19, 1657), Pilgrim Father, was born at Austerfield, Yorkshire, into a family of substantial yeomen. His father, William Bradford (d. 1591), married Alice Hanson, daughter of the village shopkeeper, June 21/31, 1584. Their third child and only son, the future governor, was baptized at the parish church in Austerfield March 19/29, 1589/90 (*Mayflower Descendant,* VII, 65, IX, 115–17). His mother married again in 1593, after which he was brought up by his grandfather and uncles to follow the plow. The people of that region were "ignorant and licentious," but William, a puny boy, began to read the Bible at the age of twelve, and to attend the sermons of a noted non-conformist, the Rev. Richard Clyfton, at Babworth. Braving the wrath of his uncles, William joined, while still a lad, the small group which met at the house of William Brewster [*q.v.*] in Scrooby, and which became a separatist church in 1606. The attitude of their neighbors, and of the authorities, determined the Scrooby congregation "to goe into the Low-Countries, where they heard was freedome of Religion for all men." In the spring of 1609 Bradford joined the company in a stormy passage from Hull to Amsterdam, of whose hardships he gives a vivid picture. In 1609 he removed with the congregation, then under the Rev. John Robinson, to Leyden. On coming of age in 1611, Bradford converted "a comfortable inheritance left him of his honest parents" into money, which was consumed in certain "designs, by the Providence of God frowned upon" (C. Mather, *Magnalia*). He became a citizen of Leyden, is described in contemporary documents as a fustian weaver (1613) and say worker (1620), and owned a house on the Achtergracht, which he sold on a mortgage in 1619. At this period of his life Bradford must have acquired that wide knowledge of theological and general literature to which his writings bear witness. The influence of the liberal and catholic spirit of his pastor, John Robinson, and of Elder Brewster, lasted throughout his life. Bradford defines his theological position (Calvinist in theology, Congregational in polity) in his Dialogues, but like Robinson he disowned sectarian labels, and wished to retain fellowship with all reformed churches. For, as he wrote, "it is too great arrogancie for any man or church to thinke that he or they have so sounded the word of God to the bottome." His liberalism much impressed the Jesuit, Father Druillette, who was entertained by him with a fish dinner at Plymouth, one Friday in 1650. Of Bradford's personal appearance or peculiarities not the slightest hint has come down to us, except that in the inventory of his estate, beside various "sad-colored" clothes, we find a red waistcoat, silver buttons, a colored hat, a violet cloak, and a Turkey grogram suit.

Bradford took a responsible part in the preparations for removal to the new world. He was probably one of those chosen tc dispose "the commone stock . . . for the making of general provision." He signed a letter to Carver and Cushman, the agents at London, ordering them not to deviate from the original terms, in dealing with the merchant adventurers; this attitude he stoutly maintained amid the embarrassments of the final embarkation at Southampton.

From the sailing of the *Speedwell* from Delfshaven (*c.* Aug. 1, 1620), Bradford's life is inseparable from the history of the Pilgrim colony. He signed the Mayflower Compact on Nov. 11/21. Later in the same day the *Mayflower* anchored in Cape Cod (Provincetown) harbor. Bradford was "adjoined for council and advice" to the first exploring expedition which started out on Nov. 15/25, under Miles Standish. He was of the company of twenty who left Cape Cod harbor in the shallop, had the first encounter with the Indians, scudded into Plymouth harbor before a snow storm, rested the Sabbath on Clark's Island, landed at Plymouth (traditionally on the rock) on Dec. 11/21, and decided to settle there. He was taken ill during the first winter, but recovered; and in April 1621, on the death of John Carver, William Bradford was elected governor of the colony.

The situation of the Pilgrims when they arrived at Cape Cod, so eloquently described by Bradford in his ninth chapter, was much worse when the young governor took office. The great sickness had taken thirteen out of the twenty-four heads of families, all but four of their wives, and all but six of the unattached bachelors. The *Mayflower* had returned to England, provisions were running low, and there would be no harvest for four months. There were only twenty-one men and six big boys to do the planting; and they had no cattle until 1624. They knew nothing about deep-sea fishing and fur-trading, and had no means to do either. In like circumstances, many other colonies had perished. In Bradford's opinion, only the guiding hand of God kept Plymouth Colony alive. The presence of Samoset and Squanto [*qq.v.*], the windfalls of corn from unexpected quarters, the mysterious voice that warned them of the store-house fire, the messenger losing his way and thereby delivering his warning, the "sweet and gentle showers" that came out of a clear sky just in time to save the crop, the turning back of the ship which was sent out to foreclose the colony for the creditors; of such interventions Bradford is so certain of the source that he simply remarks, "Behold now another providence of God." Yet other events, no less necessary than these to save the colony, were due primarily to the inspired leadership of the Governor, and of men like Brewster, Winslow, and Standish, on whom he leaned. By sheltering both Hobbomock and Squanto, and playing them off against one another, Bradford obtained the best intelligence as to movements of the Indian tribes; and his Indian policy, a nice balance of kindness and firmness, obtained their friendship and secured his people.

Bradford urged rotation in office in 1624, but the freemen would not let him off; and he was reelected governor of the colony thirty times: every year from 1622 to 1656 with the exception of 1633, 1634, 1636, 1638, and 1644; when he "by importunity gat off" (Winthrop, *Journal,* Jan. 1, 1633); and on those occasions he was elected an assistant. Until 1639, when he was voted £20, he received no salary; and until 1651 had the privilege of dining the court of assistants at his own expense during their monthly sessions. In 1645 he was granted "a guard of two halbertes" to attend him at the General Court. The Pilgrims had slight opportunity to show political genius in their little colony; but their experience in church affairs had given them training for self-government, and they had the English instinct for majority rule. Their institutions were simple, and adapted to immediate needs rather than precedent, principles, or the terms of a charter. Bradford owned Jean Bodin's *Republic,* whose gibes at the communistic "conceits" of Plato he repeats in describing the failure of the "common course" at Plymouth; but that is the only instance in all his writings of interest in political science. He regarded the colony as an overseas Congregational church, and conducted it as such, whenever possible. Writing to the London merchants in

1623, he wished "our friends at Leyden . . . and we be considered as one body." "And indeed if they should not come to us, we would not stay here, if we might gain ever so much wealth" (*American Historical Review,* VIII, 300). Most of them were brought over by 1630, at great expense to the poor colony. Yet the franchise was never restricted to church members, as in Massachusetts-Bay.

Bradford's difficulties during the early years of the colony were greatly augmented by "untowarde persons mixt amongst them from the first," people from various parts of England who were engaged as servants or attached to the colony by the merchants. Some of them, such as Miles Standish, John Alden, and Richard Warren, became "useful Instruments"; others failed to pull their weight, and several were lazy and seditious. Two of the merchants' protégés, Lyford the lewd parson, and Oldham the mad trader, started a dangerous faction. Weston, not content with cheating the Pilgrims in England, came to plague them at Plymouth. Thomas Morton established a disorderly house at their back door, and armed the Indians. Bradford dealt with such people as a genuine Christian and a consummate politician. After much forbearance the greedy and the factious would show themselves up, decamp or be expelled, come to grief, straggle back to Plymouth, beg forgiveness and fresh assistance, receive both, betray their benefactors again, and again come to grief. The Pilgrims always forgave the injury, and recovered from the wound. When, in 1627, Bradford and seven leading Pilgrims bought out the merchant adventurers, and so acquired title to the land, houses, cattle, and implements at Plymouth, they decided, in order to preserve peace and union, to share and share alike with the "mixt multitude"; and distributed land and cattle by a method that "gave all good contente." This stroke of statesmanship placed the colony on a sound economic basis, and assimilated the outsiders to Pilgrim ideals. It created a quasi-corporation known as the "Old Comers" or "Purchasers," which became the governing class of the colony. In religious matters, although Bradford never professed toleration as a principle, his temper was distinctly liberal, for the period. Plymouth Colony passed no law against dissenters until 1650 and was little troubled by them; but Bradford lived to take part in the first legislation against Quakers (*Publications of the Colonial Society of Massachusetts,* XVII, 383).

During his first fifteen years of office, Bradford exercised a more plenary authority than any other English colonial governor between 1619 and 1685. The freemen (signers of the compact and those admitted subsequently to their number) met as a general court, elected the governor and assistants, and passed, sparingly at first, laws and regulations; but in practise they vested almost complete discretionary authority in their governor. Democracy has been read into the Pilgrim government by later historians; it cannot be found in the records, or in Bradford's *History.* In 1623 he declared that the generality were allowed to share in the government "only in some weighty maters, when we thinke good." Twenty years later, there were only 232 freemen in the jurisdiction, out of 634 men bearing arms (*Plymouth Colony Records,* VIII, 173–177; 187–196). The Governor was principal judge, and treasurer until 1637. The right of strangers to sojourn depended largely on his personal consent. As responsible for the business management, first to the merchants and then to the "Old Comers," he superintended agriculture and trade, apportioned the proceeds, and made the annual allotments of land. No distinction was made between executive, legislative, and judicial authority. Whether the Governor should do as he thought best in a given instance, or take the advice of his assistants or other leading freemen, or submit it for discussion or decision to church meeting or general court, depended on his own tact, and on circumstances. "Surely his energy must have been vast, his discretion remarkable, his ability commanding, or those stern and uncompromising men and women would scarcely have permitted him to regulate their affairs so long" (Usher, *The Pilgrims,* 1918, p. 205).

If Bradford had had any love of power or of gain, his opportunity came in 1630, when the "Warwick patent" from the Council for New England made him, and whomsoever he chose to associate with him, proprietors both of jurisdiction and soil. Bradford at once shared his right to the soil with the "Old Comers," and allowed the government to go on as before. In 1636, he was one of a committee which drafted a body of laws, defining the duties of Governor, Assistant, and General Court, requiring trial by jury in all but petty cases, and defining seven capital offenses. These laws of 1636 placed the governorship on a quasi-constitutional basis; yet even after that his position was much more independent than that of Winthrop or Haynes. In 1639 the grand jury of Plymouth evinced some jealousy as to the Old Comers' power to allot land, the Undertakers' monopoly of trade (see below), and the want of a colony treasurer. After considerable debate in the General Court it was decided by mutual consent that Bradford and his associates surrender the Warwick patent to the freemen of the colony, reserving certain tracts of land for themselves. Apart from the Lyford faction, this is the only evidence of discontent with Bradford's rule that can be discovered.

In his business management, Bradford had the common sense to see that the colony would never prosper until its members were given a stake in its prosperity. He recognized that the merchant adventurers had a right to a return on their investment, and strove as best he could to repay them; but, in warm contact as he was with the struggle for existence, he could not altogether avoid the typical pioneer attitude toward financial backers. "At great charges in this adventure, I confess you have beene, and many losses may sustain," he writes the merchants; "but the loss of his (Carver's) and many other honest and industrious mens' lives, cannot be vallewed at any prise." In 1627 the colony's debt of £1,800 to the original merchant adventurers was assumed by Bradford, with seven Pilgrims and four London merchants. These twelve "Undertakers," in return for that burden, were assigned by the Old Comers a monopoly of fishing and trading. Under Bradford's direction the Undertakers pushed these enterprises with great vigor, but indifferent success. Isaac Allerton, their agent in London, and the London partners, corruptly converted most of the profits to their own uses; so that in 1631, after sending over hundreds of pounds' worth of beaver, the Undertakers were £5,771 in debt; and after another ten years' labor, when the Undertakers resigned their monopoly, the Plymouth group still owed £1,200 to the London men. "Thus they were abused in their simplicitie, and . . . sould," writes Bradford. The colony helped them out; but in 1648 Winslow and Prence had to sell their homes; Alden and Standish, 300 acres of land; and Bradford, a farm he owned at Rehoboth, in order to discharge the balance of £400. Bradford must have continued trading on his own account, since the principal items in the inventory of his estate (1657) are debts worth £153 upon the "Dutch account att the Westward" (the Manomet trading post), and goods and debts to the value of £256 in the trading stock at the Kennebec. His house, orchard, and sundry parcels of land at Plymouth, were valued at £45. The rest of the inventory shows that he was far from being the wealthiest man in a colony of slender estates; but had accumulated property comparable to that of the better sort of English yeomen. He left a great silver "beer bowle," two silver wine cups and thirteen spoons, four Venice glasses, sundry pewter pots and flagons, and forty-nine pewter dishes, weighing ninety-seven pounds. His library was the largest at Plymouth except Elder Brewster's. Besides theology it included "divers Duch books," and works by Peter Martyr, Guicciardini, La Primaudaye, John Speed, and Jean Bodin.

Toward new colonies such as Massachusetts-Bay, Bradford held out the hand of fellowship; and the harsh insolence which the Plymouth Colony sometimes received from the Bay authorities, was disarmed by his mild answers, and firm insistence on the rights of Plymouth. He brought the colony into all common enterprises, such as the Pequot war and the New England Confederation; and attended the synod of 1647 at Cambridge, as messenger of the Plymouth Church. He welcomed the great Puritan migration to New England; although, believing as he did in maintaining his colony as a compact community, he regretted the dispersal of population occasioned by the increase of cattle-raising (Bradford, *History,* 1912, II, 151). Probably his influence prevented the recognition as a township of Duxbury, the first offshoot of Plymouth, until 1637. He endeavored, without much success, to induce his people to give proper support to the ministry, and to establish free schools. When the Plymouth church called a distinguished non-conformist, the Rev. Charles Chauncy, to its teaching eldership, Bradford encouraged his abortive project of founding a Plymouth rival to Harvard College. The study of Hebrew, "that most ancient language, and holy tongue, in which the Law and Oracles of God were write; and in which God, and angels, spake to the holy patriarks, of old time," consoled the Governor in his old age, and thinking and writing about the heroic first decade afforded him great satisfaction. He died on May 9/19, 1657, believing that the glory was departed from Plymouth Colony.

Bradford married at Amsterdam, Dec. 10, 1613, Dorothy May, daughter of a member of the English Church there (*Mayflower Descendant,* IX, 115–17). She was drowned in Cape Cod harbor, Dec. 7/17, 1620. Their only son, John, afterward came to Plymouth, married, and died without issue. Alice (Carpenter), widow of Edward Southworth, a former member of the Leyden church, arrived at Plymouth in the *Anne* with her two small boys, in July 1623; Bradford married her on August 14. By this marriage, he had a daughter and two sons, William (1624–1704) and Joseph (1630–1715) whose descendants are now numbered by the thousand.

Bradford began to write his *History of Plimmoth Plantation* (sometimes idiotically called the "Log of the *Mayflower*"), about 1630, and probably completed Book I, down to the landing at

Plymouth, within a year or two. Book II, which carries the story through 1646, was written between that year and 1650; the list of *Mayflower* passengers at the end, in 1651. He drew chiefly upon his own memory, but used a letter-book of correspondence, and his own rough notes and journal of the first year of settlement. Bradford was not writing for publication, and included matters which even in his day could not have been printed. He probably intended the book to be handed down in his family, as a perpetual monument to a high enterprise. His English is that of an educated, though not a learned man, deeply versed in the Geneva (not the King James) version of the Bible. It is not without conscious art, for he freely employs alliteration, and other conscious devices of contemporary English literature (E. F. Bradford, in *New England Quarterly,* I, 133–56). Touches of humor and irony enliven a plain story. Certain passages are worthy of Clarendon or Milton. But the peculiar quality of the work is imparted by the beauty, simplicity, and sincerity of the author's character. Although the *History* was not printed in full until 1856, the manuscript was used by colonial historians such as Morton, Hubbard, Prince, and Hutchinson, and Book I was printed in 1841, from a manuscript copy in the Plymouth church records. Directly and indirectly, it has been responsible for giving the Pilgrims and their colony the prominent place they occupy in American history, and popular tradition. There is no authority in Bradford for the sentimental and excessive claims that have been made for the Pilgrims; but there is ample ground for his own faith in their high mission.

[Bradford's *Hist. of Plimmoth Plantation* is the principal source for his life. The cheapest complete edition is the one issued by the Commonwealth of Massachusetts in 1897 and still (1927) in print (Secretary of State's office, State House, Boston). The best is the one published by the Mass. Hist. Soc. (2 vols., 1912), with valuable notes by Worthington C. Ford. The interesting history of the MS. which now reposes in the State Lib. at Boston is told in every edition. A complete facsimile of it, edited by J. H. Doyle, was published in London, 1896. A surviving fragment of Bradford's letter-book, covering the years 1624–30, is printed in *Colls. Mass. Hist. Soc.*, ser. 1, vol. III, pp. 27–84 and as a pamphlet by the Mass. Soc. of Mayflower Descendants (1906). "Mourt's Relation" (*A Relation . . . of the English Plantation Settled at Plymouth,* London, 1622), including parts of Bradford's journal; and Winslow's *Good News from New England* (1624) are reprinted with other source material in E. Arber, *The Story of the Pilgrim Fathers* (1897), and A. Young, *Chronicles of the Pilgrim Fathers* (1841); *Good News* is also in *Mayflower Descendant,* XXV–XXVI; Bradford's letters to Governor Winthrop are printed in *Colls. Mass. Hist. Soc.*, ser. 4, vol. VI, pp. 156–61; an important letter of 1623 in *Am. Hist. Rev.*, VIII, 294–301. His first "Dialogue between some young men born in New England and sundry ancient men that came out of Holland" is printed in the Plymouth Church Records (*Pubs. Colonial Soc., Mass.*, XXII, 115–41), in Young's *Chronicles,* and in *Old South Leaflets,* II, no. 49. The second Dialogue has disappeared; the third Dialogue, together with Bradford's long descriptive poem of 1654 and "A Word to New Plymouth," is in *Proc. Mass. Hist. Soc.*, XI, 396–482. "A Word to New England" and "Of Boston in New-England" are in the *Colls. Mass. Hist. Soc.*, ser. 3, vol. VII, pp. 27–8. His will and inventory are in *Mayfl. Desc.*, II, 228–34; his marriage records *Ibid.*, IX, 115–17. The *Plymouth Colony Records* (12 vols., Boston, 1855–61) are an important source. There is no good biography of Bradford. A fresh and enlightening study of the Plymouth Colony is that of R. G. Usher, *The Pilgrims and Their History* (1918); the principal older works are listed in Channing, Hart, and Turner's Guide, §§128–31.] S.E.M.

BRADFORD, WILLIAM (May 20, 1663–May 23, 1752), pioneer printer of the English middle colonies, was the son of William and Anne Bradford, humble folk of the Established Church in the parish of Barnwell, Leicestershire, England, where he was born. He was apprenticed to Andrew Sowle, chief London Quaker printer, and united with his master's sect. On Apr. 28, 1685, in London, he married his master's daughter, Elizabeth, who died in New York, July 8, 1731, aged sixty-eight years. Bradford afterward married the widow Cornelia Smith, through whose relatives he suffered pecuniary losses. The assumption that he accompanied Penn to America in 1682 seems untenable, notwithstanding the claim on his tombstone. Hildeburn (James G. Wilson, *Memorial History of New York,* I, 572) declares that another of the name then came, who attained some local importance in Sussex (now part of Delaware) County. Our Bradford, on leaving London with Penn's consent, in 1685, brought over a letter recommendatory from George Fox. It appears that Bradford and his wife resided temporarily at Philadelphia on their arrival late that year, but that soon residence and printery were removed to Oxford township, where the domicile continued until removal to New York, whilst the press was reëstablished at Philadelphia in 1688, where Bradford added a bookstore. The first issue of his press, in 1685, was an almanac by Samuel Atkins, in which Penn was dubbed "Lord Penn," an offense for which Bradford was reprimanded and ordered to print no more without license by the council (*Pennsylvania Colonial Records,* I, 165). In 1687 he was warned not to print anything about the Quakers without their official consent. He was reprehended by Gov. John Blackwell and his council, in 1689, for printing Penn's charter. So, harassed by both civil and religious leaders and disappointed in the unproductiveness of his press and the lack of encouragement in his pet scheme to print an English Bible in 1688, he transferred his press to his "assignes" and, on receiving a certificate of removal in July 1689, returned to England. Better encouragement from the Yearly

Meeting induced him to return and resume his press. In 1690 he was associated in founding the first paper-mill in English America. In 1692 he was released from his official printing contract, and became involved in the turbulence that had arisen from the schism led by George Keith, whose propaganda he forwarded by the press. Bradford was arrested; his types, paper, and other things were seized by the sheriff. The case is enmeshed in conflicting partisan statements. A summation seems to show that he refused to furnish security for his recognizance, so was committed in a dwelling, but allowed considerable freedom. At his trial he pleaded his own cause with great skill, maintaining the right of peremptory challenge of biased jurors in a libel action, and that the burden of proof was upon his prosecutors, whilst the jurors were judges of law as well as of fact. At a subsequent term he pleaded not guilty; and the jury,—out forty-eight hours,—not agreeing, he was discharged. On Apr. 28, 1693, Gov. Fletcher ordered the restoration of his seized property. Meanwhile, on Mar. 23, 1693, the New York council, under Fletcher's direction, offered inducements for a printer to come to New York, to print the acts of assembly and other official papers, and have the benefit of serving the public. Bradford accepted the offer and was established as "Printer to King William and Queen Mary." His first warrant for salary was retroactive to Apr. 10, 1693. From 1693 to 1724 he printed more than 250 pieces, and from 1725 to 1743 about 150 more. In the beginning, his issues were mainly public documents and religious controversial pamphlets, but after 1710 they were more varied. Bradford was admitted a freeman of New York in 1695, and the same year began to print the "Votes" of the assembly, which were the earliest legislative proceedings to be printed in America. In 1694, 1710, 1713, 1716, and 1726, he printed collections of New York laws. He printed the first New York paper currency (May 31, 1709), the first American Book of Common Prayer (1710), the first drama written in English America (1714), the first history of New York (1727), and the first copperplate plan of New York (Lyne's survey, undated, but 1730). He was a vestryman of Trinity Church, 1703–10; official printer to New Jersey, 1703–33, with slight interruption, and clerk of New Jersey, 1711. In his sixty-third year, he began New York's first newspaper, the *New-York Gazette,* Nov. 8, 1725 (earliest issue extant No. 18), which apparently expired on Nov. 19, 1744. Until 1733 it was the only newspaper in New York. It was never a well-edited product. Foreign news copy predominated and advertising was sparse. Journalism was for Bradford a losing venture. Having been printer to the Crown under four reigns, he retired in 1742, in his eightieth year, succeeded by his former apprentice, James Parker. He lived in retirement with his son, William, at New York, until his sudden death on the evening of May 23, 1752. Parker (*Post-Boy,* May 25, 1752) paid high tribute to Bradford as "a Man of great Sobriety and Industry;—a real Friend to the Poor and Needy; and kind and affable to all . . . his Temperance was exceedingly conspicuous, and he was almost a Stranger to sickness all his Life." No portrait of Bradford exists. His first tombstone was damaged and removed to the New York Historical Society, whilst a new one of Italian marble was dedicated in Trinity churchyard, May 20, 1863, and that night an august celebration took place in Cooper Institute. The Bradford Club was named for him in 1859. The Grolier Club, in April 1893, paid him tribute in a "Bradford Exhibition." On Nov. 8, 1925, journalists and printers celebrated the founding of his newspaper, and in 1926 there was formed the William Bradford Memorial Fellowship in Journalism. There are historical markers on the sites of his printing shops, at 81 Pearl St., and in Hanover Square.

[A collation of a great variety of conflicting statements in the following books and articles is imperative for the elimination of error: *Antiquarian Researches,* by Nathan Kite (Manchester, 1844), reprinted from the *Friend,* vols. XVI and XVII (Phila., 1843); Memoir of Bradford in the *Home Jour.,* Feb. 14, 1852, anonymous; "Wm. Bradford," by W. B., in *Hist. Mag.,* III (1859), 171 ff.; *Address at Celebration, May 20, 1863,* by John Wm. Wallace (1863), the fullest biography, in which real facts are hidden in a mass of pedantry and irrelevancy; chapter headed "Of Persecution and Prosecution" in *News of a Trumpet sounding in the Wilderness,* by Daniel Leeds (N. Y., 1697), and for Bradford's birth date *Am. Almanack,* 1739, of Titan Leeds, under May 20. The following works of Chas. R. Hildeburn are indispensable: *A Century of Printing: the Issues of the Press in Pa.,* vol. I (1885); *List of the Issues of the Press in N. Y.* (1889); chap. XV in Wilson's *Memorial Hist. of N. Y.,* vol. I (1891), containing facts not found elsewhere; *Cat. of Books Printed by Wm. Bradford* (1893); *Sketches of Printers and Printing in Colonial N. Y.* (1895); see also I. N. P. Stokes, *The Iconography of Manhattan Island,* chronology and appendix, vol. IV (1922).] V. H. P.

BRADFORD, WILLIAM (Jan. 19, 1721/22–Sept. 25, 1791), "patriot-printer of 1776," was born in Hanover Square, New York City, the son of William Bradford and his wife Sytje, daughter of Abraham Santvoort, and the grandson of William Bradford [*q.v.*], the pioneer printer of the English middle colonies. He was also a nephew of Andrew Bradford [*q.v.*] of Philadelphia, founder of the first newspaper in the middle colonies, by whom he was taught the art of typography and then taken into a partnership (1739–40). In 1741 our Bradford went to London to visit relatives and improve his opportunities as a printer and bookseller. Upon his return to Philadelphia in 1742, having imported the furnishings for a printery as well as the stock for a bookstore he set up in business, calling it "The Sign of the Bible." On Aug. 15 of this year he married Rachel Budd, daughter of Thomas Budd, of Northampton Township, Burlington County, N. J., and thereby gained much prestige. On Dec. 2, 1742, he issued the first number of a newspaper, under the title of the *Weekly Advertiser, or Pennsylvania Journal,* which in time became one of the best printed as well as most widely circulated of newspapers in America and, save for two suspensions during the American Revolution, continued to be printed by Bradford or his son Thomas [*q.v.*], or in partnership, until Sept. 18, 1793 (last known issue, according to Brigham). In establishing this paper Bradford became a rival of Benjamin Franklin, who for some years had been publishing the *Pennsylvania Gazette,* then a rather poor affair. From 1748 to 1753 Bradford printed a number of treatises or sermons of Gilbert Tennent and Hervey's *Meditations* (1750) in two volumes. In 1754 he established at the corner of Front and Market Streets a London Coffee-House for Merchants and Traders, which for years was a noted resort and the Merchants Exchange of his city. Not deterred by an intercolonial war, Bradford established in October 1757 the *American Magazine and Monthly Chronicle,* a literary periodical representing loyalty to the British Crown and "the Church of England and the Proprietary side of things," which lasted through October 1758. Under a similar title he and his son Thomas, from January to September 1769, printed *The American Magazine, or General Repository,* edited by Lewis Nichola. Although busy as a printer, journalist, bookseller, keeper of a coffee-house, and otherwise, Bradford found time to be a social leader. In 1762, in partnership with John Kidd, he established the Philadelphia Insurance Company, a successful venture of which he was principal manager. His bookstore went to better quarters in 1764, adjoining his coffee-house, so that he then controlled a group of businesses in a number of adjoining buildings. From 1760 to 1765 some two dozen publications issued from his press, comprising politics, religion, and literature, in fairly good proportions. In 1742 to 1823, the printery he established continued under him or his family as one of the principal publishing houses of the country.

When in 1747–48 Philadelphia was threatened by war and her shipping was in danger, Bradford became a lieutenant in a volunteer company of "Associators." It was his first military connection. In 1756, the country being at war, he was again in arms and was promoted to a captaincy. He was an uncompromising opponent of the Stamp Act of 1765. The day before the act took effect he issued his newspaper (Oct. 31) in mourning, with skull and crossbones, and denounced the measure in print as "the detestable Stamp Act, which no American can mention without abhorrence." As a member of the Sons of Liberty he demanded its repeal. He was a signer of the Non-Importation Resolutions of 1765. He was an early advocate for a continental congress, and in his newspaper, July 27, 1774, expressed the need by a dissected snake device and the words "Unite or Die," which device his paper carried till October 1775. When the first Congress met at Philadelphia in September, Bradford and his son were made its printers. In January 1775 he was active in the Convention of Pennsylvania, which defended "the rights and liberties of America." Bradford realized war was inevitable. He became captain of a company of the "Associators" of 1775, advancing money for military needs. After Bunker Hill he was more defiant. In June 1776 he was despatched by the Continental Congress with wagons and money for the army in Canada. After the Declaration of Independence he joined the patriot army at Amboy. Although fifty-six years of age and really exempt, and notwithstanding he had a wife and family and large business interests of benefit to his country, he became major of the second battalion of the Pennsylvania militia (July 1776), in the brigade of Gen. John Cadwalader, and reached the rank of colonel. He was in the campaign of Trenton and was severely wounded at the battle of Princeton. In 1777 he was named chairman of the Pennsylvania State Navy Board and from January 1778 he alone conducted its affairs until the board was abolished. He retired from active service after the British evacuation of Philadelphia in June 1778. His health was shattered and his personal affairs were greatly injured by the war. It is said that "full seven-eights of his credits were worthless." On May 12, 1779, he was appointed president of the court of inquiry respecting military officers, his last army connection. By his wife Rachel (b. Jan. 7, 1720/1; d. June 25 or 26, 1780), he had six children, three sons and three daughters. Although Bradford had suffered severely in body and fortune, he frequently said to his children, "Though I bequeath you no estate I leave you in the enjoyment of liberty" (Isaiah Thomas, *History of Printing in America,* 1810, II, 50). In his latter days he was afflicted by three apoplectic strokes, affecting his mind, and on Sept. 25, 1791, "he died as a child falls asleep, and the springs of nature quite worn out, the machine stopped."

[The principal source is a good volume biography, *An Old Philadelphian,* by John W. Wallace (1884), of which only 100 copies were printed. Of secondary account are: *Bradford Family* (1873), by S. S. Purple, pp. 5–6; *Bradford Family* (1906), by Henry Darrach, p. 6; "The Bradford Family of Printers," by H. L. Bullen, in the *Am. Collector,* I (1926), pp. 166–68. Details on his newspaper are in Clarence S. Brigham's "Bibliography of Am. Newspapers," pt. XIII, *Proc. Am. Antiquarian Soc.,* 1922, pp. 168–75. C. R. Hildeburn's *A Century of Printing; the Issues of the Press in Pa.* (1885) has the fullest record of Bradford's productive press.] V. H. P.

BRADFORD, WILLIAM (Sept. 14, 1755–Aug. 23, 1795), jurist, was the great-grandson of William Bradford [*q.v.*], who introduced printing into the American middle colonies and the son of William Bradford [*q.v.*] the so-called "patriot-printer of 1776," and his wife Rachel Budd. Born in Philadelphia he was educated at Princeton, N. J., 1769–72 (A.B.)—1775 (A.M.). The following year he spent in reading and in attending the lectures of Dr. Witherspoon on theology to profit by his logical method. He studied law under Edward Shippen, afterward chief justice of Pennsylvania, writing prose and verse with Addison and Shenstone as his models, while he read his Coke. His tastes were for civil rather than for military life, but like his father he patriotically answered the call of America in the Revolution. Volunteering as a private in 1776, he soon became major of brigade to Gen. Roberdeau and later a captain in Col. Hampton's continental regiment. He was elected by Congress, Apr. 10, 1777, deputy muster-master general with the rank of colonel in the Continental Army. After serving during the critical years 1777–79 at Valley Forge, White Plains, Fredericksborough, and Raritan, his broken health forced him to resign Apr. 1, 1779. Returning to his legal studies he was admitted to the bar of the supreme court of Pennsylvania and made his home at Yorktown, Pa., in 1779. At the early age of twenty-five, and but a year after he began to practise law, he was appointed through the influence of the president of the state, Joseph Reed, to succeed Jonathan D. Sergeant as attorney-general of Pennsylvania. For eleven consecutive years and under different administrations he retained this office. His contemporaries considered him a lawyer of high tone, eloquent, and of great purity of life and purpose. With Joseph Reed, James Wilson, and J. D. Sergeant, he pleaded and won the case of Pennsylvania against Connecticut before the Congressional Commission in the Wyoming land titles contention in 1782. Promoted, Aug. 22, 1791, by Gov. Mifflin, to be justice of the supreme bench of Pennsylvania, he attracted the notice of Washington, who, on Jan. 28, 1794, made him the second attorney-general of the United States in the place of Edmund Randolph promoted to the secretaryship of state. Washington valued Bradford as a personal friend and as a lawyer, and it was upon his report as one of the commissioners appointed by the President to attempt an amicable settlement of the "Whisky Insurrection" by conferences at Pittsburgh that Washington issued his proclamation of force "to secure the execution of the laws" when these peaceful efforts failed. Bradford and his wife, Susan Vergereau Boudinot, only daughter of Elias Boudinot [*q.v.*] of New Jersey, were intimates in the Washington circle, the so-called "Republican Court," and Bradford had formed in his student days a warm friendship with James Madison. Secretaries Pickering and Wolcott sought Bradford, ill at his country home, to aid them in formulating the letter which brought Washington from Mount Vernon to consider the indiscretions of Edmund Randolph as secretary of state in his dealings with the French minister Fauchet. It was from the exhaustion of dealing with this controversy and from the arduous trips at night to "Rose Hill," the country seat of his father-in-law, that Bradford contracted the fatal fever that led to his unexpected and untimely end. He influenced the revision of the criminal jurisprudence of Pennsylvania by his report of Dec. 3, 1792, which, spread upon the journals of the Pennsylvania Senate (Feb. 22, 1793), led to the statute of Apr. 22, 1794, which substituted "imprisonment at hard labor" for the death penalty for all capital crimes "except murder of the first degree." The Report was subsequently published in book form and was widely read. Bradford was buried in St. Mary's Churchyard at Burlington, N. J.

[Horace Binney Wallace, sketch in the *Am. Law Jour.,* Apr. 1852 (reprinted in J. W. Wallace's *An Old Philadelphian,* 1884, pp. 482–87); R. W. Griswold, *The Republican Court* (1856), pp. 298n., 300, 303, 310n., 335, 338 and note, 339.] J. C. B.

BRADFORD, WILLIAM (Apr. 30, 1823–Apr. 25, 1892), marine painter, was born in Fairhaven, Mass., which is only about one mile distant from New Bedford. He was the son of Melvin and Hannah (Kempton) Bradford. The Bradfords were a Quaker family and in this faith William was brought up. All of his biographers refer to his mother as being of excellent character and strong religious convictions, and he himself is said to have attributed one of his most effective traits as an artist—patience—to the self-control and calmness which are required by the Society of Friends. In 1846 he was married to Mary Breed, an estimable and accomplished woman, the daughter of Nathan Breed of Lynn, Mass., who was also of old New England Quaker stock. From early youth Bradford had had an inclination toward art but it was not until eight years after his marriage that his career as an artist was begun. At that time he and his father, who were in business together, failed, and to make a livelihood he turned to painting pictures of ships in Lynn and other harbors. The correctness of his work and the carefulness with which it was rendered won him reputation and secured purchasers. From this he passed to studies of the coast, the rocks, and sea on the New England and Canadian shore, going as far north as Labrador. For two years he shared his studio at Fairhaven with Albert Van Beest, a Dutch painter and ex-officer of the Dutch navy—a man of education and training but of no great talent. Bradford made an Arctic expedition with Dr. Hayes and at one time he himself chartered a vessel and went to Labrador where, clad in the sealskin coat of the Eskimo, he made studies of icebergs and ice-floes. These paintings were done with great fidelity to detail, were realistic, accurate, and most carefully rendered. To-day they would be described as photographic and hard, but they brought to those who saw them then a truthful impression of what the artist himself had seen.

Exhibitions of Bradford's paintings were held in Providence and other cities in the United States and also in England. One of his paintings, "Steamer *Panther* among Icebergs and Field-Ice in Melville Bay, under the light of the Midnight Sun," was purchased by Queen Victoria and exhibited, with her permission, at the Royal Academy in 1875. Among his other patrons in England were the Marchioness of Lorne and the Baroness Burdett Coutts. One of his paintings entitled "Arctic Whaler Homeward Bound" is in the permanent collection of the Art Institute of Chicago. Another, "Tracking a Whaler through Icebergs in Baffin's Bay," is in the permanent collection of the New Bedford Free Public Library. Among his other recorded works are "Fishing Boats in the Bay of Fundy," "Ship-wreck off Nantucket," "Lighthouse in St. John's Harbor," "Fishing Boats getting Under Way," "Island of Grand Manan," "Fishing Boats at Anchor," "A Sudden Squall in the Bay of Fundy," "Swift Breeze in the Harbor of Eastport," "The Coast of Labrador," "Crushed by Icebergs," "Scenes in the North" and "Arctic Scene," the last exhibited at the National Academy of Design, New York, in 1896.

[H. T. Tuckerman, *Book of the Artists* (1867); Samuel Isham, *Hist. of Am. Painting* (1905); *Art Jour.*, XXV, 255; Austin Jones, article on Bradford in the *Am. Friend*, Dec. 20, 1900; Geneal. Records in the Free Pub. Lib., New Bedford, Mass.; *N. Y. Times*, Apr. 26, 1892.] L. M.

BRADISH, LUTHER (Sept. 15, 1783–Aug. 30, 1863), diplomat and statesman, was born in Cummington, Hampshire County, Mass., son of Col. John and Hannah (Warner) Bradish. He was descended from Robert Bradish, who settled in Cambridge, Mass., in 1635. Graduating from Williams College in 1804, he went to New York and combined teaching with the study of law until his admission to the bar. Soon after this the collection of a large claim necessitated a trip to South America, the West Indies, and the British Isles. He returned to the United States in time to serve as a volunteer in the War of 1812. In 1814 he married Helen Elizabeth, daughter of George Gibbs of Newport, R. I., but two years later both she and their only child died. In 1820 John Quincy Adams, then secretary of state, requested him to sound the disposition of the Turkish Government regarding a treaty with the United States which would open the Black Sea to American trade. Provided with no authority beyond a special passport, he crossed the Atlantic on the *Columbus*, flagship of Commodore Bainbridge, and made the circuit of the western Mediterranean with the United States squadron. Supposedly engaged on a secret mission, he was dismayed by rumors current in every port that he was authorized to negotiate a treaty with the Porte. A dispatch vessel took him from Gibraltar to Smyrna, whence he went by land to Constantinople. There he was well received in diplomatic circles and held conversations with high Turkish officials. The latter, however, were unwilling to commit themselves on the prospect of an American negotiation, and temporized until the first mutterings of the Greek Revolution destroyed all hope of a definite answer. Convinced that that indecision of the Porte was due to a desire to curry favor with European powers hostile to the entry of a new rival into the Levant trade, Bradish advised that any attempt on the part of the United States to negotiate a treaty should be made without the customary intervention of a nation already represented at Constantinople. This procedure was successfully followed by Charles Rhind in 1830. After spending several months in Constantinople, Bradish visited Egypt and became personally acquainted with Mehemet Ali, the Pasha. Crossing the desert to Palestine, he traveled through Syria, returned to Constantinople by sea, and continued to Vienna on horseback. Until 1826 he remained in Europe, extending his travels to Scandinavia and Russia, while he spent considerable time in the great capitals and studied assiduously their languages, manners, and antiquities. On his return to America he resided in Franklin County, New York, where he owned extensive properties. After playing a prominent part in Philhellene activities, he was elected to the state Assembly as a Whig. This position he held from 1827 to 1830, and again from 1835 to 1838. Chosen speaker of the Assembly in 1838, he was in the same year elected lieutenant-governor. During the two terms that he held this office he established a remarkable reputation as a parliamentarian while presiding over the Senate, and as member of the court for correction of errors came off victorious in a dispute with the supreme court of the state. In 1842 he was the unsuccessful Whig nominee for governor, but was immediately appointed assistant United States treasurer for New York by his intimate friend, President Fillmore. After two years he retired from politics and devoted himself to educational and philanthropic interests in New York City, where he made his home after 1842. In 1849 he succeeded Albert Gallatin as president of the New York Historical Society and held the office until his death. He was also for many years president of the American Bible Society. By a second marriage in 1839 to Mary Eliza Hart of New York he had one daughter. His broad culture, urbane disposition, and eminent public services gained universal respect. He died suddenly at Newport, R. I.

[Sketches in the *Eclectic Mag.*, Sept. 1863, and in *Memorial Biogs. of the New Eng. Hist. and Geneal. Soc.*, V, 268–76; Bradish's report to Adams in *House Exec. Doc. No. 250*, 22 Cong., 1 Sess.; his papers (eleven boxes) in the Lib. of the N. Y. Hist. Soc.]

W. L. W—t.

BRADLEY, CHARLES HENRY (Feb. 13, 1860–Jan. 30, 1922), educator, was born in Johnson, Vt., the son of Harmon Howe and Sarah Grout (Ferguson) Bradley, and a descendant of Stephen Bradley, of Guilford, Conn. He was educated in the local public schools and at the State Normal School in his native village. At the age of twenty, he moved to Massachusetts as instructor in the State Primary School, at Palmer, of which, in 1885, he was made assistant superintendent. In March 1888 he was made head of the Farm and Trades School, an institution established in 1814 on Thompson's Island in Boston Harbor for the purpose of providing homes and education for worthy boys in destitute circumstances. In this position he remained for thirty-four years.

The Farm and Trades School, with its 157 acres of land, was the first institution of its kind in this country to make agriculture the basis of its educational policy. It was already successful when Bradley took charge of it, but he soon, through the improvements which he initiated, gave it a national reputation. He held there the first sloyd classes in the United States. He enlarged the curriculum to include such practical subjects as iron and metal work, shoe repairing, stationary engineering, and typewriting, so that each boy was equipped to earn his living by a trade. Nearly ten years before the George Junior Republic, Bradley started a boys' government plan, called "Cottage Row City," which was in successful operation for many years. He set up, in 1905, a meteorological observatory, which was later connected with the United States Weather Bureau. In the same year he visited Europe on a tour of inspection of similar schools, only to find that he was usually the teacher instead of the listener.

Bradley's innovations drew many visitors to Thompson's Island. He was offered positions as head of the New York State Reformatory in Elmira, N. Y., and as head of the House of Refuge in New York City, but preferred to remain in Boston. He was a founder and the first president of the Vermont Association of Boston. Norwich University gave him the honorary degree of Master of Arts in 1911, and he was later one of its trustees. He was a member of many patriotic organizations, including the Society of Colonial Wars, the Sons of the American Revolution, the Bostonian Society, and the New England Historical and Genealogical Society; and active in the Masonic Order. He was married on June 7, 1883, to Mary Chilton Brewster, of Duxbury, Mass., eighth in direct descent from Elder William Brewster.

[Excellent memoir in the *New Eng. Hist. and Geneal. Reg.*, LXXVII (1923), lx; also good obituary in the *Boston Evening Transcript*, Jan. 30, 1922.] C. M. F.

BRADLEY, CHARLES WILLIAM (June 27, 1807–Mar. 8, 1865), diplomat, Sinologist, was a descendant of a family which had lived in New England at least since 1640. He was the son of Luther and Mary (Atwater) Bradley, and was born at New Haven, Conn. As a youth he began to learn printing, but abandoned this to enter Washington (now Trinity) College, Hartford, Conn., in 1825. He withdrew before graduation, however, and continued his studies at the General Theological Seminary, New York City, completing his course in 1830, and later receiving an honorary M.A. both from Trinity and from Yale, as well as an LL.D. from Hobart College in 1846. Shortly before leaving the Seminary, a fall gave a shock to his nervous system which permanently affected his health, making him a victim of restlessness, excitability, and repeated morbid depressions. Nevertheless, he was for ten years rector of Episcopal parishes in North Haven, East Haddam, Sharon, and Derby, Conn., but the work proved to be too hard for him, and he passed the next few years in enforced idleness. In 1846–47 he was secretary of state for Connecticut, and in this capacity he collated, indexed, and arranged the state records in a manner which rendered them more generally accessible, besides preparing *The Connecticut Register: being an Official State Calendar of Public Officers and Institutions in Connecticut for 1847* (1848). After two years of foreign travel (1847–49), Bradley began his real career, which centered in China and lasted fourteen years (1849–63). His first brief position with a mercantile firm was severed because of his opposition to any connection with the opium traffic, and he then entered the United States Government service, being consul at Amoy (1849–54), Singapore (1854–57), and Ningpo (1857–60), respectively. In 1857 he brought back to the United States a treaty with Siam, returning with its ratification; in 1858 he accompanied the Pei-ho expedition at the request of Mr. Reed, the United States minister to China; and in 1859 he was the senior member of the Commission on American Claims against the Chinese Government. Feeling, however, that his services had not been duly recognized by his Government, he resigned from the service in 1860 and paid a brief visit to the United States, but soon returned to China, where he was an assistant in the Imperial Chinese Customs at Hankow until 1863. In this latter year, his health utterly broken, he retired to his native city, where he died.

As his career shows, Bradley's interests and activities were rather wide. In his diplomatic career he manifested all due firmness regarding the interests of his government, while opposing whatever he regarded as infringing on Chinese rights. He collected a fairly large library, of which the Oriental section was, naturally, the more valuable; but his nervous affliction forbade any extensive literary activity, though he gave his knowledge freely to other scholars. Besides the work already mentioned, he seems to have published only two brief studies: *Patronomatology,* a portion of a treatise on the philosophy of surnames, read before the Connecticut State Lyceum, and arising from his interest in the history of proper names (Baltimore, 1842), and an "Outline of the System adopted for Romanizing the [Chinese] Dialect of Amoy" (*Journal of the American Oriental Society,* IV, 1854, pp. 335–40); and he also presented to the same society a paper on "The Kings and Kingdom of Siam" (*Ibid.,* VI, 1859, p. 583), which was never printed in full. He bequeathed his Oriental library to the American Oriental Society, to which he had already given more than 850 books and manuscripts, and for the same society he collected over $1,000, primarily for the purchase of Chinese type, which still forms the nucleus of its "Charles W. Bradley Type Fund."

[*Proc. Am. Oriental Soc.,* May 1865, pp. 60–62, Oct. 1871, p. 28; *New Eng. Hist. and Geneal. Reg.,* XXII (1868), 360–61.] L. H. G.

BRADLEY, DENIS MARY (Feb. 25, 1846–Dec. 13, 1903), Roman Catholic bishop, was born in County Kerry, Ireland, of sturdy, laboring parentage. On the death of his father, his mother in 1854 brought her young brood to Manchester, N. H., where she maintained a humble home by taking in boarders and working as a seamstress. The boy's schooling, aside from the religious training of the home, was left to New Hampshire's pioneer Catholic master, Thomas Cochran. In 1864, Bradley matriculated at Holy Cross College in Worcester, receiving his bachelor's degree three years later from Georgetown College, as Holy Cross was not chartered to give degrees. He was no "poor scholar," for his mother by scrimping had hoarded three hundred golden dollars, then at high premium, to pay his modest expenses. Inspired with a religious calling, the young man entered St. Joseph's Seminary at Troy, N. Y., where after four years in cloistered study of theology, he was ordained on July 3, 1871, by Bishop Bernard McQuade of Rochester. Bradley's superior, Rt. Rev. David W. Bacon, first bishop of Portland, named the young neophyte a curate at the cathedral; for him a pleasant location because his sister was prioress of the neighboring Mercy Convent. Interested in Father Mathew's temperance movement, Bradley won the friendship of Neal Dow, who fathered the Maine prohibition law. In 1879, Bradley said the first Mass in the State Reform School, which evidenced his popularity with the non-Catholics of Portland even more than did their generosity in subscribing a share of the purse to give the priest his first vacation. After his return from abroad, he was appointed pastor of St. Joseph's Church in Manchester by Bishop James A. Healy. During the French-Canadian influx into New England, Manchester was separated from the Portland diocese, in 1884, and was given its own episcopal see. Nominated by the New England bishops, Bradley was appointed to the new diocese and consecrated by the saintly Archbishop John J. Williams of Boston. The youngest bishop in America, Bradley was well fitted for the appointment. He knew and loved the state. Of medium height and slender build, he was of a rigorous constitution. This was well, for journeyings to and ministrations in every scattered hamlet tested his metal and vitality. He was gracious and dignified, meeting the world with a sweet smile and a bright eye. Though of deep voice, he was no orator, nor was he a scholar. His sermons, however, simple and sincere, touched his hearers. When nativist opposition or factory strife demanded attention, he met the situation with a firm moderation which satisfied his priests and co-religionists and won the approval of fair-minded men. It was as the architect of his diocese, as an administrator and builder, as a supporter of Catholic schools, as a friend of labor, and as a competent business man, that the bishop did his real service.

[M. H. Dowd, *Life of Denis M. Bradley* (n.d.); John E. Finen *et al.*, *Hist. of the Cath. Ch. in New Eng.* (1899); G. C. Delany, *Life and Writings of John B. Delany* (1911); G. F. Willey, *Book of Manchester* (1896); Henry Gabriels, *Hist. Sketch of St. Joseph's Provincial Seminary, Troy, N. Y.* (1905); *Cath. Encyc.* under "New Hampshire"; *Daily Patriot* (Concord, N. H.), Dec. 14, 1903.] R. J. P.

BRADLEY, FRANK HOWE (Sept. 20, 1838–Mar. 27, 1879), geologist, was born in New Haven, Conn., graduated at Yale in 1863, and later took special courses in natural history in the Sheffield Scientific School. His tastes early took a geological trend and in 1857, while not yet nineteen years of age, he had discovered a new species of trilobite in the Potsdam sandstone of New York and proved the existence of crinoids in beds of the same horizon. After graduation he spent more than a year at Panama and vicinity where he made large collections of coral and other zoölogical materials. During 1867 he was assistant geologist on the survey of Illinois under J. G. Norwood and in 1869 served likewise on the survey of Indiana under Edward Travers Cox. A paper prepared by him on the Carboniferous rocks of Vermillion County was commented upon by Dana as a "valuable chapter" in the report of that year. In 1872 he became a member of the National Survey under F. V. Hayden and was assigned to the Snake River division in Idaho. "Among his important results, as set forth in his excellent report, there is the identification of fossils of the Quebec group in Idaho, and also at the base of the Teton range" (J. D. Dana). From 1869 to 1875 he held the chair of geology and mineralogy in the University of Tennessee, and while there made a detailed section of the unaltered Lower Silurian formations and the beds of crystalline rocks to the east, publishing his results under the caption "On the Silurian Age of the Southern Appalachians" in the *American Journal of Science* for 1876. The same year he also published a small geological map of the United States. He eventually gave up his position at Knoxville to undertake private mining ventures in the hope of securing a competence sufficient to allow him to follow his scientific calling untrammelled by financial difficulties. It was while thus engaged that he met his tragic fate, being killed by the caving in of a gold mine near Nacoochee, Ga., in which he was at work.

He is described as "a man of profound zeal for science, of exactness in observation, of great energy, and of independent judgment and purpose." He was tall, of erect figure, neat in dress, but after a fashion dictated by his work and not by prevalent modes, in this indicating his independence of character. "His lines of action were laid down by his sense of what was just and once fixed there was no swerving." He was often accused of obstinacy, and in his work met with more opposition or friction than would otherwise have been the case. He was married in 1867 to Sarah M. Bolles of New Haven by whom he had two children, a daughter and an infant son that died on the day of his own death.

[J. D. Dana, "Frank Howe Bradley," *Am. Jour. Sci.*, May 1879, pp. 415–19.] G. P. M.

BRADLEY, JOHN EDWIN (Aug. 8, 1839–Oct. 7, 1912), college president, the son of Stephen and Hannah (Austin) Bradley, was born in Lee, Mass., and was graduated from Williams College in 1865. After three years as principal of the high school at Pittsfield, Mass., he was called in 1868 to be the first principal of the Albany Free Academy, N. Y. Here he performed what was probably his most distinctive and constructive work in the educational field. He was among the pioneeers who labored in the difficult period that marked the transition from the private academy to the free public high school. To him fell not only the lot of organizing the first public high school of the city of Albany but also the still more difficult task of winning public support for the enterprise. He remained in charge of the school for eighteen years and made it one of the leading high schools in the state. In 1876 he accepted the position of superintendent of schools in Minneapolis. In this growing city of the Northwest, also, there was much pioneer work to be done. He introduced manual training into the high schools, and promoted a movement for the better training of the younger teachers of the city school system. During his six years of service in Minneapolis, the number of public schools increased from 28 to 49; the number of teachers from 296 to 572 and the pupils from 14,194 to 23,797, the school enrolment during these years growing about twice as rapidly as the population. Having established a solid reputation as an administrator in the public school systems of both the East and the Middle West, Bradley became in 1892 the president of Illinois College, an old institution of fine traditions at Jacksonville, Ill. It was for him a new field, involving many serious difficulties. He had succeeded a very popular former president; the curriculum of the old college had to be modernized to meet the demands of a new age and the increasing competition of near-by universities. The new president went about his task with keen intelligence and firm resolution but funds could not be found to ward off annual deficits. He became discouraged over the outlook and in 1900 resigned. Subsequently he served for six years as superintendent of schools at Randolph, Mass., where he died at the age of seventy-three.

Bradley was a man of dignified bearing whose kindly disposition won the affectionate regard of students in both high school and college. His wife, Martha J. Gould, whom he married in 1870, helped to make their home an attractive social center for students. His degrees included the A.M. and LL.D. conferred by Williams and the Ph.D. awarded by the Regents of the University of New York. He represented the State of New York at the Paris Exposition of 1878; was for several years a member of the National Council of Education and was several times elected to the National Council of Congregational Churches. He published many articles on educational topics and a small volume of addresses, *Work and Play* (1900).

[For career in Albany, see Jas. M. Ruso, "Hist. of Albany H. S.," in *Albany Express,* Nov. 16, 1893; *Argus,* Aug. 10, 1886; *Hist. of the Albany H. S.,* pamphlet published in 1876; for career in Minneapolis, *Reports of Minneapolis Board of Ed.,* 1887–92, especially the last one; also, *Illustrated Minneapolis, A Souvenir of the Minneapolis Jour.,* 1891; for career at Illinois College, manuscript records of trustees and faculty.]
C.H.R.

BRADLEY, JOSEPH P. (Mar. 14, 1813–Jan. 22, 1892), justice of the Supreme Court, was born at Berne, Albany County, N. Y. (The "P" does not represent the initial letter of a name. His father's name was Philo and Joseph adopted the "P" probably as a patronymic. See Stern, *post.*) The first Bradley came to this country from England in 1645. Joseph's great-grandfather was a soldier in the War of Independence, and his grandfather served in the War of 1812. His mother was Mercy Gardner, of Rhode Island stock. The Bradleys were a race of farmers, and Joseph, the eldest of eleven children, passed a laborious youth amid straitened circumstances on a small farm in his native county. He early displayed pronounced intellectual traits and a determination to get forward. Attending school four months each year, he became at the age of sixteen a country school-teacher. Later a Lutheran parson, becoming attracted to him, gave him lessons in Greek and Latin. At the age of twenty he entered Rutgers College, from which he graduated three years later, an outstanding member of a famous class. The same year, 1836, he entered upon the study of law in the office of Archer Gifford, at that time collector of the Port of Newark. He was admitted to the New Jersey bar in November 1839. In 1844 he was married to Mary, daughter of Chief Justice Hornblower of New Jersey. At the height of his professional career he devoted himself especially to patent, commercial, and corporation cases. Having a talent for mathematics he became an actuary of the Prudential Insurance Company. He was also counsel for various railroads. His first appearance before the Supreme Court of the United States occurred in December 1860, in connection with the case of Milnor *vs.* the New Jersey R. R. and Transportation Company (see appendix to 24 *Howard* in 16 *Lawyers' Edition Extra Annotated,* pp. 799–810), Bradley's argument in which anticipated the later decision of the court in Gilman *vs.* Philadelphia (3 *Wallace,* 713).

Politically Bradley was originally a Whig; and in the winter of 1860–61 he passed several weeks in Washington for the purpose of urging upon Congress a compromise between North and South along the lines of the Corwin Amendment. The firing upon Fort Sumter, however, caused him to take up immediately a strong Unionist position. He denounced secession as treason, and urged that in crushing the rebellion the National Government was restrained only by "the laws of God and the Law of Nations." Later in championing the Thirteenth Amendment he espoused the "state suicide" doctrine of Sumner—states which had attempted secession were not entitled to be counted in amending the Constitution; and if they were to be subsequently restored to their former status in the Union, it could be only through the grace of Congress. In 1862 he ran a hopeless race for Congress in support of the Lincoln administration, and in 1868 he headed the New Jersey electoral ticket for Grant. He was nominated for the Supreme Court by President Grant, along with Judge William Strong of the Pennsylvania supreme court, on the morning of the day, Feb. 7, 1870, in the afternoon of which the Court handed down its decision in Hepburn *vs.* Griswold (8 *Wallace,* 603). This coincidence has provoked the charge that the Supreme Court was "packed" in order to bring about the later decision in Knox *vs.* Lee (12 *Wallace,* 457), when the new majority of the Court, speaking through Strong and Bradley, overturned Hepburn *vs.* Griswold. The available evidence leaves the question in some obscurity. The way for the two nominations had been paved by an Act of Congress passed in April 1869, to take effect the ensuing December, whereas the decision in Hepburn *vs.* Griswold was not settled in conference till November 1869. It cannot be seriously questioned, however, that the views of both Bradley and Strong on the legal-tender question were known to those in authority when their nominations were sent in. Strong had participated in a decision of the Pennsylvania supreme court which sustained the act set aside in Hepburn *vs.* Griswold; while Bradley's leanings both as a railroad lawyer (the general attitude of the railroad interests being strongly favorable toward the legal-tender act) and as a strong nationalist during the war were scarcely open to serious doubt. We also have the testimony of Boutwell, then secretary of the treasury, that he knew in advance what the decision in Hepburn *vs.* Griswold was to be. The order of the reconstructed Court granting a reargument of the constitutional question raised by the legal-tender act was entered Apr. 11, 1870, and precipitated an acrimonious dispute among the justices, the facts concerning which were first made known in 1902 (Charles Bradley, pp. 61–74). The charge made in a paper first filed and then withdrawn by Chief Justice Chase, that the Court had acted in the matter in derogation of a previous understanding, was apparently without foundation; while in view of the fact that the original decision was by a virtual minority of the Court, the rehearing was obviously proper even if not positively required.

In 1877 Bradley was appointed a member of the famous Electoral Commission created by Congress to pass upon the electoral votes of Florida, Louisiana, South Carolina, and Oregon. Because he was the last member chosen to the Commission and took the place in it originally proffered Justice David Davis, whose political leanings were ambiguous, it came to be assumed that he would pursue a non-partisan course in what had become a bitterly partisan contest. In point of fact his vote on all critical issues before the Commission was uniformly cast in the Republican interest, with the result that Hayes was elected. His position, however, which was that developed by William M. Evarts as counsel for Hayes, was not only quite consistent throughout, but was also strongly defensible in itself. It was in brief that, in the absence at least of legislation by Congress, the two Houses, in counting the electoral vote, were performing a purely ministerial function and had therefore no power to revise the canvass by state authorities of an election of Electors, either on the suggestion of fraud or for any other cause (Charles Bradley, pp. 165–215). A charge by Justice Field that Bradley had originally vacillated in this opinion was disavowed by the former so far as derogatory to Bradley's "honor or integrity."

In his twenty-two years on the bench Bradley was the author of many notable opinions. His concurring opinion in Knox *vs.* Lee (12 *Wallace,* 554) contains the first obvious invocation in a Supreme Court opinion of the doctrine that the national government possesses certain inherent powers—a doctrine which has been utilized by the Court since then more than once. His dissenting opinion in the Slaughter House Cases (16 *Wallace,* 36, 111) anticipates remarkably present-day concepts of "due process of law" and "liberty and property" in interpretation of the Fourteenth Amendment, and was unquestionably influential in projecting these concepts into our constitutional law. In a series of opinions he contributed more than any of his contemporaries to the elaboration of the principles which still guide the Court in drawing the line between the "exclusive" power of Congress over interstate commerce and the taxing powers of the states (see Transportation Company *vs.* Parkersburg, 107 *United States Reports,* 691; Brown *vs.* Houston, 114 *U. S. R.,* 622; Coe *vs.* Errol, 116 *U. S. R.,* 517; Robbins *vs.* Shelby Taxing Dist., 120 U. S. R., 498; Philadelphia, etc., S. S. Company *vs.* Pennsylvania, 122 *U. S. R.,* 326; Leloup *vs.* Mobile, 127 *U. S. R.,* 640). In the Mormon Church Case (136 *U. S. R.* 1), in sustaining the right of Congress to revoke the charter of this organization, he foreshadowed in a measure the doctrine, later brought to fruition in the Insular Cases (182 *U. S. R.*), of the plenary power of Congress in territories; while in Boyd *vs.* United States (116 *U. S. R.*, 616) he laid down the guiding lines of the Court's present interpretation of the Fourth and Fifth Amendments on the subject of self-incrimination by the forced production of documents.

Bradley's most notable exposition of national power is to be found in his opinion in *ex parte* Siebold (100 *U. S. R.*, 371), in which, in sustaining the right of Congress to cast penally enforceable duties upon state election officials in connection with the election of members of the House of Representatives, he asserts the territorial sovereignty of the national government, acting within the sphere of its powers "on every foot of American soil," strongly deprecates state jealousy of national power, and preaches the gospel of national and state coöperation for common purposes. At the same time, Bradley was far from wishing to see the states crowded to the wall in consequence of the outcome of the Civil War. In the Civil Rights Cases (109 *U. S. R.*, 3) he asserted the necessity of construing the War Amendments in the light of the Tenth Amendment, and on that basis arrived at the conclusion that Congress has no power under the Fourteenth Amendment to anticipate state action hostile to equality under the law or to supply the deficiencies of state laws—a view which has rendered legislative powers of Congress under the Amendment practically nugatory. His opinion in Hans *vs.* Louisiana (134 *U. S. R.*, 1), extending the immunity which is conferred upon the states by the Eleventh Amendment to suits commenced or prosecuted by their own citizens also manifests his conservative tendency as respects the traditional position of the states in the Union.

Bradley was master of a vigorous and incisive, if somewhat prolix, judicial style, in which, as well as in many of his ideas, the influence of Chief Justice Marshall can be readily detected. His last opinion from the bench was his dissent in Maine *vs.* Grand Trunk Railway Company (142 *U. S. R.*, 217, 231). The views which he therein expressed have since been substantially adopted by the court (see Galveston, etc., Railroad Company *vs.* Texas, 210 *U. S. R.*, 217).

Bradley's diversions were intellectual. While history and belles-lettres claimed his attention to some extent, his chief interest was given to mathematical and genealogical studies. In addition to the immense labor of compiling a history of his own family, which was privately published shortly following his death, he also compiled the history of his wife's family and connections, besides collecting the records of many collateral branches. A further reminder of his characteristic interests is a "Perpetual Calendar for finding the day of the week on which any day of the month falls in any year before or after Christ, old style or new" (see Charles Bradley, p. 333). His general library comprised some six thousand volumes, his law library some ten thousand volumes. The latter upon his death was secured by the Prudential Insurance Company of Newark, N. J., and is maintained in that city "complete and entire even to the pictures on the walls." He was also a man who keenly relished the intellectual exchanges of social life and cultivated many distinguished friendships.

[*Miscellaneous Writings of the Late Hon. Jos. P. Bradley . . . and a Review of His "Judicial Record" by Wm. Draper Lewis . . . and An Account of His "Dissenting Opinions" by the Late A. Q. Keasbey . . .* edited and compiled by his son Chas. Bradley (1902); sketch by Horace Stern, in Wm. D. Lewis (ed.), *Gt. Am. Lawyers,* VI (1909), 345 ff.; U. S. Supreme Court Reports from 12 *Wallace* to 142 *U. S.;* citation should also be made of pertinent pages in Chas. Warren's *Supreme Court in U. S. Hist.* (1922).] E. S. C.

BRADLEY, LYDIA MOSS (July 31, 1816–Jan. 16, 1908), philanthropist, was the daughter of Capt. Zealy Moss of Loudoun County, Va., who served in the Revolutionary army. After the war, Zealy and his wife, Jeanette (Glasscock) of Fauquier County, Va., moved to Vevay, Ind., where Lydia was born. Her father entered the Baptist ministry, but was also owner of a farm on which every one worked. It was not very long before Lydia demonstrated that she had her share of sturdy heritage. Still in her teens and slight for her age, she one day traded her saddle-horse for a tract of timber land, which she set out to clear. With some help from her father, this was accomplished, and the girl sold her land at a profit. She was married to Tobias S. Bradley of Vevay on May 11, 1837, and moved with him to Peoria, Ill., where her brother, William S. Moss, lived. Tobias was soon engaged in a number of enterprises including a steamboat line to St. Louis, a ferry boat, a saw-mill and a pottery works, and, in partnership with his brother-in-law, a distillery. He purchased a farm, constantly added to it, and bought a considerable interest in the First National Bank of Peoria, later becoming its president. Their six children all died in early youth, and the Bradleys determined to commemorate them by founding an educational institution. But Mr. Bradley died in 1867, leaving an estate of $500,000. Mrs. Bradley, still slight, almost fragile, in appearance, proceeded at once to increase her fortune to the proportions necessary for her philanthropy. She became a business woman, though without giving up her practise of making her own butter and salting down her own meat. By economy and good investments but mainly by the development of real estate, at the time of her death she had multiplied her estate fourfold. Her interest in Peoria was expressed in frequent gifts to its institutions. She relieved one church of a $30,000 mortgage and contributed handsomely to all the others; she donated a hospital site, built a Home for Aged Women, and presented the city with a park named for her daughter, Laura Bradley. Meanwhile plans for her school went forward. A representative was sent to investigate other institutions and advice was sought of such men as President Harper of Chicago University and Prof. John Dewey. In 1897 the two buildings of the Bradley Polytechnic Institute were erected on a twenty-acre campus in Peoria at a cost of $250,000 and with an endowment of $2,000,000. Horology Hall contained a school of watchmaking and allied trades which had been started on a small scale in Indiana and brought to Peoria by Mrs. Bradley in 1893. In the general department, housed in Bradley Hall, four years of academic work and two of college, embracing the usual courses in literature, science, and the arts, were taught. But special emphasis was laid on practical study, and the domestic science course for girls was among the first in the Middle West. According to its charter, the aim of the general department was "to furnish students with the means of living independent, industrious, and useful lives." Evening classes in vocational subjects, and a summer school in domestic science and manual training, were later added.

[*Bradley Polytechnic Institute, The First Decade, 1897–1907* (Peoria, 1908); *Who's Who in America*, 1908–09.] M.A.K.

BRADLEY, MILTON (Nov. 8, 1836–May 30, 1911), manufacturer, was born in Vienna, Me., the son of Lewis and Fannie (Lyford) Bradley. His father operated, at Mercer, the first starch mill in Maine, an enterprise which helped to inaugurate the potato industry in that state. In 1847 the family moved to Lowell, Mass., where Milton Bradley graduated from the high school in 1854. He then entered the office of Oliver E. Cushing, a draftsman and patent agent, making good use of his spare time by peddling stationery among the girl operatives of the Lowell mills. Having earned and saved two or three hundred dollars he entered the Lawrence Scientific School at Cambridge, commuting from Lowell and teaching at night. In 1856 the family moved to Hartford, and Milton, after completing one and a half years of a two-year course, decided to accompany them. In search of employment he found himself in Springfield, Mass., in June of 1856 and secured work as a draftsman in the locomotive works of Blanchard & Kimball (later Bemis & Company). When Bemis & Company went out of business in 1858, Bradley set up for himself as a mechanical draftsman and patent securer. His most interesting job at this time was making the drawings and superintending the construction of a private car, in the shops of T. W. Wason & Company, for the Khedive of Egypt. He became interested in lithographing in 1859, went to Providence, learned the process, brought a press to Springfield in 1860, and inaugurated the lithographing business in western Massachusetts. His first important lithographing job was a portrait of Lincoln made from an original photograph brought home from the Chicago nominating convention by Samuel Bowles of the *Springfield Republican*. Business during the war, however, was so poor that Bradley took up the idea of printing games. A parlor game, known as "The Checkered Game of Life," he peddled personally throughout New York state, and the sale was so rapid that success seemed to point in the direction of the manufacture of games. Accordingly in 1864 Milton Bradley & Company was formed by the admission of J. F. Tapley and Clark W. Bryan, and in 1870 a separate building for the enterprise was secured. Tapley and Bryan retired in 1878 and the firm was reorganized as the Milton Bradley Company. Bradley was a pioneer in America in the game business. Although the Puritan mind was averse to the idea, success was instantaneous and sustained. The "Checkered Game of Life" marked a new era in parlor pastimes. "The Wheel of Life," a scientific toy which made simple pictures printed on strips of paper become animated, has been described as the original moving picture machine. The company prospered greatly from the rise of croquet and their manuals became standard for the rules of the game. Simultaneously with the development of the manufacture of games came that of kindergarten materials. It was in 1869 that Milton Bradley fell under the spell of the Froebelian philosophy chiefly through the influence of Elizabeth Peabody, and a neighbor, Edward Wiebe. Wiebe was a Springfield music teacher and a friend of Froebel's widow, and had brought from Germany the manuscript of a book on kindergartening called the *Paradise of Childhood* (1869) which Bradley published. This book, the first manual on kindergartens published in the United States, did much to promote the interest in kindergartens in America and was followed by the manufacture of kindergarten materials and the publication of children's books. In 1893 the Milton Bradley Company purchased the *Kindergarten News* and published it as the *Kindergarten Review* with Henry W. Blake as editor, a publication which became the organ of the International Kindergarten Union. Earlier Bradley had published a children's magazine, *Work and Play*. He was particularly interested in color instruction and himself wrote and published *Color in the School Room* (1890), *Color in the Kindergarten* (1893), *Elementary Color* (1895), and *Water Colors in the Schoolroom* (1900). He was twice married: in 1860 to Villona Eaton; and in 1864 to Ellen Thayer.

[*Milton Bradley, A Successful Man; A Brief Sketch of His Career and the Growth of the Institution Which He Founded, Published by Milton Bradley Company in Commemoration of Their Fiftieth Anniversary* (Springfield, 1910); *Springfield Present and Prospective*, ed. by Jas. E. Tower (1905), p. 192; *Who's Who in America*, 1910–11; *Springfield Daily Republican*, May 31, 1911.] H. U. F.

BRADLEY, STEPHEN ROW (Feb. 20, 1754–Dec. 9, 1830), jurist, senator, was descended from Stephen Bradley, one of Cromwell's Ironsides who emigrated, about the year 1650, from England to Connecticut. S. R. Bradley was born in the town of Wallingford (later known as Cheshire), the son of Moses and Mary (Row) Bradley. He graduated from Yale College in 1775, and early in 1776 was commissioned a captain of volunteers in the American army. He served in various capacities as commissary, quartermaster, aide to Gen. Wooster, and at the end of the war retired with the rank of colonel. He studied law in the famous school of Judge Tapping Reeve, at Litchfield, Conn., and in 1779 like many other active and ambitious young men, he emigrated from Connecticut to the district known as the New Hampshire Grants, where the Green Mountain Boys sought to establish a new Commonwealth of Vermont, in opposition to the claims of New York. Bradley was one of two lawyers who were the first to be admitted to the Vermont bar. He opened a law office in Westminster. His rapid rise in influence is shown by the fact that before the end of his first year in Vermont he had been chosen as one of the agents to present Vermont's cause to the Continental Congress, and had written a pamphlet entitled *Vermont's Appeal to the Candid and Impartial World* (1780), an eloquent and militant argument for Vermont's right to statehood. By direction of Gov. Chittenden the appeal was "published to the world," and circulated throughout several states. Bradley served as a member of the legislature and as speaker, and was the second judge of the supreme court who was a lawyer, most of the early judges being laymen. He was an active member of the commission that negotiated a settlement with New York, which made possible Vermont's admission as the first state to come into the Union after the original thirteen. In the convention called to consider ratification of the United States Constitution, Bradley was one of the leaders in the debate, favoring approval, which was carried by a large majority. He was elected one of Vermont's first United States senators, drawing the four-year term. He was defeated in 1794 for a reëlection, but was chosen in 1801 to fill a vacancy and was reëlected for a full term, this period continuing from October 1801 to March 1813. He served as president *pro tempore*, 1802–03 and in 1808.

Bradley introduced the bill which established a national flag of fifteen stripes and fifteen stars and this flag, sometimes known as the Bradley flag, was used from 1795 to 1814. His leadership is indicated by the fact that he issued the call for the caucus of Republican members of Congress which nominated James Madison as a candidate for president. Bradley was not an active partisan and his independence of party ties was shown on various occasions. In the controversy between the schools of political thought represented by Chief Justice Marshall and President Thomas Jefferson, which culminated in the establishment of a powerful and independent judiciary, Bradley, although a Republican, did not support the attempt to impeach certain judges. In a speech delivered in the Senate on Apr. 25, 1812, he protested against a declaration of war before an army was organized, and S. G. Goodrich, better known by his pen name, "Peter Parley," a son-in-law of Bradley, in his *Recollections of a Lifetime* (1856), says that the senator retired from public life because of his dissatisfaction with the war policy of the Madison administration. Jeremiah Mason, one of the famous lawyers of the time, was a student in Bradley's office and in his *Memoir and Correspondence* (1873), he tells of Bradley's sagacity, his wit, and his great store of anecdotes. Other contemporaries mention his urbanity and social charm. He was thrice married: to Merab Atwater, to Thankful Taylor, and to Belinda Willard.

[A. J. Beveridge, *Life of John Marshall* (1916–19); Chas. Francis Adams, ed., *Memoirs of J. Q. Adams* (1874–77); F. B. Dexter, *Biog. Sketches Grads. Yale Coll.*, vol. III (1903); B. H. Hall, *Hist. of Eastern*

Vermont (1858); W. H. Crockett, *Vermont* (1921), vols. II, III; *Records of the Governors and Council of the State of Vermont* (1874), II, 200–22; P. C. Dodge, ed., *Encyc. of Vermont Biog.* (1912).] W. H. C.

BRADLEY, WILLIAM CZAR (Mar. 23, 1782–Mar. 3, 1867), congressman, was born in Westminster, Vt., the son of Stephen Rowe Bradley [*q.v.*] and Merab (Atwater) Bradley. His mother died during his infancy. Scarlet fever, when he was two, was probably responsible for impairing his hearing. His early youth was spent with his grandparents in Cheshire, Conn., but he fitted for college at Charlestown, N. H. During his freshman year at Yale he was expelled for a prank for which he was not responsible though he later said he was guilty of other similar acts. Upon his return home his disgusted father gave him a dung fork and set him to work at a manure heap. But he retrieved himself by deciding to become a lawyer, studying with Judge Simeon Strong of Amherst, then with a Mr. Ashmun of Blandford, Mass., and later returning to his father's office to complete his studies. At seventeen he delivered the Fourth of July oration at Westminster, the program including an ode he had written. At eighteen he was secretary of the commissioner of bankruptcy of Westminster and at twenty married Sarah Richards, daughter of Hon. Mark Richards of Westminster who was lieutenant-governor of Vermont. Admitted to the bar when but twenty (1802), because of his youth he was refused permission to practise before the supreme court of the state, but the legislature made him attorney for Windham County, thus giving him access to the supreme court. In 1806–07 he represented Westminster in the Vermont legislature. In 1812 he was a member of the Governor's Council which preceded the present state Senate. He was twice a representative in Congress,—in 1813–15, when he was an ardent supporter of Madison's war policy, and again in 1823–27. A quarrel with John Quincy Adams, which turned him to the support of Jackson, caused his retirement from public life at Washington, when but forty-five. What he himself considered his greatest public service was the surveying, as agent of the treasury department, under the Treaty of Ghent, of the northeastern boundary between the United States and Canada. In this work he spent five years (1817–22), and though Great Britain at first rejected this line it was finally adopted by the Ashburton Treaty. After his retirement from national affairs and his return to the practise of law he continued within the state of Vermont to be the actual leader of Jacksonian democracy and almost its perpetual candidate for governor. In 1848 he joined the Free-Soil party and in 1850 was a member of the state legislature. Later he was a member of the young Republican party, heading the Frémont electoral ticket in 1856. In 1857 he was a member of the state constitutional convention. In 1858 he took formal leave of the bar after fifty-six years of practise.

He seems to have more enjoyed leading the uphill fight of Vermont democracy than the actual holding of public office, and his relish of the contest was said to be in inverse proportion to his chance of being elected. Though called a "free thinker" in his day, he would now be looked upon simply as a man of independent and investigating mind. He had some reputation as a poet, especially as a writer of occasional verse, and specimens of his poetry are given by Frederick Frothingham (*In Memoriam,* 1867). Of these "A Ballad of Judgment and Mercy" is considered the best.

[In addition to Frothingham, see *A Tribute of Affection to the Memory of Hon. Wm. C. Bradley* (1869), by Bradley's grand-daughter Mrs. S. B. Willard, which is largely dependent upon Frothingham but contains some new material in the form of letters; see also obituary in the *Rutland Herald,* Mar. 7, 1867.]

C. R. W—s.

BRADLEY, WILLIAM O'CONNELL (Mar. 18, 1847–May 23, 1914), governor of Kentucky, senator, was born near Lancaster in Garrard County, Ky., and was in part descended from Irish ancestry. He was the only son and the youngest child of Robert McAfee Bradley, a noted criminal lawyer and expert in land litigation, and his wife Nancy Ellen (Totten) Bradley, who was a grand-niece of George Robertson, chief justice of the Kentucky court of appeals. When he was yet young his family moved to Somerset and there he received what schooling the town afforded. He never attended college, and often in later life mentioned the fact with pride. In 1861 he was appointed a page in the legislature at Frankfort. But coming from a family that strongly supported the Union, he wanted a more active career. Therefore, he soon joined the Federal Army as recruiting agent in Pulaski County and later volunteered for active service in Louisville. On account of his age his father both times secured his release. He now studied law under the direction of his father, and in 1865 by special enactment of the legislature he was given the right to take the examination for license to practise law, being only eighteen years of age. He entered his father's office at Lancaster, where the family had now settled. Having a liking for political advancement, he ran for prosecuting attorney for Garrard County in 1870 on the Republican ticket and won. He then began a political career in Kentucky which for almost thirty years was characterized by successive defeats on account of his having the misfortune to live in a state normally Democratic. But his party stood loyally behind him, and in time he became the preëminent Republican leader in Kentucky and ultimately won political success. Four times he was nominated by his party for United States senator and four times defeated; an equal number of times he was nominated for the United States House of Representatives, making hard but losing fights the first three times, and refusing to accept the nomination the fourth time; and twice he unsuccessfully ran for governor, in 1887 and 1891. He took an important part in the national councils of the Republican party, serving as elector in 1872 and 1876, as delegate to six national conventions and as national committeeman for twelve years. In 1888 he received 106 votes in the national convention for vice-presidential nominee and in 1896 the Kentucky Republicans endorsed him for the presidential nomination. His first important political victory and the first of any consequence for the Republican party in Kentucky came in 1895, when he was elected governor of the state by a majority of almost 10,000, due largely to the disorganization of the Democrats on the money question. In 1908 a badly torn Democratic legislature elected him to the United States Senate over J. C. W. Beckham, the Democratic candidate. He died in office in Washington in 1914. He was married on July 11, 1867, to Margaret R. Duncan.

[*Lexington Leader*, May 24, 1914; *Who's Who in America*, 1912–13; *Biog. Cyc. of the Commonwealth of Ky.* (1896); M. H. Thatcher, *Stories and Speeches of Wm. O. Bradley; with Biog. Sketch* (Lexington, 1916).]
E. M. C.

BRADSTREET, ANNE (*c.* 1612–Sept. 16, 1672), colonial poet, wife of Simon Bradstreet, came to Massachusetts Bay in 1630 with the party under Winthrop, which also included her husband and her father and mother (Deputy Governor Thomas Dudley and Dorothy Dudley). The future poet was eighteen years of age and two years a wife when the voyage was undertaken, and in America she found "new manners, at which my heart rose. But after I was convinced it was the way of God, I submitted to it." The rebellion of heart was not unnatural. Her life in England had been pleasant. She was born probably at Northampton, where her father, home from Protestant wars, was as steward retrieving the fortunes of his employer, the Puritan Earl of Lincoln. She knew a culture once compared to that of Lucy Hutchinson, who "had at one time eight tutors in . . . languages, music, dancing. . . ." Her husband, the son of a non-conformist minister, had been taken into the Earl's household as a youth of fourteen years, had received the M.A. degree at Cambridge in 1624, and had returned to the estate as steward. In Massachusetts the Bradstreets settled at Ipswich, but removed to North Andover about 1644. During these years, while Anne was writing the first book of poems by an English woman in America, she moved in the highest circles, as her father, and later her husband, both held leading administrative offices. Eight children were born to her, and among her descendants were Richard Henry Dana, Wendell Phillips, and Oliver Wendell Holmes.

In the light of her century, technique and capacity rather than content were at fault in her earlier poetry, published at London in 1650 under the title, *The Tenth Muse.* Her inspiration was chiefly literary. She was apart from the Cavalier tradition, but close to another considerable body of material, didactic and religious. She enjoyed the poetry of Francis Quarles, and imitated *La Semaine* of Du Bartas, which, translated by Joshua Sylvester and published in *Bartas His Deuine Weekes and Works* (1605), greatly influenced English men of letters. In a poem she expressed herself as enamoured of Du Bartas's learning, natural philosophy, grave divinity, physic, and astronomy. Quite natural were her own attempts to sing of physics in the "Elements," of vital forces and human characteristics in the "Humours" and "Ages" of man, and natural philosophy in the "Seasons." In a long rimed history, "The Four Monarchyes" she selectively paraphrased many pages of Raleigh's *History of the World* (1614), using the Bible, Plutarch, and Usher as contributory sources. Through the "Dialogue between Old England and New" she gave voice to her anti-ritualistic beliefs, but did not incline greatly to democracy. On the whole, these works are tedious, unleavened by imaginative power, and cramped in diction. She never mastered the pentameter couplet. "Contemplations," written later, enjoys modern appreciation. In the more intricate rime scheme of seven-line stanzas, closing with an Alexandrine, she expressed herself with a grace and beauty which brightened her time and environment. Herein, she was perhaps quickened into action by the "Spectacles" in the Sylvester volume. At least she linked herself more closely to the influence of Sidney and Spenser, and in sustained verse wrote of a spiritual passion amidst elements of nature authentic to poetic tradition, if not to New England landscape. In her own period Nathaniel Ward wrote commendatory verses for the first volume, and John Rogers and John Norton, in the second, saw poetic beauties theretofore unpenned in New England. Cotton Mather became unduly fulsome in his comment on her life in his *Magnalia Christi Americana* (1702).

[Anne Bradstreet's work has been published in five editions. The first was entitled, *The Tenth Muse Lately Sprung up in America. Or Severall Poems, Compiled with Great Variety of Wit and Learning . . . By a Gentlewoman in those Parts* (London, 1650). The second and posthumous edition, *Several Poems . . .* (Boston, 1678), included later poetry, especially "Contemplations." The third (Boston, 1758) was a reprint of the second. The fourth, *The Works of Anne Bradstreet in Prose and Verse* (Charlestown, Mass., 1867), ed. by John Harvard Ellis, is based on the second, collated with the first, and contains hitherto unpublished material and scholarly biographical and critical comment. It remains without an equal. In 1897 the Duodecimos published *The Poems of Mrs. Anne Bradstreet . . .* with spelling modernized and an introduction by Chas. Eliot Norton. Helen Campbell has written a biography, *Anne Bradstreet and Her Time* (1890). See also the *Bradstreet Geneal. Table,* and a short account by Metta Bradstreet in *Colls. Topsfield Hist. Soc.,* I, 3–9. The *Pubs. Ipswich Hist. Soc.,* XII, contain "Thos. Dudley and Simon and Ann Bradstreet: a Study of House-Lots."] L. N. R.

BRADSTREET, JOHN (*c.* 1711–Sept. 25, 1774), British and colonial officer, either was born in Nova Scotia, or immigrated at an early age. Close connection with two generations of military Bradstreets influenced him to purchase an ensign's commission in Philipps's regiment of British foot in 1735. Visits to Louisburg in 1736 and 1738, and his relationship with the famous La Tour family of Nova Scotia, gave him knowledge of French methods, while garrison duty on the frontiers of a sparsely-settled province taught him the value of irregular troops, and peculiarly fitted him for his later career. When England entered the War of the Austrian Succession, he was serving as lieutenant at Canso. Captured by Du Vivier in 1744, he was imprisoned in Louisburg, and later exchanged at Boston, where he met Gov. Shirley. His arguments as to the vulnerability of Louisburg were so forcible that Pepperell described him as the "first projector of the expedition" that resulted in the capture of the stronghold in 1745 (*Documentary History of the State of Maine,* 1908, XI, 300, 301). Bradstreet maintained that he would have had the chief command had he been a native New Englander, but he was commissioned only as second colonel of the first regiment of Massachusetts troops, Pepperell's "York Provincials" (*6 Massachusetts Historical Society Collections,* X, 497). He served during the siege with distinction, and was recommended by both Shirley and Pepperell for the lieutenant-colonelcy of Pepperell's regiment, raised in 1745 on the British establishment. The selection, however, was dictated in England, and Bradstreet obtained only a captain's commission, and the newly-created post of lieutenant-governor of St. John's, Newfoundland, which he held until his death. After commanding the provincial garrison at Louisburg, not without arousing criticism, he went to St. John's, where he remained until 1754. A driving personal ambition, which was his dominating characteristic, led him in 1747 to attempt to purchase from Pepperell the colonelcy of the regiment, wholly for the sake of rank (Usher Parsons, *The Life of Sir William Pepperell,* 1855, p. 150), and undoubtedly to inspire the unsuccessful petition of Lord Baltimore in 1753 for the reëstablishment of a seventeenth century proprietary claim to Newfoundland. The petition requested that "J. Bradstreet, Esq., a gentleman of great honour and ability," be appointed governor (Public Records Office, *Colonial Office,* 194: 13, July 26, 1753). In 1755 Braddock ordered him as captain in Pepperell's newly raised regiment, the 51st, to Oswego with two companies to reinforce the weakened garrison, and to oversee the building of boats on the lake. His extraordinary abilities with that class of irregulars known as "battoe-men" were recognized when Shirley, in 1756, gave him the command of all matters relating to transportation of supplies and provisions on the New York frontier, without, however, additional pay or rank (*Correspondence of William Shirley,* 1912, II, 419). Bradstreet performed this important work with zeal, and won contemporary renown by beating off several French attacks as he was returning, in the spring of 1756, from carrying supplies to the Oswego garrison. Commissioned in 1757 as captain in the second battalion of the Royal Americans, he was chosen by Loudoun as one of his aides-de-camp, a post in which he performed quartermaster duties. In December 1757 he offered to bear part of the expense of an expedition against Fort Frontenac, to be reimbursed and recommended for promotion if successful. When Loudoun accepted the offer, Bradstreet carried forward preparations with such energy that he completed nearly 1,500 batteaux by the end of May. Wolfe, always a severe critic of Americans, marked him out at this time for especial praise (*Historical Manuscripts Commission, Report on the Manuscripts of Mrs. Stopford-Sackville,* 1910, II, 261). Pitt's sweeping changes of December 1757, which gave Bradstreet his coveted rank of lieutenant-colonel and made him deputy quartermaster-general in America, deferred the Frontenac plan until after Abercromby's defeat at Ticonderoga, when it was adopted at a council of war. The Frontenac expedition was singularly adapted to Bradstreet's abilities, for it involved, not the strategy of a siege, but the swift transport of an army over a long and difficult wilderness water-way. Though Bradstreet quarrelled with his provincial leaders, his 3,000 men, of whom but 150 were of the regular army, easily captured Fort Frontenac (Kingston, Ontario), August 1758, destroyed the fortifications, stores, and boats, and thus broke the line of French communication between the St. Lawrence and the Ohio.

For the remainder of the war Bradstreet acted as deputy quartermaster-general, and in 1762 was promoted to be colonel in America. In the suppression of Pontiac's rebellion, in 1764, he commanded the northern of the two armies that penetrated into Indian territory. He transported his small force to Detroit, re-garrisoned posts to the westward that had been captured by Indians, but gave little evidence of understanding Indian character, and allowed himself to be duped into signing a premature peace without sufficiently drastic terms. In 1772 the rules of seniority made him major-general; two years later he died of the dropsy "at his house in Broad Street," and was buried in Trinity Church with full honors of war (*Rivington's New York Gazetteer,* Sept. 29, 1774). He left two daughters, by his wife Mary.

[Information regarding the family of Nova Scotia Bradstreets is in R. H. R. Smythies, *Hist. Records of the 40th Reg.* (1894), and more particularly in Bradstreet's will, printed in the *New Eng. Hist. and Gen. Reg.,* XVI, 315, and in 12 *Wendell's N. Y. S. C. Reports,* 602, and 5 *Peters Reports,* 402. The Pepperell Papers, partly printed in *6 Mass. Hist. Soc. Colls.,* vol. X, contain material on Bradstreet's first important command. The calendar of Bradstreet papers in *Am. Antiq. Soc. Proc.,* n.s., XIX (1908), 105–81, begins with 1755, and additional material is in the *N. Y. Col. Docs., Corres. of Wm. Shirley* (1912); *Corres. of Wm. Pitt* (ed. by G. S. Kimball, 1906); the unprinted collections of Loudoun and Abercromby papers in the possession of the Henry E. Huntington Lib., San Marino, Cal.; and *An Impartial Account of Lt. Col. Bradstreet's Expedition to Fort Frontenac, . . . by a Volunteer on the Expedition* (London, 1759). Bradstreet's letters during the Pontiac rebellion are in Hough's ed. of the *Diary of the Siege of Detroit* (1860), and in *Western Reserve Hist. Soc. Tracts,* 13, 14 (1873). For a general account see H. Baker-Crothers, *Virginia and the French and Indian War* (1928).] S. M. P.

BRADSTREET, SIMON (March 1603–March 1697), early colonial statesman, was the grandson of a Suffolk gentleman of estate and the son of a non-conformist minister living in Lincolnshire. He was educated at Emmanuel College, Cambridge, where he took the A.B. degree in 1620 and the A.M. in 1624. His connection with the New England colony began in 1629 when he was made assistant of the Company of Massachusetts Bay just as its emphasis of interest in colonizing was passing from trade to religion. He sailed to New England in 1630 with Winthrop's fleet, from which time down to 1692, with the exception of the three years of the Dominion, 1686–89, he was continuously in public employ. His two marriages brought him into close connection with the small governing group in the colony, his first wife being the well-known Puritan poet, Anne Bradstreet [*q.v.*], and his second wife Mrs. Ann (Downing) Gardner, niece of John Winthrop [*q.v.*]. He served as assistant of Massachusetts for forty-nine years, during which time he had many other public responsibilities. He was secretary of the colony from 1630 to 1636 and frequently received appointment to important committees of the General Court. His diplomatic qualities became manifest early in his public career, and marked him as one of the colony's most suitable envoys in its dealings with the outside world. He was chosen in 1643 one of five to treat with Connecticut, New Haven, and Plymouth concerning the establishment of a confederacy. As a result of their negotiations the New England Confederation was formed and he and William Hathorne were chosen commissioners the following year. Bradstreet acted in that capacity for thirty-three years, during which time his ideas were most influential in molding the development of that first colonial union ("Acts of the Commissioners of the United Colonies" in *Plymouth Colony Records,* X, 108, 187–88).

Massachusetts found it hard to accept colonial status upon the restoration of Charles II, and in 1661 appointed a commission of which Bradstreet was a member, to consider the relations of the colony to the mother country. Finally the General Court decided to send agents to England to negotiate with Charles for favor and selected Bradstreet and John Norton. Both accepted appointment reluctantly. As a result of their successful mission Charles confirmed the charter, but sent a letter making such demands on the colony that the agents were charged, upon their return to New England, with having been too mild. After the death of Leverett, Bradstreet was elected governor in 1679, in which post he served until the establishment of the Dominion under Dudley's commission in 1686. While governor, as well as earlier, he won the reputation of being "moderate" toward England, even Edward Randolph reporting him as one of the three "most popular and well principled men" in the magistracy (*Calendar of State Papers, Colonial,* 1675–

76, §§849, 1067; 1681–85, §1445). As the charter struggle drew on, this conciliatory attitude brought him increasingly into ill favor with the supporters of the old theocracy, resulting in his being declared an enemy of his country in 1684 (*Ibid.*, 1681–85, §1589). He held office however until 1686, when the Dominion of New England was established under the temporary rule of Joseph Dudley. Because of his moderate proclivities Bradstreet received appointment as councillor of the new Dominion, but refused to serve on the grounds that a government without a representative assembly was contrary to Magna Charta. Upon the revolt against the Dominion in April 1689, he and many others formed a council of safety which called a convention of representatives from the towns to settle the government until orders should come from England. The convention voted for restoration of the charter government with the officials in office in 1686. Somewhat reluctantly Bradstreet, at this time an old man of eighty-six, assumed the office of governor, continuing therein until the arrival of Sir William Phips, the new royal governor, in May 1692.

Bradstreet was one of the colony's large landowners, several tracts having been given him from time to time as a reward for his public services. He, like many of the moderate party, was interested in land speculation and colonization, and with such men as the Winthrops, Richard Wharton and others, was a member of the Atherton Company for developing a large territory in the Narragansett country. He was also interested in mercantile affairs, and belonged to a company incorporated for trading on the frontier (*Massachusetts Colony Records,* II, 138; III, 53; *Calendar of State Papers, Colonial,* 1661–68, §§493, 967; 1677–80, §837–I). He lived at various times in Cambridge, Ipswich, Andover, and Boston, but spent his last years in Salem, where he died.

[*The Records of the Gov. and Co. of the Mass. Bay in New Eng.* (1850), ed. by Nathaniel Shurtleff; and "Acts of the Commissioners of the United Colonies" (volumes IX and X of *Records of the Colony of New Plymouth in New Eng.*, 1855), also ed. by Nathaniel Shurtleff, are the best sources for a study of the life of Bradstreet. There is also material in Samuel Sewall's "Diary" (*5 Mass. Hist. Soc. Colls.*, vol. V), in the "Winthrop Papers," (*5 Mass. Hist. Soc. Colls.*, vol. VIII and *6 Mass. Hist. Soc. Colls.*, vol. II).]

V. F. B.

BRADWELL, JAMES BOLESWORTH (Apr. 16, 1828–Nov. 29, 1907), lawyer, was born at Loughborough, England, where his parents, Thomas and Elizabeth (Gutteridge) Bradwell, then resided. In 1829 when he was sixteen months old the family emigrated to the United States, first settling in Utica, N. Y. Five years later they went west to Jacksonville, Ill., and thence to Wheeling, Ill., where in May 1834 his father took up land. James spent his youth on the farm, obtained some knowledge at the local school, and, by manual labor, defrayed his expenses while attending Wilson's Academy, Chicago, and Knox College, Galesburg, Ill. He then determined to study law. This he was enabled to do by working at various trades as a journeyman in Illinois and Tennessee, reading law in his spare time. He was admitted to the Tennessee bar at Memphis in 1852. For two years he was principal of a private school in Memphis, but he returned to Chicago in 1854 and was admitted to the Chicago bar on June 3, 1855. Opening an office in that city, in a short time he acquired a substantial practise, his acquaintance with the laboring classes and their problems materially assisting him. He also took an active interest in public affairs and became favorably known through his natural gifts as an eloquent and forceful speaker. In 1861 he was elected judge of the Cook County court, and being reëlected in 1865 occupied the position for eight years. At that time the court possessed probate jurisdiction, and he made a special study of this branch of law, assembling an extensive library of works on the subject, and by his opinions establishing a reputation, which, after his retirement from office, caused him to be regarded as an expert in all matters concerning wills and administration. In 1873 he was elected to the lower house of the state legislature, and by reëlection served till 1877. There he came to the front as a zealous advocate of reforms particularly in the direction of equalizing the legal status of men and women, and procured the passage of a bill making women eligible for school offices. In 1878 he prepared and issued the first volume of a series of *Reports of the Decisions of the Appellate Courts of the State of Illinois,* which extended to twenty volumes, covering the period 1877–87 (originally known as "Bradwell's Reports," now cited as *Illinois Appellate Court Reports,* I–XX). He had in 1868 assisted his wife, Myra (Colby) Bradwell [*q.v.*], in establishing the *Chicago Legal News* of which she was the editor and publisher, and, after her death in 1894, he assumed active control and undertook the editorial work. In 1903 he was compelled to retire from practise through ill health, and died in Chicago.

Possessed of much ability and indomitable perseverance, his interests covered a wide field. He was an expert in photography and in addition invented a process for making half-tones by which he produced the first half-tone cut made in Chicago. Associating himself closely with his wife's efforts on behalf of woman suffrage and other movements having for their object the complete emancipation of women, he promoted much legislation on that subject, and presided at the organization of the American Woman Suffrage Association at Cleveland. In his later years he was of patriarchal appearance, being more than six feet tall, with a long white beard and whiskers.

[F. B. Wilkie, *Sketches and Notices of the Chicago Bar* (1871), p. 66; I. M. Palmer, ed., *The Bench and Bar of Illinois* (1899), II, 831; J. W. Leonard, ed., *The Book of Chicagoans* (1905); *Proc. Ill. State Bar Ass.*, 1909, p. 410; *Chicago Daily Tribune, Chicago Daily News,* and *Inter-Ocean* (Chicago), Nov. 29, 1907.]
H. W. H. K.

BRADWELL, MYRA (Feb. 12, 1831–Feb. 14, 1894), lawyer and editor, was descended on both sides from pioneer Puritan stock. Her father, Eben Colby, was a member of a well-known New Hampshire family, related by marriage to the Chases, and her mother, Abigail (Willey), was descended from Isaac Willey who came to Boston in 1640. She herself was born at Manchester, Vt. While she was still quite young her father moved to Portage in western New York, where her early education was obtained. In 1843 the family went to Chicago, and she attended school at Kenosha and the Ladies Seminary at Elgin. Unable to obtain a college education since all the western institutions of higher learning were closed to women at that time, she became a school teacher. In 1852 she married James B. Bradwell [*q.v.*], an Englishman of good family and attainments who had come to the United States when young and studied law at Memphis, Tenn. Settling in Memphis, they established a select private school, but two years later went back to Chicago, where Bradwell, having been admitted to the Illinois bar in 1855, opened a law office, subsequently becoming judge of the Cook County court. Mrs. Bradwell took up the study of law, in the first place merely with the idea of assisting her husband in his work, but later determined to qualify herself for practise. In 1868, in the face of much discouragement, she established the *Chicago Legal News,* the pioneer weekly legal newspaper of the West. Assuming the dual position of editor and business manager (being the first woman in the world to occupy such a post) she quickly made a success of the venture, procuring a charter from the legislature and a special act making copies of the *News* containing the laws of the state and the opinions of the supreme court judges evidence of such laws and opinions. The plant of the *News* was totally destroyed in the Chicago fire of 1871, but she promptly had the paper printed and published in Milwaukee on the regular date. In 1869 she passed the necessary examination and applied to the supreme court of Illinois for admission to the bar. This was refused, the assigned reason being that she was as a married woman under disability. The case was re-argued and again she was refused, this time on the ground that she was a woman (Bradwell *vs.* The State, 55 *Illinois,* 535). The case was carried to the Supreme Court of the United States where the decision of the Illinois court was sustained, May 1873, on the ground that it was within the power of a state to prescribe the qualifications for admission to the bar of its own courts and that with the exercise of this power the United States Supreme Court could not interfere. S. P. Chase dissented (Bradwell *vs.* The State, 16 *Wallace,* 130). In 1882 she procured the passage of an act by the Illinois legislature granting to all persons, irrespective of sex, freedom in selecting a profession. She never renewed her application, but in 1885 the Illinois supreme court *proprio motu* directed a license to practise to be issued to her on her original application. She was admitted to practise before the Supreme Court of the United States, Mar. 28, 1892. She also became a member of the Illinois State Bar Association and the Illinois Press Association—being in each case the first woman to do so.

She devoted much of her time to the promotion of legislation enlarging the sphere of women's activities. She summoned the first Woman Suffrage Convention at Chicago in 1869 and for a number of years was an active member of the executive of the Illinois Woman Suffrage Association, assisting also in the formation of the American Woman Suffrage Association at Cleveland. In 1876 she was one of the Illinois representatives at the Centennial exhibition. She took a leading part in procuring the location of the World's Fair at Chicago in 1893, was one of the lady managers and acted as chairman of the committee on law reform at the auxiliary congress. She died in Chicago, Feb. 14, 1894.

[An excellent review of her life and activities appeared in the *Am. Law Rev.*, XXVIII, 278. See also *Ill. State Bar Ass. Report,* 1894, p. 86; *Mich. Law Jour.*. III, 77, and articles in the *Chicago Legal News,* XXVII, XXVIII. An article "Women Lawyers in the United States," in the *Green Bag,* II, 14, should be consulted.]
H. W. H. K.

BRADY, ANTHONY NICHOLAS (Aug. 22, 1843–July 22, 1913), business man, promoter, of Irish parentage, the son of Nicholas and Ellen (Malone) Brady, was born at Lille, France, and was brought from that country to the United States when a child. He received an elementary education in the schools of Troy, N. Y., but was little drawn toward academic training or education even if the circumstances of his parents would have permitted it. After employment at the Delavan House in Albany during his fifteenth year he determined upon an independent venture. Business of all kinds attracted him from the outset, and various early experiments led to his first effort of a considerable sort which occurred at the age of nineteen, when he opened a tea store at Albany. The enterprise was successful and led to the establishment of other similar stores in Troy and elsewhere and then in New York. During this early period he married Marcia A. Myers, daughter of a Vermont lawyer. His tea stores furnished one of the earliest examples on a small scale of the chain store plan in American retailing. The profits, however, were not sufficiently large to retain the interest of the young promoter. He was attracted by the extensive building movement then in progress in the state of New York, and directed his attention toward operations in building materials. From this it was a natural and easy step to the taking on of contracts for public improvements, including sewers, pavements, and the like. He obtained control of large granite quarries in New York and elsewhere, and furnished material with which to carry out the contracts he had undertaken largely from his own sources of supply. From this, his attention shifted to public utility services, his earliest undertakings being in gas. By this time he had perceived the fact that the field of most immediate profit in public utility construction would undoubtedly be found in tractions. He began to direct his investment of funds, now very considerable in amount, toward the purchase of traction lines in Providence and the neighboring places. New York naturally attracted him as the most promising field of effort, and after 1880, he more and more shifted his interests to that city. He was one of the organizers of the Metropolitan Traction Company, and in 1887 participated in the reorganization of the Brooklyn Rapid Transit Company, continuing as chairman of the board of directors of that enterprise up to his death. More than any other "traction magnate" he influenced plans for the subway development of New York. Although his immediate personal activities had thus been shifted to New York, he did not surrender his general participation and direction of other traction enterprises and in his later years he was engaged in extending his ownership in the street railways of Washington and Philadelphia. Moreover, during his later life he began to expand his field of operations largely in electrical public utilities, becoming concerned in the New York Edison Company as well as in other kindred enterprises.

Public utility reorganization, however, was by no means the measure or limit of his financial ambitions. He had become interested comparatively early in his career in the field of speculation and development of oil, and was one of the first and most vigorous competitors of the Standard Oil Company. Working in conjunction with his traction associates, he succeeded in giving to the Manhattan Oil Company at Lima, Ohio, valuable contracts for the supply of a large part of the oil used by the more considerable businesses of Chicago. Later on, a fairly close junction of interest between Brady and the so called Standard Oil group was formed, and he became associated with the latter in a large number of enterprises that had only a more or less indirect connection with the oil industry. The idea of consolidation, which he had found so effective and profitable in connection with tractions and public utilities, constituted the basis of his operations in these other fields, and he attempted to carry out promotion and combination schemes, not only in oil but also in tobacco and rubber, meeting with unusual success, not merely in a financial way but also in the actual development and improvement of operating conditions. During his final years, he tended more and more to devote his attention to traction interests, and only a year before his death was instrumental in extending the control of the Brooklyn Rapid Transit so as to take in the Coney Island and Brooklyn lines, the only remaining independent mileage in that portion of New York. A list of his directorships would be a long one but the number of enterprises in which he was a real though unseen power was probably much greater than the number of those in which he appeared as an active figure. At the time of his death his interests were very diversified and estimates of his real worth varied widely, conservative figures placing it at $50,000,000. Florid in complexion and of thick-set figure he was the exemplification of the "self-made man."

[*Who's Who in America*, 1912–13; *Albany Evening Jour.*, July 23, 24, 1913; *N. Y. Tribune*, July 24, 1913; *N. Y. Times*, July 24, 1913; *Sun* (N. Y.), July 23, 24, 1913.] H. P. W.

BRADY, CYRUS TOWNSEND (Dec. 20, 1861–Jan. 24, 1920), Episcopal clergyman, novelist, was born at Allegheny, Pa., the son of Jasper Ewing Brady, Jr., a banker and expert accountant, and of Harriet Cora Townsend. The Bradys were a Scotch-Irish family that had been settled in Pennsylvania since about 1744 and from generation to generation had displayed a genius for frontier fighting and for begetting numerous sons as bellicose as their fathers. Cyrus graduated from the United States Naval Academy in 1883 and after three years in the navy went west and found employment with the Missouri Pacific and Union Pacific Railroads. Though of Presbyterian antecedents, he was confirmed, while living in Omaha, in the Episcopal Church and proceeded to study for holy orders under Bishop Worthington of Nebraska. Since he was already married to Clarissa Sidney Guthrie and had several children to support, giving up his work was out of the question. He therefore read theology on trolley cars, during noon hours, and late at night, was ordained deacon in 1889 and priest in 1890, served several small charges in Missouri and Colorado, and was archdeacon of Kansas until 1895. His duties carried him over five states and, stalwart, two-fisted descendant of Indian fighters though he was, Brady found his work strenuous. "In three years, by actual count," he wrote later, "I travelled over 91,000 miles by railroad, wagon, and on horseback, preaching or delivering addresses upward of 11,000 times, besides writing letters, papers, making calls, marrying, baptizing, and doing all the other endless work of an itinerant missionary."

He returned east to be archdeacon of Pennsylvania, 1895–99, and rector of St. Paul's, Overbrook, Philadelphia, 1899 to 1902, meanwhile acting as chaplain of the 1st Pennsylvania Volunteer Infantry in the Spanish-American War and contracting camp and typhoid fever while in the service. His first novel, a story of the American Revolution entitled *For Love of Country,* appeared in 1898 and is said to have been dictated into a phonograph. He followed it the next year with a romance of the War of 1812, *For the Freedom of the Sea,* and thereafter the overflowing energies that had gone into his archidiaconal activities were poured into authorship. During the next twenty years he published more than seventy volumes. From 1902 to 1905 he made his home in Brooklyn, giving all his time to literary work, but he was rector of Trinity, Toledo, Ohio, 1905–09, of St. George's, Kansas City, Mo., 1909–13, and of the Church of the Ascension, Mt. Vernon, N. Y., 1913–14, resigning from the last because he considered the salary too low. Thereafter he was connected with St. Stephen's in New York City, where he preached from time to time. He died of pneumonia at his home in Yonkers, N. Y., Jan. 24, 1920, after an illness of two days. He was survived by his second wife, who was a Mary Barrett, and by his three sons and three daughters.

By experience and temperament Brady was ideally fitted to be a purveyor of cheap fiction. Although he was far from being a good observer, his life at sea, in the west, and in the east had given him an abundance of raw material, while in thought and feeling he was completely in harmony with the vast public that devoured his books as they were published and later applauded them when they were translated into moving pictures. His novels have no literary merit, but they are interesting to the historian of literature as an indication of popular taste over a period of twenty years. Besides his novels, Brady wrote juvenile stories, popular biographies of Stephen Decatur (1900), John Paul Jones (1900), and Andrew Jackson (1906), an historical work, *The Conquest of the Southwest* (1905), and some miscellaneous matter. His sentimentality and lack of invention are least in evidence and his good qualities—a gift for brisk, exciting narrative and a genuine love of "red-blooded" men—are displayed to best advantage in the series of volumes called *American Fights and Fighters.*

[B. McK. H. Swope, *Hist. of the Families of Mckinney—Brady—Quigley* (1905); W. G. Murdock, *Brady Family Reunion and Fragments of Brady Hist. and Biog.* (1909); *Who's Who in America,* 1918–19; *N. Y. Times,* Jan. 25, 27, 1920; *N. Y. Tribune,* Jan. 25, 1920 (a friendly and apparently well-informed obituary). There are a few biographical details in Brady's anecdotal *Recollections of a Missionary in the Great West* (1900).]

G. H. G.

BRADY, JAMES TOPHAM (Apr. 9, 1815–Feb. 9, 1869), lawyer, politician, was of pure Irish ancestry. His parents had emigrated from Ireland in 1812, settling at first in Newark, N. J., and moving in 1814 to New York City, where he was born Apr. 9, 1815. His father, Thomas J. Brady, a man of much intellectual attainment, had opened a private preparatory school, being subsequently admitted to the New York bar, and the son was given a thorough classical education. He entered his father's law office in 1831, and while yet a student gave evidence of the possession of unusual forensic ability, assisting his father in all his court cases. He was admitted to the New York bar in 1836, and his first case brought him prominently before the public. It related to the status of a slave, Coppen, and though he was unsuccessful his handling of the matter was masterly. From that day he was in constant demand in all classes of cases. He possessed from the start a valuable asset in an innate courtesy and urbanity of manner which was charming. His briefs were always carefully prepared, nothing being left to chance, and he was tireless in his study of all conceivable contingencies. As a student he had acquired a thorough knowledge of the underlying principles of law, and in his practise he did not concern himself much with precedent. Technicalities had no attraction for him and he always strove to bring himself within some broad principle. He was endowed by nature with a facility of speech, which, assiduously cultivated and molded by long study, and embellished with felicitous classical quotations, became well-nigh irresistible with a jury, whilst his arguments, clear, logical, never verbose, were put with a force and sincerity which always impressed the court.

Shortly after the Coppen case, he appeared as junior counsel to Daniel Webster in Goodyear *vs.* Day—"the India Rubber Case"—his opening speech drawing forth unstinted praise from his celebrated colleague. Henceforth he was recognized as a leader of the New York bar, and for the next twenty years appeared on one side or the other in almost all the important law-suits of the time. In 1843 he was appointed district attorney for New York, and in 1845 became for a short period corporation counsel, but these were the only public offices he ever filled. Later in his career he was offered the position of attorney-general of the United States, but declined.

His ability was displayed over the whole field of law, civil and criminal, and his services were requisitioned in every class of litigation and before all courts, both trial and appellate. He was intensely interested in the subject of insanity, of which he made a special study in all its phases. The Parrish and Allaire will cases, and the trial of Cole for murder, in the latter of which he invoked the defense of moral insanity, are outstanding instances of his facile handling of extremely difficult problems of medical jurisprudence. In purely civil cases he was equally effective. In one case he obtained $300,000 damages, the largest verdict up to that time given in a civil court. On the criminal side his influence over juries was phenomenal. He was counsel in fifty-two murder trials, and only failed in one. In one week he defended in four homicide cases and secured acquittals in all. In 1865, toward the end of his career, he was appointed a member of the commission which sat at New Orleans to investigate the charges of maladministration against Generals Banks and Butler and the Gulf Military Department but the ensuing report was never published.

He was equally prominent in politics, but never a leader, his independent habits of thought not being those of the professional politician. Prior to the war he was an ardent Democrat and ultra state's man, and in 1860 permitted himself to be nominated as candidate for governor of New York as a supporter of Breckinridge, actuated solely by a desire to uphold the principles he believed in, and knowing well that there was not the slightest chance of his election. He was a strong supporter of the administrative measures of the Government during the war, appearing on the public platform, and making speeches, which, by their brilliance of thought and patriotic spirit, attracted national attention. He was "absolutely indifferent to the prizes of political life" (*In Memoriam,* post.). In 1861 he refused the Tammany nomination for mayor of New York City, declining also repeated invitations to enter the state legislature and Congress. Every important position in the control of the Democratic party of New York was in turn proffered him in vain. He died in New York City, Feb. 9, 1869. He never married. His brother, John R. Brady, was a judge of the supreme court of New York, 1869–91.

Of medium height, and good physique, he always attracted attention by his piercing eye and monumental head, which was larger, it is said, than that of Webster. His manner was courtly, his conversation sparkling, and he was insensibly the center of attraction in the social circles where he loved to relax. He possessed cultured tastes, particularly in literature, and contributed many fugitive pieces to the *Knickerbocker Magazine* and other current periodicals. His best known work, "A Christmas Dream," written for the *New World* in 1846 and republished in book form, was extremely popular.

[The sources of information respecting the public and professional career of Brady are extensive and easily accessible. The files of the New York press covering the period 1835–69 do ample justice to his manifold activities. *In Memoriam, James T. Brady,* being a Report of a meeting of the Bar of the City of New York, Feb. 13, 1869, testifies to the high regard entertained for him by the legal profession. An excellent summary of his life appeared in the *Am. Law Rev.,* III, 779, and *The Bench and Bar of New York* by L. B. Proctor (1870), p. 238; see also *Central Law Jour.,* I, 544, and the *Green Bag,* III, 305.] H.W.H.K.

BRADY, MATHEW B. (*c.* 1823–Jan. 15, 1896), pioneer photographer, was born, according to his statement to George Alfred Townsend, in Warren County, N. Y. His father was an Irishman; of his mother nothing is recorded. In spite of his meager schooling he managed to pick up some sort of an education. He had his own way of spelling the first part of his given name, and he appears not to have known what the initial "B." represented. At Saratoga he met William Page, the portrait painter, who encouraged him to draw and who later, in New York, introduced him to S. F. B. Morse. Brady became deeply interested in Daguerre's discovery (made known in 1839) as well as in the photographic experiments of Morse and Prof. J. W. Draper, in the fall of that year, and soon began experimenting on his own account. Improvements rapidly brought the daguerreotype to the stage of a commercial success, and in either 1842 or 1843 Brady established a portrait studio at the corner of Broadway and Fulton St. in New York. His work soon attracted attention, and his studio was patronized by thousands. At each of the annual exhibitions of the American Institute in the years 1844–48 his exhibit received the first premium award of a silver medal and in 1849 the first gold medal ever awarded to daguerreotypes. About this time he began to make tinted daguerreotypes on ivory, an innovation that brought him increased patronage. He published, in 1850, his *Gallery of Illustrious Americans,* which had a considerable circulation. In 1851 he took a collection of forty-eight portraits to the World's Fair, in London, receiving the prize medal "for American daguerreotypes," with a commendation for their "beauty of execution," and in 1853 he received the prize medal at the World's Fair in New York. About 1855 he brought over from England Alexander Gardner, an expert in the wet-plate process invented by Scott-Archer, and thereupon discarded the daguerreotype for the photograph. He established a branch studio at Washington in 1858, and in 1859 a second studio, farther uptown, in New York, subsequently abandoning the one at Fulton St. The most eminent Americans in all walks of life sat for him, and he became famous as well as prosperous.

At the beginning of the Civil War he interested President Lincoln and others, including Allan Pinkerton, the head of the secret service, in his proposal to photograph battle and camp scenes, and received permission for himself and his assistants to accompany the armies. Zealous in their work, often regardless of danger, and at all times handicapped by the vexing difficulties of the photographing process of that day, these men carried their cameras to every scene that promised an interesting picture. More than 3,500 photographs are said to have been taken—many of them scenes of actual conflict, others of places devastated by gunfire, of troops on the march or in bivouac, and of individual officers and men. After the war he sought to recover copies of those that had passed from his hands, and in a booklet published by him in 1870, *Brady's National Photographic Collection of War Views and Portraits of Representative Men,* proposed the purchase of the collection by the Government for a permanent exhibit. In 1875 the Government purchased, for $25,000, a set of 2,000 of these photographs, at present stored in the War College. Another and less complete set had gone to Anthony & Company of New York, in payment of money due for photographic supplies; and this collection, with additions from a number of private collections, has been the basis for the various photographic histories of the Civil War that have appeared. Brady lost heavily by the war; the panic of 1873 completed his financial ruin, and the money obtained from the Government soon disappeared. He continued as a photographer in Washington until he was advanced in age, but never regained the prestige of his earlier days. He spent his declining years, afflicted with rheumatism and failing eyesight, in comparative poverty. In 1895, in Washington, he was run over by a vehicle, and for months thereafter was confined to his bed. Partly recovering, he went to New York, where he was tenderly cared for by a few friends, and some money was raised for him. Taken ill, he was carried to the Presbyterian Hospital, where he died.

Brady was married, about 1860, to Julia Handy, of the Eastern Shore of Maryland, who died on May 23, 1887. He was of slight but trim and square-shouldered figure, about five feet six in height, with a face expressive of refinement and intelligence. All pictures of him present him with a mustache and pointed beard, and those of Civil War times show him wearing a broad-brimmed flat hat, "like that of a Paris art student," and a linen duster. His work as a photographer was marked by initiative, enterprise, and artistry. He was usually the first to avail himself of every improvement in technique, many of the innovations being his own; and he succeeded in a rare degree in picturing his subjects in natural and unconstrained attitudes, with their individual characters strongly revealed. His nature was improvident; he could make money, but he could not retain it. He was a genial, friendly, modest man, deferential in manner, and he bore with uncomplaining cheerfulness the pathetic poverty of his last days.

[G. A. Townsend, interview with Brady in the N. Y. *World,* Apr. 12, 1891; material furnished by Brady's nephew, L. C. Handy, of Washington; obituaries in the *Evening Star* and the *Post,* of Washington, Jan. 18, 1896.]

W. J. G.

BRAGG, BRAXTON (Mar. 22, 1817–Sept. 27, 1876), Confederate soldier, was born at Warrenton, N. C., the son of Thomas Bragg, a contractor and builder, and of Margaret Crossland, an energetic and intelligent woman. He received his early education at his home town, was appointed a cadet at West Point in 1833, and graduated four years later as a second lieutenant, 3rd Artillery. He participated in the Seminole War, and in 1845 he joined Taylor's army in Texas. In 1846 he took part in the battles at Fort Brown and Monterey, for both of which actions he was brevetted. At about the same time he was promoted to captain, of Battery C, 3rd Artillery. Bragg's most distinguished service in this war was at Buena Vista, Feb. 23, 1847, where his battery, by its extraordinary activity, filled gaps in the American lines, and broke the attack of a vastly superior Mexican force. For this Bragg was brevetted lieutenant-colonel. In 1849 he married Elisa Brooks Ellis of Louisiana, and in 1856 resigned from the army and purchased a plantation in Louisiana. He became a commissioner of public works, and designed the drainage and levee system of his adopted state.

Early in 1861 Bragg was appointed a colonel, and soon after a major-general in the Louisiana militia. On Feb. 23, he was commissioned a brigadier-general, Confederate States Army, and assigned to command the coast between Pensacola and Mobile. In January 1862 he became a major-general. On Feb. 15, 1862, he proposed to the Secretary of War that his command be in part sent to Kentucky, where he foresaw that important events would take place. His advice was accepted, and he was ordered north. At Corinth, Miss., he assisted Gen. Johnston to organize his army. Bragg was given command of the 2nd Corps, and in addition was chief of staff. He went with the army to Shiloh. On Apr. 6, at the first attack at Shiloh, the 2nd Corps was in second line, but it soon became merged into the front line, Bragg supervising the Confederate right. With great energy he assaulted the Federal lines, and captured thousands of prisoners and many guns. A considerable part of the success of this day was due to the energy and vigor of Bragg. On Apr. 7, the Federals, reënforced by Buell's fresh army, had only exhausted Confederates in front of them. Fighting bravely, the latter slowly retreated until the order was given to withdraw to Corinth whither they were not followed. On Apr. 12 Bragg was promoted to general, and on June 27 relieved Beauregard of the command of the Army of Tennessee. On July 20, Gen. Kirby Smith at Knoxville advised Bragg that the Federals were about to seize Chattanooga. Kirby Smith suggested that Bragg strike into middle Tennessee to relieve the situation. Bragg at once adopted this idea. He promptly started his command for Chattanooga where he arrived with most of his army by the end of the month, ahead of the Federals. On July 30 it was agreed that Kirby Smith, with about 18,000 men, should turn the Union forces at Cumberland Gap and advance into Kentucky. Bragg at the same time, with 30,000, was to march on and seize Munfordville, Ky., and then join Kirby Smith. This plan of action was political. It was hoped that a Confederate army in Kentucky would induce that state to join the South. The plan was defective from a military point of view, in that it failed to provide for defeating the Federal army under Buell, then in front of Chattanooga.

Due to lack of transportation, a month's delay occurred, and Bragg did not start until Aug. 27. He then moved rapidly, and captured Munfordville on Sept. 17. He was now between Buell's army and its base at Louisville, and could either have attacked the one or taken the other. But he did not feel strong enough to attack Buell, and the political nature of his expedition led him to Frankfort to install a Confederate state governor. This was fatal to the success of his campaign. Buell reached Louisville, united his forces, and set out to fight Bragg. On Oct. 8, Buell fought a part of Bragg's army at Perryville. Tactically the battle was drawn, but Bragg being unwilling to fight to a decision withdrew that night into Tennessee. Kentucky had shown no desire to join the South, and the campaign was a failure. It led to great dissatisfaction with Bragg, but he retained his command.

At the end of December a new Federal army under Rosecrans advanced on Bragg, then near Stone River, Tenn. Bragg, always energetic, attacked on Dec. 31, although he had only about 38,000 men against 47,000. The Confederate attack made great gains, but Bragg failed to force the fighting on the next day or otherwise exploit his victory. After minor fighting he judged his men were exhausted and faced by superior numbers, and on Jan. 3, 1863, withdrew to Tullahoma. This was a repetition of Shiloh and Perryville. Although full of energy, Bragg was not persistent. After Stone River he invited his subordinates to express their opinion of him, and received frank statements that his presence was not wanted. President Davis however decided to keep him in command.

In June 1863, Rosecrans maneuvered Bragg out of Tullahoma, and by Sept. 9, out of Chattanooga. Forced into the mountains, Bragg sought to destroy fractions of the Federal forces while they were separated one from another. Several combinations failed, due to lack of support by subordinate generals. This was the result of quarrels, and resentment. But on Sept.

19 and 20, Bragg attacked Rosecrans at Chickamauga. He won a notable victory, and forced the Federals with severe losses back into Chattanooga where he laid siege to them. In this he made a serious error. Had he continued his offensive he might have captured large forces, but siege operations brought him nothing. Grant, assigned to the command of the Federals confronting him, opened a line of supply, and then attacked Bragg at Chattanooga on Nov. 23 to 25. The Confederate center broke, and Bragg retreated to Dalton, Ga., where on Dec. 2, 1863, he surrendered command of his army to Johnston. This ended Bragg's important services. During 1864, he was at Richmond, nominally as commander-in-chief. Practically he was military adviser to President Davis. He had several minor commands. His last battle was on Mar. 8, 1865, at Kingston, N. C., against a part of Sherman's forces. He accompanied President Davis in his flight to Georgia, was captured on May 9, and was paroled.

After the war Bragg practised as a civil engineer at Mobile and later in Texas, was a commissioner of public works of Alabama for four years, and supervised the harbor improvements of Mobile. He died at Galveston, suddenly.

Tall, bearded, and ungainly, he was intelligent and energetic and had a stern sense of duty. Irritable and quarrelsome, he made many enemies. This prevented him from securing that loyalty from subordinates which military commanders need. He was a strict disciplinarian, and the Confederates had in the west no organizer to equal him. Bragg's greatest military fault was in not following up his successes. His victories were fruitless.

[The chief source of information for Bragg's campaigns is the *Official Records. Battles and Leaders of the Civil War* (1887–88) contains notable articles; secondary works are *Braxton Bragg,* by D. C. Seitz (1924), a complete story of his life; and the *Story of the Civil War* by John C. Ropes (1904), the latter excellent as to the 1862 campaigns.] C. H. L—a.

BRAGG, EDWARD STUYVESANT (Feb. 20, 1827–June 20, 1912), Union soldier, congressman, was descended from one of the Vermont settlers who had been ousted from his lands in the dispute between New Hampshire and New York during the Revolutionary period and who pushed out into the Chenango Valley of New York. His son, Joel Bragg (1784–1870), grew up in what was then a frontier environment, married a German woman, Margaretha Kohl of Lancaster, Pa., and became the owner of a sawmill, a grist-mill, and a tavern at Unadilla, Otsego County, N. Y. In the country made known to the world by James Fenimore Cooper, Edward Stuyvesant was born and grew to manhood. The youth attended not less than four of the neighboring academies, which in those days held the place later occupied by high schools, and then spent several years at Geneva (later Hobart) College, but from the early age of twelve he had fixed on the law as his calling and at twenty he was "reading" in the office of Judge Charles C. Noble at Unadilla. In 1848 he was admitted to the bar on court examination. He had been in practise only two years when the pioneering instinct that had moved his father and grandfather impelled him to seek his fortune in the tide of westward migration and he chose the new state of Wisconsin as the scene of his future activities. He settled at Fond du Lac, on the southern end of Lake Winnebago, and that was his home for more than six decades. Within four years he had married, on Jan. 2, 1854, Cornelia Colman, a grand-daughter of one of the founders of Rochester, N. Y., and had been elected district attorney of the county. A Douglas Democrat, he was a delegate to the Charleston Convention of 1860. The opening of the Civil War found him a "War Democrat," intensely devoted to the Union cause and eager to take the field. In June 1861 he raised a company and was commissioned captain in the 6th Wisconsin Volunteer Infantry. This regiment was destined to see as much active service in the war as any other Wisconsin organization. In its period of training it was one of the regiments whose "watch-fires of a hundred circling camps" helped to inspire Julia Ward Howe's "Battle Hymn of the Republic." Bragg's promotions to major, lieutenant-colonel, and colonel quickly followed the reports of his superiors on the battles in which the Sixth was engaged, following one another in rapid succession—Gainesville, South Mountain, Antietam (where he was severely wounded), Fredericksburg, Chancellorsville, the Wilderness (where he temporarily commanded a Pennsylvania regiment), Spotsylvania, Laurel Hill, North Anna, and Cold Harbor. On June 8, 1864, he commanded the Iron Brigade, leading in the assault on Petersburg. In this long series of engagements, his conduct and bravery had been extolled by the commanding officers and his exploit at Fitz-Hugh's Crossing, when he crossed the Rappahannock with his troops in boats under the enemy's fire and captured their works, made him a brigadier-general of volunteers. He had taken part in every one of the Iron Brigade's major battles except Gettysburg, from which he was kept by illness.

Bragg was in no sense one of the "political

generals" so numerous in the war (he did not belong to the national party that was dominant in the North); but he was always keenly interested in politics. While serving in the field he was nominated for Congress in his district and defeated. After the war he was a delegate to the Union national convention of 1866, was elected state senator in 1867, and was a delegate to the national Democratic convention that nominated Greeley for president in 1872. His district sent him to Congress for four terms (1877–83 and 1885–87). Twice (1884 and 1896) he was chairman of the Wisconsin delegation to national Democratic conventions. In seconding the nomination of Cleveland for president in 1884, "the little General" hurled at the New York delegation, controlled by Tammany, a piercing epigram that was to be remembered and repeated in three campaigns: "We love him for the enemies he has made!" In a canvass when every Democratic vote was needed it was audacity to the verge of recklessness, but it went to the heart of a situation that in Bragg's opinion required blood-letting. At such a time no consideration of political expediency had weight with him. He was a politician—and a clever one—up to the point where his convictions asserted themselves. Beyond that point politics might go to the winds. Twelve years later, when the Democrats nominated Bryan for president on a Free-Silver platform he was among the outstanding "Gold Democrats" of the country who refused Bryan their support. In 1900, again, similar reasons led Bragg, a life-long Democrat, to support McKinley and the Republican ticket. After the expiration of his last term in Congress, Bragg had been named by President Cleveland as minister to Mexico, but this appointment expired with the Cleveland Administration in 1889. In 1902 President Roosevelt appointed him consul general at Hong Kong, China. Bragg remained there four years, returned to America in 1906, supported Taft for the presidency in 1908, and died at Fond du Lac on June 20, 1912.

[F. W. Halsey, *The Pioneers of Unadilla Village* (1902); Maurice McKenna, ed., *Fond du Lac County, Wis., Past and Present* (1912); *Official Records*, ser. 1; Rufus R. Dawes, *Service with the Sixth Wisconsin Volunteers* (1890).] W. B. S.

BRAGG, THOMAS (Nov. 9, 1810–Jan. 21, 1872), lawyer, Confederate statesman, born in Warrenton, N. C., was the brother of Braxton Bragg [*q.v.*], and the son of Thomas Bragg, carpenter and contractor, and his intelligent and handsome wife, Margaret Crossland. After studying in the local academy and for three years in Capt. Partridge's military school at Middletown Conn., young Thomas read law under a supreme court judge in Warrenton and then, at twenty-three, began practise in the neighboring county of Northampton. Assiduous devotion to his profession for the next twenty-two years brought him a comfortable living and a fine reputation as a lawyer who prepared his cases thoroughly, and directed his appeals to intelligence and character. Reading in his home at night in the company of his wife, Isabella Cuthbert (married on Oct. 4, 1837), was his chief recreation, pipe-smoking his constant dissipation. But party prominence came slowly. Whiggish Northampton, liking neither his sternness and aloofness nor his Democracy, sent him but once (1842) to the legislature though he then acquitted himself well as a hard-working and level-headed chairman of the judiciary committee of the House and as a candidate for attorney-general (*House Journal,* 1842–43, pp. 513 and *passim*). But ability and energy at last triumphed. Having thrice stumped his district as candidate for elector, in 1854 he voluntarily went out to meet the able and popular Whig candidate for governor. Pleased at his showing, Democratic leaders gave him their nomination. He won then narrowly, but handsomely two years later. Voluminous "official papers" and neatly indexed letter-books speak eloquently of Bragg's attention to the state's business. True to his party's recently assumed position, he urged the immediate liberalization of the senatorial franchise and the development of the state's resources through improved banking, geological surveys, and rapid extension of the state railway system. But, constitutionally conservative, he mildly defended the past and he left unmodified the inequitable tax system. Solemnly warning against federal encroachment on the state's domain he counseled no hostile counteraction (*Legislative Documents,* 1854–55, 1856–57). "A sound and reliable statesman" was the Raleigh *Standard's* verdict (Dec. 1, 1858), and a seat in the federal Senate was his reward. Thoroughly Jeffersonian, Bragg in Washington set himself against public extravagance. Free homesteads and distribution of federal funds to the states he deemed corrupting and intended to corrupt. To the old and complicated issue of the Florida Land Claims he endeavored to apply the principles of private justice, made a speech on it in opposition to Mallory and the redoubtable Toombs, and lost no laurels in the contest (*Congressional Globe,* 36 Cong., 1 Sess., pp. 1249, 2040, 2630). Then came the Civil War. In 1856 he had counseled conservatism and in 1860 delay. In 1861 he believed secession impracticable (though justifiable), but because of popular feeling he "kept his opinions within his own breast" (Cowper). Soon he was busy, as an aid to the governor, in preparing military defense. As attorney-general of the Confederacy, Nov. 21, 1861–Mar. 18, 1862, he apparently drafted a plan of organization for the department; and he worked out the nominations submitted by the President on Mar. 19, 1862 (*Journal of the Congress of the Confederate States,* V, 26; II, 108). Then he returned to Raleigh and in the dual capacity of representative of President Davis and chairman of a strong citizens' committee sought to keep the state in line. Although in 1864 Davis rejected his proposal for deferring conscription pending the elections (Dunbar Rowland, *Jefferson Davis, Constitutionalist,* 1923, VI, 201), he was credited by Holden with chief responsibility for Gov. Vance's loyalty. After the war Bragg resumed, from financial necessity, the practise of law. Ere long, too, he was deep in the fight for decent government, his judgment ripened, his once black full beard now grizzled, his fine eyes looking out from beneath heavy brows calmly and directly as of old, but unsmilingly. His death was deemed to have been hastened by his exertions as counsel for the impeachment of Gov. Holden, once his political friend and patron, whose trial he closed with a masterly plea for a verdict free from considerations of political purposes or consequences.

[The sketch by Pulaski Cowper, Bragg's private secretary, in the *N. C. Univ. Mag.,* Jan. 1891, informing, and reasonably accurate. Ashe and Boyd in their volumes on North Carolina and J. G. de R. Hamilton, *Reconstruction in N. C.* (1914) supply background and important details. Bragg's speech against Holden is in *The Trial of Wm. W. Holden* (1871); his own report of his debate with Gilmer in 1856 is in W. J. Peele's *Lives of Distinguished North Carolinians* (1898), which also reproduces his portrait. An obituary appeared in the *Daily Sentinel* (Raleigh), Jan. 23, 1872.]

C. C. P.

BRAINARD, DANIEL (May 15, 1812–Oct. 10, 1866), surgeon and pioneer in medical education, was the fifth child of a family of nine born to Jeptha, Jr., and Catherine (Comstock) Brainard. His father, a descendant in the fifth generation from that Daniel Brainard who as a boy of eight arrived in America from England in 1649, was a farmer in Oneida County, N. Y., first at Western and later at Whitesboro (Lucy Abigail Brainard, *The Genealogy of the Brainerd-Brainard Family in America, 1649–1908*). Though accounts differ as to which of these was the birthplace of the young Daniel, evidence favors the former place. In Whitesboro, he attended the common schools and the Oneida Institute, and here, in 1829, he began the study of medicine with Dr. R. S. Sykes. Shortly afterward he moved to the near-by town of Rome, continuing his medical studies with Dr. Harold H. Pope. His medical course was taken at Fairfield Medical College, Fairfield, N. Y., followed by two courses at Jefferson Medical College in Philadelphia, where he was graduated in 1834. He early specialized in anatomy and physiology, and even before taking his medical degree, he lectured upon these subjects at Fairfield and at Whitesboro. He returned after graduation to the latter place, where though nominally in practise, he devoted two years to the study of languages and science. Early in 1836, he started for the then far west and the spring of that year found him in Chicago, a town of between two and three thousand inhabitants. Here he established himself for practise. His early bent toward medical teaching is shown by his application to the state authorities in 1837 for a charter for a medical college to be named in honor of Dr. Benjamin Rush. The time for launching the medical school was not then ripe, so Brainard contented himself temporarily with a private school of anatomy conducted in his office. In the meantime, after a somewhat discouraging start, he had won a firm footing in the medical practise of the fast-growing town.

Not yet satisfied with his preparation for teaching he went, in 1839, to Paris where he remained nearly two years. His later work and his writings show how deeply he was influenced by his contact with the French school of surgery. Returning to Chicago, he was appointed, in 1842, to the chair of anatomy in St. Louis University, where he delivered two courses of lectures. His early dreams materialized with the opening of Rush Medical College on Dec. 4, 1843, on which occasion he delivered the introductory address. He was given the chair of anatomy and surgery in the new faculty, and he remained professor of surgery until his death, always the dominating figure in the affairs of the school. In April 1844 appeared the first number of the *Illinois Medical and Surgical Journal,* which after various changes of name became the *Chicago Medical Journal.* Brainard aided in its foundation and for years contributed clinical reports and editorials to its pages. He also took part in the establishment of the first general hospital in Chicago in 1847, being one of three physicians who constituted its medical staff. In 1853 he again went to Paris where before the Academy of Science he read a paper on "The Venom of Rattlesnakes; the Effects of the Venom, and the Means of Neutralizing its Absorption." This was followed by a paper before the same society by himself and Dr. Greene on "Iodine as an Antidote for Curare." Later before the Société de Chirurgie of Paris, he read a paper entitled "On the Injection of Iodine in Tissues and Cavities of the Body for the Cure of Spina Bifida, Chronic Hydrocephalus, Edema, Fibrinous Effusions, Edematous Erysipelas, etc." At this time, he was made a corresponding member of the Société de Chirurgie. In 1854, he was elected president of the Illinois State Medical Society. In the same year he was awarded a prize by the American Medical Association for his essay entitled "An Essay on a New Method of Treating Ununited Fractures and Certain Deformities of the Osseous System" (published in the *Transactions of the American Medical Association,* 1854). This essay is one of the American medical classics. In a somewhat less complete form, it was published in Paris in French shortly before its American appearance. These essays and numerous articles on clinical surgery make up his contributions to medical literature. At the time of his death he was engaged upon an extensive surgical work which remained unfinished. It was in the fall of 1866, while cholera was epidemic in Chicago, that Brainard returned from a short visit in Paris where he had left his family. On the afternoon of Oct. 9, while lecturing to his class at the college, he devoted a portion of the hour to a discussion of the local cholera situation and of the precautions to be taken against it. That evening at his home he began an article on the same subject. Retiring in apparently good health, he was stricken with cholera early the next morning and died on the evening of that day.

Brainard was tall, well proportioned, and strongly built. His portraits show a large head with long wavy hair and a strong face with a large straight nose, clear piercing eyes, and a heavy drooping mustache. He was a man of great dignity, very reserved, and taciturn to a degree. These characteristics gave him a reputation of being short-tempered and ill-natured. As a lecturer, his command of terse English enabled him to give a maximum of instruction with a minimum of words. He was a forceful public speaker and took an active interest not only in medical society work, but also in matters relating to his city and state. For twenty years he dominated surgical thought in his city while his reputation was extended into international surgical circles. He was married to Evelyn Sleight of Naperville, Ill., on Feb. 6, 1845.

[Jas. Nevins Hyde, "Early Medical Chicago" in the *Chicago Medic. Jour. and Examiner,* 1876; E. Fletcher Ingalls, in the *Ill. Medic. Jour.,* XXII, 1912; Kelly and Burrage, *Am. Medic. Biogs.* (1920).] J. M. P.

BRAINARD, JOHN GARDINER CALKINS (Oct. 21, 1796–Sept. 26, 1828), poet, whose reputation evoked a eulogy from Whittier and a sneer from Poe, was the youngest son of Sarah (Gardiner) Brainard and Jeremiah G. Brainard, a graduate of Yale College in the class of 1779, and a judge of the superior court of Connecticut. His taste for poetry appeared early in boyhood, and at Yale, where he was graduated in the class of 1815. The traditions of his family (the Brainards or Brainerds, of Flemish origin, had come to Hartford about 1649) led into the practise of the law, a profession for which he was temperamentally unsuited. His lovable nature which had made him a favorite at college shrank from the rough professional business of the day. He studied faithfully in the office of his brother, William F. Brainard; he was admitted to the bar (1819) with honor; he developed a small clientele in Middletown, Conn.; but he was, throughout this unlucky episode, thoroughly unhappy. In his own words he could not endure the "personal altercation, contradiction and . . . hard collision" of his contemporaries. To understand this, one needs only to look at his portrait which mirrors clearly his gentle and introspective spirit. He retired from the law, and returned to his birthplace, New London, where, had he possessed energy, he might have matured his gift for verse. Yet, though his mild nature recoiled from the world, he needed its stimulus, and in the winter of 1822 he became associated with P. B. Goodsell, the Hartford publisher, as editor of the *Connecticut Mirror.* This was a compromise, for Brainard was ruffled by the severe tasks of journalism. The militant politics of the age aroused in him no enthusiasm for editorial or controversy. Yet the necessity of regular writing overcame his timidity, and he had now in the periodical a medium for his delicate poetic talent. Thus he found, in spite of recurrent indolence and excessive sensibility, his vocation: to write was, if we consider his life as a whole, his one passion. It was so in college that he had interested his classmates; even as a lawyer he had written "The Memoirs of Gabriel Gap" for a New Haven paper, the *Microscope;* and he now composed steadily for the *Connecticut Mirror.* He had all the ambition of the sensitive man, and in this period was to be the crisis of his career. It occurred in 1825, in the publication of his *Occasional Pieces of Poetry,* an attractive volume made up of some fifty pieces culled from the *Mirror.* The book made a stir, and might have stimulated any one save Brainard to further effort. He was now well-known, a clumsy little man with paddling walk, pale sensitive face, abstracted air, careless dress, and great personal charm. If not too frightened, he could display, says a contemporary, repartee of the first order. It was now that Brainard's friends rightly urged a second volume to solidify his reputation. He tried to respond to this sensible advice, but as usual procrastinated, and the only other volume brought out in his lifetime was the unimportant *Fort Braddock Letters* (1827). He had that curious temperament, often found in literary men, of extravagant ambition inhibited by the profound and disheartening conviction of failure. He could not, he told S. G. Goodrich despairingly, sustain the necessary continuity of thought to hold to his purpose. "There was," says an intimate friend, "a sad prophecy in this presentiment—a prophecy which he at once made and fulfilled." The fulfilment came in the spring of 1827 when Brainard resigned from the *Connecticut Mirror* because of ill health, and again settled in New London. Never endowed with robust animal spirits, he now fell into moods of deep dejection. These coupled with his piety lent a religious gloom to his later poetry, such as, "The Invalid on the East End of Long Island." The story of the last months before his death reads, with pathetic but rather sentimental deathbed scenes, like a page from the religious annuals during America's epoch of the mezzotint and weeping willow to which epoch Brainard, along with his admirer, Lydia Huntley Sigourney, indubitably belonged. At his father's home in New London he studied the doctrines of Christian grace; he became a communicant in the First Congregational Church; and he died of consumption, venerated for his moral verse. For the weakness of Brainard's life there is confirmation in the revised edition of his poetry (1832), in *Fugitive Tales* (1830), and in the new gleanings from his verse in the *Mirror* (1842). All that he wrote reveals his carelessness, and lack of self-control. His poetry imitated sentimental models. He wrote with the same gentle elegance of Niagara Falls which he had not seen and the Connecticut River which he beheld daily. Yet in his vein of natural pathos, as in "The dead leaves strew the forest walk," he is superior to most of his school, and in other passages on Connecticut scenery his nature, so sensitive to sorrow, shows a corresponding exaltation in the presence of beauty.

[There is no life of Brainard, and extremely little manuscript material has survived (Yale Univ. Lib.). The best biographical sketches are J. G. Whittier, *The Literary Remains of John G. C. Brainard* (1832) and Royal Robbins, *The Poems of John G. C. Brainard* (1842). Other references may be found in F. B. Dexter, *Biog. Sketches Grads. Yale Coll.*, VI (1915), 734–36; E. A. and G. L. Duyckinck, *Cyc. of Am. Lit.* (1855), II, 226–30; S. G. Goodrich, *Recollections of a Lifetime* (1856), II, 143–60; S. T. Williams, "The Lit. of Conn.," in *Hist. of Conn.* (1925), ed. by N. G. Osborn, II, 518–20.]

S. T. W.
J. A. P.

BRAINERD, DAVID (Apr. 20, 1718–Oct. 9, 1747), missionary to the Indians, though but twenty-nine at the time of his death, became widely known and influential through the autobiography of his intensely pietistic life, left in the form of a diary. He was a native of Haddam in the colony of Connecticut, the son of Hezekiah Brainerd, one of His Majesty's Council. His mother, Dorothy Hobart, was the daughter of Rev. Jeremiah Hobart, and grand-daughter of Rev. Peter Hobart who, driven out of Hingham, England, by the Puritan persecutions, settled in Hingham, Mass. Probably many of the emotional experiences which Brainerd attributed to a Divine agency were pathological in origin. Certainly by the time he entered college, and very likely earlier, he was a victim of tuberculosis. From childhood he was highly emotional, unhealthily introspective, over-conscientious, and subject to periods of dark depression. Although concerned for his soul, terrified by the thought of death, and driven to the performance of religious duties at the age of seven, it was only after many terrible struggles with their grim background of Calvinistic theology, that on July 12, 1739, he felt himself converted. In the fall of that year he entered Yale to prepare for the ministry. Here in 1742 an event occurred which long preyed upon his mind. He was sympathetic toward the Whitefield revival to which the college authorities were opposed, and in the company of two or three students of like mind remarked that a tutor, Mr. Whittelsey, had "no more grace than this chair." His utterance was reported to Rector Clap, who ordered him to apologize before faculty and students. Because he refused, and on the ground that he had attended a Separatist meeting, and made a derogatory remark regarding the Rector himself, though any memory of this he denied, he was expelled; and in spite of the fact that in 1743 he offered to make abject apology if he might receive his degree, it was denied him. This act was strongly disapproved by some of the clergy, and there is a tradition that it hastened the founding of Princeton College, the first three presidents of which had been among Brainerd's strongest supporters (D. D. Field, *Genealogy of the Brainerd Family,* 1857, p. 265, and John Maclean, *History of the College of New Jersey,* 1877, I, 55–56).

After studying with Rev. Jedediah Mills of Ripton, Conn., he was licensed to preach by the

Association of Ministers at Danbury, Conn., July 29, 1742, and the same year was appointed missionary to the Indians by the Correspondents of the Society in Scotland for the Propagation of Christian Knowledge. Beginning Apr. 1, 1743, he labored for a year at Kaunaumeek, a settlement in the woods between Stockbridge and Albany, and then persuaded the Indians to move to Stockbridge, where they could be under Rev. John Sergeant [*q.v.*]. On June 12, 1744, he was ordained by the Presbytery of New York at Newark, N. J., and took up work at the Forks of the Delaware, near what is now Easton, Pa. From here he went to Crossweeksung, not far from the present town of Freehold, N. J., where his work was notably successful. In May 1746 he removed from that place with all the Indians to Cranberry, about fifteen miles distant. Early the following year, however, the condition of his health forced him to relinquish his work, and in October he died at the home of Jonathan Edwards, to whose daughter, Jerusha, he was engaged to be married.

Brainerd was a mystic of saintly character, controlled absolutely by a sense of God and duty, indifferent to any labor or risk his devotion to these entailed, yet eminently practical in his missionary program. His religious experiences, elevations and depressions of spirit, physical weakness, travels and labors, doctrinal teachings, and methods of work, are all set forth in his diary. For years this was to many a manual of religious guidance, and down to the middle of the nineteenth century, probably no person except Henry Martyn of England and India, who himself was made a missionary by reading Brainerd's life, did more to stimulate and direct missionaries in their form of work. The Society in Scotland for Propagating Christian Knowledge published portions of the diary during Brainerd's lifetime, the first in 1746 under the title, *Mirabilia Dei inter Indicos,* and the second later in the same year under the title, *Divine Grace Displayed.* These were commonly known as *Brainerd's Journal.* In 1749 Jonathan Edwards published *An Account of the Life of the Late Reverend Mr. David Brainerd,* which contains the diary with the parts already published omitted. An abridgment of this was published in England by John Wesley in 1768. A second edition with the diary in full was published by Sereno E. Dwight in 1822, and a third with an essay on Brainerd's life and character by J. M. Sherwood in 1884.

[In addition to the above mentioned works see Wm. B. Sprague, *Annals Am. Pulpit,* vol. III (1858).]

H. E. S.

BRAINERD, ERASTUS (Feb. 25, 1855–Dec. 25, 1922), editor, was a descendant of a very old Connecticut family and the son of Norman Leslie and Leora (Campbell) Brainerd. His childhood days were spent in Middletown, Conn., his birthplace. He fitted himself for Trinity College, at Hartford, but changed his plans and entered Harvard in 1870. He received the degree of B.A. in 1874. The following year was spent in graduate study. During his college days he developed a rather fine appreciation of the arts and their masters. From October 1874 to April 1878 he worked with James R. Osgood & Company, Boston publishers, and prepared for them a series of five volumes, namely: the *Life of Titian,* the *Life of Sir John E. Millais, Great Artists, Gems of the Dresden Gallery,* and the *Gray Collection of Engravings,* the latter being the most admirable. He also was curator of engravings at the Boston Museum of Fine Arts in 1876–77. In 1878 he went to Europe, there encountering several unique experiences. In the Island of Malta he was made a member of the famous knighthood which was originally established there. In Scotland he was initiated into the Scottish Rite of Masonry by the Duke of Buccleuch. When he returned to America in 1879 he began a varied newspaper career. He was successively associated with the editorial staffs of the New York *World,* the Philadelphia *Press,* the *Atlanta Constitution* and the *Atlanta Star* and somewhat later the *Press* and *Daily News* of Philadelphia. Of the latter, he was editor-in-chief and proprietor. He was married on May 30, 1882, to Mary Bella Beale of Richmond, Va. They moved to Seattle, Wash., in 1890, and Brainerd edited the *Press* and the *Press Times* of Seattle for the three years following. In 1893 he was appointed land commissioner of Washington, serving a four-year term. When the rush to the Yukon region began in 1897 Brainerd directed a most extensive and successful advertising campaign for Seattle as the starting and outfitting point for Alaska. A complete file of fourteen volumes of correspondence including letters to and from the Seattle Chamber of Commerce and newspaper clippings was compiled by Brainerd and entitled *Alaska and the Klondyke.* Shortly after, Brainerd made a visit to Alaska and spent almost five years there. After his return he edited the *Seattle Post-Intelligencer* from 1904 to 1911, and the *San Francisco Call* from March to September 1913. He was a man of many interests and exceptionally well informed on most varied subjects. His document called *Seattle and Ship Subsidy* (1902) shows his interest in economics and politics. In 1919 he served as consul for Paraguay, his jurisdiction covering Washington, Oregon, Idaho and Alaska. His death occurred at his home in Seattle.

[*Who's Who in America*, 1922–23; *Report of the Class Sec. of the Class of 1874 of Harvard Coll.* (1894, 1899, 1924); J. P. Nichols, "Advertising and the Klondike," *Wash. Hist. Quart.*, XIII, 20–26.] M. S.

BRAINERD, EZRA (Dec. 17, 1844–Dec. 8, 1924), botanist, geologist, educator, was the son of Lawrence Robbins Brainerd and Catherine (Wood) Brainerd, and was born at St. Albans, Vt. His education was in the public schools of his native town; in 1860 he entered Middlebury College, graduating four years later with the degree of A.B. For the next two years he was a tutor there, and then for two years attended Andover Theological Seminary, duly graduating though never ordained. For the next two years he was professor of rhetoric at Middlebury College; subsequently he taught physics and applied mathematics and from 1885 to 1906 was president of the college. His first scientific inclinations showed themselves in physics and surveying. Early in his career he began the study of geology, where his ability as a surveyor stood him in good stead. His work on the geology of the Champlain valley and the origin of certain Vermont formations won the admiration of Le Conte. In 1900 he published the *Blackberries of New England*, the first of his botanical papers to attract wide notice, and in the same year he was among the trio of editors who issued the *Flora of Vermont*, considered the model of a state floral catalogue. By 1904 he had published his first paper on violets, and from then until the close of his life he was constantly at work upon the study of hybridism in the genus *Viola*. The genus contains an enormous number of natural hybrids, and their pure species parents he endeavored to discover by growing the plants under controlled conditions and by studying the unit characters as they emerged in subsequent generations, according to Mendelian laws. He traveled all over the country in the study of violets, sustained an immense correspondence, and published innumerable titles on the subject, those of most philosophical interest being the series *Hybridism in the Genus Viola*. The result was an international reputation. In conjunction with Dr. A. K. Pietersen, studies in the hybridism of the genus *Rubus* were carried on at the Vermont Experiment Station; the results were published in 1920 as *Bulletin 217* of the Vermont Experiment Station. The methods that had been employed in the study were along approved genetic principles, and the publication was warmly received by the geneticists; as an avowed study in systematic classification the work was considered a failure by some specialists in systematic botany. Brainerd's last publications were his "Violets of North America," and "Some Natural Violet Hybrids of North America," constituting *Bulletin 224* and *Bulletin 239*, respectively, of the Vermont Experiment Station. These were incomplete, largely popular expositions of the subject, as Brainerd stated in private correspondence, being essentially illustrations (by Schuyler Mathews) with some textual notes by Brainerd.

His tenancy of the president's chair marked an era of expansion from poverty and obscurity to thriving prosperity for Middlebury College. Executive detail was, however, never congenial to his temperament which was distinctly that of the scholastic. He was, from its incipiency on a field expedition, the perpetual president of the Vermont Botanical Society; throughout life a fresh and enthusiastic love of nature, such as the old-style naturalists displayed, marked his botanical interests; the subjects that he chose for monographic study were largely selected on the basis of their metaphysical significance. To the end of his life he retained a great memory and a facility with the classic tongues. He was twice married, in 1868 to Frances Viola Rockwell, and, after her death, to Mary Wright in 1897.

[The only important biographical material in print is that entitled *A Memorial of Ezra Brainerd* (privately printed at Middlebury, Vt., 1927), which includes a personal eulogy by Prof. Chas. B. Wright, and a record of Brainerd's scientific achievements compiled from material supplied by Edward Foyles, of the Am. Mus. of Nat. Hist., Dr. G. P. Burns of the Univ. of Vermont and Mr. W. W. Eggleston of the Dept. of Agriculture, Washington, D. C. To this is appended a bibliography of his publications. For further personal and academic detail the writer is indebted to the private correspondence of Prof. Chas. B. Wright, to the records of Middlebury College, and to members of Brainerd's family.] D. C. P.

BRAINERD, JOHN (Feb. 28, 1720–Mar. 18, 1781), missionary to the Indians, was born in Haddam, Conn., the son of Hezekiah and Mrs. Dorothy (Hobart) Mason Brainerd, and brother of David Brainerd [*q.v.*], whose work he continued. He graduated from Yale in 1746. The following year when failing health compelled David to leave the Indian settlement, known as Bethel, at Cranberry, N. J., the Correspondents of the Society in Scotland for the Propagation of Christian Knowledge asked the younger Brainerd to take his place. He was licensed by the New York Presbytery, Apr. 11, 1747, and in his diary under date of Apr. 14, David wrote: "This day my brother went to my people." The following October David died, and John was ordained in February 1748, and soon received his missionary commission from Edinburgh.

Although he labored with devotion and apparently with good judgment for years, the Bethel enterprise ultimately failed. A pestilence carried off a considerable number of the Indian converts; their title to the land they occupied was questioned, and it was taken from them; and Brainerd's health sometimes interfered with his activities, for like his brother he seems to have suffered from tuberculosis. Dissatisfied with conditions, the Correspondents dismissed him May 7, 1755, and he took charge of the church at Newark, N. J., lately served by President Aaron Burr [*q.v.*] of the College of New Jersey. Plans were made to buy land for the Indians near New Brunswick, N. J., and in June 1756 Brainerd was again put in charge of the undertaking, but the plan failed and in September 1757 he returned to the church in Newark. In 1754 he had been made a trustee of the College of New Jersey, and in January 1758 he journeyed to Stockbridge, Mass., with Rev. Caleb Smith to secure sanction for the removal of Jonathan Edwards [*q.v.*] from the pastorate there to the presidency of the college. In May, the government having provided land for the Indians in Burlington County, he again took charge of the mission. That summer he served as chaplain of the expedition to Crown Point, and on his return settled at the Indian town, Brotherton, N. J., with supervision over several Indian and white settlements. In 1768 he removed to Bridgetown (Mount Holly), where he built up a congregation and erected a church. His activities were now chiefly among the whites. The Revolutionary War broke up his work at Bridgetown, and he took charge of the Presbyterian church at Deerfield, N. J. Here he died, and was buried under the church.

He was twice married, first, in November 1752, to Experience Lyon, who died in 1757; and second, to Mrs. Experience Price.

[Thos. Brainerd, *The Life of John Brainerd* (1865) contains much documentary material and Brainerd's journal, Oct. 15, 1749–Nov. 21, 1759; the Jour. of John Brainerd, 1761–1762 (MS.) is in the library of Princeton University. T. Brainerd reprints *A Genuine Letter from John Brainerd to His Friend in England*, London, 1753. See also W. B. Sprague, *Annals Am. Pulpit*, III (1858); Lucy A. Brainard, *The Genealogy of the Brainerd-Brainard Family in America 1649–1908* (1908).] H. E. S.

BRAINERD, LAWRENCE (Mar. 16, 1794–May 9, 1870), capitalist, senator, one of twelve children born to Ezra and Mabel (Porter) Brainerd, was a native of East Hartford, Conn. At the age of nine years he went to Troy, N. Y., to live with Joseph S. Brainerd, an uncle. Five years later, he removed with this uncle to St. Albans, Vt. He attended the St. Albans Academy for two years and entered the store of a local merchant as clerk. At the age of twenty-two he established a mercantile business of his own in which he was very successful. He bought a large tract of swamp land near Lake Champlain, drained and improved it, and developed it into a 1,200-acre farm, one of the best in Vermont. When the Bank of St. Albans was established in 1826, he became a heavy stockholder, a director, and later its president. He was active in steamboat enterprises in the early days of that method of transportation, in 1847 superintending the building at Shelburne Harbor of the *United States*, then considered one of the finest steamboats ever built. He became interested early in railroad development and the construction of the Vermont & Canada line was due largely to his energy and aid, in coöperation with John Smith and Joseph Clark. He pledged practically his entire fortune to make possible the building of the railroad. From the construction of the road until his death he was a director and in later years was associated with his son-in-law, Gov. John Gregory Smith, in the management of the corporation. He was also engaged in railroad building in Canada and was a promoter of the Missisquoi Railroad. He took an active interest in public affairs, being particularly interested in the anti-slavery cause and in temperance reform. Originally a Democrat, he was affiliated with the Free-Soil wing of the party. In 1834 he was a member of the legislature and in 1846, 1847, 1848, 1852, and 1854, he was a candidate of the Free-Soil Democratic party for governor. He was elected United States senator in 1854 to fill the vacancy caused by the death of Senator Upham, was president of the convention called to organize the Republican party in Vermont, was a delegate to a preliminary national Republican convention at Pittsburgh in February 1856, and called to order the first Republican national convention, held at Philadelphia in June 1856. Much interested in agricultural development, he was a president of the Vermont Agricultural Society. In 1819 he married Fidelia B. Gadcomb and twelve children were born to them. He was a man of large frame and great physical strength.

[*St. Albans Daily Messenger*, May 9, 1870; W. H. Crockett, *Vermont*, vol. III (1921); H. C. Williams, ed., *Biog. Encyc. of Vermont* (1885).] W. H. C.

BRAINERD, THOMAS (June 17, 1804–Aug. 21, 1866), Presbyterian minister, editor, son of Jesse and Mary (Thomas) Brainerd, was born at Leyden, Lewis County, N. Y., but spent his childhood and early youth at Rome, N. Y. He graduated from the Academy at Louisville,

N. Y., taught school at the age of seventeen, and developed tendencies toward a professional career. His first inclination in this direction was the law, toward which he began preparatory studies; but at the age of twenty-one coming under the influence of Charles G. Finney the evangelist, and being pressed further by a distressful experience, he resolved to enter the ministry. He took his theological course at Andover Theological Seminary, graduating in 1831. He then placed himself for a brief season under the guidance of Dr. James Patterson of Philadelphia with a view to connecting himself with the Presbyterian Church. On Oct. 7, 1831, he was ordained by the Third Presbytery of New York and accepted a commission under the Home Missionary Society, going to Cincinnati to take charge of the new and struggling Fourth Church in the outskirts of the city. In this field he labored for two years. In 1833 Lyman Beecher, who was pastor of the Second Church as well as president of Lane Theological Seminary, invited him to the position of an associate in the Second Church. This he accepted. At the same time he became an associate editor of the *Cincinnati Journal* and, later, editor of the *Youth's Magazine,* and assisted in editing the *Presbyterian Quarterly Review.* During the controversy involving the trial of Lyman Beecher for heresy he stood faithfully by his chief and became a firm advocate of what were known as the "New School" views, joining in 1837 the New School Presbyterian Church when it was organized. From Cincinnati he was called to the pastorate of the Third ("Old Pine Street") Church of Philadelphia and spent the remainder of his life (1837–66) in this field. During the Civil War he loyally supported the Union, and by his earnest support of the government influenced 130 young men to enlist in the Northern army. In 1864 the New School General Assembly elected him to the position of moderator. He died at Scranton, Pa., suddenly, of apoplexy, Aug. 21, 1866. In appearance he was large and dignified; in manner gentle and amiable. He was rather popular than scholarly in his tastes; full of zeal and energy, quick and impulsive, but broad in his interests. He was twice married: on Oct. 20, 1831, to Sarah J. Langstroth, and on Oct. 29, 1836, to Mrs. Mary Whiting.

His extant literary productions are not extensive. Though he was a prolific writer, most of what he wrote was designed for use in the newspapers and periodicals for which he was responsible as editor and contributor. It concerned matters under discussion at the time and was therefore naturally of an ephemeral nature. His outstanding work is *The Life of John Brainerd* (1865), a volume of permanent value as a source of information concerning a remarkable personality.

[Mary Brainerd, *Life of Rev. Thos. Brainerd* (1870); files of the *Presbyt. Quart. Rev.*] A.C.Z.

BRAMLETTE, THOMAS E. (Jan. 3, 1817–Jan. 12, 1875), governor of Kentucky, was born in Cumberland County, Ky., a part of the state favored by nature much less than the Blue Grass section, and here he grew up with what meager schooling this section afforded. Believing the legal profession would be the easiest road to distinction, he studied law and was admitted to the bar when twenty years of age. Four years later he was elected to represent Clinton County in the legislature, and having identified himself prominently with the Whig party he secured in 1848 the appointment of commonwealth's attorney from John J. Crittenden, the incoming governor. In this position he attracted attention by his strict adherence to duty and his fearless prosecution of criminals. After two years he resigned to resume his legal practise and in 1852 he removed to Columbia, Adair County. In 1856 he was elected judge for the 6th circuit and for the next five years served with distinction, his decisions being so clear and logical as rarely to be reversed by the court of appeals. With the approach of the Civil War he assumed a strong attitude in favor of the preservation of the Union, exhibiting little sympathy or patience for the strange neutrality doctrine the state had set forth in 1861. In July of this year while Kentucky was attempting to maintain her neutral position, he accepted a commission in the Federal Army and boldly set about raising the 3rd Kentucky Infantry, which he commanded as colonel—all of which was in violation of the state's tacit agreement with the Federal Government. On account of a disagreement in 1862 as to the unit he should command, he resigned from the army, and, on being offered by President Lincoln the position of United States district attorney, accepted. Using the same vigor and energy which characterized his work as commonwealth's attorney, he sought to enforce the wartime laws passed by Kentucky against Confederates and Southern sympathizers. He succeeded in convicting of treason Thomas C. Shacklett and saw him sentenced to ten years in jail, fined $10,000, and deprived of his slaves.

But it was as governor during the last two years of the war and the two years following that Bramlette made his most lasting reputation. In 1863 he was designated as the Union Democratic candidate for governor on the rejection of the honor by Joshua F. Bell, the candidate named by the convention. On account of army supervision of the election he won by an overwhelming majority over Charles A. Wickliffe, the Peace Democrat. He began his administration with as pronounced and as loud support of the war as could be heard in the state, yet within less than a year he was one of Lincoln's most bitter critics and opponents, undergoing much the same transformation as that which characterized the vast majority of Kentuckians. In the early part of 1864 when Lincoln ordered the enlistment of negro troops, he threatened to array the state against the Federal Government, and was long and persistently charged with having written but later having amended the proclamation "to bloodily baptize the state into the Confederacy." In the national Democratic convention of 1864 he was the choice of the Kentucky Democrats for vice-president, but he refused to countenance the move. He opposed Lincoln's election and wrote him menacing letters. He bitterly quarreled with Gen. Stephen G. Burbridge, the commander of Federal troops in Kentucky, and succeeded in February 1865 in having him removed. On Lincoln's death he repented of all the harsh things he had said about the President and appointed officially a day of prayer and mourning. Never sympathizing with the Federal military régime in Kentucky, he welcomed back the returning Confederate soldiers in 1865 and 1866 and recommended the repeal of all laws against them. He favored the thirteenth amendment and, without success, urged upon the legislature its adoption. In 1867 on leaving the governorship he aspired to the United States Senate but failed of election. He thereupon settled in Louisville and practised law until his death in 1875. He was married twice, first to Sallie Travis, in 1837, and after her death to Mrs. Mary E. Adams, in 1874.

[*Ky. Yeoman*, Sept. 26, 1868; *Official Records*, ser. 1, vol. IV; *Ky. Senate Jour.*, 1865; Thos. Speed, R. M. Kelly, and A. Pirtle, *The Union Regiments of Ky.* (1897); Richard H. and Lewis Collins, *Hist. of Ky.* (1874), II; H. Levin, ed., *The Lawyers and Lawmakers of Ky.* (1897); E. M. Coulter, *The Civil War and Readjustment in Ky.* (1926).] E. M. C.

BRANCH, JOHN (Nov. 4, 1782–Jan. 4, 1863), governor of North Carolina, senator, secretary of the navy, was born at Halifax, N. C., the third child in a wealthy and prominent family. His parents were Col. John and Mary (Bradford) Branch. He was educated at the University of North Carolina, graduating in 1801; he studied law, but never actively engaged in practise, preferring the life of a wealthy planter and politician. Parton's characterization of him may be accepted: "Inheriting an ample estate, he lived for many years upon his plantations and employed himself in superintending their culture. He was a man of respectable talents, good presence, and high social position." A leader in society, he was famous for his dinners and entertainments. His long public career was uneven in that it did not show an orderly progression from offices of lesser to those of higher importance, as the following analysis will demonstrate: state senator, 1811, 1813–17, 1822, 1834; speaker of the state Senate, 1815–17; governor, 1817–20; United States senator, 1823–29; secretary of the navy, 1829–31; representative in Congress, 1831–33; member of the North Carolina constitutional convention, 1835; governor of Florida Territory, 1834–45. He was a faithful member of the Democratic party, abandoning it only once in order to oppose Van Buren in 1836. He seemed to have the confidence of the party and the people, for he suffered only one defeat—that in his candidacy against Dudley, a Whig, for governor in 1838. The evidence is convincing that he was a man of firmness and integrity, although a biographer of Jackson alluded to him as "weak-willed" (J. S. Bassett, *Life of Andrew Jackson*, II, 414), McLane referred to him in a letter to Van Buren as a "miserable old woman" (*Ibid.*), and Archibald D. Murphey wrote slightingly of him as one of three in control of the Assembly in 1814 (W. H. Hoyt, ed., *The Papers of Archibald D. Murphey*, 1914, I, 75). In the last case, Murphey changed his opinion and dedicated his important "Memoir on Internal Improvements" to Branch. As governor Branch favored state aid to education, internal improvements, reorganization of the supreme court, abolition of imprisonment for debt, and elimination and punishment of impostors in the medical profession. His messages on education were notable pronouncements as to the "imperious duty" to republican institutions and civilization that rested upon the state. In 1819 he acted as president of the North Carolina branch of the American Colonization Society. In the United States Senate, to which he was elected after a long contest, Branch was allied with the "Jackson men," signalizing his union with this group by opposing the nomination of Henry Clay as secretary of state. In debate he made speeches in advocacy of the abolition of imprisonment for debt, in favor of pensions for privates as well as for officers, and in opposition to internal improvements financed by the general government. Perhaps due to the friendship of Eaton, or it may have been in order to give social tone to the cabinet, he was, when Jackson became President, made secretary of the navy,—the first of five North Carolinians to hold this place. His service in this office, although described by Jackson as satisfactory, was unimportant. His reports urged a naval school, revision of the law respecting the Marine Corps, and equalization of pay. An investigation was made, on order of Congress, of the use of liquor by officers. The chief interest in connection with Branch's membership in Jackson's first cabinet was the manner of his retirement. Like Berrien and Ingham, he was involved in the complications and embarrassments incident to the Eaton affair. With the "reorganization" of the cabinet, he was forced to resign. He declined appointment to a foreign mission and to the territorial governorship of Florida and severed relations with Jackson, becoming a supporter of Calhoun. The details in the chain of events leading to his resignation were revealed in a letter to Edward B. Freeman, published in *Niles' Register* (Sept. 3, 1831) and elsewhere. One important statement in it was that Jackson, shortly before the purging of the cabinet, had stated that he "did not claim the right to dictate" to his official household as to "social relations." Branch characterized Jackson's decision to dismiss as "arbitrary and unjust." In the bitter feelings and controversies provoked by the dismissals, Branch came near being involved in a duel with Senator Forsyth of Georgia. As a mark of public confidence and as a popular justification, he was unanimously elected to the House of Representatives in 1831. During his one term, he spoke on such topics as the bank, Indian affairs, the tariff, and the navy. Retiring voluntarily from Congress, his last public service to North Carolina was rendered as a member of the state constitutional convention of 1835, wherein he advocated annual sessions of the legislature and removal of all religious qualifications for office-holding. On several occasions he chose to uphold the rights of the states, endangered in his opinion by the Jackson administration. In 1836, he acquired large estates in Florida, to which territory his family moved and in which he spent most of his time until the death of his first wife in 1851, when he returned to North Carolina. During this period, by appointment of President Tyler, he was governor of the territory, 1843–45, in which term Florida became a state. He was married twice: first, to Elizabeth Foort, by whom he had nine children, and second, to Mrs. Eliza (Jordan) Bond. He died at Enfield.

[For documentary sources there are Gov. Branch's Letter-Book (N. C. Hist. Commission); *Reports of the Sec. Navy*, 1830–31; and the *Annals of Congress*, 1823–29. Letters concerning the disruption of the cabinet were published in the *Raleigh Register* (Sept. 1, 1831). A monograph by Marshall DeLancey Haywood "John Branch, 1782–1863" (*N. C. Booklet*, Oct. 1915), may be read with profit. See also study of John Branch by R. D. W. Connor in *N. C. Rev.*, Apr. 1913. There is a review of Branch's administration as governor of North Carolina in S. A. Ashe, *Hist. of N. C.*, II (1925), 255–77.]

W. W. P.

BRANCH, LAWRENCE O'BRYAN (Nov. 28, 1820–Sept. 17, 1862), lawyer, congressman, Confederate soldier, born at Enfield, N. C., of a prominent and wealthy family, was at an early age left an orphan when his parents (Joseph and Susan Simpson O'Bryan Branch) died. Brought back from Tennessee, where his father had been living, he became a member of the household of his uncle and guardian, John Branch [*q.v.*]. After being tutored by William J. Bingham and Salmon P. Chase, he studied for a part of one year at the University of North Carolina. He then entered Princeton, from which institution he graduated with distinction in 1838. While editing a newspaper in Tennessee, he studied law, and when he soon moved to Florida, under special act of the territorial legislature he was admitted to practise, though not then of age. The Seminole war breaking out shortly thereafter, he volunteered, serving throughout as aide-de-camp to Gen. Reid. In 1844 he was married to Nancy Haywood Blount, daughter of Gen. William Augustus Blount. Despite his success as a lawyer in Florida, he returned to North Carolina in 1848 and there supplemented his professional activities by management of his estates and by engaging in industrial undertakings, especially in railroads. In the last connection, he became (1852–55) president of the Raleigh and Gaston Railroad Company. His participation in politics began in 1852, when he was chosen presidential elector on the Pierce ticket. Effectively active in the Democratic party, he was, in 1854, elected—although an unwilling candidate—to the House of Representatives, in which body he was a member continuously from 1855 to 1861. A partisan, Southern Democrat, he was not an extremist. While speaking frankly for his district, state, and section, he repeatedly cautioned the South against immoderation. Not one of the foremost leaders, he was a forceful speaker and won sufficient distinction to be placed upon the then important Committee on Territories. He made speeches on finance, party politics, the Brooks-Sumner affair, the acquisition of Cuba, and various phases of the slavery dispute. Favoring low tariffs and the "depositing" among the states of the proceeds of the sale of public land, he opposed the "distribution" of these funds and the proposed Homestead Act. His speeches on the Kansas-Nebraska Act and its operation are valuable sources of information for those seeking the views and attitude of moderate Southerners. An admirer and consistent supporter of President Buchanan and an exponent of party policy in public finance, he was offered, on the resignation of Howell Cobb, the place of secretary of the treasury. Earlier he had declined Buchanan's offer of the position of postmaster general. Feeling that the secession of North Carolina was imminent, he again refused. His good sense and practical comprehension of politics were at no time better demonstrated than in the campaign of 1860. In a letter to his constituents of May 15, 1860, he opposed the plan of the "fire-eaters" and the inclusion in the party platform of the new doctrine of "Congressional protection to slavery in the Territories." The disruption of the party, its defeat for the sake of an abstraction, and the surrender of "all the fruits of twenty years of successful struggle with Freesoilism and Abolitionism"—*i.e.*, the principle of non-intervention by Congress—were results he saw and stated. When it was clear that seceded states were to be "coerced," he withdrew from Congress to advocate the secession of North Carolina. When that state called for troops, he volunteered as a private, but was, upon the governor's appointment, promptly given the joint office of quartermaster and paymaster-general. Wishing active service, he resigned to become colonel of the 33rd North Carolina Regiment. Later, on Jan. 17, 1862, he was commissioned brigadier-general by President Davis and was placed in command of the Confederate forces around New Bern. Operating against the greatly superior army of Gen. Burnside, he was forced to retreat, skilfully withdrawing his troops from the peninsula—a feat highly praised. He was then ordered to join Stonewall Jackson. Between January and September of 1862, he took part creditably in the battles of Hanover Court House, the Seven Days battles around Richmond, Cedar Run, Second Manassas, Fairfax Court House, Ox Hill, Harper's Ferry, and Antietam. At the last battle, after leading his brigade successfully, he was shot through the head and killed. He had been complimented by Gen. Lee and his death occurred, it is thought, on the eve of a career of higher military responsibility.

[For Branch's speeches in Congress, see *Cong. Globe*, 1855–61. The important *Letter to his Constituents*, May 15, 1860, is preserved in the Weeks Collection at the Univ. of N. C. Sketches are printed in S. A. Ashe, *Biog. Hist. of N. C.*, VII, 55 ff., and in *Confed. Mil. Hist.*, ed. by C. A. Evans (1899), IV, 298–300. An excellent short biography is that of John Hughes—*Laurence O'Bryan Branch, An Oration* (1884). For his military service, see W. Clark, *Histories of the Several Regiments and Battalions from N. C.* (1901), IV, 465–79, and D. H. Hill, *Bethel to Sharpsburg* (in press, 1927).]

W. W. P.

BRANDEGEE, FRANK BOSWORTH (July 8, 1864–Oct. 14, 1924), politician, was born in New London, son of Augustus and Nancy Christian (Bosworth) Brandegee. Having been graduated from Yale in 1885, he spent a year of travel in Great Britain and on the Continent. Upon his return he studied law, was admitted to the New London County bar, and commenced practise in New London as a member of the firm of Brandegee, Noyes & Brandegee. In 1888, the year of his admission to the bar, he also entered politics, going as a delegate to the Republican national convention at Chicago in June; and in November following he was elected to the state House of Representatives. To three other national conventions—those of 1892, 1900, and 1904—he was a delegate. With the exception of two years, he was corporation counsel of New London from 1889 to 1902, when he resigned; and for a time he also served as United States attorney in his district. In 1898 he was again elected to the Connecticut House of Representatives, of which he was speaker during the session of 1899. Chosen in 1902 as representative from the third Connecticut district in the Fifty-seventh Congress, for the unexpired term of Charles A. Russell (to Mar. 4, 1903), he was twice reëlected (Fifty-eighth and Fifty-ninth Congresses). In 1905 he resigned from the House of Representatives on being elected (May 9) United States senator for the unexpired term (1905–09) of Orville H. Platt, who had been a Connecticut senator since 1879. Brandegee was three times reëlected—in 1909, 1915, and 1921—and was a member of the committees on Foreign Relations, Judiciary, Library, and Patents. He was found dead on Oct. 14, 1924, in his house in Washington, where he had ended his life by inhaling gas. Financial difficulties, caused by unfortunate investments in real estate, were assigned as the probable cause of his suicide. For some months previous, he had been living in comparative seclusion.

An indifferent speaker, Brandegee made no particular impression by his utterances in the Senate, and outside of it he was rarely heard in public address. It was through his service on committees and through his private counsels that for a time he exerted a considerable influence—an influence largely negative, if not reactionary, in effect. He delighted in obstructive tactics, and he opposed and voted against all of the following measures alike: direct election of senators; extension of the parcel post; federal regulation of child labor; the Federal Reserve system; the income tax; prohibition; woman suffrage. He objected to any inquiry regarding William Lorimer of Illinois, whose election to the Senate was finally (1912) declared invalid; or regarding Truman H. Newberry of Michigan, whose seat was retained by a vote of 46 to 41 (1922). "In what many of us might consider a sort of consistent wrong-headedness," commented the *New York Times* (editorial of Oct. 15, 1924), "kinder observers might find a consistent disregard of political consequences." During the controversy over the League of Nations, in the Senate discussion of the peace treaty with Germany, Brandegee was a bitter irreconcilable. "I shall never vote for it," he was quoted as saying, "until hell freezes over, and I think that event is probably somewhat remote. I am not to be buncoed by any oleaginous lingo about 'humanity' or 'men everywhere'" (*New York Times,* Oct. 15, 1924). One bill to which he lent his support was that for the soldiers' bonus (adjusted compensation). He was accounted a lawyer of ability and in many respects a cultivated man.

[*Geneal. and Biog. Record of New London County, Conn.* (1905); Dwight Loomis and J. G. Calhoun, *The Judicial and Civil Hist. of Conn.* (1895); *N. Y. Times,* Oct. 15, 18, 23, and 26, 1924; N. G. Osborn, *Men of Mark in Conn.* (1906); *Who's Who in America,* 1924–25.]

G. S. B.

BRANDEGEE, TOWNSHEND STITH (Feb. 16, 1843–Apr. 7, 1925), botanist, the son of Elishama and Florence (Stith) Brandegee, was born in Berlin, Conn., where his father was a physician with a taste for natural history. His early education was inculcated, he wrote, in a "little red schoolhouse where they hired a new teacher every term, who always made the pupils begin at the first lesson. Consequently in geography we never reached Asia or Oceania. . . . My father owned a small farm, of which I have ploughed the field with oxen, cut the grass with a scythe, etc. . . . At the age of 19 I enlisted in First Regiment Conn., Artillery, Co. G, and served two years until discharged as private in the rear rank. Gen. Grant and I took Richmond." In 1866 he entered the Sheffield Scientific School of Yale, graduating in 1870. Primarily he was preparing to be an engineer, but he pursued botanical studies under Prof. A. A. Eaton, having as a boy devoted especial attention to ferns. He is mentioned in reports on the flora of Connecticut as "having made rare finds" in the vicinity of Yale. In 1871 he was made county surveyor and city engineer of Cañon City, Colo., where he spent spare time in collecting ferns for the well known Connecticut botanist, John Redfield. His specimens at length reached Asa Gray who in 1875 recommended him as botanical collector and assistant topographer to Hayden's exploring expedition of southwestern Colorado and adjacent Utah. He was successively attached as engineer to the survey of the Royal Gorge, the Santa Fé surveys in New Mexico and Arizona, and the Northern Transcontinental survey through Wyoming to Washington and Oregon. In spare hours he discovered many new western species, and assembled for Prof. C. S. Sargent several splendid collections of western timbers, first in connection with the United States Census work and later for the Jesup collection of the American Museum of Natural History.

Carrying out a commission, in 1886, to obtain certain rare timbers, he visited Santa Cruz Island off Santa Barbara, Cal., which turned his attention to the peculiar fascination of the biology of islands. This determined him definitely to devote his life to botany, and so he relinquished his engineering work, although on subsequent occasions he prepared forest maps of various western regions, combining his engineering training with his botanical knowledge. In 1889 he made a memorable trip to Magdalena Bay, Baja California, Mexico, as a volunteer in the California Academy of Sciences expedition. From that time until the close of his life he was intermittently active as a botanist of Baja California and was indeed the leading authority upon its flora, as upon that of the islands of the Gulf of California. His explorations extended into Sonora, Sinaloa, Puebla, and Vera Cruz. At the same time he pursued assiduously his explorations of California itself, especially its southern half. At first he sent his specimens to Eastern authorities, for identification, but as he gained confidence he began publishing his own species and many notes (some ninety in all), contributory to the habits, habitats, and life histories of the plants of the western states and Mexico. From 1909 to 1924 he was engaged upon his most important undertaking, *Plantæ Mexicanæ Purpusianæ,* of which twelve fascicles appeared (1909–24) through the *University of California Publications.* These were descriptions of new species collected by Dr. C. A. Purpus in Mexico.

On May 29, 1889, he married Dr. Mary Katherine (Layne) Curran (Oct. 28, 1844–Apr. 3, 1920), best known to science as Katherine Brandegee, curator of the herbarium of the California Academy of Sciences. Their wedding trip took the form of a botanical collecting journey afoot from San Diego to San Francisco. Brandegee was a man of retiring manner, reticent of his opinions but holding them staunchly. He was among the last of the old, self-trained botanists, as he was among the first of the pioneer collectors of the West. Throughout most of his life he retained the bodily vigor of his early days as a plowboy and as a mountain surveyor, and his love of sports was unquenchable; his death at Berkeley, Cal., from pneumonia released him from the rather pitiful last years of his life, when deafness, blindness, and partial paralysis had put a stop to his long activity.

[The sole authority on the lives of the two Brandegees is W. A. Setchell's "Townshend Stith Brandegee and Mary Katherine (Layne) (Curran) Brandegee," in *Univ. of Cal. Pubs. in Botany*, XIII (1926), pp. 155–78, with bibliographies. Fragments of autobiographic notes left by the subjects of the memoir are printed therein.] D. C. P.

BRANDON, GERARD CHITTOCQUE (Sept. 15, 1788–Mar. 28, 1850), lawyer, planter, governor of Mississippi, was born at Selma Plantation, near Natchez, when the Natchez District was under the dominion of Spain, the eldest son of Gerard Brandon and his wife, Dorothy Nugent. Gerard Brandon was a native of County Donegal, Ireland. He was a follower of Robert Emmet and escaped to America on the failure of his cause, settling in Charleston, S. C. He served in the War of the Revolution under Marion and in Col. Washington's cavalry and took part in the battles of Cowpens and King's Mountain. He migrated to West Florida about 1782.

Gerard C. Brandon was educated at Princeton and William and Mary and was graduated at the latter institution, dividing honors with William Cabell Rivers. He began the practise of law at Washington, the capital of Mississippi Territory, in 1812, and was also a soldier in the War of 1812. He was elected to the legislature of Mississippi Territory in 1815. In 1816 he married Margaret Chambers of Bardstown, Ky., and abandoned the law for the life of a planter, living near Fort Adams in Wilkinson County, Miss. A member of the constitutional convention of 1817 and speaker of the House of Representatives in 1822, he was lieutenant-governor under Governors Holmes and Leake in 1825–26 and was elected governor in 1827, being the first native Mississippian to hold the office. He served for two terms of two years each and his administrations were successful from a political, as well as from an economic, point of view. He was solicited to accept the United States senatorship on the expiration of his last term as governor, but declined the honor. Elected to the constitutional convention of 1832, he was the only member who had served in the convention of 1817. He was opposed to the further introduction of slaves into Mississippi, and was opposed to the election of the judiciary by the people,—which was the main issue in the election of delegates to the convention. After the adoption of an elective judiciary system, which was the first departure from the appointive system, he resigned, and returned to Wilkinson County. Thereafter he would never allow himself to be elected to public office. He was a typical Southern planter, cultured, genial, and hospitable, and though he filled with credit and ability every official position that he ever occupied, and enjoyed the distinction that a life in the public service gave, he did not undervalue the blessings of private life, and in no occupation took a keener interest than in that of a planter. He was twice married. By his first marriage he had two children, Gerard and John C. Brandon. In 1824 he married Elizabeth Stanton of Natchez and they had six sons and two daughters. He died at his Columbia Springs plantation, near Fort Adams, Mar. 28, 1850.

[The best sources of information are: Brandon's letter-book as governor, the Mississippi archives; *Mississippi Official and Statistical Register of 1908*, pp. 131–32; letters to Gov. Brandon (1825–32), Mississippi archives; sketch in Dunbar Rowland's *Mississippi*, I (1907), 287–93.] D. R.

BRANNAN, JOHN MILTON (July 1, 1819–Dec. 16, 1892), Union soldier, was born in the District of Columbia, near the city of Washington. He early took an interest in military affairs, and in 1837 secured appointment to the United States Military Academy from the state of Indiana, graduating with the class of 1841, number twenty-three in a class of fifty-two members. On July 1, following graduation, he was commissioned a brevet second lieutenant of artillery, and went for his first station to Plattsburg, N. Y., where he had considerable field service during the border disturbances of 1841–42. He received his full second lieutenancy, May 16, 1842. The outbreak of war with Mexico found Brannan a first lieutenant of artillery, and on Apr. 17, 1847, he was appointed adjutant of his regiment, the historic 1st Artillery. It is interesting to note that at this time the commissioned roster of Brannan's regiment included such names as Joseph Hooker, Irvin McDowell, John B. Magruder, Ambrose P. Hill, and Thomas J. ("Stonewall") Jackson, all of whom distinguished themselves during the Civil War. Brannan took part with his regiment in the siege and occupation of Vera Cruz, and in the subsequent battles of Cerro Gordo, La Hoya, Contreras, and Churubusco, the regiment suffering severe losses in both officers and men. At Churubusco especially, the 1st Artillery was subjected to Mexican artillery fire of round-shot and grape, and to rifle fire from hostile infantry, stationed on the roof and in the windows of the Convent of San Pablo. The Mexican position was gallantly assaulted and taken, and official records show that Lieutenants Brannan and Seymour were the first officers of their regiment to enter the enemy's works (C. M. Wilcox, *History of the Mexican War*, 1892, pp. 384–89). For this and for similar gallantry in the previous battle of Contreras, Brannan was brevetted captain, Aug. 20, 1847. In the final operations against the Mexican capital, he also took part in the historic assault on the Belen Gate, which led to the capture of the castle of Chapultepec. Here he was severely wounded. After the surrender of the city, the 1st Artillery formed, for a time, part of the American army of occupation; and Brannan's name is found in the list of the original members of the Aztec Society, organized in the City of Mexico by American officers, to commemorate the successful termination of their country's first great war on foreign soil. Returning to the United States, Brannan was promoted captain, Nov. 4, 1854; served at various frontier stations with organizations of his regiment; and in 1856–58 engaged in military operations against the hostile Seminole Indians in Florida.

With the outbreak of the Civil War, Brannan was appointed brigadier-general of volunteers, and as commander of the difficult Department of Key West, Fla., directed operations on the St. John's River, involving the enemy's evacuation of Jacksonville and the action of Pocotaligo, S. C., Oct. 24, 1862. For his services at Jacksonville, Brannan was brevetted lieutenant-colonel in the regular army, Sept. 25, 1862. Promoted a major in the regular service, Aug. 1, 1863, he was actually commanding a division in the action of Hoover's Gap, the advance of the Army of the Cumberland on Tullahoma, the action at Elk River, and the battle of Chickamauga. For services in this battle, he was brevetted a colonel, Sept. 20, 1863. He was chief of artillery, Army of the Cumberland, and commanded the Artillery Reserve with supervision of the defenses of Chattanooga until the summer of 1864. Meanwhile, he was present at the battle of Missionary Ridge, Nov. 25, 1863, and accompanied Gen. Sherman on his Georgia campaign, with engagements at Resaca, Dallas, and Kenesaw Mountain. In the siege and surrender of the city of Atlanta, he commanded the Union artillery with distinction. On Jan. 23, 1865, he was brevetted a major-general of volunteers, and on Mar. 13 of the same year brigadier-general, United States Army, for gallant and meritorious services in the Atlanta campaign. On the latter date, too, he received the brevet of major-general in the regular army, for gallant and meritorious services in the field during the war. Brannan was honorably mustered out of the volunteer service, May 31, 1866, and like many distinguished officers holding important commands during the war between the states, went back to duty as a regimental field officer, in the comparatively monotonous routine of peace-time army posts. He commanded the garrison at Ogdensburg, N. Y., at the time of the threatened Fenian Raids; was promoted lieutenant-colonel, 4th Artillery, Jan. 10, 1877; was transferred back to the 1st Artillery, Mar. 16, 1877; and was in command of the troops during the Philadelphia railroad riots of the latter year. He received his long delayed promotion to colonel, 4th Artillery, Mar. 15, 1881 and was retired from active service, Apr. 19, 1882. Until his death, he resided in New York City.

Brannan's life was characterized by marked devotion to duty. His sympathetic interest in the welfare of his soldiers was particularly shown during the serious yellow fever epidemics of 1847, 1873, and 1874. During the wavering tide in the battle of Chickamauga, his buoyant optimism and inspiring words did much to snatch victory from defeat. He was a gallant, resourceful soldier, whose name is closely identified with distinguished service in two of his country's greatest wars.

[*Bull. Ass. Grads. Mil. Acad.*, 1893; J. H. Smith, *The War with Mexico* (1919); *Battles and Leaders of the Civil War* (1887–88); G. W. Cullum, *Biog. Reg.* (3rd ed., 1891); *Soc. Army of the Cumberland, Twenty-fourth Reunion* (1894), pp. 223–27.] C. D. R.

BRANNAN, SAMUEL (Mar. 2, 1819–May 5, 1889), California pioneer, was born in Saco, York County, Me., where he was educated and spent the early years of his life. When he was fourteen years old he removed with his sister to Lake County, Ohio, where he learned the trade of a printer. Completing his apprenticeship in 1836, he visited most of the states of the Union during the next five years as a journeyman printer. His conversion to the Mormon faith in 1842 proved to be the turning point in his career. In that year he moved to New York City, where he published the *New York Messenger* and later the *New York Prophet* for the Mormon church. He soon became a leading spirit in the church and was made an elder, and his ability was shortly given even larger recognition; for in November 1845, when a conference of Mormons in New York City decided to move some of their number to a new home in Mexican California, Brannan was chosen to conduct the expedition. He chartered the ship *Brooklyn,* and sailed from New York City on Feb. 4, 1846, with two hundred and thirty-eight emigrants, including seventy men, sixty-eight women, and one hundred children. After sailing around South America and making a brief stop at the Sandwich (Hawaiian) Islands, the *Brooklyn* passed through the Golden Gate and anchored before the village of Yerba Buena (San Francisco) on the last day of July 1846. By this time the Mexican War was in progress, and California had been occupied by American troops.

Though somewhat disappointed at seeing the stars and stripes floating above the adobe custom house, Brannan and his followers went ashore and made themselves at home in their new environment. They were the first Anglo-American settlers to arrive in California after its capture by the United States,—an advance contingent of the hundreds of thousands that were soon to follow. At this time Brannan is described as "deep-chested, broad-shouldered, shaggy-headed," with "flashing black eyes." "His dress was dandified, his speech bombastic, his manners coarse, his courage and generosity boundless." Shortly after his arrival, Sam, as his contemporaries called him, became a leader in the village. He performed the first non-Catholic wedding ceremony, preached the first sermon in the English language, advocated the first public school, was defendant in the first jury trial, and set up and operated the first California flour mills. On Jan. 9, 1847, he began the publication of the *California Star,* which was the first newspaper in San Francisco. In the same year he moved to Sutter's Fort, where he conducted a store until 1849. Early in 1848 gold was found at the fort; and it is claimed that Brannan was the first to carry the news of this important discovery to San Francisco. On this occasion it is said that he "bolted into San Francisco from the diggings, travel-stained with his long journey, and rushed through the old Plaza hatless, crying out with his bull-throated bellow: *'Gold!* Gold! Gold from the American River!'"

In 1849 he closed his store at Sutter's Fort and returned to San Francisco, which had grown into a thriving city. To him this offered greater opportunities for leadership. He was elected a member of the first city council, played a major part in the great fire companies, and helped to organize the Society of California Pioneers. The San Francisco Committee of Vigilance of 1851 was organized in his office. He was its second member, its first president, and its first spokesman before the public. Much of its immediate success was due to his fearless initiative; but his impetuous nature and his frequent demands for summary punishment finally led to his resignation. Meanwhile, he had made extensive investments in real estate in San Francisco and Sacramento, and became one of the wealthiest men in California. In the fifties and early sixties he used this wealth in promoting agriculture, establishing banks, organizing railway, telegraph, and express companies, and contributing large sums for philanthropic purposes. The later years of his life were marred by a too frequent indulgence in strong drink. Then his brilliant personality became "clouded by dissipation, his wealth melted away, his position was lost, and he died in poverty and obscurity, in Escondido, San Diego County." In an attempt to evaluate his services to California, H. H. Bancroft, who did not have a favorable impression of him, nevertheless wrote: "He probably did more for San Francisco and for other places than was effected by the combined efforts of scores" of other men.

[J. A. B. Scherer, *The First Forty-Niner* (1925); M. F. Williams, *Hist. of the San Francisco Committee of Vigilance of 1851* (1921); Z. S. Eldredge, *The Beginnings of San Francisco* (1912), vol. II; F. Soule, J. H. Gihon and J. Nisbet (editors), *The Annals of San Francisco* (1855); Hubert H. Bancroft, *Hist. of Cal.* (1885–86), vols. II, V, and *Popular Tribunals* (1887), vol. I; J. S. Hittell, *Hist. of the City of San Francisco* (1878); T. H. Hittell, *Hist. of Cal.* (1885–97), vols. II, III; W. A. Linn, *The Story of the Mormons* (1902); the *Cal. Star,* 1847–48.] R. P. Bi—r.

BRANNER, JOHN CASPER (July 4, 1850–Mar. 1, 1922), geologist, was born at New Market in Jefferson County, Tenn., the son of Michael T. Branner and his wife Elsie (Baker) Branner. The family was among the early settlers in the Shenandoah Valley of Virginia, where Casper Branner received a grant of land in 1760 from Lord Fairfax. About 1799, Michael Branner moved to Jefferson County, Tenn., where his great-grandson, John Casper Branner, passed his youth. The latter's education was acquired in the local schools which were not of a high grade, but of which he made the most, being of an active, energetic, and inquiring disposition. In 1866 he entered Maryville College, near Knoxville, where he remained two years, and in 1870 he entered Cornell University at Ithaca, N. Y. Here his natural scientific tendency developed rapidly and he early attracted the attention of Prof. C. F. Hartt, who invited him, though as yet an undergraduate, to accompany him on a trip to Brazil. Such an opportunity could not be overlooked and he sailed in 1874 for Rio de Janeiro, where he remained for six years. Brazil was at this time a country little known geologically and the expedition was of importance in being the first serious attempt at systematic work. A result was the establishment on the part of the Brazilian government of a *Commissão Geologico do Imperio do Brazil* of which Dr. Hartt was director and Branner assistant. This organization was discontinued in 1877 when Branner became associated with J. E. Mills in operating gold mines in the state of Minas Geraes. He returned to New York in 1880, but a few months later was again in Brazil, in the employ of Thomas Edison, searching for a vegetable fiber of a quality suitable for incandescent lights. He returned in 1881, and a year later was commissioned by the United States Department of Agriculture to study the question of cotton culture in Brazil, a duty with which he was occupied until the spring of 1884, when he returned again to the States and shortly after received an appointment as topographer on the Geological Survey of Pennsylvania under J. P. Lesley. In the spring of 1885 he was elected professor of geology in Indiana University of which David Starr Jordan was then president. In 1887 he was appointed state geologist of Arkansas, and in 1891 he followed Dr. Jordan to the newly established Stanford University in California, where he remained as professor of geology through the rest of his active career, though elected vice-president of the university in 1898 and president in 1913. He retired with the title of president emeritus in 1916 and died at Stanford, Cal., in 1922. Notwithstanding his many official duties in connection with the university, he had three times visited Brazil: in 1899 to study the ocean reefs lying off the coast of Pernambuco; in 1907 to study the black diamond areas of Bahia and the geology of the states of Alagôas and Sergipe, and in 1911 for a further study of the Brazilian coast.

Branner's reports of the Survey were monographic in character and are in themselves sufficiently indicative of the administrative ability and industry of the man. His work in Brazil was largely in the nature of reconnaissance but sufficiently stimulating to cause the Brazilian government to follow it up, and it made a place for another American, Dr. O. A. Derby, who for many years, or until 1915, was employed as government geologist in the state of São Paulo. The final work of geological importance of Branner's life was consummated after his retirement from the presidency of Stanford University and consisted in the compilation of a geological map, with explanatory text, of Brazil, which was published in both English and Portuguese by the Geological Society of America. A good linguist, he translated from the Portuguese Herculano's *History of the Origin and Establishment of the Inquisition in Portugal.* Tall and robust and of imposing appearance, he had sufficient independence of thought to regard self-respect as of more importance than the respect of one's neighbors, but he was without egotism. He combined the faculty of investigator with that of teacher, in the latter calling being highly successful, rarely failing to arouse an enthusiastic interest among his pupils. He was married in 1883 to Susan D. Kennedy of Oneida, N. Y., by whom he had three children.

[R. A. F. Penrose, "Memorial to John Casper Branner," *Bull. Geol. Soc. of America,* XXXVI, 15–44, containing bibliography; C. R. Keyes, "John Casper Branner," *Pan American Geologist,* XXXVII, 261; R. A. F. Penrose, "John Casper Branner," *Memoirs Nat. Acad. Sci.,* vol. XXI (1927), containing bibliography.]

G. P. M.

BRANNON, HENRY (Nov. 26, 1837–Nov. 24, 1914), jurist, was a younger son of Robert and Catherine (Copenhaver) Brannon. Of Irish descent, his father was a native of Winchester, Va., where he himself was born. His youth was spent on his father's farm in the Shenandoah Valley, and his early education was obtained at private schools and the Winchester Academy. Entering the University of Virginia in 1854, he graduated in 1858 and then moved to Weston, Lewis County, in the western part of the state, where his elder brother, John, was practising law. He read law in his brother's office, was admitted to the Virginia bar in 1859, and commenced practise at Weston. In 1860 he was elected prosecuting attorney for Lewis County, occupying that position for four years. An efficient official, he acquired a wide practise, and took an active part in local politics, being a strong Republican. Though too young to be prominent in the movement which resulted in the formation of the State of West Virginia, he was elected in 1870 as representative of Lewis County in the House of Delegates, and served two terms, acting as chairman of the legislative committee on education. In 1880 he was nominated and elected judge of the 11th judicial circuit, succeeding his brother in that office. His practical acquaintance with rural conditions combined with a thorough knowledge of *nisi prius* law made him an excellent circuit judge, and at the end of his term in 1888 he was nominated and elected an associate justice of the supreme court of appeals. This office he filled for twenty-four years, being reelected in 1900 on the expiration of his first term. He retired from the bench Dec. 31, 1912, declining a renomination. During his long occupancy of the appellate court bench, he had a preponderant share in shaping the law of West Virginia in its initial stages, and by his strong common sense and freedom from tradition made an admirable interpreter of the law of a new state. New problems had to be faced, particularly those arising in regard to oil-bearing properties, and his decisions on questions of leaseholds commanded the respect and approval of other jurisdictions wherein oil development occurred at periods subsequent to its appearance in West Virginia. Though not erudite, and having no pretense to scientific legal training, his mental equipment was such that he instinctively grasped the vital points of the cases before him, his capacity for exhaustive analysis was keen, and his opinions were invariably expressed with singular clarity and force. He wrote a treatise, *Rights and Privileges Guaranteed by the Fourteenth Amendment to the Constitution of the United States* (1901), which, by its depth of thought and scholarly style, is a distinct contribution to political science. He was a great lover of literature, having an intimate knowledge of French and Spanish, and possessing an extensive library of the best authors in those languages. He was married to Hetta J. Arnold of Weston.

[His career and characteristics are well summarized in *Proc. of the W. Va. Bar Ass.*, 1914, p. 133. See also *Hist. of Lewis Co., W. Va.*, by E. C. Smith (1920); *Prominent Men of W. Va.*, by G. W. Atkinson and A. F. Gibbens (1890), p. 995; *Contemporary Biography of W. Va.* (1894), p. 204; *W. Va. Reports,* vols. LXXI and LXXIII.] H. W. H. K.

BRANT, JOSEPH (1742–Nov. 24, 1807), Mohawk chief, whose Indian name was Thayendanegea, was the son of a Mohawk chief, probably the one known as "Nickus Brant." Apparently his mother was not a Mohawk and certainly was not of sachem stock, hence (Iroquois rank descending through the females) Joseph never became a sachem though he won the lesser rank of chief. His rise was facilitated by his sister Molly's relations with Sir William Johnson [*q.v.*]. At the age of thirteen Brant accompanied Johnson in the campaign of 1755. Six years later he and two other Mohawks entered Moor's Charity School in Lebanon, Conn. He left school in 1763 to act as interpreter for a missionary, but soon entered the Iroquois contingent aiding the whites against Pontiac. A convert to the Anglican church, Brant aided the Rev. John Stewart in translating various religious works into the Mohawk tongue. Guy Johnson, son-in-law of Sir William, became superintendent of Indian Affairs in 1774, and made Brant his secretary. The latter strove hard to bring the Iroquois to the aid of the British in the Revolution, trying to discredit Samuel Kirkland, missionary to the Oneidas, who succeeded in winning the Oneidas and Tuscaroras to the American side. Now a war chief, Brant appeared at Montreal as Mohawk spokesman in a conference with Sir Guy Carleton. He was given a captain's commission and sent to England. Here he was presented at court, was entertained by Boswell and other notables, and was painted in Mohawk regalia by Romney. Back in America, he plunged into the conflict. Soon his name awoke terror throughout New York, especially in the Mohawk Valley. Commanding with skill the Indians of St. Leger's expedition, Brant displayed desperate courage at the battle of Oriskany (Aug. 6, 1777). Thereafter his Indians, sometimes alone, sometimes in conjunction with Tories under the Butlers and Johnsons, harried the Mohawk Valley, southern New York, and northern Pennsylvania. Though he certainly directed the Cherry Valley Massacre of 1778 and numerous others, his biographers assert that he did not participate in that of Wyoming (1779). Denying that he was "a monster of cruelty," he and his defenders claimed that he sought to protect women, children, prisoners, and wounded. If so, he did not always succeed. He frustrated the efforts of Red Jacket to induce the Iroquois to make a separate peace with the Americans. At the close of the struggle the Mohawks retired west of the Niagara River, whence Brant sought to procure a settlement with the United States. Failing, he induced Gov. Haldimand of Canada to assign them land. Visiting England again in 1785, he procured funds to indemnify the Iroquois for their losses in war and to purchase new lands. Following further efforts to arrange matters with the United States, including a vain trip to Philadelphia, Brant devoted most of his energies to the domestic welfare of his fellows in the Grand River settlement. He had helped establish "the Old Mohawk Church" and now translated religious works into that dialect. He opposed successfully the attempts of land speculators to preempt the lands of the Mohawks. But his old age was saddened by the dissoluteness of his eldest son and the intrigues of his old enemy, Red Jacket.

[The chief manuscript sources are the Haldimand Papers and the Kirkland MSS. The most essential printed sources are B. F. Stevens' *Fac-Similes of Manuscripts in European Archives Relating to America, 1773–83* (1889–95); Jas. Sullivan and A. C. Flick, *The Papers of Sir Wm. Johnson* (1921–27); Adam Shortt and A. G. Doughty, *Docs. Relating to the Constitutional Hist. of Canada, 1759–91* (1907); *Jours. of the Provincial Congress, Provincial Convention, Committee of Safety and Council of Safety of the State of New*

York (1842); Eleazar Wheelock, *Narrative of the Original Design, Rise, Progress and Present State of the Indian Charity-School at Lebanon in Conn.* (1763), and *A Brief Narrative of the Indian Charity School* (1766). W. L. Stone's *Life of Joseph Brant* (1838), the chief secondary authority, should be supplemented by L. A. Wood's *War Chief of the Six Nations* (1914); L. H. Morgan, *League of the Ho-de-no-sau-nee or Iroquois* (1904); S. G. Drake, *The Aboriginal Races of America* (1860); Nelson Greene, *Hist. of the Mohawk Valley* (1925); and the biographies of Johnson, Burgoyne, St. Leger, and Red Jacket.] M.L.B.

BRANTLEY, THEODORE (Feb. 12, 1851–Sept. 16, 1922), judge, born in Wilson County, Tenn., was the son of Eliza (Brown) Brantley and Edwin T. Brantley, a Presbyterian minister. In 1870 he entered Stewart College (now Southwestern-Presbyterian University) at Clarksville, Tenn., where he graduated in 1874. He then began the study of law while teaching, and from time to time attended sessions of Cumberland University at Lebanon, Tenn., which awarded him the degree of bachelor of laws in 1880. For the next three years he practised law and then became professor of ancient languages in Lincoln University, Lincoln, Ill. In 1887 he accepted a similar position at the College of Montana, Deer Lodge, Mont., which he relinquished after two years to resume the practise of law. On June 9, 1891, he was married to Lois Reat. In 1893 the Republican party drafted him as candidate for judge in a district overwhelmingly Democratic, and he was elected. In 1898 he was elected chief justice of the state supreme court, and was reëlected in 1904, 1910, and 1916. He came into office when the Constitution was new, and most of its provisions had not yet been interpreted. The mining interest which dominated the politics of the state had written it, and they held that the legislature had only delegated powers. A farmer and labor movement directed against this control was arising. The whole of Brantley's tenure was one of political agitation, and out of his court decisions came a reformed constitution and a new system of law. In 1909 the court held: "No Act of the legislature will be declared invalid as repugnant to the fundamental law except in the clearest cases" (39 *Montana Reports,* 200). While the constitution definitely restricted the taxation of mines as such, Brantley's opinion left the way open for heavy taxes upon their proceeds. It also paved the way to approval of a long line of social legislation.

When Brantley came to the supreme bench water and irrigation rights were vaguely defined. Common law practise was generally acknowledged in principle, but there were laws reflecting the California and Colorado codes. In a country of little rainfall the right to use the water in streams creates the value of real estate. It was the work of the courts to define these rights and the important decisions numbered more than a hundred. Brantley's early decisions prepared the way for the great decision in 1921 that the common law doctrine of riparian rights does not prevail, but that water rights depend upon prior appropriation for beneficial use (61 *Montana,* 152). This decision was essential to the agricultural development of the state. When an attack was made on the primary law in 1900, Brantley supported the law on the ground that the constitution stated that "all political power is vested in and derived from the people" (24 *Montana,* 3911). In 1914 the constitutionality of the initiative and referendum amendment was attacked on technical grounds. The court held that in view of the overwhelming majority in favor of the amendment the irregularities if corrected would not change the decision of the people, and brushed them all aside (49 *Montana,* 419). In spite of his philosophical view of the law and his interpretations influenced by ideals of economic and social development, Brantley preserved throughout his career the admiration of both liberals and conservatives. All had confidence in his fairness and ability, and his most startling opinions were received with respect. At his death all were willing to acknowledge the new order in Montana which had been so largely the result of his work.

[*Who's Who in America,* 1922–23; "In Memoriam," 64 *Montana Reports,* pp. viii–xxxiii; *Helena Independent,* Sept. 17, 1922; Brantley's judicial opinions are found in *Montana Reports,* XXII–LXIV.] P.C.P.

BRASHEAR, JOHN ALFRED (Nov. 24, 1840–Apr. 8, 1920), scientist, maker of astronomical lenses, belonged to a family of French Huguenots named Brasseuir who emigrated to America and settled in Calvert County, Md., in 1658. In 1775 a descendant of this family, Otho Brashear (the original Brasseuir had undergone several changes in spelling), emigrated from Maryland to the present site of Brownsville, Pa. Here his grandson, Basil Brown Brashear, a saddler by trade, married a school-teacher, the daughter of one Nathaniel Smith, who had emigrated to Brownsville probably from Massachusetts. John Alfred Brashear was the first of their seven children. His maternal grandfather, who had a passion for astronomy, taught the boy the constellations by the time he was eight, presented him with his own prized volumes of Dr. Dick's *Works* (1850), and paid for John's first view of the heavens through a telescope. "Young as I was," Brashear wrote in later years, "the scenery of the moon and the rings of Saturn impressed me deeply. . . . The entrancing beauty of that first sight has never been forgotten." All of young Brashear's formal education was obtained in the common schools of Brownsville and in a four-months' course in bookkeeping at Duff's Mercantile College, Pittsburgh. During 1856–59 he served his apprenticeship in the pattern-making trade at the engine works of John Snowden & Sons in Brownsville. After working at his trade for two years in Kentucky he came to Pittsburgh in 1861 where he resided until his death. On Sept. 24, 1862, he married Phœbe Stewart. Until he suffered a physical breakdown in 1881, Brashear endured the rigors of life in the mills in conjunction with long hours of night work devoted to study. The memory of the beauty of his first vision of the heavens persisted with such compelling force throughout these difficult years that he decided, since he could not afford to buy a good object glass, that he would make a telescope for himself. He knew nothing about the polishing of lenses, but he bought a glass for a five-inch lens and some books to tell him how to go about the work. He was arising at 5:30 to go to work in the mills and not returning until 6:00 o'clock or even later. But, with the constant and invaluable aid of his wife, he labored over the polishing of the glass far into the nights. It was three years before the lens was mounted, temporarily, and stuck through an open window for its first revelation of the heavens. From this modest beginning, Brashear rose to become the peer of any maker of astronomical lenses and instruments of precision of his day. Through his first lens he made the acquaintance of Prof. Samuel Pierpont Langley who was then at the old Allegheny Observatory, and through Langley he met William Thaw who gave him the financial aid necessary in going into business for himself in 1881. It was the perfection of his work that caused the demand for his lenses by astronomers everywhere, and it is impossible to estimate accurately the progress in the science of astronomy due to his mechanical genius. To-day his glasses are still in use not only in America but in Europe, the Orient, and the Islands of the Pacific.

Brashear's great contribution to science lay in his mastery of the art of making a plane surface. Through this, he rendered invaluable aid in the work of the distinguished physicist, Henry A. Rowland of Johns Hopkins University. The speculum-metal plates from which the famous Rowland Diffraction Gratings were made required a very accurate surface, no error of even one-fifth of a light wave, or one two-hundred-thousandth of an inch. The surfaces were polished and prepared for Rowland's Ruling Engine by Brashear and his son-in-law James B. McDowell. Another great contribution to science was the Brashear Method for silvering mirrors. "Perhaps his most important achievement was in connection with the design and development of the spectroscope for astronomical uses" (*Mechanical Engineering,* XLII, 311). The mechanical genius of Brashear, though great, was overshadowed by the personality of the man. The force that dominated him was a sincere desire to share the beauty of the universe with all mankind. It made of him a unique figure, of broad sympathy and rare understanding. To literally thousands of people he was known familiarly as "Uncle John," and it was Brashear the man, rather than Brashear the scientist, who was the recipient of uncounted honors in the later years of his life. Only the genius of his personality can explain the positions of trust he held during his last twenty-five years. He was a man without formal education, and one whose entire life had demonstrated an inability to grapple successfully with business and financial problems. Yet, as chairman of the Allegheny Observatory Committee he was entrusted with the raising of the $300,000 necessary for the new observatory. It was characteristic of him that he did not stop until he had a room in the new building where anybody who wanted to could see and hear about his "starry heavens" free. For twenty-five years he served as a trustee of the Western University of Pennsylvania (University of Pittsburgh), and though he thrice refused its chancellorship he served as acting chancellor for three years. He was one of three men selected by Andrew Carnegie to draw up plans for the Carnegie Institute of Technology. And when Henry C. Frick decided to make his gift of a half million dollars to establish the Frick Educational Commission, he did it on condition that Brashear undertake the work of getting the activities of the Commission under way. On his death in 1920, Brashear was mourned not only as Pittsburgh's, but as Pennsylvania's "best loved citizen."

[The chief source is *John A. Brashear, The Autobiography of a Man Who Loved the Stars* (1925). In her work in editing this Autobiography, the author of the above sketch has had intimate contact with the published papers and countless letters left by Dr. Brashear (now in the custody of his secretary, Martha C. Hoyt, Secretary of the Frick Educational Commission) as well as the help of a committee of scientific men appointed by the American Society of Mechanical Engineers to help her obtain an accurate estimate of Brashear's life-work.]

E. Y.

BRATTLE, THOMAS (June 20, 1658–May 18, 1713), merchant, was born in Boston, the son of Thomas and Elizabeth (Tyng) Brattle. His father, a trader and landowner, held various political offices in the colony, commanded several expeditions against the Indians, and on his death in 1683 was rated the wealthiest man in New England. His son Thomas graduated from Harvard College in 1676 in a class of three students, was executor and chief beneficiary of his father's will, returned in November 1689 from travel and study abroad, and spent the rest of his life in Boston, where his public spirit, his intellectual attainments, and his liberalism in politics and in religion were of marked service to the community. He never married. Nothing is known of his business affairs except that he evidently managed them as well as he did the finances of Harvard College, of which he was treasurer from 1693 until his death. Under his intelligent, conscientious administration the resources of the College were almost tripled in value. His relations with the Harvard Corporation, however, were not entirely peaceful. His inclinations toward the forms of the Church of England led him to become the chief organizer in 1698 of the Brattle Street Church, whose members dispensed with the "relation of experiences" as a qualification for membership, used the Lord's Prayer, had the Bible read without comment as a part of the services, and deviated in other particulars from the principles of the Cambridge Platform. Thomas Brattle thus brought down on himself the enmity of Increase and Cotton Mather. Much controversy ensued. By amending the new charter of Harvard College Increase Mather succeeded in having Brattle, his brother William, and John Leverett excluded from the Harvard Corporation, but the Brattles were reinstated in 1703 when the Mather power was failing, and the long, rancorous warfare ended with the election of Leverett to the presidency in 1707. Highly honorable to Brattle was his letter dated Oct. 8, 1692, addressed to an unnamed clergyman, in which he examined the Salem witchcraft proceedings in detail and condemned them as "ignorance and folly." He took great interest in mathematics and astronomy and sent to the Royal Society of London accounts of several eclipses that he had observed. He is said to have been an F. R. S., but his name does not appear in the lists of the Society's members in T. Thomson, *History of the Royal Society* (1812) or in the *Records of the Royal Society* (2nd ed., 1901). That fact, however, is not decisive, for Brattle's status may have been similar to Cotton Mather's [G. L. Kittredge, "Cotton Mather's Election into the Royal Society" in *Publications of the Colonial Society of Massachusetts,* XIV]. Brattle owned the first organ ever brought to New England and willed it to the Brattle Street Church, which on theological grounds felt obliged respectfully to decline it. According to the provisions of the will it was thereupon offered to King's Chapel, the Episcopalian society, which accepted it. In the Boston that was witnessing the old age of Increase Mather and the childhood of Benjamin Franklin, Thomas Brattle was an admirable, and a significant, personality.

[E. D. Harris, *An Account of Some of the Descendants of Capt. Thos. Brattle* (1867); Josiah Quincy, *Hist. of Harvard Univ.* (1840); J. L. Sibley, *Biog. Sketches of Grads. of Harvard Univ.*, II (1881)—with full refs. to sources; *Diary of Samuel Sewall* 1674–1729 in *Colls. Mass. Hist. Soc.*, ser. 5, vols. V–VII; Ebenezer Turell, *Life and Character of the Rev. Benj. Colman* (1749); Justin Winsor, ed., *Memorial Hist. of Boston* (1881–83); Brattle's contributions to the Royal Society are in the *Philosophical Transactions* for July and Aug. 1704, pp. 1630–38 and for Oct., Nov., and Dec., 1707, pp. 2471–72; his letter on the Salem witchcraft trials was reprinted in *Colls. Mass. Hist. Soc.*, V, 61–80, and in G. L. Burr, *Narratives of the Witchcraft Cases 1648–1706* (1914). For interpretation of Brattle's career see Brooks Adams, *The Emancipation of Mass.* (1887) and K. B. Murdock, *Increase Mather, the Foremost Am. Puritan* (1925).] G.H.G.

BRATTLE, WILLIAM (Nov. 22, 1662–Feb. 15, 1716/17), Congregational minister, educator, was the son of the wealthy and prominent Thomas and Elizabeth (Tyng) Brattle of Boston. After graduating from Harvard College in 1680 he became a tutor, and from 1696 to 1700 was a Fellow in the Corporation. During the four years while President Increase Mather was in Europe, Brattle and John Leverett, as the principle directors and teachers in the College, followed a policy which "inclined to the order of things which was coming" (Josiah Quincy, *The History of Harvard University,* 1840, I, 66). Even Cotton Mather noted that the College flourished under their "prudent government" (Cotton Mather, *Magnalia Christi Americana,* 1702, Bk. IV, p. 131). As a tutor, Brattle was described by a student as "able, faithful, and tender," and his heroism during the smallpox epidemic, together with his "fatherly goodness" and continued benefactions, won him the title of "Father of the College." As late as 1765 his *Compendium Logicae Secundum Principia D. Renati Cartesii,* the first American text-book on logic, was used at Harvard.

In 1696, the year of his election to the Harvard Corporation, Brattle was also ordained pastor of the church in Cambridge. On this occasion he evidenced his independence regarding established ecclesiastical usages, and as the result of his unceasing exertion, his church discontinued the formal and public relation of religious experience required of candidates for church membership. This liberalism, as well as his championship of other innovations, was probably an important factor in his exclusion from the Harvard Corporation in 1700, to which position, however, he returned three years later when the influence of his group replaced that of the Mathers. Although it has been held that Brattle's doctrinal opinions were of the strict Puritan school (William B. Sprague, *Annals of the American Pulpit,* 1856, I, 236 ff.) manuscript notes taken on his sermons by John Hancock (1671–1752) indicate as strong an interest in ethical questions as in Calvinistic theology. God's delight in mercy and Christ's mission to save sinners were doctrines which apparently found an important place in his sermons. "Follow peace with all men," and "let us excite within us compassions" were mellow sentiments. His preaching, which enjoyed a high reputation, was described as "calm, and soft, and melting" (Abiel Holmes, "The History of Cambridge," *Massachusetts Historical Society Collections,* 1800, VII). Indeed, though Brattle was sympathetic with the organization of the liberal Brattle Street Church, initiated by his brother Thomas, he seems to have mingled very little in theological controversies, and "being of a catholic and pacific spirit" to have sought harmony (Dr. Benjamin Colman, quoted by Alexander McKenzie, *Lectures on the History of the Church in Cambridge,* p. 142).

From his marriage with Elizabeth Hayman one son, William, who achieved distinction in the provincial militia, survived him. Toward the end of his life Brattle married Elizabeth Gerrish. Skilful in business, he was a generous but quiet philanthropist. Urbane, scholarly, serenely tolerant, William Brattle, by his character and influence, contributed to the mellowing of orthodox Puritanism.

[Manuscript notes taken on Brattle's sermons by John Hancock (Harvard Univ. Lib.) and by John Leverett (Mass. Hist. Soc. Lib.) are indexes to Brattle's doctrinal position. Samuel Sewall's *Diary* makes frequent references to him. The best secondary accounts are those in Edward Harris, *An Account of Some of the Descendants of Capt. Thos. Brattle* (1867); Alexander McKenzie, *Lectures on the Hist. of the First Church in Cambridge* (1873); and John Langdon Sibley, *Biog. Sketches Grads. Harvard Univ.* (1885).] M. E. C.

BRATTON, JOHN (Mar. 7, 1831–Jan. 12, 1898), Confederate soldier, the son of Dr. William Bratton, Jr., and his second wife, Isabella Means, was born at Winnsboro, S. C. After preparation at Mount Zion Academy he entered the South Carolina College from which he was graduated in 1850. Three years later he received a "medical diploma" from the South Carolina Medical College and shortly afterward began the practise of medicine in Fairfield County. In 1859 he married Elizabeth, daughter of Theodore S. Du Bose. He continued in his profession with moderate success until the beginning of the Civil War when he entered the military service of South Carolina as a private in the 6th Regiment of Volunteers. He was almost immediately promoted captain. Twice subsequently, however, he reënlisted as a private at the expiration of periods of enlistment when his regiment was reorganized. In 1862 he was elected colonel of the 6th Regiment which had become a part of Micah Jenkins's Brigade, Longstreet's Corps. After the death of Jenkins, during the Battle of the Wilderness, May 6, 1864, "Old Reliable," as Bratton was now known to his men, was appointed brigadier-general (June 27, 1864). He was several times cited for gallantry and was twice wounded. On one occasion (Battle of Seven Pines, May 31, 1862) being wounded, he was taken prisoner and was held in Fortress Monroe until exchanged several months later. Of the brigades which composed the Army of Northern Virginia at Appomattox, his was the most completely manned and was the only one which left the field as an organized unit (*Official Records,* ser. I, *passim*).

After the war Bratton did not resume the practise of medicine but became a farmer and was soon drawn into active public life. He did not seek political office but was from time to time pressed into service as a member of the constitutional convention in 1865, as state senator (1865–66), and as congressman (1884–85). He was a delegate to all the Taxpayers' Conventions, was chairman of the delegates from South Carolina to the national Democratic convention of 1876, was chairman of the state Democratic committee in 1880, and was elected by the legislature to fill the vacant office of state comptroller in 1881. In politics he adhered to the conservative party which under Wade Hampton [*q.v.*] delivered the state from Republican rule in 1876. Though a farmer he did not support the Farmer's Movement in South Carolina. His feeling against this "class movement," as he characterized it, was such that he was led to become a candidate for the governorship in 1890 in opposition to B. R. Tillman [*q.v.*], the Farmers' leader. His dignified campaign, conducted amidst all manner of political excess and extravagance, won the admiration of all classes but was at no time formidable. Like many conservatives, he retired from politics after the victory of the Tillmanites. He died at Winnsboro, Jan. 12, 1898.

[Brief but accurate sketches of Bratton's life appear in the *Confed. Mil. Hist.* (1899), V, 378–80; the *Cyc. of Eminent and Representative Men of the Carolinas* (1892), I, 433–36; *News and Courier* (Charleston, S. C.), Jan. 13, 1898. A few of Bratton's letters in manuscript are contained in the W. G. Hinson Collection owned by the Charleston (S. C.) Lib. Soc. This also includes a scrapbook of clippings from leading newspapers of the state relating to the gubernatorial campaign of 1890.] J. H. E—y.

BRAWLEY, WILLIAM HIRAM (May 13, 1841–Nov. 15, 1916), congressman and federal judge, son of Hiram Brawley and Harriet Foote, was born in Chester, S. C., and was educated in the preparatory schools of his native town and in the South Carolina College. He was a college graduate and a Confederate soldier before he was twenty years of age, was with the 6th South Carolina Volunteers in the attack on Fort Sumter, fought with his regiment in the battles in Virginia, and was wounded at the battle of Seven Pines, May 31, 1862. This wound necessitated the amputation of his left arm. After a short time spent in managing his father's plantation in April 1864, he successfully ran the blockade to England, where he completed his studies in law and literature. He returned home in November 1865, was admitted to the bar in 1866, elected solicitor of the sixth circuit in 1868, and in 1874 resigned that office to move to Charleston, where he practised law in association with Hon. W. D. Porter, and later with Hon. Joseph Barnwell. He was elected to the state legislature in 1882 and served continuously till 1890. In this year he was elected to the Fifty-first Congress where he served till February 1894 when he was appointed by President Cleveland district judge for South Carolina. He was married twice: in 1868 to Marion E. Porter, daughter of his law partner, and July 11, 1907, to Mildred Frost. He died in Charleston, Nov. 15, 1916.

Brawley's early and continued success in law practise was due to his high power of clearly stating and analyzing current issues as well as legal principles. His personal influence and his position as chairman of the judiciary committee made him the acknowledged leader in the South Carolina legislature. Added to this was oratorical ability marked even in a state much given to oratory. His appeal to the legislature in 1886 in behalf of the sufferers from the Charleston earthquake of that year was one of the bursts of impassioned eloquence heard only from gifted speakers on rare occasions. His address on the causes of the Civil War, delivered at Chester, S. C., May 10, 1905, on the occasion of the laying of the cornerstone of a monument to the Confederate dead, awakened interest in the whole country and formed the subject of an editorial in *Harper's Weekly*. Probably his greatest service as a speaker was in opposition to the Free Silver movement. His speech against the Bland Silver Bill was one of three opposition speeches from Southern members, and he was the only Southern member to vote against the bill. He spoke with equal ability on the bill to repeal the Sherman Silver Purchase Act, and it was doubtless in recognition of this service that President Cleveland offered him without solicitation the post of federal judge. Polished in manners, widely read, courteous but forceful in address, striking in appearance, and courageously honest in his convictions, he won to his support even those who differed from his financial views.

[*Who's Who in America*, 1912–13; W. R. Brooks, *S. C. Bench and Bar*, I (1908), 351–65; J. C. Hemphill, sketch in *Men of Mark in S. C.* (1906); *News and Courier* (Charleston, S. C.), Nov. 16, 1916.] J. E. W—y.

BRAXTON, CARTER (Sept. 10, 1736–Oct. 10, 1797), Revolutionary statesman, born at Newington, King and Queen County, Va., inherited wealth and gentle blood. His father, George Braxton, a planter, was sometime member of the House of Burgesses and president of the Colonial Council. His mother, Mary, was the daughter of Councilor Robert Carter (called, because of his wealth and power, King Carter). Braxton was educated at the College of William and Mary, and was later a member of its board of visitors (*William and Mary Quarterly Historical Magazine*, II, 37, XXVII, 239). When nineteen, he married Judith Robinson of a prominent Middlesex County family. Upon the death of his wife in December 1757, he went to England where he remained until the fall of 1760. In May 1761 he married Elizabeth, daughter of Richard Corbin, colonial receiver-general. When only twenty-five years of age, Braxton was sent to the House of Burgesses from King William County to which he had moved. He served actively from 1761 to 1775, with the exception of a brief period in the early seventies when he was county sheriff. In the dispute with Great Britain he was loyal to Virginia, but held the more conservative views of the Tidewater leaders. His name appears, however, with those of Washington, Jefferson, Henry, Peyton Randolph, and others of the House who signed the *Resolutions* of May 1769 that the Virginia House of Burgesses had the sole right to tax the inhabitants of the colony. He also signed the non-importation agreement at that time (*Journals of the House of Burgesses of Virginia, 1766–69*, 1906, pp. xxxviii ff.). He represented his country in the Revolutionary conventions of 1774, 1775, and 1776. It was Braxton who doubtless prevented bloodshed by adjusting a dispute between Patrick Henry and Gov. Dunmore over the gunpowder taken to the latter from the Williamsburg magazine in April 1775 (John Daly Burk, *History of Virginia,* 1804–16, IV, 13 ff.). The convention of July 1775 appointed him a member of the Committee of Safety, the governing body of the colony until the state government was inaugurated (W. W. Hening, *The Statutes at Large,* 1819–23, IX, 49, 328). Upon the death of Peyton Randolph, the convention appointed Braxton as his successor in Congress. He took his seat on Feb. 23, 1776, and was one of the signers of the Declaration of Independence (for his views regarding independence see letter to his uncle, Landon Carter, in *Letters of Members of the Continental Congress,* 1921, I, 420). He was not reappointed to his seat in Congress. This was probably due in part to his address to the Virginia convention, in which he advocated a conservative form of government for Virginia, and showed little faith in democracy (Burk, *History of Virginia,* IV, 13 ff.; Charles Campbell, *History of Virginia,* 1860, pp. 641–47; text of address in Peter Force, *American Archives,* 4th ser., VI, 748–754). In any event, he was returned that year to the Virginia Assembly, where he continued to serve, in the House and in the Council, until about the time of his death (E. G. Swem and John W. Williams, *Register of the General Assembly of Virginia, 1776–1918,* 1918. *Calendar of Virginia State Papers,* IV, 1884, p. 68; *Ibid.,* VII, 1888, p. 151). He supported the act of 1785 to establish religious freedom in Virginia, and was lay delegate from his parish to the convention which reorganized the former established church. In 1786 he removed to Richmond where he died. Losses during the Revolution, his long public service, and his unfortunate commercial ventures during his last years had wrecked his fortune.

[The best early biographical account of Braxton is in John Sanderson, *Biography of the Signers of the Declaration of Independence* (1828), V. The author of the articles dealing with the Virginia signers seems to have known his ground well. He was a contemporary of many people who knew Braxton, and doubtless of Braxton himself. His article on Braxton is well written, accurate, and unbiased. There are a few references to Braxton in the *Jours. of the Continental Congress, 1774–89,* IV (1906). Frederick Horner, *Hist. of the Blair, Banister, and Braxton Families* (1898), makes some additions to the account in Sanderson.]

R. L. M.

BRAY, THOMAS (1656–Feb. 15, 1729/30), Anglican clergyman, was born at Marton, Shropshire, England, and graduated from All Souls College, Oxford, in 1678. A country rector and author of popular catechetical lectures, in 1696 he was chosen by Henry Compton, Bishop of London, to serve as his commissary in Maryland. Largely by Bray's zeal was effected the establishment of the Church of England in that colony, where the Revolution and royal government had recently strengthened the hands of the Anglican minority. Between 1696 and 1699 he unsuccessfully solicited royal assent to the provincial church act of 1692 reënacted in 1696. He then went over to Maryland to secure the passage of a revised measure. Meanwhile he had recruited missionaries for Maryland and other colonies, and had inaugurated his notable scheme for furnishing the colonial clergy —later also the English parochial clergy—with libraries, chiefly of religious books. By 1699 he had formed some thirty such collections, sixteen in Maryland; several became also lending libraries for the laity as well as the clergy. To support these activities, with episcopal aid Bray organized a voluntary society, the Society for Promoting Christian Knowledge (1699). Moreover, in 1701 he actively promoted the chartering of the Society for the Propagation of the Gospel, whose missionary enterprises were so important in colonial history.

Bray resided in Maryland only from March 1700 to the following summer. He procured a new church act, conducted a general visitation, undertook the discipline of the baser clergy, and planned the extension of Anglicanism in Pennsylvania and other colonies. Returning to England he met powerful Quaker opposition to the establishment. His pamphlets in the cause were assailed by Joseph Wyeth (Wyeth's *An Answer to a Letter from Dr. Bray,* 1700, and *Remarks on Dr. Bray's Memorial,* 1701); the Board of Trade, moreover, rejected the Act of 1700. But though the Quakers, Bray asserted, spent large sums to defeat him, he won royal approval for the Revised Act of 1702, based upon his suggestions. Previously Bray had resigned his office, but not his interest in Maryland and in the colonies generally.

In 1706 he became rector of St. Botolph's Without, Aldgate. Already distinguished for his "ecclesiastical imperialism," in his city parish he became the aggressive leader of the religious-philanthropic movement of the pre-Wesleyan era: the founder or an active member of numerous societies, for suppressing vice, founding libraries, charity schools, and hospitals, relieving proselytes, etc. In part these organizations represented merely the resurgence of the old negative Puritan morality; in other respects they gave evidence of a new social earnestness, not without its effect on the colonies. Two of Bray's societies, merged under his will, furnished the institutional basis for the Georgia

Trust. One was the Trustees of Parochial Libraries (1710–30), the other the Associates of Dr. Bray, a trust created in 1723 to assist him in administering the D'Allone legacy for converting negroes and Indians. In his *Missionalia* (1727) Bray ridiculed Berkeley's Bermuda college scheme, and presented a rival project for artisan-missions on the American frontiers. The same year he interested himself in the lot of the poor prisoners in London, anticipating Oglethorpe's prison investigations. In 1734 his parishioner, Thomas Coram [*q.v.*], wrote that in 1729 Bray had said he hoped before he died to find a way to settle English unemployed and foreign Protestants in America, but regarded Coram's projected colony between Maine and Nova Scotia as too far north. There is evidence that Bray suggested to Oglethorpe, or discussed with him, the debtor-colony scheme. In 1730 his Associates were enlarged to embrace this third charity, and petitioned for the charter of Georgia.

"He was a Great Small man," declared Coram, "and had done Great good things in his life Time."

[For further details of Bray's career and for a partial list of his writings, see *Dict. of Nat. Biog.*, VI, 239–41. The primary source for his life is [Samuel Smith], *Publick Spirit illustrated in the Life and Designs of Dr. Bray* (London, 1746; 2nd ed., ed. by H. J. Todd, London, 1808). A manuscript version in the Bodleian Lib. was printed by B. C. Steiner in *Md. Hist. Soc. Fund Pub. No. 37* (1901) but was incorrectly ascribed to Richard Rawlinson. See this volume for reprints of several of Bray's writings, as also *Thos. Bray Club Pubs.*, Nos. 1–7. Consult further: B. C. Steiner, "Rev. Thos. Bray and his American Libraries," *Am. Hist. Rev.*, II, 59–75; and "Two Missionary Schemes," *Sewanee Rev.*, XI, 289–305; A. B. Keep, *Hist. of the N. Y. Soc. Lib.* (1908); V. W. Crane, *The Southern Frontier to the Founding of Ga.* (1928), ch. XIII.]

V. W. C.

BRAYMAN, MASON (May 23, 1813–Feb. 27, 1895), editor, lawyer, Union soldier, was born in Buffalo, the son of Daniel Brayman, a young pioneer from Connecticut, and his wife, Anna English, a native of Nova Scotia, who had lived in Otsego County, N. Y., before her marriage. He early showed a bent for journalism and the year after he reached his majority, in the latter part of the Jackson administration, he became editor of the Buffalo *Bulletin.* In later years he edited several newspapers—among them the Louisville *Advertiser* and the *Illinois State Journal.* He chose the law as his profession, however, was admitted to the New York bar and, after removing to Michigan, served for a time as city attorney of Monroe in that state. In 1842 he settled in Illinois and practised law there. His introduction to the *Illinois Revised Statutes* (1845) is a survey of the conditions under which Illinois legal machinery operated during the first quarter-century of the state's existence. Brayman held a special commission from Gov. Ford to compose the difficulties between the Mormons at Nauvoo and their hostile neighbors, and censured the anti-Mormons for attempting to take vengeance on non-Mormon residents for defending Nauvoo from attack. In 1847 during the session of the state constitutional convention, his journalistic aptitude was turned to good account in reporting the proceedings for the St. Louis *Union.* His daily letters, if preserved, would have made a unique record of the work of that important body, written from the standpoint of a trained observer, thoroughly informed as to the state's institutions. Early in the construction of the Illinois Central Railroad, Brayman acted as general solicitor of that corporation (1851–55) and secured its right of way. Judge Elliott Anthony, president of the state bar association, described Brayman in those years as "a most careful, painstaking lawyer, who understood real-estate law and our statutes relating to the same as well as any man I ever knew." In the first year of the Civil War, Brayman, although nearing his fiftieth year, volunteered, was at first commissioned major in the 29th Illinois, and was under fire at Belmont, Fort Donelson, and Shiloh. Gallantry in the field won him promotion. After advancing to colonel and brigadier-general, he finally reached the rank of major-general of volunteers by brevet. He was put in command of troops at Bolivar, Tenn., in the late fall of 1862 and remained there until the following June. While at that post he repulsed a Confederate attack led by Van Dorn, the last fighting in which he was engaged during the war. To him was assigned the task of reorganizing the Ohio regiments at Camp Dennison and he presided over a military court of inquiry in the case of Gen. Sturgis. From July 1864 to the spring of 1865 he was in command at Natchez. Later he served as president of a commission on claims at New Orleans. After the close of hostilities he tried unsuccessfully to revive several railroad projects in Missouri and Arkansas in which he had been interested before the war and then returned to journalism as editor of the *Illinois State Journal,* but in 1873 he removed to Wisconsin, where he continued newspaper work until 1876. In that year he was appointed governor of Idaho Territory by President Grant. During his term of office the Nez Percé and Bannock Indian wars occurred, in which Brayman's methods of providing for the armed defense of the Territory made him locally unpopular. After the expiration of his term he moved to Wisconsin, where he had built a home on the shore of Green Lake, but after a few years he went to Kansas City where he remained for the rest of his life. He had long been a prominent layman in the Baptist denomination, was always interested in education, had been one of the regents of the University of Illinois in its early years, and a charter member of the Chicago Historical Society. He was married to Mary Williams of Chautauqua County, N. Y.

[Article in the Buffalo *Express*, Mar. 10, 1895; statement by Daniel Brayman, Feb. 24, 1864, given in *Pubs. Buffalo Hist. Soc.*, vol. IX; "The Periodical Press of Buffalo," *Ibid.*, vol. XIX; Thos. Ford, *Hist. of Ill.* (1854); Elder Brigham H. Roberts, *The Rise and Fall of Nauvoo* (1900); *Bench and Bar of Ill.* (1899), ed. by John M. Palmer, II, 628–30; H. T. French, *Hist. of Idaho*, I (1914), 80–82.] W. B. S.

BRAYTON, CHARLES RAY (Aug. 16, 1840–Sept. 23, 1910), Republican boss of Rhode Island, was born at Apponaug, a part of the town of Warwick, R. I. He was the son of William Daniel and Anna Ward (Clarke) Brayton. His father was a Republican representative in Congress from 1857 to 1861, and subsequently (1862–71) collector of internal revenue for Rhode Island. Charles entered Brown University in 1859, but left in 1861 to organize a volunteer company later merged in the 3rd Rhode Island Volunteers. Enlisting Aug. 27 as a first lieutenant, he became captain Nov. 28, 1862, lieutenant-colonel Nov. 17, 1863, and colonel Apr. 1, 1864. On Mar. 13, 1865, he was made a brigadier-general of volunteers by brevet "for faithful and meritorious services." On Mar. 7, 1867, he was made a captain in the 17th United States Infantry, but resigned on July 6. From 1870 to 1874 he held the office of United States pension agent for Rhode Island; then, until 1880, he was postmaster at Providence. In 1886 he became chief of the state police under a state prohibitory law of that year, but before long resigned and aided in the repeal of the law. In 1891, at the age of fifty-one, he was admitted to the bar. His career as a manipulator of politics began soon after the Civil War, when he allied himself with Henry B. Anthony [*q.v.*], United States senator from Rhode Island from 1859 until his death in 1884. Upon Anthony's death Brayton transferred his political allegiance to Senator Nelson W. Aldrich [*q.v.*]. The precise nature of his relations with Anthony and Aldrich is obscure, but with their coöperation and in their interest he presently became, and for more than thirty years remained, the unquestioned boss of the Republican party in the state. His task was facilitated by the lack of a veto power in the governor, and by the provision of the state constitution which gives to each town or city one senator and at least one representative in the General Assembly. As most of the towns are small, it was possible for the representatives of less than one-tenth of the population of the state to control legislation. It was an open secret that under Brayton's administration votes were regularly bought, while he himself frankly admitted the receipt of annual retainers from railway and other corporations. In 1900 he became blind, but his political activities continued. The first serious attack upon his power was made in 1902–03, when a state Lincoln party organization attempted unsuccessfully to obtain a constitutional convention. The election of a Democratic governor, James H. Higgins, in 1906, was followed by a demand by the Governor for the ousting of Brayton from his headquarters in the sheriff's office at the state capitol, and although the demand was refused, he presently withdrew. In 1896, at the earnest insistence of his supporters, he consented to become a member of the Republican national committee. He died suddenly at Providence as a result of an accident. He was married, Mar. 13, 1865, to Antoinette Percival Belden.

[The main facts of Brayton's life are given in obituaries, Sept. 24, 1910, in the *N. Y. Times*, *N. Y. Tribune*, *Sun* (N. Y.), *Providence Jour.*, and other papers. His military record is in F. B. Heitman, *Hist. Reg.* (1903). For a vivid description of the Brayton regime, including his own account of his principles and methods, see a series of articles by E. G. Lowry in the N. Y. *Evening Post*, Mar.–May 1903 (reprinted in part in a contemporary pamphlet with an introduction by Bishop W. M. McVickar); also Lincoln Steffens, "Rhode Island: A State for Sale," in *McClure's Mag.*, XXIV, 337–53 (Feb. 1905).] W. M.

BRAZER, JOHN (Sept. 21, 1789–Feb. 25, 1846), Unitarian clergyman, was born in Worcester, Mass., the son of Samuel and Betsey Brazer. Poverty forced him to postpone entering college until he was twenty-one. His academic success at Harvard was so brilliant that he led his class in scholarship. After taking his degree in 1813 and serving an apprenticeship as a tutor he was appointed in 1817 professor of Latin. According to a colleague he became one of the chief agents in "effecting a transition from the severe and ceremonial academical government of the olden time to an intercourse with the pupils more courteous and winning." His study of theology did not narrow his unusually broad intellectual interests nor warp his sound and thorough scholarship. In 1820 he resigned his professorship and was ordained pastor of the important North Church in Salem, serving this charge until his death. On Apr. 19, 1821, he was married to Anne Warren Sever. His wide and critical acquaintance with contemporary literature and thought, his classical elegance of style and chaste delivery, together with an unusual devotion to the poor of the community, explain in part his enviable success as a clergyman. Harvard gave him the degree of D.D. in 1836 and he served as a member of the Board of Overseers. His influence was broadened by contributions to the *North American Review* and the *Christian Examiner.* These covered a wide range of subjects, varying from "Ancient Modes of Burial of the Dead" to a review of Mill's *Treatise on Logic.* After a long illness he died at Charleston, S. C. (*New England Historical and Genealogical Register,* XXVI, 316). Amiable and sensitive, he was small in person, "finely turned and moulded," with a natural grace and fluency and with epicurean tastes.

Brazer's point of view was symptomatic of the forces which crystallized in Transcendentalism. His Dudleian Lecture (May 13, 1835) anticipates Emerson's *Nature* and *Divinity School Address* in denying that the great truths of religion can be ascertained through *a priori* reasonings or metaphysical assumptions. The truths of natural theology, he urged, can be attained solely in the manner by which other facts are determined, the inductive mode of reasoning. Thus he insisted that theology must be brought down to earth, and, like Emerson, found ample proof for the existence of God in "order, beauty, harmony, and the concurrence of means to ends." For Brazer it was an inevitable conclusion that God must sit enthroned "within every heart" (*Review of the Argument in Support of Natural Religion,* 1835, p. 28). This theory of man's transcendental intuitions of the perfect and absolute, essential states of human thought, was closely related to his pantheism. God's perfections, he remarked, are "recognized in every upspringing blade of grass, in every opening flower, in every passing cloud, in every beam of light" (*Sermons,* 1849, p. 46). Brazer contended that there could be no necessary opposition between "earth and heaven, things seen and things unseen, things temporal and things spiritual" (*Introductory Essay to a Good Life,* 1836). Divine influence was not, therefore, supernaturally imparted to the human soul, and the proofs for the supernatural illumination of the human mind by the spirit of God were all to be accounted for on "principles strictly natural." His individualism and egalitarianism led him to declare that the presence of God's spirit was "equally offered to all persons, in all places, and in all times" (*Essay on the Doctrine of Divine Influence,* 1835, p. 125). Brazer's lucid exposition of doctrines that have been considered Emersonian, before Emerson's own formulation of them, gives him a definite though minor place in the history of American thought.

[The best sketch of Brazer's life is that by his friend, the Rev. Samuel Gilman, in Wm. B. Sprague's *Annals of the Am. Unitarian Pulpit* (1865), pp. 504–10. Woodbridge Riley briefly discusses his significance in *Am. Philosophy, the Early Schools* (1907), p. 207.]

M. E. C.

DICTIONARY OF AMERICAN BIOGRAPHY
AMERICAN COUNCIL OF LEARNED SOCIETIES
CSS